The Elder Scrolls® V

SKYRIM™

DAWNGUARD QUESTS 505

DRAGONBORN QUESTS 583

NOTE * Quest names marked with an asterisk do not appear in your Quest Menu list, although objectives may.

THE ATLAS OF SKYRIM 685

APPENDICES 1077

SONG OF THE DRAGONBORN

(Chorus)
Dovahkiin, Dovahkiin, naal ok zin los vahriin,
Wah dein vokul mahfaeraak ahst vaal!
Ahrk fin norok paal graan fod nust hon zindro zaan,
Dovahkiin, fah hin kogaan mu draal!

(Chorus)
Dragonborn, Dragonborn, by his honor is sworn,
To keep evil forever at bay!
And the fiercest foes rout when they hear triumph's shout,
Dragonborn, for your blessing we pray!

Huzrah nu, kul do od, wah aan bok lingrah vod,
Ahrk fin tey, boziik fun, do fin gein!
Wo lost fron wah ney dov, ahrk fin reyliik do jul,
Voth aan suleyk wah ronit faal krein!

Hearken now, sons of snow, to an age, long ago,
And the tale, boldly told, of the one!
Who was kin to both wyrm, and the races of man,
With a power to rival the sun!

Ahrk fin zul, rok drey kod, nau tol morokei frod,
Rul lot Taazokaan motaad voth kein!
Sahrot Thu'um, med aan tuz, vey zeim hokoron pah,
Ol fin Dovahkiin komeyt ok rein!

And the voice, he did wield, on that glorious field,
When great Tamriel shuddered with war!
Mighty Thu'um, like a blade, cut through enemies all,
As the Dragonborn issued his roar!

(Chorus)
Dovahkiin, Dovahkiin, naal ok zin los vahriin,
Wah dein vokul mahfaeraak ahst vaal!
Ahrk fin norok paal graan fod nust hon zindro zaan,
Dovahkiin, fah hin kogaan mu draal!

(Chorus)
Dragonborn, Dragonborn, by his honor is sworn,
To keep evil forever at bay!
And the fiercest foes rout when they hear triumph's shout,
Dragonborn, for your blessing we pray!

Ahrk fin Kel lost prodah, do ved viing ko fin krah,
Tol fod zeymah win kein meyz fundein!
Alduin, feyn do jun, kruziik vokun staadnau,
Voth aan bahlok wah diivon fin lein!

And the Scrolls have foretold, of black wings in the cold,
That when brothers wage war come unfurled!
Alduin, Bane of Kings, ancient shadow unbound,
With a hunger to swallow the world!

Nuz aan sul, fent alok, fod fin vul dovah nok,
Fen kos nahlot mahfaeraak ahrk ruz!
Paaz Keizaal fen kos stin nol bein Alduin jot,
Dovahkiin kos fin saviik do muz!

But a day, shall arise, when the dark dragon's lies,
Will be silenced forever and then!
Fair Skyrim will be free from foul Alduin's maw,
Dragonborn be the savior of men!

(Chorus)
Dovahkiin, Dovahkiin, naal ok zin los vahriin,
Wah dein vokul mahfaeraak ahst vaal!
Ahrk fin norok paal graan fodnust vok zin dro zaan,
Dovahkiin, fah hin kogaan mu draal!

(Chorus)
Dragonborn, Dragonborn, by his honor is sworn,
To keep evil forever at bay!
And the fiercest foes rout when they hear triumph's shout,
Dragonborn, for your blessing we pray!

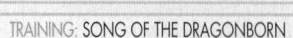

TRAINING PART 1: CHARACTER CREATION

WELCOME TO SKYRIM

We have designed the Character Creation section of the "Training" chapter to give you tactical advice in the same order as you make decisions while adventuring across the wilds of Skyrim. To begin with, we reveal the benefits of choosing a particular race. Then we thoroughly explore all 18 of the skills—and the perks associated with each—so you know what each skill does, how you increase it, and what perks to select based on your play style. Finally, we present a host of Character Archetypes—exceptional explorers tailored to a specific role, renowned heroes who use the best combinations of skills and equipment to suit a particular play style.

TIP Please read through the game's Instruction Manual and familiarize yourself with the tenets of this adventure. This training chapter assumes you have already read this information.

This guide encompasses all of Skyrim's original content and updates, as well as the Dawnguard, Hearthfire, and Dragonborn add-ons. The following icons are used to indicate new material related to an update or add-on:

Content associated with this icon is primarily related to the Dawnguard expansion.

Content associated with this icon is primarily related to the Hearthfire expansion.

Content associated with this icon is primarily related to the Dragonborn expansion.

Content associated with this icon was added or changed by a game update.

Look for these four icons throughout this book so you know what's new.

SELECTING A RACE

PART I: THE RACES OF SKYRIM

As you begin your adventure across Skyrim, the historic Elder Scrolls mantra "you are what you play" rings true: Although statistically, an Orc Wizard or a High Elven Thief may not be the optimal character choices based on starting skill bonuses and racial powers, this doesn't matter in the long run. Choose the race that most appeals to you, and don't worry about statistics and abilities.

You can overcome low starting skill values by using the skills in which you wish to become more proficient. No races have any intrinsic shortfalls that will prevent you from becoming the type of hero you want to be.

However, there are certain advantages to picking a particular race. For those adventurers who wish to maximize every advantage, it is useful to know which favored skills each race begins with bonuses to, and to understand the unique racial powers they posess; this can aid you when choosing a particular play style.

In short, this section reveals which races are best suited to a particular style of adventuring, whether that be with melee weapons, magic, stealth, or some combination of these styles.

Racial Skill Advantages

The following table shows the starting skill statistics for each race. The higher the number (over the base level of 15), the better. Values of 20 indicate this is a favored skill of the race. Values of 25 indicate this is a primary skill of the race.

RACE	SMITHING	HEAVY ARMOR	BLOCK	TWO-HANDED	ONE-HANDED	ARCHERY	LIGHT ARMOR	SNEAK	LOCKPICKING	PICKPOCKET	SPEECH	ALCHEMY	ILLUSION	CONJURATION	DESTRUCTION	RESTORATION	ALTERATION	ENCHANTING
Argonian	15	15	15	15	15	15	20	20	25	20	15	15	15	15	15	20	20	15
Breton	15	15	15	15	15	15	15	15	15	15	20	20	20	25	15	20	20	15
Dark Elf	15	15	15	15	15	15	20	20	15	15	15	20	20	15	25	15	20	15
High Elf	15	15	15	15	15	15	15	15	15	15	15	15	25	20	20	20	20	20
Imperial	15	20	20	15	20	15	15	15	15	15	15	15	15	15	20	25	15	20
Khajiit	15	15	15	15	20	20	15	25	20	20	15	20	15	15	15	15	15	15
Nord	20	15	20	25	20	15	20	15	15	15	20	15	15	15	15	15	15	15
Orc	20	25	20	20	20	15	15	15	15	15	15	15	15	15	15	15	15	20
Redguard	20	15	20	15	25	20	15	15	15	15	15	15	15	15	20	15	20	15
Wood Elf	15	15	15	15	15	25	20	20	20	20	15	20	15	15	15	15	15	15

NOTE For example, if you chose a Khajiit character, you'd receive a +5 bonus to your One-Handed, Archery, Lockpicking, Pickpocket, and Alchemy and a +10 to your Sneak skill.

Notes on Gender: There are no differences between the genders of a particular race; they share the same set of starting skill values, spells, powers, and abilities. Feel free to create the character that most appeals to you without penalty.

Starting Spells, Racial Powers, and Abilities

In addition to a slight boost to the base value of certain skills, each race has its own set of starting Spells; Racial Powers that offer a unique bonus such as the ability to regenerate or absorb Magicka; and innate Racial Abilities, such a resistance to Frost damage. A tactical overview of each race follows.

> **NOTE** **Racial Commentary:** The race you choose will affect the greetings and passing comments the citizens of Skyrim make when you speak to or pass by them.
>
> **Races and Gameplay:** Very rarely, your race may also have a small effect on gameplay. For example:
>
> When infiltrating the Thalmor Embassy dressed in the robes of that High Elf faction, High Elves (and to a lesser extent other Elves) will find it easier to sneak around undetected than will members of the other races.
>
> Orcs are welcome in Skyrim's Orc strongholds, while members of other races must first prove themselves worthy.
>
> The tone and color of some dialogue choices may change depending on your race and the situation.
>
> If your race has a noticeable effect on an interaction, that will be noted when relevant. But this isn't something to be concerned about: nothing is closed to you because of your race; indeed, you may be surprised by a positive benefit when you least expect it!

Argonians

Favored Skills: +10 Lockpicking, +5 Pickpocket, Sneak, Light Armor, Alteration, Restoration

Starting Spells: Flames, Healing

Racial Power—Histskin: You regenerate health 10x faster for 60 seconds

Racial Abilities: 50% Disease Resistance, Underwater Breathing

Ideal Play Style: Thief (Defensive)

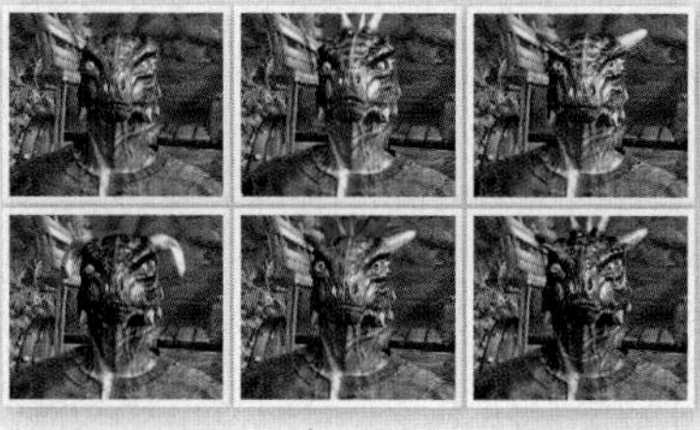

A male Argonian

A female Argonian

Little is known about the reptilian denizens of Black Marsh. Years of defending their borders have made the Argonians experts in guerilla warfare, and their natural abilities make them equally at home in water and on land. They are well suited for the treacherous swamps of their homeland and have developed natural immunity to the diseases that have doomed many would-be explorers in the region.

> **TIP** Histskin is a fantastic ability for any character, capable of quickly bringing you back from the brink of death. Even better, as a power, it allows you to keep attacking while it does its work—no concentration required.
>
> Resist Disease reduces the chance that you'll contract a disease from an animal or trap; it doesn't affect the severity of any diseases you might already have. Diseases are rarely a significant threat in Skyrim, although they can be debilitating if you let them pile up. Visit a shrine periodically, and you shouldn't have any trouble.
>
> Underwater Breathing means you'll never have to worry about drowning damage. Diving is rarely required, but this ability may allow you to claim the occasional sunken treasure or explore shipwrecks more easily.

Breton

Favored Skills: +10 Conjuration, +5 Illusion, Restoration, Speech, Alchemy, Alteration

Starting Spells: Flames, Healing, Conjure Familiar

Racial Power—Dragonskin: You absorb 50% of the Magicka from incoming spells for 60 seconds

Racial Abilities: 25% Magic Resistance

Ideal Play Style: Mage (Defensive)

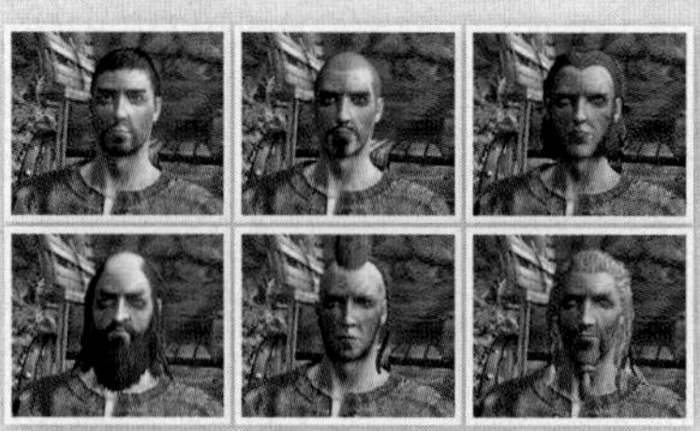

A male Breton

A female Breton

Bretons feel an instinctive bond with the mercurial forces of magic and the supernatural. Many great sorcerers have come from their home province of High Rock. In addition to their quick and perceptive grasp of spellcraft, enchantment, and alchemy, all Bretons boast a resistance to spells.

> **TIP** Bretons are fantastic at taking on other mages; both Dragonskin and Magic Resistance support this and are strong abilities even in the late game.
>
> Magic Resistance significantly increases your survivability against enemy casters, while Dragonskin is great at keeping your Magicka up; this helps you maintain the Ward spells that are your first line of defense.

Dark Elf

Favored Skills: +10 Destruction, +5 Alteration, Illusion, Sneak, Light Armor, Alchemy

Starting Spells: Flames, Sparks, Healing

Racial Power—Ancestor's Wrath: Creates a Flame Cloak that does 10 damage to nearby foes for 60 seconds.

Racial Abilities: 50% Fire Resistance

Ideal Play Style: Nightblade (Mage/Thief)

A male Dark Elf

A female Dark Elf

In the empire, "Dark Elves" is the common usage, but in their Morrowind homeland, they call themselves the "Dunmer." The dark-skinned, red-eyed Dunmer combine powerful intellect with strong and agile physiques, producing superior warriors and sorcerers. On the battlefield, Dark Elves are noted for their skilled and balanced integration of swordsmen, marksmen, and war wizards.

TIP Ancestor's Wrath is a weaker version of Flame Cloak, an Adept-level Destruction spell. While good at early levels—where you're likely to be in melee a lot—it's less valuable once you can cast the spell on your own. It's also less useful if you plan to play a ranged character, such as an archer or pure mage.

Fire Resistance is helpful against Flame Atronachs, fire-wielding casters, and fire-breathing dragons. No one enemy type uses fire spells, so it's hard to predict when exactly this ability will come into play—it's not really something you can use strategically.

High Elf

Favored Skills: +10 Illusion, +5 Alteration, Conjuration, Destruction, Restoration, Enchanting

Starting Spells: Flames, Fury, Healing

Racial Power—Highborn: For 60 seconds, you regenerate 25% of your maximum Magicka each second

Racial Abilities: Highborn Magicka (+50 Magicka)

Ideal Play Style: Mage (Offensive)

A male High Elf

A female High Elf

The High Elves, or Altmer, are the proud, tall, golden-skinned people of Summerset Isle. The common tongue of the empire, Tamrielic, is based on their speech and writing, and most of the empire's arts, crafts, and sciences are derived from High Elven traditions. High Elves are the driving force behind the rising Aldmeri Dominion, and their agents, the Thalmor, are bitterly resented by the Nords of Skyrim.

TIP Highborn will rapidly refill your Magicka, allowing you to continue casting when you need it most. Extremely strong at any level, this power is a mage's lifeline.

Highborn Magicka is like getting five free levels. It's a powerful head start for any mage—you may never need to fall back on your melee skills.

Imperial

Favored Skills: +10 Restoration, +5 Destruction, Enchanting, One-Handed, Block, Heavy Armor

Starting Spells: Flames, Healing

Racial Power—Voice of the Emperor: Calms nearby people for 60 seconds

Racial Abilities: Imperial Luck (adds a small amount of gold to most containers)

Ideal Play Style: Battlemage (Mage/Warrior)

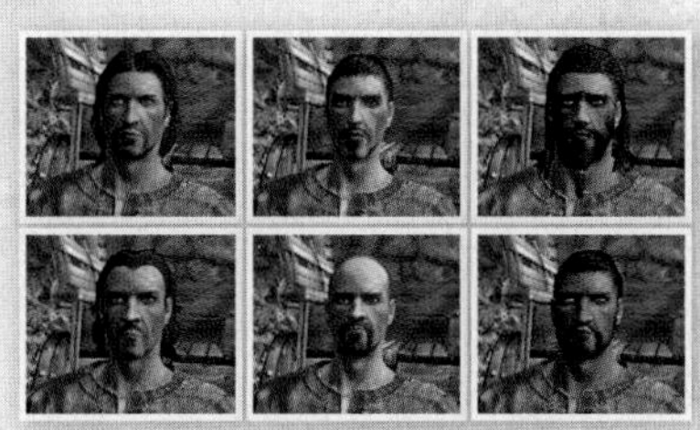

A male Imperial

A female Imperial

Natives of the civilized, cosmopolitan province of Cyrodiil, Imperials are well educated and well spoken. Though physically less imposing than the other races, Imperials are shrewd diplomats and traders. These traits, along with their remarkable skill and training as light infantry, have allowed them to rule an empire that spans the continent for centuries.

TIP Voice of the Emperor is a weaker version of the Expert-level Illusion spell Pacify, with the effect centered on your position. This can be powerful if you're surrounded by a mob of enemies, but it's less useful against smaller groups or ranged foes.

Imperial Luck adds a few extra coins to most of the chests you find. While this bonus is small (10 or less), it adds up over time. But there are plenty of other ways to make money in Skyrim.

Khajiit

Favored Skills: +10 Sneak, +5 Lockpicking, Pickpocket, Alchemy, One-Handed, Archery

Starting Spells: Flames, Healing

Racial Power—Night Eye: Improved night vision for 60 seconds

Racial Abilities: Claws (4x unarmed damage)

Ideal Play Style: Thief (Offensive)

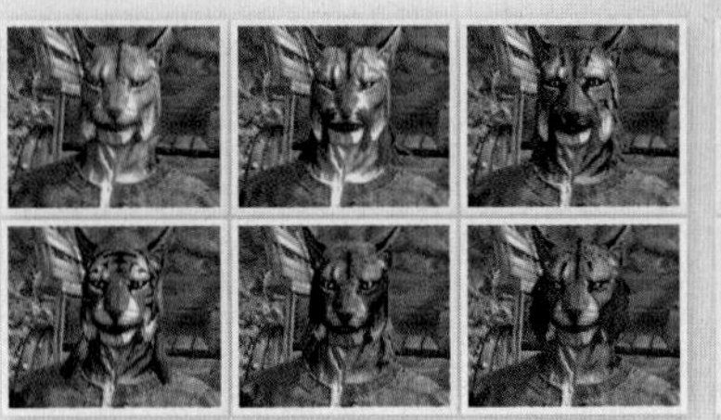

A male Khajiit

A female Khajiit

Khajiit hail from the province of Elsweyr and can vary in appearance from nearly Elven to the Cathay-raht "jaguar men" to the great Senche-Tiger. The most common breed, the Suthay-raht, is intelligent, quick, and agile. Many Khajiit disdain weapons in favor of their claws. They make excellent thieves due to their natural agility and deft hands.

TIP Night Eye allows you to see clearly in dark environments without the need for a light source that might expose your presence. This is occasionally useful, but there's usually enough light in dungeons that you can get by without it. Unlike most powers, Night Eye can be used multiple times a day without restriction.

Claws give you an overwhelming advantage in unarmed combat and brawls. Coupled with the Heavy Armor perk Fists of Steel or appropriate gear, this ability can help unarmed combat remain viable longer. But remember that unarmed combat isn't a skill, it doesn't give you skill uses, and it won't help you level up. Usually it comes into play only in the occasional brawl. But if you're a dedicated role-player who really wants to box your way through Skyrim, well, this is the ability for you.

Nord

Favored Skills: +10 Two-Handed, +5 One-Handed, Block, Smithing, Speech, Light Armor

Starting Spells: Flames, Healing

Racial Power—Battle Cry: All nearby foes flee for 30 seconds

Racial Abilities: 50% Frost Resistance

Ideal Play Style: Warrior (Offensive)

A male Nord

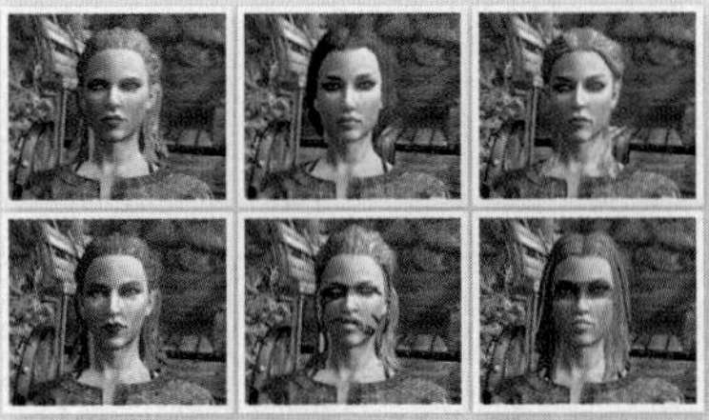

A female Nord

The natives of Skyrim are a tall and fair-haired people, aggressive and fearless in war, industrious and enterprising in trade and exploration. Strong, willful, and hardy, Nords are famous for their resistance to cold, even magical frost. Violence is an accepted and time-honored part of Nordic culture. Nords face battle with an ecstatic ferocity that shocks and appalls their enemies.

TIP Battle Cry is a weaker version of the Master-level Illusion spell Hysteria. Good against a swarm of weak foes, it buys you a few seconds to recover, reposition, or run before the fight resumes. It is useful in the right situation, though it rarely helps you win a fight outright.

Frost Resistance is good against Frost Atronachs, frost-wielding wizards, and frost dragons. But it's at its best in Skyrim's many tombs and crypts, where the undead Draugr wield frost spells almost exclusively.

Orc

Favored Skills: +10 Heavy Armor, +5 Smithing, One-Handed, Two-Handed, Block, Enchanting

Starting Spells: Flames, Healing

Racial Power—Berserk: For 60 seconds, you take half damage and inflict double damage in melee combat

Racial Abilities: None

Ideal Play Style: Warrior (Defensive)

A male Orc

A female Orc

These sophisticated barbarians of the Wrothgarian and Dragontail Mountains are noted for their unshakeable courage in war and their unflinching endurance of hardships. In the past, Orcs have been widely feared and hated by the other nations and races of Tamriel, but they have slowly won acceptance in the empire. Orcish armorers are prized for their craftsmanship, and Orc warriors in heavy armor are among the finest front-line troops in the empire.

TIP Berserk is the Orcs' only racial ability, but it's worth it—for one minute, you become an unstoppable force of destruction. Great in any combat situation, from fending off a swarm of smaller enemies to taking on a powerful dragon, and strong at any level.

Redguard

A male Redguard

A female Redguard

Favored Skills: +10 One-Handed, +5 Archery, Block, Smithing, Destruction, Alteration

Starting Spells: Flames, Healing

Racial Power—Adrenaline Rush: You regenerate Stamina 10x faster for 60 seconds

Racial Abilities: 50% Poison Resistance

Ideal Play Style: Spellsword (Warrior/Mage), Dual-Wielding

The most naturally talented warriors in Tamriel, the dark-skinned, wiry-haired Redguards of Hammerfell seem born to battle, though their pride and fierce independence of spirit makes them more suitable as scouts, skirmishers, or free-ranging heroes and adventurers than as rank-and-file soldiers. Redguards are uniquely versatile combatants, capable of switching between bow, sword, spell, or shield at will and adapting their tactics to the battle at hand.

TIP Adrenaline Rush is the Stamina version of Histskin or Highborn. Although less broadly useful than Health or Magicka regen, it will allow you to keep up your power attacks in a protracted battle—or sprint away if necessary.

Poison Resistance is helpful against the few enemies that use poison—Forsworn, Falmer, Chaurus, and spiders—and the rare poison gas trap. Not as broadly useful as most other abilities.

Wood Elf

A male Wood Elf

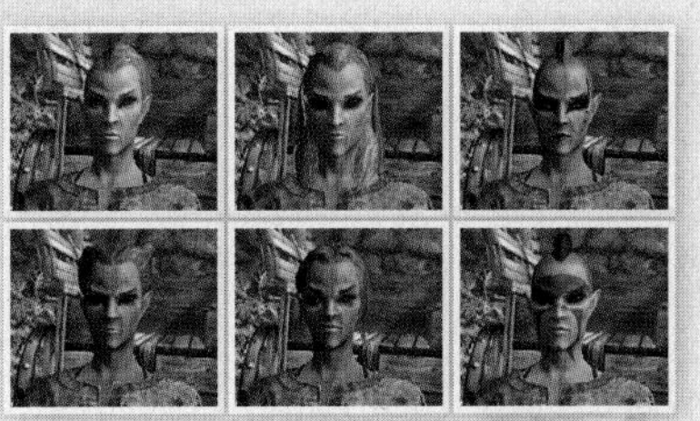

A female Wood Elf

Favored Skills: +10 Archery, +5 Sneak, Lockpicking, Pickpocket, Light Armor, Alchemy

Starting Spells: Flames, Healing

Racial Power—Command Animal: Target animal becomes your ally for 60 seconds

Racial Abilities: 50% Disease and Poison Resistance

Ideal Play Style: Thief (Archer)

The clanfolk of the Western Valenwood forests. In the empire, they are called "Wood Elves," but they call themselves the Bosmer, or the "Tree-Sap" people. Wood Elves are nimble and quick in body and wit. Their curious natures and natural agility make them good scouts, agents, and thieves, and there are no finer archers in all of Tamriel.

TIP Command Animal is a powerful, single-target version of the Animal Allegiance Shout. Its main restriction is that it works only on animals. It is good outdoors or in animal dens and caves, but not in most dungeons.

Poison and Disease Resistance is a combined version of the Argonian's Disease Resistance and the Redguard's Poison Resistance abilities. Like them, it can be useful in some situations, but it just isn't a factor most of the time.

SKILLS AND PERKS

This section is arguably the most important in terms of character development. It details every skill and perk in the game and offers advice on what perks to take based on your play style. Remember: You are what you play. You can develop any skill you want, at any time. Don't ever feel locked in to a specific path just because you've focused on it in the past.

SKILLS OVERVIEW

Skill Effects

There are 18 skills in Skyrim, divided into three major sets: Combat, Magic, and Stealth. As each skill increases, its primary effect improves; you also gain access to perks in that skill that can grant you powerful new abilities or bonuses. What does each skill do? Their primary effects are listed below:

COMBAT SKILLS: THE PATH OF MIGHT

✓	SKILL NAME	PRIMARY EFFECT(S)
☐	Smithing	Improves the value and properties of items you improve.
☐	Heavy Armor	Reduces the damage you take while wearing heavy armor.
☐	Block	Reduces the damage you take and the amount you stagger when blocking attacks.
☐	Two-Handed	Increases the damage you inflict with two-handed weapons.
☐	One-Handed	Increases the damage you inflict with one-handed weapons.
☐	Archery	Increases the damage you inflict with bows.

STEALTH SKILLS: THE PATH OF SHADOW

✓	SKILL NAME	PRIMARY EFFECT(S)
☐	Light Armor	Reduces the damage you take while wearing light armor.
☐	Sneak	Improves your ability to avoid detection while sneaking.
☐	Lockpicking	Increases your ability to pick a lock successfully. Specifically, this skill increases the arc at which the pick succeeds and reduces the chance that a pick will break.
☐	Pickpocket	Increases the chance that you can successfully pickpocket an item.
☐	Speech	Improves the prices you receive when buying or selling items, and improves your success at (Persuade), (Bribe), and (Intimidate) dialogue challenges.
☐	Alchemy	Improves the potency of potions and poisons that you craft.

MAGIC SKILLS: THE PATH OF SORCERY

✓	SKILL NAME	PRIMARY EFFECT(S)
☐	Illusion	Reduces the cost of Illusion spells.
☐	Conjuration	Reduces the cost of Conjuration spells.
☐	Destruction	Reduces the cost of Destruction spells.
☐	Restoration	Reduces the cost of Restoration spells.
☐	Alteration	Reduces the cost of Alteration spells.
☐	Enchanting	Improves the potency of items you enchant.

Improving Skills: Skill Use

In *the Elder Scrolls*, you are what you play. In Skyrim, your skill growth and level progression are determined by Skill Uses, a system that tracks the actions you perform and increases your skills accordingly. You don't have to understand how this works—just play the way you want to play, and you'll get better at it. But if you're the kind of adventurer who wants to know everything you can to maximize your potential, read on.

What Are Skill Uses?

Each of the 18 skills is "watching" for particular events to occur in the game. When one of those events occurs, the skill gains points based on the event's magnitude. What magnitude actually means varies by event and is explained in more detail below.

When the number of points in a skill passes a threshold, the skill increases. These thresholds are ever-increasing, so raising a skill from 40 to 41 takes more uses and/or higher-magnitude uses than raising that same skill from 20 to 21.

Each time a skill increases, it also contributes points toward your character's next level. The number of points depends on the level of the skill that increased, so raising a skill from 40 to 41 will take you further toward your next level than raising a skill from 20 to 21. It's important to remember two key rules:

1. Your skills improve only if you use them effectively. For example:
    - Just swinging your sword around doesn't improve your One-Handed skill. However, hitting someone with it does.
    - Just summoning an Atronach over and over again doesn't improve your Conjuration skill. But using the Atronach in combat does.
    - Just talking to everyone you meet doesn't improve your Speech skill. You have to actually buy and sell items and pass dialogue challenges.
2. Your skills generally improve faster if you use them in more challenging situations. For example:
    - Your Archery skill improves faster if you use more powerful bows that do more damage.
    - Your Illusion skill improves faster if you cast more difficult spells.
    - Your Lockpicking skill improves faster if you unlock harder chests.

Improving Skills: Training

During your journey, you will occasionally meet someone who has dedicated their lives to mastering a particular skill. These are extremely talented individuals; speak to them to request training from them in their specialty skill. Most will be happy to oblige...for a price. Each Trainer has a degree of competence—Journeyman, Expert, or Master:

Journeyman Trainers can improve your skill to a maximum of 50.

Expert Trainers can improve your skill to a maximum of 75.

Master Trainers can improve your skill to a maximum of 90.

Even the most proficient Trainers in Skyrim cannot train you past 90. You'll have to earn your way to 100!

The cost to train in a skill is based on your current skill level—the Trainer's skill has no effect. However, the Expert and Master Trainers are often members of a faction and will train you only if you're a member in good standing. Joining a faction is usually easy, so if you want access to a particular Trainer (or set of Trainers), it's worth doing early even if you don't plan to pursue that faction's quests right away.

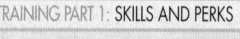

When working with a Trainer, you will receive one skill increase each time you train. You can repeat this up to five times with any combination of Trainers before you must level up. You can then return to any Trainer and pay for up to five more skill points. If you gain a level while training, go level up, then speak to the Trainer again if you want to train more.

An Example: Maximizing Your Training

Runil is happy to teach you his knowledge of Conjuration. For a price.

You wish to improve your Conjuration skill (which is 20), so you visit Runil—the Journeyman Trainer—at the graveyard in Falkreath. He offers to train you for 250 gold. Train with him, and you exchange the gold for one skill point. You can train with him four more times this level, at a slightly higher cost each time. When you're done, your skill is now 25 and you've spent a total of 1,350 gold. You must now level up before you can pay to train again. You could have received the same training from Phinis Gestor (College of Winterhold) or Falion (in Morthal) or any combination of these three, but you could never have trained your skill above 25.

If you're focused on increasing your favorite skills, be sure to visit their Trainers often, ideally just after you level up. For best results, train and then use the skill to help increase it as quickly as possible. Remember that you can visit a variety of Trainers to increase multiple skills!

Some Trainers can also be Followers, and a few of them are even candidates for marriage!

LEGENDARY DIFFICULTY AND SKILLS

Game Difficulty

Skyrim has six difficulty settings: Novice, Apprentice, Adept, Expert, Master, and Legendary. The default difficulty is Adept. The difficulty level modifies how damage is dealt in the game, as shown in the following table:

SKYRIM TABLE OF DIFFICULTY

☑ DIFFICULTY	DAMAGE RECEIVED BY THE PLAYER	DAMAGE RECEIVED BY OTHER CHARACTERS
☐ Novice	x0.5	x2
☐ Apprentice	x0.75	x1.5
☐ Adept	x1	x1
☐ Expert	x1.5	x0.75
☐ Master	x2	x0.5
☐ Legendary	x3	x0.25

What does this mean exactly? Well, think of the following example: While playing on Novice difficulty, you take only half damage from enemy attacks, and your attacks do double damage to your foes. This compares to Adept (the default difficulty).

The difficulty level affects only those two statistics. It doesn't affect the difficulty of any other challenges you may face (speech challenges, locks, etc.), and it doesn't affect the rewards you receive (such as perks or loot).

You can change the difficulty at any time in the Gameplay Settings menu (even during combat!). If you feel that the game is becoming too easy (or difficult) for you, don't hesitate to make the switch.

Are the monstrous denizens of skyrim proving too difficult to defeat? Then reduce your difficulty for fewer fraught confrontations.

Legendary Survivor

Need a challenge? Then bump up your difficulty to Legendary and face down a formidable foe!

Here are some plans for surviving on Skyrim's hardest difficulty setting: Legendary. These strategies apply to Master and Expert difficulty as well, though they may be less critical there.

For about the first ten levels, many foes will be able to kill you in a single hit. Even getting near them is dangerous, since they may perform a kill move you can't dodge. Keep your distance and used ranged attacks to wear them down.

Followers are critical to your survival. Because your Followers are actually taking less damage than normal on Legendary, they can withstand a barrage of attacks that would easily fell you. During the initial events in Helgen, stay behind your ally (Hadvar or Ralof). After making your escape, recruit a defensive, melee-focused Follower, like Vorstag, Lydia, or Farkas, and let them hold the enemy's attention while you strike from range.

Seek out additional companions whenever the opportunity presents itself. Recruit a dog, like Vigilance in Markarth or one of the Dawnguard huskies. Pick up the Conjure Familiar or Conjure Flame Atronach spells for a summoned ally. Quests that give you short-term or long-term Followers, like the Dawnguard Main Quest (Serana) or Daedric Quest: A Daedra's Best Friend (Barbas), are also worth doing early.

Defense is the best offense. Decide which armor skill you plan to use and stick to it. Focus on raising that skill, taking perks in it as soon as they become available (especially perks that increase your Armor Rating) and augmenting it with enchantments and potions. Look for other opportunities to increase your defense as well. The Lord Stone's Damage Reduction and Magic Resistance bonuses are a great asset, as are potions or enchantments that increase your other resistances.

Crowd-control abilities are much more valuable in Legendary—you simply can't survive being attacked by multiple foes at once. The Nord racial power Battle Cry is ideal for this purpose, especially early in your adventure. Illusion spells like Fear and Calm can remove a single enemy from the fight, while Shouts like Animal Allegiance, Kyne's Peace, Dismaying Shout, and Slow Time will help fend off larger groups. In Beast Form, the werewolf's Fear Howl is also very effective.

Survey the battlefield and use the terrain to your advantage. Snipe your enemies from a distance or a different elevation and force them to come to you. Maintain that distance by backing away as you continue your assault.

Early on, you may be tempted to focus on noncombat or crafting skills in order to gain some quick levels. Resist that temptation. As your level increases, the foes you face become stronger as well. If you neglect your combat skills, you may fall even further behind.

That said, don't neglect your support skills forever. If you can survive the first few levels, gradually investing in skills like Smithing, Enchanting, and Alchemy can help you gain an edge later on.

Scour the Training section of this guide for tips and advice, and take it to heart. Many tips that are only useful on a lower difficulty level—like getting "free" healing by leveling up when your health is low—are absolutely essential to your survival.

Legendary Skills

Need to be written about in Nord sagas of yore? Then truly master a skill (such as Archery) by taking it to Legendary status...and beyond!

Once one of your skills reaches 100, it cannot increase any further. You can continue to use it, taking advantage of your mastery of the skill (and its high-level perks, if you choose to acquire them). However, because you gain levels based on skill increases, continuing to use this skill will not help you progress toward the next level. Eventually, once all of your skills reach 100, you will no longer be able to gain levels at all.

When one of your skills reaches 100, a new option will appear when you highlight its constellation on the Skills menu: Legendary. To make that skill Legendary, press the Legendary button and confirm your choice. Several things will then happen:

- The skill will be marked as Legendary (an icon appears below the skill).
- The skill will be reset from 100 to 15.
- Any perks that you had in the skill will be refunded.

In effect, the Legendary skill system allows you to start over again with a skill. You can continue using it, work your way back up to 100, and gain levels as you do so (because the skill is increasing). If you reach 100, you can choose to roll it over again. This allows you to continue gaining levels and amassing perk points indefinitely!

If you reset a skill multiple times, a number will appear next to the Legendary icon below that skill, recording how many times you have reached 100 with it.

Each new level is increasingly difficult to attain, so even with multiple Legendary skills, you shouldn't expect to acquire every possible perk. Note that Legendary skills are not better than non-Legendary skills—the Legendary designation simply recognizes that you had mastered the skill and chose to start over with it again.

Legendary Skills: General Advice

Crafting the finest armor with the most impressive enchantments, and then reset your Smithing and Enchantment skills; you can still use the fruits of your labor.

Legendary skills are not for everyone. The Skill 100 perks are entertaining and powerful and reward you for the effort it took to master their skill in the first place. Try them out. Don't be too quick to throw away the chance to forge Dragonbone Armor, craft the perfect potion, or call upon a Blizzard to devastate your foes. Even without Legendary skills, you can still reach a very high level (80+), and you can always choose to make a skill Legendary later on.

While you can make a skill Legendary at any time, if you're sure you want to reset a particular skill, it's generally best to do so as soon as it reaches 100. Otherwise, you may be throwing away skill uses that could have counted toward your next level.

There is one exception to that rule: If a skill can provide you with an ongoing benefit even after you've reset it, make sure to take advantage of it. For example, use your Smithing skill to forge and improve a complete set (or two) of Dragonbone or Daedric weapons and armor. Once you reset your Smithing skill, you'll be back to working with iron weapons and armor again—but you can continue to use anything you previously crafted.

Similarly, use your Enchanting skill to enchant your best gear before you reset it, and use Alchemy to stockpile a collection of powerful potions or poisons. While you won't lose any enchantments or recipes you've learned when you reset a skill, it will be a while before you can make anything as powerful again.

The Master-level Conjuration spells allow you to permanently summon (or create) Thralls. These spells are powerful but are prohibitively costly without the Skill 100 Master Conjuration perk. Before you reset your Conjuration skill, make sure to summon a Thrall (or two, if you have the Twin Souls perk). They'll continue to follow you even after you've reset your Conjuration skill.

Some skills, especially crafting skills, can be relatively easy to build up again...if you're prepared. If your skill is approaching 100 and you plan to reset it, take some time to collect low-level raw materials like Iron Ore, Dwarven Scrap, Petty and Lesser Soul Gems, unenchanted weapons and armor, and loose ingredients you can craft with after the reset. If you plan to reset Speech, this is a great time to do it, since these crafting sessions will produce a large number of low-level items to sell.

Don't reset too many skills at once—make sure you still have enough high-level skills to be successful in combat. Otherwise, you may find yourself lowering the difficulty just to survive.

When you reset a skill, it helps to have a high-level skill of a similar type that you can fall back on while you work your old skill back up to 100. For example, before resetting an offensive skill (One Handed, Two Handed, Archery, Destruction, Conjuration), make sure you have another offensive skill at 50+ in case you find yourself in need of more attack power. Similarly, before resetting a defensive skill (Heavy Armor, Light Armor, Alteration, Restoration), make sure you have a second defensive skill ready to help you mitigate or recover from damage.

Save first. When you reset a skill, your character will suddenly become much less powerful. You may find it surprisingly difficult to cope with the loss of a combat, armor, or support skill you've come to rely on, especially if you don't have an appropriate backup skill. Since this is one choice you can't undo, make sure you have a save you can fall back on, just in case.

THE TRAINERS OF SKYRIM AND SOLSTHEIM

Combat Skills: The Path of Might

Smithing

Journeyman Trainer: Ghorza, of Markarth

Expert Trainer: Balimund, of Riften

Master Trainer: Eorlund Gray-Mane, of Whiterun

Master Trainer: Gunmar, in Fort Dawnguard (after being recruited)

Heavy Armor

There is no Journeyman Trainer for this skill.

Expert Trainer: Gharol of Dushnikh Yal, in the Reach

Master Trainer: Farkas of the Companions, in Whiterun

Master Trainer: Isran, in Fort Dawnguard

Master Trainer: Kuvar, in Thirsk Mead Hall (Solstheim)

Block

There is no Journeyman Trainer for this skill.

Expert Trainer: Njada Stonearm of the Companions, in Whiterun

Master Trainer: Larak of Mor Khazgur, in the Reach

Two-Handed

There is no Journeyman Trainer for this skill.

Expert Trainer: Torbjorn Shatter-Shield, of Windhelm

Master Trainer: Fura Bloodmouth, in Castle Volkihar

Master Trainer: Wulf Wildblood, of the Skaal Village (Solstheim)

Master Trainer: Vilkas, of the Companions, in Whiterun

One-Handed

Journeyman Trainer: Amren, of Whiterun

Expert Trainer: Athis, of the Companions in Whiterun

Master Trainer: Burguk, of Dushnikh Yal in the Reach

Archery

Journeyman Trainer: Faendal, of Riverwood

Expert Trainer: Aela the Huntress, of the Companions in Whiterun

Master Trainer: Niruin, of the Thieves Guild, in Riften

Master Trainer: Sorine Jurard, in Fort Dawnguard (after being recruited)

Stealth Skills: The Path of Shadow

Light Armor

Journeyman Trainer: Scouts-Many-Marshes, of Windhelm

Expert Trainer: Grelka, of Riften

Master Trainer: Nazir, of the Dark Brotherhood

Sneak

Journeyman Trainer: Khayla, of the Khajiit Caravans

Expert Trainer: Garvey, of Markarth

Master Trainer: Delvin Mallory, of the Thieves Guild, in Riften

Lockpicking

There is no Journeyman Trainer for this skill.

Expert Trainer: Majhad of the Khajiit Caravans.

Master Trainer: Vex, of The Thieves Guild, in Riften.

Pickpocket

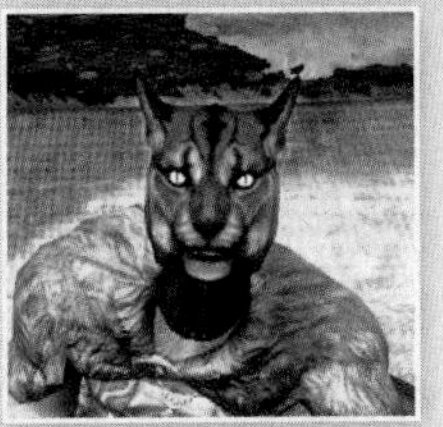

Journeyman Trainer: Ahkari, of the Khajiit Caravans

Expert Trainer: Silda the Unseen, of Windhelm

Master Trainer: Vipir, of the Thieves Guild in Riften

Speech

Journeyman Trainer: Dro'marash, of the Khajiit Caravans

Journeyman Trainer: Revyn Sadri, of Windhelm

Expert Trainer: Ogmund the Skald, of Markarth

Expert Trainer: Ronthil, in Castle Volkihar

Master Trainer: Geraud Gemaine, of the Bards College in Solitude

Alchemy

Journeyman Trainer: Lami, of Morthal

Expert Trainer: Arcadia, of Whiterun

Expert Trainer: Milore Ienth, of Raven Rock (Solstheim)

Master Trainer: Babette, of the Dark Brotherhood

Magic Skills: The Path of Sorcery

Illusion

There is no Journeyman Trainer for this skill.

Expert Trainer: Atub, of Largashbur in the Rift

Master Trainer: Drevis Neloren, of the College of Winterhold

Conjuration

Journeyman Trainer: Runil, of Falkreath

Expert Trainer: Phinis Gestor, of the College of Winterhold

Master Trainer: Falion, of Morthal

Master Trainer: Talvas Fathryon, of Tel Mithryn (Solstheim)

Destruction

Journeyman Trainer: Wuunferth the Unliving, of Windhelm

Expert Trainer: Garan Marethi, in Castle Volkihar

Expert Trainer: Sybille Stentor, of Solitude

Master Trainer: Faralda, of the College of Winterhold

Restoration

Journeyman Trainer: Aphia Velothi, in Raven Rock (Solstheim)

Expert Trainer: Keeper Carcette, in the Hall of the Vigilant

Expert Trainer: Colette Marence, of the College of Winterhold

Master Trainer: Danica Pure-Spring, of Whiterun

Master Trainer: Florentius Baenius, in Fort Dawnguard (after being rescued)

Alteration

There is no Journeyman Trainer for this skill.

Expert Trainer: Dravynea, of Kynesgrove, in Eastmarch

Master Trainer: Tolfdir, of the College of Winterhold

Enchanting

There is no Journeyman Trainer for this skill.

Expert Trainer: Sergius Turrianus, of the College of Winterhold

Master Trainer: Hamal, or Markarth

Master Trainer: Neloth, of Tel Mithryn (Solstheim)

Skill Trainers are also referenced when they relate to quests or specific Atlas locations later in this guide.

IMPROVING SKILLS: SKILL BOOKS

The Doors of Oblivion (Conjuration), one of five copies known to exist.

Scattered throughout Skyrim are several rare Skill Books, each associated with a particular skill. The first time you read each book, the associated skill increases by one. There are five different named books for each skill (90 different book titles), so a diligent collector can potentially increase each skill by 5 points.

There are multiple copies of each book in the world (usually three to five). However, you gain a skill point only the first time you read a book—rereading that book, or any of its copies, has no further effect. **For example,** those interested in the Sneak skill should look for the following books: Three Thieves (four copies), 2920, Last Seed, v8 (four copies), Sacred Witness (four copies), Legend of Krately House (three copies), and The Red Kitchen Reader (five copies). This means there is a total of 20 Sneak Skill Books, and 5 points you can add to your Sneak from reading the first copy you encounter of each tome.

Improving Skills: Scholars' Insight Power

Another way to increase your Skills is to complete Solstheim Side Quest: Black Book: The Winds of Change (page 612). Locate this Black Book inside Bloodskal Barrow (which is accessed via Raven Rock Mine). Once you find the Reward Book at the end of your expedition through Apocrypha, choose the Scholar's Insight Power; this grants you an extra skill point each time you read a Skill Book.

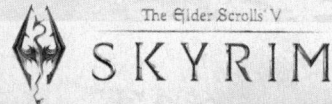

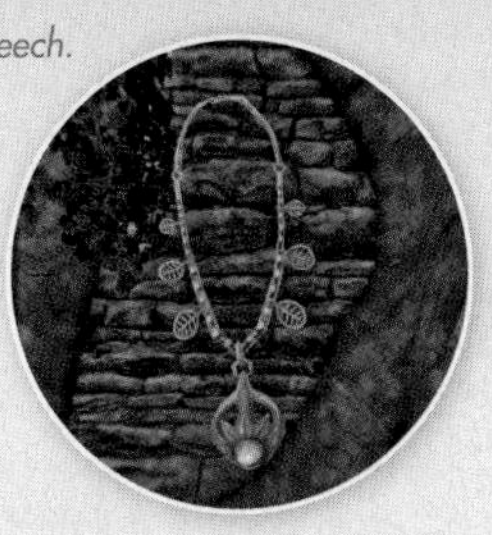

An Amulet of Dibella, which adds +15 to your Speech.

There are a variety of other ways to temporarily boost your skills (or their primary effects):

Equip enchanted items that increase that skill.

Drink a potion that boosts the skill.

Acquire a Shrine Blessing or other temporary bonus to the skill.

For example: Say you have a Speech of 40 but want to get better prices for a collection of loot you're about to sell. You could look for ways to permanently increase your skill, like completing dialogue challenges, training, or reading Skill Books. You can also equip an Amulet of Dibella (+15 Speech), pray at a Shrine of Dibella (+10% Better Prices), give a beggar a gold piece to receive the Gift of Charity (+10 Speech), or quaff a Potion of Glibness (+20 Speech). Then head over to your merchant of choice and wring out every last gold coin you can.

General Advice on Improving Skills

When improving your skills, heed the following advice:

In general, it's better to increase your skills and level up naturally, rather than trying to find ways to exploit the game. In fact, it may make your adventure harder, since you'll lack the gear and tactics needed to survive higher-level combat.

There is no fixed "maximum level" (i.e., Level 50) for you to attain. However, if you were to raise all of your skills to 100, this would take you to around Level 80. As you're able to choose only one perk each time you level up, and there are well over 200 skill-based perks, don't fixate on obtaining every single one. Instead, focus on improving the skills you're most interested in, and ignore perks you won't take advantage of, even if they're in a skill you use constantly. For those adept adventurers who reach the higher level echelons, consult the section on Legendary Skills (page 13).

Statistically, it's better to save Skill Books for higher levels, when the amount of effort or the cost of training needed to increase a skill rises dramatically. However, this tends to be difficult to do in practice, since you automatically read a book when picking it up and won't know in advance that it's a Skill Book. Unless you're intent on raising every skill to 100, it's best not to worry about this.

If you're most of the way to your next level and just need one or two more skill increases, here are some options:

If you have the gold, training is always a good option. If you're short on gold, try training in a skill you haven't used as much, as it will be less expensive (although it also won't count as much toward your next level).

Do you have any Skill Books you haven't read?

Are there any ingredients you haven't sampled? Especially at low skill levels, your Alchemy skill rises quickly just by eating common ingredients and learning their first effect.

Do you have a lot of ingredients? You may be able to make some potions. Give Alchemy a try!

Do you have any ingots or smithing supplies? You might be able to forge or improve something. Try your hand at Smithing.

SKILL CONSTELLATIONS

This section explores the entirety of the Skill Constellations. These are color-coded for combat skills: the Path of Might (red), Stealth skills; the Path of Shadow (green); and Magic skills: the Path of Magic (blue).

Dawnguard introduces Skill Constellations for Vampire Lords: The Path of Undeath (purple) and Werewolves: The Path of the Lycanthrope (orange). Seek out these minor constellations starting on page 61.

Dawnguard allows you to create Dragonbone Weapons, as part of your Smithing skill.

Dragonborn allows you to create new types of armor and weapons (Bonemold, Chitin, Nordic, and Stalhrim) as part of your Smithing skill.

Dragonborn allows you to craft and enchant staffs.

As a reward for completing Dragonborn Main Quest: At the Summit of Apocrypha (see page 601), you are able to expend a Dragon Soul to reset all of the perks in one of the Skill Constellations. So, if you decide you don't like your previous perk selections or want to try something different, this is now possible.

There are three general categories of perks that deserve special mention:

Skill-improvement perks: Many constellations offer a perk that simply makes you better at that skill's primary effect (e.g., Agile Defender for Light Armor, Juggernaut for Heavy Armor, Stealth for Sneak). Choosing these perks is akin to receiving a huge number of skill increases for that skill all at once. These perks may not be as "flashy" or instantly gratifying as some of the other perks, but they are always a strong, effective choice.

Magic rank perks: The five schools of magic each have a series of "rank" perks (Novice, Apprentice, Adept, Expert, and Master) that dramatically decrease the cost of spells from that school. These perks are absolutely critical to your ability to use magic effectively and should be a top priority for any serious mage.

Tiered perks: Some perks can be selected multiple times for increased effect. These bonuses do not stack. For example, Heavy Armor's Juggernaut 1 perk increases your armor rating by 20%, while Juggernaut 2 increases your armor rating by 40%. After taking Juggernaut 2, you will have a bonus of 40%, not 60%.

NOTE ★ = This highlights some of the best or most interesting perks in a particular Skill Constellation.

NOTE Total Perks for all Combat Skills: 91
Total Perks for all Stealth Skills: 74
Total Perks for all Magic Skills: 86

COMBAT SKILLS: THE PATH OF MIGHT – SMITHING

Smithing is the art of creating and improving weapons and armor. Smithing workstations include the blacksmith forge, grindstone (for weapons), and workbench (for armor). Any improvements made at any of these stations count toward your Smithing skill; the amount of increase is based on the value of the item you craft or improve. To increase this skill as quickly as possible, forge your own items and then improve them. You can make hide and iron items without taking any perks. You can improve any item without taking any perks. However, you need perks to create any advanced items, such as dwarven or ebony weapons and armor.

Mining, smelting, and tanning provide raw materials for smithing, although they do not count toward this skill. Smithing synergizes well with Enchanting, since it guarantees you a ready supply of items to enchant. For more information on all of these activities, see the Crafting section on page 70.

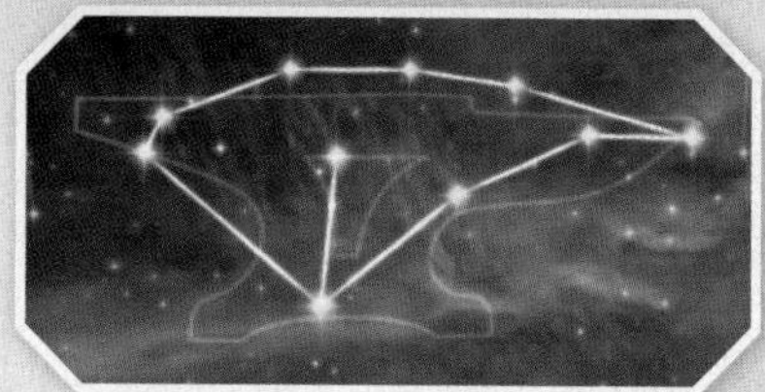

The main choice presented by your Smithing perks is obvious: Are you interested in making and improving Light Armor, like Elven, Scale, Glass, and Dragonscale? Or Heavy Armor, like Steel, Dwarven, Orcish, Ebony, Daedric, and Dragonplate? Focus on the side of the constellation that appeals most to you.

Constellation: Path of Might

Available Perks: 10

Available Smithing Perks

1. STEEL SMITHING

You can create Steel and Bonemold armor and weapons at forges and improve them twice as much.

Requires: Smithing 20

2. ARCANE BLACKSMITH ★

You can improve magical weapons and armor.

Requires: Smithing 60

This is one of the most useful Smithing perks, especially if you plan to focus on Enchanting as well. If your Enchanting skill is low, you can improve a piece of gear that has a powerful enchantment but a weak armor rating to keep it viable for longer or you can make an already great item even better. If you're a master artisan, you can make your own gear from scratch, enchant it, temper it, and then either use it or sell it for a considerable profit.

3. ELVEN SMITHING

You can create Elven armor and weapons (as well as Chitin and Heavy Chitin Armor) at forges and improve them twice as much.

Requires: Smithing 40, Steel Smithing

4. ADVANCED ARMORS

You can create Scaled and Steel Plate armor (as well as Nordic carved armor and weapons) at forges and improve them twice as much.

Requires: Smithing 50, Elven Smithing

5. GLASS SMITHING

You can create glass armor and weapons at forges and improve them twice as much.

Requires: Smithing 70, Advanced Armors

6. DWARVEN SMITHING ★

You can create dwarven armor and weapons at forges and improve them twice as much.

Requires: Smithing 30, Steel Smithing

Once you begin exploring Dwarven Ruins, you'll discover tons of scrap metal that you can smelt down into ingots. This is a great source of free, convenient crafting materials for your smithing practice. Taking this perk allows you to make better (and thus more valuable) dwarven items from these ingots, which improves your Smithing skill even more quickly and allows you to turn a nice profit too.

7. ORCISH SMITHING

You can create Orcish armor and weapons at forges and improve them twice as much.

Requires: Smithing 50, Dwarven Smithing

8. EBONY SMITHING

You can create ebony armor and weapons (as well as Stalhrim Armor, Light Stalhrim Armor, and Stalhrim Weapons*) at forges, and improve them twice as much.

Requires: Smithing 80, Orcish Smithing

> **NOTE** * If you've completed Solstheim Side Quest: A New Source of Stalhrim.

9. DAEDRIC SMITHING

You can create Daedric armor and weapons at forges and improve them twice as much.

Requires: Smithing 90, Ebony Smithing

Daedric weapons and armor are not available in shops, so the only way to get them is to find or make them.

10. DRAGON ARMOR

You can create Dragon Armor and Dragonbone Weapons at forges and improve them twice as much.

Requires: Smithing 100, Glass Smithing, OR Daedric Smithing

Dragonplate and Dragonscale armors are not available in shops, so the only way to get them is to find or make them.

Racial Benefits

+5 Smithing

- Nord
- Orc
- Redguard

Trainers

- **Journeyman:** Ghorza gra-Bagol, Blacksmith's, in Markarth.
- **Expert:** Balumund, Blacksmith's, in Riften.
- **Master:** Eorlund Gray-Mane, Skyforge, in Whiterun.
- **Master:** Gunmar, Blacksmith's, in Fort Dawnguard.

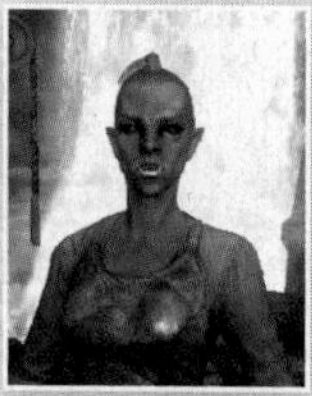

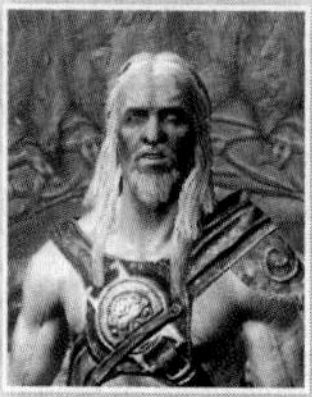

Other Resources

- For a list of Smithing Skill Books, and where to look for them, consult page 1091.
- You can find a list of Smithing Recipes later in this Training chapter, beginning on page 79.
- The following quests can also increase this skill:
  - Other Factions Quest: Rjorn's Drum (page 416).
  - Daedric Quest: Discerning the Transmundane (page 384).
  - Miscellaneous Objectives: The Reach: The Last Scabbard* (page 492).
  - Favor: Item Retrieval (Cave)* (page 500).
  - Favor: Rare Item Hunt* (page 500).

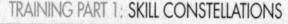

Heavy Armor allows you to make more effective use of Iron, Steel, Dwarven, Orcish, Ebony, Dragonplate, Daedric, and related armors. It offers excellent protection, though its weight will slow you down and reduce the amount of gear you can carry. High-end sets of heavy armor are especially rare, so you may wish to consider Smithing so you can craft your own when the time comes.

Your Heavy Armor skill increases when you take damage while wearing heavy armor, based on the damage of the incoming blow. If you're wearing more than one kind of armor, the incoming damage is divided up among the pieces before being used to calculate skill uses. So, the more heavy armor you're wearing, the more damage will be assigned to it, and the faster this skill will increase.

The Heavy Armor constellation has two main themes: the left arc focuses on unusual perks or those useful in specific situations, while the right arc emphasizes statistically powerful perks for Heavy Armor purists.

Constellation: Path of Might

Available Perks: 12

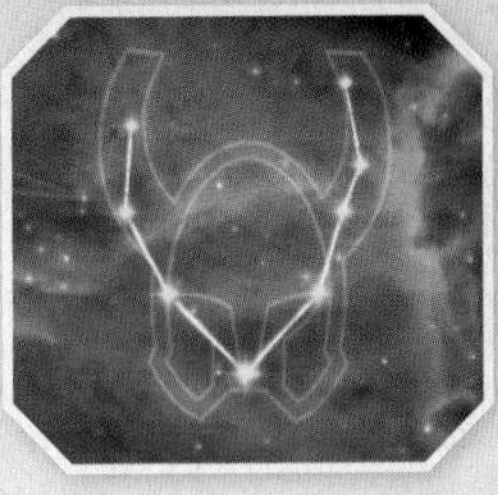

Available Heavy Armor Perks

1–5. JUGGERNAUT (5 RANKS) ★

- **Rank 1:** Increases the armor rating of your heavy armor by 20%.
  Requires: None
- **Rank 2:** Increases the armor rating of your heavy armor by 40%.
  Requires: Heavy Armor 20, Juggernaut 1
- **Rank 3:** Increases the armor rating of your heavy armor by 60%.
  Requires: Heavy Armor 40, Juggernaut 2
- **Rank 4:** Increases the armor rating of your heavy armor by 80%.
  Requires: Heavy Armor 60, Juggernaut 3
- **Rank 5:** Increases the armor rating of your heavy armor by 100%.
  Requires: Heavy Armor 80, Juggernaut 4

6. FISTS OF STEEL

Unarmed attacks with heavy armor gauntlets do their armor base rating in extra damage.
Requires: Heavy Armor 30, Juggernaut 1

Although unarmed combat doesn't increase any of your skills, it can still be a viable option, especially for Khajiits (whose Claws racial ability also improves unarmed attacks). This perk makes brawls dramatically easier.

7. WELL FITTED ★

Get a 25% Armor bonus if wearing all heavy armor: head, chest, hands, feet.
Requires: Heavy Armor 30, Juggernaut 1

This bonus stacks with Juggernaut and Matching Set—a must-have for anyone serious about using Heavy Armor.

8. CUSHIONED

Half-damage from falling if wearing all heavy armor: head, chest, hands, feet.
Requires: Heavy Armor 50, Fists of Steel

Worth considering if you enjoy climbing mountains and scampering up rocks and don't want to worry about fall damage.

9. TOWER OF STRENGTH

Get 50% less stagger when wearing only heavy armor.
Requires: Heavy Armor 50, Well Fitted

10. CONDITIONING

Heavy armor weighs nothing and doesn't slow you down.
Requires: Heavy Armor 70, Cushioned

Conditioning reduces the weight of heavy armor you're wearing (it doesn't affect the weight of armor in your inventory) and eliminates the speed penalty for wearing it. If that appeals to you but you aren't excited about having to take Fists of Steel and Cushioned to reach this perk, try out the Steed Stone ability (from one of the Standing Stones): it has almost the same effect and won't cost you any perks.

11. MATCHING SET

Additional 25% Armor bonus if wearing a matched set of heavy armor.
Requires: Heavy Armor 70, Tower of Strength

This bonus stacks with Juggernaut and Well Fitted. It's challenging to acquire a complete set of the high-end heavy armor (unless you're specializing in Smithing), so make sure you have a matching set before taking this perk.

12. REFLECT BLOWS

Gain a 10% chance to reflect melee damage back to the enemy while wearing all heavy armor: head, chest, hands, feet.
Requires: Heavy Armor 100, Matching Set

Racial Benefits

+10 Heavy Armor
- Nord

+5 Heavy Armor
- Imperial

Trainers

- **Expert:** Gharol, Dushnikh Yal, in The Reach.
- **Master:** Farkas, the Companions of Jorrvaskr, in Whiterun.
- **Master:** Isran, Fort Dawnguard, in The Rift.
- **Master:** Kuvar, Bujold's Retreat, then Thirsk Mead Hall, in Solstheim.

Other Resources

- For a list of Heavy Armor Skill Books, and where to look for them, consult page 1091.
- You can find a list of Heavy Armor items in the Inventory, beginning on page 140.
- The following quests can also increase this skill:
  - Other Factions Quest: Rjorn's Drum (page 416).
  - Daedric Quest: Discerning the Transmundane (page 384).
  - Favor: The Bandit Slayer* (page 500)
  - Solstheim Side Quest: Filial Bonds (page 621)

COMBAT SKILLS: THE PATH OF MIGHT – BLOCK

Block is the art of deflecting an enemy's blows with your shield or weapon. Your Block skill reduces the damage you take and the amount you stagger when you block an attack. Your skill increases when you successfully block damage (based on the damage of the blow before it was blocked) or when you successfully bash an enemy with a weapon or shield.

Parries with one- or two-handed weapons are also improved by your Block skill and by many Block perks—you don't have to use a shield to benefit from this skill. But remember that if you have a second weapon or spell equipped in your left hand, you can't block at all.

In the Block constellation, the left arc offers shield-specific damage-reduction perks, while the right arc focuses on Bash and Power Bash perks that work with both shield and weapon blocks.

Constellation: Path of Might

Available Perks: 13

Available Block Perks

1–5. SHIELD WALL (5 RANKS)

- **Rank 1:** Blocking is 20% more effective.
  Requires: None
- **Rank 2:** Blocking is 25% more effective.
  Requires: Block 20, Shield Wall 1
- **Rank 3:** Blocking is 30% more effective.
  Requires: Block 40, Shield Wall 2
- **Rank 4:** Blocking is 35% more effective.
  Requires: Block 60, Shield Wall 3
- **Rank 5:** Blocking is 40% more effective.
  Requires: Block 80, Shield Wall 4

6. DEFLECT ARROWS

When you block with a shield, arrows that hit the shield do no damage.

Requires: Block 30, Shield Wall 1

This perk greatly reduces the damage you take while rushing archers, but it's much less effective once you've engaged the enemy, since your shield may not be in the right place at the right time.

7. POWER BASH

Able to do a Power Bash.

Requires: Block 30, Shield Wall 1

This perk unlocks a new Power Bash move that sends enemies flying. This is a great addition to your arsenal, especially if you're employing a weapon-and-shield combat style.

8. QUICK REFLEXES

Time slows down if you are blocking during an enemy's power attack.

Requires: Block 30, Shield Wall 1

Quick Reflexes gives you a chance to react and dodge or (better yet) respond with a bash to counter the attack.

9. DEADLY BASH

Bashing does five times more damage.

Requires: Block 50, Power Bash

While this sounds powerful, bashes don't do much damage to start with. The damage bonus certainly doesn't hurt, but it's still much faster to kill enemies with your weapon than with your shield.

10. ELEMENTAL PROTECTION ★

Blocking with a shield reduces incoming fire, frost, and shock damage by 50%.

Requires: Block 50, Deflect Arrows

This perk is especially powerful when fighting mages. Combine with the Breton's Magic Resistance or the Alteration Magic Resistance perks for almost impenetrable defense, allowing you to shrug off enemy spells with ease!

11. BLOCK RUNNER

Able to move faster with a shield raised.

Requires: Block 70, Elemental Protection

Block Runner helps you close the distance with a ranged mage or archer and allows you to cover more ground when making a Shield Charge.

12. DISARMING BASH ★

Chance to disarm when power bashing.

Requires: Block 70, Deadly Bash

Disarming Bash gives you a chance to knock away an enemy's equipped weapon if he is in the middle of executing a power attack. While many enemies have backup weapons (often daggers), they're significantly less powerful, so you can usually crush a disarmed foe with ease. This is a great perk, at least until you learn the Disarm Shout, which does this more reliably. Consult the Shouts section to find out how to acquire this; you may wish to ignore this perk if the Shout becomes more useful to you.

13. SHIELD CHARGE

Sprinting with a shield raised will knock down most targets.

Requires: Block 100, Block Runner OR Disarming Bash

Shield Charge is great for forcing your way out of a mob of enemies if you get surrounded or buying a few moments to recover in the middle of a difficult battle.

Racial Benefits

+5 Block

- Imperial
- Nord
- Orc
- Redguard

Trainers

- **Expert:** Njada Stonearm, the Companions of Jorrvaskr, in Whiterun.
- **Master:** Chief Larak, Mor Khazgur, in The Reach.

Other Resources

- For a list of Block Skill Books, and where to look for them, consult page 1091.
- You can find a list of Shields and other Block-related items in the Inventory, beginning on page 140.
- The following quests can also increase this skill:
  - Other Factions Quest: Rjorn's Drum (page 416).
  - Daedric Quest: Discerning the Transmundane (page 384).
  - Miscellaneous Objectives: Haafingar Hold (Dragon Bridge): Dragon's Breath Mead* (page 490).
  - Miscellaneous Objectives: The Reach: The Ghost of Old Hroldan* (page 492).
  - Favor: Item Retrieval (Bandit Camp)* (page 500)
  - Favor: Item Retrieval (Cave)* (page 500)
  - Solstheim Side Quest: Filial Bonds (page 621)

The Two-Handed skill governs the use of large weapons such as greatswords, battleaxes, and warhammers. Those trained in this skill deliver more lethal and powerful blows. To improve this skill, damage enemies with a Two-Handed weapon. The skill improves based on the amount of damage you do (minus any enchantments), not the number of swings you take, so you get the same increase regardless of how many hits it takes to fell your foe.

A number of perks in the Two-Handed constellation improve a specific type of Two-Handed weapon. If you generally use the best weapon you can find (no matter what type it is), it's wiser to invest your perks elsewhere: better to have a bonus you can rely on than one you see only occasionally.

Constellation: Path of Might
Available Perks: 19

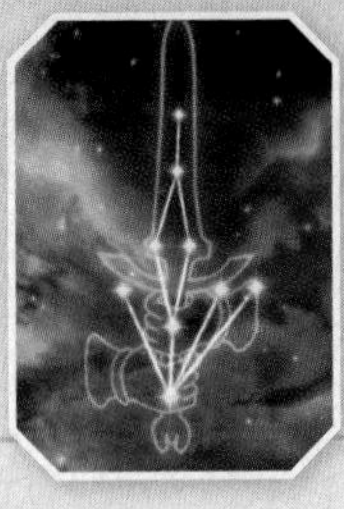

Available Two-Handed Perks

1–5. BARBARIAN (5 RANKS) ★

- **Rank 1:** Two-Handed weapons do 20% more damage.
  Requires: None
- **Rank 2:** Two-Handed weapons do 40% more damage.
  Requires: Two-Handed 20, Barbarian 1
- **Rank 3:** Two-Handed weapons do 60% more damage.
  Requires: Two-Handed 40, Barbarian 2
- **Rank 4:** Two-Handed weapons do 80% more damage.
  Requires: Two-Handed 60, Barbarian 3
- **Rank 5:** Two-Handed weapons do twice as much damage.
  Requires: Two-Handed 80, Barbarian 4

This perk provides a massive +20% bonus to your Two-Handed weapon damage with each rank. This is a huge boost; make this perk your top priority whenever your skill level permits.

6. CHAMPION'S STANCE ★

Power attacks with Two-Handed weapons cost 25% less stamina.
Requires: Two-Handed 20, Barbarian 1

In effect, this perk allows you to power attack more often. Two-Handed weapons excel at devastating power attacks, so this is a solid choice.

7–9. DEEP WOUNDS (3 RANKS)

- **Rank 1:** Attacks with greatswords have a 10% chance of doing critical damage.
  Requires: Two-Handed 30, Barbarian 1
- **Rank 2:** Attacks with greatswords have a 15% chance of doing even more critical damage.
  Requires: Two-Handed 60, Deep Wounds 1
- **Rank 3:** Attacks with greatswords have a 20% chance of doing even more critical damage.
  Requires: Two-Handed 90, Deep Wounds 2

When a weapon scores a critical hit, it deals 50% more damage, more for Ranks 2 and 3. Statistically, this perk works out to a 5% boost in your average damage over time at Rank 1 and a 15% boost by Rank 3. That's not nothing, but Barbarian is still better.

10–12. LIMBSPLITTER (3 RANKS)

- **Rank 1:** Attacks with battleaxes cause extra bleeding damage.
  Requires: Two-Handed 30
- **Rank 2:** Attacks with battleaxes cause more bleeding damage.
  Requires: Two-Handed 60, Limbsplitter 1
- **Rank 3:** Attacks with battleaxes cause even more bleeding damage.
  Requires: Two-Handed 90, Limbsplitter 2

The exact amount of bleeding damage depends on the axe, but in general, this perk causes each hit to do 1 to 3 points of damage each second for 3 to 6 seconds, with the higher ranks pushing higher into that range, making this roughly equivalent to a short-lived lingering poison.

13–15. SKULLCRUSHER (3 RANKS)

- **Rank 1:** Attacks with warhammers ignore 25% of armor.
  Requires: Two-Handed 30
- **Rank 2:** Attacks with warhammers ignore 50% of armor.
  Requires: Two-Handed 60, Skullcrusher 1
- **Rank 3:** Attacks with warhammers ignore 75% of armor.
  Requires: Two-Handed 90, Skullcrusher 2

This perk has no effect against unarmored enemies, but it can make it significantly easier to take down a heavily armored foe, such as many bosses.

16. DEVASTATING BLOW

Standing power attacks do 25% bonus damage with a chance to decapitate your enemies.
Requires: Two-Handed 50, Champion's Stance

This is a strong, reliable damage bonus. The decapitation adds a grotesquely satisfying visual touch but applies only if your attack already killed the enemy (this perk doesn't give you a chance of an instant kill).

17. GREAT CRITICAL CHARGE

You can do a Two-Handed power attack while sprinting that does double critical damage.
Requires: Two-Handed 50, Champion's Stance

Less powerful than it might appear, the "double critical damage" bonus applies only if you land a critical hit in the first place. More importantly, you have to remember to use it for it to be effective. Take this if you find yourself making "berserker rushes" on your own.

18. SWEEP

Sideways power attacks with Two-Handed weapons hit all targets in front of you.
Requires: Two-Handed 70, Devastating Blow OR Great Critical Charge

Great at clearing out swaths of enemies in a single blow.

19. WARMASTER

Backward power attacks have a 25% chance to paralyze the target.
Requires: Two-Handed 100, Sweep

Racial Benefits

+10 Two-Handed
- Nord

+5 Two-Handed
- Orc

Trainers

- **Expert:** Torbjorn Shatter-Shield, Candlehearth Hall and the streets of Windhelm.
- **Master:** Fura Bloodmouth, Castle Volkihar, in Haafingar Hold (Sea of Ghosts).
- **Master:** Vilkas, the Companions of Jorrvaskr, in Whiterun.
- **Master:** Wulf Wild-Blood, of Skaal Village, in Solstheim.

Other Resources

- For a list of Two-Handed Skill Books, and where to look for them, consult page 1091.
- You can find a list of Two-Handed items in the Inventory, beginning on page 136.
- The following quests can also increase this skill:
  - Other Factions Quest: Rjorn's Drum (page 416).
  - Daedric Quest: Discerning the Transmundane (page 384).
  - Favor: A Good Talking To* (page 499).

The One-Handed skill governs the use of weapons like the sword, war axe, mace, and dagger. Those trained in this skill deliver more deadly blows. To improve this skill, you must damage enemies with a One-Handed weapon. The skill improves based on the amount of damage you do (minus any enchantments), not the number of swings you take; therefore, while it might take 10 hits to kill a bandit with a dagger, you would get the same skill increase for killing him in three hits with a mace.

A number of perks in the One-Handed constellation improve a specific type of One-Handed weapon. If you generally use the best weapon you can find (no matter what type it is), it's wiser to invest your perks elsewhere: better to have a bonus you can rely on than one you see only occasionally.

Constellation: Path of Might

Available Perks: 21

Available One-Handed Perks

1–5. ARMSMAN (5 RANKS) ★

- **Rank 1:** One-Handed weapons do 20% more damage.
  Requires: None
- **Rank 2:** One-Handed weapons do 40% more damage.
  Requires: One-Handed 20, Armsman 1
- **Rank 3:** One-Handed weapons do 60% more damage.
  Requires: One-Handed 40, Armsman 2
- **Rank 4:** One-Handed weapons do 80% more damage.
  Requires: One-Handed 60, Armsman 3
- **Rank 5:** One-Handed weapons do twice as much damage.
  Requires: One-Handed 80, Armsman 4

This perk provides a massive +20% bonus to your One-Handed weapon damage with each rank. This is a huge boost; make this perk your top priority whenever your skill level permits.

6. FIGHTING STANCE ★

Power attacks with One-Handed weapons cost 25% less stamina.

Requires: One-Handed 20, Armsman 1

By conserving your stamina, this perk allows you to power attack or bash more often. A solid choice, especially if you dual-wield One-Handed weapons, as this bonus works well with the Dual Flurry and Dual Savagery perks.

7–9. BLADESMAN (3 RANKS)

- **Rank 1:** Attacks with swords have a 10% chance of doing critical damage.
  Requires: One-Handed 30, Armsman 1
- **Rank 2:** Attacks with swords have a 15% chance of doing more critical damage.
  Requires: One-Handed 60, Bladesman 1
- **Rank 3:** Attacks with swords have a 20% chance of doing even more critical damage.
  Requires: One-Handed 90, Bladesman 2

When a weapon scores a critical hit, it deals 50% more damage—more for ranks 2 and 3. Statistically, this perk works out to a 5% boost in your average damage over time at Rank 1 and a 15% boost by Rank 3. That's not insignificant, but Armsman is still better.

10–12. BONE BREAKER (3 RANKS)

- **Rank 1:** Attacks with maces ignore 25% of armor.
  Requires: One-Handed 30, Armsman 1
- **Rank 2:** Attacks with maces ignore 50% of armor.
  Requires: One-Handed 60, Bone Breaker 1
- **Rank 3:** Attacks with maces ignore 75% of armor.
  Requires: One-Handed 90, Bone Breaker 2

This perk has no effect against unarmored enemies, but it can make it significantly easier to take down a heavily armored foe, such as many bosses.

13–15. HACK AND SLASH (3 RANKS)

- **Rank 1:** Attacks with war axes cause extra bleeding damage.
  Requires: One-Handed 30, Armsman 1
- **Rank 2:** Attacks with war axes cause more bleeding damage.
  Requires: One-Handed 60, Hack and Slash 1
- **Rank 3:** Attacks with war axes cause even more bleeding damage.
  Requires: One-Handed 90, Hack and Slash 2

The exact amount of bleeding damage depends on the axe, but in general, this perk causes each hit to do 1 to 3 points of damage each second for 3 to 6 seconds, with the higher ranks pushing farther into that range. This is roughly equivalent to a short-lived lingering poison.

16–17. DUAL FLURRY (2 RANKS)

- **Rank 1:** Dual-wielding attacks are 20% faster.
  Requires: One-Handed 30, Armsman 1
- **Rank 2:** Dual-wielding attacks are 35% faster.
  Requires: One-Handed 50, Dual Flurry 1

18. CRITICAL CHARGE

Can do a One-Handed power attack while sprinting that does double critical damage.

Requires: One-Handed 50, Fighting Stance

This perk still requires that you land a critical hit in the first place in order to receive the damage bonus. Worth taking if you find yourself making berserker rushes on your own, if you've taken the Bladesman perks, or if you're dual-wielding (since you've got a better chance of getting a critical hit with at least one weapon).

19. SAVAGE STRIKE

Standing power attacks do 25% bonus damage with a chance to decapitate your enemies.

Requires: One-Handed 50, Fighting Stance

This is a strong, reliable damage bonus, though the decapitation only applies if you've already killed the enemy. But standing over the headless corpse of your kill is a satisfying way to temper your bloodlust!

20. DUAL SAVAGERY ★

Duel-wielding power attacks do 50% more damage.

Requires: One-Handed 70, Dual Flurry 1

A great pick if you're focused on dual wielding; this is stronger than Savage Strike or Critical Charge and stacks with both of them, making your power attacks incredibly deadly.

21. PARALYZING STRIKE

Your backward power attack has a 25% chance to paralyze the target.

Requires: One-Handed 100, Savage Strike OR Critical Charge

Paralyzing Strike is a powerful ability...if you remember to use it. When it works, you can inflict massive damage and often kill your foes outright, before they can get back on their feet. But how often do you use backward power attacks?

Racial Benefits

+10 One-Handed
- Redguard

+5 One-Handed
- Imperial
- Khajiit
- Nord
- Orc

Trainers

- **Journeyman:** Amren, in his house or the streets of Whiterun.
- **Expert:** Athis, the Companions of Jorrvaskr, in Whiterun.
- **Master:** Chief Burguk, Dushnikh Yal, in The Reach.

Other Resources

- For a list of One-Handed Skill Books, and where to look for them, consult page 1091.
- You can find a list of One-Handed items in the Inventory, beginning on page 136.
- The following quests can also increase this skill:
  - Other Factions Quest: Rjorn's Drum (page 416).
  - Daedric Quest: Discerning the Transmundane (page 384).
  - Miscellaneous Objectives: The Reach: The Ghost of Old Hroldan* (page 492).
  - Favor: Item Retrieval (Bandit Camp)* (page 500)
  - Solstheim Side Quest: Filial Bonds (page 621)

Archery represents the skill and training needed to wield a bow effectively in combat. The greater your skill, the more deadly your shots. Your Archery skill improves when you damage enemies with a bow and arrows. The amount of increase is based on the damage that you do (minus any enchantments). Of course, only shots that hit their mark will count.

Constellation: Path of Might
Available Perks: 16

Available Archery Perks

1–5. OVERDRAW (5 RANKS) ★

- **Rank 1:** Bows do 20% more damage.
  Requires: None
- **Rank 2:** Bows do 40% more damage.
  Requires: Archery 20, Overdraw 1
- **Rank 3:** Bows do 60% more damage.
  Requires: Archery 40, Overdraw 2
- **Rank 4:** Bows do 80% more damage.
  Requires: Archery 60, Overdraw 3
- **Rank 5:** Bows do twice as much damage.
  Requires: Archery 80, Overdraw 4

This perk provides a massive +20% bonus to your bow damage with each rank. This is a huge boost; make this perk your top priority whenever your skill level permits.

6–8. CRITICAL SHOT (3 RANKS)

- **Rank 1:** 10% chance of a critical hit that does extra damage.
  Requires: Archery 30, Overdraw 1
- **Rank 2:** 15% chance of a critical hit that does 25% more critical damage.
  Requires: Archery 60, Critical Shot 1
- **Rank 3:** 20% chance of a critical hit that does 50% more critical damage.
  Requires: Archery 90, Critical Shot 2

When a weapon scores a critical hit, it deals 50% more damage. Statistically, this perk works out to a 5% boost in your average damage over time at Rank 1 and a 15% boost by Rank 3. That's not insignificant, but Overdraw is still better.

9. EAGLE EYE ★

Pressing Block while aiming will zoom in your view.
Requires: Archery 30, Overdraw 1

This perk allows you to snipe enemies more accurately from a greater distance. This is a great choice for stealth archers: Since you may get only one shot, make it count!

10–11. STEADY HAND (2 RANKS)

- **Rank 1:** Zooming in with a bow slows time by 25%.
  Requires: Archery 40, Eagle Eye
- **Rank 2:** Zooming in with a bow slows time by 50%.
  Requires: Archery 60, Steady Hand 1

This perk is useful for minimizing the chance that your target will move while you line up a stealth shot or for making sure an important shot hits its mark. It's especially effective against dragons in the air; you'll still have to lead your shot a little (i.e., aim at where you think the creature will be when the arrow arrives, not where it is when you fire), but this improves your odds of hitting them significantly.

12. HUNTER'S DISCIPLINE

Recover twice as many arrows from dead bodies.
Requires: Archery 50, Critical Shot 1

A fine choice if you find yourself running out of arrows frequently or use a lot of high-end arrows. If you mainly use basic iron or steel arrows, take something else; they're so cheap and so common that recovering more of them just isn't worth the perk.

13. POWER SHOT ★

Arrows stagger all but the largest opponents 50% of the time.
Requires: Archery 50, Eagle Eye

Power Shot is surprisingly strong: In the time it takes an enemy to stagger and recover, you may be able to fire off another shot or two. The stagger will also interrupt an enemy's charge or block, briefly giving you a clear opening. Or when all else fails, take that second or two to put some space between you and your opponent.

14. RANGER

Able to move faster with a drawn bow.
Requires: Archery 60, Hunter's Discipline

15. QUICK SHOT

Can draw a bow 30% faster.
Requires: Archery 70, Power Shot

16. BULLSEYE

You have a 15% chance of paralyzing the target for 10 seconds.
Requires: Archery 100, Quick Shot OR Ranger

Bullseye gives you a chance to paralyze opponents with each shot. This is fantastic at medium and short ranges, where it can take an enemy out of a fight and allows you to finish them off quickly. It's somewhat less effective at long range, since enemies fall over when paralyzed, making it more difficult (or impossible) to hit them again from that distance.

Racial Benefits

+10 Archery
- Wood Elf

+5 Archery
- Khajiit
- Redguard

Trainers

- **Journeyman:** Faendal, of Riverwood, in Whiterun Hold.
- **Expert:** Aela the Huntress, the Companions of Jorrvaskr, in Whiterun.
- **Master:** Niruin, the Thieves Guild, The Ragged Flagon, in Riften.
- **Master:** Sorine Jurard, in Fort Dawnguard, The Rift.

Other Resources

- For a list of Archery Skill Books, and where to look for them, consult page 1091.
- You can find a list of Bows, Arrows, and other items in the Inventory, beginning on page 136.
- The following quests can also increase this skill:
  - Other Factions Quest: Rjorn's Drum (page 416).
  - Daedric Quest: Discerning the Transmundane (page 384).
  - Dungeon Quest: Angi's Camp: Composure, Speed, and Precision* (page 475).
  - Solstheim Side Quest: Filial Bonds (page 621)

Light Armor allows you to make more effective use of hide, leather, Elven, glass, Dragonscale, and related armors. Light Armor offers a good balance between weight, protection, and mobility and is recommended for stealthy characters or those with other forms of protection (such as a good shield or the occasional ward) to supplement their defenses.

Your Light Armor skill increases when you take damage while wearing light armor, based on the damage of the incoming blow. If you're wearing more than one kind of armor, the incoming damage is divided up among the pieces before being used to calculate skill uses, so wearing more light armor will allow this skill to develop faster.

Constellation: Path of Shadow
Available Perks: 10

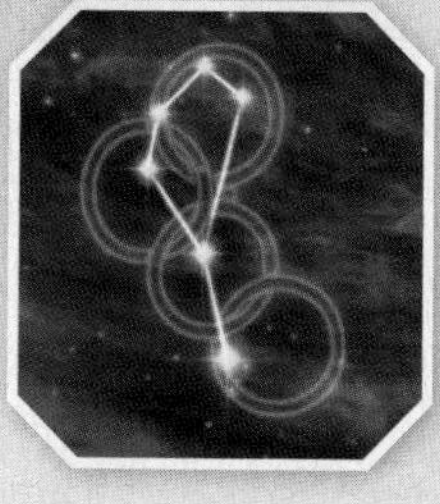

Available Light Armor Perks

1–5. AGILE DEFENDER (5 RANKS) ★

- **Rank 1:** Increase armor rating for Light Armor by 20%.
  Requires: None
- **Rank 2:** Increases the armor rating of your light armor by 40%.
  Requires: Light Armor 20, Agile Defender 1
- **Rank 3:** Increases the armor rating of your light armor by 60%.
  Requires: Light Armor 40, Agile Defender 2
- **Rank 4:** Increases the armor rating of your light armor by 80%.
  Requires: Light Armor 60, Agile Defender 3
- **Rank 5:** Increases the armor rating of your light armor by 100%.
  Requires: Light Armor 80, Agile Defender 4

6. CUSTOM FIT ★

You get a 25% armor bonus if wearing all light armor: head, chest, hands, feet.
Requires: Light Armor 30, Agile Defender 1

This bonus stacks with Agile Defender and Matching Set—a must-have for anyone serious about using light armor.

7. UNHINDERED

Light armor weighs nothing and doesn't slow you down when worn.
Requires: Light Armor 50, Custom Fit

This perk reduces the weight of the light armor you're wearing (it doesn't affect the weight of armor in your inventory) and eliminates its movement penalty. If you're not sure whether this perk is for you, try out the Steed Stone ability (from one of the Standing Stones) first: it has almost the same effect and won't cost you a perk.

8. WIND WALKER

Stamina regenerates 50% faster in all light armor: head, chest, hands, feet.
Requires: Light Armor 60, Unhindered

9. MATCHING SET

Additional 25% armor bonus if wearing a matched set of light armor.
Requires: Light Armor 70, Custom Fit

This bonus stacks with Agile Defender and Custom Fit. Make sure you have a matching set before taking this perk, though.

10. DEFT MOVEMENT

You have a 10% chance of avoiding all damage from a melee attack while wearing all light armor: head, chest, hands, feet.
Requires: Light Armor 100, Wind Walker OR Matching Set

This perk gives you a 10% chance of avoiding all damage from a hit when wearing a full set of light armor. It's a noticeable but unreliable bonus: if you're lucky, it might spare you from a lethal blow.

Racial Benefits

+5 Light Armor

- Argonian
- Dark Elf
- Nord
- Wood Elf

Trainers

- **Journeyman:** Scouts-Many-Marshes, the docks of Windhelm.
- **Expert:** Grelka, the marketplace or streets of Riften.
- **Master:** Nazir, Assassin of the Dark Brotherhood, Falkreath Hold Sanctuary.

Other Resources

- For a list of Light Armor Skill Books, and where to look for them, consult page 1091.
- You can find a list of Light Armor items in the Inventory, beginning on page 140.
- The following quests can also increase this skill:
  - Other Factions Quest: Finn's Lute (page 415).
  - Daedric Quest: Discerning the Transmundane (page 384).
  - Favor: The Bandit Slayer* (page 500)
  - Favor: Item Retrieval (Bandit Camp)* (page 500)

STEALTH SKILLS: THE PATH OF SHADOW – SNEAK

Sneak is the art of moving unseen and unheard. This skill improves when you sneak past someone or perform a successful sneak attack. You don't get credit for sneaking in an empty hallway or for just standing around—you must be sneaking (crouched) near someone who can detect you. Avoiding detection is also critical: the moment you are spotted, your sneak attempt has failed and you can no longer perform a sneak attack (until you hide again).

Constellation: Path of Shadow
Available Perks: 13

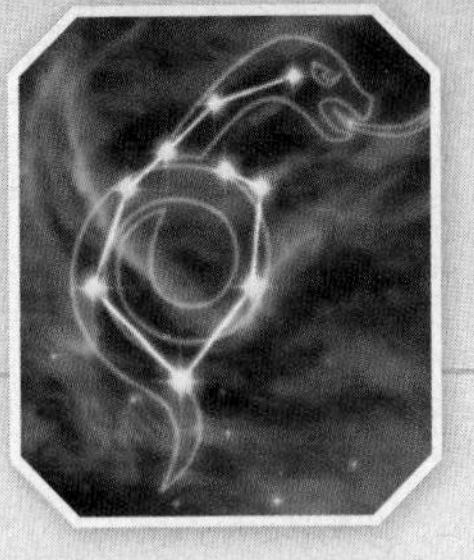

Available Sneak Perks

1–5. STEALTH (5 RANKS) ★

- **Rank 1:** You are 20% harder to detect when sneaking.
  Requires: None
- **Rank 2:** You are 25% harder to detect when sneaking.
  Requires: Sneak 20, Stealth 1
- **Rank 3:** You are 30% harder to detect when sneaking.
  Requires: Sneak 40, Stealth 2
- **Rank 4:** You are 35% harder to detect when sneaking.
  Requires: Sneak 60, Stealth 3
- **Rank 5:** You are 40% harder to detect when sneaking.
  Requires: Sneak 80, Stealth 4

This perk makes it dramatically easier to sneak past enemies unnoticed. The first rank in this skill (+20%) is absolutely critical to being able to sneak effectively. Subsequent ranks have diminishing returns but are still a good choice if you're focused on stealth and find yourself being detected too quickly. Even if Stealth isn't your focus, it's worth taking the basic Stealth perk just in case you someday need to sneak out of a dangerous situation.

6. BACKSTAB

Sneak attacks with one-handed weapons now do six times damage.
Requires: Sneak 30, Stealth 1

Backstab doubles your sneak attack damage (to 6x normal). If you're skilled enough to reliably sneak up behind enemies, this can make one-hit kills a real possibility, especially on weaker foes.

7. MUFFLED MOVEMENT

Noise from armor is reduced by 50%.
Requires: Sneak 30, Stealth 1

This perk is good at low levels but is much less useful later on, when it's eclipsed by Silence, Muffle-enchanted equipment, or the Muffle spell (Illusion skill), all of which silence your movement entirely.

8. DEADLY AIM ★

Sneak attacks with bows now do three times damage.
Requires: Sneak 40, Backstab

Deadly Aim increases the sneak attack damage done by bows (from 2x to 3x). The extra damage is noticeable, though not as dramatic as Backstab's bonus.

9. LIGHT FOOT

You won't trigger pressure plates.
Requires: Sneak 40, Muffled Movement

This perk presents an interesting dilemma. While you'll no longer have to worry about almost half the traps you encounter, your enemies and your Followers can still set them off, which generally gives you less warning than you might otherwise have had. Also, you can no longer deliberately use traps to kill enemies, which limits your options and takes some of the fun out of them. So think carefully before taking this perk, or just be cautious and avoid pressure plates in the first place.

10. ASSASSIN'S BLADE

Sneak attacks with daggers now do a total of 15 times normal damage.
Requires: Sneak 50, Deadly Aim

This perk affects only daggers, but it does make them significantly more effective at sneak attacks. With this perk, daggers do about twice the sneak attack damage of a full-sized weapon like a sword or a mace. That's a solid improvement and a good reason to choose daggers, at least for your first blow.

11. SILENT ROLL

Sprinting while sneaking executes a silent forward roll.
Requires: Sneak 50, Light Foot

Silent Roll allows you to quickly dodge behind cover while sneaking, although the drain on your Stamina prevents you from using it to roll long distances.

12. SILENCE

Walking and running does not affect detection.
Requires: Sneak 70, Silent Roll

This perk gives you a permanent Muffle effect. However, since you can receive the same effect from a spell or piece of enchanted armor, consider whether it's really worth spending one of your perk selections on.

13. SHADOW WARRIOR

Crouching stops combat for a moment and forces distant opponents to search for a target.
Requires: Sneak 100, Silence

Shadow Warrior can give you a chance to recover or make a hasty getaway if your stealth attempt goes terribly wrong. It's most effective if you can put some distance between yourself and your foes; if you use it right in front of an enemy, they'll spot you again almost immediately.

Racial Benefits

+10 Sneak
- Khajiit

+5 Sneak
- Argonian
- Dark Elf
- Wood Elf

Trainers

- **Journeyman:** Khayla, Ri'saad's Khajiit Caravans, outside Markarth or Whiterun.
- **Expert:** Garvey, the Warrens of Markarth.
- **Master:** Delvin Mallory, the Thieves Guild, The Ragged Flagon, in Riften.

Other Resources

- For a list of Sneak Skill Books, and where to look for them, consult page 1091.
- You can find a list of Sneak-related items throughout the Inventory, beginning on page 131.
- The following quests can also increase this skill:
  - Other Factions Quest: Finn's Lute (page 415).
  - Daedric Quest: Discerning the Transmundane (page 384).
  - Favor: The A Little Light Thievery* (page 499).
  - Favor: Item Retrieval (Cave)* (page 500).

Lockpicking allows you to open locked doors and containers faster, more easily, and with fewer broken lockpicks. This skill increases when you pick the lock on a door, container, or trap trigger hinge, based on the lock's difficulty. It also increases slightly if you break a pick, so if you try picking a difficult lock and fail, it isn't a total loss.

The Novice, Apprentice, Adept, Expert, and Master Locks perks decrease the difficulty of picking locks of the corresponding level. This helps save on lockpicks (and frustration), but depending on your Lockpicking skill and your own personal prowess at lockpicking, you may not find them necessary.

Note that the fabled Skeleton Key gives you the high-end Unbreakable perk while you possess it, though you must surrender the Skeleton Key as a part of the Thieves Guild questline. While you have it, take the opportunity to unlock any Expert or Master locks you wish and quickly level your Lockpicking skill.

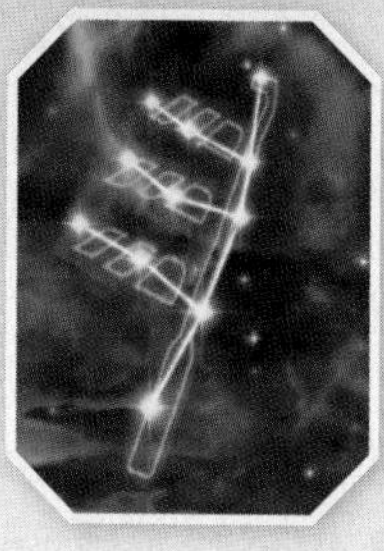

Constellation: Path of Shadow

Available Perks: 11

Available Lockpicking Perks

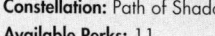

1. NOVICE LOCKS

Novice locks are much easier to pick.

Requires: None

2. APPRENTICE LOCKS

Apprentice locks are much easier to pick.

Requires: Lockpicking 25, Novice Locks

3. QUICK HANDS

Able to pick locks without being noticed.

Requires: Lockpicking 40, Apprentice Locks

Quick Hands allows you to pick locks without a crime being detected. This is sometimes useful for breaking into homes and containers without attracting too much attention, although trespass and theft will still be noticed.

4. WAX KEY

Automatically gives you a copy of a picked lock's key if it has one.

Requires: Lockpicking 50, Quick Hands

In essence, this perk allows you to automatically reopen most doors you've picked in the past. This may be useful if you find a couple of wealthy houses you can rob repeatedly (after their treasures have been replaced), or if you find yourself back in a dungeon you've been to before.

5. ADEPT LOCKS

Adept locks are much easier to pick.

Requires: Lockpicking 50, Apprentice Locks

6. GOLDEN TOUCH ★

Find more gold in chests.

Requires: Lockpicking 60, Adept Locks

Golden Touch adds a fair amount of gold to most chests (up to +100 gold pieces per chest). This stacks with the Imperial Luck racial ability, though it's significantly better.

7. TREASURE HUNTER ★

You have a 50% greater chance of finding special treasure.

Requires: Lockpicking 70, Golden Touch

This perk significantly increases your chance of finding special loot in some chests, especially large ones. What kind of loot? It could be anything, from an Iron Sword to a Dragonplate Cuirass. This is always a gamble, but it occasionally gives you something that's far better than anything you can get through any normal means. Are you feeling lucky?

8. EXPERT LOCKS

Expert locks are much easier to pick.

Requires: Lockpicking 75, Adept Locks

9. LOCKSMITH

Pick starts close to the lock opening position.

Requires: Lockpicking 80, Expert Locks

10. UNBREAKABLE

Lockpicks never break.

Requires: Lockpicking 100, Locksmith

With this perk and enough patience, you can eventually pick the lock on any chest with a single pick. Take this, and you won't need the Master Locks perk.

11. MASTER LOCKS

Master Locks are much easier to pick.

Requires: Lockpicking 100, Expert Locks

Racial Benefits

+10 Lockpicking

- Argonian

+5 Lockpicking

- Khajiit
- Wood Elf

Trainers

- **Expert:** Ma'jhad, of Ma'dran's Khajiit Caravans, outside Solitude or Windhelm.
- **Master:** Vex, the Thieves Guild, The Ragged Flagon, in Riften.

Other Resources

- For a list of Lockpicking Skill Books, and where to look for them, consult page 1091.
- You can find a list of the few available Lockpicking items, check the Inventory, beginning on page 131.
- The following quests can also increase this skill:
  - Other Factions Quest: Finn's Lute (page 415).
  - Daedric Quest: Discerning the Transmundane (page 384).
  - Favor: Item Retrieval (Bandit Camp)* (page 500).

STEALTH SKILLS: THE PATH OF SHADOW – PICKPOCKET

Pickpocket is the stealthy art of lifting gold and other valuables from an unsuspecting target. This skill increases whenever you successfully steal an item, based on the item's value. Fail to pickpocket something, and you don't receive credit for the attempt. Of course, that's probably the least of your worries at that point!

The highest-level Pickpocket perks, Misdirection and Perfect Touch, allow you to steal equipped weapons and armor off of a creature. This is an excellent trick for a stealthy assassin, as there are few more satisfying ways to take down a difficult foe than by stripping them down to their underwear before stabbing them in the back...

Constellation: Path of Shadow

Available Perks: 12

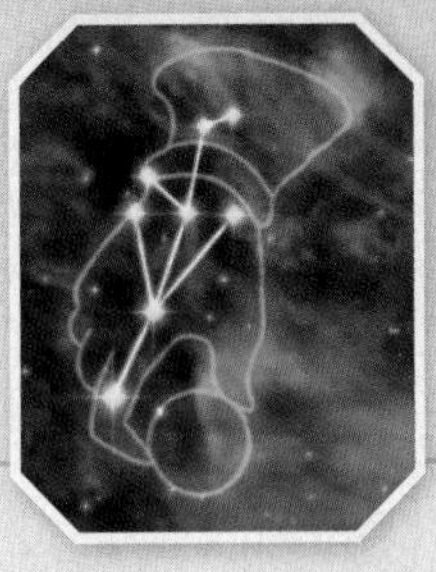

Available Pickpocket Perks

1–5. LIGHT FINGERS (5 RANKS)

- **Rank 1:** Pickpocketing bonus of 20%. Item weight and value reduce pickpocketing odds.
  Requires: None
- **Rank 2:** Pickpocketing bonus of 40%. Item weight and value reduce pickpocketing odds.
  Requires: Pickpocket 20, Light Fingers 1
- **Rank 3:** Pickpocketing bonus of 60%. Item weight and value reduce pickpocketing odds.
  Requires: Pickpocket 40, Light Fingers 2
- **Rank 4:** Pickpocketing bonus of 80%. Item weight and value reduce pickpocketing odds.
  Requires: Pickpocket 60, Light Fingers 3
- **Rank 5:** Pickpocketing bonus of 100%. Item weight and value reduce pickpocketing odds.
  Requires: Pickpocket 80, Light Fingers 4

6. NIGHT THIEF

You have a +25% chance to pickpocket if the target is asleep.
Requires: Pickpocket 20

Night Thief makes pickpocketing a sleeping character much easier. Find out where your target sleeps, hide nearby, wait for nightfall, and then rob them at your leisure. Stacks with Light Fingers.

7. CUTPURSE

Pickpocketing gold is 50% easier.
Requires: Pickpocket 40, Night Thief

8. POISONED

Silently harm enemies by placing poison in their pockets.
Requires: Pickpocket 40, Night Thief

This is a good way to sap an enemy's strength and can kill many civilians outright. This is a great tactic for some Dark Brotherhood assassinations.

9. EXTRA POCKETS ★

Carrying capacity is increased by 100 points.
Requires: Pickpocket 50, Night Thief

Increases your Max Carry weight by 100. This great for any character, especially if you've been neglecting your stamina when leveling up.

10. KEYMASTER

Pickpocketing keys always works.
Requires: Pickpocket 60, Cutpurse

Gold and items are great, but keys can be even better once you have access to a good Fence. Go rob a well-to-do character's house while they're out, and the haul will often be worth far more than what they were carrying. If you need someone to fence your stolen goods, join the Thieves Guild or take the Speech skill's Fence perk.

11. MISDIRECTION

Can pickpocket equipped weapons.
Requires: Pickpocket 70, Cutpurse

12. PERFECT TOUCH

Can pickpocket equipped items.
Requires: Pickpocket 100, Misdirection

Racial Benefits

+5 Pickpocket

- Argonian
- Khajiit
- Wood Elf

Trainers

- **Journeyman:** Ahkari, of Zaynabi's Khajiit Caravans, outside Dawnstar or Riften.
- **Expert:** Silda the Unseen, begging on the streets of Windhelm.
- **Master:** Vipir the Fleet, the Thieves Guild, The Ragged Flagon, in Riften.

Other Resources

- For a list of Pickpocket Skill Books, and where to look for them, consult page 1091.
- You can find Pickpocket-related items throughout the Inventory, beginning on page 131.
- The following quests can also increase this skill:
  - Other Factions Quest: Finn's Lute (page 415).
  - Daedric Quest: Discerning the Transmundane (page 384).

STEALTH SKILLS: THE PATH OF SHADOW – SPEECH

Speech allows you to haggle, bribe, persuade, and intimidate others to do as you ask. The higher your Speech skill, the better the prices you get when buying or selling items, and the greater your odds of success at dialogue challenges. Your Speech skill doesn't require any special effort to raise: It increases naturally when you sell items to a merchant (based on the item's value) or when you succeed at a Persuade or Intimidate challenge (based on its difficulty).

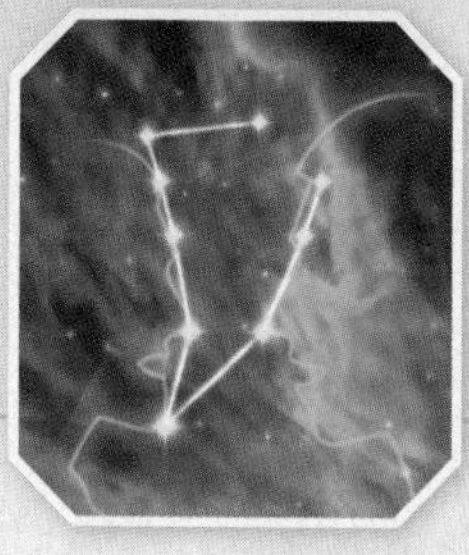

Constellation: Path of Shadow
Available Perks: 13

Available Speech Perks

1–5. HAGGLING (5 RANKS) ★

- **Rank 1:** Buying and selling prices are 10% better.
  Requires: None
- **Rank 2:** Buying and selling prices are 15% better.
  Requires: Speech 20, Haggling 1
- **Rank 3:** Buying and selling prices are 20% better.
  Requires: Speech 40, Haggling 2
- **Rank 4:** Buying and selling prices are 25% better.
  Requires: Speech 60, Haggling 3
- **Rank 5:** Buying and selling prices are 30% better.
  Requires: Speech 80, Haggling 4

Haggling significantly improves the prices you get in shops, though with diminishing returns after the first rank. Even if you don't plan to focus on Speech, it's worth picking up the first rank of this perk.

6. ALLURE

You have 10% better prices with the opposite sex.
Requires: Speech 30, Haggling 1

Allure allows you to get slightly better prices from some merchants. While this can add up over time, make sure to take advantage of it by finding merchants of the correct gender. Stacks with Haggling.

7. BRIBERY

Can bribe guards to ignore crimes.
Requires: Speech 30, Haggling 1

This perk allows you to bribe guards to overlook nonviolent crimes. The crime doesn't go away; guards just don't arrest you right now. If you're already a member of the Thieves Guild, you can do this for free, so there's no need to spend a perk on it. This is also unimportant if you're a law-abiding citizen of Skyrim.

8. MERCHANT ★

Can sell any type of item to any kind of merchant.
Requires: Speech 50, Allure

The Merchant perk makes the process of selling your loot significantly faster, since you no longer need to visit multiple vendors to sell everything.

9. PERSUASION

Persuasion attempts are 30% easier.
Requires: Speech 50, Bribery

This perk increases your effective Speech score for the purpose of Persuade challenges. This is rarely necessary, although it can help if you find yourself struggling with them.

10. INTIMIDATION

Intimidation is twice as successful.
Requires: Speech 70, Persuasion

Like Persuasion, this perk increases your effective Speech score for the purpose of Intimidate challenges. Also like Persuasion, it's rarely necessary, and there's no real reason to take both this and Persuasion, unless you have a strong role-playing preference.

11. INVESTOR

Can invest 500 gold with a shopkeeper to increase his available gold permanently.
Requires: Speech 70, Merchant

Permanently increases the amount of gold that merchants have to trade with you. Coupled with the Merchant perk, this makes it even easier to sell your loot to just one convenient merchant, reducing your downtime between quests.

12. FENCE

Can barter stolen goods with any merchant in whom you have invested.
Requires: Speech 90, Investor

If you're already a member of the Thieves Guild, you may not need another Fence, although this will make it more convenient to sell stolen items, as it increases the number of Fences to which you have access.

13. MASTER TRADER

Every merchant in the world gains 1,000 gold for bartering.
Requires: Speech 100, Fence

Racial Benefits

+5 Speech

- Breton
- Nord

Trainers

- **Journeyman:** Dro'marash, of Ahkari's Khajiit Caravans, outside Dawnstar or Riften.
- **Journeyman:** Revyn Sadri, of Sadri's Used Wares, in Windhelm.
- **Journeyman:** Ronthil, the vampire merchant in Castle Volkihar (Sea of Ghosts).
- **Expert:** Ogmund, bard of the Silver-Blood Inn, in Markarth.
- **Master:** Giraud Gemane, of the Bard's College in Solitude.

Other Resources

- For a list of Speech Skill Books, and where to look for them, consult page 1091.
- You can find Speech-related items throughout the Inventory, beginning on page 131.
- The following quests can also increase this skill:
  - Other Factions Quest: Finn's Lute (page 415).
  - Daedric Quest: Discerning the Transmundane (page 384).
  - Dungeon Quest: Bard's Leap Summit: Leap Before You Look* (page 475).
  - Favor: A Little Light Thievery* (page 499).
  - Favor: Rare Item Hunt (page 500).

MAGIC SKILLS: THE PATH OF MAGIC – RESTORATION

Restoration spells shape life energy, allowing you to heal yourself and your companions, drive back the undead, and create protective wards. Your Restoration skill increases when you use these spells effectively: to heal damage, turn undead, or shield yourself in combat. It does not increase if you heal someone who is already at full health or if you cast a Turn Undead spell when no undead are around.

Constellation: Path of Magic
Available Perks: 13

Available Restoration Perks

1. NOVICE RESTORATION ★

Cast Novice-level Restoration spells for half Magicka.

Requires: None

2. REGENERATION ★

Healing spells cure 50% more.

Requires: Restoration 20, Novice Restoration

Regeneration makes all healing spells more effective. It has a low skill requirement and is definitely worth taking early, when the concentration spell Healing may be your only restorative spell. Those few extra points of health a second can make all the difference during a particularly dangerous battle.

3. RESTORATION DUAL CASTING

Dual casting a Restoration spell overcharges the effects into an even more powerful version.

Requires: Restoration 20, Novice Restoration

Dual Casting doubles the effectiveness of some Restoration spells (Healing, Wards) and the duration of others (Turn Undead). But except in the most dire of circumstances, you're far more likely to want a weapon in your other hand than a second Restoration spell.

4. APPRENTICE RESTORATION ★

Cast Apprentice-level Restoration spells for half Magicka.

Requires: Restoration 25, Novice Restoration

5–6. RECOVERY (2 RANKS) ★

- **Rank 1:** Magicka regenerates 25% faster.
  Requires: Restoration 30, Novice Restoration
- **Rank 2:** Magicka regenerates 50% faster.
  Requires: Restoration 60, Recovery 1

A fantastic perk for any mage—after all, who can resist having more Magicka? It's also a fine choice for nonmages who still want to use magic occasionally, as it helps make up for the Magicka regeneration they miss out on by not wearing mage robes.

7. RESPITE ★

Healing spells also restore Stamina.

Requires: Restoration 40, Novice Restoration

Respite is ideal for warriors but is less effective for a pure mage, since you may not use Stamina except when sprinting away.

8. ADEPT RESTORATION ★

Cast Adept-level Restoration spells for half Magicka.

Requires: Restoration 50, Apprentice Restoration

9. WARD ABSORB

Wards recharge your Magicka when hit with spells.

Requires: Restoration 60, Novice Restoration

This perk allows your Wards to absorb 25% of the Magicka from incoming spells. This is handy if you use Wards extensively, as the additional Magicka helps to offset their cost and allows you to maintain them for longer.

10. NECROMAGE

All spells are more effective against undead.

Requires: Restoration 70, Regeneration

Necromage improves all of your spells, not just Turn Undead spells. Spells with a duration last 50% longer; spells with a magnitude are 25% stronger. So your Destruction spells now do 25% more damage to undead.

11. EXPERT RESTORATION ★

Cast Expert-level Restoration spells for half Magicka.

Requires: Restoration 75, Adept Restoration

12. AVOID DEATH

Once a day, heals 250 points automatically if you fall below 10% health.

Requires: Restoration 90

Effectively an "extra life," Avoid Death is a free, passive power that automatically activates to restore your health when you need it most. The Restoration skill requirement is steep, but if you can meet it, it's well worth your time.

13. MASTER RESTORATION ★

Cast Master-level Restoration spells for half Magicka.

Requires: Restoration 100, Expert Restoration

Racial Benefits

+10 Restoration
- Imperial

+5 Restoration
- Argonian
- Breton
- High Elf

Trainers

- **Journeyman:** Aphia Velothi, of Raven Rock, Solstheim.
- **Expert:** Colette Marence, instructor at The College of Winterhold.
- **Expert:** Keeper Carcette, Keeper of the Vigil, Hall of the Vigilant.
- **Master:** Danica Pure-Spring, priestess of Kynareth, in Whiterun.
- **Master:** Florentius Baenius, monk of Fort Dawnguard, The Rift.

Other Resources

- For a list of Restoration Skill Books, and where to look for them, consult page 1091.
- You can find a list of Restoration spells in the Inventory, beginning on page 131.
- The following quests can also increase this skill:
  - The College of Winterhold Quests: Radiant Quests: Shalidor's Insights (page 269).
  - Other Factions Quest: Pantea's Flute (page 415).
  - Daedric Quest: Discerning the Transmundane (page 384).

Alteration spells manipulate the physical world and its natural properties. This school includes some of the best defensive spells available (the Flesh spells) and a wide range of utility spells like Waterbreathing, Telekinesis, and Paralysis. Your Alteration skill increases when you cast a useful Alteration spell on a valid target. For example, you don't get credit for casting Oakflesh but never entering combat, casting Waterbreathing but never entering the water, or casting Detect Life if no one is around.

Constellation: Path of Magic
Available Perks: 14

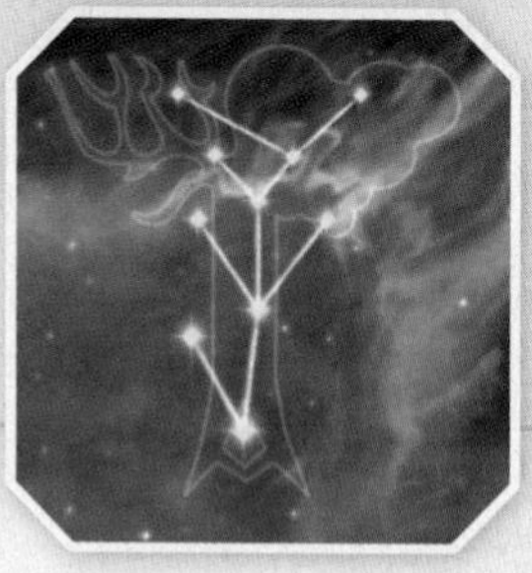

Available Alteration Perks

1. NOVICE ALTERATION ★

Cast Novice-level Alteration spells for half Magicka.

Requires: None

2. ALTERATION DUAL CASTING

Dual casting an Alteration spell overcharges the effects into an even more powerful version.

Requires: Alteration 20, Novice Alteration

Dual casting doubles the duration of most Alteration spells. Especially at early levels, this primarily affects the Flesh line of spells, so make sure you're using them frequently enough and really need that extra time before taking this perk.

3. APPRENTICE ALTERATION ★

Cast Apprentice-level Alteration spells for half Magicka.

Requires: Alteration 25, Novice Alteration

4–6. MAGE ARMOR (3 RANKS) ★

- **Rank 1:** Protection spells like Stoneflesh are twice as strong if not wearing armor.
  Requires: Alteration 30, Apprentice Alteration
- **Rank 2:** Protection spells like Stoneflesh are two and a half times as strong if not wearing armor.
  Requires: Alteration 50, Apprentice Alteration
- **Rank 3:** Protection spells like Stoneflesh are three times as strong if not wearing armor.
  Requires: Alteration 70, Apprentice Alteration

The Mage Armor perks significantly increase the effectiveness of the Flesh line of spells if you're not wearing any armor. If you're willing to commit to these spells as your primary means of defense, these perks are incredibly useful. But be sure you're willing to accept the "no armor" restriction before you invest in them.

7–9. MAGIC RESISTANCE (3 RANKS) ★

- **Rank 1:** Blocks 10% of a spell's effects.
  Requires: Alteration 30, Apprentice Alteration
- **Rank 2:** Blocks 20% of a spell's effects.
  Requires: Alteration 50, Apprentice Alteration
- **Rank 3:** Blocks 30% of a spell's effects.
  Requires: Alteration 70, Apprentice Alteration

These perks are a great way of boosting your defense against magic, instead of, or in addition to, the Restoration line of Ward spells. This is a solid choice for any caster and is especially good for Bretons, as it stacks with their racial magic resistance.

10. ADEPT ALTERATION ★

Cast Adept-level Alteration spells for half Magicka.

Requires: Alteration 50, Apprentice Alteration

11. STABILITY

Alteration spells have greater duration.

Requires: Alteration 70, Adept Alteration

Stability increases the duration of all Alteration spells by 50%. At this point in the Alteration tree, you may have begun to experiment with spells like Paralysis, where the longer duration can definitely make a difference. If you plan to use it extensively or need even longer-lasting Flesh spells, it's worth taking Stability (and possibly Alteration Dual Casting) to get the most from each cast.

12. EXPERT ALTERATION ★

Cast Expert-level Alteration spells for half Magicka.

Requires: Alteration 75, Adept Alteration

13. ATRONACH

Absorb 30% of the Magicka of any spells that hit you.

Requires: Alteration 100, Expert Alteration

This perk is worthwhile if you are running low on Magicka at high levels.

14. MASTER ALTERATION ★

Cast Master-level Alteration spells for half Magicka.

Requires: Alteration 100, Expert Alteration

Racial Benefits

+5 Alteration

- Argonian
- Breton
- Dark Elf
- High Elf
- Redguard

Trainers

- **Expert:** Dravynea the Stoneweaver, mage of Kynesgrove, Eastmarch.
- **Master:** Tolfdir, mage at The College of Winterhold.

Other Resources

- For a list of Alteration Skill Books, and where to look for them, consult page 1091.
- You can find a list of Alteration spells in the Inventory, beginning on page 131.
- The following quests can also increase this skill:
  - The College of Winterhold Quests: Radiant Quests: Shalidor's Insights (page 269).
  - Other Factions Quest: Pantea's Flute (page 415).
  - Daedric Quest: Discerning the Transmundane (page 384).
  - Miscellaneous Objectives: Eastmarch Hold: Salt for the Stoneweaver* (page 493).

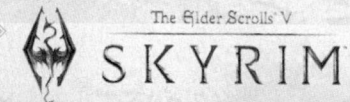

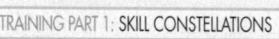

MAGIC SKILLS: THE PATH OF MAGIC – ENCHANTING

Enchanting allows you to enchant your own magic arms and armor. Your Enchanting skill increases whenever you enchant or disenchant an item (based on the value of the enchantment) and when you recharge an enchanted item.

While initially more difficult to level than Smithing or Alchemy, Enchanting is especially powerful in allowing you to maximize your potential with the right combination of enchantments. If you plan to explore Enchanting later in your adventure, it's worth disenchanting the magic items you find early on to build up your Enchanting skill and learn a wide variety of effects. You may also want to develop your Smithing skill to ensure you have a ready supply of weapons and armor to work with. See the Crafting section (page 70) for more details.

In addition, Neloth of Tel Mithryn (in Solstheim) has constructed a Staff Enchanter; augmenting staffs at this crafting station also increases your Enchanting skill.

Constellation: Path of Magic

Available Perks: 13

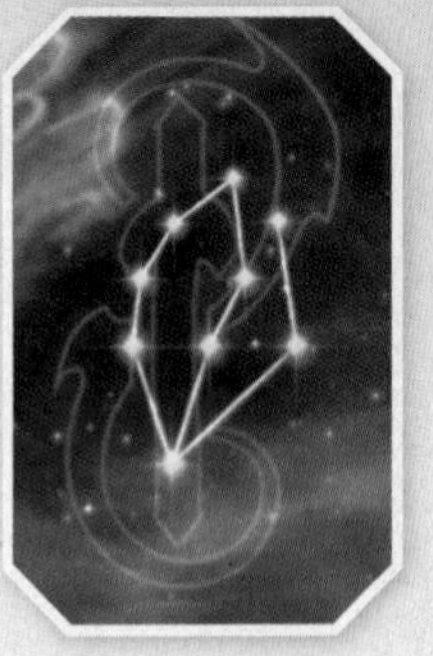

Available Enchanting Perks

1–5. ENCHANTER (5 RANKS) ★

- **Rank 1:** New enchantments are 20% stronger.
  Requires: None
- **Rank 2:** New enchantments are 40% stronger.
  Requires: Enchanting 20, Enchanter 1
- **Rank 3:** New enchantments are 60% stronger.
  Requires: Enchanting 40, Enchanter 2
- **Rank 4:** New enchantments are 80% stronger.
  Requires: Enchanting 60, Enchanter 3
- **Rank 5:** New enchantments are 100% stronger.
  Requires: Enchanting 80, Enchanter 4

The Enchanter perks increase the strength of your Enchantments across the board, making weapons use fewer charges per hit and armor enchantments more powerful. At +20% per rank, it's almost as effective as the other Enchanting perks and much more broadly useful. Take ranks in this whenever your skill level permits.

6. SOUL SQUEEZER

Soul Gems provide 250 extra energy for recharging items.

Requires: Enchanting 20, Enchanter 1

7. FIRE ENCHANTER

Fire enchantments on weapons and armor are 25% stronger.

Requires: Enchanting 30, Enchanter 1

The Fire, Frost, and Storm Enchanter perks enhance enchantments of their element. While these effects appear on both weapons and armor, they're most important on weapons. Because you need only one weapon at a time, you may want to take the Fire Enchanter perk early and save the other two for later.

8. FROST ENCHANTER

Frost enchantments on weapons and armor are 25% stronger.

Requires: Enchanting 40, Fire Enchanter

9. SOUL SIPHON

Death blows to creatures but not people trap 5% of the victim's soul, recharging the weapon.

Requires: Enchanting 40, Soul Squeezer

10. INSIGHTFUL ENCHANTER

Skill enchantments on armor are 25% stronger.

Requires: Enchanting 50, Enchanter 1

11. STORM ENCHANTER

Shock enchantments on weapons and armor are 25% stronger.

Requires: Enchanting 50, Frost Enchanter

12. CORPUS ENCHANTER

Health, Magicka, and Stamina enchantments on armor are 25% stronger.

Requires: Enchanting 70, Insightful Enchanter

13. EXTRA EFFECT ★

Can put two enchantments on the same item.

Requires: Enchanting 100, Storm Enchanter OR Corpus Enchanter

Extra Effect allows you to apply two enchantments to any item. Double-enchant everything you have, and you'll notice a tremendous leap in your power level!

Racial Benefits

+5 Enchanting

- Imperial
- High Elf
- Orc

Trainers

- **Expert:** Sergius Turrianus, instructor at The College of Winterhold.
- **Master:** Hamal, priestess of Dibella, in Markarth.
- **Master:** Neloth, enchanter of Tel Mithryn, Solstheim.

Other Resources

- For a list of Enchanting Skill Books, and where to look for them, consult page 1091.
- You can find a list of Weapon and Armor Enchantments in the Inventory, beginning on page 151.
- The following quests can also increase this skill:
  - Other Factions Quest: Pantea's Flute (page 415).
  - Daedric Quest: Discerning the Transmundane (page 384).

OVERVIEW

The following sample characters are a rogues gallery of battle-hardened adventurers, with races, skills, perks, and equipment chosen to maximize their effectiveness. They have titles like "Battlemage," "Berserker," or "Assassin," but these labels only describe their specialties; they don't appear in game. This is because you can literally create any type of character you wish, focus on any combination of skills and perks, carry and wield any weapon or spell, and choose any type of reaction to enemies and citizens of this world. But if this infinite flexibility leaves you feeling a little overwhelmed, the following Archetypes are a good place to start.

While these Archetypes have been tuned to perform well at their specific style of play, you can adapt them to suit your particular skills or interests. They are here to aid you in understanding how the choices you make can affect your character and to guide you in developing an effective play style. Remember to cross-reference the following information with the section on skills, perks, items, and Followers for more information.

Character Archetype Legend

Title: The style of play the character primarily exhibits.

Race: The character's race; picked to accentuate the play style.

Gender: This has no effect on the character, aside from occasional citizen reactions.

Statistic Focus: How to distribute the Health, Magicka, and Stamina bonuses you receive when leveling up.

Primary Skills: Two key skills that govern the character's play style; raise these as quickly as possible.

Secondary Skills: Two other skills important to the character that you should develop heavily.

Stone Ability: Which of the Standing Stones you should visit to receive an ability.

Essential Perks: The perks most critical to the character's development; you should always purchase these as they become available. Once you buy Essential perks, consider buying other perks from your primary skills and then your secondary skills.

Weapons: The type of combat to which this character is best suited (e.g., melee, spells, bow and arrows).

Armor: The type of outfits and/or armor you should seek out or craft.

Follower: A Follower or Hireling that complements this play style.

Archetype Advice: Useful tips and plans for progression as you explore Skyrim.

The Warrior

The Mage

The Archer

The Berserker

The Spellsword

The Necromancer

The Assassin

The Battlemage

The Weaponmaster

The Rogue

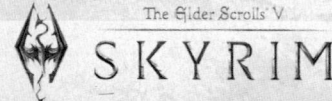

The Warrior

Race: Nord

Gender: Male

Statistic Focus: Health 60%, Stamina 40%

Primary Skills: One-Handed, Block

Secondary Skills: Light Armor, Archery

Stone Ability: Warrior Stone

Essential Perks:

- Armsman
- Fighting Stance
- Power Bash
- Disarming Bash
- Elemental Protection
- Agile Defender

Weapons: One-handed weapon and shield; bow and arrows for backup

Armor: Light armor; with your shield for defense, heavy armor will just weigh you down.

Follower: You can command the attention of your foes in melee combat, so take a ranged Follower to maximize your damage potential. Marcurio and Jenassa are both good choices.

ARCHETYPE ADVICE:

- As a Nord, you start with bonuses to your most critical skills and racial abilities that help you thrive in combat.
- Before each combat, quickly take stock of the area and decide where you want the fight to take place; give yourself enough room to maneuver but don't let your enemies surround you. Your shield is useless against attacks from behind.
- Stand your ground and let the enemy come to you. Use your bow to fire off a few shots from range before switching back to a weapon and shield for melee combat (switch using Favorites).
- Hold the attention of your foes. If enemies begin to target your Follower, take them down quickly so your Follower can return to their own attacks.
- Don't hesitate to fall back if you feel like you're getting overwhelmed or if enemies begin to flank you. A doorway or narrow hall won't leave you much room to maneuver, but it will ensure you only have to address one enemy at a time.
- If you find yourself surrounded, invoke your Battle Cry to scatter your foes and give yourself a few seconds to recover and reposition.
- Master the rhythm of combat and learn how to use your attack, power attack, and shield bash for greatest effect.
- One-Handed perks like Armsman and Fighting Stance improve your damage output, but don't forget to take Block perks as well: Power Bash, Disarming Bash, and Elemental Protection are all critical to taking full advantage of your shield's potential.
- If you can block attacks effectively, you won't take much damage, making light armor an efficient choice that allows you to remain mobile in combat. If you are struggling, you can always switch to heavy armor instead.
- While you may not take many perks in Archery, it's always a good idea to keep a bow on hand for pulling enemies or taking out a lone sniper.
- The Warrior Stone is a solid choice, helping three of your four major skills increase more quickly.

The Mage

Race: High Elf

Gender: Female

Statistic Focus: Magicka 80%, Health 20%

Primary Skills: Destruction, Conjuration

Secondary Skills: Illusion, Restoration

Stone Ability: Mage Stone

Essential Perks:

- Spellcasting Rank perks
- Destruction Dual Casting
- Augmented Flames, Frost, or Shock
- Summoner
- Elemental Potency
- Illusion Dual Casting

Weapons: Spells

Armor: Mage robes. Always take the robe with the highest Magicka Regeneration rate you can find. Then look for more gear that increases your regeneration, adds to your total Magicka, or decreases the cost of your spells.

Follower: Keep a heavily armored warrior at your side to hold foes at bay. Vorstag and Lydia are both good choices, especially early on.

ARCHETYPE ADVICE:

- As a High Elf Wizard, you'll have the highest starting Magicka of any race and can maintain that advantage by focusing on Magicka bonuses as you level.
- When even that's not enough, call on your Highborn Racial power to sustain your casting in even the longest battles. Highborn is your lifeline; make sure it's your active power (and a Favorite) unless you need to use something else, and switch back to it when you're done.
- Prepare for each battle by summoning a creature, then start the fight with your best Destruction spell from range.
- In combat, expect to spend most of your time casting Destruction and Restoration spells.
- Learn what each type of Destruction spell is best at and how to use them effectively.
- Take advantage of the spells' secondary effects; spray a room with flames to set your foes on fire, or hit a foe with ice from a distance to slow them down, allowing you to keep casting as they struggle to advance.
- When not dual casting, keep a Ward on hand to deflect blows and shield yourself from enemy spells.
- This is a powerful but fragile character; while you have plenty of Magicka to cast devastating spells, your health is low and your defenses are weak, putting you in serious risk if attacked directly.
- Let your Follower and summoned creatures distract enemies and soak up damage while you focus on taking out each foe in turn. If your summoned creature is destroyed, resummon it immediately.
- Keep a close eye on your Health and cast Healing or Fast Healing when needed, or drink a potion (remember you can tag potions as Favorites).
- If an enemy closes to melee range, check their health and quickly decide whether to keep your Ward up and maintain your attack or escalate by dual casting Destruction (for a quick takedown), Fear (to send them running), or Calm (so you can escape).
- When in doubt, remember that your robes are lighter than your enemies' armor. Sprint to make a clean getaway, or tactically retreat to put some distance between yourself and your foes so you have time to finish one more spell.
- Because of your low health and ever-increasing need for Magicka, you'll use potions at a faster rate than most other characters. For this reason, consider taking up Alchemy to supplement what you find in dungeons and save your gold.
- As with all mages, buy Spell Tomes! This should always be your top shopping priority. Join the College of Winterhold early for convenient access to all the best spell vendors.
- The Mage Stone is a solid choice for this character, allowing you to quickly increase your skills and master a wide range of spells across all disciplines.

The Archer

Race: Wood Elf
Gender: Male
Statistic Focus: Health 80%, Stamina 20%
Primary Skills: Archery, Sneak
Secondary Skills: Light Armor, Block
Stone Ability: Thief Stone
Essential Perks:
- Overdraw
- Eagle Eye
- Power Shot
- Quick Shot
- Stealth
- Deadly Aim

Weapons: Bow and arrows, the best you can afford. Ideally, find a bow with a fire, frost, or shock enchantment for even more damage. Keep a one-handed weapon for backup.

Armor: Light armor, for protection without sacrificing speed and stealth.

Follower: For an aggressive choice, take Jenassa or Faendal. For a sturdier companion, try a warrior like Vorstag or Argis.

ARCHETYPE ADVICE:

- As a Wood Elf, you excel at stealth archery, with bonuses in all your critical skills.
- If you spot an enemy, drop into a stealth crouch immediately, then creep closer and start the battle with a sneak attack for maximum damage.
- Use your bow exclusively to raise your Archery skill as quickly as possible. When rushed by an enemy, bash them with your bow, then back up and keep firing.
- Every Archery perk is worthwhile for the stealth archer; the real choice is not what perks to take but when to take them.
  - Always take Overdraw whenever your skill allows it. A 20% damage bonus per shot is just too good to pass up.
  - Want more help lining up your shots? Take Eagle Eye and Steady Hand.
  - Need to increase your damage output? Grab Deadly Aim and Power Shot.
- Don't neglect your Sneak skill, either. Practice sneaking up on even low-level enemies, or your skill may not be high enough to help you when it really matters.
- Take Light Armor to gain some protection without sacrificing your ability to Sneak effectively. It also won't hamper your mobility as much, allowing you to dodge or back away as you continue to fire at an especially persistent foe.
- Block is a good choice for another skill. While you can't take advantage of its shield-specific perks, Power Bash and Disarming Bash work just as well with a bow and give you an opening to make one last shot at point-blank range.
- Stat bonuses are less important for your character than most, since many of your foes will never make it to melee range. A high Health never hurts, but take a little Stamina as well to ensure you can bash when you really need to.
- When assaulting an outdoor camp or redoubt, find a nearby predator and use Command Animal on them. If your first shot isn't quite enough to take out the sentries, your new pet wolf or bear will probably do the job, or at least keep them at bay.
- The Thief Stone is a good match for the Archer, helping your Sneak and Light Armor skills keep pace with your Archery and ensuring they remain effective.

The Berserker

Race: Orc
Gender: Male
Statistic Focus: Health 50%, Stamina 50%
Primary Skills: Two-Handed, Heavy Armor
Secondary Skills: Smithing, Block
Stone Ability: Lord Stone
Essential Perks:
- Barbarian
- Champion's Stance
- Juggernaut
- Well-Fitted
- Tower of Strength
- Power Bash

Weapons: Two-handed weapon, the strongest you can find

Armor: Heavy armor, for added defense

Follower: Find a melee Follower who can wade into combat at your side: Stenvar is an aggressive choice, while Belrand offers more versatility. When fighting in the wilderness, take along an animal companion as well; both Vigilance and Meeko will help distract your foes.

ARCHETYPE ADVICE:

- As an Orc, you have solid skill bonuses and use of the deadly Berserk power.
- Charge into combat and hit hard. Your attacks may be slow, but they connect with devastating force, staggering foes and dealing massive damage.
- Power Attacks are critical to using two-handed weapons effectively, so boost your Stamina and take perks that improve them, especially Champion's Stance.
- Your greatest risk is wading into the thick of combat and becoming surrounded. Keep a Follower and/or animal companion with you to divide your enemies' focus and keep their numbers manageable.
- If you do find yourself surrounded, invoke your Berserk power to increase your damage resistance and gain the damage bonus you need to carve a path through your foes.
- This is not a traditional berserker: Instead of hides and war paint, outfit your warrior in a full suit of heavy armor to offset the lack of a protective shield or spell. With the right Heavy Armor perks, you can shrug off even the most powerful blows.
- The Lord Stone improves your defenses even further, allowing you to endure whatever your adversaries can throw at you.
- Remember that parrying an attack with your weapon counts as a block. While the shield-based perks in the Block constellation won't be of use to you, you can still take advantage of perks like Power Bash or Disarming Bash.
- Since your combat style relies exclusively on your weapons and armor, Smithing makes a great supporting skill, allowing you to forge and improve your own gear.

The Spellsword

Race: Dark Elf
Gender: Female
Statistic Focus: Health 40%, Magicka 30%, Stamina 30%
Primary Skills: One-Handed, Destruction
Secondary Skills: Light Armor, Illusion
Stone Ability: Lover Stone
Essential Perks:

- Armsman
- Fighting Stance
- Destruction Rank perks
- Augmented Flames, Frost, or Shock
- Impact
- Agile Defender

Weapons: One-handed weapon and spell

Armor: Light armor for speed and mobility. For best results, look for enchanted armor that increases your maximum Magicka or Magicka-regeneration rate.

Follower: If you want a friend to absorb damage, find a warrior like Lydia or Vorstag. For a more ranged support, take Jenassa or Marcurio.

ARCHETYPE ADVICE:

- As a Dark Elf, you may have to work a little harder to increase your One-Handed skill (which doesn't start with a bonus), but your other skills are an excellent fit.
- A Spellsword is all about flexibility, switching between weapons and spells as the situation demands, aggressively creating and exploiting enemy weaknesses.
- Use Destruction spells to soften up foes from a distance before they can close to melee range. Hit weaker enemies with fire spells to quickly cut down their health, use frost on stronger foes to slow their approach, and target mages with shock spells.
- In melee combat, your best defense is a good offense.
  - Early on, spray flames or sparks with one hand while you hack away with your weapon; you'll be surprised at how quickly your enemies fall.
  - As time goes on, staggering foes becomes increasingly important. Take Fighting Stance (which allows you to power attack more frequently) and Impact (to allow your spells to stagger enemies as well).
- Use your Ancestor's Wrath racial power to inflict even more damage in close combat. At later levels, Destruction's line of Cloak spells is more powerful, but Ancestor's Wrath may still be useful if you need to conserve Magicka.
- Although most of your attention will be on offense, learn a Ward spell for better protection when fighting mages or a Flesh spell (Oakflesh, Ironflesh, etc.) for an armor boost against hard-hitting warriors. Both will supplement your defenses without slowing you down.
- Try to balance your One-Handed and Destruction skills. If either falls too far behind, you may not be able to rely on it when you need it most.
- Don't neglect Light Armor perks, either. Without a shield or the ability to block, you're reliant on your armor and spells for protection.
- Illusion spells like Fear and Frenzy are helpful at disrupting large groups of foes, allowing you to concentrate on each enemy in turn without becoming overwhelmed.
- Since your skills are so wide-ranging, the Lovers Stone is a good choice to help all of them advance quickly. If you notice any of them starting to fall behind, switch to a more specific stone (Warrior, Mage, or Thief) to balance them out again.

The Necromancer

Race: Breton
Gender: Male
Statistic Focus: Magicka 70%, Health 30%
Primary Skills: Conjuration, Illusion
Secondary Skills: Alteration, Restoration
Stone Ability: Ritual Stone
Essential Perks:

- Spellcasting Rank perks
- Conjuration Dual Casting
- Necromancy
- Dark Souls
- Mystic Binding
- Mage Armor

Weapons: Spells, bound weapons

Armor: Mage robes. Always take the robe with the highest Magicka-regeneration rate you can find. Then look for more gear that increases your regeneration, adds to your total Magicka, or decreases the cost of your spells.

Follower: Bring a tough, high-damage Follower to create corpses you can resurrect. Stenvar or Ahtar are good choices.

ARCHETYPE ADVICE:

- As a Breton, you have strong skill bonuses and a fantastic resistance to magic.
- Prepare for each fight by casting your best Flesh spell (Oakflesh, Ironflesh, etc.). Early on, this is expensive—you may want to wait a few seconds to let your Magicka recover—but it becomes less of an issue as your Magicka improves.
- Necromancy has one major drawback: you need fresh corpses to resurrect. When you approach a fight, quickly size up your options and decide how to proceed:
  - If there are any dead bodies lying around, exploit them! Raise the corpse, and your new zombie will charge in ahead of you.
  - Against a group of foes, try an Illusion spell like Frenzy. One enemy may well kill another, giving you fresh zombie material.
  - Or conjure a bound weapon and attack. Work with your Follower to quickly take down the first enemy, resurrect them, and then confront the remaining foes with your new ally.
- With only your Flesh spells to protect you, you're susceptible to damage in melee combat. If an enemy rushes you, use Illusion spells like Fear or Calm to stop their attack and escape, or conjure a bound weapon to quickly cut them down.
- When confronting mages, call on your Dragonskin power to absorb their spells as Magicka, and use it to power your own spells. For even more resilience, cast a Ward; combined with your innate magic resistance, this can make you almost invulnerable.
- If a battle is taking a long time to conclude, rush into the center of the battlefield and invoke the Ritual Stone's power to raise all the surrounding dead at once, creating a zombie army to quickly overrun your opposition!
- When combat has ended, your work has not—resurrect one final zombie before moving on. You never know what lurks around the next corner.
- As with all mages, buy Spell Tomes! This should always be your top shopping priority. Join the College of Winterhold early for convenient access to all the finest spell vendors.

The Assassin

Race: Khajiit

Gender: Female

Statistic Focus: Health 60%, Magicka 20%, Stamina 20%

Primary Skills: Sneak, One-Handed

Secondary Skills: Alchemy, Pickpocket

Stone Ability: Shadow Stone

Essential Perks:

Stealth	Armsman
Backstab	Dual Flurry
Assassin's Blade	Dual Savagery

Weapons: Dual one-handed weapons (move to daggers once you take Assassin's Blade). Keep a bow on hand for situations where no good stealth route is available and for misdirecting foes.

Armor: Light armor, for protection without sacrificing speed and stealth

Follower: None, or take a warrior such as Iona or Vorstag, but have them wait at a distance in case you need the backup. Stealth is tricky enough without having to worry about a Follower.

ARCHETYPE ADVICE:

- As a Khajiit, you start with the Sneak and One-Handed skills needed to be an effective assassin and with bonuses to your Archery, Alchemy, and Lockpicking skills for support.
- For you, every encounter is a puzzle waiting to be solved. If you spot an enemy, drop into a stealthy crouch immediately, then look for a way to sneak up behind them for a lethal backstab.
- When assaulting an exterior camp or ruin, you may have better luck at night, when the cover of darkness provides better concealment. Weather matters, too: a stormy night offers better concealment than a clear one.
- In dungeons, look for alternate paths and ways to get the drop on your foes.
- In crypts and catacombs, your high Sneak skill may allow you to slip past the Draugr without disturbing their rest. But don't hesitate to lash out with a preemptive attack; few things are more satisfying than ambushing a foe before they can ambush you.
- Sneak is your most critical skill. At early levels, it may be difficult to sneak up on an enemy without being spotted, but keep practicing! You'll be amazed at how well you can avoid detection once your skill is high enough.
- As an Assassin, you need a fast, powerful offense to cut down your foes before they can retaliate. Take perks in One-Handed and Sneak to increase your damage output as much as possible.
- Alchemy is a great supporting skill; poisons make every strike count, while potions can restore your health and shore up your otherwise-fragile defenses. Don't forget to add both potions and poisons to your Favorites.
- Pickpocket is also worth exploring. With your high Sneak skill, you should have little trouble concealing yourself from townsfolk (which improves your odds of success). At low levels, you can pilfer items for a little extra gold or the occasional enchanted treasure. But the real reward comes at higher levels, where you can steal the weapons and armor off your foes before stabbing them in the back.
- Use your racial Night Eye power whenever you want better visibility. This is ideal for a stealthy character; it is free, unrestricted, and absolutely silent.
- The Shadow Stone's power gives you free use of Invisibility once per day. Even if you learn the Invisibility spell, this can still be useful, giving you a chance to disengage from foes and escape, or set up another sneak attack.

The Battlemage

Race: Imperial

Gender: Male

Statistic Focus: Magicka 60%, Health 40%

Primary Skills: Destruction, Restoration

Secondary Skills: Illusion, Heavy Armor

Stone Ability: Apprentice Stone

Essential Perks:

- Spellcasting Rank Perks
- Illusion Dual Casting
- Destruction Dual Casting
- Augmented Flames, Frost, or Shock
- Recovery
- Juggernaut

Weapons: Spells, supplemented by staffs or a one-handed weapon as needed

Armor: Heavy armor, ideally enchanted to increase your Magicka or Magicka regeneration

Follower: As a spellcaster who can stand up to melee combat, almost any Follower can complement your skills. Belrand or Stenvar are both good choices for a more aggressive melee companion.

ARCHETYPE ADVICE:

- As an Imperial, you have the right mixture of magic and martial skills needed to succeed as a Battlemage.
- Long a respected profession in Tamriel, the Battlemage combines the mage's power and versatility with a warrior's durability. Though magic is your primary focus, you can endure the rigors of melee combat if needed.
- As a Battlemage, you can choose your own approach to any combat situation:
  - Use Destruction spells to blast foes from a distance, or pull them in, where you can switch to a Dual Cast spell to finish them off.
  - Use Restoration spells to sustain yourself or strengthen your allies.
  - Use Wards to protect yourself from mages, while countering their elemental magic with your own.
  - Use Illusion spells to weaken and disrupt groups of foes at range.
  - Dabble in Conjuration to summon allies or raise the dead, or try Alteration for an even stronger defense in melee.
- Without the benefit of enchanted robes, your Magicka will regenerate far more slowly than a pure mage's, severely restricting your spellcasting. You have options here, too:
  - Take more Magicka bonuses when leveling up to increase your maximum Magicka.
  - Invest in (or make) armor and items that fortify your Magicka or Magicka regeneration.
  - Take Restoration's line of Recovery perks, which increase your regeneration rate.
  - Draw on the Apprentice Stone's power to increase your Magicka-regeneration rate, and offset the lower magic resistance with other items or Wards.
  - Keep staffs, scrolls, or a melee weapon as backup, just in case.
- Destruction is your primary means of damaging your foes. Take new ranks in Destruction as they become available, as well as any other perks you can use to increase your damage output.
- Restoration provides you with magical Wards to supplement your armor and healing spells to sustain yourself and your allies.
- Illusion spells allow you to disrupt larger groups of foes and fortify your companions in battle.
- Heavy Armor is what sets a Battlemage apart from any other wizard. While the Juggernaut perks are important, you will probably need to put spellcasting rank perks ahead of the other Heavy Armor perks.
- If you find yourself surrounded, don't forget to use your Voice of the Emperor ability to pacify nearby foes, giving you time to make a tactical retreat.
- You might also consider a different race: A Breton Battlemage can take the Apprentice Stone with less of a penalty due to their innate magic resistance, while a High Elf Battlemage will have a higher starting Magicka and the benefit of their racial Highborn ability.

The Weaponmaster

Race: Redguard

Gender: Female

Statistic Focus: Health 60%, Stamina 40%

Primary Skills: One-Handed, Heavy Armor

Secondary Skills: Archery, Enchanting

Stone Ability: Steed Stone

Essential Perks:

- Armsman
- Fighting Stance
- Dual Flurry
- Dual Savagery
- Juggernaut
- Well Fitted

Weapons: Two one-handed weapons (dual-wielding), bow and arrows for backup

Armor: Heavy armor for maximum defense

Follower: You can hold your own in melee combat, so bring a ranged Follower like Marcurio or Illia for ranged support.

ARCHETYPE ADVICE:

- As a Redguard, your One-Handed skill bonus is magnified by a dual-wielding combat style, making you a whirlwind of destruction in close combat.
- Choose how to address each battle.
  - In some cases, you may be better off rushing your foes to engage them as quickly as possible, before they can ready their defenses.
  - At other times, you may want to find a defensible position (such as a doorway or higher ground) and let your enemies come to you. Use a bow to draw your foes to you, then switch back to your weapons as your foes close in.
- Attack relentlessly. One-Handed perks like Dual Flurry allow you to strike more quickly, while Dual Savagery improves the strength of your Dual Power attack.
- Since you can't block while wielding two weapons, take heavy armor for the extra defense; you'll appreciate the additional resilience in combat.
- Enchanting is especially effective for a dual-wielding warrior, since you can apply a different enchantment to each weapon, or double up for a stronger effect. You may also want to consider Smithing to forge and improve your own weapons and armor.
- Early on, the Steed Stone is a great choice for offsetting the weight and movement penalties of Heavy Armor. If you decide to take Heavy Armor's Conditioning perk, switch to the Lord or Lady Stones for more active combat bonuses.
- Don't forget about your Adrenaline Rush power, which can rapidly refill your Stamina during an extended battle, allowing you to sustain a flurry of power attacks.

The Rogue

Race: Argonian

Gender: Female

Statistic Focus: Health 40%, Magicka 40%, Stamina 20%

Primary Skills: Sneak, Illusion

Secondary Skills: Archery, One-Handed

Stone Ability: Serpent Stone

Essential Perks:

- Stealth
- Illusion Rank Perks
- Illusion Dual Casting
- Quiet Casting
- Overdraw
- Armsman

Weapons: Spells, bow and arrows, one-handed weapon for backup

Armor: Light armor, ideally with enchantments to improve your Magicka or Magicka regeneration

Follower: Seek out a stealthy archer like Jenassa or Faendal.

ARCHETYPE ADVICE:

- As an Argonian, your natural abilities skills provide a solid foundation for a stealthy character, though your magic skills will take a little more time to build up.
- The Rogue is a hybrid mage-thief. Less narrowly focused than most of the other archetypes, it offers a great deal of versatility and is a fun choice if you enjoy toying with your enemies instead of assaulting them directly.
- When you spot a foe, drop into a stealthy crouch and creep closer to assess the situation. You have a range of options at your disposal:
  - Cast Invisibility and Muffle and sneak past your foes undetected.
  - Cast Frenzy or Fear to disrupt and disorient them.
  - Fire a well-placed arrow to catch a foe's attention and lure them into a trap.
  - Snipe a foe from range, starting combat with a devastating sneak attack.
  - Creep closer and backstab for maximum damage.
- Once combat begins, don't hesitate to attack with bow or blade. If you want to take on a foe directly, draw a second weapon to deal even more damage.
- If you feel yourself getting overwhelmed, pull out an ace:
  - Cast Fear to send your enemies running, then pelt them with arrows as they flee.
  - Cast Calm to stop combat for a moment, giving yourself time to quaff a potion or make a tactical retreat.
  - Call on the Serpent Stone's power to paralyze a foe and take them out of the fight completely. This gives you time to heal, deal with other enemies, or slaughter the now-helpless foe at your leisure.
- Your Histskin power is an amazing racial ability, capable of pulling you back from the brink of death. Give it a few seconds to do its work, then wade back into the thick of combat.
- With such a wide array of tactics at your disposal, you can find a solution to any challenge. Focus on the core improvement perks for each skill (Stealth, Illusion Ranks, Armsman, and Overdraw) to make sure each tactic remains viable, then branch out depending on what seems most useful to you.
- If you have any perks left over, explore Lockpicking or Pickpocket to take advantage of your racial skill bonuses and complete your stealthy arsenal.

TRAINING PART 2: COMBAT, DEVELOPMENT, AND CRAFTING

This section explores the vast array of actions and activities you can perform in Skyrim. We provide advice on how to improve your character as you level up and give you crucial tactical details on all facets of combat and exploration (including Shouts). We also thoroughly explain Crafting systems.

Color-coding: In the tables in this chapter, elements from the original game are in white and gray. Elements from the Dawnguard, Hearthfire, and Dragonborn add-ons have been color-coded as follows:

Soul Tear	Dawnguard/Hearthfire
Battle Fury	Dragonborn

CHARACTER ADVANCEMENT

Leveling Advice

Tactically level up during a particularly frightening combat, as shown.

As your skills increase, you gradually make progress toward gaining a level. There are several aspects of this process worth taking a closer look at:

Improve what you use: The skills you use will improve naturally as you use them. There is no need to go out of your way to improve a skill you never plan to use; this doesn't level your character any faster and won't make your character any stronger or more effective.

Use what you improve: When selecting perks, be sure you're ready to take full advantage of them. For example, don't purchase Adept-level Magic perks until you have Adept-level spells to cast. Don't take Enchanting perks unless you're planning on enchanting something in the immediate future.

Patience and perks: If you aren't sure which perk to choose when you level up or if find yourself a few skill points away from a perk you really want, it is usually better to save the choice for later. This gives you more flexibility and allows you to change your mind. Remember, once you select a perk, you can't take it back!

Tactical leveling: Leveling up fully restores your Health, Magicka, and Stamina. This can literally save your life if you find yourself bereft of potions during a difficult battle. For example, if you gain a level while exploring a dungeon, you may want to wait and level up during the final (or most difficult) fight. Conversely, there's no point in hoarding levels; once you begin leveling up, you must claim all of the levels you've earned.

COMBAT IMPROVEMENT

By now, you should have skills that aid you in dispatching enemies through melee, ranged, or magical attacks. This section offers advice on maximizing your combat potential no matter how you decide to fight your foes.

General Advice

Don't overlook your Shouts or powers; they can win the fight for you!

As you set off to explore the realm, you may be overwhelmed with the choices you can make. But remember this sage advice, and you'll thrive in the wilds of Skyrim:

Conserve your resources: Your three statistics—Health, Magicka, and Stamina—are all resources you need to conserve. If you sprint into battle (using Stamina), recast your spells right before heading into battle (Magicka), or push on after a difficult battle without pausing to recover your Health, you're at a disadvantage. Stop and wait for a moment (optionally swigging down a potion) to ensure all three stats have recovered fully before you continue.

Remember your Shouts and powers: While most of your attention will be on the weapons, spells, or shield in your hands, remember that you have a third option at your disposal. Shouts and powers are among your most devastating abilities: They don't cost anything to use, and they can dramatically turn the tide of battle in your favor. Make sure to Favorite them, and always know which one you have equipped. Then call on them whenever you need some additional offensive firepower.

Consumable consumption: Do you find yourself struggling against a particularly troublesome set of foes? Then stop, rummage around in your inventory, and see if you have an item that might help. This could be a healing or fortifying potion, a poison for your weapon, or a scroll with a powerful magic effect. Don't hoard scrolls; use them!

Active effects: It's easy to forget about the Brain Rot you contracted a few hours ago or not to notice when a blessing or buff has worn off. Check the Active Effects list in the Magic menu periodically to ensure you know what is ailing or enhancing you.

The Favorites menu: This menu allows you to quickly switch between weapons and spells, and it pauses time when you open it, without blocking your view. This gives you a moment to consider your next move.

Save early, save often! Although the game saves your progress automatically, it's always prudent to save before trying something dangerous, like running down a hallway lined with swinging blades or investigating that ominous-looking tomb.

Tuning in the difficulty: The System > Settings > Gameplay menu allows you to change the game's difficulty at any time—even during combat—which you should try if you're really struggling or if you're having too easy a time.

Melee Combat

To maximize your potential in melee combat, choose a weapon you like, learn its rhythm, improve the associated perks, and try to find (or forge) the most potent version of it that you can. If you have problems effectively bringing down foes, be sure you know how to respond to and counter their attacks.

Choose your weapon: Early in your adventure, try out a variety of weapons and combat styles and see what works best for you. Do you prefer one- or two-handed weapons? If you enjoy wielding a one-handed weapon, do you want a shield, spell, or another weapon in your free hand? Then figure out whether daggers (fast, lowest damage), swords, axes, or maces (slow, highest damage) are your favorite. By learning what you're most comfortable wielding, you can choose the perks that complement that style.

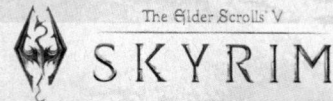

The rhythm of combat: Once you've settled on a weapon or combat style, practice your tactics. Remember that you and your opponent have a regular attack, a power attack (holding the Attack button down for a slower but more damaging strike), a block (raising your shield or weapon to deflect an enemy blow), and a bash (hitting your foe with a shield or the flat of a weapon). Try to get a feel for how long it takes you to perform these actions with your chosen weapon and how long it takes for your enemies to do the same. As your sense of timing improves, you can better decide whether to attack or defend during a fight, and choose your tactics more strategically.

Observe and counter: Combat involves more than just attacking. You can take down enemies faster and more effectively by observing their actions and choosing the appropriate counter.

◊ **Block** if your enemy uses a regular attack.

◊ **Bash** if your enemy uses a power attack to quickly interrupt and stagger them.

◊ **Power attack** if your enemy is blocking to break their block and stagger them.

◊ **Attack swiftly** if your enemy is staggered to cut them down.

Wearing a Cloak: The Destruction line of Cloak spells (Flame, Frost, and Lightning) are ideal if you plan to engage in close combat—even if you're primarily a warrior with little interest in magic. These spells allow you to damage enemies with both your weapons and the cloak's magical effects, without requiring much attention (or Magicka expenditure). Cloak spells also don't damage your Followers, so there's no need to worry in close quarters.

Ranged Combat

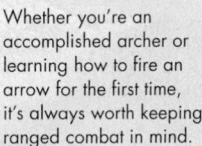

A Dragon attack: If you focus only on melee combat, your options against dragons are limited.

Whether you're an accomplished archer or learning how to fire an arrow for the first time, it's always worth keeping ranged combat in mind.

The backup bow: It always pays to keep a bow and some arrows on hand, even if you don't plan on specializing in it. You never know when you might encounter a dragon or need to soften up a particularly difficult foe from range.

Arrow gathering: Be sure to grab arrows at every opportunity. Since they have no weight, there's no reason not to take and keep every arrow you can find. There's nothing more frustrating than running out of arrows in the middle of a dungeon, especially if you're focused on archery.

Remember to bash: Don't forget that you can bash with your bow. This usually gives you enough time to fire off one more shot or to sprint away while your enemy recovers so you can line up and fire again.

Perks of power: Archery perks have a significant effect on your ranged combat repertoire, giving you the ability to zoom in, slow time, and stagger enemies after a successful hit. Just relying on archery can be a very satisfying way to play and can make hunting certain skittish animals, such as elk and deer, a lot easier.

Ranged combat only: Rarely, you may encounter a foe that can't be reached by melee weapons. On these occasions, a bow and arrow is imperative, unless you have a ranged spell.

Combat Tactics

Get the gear: Be sure you're searching for the correct gear. If you plan to focus on archery, dual-wielding, or another aggressive combat style, then offense is your best defense: Look for enchanted weapons and armor that increase your damage-dealing potential. It is often worth wearing a "weaker" piece of armor if it carries an enchantment that helps your damage output.

Prepare poisons: Poisons are a great way of quickly increasing your damage potential. Keeping some poisons on hand (via Favorites) is an excellent way to deal with heavily armored warriors or mages using Wards. Even if your weapon doesn't strike for maximum damage, the poison will.

Speed and sidestepping: Use speed to your advantage. When wearing light armor or robes, you're more agile than most of your opponents. This allows you to sidestep their power attacks (and then counter) or to sprint away if you need some space to recover and regroup.

Staggering attempts: A staggered enemy is much easier to cut down with a flurry of attacks. Power attacks and bashes stagger most foes, but look for other effects that can achieve this, too, such as the Unrelenting Force Shout.

Magic-Based Combat

The dead rise again: There's something satisfying about raising recently slain enemies to attack their own!

The five schools of magic offer a wide range of offensive and defensive spells to help crush your foes, shield yourself, or augment other combat styles.

The blended approach: In Skyrim, you don't have to be a "pure" mage to enjoy spellcasting. Any warrior can benefit from a conjured ally, healing spell, or elemental cloak, and thieves can especially appreciate the benefits of Invisibility. Even if you don't plan to focus on magic, look for spells that can enhance your combat style.

Spell-casting Rank perks: Each school of magic has a series of "Rank" perks (Novice, Apprentice, Adept, Expert, and Master) that dramatically decrease the cost of spells from that school. These perks are critical to your ability to effectively use spells from that school and should be a top priority for any serious mage.

Offensive Spells

Know your area of effect: Many spells damage anything in a wide area. While you can't be hurt by your own spells, your Followers can be, so use them with care to avoid any *unintended consequences*. On the other hand, if your only Follower is a summoned Atronach, use spells that match their element at will, since they're immune to them.

Set your own traps: Rune traps allow you to turn the environment to your advantage. Set one in a narrow space enemies will have to run through or drop one in a hall you can retreat past if combat goes poorly. In a pinch, you can also cast them directly at an enemy, although your other spells are much more cost-effective.

Raising the walls: Though initially somewhat weak, Wall spells become dramatically more powerful at higher levels. Cast them at the feet of a waking Draugr to kill it before it can finish standing up, or back down a hall as you cast a wall out in front of you. Any enemies that advance will blindly race through your death zone.

Conjuring up companions: Be sure to summon a creature or raise a zombie before heading into any major battle. When summoning a creature, pick the one that's best for your situation. Do you need the ranged offense of a Flame Atronach or the melee toughness of a Frost Atronach? When raising a zombie from those you've recently slain, pick someone you haven't looted already; even zombies are more powerful when well armed and armored.

Defensive Spells

Know your defenses: Both the Restoration line of Ward spells and the Alteration line of Flesh spells offer defensive options for spellcasters. Wards require concentration (tying up a hand) and have a per-second cost, but they are more effective against spells. Flesh spells have a higher initial cost but don't require concentration. Use Wards when fighting mages, Flesh spells against melee foes, or both in large or mixed combats where you need the extra protection.

Be ready with healing: There are a variety of healing spells to choose from; some heal a large amount of Health at once, while others heal over time at a reduced cost. Most heal only you, but some can heal your Followers as well. Learn a variety of these spells (and flag each of them as Favorites) to be prepared for any situation.

Learn spells for specific situations: Delving into a Draugr crypt? Then pick up a Turn Undead or Detect Dead spell. Exploring a shipwreck? Then grab Waterbreathing to make your diving stress-free. Whatever your need, you can probably find a spell to make your exploration easier or more entertaining.

Stealth-Based Combat

A stab in the dark (and the back): Stealthy adventurers seek to slay any foe with a swift attack their enemies never see coming.

Those who lurk in the shadows, hoping to sneak past enemies or a guard undetected, would do well to heed the following advice:

Gain the right perspective: It's dramatically easier to Sneak using third-person view, since you can see patrolling enemies more easily than in first-person.

Stay hidden: Line of sight is by far the biggest factor in determining whether an enemy can see you. Stay hidden behind walls or cover to remain out of sight. And it goes without saying that using Stealth mode (crouching) is imperative.

Seek magical aid: Invisibility and Muffle conceal you from your enemies' sight and hearing, making it much easier to sneak by unnoticed. Learn these spells, collect Invisibility potions, and look for Muffle-enchanted gear to improve your chances of a successful stealth experience. Then give the same augmentations to your Followers. Otherwise, lurk alone.

Draw out your foes: Enemies leave their posts to investigate sounds, such as an arrow impact. Place your shot carefully, and you can draw them out into the open, giving you a chance to perform a Sneak attack, fire a second arrow (this one into the enemy himself), or slip by undetected.

Lure foes into traps: For an even more devious twist, shoot an arrow near a trap, and the enemy that goes to investigate may blunder into it and set it off. Combine this with a well-placed Rune Trap spell to create your own kill zones!

> **NOTE** **Finishing Moves:** Every melee weapon you carry has a finishing flourish you can inflict on an enemy at the end of a fight. Although there's no guarantee of executing one, your best bet for seeing one is to perform a power attack on the last enemy in a battle. Most importantly, there is no tactical advantage to performing one either (e.g., they don't inflict more damage). But they are viscerally more satisfying!

Choosing Favorites

The Favorites System means less time spent rummaging through your inventory and more time spent in battle. It allows you to rapidly swap between your preferred weapons, spells, and outfits more easily and to quickly ready a power, potion, or scroll when necessary. Because it takes the hassle out of managing your inventory, it also helps you fight more effectively: you won't hesitate to change your gear when you can do so in a matter of seconds.

> **TIP** The Favorites menu also allows you to hotkey the items you use most frequently. Console players can press Left or Right to tag an item; PC players can press a number (1-8). Then press that button in game to use or switch to that item instantly!

Here is some additional advice on selecting the most effective Favorites:

Melee combat: Keep your weapon (or weapons) of choice in your Favorites menu. If you use a one-handed weapon, tag a shield as well. If you have enchanted weapons that you only use occasionally (such as weapons with Soul Trap or Paralyze enchantments), those are good choices as well.

Ranged combat: Always keep a bow in your Favorites list—even mages may need to fall back on it when battling dragons. If you're primarily focused on Archery, you may want to Favorite specific types of arrows as well—your weakest for dispatching standard enemies and your best for dragons or a particularly dangerous boss.

Spellcasting: Tag your favorite offensive and defensive spells, including your best Healing spell. Warriors should tag a Cloak spell to make sure they remember to cast it; Thieves should tag Invisibility and Muffle, and mages should tag all the key elements of their arsenal.

Shouts and powers: Don't forget to add Shouts and powers to your Favorites list! Your Racial power and Standing Stone power are both essential. Also tag the Shouts you use most frequently.

Armor and outfits: Depending on your play style, you may find it helpful to Favorite armor or sets of clothing as well. Thieves in particular may find it useful to Favorite a set of armor or clothing to use when sneaking and another to switch back to if you're discovered!

Items: Tag a set of healing potions as a Favorite so you can quickly swig them in combat without frantically fiddling with the inventory during a fraught battle. Warriors may want to do the same with stamina potions and mages with Magicka potions.

Activities: Don't forget to Favorite items depending on your current activity. If you're exploring a dungeon, you may want to Favorite a torch or staff for light. When hunting for a hidden treasure, Favorite the treasure map for quick reference.

The Nords have long practiced a unique, spiritual form of magic known as "the Way of the Voice." Nords consider themselves to be the children of the sky, and their breath and voice are their vital essence. Through the use of the Voice, this power can be articulated into a Thu'um, or Shout. Use Shouts to sharpen blades, strike enemies at a distance, or command time to stand still. Masters of the Voice are known as Tongues, and their power is legendary. The most powerful Tongues cannot speak without causing destruction and must remain gagged at all times, communicating through sign language and the scribing of runes.

NOTE The Words of Power used in Shouts are actual words from the ancient language of the dragons; for example, the Kyne's Peace Shout invokes the Words for "Kyne" "Peace" "Trust." You will learn these Words in context from ancient inscriptions found on Word Walls throughout Skyrim. To learn more about the meaning behind these words and to read translated versions of the inscriptions, see "The Language of Dragons," beginning on page 1096.

The Rule of Thu'um

A Shout is the utterance of one or more Words of Power in order to achieve a specific magical effect. Each Shout has a unique effect, such as summoning or commanding a creature, striking foes with a blast of force to stun or disarm them, or calling down a powerful lightning storm. You should frequently use these powerful special abilities; as the Dragonborn, you have an incredible gift that few heroes have ever possessed!

There are some important general points to remember regarding Shouts:

Each Shout consists of three Words of Power.

You will learn the vast majority of these Words by absorbing them, one at a time, from Word Walls found throughout Skyrim. A few Shouts are also taught to you during the Main Quest, mostly by the Greybeards of High Hrothgar. You always collect Words of Power in the order of the three-word final phrase, so it doesn't matter which Word Wall you visit first.

After you learn a Word, you must unlock it, which requires a Dragon Soul. You can only obtain Dragon Souls by slaying dragons. Since the return of the dragons only begins in earnest after Main Quest: Dragon Rising, you must complete that quest in order to begin unlocking Words and using Shouts.

You need one Dragon Soul for each Word you want to unlock. You can begin using a Shout after learning and unlocking only its first Word, but each additional Word allows you to invoke a more powerful version of the Shout.

Do you know all three Words for five Shouts? Then you'll need to slay and absorb the souls of 15 dragons to fully unlock them all. That's a tall order, so consider carefully which Shouts you really need, and spend your Dragon Souls wisely. For example, the Aura Whisper Shout (which tracks a foe's movement) is great for an assassin but is less useful for a berserker who simply charges into the fray.

Shouts can be added to your Favorites, making switching between them (and employing them for different situations) quick and easy.

Each Shout has up to three levels, corresponding to the Words of Power you've unlocked:

- **Level 1:** Tap the button. One word. Exhale. This is the weakest Shout but takes the shortest amount of time to recharge.
- **Level 2:** Briefly hold, then release the button. Two words. Inhale, then exhale. This is the midlevel Shout.
- **Level 3:** Hold the button. Three words. Inhale, inhale, then exhale. This is the highest level Shout and the most powerful, but it takes the longest to recharge.

The longer you hold the Shout button, the more powerful the shout. When you bellow a Shout, you drain your Thu'um (Shouting power), which slowly rebuilds across your compass. When the compass changes from a pulsing blue back to its regular gray, you can Shout again.

TIP If you don't have (or haven't unlocked) all three Words, holding the button uses the strongest Shout you've unlocked.

A Shout Example: Frost Breath

You begin by learning "Fo" (Frost), the first Word of this Shout, from a Word Wall. After scouring the lands for the second syllable "Krah" (Cold) and the third syllable "Diin" (Freeze), you spend three Dragon Souls to unlock all three Words. You can now use the weak, average, or strong version of this Shout.

Weak Shout: Bellow "Fo!" by tapping the Shout button.

Medium Shout: Bellow "Fo, Krah!" by briefly holding the Shout button, then releasing it.

Strong Shout: Bellow "Fo, Krah, Diin!" by holding the Shout button.

Words to Live By

Some Word Walls are set in Skyrim's exterior, such as this Wall at Shearpoint.

But most Word Walls are hidden in long-forgotten dungeons, such as the Wall in Labyrinthian.

Dawnguard and Dragonborn Word Walls are sometimes new to Skyrim's exterior, such as this Wall at Arcwind Point.

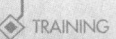

But most are learned during or after your time in other realms or during specific quests, such as this dragon summon in the Soul Cairn.

There are three additional Shouts to obtain during Dawnguard, and four additional Shouts to obtain during Dragonborn.

This section lists all of the available Shouts. Each Shout's name is followed by its three Words, the locations where you can learn them, any quests related to those locations, and some notes and tips on using each Shout. A complete table of Shouts with detailed statistics appears at the end of this section.

Animal Allegiance

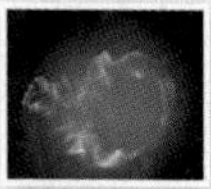

Words of Power: Raan (Animal), Mir (Allegiance), Tah (Pack)

Word Wall Locations:

Angarvunde (the Rift): Dungeon Quest: Medresi Dran and the Wandering Dead

Ancient's Ascent (Falkreath Hold): This is a dragon lair.

Ysgramor's Tomb (Winterhold Hold): The Companions Quest: Glory of the Dead

Description: A Shout for help from the beasts of the wild, who come to fight in your defense.

Notes: This Shout "charms" all nearby animals, who fight for you for a short time. You can attack them without breaking this effect, so it's easy to kill them before the Shout wears off. Note that this Shout does not affect summoned creatures (like Familiars) or creatures already under the control of someone else (like animals controlled by Spriggans).

Aura Whisper

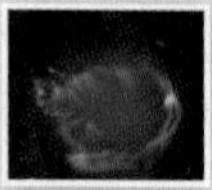

Words of Power: Laas (Life), Yah (Seek), Nir (Hunt)

Word Wall Locations:

Northwind Summit (the Rift): This is a dragon lair.

Valthume (the Reach): Dungeon Quest: Evil in Waiting. This is a dragon priest's lair.

Volunruud (the Pale): Dark Brotherhood Quest: The Silence Has Been Broken; Dungeon Quest: Silenced Tongues

Description: Your Voice is not a Shout but a whisper, revealing the life forces of any and all.

Notes: For a short time, this Shout allows you to see an aura around all living or undead creatures, even through walls. The Shout is silent, so it won't create a sound that would cause enemies to detect you. Great for thieves, archers, and assassins!

Battle Fury

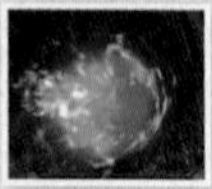

Words of Power: Mid (Loyal), Vur (Valor), Shaan (Inspire)

Word Wall locations: Vahlok's Tomb (Solstheim): Only accessible during Solstheim Side Quest: Lost Legacy.

Description: Your Thu'um enchants your nearby allies' weapons, allowing them to attack faster.

Notes: This Shout increases the attack speed of your allies, including followers and summoned creatures. The second and third words increase its potency, allowing your companions to attack up to 70% faster– and thus do up to 70% more damage for its duration. A great choice if you find yourself with several followers, or ally with a high-damage melee follower.

Become Ethereal

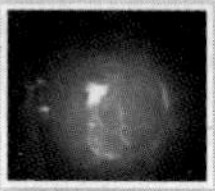

Words of Power: Feim (Fade), Zii (Spirit), Gron (Bind)

Word Wall Locations:

Ironbind Barrow (Winterhold Hold)

Lost Valley Redoubt (the Reach)

Ustengrav (Hjaalmarch): Main Quest: The Horn of Jurgen Windcaller

Description: The Thu'um reaches out to the Void, changing your form to one that cannot harm or be harmed.

Notes: While Ethereal, you are invulnerable, you can't attack or cast spells, and you recover Magicka and Stamina. This Shout gives you a few seconds to safely retreat or reposition yourself during a difficult battle. You can also use it to bypass most traps without fear of taking damage.

Bend Will

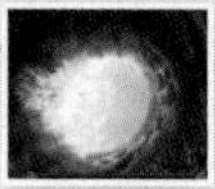

Words of Power: Gol (Stone/Earth), Hah (Mind), Dov (Dragon)

Word Wall locations:

Saering's Watch (Solstheim): The first Word of this Shout is always learned here.

Hermaeus Mora (Apocrypha): The second and third Words of this Shout are always learned from this Daedric Prince, during Dragonborn Main Quest: The Gardener of Men.

Description: Your voice bends the very stones to your will. As it gains power, animals, people, and even dragons must do your bidding.

Notes: The first Word of this Shout is used during Dragonborn Main Quest: Cleansing the Stones to remove the traces of Miraak's construction around the ancient All-Makers Stones of Solstheim. The second Word forces those around you (neutral characters and creatures) to ally themselves against an enemy you're fighting for 30 seconds. But the third Word of this Shout is the most precious, enabling you to tame and ride dragons! Consult page 108 for more information.

Call Dragon

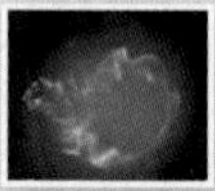

Words of Power: Od (Snow), Ah (Hunter), Viing (Wing)

Word Wall Locations:

None. You learn this Shout during Main Quest: The Fallen.

Description: Odahviing! Hear my Voice and come forth. I summon you in my time of need.

Notes: This Shout summons the dragon Odahviing to battle during Main Quest: The Fallen. After you complete the main quest, you can summon Odahviing to aid you (in most exterior areas). Note that this Shout has no effect unless all three words are used.

Call of Valor

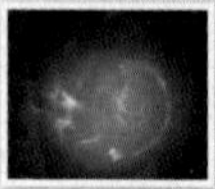

Words of Power: Hun (Hero), Kaal (Champion), Zoor (Legend)

Word Wall Locations:

None. You learn this Shout at the end of the main quest.

Description: The valiant of Sovngarde hear your Voice, and journey beyond space and time to lend their aid.

Notes: Each level of this Shout summons a different hero from Sovngarde, each with unique equipment and abilities. Choose the one that best meets your needs for the current battle.

"Hun" summons Gormlaith Golden-Hilt, who wields a bow, sword, shield, and a few Shouts.

"Hun, Kaal" summons Felldir the Old, who wields a greatsword and has a number of damaging Shouts.

"Hun, Kaal, Zoor" summons Hakon One-Eye, who wields a battleax and uses melee Shouts.

Clear Skies

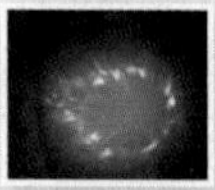

Words of Power: Lok (Sky), Vah (Spring), Koor (Summer)

Word Wall Locations:

None. You learn this Shout from the Greybeards during Main Quest: The Throat of the World.

Description: Skyrim itself yields before the Thu'um, as you clear away fog and inclement weather.

Notes: This clears the weather and disperses fog, and it dispels poison gas traps.

Cyclone

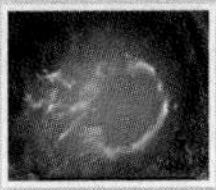

Words of Power: Ven (Wind), Gaar (Unleash/Release), Nos (Strike)

Word Wall locations:

Benkongerike (Solstheim)

White Ridge Barrow (Solstheim)

Kolbjorn Barrow (Solstheim): During Solstheim Side Quest: Unearthed

Description: Your Thu'um creates a whirling cyclone that sows chaos among your enemies.

Notes: This Shout conjures up a maelstrom of wind that departs your presence, striking enemies and throwing them up into the skies, where they're inflicted with blasts of wind and damage as they land. The pain caused and range increases as you learn the Words. This is helpful when facing foes you wish to keep from close combat (like Giants) or multiple foes bunched together.

Disarm

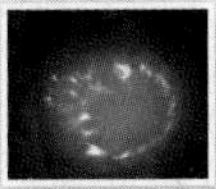

Words of Power: Zun (Weapon), Haal (Hand), Viik (Defeat)

Word Wall Locations:

Eldersblood Peak (Hjaalmarch): This is a dragon lair.

Silverdrift Lair (the Pale)

Snow Veil Sanctum (Winterhold Hold): Thieves Guild Quest: Speaking with Silence

Description: Shout defies steel as you rip the weapon from an opponent's grasp.

Notes: This Shout only affects enemies up to a specific level, with higher levels of the Shout allowing you to disarm higher-level foes. Refer to the chart at the end of this section for details. Note that some enemies cannot be disarmed.

Dismaying Shout

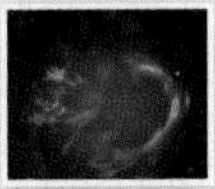

Words of Power: Faas (Fear), Ru (Run), Maar (Terror)

Word Wall Locations:

Dead Crone Rock (the Reach): Daedric Quest: Pieces of the Past

Labyrinthian (Hjaalmarch): In Shalidor's Maze

Lost Tongue Overlook (the Rift): This is a dragon lair.

Description: And the weak shall fear the Thu'um, and flee in terror.

Notes: This Shout only affects enemies up to a specific level, with higher levels of the Shout allowing you to affect higher-level foes. See the chart at the end of this section for details.

Dragonrend

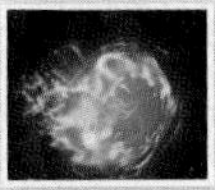

Words of Power: Joor (Mortal), Zah (Finite), Frul (Temporary)

Word Wall Locations:

None. You learn this shout during Main Quest: Alduin's Bane.

Description: Your Voice lashes out at a dragon's very soul, forcing the beast to land.

Notes: This Shout is extremely useful for fighting Alduin or other dragons if you prefer to face them in melee combat.

Drain Vitality

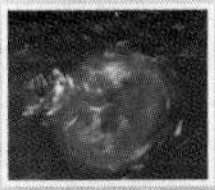

Words of Power: Gaan (Stamina), Lah (Magicka), Haas (Health)

Word Wall locations:

Arcwind Point (the Rift)

Dimhollow Crypt (the Pale)

The Frozen lake (Forgotten vale): This is a large rock, rather than a Word Wall.

Description: Coax both magical and mortal energies from your hapless opponent.

Notes: This Shout absorbs Stamina, then Magicka and Stamina, then finally Health, Magicka, and Stamina from a foe or character you hit with it (5 points per second, for 30 seconds). You learn this Shout one word at a time via Word Walls, in the usual manner. It allows you to claw back energies from foes to endure a long combat and lessen your dependency on healing magic and potions, while at the same hindering your foe considerably.

Dragon Aspect

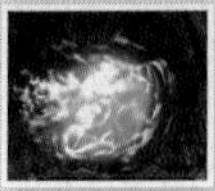

Words of Power: Mul (Strength), Qah (Armor), Diiv (Wyrm)

Word Wall locations:

Raven Rock Mine (Solstheim): During Solstheim Side Quest: The Final Descent

Temple of Miraak (Solstheim): During Dragonborn Main Quest: The Temple of Miraak

Waking Dreams of a Starless Sky (Apocrypha): During Dragonborn Main Quest: At the Summit of Apocrypha

Description: Once a day, take on the mighty aspect of a dragon, delivering colossal blows and possessing an armored hide and more powerful Shouts.

Notes: You are bound in ethereal armor for 300 seconds, and once you learn two or three Words, an Ancient Dragonborn appears by you when your Health is reduced to half or lower. Your Armor Rating (+25) and Power Attacks are increased (+25%), and at two Words, +25% Fire and Frost Resistance is available, as well as an increased Armor Rating (+100). The third Word reduces your Shout regeneration time by 20%. You may use this powerful Thu'um only once per day.

Elemental Fury

Words of Power: Su (Air), Grah (Battle), Dun (Grace)

Word Wall Locations:

Dragontooth Crater (the Reach): This is a dragon lair.

Kilkreath Ruins (Haafingar): Daedric Quest: The Break of Dawn

Shriekwind Bastion (Falkreath Hold)

Description: The Thu'um imbues your arms with the speed of wind, allowing for faster weapon strikes.

Notes: This Shout lasts only a short time, but increases your damage output by 30-70%. Time it well, and you can do some serious damage.

Fire Breath

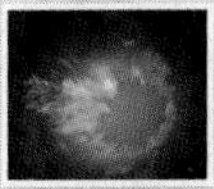

Words of Power: Yol (Fire), Toor (Inferno), Shul (Sun)

Word Wall Locations:

Dustman's Cairn (Whiterun Hold): The Companions Quest: Proving Honor

Sunderstone Gorge (Falkreath Hold)

Throat of the World (Whiterun Hold): Main Quest: The Throat of the World.

Description: Inhale air, exhale flame, and behold the Thu'um as inferno.

Notes: Fire Breath does high damage in a quick burst and sets enemies on fire. Great against foes already susceptible to fire damage (such as Vampires or Frost Atronachs).

Frost Breath

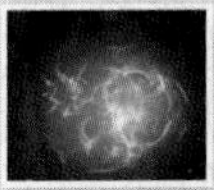

Words of Power: Fo (Frost), Krah (Cold), Diin (Freeze)

Word Wall Locations:

Bonestrewn Crest (Eastmarch): This is a dragon lair.

Folgunthur (Hjaalmarch): Side Quest: Forbidden Legend

Skyborn Altar (Hjaalmarch): This is a dragon lair.

Description: Your breath is winter, you Thu'um a blizzard.

Notes: Frost Breath does about the same damage over time as Fire Breath but slows your enemies instead of setting them on fire. If your foes are more susceptible to frost than flame (such as Fire Atronachs), or if you can take advantage of the slowing effect, this is a good choice.

Ice Form

Words of Power: Iiz (Ice), Slen (Flesh), Nus (Statue)

Word Wall Locations:

Frostmere Crypt (the Pale): Dungeon Quest: The Pale Lady

Mount Anthor (Winterhold Hold): This is a dragon lair.

Saarthal (Winterhold Hold): College of Winterhold Quest: Under Saarthal; Side Quest: Forbidden Legend

Description: Your Thu'um freezes an opponent solid.

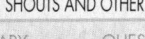

Notes: This Shout takes the form of a wave of frost that freezes your enemies solid. Foes struck by this Shout are encased in ice and effectively paralyzed, and they take frost damage over time. If an enemy encased in ice is struck by an attack, the ice shatters, allowing them to recover. Use this Shout to take one or more foes out of the fight temporarily or to buy yourself a few free attacks before they can recover.

Kyne's Peace

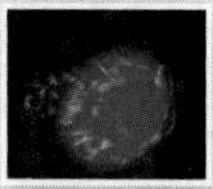

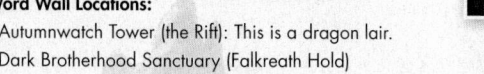

Words of Power: Kaan (Kyne), Drem (Peace), Ov (Trust)

Word Wall Locations:

Ragnvald (the Reach): This is a dragon priest's lair.

Rannveig's Fast (Whiterun Hold)

Shroud Hearth Barrow (The Rift): Dungeon Quest: Wilhelm's Scream

Description: The Voice soothes wild beasts, who lose their desire to fight of flee.

Notes: This Shout only affects wild animals, with the radius and duration of the Shout increasing at higher levels. This allows you to navigate animal dens without fighting or pacify a pack of animals before picking them off one by one.

Marked for Death

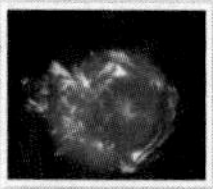

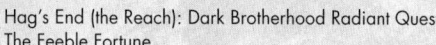

Words of Power: Krii (Kill), Lun (Leech), Aus (Suffer)

Word Wall Locations:

Autumnwatch Tower (the Rift): This is a dragon lair.

Dark Brotherhood Sanctuary (Falkreath Hold)

Forsaken Cave (the Pale): Side Quest: The White Phial

Description: Speak, and let your Voice herald doom, as an opponent's armor and life force are weakened.

Notes: This Shout saps your foes' armor and causes damage over time, allowing you to kill them more quickly. Good to use on bosses.

Slow Time

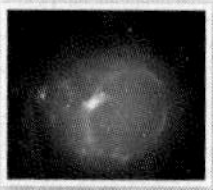

Words of Power: Tiid (Time), Klo (Sand), Ul (Eternity)

Word Wall Locations:

Hag's End (the Reach): Dark Brotherhood Radiant Quest: The Feeble Fortune

Korvanjund (The Pale): Civil War Quest: The Jagged Crown

Labyrinthian (Hjaalmarch): College of Winterhold Quest: The Staff of Magnus; this is a Dragon Priest's lair.

Description: Shout at time, and command it to obey, as the world around you stands still.

Notes: This Shout buys you extra time, which you can use for any purpose: to rush in and assault a helpless enemy, to line up a perfect sniper shot, or to easily outrun any foe. Incredibly useful!

Soul Tear

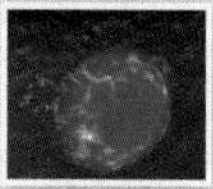

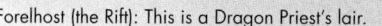

Words of Power: Rii (Essence), Vaaz (Tear), Zol (Zombie)

Word Wall Locations: None, the Soul Tear is learned one Word at a time, every time you succeed in summoning Durnehviir to Tamriel using the Summon Durnehviir Shout (below). Summon this dragon three times to learn all three words, expend three Dragon Souls, and claim this Shout as your own. Consult Side Quest: Durnehviir (page 564) for more information.

Description: Your Thu'um cuts through flesh and shatters souls, commanding the will of the fallen.

Notes: Does 300 damage, soul-traps your target, and reanimates slain foes for 60 seconds. A truly devastating Shout, and one that can critically wound even the hardiest of foes. Slain foes are resurrected within the Shout's blast radius and can augment your fighting prowess considerably. However, this Shout has no effect until you learn all three words. Simply yelling "Rii vaaz!" may get you funny looks but no devastating combat victories.

Storm Call

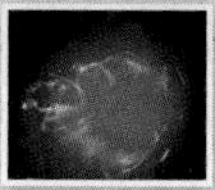

Words of Power: Strun (Storm), Bah (Wrath), Qo (Lightning)

Word Wall Locations:

Forelhost (the Rift): This is a Dragon Priest's lair.

High Gate Ruins (the Pale): This is a Dragon Priest's lair.

Skuldafn (Other Realm): Main Quest: The World-Eater's Eyrie. This is a Dragon Priest's lair.

Description: A Shout to the skies, a cry to the clouds, that awakens the destructive force of Skyrim's lightning.

Notes: Summons a thunderstorm with powerful lightning that lashes out at anything and anyone. Only works outdoors. It's fantastic against dragons, but be careful—the lightning can and will kill civilians and your Followers.

Summon Durnehviir

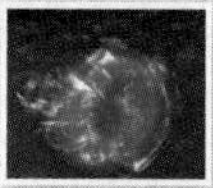

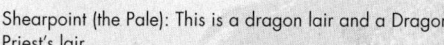

Words of Power: Dur (Curse), Neh (Never), Viir (Dying)

Word Wall Locations: None. You must enter the Soul Cairn, defeat Durnehviir in combat, meet this undead dragon as you depart the Boneyard, and learn all three Words from him so you can summon him in Tamriel. See Side Quest: Durnehviir (page 564) for more information.

Description: Durnehviir! Hear my voice and come forth from the Soul Cairn. I summon you in my time of need.

Notes: Remember to expend three Dragon Souls to learn all parts of the Word and summon the dragon. Simply yelling "Dur neh!" won't break the bonds holding the dragon in the Soul Cairn. In addition to summoning a powerful dragon to fight for you, this Shout also advances your pact with Durnehviir: each time you summon him, he teaches you the next Word of the Soul Tear Shout (above).

Throw Voice

Words of Power: Zul (Voice), Mey (Fool), Gut (Far)

Word Wall Locations:

Shearpoint (the Pale): This is a dragon lair and a Dragon Priest's lair.

Description: The Thu'um is heard, but its source unknown, fooling those into seeking it out.

Notes: This Shout produces no sound at your location, instead throwing your voice to the target. Enemies will detect the sound and investigate, allowing you to lure them away from their posts or into traps or other hazards. This is immensely useful when sneaking. Throw Voice is unique in that its Word Wall teaches you all three Words of the Shout.

Unrelenting Force

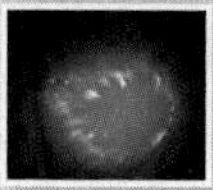

Words of Power: Fus (Force), Ro (Balance), Dah (Push)

Word Wall Locations:

Bleak Falls Barrow (Falkreath Hold): Main Quest: Bleak Falls Barrow; Side Quest: The Golden Claw

High Hrothgar (Whiterun Hold): Main Quest: The Way of the Voice. You learn both the second and third Words from the Greybeards.

Description: Your Voice is raw power, pushing aside anything—or anyone—who stands in your path.

Notes: This Shout staggers enemies or sends them flying, and does some light damage. Aim carefully to push your foes into traps, or follow up with a swift melee or ranged attack to take advantage of the stagger.

Whirlwind Sprint

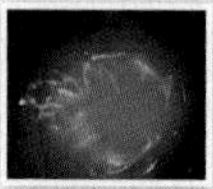

Words of Power: Wuld (Whirlwind), Nah (Fury), Kest (Tempest)

Word Wall Locations:

Dead Men's Respite (Hjaalmarch): The Bards College Quest: Tending the Flames

High Hrothgar (Whiterun Hold): Main Quest: The Way of the Voice. Learned from the Greybeards.

Volskygge (Haafingar): This is a Dragon Priest's lair.

Description: The Thu'um rushes forward, carrying you in its wake with the speed of a tempest.

Notes: This surge forward is useful for reaching otherwise-inaccessible ledges or platforms.

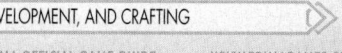

The Shouting Table

The following table provides a summary of all the Shouts and their effects:

SHOUTS

Shout Name	Word	Rebuild Time	Description	Quest / Special Restrictions
Animal Allegiance	Raan	50	Command Animal, Small Radius, Max Lv20, 30s	
	Mir	60	Command Animal, Medium Radius, Max Lv20, 45s	
	Tah	70	Command Animal, Large Radius, Max Lv20, 60s	
Aura Whisper	Laas	30	Detect Life & Undead, 10s	
	Yah	40	Detect Life & Undead, 20s	
	Nir	50	Detect Life & Undead, 30s	
Battle Fury	Mid	30	Allies attack 30% faster, 15s	Learned during Dragonborn Side Quest: Lost Legacy
	Vur	40	Allies attack 50% faster, 15s	Learned during Dragonborn Side Quest: Lost Legacy
	Shaan	50	Allies attack 70% faster, 15s	Learned during Dragonborn Side Quest: Lost Legacy
Become Ethereal	Feim	20	Ethereal, 8s	
	Zii	30	Ethereal, 13s	
	Gron	40	Ethereal, 18s	
Bend Will	Gol	10	Command Stones	Learned at Saering's Watch
	Hah	90	Command Mortals (30s), or Stones	Learned during Dragonborn Main Quest: The Gardener of Men
	Dov	90	Command Dragons, Mortals, or Stones	Learned during Dragonborn Main Quest: The Gardener of Men
Call Dragon	Od	5	-No effect-	Learned during Main Quest: The Fallen
	Ah	5	-No effect-	Learned during Main Quest: The Fallen
	Viing	300	Summons Odahviing	Learned during Main Quest: The Fallen
Call of Valor	Hun	180	Summons Gormlaith Golden-Hilt, 1m	Learned during Main Quest: Epilogue
	Kaal	180	Summons Felldir the Old, 1m	Learned during Main Quest: Epilogue
	Zoor	180	Summons Hakon One-Eye, 1m	Learned during Main Quest: Epilogue
Clear Skies	Lok	5	Clear Skies, 25s	Learned during Main Quest: The Throat of the World
	Vah	10	Clear Skies, 40s	Learned during Main Quest: The Throat of the World
	Koor	15	Clear Skies, 60s	Learned during Main Quest: The Throat of the World
Cyclone	Ven	20	Small Cyclone, 20 Damage/s	
	Gaar	40	Medium Cyclone, 40 Damage/s	
	Nos	60	Large Cyclone, 60 Damage/s	
Disarm	Zun	30	Disarm, Max Lv12	
	Haal	35	Disarm, Max Lv20	
	Viik	40	Disarm, Max Lv30	
Dismay	Faas	40	Fear, Max Lv7	
	Ru	45	Fear, Max Lv15	
	Maar	50	Fear, Max Lv24	
Dragonrend	Joor	10	Force Dragons to land; 15s	Learned during Main Quest: Alduin's Bane
	Zah	12	Force Dragons to land; 18s	Learned during Main Quest: Alduin's Bane
	Frul	15	Force Dragons to land; 22s	Learned during Main Quest: Alduin's Bane
Drain Vitality	Gaan	30	Absorb Stamina; 5/s, 30s	
	Lah	60	Absorb Magicka & Stamina; 5/s, 30s	
	Haas	90	Absorb Health, Magicka, & Stamina; 5/s, 30s	
Dragon Aspect	Mul	5	Once per day for 5m, +25 Armor, +25% Power Attack Damage.	Learned in Raven Rock Mine

SHOUTS

Shout Name	Word	Rebuild Time	Description	Quest / Special Restrictions
	Qah	5	Once per day for 5m, +25% Fire and Frost Resistance, +75 Armor, +25% Power Attack Damage, Summons an Ancient Dragonborn if your health falls below 50%.	Learned during Dragonborn Main Quest: The Temple of Miraak
	Diiv	5	Once per day for 5m, Increased Shout Effectiveness, Shouts recover 20% faster, +25% Fire and Frost Resistance, +100 Armor, +25% Power Attack Damage, Summons an Ancient Dragonborn if your health falls below 50%.	Learned during Dragonborn Main Quest: At the Summit of Apocrypha
Elemental Fury	Su	30	Increase Attack Speed (1.3x), 15s	
	Grah	40	Increase Attack Speed (1.5x), 15s	
	Dun	50	Increase Attack Speed (1.7x), 15s	
Fire Breath	Yol	30	Fire Breath; 50 Fire Damage	
	Toor	50	Fire Breath; 70 Fire Damage	
	Shul	100	Fire Breath; 90 Fire Damage	
Frost Breath	Fo	30	Frost Breath, Frost Damage 10/s for 5s, Slow	
	Krah	50	Frost Breath, Frost Damage 14/s for 5s, Slow	
	Diin	100	Frost Breath, Frost Damage 18/s for 5s, Slow	
Ice Form	Iiz	60	Ice Form Paralyze, Frost Damage 2/s, 15s	
	Slen	90	Ice Form Paralyze, Frost Damage 2/s, 30s	
	Nus	120	Ice Form Paralyze, Frost Damage 2/s, 60s	
Kyne's Peace	Kaan	40	Calm Animal, Small Area, Max Lv20, 60s	
	Drem	50	Calm Animal, Medium Area, Max Lv20, 120s	
	Ov	60	Calm Animal, Large Area, Max Lv20, 180s	
Marked for Death	Krii	20	-25 Armor, Damage Health 1/s, 60s	
	Lun	30	-50 Armor, Damage Health 2/s, 60s	
	Aus	40	-75 Armor, Damage Health 3/s, 60s	
Slow Time	Tiid	30	Slow Time (70%), 8s	
	Klo	45	Slow Time (80%), 12s	
	Ul	60	Slow Time (90%), 16s	
Soul Tear	Rii	5	-No effect-	Learned during Dawnguard Side Quest: Durnehviir
	Vaaz	5	-No effect-	Learned during Dawnguard Side Quest: Durnehviir
	Zol	90	Soul Tear, 300 Damage & Reanimate slain foes for 60s	Learned during Dawnguard Side Quest: Durnehviir
Storm Call	Strun	300	Call Storm, 60s	
	Bah	480	Call Storm, 120s	
	Qo	600	Call Storm, 180s	
Summon Durnehviir	Dur	5	-No effect-	Learned during Dawnguard Main Quest: Beyond Death
	Neh	5	-No effect-	Learned during Dawnguard Main Quest: Beyond Death
	Viir	300	Summons Durnehviir	Learned during Dawnguard Main Quest: Beyond Death
Throw Voice	Zul	30	Throw Voice	
	Mey	15	Throw Voice	
	Gut	5	Throw Voice	
Unrelenting Force	Fus	15	Unrelenting Force (Weak), 2 Damage	Learned in Bleak Falls Barrow.
	Ro	20	Unrelenting Force (Med), 5 Damage	Learned during Main Quest: The Way of the Voice
	Dah	45	Unrelenting Force (Strong), 10 Damage	Learned during Main Quest: The Way of the Voice
Whirlwind Sprint	Wuld	20	Whirlwind Sprint (Short)	
	Nah	25	Whirlwind Sprint (Med)	
	Kest	35	Whirlwind Sprint (Long)	

Other Powers and Abilities

Powers

As Dragonborn, Shouts are your most numerous type of power, but there are many other powers and abilities that you can acquire during your time in Skyrim. These are listed in the following table, and include:

Racial powers, also described in this chapter (page 7).

Standing Stone powers, also described in this chapter (page 93).

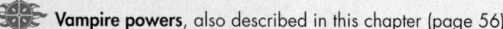

Vampire powers, also described in this chapter (page 56).

Werewolf powers, also described in this chapter (page 62).

Sacred Stone powers, also described in this chapter (page 94).

Apocrypha powers, also described in this chapter (page 96).

Nightingale powers, also described at the end of the Thieves Guild questline, on page 300.

A Dark Brotherhood power, your reward for Dark Brotherhood Quest: Bound Until Death, as described on page 324.

All Powers are found in the Magic > Powers part of your Inventory Menu. Equip a power by assigning it to the button or key you use for your Dragon Shout.

AVAILABLE POWERS

✓	NAME	DESCRIPTION	USE	ASSOCIATED LOCATION, QUEST, OR RACE
		RACIAL POWERS		
☐	Adrenaline Rush	Stamina regenerates 10x faster for 60 seconds.	Once per day	Redguard racial power
☐	Ancestor's Wrath	For 60 seconds, opponents that get too close take 8 points per second of fire damage.	Once per day	Dark Elf racial power
☐	Battle Cry	Targets flee for 30 seconds.	Once per day	Nord racial power
☐	Berserker Rage	You take half damage and do double damage for 60 seconds.	Once per day	Orc racial power
☐	Command Animal	Make an animal an ally for 60 seconds.	Once per day	Wood Elf racial power
☐	Dragonskin	Absorb 50% of the Magicka from hostile spells for 60 seconds.	Once per day	Breton racial power
☐	Highborn	Regenerate Magicka faster for 60 seconds.	Once per day	High Elf racial power
☐	Histskin	Invoke the power of the Hist to recover health ten times faster for 60 seconds.	Once per day	Argonian racial power
☐	Night Eye	Improved night vision for 60 seconds.	Unlimited times per day	Khajiit racial power
☐	Voice of the Emperor	Calms nearby people for 60 seconds.	Once per day	Imperial racial power
		STANDING STONE POWERS		
☐	The Ritual Stone	Temporarily reanimates corpses in the immediate area.	Once per day	Activate the Ritual Standing Stone
☐	The Serpent Stone	Target is paralyzed for 5 seconds and takes 25 points of damage over 5 seconds.	Once per day	Activate the Serpent Standing Stone
☐	The Shadow Stone	Invisibility for 60 seconds. Activating an object or attacking will break the spell.	Once per day	Activate the Shadow Standing Stone
☐	The Tower Stone	Unlock any expert or lower lock once per day.	Once per day	Activate the Tower Standing Stone
		VAMPIRE POWERS		
☐	Embrace of Shadows	You can become invisible. Improved night vision for 180 seconds.	Once per day	Vampire power
☐	Vampiric Drain	Absorb a set number of points of health per second from the target.	Unlimited times per day	Vampire Lord Power
☐	Vampire Lord	Transform into a Vampire Lord. Use the Revert Form power to change back.	Unlimited times per day	Vampire Lord power
☐	Vampire's Seduction	Creatures and people up to Level 8 won't fight for 30 seconds.	Once per day	Vampire power
☐	Vampire's Servant	Reanimate a dead body to fight for you for 60 seconds.	Once per day	Vampire power
☐	Vampire's Sight	Improved night vision for 60 seconds.	Unlimited times per day	Vampire power
		WEREWOLF POWERS		
☐	Beast Form	Take on the form of a werewolf.	Once per day	Werewolf power
☐	Ring of Hircine	Take on the form of a werewolf.	Once per day	Werewolf power
☐	Totem of Brotherhood	Summons two wolf spirits to aid in battle	Unlimited times per day	Werewolf power (Reward from Companions Radiant Quest: Totems of Hircine)
☐	Totem of Fear	Casts Fear against nearby enemies	Unlimited times per day	Werewolf power (reward from Companions Radiant Quest: Totems of Hircine)
☐	Totem of the Hunt	Casts a Detect Life spell.	Unlimited times per day	Werewolf power (Reward from Companions Radiant Quest: Totems of Hircine)
		SACRED STONE POWERS		
☐	Bones of the Earth	Caster ignores 80% of all physical damage for 30 seconds	Single use, then must be reacquired at the Earth Stone	Earth Stone Power (Solstheim)
☐	Conjure Werebear	Summons a werebear for 60 seconds wherever the caster is pointing	Single use, then must be reacquired at the Beast Stone	Beast Stone Power (Solstheim)
☐	North Wind	Target takes 20 points of frost damage for 10 seconds, plus stamina damage	Single use, then must be reacquired at the Wind Stone	Wind Stone Power (Solstheim)
☐	Root of Power	Spells cost 75% less Magicka for 60 seconds.	Single use, then must be reacquired at the Tree Stone	Tree Stone Power (Temple of Miraak, Solstheim)
☐	Sun Flare	A 100-point fiery explosion centered on the caster, inflicting more damage to closer targets.	Single use, then must be reacquired at the Sun Stone.	Sun Stone power (Solstheim)

AVAILABLE POWERS, CONTINUED

✓	NAME	DESCRIPTION	USE	ASSOCIATED LOCATION, QUEST, OR RACE
☐	Waters of Life	Heals everyone close to the caster 300 points.	Single use, then must be reacquired at the Water Stone	Water Stone power (Solstheim)
		APOCRYPHA POWERS		
☐	Bardic Knowledge	Summons a spectral drum that plays for 300 seconds, improving Stamina Regen for you and nearby allies	Unlimited times per day	Black Book: Untold Legends
☐	Black Market	Summons a Dremora merchant for 15 seconds	Unlimited times per day	Black Book: Untold Legends
☐	Secret Servant	Summons a Dremora butler for 15 seconds to carry your excess items	Unlimited times per day	Black Book: Untold Legends
☐	Mora's Agony	Summons a field of writhing tentacles that poisons foes	Once per day	Black Book: The Hidden Twilight
☐	Mora's Boon	Fully restores your Health, Stamina, and Magicka	Once per day	Black Book: The Hidden Twilight
☐	Mora's Grasp	Freezes the target between Oblivion and Tamriel for 30 seconds, making them immune to all damage.	Once per day	Black Book: The Hidden Twilight
☐	Secret of Arcana	Spells cost no Magicka for 30 seconds	Once per day	Black Book: Filament and Filigree
☐	Secret of Protection	You take half damage for 30 seconds from all physical attacks and most magical attacks	Once per day	Black Book: Filament and Filigree
☐	Secret of Strength	Power attacks cost no Stamina for 30 seconds	Once per day	Black Book: Filament and Filigree
		OTHER POWERS		
☐	Breath of Nchuak	Draws upon stamina to release a scorching blast of steam that deals 15 points of damage per second.	Unlimited times per day	Reward from collecting Unique Item: Visage of Mzund from Fahlbtharz (Solstheim)
☐	Nightingale Strife	Instantly absorb 100 points of Health from the target.	Once per day	Reward from Thieves Guild Quest: Darkness Returns.
☐	Nightingale Subterfuge	People and creatures in the spell's area of effect will attack anyone nearby for 30 seconds.	Once per day	Reward from Thieves Guild Quest: Darkness Returns.
☐	Shadowcloak of Nocturnal	For 120 seconds you automatically become invisible while sneaking.	Once per day	Reward from Thieves Guild Quest: Darkness Returns.
☐	Summon Karstaag	Summon Karstaag to fight for you for 120 seconds.	You may use this ability only three times and only while outdoors	Reward from Solstheim Side Quest: Karstaag's Resurrection*
☐	Summon Spectral Assassin	Summons the ghost of the legendary assassin Lucien Lachance to fight by your side, until he's defeated.	Once per day	Reward from Dark Brotherhood Quest: Bound Until Death.

Abilities

Most special abilities are offered as rewards for quests or for performing specific actions. They typically appear in your Active Effects list. Note that some are presented explicitly (with dialogue and/or onscreen text), while others may not be. A few are not visible to you at all, so learn when you can obtain them and how long they last. These are listed in the following table and include:

- Permanent Abilities (Nonskill Perks)
- Racial Abilities (innate to each race)
- Standing Stone Abilities (Skyrim's Standing Stones)
- Temporary Abilities (Buffs)
- Blessings (and Disease Curing): From shrines (see next section)

AVAILABLE ABILITIES

✓	NAME	DESCRIPTION	ASSOCIATED QUEST OR SPECIAL INSTRUCTIONS
		PERMANENT ABILITIES (NONSKILL PERKS)	
☐	Agent of Dibella	+10% melee damage to the opposite sex.	Temple Quest: The Heart of Dibella
☐	Agent of Mara	+15% Resist Magic.	Temple Quest: The Book of Love
☐	Ahzidal's Genius	+10 Enchanting while wearing four or more Relics of Ahzidal.	Solstheim Side Quest: Unearthed
☐	Ancient Knowledge	+25% Armor if wearing all Dwarven armor. Your Smithing skill increases 15% faster.	Side Quest: Unfathomable Depths
☐	Archmage's Authority	Better prices from members of the College (50% Enthir, 10% others).	College of Winterhold Quest: The Eye of Magnus
☐	Assassin's Aegis	+25% Armor if wearing all Dark Brotherhood Armor.	Dark Brotherhood Quest: Sanctuary
☐	Boethiah's Blessing	You are able to move more quietly, and close opponents receive 5 poison damage per second.	Wear Ebony Mail
☐	Blessing of the Stag Prince	Receive additional Health and Stamina while the Bow of the Stag Prince is equipped (increases as you slay more animals).	Equip Glass Bow of the Stag Prince (Solstheim)
☐	Deathbrand Instinct	+100 Armor if wearing all Deathbrand Armor.	Solstheim Side Quest: Deathbrand
☐	Dragon Infusion	You take 25% less melee damage from dragons.	Blades (Other Faction) Quest: Dragon Research
☐	Eternal Spirit	While ethereal, you recover health 25% faster.	Greybeards (Other Faction) Quest: Meditations on the Words of Power
☐	Force Without Effort	You stagger 25% less, and foes stagger 25% more.	Greybeards (Other Faction) Quest: Meditations on the Words of Power
☐	Gift of the Gab	Your Speech skill increases 15% faster.	Bards College (Other Faction) Quest: Tending the Flames

AVAILABLE ABILITIES, CONTINUED

✓	NAME	DESCRIPTION	ASSOCIATED QUEST OR SPECIAL INSTRUCTIONS
☐	Nightingale's Aegis	+25% Armor if wearing all Nightingale Armor.	Thieves Guild Quest: Trinity Restored
☐	Prowler's Profit	Chance of finding additional gems in chests.	Thieves Guild Quest: No Stone Unturned
☐	Sailor's Repose	Healing spells restore 10% more health.	Dungeon Quest (Frostflow Lighthouse): What Lies Beneath
☐	Sinderion's Serendipity	When you make a potion, you have a 25% chance of creating a second, duplicate potion.	Side Quest: A Return to Your Roots
☐	The Fire Within	Your Fire Breath Shout deals 25% more damage.	Greybeards (Other Faction) Quest: Meditations on the Words of Power

✓	NAME	DESCRIPTION	NOTES
	PERMANENT ABILITIES (INNATE RACIAL ABILITIES)		
☐	Resist Disease (Argonian)	Your Argonian blood is 50% resistance to disease.	Argonian race
☐	Waterbreathing	Your Argonian lungs can breathe underwater.	Argonian race
☐	Magic Resistance	Your Breton blood grants 25% resistance to magic.	Breton race
☐	Resist Fire	Your Dunmer blood gives you 50% resistance to Fire.	Dark Elf race
☐	Highborn	High Elves are born with 50 additional Magicka.	High Elf race
☐	Imperial Luck	Anywhere gold coins might be found, Imperials always seem to find a few more.	Imperial race
☐	Khajiit claws	Inflict 4x unarmed damage.	Khajiit race
☐	Resist Frost	Your Nord blood gives you 50% resistance to Frost.	Nord race
☐	Resist Poison (Redguard)	Your Redguard blood gives you 50% resistance to poison.	Redguard race
☐	Champion of the Night	Illusion spells cast by a vampire are 25% more powerful	Vampire race
☐	Resist Disease (Vampire)	Your vampiric blood gives you 100% resistance to disease.	Vampire race
☐	Resist Disease (Werewolf)	Your beast blood gives you 100% resistance to disease.	Vampire race
☐	Resist Poison (Vampire)	Your vampiric blood gives you 100% resistance to poison.	Vampire race
☐	Resist Disease and Poison	Your Bosmer blood gives you 50% resistance to disease and poison.	Wood Elf race

✓	NAME	DESCRIPTION	NOTES
	STANDING STONES ABILITIES (NONSKILL PERKS)		
☐	The Apprentice Stone	Those under the sign of the Apprentice recover Magicka faster but are more susceptible to Magicka damage.	100% Magicka regeneration, 100% weakness to Magicka
☐	The Atronach Stone	Those under the sign of the Atronach absorb a portion of incoming spell damage and have a larger pool of Magicka but recover it more slowly.	50% Spell Absorption, +50 Magicka, Magicka regenerates 50% slower
☐	The Lady Stone	Those under the sign of the Lady regenerate Health and Stamina more quickly.	Regenerate health and stamina 25% faster
☐	The Lord Stone	Those under the sign of the Lord are more resistant to both Magicka and physical damage.	50 Armor, 25% Magic Resistance
☐	The Lover Stone	Those under the sign of the Lover always feel a Lover's Comfort (all skills improve faster).	Learn all skills 15% faster
☐	The Mage Stone	Those under the sign of the Mage will learn all Magic skills 20% faster.	Learn Mage skills 20% faster
☐	The Steed Stone	Those under the sign of the Steed can carry more and do not suffer a movement penalty from armor.	100 extra carrying capacity; no movement penalty is applied due to armor; equipped armor is weightless
☐	The Thief Stone	Those under the sign of the Thief will learn all Stealth skills 20% faster.	Learn Thief skills 20% faster
☐	The Warrior Stone	Those under the sign of the Warrior will learn all combat skills 20% faster.	Learn Warrior skills 20% faster

✓	NAME	DESCRIPTION	ASSOCIATED ACTIVITY
	TEMPORARY ABILITIES (BUFFS)		
☐	Blood of the Ancients	Your Vampiric Drain spell absorbs Magicka and Stamina from your victim for several days.	Dawnguard Main Quest: The Bloodstone Chalice, then drink from the Bloodstone Chalice
☐	Tainted Blood of the Ancients	Your Vampiric Drain spell absorbs Magicka and Stamina from your victims for 1 day, but at the cost of 30 less health.	Dawnguard Main Quest: The Bloodstone Chalice, drink from the Bloodspring in Redwater Den
☐	Dragonslayer's Blessing	+10% Critical Hit Chance vs. Dragons; lasts 5 days.	Blades (Other Faction) Quest: Dragonslayer's Blessing
☐	Voice of the Sky	Animals will neither attack nor flee from you; lasts 1 day.	Complete the Pilgrimage of the Seven Thousand Steps (Secondary Location [6.x])
☐	Rested	All skills improve 5% faster; lasts 8 hours.	Sleep in any bed
☐	Well Rested	All skills improve 10% faster; lasts 8 hours.	Sleep in a bed you own or rent.
☐	Vampiric Blood Rested	10% Resist Magic; lasts 8 hours.	Vampire only; sleep in any coffin
☐	Lover's Comfort	All skills improve 15% faster; lasts 8 hours.	Sleep in the same location as your spouse.
☐	Father's Love	Healing spells and potions add 25% extra health; lasts 8 hours.	Male adventurer. Hearthfire: Adopt a child
☐	Mother's Love	Healing spells and potions add 25% extra health; lasts 8 hours.	Female adventurer. Hearthfire: Adopt a child
☐	The Gift of Charity	+10 Speech; lasts 1 hour.	Give a coin to any beggar.

Catching a Disease: Dirty Vermin!

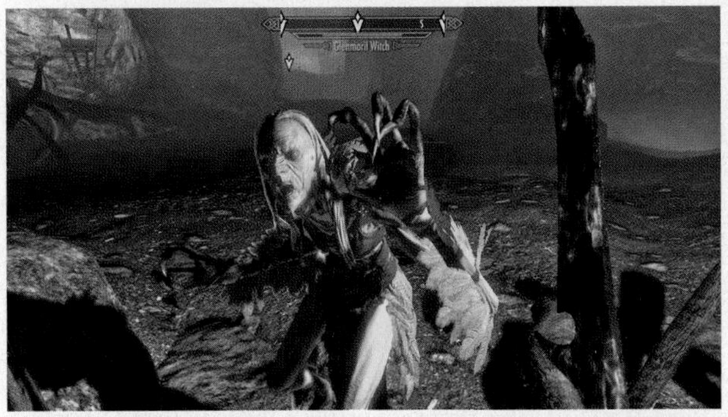

Clawed by a Hagraven? Then you may have Brain Rot!

Adventuring is dangerous, especially when battling diseased foes. Every time one of these enemies strikes you, there is a chance that you may contract the disease they carry. If you have a resistance to disease (thanks to your race or equipment), this chance is lessened, but under most circumstances, the chance of catching something is around 5% to 10% per wound you suffer. The following table lists the possible diseases, their effects, and how you can contract them.

✓ NAME	EFFECT	CONTRACTED FROM
Ataxia	Lockpicking & Pickpocket 25% harder	Traps, Skeevers
Bone Break Fever	-25 Stamina	Traps, Bears
Brain Rot	-25 Magicka	Traps, Hagravens
Droops	15% less effective with melee weapons.	Ash Hoppers
Rattles	Stamina recovers 50% slower	Traps, Chaurus
Rockjoint	25% less effective with melee weapons	Traps, wolves, foxes
Sanguinare Vampiris	-25 Health, progresses to vampirism	Vampires
Witbane	Magicka recovers 50% slower	Traps, Sabre Cats

Curing a Disease: By Potion

Drinking a Cure Disease potion is the fastest and easiest way to rid yourself of pox. You can buy these potions in many shops, find them in the wild, or make them yourself.

Curing Disease: The Shrines of Skyrim

The Temple of the Eight Divines in Solitude. Only Talos—outlawed by the Thalmor—is not worshiped here.

Most people in Skyrim follow the religion of the Divines. Shrines to the Divines can be found throughout the land: in cities, in settlements, and in the wilderness. Their locations are detailed throughout the Atlas. Praying at a Shrine cures any diseases you may have and confers a unique blessing that lasts eight hours. Only one blessing can be active at a time; praying at a different Shrine will remove any prior blessings.

CAUTION

The worship of Talos is a major factor in the civil war that currently rages across Skyrim. His worship has been outlawed in areas controlled by the empire, though Shrines to Talos may will still appear in Stormcloak strongholds. If the Stormcloaks are victorious, Shrines to Talos will return to the cities of Skyrim.

Akatosh: Cure all diseases, +10% Magicka Regeneration Rate

Arkay: Cure all diseases, +25 Health

Auriel: Cure all diseases, +10 Archery

Azura: Cure all diseases, +10 Magic Resistance

Boethiah: Cure all diseases, +10 One-Handed damage

Dibella: Cure all diseases, +10 Speechcraft

Julianos: Cure all diseases, +25 Magicka

Kynareth: Cure all diseases, +25 Stamina

Mara: Cure all diseases, +10% healing effects

Mephala: Cure all diseases, +10 Better Prices (Bartering)

Nocturnal: Cure all diseases, +10 Sneak

Stendarr: Cure all diseases, +10% blocking effectiveness

Talos: Cure all diseases, +20% Shout recovery

Zenithar: Cure all diseases, 10% better prices (bartering)

Curing Disease: Additional Shrines of Skyrim

You can also receive blessings at two rare shrines if you know where to look:

Shrine to Auriel: There are only two of these shrines believed to exist in the whole of Skyrim. One is found at the great Chantry of Auri-el, a Snow Elf Sanctuary within Darkfall Cave. The other is in the Inner Sanctum, at the pinnacle of the Forgotten Vale. Check the Atlas for exact location information.

Shrine to Nocturnal: This is an effigy of Nocturnal herself, found in the Ragged Flagon Cistern area once you complete Thieves Guild Quest: Darkness Returns. See page 300 for details on that quest.

Curing Disease: Shrines of Solstheim

If you visit the dusty realm of southern Solstheim and dock at Raven Rock, you can inspect and enter the town's temple. Inside are shrines to Daedric entities worshipped by the Dunmer: Azura, Boethiah, and Mephala. Check the Atlas for exact location information.

Curing Disease: Other Means

The Vigilants of Stendarr are a relatively new religious order. Zealous followers of the god of justice and mercy, they seek to wipe out abominations like vampires and werewolves and to purge the land of Daedra worship. If you encounter them in one of their strongholds (like the Hall of the Vigilant [3.09] or Stendarr's Beacon [9.46]), or elsewhere in the wilderness, you can ask them to cure your diseases.

NOTE The process of transforming into a vampire or werewolf will also cure any diseases you might have... though those diseases are probably the least of your concerns!

VAMPIRISM

NOTE This section includes changes to Vampirism from the Dawnguard add-on. If you do not have Dawnguard, note that your resistances and powers will be slightly different, and appearing in public as a Stage 4 Vampire is considered a crime.

Contracting Vampirism

A Vampire, attacking with Drain Life. Note the distinct complexion and garb.

Facing those who feed on the blood of the living presents several perils. In addition to their terrifying visage, zombified thralls, and skill at both melee and magical combat, vampires have a unique Drain Life ability. This can rapidly sap your health while restoring theirs each time it strikes you, and it gives you a 10 percent chance of contracting *Sanguinare Vampiris*, a disease that will eventually cause you to join their ranks.

After any battle with vampires, check your Active Effects list. If you see *Sanguinare Vampiris*, quickly drink a Cure Disease potion or make haste to a shrine for healing. As the disease runs its course, you'll receive a message at twilight that reads, "You feel a strange thirst as the sun sets," and you'll receive a second notification the following dawn that says, "You feel weaker as the sun rises." After three days of this, the disease takes over completely, and you transform into a vampire!

Remember that being infected by a "regular" vampire leads only to normal Vampirism. To become a Vampire Lord, you must be bitten by Lord Harkon or a member of his bloodline (see below).

Wanting to give yourself over to this disease? Then seek out a Vampire habitat, such as Movarth's Lair, in Hjaalmarch Hold.

Stages of Vampirism

Becoming a vampire (before and after) changes your appearance dramatically.

As a vampire, you must feed on human blood! Vampirism has four distinct stages, based on how long it has been since you last fed. The more time has elapsed, the more severe the advantages and disadvantages of this condition become. To survive as a vampire, you should know exactly what these benefits and drawbacks are.

Advantages

Immune to disease: You are completely immune to disease. Any diseases you had upon becoming a vampire are instantly cured.

Immune to poison: You are completely immune to all forms of poison.

Champion of the Night: Illusion spells that you cast are 25 percent more powerful.

Nightstalker's Footsteps: You are 25 percent harder to detect while Sneaking.

Resist Frost: The stage of your vampirism adds to your Frost Resistance:

Stage 1 vampirism: Resist Frost 20%
Stage 2 vampirism: Resist Frost 30%
Stage 3 vampirism: Resist Frost 40%
Stage 4 vampirism: Resist Frost 50%

Disadvantages

Hatred: Citizens of Skyrim and guards will not recognize you as a vampire but may (25 percent of the time) remark that you're looking distinctly "pale" or "hungry." However, even when vampirism has fully consumed you, they will not attack you on sight.

Weakness to Sunlight: When outdoors between the hours of 5:00 a.m. and 7:00 p.m., your Health, Magicka, and Stamina will not regenerate. Their maximum values are also reduced:

Stage 1 vampirism: Health, Magicka, and Stamina are reduced by 15 points.

Stage 2 vampirism: Health, Magicka, and Stamina are reduced by 30 points.

Stage 3 vampirism: Health, Magicka, and Stamina are reduced by 45 points.

Stage 4 vampirism: Health, Magicka, and Stamina are reduced by 60 points.

Weakness to Fire: The stage of your vampirism also gives you a Weakness to Fire:

Stage 1 vampirism: Weakness to Fire 20%
Stage 2 vampirism: Weakness to Fire 30%
Stage 3 vampirism: Weakness to Fire 40%
Stage 4 vampirism: Weakness to Fire 50%

Powers

As your vampirism progresses, you gain an increasingly powerful set of additional abilities.

Stage 1 Vampirism

Vampire's Sight: For one minute, you can see better in dark environments. Use this power as often as you like. It has no cost.

Vampiric Drain: A special Destruction spell, Vampiric Drain absorbs 2 Health per second from your target.

Vampire's Servant: Once per day, you can reanimate a dead creature to fight for you for 60 seconds. Only works on creatures of Level 6 or less.

Stage 2 Vampirism

All powers from Stage 1, plus:

Vampire's Seduction: Creatures and people up to Level 10 won't fight or flee for 30 seconds.

Vampiric Drain: Increases to 3 Health drained per second.

Vampire's Servant: Now affects creatures of Level 13 or lower.

Stage 3 Vampirism

All powers from Stages 1 and 2, plus:

Vampiric Drain: Increases to 4 Health drained per second.

Vampire's Servant: Now affects creatures of Level 21 or lower.

Stage 4 Vampirism

All powers from Stages 1, 2, and 3, plus:

Embrace of Shadows: Once per day, you can invoke this power to gain Vampire's Sight and Invisibility for 3 minutes.

Vampiric Drain: Increases to 5 Health drained per second.

Vampire's Servant: Now affects creatures of Level 30 or lower.

Un-Living as a Vampire

Maintaining Vampirism: Resting

Tomb, sweet tomb: Gain an additional benefit from sleeping in a coffin.

All vampires may use coffins to sleep in. There are benefits for sealing yourself away in a wooden tomb:

Sleeping in a coffin grants you all your usual resting bonuses.

You receive the Vampiric Blood bonus: This grants you 10 percent Magic Resistance for 12 hours.

Vampires can also sleep in a bed as most humans do, and they receive the usual resting bonuses. However, the Vampiric Blood bonus will not be given. If you aren't a vampire but want to see what the inside of a coffin looks like, you can sleep in one but you only receive the usual resting bonuses.

Maintaining Vampirism: Feeding

Feed your insatiable appetite using Vampire's Seduction.

Locate these ornate potions of blood as a bottled alternative to fresh blood.

The Vampire's "Cattle" of Castle Volkihar are here to serve you and your thirst.

As a vampire, you can stave off the disadvantages of your new form by feeding. Feasting on the blood of the living can be tricky. There are four basic approaches:

Sleeping Victims: Find a sleeping human (citizens and guards tend to be the easiest, though a sleeping soldier, bandit, or warlock will work as well); then activate them to feed on their blood. Doing so reverts your disease back to Stage 1.

Vampire's Seduction: If you succeed in using this power on a person, you can feed on them even if they're awake. This tactic works well on civilians, as all but the weakest foes are too high a level for Vampire's Seduction to affect them.

Blood Potion: As an alternative to feeding, you can also drink a Blood Potion, which has the same effect. Alas, these are rare; only a handful can be found in Castle Volkihar, although you may receive a few more as rewards for the Vampire Radiant Quests. They can't be Crafted.

Vampire Cattle: If you join with the vampires of Castle Volkihar, one of the benefits is a supply of "cattle," thralls kept in squalid conditions and brought out during feasting sessions. You can sate your hunger on them whenever you wish, without fear or shunning.

Feeding Is Frowned Upon: Criminality

It is important to know how the guards of each Hold are likely to treat you if you're caught feeding. In general, the following applies:

If you feed on a citizen or guard and the victim detects you, this is seen as a Crime (Bounty +40).

If you feed on a citizen or guard and someone else (who isn't a friend or ally) detects you, the same Bounty accrues.

There are some exceptions, however:

If your Sneak skill is high enough, you may not be detected.

If your victim is under the influence of Vampire's Seduction, they won't consider your teeth and slobbering a crime. However, if someone else (not a friend or ally) sees you, the Bounty increase occurs.

If you're feeding on the Vampire Cattle in Castle Volkihar, they won't object to your bloodthirsty appetite.

Life as a Vampire

The life of a vampire is far less arduous if the lands are plunged into permanent darkness....

Aside from the panic and hostility you may create during bouts of bloodletting hunger, the main problems you encounter are your weaknesses to sunlight and fire. Minimize these risks by exploring subterranean catacombs and dungeons during the daytime, and prowl the countryside at night. You may also want to draw on the power of the Lady Stone (see Standing Stones, page 93), which helps to offset the lack of normal Health or Stamina regeneration during daylight.

However, once you've completed the Dawnguard Main Quest and are able to notch a Bloodcursed Arrow to Auriel's Bow and fire it into the sun, you can create a perpetual darkness across Skyrim, effectively negating the ill effects of daylight entirely! Find out more on page 549.

As a vampire, you receive several bonuses that improve your stealth abilities, making vampirism a blessing for Thieves, Archers, and Assassins. You will also find it significantly easier to explore Falmer Hives (since you're immune to the poisons that they, their Chaurus, and their spiders use), Nordic Ruins (since the Draugr use Frost Magic almost exclusively), and Vampire Lairs (since you no longer need fear contracting the disease). You also have a dramatic advantage when fighting frost-breathing dragons, though you have a corresponding weakness to fire-breathing dragons. Keep some potions of Fire Resistance on hand, just in case!

PRINCES AMONG THE UNDEAD: VOLKIHAR VAMPIRES

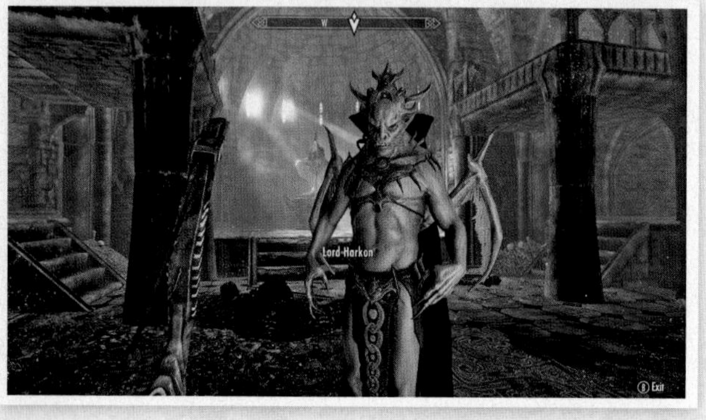

A Volkihar Vampire Lord, in all his powerful glory.

Lord Harkon is the progenitor of the Volkihar Vampire bloodline. If, during the course of the Dawnguard Main Quest, you agree to accept his "gift," his bite imbues you with an incredible and terrifying new aspect: In addition to all the standard effects of vampirism, Volkihar Vampires can assume the powerful Vampire Lord Form.

Becoming a Volkihar Vampire

During Dawnguard Main Quest: Bloodline, you'll enter Castle Volkihar for the first time and gain an audience with Lord Harkon. A conversation with the vampire king ends with Harkon offering you the power of vampirism. Accept, and you ally yourself with the vampires and become a Volkihar Vampire. This is the usual way to achieve this transformation for the first time.

If you were already a werewolf, Harkon's gift purges you of Lycanthropy. If you desire to become a werewolf again, speak with Aela the Huntress of the Companions, and consult the Werewolf section later in this chapter.

Lord Harkon's daughter, Serana, can also turn you into a Volkihar Vampire under certain conditions. This is helpful if you side with the Dawnguard but later want to rule the night as a Volkihar nightstalker!

During Dawnguard Main Quest: Chasing Echoes, if you aren't a vampire, Serana offers to turn you into a Volkihar Vampire so you're able to enter the Soul Cairn without suffering any ill effects. This is one more way to transform.

After you complete Dawnguard Main Quest: Kindred Judgment, Serana will turn you into a Volkihar Vampire if you request it, provided you haven't ordered Serana to cure herself of vampirism.

You can be cured of this strain of vampirism, too. If you crave it again, speak to Harkon or Serana to restore your Volkihar Vampire powers.

Vampire Lord Form

Overview

Fear strikes Falkreath Hold as a Vampire Lord flits silently across the still water of Lake Ilinalta....

Becoming a floating, eight-foot demonic vampire with incredible powers is certainly helpful when dealing with enemies, but it has its drawbacks—for example, you won't be bartering at shops. But there are some important elements to this form you must be aware of:

- Remember that "base" vampires don't have the correct bloodline to call upon the power of the Vampire Lord Form, so don't expect to become a Lord if you've been infected by them. You must become a Volkihar Vampire in order to use this ability.
- The Vampire Lord Form is a transformation state, much like the Beast Form for Werewolves. You access it in the Magic menu by selecting Magic > Powers > Vampire Lord. It's a good idea to make this a Favorite so you can quickly call upon it in the midst of combat. You continue to exist in your Vampire Lord form for as long as you wish (unlike Beast Form). To transform back, access your Favorites menu, select "Revert Form," and invoke it.

You are fortunate that, upon returning to your regular form, all the weapons, armor, spells, and powers you've equipped are automatically reinstated.

Vampire Lord: Advantages

Your imposing posture and terrifying form are the least of your advantages as a Volkihar Vampire. When in Vampire Lord Form:

- You retain all of the advantages associated with being a vampire (including the immunity to poison and disease and a resistance to frost).
- You gain a Water Walking ability, enabling you to walk (or float) across the surface of any body of water. You're unable to swim while in this form.

Finally, you receive an impressive number of enhancements to your statistics, based on your level:

LEVEL	ATTACK BONUS	HEALTH BONUS	MAGICKA BONUS	STAMINA BONUS	ARMOR BONUS
Level 10 or below	+0	+50	+40	+0	+100
Levels 11–15	+5	+75	+60	+10	+125
Levels 16–20	+10	+100	+80	+20	+150
Levels 21–25	+15	+125	+100	+30	+175
Levels 26–30	+20	+150	+120	+40	+200
Levels 31–35	+25	+175	+140	+50	+225
Levels 36–40	+30	+200	+160	+60	+250
Levels 41–45	+35	+225	+180	+80	+275
Level 45 and up	+40	+250	+200	+100	+300

Vampire Lord: Disadvantages

Your gangly frame and penchant for striking fear into the hearts of citizens across Skyrim can also be a hindrance. Here are the key problems associated with this form:

You retain all of the disadvantages of being a "base" vampire (including weaknesses to fire and sunlight).

You can't loot any corpses you slay.

You can't pick up or use any items you find. Since this includes keys, you may find your progress blocked in some dungeons.

You can't equip or use any of your normal weapons, spells, items, equipment, Shouts, or powers.

Your towering frame may have trouble fitting through some narrow passages and doors.

You can't speak with anyone, even your own vampire brethren.

Citizens of Skyrim are terrified of you; some of them flee, while the battle-hardened, brave, or foolish may stand their ground and attack you.

If anyone sees you transform to or from a Volkihar Vampire, the transformation is considered a Major Crime. Consult the Crime and Punishment section on page 64.

Vampire Lord: Powers

While in Vampire Lord Form, you have a variety of powers at your disposal. Most give you an advantage in combat and are divided into the following categories:

Abilities

These are general or basic movement options and strikes:

Revert Form: This allows you to change back to your human form.

Ascend and Descend: Press Sneak to switch between ground and hovering states. While on the ground, you can attack with powerful claws and bite attacks. When hovering, you can invoke Blood Magic spells (such as Drain Life). You can use Night Powers in either form.

Melee Attacks: When standing on the ground, you can rend the flesh of your foes with powerful claw attacks. Inflict a killing blow on your enemy with a power attack, and you perform a bite that devours them, snuffing out their life and draining their lifeblood.

Blood Magic: Your left and right hands, when hovering, allow you to cast Blood Magic spells.

- You have innate knowledge of two Blood Magic spells: Drain Life and Raise Dead.
- Additional Blood Magic spells can be unlocked by selecting Vampire Lord Perks (see below).
- Drain Life is always equipped in your right hand and doesn't change. You can, however, choose any Blood Magic Spell to equip in your left hand (via the Favorites menu).

Night Powers: These special states are available no matter your combat state:

- You have innate knowledge of two Night Powers: Bats and Vampire's Sight.
- Additional Night Powers can be unlocked by selecting Vampire Lord Perks (see below).
- You can change the Night Power you are using through the Favorites menu.

NOTE Remember that you can practice some of these powers and learn about the benefits of vampirism by training under Lord Harkon as part of Dawnguard Main Quest: Power of the Blood.

Blood Magic: Drain Life

Suck the very life force from your foes to replenish your own.

Volkihar Vampires are particularly adept at draining the life essence from their foes; their Drain Life is significantly more powerful than the spell a "base" vampire uses. It has additional benefits too:

It automatically increases in strength based on your level.

Instead of a close-range concentration spell, it is now a long-range projectile spell that affects all targets near the point of impact.

It now affects undead. Only Daedra and Dwarven Automatons are immune to it.

You can empower it even further by drinking from the Bloodstone Chalice, an artifact you fill during the Dawnguard Main Quest of the same name. This effect, Blood of the Ancients, wears off after a few days. The following table details how powerful Drain Life can become:

DRAIN LIFE PROGRESSION	DRAIN LIFE	DRAIN LIFE W/ BLOOD OF THE ANCIENTS	MAGICKA COST
Level 10 or below	Inflicts 50 Damage and absorbs 15 Health from all targets in range.	Also absorbs 15 Magicka and Stamina.	18
Levels 11–20	Inflicts 70 Damage and absorbs 17.5 Health from all targets in range.	Also absorbs 17.5 Magicka and Stamina.	18
Levels 21–30	Inflicts 90 Damage and absorbs 20 Health from all targets in range.	Also absorbs 20 Magicka and Stamina.	18
Levels 31–40	Inflicts 120 Damage and absorbs 22.5 Health from all targets in range.	Also absorbs 22.5 Magicka and Stamina.	18
Level 41 and up	Inflicts 150 Damage and absorbs 25 Health from all targets in range.	Also absorbs 25 Magicka and Stamina.	18

TIP The Blood of the Ancients causes your Drain Life to also absorb Magicka and Stamina. The duration of this ability grows each time you complete Vampire Faction Quest: Ancient Power.

Blood Magic: Raise Dead

The recently slain rise again to serve you!

Reanimating the corpses of the recently slain to act as your guard is a powerful spell, one you should employ to turn the tide of combat in your favor. Unlike a base vampire, the power of your Raise Dead spell depends on your level, not how recently you have fed or how powerful the spell is in your regular form. The following table details how powerful Raise Dead can become:

✓	RAISE DEAD PROGRESSION	RAISE DEAD	MAGICKA COST
	Level 10 or below	Reanimates a dead body to fight for you. Works on targets up to Level 8.	50
	Levels 11–20	Reanimates a dead body to fight for you. Works on targets up to Level 16.	50
	Levels 21–30	Reanimates a dead body to fight for you. Works on targets up to Level 24.	50
	Levels 31–40	Reanimates a dead body to fight for you. Works on targets up to Level 30.	50
	Level 41 and up	Reanimates a dead body to fight for you. Works on targets up to Level 36.	50

Blood Magic: Other Spells

Summon gargoyles to tear foes asunder with terrible punishment.

If giving the dead life to do your bidding isn't your main method of foe disposal, you can also learn the following Blood Magic spells by obtaining perks (see below). These take the place of the Raise Dead spell in your left hand, although you can switch between them at any time. The following table lists all of the Blood Magic spells you can learn:

✓	BLOOD MAGIC SPELL	PREREQUISITES	DESCRIPTION	MAGICKA COST
	Vampiric Grip	Vampiric Grip Perk	Pulls a living creature toward you, then chokes them, absorbing 5 Health/second. Once released, your target is sent flying.	65 per second
	Summon Gargoyle	Summon Gargoyle Perk	Summons a gargoyle for 60 seconds.	50
	Improved Summon Gargoyle	Summon Gargoyle Perk, Amulet of the Gargoyle Item	Summons two gargoyles. One lasts for 60 seconds, the other for 30 seconds.	50
	Corpse Curse	Corpse Curse Perk	Paralyzes a living creature.	100

Night Powers

Night Powers such as Bats are helpful when the tide of combat turns against you.

As if your astonishing array of abilities wasn't enough, you also have a number of Night Powers you can use in a more defensive posture during combat and switch between at any time. You begin with the Bats and Vampire's Sight Powers and can learn the rest as perks. The following table reveals all of the Night Powers you can acquire.

✓	NIGHT POWER	PREREQUISITES	USE LIMIT	DESCRIPTION
	Bats	None	Up to twice per 30 seconds.	You transform into a swarm of bats that surges forward, then re-forms at your destination.
	Improved Bats	Amulet of Bats Item	Up to twice per 30 seconds.	Your swarm of bats absorbs 15 Health/second from nearby enemies.
	Vampire's Sight	None	None	Nighteye for 60 seconds.
	Detect All Creatures	Detect All Creatures Perk	None	Sends out a brief pulse that reveals all creatures for two seconds. This affects all creatures, including the living, undead, Daedra, and automatons.
	Mist Form	Mist Form Perk	60-second cooldown	You transform into a cloud of mist. For 15 seconds, you are invulnerable and unable to attack or be attacked. During this time, your Health, Magicka, and Stamina regenerate rapidly.
	Supernatural Reflexes	Supernatural Reflexes Perk	60-second cooldown	Slows time for 10 seconds.
	Night Cloak	Night Cloak Perk	Continuous	While in Vampire Lord Form, you are surrounded by a cloud of bats that absorb 4 Health/second from all nearby enemies. This power is always active.

KINECT SUPPORT (XBOX ONLY)

For adventurers with a Kinect, there are several unique actions and commands you can employ without normal controller use. These are designed to help you more thoroughly immerse yourself in the action. The following section details all the different commands, along with tips on using Shouts, managing your inventory, and so on:

CONTROLS

When Kinect is disabled:

Right Bumper Button: Shout/Powers

When Kinect is enabled:

Right Bumper Button: Enable Dragon Language Shouts
Left Bumper Button and **Right Bumper Button:** Shout/Powers

VOICE COMMAND LIST

Gameplay

These are usable only during gameplay:

Quick Items: Opens the Inventory menu

Quick Magic: Opens the Magic menu

Quick Stats: Opens the Stats menu

Quick Map: Opens the Map menu

Quick Save: Quick-saves the game

Quick Load: Quick-loads the game

New Save: Saves the game into a new save slot

Pause Game: Pauses the game

Character Menu

This is usable only in the Character menu.

Items: Opens the Inventory menu

Magic: Opens the Magic menu

Skills: Opens the Skills menu

Map: Opens the Map menu

Favorites Menu

This is usable only in the Favorites menu.

Assign [hot key command]: Sets the selected item to the spoken hot key

Health Potion	Battleaxe
Magicka Potion	Warhammer
Stamina Potion	Fire Spell
Poison	Frost Spell
Sword	Lightning Spell
Mace	Ward Spell
Axe	Ritual Spell
Dagger	Bound Weapon
Bow	Summon Spell
Shield	Armor Spell
Dual-Wield Left	Calm Spell
Dual-Wield Right	Frenzy Spell
Soul Trap	Healing Spell
Greatsword	Light

Hot Key Equipping

This is usable only during gameplay and equips a [hot key command] (such as Summon Spell or Heath Potion) that you have previously assigned in the Favorites menu:

Equip [hot key command]: Equips item in the default hand

Equip Left [hot key command]: Equips item in the left hand, if possible.

Equip Right [hot key command]: Equips item in the right hand, if possible.

Equip Dual [hot key command]: Equips the item in both hands, if possible.

Equip Sword and Shield: Equips the item with the Sword hot key in the right hand and the item with the Shield hot key in the left hand.

Also: Equip Mace and Shield, Equip Axe and Shield, Equip Dagger and Shield.

Equip Dual Weapons: Equips the item with the DualWieldLeft hot key in the left hand and the item with the DualWieldRight hot key in the right hand.

TIP Use Voice hot keys efficiently: Voice hot key names cover a wide range of uses, but they don't restrict what you can assign to them. For example, you don't have to assign a fire spell to "Fire Spell"; you can assign a Health Potion to it if you wanted to. If you never, say, use a Warhammer, don't hesitate to assign "Warhammer" to something you will use, like a staff or custom potion.

Follower Commands

There are usable only during gameplay and are valid only if you have a Follower.

Ally Follow: Your ally follows you as if you told them, "Follow me."
Ally Follow Me does the same thing.

Ally Wait: Your ally stays where they are.
Ally Wait Here does the same thing.

Ally Trade: Opens your ally's inventory.
Ally Items does the same thing.

Ally Open: Commands your ally to open the container/door you're looking at.

Ally Stand: Commands your ally to stand at the spot you're looking at.

Ally Retrieve: Commands your ally to pick up the item you're looking at.

Ally Attack: Commands your ally to attack the character or enemy you're looking at.

Ally Interact: Does a generic Interact command with the ally. This is the same as if you entered Command mode and pressed the A Button. What the ally does depends on what you're looking at.
Ally Interact and Ally Use do the same thing.

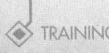

Using Shouts

You are now able to use Shouts in three different ways during gameplay:

Shout Names (or English Names): Without pressing any buttons, you can just say the name of the Shout. For example, if you say "Unrelenting Force," that Shout is used. This uses the highest level of the Shout you have unlocked.

Dragon Language Shouts: By holding down the **Right Bumper Button**, you unlock Dragon Language mode. While holding the button, you can say one, two, or three Words of a Shout to trigger that shout. "Fus," "Fus Ro," and "Fus Ro Dah" will all trigger their corresponding power levels (but remember, you can only use the Words you've unlocked).

Button Pressing: While Kinect is enabled, the **Left and Right Buttons** together can be used to trigger Shouts or Powers without the use of voice commands, if you prefer.

Unrelenting Force: "Fus Ro Dah"
Dismaying Shout: "Faas Ru Maar"
Become Ethereal: "Feim Zii Gron"
Whirlwind Sprint: "Wuld Nah Kest"
Elemental Fury: "Su Grah Dun"
Clear Skies: "Lok Vah Koor"
Fire Breath: "Yol Toor Shul"
Dragonrend: "Joor Zah Frul"
Call of Valor: "Hun Kaal Zoor"
Call Dragon: "Od Ah Viing" (no first- or second-level variations of this Shout)

Animal Allegiance: "Raan Mir Tah"
Aura Whisper: "Laas Yah Nir"
Disarm: "Zun Haal Viik"
Marked for Death: "Krii Lun Aus"
Frost Breath: "Fo Krah Diin"
Storm Call: "Strun Bah Qo"
Kyne's Peace: "Kaan Drem Ov"
Slow Time: "Tiid Klo Ul"
Throw Voice: "Zul Mey Gut"
Ice Form: "Iiz Slen Nus"

Drain Vitality: "Gaan Lah Haas"
Soul Tear: "Rii Vaaz Zol"
Summon Durnehviir: "Dur Neh Viir"

Battle Fury: "Mid Vur Shaan"
Bend Will: "Gol Hah Dov"
Cyclone: "Ven Gaar Nos"
Dragon Aspect: "Mul Qah Diiv" (no first- or second-level variations of this Shout)

Inventory Menu

This is usable only in the Inventory menu. The Inventory Sorting commands are unique to Kinect and make deciding what to sell (or drop) a snap.

[Category name]: Opens the menu to that category

Favorites
All
Weapons
Apparel
Also: Armor
Potions
Scrolls
Food
Ingredients
Books
Keys
Miscellaneous

Sort by Name: Sorts the item list by name, increasing. If the list is already sorted by name increasingly, it sorts it decreasingly.
Sort by Weight: Sorts the item list by weight, decreasing. If the list is already sorted by weight decreasingly, it sorts it increasingly.
Sort by Value: Sorts the item list by value, decreasing. If the list is already sorted by value decreasingly, it sorts it increasingly.
Close Menu: Closes the menu

Barter Menu

This is usable only in the Barter menu.

Vendor categories: Opens the item list for the spoken vendor category.

Their Items
Their Weapons
Their Apparel
Their Potions
Their Scrolls
Their Food
Their Ingredients
Their Books
Their Keys
Their Miscellaneous

Player categories: Opens the item list for the spoken player category.

My Items
Also: All
My Weapons
Also: Weapons
My Apparel
Also: Apparel, Armor
My Potions
Also: Potions
My Scrolls
Also: Scrolls
My Food
Also: Food
My Ingredients
Also: Ingredients
My Books
Also: Books
My Keys
Also: Keys
My Miscellaneous
Sort by Name
Sort by Value
Sort by Weight
Close Menu

Container Menu

This is only usable in the Container menu.

Container categories: Opens the item list for the spoken container category.

Their Items
Their Weapons
Their Apparel
Also: Their Armor
Their Potions
Their Scrolls
Their Food
Their Ingredients
Their Books
Their Keys
Their Miscellaneous

Player categories: Opens the item list for the spoken player category.

My Items
Also: All
My Weapons
Also: Weapons
My Apparel
Also: Apparel, Armor
My Potions
Also: Potions
My Scrolls
Also: Scrolls
My Food
Also: Food
My Ingredients
Also: Ingredients
My Books
Also: Books
My Keys
Also: Keys

Managing Your Loot Limit

When looking at a chest, corpse, or other container, use the command "Loot Items" to take all of the items with a value-to-weight ratio greater than or equal to your Loot Limit. This is less complicated than it sounds, as it's mimicking what you do naturally when trying to decide whether it's really worth lugging that heavy armor or iron sword back to a settlement to sell or craft. Plus, you can set a limit depending on how much you want to carry by saying the following:

"Set Loot Limit 0" (default): The most restrictive setting. You'll take only weightless items (gold, arrows, keys, notes, some quest items).

"Set Loot Limit 5": The most permissive setting. You take virtually all items, including some steel weapons (and up), steel armor (and up), and pretty much everything else.

"Set Loot Limit 10": At a 10:1 ratio, you'll start to leave more items. This is the highest limit at which you can still expect to get most Alchemy ingredients.

"Set Loot Limit 25": At a 25:1 ratio, you begin to exclude midlevel items like Elven weapons and steel plate armor.

"Set Loot Limit 50": At a 50:1 ratio, you take very little, leaving behind even glass weapons and ebony armor. This is the highest limit at which you'll take Skill Books.

"Set Loot Limit 100": At 100:1 ratio, even some Daedric and Dragonplate items will be passed over.

Other loot limit commands:

Sort by Name   Sort by Value   Sort by Weight   Close Menu

Magic Menu

This is usable only in the Magic menu.

[Category name]: Opens menu to that category.

Favorites	Illusion	Restoration	Active Effects
All	Destruction	Shouts	Also: Effects
Alteration	Conjuration	Powers	

Map Menu

This is usable only in the Map menu. Use Map Menu Commands to navigate more quickly. The "Quest Marker" command is especially helpful in finding your next destination without having to scroll around. When you're done there, say the name of a Hold Capital to quickly jump back to town:

[City name]: Centers the camera on that city. You can say:

Windhelm	Markarth
Falkreath	Riften
Dawnstar	Whiterun
Morthal	Winterhold
Solitude	

Player: Centers camera on the player.
Also: Where Am I

Waypoint: Centers camera on player-set marker, if applicable.

Quest Marker: Centers camera on active quest target. Saying it multiple times will cycle through targets.
Also: Quest

Stats Menu

This is usable only in the Stats menu.

[Skill name]: Instantly sets the camera to center on that skill's perk tree. All the skills are accounted for:

One-Handed	Heavy Armor	Alchemy	Illusion
Two-Handed	Light Armor	Speech	Restoration
Archery	Pickpocket	Alteration	Enchanting
Block	Lockpicking	Conjuration	
Smithing	Sneak	Destruction	

CRAFTING

When not delving into crumbling ruins in search of treasure, there are several other skills any would-be adventurer should explore. This section reveals just how rewarding the skills of alchemy, enchanting, smithing, and the lesser crafting activities can be.

The Dragonborn expansion adds the ability to create a variety of spiders, which you can "cast" (i.e., throw them) and are treated a little like scrolls in your inventory. Like the Atronach Forge in the College of Winterhold (see page 270), all the information regarding this crafting activity is detailed in the specific quest, on page 666.

ALCHEMY

NOTE For advice on which Alchemy perks to take, and general information on improving your Alchemy skill, consult the Skills and Perks section, back on page 12.

TIP If you plan to focus on your Alchemy skill, scour the world collecting everything you see: Pick flowers, catch insects, hunt, and fish (i.e., grab fish while swimming, rather than casting a line). Steal any ingredients you see lying around in buildings, if you can get away with it—potions made with stolen ingredients are not treated as stolen. The more (and wider variety) of ingredients you have, the quicker your skills will advance.

If foraging isn't something you want to do, you can always purchase your ingredients from merchants. The best selections can be found in Alchemist shops, located in all the major cities. However, this makes alchemy a much more expensive prospect.

Alchemic Experimentation: An Overview

With an Alchemy Lab, combinations of ingredients become great elixirs or potent poisons.

Alchemy is the craft of combining ingredients to create beneficial potions or debilitating poisons. The key to mastering this art is experimentation: When you smith or enchant an item, you already know what the end result of what the crafting process is going to be; the recipes or combinations of materials are clearly laid out in advance. Not so with alchemy; you often have no idea what you're making, and discovering a powerful new potion or effect is a thrill unto itself.

In short: The process of alchemy involves **foraging for ingredients**, **learning their effects**, and then **experimenting by combining them with other ingredients** to make **potions and poisons**.

Foraging for Ingredients

The Foraging Process

Living off the land is more than just farming crops: Scour Skyrim for ingredients.

The realm of Skyrim is filled with dozens of unique ingredients, which can be categorized into three major groups: those that are grown (such as flowers, mushrooms, and crops), those that are alive (such as dragonflies or butterflies), and those taken from an enemy's corpse (such as Falmer Ears, Hagraven Feathers, or Troll Fat). All of these are stored in the Ingredients menu in your inventory.

Learning Ingredient Effects

Once you've collected one or more ingredients, you can study it in your inventory. Notice that under its weight and value, there are four effects—the ingredient's alchemic properties—which are all initially "unknown." Your ongoing task is to learn what all four of these effects are. Until you do, your initial attempts at crafting potions can be a little hit or miss.

Ingredient digestion: The easiest way to learn the properties of an ingredient is to eat it! This always reveals the first effect, and depending on your Alchemy perks, it may reveal more. The advantage of eating ingredients is that you always receive the first property; it always works. The downside is that for rare items, you'll have to consume the item for no directly beneficial effect.

Experimental potions: Or you can learn an ingredient's properties by attempting to craft a potion with the ingredient. Constant use of a particular ingredient will gradually allow you to learn its effects and discover good combinations with other ingredients.

Crib sheets: Or you can consult this guide, which helpfully lists the four alchemic properties for every ingredient in Skyrim.

AN EXAMPLE: GIANT'S TOE

After wiping out a camp of giants, you salvage three Giant Toes from their corpses. You eat one and learn that its first effect is "Damage Stamina." Easy!

A little later, you return to an Alchemy Lab and try combining it with Bone Meal, another ingredient that has the "Damage Stamina" effect. It works, creating a Damage Stamina Poison, but since you already knew both ingredients had that effect, you don't learn anything new.

You then decide to be a little more adventurous and try combining it with Wheat, an ingredient you know nothing about. Success! Both the Giant Toe and Wheat have two effects in common: "Fortify Health" (the second effect on both ingredients) and "Damage Stamina Regen" (the third effect on Wheat and the fourth on Giant Toe). You learn the four new effects and acquire an interesting potion that fortifies your health at the cost of reducing your stamina regen.

Crafting Potions

In order to craft potions, you must use an Alchemy Lab. If you plan to focus on alchemy, you'll want to find an Alchemy Lab that you can access quickly and return to it frequently. Near the start of your adventure, one good location is the Alchemy Lab inside the Sleeping Giant Inn in Riverwood. Later on, you may want to purchase a house (see page 98) for convenient access to your own Alchemy Lab and plenty of storage space for ingredients.

Selecting ingredients: Step up to the Alchemy Lab, pick two distinct ingredients (you cannot combine two identical ingredients), and mix them together. You can optionally add a third ingredient if you wish (and want to further experiment).

Experimental potions: If you don't know what effects the ingredients share, the Alchemy Lab will caution you that the result is a "Potion of Unknown Effect," but you can still try it.

When you combine ingredients, the Alchemy Lab checks the complete list of the two (or three) ingredients' effects. If none of those effects match, the crafting fails. If there is one or more match, it succeeds.

Failure: If there were no matches, you receive nothing and use up the ingredients, but still receive a small Alchemy skill improvement. The Alchemy Lab remembers that the combination failed and grays it out, indicating you don't need to try it again.

Success: If there was a match, the resulting potion or poison has all of the effects that matched, in a much more potent form than simply eating one of the ingredients would have given you. Most of the time, you receive an item with only one effect, but you may end up with two, three, or even four matches.

Potion or poison? The resulting mixture is classified as a potion if its primary effect is beneficial; it's a poison if its primary effect is harmful. You can have potions with lesser negative effects and poisons with lesser positive effects, although these aren't usually worth making more than once during experimentation. The Purity perk allows you to remove these side effects from your mixtures, creating wholly positive potions and negative poisons.

Effect reference: The Alchemy Lab menu handles all the bookkeeping for you—it knows which ingredients you have, which effects you've learned, and which combinations you've tried before without success. Based on this information, it even recommends ingredients that you know you can combine to produce a specific result, like "Restore Health." While these recommendations are great for quickly creating just the potion you need, don't forget to experiment to continue learning new effects.

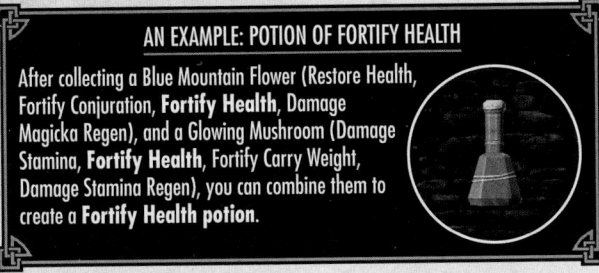

AN EXAMPLE: POTION OF FORTIFY HEALTH

After collecting a Blue Mountain Flower (Restore Health, Fortify Conjuration, **Fortify Health**, Damage Magicka Regen), and a Glowing Mushroom (Damage Stamina, **Fortify Health**, Fortify Carry Weight, Damage Stamina Regen), you can combine them to create a **Fortify Health potion.**

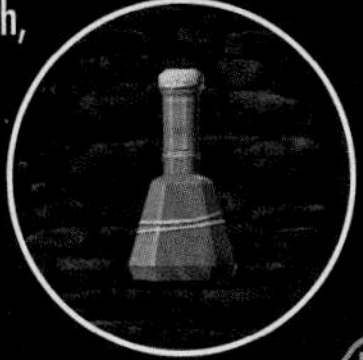

Advanced Alchemy

Alchemy Skill and Potion Creation

Your Alchemy skill improves the effectiveness of the potions and poisons your craft:

- If an effect has only a magnitude (e.g., Restore 50 Health), your skill increases it.
- If an effect has only a duration (e.g., Invisibility for 30 seconds), your skill extends it.
- If an effect has both a magnitude and a duration, only one of the two values will increase, never both. For potions and poisons that affect regeneration rate, the duration increases; for everything else, the magnitude increases.

In addition to your raw skill, the perks in the Alchemy tree dramatically increase the effectiveness of potions you craft. Because of the number of factors that can affect the potency of these potions, exact statistics are not listed in this guide. Consult the exact values in the Alchemy Lab to see what you can create given your current skill and perks. Your Alchemy skill increases when:

- You learn a new effect for an ingredient.
- You successfully craft a potion.
- You attempt to craft a potion but fail (a very small increase).

Three-Ingredient Potions

Potions with three ingredients are more likely to succeed (with 12 effects between them, there's a greater chance of at least one match). However, they are also more likely to produce results with multiple effects...which may or may not be a good thing. You might end up with an excellent potion that has three or even four positive effects—or one that has a bizarre mix of positive and negative properties. These can still be helpful when trying to learn ingredient effects as quickly as possible, but you may not be able to get much use out of the resulting potion.

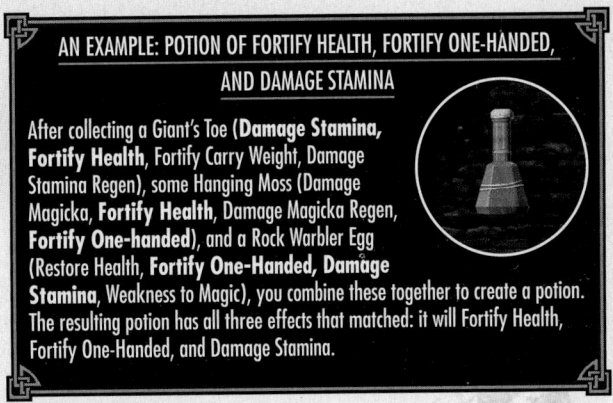

AN EXAMPLE: POTION OF FORTIFY HEALTH, FORTIFY ONE-HANDED, AND DAMAGE STAMINA

After collecting a Giant's Toe (**Damage Stamina, Fortify Health**, Fortify Carry Weight, Damage Stamina Regen), some Hanging Moss (Damage Magicka, **Fortify Health**, Damage Magicka Regen, **Fortify One-handed)**, and a Rock Warbler Egg (Restore Health, **Fortify One-Handed, Damage Stamina**, Weakness to Magic), you combine these together to create a potion. The resulting potion has all three effects that matched: it will Fortify Health, Fortify One-Handed, and Damage Stamina.

Alchemic Recipes and Combinations

Novice Recipes

If you're just starting out on your adventure, here are a few good recipes to try:

✓	POTION EFFECT	INGREDIENT #1	INGREDIENT #2†
	HEALTH POTIONS		
☐	Restore Health	Blue Mountain Flower	Butterfly Wing
☐	Fortify Health	Giant's Toe	Hanging Moss
☐	Regenerate Health	Juniper Berries	Nordic Barnacle
	MAGICKA POTIONS		
☐	Restore Magicka	Creep Cluster	Red Mountain Flower
☐	Fortify Magicka	Red Mountain Flower	Tundra Cotton
☐	Regenerate Magicka	Garlic	Salt Pile
	STAMINA POTIONS		
☐	Restore Stamina	Pine Thrush Egg	Purple Mountain Flower
☐	Fortify Stamina	Garlic	Lavender
☐	Regenerate Stamina	Bee	Mora Tapinella
	RESISTANCE POTIONS		
☐	Resist Fire	Fly Amanita	Snowberries
☐	Resist Frost	Snowberries	Thistle Branch
☐	Resist Shock	Glowdust	Snowberries
	UTILITY POTIONS		
☐	Invisibility	Chaurus Eggs	Nirnroot
☐	Waterbreathing	Chicken's Egg	Nordic Barnacle
	POISONS		
☐	Damage Health (Weak)	Falmer Ear	Imp Stool
☐	Damage Health (Strong)	Falmer Ear	River Betty
☐	Damage Magicka	Butterfly Wing	Hanging Moss
☐	Paralysis	Canis Root	Imp Stool

Advanced Recipes

At higher levels, once you have a wider range of ingredients at your disposal, you can begin to construct potions with more and more complex effects. Here are just a few examples:

✓	POTION EFFECT	INGREDIENT #1	INGREDIENT #2	INGREDIENT #3†
	TWO-EFFECT POTIONS			
☐	Restore Health and Fortify Health	Blue Mountain Flower	Wheat	None
☐	Invisibility and Regen Health	Luna Moth Wing	Vampire Dust	None
☐	Paralysis and Damage Health	Canis Root	Imp Stool	River Betty
	THREE-EFFECT POTIONS			
☐	Fortify Heavy Armor, Fortify Block, Resist Frost	Briar Heart	Slaughterfish Scales	Thistle Branch
☐	Fortify One-handed, Fortify Sneak, Fortify Light Armor	Beehive Husk	Hawk Feathers	Rock Warbler Egg
☐	Fortify Magicka, Fortify Destruction, Restore Magicka	Briar Heart	Ectoplasm	Glowdust
☐	Regen Magicka, Fortify Magicka, Restore Magicka	Briar Heart	Jazbay Grapes	Moon Sugar
	FOUR-EFFECT POTIONS			
☐	Regen Magicka, Resist Frost, Resist Fire, Restore Magicka	Fire Salts	Moon Sugar	Snowberries
☐	Invisibility, Regen Health, Fortify Light Armor, Cure Disease	Hawk Feathers	Luna Moth Wing	Vampire Dust

NOTE † The order in which you mix the ingredients doesn't matter.

Please see the Inventory chapter for tables listing all of the available ingredients and their properties (weight, value, effects). In addition, three sample locations are given where each ingredient can be found (usually in abundance). There is also an Alchemy Effects list, which reveals every effect of an ingredient and which ingredients have these effects.

Dragonborn adds almost a dozen new ingredients, from Ash Hopper Jelly to Trama Roots. The Inventory chapter of this book details them all (page 146).

ENCHANTING

NOTE For advice on which Enchanting perks to take and general information on improving your Enchanting skill, consult the "Skills and Perks" section, back on page 12.

Arcane Enchanting: An Overview

With an Arcane Enchanter, items are both ruined and reborn as new and more powerful objects.

Enchanting requires you to make short-term sacrifices for long-term rewards. The important (and sometimes difficult) choices you make throughout this process determine what items you can create and how powerful they will be. **In short,** enchanting is the art of **imbuing an item** with **magical enchantments** powered by **soul energy**. However, this is done **at the expense of other enchanted items**. To enchant an item, you need:

- **An enchantment.** Before you can imbue an item with an enchantment, you must first learn that enchantment by disenchanting an item with the same base effect.
- **A filled Soul Gem.** While you can find filled Soul Gems in the world, you can also create them by using an empty Soul Gem and the Soul Trap spell (Conjuration) or a weapon enchanted with the Soul Trap enchantment.
- **An unenchanted item.** These are easy to find, though you may wish to smith your own in order to have a ready supply of items to enchant.
- **The Arcane Enchanter:** To enchant an item, you will also need to use an Arcane Enchanter. If you plan to focus on enchanting, locate an Arcane Enchanter you can return to quickly and easily and make a point of visiting it often. Two locations close to your starting point of Helgen are Anise's Cabin, across the river from Riverwood, and Farengar's study in Whiterun's palace of Dragonsreach. Later on, you may want to purchase a house with an Arcane Enchanter (see page 98).

Disenchanting Items

The only way to learn new enchantments is to disenchant an existing enchanted item. The disenchanting process destroys the original item and teaches you the item's base enchantment—that is, its fundamental ability (e.g., Fortify Health), not its specific value (e.g., Fortify Health 50). Once you learn an enchantment, you can apply it to as many other items as you wish.

Early on, disenchanting may be a difficult, even painful decision. Enchanted items are both useful and extremely valuable, while the enchantment you learn does nothing in and of itself. You should definitely use enchanted items you find, rather than rush to disenchant them all. But when you outgrow an item or find something you aren't interested in, consider disenchanting it instead of selling it—you're making an investment in your future.

It is important to remember that you learn only the base (or general) enchantment and not the specific enchantment that appears on the item. Because of this, disenchanting a more valuable item doesn't give you a better enchantment, as these examples show:

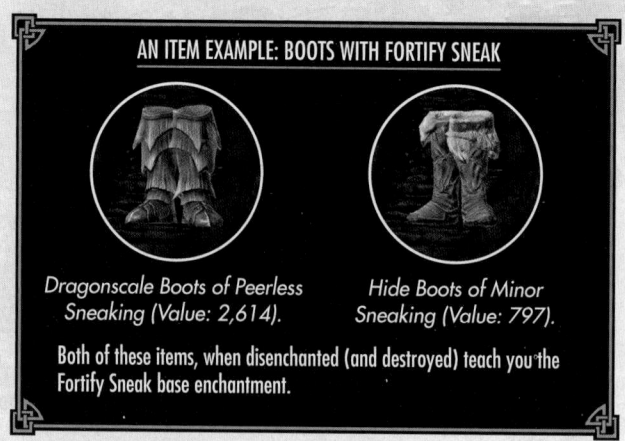

AN ITEM EXAMPLE: BOOTS WITH FORTIFY SNEAK

Dragonscale Boots of Peerless Sneaking (Value: 2,614).

Hide Boots of Minor Sneaking (Value: 797).

Both of these items, when disenchanted (and destroyed) teach you the Fortify Sneak base enchantment.

While you can make money by forging your own items and then selling them, you need to be careful in how you go about it. Purchasing materials from a merchant, taking them to a forge to create an item, and then returning to sell the item back to the merchant may help you improve your Smithing skill, but financially, it's always a losing proposition. If you want to use Smithing to make money, it's always better to gather materials from the wild, although that can be time-consuming.

If you decide to focus on smithing, you'll occasionally find you require certain materials before they're commonly available from merchants. Once again, this is when foraging in the wilderness or swinging a pickaxe at an ore vein is your best option. Check the "Mining" section on page 84 for locations where you can find rare ore.

NOTE For the most part, all Blacksmith forges allow you to forge the same weapons and armor. There are a handful of exceptions:

1. After completing The Companions Quest: Glory of the Dead, you can craft Ancient Nord Armor and Nord Hero Weapons at Eorlund Gray-Mane's Skyforge in Whiterun.
2. After completing Dawnguard Main Quest: A New Order, you can forge crossbows and advanced bolts at Gunmar's Forge in Fort Dawnguard.
3. After completing Side Quest: Lost to the Ages, you can forge an Aetherium Item at the Aetherium Forge.

Improving Items

The Grindstone: Sharpen a blade to improve its damage and value.

The Workbench: Temper armor into defensive and wearable works of art.

Contrary to what you might believe, the heart of smithing lies not in crafting items but in improving them. As with forging, these improvements are simple and result in equally straightforward bonuses to your attack (weapons) and defense (armor) that can significantly improve your combat effectiveness. As you might expect, arms and armor improved in this way also command a premium when sold to merchants.

TIP A Master Blacksmith can improve plain steel armor to make it almost as strong as Dragonplate. And if he's improving Dragonplate? The results are even more spectacular!

The grindstone: You improve weapons by sharpening them at a grindstone.

The workbench: You improve armor by tempering it at a workbench.

When interacting with either of these crafting stations, you are given a complete list of the items you have (whether they were found, bought, stolen, or made by you) that can be improved, along with the materials you need to improve each of them. Improving a weapon or piece of armor always requires one piece of that item's primary material, so sharpening an iron sword requires one Iron Ingot, while tempering a Dragonscale Cuirass requires one Dragon Scale. The clue is in the name!

In exchange for using this material, you receive a bonus to your weapon's damage or armor's defense rating based on your Smithing skill and perks. As your Smithing skill improves, you're able to return to a grindstone or workbench and improve the same item again (at the cost of one material each time), to increase that bonus still further, if you wish.

Rules to Remember

Bonuses are not cumulative: Having sharpened an iron sword with a Smithing skill of 25 (using an Iron Ingot), you return to the grindstone with a Smithing skill of 50 (and expend another Iron Ingot) to receive a better bonus. However, if you'd waited and brought the sword to the grindstone for the first time at Skill 50, the bonus would be the same.

Bonuses stack with enchantments: However, if you're a skilled craftsman in the arts of smithing and enchanting, you can forge an item, then both improve and enchant it for maximum damage. Note that you need the Arcane Blacksmith perk in order to improve enchanted weapons and armor, so if you don't have it, make sure to sharpen or temper the item before you enchant it! Otherwise, the order doesn't matter.

Nomenclature: When you improve an item, it receives a modifier that indicates the amount of improvement you've made to the weapon. This modifier is based on your Smithing skill and perks. After you've improved an item, you can only improve it again once your Smithing skill and perks will allow you to raise it to the next modifier rank. For example:

If you have a Smithing skill of 39 and the Steel Smithing perk, and you improve a steel sword at a grindstone, the sword will receive the "Superior" modifier and a [+3] damage bonus.

Return with a Smithing skill of 40, and your skill has reached the next threshold, allowing you to improve the sword again. This gives it the "Exquisite" modifier and a better bonus, [+5].

If you come back with a Smithing skill of 55, your skill has not yet reached the next threshold, so you can't improve that sword again. If you have a different steel sword you want to improve, it will also receive the "Exquisite" modifier and a [+5] bonus.

There are no perks that improve iron weapons—only weapons of other metal types. **CAUTION**

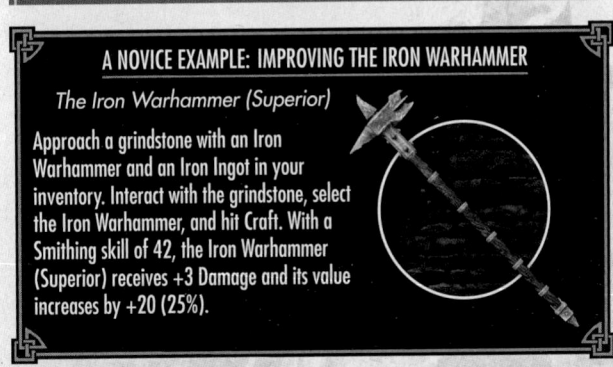

A NOVICE EXAMPLE: IMPROVING THE IRON WARHAMMER

The Iron Warhammer (Superior)

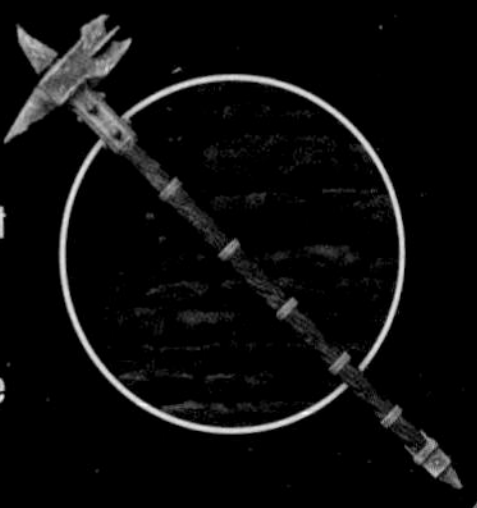

Approach a grindstone with an Iron Warhammer and an Iron Ingot in your inventory. Interact with the grindstone, select the Iron Warhammer, and hit Craft. With a Smithing skill of 42, the Iron Warhammer (Superior) receives +3 Damage and its value increases by +20 (25%).

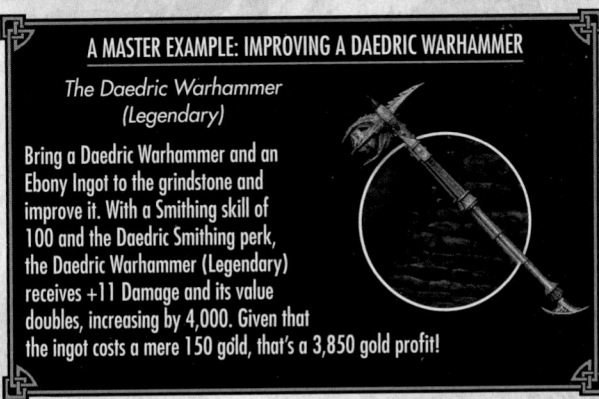

A MASTER EXAMPLE: IMPROVING A DAEDRIC WARHAMMER

The Daedric Warhammer (Legendary)

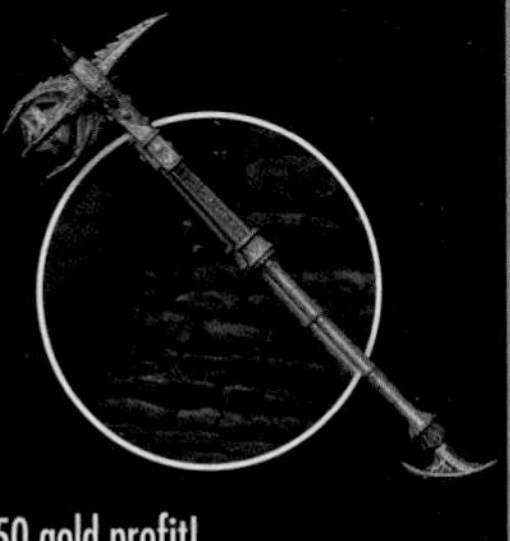

Bring a Daedric Warhammer and an Ebony Ingot to the grindstone and improve it. With a Smithing skill of 100 and the Daedric Smithing perk, the Daedric Warhammer (Legendary) receives +11 Damage and its value doubles, increasing by 4,000. Given that the ingot costs a mere 150 gold, that's a 3,850 gold profit!

The Economics of Improvements

Improving the items you find (and those you forge) is simple, quick, and relatively inexpensive, making this an excellent way to both increase your Smithing skill and earn some extra gold. Simply collect weapons and armor throughout your travels, then improve them before selling them for a profit.

At lower levels, this yields dividends, as you're constantly using your skill and may even make your money back (especially if you mine, smelt, or tan your own materials). At higher levels, with good smithing (and Speech skills for bartering), you can easily rake in hundreds or even thousands of additional gold for each haul of loot.

General Advice

Improve and sharpen everything. As discussed above, this is one of the fastest and easiest ways to make money, especially later in the game, with high Smithing and Speech skills.

Stop overpaying for materials. Smithing can be an expensive hobby if you have to buy all your components from local merchants. If you're tired of paying a premium on leather or ingots, and you have some time to spare, make them yourself!

Delve into Dwarven Ruins. One of the easiest ways to level your Smithing skill is to clear out a Dwarven Ruin, then go back and make a second trip to haul out all of the scrap metal you can carry. Smelt it down into Dwarven Metal Ingots, and you'll have more materials than you know what do to with.

Save those Daedra Hearts. These are among the rarest ingredients, but they're essential for forging Daedric weapons and armor. If you find any early in your adventure, save them until you're ready for them. Otherwise, you'll have to make them yourself with an equally rare ingredient (in College of Winterhold Radiant Quest: The Atronach Forge) or track down the one merchant who sells them (Enthir, also at the College of Winterhold) and pay an outrageous premium.

Dawnguard: Smithing

Arrow Crafting

You can now construct arrows at any forge, meaning you no longer have to search for or buy them if you don't wish to. However, for arrows of a particular type (such as Orcish or Glass Arrows, as shown), you need to have the appropriate Smithing Perk (such as Orcish Smithing or Glass Smithing).

Dragonbone Weapons

You are now able to construct Dragonbone weapons at any forge, as long as you have the Dragon Armor Perk. Dragonbone weapons (such as the one shown above) inflict more damage than Daedric weapons, although they are (very slightly) heavier. Dragonbone weapons are extremely rare; they are almost never found as loot, so smithing them is by far the easiest and most reliable method for master Blacksmiths to acquire them.

Crossbows and Crossbow Bolts

Provided you meet several requirements, you are now able to construct Crossbows and Crossbow Bolts. For this to occur, you must first complete Dawnguard Main Quest: A New Order. As only adventurers allied with the Dawnguard can finish this quest, only Dawnguard-allied players can forge these weapons. However, anyone can loot them from Dawnguard agents or occasionally purchase bolts from some vendors.

Once you complete this quest, speak to Sorine Jurard in Fort Dawnguard about making a Crossbow; this unlocks the ability to forge the basic Crossbow and Steel Bolts. Then, through repeated completion of Dawnguard Faction Quest: Ancient Technology, you and Sorine can unlock "recipes" (schematics) for a variety of improved weapons and bolts, including Dwarven Crossbows, Dwarven Bolts, Enhanced Crossbows, and Exploding Bolts (inflicting Fire, Frost, or Shock damage).

You still need to have the correct tools for making these weapons and bolts: Although you can forge basic Steel Bolts and (once learned) Dwarven Bolts at any forge, you can construct only Crossbows and the explosive advanced bolts at Gunmar's Forge inside Fort Dawnguard. In addition, you need the Steel Smithing Perk to fashion basic Crossbow and Steel Bolts (they are found in the "Steel" Smithing Menu). Similarly, you need the Dwarven Smithing Perk to make the Dwarven Crossbow and Dwarven Bolts (they are found in the "Dwarven" Smithing menu).

Miscellaneous and Jewelry Recipes

There are also two Miscellaneous Recipes that you can craft—the Shellbug Helmet (shown) and Bone Hawk Amulet—which are listed on page 81.

Aetherium Items

At the end of Side Quest: Lost to the Ages, your reward is the crafting of one of three unique Aetherium items at the Aetherium Forge, located deep below the Ruins of Bthalft in the Rift. Aetherium is an incredibly rare material, so much so that only one item—the Aetherial Crown, Shield, or Staff—can be made. A Smithing skill isn't necessary for this creation.

Hearthfire: Smithing

Building Materials

Hearthfire adds Building Materials to your Smithing menu list. These are small items needed in the construction of a house, such as nails, fittings, hinges, and locks. Most require Iron Ingots to make (and locks require Corundum). None of these items require any Smithing Perk prerequisites, so you can forge them even without a prior knowledge of Smithing.

Dragonborn: Smithing

Dragonborn adds four new sets of recipes: Bonemold, Chitin, Nordic, and Stalhrim.

Bonemold Smithing

Bonemold items require the Steel Smithing perk to create. Basic Bonemold items have no special prerequisites, but improved Bonemold items, a variant with better statistics, can be crafted only after you complete both Thieves Guild Quest: Meet the Family (see page 287) and Solstheim Regional Activity: Thievery and the Karstaag Connection* (see page 669). The ability to craft these items is part of your reward for the quest. The armor has a rating similar to Steel armor but is lighter.

Chitin Smithing

Chitin items require the Elven Smithing perk to create. They have no special prerequisites. The armor has a rating similar to Steel armor but it weighs less. There is also a rare variant—Morag Tong Armor—worn by the infamous clan of Dunmeri assassins.

Nordic Smithing

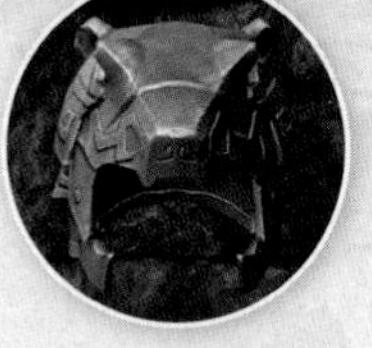

Nordic Carved items require the Advanced Armors perk to create. They have no special prerequisites. Note that these items are distinct from Ancient Nord (Draugr) items, which can't be crafted, and from Nord Hero items, which are a reward for completing the Companions Quest: Glory of the Dead (see page 245). It has a similar rating to Ebony and Orcish armor but is lighter.

Stalhrim Smithing

Stalhrim items require the Ebony Smithing perk to create. You must also complete Solstheim Side Quest: A New Source of Stalhrim (see page 633) to unlock the ability to craft them. Stalhrim items require Stalhrim Ore, a rare material found only on Solstheim. Think of Stalhrim armor as being like Dragonplate Armor but lighter.

Note that these recipes require ore, not ingots. Stalhrim, a type of elemental ice, can't be smelted into ingots. You can buy Stalhrim from Halbarn (the blacksmith in Skaal village) or mine it yourself (see below). All Stalhrim items have an innate property: any Frost enchantments placed on them (e.g., frost damage for weapons, frost resistance for armor) are 10% stronger than normal.

Smithing Recipes

NOTE The following table lists the recipes for forging each weapon and piece of armor. Since the Tempering recipes are straightforward (always one item of the primary material), they aren't necessary to show. After this, there are additional recipe tables for Dawnguard, Hearthfire, and Dragonborn smithing.

SMITHING IMPROVEMENT MODIFIERS

✓	NAME	SKILL (WITH PERKS)	✓	NAME	SKILL (WITH PERKS)
☐	Fine	0–19	☐	Flawless	60–79
☐	Superior	20–39	☐	Epic	80–99
☐	Exquisite	40–59	☐	Legendary	100

✓	INGREDIENTS	NAME	DMG/AMR	WEIGHT	VALUE
	HIDE				
☐	3 Leather Strips, 4 Leather	Hide Armor	20	5	50
☐	2 Leather Strips, 2 Leather	Hide Boots	5	1	10
☐	2 Leather Strips, 1 Leather	Hide Bracers	5	1	10
☐	1 Leather Strips, 2 Leather	Hide Helmet	10	2	25
☐	2 Leather Strips, 4 Leather	Hide Shield	15	4	25
	IRON				
☐	3 Leather Strips, 5 Iron Ingot, Corundum Ingot	Banded Iron Armor	28	35	200
☐	1 Leather Strip, 4 Iron Ingot, Corundum Ingot	Banded Iron Shield	22	12	100
☐	3 Leather Strips, 5 Iron Ingot	Iron Armor	25	30	125
☐	2 Leather Strips, 4 Iron Ingot	Iron Battleaxe	16	20	55
☐	2 Leather Strips, 3 Iron Ingot	Iron Boots	10	6	25
☐	1 Leather Strip, 1 Iron Ingot	Iron Dagger	4	2	10
☐	2 Leather Strips, 2 Iron Ingot	Iron Gauntlets	10	5	25
☐	2 Leather Strips, 4 Iron Ingot	Iron Greatsword	15	16	50
☐	2 Leather Strips, 3 Iron Ingot	Iron Helmet	15	5	60
☐	2 Leather Strips, 3 Iron Ingot	Iron Mace	9	13	35
☐	1 Leather Strip 4 Iron Ingot	Iron Shield	20	12	60
☐	1 Leather Strip, 2 Iron Ingot	Iron Sword	7	9	25
☐	2 Leather Strips, 2 Iron Ingot	Iron War Axe	8	11	30
☐	3 Leather Strips, 4 Iron Ingot	Iron Warhammer	18	24	60
	STUDDED				
☐	3 Leather Strips, 4 Leather, 1 Iron Ingot	Studded Armor	23	6	75
	IMPERIAL				
☐	3 Leather Strips, 2 Leather, 4 Steel Ingot	Imperial Armor	25	35	100
☐	2 Leather Strips, 1 Leather, 2 Steel Ingot	Imperial Boots	10	8	20
☐	2 Leather Strips, 1 Leather, 2 Steel Ingot	Imperial Bracers	10	4	15
☐	1 Leather Strip, 1 Leather, 2 Steel Ingot	Imperial Helmet	15	5	50
☐	2 Leather Strips, 4 Steel Ingot	Imperial Shield	20	12	50
	STEEL				
☐	3 Leather Strips, 2 Leather, 3 Steel Ingot, 2 Corundum Ingot	Scaled Armor	32	6	350
☐	2 Leather Strips, 1 Leather, 2 Steel Ingot, 1 Corundum Ingot	Scaled Boots	9	2	70
☐	2 Leather Strips, 1 Leather, 1 Steel Ingot, 1 Corundum Ingot	Scaled Bracers	9	2	70
☐	1 Leather Strip, 1 Leather, 2 Steel Ingot, 1 Corundum Ingot	Scaled Helmet	14	2	175
☐	3 Leather Strips, 4 Steel Ingot, 1 Iron Ingot	Steel Armor	31	35	275
☐	2 Leather Strips, 4 Steel Ingot, 1 Iron Ingot	Steel Battleaxe	18	21	100
☐	2 Leather Strips, 3 Steel Ingot, 1 Iron Ingot	Steel Cuffed Boots	12	8	55
☐	1 Leather Strip, 1 Steel Ingot, 1 Iron Ingot	Steel Dagger	5	2.5	18
☐	3 Leather Strips, 4 Steel Ingot, 2 Iron Ingot	Steel Greatsword	17	17	90
☐	2 Leather Strips, 2 Steel Ingot, 1 Iron Ingot	Steel Helmet	17	5	125
☐	2 Leather Strips, 2 Steel Ingot, 1 Iron Ingot	Steel Horned Helmet	17	5	125
☐	2 Leather Strips, 2 Steel Ingot, 1 Iron Ingot	Steel Imperial Gauntlets	12	4	55
☐	1 Leather Strip, 3 Steel Ingot, 1 Iron Ingot	Steel Mace	10	14	65
☐	2 Leather Strips, 2 Steel Ingot, 1 Iron Ingot	Steel Nordic Gauntlets	12	4	55
☐	3 Leather Strips, 3 Steel Ingot, 1 Iron Ingot, 1 Corundum Ingot	Steel Plate Armor	40	38	625
☐	2 Leather Strips, 2 Steel Ingot, 1 Iron Ingot, 1 Corundum Ingot	Steel Plate Boots	14	9	125
☐	2 Leather Strips, 2 Steel Ingot, 1 Iron Ingot, 1 Corundum Ingot	Steel Plate Gauntlets	14	6	125
☐	2 Leather Strips, 2 Steel Ingot, 1 Iron Ingot, 1 Corundum Ingot	Steel Plate Helmet	19	6	300
☐	1 Leather Strips, 3 Steel Ingot, 1 Iron Ingot	Steel Shield	24	12	150
☐	2 Leather Strips, 3 Steel Ingot, 1 Iron Ingot	Steel Shin Boots	12	8	55
☐	1 Leather Strip, 2 Steel Ingot, 1 Iron Ingot	Steel Sword	8	10	45
☐	2 Leather Strips, 2 Steel Ingot, 1 Iron Ingot	Steel War Axe	9	12	55
☐	3 Leather Strips, 4 Steel Ingot, 1 Iron Ingot	Steel Warhammer	20	25	110
	LEATHER				
☐	3 Leather Strips, 4 Leather	Leather Armor	26	6	125
☐	2 Leather Strips, 2 Leather	Leather Boots	7	2	25
☐	2 Leather Strips, 1 Leather	Leather Bracers	7	2	25
☐	1 Leather Strip, 2 Leather	Leather Helmet	12	2	60
	DWARVEN				
☐	3 Leather Strips, 3 Dwarven Metal Ingot, 1 Iron Ingot, 1 Steel Ingot	Dwarven Armor	34	45	400
☐	2 Leather Strips, 2 Dwarven Metal Ingot, 1 Iron Ingot, 2 Steel Ingot	Dwarven Battleaxe	20	23	300
☐	2 Leather Strips, 2 Dwarven Metal Ingot, 1 Iron Ingot, 1 Steel Ingot	Dwarven Boots	13	10	85
☐	2 Dwarven Metal Ingot, 1 Iron Ingot	Dwarven Bow	12	10	270
☐	1 Leather Strip, 1 Dwarven Metal Ingot, 1 Iron Ingot, 1 Steel Ingot	Dwarven Dagger	7	3.5	55
☐	2 Leather Strips, 1 Dwarven Metal Ingot, 1 Iron Ingot, 1 Steel Ingot	Dwarven Gauntlets	13	8	85
☐	3 Leather Strips, 2 Dwarven Metal Ingot, 2 Iron Ingot, 2 Steel Ingot	Dwarven Greatsword	19	19	270
☐	2 Leather Strips, 2 Dwarven Metal Ingot, 1 Iron Ingot, 1 Steel Ingot	Dwarven Helmet	18	12	200
☐	1 Leather Strip, 2 Dwarven Metal Ingot, 1 Iron Ingot, 1 Steel Ingot	Dwarven Mace	12	16	190
☐	1 Leather Strip, 2 Dwarven Metal Ingot, 1 Iron Ingot, 1 Steel Ingot	Dwarven Shield	26	12	225
☐	1 Leather Strip, 1 Dwarven Metal Ingot, 1 Iron Ingot, 1 Steel Ingot	Dwarven Sword	10	12	135
☐	2 Leather Strips, 1 Dwarven Metal Ingot, 1 Iron Ingot, 1 Steel Ingot	Dwarven War Axe	11	14	165
☐	3 Leather Strips, 2 Dwarven Metal Ingot, 1 Iron Ingot, 2 Steel Ingot	Dwarven Warhammer	22	27	325
	ELVEN				
☐	3 Leather Strips, 1 Leather, 4 Refined Moonstone, 1 Iron Ingot	Elven Armor	29	4	225
☐	2 Leather Strips, 2 Refined Moonstone, 2 Iron Ingot, 1 Quicksilver Ingot	Elven Battleaxe	21	24	520

✓	INGREDIENTS	NAME	DMG/AMR	WEIGHT	VALUE
☐	2 Leather Strips, 1 Leather, 2 Refined Moonstone, 1 Iron Ingot	Elven Boots	8	1	45
☐	2 Refined Moonstone, 1 Quicksilver Ingot	Elven Bow	13	12	470
☐	1 Leather Strips, 1 Refined Moonstone, 1 Iron Ingot, 1 Quicksilver Ingot	Elven Dagger	8	4	95
☐	2 Leather Strips, 1 Leather, 1 Refined Moonstone, 1 Iron Ingot	Elven Gauntlets	8	1	45
☐	3 Leather Strips, 4 Refined Moonstone, 1 Iron Ingot, 1 Quicksilver Ingot	Elven Gilded Armor	35	4	550
☐	3 Leather Strips, 2 Refined Moonstone, 2 Iron Ingot, 1 Quicksilver Ingot	Elven Greatsword	20	20	470
☐	1 Leather Strips, 1 Leather, 2 Refined Moonstone, 1 Iron Ingot	Elven Helmet	13	1	110
☐	1 Leather Strips, 2 Refined Moonstone, 1 Iron Ingot, 1 Quicksilver Ingot	Elven Mace	13	17	330
☐	2 Leather Strips, 4 Refined Moonstone, 1 Iron Ingot	Elven Shield	21	4	115
☐	1 Leather Strips, 1 Refined Moonstone, 1 Iron Ingot, 1 Quicksilver Ingot	Elven Sword	11	13	235
☐	2 Leather Strips, 1 Refined Moonstone, 1 Iron Ingot, 1 Quicksilver Ingot	Elven War Axe	12	15	280
☐	3 Leather Strips, 2 Refined Moonstone, 2 Iron Ingot, 1 Quicksilver Ingot	Elven Warhammer	23	28	565
	ORCISH				
☐	3 Leather Strips, 4 Orichalcum Ingot, 1 Iron Ingot	Orcish Armor	40	35	1000
☐	2 Leather Strips, 4 Orichalcum Ingot, 1 Iron Ingot	Orcish Battleaxe	19	25	165
☐	2 Leather Strips, 3 Orichalcum Ingot, 1 Iron Ingot	Orcish Boots	15	7	200
☐	2 Orichalcum Ingot, 1 Iron Ingot	Orcish Bow	10	9	150
☐	1 Leather Strips, 1 Orichalcum Ingot, 1 Iron Ingot	Orcish Dagger	6	3	30
☐	2 Leather Strips, 2 Orichalcum Ingot, 1 Iron Ingot	Orcish Gauntlets	15	7	200
☐	3 Leather Strips, 4 Orichalcum Ingot, 2 Iron Ingot	Orcish Greatsword	18	18	75
☐	2 Leather Strips, 2 Orichalcum Ingot, 1 Iron Ingot	Orcish Helmet	20	8	500
☐	1 Leather Strip, 3 Orichalcum Ingot, 1 Iron Ingot	Orcish Mace	11	15	105
☐	1 Leather Strip, 3 Orichalcum Ingot, 1 Iron Ingot	Orcish Shield	30	14	500
☐	1 Leather Strip, 2 Orichalcum Ingot, 1 Iron Ingot	Orcish Sword	9	11	75
☐	2 Leather Strips, 2 Orichalcum Ingot, 1 Iron Ingot	Orcish War Axe	10	13	90
☐	3 Leather Strips, 4 Orichalcum Ingot, 1 Iron Ingot	Orcish Warhammer	21	26	180
	EBONY				
☐	3 Leather Strips, 5 Ebony Ingot	Ebony Armor	43	38	1,500
☐	2 Leather Strips, 5 Ebony Ingot	Ebony Battleaxe	23	26	1,585
☐	2 Leather Strips, 3 Ebony Ingot	Ebony Boots	16	7	275
☐	3 Ebony Ingot	Ebony Bow	17	16	1,440
☐	1 Leather Strip, 1 Ebony Ingot	Ebony Dagger	10	5	290
☐	2 Leather Strips, 2 Ebony Ingot	Ebony Gauntlets	16	7	275
☐	3 Leather Strips, 5 Ebony Ingot	Ebony Greatsword	22	22	1,440
☐	2 Leather Strips, 3 Ebony Ingot	Ebony Helmet	21	10	750
☐	1 Leather Strip, 3 Ebony Ingot	Ebony Mace	16	19	1,000
☐	1 Leather Strip, 4 Ebony Ingot	Ebony Shield	32	14	750
☐	1 Leather Strip, 2 Ebony Ingot	Ebony Sword	13	15	720
☐	2 Leather Strips, 2 Ebony Ingot	Ebony War Axe	15	17	865

✓	INGREDIENTS	NAME	DMG/AMR	WEIGHT	VALUE
☐	3 Leather Strips, 5 Ebony Ingot	Ebony Warhammer	25	30	1,725
	GLASS				
☐	3 Leather Strips, 1 Leather, 4 Refined Malachite, 2 Refined Moonstone	Glass Armor	38	7	900
☐	2 Leather Strips, 2 Refined Malachite, 2 Refined Moonstone	Glass Arrow	18	0	6
☐	2 Leather Strips, 1 Leather, 2 Refined Malachite, 1 Refined Moonstone	Glass Battleaxe	22	25	900
☐	2 Refined Malachite, 1 Refined Moonstone	Glass Boots	11	2	190
☐	1 Leather Strip, 1 Refined Malachite, 1 Refined Moonstone	Glass Bow	15	14	820
☐	2 Leather Strips, 1 Leather, 1 Refined Malachite, 1 Refined Moonstone	Glass Dagger	9	4.5	165
☐	3 Leather Strips, 2 Refined Malachite, 2 Refined Moonstone	Glass Gauntlets	11	2	190
☐	1 Leather Strip, 1 Leather, 2 Refined Malachite, 1 Refined Moonstone	Glass Greatsword	21	22	820
☐	3 Leather Strips, 2 Refined Malachite, 1 Refined Moonstone	Glass Helmet	16	2	450
☐	1 Leather Strip, 2 Refined Malachite, 1 Refined Moonstone	Glass Mace	14	18	575
☐	2 Leather Strips, 4 Refined Malachite, 1 Refined Moonstone	Glass Shield	27	6	450
☐	1 Leather Strip, 1 Refined Malachite, 1 Refined Moonstone	Glass Sword	12	14	410
☐	2 Leather Strips, 1 Refined Malachite, 1 Refined Moonstone	Glass War Axe	13	16	490
☐	3 Leather Strips, 3 Refined Malachite, 2 Refined Moonstone	Glass Warhammer	24	29	985
	DRAGON				
☐	3 Leather Strips, 3 Dragon Scales, 2 Dragon Bone	Dragonplate Armor	46	40	2,125
☐	2 Leather Strips, 3 Dragon Scales, 1 Dragon Bone	Dragonplate Boots	17	8	425
☐	2 Leather Strips, 2 Dragon Scales, 1 Dragon Bone	Dragonplate Gauntlets	17	8	425
☐	2 Leather Strips, 2 Dragon Scales, 1 Dragon Bone	Dragonplate Helmet	22	8	1,050
☐	1 Leather Strip, 3 Dragon Scales, 1 Dragon Bone	Dragonplate Shield	34	15	1,050
☐	3 Leather Strips, 1 Leather, 4 Dragon Scales, 2 Iron Ingot	Dragonscale Armor	41	10	1,500
☐	2 Leather Strips, 1 Leather, 2 Dragon Scales, 1 Iron Ingot	Dragonscale Boots	12	3	300
☐	2 Leather Strips, 1 Leather, 2 Dragon Scales, 1 Iron Ingot	Dragonscale Gauntlets	12	3	300
☐	1 Leather Strip, 1 Leather, 2 Dragon Scales, 1 Iron Ingot	Dragonscale Helmet	17	4	750
☐	2 Leather Strips, 4 Dragon Scales, 2 Iron Ingot	Dragonscale Shield	29	6	750
	DAEDRIC				
☐	3 Leather Strips, 5 Ebony Ingot, 1 Daedra Heart	Daedric Armor	49	50	3,200
☐	2 Leather Strips, 5 Ebony Ingot, 1 Daedra Heart	Daedric Battleaxe	25	27	2750
☐	2 Leather Strips, 3 Ebony Ingot, 1 Daedra Heart	Daedric Boots	18	10	625
☐	3 Ebony Ingot, 1 Daedra Heart	Daedric Bow	19	18	2,500
☐	1 Leather Strip, 1 Ebony Ingot, 1 Daedra Heart	Daedric Dagger	11	6	500
☐	2 Leather Strips, 2 Ebony Ingot, 1 Daedra Heart	Daedric Gauntlets	18	6	625
☐	3 Leather Strips, 5 Ebony Ingot, 1 Daedra Heart	Daedric Greatsword	24	23	2,500
☐	2 Leather Strips, 3 Ebony Ingot, 1 Daedra Heart	Daedric Helmet	23	15	1,600
☐	1 Leather Strip, 3 Ebony Ingot, 1 Daedra Heart	Daedric Mace	16	20	1,750

The Elder Scrolls V

SKYRIM

✓	INGREDIENTS	NAME	DMG/AMR	WEIGHT	VALUE
☐	1 Leather Strip, 4 Ebony Ingot, 1 Daedra Heart	Daedric Shield	36	15	1,600
☐	1 Leather Strip, 2 Ebony Ingot, 1 Daedra Heart	Daedric Sword	14	16	1,250
☐	2 Leather Strips, 2 Ebony Ingot, 1 Daedra Heart	Daedric War Axe	15	18	1,500
☐	3 Leather Strips, 5 Ebony Ingot, 1 Daedra Heart	Daedric Warhammer	27	31	4,000
	JEWELRY				
☐	1 Flawless Diamond, 1 Gold Ingot	Gold Diamond Necklace	0	0.5	1,200
☐	1 Diamond, 1 Gold Ingot	Gold Diamond Ring	0	0.25	900
☐	1 Emerald, 1 Gold Ingot	Gold Emerald Ring	0	0.25	700
☐	2 Flawless Amethyst, 1 Gold Ingot	Gold Jeweled Necklace	0	0.5	485
☐	1 Gold Ingot	Gold Necklace	0	0.5	120
☐	1 Gold Ingot	2 Gold Ring	0	0.25	75
☐	1 Flawless Ruby, 1 Gold Ingot	Gold Ruby Necklace	0	0.5	550
☐	1 Sapphire, 1 Gold Ingot	Gold Sapphire Ring	0	0.25	500
☐	1 Amethyst, 1 Silver Ingot	Silver Amethyst Ring	0	0.25	180
☐	1 Flawless Emerald, 1 Silver Ingot	Silver Emerald Necklace	0	0.5	830
☐	1 Garnet, 1 Silver Ingot	Silver Garnet Ring	0	0.25	160
☐	1 Flawless Garnet, 1 Silver Ingot	Silver Jeweled Necklace	0	0.5	380
☐	1 Silver Ingot	Silver Necklace	0	0.5	60
☐	1 Silver Ingot	2 Silver Ring	0	0.25	30
☐	1 Ruby, 1 Silver Ingot	Silver Ruby Ring	0	0.25	260
☐	1 Flawless Sapphire, 1 Silver Ingot	Silver Sapphire Necklace	0	0.5	580
	DRAUGR (SKYFORGE ONLY, AFTER GLORY OF THE DEAD)				
☐	3 Leather Strips, 3 Steel Ingot, 1 Ancient Nord Battleaxe	Nord Hero Battleaxe	32	20	239
☐	3 Leather Strips, 3 Steel Ingot, 1 Ancient Nord Greatsword	Nord Hero Greatsword	30	16	199
☐	2 Leather Strips, 2 Steel Ingot, 1 Ancient Sword	Nord Hero Sword	30	9	107
☐	2 Leather Strips, 2 Steel Ingot, 1 Ancient Nord War Axe	Nord Hero War Axe	32	11	131
☐	4 Leather Strips, 2 Leather, 2 Iron Ingot, 5 Steel Ingot	Ancient Nord Armor	25	28	125
☐	3 Leather Strips, 2 Leather, 2 Iron Ingot, 4 Steel Ingot	Ancient Nord Boots	10	5	25
☐	3 Leather Strips, 2 Leather, 2 Iron Ingot, 3 Steel Ingot	Ancient Nord Gauntlets	10	4	25
☐	3 Leather Strips, 2 Leather, 2 Iron Ingot, 3 Steel Ingot	Ancient Nord Helmet	15	4	60

Dawnguard Smithing Recipes

This table lists the recipes for forging the new items available in Dawnguard.

✓	INGREDIENTS	NAME	DMG/AMR	WEIGHT	VALUE
	ARROWS				
☐	1 Firewood, 1 Iron Ingot	Iron Arrow (24)	8	0	1
☐	1 Firewood, 1 Steel Ingot	Steel Arrow (24)	10	0	2
☐	1 Firewood, 1 Dwarven Metal Ingot	Dwarven Arrow (24)	14	0	4
☐	1 Firewood, 1 Refined Moonstone	Elven Arrow (24)	16	0	5
☐	1 Firewood, 1 Orichalcum Ingot	Orcish Arrow (24)	12	0	3
☐	1 Firewood, 1 Ebony Ingot	Ebony Arrow (24)	20	0	7
☐	1 Firewood, 1 Malachite Ingot	Glass Arrow (24)	18	0	6
☐	1 Firewood, 1 Ebony Ingot, 1 Daedra Heart	Daedric Arrow (24)	24	0	8

✓	INGREDIENTS	NAME	DMG/AMR	WEIGHT	VALUE
☐	1 Firewood, 1 Dragon Bone	Dragonbone Arrow (24)	25	0	9
	DRAGON				
☐	2 Leather Strips, 2 Ebony Ingot, 3 Dragon Bone	Dragonbone Battleaxe	26	30	3,000
☐	1 Ebony Ingot, 2 Dragon Bone	Dragonbone Bow	20	20	2,725
☐	1 Leather Strip, 1 Dragon Bone	Dragonbone Dagger	12	6.5	600
☐	3 Leather Strips, 1 Ebony Ingot, 4 Dragon Bone	Dragonbone Greatsword	25	27	2,725
☐	1 Leather Strip, 1 Ebony Ingot, 2 Dragon Bone	Dragonbone Mace	17	22	2,000
☐	1 Leather Strips, 1 Ebony Ingot, 1 Dragon Bone	Dragonbone Sword	15	19	1,500
☐	2 Leather Strips, 1 Ebony Ingot, 1 Dragon Bone	Dragonbone War Axe	16	21	1,700
☐	3 Leather Strips, 2 Ebony Ingots, 3 Dragon Bones	Dragonbone Warhammer	28	33	4275
	MISCELLANEOUS				
☐	2 Leather Strips, 1 Bone Hawk Skull, 6 Bone Hawk Feathers	Bone Hawk Amulet	0	1	100
☐	2 Shellbug Chitin, 2 Iron Ingot	Shellbug Helmet	22	6	600
	CROSSBOWS AND BOLTS				
☐	3 Firewood, 3 Steel Ingot	Crossbow	19	14	120
☐	1 Steel Crossbow, 2 Corundum Ingots	Enhanced Crossbow	19	15	200
☐	5 Dwarven Ingots	Dwarven Crossbow	22	20	350
☐	Dwarven Crossbow, 2 Quicksilver Ingots	Enhanced Dwarven Crossbow	22	21	550
☐	1 Firewood, 1 Steel Ingot	Steel Bolt (10)	10	0	1
☐	10 Steel Bolts, 1 Fire Salts	Exploding Steel Bolt of Fire (10)	10	0	5
	Explodes for 10 points of fire damage.				
☐	10 Steel Bolts, 1 Frost Salts	Exploding Steel Bolt of Ice (10)	10	0	5
	Explodes for 10 points of frost damage to Health and Stamina.				
☐	10 Steel Bolts, 1 Void Salts	Exploding Steel Bolt of Shock (10)	10	0	5
	Explodes for 10 points of shock damage to Health and half that to Magicka.				
☐	1 Firewood, 1 Dwarven Ingot	Dwarven Bolt (10)	14	0	3
☐	1 Dwarven Bolt, 1 Fire Salts	Exploding Dwarven Bolt of Fire (10)	14	0	15
	Explodes for 10 points of fire damage.				
☐	1 Dwarven Bolt, 1 Frost Salts	Exploding Dwarven Bolt of Ice (10)	14	0	15
	Explodes for 10 points of frost damage to Health and Stamina.				
☐	1 Dwarven Bolt, 1 Void Salts	Exploding Dwarven Bolt of Shock (10)	14	0	15
	Explodes for 10 points of shock damage to Health and half that to Magicka.				
	AETHERIUM (AETHERIUM FORGE ONLY)				
☐	1 Aetherium Crest, 2 Flawless Sapphires, 2 Dwarven Ingots, 2 Gold Ingots	Aetherial Crown	0	2	2250
☐	1 Aetherium Crest, 4 Dwarven Ingots, 2 Malachite Ingots	Aetherial Shield	26	12	2000
☐	1 Aetherium Crest, 2 Dwarven Ingots, 2 Ebony Ingots, 1 Gold Ingot	Aetherial Staff	0	8	1970

Hearthfire Smithing Recipes

	BUILDING MATERIALS (HEARTHFIRE ONLY)				
☐	1 Iron Ingot	Iron Fittings		1	4
☐	1 Iron Ingot	Hinge (2)		0.5	4
☐	1 Iron Ingot	Nails (10)		0.1	1
☐	1 Iron Ingot, 1 Corundum Ingot	Lock		0.5	10

Dragonborn Smithing Recipes

This table lists the additional recipes for forging the new items available in Dragonborn. You should also reference the previous Smithing recipes for a complete list.

✓	INGREDIENTS	NAME	DMG/AMR	WEIGHT	VALUE
	BONEMOLD				
☐	2 Netch Leather, 10 Bone Meal, 1 Iron Ingot	Bonemold Armor	32	34	290
☐	1 Netch Leather, 1 Iron Ingot, 6 Bone Meal	Bonemold Boots	12	7	60
☐	1 Netch Leather, 4 Bone Meal, 1 Iron Ingot	Bonemold Gauntlets	12	3.5	60
☐	1 Netch Leather, 6 Bone Meal, 1 Iron Ingot	Bonemold Helmet	17	4.5	135
☐	1 Netch Leather, 8 Bone Meal, 1 Iron Ingot	Bonemold Shield	22	8	95
☐	2 Netch Leather, 10 Bone Meal, 1 Iron Ingot, 1 Void Salts, 1 Stalhrim Ore, 1 Netch Jelly	Improved Bonemold Armor	35	43	290
☐	1 Netch Leather, 6 Bone Meal, 1 Iron Ingot, 1 Void Salts, 1 Stalhrim Ore, 1 Netch Jelly	Improved Bonemold Boots	13	9	60
☐	1 Netch Leather, 4 Bone Meal, 1 Iron Ingot, 1 Void Salts, 1 Stalhrim Ore, 1 Netch Jelly	Improved Bonemold Gauntlets	13	7	60
☐	1 Netch Leather, 6 Bone Meal, 1 Iron Ingot, 1 Void Salts, 1 Stalhrim Ore, 1 Netch Jelly	Improved Bonemold Helmet	18	11	135
☐	1 Netch Leather, 8 Bone Meal, 1 Iron Ingot, 1 Void Salts, 1 Stalhrim Ore, 1 Netch Jelly	Improved Bonemold Shield	26	11	95
	CHITIN				
☐	2 Netch Leather, 5 Chitin Plate, 1 Iron Ingot	Chitin Armor	30	4	240
☐	1 Netch Leather, 3 Chitin Plate, 1 Iron Ingot	Chitin Boots	9	1	50
☐	1 Netch Leather, 2 Chitin Plate, 1 Iron Ingot	Chitin Bracers	9	2	50
☐	2 Netch Leather, 6 Chitin Plate, 1 Corundum Ingot	Chitin Heavy Armor	40	35	650
☐	1 Netch Leather, 4 Chitin Plate, 1 Corundum Ingot	Chitin Heavy Boots	14	6	135
☐	1 Netch Leather, 3 Chitin Plate, 1 Corundum Ingot	Chitin Heavy Gauntlets	14	5	135
☐	1 Netch Leather, 4 Chitin Plate, 1 Corundum Ingot	Chitin Heavy Helmet	19	5	135
☐	1 Netch Leather, 3 Chitin Plate, 1 Iron Ingot	Chitin Helmet	14	1	125
☐	1 Netch Leather, 4 Chitin Plate, 1 Iron Ingot	Chitin Shield	25	8	215
	NORDIC				
☐	1 Firewood, 1 Steel Ingot, 1 Quicksilver Ingot	Nordic Arrow (24)	12	0	3
☐	5 Steel Ingot, 2 Leather Strips, 1 Quicksilver Ingot	Nordic Battleaxe	21	23	650
☐	3 Steel Ingot, 1 Quicksilver Ingot	Nordic Bow	13	11	580
☐	3 Leather Strips, 6 Steel Ingot, 1 Ebony Ingot, 1 Quicksilver Ingot	Nordic Carved Armor	43	37	1600

✓	INGREDIENTS	NAME	DMG/AMR	WEIGHT	VALUE
☐	2 Leather Strips, 4 Steel Ingot, 1 Ebony Ingot, 1 Quicksilver Ingot	Nordic Carved Boots	15	6	220
☐	2 Leather Strips, 3 Steel Ingot, 1 Ebony Ingot, 1 Quicksilver Ingot	Nordic Carved Gauntlets	15	6	220
☐	2 Leather Strips, 4 Steel Ingot, 1 Ebony Ingot, 1 Quicksilver Ingot	Nordic Carved Helmet	20	7	550
☐	1 Steel Ingot, 1 Leather Strips, 1 Quicksilver Ingot	Nordic Dagger	8	3.5	115
☐	5 Steel Ingot, 3 Leather Strips, 1 Quicksilver Ingot	Nordic Greatsword	20	19	585
☐	1 Leather Strips, 1 Steel Ingot, 1 Quicksilver Ingot	Nordic Mace	13	16	410
☐	1 Leather Strips, 4 Steel Ingot, 1 Quicksilver Ingot	Nordic Shield	27	10	335
☐	2 Steel Ingot, 1 Leather Strips, 1 Quicksilver Ingot	Nordic Sword	11	12	290
☐	2 Steel Ingot, 2 Leather Strips, 1 Quicksilver Ingot	Nordic War Axe	12	14	350
☐	5 Steel Ingot, 3 Leather Strips, 1 Quicksilver Ingot	Nordic Warhammer	23	27	700
	STALHRIM				
☐	3 Leather Strips, 6 Stalhrim Ore, 1 Quicksilver Ingot	Stalhrim Armor	46	38	2200
☐	1 Firewood, 1 Stalhrim Ore	Stalhrim Arrow (24)	20	0	7
☐	5 Stalhrim Ore, 2 Leather Strips	Stalhrim Battleaxe	24	25	2150
☐	2 Leather Strips, 1 Quicksilver Ingot, 4 Stalhrim Ore	Stalhrim Boots	17	7	450
☐	3 Stalhrim Ore	Stalhrim Bow	17	15	1800
☐	1 Stalhrim Ore, 1 Leather Strips	Stalhrim Dagger	10	4.5	395
☐	2 Leather Strips, 3 Stalhrim Ore, 1 Quicksilver Ingot	Stalhrim Gauntlets	17	7	450
☐	5 Stalhrim Ore, 3 Leather Strips	Stalhrim Greatsword	23	21	1970
☐	2 Leather Strips, 4 Stalhrim Ore, 1 Quicksilver Ingot	Stalhrim Helmet	22	7	1135
☐	3 Leather Strips, 5 Stalhrim Ore, 1 Steel Ingot	Stalhrim Light Armor	39	7	925
☐	2 Leather Strips, 1 Steel Ingot, 3 Stalhrim Ore	Stalhrim Light Boots	12	2	215
☐	2 Leather Strips, 2 Stalhrim Ore, 1 Steel Ingot	Stalhrim Light Gauntlets	12	2	215
☐	2 Leather Strips, 3 Stalhrim Ore, 1 Steel Ingot	Stalhrim Light Helmet	17	2	465
☐	3 Stalhrim Ore, 1 Leather Strips	Stalhrim Mace	16	18	1375
☐	1 Leather Strips, 4 Stalhrim Ore, 1 Steel Ingot	Stalhrim Shield	30	10	600
☐	2 Stalhrim Ore, 1 Leather Strips	Stalhrim Sword	13	14	985
☐	2 Stalhrim Ore, 2 Leather Strips	Stalhrim Waraxe	15	16	1180
☐	5 Stalhrim Ore, 3 Leather Strips	Stalhrim Warhammer	26	29	2850

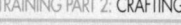

Cooking

NOTE Cooking meats, soups, and stews does not increase any skill.

Throw the meat, plants, and other ingredients (often mead-related) into a pot. Stir and stave off the hunger pangs.

Cooking allows you to transform meat, vegetables, and other ingredients into better-tasting, higher-quality food. Cooking is a rudimentary method of living off the land and is far surpassed by alchemy (which is a skill and creates potions that are much more potent).

Cooking requires a cooking pot or cooking spit, which can easily be found in every town and village across Skyrim—almost every house has one by the fireplace. You can also find them in other inhabited locations like forts or bandit camps.

Interact with a cooking pot (or cooking spit) to bring up the Cooking menu, which lists the food you can cook. All of the cooking recipes are readily available at any cooking pot or spit, as long as you have the ingredients for them. If you're missing ingredients, the recipe is still shown but grayed out.

Most of the food you can cook isn't all that helpful, typically restoring 5 to 10 points of Health or Stamina—less than you'd receive from even the cheapest of potions. Moreover, the ingredients are often the same price or more expensive than the resulting food and can often be put to better use in alchemy instead.

However, for a new adventurer embarking on their travels across the realm and scrabbling to get by, cooked food is a way to recover a little health in a pinch. For those who wish to live as the Nords do, killing their own meats, harvesting their own vegetables, and cooking the resulting ingredients into a somewhat murky-looking stew, this is an authentic way to satiate hunger and fatigue. But for everyone else, alchemy is a better bet, as it helps to advance your level and makes significantly better restorative items...with one delicious exception: the Elsweyr Fondue is excellent.

A COOKING EXAMPLE: THE ELSWEYR FONDUE

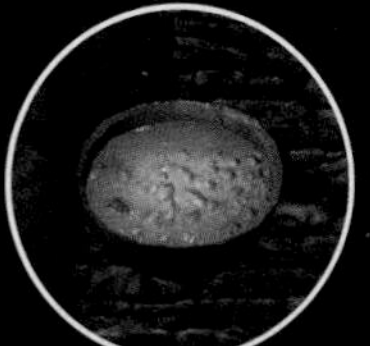

Approach a cooking pot to learn the recipe for Elsweyr Fondue. It requires:

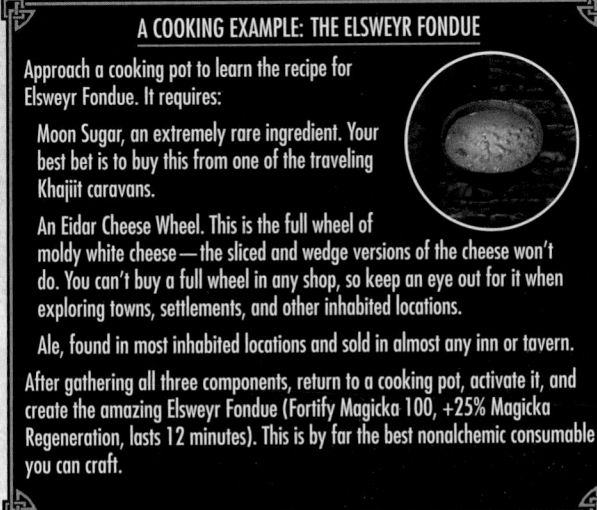

Moon Sugar, an extremely rare ingredient. Your best bet is to buy this from one of the traveling Khajiit caravans.

An Eidar Cheese Wheel. This is the full wheel of moldy white cheese—the sliced and wedge versions of the cheese won't do. You can't buy a full wheel in any shop, so keep an eye out for it when exploring towns, settlements, and other inhabited locations.

Ale, found in most inhabited locations and sold in almost any inn or tavern.

After gathering all three components, return to a cooking pot, activate it, and create the amazing Elsweyr Fondue (Fortify Magicka 100, +25% Magicka Regeneration, lasts 12 minutes). This is by far the best nonalchemic consumable you can craft.

Hearthfire and Dragonborn: Cooking

Recipes

Hearthfire adds the following additions to your cooking:

Cooking Recipes: There are two new recipes (Steamed Mudcrab Legs and Clam Chowder) that can be made at any cookpot.

Baking Recipes: When you build your own house, you can construct a kitchen in the east wing addition. One of its unique furnishings is an oven. This allows you to bake any of these recipes (including the delicious apple pie and the ubiquitous sweetroll). The oven is the only place you can bake. The only way you can gain access to one is to build it.

Milling Recipes: If you purchase land in the Pale and build Heljarchen Hall, you can construct the unique mill outbuilding. The mill allows you to convert wheat into a sack of flour. Flour is required for most baking recipes, so you might want to add a kitchen (and oven) to Heljarchen Hall and make it the epicenter of your pastry-based antics.

NOTE Dawnguard adds no additional cooking recipes. Dragonborn adds two new cooking recipes. These have no special requirements.

Cooking Recipes

The following tables show every recipe you can make, including the ingredients and the effects of the food once mixed together. After that is a table of baking recipes (requiring the Hearthfire Oven) and the single milling recipe (requiring the Hearthfire Flour Mill).

✓	INGREDIENTS	PRODUCES	WEIGHT	VALUE	EFFECT
☐	Cabbage, Red Apple, Salt Pile	Apple Cabbage Stew	0.5	8	Restore Health 10, Restore Stamina 15
☐	Carrot, Garlic, Raw Beef, Salt Pile	Beef Stew	0.5	8	Fortify Stamina 25/12m, Regenerate Stamina 2/12m
☐	Cabbage, Leek, Potato, Salt Pile	Cabbage Potato Soup	0.5	5	Restore Health 10, Restore Stamina 10
☐	1 Cabbage, 1 Salt Pile	Cabbage Soup	0.5	5	Restore Health 10, Restore Stamina 8
☐	1 Clam Meat, 1 Potato, 1 Jug of Milk, 1 Butter	Clam Chowder	0.5	5	Restore Health 10, Restore Stamina 10
☐	Raw Beef, Salt Pile	Cooked Beef	0.5	5	Restore Health 10
☐	Ale, Eidar Cheese Wheel, Moon Sugar	Elsweyr Fondue	0.5	5	Fortify Magicka 100/12m, Regenerate Magicka 25%/12m
☐	Chicken Breast, Salt Pile	Grilled Chicken Breast	0.2	4	Restore Health 5
☐	1 Ash Yam, 1 Garlic, 1 Horker Meat	Horker and Ash Yam Stew	0.5	8	Restore Health 15, Restore Stamina 15, Regenerate Health 1/12m
☐	Horker Meat, Salt Pile	Horker Loaf	1	4	Restore Health 10
☐	Garlic, Horker Meat, Lavender, Tomato	Horker Stew	0.5	8	Restore Health 15, Restore Stamina 15, Regenerate Health 1/12m
☐	Horse Meat, Salt Pile	Horse Haunch	2	4	Restore Health 10
☐	Leg of Goat, Salt Pile	Leg of Goat Roast	1	4	Restore Health 10
☐	Mammoth Snout, Salt Pile	Mammoth Steak	2	8	Restore Health 10
☐	Pheasant Breast, Salt Pile	Pheasant Roast	0.2	4	Restore Health 5
☐	Raw Rabbit Leg, Salt Pile	Rabbit Haunch	0.1	3	Restore Health 5
☐	Salmon Meat, Salt Pile	Salmon Steak	0.1	4	Restore Health 5

✓	INGREDIENTS	PRODUCES	WEIGHT	VALUE	EFFECT
	1 Mudcrab Legs, 1 Butter	Steamed Mudcrab Legs	0.1	4	Restore Health 12
	Garlic, Leek, Tomato, Salt Pile	Tomato Soup	0.5	5	Restore Health 10, Restore Stamina 10
	Cabbage, Leek, Potato, Tomato	Vegetable Soup	0.5	5	Regenerate Health 1/12m, Regenerate Stamina 1/12m
	Venison, Salt Pile	Venison Chop	2	5	Restore Health 5
	Leek, Potato, Salt Pile, Venison	Venison Stew	0.5	8	Restore Stamina 15, Regenerate Health 1/12m, Regenerate Stamina 1/12m

BAKING RECIPES (REQUIRES HEARTHFIRE OVEN)

✓	INGREDIENTS	PRODUCES	WEIGHT	VALUE	EFFECT
	1 Sack of Flour, 1 Green Apple, 1 Red Apple	Apple Dumpling	0.1	2	Restore Health 5, Fortify Archery 5%/60s
	1 Sack of Flour, 1 Salt Pile, 1 Butter, 1 Chicken's Egg, 2 Green Apples, 2 Red Apples	Apple Pie	0.5	5	Restore Health 10
	1 Sack of Flour, 1 Salt Pile	Braided Bread	0.2	2	Restore Health 2, Fortify Carry Weight 5/30s
	1 Sack of Flour, 1 Salt Pile, 1 Jug of Milk, 1 Chicken's Egg	Bread	0.2	2	Restore Health 2
	1 Sack of Flour, 1 Salt Pile, 1 Chicken Meat, 1 Garlic, 1 Leek	Chicken Dumpling	0.1	2	Restore Health 15, Regenerate Health 1/2m
	1 Loaf of Bread, 1 Butter, 1 Garlic	Garlic Bread (2)	0.1	2	Restore Health 1, Cure Disease
	1 Sack of Flour, 2 Jazbays, 1 Butter	Jazbay Crostata	0.2	2	Restore Health 10, Fortify Magicka 4/60s
	1 Sack of Flour, 3 Juniper Berries, 1 Butter	Juniper Berry Crostata	0.2	2	Restore Health 4, Regen Health 2/60s
	1 Sack of Flour, 1 Moon Sugar, 2 Snowberries, 1 Lavender	Lavender Dumpling	0.1	2	Restore Health 5, Fortify Magicka 10/60s, Resist Magic 10%/60s
	1 Sack of Flour, 1 Jug of Milk, 1 Salt Pile, 1 Potato, 1 Chicken's Egg	Potato Bread	0.2	2	Restore Health 3
	1 Sack of Flour, 2 Snowberries, 1 Butter	Snowberry Crostata	0.2	2	Restore Health 10, Resist Fire 4%/60s
	1 Sack of Flour, 1 Jug of Milk, 1 Salt Pile, 1 Butter, 1 Chicken's Egg	Sweetroll	0.1	2	Restore Health 5

MILLING RECIPES (REQUIRES HEARTHFIRE FLOUR MILL)

✓	INGREDIENTS	PRODUCES	WEIGHT	VALUE	EFFECT
	3 Wheat	Sack of Flour	0.5	1	Restore Health 1

Construct an Oven in your Hearthfire abode and bake some delicious treats!

Mining

NOTE Mining minerals and gems does not increase any skill.

Assaulting an ore vein with dual-wielded pickaxes is the quickest (and craziest) way to mine.

Throughout Skyrim, there are a variety of natural mineral deposits, concentrated in ore veins. Extracting minerals and gems from these veins can make you a small amount of gold, but more importantly, it helps you gather raw materials for smithing (which can save you a huge amount of money if you aim to craft your own items). To extract the ore, you first need a pickaxe. You can purchase one from almost any Blacksmith or general store merchant, or find them (for free) in any mine.

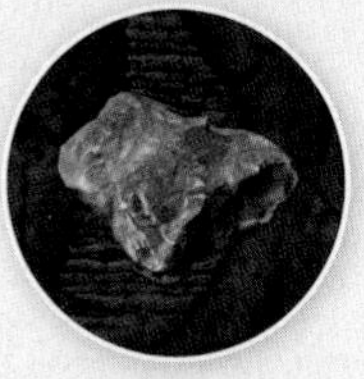

To mine ore, approach an ore vein with a pickaxe in your inventory and interact with it. Typically, a vein produces around three pieces of ore before becoming depleted. Along with each piece of ore, you also have a 10% chance of extracting a (random) gemstone.

TIP **Ore attack!** Instead of activating an ore vein and waiting for your character to mine the ore, you can also attack the ore with a pickaxe instead, which mines it at a slightly faster rate. Dual-wield pickaxes for even faster ore removal, if you really must.

Once mined, ore can be sold for a (generally small) amount of gold, or smelted down to make ingots (a slightly better way to earn money from your digging).

TIP Have you exhausted all the veins in a mine? Then wait about a month, and the veins will reset and can be mined again.

A MINING EXAMPLE: ORICHALCUM AT MOR KHAZGUR

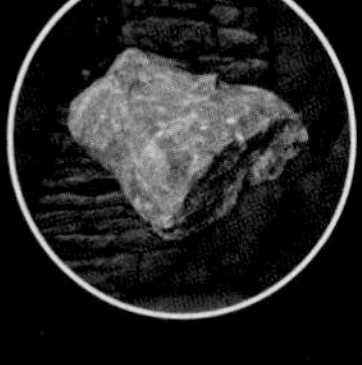

After becoming blood-kin with the Orcs of Mor Khazgur, enter the mine above their longhouse and grab a pickaxe from the table. Approach an Orichalcum ore vein and activate it. After a few seconds, you'll mine three pieces of Orichalcum Ore (each Weight 1, Value 20). Then use the smelter just outside the mine to smelt two pieces of ore into an Orichalcum Ingot (Weight 1, Value 45).

Where to Mine?

You can look for minerals in the wilderness of Skyrim's windswept Holds, though the best and most reliable sources can be found inside the realm's many mines. A few general tips if you plan to delve into mining:

- **Keep a pickaxe handy.** You never know where you might run into some valuable ore, whether out in the wilds or in the depths of a dungeon.
- **Look for mines.** Many settlements have mines, which give you easy access to a specific type of ore. When you befriend the Orc strongholds, you also get access to their rich Orichalcum and Ebony mines.
- **Plan your return trip.** Every in-game month or so, ore veins that have been depleted will replenish. Check back occasionally to strip them of their new ore.

The Holds of Skyrim and Beyond

If you're scouring the landscape, here are some general tips for finding ore deposits:

Falkreath Hold (near Helgen and Riverwood) has a slightly higher concentration of iron ore veins than usual.

The central tundra of Whiterun Hold is a good place to look for Corundum ore.

More valuable ores (Gold, Silver, Moonstone, Oricalchum, and Quicksilver) are most often found in more extreme environments, such as deep in the mountains or along the northern coast.

The Forgotten Vale has deposits of rarer minerals (such as Gold and Quicksilver), as well as Shellbugs (Falmer beasts bred for their hard coatings). Check the Atlas (page 995) for further information.

Dragonborn: Mining

Dragonborn adds several new types of materials to mine:

Geodes are a special type of ore vein that produces gems of a particular type. You can find Amethyst, Emerald, Ruby, and Sapphire Geodes on Solstheim.

Heart Stone is a rare material used in Staff Enchanting (see above) and as a reagent for the Ash Guardian spell.

Stalhrim is a type of elemental ice found in the tombs of the ancient Nords buried on Solstheim. The Skaal of northern Solstheim use it in crafting weapons and armor.

In order to mine it, you need an Ancient Nord Pickaxe—normal pickaxes won't work. These can be found randomly in chests or obtained as part of Solstheim Regional Activity: Take Your Pick* (which sends you to fetch one; see page 669) or Solstheim Side Quest: Unearthed (Ralis's unique pickaxe, Hoarfrost, is one; see page 645).

The Minerals of Skyrim and Solstheim

The following tables reveal locations where minerals can be mined from veins, as well as where ore appears (having already been mined). Only the major locations, usually with two or more deposits, are shown. Note that some veins may be in the immediate vicinity of the location, and may require you to search for them.

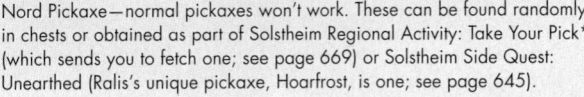

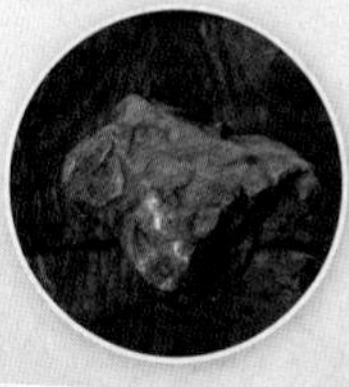
Iron Ore

Orichalcum Ore

Silver Ore

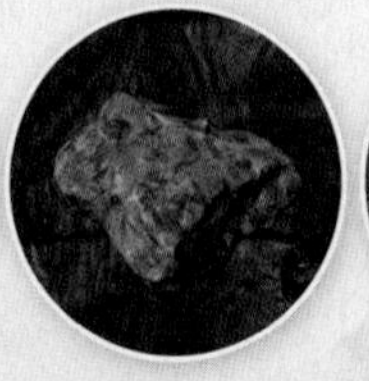
Corundum Ore

Ebony Ore

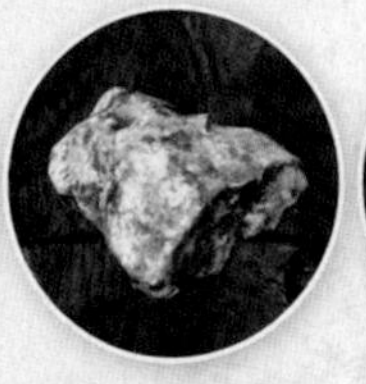
Gold Ore

Moonstone Ore

Malachite Ore

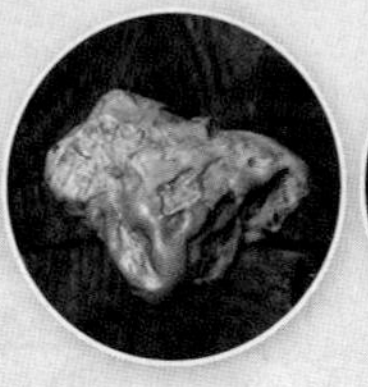
Quicksilver Ore

Shellbug

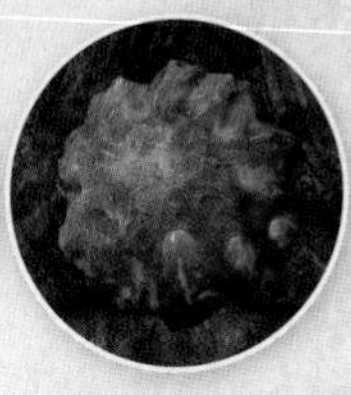
Heart Stone

Gem Geode

Stalhrim Deposit

MINERALS

✓	HOLD	LOCATION	VEINS	ORE
	IRON VEINS AND ORE			
☐	Whiterun	Halted Stream Camp	16	4
☐	Winterhold	Fort Fellhammer	10	10
☐	Falkreath Hold	Embershard Mine	9	2
☐	The Rift	Treva's Watch	1	3
☐	Falkreath Hold	Knifepoint Ridge	6	3
☐	The Reach	Blind Cliff Cave	6	0
☐	Eastmarch	Gloombound Mine	6	0
☐	The Pale	Iron-Breaker Mine	6	1
☐	The Reach	Left Hand Mine	5	0
☐	The Reach	Nchuand-Zel	4	0
☐	Hjaalmarch	Rockwallow Mine	4	0
☐	Eastmarch	Lost Knife Hideout	3	0
☐	The Rift	Northwind Mine	3	0
☐	Solstheim	Damphall Mine	2	0

✓	HOLD	LOCATION	VEINS	ORE
	ORICHALCUM VEINS AND ORE			
☐	Falkreath Hold	Bilegulch Mine	9	6
☐	The Reach	Dushnikh Yal Mine	7	6
☐	The Reach	Mor Khazgur Mine	7	1
☐	The Rift	Giant's Grove	4	0
☐	Winterhold	Blackreach	3	0
☐	Solstheim	Highpoint Tower	3	0
☐	Hjaalmarch	Skyborn Altar	3	0
☐	The Rift	Fallowstone Cave	2	0
☐	Hjaalmarch	Chillwind Depths	2	0
☐	The Pale	High Gate Ruins	2	0
☐	Solstheim	Haknir's Shoal	2	0
☐	The Pale	Nightgate Inn	2	0
☐	Whiterun Hold	Guldun Rock	2	0
☐	The Rift	Largashbur	1	2

MINERALS, CONTINUED

✓	HOLD	LOCATION	VEINS	ORE
	SILVER VEINS AND ORE			
☐	The Reach	Sanuarach Mine	7	4
☐	Markarth	Cidhna Mine	6	0
☐	Solstheim	Benkongerike	4	0
☐	Falkreath Hold	Sunderstone Gorge	4	0
☐	The Rift	Fallowstone Cave	3	0
☐	Whiterun Hold	Silent Moons Camp	2	0
☐	Solstheim	Secondary Location: Shrine of Zenithar	2	0
	CORUNDUM VEINS AND ORE			
☐	Falkreath Hold	Knifepoint Ridge	19	0
☐	Winterhold	Blackreach	14*	2
☐	Eastmarch	Goldenrock Mine	4	6
☐	The Reach	Liar's Retreat	4	0
☐	The Rift	Broken Helm Hollow	3	0
☐	The Reach	Gloomreach	3	0
☐	Eastmarch	Lost Knife Hideout	3	0
☐	Whiterun Hold	Battle-Born Farm	2	0
☐	Whiterun Hold	Cold Rock Pass	2	0
☐	Eastmarch	Eldergleam Sanctuary	2	0
☐	Haafingar	Ironback Hideout	2	0
☐	Hjaalmarch	Ustengrav	2	0
☐	Solstheim	Secondary Location: Shrine of Zenithar	1	2

NOTE * There are 13 more Geode Ore Veins in Blackreach that can be mined for Corundum.

✓	HOLD	LOCATION	VEINS	ORE
	EBONY VEINS AND ORE			
☐	Eastmarch	Gloombound Mine	16	16
☐	Solstheim	Raven Rock Mine	9	0
☐	Winterhold	Blackreach	6	0
☐	The Rift	Redbelly Mine	3	3
☐	Whiterun Hold	Throat of the World	2	0
	GOLD VEINS AND ORE			
☐	The Reach	Kolskeggr Mine	17	3
☐	Hjaalmarch	Labyrinthian	2	6
☐	The Pale	Raldbthar	5	2
☐	Whiterun Hold	Darkshade	4	0
☐	Solstheim	Frossel	4	0
☐	Winterhold	Blackreach	3	1
☐	Solstheim	Fort Frostmoth	3	0
☐	The Rift	Lost Prospect Mine	3	0
☐	The Reach	Bthardamz	3	0
☐	Solstheim	Secondary Location: The Miner's Lament	2	5
☐	Solstheim	Secondary Location: Gold Miners' Floodgate	0	6
	MOONSTONE VEINS AND ORE			
☐	The Reach	Soljund's Sinkhole	5	3
☐	Eastmarch	Mzulft	7	0
☐	Falkreath Hold	Southfringe Sanctum	3	0
☐	Winterhold	Blackreach	2	0
☐	The Reach	Darkfall Cave	2	0
☐	Eastmarch	Kagrenzel	2	0
☐	Whiterun Hold	Silent Moons Camp	2	0
☐	Eastmarch	Stony Creek Cave	2	0
	MALACHITE VEINS AND ORE			
☐	Eastmarch	Steamscorch Mine	7	2
☐	Whiterun Hold	Throat of the World	2	0
☐	The Pale	Dimhollow Crypt	8	0
☐	Solstheim	Nchardak	4	0
☐	The Rift	Ruunvald Excavation	4	0
☐	Solstheim	Glacial Cave	2	0
	QUICKSILVER VEINS AND ORE			
☐	The Pale	Quicksilver Mine	5	2
☐	The Reach	Blind Cliff Cave	3	0
☐	Winterhold	Blackreach	3	0
☐	Solstheim	Altar of Thrond	2	0
☐	The Rift	Arcwind Point	2	0
☐	Falkreath Hold	Bloodlet Throne	2	0
☐	The Reach	Druadach Redoubt	2	0
☐	Whiterun Hold	Shimmermist Cave	2	0
☐	The Pale	Silverdrift Lair	2	0
☐	The Rift	Tolvald's Cave	2	0
☐	Winterhold	The Tower Stone	2	0

✓	HOLD	LOCATION	SHELLBUGS
	SHELLBUGS (DAWNGUARD ONLY)		
☐	Forgotten Vale	Forgotten Vale Cave	1
☐	Forgotten Vale	Sharpslope Cave	1

✓	LOCATION	DEPOSITS
	HEART STONE DEPOSITS (SOLSTHEIM ONLY)	
☐	Brodir Grove	3
☐	Broken Tusk Mine	2
☐	Fort Frostmoth	2
☐	Hrodulf's House	2
☐	White Ridge Barrow	2
☐	Secondary Location: Impact Crater (Burnt Spriggan)	2
☐	Secondary Location: Miner Immolation	2
☐	Secondary Location: Impact Crater (Tel Mithryn)	1
☐	Secondary Location: Reavers' Folly	1

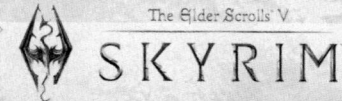

✓	LOCATION	TYPE	GEODES
	GEM GEODES (SOLSTHEIM ONLY)		
☐	Highpoint Tower	Amethyst	1
☐	Secondary Location: The Miner's Lament	Emerald	2
☐	Highpoint Tower	Emerald	1
☐	Kolbjorn's Barrow	Emerald	1
☐	White Ridge Barrow	Ruby	13
☐	Fort Frostmoth	Ruby	3
☐	Highpoint Tower	Ruby	2
☐	Secondary Location: Spider Nest (Kagrumez)	Ruby	1
☐	Highpoint Tower	Sapphire	4
☐	White Ridge Barrow	Sapphire	2
☐	Secondary Location: Shrine of Zenithar	Sapphire	2
☐	Secondary Location: White Ridge Barrow Hut	Sapphire	2
	STALHRIM DEPOSITS (SOLSTHEIM ONLY)		
☐	Stalhrim Source	10	0
☐	Gyldenhul Barrow	2	0
☐	Kolbjorn Barrow	2	0
☐	Secondary Location: Horker Iceberg	2	0

Smelting

NOTE Smelting ore and scrap metal into ingots does not increase any skill.

Approach the domed smelter, withstand the great heat, and transform your ore into ingots.

You can purchase ore from most Blacksmiths, or mine it yourself if money is a concern. But what do you do with the ore?

Raw ore isn't useful on its own and doesn't sell for many gold pieces. However, if you bring your ore to a smelter, you can smelt it into metal ingots, which you can then sell for more gold pieces or use it to smith your own weapons and armor.

An Ebony Ingot, smelted from two clumps of Ebony Ore.

TIP Make sure you mine and smelt the minerals you're proficient in making items with!

Also, scour Dwarven Ruins in search of scrap metal. You can find a lot of loose metal lying around, and even more in the remains of Dwarven Automatons (such as Dwarven Spheres) once you've reduced them to scrap. Dwarven scrap can be smelted down into Dwarven Metal Ingots. This may cause Calcelmo, the Dwarven researcher in Markarth, a slight case of conniptions, but it increases their value significantly. Pick up everything you can carry and haul it back to town. You can forge weapons and armor with the ingots to rapidly improve your Smithing skill, or sell it to recoup the cost of other materials.

NOTE Ingots can be found in your Misc Inventory menu.

Smelting Recipes

The following table lists all of the available smelting recipes and the type of ingots produced by each. All of these recipes are available to you immediately; you just need the ore or scrap metal required for them.

✓	INGREDIENTS	PRODUCES	WEIGHT	VALUE
☐	2 Corundum Ore	Corundum Ingot	1	40
☐	Large Decorative Dwemer Strut	Dwarven Metal Ingot (2)	1	30
☐	Small Dwemer Plate Metal	Dwarven Metal Ingot (3)	1	30
☐	Bent Dwemer Scrap Metal	Dwarven Metal Ingot (3)	1	30
☐	Large Dwemer Strut	Dwarven Metal Ingot (3)	1	30
☐	Large Dwemer Plate Metal	Dwarven Metal Ingot (3)	1	30
☐	Solid Dwemer Metal	Dwarven Metal Ingot (5)	1	30
☐	2 Ebony Ore	Ebony Ingot	1	150
☐	2 Gold Ore	Gold Ingot	1	100
☐	1 Iron Ore	Iron Ingot	1	7
☐	2 Orichalcum Ore	Orichalcum Ingot	1	45
☐	2 Quicksilver Ore	Quicksilver Ingot	1	60
☐	2 Malachite Ore	Refined Malachite	1	100
☐	2 Moonstone Ore	Refined Moonstone	1	75
☐	2 Silver Ore	Silver Ingot	1	50
☐	2 Iron Ore	Steel Ingot	1	20

Tanning

NOTE Tanning animal hides into leather and leather strips does not increase any skill.

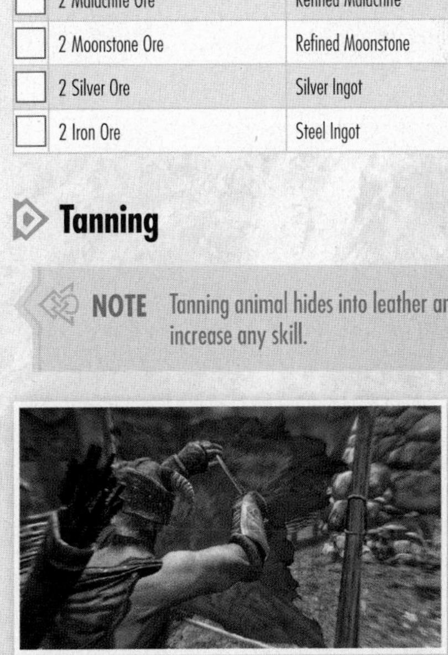

Approach a tanning rack and transform a wild animal hide into leather or leather strips.

Tanning is a simple process; it allows you to transform animal hides into leather or leather strips. These can then be sold or used in your own smithing. Larger pelts produce more leather...but are often more valuable as pelts, rather than broken down into their leather components. Therefore, it is wise to think twice before tanning everything you've skinned!

TIP Keep an eye on value. Depending on your Speech skill, you may be better off selling a valuable pelt and then buying leather from a merchant, rather than tanning that same pelt into leather.

Tanning Recipes

The following table lists all of the available tanning recipes. All of these recipes are available to you immediately; you just need the hides for them.

✓	INGREDIENTS	PRODUCES	WEIGHT	VALUE
	Leather	Leather Strips (4)	0.1	10
	2 Goat Hide	Leather	2	10
	Fox Pelt	Leather	2	10
	Snow Fox Pelt	Leather	2	10
	Wolf Pelt	Leather	2	10
	Ice Wolf Pelt	Leather	2	10
	Deer Hide	Leather (2)	2	10
	Cow Hide	Leather (3)	2	10
	Horse Hide	Leather (3)	2	10
	Bear Pelt	Leather (4)	2	10
	Cave Bear Pelt	Leather (4)	2	10
	Sabre Cat Pelt	Leather (4)	2	10
	Sabre Cat Snow Pelt	Leather (4)	2	10
	Snow Bear Pelt	Leather (4)	2	10
	Vale Deer Hide	Leather (2)	2	10
	Vale Sabre Cat Hide	Leather (4)	2	10

Wood Chopping

NOTE This manual labor does not increase any skill.

Swing a woodcutter's axe, cleaving a small log in twain. Now repeat until you've had enough.

There are several wood-chopping blocks throughout Skyrim, which allow you to execute this most simple of all crafting exercises: chopping wood. For this, you need a woodcutter's axe, which you can purchase from almost any general store merchant or find (for free) at any lumber mill. Simply approach the wood-chopping block, interact with it, and you begin chopping. For each chop, two pieces of firewood are added to your Misc Inventory. When you're finished, sell the firewood to any lumber foreman for 5 gold per piece of wood. You won't get a better deal from any merchant.

NOTE Chopping firewood is a slow and methodical way to earn a tiny amount of gold. While it is something you can do to eke out the last few coins you need for a piece of armor, it's mostly just a small way of interacting with the world. You can also load lumber logs onto the wooden conveyor belt at lumber mills and watch as they're sliced with a vertical saw. This manual labor is free, just something to pass the time.

Lumber Mill Locations

If you're determined to sell your firewood for the best possible prices, do so at the following locations, where you can speak to (and obtain payment from) the lumber mill owner or operator. Note that not all of these lumber mills have a wood-chopping block.

✓	LUMBER MILL	LOCATION (HOLD)
	Dragon Bridge	Haafingar
	Solitude Sawmill	Haafingar
	Morthal	Hjaalmarch
	Anga's Mill	The Pale
	Riverwood	Whiterun

✓	LUMBER MILL	LOCATION (HOLD)
	Mixwater Mill	Eastmarch
	Falkreath	Falkreath
	Half-moon Mill	Falkreath
	Heartwood Mill	The Rift

TRAINING PART 3: ADVENTURING ACROSS SKYRIM

This section looks at the broader aspects of adventuring in Skyrim. There's information on how Skyrim is segmented so you can grasp how where you are within this giant realm. We explain the different types of map locations and the kinds of enemies and challenges that await you. Finally, we provide a range of tips on mapping, what to expect when exploring dungeons, who to speak to in Skyrim and why, and what services, areas of interest, and collectibles you should look for.

THE HOLDS OF SKYRIM

Skyrim is divided into nine separate Holds: Haafingar, Hjaalmarch, the Pale, Winterhold Hold, the Reach, Whiterun Hold, Eastmarch, Falkreath Hold, and the Rift. Each of these Holds has a distinct atmosphere to it, from the Autumnal Forest of the Rift, to the Tundra Plains of Whiterun Hold, to the ragged and rugged Northern Coast of the Pale. You can't see the borders of these Holds on your world map, but we show them in this guide's maps. Wherever possible, cartographers have used rivers, roads, and treacherous mountains to separate Holds so it's easier to find a location in this guide.

Each Hold has a capital city: Solitude, Morthal, Dawnstar, Winterhold, Markarth, Whiterun, Windhelm, Falkreath, and Riften. These are the nine shields (crests) that you can see on your world map. While most Holds contain smaller towns and settlements as well, the capital is always the most important and highly populated location within the Hold and is among the safest places to be (unless it's under siege during the Civil War, of course).

Habitations

A city, town, or dwelling populated with citizens who are almost always neutral, if not civil and friendly, toward you.

Windhelm, capital of Eastmarch

Habitations range in size from a small group of Khajiit Caravaneers to the rugged majesty of Solitude, the sprawling capital of Haafingar Hold. Here, you're likely to find citizens in need of help (or at least a Favor or two) or who have rumors to share, tasks to accomplish, quests to start, and interactions that test your social skills more than your skill at arms. The major types of habitations are listed in this guide's Atlas.

Dungeons

A location populated with hostile people or creatures that typically attack you on sight.

High Gate Ruins, in the Pale

A "dungeon" is a place where you will find exploration and combat. It is an all-encompassing term for a location with usually no friendly faces, a place where you encounter wild animals, brigands, or worse. When you fully explore a dungeon, you typically leave with a reward that makes the harrowing trek worth your time and sanity. Dungeons vary widely in size, from small caves to massive, multistoried ruins. Most have a high-level foe you most defeat (a "boss"), and some even have their own small quests. Others are woven into the larger quests that dominate your adventure.

When you clear a dungeon—that is, explore it and defeat all of the major foes within—your map typically marks it as "cleared." Some locations cannot be cleared, and others can be cleared only under special circumstances.

Most dungeons will repopulate over time. This can happen in as little as a week for a location you left midway through and may not happen for a month or more (if ever) for a dungeon you have cleared. Note that your map will not indicate when a location has repopulated (once cleared, always cleared), so be careful—you may find enemies where you least expect them.

Other Locations

There are also many minor locations and encounters not flagged on your in-game world map, but all of them are listed on this guide's map. These are Secondary Locations, usually small shrines, lost treasure chests, tiny campsites, dragon burial mounds, or other odd occurrences that you can stumble upon. There are also World Encounters, small events that occur randomly. This could be anything from a fox chasing some chickens, to a challenge from an Orc, to a Khajiit with a penchant for being economical with the truth....

NOTE All of these locations are noted on this guide's maps and are detailed in the Atlas. Although this guide's map is exhaustive, there are several scattered cases, satchels, and other loot hidden throughout this realm that are not shown, as there are much easier places to find identical items.

Mapping and Movement

The realm of Skyrim is vast and foreboding and at times almost overwhelming—there are over 350 Primary Locations to discover! Although you can go where you want, do what you want, and see what you want, it is worth considering the following plans to explore a location more logically:

Plan 1—The Base Camp: Use a location you've cleared out or a location you know is safe (such as Riverwood) as a base camp until you're familiar with your surroundings. Learn how far a new location is from this safe place.

Plan 2—The Landmarks: Look for landmarks when you travel. No matter where you are in Skyrim, you should be able to spin around slowly and spot two familiar landmarks to get your bearings. This is easier in some Holds (such as Whiterun, with its capital and the towering Throat of the World mountain) and more difficult in others (such as the craggy Reach). However, once you know the locations around a big landmark, you can investigate other locations close to it without becoming lost. Also use smaller landmarks such as roadside shrines, bridges, or signposts to remember where you've been.

Plan 3—Roads and Paths: You may be tempted to charge off into the wilderness, and this is perfectly fine. But to efficiently discover everything in the area of a Hold, it is worth using the network of roads (cobblestones, with signposts) and pathways (tracks, goat trails, and even foot-tracked snow). These almost always lead you close or directly to a Primary Location. Follow the roads to make a circular trek around a Hold, then return and methodically search areas off this beaten track.

Plan 4—Your Destination Marker: If you select an empty spot on the world map, you can place your own destination marker there. This is extremely useful when used in conjunction with this guide's Atlas, as there are close to

200 Secondary Locations, which don't show up on your world map! Simply gauge where a Secondary Location is by comparing the world map to the guide map, place the marker, and head there.

Plan 5—Use the Atlas: This guide has a sizable section revealing every location in Skyrim. Reference the locations and maps in that giant chapter to help you on your way.

DUNGEON EXPLORATION

Finding Your Way

Whether you're assaulting a ruined fortress filled with bandits or stealthily creeping through some long-forgotten crypt, dungeons are at the heart of your adventuring experience. Although they may appear confusing at first, the winding tunnels and twisting corridors generally lead to a final chamber, where you must defeat a powerful foe to claim your reward. In Skyrim, many dungeons also have a secret exit or shortcut—a hidden passage, barred door, elevated tunnel, or dwarven elevator that leads back to the entrance. This allows you to exit a dungeon without having to backtrack.

Lighting Your Way

Carrying a torch or employing a staff or spell to light your way makes the frightening darkness of dungeons a little less intimidating. Be sure to have a light source tagged as a Favorite so you can quickly switch between it and your combat weapons as needed.

Khajiit and vampires can call on their Nighteye power to see in the dark, allowing them to more easily slip through the darkness undetected.

Also note the positions of lanterns, torches, and braziers inside dungeons, as they are almost always visual cues that point you in the correct direction. If you're lost, look for these light sources to guide you.

Dungeon Puzzles

MINOR SPOILERS

Many dungeons were sealed for a reason—they contain the dormant (and often undead) remains of a once-powerful entity. To protect these tombs from grave robbers and brigands, the ancient Nords concocted many puzzles to flummox and foil the unwary. The same is true inside Dwarven Ruins, but on a far grander scale. Here is what you can expect:

Switches, Levers, Chains, and Handles

If you're stuck in a chamber, look for any of these devices to open the doors, gates, and portcullises that prevent your progress. Chains are usually the most difficult to spot, hanging on a gloomy wall. Sometimes, these must be triggered in a specific order to open the path forward.

Nordic Puzzle Door

A series of concentric metal rings are embedded in an impenetrable door, each embossed with three animal glyphs. Explore the dungeon to find the Dragon Claw associated with the door—a precious artifact that holds the key to this puzzle. In your inventory, inspect the palm of the claw to find the solution to the door. Line up the three animals glyphs in the correct order, then activate the central "keyhole" with the Dragon Claw to unlock the door.

Nordic Puzzle Pillars and Petroglyphs

Many chambers require you to rotate two or more stone pillars to face the correct direction in order to open a path forward. These pillars have been inscribed with a set of animal petroglyphs, which correspond to another set of glyphs somewhere in the surrounding chamber. Match the two sets of animal carvings to solve the puzzle.

Rotating Walls

Stone walls controlled by a hidden mechanism can rotate to open or close paths in a dungeon. When you encounter them, look for a set of Nordic Puzzle Pillars or a lever, chain, or switch you can use to open the way forward.

Dwarven Puzzles

Long ago, the ancient dwarves constructed immense clockwork mechanisms and complex steamworks. The ruins of this long-lost race still yield a variety of intricate and unique puzzles, from trying to stop the flow of poisonous gas into a chamber, to carefully aligning a system of mirrors in an Oculory, to inserting an otherworldly key into a strange slot. In some cases, you may need to find the "key" object beforehand, or your progress will be limited at best.

Other Puzzles

There are occasionally other puzzles that are more complicated, requiring a Shout or other technique to solve. These are duly noted.

TIP Every puzzle has a solution; for more details, check the Atlas location of the dungeon in question or the quest you've embarked on.

Traps and Triggers

The infamous oil lamp trap: Turn the burn on your enemies, if you're quick and clever!

The unpleasant Poison Bloom Trap: What pretty lattice-like petals. What a heady aroma...Gak!!

Dungeon exploration would be nowhere near as terrifying without the uncertainty of possibly stumbling over a tripwire and being pincushioned by a dozen rusty darts! Throughout your adventure, expect to run into, step on, or trigger any of 30 different traps. The following chart lists every major type of trap and trigger, along with advice on how best to avoid them.

Note that most traps have a small chance of infecting you with a random disease. It might be worth keeping around a Cure Disease potion just in case...

TRAP	DAMAGE	THREAT LEVEL	MOST COMMON IN...	TIPS
Apocrypha Tentacles	Average	Average	Apocrypha	Yet another reason to avoid the water. As you explore Apocrypha, tentacles will frequently rise up from the inky depths to lash out at you, doing damage and possibly afflicting you with disease. You can often avoid them entirely by hugging the walls and keeping well away from the edge of the platforms.
Apocrypha Water	Low	Average	Apocrypha	The roiling black waters of Apocrypha are lethal to mortals, although "dying" will merely return your spirit to Tamriel. Avoid the water at all costs, and be careful that your foes don't knock you into it.
Bear Trap	Average	Nuisance	Bandit Camps, Outdoors	Watch where you step! Bear Traps are often hidden in the bushes or under low grass, ready to snap if you aren't careful. You can often lure enemies into stepping on them. Interacting with the trap will also allow you to close or open them.
Battering Ram Trap	High	High	Nordic Ruins	Talk about a headache! Battering Ram traps cover a long arc, and at higher levels, can kill you or your foes in a single hit. Look out for the triggers that set them off, and keep an eye on the ceiling for them. Lure enemies into them to take them out in one shot.
Bone Alarm Trap	None	Nuisance	Bandit Camps, Forsworn Redoubts	Bone Alarm traps don't do any damage, but alert enemies to your presence. If you aren't sneaking anyway, they won't make much difference. If you are, watch your step and try to avoid them if you can. Shooting them with a bow will draw unaware enemies to them, allowing you to set up an ambush.
Crossbow Trap	Average	Average	Dawnguard/Vigilant Bases	Crossbow Traps fire fast and hit hard, like any other crossbow. However, they fire only a single shot and are relatively easy to disarm. Avoid their trigger mechanism, approach the crossbow, and activate it to pick it up. You can also place a standard crossbow and steel bolt into the mechanism if you want to use it against your foes.
Dart Trap	Average	Average	Nordic Ruins, Dwarven Ruins	The most common kind of trap, dart traps are also among the most avoidable. Even if you trigger them by accident, you can often just jump out of the way to minimize the damage you take. They deal a small amount of poison damage.
Dwarven Ballista Trap	High	Low	Dwarven Ruins	Dwarven Ballistas shoot a large bolt that explodes on impact, doing massive damage to anything in the blast radius. Functional ballistas are extremely rare, and often something you can turn to your advantage- look for a valve or lever you can use to turn the trap on your enemies.
Dwarven Fire Pillar Trap	Average	Average	Dwarven Ruins	Initially resembling a pressure plate, Dwarven Fire Pillars rise from the ground and rotate, spewing gouts of flame. Spotting these traps in advance is key to avoiding them.
Dwarven Piston Trap	None	Nuisance	Dwarven Ruins	Dwarven Pistons shove anything in front of them away. They don't do any damage, but they hit hard, and have a habit of pushing you (or your enemies) into something nasty.
Dwarven Thresher	Average	High	Dwarven Ruins	Dwarven Threshers are a pair of whirling blades that rise from the floor, sometimes remaining in place and sometimes moving along a track built into the ground. Often appearing in narrow corridors, they are highly dangerous, capable of killing you, your followers, or your enemies with a few solid hits. If you see one, get out of the way!
Explosive Gas Trap	Average	Low	Nordic Ruins, Caves	See that ripple in the air? It might be a cloud of flammable, explosive gas. Put away your torch, keep your Flames spell in check, and you shouldn't have any problems with them. Explosive Gas is extremely rare.
Flail Trap	High	Average	Bandit Camps	Also fairly rare, Flail traps tend to be located on the ceiling, ready to drop a large, spiked sphere into your head. If you see it coming, back away- once the trap has come to a full and complete stop, it's harmless.
Flamethrower Trap	Average	Average	Any Dungeon	Often built into the mouths of Nordic dragon statues or set into pressure plates, flamethrower traps are a threat most adventurers will see from time to time. Because their flame travels in a narrow, focused beam, your best bet is to quickly step out of the way and let the trap subside.
Infected Spike Trap	Average	Nuisance	Vampire Lairs	These hanging ropes are strung with bloody caltrops that pierce the skin and inflict you with disease. If you're careful, you can usually avoid them entirely or even lure enemies through them.
Magic Caster Trap	Varies	Varies	Any Dungeon	Magic Casters consist of a runed pedestal powered by a Soul Gem. When triggered, the Soul Gem casts a preset spell, which could be anything from Flames to Ice Storm. If you can't avoid the trap altogether, you can disarm it by removing the Soul Gem- taking it directly works, but you can also hit it with an arrow from a safe distance, or grab it with Telekinesis.
Mammoth Skull Trap	High	Low	Any Dungeon	When triggered, this huge mammoth skull swings forward on its support ropes, slamming into anything in front of it with lethal force. This trap tends to be easy to spot- you can't exactly overlook a giant mammoth skull- so it's rarely much of a threat to you, though you can lure your enemies into it.
Oil Lamp Trap	Low	Low	Nordic Ruins	The oil lamp itself isn't usually a problem. It's the pool of oil that often sits under the lamp that you should keep an eye on, and lure your enemies into if possible. Then hit or shoot down the lamp to set the oil ablaze. They are often triggered by tripwires, but shooting or attacking them will also cause the lamp to drop.
Oil Pool Trap	Average	Low	Any Dungeon	Oil Pools are easily turned against your foes- just lure them into the oil and light it with any fire source. Oil Lamp traps are often conveniently nearby, but lacking one of those a Flames Spell, or Fire Atronach will work just as well.
Poison Blooms	None	Varies	Falmer Hives	Poison Blooms are easy to identify by their large, white, lattice-like petals. When you approach them, they begin to shudder. Quickly activate them to pluck the bloom, or they will open, spewing a cloud of poison gas.
Poison Gas Trap	Average	Average	Dwarven Ruins	Poison Gas does steady damage over time if you stand in it. When you find a patch of poison gas, look around for a way to turn it off. Failing that, make a run for it, using a Healing spell or potions to keep your health up. The Clear Skies Shout can also be used to dissipate the gas.
Rockfall Trap	Average	Average	Bandit Camps, Nordic Ruins, Mines, Caves	Rockfall traps are fairly rare, but the sheer number of rocks they contain can make them a threat if you're standing in the wrong place. If you see one, your best bet is to get out of the way.
Rune Trap	Average	High	Any Dungeon	Rune Traps look much like the Fire, Frost, and Shock Runes that you can place with the Destruction spells of the same name. And like those spells, these traps pack a quite a punch, exploding automatically if you get close enough. Your best bet is to lure an enemy to run across them and set them off. Failing that, you can shoot them with a spell to set them off, but keep your distance.
Spear Trap	Average	High	Any Dungeon	A single spear trap is no threat... but spear traps tend to come in groups of five or more, lashing out unexpectedly from the floor or walls. Your best bet is to look for the ports from which they emerge and try to avoid setting them off in the first place.
Swinging Blade Trap	Average	Average	Nordic Ruins	Blade traps often appear in sets in long, narrow hallways. They're usually easy enough for you to dodge, although enemies (and your followers) have a harder time, making them a great kill zone. When you're ready to go through, tell your follower to stay behind, time your run carefully, and look for a lever on the far side to disable them.
Swinging Wall Trap	High	High	Any Dungeon	Swinging wall traps come in a variety of shapes and sizes, from the heavy spiked-iron walls in forts to the netting and tusk traps of Riekling dens. But all are fast, lethal, and difficult to distinguish from other wood or metal beams in a dungeon. If you notice a freestanding beam that doesn't quite reach the ceiling, be careful. Try to snare an enemy with it if possible—few things are as satisfying as watching a foe get hurled into the wall by this trap.
Hinge Trigger	None	Varies	Any Dungeon	Find a suspicous-looking chest or door? Then look for this little metal hinge and wire on the side. Carefully activate it, and you can pick its lock to safely disable it before opening the object it was attached to. You can also hit it with an attack from a distance to break it and set off the trap in (relative) safety.
Pressure Pedestal	None	Varies	Nordic Ruins	If you see a flat-topped pedestal with a tantilizing item on it, be careful- it could be a pressure pedestal trap. If the pedestal isn't weighted down, a trap will be set off. Grab the item from a distance (Telekenesis is great for this), or drop something else on the pedestal to keep it weighed down. Or just grab the item and run for it.

TRAP	DAMAGE	THREAT LEVEL	MOST COMMON IN...	TIPS
Pressure Plate	None	Varies	Any Dungeon	By far the most common trap-triggering mechanism, Pressure Plates can be found in almost any dungeon– just look for suspicious raised stones and avoid them. Or take the Sneak Skill's Light Foot Perk to avoid setting these off altogether.
Tripwire	None	Varies	Any Dungeon	See a low-lying white wire? That's a tripwire. Leap over it or skirt around it to avoid setting it off. Or edge forward very carefully to see what happens when it breaks. You can also interact with the tripwire to disarm it. Tripwire-triggered traps only fire once.

NOTE Throughout the Quest and Atlas chapters, traps are mentioned when they are a major obstacle or block your path to finishing an objective or location walkthrough. However, due to their sheer number, traps are not tracked in this guide.

OTHER SITES OF INTEREST

Dragon Mounds

Dotted across the fells and forests and the plains and snowlines of Skyrim are strange circular mounds, surrounded by a scattering of standing stones. These are ancient dragon burial mounds, the final resting places of these creatures when they were slain centuries ago. But now the dragons are back! Alduin the World-Eater, a terror out of the most ancient legends, has returned to Skyrim, and over the course of the Main Quest, he opens these mounds and resurrects the dragons within, calling them forth to wreak havoc once more!

How Dragon Mounds Open

There are 22 Dragon Mounds scattered throughout the Nine Holds of Skyrim, and two more on the isle of Solstheim. When you encounter one (all are listed in the Atlas and marked on the Hold maps), it will be in one of four states. Over the course of the Main Quest, these mounds gradually open, releasing the dragons trapped within.

State I: Dormant

Each Dragon Mound opens in response to a specific objective in the Main Quest. Before that point, the Dragon Mound is dormant. The ground is covered, and the site could easily be mistaken for an ancient Nordic burial mound, as the two are quite similar.

State II: Deserted

As the Main Quest develops, you may find some mounds that have been opened but have no dragon nearby. This means Alduin has visited this site, resurrected a dragon from the mound, and both creatures have flown away. There is little for you to do here. But look around carefully—you may well spot the dragon at a nearby Dragon Lair!

State III: Awakened

As the Main Quest goes on, you will find more and more mounds in this state. Alduin has visited the site, resurrected the dragon from the mound, and flown away. Meanwhile, the reborn dragon remains here, gathering its strength and waiting for a chance to strike. Slay the beast and claim its soul to unlock your power as Dragonborn!

State IV: Resurrection

And in a few cases, if you stumble across just the right mound at just the right time, you may encounter Alduin himself! If you watch, Alduin will resurrect the dragon before your eyes, then fly off to his next destination. Attack, and Alduin roars into the skies, mocking you, before making his escape (he cannot be harmed). Meanwhile, the resurrected dragon will turn and attack! If you miss this opportunity, the mound will change to State III, with the newly resurrected dragon remaining near its mound until you arrive to challenge it.

Dragon Mound Stages Chart

The following chart lists (by Hold) all of the Dragon Mounds, when they are opened, and what state the mound will be in when it opens.

NAME OF DRAGON MOUND	HOLD LOCATION	STATE	DRAGON?	MAIN QUEST NOTES
[2.C] Dragon Mound: Karth River Forest	Hjaalmarch	II	No	Opens during Act II: Diplomatic Immunity
[2.G] Dragon Mound: Robber's Gorge Bluffs	Hjaalmarch	III	Yes	Opens during Act II: Diplomatic Immunity
[2.P] Dragon Mound: Labyrinthian Peaks	Hjaalmarch	II	No	Opens during Act II: Elder Knowledge
[3.D] Dragon Mound: Sea Shore Foothills	The Pale	III	Yes	Opens during Act II: Elder Knowledge
[3.M] Dragon Mound: Shimmermist Hills	The Pale	III	Yes	Opens during Act II: Elder Knowledge
[3.Q] Dragon Mound: Yorgrim Resurrection	The Pale	IV	Yes	Opens during Act II: Elder Knowledge. Visit this location before Act II: Alduin's Bane is complete in order to witness the resurrection!
[5.B] Dragon Mound: Reachwater Pass	The Reach	III	Yes	Opens during Act II: Elder Knowledge
[5.I] Dragon Mound: Ragnvald Vale	The Reach	III	Yes	Opens during Act II: Elder Knowledge
[5.T] Dragon Mound: Karthspire Bluffs	The Reach	III	Yes	Opens during Act II: Alduin's Wall
[6.B] Dragon Mound: Rorikstead Resurrection	Whiterun Hold	IV	Yes	Opens during Act II: Alduin's Wall. Visit this location before Act II: Elder Knowledge begins in order to witness the resurrection!
[6.K] Dragon Mound: Great Henge Resurrection	Whiterun Hold	IV	Yes	Opens during Act II: Diplomatic Immunity. Visit this location before Act II: Alduin's Wall begins in order to witness the resurrection!
[6.O] Dragon Mound: Lone Mountain	Whiterun Hold	III	Yes	Opens during Act II: Alduin's Wall
[7.H] Dragon Mound: Kynesgrove Resurrection	Eastmarch	IV	Yes	Opens during Act I: A Blade in the Dark. You will visit this location during Main Quest: A Blade in the Dark, witness the resurrection, and kill resurrected dragon.
[7.L] Dragon Mound: Bonestrewn Crest	Eastmarch	II	No	Opens during Act I: Dragon Rising
[7.N] Dragon Mound: Witchmist Grove	Eastmarch	II	No	Opens during Act I: The Way of the Voice
[7.T] Dragon Mound: Mzulft Foothills	Eastmarch	II	No	Opens during Act I: Dragon Rising
[8.A] Dragon Mound: Bilegulch Ridge	Falkreath Hold	II	No	Opens during Act II: Alduin's Wall
[8.L] Dragon Mound: Evergreen Woods	Falkreath Hold	III	Yes	Opens during Act II: Alduin's Wall
[8.AI] Dragon Mound: Bloodlet Peaks	Falkreath Hold	II	No	Opens during Act II: Alduin's Wall
[9.F] Dragon Mound: Autumnwatch Woods	The Rift	II	No	Opens during Act II: Diplomatic Immunity
[9.M] Dragon Mound: Autumnshade Woods	The Rift	II	No	Opens during Act I: Bleak Falls Barrow
[9.Q] Dragon Mound: Lost Tongue Pass	The Rift	II	No	Opens during Act II: Diplomatic Immunity
[S.NN] Dragon Mound: Frozen Shoals	Solstheim	III	Yes	Opens during Act I: Dragon Rising
[S.SK] Dragon Mound: Temple Foothills	Solstheim	III	Yes	Opens during Act I: Dragon Rising

TIP Want to face a dragon or see Alduin before he flies away? Then simply complete your current Main Quest, consult this chart, and head off to find any mounds that have triggered.

Standing Stones

Throughout the wilderness of Skyrim, you can find 13 of these ancient and powerful standing stones. Etched into each is the sign of one of the major constellations known throughout Tamriel. Touch the stone, and you can choose to receive its blessing. You'll focus the stone, and a bolt of pure magic arcs to the heavens. This blessing is now permanent, until you visit a different stone and receive its blessing, which supersedes the previous one. You may have only one blessing at a time. Standing stones can be divided into two major sets: 4 Skill Improvement stones, and 9 other stones.

Skill Improvement Stones

The Warrior Stone: Located at the Guardian Stones (Falkreath Hold). Combat skills increase 20% faster.

The Mage Stone: Located at the Guardian Stones (Falkreath Hold). Magic skills improve 20% faster.

The Thief Stone: Located at the Guardian Stones (Falkreath Hold). Stealth skills increase 20% faster.

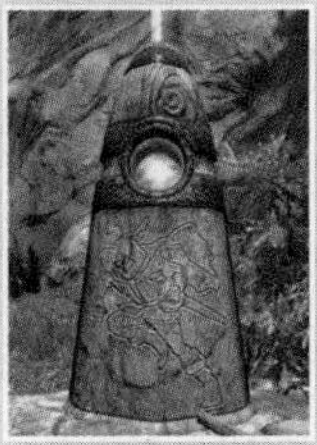

The Lover Stone: Located in the Reach. All skills improve 15% faster.

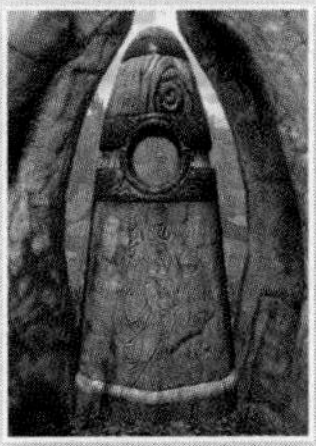

Four standing stones—Warrior, Thief, Mage, and Lover—increase the rate at which your skills improve. The choice to use or not to use these stones is more important than you may think.

Accept one of these stones' blessings if:

You crave high-level spells and perks and want access to them as quickly as possible.

You want to trek through high-level dungeons (such as Dwarven Ruins and Dragon Priest crypts) as soon as you can.

You're trying to maintain a second set of skills that you don't use as often: For example, your primary focus might be as a warrior, with a secondary interest in stealth. You may want to take the Thief Stone just to help your stealth-based skills keep pace.

You want to quickly increase a skill or set of skills that you haven't used before or that you've neglected: For example, if you decide to add Restoration spells to your Warrior's repertoire or if you want to pick up some Illusion Magic to complement your Thief's skills, the Mage Stone will help you master them more quickly.

Resist these stones' blessings (and choose one of the other stones) if:

You want to make your adventure as long and rewarding as possible and want to see and do everything you possibly can in Skyrim. Your adventure is most entertaining when you're below Level 50. Impatience isn't rewarded....

You're more interested in experimenting with the dramatic and varied effects that the other stones can have on your style of play, rather than accepting these "hidden" bonuses.

NOTE A few points to remember:

The Warrior, Mage, and Thief Stones provide bonuses to skill growth in their respective skills, while the Lover's Stone provides a slightly smaller bonus to skill growth in all skills. This is great if you like to try a little of everything or have a character that draws heavily on skills across multiple disciplines.

Don't expect to crush your foes just because your skills increase more quickly. In fact, these Stones may make your adventure slightly more difficult, since you'll have less time per level to find and upgrade your equipment and master advanced combat tactics.

Don't feel "locked in" to any particular stone blessing. If you want to try out one of the others, you can always change back later—just Fast-Travel back to your stone of choice and touch it again. It's that simple.

Other Stones

The Apprentice Stone, located in Hjaalmarch Hold: Recover Magicka twice as fast; twice as vulnerable to magic.

This stone offers a slightly risky option for Mages who find themselves running out of Magicka too frequently or for Battlemages who don't want to sacrifice the protection of their armor for the Magicka Regeneration bonuses of mage robes. The weakness to Magicka is a real liability—especially in warlock or vampire dungeons, where almost all of your foes cast spells—but it can be offset by having a summoned creature or Follower to help soak up the damage. For Bretons, this weakness is also offset by your racial Magic Resistance, making it much more palatable.

The Atronach Stone, located in Eastmarch Hold: 50 extra points of Magicka, 50% absorb spells, -50% Magicka Regen.

This gives you the benefits of two of the best racial abilities—the High Elves' Highborn Magicka and the Breton's Dragonskin (as a constant effect)—with the huge drawback of halved Magicka Regen. You can easily offset or overcome this drawback by equipping mage robes or other items that increase your Magicka regeneration rate.

The Lady Stone, located in Falkreath Hold: Regenerate Health and Stamina 25% faster.

This is a solid, effective choice for offensive warriors. The bonus isn't spectacular, but it will give you more staying power in combat. It's also an excellent choice for vampires, as it can offset your Health and Stamina regeneration penalties while in sunlight.

The Lord Stone, located in the Pale: 50 points of damage resistance, 25% magic resistance.

This grants you two excellent resistance bonuses in one! The damage resistance bonus is the equivalent to 50 points of armor, which is like giving your robed mage a Daedric Cuirass (and makes an already well-armored warrior even more resilient)! The magic resistance bonus is also solid, cutting spell damage by a quarter. Overall, this is a good choice for any character who wants to shore up their defenses.

The Ritual Stone, located in Whiterun Hold. Raises all dead around you to fight for you.

Arguably the most entertaining, and one of the most useful blessings, the Ritual Stone grants you a power that raises all the dead around you—from the mightiest Draugr Deathlord to the lowliest chicken—and causes them to fight for you. Useful in a wide range of situations, this power really shines in the large-scale battles at the end of many dungeons, where you can find yourself quickly raising 5 to 10 corpses to take on their former allies!

The Serpent Stone, located in Winterhold Hold: Paralyze the target for 5 seconds and do 25 points of damage.

Paralyze is a useful ability to have on hand, allowing you to quickly score multiple hits on a foe before they can recover, take one enemy out of the fight so you can deal with others, or simply buy yourself a few seconds to retreat and regroup. It's especially useful when fighting individual, high-level foes. However, you can achieve the same effect with a spell or poison, so this power may be less useful at higher levels once you have other options at your disposal.

The Shadow Stone, located in the Rift: Invisibility for 60 seconds.

This power is exceptionally useful for a stealthy character. It can be invoked instantly, silently, with no Illusion skill or casting time required. You can achieve the same effect with a spell—and you definitely want that spell—but even after obtaining it, the Shadow Stone's power can still be useful to keep around as a backup.

The Steed Stone, located in Haafingar Hold: Carry weight +100, no movement penalty from armor.

Although this blessing doesn't bring you the instant gratification or protection of those that help you in combat, it is worth considering the Steed Stone's ability if you rely on heavy armor: You'll appreciate the extra mobility and Carry Weight it affords you. It's also worth trying this ability before taking the Conditioned (Heavy Armor) or Unhindered (Light Armor) perks; you may even want to take it instead of those perks and select another perk.

The Tower Stone, located in Winterhold Hold. Unlock any Expert-level lock (or lower) once per day.

If you constantly find yourself out of lockpicks or simply don't enjoy lockpicking, the Tower Stone's power will help you open one locked door or treasure chest per day. For everyone else, there are more useful abilities to choose from.

NOTE Standing Stones are all Primary Locations, and their locations are shown throughout the Atlas. For a table showing the effects of all Standing Stones, consult the Shouts and Other Powers section (page 54), earlier in Training.

Sacred Stones (All-Maker Stones)

The Skaal of Solstheim revere six Sacred Stones, symbols of their bond with nature and the All-Maker. These places of power are being corrupted by Miraak, who is compelling the people of Solstheim to rebuild them to strengthen his own power.

CAUTION Interacting with any Sacred Stone before cleansing it puts you under Miraak's influence. You actually help with the construction!

In order to draw upon their magic, you must first cleanse them of Miraak's influence by using the Bend Will Shout on them. Doing so destroys the shrine, frees the people enslaved by Miraak's power, and releases a powerful Lurker that attacks you.

NOTE There is one exception: The Tree Stone, located in the heart of Miraak's Temple, cannot be cleansed in this way. The only way to free it is to defeat Miraak in Dragonborn Main Quest: At the Summit of Apocrypha.

Blessings of the Sacred Stones

Thereafter, you can interact with each Sacred Stone once per day to receive its blessing: it fully heals you and grants you a potent single-use power. Once you expend it, you must return to the Sacred Stone to acquire this power again.

Beast Stone: Grants you the Conjure Wearbear power, which summons a werebear for 60 seconds wherever the caster is pointing.

Earth Stone: Grants you the Bones of the Earth power, which protects you from 80% of all physical damage for 30 seconds.

Sun Stone: Grants you the Sun Flare power, a 100-point fiery explosion centered on the caster. Does more damage to closer targets.

Tree Stone: Grants you the Root of Power, which causes all spells to cost 75% less for 60 seconds.

Water Stone: Grants you the Waters of Life power, which heals everyone close to you for 200 points.

Wind Stone: Grants you the North Wind power, which does 20 points of frost damage to all enemies within range for 10 seconds.

SHADOWMARKS

A strange rune on a building in Solitude. It has a meaning to those in the know.

Eagle-eyed adventurers may notice that some locations across Skyrim are marked with strange glyphs. Unbeknownst to most, these runes are actually symbols used by the Thieves Guild to indicate locations that members feel are particularly wealthy targets, safe, dangerous, or have inhabitants that may be helpful or problematic. These symbols are known as Shadowmarks. To learn more about Shadowmarks, search the Thieves Guild for a book written by Delvin Mallory called Shadowmarks, which lists all of the markings that the Thieves Guild uses. For more information on Shadowmarks, see page 304.

BOOKS

Voracious readers will be pleased to learn that a wealth of knowledge is located in dozens of different books. These fall into one of six general categories: Skill Books, Spell Tomes, functional books, common books, notes and journals, and Black Books of Hermaeus Mora.

Skill Books

The Doors of Oblivion (Conjuration), one of only five copies of this rare book.

When read, these books increase one of your skills by a single point. There are five different Skill Books associated with each skill (meaning 90 different book titles), but there are multiple copies of each book (usually 3 to 5 each), bringing the total number of Skill Books to well over 400. However, you only receive a skill increase the first time you read any particular title; rereading that book or any of its copies has no further effect. This means you can only use Skill Books to increase each skill by a maximum of five points.

For example: Those interested in the Sneak skill should look for Three Thieves (four copies), 2920, Last Seed, v8 (four copies), Sacred Witness (four copies), Legend of Krately House (three copies), and The Red Kitchen Reader (five copies). This means there are 20 Sneak Skill Books and five points you can add to your Sneak from reading the first copy you encounter of each tome.

Spell Tomes

Spell Tome: Ice Storm (Destruction), which is located in the world or purchased from select vendors.

Spell Tomes are books of magic with the sigil of their school embossed on the front cover. When you read them, the book is consumed and you instantly learn the spell it contained. If you later find another copy of the same Spell Tome, sell it, as it isn't of any use to you anymore. You can purchase Spell Tomes from a few select vendors, the Court Wizards in each of the major Hold capitals, and the mages of the College of Winterhold. You can also find Spell Tomes randomly in dungeons.

Functional Books

Lost Legends of Skyrim hints at an ancient mystery.

Functional books describe actual locations, legends, or mysteries to be discovered in the wilds of Skyrim. When read, they add locations to your world map and might trigger a quest or objective related to the contents of the book. There are seven of these types of books, each with several copies. Once you've read one copy, you never need to read another copy of the same book, as the information is identical.

Common Books

The Lusty Argonian Maid, v2, one of only three copies of this scandalous work.

There are a wide variety of other books in Skyrim. They provide stories, histories, advice on battle, fiction, and many other types of reading material to add a little flavor to your adventure. Many of these books provide interesting asides to locations you visit. However, none of these books grant you any kind of bonus; they are simply there to be read. Across Skyrim and Solstheim, there are 263 different books to read (or collect, if you like). Some are quite common, while others are rare and valuable.

Notes and Journals

A Note from Falk Firebeard of Solitude, delivered by courier during Side Quest: The Wolf Queen Awakened.

In addition to books, there are a wide variety of notes and journals used throughout your adventure to convey shorter or more personal messages, from the important to the trivial. Some are given or found during quests, while others can be picked up in houses and dungeons. Quest notes are listed in the appropriate quests, while most other notes simply aren't important enough to be tracked in this guide. But they're all worth a read, if you have the time.

> **NOTE** Sample locations of every functional and common book are shown in the Inventory chapter (page 157). The two easiest locations to find every type of the Skill Book are also presented in the Appendices and across the Atlas.

Black Books and Apocrypha Powers

One of seven known Black Books, with the power to transport you into a realm of Oblivion.

On the isle of Solstheim, you may come across one of seven Black Books—tomes of forbidden knowledge that transport you into the realm of Oblivion controlled by the Daedric Prince Hermaeus Mora. This realm is known as Apocrypha. Two of these are found and used as part of the Dragonborn Main Quest.

The other five are located in specific dungeons across the island and can be found through normal exploration (even before the Dragonborn Main Quest). For example, the Black Book: Filament and Filigree can be found in Kolbjorn Barrow.

If you are on Solstheim (and not Skyrim), and you aren't engaged in combat, reading a Black Book will transport you to the book's corresponding Apocrypha realm. If you are not on Solstheim or are in combat, the book doesn't work.

Each book takes you to a specific Apocrypha realm (a dungeon you can explore). While all seven of these dungeons are known as "Apocrypha," they are all distinct areas. For clarity, this guide has subtitled each distinct area with the name of the book that sends you there. For example, when you read Black Book: Filament and Filigree, you are transported to a specific part of Apocrypha. You cannot move into areas served by other Black Books.

Consult the Apocrypha section of the Solstheim Atlas (starting on page 1065) for further details, and search out Dragonborn Main Quests (starting on page 583) and Solstheim Side Quests (starting on page 606) for more information on these locations.

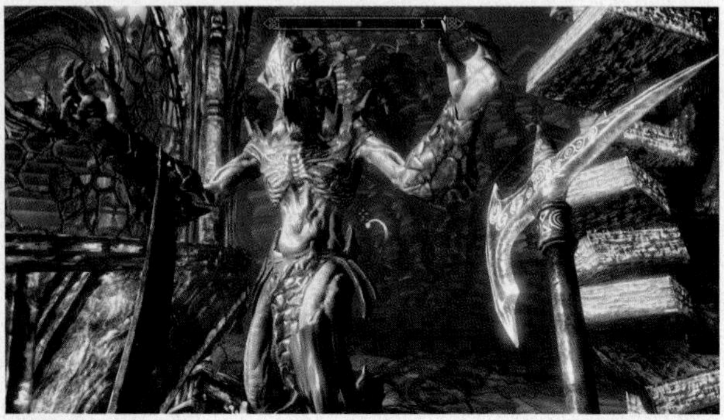

Your arrival into the churning, burning skies of Apocrypha, where all forbidden knowledge is learned...

Upon arriving in Apocrypha, you receive a quest to finish the Black Book you've just read. Exactly what happens next varies depending on the book you opened (which you can open as many times as you like by accessing it in your inventory). The variations are as follows:

For the Main Quest book Waking Dreams..., you read the book as part of Dragonborn Main Quest: The Temple of Miraak, but you don't obtain a quest because Miraak confronts you and throws you out of the realm. You can't complete this book until you do so as a part of Dragonborn Main Quest: At the Summit of Apocrypha.

For the Main Quest book Epistolary Acumen, you read the book as part of Dragonborn Main Quest: The Gardener of Men. Completing it is required by that quest.

For the other five books, you receive the corresponding Solstheim Side Quest (named the same as the book) as a reminder that you need to complete it.

When you appear in Apocrypha for the first time, you are confronted by an apparition of Hermaeus Mora, who beckons you into the realm, explaining it a little more clearly. This occurs only once.

As you progress through each Apocrypha realm, specific checkpoints are invisibly set as you complete certain actions or events. If you leave the realm and return, you will arrive at the last checkpoint—you don't have to start all over again. These checkpoints are never seen or known, but you're likely to appear just after the chapter you've reached in a previous exploration.

To leave Apocrypha and return to Solstheim, you can:

Die. Dying in Apocrypha simply transports you out; it doesn't actually kill you.

Read any Black Book in your inventory.

Complete the Apocrypha realm, reach the Reward Book, claim your reward, and then interact with the Reward Book again to leave.

When you leave Apocrypha, you return to Solstheim exactly where you were when you read the Black Book.

At the end of each Apocrypha realm, you will find a Reward Book. There are large tomes matching the name of the book you read to enter the realm. Interacting with the book opens it, causing three orbs to emerge, each representing a power or ability that the book can bestow.

Each book has a specific and distinct set of rewards (see page 53 for the powers and the following table for a complete list). Some are passive abilities that are always "on" while you have them. Some are powers, which you can use only once a day. Some are lesser powers, which you can use as often as you like.

Once you select a reward, interacting with the Reward Book again will return you to Solstheim. However, since you can always read the Black Book in your inventory to return to Apocrypha, you can return here and choose a different power whenever you want. You can have only one power from each book at a time.

NOTE Note that the Waking Dreams Reward Book (found at the end of Dragonborn Main Quest: At the Summit of Apocrypha) works differently: It displays images of the 18 Constellations. You can interact with these images to reset your perks in that constellation, allowing you to retool your skills.

Dragonborn Black Books and Apocrypha Powers List

The following table shows the rewards for each of the seven Black Books available in Apocrypha.

		BLACK BOOK: WAKING DREAMS	
✓	**BLACK BOOK LOCATED IN**	**BLACK BOOK DUNGEON**	**ASSOCIATED QUEST(S)**
☐	[S.N24] Temple of Miraak	[S.A07] Apocrypha: Waking Dreams of a Starless Sky	Dragonborn Main Quest: The Temple of Miraak, At the Summit of Apocrypha
✓	**POWER NAME**	**DESCRIPTION**	**NOTES AND TIPS**
☐	Shadow Constellations	Activated Object. You may spend a Dragon Soul to reset all of the Perks in a skill constellation.	You can spend as many Dragon Souls in this way as you like, allowing you to completely retool your character's perks whenever you want. This is great for experimenting with different combinations of perks, or for changing the feel of the game when you want a new challenge.
		BLACK BOOK: EPISTOLARY ACUMEN	
✓	**BLACK BOOK LOCATED IN**	**BLACK BOOK DUNGEON**	**ASSOCIATED QUEST(S)**
☐	[S.S14] Nchardak	[S.A01] Apocrypha: Epistolary Acumen	Dragonborn Main Quest: The Gardener of Men
✓	**POWER NAME**	**DESCRIPTION**	**NOTES AND TIPS**
☐	Dragonborn Force	Passive Ability. Your Unrelenting Force Shout does more damage, and using all three words may disintegrate enemies.	Increases the damage of Unrelenting Force to 10/25/50. Enemies will only be disintegrated if you use the complete shout (all three words), and only if the damage would have killed them anyway.
☐	Dragonborn Flame	Passive Ability. When your Fire Breath Shout kills an enemy, a fire wyrm emerges from their corpse to fight for you for 60s.	Fire Wyrms fight in melee, doing modest damage and setting foes on fire; see the Bestiary for complete details. They do not count as or replace any summoned creatures you may have. They remain at the spot where they were created (instead of following you), making this much more useful early in a battle.
☐	Dragonborn Frost	Passive Ability. Your Frost Breath Shout encases foes in ice for 15s.	Foes encased in ice are paralyzed and unable to attack (just as with the Ice Form Shout), although it's worth noting that, unlike Ice Form, they do not take additional damage over time. Enemies immune to paralysis are immune to this effect as well.

BLACK BOOK: FILAMENT AND FILIGREE

☑	BLACK BOOK LOCATED IN	BLACK BOOK DUNGEON	ASSOCIATED QUEST(S)
☐	[S.S04] Kolbjorn Barrow	[S.A02] Apocrypha: Filament and Filigree	Solstheim Side Quest: Black Book: Filament and Filigree, Solstheim Side Quest: Unearthed

☑	POWER NAME	DESCRIPTION	NOTES AND TIPS
☐	Secret of Strength	Power. Power attacks cost no Stamina for 30s.	Combined with a good weapon and the Elemental Fury Shout, this power allows you to inflict incredible amounts of damage.
☐	Secret of Arcana	Power. Spells cost no Magicka for 30s.	This power actually reduces the cost of all of your spells to 0, potentially allowing you to cast high-cost Ritual spells you normally couldn't afford at all. Care to summon a Storm Thrall? Or maybe blast your enemy with Lightning Storm for 30 seconds straight?
☐	Secret of Protection	Power. You take half damage for 30s from all physical and most magical attacks.	If you prefer defense to offense, Secret of Protection can make a huge difference against enemies with a high damage output (such as dragons or Karstaag), halving all incoming damage for its duration.

BLACK BOOK: THE HIDDEN TWILIGHT

☑	BLACK BOOK LOCATED IN	BLACK BOOK DUNGEON	ASSOCIATED QUEST(S)
☐	[S.S00] Tel Mithryn	[S.A03] Apocrypha: The Hidden Twilight	Solstheim Side Quest: Black Book: The Hidden Twilight, Solstheim Side Quest: The Reluctant Steward

☑	POWER NAME	DESCRIPTION	NOTES AND TIPS
☐	Mora's Agony	Power. Summons a field of writhing tentacles that lasts 30 seconds and poisons foes who enter it.	In addition to poisoning foes (5dmg/s for 3s), the tentacles also stagger enemies, who may stumble into them repeatedly and suffer the poison effect multiple times. This makes Mora's Agony an effective way of stopping humanoid pursuers in their tracks (though don't expect it to stop a Dragon or a Mammoth). Consult the Bestiary to make sure your foes are not immune to poison.
☐	Mora's Grasp	Power. Target is frozen between Oblivion and Tamriel for 30 seconds, and immune to all damage.	Mora's Grasp affects a much wider range of targets than most paralysis-type spells: only Dragons and some boss enemies are unaffected by it. Just be careful not to miss– you only get one shot per day.
☐	Mora's Boon	Power. Fully restores your Health, Magicka, and Stamina.	It may not be flashy, but having a full heal on hand can make all the difference if you find yourself in a close battle and run out of potions.

BLACK BOOK: THE SALLOW REGENT

☑	BLACK BOOK LOCATED IN	BLACK BOOK DUNGEON	ASSOCIATED QUEST(S)
☐	[S.N17] White Ridge Barrow	[S.A04] Apocrypha: The Sallow Regent	Solstheim Side Quest: Black Book: The Sallow Regent

☑	POWER NAME	DESCRIPTION	NOTES AND TIPS
☐	Seeker of Might	Passive Ability. Improves all of your combat skills by 10%.	This ability increases the damage you do with all weapons by 10%, increases the amount of damage blocking will prevent by 10%, increases the armor rating of your Heavy Armor by 10%, and increases the bonuses you get from tempering items by 10%.
☐	Seeker of Sorcery	Passive Ability. Improves all of your magic skills by 10%.	This ability reduces the cost of all spells by 10%, and increases the strength of your enchantments by 10%.
☐	Seeker of Shadows	Passive Ability. Improves all of your stealth skills by 10%.	This ability increases the armor rating of your Light Armor by 10%, makes it 10% easier to sneak, pick locks, or pick pockets, and improves the prices you get from buying or selling items by 10%.

BLACK BOOK: UNTOLD LEGENDS

☑	BLACK BOOK LOCATED IN	BLACK BOOK DUNGEON	ASSOCIATED QUEST(S)
☐	[S.N16] Benkongerike	[S.A05] Apocrypha: Untold Legends	Solstheim Side Quest: Black Book: Untold Legends

☑	POWER NAME	DESCRIPTION	NOTES AND TIPS
☐	Black Market	Lesser Power. Summons a Dremora merchant for 15s.	Black Market allows you to summon a merchant anytime, anywhere. The Dremora Merchant has 2000 gold and a small selection of rare and enchanted items to sell. However, he drives a hard bargain– expect to pay more, and get less, than you would from any other merchant.
☐	Secret Servant	Lesser Power. Summons a Dremora butler for 15s.	If you'd prefer to save your loot and sort it out when you get back to town, Secret Servant summons a dremora butler who can carry up to 150-weight of items for you.
☐	Bardic Knowledge	Lesser Power. Summons a spectral drum to play for you, increasing Stamina regeneration for you and nearby allies for 240s.	More of a fun choice, the drum summoned by Bardic Knowledge just follows you around and plays instrumental music. It does provide a significant (50%) boost to your Stamina regeneration, and doesn't count as or replace any summoned creatures you may have.

BLACK BOOK: THE WINDS OF CHANGE

☑	BLACK BOOK LOCATED IN	BLACK BOOK DUNGEON	ASSOCIATED QUEST(S)
☐	[S.S00] Raven Rock (Mine)	[S.A06] Apocrypha: The Winds of Change	Solstheim Side Quest: Black Book: The Winds of Change

☑	POWER NAME	DESCRIPTION	NOTES AND TIPS
☐	Scholar's Insight	Passive Ability. Reading Skill Books gives you an extra Skill Point.	Scholar's Insight is great for getting maximum value out of the Skill Books you find. For best results, avoid reading skill books until you hit 90 in a skill, then read all five for a quick boost to 100.
☐	Companion's Insight	Passive Ability. Your attacks, shouts, and destruction spells do no damage to your followers in combat.	If you prefer ranged combat or (especially) spells with large areas of effect, you may have accidentally killed your own followers on occasion. Take this ability, and you'll never have to worry about that again.
☐	Lover's Insight	Passive Ability. Do 10% more damage and get 10% better prices from people of the opposite sex.	This is a more subtle bonus, but its effects do add up over time. Consult the Traders list in the appendix to identify vendors of the opposite sex.

▷ Apocrypha Fonts

In Apocrypha, you can find sculptures with blue and green orbs set into them. Interacting with them will fully restore your Magicka or Stamina, respectively. You can use each font only once per visit to Apocrypha.

A font of Magicka

A font of Stamina

Quests

Quests are a series of related objectives that make up a single mission or story. These range from the simple to the epic, and a large amount of this guide is spent detailing every one of them! In game, the Quest Journal tracks all of your current and former quests, while the General Stats page keeps track of how many quests you've completed. Remember that there are dozens of Miscellaneous Objectives, Favor Quests, and World Encounters and Interactions to discover as well. Every quest is documented later in this guide.

> **TIP** The Quest Target Marker is exceptionally useful, and you should always keep the target for your current quest(s) turned on. Remember to set your quest or objective as "Active" first, then highlight the quest and press "Show on Map" to display the world map centered on the location you need to reach. The marker will also appear on your compass to guide you.

Favors and Friendship

Ingratiate yourself with important folks, such as Jarl Laila Law-Giver of Riften, to gain social standing and power.

When visiting a city, town, or settlement, take a moment to speak with everyone you meet. In addition to learning more about the area, they often have a Favor or other task they could use your help with. Complete it, and they react to you much more favorably. Keep this up among folks in the same settlement, and you'll soon hear the guards mention your pleasant reputation. Consult the Miscellaneous Objectives and Favor Quest chapters, beginning on page 489, for a list of the huge number of favors you can perform.

Making friends has several useful benefits:

- Your friends will often be willing to help you in return.
- They will occasionally give you gifts.
- They may allow you to take items from their house, shop, or market stall without paying for them (you'll notice that many items are no longer marked "steal," so help yourself!).
- They're willing to put you up for the night. When in their home, you are no longer trespassing, and you can sleep in any bed they own. An unscrupulous "friend" could take advantage of this hospitality to rob them blind...
- Some may even be willing to join you on your adventure if you ask! Consult the Followers list later in this section for details.

> **NOTE** Completing Favors for a Hold's inhabitants also wins you the Jarl's attention. Complete the Jarl's quest or Favors, and you will be given the title of Thane. Thanes are granted the services of a housecarl (see Followers, page 100) and receive more lenient treatment for crimes they commit (see Crime, page 64). You can become the Thane of any or all of the nine Holds.

Houses

Buying a House

When the time comes to establish yourself as more than just a wandering dragon-slayer, you can put down roots in any (or all) of Skyrim's major capitals by purchasing a House. You can't just saunter into town with a hefty bag of gold and demand a dwelling, though: You must first win the Jarl's trust. Speak to them and complete the quests or Favors they assign until you earn their friendship and permission to buy a house in the city. For more details on what you need to do, see the appropriate Thane task in the Favors section (see page 502).

> **TIP** Remember, the Civil War affects who controls each of the five major cities. If your faction takes control of a city, you can be sure the newly installed Jarl will reward your efforts and may give you permission to purchase a house immediately!

With the Jarl's approval, you can now approach the steward (who is usually nearby) and ask about purchasing a home. The price is displayed and is not negotiable. Pay the steward, and you receive the key to the dwelling.

Decorating Your Property

Furnish your house with a variety of accoutrements, ideally keeping your areas tidy.

Once you've purchased a house, you can leave it in its current (usually sparse and cobwebbed) state or speak to the steward again to begin decorating it. Each house comes with a Home Decorating Guide that describes the options available to you, so you can make an informed decision about which furnishings to purchase. In addition to purely cosmetic items like chairs or cupboards, decorations also include such useful things as crafting stations, weapon racks, mannequins, and bookshelves. Simply return to the steward and buy the decorations you want; when you return to your house, they have been installed.

Benefits of Home Ownership

Owning a house gives you a variety of useful benefits:

- You have a convenient base of operations in the city, with several easily accessible crafting stations and a bed you own (for the Well Rested or Lover's Comfort bonuses, see page 54).
- You can store any weapons, armor, crafting materials, or other items you have in your house, knowing they will always be there when you return.
- You can prominently display the weapons, artifacts, and items that you've collected on a variety of weapon racks, weapon plaques, mannequins, and bookshelves.
- If you've been named Thane of the Hold, you can find your housecarl in your house, ready to join you at a moment's notice.
- If you're married (see Side Quest: The Bonds of Matrimony, page 423), you can also ask your spouse to move in with you, instead of meeting them in the inn or bedding down in their (often rudimentary) place!

Available Properties

Proudspire Manor, Solitude (Haafingar Hold)

Price: 25,000 gold
Jarl (in Solitude): Jarl Elisif the Fair
Steward: Falk Firebeard
Available Decorations:

- Bedroom (2,000)
- Living Room (2,000)
- Alchemy Laboratory (2,500)
- Enchanting Laboratory (2,500)
- Patio Decorations (500)
- Kitchen (1,500)

Total Cost: 36,000 gold

Windstad Manor (Hjaalmarch Hold)

Price: 5,000 gold (for land and deeds only)
Jarl (in Morthal): Jarl Igrod Ravencrone
Steward: Aslfur
Available Decorations:

See the Hearthfire section of Training, starting on page 112.

Heljarchen Hall (The Pale)

Price: 5,000 gold (for land and deeds only)
Jarl (in Dawnstar): Jarl Skald the Elder
Steward: None
Available Decorations:

See Hearthfire section of Training, starting on page 112.

Vlindrel Hall, Markarth (The Reach)

Price: 8,000 gold
Jarl (in Markarth): Jarl Igmund or Jarl Thongvor Silverfish
Steward: Raerek or Reburrus Quintilius
Available Decorations:

- Bedroom (800)
- Living Room (900)
- Alchemy Laboratory (1,000)
- Enchanting Laboratory (1,000)
- Entrance Hall (500)

Total Cost: 12,200 gold

Breezehome, Whiterun (Whiterun Hold)

Price: 5,000 gold
Jarl (in Whiterun): Jarl Balgruuf the Greater or Jarl Vignar the Revered
Steward: Proventus Avenicci or Brill
Available Decorations:

- Alchemy Laboratory (500)
- Bedroom (300)
- Loft (200)
- Dining Room (250)

Total Cost: 6,250 gold

Hjerim, Windhelm (Eastmarch)

Price: 12,000 gold
Jarl (in Windhelm): Jarl Ulfric Stormcloak or Jarl Brunwulf Free-Winter
Steward: Jorleif or Captain Lonely-Gale
Available Decorations:

- Kitchen (1,000)
- Bedroom (1,000)
- Living Room (1,500)
- Alchemy Laboratory (1,500)
- Enchanting Laboratory (1,500)
- Armory (2,000)
- Clean up that murderer's mess (500)

Total Cost: 21,000 gold

NOTE To purchase Hjerim, you must complete the first part of Side Quest: Blood on the Ice.

Lakeview Manor (Falkreath Hold)

Price: 5,000 gold (for land and deeds only)
Jarl (in Falkreath): Jarl Siddgeir
Steward: Nenya
Available Decorations:

See Hearthfire section of Training, starting on page 112.

Honeyside, Riften (The Rift)

Price: 8,000 gold
Jarl (in Riften): Jarl Laila Lawgiver or Jarl Maven Black-Briar
Steward: Anuriel or Hemming Black-Briar
Available Decorations:

- Bedroom (600)
- Kitchen (500)
- Alchemy Laboratory (1,000)
- Enchanting Laboratory (1,000)
- Garden (800)
- Porch (400)

Total Cost: 12,200 gold pieces

Severin Manor (Raven Rock, Solstheim)

Price: Complementary, after completing Solstheim Side Quest: Served Cold
Councilor (in Raven Rock): Lleril Morvayn
Second Councilor: Adril Arano
Available Decorations:

None. It comes fully furnished and cannot be decorated.

Your spouse and children cannot live here either.

NOTE The precise location of every house you can buy is indicated in the Atlas. The exact method of purchasing each house is detailed in the Thane's Tasks part of the Favors section of the quests chapter, on page 502.

MINOR SPOILERS

Throughout the realm, there are those who stand ready to join you in your adventure and are prepared to lay down their lives in your service. These selfless companions are broadly known as Followers. Followers may join you for any number of reasons, whether because you've hired their services, helped them in the past, or are simply taking on a charge that they have an interest in. Some join you only for the duration of a specific quest, while others will follow you indefinitely. This section explores these and other details about your Followers.

NOTE Typically, you can have only one human Follower and one animal (dog) Follower at a time, although additional Followers may join you temporarily for a quest that they have an interest in.

General Traits

Your Follower normally acts as a shadow, bodyguard, item repository, and friend.

When a Follower has agreed to join you on your adventure, there are several advantages they bring and help you can expect from them:

Equipment: Your Followers will always equip the best weapons, armor, and items they have available and will try to use staffs and other items effectively. They take their own skills and proficiencies into account when making these decisions, so all else being equal, expect Jenassa (an archer) to prefer a bow to a two-handed sword and light armor to heavy plate.

Skills: All Followers have a specific set of favored skills (listed below), which improve as their level increases. Unlike your character, Followers do not become better at the skills they use—for example, no matter how hard you try to force Marcurio (a mage) to be a greatsword-wielding warrior, he'll always be better with magic. Make sure to select a Follower whose skill set meets your needs.

Levels: Most Followers automatically level up when you do, so there's no need to worry about a Follower "falling behind" if you go off and adventure on your own or want to work with someone else for a while.

Tactics: Followers will try to follow your lead whenever possible:

When you sneak, they will sneak as well and will stop when you do. Don't expect them to take cover on their own, though—if you want them to hide in a particular location, order them to move to it.

When you draw or sheathe your weapons, so will they.

When attacked, they will use their best weapons, spells, and tactics to defend both themselves and you.

Catching Up: If you travel on horseback (or with the great loping strides of a werewolf), you may find that your Followers fall behind. Don't worry about losing them; there are several ways you can help them catch up:

Just Wait (using the Wait System), and they'll use the time to catch up.

Load into any new space, and they'll be right behind you.

Fast-Travel anywhere, and they'll arrive next to you.

Heading Home: If you dismiss a Follower, they will return home and take up their original routine. Most Followers will rejoin you if you ask, though you may need to pay for the services of hirelings again if too much time has passed.

Death and Dying: When a Follower's health is exhausted, they will collapse. Heal them or finish the combat and wait for their health to regenerate, and they will recover, none the worse for wear.

CAUTION Be careful, though—if you inflict lethal damage on a Follower, either directly (e.g., by hitting them with an errant attack) or indirectly (e.g., from the blast of a fireball), they will die. Permanently.

At Your Command

You can also issue orders to your Followers. To do this, either speak to them or enter Command mode (target them, then press and hold the Activate button until the cursor changes). The available orders are:

Wait/Follow: If you want to explore an area on your own or try a stealthy approach, use the Wait command to tell your Follower to stop shadowing you. Once you're done, return to your Follower and tell them to accompany you again. Note there are some situations and locations where Followers can't accompany you (such as to jail, if you're arrested). If you leave a Follower at a location and don't return, they eventually return home.

Do Something: You can order your Follower to do something specific, which can be helpful in all kinds of situations. Move your target crosshairs onto something you want your Follower to use, take, steal, or attack, then press Activate to give the order.

Trade Items: This allows you to exchange items between your inventory and your Follower's. Some notes:

All Followers start with some basic equipment. You can't take these items from them. You can, however, give your Followers better gear, such as items that you've improved, enchanted, or think your Follower might be more adept at using. If they judge the item is better than what they currently have, they'll equip it immediately.

You can have your Follower carry their share of the treasure, effectively turning them into a pack mule. This roughly doubles the amount of loot you can carry, which is handy if you're trying to gather as much as you can from a dungeon before returning to town and selling it off. Note that your Followers do have a maximum carry weight (not shown), so there is a limit to what they can carry as well.

Part Ways: If this relationship just isn't working out, you can tell your Follower that you no longer need their services. They'll head home, and you can then acquire a different Follower or set off on your own.

Other Notes and Tips

When choosing a Follower, pick one that complements your play style. If you're adept at sneaking and silent ranged takedowns with a bow, find someone with similar prowess. If you're a robed mage, seek the company of a powerful warrior to hold your foes at bay. Experiment around with the available Followers until you find one you enjoy adventuring with. Then add a dog!

It's almost always a good idea to bring a Follower along; they can distract foes, soak up damage on your behalf, and help you to take down enemies more quickly. However, there are two cases to be wary of:

If you plan to take a stealthy approach to your next mission, Followers can be more of a hindrance than a help. Even with a well-outfitted stealthy Follower, they can't use cover and concealment as effectively as you can. When stealth is essential, you may want to go it alone.

If you're a Mage with a lot of area-of-effect spells, the collateral damage can be lethal to your Followers. Control your casting carefully, or leave your Follower at home and take up Conjuration instead—Atronachs are immune to spells of their element, and Zombies are, well, dead anyway.

NOTE Many Followers are also Trainers. Bring them with you, and you will be able to train whenever you like, so long as you have the funds.

You can also be romantically tied to many Followers. Consult Side Quest: The Bonds of Matrimony (page 423) for more details.

Types of Followers

This section identifies all of the characters who can become your Followers. We detail each Follower's primary combat style (e.g., Warrior) and their favored skills. We also note any prerequisites for obtaining them.

In general, Followers can be classified into these major categories:

Hirelings: Mercenaries who will accompany you if you hire them.

Housecarls: If you are named Thane of a Hold, the Jarl will appoint a Housecarl as your bodyguard.

Guildmates: If you join one of the major guilds, you may be able to ask your fellow guild members to follow you.

Quest or Dungeon Followers: These characters will follow you once you complete their quest or dungeon.

Favor Followers: Friends you have completed Favors for may join you if you ask.

Animal Companions: Loyal dogs who will fight at your side in combat. The following are also available:

Armored Trolls, Armored Frost Trolls, Death Hounds, and Huskies

A Steadfast Dwarven Spider and a Steadfast Dwarven Sphere

TIP To find the exact location of every Follower, simply look up the settlement mentioned in their description in the Atlas.

Hirelings

The following are mercenaries for hire, each with their own unique combat style. To purchase their services, you must pay a flat fee of 500 gold pieces. If you dismiss them, they may charge you that fee again.

Belrand, in Solitude (Haafingar)

Spellsword: One-Handed, Light Armor, Destruction, Restoration

Vorstag, in Markarth (the Reach)

Warrior: One-Handed, Heavy Armor, Archery, Block

Jenassa, in Whiterun (Whiterun Hold)

Archer: Archery, Light Armor, One-Handed, Block, Sneak

Stenvar, in Windhelm (Eastmarch)

Knight: Two-Handed, Heavy Armor, Archery, Block

Marcurio, in Riften (the Rift)

Mage: Destruction, Restoration, Alteration, Conjuration, Sneak

Erik the Slayer, in Rorikstead (Whiterun Hold)

Barbarian: Two-Handed, Light Armor, Archery, Block. (You must complete Miscellaneous Objective: Erik the Slayer before you can hire Erik.)

Teldryn Sero, in Raven Rock (Solstheim)

Spellsword—One-Handed, Destruction, Light Armor, Conjuration, Restoration

Housecarls

The following Housecarls are bodyguards sworn to your service as Thane. For advice on becoming the Thane of one or more Holds, consult page 502. You do not receive a Housecarl for becoming Thane of Winterhold.

Jordis the Sword-Maiden, Housecarl of Solitude (Haafingar)

Housecarl: One-Handed, Heavy Armor, Archery, Block

Valdimar, Housecarl of Windstad Manor (Hjaalmarch)

Housecarl: Heavy Armor, One-Handed, Archery, Block

Gregor: Housecarl of Heljarchen Hall (The Pale)

Housecarl: Heavy Armor, One-Handed, Archery, Block

Argis the Bulwark, Housecarl of Markarth (the Reach)

Housecarl: One-Handed, Heavy Armor, Archery, Block

Lydia, Housecarl of Whiterun (Whiterun Hold)

Housecarl: One-Handed, Heavy Armor, Archery, Block

Calder, Housecarl of Windhelm (Windhelm Hold)

Housecarl: One-Handed, Heavy Armor, Archery, Block

Rayya, Housecarl of Lakeview Manor (Falkreath Hold)

Housecarl: One-Handed, Heavy Armor, Archery, Block

Iona, Housecarl of Riften (the Rift)

Housecarl: One-Handed, Heavy Armor, Archery, Block

The Companions

This ancient and renowned order of warriors is headquartered in Whiterun. Companions have an extremely close bond, referring to each other as Shield-Siblings. Once you complete their questline, the following Companions become available as Followers. Visit Jorrvaskr in Whiterun to find them.

Aela the Huntress

Archer: Archery, Light Armor, Sneak, Speech, One-Handed

Expert Trainer: Archery

Athis

Warrior: One-Handed, Block, Archery, Light Armor

Expert Trainer: One-Handed

Farkas

Warrior: One-Handed, Heavy Armor, Smithing, Speech

Master Trainer: Heavy Armor

Njada Stonearm

Warrior: One-Handed, Block, Speech

Expert Trainer: Block

Ria

Warrior: One-Handed, Heavy Armor, Archery, Block

Torvar

Warrior: One-Handed, Heavy Armor, Archery, Block

Vilkas

Knight: Two-Handed, Heavy Armor, Archery, Block

Master Trainer: Two-Handed

The College of Winterhold

Your fellow students at the College of Winterhold will join you once you are a member of the College and complete their specific College of Winterhold Radiant Quest:

Onmund

Sorcerer: Destruction, Illusion, One-Handed, Heavy Armor

J'Zargo

Sorcerer: Destruction, Illusion, One-Handed, Heavy Armor

Brelyna Maryon

Mage: Alteration, Illusion, Conjuration, Sneak

Dark Brotherhood Assassins

After completing the Dark Brotherhood questline, two new initiates and a strange jester are available to aid and abet you in your adventures. You'll find them at the Dawnstar Sanctary in the Pale:

Dark Brotherhood Initiate (Male and Female)

Assassin: Sneak, One-Handed, Archery, Light Armor

Cicero, the Fool of Hearts, Jester and Keeper of the Night Mother

Assassin: Sneak, One-Handed, Archery, Light Armor

Quest-Related Followers

The following citizens of Skyrim and Solstheim sometimes accompany you on specific quests and are willing to join you after you finish the quest they are involved in (providing they survive the quest as well). Consult each quest for more information.

Adelaisa Vendicci (Side Quest: Rise in the East)

Townsperson: Alchemy, Enchanting, Smithing, Speech

Aranea (Daedric Quest: The Black Star)

Mage: Destruction, Restoration, Conjuration, Alteration

Eola (Daedric Quest: The Taste of Death)

Nightblade: Destruction, One-Handed, Alteration, Sneak

Erandur (Daedric Quest: Waking Nightmare)

Healer: Restoration, Conjuration, Speech, Alchemy

Frea (Dragonborn Main Quest: The Temple of Miraak)

Shaman: One-Handed, Alteration, Light Armor, Restoration, Archery

Lob (Daedric Quest: The Cursed Tribe)

Archer: Archery, Light Armor, One-Handed, Block, Sneak

Ogol (Daedric Quest: The Cursed Tribe)

Warrior: One-Handed, Heavy Armor, Archery, Sneak

Ralis Sedarys (Solstheim Side Quest: Unearthed)

Warrior: One-Handed, Light Armor, Block, Sneak

Rieklings (Solstheim Side Quest: The Chief of Thirsk Hall)

Riekling: Archery, Two-Handed, Light Armor, Sneak (see the Bestiary on page 187 for complete details)

Ugor (Daedric Quest: The Cursed Tribe)

Archer: Archery, Light Armor, One-Handed, Block, Sneak

Dawnguard Followers

The characters listed below are willing to join you on your adventures if you meet their requirements. However, for most of the Dawnguard Main Quest, you will be fighting alongside Serana, who is vehemently opposed to leaving your side. You can have an animal companion and Serana with you, but not another higher-functioning bipedal Follower. For these Followers, request their presence after the Dawnguard Main Quest is over.

Agmaer

Dawnguard Recruit: One-Handed, Two-Handed, Block, Light Armor, Heavy Armor.

You must be allied with the Dawnguard and complete Dawnguard Main Quest: Prophet.

Beleval

Dawnguard Recruit: One-Handed, Two-Handed, Block, Light Armor, Heavy Armor.

You must be allied with the Dawnguard and complete Dawnguard Main Quest: Prophet.

Celann

Dawnguard Warrior: One-Handed, Heavy Armor, Archery, Block.

You must be allied with the Dawnguard and complete Dawnguard Main Quest: Prophet.

Durak

Dawnguard Hunter: Archery, One-Handed, Light Armor, Block.

You must be allied with the Dawnguard and complete Dawnguard Main Quest: Prophet.

Ingjard

Dawnguard Warrior: Two-Handed, Heavy Armor, Archery, Block.

You must be allied with the Dawnguard and complete Dawnguard Main Quest: Prophet.

Serana

Vampire Mage: Sneak, One-handed, Light Armor, Conjuration, Destruction, Alteration.

Available once Dawnguard Main Quest: Awakening is complete. For a full rundown of Serana's abilities and strengths, consult the introduction to the Dawnguard Main Quests, on page 512.

Dungeon-Related Followers

The following denizens of the dungeons of Skyrim are available to help your cause once you clear the dungeon in which you find them. Providing they survive. Consult the Dungeon Quests on page 473 for more information.

Illia, Darklight Tower (the Rift)

Mage: Destruction, Restoration, Conjuration, Alteration

Golldir, Hillgrund's Tomb (Whiterun Hold)

Warrior: One-Handed, Heavy Armor, Archery, Block

Favor Followers

The following inhabitants of Skyrim agree to join you once you've befriended them by completing a task or Favor they set for you. Consult Favors (on page 497) for more information.

Ahtar the Jailor, in Solitude's Castle Dour (Haafingar)

Knight: Two-Handed, Heavy Armor, Archery, Block

Benor, the guard lieutenant of Morthal (Hjaalmarch)

Knight: Two-Handed, Heavy Armor, Archery, Block

Cosnach, the drunkard in Markarth (the Reach)

Warrior: One-Handed, Heavy Armor, Archery, Block

Borgakh, the daughter of Bagrak, in Mor Khazgur (the Reach)

Warrior: One-Handed, Heavy Armor, Archery, Sneak

Ghorbash, the brother of the Orc Chief of Dushnikh Yal (the Reach)

Archer: Archery, Light Armor, One-Handed, Block, Sneak

Uthgerd the Unbroken, the brawling warrior of Whiterun (Whiterun Hold)

Warrior: One-Handed, Heavy Armor, Archery, Block

Sven, the minstrel and lumberjack of Riverwood (Whiterun Hold)

Townsperson: Alchemy, Enchanting, Smithing, Archery

Faendal, the hunter and lumberjack of Riverwood (Whiterun Hold)

Archer: Archery, Light Armor, One-Handed, Sneak

Journeyman Trainer: Archery

Roggi Knot-Beard, the Nord miner of Kynesgrove (Eastmarch)

Townsperson: Alchemy, Enchanting, Smithing, One-Handed

Derkeethus, the kidnapped fisherman, held in Darkwater Pass (Eastmarch)

Archer: Archery, Light Armor, One-Handed, Block, Sneak

Annekke Crag-Jumper, the adventuress of Darkwater Crossing (Eastmarch)

Archer: Archery, Light Armor, One-Handed, Block, Sneak

Mjoll the Lioness, adventuress, in Riften (the Rift)

Knight: Two-Handed, Heavy Armor, Archery, Block

Kharjo, the bodyguard for Ahkari's Caravan (Khajiit Caravans)

Warrior: One-Handed, Heavy Armor, Archery, Block

Talvas Fathryon, Master Neloth's apprentice in Tel Mithryn (Solstheim)

Mage: Conjuration, Restoration, Destruction, Alteration, Sneak

Animal Companions

Two-legged, higher-functioning Followers aren't the only ones you can bring with you on adventures. Four-legged friends and other beast or mechanical Followers are also available. The following animal companions can follow, stay, and attack, but they can't carry items:

Vigilance: A war dog you can purchase from Banning at Markarth Stables (in the Reach) for 500 gold.

Meeko: A dog you find in the wilderness close to Meeko's Shack, in Hjaalmarch.

Stray dog: A dog you can meet in a random World Encounter (Corpses in the Aftermath of a Dragon Attack or Dog Fending Off a Pair of Wolves; see page 677).

Armored Frost Troll

In Fort Dawnguard

Frost Troll: Claw and Bite attacks. Animal companion. You must be allied with the Dawnguard and complete Dawnguard Main Quest: A New Order to hire this troll from Gunmar for 500 gold.

Armored Troll

In Fort Dawnguard

Troll: Claw and Bite attacks. Animal companion. You must be allied with the Dawnguard and complete Dawnguard Main Quest: A New Order to hire this troll from Gunmar for 500 gold.

Bran

In Fort Dawnguard

Dawnguard Husky: Bite attacks. Animal companion. You must be allied with the Dawnguard and complete Dawnguard Main Quest: A New Order.

CuSith

In Castle Volkihar

Death Hound: Claw and Bite attacks. Animal Companion. You must be allied with the Volkihar Vampires and complete Dawnguard Main Quest: The Bloodstone Chalice.

Garmr

In Castle Volkihar

Death Hound: Claw and Bite attacks. Animal companion. You must be allied with the Volkihar Vampires and complete Dawnguard Main Quest: The Bloodstone Chalice.

Sceolang

In Fort Dawnguard.

Dawnguard Husky: Claw and Bite attacks. Animal companion. You must be allied with the Dawnguard and complete Dawnguard Main Quest: A New Order.

Steadfast Dwarven Spider: Your prize for completing the first battle in Kagrumez, as part of Solstheim Side Quest: The Challenges of Kagrumez* (see page 650).

Steadfast Dwarven Sphere, your prize for completing the second battle in Kagrumez, as part of Solstheim Side Quest: The Challenges of Kagrumez* (see page 650).

Pets

Finally, if you've built your own dwelling and adopted a small child, they may bring home an animal to play with. These pets aren't cut out for adventuring. See page 130 for more information.

Hares
(adopted girls only)

Mudcrabs
(adopted boys only)

Red Foxes
(adopted girls only)

Skeevers
(adopted boys only)

White Foxes
(adopted girls only)

HORSES

Shadowmere: The ultimate steed of Skyrim?

Horses can be purchased and used by adventurers to quickly travel between far-flung destinations. There are several ways in which you can acquire a horse:

Buying a Horse

You can purchase a horse at the stables adjacent to each of the five major Hold capitals; the four minor Hold capitals (Morthal, Dawnstar, Winterhold, and Falkreath) do not have stables.

Each stable sells a particular type of horse. The price of each horse, regardless of its type, is 1,000 gold pieces. This price is fixed and isn't affected by your Speech skill, Speech perks, or other effects (such as a Potion of Haggling). Horses are all identical in terms of speed, health, and performance; the only difference is their color.

AVAILABLE HORSES

✓	HORSE TYPE	HOLD NAME	LOCATION OF PURCHASE	PRICE
☐	Black	Whiterun Hold	Whiterun Stables	1,000
☐	Brown	Eastmarch	Windhelm Stables	1,000
☐	Gray	The Rift	Riften Stables	1,000
☐	Paint	The Reach	Markarth Stables	1,000
☐	Palomino	Haafingar	Katla's Farm (Solitude)	1,000
☐	Frost	The Rift	Special	N/A
☐	Shadowmere	Falkreath	Special	N/A
☐	Arvak	Soul Cairn	Special	N/A

Owning a Horse

Horses you own are always saddled and have your name added to their title (e.g., "Prisoner's Horse"). This helps you differentiate between your horse and any others that may be around—just look for the name and saddle.

You can own all five types of horses, providing you have the gold to pay for each of them. If you own more than one horse, the horse you've most recently ridden travels with you if you decide to Fast-Travel to a location. All of your other horses return to the stables where you purchased them and wait for you there (you can return and use them whenever you wish).

Borrowing or Stealing a Horse

You can steal horses from several different locations. The best places to look are the stables where you can purchase a steed, any military camp or military fort, and in World Encounters. To steal a horse, simply walk up to it and mount it. Stealing a horse adds 50 to your bounty for that Hold. Dismounting from a stolen steed and then mounting it again counts as a separate theft, adding 50 more gold to your bounty. Horse rustling can get expensive fast.

Occasionally, you can "borrow" an unowned horse (one not marked "Steal") from a location, World Encounter, or military fort. Unowned horses behave in the same manner as stolen horses, except that riding them isn't a crime and your bounty won't increase.

Using a Horse

It is important to learn what you and your steed are capable of. Horses can move at a canter (run) and gallop (sprint) speed equal to your very best run and sprint speeds while on foot. However, horses aren't weighed down by your armor, and they likely have more stamina than you do, making them a faster way to travel overall. Plus, you get to conserve your stamina so you won't be worn out if you find yourself ambushed by brigands on the road.

Horses can charge through or leap over low or small obstacles (essentially anything you could jump across when on foot). Larger obstacles can't be jumped, so avoid them or move around them.

By nature, horses are not aggressive, and although able to attack, they generally flee from combat once you dismount.

Your Followers can't ride horses. If you ride off on horseback, your Follower will run after you but is likely to fall behind. When you approach your destination, you may want to stop and use the Wait command, which will give them a chance to catch up.

Controlling a Horse

When riding a horse, it's important to note the following controls:

The camera is locked into a third-person view, and the View-Switch button centers the camera behind you.

The Activate button allows you to dismount. You must dismount in order to activate objects or speak to others.

The Jump button causes your horse to rear dramatically. You can jump while riding a horse if you're running at a moderate pace.

The Sprint button allows you to gallop.

Fast-Traveling and Horses

If you own one or more horses, the horse you most recently rode will Fast-Travel with you. This is handy if you've lost your horse after a fight or emerged from a dungeon in a different location. Simply Fast-Travel somewhere nearby, and your horse will be standing next to you.

If you're riding a stolen or borrowed horse, your horse will only Fast-Travel with you if you're riding it when you trigger the Fast-Travel. Otherwise, you'll leave it behind.

Horses won't accompany you into cities, dungeons, or other interiors. If you Fast-Travel to a city, your horse will be left at the stables just outside.

The Death of a Horse

While riding a horse, most of the damage from falls and enemy attacks will be absorbed by your horse. When a horse is reduced to 10% of its health or less, it drops you and tries to flee. If your horse takes lethal damage, it will die.

If you own a horse and it expires, a new horse of the same type will become available for purchase at the same stables as previously indicated. The same cannot be said for Frost or Shadowmere; when they expire, it is usually permanent.

Mounted Combat

This information is designed to be read after you've familiarized yourself with the section on Horses (see above).

The ultimate steed and rider of Skyrim: Arvak attacks!

For the warrior, charging a group of bandits on the Whiterun tundra has never been so epic, especially if you're riding a steed and bloodying your blade while on horseback!

The Basics of Mounted Combat

Before you ride off with bludgeoning from horseback on your mind, it's worth having a small amount of practice first and learning the rudimentary rules for fighting from a horse:

You're able to use one-handed weapons, two-handed weapons, or archery (bows/crossbows) in mounted combat. You can't use staffs, torches, shields, or spells of any kind.

Only the weapon equipped in your right hand is used for mounted combat. If you equip a weapon in your left hand, it can't be used.

In mounted combat, you wield two-handed weapons with one hand, but they swing much more slowly than one-handed weapons do. You still can't equip anything in your left hand while using them.

Weapon Attacks

The Left Hand button will use your equipped weapon to attack to the left of the horse. The Right Hand button will use your equipped weapon to attack to the right of the horse. If you hold either the Left or Right Hand buttons, you will draw back and hold your attack until you release the button. This makes it easier to time a "ride-by" attack. This strike is also a power attack (which costs Stamina, hits harder, and does more damage). If you don't have enough Stamina to perform the power attack, you'll just perform a regular attack instead, as you would if fighting on foot.

Bow Attacks

Bow attacks work as usual, although you cannot aim behind you. Archery Perks like Eagle Eye (zoom) and Steady Hand (slow time while aiming) will still work, although Ranger (faster movement speed) will not increase your speed while riding a horse.

The Subtleties of Mounted Combat

Once you're able to maneuver around a group of foes and rip them apart from your steed, consider the following advanced tactics:

If you're wielding a one-handed weapon, equip a shield. Even though you can't actively block with it, the shield still increases your armor rating.

If you're a dual-wielding specialist, don't despair! You may not be able to use your left-hand weapon in mounted combat, but just having it equipped will still allow you to take advantage of the Dual Flurry (faster attack speed) and Dual Savagery (higher power attack damage) Perks, if you have them.

More generally, any One-Handed, Two-Handed, or Archery Perks you have will still apply during mounted combat, although you may not be able to perform certain attacks (such as directional power attacks) while mounted.

You can sprint on the horse while attacking. This doesn't affect your attack in any way (damage, stagger chance, etc.), but it will make it a little easier for you to flee.

During mounted combat, virtually all incoming damage will be absorbed by your horse. While horses have a fair amount of Health (around 300 points), this damage adds up quickly, and you have no way to heal your horse while mounted. If you aren't careful, your horse will die, and replacing horses can get expensive fast. If you plan to use mounted combat extensively, you may wish to consider a more sturdy beast (Shadowmere) or one you can recall if he should die (Arvak).

Mounted combat keeps you and your horse together. Particularly when riding Shadowmere, you may want to consider whether you could be more effective fighting separately.

Advantages of Mounted Combat

Your horse acts as a damage shield, taking almost all of the damage that you would otherwise suffer.

Remaining on horseback allows you to move quickly and make a getaway if the combat turns against you.

Disadvantages of Mounted Combat

Your combat options are much more limited, since you can't block or cast spells. You may find it more difficult to time and aim your attacks.

Once you dismount, most horses will usually flee, although this does distract enemies and absorbs damage from anyone who attacks them.

However, once you dismount, if you're riding Shadowmere (the Dark Brotherhood's special horse), he is free to attack, giving you an extra ally in your fight.

Unique Horses: Arvak, Frost, and Shadowmere

There are three unique horses you may wish to seek out:

Frost: As part of Side Quest: Promises to Keep (page 459), you're tasked with stealing Frost from the Black-Briar Lodge in the Rift. At the end of this quest, you have the option to betray the man who sent you on that mission, Louis Letrush, and keep Frost for yourself. If you do, you gain legal ownership of Frost. Aside from the fact this didn't cost you any gold, Frost is a normal horse in every other respect.

Shadowmere: At the start of Dark Brotherhood Quest: The Cure for Madness (page 327), Astrid—the leader of the Dark Brotherhood—summons Shadowmere, a powerful steed. From this point forward, you have ownership of Shadowmere. In addition to this not costing you any gold, Shadowmere has other advantages:

He has twice the stamina and almost five times the health of a normal horse.

When injured, his health regenerates rapidly, making him extremely difficult for foes to kill.

He is much more aggressive than a normal horse, fighting with you instead of fleeing from danger.

With glowing eyes, a unique saddle, and a jet-black mane, Shadowmere is one of the ultimate steeds of Skyrim!

Arvak: Complete Regional Activities: Soul Cairn: Arvak the Spectral Steed* (see page 573), and find Arvak's Skull within this realm. Return it to the lost soul in the cairn. In gratitude, the soul teaches you a spell that causes Arvak to appear before you.

Summon Arvak to aid you on your travels. Select Magic > Conjuration > Summon Arvak, and with enough Magicka, you can conjure the spectral horse in the Skyrim Exterior, Blackreach, Forgotten Vale Exterior, Soul Cairn, Dayspring Canyon, and Solstheim Exterior.

CARRIAGES AND FERRIES

Carriages: Hold Capital Travel

Travel between Hold capitals in some style and comfort.

If you can't afford a horse, carriages are another good way to quickly travel around Skyrim. Outside each of the five major Hold capitals (generally near the stables), you can find a horse cart hitched up and ready to go. Speak to the driver to learn that he offers a carriage service and will gladly ferry you to any of Skyrim's capitals for a nominal fee:

20 gold for a ride to the major Hold capitals: Solitude, Markarth, Whiterun, Windhelm, or Riften.

50 gold for a ride to the minor Hold capitals: Morthal, Dawnstar, Winterhold, or Falkreath.

If you've constructed Windstad Manor, Heljarchen Hall, or Lakeview Manor, and hired a carriage driver, you can travel between your properties and the Hold capitals free of charge. These carriage drivers can also take you to the smaller settlements (any village, town, or Hold capital).

Pay the fee, then head around back and activate the carriage to climb aboard. The driver will mention a piece of lore as you set off. A moment later, you'll find yourself at your destination.

TIP Is this a good deal? It depends on your play style. If you'd rather walk or ride from one location to another, you may find the journey as rewarding as the destination, with dozens of locations to explore and challenges to face along the way. If you simply want to reach your goal as quickly as possible, a carriage ride will take you to the nearest city in record time. Spend 300 gold, and you can quickly unlock all of the capital cities, allowing you to Fast-Travel to them whenever you wish.

Ferries: Setting Sail

Gort waits patiently on the icy docks of Windhelm for a paying customer.

Are the carriage drivers of Skyrim giving you a bit of backchat? Fed up of buying a horse and having it die in the wilderness? Then why not travel through Skyrim by sea (and specifically, the Sea of Ghosts), courtesy of Skyrim's fledgling Ferry system? Recently launched, there are now ferry boats moored at the docks in Solitude, Dawnstar, and Windhelm:

Jolf is tending to his boat on the edge of the docks at the East Empire Company Warehouse, just south of Solitude.

Harlaug has moored his vessel on the shallow beach close to Silus Vesuius's House in Dawnstar.

Gort is waiting for a paying customer outside Windhelm's gates, down in the dock area, just outside the Clan Shatter-Shield Office.

Speak to the ferryman by each boat, and you're offered a ride to either of the other two cities. The cost is 50 gold. Agree, climb into the boat and sit down, and you appear at the docks (described above) at the city you chose.

In addition, once you complete Dawnguard Main Quest: Awakening, you can ask any ferryman to bring you to Castle Volkihar (Serana's home), although it's described as "an island near the border of High Rock." This startles the ferryman, as they believe the place is cursed and won't take you all the way there; they take you only to Icewater Jetty. The fee for this dangerous journey is 500 gold!

If you haven't already visited Northwatch Keep (for Side Quest: Missing in Action) and can't Fast-Travel anywhere close to Icewater Jetty, the cost may be worth it. Otherwise, you can trek there on foot (although this takes time). From Icewater Jetty, you can take the rowboat out to Castle Volkihar.

The Northern Maiden

Launching from Windhelm Docks, the Northern Maiden makes Raven Rock on the isle of Solstheim its port, transporting people and cargo to and from the mainland. This is the only method of entering the island, and safe passage must be obtained by speaking with the ship's captain, Gjalund Salt-Sage.

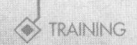

Dragon Taming

Once the Bend Will Shout is learned, you may summon a Dragon instead of battling it. This occurs throughout Skyrim or Solstheim

In order to tame and ride a dragon, you must learn all three words of the Bend Will Shout by completing Dragonborn Main Quest: The Gardener of Men; then unlock them with Dragon Souls in the usual manner. After that, you need to find a dragon:

If you have completed the Main Quest, you can call upon Odahviing, using the Call Dragon Shout.

You can also tame almost any dragon you find in the wild. Dragon lairs or dragon mounds are often the best places to look for them.

The following dragons cannot be tamed or ridden:

- Alduin
- Paarthurnax
- Durnehviir

Use the complete Bend Will Shout on the dragon to tame it. You must use the full Shout (all three words), or it will have no effect.

Dragon Riding

Dragons offer great protection, swift travel, and the ability to Fast-Travel, even during combat!

After you successfully tame a dragon, it will land nearby. Press your **Activate** button or key to mount up and begin riding. While riding a dragon, you can:

Orbit: By default, the dragon will simply begin flying around the immediate area. Enjoy the view—it's often spectacular.

Lock Targets: You can press the **Jump** button or key to enter or exit target-lock mode. While you are in target lock mode:

The name of your current target will be displayed below the compass. Your camera will remain focused on this target as the dragon flies around.

You can cycle between targets with the left and right arrows on your D-pad.

You can order your dragon to attack by pressing the **Sneak** button or key.

You can equip and use most spells and Shouts (those that can't be used will be grayed out). Given the dragon's high rate of speed, only projectile spells and Shouts tend to be effective, though.

Fly to a Destination: While your dragon is flying, you can call up the map to Fast-Travel to almost any location you have discovered. You will arrive still mounted and ready to engage in combat.

While riding a dragon, you can Fast-Travel even while in combat. This makes it easy to escape if the battle is going badly for you. However, you cannot Fast-Travel to some destinations, such as Dragonsreach, in this way and that location will be hidden on your map.

Dismount: When you're ready to move on, press the **Activate** button or key button to order the dragon to land. If you change your mind, you can press the **Activate** button or key again to cancel the landing.

Death from Above: Advice for Proficient Dragon Combat

The might of the Dragonborn wins over this most terrifying of beasts: Sky-bound to victory!

If you use Bend Will on a dragon but decide not to ride it or are at a location where the dragon can't find room to land (such as Deepwood Vale), the dragon will just orbit your position and engage your foes in combat. This is often as (or more) useful than actually riding it—you can't ask for a better ally than a dragon.

If you decide not to ride your dragon, then change your mind, just aim Bend Will at it to get it to land again and allow you to climb on. However, this does **not** extend the duration of the Bend Will effect.

If you choose not to enter Target Lock mode, your dragon can still fight on its own. It will initiate combat if attacked, pick its own targets, and continue fighting until they are defeated. Leaving Target Lock mode does not cause your dragon to break off combat.

When you first enter Target Lock mode, your initial target is either your dragon's current combat target or the nearest available target (if your dragon isn't in combat). The list of available targets does not update, so if more foes join the fray, exit and reenter Target Lock mode to acquire them.

When you use projectile spells or Shouts while in Target Lock mode, you automatically lead your target (aim your shot based on their current movement). Your shots are most accurate when both your target and your dragon are flying in a straight line (or your target is standing still). If you have trouble connecting, choose a spell with an explosive impact, like Fireball.

If your dragon loses too much health, it will land and remain on the ground until it dies or its health recovers enough for it to fly again. If you have the Restoration spell Grand Healing, you can use it to heal both the dragon and yourself.

If you are not riding your dragon, it will fight for you until the Bend Will Shout expires; then it will fly away. If you are riding it, the dragon will never become "untamed," even if the Bend Will effect expires—it will wait until the next time you land, at which point it will immediately fly away.

Once your dragon departs, if you wait around long enough, it may return to its original location (e.g., to its lair), although it will no longer be friendly with you.

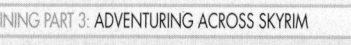

The Gift of Charity

If you give your child an allowance or gift (see below), you receive the Gift of Charity blessing, just as if you had given a coin to a beggar. This is in addition to any other effects the gift may have.

Your Child's Basic Behaviors

Unless you choose to give your child some orders, which supersede these antics, your child makes him or herself at home in your dwelling in a variety of ways: They spend their mornings around the house, sweeping, reading, practicing their instruments, and exploring their new home. After lunch, they go outside and play until dinnertime. In the evenings, if you've given your child a weapon and your house has a practice dummy, they often spar with it. If your child has a doll, they may play with it, too.

Giving Orders: Basic Discipline

When you begin a conversation with your child, you can "request" that he or she follow one particular order. When that order is given, the child obeys it for three hours or until you give them another one. Sometimes, if the order isn't something your child wants to do (such as "chores"), expect a small tantrum or whine. You can relent or insist they complete the task you've given them.

> **NOTE** Orders have a priority: If you give the child a low-priority order ("Go outside"), giving them a higher-priority order ("Go to bed") overrides the lower one. If you give the child a high-priority order, you won't be able to give them a lower-priority order until the higher-priority one expires.

The orders you have available and how they are carried out (along with their priorities) are as follows:

1. **Go Outside:** Available from 6:00 a.m. to 9:00 p.m., if the child is in the house. The child leaves the house and plays outside.
2. **Go Inside:** Available whenever the child is not in the house. The child heads back inside and mopes around.
3. **Do Your Chores:** Available from 6:00 a.m. to 9:00 p.m. The child begins a sweeping regimen throughout the house.
4. **Go to Bed:** Available from 6:00 p.m. to 8:00 a.m., if the child is not already asleep. The child goes to sleep in their bed.

Giving Orders: Games

All work and no play may make your child more prone to tantrums, so it's important to play games with them. This is one of the conversation options and works as follows:

Ask them if they want to play a game. If this occurs at night, your child asks if this is really okay.

Then you can choose either a game of tag or hide-and-seek.

Follow the Miscellaneous Objective prompts and watch out; if other children are present, they can get roped into the game, too!

Asking your child to play a game cancels anything else they are doing; this order has the highest priority. However, once the game is under way, giving your child another order ends the game.

Giving Gifts

Samuel looks smart in his new tunic, but he'd rather be wielding a wooden sword.

Children are happiest when they're preoccupied, ideally with a gift you've picked up on your travels. Such items include:

Children's weapons (daggers or the wooden sword)

Children's clothes (these are gender-specific miscellaneous items)

Children's books (yellow book of riddles, etc.)

Children's toys (a doll)

Sweets (such as a sweetroll or taffy)

Such items are mostly found in shops, though you may find them in cupboard or other containers on your travels. If you're searching for a gift you want to give your child with some urgency, try the following:

Most general goods vendors and miscellaneous containers (such as cupboards) have a chance of having a wooden sword, doll, or children's clothes.

If you visit Radiant Raiment in Solitude, Endarie always has a complete set of children's clothes in stock.

Visit any of the three Khajiit Caravans if you want to buy a wooden sword, doll, or children's clothes.

When you return and give the gift to your child (through conversation), he or she reacts differently depending on the type of gift:

Weapons: They take it immediately (any previously equipped weapon is placed in their bedroom chest). If you have a practice dummy in your house, they run off to spar with it immediately and practice for about an hour. This sparring practice becomes a part of their evening routine.

Clothing: They wear it immediately, and their former clothing is placed in their bedroom chest.

Dolls (girls only): Boys aren't interested in this gift. Your girl plays with the doll for about an hour. It reappears from time to time as a basic behavior as your girl plays with it.

Books: The book is placed in their bedroom chest.

Food: If you hand over some food, they eat it immediately.

> **NOTE** Every gift has an intrinsic value to it. Sometimes your child wants to give you a gift, and the more gifts you give, the better the likelihood of receiving a more impressive gift in return.

Regardless of the gift you hand over, you're rewarded the Gift of Charity blessing: +10 to Speech for one hour.

Your Child's Bedroom Chest

Your child keeps their belongings in a bedroom chest or dresser, which over time fills with items they've collected or that you've given them. You can take whatever you wish from this chest. The child's own items tend to be rudimentary (but sometimes rare) ingredients, small trinkets, and occasionally a valuable [random] item. The quality of their trinkets and the chance of finding a valuable item increases based on the value of the gifts you've given them.

Check this chest once every five days so it keeps refilling. If you move to a different home, your child will start a new collection there (any items in the chest in your old home remain there).

Returning Home and Other Antics

After a particularly arduous quest, returning home to your child (and perhaps your spouse) should be a joy. Or at least a passable way to continue your existence before you're inevitably slain by bandits. Upon your return, expect your child to be eager to interact with you in one of the following (usually randomly determined) ways:

Thanks for Adopting Me!: Your child rushes in to say hello and thanks you for adopting him or her.

Thanks for Adopting Me, Look What I Found!: Your child rushes in to greet you, thanks you for adopting them, and then tells you there's a few items they've collected in their bedroom chest. You can take one or all of them if you'd like.

Look What I Found!: Your child rushes in to tell you he or she has been collecting items and has placed them in their bedroom chest. You can take any of them if you want.

Can We Keep Him?: If your family doesn't already have an animal companion, and you haven't previously banned them and you bring home an animal companion, your child may ask if they can keep the animal when you don't need it. Consult the Hearthfire Pets section below for more details.

It Followed Me Home!: If your family doesn't already have a pet and you haven't previously banned them, there's a chance that your child is waiting for you with a small animal. Your child asks if they can keep it. Consult the Hearthfire Pets section below for more details.

Mudcrabs are smarter than you!: If you have two children, when you arrive home, your children may be calling each other names. If you don't intervene, the argument ends with both children beginning a game of tag. Speak to either child to:

- Break up the argument.
- Order the child you're speaking with to their room.
- Or back off and let the argument continue. The more aggressive child always wins the argument, just like Braith does when she harangues Lars in Whiterun.

You Smell Like a Hagraven!: If you have two children, when you arrive home, they may be calling each other names. If you don't intervene, the argument ends with one of the children running off and crying. They head to their room for an hour. You can:

- Break up the argument.
- Order the child you're speaking with to their room.
- Or back off and let the argument continue.

Can I Have My Allowance?: Your child may run up to you and ask for money. Respond to this mini-shakedown by handing over some of your current gold, which can range from nothing all the way up to 1,000 coins. Any gold is added to your child's personal collection and will raise the value of any items they subsequently find and gift to you.

If you give your child one or more gold, you receive the Gift of Charity blessing. If you fail to give your child any money on three consecutive occasions, the next present they get you may be especially disappointing. They've come to the conclusion that your family is poor, and hand over some beggar's clothing. The cheek of it!

I Got You a Present!: Your child may dash up to you and hand over a gift they've found or bought for you. There's a small [10 percent] chance you'll receive two of the same item. The value of the item depends on the child's personal funds: The larger their allowance, the better the items they get for you. The value of these gifts is also deducted from their savings, so don't expect a one-time allowance to support pricey gifts for long. Over time, this always works out in your favor, so giving your child 30 gold always results in them giving you items worth more than 30 gold.

I Want a Present!: Your child may dash up to you and ask if you've brought them a present. You can:

- Ask what they want, and they point you in the direction of a vendor with the item (usually Radiant Raiment or one of the Khajiit Caravans).
- You can give them a gift, and your child takes it with a gleeful exclamation.
- Or you can refuse to give them a gift, and your child leaves you feeling a little insulted.

Can We Play a Game?: Your child may dash up to you ask if you want to play a game with them. You can answer yes and begin a game of either tag or hide-and-seek. Or, you can answer no (mentioning the hour if it's between 10:00 p.m. and 6:00 a.m.) and your child leaves you feeling a little put out.

Hearthfire Animal Adoption

An added benefit of adoption is that your children can take care of your animals. There are two types of animals they can "adopt": animal companions and pets.

Animal Companions

Bring home a four-legged friend and your child will love him and hug him and squeeze him....

If you bring home an animal companion (such as a dog), your children may ask if they can keep it. You have three options at this point:

If you agree, then later dismiss your animal companion, they will return to the house your children are living in and wait for you there. You can ask them to rejoin you at any time.

If you decline, your children won't ask again for at least 15 days.

If you put your foot down and say no pets, your children will never ask again and will never try to adopt a house pet, either.

You can adopt only one animal companion at a time. If your adopted animal companion is killed, you can adopt a replacement.

> **TIP** If you're trying to get your children to adopt your animal companion but they are engaged in another activity instead, try leaving town and coming back in another day or two. You can't force this.

> **NOTE** Note that some animal companions, such as Armored Trolls and Death Hounds, don't make good pets for children. Your children may react, but they won't ask to keep them.

The following animal companions are available for adoption by your children:

Common dogs: Vigilance, Meeko, Stray Dog.

Dawnguard Huskies: Bran or Sceolang.

Pets

Meet Samuel's pet mudcrab, Mr. Snapper. He was recently saved from the cooking pot.

You're not the only one with a plan to bring home an animal; your children may also be spotted playing with a stray and (as mentioned previous) may ask you whether they can keep them. Your decisions are as follows:

You can agree, and the animal lives in your house, following your child around.

You can refuse, and your child sends the animal away. They won't try to adopt another pet for at least 15 days.

You can refuse with vigor, saying "no pets" firmly. Your child never asks again and won't show interest in adopting an animal companion either! Fine, be like that!

> **NOTE** You can adopt only one pet at a time. If your current pet is killed, you can adopt a replacement. This event has a random chance of occurring, so you can't force it.

The following pets are available for adoption if your children brings one home:

Hares (girls only)	Skeevers (boys only)
Mudcrabs (boys only)	White foxes (girls only)
Red foxes (girls only)	

> Don't kill your pets. If you do, your children will "Never speak to you again." Well, for a day or two. **CAUTION**

THE INVENTORY

INVENTORY OVERVIEW

Behold the charts and tables of Skyrim! The following pages deluge you with information on the thousands of spells, weapons, armor sets, and items that you can acquire during your adventure. If you're interested in the properties of an item you haven't found yet, want to compare it to another item, or simply want to see everything that is possible to find, you'll find the information here.

There are a few general rules you should be aware of before digging in:

As described in the skills section of Training (see page 12), many skills, perks, and enchantments affect the damage you do with weapons, the protection you receive from armor, and the cost of your spells. To account for this, the game automatically calculates those effects and applies them to the spells and items you see in game. The values listed below are the base values for the item in question: you will rarely, if ever, see these exact numbers because of the impact of your skills. But this list is still an effective way of comparing two items to gauge the relative differences between them.

Some items, especially unique weapons and armor, are marked as being Leveled. This means that the actual item you receive in game will be dependent on your level, and may have better statistics and stronger versions of the enchantments listed here.

Some enchantments and effects are said to Stack with others. This means that the benefits of those effects are cumulative; they combine to give you a stronger result.

Color-coding: In the following tables, elements from the original game are in white and gray. Elements from the Dawnguard, Hearthfire, and Dragonborn add-ons have been color-coded as follows:

Wooden Sword Dawnguard/Hearthfire   Ash Shell Dragonborn

SPELLS

Table I: Spells

Spells are an essential tool for many characters, from Arch-mages who have mastered the intricacies of all five Schools of Magic to those that merely dabble in sorcery to suit their needs, such as a Thief who relies on Invisibility, or a Warrior who invokes a healing spell to cure his wounds. This section lists all of the spells available to you. You will find or buy most of these in the form of Spell Tomes, although you may be taught a few of them directly.

Spell List Notes

Only spells that can be used by your character are included on this list. It does not include Powers, such as a Vampire's Embrace of Shadows or a Werewolf's Beast Form, or enemy spells or spell-like effects that you can't acquire.

All Destruction Spells have secondary effects based on their element, regardless of whether those effects are listed in the spell description.

All Fire spells can light enemies on fire, causing your foes to take additional damage for several seconds. This makes fire spells especially effective against foes with high health.

All Frost spells do Stamina damage equal to their Health damage, and slow targets by 50% for several seconds (the exact duration varies by spell). This makes them especially effective against berserkers and other foes who rely on power attacks, shield bashes, and other tactics that depend on stamina.

All Shock spells do Magicka damage equal to half their Health damage (except where otherwise noted). This makes them ideal for crippling enemy mages.

Spell List Key

Spell Name: The name of the spell as it appears in your Magic Menu.

Level: The level of the spell (Novice - Master). Unique or quest-based spells in each School of Magic are included in a 'Special' category at the bottom of the list.

Standard Cost: The cost of the spell after taking the relevant spell level perk, with the minimum skill required to do so. So Novice Spells are displayed at Skill 15, Apprentice at 25, etc. This is the most useful number, as it provides the most realistic basis for cost comparison among spells.

Base Cost: The cost of the spell at skill level 15, with no perks.

Skill 100 Cost: The cost of the spell at skill level 100, after taking all of the spell level perks. This is provided for comparison so you can see how the costs diminish as you become more proficient.

Description: The description of the spell as it appears in your Magic Menu.

Notes and Restrictions: Lists any quests or other significant limiting factors that govern when you can acquire the spell. Also provides clarifications on how the spell works, and tips on using it effectively.

✓	SPELL NAME	LEVEL	STANDARD COST	BASE COST	SKILL 100 COST	DESCRIPTION	NOTES AND RESTRICTIONS
						ALTERATION	
☐	Candlelight	Novice	9	18	6	Creates a hovering light that lasts for 60s.	
☐	Oakflesh	Novice	45	91	30	Improves the caster's armor rating by 40 points for 60s.	
☐	Magelight	Apprentice	35	74	25	Ball of light that lasts 60s and sticks where it strikes.	
☐	Stoneflesh	Apprentice	81	171	57	Improves the caster's armor rating by 60 points for 60s.	
☐	Ash Shell	Adept	93	221	74	Targets that fail to resist are immobilized in hardened ash for 30s.	Sold by Talvas in Tel Mithryn. Ash Shell is effectively a cheaper and weaker form of Paralyze. Foes encased in ash are taken out of the fight, but become immune to damage, preventing you from killing them for the duration.
☐	Detect Life	Adept	37/s	88/s	29/s	Nearby living creatures, but not undead, machines, or daedra, can be seen through walls.	Excellent in stealth situations for keeping track of patrolling guards. The color of the glow indicates whether the creature is hostile towards you.
☐	Ironflesh	Adept	98	235	79	Improves the caster's armor rating by 80 points for 60s.	
☐	Telekenesis	Adept	63/s	149/s	50/s	Can pull an object to you from a distance. Add it to your inventory or throw it.	Great for pulling items off pressure plates from a safe distance, or rearranging items (say, in your house).
☐	Waterbreathing	Adept	82	196	66	Can breathe water for 60s.	Watch for the glow around your body to fade, indicating that the spell has worn off. When it does, you have the equivalent of a full breath (as if you'd just surfaced) before you begin to drown.
☐	Ash Rune	Expert	138	369	124	Cast on a nearby surface, it explodes when enemies are nearby, immobilizing them in hardened ash for 30s.	Sold by Talvas in Tel Mithryn. Ash Rune effectively casts Ash Shell on all enemies within range of the Rune's explosion. Cast it in a hallway before battle to stall pursuers if you need to retreat, or to take a tightly-clustered group of foes out of a larger fight. The Destruction skill's Rune Master perk increases the range of this spell.
☐	Detect Dead	Expert	49/s	130/s	43/s	Nearby dead can be seen through walls.	This spell detects undead and corpses. Great for spotting Draugr lurking in dark catacombs.
☐	Ebonyflesh	Expert	113	300	101	Improves the caster's armor rating by 100 points for 60s.	
☐	Paralyze	Expert	149	396	133	Targets that fail to resist are paralyzed for 10s.	Paralyzed creatures near a ledge will often fall to their deaths.
☐	Dragonhide	Master	248	738	248	Caster ignores 80% of all physical damage for 30s.	Reward for College of Winterhold Radiant Quest: Alteration Ritual Spell.
☐	Mass Paralysis	Master	278	826	278	All targets in the area that fail to resist are paralyzed for 15s.	Sold by Tolfdir, after completing College of Winterhold Radiant Quest: Alteration Ritual Spell.
☐	Equilibrium	Special - Novice	0	0	0	Converts 25 points of health into magicka per second. Caster can be killed by this effect.	Can only be found in Labyrinthian Chasm, during College of Winterhold Quest: The Staff of Magnus, in a side chamber. A risky spell, but it is a fast, low-cost way to recover a lot of Magicka in a hurry.
☐	Transmute	Special - Adept	37	88	29	Transmute one piece of unrefined Iron Ore to Silver, or Silver Ore to Gold, if the caster is carrying any.	This spell is sometimes sold by Enthir, though you can also find copies in Halted Stream Camp, Ansilvund Burial Chamber, and Knifepoint Ridge Mine. Cast this spell twice to transform a piece of Iron Ore (2 gold) to Gold Ore (50 gold). Profit!
						CONJURATION	
☐	Bound Dagger	Novice	23	47	15	Creates a magic dagger for 120s. Sheathe it to dispel.	Sold by Talvas in Tel Mithryn. For half the cost of a Bound Sword, you can get a Bound Dagger that does 2/3 the damage (or more, if you have the dagger-oriented Sneak perks). As with Bound Sword, cast this spell seperately in each hand if you want to dual-wield bound daggers.
☐	Bound Sword	Novice	41	82	27	Creates a magic sword for 120s. Sheathe it to dispel.	Dualcasting this spell does not give you dual bound swords. If that's what you want, cast the spell seperately in each hand.
☐	Conjure Familiar	Novice	47	94	31	Summons a Familiar for 60s wherever the caster is pointing.	
☐	Raise Zombie	Novice	45	90	30	Reanimate a weak dead body to fight for you for 60s.	Works on creatures up to Lv6.
☐	Bound Battleaxe	Apprentice	70	149	50	Creates a magic battle axe for 120s. Sheathe it to dispel.	
☐	Conjure Flame Atronach	Apprentice	62	132	44	Summons a Flame Atronach for 60s wherever the caster is pointing.	Flame Atronachs do good ranged damage, but are fairly weak in melee.
☐	Conjure Boneman	Apprentice	53	113	38	Summons a Boneman Archer from the Soul Cairn for 60s wherever the caster is pointing.	Bonemen have slightly more health than Flame Atronachs but generally do less damage. They are cheaper to cast, though.
☐	Reanimate Corpse	Apprentice	60	127	42	Reanimate a more powerful dead body to fight for you for 60s.	Works on creatures up to Lv13.
☐	Soul Trap	Apprentice	44	94	31	If a target dies within 60s, fills a soul gem.	This spell always places the soul into the smallest soul gem that can hold it. But keep an eye on your soul gem inventory– you don't want to waste a Grand Soul Gem on a Skeever's soul. Remember that human souls can only be captured in Black Soul Gems.
☐	Banish Daedra	Adept	72	173	58	Weaker summoned daedra are sent back to Oblivion.	Only works on conjured daedra (not on 'permanent' ones, like those in some Warlock dungeons). Works on Daedra up to Lv15 (Familiars and Flame Atronachs). In addition to its stated effect, this spell will also stagger any Daedra it hits, making it useful in buying you some space against even higher-level foes.
☐	Bound Bow	Adept	76	183	61	Creates a magic bow for 120s. Sheathe it to dispel.	In addition to the bow, this spell also creates bound arrows that last for the life of the bow.
☐	Conjure Mistman	Adept	71	170	57	Summons a Mistman from the Soul Cairn for 60s wherever the caster is pointing.	Mistmen are frost-based spellcasters with high health.
☐	Conjure Seeker	Adept	58	139	46	Summons a Seeker for 60s wherever the caster is pointing.	Found only in Apocrypha. Seekers attack from range with non-elemental spells that can't be resisted. They are also very durable, with high health and the ability to create distracting illusions.
☐	Conjure Frost Atronach	Adept	79	189	63	Summons a Frost Atronach for 60s wherever the caster is pointing.	Frost Atronachs do good melee damage and have high health, but lack a ranged attack.
☐	Revenant	Adept	68	162	54	Reanimate a powerful dead body to fight for you for 60s.	Works on creatures up to Lv21.
☐	Command Daedra	Expert	80	214	72	Powerful summoned and raised creatures are put under your control.	Only works on conjured daedra (not on 'permanent' ones, like those in many Warlock dungeons). Works on Daedra up to Lv20 (Frost Atronachs and lower).

✓	SPELL NAME	LEVEL	STANDARD COST	BASE COST	SKILL 100 COST	DESCRIPTION	NOTES AND RESTRICTIONS
☐	Conjure Ash Guardian	Expert	112	300	101	Creates an Ash Guardian that guards that location until destroyed. Consumes a heart stone from your inventory, without which it will be hostile.	Sold by Talvas in Tel Mithryn. Ash Guardians are primarily melee combatants, although they do have a short-range ash cloud attack. Make sure you have a Heart Stone in your inventory before casting this spell (or the Guardian will attack you), and be aware that the Guardian will guard the location where you summon it instead of following you.
☐	Conjure Dremora Lord	Expert	118	316	106	Summons a Dremora Lord for 60s.	Dremora Lords are powerful melee combatants with a number of fire spells at their disposal.
☐	Conjure Storm Atronach	Expert	107	284	95	Summons a Storm Atronach for 60s wherever the caster is pointing.	Storm Atronachs are powerful ranged combatants.
☐	Dread Zombie	Expert	100	266	89	Reanimate a very powerful dead body to fight for you for 60s.	Works on creatures up to Lv30.
☐	Expel Daedra	Expert	71	190	64	Powerful summoned daedra creatures are sent back to Oblivion.	Only works on conjured daedra (not on 'permanent' ones, like those in many Warlock dungeons). Works on Daedra up to Lv20 (Frost Atronachs and lower). Staggers any Daedra it hits.
☐	Conjure Wrathman	Expert	99	265	89	Summons a Wrathman from the Soul Cairn for 60s wherever the caster is pointing.	Wrathmen are powerful warriors with almost four times as much health as a Storm Atronach.
☐	Dead Thrall	Master	296	881	296	Reanimate a dead body permanently to fight for you. Only works on people.	Works on creatures up to Lv40.
☐	Flame Thrall	Master	267	793	267	Summons a Flame Atronach permanently.	Reward for College of Winterhold Radiant Quest: Conjuration Ritual Spell. Thralls are stronger versions of the standard atronachs. After casting this spell, consider resting or waiting to recover your magicka.
☐	Frost Thrall	Master	326	969	326	Summons a Frost Atronach permanently.	Sold by Phinis, after completing College of Winterhold Radiant Quest: Conjuration Ritual Spell.
☐	Storm Thrall	Master	356	1057	356	Summons a Storm Atronach permanently.	Sold by Phinis, after completing College of Winterhold Radiant Quest: Conjuration Ritual Spell.
☐	Flaming Familiar	Special - Apprentice	24	50	17	Summons a Flaming Familiar which will charge into battle and explode.	Reward for Dungeon Quest: A Scroll for Anska. The Flaming Familiar will behave like a standard Familiar for a few seconds, then explode for 40 points of damage.
☐	Summon Arniel's Shade	Special - Apprentice	0	0	0	Summons the Shade of Arniel Gane for 60s wherever the caster is pointing.	Reward for College of Winterhold Radiant Quest: Arniel's Endeavor. Arniel's Shade is physically weak, but a powerful spellcaster.
☐	Summon Unbound Dremora	Special - Novice	88	176	59	Summons an unbound Dremora.	Quest spell for College of Winterhold Radiant Quest: Conjuration Ritual Spell. Summons an Unbound Dremora in a specific location for the quest. Otherwise, no effect.
	DESTRUCTION						
☐	Flames	Novice	6/s	13/s	4/s	A gout of fire that does 8 points per second. Targets on fire take extra damage.	Targets on fire take more damage because they're burning; the spell doesn't do bonus damage if they're burning.
☐	Frostbite	Novice	7/s	14/s	4/s	A blast of cold that does 8 points of damage per second to Health and Stamina.	
☐	Sparks	Novice	8/s	16/s	5/s	Lightning that does 8 points of shock damage to Health and Magicka per second.	
☐	Fire Rune	Apprentice	98	207	69	Cast on a nearby surface, it explodes for 50 points of fire damage when enemies come near.	Runes last indefinately, but you can only place one at a time. For best results, place them in a corridor the enemy will have to use, then pull them towards you. In a pinch, you can also cast a rune directly under an enemy to trigger the explosion immediately, although that's less efficient than your other spells.
☐	Firebolt	Apprentice	17	36	12	A blast of fire that does 25 points of damage. Targets on fire take extra damage.	
☐	Freeze	Apprentice	12	26	8	A spike of ice that does 20 points of frost damage to Health and Stamina and slows the target for 15s.	You can only cast this spell while wearing Ahzidal's Ring of Arcana, found in Kolbjorn Barrow. While it does slightly less damage than Ice Spike, it costs only half as much, and slows the target for long enough for you to get away (or back up and cast again). The slow effect does not stack– casting it again on the same enemy just resets the clock.
☐	Frost Rune	Apprentice	122	258	87	Cast on a nearby surface, it explodes for 50 points of frost damage when enemies come near.	
☐	Ice Spike	Apprentice	25	42	14	A spike of ice that does 25 points of frost damage to Health and Stamina.	
☐	Ignite	Apprentice	12	26	8	A blast of flame that sets the target on fire, doing 4 damage per second for 15s.	You can only cast this spell while wearing Ahzidal's Ring of Arcana, found in Kolbjorn Barrow. This spell costs less than Firebolt, and by the end of its duration, does more than twice the damage. This effect does stack (allowing you to accelerate the damage by casting it repeatedly). Ignite also prevents enemies with health regeneration (like Trolls or Karstaag) from regenerating while it lasts.
☐	Lightning Bolt	Apprentice	21	45	15	A bolt of lightning that does 25 points of shock damage to Health and half that to Magicka.	
☐	Lightning Rune	Apprentice	134	284	95	Cast on a nearby surface, it explodes for 50 points of shock damage when enemies come near.	

Alteration Spell: Detect Dead

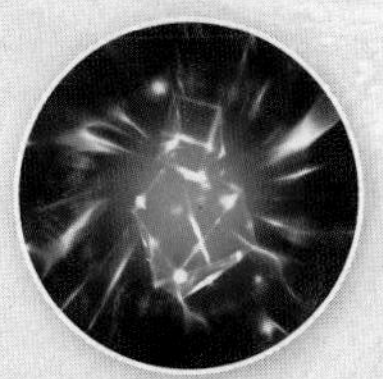
Alteration Spell: Dragonhide

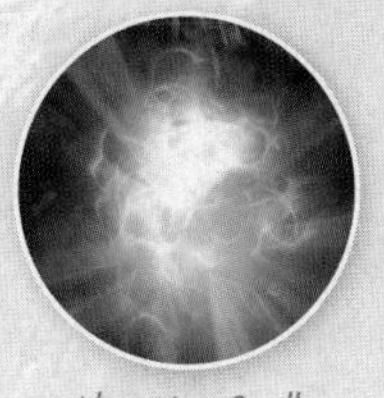
Alteration Spell: Mass Paralysis

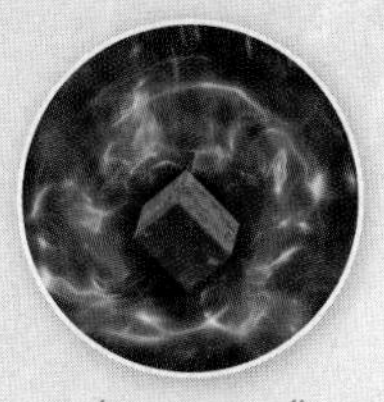
Alteration Spell: Telekinesis

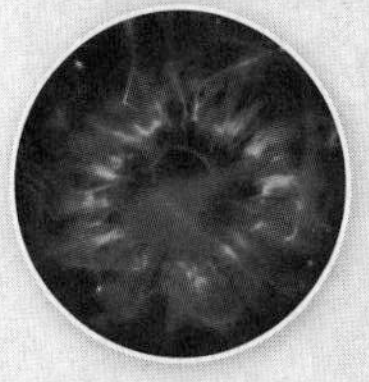
Conjuration Spell: Command Daedra

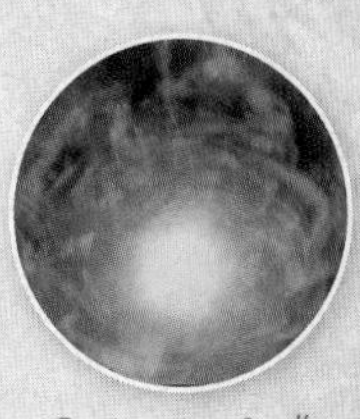
Conjuration Spell: Conjure Ash Guardian

✓	SPELL NAME	LEVEL	STANDARD COST	BASE COST	SKILL 100 COST	DESCRIPTION	NOTES AND RESTRICTIONS
	Chain Lightning	Adept	57	137	46	Lightning bolt that does 40 points of shock damage to Health and half to Magicka, then leaps to a new target.	
	Fireball	Adept	40	117	39	A fiery explosion for 40 points of damage in a 15 foot radius. Targets on fire take extra damage.	
	Flame Cloak	Adept	107	254	85	For 60s, opponents in melee range take 8 points of fire damage per second. Targets on fire take extra damage.	Cloak spells are great if you expect to be in melee frequently, or prefer short-range spells (Flames, Wall of Flames, etc.), as they significantly increase your damage output.
	Frost Cloak	Adept	117	278	93	For 60s, opponents in melee range take 8 points of frost damage and Stamina damage per second.	
	Ice Storm	Adept	53	127	42	A freezing whirlwind that does 40 points of frost damage per second to Health and Stamina.	
	Lightning Cloak	Adept	137	326	110	For 60s, nearby opponents take 8 points of shock damage and half magicka damage.	
	Whirlwind Cloak	Adept	125	298	100	For 60s, opponents in melee range have a chance of being flung away.	Sold by Talvas in Tel Mithryn.
	Icy Spear	Expert	106	282	95	A spear of ice that does 60 points of frost damage to Health and Stamina.	
	Incinerate	Expert	98	262	88	A blast of fire that does 60 points of damage. Targets on fire take extra damage.	
	Thunderbolt	Expert	113	302	101	A Thunderbolt that does 60 points of shock damage to Health and half that to Magicka.	
	Wall of Flames	Expert	39/s	104/s	35/s	Sprayed on the ground, it creates a wall of fire that does 50 points of fire damage per second.	
	Wall of Frost	Expert	45/s	121/s	40/s	Sprayed on the ground, it creates a wall of frost that does 50 points of frost damage per second.	
	Wall of Storms	Expert	48/s	128/s	43/s	Sprayed on the ground, it creates a wall of lightning that does 50 points of shock damage per second.	
	Blizzard	Master	328	975	328	Targets take 20 points of frost damage for 10s, plus Stamina damage.	Sold by Faralda, after completing College of Winterhold Radiant Quest: Destruction Ritual Spell. Damages everything in a large radius around the caster for 10s.
	Fire Storm	Master	423	1257	423	A 100 point firey explosion centered on the caster. Does more damage to closer targets.	Reward for College of Winterhold Radiant Quest: Destruction Ritual Spell. Does extra damage to things closer to the caster.
	Lightning Storm	Master	41/s	122/s	41/s	Target takes 75 points of shock damage per second to Health, and half that to Magicka.	Sold by Faralda, after completing College of Winterhold Radiant Quest: Destruction Ritual Spell. Not an area-of-effect spell, Lightning Storm is a single concentrated bolt that does massive damage and disintegrates targets.
	Arniel's Convection	Special - Novice	1	1	1	Burns the target 1 points per second. Targets on fire take extra damage.	Quest spell for College of Winterhold Radiant Quest: Arniel's Endeavor. Heats Dwarven Convectors for the quest. Otherwise, not especially useful.
	Vampiric Drain	Special - Novice	Varies	Varies	Varies	Absorb health from the target.	A spell unique to Vampires, Vampiric Drain both damages your foes and restores your own health.
						ILLUSION	
	Courage	Novice	17	35	11	Target won't flee for 60s and gets some extra health and stamina.	Best used to strengthen a follower. In a pinch, you can also use it as a cheap way to stop weak enemies from fleeing.
	Clairvoyance	Novice	11/s	22/s	7/s	Shows the path to the current goal.	Clairvoyance isn't a spell you'll need very often, but it can be a real help if you get lost in a dungeon.
	Fury	Novice	29	59	20	Creatures and people up to Lv6 will attack anything nearby for 30s.	Targets a single foe. Best cast at range, since they'll attack anyone nearby indiscriminately, including you.
	Calm	Apprentice	61	129	43	Creatures and people up to Lv9 won't fight for 30s.	Targets a single foe.
	Fear	Apprentice	64	135	45	Creatures and people up to Lv9 flee from combat for 30s.	Targets a single foe.
	Muffle	Apprentice	60	127	42	You move more quietly for 180s.	Silences your movement. Important for stealthy characters, or anyone who wants to try sneaking around while wearing armor.
	Frenzy	Adept	77	184	62	Creatures and people up to Lv14 will attack anyone nearby for 60s.	Targets a single foe.
	Frenzy Rune	Adept	103	245	82	Targets up to Lv20 that fail to resist are frenzied for 30s.	Sold by Talvas in Tel Mithryn. All enemies within range of the Rune's explosion will be frenzied, making this great for getting a tightly-grouped band of enemies to start fighting. Note that the Destruction skill's Rune Master perk increases the range of this spell.
	Rally	Adept	42	100	33	Targets won't flee for 60s and get extra health and stamina.	Targets a single foe.
	Invisibility	Expert	111	295	99	Caster is invisible for 30s. Activating an object or attacking will break the spell.	Another important spell for stealthy characters. Combined with Muffle, you should be able to sneak by most foes without too much difficulty.
	Pacify	Expert	96	256	86	Creatures and people up to Lv20 won't fight for 60s.	Affects all foes in a small area.

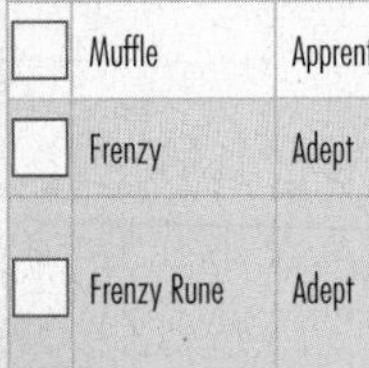

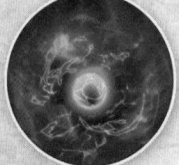

Conjuration Spell: Dead Thrall

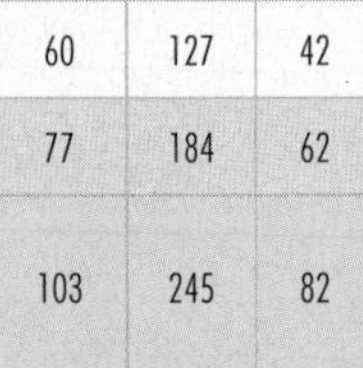

Destruction Spell: Blizzard

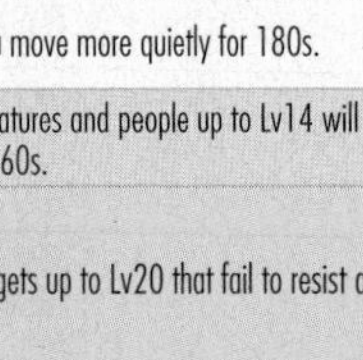

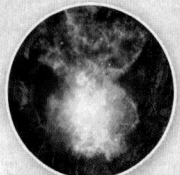

Destruction Spell: Fire Storm

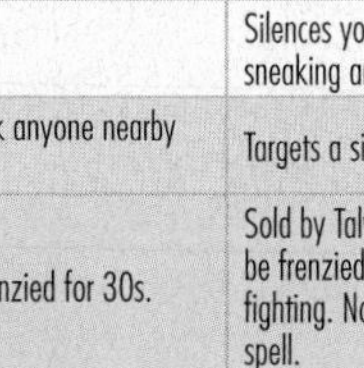

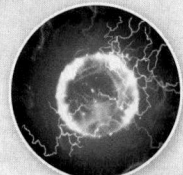

Destruction Spell: Lightning Storm

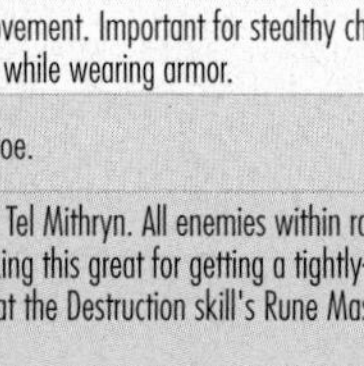

Destruction Spell: Vampiric Drain

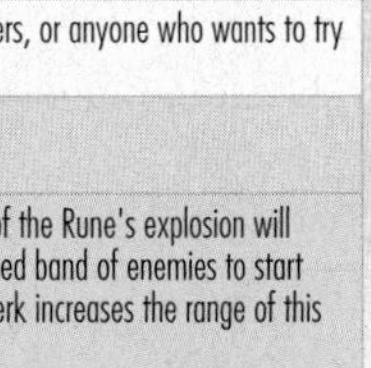

Illusion Spell: Invisibility

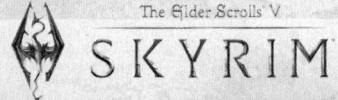

✓	SPELL NAME	LEVEL	STANDARD COST	BASE COST	SKILL 100 COST	DESCRIPTION	NOTES AND RESTRICTIONS
☐	Rout	Expert	104	278	93	Creatures and people up to level 20 flee from combat for 30s.	Affects all foes in a small area.
☐	Call to Arms	Master	194	577	194	Targets have improved combat skills, health, and stamina for 10m.	Sold by Drevis, after completing College of Winterhold Radiant Quest: Illusion Ritual Spell. Affects all allies in a large area.
☐	Harmony	Master	312	927	312	Creatures and people up to Lv25 nearby won't fight for 60s.	Sold by Drevis, after completing College of Winterhold Radiant Quest: Illusion Ritual Spell. Affects all foes in a large area.
☐	Hysteria	Master	257	763	257	Creatures and people up to Lv25 flee from combat for 60s.	Sold by Drevis, after completing College of Winterhold Radiant Quest: Illusion Ritual Spell. Affects all foes in a large area.
☐	Mayhem	Master	294	873	294	Creatures and people up to Lv25 will attack anyone nearby for 60s.	Reward for College of Winterhold Radiant Quest: Illusion Ritual Spell. Affects all foes in a large area.
☐	Vision of the Tenth Eye	Special - Novice	0	0	0	See what others cannot.	Quest spell for College of Winterhold Radiant Quest: Illusion Ritual Spell. Reveals the location of the four Master Illusion Texts needed for the quest; otherwise useless.
						RESTORATION	
☐	Healing	Novice	5/s	11/s	3/s	Heals the caster 10 points per second.	If someone is attacking you, Healing rarely heals enough to keep you from dying. Back away and let a follower or summoned creature step in to buy you some time.
☐	Lesser Ward	Novice	15/s	30/s	10/s	Increases armor rating by 40 points and negates up to 40 points of spell damage or effects.	A Ward's armor bonus stacks with the Alteration line of 'flesh' spells for an even stronger defense. Wards are far more effective against spells, although they tie up a hand and cost more to maintain.
☐	Fast Healing	Apprentice	30	65	21	Heals the caster 50 points.	Direct healing spells are less efficient than heal-over-time spells, but they're faster, and may be fast enough to pull you back from the brink of death in a close battle.
☐	Healing Hands	Apprentice	10/s	22/s	7/s	Heals the target 10 points per second, but not undead, atronachs, or machines.	
☐	Necromantic Healing	Apprentice	15/s	33/s	11/s	Heals the undead target 10 points per second, but not the living, Atronachs, or machines.	Allows you to heal Serana or your resurrected minions.
☐	Steadfast Ward	Apprentice	24/s	51/s	17/s	Increases armor rating by 60 points and negates up to 60 points of spell damage or effects.	
☐	Sun Fire	Apprentice	10	21	7	Ball of sunlight that does 25 points of damage to undead.	Firebolt costs about the same as Sun Fire and generally does more damage to undead because of their weakness to fire.
☐	Turn Lesser Undead	Apprentice	35	74	24	Undead up to Lv6 flee for 30s.	Targets a single foe.
☐	Close Wounds	Adept	46	111	37	Heals the caster 100 points.	
☐	Greater Ward	Adept	32/s	76/s	25/s	Increases armor rating by 80 points and negates up to 80 points of spell damage or effects.	
☐	Heal Other	Adept	29	71	24	Heals the target 75 points, but not undead, atronachs, or machines.	
☐	Heal Undead	Adept	42	101	34	Heals the undead target 75 points but not the living, Atronachs, or machines.	Heal Undead has a higher casting cost but is significantly more efficient than Necromantic Healing.
☐	Poison Rune	Adept	91	217	73	Targets that fail to resist take 3 poison damage per second for 30s.	Sold by Talvas in Tel Mithryn. Before using this spell, consult the Bestiary for more information on which enemies are immune or resistant to poison. Note that the Destruction skill's Rune Master perk increases the range of this spell.
☐	Repel Lesser Undead	Adept	42	101	34	All affected undead up to level 8 flee for 30s.	Affects all undead in the arc of fire.
☐	Stendarr's Aura	Adept	92	219	73	For 60s, undead in melee range take 10 points of sun damage per second.	A slightly cheaper alternative to Flame Cloak if you're fighting undead.
☐	Turn Undead	Adept	62	148	50	Undead up to Lv13 flee for 30s.	Targets a single foe.
☐	Vampire's Bane	Adept	26	63	21	Sunlight explosion that does 40 points of damage in a 15-foot radius to undead.	Fireball is slightly more expensive but has the same radius and generally does more damage to undead.
☐	Circle of Protection	Expert	56	151	50	Undead up to Lv30 entering the circle will flee.	Creates a warding circle around the location where the spell is cast.
☐	Grand Healing	Expert	84	224	75	Heals everyone close to the caster 200 points.	Does not heal Daedra, Automatons, or Undead. But it can heal other enemies, so use this carefully.
☐	Repel Undead	Expert	117	311	105	All affected undead up to Lv16 flee for 30s.	Affects all undead in the arc of fire.
☐	Turn Greater Undead	Expert	88	235	79	Undead up to Lv21 flee for 30s.	Targets a single foe.
☐	Bane of the Undead	Master	293	871	293	Sets undead up to Lv30 on fire and makes them flee for 30s.	Reward for College of Winterhold Radiant Quest: Restoration Ritual Spell. Affects all nearby undead in a large area.
☐	Guardian Circle	Master	212	632	212	Undead up to Lv35 entering the circle will flee. Caster heals 20 health per second inside it.	Sold by Colette, after completing College of Winterhold Radiant Quest: Restoration Ritual Spell. Creates a warding circle around the location where the spell is cast.

Illusion Spell: Mayhem

Illusion Spell: Muffle

Restoration Spell: Bane of the Undead

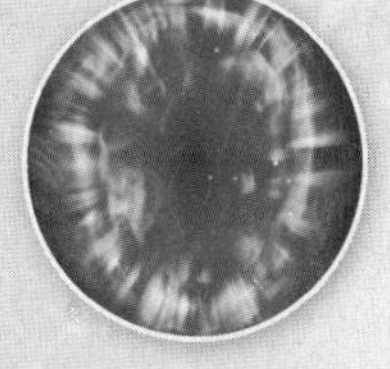
Restoration Spell: Greater Ward

Restoration Spell: Guardian Circle

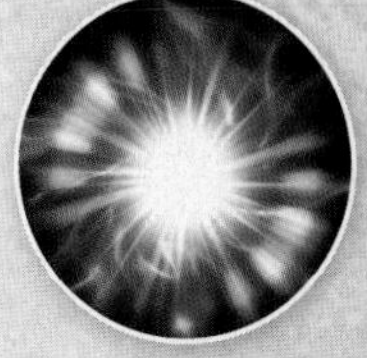
Restoration Spell: Vampire's Bane

Table II: General Data

Weapon Base Properties

This section lists the relative speed and stagger chance for each type of weapon, allowing you to choose the one best suited to your needs.

Standard Weapon, Heavy Armor, and Light Armor Progression

This section lists the standard weapon and armor materials in order of increasing value and damage/armor rating.

For each material, the table identifies the level at which it normally begins to appear.

- You can obtain items earlier than the indicated level in a variety of ways, such as aggressively increasing your Smithing Skill, discovering an exceptional item in a treasure chest, or clearing a dungeon well above your current level.
- Non-enchanted items show up at lower levels than their enchanted versions. Typically, enchanted items show up ~1-5 levels after the stated 'Commonly Available' level.

For each material, the level of the enchantments typically found on it are also listed. This is always a range, corresponding to the 'Enchantment Level' column in the Derived Enchantments Table. So, for example:

- Orcish Swords can be found with Ench Level 2-4 enchantments. So you might find an Orcish Sword of Flames (Fire Damage Ench Level 4), but never an Orcish Sword of the Inferno (Fire Damage Ench Level 6).
- Dragonscale Boots can be found with level 4-6 enchantments. So you might find a Dragonscale Boots of the Ox (Carry Weight Ench Level 5), but never a Dragonscale Boots of Lifting (Carry Weight Ench Level 1).

This range does not restrict the kinds of items you can enchant. So while you're never given an Orcish Sword of the Inferno, you could enchant an Orcish Sword with a comparable fire enchantment if you really wanted to.

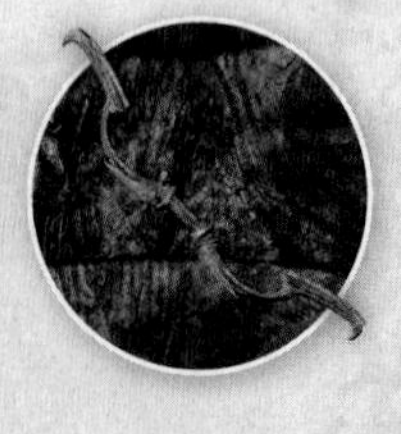

Bow: Dwarven Black Bow of Fate

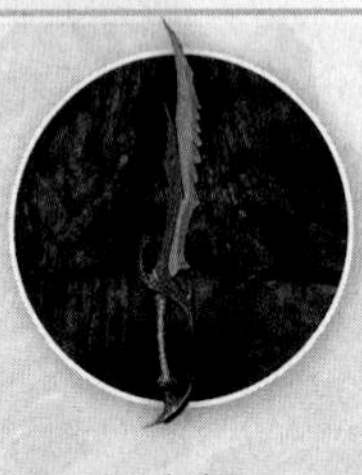

One-Handed Weapon: Daedric Sword

One-Handed Weapon: Dragonborn Mace

One-Handed Weapon: Glass War Axe

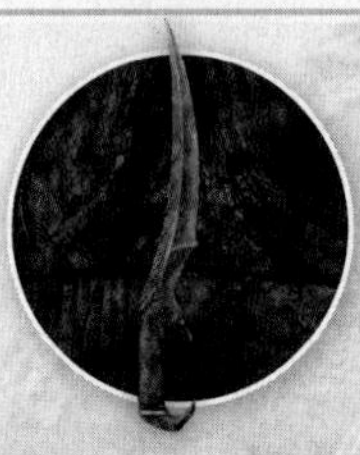

One-Handed Weapon: Blade of Woe

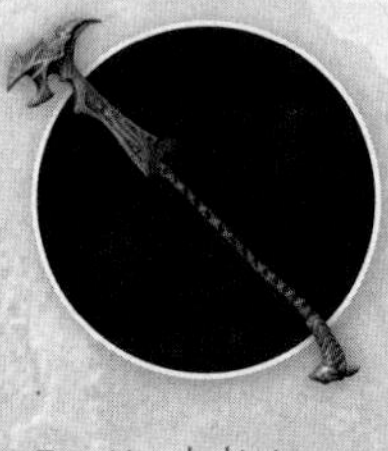

Two-Handed Weapon: The Longhammer

Weapon Type	Relative Speed	Stagger Chance
WEAPON BASE PROPERTIES		
Dagger	Fastest	None
Sword	↓	Lowest
War Axe		↑
Mace		
Greatsword		
Battleaxe		
Warhammer	Slowest	Highest

Material	Commonly Available	Enchantment Levels
STANDARD HEAVY ARMOR PROGRESSION		
Iron	Lv 1	1-3
Bonemold	Lv 1	1-3
Steel	Lv 6	1-3
Dwarven	Lv 12	2-4
Chitin Heavy	Lv 17	2-4
Steel Plate	Lv 18	2-4
Nordic	Lv 24	3-5
Orcish	Lv 25	3-5
Ebony	Lv 32	3-5
Stalhrim	Lv 39	4-6
Dragonplate	Lv 40	4-6
Daedric	Lv 48	4-6

Material	Commonly Available	Enchantment Levels
STANDARD WEAPON PROGRESSION		
Iron	Lv 1	1-3
Steel	Lv 2	1-3
Orcish	Lv 6	2-4
Dwarven	Lv 12	2-4
Nordic	Lv 18	3-5
Elven	Lv 19	3-5
Glass	Lv 27	3-5
Stalhrim	Lv 35	4-6
Ebony	Lv 36	4-6
Daedric	Lv 46	4-6
Dragonbone	Lv 46	None

Material	Commonly Available	Enchantment Levels
STANDARD LIGHT ARMOR PROGRESSION		
Hide	Lv 1	1-3
Leather	Lv 6	1-3
Chitin	Lv 11	2-4
Elven	Lv 12	2-4
Scaled	Lv 27	2-4
Stalhrim Light	Lv 35	3-5
Glass	Lv 36	3-5
Dragonscale	Lv 48	4-6

Table III: Weapons

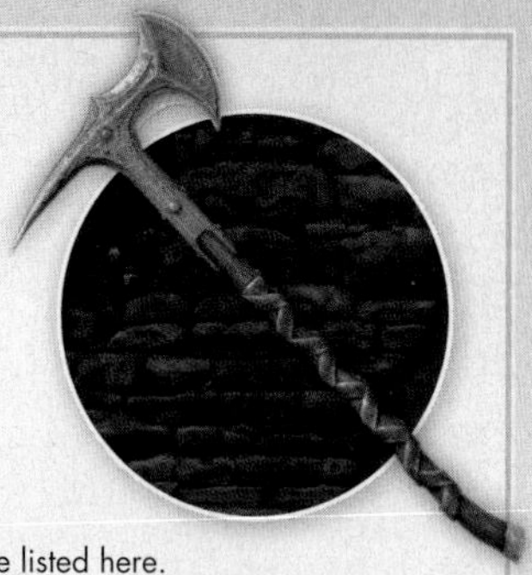

This section lists all of the weapons in the game and their properties.

The critical damage of all weapons is always equal to half their base damage, rounded down.

Weapons marked "Uses [Material] enchant list" have the same enchantment levels as an item of the indicated material type.

Enchanted weapons will have a higher value than shown here. The additional value added by the enchantment depends on the type and strength of the enchantment.

Weapons marked "Leveled" have several different leveled variants; you will always receive the one most appropriate to your level. Higher-level versions may have better statistics and stronger enchantments than the example listed here.

All weapons with the exception of Unique Weapons (of any type) can be found in a variety of locations throughout the world. Unique Weapons are tracked in the Atlas Chapter (page 685) and Appendices of this guide. Note that unique items typically can't be disenchanted unless their enchantment is one of the base enchantments.

✓	NAME	DAMAGE	WEIGHT	VALUE
	STANDARD ONE-HANDED WEAPONS			
	Iron Dagger	4	2	10
	Iron Mace	9	13	35
	Iron Sword	7	9	25
	Iron War Axe	8	11	30
	Steel Dagger	5	2.5	18
	Steel Mace	10	14	65
	Steel Sword	8	10	45
	Steel War Axe	9	12	55
	Orcish Dagger	6	3	30
	Orcish Mace	11	15	105
	Orcish Sword	9	11	75
	Orcish War Axe	10	13	90
	Dwarven Dagger	7	3.5	55
	Dwarven Mace	12	16	190
	Dwarven Sword	10	12	135
	Dwarven War Axe	11	14	165
	Elven Dagger	8	4	95
	Elven Mace	13	17	330
	Elven Sword	11	13	235
	Elven War Axe	12	15	280
	Nordic Dagger	8	3.5	115
	Nordic Mace	13	16	410
	Nordic Sword	11	12	290
	Nordic War Axe	12	14	350
	Glass Dagger	9	4.5	165
	Glass Mace	14	18	575
	Glass Sword	12	14	410
	Glass War Axe	13	16	490
	Ebony Dagger	10	5	290
	Ebony Mace	16	19	1000
	Ebony Sword	13	15	720
	Ebony War Axe	15	17	865
	Stalhrim Dagger	10	4.5	395
	Stalhrim Mace	16	18	1375
	Stalhrim Sword	13	14	985
	Stalhrim War Axe	15	16	1180
	Daedric Dagger	11	6	500

✓	NAME	DAMAGE	WEIGHT	VALUE
	Daedric Mace	16	20	1750
	Daedric Sword	14	16	1250
	Daedric War Axe	15	18	1500
	Dragonbone Dagger	12	6.5	600
	Dragonbone Mace	17	22	2000
	Dragonbone Sword	15	19	1500
	Dragonbone War Axe	16	21	1700
	STANDARD TWO-HANDED WEAPONS			
	Iron Battleaxe	16	20	55
	Iron Greatsword	15	16	50
	Iron Warhammer	18	24	60
	Steel Battleaxe	18	21	100
	Steel Greatsword	17	17	90
	Steel Warhammer	20	25	110
	Orcish Battleaxe	19	25	165
	Orcish Greatsword	18	18	75
	Orcish Warhammer	21	26	180
	Dwarven Battleaxe	20	23	300
	Dwarven Greatsword	19	19	270
	Dwarven Warhammer	22	27	325
	Elven Battleaxe	21	24	520
	Elven Greatsword	20	20	470
	Elven Warhammer	23	28	565
	Nordic Battleaxe	21	23	650
	Nordic Greatsword	20	19	585
	Nordic Warhammer	23	27	700
	Glass Battleaxe	22	25	900
	Glass Greatsword	21	22	820
	Glass Warhammer	24	29	985
	Ebony Battleaxe	23	26	1585
	Ebony Greatsword	22	22	1440
	Ebony Warhammer	25	30	1725
	Stalhrim Battleaxe	24	25	2150
	Stalhrim Greatsword	23	21	1970
	Stalhrim Warhammer	26	29	2850
	Daedric Battleaxe	25	27	2750
	Daedric Greatsword	24	23	2500
	Daedric Warhammer	27	31	4000

✓	NAME	DAMAGE	WEIGHT	VALUE
	Dragonbone Battleaxe	26	30	3000
	Dragonbone Greatsword	25	27	2725
	Dragonbone Warhammer	28	33	4275
	STANDARD BOWS			
	Long Bow	6	5	30
	Hunting Bow	7	7	50
	Orcish Bow	10	9	150
	Dwarven Bow	12	10	270
	Elven Bow	13	12	470
	Nordic Bow	13	11	580
	Glass Bow	15	14	820
	Ebony Bow	17	16	1440
	Stalhrim Bow	17	15	1800
	Daedric Bow	19	18	2500
	Dragonbone Bow	20	20	2725
	ARROWS			
	Iron Arrow	8	0	1
	Steel Arrow	10	0	2
	Orcish Arrow	12	0	3
	Nordic Arrow	12	0	3
	Dwarven Arrow	14	0	4
	Elven Arrow	16	0	5
	Glass Arrow	18	0	6
	Ebony Arrow	20	0	7
	Stalhrim Arrow	20	0	7
	Daedric Arrow	24	0	8
	Dragonbone Arrow	25	0	9
	CROSSBOWS			
	Crossbow	19	14	120
	*Note: Uses Iron enchant list.			
	Enhanced Crossbow	19	15	200
	*Note: Attacks with this crossbow ignore 50% of armor. Can still be enchanted.			
	Dwarven Crossbow	22	20	350
	*Note: Uses Elven enchant list.			
	Enhanced Dwarven Crossbow	22	21	550
	*Note: Attacks with this crossbow ignore 50% of Armor. Can still be enchanted.			

✓	NAME	DAMAGE	WEIGHT	VALUE
	BOLTS			
	Steel Bolt	10	0	1
	Exploding Steel Bolt of Fire	10	0	5
	*Note: Explodes for 10 points of fire damage.			
	Exploding Steel Bolt of Ice	10	0	5
	*Note: Explodes for 10 points of frost damage to Health and Stamina.			
	Exploding Steel Bolt of Shock	10	0	5
	*Note: Explodes for 10 points of shock damage to Health and half that to Magicka.			
	Dwarven Bolt	14	0	3
	Exploding Dwarven Bolt of Fire	14	0	15
	*Note: Explodes for 15 points of fire damage.			
	Exploding Dwarven Bolt of Ice	14	0	15
	*Note: Explodes for 15 points of frost damage to Health and Stamina.			
	Exploding Dwarven Bolt of Shock	14	0	15
	*Note: Explodes for 15 points of shock damage to Health and half that to Magicka.			
	SKYFORGE WEAPONS			
	Skyforge Steel Battleaxe*	23	23	150
	Skyforge Steel Dagger*	8	2.5	25
	Skyforge Steel Greatsword*	19	17	140
	Skyforge Steel Sword*	10	10	70
	Skyforge Steel War Axe*	14	12	80
	*Note: Sold only at Skyforge.			
	Nord Hero Battle Axe*	18	22	28
	Nord Hero Bow*	8	12	45
	Nord Hero Greatsword*	17	18	35
	Nord Hero Sword*	8	12	13
	Nord Hero War Axe*	9	14	15
	*Note: Can forge at Skyforge after Glory of the Dead.			
	ENEMY / FACTION-SPECIFIC WEAPONS			
	Ancient Nord Battle Axe*	18	22	28

✓	NAME	DAMAGE	WEIGHT	VALUE
☐	Ancient Nord Greatsword*	17	18	35
☐	Ancient Nord Sword*	8	12	13
☐	Ancient Nord War Axe*	9	14	15
☐	Ancient Nord Bow*	8	12	45
☐	Dawnguard War Axe	11	13	55
	*Note: Does additional damage to vampires (+5). Can still be enchanted.			
☐	Dawnguard Warhammer	22	26	110
	*Note: Does additional damage to vampires (+5). Can still be enchanted.			
☐	Honed Ancient Nord Battle Axe*	21	25	50
☐	Honed Ancient Nord Greatsword*	20	21	63
☐	Honed Ancient Nord Sword*	11	15	23
☐	Honed Ancient Nord War Axe*	12	16	27
☐	Supple Ancient Nord Bow*	14	18	235
	*Note: Uses Iron enchant list.			
☐	Ancient Nord Arrow	10	0	1
☐	Dragon Priest Dagger	6	5	9
☐	Falmer Bow	12	15	135
☐	Falmer Sword	10	18	67
☐	Falmer War Axe	11	21	82
☐	Falmer Supple Bow	15	20	410

✓	NAME	DAMAGE	WEIGHT	VALUE
☐	Falmer Arrow	7	0	1
☐	Honed Falmer Sword	12	18	205
☐	Honed Falmer War Axe	13	21	245
☐	Forsworn Axe	14	14	81
☐	Forsworn Bow	8	9	95
☐	Forsworn Sword	8	12	5
☐	Forsworn Arrow	7	0	1
☐	Riekling Spear	10	0	2
☐	Silver Greatsword	17	12	160
☐	Silver Sword	8	7	100
☐	Imperial Bow*	9	8	90
☐	Imperial Sword*	8	10	23
	*Note: Uses Iron enchant list.			
	OTHER WEAPONS & TOOLS			
☐	Ancient Nordic Pickaxe	5	10	500
☐	Blades Sword	11	10	300
☐	Pickaxe	5	10	5
	Note: Required to mine ore.			
☐	Scimitar	11	10	5
☐	Woodcutter's Axe	5	10	5
	Note: Required to chop wood.			
	CHILDREN'S TOYS (HEARTHFIRE)			
☐	Wooden Sword	2	3	25

✓	NAME	DAMAGE	WEIGHT	VALUE	ENCHANTMENT	NOTES
	STAFFS					
☐	Forsworn Staff	0	8	183	Flames	
☐	Grand Staff of Charming	0	8	1393	Calm	
☐	Grand Staff of Repulsion	0	8	1289	Repel Undead	
☐	Grand Staff of Turning	0	8	1520	Turn Greater Undead	
☐	Minor Staff of Turning	0	8	556	Turn Lesser Undead	
☐	Staff of Banishing	0	8	926	Banish Daedra	
☐	Staff of Chain Lightning	0	8	1494	Chain Lightning	
☐	Staff of Chain Lightning, Falmer	0	8	1,494	Chain Lightning	
☐	Staff of Calm	0	8	1153	Calm	
☐	Staff of Courage	0	8	79	Courage	
☐	Staff of Daedric Command	0	8	2307	Command Daedra	
☐	Staff of Dread Zombies	0	8	1248	Dread Zombie	
☐	Staff of Expulsion	0	8	2092	Expel Daedra	
☐	Staff of Fear	0	8	2443	Fear	
☐	Staff of Fireballs	0	8	1309	Fireball	
☐	Staff of Fireballs, Falmer	0	8	1,309	Fireball	
☐	Staff of Firebolts	0	8	456	Firebolt	
☐	Staff of Firebolts, Falmer	0	8	396	Firebolt	
☐	Staff of the Flame Atronach, Falmer	0	8	727	Conjure Flame Atronach	
☐	Staff of Flames	0	8	183	Flames	
☐	Staff of Frenzy	0	8	1149	Frenzy	
☐	Staff of Frostbite	0	8	198	Frostbite	
☐	Staff of Fury	0	8	803	Fury	

✓	NAME	DAMAGE	WEIGHT	VALUE	ENCHANTMENT	NOTES
☐	Staff of Ice Spikes	0	8	511	Ice Spike	
☐	Staff of Ice Storms	0	8	1401	Ice Storm	
☐	Staff of Icy Spear	0	8	2931	Icy Spear	
☐	Staff of Ice Spikes, Falmer	0	8	511	Ice Spike	
☐	Staff of Ice Storms, Falmer	0	8	1,401	Ice Storm	
☐	Staff of Incineration	0	8	2750	Incinerate	
☐	Staff of Inspiration	0	8	317	Rally	
☐	Staff of Lightning Bolts	0	8	538	Lightning Bolt	
☐	Staff of Lightning Bolts, Falmer	0	8	538	Lightning Bolt	
☐	Staff of Magelight	0	8	239	Magelight	
☐	Staff of Mending	0	8	613	Heal Other	
☐	Staff of Paralysis	0	8	3965	Paralyze	
☐	Staff of Reanimation	0	8	949	Reanimate Corpse	
☐	Staff of Repulsion	0	8	675	Repel Lesser Undead	
☐	Staff of Revenants	0	8	824	Revenant	
☐	Staff of Soul Trapping	0	8	986	Soul Trap	
☐	Staff of Sparks	0	8	218	Sparks	
☐	Staff of the Familiar	0	8	926	Conjure Familiar	
☐	Staff of the Flame Atronach	0	8	727	Conjure Flame Atronach	
☐	Staff of the Flame Wall	0	8	1310	Wall of Flames	
☐	Staff of the Frost Atronach	0	8	1106	Conjure Frost Atronach	
☐	Staff of the Frost Atronach, Falmer	0	8	1,106	Conjure Frost Atronach	
☐	Staff of the Frost Wall	0	8	1468	Wall of Frost	
☐	Staff of the Healing Hand	0	8	198	Healing Hands	
☐	Staff of the Storm Atronach	0	8	1656	Conjure Storm Atronach	
☐	Staff of the Storm Wall	0	8	1531	Wall of Storms	
☐	Staff of Thunderbolts	0	8	778	Thunderbolt	
☐	Staff of Turning	0	8	1036	Turn Undead	
☐	Staff of Vanquishment	0	8	1807	Rout	
☐	Staff of Zombies	0	8	449	Raise Zombie	
	UNIQUE WEAPONS - DUNGEONS					
☐	Aegisbane	18	24	135	Frost Damage 5	
☐	Angi's Bow	7	7	50		
☐	Bloodthorn	5	2.5	183	Soul Trap	
☐	Bolar's Oathblade	11	10	1014	Damage Stamina 25, Fear	
☐	Borvir's Dagger	8	4	18		
☐	Bow of the Hunt	10	7	434	+20 Damage to Animals	
☐	Ceremonial Axe	9	14	5		
☐	Ceremonial Sword	8	12	5		
☐	Dragon Priest Staff	0	8	1570	Wall of Flames	
☐	Dragon Priest Staff	0	8	1431	Wall of Storms	
☐	Drainblood Battleaxe	21	5	266	Absorb Health 15	
☐	Drainheart Sword	11	3	73	Absorb Stamina 15	
☐	Drainspell Bow	14	6	458	Absorb Magicka 15	
☐	Eduj	11	9	300	Frost Damage 10	
☐	Eye of Melka	0	8	1234	Fireball	
☐	Froki's Bow	6	5	307	Damage Stamina 10	
☐	Gadnor's Staff of Charming	0	8	803	Fury	
☐	Gauldur Blackblade	8	12	234	Absorb Health	Leveled
☐	Gauldur Blackbow	14	18	750	Absorb Magicka	Leveled
☐	Ghostblade	8	1	300	+3 Damage (Ignores Armor)	
☐	Halldir's Staff	0	8	1874	Calm & Soul Trap	

✓	NAME	DAMAGE	WEIGHT	VALUE	ENCHANTMENT	NOTES
☐	Hevnoraak's Staff	0	8	1791	Wall of Storms	
☐	Lunar Iron Mace	9	13	99	Bonus Fire Damage at Night	Leveled
☐	Lunar Iron Sword	7	9	89	Bonus Fire Damage at Night	Leveled
☐	Lunar Iron War Axe	8	11	94	Bonus Fire Damage at Night	Leveled
☐	Lunar Steel Mace	10	14	129	Bonus Fire Damage at Night	Leveled
☐	Lunar Steel Sword	8	10	69	Bonus Fire Damage at Night	Leveled
☐	Lunar Steel War Axe	9	12	119	Bonus Fire Damage at Night	Leveled
☐	Notched Pickaxe	5	10	303	Fortify Smithing 5, Shock Damage 5	Can be used to mine ore.
☐	Okin	12	11	320	Frost Damage 10	
☐	Poacher's Axe	5	10	31	+3 Damage to Animals	
☐	Red Eagle's Bane	11	15	345	Burn Undead, Turn Undead	
☐	Red Eagle's Fury	8	12	97	Fire Damage 5	
☐	Rundi's Dagger	5	2.5	18		
☐	Spider Control Rod	1	8	153	Place Spider Beacon	
☐	Staff of Hag's Wrath	0	8	1310	Wall of Flames	
☐	Staff of Jyrik Gauldurson	0	8	594	Lightning Bolt	
☐	Steel Battleaxe of Fiery Souls	18	21	320	Soul Trap, Fire Damage 10	
☐	The Longhammer	21	18	90	Faster swings	
☐	The Pale Blade	8	12	169	Frost Damage, Fear	Leveled
☐	The Woodsman's Friend	17	20	28		
☐	Trollsbane	20	25	121	Fire Damage 15 to Trolls	
☐	Windshear	11	10	40	Knockdown on Bash 60%	
	UNIQUE WEAPONS - QUEST REWARDS					
☐	Blade of Woe	12	7	880	Absorb Health 10	
☐	Chillrend	10	11	552	Frost Damage, Paralyze	Leveled
☐	Dragonbane	10	10	789	Shock Damage, Bonus Damage to Dragons	Leveled
☐	Firiniel's End	13	12	785	Frost Damage 20	

✓	NAME	DAMAGE	WEIGHT	VALUE	ENCHANTMENT	NOTES
☐	Keening	8	4	13	Absorb Health, Magicka, Stamina 10	
☐	Nightingale Blade	10	11	426	Absorb Health, Absorb Stamina	Leveled
☐	Nightingale Bow	12	9	493	Frost Damage, Shock Damage	Leveled
☐	Shiv	5	2	5		
☐	Staff of Magnus	0	8	1468	Absorb Magicka, then Health	
☐	The Rueful Axe	22	10	1183	Damage Stamina 20	
☐	Valdr's Lucky Dagger	5	2.5	15	25% Critical Hit Chance	
☐	Wuuthrad	25	25	2000	1.2x Damage to Elves	
	UNIQUE WEAPONS - QUEST ITEMS					
☐	Alessandra's Dagger	5	1	10		
☐	Amren's Family Sword	7	9	25		
☐	Balgruuf's Greatsword	17	17	200		
☐	Blade of Sacrifice	10	4	144		
☐	Broken Staff	17	10	5		
☐	Dravin's Bow	8	7	50		
☐	Ghorbash's Ancestral Axe	8	11	30		
☐	Grimsever	12	14	727	Frost Damage 15	
☐	Headsman's Axe	17	11	15		
☐	Hjalti's Sword	8	12	13		
☐	Kahvozein's Fang	6	5	9		
☐	Nettlebane	6	10	5		
☐	Queen Freydis's Sword	8	10	45		
☐	Rusty Mace	7	13	5		
☐	Shagrol's Warhammer	21	26	200		
☐	Staff of Arcane Authority	0	8	2443	Fear	
☐	Staff of Tandil	0	8	2530	Mass Calm	
☐	Steel Sword	8	10	23		

✓	NAME	DAMAGE	WEIGHT	VALUE	ENCHANTMENT
	UNIQUE WEAPONS - DAWNGUARD				
☐	Aetherial Staff	0	8	1,970	Summon a Dwarven Spider or Sphere for 60 seconds wherever the caster is pointing.
☐	Auriel's Bow	13	11	1,436	Undead take 20 points of sun damage; other targets take half that. Bloodcursed Arrows also cause you to absorb health from your victim.
☐	Bloodcursed Elven Arrow	16	0	6	Shrouds the sun in darkness if shot with Auriel's Bow.
☐	Sunhallowed Elven Arrow	16	0	16	Causes sunburst attacks to nearby targets if shot at the sun with Auriel's Bow.
☐	Dawnguard Rune Axe	11	13	175	For every 10 undead you kill with this axe, the axe will do +10 Sun Damage to undead (up to +100).
☐	Dawnguard Rune Hammer	22	26	500	Bashing places a rune on a nearby surface; the rune explodes for 50 points of fire damage when enemies come near.
☐	Harkon's Sword	8	9	1,472	Absorbs 15 points of Health, Magicka, and Stamina if wielded by a vampire.
☐	Staff of Ruunvald	0	8	1,393	Calm targets up to Lv 8 for 30s.
☐	Zephyr	12	10	670	Fires 30% faster than a standard bow.

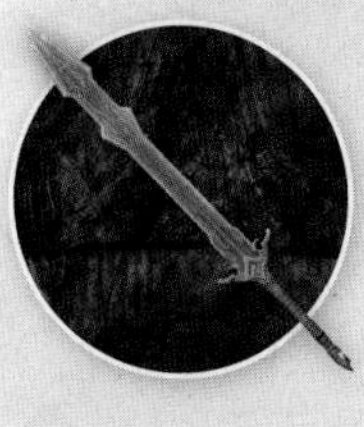

Two-Handed Weapon: Nord Hero Greatsword

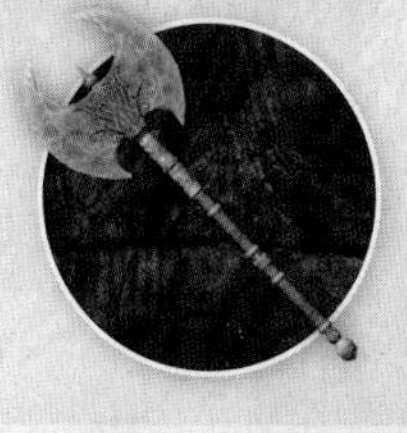

Two-Handed Weapon: Stalhrim Battleaxe

✓	NAME	DAMAGE	WEIGHT	VALUE	ENCHANTMENT	NOTES
	UNIQUE WEAPONS - DRAGONBORN					
☐	Bloodscythe	13	10	1859	When dual-wielded with Soulrender, Absorb Health 15, 25% chance of Reduce Armor 100 for 15s	
☐	Bloodskal Blade	21	16	500	Power Attacks release an energy blast that does 30 Magic Damage	
☐	Glass Bow of the Stag Prince	16	14	375	+5 Health and Stamina per 20 Animals Killed, up to +25	
☐	Champion's Cudgel	24	27	1767	50% chance each of +25 fire, +25 frost, and +25 shock damage	
☐	Dwarven Black Bow of Fate	13	10	1446	50% chance each of Absorb Health 25, Absorb Magicka 25, Absorb Stamina 25	
☐	Hoarfrost	5	10	946	Frost Damage 15, 3% chance of Ice Form Paralysis	Counts as an Ancient Nordic Pickaxe
☐	Horksbane	10	14	250	+20 Damage vs. Horkers	
☐	Miraak's Staff	0	8	1130	Summons tentacles that stagger and poison foes	Leveled
☐	Miraak's Sword	12	3	427	Tentacle Lash, Absorb Stamina	Leveled
☐	Soulrender	13	10	1892	When dual wielded with Bloodscythe, Absorb Magicka 15, 25% chance of Dispel Magic	
☐	Stormfang	17	17	1175	Shock Damage 30	

Table IV: Armor

This section lists all of the armor, robes, and other clothing available to you, and their properties.

Armor and Clothing marked "Uses [Material] enchant list" has the same enchantment levels as an item of the indicated material type.

Circlets, Rings, and Necklaces may appear with armor enchantments of any level.

Enchanted armor will have a higher value than shown here. The additional value added by the enchantment depends on the type and strength of the enchantment.

Armor and Clothing marked "Leveled" has several different leveled variants; you will always receive the one most appropriate to your level. Higher-level versions may have better statistics and stronger enchantments than the example listed here.

All shields are listed as being 'Heavy Armor'. However, they don't count as Heavy Armor for the purposes of skills or perks. For example:

- Your Heavy Armor skill doesn't make you any better with a shield.
- If you have perks that only work if you're wearing a full set of light armor or no armor, holding a shield doesn't count against you.

Clothing often comes in a variety of appearances that aren't distinguished by name (there are at least a half-dozen 'boots', for example). So a representative item from each set has been listed here. Be aware that an item's appearance and properties may vary slightly between instances of these items.

All Armor and Clothing, with the exception of Unique Armor (of any type) can be found in a variety of locations throughout the world. Unique Armor and Outfits are tracked in the Atlas Chapter (page 685) and Appendices of this guide.

✓	NAME	ARMOR	WEIGHT	VALUE	TYPE
	STANDARD HEAVY ARMOR SETS				
☐	Iron Armor	25	30	125	Heavy
☐	Iron Boots	10	6	25	Heavy
☐	Iron Gauntlets	10	5	25	Heavy
☐	Iron Helmet	15	5	60	Heavy
☐	Iron Shield	20	12	60	Heavy
☐	Bonemold Armor	32	34	290	Heavy
☐	Bonemold Pauldron Armor	36	33	290	Heavy
☐	Bonemold Boots	12	7	60	Heavy
☐	Bonemold Gauntlets	12	3.5	60	Heavy
☐	Bonemold Helmet	17	4.5	135	Heavy
☐	Bonemold Shield	22	8	95	Heavy
☐	Improved Bonemold Armor	35	43	290	Heavy
☐	Improved Bonemold Boots	13	9	60	Heavy
☐	Improved Bonemold Gauntlets	13	7	60	Heavy
☐	Improved Bonemold Helmet	18	11	135	Heavy
☐	Improved Bonemold Shield	26	11	95	Heavy
☐	Steel Armor	31	35	275	Heavy
☐	Steel Cuffed Boots	12	8	55	Heavy
☐	Steel Shin Boots	12	8	55	Heavy
☐	Steel Nordic Gauntlets	12	4	55	Heavy
☐	Steel Imperial Gauntlets	12	4	55	Heavy
☐	Steel Helmet	17	5	125	Heavy
☐	Steel Horned Helmet	17	5	125	Heavy
☐	Steel Shield	24	12	150	Heavy
☐	Dwarven Armor	34	45	400	Heavy
☐	Dwarven Boots	13	10	85	Heavy
☐	Dwarven Gauntlets	13	8	85	Heavy
☐	Dwarven Helmet	18	12	200	Heavy
☐	Dwarven Shield	26	12	225	Heavy
☐	Chitin Heavy Armor	40	35	650	Heavy
☐	Chitin Heavy Boots	14	6	135	Heavy
☐	Chitin Heavy Gauntlets	14	5	135	Heavy
☐	Chitin Heavy Helmet	19	5	135	Heavy
☐	Steel Plate Armor	40	38	625	Heavy
☐	Steel Plate Boots	14	9	125	Heavy
☐	Steel Plate Gauntlets	14	6	125	Heavy
☐	Steel Plate Helmet	19	6	300	Heavy
☐	Steel Plate Shield	28	14	325	Heavy
☐	Nordic Carved Armor	43	37	1600	Heavy
☐	Nordic Carved Boots	15	6	220	Heavy
☐	Nordic Carved Gauntlets	15	6	220	Heavy
☐	Nordic Carved Helmet	20	7	550	Heavy
☐	Nordic Shield	27	10	335	Heavy
☐	Orcish Armor	40	35	1000	Heavy
☐	Orcish Boots	15	7	200	Heavy
☐	Orcish Gauntlets	15	7	200	Heavy
☐	Orcish Helmet	20	8	500	Heavy
☐	Orcish Shield	30	14	500	Heavy
☐	Ebony Armor	43	38	1500	Heavy
☐	Ebony Boots	16	7	275	Heavy
☐	Ebony Gauntlets	16	7	275	Heavy
☐	Ebony Helmet	21	10	750	Heavy
☐	Ebony Shield	32	14	750	Heavy
☐	Stalhrim Armor	46	38	2200	Heavy
☐	Stalhrim Boots	17	7	450	Heavy
☐	Stalhrim Gauntlets	17	7	450	Heavy
☐	Stalhrim Helmet	22	7	1135	Heavy
☐	Dragonplate Armor	46	40	2125	Heavy
☐	Dragonplate Boots	17	8	425	Heavy
☐	Dragonplate Gauntlets	17	8	425	Heavy
☐	Dragonplate Helmet	22	8	1050	Heavy
☐	Dragonplate Shield	34	15	1050	Heavy
☐	Daedric Armor	49	50	3200	Heavy
☐	Daedric Boots	18	10	625	Heavy
☐	Daedric Gauntlets	18	6	625	Heavy
☐	Daedric Helmet	23	15	1600	Heavy
☐	Daedric Shield	36	15	1600	Heavy
	STANDARD LIGHT ARMOR SETS				
☐	Hide Armor	20	5	50	Light
☐	Hide Boots	5	1	10	Light
☐	Hide Bracers	5	1	10	Light
☐	Hide Helmet	10	2	25	Light
☐	Hide Shield	15	4	25	Light
☐	Leather Armor	26	6	125	Light
☐	Leather Boots	7	2	25	Light
☐	Leather Bracers	7	2	25	Light
☐	Leather Helmet	12	2	60	Light
☐	Chitin Armor	30	4	240	Light
☐	Chitin Boots	9	1	50	Light
☐	Chitin Bracers	9	2	50	Light
☐	Chitin Helmet	14	1	125	Light
☐	Chitin Shield	25	8	215	Light
☐	Elven Armor	29	4	225	Light
☐	Elven Boots	8	1	45	Light
☐	Elven Gauntlets	8	1	45	Light
☐	Elven Helmet	13	1	110	Light
☐	Elven Shield	21	4	115	Light
☐	Scaled Armor	32	6	350	Light
☐	Scaled Horn Armor	32	6	350	Light
☐	Scaled Boots	9	2	70	Light
☐	Scaled Bracers	9	2	70	Light
☐	Scaled Helmet	14	2	175	Light
☐	Stalhrim Light Armor	39	7	925	Light
☐	Stalhrim Light Boots	12	2	215	Light
☐	Stalhrim Light Bracers	12	2	215	Light
☐	Stalhrim Light Helmet	17	2	465	Light
☐	Stalhrim Shield	30	10	600	Light
☐	Glass Armor	38	7	900	Light

☑	NAME	ARMOR	WEIGHT	VALUE	TYPE
☐	Glass Boots	11	2	190	Light
☐	Glass Gauntlets	11	2	190	Light
☐	Glass Helmet	16	2	450	Light
☐	Glass Shield	27	6	450	Light
☐	Dragonscale Armor	41	10	1500	Light
☐	Dragonscale Boots	12	3	300	Light
☐	Dragonscale Gauntlets	12	3	300	Light
☐	Dragonscale Helmet	17	4	750	Light
☐	Dragonscale Shield	29	6	750	Light

STANDARD ARMOR PIECES

These pieces are not part of a complete set, but use enchantments from the standard list.

☑	NAME	ARMOR	WEIGHT	VALUE	TYPE
☐	Banded Iron Armor	28	35	200	Heavy
	Note: Uses Iron enchant list.				
☐	Banded Iron Shield	22	12	100	Heavy
	Note: Uses Iron enchant list.				
☐	Studded Armor	23	6	75	Light
	Note: Uses Leather enchant list.				
☐	Elven Gilded Armor	35	4	550	Light
	Note: Uses Glass enchant list.				

SOLDIER AND GUARD ARMOR

☑	NAME	ARMOR	WEIGHT	VALUE	TYPE
☐	Imperial Light Armor*	23	6	75	Light
☐	Imperial Light Boots*	6	2	15	Light
☐	Imperial Light Bracers*	6	1	15	Light
☐	Imperial Light Helmet*	11	2	35	Light
☐	Imperial Light Shield*	19	4	40	Light
☐	Studded Imperial Armor*	23	6	125	Light
	*Note: Uses Leather enchant list.				
☐	Imperial Armor*	25	35	100	Heavy
☐	Imperial Boots*	10	8	20	Heavy
☐	Imperial Bracers*	10	4	15	Heavy
☐	Imperial Helmet*	15	5	50	Heavy
	*Note: Uses Steel enchant list.				
☐	Imperial Helmet	18	5	30	Heavy
☐	Imperial Officer's Helmet	17	4	30	Heavy
☐	Imperial Shield	20	12	50	Heavy
☐	Stormcloak Cuirass	21	8	25	Light
☐	Stormcloak Helmet	10	2	12	Light
☐	Fur Boots	5	2	5	Light
☐	Fur Gauntlets	5	2	5	Light
☐	Stormcloak Officer Armor	27	8	35	Light
☐	Stormcloak Officer Boots	7	2	7	Light
☐	Stormcloak Officer Bracers	7	2	7	Light
☐	Stormcloak Officer Helmet	12	2	15	Light
☐	Eastmarch Guard Helmet	12	2	12	Light
☐	Falkreath Guard's Armor	23	6	75	Light
☐	Falkreath Guard's Helmet	11	2	35	Light
☐	Falkreath Guard's Shield	17	3	40	Heavy
☐	Hjaalmarch Guard's Armor	23	6	75	Light
☐	Hjaalmarch Guard's Helmet	11	2	35	Light
☐	Hjaalmarch Guard's Shield	17	3	40	Heavy
☐	Markarth Guard's Armor	23	6	75	Light
☐	Markarth Guard's Helmet	11	2	35	Light
☐	Markarth Guard's Shield	17	3	40	Heavy
☐	Pale Guard's Armor	23	6	75	Light
☐	Pale Guard's Helmet	11	2	35	Light
☐	Pale Guard's Shield	17	3	40	Heavy
☐	Riften Guard's Armor	23	6	75	Light
☐	Riften Guard's Helmet	11	2	35	Light
☐	Riften Guard's Shield	17	3	40	Heavy
☐	Solitude Guard's Armor	23	6	75	Light
☐	Solitude Guard's Helmet	11	2	35	Light
☐	Solitude Guard's Shield	17	3	40	Heavy
☐	Whiterun Guard's Armor	23	6	75	Light
☐	Whiterun Guard's Helmet	11	2	35	Light
☐	Whiterun Guard's Shield	17	3	40	Heavy
☐	Windhelm Guard's Shield	17	3	40	Heavy
☐	Winterhold Guard's Armor	23	6	75	Light
☐	Winterhold Guard's Helmet	11	2	35	Light
☐	Winterhold Guard's Shield	17	3	40	Heavy

DAWNGUARD ARMOR

☑	NAME	ARMOR	WEIGHT	VALUE	TYPE
☐	Dawnguard Armor	29	6	220	Light
☐	Dawnguard Boots	8	1.5	25	Light
☐	Dawnguard Gauntlets	8	1.5	40	Light
☐	Dawnguard Helmet	16	1.5	100	Light
	Note: 25% less damage from vampire attacks and Drain Life spells while wearing a complete set of Dawnguard armor.				
☐	Dawnguard Heavy Armor	34	42	425	Heavy
☐	Dawnguard Heavy Boots	13	9	85	Heavy
☐	Dawnguard Heavy Gauntlets	13	7	85	Heavy
☐	Dawnguard Full Helmet	18	10	220	Heavy
	Note: 25% less damage from vampire attacks and Drain Life spells while wearing a complete set of Dawnguard armor.				
☐	Dawnguard Shield	26	10	240	Heavy
	Note: +10 Bash damage against vampires.				

VAMPIRE ARMOR

☑	NAME	ARMOR	WEIGHT	VALUE	TYPE
☐	Vampire Robes	0	1	5	
☐	Vampire Gloves	0	0.5	1	
☐	Vampire Hood	0	0.5	1	
☐	Vampire Boots	0	1	2	
☐	Vampire Armor	25	5	175	Light
☐	Vampire Boots	7	2	25	Light
☐	Vampire Gauntlets	8	1.5	25	Light
☐	Vampire Armor of Minor Conjuration	25	5	195	Light
	Note: +50% Magicka Regen, Fortify Conjuration 12%				
☐	Vampire Armor of Conjuration	25	5	225	Light
	Note: +50% Magicka Regen, Fortify Conjuration 15%				
☐	Vampire Armor of Major Conjuration	25	5	250	Light
	Note: +50% Magicka Regen, Fortify Conjuration 17%				
☐	Vampire Armor of Eminent Conjuration	25	5	275	Light
	Note: +50% Magicka Regen, Fortify Conjuration 20%				
☐	Vampire Armor of Extreme Conjuration	25	5	325	Light
	Note: +50% Magicka Regen, Fortify Conjuration 22%				
☐	Vampire Armor of Peerless Conjuration	25	5	375	Light
	Note: +50% Magicka Regen, Fortify Conjuration 25%				
☐	Vampire Armor of Minor Destruction	25	5	195	Light
	Note: +50% Magicka Regen, Fortify Destruction 12%				
☐	Vampire Armor of Destruction	25	5	225	Light
	Note: +50% Magicka Regen, Fortify Destruction 15%				
☐	Vampire Armor of Major Destruction	25	5	250	Light
	Note: +50% Magicka Regen, Fortify Destruction 17%				
☐	Vampire Armor of Eminent Destruction	25	5	275	Light
	Note: +50% Magicka Regen, Fortify Destruction 20%				
☐	Vampire Armor of Extreme Destruction	25	5	325	Light
	Note: +50% Magicka Regen, Fortify Destruction 22%				
☐	Vampire Armor of Peerless Destruction	25	5	375	Light
	Note: +50% Magicka Regen, Fortify Destruction 25%				
☐	Vampire Armor of Quickening	25	5	225	Light
	Note: +75% Magicka Regen				
☐	Vampire Armor of Recharging	25	5	250	Light
	Note: +100% Magicka Regen				
☐	Vampire Armor of Replenishing	25	5	275	Light
	Note: +125% Magicka Regen				
☐	Vampire Armor of Resurgence	25	5	325	Light
	Note: +150% Magicka Regen				

ENEMY / FACTION-SPECIFIC ARMOR

☑	NAME	ARMOR	WEIGHT	VALUE	TYPE
☐	Ancient Nord Armor	25	28	125	Heavy
☐	Ancient Nord Boots	10	5	25	Heavy
☐	Ancient Nord Gauntlets	10	4	25	Heavy
☐	Ancient Nord Helmet	15	4	60	Heavy
☐	Blades Armor	44	45	400	Heavy
☐	Blades Boots	13	10	85	Heavy
☐	Blades Gauntlets	13	8	85	Heavy
☐	Blades Helmet	18	12	200	Heavy
☐	Blades Shield	26	12	225	Heavy
☐	Cultist Mask	17	5	50	Heavy
☐	Cultist Robes	0	1	331	
	Enchantment: Magicka regenerates 75% faster.				
☐	Cultist Boots	0	1	25	
☐	Cultist Gloves	7	1.5	30	Light
☐	Dented Iron Shield	15	12	30	Heavy
☐	Falmer Armor	31	20	275	Heavy
☐	Falmer Boots	12	4	55	Heavy
☐	Falmer Gauntlets	12	4	55	Heavy
☐	Falmer Helmet	10	5	25	Heavy
☐	Falmer Hardened Armor	34	40	250	Heavy

✓	NAME	ARMOR	WEIGHT	VALUE	TYPE
☐	Falmer Hardened Boots	13	8	50	Heavy
☐	Falmer Hardened Gauntlets	13	7	60	Heavy
☐	Falmer Hardened Helm	18	10	150	Heavy
☐	Falmer Heavy Armor	43	35	1,200	Heavy
☐	Falmer Heavy Boots	16	6	225	Heavy
☐	Falmer Heavy Gauntlets	16	6	225	Heavy
☐	Falmer Heavy Helm	21	8	600	Heavy
☐	Falmer Shield	28	15	10	Heavy
☐	Forsworn Armor	26	6	100	Light
☐	Forsworn Boots	7	2	20	Light
☐	Forsworn Gauntlets	7	2	20	Light
☐	Forsworn Headdress	12	2	50	Light
☐	Fur Armor	23	6	50	Light
☐	Fur Bracers	6	1	10	Light
☐	Fur Helmet	11	1	23	Light
☐	Fur Shoes	6	2	4	Light
☐	Morag Tong Armor	26	5	150	Light
☐	Morag Tong Boots	8	2	35	Light
☐	Morag Tong Bracers	7	2	25	Light
☐	Morag Tong Hood	12	1.5	2	Light
☐	Penitus Oculatus Armor	23	6	75	Light
☐	Penitus Oculatus Boots	6	1	15	Light
☐	Penitus Oculatus Bracers	6	1	15	Light
☐	Penitus Oculatus Helmet	11	1	35	Light
☐	Thalmor Boots	5	1	10	
☐	Thalmor Gloves	5	1	10	
☐	Thalmor Hood	5	1	10	
☐	Thalmor Robes*	0	4	410	
☐	Hooded Thalmor Robes*	20	5	410	
*Note: Destruction spells cost 12% less to cast.					
☐	Elven Light Armor	26	4	125	Light
☐	Elven Light Boots	7	1	25	Light
☐	Elven Light Gauntlets	7	1	25	Light
☐	Elven Light Helmet	12	1	60	Light
☐	Wolf Armor	31	20	55	Heavy

✓	NAME	ARMOR	WEIGHT	VALUE	TYPE
☐	Wolf Boots	12	4	11	Heavy
☐	Wolf Gauntlets	12	4	11	Heavy
☐	Wolf Helmet	17	4	125	Heavy
☐	Vaermina Robes	8	5	10	
STANDARD ROBES & HOODS					
Some robes come in several visual styles that do not affect their names or other properties.					
☐	Black Robes	0	1	5	
☐	Blue Robes	0	1	5	
☐	College Robes	0	1	10	
☐	Hooded Black Robes	0	1	5	
☐	Hooded Blue Robes	0	1	5	
☐	Mantled College Robes	0	1	5	
☐	Black Mage Robes*	0	1	153	
☐	Hooded Black Mage Robes*	0	1	55	
☐	Necromancer Robes*	0	1	55	
☐	Hooded Necromancer Robes*	0	1	55	
*Note: +50% Magicka Regen.					
☐	Robes	0	1	5	
Note: Uses Warlock Robes enchant list.					
☐	Novice Robes	0	1	153	
Note: +50% Magicka Regen; additionally uses College Robes enchant list.					
☐	Apprentice Robes	0	1	539	
Note: +75% Magicka Regen; additionally uses College Robes enchant list.					
☐	Adept Robes	0	1	977	
Note: +100% Magicka Regen; additionally uses College Robes enchant list.					
☐	Expert Robes	0	1	1517	
Note: +125% Magicka Regen; additionally uses College Robes enchant list.					
☐	Master Robes	0	1	2298	
Note: +150% Magicka Regen; additionally uses College Robes enchant list.					
☐	Novice Hood	0	1	305	
Note: +30 Magicka					
☐	Apprentice Hood	0	1	415	
Note: +40 Magicka					

✓	NAME	ARMOR	WEIGHT	VALUE	TYPE
☐	Adept Hood	0	1	528	
Note: +50 Magicka					
JEWELRY - CIRCLETS					
☐	Copper and Onyx Circlet	0	2	50	
☐	Copper and Moonstone Circlet	0	2	100	
☐	Copper and Ruby Circlet	0	2	150	
☐	Copper and Sapphire Circlet	0	2	200	
☐	Silver and Moonstone Circlet	0	2	250	
☐	Jade and Sapphire Circlet	0	2	300	
☐	Jade and Emerald Circlet	0	2	350	
☐	Silver and Sapphire Circlet	0	2	400	
☐	Gold and Ruby Circlet	0	2	450	
☐	Gold and Emerald Circlet	0	2	500	
JEWELRY - RINGS					
☐	Silver Ring	0	0.25	30	
☐	Gold Ring	0	0.25	75	
☐	Silver Garnet Ring	0	0.25	160	
☐	Silver Amethyst Ring	0	0.25	180	
☐	Silver Ruby Ring	0	0.25	260	
☐	Gold Sapphire Ring	0	0.25	500	
☐	Gold Emerald Ring	0	0.25	700	
☐	Gold Diamond Ring	0	0.25	900	
JEWELRY - NECKLACES & AMULETS					
☐	Silver Necklace	0	0.5	60	
☐	Gold Necklace	0	0.5	120	
☐	Silver Jeweled Necklace	0	0.5	380	
☐	Gold Jeweled Necklace	0	0.5	485	
☐	Gold Ruby Necklace	0	0.5	550	
☐	Silver Sapphire Necklace	0	0.5	580	
☐	Silver Emerald Necklace	0	0.5	830	
☐	Gold Diamond Necklace	0	0.5	1200	
☐	Ancient Nord Amulet	0	1	100	

✓	NAME	ARMOR	WEIGHT	VALUE	TYPE	ENCHANTMENT
JEWELRY - DIVINES AMULETS						
☐	Amulet of Akatosh	0	1	89		+25% Magicka Regen
☐	Amulet of Arkay	0	1	114		+10 Health
☐	Amulet of Dibella	0	1	118		+15 Speechcraft
☐	Amulet of Julianos	0	1	108		+10 Magicka
☐	Amulet of Kynareth	0	1	96		+10 Stamina
☐	Amulet of Mara	0	1	316		Restoration spells cost 10% less to cast.
☐	Amulet of Stendarr	0	1	196		Shields block 10% more damage.
☐	Amulet of Talos	0	1	25		Time between Shouts reduced by 20%.
☐	Amulet of Zenithar	0	1	511		Prices are 10% better.
UNIQUE ARMOR - DUNGEON REWARDS						
☐	Ancient Helmet of the Unburned	15	4	841	Heavy	Resist Fire 40%
☐	Diadem of the Savant	7	4	1201	Light	All spells cost 5% less to cast.

✓	NAME	ARMOR	WEIGHT	VALUE	TYPE	ENCHANTMENT
☐	Fjola's Wedding Band	0	0.3	150		
☐	Gloves of the Pugilist	5	2	194	Light	+10 Unarmed damage
☐	Helm of Yngol	21	8	565	Heavy	Resist Frost 30%
☐	Ironhand Gauntlets	12	4	444	Heavy	Improve Two-Handed 15%
☐	Kyne's Token	0	1	325		Improve Archery 5%, Damage from Animals -10%
☐	Movarth's Boots	5	1	792	Light	Improve Sneaking 15
☐	Predator's Grace	5	1	117	Light	Muffle, Stamina Regenerates Faster
☐	Targe of the Blooded	20	8	300	Heavy	Bashes do 3 Bleeding Damage / 5s.
UNIQUE ARMOR - DRAGON PRIEST MASKS						
☐	Hevnoraak	23	9	891	Heavy	+40 Heavy Armor
☐	Konahrik	24	7	3200	Heavy	Heal wearer and damage enemies when health is low. Chance to summon a Dragon Priest.
☐	Krosis	21	5	1615	Light	Improve Lockpicking 20%, Archery 20%, Alchemy 20%

✓	NAME	ARMOR	WEIGHT	VALUE	TYPE	ENCHANTMENT
☐	Morokei	5	4	637	Light	+100% Magicka Regen
☐	Nahkriin	23	9	2173	Heavy	+50 Magicka; Improve Destruction 20%, Restoration 20%
☐	Otar	23	9	1521	Heavy	Resist Fire 30%, Resist Frost 30%, Resist Shock 30%
☐	Rahgot	23	9	962	Heavy	+70 Stamina
☐	Vokun	23	9	2182	Heavy	Improve Conjuration 20%, Illusion 20%, Alteration 20%
☐	Volsung	23	9	4611	Light	+20 Carry Weight, Improve Prices 20%, Waterbreathing
☐	Wooden Mask	2	2	40	Light	Timeshift the Labyrinthian Sanctuary

UNIQUE ARMOR - QUEST REWARDS

✓	NAME	ARMOR	WEIGHT	VALUE	TYPE	ENCHANTMENT
☐	Amulet of Articulation	2	1	1067	Light	Improve Speech, Persuade checks always succeed
Note: Leveled						
☐	Ancient Shrouded Armor	33	5	617	Light	Resist Poison 100%
☐	Ancient Shrouded Boots	12	0.5	355	Light	Muffle
☐	Ancient Shrouded Cowl	15	1	1199	Light	Improve Archery 35%
☐	Ancient Shrouded Gloves	12	1	175	Light	Double One-Handed sneak attack damage
☐	Archmage's Robes	0	1	2409		All spells cost 15% less to cast
☐	Armor of the Old Gods	24	3	611	Light	Destruction spells cost 15% less to cast
☐	Asgeir's Wedding Band	0	0.3	100		
☐	Boots	0	1	603		Resist Shock 40%
☐	Boots of the Old Gods	7	1.5	1104	Light	Improve Sneak 20%
☐	Cicero's Boots	0	0.5	355		Muffle
☐	Cicero's Clothes	0	1	1946		Improve One-Handed 20%, Improve Prices 20%
☐	Cicero's Gloves	0	0.5	175		Double One-Handed sneak attack damage
☐	Cicero's Hat	0	0.5	2168		Improve Sneak 35%
☐	Gauldur Amulet Fragment (Folgunthur)	0	0.5	816		+30 Health
☐	Gauldur Amulet Fragment (Geirmund's Hall)	0	0.5	753		+30 Stamina
☐	Gauldur Amulet Fragment (Saarthal)	0	0.5	795		+30 Magicka
☐	Gauntlets of the Old Gods	8	0.5	592	Light	Improve Archery 20%
☐	Guild Master's Armor	38	10	1779	Light	+50 Carry Weight
☐	Guild Master's Boots	11	2	649	Light	Improve Pickpocket 35%
☐	Guild Master's Gloves	11	2	599	Light	Improve Lockpick 35%
☐	Guild Master's Hood	16	3	1252	Light	Improve Speech 20%
☐	Helm of Winterhold	17	5	125	Heavy	
☐	Helmet of the Old Gods	12	1	345	Light	+30 Magicka
☐	Jester's Boots	0	1	305		Muffle
☐	Jester's Clothes	0	1	1163		Improve One-Handed 12%, Improve Prices 12%
☐	Jester's Gloves	0	0.5	125		Double One-Handed sneak attack damage
☐	Jester's Hat	0	0.5	1806		Improve Sneak 30%
☐	Jeweled Amulet	0	0.5	1000		
☐	Linwe's Armor	31	8	368	Light	+15 Stamina
☐	Linwe's Boots	11	2	837	Light	Improve Sneak 15%
☐	Linwe's Gloves	11	2	483	Light	Improve One-Handed 15%
☐	Linwe's Hood	16	2	563	Light	Improve Archery 15%
☐	Mage's Circlet	0	2	509		Improve Magicka
Note: Leveled						
☐	Muiri's Ring	0	0.3	434		Improve Alchemy 15%
Note: Bonus reward for Dark Brotherhood Quest Mourning Never Comes.						
☐	Necromancer Amulet	0	0.5	2635		+50 Magicka, Improve Conjuration 25%, -75% Health and Stamina Regen

✓	NAME	ARMOR	WEIGHT	VALUE	TYPE	ENCHANTMENT
☐	Nightingale Armor*	34	12	1249	Light	+ Stamina, Resist Frost
☐	Nightingale Boots*	10	2	295	Light	Muffle
☐	Nightingale Gloves*	10	2	819	Light	Improve Lockpick, Improve One-Handed
☐	Nightingale Hood*	15	2	804	Light	Imrove Illusion
*Note: Leveled						
☐	Nightweaver's Band	0	0.3	1131		Improve Sneak 10%, Destruction 10%
☐	Savos Aren's Amulet	0	1	818		+50 Magicka
☐	Shield of Solitude	26	12	555	Heavy	Resist Magic, Improve Block
Note: Leveled						
☐	Shield of Ysgramor	30	12	1715	Heavy	+20 Health, Resist Magic 20%
☐	Shrouded Armor	29	7	373	Light	Resist Poison 50%
☐	Shrouded Boots	8	2	305	Light	Muffle
☐	Shrouded Cowl	13	2	677	Light	Improve Archery 20%
☐	Shrouded Cowl Maskless	13	2	677	Light	Improve Archery 20%
☐	Shrouded Gloves	8	2	125	Light	Backstab does double damage
☐	Shrouded Hand Wraps	0	0.5	50	Light	Double One-Handed sneak attack damage
☐	Shrouded Hood	0	0.5	1485	Light	Improve Sneak 25%
☐	Shrouded Robes	0	0.5	711	Light	Improve Destruction 15%
☐	Shrouded Shoes	0	0.5	150		Muffle
☐	Silver-Blood Family Ring	0	0.3	772		Improve Smithing 20%
☐	The Bond of Matrimony	0	0.3	496		Improve Restoration 10%
☐	The Gauldur Amulet	0	0	1864		+30 Health, +30 Magicka, +30 Stamina
☐	Thieves Guild Armor	29	7	665	Light	+20 Carry Weight
☐	Thieves Guild Armor (Improved)	30	6	1299	Light	+35 Carry Weight
☐	Thieves Guild Boots	9	1.5	241	Light	Improve Pickpocket 15%
☐	Thieves Guild Boots (Improved)	10	1	479	Light	Improve Pickpocket 25%
☐	Thieves Guild Gloves	9	1	222	Light	Improve Lockpick 15%
☐	Thieves Guild Gloves (Improved)	10	1	445	Light	Improve Lockpick 25%
☐	Thieves Guild Hood	13	1.5	551	Light	Improve Prices 10%
☐	Thieves Guild Hood (Improved)	15	1	967	Light	Improve Prices 15%
☐	Tumblerbane Gloves	7	2	325	Light	Improve Lockpick 20%
☐	Vittoria's Wedding Band	0	0.3	100		
☐	Worn Shrouded Armor	20	6	80	Light	
☐	Worn Shrouded Boots	3	2	45	Light	
☐	Worn Shrouded Cowl	8	2	50	Light	
☐	Worn Shrouded Gloves	4	2	50	Light	Backstab does double damage

UNIQUE ARMOR - QUEST ITEMS

✓	NAME	ARMOR	WEIGHT	VALUE	TYPE	ENCHANTMENT
☐	Andurs' Amulet of Arkay	0	1	294		+10 Health
☐	Calcelmo's Ring	0	0.3	20		
☐	Charmed Necklace	0	0.5	790		+25 Carry Weight
☐	Cursed Ring of Hircine	0	0.3	50		Random werewolf transformations.
Note: No effect except on werewolves.						
☐	Enchanted Ring	0	0.3	207		+20 Health
☐	Execution Hood	0	0.5	5		
☐	Fjotli's Silver Locket	0	0.5	30		
☐	Focusing Gloves	0	0	0		
☐	Hrolfdir's Shield	24	12	60	Heavy	
☐	Ilas-Tei's Ring	0	0.3	40		
☐	Jagged Crown	23	9	5000	Heavy	
☐	Leather Hood	0	1	10		
☐	Madesi's Silver Ring	0	0.3	10		
☐	Moon Amulet	0	0.5	250		

✓	NAME	ARMOR	WEIGHT	VALUE	TYPE	ENCHANTMENT
	Noster's Helmet	11	2	35	Light	
	Ogmund's Amulet of Talos	0	1	25		Time between Shouts reduced by 20%
	Party Boots	0	0	25		
	Party Clothes	0	1	25		
	Raerek's Inscribed Amulet of Talos	0	1	205		Time between Shouts reduced by 20%
	Reyda's Necklace	0	0.5	30		
	Ring of Pure Mixtures	0	0.3	337		Improve Alchemy 12%

✓	NAME	ARMOR	WEIGHT	VALUE	TYPE	ENCHANTMENT
	Roggi's Ancestral Shield	20	12	60	Heavy	
	Saarthal Amulet	0	0.8	184		Spells cost 3% less to cast.
	Shahvee's Amulet of Zenithar	0	1	691		Improve Prices 10%
	Strange Amulet	0	0	1000		
	The Forgemaster's Fingers	10	5	394	Heavy	Improve Smithing 15%
	Viola's Gold Ring	0	0.3	75		
	Yisra's Necklace	0	0.5	50		

✓	NAME	ARMOR	WEIGHT	VALUE	TYPE	ENCHANTMENT
UNIQUE ARMOR - DAWNGUARD						
	Aetherial Crown	0	2	2,250		Retains the last Standing Stone ability you held, granting you its effects in addition to those of your current Stone.
	Aetherial Shield	26	12	2,000		Enemies struck by this shield become ethereal for 15 seconds, making them unable to attack or be attacked.
	Amulet of Bats	0	0.5	1,000		Your Bats Power drains life from nearby enemies.
Note: No effect unless you are in Vampire Lord Form.Note:						
	Amulet of the Gargoyle	0	0.5	1,000		Your Summon Gargoyle spell summons an additional gargoyle for 30 seconds.
Note: No effect unless you are in Vampire Lord Form.						
	Ancient Falmer Boots	9	2	190	Light	
	Ancient Falmer Cuirass	32	5	900	Light	
	Ancient Falmer Gauntlets	9	2	190	Light	
	Auriel's Shield	32	14	755		Stores the energy of blocked attacks. Performing a power bash will release the stored energy.
	Bone Hawk Amulet	0	1	100		
	Bone Hawk Ring	0	0.3	75		
	Dawnguard Rune Shield	27	6	450		+10 Bash damage against vampires, and sustained blocking creates a minor sun shield doing 10 points of damage while draining the wielder's stamina.
	Locket of Saint Jiub	5	0.5	2,422		+50 Stamina, +50 Carry Weight
	Ring of the Beast	0	0.3	1,927		+100 Health. Unarmed attacks do an additional 20 damage.
Note: No effect unless you are in Vampire Lord Form.						
	Ring of the Erudite	0	0.3	1,803		+100 Magicka, Regenerate +2 Magicka/second.
Note: No effect unless you are in Vampire Lord Form.						
	Shellbug Helmet	22	6	600	Heavy	
	Taron Dreth's Robes	0	1	1,113		+75% Magicka Regen, Fortify Destruction 15%
	Vampire Royal Armor	30	9	655	Light	+125% Magicka Regen

✓	NAME	ARMOR	WEIGHT	VALUE	TYPE	ENCHANTMENT
UNIQUE ARMOR - DRAGONBORN ACOLYTE PRIEST MASKS						
	Ahzidal	23	9	1165	Heavy	-Ahzidal: "Increases Fire Resistance by 50% and Fire spell damage by 25%".
	Dukaan	23	9	1202	Heavy	-Dukaan: "Increases Frost Resistance by 50% and Frost spell damage by 25%".
	Zahkriisos	23	9	1239	Heavy	-Zahkriisos: "Increases Shock Resistance by 50% and Shock spell damage by 25%".
UNIQUE ARMOR - DRAGONBORN DUNGEON REWARDS						
	Visage of Mzund	24	12	1542	Heavy	+60 Stamina, Breath of Nchuak Power
UNIQUE ARMOR - DRAGONBORN QUEST REWARDS						
	Ahzidal's Armor of Retribution	40	38	2750	Heavy	5% chance of paralyzing enemies when struck in melee
	Ahzidal's Boots of Waterwalking	14	9	1125	Heavy	Waterwalking
	Ahzidal's Gauntlets of Warding	14	6	1750	Heavy	Wards are 25% weaker, absorb 50% of magicka from incoming spells
	Ahzidal's Helm of Vision	19	6	1250	Heavy	Conjuration and Rune spells cost 25% more, but can be cast at +1 Range Increment
	Ahzidal's Ring of Arcana	0	0.3	1425		Allows you to cast Ignite and Freeze
	Ahzidal's Ring of Necromancy	0	0.3	1100		Reanimated creatures explode for 50 Frost Damage when hit
	Blackguard's Armor	33	7	2079	Light	+50 Carry Weight
	Blackguard's Boots	13	2	836	Light	Improve Pickpocket 40%
	Blackguard's Gloves	8	2	778	Light	Improve Lockpick 40%
	Blackguard's Hood	18	2	1745	Light	Improve Prices 25%
	Deathbrand Armor	39	7	1600	Light	+15 Stamina per Deathbrand Item
	Deathbrand Boots	12	2	2000	Light	+10 Carry Weight per Deathbrand Item
	Deathbrand Gauntlets	12	2	3571	Light	+10% Dual Wielding per Deathbrand Item
	Deathbrand Helm	16.5	2	750	Light	Waterbreathing; +100 Armor if wearing all Deathbrand Items
	Miraak's Boots	11	2	25		When worn with Miraak's Gloves and Robes, increases Magicka Absorbtion to 15%.

Heavy Armor: Dwarven Armor

Heavy Armor: Orcish Armor

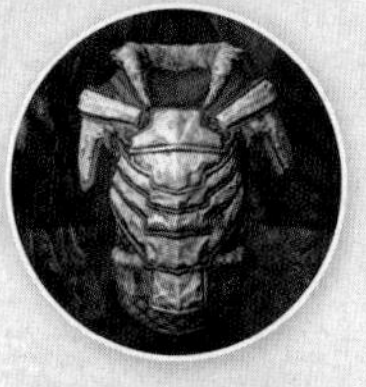
Heavy Armor: Stalhrim Armor

Light Armor: Ancient Shrouded Armor

Light Armor: Armor of the Old Gods

Light Armor: Elven Gilded Armor

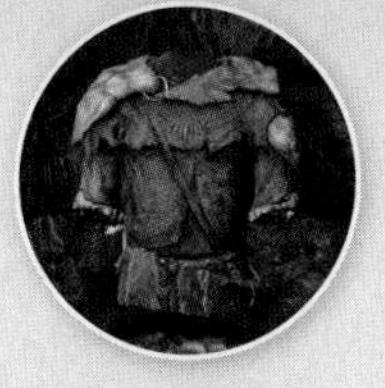
Light Armor: Fur Armor

Light Armor: Glass Armor

Shield: Auriel's Shield

Shield: Orcish Shield

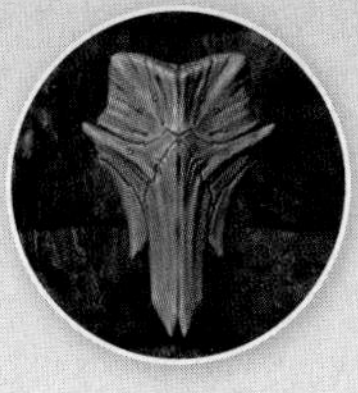
Shield: Dragonplate Shield

Shield: Shield of Ysgramor

NAME	ARMOR	WEIGHT	VALUE	TYPE	ENCHANTMENT
Miraak's Gloves	7	1.5	30	Light	When worn with Miraak's Boots and Robes, increases Magicka Absorbtion to 15%.
Miraak's Mask	23	9	739	Heavy	Magic Resistance
Note: Leveled					
Miraak's Robes	0	1	100		Absorb Magicka 5% from Spells and Dragon Breath Shouts, Chance of Tentacle Explosions when struck in melee
Ring of Bloodlust	0	0.3	1500		While in Beast Form, +50% Outgoing Damage, +50% Incoming Damage

NAME	ARMOR	WEIGHT	VALUE	TYPE	ENCHANTMENT
Ring of Instinct	0	0.3	3000		When entering Beast Form, Slow Time 20s
Ring of the Hunt	0	0.3	3500		While in Beast Form, your health regenerates
Ring of the Moon	0	0.3	2250		While in Beast Form, +50% Howl Duration
Telvanni Robes	0	2	75		Magicka regenerates 75% faster.
UNIQUE ARMOR - DRAGONBORN QUEST ITEMS					
Bera's Necklace	0	0.5	580		
Neloth's Ring of Tracking	0	0.3	100		

NAME	ARMOR	WEIGHT	VALUE	TYPE
CLOTHING - STANDARD OUTFITS				
Common clothes worn by people throughout Skyrim. Most outfits have several visual styles, but similar or identical names.				
Arm Bandages	0	0.5	1	
Belted Tunic	0	1	2	
Blacksmith's Apron	0	1	8	
Boots	0	1	3	
Brown Robes	0	1	5	
Child's Clothes	0	1	4	
Clothes	0	1	5	
College Boots	8	0	0	Light
Cowl	0	1	1	
Cuffed Boots	0	1	25	
Dunmer Outfit	0	2	75	
+75% Magicka Regen				
Dunmer Shoes	0	2	25	
Embellished Robes	2	3	100	
Embroidered Garment	0	1	100	
Fine Armguards	7	0.5	25	Light
Fine Boots	0	0	20	
Fine Boots	0	1	25	
Fine Clothes	0	1	50	
Fine Clothes	0	1	35	
Fine Hat	0	0.5	25	
Fine Raiment	0	1	100	
Footwraps	0	1	1	
Fur-lined Boots	0	1	25	
Fur-Trimmed Cloak	0	1	100	
Gilded Wristguards	7	0.5	21	Light
Gloves	0	0.5	1	
Green Robes	0	1	5	
Grey Robes	0	1	5	
Hammerfell Garb	0	1	5	
Hat	0	0.5	1	
Head bandages	5	0	0	
Hooded Brown Robes	0	1	5	
Hooded Green Robes	0	1	5	
Hooded Grey Robes	0	1	5	
Hooded Monk Robes	0	1	5	
Hooded Necromancer Robes	0	1	5	
Hooded Red Robes	0	1	5	
Mage Hood	0	1	1	
Mantled College Robes	0	1	5	
Miner's Clothes	0	1	2	
Monk Robes	0	1	5	
Necromancer Robes	0	1	5	
Moth Priest Robes	0	1	5	
Moth Priest Sandals	0	1	5	
Noble Clothes	2	3	100	
Pleated Shoes	0	1	25	
Radiant Raiment Fine Clothes	0	1	55	
Ragged Boots	0	1	1	
Ragged Cap	0	0.5	1	
Ragged Robes	1	1	1	
Ragged Trousers	0	1	1	
Red Robes	0	1	5	
Redguard Boots	0	1	3	
Refined Tunic	2	3	100	
Roughspun Tunic	0	1	1	
Shoes	1	0	2	
Skaal Boots	7	1.5	30	Light
Skaal Coat	26	5	100	Light
Skaal Gloves	7	1.5	30	Light
Skaal Hat	6	1.5	400	Light
Temple Priest Boots	0	1	25	
Temple Priest Hood	0	2	25	
Temple Priest Robes	0	2	75	
+75% Magicka Regen				
Chef's Tunic	0	1	8	
Chef's Hat	0	0.5	1	
Mourner's Hat	0	0.5	1	
Mourner's Clothes	0	1	2	
Alik'r Hood	0	0.5	2	
QUEST / UNIQUE OUTFITS				
Unique outfits worn by important characters or during special events.				
Emperor's Robes	0	1	100	
Mythic Dawn Boots	0	1	15	
Mythic Dawn Gloves	0	1	25	
Mythic Dawn Robes	0	2	25	
Mythic Dawn Robes	0	2	25	
Ulfric's Clothes	0	1	100	
Ulfric's Boots	0	1	25	
Ulfric's Bracers	5	0.5	25	Light
Wedding Dress	0	1	50	
Wedding Sandals	0	1	20	
Wedding Wreath	0	0.5	10	
General Tullius' Armor	31	18	65	Heavy

Table V: Ingredients

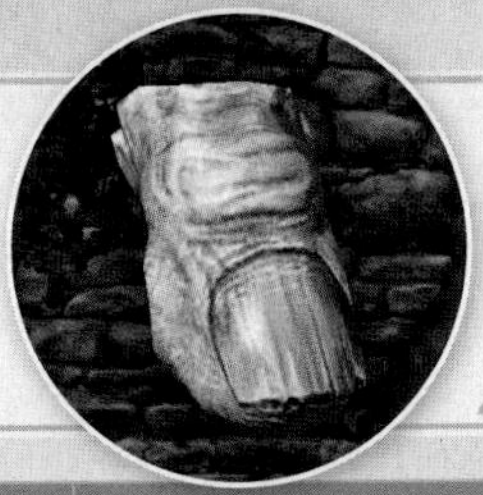

This table lists all the available ingredients and their properties (weight, value, effects). In addition, three sample locations are shown where the ingredients can be found (usually in abundance, although this varies as some ingredients are only encountered as a single item rather than in clusters).

✓	Ingredient Name	Weight	Value	Effect 1	Effect 2	Effect 3	Effect 4	Location A (Amount if Applicable)	Location B (Amount if Applicable)	Location C (Amount if Applicable)	Notes
	Abecean Longfin	0.5	15	Weakness to Frost	Fortify Sneak	Weakness to Poison	Fortify Restoration	[9.00] Riften (Plankside)	[7.00] Windhelm (Docks)	[-]	Catch these fish randomly in lakes, rivers, and the ocean.
	Ancestor Moth Wing	0.1	2	Damage Stamina	Fortify Conjuration	Damage Magicka Regen	Fortify Enchanting	[DG.03] Ancestor Glade			Only available inside the Ancestor Glade.
	Ash Creep Cluster	0.3	20	Damage Stamina	Invisibility	Resist Fire	Fortify Destruction	[S.S00] Raven Rock Mine (near Alchemy Lab)	[S.S02] Bloodskal Barrow (exterior)	[S.SU] Impact Crater (west of Tel Mithryn)	Found in the exterior of Southern Ash Lands.
	Ash Hopper Jelly	0.3	20	Restore Health	Fortify Light Armor	Resist Shock	Weakness to Frost	[S.SC] Reavers' Folly (Secondary Location)	[S.S04] Kolbjorn Barrow (northeastern exterior)	[S.S15] Sun Stone (western exterior)	Found on the bodies of Ash Hoppers.
	Ashen Grass Pod	0.1	1	Resist Fire	Weakness to Shock	Fortify Lockpicking	Fortify Sneak	[S.S05] Wreck of the Strident Squall (north exterior)	[S.S06] Hrodulf's House (south exterior)	[S.S11] Fort Frostmoth (southern exterior)	Found on Spiky Grass the exterior of Southern Ash Lands.
	Bear Claws	0.1	2	Restore Stamina	Fortify Health	Fortify One-handed	Damage Magicka Regen	[9.33] Fallowstone Cave	[8.05] Moss Mother Cavern	Pine Forest Exterior (hunt the animal)	Found on bear corpses. Check the Atlas for locations that have bears or predators.
	Bee	0.1	3	Restore Stamina	Ravage Stamina	Regenerate Stamina	Weakness to Shock	[9.10] Honeystrand Cave	[9.29] Goldenglow Estate	[-]	Commonly found near beehives, which are plentiful here.
	Beehive Husk	1	5	Resist Poison	Fortify Light Armor	Fortify Sneak	Fortify Destruction	[9.10] Honeystrand Cave	[9.29] Goldenglow Estate	[-]	Commonly found near beehives, which are plentiful here.
	Bleeding Crown	0.3	10	Weakness to Fire	Fortify Block	Weakness to Poison	Resist Magic	[1.10] Pinemoon Cave (45)	[2.02] Chillwind Depths (34)	[9.04] Geirmund's Hall (34)	Plentiful in these caves.
	Blisterwort	0.2	12	Damage Stamina	Frenzy	Restore Health	Fortify Smithing	[2.02] Chillwind Depths (59)	[8.21] Halldir's Cairn (9)	[9.34] Lost Prospect Mine (9)	Plentiful in these caves.
	Blue Butterfly Wing	0.1	2	Damage Stamina	Fortify Conjuration	Damage Magicka Regen	Fortify Enchanting	[7.00] Windhelm (Wuunferth's Quarters)	[8.10] Evergreen Grove	Pine Forest Exterior	Catch butterflies from midair to pluck their wings.
	Blue Dartwing	0.1	1	Resist Shock	Fortify Pickpocket	Restore Health	Fear	[6.01] Lund's Hut (3)	[7.21] Steamcrag Camp	Any wilderness.	These blue dragonflies are common in the wilderness, especially around shallow ponds.
	Blue Mountain Flower	0.1	2	Restore Health	Fortify Conjuration	Fortify Health	Damage Magicka Regen	[1.00] Solitude (7)	[9.00] Riften (7)	Any wilderness.	Plentiful around these Capitals.
	Boar Tusk	0.5	20	Fortify Stamina	Fortify Health	Fortify Block	Frenzy	[S.N06] Bristleback Cave	[S.N08] Broken Tusk Mine	[S.N19] Moesring Pass	Found on the bodies of Tusked Bristlebacks
	Bone Meal	0.5	5	Damage Stamina	Resist Fire	Fortify Conjuration	Ravage Stamina	[8.18] Bleak Falls Barrow	[5.42] Valthume (4)	Any Draugr Dungeon	Found on Skeletons and Draugr. Check the Atlas for references to this creature.
	Briar Heart	0.5	20	Restore Magicka	Fortify Block	Paralysis	Fortify Magicka	[5.44] Lost Valley Redoubt	[5.26] Red Eagle Redoubt	[5.18] Broken Tower Redoubt	Found on Forsworn Briar-Hearts, the leaders of most Forsworn Redoubts. Check the Atlas for locations.
	Burnt Spriggan Wood	0.5	20	Weakness to Fire	Fortify Alteration	Damage Magicka Regen	Slow	[S.S06] Hrodulf's House (south exterior)	[S.S07] Brodir Grove (exterior surroundings)	[S.S09] Ramshackle Trading Post (exterior surroundings)	Found on the bodies of Burnt Spriggan
	Butterfly Wing	0.1	3	Restore Health	Fortify Barter	Lingering Damage Stamina	Damage Magicka	[3.06] Nightcaller Temple (4)	[1.20] Shadowgreen Cavern	Pine Forest Exterior	Catch butterflies from midair to pluck their wings.
	Canis Root	0.1	5	Damage Stamina	Fortify One-handed	Fortify Marksman	Paralysis	[2.08] Swamp ground southeast of Folgunthur (9)	[2.K] Summoning Stones (close by) (5)	[2.00] Morthal (5)	Usually grows in frozen coast or marshland.
	Charred Skeever Hide	0.5	1	Restore Stamina	Cure Disease	Resist Poison	Restore Health	[3.10] Fort Dunstad (2)	[6.08] Sleeping Tree Camp (2)	[3.07] Red Road Pass (2)	Usually roasting on bonfires. This cannot be cooked.
	Chaurus Eggs	0.2	10	Weakness to Poison	Fortify Stamina	Damage Magicka	Invisibility	[4.06] Frostflow Lighthouse (Abyss) (200+)	[2.02] Chillwind Depths (150+)	[9.23] Tolvald's Cave (100+)	Found on this enemy, as well as across these Caves.
	Chaurus Hunter Antennae	0.1	2	Damage Stamina	Fortify Conjuration	Damage Magicka Regen	Fortify Enchanting	[DG.11] Darkfall Passage	[DG.12] [FV1.E] Forgotten Vale Cave	[DG.12] [FV3.F] Sharpslope Cave	Sometimes harvested from a dead Chaurus Hunter.
	Chicken's Egg	0.5	2	Resist Magic	Damage Magicka Regen	Waterbreathing	Lingering Damage Stamina	[5.20] Salvius Farm (3)	[7.15] Mixwater Mill (3)	[8.11] Half-Moon Mill (2)	Usually found in Chicken Nests.
	Creep Cluster	0.2	1	Restore Magicka	Damage Stamina Regen	Fortify Carry Weight	Weakness to Magic	[7.20] Bonestrewn Crest (7)	[7.05] Kynesgrove (close by) (6)	[7.17] Cronvangr Cave (6)	Mainly found in Eastmarch Hold.
	Crimson Nirnroot	0.2	10	Damage Health	Damage Stamina	Invisibility	Resist Magic	[10.02] Blackreach (44)	[-]	[-]	Only found in Blackreach. See Blackreach map for more information.

✓	INGREDIENT NAME	WEIGHT	VALUE	EFFECT 1	EFFECT 2	EFFECT 3	EFFECT 4	LOCATION A (AMOUNT IF APPLICABLE)	LOCATION B (AMOUNT IF APPLICABLE)	LOCATION C (AMOUNT IF APPLICABLE)	NOTES
☐	Cyrodilic Spadetail	0.3	15	Damage Stamina	Fortify Restoration	Fear	Ravage Health	[9.00] Riften (Plankside)	[7.00] Windhelm (Docks)	[-]	Catch these fish randomly in lakes, rivers, and the ocean.
☐	Daedra Heart	0.5	250	Restore Health	Damage Stamina Regen	Damage Magicka	Fear	[3.06] Nightcaller Temple (2)	Daedric Quests: The Black Star or Pieces of the Past	College of Winterhold Radiant Quest: The Atronach Forge	Found on Dremora. Cannot be obtained from summoned Dremora. Check the Atlas for references to this creature.
☐	Deathbell	0.1	4	Damage Health	Ravage Stamina	Slow	Weakness to Poison	[2.23] Labyrinthian (Shalidor's Maze) (5)	[2.08] Folgunthur (5+)	[1.00] Solitude (inside Bards' College) (5)	Usually grows in frozen coast or marshland.
☐	Dragon's Tongue	0.1	5	Resist Fire	Fortify Barter	Fortify Illusion	Fortify Two-handed	[7.20] Bonestrewn Crest (15+)	[7.05] Kynesgrove (7)	[7.30] Eldergleam Sanctuary (5+)	A plant that looks like a dragon's tongue, not actually the tongue of a dragon! Usually found in Eastmarch.
☐	Dwarven Oil	0.3	15	Weakness to Magic	Fortify Illusion	Regenerate Magicka	Restore Magicka	[2.18] Mzinchaleft (8)	[3.31] Irkngthand (2)	[4.13] Alftand (1)	Found on many Dwarven Automatons. Otherwise, very rare.
☐	Ectoplasm	0.1	25	Restore Magicka	Fortify Destruction	Fortify Magicka	Damage Health	[6.09] Rannveig's Fast	[4.00] College of Winterhold (5)	[4.02] Yngvild	Found on Ghosts. Check the Atlas for references to this creature.
☐	Elves Ear	0.1	10	Restore Magicka	Fortify Marksman	Weakness to Frost	Resist Fire	[1.00] Riften (Bee and Barb) (7)	[6.00] Whiterun (Dragonsreach) (9)	[9.35] Black-Briar Lodge (7)	Dried Elves Ear can be found in most dwellings.
☐	Emperor Parasol Moss	0.3	1	Damage Health	Fortify Magicka	Regenerate Health	Fortify Two-handed	[S.S15] Sun Stone (exterior giant mushrooms)	[S.S00] Tel Mithryn (exterior giant mushrooms)	None	Usually hangs from Emperor Parasol (giant mushroom)
☐	Eye of Sabre Cat	0.1	2	Restore Stamina	Ravage Health	Damage Magicka	Restore Health	[5.29] Karthspire Camp (2)	Pine Forest Exterior (hunt the animal)	Snowy mountains (hunt the animal)	Found on Sabre Cats, regardless of pelt type. Check the Atlas for references to this creature.
☐	Falmer Ear	0.2	10	Damage Health	Frenzy	Resist Poison	Fortify Lockpicking	[4.13] Alftand (7)	[4.00] College of Winterhold (3+)	Any Dwarven Dungeon.	Found on Falmer. Check the Atlas for references to this creature.
☐	Felsaad Tern Feathers	0.1	15	Restore Health	Fortify Light Armor	Cure Disease	Resist Magic	[S.S00] Raven Rock (interior houses)	[S.S00] Raven Rock (skies above)	[S.SN00] Skaal Village (skies above)	Found on the bodies of Felsaad Terns; shoot the birds from the sky with arrows, bolts, magic, or Shouts.
☐	Fire Salts	0.3	50	Weakness to Frost	Resist Fire	Restore Magicka	Regenerate Magicka	[8.02] Sunderstone Gorge (3)	[3.06] Nightcaller Temple (3)	[4.20] Septimus Signus' Outpost	Found on Flame Atronachs, but cannot be obtained from summoned Atronachs. Check the Atlas for references to this creature.
☐	Fly Amanita	0.1	2	Resist Fire	Fortify Two-handed	Frenzy	Regenerate Stamina	[1.10] Pinemoon Cave (60+)	[9.04] Geirmund's Hall (40+)	[2.02] Chillwind Depths (30+)	Plentiful in these caves.
☐	Frost Mirriam	0.1	1	Resist Frost	Fortify Sneak	Ravage Magicka	Damage Stamina Regen	[9.35] Black-Briar Lodge (5)	[9.00] Riften (Temple of Mara) (4)	[5.00] Markarth (Vindrell Hall) (3)	Many buildings in Riften contain Dried Frost Mirriam.
☐	Frost Salts	0.3	100	Weakness to Fire	Resist Frost	Restore Magicka	Fortify Conjuration	[9.00] Riften (Mistveil Keep and Honeyside) (5)	[4.00] College of Winterhold (4+)	[5.09] Harmugstahl	Found on Frost Atronachs, but cannot be obtained from summoned Atronachs. Check the Atlas for references to this creature.
☐	Garlic	0.3	1	Resist Poison	Fortify Stamina	Regenerate Magicka	Regenerate Health	[1.24] East Empire Warehouse (9)	[1.00] Solitude (Vittoria Vici's House_ (8)	[3.10] Fort Dunstad (7)	Usually found in many dwellings.
☐	Giant Lichen	0.3	5	Weakness to Shock	Ravage Health	Weakness to Poison	Restore Magicka	[2.10] Fort Snowhawk (marsh exterior) (14)	[2.21] Kjenstag Ruins (west of location) (9)	[2.16] Ustengrav (8)	Mostly found outside.
☐	Giant's Toe	1	20	Damage Stamina	Fortify Health	Fortify Carry Weight	Damage Stamina Regen	[2.07] Talking Stone Camp	[6.08] Sleeping Tree Camp	[8.17] Secunda's Kiss	Found on Giants. Check the Atlas for references to this creature.
☐	Gleamblossom	0.1	5	Resist Magic	Fear	Regenerate Health	Paralysis	[DG.11] Darkfall Passage	[DG.11] Darkfall Grotto	None	Only found in the Darkfall cave system.
☐	Glow Dust	0.5	20	Damage Magicka	Damage Magicka Regen	Fortify Destruction	Resist Shock	[3.11] Shrine of Mehrunes Dagon (3)	[7.00] Windhelm (Palace of the Kings) (3)	[3.08] Frostmere Crypt	Found on Wispmothers. Check the Atlas for references.
☐	Glowing Mushroom	0.2	5	Resist Shock	Fortify Destruction	Fortify Smithing	Fortify Health	[9.23] Tolvald's Cave (250+)	[4.06] Frostflow Lighthouse (90+)	[1.06] Lost Echo Cave (57)	Plentiful in these caves.
☐	Grass Pod	0.1	1	Resist Poison	Ravage Magicka	Fortify Alteration	Restore Magicka	[10.04] Japhet's Folly	[3.00] Dawnstar (coastal plain to the northwest)	Northern coastline	Plentiful along the marshy northern coastline.
☐	Hagraven Claw	0.3	20	Resist Magic	Lingering Damage Magicka	Fortify Enchanting	Fortify Barter	[5.03] Hag's End	[5.36] Dead Crone Rock	[8.03] Glenmoril Coven	Found on Hagravens. Check the Atlas for references to this creature.
☐	Hagraven Feathers	0.1	20	Damage Magicka	Fortify Conjuration	Frenzy	Weakness to Shock	[5.03] Hag's End	[5.36] Dead Crone Rock	[8.03] Glenmoril Coven	Found on Hagravens. Check the Atlas for references to this creature.
☐	Hanging Moss	0.3	1	Damage Magicka	Fortify Health	Damage Magicka Regen	Fortify One-handed	[1.00] Solitude (Hall of the Dead) (60+)	[6.12] Dustman's Cairn (45+)	[8.02] Sunderstone Gorge (22+)	Usually found clinging to stone buildings, and the rocky outcrops across The Reach.
☐	Hawk Beak	0.3	15	Restore Stamina	Resist Frost	Fortify Carry Weight	Resist Shock	[1.00] Solitude (Exterior, Docks)	[8.12] Bloated Man's Grotto	Any Silver Hand Location	Shoot hawks from the sky to claim this ingredient from them, or from Silver Hand Members during The Companions Quests.
☐	Hawk Feathers	0.1	15	Cure Disease	Fortify Light Armor	Fortify One-handed	Fortify Sneak	[1.00] Solitude (Exterior, Docks)	[8.12] Bloated Man's Grotto	Any Silver Hand Location	Shoot hawks from the sky to claim this ingredient from them, or from Silver Hand Members during The Companions Quests.
☐	Histcarp	0.3	6	Restore Stamina	Fortify Magicka	Damage Stamina Regen	Waterbreathing	[9.00] Riften (Plankside)	[7.00] Windhelm (Docks)	[-]	Catch these fish randomly in lakes, rivers, and the ocean.
☐	Honeycomb	1	5	Restore Stamina	Fortify Block	Fortify Light Armor	Ravage Stamina	[9.10] Honeystrand Cave	[9.29] Goldenglow Estate	[-]	Commonly found near beehives, which are plentiful here.

✓	Ingredient Name	Weight	Value	Effect 1	Effect 2	Effect 3	Effect 4	Location A (Amount if Applicable)	Location B (Amount if Applicable)	Location C (Amount if Applicable)	Notes
☐	Human Flesh	0.3	1	Damage Health	Paralysis	Restore Magicka	Fortify Sneak	[4.13] Aftand (3)	[9.23] Tolvald's Cave (3)	[5.41] Reachcliff Cave (2)	Very rare.
☐	Human Heart	1	0	Damage Health	Damage Magicka	Damage Magicka Regen	Frenzy	[5.44] Lost Valley Redoubt (1)	[8.02] Sunderstone Gorge (1)	[8.13] North Brittle Shin Pass (1)	Very rare, usually found in Dungeons.
☐	Ice Wraith Teeth	0.3	30	Weakness to Frost	Fortify Heavy Armor	Invisibility	Weakness to Fire	[4.00] College of Winterhold (5)	[6.00] Whiterun (Jorrvasker) (5)	[3.00] Dawnstar (The White Hall) (4)	Found on Ice Wraiths. Check the Atlas for references to this creature.
☐	Imp Stool	0.3	0	Damage Health	Lingering Damage Health	Paralysis	Restore Health	[2.02] Chillwind Depths (50+)	[8.21] Halldir's Cairn (20+)	[6.26] White River Watch (19)	Plentiful in these caves.
☐	Jarrin Root	0.5	10	Damage Health	Damage Magicka	Damage Stamina	Damage Magicka Regen	Dark Brotherhood Quest: To Kill an Empire	[-]	[-]	Unique Ingredient: The only Jarrin Root in Skyrim is given to you by Astrid during Dark Brotherhood Quest: To Kill an Empire. You can use it for the quest, but don't have to. Eating it will kill you instantly. It makes by far the strongest poisons of any ingredient.
☐	Jazbay Grapes	0.2	1	Weakness to Magic	Fortify Magicka	Regenerate Magicka	Ravage Health	[7.Q] Mistwatch Folly (8)	[8.33] South Skybound Watch (Interior) (8)	[7.32] The Atronach Stone (5)	Mainly found in Eastmarch Hold.
☐	Juniper Berries	0.1	1	Weakness to Fire	Fortify Marksman	Regenerate Health	Damage Stamina Regen	[5.00] Markarth (exterior and Cidhna Mines) (15+)	[5.Z] Shrine of Dibella: Bridge at Old Hroldan (8)	[5.X] Reachwind Burial Mound (8)	Mainly found in The Reach.
☐	Large Antlers	0.1	2	Restore Stamina	Fortify Stamina	Slow	Damage Stamina Regen	Pine Forest Exterior (hunt the animal)	The Rift (hunt the animal)	Tundra Plains (hunt the animal)	Found on Elk. Check the Atlas for references to this creature.
☐	Lavender	0.1	1	Resist Magic	Fortify Stamina	Ravage Magicka	Fortify Conjuration	[6.00] Whiterun (Temple of Kynareth, Wind District, and Dragonsreach) (40+)	[5.12] Cliffside Retreat (east of location) (8)	[5.28] Rebel's Cairn (5)	Grows across the Tundra plains of Whiterun Hold.
☐	Luna Moth Wing	0.1	5	Damage Magicka	Fortify Light Armor	Regenerate Health	Invisibility	[3.06] Nightcaller Temple (5)	[1.20] Shadowgreen Cavern	[6.08] Sleeping Tree Camp	Catch butterflies from midair to pluck their wings. Pale-winged Luna Moths can be found most easily at night.
☐	Moon Sugar	0.3	50	Weakness to Fire	Resist Frost	Restore Magicka	Regenerate Magicka	[9.00] Riften (Warehouse) (6)	[7.37] Cragslane Cavern (2)	[8.02] Sunderstone Gorge (1)	Sold by Khajiit Caravans. Otherwise, very rare.
☐	Mora Tapinella	0.3	4	Restore Magicka	Lingering Damage Health	Regenerate Stamina	Fortify Illusion	[3.08] Frostmere Crypt (4+)	"[2.H] Swamp Pond Massacre (ground to the north) (3)"	[2.03] Robber's Gorge (Exterior) (3)	This species of mushroom grows on dead tree stumps, mainly outside across pine forests.
☐	Mudcrab Chitin	0.3	2	Restore Stamina	Cure Disease	Resist Poison	Resist Fire	[6.27] Riverwood (river banks)	[6.H] King of the Mudcrabs	The banks of most rivers and lakes.	Found on Mudcrabs. Check the Atlas for references to this creature.
☐	Namira's Rot	0.3	0	Damage Magicka	Fortify Lockpicking	Fear	Regenerate Health	[2.02] Chillwind Depths (60)	[8.21] Halldir's Cairn (18+)	[5.11] Liar's Retreat (10)	Reasonably plentiful in these caves.
☐	Netch Jelly	0.5	20	Paralysis	Fortify Carry Weight	Restore Stamina	Fear	[S.NC] Waterfall and Grazing Netch	[S.S00] Coast around Tel Mithryn	[S.S00] Raven Rock Mine (Bloodskal Barrow)	Usually found on the remains of Netch.
☐	Nightshade	0.1	8	Damage Health	Damage Magicka Regen	Lingering Damage Stamina	Fortify Destruction	[2.23] Labyrinthian (10+)	[8.00] Falkreath (10+)	[1.00] Solitude (Arch) (7)	Reasonably plentiful in these areas. Grows outside (mainly in pine forests) and inside some dungeons.
☐	Nirnroot	0.2	10	Damage Health	Damage Stamina	Invisibility	Resist Magic	[9.06] Sarethi Farm (8)	[8.K] Alchemist's Camp: Evergreen Woods (3)	[3.00] Dawnstar (coast) (3)	Aside from Sarethi's Farm, these are found along river banks.
☐	Nordic Barnacle	0.2	5	Damage Magicka	Waterbreathing	Regenerate Health	Fortify Pickpocket	[1.07] Orphan's Tear (19)	[4.01] Hela's Folly (19)	[2.05] Crabber's Shanty (coast nearby)	Usually found on shipwrecks, or along the coast.
☐	Orange Dartwing	0.1	1	Restore Stamina	Ravage Magicka	Fortify Pickpocket	Lingering Damage Health	[1.00] Solitude (Hall of the Dead) (6)	[3.27] Forsaken Cave (5)	Any wilderness.	These orange dragonflies are common in the wilderness, especially around shallow ponds.
☐	Pearl	0.1	2	Restore Stamina	Fortify Block	Restore Magicka	Resist Shock	[9.04] Geirmund's Hall (3)	[4.13] Alftand (1)	[-]	Easier to purchase from Apothecary traders. Otherwise very rare.
☐	Pine Thrush Egg	0.5	2	Restore Stamina	Fortify Lockpicking	Weakness to Poison	Resist Shock	[9.25] Shor's Stone (Sylgja's House) (6)	[6.02] Rorikstead (Lemkil's House) (5)	[9.18] Avanchnzel (exterior)	Look for birds' nests with these mottled brown eggs, mainly in forested areas.
☐	Poison Bloom	0.3	5	Damage Health	Slow	Fortify Carry Weight	Fear	[DG.03] Ancestor Glade	[DG.11] Darkfall Passage	[DG.11] Darkfall Grotto	None
☐	Powdered Mammoth Tusk	0.1	2	Restore Stamina	Fortify Sneak	Weakness to Fire	Fear	[2.07] Talking Stone Camp	[6.08] Sleeping Tree Camp	[8.17] Secunda's Kiss	Found on a Mammoth. Check the Atlas for references to this creature.
☐	Purple Mountain Flower	0.1	2	Restore Stamina	Fortify Sneak	Lingering Damage Magicka	Resist Frost	[1.17] Dragon Bridge (11)	[5.13] Dragon Bridge Overlook (7)	Any wilderness.	Plentiful around these areas.
☐	Red Mountain Flower	0.1	2	Restore Magicka	Ravage Magicka	Fortify Magicka	Damage Health	[6.00] Whiterun (10)	[1.20] Shadowgreen Cavern (10)	Any wilderness.	Plentiful around the Capital of Whiterun and within the spacious Shadowgreen Cavern.
☐	River Betty	0.3	15	Damage Health	Fortify Alteration	Slow	Fortify Carry Weight	[9.00] Riften (Plankside)	[7.00] Windhelm (Docks)	[-]	Catch these fish randomly in lakes, rivers, and the ocean.
☐	Rock Warbler Egg	0.5	2	Restore Health	Fortify One-handed	Damage Stamina	Weakness to Magic	[5.00] Markarth (Warrens) (3)	[5.42] Valthume (rocks east of entrance)	[5.20] Salvius Farm (nearby ridges)	Look for birds' nests with these large, green eggs, mainly in the Reach.
☐	Sabre Cat Tooth	0.1	2	Restore Stamina	Fortify Heavy Armor	Fortify Smithing	Weakness to Poison	[6.10] Drelas' Cottage (2)	Pine Forest Exterior (hunt the animal)	Snowy mountains (hunt the animal)	Found on a Sabre Cat. Check the Atlas for references to this creature.
☐	Salt Pile	0.2	2	Weakness to Magic	Fortify Restoration	Slow	Regenerate Magicka	[4.00] College of Winterhold (Midden) (7)	[6.29] Fellglow Keep (5)	[3.10] Fort Dunstad (5)	Most merchants carry this.

✓	Ingredient Name	Weight	Value	Effect 1	Effect 2	Effect 3	Effect 4	Location A (Amount if Applicable)	Location B (Amount if Applicable)	Location C (Amount if Applicable)	Notes
☐	Scaly Pholiota	0.3	4	Weakness to Magic	Fortify Illusion	Regenerate Stamina	Fortify Carry Weight	[9.B] Wood Cutter's Camp: Lake Geir (3)	[9.L] Altar in the Woods: Autumnshade (3)	[9.37] Darklight Tower (north, closer to the lake) (3)	Usually found on or near fallen trees or stumps.
☐	Scathecraw	0.1	1	Ravage Health	Ravage Stamina	Ravage Magicka	Lingering Damage Health	[S.S00] Raven Rock	[S.S05] Wreck of the Strident Squall	[S.S00] Tel Mithryn (southwest exterior)	Plentiful in the Southern Ash Lands
☐	Silverside Perch	0.3	15	Restore Stamina	Damage Stamina Regen	Ravage Health	Resist Frost	[9.00] Riften (Plankside)	[7.00] Windhelm (Docks)	[-]	Catch these fish randomly in lakes, rivers, and the ocean.
☐	Skeever Tail	0.2	3	Damage Stamina Regen	Ravage Health	Damage Health	Fortify Light Armor	[3.10] Fort Dunstad (8)	[3.06] Nightcaller Temple (4)	[5.11] Liar's Retreat (4)	Found on Skeevers. Check the Atlas for references to this creature.
☐	Slaughterfish Egg	0.2	3	Resist Poison	Fortify Pickpocket	Lingering Damage Health	Fortify Stamina	[3.A] Horker Standing Stones (15)	[3.02] Wreck Of The Brinehammer (ocean) (10)	[9.45] Forelhost (7+)	Usually found close to water, or Slaughterfish.
☐	Slaughterfish Scales	0.1	3	Resist Frost	Lingering Damage Health	Fortify Heavy Armor	Fortify Block	[8.03] Glenmoril Coven (6)	[9.23] Tolvald's Cave (4)	Any lake in Skyrim where Slaughterfish dwell.	Found on Slaughterfish. Check the Atlas for references to this creature.
☐	Small Antlers	0.1	2	Weakness to Poison	Fortify Restoration	Lingering Damage Stamina	Damage Health	Pine Forest Exterior (hunt the animal)	The Rift (hunt the animal)	Tundra Plains (hunt the animal)	Found on Deer. Check the Atlas for references to this creature.
☐	Small Pearl	0.1	2	Restore Stamina	Fortify One-handed	Fortify Restoration	Resist Frost	[9.04] Geirmund's Hall (3)	[4.13] Alftand (1)	[-]	Easier to purchase from Apothecary traders. Otherwise very rare.
☐	Snowberries	0.1	4	Resist Fire	Fortify Enchanting	Resist Frost	Resist Shock	[4.07] Driftshade Refuge (25)	[7.10] Traitor's Post (12)	[4.00] College of Winterhold (11)	Find these outside, where snow is on the ground.
☐	Spawn Ash	0.1	20	Ravage Stamina	Resist Fire	Fortify Enchanting	Ravage Magicka	[S.S03] Old Attius Farm	[S.S10] Highpoint Tower	[S.S11] Fort Frostmoth	Found on the remains of Ash Spawn.
☐	Spider Egg	0.2	5	Damage Stamina	Damage Magicka Regen	Fortify Lockpicking	Fortify Marksman	[4.15] Ironbind Barrow (11)	[5.09] Harmugstah (8)	[6.00] Whiterun (Jorrvaskr) (7)	Found on some Frostbite Spiders, or close by their lairs. Check the Atlas for references to this creature.
☐	Spriggan Sap	0.2	15	Damage Magicka Regen	Fortify Enchanting	Fortify Smithing	Fortify Alteration	[8.05] Moss Mother Cavern	[1.20] Shadowgreen Cavern	[4.00] College of Winterhold (2)	Found on Spriggans. Check the Atlas for references to this creature.
☐	Swamp Fungal Pod	0.3	5	Resist Shock	Lingering Damage Magicka	Paralysis	Restore Health	[2.19] Movarth's Lair (Exterior) (10)	[2.00] Morthal (swamp to the northwest and west) (15+)	[-]	Mainly found in the wet ground of Hjaalmarch Hold.
☐	Taproot	0.5	15	Weakness to Magic	Fortify Illusion	Regenerate Magicka	Restore Magicka	[8.05] Moss Mother Cavern	[1.20] Shadowgreen Cavern	[1.11] Clearpine Pond	Found on Spriggans. Check the Atlas for references to this creature.
☐	Thistle Branch	0.1	1	Resist Frost	Ravage Stamina	Resist Poison	Fortify Heavy Armor	[1.00] Solitude (Arch and Blue Palace)	[1.17] Dragon Bridge (7)	[6.27] Riverwood (7)	Mainly found in scrubland and around settlements.
☐	Torchbug Thorax	0.1	1	Restore Stamina	Lingering Damage Magicka	Weakness to Magic	Fortify Stamina	[4.00] College of Winterhold (10+)	[3.27] Forsaken Cave (5+)	[3.00] Dawnstar (The White Hall) (3)	Look for these glowing insects at dusk or night, across the wilderness (but not at altitude).
☐	Trama Root	0.2	1	Weakness to Shock	Fortify Carry Weight	Damage Magicka	Slow	[S.S09] Ramshackle Trading Post	[S.S12] Ashfallow Citadel	[S.S15] Sun Stone	Found in the exterior of Southern Ash Lands.
☐	Troll Fat	1	15	Resist Poison	Fortify Two-handed	Frenzy	Damage Health	[1.24] East Empire Warehouse (15+)	[6.30] Graywinter Watch	Animal Dens across the wilderness.	Found on Trolls. Check the Atlas for references to this creature.
☐	Tundra Cotton	0.1	1	Resist Magic	Fortify Magicka	Fortify Block	Fortify Barter	[1.00] Solitude (Buildings in The Avenues District)	[6.14] Redoran's Retreat (13)	[8.12] Bloated Man's Grotto (10)	Found growing outside, at low altitudes.
☐	Vampire Dust	0.2	25	Invisibility	Restore Magicka	Regenerate Health	Cure Disease	[8.25] North Shriekwind Bastion	[6.07] Broken Fang Cave	Any Court Wizard's Quarters, or your house's Alchemy Lab.	Found on Vampires. Check the Atlas for references to this creature.
☐	Void Salts	0.2	125	Weakness to Shock	Resist Magic	Damage Health	Fortify Magicka	[1.00] Solitude (Proudspire Manor Alchemy Lab) (4)	[9.00] Riften (Honeyside Alchemy Lab) (3)	[4.00] College of Winterhold (Archmage's Quarters)	Found on Storm Atronachs, but cannot be obtained from summoned Atronachs. Check the Atlas for references to this creature.
☐	Wheat	0.1	5	Restore Health	Fortify Health	Damage Stamina Regen	Lingering Damage Magicka	[1.23] Katla's Farm	[6.02] Rorikshead	[6.24] Battle-Born Farm	Check the larger towns (such as Rorikshead), or consult Favor (Activity): Harvesting Crops†.
☐	White Cap	0.3	0	Weakness to Frost	Fortify Heavy Armor	Restore Magicka	Ravage Magicka	[2.02] Chillwind Depths (40+)	[8.21] Halldir's Cairn (20+)	[6.26] White River Watch (15+)	Plentiful in these locations.
☐	Wisp Wrappings	0.1	2	Restore Stamina	Fortify Destruction	Fortify Carry Weight	Resist Magic	[3.08] Frostmere Crypt	[2.23] Labyrinthian	[5.J] Dwarven Ruins: Lair of the Wispmother	Found on Wispmothers. Check the Atlas for references.
☐	Yellow Mountain Flower	0.1	2	Resist Poison	Fortify Restoration	Fortify Health	Damage Stamina Regen	[DG.11] Darkfall Cave	[DG.03] Ancestor Glade	[DG.09] Castle Volkihar (Courtyard)	None.

Blisterwort

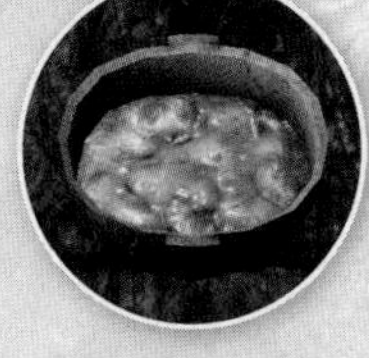
Ectoplasm

Poison Bloom

River Betty

Slaughterfish Egg

Yellow Mountain Flower

Table VI: Alchemy Effects List

This list that reveals every Alchemic Effect, and which ingredients have those effects.

Effect Name	Ingredients with this Effect
Cure Disease	Charred Skeever Hide, Felsaad Tern Feathers, Hawk Feathers, Mudcrab Chitin, Vampire Dust
Damage Health	Crimson Nirnroot, Deathbell, Ectoplasm, Emperor Parasol Moss, Falmer Ear, Human Flesh, Human Heart, Imp Stool, Jarrin Root, Nightshade, Nirnroot, Poison Bloom, Red Mountain Flower, River Betty, Skeever Tail, Small Antlers, Troll Fat, Void Salts
Damage Magicka	Butterfly Wing, Chaurus Eggs, Daedra Heart, Eye of Sabre Cat, Glow Dust, Hagraven Feathers, Hanging Moss, Human Heart, Jarrin Root, Luna Moth Wing, Namira's Rot, Nordic Barnacle, Trama Root
Damage Magicka Regen	Ancestor Moth Wing, Bear Claws, Blue Butterfly Wing, Blue Mountain Flower, Burnt Spriggan Wood, Chaurus Hunter Antennae, Chicken's Egg, Glow Dust, Hanging Moss, Hawk's Egg, Human Heart, Jarrin Root, Nightshade, Spider Egg, Spriggan Sap
Damage Stamina	Ancestor Moth Wing, Ash Creep Cluster, Blisterwort, Blue Butterfly Wing, Bone Meal, Canis Root, Chaurus Hunter Antennae, Crimson Nirnroot, Cyrodilic Spadetail, Giant's Toe, Jarrin Root, Nirnroot, Rock Warbler Egg, Spider Egg
Damage Stamina Regen	Creep Cluster, Daedra Heart, Frost Mirriam, Giant's Toe, Histcarp, Juniper Berries, Large Antlers, Silverside Perch, Skeever Tail, Wheat, Yellow Mountain Flower
Fear	Blue Dartwing, Cyrodilic Spadetail, Daedra Heart, Gleamblossom, Namira's Rot, Netch Jelly, Poison Bloom, Powdered Mammoth Tusk
Fortify Alteration	Burnt Spriggan Wood, Grass Pod, River Betty, Spriggan Sap
Fortify Barter	Butterfly Wing, Dragon's Tongue, Hagraven Claw, Tundra Cotton
Fortify Block	Bleeding Crown, Boar Tusk, Briar Heart, Honeycomb, Pearl, Slaughterfish Scales, Tundra Cotton
Fortify Carry Weight	Creep Cluster, Giant's Toe, Hawk Beak, Netch Jelly, Poison Bloom, River Betty, Scaly Pholiota, Trama Root, Wisp Wrappings
Fortify Conjuration	Ancestor Moth Wing, Blue Butterfly Wing, Blue Mountain Flower, Bone Meal, Chaurus Hunter Antennae, Frost Salts, Hagraven Feathers, Lavender
Fortify Destruction	Ash Creep Cluster, Beehive Husk, Ectoplasm, Glow Dust, Glowing Mushroom, Nightshade, Wisp Wrappings
Fortify Enchanting	Ancestor Moth Wing, Blue Butterfly Wing, Chaurus Hunter Antennae, Hagraven Claw, Snowberries, Spawn Ash, Spriggan Sap
Fortify Health	Bear Claws, Blue Mountain Flower, Boar Tusk, Giant's Toe, Glowing Mushroom, Hanging Moss, Wheat, Yellow Mountain Flower
Fortify Heavy Armor	Ice Wraith Teeth, Sabre Cat Tooth, Slaughterfish Scales, Thistle Branch, White Cap
Fortify Illusion	Dragon's Tongue, Dwarven Oil, Mora Tapinella, Scaly Pholiota, Taproot
Fortify Light Armor	Ash Hopper Jelly, Beehive Husk, Felsaad Tern Feathers, Hawk Feathers, Honeycomb, Luna Moth Wing, Skeever Tail
Fortify Lockpicking	Ashen Grass Pod, Falmer Ear, Namira's Rot, Pine Thrush Egg, Spider Egg
Fortify Magicka	Briar Heart, Ectoplasm, Emperor Parasol Moss, Histcarp, Jazbay Grapes, Red Mountain Flower, Salmon Roe, Tundra Cotton, Void Salts
Fortify Marksman	Canis Root, Elves Ear, Juniper Berries, Spider Egg
Fortify One-handed	Bear Claws, Canis Root, Hanging Moss, Hawk Feathers, Rock Warbler Egg, Small Pearl
Fortify Pickpocket	Blue Dartwing, Nordic Barnacle, Orange Dartwing, Slaughterfish Egg
Fortify Restoration	Abecean Longfin, Cyrodilic Spadetail, Salt Pile, Small Antlers, Small Pearl, Yellow Mountain Flower
Fortify Smithing	Blisterwort, Glowing Mushroom, Sabre Cat Tooth, Spriggan Sap
Fortify Sneak	Abecean Longfin, Ashen Grass Pod, Beehive Husk, Frost Mirriam, Hawk Feathers, Human Flesh, Powdered Mammoth Tusk, Purple Mountain Flower
Fortify Stamina	Boar Tusk, Chaurus Eggs, Garlic, Large Antlers, Lavender, Slaughterfish Egg, Torchbug Thorax
Fortify Two-handed	Dragon's Tongue, Emperor Parasol Moss, Fly Amanita, Troll Fat
Frenzy	Blisterwort, Boar Tusk, Falmer Ear, Fly Amanita, Hagraven Feathers, Human Heart, Troll Fat
Invisibility	Ash Creep Cluster, Chaurus Eggs, Crimson Nirnroot, Ice Wraith Teeth, Luna Moth Wing, Nirnroot, Vampire Dust
Lingering Damage Health	Imp Stool, Mora Tapinella, Orange Dartwing, Scathecraw, Slaughterfish Egg, Slaughterfish Scales
Lingering Damage Magicka	Hagraven Claw, Purple Mountain Flower, Swamp Fungal Pod, Torchbug Thorax, Wheat
Lingering Damage Stamina	Butterfly Wing, Chicken's Egg, Hawk's Egg, Nightshade, Small Antlers
Paralysis	Briar Heart, Canis Root, Gleamblossom, Human Flesh, Imp Stool, Netch Jelly, Swamp Fungal Pod
Ravage Health	Cyrodilic Spadetail, Eye of Sabre Cat, Giant Lichen, Jazbay Grapes, Scathecraw, Silverside Perch, Skeever Tail
Ravage Magicka	Frost Mirriam, Grass Pod, Lavender, Orange Dartwing, Spawn Ash, Red Mountain Flower, Scathecraw, White Cap
Ravage Stamina	Bee, Bone Meal, Deathbell, Honeycomb, Spawn Ash, Scathecraw, Thistle Branch
Regenerate Health	Emperor Parasol Moss, Garlic, Gleamblossom, Juniper Berries, Luna Moth Wing, Namira's Rot, Nordic Barnacle, Vampire Dust
Regenerate Magicka	Dwarven Oil, Fire Salts, Garlic, Jazbay Grapes, Moon Sugar, Salmon Roe, Salt Pile, Taproot
Regenerate Stamina	Bee, Fly Amanita, Mora Tapinella, Scaly Pholiota
Resist Fire	Ash Creep Cluster, Ashen Grass Pod, Bone Meal, Dragon's Tongue, Elves Ear, Fire Salts, Fly Amanita, Mudcrab Chitin, Snowberries, Spawn Ash
Resist Frost	Frost Mirriam, Frost Salts, Hawk Beak, Moon Sugar, Purple Mountain Flower, Silverside Perch, Slaughterfish Scales, Small Pearl, Snowberries, Thistle Branch
Resist Magic	Bleeding Crown, Chicken's Egg, Crimson Nirnroot, Felsaad Tern Feathers, Gleamblossom, Hagraven Claw, Hawk's Egg, Lavender, Nirnroot, Tundra Cotton, Void Salts, Wisp Wrappings
Resist Poison	Beehive Husk, Charred Skeever Hide, Falmer Ear, Garlic, Grass Pod, Mudcrab Chitin, Slaughterfish Egg, Thistle Branch, Troll Fat, Yellow Mountain Flower
Resist Shock	Ash Hopper Jelly, Blue Dartwing, Glow Dust, Glowing Mushroom, Hawk Beak, Pearl, Pine Thrush Egg, Snowberries, Swamp Fungal Pod
Restore Health	Ash Hopper Jelly, Blisterwort, Blue Dartwing, Blue Mountain Flower, Butterfly Wing, Charred Skeever Hide, Daedra Heart, Eye of Sabre Cat, Felsaad Tern Feathers, Imp Stool, Rock Warbler Egg, Swamp Fungal Pod, Wheat
Restore Magicka	Briar Heart, Creep Cluster, Dwarven Oil, Ectoplasm, Elves Ear, Fire Salts, Frost Salts, Giant Lichen, Grass Pod, Human Flesh, Moon Sugar, Mora Tapinella, Pearl, Red Mountain Flower, Taproot, Vampire Dust, White Cap
Restore Stamina	Bear Claws, Bee, Charred Skeever Hide, Eye of Sabre Cat, Hawk Beak, Histcarp, Honeycomb, Large Antlers, Mudcrab Chitin, Netch Jelly, Orange Dartwing, Pearl, Pine Thrush Egg, Powdered Mammoth Tusk, Purple Mountain Flower, Sabre Cat Tooth, Salmon Roe, Silverside Perch, Small Pearl, Torchbug Thorax, Wisp Wrappings
Slow	Burnt Spriggan Wood, Deathbell, Large Antlers, Poison Bloom, River Betty, Salt Pile, Trama Root
Waterbreathing	Chicken's Egg, Hawk's Egg, Histcarp, Nordic Barnacle, Salmon Roe
Weakness to Fire	Bleeding Crown, Burnt Spriggan Wood, Frost Salts, Ice Wraith Teeth, Juniper Berries, Moon Sugar, Powdered Mammoth Tusk
Weakness to Frost	Abecean Longfin, Ash Hopper Jelly, Elves Ear, Fire Salts, Ice Wraith Teeth, White Cap
Weakness to Magic	Creep Cluster, Dwarven Oil, Jazbay Grapes, Rock Warbler Egg, Salt Pile, Scaly Pholiota, Taproot, Torchbug Thorax
Weakness to Poison	Abecean Longfin, Bleeding Crown, Chaurus Eggs, Deathbell, Giant Lichen, Pine Thrush Egg, Sabre Cat Tooth, Small Antlers
Weakness to Shock	Ashen Grass Pod, Bee, Giant Lichen, Hagraven Feathers, Trama Root, Void Salts

Potion: Lingering Stamina Poison

Potion of Deadly Poison

Table VII: Soul Gems

A list of soul gems and their properties. Note that the Filled Soul Gems listed here are the 'standard' filled soul gems you can find in the world. If you Soul Trap a weaker creature into a larger gem, the resulting value will be reduced.

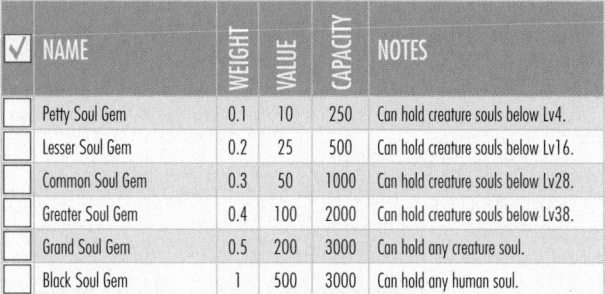

✓	NAME	WEIGHT	VALUE	CAPACITY	NOTES
☐	Petty Soul Gem	0.1	10	250	Can hold creature souls below Lv4.
☐	Lesser Soul Gem	0.2	25	500	Can hold creature souls below Lv16.
☐	Common Soul Gem	0.3	50	1000	Can hold creature souls below Lv28.
☐	Greater Soul Gem	0.4	100	2000	Can hold creature souls below Lv38.
☐	Grand Soul Gem	0.5	200	3000	Can hold any creature soul.
☐	Black Soul Gem	1	500	3000	Can hold any human soul.

✓	NAME	WEIGHT	VALUE	CAPACITY	NOTES
☐	Petty Soul Gem (Filled)	0.1	40	250	Holds a petty soul.
☐	Lesser Soul Gem (Filled)	0.2	80	500	Holds a lesser soul.
☐	Common Soul Gem (Filled)	0.3	150	1000	Holds a common soul.
☐	Greater Soul Gem (Filled)	0.4	350	2000	Holds a greater soul.
☐	Grand Soul Gem (Filled)	0.5	500	3000	Holds a grand soul.
☐	Black Soul Gem (Filled)	1	1200	3000	Holds a human soul.

Table VIII: Base Enchantments

The two tables below list all of the base weapon and armor enchantments.

When Disenchanting an item, you always learn its Base Enchantment.

- So disenchanting a Daedric Mace of the Inferno teaches you 'Fire Damage'.
- But disenchanting an Iron Sword of Embers also teaches you 'Fire Damage'. Despite the cheaper item, you learn the same effect.

When Enchanting an item:

- You can apply any weapon enchantment to any weapon.
- You can apply armor enchantments only to a subset of armor pieces, as shown below.

Examples:

You can enchant any weapon with Fire Damage, from a dagger to a warhammer.

You can apply Waterbreathing to any Helm, Ring, or Necklace.

You can put Muffle on any pair of Boots, but only on Boots.

✓	BASE ENCHANTMENT	EFFECT
	WEAPON BASE ENCHANTMENTS	
☐	Absorb Health	Absorb # Health.
☐	Absorb Magicka	Absorb # Magicka.
☐	Absorb Stamina	Absorb # Stamina.
☐	Banish	Banishes summoned daedra below level #.
☐	Chaos	50% chance each of +# fire, +# frost, and +# shock damage
☐	Fear	Creatures below level # flee for 30s.
☐	Fire Damage	+# fire damage.
☐	Frost Damage	+# frost damage.
☐	Magicka Damage	+# magicka damage.
☐	Paralyze	Paralyzes creatures below level #.
☐	Shock Damage	+# shock damage.
☐	Soul Trap	Soul traps creatures that die within # seconds.
☐	Stamina Damage	+# magicka damage.
☐	Turn Undead	Undead below level # flee for 30s.

Stalhrim War Axe of Terror

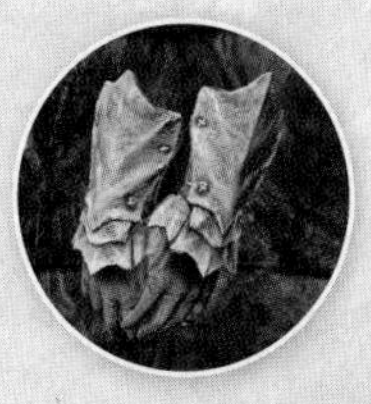

Bonemold Gauntlets of Alteration

✓	MODIFIER	BASE ENCHANTMENT	HEAD	CHEST	HANDS	FEET	SHIELD	RING	NECKLACE
		STANDARD ARMOR ENCHANTMENTS							
☐	Fortify Alchemy	Potions and poisons you craft are #% stronger.	X		X			X	X
☐	Fortify Alteration	Alteration spells cost #% less to cast.	X	X				X	X
☐	Fortify Archery	Increases bow damage by #%.	X		X			X	X
☐	Fortify Block	When blocking, you block #% more damage.			X		X	X	X
☐	Fortify Carry Weight	+# Carry Weight			X	X		X	X
☐	Fortify Conjuration	Conjuration spells cost #% less to cast.	X	X				X	X
☐	Fortify Destruction	Destruction spells cost #% less to cast.	X	X				X	X
☐	Fortify Healing Rate	Increases your health regeneration rate by #%.		X				X	X
☐	Fortify Health	+# Health		X			X	X	X
☐	Fortify Heavy Armor	Increases your Heavy Armor skill by #.		X	X			X	X
☐	Fortify Illusion	Illusion spells cost #% less to cast.	X	X				X	X
☐	Fortify Light Armor	Increases your Light Armor skill by #.		X	X			X	X
☐	Fortify Lockpicking	Locks are #% easier to pick.	X		X			X	X
☐	Fortify Magicka	+# Magicka	X		X			X	X

✓	MODIFIER	BASE ENCHANTMENT	HEAD	CHEST	HANDS	FEET	SHIELD	RING	NECKLACE
☐	Fortify Magicka Rate	Increases your magicka regeneration rate by #%.	X	X				X	
☐	Fortify One-Handed	Increases one-handed weapon damage by #%.			X	X		X	X
☐	Fortify Pickpocket	Pickpocketing items is #% easier.			X	X		X	X
☐	Fortify Restoration	Restoration spells cost #% less to cast.	X	X				X	X
☐	Fortify Smithing	Weapons and armor improvements are #% stronger.		X	X			X	X
☐	Fortify Sneak	Sneaking is #% easier.			X	X		X	X
☐	Fortify Speech	Prices you get are #% better.							X
☐	Fortify Stamina	+# Stamina		X		X		X	X

✓	MODIFIER	BASE ENCHANTMENT	HEAD	CHEST	HANDS	FEET	SHIELD	RING	NECKLACE
☐	Fortify Stamina Rate	Increases your stamina regeneration rate by #%.		X		X			X
☐	Fortify Two-Handed	Increases two-handed weapon damage by #%.			X	X		X	X
☐	Muffle	You move silently when sneaking.				X			
☐	Resist Disease	+#% Disease Resistance		X			X	X	X
☐	Resist Fire	+#% Fire Resistance				X	X	X	X
☐	Resist Frost	+#% Frost Resistance				X	X	X	X
☐	Resist Magic	+#% Magic Resistance (all forms of magic)					X	X	X
☐	Resist Poison	+#% Poison Resistance		X			X	X	X
☐	Resist Shock	+#% Shock Resistance				X	X	X	X
☐	Waterbreathing	You do not drown when swimming.	X					X	X

Table IX: Derived Enchantments

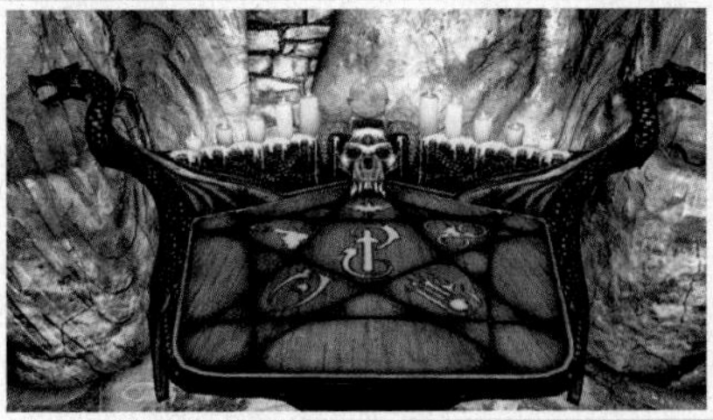

This table lists all of the Enchantments that can appear on items you find in the world.

Derived Enchantments Key

Modifier: The item suffix (or, occasionally, prefix) that identifies the enchantment.

Base Enchantment: The enchantment that you learn if you disenchant the item. Cross-reference this with the Base Enchantments Table for a complete description of the enchantment.

Ench Level: The level of this particular enchantment. Cross-reference this with the General Data Table to identify which material types this enchantment can appear on.

Magnitude: The "strength" of this particular enchantment, which might be expressed as a percentage, duration, level, or raw modifier. Plug this into the "#" in the base enchantment's description.

Not every possible combination of weapon, material, and enchantment permitted under this system exists in Skyrim... but the vast majority do.

For Example: You find an Elven Mace of Enervating. Looking it up on this table, you find that its Base Enchantment is "Magicka Damage", and its magnitude is "50". Cross-referencing this with the Base Enchantments Table tells you that it does "+50 Magicka Damage".

Note that the College of Winterhold Robes work a little differently:

There are five basic robes: Novice, Apprentice, Adept, Expert, Master. Each of these robes has a specific Fortify Magicka Rate enchantment on it, as listed on the Armor page.

In addition to that enchantment, these robes may also have an additional enchantment related to one of the five schools of magic. The modifier is just the name of the school, since the magnitude is determined by the type of robe. So, for example, you can find:

Novice Robes of Conjuration [+50% Magicka Regen; 12% Conjuration]

Apprentice Robes of Conjuration [+75% Magicka Regen; 15% Conjuration]

Apprentice Robes of Destruction [+75% Magicka Regen; 15% Destruction]

✓	MODIFIER	BASE ENCHANTMENT	ENCH LEVEL	MAGNITUDE
	STANDARD WEAPON ENCHANTMENTS			
☐	of Absorption	Absorb Health	2	5
☐	of Consuming	Absorb Health	3	10
☐	of Devouring	Absorb Health	4	15
☐	of Leeching	Absorb Health	5	20
☐	of the Vampire	Absorb Health	6	25
☐	of Siphoning	Absorb Magicka	2	10
☐	of Harrowing	Absorb Magicka	3	15
☐	of Winnowing	Absorb Magicka	4	20
☐	of Evoking	Absorb Magicka	5	25
☐	of the Sorcerer	Absorb Magicka	6	30
☐	of Gleaning	Absorb Stamina	2	10
☐	of Reaping	Absorb Stamina	3	15
☐	of Harvesting	Absorb Stamina	4	20
☐	of Garnering	Absorb Stamina	5	25
☐	of Subsuming	Absorb Stamina	6	30
☐	of Banishing	Banish	4	Lv12
☐	of Expelling	Banish	5	Lv20
☐	of Annihilating	Banish	6	Lv36
☐	of Chaos	Chaos	3	15
☐	of High Chaos	Chaos	4	20
☐	of Extreme Chaos	Chaos	5	25
☐	of Ultimate Chaos	Chaos	6	30
☐	of Dismay	Fear	1	Lv5
☐	of Cowardice	Fear	2	Lv7
☐	of Fear	Fear	3	Lv10
☐	of Despair	Fear	4	Lv13
☐	of Dread	Fear	5	Lv16
☐	of Terror	Fear	6	Lv20
☐	of Embers	Fire Damage	1	5
☐	of Burning	Fire Damage	2	10
☐	of Scorching	Fire Damage	3	15
☐	of Fire / Flames	Fire Damage	4	20
☐	of the Blaze	Fire Damage	5	25
☐	of the Inferno	Fire Damage	6	30
☐	of Cold / Chills	Frost Damage	1	5
☐	of Frost	Frost Damage	2	10
☐	of Ice	Frost Damage	3	15
☐	of Freezing	Frost Damage	4	20

MODIFIER	BASE ENCHANTMENT	ENCH LEVEL	MAGNITUDE
of Blizzards	Frost Damage	5	25
of Winter	Frost Damage	6	30
of Sapping	Magicka Damage	1	10
of Draining	Magicka Damage	2	20
of Diminishing	Magicka Damage	3	30
of Depleting	Magicka Damage	4	40
of Enervating	Magicka Damage	5	50
of Nullifying	Magicka Damage	6	60
of Stunning	Paralyze	4	2s
of Immobilizing	Paralyze	5	4s
of Petrifying	Paralyze	6	6s
of Sparks	Shock Damage	1	5
of Arcing	Shock Damage	2	10
of Shocks	Shock Damage	3	15
of Thunderbolts	Shock Damage	4	20
of Lightning	Shock Damage	5	25
of Storms	Shock Damage	6	30
of Souls	Soul Trap	1	3s
of Soul Snares	Soul Trap	2	5s
of Binding	Soul Trap	3	7s
of Animus	Soul Trap	4	10s
of Malediction	Soul Trap	5	15s
of Damnation	Soul Trap	6	20s
of Fatigue	Stamina Damage	1	5
of Weariness	Stamina Damage	2	10
of Torpor	Stamina Damage	3	15
of Debilitation	Stamina Damage	4	20
of Lethargy	Stamina Damage	5	25
of Exhaustion	Stamina Damage	6	30
Blessed	Turn Undead	1	Lv3
Sanctified	Turn Undead	2	Lv7
Reverent	Turn Undead	3	Lv13
Hallowed	Turn Undead	4	Lv21
Virtuous	Turn Undead	5	Lv30
Holy	Turn Undead	6	Lv40

STANDARD ARMOR ENCHANTMENTS

MODIFIER	BASE ENCHANTMENT	ENCH LEVEL	MAGNITUDE
of Minor Alchemy	Fortify Alchemy	1	12%
of Alchemy	Fortify Alchemy	2	15%
of Major Alchemy	Fortify Alchemy	3	17%
of Eminent Alchemy	Fortify Alchemy	4	20%
of Extreme Alchemy	Fortify Alchemy	5	22%
of Peerless Alchemy	Fortify Alchemy	6	25%
of Minor Alteration	Fortify Alteration	1	12%
of Alteration	Fortify Alteration	2	15%
of Major Alteration	Fortify Alteration	3	17%
of Eminent Alteration	Fortify Alteration	4	20%
of Extreme Alteration	Fortify Alteration	5	22%
of Peerless Alteration	Fortify Alteration	6	25%
of Minor Blocking	Fortify Block	1	15%
of Blocking	Fortify Block	2	20%
of Major Blocking	Fortify Block	3	25%
of Eminent Blocking	Fortify Block	4	30%
of Extreme Blocking	Fortify Block	5	35%
of Peerless Blocking	Fortify Block	6	40%
of Lifting	Fortify Carry Weight	1	+25
of Hauling	Fortify Carry Weight	2	+30
of Strength	Fortify Carry Weight	3	+35
of Brawn	Fortify Carry Weight	4	+40
of the Ox	Fortify Carry Weight	5	+45
of the Mammoth	Fortify Carry Weight	6	+50
of Minor Conjuring / Conjuration	Fortify Conjuration	1	12%
of Conjuring / Conjuration	Fortify Conjuration	2	15%
of Major Conjuring / Conjuration	Fortify Conjuration	3	17%
of Eminent Conjuring / Conjuration	Fortify Conjuration	4	20%
of Extreme Conjuring / Conjuration	Fortify Conjuration	5	22%
of Peerless Conjuring / Conjuration	Fortify Conjuration	6	25%
of Minor Destruction	Fortify Destruction	1	12%
of Destruction	Fortify Destruction	2	15%
of Major Destruction	Fortify Destruction	3	17%
of Eminent Destruction	Fortify Destruction	4	20%
of Extreme Destruction	Fortify Destruction	5	22%
of Peerless Destruction	Fortify Destruction	6	25%
of Remedy	Fortify Healing Rate	3	20%
of Mending	Fortify Healing Rate	4	30%
of Regeneration	Fortify Healing Rate	5	40%
of Revival	Fortify Healing Rate	6	50%
of Minor Health	Fortify Health	1	+20
of Health	Fortify Health	2	+30
of Major Health	Fortify Health	3	+40
of Eminent Health	Fortify Health	4	+50
of Extreme Health	Fortify Health	5	+60
of Peerless Health	Fortify Health	6	+70
of the Minor Knight	Fortify Heavy Armor	1	12
of the Knight	Fortify Heavy Armor	2	15
of the Major Knight	Fortify Heavy Armor	3	17
of the Eminent Knight	Fortify Heavy Armor	4	20
of the Extreme Knight	Fortify Heavy Armor	5	22
of the Peerless Knight	Fortify Heavy Armor	6	25
of Minor Illusion	Fortify Illusion	1	12%
of Illusion	Fortify Illusion	2	15%
of Major Illusion	Fortify Illusion	3	17%
of Eminent Illusion	Fortify Illusion	4	20%
of Extreme Illusion	Fortify Illusion	5	22%
of Peerless Illusion	Fortify Illusion	6	25%
of the Minor Squire	Fortify Light Armor	1	12
of the Squire	Fortify Light Armor	2	15
of the Major Squire	Fortify Light Armor	3	17
of the Eminent Squire	Fortify Light Armor	4	20
of the Extreme Squire	Fortify Light Armor	5	22
of the Peerless Squire	Fortify Light Armor	6	25
of Minor Lockpicking	Fortify Lockpicking	1	15%
of Lockpicking	Fortify Lockpicking	2	20%
of Major Lockpicking	Fortify Lockpicking	3	25%
of Eminent Lockpicking	Fortify Lockpicking	4	30%
of Extreme Lockpicking	Fortify Lockpicking	5	35%
of Peerless Lockpicking	Fortify Lockpicking	6	40%
of Magicka	Fortify Magicka	1	+20
of Magicka	Fortify Magicka	2	+30
of Major Magicka	Fortify Magicka	3	+40
of Eminent Magicka	Fortify Magicka	4	+50
of Extreme Magicka	Fortify Magicka	5	+60
of Peerless Magicka	Fortify Magicka	6	+70
of Recharging	Fortify Magicka Rate	3	40%
of Replenishing	Fortify Magicka Rate	4	60%
of Resurgence	Fortify Magicka Rate	5	80%
of Recovery	Fortify Magicka Rate	6	100%
of Minor Archery	Fortify Archery	1	15%
of Archery	Fortify Archery	2	20%
of Major Archery	Fortify Archery	3	25%
of Eminent Archery	Fortify Archery	4	30%
of Extreme Archery	Fortify Archery	5	35%
of Peerless Archery	Fortify Archery	6	40%
of Minor Wielding	Fortify One-Handed	1	15%
of Wielding	Fortify One-Handed	2	20%
of Major Wielding	Fortify One-Handed	3	25%
of Eminent Wielding	Fortify One-Handed	4	30%
of Extreme Wielding	Fortify One-Handed	5	35%
of Peerless Wielding	Fortify One-Handed	6	40%
of Minor Deft Hands	Fortify Pickpocket	1	15%
of Deft Hands	Fortify Pickpocket	2	20%
of Major Deft Hands	Fortify Pickpocket	3	25%
of Eminent Deft Hands	Fortify Pickpocket	4	30%
of Extreme Deft Hands	Fortify Pickpocket	5	35%
of Peerless Deft Hands	Fortify Pickpocket	6	40%
of Minor Restoration	Fortify Restoration	1	12%
of Restoration	Fortify Restoration	2	15%
of Major Restoration	Fortify Restoration	3	17%
of Eminent Restoration	Fortify Restoration	4	20%
of Extreme Restoration	Fortify Restoration	5	22%
of Peerless Restoration	Fortify Restoration	6	25%
of Minor Smithing	Fortify Smithing	1	12%
of Smithing	Fortify Smithing	2	15%
of Major Smithing	Fortify Smithing	3	17%

✓	MODIFIER	BASE ENCHANTMENT	ENCH LEVEL	MAGNITUDE
	of Eminent Smithing	Fortify Smithing	4	20%
	of Extreme Smithing	Fortify Smithing	5	22%
	of Peerless Smithing	Fortify Smithing	6	25%
	of Minor Sneaking	Fortify Sneak	1	15%
	of Sneaking	Fortify Sneak	2	20%
	of Major Sneaking	Fortify Sneak	3	25%
	of Eminent Sneaking	Fortify Sneak	4	30%
	of Extreme Sneaking	Fortify Sneak	5	35%
	of Peerless Sneaking	Fortify Sneak	6	40%
	of Minor Haggling	Fortify Speech	1	12%
	of Haggling	Fortify Speech	2	15%
	of Major Haggling	Fortify Speech	3	17%
	of Eminent Haggling	Fortify Speech	4	20%
	of Extreme Haggling	Fortify Speech	5	22%
	of Peerless Haggling	Fortify Speech	6	25%
	of Minor Stamina	Fortify Stamina	1	+20
	of Stamina	Fortify Stamina	2	+30
	of Major Stamina	Fortify Stamina	3	+40
	of Eminent Stamina	Fortify Stamina	4	+50
	of Extreme Stamina	Fortify Stamina	5	+60
	of Peerless Stamina	Fortify Stamina	6	+70
	of Recuperation	Fortify Stamina Rate	3	20%
	of Rejuvenation	Fortify Stamina Rate	4	30%
	of Invigoration	Fortify Stamina Rate	5	40%
	of Renewal	Fortify Stamina Rate	6	50%
	of Minor Sure Grip	Fortify Two-Handed	1	15%
	of Sure Grip	Fortify Two-Handed	2	20%
	of Major Sure Grip	Fortify Two-Handed	3	25%
	of Eminent Sure Grip	Fortify Two-Handed	4	30%
	of Extreme Striking	Fortify Two-Handed	5	35%
	of Peerless Sure Grip	Fortify Two-Handed	6	40%
	of Muffling	Muffle	3 & 4	–
	of Disease Resistance	Resist Disease	[Neck Only]	50%
	of Disease Immunity	Resist Disease	[Neck Only]	100%
	of Resist Fire	Resist Fire	1	15%
	of Waning Fire	Resist Fire	2	30%

✓	MODIFIER	BASE ENCHANTMENT	ENCH LEVEL	MAGNITUDE
	of Dwindling Fire / Flames	Resist Fire	3	40%
	of Fire / Flame Suppression	Resist Fire	4	50%
	of Fire Abatement	Resist Fire	5	60%
	of the Firewalker	Resist Fire	6	70%
	of Resist Frost	Resist Frost	1	15%
	of Waning Frost	Resist Frost	2	30%
	of Dwindling Frost	Resist Frost	3	40%
	of Frost Suppression	Resist Frost	4	50%
	of Frost Abatement	Resist Frost	5	60%
	of Warmth	Resist Frost	6	70%
	of Resist Magic	Resist Magic	1	10%
	of Waning Magic	Resist Magic	2	12%
	of Dwindling Magic	Resist Magic	3	15%
	of Magic Suppression	Resist Magic	4	17%
	of Magic Abatement	Resist Magic	5	20%
	of Nullification	Resist Magic	6	22%
	of Poison Resistance	Resist Poison	[Neck Only]	50%
	of Poison Immunity	Resist Poison	[Neck Only]	100%
	of Resist Shock	Resist Shock	1	15%
	of Waning Shock	Resist Shock	2	30%
	of Dwindling Shock	Resist Shock	3	40%
	of Shock Suppression	Resist Shock	4	50%
	of Shock Abatement	Resist Shock	5	60%
	of Grounding	Resist Shock	6	70%
	of Waterbreathing	Waterbreathing	3 & 4	–

WARLOCK ROBE ENCHANTMENTS

All Warlock Robes have an additional [Fortify Magicka Rate 50%] enchantment that can't be learned by disenchanting the robe. The only robes you can learn that enchantment from are the [Fortify Magicka Rate] ones below, which have their stated rate instead of this default.

✓	MODIFIER	BASE ENCHANTMENT	ENCH LEVEL	MAGNITUDE
	of Minor Alteration	Fortify Alteration		12%
	of Alteration	Fortify Alteration		15%
	of Major Alteration	Fortify Alteration		17%
	of Eminent Alteration	Fortify Alteration		20%
	of Extreme Alteration	Fortify Alteration		22%
	of Peerless Alteration	Fortify Alteration		25%
	of Minor Conjuration	Fortify Conjuration		12%
	of Conjuration	Fortify Conjuration		15%
	of Major Conjuration	Fortify Conjuration		17%
	of Eminent Conjuration	Fortify Conjuration		20%
	of Extreme Conjuration	Fortify Conjuration		22%
	of Peerless Conjuration	Fortify Conjuration		25%
	of Minor Destruction	Fortify Destruction		12%
	of Destruction	Fortify Destruction		15%
	of Major Destruction	Fortify Destruction		17%
	of Eminent Destruction	Fortify Destruction		20%
	of Extreme Destruction	Fortify Destruction		22%
	of Peerless Destruction	Fortify Destruction		25%
	of Minor Illusion	Fortify Illusion		12%
	of Illusion	Fortify Illusion		15%
	of Major Illusion	Fortify Illusion		17%
	of Eminent Illusion	Fortify Illusion		20%
	of Extreme Illusion	Fortify Illusion		22%
	of Peerless Illusion	Fortify Illusion		25%
	of Minor Restoration	Fortify Restoration		12%
	of Restoration	Fortify Restoration		15%
	of Major Restoration	Fortify Restoration		17%
	of Eminent Restoration	Fortify Restoration		20%
	of Extreme Restoration	Fortify Restoration		22%
	of Peerless Restoration	Fortify Restoration		25%
	of Quickening	Fortify Magicka Rate		75%
	of Recharging	Fortify Magicka Rate		100%
	of Replenishing	Fortify Magicka Rate		125%
	of Resurgence	Fortify Magicka Rate		150%

COLLEGE OF WINTERHOLD ROBE ENCHANTMENTS

✓	MODIFIER	BASE ENCHANTMENT	ENCH LEVEL	MAGNITUDE
	[Novice Robes] of Alteration	Fortify Alteration		12%
	[Apprentice Robes] of Alteration	Fortify Alteration		15%
	[Adept Robes] of Alteration	Fortify Alteration		17%
	[Expert Robes] of Alteration	Fortify Alteration		20%
	[Master Robes] of Alteration	Fortify Alteration		22%
	[Novice Robes] of Conjuration	Fortify Conjuration		12%
	[Apprentice Robes] of Conjuration	Fortify Conjuration		15%
	[Adept Robes] of Conjuration	Fortify Conjuration		17%
	[Expert Robes] of Conjuration	Fortify Conjuration		20%
	[Master Robes] of Conjuration	Fortify Conjuration		22%
	[Novice Robes] of Destruction	Fortify Destruction		12%
	[Apprentice Robes] of Destruction	Fortify Destruction		15%
	[Adept Robes] of Destruction	Fortify Destruction		17%
	[Expert Robes] of Destruction	Fortify Destruction		20%
	[Master Robes] of Destruction	Fortify Destruction		22%
	[Novice Robes] of Illusion	Fortify Illusion		12%
	[Apprentice Robes] of Illusion	Fortify Illusion		15%
	[Adept Robes] of Illusion	Fortify Illusion		17%
	[Expert Robes] of Illusion	Fortify Illusion		20%
	[Master Robes] of Illusion	Fortify Illusion		22%
	[Novice Robes] of Restoration	Fortify Restoration		12%
	[Apprentice Robes] of Restoration	Fortify Restoration		15%
	[Adept Robes] of Restoration	Fortify Restoration		17%
	[Expert Robes] of Restoration	Fortify Restoration		20%
	[Master Robes] of Restoration	Fortify Restoration		22%

NOTE For Smithing Recipes, consult the Training Section on Smithing, beginning on page 76.

Nordic Warhammer of Extreme Chaos

Table X: Staff Enchantments

This table lists all of the Staffs you can create using the Staff Enchanter in Tel Mithryn on the isle of Solstheim. In order to use this device, you must complete Solstheim Side Quest: Reluctant Steward for Neloth; see page 637 for further details. Note that unenchanted staffs are given to you by Neloth, and must be imbued with Heart Stones.

✓	INGREDIENTS	PRODUCES	WEIGHT	VALUE
	ALTERATION STAFFS			
☐	1 Unenchanted Alteration Staff, 2 Heart Stones	Staff of Magelight	8	239
☐	1 Unenchanted Alteration Staff, 4 Heart Stones	Staff of Paralysis	8	3965
	CONJURATION STAFFS			
☐	1 Unenchanted Conjuration Staff, 1 Heart Stones	Staff of Zombies	8	449
☐	1 Unenchanted Conjuration Staff, 1 Heart Stones	Staff of the Familiar	8	926
☐	1 Unenchanted Conjuration Staff, 2 Heart Stones	Staff of Reanimation	8	949
☐	1 Unenchanted Conjuration Staff, 2 Heart Stones	Staff of the Flame Atronach	8	727
☐	1 Unenchanted Conjuration Staff, 2 Heart Stones	Staff of Soul Trapping	8	986
☐	1 Unenchanted Conjuration Staff, 3 Heart Stones	Staff of the Frost Atronach	8	1106
☐	1 Unenchanted Conjuration Staff, 3 Heart Stones	Staff of Revenants	8	824
☐	1 Unenchanted Conjuration Staff, 3 Heart Stones	Staff of Banishing	8	926
☐	1 Unenchanted Conjuration Staff, 4 Heart Stones	Staff of the Storm Atronach	8	1656
☐	1 Unenchanted Conjuration Staff, 4 Heart Stones	Staff of Dread Zombies	8	1248
☐	1 Unenchanted Conjuration Staff, 4 Heart Stones	Staff of Expulsion	8	2092
☐	1 Unenchanted Conjuration Staff, 4 Heart Stones	Staff of Daedric Command	8	2307
	DESTRUCTION STAFFS			
☐	1 Unenchanted Destruction Staff, 1 Heart Stones	Staff of Flames	8	183
☐	1 Unenchanted Destruction Staff, 1 Heart Stones	Staff of Frostbite	8	198
☐	1 Unenchanted Destruction Staff, 1 Heart Stones	Staff of Sparks	8	218
☐	1 Unenchanted Destruction Staff, 2 Heart Stones	Staff of Lightning Bolts	8	538
☐	1 Unenchanted Destruction Staff, 2 Heart Stones	Staff of Firebolts	8	456
☐	1 Unenchanted Destruction Staff, 2 Heart Stones	Staff of Ice Spikes	8	511
☐	1 Unenchanted Destruction Staff, 3 Heart Stones	Staff of Fireballs	8	1309

✓	INGREDIENTS	PRODUCES	WEIGHT	VALUE
☐	1 Unenchanted Destruction Staff, 3 Heart Stones	Staff of Chain Lightning	8	1494
☐	1 Unenchanted Destruction Staff, 3 Heart Stones	Staff of Ice Storms	8	1401
☐	1 Unenchanted Destruction Staff, 4 Heart Stones	Staff of Icy Spear	8	2931
☐	1 Unenchanted Destruction Staff, 4 Heart Stones	Staff of Inceration	8	2750
☐	1 Unenchanted Destruction Staff, 4 Heart Stones	Staff of the Flame Wall	8	1310
☐	1 Unenchanted Destruction Staff, 4 Heart Stones	Staff of the Frost Wall	8	1468
☐	1 Unenchanted Destruction Staff, 4 Heart Stones	Staff of the Storm Wall	8	1531
☐	1 Unenchanted Destruction Staff, 4 Heart Stones	Staff of Thunderbolts	8	778
	ILLUSION STAFFS			
☐	1 Unenchanted Illusion Staff, 1 Heart Stones	Staff of Courage	8	79
☐	1 Unenchanted Illusion Staff, 2 Heart Stones	Staff of Fear	8	2443
☐	1 Unenchanted Illusion Staff, 2 Heart Stones	Staff of Calm	8	1153
☐	1 Unenchanted Illusion Staff, 2 Heart Stones	Staff of Fury	8	803
☐	1 Unenchanted Illusion Staff, 3 Heart Stones	Staff of Frenzy	8	1149
☐	1 Unenchanted Illusion Staff, 3 Heart Stones	Staff of Inspiration	8	317
☐	1 Unenchanted Illusion Staff, 4 Heart Stones	Staff of Vanquishment	8	1807
	RESTORATION STAFFS			
☐	1 Unenchanted Restoration Staff, 2 Heart Stones	Staff of the Healing Hand	8	198
☐	1 Unenchanted Restoration Staff, 2 Heart Stones	Minor Staff of Turning	8	556
☐	1 Unenchanted Restoration Staff, 3 Heart Stones	Staff of Repulsion	8	675
☐	1 Unenchanted Restoration Staff, 3 Heart Stones	Staff of Mending	8	613
☐	1 Unenchanted Restoration Staff, 3 Heart Stones	Staff of Turning	8	1036
☐	1 Unenchanted Restoration Staff, 4 Heart Stones	Grand Staff of Repulsion	8	1289
☐	1 Unenchanted Restoration Staff, 4 Heart Stones	Grand Staff of Turning	8	1520

Staff:
Staff of Vanquishment

Book:
Heavy Armor Forging

Book:
Jornibret's Last Dance

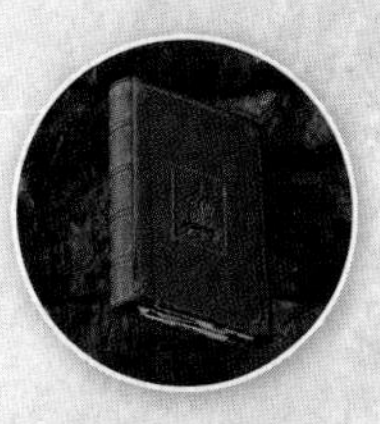

Book:
The Red Kitchen Reader

Book:
Unknown Book, vol. IV

Book:
Black Book: Untold Legends

Scroll:
Scroll of Soul Trap

Gem:
Flawless Diamond

Food:
Eidar Cheese Wheel

Food:
Apple Cabbage Stew

Miscellaneous Items:
Skull (Runic)

Quest Item:
Karstaag's Skull

Table XI: Daedric Artifacts

A list all of the Daedric Artifacts and their abilities. Daedric Artifacts can only be obtained by completing the relevant Daedric Quest. See the Daedric Quests chapter or the Atlas for more details.

NAME	ITEM TYPE	DAMAGE	WEIGHT	VALUE	ENCHANTMENT	NOTES
DAEDRIC ARTIFACTS - WEAPONS						
Dawnbreaker	Sword	12	10	740	+10 Fire Damage; Casts Bane of the Undead on killing an undead	
Ebony Blade	Sword	13	10	2000	Absorb Health 10-30.	
Mace of Molag Bal	Mace	16	18	1257	25 Magicka Damage, 25 Stamina Damage, Soul Trap	Begins at 10, increases to 30 as you kill 10 friends.
Mehrunes' Razor	Dagger	11	3	860	1% Instant Kill	
Sanguine Rose	Staff	0	10	2087	Summons a Dremora for 60s.	
Skull of Corruption	Staff	0	10	1680	20 Damage, or 50 if powered with dreams from sleeping people	A Dremora Lord.
Volendrung	Warhammer	25	26	1843	Absorb Stamina 50	
Wabbajack	Staff	0	10	1565	Change target creature into another random creature	
DAEDRIC ARTIFACTS - ARMOR						
Ebony Mail	Armor	45	28	5000	Muffle while sneaking, Poison Cloak when in combat	
Ring of Hircine	Ring	0	0.3	400	+1 Werewolf Transform / Day	Must already be a werewolf to use this.
Ring of Namira	Ring	0	0.3	870	+50 Stamina. Feeding from NPC corpses raises Health by 50 and Health Regen by 50% for 4 hours	
Savior's Hide	Armor	26	6	2679	Resist Magic 15%, Resist Poison 50%	
Spellbreaker	Shield	38	12	277	Automatic Strength-50 spell ward while blocking	
DAEDRIC ARTIFACTS - OTHER ITEMS						
Azura's Star	Soul Gem		0	1000	Reusable Grand Soul Gem	
Oghma Infinium	Book		1	2500	Once only, +5 Skill Increases to your choice of Combat, Magic, or Stealth Skills.	Black Soul Gems store human souls.
Skeleton Key	Lockpick		0.5	0	Unbreakable Lockpick	
The Black Star	Soul Gem		0	1000	Reusable Black Soul Gem	

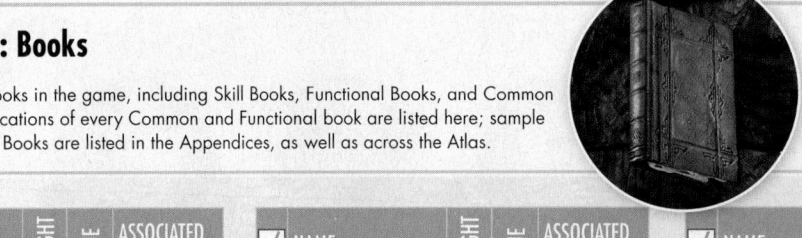

Table XII: Books

A list of all the books in the game, including Skill Books, Functional Books, and Common Books. Sample locations of every Common and Functional book are listed here; sample locations for Skill Books are listed in the Appendices, as well as across the Atlas.

NAME	WEIGHT	VALUE	ASSOCIATED SKILL
SKILL BOOKS			
The Armorer's Challenge	1	70	Smithing
Last Scabbard of Akrash	1	70	Smithing
Light Armor Forging	1	70	Smithing
Cherim's Heart	1	70	Smithing
Heavy Armor Forging	1	70	Smithing
Death Blow of Abernanit	1	50	Block
The Mirror	1	50	Block
A Dance in Fire, v2	1	50	Block
Warrior	1	50	Block
Battle of Red Mountain	1	50	Block
Hallgerd's Tale	1	70	Heavy Armor
2920, MidYear, v6	1	70	Heavy Armor
Chimarvamidium	1	70	Heavy Armor

NAME	WEIGHT	VALUE	ASSOCIATED SKILL
Orsinium and the Orcs	1	70	Heavy Armor
The Knights of the Nine	1	70	Heavy Armor
The Rear Guard	1	50	Light Armor
Ice and Chitin	1	50	Light Armor
Jornibret's Last Dance	1	50	Light Armor
The Refugees	1	50	Light Armor
Rislav The Righteous	1	50	Light Armor
The Importance of Where	1	50	One-Handed
2920, Morning Star, v1	1	50	One-Handed
Fire and Darkness	1	50	One-Handed
Night Falls on Sentinel	1	50	One-Handed
Mace Etiquette	1	50	One-Handed
Words and Philosophy	1	50	Two-Handed
The Legendary Sancre Tor	1	50	Two-Handed

NAME	WEIGHT	VALUE	ASSOCIATED SKILL
King	1	50	Two-Handed
Song Of Hrormir	1	50	Two-Handed
Battle of Sancre Tor	1	50	Two-Handed
Enchanter's Primer	1	50	Enchanting
A Tragedy in Black	1	50	Enchanting
Twin Secrets	1	50	Enchanting
Catalogue of Weapon Enchantments	1	50	Enchanting
Catalogue of Armor Enchantments	1	50	Enchanting
Daughter of the Niben	1	60	Alteration
Breathing Water	1	60	Alteration
Sithis	1	60	Alteration
Reality & Other Falsehoods	1	60	Alteration
The Lunar Lorkhan	1	60	Alteration

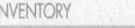

✓	NAME	WEIGHT	VALUE	ASSOCIATED SKILL
☐	The Doors of Oblivion	1	50	Conjuration
☐	Liminal Bridges	1	50	Conjuration
☐	2920, Hearth Fire, v9	1	50	Conjuration
☐	2920, Frostfall, v10	1	50	Conjuration
☐	The Warrior's Charge	1	50	Conjuration
☐	Horrors of Castle Xyr	1	55	Destruction
☐	Response to Bero's Speech	1	55	Destruction
☐	A Hypothetical Treachery	1	55	Destruction
☐	The Art of War Magic	1	55	Destruction
☐	Mystery of Talara, v3	1	55	Destruction
☐	Incident at Necrom	1	60	Illusion
☐	2920, Sun's Dawn, v2	1	60	Illusion
☐	The Black Arts On Trial	1	60	Illusion
☐	Before the Ages of Man	1	60	Illusion
☐	Mystery of Talara, Part 4	1	60	Illusion
☐	Withershins	1	55	Restoration
☐	Racial Phylogeny	1	55	Restoration
☐	The Exodus	1	55	Restoration

✓	NAME	WEIGHT	VALUE	ASSOCIATED SKILL
☐	2920, Rain's Hand, v4	1	55	Restoration
☐	Mystery of Talara, v 2	1	55	Restoration
☐	A Game at Dinner	1	55	Alchemy
☐	Mannimarco, King of Worms	1	55	Alchemy
☐	Song of the Alchemists	1	55	Alchemy
☐	De Rerum Dirennis	1	55	Alchemy
☐	Herbalist's Guide to Skyrim	1	55	Alchemy
☐	The Locked Room	1	75	Lockpicking
☐	The Wolf Queen, v1	1	75	Lockpicking
☐	Proper Lock Design	1	75	Lockpicking
☐	Advances in Lockpicking	1	75	Lockpicking
☐	Surfeit of Thieves	1	75	Lockpicking
☐	The Gold Ribbon of Merit	1	65	Archery
☐	The Marksmanship Lesson	1	65	Archery
☐	Vernaccus and Bourlor	1	65	Archery
☐	Father Of The Niben	1	65	Archery
☐	The Black Arrow, v2	1	65	Archery

✓	NAME	WEIGHT	VALUE	ASSOCIATED SKILL
☐	Purloined Shadows	1	60	Pickpocket
☐	Thief	1	60	Pickpocket
☐	Aevar Stone-Singer	1	60	Pickpocket
☐	Beggar	1	60	Pickpocket
☐	Wulfmare's Guide to Better Thieving	1	60	Pickpocket
☐	Three Thieves	1	75	Sneak
☐	2920, Last Seed, v8	1	75	Sneak
☐	Sacred Witness	1	75	Sneak
☐	Legend of Krately House	1	75	Sneak
☐	The Red Kitchen Reader	1	75	Sneak
☐	A Dance in Fire, v6	1	60	Speech
☐	A Dance in Fire, v7	1	60	Speech
☐	2920, Second Seed, v5	1	60	Speech
☐	The Buying Game	1	60	Speech
☐	Biography of the Wolf Queen	1	60	Speech

✓	NAME	WEIGHT	VALUE	SAMPLE LOCATION	APPROX NUMBER ACROSS SKYRIM
	FUNCTIONAL BOOKS				
☐	An Explorer's Guide to Skyrim	1	8	[1.00] Solitude (The Bards' College)	16
	Adds Map Markers to several Standing Stones.				
☐	The Aetherium Wars	1	15	Fort Dawnguard or Castle Volkihar	20
	Starts Side Quest: Lost to the Ages				
☐	Ahzidal's Descent	1	16	Tel Mithryn	9
	Starts Solstheim Side Quest: Unearthed.				
☐	Deathbrand	1	22	Tel Mithryn	11
	Starts Solstheim Side Quest: Deathbrand if you are Level 36+.				
☐	The Legend of Red Eagle	1	5	[1.00] Solitude (The Bards' College)	38
	Starts Dungeon Quest: The Legend of Red Eagle.				
☐	Lost Legends	1	11	[1.00] Solitude (The Bards' College)	24
	Starts Side Quest: Forbidden Legend.				
☐	Boethiah's Proving	1	25	[4.20] Sepitmus Signus's Outpost	4
	Starts Daedric Quest: Boethiah's Calling. Only appears after you reach Level 32.				
	COMMON BOOKS				
☐	16 Accords of Madness, v. VI	1	25	[3.06] Nightcaller Temple	1
☐	2920, Evening Star, v12	1	11	[1.00] Solitude (Angleine's Aromatics)	3
☐	2920, First Seed, v3	1	11	[7.00] Windhelm (Palace of the Kings)	3
☐	2920, Sun's Dusk, v11	1	11	[1.00] Solitude (Angleine's Aromatics)	3
☐	2920, Sun's Height, v7	1	3	[9.16] Treva's Watch	2
☐	A Children's Anuad	1	6	[1.00] Solitude (The Bards' College)	21
☐	A Dance in Fire, v1	1	3	[1.00] Solitude (The Bards' College)	16
☐	A Dance in Fire, v3	1	3	[1.00] Solitude (The Bards' College)	5
☐	A Dance in Fire, v4	1	4	[1.00] Solitude (The Bards' College)	14
☐	A Dance in Fire, v5	1	30	[9.00] Riften (Mistveil Keep)	1
☐	A Dream of Sovngarde	1	8	[1.00] Solitude (The Bards' College)	15
☐	A Gentleman's Guide to Whiterun	1	3	[1.00] Solitude (The Bards' College)	21
☐	A Kiss, Sweet Mother	1	6	[1.00] Solitude (The Bards' College)	20
☐	A Minor Maze	1	8	[1.00] Solitude (The Bards' College)	14
☐	Aedra and Daedra	1	5	[1.00] Solitude (The Bards' College)	29

✓	NAME	WEIGHT	VALUE	SAMPLE LOCATION	APPROX NUMBER ACROSS SKYRIM
☐	Ahzirr Traajijazeri	1	4	[7.00] Windhelm (Palace of the Kings)	2
☐	Alduin is Real	1	8	[1.00] Solitude (The Bards' College)	17
☐	Amongst the Draugr	1	14	[1.00] Solitude (The Winking Skeever)	1
☐	Ancestors and the Dunmer	1	8	[1.00] Solitude (Angleine's Aromatics)	24
☐	Antecedants of Dwemer Law	1	5	[1.00] Solitude (The Bards' College)	40
☐	Arcana Restored	1	25	[4.00] College of Winterhold (Arcanaeum)	2
☐	Argonian Account, Book 1	1	2	[1.00] Solitude (The Bards' College)	17
☐	Argonian Account, Book 2	1	12	[1.00] Solitude (Temple of the Divines)	3
☐	Argonian Account, Book 3	1	3	[1.00] Solitude (The Bards' College)	21
☐	Argonian Account, Book 4	1	12	[4.07] Driftshade Refuge	2
☐	Azura and the Box	1	10	[4.00] College of Winterhold (Hall of Attainment)	6
☐	Beggar Prince	1	5	[1.00] Solitude (The Bards' College)	45
☐	Biography of Barenziah, v1	1	3	[1.00] Solitude (The Bards' College)	44
☐	Biography of Barenziah, v2	1	3	[1.00] Solitude (The Bards' College)	40
☐	Biography of Barenziah, v3	1	3	[1.00] Solitude (The Bards' College)	49
☐	Bone, Part I	1	6	Tel Mithryn	9
☐	Bone, Part II	1	6	Raven Rock (Bulwark)	6
☐	Brief History of the Empire, v1	1	2	[1.00] Solitude (The Bards' College)	56
☐	Brief History of the Empire, v2	1	2	[1.00] Solitude (The Bards' College)	57
☐	Brief History of the Empire, v3	1	2	[1.00] Solitude (The Bards' College)	48
☐	Brief History of the Empire, v4	1	2	[1.00] Solitude (The Bards' College)	46
☐	Brothers of Darkness	1	30	[1.28] Katariah (Dark Brotherhood Quest: Hail Sithis!)	1
☐	Cats of Skyrim	1	7	[4.00] College of Winterhold (Arcanaeum)	15
☐	Chance's Folly	1	6	[4.00] College of Winterhold (Arcanaeum)	34
☐	Changed Ones	1	11	Tel Mithryn (Steward's House)	2
☐	Charwich-Koniinge Letters, v1	1	13	[1.00] Solitude (The Bards' College)	3
☐	Charwich-Koniinge Letters, v3	1	13	[1.00] Solitude (Vittoria Vici's House)	1
☐	Charwich-Koniinge, v2	1	13	[4.07] Driftshade Refuge	1

✓	NAME	WEIGHT	VALUE	SAMPLE LOCATION	APPROX NUMBER ACROSS SKYRIM
	Chaurus Pie: A Recipe	1	11	[5.00] Markarth (Endon's House)	1
	Children of the All-Maker	1	11	Skaal Village (Shaman's Hut)	2
	Children of the Sky	1	25	[9.00] Riften (Ratway Warrens: Esbern's Hideout)	2
	Chimarvamidium	1	20	[4.20] Septimus Signus's Outpost	4
	Chronicles of Nchuleft	1	30	[5.00] Markarth (Dwemer Museum)	1
	Cleansing of the Fane	1	20	[Random Dungeon] (College of Winterhold Radiant Quest: Valuable Book Procurement)	1
	Confessions of a Dunmer Skooma Eater	1	3	Raven Rock (Bulwark)	5
	Confessions of a Khajiit Fur Trader	1	11	Dead Drop Falls	1
	Darkest Darkness	1	5	[1.00] Solitude (The Bards' College)	47
	Death of a Wanderer	1	12	[1.00] Solitude (Castle Dour, Thalmor Headquarters)	1
	Diary of Faire Agarwen	1	20	College of Winterhold (Arcanaeum)	1
	Translated version of Unknown Book, vol. III.				
	Dragon Language: Myth no More	1	14	[5.31] Sky Haven Temple	1
	Dunmer of Skyrim	1	7	[1.00] Solitude (The Bards' College)	16
	Dwarves, v1	1	10	[5.00] Markarth (Dwemer Museum Bookshelf)	6
	Dwarves, v2	1	10	[5.00] Markarth (Dwemer Museum Bookshelf)	5
	Dwarves, v3	1	10	[5.00] Markarth (Arnleif and Sons)	2
	Dwemer History and Culture	1	13	[1.00] Solitude (Castle Dour)	9
	Dwemer Inquiries Vol I	1	6	[5.00] Markarth (Dwemer Museum Bookshelf)	19
	Dwemer Inquiries Vol II	1	6	[1.00] Solitude (The Bards' College)	16
	Dwemer Inquiries Vol III	1	6	[5.00] Markarth (Dwemer Museum Bookshelf)	21
	Effects of the Elder Scrolls	1	25	[4.00] College of Winterhold (Arcanaeum)	3
	Fall from Glory	1	8	[4.00] College of Winterhold (Arcanaeum)	20
	Fall of the Snow Prince	1	11	[1.00] Solitude (Radiant Raiment)	2
	Feyfolken I	1	12	[1.00] Solitude (The Bards' College)	2
	Feyfolken II	1	12	[1.00] Solitude (The Bards' College)	3
	Feyfolken III	1	12	[4.00] Winterhold (Jarl's Longhouse)	2
	Final Lesson	1	14	[5.34] Old Hroldan Inn	1
	Five Songs of King Wulfharth	1	30	[7.00] Windhelm (Palace of the Kings)	1
	Flight from the Thalmor	1	13	[5.31] Sky Haven Temple	2
	Forge, Hammer and Anvil	1	14	[4.07] Driftshade Refuge	1
	Fragment: On Artaeum	1	20	[6.29] Fellglow Keep (College of Winterhold Quest: Hitting the Books)	1
	Frontier, Conquest	1	5	[1.00] Solitude (The Bards' College)	29
	Galerion The Mystic	1	6	[1.00] Solitude (The Bards' College)	34
	Ghosts in the Storm	1	13	[8.00] Falkreath (Jarl's Longhouse)	2
	Glories and Laments	1	25	[1.28] Katariah (Dark Brotherhood Quest: Hail Sithis!)	1
	Gods and Worship	1	5	[1.00] Solitude (The Bards' College)	31
	Great Harbingers	1	13	[6.00] Whiterun (Jorrvaskr)	1
	Hanging Gardens	1	30	[9.36] Largashbur	2
	Harvesting Frostbite Spider Venom	1	7	[1.00] Solitude (The Bards' College)	14
	Herbane's Bestiary: Automatons	1	14	[4.00] College of Winterhold (Arcanaeum)	2
	Herbane's Bestiary: Hagravens	1	6	[1.00] Solitude (The Bards' College)	18
	Herbane's Bestiary: Ice Wraiths	1	7	[1.00] Solitude (The Bards' College)	16
	History of Raven Rock, Vol. I	1	7	Raven Rock (The Retching Netch)	11

✓	NAME	WEIGHT	VALUE	SAMPLE LOCATION	APPROX NUMBER ACROSS SKYRIM
	History of Raven Rock, Vol. II	1	7	Raven Rock (The Retching Netch)	8
	History of Raven Rock, Vol. III	1	7	Raven Rock (The Retching Netch)	6
	Horker Attacks	1	4	[1.00] Solitude (The Bards' College)	19
	Immortal Blood	1	4	[1.00] Solitude (The Bards' College)	18
	Imperial Report on Saarthal	1	13	[4.00] College of Winterhold (Arcanaeum)	3
	Invocation of Azura	1	20	[1.00] Solitude (The Bards' College)	1
	Journal of Mirtil Angoth	1	20	College of Winterhold (Arcanaeum)	1
	Translated version of Unknown Book, vol. II.				
	Killing - Before You're Killed	1	3	[1.00] Solitude (The Bards' College)	20
	Kolb & the Dragon	1	2	[1.00] Solitude (The Bards' College)	18
	Last King of the Ayleids	1	25	[6.29] Fellglow Keep (College of Winterhold Quest: Hitting the Books)	1
	Life of Uriel Septim VII	1	5	[1.00] Solitude (The Bards' College)	47
	Lives of the Saints	1	5	Tel Mithryn	2
	Lusty Argonian Maid Folio	1	25	Wreck of the Strident Squall	1
	Lycanthropic Legends of Skyrim	1	20	[6.00] Whiterun (Jorrvaskr)	1
	Magic from the Sky	1	12	[9.02] Shroud Hearth Barrow	3
	Mixed Unit Tactics	1	5	[1.00] Solitude (The Bards' College)	48
	Mysterious Akavir	1	5	[4.00] College of Winterhold (Arcanaeum)	30
	Mystery of Talara, v 1	1	3	[1.00] Solitude (The Bards' College)	17
	Mystery of Talara, v5	1	11	[1.00] Solitude (The Bards' College)	2
	Myths of Sheogorath	1	2	[1.00] Solitude (The Bards' College)	31
	Nchunak's Fire and Faith	1	20	Fahlbtharz (Exterior)	1
	Nerevar Moon and Star	1	30	[5.00] Markarth (Dwemer Museum)	1
	Nerevar at Red Mountain	1	30	Tel Mithryn	1
	N'Gasta! Kvata! Kvakis!	1	20	[1.00] Solitude (The Bards' College)	1
	Nightingales: Fact or Fiction?	1	3	[4.00] College of Winterhold (Arcanaeum)	10
	Nords Arise!	1	4	[1.00] Solitude (The Bards' College)	19
	Nords of Skyrim	1	6	[1.00] Solitude (The Bards' College)	16
	Ode To The Tundrastriders	1	8	[1.00] Solitude (The Bards' College)	13
	Of Crossed Daggers	1	5	[1.00] Solitude (The Bards' College)	17
	Of Fjori and Holgeir	1	6	[1.00] Solitude (The Bards' College)	16
	Olaf and the Dragon	1	2	[1.00] Solitude (The Bards' College)	19
	On Apocrypha: Boneless Limbs	1	100	[S.A07] Waking Dreams	1
	On Apocrypha: Delving Pincers	1	100	[S.A07] Waking Dreams	1
	On Apocrypha: Gnashing Blades	1	100	[S.A07] Waking Dreams	1
	On Apocrypha: Prying Orbs	1	100	[S.A07] Waking Dreams	1
	On Oblivion	1	10	[1.00] Solitude (The Bards' College)	4
	On Stepping Lightly	1	12	[1.00] Solitude (The Bards' College)	1
	On the Great Collapse	1	12	[5.00] Markarth (Dwemer Museum Bookshelf)	6
	Palla, volume 1	1	3	[1.00] Solitude (Castle Dour Dungeons)	6
	Palla, volume 2	1	10	[9.00] Riften (Elgrim's Elixirs)	1
	Pension of the Ancestor Moth	1	8	[1.00] Solitude (The Bards' College)	15
	Physicalities of Werewolves	1	14	[8.11] Half-Moon Mill	2
	Pirate King of the Abecean	1	6	[1.00] Solitude (The Bards' College)	19
	Remanada	1	20	[5.31] Sky Haven Temple	3
	Report: Disaster at Ionith	1	3	[1.00] Solitude (The Bards' College)	25
	Rising Threat, Vol. I	1	6	[1.00] Solitude (The Bards' College)	13
	Rising Threat, Vol. II	1	6	[1.00] Solitude (The Bards' College)	14
	Rising Threat, Vol. III	1	6	[1.00] Solitude (The Bards' College)	16

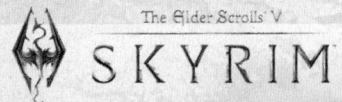

☑	NAME	WEIGHT	VALUE	SAMPLE LOCATION	APPROX NUMBER ACROSS SKYRIM
☐	Rising Threat, Vol. IV	1	6	[1.00] Solitude (The Bards' College)	14
☐	Ruins of Kemel-Ze	1	7	[6.00] Whiterun (Jorrvaskr)	22
☐	Saint Jiub's Opus	1	1,250	Soul Cairn	1
	Reward for Side Quest: Impatience of a Saint.				
☐	Scourge of the Gray Quarter	1	8	[1.00] Solitude (The Bards' College)	16
☐	Shadowmarks	1	30	[9.00] Riften (The Ratway Cistern)	4
☐	Shezarr and the Divines	1	11	[1.00] Solitude (The Winking Skeever)	3
☐	Short History of Morrowind	1	15	[1.00] Solitude (The Blue Palace)	4
☐	Song of the Askelde Men	1	5	[1.00] Solitude (The Bards' College)	16
☐	Songs of Skyrim	1	10	[7.05] Kynesgrove (Braidwood Inn)	1
☐	Songs of Skyrim: Revised	1	14	[6.21] Pelagia Farm	1
☐	Songs of the Return, Vol 19	1	6	[1.00] Solitude (The Bards' College)	18
☐	Songs of the Return, Vol 2	1	6	[1.00] Solitude (The Bards' College)	21
☐	Songs of the Return, vol 24	1	30	[6.00] Whiterun (Jorrvaskr)	1
☐	Songs of the Return, Vol 56	1	6	[1.00] Solitude (The Bards' College)	20
☐	Songs of the Return, Vol 7	1	6	[1.00] Solitude (The Bards' College)	17
☐	Souls, Black and White	1	20	[4.00] College of Winterhold (Hall of Attainment)	1
☐	Sovngarde: A Reexamination	1	12	[9.00] Riften (Riften Jail)	2
☐	Spirit of Nirn	1	6	[1.00] Solitude (The Bards' College)	33
☐	Spirit of the Daedra	1	25	[6.02] Rorikshead (Rorik's Manor)	1
☐	The "Madmen" of the Reach	1	7	[1.00] Solitude (The Bards' College)	18
☐	The Adabal-a	1	25	[1.28] Katariah (Dark Brotherhood Quest: Hail Sithis!)	2
☐	The Alduin/Akatosh Dichotomy	1	8	[1.00] Solitude (The Bards' College)	12
☐	The Amulet of Kings	1	6	[1.00] Solitude (The Bards' College)	22
☐	The Apprentice's Assistant	1	12	[8.00] Falkreath (Corpslight Farm)	2
☐	The Anticipations	1	14	[S.A07] Waking Dreams (Chapter IV)	1
☐	The Arcturian Heresy	1	6	[1.00] Solitude (The Bards' College)	22
☐	The Axe Man	1	6	Raven Rock (Bulwark)	7
☐	The Bear of Markarth	1	8	[1.00] Solitude (The Bards' College)	17
☐	The Beginner's Guide to Homesteading	1	10	Any of the three plots of land, on the Carpenter's Workbench	3
	Accessible once Hearthfire begins.				
☐	The Betrayed	1	20	College of Winterhold (Arcanaeum)	1
	Translated version of Unknown Book, vol. 1.				
☐	The Black Arrow, v1	1	2	[1.00] Solitude (The Bards' College)	9
☐	The Book of Daedra	1	5	[1.00] Solitude (The Bards' College)	42
☐	The Book of Life and Service	1	35	Soul Cairn [SC1.1] Steps of the Barrier Walls (South).	6
☐	The Book of the Dragonborn	1	12	[4.00] College of Winterhold (Arcanaeum)	4
☐	The Cabin in the Woods	1	8	[1.00] Solitude (The Bards' College)	13
☐	The Cake and The Diamond	1	5	[1.00] Solitude (The Bards' College)	47
☐	The City of Stone	1	4	[1.00] Solitude (The Bards' College)	24
☐	The Code of Malacath	1	2	[1.00] Solitude (The Bards' College)	23
☐	The Doors of the Spirit	1	5	Tel Mithryn	2
☐	The Dowry	1	11	[9.00] Riften (Mistveil Keep)	1
☐	The Dragon Break	1	14	[9.00] Riften (Ratway Warrens: Esbern's Hideout)	2
☐	The Dragon War	1	12	[9.00] Riften (Ratway Warrens: Esbern's Hideout)	3
☐	The Falmer: A Study	1	11	[4.00] College of Winterhold (Arcanaeum)	3
☐	The Firmament	1	5	[1.00] Solitude (The Bards' College)	54
☐	The Firsthold Revolt	1	7	[1.00] Solitude (The Bards' College)	32
☐	The Five Far Stars	1	7	Raven Rock (Bulwark)	6

☑	NAME	WEIGHT	VALUE	SAMPLE LOCATION	APPROX NUMBER ACROSS SKYRIM
☐	The Great War	1	6	[1.00] Solitude (The Bards' College)	15
☐	The Guardian and the Traitor	2	20	Skaal Village (Greathall)	2
☐	The Holds of Skyrim	1	3	[1.00] Solitude (The Bards' College)	19
☐	The Hope of the Redoran	1	5	[1.00] Solitude (The Bards' College)	31
☐	The House of Troubles	1	7	Raven Rock (Bulwark)	9
☐	The Legendary Scourge	1	30	[Random Dungeon] (College of Winterhold Radiant Quest: Valuable Book Procurement)	1
☐	The Lusty Argonian Maid, v1	1	14	[9.00] Riften (Haelga's Bunkhouse)	4
☐	The Lusty Argonian Maid, v2	1	14	[9.00] Riften (Haelga's Bunkhouse)	3
☐	The Madness of Pelagius	1	12	[6.00] Whiterun (Dragonsreach Jarl's Quarters)	1
☐	The Monomyth	1	8	[1.00] Solitude (The Bards' College)	13
☐	The Night Mother's Truth	1	25	[8.00] Falkreath (Jarl's Longhouse)	2
☐	The Oblivion Crisis	1	6	[1.00] Solitude (The Bards' College)	17
☐	The Old Ways	1	30	[4.19] Fort Kastav	1
☐	The Pig Children	1	20	[1.00] Solitude (The Bards' College)	1
☐	The Poison Song, Book I	1	3	Raven Rock (Alor House)	6
☐	The Poison Song, Book II	1	3	Raven Rock (Alor House)	5
☐	The Poison Song, Book III	1	3	Raven Rock (Alor House)	5
☐	The Poison Song, Book IV	1	3	Raven Rock (Alor House)	4
☐	The Poison Song, Book V	1	3	Raven Rock (Alor House)	2
☐	The Poison Song, Book VI	1	3	Raven Rock (Alor House)	3
☐	The Poison Song, Book VII	1	3	Raven Rock (Alor House)	2
☐	The Ransom of Zarek	1	2	[1.00] Solitude (The Bards' College)	14
☐	The Real Barenziah, v1	1	5	[1.00] Solitude (The Bards' College)	21
☐	The Real Barenziah, v2	1	5	[1.00] Solitude (The Bards' College)	41
☐	The Real Barenziah, v3	1	5	[1.00] Solitude (The Bards' College)	37
☐	The Real Barenziah, v4	1	5	[1.00] Solitude (The Bards' College)	37
☐	The Real Barenziah, v5	1	5	[6.00] Whiterun (Jorrvaskr)	25
☐	The Reclamations	1	6	Raven Rock (Temple)	4
☐	The Red Book of Riddles	1	30	[3.25] Nightgate Inn (Carried by Fultheim)	1
☐	The Red Year, Vol. I	1	6	Raven Rock (Temple)	9
☐	The Red Year, Vol. II	1	6	Raven Rock (Temple)	5
☐	The Rise and Fall of the Blades	1	11	[4.00] College of Winterhold (Arcanaeum)	5
☐	The Seed	1	10	[1.00] Solitude (The Bards' College)	3
☐	The Song of Pelinal, v1	1	5	[9.00] Riften (Temple of Mara)	15
☐	The Song of Pelinal, v2	1	5	[1.00] Solitude (The Bards' College)	18
☐	The Song of Pelinal, v3	1	5	[1.00] Solitude (The Bards' College)	15
☐	The Song of Pelinal, v4	1	5	[1.00] Solitude (The Bards' College)	14
☐	The Song of Pelinal, v5	1	5	[1.00] Solitude (The Bards' College)	18
☐	The Song of Pelinal, v6	1	5	[1.00] Solitude (The Bards' College)	12
☐	The Song of Pelinal, v7	1	5	[1.00] Solitude (The Bards' College)	11
☐	The Song of Pelinal, v8	1	5	[1.00] Solitude (The Bards' College)	12
☐	The Sultry Argonian Bard, v1	1	14	Dead Drop Mine	1
☐	The Tale of Dro'Zira	1	11	[8.00] Falkreath (Dengeir's House)	2
☐	The Talos Mistake	1	7	[1.00] Solitude (The Blue Palace)	18
☐	The Third Door	1	11	[5.00] Markarth (Vlindrell Hall)	1
☐	The Third Era Timeline	1	8	[1.00] Solitude (The Bards' College)	16
☐	Touching the Sky	1	20	College of Winterhold (Arcanaeum)	1
	Translated version of Unknown Book, vol. IV.				
☐	The True Nature of Orcs	1	20	[5.38] Dushnikh Yal	4
☐	The True Noble's Code	1	7	Tel Mithryn	4

NAME	WEIGHT	VALUE	SAMPLE LOCATION	APPROX NUMBER ACROSS SKYRIM
Unknown Book, vol. I	1	20	The Forgotten Vale [FV2.A] Snow Lake Entrance: The Sprawled Skeleton.	1
Urag will buy this book and give you its translation, The Betrayed.				
Unknown Book, vol. II	1	20	The Forgotten Vale [FV2.H] Forgotton Vale Overlook: Vista.	1
Urag will buy this book and give you its translation, Journal of Mirtil Angoth.				
Unknown Book, vol. III	1	20	The Forgotten Vale [FV3.M] Falmer Hut, Dead-End Ledge.	1
Urag will buy this book and give you its translation, Diary of Faire Agarwen.				
Unknown Book, vol. IV	1	20	The Forgotten Vale [FV4.G] Falmer Fissure Village (Part 3).	1
Urag will buy this book and give you its translation, Touching the Sky.				
The Waters of Oblivion	1	30	[Random Dungeon] (College of Winterhold Radiant Quest: Valuable Book Procurement)	1
The Wild Elves	1	25	[1.00] Solitude (The Bards' College)	1
The Windhelm Letters	1	7	[1.00] Solitude (The Bards' College)	15
The Wispmother	1	8	[4.00] College of Winterhold (Arcanaeum)	15
The Wolf Queen, v2	1	4	[1.00] Solitude (The Bards' College)	22
The Wolf Queen, v3	1	4	[1.00] Solitude (The Bards' College)	27
The Wolf Queen, v4	1	4	[1.00] Solitude (The Bards' College)	17
The Wolf Queen, v5	1	4	[1.00] Solitude (The Bards' College)	21
The Wolf Queen, v6	1	30	[6.00] Whiterun (Dragonsreach)	2
The Wolf Queen, v7	1	4	[1.00] Solitude (The Bards' College)	19
The Wolf Queen, v8	1	12	[1.00] Solitude (Proudspire Manor)	2
The Woodcutter's Wife	1	8	[1.00] Solitude (The Bards' College)	14
There Be Dragons	1	11	[6.27] Riverwood (Sleeping Giant Inn)	1
Thief of Virtue	1	5	[1.00] Solitude (The Bards' College)	42
Thirsk, A Revised History	1	3	[S.A07] Waking Dreams (Chapter IV)	2
Trap	1	13	[S.S02] Blood Skal Barrow (Exterior)	1
Treatise on Ayleidic Cities	1	25	[3.00] Dawnstar (The White Hall)	1
Trials of St. Alessia	1	5	[1.00] Solitude (The Bards' College)	13
Troll Slaying	1	8	[1.00] Solitude (The Bards' College)	15
Uncommon Taste	1	3	[1.00] Solitude (The Bards' College)	28
Varieties of Daedra	1	11	[3.06] Nightcaller Temple (Daedric Quest: Waking Nightmare)	2
Varieties of Faith in the Empire	1	13	Tel Mithryn	1
Vernaccus and Bourlor	1	6	[1.00] Solitude (The Bards' College)	19
Wabbajack	1	7	[1.00] Solitude (The Bards' College)	15
Walking the World, Vol XI	1	8	[1.00] Solitude (The Bards' College)	15
War of the First Council	1	25	[5.00] Markarth (Dwemer Museum)	1
Watcher of Stones	1	8	[1.00] Solitude (The Bards' College)	16
Where Were You When the Dragon Broke?	1	13	[S.N03] Fahlbtharz	1
Wind and Sand	1	100	[Random dungeon]	1
Words of the Wind	1	5	Tel Mithryn	6
Words of Clan Mother Ahnissi	1	14	[4.00] Winterhold (The Frozen Hearth)	1
Wraith's Wedding Dowry	1	10	[1.25] Brinewater Grotto	2
Yellow Book of Riddles	1	3	[1.00] Solitude (The Bards' College)	31
Yngol and the Sea-Ghosts	1	5	[1.00] Solitude (The Bards' College)	37

NAME	WEIGHT	VALUE	NOTES
BLACK BOOKS			
Black Book: Epistolary Acumen	1	2000	Found in Nchardak Reading Room.
Black Book: Filament and Filigree	1	2000	Found in Kolbjorn Barrow.
Black Book: The Hidden Twilight	1	2000	Found in Tel Mithryn.
Black Book: The Sallow Regent	1	2000	Found in White Ridge Barrow Sanctum.
Black Book: The Winds of Change	1	2000	Found in Raven Rock Mine.
Black Book: Untold Legends	1	2000	Found in Benkongerike Great Hall.
Black Book: Waking Dreams	1	2000	Found in The Temple of Miraak Sanctum.

Table XIII: Spell Tomes

A list of spell tomes. Cross-reference this list with the Spell Table (on page 132) to identify any restrictions.

NAME	WEIGHT	VALUE	TEACHES SPELL
SPELL TOMES			
Spell Tome: Ash Rune	1	635	Ash Rune
Spell Tome: Ash Shell	1	425	Ash Shell
Spell Tome: Bane of the Undead	1	1200	Bane of the Undead
Spell Tome: Banish Daedra	1	346	Banish Daedra
Spell Tome: Blizzard	1	1350	Blizzard
Spell Tome: Bound Battleaxe	1	99	Bound Battleaxe
Spell Tome: Bound Bow	1	335	Bound Bow
Spell Tome: Bound Dagger	1	38	Bound Dagger
Spell Tome: Bound Sword	1	49	Bound Sword
Spell Tome: Call To Arms	1	1150	Call to Arms
Spell Tome: Calm	1	91	Calm
Spell Tome: Candlelight	1	44	Candlelight
Spell Tome: Chain Lightning	1	390	Chain Lightning
Spell Tome: Circle Of Protection	1	650	Circle of Protection
Spell Tome: Clairvoyance	1	50	Clairvoyance
Spell Tome: Close Wounds	1	360	Close Wounds
Spell Tome: Command Daedra	1	660	Command Daedra
Spell Tome: Conjure Ash Guardian	1	720	Conjure Ash Guardian
Spell Tome: Conjure Boneman	1	75	Conjure Boneman
Spell Tome: Conjure Dremora Lord	1	730	Conjure Dremora Lord
Spell Tome: Conjure Familiar	1	49	Conjure Familiar
Spell Tome: Conjure Flame Atronach	1	99	Conjure Flame Atronach
Spell Tome: Conjure Frost Atronach	1	347	Conjure Frost Atronach
Spell Tome: Conjure Mistman	1	75	Conjure Mistman
Spell Tome: Conjure Seeker	1	307	Conjure Seeker
Spell Tome: Conjure Storm Atronach	1	690	Conjure Storm Atronach
Spell Tome: Conjure Wrathman	1	75	Conjure Wrathman
Spell Tome: Courage	1	46	Courage
Spell Tome: Dead Thrall	1	1270	Dead Thrall
Spell Tome: Detect Life	1	332	Detect Life
Spell Tome: Detect Undead	1	600	Detect Dead
Spell Tome: Dragonhide	1	1389	Dragonhide
Spell Tome: Dread Zombie	1	630	Dread Zombie

✓	NAME	WEIGHT	VALUE	TEACHES SPELL
	Spell Tome: Ebonyflesh	1	650	Ebonyflesh
	Spell Tome: Expel Daedra	1	620	Expel Daedra
	Spell Tome: Fast Healing	1	94	Fast Healing
	Spell Tome: Fear	1	80	Fear
	Spell Tome: Fire Rune	1	90	Fire Rune
	Spell Tome: Fire Storm	1	1290	Fire Storm
	Spell Tome: Fireball	1	345	Fireball
	Spell Tome: Firebolt	1	96	Firebolt
	Spell Tome: Flame Cloak	1	325	Flame Cloak
	Spell Tome: Flame Thrall	1	1260	Flame Thrall
	Spell Tome: Flames	1	50	Flames
	Spell Tome: Frenzy	1	330	Frenzy
	Spell Tome: Frenzy Rune	1	310	Frenzy Rune
	Spell Tome: Frost Cloak	1	340	Frost Cloak
	Spell Tome: Frost Rune	1	92	Frost Rune
	Spell Tome: Frost Thrall	1	1300	Frost Thrall
	Spell Tome: Frostbite	1	47	Frostbite
	Spell Tome: Fury	1	43	Fury
	Spell Tome: Grand Healing	1	680	Grand Healing
	Spell Tome: Greater Ward	1	341	Greater Ward
	Spell Tome: Guardian Circle	1	1220	Guardian Circle
	Spell Tome: Harmony	1	1220	Harmony
	Spell Tome: Heal Other	1	300	Heal Other
	Spell Tome: Heal Undead	1	370	Heal Undead
	Spell Tome: Healing	1	50	Healing
	Spell Tome: Healing Hands	1	89	Healing Hands
	Spell Tome: Hysteria	1	1240	Hysteria
	Spell Tome: Ice Spike	1	96	Ice Spike
	Spell Tome: Ice Storm	1	360	Ice Storm
	Spell Tome: Icy Spear	1	725	Icy Spear
	Spell Tome: Incinerate	1	710	Incinerate
	Spell Tome: Invisibility	1	625	Invisibility
	Spell Tome: Ironflesh	1	341	Ironflesh
	Spell Tome: Lesser Ward	1	45	Lesser Ward
	Spell Tome: Lightning Bolt	1	95	Lightning Bolt
	Spell Tome: Lightning Cloak	1	355	Lightning Cloak
	Spell Tome: Lightning Rune	1	93	Lightning Rune
	Spell Tome: Lightning Storm	1	1400	Lightning Storm
	Spell Tome: Magelight	1	87	Magelight
	Spell Tome: Mass Paralysis	1	1280	Mass Paralysis
	Spell Tome: Mayhem	1	1250	Mayhem
	Spell Tome: Muffle	1	88	Muffle
	Spell Tome: Necromantic Healing	1	115	Necromantic Healing
	Spell Tome: Oakflesh	1	44	Oakflesh
	Spell Tome: Pacify	1	610	Pacify
	Spell Tome: Paralyze	1	685	Paralyze
	Spell Tome: Poison Rune	1	290	Poison Rune
	Spell Tome: Raise Zombie	1	49	Raise Zombie
	Spell Tome: Rally	1	300	Rally
	Spell Tome: Reanimate Corpse	1	99	Reanimate Corpse
	Spell Tome: Repel Lesser Undead	1	333	Repel Lesser Undead
	Spell Tome: Repel Undead	1	655	Repel Undead
	Spell Tome: Revenant	1	340	Revenant
	Spell Tome: Rout	1	653	Rout
	Spell Tome: Soul Trap	1	100	Soul Trap
	Spell Tome: Sparks	1	46	Sparks
	Spell Tome: Steadfast Ward	1	92	Steadfast Ward
	Spell Tome: Stendarr's Aura	1	335	Stendarr's Aura
	Spell Tome: Stoneflesh	1	95	Stoneflesh
	Spell Tome: Storm Thrall	1	1350	Storm Thrall
	Spell Tome: Sun Fire	1	80	Sun Fire
	Spell Tome: Telekinesis	1	326	Telekinesis
	Spell Tome: Thunderbolt	1	750	Thunderbolt
	Spell Tome: Transmute Mineral Ore	1	900	Transmute
	Spell Tome: Turn Greater Undead	1	664	Turn Greater Undead
	Spell Tome: Turn Lesser Undead	1	89	Turn Lesser Undead
	Spell Tome: Turn Undead	1	323	Turn Undead
	Spell Tome: Vampire's Bane	1	340	Vampire's Bane
	Spell Tome: Wall of Flames	1	680	Wall of Flames
	Spell Tome: Wall of Frost	1	700	Wall of Frost
	Spell Tome: Wall of Storms	1	725	Wall of Storms
	Spell Tome: Waterbreathing	1	340	Waterbreathing
	Spell Tome: Whirlwind Cloak	1	395	Whirlwind Cloak

Table XIV: Potions

A list of all the standard potions and poisons in the realm, including usable potions acquired as part of a quest (like Vaermina's Torpor). Non-usable potions (for example, potions you are asked to deliver to someone) are listed on a table in the Other Items section.

✓	POTION NAME	WEIGHT	VALUE	EFFECT
	POTIONS			
	Ice Wraith Essence	0.5	96	+20% Frost Resistance, 60s
	Potion of Cure Disease	0.5	79	Cures all active diseases.
	Cure Poison	0.5	31	Cures all active poisons.
	Potion of Strength	0.5	170	+20 Carry Weight, 5m
	Draught of Strength	0.5	266	+30 Carry Weight, 5m
	Solution of Strength	0.5	365	+40 Carry Weight, 5m
	Philter of Strength	0.5	467	+50 Carry Weight, 5m
	Elixir of Strength	0.5	571	+60 Carry Weight, 5m
	Potion of Regeneration	0.5	311	+50% Health Regen, 5m
	Draught of Regeneration	0.5	380	+60% Health Regen, 5m
	Solution of Regeneration	0.5	451	+70% Health Regen, 5m
	Philter of Regeneration	0.5	522	+80% Health Regen, 5m
	Elixir of Regeneration	0.5	668	+100% Health Regen, 5m
	Potion of Health	0.5	67	+20 Max Health, 60s
	Draught of Health	0.5	145	+40 Max Health, 60s
	Solution of Health	0.5	226	+60 Max Health, 60s
	Philter of Health	0.5	311	+80 Max Health, 60s
	Elixir of Health	0.5	398	+100 Max Health, 60s
	Potion of Extra Magicka	0.5	58	+20 Max Magicka, 60s
	Draught of Extra Magicka	0.5	124	+40 Max Magicka, 60s
	Solution of Extra Magicka	0.5	194	+60 Max Magicka, 60s
	Philter of Extra Magicka	0.5	266	+80 Max Magicka, 60s
	Elixir of Extra Magicka	0.5	341	+100 Max Magicka, 60s
	Potion of Lasting Potency	0.5	311	+50% Magicka Regen, 5m
	Draught of Lasting Potency	0.5	380	+60% Magicka Regen, 5m
	Solution of Lasting Potency	0.5	451	+70% Magicka Regen, 5m
	Philter of Lasting Potency	0.5	522	+80% Magicka Regen, 5m
	Elixir of Lasting Potency	0.5	668	+100% Magicka Regen, 5m
	Potion of Alteration	0.5	49	+25% Alteration, 60s
	Draught of Alteration	0.5	106	+50% Alteration, 60s
	Philter of Alteration	0.5	165	+75% Alteration, 60s
	Elixir of Alteration	0.5	227	+100% Alteration, 60s
	Potion of Haggling	0.5	84	+10% Better Prices, 30s
	Draught of Haggling	0.5	131	+15% Better Prices, 30s
	Philter of Haggling	0.5	180	+25% Better Prices, 30s
	Elixir of Haggling	0.5	230	+30% Better Prices, 30s
	Potion of the Defender	0.5	45	+10% Block, 60s

POTION NAME	WEIGHT	VALUE	EFFECT
Draught of the Defender	0.5	70	+15% Block, 60s
Philter of the Defender	0.5	96	+20% Block, 60s
Elixir of the Defender	0.5	123	+25% Block, 60s
Conjurer's Potion	0.5	61	+25% Conjuration, 60s
Conjurer's Draught	0.5	132	+50% Conjuration, 60s
Conjurer's Philter	0.5	207	+75% Conjuration, 60s
Conjurer's Elixir	0.5	284	+100% Conjuration, 60s
Potion of Destruction	0.5	96	+20% Destruction, 60s
Draught of Destruction	0.5	151	+30% Destruction, 60s
Philter of Destruction	0.5	207	+40% Destruction, 60s
Elixir of Destruction	0.5	265	+50% Destruction, 60s
Enchanter's Potion	0.5	54	+10% Enchanting, 60s
Enchanter's Draught	0.5	84	+15% Enchanting, 60s
Enchanter's Philter	0.5	116	+20% Enchanting, 60s
Enchanter's Elixir	0.5	148	+25% Enchanting, 60s
Potion of the Knight	0.5	45	+10 Heavy Armor, 60s
Draught of the Knight	0.5	70	+15 Heavy Armor, 60s
Philter of the Knight	0.5	96	+20 Heavy Armor, 60s
Elixir of the Knight	0.5	123	+25 Heavy Armor, 60s
Potion of Illusion	0.5	99	+25% Illusion, 60s
Draught of Illusion	0.5	212	+50% Illusion, 60s
Philter of Illusion	0.5	331	+75% Illusion, 60s
Elixir of Illusion	0.5	455	+100% Illusion, 60s
Skirmisher's Potion	0.5	45	+10 Light Armor, 60s
Skirmisher's Draught	0.5	70	+15 Light Armor, 60s
Skirmisher's Philter	0.5	96	+20 Light Armor, 60s
Skirmisher's Elixir	0.5	123	+25 Light Armor, 60s
Potion of Lockpicking	0.5	45	+20% Lockpicking, 30s
Draught of Lockpicking	0.5	70	+30% Lockpicking, 30s
Philter of Lockpicking	0.5	96	+40% Lockpicking, 30s
Elixir of Lockpicking	0.5	123	+50% Lockpicking, 30s
Potion of True Shot	0.5	96	+20% Bow Damage, 60s
Draught of True Shot	0.5	151	+30% Bow Damage, 60s
Philter of True Shot	0.5	207	+40% Bow Damage, 60s
Elixir of True Shot	0.5	265	+50% Bow Damage, 60s
Potion of the Warrior	0.5	96	+20% One-Handed Damage, 60s
Draught of the Warrior	0.5	151	+30% One-Handed Damage, 60s
Philter of the Warrior	0.5	207	+40% One-Handed Damage, 60s
Elixir of the Warrior	0.5	265	+50% One-Handed Damage, 60s
Potion of Glibness	0.5	96	+20 Speech, 60s
Draught of Glibness	0.5	151	+30 Speech, 60s
Philter of Glibness	0.5	207	+40 Speech, 60s
Elixir of Glibness	0.5	265	+50 Speech, 60s
Potion of Pickpocketing	0.5	96	+20% Pickpocket, 60s
Draught of Pickpocketing	0.5	151	+30% Pickpocket, 60s
Philter of Pickpocketing	0.5	207	+40% Pickpocket, 60s
Elixir of Pickpocketing	0.5	265	+50% Pickpocket, 60s
Potion of the Healer	0.5	96	+20% Restoration, 60s
Draught of the Healer	0.5	151	+30% Restoration, 60s
Philter of the Healer	0.5	207	+40% Restoration, 60s
Elixir of the Healer	0.5	265	+50% Restoration, 60s
Blacksmith's Potion	0.5	67	+20% Smithing, 30s
Blacksmith's Draught	0.5	105	+30% Smithing, 30s
Blacksmith's Philter	0.5	145	+40% Smithing, 30s
Blacksmith's Elixir	0.5	185	+50% Smithing, 30s
Potion of Light Feet	0.5	45	+10% Sneak, 60s
Draught of Light Feet	0.5	70	+15% Sneak, 60s
Philter of Light Feet	0.5	96	+20% Sneak, 60s
Elixir of Light Feet	0.5	123	+25% Sneak, 60s
Potion of the Berserker	0.5	96	+20% Two-Handed Damage, 60s
Draught of the Berserker	0.5	151	+30% Two-Handed Damage, 60s
Philter of the Berserker	0.5	207	+40% Two-Handed Damage, 60s
Elixir of the Berserker	0.5	265	+50% Two-Handed Damage, 60s
Potion of Enhanced Stamina	0.5	341	+20 Max Stamina, 5m
Draught of Enhanced Stamina	0.5	731	+40 Max Stamina, 5m
Solution of Enhanced Stamina	0.5	1142	+60 Max Stamina, 5m
Philter of Enhanced Stamina	0.5	1568	+80 Max Stamina, 5m
Elixir of Enhanced Stamina	0.5	341	+100 Max Stamina, 5m
Potion of Vigor	0.5	311	+50% Stamina Regen, 5m
Draught of Vigor	0.5	380	+60% Stamina Regen, 5m
Solution of Vigor	0.5	451	+70% Stamina Regen, 5m
Philter of Vigor	0.5	522	+80% Stamina Regen, 5m
Elixir of Vigor	0.5	668	+100% Stamina Regen, 5m
Potion of Brief Invisibility	0.5	214	Invisibility 20s
Potion of Extended Invisibility	0.5	334	Invisibility 30s
Potion of Enduring Invisibility	0.5	459	Invisibility 40s
Potion of Prolonged Invisibility	0.5	587	Invisibility 50s
Elixir of Fire Resistance	0.5	265	+50% Fire Resistance
Potion of Fire Resistance	0.5	96	+20% Fire Resistance
Draught of Fire Resistance	0.5	151	+30% Fire Resistance
Philter of Fire Resistance	0.5	207	+40% Fire Resistance
Elixir of Resistance Cold	0.5	265	+50% Frost Resistance
Potion of Resistance Cold	0.5	96	+20% Frost Resistance
Draught of Resistance Cold	0.5	151	+30% Frost Resistance
Philter of Resistance Cold	0.5	207	+40% Frost Resistance
Elixir of Magic Resistance	0.5	247	+25% Magic Resistance
Potion of Magic Resistance	0.5	90	+10% Magic Resistance
Draught of Magic Resistance	0.5	141	+15% Magic Resistance
Philter of Magic Resistance	0.5	193	+20% Magic Resistance
Elixir of Shock Resistance	0.5	265	+50% Shock Resistance
Potion of Shock Resistance	0.5	96	+20% Shock Resistance
Draught of Shock Resistance	0.5	151	+30% Shock Resistance
Philter of Shock Resistance	0.5	207	+40% Shock Resistance
Potion of Minor Healing	0.5	17	Restore Health 25
Potion of Healing	0.5	36	Restore Health 50
Potion of Plentiful Healing	0.5	57	Restore Health 75
Potion of Vigorous Healing	0.5	79	Restore Health 100
Potion of Extreme Healing	0.5	123	Restore Health 150
Potion of Ultimate Healing	0.5	251	Restore Health Full
Potion of Minor Magicka	0.5	20	Restore Magicka 25
Potion of Magicka	0.5	44	Restore Magicka 50
Potion of Plentiful Magicka	0.5	69	Restore Magicka 75
Potion of Vigorous Magicka	0.5	95	Restore Magicka 100
Potion of Extreme Magicka	0.5	148	Restore Magicka 150
Potion of Ultimate Magicka	0.5	150	Restore Magicka Full
Potion of Minor Stamina	0.5	20	Restore Stamina 25
Potion of Stamina	0.5	44	Restore Stamina 50
Potion of Plentiful Stamina	0.5	69	Restore Stamina 75
Potion of Vigorous Stamina	0.5	95	Restore Stamina 100
Potion of Extreme Stamina	0.5	148	Restore Stamina 150
Potion of Ultimate Stamina	0.5	150	Restore Stamina Full

POISONS

POTION NAME	WEIGHT	VALUE	EFFECT
Weak Poison	0.5	58	Damage Health 15
Poison	0.5	103	Damage Health 25
Potent Poison	0.5	149	Damage Health 35
Virulent Poison	0.5	221	Damage Health 50
Deadly Poison	0.5	296	Damage Health 65
Weak Lingering Poison	0.5	12	Damage Health 1/s, 10s
Lingering Poison	0.5	18	Damage Health 1/s, 15s
Potent Lingering Poison	0.5	40	Damage Health 2/s, 15s
Malign Lingering Poison	0.5	55	Damage Health 2/s, 20s
Deadly Lingering Poison	0.5	86	Damage Health 3/s, 20s
Weak Magicka Poison	0.5	92	Damage Magicka 30
Magicka Poison	0.5	162	Damage Magicka 50
Potent Magicka Poison	0.5	235	Damage Magicka 70
Malign Magicka Poison	0.5	348	Damage Magicka 100
Deadly Magicka Poison	0.5	465	Damage Magicka 130
Lingering Magicka Poison	0.5	10	Damage Magicka 1/s, 10s

POTION NAME	WEIGHT	VALUE	EFFECT
Enduring Magicka Poison	0.5	15	Damage Magicka 1/s, 15s
Lasting Magicka Poison	0.5	33	Damage Magicka 2/s, 15s
Persisting Magicka Poison	0.5	45	Damage Magicka 2/s, 20s
Unceasing Magicka Poison	0.5	71	Damage Magicka 3/s, 20s
Weak Recovery Poison	0.5	79	-100% Magicka Regen, 10s
Magicka Recovery Poison	0.5	169	-100% Magicka Regen, 20s
Potent Recovery Poison	0.5	265	-100% Magicka Regen, 30s
Malign Recovery Poison	0.5	414	-100% Magicka Regen, 45s
Deadly Recovery Poison	0.5	568	-100% Magicka Regen, 60s
Weak Stamina Poison	0.5	75	Damaga Stamina 30
Stamina Poison	0.5	133	Damage Stamina 50
Potent Stamina Poison	0.5	192	Damage Stamina 70
Virulent Stamina Poison	0.5	285	Damage Stamina 100
Deadly Stamina Poison	0.5	380	Damage Stamina 130
Lingering Stamina Poison	0.5	6	Damage Stamina 1/s, 30s
Enduring Stamina Poison	0.5	12	Damage Stamina 2/s, 30s
Lasting Stamina Poison	0.5	20	Damage Stamina 3/s, 30s
Persisting Stamina Poison	0.5	27	Damage Stamina 4/s, 30s
Unceasing Stamina Poison	0.5	35	Damage Stamina 5/s, 30s
Weak Vigor Poison	0.5	74	-100% Stamina Regen, 15s
Vigor Poison	0.5	159	-100% Stamina Regen, 30s
Potent Vigor Poison	0.5	248	-100% Stamina Regen, 45s
Malign Vigor Poison	0.5	341	-100% Stamina Regen, 60s
Weak Fear Poison	0.5	98	Fear (up to Lv5), 30s
Fear Poison	0.5	164	Fear (up to Lv8), 30s
Potent Fear Poison	0.5	281	Fear (up to Lv13), 30s
Virulent Fear Poison	0.5	402	Fear (up to Lv18), 30s
Deadly Fear Poison	0.5	526	Fear (up to Lv23), 30s
Weak Frenzy Poison	0.5	88	Frenzy (up to Lv5), 10s
Frenzy Poison	0.5	147	Frenzy (up to Lv8), 10s
Potent Frenzy Poison	0.5	252	Frenzy (up to Lv13), 10s
Virulent Frenzy Poison	0.5	360	Frenzy (up to Lv18), 10s
Deadly Frenzy Poison	0.5	472	Frenzy (up to Lv23), 10s
Weak Paralysis Poison	0.5	132	Paralysis, 3s
Paralysis Poison	0.5	233	Paralysis, 5s
Potent Paralysis Poison	0.5	337	Paralysis, 7s
Virulent Paralysis Poison	0.5	500	Paralysis, 10s
Deadly Paralysis Poison	0.5	781	Paralysis, 15s
Weak Aversion to Fire	0.5	116	-40% Fire Resistance, 30s
Aversion to Fire	0.5	164	-55% Fire Resistance, 30s
Potent Aversion to Fire	0.5	215	-70% Fire Resistance, 30s
Malign Aversion to Fire	0.5	266	-85% Fire Resistance, 30s
Deadly Aversion to Fire	0.5	318	-100% Fire Resistance, 30s
Weak Aversion to Frost	0.5	96	-40% Frost Resistance, 30s
Aversion to Frost	0.5	137	-55% Frost Resistance, 30s
Potent Aversion to Frost	0.5	179	-70% Frost Resistance, 30s
Malign Aversion to Frost	0.5	221	-85% Frost Resistance, 30s
Deadly Aversion to Frost	0.5	265	-100% Frost Resistance, 30s
Weak Aversion to Magic	0.5	193	-40% Magic Resistance, 30s
Aversion to Magic	0.5	274	-55% Magic Resistance, 30s
Potent Aversion to Magic	0.5	358	-70% Magic Resistance, 30s
Malign Aversion to Magic	0.5	443	-85% Magic Resistance, 30s
Deadly Aversion to Magic	0.5	530	-100% Magic Resistance, 30s
Weak Aversion to Shock	0.5	135	-40% Shock Resistance, 30s
Aversion to Shock	0.5	192	-55% Shock Resistance, 30s
Potent Aversion to Shock	0.5	250	-70% Shock Resistance, 30s
Malign Aversion to Shock	0.5	310	-85% Shock Resistance, 30s
Deadly Aversion to Shock	0.5	371	-100% Shock Resistance, 30s
Frostbite Venom	0.5	21	Damage Health 5/s, Damage Magicka 5/s, 4s

THIEVES' GUILD COMPOUND POTIONS

POTION NAME	WEIGHT	VALUE	EFFECT
Potion of Conflict	0.5	115	+10 Light Armor, +15% One-Handed Damage, 60s
Draught of Conflict	0.5	166	+15 Light Armor, +20% One-Handed Damage, 60s
Philter of Conflict	0.5	219	+20 Light Armor, +25% One-Handed Damage, 60s
Elixir of Conflict	0.5	330	+30 Light Armor, +35% One-Handed Damage, 60s
Grand Elixir of Conflict	0.5	443	+40 Light Armor, +45% One-Handed Damage, 60s
Prime Elixir of Conflict	0.5	559	+50 Light Armor, +55% One-Handed Damage, 60s
Potion of Escape	0.5	351	Invisibility 30s, Restore Health 25
Draught of Escape	0.5	495	Invisibility 40s, Restore Health 50
Philter of Escape	0.5	580	Invisibility 45s, Restore Health 75
Elixir of Escape	0.5	666	Invisibility 50s, Restore Health 100
Grand Elixir of Escape	0.5	753	Invisibility 55s, Restore Health 125
Prime Elixir of Escape	0.5	840	Invisibility 60s, Restore Health 150
Potion of Keenshot	0.5	74	+15% Bow Damage, +5% Stamina Regen, 60s
Draught of Keenshot	0.5	102	+20% Bow Damage, +7% Stamina Regen, 60s
Philter of Keenshot	0.5	131	+25% Bow Damage, +9% Stamina Regen, 60s
Elixir of Keenshot	0.5	161	+30% Bow Damage, +11% Stamina Regen, 60s
Grand Elixir of Keenshot	0.5	191	+35% Bow Damage, +13% Stamina Regen, 60s
Prime Elixir of Keenshot	0.5	221	+40% Bow Damage, +15% Stamina Regen, 60s
Potion of Larceny	0.5	140	+15% Lockpicking, +15% Pickpocket
Draught of Larceny	0.5	192	+20% Lockpicking, +20% Pickpocket
Philter of Larceny	0.5	246	+25% Lockpicking, +25% Pickpocket
Elixir of Larceny	0.5	302	+30% Lockpicking, +30% Pickpocket
Grand Elixir of Larceny	0.5	358	+35% Lockpicking, +35% Pickpocket
Prime Elixir of Larceny	0.5	414	+40% Lockpicking, +40% Pickpocket
Potion of Plunder	0.5	511	+20 Carry Weight, +20 Max Stamina, 5m
Draught of Plunder	0.5	799	+30 Carry Weight, +30 Max Stamina, 5m
Philter of Plunder	0.5	1096	+40 Carry Weight, +40 Max Stamina, 5m
Elixir of Plunder	0.5	1402	+50 Carry Weight, +50 Max Stamina, 5m
Grand Elixir of Plunder	0.5	1713	+60 Carry Weight, +60 Max Stamina, 5m
Prime Elixir of Plunder	0.5	2029	+70 Carry Weight, +70 Max Stamina, 5m

QUEST POTIONS

POTION NAME	WEIGHT	VALUE	EFFECT
Lotus Extract	0.5	86	Damage Health 6/s, 10s
Ice Wraith Bane	0.5	221	Damage Health 50
Nightshade Extact	0.5	12	Damage Health 1, 10s
Sleeping Tree Sap	0.5	100	+100 Max Health, Slow 25%, 45s
Esbern's Potion	0.5	250	Dragons do 25% less damage.
Vaermina's Torpor	0.5	0	Enter the dreams of those around you.
The White Phial (Full)	0.5	341	Varies by effect.
Philter of the Phantom	0.5	50	Look like a ghost for 30s.
Falmer Blood Elixir	0.5	1	Restore Health 1
Velvet LeChance	0.5	5	Restore Stamina 25
White-Gold Tower	0.5	5	Restore Stamina 25
Cliff Racer	0.5	5	Restore Stamina 25

Potion: Persisting Stamina Poison

✓	POTION NAME	WEIGHT	VALUE	EFFECT
	POTIONS - DAWNGUARD			
☐	Potion of Blood	0.5	75	Equivalent to feeding on human blood for vampires. Vampires also recover 100 Health.
☐	Soul Husk Extract	0.5	254	For 60s, you gain 25% Magic Resistance and are protected from Soul Drain effects in the Soul Cairn.
☐	Redwater Skooma	0.5	35	Restore Stamina 40, slow 50% for 48s.

✓	POTION NAME	WEIGHT	VALUE	EFFECT
	POTIONS - DRAGONBORN			
☐	Potion of Minor Well-being	0.5	33	Restore Health, Magicka, and Stamina 15
☐	Potion of Well-being	0.5	84	Restore Health, Magicka, and Stamina 35
☐	Potion of Plentiful Well-being	0.5	139	Restore Health, Magicka, and Stamina 55
☐	Potion of Vigorous Well-being	0.5	196	Restore Health, Magicka, and Stamina 75

✓	POTION NAME	WEIGHT	VALUE	EFFECT
☐	Potion of Extreme Well-being	0.5	239	Restore Health, Magicka, and Stamina 90
☐	Potion of Ultimate Well-being	0.5	269	Restore Health, Magicka, and Stamina 100
☐	Potion of Waterwalking	0.5	500	Waterwalking 60s

Table XV: Other Items

This section lists all of the other major items you can find in Skyrim.

✓	NAME	WEIGHT	VALUE	EFFECT
	SCROLLS			
	While these scrolls are the most common, you may occasionally find a scroll that casts a lesser spell.			
☐	Scroll of Bane of the Undead	0.5	500	Bane of the Undead
☐	Scroll of Blizzard	0.5	500	Blizzard
☐	Scroll of Call to Arms	0.5	500	Call to Arms
☐	Scroll of Dead Thrall	0.5	500	Dead Thrall
☐	Scroll of Dragonhide	0.5	250	Dragonhide
☐	Scroll of Fire Storm	0.5	500	Fire Storm
☐	Scroll of Flame Thrall	0.5	500	Flame Thrall
☐	Scroll of Frost Thrall	0.5	500	Frost Thrall
☐	Scroll of Guardian Circle	0.5	250	Guardian Circle
☐	Scroll of Harmony	0.5	500	Harmony
☐	Scroll of Hysteria	0.5	500	Hysteria
☐	Scroll of Mass Paralysis	0.5	500	Mass Paralysis
☐	Scroll of Mayhem	0.5	500	Mayhem
☐	Scroll of Storm Thrall	0.5	500	Storm Thrall
☐	Shalidor's Insights: Alteration*	0.5	50	For 2m, Alteration spells cost 50% less and last 100% longer.
☐	Shalidor's Insights: Conjuration*	0.5	50	For 2m, Conjuration spells cost 50% less and last 100% longer.
☐	Shalidor's Insights: Destruction*	0.5	50	For 2m, Destruction spells cost 50% less and last 100% longer.
☐	Shalidor's Insights: Illusion*	0.5	50	For 2m, Illusion spells cost 50% less and last 100% longer.
☐	Shalidor's Insights: Magicka*	0.5	50	For 2m, +100 Magicka and +100% Magicka Regeneration.
☐	Shalidor's Insights: Restoration*	0.5	50	For 2m, Restoration spells cost 50% less and last 100% longer.
	*Note: Reward for College of Winterhold quest Shalidor's Insight.			
☐	J'zargo's Flame Cloak Scroll	0.5	100	Flame Cloak, explodes near undead.
	Note: Quest item for College of Winterhold quest J'zargo's Experiment.			

Food: Sujamma

Dragon Claw: Ruby Dragon Claw

Quest Item: Skeleton Key

✓	NAME	WEIGHT	VALUE	EFFECT
	SPIDERS			
☐	Exploding Flame Spider	0.5	100	Tosses a dead spider on the ground which explodes for 16-96 physical damage and 26-106 fire damage (based on your level) when an enemy gets close.
☐	Exploding Frost Spider	0.5	100	Tosses a dead spider on the ground which explodes for 16-96 physical damage and 26-106 frost damage (based on your level) when an enemy gets close.
☐	Exploding Poison Spider	0.5	100	Tosses a dead spider on the ground which explodes for 16-96 physical damage and 26-106 poison damage (based on your level) when an enemy gets close.
☐	Exploding Shock Spider	0.5	100	Tosses a dead spider on the ground which explodes for 16-96 physical damage and 26-106 shock damage (based on your level) when an enemy gets close.
☐	Flame Cloaked Spider	0.5	100	Tosses a Flame Cloaked spider on the ground that will follow you and cause 15-40 fire damage per second to enemies that get too close.
☐	Frost Cloaked Spider	0.5	100	Tosses a Frost Cloaked spider on the ground that will follow you and cause 15-40 frost damage per second to enemies that get too close.
☐	Glowing Spider	0.5	100	Spawns a glowing spider that will follow you, lighting the surrounding area. Only one can be spawned at a time.
☐	Jumping Flame Spider	0.5	100	Tosses a Jumping Flame spider on the ground that will follow you and launch itself at nearby enemies, exploding for 16-96 physical damage and 26-106 fire damage (based on your level).
☐	Jumping Frost Spider	0.5	100	Tosses a Jumping Frost spider on the ground that will follow you and launch itself at nearby enemies, exploding for 16-96 physical damage and 26-106 frost damage (based on your level).
☐	Jumping Poison Spider	0.5	100	Tosses a Jumping Poison spider on the ground that will follow you and launch itself at nearby enemies, exploding for 16-96 physical damage and 26-106 poison damage (based on your level).
☐	Jumping Shock Spider	0.5	100	Tosses a Jumping Shock spider on the ground that will follow you and launch itself at nearby enemies, exploding for 16-96 physical damage and 26-106 shock damage (based on your level).
☐	Mind Control Spider	0.5	100	Creatures and people that this spider attaches to will fight for you for 30s.
☐	Oil Spider	0.5	100	Spawns a spider that secretes a flammable oil when it feels threatened.
☐	Poison Cloaked Spider	0.5	100	Tosses a Poison Cloaked spider on the ground that will follow you and cause 15-40 poison damage per second to enemies that get too close.
☐	Shock Cloaked Spider	0.5	100	Tosses a Shock Cloaked spider on the ground that will follow you and cause 15-40 shock damage per second to enemies that get too close.

☑	NAME	WEIGHT	VALUE
	INGOTS		
☐	Iron Ingot	1	7
☐	Steel Ingot	1	20
☐	Dwarven Metal Ingot	1	30
☐	Corundum Ingot	1	40
☐	Orichalcum Ingot	1	45
☐	Silver Ingot	1	50
☐	Quicksilver Ingot	1	60
☐	Refined Moonstone	1	75
☐	Gold Ingot	1	100
☐	Refined Malachite	1	100
☐	Ebony Ingot	1	150
	ORE		
☐	Iron Ore	1	2

☑	NAME	WEIGHT	VALUE
☐	Corundum Ore	1	20
☐	Heart Stone	1	100
☐	Orichalcum Ore	1	20
☐	Quicksilver Ore	1	25
☐	Silver Ore	1	25
☐	Malachite Ore	1	30
☐	Moonstone Ore	1	30
☐	Gold Ore	1	50
☐	Ebony Ore	1	60
☐	Stalhrim	1	200
	GEMS		
☐	Garnet	0.1	100
☐	Amethyst	0.1	120
☐	Flawless Garnet	0.1	150

☑	NAME	WEIGHT	VALUE
☐	Flawless Amethyst	0.1	180
☐	Ruby	0.1	200
☐	Flawless Ruby	0.1	350
☐	Sapphire	0.1	400
☐	Flawless Sapphire	0.1	500
☐	Emerald	0.1	600
☐	Flawless Emerald	0.1	750
☐	Diamond	0.1	800
☐	Flawless Diamond	0.1	1000
☐	Exquisite Sapphire	0.2	5000
	LEATHER & HIDES		
☐	Leather	2	10
☐	Leather Strips	0.1	3
☐	Goat Hide	1	5

☑	NAME	WEIGHT	VALUE
☐	Fox Pelt	0.5	5
☐	Snow Fox Pelt	0.5	7
☐	Wolf Pelt	1	10
☐	Ice Wolf Pelt	1	15
☐	Deer Hide	2	10
☐	Cow Hide	2	10
☐	Horse Hide	2	15
☐	Bear Pelt	3	50
☐	Cave Bear Pelt	3	60
☐	Sabre Cat Pelt	2	25
☐	Sabre Cat Snow Pelt	2	40
☐	Snow Bear Pelt	3	75
☐	Chitin Plate	1	5
☐	Netch Leather	2	10

☑	NAME	WEIGHT	VALUE	EFFECT
	FOOD			
☐	Alto Wine	0.5	12	Restore Stamina 15
☐	Apple Cabbage Stew	0.5	8	Restore Health 10, Restore Stamina 15
☐	Apple Dumpling	0.1	3	Restore Health 5, Fortify Archery 5%/60s (Hearthfire).
☐	Apple Pie	0.5	5	Restore Health 10
☐	Argonian Bloodwine	0.5	100	Resist Poison 40%/50s, Waterbreathing 50s, Damage Stamina Regeneration 30%/30s (Hearthfire).
☐	Ash Hopper Leg	1	2	Restore Health 2
☐	Ash Hopper Meat	0.5	2	Restore Health 2
☐	Ash Yam	0.1	1	Restore Health 1
☐	Ashfire Mead	0.5	50	Restore Stamina 40. Regenerate Stamina 50% slower for 30s.
☐	Baked Potatoes	0.1	2	Restore Health 5
☐	Beef Stew	0.5	8	+25 Max Stamina/12m, Regenerate Stamina 2/s for 12m
☐	Black-Briar Mead	0.2	25	Restore Stamina 20
☐	Black-Briar Reserve	0.5	100	Restore Stamina 30
☐	Boar Meat	1	2	Restore Health 2
☐	Boiled Creme Treat	0.5	4	Restore Health 10
☐	Braided Bread	0.2	2	Restore Health 2, Fortify Carry Weight 5/30s (Hearthfire).
☐	Bread	0.2	2	Restore Health 2
☐	Bread	0.2	2	Restore Health 2
☐	Butter	0.1	1	Restore Health 2 (Hearthfire)
☐	Cabbage	0.25	2	Restore Health 1
☐	Cabbage Potato Soup	0.5	5	Restore Health 10, Restore Stamina 10
☐	Cabbage Soup	0.5	5	Restore Health 10, Restore Stamina 10
☐	Cabbage Soup	0.5	5	Restore Health 10, Restore Stamina 8
☐	Carrot	0.1	1	Restore Health 1
☐	Charred Skeever Meat	0.2	4	Restore Health 2

☑	NAME	WEIGHT	VALUE	EFFECT
☐	Chicken Breast	0.2	3	Restore Health 2
☐	Chicken Dumpling	0.1	3	Restore Health 15, Regenerate Health 1/2m (Hearthfire).
☐	Clam Chowder	0.5	5	Restore Health 10, Restore Stamina 10 (Hearthfire).
☐	Clam Meat	0.1	1	Restore Health 1
☐	Cooked Boar Meat	1	15	Restore Health 12
☐	Cooked Beef	0.5	5	Restore Health 10
☐	Dog Meat	0.2	3	Restore Health 2
☐	Eidar Cheese Wedge	0.25	5	Restore Health 1
☐	Eidar Cheese Wheel	2	13	Restore Health 15
☐	Elsweyr Fondue	0.5	5	+100 Max Magicka/12m, +25% Magicka Regen/12m
☐	Flin	0.5	15	Restore Stamina 20. Regenerate Stamina 20% slower for 120s.
☐	Garlic Bread	0.1	2	Restore Health 1, Cure Disease (Hearthfire).
☐	Goat Cheese Wedge	0.25	4	Restore Health 1
☐	Goat Cheese Wheel	2	10	Restore Health 15
☐	Gourd	0.2	1	Restore Health 1
☐	Green Apple	0.1	3	Restore Health 2
☐	Grilled Chicken Breast	0.2	4	Restore Health 5
☐	Grilled Leeks	0.1	2	Restore Health 6
☐	Homecooked Meal	5	1	+25% Health, Magicka, and Stamina Regen/10m
☐	Honey	0.1	2	Restore Health 2
☐	Honey Nut Treat	0.1	2	Restore Health 5
☐	Honningbrew Mead	0.5	20	Restore Stamina 20
☐	Horker and Ash Yam Stew	0.5	8	Restore Health 15, Restore Stamina 15, Regenerate Health 1/12m
☐	Horker Loaf	1	4	Restore Health 10
☐	Horker Meat	1	3	Restore Health 1
☐	Horker Stew	0.5	8	Restore Health 15, Restore Stamina 15, Regenerate Health 1/s /12m

☑	NAME	WEIGHT	VALUE	EFFECT
☐	Horse Haunch	2	4	Restore Health 10
☐	Horse Meat	2	3	Restore Health 2
☐	Jazbay Crostata	0.2	5	Restore Health 10, Fortify Magicka 4/60s (Hearthfire).
☐	Jug of Milk	1	2	Restore Health 2 (Hearthfire).
☐	Juniper Berry Crostata	0.2	5	Restore Health 4, Regenerate Health 2/60s (Hearthfire).
☐	Lavender Dumpling	0.1	3	Restore Health 5, Fortify Magicka 10/60s, Resist Magic 10%/60s (Hearthfire).
☐	Leek	0.1	1	Restore Health 1
☐	Leg of Goat	1	3	Restore Health 2
☐	Leg of Goat Roast	1	4	Restore Health 10
☐	Long Taffy Treat	0.1	3	Restore Health 10
☐	Mammoth Cheese Bowl	0.5	3	Restore Health 10
☐	Mammoth Snout	3	6	Restore Health 5
☐	Mammoth Steak	2	8	Restore Health 10
☐	Matze	0.5	5	Restore Stamina 10, Resist Frost 20% for 60s, Regenerate Magicka 25% slower for 60s.
☐	Mudcrab Legs	0.1	3	Restore Health 1 (Hearthfire).
☐	Nord Mead	0.5	5	Restore Stamina 15
☐	Pheasant Breast	0.2	3	Restore Health 2
☐	Pheasant Roast	0.2	4	Restore Health 5
☐	Potato	0.1	1	Restore Health 1
☐	Potato Bread	0.2	2	Restore Health 3 (Hearthfire).
☐	Rabbit Haunch	0.1	3	Restore Health 5
☐	Raw Beef	0.2	4	Restore Health 2
☐	Raw Rabbit Leg	0.1	2	Restore Health 2
☐	Red Apple	0.1	3	Restore Health 2
☐	Sack of Flour	0.5	1	Restore Health 1 (Hearthfire).
☐	Salmon Meat	0.1	3	Restore Health 2
☐	Salmon Steak	0.1	4	Restore Health 5

✓	NAME	WEIGHT	VALUE	EFFECT
	Salmon Steak	0.1	4	Restore Health 5 (Hearthfire).
	Seared Slaughterfish	0.1	5	Restore Health 5
	Shein	0.5	10	Restore Stamina 25. Regenerate Stamina 30% slower for 60s.
	Sliced Eidar Cheese	2	10	Restore Health 15
	Sliced Goat Cheese	2	8	Restore Health 15
	Snowberry Crostata	0.2	5	Restore Health 10, Resist Fire 4%/60s (Hearthfire).
	Soul Husk	0.1	1	For 10s, you gain 10% Magic Resistance and are protected from Soul Drain effects in the Soul Cairn (Dawnguard).

✓	NAME	WEIGHT	VALUE	EFFECT
	Spiced Wine	0.5	7	Restore Stamina 25
	Steamed Mudcrab Legs	0.1	4	Restore Health 12 (Hearthfire).
	Sujamma	0.5	10	Restore Stamina 15. Regenerate Stamina 30% slower for 60s.
	Surilie Brothers Wine	0.5	40	Restore Stamina 15, Damage Stamina Regeneration 30/30s (Hearthfire).
	Sweet Roll	0.1	2	Restore Health 5
	Tomato	0.1	4	Restore Health 1

✓	NAME	WEIGHT	VALUE	EFFECT
	Tomato Soup	0.5	5	Restore Health 10, Restore Stamina 10
	Vegetable Soup	0.5	5	Regenerate Health 1/12m, Regenerate Stamina 1/12m
	Venison	2	4	Restore Health 2
	Venison Chop	2	5	Restore Health 5
	Venison Stew	0.5	8	Restore Stamina 15, Regenerate Health 1/12m, Regenerate Stamina 1/12m
	Wine	0.5	7	Restore Stamina 15

✓	ZONE #	CLOSEST LOCATION	NAME	GLYPH SEQUENCE	VALUE
			DRAGON CLAWS		
	[SS.13]	Vahlok's Tomb	Amethyst Claw (Left)	Special	200
	[SS.13]	Vahlok's Tomb	Amethyst Claw (Right)	Special	200
	[10.05]	Skuldafn	Diamond Claw	Fox, Moth, Dragon	1000
	[2.04]	Dead Men's Respite	Ruby Dragon Claw	Wolf, Hawk, Wolf	400
	[2.08]	Folgunthur	Ivory Dragon Claw	Hawk, Hawk, Dragon	200
	[3.22]	Korvanjund	Ebony Claw	Fox, Moth, Dragon	800
	[4.30]	Yngol Barrow	Coral Dragon Claw	Snake, Wolf, Moth	150
	[5.39]	Reachwater Rock	Emerald Dragon Claw	Bear, Whale, Snake	600
	[5.42]	Valthume	Iron Claw	Dragon, Hawk, Wolf	75
	[8.18]	Bleak Falls Barrow	Golden Claw	Bear, Moth, Owl	100
	[9.01]	Ivarstead	Sapphire Dragon Claw	Moth, Owl, Wolf	500
	[9.45]	Forelhost	Glass Claw	Fox, Owl, Snake	700
			CAPTURED CRITTERS		
	[3.19]	Duskglow Crevice	Moth in a Jar	1	1
	[4.06]	Frostflow Lighthouse	Torchbug in a Jar	1	1
	[5.38]	Dushnikh Yal	Dragonfly in a Jar	1	1
	[9.09]	Alchemist's Shack	Butterfly in a Jar	1	1
	[9.29]	Goldenglow Estate	Bee in a Jar	1	1

✓	NAME	WEIGHT	VALUE
	CHILDREN'S CLOTHES (HEARTHFIRE)		
	Boy's Blue Tunic	2	6
	Boy's Green Tunic	2	4
	Boy's Gray Tunic	2	8
	Boy's Red Tunic	2	5
	Boy's Yellow Tunic	2	10
	Girl's Blue Dress	2	6
	Girl's Green Dress	2	4
	Girl's Gray Dress	2	8
	Girl's Red Dress	2	5
	Girl's Yellow Dress	2	10
	CHILDREN'S TOYS (HEARTHFIRE)		
	Child's Doll	2	10

✓	NAME	WEIGHT	VALUE
	HOUSE COMPONENTS (HEARTHFIRE)		
	Clay	1	1
	Iron Fittings	1	4
	Glass	1	5
	Hinge	0.5	4
	Goat Horns	1	5
	Lock	0.5	10
	Nails	0.1	1
	Quarried Stone	1	2
	Straw	1	1
	PARAGON STONES (DAWNGUARD)		
	Amethyst Paragon	0.3	360
	Diamond Paragon	0.3	2,000
	Ruby Paragon	0.3	700
	Sapphire Paragon	0.3	1,000
	Emerald Paragon	0.3	1,500

✓	NAME	WEIGHT	VALUE
	MISCELLANEOUS ITEMS		
	Many items have variants with different weights and values than those listed below.		
	Albino Spider Pod	1	10
	Basket	0.5	1
	Bellows	1	1
	Bent Dwemer Scrap Metal	2	15
	Bloody Rags	1	1
	Bloody Tankard	0.5	1
	Bone Hawk Claw	1	7
	Bone Hawk Feathers	1	7
	Bone Hawk Skull	1	7
	Bowl	0.5	5
	Broken Iron Mace Handle	5	5
	Broken Iron Mace Head	8	5
	Broken Iron Sword Blade	6	5
	Broken Iron Sword Handle	3	5
	Broken Iron War Axe Handle	5	5
	Broken Iron War Axe Head	6	5
	Broken Steel Battle Axe Handle	9	10
	Broken Steel Battle Axe Head	12	10
	Broken Steel Greatsword Blade	10	10
	Broken Steel Greatsword Handle	7	10
	Broken Steel Sword Blade	6	10
	Broken Steel Sword Handle	4	10
	Broken Steel Warhammer Handle	10	10
	Broken Steel Warhammer Head	15	10
	Broom	1	1
	Bucket	0.5	1
	Burned Book	2	0
	Candlestick	1	25
	Candlestick	1	25
	Cast Iron Pot	6	8
	Charcoal	0.5	2
	Chaurus Chitin	4	50

✓	NAME	WEIGHT	VALUE
	Clothes Iron	3	7
	Cup	0.5	5
	Damaged Albino Spider Pod	1	10
	Death Hound Collar	2	50
	Dragon Bone	15	500
	Dragon Scales	10	250
	Drum	4	10
	Dwemer Cup	0.5	6
	Dwemer Dish	0.5	8
	Dwemer Gear	2	15
	Dwemer Gyro	2	15
	Dwemer Lever	2	15
	Dwemer Pan	0.5	8
	Dwemer Pan	3	10
	Dwemer Plate	1	8
	Dwemer Scrap Metal	2	15
	Embalming Tool	0.5	3
	Empty Wine Bottle	0.5	1
	Firewood	5	5
	Flagon	0.5	1
	Flower Basket	1	5
	Flute	2	25
	Goblet	0.5	5
	Hammer	3	1
	Horker Tusk	1	15
	Imperial War Horn	5	70
	Inkwell	0.3	1
	Jug	2	10
	Kettle	2	4
	Knife	0.5	6
	Lantern	2	1
	Large Decorative Dwemer Strut	15	10
	Large Dwemer Plate Metal	2	15
	Large Dwemer Strut	20	15
	Linen Wrap	3	2
	Lockpick	0	2
	Lute	4	25

✓	NAME	WEIGHT	VALUE
	Mammoth Tusk	5	150
	Nord War Horn	5	70
	Pitchfork	4	1
	Pitchfork	4	1
	Plate	0.5	1
	Platter	0.5	5
	Pot	3	5
	Quill	0.5	1
	Roll of Paper	1	4
	Ruined Book	2	5
	Saw	2	3
	Silver Jug	2	30
	Torture Tool	1	2
	Shovel	4	3
	Skull	2	5
	Skull (Runic)	2	50
	Small Dwemer Lever	2	15
	Small Dwemer Plate Metal	2	15
	Solid Dwemer Metal	25	25
	Soul Gem Fragment	0.1	5
	Spigot	2	1
	Spoon	0.5	6
	Tankard	0.5	1
	Tongs	1	1
	Torture Tool	1	2
	Troll Skull	3.5	5
	Vale Deer Hide	2	10
	Vale Sabre Cat Hide	2	10
	Wooden Bowl	0.5	1
	Wooden Ladle	0.5	1
	Wooden Plate	0.5	1
	Fork	0.5	3

QUEST ITEMS

✓	NAME	WEIGHT	VALUE
	Aetherium Crest	1	1,000
	Aetherium Shard	0.25	100
	Ancient Traveler's Skull	5	0
	Ancient Vampire Arm	1	250
	Ancient Vampire Hands	1	250
	Ancient Vampire Head	1	250
	Ancient Vampire Leg	2	250
	Ancient Vampire Rib Cage	1	250
	Aretino Family Heirloom	0.5	100
	Argonian Ale	0.5	5
	Attunement Sphere	0	0
	Arvak's Skull	4	0
	Ash Extractor	0.5	1
	Ash Spawn Sample	1	100
	Balmora Blue	0.5	67
	Balwen's Ornamental Ring	3	0
	Barenziahs Crown	0	0
	Black-Briar Mead Keg	20	0
	Blank Lexicon	0	0
	Bloodstone Chalice	11	0
	Briar Heart	1	0
	Broken Azura's Star	0.5	0
	Burial Urn	1	0
	Bust of the Gray Fox	0	0
	Calcelmo's Stone Rubbing	0.5	0
	Canticle Bark	0	350
	Centurion Dynamo Core	4	131
	Coinpurse	0	0
	Colovian Brandy	0.5	100
	Control Cube	0.5	50
	Cracked White Phial	0.5	0
	Crescent Moon Crest	0	0
	Crown of Barenziah	0	0
	Curious Silver Mold	1	250
	Cyrodilic Brandy	0.5	150
	Deathbrand Treasure Map	0	500
	Dibella Statue	2	100
	Double-Distilled Skooma	0.5	44
	Dragon Heartscales	10	250
	Dragon's Breath Mead	0.5	5
	Dragonstone	25	0
	Draw Knife	5	0
	Dwarven Crossbow Schematic	0	100
	Dwemer Bowl	2	20
	Dwemer Cog	10	5
	Dwemer Exploding Fire Bolt Schematic	0	100
	Dwemer Exploding Ice Bolt Schematic	0	100
	Dwemer Exploding Shock Bolt Schematic	0	100
	Dwemer Puzzle Cube	0	0
	East Empire Shipping Map	0	0
	Elder Scroll	0	20
	Elder Scroll (Blood)	20	0
	Elder Scroll (Dragon)	20	0
	Elder Scroll (Sun)	20	0
	Eldergleam Sap	1	0
	Eldergleam Sapling	1	0
	Emberbrand Wine	0.5	15
	Empty Skooma Bottle	0.5	0
	Enhanced Crossbow Schematic	0	100
	Enhanced Dwarven Crossbow Schematic	0	100
	Essence Extractor	1	0
	Exquisite Sapphire	0.2	5000
	Finely Ground Bone Meal	0.1	0
	Finn's Lute	4	25
	Firebrand Wine	0.5	137
	Firebrand Wine Case	6	0
	Focusing Crystal	1	10
	Fragment of Wuuthrad	2	0
	Fragments of Wuuthrad	0	0
	Full Moon Crest	0	0
	Gildergreen Sapling	8	0
	Glenmoril Witch Head	4	0
	Glowing Crystal Shard	0.25	100
	Golden Claw	0.5	100
	Golden Ship Model	0	0
	Golden Urn	0	0
	Habd's Remains	1	0
	Half Moon Crest	0	0
	Heart of Winter	0.5	100
	Hilt of Mehrunes' Razor	2	0
	Honey Jar	1	0
	Honningbrew Decanter	0	0
	Horn of Jurgen Windcaller	4	0
	Imperial Documents	0	0
	Initiate's Ewer	1.5	1,500
	Iron Claw	0.5	75
	Jarrin Root	0.5	100
	Jessica's Wine	0.5	12
	Jeweled Amulet	0.5	100
	Jeweled Candlestick	0	0
	Jeweled Flagon	0	0
	Jeweled Goblet	0	0
	Jeweled Pendant	0.5	200
	Jeweled Pitcher	0	0
	Kagrumez Resonance Gem	0.2	500
	Karstaag's Skull	3	25
	Katarina's Ornamental Ring	3	0
	Klimmek's Supplies	0	0
	Kordir's Skooma	0.5	20
	Left Eye of the Falmer	5	2500
	Lexicon	0	0
	Malyn's Black Soul Gem	0.5	0
	Mammoth Tusk Powder	0.5	0
	Map of Dragon Burials	0	0
	Mark of Dibella	0.5	0
	Mead with Juniper Berry	0.5	5
	Mercer's Plans	0.5	0
	Meridia's Beacon	0.5	0
	Michaela's Flagon	0.5	1
	Model Ship	0	0
	Nurelion's Mixture	5	15
	Olava's Token	0.5	100
	Opaque Vessel	0	0
	Ornate Drinking Horn	0	0
	Package for Grelka	2	0
	Package for Verner	2	0
	Pantea's Flute	2	25
	Pelagius' Hip Bone	1	250
	Pest Poison	0.5	0
	Petty Soul Gem	0.5	0
	Pithi's Ornamental Ring	3	0
	Pommel Stone of Mehrunes' Razor	2	0
	Potema's Skull	0	0
	Purified Void Salts	0.1	0
	Queen Bee Statue	0	0
	Quicksilver Ore	1	25
	Quill of Gemination	0.1	150
	Reaper Gem Fragment	0.1	5
	Right Eye of the Falmer	5	2500
	Rjorn's Drum	4	10
	Runed Lexicon	0	0
	Sadri's Sujamma	0.3	0
	Saerek's Skull Key	0.3	100
	Sapphire Dragon Claw	0.5	500
	Satchel of Moon Sugar	0	0
	Scabbard of Mehrunes' Razor	3	0
	Sealed Letter	0.5	100
	Sealed Scroll	0.5	0
	Shards of Mehrunes' Razor	6	0
	Sigil Stone	0	0
	Silver Candlestick	1	75
	Silver Hand Stratagem	0	0
	Sinding's Skin	4	0
	Skeleton Key	0.5	0
	Skooma	0.5	20
	Soaked Taproot	2	1
	Soul Essence Gem (Full)	0.5	250
	Soul Gem Shards	0.1	0
	Spiced Beef	0.5	4
	Stallion's Potion	0.5	341
	Statue of Dibella	3	100
	StormCloak Documents	0	0
	Strange crystal	1	10
	Strange Gem	0.5	0
	Stros M'Kai Rum	0.5	12
	Sylgja's Satchel	0	0
	The Dancer's Flute	2	3
	The White Phial (Empty)	0.5	0
	Tolfdir's Alembic	2	0
	Torc of Labyrinthian	1	10
	Torsten's Skull Key	0.3	100
	Torture Tools	2	15
	Torygg's War Horn	5	0
	Treoy's Ornamental Ring	3	0
	Unmelting Snow	1	0
	Unusual Gem	0.5	200
	Verner's Satchel	0	0
	Warped Soul Gem	0.5	0
	Wedding Ring	0.5	0
	Werewolf Totem	0.5	1
	Weystone Focus	0.3	300
	Wylandriah's Spoon	0	0
	Ysgramor's Soup Spoon	0.5	3

THE BESTIARY

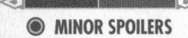

MINOR SPOILERS

The wild and untamed lands of Skyrim are teeming with adversaries, from the wretched to the powerful, and the monstrous to the meek. This chapter presents them alphabetized by type, so you can identify the foes you're about to engage in battle. This allows you to identify weaknesses that you can exploit, bolster your defenses against the spells and abilities your enemies will use, and know what kind of loot to expect. Heed the following notes before exploring the Bestiary in detail.

BESTIARY ADVICE

Enemies

Enemies that are members of one of the ten races that you can choose from have all the benefits of their race (which you can read about at the start of the Training chapter) in addition to any statistics indicated in the Bestiary below.

For example, a High Elf Warlock has a higher Magicka than indicated due to their Highborn Magicka racial ability. A Breton Warlock will be more resistant to spells because of their Magic Resistance ability. A Nord Warlock will shrug off frost spells (Frost Resistance), while a Dark Elf Warlock will be more resistant to fire (Fire Resistance).

As your level increases, the difficulty of the enemies you encounter will typically increase in stages. This is most visible when you read the name of your adversaries, which usually indicates their level. For example, a "Novice Necromancer" (Level 1) is noticeably weaker than an "Apprentice Necromancer" (Level 6) or a "Master Necromancer" (Level 36). A few characters (such as your Followers) work differently: Their level will gradually increase as your level does, though possibly at a slower rate.

Ordinary citizens of Skyrim and unique enemies for particular quests are not listed in this section. The vast majority of unique enemies borrow their statistics from a related creature that is on the chart, perhaps with a slight change to their weapons, armor, or spells. For example, all of the Civil War military camps have a commander with a unique name. However, these are simply named versions of the "Imperial Legate" or "Stormcloak Commander" characters in the Bestiary.

Items and Spells

(Parenthesis) indicate that an item may or may not be present—random chance per creature.

A / Slash indicates that one of the items will be present, the others will not.

[Brackets] indicate that the version of the item carried by the creature cannot be looted from their body. For example, most Skeleton armor can't be taken from Skeletons.

Many creatures have some form of Loot Item (eg. Skeleton Loot). These are typically lists of small items (food, ingredients, etc.) that the creature may be carrying; a creature may have none, one, or several of these items on them when killed. For each creature type, we've provided a quick summary of the kinds of things they're likely to be carrying.

THE BESTIARY CHART LEGEND

COLUMN	NOTES
Name	Name of the creature as it appears in the game.
Subtype	Not visible in game; provides some additional notes to help identify the creature if the name isn't sufficient on its own.
Lv	Level of the creature; roughly suggests the level at which you should be able to reasonably defeat it. Depending on your particular mix of skills and perks, your actual experience may vary.
Health	The creature's base health.
Magicka	The creature's base magicka.
Stamina	The creature's base stamina.
Weapons	The weapon(s) the creature possesses, in addition to its unarmed attacks.
Armor	The armor the creature wears.
Items	Any loose items the creature carries.
Spells	The creature's list of spells or spell-like special abilities.
Notes	Any special properties, such as elemental weaknesses or resistances that may affect how you choose to fight the creature.

NOTE * If a Level number is starred (for example, "30*"), this creature is one that levels with you: As your level and statistics increase, so will its level and statistics. The values in the table represent the creature's stats for the indicated level, which is often the creature's lowest possible level.

NOTE **A Note on Ghosts**

All ghosts use the statistics, spells, and abilities of their original forms (often Bandits or Draugr). They disintegrate into Ectoplasm when killed.

Color-coding: In the following tables, elements from the original game are in white and gray. Elements from the Dawnguard, Hearthfire, and Dragonborn add-ons have been color-coded as follows:

Chaurus Hunter	Dawnguard/Hearthfire
Reaver Lord	Dragonborn

Afflicted

The Afflicted of Peryite have a damaging Vile Vapor ability in addition to their normal attacks.

AFFLICTED – ARCHERS

NAME	SUBTYPE	LV	HEALTH	MAGICKA	STAMINA	WEAPONS	ARMOR	ITEMS	SPELLS
Afflicted	Archer	1	30	25	70	Bow, Arrows	Clothes, Gloves, Hat, Boots	(Lockpick), (Gold)	Vile Vapor
Afflicted	Archer	5	74	25	86	Bow, Arrows, Iron Dagger	Clothes, Gloves, Hat, Boots	(Lockpick), (Gold)	Vile Vapor
Afflicted	Archer	9	118	25	102	Bow, Arrows, Steel Dagger	Clothes, Gloves, Hat, Boots	(Lockpick), (Gold)	Vile Vapor
Afflicted	Archer	14	173	25	122	Bow, Arrows, Steel Dagger	Clothes, Gloves, Hat, Boots	(Lockpick), (Gold)	Vile Vapor
Afflicted	Archer	19	228	25	142	Bow, Arrows, Steel Dagger	Clothes, Gloves, Hat, Boots	(Lockpick), (Gold)	Vile Vapor
Afflicted	Archer	24	283	25	162	Bow, Arrows, Steel Dagger	Clothes, Gloves, Hat, Boots	(Lockpick), (Gold)	Vile Vapor

Afflicted

AFFLICTED – GUARDIANS

NAME	SUBTYPE	LV	HEALTH	MAGICKA	STAMINA	WEAPONS	ARMOR	ITEMS	SPELLS
Afflicted	Guardian	1	30	25	70	1H Weapon	(Heavy Cuirass / Light Cuirass / Clothes), Heavy Gauntlets, Heavy Boots, Heavy Helmet, Heavy Shield	(Lockpick), (Gold)	Vile Vapor
Afflicted	Guardian	5	94	25	86	1H Weapon	(Heavy Cuirass / Light Cuirass / Clothes), Heavy Gauntlets, Heavy Boots, Heavy Helmet, Heavy Shield	(Lockpick), (Gold)	Vile Vapor
Afflicted	Guardian	9	118	25	102	1H Weapon	(Heavy Cuirass / Light Cuirass / Clothes), Heavy Gauntlets, Heavy Boots, Heavy Helmet, Heavy Shield	(Lockpick), (Gold)	Vile Vapor
Afflicted	Guardian	14	173	25	122	1H Weapon	(Heavy Cuirass / Light Cuirass / Clothes), Heavy Gauntlets, Heavy Boots, Heavy Helmet, Heavy Shield	(Lockpick), (Gold)	Vile Vapor
Afflicted	Guardian	19	228	25	142	1H Weapon	(Heavy Cuirass / Light Cuirass / Clothes), Heavy Gauntlets, Heavy Boots, Heavy Helmet, Heavy Shield	(Lockpick), (Gold)	Vile Vapor
Afflicted	Guardian	24	283	25	162	1H Weapon	(Heavy Cuirass / Light Cuirass / Clothes), Heavy Gauntlets, Heavy Boots, Heavy Helmet, Heavy Shield	(Lockpick), (Gold)	Vile Vapor

AFFLICTED – MAGES

NAME	SUBTYPE	LV	HEALTH	MAGICKA	STAMINA	WEAPONS	ARMOR	ITEMS	SPELLS
Afflicted	Mage	1	30	100	70	Iron Dagger	Mage Robes, Boots	(Lockpick), (Gold)	(Frostbite / Flames / Sparks), Healing, Oakflesh, Lesser Ward, Vile Vapor
Afflicted	Mage	5	66	124	70	Iron Dagger	Mage Robes, Boots	(Lockpick), (Gold)	(Frostbite / Flames / Sparks), Healing, Oakflesh, Lesser Ward, Vile Vapor
Afflicted	Mage	9	102	123	70	Steel Dagger	Mage Robes, Boots	(Lockpick), (Gold)	(Ice Spike / Firebolt / Lightning Bolt), Fast Healing, Stoneflesh, Steadfast Ward, Vile Vapor
Afflicted	Mage	14	147	153	70	Dwarven Dagger, Iron Dagger	Mage Robes, Boots	(Lockpick), (Gold)	(Ice Spike / Firebolt / Lightning Bolt), Fast Healing, Stoneflesh, Steadfast Ward, Vile Vapor
Afflicted	Mage	19	192	183	70	Dwarven Dagger, Iron Dagger	Mage Robes, Boots	(Lockpick), (Gold)	(Ice Spike / Firebolt / Lightning Bolt), Fast Healing, Stoneflesh, Steadfast Ward, Vile Vapor

AFFLICTED – WARRIORS

NAME	SUBTYPE	LV	HEALTH	MAGICKA	STAMINA	WEAPONS	ARMOR	ITEMS	SPELLS
Afflicted	Warrior	1	30	25	70	1H Weapon	(Light Cuirass / Heavy Cuirass / Clothes), Light Boots, Light Gauntlets, (Light Helmet), (Light Shield)	(Lockpick), (Gold)	Vile Vapor
Afflicted	Warrior	5	94	25	86	1H Weapon	(Light Cuirass / Heavy Cuirass / Clothes), Light Boots, Light Gauntlets, (Light Helmet), (Light Shield)	(Lockpick), (Gold)	Vile Vapor
Afflicted	Warrior	9	118	25	102	1H Weapon	(Light Cuirass / Heavy Cuirass / Clothes), Light Boots, Light Gauntlets, (Light Helmet), (Light Shield)	(Lockpick), (Gold)	Vile Vapor
Afflicted	Warrior	14	173	25	122	1H Weapon	(Light Cuirass / Heavy Cuirass / Clothes), Light Boots, Light Gauntlets, (Light Helmet), (Light Shield)	(Lockpick), (Gold)	Vile Vapor
Afflicted	Warrior	19	228	25	142	1H Weapon, Orcish Dagger	(Light Cuirass / Heavy Cuirass / Clothes), Light Boots, Light Gauntlets, (Light Helmet), (Light Shield)	(Lockpick), (Gold)	Vile Vapor
Afflicted	Warrior	24	283	25	162	1H Weapon, Orcish Dagger	(Light Cuirass / Heavy Cuirass / Clothes), Light Boots, Light Gauntlets, (Light Helmet), (Light Shield)	(Lockpick), (Gold)	Vile Vapor

Alik'r

ALIK'R – ARCHERS

NAME	SUBTYPE	LV	HEALTH	MAGICKA	STAMINA	WEAPONS	ARMOR	ITEMS	SPELLS
Alik'r Warrior	Archer	1	40	25	25	Bow, Arrows, Iron Dagger	Hammerfell Garb, Redguard Hood, Redguard Boots	Gold, (Lockpick)	
Alik'r Warrior	Archer	6	85	25	45	Bow, Arrows, Iron Dagger	Hammerfell Garb, Redguard Hood, Redguard Boots	Gold, (Lockpick)	
Alik'r Warrior	Archer	14	173	25	77	Bow, Arrows, Steel Dagger	Hammerfell Garb, Redguard Hood, Redguard Boots	Gold, (Lockpick)	
Alik'r Warrior	Archer	24	283	25	117	Bow, Arrows, Steel Dagger	Hammerfell Garb, Redguard Hood, Redguard Boots	Gold, (Lockpick)	
Alik'r Warrior	Archer	34	393	25	157	Bow, Arrows, Steel Dagger	Hammerfell Garb, Redguard Hood, Redguard Boots	Gold, (Lockpick)	
Alik'r Warrior	Archer	44	503	25	197	Bow, Arrows, Steel Dagger	Hammerfell Garb, Redguard Hood, Redguard Boots	Gold, (Lockpick)	

Alik'r (Berserker)

ALIK'R – BERSERKERS

NAME	SUBTYPE	LV	HEALTH	MAGICKA	STAMINA	WEAPONS	ARMOR	ITEMS	SPELLS
Alik'r Warrior	Berserker	1	40	25	25	Iron Dagger	Hammerfell Garb, Redguard Hood, Redguard Boots	Gold, (Lockpick)	
Alik'r Warrior	Berserker	6	85	25	45	Iron Dagger	Hammerfell Garb, Redguard Hood, Redguard Boots	Gold, (Lockpick)	
Alik'r Warrior	Berserker	14	173	25	77	Steel Dagger	Hammerfell Garb, Redguard Hood, Redguard Boots	Gold, (Lockpick)	
Alik'r Warrior	Berserker	24	283	25	117	Steel Dagger	Hammerfell Garb, Redguard Hood, Redguard Boots	Gold, (Lockpick)	
Alik'r Warrior	Berserker	34	393	25	157	Orcish Dagger	Hammerfell Garb, Redguard Hood, Redguard Boots	Gold, (Lockpick)	
Alik'r Warrior	Berserker	44	503	25	197	Orcish Dagger	Hammerfell Garb, Redguard Hood, Redguard Boots	Gold, (Lockpick)	

Alik'r (Mage)

ALIK'R – MAGES

NAME	SUBTYPE	LV	HEALTH	MAGICKA	STAMINA	WEAPONS	ARMOR	ITEMS	SPELLS
Alik'r Warrior	Mage	1	40	25	25	Iron Dagger	Hammerfell Garb, Redguard Hood, Redguard Boots	Gold, (Lockpick)	(Frostbite, Flames, Shock), Healing, Lesser Ward
Alik'r Warrior	Mage	6	75	55	25	Iron Dagger	Hammerfell Garb, Redguard Hood, Redguard Boots	Gold, (Lockpick)	(Frostbite, Flames, Shock), Healing, Lesser Ward
Alik'r Warrior	Mage	14	147	103	25	Iron Dagger	Hammerfell Garb, Redguard Hood, Redguard Boots	Gold, (Lockpick)	(Ice Spike / Firebolt / Lightning Bolt), Fast Healing, Steadfast Ward
Alik'r Warrior	Mage	24	237	163	25	Iron Dagger	Hammerfell Garb, Redguard Hood, Redguard Boots	Gold, (Lockpick)	(Ice Spike / Firebolt / Lightning Bolt), Fast Healing, Steadfast Ward
Alik'r Warrior	Mage	34	327	223	25	Iron Dagger	Hammerfell Garb, Redguard Hood, Redguard Boots	Gold, (Lockpick)	(Ice Spike / Firebolt / Lightning Bolt), Fast Healing, Steadfast Ward
Alik'r Warrior	Mage	44	417	283	25	Iron Dagger	Hammerfell Garb, Redguard Hood, Redguard Boots	Gold, (Lockpick)	(Ice Spike / Firebolt / Lightning Bolt), Fast Healing, Steadfast Ward

ALIK'R – WARRIORS

NAME	SUBTYPE	LV	HEALTH	MAGICKA	STAMINA	WEAPONS	ARMOR	ITEMS	SPELLS
Alik'r Warrior	Warrior	1	40	25	25	Scimitar, Iron Dagger	Hammerfell Garb, Redguard Hood, Redguard Boots	Gold, (Lockpick)	
Alik'r Warrior	Warrior	6	85	25	45	Scimitar, Iron Dagger	Hammerfell Garb, Redguard Hood, Redguard Boots	Gold, (Lockpick)	
Alik'r Warrior	Warrior	14	173	25	77	Scimitar, Steel Dagger	Hammerfell Garb, Redguard Hood, Redguard Boots	Gold, (Lockpick)	
Alik'r Warrior	Warrior	24	283	25	117	Scimitar, Steel Dagger	Hammerfell Garb, Redguard Hood, Redguard Boots	Gold, (Lockpick)	
Alik'r Warrior	Warrior	34	393	25	157	Scimitar, Orcish Dagger	Hammerfell Garb, Redguard Hood, Redguard Boots	Gold, (Lockpick)	
Alik'r Warrior	Warrior	44	503	25	197	Scimitar, Orcish Dagger	Hammerfell Garb, Redguard Hood, Redguard Boots	Gold, (Lockpick)	

Alik'r (Warrior)

Animals

This list includes wild and domesticated animals that appear only appear in one or two forms. Minor Treasure includes a tiny chance of: A few gold, a gem, or a ring.

Domesticated Animal (Cow)

DOMESTICATED ANIMALS

NAME	SUBTYPE	LV	HEALTH	MAGICKA	STAMINA	WEAPONS	ARMOR	ITEMS	SPELLS	NOTES
Chicken		1	5	0	25	2 Dmg		Chicken Breast		
Cow		3	87	0	33	10 Dmg		Raw Beef, Cow Hide, (Minor Treasure)		
Goat		3	22	0	8	7 Dmg		Goat Hide, Leg of Goat, (Minor Treasure)		Resist Frost 50%

WILD PREDATORS

NAME	SUBTYPE	LV	HEALTH	MAGICKA	STAMINA	WEAPONS	ARMOR	ITEMS	SPELLS	NOTES
Skeever		1	15	0	15	5 Dmg		Skeever Tail, (Minor Treasure)		
Wolf		2	22	0	205	5 Dmg		Wolf Pelt, (Minor Treasure)		
Ash Hopper		4	155	0	135	30 Dmg		Ash Hopper Jelly, Ash Hopper Meat, Chitin Plate, (Minor Treasure)		Resist Poison 50%
Ice Wolf		6	137	0	255	20 Dmg		Ice Wolf Pelt, (Minor Treasure)		Resist Frost 50%
Sabre Cat		6	150	0	225	35 Dmg		Sabre Cat Pelt, (Sabre Cat Eyeball / Sabre Cat Tooth), (Minor Treasure)		
Sabre Cat, Snowy		11	275	0	300	45 Dmg		Sabre Cat Snow Pelt, (Sabre Cat Eyeball / Sabre Cat Tooth), (Minor Treasure)		Resist Frost 50%
Bear		12	260	0	225	35 Dmg		Bear Pelt, Bear Claws, (Minor Treasure)		
Bear, Cave		16	450	0	425	30 Dmg		Bear Pelt, Bear Claws, (Minor Treasure)		
Bear, Snow		20	550	0	400	45 Dmg		Bear Pelt, Bear Claws, (Minor Treasure)		Resist Frost 50%
Mudcrab		1	5	0	25	5 Dmg		Mudcrab Chitin, (Minor Treasure)		Waterbreathing
Mudcrab, Solstheim		1	5	0	25	5 Dmg		Mudcrab Chitin, (Minor Treasure)		Waterbreathing
Mudcrab	Large	2	35	0	30	20 Dmg		Mudcrab Chitin, (Minor Treasure)		Waterbreathing
Mudcrab	Giant	3	55	0	35	25 Dmg		2 Mudcrab Chitin, (Minor Treasure)		Waterbreathing
Slaughterfish		1	35	0	25	5 Dmg		Slaughterfish Scales, (Minor Treasure)		Waterbreathing
Horker		3	175	0	185	15 Dmg		Horker Meat, Horker Tusk, (Minor Treasure)		
Ice Wraiths		9	193	50	227	40 Dmg + Frost 7/s for 3s		Ice Wraith Teeth, Ice Wraith Essence		Immune to Frost, Weak to Fire 25%, Waterwalking

Wild Predator (Snow Bear)

WILD PREY

NAME	SUBTYPE	LV	HEALTH	MAGICKA	STAMINA	WEAPONS	ARMOR	ITEMS	SPELLS	NOTES
Deer		1	50	0	25	5 Dmg		Venison, Deer Hide, (Minor Treasure)		
Elk	Male	1	50	0	25	5 Dmg		Venison, Deer Hide, (Minor Treasure)		
Elk	Female	1	50	0	25	5 Dmg		Venison, Deer Hide, (Minor Treasure)		
Goat	Wild	1	25	0	25	7 Dmg		Goat Hide, Leg of Goat, (Minor Treasure)		Resist Frost 50%
Hare		1	5	0	25	2 Dmg		Raw Rabbit Leg		
Fox		2	22	0	25	5 Dmg		Fox Pelt		
Snow Fox		2	22	0	25	5 Dmg		Snow Fox Pelt		Resist Frost 50%
Mammoth		38	931	0	424	65 Dmg		Mammoth Meat, Mammoth Tusk, (Minor Treasure)		Resist Frost 33%

Wild Prey (Mammoth)

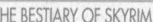

UNIQUE ANIMALS

NAME	SUBTYPE	LV	HEALTH	MAGICKA	STAMINA	WEAPONS	ARMOR	ITEMS	SPELLS	NOTES
Old Salty	Mudcrab	3	55	0	35	25 Dmg		2 Mudcrab Chitin, (Minor Treasure)		Waterbreathing
Lord Tusk	Horker	25	445	0	275	15 Dmg		Horker Meat, Horker Tusk, (Minor Treasure)		

Unique Animal (Old Salty)

Domesticated Animal (Chicken)

Wild Predator (Ice Wolf)

Wild Predator (Sabre Cat)

Wild Prey (Elk)

Apocrypha Keepers

Apocrypha is the plane of Oblivion ruled by Hermeus Mora, lord of fate and keeper of forbidden knowledge. The Daedra of this realm come in two forms: Seekers are masters of illusion, who use invisibility and mirror images as distractions while they sap your strength; use a quick area-of-effect attack to break through their decoys and find the real Seeker. Lurkers are towering monstrosities with powerful physical and poison-based attacks; poison resistance is effective against them, but your best defense may be to simply keep your distance and attack them from range.

SEEKERS

NAME	SUBTYPE	LV	HEALTH	MAGICKA	STAMINA	WEAPONS	ARMOR	ITEMS	SPELLS	NOTES
Seeker		21	550	300	0			(Books), (Spellbook), Scroll	Seeker Drain, Knowledge Drain, Mirror, Invisibility	Waterwalking, Regenerates Health, Immune to Paralysis, Resist Shock 33%
Seeker	Mirror Image	21	20	300	0			(Books), (Spellbook), Scroll	Seeker Drain, Knowledge Drain, Mirror, Invisibility	Waterwalking, Regenerates Health, Immune to Paralysis, Resist Shock 33%
Seeker	Conjured	21	550	300	0				Seeker Drain, Knowledge Drain, Mirror, Invisibility	Waterwalking, Regenerates Health, Immune to Paralysis, Resist Shock 33%
Seeker Aspirant		32	660	355	0			(Books), (Spellbook), Scroll	Seeker Drain, Knowledge Drain, Mirror, Invisibility	Waterwalking, Regenerates Health, Immune to Paralysis, Resist Shock 33%
Seeker Aspirant	Mirror Image	32	60	303	104				Seeker Drain, Knowledge Drain, Mirror, Invisibility	Waterwalking, Regenerates Health, Immune to Paralysis, Resist Shock 33%
High Seeker		42	760	405	0			(Books), (Spellbook), Scroll	Seeker Drain, Knowledge Drain, Mirror, Invisibility	Waterwalking, Regenerates Health, Immune to Paralysis, Resist Shock 33%
High Seeker	Mirror Image	42	100	337	137				Seeker Drain, Knowledge Drain, Mirror, Invisibility	Waterwalking, Regenerates Health, Immune to Paralysis, Resist Shock 33%

Seeker (High Seeker)

LURKERS

NAME	SUBTYPE	LV	HEALTH	MAGICKA	STAMINA	WEAPONS	ARMOR	ITEMS	SPELLS	NOTES
Lurker		25	818	15	277	60 Dmg		Gold, (Ingredients), (Jewelry), (Soul Gems)	Giant Stomp, Tentacle Burst, Tentacle Spray	Regenerates Health, Resist Poison 33%, Resist Magic 25%, Resist Frost 25%
Lurker Guardian		35	1135	15	410	90 Dmg		Gold, (Ingredients), (Jewelry), (Soul Gems)	Giant Stomp, Tentacle Burst, Tentacle Spray	Regenerates Health, Resist Poison 33%, Resist Magic 25%, Resist Frost 25%
Lurker Sentinel		45	1451	15	444	120 Dmg		Gold, (Ingredients), (Jewelry), (Soul Gems)	Giant Stomp, Tentacle Burst, Tentacle Spray	Regenerates Health, Resist Poison 33%, Resist Magic 25%, Resist Frost 25%
Lurker Vindicator		55	1768	15	477	140 Dmg		Gold, (Ingredients), (Jewelry), (Soul Gems)	Giant Stomp, Tentacle Burst, Tentacle Spray	Regenerates Health, Resist Poison 33%, Resist Magic 25%, Resist Frost 25%

Lurker Vindicator

Ash Spawn

Born from bones of Solstheim's dead infused with the ash of Red Mountain, Ash Spawn roam the southern wastes of Solstheim. They are immune to poison and highly resistant to fire, but have no particular weaknesses.

ASH SPAWN WARRIORS

NAME	SUBTYPE	LV	HEALTH	MAGICKA	STAMINA	WEAPONS	ARMOR	ITEMS	SPELLS	NOTES
Ash Spawn	Warrior	20	440	50	175	[Ashen Battleaxe]		(Ore), (Gems), Spawn Ash		Waterbreathing, Immune to Poison, Resist Fire 75%
Ash Spawn Skirmisher	Warrior	30	690	75	275	[Ashen Battleaxe]		(Ore), (Gems), Spawn Ash		Waterbreathing, Immune to Poison, Resist Fire 75%
Ash Spawn Immolator	Warrior	40	940	100	375	[Ashen Battleaxe]		(Ore), (Gems), Spawn Ash		Waterbreathing, Immune to Poison, Resist Fire 75%

Ash Spawn Warrior (Ash Spawn Skirmisher)

ASH SPAWN SPELLSWORDS

NAME	SUBTYPE	LV	HEALTH	MAGICKA	STAMINA	WEAPONS	ARMOR	ITEMS	SPELLS	NOTES
Ash Spawn	Spellsword	20	440	50	175	[Ashen War Axe]		(Ore), (Gems), Spawn Ash	Firebolt	Waterbreathing, Immune to Poison, Resist Fire 75%
Ash Spawn Skirmisher	Spellsword	30	690	75	275	[Ashen War Axe]		(Ore), (Gems), Spawn Ash		Waterbreathing, Immune to Poison, Resist Fire 75%
Ash Spawn Immolator	Spellsword	40	940	100	375	[Ashen War Axe]		(Ore), (Gems), Spawn Ash		Waterbreathing, Immune to Poison, Resist Fire 75%

Ash Spawn Spellsword (Ash Spawn Immolator)

ASH SPAWN MAGES

NAME	SUBTYPE	LV	HEALTH	MAGICKA	STAMINA	WEAPONS	ARMOR	ITEMS	SPELLS	NOTES
Ash Spawn	Mage	20	440	145	80			(Ore), (Gems), Spawn Ash	Flame Cloak, Firebolt	Waterbreathing, Immune to Poison, Resist Fire 75%
Ash Spawn Skirmisher	Mage	30	690	220	80			(Ore), (Gems), Spawn Ash	Flame Cloak, Firebolt	Waterbreathing, Immune to Poison, Resist Fire 75%
Ash Spawn Immolator	Mage	40	940	295	80			(Ore), (Gems), Spawn Ash	Flame Cloak, Firebolt	Waterbreathing, Immune to Poison, Resist Fire 75%

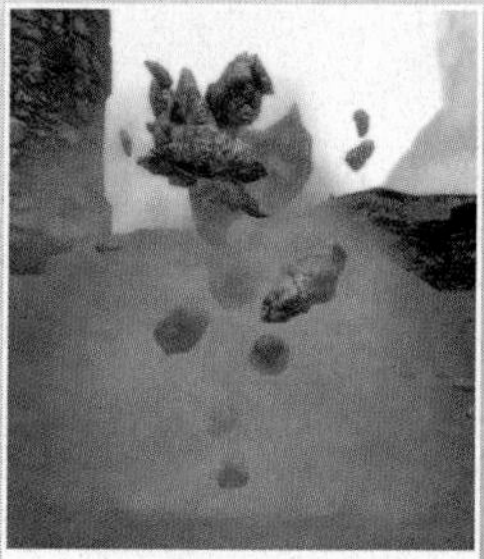

Conjured Ash Spawn (Ash Guardian)

CONJURED ASH SPAWN

NAME	SUBTYPE	LV	HEALTH	MAGICKA	STAMINA	WEAPONS	ARMOR	ITEMS	SPELLS	NOTES
Ash Spawn	Spellsword	20	440	50	175	[Ashen War Axe]			Firebolt	Waterbreathing, Immune to Poison, Resist Fire 75%
Ash Guardian		30	441	197	247	50 Dmg			Searing Embers	Waterwalking, Immune to Poison, Immune to Paralysis

Bandits

Bandits are among the most common threats in Skyrim, and include members of every race.

BANDIT ARCHERS

NAME	SUBTYPE	LV	HEALTH	MAGICKA	STAMINA	WEAPONS	ARMOR	ITEMS	SPELLS	NOTES
Bandit	Archer	1	35	25	70	Bow, Arrows, Dagger	Light Cuirass, Light Boots, (Light Gauntlets)	(Gold)		
Bandit Outlaw	Archer	5	109	25	86	Bow, Arrows, Dagger	Light Cuirass, Light Boots, (Light Gauntlets)	(Gold)		
Bandit Thug	Archer	9	238	25	107	Bow, Arrows, Dagger	Light Cuirass, Light Boots, (Light Gauntlets)	(Gold)		
Bandit Highwayman	Archer	14	318	25	122	Bow, Arrows, Dagger	Light Cuirass, Light Boots, (Light Gauntlets)	(Gold)		
Bandit Plunderer	Archer	19	398	25	172	Bow, Arrows, Dagger	Light Cuirass, Light Boots, (Light Gauntlets)	Gold, (Lockpick)		
Bandit Marauder	Archer	25	489	25	246	Bow, Arrows, Dagger	Light Cuirass, Light Boots, (Light Gauntlets)	Gold, (Lockpick)		

Bandit (Warrior)

BANDIT BERSERKERS

NAME	SUBTYPE	LV	HEALTH	MAGICKA	STAMINA	WEAPONS	ARMOR	ITEMS	SPELLS	NOTES
Bandit	Berserker	1	35	25	70	2H Weapon	Light Cuirass, Light Boots, (Light Gauntlets)	(Gold), (Lockpick)		
Bandit Outlaw	Berserker	5	109	25	86	2H Weapon	Light Cuirass, Light Boots, (Light Gauntlets)	(Gold), (Lockpick)		
Bandit Thug	Berserker	9	238	25	107	2H Weapon	Light Cuirass, Light Boots, (Light Gauntlets)	(Gold), (Lockpick)		
Bandit Highwayman	Berserker	14	318	25	122	2H Weapon	Light Cuirass, Light Boots, (Light Gauntlets)	(Gold), (Lockpick)		
Bandit Plunderer	Berserker	19	398	25	172	2H Weapon, Orcish Dagger	Light Cuirass, Light Boots, (Light Gauntlets)	Gold		
Bandit Marauder	Berserker	25	489	25	246	2H Weapon, Orcish Dagger	Light Cuirass, Light Boots, (Light Gauntlets)	Gold		

Bandit (Berserker)

BANDIT GUARDIANS

NAME	SUBTYPE	LV	HEALTH	MAGICKA	STAMINA	WEAPONS	ARMOR	ITEMS	SPELLS	NOTES
Bandit	Guardian	1	35	25	70	1H Weapon	Heavy Cuirass, Heavy Boots, (Heavy Gauntlets), Heavy Helmet, Shield	(Gold), (Lockpick)		
Bandit Outlaw	Guardian	5	109	25	86	1H Weapon	Heavy Cuirass, Heavy Boots, (Heavy Gauntlets), Heavy Helmet, Shield	(Gold), (Lockpick)		
Bandit Thug	Guardian	9	238	25	107	1H Weapon	Heavy Cuirass, Heavy Boots, (Heavy Gauntlets), Heavy Helmet, Shield	(Gold), (Lockpick)		
Bandit Highwayman	Guardian	14	318	25	122	1H Weapon	Heavy Cuirass, Heavy Boots, (Heavy Gauntlets), Heavy Helmet, Shield	(Gold), (Lockpick)		
Bandit Plunderer	Guardian	19	398	25	172	1H Weapon, Orcish Dagger	Heavy Cuirass, Heavy Boots, (Heavy Gauntlets), Heavy Helmet, Shield	Gold		
Bandit Marauder	Guardian	25	489	25	246	1H Weapon, Orcish Dagger	Heavy Cuirass, Heavy Boots, (Heavy Gauntlets), Heavy Helmet, Shield	Gold		

BANDIT WARRIORS – 1H

NAME	SUBTYPE	LV	HEALTH	MAGICKA	STAMINA	WEAPONS	ARMOR	ITEMS	SPELLS	NOTES
Bandit	1H Warrior	1	35	25	70	1H Weapon	Light Cuirass, Light Boots, (Light Gauntlets), (Shield)	(Gold)		
Bandit Outlaw	1H Warrior	5	109	25	86	1H Weapon	Light Cuirass, Light Boots, (Light Gauntlets), (Shield)	(Gold)		
Bandit Thug	1H Warrior	9	238	25	107	1H Weapon	Light Cuirass, Light Boots, (Light Gauntlets), (Shield)	(Gold)		
Bandit Highwayman	1H Warrior	14	318	25	122	1H Weapon	Light Cuirass, Light Boots, (Light Gauntlets), (Shield)	(Gold)		
Bandit Plunderer	1H Warrior	19	398	25	172	1H Weapon	Light Cuirass, Light Boots, (Light Gauntlets), (Shield)	Gold		
Bandit Marauder	1H Warrior	25	489	25	246	1H Weapon	Light Cuirass, Light Boots, (Light Gauntlets), (Shield)	Gold		

Bandit (Wizard)

BANDIT WARRIORS – 2H

NAME	SUBTYPE	LV	HEALTH	MAGICKA	STAMINA	WEAPONS	ARMOR	ITEMS	SPELLS	NOTES
Bandit	2H Warrior	1	35	25	70	2H Weapon	Light Cuirass, Light Boots, (Light Gauntlets)	(Gold), (Lockpick)		
Bandit Outlaw	2H Warrior	5	109	25	86	2H Weapon	Light Cuirass, Light Boots, (Light Gauntlets)	(Gold), (Lockpick)		
Bandit Thug	2H Warrior	9	238	25	107	2H Weapon	Light Cuirass, Light Boots, (Light Gauntlets)	(Gold), (Lockpick)		
Bandit Highwayman	2H Warrior	14	318	25	122	2H Weapon	Light Cuirass, Light Boots, (Light Gauntlets)	(Gold), (Lockpick)		
Bandit Plunderer	2H Warrior	19	398	25	172	2H Weapon, Orcish Dagger	Light Cuirass, Light Boots, (Light Gauntlets)	Gold, (Lockpick)		
Bandit Marauder	2H Warrior	25	489	25	246	2H Weapon, Orcish Dagger	Light Cuirass, Light Boots, (Light Gauntlets)	Gold, (Lockpick)		

Bandit (Warrior)

BANDIT WIZARDS

NAME	SUBTYPE	LV	HEALTH	MAGICKA	STAMINA	WEAPONS	ARMOR	ITEMS	SPELLS	NOTES
Bandit	Wizard	1	35	100	50	Iron Dagger	Fur Armor, Boots	(Gold)	Healing, (Frostbite / Flames / Sparks), Oakflesh, Lesser Ward	
Bandit Outlaw	Wizard	5	101	124	70	Iron Dagger	Fur Armor, Boots	(Gold)	Healing, (Frostbite / Flames / Sparks), Oakflesh, Lesser Ward	
Bandit Thug	Wizard	9	222	173	75	Steel Dagger	Fur Armor, Boots	(Gold)	Fast Healing, Stoneflesh, (Ice Spike, Firebolt, Lightning Bolt), Steadfast Ward	
Bandit Highwayman	Wizard	14	292	153	70	Dagger	Fur Armor, Boots	(Gold)	Fast Healing, Stoneflesh, (Ice Spike, Firebolt, Lightning Bolt), Steadfast Ward	
Bandit Plunderer	Wizard	19	362	183	70	Dagger	Fur Armor, Boots	Gold, (Lockpick)	Fast Healing, Stoneflesh, (Ice Storm / Fireball / Chain Lightning), (Ice Spike, Firebolt, Lightning Bolt), Steadfast Ward	
Bandit Marauder	Wizard	25	441	294	150	Dagger	Fur Armor, Boots	Gold, (Lockpick)	Close Wounds, Fast Healing, Ironflesh, (Ice Storm / Fireball / Chain Lightning), (Ice Spike, Firebolt, Lightning Bolt), Steadfast Ward	

BANDIT CHIEFS – 1H

NAME	SUBTYPE	LV	HEALTH	MAGICKA	STAMINA	WEAPONS	ARMOR	ITEMS	SPELLS	NOTES
Bandit Chief	1H Warrior	6	155	25	95	1H Weapon, Steel Dagger	Heavy Cuirass, Heavy Boots, (Heavy Gauntlets), Heavy Helmet, Shield	Gold		
Bandit Chief	1H Warrior	10	224	25	126	1H Weapon, Steel Dagger	Heavy Cuirass, Heavy Boots, (Heavy Gauntlets), Heavy Helmet, Shield	Gold		
Bandit Chief	1H Warrior	16	315	25	160	1H Weapon, Orcish Dagger	Heavy Cuirass, Heavy Boots, (Heavy Gauntlets), Heavy Helmet, Shield	Gold		
Bandit Chief	1H Warrior	21	395	25	195	1H Weapon, Elven Dagger	Heavy Cuirass, Heavy Boots, (Heavy Gauntlets), Heavy Helmet, Shield	Gold		
Bandit Chief	1H Warrior	28	497	25	258	1H Weapon, Elven Dagger	Heavy Cuirass, Heavy Boots, (Heavy Gauntlets), (Heavy Helmet), Shield	Gold		

Bandit (Bandit Chief)

BANDIT CHIEFS – 2H

NAME	SUBTYPE	LV	HEALTH	MAGICKA	STAMINA	WEAPONS	ARMOR	ITEMS	SPELLS	NOTES
Bandit Chief	1H Warrior	6	155	25	95	2H Weapon, Steel Dagger	Heavy Cuirass, Heavy Boots, (Heavy Gauntlets), Heavy Helmet, (Shield)	Gold		
Bandit Chief	1H Warrior	10	224	25	126	2H Weapon, Steel Dagger	Heavy Cuirass, Heavy Boots, (Heavy Gauntlets), Heavy Helmet, (Shield)	Gold		
Bandit Chief	1H Warrior	16	315	25	160	2H Weapon, Orcish Dagger	Heavy Cuirass, Heavy Boots, (Heavy Gauntlets), Heavy Helmet, (Shield)	Gold		
Bandit Chief	1H Warrior	21	395	25	195	2H Weapon, Elven Dagger	Heavy Cuirass, Heavy Boots, (Heavy Gauntlets), Heavy Helmet, (Shield)	Gold		
Bandit Chief	1H Warrior	28	497	25	258	2H Weapon, Elven Dagger	Heavy Cuirass, Heavy Boots, (Heavy Gauntlets), Heavy Helmet, (Shield)	Gold		

Bandit (Bandit Chief)

Chaurus

The insectoid Chaurus often fight alongside their Falmer masters. Their high health and lingering poison attack makes them dangerous opponents. Be sure to increase your resistance to poison with potions or enchantments before facing them.

When a Chaurus reaches the end of its natural lifespan, it forms a cocoon and is reborn as a flying Chaurus Hunter. Hunters have more powerful attacks, greater health, and stronger chitin that resists physical damage, making magic a more effective choice against them. Minor Treasure includes a tiny chance of: A few gold, a gem, or a ring.

Chaurus

CHAURUS

NAME	SUBTYPE	LV	HEALTH	MAGICKA	STAMINA	WEAPONS	ARMOR	ITEMS	SPELLS	NOTES
Chaurus		12	253	0	137	20 Dmg + Poison 5/s for 5s		Chaurus Chitin, (Chaurus Eggs), (Minor Treasure)	Poison Spit Attack	Resist Poison 50%
Chaurus Hunter Fledgling		16	375	50	150	32 + Poison 10/s for 5s		Chaurus Chitin, Chaurus Hunter Antennae, (Chaurus Eggs), (Minor Treasure)	Poison Spit Attack	Resist Poison 50%, 100 Armor
Chaurus Reaper		20	371	0	214	55 Dmg + Poison 7/s for 7s		Chaurus Chitin, (Chaurus Eggs), (Minor Treasure)	Poison Spit Attack	Resist Poison 50%
Chaurus Hunter		32	636	50	204	96 + Poison 10/s for 5s		Chaurus Chitin, Chaurus Hunter Antennae, (Chaurus Eggs), (Minor Treasure)	Poison Spit Attack	Resist Poison 50%, 100 Armor

Chaurus Hunter

Cultists

Miraak's human followers, the Cultists, oversee his plans on Solstheim and carry out their master's will across Tamriel. Cultists are powerful conjurers, with the ability to command or banish your summoned creatures, and often to summon creatures of their own, including Seekers from Apocrypha. Cultist loot includes a chance of: Gold, Ingredients, Potions, Scrolls, Soul Gems, Spell Tomes, or Recipes.

Miraak's strongest servants are his three Acolytes, powerful Dragon Priests who followed him to Solstheim in the distant past. Each Acolyte uses spells from one element exclusively, so prepare for battle by using potions or equipping gear that gives you resistance to their element. They have no special weaknesses.

CULTISTS

NAME	SUBTYPE	LV	HEALTH	MAGICKA	STAMINA	WEAPONS	ARMOR	ITEMS	SPELLS	NOTES
Cultist		12	192	198	25	Dagger, (Staff)	Cultist Robes, Cultist Mask, Cultist Boots, Cultist Gloves	(Cultist Loot)	(Conjure Flame Atronach), Fast Healing, Firebolt, Flames, Stoneflesh, Steadfast Ward	
Cultist Adept		19	525	270	25	Dagger, (Staff)	Cultist Robes, Cultist Mask, Cultist Boots, Cultist Gloves	(Cultist Loot)	(Conjure Seeker), Banish Daedra, Close Wounds, Fast Healing, Lightning Bolt, Sparks, Stoneflesh, Steadfast Ward	
Ascendant Cultist		27	767	323	25	Dagger, (Staff)	Cultist Robes, Cultist Mask, Cultist Boots, Cultist Gloves	(Cultist Loot)	(Conjure Seeker), Chain Lightning, Close Wounds, Command Daedra, Expel Daedra, Fast Healing, Lightning Bolt, Stoneflesh, Steadfast Ward	
Master Cultist		36	942	383	25	Dagger, (Staff)	Cultist Robes, Cultist Mask, Cultist Boots, Cultist Gloves	(Cultist Loot)	(Conjure Seeker), Chain Lightning, Close Wounds, Command Daedra, Expel Daedra, Ironflesh, Lightning Bolt, Greater Ward	
Arch Cultist		46	1325	500	50	Dagger, (Staff)	Cultist Robes, Cultist Mask, Cultist Boots, Cultist Gloves	(Cultist Loot)	(Conjure Seeker), Chain Lightning, Close Wounds, Command Daedra, Expel Daedra, Ironflesh, Thunderbolt, Greater Ward	

Cultist (Arch Cultist)

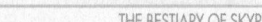

ACOLYTES

NAME	SUBTYPE	LV	HEALTH	MAGICKA	STAMINA	WEAPONS	ARMOR	ITEMS	SPELLS	NOTES
Ahzidal		60	2000	595	0		Ahzidal, [Acolyte Robes]		Fire Stream, Ebonyflesh, Flame Cloak, Raise Zombie, Revenant, Greater Ward	Waterwalking, Immune to Poison, Immune to Paralysis
Dukaan		60	2000	595	0		Dukaan, [Acolyte Robes]		Conjure Seeker, Frost Stream, Ebonyflesh, Frost Cloak, Greater Ward	Waterwalking, Immune to Poison, Immune to Paralysis
Zahkriisos		60*	2000	495	0		Zahkriisos, [Acolyte Robes]		Conjure Seeker, Ebonyflesh, Lightning Cloak, Greater Ward, (Thunderbolt/Lightning Storm)	Waterwalking, Immune to Poison, Immune to Paralysis

Acolyte (Zahkriisos)

MIRAAK

NAME	SUBTYPE	LV	HEALTH	MAGICKA	STAMINA	WEAPONS	ARMOR	ITEMS	SPELLS	NOTES
Miraak		35*	747	378	335	Miraak's Sword, Miraak's Staff	Miraak's Mask, Miraak's Robes, Miraak's Boots, Miraak's Gloves		Dragon Aspect Shout, Become Ethereal Shout, Cyclone Shout, Fire Breath Shout, Frost Breath Shout, Souleater Shout, Unrelenting Force Shout, Whirlwind Sprint Shout, Chain Lightning, Fast Healing, Greater Ward, Lightning Bolt, Lightning Cloak, Sparks	
Miraak		60*	966	471	398	Miraak's Sword, Miraak's Staff	Miraak's Mask, Miraak's Robes, Miraak's Boots, Miraak's Gloves		Dragon Aspect Shout, Become Ethereal Shout, Cyclone Shout, Fire Breath Shout, Frost Breath Shout, Souleater Shout, Unrelenting Force Shout, Whirlwind Sprint Shout, Chain Lightning, Fast Healing, Greater Ward, Lightning Bolt, Lightning Cloak, Sparks	

Daedra

Daedra include all manner of creatures native to Oblivion, from elemental Atronachs to the powerful Dremora. All of the Daedra in this list will be affected by Daedra-banishing spells and effects (Banish Daedra, Expel Daedra, etc.). Don't bother using Illusion spells against Daedra, but do take advantage of the Atronachs' elemental weaknesses—obviously, fire spells are best against Frost Atronachs, and frost spells against Flame Atronachs.

Note that Atronachs summoned by the common conjuration spells are generally weaker than those bound in more permanent ways (such as the ones you often find in Warlock dungeons). You can claim Daedra Hearts from the bodies of slain Dremora; these are one of the rarest ingredients in the game, and essential for smithing Daedric items.

Daedra (Flame Atronach)

DAEDRA

NAME	SUBTYPE	LV	HEALTH	MAGICKA	STAMINA	WEAPONS	ARMOR	ITEMS	SPELLS	NOTES
Familiar	Conjured	2	32	0	205	5 Dmg				
Flame Atronach	Conjured	5	111	174	50	5 Dmg + 10 Fire			Firebolt	Immune to Fire, Weak to Frost 33%, Flame Cloak, Waterwalking, Death Explosion (Flame)
Flame Atronach		5	111	174	50	5 Dmg + 10 Fire		Flame Salts	Firebolt	Immune to Fire, Weak to Frost 33%, Flame Cloak, Waterwalking, Death Explosion (Flame)
Firev Wyrm	Conjured	11	316	50	234	15 Dmg + 20 Fire				Immune to Fire, Weak to Frost 25%, Waterwalking, Death Explosion (Fire)
Frost Atronach	Conjured	16	300	25	125	20 Dmg + 25 Frost				Immune to Frost, Weak to Fire 33%, Frost Cloak, Waterbreathing, Death Explosion (Frost)
Frost Atronach		16	400	25	250	20 Dmg + 25 Frost		Frost Salts		Immune to Frost, Weak to Fire 33%, Frost Cloak, Waterbreathing, Death Explosion (Frost)
Storm Atronach	Conjured	30	241	197	147	30 Dmg + 20 Shock			Chain Lightning, Lightning Bolt	Immune to Shock, Shock Cloak, Waterwalking, Death Explosion (Shock)
Storm Atronach		30	441	197	247	30 Dmg + 20 Shock		Void Salts	Chain Lightning, Lightning Bolt	Immune to Shock, Shock Cloak, Waterwalking, Death Explosion (Shock)

DREMORA

NAME	SUBTYPE	LV	HEALTH	MAGICKA	STAMINA	WEAPONS	ARMOR	ITEMS	SPELLS	NOTES
Dremora		25*	289	25	121	Sword, Iron Dagger	[Dremora Armor]	Daedra Heart	Conjure Flame Atronach, Fire Storm, Wall of Flames	
Dremora Churl		6	92	183	50	(1H/2H Weapon), Iron Dagger	[Dremora Robes]	Daedra Heart	Fast Healing, Flames, Oakflesh, Lesser Ward	
Dremora Caitiff		12	142	223	50	(1H/2H Weapon), Iron Dagger	[Dremora Robes]	Daedra Heart	Fast Healing, Firebolt, Stoneflesh, Lesser Ward	
Dremora Kynval		19	200	270	50	(1H/2H Weapon), Iron Dagger	[Dremora Robes]	Daedra Heart	Close Wounds, Fireball, Firebolt, Flame Cloak, Stoneflesh, Steadfast Ward	
Dremora Kynreeve		27	267	323	50	(1H/2H Weapon), Iron Dagger	[Dremora Robes]	Daedra Heart	Close Wounds, Fireball, Firebolt, Flame Cloak, Ironflesh, Steadfast Ward	
Dremora Markynaz		36	342	383	50	(1H/2H Weapon), Iron Dagger	[Dremora Robes]	Daedra Heart	Close Wounds, Fireball, Flame Cloak, Incinerate, Ironflesh, Steadfast Ward	
Dremora Valkynaz		46	425	450	50	(1H/2H Weapon), Iron Dagger	[Dremora Robes]	Daedra Heart	Close Wounds, Fireball, Flame Cloak, Incinerate, Ironflesh, Steadfast Ward	
Dremora Lord	Conjured	30	491	247	197	[Daedric Greatsword of the Inferno]	[Dremora Armor]		Firebolt, Flame Cloak, Incinerate, Steadfast Ward	

Daedra (Dremora Lord)

Dawnguard

Long ago, the Dawnguard were an organization of elite Vampire Hunters. Under the leadership of Isran, they have begun to rebuild their base in Skyrim's eastern mountains, and their agents are beginning to spread throughout the Nine Holds. Dawnguard loot includes a chance of food or drink, lockpicks, jewelry, gems, tools, or ingots.

DAWNGUARD WARRIORS

NAME	SUBTYPE	LV	HEALTH	MAGICKA	STAMINA	WEAPONS	ARMOR	ITEMS	SPELLS	NOTES
Dawnguard	Warrior	1	35	25	70	(Dawnguard Axe/ Dawnguard Hammer)	Dawnguard Armor, Dawnguard Boots, Dawnguard Gloves (Dawnguard Helmet)	Dawnguard Loot, (Gold)		
Dawnguard	Warrior	5	109	25	86	(Dawnguard Axe/ Dawnguard Hammer)	Dawnguard Armor, Dawnguard Boots, Dawnguard Gloves, (Dawnguard Helmet)	Dawnguard Loot (Gold)		
Dawnguard	Warrior	9	238	25	107	(Dawnguard Axe/ Dawnguard Hammer)	Dawnguard Armor, Dawnguard Boots, Dawnguard Gloves, (Dawnguard Helmet)	Dawnguard Loot (Gold)		
Dawnguard	Warrior	14	318	25	152	(Dawnguard Axe/ Dawnguard Hammer)	Dawnguard Armor, Dawnguard Boots, Dawnguard Gloves, (Dawnguard Helmet)	Dawnguard Loot (Gold)		
Dawnguard	Warrior	19	398	25	172	(Dawnguard Axe/ Dawnguard Hammer)	Dawnguard Armor, Dawnguard Boots, Dawnguard Gloves, (Dawnguard Helmet)	Dawnguard Loot (Gold)		
Dawnguard	Warrior	25	489	25	246	(Dawnguard Axe/ Dawnguard Hammer)	Dawnguard Armor, Dawnguard Boots, Dawnguard Gloves, (Dawnguard Helmet)	Dawnguard Loot (Gold)		

Dawnguard Crossbowman

DAWNGUARD CROSSBOWMEN

NAME	SUBTYPE	LV	HEALTH	MAGICKA	STAMINA	WEAPONS	ARMOR	ITEMS	SPELLS	NOTES
Dawnguard	Crossbowman	1	35	25	70	Crossbow, Steel Bolts, Dawnguard Axe	Dawnguard Armor, Dawnguard Boots, Dawnguard Gloves, (Dawnguard Helmet)	(Gold)		

Dawnguard Warrior (One-Handed)

DAWNGUARD LEADERS

NAME	SUBTYPE	LV	HEALTH	MAGICKA	STAMINA	WEAPONS	ARMOR	ITEMS	SPELLS	NOTES
Dawnguard	Warrior	10*	149	50	86	Dawnguard Axe	Dawnguard Armor, Dawnguard Boots, Dawnguard Gloves (Dawnguard Helmet)	(Gold)		
Dawnguard	Mage	10*	131	104	50	Dawnguard Axe	Dawnguard Armor, Dawnguard Boots, Dawnguard Gauntlets	(Gold)	(Flames/Frostbite/Shock), (Firebolt/Ice Spike/Lightning Bolt), (Fireball/Ice Storm/Chain Lightning)	
Dawnguard	Crossbowman	10*	149	50	86	Dawnguard Axe, Crossbow, Steel Bolts	Dawnguard Armor, Dawnguard Boots, Dawnguard Gloves (Dawnguard Helmet)	(Gold)		

Dawnguard Warrior (Two-Handed)

Death Hounds

With a fearsome bite and bloodlust the equal of any vampire, these undead dogs will rend the flesh of any who oppose their masters. As allies, their bite and ever-present Frost Cloak mean they do significantly more damage than a common dog, although common dogs will have more Health at higher levels. When facing them, consider increasing your Frost Resistance to minimize the damage from their Frost Cloak. Spells that damage or turn undead also work well against them.

Minor treasure includes a tiny chance of a few gold, a gem, or a ring.

Death Hound

DEATH HOUNDS

NAME	SUBTYPE	LV	HEALTH	MAGICKA	STAMINA	WEAPONS	ARMOR	ITEMS	SPELLS	NOTES
Death Hound		5	115	0	120	13 Dmg		Death Hound Collar, Dog Meat (Minor Treasure)		33% Resist Frost, Frost Cloak

Dogs

While dogs are a common sight in Skyrim, purebreeds like Huskies are rare. The Dawnguard train them as war dogs, using them to seek out vampires and hunt them down. With almost twice the Health, Stamina, and attack power of an average dog, the armored Huskies are a worthy companion for any warrior. Minor treasure includes a tiny chance of a few gold, a gem, or a ring.

DOGS

NAME	SUBTYPE	LV	HEALTH	MAGICKA	STAMINA	WEAPONS	ARMOR	ITEMS	SPELLS	NOTES
Dog		2	21	0	24	8 Dmg		Dog Meat (Minor Treasure)		
Dog	Trained	10*	100	0	65	8 Dmg		Dog Meat (Minor Treasure)		
Husky	Unarmored	2	21	0	24	13 Dmg		Dog Meat (Minor Treasure)		
Dawnguard Husky	Armored	10*	190	0	145	20 Dmg		Dog Meat (Minor Treasure)		

Dawnguard Husky

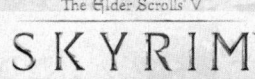

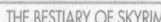

Dragons

Dragons are among the most formidable foes, with powerful attacks and vast reserves of health. A dragon's color usually indicates their difficulty, allowing you to choose whether to fight or flee as soon as you spot them. When fighting a dragon, stay on the move– patience and ranged attacks work best. Be especially careful of Revered and Legendary Dragons, who have a powerful shout that drains your Health, Magicka, and Stamina.

Dragon Loot includes a chance of: Dragon Bones, Dragon Scales, Gold, Gems, Weapons, or Armor; Dragons usually have several of these items. If you intend to smith dragon weapons or armor, make sure to save a couple dozen Dragon Scales, or a few Dragon Bones.

Ancient Dragon

Blood Dragon

Legendary Dragon (Fire)

DRAGONS

NAME	SUBTYPE	LV	HEALTH	MAGICKA	STAMINA	WEAPONS	ARMOR	ITEMS	SPELLS	NOTES
Dragon	Brown, Fire	10	905	150	130			(Dragon Loot), Dragon Bone, Dragon Scales	Fire Breath Shout, Fireball Shout	Resist Fire 50%, Weak to Frost 25%
Dragon	Brown, Frost	10	905	150	130			(Dragon Loot), Dragon Bone, Dragon Scales	Frost Breath Shout, Ice Storm Shout	Resist Frost 50%, Weak to Fire 25%
Blood Dragon	Green, Fire	20	1421	150	164			(Dragon Loot), Dragon Bone, Dragon Scales	Fire Breath Shout, Fireball Shout, Unrelenting Force Shout	Resist Fire 50%, Weak to Frost 25%
Blood Dragon	Green, Frost	20	1421	150	164			(Dragon Loot), Dragon Bone, Dragon Scales	Frost Breath Shout, Ice Storm Shout, Unrelenting Force Shout	Resist Frost 50%, Weak to Fire 25%
Frost Dragon	White, Frost	30	1860	150	197			(Dragon Loot), Dragon Bone, Dragon Scales	Frost Breath Shout, Ice Storm Shout, Unrelenting Force Shout	Resist Frost 50%, Weak to Fire 25%
Elder Dragon	Bronze, Fire	40	2255	150	230			(Dragon Loot), Dragon Bone, Dragon Scales	Fire Breath Shout, Fireball Shout, Unrelenting Force Shout	Resist Fire 50%, Weak to Frost 25%
Elder Dragon	Bronze, Frost	40	2255	150	230			(Dragon Loot), Dragon Bone, Dragon Scales	Frost Breath Shout, Ice Storm Shout, Unrelenting Force Shout	Resist Frost 50%, Weak to Fire 25%
Ancient Dragon	Red/Black, Fire	50	3071	150	264			(Dragon Loot), Dragon Bone, Dragon Scales	Fire Breath Shout, Fireball Shout, Unrelenting Force Shout	Resist Fire 50%, Weak to Frost 25%
Ancient Dragon	Red/Black, Frost	50	3071	150	264			(Dragon Loot), Dragon Bone, Dragon Scales	Frost Breath Shout, Ice Storm Shout, Unrelenting Force Shout	Resist Frost 50%, Weak to Fire 25%
Serpentine Dragon	Serpentine, Fire	58	3565	150	290			(Dragon Loot), Dragon Bone, Dragon Scales	Fire Breath Shout, Fireball Shout, Unrelenting Force Shout	Resist Fire 50%, Weak to Frost 25%
Serpentine Dragon	Serpentine, Frost	58	3565	150	290			(Dragon Loot), Dragon Bone, Dragon Scales	Frost Breath Shout, Ice Storm Shout, Unrelenting Force Shout	Resist Frost 50%, Weak to Fire 25%
Revered Dragon	Orange, Fire	62	3511	150	304			(Dragon Loot), (Daedric Weapons/Armor), Dragon Bone, Dragon Scales	Fire Breath Shout, Drain Vitality Shout, Unrelenting Force Shout	Resist Fire 50%, Weak to Frost 25%
Legendary Dragon	Purple, Fire	75	4163	150	347			(Dragon Loot), (Daedric Weapons/Armor), Dragon Bone, Dragon Scales	Fire Breath Shout, Drain Vitality Shout, Unrelenting Force Shout	Resist Fire 50%, Weak to Frost 25%
Legendary Dragon	Purple, Frost	75	4163	150	347			(Dragon Loot), (Daedric Weapons/Armor), Dragon Bone, Dragon Scales	Frost Breath Shout, Drain Vitality Shout, Unrelenting Force Shout	Resist Frost 50%, Weak to Fire 25%

UNIQUE DRAGONS

NAME	SUBTYPE	LV	HEALTH	MAGICKA	STAMINA	WEAPONS	ARMOR	ITEMS	SPELLS	NOTES
Durnehviir	Ichor	30*	1969	150	266			Dragon Bones	Frost Breath Shout, Raise Dead Shout, Drain Vitality Shout	Resist Frost 50%, Weak to Fire 25%
Naaslaarum	Orange, Fire	27*	1421	150	164			(Dragon Loot), Dragon Bone, Dragon Scales	Fire Breath Shout, Fireball Shout, Unrelenting Force Shout	Resist Fire 50%, Weak to Frost 25%
Vaslaarum	Orange, Fire	27*	1421	150	164			(Dragon Loot), Dragon Bone, Dragon Scales	Fire Breath Shout, Fireball Shout, Unrelenting Force Shout	Resist Fire 50%, Weak to Frost 25%

ALDUIN

NAME	SUBTYPE	LV	HEALTH	MAGICKA	STAMINA	WEAPONS	ARMOR	ITEMS	SPELLS	NOTES
Alduin	Alduin's Bane	20*	2471	50	114				Meteor Storm Shout, Unrelenting Force Shout, Fire Breath Shout, Frost Breath Shout, Fireball Shout, Ice Storm Shout	Resist Fire 50%, Weak to Frost 25%. This is Alduin as he appears during Main Quest: Alduin's Bane. Alduin is invulnerable unless weakened by the Dragonrend Shout.
Alduin	Dragonslayer	20*	2671	50	114				Meteor Storm Shout, Unrelenting Force Shout, Fire Breath Shout, Frost Breath Shout, Fireball Shout, Ice Storm Shout	Resist Fire 50%, Weak to Frost 25%. This is Alduin as he appears during Main Quest: Dragonslayer. Alduin is invulnerable unless weakened by the Dragonrend Shout.
Alduin	Dragonslayer	40*	2905	50	180				Meteor Storm Shout, Unrelenting Force Shout, Fire Breath Shout, Frost Breath Shout, Fireball Shout, Ice Storm Shout	See above; this just illustrates his stats at a different level.
Alduin	Dragonslayer	60*	3138	50	247				Meteor Storm Shout, Unrelenting Force Shout, Fire Breath Shout, Frost Breath Shout, Fireball Shout, Ice Storm Shout	See above; this just illustrates his stats at a different level.

Draugr

Draugr are among the most common foes in Skyrim's many crypts and catacombs. Fire is your best weapon against them. High-level Draugr, like Dragon Priests and Deathlords, are especially deadly foes– don't go toe-to-toe with Deathlords unless you can withstand some serious damage. Draugr Loot includes a chance of jewelry, gems, soul gems, ingots, or potions. Note that you can't loot their armor (would you really want it?).

Draugr (Draugr Wight)

Draugr (Draugr Deathlord)

Draugr (Dragon Priest)

DRAUGR ARCHERS

NAME	SUBTYPE	LV	HEALTH	MAGICKA	STAMINA	WEAPONS	ARMOR	ITEMS	SPELLS	NOTES
Draugr	Archer	1	50	0	80	Ancient Nord Bow, Ancient Nord Arrows, Ancient Nord War Axe	[Draugr Armor]	Draugr Loot		
Restless Draugr	Archer	6	175	0	205	Ancient Nord Bow, Ancient Nord Arrows, Ancient Nord War Axe	[Draugr Armor]	Draugr Loot		
Draugr Wight	Archer	13	400	0	340	Ancient Nord Bow, Ancient Nord Arrows, Ancient Nord War Axe	[Draugr Armor]	Draugr Loot		
Draugr Scourge	Archer	21	900	0	480	Ancient Nord Bow, Ancient Nord Arrows, Ancient Nord War Axe	[Draugr Armor]	Draugr Loot	Unrelenting Force Shout	
Draugr Deathlord	Archer	30	1000	10	575	Ancient Nord Bow, Orcish Arrows, Ancient Nord War Axe	[Draugr Armor]	Draugr Loot	Frost Cloak, Disarm Shout, Unrelenting Force Shout	
Draugr Deathlord	Archer	40	1300	10	625	Ebony Bow, Ebony Arrows, Ancient Nord War Axe	[Draugr Armor]	Draugr Loot	Frost Cloak, Disarm Shout, Unrelenting Force Shout	Immune to Poison, Resist Frost 50%

DRAUGR WARRIORS – 1H

NAME	SUBTYPE	LV	HEALTH	MAGICKA	STAMINA	WEAPONS	ARMOR	ITEMS	SPELLS	NOTES
Draugr	1H Warrior	1	50	0	80	1H Ancient Nord Weapon	[Draugr Armor], (Iron Shield)	Draugr Loot		
Restless Draugr	1H Warrior	6	150	0	204	1H Ancient Nord Weapon	[Draugr Armor], (Iron Shield)	Draugr Loot		
Draugr Wight	1H Warrior	13	320	0	340	1H Ancient Nord Weapon	[Draugr Armor], (Iron Shield)	Draugr Loot		
Draugr Scourge	1H Warrior	21	700	0	480	1H Ancient Nord Weapon	[Draugr Armor], (Iron Shield)	Draugr Loot	Unrelenting Force Shout	
Hulking Draugr	1H Warrior	26	800	0	505	1H Ancient Nord Weapon	[Draugr Armor], (Dented Iron Shield)	Draugr Loot	Unrelenting Force Shout	
Draugr Deathlord	1H Warrior	30	1000	10	575	1H Ebony Weapon	[Draugr Armor], (Iron Shield)	Draugr Loot	Frost Cloak, Disarm Shout, Unrelenting Force Shout	
Draugr Deathlord	1H Warrior	30	1000	10	575	1H Ebony Weapon	[Draugr Armor], (Ebony Shield)	Draugr Loot	Frost Cloak, Disarm Shout, Unrelenting Force Shout	

DRAUGR WARRIORS – 2H

NAME	SUBTYPE	LV	HEALTH	MAGICKA	STAMINA	WEAPONS	ARMOR	ITEMS	SPELLS	NOTES
Draugr	2H Warrior	1	50	0	80	2H Ancient Nord Weapon	[Draugr Armor]	Draugr Loot		
Restless Draugr	2H Warrior	6	150	0	204	2H Ancient Nord Weapon	[Draugr Armor]	Draugr Loot		
Draugr Wight	2H Warrior	13	320	0	340	2H Ancient Nord Weapon	[Draugr Armor]	Draugr Loot		
Draugr Scourge	2H Warrior	21	700	0	480	2H Ancient Nord Weapon	[Draugr Armor]	Draugr Loot	Unrelenting Force Shout	
Draugr Deathlord	2H Warrior	30	1000	10	575	2H Ancient Nord Weapon	[Draugr Armor]	Draugr Loot	Frost Cloak, Disarm Shout, Unrelenting Force Shout	
Draugr Deathlord	2H Warrior	30	1000	10	575	2H Ebony Weapon	[Draugr Armor]	Draugr Loot	Frost Cloak, Disarm Shout, Unrelenting Force Shout	

DRAUGR WARLOCKS

NAME	SUBTYPE	LV	HEALTH	MAGICKA	STAMINA	WEAPONS	ARMOR	ITEMS	SPELLS	NOTES
Restless Draugr	2H Warrior	6	150	50	180	1H Ancient Nord Weapon	[Draugr Armor]	Draugr Loot	Frostbite	
Draugr Wight	2H Warrior	13	490	100	280	1H Ancient Nord Weapon	[Draugr Armor]	Draugr Loot	Frostbite, Ice Spike	
Draugr Scourge	2H Warrior	21	700	160	380	1H Ancient Nord Weapon	[Draugr Armor]	Draugr Loot	Conjure Frost Atronach, Frostbite, Ice Spike	

DRAUGR OVERLORDS

NAME	SUBTYPE	LV	HEALTH	MAGICKA	STAMINA	WEAPONS	ARMOR	ITEMS	SPELLS	NOTES
Draugr Overlord		7	210	0	260	1H/2H Enchanted Ancient Nord Weapon	[Draugr Armor], (Iron Shield)	Draugr Loot	Unrelenting Force Shout	
Draugr Wight Overlord		15	490	0	450	1H/2H Enchanted Ancient Nord Weapon	[Draugr Armor], (Iron Shield)	Draugr Loot	Disarm Shout, Unrelenting Force Shout	
Draugr Scourge Lord		24	880	0	595	1H/2H Enchanted Ancient Nord Weapon	[Draugr Armor], (Iron Shield)	Draugr Loot	Disarm Shout, Unrelenting Force Shout, Frost Breath Shout	
Draugr Death Overlord		34	1290	10	645	1H/2H Enchanted Ancient Nord Weapon	[Draugr Armor], (Iron Shield)	Draugr Loot	Frost Cloak, Disarm Shout, Unrelenting Force Shout, Frost Breath Shout	
Draugr Death Overlord		45	1400	10	700	1H/2H Ebony Weapon	[Draugr Armor], (Iron Shield)	Draugr Loot	Frost Cloak, Disarm Shout, Unrelenting Force Shout, Frost Breath Shout	

DRAGON PRIESTS

NAME	SUBTYPE	LV	HEALTH	MAGICKA	STAMINA	WEAPONS	ARMOR	ITEMS	SPELLS	NOTES
Dragon Priest	Fire	50	1490	545	0		[Dragon Priest Robes]	Bone Meal, Gold	Greater Ward, Conjure Flame Atronach, Fireball, Ebonyflesh, Command Daedra, Incinerate	
Dragon Priest	Frost	50	1490	545	0		[Dragon Priest Robes]	Bone Meal, Gold	Ice Storm, Greater Ward, Conjure Frost Atronach, Command Daedra, Ebonyflesh, Icy Spear	
Dragon Priest	Shock	50	1490	545	0		[Dragon Priest Robes]	Bone Meal, Gold	Greater Ward, Conjure Storm Atronach, Chain Lightning, Thunderbolt, Command Daedra, Ebonyflesh	

Dwarven Automatons

Automatons are the mechanical constructs left behind by the Dwarves who once inhabited Skyrim. As constructs, most Automatons are immune to poison, Illusion spells, Frost spells, and Soul Trap, and have 25% Magic Resistance. Dwarven Loot includes a chance of: arrows, scrap metal, oil, ore, gems, or soul gems. Spheres give more (and more valuable) loot than Spiders, and Centurions more than Spheres.

DWARVEN SPIDERS

NAME	SUBTYPE	LV	HEALTH	MAGICKA	STAMINA	WEAPONS	ARMOR	ITEMS	SPELLS	NOTES
Warped Dwarven Spider		5	94	3	116	8 Dmg		Dwarven Loot		Automaton Resistances
Dwarven Spider Worker		12	125	3	120	11 Dmg		Dwarven Loot		Automaton Resistances
Dwarven Spider		16	175	3	160	15 Dmg		Dwarven Loot	Electrical Shock	Automaton Resistances, Explode on death (shock damage)
Dwarven Spider Guardian		22	225	3	200	22 Dmg		Dwarven Loot	Electrical Shock	Automaton Resistances, Explode on death (shock damage)

Dwarven Automatons (Centurion)

Warped Dwarven Sphere

DWARVEN SPHERES

NAME	SUBTYPE	LV	HEALTH	MAGICKA	STAMINA	WEAPONS	ARMOR	ITEMS	SPELLS	NOTES
Warped Dwarven Sphere		7	141	0	134	23 Dmg		Dwarven Loot		Automaton Resistances
Dwarven Sphere		16	315	0	170	55 Dmg		Dwarven Loot		Automaton Resistances
Dwarven Sphere Guardian		24	453	0	262	55 Dmg		Dwarven Loot		Automaton Resistances
Dwarven Sphere Master		30	619	0	301	82 Dmg		Dwarven Loot		Automaton Resistances

DWARVEN BALLISTAS

NAME	SUBTYPE	LV	HEALTH	MAGICKA	STAMINA	WEAPONS	ARMOR	ITEMS	SPELLS	NOTES
Dwarven Ballista		20	409	0	186	45 Dmg		Dwarven Loot		Automaton Resistances, Armor-Piercing Bolts
Dwarven Ballista Guardian		28	530	0	218	90 Dmg		Dwarven Loot		Automaton Resistances, Armor-Piercing Bolts
Dwarven Ballista Master		33	700	0	238	135 Dmg		Dwarven Loot		Automaton Resistances, Armor-Piercing Bolts

DWARVEN CENTURION

NAME	SUBTYPE	LV	HEALTH	MAGICKA	STAMINA	WEAPONS	ARMOR	ITEMS	SPELLS	NOTES
Dwarven Centurion		24	653	15	292	75 Dmg		Dwarven Loot	Steam Breath	Automaton Resistances
Dwarven Centurion Guardian		30	819	15	416	100 Dmg		Dwarven Loot	Steam Breath	Automaton Resistances
Dwarven Centurion Master		36	1000	15	540	112 Dmg		Dwarven Loot	Steam Breath	Automaton Resistances

UNIQUE AUTOMATONS

NAME	SUBTYPE	LV	HEALTH	MAGICKA	STAMINA	WEAPONS	ARMOR	ITEMS	SPELLS	NOTES
The Forgemaster		24*	853	15	292	100 Dmg		Dwarven Loot	Fire Breath, Fireball Breath	Flame Cloak, Immune to Fire, Immune to Poison, Immune to Illusion, Immune to Soul Trap, 25% Resist Magic, 25% Resist Shock, Weak to Frost 50%
The Forgemaster		50*	1289	265	596	112 Dmg		Dwarven Loot	Fire Breath, Fireball Breath	Flame Cloak, Immune to Fire, Immune to Poison, Immune to Illusion, Immune to Soul Trap, 25% Resist Magic, 25% Resist Shock, Weak to Frost 50%

Ebony Warrior

The Ebony Warrior is a unique and powerful foe, with high health and some of the best weapons and armor to be found anywhere. He is marginally more vulnerable to Fire than the other elements, since only his shield confers Fire Resistance, and he won't have it equipped if you fight him from range. Defeat him, and you can claim his gear for your own.

EBONY WARRIOR

NAME	SUBTYPE	LV	HEALTH	MAGICKA	STAMINA	WEAPONS	ARMOR	ITEMS	SPELLS	NOTES
Ebony Warrior		80	1971	100	364	Ebony Sword of the Vampire, Ebony Bow of Storms, Ebony Arrows, Iron Arrows	Ebony Armor of Regeneration, Ebony Boots of Frost Suppression, Ebony Helmet of Waterbreathing, Ebony Gauntlets of Extreme Wielding, Ebony Shield of Fire Suppression	Potion of Vigorous Healing, Gold Necklace of Shock Suppression, Ring of Peerless Wielding, Gems x6, Black Soul Gem, Daedra Heart, Human Heart		

The Ebony Warrior

Falmer

Falmer inhabit the deep caves and dwarven ruins of Skyrim, as well as the Forgotten Vale. Most poison their weapons for added damage and charge into battle with their pet Chaurus and spiders. Since Falmer are blind, you can use light spells and torches without being detected. They have excellent hearing, though, so keep your distance and move slowly if you plan a stealthy approach. Falmer Loot includes a chance of Falmer Ears, poisons, or gold.

Falmer (Shadowmaster)

Falmer Warmonger

FERAL FALMER

NAME	SUBTYPE	LV	HEALTH	MAGICKA	STAMINA	WEAPONS	ARMOR	ITEMS	SPELLS	NOTES
Feral Falmer		9	180	177	163	2 Dmg		Falmer Loot, Gold		5 Poison Damage/3s on hit.

FALMER ARCHER

NAME	SUBTYPE	LV	HEALTH	MAGICKA	STAMINA	WEAPONS	ARMOR	ITEMS	SPELLS	NOTES
Falmer	Archer	9	180	177	163	Falmer Bow, Falmer Sword, Falmer Arrows (Arrows)		Falmer Loot, Gold		5 Poison Damage/3s on hit.
Falmer Skulker	Archer	15	290	247	198	Falmer Bow, Falmer Arrows (Arrows)		Falmer Loot, Gold		6 Poison Damage/3s on hit.
Falmer Gloomlurker	Archer	22	410	220	210	Falmer Bow, Falmer Arrows (Arrows)	Falmer Helmet	Falmer Loot, Gold		7 Poison Damage/3s on hit.
Falmer Nightprowler	Archer	30	550	197	300	Falmer Bow, Falmer Arrows (Arrows)	Falmer Helmet	Falmer Loot, Gold		9 Poison Damage/3s on hit.
Falmer Shadowmaster	Archer	38	700	273	362	Falmer Bow, Falmer Arrows (Arrows)	Falmer Helmet	Falmer Loot, Gold		12 Poison Damage/3s on hit.
Falmer Warmonger	Archer	48	920	307	378	Falmer Bow, Falmer Arrows (Arrows)	(Falmer Armor), (Falmer Boots), (Falmer Helmet), (Falmer Gauntlets), Falmer Shield	Falmer Loot, Gold		12 Poison Damage/4s on hit.

FALMER SHAMAN

NAME	SUBTYPE	LV	HEALTH	MAGICKA	STAMINA	WEAPONS	ARMOR	ITEMS	SPELLS	NOTES
Falmer	Shaman	5	133	120	157	(Staff)		Falmer Loot, Gold	Bound Sword, Fast Healing, Ice Spike, Oakflesh, Sparks, Lesser Ward	
Falmer Skulker	Shaman	8	183	185	187	(Staff)		Falmer Loot, Gold	Bound Sword, Frostbite, Lightning Bolt, Stoneflesh, Steadfast Ward	
Falmer Gloomlurker	Shaman	14	258	265	197	(Staff)		Falmer Loot, Gold	Bound Sword, Fast Healing, Frostbite, Ice Spike, Lightning Cloak, Steadfast Ward	
Falmer Nightprowler	Shaman	19	350	340	230	(Staff)		Falmer Loot, Gold	Bound Sword, Fast Healing, Ice Spike, Sparks, Stoneflesh, Steadfast Ward	
Falmer Shadowmaster	Shaman	25	400	420	240	(Staff)		Falmer Loot, Gold	Bound Sword, Fast Healing, Frost Cloak, Ironflesh, Lightning Bolt, Steadfast Ward	
Falmer Warmonger	Shaman	35	533	470	257	(Staff)		Falmer Loot, Gold	Bound Sword, Chain Lightning, Fast Healing, Frost Cloak, Ironflesh, Lightning Bolt, Steadfast Ward	

FALMER SPELLSWORDS

NAME	SUBTYPE	LV	HEALTH	MAGICKA	STAMINA	WEAPONS	ARMOR	ITEMS	SPELLS	NOTES
Falmer	Spellsword	9	180	177	163	1H Falmer Weapon		Falmer Loot, Gold	Frostbite, Healing	5 Poison Damage/3s on hit.
Falmer Skulker	Spellsword	15	290	197	198	1H Falmer Weapon		Falmer Loot, Gold	Healing, Ice Spike, Sparks	6 Poison Damage/3s on hit.
Falmer Gloomlurker	Spellsword	22	410	220	210	1H Falmer Weapon	Falmer Helmet	Falmer Loot, Gold	Frostbite, Frost Cloak, Healing, Lightning Bolt	7 Poison Damage/3s on hit.
Falmer Nightprowler	Spellsword	30	550	197	300	1H Falmer Weapon	Falmer Helmet	Falmer Loot, Gold	Chain Lightning, Healing, Ice Spike, Sparks	9 Poison Damage/3s on hit.
Falmer Shadowmaster	Spellsword	38	700	273	362	1H Falmer Weapon	Falmer Helmet	Falmer Loot, Gold	Chain Lightning, Healing, Ice Spike, Wall of Frost	12 Poison Damage/3s on hit.
Falmer Warmonger	Spellsword	48	920	307	378	1H Falmer Weapon	(Falmer Armor), (Falmer Boots), (Falmer Helmet), (Falmer Gauntlets)	Falmer Loot, Gold	Chain Lightning, Healing, Ice Spike, Wall of Frost	12 Poison Damage/4s on hit.

FALMER WARRIORS

NAME	SUBTYPE	LV	HEALTH	MAGICKA	STAMINA	WEAPONS	ARMOR	ITEMS	SPELLS	NOTES
Falmer	Warrior	9	180	177	163	1H Falmer Weapon	Falmer Shield	Falmer Loot, Gold		5 Poison Damage/3s on hit.
Falmer Skulker	Warrior	15	290	247	198	1H Falmer Weapon	Falmer Shield	Falmer Loot, (Restore Health Potion), Gold		6 Poison Damage/3s on hit.
Falmer Gloomlurker	Warrior	22	410	220	210	1H Falmer Weapon	Falmer Helmet, Falmer Shield	Falmer Loot, (Restore Health Potion), Gold		7 Poison Damage/3s on hit.
Falmer Nightprowler	Warrior	30	550	197	300	1H Falmer Weapon	Falmer Helmet, Falmer Shield	Falmer Loot, (Restore Health Potion), Gold		9 Poison Damage/3s on hit.
Falmer Shadowmaster	Warrior	38	700	273	362	1H Falmer Weapon	Falmer Helmet, Falmer Shield	Falmer Loot, Restore Health Potion, Gold		12 Poison Damage/3s on hit.
Falmer Warmonger	Warrior	48	920	307	378	1H Falmer Weapon	(Falmer Armor), (Falmer Boots), (Falmer Helmet), (Falmer Gauntlets), Falmer Shield	Falmer Loot, Restore Health Potion, Gold		12 Poison Damage/4s on hit.

FALMER BOSS: SPELLSWORD										
NAME	SUBTYPE	LV	HEALTH	MAGICKA	STAMINA	WEAPONS	ARMOR	ITEMS	SPELLS	NOTES
Falmer Skulker	Spellsword	18	370	257	203	1H Falmer Weapon		Falmer Loot, Gold	Healing, Ice Spike, Sparks	6 Poison Damage/3s on hit.
Falmer Gloomlurker	Spellsword	26	500	283	242	1H Falmer Weapon	Falmer Helmet	Falmer Loot, Gold	Frostbite, Frost Cloak, Healing, Lightning Bolt	7 Poison Damage/3s on hit.
Falmer Nightprowler	Spellsword	35	640	313	307	1H Falmer Weapon	Falmer Helmet	Falmer Loot, Gold	Chain Lightning, Healing, Ice Spike, Sparks	9 Poison Damage/3s on hit.
Falmer Shadowmaster	Spellsword	44	830	403	272	1H Falmer Weapon	Falmer Helmet	Falmer Loot, Gold	Chain Lightning, Healing, Ice Spike, Wall of Frost	12 Poison Damage/3s on hit.
Falmer Warmonger	Spellsword	54	930	437	288	1H Falmer Weapon	(Falmer Armor), (Falmer Boots), (Falmer Helmet), (Falmer Gauntlets)	Falmer Loot, Gold	Chain Lightning, Healing, Ice Spike, Wall of Frost	12 Poison Damage/4s on hit.

FALMER BOSS: WARRIOR										
NAME	SUBTYPE	LV	HEALTH	MAGICKA	STAMINA	WEAPONS	ARMOR	ITEMS	SPELLS	NOTES
Falmer Skulker	Warrior	18	370	182	228	1H Falmer Weapon	Falmer Shield	Falmer Loot, Gold	Healing	6 Poison Damage/3s on hit.
Falmer Gloomlurker	Warrior	26	500	233	242	1H Falmer Weapon	Falmer Helmet, Falmer Shield	Falmer Loot, Gold	Healing	7 Poison Damage/3s on hit.
Falmer Nightprowler	Warrior	35	640	213	357	1H Falmer Weapon	Falmer Helmet, Falmer Shield	Falmer Loot, Gold	Healing	9 Poison Damage/3s on hit.
Falmer Shadowmaster	Warrior	44	830	293	372	1H Falmer Weapon	Falmer Helmet, Falmer Shield	Falmer Loot, Gold	Healing	12 Poison Damage/3s on hit.
Falmer Warmonger	Warrior	54	930	327	388	1H Falmer Weapon	(Falmer Armor), (Falmer Boots), (Falmer Helmet), (Falmer Gauntlets), Falmer Shield	Falmer Loot, Gold	Healing	12 Poison Damage/4s on hit.

UNIQUE FALMER										
NAME	SUBTYPE	LV	HEALTH	MAGICKA	STAMINA	WEAPONS	ARMOR	ITEMS	SPELLS	NOTES
Arch-Curate Vyrthur		15*	340	220	50	Elven Dagger of Blizzards	Ancient Falmer Cuirass, Ancient Falmer Boots, Ancient Falmer Gauntlets	Gems, Potions	Drain Health, Conjure Frost Atronach, Invisibility, Lightning Bolt, Ice Storm, Icy Spear, Frost Cloak, Banish Daedra, Command Daedra	50% Resist Frost, 20% Resist Magic, Weak to Fire 50%, Undead
Arch-Curate Vyrthur		50*	690	395	50	Elven Dagger of Blizzards	Ancient Falmer Cuirass, Ancient Falmer Boots, Ancient Falmer Gauntlets	Gems, Potions	Drain Health, Conjure Frost Atronach, Invisibility, Lightning Bolt, Ice Storm, Icy Spear, Frost Cloak, Banish Daedra, Command Daedra	50% Resist Frost, 20% Resist Magic, Weak to Fire 50%, Undead

Forgotten Vale Animals

In the centuries that the Forgotten Vale has been isolated from the outside world, its animals have grown to be very different than those in Skyrim. Despite their appearance, these creatures have no special resistances or weaknesses, so the same tactics for fighting them still apply. Minor Treasure includes a tiny chance of a few gold, a gem, or a ring.

Vale Sabre Cat

FORGOTTEN VALE ANIMALS										
NAME	SUBTYPE	LV	HEALTH	MAGICKA	STAMINA	WEAPONS	ARMOR	ITEMS	SPELLS	NOTES
Vale Deer		1	50	0	25			Vale Deer Hide, Venison, (Large Antlers), (Minor Treasure)		
Vale Sabre Cat		6	150	0	225	52 Dmg		Vale Sabre Cat Hide, (Sabre Cat Eyeball/Sabre Cat Tooth), (Minor Treasure)		

Forgotten Vale Frozen Creatures

Deep within the Forgotten Vale, you may find creatures that have been transformed into living ice. They have the statistics, abilities, and resistances of their living forms (as listed in this section) but are additionally [Immune to Frost, Weak to Fire 25%]. They shatter when killed, making any items they carry unrecoverable.

The one exception is the Ancient Frost Atronach, whose power has been amplified by the ice. Keep your distance from him to avoid his persistent Frost Cloak and powerful melee attacks, and use fire spells or weapons with a flame enchantment to bring him down.

Frozen Falmer

FORGOTTEN VALE FROZEN CREATURES										
NAME	SUBTYPE	LV	HEALTH	MAGICKA	STAMINA	WEAPONS	ARMOR	ITEMS	SPELLS	NOTES
Ancient Frost Atronach		20*	440	32	263	30 Dmg				Immune to Frost, Immune to Paralysis, Weak to Fire 33%, Frost Cloak
Ancient Frost Atronach		50*	890	107	413	50 Dmg				Immune to Frost, Immune to Paralysis, Weak to Fire 33%, Frost Cloak

Forsworn

The tribal natives of the Reach, Forsworn revere Hagravens and fight to drive invaders from their lands. Forsworn Wizard Loot includes a chance of ingredients, potions, soul gems, or a forsworn weapon.

FORSWORN ARCHER

NAME	SUBTYPE	LV	HEALTH	MAGICKA	STAMINA	WEAPONS	ARMOR	ITEMS	SPELLS	NOTES
Forsworn	Archer	1	50	50	50	Forsworn Bow, Forsworn Arrows, Dagger	Forsworn Cuirass, Forsworn Boots, (Forsworn Helmet), (Forsworn Gauntlets)	(Gold)	Healing	
Forsworn Forager	Archer	6	95	60	70	Forsworn Bow, Forsworn Arrows, Dagger	Forsworn Cuirass, Forsworn Boots, (Forsworn Helmet), (Forsworn Gauntlets)	(Gold)	Healing	
Forsworn Looter	Archer	14	192	76	152	Forsworn Bow, Forsworn Arrows, Dagger	Forsworn Cuirass, Forsworn Boots, (Forsworn Helmet), (Forsworn Gauntlets)	(Gold)	Fast Healing	
Forsworn Pillager	Archer	24	357	96	192	Forsworn Bow, Forsworn Arrows, Dagger	Forsworn Cuirass, Forsworn Boots, (Forsworn Helmet), (Forsworn Gauntlets)	(Gold)	Fast Healing	
Forsworn Ravager	Archer	34	447	116	182	Forsworn Bow, Forsworn Arrows, Dagger	Forsworn Cuirass, Forsworn Boots, (Forsworn Helmet), (Forsworn Gauntlets)	(Gold)	Fast Healing	
Forsworn Warlord	Archer	46	455	140	230	Forsworn Bow, Forsworn Arrows, Dagger	Forsworn Cuirass, Forsworn Boots, (Forsworn Helmet), (Forsworn Gauntlets)	(Gold)	Close Wounds	

Forsworn (Archer)

FORSWORN BERSERKERS

NAME	SUBTYPE	LV	HEALTH	MAGICKA	STAMINA	WEAPONS	ARMOR	ITEMS	SPELLS	NOTES
Forsworn	Berserker	1	50	50	50	2x (Forsworn Axe / Forsworn Sword)	Forsworn Cuirass, Forsworn Boots, (Forsworn Helmet), (Forsworn Gauntlets)	(Gold)		
Forsworn Forager	Berserker	6	95	70	85	2x (Forsworn Axe / Forsworn Sword)	Forsworn Cuirass, Forsworn Boots, (Forsworn Helmet), (Forsworn Gauntlets)	(Gold)		
Forsworn Looter	Berserker	14	192	102	126	2x (Forsworn Axe / Forsworn Sword)	Forsworn Cuirass, Forsworn Boots, (Forsworn Helmet), (Forsworn Gauntlets)	(Gold)		
Forsworn Pillager	Berserker	24	357	142	146	2x (Forsworn Axe / Forsworn Sword)	Forsworn Cuirass, Forsworn Boots, (Forsworn Helmet), (Forsworn Gauntlets)	(Gold)		
Forsworn Ravager	Berserker	34	447	182	116	2x (Forsworn Axe / Forsworn Sword)	Forsworn Cuirass, Forsworn Boots, (Forsworn Helmet), (Forsworn Gauntlets)	(Gold)		
Forsworn Warlord	Berserker	46	455	230	140	2x (Forsworn Axe / Forsworn Sword)	Forsworn Cuirass, Forsworn Boots, (Forsworn Helmet), (Forsworn Gauntlets)	(Gold)		

FORSWORN SHAMAN

NAME	SUBTYPE	LV	HEALTH	MAGICKA	STAMINA	WEAPONS	ARMOR	ITEMS	SPELLS	NOTES
Forsworn	Shaman	1	50	100	50	Dagger	Forsworn Cuirass, Forsworn Boots, (Forsworn Helmet), (Forsworn Gauntlets)	Forsworn Wizard Loot	Flames, Healing, Lesser Ward	
Forsworn Forager	Shaman	6	95	130	50	Dagger	Forsworn Cuirass, Forsworn Boots, (Forsworn Helmet), (Forsworn Gauntlets)	Forsworn Wizard Loot	Conjure Flame Atronach, Flames, Healing, Lesser Ward	
Forsworn Looter	Shaman	14	192	178	50	Dagger	Forsworn Cuirass, Forsworn Boots, (Forsworn Helmet), (Forsworn Gauntlets)	Forsworn Wizard Loot	Conjure Flame Atronach, Firebolt, Flames, Healing, Lesser Ward	
Forsworn Pillager	Shaman	24	357	288	50	Dagger	Forsworn Cuirass, Forsworn Boots, (Forsworn Helmet), (Forsworn Gauntlets)	Forsworn Wizard Loot	Conjure Frost Atronach, Fast Healing, Ice Spike, Ice Storm, Stoneflesh, Steadfast Ward	
Forsworn Ravager	Shaman	34	447	248	50	Dagger	Forsworn Cuirass, Forsworn Boots, (Forsworn Helmet), (Forsworn Gauntlets)	Forsworn Wizard Loot	Conjure Frost Atronach, Frost Cloak, Ice Spike, Ice Storm, Icy Spear, Stoneflesh, Steadfast Ward	
Forsworn Warlord	Shaman	46	455	320	50	Dagger	Forsworn Cuirass, Forsworn Boots, (Forsworn Helmet), (Forsworn Gauntlets)	Forsworn Wizard Loot	Chain Lightning, Close Wounds, Conjure Storm Atronach, Expel Daedra, Ironflesh, Lightning Bolt, Lightning Cloak, Thunderbolt, Greater Ward	

Forsworn (Berserker)

Forsworn (Shaman)

FORSWORN BOSS – BERSERKER

NAME	SUBTYPE	LV	HEALTH	MAGICKA	STAMINA	WEAPONS	ARMOR	ITEMS	SPELLS	NOTES
Forsworn Briarheart	Warrior	7	104	74	112	2x 1H Forsworn Weapon	[Briarheart Armor], Forsworn Boots, Forsworn Helmet	(Gold), Briarheart		
Forsworn Briarheart	Warrior	16	235	110	130	2x 1H Forsworn Weapon	[Briarheart Armor], Forsworn Boots, Forsworn Helmet	(Gold), Briarheart		
Forsworn Briarheart	Warrior	27	434	154	152	2x 1H Forsworn Weapon	[Briarheart Armor], Forsworn Boots, Forsworn Helmet	(Gold), Briarheart		
Forsworn Briarheart	Warrior	38	533	198	174	2x 1H Forsworn Weapon	[Briarheart Armor], Forsworn Boots, Forsworn Helmet	(Gold), Briarheart		
Forsworn Briarheart	Warrior	51	623	350	195	2x 1H Forsworn Weapon	[Briarheart Armor], Forsworn Boots, Forsworn Helmet	(Gold), Briarheart		

Forsworn (Briarheart)

FORSWORN BOSS – SHAMAN										
NAME	SUBTYPE	LV	HEALTH	MAGICKA	STAMINA	WEAPONS	ARMOR	ITEMS	SPELLS	NOTES
Forsworn Briarheart	Shaman	7	104	86	50	Dagger	[Briarheart Armor], Forsworn Boots, Forsworn Helmet	Forsworn Wizard Loot, Briarheart	Conjure Flame Atronach, Flames, Healing, Lesser Ward	
Forsworn Briarheart	Shaman	16	235	110	50	Dagger	[Briarheart Armor], Forsworn Boots, Forsworn Helmet	Forsworn Wizard Loot, Briarheart	Conjure Flame Atronach, Firebolt, Flames, Healing, Lesser Ward	
Forsworn Briarheart	Shaman	27	434	306	50	Dagger	[Briarheart Armor], Forsworn Boots, Forsworn Helmet	Forsworn Wizard Loot, Briarheart	Conjure Frost Atronach, Fast Healing, Ice Spike, Ice Storm, Stoneflesh, Steadfast Ward	
Forsworn Briarheart	Shaman	38	533	272	50	Dagger	[Briarheart Armor], Forsworn Boots, Forsworn Helmet	Forsworn Wizard Loot, Briarheart	Conjure Frost Atronach, Frost Cloak, Ice Spike, Ice Storm, Icy Spear, Stoneflesh, Steadfast Ward	
Forsworn Briarheart	Shaman	51	620	350	50	Dagger	[Briarheart Armor], Forsworn Boots, Forsworn Helmet	Forsworn Wizard Loot, Briarheart	Chain Lightning, Close Wounds, Conjure Storm Atronach, Expel Daedra, Ironflesh, Lightning Bolt, Lightning Cloak, Thunderbolt, Greater Ward	

Gargoyles

Gargoyles are predatory creatures with a stony skin that allows them to protect themselves and helps ambush their prey. Gargoyles in statue form are immune to all damage and magical effects. Once they emerge, gargoyles are still highly resistant to physical attacks and drain health from their victims with each hit. Keep your distance and use magic or enchanted weapons to bring them down.

Gargoyle Sentinel

GARGOYLES										
NAME	SUBTYPE	LV	HEALTH	MAGICKA	STAMINA	WEAPONS	ARMOR	ITEMS	SPELLS	NOTES
Gargoyle		13	240	0	90	25 Dmg + 5 Drain Health		Ore, Gems		Immune to Poison, Immune to Paralysis, 250 Armor
Gargoyle	Conjured	13	240	0	90	25 Dmg + 5 Drain Health				Immune to Poison, Immune to Paralysis, 250 Armor
Gargoyle Brute		25	580	0	180	35 Dmg + 12 Drain Health		Ore, Gems		Immune to Poison, Immune to Paralysis, 250 Armor
Gargoyle Sentinel		43	890	0	290	55 Dmg + 16 Drain Health		Ore, Gems		Immune to Poison, Immune to Paralysis, 250 Armor

Giants

The nomadic Giants shepherd their mammoth herds across the Tundra of central Skyrim. While powerful, they are generally peaceful if left alone. Their cousins, the Frost Giants of the Forgotten Vale, are even more formidible, with hard-hitting attacks and huge reserves of health. When fighting giants, don't let them get within melee range—they are deceptively fast, so don't get caught out in the open. Use cover and obstacles to your advantage, and wear them down with ranged attacks. Giant Loot typically includes several of: Giant Toes, Giant Weapons, Giant Armor, Gold, Gems, Soul Gems, and Animal Parts.

Giant

GIANT										
NAME	SUBTYPE	LV	HEALTH	MAGICKA	STAMINA	WEAPONS	ARMOR	ITEMS	SPELLS	NOTES
Giant		32	591	0	374	[Giant Club]		Giant Toe, (Giant Loot)	Giant Stomp	Resist Magic 33%
Frost Giant		50	1039	0	446	[Giant Club]		Giant Toe, (Giant Loot)	Giant Stomp	Resist Magic 33%, Immune to Frost, Weak to Fire 50%

Frost Giant

UNIQUE GIANTS										
NAME	SUBTYPE	LV	HEALTH	MAGICKA	STAMINA	WEAPONS	ARMOR	ITEMS	SPELLS	NOTES
Karstaag		60	4000	0	1000	[Giant Club]		Grand Soul Gem, Ectoplasm	Conjure Ice Wraiths, Blizzard Stomp, Frost Cloak	Immune to Frost, Immune to Poison, Immune to Disease, Immune to Fear, Resist Shock 75%, Weak to Fire 25%, Regenerates Health, Frost Attacks

Hagravens

Witches who surrender their humanity become Hagravens, creatures of corruption and decay revered by the Forsworn of the Reach. Before fighting them, do what you can to bolster your fire resistance. Warriors should close to melee range rather than try to take them on at a distance.

Hagraven

HAGRAVENS

NAME	SUBTYPE	LV	HEALTH	MAGICKA	STAMINA	WEAPONS	ARMOR	ITEMS	SPELLS	NOTES
Hagraven		20	471	314	50			Hagraven Feathers	Close Wounds, Fast Healing, Fireball, Firebolt	

Horses

Horses are a common mode of transportation in Skyrim, at least for those able to afford them. You can obtain a number of unique horses through quests. For example, during your time in the Soul Cairn, you may learn how to summon the skeletal horse Arvak.

Horse (Brown)

Arvak

HORSES

NAME	SUBTYPE	LV	HEALTH	MAGICKA	STAMINA	WEAPONS	ARMOR	ITEMS	SPELLS	NOTES
Horse	Black	4	289	0	106			Horse Meat, Horse Hide, (Minor Treasure)		
Horse	Paint	4	289	0	106			Horse Meat, Horse Hide, (Minor Treasure)		
Horse	Brown	4	289	0	106			Horse Meat, Horse Hide, (Minor Treasure)		
Horse	Gray	4	289	0	106			Horse Meat, Horse Hide, (Minor Treasure)		
Horse	Palomino	4	289	0	106			Horse Meat, Horse Hide, (Minor Treasure)		
Arvak	Conjured	4	289	0	106					
Frost		4	289	0	106			Horse Meat, Horse Hide, (Minor Treasure)		
Shadowmere		50	1637	0	198			Horse Meat, Horse Hide, (Minor Treasure)		Regenerates Health, Aggressive

Hunters

Skyrim's vast forests are home to any number of hunters, who prefer the wilderness to life in the cities. Orcs in particular often take up this nomadic lifestyle. Most are glad to barter with a passing adventurer.

Hunter

HUNTERS

NAME	SUBTYPE	LV	HEALTH	MAGICKA	STAMINA	WEAPONS	ARMOR	ITEMS	SPELLS	NOTES
Hunter		5*	79	25	41	Bow, Arrows, Dagger	Hide Cuirass, Gloves, (Hat), Clothes	(Meat), (Animal Parts), (Gold)		
Orc Hunter		1	30	25	70	Bow, Arrows, Dagger	Light Cuirass, Light Boots, (Gauntlets)	(Lockpick), (Meat), (Animal Parts), (Gold)		

Morag Tong

The Morag Tong are an ancient guild of assassins, legally sanctioned to carry out 'writs' of execution against their targets. They have a long and bitter rivalry with the Dark Brotherhood, which split from the Morag Tong centuries ago. When fighting the Morag Tong, be sure you finish off your target, as most will try to use Invisibility to escape and recover. Morag Tong Loot includes a chance of: Food, Drink, Jewelry, Lockpicks, Gems, or Tools.

MORAG TONG

NAME	SUBTYPE	LV	HEALTH	MAGICKA	STAMINA	WEAPONS	ARMOR	ITEMS	SPELLS	NOTES
Morag Tong Assassin	Assassin	5*	109	25	86	1H Weapon	Morag Tong Armor, Morag Tong Hood, Morag Tong Bracers, Morag Tong Boots	Gold	Fast Healing, Invisibility	
Morag Tong Assassin	Sniper	5*	109	25	86	Bow, Arrows, Dagger	Morag Tong Armor, Morag Tong Hood, Morag Tong Bracers, Morag Tong Boots	Gold, (Morag Tong Loot)	Invisibility	

Morag Tong Assassin

Netch

Netch are a wild species native to Morrowind that resemble floating jellyfish. They are generally peaceful, and are often kept and herded like cattle by Dark Elven farmers. But be warned: if provoked, they are highly dangerous. All Netch are resistant to shock, and their tentacles do shock damage, so plan accordingly. Minor Treasure includes a tiny chance of: A few gold, a gem, or a ring.

NETCH

NAME	SUBTYPE	LV	HEALTH	MAGICKA	STAMINA	WEAPONS	ARMOR	ITEMS	SPELLS	NOTES
Netch Calf		25	430	0	130	27 Dmg + 25 Shock		Netch Jelly		Waterwalking, Resist Shock 50%, Shock Attacks
Bull Netch		36	908	0	267	45 Dmg + 70 Shock		Netch Jelly, Netch Leather, (Minor Treasure)		Waterwalking, Resist Shock 50%, Shock Attacks
Betty Netch		40	1055	0	280	45 Dmg + 70 Shock		Netch Jelly, Netch Leather, (Minor Treasure)		Waterwalking, Resist Shock 50%, Shock Attacks

Betty Netch

Penitus Oculatus

After the fall of the Blades, the Penitus Oculatus were created to serve as the Emperor's personal security force. They have an outpost in Dragon Bridge.

PENITUS OCULATUS ARCHERS

NAME	SUBTYPE	LV	HEALTH	MAGICKA	STAMINA	WEAPONS	ARMOR	ITEMS	SPELLS	NOTES
Penitus Oculatus Agent	Battlemage	1	50	50	50	Imperial Bow, Arrows, Iron Dagger	Penitus Oculatus Armor, Penitus Oculatus Boots, Penitus Oculatus Bracers	Gold		
Penitus Oculatus Agent	Battlemage	4	85	60	60	Imperial Bow, Arrows, Iron Dagger	Penitus Oculatus Armor, Penitus Oculatus Boots, Penitus Oculatus Bracers	Gold		
Penitus Oculatus Agent	Battlemage	8	128	73	74	Imperial Bow, Arrows, Iron Dagger	Penitus Oculatus Armor, Penitus Oculatus Boots, Penitus Oculatus Bracers	Gold		
Penitus Oculatus Agent	Battlemage	13	180	90	90	Imperial Bow, Arrows, Iron Dagger	Penitus Oculatus Armor, Penitus Oculatus Boots, Penitus Oculatus Bracers	Gold		
Penitus Oculatus Agent	Battlemage	18	231	107	107	Imperial Bow, Arrows, Iron Dagger	Penitus Oculatus Armor, Penitus Oculatus Boots, Penitus Oculatus Bracers	Gold		
Penitus Oculatus Agent	Battlemage	23	283	123	124	Imperial Bow, Arrows, Iron Dagger	Penitus Oculatus Armor, Penitus Oculatus Boots, Penitus Oculatus Bracers	Gold		

Penitus Oculatus

PENITUS OCULATUS BATTLEMAGES

NAME	SUBTYPE	LV	HEALTH	MAGICKA	STAMINA	WEAPONS	ARMOR	ITEMS	SPELLS	NOTES
Penitus Oculatus Agent	Battlemage	1	50	50	50	2x Imperial Sword	Penitus Oculatus Armor, Penitus Oculatus Boots, Penitus Oculatus Bracers, Penitus Oculatus Helmet		Fast Healing, (Flames/Sparks), Lesser Ward	
Penitus Oculatus Agent	Battlemage	4	85	60	60	2x Imperial Sword	Penitus Oculatus Armor, Penitus Oculatus Boots, Penitus Oculatus Bracers, Penitus Oculatus Helmet		Fast Healing, (Firebolt/Lightning Bolt), Lesser Ward	
Penitus Oculatus Agent	Battlemage	8	128	73	74	2x Imperial Sword	Penitus Oculatus Armor, Penitus Oculatus Boots, Penitus Oculatus Bracers, Penitus Oculatus Helmet		Fast Healing, (Firebolt/Lightning Bolt), Lesser Ward	
Penitus Oculatus Agent	Battlemage	13	180	90	90	2x Imperial Sword	Penitus Oculatus Armor, Penitus Oculatus Boots, Penitus Oculatus Bracers, Penitus Oculatus Helmet		Fast Healing, (Firebolt/Lightning Bolt), Lesser Ward	
Penitus Oculatus Agent	Battlemage	18	231	107	107	2x Imperial Sword	Penitus Oculatus Armor, Penitus Oculatus Boots, Penitus Oculatus Bracers, Penitus Oculatus Helmet		Fast Healing, (Fireball/Chain Lightning), Lesser Ward	
Penitus Oculatus Agent	Battlemage	23	283	123	124	2x Imperial Sword	Penitus Oculatus Armor, Penitus Oculatus Boots, Penitus Oculatus Bracers, Penitus Oculatus Helmet		Fast Healing, (Fireball/Chain Lightning), Lesser Ward	

PENITUS OCULATUS WARRIORS

NAME	SUBTYPE	LV	HEALTH	MAGICKA	STAMINA	WEAPONS	ARMOR	ITEMS	SPELLS	NOTES
Penitus Oculatus Agent	Battlemage	1	50	50	50	Imperial Sword, Imperial Shield	Penitus Oculatus Armor, Penitus Oculatus Boots, Penitus Oculatus Bracers, Penitus Oculatus Helmet	Gold		
Penitus Oculatus Agent	Battlemage	4	85	60	60	Imperial Sword, Imperial Shield	Penitus Oculatus Armor, Penitus Oculatus Boots, Penitus Oculatus Bracers, Penitus Oculatus Helmet	Gold		
Penitus Oculatus Agent	Battlemage	8	128	73	74	Imperial Sword, Imperial Shield	Penitus Oculatus Armor, Penitus Oculatus Boots, Penitus Oculatus Bracers, Penitus Oculatus Helmet	Gold		
Penitus Oculatus Agent	Battlemage	13	180	90	90	Imperial Sword, Imperial Shield	Penitus Oculatus Armor, Penitus Oculatus Boots, Penitus Oculatus Bracers, Penitus Oculatus Helmet	Gold		
Penitus Oculatus Agent	Battlemage	18	231	107	107	Imperial Sword, Imperial Shield	Penitus Oculatus Armor, Penitus Oculatus Boots, Penitus Oculatus Bracers, Penitus Oculatus Helmet	Gold		
Penitus Oculatus Agent	Battlemage	23	283	123	124	Imperial Sword, Imperial Shield	Penitus Oculatus Armor, Penitus Oculatus Boots, Penitus Oculatus Bracers, Penitus Oculatus Helmet	Gold		

Reavers

'Reavers' are the bandits and pirates that ply the waters of the eastern Sea of Ghosts. They are almost exclusively Dark Elves (with the Dark Elves' innate resistance to fire), and tend to be slightly more challenging than typical bandits: they have a chance of having better armor, and their leaders, the Reaver Lords, can wield spells and weapons with equal finesse. Reaver Loot includes a chance of: Food, Drink, Jewelry, Lockpicks, Gems, or Tools. Reaver Wizard Loot additionally includes a chance of: Soul Gems, Ingredients, Books, Spell Tomes, and Staffs.

REAVER ARCHERS

NAME	SUBTYPE	LV	HEALTH	MAGICKA	STAMINA	WEAPONS	ARMOR	ITEMS	SPELLS	NOTES
Reaver	Archer	1	35	25	70	Bow, Arrows, Dagger	Light Armor, Light Boots, (Light Gauntlets), (Light Helmet), (Light Shield)	(Gold)		
Reaver Outlaw	Archer	5	109	25	86	Bow, Arrows, Dagger	Light Armor, Light Boots, (Light Gauntlets), (Light Helmet), (Light Shield)	(Gold)		
Reaver Thug	Archer	9	238	25	107	Bow, Arrows, Dagger	Light Armor, Light Boots, (Light Gauntlets), (Light Helmet), (Light Shield)	(Gold)		
Reaver Highwayman	Archer	14	318	25	122	Bow, Arrows, Dagger	Light Armor, Light Boots, (Light Gauntlets), (Light Helmet), (Light Shield)	(Gold)		
Reaver Plunderer	Archer	19	398	25	172	Bow, Arrows, Dagger	Light Armor, Light Boots, (Light Gauntlets), (Light Helmet), (Light Shield)	Gold, (Lockpick)		
Reaver Marauder	Archer	25	489	25	246	Bow, Arrows, Dagger	Light Armor, Light Boots, (Light Gauntlets), (Light Helmet), (Light Shield)	Gold, (Lockpick)		

Reaver Marauder

REAVER WARRIORS

NAME	SUBTYPE	LV	HEALTH	MAGICKA	STAMINA	WEAPONS	ARMOR	ITEMS	SPELLS	NOTES
Reaver	1H Warrior	1	35	25	70	1H Weapon	Light Armor, Light Boots, (Light Gauntlets), (Light Helmet), (Shield)	Reaver Loot, (Gold)		
Reaver Outlaw	1H Warrior	5	109	25	86	1H Weapon	Light Armor, Light Boots, (Light Gauntlets), (Light Helmet), (Shield)	Reaver Loot, (Gold)		
Reaver Thug	1H Warrior	9	238	25	107	1H Weapon	Light Armor, Light Boots, (Light Gauntlets), (Light Helmet), (Shield)	Reaver Loot, (Gold)		
Reaver Highwayman	1H Warrior	14	318	25	152	1H Weapon	Light Armor, Light Boots, (Light Gauntlets), (Light Helmet), (Shield)	Reaver Loot, (Gold)		
Reaver Plunderer	1H Warrior	19	398	25	172	1H Weapon	Light Armor, Light Boots, (Light Gauntlets), (Light Helmet), (Shield)	Reaver Loot, (Gold)		
Reaver Marauder	1H Warrior	25	489	25	246	1H Weapon	Light Armor, Light Boots, (Light Gauntlets), (Light Helmet), (Shield)	Reaver Loot, (Gold)		

Reaver Lord

REAVER WIZARDS

NAME	SUBTYPE	LV	HEALTH	MAGICKA	STAMINA	WEAPONS	ARMOR	ITEMS	SPELLS	NOTES
Reaver	Wizard	1	35	100	50	Iron Dagger	Fur Armor, Boots	Reaver Wizard Loot, (Gold)	Healing, (Frostbite / Flames / Sparks), Oakflesh, Lesser Ward	
Reaver Outlaw	Wizard	5	101	124	70	Iron Dagger	Fur Armor, Boots	Reaver Wizard Loot, (Gold)	Healing, (Frostbite / Flames / Sparks), Oakflesh, Lesser Ward	
Reaver Thug	Wizard	9	222	173	75	Steel Dagger	Fur Armor, Boots	Reaver Wizard Loot, (Gold)	Fast Healing, Stoneflesh, (Ice Spike, Firebolt, Lightning Bolt), Steadfast Ward	
Reaver Highwayman	Wizard	14	292	153	70	Dagger	Fur Armor, Boots	Reaver Wizard Loot, (Gold)	Fast Healing, Stoneflesh, (Ice Spike, Firebolt, Lightning Bolt), Steadfast Ward	
Reaver Plunderer	Wizard	19	362	183	70	Dagger	Fur Armor, Boots	Reaver Wizard Loot, (Gold)	Fast Healing, Stoneflesh, (Ice Storm / Fireball / Chain Lightning), (Ice Spike, Firebolt, Lightning Bolt), Steadfast Ward	
Reaver Marauder	Wizard	25	441	294	150	Dagger	Fur Armor, Boots	Reaver Wizard Loot, (Gold)	Close Wounds, Fast Healing, Ironflesh, (Ice Storm / Fireball / Chain Lightning), (Ice Spike, Firebolt, Lightning Bolt), Steadfast Ward	

REAVER LORDS

NAME	SUBTYPE	LV	HEALTH	MAGICKA	STAMINA	WEAPONS	ARMOR	ITEMS	SPELLS	NOTES
Reaver Lord	Spellsword	6	155	45	75	1H Weapon, Steel Dagger	Heavy Armor, Heavy Boots, Heavy Gauntlets, Heavy Helmet	Reaver Loot, Gold	Healing, Oakflesh, Lesser Ward	
Reaver Lord	Spellsword	10	224	61	90	1H Weapon, Steel Dagger	Heavy Armor, Heavy Boots, Heavy Gauntlets, Heavy Helmet	Reaver Loot, Gold	Stoneflesh, Steadfast Ward, Fast Healing, (Ice Spike / Firebolt / Lightning Bolt)	
Reaver Lord	Spellsword	16	315	85	100	1H Weapon, Orcish Dagger	Heavy Armor, Heavy Boots, Heavy Gauntlets, Heavy Helmet	Reaver Loot, Gold	Stoneflesh, Steadfast Ward, Fast Healing, (Ice Spike / Firebolt / Lightning Bolt)	
Reaver Lord	Spellsword	21	395	105	115	1H Weapon, Elven Dagger	Heavy Armor, Heavy Boots, Heavy Gauntlets, Heavy Helmet	Reaver Loot, Gold	Stoneflesh, Steadfast Ward, Fast Healing, (Ice Storm / Fireball / Chain Lightning), (Ice Spike / Firebolt / Lightning Bolt)	
Reaver Lord	Spellsword	28	497	133	150	1H Weapon, Elven Dagger	Heavy Armor, Heavy Boots, Heavy Gauntlets, Heavy Helmet	Reaver Loot, Gold	Close Wounds, Ironflesh, Steadfast Ward, Fast Healing, (Ice Storm / Fireball / Chain Lightning), (Ice Spike / Firebolt / Lightning Bolt)	

Rieklings

Rieklings are small, blue-skinned humanoids that inhabit the icy northern regions of Solstheim. They tend to live in small clans, stealing or scavenging whatever they can to survive. Some clans raise and keep Bristleback Boars, which their best warriors use as mounts. Riekling Loot includes a chance of: Junk, Ingredients, Gems, Jewelry, Potions, or Gold. Boar Loot includes a chance of: Boar Tusks, Boar Meat, Potions, Gold, or Mushrooms.

Riekling Charger

Riekling Chief

RIEKLING WARRIORS

NAME	SUBTYPE	LV	HEALTH	MAGICKA	STAMINA	WEAPONS	ARMOR	ITEMS	SPELLS	NOTES
Riekling	Warrior	6	130	0	120	[Riekling Spear]		Riekling Loot		Resist Frost 25%
Riekling Scout	Warrior	11	200	0	140	[Riekling Spear]		Riekling Loot		Resist Frost 25%
Riekling Hunter	Warrior	16	250	0	160	[Riekling Spear]		Riekling Loot		Resist Frost 25%
Riekling Warrior	Warrior	23	352	0	188	[Riekling Spear]		Riekling Loot		Resist Frost 25%

RIEKLING SPEAR-THROWERS

NAME	SUBTYPE	LV	HEALTH	MAGICKA	STAMINA	WEAPONS	ARMOR	ITEMS	SPELLS	NOTES
Riekling	Spear-Thrower	6	130	0	120	Riekling Spears		Riekling Loot		Resist Frost 25%
Riekling Scout	Spear-Thrower	11	200	0	140	Riekling Spears		Riekling Loot		Resist Frost 25%
Riekling Hunter	Spear-Thrower	16	250	0	160	Riekling Spears		Riekling Loot		Resist Frost 25%
Riekling Warrior	Spear-Thrower	23	352	0	188	Riekling Spears		Riekling Loot		Resist Frost 25%

BRISTLEBACK BOARS

NAME	SUBTYPE	LV	HEALTH	MAGICKA	STAMINA	WEAPONS	ARMOR	ITEMS	SPELLS	NOTES
Bristleback		7	260	0	80	50 Dmg		Boar Loot		Resist Frost 25%

UNIQUE RIEKLINGS

NAME	SUBTYPE	LV	HEALTH	MAGICKA	STAMINA	WEAPONS	ARMOR	ITEMS	SPELLS	NOTES
Riekling Chief		22	401	0	184	[Riekling Spear]		Riekling Loot		Resist Frost 25%

MOUNTED RIEKLINGS

NAME	SUBTYPE	LV	HEALTH	MAGICKA	STAMINA	WEAPONS	ARMOR	ITEMS	SPELLS	NOTES
Riekling Rider		25	605	0	246	[Riekling Spear]		Boar Loot, Riekling Loot		Resist Frost 25%
Riekling Courser		32	755	0	274	[Riekling Spear]		Boar Loot, Riekling Loot		Resist Frost 25%
Riekling Charger		40	1055	0	306	[Riekling Spear]		Boar Loot, Riekling Loot		Resist Frost 25%

Sailor

Solitude, Dawnstar, and Windhelm are all important Imperial ports, and many sailors from those cities crew the ships that ply the waters along the Sea of Ghosts.

Sailor

SAILOR

NAME	SUBTYPE	LV	HEALTH	MAGICKA	STAMINA	WEAPONS	ARMOR	ITEMS	SPELLS	NOTES
Sailor		1	10	25	25	Dagger	Clothes	(Gold)		

Skeletons

The skeletal remains of the dead are a constant threat around Necromancers and Vampires. Unarmored skeletons tend to be weak, while armored skeletons present a much more difficult challenge. As with all undead, use fire magic or spells that damage or repel the undead to deal with them. Skeleton Loot includes a chance of: Jewelry, Gems, Soul Gems, Ingots, or Potions.

Skeleton

UNARMORED SKELETONS

NAME	SUBTYPE	LV	HEALTH	MAGICKA	STAMINA	WEAPONS	ARMOR	ITEMS	SPELLS	NOTES
Skeleton	1H Warrior	1	20	0	80	1H Ancient Nord Weapon, (Shield)		Bone Meal, (Skeleton Loot)		
Skeleton	2H Warrior	1	20	0	80	2H Ancient Nord Weapon		Bone Meal		
Skeleton	Archer	1	20	0	80	Ancient Nord Bow, Ancient Nord Arrows		Bone Meal, (Skeleton Loot)		
Skeleton	Robed	1	20	0	80	Ancient Nord Sword	[Warlock Hood]	Bone Meal, (Skeleton Loot), (Spellbook)		
Corrupted Shade		1	30	0	80	1H Ancient Nord Weapon, (Shield)		Bone Meal		

SKELETON ARCHERS

NAME	SUBTYPE	LV	HEALTH	MAGICKA	STAMINA	WEAPONS	ARMOR	ITEMS	SPELLS	NOTES
Skeleton	Archer	1	50	0	80	Ancient Nord Bow, Ancient Nord Arrows	[Skeleton Archer Armor]	Bone Meal, (Skeleton Loot)		50% Resist Frost, Immune to Poison
Skeleton	Archer	6	175	0	205	Ancient Nord Bow, Ancient Nord Arrows	[Skeleton Archer Armor]	Bone Meal, (Skeleton Loot)		50% Resist Frost, Immune to Poison
Skeleton	Archer	13	400	0	340	Ancient Nord Bow, Ancient Nord Arrows	[Skeleton Archer Armor]	Bone Meal, (Skeleton Loot)		50% Resist Frost, Immune to Poison
Skeleton	Archer	21	900	0	480	Ancient Nord Bow, Ancient Nord Arrows	[Skeleton Archer Armor]	Bone Meal, (Skeleton Loot)		50% Resist Frost, Immune to Poison
Skeleton	Archer	30	1000	10	575	Ancient Nord Bow, Ancient Nord Arrows	[Skeleton Archer Armor]	Bone Meal, (Skeleton Loot)		50% Resist Frost, Immune to Poison
Skeleton	Archer	40	1300	10	625	Ebony Bow, Ebony Arrows, Ancient Nord War Axe	[Skeleton Archer Armor]	Bone Meal, (Skeleton Loot)		50% Resist Frost, Immune to Poison

SKELETON WARLOCKS

NAME	SUBTYPE	LV	HEALTH	MAGICKA	STAMINA	WEAPONS	ARMOR	ITEMS	SPELLS	NOTES
Skeleton	Warlock	6	150	50	180	Ancient Nord Sword	[Skeleton Warlock Armor], [Warlock Hood]	Bone Meal, (Skeleton Loot), (Spellbook)	Ice Spike, Ice Storm, Reanimate Corpse	50% Resist Frost, Immune to Poison
Skeleton	Warlock	13	490	100	280	Ancient Nord Sword	[Skeleton Warlock Armor], [Warlock Hood]	Bone Meal, (Skeleton Loot), (Spellbook)	Ice Spike, Ice Storm, Reanimate Corpse	50% Resist Frost, Immune to Poison
Skeleton	Warlock	21	700	160	380	Ancient Nord Sword	[Skeleton Warlock Armor], [Warlock Hood]	Bone Meal, (Skeleton Loot), (Spellbook)	Ice Spike, Ice Storm, Reanimate Corpse	50% Resist Frost, Immune to Poison

Skeleton Warlock

SKELETON WARRIORS

NAME	SUBTYPE	LV	HEALTH	MAGICKA	STAMINA	WEAPONS	ARMOR	ITEMS	SPELLS	NOTES
Skeleton	1H Warrior	1	50	0	80	Ancient Nord Sword	[Skeleton Warrior Armor]	Bone Meal, (Skeleton Loot)		50% Resist Frost, Immune to Poison
Skeleton	1H Warrior	6	150	0	205	Ancient Nord Sword	[Skeleton Warrior Armor]	Bone Meal, (Skeleton Loot)		50% Resist Frost, Immune to Poison
Skeleton	1H Warrior	13	320	0	340	Ancient Nord Sword	[Skeleton Warrior Armor]	Bone Meal, (Skeleton Loot)		50% Resist Frost, Immune to Poison
Skeleton	1H Warrior	21	700	0	480	Ancient Nord Sword	[Skeleton Warrior Armor]	Bone Meal, (Skeleton Loot)		50% Resist Frost, Immune to Poison
Skeleton	1H Warrior	30	1000	10	575	Ancient Nord Sword	[Skeleton Warrior Armor]	Bone Meal, (Skeleton Loot)		50% Resist Frost, Immune to Poison

Skeleton Warrior

SKELETON WARLORDS

NAME	SUBTYPE	LV	HEALTH	MAGICKA	STAMINA	WEAPONS	ARMOR	ITEMS	SPELLS	NOTES
Skeleton	2H Warrior	1	50	0	80	(Ancient Nord Greatsword / Battleaxe / Warhammer)	[Skeleton Warlord Armor]	Bone Meal, (Skeleton Loot)		50% Resist Frost, Immune to Poison
Skeleton	2H Warrior	6	150	0	204	(Ancient Nord Greatsword / Battleaxe / Warhammer)	[Skeleton Warlord Armor]	Bone Meal, (Skeleton Loot)		50% Resist Frost, Immune to Poison
Skeleton	2H Warrior	13	320	0	340	(Ancient Nord Greatsword / Battleaxe / Warhammer)	[Skeleton Warlord Armor]	Bone Meal, (Skeleton Loot)		50% Resist Frost, Immune to Poison
Skeleton	2H Warrior	21	700	0	480	(Ancient Nord Greatsword / Battleaxe / Warhammer)	[Skeleton Warlord Armor]	Bone Meal, (Skeleton Loot)		50% Resist Frost, Immune to Poison
Skeleton	2H Warrior	30	1000	10	575	(Ancient Nord Greatsword / Battleaxe / Warhammer)	[Skeleton Warlord Armor]	Bone Meal, (Skeleton Loot)		50% Resist Frost, Immune to Poison

Soul Guards

The Soul Cairn is the plane of undeath, home to lost and accursed souls forced to wander there for eternity. All Soul Guards are undead, so spells that damage or repel undead work well against them, as does fire magic. Soul Guard Loot includes a random chance of Soul Gems, Soul Husks, gold, gems, jewelry, or ingredients.

BONEMAN ARCHER

NAME	SUBTYPE	LV	HEALTH	MAGICKA	STAMINA	WEAPONS	ARMOR	ITEMS	SPELLS	NOTES
Boneman	Archer	1	50	0	80	Ancient Nord Bow, Ancient Nord Arrows		Soul Guard Loot		25% Resist Frost, Immune to Poison, Immune to Paralysis
Boneman	Archer	6	175	0	205	Ancient Nord Bow, Ancient Nord Arrows		Soul Guard Loot		25% Resist Frost, Immune to Poison, Immune to Paralysis
Boneman	Archer	13	400	0	340	Ancient Nord Bow, Ancient Nord Arrows		Soul Guard Loot		25% Resist Frost, Immune to Poison, Immune to Paralysis
Boneman	Archer	21	900	0	480	Ancient Nord Bow, Ancient Nord Arrows		Soul Guard Loot		25% Resist Frost, Immune to Poison, Immune to Paralysis
Boneman	Archer	30	1000	10	575	Ancient Nord Bow, Ancient Nord Arrows		Soul Guard Loot		25% Resist Frost, Immune to Poison, Immune to Paralysis
Boneman	Archer	40	1300	10	625	Ancient Nord Bow, Ancient Nord Arrows		Soul Guard Loot		25% Resist Frost, Immune to Poison, Immune to Paralysis

Boneman

BONEMAN WARRIORS

NAME	SUBTYPE	LV	HEALTH	MAGICKA	STAMINA	WEAPONS	ARMOR	ITEMS	SPELLS	NOTES
Boneman	1H Warrior	1	50	0	80	1H Ancient Nord Weapon	(Iron Shield)	Soul Guard Loot		25% Resist Frost, Immune to Poison, Immune to Paralysis
Boneman	1H Warrior	6	150	0	205	1H Ancient Nord Weapon	(Iron Shield)	Soul Guard Loot		25% Resist Frost, Immune to Poison, Immune to Paralysis
Boneman	1H Warrior	13	320	0	340	1H Ancient Nord Weapon	(Iron Shield)	Soul Guard Loot		25% Resist Frost, Immune to Poison, Immune to Paralysis
Boneman	1H Warrior	21	700	0	480	1H Ancient Nord Weapon	(Iron Shield)	Soul Guard Loot		25% Resist Frost, Immune to Poison, Immune to Paralysis
Boneman	1H Warrior	30	1000	10	575	1H Ancient Nord Weapon	(Iron Shield)	Soul Guard Loot		25% Resist Frost, Immune to Poison, Immune to Paralysis

Keeper

MISTMEN

NAME	SUBTYPE	LV	HEALTH	MAGICKA	STAMINA	WEAPONS	ARMOR	ITEMS	SPELLS	NOTES
Mistman	Warlock	6	150	50	180			Soul Guard Loot	Frostbite, Ice Spike	25% Resist Frost, Immune to Poison, Immune to Paralysis
Mistman	Warlock	13	490	100	280			Soul Guard Loot	Frostbite, Ice Spike	25% Resist Frost, Immune to Poison, Immune to Paralysis
Mistman	Warlock	21	700	160	380			Soul Guard Loot	Frostbite, Ice Spike	25% Resist Frost, Immune to Poison, Immune to Paralysis

WRATHMEN

NAME	SUBTYPE	LV	HEALTH	MAGICKA	STAMINA	WEAPONS	ARMOR	ITEMS	SPELLS	NOTES
Wrathman	2H Warrior	1	50	0	80	2H Ancient Nord Weapon		Soul Guard Loot		50% Resist Frost, Immune to Poison, Immune to Paralysis
Wrathman	2H Warrior	6	150	0	204	2H Ancient Nord Weapon		Soul Guard Loot		50% Resist Frost, Immune to Poison, Immune to Paralysis
Wrathman	2H Warrior	13	320	0	340	2H Ancient Nord Weapon		Soul Guard Loot		50% Resist Frost, Immune to Poison, Immune to Paralysis
Wrathman	2H Warrior	21	700	0	480	2H Ancient Nord Weapon		Soul Guard Loot		50% Resist Frost, Immune to Poison, Immune to Paralysis
Wrathman	2H Warrior	30	1000	10	575	2H Ancient Nord Weapon		Soul Guard Loot		50% Resist Frost, Immune to Poison, Immune to Paralysis

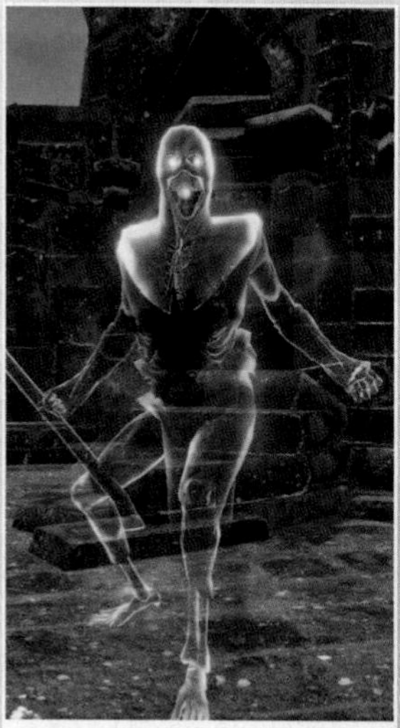

Reaper

UNIQUE SOUL GUARDS

NAME	SUBTYPE	LV	HEALTH	MAGICKA	STAMINA	WEAPONS	ARMOR	ITEMS	SPELLS	NOTES
Keeper	1H Warrior	10*	340	0	225	(Dragonbone Mace)	(Dragonplate Armor), (Dragonplate Gauntlets), (Dragonplate Boots), (Dragonplate Shield)	(Dragonbone Mace), Black Soul Gem		25% Resist Frost, 10% Resist Magic, Immune to Poison, Immune to Paralysis
Keeper	2H Warrior	10*	390	0	225	(Dragonbone Battleaxe)	(Dragonplate Armor), (Dragonplate Gauntlets), (Dragonplate Boots), (Dragonplate Shield)	(Dragonbone Battleaxe), Black Soul Gem		25% Resist Frost, 10% Resist Magic, Immune to Poison, Immune to Paralysis
Keeper	Archer	10*	340	0	225	(Dragonbone Bow, Dragonbone Arrows)	(Dragonplate Armor), (Dragonplate Gauntlets), (Dragonplate Boots), (Dragonplate Shield)	(Dragonbone Bow), (Dragonbone Arrows), Black Soul Gem		25% Resist Frost, 10% Resist Magic, Immune to Poison, Immune to Paralysis
Reaper		10*	325	0	110	Executioner's Axe	(Reaper Robe), (Reaper Hood), (Reaper Bracers)	Daedra Heart, Black Soul Gem	Vile Vapor, Unrelenting Force Shout	25% Resist Frost, Immune to Poison, Immune to Paralysis

CONJURED SOUL GUARDS

NAME	SUBTYPE	LV	HEALTH	MAGICKA	STAMINA	WEAPONS	ARMOR	ITEMS	SPELLS	NOTES
Boneman	Archer, Conjured	6	140	0	205	[Ancient Nord Bow], [Ancient Nord Arrows], [Ancient Nord War Axe]				25% Resist Frost, Immune to Poison, Immune to Paralysis
Mistman	Warlock, Conjured	13	490	210	280				Frostbite, Ice Spike	25% Resist Frost, Immune to Poison, Immune to Paralysis
Wrathman	2H Warrior, Conjured	30	800	10	475	[2H Ancient Nord Weapon]				50% Resist Frost, Immune to Poison, Immune to Paralysis

Spiders

Frostbite Spiders are giant arachnids often found in Skyrim's caves and ruins. They have a dangerous poison spit attack, though their bite is just as poisonous—try to keep your distance and focus on ranged attacks. Despite their name, they are not actually resistant to frost. The white variety of spiders is somewhat tougher than the red variety for each size category. Minor Treasure includes a tiny chance of: A few gold, a gem, or a ring.

Solstheim Spiders are a unique species of spider that has recently been discovered on Solstheim. Prolonged exposure to certain minerals (particularly gemstones) seems to cause the 'standard' Albino Spider to take on new and volatile forms. When fighting these spiders, observe their coloration and prepare yourself with Fire, Frost, Shock, or Poison Resistance accordingly. The damage from the jumping and exploding variants is half physical and half elemental, so while resistance will help, it won't mitigate the damage completely.

Frostbite Spider

FROSTBITE SPIDERS

NAME	SUBTYPE	LV	HEALTH	MAGICKA	STAMINA	WEAPONS	ARMOR	ITEMS	SPELLS	NOTES
Frostbite Spider	Small, Red	1	15	0	25	6 + 3/s for 3s		Frostbite Venom, (Minor Treasure)	Poison Spit	
Frostbite Spider	Small, White	3	35	0	35	6 + 3/s for 3s		Frostbite Venom, (Minor Treasure)	Poison Spit	
Frostbite Spider	Large, Red	6	150	0	200	45 + 5/s for 3s		Frostbite Venom, (Minor Treasure)	Poison Spit	
Frostbite Spider	Large, White	8	220	0	235	45 + 5/s for 3s		Frostbite Venom, (Minor Treasure)	Poison Spit	
Giant Frostbite Spider	Giant, Red	14	380	0	315	135 + 10/s for 3s		2x Frostbite Venom, (Minor Treasure)	Poison Spit	
Giant Frostbite Spider	Giant, White	17	510	0	430	135 + 10/s for 3s		2x Frostbite Venom, (Minor Treasure)	Poison Spit	

Jumping Shock Spider

SOLSTHEIM SPIDERS

NAME	SUBTYPE	LV	HEALTH	MAGICKA	STAMINA	WEAPONS	ARMOR	ITEMS	SPELLS	NOTES
Albino Spider		5	41	4	45	2 Dmg + 3/s for 3s		Albino Spider Pod, Damaged Albino Spider Pod		
Oil Spider		6	51	4	50	None			Excrete Oil	
Flame Cloaked Spider		6	51	4	50	2 Dmg + 3/s for 3s			Flame Cloak	Immune to Fire
Frost Cloaked Spider		6	51	4	50	2 Dmg + 3/s for 3s			Frost Cloak	Immune to Frost
Poisonous Cloaked Spider		6	51	4	50	2 Dmg + 3/s for 3s			Poison Cloak	Immune to Poison
Shock Cloaked Spider		6	51	4	50	2 Dmg + 3/s for 3s			Shock Cloak	Immune to Shock
Jumping Flame Spider		10*	91	4	70	2 Dmg + 3/s for 3s			Fire Spit, Fire Explosion	Immune to Fire
Jumping Frost Spider		10*	91	4	70	2 Dmg + 3/s for 3s			Frost Spit, Frost Explosion	Immune to Frost
Jumping Poisonous Spider		10*	91	4	70	2 Dmg + 3/s for 3s			Poison Spit, Poison Explosion	Immune to Poison
Jumping Shock Spider		10*	91	4	70	2 Dmg + 3/s for 3s			Shock Spit, Shock Explosion	Immune to Shock

Soldiers & Guards

Each of Skyrim's Nine Holds maintains its own standing force of guards, who owe their loyalty to the Jarl. As the Civil War rages between the Imperial Legion and the Stormcloaks, their soldiers will take posession of the military camps, forts, towns, and cities of Skyrim, replacing some of the local guards.

HOLD GUARDS

NAME	SUBTYPE	LV	HEALTH	MAGICKA	STAMINA	WEAPONS	ARMOR	ITEMS	SPELLS	NOTES
[Hold] Guard		20*	252	50	183	(Imperial/ Stormcloak Weapon)	[Hold] Armor, [Hold] Shield, Boots, Helmet	(Torch), (Food), (Drink), (Amulet), (Gold)		Guards use the weapons of the faction their Hold is loyal to.

Redoran Guard

Soldiers & Guard (Hold Guard)

SOLSTHEIM GUARDS

NAME	SUBTYPE	LV	HEALTH	MAGICKA	STAMINA	WEAPONS	ARMOR	ITEMS	SPELLS	NOTES
Redoran Guard		20*	252	50	183	Elven Sword, Elven Bow, Elven Arrows	Bonemold Armor, Bonemold Helm, Bonemold Gauntlets, Bonemold Boots, Bonemold Shield	Gold		Guards use the weapons of the faction their Hold is loyal to.

IMPERIAL LEGION

NAME	SUBTYPE	LV	HEALTH	MAGICKA	STAMINA	WEAPONS	ARMOR	ITEMS	SPELLS	NOTES
Imperial Soldier	Guard	20*	252	50	183	Imperial Sword, Imperial Bow, Steel Arrows, Steel Dagger	Imperial Light Armor, Imperial Light Boots, Imperial Light Gauntlets, Imperial Light Helmet	(Torch), (Food), (Drink), (Amulet), (Gold)		
Imperial Soldier	Fort / Siege	5*	74	50	71	Imperial Sword, Imperial Bow, Steel Arrows, Steel Dagger	Imperial Light Armor, Imperial Light Boots, Imperial Light Gauntlets, Imperial Light Helmet	(Torch), (Food), (Drink), (Amulet), (Gold)		
Fort Commander		5*	74	50	71	Imperial Sword, Imperial Bow, Steel Arrows, Steel Dagger	Imperial Light Armor, Imperial Light Boots, Imperial Light Gauntlets, Imperial Light Helmet	(Torch), (Food), (Drink), (Amulet), (Gold)		
Imperial Legate		5*	74	50	71	Imperial Sword, Imperial Bow, Steel Arrows, Steel Dagger	Imperial Heavy Armor, Imperial Heavy Boots, Imperial Heavy Gauntlets			
Imperial General		5*	74	50	71	Imperial Sword, Imperial Bow, Steel Arrows, Steel Dagger	Imperial Heavy Armor, Imperial Heavy Boots, Imperial Heavy Gauntlets, Imperial Light Shield	(Torch), (Food), (Drink), (Amulet), (Gold)		

STORMCLOAKS

NAME	SUBTYPE	LV	HEALTH	MAGICKA	STAMINA	WEAPONS	ARMOR	ITEMS	SPELLS	NOTES
Stormcloak Soldier	Guard	20*	252	50	183	(1H Weapon & Shield / 2H Weapon), Hunting Bow, Arrows	Stormcloak Armor, Fur Boots, Fur Gauntlets, Stormcloak Helmet	(Torch), (Food), (Drink), (Amulet), (Gold)		
Stormcloak Soldier	Fort / Siege	5*	74	50	71	(1H Weapon & Shield / 2H Weapon), Hunting Bow, Arrows	Stormcloak Armor, Fur Boots, Fur Gauntlets, Stormcloak Helmet	(Torch), (Food), (Drink), (Amulet), (Gold)		
Fort Commander		5*	74	50	71	(1H Weapon & Shield / 2H Weapon), Hunting Bow, Arrows	Stormcloak Armor, Fur Boots, Fur Gauntlets, Stormcloak Helmet	(Torch), (Food), (Drink), (Amulet), (Gold)		
Stormcloak Commander		5*	74	50	71	(1H Weapon & Shield / 2H Weapon), Hunting Bow, Steel Arrows, Steel Dagger	Stormcloak Officer Armor, Stormcloak Officer Boots, Stormcloak Officer Gauntlets			
Stormcloak General		5*	74	50	71	(1H Weapon & Shield / 2H Weapon), Hunting Bow, Arrows	Stormcloak Officer Armor, Stormcloak Officer Boots, Stormcloak Officer Gauntlets, Stormcloak Officer Helmet, Steel Shield	(Torch), (Food), (Drink), (Amulet), (Gold)		

Imperial Legion (General)

Stormcloaks (General)

Spriggan

Burnt Spriggan

Spriggan

Spriggans are spirits of the forest, often dwelling in secluded groves and grottos. They are just as tough in melee as with ranged attacks, and are often are accompanied by bears, wolves, and sabre cats that will fight to protect them. Most Spriggans are vulnerable to fire, so use it against them whenever possible.

The Burnt Spriggans of Solstheim are another matter. These tortured creatures are immune to fire (and actually use it against you), but they lack the allies of other Spriggans. Use ranged weapons or magic to take them out from a distance when possible.

SPRIGGAN

NAME	SUBTYPE	LV	HEALTH	MAGICKA	STAMINA	WEAPONS	ARMOR	ITEMS	SPELLS	NOTES
Spriggan		8	195	150	85	25 Dmg + Poison 2/s for 10s		Taproot	Leaf Blast, Call Creatures, Heal	Weak to Fire 33%
Spriggan Matron		18	445	250	135	30 Dmg + Poison 2/s for 10s		Taproot	Leaf Blast, Call Creatures, Heal	Weak to Fire 33%
Spriggan Earth Mother		30	765	250	195	30 Dmg + Poison 2/s for 10s		Taproot	Leaf Blast, Call Creatures, Heal	Weak to Fire 25%
Burnt Spriggan		30	945	300	185	51 Dmg + Poison 2/s for 10s		Burnt Spriggan Wood	Flames	Immune to Fire

Thalmor

The Thalmor are the agents of the elven Aldmeri Dominion, charged with overseeing the implementation of the White-Gold Concordat, the peace treaty between the Dominion and the Empire. Most view them as spies, or worse. Thalmor Loot includes a chance of gems, food, or drink. Thalmor Wizard Loot includes a chance of gems, soul gems, potions, or ingredients.

Thalmor (Guardian) Thalmor

(Spellsword)

Thalmor (Warrior)

Thalmor (Wizard)

THALMOR ARCHER

NAME	SUBTYPE	LV	HEALTH	MAGICKA	STAMINA	WEAPONS	ARMOR	ITEMS	SPELLS	NOTES
Thalmor Soldier	Archer	4	127	56	62	Bow, Arrows, Dagger	Cuirass, Boots, Helmet, Gauntlets	Thalmor Loot	Bound Sword, Fast Healing	
Thalmor Soldier	Archer	12	249	72	94	Bow, Arrows, Dagger	Cuirass, Boots, Helmet, Gauntlets	Thalmor Loot	Bound Sword, Fast Healing	
Thalmor Soldier	Archer	20	371	88	126	Bow, Arrows, Dagger	Cuirass, Boots, Helmet, Gauntlets	Thalmor Loot	Bound Sword, Fast Healing	
Thalmor Soldier	Archer	28	493	104	158	Bow, Arrows, Dagger	Cuirass, Boots, Helmet, Gauntlets	Thalmor Loot	Bound Sword, Fast Healing	
Thalmor Soldier	Archer	36	565	120	190	Bow, Arrows, Dagger	Cuirass, Boots, Helmet, Gauntlets	Thalmor Loot	Bound Sword, Fast Healing	

THALMOR GUARDIAN

NAME	SUBTYPE	LV	HEALTH	MAGICKA	STAMINA	WEAPONS	ARMOR	ITEMS	SPELLS	NOTES
Thalmor Soldier	Guardian	4	127	56	62	1H Weapon, Dagger	Cuirass, Boots, Helmet, Gauntlets, Shield			
Thalmor Soldier	Guardian	12	249	72	94	1H Weapon, Dagger	Cuirass, Boots, Helmet, Gauntlets, Shield			
Thalmor Soldier	Guardian	20	371	88	126	1H Weapon, Dagger	Cuirass, Boots, Helmet, Gauntlets, Shield			
Thalmor Soldier	Guardian	28	493	104	158	1H Weapon, Dagger	Cuirass, Boots, Helmet, Gauntlets, Shield			
Thalmor Soldier	Guardian	36	565	120	190	1H Weapon, Dagger	Cuirass, Boots, Helmet, Gauntlets, Shield			

THALMOR SPELLSWORD

NAME	SUBTYPE	LV	HEALTH	MAGICKA	STAMINA	WEAPONS	ARMOR	ITEMS	SPELLS	NOTES
Thalmor Soldier	Spellsword	4	127	56	62	1H Weapon, Dagger	Cuirass, Boots, Helmet, Gauntlets		Flames, Fast Healing	
Thalmor Soldier	Spellsword	12	249	72	94	1H Weapon, Dagger	Cuirass, Boots, Helmet, Gauntlets		Flames, Fast Healing	
Thalmor Soldier	Spellsword	20	371	88	126	1H Weapon, Dagger	Cuirass, Boots, Helmet, Gauntlets		Flames, Fast Healing	
Thalmor Soldier	Spellsword	28	493	104	158	1H Weapon, Dagger	Cuirass, Boots, Helmet, Gauntlets		Flames, Fast Healing	
Thalmor Soldier	Spellsword	36	565	120	190	1H Weapon, Dagger	Cuirass, Boots, Helmet, Gauntlets		Flames, Fast Healing	

THALMOR WARRIOR

NAME	SUBTYPE	LV	HEALTH	MAGICKA	STAMINA	WEAPONS	ARMOR	ITEMS	SPELLS	NOTES
Thalmor Soldier	Warrior	4	127	56	62	1H Weapon	Cuirass, Boots, Helmet, Gauntlets, (Shield)		Bound Sword	
Thalmor Soldier	Warrior	12	249	72	94	1H Weapon	Cuirass, Boots, Helmet, Gauntlets, (Shield)		Bound Sword	
Thalmor Soldier	Warrior	20	371	88	126	1H Weapon	Cuirass, Boots, Helmet, Gauntlets, (Shield)		Bound Sword	
Thalmor Soldier	Warrior	28	493	104	158	1H Weapon	Cuirass, Boots, Helmet, Gauntlets, (Shield)		Bound Sword	
Thalmor Soldier	Warrior	36	565	120	190	1H Weapon	Cuirass, Boots, Helmet, Gauntlets, (Shield)		Bound Sword	

THALMOR WIZARD

NAME	SUBTYPE	LV	HEALTH	MAGICKA	STAMINA	WEAPONS	ARMOR	ITEMS	SPELLS	NOTES
Thalmor Wizard		4	127	118	50	Dagger	Thalmor Robes, Thalmor Boots, Thalmor Gloves, Thalmor Hood	Thalmor Wizard Loot	Flames, Frostbite, Healing, Oakflesh, Sparks, Lesser Ward	
Thalmor Wizard		12	249	166	50	Dagger	Thalmor Robes, Thalmor Boots, Thalmor Gloves, Thalmor Hood	Thalmor Wizard Loot	Conjure Flame Atronach, Fast Healing, Firebolt, Lightning Bolt, Oakflesh, Lesser Ward	
Thalmor Wizard		20	371	239	50	Dagger	Thalmor Robes, Thalmor Boots, Thalmor Gloves, Thalmor Hood	Thalmor Wizard Loot	Banish Daedra, Chain Lightning, Conjure Flame Atronach, Fast Healing, Fireball, Lightning Bolt, Oakflesh, Steadfast Ward	
Thalmor Wizard		28	493	312	50	Dagger	Thalmor Robes, Thalmor Boots, Thalmor Gloves, Thalmor Hood	Thalmor Wizard Loot	Chain Lightning, Conjure Storm Atronach, Fast Healing, Incinerate, Stoneflesh, Thunderbolt, Turn Lesser Undead, Steadfast Ward	
Thalmor Wizard		36	565	385	50	Dagger	Thalmor Robes, Thalmor Boots, Thalmor Gloves, Thalmor Hood	Thalmor Wizard Loot	Banish Daedra, Chain Lightning, Close Wounds, Conjure Storm Atronach, Expel Daedra, Fast Healing, Incinerate, Stoneflesh, Thunderbolt, Turn Undead, Steadfast Ward	
Thalmor Wizard		44	637	458	50	Dagger	Thalmor Robes, Thalmor Boots, Thalmor Gloves, Thalmor Hood	Thalmor Wizard Loot	Banish Daedra, Chain Lightning, Close Wounds, Conjure Storm Atronach, Expel Daedra, Fast Healing, Incinerate, Ironflesh, Thunderbolt, Turn Undead, Steadfast Ward	

THALMOR WIZARD – BOSS

NAME	SUBTYPE	LV	HEALTH	MAGICKA	STAMINA	WEAPONS	ARMOR	ITEMS	SPELLS	NOTES
Thalmor Wizard	Boss	14	317	228	50	Dagger	Thalmor Robes, Thalmor Boots, Thalmor Gloves, Thalmor Hood	Thalmor Wizard Loot	Conjure Flame Atronach, Fast Healing, Firebolt, Lightning Bolt, Oakflesh, Lesser Ward	
Thalmor Wizard	Boss	23	448	282	50	Dagger	Thalmor Robes, Thalmor Boots, Thalmor Gloves, Thalmor Hood	Thalmor Wizard Loot	Banish Daedra, Chain Lightning, Conjure Flame Atronach, Fast Healing, Fireball, Lightning Bolt, Oakflesh, Steadfast Ward	
Thalmor Wizard	Boss	32	579	386	50	Dagger	Thalmor Robes, Thalmor Boots, Thalmor Gloves, Thalmor Hood	Thalmor Wizard Loot	Chain Lightning, Conjure Storm Atronach, Fast Healing, Incinerate, Stoneflesh, Thunderbolt, Turn Lesser Undead, Steadfast Ward	
Thalmor Wizard	Boss	40	651	434	50	Dagger	Thalmor Robes, Thalmor Boots, Thalmor Gloves, Thalmor Hood	Thalmor Wizard Loot	Banish Daedra, Chain Lightning, Close Wounds, Conjure Storm Atronach, Expel Daedra, Fast Healing, Incinerate, Stoneflesh, Thunderbolt, Turn Undead, Steadfast Ward	
Thalmor Wizard	Boss	50	791	544	50	Dagger	Thalmor Robes, Thalmor Boots, Thalmor Gloves, Thalmor Hood	Thalmor Wizard Loot	Banish Daedra, Chain Lightning, Close Wounds, Conjure Storm Atronach, Expel Daedra, Fast Healing, Incinerate, Ironflesh, Thunderbolt, Turn Undead, Steadfast Ward	

Trolls

Trolls are among the most feared of Skyrim's predators. They regenerate health, so attack aggressively—it's worth taking some punishment to keep the attacks up. Trolls are notably weak to fire. Minor Treasure includes a tiny chance of a few gold, a gem, or a ring.

Recently, the Dawnguard's beastmasters have found a way to tame these fearsome creatures. Properly trained and outfitted with heavy iron plates, their Armored Trolls are fearsome allies in the fight against the vampire menace.

Troll (Frost Troll)

TROLLS

NAME	SUBTYPE	LV	HEALTH	MAGICKA	STAMINA	WEAPONS	ARMOR	ITEMS	SPELLS	NOTES
Troll		14	280	0	340	35 Dmg		Troll Fat, (Minor Treasure)		Regenerate Health, Weak to Fire 50%
Frost Troll		22	460	0	480	65 Dmg		Troll Fat, (Minor Treasure)		Regenerate Health, Weak to Fire 50%

Armored Troll

DAWNGUARD ARMORED TROLLS

NAME	SUBTYPE	LV	HEALTH	MAGICKA	STAMINA	WEAPONS	ARMOR	ITEMS	SPELLS	NOTES
Armored Troll		14	280	0	340	35 Dmg		Troll Fat, (Minor Treasure)		Regenerate Health, Weak to Fire 50%, 200 Armor
Armored Frost Troll		22	460	0	480	65 Dmg		Troll Fat, (Minor Treasure)		Regenerate Health, Weak to Fire 50%, 200 Armor

Vampires

Vampirism begins as a disease, Sanguinare Vampiris, but quickly progresses to something much worse if left untreated. Vampires tend to congregate in clans, and their fearsome reputation is well deserved. It's worth spending those scrolls and potions you've been hoarding to defeat higher-level vampires. You can't let the fight drag on, because their primary attack heals them while hurting you. Vampire Loot includes a chance of lockpicks, potions, jewelry, gems, gold, books, or staffs.

Vampire

Nightlord Vampire

VAMPIRES

NAME	SUBTYPE	LV	HEALTH	MAGICKA	STAMINA	WEAPONS	ARMOR	ITEMS	SPELLS	NOTES
Vampire Fledgling		1	35	75	50	(1H Sword/1H Axe)	(Vampire Armor/Vampire Robes), Vampire Boots	Vampire Loot, (Gold)	Vampire Drain Life, Invisibility	50% Resist Frost, 50% Weak to Fire, No Regen in Sunlight
Vampire		6	120	120	90	(1H Sword/1H Axe)	(Vampire Armor/Vampire Robes), Vampire Boots	Vampire Loot, (Gold)	Vampire Drain Life, Invisibility, (Raise Zombie)	50% Resist Frost, 50% Weak to Fire, No Regen in Sunlight
Blooded Vampire		12	224	169	112	(1H Sword/1H Axe)	(Vampire Armor/Vampire Robes), Vampire Boots	Vampire Loot, (Gold)	Vampire Drain Life, Invisibility, (Raise Zombie)	50% Resist Frost, 50% Weak to Fire, No Regen in Sunlight
Vampire Mistwalker		20	331	226	148	(1H Sword/1H Axe)	(Vampire Armor/Vampire Robes), Vampire Boots	Vampire Loot, (Gold)	Vampire Drain Life, Invisibility, Ice Spike, (Reanimate Corpse)	50% Resist Frost, 50% Weak to Fire, No Regen in Sunlight
Vampire Nightstalker		28	413	283	179	(1H Sword/1H Axe)	(Vampire Armor/Vampire Robes), Vampire Boots	Vampire Loot, (Gold)	Vampire Drain Life, Invisibility, Ice Spike, Lightning Bolt, (Reanimate Corpse)	50% Resist Frost, 50% Weak to Fire, No Regen in Sunlight
Ancient Vampire		38	583	348	224	(1H Sword/1H Axe)	(Vampire Armor/Vampire Robes), Vampire Boots	Vampire Loot, (Gold)	Vampire Drain Life, Invisibility, Ice Spike, Lightning Bolt, (Revenant)	50% Resist Frost, 50% Weak to Fire, No Regen in Sunlight
Volkihar Vampire		48	823	413	294	(1H Sword/1H Axe)	(Vampire Armor/Vampire Robes), Vampire Boots	Vampire Loot, (Gold)	Vampire Drain Life, Invisibility, Chain Lightning, Ice Storm, (Revenant)	50% Resist Frost, 50% Weak to Fire, No Regen in Sunlight
Nightlord Vampire		60	1031	486	318	(1H Sword/1H Axe)	(Vampire Armor/Vampire Robes), Vampire Boots	Vampire Loot, (Gold)	Vampire Drain Life, Invisibility, Chain Lightning, Thunderbolt, Ice Storm, Icy Spear, Revenant	50% Resist Frost, 50% Weak to Fire, No Regen in Sunlight

MASTER VAMPIRES

NAME	SUBTYPE	LV	HEALTH	MAGICKA	STAMINA	WEAPONS	ARMOR	ITEMS	SPELLS	NOTES
Vampire		1	35	75	50	(1H Sword/1H Axe)	(Vampire Armor/Vampire Robes), Vampire Boots	Vampire Loot, (Gold)	Vampire Drain Life, Invisibility	50% Resist Frost, 50% Weak to Fire, No Regen in Sunlight
Vampire		6	120	120	90	(1H Sword/1H Axe)	(Vampire Armor/Vampire Robes), Vampire Boots	Vampire Loot, (Gold)	Vampire Drain Life, Invisibility, (Raise Zombie)	50% Resist Frost, 50% Weak to Fire, No Regen in Sunlight
Master Vampire		14	252	177	126	(1H Sword/1H Axe)	(Vampire Armor/Vampire Robes), Vampire Boots	Vampire Loot, (Gold)	Vampire Drain Life, Invisibility, (Raise Zombie)	50% Resist Frost, 50% Weak to Fire, No Regen in Sunlight
Master Vampire		23	378	238	169	(1H Sword/1H Axe)	(Vampire Armor/Vampire Robes), Vampire Boots	Vampire Loot, (Gold)	Vampire Drain Life, Invisibility, Ice Spike, (Reanimate Corpse)	50% Resist Frost, 50% Weak to Fire, No Regen in Sunlight
Master Vampire		31	500	310	210	(1H Sword/1H Axe)	(Vampire Armor/Vampire Robes), Vampire Boots	Vampire Loot, (Gold)	Vampire Drain Life, Invisibility, Ice Spike, Lightning Bolt, (Reanimate Corpse)	50% Resist Frost, 50% Weak to Fire, No Regen in Sunlight
Master Vampire		42	669	414	257	(1H Sword/1H Axe)	(Vampire Armor/Vampire Robes), Vampire Boots	Vampire Loot, (Gold)	Vampire Drain Life, Invisibility, Ice Spike, Lightning Bolt, (Revenant)	50% Resist Frost, 50% Weak to Fire, No Regen in Sunlight
Volkihar Master Vampire		53	968	458	354	(1H Sword/1H Axe)	(Vampire Armor/Vampire Robes), Vampire Boots	Vampire Loot, (Gold)	Vampire Drain Life, Invisibility, Chain Lightning, Ice Storm, (Revenant)	50% Resist Frost, 50% Weak to Fire, No Regen in Sunlight
Nightmaster Vampire		65	1226	531	378	(1H Sword/1H Axe)	(Vampire Armor/Vampire Robes), Vampire Boots	Vampire Loot, (Gold)	Vampire Drain Life, Invisibility, Chain Lightning, Thunderbolt, Ice Storm, Icy Spear, Revenant	50% Resist Frost, 50% Weak to Fire, No Regen in Sunlight

CASTLE VOLKIHAR COURT VAMPIRES

NAME	SUBTYPE	LV	HEALTH	MAGICKA	STAMINA	WEAPONS	ARMOR	ITEMS	SPELLS	NOTES
Court Vampire	Mage	10*	131	104	50	(1H Sword/1H Axe/1H Mace)	Vampire Armor, Vampire Boots	Vampire Loot, (Gold)	Vampire Drain Life, Invisibility, (Flames/Frostbite/Sparks), (Firebolt/Ice Spike/Lightning Bolt), (Ice Storm/Fireball/Chain Lightning)	50% Resist Frost, 50% Weak to Fire, Immune to Poison, No Regen in Sunlight, Increased Unarmed Damage
Court Vampire	Warrior	10*	131	86	68	(1H Sword/1H Axe/1H Mace)	Vampire Armor, Vampire Boots	Vampire Loot, (Gold)	Vampire Drain Life, Invisibility	50% Resist Frost, 50% Weak to Fire, Immune to Poison, No Regen in Sunlight, Increased Unarmed Damage

LORD HARKON

NAME	SUBTYPE	LV	HEALTH	MAGICKA	STAMINA	WEAPONS	ARMOR	ITEMS	SPELLS	NOTES
Harkon	Human Form	10*	331	186	68	Harkon's Sword	Vampire Royal Armor, Vampire Boots	Necklace of Magic Suppression, Ring of Eminent Destruction, Vampire Dust, Potions, Jewelry, Black Soul Gem	Conjure Gargoyle, Drain Life, Invisibility, [Level-Dependent Spells]	50% Resist Frost, 50% Weak to Fire, No Regen in Sunlight
Harkon	Vampire Lord	10*	331	186	68	Harkon's Sword	Vampire Royal Armor, Vampire Boots, (Vampire Lord Cape)	Necklace of Magic Suppression, Ring of Eminent Destruction, Vampire Dust, Potions, Jewelry, Black Soul Gem	Conjure Gargoyle, Drain Life, Invisibility, [Level-Dependent Spells]	50% Resist Frost, 50% Weak to Fire, No Regen in Sunlight, Immune to Paralysis
Harkon	Vampire Lord (Boss)	10*	331	186	68	Harkon's Sword	Vampire Royal Armor, Vampire Boots, (Vampire Lord Cape)	Necklace of Magic Suppression, Ring of Eminent Destruction, Vampire Dust, Potions, Jewelry, Black Soul Gem	Shadow Shield, Swarm of Bats, Mistform, Conjure Gargoyle, Revenant, Reanimate Corpse, Raise Zombie, Vampiric Drain, Drain Life	50% Resist Frost, 50% Weak to Fire, No Regen in Sunlight, Immune to Paralysis
Harkon	Vampire Lord (Boss)	50*	691	346	148	Harkon's Sword	Vampire Royal Armor, Vampire Boots, (Vampire Lord Cape)	Necklace of Magic Suppression, Ring of Eminent Destruction, Vampire Dust, Potions, Jewelry, Black Soul Gem	Shadow Shield, Swarm of Bats, Mistform, Conjure Gargoyle, Revenant, Reanimate Corpse, Raise Zombie, Vampiric Drain, Drain Life	50% Resist Frost, 50% Weak to Fire, No Regen in Sunlight, Immune to Paralysis

Vigilants of Stendarr

The Vigilants of Stendarr are priests in the service of Stendarr, the Divine of Mercy. They will gladly lend their aid to a hero who fits their ideals of virtue. But werewolves, vampires, and daedra worshippers have reason to fear their wrath.

VIGILANTS OF STENDARR

NAME	SUBTYPE	LV	HEALTH	MAGICKA	STAMINA	WEAPONS	ARMOR	ITEMS	SPELLS	NOTES
Vigilant of Stendarr		5	90	57	63	Mace, Torch	Steel Boots, Steel Gauntlets, Mage Robes, Mage Hood, Amulet of Stendarr	Potions, Books	Healing, Oakflesh, Lesser Ward	
Vigilant of Stendarr		9	130	63	77	Mace, Torch	Steel Boots, Steel Gauntlets, Mage Robes, Mage Hood, Amulet of Stendarr	Potions, Books	Healing, Oakflesh, Lesser Ward	
Vigilant of Stendarr		14	180	72	93	Mace, Torch	Steel Boots, Steel Gauntlets, Mage Robes, Mage Hood, Amulet of Stendarr	Potions, Books	Healing, Oakflesh, Lesser Ward	
Vigilant of Stendarr		19	230	80	110	Mace, Torch	Steel Boots, Steel Gauntlets, Mage Robes, Mage Hood, Amulet of Stendarr	Potions, Books	Healing, Oakflesh, Lesser Ward	
Vigilant of Stendarr		25	290	90	130	Mace, Torch	Steel Boots, Steel Gauntlets, Mage Robes, Mage Hood, Amulet of Stendarr	Potions, Books	Healing, Oakflesh, Lesser Ward	

Vigilant of Stendarr

Warlocks

Warlocks is a catchall term for the mages, wizards, conjurers, and necromancers that you may face on your journey. Warlocks encountered as bosses have more magicka than their non-boss counterparts, and are more likely to carry a staff. Warlock Loot includes a chance of: soul gems, potions, recipes, and alchemy ingredients.

Storm Mage (Arch Electromancer)

Warlock (Arch Necromancer)

FIRE MAGES

NAME	SUBTYPE	LV	HEALTH	MAGICKA	STAMINA	WEAPONS	ARMOR	ITEMS	SPELLS	NOTES
Novice Fire Mage		1	50	100	25	Dagger, (Staff)	Mage Robes, Boots	(Warlock Loot)	Flames, Lesser Ward	
Apprentice Fire Mage		6	142	158	25	Dagger, (Staff)	Mage Robes, Boots	(Warlock Loot)	Firebolt, Flames, Healing, Oakflesh, Lesser Ward	
Fire Mage Adept		12	192	198	25	Dagger, (Staff)	Mage Robes, Boots	(Warlock Loot)	Fast Healing, Firebolt, Flames, Stoneflesh, Steadfast Ward	
Fire Mage		19	275	270	25	Dagger, (Staff)	Mage Robes, Boots	(Warlock Loot)	Fast Healing, Fireball, Firebolt, Flame Cloak, Stoneflesh, Steadfast Ward	
Fire Wizard		27	367	323	25	Dagger, (Staff)	Mage Robes, Boots	(Warlock Loot)	Close Wounds, Fast Healing, Fireball, Firebolt, Flame Cloak, Ironflesh, Steadfast Ward	
Pyromancer		36	467	383	25	Dagger, (Staff of Fireballs)	Mage Robes, Boots	(Warlock Loot)	Close Wounds, Fireball, Flame Cloak, Grand Healing, Incinerate, Ironflesh, Greater Ward	
Arch Pyromancer		46	575	500	50	Dagger, (Staff of Fireballs)	Mage Robes, Boots	(Warlock Loot)	Close Wounds, Fireball, Flame Cloak, Grand Healing, Incinerate, Ironflesh, Greater Ward	

ICE MAGES

NAME	SUBTYPE	LV	HEALTH	MAGICKA	STAMINA	WEAPONS	ARMOR	ITEMS	SPELLS	NOTES
Novice Ice Mage		1	50	100	25	Dagger, (Staff)	Mage Robes, Boots	(Warlock Loot)	Frostbite, Lesser Ward	
Apprentice Ice Mage		6	142	158	25	Dagger, (Staff)	Mage Robes, Boots	(Warlock Loot)	Frostbite, Healing, Ice Spike, Oakflesh, Lesser Ward	
Ice Mage Adept		12	192	198	25	Dagger, (Staff)	Mage Robes, Boots	(Warlock Loot)	Fast Healing, Frostbite, Ice Spike, Stoneflesh, Steadfast Ward	
Ice Mage		19	275	270	25	Dagger, (Staff)	Mage Robes, Boots	(Warlock Loot)	Fast Healing, Frost Cloak, Ice Spike, Ice Storm, Stoneflesh, Steadfast Ward	
Ice Wizard		27	367	323	25	Dagger, (Staff)	Mage Robes, Boots	(Warlock Loot)	Close Wounds, Fast Healing, Frost Cloak, Ice Spike, Ice Storm, Ironflesh, Steadfast Ward	
Cryomancer		36	467	383	25	Dagger, (Staff of Ice Storm)	Mage Robes, Boots	(Warlock Loot)	Close Wounds, Frost Cloak, Grand Healing, Ice Storm, Icy Spear, Ironflesh, Greater Ward	
Arch Cryomancer		46	575	500	50	Dagger, (Staff of Ice Storm)	Mage Robes, Boots	(Warlock Loot)	Close Wounds, Frost Cloak, Grand Healing, Ice Storm, Icy Spear, Ironflesh, Greater Ward	

STORM MAGES

NAME	SUBTYPE	LV	HEALTH	MAGICKA	STAMINA	WEAPONS	ARMOR	ITEMS	SPELLS	NOTES
Novice Storm Mage		1	50	100	25	Dagger, (Staff)	Mage Robes, Boots	(Warlock Loot)	Sparks, Lesser Ward	
Apprentice Storm Mage		6	142	158	25	Dagger, (Staff)	Mage Robes, Boots	(Warlock Loot)	Fast Healing, Lightning Bolt, Oakflesh, Sparks, Lesser Ward	
Storm Mage Adept		12	192	198	25	Dagger, (Staff)	Mage Robes, Boots	(Warlock Loot)	Fast Healing, Lightning Bolt, Sparks, Stoneflesh, Steadfast Ward	
Storm Mage		19	275	270	25	Dagger, (Staff)	Mage Robes, Boots	(Warlock Loot)	Chain Lightning, Fast Healing, Lightning Bolt, Lightning Cloak, Stoneflesh, Steadfast Ward	
Storm Wizard		27	367	323	25	Dagger, (Staff)	Mage Robes, Boots	(Warlock Loot)	Chain Lightning, Close Wounds, Fast Healing, Ironflesh, Lightning Bolt, Lightning Cloak, Steadfast Ward	
Electromancer		36	467	383	25	Dagger, (Staff of Chain Lightning)	Mage Robes, Boots	(Warlock Loot)	Chain Lightning, Close Wounds, Grand Healing, Ironflesh, Lightning Cloak, Thunderbolt, Greater Ward	
Arch Electromancer		46	575	500	50	Dagger, (Staff of Chain Lightning)	Mage Robes, Boots	(Warlock Loot)	Chain Lightning, Close Wounds, Grand Healing, Ironflesh, Lightning Cloak, Thunderbolt, Greater Ward	

CONJURERS

NAME	SUBTYPE	LV	HEALTH	MAGICKA	STAMINA	WEAPONS	ARMOR	ITEMS	SPELLS	NOTES
Novice Conjurer		1	50	100	25	Dagger, (Staff)	Mage Robes, Boots	(Warlock Loot)	Conjure Familiar, Flames, Oakflesh, Lesser Ward	
Apprentice Conjurer		6	142	158	25	Dagger, (Staff)	Mage Robes, Boots	(Warlock Loot)	Conjure Flame Atronach, Fast Healing, Flames, Oakflesh, Lesser Ward	
Conjurer Adept		12	192	198	25	Dagger, (Staff)	Mage Robes, Boots	(Warlock Loot)	Conjure Flame Atronach, Fast Healing, Firebolt, Flames, Stoneflesh, Steadfast Ward	
Conjurer		19	275	270	25	Dagger, (Staff)	Mage Robes, Boots	(Warlock Loot)	Banish Daedra, Close Wounds, Conjure Frost Atronach, Fast Healing, Frostbite, Ice Spike, Stoneflesh, Steadfast Ward	
Ascendant Conjurer		27	367	323	25	Dagger, (Staff)	Mage Robes, Boots	(Warlock Loot)	Close Wounds, Command Daedra, Conjure Storm Atronach, Expel Daedra, Fast Healing, Ice Spike, Ice Storm, Stoneflesh, Steadfast Ward	
Master Conjurer		36	467	383	25	Dagger, (Staff)	Mage Robes, Boots	(Warlock Loot)	Chain Lightning, Close Wounds, Command Daedra, Conjure Storm Atronach, Expel Daedra, Ironflesh, Thunderbolt, Greater Ward	
Arch Conjurer		46	575	500	50	Dagger, (Staff)	Mage Robes, Boots	(Warlock Loot)	Chain Lightning, Close Wounds, Command Daedra, Conjure Storm Atronach, Expel Daedra, Ironflesh, Thunderbolt, Greater Ward	

NECROMANCERS										
NAME	SUBTYPE	LV	HEALTH	MAGICKA	STAMINA	WEAPONS	ARMOR	ITEMS	SPELLS	NOTES
Novice Necromancer		1	50	100	25	Dagger	Necromancer Robes, Necromancer Boots	(Warlock Loot)	Frostbite, Raise Zombie, Lesser Ward	
Apprentice Necromaner		6	142	158	25	Dagger, (Soul Gems)	Necromancer Robes, Necromancer Boots	(Warlock Loot)	Fast Healing, Frostbite, Ice Spike, Oakflesh, Raise Zombie, Lesser Ward	
Necromancer Adept		12	192	198	25	Dagger, (Soul Gems)	Necromancer Robes, Necromancer Boots	(Warlock Loot)	Fast Healing, Frostbite, Ice Spike, Reanimate Corpse, Stoneflesh, Steadfast Ward	
Necromage		19	275	270	25	Dagger, (Soul Gems)	Necromancer Robes, Necromancer Boots	(Warlock Loot)	Fast Healing, Ice Spike, Reanimate Corpse, Revenant, Stoneflesh, Turn Undead, Steadfast Ward	
Ascendant Necromancer		27	367	323	25	Dagger, (Soul Gems)	Necromancer Robes, Necromancer Boots	(Warlock Loot)	Close Wounds, Dread Zombie, Fast Healing, Ice Spike, Ice Storm, Ironflesh, Revenant, Turn Undead, Steadfast Ward	
Master Necromancer		36	467	383	25	Dagger, (Staff), (Soul Gems)	Necromancer Robes, Necromancer Boots	(Warlock Loot)	Close Wounds, Dread Zombie, Grand Healing, Ice Spike, Ice Storm, Ironflesh, Revenant, Turn Greater Undead, Greater Ward	
Arch Necromancer		46	575	500	50	Dagger, (Staff), (Soul Gems)	Necromancer Robes, Necromancer Boots	(Warlock Loot)	Close Wounds, Dread Zombie, Grand Healing, Ice Spike, Ice Storm, Ironflesh, Revenant, Turn Greater Undead, Greater Ward	

Werebears

Among the most fearsome of lycanthropes, Werebears are tough and vicious predators who have sacrificed almost all of their humanity. If possible, kill them before they have a chance to transform, as their health and resistances are far stronger once in beast form. Fighting a transformed Werebear in melee can be difficult– they move quickly, hit hard, and can endure a huge amount of damage before they fall. But like Werewolves, they lack a ranged attack, so archery and spells are effective against them if you can keep your distance. Werebear loot includes a small chance of: Gold, Ingredients, Gems, or Jewelry.

Werebear (Beast Form)

Werebear (Human)

WEREBEARS										
NAME	SUBTYPE	LV	HEALTH	MAGICKA	STAMINA	WEAPONS	ARMOR	ITEMS	SPELLS	NOTES
Werebear	Human	17	241	25	134		Ragged Trousers	Food, Ingredients		
Werebear	Beast Form	25	740	0	370	42 Dmg		Bear Pelt, Bear Claws, (Werebear Loot)		Immune to Paralysis, Immune to Disease, Resist Frost 75%, Resist Poison 50%
Werebear	Conjured	25	740	0	370	42 Dmg				Immune to Paralysis, Immune to Disease, Resist Frost 75%, Resist Poison 50%

Werewolves

Werewolves have always held a place in Skyrim's darker legends and tales. Despite their bulk, these hulking beasts move quickly and have fast, powerful melee attacks, but they lack any kind of ranged attack. Should you find yourself facing a werewolf, take advantage of this by keeping your distance, using obstacles and cover to your advantage, and attacking with ranged weapons and spells. Minor Treasure includes a tiny chance of a few gold, a gem, or a ring.

Werewolf Vargr

WEREWOLVES										
NAME	SUBTYPE	LV	HEALTH	MAGICKA	STAMINA	WEAPONS	ARMOR	ITEMS	SPELLS	NOTES
Werewolf		1	150	0	200	20 Dmg		Wolf Pelt, Human Flesh, (Clothes), (Minor Treasure)		Immune to Disease, Immune to Paralysis, No Health Regen
Werewolf Savage		6	200	0	225	25 Dmg		Wolf Pelt, Human Flesh, (Clothes), (Minor Treasure)		Immune to Disease, Immune to Paralysis, No Health Regen
Werewolf Brute		12	260	0	255	30 Dmg		Wolf Pelt, Human Flesh, (Clothes), (Minor Treasure)		Immune to Disease, Immune to Paralysis, No Health Regen
Werewolf Skinwalker		20	340	0	295	35 Dmg		Wolf Pelt, Human Flesh, (Clothes), (Minor Treasure)		Immune to Disease, Immune to Paralysis, No Health Regen
Werewolf Beastmaster		28	420	0	335	40 Dmg		Wolf Pelt, Human Flesh, (Clothes), (Minor Treasure)		Immune to Disease, Immune to Paralysis, No Health Regen
Werewolf Vargr		38	520	0	385	45 Dmg		Wolf Pelt, Human Flesh, (Clothes), (Minor Treasure)		Immune to Disease, Immune to Paralysis, No Health Regen
Pack Member	Conjured	12	210	0	185	30 Dmg				Immune to Disease, Immune to Paralysis, No Health Regen

Wisps

Wispmothers are always found with a group of Wisps (typically 3). While the Wisps live, each grants the Wispmother a bonus to her Health, Magicka, or Stamina. Make sure to kill the Wisps before attacking the Wispmother directly; she is much weaker without them. When her health is low, the Wispmother will conjure two illusory Shades as a distraction.

Wisp (Wispmother)

WISPS

NAME	SUBTYPE	LV	HEALTH	MAGICKA	STAMINA	WEAPONS	ARMOR	ITEMS	SPELLS	NOTES
Wisp		1	50	50	50				Energy Sap	Waterwalking
Shade		5	36	224	50				Frostbite	Waterwalking
Wispmother		28	600	300	50			Glowdust, Wisp Wrappings	Ice Volley, Conjure Shades	Speed Burst, Regeneration, Waterwalking

Witches

Witches are female sorcerers training to become Hagravens, and often serve under them.

Witch

WITCHES

NAME	SUBTYPE	LV	HEALTH	MAGICKA	STAMINA	WEAPONS	ARMOR	ITEMS	SPELLS	NOTES
Witch	Fire	4	75	70	25	Dagger	Mage Robes, Boots		Firebolt, Flames, Oakflesh, Lesser Ward	
Witch	Frost	4	75	70	25	Dagger	Mage Robes, Boots		Frostbite, Ice Spike, Oakflesh, Lesser Ward	
Witch	Shock	4	75	70	25	Dagger	Mage Robes, Boots		Lightning Bolt, Sparks, Oakflesh, Lesser Ward	
Hag	Fire	8	109	96	25	Dagger	Mage Robes, Boots		Flames, Firebolt, Stoneflesh, Steadfast Ward	
Hag	Frost	8	109	96	25	Dagger	Mage Robes, Boots		Frostbite, Ice Spike, Stoneflesh, Steadfast Ward	
Hag	Shock	8	109	96	25	Dagger	Mage Robes, Boots		Lightning Bolt, Sparks, Stoneflesh, Steadfast Ward	

QUESTS

MAIN QUEST

OVERVIEW

The Main Quest begins the moment you start your adventure. Over the course of three acts, these quests involve some of the most important and wide-ranging events in Skyrim. Once you escape the town of Helgen, you are free to continue or ignore the Main Quest whenever you wish. However, it is recommended that you complete most of the first act sooner rather than later, as you're rewarded with several important powers (including Shouts) that can make your other adventures less fraught and more entertaining. Remember that you can completely finish the Main Quest and then return to tackle any other quests (or just explore) without penalty.

NOTE **Cross-Referencing:** Do you want to see maps and learn more about the traps, non-quest-related items, collectibles, crafting areas, and other important rooms of note in every location during these quests? Then cross-reference the location you travel to with the information on that location contained in this guide's Atlas.

NOTE The main quest also involves a number of Skyrim's other factions. For more information, consult their Quest listings. For information on Hadvar, Ralof, General Tullius, and Ulfric Stormcloak, consult the Civil War Quest Introduction.

AVAILABLE QUESTS

There are a total of 20 different Main Quests in three acts. Each quest leads directly into the next, as shown in the following table:

✓	QUEST NAME	PREREQUISITES
	ACT I	
☐	Main Quest: Unbound	None
☐	Main Quest: Before the Storm	Complete Main Quest: Unbound
☐	Main Quest: Bleak Falls Barrow	Complete Main Quest: Before the Storm
☐	Main Quest: Dragon Rising	Complete Main Quest: Bleak Falls Barrow
☐	Main Quest: The Way of the Voice	Complete Main Quest: Dragon Rising
☐	Main Quest: The Horn of Jurgen Windcaller	Complete Main Quest: The Way of the Voice
☐	Main Quest: A Blade in the Dark	Complete Main Quest: The Horn of Jurgen Windcaller

✓	QUEST NAME	PREREQUISITES
	ACT II	
☐	Main Quest: Diplomatic Immunity	Complete Main Quest: A Blade in the Dark
☐	Main Quest: A Cornered Rat	Complete Main Quest: Diplomatic Immunity
☐	Main Quest: Alduin's Wall	Complete Main Quest: A Cornered Rat
☐	Main Quest: The Throat of the World	Complete Main Quest: Alduin's Wall
☐	Main Quest: Elder Knowledge	Complete Main Quest: The Throat of the World
☐	Main Quest: Alduin's Bane	Complete Main Quest: Elder Knowledge

✓	QUEST NAME	PREREQUISITES
	ACT III	
☐	Main Quest: The Fallen	Complete Main Quest: Alduin's Bane
☐	Main Quest: Paarthurnax†	Complete Main Quest: Alduin's Bane
☐	Main Quest: Season Unending‡	Complete Main Quest: Alduin's Bane
☐	Main Quest: The World-Eater's Eyrie	Complete Main Quest: The Fallen
☐	Main Quest: Sovngarde	Complete Main Quest: The World-Eater's Eyrie
☐	Main Quest: Dragonslayer	Complete Main Quest: Sovngarde
☐	Main Quest: Epilogue	Complete Main Quest: Dragonslayer

NOTE † This quest is optional and can be completed at any point after Alduin's Bane, even after the Main Quest is over.

‡ This quest occurs only if the Civil War still rages across Skyrim. See its description for more details.

The Greybeards and the Blades have their own Faction Radiant Quests. Consult the section marked "Other Factions: Quests" on page 408 for more information.

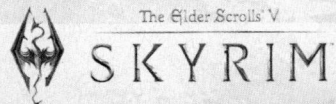

UNBOUND

INTERSECTING QUESTS: Main Quest: Before the Storm

LOCATIONS: Helgen

CHARACTERS: Alduin, Elenwen, General Tullius, Gunjar, Gunnar, Hadvar, Haming, Imperial Captain, Imperial Soldier, Ingrid, Lokir, Matlara, Priestess of Arkay, Ralof, Stormcloak Soldier, Thalmor Soldier, Torolf, Torturer, Torturer's Assistant, Ulfric Stormcloak, Vilod

ENEMIES: Cave Bear, Frostbite Spider, Imperial Soldier, Stormcloak Soldier, Torturer, Torturer's Assistant

◊ **OBJECTIVES:** Make your way to the Keep, Enter the Keep with Hadvar or Ralof, Escape Helgen, Find some equipment, Loot Gunjar's body, (Optional) Search the barrel for potions, (Optional) Attempt to pick the lock to the cage

Bound for the Block

The clattering of hooves against cobblestone and the sway of the prison cart wakes you. Ralof, a Stormcloak rebel, wastes no time in talking to you. You're joined on this condemned wagon by a horse rustler named Lokir who hails from a town called Rorikstead and a large, imposing man who is bound and gagged. After Lokir addresses the man without proper respect, Ralof tells him to watch his tongue: he's speaking to Ulfric Stormcloak, the true High King of Skyrim and leader of the Stormcloak Rebellion against the Empire!

The convoy continues toward the gates of Helgen, a fortified hamlet in Falkreath Hold. You pass by General Tullius, leader of the Imperial forces in Skyrim, and his Thalmor advisors. Ralof looks around the settlement, remembering his youthful indiscretions. You pass a boy named Haming, who wants to watch the soldiers parading in his town. His father quickly herds him back indoors. The wagon stops. This is the end of the line. The prisoners disembark, and their names are recorded. Lokir attempts to flee but is cut down by Imperial archers. An Imperial Soldier named Hadvar beckons you forward and asks for your name.

> **NOTE** At this point, you should create the precise character you wish to adventure as. You need only choose your character's race, gender, and distinguishing features (from the size of your nose to the scars on your face). The only choice that affects your adventure is your race, as each race has specific strengths and powers. Consult the Training section of this guide on page 6 for more insight. For the purposes of this guide, a Male Nord named Dovahkiin was created.

Hadvar turns to his superior and asks her what to do with you, as you're not on the list of captured rebels. The Imperial Captain tells Hadvar to ignore the list; you're going to the block. You step forward, where General Tullius has a rather one-sided discussion with Ulfric Stormcloak, interrupted only by a strange guttural sound in the distance. A Priestess of Arkay attempts to bless the rebels before they're put to death, mentioning the "Eight Divines" (Thalmor law prohibits the worship of the Nordic god Talos, Tiber Septim; this infuriates the Stormcloaks). After the headsman swings his axe, the first rebel is beheaded, and you're summoned to the block just as another bellow echoes through the mountains. Resting your head on the block, the headsman raises his axe...and a gigantic black creature arcs through the skies, landing heavily on Helgen's central tower and unleashing a Thu'um (or Shout) that scatters everyone, both rebel and Imperial alike!

◊ **OBJECTIVE:** Make your way to the Keep

The World-Eater Returns

Amid the chaos, Ralof yells for you to follow him. Oblige him (as you're still bound, and dashing about in a panic doesn't further your cause). Follow Ralof as he reconvenes with Ulfric Stormcloak inside the Keep and beckons you to follow him up the steps. As you reach the Keep's second landing, a section of exterior wall comes crashing down, and the black dragon roasts the area with fire before flying out of view. Ralof tells you to leap across to the ruins of the town's inn. Jump across, landing in the upstairs area, then head down to ground level.

The streets are filled with fire, wreckage, and panicked citizens. Hadvar is removing the boy Haming from danger, before recommending you follow him to (relative) safety. Shadow Hadvar as you both weave through the ruins of Helgen, briefly pausing to watch hapless Imperial forces trying to bring down the dragon. You can't help or search corpses, as your hands are still tied. Eventually, Hadvar brings you to the main Keep, where you both run into Ralof. After a short but tense standoff, they run to separate doors of the Keep and shout for you to head inside with them.

◊ **OBJECTIVE:** Enter the Keep with Hadvar or Ralof

> **NOTE** This quest splits into two parallel paths at this point. The general route out of Helgen through the Keep is the same, but your allies and enemies will be different. The person you join with here affects who you journey with in the next quest and sets you up with an alliance for the Civil War Quests to come. However, you can still switch sides after this quest, so it doesn't matter who you escape with.

◊ **OBJECTIVE:** Escape Helgen

Battle Through the Keep

Path A: Helping Hadvar

Follow Hadvar into Helgen's Keep, where he removes your bindings and recommends you search the barracks for any weapons and items you can find. Step over to the Warden's Chest, which has what you need.

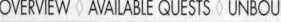

◊ OBJECTIVE: Find some equipment

- ➤ Imperial Light Armor
- ➤ Imperial Light Boots
- ➤ Iron Sword
- ➤ Helgen Keep Key

After searching the room (there's a weapon on the weapon rack by the wall and more items in one of the other chests), Hadvar opens the wooden grating, allowing you to continue down a corridor to a second pull chain and grating. Equip your new weapons and armor, and then slaughter the Stormcloak Soldiers in the room beyond. When they are both dead, you can ransack their bodies for items and different equipment. Unlock the gate to the west and proceed.

Path B: Rendezvous with Ralof

Follow Ralof into Helgen's Keep, where he encounters the remains of his comrade, Gunjar. After wishing him a quick journey to Sovngarde, he cuts your bonds and instructs you to take Gunjar's gear.

◊ OBJECTIVE: Loot Gunjar's body

- ➤ Iron War Axe
- ➤ Stormcloak Cuirass
- ➤ Fur Boots

After inspecting both exits (which are locked), Ralof notices some incoming Imperials and crouches down ready to ambush them. Equip your new weapons and armor, and then slaughter the Imperial Captain and Soldier. When they are both dead, you can ransack their corpses for items and different equipment. You'll find the Helgen Keep Key on the Captain's body. Unlock the gate to the west and proceed.

- ➤ Helgen Keep Key

> **TIP** **Character Development:** During either Path A or Path B, you should be learning all of the following:
>
> How to loot corpses, learning what to take and leave behind and seeing which items give you the best stat increases. The small triangle next to items in your inventory signifies that they are better than the ones you currently have equipped.
>
> How to equip weapons and armor, as well as any spells or powers you may have because of your race.
>
> What it feels like to wield a weapon, a spell, a weapon and shield, or two weapons. Or, take the two-handed weapon one of your enemies was carrying and use it. These help to increase different skills, which you can start doing right now!
>
> How to ready and sheathe your weapon(s), perform regular and power attacks, and block (either with a weapon or a shield).
>
> You can set your Favorites to a combination of weapons and powers that you enjoy, and then a second set to switch between.
>
> You can switch between first- and third-person views to see which you prefer.

Merged Path: Helgen Escape

Follow your ally through the gate and down the steps. The dragon causes the roof to collapse, forcing you left and into a storage room. Two enemies (of the opposing faction) are in this chamber. Bring them both down, helping your ally as much or as little as you wish. He recommends you look around the room for potions; you'll need them!

◊ OBJECTIVE: (Optional) Search the barrel for potions

You can search for whatever you wish. However, simply look in the barrel indicated, collect the potions, and meet up again with your ally.

- ➤ Potions

Head back out into the main corridor (on the other side of the roof collapse), and follow your friend down into the torture chamber. The Torturer and his assistant (both Imperials) are fighting Stormcloaks in here. After the commotion is over, grab the items from the knapsack on the table, read or take the *Book of the Dragonborn*, and steal a dagger and any other weapons from the chamber. Your ally notices that one of the torturer's cages houses the corpse of a mage and suggests you pry open the lock. You're given lockpicks for this purpose. Open the lock (Novice), and take the mage's clothing and your first Spell Tome. Then head out of the chamber.

- ➤ The Book of the Dragonborn
- ➤ Novice Hood
- ➤ Lockpick (12)
- ➤ Novice Robes
- ➤ Loose gear
- ➤ Spell Tome: Sparks

> **TIP** **Character Development:** At this point, you should be:
>
> Swapping, dropping, and equipping weapons that you find interesting.
>
> Opening the two other cells to further improve your Lockpicking skill.
>
> Reading both books and learning the Sparks spell from the Tome. Now equip this spell in one of your hands if you want to try it out.
>
> Donning the mage's Novice Hood and Robes if their enchantment suits you better than your previous outfit.

Wind your way past the prison cells and down the steps, and be ready to combat enemies in the two-level lower dungeon. You can leave your ally to soak up most of the damage or wade in yourself. There are some particular methods of tackling the foes in here:

The terrain is narrow, meaning movement is restricted. So watch your step, as well as the foes armed with bows.

Quickly take down a foe and grab a bow and some arrows. Use those on the enemy, ideally from range and the upper level.

If you have a fire-based spell (because of your race), you can set fire to the pool of oil on the opposite side, burning some foes.

Or you can use Sparks and weaken enemies with electrical damage from a distance.

Follow your ally out of the lower dungeon to a bridge that he lowers using the lever (or you can do this if you're impatient). After crossing the bridge, a giant slab of stone crushes the structure, stopping you from backtracking. However, you can drop through the wreckage and follow the path down the rushing subterranean stream. Follow the flow of water past a skeleton (take its coin purse) and down into a cobweb-filled cave. It is here that you're set upon by around six Frostbite Spiders. Use ranged attacks to weaken them, followed by melee strikes to finish them; this is the best way to battle them.

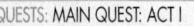

Leave your ally to attack his own arachnids, or team up and make quick work of them.

After crossing a small natural bridge, your ally crouches and indicates the presence of a bear just ahead. He suggests two ways to get past her: sneaking so as not to disturb her, or hitting her with an arrow from the bow he gives you. The choice is yours. You can:

Crouch (which means you're sneaking) and quietly head left (southeast) down the cave into a tunnel, avoiding the bear completely.

Equip the bow (you may wish to have already set up a melee weapon or weapon and spell in your Favorites to quickly swap to), fire up to three shots before she reaches you, and then finish her off with your ally's help.

Use the weapons or spells you prefer to take down the bear. You may want to invoke your racial power in this fight, if it helps. Wood Elves, in particular, can use Command Animal to simply turn the bear into an ally and walk right by.

Or simply sprint past the bear and down the tunnel as quickly as possible.

➤ **Long Bow** ➤ **Iron Arrow (12)**

Quest Conclusion

After the bear encounter, the cave narrows to a winding tunnel, with light streaming from the far end. This is the way out! Main Quest: Before the Storm begins immediately.

BEFORE THE STORM

PREREQUISITES: Character Generation, Complete Main Quest: Unbound

INTERSECTING QUESTS: Main Quest: Unbound, Main Quest: Bleak Falls Barrow, Side Quest: The Golden Claw

LOCATIONS:, Helgen, Riverwood, Alvor and Sigrid's House, Hod and Gerdur's House, Whiterun, Dragonsreach

CHARACTERS: Alvor, Dorthe, Frodnar, Gerdur, Hadvar, Hilde, Hod, Irileth, Jarl Balgruuf the Greater of Whiterun, Proventus Avenicci, Ralof, Sigrid, Sven

ENEMIES: Rabbit, Wolf

◊ **OBJECTIVES:** Talk to Alvor in Riverwood, Talk to Gerdur in Riverwood, Talk to the Jarl of Whiterun

◊ **OBJECTIVE:** Talk to Alvor in Riverwood

◊ **OBJECTIVE:** Talk to Gerdur in Riverwood
♦ **TARGET:** Your friend's contact, in the town of Riverwood

A Wander Down to Riverwood

You emerge into the bright light of Falkreath Hold, north of the still-shouldering ruin of Helgen. You and your companion watch as the dragon responsible for disrupting your execution flies away to the north.

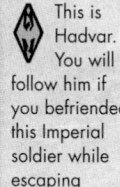

This is Hadvar. You will follow him if you befriended this Imperial soldier while escaping Helgen.

This is Ralof. You will follow him if you befriended this Stormcloak operative while escaping Helgen.

Speak to him so the objective updates. At this point, you can:

◊ Follow him down the hillside, which is advisable if you want to complete this quest.

◊ Head off alone, ignoring him: To continue this quest, simply meet up with Hadvar's or Ralof's contact in Riverwood, or journey to Whiterun and speak to the Jarl there.

Civil War: The lands of Skyrim are engaged in a fierce Civil War between the Imperials and Stormcloaks. In fact, if you decide to begin the long and bloody routing of the faction you oppose, consult the Civil War Quests elsewhere in this guide. The Civil War can affect some of the Main Quest after this quest, but only if you've made decisions during the Civil War Quests. Such variations are flagged throughout the Main Quest. If applicable, they give you ample time to side with your Faction if you wish.

Follow your friend down the hillside. He points out the ominous ruins on the river's opposite side: Bleak Falls Barrow. Continue to the edge of the White River, which flows from Lake Ilinalta to the west. Your friend is talking about the current situation regarding your chosen Faction when a couple of wolves interrupt him. Join in the attack, or watch your friend defeat them. Then follow the path along the riverbank and into Riverwood, which is on the edge of Whiterun Hold.

TIP **Roaming Around:** Investigate any nearby Primary Locations on your way to Riverwood. Either before or after you reach Riverwood, be sure to inspect the Guardian Stones and perhaps fight off a few bandits inside Embershard Mine. You can also spot salmon leaping the rapids, try the bow and shoot a rabbit or two, and pick any wildflowers or other ingredients growing nearby. Consult the guide's Atlas Chapter (beginning on page 685) to see every nearby location, and what each contains.

NOTE **Compass:** Nearby Primary Locations are black on your compass. After you discover them, they change to white. Once you "clear" them, this is flagged on your world map. Remember that "cleared" doesn't mean "ransacked"; you can leave the treasures inside a dungeon, and your map will still mark it as cleared.

Imperials: Alvor and Sigrid

Enter Riverwood, where Hadvar beckons you to meet his uncle. Head to the blacksmith's, where Uncle Alvor is hammering away in his forge. He seems confused and troubled by his nephew's appearance and is convinced to head inside his house to talk. Sigrid (Alvor's wife) will prepare some vittles; it looks like you could use some sustenance.

Head inside Alvor and Sigrid's House. Hadvar tells of his assignment to General Tullius's guard and the dragon attack in Helgen. Alvor accuses Hadvar of being drunk, saying the dragons were wiped out long ago. Hadvar finishes the story, telling Alvor that he owes his life to you. Hadvar wishes to leave for Solitude, but you both need food and a place to stay. Alvor offers you a gift, while his daughter Dorthe watches silently. You can take any or all of the items offered. Then Alvor turns to you: Riverwood needs your help. Jarl Balgruuf of Whiterun needs to know if there's a dragon on the loose, as Riverwood is defenseless against it. Soldiers must be sent here. Your Quest Objective updates, along with your map, and you can ask Alvor, Sigrid, or anyone else further questions before you leave.

➤ **Gift**

Stormcloaks: Gerdur and Hod

Enter Riverood, where Ralof walks around the left (northern) side of the Blacksmith's to meet his sister. Sven and his mother, Hilde, can be heard arguing about the dragon she saw. Ralof shouts a greeting to his sister Gerdur, who is delighted to see him. She seems concerned, especially after learning that Ulfric Stormcloak had been captured. She is convinced to move to a quieter area away from eavesdroppers. She yells for her husband, Hod.

By the river, Hod and Gerdur (and later, Gerdur's son Frodnar) listens to Ralof as he recalls the ambush by the Imperials outside Darkwater Crossing. It was as if they knew the Stormcloaks were there. After narrowly escaping the headsman's block, and after a mistrial for Ulfric, a dragon appeared over Helgen and inadvertently saved them! Now you both need food and a place to say. Gerdur offers you a key to her home, and a gift. Then she tells you that Riverwood is defenseless, and Jarl Balgruuf of Whiterun needs to know if there's a dragon on the loose. While Ralof and his relatives head back to Gerdur's home, you can follow them or set off. Your Quest Objective updates, along with your map. You may also ask Gerdur, Hod, or anyone else further questions before you leave.

➤ **Key to Gerdur's House** ➤ **Gift**

TIP Although you may choose one gift, it is advisable to take everything: The items you don't need you can sell at the Riverwood Trader across the thoroughfare. At the very least, take the Potions of Minor Healing; they are most useful.

NOTE **Talk Is Cheap:** You are encouraged to speak to any of the townsfolk. Some have problems or tasks you can solve (known as Favors). Some offer a background to this realm. A few may embroil you in local politics. Others won't even give you the time of day. All of these conversations are optional.

Sleep Is Cheaper: You are fortunate that your friend's relatives have a place in Riverwood that you can return to. Sleep in a bed to refresh you, until you find other accommodation. Fast-Travel back to Riverwood to relieve your fatigue, aches, and pains.

Crafting Makes You Money: Alvor has a forge and other blacksmithing tools. Or try out the Alchemy Lab in the Sleeping Giant Inn just up the road.

Quest Objectives: The Quest menu lists the active quests and the related objectives, and it keeps track of miscellaneous objectives, or more minor tasks you can optionally try. To prevent confusion, use the Toggle Active feature in the Quest menu, and select only the quests you're interested in. Also, you can click over to the Objectives submenu and use the Show on Map feature so you know exactly where you're going.

Intersecting Quest: These are quests that take place in the main location you're currently in or will be visiting. We list them in this guide so you don't have to backtrack much. In this particular case, Side Quest: The Golden Claw is available if you visit the Riverwood Trader and speak to Lucan or Camilla Valerius. You can do this before or after the start of the next Main Quest: Bleak Falls Barrow.

The Fortress-City of Whiterun

◊ **OBJECTIVE:** Talk to the Jarl of Whiterun
♦ **TARGET:** Jarl Balgruuf, inside Dragonsreach, in Whiterun

You must now make your way to Whiterun, the capital to the north. The optimal route is to cross the bridge as you exit Riverwood, follow the path with the waterfall rapids to your right (east), and begin a hill descent. You may have a World Encounter on the way down. Take the left (west) path at the two bridges, on the opposite side of the stream to Chillfurrow Farm, and pass the Honningbrew Meadery. You may hear the sounds of combat coming from the outskirts of Pelagia Farm; a giant has lumbered into this area, and a group of fighters called The Companions is fighting it.

NOTE You can help the fighters out and begin The Companions Quests if you wish.

Make your way past the Whiterun Stables and then up the hill, over the drawbridge, and to the main Whiterun gate. As you approach, a guard stops you; the city is closed with the news of the dragons spreading faster than you can travel. You can:

◊ Tell the guard that Riverwood calls for the Jarl's aid. This is the optimal plan, and only available with this quest active.

◊ (Persuade) Or you can tell the guard you have news from Helgen about the dragon attack.

◊ (Bribe) Or bribe the guard with a portion of your collected gold.

◊ (Intimidate) Or order the guard to stand aside.

Once you're inside the walls of Whiterun, there is much to do and see. Don't worry about roaming this city, entering buildings, and interacting with the locals. But once you decide to complete this quest, head north, up to the hilltop that the city sits on, past the Gildergreen Tree (part of the Kynareth Temple), and the Shrine to Talos. Climb the stone steps to discover Dragonsreach, home of the Jarl.

Walk toward the huge central fire on either side of the banquet tables. The inhabitants of Dragonsreach are a little on edge. As you step forward, you are met by Irileth, Jarl Balgruuf's Housecarl. Explain to her that you're here to see the Jarl; you can be as forthright or secretive with the information, depending on how annoyed you wish Irileth to be. After a stare-down, the Jarl requests your presence. Speak to him about the dragon that destroyed Helgen.

Begin to tell the Jarl your tale; your responses result in the same course of action (assuming you don't go mad and launch into an attack inside Dragonsreach):

If you mention Alvor, Jarl Balgruuf notes that he's a reliable, solid fellow and not prone to flights of fancy.

If you mention Gerdur, Jarl Balgruuf says that she's a pillar of the community and not prone to flights of fancy.

This gives more credence to your story. You can give the Jarl as many personal details as you wish in the course of his questioning and your story. After a discussion in which Irileth wisely asks for troops to be sent to Riverwood immediately, Proventus Avenicci (the Jarl's steward) warns that the Jarl of Falkreath may see this as provocation.

CAUTION

The Jarl of Whiterun and his court can be attacked but not killed. It is unwise to shed their blood, as you're likely to be overwhelmed. If you employ violence, accidental or otherwise, return here after three 3 (or more) days to recommence talks.

Quest Conclusion

After Avenicci slinks off to tend to other duties, Jarl Balgruuf thanks you for your initiative and gives you a small token of his esteem, based on whichever Armor Skill (Light or Heavy) is higher.

➤ **Leveled Armor**

Postquest Activities

Main Quest: Bleak Falls Barrow begins immediately.

BLEAK FALLS BARROW

PREREQUISITES: Complete Main Quest: Before the Storm

INTERSECTING QUESTS: Main Quest: Before the Storm, Main Quest: Dragon Rising, Side Quest: The Golden Claw

LOCATIONS: Bleak Falls Barrow, Bleak Falls Temple, Bleak Falls Sanctum, Riverwood, Sleeping Giant Inn, Whiterun, Dragonsreach

CHARACTERS: Camilla Valerius, Delphine, Farengar Secret-Fire, Jarl Balgruuf the Greater of Whiterun, Lucan Valerius

ENEMIES: Arvel the Swift, Bandits, Draugr, Frostbite Spider, Frost Troll, Skeever

◊ **OBJECTIVES:** Talk to Farengar , Retrieve the Dragonstone, Deliver the Dragonstone to Farengar

Reliable Sources

◊ **OBJECTIVE:** Talk to Farengar

At the end of your conversation with Jarl Balgruuf the Greater, he asks you to consult with his court wizard, Farengar Secret-Fire. Follow the Jarl into Farengar's study, where the Jarl introduces you. Farengar has a job for you almost immediately: to delve into a dangerous ruin in search of an ancient stone tablet. Ask for further information, and Farengar explains you're to look for something called a "Dragonstone," a tablet said to contain a map of the dragon burial sites across Skyrim. Farengar believes the stone is interred in the main chamber of Bleak Falls Barrow, and he has "reliable sources" that have confirmed as much. Before you leave, you can speak to Farengar about a variety of topics to gain a deeper understanding of his role in the Jarl's court.

NOTE If you've already explored Bleak Falls Barrow and found the Dragonstone, you can simply inform Farengar and hand it over, shortening this quest considerably. Skip to the "Quest Conclusion" section for your next actions.

◊ **OBJECTIVE:** Retrieve the Dragonstone

♦ **TARGET:** Dragonstone, on Draugr Lord, inside Bleak Falls Barrow

NOTE **Traveling Options:** At this point, you have three possible options to reach Riverwood, which is the closest place to Bleak Falls Barrow that you've already visited. You can:

◊ Trek there on foot. This takes longer, but you receive more experience from any encounters along the way.

◊ Head down to the Whiterun Stables and purchase a horse. This is faster, and occurs in "real time," but horses are pricey.

◊ Or bring up your world map and Fast-Travel back to Riverwood. The last option avoids combat but also any encounters.

Taking a carriage from Whiterun Stables is not an option, as these trips only take you to Hold Capitals.

TIP **Intersecting Quest:** Bleak Falls Barrow is the main location for Side Quest: The Golden Claw. You actually begin this quest, too, once you enter the Barrow. For more information, consult the "Side Quest: The Golden Claw" section later in this guide; begin at the Riverwood Trader and speak to the proprietors, Lucan and his sister Camilla Valerius.

Unreliable Bandits

Head up the mountain path north of Riverwood, passing the Riverwood Folly (where bandits roam). At the summit, the Nord tomb appears through the blizzard. Expect more bandit activity in this area. Locate the arched carved door leading into Bleak Falls Temple. Inside the first chamber, you hear two bandits around a campfire talking about a Dark Elf heading farther into the Barrow. End their conversation swiftly before venturing down the stairs.

Pass through the spiderwebs and the burial urns, and around the dead Skeever. Engage another bandit on your way to a ceremonial entrance room. A portcullis blocks your path, and the lever nearby is currently inactive. In the alcoves to the left are a trio of three-sided pillars. Approach the first; they can be activated. Each side has a different animal carving: the Hawk, Whale, and Snake.

Puzzle Solution: Rotate the pillars so a Snake, Snake, and Whale face out. The carved Nord heads above the portcullis (and the fallen middle one) hold the answer in their maws.

> **NOTE** (Sneak) If you're remaining unseen as you move through this Barrow, you can follow the third bandit into the ceremonial entrance room and activate the lever on the ground. He succumbs to the dart trap immediately.

Descend the spiral steps beyond, battling a few Skeevers on your way down. As the thick spider silk begins to cover the walls, you hear a voice up ahead and to your left. Cut through the doorway covered in webbing, and enter the lair of a Giant Frostbite Spider. Attack the arachnid before venturing toward the trussed-up Dark Elf—one of the bandits from the raiding party you slaughtered previously. This is Arvel the Swift, who is carrying a Golden Claw, which is pertinent to both this quest and the Side Quest. He quickly tells you he knows how it fits into the door in the Hall of Stories. The bandit is babbling. But he needs cutting down first. Oblige him.

After a couple of weapon swipes (or magical blasts), Arvel's sticky prison gives way. He immediately flees, laughing that he won't be sharing his treasure with the likes of you. This is correct, but that's due to his imminent departure from this realm. This can be by your hands—a quick arrow or two in the back or other ranged attack—or by the denizens that lurk deeper in this crypt.

> **CAUTION** It isn't wise to rush after Arvel; you'll soon catch up with him, and it is better to be prepared rather than rush headlong into an unknown chamber.

Knee-Deep in the Nordic Dead

Follow Arvel, passing through the crypt entrance and down into the catacombs. The Swift soon meets the dead, as Arvel falls under a flurry of Draugr attacks. The Nord undead now turn their attention to you. Battle them back or run north toward the open spiked gate and pressure plate. Keep to the extreme left, and you can activate the swinging gate trap without being hit. Use it as a skewering device against the Draugr; then search Arvel. Among his belongings are the Golden Claw and the Dark Elf's journal. Read it for more clues on this Barrow's secret.

- **Golden Claw**
- **Arvel's Journal**

Continue downward, battling Draugr and searching corpses, both resting and animated, as you go. At the swinging blades, sprint forward the moment the closest blade swings past you. Brandish your weaponry but don't be overzealous with fire in the passageway with puddles; this is actually oil leaking from a hanging lamp, and the corridor erupts if flames touch the ground. Use this as a trap against your bony foes.

Eventually, you climb steps into a tall chamber with a waterfall, and another Draugr. The Barrow's secret lies past a portcullis above the rushing stream. Locate the chain next to the portcullis and activate it before splashing down the stream and into a larger cavern with an opening at the far end. Head to a natural bridge below the waterfall, or stand atop the waterfall and fire down on the enemy below (this is either a Draugr or a Frost Troll). By the bridge, optionally scavenge on the curved path below. Then follow the path into the illuminated entrance to Bleak Falls Sanctum.

Open the Sanctum doors, and weave your way to a bladed corridor. Coax the Draugr beyond into this trap before dashing through it, into the Great Chamber. Expect attacks from Draugr bowmen on the bridge above and melee strikes from the ground. Remember you can drop oil lamps and burn these foes as you head over the bridge and to the Iron Door leading into the long Hall of Stories and to a Nordic Puzzle Door.

Puzzle Solution: The door consists of three "rings" that rotate when you activate them. Each of them has three animals plated into the structure, and you unlock the central keyhole by using the Golden Claw itself. This puzzle is inaccessible without it. The puzzle solution is actually on the palm of the Golden Claw; rotate it in your inventory to see the three circular petroglyph carvings on the Claw's palm. Move the rings so the Bear, Moth, and Owl appear on the outer, middle, and inner rings, respectively. Then insert the Golden Claw into the keyhole.

Guardian of the Dragonstone

This reveals the Barrow's secret at last: a ceremonial burial grotto with waterfalls surrounding the long-forgotten chamber. Move to the carved stone center, and check the chest and scavenge what you need; then inspect the Word Wall, where you're granted a Word of Power! However, this stirs a toughened Draugr from his rest, and you must defend yourself from this final Barrow guardian. After the fight, inspect the corpse of the Draugr; he is carrying the Dragonstone you seek! Grab this before taking the staircase on the chamber's left side, activating the handle to raise a secret stone slab door out in an upper Barrow alcove, and then exit out into Skyrim.

➤ **Word of Power:** Unrelenting Force ➤ **Dragonstone**

◊ **OBJECTIVE:** Deliver the Dragonstone to Farengar
♦ **TARGET:** Farengar Secret-Fire, Dragonsreach, in Whiterun

TIP **The Golden Claw:** Remember you still have it! If you want to complete the Side Quest, too, return it to Lucan in the Riverwood Trader first. He rewards you with a large sum of gold (the amount you receive depends on your level).

NOTE Shouts are made up of Words of Power, and the one you've absorbed from the Word Wall may be your first. If you open the Magic Menu, you'll see that you can't use or equip it until you've absorbed a Dragon Soul from a dragon you've killed. Be patient—that will happen soon enough.

TIP **Equipping for Adventure:** At this point, it is worth learning how to strengthen your resolve, spend your gold, or barter your unwanted equipment. You can:

- ◊ Visit Riverwood and purchase or barter at the Riverwood Trader. Locate Alvor the Blacksmith for all your smithing needs. Visit the Sleeping Giant Inn and locate the Alchemy Lab Lab to craft some potions.
- ◊ Visit Whiterun and peruse the market area, which has various stalls, shops, and a Blacksmith. Farengar Secret-Fire also has a handy Enchanting Workbench and sells spells.

Quest Conclusion

Return to Dragonsreach (the quickest way is to Fast-Travel directly to it), and immediately consult with Farengar. If this is the second time you've visited him, he is joined in his study by a mysterious hooded figure named Delphine—possibly the "reliable source" he referred to earlier. He is talking about the cross-referencing of texts that mention dragons. Finally, Farengar turns to you, impressed that you didn't die in the Barrow. As you hand over the Dragonstone, he says that you're a cut above the usual brutes the Jarl sends his way. Speak to the Jarl for your reward, which occurs during the initial conversations of the next quest.

NOTE If you already had the Dragonstone prior to this quest and visited Farengar only once, Delphine isn't here. Don't worry—you'll meet her soon enough!

Postquest Activities

Main Quest: Dragon Rising begins immediately.

DRAGON RISING

PREREQUISITES: Complete Main Quest: Bleak Falls Barrow
INTERSECTING QUESTS: Main Quest: Bleak Falls Barrow, Main Quest: The Way of the Voice
LOCATIONS: Western Watchtower, Whiterun, Dragonsreach
CHARACTERS: Farengar, Hrongar, Irileth, Jarl Balgruuf the Greater, Proventus Avenicci, Whiterun Guard
ENEMY: Mirmulnir ("Loyal Mortal Hunter")
◊ **OBJECTIVES:** Talk to Jarl Balgruuf, Meet Irileth near the Western Watchtower, Kill the dragon, Investigate the dragon, Report back to Jarl Balgruuf, (Optional) Use your new Shout power

All Along the Watchtower

◊ **OBJECTIVE:** Talk to Jarl Balgruuf

As you finish your conversation about the Dragonstone with Farengar, Irileth interrupts you with some troubling news: A dragon has been sighted nearby! Farengar seems positively giddy, while Irileth seems unsure if they could stop an attack on Whiterun. Locate the Jarl, who is questioning the Whiterun Guard who reported seeing the beast. Jarl Balgruuf orders Irileth to bolster the Western Watchtower with more men, a plan Irileth is already undertaking. Then the Jarl turns to you, seeking your help once again. Your experience at Helgen means you're most experienced in dealing with dragons. As a token of his esteem, he's instructed Avenicci that you're permitted to purchase property in Whiterun. Assuming you're alive and have enough gold! You're also gifted something from the Jarl's personal armory:

➤ **Leveled Armor**

◊ **OBJECTIVE:** Meet Irileth near the Western Watchtower

NOTE **Property Purchasing:** Locate Avenicci (he's usually within the walls of Dragonsreach, and within whispering distance of the Jarl), ideally after you return from your dragon slaying. A house is quite expensive—5,000 gold pieces—so be sure to have enough funds. Consult the Thane Tasks for further information.

TIP **Weaponry Purchasing:** At this point, consider purchasing additional supplies, especially Healing potions (if you aren't using Healing spells), and utilizing your "Favorites" to set up both long- and melee-range offense.

As the Jarl prevents Farengar from viewing the dragon, exit Dragonsreach. If you stride through Whiterun with Irileth, she gathers some Whiterun Guards and explains the situation. Or you can leave Whiterun. Follow the stone path that winds between the tundra plains, heading for the lone tower in the middle distance. As you get close, step up to Irileth who is hiding behind a rocky outcrop. If Irileth is behind you, you can either wait for her (and the soldiers) to arrive, or investigate the Watchtower on your own.

NOTE In fact, you can skip talking to the Jarl entirely. As soon as Irileth interrupts Farengar, you can go directly to the Watchtower and trigger the dragon attack after approaching the survivor. Irileth will arrive with troops as the battle begins.

If she's with you, Irileth notes that the Western Watchtower looks to have been ferociously attacked. The small fires and rubble confirm this assertion. She believes the dragon is still skulking nearby and orders you to spread out and look for survivors.

A closer inspection supports Irileth's summation; the place has been struck and lives lost. Move into the tower. As you enter, a fearful Whiterun Guard yells that the beast is still out there and has already taken two guards named Hroki and Tor when they tried to flee! Moments later, a bone-shaking roar announces the return of the dragon!

◊ **OBJECTIVE:** Kill the dragon

Dragonborn Rising

There's little time to watch the giant lizard circling overhead; you must try to kill the creature as proficiently as possible.

Dragon Slaying: Switch to whatever long-range offensive weaponry you have, ideally ranged magic or a bow and arrow.

You are fortunate that Irileth and a few Whiterun Guards are attempting to strike the dragon, too, thus keeping it from predominantly attacking you. Irileth's magic is strong, so aid her by attacking from an opposite direction. Split up so there are fewer of you to fry at once!

If you're using a bow and arrow, remember to aim (and slow time, if you have the perk) for a better chance to hit.

This dragon breathes fire, so consuming potions or casting magic that lessens fire-based damage (see The Inventory Chapter on page 131) is a good idea.

When the dragon drops to a hover, it is usually preparing a gout of fiery breath. Take as many ranged shots as you deem safe, and then rush under or around the creature. Fire again as the dragon flies off.

When the dragon lands, attack from the sides; ranged attacks are still just as strong, but melee attacks are now possible, as long as you try cutting down the dragon between breath attacks or from the side.

If worse comes to worst, flee into the tower and use some Health potions. You can also attack from the tower's top or use the stairs to head down, out of the dragon's breath attacks.

◊ **OBJECTIVE:** Investigate the dragon

Approach the dead dragon. As you get close, it begins to burn! Fortunately, this isn't harmful; in fact, the crackling flesh merges into the ethereal soul of the dragon, and a maelstrom of energy and light whirls around you. You're actively absorbing the soul of Mirmulnir! Once the light subsides, search the dragon for some valuables. Now approach Irileth. The normally stoic Dark Elf is showing a little emotion after this battle.

➤ **Dragon Soul Absorbed**

◊ **OBJECTIVE:** Report back to Jarl Balgruuf
◊ **OBJECTIVE:** (Optional) Use your new Shout power

CAUTION With a keen eye, it appears the dragon that attacked Helgen is not the one you just fought. This means that more than one dragon has returned—a bigger problem than first thought!

Access your Magic menu, scroll down to Shouts, and equip the Unrelenting Force Shout. You have the Dragon Soul necessary to conjure this Shout, so try it out. It isn't wise to do this on your allies (although they won't attack back), so try staggering a nearby enemy or just yelling at the tundra itself. Your Shout then recharges; note the Compass gradually fills from blue to bright white before becoming a normal white color. With Irileth taking command at the Watchtower, you should leave for Jarl Balgruuf's at once.

Quest Conclusion

Return to Dragonsreach and approach the Jarl, who has recently been joined by his equally imposing brother, Hrongar. Explain to the Jarl that you're actually "Dragonborn" and that you absorbed some of the dragon's power when it was slain. Jarl Balgruuf is shocked; it appears that the Masters of the Way of the Voice—known colloquially as the Greybeards—were not only correct in their predictions, but also are actively summoning you. Your reward? A trek to meet them!

Postquest Activities

Continue the conversation with Jarl Balgruuf as Main Quest: The Way of the Voice begins.

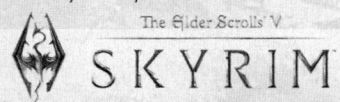

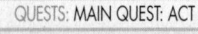

PREREQUISITES: Complete Main Quest: Dragon Rising

INTERSECTING QUESTS: Main Quest: Dragon Rising, Main Quest: The Horn of Jurgen Windcaller

LOCATIONS: High Hrothgar, Ivarstead, High Hrothgar Courtyard, Whiterun, Dragonsreach

CHARACTERS: Hrongar, Jarl Balgruuf the Greater, Lydia, Master Arngeir, Master Borri, Master Einarth, Master Wulfgar, Proventus Avenicci

ENEMIES: Bandit, Frost Troll, Sabre Cat, Wolf

◊ **OBJECTIVES:** Speak to the Greybeards, Demonstrate your "Unrelenting Force" Shout, Speak to Arngeir, Learn the Word of Power from Einarth, Demonstrate your "Unrelenting Force" Shout (3), Learn the Word of Power from Borri, Demonstrate your "Whirlwind Sprint" Shout, Speak to Arngeir for further training

Arise, Thane of Whiterun

◊ **OBJECTIVE:** Speak to the Greybeards

Continue to speak with Jarl Balgruuf about the Greybeards. He informs you that these venerable monks live in secluded isolation high on the slopes of the Throat of the World (the largest mountain in Skyrim). They have the ability to focus your vital essence into a Thu'um, or Shout, and they give you the location of their monastery in High Hrothgar—atop a 7,000-step climb! After a verbal altercation between Hrongar and Proventus Avenicci over Nordic sacred traditions, Jarl Balgruuf grants you the greatest honor within his power: You are named Thane of Whiterun. You also receive a weapon from the Jarl's armory and a Housecarl of your own.

➤ **Axe of Whiterun** ➤ **Follower:** Lydia (Housecarl)

NOTE **Followers:** Lydia may be your first Follower. You may take her with you on your trek or journey there alone. Lydia remains in Dragonsreach until you instruct her to accompany you on any adventure. Although you have an adept bodyguard, your Follower requires armor and weaponry. For more information on Followers, consult page 100.

Becoming Thane: This is an accomplishment to be proud of. Your new title means you're treated with the utmost respect by the guards and many inhabitants of the city of which you're Thane. You can also purchase property in the city. For more information, consult page 502.

If you ignored this meeting with the Jarl and trekked to High Hrothgar first, the Jarl will be here to reward you when you return. However, you do not witness the tension between Hrongar and Proventus Avenicci.

Journeying to Ivarstead

The route to High Hrothgar involves a lengthy, spiraling journey clockwise around the base of the throat of the World. the first stop along this path is at the base of the 7,000 steps, in the town of Ivarstead. exit Whiterun and trek east, passing the Honningbrew Meadery. Cross the stone bridge over the White River, and follow the marked signpost to ivarstead. Continue along this stone path past a few encounters with wolves to a fork in the paths. At this point, you can choose one of two recommended routes to Ivarstead: the long and winding road or the short and steep trail.

The Long and Winding Road

You may continue along the marked path, ignoring the track up to the Giants of Guldun Rock. Prepare to pay a toll (or fight) at the bandit-infested Valtheim Towers. Then descend past the waterfall, along the same path past some drystone walls and the stone trilithon at the base of a stepped side path indicating the entrance to Hillgrund's Tomb. Cross the bridge over Darkwater River and journey south (and southeast), right past Fort Amol. Head over another bridge close to a waterfall and continue along the stone path. Beware of more animal encounters, including a Sabre Cat or two! Head over another bridge, next to an even-more impressive waterfall, and trek east up a hill, where the stone path deteriorates.

The path soon turns southwest, up a long, steep slope, past Snapleg Cave. Continue southwest, ignoring the bridge. Head into birch woodland where Sarethi Farm is located. Expect elk, deer, a hunter's tent or two, and a view of Lake Geir from the bridge over the Treva River. Continue farther into the forest as the path winds west, past a junction and more drystone walls. Then turn right (northwest) at the small stone ruins near Honeystrand Cave. You finally reach Ivarstead after crossing another stone bridge.

The Short and Steep Trail

Or you can try this shortcut. Follow the path around to the right (east) just after you pass White River Watch, and come up to The Ritual Stone on your left. Cut south close to the Whiterun stormcloak camp, and up through the snowy foothills of the mountain, up an unmarked goat trail. Be sure you're traveling southeast up a steep embankment and into the snow. This levels out eventually, after you make several zigzags up very steep terrain above the snow line. Pass a few goats as the trail levels out and then quickly descends, joining a more recognizable trail. Head southeast and over the brow of the hill and past a copse of birch trees to the rushing rapids of Darkwater River. Cross the river, listening for the strange chime of a Nimroot growing around the corpses of a Troll's victims at Darkwater Overhang. Fight or flee from the Troll, then trek up the left side of the roaring waterfalls and into Ivarstead.

CAUTION Climbing directly up the mountain's side to reach High Hrothgar quickly results in you becoming stuck or falling to your death.

> **TIP** **Making Inroads:** At this point, you should have learned that taking a long road to an important objective (in this case, Ivarstead) isn't a journey wasted, as you uncover several Primary Locations along the way. You can explore these immediately or at your leisure. You should also learn that using the paths, trails, and rivers is the best way to understand and remember where you are in the rugged lands of Skyrim.
>
> **Road Markings:** Both signposts and markers (the collections of stacked flat stones, sometimes with a primitive flag attached to them) are visual notes that indicate a nearby area of interest. Look for them.

7,000 Steps Above Ivarstead

Ivarstead is a slightly depressing place. The inhabitants are leaving for the greener (or at least, less snowy) pastures of Riften. You can stay and chat with the locals (mainly about their troubles or the supplies they need to send up to the Greybeards), or listen to them talk about the path up to High Hrothgar; they don't think the 7,000 steps are safe. You'll find out soon enough!

Your pilgrimage begins at the other side of the stone bridge. Almost immediately, you spot a small shrine. Inspect it more closely, and you'll see an Etched Tablet carved into the shrine arch. Read the emblem for the first of ten verses detailing the history of dragons and man.

Follow the winding path: At the second shrine, you may find a hunter named Barknar praying. He tells you to watch for wolves. You're now at the edge of the snow level. Continue up the precarious path: Expect a couple of wolf attacks along the way. The third shrine is nestled on a small snowy plateau. Follow the path down and up two sets of snowbound steps; remain on the side of the mountain, as the drop is precipitous. The fourth shrine is near some stab stones and a small copse of fir trees. You may find another traveler at this shrine, a pilgrim named Karita.

Use the marker stones as you wander up, into a granite gully. A Frost Troll is likely to be guarding this area, leaping down to maul you. Retaliate or run. The fifth shrine is just beyond the Frost Troll ambush. The blizzard is worsening; trek north down the snow steps, passing a few windswept trees to the sixth shrine, in front of a stone marker. Continue north and locate the seventh shrine jutting out to the west, on a precarious promontory. If you could see it, you'd be looking out across southern Eastmarch. Turn north, and look for the eighth shrine in front of a rocky outcrop, to your left (northwest).

The ninth shrine is below a stone statue to Talos. You'll see this as you round the bend in the path and come across the High Hrothgar monastery. As you close in on the final set of steps (did you count 7,000?), the final shrine is set off to the right (southeast) side, by the entrance stairs. Climb the entrance steps, grab any supplies and offerings at the base of the stairs, and then ascend the left set of stairs to enter High Hrothgar.

Something to Shout About

The monastery is adorned with carvings from ancient times and banners bearing the strange symbols of the dragon language. An old monk in a long robe steps forward; this is Arngeir, the leader of the Greybeards. He knows who you are. Speak with him, and he asks for a taste of your voice. Oblige him.

> ◊ **OBJECTIVE:** Demonstrate your "Unrelenting Force" Shout
> ◊ **OBJECTIVE:** Speak to Arngeir
> ♦ **TARGET:** Arngeir, inside High Hrothgar

Select the Unrelenting Force Shout from your Magic menu, and bellow at or near Arngeir. The other Greybeards, Borri, Einarth, and Wulfgar come to watch. Your fate is confirmed; speak with him again, and he welcomes you to the monastery. Master Arngeir speaks for the Greybeards and asks why you have come. Answer any way you wish (questions lead to more information on the monastery and the Greybeards' existence). When you are ready, tell Arngeir that you're "ready to learn." Arngeir wishes to train you so you're better able to execute a Thu'um, or Shout.

> ◊ **OBJECTIVE:** Learn the Word of Power from Einarth

Master Arngeir explains that all Shouts are made up of three Words of Power. As you master each Word, your Shout becomes progressively stronger. Currently, you have only learned *Fus* (or "Force"), the first Word of your Unrelenting Force Shout. Master Einarth now teaches you *Ro* (or "Balance"), the second Word. This allows you to focus your Thu'um more sharply. Einarth Shouts into the hallowed stone of the monastery. Step onto the dragon runes that glow from the Shout, and absorb this second word.

➤ **Word of Power:** Balance, Unrelenting Force

Your learning impresses Arngeir, but he warns you that to unlock its meaning, you must constantly practice. As part of your initiation, Master Einarth allows you to tap into his understanding of Ro. Einarth glows with an orange light, imparting his knowledge onto you, in the same way you absorb the soul of a dragon. Now comes the real test: to see how quickly you've mastered the entire Shout!

> ◊ **OBJECTIVE:** Demonstrate your Unrelenting Force Shout (3x)

The monks have three targets for you to bellow your Shout toward. As the first ghostly monk figure is conjured, execute your Shout. The trick to this Shout's strength is the length of time that you hold the Shout button down. Continuously hold the button until the Shout is omitted. Tap the button if you wish to lessen the stagger you inflict upon your foes (or in this case, your ghostly Greybeard). After you complete three Shouts to Arngeir's satisfaction, he congratulates you and motions for you to follow Master Borri into the courtyard.

> **TIP** Play around with the length of time you hold the button down before releasing it to strengthen or weaken your Shout, so you know how long to attempt this ability.

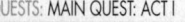

◊ **OBJECTIVE:** Learn the Word of Power from Borri

Follow Master Borri to the door to High Hrothgar Courtyard and step outside, stopping next to Borri, who is ready to teach you a new Shout—the *Wuld* (or "Whirlwind"). Stand over the snow that Borri has projected the Shout into, and absorb the Shout. Then approach Borri and he glows, gifting you his knowledge of the Word.

> **NOTE** The Word of Power that Borri teaches you may be different if (during the course of your adventures) you've found a Word Wall and absorbed one or two of the other parts of the phrase for the Whirlwind Sprint Shout. If you have all three Words of Power, this Shout (like all others) is much more potent. Check the Appendices (page 1077) for a list of locations where all Shouts can be found.

➤ **Word of Power:** Whirlwind, Whirlwind Sprint

◊ **OBJECTIVE:** Demonstrate your "Whirlwind Sprint" Shout

Master Borri walks toward an iron gate. Before following him, enter the Magic > Shouts menu to change your Shout to Whirlwind Sprint (you don't want to bellow Unrelenting Force at the gate!). Stand between the two stone columns facing the gate, with Master Wulfgar in view. He demonstrates the Whirlwind Sprint, rushing at an amazing speed through the gate before it closes. Now it is your turn: The moment the gate opens, execute the Shout and rush forward, aiming for the single stone column by the cliff edge. You should easily pass through before the gate closes. If you don't, try again.

◊ **OBJECTIVE:** Speak to Arngeir for further training

Quest Conclusion

Master Arngeir is astonished at your quick mastery of a new Thu'um. He tells you that the gods gave you this gift for a reason, but it is up to you to figure out how best to utilize it. For now, though, you are ready for the final part of your trial: Retrieve the Horn of Jurgen Windcaller, the founder of the Greybeards. Arngeir tells you that the horn is in Windcaller's tomb in the ancient fane (temple) of Ustengrav. If you remain true to the Way of the Voice, you will return.

Postquest Activities

Continue to ask Arngeir questions if you wish. Main Quest: The Horn of Jurgen Windcaller has already begun!

THE HORN OF JURGEN WINDCALLER

PREREQUISITES: Complete Main Quest: The Way of the Voice, 10 gold pieces

INTERSECTING QUESTS: Main Quest: The Way of the Voice, Main Quest: The Horn of Jurgen Windcaller

LOCATIONS: High Hrothgar, High Hrothgar Courtyard, Riverwood, Sleeping Giant Inn, Ustengrav, Ustengrav Depths

CHARACTERS: Delphine, Master Arngeir, Master Borri, Master Einarth, Master Wulfgar, Orgnar

ENEMIES: Bandit, Bandit Thrall, Conjurer, Draugr, Fire Mage, Frostbite Spider, Necromancer , Skeleton

◊ **OBJECTIVES:** Retrieve the horn, Meet with whoever took the horn, Return the horn to Arngeir, Learn the Word of Power from Wulfgar, Receive the Greybeards' greeting

Underground in Ustengrav

◊ **OBJECTIVE:** Retrieve the horn

♦ **TARGET:** Horn of Jurgen Windcaller, inside Ustengrav

Once Arngeir gives you this quest, you may ask him about the Greybeards, why dragons are returning, who Jurgen Windcaller is, and other conversation topics. Turn to your world map and locate Ustengrav on the eastern edge of the great marsh, northeast of Morthal in Hjaalmarch Hold. Your first task is to descend from High Hrothgar.

> **TIP** Your descent can be done on foot or by horse (if you came on a steed), but a much quicker plan is to halve the distance between here at Ustengrav and Fast-Travel to Whiterun, the Western Watchtower, or any location closest to the temple tomb. Don't forget to use your new Whirlwind Sprint Shout to cover distances more swiftly than before!

When you finally reach Ustengrav, you may find a small campfire and lean-to by the circular barrow entrance. Expect a confrontation with bandits and a necromancer. Then descend the barrow steps and open the door to Ustengrav.

Heading down the wide steps, into the gloom of the ancient temple, you stumble upon a group of mages and conjurers picking clean the remains of a thwarted bandit attack. You can slink by using Sneak or engage the magicians in combat.

> **TIP** The Bandit Thralls are being controlled by a necromancer—kill him, and the thralls die too.

Locate the opening in the northeast wall of the temple entrance, and follow the trail of lanterns down the steps. This soon becomes a trail of mage corpses, as you watch a group of Draugr demolish the wizards and make a run at you. Cut down the Draugr, or use whatever cunning magic or sneaking you wish, before continuing into the first burial crypt. Scavenge whatever you wish, then head east and turn south, down a passage lit by candles.

There are steps down to your right (west), leading to a small crypt. Grab the items and yank the pull-chain. A section of wall rumbles open, leading you down a cramped tunnel to a secret dead-end chamber and a treasure chest. Retrace your steps. Enter the great hall, with a stone bridge ahead of and above you. Fend off the Draugr that clamber out of their vertical tombs. Then climb the interior stairwell, and cross the bridge you just passed under. Locate the iron door and enter the Ustengrav Depths.

Head down the winding tunnel until it opens into a gigantic, multilevel grotto. It is immense enough to have trees, a waterfall, and a Word Wall! Continue down the tree-root ledge and tunnel, heading south and then east. You appear on a bridge overlooking an ancient banqueting hall. Follow the steps down, eliminating Draugr as you go. To the east are the remains of a food-preparation area running parallel to the hall. Head south, up more stairs, and cross a second bridge to exit the hall.

The tunnel to the southwest widens into an entrance room with a middle pillar. To the left is a double portcullis (open it with two wall handles; one is farther along the southwest wall) behind which is a small room with treasure. Take this and optionally shoot the lamp down onto the oil below to burn any Draugr that come to investigate you. Head west through a gap in the wall. Here, there are steps up to a small preparation alcove, and more importantly, an earthen and rock corridor that leads into the gigantic grotto.

Follow the collapsed bridge down to the massive pillars under the chamber, where parts of an ancient fire trap still burn and skeletons roam. Cut down all the bony fiends in this two-floor area, inspect the throne area (with another skeleton to slaughter), and then run northeast around the perimeter wall ledge, down to the rocky base of the grotto. Moments later, you learn a word from the Become Ethereal Shout. Afterward, you fight with a Draugr over a treasure chest behind the waterfall. Before you leave, try your Whirlwind Sprint Shout and traverse the collapsed bridges in this area, leading to a small chamber you can loot.

➤ **Word of Power:** Become Ethereal

The Tomb Raider

Backtrack to the throne area where you fought the skeletons, and look to your east. Cross the large natural bridge that spans the grotto, to a second two-floor underchamber on the eastern side. First, clear out the skeletons from the balcony above, and then inspect a set of three strange stones back on the lower underchamber area.

Puzzle Solution: If you stand close to each one of the three stones, they pulse with an eerie, magical glow. This has the added effect of opening one of three portcullises in the tunnel to the east. However, after a second or two, the light switches off, blocking your path. This is the only way the portcullises open. If you get through one or two of them, you must turn back; all three must be raised for you to continue. The trick here is to line yourself up on the western side of the stones, as shown in the preceding picture with the stones between you and the portcullises. Then execute a Whirlwind Sprint Shout, followed by another to make sure you dash past the stones and the opening portcullises immediately.

Continue east, jumping to the natural rock on either side of the circular floor tiles, as they blast gouts of fire when you stand on them. This can prove handy when you reach the raised section of floor in the room of alcoves—a pack of Frostbite Spiders descends from the ceiling to attack. Optionally back up so the spiders scuttle onto the floor tiles and are burned along with your own attacks. Exit by hacking the cobwebs from the doorway to the east. Then open the wooden door.

Pull the chain to raise the portcullis that leads into the final resting place of Jurgen Windcaller. As you step forward, four dragon statue heads rumble up from the water. Continue across the bridge over the flooded lower floor and approach the ornate tomb. The horn should be still clutched by the carved arm of Jurgen in his sarcophagus...but it isn't! Instead, there's a small piece of paper. Take and read it. The damned thief who took the horn has left you a note; it requests that you rent the attic room at the Sleeping Giant Inn in Riverwood, and it is signed "A friend."

➤ **Mysterious Note**

◊ **OBJECTIVE FAILED:** Retrieve the horn
◊ **OBJECTIVE:** Meet with whoever took the horn
♦ **TARGET:** "A friend" inside Sleeping Giant Inn, in Riverwood

CAUTION

This may be the first time that you've failed an objective. This is mandatory; you cannot succeed at this particular objective at the moment.

A Mysterious Stranger

You'd think "a friend" wouldn't want you risking your life in a Draugr dungeon! Stifle any indignant rage you may be experiencing, and console yourself with any treasure you find through the wooden door behind the sarcophagus. There is an exit tunnel in the left (north) wall, offering a shortcut to an iron door, and a lever that lowers a section of stone wall, allowing you to step into the initial crypt, up into the temple entrance, and out of Ustengrav.

Fast-Travel (or trek back) to Riverwood, and follow the instructions of the Mysterious Note. Locate the Sleeping Giant Inn, enter, and locate Delphine, who owns the place with her slightly dense friend Orgnar. Step up to Delphine and ask to rent the attic room for 10 gold. After the money changes hands, she tells you the Sleeping Giant doesn't have an attic room, but you can take the room on the left. Enter the room, and after a few moments, Delphine joins you. Apparently you're the Dragonborn she's been hearing so much about. As a way of a peace offering, she hands you the horn that you seek.

➤ **Horn of Jurgen Windcaller**

◊ **MAIN QUEST:** A Blade in the Dark begins
◊ **OBJECTIVE:** Return the horn to Arngeir
♦ **TARGET:** Master Arngeir, in High Hrothgar

TIP You now have two Main Quests active. In order to finish this one, you must return to High Hrothgar. You can attempt this at any time, but it is usually advisable to speak with Delphine first (the initial part of the next Main Quest). Once you leave the Sleeping Giant, trek (or Fast-Travel) back to High Hrothgar.

Quest Conclusion

Enter High Hrothgar, and head through the monastery until you spot Arngeir. He already knows you have returned with the Horn of Jurgen Windcaller and remarks that the time has come for the Greybeards to recognize you formally as Dragonborn.

◊ **OBJECTIVE:** Learn the Word of Power from Wulfgar
♦ **TARGET:** Master Wulfgar, in High Hrothgar

Return to the central chamber inside High Hrothgar as the Greybeards assemble. Master Wulfgar approaches the center of the floor and bellows the word *Dah* ("Push") into the granite. Step onto the glowing runes and absorb the Word of Power. You can now utilize the Shout Unrelenting Force with maximum potency! Absorb the learning from Wulfgar as well.

➤ **Word of Power:** Push, Unrelenting Force

◊ **OBJECTIVE:** Receive the Greybeards' greeting

Remain in the center of the room. The Greybeards stand at each point of the diamond paving, and Arngeir greets you with a ferocious chant in dragon tongue. You withstand the blast, which pleases and impresses Arngeir. You've tasted the Voice of the Greybeards and passed through unscathed. High Hrothgar is now open to you!

Postquest Activities

There are two tasks you can attempt with the Greybeards from this point on. Look up the Other Faction Quests on page 408. Also remember that Main Quest: A Blade in the Dark is already under way!

Return to Ustengrav and activate Jurgen Windcaller's tomb. The horn returns to its rightful resting place, and you receive a bonus Dragon Soul.

➤ **Dragon Soul**

A BLADE IN THE DARK

PREREQUISITES: Complete Main Quest: The Horn of Jurgen Windcaller

◉ MINOR SPOILERS

INTERSECTING QUESTS: Main Quest: The Horn of Jurgen Windcaller, Main Quest: Diplomatic Immunity

LOCATIONS: Kynesgrove, Kynesgrove Dragon Mound, Riverwood, Sleeping Giant Inn

CHARACTERS: Delphine, Iddra, Orgnar

ENEMIES: Alduin ("World Eater"), Sahloknir ("Phantom Sky Hunter")

◊ **OBJECTIVES:** Talk to Delphine, Locate the dragon burial site, Kill the dragon Sahloknir, Talk to Delphine

Grave Concerns

◊ **OBJECTIVE:** Talk to Delphine
♦ **TARGET:** Delphine, the Sleeping Giant Inn, in Riverwood

Once Delphine has given you the Horn of Jurgen Windcaller, she requests that you follow her. Oblige her, walking across the inn to the bedroom opposite, where Delphine opens a cabinet and pushes the fake back, revealing a secret set of cellar steps. This leads to a war room of sorts, complete with a map of Skyrim on a central table and various potions and items you can take. Delphine mentions the Dragonborn, and through conversation choices (answer as you wish), you realize Delphine was the one who took the horn (she was Farengar Secret-Fire's "reliable source" back in Dragonsreach who found the location of the Dragonstone). She knows that Thalmor spies are everywhere, so she took precautions to arrange this meeting.

Delphine is part of a group that has been searching for someone like you—a Dragonborn—for a very long time. Delphine needs to know if you can devour a dragon's soul, as you'll have a chance to prove it soon enough. She also holds a low opinion of the Greybeards. Finally, she reveals the reasons for her agitation: She's discovered that dragons aren't just coming back—they're coming back to life! It seems that the dragons weren't banished; they were extinguished from this land, and now something is bringing them back from the dead. Using a pattern she discovered on the Dragonstone you found, Delphine has deciphered the location where she believes the next dragon will rise from the dead, and she needs you to help her stop it. The location is Kynesgrove in Eastmarch.

◊ **OBJECTIVE:** Locate the dragon burial site
♦ **TARGET:** Dragon mound above Kynesgrove

TIP After speaking with Delphine, you should head to High Hrothgar once you emerge from the Sleeping Giant Inn so you complete the previous Main Quest as quickly as possible.

Use the annotated map bearing all of the dragon burial sites as the basis for tracking and killing all the dragons that may return to Skyrim.

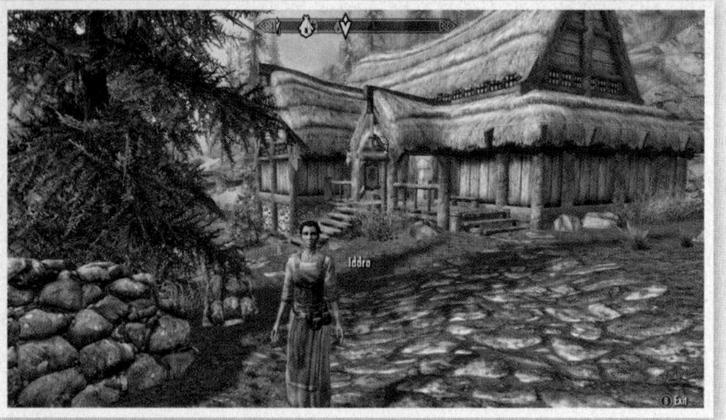

Once you tell Delphine that you're ready, she dons her leathers, informs Orgnar that she's traveling, and sets off on the long walk to Kynesgrove. This settlement is in the northern part of Eastmarch Hold, just southwest of Windhelm. To reach there, you can do the following:

Take the journey on foot. You can either keep up with Delphine or you can fight your way alone. Stay on the roads, prepare for world encounters, and discover as many Primary Locations along the way as possible (that you can return to and explore later). Remember to also use your Whirlwind Sprint for a faster pace.

Or, if you've already made some discoveries in the area in and around Kynesgrove (by visiting Windhelm, for example), you may wish to Fast-Travel to the nearest unlocked location and then travel to Kynesgrove.

Or, you can take a horse for a slightly faster journey.

When you reach Kynesgrove, Delphine should be ahead of you (if she isn't, wait for her). She senses something is wrong; this is soon proven correct when Iddra (a resident of the hamlet) runs over, shouting that there's a dragon attacking at the top of the hill! Delphine starts sprinting.

A Terrible Resurrection

Delphine slows to an incredulous stumble as a huge black dragon with piercing red eyes hovers above a dragon mound at the top of the hill. It bellows a guttural roar in dragon tongue. The dragon mound where Alduin concentrated his Shout begins to swirl with a strange energy, not unlike the ethereal material you've absorbed during previous dragon confrontations. The next moment, the mound bursts open, and a huge skeletal dragon begins to emerge from deathly slumber. The dragons speak quickly to each other, before Alduin turns, mocks your claim to be "dovahkiin," and departs the area as quickly as he arrives.

> **TIP** You may interrupt this resurrection and attack the newly returned dragon as quickly as you wish.

◊ **OBJECTIVE:** Kill the dragon Sahloknir

The skeletal Sahloknir clambers out of his grave and is resurrected by Alduin's powerful magic. Before Sahloknir's skin can gather around his bones and he regains his powers, race in with your most impressive melee implements and deliver a series of attacks to weaken the dragon's health.

> **TIP** Remember! Attacking a skeletal dragon before it grows flesh and wings to fly is a much easier battle: Get in early and quickly with your weapons.

Delphine fires arrows, then rushes in with melee attacks when the dragon lands; you should demonstrate your offensive powers too. Follow the same set of tactics laid out during Main Quest: Dragon Rising, when you faced Mirmulnir the "Loyal Mortal Hunter." One overriding plan is to ensure that Sahloknir's life is as short as possible!

When Sahloknir has been reduced back into a pile of bones, the beast splits apart into hundreds of scaly shards, and you absorb another Dragon Soul. Search the dragon, and then head over to Delphine for her promised revelations.

➤ **Dragon Soul absorbed**

◊ **OBJECTIVE:** Talk to Delphine

Quest Conclusion

Delphine lives up to her promise and answers any questions you have. Most importantly, she reveals herself to be one of the last members of the Blades. Long ago, the Blades were dragonslayers, serving the Dragonborn, the greatest dragonslayer. For 200 years, the Blades have been searching for a purpose. Now that purpose is clear. You may mention that you've seen Alduin before; he rampaged through Helgen and prevented your execution. Delphine finds this interesting but is annoyed that she's still blundering around in the dark.

Your next move is to find out who is controlling these dragons, and the Thalmor—the faction that rules the Aldmeri Dominion—are the best lead. Even if they aren't involved, they'll know who is. Delphine believes that there are no worse enemy to humankind than the Thalmor. She also has some ideas for getting you into the Thalmor Embassy, but she needs time to plan. You receive her secret Key and are told to meet her back in Riverwood.

➤ **Delphine's Secret Door Key**

Postquest Activities

Delphine's Secret Door Key opens the cabinet in her room in the Sleeping Giant Inn. Return to Riverwood when you wish to begin Main Quest: Diplomatic Immunity. Act I now concludes.

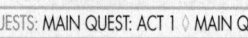

PREREQUISITES: Complete Main Quest: Diplomatic Immunity

INTERSECTING QUESTS: Main Quest: Diplomatic Immunity, Main Quest: Alduin's Wall, Thieves Guild Quest: A Chance Arrangement

LOCATIONS: Riften, The Bee and Barb, The Ragged Flagon, The Ratway, The Ratway Vaults, The Ratway Warrens, Riftweald Manor, Riverwood, Sleeping Giant Inn

CHARACTERS: Brand-Shei, Brynjolf, Delphine , Esbern , Keerava, Madesi, Riften Guard, Salvianus, Vekel the Man

ENEMIES: Drahff, Gissur, Hefid the Deaf, Hewnon Black-Skeever, Knjakr, Shavari, Skeever, Thalmor Soldier, Thalmor Wizard

◊ **OBJECTIVES:** Talk to Brynjolf, Search the Ratway for Esbern's hideout, Find Esbern in the Ratway Warrens, Talk to Esbern

A Den of Iniquity

◊ **OBJECTIVE:** Talk to Brynjolf
♦ **TARGET:** Brynjolf, in Riften

Delphine instructs you to meet with her contact, a member of the Thieves Guild named Brynjolf. However, before you go, ask her about your birthright. You can also ask why the Blades are on the run. Turns out it's because the Thalmor were systematically hunting them down thanks to the White-Gold Concordat, which was signed with the Empire. It ended the war but gave the Thalmor free rein to stomp out the worship of Talos. You may also ask about the Thalmor, the arrogant and extreme rulers of the Aldmeri Dominion, or what used to be the Imperial provinces of Summerset Isle and Valenwood. When you've heard enough, leave the Sleeping Giant Inn and travel to Riften.

> **TIP** Remember the equipment you just gathered from where Delphine deposited it? If you need to equip any of it or arrange your Favorites, do this right now.

When you arrive at either of the city's gates for the first time, a guard halts you and attempts to shake you down for a "visitor's tax." You can:

(Persuade) Realize this for what it is.

(Gold) Realize this for what it is but pay up (the amount varies, depending on how poor you are)

(Intimidate) Threaten that you kill thieves

Any of these options (if successful) allows the guard to open the door. Butchering the guard also gets you into Riften, after dramatically increasing your bounty and forcing you to spend time in the jail.

You meet a mysterious character in the Grand Plaza (during daylight hours) or inside the Bee and Barb the first time you look around the Grand Plaza in Riften.

First-time Thief: If you're meeting Brynjolf for the first time, and if you have some general skills in concealment or silent stealth or you've dealt with the guard at the Riften gate without resorting to violence, a man named Brynjolf strikes up a conversation with you. He may have an errand for you to perform to test your skills and may reward you with gold. Thieves Guild Quest: A Chance Arrangement must now be completed before Brynjolf releases the knowledge of where Esbern is hiding out.

(Persuade) Or you can use your verbal charms to reveal the location of Esbern, without playing Brynjolf's little game. If so, you can skip A Chance Arrangement.

Guild Member: If you're meeting Brynjolf and you've already proved yourself skilled by completing Thieves Guild Quest: A Chance Arrangement, Brynjolf is happy to point you in the direction of where Esbern is hiding out, once you ask him about these matters.

> **TIP** You don't have to play along with Brynjolf's schemes, though.
>
> (Persuade) You can speak to Keerava inside the Bee and Barb to learn about the Ragged Flagon, which gets you partway there.
>
> Or you can skip ahead to 'The Ratway Hidey-hole' and just follow the directions straight to Esbern.

Interlude: A Chance Arrangement

He tells you to pilfer a silver ring from a stall owned by Madesi in the marketplace while he creates a distraction. Place it in the pocket of a Dark Elf vendor named Brand-Shei. If you're caught, you're on your own, but if you succeed, he'll have some better-paying schemes. If you've met Brynjolf during the evening or night, he'll be waiting between eight in the morning and eight in the evening for you. If you met Brynjolf at night, wait until daylight and meet up again.

◊ **A CHANCE ARRANGEMENT OBJECTIVE:** Meet Brynjolf during daytime
♦ **TARGET:** Brynjolf, Grand Plaza in Riften
◊ **A CHANCE ARRANGEMENT OBJECTIVE:** Steal Madesi's Ring
♦ **TARGET:** Madesi's stand, Grand Plaza in Riften

Brynjolf is waiting for you by his own plaza stand, where he's about to hawk his "amazing" Falmerblood Elixir. Naturally, this patter is designed to draw a crowd (including Madesi and Brand-Shei), allowing you to quickly move around the plaza's perimeter via the stone wall and crouch behind Madesi's stall.

(Lockpick [Novice]) Produce your lockpicks, and unlock the sliding door under the stall counter. Quickly rummage around inside Madesi's strongbox. You can happily help yourself to any of the items here, but the valuable you're concerned with is the Silver Ring. Steal it quickly, before any of the city guards spot you.

> **CAUTION** You must attempt to pick this lock only after any city guards pass you, and you're hidden from view while sneaking.

➤ **Madesi's Silver Ring**

◊ **A CHANCE ARRANGEMENT OBJECTIVE:** Plant Madesi's Ring
♦ **TARGET:** Brand-Shei, Grand Plaza in Riften

Creep around so the assembled beggars and storekeepers don't see you, and position yourself behind Brand-Shei.

(Sneak) You must now "reverse-pickpocket" the Dark Elf. This involves pickpocketing, choosing your own Apparel menu, selecting Madesi's Silver Ring, and giving it to Brand-Shei to finish the technique. Remember, no one must see you attempt this!

If you're successful, Brand-Shei is mistaken for a thief and hauled away to Riften prison. Your paths may cross again in the future....

◊ **A CHANCE ARRANGEMENT OBJECTIVE:** Speak to Brynjolf
♦ **TARGET:** Brynjolf, Grand Plaza in Riften

> **CAUTION** If you're arrested, or you leave Riften and wait more than half a day to complete Brynjolf's Objective, or you murder someone during his distraction, Thieves Guild Quest: A Chance Arrangement still completes. However, this is no reward, and Brynjolf isn't pleased with your inadequacies. This is not the way to impress a future mentor!

Speak to Brynjolf after the ring-plant misdirection, and he congratulates (and rewards) you. You receive no monetary gain if you failed. Then he mentions his organization has been having some bad luck but mentions that there's more money to earn if you can handle it. Reply that you can, and Brynjolf recommends you meet him at the Ragged Flagon tavern, deep inside Riften's subterranean Ratway. He also points you in the direction of Esbern when you ask him; he's down in the Ratway.

➤ **100 gold pieces**

◊ **OBJECTIVE:** Search the Ratway for Esbern's hideout
♦ **TARGET:** Ragged Flagon, inside the Ratway, in Riften

> **TIP** This is an optimal time to strike up a friendship with other members of the Thieves Guild and perhaps begin a series of quests with them. Consult the Thieves Guild Quests starting on page 278 for all the pertinent information.

The Ratway Hidey-hole

Open the barred gate by the water's edge and go into the sewers that run the length and breadth of Riften. Down the first tunnel, you may stumble across two equally odious characters: Drahff and Hewnon Black-Skeever. They attempt to mug you for all your equipment. You can:

(Persuade) Try to let Drahff know that you've killed dozens like him.

Any other option results in violence. This doesn't impact your standing in Riften and is the recommended choice.

Now continue through this small maze of interlocking sewage tunnels. Watch for hanging oil traps, and a bear trap along the way. If your Lockpick skill is high enough, there's a chamber to check out, but your main purpose is finding the Ragged Flagon.

The tavern is unique, being constructed on and above a sewage conduit chamber. When you spot Brynjolf, he is talking with the barkeep (Vekel the Man), speaking about Brynjolf's predicament with his "organization." Speak to Vekel the Man, or seek out another Thieves Guild member named Dirge and ask either of them if they've seen "an old guy, hiding out" somewhere in Riften. Both Vekel's and Dirge's minds are cloudy, so you may need to clear them by:

(Persuade) Appealing to his sense of urgency and telling your contact that Esbern's life is in danger.

(Gold) Appealing to his sense of greed and offering gold so he remembers.

(Brawl) Appealing to his boisterous side and proving your might with a bare-knuckle fight. No weapons, or this suddenly gets a lot less friendly!

When one of these choices succeeds, Vekel or Dirge tells you that Esbern is holed up in the Ratway Warrens and hardly ever leaves the place.

If you're already a full-fledged member of the Thieves Guild, which requires you to have Thieves Guild Quest: Loud and Clear active and to have been awarded your thief's clothing, Vekel and Dirge also point you in the direction of the Ratway Warrens.

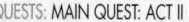

◊ **OBJECTIVE:** Find Esbern in the Ratway Warrens
♦ **TARGET:** Esbern, inside the Ratway, in Riften

CROSSING THE THALMOR: GISSUR'S REVENGE

Dispatching Gissur back at the Embassy prevents him from shadowing your movements.

If you left Spymaster Rulindil's spy Gissur alive during the previous quest, you may spot him in the Ragged Flagon. You can slay him or leave him alone. If you speak with either Dirge or Vekel, Gissur eavesdrops and sneaks out of the Ragged Flagon, into the Ratway. If you (carefully) follow him, you can eavesdrop as he tells the Thalmor troops where you are. You may wish to attack at any time, or:

You can remain hidden, as the Thalmor enter the Ragged Flagon, confront Dirge or Vekel, and are given a menacing brush-off by the Thieves Guild.

Or, you can reveal yourself (accidentally or otherwise) and turn the Ragged Flagon into a slaughterhouse. Leave no Thalmor alive!

CROSSING THE THALMOR: SHAVARI THE ASSASSIN

The Thalmor are hiring proficient assassins to track and kill you.

Unbeknownst to you, once you escaped the Thalmor Embassy, Elenwen placed a bounty on your head, which attracted the attention of a Khajiit assassin named Shavari. As soon as you enter the Ragged Flagon or the Ratway Vaults, she enters the Ratway after you. Be quick if you spot an unknown Khajiit in these parts; slay her before she can fulfill her task. Inspect her corpse for a note from "E" that proves the Thalmor plot against you.

➤ **Shavari's Note**

Remembering the 30th of Frostfall

If you were directed into the Ratway Warrens or even stumbled here on your own, the Thalmor are already prowling this maze of connecting corridors around a central hub room (which you've just entered).

However, if Dirge or Vekel directed you to the Warrens, you are forewarned about the Thalmor ambush, allowing you to expect any attacks and even trying to ambush the guards and gain the upper hand. Either way, unless your sneaking ability is exceptional, expect to fight around four of these enemies throughout your navigation of the Warrens.

From either entrance into the Warrens, there are two possible routes:

The first is to navigate around the interconnected corridors and chambers, sneaking past or fighting Thalmor enemies and a few Skeever along the way. This is the long route, but it allows you to remain hidden, or at least clear the Warrens of foes for the moment.

Or, you can appear on the upper balcony of the multifloored central hub room, which is well lit and has a cart and hay bale at the base of it. Drop to the open gate on the eastern side of the bottom floor. The entrance to the Ratway Vaults is just south of this point, at the bottom of the Warrens.

Open the wooden door and enter the Ratway Vaults. The Thalmor haven't found this area yet, and it is rarely trafficked. One of the reasons may be the lunatics who populate the chambers here. Beware of Hefid the Deaf, and Knjakr the mad chef, as both of them get violent when they spot you. You'll also have to contend with a brain-addled man named Salvianus, who talks to himself. But you're actually here to locate the well-locked door on the upper balcony of the hub chamber, in the southwest corner.

Sidle up to the door and activate it, and you'll hear an old man shouting for you to go away. Persist, and the door's shutter slides open and a pair of eyes peer out. They are attached to a man who claims to not know who Esbern is.

No amount of persuasion or pleading gets the man to unlock the door. Use the quote Delphine told you to tell the man: "remember the 30th of Frostfall." Only then does the man reveal himself to be Esbern and unlock the door.

If you haven't spoken to Delphine after escaping the Thalmor Embassy, you can inform Esbern that you're Dragonborn, which is enough to pique his interest.

◊ **OBJECTIVE:** Talk to Esbern

Quest Conclusion

Once you're inside Esbern's hidey-hole, he asks how Delphine is after all these years, regarding the situation as "hopeless." He tells you that Alduin has returned, just as the prophecy said. Esbern believes it to be the end of the world. In fact, the only glimmer of hope would be if a Dragonborn returned....

Postquest Activities

During the conversation, Main Quest: Alduin's Wall begins immediately.

PREREQUISITES: Complete Main Quest: A Cornered Rat

MINOR SPOILERS

INTERSECTING QUESTS: Main Quest: A Cornered Rat, Main Quest: The Throat of the World

LOCATIONS: Karthspire, Riften, The Ragged Flagon, The Ratway, The Ratway Warrens, Riverwood, Sleeping Giant Inn, Sky Haven Temple, Alduin's Wall

CHARACTERS: Delphine, Esbern, Orgnar

ENEMIES: Forsworn, Thalmor Soldier, Thalmor Wizard

◊ **OBJECTIVES:** Escort Esbern to Riverwood, Talk to Esbern, Gain entrance to Sky Haven Temple, Learn the secret of Alduin's Wall

History and Prophecy

◊ **OBJECTIVE:** Escort Esbern to Riverwood

♦ **TARGET:** The Sleeping Giant Inn, in Riverwood

Now that Brynjolf and the Thieves Guild have helped you locate the slightly deranged Esbern, it is your job to chaperone him to Riverwood. Ask him if he knows the way out of here, and he sets off running. Follow him out of his hidey-hole or request that he follow you. Head down the stairs in the sewer junction chamber. As you both enter the sewer passages, Thalmor agents begin to appear. Defeat them. Combat continues as you push up the stairs and into the Ratway Warrens. Let Esbern fight the Thalmor Soldiers that may appear; Esbern is a powerful wizard and can handle himself in a fight.

Head west, through the open gate in the hub room and into the connecting sewer tunnel. Go north past the tree routes and up the stairs by the dining chamber. Next, travel around to the south, above the hub room. Cross the middle balcony of the hub room, and go to the upper balcony overlooking this same hub room chamber. Head west into the Ragged Flagon. From here, head west, into the Ratway mead-tasting room; then turn right (north) and use the wall lever to lower the wooden bridge if you haven't done this already. From here, you're one winding corridor away from exiting into Riften. At this point, you can Fast-Travel or trek back to Riverwood and the Sleeping Giant Inn.

TIP Esbern simply crouches when overwhelmed by enemy attacks and then rises again. Don't worry about him being killed.

◊ **OBJECTIVE:** Talk to Esbern

Inform Delphine that you've found Esbern, and she's most thankful, taking you both down into her secret cellar. Esbern reveals a particularly important historical location: Sky Haven Temple, constructed around one of the main Akaviri military camps in the Reach, during the conquest of Skyrim. He also places a book on the table. Read it at your leisure for some history.

➤ **Annals of the Dragonguard**

Delphine isn't impressed until Esbern informs you both that the Sky Haven Temple is where Alduin's Wall was built to set in stone all their accumulated dragonlore. But the location of the wall, one of the wonders of the ancient world, was lost. Fortunately, Esbern knows where it is and why the three of you should journey there: The ancient Blades recorded both history and prophecy on Aduin's Wall. With any luck, it may reveal how to defeat Alduin himself.

◊ **OBJECTIVE:** Gain entrance to Sky Haven Temple

Forsworn and Forsaken

Delphine knows that Esbern's description fits an area of Skyrim called Karthspire, in the Karth River Canyon. She asks whether you should all travel there together or whether you should meet them at the Sky Haven Temple entrance. The choice is yours. You can:

Fast-Travel to the nearest location closest to the temple, and then walk there. Or Fast-Travel to the temple entrance itself, if you've already discovered it.

Travel the path along Falkreath Hold, which involves fending off any enemies along the way and fighting as a trio. This takes longer but allows you to raise levels and watch your teammates' considerable fighting talents. Neither of them can die from enemy attacks, so you can back them up in combat if that's your style.

Take the same, lengthy route on your own or on horseback. You won't need to wait around, but you have no backup during any fights.

Catch a carriage from Whiterun to Markarth, and then approach on foot from the west, as Delphine recommends.

After the meeting, Delphine says her last good-byes to Orgnar the barkeep and leaves the Sleeping Giant Inn for good.

The Forsworn—primitive tribesmen fighting to drive the Nords out of this western hold—are active in this area. They are formidable warriors and mages, especially in groups as large as those you find at the Karthspire exterior. Depending on your play style and whether you're traveling alone or with Delphine and Esbern, expect a protracted and furious battle across the sprawling wooden and stone battlements as you cross the platforms spanning the Karth River. After some fine sneaking or impressive combat, seek the inky-black cave entrance and enter Karthspire interior.

TIP If you lose Delphine and Esbern during the journey to the Sky Haven Temple, they appear when you enter the Karthspire interior. If you told them to go ahead, they will be waiting on the road close to the entrance, near the Karthspire Forsworn Camp (unless you reach there first).

Fighting continues inside Karthspire as you head through a Forsworn camp and into a narrow ascension chamber, with stone buttresses and temple columns carved by the early Akaviri. There is an entrance high above you to the west, but it is currently impassable. There is a trick to releasing the two raised bridges that cross the width of the chamber. Move up to the three tricornered small pillars atop the dirt ramp.

Puzzle Solution: The square tile in the middle of each column is significant; study the hieroglyph in each one. One looks like an eye with a pair of horns above it. One looks like a ceremonial bowl with stylized fire. The third looks like two dragon heads facing each other and an arrow pointing down. This is the symbol of the Dragonborn. Activate the pillars so the "Dragonborn" tile is shown and the line atop each pillar points east to west. The bridge to your left (south) lowers with a rumble.

Cross the bridge and wait for Esbern to give his opinion on the tiled floor in the connecting chamber. Expect a fiery death if you step on the incorrect pressure plate. But there is a method to this madness:

Puzzle Solution: Look for the plates that have the "Dragonborn" hieroglyph on them. Step only on those plates to wind your way across the floor, before you finally reach a carved dragon head and a lever. Pull the lever, and the second crossing lowers. This has the added bonus of switching off the pressure-plate trap.

Allegory and Mythic Symbolism

Head north across the two lowered bridges and into the Sky Haven Temple entrance, a large and remarkably well-preserved chamber. Esbern strides toward a big stone head at the far (west) end.

Speak to Esbern about the entrance. He studies the circular floor carvings, murmuring something about them being a "blood seal." The mechanism needs blood to activate: your blood. The ancient Blades revered Reman Cyrodiil, and the whole place appears to be a shrine to him. Esbern explains the historical significance of this site. Listen for as long as you wish, but when you are ready, stand in the center of the circular floor carving and activate the blood seal. You cut your palm, dripping blood into the floor seal, and Reman Cyrodiil's giant carved head lifts open.

◊ **OBJECTIVE:** Learn the secret of Alduin's Wall

Quest Conclusion

You may wish to run on ahead or witness Esbern's excited discovery of Akaviri bas-reliefs. But the main chamber holds the real prize. While Delphine waits impatiently, Esbern explores the entirety of Alduin's Wall, which dominates this chamber. In the middle of the wall, Esbern discovers that the ancient Nords used a Shout to defeat Alduin. Delphine asks if you know of such a Shout. Answer that the Greybeards might know. Delphine responds with a few choice words about the Greybeards; she believes they shrank from their responsibilities and destiny. She recommends you head off to see them while she remains; Esbern is likely to be here a while.

"When misrule takes its place at the eight corners of the world,
When the Brass Tower walks and Time is reshaped,
When the thrice-blessed fail and the Red Tower trembles,
When the Dragonborn Ruler loses his throne, and the White Tower falls,
When the Snow Tower lies sundered, kingless, bleeding,
The World-Eater wakes, and the Wheel turns upon the Last Dragonborn."

Postquest Activities

Esbern continues to inspect Alduin's Wall as Main Quest: The Throat of the World begins. In addition, you can start to befriend Delphine and Esbern inside the Sky Haven Temple and complete the four Blades Factions Quests, earning you Followers, items, dragons to kill, and blessings from Esbern. Consult that Chapter for details.

THE THROAT OF THE WORLD

PREREQUISITES: Complete Main Quest: Alduin's Wall

◉ **MINOR SPOILERS**

INTERSECTING QUESTS: Main Quest: Alduin's Wall, Main Quest: Elder Knowledge Favorites, Main Quest: Paarthurnax

LOCATIONS: High Hrothgar, High Hrothgar Courtyard, Sky Haven Temple, Throat of the World

CHARACTERS: Delphine, Esbern, Master Arngeir, Master Einarth, Paarthurnax

ENEMIES: Ice Wraith, Troll

◊ **OBJECTIVES:** Talk to Arngeir, Learn the Clear Skies Shout, Use the Clear Skies Shout to open the path, Talk to Paarthurnax, Learn the Word of Power from Paarthurnax, Use your Fire Breath Shout on Paarthurnax, Talk to Paarthurnax

Sky Above, Voice Within

◊ **OBJECTIVE:** Talk to Arngeir
♦ **TARGET:** Master Arngeir, High Hrothgar

While Esbern inspects the third panel of Alduin's Wall (and offers his opinion of it if you wish to listen), you should exit Sky Haven Temple. Head up and north, and exit through any of the "dragon arrow" doors to an outside ruin offering excellent views over the Reach. You have a long trek back toward Whiterun, and then must navigate the 7,000 steps again to High Hrothgar. You should Fast-Travel if you're feeling impatient. Seek out Master Arngeir, and inform him that you need to learn the Shout that was used to defeat Alduin. The Greybeard is angered by your request, blaming the meddling Blades for their reckless arrogance. Arngeir ends the conversation (no matter what you say) by admonishing you for straying from the path of wisdom.

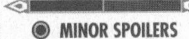

Master Einarth murmurs something to Arngeir in dragon tongue, and Arngeir calls for you to stop. He apologizes for his outburst and informs you that the Shout is called "Dragonrend." It is unknown, even to the Greybeards of High Hrothgar, as it is deemed evil. Only the master of the Greybeards—Paarthurnax—can answer your questions. You are beckoned into the courtyard and are taught another Shout that will open the way to Paarthurnax.

◊ **OBJECTIVE:** Learn the Clear Skies Shout
♦ **TARGET:** Master Arngeir, High Hrothgar Courtyard

Follow Arngeir toward the ceremonial fire pit on the raised area of the courtyard, where he bellows three glowing, runic words into the carved stone on the ground below. Step onto and absorb each of them, so your Clear Skies Shout is the strongest it can be. Then absorb the knowledge from the glowing Master Arngeir. You learn Lok ("Sky"), Vah ("Spring"), and Koor ("Summer"). Then enter your Magic > Shout Inventory menu, and select this Shout.

- **Word of Power:** Sky, Clear Skies
- **Word of Power:** Spring, Clear Skies
- **Word of Power:** Summer, Clear Skies

◊ **OBJECTIVE:** Use the Clear Skies Shout to open the path
♦ **TARGET:** The mountain fog, atop the High Hrothgar steps

Clearing the Throat

With the Shout selected, turn and depart from High Hrothgar, heading up the steps from the fire pit to the southeast. You are greeted by a perimeter arch, through which is an impenetrable fog. Execute the Clear Skies Shout and the fog dissipates for a few seconds before blanketing the mountain again. This gives you a clear view of the path to the mountaintop.

◊ **OBJECTIVE:** Talk to Paarthurnax
♦ **TARGET:** Paarthurnax, the Throat of the World summit

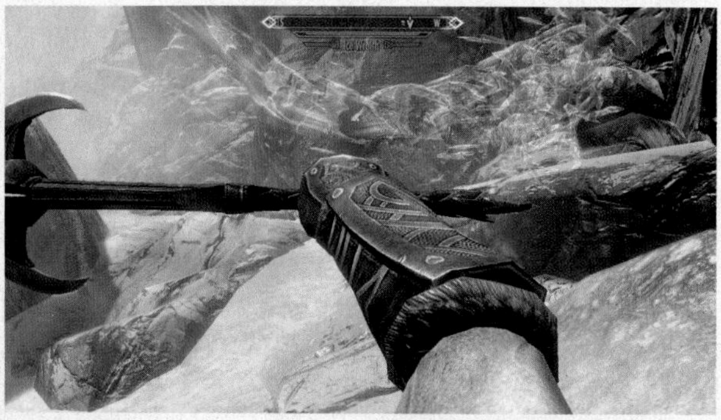

Continue up the path until you reach the edge of the fog bank. If the fog returns, then Shout again. As you progress up the zigzagging path, look out for the marker stones and the flags affixed to them. The pace is slow, but you eventually emerge above the fog bank and discover the Throat of the World—the summit of the largest mountain in Skyrim.

> **CAUTION**
> Don't wander around blindly in the gray mist; this is dangerous. Lingering in the fog can drain your Stamina, and you'll have to contend with Ice Wraiths and possibly a troll along the way.

A deep booming voice echoes around the giant rocks and snowbanks atop the mountain. Paarthurnax greets you. Speak to this giant white dragon, who asks why you intrude upon his meditation. Explain that you need to learn the Dragonrend Shout. He responds that patience is required and that formalities must be observed. Paarthurnax lands on the ground nearby and encourages you to hear his Thu'um and respond—if you are truly Dovahkiin! He opens his maw and scorches a nearby rock in a great gout of fire!

◊ **OBJECTIVE:** Learn the Word of Power from Paarthurnax

The rock soon glows with a runic Word of Power. Take this as the gift it is intended to be, and absorb another new Word of the Fire Breath Shout. You then absorb Paarthurnax's knowledge of the Word...except the beast is still alive and doesn't need slaying.

- **Word of Power:** Fire Breath

◊ **OBJECTIVE:** Use your Fire Breath Shout on Paarthurnax

Paarthurnax now wishes you to greet him, not as a mortal but as a dovah ("dragon"). Select the Fire Breath Shout from your inventory, and yell it directly into the dragon, bathing him in your fiery blast. Paarthurnax doesn't become hostile; this is the ceremonial greeting he was expecting.

> **CAUTION**
> Of course, don't follow this up with actual combat, or Paarthurnax actually becomes hostile, and you can't kill him now.

◊ **OBJECTIVE:** Talk to Paarthurnax

Watcher at the Time-Wound

Paarthurnax is happy to make your acquaintance and asks what you wish of him. When you repeat your request to learn the Dragonrend Shout, Paarthurnax has been expecting this. After further conversation, the great dragon says that even he does not know the Thu'um that you seek. After another question, he asks why you want to learn the Shout. Reply with any answer you wish, but do tell him you need to stop Alduin. Paarthurnax describes his elder brother as "troublesome." This hermit soon asks you why he lives up here.

Your answers won't be correct, so he tells you he meditates at this spot, as it was where Alduin was defeated by the ancient Tongues. But even the Dragonrend Shout wasn't enough; they had to employ the Kel—or Elder Scroll—to create a Tiid-Ahraan, or Time-Wound, and cast him adrift on the currents of Time. If you ask, he explains what an Elder Scroll is and reveals he has been waiting: For thousands of years, until Alduin began to emerge from Time. This is important to your cause. If you found an Elder Scroll at this exact location, you might be able to cast yourself back to the other end of the time break—and learn Dragonrend from those who created it!

Quest Conclusion

You're left with one overwhelming question...

Postquest Activities

...which is answered during Main Quest: Elder Knowledge!

PREREQUISITES: Complete Main Quest: The Throat of the World

MINOR SPOILERS

INTERSECTING QUESTS: Main Quest: The Throat of the World, Main Quest: Alduin's Bane, Main Quest: Paarthurnax, Daedric Quest: Discerning the Transmundane, Other Faction Quests (The Greybeards Quests): Word Wall Revelations*, Other Faction Quests (The Greybeards Quests): Meditations on Words of Power*, College of Winterhold Quest: First Lessons

LOCATIONS: Alftand, Alftand Animonculory, Alftand Cathedral, Alftand Glacial Ruins, Alftand Ruined Tower , Blackreach, College of Winterhold, Hall of the Elements, The Arcanaeum, High Hrothgar , High Hrothgar Courtyard, Septimus Signus's Outpost, Sky Haven Temple, Throat of the World, Tower of Mzark, Oculory

CHARACTERS: Esbern, Faralda, Master Arngeir, Paarthurnax, Septimus Signus, Urag gro-Shub

ENEMIES: Dwarven Centurion, Dwarven Sphere, Dwarven Spider, Falmer, Frostbite Spider, Horker, Ice Wolf, J'darr, Skeever, Wolf

◊ OBJECTIVES: Learn the location of the Elder Scroll, (Optional) Talk to Esbern, OR (Optional) Talk to Arngeir, Objective: Recover the Elder Scroll

NOTE * Quest names marked with this symbol do not appear in your Quest Menu list, although objectives may.

Higher Learning

◊ OBJECTIVE: Learn the location of the Elder Scroll
♦ TARGET: College of Winterhold
◊ OBJECTIVE: (Optional) Talk to Esbern
♦ TARGET: Esbern, at the Sky Haven Temple
◊ OBJECTIVE: OR (Optional) Talk to Arngeir
♦ TARGET: Master Arngeir, at High Hrothgar

Finish your conversation with Paarthurnax by asking him to impart all the information about the Elder Scroll that he can. According to him, when you return with the Scroll, you shall meet Hakon, Gormlaith, and Felldir—the first mortals to whom Paarthurnax taught the Thu'um and who led the rebellion against Alduin. Complete your talk with Paarthurnax, and then leave to locate the Elder Scroll, if you haven't found it yet. There are two optional clues that point you in the correct direction.

NOTE Do you already have the Elder Scroll in your possession? This is possible, if you've completed Daedric Quest: Discerning the Transmundane. If so, you can skip this quest and begin Main Quest: Alduin's Bane.

NOTE Remember that, you can still return to him to meditate on Words of Power. Consult Other Factions Quests (The Greybeards Quests): Meditations on Words of Power for more details. This quest becomes available once you complete Main Quest: The Horn of Jurgen Windcaller.

Talking to Esbern: To learn more about your Elder Scroll search, you may wish to return to the Sky Haven Temple. Esbern is usually standing outside, atop the mountain the temple is dug into, gazing over the Reach. Approach the temple pavilion and speak to him. He recommends you visit the College of Winterhold. Your map updates.

Talking to Arngeir: To learn more about your Elder Scroll search, you can visit High Hrothgar and speak with Master Arngeir. The Greybeards do not concern themselves with the Scrolls, but such blasphemies have always been the stock-in-trade of the mages of Winterhold. He suggests you try their College. Your map updates.

NOTE At this point, you can speak to Arngeir and learn the locations of additional Words of Power. Consult Other Factions Quests (The Greybeards Quests): Word Wall Revelations for more details.

Insane Ruminations

Begin your journey to the city of Winterhold. The College is linked to it by a bridge. At the bridge's near end, a High Elf wizard guards the entrance. She stops you, warning that it's not safe to cross the bridge and that you will be denied entrance to the city. She will become hostile if you take a swing at her. Although she has some complaints about the College, which you can ask her about, you really just want to enter the College. Ask if this is possible, and she asks why. Choose the answer that best suits your demeanor. She requires that you take a test to show you're at least competent in the use of magic. You can:

Walk right in without dealing with Faralda, if you're already a member of the College of Winterhold and started that line of Side Quests.

(Persuade) Tell her that you both know you'll be successful.

Agree to take the test. When the test begins, Faralda requests you aim a spell at the seal on the ground near to her.

Ask if she would grant entry to the Dragonborn. Faralda asks if you really have the Voice. Show her any Shout you have.

Spell Casting: Bring up your Magic menu and choose the spell Faralda has requested. She can choose Firebolt, Magelight, Fury, Conjure Flame Atronach, or Healing Hands, depending on your available spells and knowledge of particular magic styles. Aim at the seal and cast the spell. After a successful casting, Faralda tells you to find Mirabelle Ervine inside the College.

Dragon Shouting: Bring up your Shout inventory, choose any Shout (a good choice is Fire Breath), aim it at the seal, and bellow. After you strike the seal, Faralda tells you that there is much you both can learn from each other and that you'd be a superb addition to the College.

You can now ask Faralda more questions about Mirabelle and the College, or even receive training in the arts of Destruction Magic. College of Winterhold Quest: First Lessons is now active, and you are told to report to Mirabelle Ervine. However, this objective is not required or part of the Main Quest. Cross the bridge, enter the College's exterior courtyard, open the grand doors, and enter the Hall of the Elements. Immediately make a right (east) turn and enter the Arcanaeum.

CAUTION Be extremely careful where you wave your fingers! Don't aim (accidentally or otherwise) at Faralda or choose a spell (or Shout) that has a large area of effect. If you cast a wider flame-based attack, you risk setting Faralda on fire, effectively ending your tryout as an apprentice mage!

TIP Do you want to mingle with other mages? Then consult the College of Winterhold Quests for further information on the denizens of this epicenter of magic in Skyrim. This is also a great time to start their quests, if you haven't done so already.

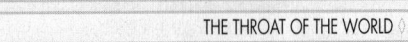

Look for the Orc Mage named Urag gro-Shub, who runs the Arcanaeum. Although you can ask to assist him in College business (which allows you to accomplish several College-related tasks unrelated to this quest) and can ask about the Arcanaeum library, you're here to ask him about the Elder Scroll. Urag isn't too happy with you offhandedly asking about such a powerful artifact. You may listen to an overview of the Scrolls before asking if there's an Elder Scroll you could use. Urag laughs at this question; he wouldn't show the likes of you, even if he obtained one. Ask if he at least has any information on them. He agrees to locate a couple of arcane tomes that may have some clues. But mostly they contain lies leavened with rumors.

Urag gro-Shub locates and places two tomes on the nearby desk: *Effects of the Elder Scrolls* and *Ruminations on the Elder Scrolls*. After reading both books (which you may keep or leave on the desk), you find that the Ruminations tome is the work of a madman. Daedric Quest: Discerning the Transmundane now begins.

➤ *Effects of the Elder Scrolls* ➤ *Ruminations on the Elder Scrolls*

◊ **DAEDRIC QUEST OBJECTIVE:** Ask Urag about the insane book

Return to Urag and let him know that the Ruminations book is incomprehensible. He doesn't seem surprised; after all, this book was the work of Septimus Signus. Although Signus is the world's master of the nature of Elder Scrolls, Urag tells you he's "been gone for a long while." You suspect he means both mentally and physically. He currently resides north of the College in the treacherous Ice Fields.

◊ **DAEDRIC QUEST OBJECTIVE:** Find Septimus Signus
♦ **TARGET:** Septimus Signus's Outpost

The Hermit of Hermaeus Mora

The giant chunks of ice floating off the Northern Coast are your next destination. Exit the College and run down to the frigid coastal waters. Hop across any floating ice that you can, navigating your way north. Expect to slice into a few Horkers along the way, and you may encounter wolves and Ice Wolves.

Septimus Signus's Outpost is cut into one of the hill-sized icebergs, close to a moored rowing boat. Climb down the ladder and the slope to reach a lone mage in a chamber of ice. He appears to be guarding some kind of Dwemer box about the size of a house.

Asking Septimus about the Elder Scrolls results in a torrent of knowledge. Ask where the Scroll is, and after receiving moderately useless information, ask once more (either pleasantly or with a more threatening tone). Septimus agrees to tell you, but in return, you must venture into Blackreach, a strange underground Dwemer city that lies below Alftand.

Ask about getting into Blackreach. Septimus keeps up his riddle-based prattling and hands you two items: The first is an odd-edged lexicon, used by the Dwemer for inscribing. The second is an Attunement Sphere, which apparently "sings" when you near an important Dwemer door. Once these are in your grasp, your Main Quest updates. Stay and speak further with Septimus if your sanity can stand it.

➤ **Attunement Sphere** ➤ **Blank Lexicon**

◊ **DAEDRIC QUEST OBJECTIVE:** Transcribe the Lexicon
♦ **TARGET:** Tower of Mzark
◊ **OBJECTIVE:** Recover the Elder Scroll
♦ **TARGET:** Tower of Mzark

Trek to the Tower

TIP You must have the Attunement Sphere on your person in order to continue; otherwise, you cannot access the route necessary to reach the Elder Scroll. The following location is one of a few entrances to a giant underground city called Blackreach. This is the optimal path, but there are others. Consult the Atlas to see all the ways to enter this subterranean citadel and the Tower of Mzark.

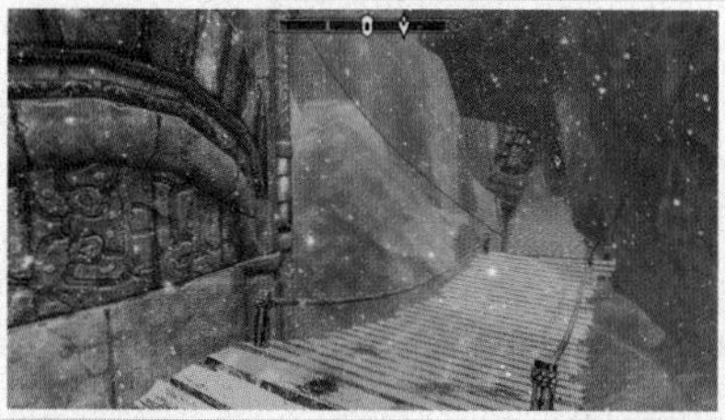

Alftand is located on the glacial mountains southwest of Winterhold. Your trek there is usually interrupted by wild animal attacks. The exterior of Alftand is a series of dotted structures, both Dwarven and Nordic in nature. Below the glaciers is the Alftand Ruined Tower, which offers a dangerous route to the glacier's top. A much better way is to stay outside to reach the two windswept huts, an inaccessible Dwarven tower, and a precarious platform that winds down and around the rooftops, on the side of the glacier. Head down the planked bridges until you reach the entrance to the Alftand Glacial Ruins. This is the way to go.

Wind through the glacial tunnels that have been mined out and left in a real mess, with debris and cooking equipment strewn about, and the signs of fighting everywhere you look. Follow the tunnel down until you reach the beginnings of the Dwarven architecture, a stone tunnel that ends in a connecting room with a stone table, and a large barred doorway to the north. This can only be unlocked from the other side. On the nearby table you'll find Research Notes. Whoever wrote it thought he saw a strange human figure on the other side of the barred doorway.

➤ **Research Notes**

At this point, the passage west heads up a ramp and down the other side, into another glacial intrusion. Watch for attacks from a Dwarven Spider as you go. A Skooma-addled Khajiit is shouting about being trapped here and attacks if he sees you. Drop him, and continue down into the start of the main Dwarven ruins. The ceilings tower above you as you reach a cog and piston room with a raised center and two Dwarven Spheres appearing from their wall holes to attack. Continue north to a vent chamber with a locked gate (Novice) leading to a few scraps of treasure. Head through the gold door and up to a Dwarven Spider–infested passage stretching south. This leads to a locked (Apprentice) gold door with items to steal behind it, and a main path around to the east, which brings you back into the cog and piston room. This time, you're above the raised center. Navigate the pistons (jump over them, or you risk being pushed off by them) in a counterclockwise route to the short corridor and door to the Alftand Animonculory.

TIP There are many trinkets of Dwemer origin to pick up (and sell once you leave). Among the vendors across Skyrim, a wizard named Calcelmo in Markarth's Understone Keep is most interested in these items and gives a good price, although you can sell them to any merchant or vendor who wants them.

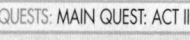

Move through the green-tinged corridor to an opening on your left (east). This leads to a large pipeworks corridor. Avoid two Dwarven Spheres by staying on the low ground, and head through the gap in the gold fencing to the left of the stone steps. Otherwise, head up the steps, over the pipes, and up the ramp with the central slit. Walk on the slit so you don't trigger a blade trap by stepping on the pressure plates. At the barred doorway, use the lever on your right to lower the bars. The lever behind the bars raises them, which isn't necessary unless you're being pursued and want to halt your attackers. Step out into the grand Animonculory shaft—a long vertical drop you need to descend without falling. Remove any Dwarven Spider threats, and head down the sloping stone walkway to an arched entrance platform. The gold door here (Apprentice) just leads to a dead end and more treasure.

Peer over the edge of the stone platform facing into the shaft. The walkway below has crumbled, forcing you to drop onto the jutting gold pipe and then the rubble platform. There is a walkway to the west, heading up to a precarious ledge, a Dwarven Spider battle, and a piston that can push you over the edge. The way forward and downward is to the northeast. Look for the lantern and falling water, as the sloping walkway is hidden.

As you descend, something horrific shuffles out of the shadows: an eyeless figure, thought to be myth. These are Falmer, the degenerate remnants of the original Elven inhabitants of Skyrim! Dispatch four of them as you follow the winding platform down. Take care not to lose your footing and fall to your death. Next, face the jet of fire blasting the entrance to a gold door. Dart through or around, and enter a Falmer nest.

Falmer appear from their huts, forcing you to fight or sneak by. Follow the passage down to a second set of Falmer in a boiler chamber. Watch for those rattling, hanging bones if you're sneaking, as these startle the Falmer into finding you. Head down the steps, watching for Skeever attacks, and look for a gold door on the southeast wall. This is the way onward, but you may wish to turn to the northwest, open a gate, and enter an ancient Dwarven Elevator. Pull the lever and you ascend to the Alftand Glacial Ruins.

Step around the rubble and to the barred doorway where you found the Research Notes. Pull a wall lever here, so the bars retract. This allows you to easily navigate up and down the Animonculory if you explore here in the future. For now, use the elevator to head back down, and open the gold door in the southeast wall. This leads down the sloping walkway to the shaft's bottom, where you encounter another Falmer attack and face a Frostbite Spider. From here, you have only one set of corridor steps and a claw trap (move around the trip wire) before you enter the Alftand Cathedral.

Battle a Falmer and navigate some floor trigger plates to reach a gold door that leads out into the main cathedral chamber—a massive echoing cavern with a central structure and a doorway barred with spears. Check the area for Falmer and the steps to your left (south) before heading to a gold lever above the entrance from which you came. This raises the spears, enabling you to enter the cathedral platform, where a giant steam-powered mechanical monster roars into life. This Dwarven Centurion is a frightening form, but you should defeat it, as it carries a handy key.

➤ **Key to Alftand Lift**

Climb to the gate (southwest) at the platform's top, open it, and then listen to the arguments of two thieves, Sulla and Umana. You must slay them, as there's no reasoning with them. Now open the gate beyond the strange Dwarven Mechanism. This leads up to the top of the Alftand glacier, and a tower you couldn't access when you first reached here. Open the gate from the inside using the wall lever (so you can access the cathedral directly from the surface during future adventures); then travel back down to the cathedral. Approach the Dwarven Mechanism now, and insert the Attunement Sphere Septimus gave you. The floor parts, revealing stairs down to a hidden gold door and an entrance into the mysterious undercity of Blackreach.

> **NOTE** Take a moment to adjust to the vastness of this cavern. Aside from firing a Dwarven crossbow using an adjacent lever and investigating the small stone building to the southwest (Sinderion's Field Laboratory, where you can start collecting Crimson Nirnroot and begin Side Quest: A Return to Your Roots), there is a sprawling area to adventure through. Consult the Atlas for information on the entire area; this walkthrough points you directly to the exit necessary to reach the Elder Scroll.

Exiting Blackreach using the appropriate Dwarven Elevator involves a romp west. First, though, you may wish to head southeast, to a golden button encased on a Dwarven head pedestal. Press it, and the elevator behind lights up, allowing you to ascend and exit back outside. Open the gate, allowing you to enter from the Great Lift of Alftand (a new tower entrance northeast of Nightgate Inn). Return to Blackreach and find the cobblestone path heading roughly west. Follow it past ancient structures and towering luminescent fungi. Continue with a giant lake and cascading waterfalls to your left (south), heading over a stone bridge. Go west and turn left (south) to reach a colossal elevator that allows you to ascend into the Tower of Mzark, your destination.

Oculory Operation

Venture along a corridor with a burst steam pipe and small camping area, and through gold doors into a gigantic, circular Aedrome chamber. The chamber is dominated by a huge sphere. This appears to be some kind of massive Oculory, with a variety of focusing lenses and other golden machinery attached. Head to the cluster of controls on the platform above the Oculory. The controls are comprised of five cylindrical devices: a Lexicon Receptacle and four positioning buttons embedded in pedestals. There is a certain way to use these devices to produce something hidden in one of the lenses.

Puzzle solution: Activate the Lexicon Receptacle, so the Blank Lexicon rests on top of it. The two pedestals to the Receptacle's right—the only ones currently active—open and close the Oculory lenses. Press the taller of the two pedestals (right of the middle one with the lens chart on it) three or four times, until the pedestal with the blue button to the left of the middle one starts to glow. Move to this new pedestal (at this point, the Blank Lexicon may be glowing blue). The two pedestals to the left of the Receptacle—the taller of which is now active—control the ceiling lens array. Press the button of the taller, left pedestal twice, until the button on the far left, smaller pedestal begins to glow. Now press that button, and a large set of lens crystals descends from the ceiling and stops. The main crystal rotates and splits apart to reveal a tubelike carrying device.

Quest Conclusion

Drop down from the balcony controls and approach the open lens crystal. Take the Elder Scroll from its elaborate compartment. Then exit using the door under the Lexicon Receptacle. This leads to one final Dwarven Elevator, which allows you to open the gate from the Tower of Mzark, step out into the exterior, and add another possible entrance to Blackreach, if you decide to return.

➤ **Elder Scroll**

Postquest Activities

As soon as you take the Elder Scroll, Main Quest: Alduin's Bane begins. In addition, you are able to return to the giant underground city of Blackreach and can continue Daedric Quest: Discerning the Transmundane from this point on. Consult that quest for further information.

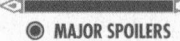

ALDUIN'S BANE

PREREQUISITES: Complete Main Quest: Elder Knowledge

MAJOR SPOILERS

INTERSECTING QUESTS: Main Quest: Elder Knowledge, Main Quest: The Fallen, Main Quest: Paarthurnax, Other Faction Quests (The Greybeards Quests): Meditations on Words of Power*, Other Faction Quests (The Greybeards Quests): Words of Power*, College of Winterhold Quest: First Lessons

LOCATIONS: Throat of the World, Tower of Mzark, Oculory

CHARACTERS: Felldir, Gormlaith, Hakon, Paarthurnax

ENEMIES: Alduin

◊ **OBJECTIVES:** Read the Elder Scroll at the Time-Wound , Learn the Dragonrend Shout from the Nord heroes, Defeat Alduin

NOTE * Quest names marked with this symbol do not appear in your Quest Menu list, although objectives may.

A Blast from the Past

◊ **OBJECTIVE:** Read the Elder Scroll at the Time-Wound
♦ **TARGET:** Throat of the World (mountain summit)

Once you've taken the Elder Scroll from the Oculory inside the Tower of Mzark, simply return to the Dwarven Elevator and head outside. Once you're back on Skyrim's surface, you can travel (by your preferred means) to the Throat of the World, where Paarthurmax is perched on his rock, watching you intently. Move near the Time-Wound, which glows brighter as you advance upon it, and read the Elder Scroll from your inventory.

◊ **OBJECTIVE:** Learn the Dragonrend Shout from the Nord heroes
♦ **TARGET:** Hakon, Gormlaith, and Felldir, through the Elder Scroll

Your vision pitches back into the past, thousands of years ago, when the Nord heroes of old first fought Alduin and his dragon brethren. But Gormlaith, Hakon, and Felldir are seen as if you could reach out and touch them. You cannot move while watching this memory play out. You watch as Gormlaith and Hakon deliver a series of killing blows to a dragon, with Hakon worrying that Alduin may not appear and fall into the trap they have set for him. Felldir has seen none of his kin stand against Alduin, not Galthor, Sorri, or Birkir. Gormlaith replies that they did not have Dragonrend. But as Alduin cannot be slain like a lesser dragon, Felldir has brought something to even the odds—an Elder Scroll!

The giant black dragon soon descends on the trio of Nord warriors. As planned, the three heroes bellow out Joor ("Mortal"), Zah ("Finite"), Frul ("Temporary")! At the same moment in present time, you absorb the knowledge of this Shout yourself. Alduin is confused, and sees fear for the first time. While Gormlaith is torn and tossed about by an enraged Alduin, Hakon yells to Felldir to use the Elder Scroll. After Felldir yells the incantation, Alduin is consumed by a massive ball of energy, sucked into the Elder Scroll, and is banished from the world of Skyrim...of the past. But what of the present?

➤ **Word of Power:** Mortal, Dragonrend

➤ **Word of Power:** Finite, Dragonrend

➤ **Word of Power:** Temporary, Dragonrend

◊ **OBJECTIVE:** Defeat Alduin
♦ **TARGET:** Alduin, Throat of the World

Rending the World-Eater Asunder

Something black and jagged arcs through the blizzard. Alduin has seen your attempts at reading the Elder Scroll but arrives too late to prevent you from learning the Shout that may be his downfall. Paarthurnax attempts to intercept Alduin's attack but is cut down and lands heavily near you. He tells you to use the Dragonrend Shout if you can.

Dragon Slaying: Immediately select Dragonrend from the Shouts, and target the Thu'um directly at Alduin as he flies down to a hover, swoops past, or lands.

Try to lengthen the attack of the Shout (by holding down the Shout button). When he lands heavily, utilize your favored attack (which can be a second or third Shout as well as your magic and ranged or melee weapons).

If Alduin takes to the skies, use Dragonrend again; it is the only guaranteed way of dropping him back down to earth.

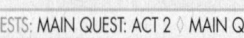

> **CAUTION**
> Warning! Alduin is completely invincible except when he's affected by Dragonrend!

Continue combat, which is the most difficult that you've likely faced, and make use of any Health, Magicka, or Stamina potions that you've acquired for this battle.

Quest Conclusion

The battle ends only after you've depleted Alduin's health, or he's savaged you to death; there is no respite. Kill or be killed!

Postquest Activities

Once you've dealt a final blow to Alduin, Main Quest: The Fallen begins.

MAIN QUEST: ACT III

THE FALLEN

PREREQUISITES: Complete Main Quest: Alduin's Bane

INTERSECTING QUESTS: Main Quest: The Fallen, Main Quest: Paarthurnax, Other Faction Quests (The Greybeards Quests): Word Wall Revelations*, Other Faction Quests (The Greybeards Quests): Meditations on Words of Power*

LOCATIONS: Whiterun, Dragonsreach

CHARACTERS: Esbern, General Tullius, Jarl Balgruuf the Greater, Jarl Vignar the Revered, Master Arngeir, Paarthurnax, Ulfric Stormcloak

ENEMIES: Alduin, Odahviing

◊ **OBJECTIVES:** Talk to Paarthurnax, OR Talk to Arngeir, OR Talk to Esbern, Talk to the Jarl of Whiterun, Learn Shout to call Odahviing, Prepare trap for Odahviing, Call Odahviing to Dragonsreach, Defeat and trap Odahviing, Interrogate Odahviing

> **NOTE** * Quest names marked with this symbol do not appear in your Quest Menu list, although objectives may.

Part 1: Expert Mediation

◊ **OBJECTIVE:** Talk to Paarthurnax
♦ **TARGET:** Throat of the World
◊ **OBJECTIVE:** OR Talk to Arngeir
♦ **TARGET:** High Hrothgar
◊ **OBJECTIVE:** OR Talk to Esbern
♦ **TARGET:** Sky Haven Temple

Alduin collapses to the ground after you deal him a particularly impressive blow. But the arch-dragon isn't some common serpent; he is firstborn of Akatosh! He cannot be slain here, even by you. He takes to the skies, and even your Dragonrend cannot stop him. He seems weakened; he's down but not out. Now you must seek the guidance of your chosen ally. You have three to choose from:

1. Paarthurnax

If you are favoring the kinship of the Greybeards over the Blades, you may seek council with Paarthurnax. Mention that you need to find out where Alduin went, and the dragon ponders this. Perhaps an ally of his could be convinced to betray him. Paarthurnax mentions that the palace in Whiterun—Dragonsreach—was originally built to house a captive dovah (dragon). It would be a fine place to trap an Alduin ally. You mention that the Jarl might need some convincing (as the quest updates). Then Paarthurnax tells you the story of how the place came to be named Dragonsreach.

2. Arngeir

You may visit Master Arngeir, who heard the Dragonrend Shout from High Hrothgar. Arngeir tells you that Alduin can travel to Sovngarde to devour the souls of the dead, but no one knows how this is achieved. You reply that one of his dragon allies might reveal this. But there is one possibility: Dragonsreach, which was originally built to hold a captive dragon. This did indeed occur in the time of Olaf One-Eye, thousands of years ago. You might be able to trap a dragon there, once you have the Jarl's cooperation.

3. Esbern

Or you can return to Esbern at the Sky Temple pavilion outside, and he asks what happened. He believes Alduin returned to Sovngarde to feed on the souls of the dead, and if you don't find him soon, he'll return stronger than ever. When you mention that his dragon allies might know where the portal to Sovngarde is, Esbern agrees and asks you about Dragonsreach. Apparently it was built to hold a captive dragon, back before the Akaviri crusaders cleansed Skyrim of dragons. You could trap a dragon there, but getting the Jarl to use his palace as a dragon trap might be impossible.

◊ **OBJECTIVE:** Talk to the Jarl of Whiterun
♦ **TARGET:** The Jarl of Whiterun, in Dragonsreach, in Whiterun

> **NOTE** Esbern has another problem if you speak with him. He's discovered who the Greybeards' leader really is—a dragon responsible for many atrocities during the ancient Dragon War. On behalf of the Blades, he demands that Paarthurnax die for these crimes. Furthermore, Esbern's oath as a Blade prevents him from offering you aid or comfort until this dragon is slain.
>
> Main Quest: Paarthurnax begins officially at this point. Consult Main Quest: Paarthurnax for further information. It can also occur if you speak to Delphine. You must complete this quest to access help at the Sky Haven Temple from the Blades; otherwise Delphine and Esbern will speak but offer no assistance to you, which takes the form of the four Other Factions Quests involving the Blades.

Return to Whiterun and visit Dragonsreach within its walls. Approach the Jarl, who is usually sitting under Numinex's skull. Numinex is the dragon that Jarl Olaf One-Eye brought back to Whiterun. Request that the Jarl help you, as you require a trap to snare a dragon in the Jarl's palace. The Jarl's responses, and even the Jarl himself differs, depending on how the Civil War is progressing:

Jarl Balgruuf the Greater is the Jarl if the Imperials still have this Hold during the Civil War or if you haven't decided to start the Civil War.

If the Stormcloaks have one Hold left or have been completely wiped out, and the Imperials (to which Jarl Balgruuf has pledged loyalty) have emerged victorious in the Civil War, the Jarl begrudgingly agrees to let you try out your insane dragon-trapping plan. You can skip Main Quest: Season Unending (which occurs in the middle of this quest), and continue your plan on the Dragonsreach balcony. Main Quest: The Fallen (Part 2) begins.

If the Stormcloaks have more than one Hold left during the Civil War, or you haven't started any of the Civil War Quests yet, the Jarl has more pressing matters than your lunatic schemes: Quest Conclusion Part 1 begins.

Jarl Vignar the Revered is the Jarl if you've attacked Whiterun and driven out the forces loyal to Jarl Balgruuf and the Imperials and slaughtered those who defended the city.

If the Imperials have one Hold left or have been completely obliterated from the Holds' major cities, and the Stormcloaks (who have installed this newly appointed Jarl) are victorious in the Civil War, the Jarl reluctantly agrees to let you perform your dragon-snaring act. You can skip Main Quest: Season Unending (which occurs in the middle of this quest), and continue the plan on the Dragonsreach balcony. Main Quest: The Fallen (Part 2) begins.

If the Imperials have more than one Hold left during the Civil War, but the Civil War is under way and Whiterun has fallen to the Stormcloaks, the Jarl has problems with the ongoing Civil War conflict. Quest Conclusion Part 1 begins.

Quest Conclusion Part 1

The Jarl has no time (or additional men) to spare to trap a dragon. Explain that this is the only way to find Alduin. The Jarl says he wants to help, but he requires your aid first. Ulfric Stormcloak and General Tullius are both waiting for the Jarl to make the wrong move, and the Jarl's enemies won't sit idly by while a dragon slaughters the Jarl's forces. The Jarl cannot weaken the city while the threat of enemy attacks is looming. That threat would have to be nullified, even temporarily, for the Jarl to agree to your plan. For this to happen, both sides must agree to a truce, but the Jarl feels the bitterness runs too deep.

But all is not lost. The Greybeards might be willing to hold a peace council, and then perhaps Ulfric and Tullius will listen. You're told to negotiate a peace deal, and so begins Main Quest: Season Unending.

◊ **MAIN QUEST:** Season Unending
◊ **OBJECTIVE:** Get Greybeards' help in negotiating a truce
♦ **TARGET:** Master Arngeir, in High Hrothgar

Part 2: Epic Entanglement

◊ **OBJECTIVE:** Learn Shout to call Odahviing
♦ **TARGET:** Esbern, in the Sky Haven Temple
♦ **TARGET:** OR Paarthurnax, at the Throat of the World

Once you have convinced the Jarl to aid you, you still need a way to lure a dragon into your trap. You have a choice of teachers:

Esbern: who has been busy in the Sky Haven Temple library. It appears that the ancient Blades recorded many of the names of the dragons they slew. By cross-referencing the burial-site map that Delphine created from the Dragonstone, Esbern has identified one of Alduin's raised dragons.

Paarthurnax: whose arcane knowledge and commanding expertise of Shouts enables him to easily inform you of the Shout that you seek.

Because the names of dragons are always three Words of Power (Shouts), the dragon will hear and come to you when his name is bellowed. Your teacher has the name of Od-Ah-Viing ("Winged Snow Hunter"), and you learn the Shout to call Odahviing.

- **Word of Power:** Snow, Call Dragon
- **Word of Power:** Hunter, Call Dragon
- **Word of Power:** Wing, Call Dragon

NOTE Delphine, if she's with Esbern, now has a bone to pick with you. She assures you that the Blades won't be nearly as accommodating if you don't slay Paarthurnax up at the Throat of the World. This is another hint to start Main Quest: Paarthurnax. Once again, it is purely optional. Consult that quest for more information.

◊ **OBJECTIVE:** Prepare trap for Odahviing
♦ **TARGET:** Jarl of Whiterun, in Dragonsreach

Now that you've learned the Call Dragon Shout, you can try it out anywhere. Odahviing appears in the skies, but he's too far away to bring down using Dragonrend. As there's no way to capture Odahviing until you reach Dragonsreach, return to Whiterun and speak with the Jarl. He is ready, so inform him you're prepared to catch a dragon. Follow the Jarl up the steps to the side of his throne and out the doors to the northeast.

◊ **OBJECTIVE:** Call Odahviing to Dragonsreach
♦ **TARGET:** Battlements, atop Dragonsreach

You emerge on the large stone battlements, which have a dragon-sized porch area. Move to the crenellations at the structure's northeast edge, where the Jarl tells you to call; his men are ready. Execute the Call Dragon Shout and wait a few moments. The ominous sound of leathery wings echoes across the tundra.

◊ **OBJECTIVE:** Defeat and trap Odahviing

The mighty red beast soars up and attacks the battlements. At this point, you must bring Odahviing down and spring the trap:

Dragon Trapping: It is important to note that you're trapping—and not killing—Odahviing. Attacking with ranged spells or arrows usually annoys Odahviing enough for him to swoop and land on the battlements.

An easier plan is to yell the Dragonrend Shout at Odahviing. This hampers his flying and makes him drop onto the battlements without having to lengthen this already-difficult battle.

When he drops onto Dragonsreach, Odahviing advances on his wings, furious at being forced to land. Back up (to the southwest) so Odahviing enters the giant hallway and passes between the two huge chains attached to the giant stocks contraption. When the dragon moves forward, the stocks slam down, trapping Odahviing!

◊ **OBJECTIVE:** Interrogate Odahviing

CAUTION
Remember, you're interrogating, not killing, Odahviing. You cannot dispatch him, so concentrate on trapping him.

Odahviing feels humiliated and is perhaps a little impressed by your trapping talents. Ask where Alduin is hiding (and then ask again), and Odahviing reveals Alduin has traveled to Sovngarde to regain his strength. The door to Sovngarde is located at Skuldafn, one of his ancient fanes (temples) high in the eastern mountains. After answering your questions, Odahviing asks to be freed. Answer that he must serve you. Odahviing initially refuses but remembers one important detail he forgot to mention...

Quest Conclusion Part 2

It seems that Skuldafn can be entered only by flying. Odahviing offers to fly you there, but only after you free him. This conundrum is concluded at the start of the next quest.

Postquest Activities

Once you're pondering how to reach Skuldafn and setting Odahviing free, Main Quest: The World-Eater's Eyrie begins.

PAARTHURNAX

PREREQUISITES: Complete Main Quest: Alduin's Bane

◉ MINOR SPOILERS

INTERSECTING QUESTS: Main Quest: Alduin's Bane, Other Faction Quests (The Greybeards Quests): Word Wall Revelations* , Other Faction Quests (The Greybeards Quests): Meditations on Words of Power*, College of Winterhold Quest: First Lessons

LOCATIONS: Riverwood, Sleeping Giant Inn, Sky Haven Temple, Throat of the World

CHARACTERS: Delphine, Esbern, Master Arngeir

ENEMIES: Paarthurnax

◊ **OBJECTIVES:** Kill Paarthurnax, Talk to Delphine or Esbern

NOTE * Quest names marked with this symbol do not appear in your Quest Menu list, although objectives may.

Slaying the Summit's Hermit

◊ **OBJECTIVE:** Kill Paarthurnax
♦ **TARGET:** Throat of the World (mountain summit)

Your alliance with the Blades sits uneasily upon a knife edge. They refuse to help you (which basically means you cannot access their Other Faction Quests) until you've defeated the monster at the Throat of the World. Reasoning with them that Paarthurnax has changed his ways and now embodies peace and meditation falls on deaf ears. They simply want you to remove Paarthurnax, as they perceive him to be partly responsible for the many deaths of their ancestral clan members.

CAUTION
Remember! This quest is completely optional. You will lose standing with the Greybeards if you complete this task, so it is time to pick a side.

NOTE Killing Paarthurnax does not affect the future Main Quests; you will still be able to complete your task of killing Paarthurnax's brother, Alduin, without any complications.

Return to the Throat of the World (or remain here after the end of Main Quest: Alduin's Bane) and approach Paarthurnax. Kill him using your favorite weaponry. One method is to launch Fire Breath (the Shout he actually taught you) into him until he starts to flinch and takes to the skies. Then wound and bring him down to the ground with Dragonrend. Finish with your other attacks, using a bow, magic, or melee weapons. Gather the gold and bones from Paarthurnax's corpse, but only after absorbing his soul.

➤ **Dragon's Soul**

◊ **OBJECTIVE:** Talk to Delphine or Esbern
♦ **TARGET:** Riverwood or Sky Haven Temple

Quest Conclusion

Return to Delphine or to Esbern. Depending on when you killed Paarthurnax or who gave you this quest, expect a similar response from either of them: They are extremely happy; the ancient evil is avenged, and the shades of many Blades salute you this day!

Return to Master Arngeir, and the greeting is slightly colder. You are lucky the Greybeards are men of peace, as you've tested their philosophy beyond the breaking point. You've thrown your lot in with a cabal of Akaviri barbarians. You are no longer welcome in High Hrothgar.

TIP To gain the most knowledge and help from both the Greybeards and the Blades, complete both of the Other Factions Greybeards Quests to your satisfaction, and then complete this quest. After that, you have limited contact with the Greybeards but are on excellent terms with the Blades. You can complete the four different (and some repeatable) Other Factions Blade Quests afterward.

Postquest Activities

Your other Main Quests continue as normal. Contact with the Greybeards is now kept to a minimum; they want nothing more to do with the likes of you. The Blades welcome you into their fold. You may begin any of their Other Faction Quests after speaking to Esbern or Delphine.

SEASON UNENDING

PREREQUISITES: Partial Complete Main Quest: The Fallen

INTERSECTING QUESTS: Main Quest: The Fallen, Main Quest: Paarthurnax, Other Faction Quests (The Greybeards Quests): Word Wall Revelations*, Other Faction Quests (The Greybeards Quests): Meditations on Words of Power*

LOCATIONS: High Hrothgar, Solitude, Castle Dour, Whiterun, Dragonsreach, Windhelm, Palace of the Kings

CHARACTERS: Delphine, Elenwen, Esbern, Galmar Stone-Fist, General Tullius, Jarl Balgruuf the Greater, Jarl Elisif the Fair, Jarl Vignar the Revered , Legate Rikke, Master Arngeir, Ulfric Stormcloak

ENEMIES: None

◊ **OBJECTIVES:** Get Greybeards' help in negotiating a truce, Talk to Arngeir, Talk to General Tullius, Talk to Ulfric Stormcloak, Talk to Arngeir, Take your seat, Negotiate a truce

NOTE Season Unending only occurs if the Civil War still rages across Skyrim; consult the previous quest for more details. In order to convince General Tullius and Jarl Ulfric to attend, you may need to finish your current Civil War quest. Once both have agreed to attend the council, the Civil War effectively comes to a halt, and you cannot obtain any more Civil War Quests until you finish the Main Quest.

A Modicum of Civility

◊ **OBJECTIVE:** Get Greybeards' help in negotiating a truce
◊ **OBJECTIVE:** Talk to Arngeir
♦ **TARGET:** Master Arngeir, in High Hrothgar

Return to High Hrothgar and seek out Master Arngeir. Initially, he talks about the difficulties in capturing a dragon. Inform him that you're actually here to get his help stopping the Civil War. Arngeir reluctantly agrees to this and requests that you journey to Ulfric Stormcloak and General Tullius, and tell them that the Greybeards wish to speak to them. You may approach the leader of the Stormcloaks and the Imperials in either order.

◊ **OBJECTIVE:** Talk to General Tullius
♦ **TARGET:** Castle Dour, in Solitude
◊ **OBJECTIVE:** Talk to Ulfric Stormcloak
♦ **TARGET:** Palace of the Kings, in Windhelm

General Tullius: Plot a path and trek to Solitude. Enter the walled city. Progress to the entrance to Castle Dour, where the high-ranking Imperials command the ongoing war efforts. Approach General Tullius. He has a different greeting depending on how the Civil War is progressing and whose side you've chosen, but he certainly remembers you from Helgen.

Speak to the general again if he fobs you off and tell him you have a message from the Greybeards—they are convening a peace council at High Hrothgar. You can attempt to persuade Tullius, tell him that Ulfric has already agreed (if this is the case) or convince him with answers that you choose: Eventually he agrees to the treaty.

Ulfric Stormcloak: Figure out a favored route and journey to Windhelm. Step inside the walled city. Move to the entrance to the Palace of the Kings, where the Stormcloak chieftains plan their ongoing raids. Approach Ulfric Stormcloak. His opinion on you differs, depending on how the Civil War is progressing and the side you've chosen, but he can't forget his time at Helgen. Inform him of the message from the Greybeards, that they have requested a peace council at High Hrothgar. You can try persuading Ulfric, letting him know Tullius has already agreed (if this has happened), or bring him around with answers of your choosing. Finally, he agrees to the sit-down treaty meeting.

◊ **OBJECTIVE:** Talk to Arngeir
♦ **TARGET:** Master Arngeir, in High Hrothgar

War and Peace

Journey back to High Hrothgar and locate Master Arngeir. As you arrive, Delphine and Esbern are having a heated discussion with the Greybeards, demanding to be part of the meeting. If you've completed Main Quest: Paarthurnax, the conversation is slightly different, depending on how you've dealt with the dragon. The conversation ends, Arngeir expresses further concerns to you—especially that this place was built and dedicated to peace—before all parties are requested to take their seats for the council.

◊ **OBJECTIVE:** Take your seat

Enter the grand hall in High Hrothgar, and take your seat opposite the entrance. The various members of the factions attending this meeting are as follows:

- Legate Rikke, a loyal and disciplined second-in-command and a true believer in the rightness of the Imperial cause.
- Jarl Elisif the Fair, the figurehead of Solitude who defers to Tullius.
- General Tullius, the leader of the Imperial forces in Skyrim. He is practical but impatient and unimaginative.
- Jarl Balgruuf the Greater, of Whiterun. A strong, noble, and valiant leader, he attends if he still rules his city.

Elenwen, a steely, determined, and ruthless head of the Thalmor observers. She sits near the Imperials, but her machinations are more complex.

Arngeir, Delphine, and Esbern sit in the adjacent chairs, opposite you. Their alliances are disparate but well known to you.

- Ulfric Stormcloak, the fiery and charismatic Jarl of Windhelm, is attempting to win Skyrim's independence.
- Galmar Stone-Fist is Ulfric's grizzled, hard-bitten, and fearless housecarl. Importantly, he is also completely loyal.
- Jarl Vignar of Whiterun, if the Civil War has progressed and the Stormcloaks have Whiterun under their control.

◊ **OBJECTIVE:** Negotiate a truce

Opening Remarks

The negotiations now begin. Due to the variations that your previous choices have already had on this peace process, there are several variations and discussions. But it is vitally important for your own machinations that you understand what you should be seeking to accomplish from this:

Failure is not an option

The good news is, unless you start brandishing a weapon and slashing dignitaries, there is no way to "fail" in this meeting. But you must tailor the agreements to your personal wishes. Here's how this all breaks down:

Every time you're asked your opinion, you need to favor a faction, either the Imperials or the Stormcloaks. Logically, you should side with the faction you are helping (or wanting to help) in the Civil War; strongly agree with all their statements.

Or, you can favor the opposing faction. This is counterintuitive, as it will only anger your allies and (if you're interested in the Civil War) will force you to retake any Holds you gave away thanks to your terrible negotiations.

You can favor one faction a little or a lot. Read the answers you're about to give to determine what are strongly or weakly favored responses.

Or, you can favor neither side if the Civil War doesn't interest you, the Civil War Quests haven't started yet, or you wish to simply be impartial. This has no real effects on the faction you may be leaning toward.

Negotiations Begin: Whose Side Are You On?

Hold Importance

First, you should understand how the Holds of Skyrim are broken down, in terms of "type," for this meeting. The following table shows which Holds are strongholds (the base of operations for a faction), which are major Holds (important), and which are minor Holds (less important):

✓	NAME OF HOLD	CAPITAL CITY	HOLD TYPE
☐	Haarfingar	Solitude	Stronghold: Imperials
☐	Hjaalmarch	Morthal	Minor
☐	The Pale	Dawnstar	Minor
☐	Winterhold	Winterhold	Minor
☐	The Reach	Markarth	Major
☐	Whiterun	Whiterun	Major
☐	Eastmarch	Windhelm	Stronghold: Stormcloaks
☐	Falkreath	Falkreath	Minor
☐	The Rift	Riften	Major

Negotiation 1: Elenwen

As soon as the negotiations begin, Ulfric raises objections about Elenwen even being involved in this council. Tullius or Ulfric asks you what your thoughts are:

- To agree with Ulfric and kick out this unwanted entity
- To disagree with Ulfric and keep Elenwen in the meeting

Negotiation 2: Markarth or Riften

The next item to discuss is giving up a major Hold. If you take the Stormcloak side, General Tullius will demand that Riften be turned over to the Empire. Otherwise, Ulfric will demand Markarth be surrendered to the Stormcloaks. The opposing faction's reaction depends on the state of the Civil War:

The faction that controls Markarth or Riften asks you what you think is a fair trade for the city. Your answer is always one of two choices:

◊ An exchange of a major Hold the opposition has

◊ An exchange of a minor Hold the opposition has

The council goes along with whatever choice you make. Bear in mind that the side that controls Markarth or Riften will be unhappy if it is bargained for a minor Hold!

Negotiation 3: The Archivist Speaks

At this point, one of the factions threatens to leave the bargaining table. This is always the faction that is most unhappy at the moment (the one you have favored the least). Esbern restores order with an impassioned speech about the greater danger, and both sides grudgingly agree to continue.

Negotiation 4: Concessions

It is now time for the faction that you've favored less (and thus "losing" the negotiations) to ask for additional concessions.

For each demand, you can choose whether to agree to the concession. This continues until the side demanding a concession from you receives it or they run out of concessions to ask for (which requires you to refuse all their demands).

TIP This is an excellent opportunity to really stick it to the side you aren't allied with! Remember that any changes you agree to (such as a hold changing hands) from here on will affect any Civil War Quests that are currently active.

Quest Conclusion

The council now concludes. If you've favored the enemy over your initial allies, you will be scolded by your allies. The quest then concludes.

Postquest Activities

At this point, Main Quest: The Fallen begins. Consult Part 2 of this quest (shown previously) for more information.

PREREQUISITES: Complete Main Quest: The Fallen

MINOR SPOILERS

INTERSECTING QUESTS: Main Quest: The Fallen, Main Quest: Sovngarde, Main Quest: Paarthurnax, Other Faction Quests (The Greybeards Quests): Word Wall Revelations* , Other Faction Quests (The Greybeards Quests): Meditations on Words of Power*, Side Quest: Masks of the Dragon Priests*

LOCATIONS: Skuldafn, Skuldafn North Tower, Skuldafn South Tower , Skuldafn Temple, Whiterun, Dragonsreach

CHARACTERS: Jarl Balgruuf the Greater, Jarl Vignar the Revered, Odahviing ("Winged Snow Hunter"), Whiterun Guard

ENEMIES: Dragon, Draugr, Frostbite Spider, Nahkriin the Dragon Priest

◊ **OBJECTIVES:** Set Odahviing free, Talk to Odahviing, Reach Alduin's portal to Sovngarde, Enter Sovngarde

NOTE * Quest names marked with this symbol do not appear in your Quest Menu list, although objectives may.

Eastward, to the Afterlife

◊ **OBJECTIVE:** Set Odahviing free
♦ **TARGET:** Odanviing, Dragonsreach in Whiterun

Although you're right to be suspicious, the only way to reach Skuldafn is to agree to free Odahviing, on the condition that he transport you there. You may also witness Irileth's and Farengar Secret-Fire's reactions and questioning of the dragon. Then climb the steps to the side of the hall where Odahviing is waiting. Instruct the guard to open the trap. The guard isn't too happy, so confirm these are your wishes. If you don't wish to wait, you may activate the pull-chain yourself.

◊ **OBJECTIVE:** Talk to Odahviing

When you return to the dragon, he turns and lumbers to the parapet and waits for your arrival. Odahviing is awaiting your command. When you are ready (and fully equipped for this final adventure), tell Odahviing you're ready to be taken to Skuldafn. You clamber aboard the dragon and set off for a flight across the eastern mountains.

◊ **OBJECTIVE:** Reach Alduin's portal to Sovngarde
♦ **TARGET:** Exterior portal, the roof of Skuldafn Temple

Odahviing deposits you on the edge of the Skuldafn fane (temple) and departs; this is as far as he can take you. Bring up your map; you're on the eastern side of the Velothi Mountains, out of the Skyrim realm.

Edge through the first of two giant stone arches and cross the bridge. You're likely to be set upon by a dragon at this point, but it may depart the area before you can take it down (or utilize Dragonrend). Don't overstretch yourself fighting it if it flees (or use Dragonrend if you want it to flee). After passing through the second archway on the bridge's opposite side, there are other foes to concern yourself with.

The first of these are Draugr that clatter down the stone steps as you intercept (or sneak past) them. Continue south, into a cracked courtyard with temple outbuildings to investigate. But first, the dragon returns to try and finish you. As with your other dragon battles, employ the tactics already learned: down the beast with Dragonrend, and then dispatch it with your favorite killing implements or augmentations. You absorb the Dragon Soul after you slay the creature. There is little time to rest; another dragon attacks only moments later. Deal with it in a similar fashion. Should you wish to flee, the only areas suitable are the side temples, filled with Draugr. Absorb another Dragon Soul before continuing your Draugr dispatching.

➤ Dragon Soul (2)

Take a moment to survey the scenery: This sprawling fane is comprised of a South Temple Tower, a north temple tower, and a main temple interior, which is the likely location to head to when looking for Alduin's Portal. Before you climb the main stone stairs, split by a torch and a stone column, inspect the Skuldafn South Tower. Inside is a spiral staircase and a small chamber with items to gather. A second chamber is atop the stairs and has a chest and a few other items. Expect at least six Draugrs as you battle through this tower. Two upper exits allow you to safely check the main temple and the courtyard from which you just came.

Head back down to the courtyard. Move east up either of the two stone staircases and under either arch to a small open folly with a treasure chest at the top. Next, head north, under another arch, before beginning a pitched battle (or a sneaking maneuver) against the remains of the Nord dead. The Draugr continue to appear as you encroach up the main stairs toward the main temple sanctum. When you're fighting up the stairs, beware of Draugr perched atop the temple's roof, as they can strike you with ranged fire. Fight back using your own projectile attacks, or move to the door so the rooftop foes can't aim at you.

Before entering the main temple, you can optionally turn around and head south, down the eastern platform overlooking the ruined outer buildings you just navigated, to the entrance of Skuldafn North Tower. This provides more Draugr for you to defeat. Take the spiral staircase to an upper chamber and exterior balcony. The balcony leads back to an otherwise-inaccessible interior corridor with a treasure chest to raid. After you emerge back on the eastern platform, investigate the exterior steps to the southwest, which leads to an altar and a battle with a particularly powerful Draugr. Open the treasure chest on the altar, then use the aqueduct bridge and head north. Finally you reach and open the door to Skuldafn Temple.

Prelude to the Maelstrom

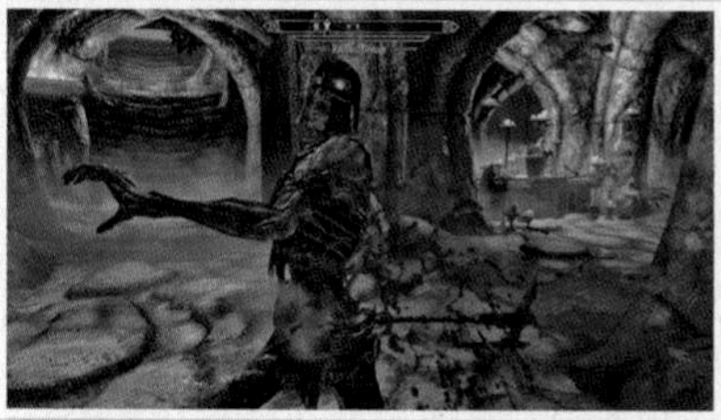

You are greeted by ancient Nordic architecture and a central ceremonial buttress with an embalming table to your right. Venture down either corridor (the right has a chest to open, while the left as a floor trigger and a dart trap). Engage the Draugr guarding the connecting passages ahead of you, surrounding a second embalming table. Ascend either set of steps to an upper chamber, where the vertical Draugr coffin lids fly open, and out spills more emaciated bags of bones for you to thwart. After eliminating the Draugr, you'll notice the two archways ahead are blocked by portcullises. Investigate the pillars and lever to continue your progress.

Puzzle Solution Part 1: A lever raises the portcullises, but it is currently not attached to the mechanism. In the upper chamber, there are three pillars with carved animal petroglyphs on them. Investigate the two outer pillars first. On the outside of the ceremonial arch structure they are sitting under is a second carving, which is resting in the mouth of a stone head. Move the pillar on the western side so the Whale glyph is facing the chamber's western side (in the same direction as the carving above the pillar). Move the pillar on the eastern side so the Snake glyph is facing the chamber's eastern side. The mechanism is now attached.

Puzzle Solution Part 2: Before you move the middle pillar, peer at the two portcullises. Above each is a stone head, and in the mouth of each head is another glyph, partially obscured by the stone crossbeam. The left (northwest) mouth has a Snake. The right (northeast) has a Hawk. Now rotate the middle pillar so the Snake or the Hawk faces the lever pedestal. Then pull the lever, and the portcullis corresponding to the Snake or Hawk opens. You can have only one portcullis open at a time.

Take the steps through the left portcullis up to a hallway (as the right one leads to a blocked area and small chest), and drop to the altar and embalming table below. Fight through cobwebs and Frostbite Spiders, and climb some stairs (some cobwebbed alcoves reveal a hidden chest or some egg sacs). Locate an iron double door leading to a second puzzle chamber. Clear the chamber of Draugr and ransack any treasure chests before you concentrate on the animal petroglyphs.

Puzzle Solution: Begin on the ground floor. Head east, and walk around the room until you spot a carved head with a Snake petroglyph in its mouth. Return to the pillar facing the double doors you entered, and turn it so the Snake faces the doors (west). Ascend to the bridge area above. Locate the second carved head with a Hawk in its mouth. Match that so the Hawk is facing the same direction (outward or to the north) in the alcove underneath this head. Turn around (to the north), and match the Whale on the pedestal in the opposite alcove, with the final head above it. Then pull the lever on the pedestal. This lowers the bridge, allowing you to exit.

Follow the corridor around to another embalming room with steps up to a gallery and a bridge to cross into the next chamber. Demolish Draugr along the way. Beware of the spiral steps; there's a pressure plate directly in front of you that releases darts and an oil lamp that falls onto flammable oil. Gather any items before climbing the steps, bring down more Draugr in the connecting chamber with the blocked portcullis exit, and then enter the antechamber with a chest and a lever pedestal to raise the portcullis.

Now follow the wide ceremonial corridor up, watching for oil-lamp traps. Continue toward a Nordic Puzzle Door, guarded by a high-ranking Draugr. Fight this fiend until he collapses; his corpse holds the Diamond Claw, the key to exiting this place.

➤ **Diamond Claw**

Puzzle Solution: Approach the Nordic Puzzle Door, but first inspect the palm of the Diamond Claw you just picked up. The three symbols etched into the palm are Wolf, Moth, and Dragon. These correspond to the animal symbols on the door's outer, middle, and inner rings, respectively.

The door rumbles down, allowing you to step into a huge main crypt. The place is silent compared to the Draugr infestations you've beaten back previously. Approach the Word Wall at the crypt's far end and absorb another—and extremely potent—Word of Power. Then depart the temple interior, optionally checking an embalming chamber to the side, before opening the double wooden doors to the temple exterior.

➤ **Word of Power:** Storm Call

You appear on the roof of the temple you've just navigated. Deliver some killing blows to any remaining Draugr you failed to cull while on the lower ground. Although there's some side battlements to investigate, there's little to find. Instead, locate the stone steps and the jet of molten fire roaring into the skies.

◊ **OBJECTIVE:** Enter Sovngarde

Two large dragons flank you, sitting atop carved columns to your left and right. In the courtyard's center are steps where a Dragon Priest is attempting to close the portal using dragon tongue incantations. The priest's name is Nahkriin, and he carries a staff that opens the maw he's just closed (although it is possible to kill him before this chant is completed). Engage Nahkriin in battle, but beware of his electrical prowess; use the arches and stairs as cover if you need to, and watch for the dragons that intermittently swoop in to attack. Fight back with Dragonrend, and slay each dragon before turning your attention to the priest. Fight him until all that remains is a pile of dust. Aside from some sizable gold, you receive Nahkriin's Mask (useful for Side Quest: Masks of the Dragon Priests*) and the Dragon Priest Staff.

➤ **Dragon Soul (2)** ➤ **Dragon Priest Staff** ➤ **Nahkriin**

Quest Conclusion

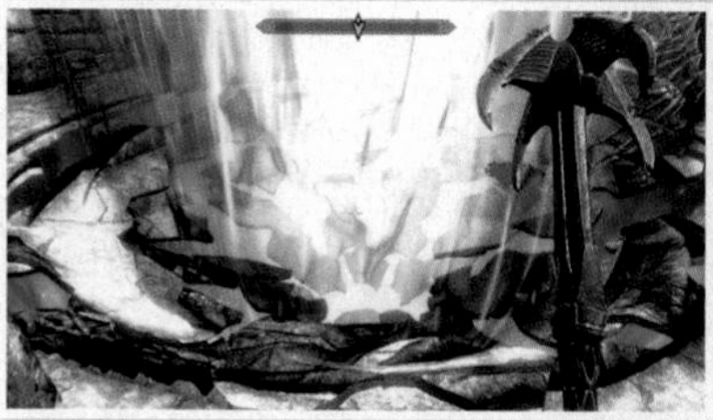

Ascend the ceremonial steps. Activate the Dragon Seal at the top of the steps, and you jam the staff's shaft into the seal's center. A great gout of fire blasts forth from a whirling vortex—a gateway to the Aetherius, where Alduin cheats death and feeds off the souls of heroes past. Step down into the light and into Sovngarde!

Postquest Activities

After you step into this writhing gateway, Main Quest: Sovngarde begins. Before you enter, know that you can never explore Skuldafn again. If there are items you wish to collect, do so before entering the gateway.

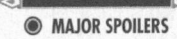

PREREQUISITES: Complete Main Quest: The World-Eater's Eyrie

MAJOR SPOILERS

INTERSECTING QUESTS: Main Quest: The World-Eater's Eyrie, Main Quest: Dragonslayer

LOCATIONS: Sovngarde, Hall of Valor, Shadowed Vale, Whalebone Bridge

CHARACTERS: Erlendr the Quick, Felldir, Gormlaith Golden-Hilt, Hakon, Hunroor the Agile, Jurgen Windcaller ("The Calm"), Olaf One-Eye, Stormcloak Soldier, Tsun, Ulfgar the Unending, Ysgramor, and many others.

ENEMIES: Alduin

◊ **OBJECTIVES:** Find out how to defeat Alduin, Gain admittance to the Hall of Valor, Talk to the heroes of Sovngarde

Terror in the Shadowed Vale

◊ **OBJECTIVE:** Find out how to defeat Alduin

♦ **TARGET:** Lost soul, in the Shadowed Vale

You have crossed the threshold of the living and entered the afterlife, the realm of Aetherius. Alduin's presence is powerful here; indeed, you can see the dragon in the distance, below the red glow of the eternal sunset. Follow the pathway down (north), passing between the mammoth tusks and the monolithic cowled statues and into the valley of mists—the Shadowed Vale.

The mists—created by Alduin—begin to thicken, impeding your path and vision. Use the Clear Skies Shout to clear the fog back for a few moments. Look at the winding path through the misty valley, which is interspersed with runic stones and blue torchlight that indicates the main route to take. Soon you make out a figure, a Stormcloak Soldier, lost and terrified. He pleads with you to turn back. The fellow splutters out a riddle: "vain is all courage against the peril that guards the way." You surmise he's talking about Alduin.

He tells the tale of his own demise but is even more terrified of Alduin, whose hunger is insatiable. The dragon hunts the lost souls snared within this shadowed valley, feasts upon them to regain his power, and returns to Tamriel. The soldier pleads with you to take him to Shor's Hall, where the heroes of old await their eternity in safety from Alduin's hunt. Answer him in any way you wish. Perhaps you might seek some help inside this Hall of Valor?

◊ **OBJECTIVE:** Gain admittance to the Hall of Valor

♦ **TARGET:** Tsun, in Sovngarde

Execute the Clear Skies Shout once more to spot the Hall of Valor silhouetted against the gloomy skies in the distance to the north. Venture farther into the valley, and the path splits, continuing around both sides of a central rock outcrop. You can climb the steps cut into the outcrop. Watch Alduin as he swoops about in the middle distance, plucking souls lost in the fog and devouring them. Atop this central outcrop, above the fog, you can also view the entrance to the Hall of Valor, a gigantic whale skeleton that spans a bottomless chasm void.

Seeking Valor

Return to the path below. No matter which path to the whalebone bridge that you take, expect to encounter two or three lost souls caught forever in the fog. Expect both Stormcloaks and Imperials here, along with those you may have dispatched during your adventure. Along the left-hand path, you can also meet High King Torygg, whose death at the hands of Ulfric Stormcloak plunged Skyrim into civil war. All fear the World-Eater. Emerge from Shadowed Vale and approach the steps leading to the whalebone bridge, where a mighty figure stands before you.

Approach Tsun. If you've studied your Tamriel history, you'll know he is a hero of ancient times, the brother of Stendarr, shield-thane to Shor, and a warrior of supreme quality. To Nords, he is revered as the greatest warrior who ever lived. As you approach, he asks what brings you to Sovngarde. You can:

Ignore him and attempt to cross the bridge without his permission. It takes but a moment for Tsun to catch you in this maneuver, and lightning is summoned from the skies. It strikes you repeatedly, forcing you to stop, die, or leap from the bridge and to your death.

Speak to Tsun. When you ask, he tells you that he judges those fit to join the fellowship of honor inside the Hall of Valor. After further posturing, inform Tsun that you seek to enter the Hall and that you have a right of birth; you are Dragonborn.

Tsun greets you with a series of verses. This warrior poetry is filled with illuminating, rugged beauty. You receive a separate response if you've achieved any (or all) of the following:

- ◊ Become the leader of the Companions.
- ◊ Become the head of the College of Winterhold.
- ◊ Achieved the status as the head of the Dark Brotherhood.
- ◊ Achieved the status as the leader of the Thieves Guild.

Tsun agrees to let you into the Hall, but only after you pass the warrior's test. Tsun unsheathes his two-handed battleaxe and advances upon you!

This battle need not be difficult. You may utilize any of the Shouts that you've learned that damage foes in combat (Fire Breath is a good choice). Back these ranged attacks with your favored offensive weaponry. Once you wound Tsun enough, he halts the attack, judges that you fought well, and steps aside, allowing you to cross the Whalebone Bridge. Don't fall off the bridge as you cross!

◊ **OBJECTIVE:** Talk to the heroes of Sovngarde

♦ **TARGETS:** Gormlaith Golden-Hilt, Felldir, and Hakon, in the Hall of Valor

The giant doors to the Hall of Valor appear before you. Push one open and enter the grand hall. Heroes from Tamriel's recent and distant past walk this Hall, which is dominated by mead and meat: A banquet, including a huge spit-roast is underway, and Shor's subjects make merry, awaiting his summons to the last battle. You are greeted by the mighty warrior who adapted Nordic writing from the elves, Ysgramor. This revered ancestor of the Companions tells you that three warriors stand ready, awaiting your word to loose their fury upon the perilous foe. Their names are Gormlaith the Fearless, Hakon the Valiant, and Felldir the Old. You may remember them as the Nordic warriors you saw in your Elder Scrolls vision. Seek them out among the other heroes of Sovngarde.

The following heroic fighters from yore are among the honored guests in the Hall of Valor:

Erlendr the Quick, a friend of Ulfgar, who was turned into a stone pillar by a mage named Grimkell.

Jurgen Windcaller ("The Calm"), the founder of the Way of the Voice. The Greybeards honor him.

Hunroor the Agile, a companion of Ulfgar, who was turned into a stone pillar by a mage called Grimkell.

Ulfgar the Unending, a Nord barbarian who has finally found his way home, along with his brethren.

Olaf One-Eye, a first-era king who helped capture a mighty dragon named Numinex and housed him in Dragonsreach.

Quest Conclusion

When you're done wandering among the heroes, locate the three Nordic warriors who defeated Alduin the first time around: Gormlaith Golden-Hilt, Hakon One-Eye, and Felldir the Old. Gormlaith is raring to seal Alduin's doom, but hold council before the battle begins. They agree that Alduin's mist is more than a snare; it is his shield and cloak. With the four voices of the heroes and Dragonborn joined in unison, the mist can be removed and Alduin brought to battle. The World-Eater fears you, Dragonborn!

Postquest Activities

Once the Nordic heroes agree to fight Alduin, Main Quest: Dragonslayer begins.

DRAGONSLAYER

PREREQUISITES: Complete Main Quest: Sovngarde

MAJOR SPOILERS

INTERSECTING QUESTS: Main Quest: Sovngarde, Main Quest: Epilogue

LOCATIONS: Sovngarde, Hall of Valor, Shadowed Vale, Whalebone Bridge

CHARACTERS: Gormlaith Golden-Hilt, Hakon One-Eye, and Felldir the Old

ENEMIES: Alduin

◊ **OBJECTIVES:** Help the heroes of Sovngarde dispel Alduin's mist, Defeat Alduin

"I've Waited an Eternity for This Day"

◊ **OBJECTIVE:** Help the heroes of Sovngarde dispel Alduin's mist

♦ **TARGET:** Nordic heroes, Shadowed Vale, in Sovngarde

Leave the Hall of Valor and cross the Whalebone Bridge to the edge of the Shadowed Vale, where your Nordic brethren are gathered. They are eager to slay Alduin for a second time, while the World-Eater roars away in this mist. When the three heroes have assembled, use your Clear Skies Shout to blow away the nearby mist – your allies will join you. Alduin bellows back with a Shout of his own, and the mist descends once again. Continue your Shouts until Alduin's might is broken.

TIP Have all your favorite weapons, spells, and Shouts set up so you can switch between them quickly, depending on how combat goes.

◊ **OBJECTIVE:** Defeat Alduin

With the mists permanently dispelled, Alduin's massive, jagged form swoops down into the vale. He begins to launch a barrage of fire attacks at you, the Nords, and any of the lost souls that have been freed from their permanent fog. The time has come to finish Alduin forever!

Dragon Slaying: Alduin is a lot less mobile when he's writhing in agony and having to land after a Dragonrend attack strikes him. Make this your earliest priority, and dodge any attacks he launches from his mouth.

Utilizing the Dragonrend is imperative; Alduin is invulnerable unless he's writhing and descending to the ground or unless he's on the ground after being affected by Dragonrend. If he isn't bathed in the blue light from this attack, he's impervious to your weapons.

Stand close to your fellow fighters so you can vary the attacks and so you don't face Alduin on your own. If your coordinated attacks come from different directions, Alduin won't focus all his attention on you. Meanwhile, you have the luxury of striking only him.

You need only one Dragonrend to down Alduin; you can switch to another Shout (such as Fire Breath) and attack with that and with your favored weapons. Use any that you've employed successfully against dragons in the past. But remember to attempt this only when Dragonrend is still affecting him.

Quest Conclusion

After you strike the killing blow, Alduin writhes in agony and his soul begins to dissipate....

Postquest Activities

After you strike the killing blow, Main Quest: Epilogue begins.

EPILOGUE

MAJOR SPOILERS

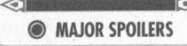

PREREQUISITES: Complete Main Quest: Dragonslayer

INTERSECTING QUESTS: Main Quest: Dragonslayer, Main Quest: Paarthurnax

LOCATIONS: High Hrothgar, Sky Haven Temple, Sovngarde, Hall of Valor, Shadowed Vale, Whalebone Bridge, Throat of the World

CHARACTERS: Delphine, Esbern, Felldir, Gormlaith Golden-Hilt, Hakon, Master Arngeir, Odahviing, Paarthurnax, Tsun

ENEMIES: Alduin

◊ **OBJECTIVES:** Speak to Tsun to return to Skyrim

Banishment: Ziil gro dovah ulse!

NOTE Once you complete Main Quest: Dragonslayer, this quest automatically begins.

◊ **OBJECTIVE:** Speak to Tsun to return to Skyrim
♦ **TARGET:** Tsun, Whalebone Bridge, in Sovngarde

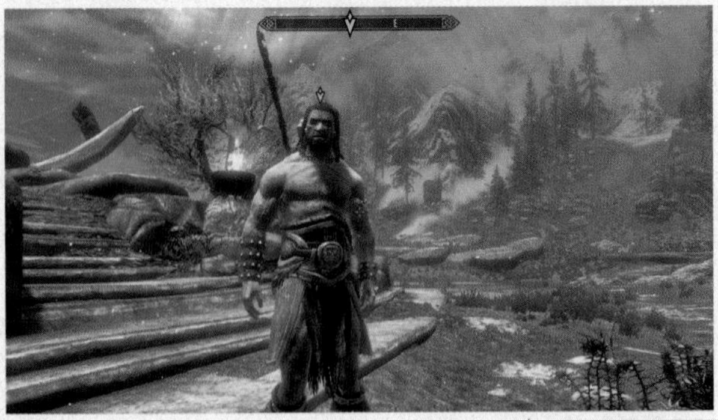

Alduin thrashes on the ground as his soul leaves his corporeal form. With a final, thunderous spasm, Alduin is torn apart; not even his skeleton remains in this afterlife. Tsun is the first to congratulate you on your mighty deed; you have cleansed Sovngarde of Alduin's evil snare. They will sing of this battle in the Hall of Valor! You may speak to any of the heroes who helped you in battle. When you're ready to leave, only Tsun can transport you from this place. Tsun summons Shor's Might and returns you to the Throat of the World. First, though, he grants you a Shout, one that brings a hero from Sovngarde to your side in your hour of need.

- **Word of Power:** Hero, Call of Valor
- **Word of Power:** Champion, Call of Valor
- **Word of Power:** Legend, Call of Valor

Quest Conclusion

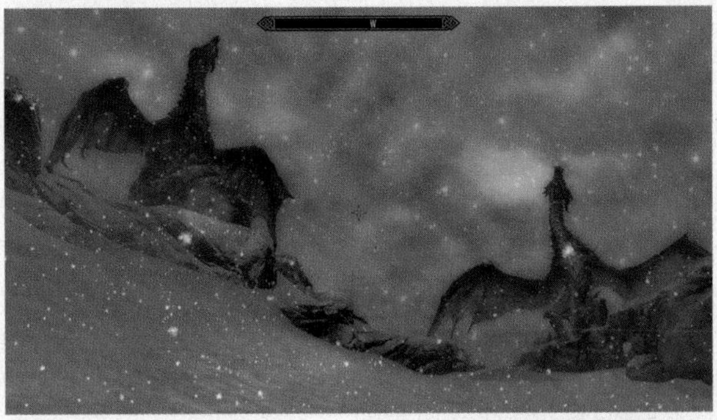

You return to the Throat of the World, with a full complement of dragons perched on the mountaintop at your arrival. The two recognizable beasts are Odahviing and Paarthurnax (if he is still alive). These beasts roar in a death chant for their fallen god—their leader, Alduin, and then take to the skies. Should you attack, they depart without fighting back. Paarthurnax greets you, impressed by your feats. Then he, too, flies away, leaving only Odahviing. Speak with him, and he informs you that he is now in your service.

NOTE The Call Dragon Shout now summons him to do your bidding.

Return to High Hrothgar and speak with Master Arngeir. Inform him of your actions; he believes Alduin may yet rise again, but that is for the gods to decide.

If you return to Sky Haven Temple, Delphine asks whether you have good news. But there's still the matter of Paarthurnax, if he lives. The Blades are grateful but are certainly more appreciative if Alduin's brother is also slain.

Postquest Activities

Once you return to the Throat of the World, you can continue exploring Skyrim and finish any other quests.

THE COMPANIONS QUESTS

OVERVIEW

Optimal Quest Start

You can start the Companions Quests when you arrive at Whiterun for the first time, or at any point thereafter. Warriors may wish to join sooner rather than later for access to a wide range of combat skill trainers.

NOTE **Cross-Referencing:** Do you want to see maps and learn more about the traps, non-quest-related items, collectibles, crafting areas, and other important rooms in every location during these quests? Then remember to cross-reference the location you travel to with the information contained in the Atlas.

Sanctuary: Jorrvaskr, in Whiterun

Jorrvaskr exterior, as seen from the Whiterun Plaza.

Jorrvaskr interior, during a drinking session.

The Companions' sanctuary is the Nordic longhouse adjacent to Dragonsreach, on the upper end of Whiterun. This is an ancient and honored mead hall where generations of Companions have met. According to local legend, Jorrvaskr is actually the oldest building in all of Whiterun. It existed alone on the mountain while the city was built up around it over the centuries. It features a main dining area, below which are the living quarters for the whelps and for the Circle and Harbinger.

Outside, there is a training area, and close by is the Skyforge, where the Companions' weapons are formed. The forge itself is large, ancient, and built outside on a mountain, close to the sky. Below the Skyforge is a ceremonial area known as the Underforge, which is out of bounds except on rare occasions.

Important Characters

Founder: Ysgramor

Ysgramor was born in Atmora, the ancestral land for all humans. He and two of his sons were the only survivors of the Night of Tears, when the elves attacked Saarthal and killed all the other inhabitants. Ysgramor retreated to Atmora, rallied an army of Five Hundred Companions, and led them to vanquish the elves and drive them out of Skyrim.

Harbinger: Kodlak Whitemane

For 20 years now, Kodlak has commanded the Companions, balancing his tactical skill, ferocity in combat, and commanding presence. But those days are drawing to a close. A year ago, Kodlak contracted the rot and his condition has rapidly diminished. He has become weak in body, and his frustration shows. He's taken to locking himself behind closed doors, poring over old documents, desperate to cure himself of lycanthropy.

The Circle: Aela the Huntress

Aela is the latest in a long family of women in the Companions. Her mother was a member, as was her grandmother and every woman in her family for generations. Aela claims that her line runs back to Hrotti Blackblade, one of the original Five Hundred Companions. Aela was not raised in the Companions like Vilkas and Farkas were, but it has been a fixture in her life from a very early age.

➤ **Trainer (Archery: Expert):** Aela the Huntress

The Circle: Farkas

Farkas and his twin brother, Vilkas, were both raised in the Companions by a man named Jergen, who rescued them from a circle of necromancers. Farkas is a bit cavalier with his Beast Form and a bit loose with his tongue, even to his superiors. This is not a big deal in the Companions, but he shows more disrespect to the older members than others do. Farkas is also...a bit slow.

➤ **Trainer (Heavy Armor: Master):** Farkas

The Circle: Vilkas

Vilkas and his twin brother, Farkas, were raised in Jorrvaskr—a place not accustomed to the sight of children. Only Tilma the Haggard offered them anything in the way of comfort. Several years ago, Jergen was killed in a battle with brigands near Dawnstar. Vilkas serves as the Master at Arms and is in charge of training younger members in weapon combat. He is hard on his students but is an excellent teacher.

➤ **Trainer (Two-Handed: Master):** Vilkas

The Circle: Skjor the Scarred

Skjor's early life was one common among the Companions. He fought in the Great War and returned to Skyrim after the Empire's defeat. He earned a reputation as being a sword for hire and was eventually recruited by the Companions. Skjor has always seen his role as the steady and loyal friend to those in power. He has few ambitions of his own, beyond supporting and standing by those to whom he has sworn loyalty. There is no one in the Companions with a greater sense of duty and honor.

Member: Athis

Adept in one-handed weaponry, Athis is a Dark Elf who keeps quiet most of the time. He is civil and loyal, but never at the forefront of any battles.

➤ **Trainer (One-Handed: Expert):** Athis

Member: Njada Stonearm

An impressive brawler and expert at blocking, but with an unpleasant attitude and uncaring disposition, Njada has few friends, which is just how she likes it.

➤ **Trainer (Block: Expert):** Njada Stonearm

Member: Ria

Ria is the youngest of the whelp recruits and is determined to fight and die alongside her Shield-Brothers. She is especially in awe of Aela the Huntress.

Member: Torvar

Torvar is a recent whelp and isn't taking well to the intensive training. He grows ever weary and anxious; the thought of dying in battle terrifies him.

Member: Vignar the Revered

Vignar the Revered was once a general and commander in the Legion during the Great War. He led brave warriors for nearly 30 years. That was a long time, though, and now Vignar lives a life of peace and relative quiet. He holds a place of honor among the Companions, and the group welcomes his council.

Housekeeper: Tilma the Haggard

Tilma the Haggard has been the single servant of Jorrvaskr for as long as anyone can remember. The Companions joke that they built the mead hall around her. To an outsider, it may seem as if Tilma is little more than a slave. But she is definitely there by choice and is committed to her duties and the warriors of Jorrvaskr.

Blacksmith: Eorlund Gray-Mane

Eorlund Gray-Mane is the patriarch of Clan Gray-Mane, one of the oldest, most respected families in Whiterun. Eorlund is widely known to be the best blacksmith in all of Skyrim. Although not a Companion himself, his wares have become the stuff of legend and are especially prized by the Companions. Eorlund is very old (and has a brilliant mane of long gray hair), but his long hours working the Skyforge have kept him incredibly fit.

➤ **Trainer (Smithing: Master):** Eorlund Gray-Mane

TIP **Forging Ahead:** Once you complete Companions Quest: Glory of the Dead, the Skyforge can forge a unique set of Nord Hero weapons. Skyforge steel weaponry is slightly better than normal steel.

NOTE **Intimate Companionship:** Farkas, Vilkas, Aela, Athis, Ria, Njada, and Torvar are all able to be married once Companions Quest: Glory of the Dead is over. Consult Temple Side Quest: The Bonds of Matrimony (page 423) for more details.

Training

The main members of this guild of fighters are extremely talented in a particular skill. Speak to each of them and increase the chosen skill by a point, to a maximum of five points before you level up. If you have enough gold, you can complete this numerous times:

☑	SKILL	RANK	TRAINER
☐	Archery	Expert	Aela the Huntress
☐	Block	Expert	Njada Stonearm
☐	Heavy Armor	Master	Farkas
☐	One-Handed	Expert	Athis
☐	Smithing	Master	Eorlund Gray-Mane
☐	Two-Handed	Master	Vilkas

Available Quests

There are a total of 19 quests available with the Companions. Six of these are Critical Path Quests, and 13 are Radiant Quests.

Critical Path Quests

Simply referred to as "quests," these are the main quests you attempt with the Companions. All but the first quest have one or more prerequisites, as shown in the following table:

☑	QUEST NAME	PREREQUISITES
☐	Companions Quest: Take Up Arms	None
☐	Companions Quest: Proving Honor	Complete Companions Quest: Take Up Arms, and one or more Radiant Quests.
☐	Companions Quest: The Silver Hand	Complete Companions Quest: Proving Honor, and one or more Radiant Quests.
☐	Companions Quest: Blood's Honor	Complete Companions Quest: The Silver Hand, and three or more Radiant Quests.
☐	Companions Quest: Purity of Revenge	Complete Companions Quest: Blood's Honor.
☐	Companions Quest: Glory of the Dead	Complete Companions Quest: Purity of Revenge.

Radiant Quests

These are usually smaller quests that require you to complete a task for a particular Companion. The Initial Wave Radiant Quests are available first, and remain available after the critical path quests are complete. The Second Wave quests are next; you must complete two to begin Companions Quest: Blood's Honor. The Final Wave quests only become available after all of the critical path quests are complete.

In each case, the objectives of a Radiant Quest are usually random. They are listed in more detail after the Critical Path Quests, but consult the following table to learn the prerequisites required to begin every Radiant Quest:

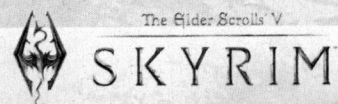

✓	CHRONOLOGY	QUEST GIVER	RADIANT QUEST NAME	PREREQUISITES
☐	Initial Wave	Aela	Animal Extermination (I)	Once the Companions Quest: Take Up Arms has been completed.
☐	Initial Wave	Aela	Animal Extermination (II)	Once the Companions Quest: Take Up Arms has been completed.
☐	Initial Wave	Farkas	Hired Muscle	Once the Companions Quest: Take Up Arms has been completed.
☐	Initial Wave	Farkas	Trouble in Skyrim	Once the Companions Quest: Take Up Arms has been completed.
☐	Initial Wave	Skjor or Vilkas	Family Heirloom	Once the Companions Quest: Take Up Arms has been completed.
☐	Initial Wave	Skjor or Vilkas	Escaped Criminal	Once the Companions Quest: Take Up Arms has been completed.
☐	Initial Wave	Skjor or Vilkas	Rescue Mission	Once the Companions Quest: Take Up Arms has been completed.
☐	Second Wave	Aela	Striking the Heart	Once the Companions Quest: The Silver Hand has been completed but before Blood's Honor begins.
☐	Second Wave	Aela	Stealing Plans	Once the Companions Quest: The Silver Hand has been completed but before Blood's Honor begins.
☐	Second Wave	Aela	Retrieval	Once the Companions Quest: The Silver Hand has been completed but before Blood's Honor begins.
☐	Final Wave	Aela	Totems of Hircine	Once the Companions Quest: Glory of the Dead has been completed.
☐	Final Wave	Farkas or Vilkas	Purity	Once the Companions Quest: Glory of the Dead has been completed.
☐	Final Wave	Farkas or Vilkas	Dragon Seekers	Once both the Companions Quest: Glory of the Dead and Main Quest: A Blade in the Dark have been completed.

TAKE UP ARMS

PREREQUISITES: None

INTERSECTING QUESTS: Companions Quest: Proving Honor, Companions Radiant Quests

LOCATIONS: Pelagia Farm, Whiterun, Jorrvaskr, Living Quarters, Skyforge

CHARACTERS: Aela the Huntress, Athis, Eorlund Gray-Mane, Farkas, Kodlak Whitemane, Njada Stonearm, Ria, Skjor, Vilkas

ENEMIES: Giant

◊ **OBJECTIVES:** Speak to Kodlak Whitemane, Train with Vilkas, Give Vilkas's sword to Eorlund, Bring Aela her shield, Follow Farkas to your quarters

Training the Whelp

You hear the sounds of a pitched battle across the plains, close to Pelagia Farm, within the outskirts of Whiterun. Come closer to the fight, and you'll witness two warriors attempting to topple a giant who was trespassing too far into the farmland. You may watch or join the fracas. After the giant is killed (you can search him without penalty), you may speak with Aela the Huntress, Ria, or Farkas, the warriors who slew the giant. They explain who the Companions are and how you may join their Guild: Head to Jorrvaskr if you're worth anything in a fight.

Enter the city of Whiterun and climb the streets until you reach the steps leading up to Jorrvaskr, the Companions' longhouse. When you step inside, you'll likely see a training fight in progress, with two recruits (Athis and Njada Stonearm) brawling. The other Companions watching the melee offer words of encouragement. The sparring is overseen by an intimidating, one-eyed man named Skjor. Speak to him when you wish to proceed with important knowledge about this Guild. He explains the Companions are known by many names, and not all of them complimentary. The battle switches to fists, and Njada Stonearm lives up to her last name, finishing her opponent and ending the fight.

You may speak with her and listen to her rude replies. But when you ask her (or other Companions) who is in charge, she mentions someone named Kodlak Whitemane, who is the Harbinger; this is the closest to a leader this rabble have and to whom they pledge their loyalty. Once you learn about Kodlak, this quest officially commences.

◊ **OBJECTIVE:** Speak to Kodlak Whitemane

Head to the longhouse's south end, down the stairs, and open the doors to the Living Quarters. Head along the main lower-floor corridor to reach Kodlak. He is usually speaking with Vilkas, who still hears the call of the blood, which Kodlak calls "a burden to bear." They finish speaking and look at you: There is a stranger in their hall.

You can ask Kodlak who the Companions are, why he joined them, where they stand on the Civil War, and, most importantly for this quest, if you can join them. Although Vilkas voices his disapproval, Kodlak says that Jorrvaskr has some empty beds for those with a fire burning in their hearts. He then asks how you are in battle. You may answer how you wish; it results in Kodlak requesting that Vilkas take you outside to see how you handle yourself.

◊ **OBJECTIVE:** Train with Vilkas

Exit Jorrvaskr and head into the courtyard to the structure's rear. Vilkas instructs you to take a few swings at him. Oblige by unsheathing your favored melee weapon and striking Vilkas, who expertly blocks with his shield. Stop your attacks when instructed (or you'll soon learn why crossing the Companions isn't a good idea). Vilkas seems to think you have an inkling of promise, but you're still considered a whelp to them. In the meantime, you have some orders to take care of: Vilkas wants you to take his sword up to Eorlund Gray-Mane, who is waiting to sharpen it.

➤ **Skyforge Steel Sword**

◊ **OBJECTIVE:** Give Vilkas's sword to Eorlund
♦ **TARGET:** Skyforge, in Whiterun

Take the sword (optionally testing it out in an unrelated adventure or two), and bring it up the steps hewn into the rocky outcrop to the north of Jorrvaskr. You reach the Skyforge, an impressively large forge where Eorlund Gray-Mane works the steel. Inform Eorlund of your errand. Depending on your answers, Eorlund tells you to remember that nobody rules anyone in the Companions, so subservient attitudes aren't necessary. They haven't had any leaders since Ysgramor. Eorlund isn't a Companion, but he's an expert in working the Skyforge, which produces the best steel in all of Skyrim. Before you go, Eorlund has a request: He wants you to take a shield to Aela the Huntress. Seeing the irony of this request is optional.

➤ **Steel Shield**

◊ **OBJECTIVE:** Bring Aela her shield
♦ **TARGET:** Aela the Huntress, in Jorrvaskr in Whiterun

Return to Jorrvaskr, and search the hall or the Living Quarters for Aela the Huntress, who is usually speaking with Skjor. Tell her you have her shield, and she gratefully receives it. She learns who you are and of your fight with Vilkas. She asks how you'd handle yourself in a real fight with him. Answer how you wish, although she won't like it if you threaten violence to a Shield-Brother. She tells you to speak to Farkas, who arrives at the end of this conversation.

◊ **OBJECTIVE:** Follow Farkas to your quarters

Quest Conclusion

Farkas seems pleasant enough; in fact, he's glad of the company. He takes you down the main hall of the Living Quarters, to the dormitory you'll be sharing. You can pick any bed that isn't being slept in. The quest concludes.

Postquest Activities

Farkas ends the conversation, asking whether you might help with a problem they are having. You may speak to him or ignore him and seek out employment from another Companion: And so begins your Faction Radiant Quests (consult the quest name that appears after agreeing to the task, and cross-reference it with the Radiant Quest in this chapter). You'll need to complete at least one of these before Companions Quest: Proving Honor begins.

PROVING HONOR

MINOR SPOILERS

PREREQUISITES: Complete the Companions Quest: Take up Arms, Complete one Faction Radiant Quest

INTERSECTING QUESTS: The Companions Quest: Take up Arms, The Companions Quest: Proving Honor , The Companions Quest: Brotherhood, The Companions Quest: The Silver Hand, The Companions Radiant Quests

LOCATIONS: Dustman's Cairn, Whiterun, Jorrvaskr

CHARACTERS: Farkas, Skjor

ENEMIES: Draugr, Frostbite Spider, Giant Frostbite Spider, Silver Hand, Skeever

◊ **OBJECTIVES:** Talk to Skjor, Speak to Farkas, Retrieve the fragment, Return to Jorrvaskr

Trial of the Cohort

◊ **OBJECTIVE:** Talk to Skjor

The Companions have witnessed your previous work ethic, and once you revisit Whiterun, enter Jorrvaskr, and search out Skjor, you are greeted more warmly. He has a more interesting task for you to help with. It appears a scholar visited the Companions a week ago, explaining where they could find another fragment of Ysgramor's Blade. Seeking out the fragment is considered a trial; do well, and you can consider yourself a member of the Companions. Farkas is your Shield-Sibling for this adventure.

◊ **OBJECTIVE:** Speak to Farkas

Farkas is usually within Jorrvaskr and is ready to retrieve the fragment when you are. You may speak also to Farkas about personal matters if you wish.

◊ **OBJECTIVE:** Retrieve the fragment
♦ **TARGET:** Fragment of Ysgramor's Blade, inside Dustman's Cairn

Ysgramor's Blessing

After a trek through the wilderness with Farkas, navigate northwest of Whiterun and up to Dustman's Cairn. Drop below the standing stones. Arm yourself and begin to navigate through these catacombs, and listen for Farkas's advice. Take any treasure as you descend past the loose burial stones. Continue deeper into a ceremonial hub chamber with multiple archways and a couple of thrones.

The way forward is blocked. The only area of interest is an archway with a raised portcullis, which leads to a small alcove with a lever. Activate it, and the portcullis drops, trapping you inside but raising the portcullis of a nearby archway. Farkas looks in and tells you he'll find the release, but as he does, he is surrounded by the members of the Silver Hand! Severely outnumbered, Farkas backs up before letting out a guttural growl and transforming into a massive werewolf that slaughters the Silver Hand where they cower! After freeing you, speak to Farkas, who explains his metamorphosis (known colloquially as his Beast Form)is a blessing bestowed upon some of the Companions.

Press on through the archway Farkas just opened. You face multiple Draugr and Silver Hand as you descend into this elongated crypt. Beware of occasional dart traps (watch for pressure stones beneath your feet that trigger them), and continue the slaughtering up until you reach the large crypt chamber with a locked iron door at the eastern end. Check the burial urns nearby for a key that opens this door.

➤ **Dustman's Cairn Key**

Quickly deal with the Skeever problem once you're through the door, passing interconnecting chambers and stone passageways. A battle against a Giant Frostbite Spider occurs soon afterward. Continue through another bank of crypts, until you reach the major tomb room, where a Draugr Wight is buried. Strange chanting draws you to the area behind the raised tomb; this is a Word Wall, and a Word of Power is drummed into your subconscious! With the chant fresh in your memory, inspect the raised tomb and take the fragment lying on top of it (along with any other spoils you wish).

➤ **Word of Power:** Fire Breath ➤ **Fragment of Ysgramor's Blade**

◊ **OBJECTIVE:** Return to Jorrvaskr
♦ **TARGET:** Jorrvaskr, in Whiterun

If you check your map (or the map provided in the Atlas), you'll spot an exit corridor off to the side of this tomb room, behind the raised stone alcove. Alas, when you attempt to breach it, the burial stones will not shift, but the Draugr begin to attack. Drop into the main chamber, where a protracted battle with at least 20 Draugr (including a dreaded high-ranking Draugr that clambers out of the raised tomb) takes place. Keep moving, retreat to safety if you need to, and don't leave Farkas to fend for himself! A final Draugr crashes through the burial stone, allowing access up a tight side tunnel. At the tunnel's end is a lever, which opens a secret rock door leading back to the cairn's entrance.

Quest Conclusion: Brotherhood

From here, it is a simple matter of returning to Jorrvaskr and seeking out Skjor, who gladly takes the fragment of Ysgramor's Blade from you. Vilkas is also waiting, having heard how well you did as a Shield-Sibling. The Companions are assembled in the rear courtyard. They are concluding a circle of judgment, and Kodlak informs you that you are now a member of the Companions. You are welcomed into the fold, but you still need to prove yourself.

Postquest Activities

Speak to Aela, Farkas, Skjor, or Vilkas, and tell them you're looking for work to begin any other Faction Radiant Quests.

MINOR SPOILERS

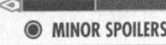

PREREQUISITES: Complete the Companions Quest: Proving Honor, Complete one Faction Radiant Quest

INTERSECTING QUESTS: The Companions Quest: Proving Honor, The Companions Radiant Quests

LOCATIONS: Gallows Rock, Whiterun, Jorrvaskr, Skyforge, Underforge

CHARACTERS: Aela the Huntress, Farkas, Skjor, Werewolf

ENEMIES: Krev the Skinner, Silver Hand, Skeever

◊ **OBJECTIVES:** Talk to Skjor, Meet with Skjor at night, Enter the Underforge, Participate in the blood ritual, Talk to Aela, Kill the werewolf hunters, Talk to Aela

Forging the Lycanthrope

◊ **OBJECTIVE:** Talk to Skjor

After completing the Companions Quest: Proving Honor, Skjor has spent enough time judging your worthiness to become one of the Companions. When you find Skjor, he says he has something a little different planned for your next task and requests you meet him at the entrance to the Underforge after nightfall.

◊ **OBJECTIVE:** Meet with Skjor at night
◊ **OBJECTIVE:** Enter the Underforge
♦ **TARGET:** Underforge, in Whiterun

Once the sun has set (any time between 06:00 p.m. and 08:00 a.m.), head around the left (north) side of Jorrvaskr building and meet with Skjor by a massive protrusion of stone, below the Skyforge. Skjor explains this is the most ancient part of Whiterun and that the Underforge taps a vein of magic older than men or elves. Skjor beckons for you to open the rock wall that shifts apart, allowing entrance into the Underforge.

Skjor enters the Underforge with you. Aela the Huntress has taken a lupine form and is waiting around the Sacred Font. Skjor explains the ceremony you will undertake is to be done in secret, as Kodlak is busy trying to throw away the gift the Companions have been granted; he thinks it a curse rather than a blessing. Now join in the shared blood of the wolf and activate the Sacred Font.

◊ **OBJECTIVE:** Participate in the blood ritual

You experience a tremendous change in your body structure. Your vision is much improved. Your speed is like that of the wolf. Your social standing with the locals is possibly not worth testing out at the moment. Soon, your eyes close and everything turns to black.

◊ **OBJECTIVE:** Talk to Aela
♦ **TARGET:** Aela the Huntress, on the moors outside Gallows Rock

> **TIP** As a werewolf, any crime you commit will not count against you, as your identity is not known. However, everyone (except for the Companions) is hostile and will fight or flee from you. If you kill anyone, they remain dead (so don't slay a merchant accidentally!). You can howl and sprint places on all fours for an even quicker dash. You may turn into a werewolf once per day.

Clawing the Silver Hand

You wake up on the moors, clad in little more than your modesty. Aela the Huntress is with you and explains that your transformation was not easy but successful. To celebrate becoming part of the Companions, you are to slaughter a pack of werewolf hunters known as the Silver Hand, who are camped nearby. But first, ask Aela any questions about your "condition" that you wish. Then place your armor and clothing back on, and arm up for the assault.

◊ **OBJECTIVE:** Kill the werewolf hunters
♦ **TARGET:** Silver Hand clan, in Gallows Rock

Charge or prowl around the exterior battlements of the Gallows Rock fortification before slaying the two Silver Hand guarding the entrance. Then step inside. Judging by the spear bars on the doorway, the Silver Hand must have locked the place down once Skjor charged in. Activate the lever and head down the stairs. Make sure Aela accompanies you, as she's helpful in combat as a Shield-Sibling. Continue through this complex of stone corridors, removing Skeever vermin and Silver Hand as you go.

> **TIP** Remember you can use your Beast Form during this quest. Access it via your Magic menu.

Many of your brethren lie dead in the cells; release any who are alive so they can savage their captors. Then push down the stairs, into a stone hall with skinned pelt hangings. Battle through and down the stairs to the circular chamber with the columns. This is the lair of Krev the Skinner, the Silver Hand leader in these parts. He is flanked by two lackeys. Muster your combat potential and savagely dispatch them all. Then ransack the chamber (and optionally, the entire area) for loot.

◊ **OBJECTIVE:** Talk to Aela

Quest Conclusion

There are no rewards here, only sadness. Alas, Aela has seen the body of Skjor. He is dead; he should not have come here without a Shield-Brother. Skjor will be avenged. The plot to kill all of those responsible for this outrage begins now!

Postquest Activities

You must now complete two additional Radiant Quests for Aela (and her only) to begin The Companions Quest: Blood's Honor.

BLOOD'S HONOR

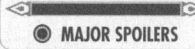

PREREQUISITES: Complete the Companions Quest: The Silver Hand, Complete two Companions Radiant Quests

◉ MAJOR SPOILERS

INTERSECTING QUESTS: The Companions Quest: The Silver Hand, The Companions Quest: Purity of Revenge, The Companions Radiant Quests

LOCATIONS: Glenmoril Coven, Whiterun, Jorrvaskr, Jorrvaskr Living Quarters

CHARACTERS: Aela the Huntress, Kodlak Whitemane, Vilkas

ENEMIES: Frostbite Spider, Glenmoril Witch, Silver Hand, Skeever

◊ **OBJECTIVES:** Collect a Glenmoril Witch's head, (Optional) Wipe out the Glenmoril Witches, Return to Kodlak

Hircine's Curse

After completing the Companions Quest: Proving Honor and then tending to other business, visit Kodlak, who is usually down in his Living Quarters in Jorrvaskr. Sit next to him and begin to talk. After telling him what you've been up to, Kodlak asks if you've heard the story of how the Companions became werewolves. The Order of the Companions is almost 5,000 years old, but the beastblood has only "troubled" them for a few hundred. One of Kodlak's predecessors made a bargain with the witches of Glenmoril Coven; if the Companions were to hunt in the name of their lord, Hircine, they would be granted great power. But there was deception!

Although in wolf form the Companions are powerful, the disease of lycanthropy seeps into the spirit, and upon death, werewolves are claimed by Hircine for his Hunting Grounds. For some, the eternal chase and capture is a boon, but for a true Nord like Kodlak, it is a curse, for he wishes Sovngarde to be his spirit home. Rather than resigning himself to a wolf's death, Kodlak has spent his twilight years trying to find a cure. The answer lies in the same magic that the witches used to ensnare the Companions. You are to go to their coven and strike down all witches. Return with their heads—the seat of their abilities.

◊ **OBJECTIVE:** Collect a Glenmoril Witch's head
◊ **OBJECTIVE:** (Optional) Wipe out the Glenmoril Witches
♦ **TARGET:** Glenmoril Witch, in Glenmoril Coven

Trek across the tundra plains and southwest, into the mountains, keeping below the snow line. The trappings of witchcraft hang from the gnarled trees at the Coven's entrance.

Enter the Coven, which is formed around a central hub cavern, where a Glenmoril Witch awaits. Strike her with sneak, ranged, or melee attacks. Beware of her frost spells and her familiar. Continue combat until one of you falls—be sure it's the crone! Then inspect the withered corpse and collect the head (as well as any Hagraven Feathers you may need for crafting).

➤ **Glenmoril Witch Head**

◊ **OBJECTIVE:** Return to Kodlak

At this point, you are prompted to return to Kodlak. Before you return (which is a critical part of this quest), you can also hunt down the four other Glenmoril Witches who inhabit this coven.

TIP If you're having trouble locating any of the witches' chambers, carefully inspect the hub chamber (where the first witch was), as some connecting tunnels can be hard to spot.

Journey back to Whiterun, and head toward Jorrvaskr. Judging from the onlookers, Aela's drawn weapon, and the slaughtered Silver Hand at her feet, the longhouse was the scene of a vicious Silver Hand attack while you were away. Enter Jorrvaskr and speak with Vilkas. He has some sorrowful news; Kodlak was killed during the fighting.

Quest Conclusion

The Silver Hand made off with all the fragments of Wuuthrad that you had collected. Vilkas vows that you and he will bring the battle to their chief camp. Kodlak will be avenged.

Postquest Activities

The Companions Quest: Purity of Revenge begins immediately. There are now no Radiant Quests available, due to the recent Silver Hand attack. Although you may think the Witch Heads aren't of use, they become important during Companions Quest: Glory of the Dead and afterward.

PURITY OF REVENGE

PREREQUISITES: Complete the Companions Quest: Blood's Honor

◉ MINOR SPOILERS

INTERSECTING QUESTS: The Companions Quest: Blood's Honor, The Companions Quest: Glory of the Dead, The Companions Radiant Quests

LOCATIONS: Driftshade Refuge, Driftshade Cellar, Whiterun, Jorrvaskr

CHARACTERS: Vilkas, Werewolf

ENEMIES: Silver Hand

◊ **OBJECTIVES:** Retrieve the fragments of Wuuthrad, (Optional) Wipe out the Silver Hand, Return to Jorrvaskr

Severing the Silver Hand

◊ **OBJECTIVE:** Retrieve the fragments of Wuuthrad

◊ **OBJECTIVE:** (Optional) Wipe out the Silver Hand

♦ **TARGET:** Wuuthrad fragments, inside Driftshade Refuge

Vilkas wishes to immediately depart for the Silver Hand stronghold of Driftshade Refuge and accompanies you as your Shield-Brother. Purchase any equipment if necessary, and then journey north into the Mountains of Winterhold, to the southeast of Dawnstar. Combat begins immediately. Sneaking is inadvisable for a Companion, especially one with an optional objective to fulfill and a recently slain advisor. Dispatch the foes guarding the entrance to the Refuge. Kill the one on the roof with ranged weapons, or sneak up the steps to the rear of the entrance.

Descend the stone-stepped corridor and into a lower shrine room, with moss-covered pillars and Silver Hand to cut down with speed and ferociousness. Make a systematic sweep of every chamber via the connecting corridors, culling foes as you go. Leave no one alive, lest you mock the death of the beloved Kodlak! Eventually, you reach a chamber with vertical spears blocking an entrance. Activate the lever just to the right of the spears, and they retract, allowing you into Driftshade Cellar.

Fight your way past the stacked wood and barrels, watching for the pressure plate lest you receive a swinging gate trap in the face—a fate you can attempt for any foes if you wish. Venture farther into the cellar, and split open the Silver Hand guarding a large distillery tank of mead. Exit via a hole in the stone wall and into a snow tunnel. You appear in a small cavern complete with holding cells. Release any werewolves still alive (they are locals afflicted with lycanthropy, rather than Companions). The snow tunnel connects back into the cellar.

Pass the remains of a werewolf and shred the foes in the torture room. Enter the remains of the cellar's grand hall, now full of collapsed masonry. After more Silver Hand slaughtering, head south, up the steps and back into the refuge area. Enter the small dungeon room, then turn left and bound up the stairs. The remaining Silver Hand are in this chamber. Kill them all. Your optional objective should complete at this point. Then inspect the table on the elevated dining area, where all the fragments of Ysgramor's Blade can be found...again. Take them before resting for a moment with Vilkas, who seems to have finally realized your prowess as a fighter.

➤ **Fragments of Wuuthrad**

◊ **OBJECTIVE:** Return to Jorrvaskr

Quest Conclusion

Head south out of Driftshade Refuge, back outside, and then to Whiterun and your longhouse home. As you near Jorrvaskr, Vilkas remarks that your brethren should have finished preparing the funeral of Kodlak by now.

Postquest Activities

The Companions Quest: Glory of the Dead begins immediately. There are now no Radiant Quests available, due to the preparations for Kodlak's departure.

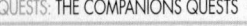

PREREQUISITES: Complete the Companions Quest: Purity of Revenge

MAJOR SPOILERS

INTERSECTING QUESTS: The Companions Quest: Purity of Revenge, The Companions Radiant Quests

LOCATIONS: Whiterun, Jorrvaskr, Jorrvaskr Living Quarters, Skyforge, Underforge, Ysgramor's Tomb

CHARACTERS: Aela the Huntress, Danica Pure-Spring, Eorlund Gray-Mane, Farkas, Jarl of Whiterun, Kodlak Whitemane, Vilkas

ENEMIES: Companion Ghost, Frostbite Spider, Kodlak's Wolf Spirit, Skeever

◊ **OBJECTIVES:** Attend Kodlak's funeral, Retrieve Kodlak's fragment, Give the final fragment to Eorlund, Meet the Circle, Go to Ysgramor's Tomb with the Circle, Return Wuuthrad to Ysgramor, Get to the burial chamber, Speak to Kodlak, Put witch head into fire, Defeat the wolf spirit, Speak to Kodlak

Out of the Strong Comes Forth Steel

◊ **OBJECTIVE:** Attend Kodlak's funeral
♦ **TARGET:** Skyforge, north of Jorrvaskr, in Whiterun

Upon your return to Jorrvaskr, there is no one inside the building; they are all at the Skyforge, where Eorlund has prepared the pyre for Kodlak's funeral. The Companions are there, along with some of Whiterun's population, including the Jarl and the priestess Danica Pure-Spring. Aela steps forward to join Eorlund and Vilkas in a simple, strong-hearted eulogy. Aela lights the pyre, and Kodlak's body is set ablaze. With his spirit departed, she requests that the members of the Circle should withdraw to the Underforge to grieve together. Before you leave with them, Eorlund asks whether you have the Fragments of Wuuthrad; he needs to prepare them for mounting back in Jorrvaskr. There is a final piece of the Wuuthrad that Kodlak always kept close. Eorlund requests that you go to Kodlak's chambers and bring the piece back for him.

◊ **OBJECTIVE:** Retrieve Kodlak's fragment
♦ **TARGET:** Living Quarters, in Jorrvaskr in Whiterun

Enter Jorrvaskr and descend into the Living Quarters. Head north, past the chair where you and Kodlak sat and talked. His bedroom is to the right (east). Check the bedside table and grab the two items within. One is the fragment Eorlund mentioned, and the other is Kodlak's Journal. You may optionally read it. Kodlak's wishes for your role within the Companions are detailed in it.

➤ **Fragment of Ysgramor's Blade** ➤ **Kodlak's Journal**

◊ **OBJECTIVE:** Give the final fragment to Eorlund

Return to Eorlund, who is usually at the Skyforge, and hand over the fragment. He thanks you and says the Companions are waiting for you inside the Underforge.

◊ **OBJECTIVE:** Meet the Circle
♦ **TARGET:** Underforge, in Whiterun

Open the loose rock wall below the Skyforge and enter the place where you were once baptized into the moon-born. Vilkas and Aela are having a heated discussion over Kodlak's final wishes. Although Aela is at one with her Beast Form, Vilkas knows that Kodlak wished to meet Ysgramor and know the glories of Sovngarde and the Hall of Valor. The curse of lycanthropy took that from him. Aela relents, understanding that Kodlak's wishes are to be respected.

Vilkas then tells you of the Tomb of Ysgramor, where the souls of Harbingers past heed the call of northern steel. But the tomb cannot be entered because Ysgramor's Blade is in pieces. Eorlund informs them that tools are meant to be broken...and repaired! This is the first time that all pieces of the Blade have been returned together, and the flames of Kodlak fuel the rebirth of Wuuthrad! Eorlund hands you the blade, which is now in one piece, and the Circle of Companions set off to enter the tomb and help cast Kodlak off into the Nordic realm of the afterlife.

➤ **Wuuthrad**

◊ **OBJECTIVE:** Go to Ysgramor's Tomb with the Circle
♦ **TARGET:** Entrance to Ysgramor's Tomb

TIP Wuuthrad the Elf-Slayer is a powerful two-handed weapon that does 20% more damage to elven foes. It is a suitable reward for someone who has brought honor to the Companions.

Taming the Wolf

Northwest of Winterhold, in the ice fields of the Sea of Ghosts, lies the Nordic cairn indicating the entrance to Ysgramor's Tomb. Climb over the lip of the cairn and open the iron door that leads into the tomb interior. Your Shield-Siblings are already inspecting the weaponless statue at the tomb's entrance plinth. Vilkas says this is the resting place of Ysgramor and his most trusted generals, and you should be cautious. Then Vilkas reveals that he won't be accompanying you on this final mission; his mind is too fogged and his heart grieved. He then instructs you to grant Ysgramor's statue its rightful blade.

◊ **OBJECTIVE:** Return Wuuthrad to Ysgramor

Approach the statue of Ysgramor and place the Wuuthrad in the statue's grip. The tomb entrance behind (north of) the statue slides open. You, Farkas, and Aela the Huntress will now meet Ysgramor's guardians and fight your way to the resting place of Ysgramor.

◊ **OBJECTIVE:** Get to the burial chamber

Brush aside the cobwebs and investigate the tunnel beyond, which turns west and ends at a double door with an alcove on either side. From each alcove, a Companion Ghost appears, ready to test your mettle. Slay them as if they were enemies; you are proving yourself to them in battle, and there is no greater honor. Open the double doors and enter the entrance hall, where three more ghosts appear to thwart you. Tackle them, checking on your Shield-Siblings in case they need your support.

Head south, down another level, and into the hall of crypts. Return several more Companion Ghosts to Sovngarde as they emerge from their vertical tombs, then head south, hacking at the entrance filled with cobwebs. Farkas parts company with you at this point. The cobwebs lead to two connected chambers filled with Frostbite Spiders (expect at least one to be Giant). Dispatch them all before activating the chain by the portcullis to the south. Venture into the main tomb. At least six more Companion Ghosts appear to stop you between here and the corridor and the steps up to an iron door.

Open the door to reach a long hall with a pedestal at its far end. Atop the pedestal is a handle. Pull it to open the portcullis in the sunken corridor on your left (north). Head down into a giant ceremonial chamber, with the skull of a mammoth dominating the central embalming table. At least four more Companion Ghosts appear. Stick your bladed weapon into their ethereal forms. When the fight is over, you may climb the final steps, open the double doors, and enter Ysgramor's burial chamber.

◊ **OBJECTIVE:** Speak to Kodlak

And So Slain the Beast Inside

Stride over to meet the spirit of Kodlak, who (along with his fellow Harbingers from history) have been warming themselves in this chamber and trying to evade Hircine. Although you can see only Kodlak's spirit, he assures you his predecessors are with you, in this most sacred of chambers. Tell Kodlak that Vilkas mentioned a cure was still possible, and Kodlak instructs you to take one of the witches' heads and throw it into the blue fire. It will release their magic—for him at least.

◊ **OBJECTIVE:** Put witch head into fire
◊ **OBJECTIVE:** Defeat the wolf spirit

Approach the Flame of the Harbinger and drop a witch's head into it. The moment the blue flames begin to devour the head and the witch's magical grip loosens, Kodlak's Wolf Spirt appears. You must destroy it in combat.

◊ **OBJECTIVE:** Speak to Kodlak

Quest Conclusion

Return to Kodlak's spirit and tell him you killed his beast spirit. He thanks you for this gift, one tainted by sadness that the other Harbingers remain trapped by Hircine. Perhaps a battle for their souls could be waged from Sovngarde. For today, however, you must triumph in your victory and lead the Companions to further glory!

Postquest Activities

Locate any treasure chests you wish to plunder. Pull the chain and exit via the raised area on the chamber's eastern side. Head up the spiral stairs to a second chain that removes a section of rock wall. Return to the entrance chamber where Ysgramor's statue is standing. You may now return to Jorrvaskr at your leisure. Although your critical Companions Quests are over, there are now three additional Radiant Quests available (along with the initial ones). You enjoy the companionship of your Shield-Brothers and Sisters as you return, victorious, as Harbinger!

➤ **Word of Power:** Animal Allegiance

TIP You may wish to take Wuuthrad from Ysgramor's statue before you leave, and use this weapon.

TIP **Forging Ahead:** The Skyforge, burning with Kodlak's Spirit, can now forge a unique set of Nord Hero weapons if you have the skill to craft them.

NOTE **Intimate Companionship:** Farkas, Vilkas, Aela, Athis, Ria, Njada, and Torvar are all able to be married once Companions Quest: Glory of the Dead is over. Consult Temple Side Quest: The Bonds of Matrimony (page 423) for more details.

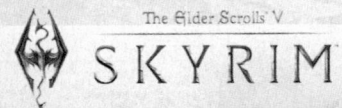

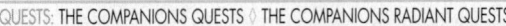

FINAL WAVE: PURITY

Quest giver: Farkas **Quest giver: Vilkas**

Talk to Farkas or Vilkas. They are worried that when they pass from this realm, they, too, will share the same fate that befell Kodlak—trapped in a purgatory and desperately avoiding Hircine's Hunting Grounds. The quest giver wants the curse of lycanthropy to be purged from his spirit and asks for your help in acquiring the necessary ingredients to make this possible.

◊ **OBJECTIVE:** Collect a Glenmoril Witch Head
♦ **TARGET:** Glenmoril Witch Head, Glenmoril Coven

There are two options at this point: If you have already culled the Glenmoril Coven of all five witches, you should have a spare Witch Head in your inventory. If you don't, you should journey to the Glenmoril Coven, sever another Witch Head, and return to Farkas's or Vilkas's location.

➤ **Glenmoril Witch Head**

◊ **OBJECTIVE:** Cleanse [the quest giver] of beastblood

Only one location has the necessary magic to thwart the power of Hircine, and that is Ysgramor's Tomb. Follow the route set out in the Companions Quest: Glory of the Dead (with the quest giver as your Shield-Brother) until you reach the chamber with the Flame of the Harbinger.

◊ **OBJECTIVE:** Kill [the quest giver's] wolf spirit

Quest Conclusion

Place one of the Witch Heads into the flickering blue flame, and then defeat the wolf spirit that leaves the body. Once this combat is over, Farkas or Vilkas is effectively "cured" of lycanthropy. You can also drop a head into the flames and cure yourself. But be warned: Once cured, you lose your Beast Form ability forever.

Postquest Activities

You may now speak to another Companion and begin another Radiant Quest.

FINAL WAVE: DRAGON SEEKERS

Quest giver: Farkas **Quest giver: Vilkas**

Either Farkas or Vilkas tells you that a dragon is terrorizing a nearby Hold. The exact details are scarce, but this would be a fine and victorious combat victory and would help keep the denizens of Skyrim safe. You are given instructions on where this dragon's lair may be.

◊ **OBJECTIVE:** Kill the dragon at [a random dragon's lair]

Walk the path to the dragon's location (with the quest giver as your Shield-Brother), and begin combat with this monstrous beast. Depending on how far through the Main Quest you are, the Shouts you have learned can very much help in this epic confrontation. Defeat the dragon and claim its soul for your own.

TIP If you require more information on how to defeat the dragon, consult the tactics listed in Main Quest: Dragon Rising or Main Quest: A Blade in the Dark. If you've learned the Dragonrend Shout (after completing Main Quest: Alduin's Bane), fighting with melee weapons suddenly becomes a whole lot easier.

➤ **Dragon Soul**

◊ **OBJECTIVE:** Talk to [the quest giver]

Quest Conclusion

Farkasor Vilkas are impressed by your dragon-slaying abilities. You are truly the Harbinger of the Companions!

Postquest Activities

You may now speak to another Companion and begin another Radiant Quest.

THE COLLEGE OF WINTERHOLD QUESTS

OVERVIEW

Optimal Quest Start

The College of Winterhold Quests begin when you arrive at the College for the first time. They give you access to trainers and vendors that considerably increase your magical abilities and skills. You can join the College whenever you like, although Magic-focused characters may want to join sooner rather than later to gain access to this ready source of spells. Most other characters will come to the College much later, as part of Main Quest: Elder Knowledge.

> **NOTE** **Cross-Referencing:** Do you want to see maps and learn more about the traps, non-quest-related items, collectibles, crafting areas, and other important rooms of note in every location during these quests? Then cross-reference the location you travel to with the information on that location contained in this guide's Atlas.

Sanctuary: College of Winterhold

The College of Winterhold, perched on its pillar of rock.

Inside the College, where mages perfect their magic.

The threadbare Hold City of Winterhold has seen most of its population driven away. The center of life in these parts nowadays is the College of Winterhold. Once a prominent, influential location in Skyrim, Winterhold has fallen on hard times but is still a haven for mages in Skyrim, a safe refuge from distrustful Nords. Largely self-sufficient, the College of Winterhold is quite content to be isolated from the rest of the province, although a more peaceful coexistence with the outside world is always preferred.

The College of Winterhold is situated on a cliff overlooking the Sea of Ghosts. Over the years, the cliff has fallen into the sea, taking nearly all of the original city with it. Only a few buildings remain, though somehow the College of Winterhold has largely been untouched by the damage. It now resides on a free-standing crag of rock and ice. Inside, the College is split into three distinctive towers: Halls of Countenance and Attainment where apprentices and senior mages reside; the Hall of the Elements, where the Arch-Mage resides, gatherings are held, and the Arcanaeum (the College's great library) is kept. Below the College lies the Midden, a warren of icy tunnels where the remnants of long-forgotten experiments reside.

Important Characters

Arch-Mage: Savos Aren

Savos has been the Arch-Mage of the College for a very long time and tried to assure the people that the College was not responsible for the Great Collapse. He took threats seriously after the White-Gold Concordat and helped secure the grounds of the College. Through it all, he's managed to maintain his good demeanor and his faith in humanity. He has little concern for public perception these days, believing that if the mages of the College keep to themselves, no one will bother them. As such, he has every intention of staying out of the Civil War and the Thalmor's rise to power.

Thalmor Advisor: Ancano

A Thalmor agent currently residing at the College of Winterhold, acting in an "advisory" position, Ancano's patronizing tone and haughtiness have made this High Elf into a hated figure. Feeling he has no one to answer to, Ancano is using his time at the College to find out any secrets he can and relay them to his masters back at the Embassy in Haafingar. He isn't winning any popularity awards in the College.

Master-Wizard: Mirabelle Ervine

Mirabelle may be second-in-command, but she's the one who really runs the College. The day-to-day operations are under her jurisdiction, which doesn't make her popular, but she knows someone has to do the job. Mirabelle is frustrated that the College is seen as a black mark, that magic in general is shunned, and takes very seriously any allegations of wrongdoing leveled at the College or its members. She has no use for either the Psijics or the Thalmor—they're all just getting in the way and giving the College a bad reputation.

Wizard: Sergius Turrianus

Well aware of the contempt Nirya and Faralda have for one another, Sergius takes time from his duties as Enchanting instructor to instigate conflict between the two women, in the hopes that Faralda will turn to him for comfort. While he's sure this is going to backfire on him eventually, he's going to enjoy it while he can.

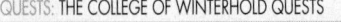

➤ **Trainer (Enchanting: Expert):** Sergius Turrianus

Wizard: Drevis Neloren

Drevis is a strange duck. Quite versed in Illusion, he's well liked by the apprentices but has little presence outside his class. His colleagues barely seem to acknowledge him; he floats through the day leaving little mark on anything. If they were paying attention, one might question whether he's really there at all....Drevis has a habit of wandering into the Arcanaeum and talking Urag gro-Shub's ear off, largely because Urag can't get away.

➤ **Vendor:** Illusion spells

➤ **Trainer (Illusion: Master):** Drevis Neloren

Wizard: Faralda

Faralda has her eye on Mirabelle Ervine's position, a stepping stone on her way to being Arch-Mage. Recently she's noticed that Nirya seems to have her sights set on the same position, and the two have developed a bitter rivalry over it. Rumors of sabotaged experiments and undermined research provide plenty of gossip for the other mages. When upset over something Nirya has done, Faralda goes running to Sergius Turrianus, who is in fact playing up both sides of this conflict to get close to Faralda.

➤ **Vendor:** Destruction spells

➤ **Trainer (Destruction: Expert):** Faralda

Wizard: Phinis Gestor

Phinis has little concern for the affairs of mortals. He's a wizard who conjures creatures from the Beyond—what else matters? Phinis is also interested in Necromancy and takes solace in the notion that the College is one of the few places he can get away with honing his art without being stoned to death in the process. He regularly relies on Enthir to procure some of the more sensitive items his conjurations require, but only interacts socially with Arniel Gane, the one person in the College who doesn't seem nervous when speaking to him.

➤ **Vendor:** Conjuration spells

➤ **Trainer (Conjuration: Expert):** Phinis Gestor

Scholar: Arniel Gane

Arniel is a small, frail little man who's never been entirely comfortable in his own skin. He feels weak and helpless, and while turning to magic has alleviated some of that, he wants to take it a step further. His ultimate (and very secret) goal is to research dwarven artifacts and figure out why the civilization disappeared. To that end, he occasionally procures the services of Enthir for some controversial items.

Scholar: Colette Marence

Colette is the Restoration teacher at the College and is well aware that she's been labeled as a peace-loving star-gazing Spriggan-hugger. Having made repeated attempts to break out of that role and finding that everyone treated her even worse when she no longer fit the image they'd created for her, she's finally given in and accepted that no one will ever see her differently.

➤ **Vendor:** Restoration spells

➤ **Trainer (Restoration: Expert):** Colette Marence

Scholar: Enthir

Enthir is the "man who knows how to obtain materials" in the College. While the College has very flexible rules on what's acceptable research and what's not, there are some reagents and spell components that just can't be acquired through legal means. Enthir, working with Birna in Winterhold, is the elf who takes care of that. He also becomes a Fence in Winterhold during the Thieves Guild Quests.

➤ **Fence (Thieves Guild)**

Scholar: Nirya

Nirya is supremely confident of her abilities and is far more interested in jostling for a leadership position than improving her skills. As Faralda seems to be the only other mage to share these ambitions, she's decided to take her down. Sergius provides insight as to how to go about doing this, and while Nirya has a sense that he may be using her, she can't imagine what his motivation is and so she doesn't worry about it.

Wizard: Tolfdir

Tolfdir is old. Very old. And while it's easy for the others to write him off as a doddering old fool, he is actually one of the few real masters of Alteration magic. He loves his work, offering to give new apprentices their first taste of the College, and is always available to help if it's needed and if it doesn't involve too much physical activity. Despite his elderly nature, those with perceptive qualities know to treat him as the venerable mentor and advisor that his years have taught him to be.

➤ **Vendor:** Alteration spells

➤ **Trainer (Alteration: Master):** Tolfdir

Lorekeeper: Urag gro-Shub

Urag's never been a "normal" Orc, preferring books and spells to blades and war paint. He put on a good show for as long as he could, then quietly snuck off to the College of Winterhold when he had the chance. While he's very good at what he does and loves it, he's still somewhat conflicted by how contrary this is to what's perceived as typical Orc behavior. As such, he feels it necessary to attempt to maintain a gruff, serious exterior. He's actually developed a close relationship with Savos Aren and with Drevis Neloren (against his better judgment), largely because Drevis seems oblivious at Urag's attempts to drive him away.

➤ **Vendor:** Books

Apprentice: Brelyna Maryon

Brelyna comes from a line of Telvanni wizards, well known for their proficiency. However, she is struggling with magic and has opted to study at the College, out of sight of her friends and relatives. Her plan is to get over whatever problem she's having and then return to Solstheim to finish her studies—and do so as quickly as possible.

➤ **Follower:** Brelyna Maryon

Apprentice: J'Zargo

Encouraged by his peers to seek greater magical knowledge, he's traveled to Skyrim to learn what the Nords have to offer about magic. J'Zargo is not intimidated to be the only of his kind at the College; rather, he takes this as a sign that he's an exceptional mage. He believes himself superior to his fellow apprentices and thinks the only reason he hasn't already been made a scholar (or higher) is protocol.

➤ **Follower:** J'Zargo

Apprentice: Onmund

As a Nord, Onmund's natural magical ability was seriously frowned upon by his family. Coming from a difficult childhood as a result, he's happy to finally be someplace where everyone is more like him. Unfortunately, no one seems quite as happy as he is, which he finds to be very puzzling. His frequent attempts to make friends and engage in social activities often fall flat, but this has not dampened his enthusiasm.

➤ **Follower:** Onmund

Augur of Dunlain

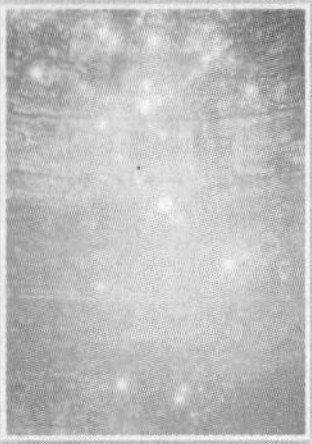

Formerly a mage from Dunlain in High Rock, Augur was working on some unapproved experiments in the Midden and wound up fused to the magical energies that flow through the College. Now incorporeal, he has sequestered himself in a locked room in the Midden but keeps tabs on everything going on in the College.

Psijic Monk: Quaranir

Quaranir is a member of the Psijic Order, a group that teaches a philosophy called the Elder Way, peaceful meditation to reach a higher state of consciousness and manipulation of the living world. These monks have been known to guide particularly adept mages, and Quaranir believes that his guidance is needed now.

Training and other Notes

In addition to a warm bed and like-minded brethren, some of the members of this College of mages are extremely talented in a particular skill. Speak to each of them and increase the chosen skill by a point, to a maximum of five points before you level up. If you have enough gold, you can complete this numerous times:

✓	SKILL	RANK	TRAINER
	Alteration	Master	Tolfdir
	Conjuration	Expert	Phinis Gestor
	Destruction	Master	Faralda
	Illusion	Master	Drevis Neloren
	Restoration	Expert	Colette Marence
	Enchanting	Expert	Sergius Turrianus

Followers and Marriage

Any of the three Apprentices—Brelyna, Onmund, and J'Zargo—can become Followers once you complete their Faction Radiant Quests. In addition, Onmund and Brelyna are candidates for marriage. Consult Side Quest: The Bonds of Matrimony for more details on the nuptials.

Magic Robes

Scour the College for a series of different-colored variations of College Robes; these are the finest premade enchanted robes you can obtain and are rarely found as loot. You can find them from merchants and randomly lying around in chests, wardrobes, or other containers.

Available Quests

There are 31 different quests available with the College of Winterhold. Eight of these are Critical Path Quests; 23 are Radiant Quests.

Critical Path Quests

Simply referred to as "quests," these are the main quests you attempt. All but the first quest have one or more prerequisites, as shown in the following table:

✓	QUEST NAME	PREREQUISITES
	College of Winterhold Quest: First Lessons	None
	College of Winterhold Quest: Under Saarthal	Complete College of Winterhold Quest: First Lessons
	College of Winterhold Quest: Hitting the Books	Complete College of Winterhold Quest: Under Saarthal
	College of Winterhold Quest: Good Intentions	Complete College of Winterhold Quest: Hitting the Books
	College of Winterhold Quest: Revealing the Unseen	Complete College of Winterhold Quest: Good Intentions
	College of Winterhold Quest: Containment	Complete College of Winterhold Quest: Revealing the Unseen
	College of Winterhold Quest: The Staff of Magnus	Complete College of Winterhold Quest: Containment
	College of Winterhold Quest: The Eye of Magnus	Complete College of Winterhold Quest: The Staff of Magnus

Radiant Quests

Also known as "Faction Radiant Quests," these are usually smaller quests that require you to complete an objective for a particular person. New quests of this nature appear as you progress through the Critical Path Quests. In most cases, the objectives of a Radiant Quest are randomized. They are listed in more detail after the Critical Path Quests, but for the prerequisites required to begin every Radiant Quest, consult the following table:

✓	QUEST NAME	QUEST GIVER	PREREQUISITES
	Radiant Quest: Rejoining the College	N/A	Complete College of Winterhold Quest: First Lessons, violence against a member
	Radiant Quest: Tolfdir's Alembic*	Tolfdir	Complete College of Winterhold Quest: First Lessons
	Radiant Quest: Out of Balance*	Drevis Neloren	Complete College of Winterhold Quest: First Lessons
	Radiant Quest: An Enchanted Journey*	Sergius Turrianus	Complete College of Winterhold Quest: First Lessons
	Radiant Quest: Restocking Soul Gems*	Sergius Turrianus	Complete College of Winterhold Quest: First Lessons
	Radiant Quest: Valuable Book Procurement*	Urag gro-Shub	Complete College of Winterhold Quest: First Lessons
	Radiant Quest: Shalidor's Insights	Urag gro-Shub	Complete College of Winterhold Quest: First Lessons
	Radiant Quest: The Atronach Forge*	N/A	Complete College of Winterhold Quest: First Lessons; Ritual Spell Quests: Conjuration Ritual Spell to unlock the forge's full potential.
	Radiant Quest: Forgotten Names*	N/A	Complete College of Winterhold Quest: First Lessons
	Radiant Quest: Aftershock	Tolfdir	Complete College of Winterhold Quest: The Eye of Magnus
	Radiant Quest: Rogue Wizard	Tolfdir	Complete College of Winterhold Quest: The Eye of Magnus
	Arniel's Endeavors: Arniel's Endeavor (Part 1)	Arniel Gane	Complete College of Winterhold: Under Saarthal
	Arniel's Endeavors: Arniel's Endeavor (Part 2)	Arniel Gane	Complete College of Arniel's Endeavors: Arniel's Endeavor (Part 1)
	Arniel's Endeavors: Arniel's Endeavor (Part 3)	Arniel Gane	Complete College of Arniel's Endeavors: Arniel's Endeavor (Part 2), and College of Winterhold Quest: The Eye of Magnus
	Arniel's Endeavors: Arniel's Endeavor (Part 4)	Arniel Gane	Complete College of Arniel's Endeavors: Arniel's Endeavor (Part 3) and College of Winterhold Quest: The Eye of Magnus
	Apprentice Radiant Quest: Brelyna's Practice	Brelyna Maryon	Complete College of Winterhold: Under Saarthal

✓	QUEST NAME	QUEST GIVER	PREREQUISITES
☐	Apprentice Radiant Quest: J'Zargo's Experiment	J'Zargo	Complete College of Winterhold: Under Saarthal
☐	Apprentice Radiant Quest: Onmund's Request	Onmund	Complete College of Winterhold: Under Saarthal
☐	Ritual Spell Quests: Destruction Ritual Spell	Faralda	Destruction Skill of 90
☐	Ritual Spell Quests: Illusion Ritual Spell	Drevis Neloren	Illusion Skill of 90
☐	Ritual Spell Quests: Conjuration Ritual Spell	Phinis Gestor	Conjuration Skill of 90
☐	Ritual Spell Quests: Restoration Ritual Spell	Colette Marence	Restoration Skill of 90
☐	Ritual Spell Quests: Alteration Ritual Spell	Tolfdir	Alteration Skill of 90

NOTE * Indicates the quest name does not appear in your Quest menu; check the "Miscellaneous" area for objectives that may appear.

FIRST LESSONS

PREREQUISITES: None

INTERSECTING QUESTS: The College of Winterhold Quest: Under Saarthal, Main Quest: Elder Knowledge

LOCATIONS: College of Winterhold, Hall of Attainment, Hall of Countenance, Hall of the Elements, Winterhold

CHARACTERS: Brelyna Maryon, Faralda, J'Zargo, Mirabelle Ervine, Onmund, Tolfdir

ENEMIES: None

◊ **OBJECTIVES:** Visit the College of Winterhold, Cast a [chosen] spell, Report to Mirabelle Ervine, Tour the College of Winterhold, Listen to Tolfdir

A Cold to a Warm Reception

During your adventuring, you soon learn of a great college to the north, adjacent to the Hold City of Winterhold. You can speak to various folk across Skyrim and receive the following objective. Denizens include:

- Innkeepers or barkeeps in each of the Hold's inns or taverns
- Court wizards in the Jarl's service in each Hold City, where available
- Ambarys Rendar in Windhelm
- Corpulus Vinius in Solitude
- Dagur in Winterhold
- Dravynea in Kynesgrove
- Elda in Windhelm
- Faida in Dragon Bridge
- Frabbi in Markarth
- Hadring in Nightgate Inn
- Haelga in Riften
- Hulda in Whiterun
- Iddra in Kynesgrove
- Jonna in Morthal
- Keerava in Riften
- Kleppr in Markarth
- Madena in Dawnstar
- Melaran in Solitude
- Mralki in Rorikstead
- Orgnar in Riverwood
- Skuli in Old Hroldan Inn
- Sybille Stentor in Solitude
- Valga Vinicia in Falkreath
- Vilod in Helgen
- Wilhelm in Ivarstead
- Wylandriah in Riften

◊ **OBJECTIVE:** Visit the College of Winterhold

Alternatively, you can simply journey to Winterhold and approach the bridge spanning from the city to the College.

At the near end of the bridge that links Winterhold to the College, a High Elf wizard guards the entrance. She stops you (and warns you to stop if you ignore her or try to gain entry into the sealed College without her approval). Although she has some complaints about the College (which you can ask her about), your real reason for being here is to enter the College. Ask if this is possible, and she asks why. Choose the answer that best suits you. She requires that you take a test to show you're at least possibly competent in the use of magic. You can:

(Persuasion) Attempt to gain entry without completing her unnecessary test.

Agree to take the test. When the test begins, Faralda requests you aim a spell at the seal on the ground near her.

◊ **OBJECTIVE:** Cast a [chosen] spell
♦ **TARGET:** Marker stone, College of Winterhold entrance

Ask if she would grant entry to the Dragonborn. Faralda asks if you really have the Voice. Show her using your Fire Breath (or any other) Shout.

Spell-casting: Bring up your Magic menu and choose the spell Faralda has requested. She can choose Firebolt, Magelight, Fury, Conjure Flame Atronach, or Healing Hands, depending on your available spells and knowledge of particular Magic styles. Aim at the seal, and cast the spell. After your successful casting, Faralda tells you to find Mirabelle Ervine inside the College.

TIP If you don't have any spells, Faralda offers to sell you one for 30 gold pieces. This is a great way to obtain an Apprentice-level spell for a cheap price!

CAUTION Be extremely careful where you're waving your fingers! Don't aim at Faralda or choose a spell (or Shout) that has a large area of effect. If you cast a wider flame-based attack, you risk setting Faralda on fire, effectively ending your tryout as an apprentice mage!

Dragon Shouting: Bring up your Shout inventory, choose any Shout (a good choice is Fire Breath), and bellow. After you strike the seal, Faralda walks over and tells you that there is much you both can learn from each other and that you'd be a superb addition to the College.

You can now ask Faralda more questions about Mirabelle and the College, and you can even receive training in the arts of Destruction magic. College of Winterhold Quest: First Lessons is now active, and you are told to report to Mirabelle Ervine.

◊ **OBJECTIVE:** Report to Mirabelle Ervine.
♦ **TARGET:** Mirabelle Ervine, College of Winterhold courtyard

The Makings of a Mage

Walk across the bridge to the impressive stone edifice, a fortress both highly defensible and remote enough for its students to concentrate on their studies. Head into the outer exterior courtyard, and meet with Mirabelle Ervine. She greets you and hands you the garb of a mage (which you can wear if you wish). She then begins a tour of the College, and you are most definitely encouraged to follow her.

- **Apprentice Hood of Magicka**
- **Boots**
- **Apprentice Robes of Destruction**

◊ **OBJECTIVE:** Tour the College of Winterhold

Mirabelle explains that the Hall of the Elements is the primary location for lectures, practice sessions, and meetings. She also points out that the Arch-Mage's quarters are adjacent but are strictly off-limits to students. Follow Mirabelle to the living quarters. She talks about recent problems the College has been having with Nords. Newest members stay in the Hall of Countenance, where students may be working on spell-casting or experiments. Mirabelle then takes you to the Hall of the Elements.

She tells you that your teacher is likely to be Tolfdir, who is probably already addressing the new Apprentices. She encourages you to report any problems to a senior member before handing you off to Tolfdir.

- **College of Winterhold:** Bed

◊ **OBJECTIVE:** Listen to Tolfdir
♦ **TARGET:** Tolfdir, in the Hall of the Elements

NOTE The entire tour of the College is optional; you can ignore it and run straight into the Hall of the Elements and find Tolfdir.

Find Tolfdir, who tells you that the lesson has just started. Mingle with the other students —Brelyna Maryon, J'Zargo, and Onmund—and heed Tolfdir's advice, although a few of the apprentices are more keen on mage dueling than on hearing a verbal lesson. Tolfdir advises them against impulsive behavior and seeks your thoughts. You may answer with an unsure, practical, or safety-based response. Soon enough, Tolfdir agrees to a practical lesson in the art of Wards.

Wards are protective spells that block magic. Tolfdir has made sure no one within the Hall of the Elements will be hurt and then turns to you and asks if you know a Ward spell. You can answer with one of these options:

You don't have a Ward spell; Tolfdir immediately teaches you Lesser Ward.

You have a Ward spell but don't know how to use it. Tolfdir then explains how they work.

You have a Ward spell and know how to use it. Tolfdir begins a practical demonstration, which eventually happens no matter which answer you choose.

- **Spell:** Lesser Ward

Select a Ward spell from your list and activate it. Tolfdir throws a fire-based spell at you, which you absorb. Once you complete this, Tolfdir seems more confident in the newcomers' abilities and says that he will be leaving soon and taking the Apprentices to Saathal, a Draugr tomb and the site of an ongoing excavation by the College of Winterhold. He expects you to meet him there in a few hours. The lesson now ends.

Quest Conclusion

You are now a member of the College and are free to roam the College of Winterhold.

Postquest Activities

The College of Winterhold Quest: Under Saarthal begins immediately. You can also begin to complete Faction Radiant Quests for the College's many mages.

UNDER SAARTHAL

MINOR SPOILERS

PREREQUISITES: Complete the College of Winterhold Quest: First Lessons

INTERSECTING QUESTS: The College of Winterhold Quest: First Lessons, The College of Winterhold Quest: Hitting the Books, Side Quest: Forbidden Legend

LOCATIONS: College of Winterhold, Hall of Countenance, Hall of the Elements, Saarthal, Saarthal Excavation

CHARACTERS: Arniel Gane, Brelyna Maryon, J'Zargo, Onmund, Nerien, Savos Aren, Tolfdir

ENEMIES: Draugr, Jyrik Gauldurson

◊ **OBJECTIVES:** Meet Tolfdir outside Saarthal, Follow Tolfdir, Find Arniel Gane, Search for magical artifacts (4), Use the Saarthal Amulet to escape the trap, Follow Tolfdir, Tell Tolfdir about the vision, Follow Tolfdir, Find the danger within Saarthal, Talk to the Arch-Mage

A New Vision for Saarthal

This quest begins immediately after you complete the College of Winterhold Quest: First Lessons. Completing this is also part of Side Quest: Forbidden Legend. Check that quest for more information.

◊ **OBJECTIVE:** Meet Tolfdir outside Saarthal

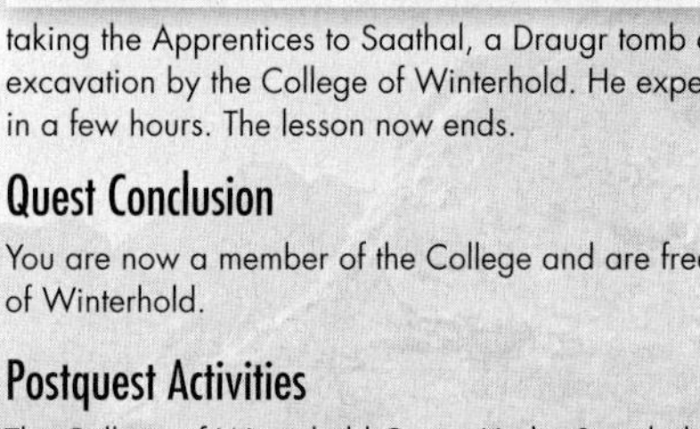

Tolfdir has already made preparations to take his Apprentices (including you) to Saarthal—the remains of an ancient Nordic burial site of great importance and unknown depths and the site of an ongoing excavation by the College. Saarthal is southwest of Winterhold, in a treacherous part of the mountains where wolves like to roam. If you reach the entrance first, wait for the others; they may have been held up by an unexpected encounter. You may converse with any or all of them, but let Tolfdir know when you're ready to begin the exploration. Find out more about the site by asking him, too. Then follow him into the Saarthal Excavation.

◊ **OBJECTIVE:** Follow Tolfdir

NOTE The Saarthal Excavation door is firmly sealed and opened only during this quest.

Tolfdir descends the rickety steps into the entrance chamber, explaining that Saarthal was one of the earliest Nord settlements in Skyrim, and the largest. It was sacked during the infamous Night of Tears, but little else is known about what happened to the settlement. After some further instruction, ask Tolfdir what he needs, and he asks you to help Arniel Gane catalog some finds and locate enchanted items.

◊ **OBJECTIVE:** Find Arniel Gane

Follow the path of lanterns along the passages and into a multifloored chamber with wooden scaffolding. Drop from the bridge, and find Arniel Gane in a side corridor. He instructs you to look around the chambers to his north and to be careful.

◊ **OBJECTIVE:** Search for magical artifacts (4)

The intersecting passages north of Arniel Gane aren't dangerous, but the enchanted items dotted around here may be difficult to spot. Make slow, deliberate sweeps of each area until you find the items in question. Once you have the first three easy-to-spot items, head to this strange, torch-lit carved arch with the Saarthal Amulet on it. Grab it, and you immediately hear strange, scraping sounds. You triggered a spear trap. Tolfdir appears to see if you're all right. Explain what happened, and he suggests using it in some way.

➤ **Enchanted Ring (3)** ➤ **Saarthal Amulet**

◊ **OBJECTIVE:** Use the Saarthal Amulet to escape the trap
◊ **OBJECTIVE:** Follow Tolfdir

Select the Saarthal Amulet from your inventory and wear it. Tolfdir remarks that the wall from which you took the amulet may be susceptible to your magic. Launch a Firebolt (or other target-based spell) at the carved wall section, and it shatters back into an unexplored passage. The spear trap recedes. Instead of rushing through, wait for Tolfdir to approach, and follow him into the rocky tunnel. As Tolfdir plods ahead, he wonders why this place was sealed off. You both step into a small mausoleum chamber, where Tolfdir tells you to be on your guard.

The Saarthal Discovery

A moment later, an apparition named Nerien appears in a startling vision. He is unknown to you, and you appear to be the only one who is communicating with him. He mutters a warning that the events you've set in motion cannot be undone. But judgment on you will be based on your forthcoming actions and how you deal with the dangers ahead. The Psijic Order believes in you. You alone have the ability to prevent disaster. Take great care, and know that the Order is watching....

◊ **OBJECTIVE:** Tell Tolfdir about the vision
◊ **OBJECTIVE:** Follow Tolfdir

Immediately inform Tolfdir about your vision, and the message. Tolfdir thinks this is all very odd, as the Psijics have no connection to these ruins, and no one has seen their order in a long time. He suspects the coffins embedded around this room are connected to deeper chambers. His excavation techniques are quickly abandoned as a Draugr breaks through from the other side. After dispatching the Draugr, follow Tolfdir into another newly discovered passage beyond.

Pull the lever at the bottom of the passage to open the portcullis. This leads into a grand, circular chamber with a bridge crossing a chasm. Fortunately, grating prevents you from plummeting to your death. Around the chamber are coffin alcoves. The Draugr start to stir. Back Tolfdir up as you bring your magic (or other attacks) to bear on the advancing undead. Once you down the Draugr, Tolfdir begins inspecting the chamber in greater detail and wishes to remain here. You're tasked with finding out what terrible dangers the Psijic Order mentioned in your vision. On your own...

◊ **OBJECTIVE:** Find the danger within Saarthal

Awakening the Scourge of Skyrim

Head north, removing the spear bars and portcullis from the iron door by activating a lever on both sides of the door. Step into Saarthal itself, and work your way through a grand burial crypt. You awaken the Draugr, so expect them to step out of their wall coffins as you progress. Head up the wooden steps, inspect the raised sarcophagus near the iron door, and pass through into a sloping stone burial tunnel. Watch for traps of a flame and dart-based nature. Then enter the crypt corridor of carvings.

At this corridor's far end is a barred archway with a lever on a pedestal. Activate the lever, and you're struck by darts. Along the sides of the corridor are a total of six pillars, each with a trio of animal petroglyphs carved into them.

Puzzle solution: The trick here is to notice a smaller carving above each pillar. Make sure that the pillar below matches this smaller carving. Along the north wall from left to right, adjust the pillars so the following animal forms are facing out: Whale, Snake, and Hawk. Along the south wall from left to right: Hawk, Hawk, and Whale.

Inside the two-level ceremony room beyond, you encounter a power Draugr close to the wooden side steps. Battle it, then take the upper door exit past the treasure chest. Avoid the runic traps and reach a second puzzle passage. Expect a dart trap if you pull the lever before correctly positioning the four carved pillars.

Puzzle solution: The four correct positions are displayed in the large carved mouths on each side of the passage and behind each movable pillar. On the west wall from left right: Hawk and Whale. On the east wall from left to right: Snake and Whale. Each pillar makes several other pillars move too. This causes no end of adjustment problems if you don't know how many pillars move during each activation (look at the nearby picture, which has each pillar numbered):

Pillar 1 (Whale): Activate it to move all four pillars.

Pillar 2 (Snake): Activate it to move pillars 2, 3, and 4.

Pillar 3 (Hawk): Activate it to move pillars 3 and 4.

Pillar 4 (Whale): Activate it and only it moves.

The solution is deceptively simple: Turn the pillar that rotates the most number of pillars first, and continue activating pillars that rotate consecutively fewer pillars until the puzzle is solved. That way you affect fewer pillars as you go. Face the portcullis archway (to the south):

Activate pillar 1 to show the Whale.

Activate pillar 2 to show the Snake.

Activate pillar 3 to show the Hawk.

Activate pillar 4 to show the Whale.

Watch for more runic and dart traps as Tolfdir catches up with you. He finds all of this fascinating. You can ask him further questions about the Psijic Order and then continue exploring. Open the iron door and enter the chamber of Jyrik Gauldurson. Tolfdir is transfixed by a massive ten-foot glowing orb, floating in a bubble of writhing magic, at the room's opposite end. It is pulsing and made of some strange, unknown material. Tolfdir averts his gaze when a ferocious-looking Draugr rises from his eternal throne chair; you're about to face Jyrik Gauldurson. This most evil of Nords was sealed down here to prevent his reanimation. Not anymore!

Jyrik Gauldurson is coursing with evil magic, and for the first ten seconds of the battle, he is utterly impervious to any attacks. Use this time to step behind cover, or let any summoned creatures or Followers bear the brunt of his attacks. Eventually, Tolfdir realizes that all your combined offensive capabilities aren't having an effect, so he turns to the Eye and focuses his attacks on the crackling globe. A few seconds later, he yells that Jyrik is vulnerable. Attack!

To further complicate matters, Jyrik is bathed in an elemental shield that cycles through the different elements; he is impervious to attacks from the same element. So, if he's bathed in fire, then any Flame-based spells have no effect on him. Use attacks from any other element instead. If you have only one type of elemental magic (i.e., only Fire), wait a few seconds until Jyric's shielding changes elements and then strike!

TIP Jyrik is extremely vulnerable to frost damage when he's on fire, and when encased in a frost shield, he's very vulnerable to fire. Use this to your advantage!

◊ **OBJECTIVE:** Talk to the Arch-Mage

Quest Conclusion

With Jyrik Gauldurson gurgling his last curse, turn your attention to the giant orb. Tolfdir agrees that the Arch-Mage at the College of Winterhold should be informed immediately. Use the iron door behind the orb to exit the chamber, which leads to a fern-filled grotto and an ancient Word Wall. Absorb the power before you return to the excavation site, releasing the portcullis exit with a wall handle, and leave Saarthal.

- **Gauldur Amulet Fragment**
- **Writ of Sealing**
- **Word of Power:** Ice Storm
- **Staff of Jyrik Gauldurson**

TIP Be sure to take the Gauldur Amulet Fragment, as it imbues you with +30 Magicka! Read the Writ of Sealing, and you begin Side Quest: Forbidden Legend. It seems there are two other Gauldurson brothers to face elsewhere in Skyrim! Consult Side Quest: Forbidden Legend quest (on page 431) for more information.

Return to the College and seek out Savos Aren, either in the Hall of Countenance or Hall of the Elements. You may ask him about the Psijic Order, but you're here to speak to him about the Saarthal discovery. Savos Aren is taken aback by your findings and believes more research is needed while he journeys to Saarthal to inspect the orb. You are rewarded for your efforts.

- **Staff of Magelight**

Postquest Activities

The College of Winterhold Quest: Hitting the Books begins immediately. You can now speak to each of Tolfdir's three students and Arniel, and engage in some more Radiant Quests from this point on.

HITTING THE BOOKS

PREREQUISITES: Complete the College of Winterhold Quest: Under Saarthal

INTERSECTING QUESTS: The College of Winterhold Quest: Under Saarthal, The College of Winterhold Quest: Good Intentions, The College of Winterhold Faction Radiant Quests

LOCATIONS: College of Winterhold, Arcanaeum, Hall of Countenance, Hall of the Elements, Fellglow Keep, Fellglow Keep Dungeons, Fellglow Keep Ritual Chamber

CHARACTERS: Orthorn, Savos Aren, Urag gro-Shub

ENEMIES: Atronach, The Caller, Conjurer, Fire Mage, Frost Atronach, Frostbite Spider, Ice Mage, Necromancer, Skeleton, Storm Atronach, Storm Mage, Vampire, Wolf

◊ **OBJECTIVES:** Speak with Urag gro-Shub, Find the stolen books (3), (Optional) Free Orthorn, Return the books

Tardy Bookkeeping

This quest begins immediately after you complete the College of Winterhold Quest: Under Saarthal.

◊ **OBJECTIVE:** Speak with Urag gro-Shub

♦ **TARGET:** Urag gro-Shub, in the Arcanaeum

Arch-Mage Savos Aren will form a plan for dealing with the large undulating orb you found in the depths of Saarthal. In the meantime, locate the Arcanaeum off the Hall of the Elements. Seek out Urag gro-Shub the Lorekeeper in his library. There are several questions you can ask him, and you can help him find special books (aside from this quest). But to further this quest, tell him you need to learn about the orb that was found in Saarthal. Urag has no information on the matter.

Guild Fence (Windhelm): Niranye

A beautiful High Elf who runs a stall in the Stone Quarter, many attribute her fortune to membership in the Thieves Guild, so they keep a wide berth. In actuality, Niranye is the Fence for the Summerset Shadows Thieves Guild. Linwe is the leader, and they maintain a small headquarters of about a dozen Altmer thieves in Uttering Hills Cave.

➤ **Fence (Windhelm)**

> **NOTE** Niranye becomes a Fence if she survives (and once you complete) City Influence Quest: Summerset Shadows.

Guild Fence (Markarth): Endon

Endon is a silversmith in Markarth, like his forefathers and mothers before him. He is proud of the long cosmopolitan tradition in Markarth (unlike most of the rest of Skyrim), which is not widely known, and he deplores the sad state that the feuding of the Nords and Reachmen (known as the Forsworn) has brought the city. Endon works out of his small but tidy house in Dryside. His wife, Kerah, works with him, and also sells their jewelry in the market during the day. His daughter Adara is his apprentice.

➤ **Fence (Markarth)**

> **NOTE** Endon becomes a Fence if he survives (and once you complete) City Influence Quest: Silver Lining.

Guild Fence (Caravan): Ri'saad

Ri'saad is the patriarch of Skyrim's Khajiit Caravans. A skilled merchant and gifted leader, he has organized a small syndicate of independent merchant caravans that travel the roads and cities of Skyrim.

Guild Fence (Caravan): Atahba

Ri'saad's first wife is a shrewd businesswoman in her own right. She's with Ri'saad mostly because he's the shrewdest Khajiit in Skyrim and had more money than anyone else she knew, but she's also grown to love him over the years. She refuses to talk about her past.

➤ **Fence (Caravan)**

> **NOTE** Ri'saad and Atahba become a Fence once your Thieves Guild growth reaches Stage 3‡ and you complete Quest: Moon Sugar Rush*.

Guild Fence (Caravan): Ma'jhad

Ma'jahd is a bodyguard in Ma'dran's caravan, which travels the roads between Windhelm and Solitude. He is a seasoned safecracker, and is always willing to train customers in the fine art of Lockpicking.

➤ **Fence (Caravan)**

➤ **Trainer (Lockpicking: Expert):** Ma'jhad

> **NOTE** Ma'jhad becomes a Fence once your Thieves Guild growth reaches Stage 3‡ and you complete Quest: Moon Sugar Rush*.

Guild Fence (Caravan): Zaynabi

Struck by wanderlust, Zaynabi has traveled far and wide. She's seen her fair share of troubles, but nothing seems to phase her go-lucky attitude. She has become quite the archer. She occasionally freelances out her scouting services and offers her services as a bowyer and fletcher.

➤ **Fence (Caravan)**

> **NOTE** Zaynabi becomes a Fence once your Thieves Guild growth reaches Stage 3‡ and you complete Quest: Moon Sugar Rush*.

Associate: Maul

Maul is a close friend of Hemming Black-Briar, having met each other during a bandit ambush: Maul happened by and dove into the fray to save him. Ever since then, they have been literally partners in crime, with Maul assisting Hemming in his more nefarious activities assigned by Maven Black-Briar. Whenever Hemming needs "wet work" done, Maul is the go to for these things. Maul's brother is Dirge. Maul is quite fond of his brother (as they grew up alone together) and would seek vengeance on anyone that harmed him.

Associate: Galathil

Assuming you've learned of her presence via Dawnguard Side Quest: Face to Face* (see page 585), the water deck of the Ragged Flagon becomes home to a mysterious Dunmer named Galathil, who utilizes a mixture of magic and deft cutting to rearrange your features for a (potentially) reasonable fee of 1,000 gold. Nothing is known about her, except for her services: You can completely change your facial appearance, just like you did prior to your escape from Helgen at the very start of your adventure. You cannot change your race or sex. if you're a female Khajiit, you stay one. If you've contracted vampirism, Galathil notices this straightaway. Her techniques work only on the living, so you'll have to seek a cure before she agrees to work on you.

Associate: Glover Mallory

Glover Mallory is one of the most prominent non-Dunmer citizens in Raven Rock. He's jovial, warm and when he isn't at his anvil, can be found hoisting a mug at the Retching Netch. In actuality, Glover Mallory is a member of Skyrim's Thieves Guild and brother to Delvin Mallory. Glover was sent to Solstheim by Mercer Frey in order to establish a base of operations there. Unbeknownst to Glover, this was Mercer's way of separating Delvin from his brother, who he feared might tip the scales against him if his true nature was ever revealed. Glover (who possesses superior smithing skills) was more than happy to assist the Guild and make some extra money on the side and gladly accepted the funding that Mercer provided so he could establish a front on Solstheim. Pickings have been quite scarce in Raven Rock, but due to his cheery disposition, Glover's made the most of it. Absolutely no one on the island is aware of his past.

AN INFLUX OF IMMIGRANTS

The following table details the names, occupations, and quest prerequisites (or Stage that the Thieves Guild needs to be at) for allies of the Thieves Guild to arrive at the Ragged Flagon or Cistern or to set up in a Hold City:

✓	NAME OF NEW GUILD MEMBER (AND LOCATION)	OCCUPATION	PREREQUISITE
☐	Tonilia	Fence	Thieves Guild Quest: Loud and Clear
☐	Gulum-Ei (in Solitude)	Fence	Thieves Guild Quest: Scoundrel's Folly
☐	Mallus Maccius (in Whiterun)	Fence	Thieves Guild Quest: Dampened Spirits
☐	Enthir (Winterhold)	Fence	Thieves Guild Quest: Hard Answers
☐	Niranye (Windhelm)	Fence	City Influence Quest: Summerset Shadows
☐	Endon (Markarth)	Fence	City Influence Quest: Silver Lining
☐	Syndus	Vendor (Fletcher)	Stage 1
☐	Herluin Lothaire	Vendor (Apothecary)	Stage 2

✓	NAME OF NEW GUILD MEMBER (AND LOCATION)	OCCUPATION	PREREQUISITE
☐	Arnskar Ember-Master	Vendor (Blacksmith)	Stage 3
☐	Atahba (Caravan)	Fence	Stage 3
☐	Garthar	Member	Stage 3
☐	Ma'jhad (Caravan)	Fence	Stage 3
☐	Ri'saad (Caravan)	Fence	Stage 3
☐	Zaynabi (Caravan)	Fence	Stage 3
☐	Ravyn Imyan	Member	Stage 4
☐	Vanryth Gatharian	Vendor (Light Armor)	Stage 4
☐	Galathil	Face Sculptor	Dawnguard Side Quest: Face to Face*

TRAINING

In addition to a warm bed and companionship, the main members of this guild of thieves and their associates are extremely talented in particular skills.

✓	SKILL	RANK	TRAINER
☐	Archery	Master	Niruin
☐	Pickpocket	Master	Vipir the Fleet
☐	Lockpicking	Master	Vex

✓	SKILL	RANK	TRAINER
☐	Lockpicking	Expert	Ma'jhad
☐	Sneak	Master	Delvin Mallory

OTHER ADVANTAGES

Guild Chests

In addition to your kinsmen and an influx of like-minded ne'er-do-wells joining the Guild as news spreads of its power and influence, there are other advantages of being a Thieves Guild member. In the Cistern, there are a group of "Guild Chests" that you can loot: They contain useful items such as lockpicks, potions, and gold. But the real advantage is that you can use the chests to store your items, without fear of them being lost. Use this as a dumping ground for extra equipment you wish to sell, craft, or otherwise dispose of.

Mercer's Bookcases

The shelving behind Mercer's desk in the Cistern slowly fills with trophies relevant to your exploits and with any Larceny Targets you may recover and sell to Delvin. As you finish the Additional Jobs that Vex and Delvin give you, trophies of recovered items begin to fill the shelves too:

Jeweled Candlesticks appear after you complete five jobs.

An Ornate Drinking Horn appears after you complete 15 jobs.

A Golden Ship Model appears after you complete 25 jobs.

A Golden Urn appears after you complete 35 jobs.

A Jeweled Goblet appears after you complete 45 jobs.

A Jeweled Pitcher appears after you complete 55 jobs.

A Jeweled Flagon appears after you complete 75 jobs.

A safe appears along the back wall, next to the bookcases, after you complete 125 jobs. It contains gems, gold, and some very useful customized Thief potions!

If you complete Thieves Guild Radiant Quest: No Stone Unturned, the Crown will appear on the bust and pedestal behind the desk, between the bookshelves.

Additional Accouterments

If you complete Thieves Guild Quest: Darkness Returns, a Shrine of Nocturnal appears in the Cistern. This is the same as the other temple shrines scattered across Skyrim, which cure diseases. This bestows a Sneak Blessing.

If you become the Guild Master, a tribute chest appears in front of the desk in the Cistern. It contains gold and gems and is periodically restocked.

The Guild has four visible Stages of growth. As the Stages progress, you will witness more opulent furnishings; additional boxes, barrels, and banners; and the occasional new Guild member. A new vendor appears in the Ragged Flagon in an empty niche, one per Stage.

Alas, no one in the Thieves Guild is the marrying type.

AVAILABLE QUESTS

There are 29 different quests available within the Thieves Guild. Twelve of these are Critical Path Quests, while 17 are Radiant Quests or Additional Objectives.

Critical Path Quests

Simply referred to as "quests," these are the main quests you attempt. All but the first quest require one or more prerequisites, as shown in the following table:

✓	QUEST NAME	PREREQUISITES
☐	Thieves Guild Quest: A Chance Arrangement	None
☐	Thieves Guild Quest: Taking Care of Business	Complete Thieves Guild Quest: A Chance Arrangement
☐	Thieves Guild Quest: Loud and Clear	Complete Thieves Guild Quest: Taking Care of Business
☐	Thieves Guild Quest: Meet the Family*	Complete Thieves Guild Quest: Loud and Clear
☐	Thieves Guild Quest: Dampened Spirits	Complete Thieves Guild Quest: Loud and Clear
☐	Thieves Guild Quest: Scoundrel's Folly	Complete Thieves Guild Quest: Dampened Spirits
☐	Thieves Guild Quest: Speaking with Silence	Complete Thieves Guild Quest: Scoundrel's Folly
☐	Thieves Guild Quest: Hard Answers	Complete Thieves Guild Quest: Speaking with Silence
☐	Thieves Guild Quest: The Pursuit	Complete Thieves Guild Quest: Hard Answers
☐	Thieves Guild Quest: Trinity Restored	Complete Thieves Guild Quest: The Pursuit
☐	Thieves Guild Quest: Blindsighted	Complete Trinity Restored
☐	Thieves Guild Quest: Darkness Returns	Complete Blindsighted

Radiant Quests

These are usually smaller quests and are split into three subsections. There are "Radiant Quests," which you can opt to attempt and are grouped together as they affect your relationships with the Guild. There are additional objectives that you can complete to strengthen the ties the Thieves Guild have across Skyrim. Finally, there are City Influence Quests (culminating in you becoming the Guild Leader), which complete your Guild domination across this realm, as merchants and new thieves flock to your sewer.

In some cases, the Additional Objectives are randomized. The prerequisites required to begin every Radiant Quest is in the following table:

✓	QUEST NAME	PREREQUISITES
☐	Radiant Quest: No Stone Unturned	None
☐	Radiant Quest: Reparations‡	Complete Thieves Guild Quest: Taking Care of Business
☐	Radiant Quest: Moon Sugar Rush*	Complete Thieves Guild Quest: Meet the Family
☐	Radiant Quest: Armor Exchange*	Complete Thieves Guild Quest: Scoundrel's Folly
☐	Radiant Quest: The Litany of Larceny*	Complete Thieves Guild Quest: Meet the Family (and finding a Larceny Target in a subsequent quest)
☐	Additional Job: The Numbers Job	Complete Thieves Guild Quest: Meet the Family
☐	Additional Job: The Fishing Job	Complete Thieves Guild Quest: Meet the Family
☐	Additional Job: The Bedlam Job	Complete Thieves Guild Quest: Meet the Family
☐	Additional Job: The Burglary Job	Complete Thieves Guild Quest: Meet the Family
☐	Additional Job: The Shill Job	Complete Thieves Guild Quest: Meet the Family
☐	Additional Job: The Sweep Job	Complete Thieves Guild Quest: Meet the Family
☐	Additional Job: The Heist Job	Complete Thieves Guild Quest: Meet the Family
☐	City Influence Quest: Silver Lining	Complete Thieves Guild Quest: Meet the Family and 5 Additional Jobs in Markarth
☐	City Influence Quest: The Dainty Sload	Complete Thieves Guild Quest: Meet the Family and 5 Additional Jobs in Solitude
☐	City Influence Quest: Imitation Amnesty	Complete Thieves Guild Quest: Meet the Family and 5 Additional Jobs in Whiterun
☐	City Influence Quest: Summerset Shadows	Complete Thieves Guild Quest: Meet the Family and 5 Additional Jobs in Windhelm
☐	Leadership Quest: Under New Management	Complete Thieves Guild Quest: Darkness Returns and all four City Influence Quests

NOTE ‡ Indicates you must have been kicked out of the Guild to begin this Radiant Quest.

NOTE * = Indicates the quest name does not appear in your Quest menu; check the "Miscellaneous" area for objectives that may appear.

A CHANCE ARRANGEMENT

PREREQUISITES: None

INTERSECTING QUESTS: Main Quest: A Cornered Rat, Thieves Guild Quest: Taking Care of Business, Thieves Guild Quest: No Stone Unturned

LOCATIONS: Riften, The Bee and Barb, Marketplace

CHARACTERS: Brand-Shei, Brynjolf, Madesi,

ENEMIES: None

◊ **OBJECTIVES:** Meet Brynjolf during daytime, Steal Madesi's Ring, Plant Madesi's Ring, Speak to Brynjolf

Sizing up Your Mark

The first time you visit the Bee and Barb or look around the marketplace in Riften, a man named Brynjolf strikes up a conversation with you. He has an errand he wants your help with, and will reward you with gold.

He tells you to pilfer a silver ring from Madesi's stall in the marketplace while he creates a distraction. You are then to place it in the pocket of a Dark Elf vendor named Brand-Shei. If you're caught, you're on your own; if you succeed, Brynjolf will have some better-paying schemes. If you've met Brynjolf during the evening or night, he'll be waiting between eight in the morning and eight in the evening for you. If you met Brynjolf during the night, wait until daylight and meet up again.

◊ **OBJECTIVE:** Meet Brynjolf during daytime
♦ **TARGET:** Brynjolf, marketplace in Riften
◊ **OBJECTIVE:** Steal Madesi's Ring
♦ **TARGET:** Madesi's stand, marketplace in Riften

Making Your Mark

Brynjolf is waiting for you by his plaza stand, where he's about to hawk his "amazing" Falmerblood Elixir. Naturally, this patter is designed to draw a crowd (including Madesi and Brand-Shei), allowing you to quickly move around the plaza's perimeter stone wall and crouch behind Madesi's stall.

(Lockpick [Novice]) Produce your lockpicks and unlock the sliding door under the stall counter; then unlock Madesi's strongbox and quickly rummage around inside. You can help yourself to any of the items here, but the valuable you're concerned with is Madesi's Silver Ring. Steal it quickly, before any of the city guards spot you.Attempt this Lockpick only after any city guards pass you by, and you're hidden from view while sneaking.

➤ **Madesi's Silver Ring**

◊ **OBJECTIVE:** Plant Madesi's Ring
♦ **TARGET:** Brand-Shei, marketplace in Riften

Creep around so you're unseen by most of the assembled beggars and storekeepers, and position yourself behind Brand-Shei.

(Sneak and Pickpocket) You must now "reverse-pickpocket" the Dark Elf. This involves Pickpocketing, choosing your own Apparel menu, selecting Madesi's Silver Ring, and giving it to Brand-Shei to finish the technique, without being seen by anyone. As this is likely your first attempt at such an action, you have a slight boost to your Pickpocket skill, but don't expect this to happen again!

If you're successful, Brand-Shei is mistaken for a thief and hauled away to Riften prison. Your paths may cross again in the future....

◊ **OBJECTIVE:** Speak to Brynjolf
♦ **TARGET:** Brynjolf, marketplace in Riften

CAUTION

If you're arrested, you leave Riften, wait more than half a day to complete Brynjolf's objective, or you murder someone during his distraction. Thieves Guild Quest: A Chance Arrangement still completes. However, there is no reward, and Brynjolf isn't pleased with your inadequacy. This is not the way to impress a future mentor!

Quest Conclusion

Speak to Brynjolf after the misdirection goes down, and he congratulates (and rewards) you if the plan was a success. You receive no monetary gain if you failed. Then he mentions his organization has been having a run of bad luck, but quickly mentions that there's more money to earn if you can handle it. Reply that you can, and Brynjolf recommends you meet him at the Ragged Flagon tavern, deep inside Riften's subterranean Ratway.

➤ **100 gold pieces**

Postquest Activities

Thieves Guild Quest: Taking Care of Business is now active. After this quest concludes, stay for a moment and watch the guard arrest Brand-Shei. He's hauled off toward Mistveil Keep and spends a week there before being released back into Riften. Visit him during this time if you like, but he doesn't have much to say to the likes of you!

If you encountered a man named Maul close to Riften's north gate, you have another chance to get to know the Thieves Guild, but only if you're carrying an Unusual Gem you may have found scattered around Skyrim. Consult Thieves Guild Quest: No Stone Unturned for more information. Maul points you toward Brynjolf if you're not yet a member of the Thieves Guild.

TAKING CARE OF BUSINESS

PREREQUISITES: Complete Thieves Guild Quest: A Chance Arrangement
INTERSECTING QUESTS: Thieves Guild Quest: Loud and Clear
LOCATIONS: Riften, The Bee and Barb, Haelga's Bunkhouse, Pawned Prawn, Ragged Flagon, Ratway
CHARACTERS: Bersi Honey-Hand, Brynjolf, Haelga, Keerava, Talen-Jei, Vekel the Man,
ENEMIES: Drahff, Hewnon Black-Skeever
◊ **OBJECTIVES:** Locate Brynjolf at the Ragged Flagon, Collect Keerava's debt, Collect Bersi Honey-Hand's debt, Collect Haelga's debt, (Optional) Use Talen-Jei to get to Keerava, (Optional) Smash Bersi's prized Dwarven Urn, (Optional) Steal Haelga's Statue of Dibella, Return to Brynjolf

To the Tavern

◊ **OBJECTIVE:** Locate Brynjolf at the Ragged Flagon
♦ **TARGET:** Ragged Flagon, in the Ratway in Riften

Begin with this objective already active. Search for the entrance to the Ratway, which is under the Grand Plaza by the water's edge, on the town's south side. Once you're through the iron gate, prepare to stumble across a couple of inept thugs looking for a victim to mug. You can sneak by them if you wait until Drahff patrols the Ratway entrance and Hewnon has his back to you.

Now continue through this small maze of interlocking sewage tunnels. Watch for a hanging oil trap and a bear trap along the way. If your Lockpick skill is high enough, there's a chamber to check out, but your main purpose is finding the Ragged Flagon.

The tavern has a unique floorplan, being constructed within the space below Riften's central well. When you spot Brynjolf, he is conversing with the barkeep, Vekel the Man, about Brynjolf's predicament with his "organization." Speak to Brynjolf, and he asks if you'd be interested in handling a few deadbeats for him. Do a good job, and Brynjolf predicts a permanent place in his guild. Ask how to collect the dues owed, and Brynjolf recommends anything short of killing them.

◊ **OBJECTIVE:** Collect Keerava's debt
♦ **TARGET:** Keerava, in the Bee and Barb in Riften
◊ **OBJECTIVE:** Collect Bersi Honey-Hand's debt
♦ **TARGET:** Bersi Honey-Hand, in the Pawned Prawn, in Riften
◊ **OBJECTIVE:** Collect Haelga's debt
♦ **TARGET:** Haelga, in Haelga's Bunkhouse in Riften

(Optional) Remain in the Ragged Flagon for a moment and quiz Brynjolf on each of the targets to gain more information. You learn about Keerava's lover Talen-Jei, Bersi's love of dwarven pottery, and Haelga's devotion to the goddess Dibella. Be sure your quest updates with the following:

◊ **OBJECTIVE:** (Optional) Use Talen-Jei to get to Keerava
◊ **OBJECTIVE:** (Optional) Smash Bersi's prized Dwarven Urn
◊ **OBJECTIVE:** (Optional) Steal Haelga's Statue of Dibella

Shopkeeper Shakedowns

Return to the surface, ensuring you activate the lever in the Ratway that lowers the bridge, enabling a fast exit. Now visit each of the three shopkeepers on Brynjolf's list, while remembering the following:

1. You can approach any of the three shopkeepers in any order. Apply the information you've learned...
2. You may impose your unarmed prowess against them but can do so only the first time you talk to your target. Be sure you begin this from a conversation, or you'll have the whole town against you!
3. Once two of the three shopkeepers have paid up, the third has heard of your intimidation and hands over their payment without any fuss.
4. You must collect all three payments before returning to Brynjolf to complete the quest. Brynjolf is essentially expecting 300 gold. If you spend some of the payments the shopkeepers gave you (dropping your total below 300), Brynjolf won't be satisfied until you bring the entire amount. No skimming!

Keerava's Comeuppance

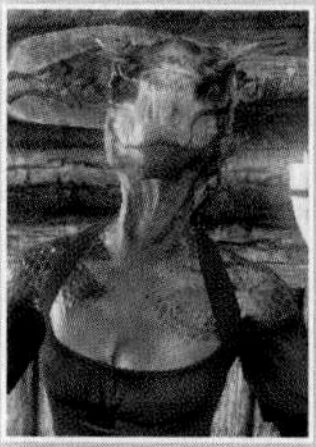

Enter the Bee and Barb, and venture toward Keerava. You may:

(Brawl) Speak to her before pummeling her with your fists. Once she's knocked down, she pays up.

Or tell her you've finished wasting your time talking to her. Then seek out Talen-Jei.

Talen-Jei is usually inside the tavern, close to his lover. Converse with him and tell him to talk some sense into Keerava. He lets you in on the location of Keerava's family. This is something you can use to your advantage. Return to her and threaten to visit "that farm in Morrowind." Her bravery falters. She begs you not to hurt her family and then pays up.

➤ **100 gold pieces**

Bersi's Reimbursement

Enter the Pawned Prawn and locate Bersi Honey-Hand at the counter. You can:

(Brawl) Tell him to shut his mouth, and beat him down with your fists until he pays his dues.

Or tell him you've had enough of this banter and look around the room for something to break.

Behind you is a rather fine example of dwarven pottery. Produce your favored smashing implement and strike the urn until it shatters. Ignore the yells from Bersi and his wife. When the pottery is in pieces, return to Bersi and ask if he wants anything else broken. This does the trick, and he hands over the gold he owes.

➤ **100 gold pieces**

Haelga's Hostage

Step into Haelga's Bunkhouse and find the proprietor. You're able to:

(Brawl) Tell her that she'll have to pay in more than just coin, and beat her into agreement.

Or inform her that the Guild has run out of patience with her. Gaze around the interior for something to steal.

On the wall near the door is a small shrine dedicated to the goddess of women, Dibella. Steal the Statue of Dibella, then return to Haelga and threaten to drop it down a well. Soon the monies owed appears in your hands.

➤ **100 gold pieces**

Quest Conclusion

Find Brynjolf back in the Ragged Flagon. He's impressed you managed to both acquire the gold and keep it "clean"—not resorting to bloodshed. In return for your services, he gives you a cut of the gold you've collected and offers you the following:

➤ **One Poison [random]**

➤ **One Healing potion [random and leveled]**

➤ **Fortify Stealth Skill potion [random and leveled]**

◊ **OBJECTIVE:** Return to Brynjolf
♦ **TARGET:** Ragged Flagon, in the Ratway in Riften

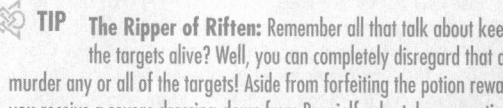

TIP **The Ripper of Riften:** Remember all that talk about keeping the targets alive? Well, you can completely disregard that and murder any or all of the targets! Aside from forfeiting the potion rewards, you receive a severe dressing-down from Brynjolf, who takes exception to your actions. But the quest still completes.

Brynjolf recognizes the telltale signs of a practiced thief in you and thinks you'll fit in with the rest of the team. After telling you not to worry about the rough patch the Guild has been in, Brynjolf offers to show you what the Thieves Guild is all about.

Postquest Activities

Thieves Guild Quest: Loud and Clear is now active.

PREREQUISITES: Complete Thieves Guild Quest: Taking Care of Business

INTERSECTING QUESTS: Thieves Guild Quest: Additional Jobs, Thieves Guild Quest: Larceny Targets, Thieves Guild Quest: Dampened Spirits

LOCATIONS: Goldenglow Estate, Goldenglow Estate Basement, Goldenglow Estate Second Floor, Riften, Ragged Flagon, Cistern, Ratway

CHARACTERS: Brynjolf, Delvin Mallory, Maven Black-Briar, Mercer Frey, Tonilia, Vex,

ENEMIES: Aringoth, Mercenaries, Skeevers

◊ **OBJECTIVES:** Follow Brynjolf, Listen to Mercer Frey, Talk to Brynjolf, Burn three beehives, Clear out Aringoth's safe, (Optional) Speak to Vex about, Goldenglow Estate, Meet the Family: Learn more about the Thieves Guild from Vex, Meet the Family: Learn more about the Thieves Guild from Delvin, Meet the Family: Retrieve your Thieves Guild Armor from Tonilia, (Optional) Enter Goldenglow using the sewer, (Optional) Obtain the key to Aringoth's safe, Return to Brynjolf

Do as You're Told, and Keep Your Blade Clean

◊ **OBJECTIVE:** Follow Brynjolf

♦ **TARGET:** Ragged Flagon, in the Ratway in Riften

You begin this quest with the previous objective already active. Follow Brynjolf into the Ragged Flagon's Cistern. The time has come to meet the rest of his team, including the leader of this small operation—Mercer Frey.

◊ **OBJECTIVE:** Listen to Mercer Frey

◊ **OBJECTIVE:** Talk to Brynjolf

♦ **TARGET:** Mercer Frey and Brynjolf, in the Cistern in Riften

Mercer Frey is initially suspicious of you and tells you that acting like a maverick will result in a docking of your pay. You may be with thieves, but there is a code to uphold. Once you agree, Mercer Frey has a job for you, one that Brynjolf is worried may be much too difficult. It involves infiltrating Goldenglow Estate, just outside of town; even one of Mercer's own found this job too dangerous. The farm's proprietor is no longer honoring his bargain with the Guild; you must go there to teach him a lesson. Brynjolf suggests you speak to more of the Guild members to gain a better perspective of both your task and the Guild in general.

◊ **OBJECTIVE:** Burn three beehives

◊ **OBJECTIVE:** Clear out Aringoth's safe

♦ **TARGET:** Beehives, Goldenglow Estate

Ask Brynjolf about the Goldenglow job. The farm is owned by some smart-mouthed Wood Elf named Aringoth. Honey production is a valuable commodity on the farm, so setting fire to some of the hives there is your first instruction. Then clear out the safe inside the main house. You can't set the whole place ablaze, though, as an important client with ties to Goldenglow Estate would be furious. Ask for more information, and Brynjolf mentions the estate is guarded by mercenaries; the entire island is fortified, and Brynjolf recommends you find out more from Vex, who already scouted the area and narrowly missed being killed.

◊ **OBJECTIVE:** (Optional) Speak to Vex about Goldenglow Estate

◊ **OBJECTIVE:** Meet the Family: Learn more about the Thieves Guild from Vex

◊ **OBJECTIVE:** Meet the Family: Learn more about the Thieves Guild from Delvin

◊ **OBJECTIVE:** Meet the Family: Retrieve your Thieves Guild Armor from Tonilia

♦ **TARGET:** Ragged Flagon, in the Ratway in Riften

Back in the Ragged Flagon, seek out Vex, who sees the recent Guild problems as a run of bad luck. You can speak to her about some extra work: This starts the Thieves Guild Quest: Additional Jobs (consult this quest for more information). You can also pay her to train you in Lockpicking if you have the coin. Lastly, if you ask her about Goldenglow, she mentions a sewer access point running under the estate, which could be a more clandestine way of entering the premises.

◊ **OBJECTIVE:** (Optional) Enter Goldenglow using the sewer

♦ **TARGET:** Goldenglow Estate

A few years ago, the Ragged Flagon was as busy as an Imperial City, but speak to Delvin Mallory and he firmly believes a curse was responsible for the Guild's downfall. Speak to him, and he offers you the chance to earn more coin: This starts the Thieves Guild Quest: Additional Jobs (consult this quest for more information). He can also train you in the art of Sneaking, provided you have the gold to pay him.

Speak with Tonilia, who gives a "warts and all" review of this little Guild—you're only as good as the gold you're bringing in. She buys and sells, but on this one occasion, she has something for free; you're given your Thieves Guild attire. You can now begin your first major infiltration!

- **Thieves Guild Boots (Fortify Pickpocket)**
- **Thieves Guild Armor (Fortify Carry)**
- **Thieves Guild Gloves (Fortify Lockpicking)**
- **Thieves Guild Hood (Fortify Speech)**

Compare the statistical increases of this attire to your normal apparel and see which you favor; the magical bonuses offered by the Thieves Guild clothing makes them extremely useful.

Goldenglow Estate: Reconnoiter

The Goldenglow Estate consists of three connected islands in the middle of a lake. How you choose to access this location influences how dangerous this task becomes. Bear in mind any or all of the following plans before you set foot on Aringoth's property.

To enter the property, you can:

Slay the gate guard at the main gates and search his corpse for the key to the main gates. Use this to unlock the main gates for an easier way onto the island.

Fire on the mercenaries from a distance and take down any you can before setting foot on the islands.

Swim around to the jetty behind the main building, and sneak up to the house from this point.

Locate the sewer entrance on the northwest side as Vex described. Drop down and follow it to the back entrance of the estate house.

There are other helpful methods of completing this task. You can:

Infiltrate the estate under cover of darkness; this makes you less likely to be spotted by the mercenary guards.

Complete the beehive destruction first, as this lures more mercenaries out of the estate house, helping your main infiltration.

Throw caution to the wind and wade into the establishment. Although not normally tolerated, killing any mercenaries. This isn't a problem.

(Sneak) You may also utilize Sneak throughout this task, creeping around to either estate entrance and moving through the house, launching Sneak attacks on enemies you cannot pass before hiding and continuing on. There is a locked rear entrance to the estate building just near the exit from the sewers. It's a difficult lock but a great way to slip inside unseen.

Beehive Burn

Set the bees ablaze, but don't snuff out all the hives. Do this at any time, but coaxing more mercenaries out of the house before you enter the dwelling means you can fight them in an open area and at distance, which is easier. Burn the hives before or after alerting the mercenaries. You can:

Use a ranged fire attack (such as a fireball or arrow fired from a flame-enchanted bow).

Use a melee-range fire attack (such as a torch).

Continue with this ransacking until three of the hives are alight. Ignore the other hives or face a dock in your reward and an annoyed Brynjolf if you set more than three ablaze.

Sneak to the Safe

◊ **OBJECTIVE:** (Optional) Obtain the key to Aringoth's safe
♦ **TARGET:** Aringoth, Goldenglow Estate

No matter which route (or entrance) you took to infiltrate the estate house, once inside, an additional objective becomes available: As Aringoth's safe is tricky to unlock, you may wish to seek out Aringoth and take both of his keys. If you want them, head up to the second floor and search for the Wood Elf. You may be able to avoid further bloodshed. You can:

(Persuade) Try a little light threatening to make him hand over the key.

(Fight) Or use violent bloodshed, a normally frowned-upon plan but one sanctioned for this task.

(Sneak) You may also be able to sneak up to his room and pickpocket the key from him.

➤ **Goldenglow Cellar Key** ➤ **Goldenglow Safe Key**

QUEST: LARCENY TARGET

Aside from helping yourself to any valuables you find throughout your estate infiltration, keep a lookout for your first Larceny Target: The Queen Bee Statue is found on a bedside table upstairs in Aringoth's bedroom. Sell it to Delvin or keep it if you wish. Consult the Thieves Guild Quest: Larceny Targets for further information.

➤ **Queen Bee Statue**

If you don't want the hassle of confronting Aringoth for the keys, head to the gate door that leads to the cellar. You can:

(Lockpick [Novice]) Unlock it using your skills.

Or utilize the Goldenglow Cellar Key.

After navigating down more steps and encountering additional mercenaries, you finally locate the safe. You can:

(Lockpick [Expert]) Utilize your talents and open the safe.

Or use the Goldenglow Safe Key, which you pried from Aringoth.

Inside the safe is the Goldenglow Bill of Sale and some gold. Take everything!

➤ **Goldenglow Bill of Sale**

◊ **OBJECTIVE:** Return to Brynjolf
♦ **TARGET:** Ragged Flagon, in the Ratway in Riften

Quest Conclusion

Locate Brynjolf in the Ragged Flagon and hand the Bill of Sale over to him. Assuming you burned the correct number of beehives, he rewards you with gold for your troubles. The Bill of Sale is of particular interest, as it reveals that the estate was purchased by an unidentified buyer who seems to be aligning against the Thieves Guild! The note has a strange dagger symbol on it, but no one is certain what it means. Maven Black-Briar will be furious now that she's been cut out of a deal. Brynjolf rewards you and then tells you it is time to meet the real power behind the Guild.

➤ **Leveled gold pieces**

Postquest Activities: Meet the Family

Thieves Guild Quest: Dampened Spirits is now active. After your induction into the Thieves Guild, you are requested to speak to Vex and Delvin Mallory about Thieves Guild Quest: Additional Jobs.

NOTE * Quest names marked with this symbol do not appear in your Quest Menu list, although objectives may.

Now that Mercer Frey has fully inducted you into the Thieves Guild, there are now several benefits of having close ties to this organization, which are available to you from this point on:

- ◊ The Caches hidden in Riften are now available. Consult the City Influence Quests: Ultimate Rewards table on page 312 to learn more about these.
- ◊ The hidden Hall of the Dead Mausoleum entrance for the Thieves Guild is now accessible from the graveyard. Press the button on the face of the mausoleum. The entire slab slides into the wall, leading to some steps to a hatch and into the Cistern. This means you need not traverse the Ratway any longer and can Fast-Travel directly to this location, as it becomes a map marker!
- ◊ You can now bribe and pay off Guards in The Rift, giving you more options for dealing with any bounties you may acquire. See the Crime and Punishment section on page 64 for details.
- ◊ You are now part of the Thieves Guild faction! Everything contained within the Cistern (including Guild chests, books, and anything else you may have wanted to steal) can now be looted!

DAMPENED SPIRITS

PREREQUISITES: Complete Thieves Guild Quest: Loud and Clear

INTERSECTING QUESTS: Thieves Guild Quest: Additional Jobs, Thieves Guild Quest: Larceny Targets, Thieves Guild Quest: Scoundrel's Folly

LOCATIONS: Honningbrew Meadery, Honningbrew Basement, Honningbrew Boilery, Riften, The Bee and Barb, Black-Briar Manor, Cistern, Ratway, The Ragged Flagon, Whiterun, The Bannered Mare

CHARACTERS: Brynjolf, Commander Caius (if Imperials hold Whiterun), Mallus Maccius, Maven Black-Briar, Sabjorn, Sinmir (if Stormcloaks hold Whiterun)

ENEMIES: Frostbite Spider, Hamelyn, Venomfang Skeever,

◊ **OBJECTIVES:** Speak to Maven Black-Briar, Speak to Mallus Maccius, Speak to Sabjorn, Poison the Nest, Poison the Honningbrew Vat, Return to Sabjorn, Attend the tasting ceremony, Speak to Mallus Maccius, Identify Sabjorn's silent partner, Return to Maven Black-Briar, Return to Brynjolf

A Plan Is Brewing

◊ **OBJECTIVE:** Speak to Maven Black-Briar
♦ **TARGET:** Black-Briar Manor or the Bee and Barb in Riften

You begin this quest with the previous objective already active. Leave the Ragged Flagon and find Maven. You can be as flippant or sycophantic as you like in your responses to this ale baroness; she still has a particular role for you to undertake once you agree to it. This involves her only real competition in Skyrim: the Honningbrew Meadery located close to Whiterun. With the mead production of the Goldenglow Farm being interrupted, this has a knock-on effect with her production too. Her rival, a Nord named Sabjorn who owns the Honningbrew Meadery, cannot be allowed to up his production and cut into her profits. You're to head to Whiterun and seek out Mallus Maccius, Sabjorn's disgruntled assistant (and unofficial contact for Maven), and hatch a plan to bring Sabjorn down. Maven is also keen to learn who backed Sabjorn financially.

◊ **OBJECTIVE:** Speak to Mallus Maccius
♦ **TARGET:** The Bannered Mare in Whiterun

Enter Whiterun and the Bannered Mare, before locating the weasel-like Mallus Maccius. He has already formulated a plan to bring Sabjorn down: The Honningbrew Meadery has a well-known Skeever infestation (partly because he told the townsfolk about it). The vermin are interfering with Sabjorn's latest batch of "Honningbrew Reserve," which is being readied for Whiterun's Captain of the Guard. A tasting ceremony cannot be held until the meadery is cleared of Skeevers. This is where you come in. You're to pose as a helper, ready to poison the rodents, but you'll also sabotage the brewing vats too.

◊ **OBJECTIVE:** Speak to Sabjorn
♦ **TARGET:** Honningbrew Meadery

CAUTION

This upcoming plan is one of infiltration, not violence: Do not target Sabjorn or Mallus in battle.

Sabjorn's Subjugation

You can ask Mallus further questions to gain more understanding of the situation if you wish. Then travel a short distance to the meadery and enter the main building. Sabjorn is just inside, worried about his Skeever problem and annoyed that his no-good assistant Mallus isn't around to help. After agreeing to help, you can:

(Persuade) Request payment in advance.

(Intimidate) Threaten him to obtain a payment in advance.

Agree to receive the payment once the job is done. This isn't the most prudent of options.

If you're successful in your Persuasion or Intimidation, Sabjorn agrees to pay you half your reward (500 gold pieces) now.

➤ **Honningbrew Meadery Key** ➤ **500 gold pieces**

➤ **Pest Poison**

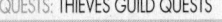

◊ **OBJECTIVE:** Poison the Nest
◊ **OBJECTIVE:** Poison the Honningbrew Vat
♦ **TARGET:** Nest and vat, inside Honningbrew Meadery

Aicantar's chamber offers one final set of options. Once again, sneaking here is difficult: Aicantar keeps close watch on the exit. You can certainly fight him, the guard, and a pair of reinforcements (optionally with your spider). But a better option is to sneak into the control booth on the walkway and turn the valve.

Chaos breaks out below. All the traps in the room turn on, and Aicantar and the guard panic, yelling for everyone to flee the Laboratory. They and any surviving guards in the Laboratory make a break for the Museum. They may not get far, as Aicantar's robes have a nasty tendency to get caught in the thresher....

QUEST: LARCENY TARGET

Before you struggle out of the Laboratory, check the alcove on your right, which has a Dwemer Puzzle Box on display. Snag it now, as you won't be returning this way. Hand it to Delvin Mallory for a cash reward. Consult the Thieves Guild Quest: Larceny Targets for further information.

➤ **Dwemer Puzzle Cube**

Continue out onto the Markarth wizards' balcony.

There's the Rub

After marveling at the impressive vista, clamber up the steps and enter Calcelmo's Tower. On this room's upper level, you can see an ornate stone covered in hieroglyphics: there appear to be verses written in Ancient Falmer and Dwemer. This looks to be the guide to translating Gallus's Journal! However, getting it back may pose a challenge....

Continue up the stairs on the left (east) and enter Calcelmo's private office, packed with artifacts and rubbings. A door from the office leads out to the stone. But interacting with it won't get you far: The stone is much too heavy to lift.

◊ **OBJECTIVE:** Duplicate the writing on Calcelmo's Stone
♦ **TARGET:** Calcelmo's Tower, in Understone Keep in Markarth

Puzzle Solution: Sift through the valuables and check the main table. Calcelmo has been making some rubbings on paper, and these are scattered everywhere. Take a roll of paper and some charcoal from a side table. Return to Calcelmo's Stone and make a rubbing of the text there. (It's possible to find the roll of paper and charcoal in the world prior to this quest, but it isn't necessary; there's plenty of it around.)

➤ **Roll of Paper** ➤ **Charcoal** ➤ **Calcelmo's Stone Rubbing**

◊ **OBJECTIVE:** Return to Enthir
♦ **TARGET:** The Frozen Hearth in Winterhold

Nocturnal's Quisling

Now for the small matter of an escape plan. Mere moments after you make the rubbing, the doors to the tower open and a group of soldiers enter, led by Captain Aquilius of the Wizards' Guard. They are joined by Aicantar (if he's still alive). After a brief argument, they spread out to scour the tower.

You can try to fight or run past them. With an excellent Sneak skill, you may even be able to get out undetected: drop onto the platform to the west and head up the stairs. At the gap, leap onto the narrow metal catwalk and race for the door.

Out on the balcony, you have a choice: You can try to backtrack through the Laboratory, Museum, and Keep, but between the Wizards' Guards and the city guard, you've probably made some enemies by now. Your quest target suggests a better option: On the balcony's east side, some of the stonework has fallen away, exposing a narrow stone path. Follow it, leap into the waterfall at the end, and make your getaway. Fast-Travel back to Winterhold at your earliest convenience.

Back inside the Frozen Hearth, hand the stone rubbing to Enthir and tell him it should help with the translation. Karliah will be here when you arrive with the rubbing. As Enthir pores over the rubbing and Gallus's Journal, he reveals the disturbing truth: Gallus suspected Mercer's wavering allegiance to the Thieves Guild for months; this included a vast expenditure on a lavish lifestyle of gold and trinkets. Mercer was apparently paying for this by removing valuables from the Guild's treasure vaults without anyone's knowledge! There is also talk of Mercer desecrating something known as the Twilight Sepulcher, which disgusts Karliah.

◊ **OBJECTIVE:** Speak to Enthir
◊ **OBJECTIVE:** Speak to Karliah
♦ **TARGET:** The Frozen Hearth, in Winterhold

Quest Conclusion

Speak to Enthir again, and he urges you to help Karliah and reveal the traitor to your brethren. He also thanks you for your help and tells you that if you're ever in this area again, he can fence any goods you may have gathered via slightly nefarious means.

➤ **Gallus's Translated Journal (Item)**

➤ **Vendor (Fence):** Enthir

Locate Karliah nearby, who tells you the Twilight Sepulcher is the sacred temple to Nocturnal, the patron of thieves and gamblers. Defiling the sacred ground he swore to protect, Mercer is now revealed as an insidious fiend. But getting the rest of the Guild on your side may require more than simple guile. For your part, Karliah rewards you with Gallus's old weapon.

➤ **Nightingale Blade**

Postquest Activities

The Nightingale Blade is a leveled weapon, with an Absorb Health and Drain Stamina enchantment on it. After some optional additional questions, Thieves Guild Quest: The Pursuit commences. Build up influence in more cities by continuing Thieves Guild Quest: Additional Jobs. You may want to return to Markarth, especially if you've slain the museum guards, and brush up on your Lockpicking before cleaning the place out, as there's a wealth of loot to pick over.

PREREQUISITES: Complete Thieves Guild Quest: Hard Answers

MAJOR SPOILERS

INTERSECTING QUESTS: Thieves Guild Quest: Additional Jobs, Thieves Guild Quest: Larceny Targets, Thieves Guild Quest: Trinity Restored

LOCATIONS: Lake Honrich, Riften, The Bee and Barb, Black-Briar Manor, Mercer's House, The Ratway, Cistern, The Ragged Flagon, The Ratway Sewers, Riftweald Manor

CHARACTERS: Brynjolf, Delvin Mallory, Karliah, Maven Black-Briar, Vex

ENEMIES: Bandit, Mjoll the Lioness, Thug, Vald

◊ **OBJECTIVES:** Meet Karliah at the Ragged Flagon, Follow Karliah, Speak to Brynjolf, Infiltrate Mercer's House, (Optional) Shoot the mechanism to lower the ramp, (Optional) Speak to Vex about Vald, Miscellaneous Objective: (Optional) Talk to Maven about Vald's debt, Miscellaneous Objective: Locate the Quill of Gemination under Lake Honrich, Miscellaneous Objective: Bring the Quill of Gemination to Maven, Discover evidence of Mercer's location, Speak to Brynjolf

NOTE The quests listed as "Miscellaneous Objective" do not appear within "The Pursuit" quest but are here in case you wish to perform this optional plan.

A Perfect Heist

◊ **OBJECTIVE:** Meet Karliah at the Ragged Flagon
◊ **OBJECTIVE:** Follow Karliah
♦ **TARGET:** Inside the Ratway, in Riften

This quest begins with the first objective already in play. Return to the familiar grounds of the Thieves Guild, and you'll find your usual entrance point by the Hall of the Dead Mausoleum is locked. You must navigate the sights (and smells) of the Ratway, down to the Ragged Flagon, where you'll meet Karliah. She has Gallus's translated journal ready to show the Guild members who require convincing. Agree to back her up and move into the Cistern. As expected, Brynjolf (flanked by Vex and Delvin Mallory) draws his blade and sharply asks why you're here with "a murderer." Armed with proof of Mercer's betrayal, Karliah hands over Gallus's Journal.

◊ **OBJECTIVE:** Speak to Brynjolf

Brynjolf cannot believe Mercer has been stealing from the Guild, so he orders Delvin to open the vault. The gold, the jewels...they're all gone! It takes two keys to unlock the vault. Delvin, Brynjolf, and Mercer are the only ones who carry such keys, so how did Mercer break into the vault alone? The answer is a mystery (even though Karliah quietly has her suspicions). Although vindicated, Karliah is just as angered by this as the rest of the Guild, except perhaps for the seething Vex, who vows to kill Mercer immediately. Brynjolf's cooler head prevails, and he orders Vex and Delvin to guard the Ragged Flagon. Then he turns to you and asks what you've learned from Karliah.

Explain that Mercer killed Gallus, that the three of them were Nightingales, and that Karliah was behind Goldenglow and Honningbrew (a cunning plan to try and make Mercer look weak in front of Maven Black-Briar). Then Brynjolf has an important task for you: Break into Mercer's Riften house—Riftweald Manor—and gather any information that may indicate where the traitor has gone. Before you leave Brynjolf, ask him what is the best way into Riftweald Manor. You receive information about a "watchdog" and an exterior ramp with a mechanism to lower it, which could aid in your escape. Then ask about the "watchdog" named Vald. Brynjolf indicates Vex may have more information to provide. These grant you two optional objectives.

◊ **OBJECTIVE:** Infiltrate Mercer's House
◊ **OBJECTIVE:** (Optional) Shoot the mechanism to lower the ramp
◊ **OBJECTIVE:** (Optional) Speak to Vex about Vald
♦ **TARGET:** Riftweald Manor, in Riften

Locate Vex in the Cistern or Ragged Flagon, and ask her about Vald. She tells you he's only interested in gold, so buying him off is a possibility. But even Vald might not betray Mercer Frey (as he wouldn't live long enough to spend his bribe). Instead, Vex suggests you speak to Maven Black-Briar about erasing Vald's debt. Or you could run him through with your blade...Vex doesn't care either way.

◊ **OBJECTIVE:** (Optional) Talk to Maven about Vald's debt
♦ **TARGET:** Maven Black-Briar, in Riften

OPTIONAL: ERASING VALD'S DEBT

Locate Maven Black-Briar in the Bee and Barb, the marketplace, or Black-Briar Manor. Tell her you'd like to remove Vald's debt. Maven isn't receptive to this; she tells you she commissioned a unique Quill, and Vald was hired to ensure it reached her safely. Because of his blundering, it ended up at the bottom of Lake Honrich, and she's very keen to have it retrieved. She'll call the debt satisfied if you'll fish it out. You can also ask her about the properties of this fabled Quill and how it ended up in the lake. Finally, Maven can also give you vague directions to the Quill's location if you ask if she has ideas where to look for it: underwater, and close to one of the small islands in the lake.

◊ **OBJECTIVE:** Locate the Quill of Gemination under Lake Honrich
♦ **TARGET:** Beneath a small island, in Lake Honrich

The sunken rowboat's location isn't on your world or local maps, so consult the adjacent picture. The "current location" shows the exact spot where the rowboat sank, south of a small island and halfway between Riften (to the east) and Goldenglow Farm (to the west). The murky water makes finding this extremely tricky, but it isn't that far down. When you find the half-embedded boat, search for Vald's Strongbox [Average], and use your Lockpick skill to open it. Grab the gold and the Quill, and swim back to Riften.

➤ **Quill of Gemination**

◊ **OBJECTIVE:** Bring the Quill of Gemination to Maven

Find Maven and hand over the Quill. She gives you a document absolving Vald of his debt, but she doesn't want to ever see him in Riften again. Rejoin the main part of this quest.

➤ **Vald's Debt**

NOTE If you wish, you can keep this Quill, complete this quest, and then sell it for around 150 gold pieces.

Ransacking Riftweald Manor

Whether or not you went swimming for a Quill, you should figure out how best to enter Mercer Frey's abode. All of the ground-level doors are barred from the inside and are never accessible. The only way in is the door off the balcony.

Head to the rear gate and speak to Vald. He is immune to Bribery or Intimidation, and ignores you unless you present him with Vald's debt document. He agrees to flee the area, unlocks the (otherwise impassable) side gate, and gives you the key to Mercer's house.

A successful Persuade will trick him into leaving you to guard the house, and he'll present you with the key to the house. He'll then walk away from the house and you are free to bring down the ramp.

(Lockpick [Expert]) Or, you can lockpick the rear gate. You need to deal with Vald, but remember that killing him in cold blood doesn't win over the local guards and increases your Bounty. The moment you enter the backyard in this manner, Vald will become hostile and attack.

For those less inclined to lockpick: Vald's patrol causes him to pause with his back to the gate. It's possible to pick his pocket and grab the key right off of him, but you may still have to deal with him if he detects you once you pop the lock and enter the yard!

➤ **Mercer's House Key**

NOTE This key unlocks the upper rear entrance to Mercer's House and both the side and rear gates.

Time for a spot of precision archery: Aim your arrow at the mechanism just below and to the left of the upper balcony, and fire. This releases the ramp, allowing you a much more stealthy way into the residence, instead of through the front door. Climb the ramp, and use the house key to unlock the otherwise-difficult-to-open door (Lockpick [Expert]).

◊ **OBJECTIVE:** Discover evidence of Mercer's location
♦ **TARGET:** Mercer's House, in Riften

Head through Mercer's House, electing to sneak by or slaughter any bandits guarding the location. Progress downstairs and find the room with the bench table and single chair. Adjacent to the barred door is a suspicious cabinet. Open it and activate the false back panel. Step into a secret room with stairs leading down into a subterranean cellar; this is part of the sewer system linking to the Ratway. Head through, watching for dart, fire, and swinging traps, and open the door into Mercer's hidden office. Gather some gold and his plans. Before you leave, attempt to open the display case (Master), which houses Mercer's exceptional frost sword!

➤ **Mercer's Plans** ➤ **Chillrend**

QUEST: LARCENY TARGET

While you're rummaging around in Mercer's private office, snag that expensive-looking bust up onto the bookshelf. Consult the Thieves Guild Quest: Larceny Targets for further information.

➤ **Bust of the Gray Fox**

◊ **OBJECTIVE:** Speak to Brynjolf
♦ **TARGET:** The Ragged Flagon or Cistern, in the Ratway

Either retrace your steps back to the surface or (better yet) head into the Ratway Sewers, which offer you a quick route back to the Ragged Flagon.

Quest Conclusion

Return to Brynjolf, who hasn't had any luck in tracking Mercer down. But after you produce the plans, these reveal that Mercer is intent on taking the Eyes of the Falmer, a heist Gallus had been planning for years. The only course of action is clear: to pursue this cur into an ancient Falmer dungeon and intercept him before he can take this invaluable item! Aside from Chillrend, there are no other rewards, only a summoning to meet Karliah at once.

Postquest Activities

Thieves Guild Quest: Trinity Restored now commences.

PREREQUISITES: Complete Thieves Guild Quest: The Pursuit

MAJOR SPOILERS

INTERSECTING QUESTS: Thieves Guild Quest: Additional Jobs, Thieves Guild Quest: Larceny Targets, Thieves Guild Quest: Blindsighted

LOCATIONS: Nightingale Hall , Twilight Sepulcher , Riften, The Ragged Flagon, Cistern, The Ratway

CHARACTERS: Brynjolf, Karliah

◊ **OBJECTIVES:** Listen to Karliah, Meet Karliah at the Standing Stone, Follow Karliah, Activate the Armor Stone, Equip the Nightingale Armor, Follow Karliah, Stand on vacant floor glyph, Speak to Karliah, Speak to Brynjolf

An Audience with Lady Nocturnal

◊ **OBJECTIVE:** Listen to Karliah
♦ **TARGET:** Inside the Ratway, in Riften

This quest begins with the first objective already under way. Although Karliah is a Nightingale, it falls to the current acting leader of the Thieves Guild to order the murder of Mercer. Brynjolf has no qualms about this, but Karliah points out that great care must be taken; after all, Mercer is a Nightingale, and an agent of Nocturnal. She suggests meeting Mercer on equal footing. Just outside Riften is a clearing and an old standing stone. She cryptically asks that you meet there.

◊ **OBJECTIVE:** Meet Karliah at the Standing Stone
♦ **TARGET:** Nightingale Hall, just southwest of Riften

Take the southwest exit from Riften and walk the path until you see the large petroglyph stone among the silver birch trees. Both Brynjolf and Karliah are waiting for you. Karliah explains this is the headquarters of the Nightingales, and you're here to seek an edge in the forthcoming fight with Mercer. You may ask her further questions, but she says she'll tell you more once you're inside Nightingale Hall. Follow her inside. A secret door in the face of the rocky cliff will open, revealing a door into Nightingale Hall.

◊ **OBJECTIVE:** Follow Karliah

Step through the still air of the entrance tunnel. Brynjolf can't believe this place existed but doesn't know why he's here. Karliah reveals you are the first of the uninitiated to set foot in here in over a century. You are to accompany Karliah to the armory to don the armor of a Nightingale and begin the oath. Your roles should now become increasingly clear.

◊ **OBJECTIVE:** Activate the Armor Stone
◊ **OBJECTIVE:** Equip the Nightingale Armor

Cross the bridge, and through the archway are plinths with the same petroglyph carvings—that of the Nightingale and dark moon. Activate the Armor Stone, and the armor will be added to your inventory. Then go into your apparel and equip the armor to continue.

- Nightingale Armor
- Nightingale Gloves
- Nightingale Boots
- Nightingale Hood

◊ **OBJECTIVE:** Follow Karliah
◊ **OBJECTIVE:** Stand on vacant floor glyph

Nocturnal at Our Backs

Stride toward the entrance to the Welkinsight Chamber, where Karliah explains the steps to becoming a Nightingale. After some hesitation on Brynjolf's part, follow the procession forward as the gate opens, and stand on the ancient circle glyph inscribed into the ground. Karliah performs the oath, and a dialogue with Lady Nocturnal begins. (Her voice emanates from a ball of energy. She doesn't appear in person at this point.)

◊ **OBJECTIVE:** Speak to Karliah
◊ **OBJECTIVE:** Speak to Brynjolf

Once the ceremony is over, Karliah reveals the last secret of the Nightingales: Their purpose is to guard not only the Twilight Sepulcher, but also the secret kept within—the Skeleton Key of Nocturnal. Mercer stole this key, which opens any lock (indeed, the artifact allowed him to bypass the otherwise-sealed locks on the Guild's vault doors), and the powers of the key may have imbued him with powers beyond normal reckoning.

Quest Conclusion

Brynjolf tells you that due to the circumstances that have befallen the Thieves Guild, there is no one qualified to lead the forces except for you.

At this point, if you've completed all of the City Influence Quests, Brynjolf indicates that after this whole sorry affair is over, you are to become Guild Master.

At this point, if you haven't completed all of the City Influence Quests, Brynjolf says that as soon as Delvin tells him the Guild has regained a foothold in Skyrim, you are to become Guild Master.

Postquest Activities

Thieves Guild Quest: Blindsighted begins now!

PREREQUISITES: Complete Thieves Guild Quest: Trinity Restored

MAJOR SPOILERS

INTERSECTING QUESTS: Thieves Guild Quest: Additional Jobs, Thieves Guild Quest: Larceny Targets, Thieves Guild Quest: Trinity Restored

LOCATIONS: Bronze Water Cave, Irkngthand, Irkngthand Arcanex, Irkngthand Grand Cavern, Irkngthand Sanctuary, Irkngthand Slave Pens

CHARACTERS: Brynjolf, Karliah

ENEMIES: Bandit, Chaurus, Dwarven Centurion, Dwarven Sphere, Dwarven Spider, Falmer, Frostbite Spider, Mercer Frey

◊ OBJECTIVES: Travel to Irkngthand, Speak to Karliah, Locate Mercer Frey, Slay Mercer Frey, Retrieve the Skeleton Key, Escape from Irkngthand, Speak to Karliah

Infiltration of Irkngthand

◊ **OBJECTIVE:** Travel to Irkngthand
♦ **TARGET:** Entrance to Irkngthand Arcanex

This quest begins with the first objective already under way. Head to Irkngthand, in the mountains above Lake Yorgrim. The exterior is a sprawling jumble of fallen dwarven ruins, a sealed gate, and a complement of bandits you must sneak past or slay. Ignore the gate with the bars and instead head right (west), under the fallen columns, and to the stone steps near some bear traps. Step onto the upper ledge next to the dwarven exterior, and head southeast. Follow the ledge to a corridor in the right wall, watching for the spear trap as you exit. Find the rickety wooden steps and follow this precarious path across the domed rooftops and over two wood bridges to the upper entrance of the main structure, Irkngthand Arcanex. Another option is to locate a lever along the path that drops the gate, allowing an easier access in and out.

◊ **OBJECTIVE:** Speak to Karliah
♦ **TARGET:** Entrance to Irkngthand Grand Cavern

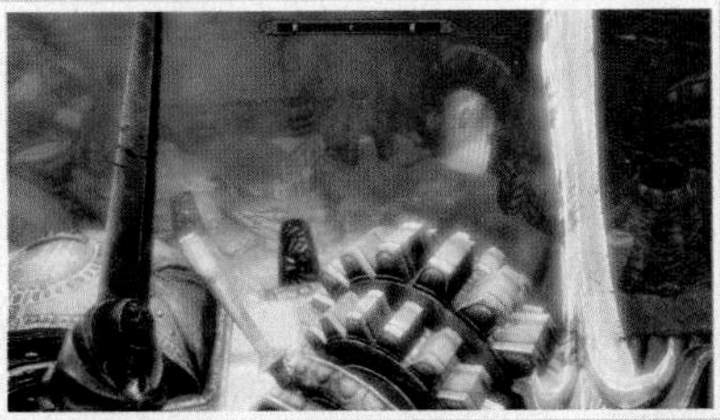

Step into the golden gloom. Pass the bloodstained camp, moving southwest into a ceremonial pool chamber with more strewn dwarven machinery. A sphere springs to life here. Head into a chamber of faint green mist, and quickly avoid the numerous fire pillars, following the path among the rubble to the southeast gate. Once through the gate, locate the Dwarven Elevator and ride it down to the Grand Cavern. You meet Karliah and Brynjolf down the steps. Mention the bandits Mercer slew, and commence your hunt for Mercer Frey.

◊ **OBJECTIVE:** Locate Mercer Frey
♦ **TARGET:** Irkngthand Sanctuary

Moving around to the large balcony overlooking the last chamber in this area, Karliah spots Mercer Frey skulking close to the exit. You can't directly access this lower stepped chamber, so head through the door and along the winding corridors to a giant chamber of dwarven ruins. Cut down the Falmer that inhabit these parts before moving west along the ledge. There's a locked (Master) cage where an ancient ballista can be fired on foes down below. Head to a ledge with a lever. There is a second lever on the room's opposite side. Brynjolf mentions that these levers hold the key to your progress:

Puzzle Solution: Both the levers must be pulled to lower the bars that block your passage. Each lever is on either side of the raised area. If you aren't quick enough, the levers reset, so remove the enemy threats first. Then pull the lever farthest from the exit, and quickly rush to the opposite side and pull the other. This gives you the most amount of time to reach the exit. Both lamps by the door should be lit for you to proceed.

Now descend to the earthen floor, fighting Falmer and Dwarven Spheres, and head through the exit you created.

> **TIP** You can run off on your own if you wish; Karliah and Brynjolf will join you in a subsequent section of this place. If you get too far from them, they will attempt to catch up.

The subsequent chamber is in an even more dilapidated state. Climb atop the rubble and rooftops, fighting Falmer as you go. Head west to the stone ramps and up to the gold door. Beyond is a small study area and a gate to the southeast. Although Mercer has already ransacked this area, he neglected to grab a couple of Detect Life Scrolls strewn in this room; grab them, as they are useful later during your battle with him.

➤ **Scroll:** Detect Life (3)

Enter the gate, and your route opens up into a massive grand cavern. This is actually the location you saw from the balcony, which is in this chamber. Now you can battle through the Falmer to the opposite side, optionally challenging a Dwarven Centurion to fight if you wish or jumping off the small bridge and pressing the button on the console to release the Centurion on the hapless Falmer. Climb the stone ramp and run across the ledge to reach the upper Falmer camp. Exit into the Irkngthand Slave Pens.

Brynjolf notices the stench in these parts; you're going to be encountering several Falmer and their nasty pets, the Chaurus. First, though, destroy a Dwarven Spider or two, pass a locked gate (Apprentice), and head down the steps into a Dwarven Torture Chamber with bone chimes that alert the Falmer of your movements. If you sneak up on them, you can use the lever on the overlook to unleash a dwarven thresher trap on the Falmer below.

Journey down the corridor, turning right (south) into a Falmer camp. Slaughter (or sneak) your way east and south, opening the Chaurus pens to reach a chamber of pipes. Take the low road or high ledge to the drop-down at the eastern end, which leads to your ultimate destination: the Irkngthand Sanctuary. Or you can sneak across the dwarven pipes that run along the ceiling in one area, allowing you to cross most of this large expanse undetected.

No Mercy: Into the Frey!

A giant Falmer statue greets you from the opposite side of this huge Sanctuary chamber. Mercer has set about defiling it already, and Falmer blood has been spilled. Although Karliah and Brynjolf attempt silence, Mercer Frey finishes prying out the statue's massive eyes, notices you all, and casts a shock-wave-type spell that disrupts and destabilizes the massive chamber. The pipes in the ceiling burst, and water floods the chamber to about ankle depth. There's an immediate rumbling as you tumble down from the ledge, which splits apart, leaving your brethren stranded. You must face Mercer Frey alone! He speaks to you from your fallen position. You can speak to Frey about Nocturnal and the key, but there's only one way this ends: with one of you at the end of a blade!

◊ **OBJECTIVE:** Slay Mercer Frey

Target: Mercer Frey. Mercer is a vicious swordsman. He is nimble and dextrous and can turn himself invisible. Even before you fight him, he uses one of his stolen Nightingale powers to Frenzy Brynjolf, who turns on Karliah, effectively keeping them from helping you in this battle. This causes no end of problems, especially as the chamber you're on is getting wetter and is very steep. There are steps around the statue, and you can cross the statue's lap.

Mercer Frey may be invisible for most of the fight, but keep an eye on the water, as it will ripple when Mercer runs through it.

If you grabbed the Detect Life Scrolls or have a spell of the same name, now would be an exceptionally good time to use it!

Strike Mercer with your Nightingale Blade. This drains him and leaves a shimmering trail from him, even when he's invisible. Use that to your advantage. Keep moving so he can't sneak up on you, and keep your back to a wall so he can't hit you from behind.

Mercer's form is shimmering and isn't completely invisible; strike out quickly when you see this shape. If you're attacking at melee range, remember you can still block and then counterattack immediately. This helps when fighting blind. Spells with ongoing effects also help, such as Flames, which coat Mercer in fire, allowing you to see him more clearly.

After the shadows take him, search Mercer Frey quickly. Among his belongings, you can claim the two Eyes of the Falmer and the Skeleton Key Karliah spoke of. Now is the time to make good your escape!

◊ **OBJECTIVE:** Retrieve the Skeleton Key
◊ **OBJECTIVE:** Escape from Irkngthand
♦ **TARGET:** Bronze Water Cave

➤ Eye of the Falmer (2) ➤ Skeleton Key

QUEST: LARCENY TARGET

Make sure to bring these enormous gems to Delvin. Consult Thieves Guild Quest: Larceny Targets for more information.

The statue chamber becomes increasingly unstable, with torrents of water cascading down from an increasing number of holes in the ceiling. Karliah yells that there must be a way out, and yet the water still rises. Stay calm, and after snagging your final Larceny Target, turn and face the chamber's southeastern side, just above the head of the Falmer Statue. Right before the cavern completely fills with water, a cluster of rocks dislodge, revealing a tunnel opening—but only if you have the power of the Skeleton Key, so be sure to grab it off Mercer's corpse. Don't waste any more time; scramble up into the tunnel and escape!

◊ **OBJECTIVE:** Speak to Karliah

Quest Conclusion

You emerge into the Bronze Water Cave, on the shore of Lake Yorgrim. Brynjolf has matters to attend to, but Karliah speaks with you for a few moments, realizing her 25-year exile is over and presenting you with a token of her esteem. Now it is time to return the Skeleton Key to its rightful place, by traversing the Pilgrim's Path in the Twilight Sepulcher. This is a journey you'll be taking alone.

➤ Nightingale Bow

Postquest Activities

This is a leveled bow that deals Frost and Shock damage and slows the target slightly. Thieves Guild Quest: Darkness Returns begins now!

TIP From the point you obtain the Skeleton Key to the end of the next quest, you have an unbreakable Lockpick! This means you can try your hand to any lock for as long as you like with no fear of snapping a pick! You may wish to unlock some particularly troublesome locks across Skyrim before continuing!

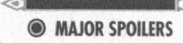

DARKNESS RETURNS

PREREQUISITES: Complete Thieves Guild Quest: Blindsighted

MAJOR SPOILERS

INTERSECTING QUESTS: Thieves Guild Quest: Additional Jobs, Thieves Guild Quest: Larceny Targets, Thieves Guild Quest: Under New Management

LOCATIONS: Twilight Sepulcher, Ebonmere, Twilight Sepulcher Inner Sanctum

CHARACTERS: Gallus, Karliah, Nocturnal

ENEMIES: Nightingale Sentinel

◊ **OBJECTIVES:** Enter the Twilight Sepulcher, Speak to the Nightingale Sentinel, Follow the Pilgrim's Path, (Optional) Retrieve Nystrom's Journal , Return the Skeleton Key to the Ebonmere, Listen to Nocturnal, Speak to Karliah, Choose Nightingale Role

A Dark Journey: Pilgrim's Path

◊ **OBJECTIVE:** Enter the Twilight Sepulcher
◊ **OBJECTIVE:** Speak to the Nightingale Sentinel

This quest begins with the first objective already under way. Journey to the mountains to the west of Falkreath, and find the entrance to the Twilight Sepulcher, close to a rushing mountain stream. Open the ornate Iron Door, and step into this sacred site. The large entrance cavern is dominated by an arched entrance ahead (south) of you. Waiting for you at the steps below the entrance is a ghostly figure. Speak to the last of the Nightingale Sentinels, who blames himself for this predicament after allowing Mercer Frey to lure him to his fate and steal the Skeleton Key.

You recognize this entity to be Gallus, although this spirit hasn't gone by that name in a long time. Explain you have the key. Continue the conversation, mentioning Karliah is still alive and telling him the key has been returned. Alas, Gallus cannot help you, as this place holds the Ebonmere—a conduit to Nocturnal's realm of Evergloam. When Mercer removed the key, it closed the conduit, weakening the guardians of this place and causing them to forget their true purpose. To rectify this situation, you must take the Pilgrim's Path.

◊ **OBJECTIVE:** Follow the Pilgrim's Path
♦ **TARGET:** Entrance to Evergloam, in Twilight Sepulcher Inner Sanctum

You can ask Gallus more questions about what is wrong with the other Sentinels, how the Ebonmere affects you, and what you'll face along Pilgrim's Path. For this question, the spirit recommends you read the journal of a long-dead adventurer who had hoped to take the Path.

◊ **OBJECTIVE:** (Optional) Retrieve Nystrom's Journal

Nystrom's skeletal remains lie in this chamber, to the east. Search him and check out his weapon, but the real prize is the journal on his corpse.

➤ **Nystrom's Journal**

THE FIVE TESTS OF PILGRIM'S PATH

The journal mentions five tests, giving obtuse advice on each of them:

1. "Shadows of their former selves, sentinels of the dark. They wander ever more and deal swift death to defilers."
2. "Above all they stand, vigilance everlasting. Beholden to the murk yet contentious of the glow."
3. "Offer what She desires most, but reject the material. For her greatest want is that which cannot be seen, felt or carried."
4. "Direct and yet indirect. The path to salvation a route cunning with fortune betraying the foolish."
5. "The journey is complete, the Empress's embrace awaits the fallen. Hesitate not if you wish to gift her your eternal devotion."

Puzzle Solution: The five clues refer to the following sections of your forthcoming quest:

1. This refers to the Sentinels guarding this place.
2. This refers to the chamber with the areas of light and darkness and the archers that fire upon you, and that the light is damaging.
3. This refers to the offering room with the basin; Nocturnal desires darkness more than anything else, so the basin is a red herring; extinguish all of the braziers to create darkness.
4. This refers to the long gauntlet of traps in the narrow passage that can be bypassed by picking the lock and avoiding it.
5. This refers to the shaft with no exit.

Party of the First Part: Sentinels

Head up the stairs, weaving your way past a sealed grating and down through an Iron Door, into a candlelit crypt. Nightingale Sentinels are poised here to repel intruders and cannot be reasoned with. Slay those you encounter, pausing only to sift through any books in the upper library. Next, squeeze past the central pedestal, past a floor trigger in the next corridor, and head west to an Iron Door.

Party of the Second Part: Shadows

CAUTION

Beware! This chamber of shadows can burn you to a crisp in moments. You may wish to save your game before proceeding!

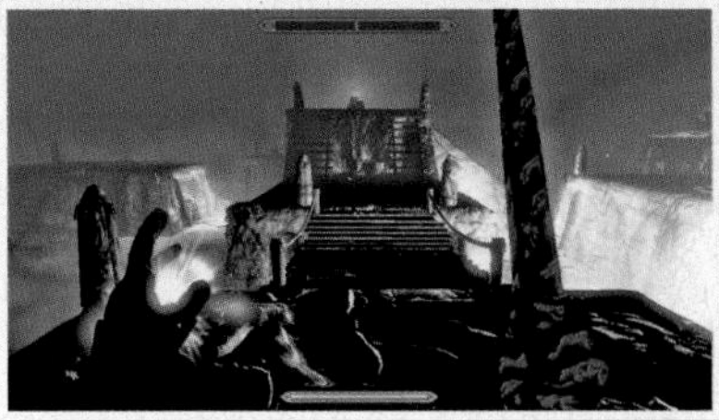

Enter a chamber of shadows. Urns glow with inhuman light. Stone plateaus and a weaving path coax you forward. Then the burning starts! You begin to lose health at an alarming rate as you walk through this collection of cursed passages and platforms.

Puzzle Solution: Walk into the lit areas, and your health plummets. The darker the areas, the less your health diminishes. As you enter, run west (and slightly north, to the right) and climb atop the first platform, dodging any dart traps you trigger. Wait up here to regain your health. Turn southwest and rush *behind* the next structure, and use the wooden steps to climb up after a sharp left (east) turn. Next, rush over the wooden bridge, stepping to the right to avoid more darts. Run up the wooden steps, past the cauldron of light, to the dark edge of the ledge. Regain your health and look southwest. Drop down, running south up the dark middle of the steps to the exit door.

Party of the Third Part: Struck

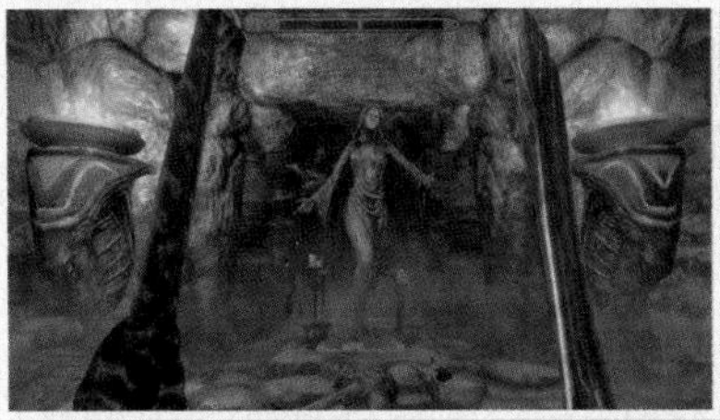

Walk through the crypt to a pedestal of Nocturnal with a dead bandit at the foot of it. The two ornate wall torches are each hiding the pull chain; yank this to reveal a false wall that rumbles open. Weave through the corridor, heading west, to a group of swinging axes blocking your path. Look left to see a locked door. Pick the lock (Lockpick [Master]) and you can bypass all the traps and head straight to the fourth part). Or, watch for a floor trigger that launches darts. Sprint between them to the Iron Door, avoiding another floor trigger that skewers you with spears by the door. Wait as the door opens and a battering ram swings at you. Step to the right to avoid it, and run under it as it repositions. You can enter the Inner Sanctum from here, or optionally investigate a ghostly banquet hall with items to scavenge and two more Sentinels to dispatch.

Party of the Fourth Part: Skeleton

Amble through a candlelit hallway with a faint purple mist in the air. This leads to a nasty drop down a circular well. At the bottom are the skeletal remains of Anders, an adventurer. Read his message if you wish, before realizing you're well and truly stuck down this well.

Puzzle solution: After a few moments of sweating, you produce the Skeleton Key automatically; the arcane device seems to "know" what you want to unlock and allows you to pass through the floor and into the Ebonmere chamber.

➤ **Anders's Message**

Party of the Fifth Part: Summoning

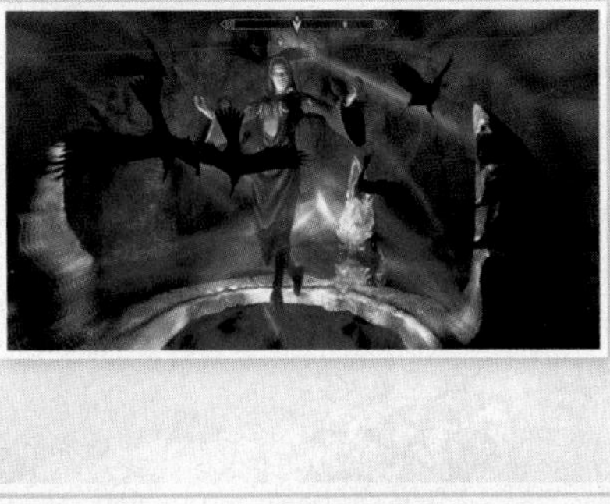

After producing the Skeleton Key and dropping the down the well and into the entrance to Evergloam, you have but one choice: Return the Skeleton Key to the Ebonmere.

◊ **OBJECTIVE:** Return the Skeleton Key to the Ebonmere
◊ **OBJECTIVE:** Listen to Nocturnal
◊ **OBJECTIVE:** Speak to Karliah

A circle of impossibly deep blue vapors congeals around the Ebonmere, a three-pronged portal to Evergloam. A flock of black nightingales departs, announcing the arrival of Nocturnal. She notes that a champion has returned the Skeleton Key to the Sepulcher and the Ebonmere is restored. You shall have your trinkets of reward and must drink deeply from the Ebonmere to become an Agent of Nocturnal! It seems this Skeleton Key unlocks more than just doors; it also reveals inner potential.

Once you choose the power, you can now freely and quickly leave the temple. This ends the Thieves Guild critical path quests.

Quest Conclusion

You have done well in the eyes of Nocturnal. Karliah has also appeared. She is visited by the spirit of Gallus one final time; his tormented imprisonment has been lifted, and he leaves his love to walk with the shadows. Speak with Karliah, and she gives you more information about the circles at the base of the Ebonmere. These imbue you with powers befitting a Nightingale Agent. The symbol is of the waxing and waning moon. You can return here once every 24 hours to change your ability, and one day you may be forced back to defend this place; this is your pact with Nocturnal. For now, though, there are pockets brimming with coin and coffers ripe for the picking all across Skyrim!

◊ **OBJECTIVE:** Choose Nightingale Role

- **Agent of Shadow:** For two minutes, you are invisible when sneaking. Note that attacking or activating something makes you appear, just as with standard invisibility. You simply need to begin to sneak again, and the invisibility will instantly reactivate. This is a power, so you can use it only once per day.
- **Agent of Subterfuge:** You can cast a massive Fury spell that can Frenzy any target regardless of its level. This is a power, so you can use it only once per day.
- **Agent of Strife:** You can cast a huge blast of energy that damages the health of the target for 100 points and grants this same health to you. This is a power, so you can use it only once per day.

Postquest Activities

Karliah makes Nightingale Hall her home, and you can visit her there. Activate the portal to reach the Sepulcher's entrance hall, and head back to finish any remaining additional jobs. This allows you to finally assume the leadership of the Thieves Guild. But your Critical Path Quests are now over.

THIEVES GUILD RADIANT QUESTS

The following 18 Radiant Quests, Additional Jobs, and City Influence Quests occur throughout (and between) the critical Thieves Guild Quests and offer you a different task to accomplish, usually with a sizable reward. Additional Jobs can be completed multiple times. These are available depending on how far along through the critical quests you are. For a complete list of how to unlock each quest, consult the Introduction to the Thieves Guild Quests, at the start of this chapter.

NO STONE UNTURNED

PREREQUISITES: None

INTERSECTING QUESTS: Dark Brotherhood Quest: With Friends Like These..., Dark Brotherhood Quest: Destroy the Dark Brotherhood!, Main Quest: Diplomatic Immunity, Thieves Guild City Influence Quest: Silver Lining

◊ **OBJECTIVES:** Objective: Bring the Unusual Gem to an appraiser of stolen goods, Objective: Bring the Unusual Gem to Vex in the Thieves Guild, Objective: Recover the Stones of Barenziah (24), Objective: Recover the Crown of Barenziah, Objective: Return to Vex

A Crowning Achievement

During your adventures, you may stumble upon an odd-looking but possibly extremely valuable gemstone. This particular valuable stands out from the rest and is called an "Unusual Gem." Any other precious stone is irrelevant to this quest. Once you take (or steal) the gem, the quest begins and one of two objectives appear. The first occurs if you haven't yet joined the Thieves Guild.

- **Unusual Gem**

◊ **OBJECTIVE:** Bring the Unusual Gem to an appraiser of stolen goods
◊ **OBJECTIVE:** Bring the Unusual Gem to Vex in the Thieves Guild

NOTE If you haven't met any Thieves Guild members yet, journey to Riften's Stables and enter via the northern gate. A lout named Maul (the brother of Guild member Dirge) accosts you as you enter Riften. You can speak with him, using Persuasion, Bribing, or Brawling to test his mettle. Then ask about the Unusual Gem you have, and you're directed toward Vex (although he doesn't mention her by name until you're a full member of the Thieves Guild). If Maul has died or you've angered him to the point that you're not on speaking terms, you must simply stumble upon Vex.

Once you know to speak with Vex, meet her at the Ragged Flagon in Riften. Ask her if the Unusual Gem you found is worth anything, and she tells you the gem is a Stone of Barenziah. Although it isn't worth anything in its current state, it is one of 24 prized gems pried off Barenziah's ceremonial crown. Many have attempted to collect all the gems but have failed. Until now! She will pay for a full set of gems and asks you to talk to her again once you've found all 24.

◊ **OBJECTIVE:** Recover the Stones of Barenziah (24)

NOTE Any Unusual Gems (including any you've already found) are called "Stones of Barenziah."

You must now begin to collect the remaining Stones of Barenziah. There are 24 total, minus any you've already found (which must be a minimum of one to trigger this quest). Consult the following table for guidance regarding every Stone's location:

✓	NUMBER	ZONE #	LOCATION	DESCRIPTION	PREREQUISITE
☐	[1/24]	[1.00]	Solitude (Proudspire Manor)	In the master bedroom of Proudspire Manor	Proudspire Manor purchased
☐	[2/24]	[1.00]	Solitude (Blue Palace)	On a shelf in Jarl Elisif the Fair's quarters.	None
☐	[3/24]	[1.21]	Thalmor Embassy (Reeking Cave)	Inside the cave, near a Frost Troll.	None (access this during Main Quest: Diplomatic Immunity, or access the cave instead)
☐	[4/24]	[1.27]	Dainty Sload	On a small table in the Captain's Quarters of the Dainty Sload, moored near Solitude.	None
☐	[5/24]	[4.00]	College of Winterhold	On a shelf in the Arch-Mage's Quarters.	None
☐	[6/24]	[4.02]	Yngvild	In the Throne Room area of Yngvild, in the chamber behind the throne.	None
☐	[7/24]	[4.05]	Hob's Fall Cave	In the necromancers' sleeping area.	None
☐	[8/24]	[5.00]	Markarth (Treasury House)	On a nightstand next to the bed in the master bedroom.	None
☐	[9/24]	[5.00]	Markarth (Understone Keep)	On a table in a locked side room of the Dwemer Museum.	None
☐	[10/24]	[5.36]	Dead Crone Rock	On a makeshift altar at Dead Crone Rock.	None
☐	[11/24]	[6.00]	Whiterun (Jorrvaskr)	In Kodlak Whitemane's bedroom.	None
☐	[12/24]	[6.00]	Whiterun (Hall of the Dead)	In one of the wall crypts at the foot of a skeleton.	None
☐	[13/24]	[6.00]	Whiterun (Dragonsreach)	In the Jarl's bedroom area of the Jarl's Quarters.	None
☐	[14/24]	[6.09]	Rannveig's Fast	On a table near the watery prison within Rannveig's Fast.	None
☐	[15/24]	[6.29]	Fellglow Keep	On a counter in the workroom at the top of the front foyer.	None
☐	[16/24]	[7.00]	Windhelm (House of Clan Shatter-Shield)	In a bedroom of the Shatter-Shield home.	None
☐	[17/24]	[7.00]	Windhelm (Palace of the Kings)	On a table in Wuunferth the Unliving's quarters.	None
☐	[18/24]	[7.36]	Stony Creek Cave	In the Bandit Wizard's cavern in Stony Creek Cave.	None
☐	[19/24]	[7.38]	Ansilvund	Near Fjori's ghost in the burial chambers of Ansilvund.	None
☐	[20/24]	[8.02]	Sunderstone Gorge	On the altar in front of the Word Wall.	None
☐	[21/24]	[8.22]	Dark Brotherhood Sanctuary	On the dresser in Astrid's room.	During or after Dark Brotherhood Quest: With Friends Like These... OR Dark Brotherhood Quest: Destroy the Dark Brotherhood!
☐	[22/24]	[8.28]	Pinewatch	In a locked treasure room in the Pinewatch Bandit Sanctuary.	None
☐	[23/24]	[9.00]	Riften (Mistveil Keep)	In the Jarl's Chambers in Mistveil Keep, on the bedside table.	None
☐	[24/24]	[9.35]	Riften (Black-Briar Lodge)	In the upstairs master bedroom of Black-Briar Lodge.	None

◊ **OBJECTIVE:** Recover the Crown of Barenziah

After you collect all 24 Stones of Barenziah, return to Vex, and she lets you in on a little secret: She knows the location of the Crown of Barenziah, and she'll pay handsomely if you bring it back. Naturally, this involves a long and dangerous trek through Tolvald's Cave, to the southwest of Riften. This place is infested with wild animals and worse—Falmer and their horrific pets, the Chaurus. Battle through this maze of caves to Tolvald's Crossing, moving to a large, dead-end chamber. There's a refuse pile at the end of the path that winds to the right, just after the waterfall. Sort through the pile for the crown.

➤ **Crown of Barenziah**

◊ **OBJECTIVE:** Return to Vex

Quest Conclusion

Back at the Ragged Flagon, tell Vex you've found the Crown of Barenziah. She's suitably impressed and rewards you with the Prowler's Profit perk, which vastly increases the chances of finding gems while scavenging dungeons. You can then sell these for substantial sums of gold. The completed crown with gems is in the Guild behind Mercer's desk once you complete the quest.

➤ **Perk:** Prowler's Profit

REPARATIONS

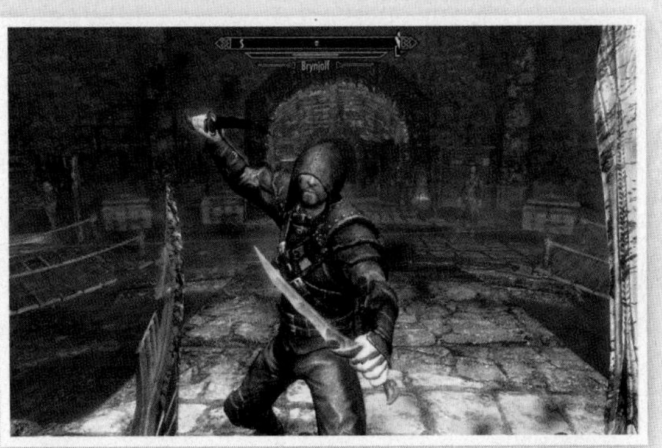

If you commit a minor crime, such as accidentally striking a Guild member or pickpocketing them, you're usually let off with a warning (if you're caught). However, if you commit a serious crime, such as assaulting or murdering a Thieves Guild member, all of them become hostile and will attack you. At this point, you can:

Continue on the killing spree, which doesn't result in much else besides dead bodies and fewer places to sell or train. Note that Vex, Delvin, Brynjolf, and Mercer are essential, so surviving in this state is going to be exceedingly difficult!

Yield by sheathing your weapons, or flee the Ragged Flagon, wait three days, and return. Expect the Guild to be unfriendly but not hostile toward you.

Speak to Vex. She requires the princely sum of 1,000 gold pieces paid to the Guild as reparations. Pay up, and you become firm friends again. Refuse, and expect to be ostracized until you pay the fine. This halts all quest progress, including Additional Quests and City Influence Quests. Until reparations are made, you are all alone.

SHADOWMARKS*

NOTE * Quest names marked with this symbol do not appear in your Quest Menu list, although objectives may.

Eagle-eyed members of the Thieves Guild may notice certain locations across Skyrim are marked with strange little pictorial signs. These inscriptions, which are unknown markings to outsiders, are actually a cryptolect that the Guild uses to flag locations that members feel are particularly safe or dangerous or that have entities that may be helpful or problematic. The symbols are known as Shadowmarks.

To learn more about Shadowmarks, search the Thieves Guild premises for a particularly well-researched book called *Shadowmarks*, written by Delvin Mallory. It contains all the markings the Thieves Guild uses.

➤ **Shadowmarks**

GLOSSARY OF SHADOWMARKS

The following Shadowmarks appear throughout the realm of Skyrim. Here's what they mean:

✓		SHADOWMARK	DESCRIPTION
☐		"The Guild"	This place is as safe as the Flagon's Cistern. Someone from the Guild is nearby for certain.
☐		"Safe"	A safe way around an obstacle, such as a hallway without traps or a house already cleared out. Head the way it is pointing to be safe.
☐		"Danger"	Head the other way or take your life in your hands. Danger lurks beyond this point!
☐		"Escape Route"	If you find yourself in jail, look for this marking and find an escape route nearby.
☐		"Protected"	Don't go here when thieving; the people at this location are under the Guild's protection and should never be robbed or assaulted.
☐		"Fence"	This should become your favorite landmark; expect to sell your hard-earned stolen goods here at a fair price.
☐		"Thieves' Cache"	Find this on a chest or barrel; expect a gift. Membership has its privileges.
☐		"Loot"	There's something near here worth stealing.
☐		"Empty"	Pass over this place, as there's nothing of note inside.

These markings can reveal (for example) who they consider a Fence, so if you're prowling a new town, you can learn where friends, foes, thieving opportunities, and like-minded souls reside. This can also help during certain Jobs so you know what's likely to be inside a house before you enter it; every one of the five largest Hold Cities (Solitude, Markarth, Whiterun, Windhelm, and Riften) has these markings to find. Also note that Guild Cache barrels are clearly emblazoned with the Thieves Cache Shadowmark, making them easier to spot for eagle-eyed thieves exploring the five largest capitals.

MOON SUGAR RUSH*

When you speak with Tonilla after being inducted into the Guild, she tells you that she has something for you to do. The Guild is lacking a reliable way to transport merchandise across Skyrim. Tonilia reckons the shrewd Khajiit caravaneers might want a cut of the profits for selling (and fencing) for the Guild. Their leader, Ri'saad, should make a deal if you present him with the satchel of Moon Sugar she gives you.

➤ **Satchel of Moon Sugar**

◊ **OBJECTIVE:** Deliver Moon Sugar to Ri'saad

Take this unrefined narcotic to Ri'saad, and tell him you bring an offer from the Thieves Guild. Hand over the Moon Sugar, and he's swayed into an agreement. From this point on, any Khajiit Caravan you meet across Skyrim will be happy to purchase your stolen goods for a fair sum. Ask him further questions and barter with him if you wish.

◊ **OBJECTIVE:** Return to Tonilia

Head back to the Ragged Flagon, inform Tonilia of your success, and she gives you some gold for your troubles. Much more importantly, you can sell stolen property to the following Fences, in each of the Caravans!

➤ **Leveled gold pieces**

➤ **Fence (Caravan):** Atahba

➤ **Fence (Caravan):** Majhad

➤ **Fence (Caravan):** Zaynabi

➤ **Fence (Caravan):** Ri'saad

ARMOR EXCHANGE*

Once you successfully complete Thieves Guild Quest: Scoundrel's Folly, Brynjolf mentions that Tonilia has a special piece of armor that you can exchange. When you speak to her, she offers to exchange one of your four pieces of Thieves Armor for a piece that's more enhanced. Choose from the hood, cuirass, gloves, or boots. You can choose only one and can't go back on your choice. The quest then concludes.

➤ **Thieves Guild Armor (+35 Carry Weight)**

➤ **Thieves Guild Boots (Improve Pickpocket 25%)**

➤ **Thieves Guild Gloves (Improve Lockpick 25%)**

➤ **Thieves Guild Hood (Improve Prices 15%)**

LARCENY TARGETS*

Throughout almost all of the Thieves Guild Critical Path Quests, you'll find a valuable item to steal, with the express intention of making a little money from it. The exact location of each Larceny Target is detailed in each specific quest. Return and speak to Delvin about cashing in your stolen goods for gold. The following table lists all available Larceny Targets and the quests they appear in:

Queen Bee Statue

Honningbrew Decanter

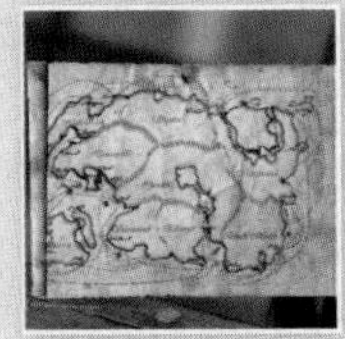
East Empire Shipping Map

Model Ship

Dwemer Puzzle Cube

Bust of the Gray Fox

Eye of the Falmer (Second Gem)

✓ LARCENY TARGET	THIEVES GUILD QUEST	LOCATION	DESCRIPTION
☐ Queen Bee Statue	Loud and Clear	Goldenglow Estate second floor	On a bedside table upstairs in Aringoth's bedroom
☐ Honningbrew Decanter	Dampened Spirits	Honningbrew Meadery	Locked upstairs office belonging to Sabjorn
☐ East Empire Shipping Map	Scoundrel's Folly	East Empire Trading Company Warehouse	In the dock overseer's hut, northwest corner
☐ Model Ship	Speaking with Silence	Snow Veil Sanctum	Fallen from a pedestal, deep in the dungeon
☐ Dwemer Puzzle Cube	Hard Answers	Calcelmo's Laboratory	In an alcove, near Calcelmo's assistant Aicantar
☐ Bust of the Gray Fox	The Pursuit	Mercer's House	In Mercer Frey's cellar office, in his house in Riften
☐ Eye of the Falmer (Second Gem)	Blindsighted	Irkngthand Sanctuary	Taken from Mercer Frey's corpse.

TIP Did you miss one of these trinkets? Then return to the location and snag it; all should still be there. Also look for sold Larceny Targets to appear as trophies on one of the bookcases behind Mercer's desk in the Cistern and for the bust of the Gray Fox on the desk.

➤ **150 to 300 gold pieces (per item)**

ADDITIONAL JOBS

PREREQUISITES: Complete Thieves Guild Quest: Taking Care of Business

AN OVERVIEW

Ready for some extra work? Once Brynjolf instructs you to speak with Vex and Delvin Mallory about additional work they may have for you (after you complete Thieves Guild Quest: Taking Care of Business and you "officially" join the Guild), immediately chat with either of your new brethren. Aside from offering you training in Lockpicking (Vex) and Sneaking (Delvin), ask them to explain the jobs they have to offer you, and then begin any you wish. You can have one Additional Job from each of them active at any given time. The Guild frowns on you quitting jobs you may be finding too difficult, but this is possible too. When you successfully finish a certain number (and variety) of Additional Jobs, Part 3: City Influence Quests become accessible (see below).

➤ **Leveled gold pieces**

✓ JOB GIVER	TYPE OF JOB
☐ Delvin Mallory	The Numbers Job
☐ Delvin Mallory	The Fishing Job
☐ Delvin Mallory	The Bedlam Job
☐ Vex	The Burglary Job

✓ JOB GIVER	TYPE OF JOB
☐ Vex	The Shill Job
☐ Vex	The Sweep Job
☐ Vex	The Heist Job

NOTE The following gives general information on all seven types of jobs and provides a particular example of each. You can continue to choose jobs for as long as you like; there's no upper limit.

CAUTION Be warned! Killing witnesses or the owners of any object you are pilfering is against the Thieves Guild code and fails the active job. Thieves steal valuables, not lives! Even worse, once the job fails, there is no gold reward, and the job does not count toward unlocking the City Influence Quests!

DELVIN'S ADDITIONAL JOBS

The Numbers Job

◊ **OBJECTIVE:** Make changes in the ledger at [business name] in a Hold City
◊ **OBJECTIVE:** Return to Delvin

Delvin is concerned with skimming a little off the top: To this end, he requires you to visit a store somewhere in the realm and make some subtle changes to the ledger. Enter the establishment, find the ledger, and fix it. You only need to complete the ledger changes without being spotted, although some ledgers are in the same room as a vendor, meaning you need to enter at night or use Sneak abilities.

The Fishing Job

◊ **OBJECTIVE:** Retrieve [item] from [mark] in [Hold City].
◊ **OBJECTIVE:** Return the valuable to Delvin.

Delvin has numerous jobs to test one of the oldest and most important skills that a thief must possess: a penchant for pickpocketing! Move to the location indicated and observe the person. Check the route they take and be patient; then quickly crouch and follow them. Swipe the valuable before they can react or even know it's gone! Augmentations both magical and skillful help here.

The Bedlam Job

◊ **OBJECTIVE:** Steal [a set amount of] gold in goods, from a Hold city
◊ **OBJECTIVE:** Return the valuables to Delvin

Delvin's third job involves surreptitiously entering a city and emptying it of a set number of valuables up to a value in gold pieces that Delvin has determined. The trick here is to know where in the city you can pillage (everywhere within the local map but not adjacent locations such as the Blue Palace in Solitude or Understone Keep in Markarth) and to take items only while you're hidden; therefore, crouch and check every time, just before you make the snatch. If you are seen taking an object, it doesn't count toward the total, so make sure you are completely hidden. Basically, keep stealing until the quest triggers that you're done!

TIP The best locations to pilfer from are stores, marketplaces, and private residences. The Dwemer Museum in Markarth does not count. Any additional stolen goods can be sold to Tonilia, as this is the one job where you're allowed to keep the items at the end!

VEX'S ADDITIONAL JOBS

The Burglary Job

◊ **OBJECTIVE:** Retrieve [an item] from [a wealthy home] somewhere in a Hold city
◊ **OBJECTIVE:** Return the valuable to Vex

Vex requires you to break into a location (usually the residence of a high-ranking or wealthy person) and steal a valuable object that the Thieves Guild can sell. This almost always requires you to wait until any residents of the location have left or to utilize your Sneak and Lockpick talents to unlock one of the location's doors, steal the valuable, and leave quickly.

The Shill Job

◊ **OBJECTIVE:** Plant [evidence] in [a wealthy home] somewhere in a Hold City
◊ **OBJECTIVE:** Return to Vex

Vex wants you to take a stolen item acquired by the Guild and place it inside the home of a high-ranking person, in order to implicate them in a crime. Aside from taking the usual precautions when entering and exiting the building (ensuring no one sees you inside or out), you must locate a chest or other object that holds items and place the stolen item in it. Remember; only place the specific item you're carrying!

The Sweep Job

◊ **OBJECTIVE:** Clear [a wealthy home], somewhere in a Hold City, of [valuables]
◊ **OBJECTIVE:** Return the valuables to Vex

Vex orders you to head to a location the Guild has staked out and believes has numerous high-quality items. You must enter the premises unseen. Once inside, you are to clear the house of a specific number of valuables (and optionally, anything else you can get away with, although this isn't necessary for this quest). Then return to Vex without arousing suspicion at any time.

The Heist Job

◊ **OBJECTIVE:** Steal [an item] from [a store] in a Hold City
◊ **OBJECTIVE:** Return [the item] to Vex

The last type of job Vex has is similar to burglary but with an important difference: You're taking a valuable item from a store rather than a private residence. As there's usually someone in a store and in a storeroom where a strongbox usually holds the valuable item, proficient sneaking, usually at nighttime, is the only way to avoid angering the locals and increasing your Bounty (which can occur but is not recommended).

TIP Common sense should prevail when you're trying to complete jobs without being caught:

Burglarize stores when they are closed so the vendors don't see you.

Stake out private residences and watch when the inhabitants leave; when the house is empty, pick the lock and steal without the possibility of discovery.

The more risk you take by attempting crimes with vendors or residents gazing at you, the harder you're making it for yourself.

There's no reason to rush; spend time staking places out and learning where the targets are, and come back later to attempt the deed.

CITY INFLUENCE QUESTS

GROWING THE GUILD AND GAINING INFLUENCE

An Overview

As you become continuously successful with your jobs, you can inquire during conversations with Delvin Mallory or Vex about the reasons for these jobs and how they help the Guild. The reasons are simple: Years ago, the Guild had a foothold in every major city in Skyrim—folks wouldn't dare lifting an apple without checking with the Guild first—but as the Guild collapsed, they lost Fences, influential contacts, and, most importantly, respect. With your help, the Guild can be taken seriously and start to take the cities back again.

Thanks to Maven Black-Briar, you have some pull in Riften, but if you're caught in a nefarious act in Whiterun or another Skyrim city, you should expect an extended jail stay. But once you complete a unique job for an influential and powerful individual within each prominent city, you can expect a much more lenient attitude. However, these city leaders won't approach the Guild until numerous smaller "jobs" have been completed—the tasks you're undertaking already.

To activate the following City Influence Quests (one per city), you must complete a total of 5 Additional Jobs within that city. After you successfully finish 5 Additional Jobs in a particular city, contact Delvin Mallory inside the Ragged Flagon and begin one or more of the following jobs. Continue to complete Additional Jobs until you successfully finish 5 or more in every city. Obviously, with the random nature of the jobs, you may have to complete more than 10 before receiving a job for a city you haven't finished all the necessary jobs in yet. The cities that the Thieves Guild wishes to gain influence in are:

✓	NAME OF CITY	ADDITIONAL JOBS COMPLETED?	AVAILABLE QUEST
☐	Markarth	5	Silver Lining
☐	Solitude	5	The Dainty Sload
☐	Whiterun	5	Imitation Amnesty
☐	Windhelm	5	Summerset Shadows
☐	Riften	0	None†

NOTE † Additional Jobs are available but no additional quest is available. You can perform jobs there, but they don't contribute to the City Influence Quests.

The rewards you receive for spreading the Thieves Guild's influence across Skyrim are detailed after the following four City Influence Quests.

PREREQUISITES: Complete Thieves Guild Quests: Additional Jobs in Markarth (5)

INTERSECTING QUESTS: All further Thieves Guild Quests

LOCATIONS: Pinewatch, Pinewatch Bandit's Sanctuary, Riften, Ratway, Cistern, The Ragged Flagon

CHARACTERS: Adora, Delvin Mallory, Endon, Rhorlak

ENEMIES: Bandit, Rigel Strong-Arm

◊ **OBJECTIVES:** Speak to Endon the Silversmith, Enter Pinewatch, Recover Endon's Silver Mold, Return to Endon

Molding Endon's Alliance

◊ **OBJECTIVE:** Speak to Endon the Silversmith

♦ **TARGET:** Endon, in Markarth

After you complete 5 (or more) successful Additional Jobs in Markarth, Delvin Mallory receives word that one of the finest Silversmiths in all of Skyrim, a man named Endon, has ordered a special mold from far-off Valenwood but it never arrived at his shop. Meet Endon (and his daughter, Adora) and tell him Delvin sent you. He informs you that bandits were most likely to blame. As Markarth's other resources are stretched thin, he has requested that the Thieves Guild handle this. Endon promises both his loyalty and some of his wealth in exchange for returning the invaluable mold.

◊ **OBJECTIVE:** Enter Pinewatch

Journey to the remote farmhouse known as Pinewatch in the middle of the pine forest, and pick the lock of the door (Average). Step inside, and your objective updates.

◊ **OBJECTIVE:** Recover Endon's Silver Mold

♦ **TARGET:** Inside the Pinewatch Bandit's Sanctuary, in Pinewatch

The lone farmhouse is deceptively small. Head to the cellar and locate (or wake up) Rhorlak. To progress further, try one of the following:

Choose to kill him. Search the cellar, find the note on the table and read it, and locate the secret trigger button.

(Bribe) Offer to loosen his tongue with money. He mentions a secret trigger button in the cellar wall.

Or simply ignore Rhorlak (the cheapest, nonviolent option) and simply find the button in the wall, with or without reading the note.

Or find the note tacked onto the wall with a dagger, by the door to the wilderness.

Across from the cellar fireplace is a suspiciously empty shelving cabinet. Check to the right of it for a button, above a basket. Press it. The cabinet swings out, revealing a tunnel behind it.

➤ **Note to Rhorlak**

Cross the wooden bridges and through the roughly hewn connecting tunnels, as Pinewatch's underground maze opens up before you. Bandits are guarding this area, so approach each chamber with your armaments at the ready. Continue past a large collection of barrels, down the craggy path, and fight more bandits to reach a door leading to the Pinewatch Bandit's Sanctuary.

In the first Sanctuary chamber, use the stacked barrels as cover when fighting off (or sneaking past) another group of bandits. Look for the opening in the upper western wall. Go past the cage room and up the stone steps to a wooden door and a small crypt room. The dead Draugr inform you that bandits are farther inside these catacombs; travel into the makeshift camp where you'll encounter more fighting. Head into the chamber with the hanging bone chimes; brush into them if you wish to alert Rigel Strong-Arm, the leader of this motley crew. Search (or pickpocket) her for the necessary keys to enter all additional chambers.

➤ **Pinewatch Key** ➤ **Pinewatch Treasure Room Key**

At the next wooden door, pick the lock (Very Hard) or use the Pinewatch Treasure Room Key. Just beyond is an iron door leading across a precarious pair of wooden beams with dart traps on either side. Sprint across, open another wooden door, and watch for two trigger stones in the floor; they both release traps—swinging blades and a battering ram, respectively—as you progress to the main crypt. You're greeted with a mace trap to the face, so take a step back and duck into the chamber. Sitting in the despoiled sarcophagus is the unique item you've been tasked to find. Take it, any coin, and the Silver Candlestick (which you can fence back at the Ragged Flagon). The treasure chest is worth prying open, too!

➤ **Endon's Silver Mold** ➤ **Silver Candlestick**

◊ **OBJECTIVE:** Return to Endon

♦ **TARGET:** Endon, in Markarth

TIP Pinewatch is not locked prior to this quest, and you can actually obtain the Silver Mold at any time, carrying it with you throughout your adventures until this quest begins. In this event, you can immediately give the item to Endon when you first meet him, completing the quest almost immediately.

Quest Conclusion

Open the door with the bar on it, which is a shortcut back to the cellar and out into Skyrim. Travel back to Markarth, and speak with Endon. He takes the mold and is now an influential ally in Markarth and a Fence in the city if you wish to sell stolen goods.

➤ **Fence:** Endon ➤ **Leveled Enchanted Light Armor**

PREREQUISITES: Complete Thieves Guild Quests: Additional Jobs in Solitude (5)

INTERSECTING QUESTS: All further Thieves Guild Quests

LOCATIONS: The Dainty Sload, East Empire Company Warehouse, Red Wave, Riften, Ratway, Cistern, The Ragged Flagon, Solitude, Blue Palace, Erikur's House

CHARACTERS: Delvin Mallory, Erikur, Sabine Nytte

ENEMIES: First Mate, Sailor

◊ **OBJECTIVES:** Speak to Erikur, Acquire Balmora Blue, Plant the Balmora Blue, Return to Erikur

Erikur's Devious Delivery

◊ **OBJECTIVE:** Speak to Erikur
♦ **TARGET:** Erikur, in Solitude

After completing 5 (or more) Additional Jobs in Solitude, Delvin Mallory informs you about a matter regarding Erikur, a businessman in Solitude. Find this Thane in the Blue Palace or near his impressive home. Whether it is by hook or by crook, as long as his business affairs flourish, Erikur is not afraid to get a little dirty. Recently, Captain Volf of the cargo ship *The Dainty Sload* has defaulted on a trade agreement he had with the Thane. The details of the agreement aren't clear, but whatever happened, Erikur stands to lose quite a bit of money. This, and the Captain's stubbornness, have made Erikur decide to contact the Thieves Guild for assistance on the matter.

The Guild has worked with Erikur before, and matters usually ended mutually beneficial for both parties. Trying to resolve the matters through legal channels would prove difficult, as the Captain of the vessel has covered his bases. To this end, Erikur has requested that you plant a substance known as "Balmora Blue" aboard the ship, framing the Captain as a smuggler. You'll find the source of the contraband close to a second vessel, the *Red Wave*, moored in the harbor below Solitude.

◊ **OBJECTIVE:** Acquire Balmora Blue
♦ **TARGET:** Sabine Nytte, on the *Red Wave*, East Empire Company Warehouse

Your contact is a deckhand named Sabine Nytte. Travel to the East Empire Company Warehouse, and look for a large ship moored off the jetty outside the East Empire store. Board the ship and speak to Sabine (she'll always be up on deck during this quest). She has the merchandise you require, but it's going to cost you! You can:

(1,500 gold) Pay Sabine a large amount of gold and receive the Balmora Blue immediately.

Ask if there's another way to earn it. There isn't.

(Pickpocket) Oh, but there is! Carefully pick her pockets and obtain the key.

Protest at the price. Sabine isn't budging, and she isn't stupid. She isn't carrying the contraband for you to steal!

(Sneak, Pickpocket) Or, you can find a second key on Sabine, pickpocket it, and then head into the bowels of the *Red Wave* to a safe. Inside the safe is a note pinpointing the location of the Balmora Blue Chest. Execute this plan if you've annoyed Sabine to the point of her refusing to speak to you or if you prefer a stealthy route to reach this objective.

Or you can ignore Sabine completely and use this guide to pinpoint the hidden footlocker, swim down, and save yourself some coin!

Once you pay the money, Sabine hands you a key and explains where the stash is located: underwater, and close by.

➤ **Sabine's Footlocker Key** ➤ **Sabine's Red Wave Key**

Sabine's contraband is sealed inside a footlocker below the jetty adjacent to the *Red Wave*. Dive down and locate the chest, using either Lockpick (Hard) or your key to open it.

➤ **Balmora Blue**

◊ **OBJECTIVE:** Plant the Balmora Blue
♦ **TARGET:** Captain's Chest, below deck aboard the *Dainty Sload*

Journey to the *Dainty Sload* and attempt to sneak aboard, or utilize your magic to enter the hold. The sailors stationed here will attack on sight. Sprint past the sailors as you head counterclockwise through the ship's interior to the hold stairs. Or simply use Invisibility and Pacify. Once inside the hold, cross to the opposite side, pass the first mate, and drop the Balmora Blue into the Captain's Chest after you first unlock it (Average).

◊ **OBJECTIVE:** Return to Erikur
♦ **TARGET:** Erikur, in Solitude

Quest Conclusion

When you return to Erikur to announce your success, he has already heard about it. He gives you something for your troubles and is now happy to reopen any doors the Guild needs in the city of Solitude. You receive the following from him:

➤ **Spell Tome (Leveled)**

PREREQUISITES: Complete Thieves Guild Quests: Additional Jobs in Whiterun (5)

INTERSECTING QUESTS: All further Thieves Guild Quests

LOCATIONS: Riften, Ratway, Cistern, The Ragged Flagon, Whiterun, Dragonsreach, Dragonsreach Jarl's Quarters

CHARACTERS: Irileth, Olfrid Battle-Born

ENEMIES: None

◊ **OBJECTIVES:** Speak to Olfrid Battle-Born, Steal the letter incriminating Arn, Forge the prison registry, Return to Olfrid Battle-Born

Letter of Intent

◊ **OBJECTIVE:** Speak to Olfrid Battle-Born

♦ **TARGET:** Olfrid Battle-Born, in Whiterun

After finishing 5 (or more) successful Additional Jobs in Whiterun, Delvin Mallory receives an urgent missive from Olfrid Battle-Born, a wealthy Nord residing in Whiterun. It appears that Arn, an old friend of Olfrid, was incarcerated inside Whiterun's prison for a serious crime he committed in Solitude, a crime that will result in his execution. Fortunately, the Whiterun authorities are not aware of his friend's identity; he was arrested on the simple charge of drunken and lewd behavior. The problem is that the authorities in Solitude recently dispatched a letter to the Jarl of Whiterun, outlining criminals for whom they are searching. If the Jarl reads the letter and makes the connection with Olfrid's friend, he'll be sent to his death. Olfrid proposes that you infiltrate the Jarl's private quarters in Whiterun and steal the letter. While you're at it, you might as well make a change in the prison logbook with his friend's identity written inside.

◊ **OBJECTIVE:** Steal the letter incriminating Arn

♦ **TARGET:** Bedroom, in the Dragonsreach Jarl's Quarters

◊ **OBJECTIVE:** Forge the prison registry

♦ **TARGET:** Study, in the Dragonsreach Jarl's Quarters

Such a brazen act of trespass won't be tolerated by the leaders of Whiterun, so be sure you're carrying the proper cloaking attire or magical accoutrements to make your infiltration successful. After some additional conversation with Olfrid to pinpoint the letter's location (and other, optional information), head into the imposing Dragonsreach.

Once inside, if you're simply wandering around in full view of the guards, Irileth usually stops you. Simply mention that you want to see the Jarl, and you're given a very temporary reprieve. If the guards or other dwellers turn hostile, do not engage them in battle, as killing those you seek to win the influence of is a terrible idea.

Head northwest from the great hall's entrance stairs. Go down the side steps and into the Dragonsreach Jarl's Quarters. The prison registry is on a table in the corner of a bedroom on the other side.

Continue through the Jarl's personal chambers, heading in a roughly southwest direction until you open the doors into the Jarl's study. On the table is a letter from Solitude. Grab that, and then flee the area, ideally without being spotted or murdering anyone.

➤ **Letter from Solitude**

◊ **OBJECTIVE:** Return to Olfrid Battle-Born

♦ **TARGET:** Olfrid Battle-Born, in Whiterun

CAUTION

You're taking your life into your own hands thinking you'll better the sheer number of guards and tough folks roaming these parts; it is better to remain with weapons sheathed, and exit without combat.

Quest Conclusion

Scour the streets of Whiterun for Olfrid Battle-Born, who may be wandering about or hanging inside a dwelling. Although he keeps quiet about Arn, he's happy to receive the letter and tells you to let Delvin know the Guild will be "quite pleased" with what Olfrid can do to influence the powers that run this city. You are also given the an Enchanted Ring.

➤ **Enchanted Ring (Leveled)**

Keeper: Cicero

Cicero, the "Fool of Hearts," is a psychotic, singsong speaking, knife-wielding jester. He is also the Keeper of the Night Mother and arrives at the Sanctuary with her body. Overly paranoid, he constantly speaks with "Mother" and furiously protects her. If he ever hears of a threat to the Brotherhood, he acts quickly and impulsively.

Shadowscale: Veezara

Veezara is a Shadowscale, an Argonian born under the sign of the Shadow. For years he served the king of High Marsh. When he was honorably released from service, he wandered Tamriel and eventually made his way to the Sanctuary in Skyrim. He is friendly and somewhat quiet, but extremely skilled.

Assassin and Blacksmith: Arnbjorn

Arnbjorn is a boisterous Nordic barbarian and husband to Astrid, who's been the only one to tame him—since he also happens to be a werewolf. His loyalty to her is unwavering and unquestioning. He was once a Companion, but his barbaric ways and eagerness for killing made it an uneasy association. After wandering the paths of Skyrim, he found this shadowy organization a much better fit for him. He sometimes works the forge inside the Sanctuary.

➤ **Blacksmith:** Arnbjorn

Familiar: Lis

More of a pet than a familiar, Gabriella's Frostbite Spider, Lis, is a permanent resident and unofficial mascot of the Dark Brotherhood Sanctuary. Don't confuse this with a wild spider; it is friendly to members, and it would be a shame if someone slew it out of spite or perverse amusement...especially as all the other Dark Brotherhood members turn hostile if you're foolish enough to slay such a fine and furry beast!

ASSASSINATIONS: A TACTICAL OVERVIEW

Assassination Effects

Before you enter the world of clandestine murder, check the targets you are terminating. Some of them may have other quest-related objectives that change or disappear completely after you assassinate them. Although this never prevents you from completing essential quests, checking the Atlas and the Index prior to taking a victim down is worthwhile.

Skills to Learn

Entering buildings, finding a target, quietly slaying them, and leaving without raising the alarm (or even being seen) requires proficiency in the following skills, which you should think about improving through training and constant use:

One-Handed: for daggers and stealth attacks

Archery: for removing foes from long range without causing a ruckus

Light Armor: so you can sneak and still take damage

Sneak: arguably the most important skill if you're taking a clandestine approach to assassinations

Lockpicking: helpful when trespassing in a locked a building

Illusion spells: such as Invisibility to help you sneak, and Fear or Pacify for an easier getaway

Alchemy: for creating poisons to tip your weapons with

Occasional other spells: such as Detect Life when you're looking for foes, friends, or targets

The Assassination Itself

The following are some overall tactics that are worth thinking about employing:

The basic kill: Find the target. Produce your preferred melee weapon. Hit the target with it until he or she expires. Then fight or flee out of the location (if you're spotted), and damn the consequences!

The ranged kill: If you prefer longer-ranged magic or bows, utilize them when attacking the target. If you can fire from cover and without being seen (crouch to check), so much the better.

The stealth kill: Increase your Sneak using augmentations to decrease your visibility, attack in the dead of night and from behind, and then merge back into the shadows if you're spotted.

The poison kill: When culling your target, you obviously want to complete the task as quickly as possible, so coat your assassination weapon in poison so your target dies with one swipe.

TRAINING

In addition to a comfy bed and like-minded attitudes, the main members of this assassin guild are dazzlingly proficient in a particular skill. Speak to each of them, and increase the chosen skill by a point. If you have the gold, you can complete this numerous times:

☑	SKILL	RANK	TRAINER
☐	Light Armor	Master	Nazir
☐	Alchemy	Master	Babette

AVAILABLE QUESTS AND TASKS

There are 37 different quests available with the Dark Brotherhood. Thirteen of these are Critical Path Quests (plus an additional introductory quest involving Cicero). Twelve are Side Contract Quests. The remaining 11 are additional quests.

Critical Path Quests

Simply referred to as "quests," these are the main missions you attempt for the Dark Brotherhood. All but the first quest have one or more prerequisites, as shown in the following table:

☑	QUEST NAME	PREREQUISITES
☐	Dark Brotherhood Quest: Delayed Burial	None
☐	Dark Brotherhood Quest: Innocence Lost	None
☐	Dark Brotherhood Quest: With Friends Like These...	Complete Dark Brotherhood Quest: Innocence Lost
☐	Dark Brotherhood Quest: Sanctuary	Complete Dark Brotherhood Quest: With Friends Like These...
☐	Dark Brotherhood Quest: Mourning Never Comes	Complete Dark Brotherhood Quest: Sanctuary
☐	Dark Brotherhood Quest: Whispers in the Dark	Complete Dark Brotherhood Quest: Mourning Never Comes
☐	Dark Brotherhood Quest: The Silence Has Been Broken	Complete Dark Brotherhood Quest: Whispers in the Dark

✓	QUEST NAME	PREREQUISITES
☐	Dark Brotherhood Quest: Bound Until Death	Complete Dark Brotherhood Quest: The Silence Has Been Broken
☐	Dark Brotherhood Quest: Breaching Security	Complete Dark Brotherhood Quest: Bound Until Death
☐	Dark Brotherhood Quest: The Cure for Madness	Complete Dark Brotherhood Quest: Breaching Security
☐	Dark Brotherhood Quest: Recipe for Disaster	Complete Dark Brotherhood Quest: The Cure for Madness
☐	Dark Brotherhood Quest: To Kill an Empire	Complete Dark Brotherhood Quest: Recipe for Disaster
☐	Dark Brotherhood Quest: Death Incarnate	Complete Dark Brotherhood Quest: To Kill an Empire
☐	Dark Brotherhood Quest: Hail Sithis!	Complete Dark Brotherhood Quest: Death Incarnate

Side Contract Quests

Referred to as "Side Contracts," these are assassinations you complete for Nazir, in six parts. Sometimes you are given two or more targets and sometimes only one. Here's how you access them:

✓	QUEST NAME	PREREQUISITES
☐	Side Contract: Kill Narfi	Complete Dark Brotherhood Quest: Sanctuary. Unavailable during Dark Brotherhood Quest: Death Incarnate.
☐	Side Contract: Kill Ennodius Papius	Complete Dark Brotherhood Quest: Sanctuary. Unavailable during Dark Brotherhood Quest: Death Incarnate.
☐	Side Contract: Kill Beitild	Complete Dark Brotherhood Quest: Sanctuary. Unavailable during Dark Brotherhood Quest: Death Incarnate.
☐	Side Contract: Kill Hern	Complete first three Side Contracts. Available during Dark Brotherhood Quest: Whispers in the Dark. Unavailable during Dark Brotherhood Quest: Death Incarnate.
☐	Side Contract: Kill Lurbuk	Complete first three Side Contracts. Available during Dark Brotherhood Quest: Whispers in the Dark. Unavailable during Dark Brotherhood Quest: Death Incarnate.
☐	Side Contract: Kill Deekus	Complete first five Side Contracts. Available during Dark Brotherhood Quest: The Silence Has Been Broken. Unavailable during Dark Brotherhood Quest: Death Incarnate.
☐	Side Contract: Kill Ma'randru-jo	Complete first five Side Contracts. Available during Dark Brotherhood Quest: The Silence Has Been Broken. Unavailable during Dark Brotherhood Quest: Death Incarnate.
☐	Side Contract: Kill Anoriath	Complete first five Side Contracts. Available during Dark Brotherhood Quest: The Silence Has Been Broken. Unavailable during Dark Brotherhood Quest: Death Incarnate.
☐	Side Contract: Kill Agnis	Complete the eight previous Side Contracts. Available after completion of Dark Brotherhood Quest: The Silence Has Been Broken. Unavailable during Dark Brotherhood Quest: Death Incarnate.
☐	Side Contract: Kill Maluril	Complete the nine previous Side Contracts. Unavailable during Dark Brotherhood Quest: Death Incarnate.
☐	Side Contract: Kill Helvard	Complete the nine previous Side Contracts. Unavailable during Dark Brotherhood Quest: Death Incarnate.
☐	Side Contract: Kill Safia	Complete all previous Side Contracts. Unavailable during Dark Brotherhood Quest: Death Incarnate.

Radiant Quests

Any other objectives or jobs with the Dark Brotherhood are listed here. A few of them have random targets, items, or other interactions. They are listed in more detail after the Critical Path Quests, but for the prerequisites required to begin every additional quest, consult the following table:

✓	RADIANT QUESTS	PREREQUISITES
☐	Destroy the Dark Brotherhood!	Complete Dark Brotherhood Quest: Innocence Lost, and kill Astrid
☐	Honor Thy Family	Complete Dark Brotherhood Quest: With Friends Like These...
☐	The Feeble Fortune*	Complete Dark Brotherhood Quest: Breaching Security, and earn the bonus
☐	Where You Hang Your Enemy's Head...	Complete Dark Brotherhood Quest: Hail Sithis!
☐	Welcome to the Brotherhood†	Complete Dark Brotherhood Quest: Hail Sithis!
☐	Cicero's Return*	Complete Dark Brotherhood Quest: Hail Sithis!
☐	The Dark Brotherhood Forever!	Complete Dark Brotherhood Quest: Hail Sithis!
☐	The Torturer's Treasure: Part I*	Complete Radiant Quest: Where You Hang Your Enemy's Head...
☐	The Torturer's Treasure: Part II*	Complete Radiant Quest: Where You Hang Your Enemy's Head...
☐	The Torturer's Treasure: Part III*	Complete Radiant Quest: Where You Hang Your Enemy's Head...
☐	The Torturer's Treasure: Part IV*	Complete Radiant Quest: Where You Hang Your Enemy's Head...

NOTE * = Indicates the quest name does not appear in your menu; check the "Miscellaneous" area for objectives that may appear.

DELAYED BURIAL

PREREQUISITES: None
INTERSECTING QUESTS: Dark Brotherhood Quest: Innocence Lost
LOCATIONS: Loreius Farm
CHARACTERS: Cicero, Curwe, Roadside Guard, Vantus Loreius
ENEMIES: None
◊ **OBJECTIVES:** Convince Loreius to fix the wheel, Convince Loreius OR report Cicero, Talk to Cicero, OR talk to Loreius

TIP It is recommended you complete this quest before beginning Dark Brotherhood Quest: With Friends Like These... and joining the Dark Brotherhood, as Cicero has some additional words for you, depending on your actions during this quest. You may also gain additional flavor depending on your actions here.

Surely You Jest

The road north of Whiterun is sometimes treacherous. Should you follow this path north from the city or visit Shimmermist Cave and journey due northwest from that location, you encounter a strange little man dressed as a jester, standing by a horse-drawn cart. Inspect the cart, and you'll see one of its wheels has detached from the axle. On the cart is a hefty-looking wooden crate.

The jester is named Cicero. He seems to be a little crazy but does need some help. He says the crate contains the body of his dear, departed mother. They were on their way from Cyrodiil to her new resting place, but the wheel on the cart broke. Although the farmer nearby must have proper tools to repair the cart, he refuses to, likely because of Cicero's strange demeanor and dress. Cicero asks you to speak with Vantus Loreius the farmer on his behalf. There's coin in it for you, too.

◊ **OBJECTIVE:** Convince Loreius to fix the wheel
♦ **TARGET:** Vantus Loreius, in Loreius Farm

Head roughly west toward the Loreius Farm and locate the farmer and his wife, Curwe. Speak with Vantus Loreius and explain Cicero's predicament. Loreius is extremely suspicious of Cicero, from his outfit to the contents of the crate he insists is his mother, and he doesn't want to be caught up in anything. You can steer the conversation toward siding with Loreius or talking him into helping Cicero. As the conversation progresses, you realize you have two choices: convincing Loreius or reporting Cicero.

◊ **OBJECTIVE:** Convince Loreius OR report Cicero
♦ **TARGET:** Vantus Loreius, OR Roadside Guard

Convincing Loreius: Vantus Loreius is easily convinced that his suspicions are unfounded and that Cicero is simply an unfortunate character in need of his wheelwright prowess. Be sure Loreius agrees to this, and then return to Cicero to tell him the good news.

Reporting Cicero: If Loreius has convinced you that Cicero is a suspicious character, head back down to the road and locate the Roadside Guard patrolling close by. Speak to the guard and make up any tall tale that is detrimental to Cicero's character. The guard promptly strides off to arrest Cicero, and you can return to Loreius to celebrate framing a weird (but possibly innocent) man.

◊ **OBJECTIVE:** Talk to Cicero, OR Talk to Loreius

Quest Conclusion

You receive gold as a reward no matter who you side with.

➤ **50 gold pieces**

Postquest Activities

If you side with Loreius and inform the guard, once you join the Dark Brotherhood and return to see Vantus Loreius and his wife again, you'll find them murdered on their farm. The culprit is unknown, although you have your suspicions....

INNOCENCE LOST

PREREQUISITES: None

INTERSECTING QUESTS: Dark Brotherhood Quest: With Friends Like These...

LOCATIONS: Riften, Honorhall Orphanage, Windhelm, Aretino Residence

CHARACTERS: Aventus Aretino, Constance Michel, Francois Beaufort, Grimvar Cruel-Sea, Hroar, Idesa Sadri, Runa Fair-Shield, Samuel

ENEMIES: Grelod the Kind

◊ **OBJECTIVES:** Talk to Aventus Aretino, Kill Grelod the Kind, Tell Aventus Aretino that Grelod is dead

The Black Sacrament Enacted

Begin this quest in a number of different ways:

1. You can hear a rumor that mentions a boy named Aventus Aretino if you visit any of the inns or taverns across Skyrim. The nearest to your starting location in Helgen is the Sleeping Giant Inn in Riverwood. The one closest to this quest is Candlehearth Hall in Windhelm. Keep asking about rumors until Aventus's name is mentioned; then follow up on this information.

2. Or, you can visit the Honorhall Orphanage in Riften. Enter the premises and watch as Grelod the Kind doesn't live up to her name. Once the harridan has ordered her children to bed, speak with any of the "guttersnipes." Francois Beaufort, Samuel, Runa Fair-Shield, or Hroar all point you in the direction of the escaped orphan, Aventus Aretino, and his location in Windhelm.

3. Or, if you're already in Windhelm, the first city guard you speak to mentions something about the ritual going on in a building inside this settlement. If you're close to the Aretino Residence, you can witness a conversation between Grimvar Cruel-Sea and Idesa Sadri; speak to them about this "cursed" child who some have heard reciting the "Black Sacrament." As the house is close by, you can easily check whether these stories hold weight.

◊ **OBJECTIVE:** Talk to Aventus Aretino
♦ **TARGET:** Aretino Residence, in Windhelm

The Sadist Headmistress Redacted

It appears the rumors are true; Aventus Aretino, a recently orphaned child, has fled from Riften and headed back to his family home.

(Lockpick [Novice]) The only way into the dwelling is to pick the lock. Once inside, you find Aventus in a trancelike state, reciting the Black Sacrament—the means by which those wishing revenge are said to contact the Dark Brotherhood. Aventus isn't concerned that you've found him out; in fact, he's thrilled that a Dark Brotherhood assassin has come to arrange a murder! Even if this wasn't your intention, Aventus doesn't listen; he wants the cruel and sadistic headmistress of the Honorhall Orphanage dead, mainly to save the other children from her violence and so her more compassionate subordinate, Constance Michel, can take over.

◊ **OBJECTIVE:** Kill Grelod the Kind
♦ **TARGET:** Honorhall Orphanage, in Riften

Travel to the Honorhall Orphanage and speak with Grelod the Kind. You may reveal as little or as much of your plan as you want. Immediately afterward, you must kill her for her crimes against children.

◊ **OBJECTIVE:** Tell Aventus Aretino that Grelod is dead
♦ **TARGET:** Aretino Residence, in Windhelm

CAUTION Beware that once you murder Grelod the Kind, your bounty level in this Hold is raised significantly if anyone witnessed this dark deed.

(Sneak) Just like any murder you commit as part of the Dark Brotherhood, slaying your target while remaining stealthy is preferred so nobody witnesses the crime. With Grelod, this can involve waiting until she's sleeping. However, Grelod will scream when she dies, alerting the children and Constance, and everyone becomes suspicious of you, even if your Bounty hasn't increased in the Rift.

Quest Conclusion

Travel back to Aventus and inform him that the assassination is complete. He is thrilled and rewards you with a fancy family trinket. It appears this quest is over.

➤ **Aretino Family Heirloom**

Postquest Activities

An odd occurrence gives you pause. Once you leave Windhelm and enter any other city in Skyrim, a courier approaches you (assuming you don't run past him). He was told to deliver a message. Examine the black handprint and the words inside that state simply, "We know." The commencement of Dark Brotherhood Quest: With Friends Like These... will follow.

TIP You don't have to wait for a courier to appear for the next quest to commence: Simply find a bed to sleep in (outside Windhelm) and have your dreams interrupted by an assassin named Astrid.

PREREQUISITES: Complete Dark Brotherhood Quest: Innocence Lost

INTERSECTING QUESTS: Dark Brotherhood Quest: Innocence Lost, Dark Brotherhood Quest: Sanctuary

LOCATIONS: Abandoned Shack, Dark Brotherhood Sanctuary

CHARACTERS: Alea Quintus, Astrid, Fultheim the Fearless, Nazir, Vasha

ENEMIES: None

◊ **OBJECTIVES:** Kill one of the captives, Enter the Dark Brotherhood Sanctuary

A Waking Nightmare

This quest begins once you complete Dark Brotherhood Quest: Innocence Lost.

The Dark Brotherhood has their eye on you. You cannot flee from their gaze, a fact that becomes increasingly obvious the next time you decide to sleep. Instead of waking up where you were, you appear inside a strange shack in the northern reaches of Skyrim. Your only option is to converse with a mysterious veiled figure in black.

The woman introduces herself as Astrid, representative for the Dark Brotherhood. Although you've demonstrated an aptitude for deathcraft and would be an asset to the Brotherhood, you've created a problem. The person you slew—Grelod the Kind—was one of the Brotherhood's legitimate targets. Therefore, you owe the Dark Brotherhood a kill.

Astrid tells you there are three bound captives in this shack. One of them has a contract on their life. You're tasked with figuring out which one and then slaying them. Only after the bloodshed will Astrid give you the necessary key to unlock the Abandoned Shack, allowing you to leave.

◊ **OBJECTIVE:** Kill one of the captives

♦ **TARGET:** Any captive in Abandoned Shack

CAUTION

As soon as Astrid finishes her speech, you can attack and kill her, obtaining the Shack Key and fleeing the scene; however, you won't be able to continue any further down this line of quests. This begins a new task: Dark Brotherhood Quest: Destroy the Dark Brotherhood! Consult page 338 for more information.

(Intimidate; Persuade) With each captive, you have a possible Intimidate or Persuade check you can make. Then make your choice and kill the captive you think is guilty:

Captive 1: Fultheim the Fearless. This giant Nord warrior becomes more of a sniveling coward the more you question him.

Captive 2: Alea Quintus. This mother of six children has certain anger issues. She'd kill you with her bare hands if given the chance.

Captive 3: Vasha: A Khajiit crime lord who utilizes both threats and negotiation in order to win his release.

Guilt. Innocence. Right. Wrong. Irrelevant?

Spoiler Alert: Return to Astrid after killing the captive, and she's impressed by your deductions. But the guilt of the victim you chose wasn't important—after all, each captive was innocent. It was the loyalty and unquestioning nature of your kill that has repaid your debt. You are free to leave. But why part ways? Astrid officially extends an invitation to join her family and gives you a passphrase to use to enter the Dark Brotherhood's Sanctuary.

➤ **Abandoned Shack Key**

◊ **OBJECTIVE:** Enter the Dark Brotherhood Sanctuary

Quest Conclusion

Journey south to the Pine Forest and locate the door marked with the skull. When prompted, reply with, "Silence, my brother." The door unlocks, allowing you under the road and into the Sanctuary. Astrid welcomes you as part of the Family and hands you the Shrouded Armor. She is preparing a target for you, as well as the arrival of the Night Mother, but for now Nazir has some side missions to undertake for fun and profit. Head deeper into the Sanctuary and meet your new brethren. You can listen in on a conversation where the Family members share some of their exploits.

➤ **Shrouded Armor**

➤ **Shrouded Boots**

➤ **Shrouded Gloves**

➤ **Shrouded Helmet**

Postquest Activities

Dark Brotherhood Quest: Sanctuary begins immediately.

TIP **Shrouded Armor:** This is arguably the ultimate attire for an assassin, as it has enchantments that boost those murderous skills you'll be using. There's some ancient Shrouded Armor (which is even more impressive) available in Hag's End, but you'll have to complete more missions for this organization before you can attempt to find it. See Dark Brotherhood Quest: The Feeble Fortune* on page 341 for more information.

NOTE * Quest names marked with this symbol do not appear in your Quest Menu list.

SANCTUARY

PREREQUISITES: Complete Dark Brotherhood Quest: With Friends Like These...

INTERSECTING QUESTS: Dark Brotherhood Quest: With Friends Like These..., Dark Brotherhood Quest: Side Contract: Kill Narfi, Dark Brotherhood Quest: Side Contract: Kill Ennodius Papius, Dark Brotherhood Quest: Side Contract: Kill Beitild, Dark Brotherhood Quest: Mourning Never Comes

LOCATIONS: Dark Brotherhood Sanctuary

CHARACTERS: Arnbjorn , Astrid, Babette, Cicero , Festus Krex, Gabriella , Nazir , The Night Mother, Veezara

ENEMIES: None

◊ **OBJECTIVES:** Speak with Nazir, Receive the first set of contracts from Nazir

Your Brotherhood Brethren

This quest begins once you complete Dark Brotherhood Quest: With Friends Like These....

◊ **OBJECTIVE:** Speak with Nazir

Heed Astrid's instructions, and venture deeper into the Dark Brotherhood's Sanctuary, where Nazir and the rest of the Brotherhood are talking about their clandestine activities with an air of mirth. You can speak to the other members, but your only critical contact is Nazir. This man has some side contracts you may be interested in fulfilling. Nazir is also a Trainer and can teach you how to be more effective when wearing Light Armor.

➤ **Trainer (Light Armor):** Nazir

◊ **OBJECTIVE:** Receive the first set of contracts from Nazir

MEETING THE BROTHERHOOD

In addition to Astrid and Nazir, you can converse with (and inquire about) other Brotherhood members—Arnbjorn, Babette, Cicero, Festus Krex, Gabriella, Nazir, the Night Mother, and Veezara—who offer you advice on any future quest related to this faction (speak to each between Dark Brotherhood Quests). For more information on these Dark Brotherhood members, check the "Overview" section at the start of this chapter.

NOTE At this point, the Dark Brotherhood Quest: Side Contracts also begin. They are given by Nazir. Consult the "Dark Brotherhood Radiant Quests" and "Dark Brotherhood Quest: Side Contracts" sections of this chapter. These detail every contract and how to obtain them.

Quest Conclusion

After completing one or more of Nazir's side contracts, when you return to the Dark Brotherhood Sanctuary and move into the grotto area, there's a flurry of activity as Cicero has arrived with his mother; check the next quest for all of the details. After speaking with Astrid, head to Nazir if you're collecting payment for any of the first three contracts.

Postquest Activities

You usually return to Nazir once Dark Brotherhood Quest: Mourning Never Comes has already begun.

MOURNING NEVER COMES

PREREQUISITES: Complete Dark Brotherhood Quest: Sanctuary

INTERSECTING QUESTS: Dark Brotherhood Quest: Sanctuary, Dark Brotherhood Quest: Whispers in the Dark

LOCATIONS: Dark Brotherhood Sanctuary , Markarth, The Hag's Cure, Raldbthar, Raldbthar Consortium, Windhelm, The White Phial, Blacksmith Quarters

CHARACTERS: Arnbjorn, Astrid, Babette, Cicero, Festus Krex, Gabriella, Muiri, Nazir, The Night Mother, Veezara

ENEMIES: Alain Dufont , Bandits, Nilsine Shatter-Shield

◊ **OBJECTIVES:** Talk to Muiri, Kill Alain Dufont, (Optional) Kill Nilsine Shatter-Shield, Talk to Muiri, Report back to Astrid

Clowning Around

This quest begins once you complete Dark Brotherhood Quest: Sanctuary.

After returning from your first side contract (or later), it appears the Dark Brotherhood are welcoming a new visitor. Cicero and his oversized coffin have arrived; you'll find them in the grotto. Cicero is engaged in a slightly tense conversation with Arnbjorn. Astrid isn't overly fond of the jester but still welcomes him into the fold, along with his cargo. Ask Astrid about a contract, and she gives you instructions. An Apothecary's Apprentice over in Markarth has completed the Black Sacrament. Find her and follow her wishes. You can ask Astrid about the Night Mother (the corpse Cicero has hauled in with him), advice on the contracts, and other rules to follow if you desire.

◊ **OBJECTIVE:** Talk to Muiri

♦ **TARGET:** The Hag's Cure, in Markarth

Cicero is a psychotic, knife-wielding jester. He is also the Keeper of the Night Mother. He is grateful if you helped convince Vantus Loreius to fix his wagon during Dark Brotherhood Quest: Delayed Burial but is most put out if you didn't. You can ask him about himself, the Night Mother, and a variety of other topics, but you may wish to watch this fellow; he could be unpredictable.

CAUTION

The Hag's Helper

Journey to Markarth and seek out Muiri, who may be hanging around inside the Silver-Blood Inn, walking nearby, or heading toward the Hag's Cure apothecary shop (or already inside). Tell her that you've come, and she speaks conspiratorially about her problem: While visiting the wealthy Shatter-Shield family in Windhelm—who were old and dear friends and recently lost their daughter to a murderer—Muiri went to the local tavern to drown her sorrows; there she fell in love with a dashing stranger named Alain Dufont. What Muiri didn't know at the time was that Alain was actually using her so he could infiltrate the family and rob them blind. Alain, who turned out to be a local bandit leader, made off with an impressive haul.

The Shatter-Shields blame Muiri, and the family matriarch (who once viewed Muiri as another daughter) now wants nothing more to do with her. So, not only has Muiri been betrayed by the man she thought loved her, but she's also been disowned by the Shatter-Shields. What does Muiri want? Revenge. Twice over! She wants you to travel to where Alain and his bandits are holded up and kill the thieving liar. But she also offers you an optional objective: to kill Nilsine Shatter-Shield. With both of her real daughters now dead, family matriarch Tova will surely accept Muiri once more as her surrogate daughter. Or so her addled mind believes. Before you go, Muiri offers you some doses of a particularly potent poison, which you can use on your targets if you wish.

➤ **Lotus Extract (2)**

◊ **OBJECTIVE:** Kill Alain Dufont
♦ **TARGET:** Alain Dufont, in Raldbthar
◊ **OBJECTIVE:** (Optional) Kill Nilsine Shatter-Shield
♦ **TARGET:** Nilsine Shatter-Shield, in Windhelm

NOTE The following two assassinations may occur in whichever order you wish.

Contract: Alain Dufont

Plod through the snow until you reach the spectacular carved dwarven stronghold. If you aren't being particularly sneaky (and you don't need to be), prepare for bandit attacks as you ascend the outer stairs. Deal with these light threats and open the door leading to Raldbthar Consortium.

Enter the Consortium level. Cut down the bandits you see as you navigate the fire trap and head down the sloping corridor to a giant chamber of crumbling columns. Alain Dufont's bandit clan are having a conference. A single arrow dipped in Lotus Extract is a professional method of taking Alain out, or you can wade in with your favored offensive spells or melee weapons. Don't forget to poison your weapon before it strikes Alain to drop him in a single strike. Afterward, take his unique weapon, Aegisbane, before you depart. This weapon is the stolen family symbol of Clan Shatter-Shield. You can:

- Continue to explore this stronghold (consult the Atlas starting on page 685 for more details)
- Journey back to Muiri
- Or continue your assassinations by tackling the optional target, Nilsine Shatter-Shield.

➤ **Unique Weapon:** Aegisbane

Nilsine Shatter-Shield (Optional)

Set off to Windhelm and search out the location of Nilsine, who is usually in the market area between the White Phial and the Blacksmith Quarters. You can speak to her about the recent death of her twin sister, but that isn't the reason you're here. You're here to kill her (ideally after coating your blade or arrow with a dose of Lotus Extract). If you're spotted, it is usually better to flee than be overwhelmed by the city guard.

TIP **In the Shadows:** It is safer to wait until nightfall and follow Nilsine to a secluded location, such as her home or an area en route to her house with no other onlookers, before completing the despicable deed.

◊ **OBJECTIVE:** Talk to Muiri
♦ **TARGET:** The Hag's Cure, in Markarth

Quest Conclusion

Trek back to Markarth and explain to Muiri who you've killed. She is pleased with the demise of Alain Dufont and is ecstatic if you also carried out her optional wishes. She rewards you accordingly:

➤ **50 gold pieces (Alain Dufont)**

➤ **Muiri's Ring (Nilsine Shatter-Shield)**

◊ **OBJECTIVE:** Report back to Astrid
♦ **TARGET:** Dark Brotherhood Sanctuary

Postquest Activities

Return to the Dark Brotherhood Sanctuary and locate Astrid. She is happy that you finished your contract, but she needs your help with a matter of a more personal nature. Although she may be paranoid, you're sure that jester is part of it! Dark Brotherhood Quest: Whispers in the Dark now begins.

WHISPERS IN THE DARK

PREREQUISITES: Complete Dark Brotherhood Quest: Mourning Never Comes

MINOR SPOILERS

INTERSECTING QUESTS: Dark Brotherhood Quest: Mourning Never Comes, Dark Brotherhood Quest: Side Contract: Kill Hern, Dark Brotherhood Quest: Side Contract: Kill Lurbuk, Dark Brotherhood Quest: The Silence Has Been Broken

LOCATIONS: Dark Brotherhood Sanctuary

CHARACTERS: Astrid, Cicero, Nazir, Night Mother

ENEMIES: None

◊ **OBJECTIVES:** Hide in the Night Mother's coffin, Talk to Cicero, Talk to Astrid, Receive a side contract from Nazir

Listen to Your Mother

This quest begins once you complete Dark Brotherhood Quest: Mourning Never Comes.

Back at the Dark Brotherhood Sanctuary, Astrid tells you about a personal matter she's worried about: It seems Cicero is acting erratically, locking himself inside the chamber where the Night Mother is stored, and she hears whispering voices. She fears a conspiracy, but who is he talking to? Feel free to ask more questions after you agree to eavesdrop from the most secure location in the room: inside the Night Mother's coffin!

◊ **OBJECTIVE:** Hide in the Night Mother's coffin
♦ **TARGET:** Dark Brotherhood Sanctuary

The coffin is now out of its carrying crate and is installed just behind the circular stained-glass window. Unlock it and step inside; there's just enough room between you and the Night Mother's remains. With the doors shut behind you, you can hear Cicero engaged in conversation with the corpse. There's no conspiracy talk here, just one-sided chatter from the jester about keeping the Night Mother safe and finding the "Listener." Then something odd happens; the face of the Night Mother begins to glow, and a voice appears inside your head! She informs you that "you're the one," and the coffin doors swing open.

◊ **OBJECTIVE:** Talk to Cicero
◊ **OBJECTIVE:** Talk to Astrid

MEETING THE BROTHERHOOD

The Night Mother

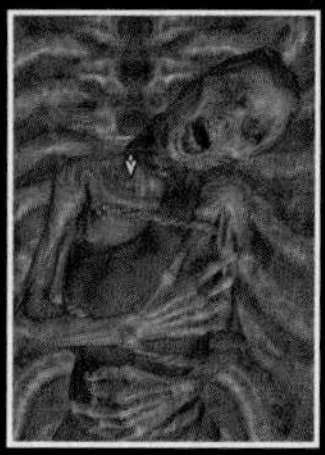

In the physical realm, the Night Mother exists as a mummified corpse, resting inside a large sarcophagus. Her Keeper, Cicero, brought her here. She exists as a voice inside your head; at first it's just fragmented snippets, but later you receive more structured communications.

"Defiler!" Cicero stops short of an all-out attack but is alarmed at your subterfuge. However, as you relate what the Night Mother has told you, the jester's anger dissipates and is replaced with excitement that he's found "the Listener." After you convince Cicero, Astrid enters the chamber, wanting to know what the commotion is about. You relay the events and the Night Mother's request that you speak with someone named Amaund Motierre in Volunruud. Astrid needs time to think about this possible contract from a long-dead matriarch and instructs you to attempt other work in the meantime.

◊ **OBJECTIVE:** Receive a side contract from Nazir

NOTE You can visit Amaund in Volunruud before speaking to Astrid, and receive the items you need to hand over to her, but you must speak with Astrid eventually (during the next Quest).

You may tell Nazir about the recent occurrences, but be sure to ask about some additional work. You must finish the previous three side contracts before receiving information on two more targets for you to swiftly dispatch: a fearsome vampire named Hern and a bard called Lurbuk. Tackle either target in any order you wish.

NOTE Consult the "Dark Brotherhood Radiant Quests" and "Dark Brotherhood Quest: Side Contracts" sections of this chapter. These detail every contract and how to obtain them.

Quest Conclusion

Return to the Dark Brotherhood Sanctuary. After a conversation with Astrid (detailed in the next quest), locate Nazir to collect any additional payments for side contracts you've finished. You may wish to finish any outstanding assassinations at this point, too.

Postquest Activities

You usually return to Nazir once Dark Brotherhood Quest: The Silence Has Been Broken begins.

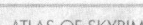

PREREQUISITES: Complete Dark Brotherhood Quest: Whispers in the Dark

INTERSECTING QUESTS: Dark Brotherhood Quest: Whispers in the Dark, Dark Brotherhood Quest: Bound Until Death

LOCATIONS: Dark Brotherhood Sanctuary, Riften, Ratway, The Ragged Flagon, Volunruud

CHARACTERS: Amaund Motierre, Astrid, Delvin Mallory, Nazir, Rexus

ENEMIES: Draugr

◊ **OBJECTIVES:** Speak with Amaund Motierre, Talk to Rexus, Deliver the letter and amulet to Astrid, Show the amulet to Delvin Mallory, Report back to Astrid

Dark Machinations

This quest begins once you complete Dark Brotherhood Quest: Whispers in the Dark and the two side contracts, and after you speak with Astrid.

The next time you visit the Dark Brotherhood Sanctuary, Astrid stops you to talk. Although she isn't sure what's happening with you and the voices inside your head, she feels it would be beneficial for you to complete the liaison with the contact the Night Mother mentioned to you. You're to set off for Volunruud, a crypt to the northeast, at your earliest convenience. Afterward, conclude any business you may have with your side contracts by visiting Nazir. Talk to the Brotherhood members about this quest if you wish, and then set off.

◊ **OBJECTIVE:** Speak with Amaund Motierre
◊ **OBJECTIVE:** Talk to Rexus
♦ **TARGET:** Inside Volunruud

Travel to the earthen mound with the entrance over the embankment guarded by standing stones, and ready your weapon for a small altercation with Draugr warriors. Although there are many rooms and tunnels throughout this complex, you need only reach the bottom of the first set of stairs, turn left, and walk southwest to a small antechamber with Draugr corpses among the ferns. In the room beyond is Amaund Motierre and his bodyguard, Rexus. Motierre's revelations are astonishing; he wishes to hire the Dark Brotherhood to remove several people, culminating with an assassination of the Emperor of Tamriel! He ends his diatribe by motioning to Rexus, who strides forward to hand over the following items:

➤ **Sealed Letter** ➤ **Jeweled Amulet**

◊ **OBJECTIVE:** Deliver the letter and amulet to Astrid
♦ **TARGET:** Dark Brotherhood Sanctuary

Motierre explains the Amulet can be used for purchasing necessities for the forthcoming contracts, and the Sealed Letter is an agreement with the Dark Brotherhood; both are for Astrid. Optionally investigate further into Volunruud, then exit and return to Astrid. She's understandably incredulous. Show her the items, and she begins to believe. Surely the Night Mother wouldn't misdirect the Brotherhood....

For the moment, Astrid will take the letter, while you journey to Riften and locate a fence and friend of the Brotherhood called Delvin Mallory, who should be able to appraise the Amulet. He's a trusted ally and is holed up in the underbelly of the town.

◊ **OBJECTIVE:** Show the amulet to Delvin Mallory
♦ **TARGET:** The Ragged Flagon, inside the Ratway in Riften

On the Fence

Trek to Riften and find the entrance to the Ratway, by the water's edge underneath the Scorched Hammer. Navigate the maze of sewer tunnels until you find the door into the Ragged Flagon, and then tell Delvin Mallory that the Dark Brotherhood requires his services. He asks how Astrid is, and then you hand over the Jeweled Amulet (via conversation rather than inventory access). Mallory inspects the Amulet and identifies it as belonging to the Emperor's Elder Council. Although worried about who the Brotherhood had to murder to obtain it, when you ask him to purchase it, he eagerly hands over a letter of credit to cover any expenses Astrid requires.

➤ **Letter of Credit**

NOTE You may already be familiar with Delvin Mallory if you're engaged in the Thieves Guild Faction Quests. He has some additional dialogue if you're partway through those missions.

◊ **OBJECTIVE:** Report back to Astrid
♦ **TARGET:** The Dark Brotherhood Sanctuary

Quest Rewards

Back in the Sanctuary, once you explain the credit Delvin Mallory just opened, your only reward from Astrid are the beginnings of Amaund Motierre's most devious of plans, which are now being put into action: She hopes you have something fancy to wear; you're going to a wedding....

NOTE Astrid reprimands you at this point if you broke the seal to read the letter, which contains a list of forthcoming targets, but this doesn't have a lasting effect on your relationship.

Postquest Activities

Dark Brotherhood Quest: Bound Until Death begins immediately. In addition, more side contracts are now available from Nazir.

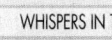

PREREQUISITES: Complete Dark Brotherhood Quest: The Silence Has Been Broken

MINOR SPOILERS

INTERSECTING QUESTS: Dark Brotherhood Quest: The Silence Has Been Broken, Dark Brotherhood Quest: Breaching Security

LOCATIONS: Dark Brotherhood Sanctuary, Solitude, Temple of the Divines

CHARACTERS: Alexia Vici, Asgeir Snow-Shod, Astrid, Babette, Gabriella, Jarl Elisif the Fair, Kayd, Lodi, Noster Eagle-Eye, Nura Snow-Shod, Pantea Ateia, Veezara, Vivienne Onis, Vuwulf Snow-Shod

ENEMIES: Vittoria Vici

◊ **OBJECTIVES:** Kill Vittoria Vici, Report back to Astrid

A Marriage of Inconvenience

This quest begins once you complete Dark Brotherhood Quest: The Silence Has Been Broken.

Upon completion of your previous Dark Brotherhood Quest, a rendezvous with Astrid reveals more about the first of Amaund Motierre's list of targets: Vittoria Vici, an Imperial with pro-Empire sentiments. She is set to be married to her Nord fiancé, Asgeir Snow-Shod, who has strong ties to the Stormcloaks. Although invited, the Emperor respectfully declined. But no matter; his family will be directly affected, for Vittoria Vici is the Emperor's first cousin. The current animosity in the region means that the assassination of the Emperor's cousin will force him into involvement in the Civil War.

◊ **OBJECTIVE:** Kill Vittoria Vici
♦ **TARGET:** Vittoria Vici, Temple of the Divines, in Solitude

TIP Converse with Astrid, Babette, and Gabriella. Astrid insists that this assassination must be a daring public display, messy and loud. There is no hiding in the shadows on this occasion! Babette and Gabriella mention two different ways you can slay Vittoria. Consult the next section for more information.

Divines Retribution

Locate the imposing rock fortress of Solitude and enter the city. Pass through the outer bailey of market shops and houses and into the large inner courtyard to the northeast, which is adjacent to the Temple of the Divines. Step through either archway, and you'll see the ceremony reception is already under way. You can chat with any number of guests: Noster Eagle-Eye, Vivienne Onis, Vuwulf Snow-Shod, Kayd, Alexia Vici, Nura Snow-Shod, Jarl Elisif the Fair, Pantea Ateia, and Lodi. You may even wish to give your regards to the bride and groom for flavor and fun.

TIP Consult the map of Solitude in the Atlas (page 692), and trace a route back to an exit. Run back there once or twice before you make the kill so you know exactly where to escape.

With the ceremony under way, you have numerous methods of removing Vittoria Vici:

Fire from afar: Take to the battlements via the stone steps in the adjacent courtyard, working your way up and around to the crenellations above the temple and then striking Vittoria with a well-aimed arrow or magical attack (dip an arrow in Lotus Extract to ensure a one-hit kill). This allows you to escape more easily.

Babette's advice: She mentions an old statue that rests rather precariously over the balcony where Vittoria will be giving her speech. Take one of the side doors or the crenellations to the statue and push it off so it lands on Vittoria's head.

Gabriella's advice: She tells you of a small parapet (accessed via a side door near the reception courtyard) directly across from the balcony where the speech will be given. She's already left a present: arrows and a special enchanted bow named Firiniel's End. Locate the parapet, and use this bow instead of your own.

A more messy death: Of course, you can run her through with your pointy weapon, bludgeon her to death with a warhammer, or attack her from close quarters. This has few advantages other than seeing your victim die in close proximity to you.

TIP Remember to time your killing so that Vittoria collapses during her speech, where the assembled throng is at its most attentive: There's a bonus in it for you.

➤ **Firiniel's End**

◊ **OBJECTIVE:** Report back to Astrid
♦ **TARGET:** Dark Brotherhood Sanctuary

CAUTION As you might expect, your bounty in Haafingar has risen considerably. Expect all guards to be hostile as you flee Solitude.

Escaping Solitude

Now that the marriage is over and the reception ruined, you must make good your escape. Along the way, you may run into Veezara, who Astrid has sent to keep an eye on you. He tells you to run while he holds off the enemy. Oblige him rather than sticking around to face overwhelming odds; Veezara can take care of himself. Rush to an exit, flee the city, and continue into the countryside until you aren't chased anymore. Fast-Travel (or trek) back to the Dark Brotherhood Sanctuary.

Quest Conclusion

Rendezvous with Astrid, and once you confirm the bride's demise, Astrid seems quite excited at the path you've trodden and rewards you with an impressive spell. If you killed Vittoria as she addressed the crowd, you are given additional gold pieces. Then Astrid requests you go speak to Gabriella; she has some information on your next quest.

- **Summon Spectral Assassin (Power)**
- **Gold pieces (bonus)**

Postquest Activities

Dark Brotherhood Quest: Breaching Security begins immediately.

> **TIP** **A Ghost of LaChance:** The Spectral Assassin you're now able to conjure from the afterlife is none other than Lucien LaChance, the Dark Brotherhood speaker from Oblivion! Not only will he fight by your side (summon him once per day), but also you can converse with him. He'll offer advice on your current quest or the location you're visiting. Be sure to meet this legend!

BREACHING SECURITY

PREREQUISITES: Complete Dark Brotherhood Quest: Bound Until Death

INTERSECTING QUESTS: Dark Brotherhood Quest: Bound Until Death, Dark Brotherhood Quest: The Cure for Madness

LOCATIONS: Dark Brotherhood Sanctuary, Dragon Bridge, Penitus Oculatus Outpost, Markarth, Guard Tower, Understone Keep, Riften, Mistveil Keep, Solitude, Castle Dour, Emperor's Tower, Windhelm, Bloodworks, Palace of the Kings, Whiterun, The Bannered Mare, Dragonsreach

CHARACTERS: Astrid, Cicero, Gabriella

ENEMIES: Gaius Maro

◊ **OBJECTIVES:** Speak with Gabriella, Kill Gaius Maro, (Optional) Steal Gaius Maro's travel schedule, Plant the Incriminating Letter on Gaius Maro's body, Report back to Gabriella

Eyes on the Penitus Oculatus

This quest begins once you complete Dark Brotherhood Quest: Bound Until Death.

◊ **OBJECTIVE:** Speak with Gabriella

After your talk with Astrid, she recommends you speak with Gabriella, who was also working on the details of the next contract while you were away. Optionally pass by Veezara (who you can speak with regarding his help during the escape from Solitude); then converse with Gabriella, who tells you your next target, a man named Gaius Maro—apparently an agent of the Emperor's security force known as the Penitus Oculatus. Gaius's superior officer (and father)—Commander Maro—has given his son instructions to check the security of every major settlement in Skyrim, in preparation for the Emperor's visit.

Your task is to implicate him in a plot to kill the Emperor by dispatching him and planting an incriminating letter on his corpse. This should distract Commander Maro and make the Penitus Oculatus think the only threat to the Emperor has been quashed. Gaius Maro is also the only man who knows the identity of the "Gourmet," a famous chef scheduled to cook for the Emperor at a private dinner. Gabriella also reveals the possibility of a travel schedule, allowing you to kill Gaius while he is away from the garrison town of Dragon Bridge and earn a bonus. Speak to her for a little more information.

- **Incriminating Letter**

◊ **OBJECTIVE:** Kill Gaius Maro
◊ **OBJECTIVE:** (Optional) Steal Gaius Maro's travel schedule
♦ **TARGET:** Gaius Maro, in Dragon Bridge (or various locations)

> **NOTE** At this point, there are two plans to try. The first is easier but does not net you a bonus. The second is longer, requires some waiting, and could take multiple days to accomplish, but it is more rewarding. In either plan, you must travel to Dragon Bridge. Note that the "quest target" on your in-game compass and map appears differently depending on your actions: If you steal the travel schedule, you can see where Gaius Maro is, wherever you are. If you haven't, his quest target marker appears only when you're in his general vicinity.

Plan A: Death at Dragon Bridge

When you reach the spectacular carved bridge over the Karth River, stop and survey the settlement. If you journeyed here from the Dark Brotherhood Sanctuary, Gaius Maro is usually on the main thoroughfare, talking with his father, Commander Maro, and then his "love," Faida. He then sets off on foot. Simply plant an arrow or melee strike into him, poison-tipped or not. Then promptly flee the scene. You don't need the travel schedule if you aren't interested in the bonus.

THE SCHEDULE OF GAIUS MARO

Snagging the schedule allows you to plan an assassination based on the day of the week and your other active quests. Use the list below to see the general time and location of Gaius Maro:

DAY OF THE WEEK	LOCATION	BUILDING NAME
Morndas	Solitude	The Emperor's Tower
Morndas evening	Solitude	Castle Dour (food and sleep)
Tirdas	Windhelm	The Palace of the Kings
Tirdas evening	Windhelm	Barracks (food and sleep)
Middas	Riften	Mistveil Keep
Turdas	Whiterun	Dragonsreach
Turdas evening	Whiterun	The Bannered Mare (food and sleep)
Fredas	Markarth	Understone Keep
Fredas evening	Markarth	Guard Tower (food and sleep)
Loredas and Sundas	Riften	The Bee and Barb

Plan B: The Stalking Assassin

Your first task is to try locating the travel schedule, which is on a table inside the Penitus Oculatus Outpost. You can sneak in there; the guards will say you are in the wrong place but won't attack you. Be sure to read and take the schedule so you can refer to it during your stalking of Maro.

➤ **Gaius Maro's Schedule**

> **TIP** When you rest or sleep, the Rest menu displays the exact day, time, and date. Figure out when to strike based off this information. For the exact locations of each structure within a city, consult this guide's Atlas (page 685).

With the schedule in hand, you can now time your arrival at any of the major cities in Skyrim to coincide with Gaius's visit. You may, for example, wish to complete other quests or business, or simply wait (or sleep) until the appropriate day and time. When you finally wish to face Gaius, there are a few matters to bear in mind:

To gain the bonus, do not kill Gaius Maro in Dragon Bridge or on the road as he travels between cities.

The various assassination techniques listed when you started the side contracts during Dark Brotherhood Quest: Sanctuary apply here, too. Check that section for possible execution plans.

Find the unlocked chamber where Gaius is, and then murder him while he sleeps. This is one reason why nighttime assassinations are recommended.

Or, use simple combat followed by placing the letter and then fleeing from authorities.

Finally, you can head to Dragon Bridge and follow him at a discreet distance as he walks to a Hold City. To be sure of claiming your bonus, wait until he enters the city to kill him. You may be able to kill him just outside the gates… but if he runs, you'll lose credit for the bonus.

> ◊ **OBJECTIVE:** Plant the Incriminating Letter on Gaius Maro's body

No matter where Gaius finally rests, be sure you stop to place on his body the Incriminating Letter that Gabriella gave you.

> ◊ **OBJECTIVE:** Report back to Gabriella
> ♦ **TARGET:** Gabriella, in Dark Brotherhood Sanctuary

Quest Conclusion

Gabriella is anxiously awaiting your return. She already knows you did the deed and quickly rewards you accordingly. Then she immediately informs you of a more pressing matter. There has been an "incident" involving Cicero. Astrid will explain.

➤ **100 gold pieces**

> ◊ **DARK BROTHERHOOD QUEST:** The Feeble Fortune* begins (Bonus)

> **NOTE** * Quest names marked with this symbol do not appear in your Quest Menu list, although objectives may.

Postquest Activities

Dark Brotherhood Quest: The Cure for Madness begins immediately. Remember to consult with Olava the Feeble in Whiterun and listen to your fortune; this quest information is on page 341.

PREREQUISITES: Complete Dark Brotherhood Quest: Breaching Security

MINOR SPOILERS

INTERSECTING QUESTS: Dark Brotherhood Quest: Breaching Security, Dark Brotherhood Quest: Side Contract: Kill Deekus, Dark Brotherhood Quest: Side Contract: Kill Ma'randru-jo, Dark Brotherhood Quest: Side Contract: Kill Anoriath, Dark Brotherhood Quest: Side Contract: Kill Agnis, Dark Brotherhood Quest: Side Contract: Kill Maluril, Dark Brotherhood Quest: Side Contract: Kill Helvard, Dark Brotherhood Quest: Side Contract: Kill Safia, Dark Brotherhood Quest: Recipe for Disaster

LOCATIONS: Dark Brotherhood Sanctuary, Dawnstar Sanctuary

CHARACTERS: Arnbjorn, Astrid, Festus Krex, Gabriella, Nazir, Shadowmere, Veezara

ENEMIES: Cicero, Sanctuary Guardian, Udefrykte

◊ **OBJECTIVES:** Talk to Astrid, Search Cicero's Room, Talk to Astrid, Behold Shadowmere, Locate Arnbjorn, Talk to Arnbjorn, Enter the Dawnstar Sanctuary, Kill Cicero , Kill Cicero or leave the Sanctuary, Report back to Astrid

The Savagery of Cicero

This quest begins once you complete Dark Brotherhood Quest: Breaching Security.

◊ **OBJECTIVE:** Talk to Astrid

Inside the main grotto chamber of the Sanctuary, the Dark Brotherhood are gathered around Veezara, who was bleeding from a deep wound. Speak to Astrid, and she reveals that Cicero has gone mad. She says the maniac didn't like some remarks Astrid had made regarding the Night Mother and attempted to kill her. Veezara stopped him but was wounded. Cicero fled into the forest. Arnbjorn gave chase and hasn't been seen since. Astrid is worried for her husband's safety. She is also calling on you to kill Cicero for this treachery! She suggests you find evidence in Cicero's chamber.

NOTE Although this may not seem like the most opportune time to start some side contracts, all the remaining targets are now available. There are three active targets, followed by one, then another two, and then the final assassination. Advice on these seven tasks are listed after Cicero has been dealt with, in the "Dark Brotherhood Quest: Side Contracts" section.

◊ **OBJECTIVE:** Search Cicero's Room

Search the Sanctuary until you find Cicero's chamber and the Journal on top of the barrel. Pick up the Journal to read about Cicero's exploits upon his arrival in Skyrim and his knowledge of another, older Sanctuary near Dawnstar. The book also has the passphrase to enter the Sanctuary and some evidence of what (and who) resides inside. Also revealed is Cicero's distaste for Astrid and her "new ways."

➤ **Cicero's Journal, Final Volume**

◊ **OBJECTIVE:** Talk to Astrid

Return to Astrid, and she orders you to the Dawnstar Sanctuary as quickly as possible; in fact, she has secured a steed named Shadowmere to quicken your progress to your destination if you wish.

◊ **OBJECTIVE:** Behold Shadowmere
♦ **TARGET:** Fetid pond, outside Dawnstar Sanctuary
◊ **OBJECTIVE:** Locate Arnbjorn
◊ **OBJECTIVE:** Talk to Arnbjorn
♦ **TARGET:** Dawnstar Sanctuary

Race, by foot, horse, or Fast-Travel to Dawnstar, to the Black Door cut into the beachside cliffs. Just outside you'll find the crumpled form of Arnbjorn. It seems the jester is a deft hand with his "butter knife," as Arnbjorn calls it, indicating the nasty wound. Arnbjorn reckons he wounded Cicero, too, judging by the trail of blood the fool left behind as he entered the Dawnstar Sanctuary. Arnbjorn would have followed but couldn't open the Black Door. Convince Arnbjorn to return to Astrid, while you follow the blood.

Puzzle Solution: At the Black Door, when it asks, "What is life's greatest illusion?" answer "Innocence, by Brother." You'll know this if you read Cicero's Journal.

◊ **OBJECTIVE:** Enter the Dawnstar Sanctuary
◊ **OBJECTIVE:** Kill Cicero

A Fool's Errand

Head down the stairs, and you can hear Cicero deeper in the maze of connecting chambers, saying that Astrid has "sent the best" to defeat him. He is hurt; notice the intermittent puddles and drops of blood on the floor and walls. Follow the trail to Cicero. Draw your weapons as you move through the rooms; there are Sanctuary Guardians to kill as you continue deeper down. Note the gold haul you usually find in their remains. Then ready yourself for the traps:

Spear Trapped Bridge: Approach this bridge carefully; three spears shoot out from the right. You should also strike the hanging oil lamps either side of the bridge to lessen the severity of a trap in the oil room directly below.

Oil Room: Set fire to the oil on the floor before you enter this room, or the oil lamps on either side of the bridge drop and roast you alive. Deal with the Sanctuary Guardians from a distance, coaxing them into frying in the room.

Bear Traps: Pass through the broken circular window into the ice tunnels, but watch yourself by the dead goat; there are bear traps to maneuver over or around.

Udefrykte: The beast Cicero wrote about in his journal waits for you inside the ice tunnels. Slay this demented troll with a mixture of ranged attacks, swipes, and dodges around the narrow cave with the chest in it.

Sanctuary Crypt: Retract the vertical spears by using the pull chain. Head down the stairs and face more Sanctuary Guardians as Cicero asks whether you'll let bygones by bygones. Then climb the stairs opposite, lift the door bar so you can easily exit the Sanctuary after facing Cicero, then open the door to the torture room.

Keeper of the Old Ways

Flanked by two dead skeletons, Cicero awaits your fury. You can immediately attack or remain silent and let Cicero explain himself; after all, you are the Listener. While lacking in clarity, Cicero tells you Astrid is a "pretender" who had no right to "blaspheme" the Night Mother; he was simply compelled through his sense of duty as the Keeper. Or this could be the rambling nonsense of a Fool of Hearts. You have a choice to make: kill him or leave the Sanctuary.

◊ **OBJECTIVE:** Kill Cicero, or leave the Sanctuary

Choose to slay this battle-hardened fool, who isn't quite as wounded as he may have let on; you have a real fight on your hands! Or, follow Cicero's advice and leave the Sanctuary, lifting the door bar and exiting quickly via the central chamber. As you step out onto the beach, your quest updates.

◊ **OBJECTIVE:** Report back to Astrid

Quest Conclusion

Back at the first Sanctuary, Astrid is anxious about the news of Cicero's demise. You let her know the jester is dead, either telling her the truth (if you killed him) or lying (if you left him alone). Leave Cicero alive, and an additional quest, Cicero's Return, can occur at the end of this series of quests. For now, there are other matters to attend to and important fellows to murder. Consult with Festus Krex for further details.

Postquest Activities

Dark Brotherhood Quest: Recipe for Disaster begins immediately. Your remaining side contracts are also available, and it is wise to attempt as many of these as you wish as early as possible.

PREREQUISITES: Complete Dark Brotherhood Quest: The Cure for Madness

INTERSECTING QUESTS: Dark Brotherhood Quest: The Cure for Madness, Dark Brotherhood Side Contract Quests, Dark Brotherhood Quest: To Kill an Empire, Side Quest: No One Escapes Cidhna Mine, Thane of the Reach

LOCATIONS: Dark Brotherhood Sanctuary, Markarth, Understone Keep, Nightgate Inn, Nightgate Inn Cellar

CHARACTERS: Astrid, Festus Krex

ENEMIES: Anton Virane, Balagog gro-Nolob, Markarth Guard

◊ **OBJECTIVES:** Report to Festus Krex, Question Anton Virane, Kill Anton Virane, Kill Balagog gro-Nolob, (Optional) Drag Balagog's body to a hiding place, Report back to Festus Krex

Carving the Cook

This quest begins once you complete Dark Brotherhood Quest: The Cure for Madness.

◊ **OBJECTIVE:** Report to Festus Krex

Astrid mentions there is one more target for you before the strike against the Emperor; she asks if you've heard of the "Gourmet," a chef and author of a realm-famous cookbook. The Gourmet is scheduled to cook for the Emperor. But not after you kill him, steal his Writ of Passage, and assume his role of master chef. Follow Astrid's advice and talk to Festus Krex for further details. When you visit Krex deeper in the Sanctuary, he tells you the mission is slightly more tricky than a simple slice-and-dice; the Dark Brotherhood don't actually know who the Gourmet is.

Krex then shows you a cookbook signed by the Gourmet; it is signed to a man named Anton Virane, who has been tracked to the keep in Markarth. Virane is the cook there. You are to find Virane, have him tell you who and where the Gourmet really is, and then tie up any "loose ends": You'll be assassinating two cooks for this task. After you kill the Gourmet, Krex hopes that you'll hide the body so any authorities take longer to reveal the Gourmet's identity and what you've done. You can ask any additional questions you wish (more about the Gourmet, the cookbook, or the Gourmet's location in Skyrim) before departing.

➤ **Uncommon Taste—Signed**

◊ **OBJECTIVE:** Question Anton Virane
♦ **TARGET:** Anton Virane, Understone Keep, in Markarth

NOTE Technically, you can head to the Gourmet's hiding place right away and kill him. However, when you return to Festus Krex, he still requires you to assassinate Anton Virane, so attempting this in order is recommended.

Travel to Markarth, enter the canyon city, and scale the precarious stone steps to the Understone Keep. Head west, between the two guards, and turn left before you reach the stairs to the Jarl's chamber. Enter the kitchens to the south, where Anton Virane and his two helpers are located.

When you speak with Anton (you must pry information from him before the murder), he insists he's a Breton; he's been previously accused of being a Reachman—and with the Forsworn activity in this Hold, this isn't the highest of compliments. But no matter; you're here to ask Anton who and where the Gourmet is.

After initially refusing to divulge this information, Anton changes his tune after you intimidate him and he realizes who you work for. He reveals the Gourmet is an Orc named Balagog gro-Nolob, who is staying at the Nightgate Inn. Then Anton nervously asks that you let him go. You can lie and tell him he's safe, or begin the execution right away. The only reason to lie is if you aren't quite prepared to assassinate Anton or if you want to mess with him.

◊ **OBJECTIVE:** Kill Anton Virane

Draw your blade and plunge it into Anton. Don't stop until he's dead. Do this only after he imparts the necessary information. You may use any weapon you wish (including magic or Shouts), and from your previous assassination experience, you should be aware that this attack is going to cause you problems within Markarth's walls. You can get around this by completing one of the following:

Kill Anton and then flee the city. Keep going until you outrun the guards. However, your bounty will still be high, and Markarth's guards will remember you if you return.

Become Thane of Markarth by completing the Thane Quest at this Capital City (detailed later in this guide). After the murder, you can explain to the guard who you are, and they let you off with a warning.

Elect to pay off your debts or give yourself up, since killing every guard in Markarth is impossible.

Or, you can rely on your trusted Sneak, attacking from behind or waiting and attacking him while he sleeps or when he's on his own.

NOTE For further details on committing murder in a Hold City, consult the Crime and Punishment section of this guide (page 64).

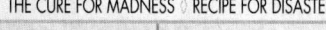

◊ **OBJECTIVE:** Kill Balagog gro-Nolob
♦ **TARGET:** Balagog gro-Nolob, Nightgate Inn Cellar

Needs More Assault

Offering pristine views of Yorgrim Lake to the west of Windhelm, Nightgate Inn is a perfect spot for a reclusive chef to write his books. Or for an assassin to commit murder. Journey to this out-of-the-way spot and search the side of the building for a trapdoor. Open it and drop into the Nightgate Inn Cellar. Balagog gro-Nolob is usually sitting in the bedroom down here, close to the mead barrels.

Frighten him with a flourish of prose or cut him down without conversation. Whatever you choose, your fight ends with Balagog gro-Nolob dying on the stone cellar floor. With no one else about, this murder is far easier to commit than that of Anton Virane. Pocket the Writ of Passage when you search his corpse. Balagog also goes outside and stands by the lake, so you can kill him outside as well. Do that, and the hiding place for the body is the lake.

➤ **Gourmet's Writ of Passage**

◊ **OBJECTIVE:** (Optional) Drag Balagog's body to a hiding place
♦ **TARGET:** Hiding place, Nightgate Inn Cellar

Hiding the corpse is an optional but recommended objective to complete, as it is straightforward and nets you a bonus at the end of this quest. Simply grab the corpse and move it to any of the indicated target spots in the cellar: behind a mead barrel or in an alcove. Your objective updates after you place it in a correct spot, of which there are plenty.

◊ **OBJECTIVE:** Report back to Festus Krex
♦ **TARGET:** Festus Krex, Dark Brotherhood Sanctuary

Quest Conclusion

Return to Festus Krex at the Dark Brotherhood Sanctuary, and inform him the deed has been done. Depending on your actions, he is impressed by your competence (if you killed both cooks and hid Balagog's corpse), and a little less so if Balagog's body is still lying where you killed him. Festus offers you a reward: gold for completing the quest, and the bonus of a ring if you hid the corpse. Then he suggests you see Astrid to commence the final stage of this grand and glorious operation.

➤ **300 gold pieces** ➤ **Nightweaver's Band (Bonus only)**

Postquest Activities

Dark Brotherhood Quest: To Kill an Empire begins immediately. Your remaining side contracts are also available.

TO KILL AN EMPIRE

PREREQUISITES: Complete Dark Brotherhood Quest: Recipe for Disaster

MAJOR SPOILERS

INTERSECTING QUESTS: Dark Brotherhood Quest: Recipe for Disaster, Dark Brotherhood Side Contract Quests, Dark Brotherhood Quest: Death Incarnate, Thane of Haafingar

LOCATIONS: Dark Brotherhood Sanctuary, Solitude, Castle Dour, Castle Dour, Emperor's Tower

CHARACTERS: Astrid, Festus Krex, Gianna, Nobleman

ENEMIES: Commander Maro, Emperor Titus Mede II, Penitus Oculatus Agent, Solitude Guard

◊ **OBJECTIVES:** Report to Astrid, Report to Commander Maro, Report to Gianna, Report to Gianna while wearing a chef's hat, Make the Potage le Magnifique, Follow Gianna to the dining room, Kill the Emperor, Escape the Tower!, Return to the Sanctuary

The Last Supper

This quest begins once you complete Dark Brotherhood Quest: Recipe for Disaster.

◊ **OBJECTIVE:** Report to Astrid

TIP Don't forget to wear the Nightweaver's Band if you acquired it during the previous quest!

Astrid realizes what you've accomplished and prepares you for the honor of assassinating the Emperor. You're to head to Castle Dour in Solitude and present the Gourmet's Writ of Passage to the officer in charge, Commander Maro. Astrid then tells you that you're going to prepare a special meal for the Emperor, with an extra ingredient that she hands you. Before you depart, you can ask for more details on Jarrin Root and other information. (Astrid tells you one taste of Jarrin Root is deadly, and she means it. Go to your inventory and eat it, and you'll drop dead.)

➤ **Jarrin Root**

◊ **OBJECTIVE:** Report to Commander Maro
♦ **TARGET:** Castle Dour courtyard, in Solitude

Journey to Solitude and locate the sprawling Castle Dour atop the hill. Step into the large courtyard and find Commander Maro waiting by the tower entrance. He certainly isn't going to let anyone in with the Emperor staying. There's no need to use violence or sneaking; instead, speak to Maro and show him the Gourmet's Writ of Passage. Maro reads the missive and is promptly most apologetic, realizing you're the "Gourmet." He allows you into the Emperor's Tower and requests you meet the castle chef, Gianna. Outside you can also eavesdrop on a conversation between two Penitus Oculatus Agents, talking about Commander Maro and his state of mind, now that his son is not only dead, but also apparently a traitor.

◊ **OBJECTIVE:** Report to Gianna
♦ **TARGET:** Castle Dour kitchens, in Solitude

This Soup Is to Die For

Enter the tower. Head left (east) and then right along (south) the corridor to reach the kitchens. Gianna is busily preparing the banquet feast and mistakes you for a delivery person. She is extremely apologetic when you reveal that you are the "Gourmet"! She requests that you don the proper attire; you can't very well cook without a chef's hat.

◊ **OBJECTIVE:** Report to Gianna while wearing a chef's hat

The shelves with the hanging garlic to your left (east) have a selection of chef's hats you can wear. Take one, and then replace your current headgear with it. Then speak to Gianna again. She would be honored to prepare your signature dish, the *Potage le Magnifique*, to your exacting specifications. Gianna now asks you for a series of ingredients you can add to the base broth.

➤ **Chef's Hat**

◊ **OBJECTIVE:** Make the Potage le Magnifique

Begin to choose the ingredients. You can:

Answer with expected ingredients, such as carrots, a splash of mead, Nirnroot, or diced Horker meat.

Answer with more "esoteric" ingredients, such as a sweetroll, Vampire Dust, a Giant Toe, or a septim.

Or remain silent and let Gianna figure out what she would add, as a "test" for her.

You can add as many expected or odd ingredients as you wish. When she asks whether the soup is done, tell her there is one final ingredient and hand over the Jarrin Root. Although she's unsure, your "special ingredient" makes it into the broth. She takes the soup in a stew pot to the dining room.

TIP You may elect not to poison the soup and plan a (usually) more violent method of slaying the Emperor, once the soup is served.

◊ **OBJECTIVE:** Follow Gianna to the dining room

Follow Gianna across the throne room, up the stairs, and along to the dining room, where you can hear Emperor Titus Mede II talking to three noble guests and taking a rather blasé attitude toward the murder of his cousin, Vittoria Vici. After Gianna takes a deep breath and prepares to present the Potage, you have this opportunity to strike.

◊ **OBJECTIVE:** Kill the Emperor

The Emperor prepares to have the first taste of the Potage le Magnifique, takes a few slurps, comments on its deliciousness, and then keels over dead. The same effect can be achieved if you quickly attack him. Either way, your bounty suddenly skyrockets, the Penitus Oculatus Agent yells for some help, and general pandemonium breaks out. If you've poisoned the Potage, when the Emperor dies, one of the Penitus Oculatus Agents yells that you and the cook have done the dirty deed, and poor Gianna is also attacked in the confusion. Fortunately, this can serve as a distraction while you escape.

◊ **OBJECTIVE:** Escape the Tower!
♦ **TARGET:** Tower battlements, above Solitude

Dupe le Magnifique

In the midst of the commotion, dodge any of the guests milling about and disappear out of the entrance to the south, which is only a few steps away. You appear on the Tower battlements, where a cluster of guards and a greeting from Commander Maro stops you. Instead of fury, Maro greets you with a contemptible glee. It appears you've killed a decoy of the Emperor; a member of your "Family" tipped off Maro about the operation! You were traded for the Dark Brotherhood's continued well-being, but Maro has grown tired of this little operation and now vows to butcher all of your clan—starting with you.

◊ **OBJECTIVE:** Return to the Sanctuary
♦ **TARGET:** Dark Brotherhood Sanctuary

To flee Solitude, you can simply dash past the Penitus Oculatus on the stairs, and then quickly descend the tower's spiral stairs to the ground level (don't exit into Solitude itself, unless you're trying to hide and blend in with the population, or you're using a spell or Sneak to obscure yourself). Continue down the stairs until you reach a lower exit out into Skyrim and the harbor under the gigantic stone arch.

Quest Conclusion

The Brotherhood Sanctuary has disappeared from your world map, making a direct Fast-Travel impossible. Instead, Fast-Travel to Falkreath and head along the road until you spot Penitus Oculatus carts on the road. Or, sneak through the backwoods for a stealthier approach. This quest concludes as you approach the hidden entrance. You hear the sounds of fighting, and Imperials swarm the area. Has the Sanctuary been compromised?

NOTE Remember that the Penitus Oculatus is a separate and distinct faction from the Imperial Legion. Your dealings with the Penitus Oculatus will not harm your standing with the Legion if you're siding with them during the Civil War.

Postquest Activities

Dark Brotherhood Quest: Death Incarnate begins immediately.

DEATH INCARNATE

PREREQUISITES: Complete Dark Brotherhood Quest: To Kill an Empire

◉ MAJOR SPOILERS

INTERSECTING QUESTS: Dark Brotherhood Quest: To Kill an Empire, Dark Brotherhood Quest: Hail Sithis!

LOCATIONS: Dark Brotherhood Sanctuary

CHARACTERS: Babette, Nazir, The Night Mother

ENEMIES: Arcturus, Penitus Oculatus Agent

◊ **OBJECTIVES:** Enter the Sanctuary, Search for survivors, Kill Nazir's attacker!, Speak with Nazir, Escape the Sanctuary, Embrace the Night Mother, Talk to Astrid, Kill Astrid, (Optional) Retrieve the Blade of Woe, Return to the Night Mother

The Brotherhood Burns

This quest begins once you complete Dark Brotherhood Quest: To Kill an Empire.

◊ **OBJECTIVE:** Enter the Sanctuary

Commander Maro's men have found your secret sanctuary and are currently ransacking it. This terrible sight becomes all-too real as you enter the road close by the Sanctuary entrance, where at least four Penitus Oculatus Agents are milling about. You can:

Engage them in furious and brutal combat, slaying them all where they stand for desecrating your home.

(Sneak) Or, you can sneak to the Sanctuary entrance without being spotted, ignoring the enemy so you can save your fury for the foes inside the Sanctuary. Head for the Black Door and quickly enter your home.

◊ **OBJECTIVE:** Search for survivors

There is a thick sheen to the air. Force (or sneak) your way down to where you usually meet Astrid. Here, you'll face two Penitus Oculatus Agents. If you're silent, you can overhear them talking about the spreading fire inside the Sanctuary and how an agent named Arcturus led some men deeper into the Sanctuary. Kill the foes quickly, and watch out when you're using fire-based attacks; the area is awash in spilled oil. The only way is down, into the flaming grotto, with more fighting against agents. You'll see the last moments of Arnbjorn's life; now in werewolf form, he tears into two agents before being felled by arrows. There is nothing you can do to save him. Quickly locate the dining hall, where Nazir (the only remaining Dark Brotherhood member you've found alive so far) is battling with more agents.

◊ **OBJECTIVE:** Kill Nazir's attacker!

◊ **OBJECTIVE:** Speak with Nazir

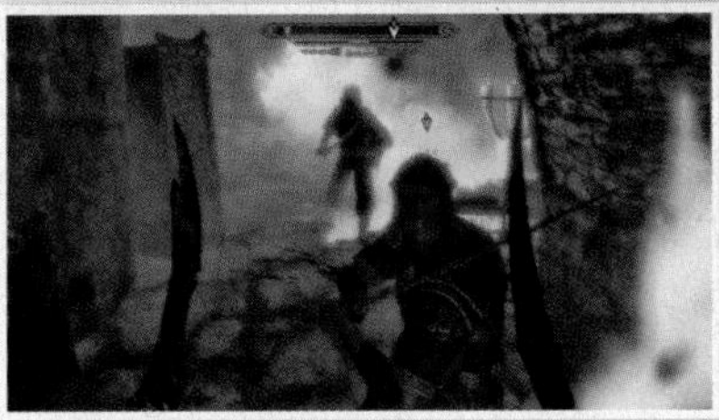

Arcturus, one of Maro's henchmen, is attempting to murder Nazir, so bound over to Nazir's location and help him dispatch this Imperial swine. Show no mercy! Next, kill any other agents who are near to either of you; then quickly stop to tell Nazir about the setup. Nazir had already figured this out. There's little time for chitchatting; you need to flee the Sanctuary before you're roasted alive!

◊ **OBJECTIVE:** Escape the Sanctuary

◊ **OBJECTIVE:** Embrace the Night Mother

Follow Nazir to the southeast, into the connecting corridor above the stained-glass window. Amid the turmoil and flames, the Night Mother calls to you. She tells you to embrace her, as she is your only salvation. Cut down any foes on your way to opening the iron door to the south, and enter the Night Mother's chamber. Open her sarcophagus, step inside, and fall asleep. The Night Mother causes her coffin to fall through the window. You survive in the coffin, and that gives Nazir a way out. It appears Nazir and Babette are maneuvering the coffin into an upright position. Just before the doors open, the Night Mother tells you to speak with Astrid, here in the Sanctuary.

◊ **OBJECTIVE:** Talk to Astrid

The Dread Lord Beckons

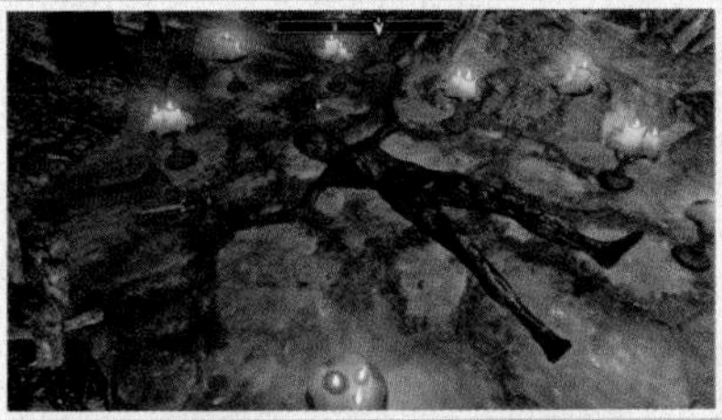

As you step out of the coffin, Nazir tells you to slow down. You can reply in whatever way you wish, but moments later, you should move out of the grotto and up the stone stairs to the south, past the charred remains of the entrance chamber. Turn right (west) and head north, where Astrid is waiting. Or more accurately, burned beyond recognition, surrounded by a flickering candle configuration used in the Black Sacrament. Astrid is almost unrecognizable but has much to say, and only moments left to say it. She betrayed you to the Penitus Oculatus, in return for their promise to spare the Dark Brotherhood.

You may react with seething rage, pity, or silence. Astrid knows what she has done was an unforgiveable mistake, and the Dread Lord Sithis shall judge her accordingly. She also knows that there is still a chance, that you could rebuild the Dark Brotherhood and start over again. She enacted a Black Sacrament and prayed for a contract. You lead this family now. Her Blade of Woe is yours, to see through the transfer of power, which is achieved by killing her.

◊ **OBJECTIVE:** Kill Astrid

◊ **OBJECTIVE:** (Optional) Retrieve the Blade of Woe

◊ **OBJECTIVE:** Return to the Night Mother

Quest Conclusion

Step over to Astrid's ruined form and swiftly end her life. Although she wishes you to take the Blade of Woe, it isn't necessary to kill her with it (but the weapon is well worth using from this point on). Once Astrid has found redemption in the Void, return to the Night Mother's sarcophagus. Your rebuilding of the Dark Brotherhood begins now.

➤ Blade of Woe

Postquest Activities

Dark Brotherhood Quest: Hail Sithis! begins immediately. Alas, all the members of the Dark Brotherhood, save for Babette and Nazir, perished in the battle.

HAIL SITHIS!

PREREQUISITES: Complete Dark Brotherhood Quest: Death Incarnate

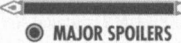

MAJOR SPOILERS

INTERSECTING QUESTS: Dark Brotherhood Quest: Death Incarnate, Dark Brotherhood Quest: Where You Hang Your Enemy's Head...

LOCATIONS: Dark Brotherhood Sanctuary, East Empire Company Warehouse, Katariah, Volunruud , Whiterun, Bannered Mare

CHARACTERS: Amaund Motierre, Babette, Nazir, The Night Mother

ENEMIES: Captain Avidius, Commander Maro, Emperor Titus Mede II, Lieutenant Salvarus, Penitus Oculatus Agent, Sailor, Solitude Guard

◊ **OBJECTIVES:** Talk to Nazir, Talk to Amaund Motierre, Board the Katariah, (Optional) Kill Commander Maro, Kill the Emperor!, Report to Amaund Motierre, Retrieve the payment, (Optional) Kill Amaund Motierre, Report to Nazir

Death to the Emperor

This quest begins once you complete Dark Brotherhood Quest: Death Incarnate.

◊ **OBJECTIVE:** Talk to Nazir

Only Nazir and Babette remain, as you come to grips with your Family's slaughter. Babette will follow Nazir's lead, so speak with him; he dejectedly believes this is the end for the Dark Brotherhood. But tell him the Night Mother has spoken to you again, and the original contract must be carried out. You're to speak with Amaund Motierre, and the true Emperor must be assassinated. While you muster a second attempt at regicide, Nazir recommends moving the Dark Brotherhood's Sanctuary to the one near Dawnstar, where you followed Cicero. You'll meet Nazir there afterward, ideally with a barrel full of gold.

◊ **OBJECTIVE:** Talk to Amaund Motierre

♦ **TARGET:** Amaund Motierre, Bannered Mare, in Whiterun

Amaund Motierre has taken up residence in the Bannered Mare, over in Whiterun. Travel there, and open the door to the room at the rear of the tavern. He's more than a little startled at your arrival, considering the news about the sacking of the Sanctuary. He babbles about having nothing to do with the violence to your Family and still wants the Emperor dead. You are here to honor your contract, so ask him where the Emperor is. Amaund tells you he's aboard his ship, the *Katariah*, now moored in the Solitude inlet. Upon your return after a successful assassination, Amaund will reveal the location of the dead drop that holds your payment. Ask him additional questions (about security and getting aboard the ship) if you wish. Demanding to know where Commander Maro is nets you an optional objective.

◊ **OBJECTIVE:** Board the *Katariah*

♦ **TARGET:** *Katariah* ship, Solitude inlet

◊ **OBJECTIVE:** (Optional) Kill Commander Maro

♦ **TARGET:** Wharf of Solitude docks, near East Empire Company Warehouse

(Optional) Additional Executions I

NOTE You may optionally kill Commander Maro at any point before the end of this quest, ideally before or after you assassinate the real Emperor.

Travel to Solitude's docks, close to the East Empire Company Warehouse, and search the wharf for the Commander. There's no time or point in talking; simply approach and kill him with a charge, sneak attack, long-range magic, or bow fire. Expect the nearby Solitude Guards to try and stop you. Fleeing the scene is usually the best option if you're spotted; the alternatives are to give up and go to jail or raise your bounty in this Hold considerably.

Bringing Down an Empire

Travel to Solitude's inlet, under the giant arch that the city rests upon, and locate the impressive galleon moored in the waters here. Swim alongside the vessel, dipping down underwater as you search for the anchor chain. Grab this, and haul yourself aboard the *Katariah*. You actually load *into* the cargo hold; don't climb the chain to the deck.

◊ **OBJECTIVE:** Kill the Emperor!

♦ **TARGET:** Emperor Titus Mede II, Emperor's Quarters, on the *Katariah*

TIP The *Katariah* is anchored in the Solitude inlet when this quest began and remains here for the rest of your adventure. You may wish to give the ship a thorough search for valuable items. Consult the Atlas for the important areas to check.

You clamber into the hold of the *Katariah*, and your quest updates. At this point, your usual infiltration plans commence. You may explore this ship using magical augmentations that make you harder to see or the enemies less alert. You can also sneak (see below) or simply wade through and clobber anyone who gets it your way.

You don't need to return to this ship, so inspect every chamber for items you may wish to claim. Work your way south along the lower deck, into the large central dining galley. Climb the steps and expect more enemies as you reach the jail area. You're attacking both sailors and Penitus Oculatus Agents. This floor also has a small armory and dormitories; additional foes and items can be found here.

Your first critical foe to face is Captain Avidius, who is usually in his cabin by the storeroom and ladder. Kill (or pickpocket) them, and secure the Katariah Master Key from his corpse; this makes navigating the locked doors much more straightforward. Otherwise, you'll need extremely impressive Lockpick abilities.

➤ **Katariah Master Key**

The ladder up to the deck isn't necessary; instead, move north to the gold door that was locked previously (Expert), and open it—either with your Lockpick ability or the Key. Repel the foes in this dormitory area, and sneak past or destroy Lieutenant Salvarus, who is stationed behind the gold door at the northern end of this floor. Climb up the nearby steps, and you're a room away from meeting the Emperor. The real one this time!

> **TIP** **Sneaking to the Emperor's Quarters:** From the initial room, follow the sailor as he meets his friend and wanders into the galley. When they enter, wait for another sailor to exit from the barracks at the hall's end, and head into the galley as well. Now wait for the guard to move away from the bar, and then sneak around to the chamber's right side. The bard with the flute moves out of the way, allowing a clear path to the stairs. At the top of the stairs, pick the locked door (Expert). You don't have to deal with the captain or the two soldiers in the central room!

> **TIP** **Further Fighting:** If you're in the mood for more combat, use the ladder up to the trapdoor near Captain Avidius's cabin, or the gold door opposite the door to the Emperor's Quarters. Exit out onto the *Katariah's* exterior deck. Here, you can slice into the Emperor's agents if you wish. This is one option as an escape route, too. If you want to avoid fighting the captain, you can sneak across the deck. It's much harder (try it at night), but you can go this way if you want to.

Approach the door to the Emperor's Quarters (Master). This requires an impressive Lockpick or the use of the Katariah Master Key. (If you didn't get it from the captain, Lieutenant Salvarus downstairs has another.) Step forward, and the Emperor greets you: Not with a blade or a string of curses but with a well-mannered speech. He knew Commander Maro to be a fool; one cannot stop the Dark Brotherhood!

You can:

Execute the Emperor immediately.

Or speak with him and give him a moment to say a few words before you run him through. He asks for a favor. Not as part of a Black Sacrament, but as an old man's dying wish. There is one who set this assassination forth, and the Emperor wants him punished for his treachery. You are to kill that person. You need not commit to this deed. Now the Emperor turns and waits for death. Oblige him.

➤ **Emperor's Robes** ➤ **Katariah Master Key**

> ◊ **OBJECTIVE:** Report to Amaund Motierre
> ♦ **TARGET:** Amaund Motierre, Bannered Mare, in Whiterun

Ransack the Emperor's Quarters for any books or other items you wish; the Emperor's chest in his bedroom has some good loot. Leave via the door in the northeast wall that leads to an exterior balcony, allowing you to dive into the waters and swim to safety, or backtrack and enter the deck, if you want more fighting. Whatever your route, travel back to Whiterun, enter the Bannered Mare once again. Speak with Amaund, and inform him that Titus Mede II lies dead. Amaund has just heard this information himself and is extremely pleased: As you shall be; there is a considerable payment inside an urn, in the chamber where you first met, back in Volunruud. Amaund wants you to leave now and never cross paths with him again.

> ◊ **OBJECTIVE:** Retrieve the payment
> ♦ **TARGET:** Urn, in Volunruud
> ◊ **OBJECTIVE:** (Optional) Kill Amaund Motierre

(Optional) Additional Executions II

If you wish to kill Amaund and honor the Emperor's wishes, you can tell him there's just one more matter to clear up and then tell him you're doing a favor for an honorable man. Or, you can choose to answer him differently (or remain silent) and attack him anyway! Turn your blade into him and dispatch this aloof traitor (grab his pocketful of gems). Your bounty in Whiterun skyrockets, so expect Guards to confront you moments after the murder.

Quest Conclusion

Amaund Motierre lived up to his part of the bargain; travel to Volunruud, dismantle any skeletal foes that greet you, and search the initial room where you met previously. Inside the urn is a considerable sum of gold!

➤ **20,000 gold pieces**

> ◊ **OBJECTIVE:** Report to Nazir
> ♦ **TARGET:** Nazir, Dawnstar Sanctuary

Now journey to the Darkstar Sanctuary and approach the Black Door. The door opens, allowing you down into the main chamber with the smashed circular window and large fireplace. Nazir is waiting for word on the Emperor. Inform him that you've done the deed, and tell him how much gold you were paid as a reward. You can be truthful or lie (it doesn't matter). Nazir recommends you go to Riften and search out a man named Delvin Mallory, someone Astrid already had you visit previously. This time, though, the "obtainer of goods" will refit this Sanctuary, using the money you earned, and make a true home for this Family once again.

Postquest Activities

Dark Brotherhood Quest: Where You Hang Your Enemy's Head... begins immediately, along with additional quests.

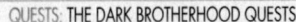

DARK BROTHERHOOD QUEST: SIDE CONTRACTS

The following 12 Side Contract Quests occur throughout the critical Dark Brotherhood Quests, and offer you several targets to assassinate. Some are accessible earlier than others, and all have a limited window of opportunity. For a complete list of how to unlock each Side Contract Quest, consult the Introduction to the Dark Brotherhood Quests, at the start of this chapter.

Side Contracts: Overview

The contracts Nazir gives you are the first in a long line of assassinations you can (and should) elect to attempt in the name of the Dark Brotherhood. Each requires you to seek out the targets, kill them, and then report back to Nazir (either in between or after completing any other quests). Although each assassination takes place in a different locale, the overall tactics detailed in the introduction to these quests on page 315 are worth employing.

> **TIP** Consult the section called Crime and Punishment on page 64 for a complete overview of how crimes, bounty, and assassinations work.

SIDE CONTRACTS: PART 1

Contract: Narfi

- ◊ **OBJECTIVE:** Kill Narfi
- ♦ **TARGET:** Narfi, in Ivarstead

Narfi is a beggar with unpaid debts. When you reach Ivarstead, cross by the rapids (or sneak around via the base of the mountain on the river's opposite side), and deliver a swift death to this unfortunate soul. You're out in the open and easily spotted, so be careful (or fleet of foot).

Contract: Ennodius Papius

- ◊ **OBJECTIVE:** Kill Ennodius Papius
- ♦ **TARGET:** Ennodius Papius, at Anga's Mill

Ennodius is usually found outside the settlement of Anga's Mill, near or inside a small tent close to the stream. You may converse with the paranoid layabout or simply end his life. Then check his corpse and possessions for items of interest, and depart.

Contract: Beitild

- ◊ **OBJECTIVE:** Kill Beitild
- ♦ **TARGET:** Beitild, in Dawnstar

Beitild is in Darkstar, either inside her house or on the thoroughfare. The guards don't take kindly to a massacre on their doorstep, so be careful (or run quickly afterward). Slay Beitild and take her house key; ransack the residence if you wish (mainly for the gold), and then leave.

➤ **Key to Beitild's House**

Quest Conclusions

- ◊ **OBJECTIVE:** Report back to Nazir

When you return to the Dark Brotherhood Sanctuary, move into the grotto area. Find Nazir to collect your payment for the first three contracts. Nazir is often in the banquet hall but could be anywhere in the Sanctuary.

➤ **Leveled gold (Narfi)**
➤ **Leveled gold (Beitild)**
➤ **Leveled gold (Ennodius Papius)**

Postquest Activities

You usually return to Nazir once Dark Brotherhood Quest: Mourning Never Comes begins.

SIDE CONTRACTS: PART 2

Contract: Hern

◊ **OBJECTIVE:** Kill Hern
♦ **TARGET:** Hern, at Half-Moon Mill

Journey to Half-Moon Mill and scout the small cluster of buildings for one with the vampire Hern in or outside it. Then deliver a quick and killing blow (ideally using any remaining Lotus Extract) for a one-strike death. Beware of Hern's vampire wife, Hert, as she fights to the death, too. Optionally ransack the Mill afterward.

> **TIP** Attacking during the day is helpful, as vampires are more powerful at night. Try to slay at least one of these bloodsuckers while they sleep, which usually requires sneaking rather than mayhem! For more information on vampirism (including a possible cure), consult the information on page 56 of the Training section of this guide.

Contract: Lurbuk

◊ **OBJECTIVE:** Kill Lurbuk
♦ **TARGET:** Lurbuk, in Morthal

Set off toward the town of Morthal, on the edge of the Karth River delta. Investigate the buildings until you reach the Moorside Inn, a known location where Lurbuk has sung before. When you find him, you can optionally request a "song of fear and death" before you run him through with an implement of your choosing.

Quest Conclusions

◊ **OBJECTIVE:** Report back to Nazir

Return to the Dark Brotherhood Sanctuary and locate Nazir. Collect your additional payments for side contracts four and five.

➤ **Leveled gold (Hern)** ➤ **Leveled gold (Lurbuk)**

Postquest Activities

You usually return to Nazir after Dark Brotherhood Quest: The Silence Has Been Broken begins.

SIDE CONTRACTS: PART 3

Contract: Deekus

◊ **OBJECTIVE:** Kill Deekus
♦ **TARGET:** Deekus, by Hela's Folly

Deekus left his old life and spends his time eking out an existence at a small camp with scattered stolen trinkets, close to the shipwreck Hela's Folly (which is near Yngvild), and braving the frigid waters of the Northern Coast. There isn't anyone near to hear Deekus's screams; this is an easy kill. Loot both the possessions, and the contents of Hela's Folly afterward, if you wish.

Contract: Ma'randru-jo

◊ **OBJECTIVE:** Kill Ma'randru-jo
♦ **TARGET:** Ma'randru-jo, near Solitude

This Khajiit is a member of Ri'saad's caravan, so the two are friends and will react accordingly if you attack. Ma'randru-jo is always found traveling with the caravan itself. Expect nearby friends of Ma'randru-jo to defend him when you pounce; longer-range assassinations are safe in this case.

Contract: Anoriath

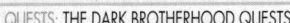

◊ **OBJECTIVE:** Kill Anoriath
♦ **TARGET:** Anoriath, in Whiterun

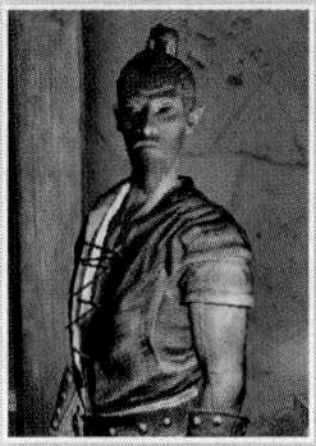

Anoriath and his brother Elrindir, have made a successful archery business in Whiterun, and they have a market store selling fresh venison. He's likely to be either hanging out at the Drunken Huntsman or selling at the marketplace close to the Bannered Mare. Although it may be fitting to kill him using your bow, melee strikes or other takedowns work, too. Beware of combat in cities; prepare to run once your bounty rises!

◊ **OBJECTIVE:** Report back to Nazir

Nazir's Rewards

Once you have fulfilled these three side contracts, return to Nazir and receive your payment. Then ask about any other contracts, and Nazir tells you about Agnis, your next kill.

- **Leveled gold (Deekus)**
- **Leveled gold (Ma'randru-jo)**
- **Leveled gold (Anoriath)**

SIDE CONTRACTS: PART 4

Contract: Agnis

◊ **OBJECTIVE:** Kill Agnis
♦ **TARGET:** Agnis, in Fort Greymoor

Set off for Fort Greymoor and assault this stronghold, which is initially teeming with bandits. Although sneaking is an option, your hunt usually degenerates into combat pretty quickly. Slay the bandits (or other enemies, should this location have been taken over) as you progress through the prison until you reach Agnis the cleaning servant, who is easily cut down.

TIP If you are ensconced in the ongoing turmoil of the Civil War Quests, this fortification is a key location. Instead of bandits, there are soldiers of the faction that controls Whiterun Hold (which starts in Imperial hands). If you're on the same side as the soldiers, you need not fight them, making this task a lot easier!

◊ **OBJECTIVE:** Report back to Nazir

Nazir's Rewards

Agnis is a single side contract; you must return to Nazir and inform him of your success before he offers you the next two contracts. Don't forget to train in Light Armor with him, if you have the coin.

- **Leveled gold (Agnis)**

SIDE CONTRACTS: PART 5

Contract: Maluril

◊ **OBJECTIVE:** Kill Maluril
♦ **TARGET:** Maluril, in Mzinchaleft

Prepare for a dungeon crawl and set off for the ancient and spectacular Mzinchaleft, introducing the assorted bandits to your style of combat and entering the giant underground structure. Battle down to a locked door and a guard outside. Search the guard for a key if you're having trouble opening the door.

(Lockpick [Average]) Use your prowess to open it, confront Maluril as he pours over Dwemer artifacts, and kill the wizard.

Contract: Helvard

◊ **OBJECTIVE:** Kill Helvard
♦ **TARGET:** Helvard, in Falkreath

Helvard is the Housecarl in the service of the Jarl of Falkreath. He is either striding about town or planning actions inside the Jarl's Longhouse with Siddgeir. Helvard doesn't feel Siddgeir is up to the task, which is probably why you're here. It may be wise to coat your blade in poison, as Helvard's quick death means you can flee without slaughtering the high-ranking town officials. Unless you want to.

> **TIP** The Jarl cannot be killed, and the only way to survive this with your integrity (and equipment) intact is to complete the assassination. And then run!

◊ **OBJECTIVE:** Report back to Nazir

Nazir's Rewards

Back at the Dark Brotherhood Sanctuary, Nazir is rapidly running out of targets for you to cull. But he has one last assassination, that of a formidable pirate known as Safia.

- **Leveled gold (Maluril)**
- **Leveled gold (Helvard)**

SIDE CONTRACTS: PART 6

Contract: Safia

◊ **OBJECTIVE:** Kill Safia
♦ **TARGET:** Safia, moored near the East Empire Company Warehouse

Journey to the East Empire Company Warehouse and look for the Red Wave, a pirate ship docked on the main jetty.

(Lockpick [Novice]) Pick the lock and enter the vessel after boarding it. Safia is in the hold at the ship's bottom. She seems to have predicted your arrival (if you speak with her) and prepares for a fight, with intermittent fleeing. Cut her down!

- **Leveled weapon**

◊ **OBJECTIVE:** Report back to Nazir

Quest Rewards

With the cutthroat defeated, you may return to Nazir and receive the final payment for your last side contract.

- **Leveled gold (Safia)**

Postquest Activities

This concludes Nazir's business for now, although once Dark Brotherhood Quest: Hail Sithis! has been completed, you may receive further work...just not from Nazir.

DESTROY THE DARK BROTHERHOOD!

PREREQUISITES: Commencement of Dark Brotherhood Quest: With Friends Like These...

INTERSECTING QUESTS: Dark Brotherhood Quest: With Friends Like These...

LOCATIONS: Abandoned Shack, Dark Brotherhood Sanctuary, Dragon Bridge, Penitus Oculatus Outpost

CHARACTERS: Alea Quintus, Commander Maro, Fultheim the Fearless, Vasha

ENEMIES: Arnbjorn, Astrid, Festus Krex, Gabriella, Lis, Nazir, Veezara

◊ **OBJECTIVES:** Report Astrid's death to a guard, Speak with Commander Maro, Kill everyone in the Sanctuary!, Report back to Commander Maro

Fail, Sithis!

> **NOTE** This quest begins only after you start Dark Brotherhood Quest: With Friends Like These...

> **CAUTION** Completing this quest will make any remaining Dark Brotherhood Quests inaccessible to you.

When Astrid first captures you and forces you to kill one of the three hostages in the Abandoned Shack, she notes that "someone isn't leaving here alive." That "someone" doesn't need to be pleading for their life with a bag on their head. Instead of spilling innocent blood, you can turn and attack Astrid. She is very strong, so ensure you get as many attacks in as possible before she drops from her perch and begins attacking you. When Astrid drops dead, gurgling "well done" as she falls, search her for the items listed here. Before you leave, you have the option to untie the three prisoners.

- **Abandoned Shack Key**
- **Blade of Woe**

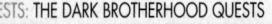

◊ **OBJECTIVE:** Report Astrid's death to a guard
♦ **TARGET:** Any Guard

Step out of the Abandoned Shack, situate yourself after your kidnap, and then decide where to journey to find a guard. One easy example is to head to Solitude and speak to any guard there. Or, if you don't want to travel, simply go to Dragon Bridge. Inform a guard that you killed the leader of the Dark Brotherhood, and they are stunned. You're told to report this action to Commander Maro immediately.

◊ **OBJECTIVE:** Speak with Commander Maro
♦ **TARGET:** Command Maro, inside the Penitus Oculatus Outpost, in Dragon Bridge

Journey to the Imperial settlement of Dragon Bridge and find the straw-roofed dwelling with Imperial banners out front, used as a Penitus Oculatus Outpost. Once inside, speak to Commander Maro, who is ecstatic at this turn of events and realizes it's time to strike against the Dark Brotherhood. He wants you to pay them a visit. Use the passphrase "Silence, my brother," and murder every assassin in that hole! Return to Maro afterward and expect considerable compensation.

◊ **OBJECTIVE:** Kill everyone in the Sanctuary!
♦ **TARGET:** All assassins, Dark Brotherhood Sanctuary

Mass Murder in the Sanctuary

Journey to the Dark Brotherhood Sanctuary in Falkreath, and step up to the Black Door. Answer the question "What is the music of life?" with the passphrase you just learned from Maro. If Maro hasn't told you the passphrase yet, this isn't available as an answer. Head down the steps into the Sanctuary, and begin the first of a series of fraught battles with each member of the Dark Brotherhood (Babette does not fight and is nowhere to be found). They instantly recognize you as an intruder and begin to attack.

CAUTION These toughened assassins are specialized fighters, and you won't just cut through them. Running through the Sanctuary is like signing your own death warrant. If you beckon more than one attacker at a time, you'll run into a large amount of trouble. Face them one at a time!

You meet the Dark Brotherhood in the following order:

Arnbjorn is in his chamber, prior to entering the grotto. He carries an enchanted warhammer and attacks with the ferocity of a wolf man.

Veezara is in the main grotto area and wields two weapons with amazing dexterity. He is a force to be reckoned with and should be approached with caution.

Gabriella (and Lis the spider) are in the laboratory area. Both are formidable foes. At this point, you can backtrack to the previously explored areas for a breather, if necessary.

Nazir carries a scimitar and isn't afraid to stick it between your ribs. He's holed up in the dining room chamber, which can be difficult to maneuver through.

Festus is the final member of the Dark Brotherhood to fall to your might. He guards the Chapel and has several nasty spells he doesn't mind casting on you.

Eventually, when the last assassin falls or between combat altercations, you may search the dead Brotherhood and ransack their hideout for more Shrouded outfits, weapons, and other common items.

- **Potions (various)**
- **Enchanted and Leveled Weapons**
- **Leveled Armor and Outfits**

CAUTION You can't waltz into the Sanctuary and carve up the Dark Brotherhood once you finish Dark Brotherhood Quest: With Friends Like These... The Dark Brotherhood simply murder you if you try an assassination within the ranks.

TIP Is this wanton carnage too much for you? Then you can flee the Sanctuary, only to return and finish the job at your leisure.

◊ **OBJECTIVE:** Report back to Commander Maro

Quest Conclusion

Head back to Dragon Bridge and inform Commander Maro of your penchant for assassination. He congratulates you on striking a blow against the Dark Brotherhood, which they aren't likely to recover from. Accept your blood money.

- **3,000 gold pieces**

Postquest Activities

All the remaining Dark Brotherhood Quests are now inaccessible to you.

PREREQUISITES: Complete Dark Brotherhood Quest: Hail Sithis!
INTERSECTING QUESTS: Dark Brotherhood Quest: Hail Sithis!
LOCATIONS: Dawnstar Sanctuary, Riften , The Ratway, The Ragged Flagon
CHARACTERS: Babette , Cicero , Delvin Mallory , Nazir
ENEMIES: None
◊ **OBJECTIVE:** Employ Delvin Mallory's services

That's Your Home

This quest begins once you complete Dark Brotherhood Quest: Hail Sithis!

◊ **OBJECTIVE:** Employ Delvin Mallory's services

Nazir says that you can use the large haul of gold you received from your previous quest to modify the Dawnstar Sanctuary. If you spend the funds on this place rather than on yourself and your inventory, set off to Riften and follow the Ratway to the Ragged Flagon, where the Thieves Guild members reside.

NOTE You may run into Cicero as you exit the Dawnstar Sanctuary for the first time after Nazir and Babette move there. Consult the Dark Brotherhood Radiant Quests: Cicero's Return for more details.

A Poisoner's Nook, along with an allotment of deadly plant-life.

Secret Entrance, shown from the exterior, overlooking Dawnstar.

The Listener's Bedroom, where clandestine and cunning plans are hatched.

Before Delvin's handiwork: The main chamber needs some attention.

Afterwards: New banners and stained-glass windows are installed.

Find Delvin and ask if he can repair and refit the Dawnstar Sanctuary. He says it will cost you, but he can help. Spruce up the place with any of the possible repairs:

IMPROVEMENT	DESCRIPTION	COST
New Banners	The black hand of the Dark Brotherhood now adorns many a wall.	1,000 gold pieces
Poisoner's Nook	An Alchemy Lab, complete with potions and special plants (that regrow and can be used in poisons) is installed near the tiny plant allotment upstairs.	5,000 gold pieces
Torture Chamber	Four prisoners hang here, shackled and ready to reveal the locations of their hidden caches.	5,000 gold pieces
Secret Entrance	Travel to and from the rocky ground above the sanctuary. The exterior entrance is next to the Dawnstar Fast-Travel marker, which makes it even easier to get in and out of the Sanctuary.	5,000 gold pieces
Master Bedroom	In addition to a place to hang your weapons and sleep, you gain some special items fit for a Listener.	3,000 gold pieces
	Total:	19,000 gold pieces

Quest Conclusion

The next time you return to the Dawnstar Sanctuary, any improvements will be made, which you can inspect.

Postquest Activities

Your critical quests are now over. As the leader of the Dark Brotherhood, there are Radiant Quests to complete from this point and an old friend to possibly meet up with....

DARK BROTHERHOOD RADIANT QUESTS

In addition to the Dark Brotherhood Contract Quests, the following jobs or quests occur throughout (and between) the critical Dark Brotherhood Quests and offer you a variety of objectives to accomplish. Some are accessible earlier than others. For a complete list of how each additional quest is unlocked, consult the Introduction to the Dark Brotherhood Quests at the start of this chapter.

NOTE Task names marked with an asterisk (*) do not appear in your Quest menu list, although objectives may.

HONOR THY FAMILY

Have you slighted a member of the Dark Brotherhood Family? They aren't concerned with you stealing anything from the Sanctuary, but they draw the line at violence. This objective triggers if you strike (accidentally or otherwise) any Family member once and then sheath your weapon. This is important; continue to brandish your weapon, and the whole Family turns hostile! After you calm down, you are instructed to speak with Nazir and pay the fine imposed for your behavior. Return with 500 gold pieces, and you may continue working with the Dark Brotherhood.

THE FEEBLE FORTUNE*

PREREQUISITES: Complete Dark Brotherhood Quest: Breaching Security (with bonus)

INTERSECTING QUESTS: Dark Brotherhood Quest: Breaching Security, Dark Brotherhood Quest: The Cure for Madness

LOCATIONS: Dark Brotherhood Sanctuary, Deepwood Redoubt, Deepwood Vale, Hag's End, Whiterun, Olava the Feeble's House

CHARACTERS: Dark Brotherhood Assassin, Gabriella, Olava the Feeble

ENEMIES: Forsworn, Frostbite Spider, Hagraven, Witch

◊ **OBJECTIVES:** Receive a reading from Olava the Feeble, Locate the assassin of old

A Token Gesture

Assuming you've killed Gaius Maro by following Gabriella's instructions to the letter and securing the bonus, when you speak to her at the Dark Brotherhood Sanctuary, she hands you a token, mentions a fortune-teller named Olava, and suggests you visit her for a reading. She quickly tells you about the problems that occur at the start of Dark Brotherhood Quest: The Cure for Madness. When you have a spare moment, head to see Olava.

◊ **OBJECTIVE:** Receive a reading from Olava the Feeble

♦ **TARGET:** Olava the Feeble's House, in Whiterun

Journey to Whiterun and locate Olava the Feeble's House, off the main path in the southern part of the city. Tell her you have a token for her, and she shakes off her bad mood, realizes you're a friend of Gabriella's, and agrees to give you a reading. She sees a Sanctuary but with snow and lit by the star of dawn. There are other shadowy figures she spies in the ether, and before you are Family, she sees a great spillage of blood. But before that, she sees a ruin ripe for the plunder—Deepwood Redoubt. Through there is a place named Hag's End, where an assassin of old bequeaths his ancient earthly possessions to you!

◊ **OBJECTIVE:** Locate the assassin of old

♦ **TARGET:** Dark Brotherhood Assassin (dead), behind rock panel inside Hag's End

Danger at Deepwood

Trek to the mountains west of Dragon Bridge, using any path to the north of Hag's End. The path disappears, forcing you to hike to the perimeter, which is flanked by a few large snow-capped stones. Head up the stairs and find the illuminated iron door in the southeast overhang dug into the mountains. There's a campfire to your left and an altar to your right. Forsworn instantly attack if they spot you. The iron door leads to Deepwood Redoubt's interior.

Pass a few tomb corpses and head through a gate and up some stairs, watching out for a dart trap (check the floor and step over the trigger plate). Turn left (southeast) and begin fighting through more Forsworn. There are bowmen on the bridge, so head right, through an old Nord crypt entrance (watching for swinging axes, which you can switch off using the lever at the end) and into a ruined embalming room. There is an iron door here and three Rune Traps. The iron door is locked (Expert); unlock it using your Lockpick skill or the key you find on the corpse of the Forsworn you must fight in the adjacent bedroom.

> **TIP** For such Rune Traps, try to avoid them or try to trigger them by coaxing an enemy onto them, dragging a body onto them, or summoning a creature onto them. In this example, the Forsworn in the bedroom is an excellent victim to lure onto the runes.

➤ **Deepwood Redoubt Key**

Once through the door, check the floor for a trigger plate to avoid getting hit by a wall trap, open the iron door, and cross the bridge you saw earlier. Head northeast. Move up the stairs to a larger iron door. This brings you into Deepwood Vale.

This hidden vale is a large, multileveled entrance to Hag's End. You'll probably face around ten Forsworn on the various balconies, turrets, and upper ledges as you progress. You may systematically check everywhere while fighting through these foes, race for the entrance to Hag's End, or take a more long-range approach, sneaking along the sides and firing your bow from range. There are wooden steps below a slightly sunken arch; use those, climb up the arch span instead, or use the stone steps farther south. Deal with the Forsworn boss on the upper level, then continue up and locate the iron door leading into Hag's End.

> **TIP** A frontal assault is highly dangerous, and the main entrance is a death trap. You're likely to be mobbed by four or five Forsworn, but this is an option for those with a thirst for blood (and health potions).
>
> Heading right, picking the lock of the lower door on the right tower, and sneaking in from the side allows you to sneak (or dash) to the stairs. Combat is safer on this side of the vale.
>
> Heading left, hop across the cliffs around the left tower and enter from this side. Although you must fight across the whole camp, the way the enemies meet you means you're in less danger than running up the middle with a sword and a death wish.

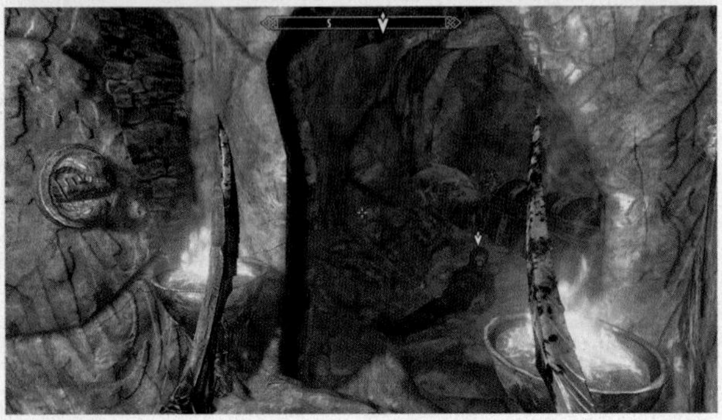

Open the double doors to the northeast and enter a witches' banqueting hall. To continue, dispatch three witches and a Hagraven. When you damage or pass the Hagraven, she will teleport away; you'll have to fight her again later. Open the door at the hall's opposite end; this leads to a dead-end room with more ice traps.

Look right (southeast) and climb the stairs, watching out for a trigger plate that launches a battering ram from the left. Disarm the hinge trigger to open the chest on the shelf in this area. Turn right (southwest), and battle your way through two more witches and the Hagraven in the alcove throne room. Ignore the raised bridge for the moment, and check for a handle on the wall behind the throne. Pull that, and a section of wall opens, revealing a hidden alcove. This is where the slain Dark Brotherhood Assassin lies. Take whatever treasure you wish from the corpse and nearby chest. The assassin's outfit is of particular interest.

➤ **Ancient Shrouded Armor** ➤ **Ancient Shrouded Gloves**
➤ **Ancient Shrouded Boots** ➤ **Ancient Shrouded Helmet**

> **CAUTION** You can't simply wander to this secret rock panel and use the handle to open it. The handle doesn't appear until Olava has read your fortune.

> **NOTE** At this point, you can finish your exploration of Hag's End or retrace your steps.

Assuming you wish to complete your investigation of Hag's End, use the lever next to the bridge to lower it. Cross and fight a witch, then ascend more stairs to a junction with a gate (Master) leading to a treasure chest and fire trap. Open this using the Hag's End Key, located on the mantel in the Hagraven's bedroom (in this hall) or on the Hagraven once you kill her.

On your right (northeast) is a handle. Pull it, and three portcullises open. Wait for the spear traps to recede before moving into a circular chamber with spilled oil. Treat the Hagraven and two witches to a burning (there's an oil lamp in the dragon statue's teeth), before yanking the chain attached to the statue, opening another portcullis, and exiting up into a grand hall, where the Nordic voices call you to a Word Wall!

➤ **Word of Power:** Slow Time

Conclusion

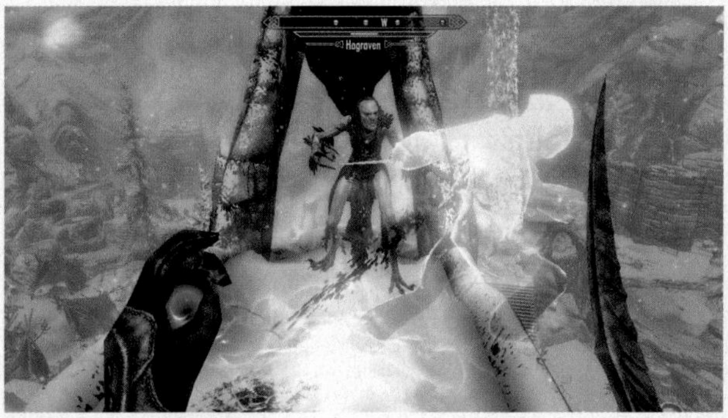

With a new Shout learned, open the door to Deepwood Vale. You emerge on a high ledge overlooking the exterior area. Your final Hagraven battle occurs here; watch for her "pets"—Skeevers, Frostbite Spiders, or even Trolls—that you must tackle before you can cut the old crone down. Inspect the Hagraven, as she carries the Hag's End Key, which can open the gate you saw earlier. Also check the sacrificed witch on the altar; here you'll find the impressive Bloodthorn dagger. Then face the waterfall, drop to the Hag's End entrance, and retrace your steps back into the wilds of Skyrim.

> **TIP** Wait! From the upper platform atop Hag's End, look for a little valley from which the waterfalls descend. Employ a Whirlwind Sprint Shout to reach this valley, and locate the chest with a pair of Unique boots.

➤ **Hag's End Key** ➤ **Predator's Grace Boots**
➤ **Bloodthorn**

WELCOME TO THE BROTHERHOOD*

NOTE This objective becomes available as soon as Dark Brotherhood Quest: Hail Sithis! concludes.

When you return to the Dawnstar Sanctuary, ideally after refurbishment, Nazir has managed to attract two Dark Brotherhood Initiates. You can select either of them to accompany you on your adventures; it would be an honor for them to serve the Listener. Further Initiates arrive if any are slain during the course of a more hectic exploration.

➤ **Follower:** Dark Brotherhood Initiate

CICERO'S RETURN*

NOTE Previously, you've had at least two opportunities to fight Cicero, most prominently during Dark Brotherhood Quest: Delayed Burial and The Cure for Madness. If you didn't defeat him during the latter quest, this is active.

If you kept Cicero alive (even if that meant lying to Astrid), he usually gives you a startling greeting outside Dawnstar Sanctuary the first time you leave the premises. After one more jest, Cicero says he's here to serve the Night Mother. From this point on, you'll find him inside the Sanctuary, where you can ignore or speak to him. You may keep him alive for the hilarity, or you may bring him on an adventure. Whether he returns from that adventure, of course, depends on what you equip him with and how helpful you are during a combat situation....

➤ **Follower:** Cicero

NOTE Cicero has a particular prowess at melee fighting. You can give him orders, and he comments when you visit certain locations and sings songs to himself.

THE DARK BROTHERHOOD FOREVER!

◊ **OBJECTIVES:** Approach the Night Mother, Speak with the contact, Kill the target

Murder for Mother

◊ **OBJECTIVE:** Approach the Night Mother

When you reach the newly claimed Dawnstar Sanctuary, the Night Mother tells you to approach her. Do as she asks, and she informs you that somewhere in Skyrim, the Black Sacrament has been completed, and someone wishes to pay the Dark Brotherhood for their services. You are to meet them and gain further information on that target.

◊ **OBJECTIVE:** Speak with the contact
♦ **TARGET:** Random person. Random location.

Travel to the location where the contact wishes to speak to you. They quickly hand over a payment, along with instructions on how to find their target and kill them. This is a simple assassination, and one that pays.

➤ **Leveled gold pieces**

◊ **OBJECTIVE:** Kill the target
♦ **TARGET:** Random person. Random location.

The contacts and targets are randomly chosen from the following lists (they won't be the same each time):

Contacts

A nervous patron at Candlehearth Hall in Windhelm

A wary outlaw at the Bee and Barb in Riften

A corrupt agent at the Penitus Oculatus Outpost in Dragon Bridge

A scheming servant at the Keep in Markarth

A desperate gambler at the Barracks in Windhelm

A blasphemous priest at the Temple of Kynareth in Whiterun

A dishonored skald at the Bards College in Solitude

An indolent farmer at the Vilemyr Inn in Ivarstead

An grief-stricken chef at the Windpeak Inn, here in Dawnstar

An unemployed laborer at the Frostfruit Inn in Rorikstead

Targets

A visiting noble at Dragonsreach in Whiterun

A big laborer at Katla's Farm

An itinerant lumberjack in Morthal, at the logging camp

A reckless mage in the Frozen Hearth Inn in Winterhold.

A seasoned hunter, just outside Falkreath

A poor fishwife, on the Riften Docks

A grim shieldmaiden walking the streets of Markarth

A traveling dignitary in Solitude

A coldhearted gravedigger, who tends to work in the Hall of the Dead in Windhelm

A beautiful barbarian, in Ivarstead

Conclusion

Approach your target, who is usually within the walls of a city or other highly populated location, and quickly dispatch them. To deal with any guards or others who see you, use the same techniques you did in previous Dark Brotherhood missions.

Postquest Activities

Once the target is dead, this objective automatically starts again. Return to the Night Mother and locate your next contact.

THE TORTURER'S TREASURE: PARTS I, II, III, IV*

Visit your newly constructed torture chamber, and you'll discover that Nazir has clamped four torture victims to the stone walls. If you speak to one of them, they give a variety of angry or frightened answers. Continue talking to the victim, and they eventually let you know of a hidden stash of treasure. Leave your victim to hang, and progress to your next victim, repeating this process until all four victims have revealed where each of their caches lie.

◊ **MISCELLANEOUS:** Take the hidden treasure

TIP There are four treasure stashes, so it's better to interrogate all four victims and collect each of the four stashes once, rather than interrogating one at a time. This treasure is accessible only after this is active.

Conclusion

NOTE Consult your Miscellaneous Quest menu and flag all four objectives so they are shown on the map. Then journey to each of them and uncover a Hollowed-Out Rock or Hollowed-Out Tree Stump at the specified location. Search this and pry out a sizable cache of gold, usually between 1,000 to 2,000 gold pieces per stash. This typically pays for the torture chamber's construction and leaves you with an extra 1,000 to 1,200 gold pieces after all four caches are cleared.

➤ **1,000 to 2,000 gold pieces (4)**

CIVIL WAR QUESTS

GENERAL OVERVIEW

The Civil War Quests automatically begin the moment you meet your ally during the escape from Helgen. From this point, you begin to make important choices with ramifications across Skyrim. You may choose to side with either the Imperial Legion or the Stormcloak Rebellion and complete quests for your chosen faction. Main Quests: The Fallen and Season Unending are affected by your actions within the Civil War; consult those quests for more information.

Picking a Side

Choosing a side can be done quickly or delayed until the very last moment. You can work with the person you escaped Helgen with—either Hadvar (Imperials) or Ralof (Stormcloaks). However, you haven't officially picked a side until you've visited the stronghold of your chosen faction and sworn an oath to the Imperials (in Solitude) or Stormcloaks (in Windhelm).

There is a last-minute change you can make after that: At the very end of Civil War Quest: The Jagged Crown, you can decide to bring the Crown itself to the enemy leader. At this point, there is no turning back!

NOTE **Cross-Referencing:** Do you want to see maps and learn more about the traps, non-quest-related items, collectibles, crafting areas, and other important rooms of note in every location during these quests? Then cross-reference the location you travel to with the information on that location contained in this guide's Atlas.

CIVIL WAR MAP

MAP LEGEND

Imperial Territory				Stormcloak Territory	
1 FORT HRAGGSTAD	5 MORTHAL	9 FORT SUNGARD	13 FALKREATH	16 WINTERHOLD	21 FORT AMOL
2 SOLITUDE	6 KARTHWASTEN	10 FORT GREYMOOR	14 HELGEN	17 DAWNSTAR	22 IVARSTEAD
3 DRAGON BRIDGE	7 MARKARTH	11 WHITERUN	15 FORT NEUGRAD	18 FORT DUNSTAD	23 SHOR'S STONE
4 FORT SNOWHAWK	8 RORIKSTEAD	12 RIVERWOOD		19 FORT KASTAV	24 FORT GREENWALL
				20 WINDHELM	25 RIFTEN

This shows the important tactical locations of Skyrim and who controls them at the start of the Civil War.

Imperial Headquarters: Castle Dour, in Solitude

Castle Dour, on approach from Solitude interior.

A strategic planning session.

Solitude is the capital of Skyrim (and Haafingar Hold) and is the one, true cosmopolitan city of Skyrim. Dominating the city's northern district is Castle Dour. Thick-walled and imposing, it protected its inhabitants from invaders. As the city grew, walls were added to surround the other, newer buildings. During a long period of peace, a palace was built for the Jarl. Castle Dour was converted into the Imperial Garrison, and the Jarl moved to the Blue Palace in the south of the city.

Important Characters: Imperial Legion

General Tullius

Tullius is a no-nonsense military man, impatient with politicians and compromise. He believes the best solution is to crush the rebellion ruthlessly. Although historically competent, his recent tactics have inflamed the tensions after he allowed the Thalmor to begin enforcing the terms of the hated White-Gold Concordat. He is practical and dedicated, but he lacks imagination and is impatient.

Legate Rikke

Rikke is widely respected by the Skyrim legions she commands and is strictly loyal to Tullius's orders even when she disagrees with them. Although from Nordic stock, she is a true believer in the rightness of the Imperial cause. She is both loyal and disciplined.

Hadvar

A loyal, brave, and enthusiastic Imperial soldier who befriends you during the escape from Helgen. He is related to Alvor the Blacksmith, in Riverwood.

Available Quests

There are a total of 12 different Critical Path Quests available during the Civil War if you side with the Imperials. One of these is an Overview Quest—the Reunification of Skyrim. All but the first quest have one or more prerequisites, as shown in the following table:

✓	QUEST NAME	PREREQUISITES
	Civil War Quest: Joining the Legion	None
	Civil War Quest: The Jagged Crown	Complete Civil War Quest: Joining the Legion
	Civil War Quest: Message to Whiterun	Complete Civil War Quest: The Jagged Crown
	Civil War Quest: Defense of Whiterun	Complete Civil War Quest: Message to Whiterun
	Civil War Quest: Reunification of Skyrim†	Complete Civil War Quest: Message to Whiterun
	Civil War Quest: A False Front	Complete Civil War Quest: Defense of Whiterun
	Civil War Quest: The Battle for Fort Dunstad	Complete Civil War Quest: A False Front
	Civil War Quest: Compelling Tribute	Complete Civil War Quest: The Battle for Fort Dunstad
	Civil War Quest: The Battle for Fort Greenwall	Complete Civil War Quest: Compelling Tribute
	Civil War Quest: Rescue from Fort Kastav	Complete Civil War Quest: The Battle for Fort Greenwall
	Civil War Quest: The Battle for Fort Amol	Complete Civil War Quest: Rescue from Fort Kastav
	Civil War Quest: Battle for Windhelm	Complete Civil War Quest: The Battle for Fort Amol

NOTE † = Civil War Quest: Reunification of Skyrim is an Overview Quest that continues until the end of Civil War Quest: Battle for Windhelm.

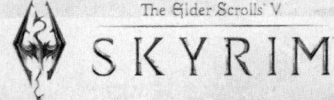

Stormcloak Sanctuary: Palace of the Kings, in Windhelm

Palace of the Kings, on approach from Windhelm interior.

The war room, during tactical planning.

Windhelm sits on the northern bank of the White River and is an imposing sight. The Palace of the Kings (also known historically as the Palace of Ysgramor) is an ancient stone fortress and the city's main keep. These days, the palace serves as the headquarters of the Stormcloaks, under the leadership of Jarl Ulfric Stormcloak, who sits upon the ancient Throne of Ysgramor. And so the Palace of the Kings is, as such, the center of the pro-Nord war effort in the Civil War.

Important Characters: Stormcloak Rebellion

Jarl Ulfric Stormcloak

Ulfric fought in the Imperial Legions during the Great War against the Aldmeri Dominion. Disillusioned over the Markarth incident, he founded the Stormcloaks as an underground group centered around now-proscribed worship of Talos. After killing the High King of Skyrim in the throne room of Solitude after declaring him a lackey of the Empire, he was arrested in surprisingly swift time, possibly aided by Thalmor agents. Only recently has he escaped the chopping block at Helgen. He is fiery and impetuous and a born leader, but he lacks the cool head of a strategist.

Galmar Stone-Fist

Galmar may be old, but he is still hale. A very experienced Nord warrior, he is also Ulfric's right-hand man and Housecarl. He served Ulfric's father and is more concerned with winning the war than the politics behind it. He is Ulfric's most trusted ally and acts as his field commander. He is a firm believer in the old ways of Talos, and distrusts High Elves. A grizzled bear of a man, he is imposing and gruff, but fair.

Ralof

A loyal, brave, and enthusiastic Stormcloak soldier who befriends you during the escape from Helgen. He is related to Gerdur the lumber mill owner, in Riverwood.

Available Quests

There are a total of 12 different Critical Path Quests available during the Civil War if you side with the Stormcloaks. One of these is an Overview Quest—the Liberation of Skyrim. All but the first quest have one or more prerequisites, as shown in the following table:

✓	QUEST NAME	PREREQUISITES
	Civil War Quest: Joining the Stormcloaks	None
	Civil War Quest: The Jagged Crown	Complete Civil War Quest: Joining the Stormcloaks
	Civil War Quest: Message to Whiterun	Complete Civil War Quest: The Jagged Crown
	Civil War Quest: Battle for Whiterun	Complete Civil War Quest: Message to Whiterun
	Civil War Quest: Liberation of Skyrim†	Complete Civil War Quest: Battle for Whiterun
	Civil War Quest: Rescue from Fort Neugrad	Complete Civil War Quest: Battle for Whiterun
	Civil War Quest: Compelling Tribute	Complete Civil War Quest: Rescue from Fort Neugrad
	Civil War Quest: The Battle for Fort Sungard	Complete Civil War Quest: Compelling Tribute
	Civil War Quest: A False Front	Complete Civil War Quest: The Battle for Fort Sungard
	Civil War Quest: The Battle for Fort Snowhawk	Complete Civil War Quest: A False Front
	Civil War Quest: The Battle for Fort Hraggstad	Complete Civil War Quest: The Battle for Fort Snowhawk
	Civil War Quest: Battle for Solitude	Complete Civil War Quest: The Battle for Fort Hraggstad

NOTE † = Civil War Quest: Liberation of Skyrim is an Overview Quest that continues until the end of Civil War Quest: Battle for Solitude.

Reconnaissance: Preliminary Planning

Halt! Before beginning a Civil War Quest that involves attacking a fortification, you may wish to employ some smart reconnaissance, visiting the any fort you'll be assaulting later in the Civil War and inspecting the exterior battlements, learning where the stairs and upper crenellations are. However, remember the following advice and caveats:

- Once you've accepted the quest that sends you to a Hold, a reconnaissance is too late; enemy soldiers attack if you approach the fort. However, if you arrive before you receive the particular quest to assault the fort, you can walk around. The soldiers will call you out as a trespasser, but they probably won't attack you on sight. For best results, sneak.
- You can visit any or all of the forts before the Civil War starts. This will give you a chance to inspect them and collect some loot from the enemies (usually warlocks or bandits) who occupy them before the soldiers move in.
- Finally, the "real" attack on the fortification doesn't start until the specific quest is running. If you arrived here earlier and tried to take out the garrison all by yourself, the enemy will be back up to full strength when the proper attack begins.

CAUTION There is one matter to be careful of: If you've been here before, you'll have a map marker to the fort. If you Fast-Travel there, the soldiers usually spot you immediately, and the battle starts early, and without your side backing you up! Therefore, it is always better to Fast-Travel to an adjacent location and meet up with your men first.

NOTE As always, study the Atlas section for each location.

Attacking Forts: A Fighting Chance

Whenever you're outside a fortified structure, attempting to get in, raze the place, and cut down the enemy guards inside, there are a few general strategies you should employ:

- Your main goal is to lead and support your soldiers. While you can attack from another entrance, you risk getting overwhelmed. You're likely better off if you stay with your men unless you're trying to achieve some tactical goal.
- Don't head into an interior part of the structure. Stay with your allies and give yourself room to maneuver.
- There's usually more than one entrance. Check the exterior walls for gaps, fallen sections you can leap over, or other debris for infiltration purposes.
- Move carefully and deliberately. If you get out too far ahead of your troops, the enemy may surround you.
- You have two basic choices: you can move through the fort and fight soldiers as you go, or find and secure one position and let the enemy come to you.
- Most entrances to strongholds are bolstered by barricades. Destroy these with magic or melee weapons if you want your allies to storm the area.
- Need a rest? Then back away and administer magic or potions before returning into the fray.
- Gain height. It is always advantageous to gain the highest ground, whether it is a turret or battlements section.
- Use any walls as cover, and attack foes grouped together with area-of-effect weapons. However, these same area-of-effect weapons can damage your own forces. Be very aware of who you're fighting!
- Stormcloaks are clad in dark blue. Those folks in red? Imperials! Make sure you know which side you're on!
- You can fight with long-range arrows or magic, or rush in with a melee or a combination of both. As long as you're killing foes, you aren't penalized for the way you're dispatching them.
- (Melee) Keep an eye out for archers on the walls. If you see one of your men fighting the enemy, help them—the enemy can't block both of your attacks at once.
- (Ranged) Find a good sniping spot, somewhere you can maximize your damage and have good sight lines. Ideally, shadow some of your soldiers so if your position is attacked, they can deal with the enemy while you back away and continue to strike from range.

Your mission is complete when the enemy garrison is all but wiped out. A few stragglers may remain, but these are optional kills.

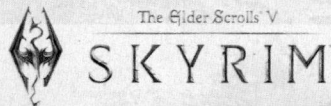

PREREQUISITES: Complete Civil War Quest: Compelling Tribute

INTERSECTING QUESTS: Civil War Quest: Compelling Tribute, Civil War Quest: Rescue from Fort Kastav

LOCATIONS: Fort Greenwall, Rift Imperial Camp, Solitude, Castle Dour

CHARACTERS: General Tullius, Legate Rikke, Imperial Soldier

ENEMIES: Stormcloak Soldier

◊ **OBJECTIVES:** Reunification of Skyrim: Regain the Rift, The Battle for Fort Greenwall: Join the men attacking Fort Greenwall, The Battle for Fort Greenwall: Take over Fort Greenwall by killing the enemy, The Battle for Fort Greenwall: Report to General Tullius, Reunification of Skyrim: Regain Winterhold Hold

Closing the Rift

◊ **REUNIFICATION OF SKYRIM CONTINUES**
◊ **OBJECTIVE:** Regain the Rift
♦ **TARGET:** Legate Rikke, Rift Imperial Camp'

Travel to the Rift Imperial Camp, and you're congratulated by Legate Rikke. Report for duty, and she says your next objective is Fort Greenwall. You are to meet the soldiers waiting near the fort for the attack orders, and then wipe out the Stormcloaks inside. Agree to the task and the quest commences.

➤ **150 gold pieces**

◊ **THE BATTLE FOR FORT GREENWALL BEGINS**
◊ **OBJECTIVE:** Join the men attacking Fort Greenwall
♦ **TARGET:** On the road, northwest of Fort Greenwall

Fort Greenwall is in the leafy woodland north of Riften. Legate Rikke's men are on the path to the fort's northwest, so approaching from the southeast can fail this objective (but not the quest). Join the detachment of Imperial forces stationed close to the fortification. After studying the Atlas entry of this place (page 958) and conversing with the leader, commence the battle, attacking from either side.

◊ **OBJECTIVE:** Take over Fort Greenwall by killing the enemy

Assault the fortification and help eliminate all the Stormcloak Soldiers. Enter from one of the following weak points or fortified positions, and note the impenetrable parts of the outer walls:

Southeast long wall: Southern end has a collapsed wall section that you can easily leap through. The middle entrance (on the road) is heavily guarded with barricades; you can maneuver easily around it.

Northwest long wall: The middle entrance (on the road) has numerous barricades, which are easily navigated around.

Southwest edge: Completely impenetrable.

Northeast edge: Completely impenetrable.

Whirlwind Sprint: If you've learned this Shout during Main Quest: The Way of the Voice, you can actually dash into this structure from the hills next to the western wall.

Greenwall Cave: Access this from under the rocky outcrop just northeast of the fort. This brings you up into the center of the fort's exterior, past the battlements, and is a good way to sneak in. Although this route allows you to slip past the enemy before your troops arrive, allowing you to bring down the barricades immediately, it is risky. Try running across the courtyard to the stairs next to the stable to gain the high ground, as you'll be right in the middle of the enemy!

Heading higher: The small courtyard on the ground is easily clustered and jammed with the influx of friends and foes. Escape this danger by heading east or west right away to the fort's higher edges. However, if you're a mage with area-effect spells, this courtyard is the place to lay waste to the enemy!

When you are victorious and the enemies routed, the Imperial forces remain to garrison this location. Meanwhile, you have other tasks to complete.

◊ **OBJECTIVE:** Report to General Tullius
♦ **TARGET:** General Tullius, Castle Dour in Solitude

Quest Conclusion

Return to Castle Dour and inform Tullius of your victory. This captures the Hold of the Rift and gives Ulfric reason to be concerned, what with the Empire so close to his doorstep. Your competence has impressed the General. You're instructed to meet Legate Rikke again; she's planning continued raids against Ulfric in Winterhold Hold.

➤ **Leveled Shield**

◊ **REUNIFICATION OF SKYRIM CONTINUES**
◊ **OBJECTIVE:** Regain Winterhold Hold
♦ **TARGET:** Legate Rikke, Winterhold Imperial Camp

Postquest Activities

Civil War Quest: Reunification of Skyrim is still ongoing. Civil War Quest: Rescue from Fort Kastav begins momentarily.

PREREQUISITES: Complete Civil War Quest: The Battle for Fort Greenwall

INTERSECTING QUESTS: Civil War Quest: The Battle for Fort Greenwall, Civil War Quest: The Battle for Fort Amol

LOCATIONS: Fort Kastav, Fort Kastav Prison, Solitude, Castle Dour, Winterhold Imperial Camp

CHARACTERS: General Tullius, Hadvar, Imperial Soldier, Legate Rikke

ENEMIES: Stormcloak Soldier

◊ **OBJECTIVES:** Reunification of Skyrim: Regain Winterhold Hold, Rescue from Fort Kastav: Meet the men near Fort Kastav, Rescue from Fort Kastav: Sneak into the fort, Rescue from Fort Kastav: Free the prisoners, Rescue from Fort Kastav: Take over the fort, Rescue from Fort Kastav: Report to General Tullius, Reunification of Skyrim: Regain Eastmarch

A Hard Fort Struggle

◊ **REUNIFICATION OF SKYRIM CONTINUES**
◊ **OBJECTIVE:** Regain Winterhold Hold
♦ **TARGET:** Legate Rikke, Winterhold Imperial Camp

TIP Stop! Before you return to Legate Rikke and begin this quest, study the Atlas entry for Fort Kastav (page 793).

Journey to Legate Rikke's newly established forward-operating base, just to the west of Dawnstar on the edge of Winterhold Hold. This camp has the same benefits as the one in the Rift. Report in with Legate Rikke, and she has your orders. You must infiltrate Fort Kastav, as the rebels are keeping some Imperial soldiers prisoner there. She aims to turn that into an advantage by using your cunning to find a way inside, free the men, and liberate the fort. This is an attack from the inside!

◊ **CIVIL WAR QUEST:** Rescue from Fort Kastav begins
◊ **OBJECTIVE:** Meet the men near Fort Kastav
♦ **TARGET:** Mountains southwest of Fort Kastav

Head up the rugged terrain of rocks and snow (Fast-Traveling from Nightgate Inn or Windhelm and then sprinting to meet your men are quick options, but without getting close enough to alert the enemy). You'll encounter a small team of four men. One of them is your old friend Hadvar, who has already had a reconnoiter of Fort Kastav, which appears particularly large and well defended in the distance, partly due to the mountain slopes keeping raiders away from the walls. However, there is a grate on the outside of the wall. It used to be buried in snow, and Hadvar reckons the enemy doesn't even know it's there. You must sneak in there, free the prisoners, and kill anyone you meet. Hadvar will wait to rush the fort as soon as they hear fighting, and you'll rendezvous in the courtyard. At this point, inform Hadvar that you're on it and begin the sneak.

◊ **OBJECTIVE:** Sneak into the fort

CAUTION Or, tell Hadvar you aren't interested in sneaking. At this point, you can take a direct (and more dangerous) approach: assault the fort via the main entrance and battle down to the prisoners inside. This is possible but isn't recommended, as it's slightly more risky.

The Enemy Within

Instead, crouch and begin heading along the snow-filled gully toward the fortification. You may wish to wait until after nightfall to minimize the enemy spotting you. Travel the gully's right (south) side, navigate easily around the barricades, pass the base of the stone tower, and follow the earthen bank until you spot a slope you can climb up, near three planks of snow-covered wood. Turn right, step over another small wooden bridge, and open the trapdoor leading to Fort Kastav Prison.

◊ **OBJECTIVE:** Free the prisoners

◊ **OBJECTIVE:** Take over Fort Sungard by killing the enemy

Assault the fortification and help eliminate all the Imperial Soldiers. Enter from one of the following weak points or fortified positions:

North wall: This is both impenetrable and treacherous, being close to extremely steep and rocky ground. However, you can scale the jagged rocks to the northeast and attack from here (ranged weapons only).

East wall: In the northeast corner, the battlements have fallen, allowing you to leap atop them. There is an often-overlooked entrance arch, too, which is perfect for a surprise attack!

Tower entrance: Located outside the walls on the fort's southeast corner, close to the oubliette tower. Enter this door and scale the spiral stairs to the tower's top. You can rain down ranged fire almost with impunity!

Oubliette tower: This isn't worth ascending, as your view isn't good for soldier dispatching.

South wall: The terrain is steep and unforgiving, but there is a fire pit balcony with an easily assaulted archway entrance here.

Southwest muster: The southwest corner wall has an exterior pipe leading into the Muster. From here you can sneak or rush through and up onto the exterior battlements.

West wall: The main entrance where your brethren usually attack from. It is the most problematic location because of the barricades and because you're fighting uphill, but it leads through an archway and eventually onto the battlements.

After you win the battle, the Stormcloak forces remain to garrison this location. Meanwhile, you have other plans.

◊ **LIBERATION OF SKYRIM CONTINUES**
◊ **OBJECTIVE:** Report to Ulfric Stormcloak
♦ **TARGET:** Ulfric Stormcloak, in Palace of the Kings in Windhelm

Quest Conclusion

Return to the Palace of the Kings and inform Ulfric of your victory. This captures the Hold of the Reach and stopped the raping of her silver mines. For your valor and battle prowess, you are named Ice-Hammer. Take the earned weapon as a gift and symbol of this new rank. You're instructed to meet Galmar again; he's planning some surprises for General Tullius in Hjaalmarch.

NOTE This title may change if you ran away from Whiterun or gained a Hold from a peace treaty during Main Quest: Season Unending. Therefore, the title noted may differ from the one you received.

➤ **Leveled Shield**

◊ **OBJECTIVE:** Liberate Hjaalmarch
♦ **TARGET:** Galmar Stone-Fist, Hjaalmarch Stormcloak Camp

Postquest Activities

Civil War Quest: Liberation of Skyrim is still ongoing. Civil War Quest: A False Front begins shortly.

LIBERATION OF SKYRIM (CONTINUED) – A FALSE FRONT

PREREQUISITES: Complete Civil War Quest: The Battle for Fort Sungard

INTERSECTING QUESTS: Civil War Quest: The Battle for Fort Sungard, Civil War Quest: The Battle for Fort Snowhawk

LOCATIONS: Dragon Bridge, Four Shields Tavern, Hjaalmarch Stormcloak Camp, Morthal, Highmoon Hall, Rorikstead, Frostfruit Inn

CHARACTERS: Faida, Galmar Stone-Fist, Legate Taurinus Duilis, Mralki

ENEMIES: Imperial Courier

◊ **OBJECTIVES:** Liberation of Skyrim: Liberate Hjaalmarch, A False Front: Find the Imperial Courier, A False Front: Retrieve the Imperial Courier's package, A False Front: Bring the documents to Galmar Stone-Fist, A False Front: Bring the forged documents to Legate Taurinus Duilis, Liberation of Skyrim: Liberate Hjaalmarch

Delivering the Doctored Documents

◊ **LIBERATION OF SKYRIM CONTINUES**
◊ **OBJECTIVE:** Liberate Hjaalmarch
♦ **TARGET:** Galmar Stone-Fist, Hjaalmarch Stormcloak Camp

Journey to Galmar's newly established forward-operating base, to the west and slightly north of Morthal, on the Hold's edge. This camp has the same benefits as the one in the Reach. Report in with Galmar, who has your orders. You are to deliver some false orders to the Imperial Legate in Morthal. But to make that happen, Galmar needs to get his hands on some Imperial orders to make forgeries. Fortunately, Imperial runners make frequent stops at the inns in Dragon Bridge and Rorikstead. Head to one of those places and convince the innkeeper to help you.

◊ **A FALSE FRONT BEGINS**
◊ **OBJECTIVE:** Find the Imperial Courier
♦ **TARGET:** Barkeep of Four Shields Tavern or Frostfruit Inn

There are two inns at the locations Galmar mentioned: The Four Shields Tavern is in Dragon Bridge, along the main road to the west of Solitude and operated by Faida. The Frostfruit Inn is one of the prominent structures of Rorikstead and has an innkeeper named Mralki. Journey to either of these locations and speak to the innkeeper, asking whether they've seen any Imperial Couriers. After an evasive response, you can:

(Persuade) Warn that the courier's life is in danger.

(Bribe) Offer some gold for the information.

(Intimidate) Mention that you can get rough if you need to.

Or wait around in the inn.

If you succeed using any of the first three options, the barkeep tells you that the courier just left and that you can probably catch him. Or you can wait in the inn for the courier to return. The courier is halfway between both the inns on the main road. Even if you're unsuccessful, you can elect to run after or wait for the courier (the only difference is the objective won't update). You must visit one of the inns before finding the courier.

◊ **OBJECTIVE:** Retrieve the Imperial Courier's package
♦ **TARGET:** Courier, inside or between either inn

The courier travels to and from each inn. He loiters at the inn for an hour, sleeps there for an hour, and then heads back to the other inn. He repeats this route until you intercept him, either by waiting inside the inn or finding him on the road. At this point, you have a three options:

(Pickpocket) Pickpocket the documents while the courier is unaware.

Speak to the courier, demanding the documents. He refuses and you must kill him.

Simply kill the courier and loot the corpse for the documents.

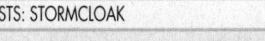

CAUTION

Watch out! Killing the courier in either town is a crime. In Dragon Bridge, you may have to contend with both the guards and the elite Penitus Oculatus. In Rorikstead, Stormcloak Guards have taken the town, and may even kill the courier if they spot him. If you prefer to do the deed yourself, meet him on the road, where his death won't arouse suspicion.

➤ **Imperial Documents**

◊ **OBJECTIVE:** Bring the documents to Galmar Stone-Fist
♦ **TARGET:** Galmar Stone-Fist, Hjaalmarch Stormcloak Camp

After returning to Galmar, he reads the documents, noting the Imperials know more about the Stormcloak plans than was expected. He "corrects" the documents with false information and orders you to present them to the Imperial Legate in Morthal, throwing him off the trail.

◊ **OBJECTIVE:** Bring the forged documents to Legate Taurinus Duilis
♦ **TARGET:** Legate Taurinus Duilis, Highmoon Hall, in Morthal

Quest Conclusion

You'll usually find the Legate inside Highmoon Hall, the Jarl's residence inside the Hold City of Morthal, although he sometimes walks the pathways around the city. Present some important documents to him. He reads over them, noting the troop movements (false) and rewarding you with a little gold for a drink at the Moorside Inn for your troubles. This quest now concludes.

➤ **5 gold pieces**

TIP There's no need to change from your Stormcloak garb when you meet Taurinus; you quickly make up a verbal ruse that it's easier to "sneak past the enemy" clad in their colors.

◊ **LIBERATION OF SKYRIM CONTINUES**
◊ **OBJECTIVE:** Liberate Hjaalmarch
♦ **TARGET:** Galmar Stone-Fist, Hjaalmarch Stormcloak Camp

Postquest Activities

Civil War Quest: Liberation of Skyrim is still ongoing. Civil War Quest: The Battle for Fort Snowhawk now begins.

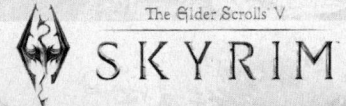

PREREQUISITES: Complete Civil War Quest: A False Front

INTERSECTING QUESTS: Civil War Quest: A False Front, Civil War Quest: The Battle for Fort Hraggstad

LOCATIONS: Fort Snowhawk , Fort Snowhawk Tower , Hjaalmarch Stormcloak Camp, Windhelm, Palace of the Kings

CHARACTERS: Galmar Stone-Fist, Jarl Ulfric Stormcloak, Stormcloak Soldier

ENEMIES: Imperial Soldier

◊ **OBJECTIVES:** Liberation of Skyrim: Liberate Hjaalmarch, The Battle for Fort Snowhawk: Join the men attacking Fort Snowhawk, The Battle for Fort Snowhawk: Take over Fort Snowhawk by killing the enemy, The Battle for Fort Snowhawk: Report to Ulfric Stormcloak, Liberation of Skyrim: Liberate Haafingar

March on Hjaalmarch

◊ **LIBERATION OF SKYRIM CONTINUES**
◊ **OBJECTIVE:** Liberate Hjaalmarch
♦ **TARGET:** Galmar Stone-Fist, Hjaalmarch Stormcloak Camp

Travel to the Hjaalmarch Stormcloak Camp, where Galmar Stone-Fist congratulates you. Report for duty, and he says your next objective is Fort Snowhawk. You are to meet your Brothers waiting nearby for the attack orders and then wipe out the Legion inside. Agree to the task, and the quest commences.

◊ **THE BATTLE FOR FORT SNOWHAWK BEGINS**
◊ **OBJECTIVE:** Join the men attacking Fort Snowhawk
♦ **TARGET:** On the road, southwest of Fort Snowhawk

Fort Snowhawk is atop a shallow hill just west of Morthal, close to craggy peaks to the southwest. This is where your band of Brothers are coming from. If you approach the fort from the northeast, you may attract the enemy's attention and commence the battle too soon. Instead, take the road from Morthal and meet up with your Brothers on the ridge south of the fort. After studying the Atlas entry of this place (on page 730) and conversing with the leader, commence the battle.

◊ **OBJECTIVE:** Take over Fort Snowhawk by killing the enemy

Assault the fortification and help eliminate all the Imperial Soldiers in the garrison. Enter from one of the following weak points or fortified positions:

Southwest wall: This is dominated by two turrets and a main entrance from the road. It is the usual place to assault and has multiple barricades to crush or dodge. It is also where the battle is fiercest. If you're specializing in melee weapons, take out those barricades and clear a path. If you're using ranged weapons, pick off foes on the walls to help your men advance.

Northwest wall: You can navigate the crumbling wall to the west by the turret if you jump precisely, and there are numerous low or ruined sections along the wall you can easily head across. This area is extremely easy to penetrate.

Northeast wall: The crumbling eastern wall has several places from which you can infiltrate. Although there's a cave into Fort Snowhawk Prison by the shallow lake, this leads to a ledge that's too high to climb onto; this is only an exit. Ignore this cave completely; you must focus on the fort's exterior and assault.

Southeast wall: There's a gap in the southeast wall at the end of the wooden fencing.

Central tower: Rush the southwest entrance and head for the door, sprinting up the interior spiral steps and taking the ladder to the exterior top of the central tower. This offers exceptional sniping views all around you.

Staying outside: Although the central tower is worth climbing if you're stealthy, the rest of the keep is highly dangerous: Don't waste time fighting foes on your own!

Upper roof: This has some excellent lines of sight and relatively few soldiers to attack you. To reach this position, head for the southeast courtyard, climbing the stairs there and heading across the walls.

When you are victorious and the enemies routed, the Stormcloak forces remain to garrison this location. Meanwhile, you have other tasks to complete.

◊ **OBJECTIVE:** Report to Ulfric Stormcloak
♦ **TARGET:** Ulfric Stormcloak, Palace of the Kings in Windhelm

Quest Conclusion

Return to the Palace of the Kings and inform Ulfric of your victory. This captures the Hold of Hjaalmarch, which makes Tullius nervous. As soon as the Stormcloaks are able, the march on Solitude will begin. Your savagery and dedication has earned Ulfric's respect, and he numbers you among his kin. You shall now be known as Stormblade. You are handed a special weapon on behalf of the Sons and Daughters of Skyrim. Then you're told to meet Galmar Stone-Fist again; he's finished setting up camp in Haafingar Hold.

NOTE This title may change if you ran away from Whiterun or gained a Hold from a peace treaty during Main Quest: Season Unending. Therefore, the title noted may differ from the one you received.

➤ **Leveled Armor**

◊ **LIBERATION OF SKYRIM CONTINUES**
◊ **OBJECTIVE:** Liberate Haafingar
♦ **TARGET:** Galmar Stone-Fist, Haafingar Imperial Camp

Postquest Activities

Civil War Quest: Liberation of Skyrim is still going. Civil War Quest: The Battle for Fort Hraggstad begins momentarily.

LIBERATION OF SKYRIM (CONTINUED) – THE BATTLE FOR FORT HRAGGSTAD

PREREQUISITES: Complete Civil War Quest: The Battle for Fort Snowhawk

INTERSECTING QUESTS: Civil War Quest: The Battle for Fort Snowhawk, Civil War Quest: Battle for Solitude

LOCATIONS: Fort Hraggstad, Haafingar Stormcloak Camp

CHARACTERS: Galmar Stone-Fist, Stormcloak Soldier

ENEMIES: Imperial Soldier

◊ **OBJECTIVES:** Liberation of Skyrim: Liberate Haafingar, The Battle for Fort Hraggstad: Join the men attacking Fort Hraggstad , The Battle for Fort Hraggstad: Take over Fort Hraggstad by killing the enemy, Liberation of Skyrim: Liberate Haafingar

Breaking Haafingar

◊ **LIBERATION OF SKYRIM CONTINUES**
◊ **OBJECTIVE:** Liberate Haafingar
♦ **TARGET:** Galmar Stone-Fist, Haafingar Stormcloak Camp

Take the main path between Dragon Bridge and Solitude. Locate Galmar's Stormcloak Camp, which overlooks the Karth River. Head into Galmar's tent and speak with him. He tells you that your objective is an enemy-held fort. You are to meet the soldiers waiting nearby for the attack orders and then wipe out the Imperial Legion forces inside. Agree to the task, and the quest commences.

◊ **THE BATTLE FOR FORT HRAGGSTAD BEGINS**
◊ **OBJECTIVE:** Join the men attacking Fort Hraggstad
♦ **TARGET:** On the road, east of Fort Hraggstad

Fort Hraggstad is perched on a snowy mountain overlooking the Sea of Ghosts, with a sheer cliff to the north. Galmar's brothers are on the flat rocks just southeast of the fortification, so approaching from the west may fail this objective (but not the ongoing quest). Join the Stormcloak Soldiers creeping up on the fort if you don't wish to assault it alone. After studying the Atlas entry of this place (page 703) and conversing with the leader, commence the battle.

◊ **OBJECTIVE:** Take over Fort Hraggstad by killing the enemy

Charge the fortification and help eliminate all of the Imperial Soldiers. Enter from one of the following weak points or fortified positions:

Northeast wall: This is mostly impenetrable, but there is a gap just east of the northern tower turret that allows easy access into the grounds.

Southeast wall: The main road and entrance (dotted with barricades) are the usual swarm points for your forces but are heavily guarded.

Southwest wall: This wall section from tower to tower is impressively impenetrable.

Northwest wall: The dangerous rocky terrain and cliff edge make this impenetrable wall well worth ignoring.

Advantage point: The cluster of rocks to the west overlooks the fort and is excellent for long-range attacks. Another option is the tall fort tower in the fort's northern section, although that requires battling to reach.

Quest Conclusion

When the enemy finally succumbs to your might and the fort falls to the Stormcloaks, your forces remain to garrison this location.

◊ **LIBERATION OF SKYRIM CONTINUES**
◊ **OBJECTIVE:** Liberate Haafingar
♦ **TARGET:** Galmar Stone-Fist, Haafingar Stormcloak Camp

Postquest Activities

Civil War Quest: Liberation of Skyrim is almost over. Civil War Quest: Battle for Solitude begins shortly.

LIBERATION OF SKYRIM (CONCLUDES) – BATTLE FOR SOLITUDE

MAJOR SPOILERS

PREREQUISITES: Complete Civil War Quest: The Battle for Fort Hraggstad

INTERSECTING QUESTS: Civil War Quest: The Battle for Fort Hraggstad

LOCATIONS: Haafingar Stormcloak Camp, Solitude, Castle Dour

CHARACTERS: Galmar Stone-Fist, Jarl Ulfric Stormcloak, Stormcloak Soldier

ENEMIES: General Tullius, Imperial Soldier, Legate Rikke

◊ **OBJECTIVES:** Liberation of Skyrim: Liberate Haafingar, Battle for Solitude: Get your orders from Ulfric Stormcloak, Battle for Solitude: Take over Solitude by killing the enemy, Battle for Solitude: Force General Tullius to surrender

The Fall of Solitude

◊ **LIBERATION OF SKYRIM CONTINUES**
◊ **OBJECTIVE:** Liberate Haafingar
♦ **TARGET:** Galmar Stone-Fist, Haafingar Stormcloak Camp

TIP Stop! Before mounting a final assault on Solitude, consider studying the streets, uncovering routes from the main gates to Castle Dour, using the route that passes by the Hall of the Dead, so you're completely familiar with the street layout. It is wise to add any helpful inventory equipment (such as Magicka-, Health-, or Stamina-augmenting items) before commencing this quest.

Maneuver back to the Haafingar Stormcloak Camp and speak with Galmar Stone-Fist. He is extremely proud of your accomplishments and rewards you accordingly. Then he tells you that the Brothers of Skyrim are gathering to attack Solitude, and you're part of it!

➤ **150 gold pieces**

◊ **BATTLE FOR SOLITUDE BEGINS**
◊ **OBJECTIVE:** Get your orders from Ulfric Stormcloak
♦ **TARGET:** Great gate of Solitude

Travel up the road toward the large entrance gate to Solitude, which the Stormcloaks have already razed. The flame catapults are bombarding the embattled city in great plumes of flame, and the air is thick with smoke and Imperial fear.

Rush forward (east) through the wreckage, to the towering gate, where Ulfric Stormcloak is yelling words of encouragement to his forces. This is the time to deliver the final blow to the hated Imperials! Fear neither pain nor darkness, for Sovngarde awaits those who die with weapons in their hands and courage in their hearts!

◊ **OBJECTIVE:** Take over Solitude by killing the enemy

The stronghold for the Imperials is on fire, and the chaos of fighting General Tullius's remaining men and navigating the various barriers can be confusing. Learn the various locations you must fight through:

Initial courtyard: The Winking Skeever and other merchant stores are closed, and the ground is littered with fire. Push forward on either side of the flaming obstacles.

East to market: The stone ramp up to the forge area is blocked by debris, forcing you to head east, passing the market stalls to your right and heading for a barricade under the arched parapet bridge.

The Hall of the Dead: You can scramble along the rocks to the left, or hack the barricade and head along the left side of the Hall of the Dead building. Debris and enemy troops are everywhere.

Castle courtyard: The eventual fight continues with a left (north) turn up the main avenue and into the flaming courtyard outside Castle Dour.

CAUTION The flow of enemy soldiers does not stop! Therefore, it is imperative you reach Castle Dour as quickly as possible.

◊ **OBJECTIVE:** Force General Tullius to surrender

A Little More Than a Rebellion

Push into Castle Dour with Galmar Stone-Fist and Ulfric Stormcloak. Both General Tullius and Legate Rikke are cornered in this castle. Ulfric turns to his old friend and tells you war always comes down to a single truth-laden moment. Rikke won't stand down, so you're forced to kill her. Race forward and begin attacking Tullius or Rikke, choosing the foe your allies aren't fighting so you can bring the Imperial leaders to their knees more quickly. Step back if you're being wounded too severely.

Tullius splutters through mouthfuls of blood that the Thalmor are to blame; they stirred up the trouble here and forced him to divert resources, quelling this rebellion. Galmar and Ulfric smile, as this is more than a rebellion now! Before Galmar runs Tullius through, Ulfric stops him and asks you to execute the General; it'll make for a better story. You can:

Agree, and plunge Ulfric's sword into the bowed form of General Tullius. Equip the sword first if you wish.

Or refuse, leaving Galmar to do the job.

Quest Conclusion

With the Imperials firmly routed and their leadership bleeding across the Castle floor, Ulfric tells Galmar that he'll step out and give a speech to his surviving Brothers and Sisters and will take care of Jarl Elisif. He has a final gift for you as a tribute to your valor; you may keep his sword.

➤ **Leveled Weapon**

Postquest Activities

Ulfric and Galmar leave the castle to address the troops to raucous cheers. Afterward, if you ask Ulfric for any other tasks, he tells you to watch for remaining Imperial camps across Skyrim. Defeat the remnants of the Empire in Skyrim as you please. The Sons and Daughers of Skyrim will rejoice once more...with the Thalmor looking on from the shadows....

NOTE If you wait a couple of days, Solitude begins to return to normal. Elisif the Fair remains as Jarl and has sworn fealty to Ulfric. Stormcloaks are stationed throughout the city, in case the Imperials send additional troops to attack (and to keep Elisif from thinking twice about where her loyalties lie).

DAEDRIC QUESTS

OVERVIEW

The Daedric Quests are unrelated to one another. Each has its own requirements, and some can only be started later in your adventure. There is no ideal time to begin one; simply seek out the ones that interest you, or complete the ones that you come across.

> **NOTE** **Cross-Referencing:** If you want to see maps and learn more about the traps, non-quest-related items, collectibles, crafting areas, and other important rooms of note in every location during these quests, then cross-reference the location you travel to with the information on that location contained in this guide's Atlas.

Daedric Lords

Azura: Queen of Dawn and Dusk

Boethiah: Prince of Plots

Clavicus Vile: Master of Insidious Wishes

Hermaeus Mora: Keeper of Forbidden Knowledge

Hircine: Lord of the Hunt

Malacath: Creator of Curses

Mehrunes Dagon: Prince of Destruction

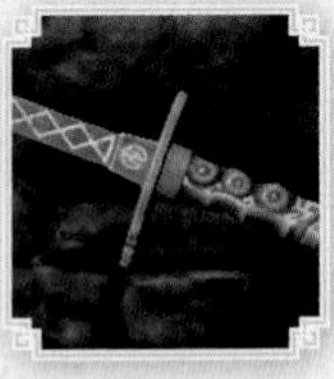

Mephala: The Webspinner

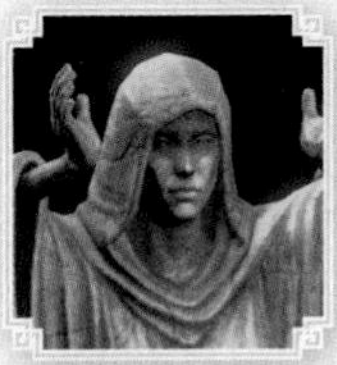

Meridia: Lady of Light

Molag Bal: Lord of Corruption

Namira: Lady of Decay

Nocturnal: Mistress of Shadows

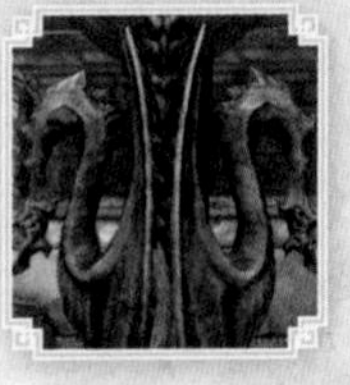

Peryite: Bringer of Pestilence

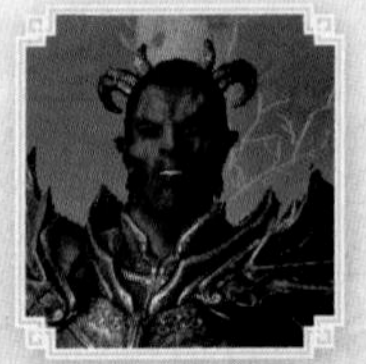

Sanguine: Lord of Revelry

Sheogorath: Prince of Madness

Vaermina: Weaver of Dreams

Available Quests

There are 15 Daedric Quests. Nocturnal's quest is part of the Thieves Guild and is detailed on page 300. Any prerequisites, as well as the Daedric Artifacts you will be rewarded with, are shown in the following table:

✓	DAEDRIC LORD	QUEST NAME	PREREQUISITES	DAEDRIC ARTIFACT
	Azura	The Black Star	None	Azura's Star or the Black Star
	Boethiah	Boethiah's Calling	Level 30	Ebony Mail
	Clavicus Vile	A Daedra's Best Friend	Level 10	Masque of Clavicus Vile
	Hermaeus Mora	Discerning the Transmundane	Level 15 (to begin Blood Harvest)	Oghma Infinium
	Hircine	Ill Met by Moonlight	None	Savior's Hide or Ring of Hircine
	Malacath	The Cursed Tribe	Level 9	Volendrung
	Mehrunes Dagon	Pieces of the Past	Level 20	Mehrunes' Razor
	Mephala	The Whispering Door	Level 20 and Complete Main Quest: Dragon Rising	Ebony Blade
	Meridia	The Break of Dawn	Level 12	Dawnbreaker
	Molag Bal	The House of Horrors	None	Mace of Molag Bal
	Namira	The Taste of Death	None	Ring of Namira
	Nocturnal	Thieves Guild Quests	None	Skeleton Key
	Peryite	The Only Cure	Level 10	Spellbreaker
	Sanguine	A Night to Remember	Level 14	Sanguine Rose
	Sheogorath	The Mind of Madness	None	Wabbajack
	Vaermina	Waking Nightmare	Level 14	Skull of Corruption

(The Skeleton Key does not count towards the Daedric Influence or Oblivion Walker achievement.)

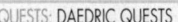

MINOR SPOILERS

PREREQUISITES: None.

INTERSECTING QUESTS: Miscellaneous Objectives: Innkeepers

LOCATIONS: The College of Winterhold, Ilinalta's Deep, Shrine of Azura, Winterhold, The Frozen Hearth Inn, Azura's Star

CHARACTERS: Aranea Ienith, Azura, Colette, Dagur, Drevis, Faralda, Mirabelle, Nelacar, Nirya, Phinis, Sergius, Tolfdir

ENEMIES: Dremora, Malyn Varen, Necromancer, Skeleton

◊ **OBJECTIVES:** Miscellaneous Objective: Visit the Shrine of Azura, Find the elven mage from Aranea's vision, Speak to Nelacar, Find Azura's Star, Bring the Star to Aranea or bring the Star to Nelacar, Tell Azura you're ready to enter the Star, Tell Nelacar you're ready to enter the Star, Destroy Malyn Varen's soul

The Lure of Azura

On your journey throughout Skyrim, you can speak to many a barkeep (such as Hulda in Whiterun) and gain much from their scuttlebutt (Miscellaneous Objective: Innkeepers). Ask for rumors until you're told of the Shrine of Azura; the Dark Elves are said to have built it after they fled from Morrowind. It's certainly a sight to see. Check your map marker now.

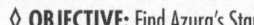

◊ **MISCELLANEOUS OBJECTIVE:** Visit the Shrine of Azura
♦ **TARGET:** Shrine of Azura

At the top of the snow-covered steps under the Shrine of Azura, a single Dunmer priestess named Aranea is praying. Speak to her, and she says your visit here was destined. Agree to help, and Aranea gives you a rather cryptic message: You're to find an elven man who came to her in a vision, one who can "turn the brightest star as black as night." She suggests you look for this enchanter in Winterhold.

◊ **OBJECTIVE:** Find the elven mage from Aranea's vision
◊ **OBJECTIVE:** Speak to Nelacar
♦ **TARGET:** Nelacar, the Frozen Hearth Inn, in Winterhold

Descend into Winterhold, and start talking to the townsfolk. Speak with Colette, Dagur, Drevis, Faralda, Mirabelle, Nirya, Phinis, Tolfdir, or Sergius; they all point to an elderly elven wizard who lives inside the Frozen Hearth Inn. Enter the building, and attempt the following:

(Persuade) Inform him that a priestess of Azura sent you.

(Bribe) Pay him for his information.

(Intimidate) Pressure him into talking. When you reach Level 6 or higher, this is an easy test to complete.

When you're successful, Nelacar begins to explain about Azura's Star. Unlike a regular Soul Gem, the Star allows any number of souls to pass through it. Nelacar discovered this the hard way while working for his master, Malyn Varen, who was experimenting with the artifact in the hope of preserving his soul and allowing him to escape his disease-ridden body. The power of the Star slowly made Malyn paranoid and impulsive (although Nelacar believes Azura was responsible for that), resulting in the deaths of several students and Malyn's banishment from the College to a place called Ilinalta's Deep.

◊ **OBJECTIVE:** Find Azura's Star
♦ **TARGET:** Ilinalta's Deep

Deep in Undeath

Locate the ruined fort known as Ilinalta's Deep, and enter via the trapdoor at the top of the sunken turret. Begin trekking through the soggy interior catacombs, brandishing your best skeleton-culling weapons. You face intermittent attacks from necromancers—the remnants of Malyn's students. Follow the waterlogged corridors and gloomy altars and alcoves until you reach a large spiral staircase.

TIP Consult the Atlas on page 908 for all the loot you can remove from this dungeon, which involves some underwater searching.

Climb the spiral stairs to the final resting place of Malyn Varen. Among the gold and grimoires, locate Azura's Star, which appears to be broken. Escape the Deep via the ladder in Varen's death chamber.

➤ **Broken Azura's Star**

◊ **OBJECTIVE:** Bring the Star to Aranea
♦ **TARGET:** Shrine of Azura
OR
◊ **OBJECTIVE:** Bring the Star to Nelacar
♦ **TARGET:** The Frozen Hearth Inn, in Winterhold

A Star of Dark or Brightness

The quest now has two possible conclusions: A communion with Azura or a chat with an old elf enchanter.

A Communion with Azura

You can journey back to the Shrine of Azura and speak with Aranea. When the Star is placed on the altar, the daedra speaks, congratulating you on locating it but warning that the artifact is useless until Malyn Varen's soul has been purged from it. Azura offers to send you into the Star to deal with Malyn directly.

◊ **OBJECTIVE:** Tell Azura you're ready to enter the Star
♦ **TARGET:** The Star of Azura

Chat with an Old Elf Enchanter

Or you can journey back to the Frozen Hearth Inn and speak to Nelacar. After examining the Star, Nelacar discovers that Malyn Varen's soul is trapped inside. He says he can repair the Star, transforming it into a vessel that stores black souls. But first, Malyn must be purged from the device; you must be soul-trapped to deal with Malyn directly.

◊ **OBJECTIVE:** Tell Nelacar you're ready to enter the Star
♦ **TARGET:** The Star of Azura

NOTE "Black souls" refer to human souls (from townsfolk, the Forsworn, or bandits) that can't ordinarily be stored in standard Soul Gems. These are used for Enchanting purposes.

No matter which of the two paths you choose, your personage is spirited away into the strange ethereal otherworld of the Star.

◊ **OBJECTIVE:** Destroy Malyn Varen's soul
♦ **TARGET:** Malyn Varen, inside the Star of Azura

After telling Malyn that he cannot escape his fate, run after him. He conjures up to three Dremora and attacks with lightning from his potent staff. Quickly nullify the enemies, and then strike down Malyn. As Malyn crumples, your spirit is transported back to Skyrim.

Malyn Varen's soul has been consigned to Oblivion. You are ready to receive an offering from either Lady Azura or Nelacar. In addition, if you're at the Shrine of Azura, you may speak with Aranea Ienith again. With her guardianship at an end, she offers to accompany you as a Follower, if you'll agree to it.

Quest Conclusion (Azura)

➤ **Follower:** Aranea Ienith ➤ **Azura's Star**

Quest Conclusion (Nelacar)

➤ **The Black Star**

Postquest Activities

The person (Nelacar or Aranea) you didn't side with has some harsh words with you, if you meet up with them again. Aranea obviously won't become your Follower if you side with Nelacar.

TIP Aranea is a very competent wizard: She has a Magic Staff of Frostbite and has focused her abilities on Conjuration and Destruction magic.

PREREQUISITES: You must be Level 30 or higher.

MINOR SPOILERS

INTERSECTING QUESTS: None

LOCATIONS: Sacellum of Boethiah, Knifepoint Mine, Knifepoint Ridge

CHARACTERS: Boethiah

ENEMIES: Bandit, Boethiah Cultist, Champion of Boethiah, Frost Troll, Priestess of Boethiah

◊ OBJECTIVES: Find the shrine of Boethiah, Find the cult of Boethiah, Lead someone to become trapped by the shrine and slay them, Speak to Boethiah's Conduit, Slay the other cultists, Slay everyone at Knifepoint Ridge stealthily, Retrieve and equip the Ebony Mail

Congealing an Empty Vapor

Once you're an experienced adventurer (Level 32 or higher), you can join the cult of the fabled Boethiah, the Prince of Plots and original god-ancestor of the Dark Elves. This is triggered via one of the following antics:

During your searching, you (randomly) uncover a book named Boethiah's Proving and read it.

During your travels, you (randomly) encounter a Boethiah Cultist, who attacks you. Slay the cultist, search the corpse, and uncover the book. Then read it.

Or, you can simply stumble upon the Sacellum of Boethiah (although you won't have the map marker to guide you, and the location is deserted until you reach Level 32).

◊ OBJECTIVE: Find the shrine of Boethiah
◊ OBJECTIVE: Find the cult of Boethiah
♦ TARGET: Sacellum of Boethiah

Brave the Frost Trolls, or other weathered adversaries, as you trek up the snowy mountains east of Windhelm. Among the rocks and snow is a rudimentary arena, where those seeking the gaze of Boethiah are engaged in bloody combat. Confront a Priestess of Boethiah without resorting to combat (yet). She explains that you are an "empty vapor," unworthy of Boethiah's attention. Tell her you're not afraid of her, and you learn about Boethiah, who only cares for those who care for themselves. You are to prove that you can lie; you must find someone, gain their trust, lead them to the shrine above, and instruct your thrall to touch the Pillar of Sacrifice. This stalls your victim, who you must slay with a ceremonial dagger. If your will is strong, Boethiah will stir and you will be one of them!

➤ Blade of Sacrifice

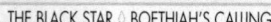

◊ OBJECTIVE: Lead someone to become trapped by the shrine and slay them
♦ TARGET: Any Follower, at the Sacellum of Boethiah

Enthralling a Willing Thrall

Leave this place of violence and ponder for a moment: Which Follower is worth sacrificing to Boethiah? One who has accompanied you on many of your adventurers or one who is waiting patiently for your return? You may choose any Follower you've met during your travels. Remember the following:

If your morals prevent you from sacrificing just anyone, then choose a Follower who has annoyed you or you don't like. This doesn't affect your standing in Skyrim; it just makes you feel better about leading a friend to their death!

You must sacrifice someone to complete this quest. If your morals prevent this, perhaps the Prince of Plots isn't right for you....

If you don't suffer from this guilt or don't care who you wish to sacrifice, then anyone stupid enough to blindly follow you will do! This can be anyone you've befriended, a hireling in your service or a Housecarl appointed to you by a Jarl.

TIP For a complete list of Followers, consult the Training chapter. This quest involves human sacrifice and an unwilling subject. To minimize any regrets you may have about leading someone to their death, simply complete the Dark Brotherhood Quests, obtain an initiate, and sacrifice one of them.

Bring your unwitting victim back to the Sacellum of Boethiah. To avoid them dying during the trek, you may wish to Fast-Travel here. Climb up the steps to the Pillar of Sacrifice, and instruct your victim to activate it. As your Follower inspects the pillar, he is trapped by magical energy. Arm yourself with the Blade of Sacrifice (given by the Priestess), and don't finish slashing until your Follower collapses in a pool of blood. Your murder soon yields results: Boethiah possesses the bloody corpse!

TIP Remember! It is more fitting to murder your Follower using the Blade of Sacrifice, but any weapon will do. Point your Follower to interact with the Pillar of Sacrifice so they are standing in the correct spot before the slaying begins.

◊ OBJECTIVE: Speak to Boethiah's Conduit
♦ TARGET: Your slain Follower, at the Sacellum of Boethiah

Boethiah enters the flesh of the recently culled. Make your answers more insulting rather than sycophantic to earn a modicum of her respect. She then addresses you and the cultists who have gathered to witness your commune. She has a special task for the one who exceeds the rest—the one who is left standing. With that, she leaves your Follower's corpse, and mayhem ensues!

◊ **OBJECTIVE:** Slay the other cultists

Draw your preferred weapon, head down to the fighting pit, and begin killing the cultists. Let the shrine be bathed in blood! There are usually around five cultists to slay. You can wade in or hang back and let your fellow cultists fight among themselves before you move in to finish the wounded. Once all are dead, Boethiah possesses the last one to die and congratulates you on your ferocity in combat. If you're able to cast aside your honor, Boethiah has one more task. Her previous champion displeases her, and she wishes him replaced in the traditional fashion: You are to kill everyone at Knifepoint Ridge, as quickly and as invisibly as possible. You are but an instrument of Boethiah; showing yourself too frequently will displease her.

◊ **OBJECTIVE:** Slay everyone at Knifepoint Ridge stealthily
◊ **OBJECTIVE:** Retrieve and equip the Ebony Mail
♦ **TARGET:** All enemies and Champion of Boethiah at Knifepoint Ridge

NOTE The area of Knifepoint Ridge where the Champion lurks is inaccessible prior to this quest's start, so you can't attempt an early reconnoiter of the area. Slaying foes before the start of this quest doesn't affect the number of enemies you face, either.

As You Will It, So It Shall Be

Knifepoint Ridge, in the southern hills equidistant between Markarth and Whiterun, is where you prove yourself to Boethiah. Approach the small collection of huts, tents, and guard towers and slay the bandits quickly and effectively. Don't charge in but try to remain hidden, although rampaging through here is still possible. Be sure no one is left on the surface before locating and opening the entrance to Knifepoint Mine.

TIP Wait for nightfall, and use the Invisibility and Muffle spells to increase your stealthiness. Instead of taking the main road to the camp's front entrance, climb the steep slope to the southeast. Work your way around and behind the guard tower (bypassing the rock trap); this route to the Blacksmith's shed is easier. Now shoot the Champion of Boethiah through a hole in the wall!

TIP If you take the side hallway that ramps down, locate a hidden path underneath the scaffolding, immediately on your left. If you sneak through here, you'll have access to a passage on the opposite side of the large chamber that winds around and exits right next to the Champion's shack. This allows you to bypass all the enemies in this area.

Once inside the mine, try the stealthy plans mentioned, sneaking and knifing foes using, for example, Sneak attacks from bows at a distance or Invisibility. There are several bottles of poison you can use, and there's an Alchemy Table in the area caged off from the large chamber; use this to make your attacks more potent or your movement more stealthy. When you reach the Champion of Boethiah, use the fire-through-the-hole tactic or approach and strike him down from behind, if you can.

Quest Conclusion

Ransack the corpse of the slain Champion for your prizes. Equip the Ebony Mail to conclude this quest. Boethiah speaks to you, exclaiming her satisfaction at the blood you spilled in her honor. Your name is to be written on Boethiah's tablet of absolute darkness, and you receive her blessing.

- Ebony Shield
- Ebony Gauntlets
- Ebony Boots
- Ebony Mail

Postquest Activities

Congratulations! Serve your new mistress well!

PREREQUISITES: You must be Level 10 or higher.

MINOR SPOILERS

INTERSECTING QUESTS: None

LOCATIONS: Falkreath, Lod's House, Haemar's Shame, Haemar's Cavern, Rimerock Burrow

CHARACTERS: Barbas, Clavicus Vile, Imperial Soldier, Lod

ENEMIES: Atronach, Frostbite Spider, Sebastian Lort, Vampire, Vampire's Thrall

◊ **OBJECTIVES:** Miscellaneous: Speak to Lod, Miscellaneous: Find the dog outside Falkreath, Travel with Barbas to the shrine of Clavicus Vile, Retrieve the Rueful Axe with Barbas, Return to the shrine of Clavicus Vile with Barbas and the Rueful Axe, Give the Rueful Axe to Clavicus Vile OR Kill Barbas with the Rueful Axe

A Shaggy Dog Story

You may begin this quest once you reach Level 10. Enter the town of Falkreath and speak to an Imperial Soldier at the entrance. He asks whether you've seen a dog. Whatever your answer, he points you toward the town's Blacksmith, Lod, who has been asking about the hound. You may also go straight to Lod to begin the quest.

◊ **OBJECTIVE:** Miscellaneous Objective: Speak to Lod
♦ **TARGET:** Lod, in Falkreath

Locate Lod either inside or outside his Blacksmith's shop, and he asks whether you'd be interested in coaxing a dog that he's seen. He spotted it on the road close to town and wants to befriend it. You can:

Agree to find the creature, and Lod gives you some meat to help you gain the dog's interest.

(Persuade) Or you can agree to find the creature...for a price. If you're successful, Lod agrees, gives you half a payment and the meat.

Then exit Falkreath and locate the wolfhound with the strange bark, a dog named Barbas. You should begin the main Daedric Quest from this point, rather than returning the dog to Lod. Otherwise, Barbas won't follow you, although you can mention to Lod that the dog was more trouble than he was worth (and receive a small reward of gold).

➤ **25 gold pieces** ➤ **Mammoth Snout**

◊ **OBJECTIVE:** Find the dog outside Falkreath
♦ **TARGET:** Barbas, on the road close to Falkreath

Speak to the dog named Barbas. Unexpectedly, the dog speaks back! The dog introduces himself as Barbas, and he has a problem you can help him with: He recently got into an argument with his master, which got a little heated, and he needs you to settle the disagreement. After his banishment, Barbas and his master can only manifest close to a shrine, and he requests you meet him there. He finishes by warning you not to trust anything his master says.

➤ **Follower:** Barbas

◊ **OBJECTIVE:** Travel with Barbas to the shrine of Clavicus Vile
♦ **TARGET:** Shrine to Clavicus Vile, inside Haemar's Shame

You and your new best friend don't have to journey to Haemar's Shrine immediately: You can commence other adventuring tasks; Barbas heads to Haemar's Shame to wait for you. Once you decide to continue this quest, trek to Haemar's Shame and enter Haemar's Cavern.

Expect a cold reception once you step into the cavern; vampires and their thralls are holed up in this maze of rock and snow. Fight or sneak your way past these creatures, until you reach a larger chamber with wooden fencing around a central hole. Head down the ramp into the hole, where you find a tunnel leading toward Haemar's Shame. Deliver a killing blow to the Frostbite Spider in the next room of jagged rocks before following lanterns and torches down a tunnel, past a room of bloodied cages, and around to a subterranean stream.

Continue up a connecting tunnel and into the main shrine chamber, where you encounter several vampires of differing strengths. Deal with them. When the area is devoid of bloodsuckers, approach the statue of Clavicus Vile, stepping over the dead offering, and activate the statue.

Vile is pleased to see you. He says that in killing his vampiric followers, you've already helped him fulfill a set of wishes—that his worshippers be cured. Mention that you're here to reunite Vile with Barbas, and the Daedric Prince's jovial nature changes. Apparently, he's sick of that "insufferable pup" but continues to listen to you, as he really doesn't want to be confined to this backwater shrine. There is a way Barbas can earn a place back at Vile's side: An incredibly powerful axe is residing somewhere deep inside Rimerock Burrow. Bring this back, and Vile insists he will grant you a reward, with "no strings attached." Agree, use the pull chain to access the exit tunnel, and exit Haemar's Shame via the quick exit.

◊ **OBJECTIVE:** Retrieve the Rueful Axe with Barbas
♦ **TARGET:** Rueful Axe, in Rimerock Burrow

A Deal with a Daedric Prince

Across the mountains, east of Solitude, is a high and precarious path carved into the side of the rocky terrain. Cross the small bridge and enter Rimerock Burrow. Draw your weapon and prepare to fight Sebastian Lort and his conjurations, who are using this remote grotto as a base. The mage and his Atronach aren't of much importance, but the Rueful Axe lying on the altar to the rear of the Burrow most certainly is. Grab it, along with any other treasure you deem valuable, and leave.

➤ **Rueful Axe**

◊ **OBJECTIVE:** Return to the shrine of Clavicus Vile with Barbas and the Rueful Axe
♦ **TARGET:** Shrine to Clavicus Vile, inside Haemar's Shame

Return to Haemar's Shame, and work your way through the chambers, polishing off any vampires you may have missed during your first exploration. Activate Clavicus Vile's shrine, and the Daedric Prince congratulates you on your accomplishment and your new loyal friend Barbas. Vile then says he could be persuaded to let you keep the Rueful Axe...if you use the weapon to strike Barbas down!

◊ **OBJECTIVE:** Give the Rueful Axe to Clavicus Vile OR Kill Barbas with the Rueful Axe

Quest Conclusion

At this point, you have a choice to make: give Vile the axe or kill Barbas. If you give Vile the axe, the deity is disappointed at your loyalty and at the fact that he now faces an eternity with Barbas. The dog waylays Vile's threats to turn you into a worm and insists that Vile keep his end of the bargain. He grants you his boon, as previously agreed. Barbas and his master are intertwined for an eternity.

➤ **Masque of Clavicus Vile**

If you give Barbas the axe right between his furry eyes, the deity is most pleased with your double-crossing and the fact that he doesn't have to spend an eternity with Barbas. He leaves you to use the Daedra-harming Rueful Axe.

➤ **Rueful Axe**

Postquest Activities

You can return to Lod and explain that Barbas was more trouble than he was worth, after which you're given a small reward for your time.

➤ **Leveled gold pieces**

DISCERNING THE TRANSMUNDANE

MINOR SPOILERS

PREREQUISITES: You must be Level 15 or higher to begin the second half of this quest, flagged as "Blood Harvest" in the guide.

INTERSECTING QUESTS: College of Winterhold Quest: First Lessons, Main Quest: Elder Knowledge, Main Quest: Alduin's Bane

LOCATIONS: Alftand, Blackreach, College of Winterhold, Arcanaeum, Hall of the Elements, Septimus Signus's Outpost, Tower of Mzark, Oculory

CHARACTERS: Septimus Signus, Urag gro-Shub, Wretched Abyss (Hermaeus Mora)

ENEMIES: Dwarven Centurion, Dwarven Sphere, Dwarven Spider, Falmer

◊ **OBJECTIVES:** Ask Urag about the insane book, Find Septimus Signus, Transcribe the Lexicon, Give the Lexicon to Septimus, Harvest High Elf blood, Harvest Wood Elf blood, Harvest Dark Elf blood, Harvest Falmer blood, Harvest Orc blood, Bring blood to Septimus, Take the Oghma Infinium

Acute Occult Ruminations

There are two ways you can begin this quest:

1. During Main Quest: Elder Knowledge, you are sent to the College of Winterhold in search of an Elder Scroll. Approach the entrance and speak to Faralda about gaining admittance.

2. Otherwise, you must locate Septimus Signus's Outpost on your own. Skip to the section marked 'Puppet of the Abyss' instead.

Enter the College and head into the Arcanaeum. Look for the Orc Mage named Urag gro-Shub, who runs the Arcanaeum. Although you can ask to assist him in College business (which allows you to accomplish several College-related tasks unrelated to this quest) and ask about the library, you're here to talk about the Elder Scroll. Urag isn't too happy with you offhandedly asking about such a powerful artifact. You may listen to an overview of the Scrolls before asking if there's an Elder Scroll you could use. Urag laughs at this question; he wouldn't show it to the likes of you, even if he obtained one. Ask if he at least has any information on them. He agrees to locate a couple of arcane tomes that may have some clues. But mostly they contain ravings leavened with rumor and conjecture.

Urag gro-Shub locates and places two tomes on the nearby desk: *Effects of the Elder Scrolls* and *Ruminations on the Elder Scrolls*. After reading both books (which you may keep or leave on the desk), you find that the *Ruminations* tome is the work of a madman. Daedric Quest: Discerning the Transmundane now begins, and your objective updates:

➤ **Effects of the Elder Scrolls** ➤ **Ruminations on the Elder Scrolls**

◊ **OBJECTIVE:** Ask Urag about the insane book

Tell Urag that the *Ruminations* book is incomprehensible. He doesn't seem surprised; after all, this book was the work of Septimus Signus. Although Signus was a master on the nature of Elder Scrolls, Urag tells you that he's "been gone for a long while." You suspect he means both mentally and physically. Signus currently resides north of the College in the treacherous Ice Fields.

◊ **OBJECTIVE:** Find Septimus Signus
♦ **TARGET:** Septimus Signus's Outpost

Puppet of the Abyss

The giant chunks of ice floating off the Sea of Ghosts are your next destination. Exit the College and run to the frigid waters. Hop across the floating ice, making your way north. Expect to slice into a few wild animals along the way. Septimus Signus's Outpost is an odd little door cut into a hill-sized iceberg, close to a moored rowboat. Climb down the ladder and the slope to reach a lone mage in a chamber of ice, alone with his books and thoughts. He appears to be studying some kind of Dwemer box about the size of a house.

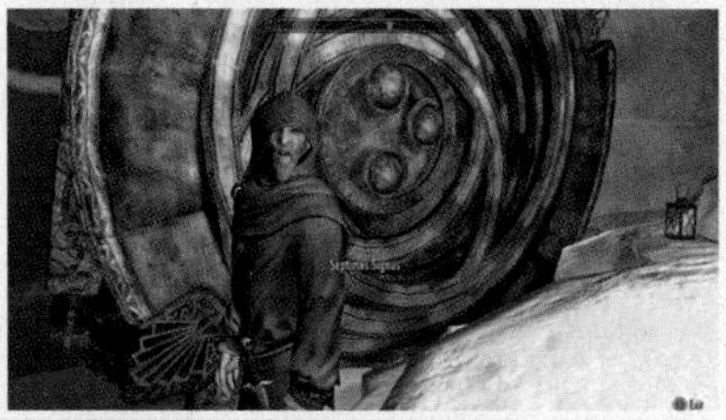

Ask Septimus about the Elder Scrolls if you want him to deliver a rapid-fire barrage of knowledge on the subject. Ask where the Scroll is again, and after receiving moderately useless information, ask once more (either pleasantly or with a more threatening tone). Septimus agrees to tell you, but in return, you must venture into Blackreach, a giant underground Dwemer city that lies below several Dwarven ruins hidden across Skyrim. Ask about getting into Blackreach, and Septimus keeps up his riddle-based prattling and hands you two items: The first is an odd-edged lexicon, used by the Dwemer for inscribing. The second is an Attunement Sphere, which apparently "sings" when you near an important Dwemer door. Once these are in your grasp, your Main Quest updates. Stay and speak further with Septimus if your sanity can stand it.

➤ **Attunement Sphere** ➤ **Blank Lexicon**

◊ **OBJECTIVE:** Transcribe the Lexicon
♦ **TARGET:** Daedric Quest, in Blackreach
◊ **MAIN QUEST OBJECTIVE:** Recover the Elder Scroll
♦ **TARGET:** Tower of Mzark

NOTE This quest continues only after you enter the gargantuan subterranean Dwemer city of Blackreach. The optimal path to reach this sprawling cavern is detailed in Main Quest: Elder Knowledge. These both require you to secure the Attunement Sphere from Septimus, which is the only way to access Blackreach.

After you secure the Attunement Sphere and Blank Lexicon from Septimus, locate Alftand on the glacial mountains southwest of Winterhold. Enter and head through the Alftand Glacial Ruins, battling Dwarven Spheres and Dwarven Spiders. Maneuver through the tower and connecting chambers of the Alftand Animonculory (opening the elevator back to the Glacial Ruins as you go), and battle the Dwarven Centurion in the Alftand Cathedral to reach an elevator (opening the exit back up to the surface first). Descend back into the cathedral and use the Attunement Sphere to activate the Dwarven Mechanism to access the hidden entrance to Blackreach.

TIP Alftand is only one of several entrances to Blackreach. Consult the Atlas to see all of the ways to enter this subterranean citadel and the Tower of Mzark.

Enter Blackreach and keep a steady pace along the cobblestone pathways, heading in a westerly direction. You're looking for a massive vertical stone elevator shaft that pierces the roof of this massive underground complex. When you find it, pull the lever and head into the Tower of Mzark. Venture into a gigantic, circular Aedrome chamber, which is dominated by a huge sphere. This appears to be some kind of massive Oculory, with a variety of focusing lenses and other golden machinery attached.

Head to the cluster of controls on the platform above the Oculory. The controls are comprised of five cylindrical devices: a Lexicon Receptacle and four positioning buttons embedded in pedestals. There is a knack to using these devices to produce something hidden in one of the lenses.

Puzzle solution: Activate the Lexicon Receptacle, so the Blank Lexicon rests on top of it. The two pedestals to the Receptacle's right—the only ones currently active—open and close the Oculory lenses. Press the taller of the two pedestals (right of the middle one with the lens chart on it) three or four times, until the pedestal with the blue button to the left of the middle one starts to glow. Move to this new pedestal. At this point, the Blank Lexicon will also be glowing blue. The two pedestals to the Receptacle's left—the taller of which is now active—control the ceiling lens array. Press the button of the taller, left pedestal twice, until the button on the far-left smaller pedestal begins to glow. Now press that button, and a large set of lens crystals descends from the ceiling, stops, and the main crystal rotates and splits apart to reveal some kind of tubelike carrying device.

Drop from the balcony controls, and approach the open lens crystal. Take the Elder Scroll from its elaborate compartment. Once you've taken the Elder Scroll, your path diverges, but only if Main Quest: Elder Knowledge is currently active. If it is, Main Quest: Alduin's Bane begins, and your next plan is to take the Scroll to the summit of the Throat of the World, and read it there. However, for this quest, Septimus is more concerned with the transcription etched onto the Lexicon. Retrieve the Lexicon from the receptacle; don't leave without it!

➤ **Elder Scroll** ➤ **Runed Lexicon**

◊ **OBJECTIVE:** Give the Lexicon to Septimus

Blood Harvest

Leave the Tower of Mzark by the elevator at the end of the corridor under the pedestals, which ascends to Skyrim's surface. Trek back to the Sea of Ghosts and enter Septimus Signus's Outpost. Septimus is still happily talking to himself; interrupt so he talks to you, and tell him you've inscribed the Lexicon. Apparently, the sealing structure interlocks in the tiniest fractals. That obviously means something to Signus, who needs Dwemer blood to loosen these interlocking hooks. However, as the Dwemer are long dead, your next task is to search for a panoply of their brethren. Septimus wants blood! He hands you an Extractor and lists the races related to the Dwemer of which he requires blood. Before you leave, you may ask him further questions about the giant box he paces beside.

➤ Essence Extractor

◊ **OBJECTIVE:** Harvest High Elf blood
◊ **OBJECTIVE:** Harvest Wood Elf blood
◊ **OBJECTIVE:** Harvest Dark Elf blood
◊ **OBJECTIVE:** Harvest Falmer blood
◊ **OBJECTIVE:** Harvest Orc blood

As you reach the Outpost exit, you see a strange mist that quickly congeals into a frightening void. This is the Wretched Abyss, and it coaxes you forward, wanting you to bask in its presence. When you ask what it is, it replies that it is but an aspect of Hermaeus Mora, who has been watching you. He tells you that once the giant Dwemer lockbox has been opened, Septimus will have outlived his usefulness. When that time comes, you may take his place as Hermaeus Mora's emissary. You can agree or refuse. Either way, you won't need to choose until after you open the box. The Abyss retracts, allowing you to leave.

At this point, you may wish to continue other quests; finding all this blood is an adventure unto itself, and one that is much easier once you realize where you can harvest with impunity! Obviously, the danger comes with slaughtering an innocent in broad daylight, and usually within a Hold City's walls, which isn't recommended at all. For this reason, there are other possible places look:

☑	RACE	OPTIMAL LOCATIONS	NOTES
☐	High Elf	Hob's Fall Cave, Yngvild, world encounters, any Warlock lair	High Elves appear as Warlocks, so slay enemies rather than townsfolk.
☐	Dark Elf	Hob's Fall Cave, Yngvild, world encounters, any Warlock lair	Dark Elves appear as Warlocks, so slay enemies rather than townsfolk.
☐	Wood Elf	Pinepeak Cavern or any hunter camp	You can find a dead Wood Elf lying on the rocks just outside the entrance to Pinepeak Cavern, across the bridge from Ivarstead. When assaulting a hunter camp, one in four hunters is a Wood Elf.
☐	Falmer	Blackreach, Falmer Hives, any Dwarven Ruins	You can return to Blackreach easily, making this blood simple to spill.
☐	Orc	Cracked Tusk Keep, Rift Watchtower, or any bandit camp	Slay the hostile Orcs in these locations, rather than the friendly Orcs in Strongholds.

TIP Double-check every figure you meet during wilderness treks, and slay them if they're one of the races mentioned.

◊ **OBJECTIVE:** Bring blood to Septimus

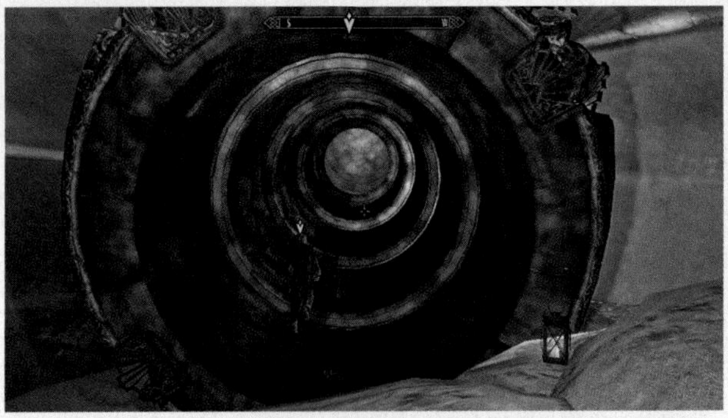

Once your blood-siphoning trek is complete, return to the iceberg on the Sea of Ghosts, and revisit Septimus once more. Inform him that you have the blood samples he requires. He takes them and quickly mixes them up before approaching the massive Dwemer box. It rotates, and telescopes open into an otherworldly passage. Septimus races up this corridor, into a chamber of circles, and approaches an odd book. He reaches out to take it but suddenly disintegrates into a pile of ash.

◊ **OBJECTIVE:** Take the Oghma Infinium

Quest Conclusion

Step into the chamber and take the book. You are instantly bombarded with a knowledge intake that could hemorrhage the brains of lesser mortals. You may look into this unspeakable tome and live, or choose to close the book. Your knowledge is increased by an impressive amount, and this translates into skill increases for associated abilities. Here's how this breaks down:

- Elect not to read: No benefits.
- Read the Path of Might: +5 in all skills of this path (Smithing, Heavy Armor, Block, Two-Handed, One-Handed, Archery)
- Read the Path of Shadow: +5 in all skills of this path (Light Armor, Sneak, Lockpicking, Pickpocket, Speech, Alchemy)
- Read the Path of Magic: +5 in all skills of this path (Illusion, Conjuration, Destruction, Restoration, Alteration, Enchanting)

As you try to leave the box, the Wretched Abyss appears. You can elect to work wonders together as Hermaeus Mora's champion or disavow any agreement with the Daedric Prince.

Postquest Activities

You can embrace Hermaeus Mora, or deny him all you want; you are still doing his will.

PREREQUISITES: None.

MINOR SPOILERS

INTERSECTING QUESTS: None

LOCATIONS: Bloated Man's Grotto, Falkreath, Falkreath Barracks, Falkreath Jail, Peak's Shade Tower,

CHARACTERS: Aspect of Hircine, Hircine, Hunters of Hircine, Indara Caerelia, Mathies Caerelia, Sinding

ENEMIES: Hunters of Hircine, Sinding, White Stag

◊ **OBJECTIVES:** Speak to Sinding, Kill the great beast, Begin the hunt, Hunt or Spare Sinding, Skin Sinding, Speak to Hircine, Kill the Hunters, Talk to Sinding

The Curse of Falkreath

For such a modest town, Falkreath has a sizable cemetery. As you enter this location, a burial ceremony is under way for a young girl. Instead of marching right in and interrogating everyone, you may listen to the townsfolk and gain some insight. Speak to the parents of the slain child—Indara Caerelia or her husband, Mathies. Either will tell you that their daughter was ripped apart by a man named Sinding, a laborer passing through this Hold. If you can stand to look upon him, you're told where he is. If you miss the burial, find Mathies or his wife tending to crops near their home.

◊ **OBJECTIVE:** Speak to Sinding
♦ **TARGET:** Sinding, inside Falkreath Barracks

Visit the Falkreath Barracks and locate Sinding in the jail. The man explains he suffers from lycanthropy and was in werewolf form during the attack. He is remorseful about his murderous infanticide. He tells you he lost control and needed to be restrained. He blames this on a cursed ring he acquired. It belongs to Hircine (the Daedric Lord of the Hunt). Sinding was told it could help him control his transformations, but instead it caused them to occur sporadically and at the most inopportune times. Sinding seeks to appease Hircine by returning the ring. He says legend holds that Hircine will appear to any who can slay a legendary beast that roams these woods. The beast in question is close by. Agree to take the ring to Hircine.

Ring of Hircine (Cursed)

◊ **OBJECTIVE:** Kill the great beast
♦ **TARGET:** The White Stag, in the woods close to Falkreath

CAUTION

Beware the power of Hircine! With the ring in your possession, it cannot be removed. It is both powerful and cursed. If you are already a werewolf (as part of the Companions Quests) and you're outside a dungeon or city, every minute there is a 10 percent chance you will turn into your wolf form.

The Lord of the Hunt Smiles on You

The great beast of the forest is usually close to the path in the woods surrounding Peak's Shade Tower, but it moves constantly. Long-range weapons, such as magic or a bow, are an obvious advantage. Pursue the White Stag, and hunt it until your shots bring it down. Approach the slain animal, and a manifestation of Hircine appears. Speak to the Aspect of Hircine, and he recognizes the ring you carry. Hircine tells you Sinding has fled and gone into hiding, and a Great Hunt has been called to slay him. Hircine charges you to find this rogue shifter, tear the skin from his body, and bring it as an offering to him. He mentions there is a spot of competition to win Hircine's favor, and there's no time to dillydally.

◊ **OBJECTIVE:** Begin the hunt
♦ **TARGET:** Bloated Man's Grotto

Sinding has fled to Bloated Man's Grotto, a cave on the southern rim of the Tundra, just north of Lake Ilinalta. Journey there, and enter the grounds of this interior forest. The sky is bloodred and swirled with clouds. The Bloodmoon looms overhead. Hircine's power is focused on this place. As the entrance cave opens up, you spot a campsite where a group of hunters lie in pools of blood. A Khajiit named J'Kier greets you as a fellow hunter. Though badly lacerated, he explains that the prey is too strong, but more hunters have come to slay the monster and gain Hircine's favor. J'Kier then passes. You can check on Batum gra-Bar, Ma'tasarr, and Hoddreid, but the rest of the hunting party has died. Sinding is a considerable force in this forest.

◊ **OBJECTIVE:** Hunt or Spare Sinding
♦ **TARGET:** Sinding, in Bloated Man's Grotto

The path to the left has been blocked by some fallen trees, so continue down the path past the pond. You hear a roar from up ahead and turn a corner to see Sinding standing atop a rocky outcrop. He doesn't attack you immediately. You can:

Charge in, ignoring any conversation Sinding attempts to have with you. This begins Path 1.

Ignore any conversation topics and attempt to kill Sinding, as Hircine has requested. This also begins Path 1.

Or, tell Sinding you've been sent to kill him. While he understands he can't stop you, he promises not to return to civilization to inadvertently murder anyone else. Spare his life (which begins Path 2), or kill him for defying Hircine (which also begins Path 1).

Path 1: Ending the Sins of Sinding

If you tell Sinding that he has to die or attack him at any time, you are fulfilling Hircine's request. Sinding flees to the ruins atop the hill, leaving you to give chase. The hunt is now on! Stalk your furry prey, using any means at your disposal. Quicken your pace by utilizing the Slow Time and Whirlwind Sprint Shouts, or you can simply run to Sinding instead (supplement your sprint with some Fortify or Restore Stamina potions). If you're only relying on your nonaugmented sprinting, you'll barely match Sinding's pace.

Continue to track and keep pace with Sinding as he clears the ruins, drops down, and slaughters two hunters in the first clearing. You may catch him here if you're swift and engage in a brief combat, but he flees after a few strikes. Pursue the beast into a second clearing, where three more hunters wait, and then into a third clearing where you find an additional three hunters. Attempt combat in all three locations.

> **TIP** They don't stand a chance against Sinding, but if you hold his attention, the damage the hunters deal can help whittle down Sinding's considerable constitution. Any hunters that survive combat when Sinding moves on will follow you into the next clearing.

In the third clearing, Sinding finally stands his ground. With the help of any surviving hunters, bring down your quarry.

> **TIP** Is Sinding becoming a problem to slay? Are you being pulverized by his sharp claws? Then check the terrain; Bloated Man's Grotto has numerous cliffs, and Sinding doesn't have any ranged attacks. If you can clamber up to the mountainous area (particularly the promontory) in the center of this grotto, you can run along the top of the cliffs, sniping Sinding to death. Which is hardly sporting, but very effective!

◊ **OBJECTIVE:** Skin Sinding
◊ **OBJECTIVE:** Speak to Hircine

After you tear the skin from Sinding's body, Hircine appears in Sinding's form and thanks you for your offering. Satisfied that Sinding has been cast from this world, the Lord of the Hunt transforms the skin into his legendary artifact, the Savior's Hide, and gives it to you as a reward.

➤ **Sinding's Skin**

Path 2: Taking the Side of Sinding

◊ **OBJECTIVE:** Kill the Hunters

Inform Sinding that you will spare his life: Sinding is thankful, but there is little time to lose; more hunters have appeared and must be defeated. Sinding waits for you on the promontory. Head up the stairs on your right and join forces with him, then head through the ruins to reach the first group of hunters. There are two in the first clearing, three in the second, and three more in the third.

> **TIP** If you side with Sinding but attack him at any time later on, Path 1 is your only option. Devious, underhanded scoundrels may wish to time their betrayal of Sinding at just the right moment—when he's badly wounded by hunters! This is far less work for you but displays appalling sportsmanship!

◊ **OBJECTIVE:** Talk to Sinding

Speak with Sinding, and he is grateful for your help. But when you leave the Grotto, you find yourself face to face with Hircine once more. No matter your answers, he is satisfied by the hunt, and removes the curse on the ring.

Quest Conclusion

If you sided with Hircine, you receive the Savior's Hide.

➤ **Savior's Hide**

If you sided with Sinding, you keep Hircine's ring.

➤ **Ring of Hircine**

Postquest Activities

If you obtained the Savior's Hide, the ring is removed. If you sided with Sinding, you keep the ring, which is no longer cursed. It grants you an additional werewolf transformation per day (but only if you're a werewolf), and you don't need to worry about uncontrollable transformations!

PREREQUISITES: You must be Level 9 or higher.

MINOR SPOILERS

INTERSECTING QUESTS: None

LOCATIONS: Fallowstone Cave, Giant's Grove, Largashbur

CHARACTERS: Atub, Chief Yamarz, Gularzob, Malacath, Ugor

ENEMIES: Cave Bear, Giant

◊ **OBJECTIVES:** Bring Troll Fat and a Daedra Heart to Atub, Observe Atub's ritual, Speak with Yamarz, Meet Yamarz at Fallowstone Cave, Protect Yamarz, Defeat the giant, Take Shagrol's Warhammer back to Largashbur, Place Shagrol's Warhammer on the shrine in Largashbur

Keeper of Oaths, Master of Curses

Largashbur is a stronghold in the southwestern corner of the Rift and is home to a tribe of distrustful Orcs. As you approach, the Orcs are engaged in a battle with a giant. You can watch as they eventually take the giant down or step in and help (but be very careful you don't target the Orcs fighting). After the skirmish, Ugor—one of the gate guards—demands that you leave at once. Her anger is tempered by the slightly more levelheaded Atub, who you should speak with. Ask her what is going on, and she quickly (and uncharacteristically) reveals that her tribe is suffering and needs help.

It seems the tribe's once-powerful chief, Yamarz, is now stricken and cursed. This weakens the tribe, and the giants sense this: The stronghold has suffered from constant giant attacks. Yamarz has demanded the tribe remain within the walls of Largashbur, and Atub wishes to petition Malacath to lift this curse. As she cannot travel to the shrine, the ritual must be performed within Largashbur, but Atub lacks some materials needed; in particular she requires Troll Fat and a Daedra Heart.

◊ **OBJECTIVE:** Bring Troll Fat and a Daedra Heart to Atub

Troll Fat Finding: This is a relatively easy material to find. Simply locate an area where trolls (regular or Frost) roam, defeat one, and then search the corpse for the Troll Fat you need. There are always a couple of these powerful beasts roaming the exterior of Labyrinthian.

➤ **Troll Fat**

Daedra Heart Hunting: This is harder. Plunging your hand into a dead Dremora is the easy part; finding one is not. Try the following places:

During Daedric Quests: The Black Star and Pieces of the Past.

These occasionally show up in a vendor's list.

Enthir in the College of Winterhold always has one or two for sale, but at an inflated price.

If stealing appeals to you, find one in Kodlak's room in Jorrvaskr (Whiterun).

Or, steal one from the altar in the Hall of the Vigilant (in the Pale Hold).

Or, steal one from the Alchemy Room of the Nightcaller Temple (during Daedric Quest: Waking Nightmare).

➤ **Daedra Heart**

◊ **OBJECTIVE:** Observe Atub's ritual

Once you return with both materials for the ritual, Atub thanks you and beckons you into Largashbur. An enraged Ugor yells at Atub for bringing an outsider into the stronghold, but Atub calms her, allowing you safe passage into the settlement. She walks across the dirt yard and into the longhouse. Chief Yamarz is usually inside and takes an immediate disliking to you. Speak with him, and he keeps the insults flowing and complains about his cursed lack of sleep. Atub approaches and tells him it is time for the ritual to begin.

After Atub commences the ritual, Malacath's booming voice soon resonates around the camp. Most of the Daedric Prince's venom is directed at Yamarz, who is called weak, small, and an embarrassment. Furthermore, the Orcs have let giants overrun Malacath's shrine. This is an outrage! Yamarz is ordered to bring back the leader's club as an offering. Only then will Malacath consider lifting the curse. The ritual concludes, and Yamarz agrees to this task. But first, he wants a word with you.

◊ **OBJECTIVE:** Speak with Yamarz

Blaming you for Malacath's task, Yamarz demands that you help him. You're to act as his bodyguard, ensuring he doesn't have any trouble reaching the giant. And just so you're clear, he'll definitely be killing the giant's leader himself; he just wants you to handle any attackers along the way. He agrees to make it worth your while. Whether you agree or not is immaterial; you are to meet Yamarz at the entrance to the giants' lair, which leads to Malacath's shrine.

◊ **OBJECTIVE:** Meet Yamarz at Fallowstone Cave

Malacath's Proving Grounds

Fallowstone Cave is nestled in the foothills of the Velothi Mountains, northeast of Riften. You may trek there with Chief Yamarz, fending off any attacks as you cross the thick forest of birch and pine trees, or you can Fast-Travel (or ride) to the cave entrance and wait for Yamarz to appear. Your chaperoning begins after you enter the cave.

> ◊ **OBJECTIVE:** Protect Yamarz
> ♦ **TARGET:** Chief Yamarz, throughout Fallowstone Cave

Enter the cave. Yamarz reluctantly sets off down the tunnel. Follow a few paces or two behind him as the tunnel opens into a gloriously immense subterranean cavern, complete with a waterfall to your left and a series of large, natural steps down to a lower lake area. Follow Yamarz over the small natural bridge and down the steps. Continue to the grotto floor. At the grotto's far end is a campfire and a giant wandering the area. Yamarz avoids the area, and heads along the rushing stream, into a connecting tunnel.

> **TIP** There's no need to confront the giant; if you wish to slay one, wait until this objective completes and backtrack to fight them, rather than risk Yamarz's health.

Head down the stream into a smaller grotto lagoon, where you see a second giant. Avoid it unless it charges you both, and then follow the cave tunnel on the southeastern wall. Enter and scramble up the dirt tunnel, to a confrontation with a couple of wild animals (usually cave bears). The bears are roaming an area of corpses and half-digested food at the entrance to a gap in the southwest tunnel wall. Follow Yamarz up here and into Giant's Grove.

Move alongside Yamarz, following a path of skeletal remains and bloodstains in the snow, until he stops and turns to you, telling you he's ready to kill the giant—that is, of course, unless you want to make some extra gold.

Yamarz has a proposition for you: If you face the giant and kill it, he'll simply return to the tribe and tell them he was responsible. They'll be none the wiser, and you'll be all the richer. You can:

Refuse, telling Yamarz that he is the one who is supposed to kill the giant to lift the curse. He reluctantly agrees and rushes toward the campfire and the giant guarding a large shrine statue of Malacath. Moments later, Yamarz is caught by the giant's club and is crushed, sprawled dead on the snow. You now need to face the giant yourself.

Agree, and rush toward the large campfire and the giant with your weapons drawn.

> ◊ **OBJECTIVE:** Defeat the giant

Kill the giant using the same techniques you've used countless times before. Remember to use the landscape to your advantage, finding cover so your Stamina recharges. After you destroy this giant leader, search the corpse for a massive hammer. This is the weapon Malacath ordered Yamarz to return to Largashbur.

➤ **Shagrol's Warhammer**

> ◊ **OBJECTIVE:** Take Shagrol's Warhammer back to Largashbur

Head back toward the exit of Giant's Grove. If you agreed to kill the giant for Chief Yamarz, he is here, ready to welch on his agreement. He can't have the likes of you usurping his authority and mentioning you were responsible for the giant's death. Yamarz attacks and must be killed.

Either way, when both Chief Yamarz and the giant leader are dead, Malacath speaks to you from his shrine effigy, impressed by your fighting prowess.

Atub greets you at the gate to Largashbur. She asks what happened to Yamarz. You can tell the truth or give a slightly skewed account of events in which Yamarz was a brave fighter instead of the sniveling backstabber he actually was. Either way, Atub walks toward the shrine, Malacath's voice ringing around the camp. The Daedric Prince is willing to give this motley band of Orcs a chance and appoints Gularzob (Yamarz's son) as chief. Malacath finally insists that you place the hammer on the shrine.

> ◊ **OBJECTIVE:** Place Shagrol's Warhammer on the shrine in Largashbur

Quest Conclusion

Approach the skull on the trunk and place the hammer on its antlers. Malacath is satisfied and replaces the hammer with an exceptional weapon named Volendrung, which you can wield!

➤ **Volendrung**

Postquest Activities

Volendrung is a massive warhammer with an Absorb Stamina enchantment. This allows you to inflict power attacks without stopping for as long as it has a charge! As Malacath's champion, you can take this. Malacath then names Gularzob as the new chief, and all the remaining Orcs are now friendly toward you. As Malacath's champion, you are also blood-kin to the other Orcs as well and don't have to complete Side Quest: Forgemaster's Fingers to gain acceptance in any Orc stronghold.

MINOR SPOILERS

PREREQUISITES: You must be Level 20 or higher

INTERSECTING QUESTS: None

LOCATIONS: Cracked Tusk Keep, Cracked Tusk Vaults, Dawnstar, Silus Vesuius's House , (aka the Museum of the Mythic Dawn), Dead Crone Rock, Hag Rock Redoubt, Hag Rock Redoubt Ruin, Morthal, Jorgen and Lami's House, Shrine of Mehrunes Dagon

CHARACTERS: Courier, Jorgen, Lami, Madena, Mehrunes Dagon, Silus Vesuius

ENEMIES: Cave Bear, Drascua, Forsworn, Forsworn Briarheart, Ghunzul, Orc Bandit, Orc Hunter, Snow Bear

◊ **OBJECTIVES:** Miscellaneous: Visit the museum in Dawnstar, Speak to Silus inside his house, Retrieve the pommel of Mehrunes' Razor, Retrieve the blade shards of Mehrunes' Razor, Retrieve the hilt of Mehrunes' Razor, Bring the pommel stone to Silus, Bring the blade shards to Silus, Bring the hilt to Silus, Meet Silus at the Shrine of Mehrunes Dagon, Speak to Mehrunes Dagon, Kill Silus, Reforge Mehrunes' Razor, Claim Mehrunes' Razor

Dead Oaths on Dead Lips

When you reach Level 20, visit any city in Skyrim; Riverwood is a fine example. When you reach the city, a courier approaches and delivers a message regarding the opening of a new museum up in Dawnstar. The owner is handing out invitations; you can visit at your earliest convenience. This doesn't begin the quest yet, just a Miscellaneous Objective that piques your interest.

◊ **MISCELLANEOUS OBJECTIVE:** Visit the museum in Dawnstar
♦ **TARGET:** Silus Vesuius's House, in Dawnstar

As you near Silus Vesuius's House in Dawnstar, he is out on the porch having a heated discussion with Dawnstar's Court Wizard, Madena. The argument centers around Silus refusing to bury his family's legacy. Madena eventually gives up talking to him and leaves, allowing you to greet Silus and visit the Museum of the Mythic Dawn. You can ask him more about it, and he reveals it contains artifacts from a group that once toppled an Empire. Silus also has a job you'd be perfect for. This quest now officially begins.

◊ **OBJECTIVE:** Speak to Silus inside his house
♦ **TARGET:** The Museum of the Mythic Dawn, in Dawnstar

The museum takes up about two-thirds of Silus's house. You are free to peruse the cabinets before speaking to Silus; he offers commentary as you inspect each display case. You discover the tapestries were hung in hideouts where the mysterious Mythic Dawn would meet and plot. The scabbard has Oblivion Gate iconography etched into it, a key symbol of Mehrunes Dagon, the patron Daedra. The case of books are commentaries on the Mysterium Xarxes, written by the cult's leader, Mankar Camoran. The burned paper is all that remains of the fabled Mysterium Xarxes, the blasphemous book written by Mehrunes Dagon. Finally, the robes were worn during the Mythic Dawn's secret meetings, where they plotted to bring Dagon into Tamriel.

With the tour over, you can speak with Silus about the Mythic Dawn and the museum. But asking about the job is the most important question. Silus tells you that after the Oblivion Crisis, groups began to appear that were dedicated to wiping out what was left of the Mythic Dawn. One of these groups found Mehrunes' Razor, the artifact of Dagon. After splitting this razor into three fragments, the pieces were dispersed. Silus wants the pieces reunited. You're here to remove the fragments from their current owners—two dangerous marauders named Ghunzul and Drascua and a resident of Morthal named Jorgen. Silus hands you notes about each of them and will gladly pay for any pieces you bring back to him.

➤ The Keepers of the Razor

◊ **OBJECTIVE:** Retrieve the pommel of Mehrunes' Razor
♦ **TARGET:** Drascua, in Dead Crone Rock
◊ **OBJECTIVE:** Retrieve the blade shards of Mehrunes' Razor
♦ **TARGET:** Ghunzul, in Cracked Tusk Keep
◊ **OBJECTIVE:** Retrieve the hilt of Mehrunes' Razor
♦ **TARGET:** Jorgen, in Morthal

Daedric Defragmentation

TIP You may have already explored these main locations and found a fragment. If you investigate the areas and the fragment isn't there, check your inventory.

Part 1: Drascua's Pommel

Far to the west, just southwest of Markarth, is Hag Rock Redoubt. Begin the long ascension, passing under a couple of buttress overhangs while tackling the Forsworn that are swarming this location. Continue up the slopes, passing under two stone arches with carved heads atop each side; beware of cave bears in these parts. At this point, you can:

Proceed directly to Dead Crone Rock by weaving through the exterior Forsworn Camp.

Or you can follow the pathway up to an old ceremonial crypt and sacrificial area sunk into the side of the mountain, and enter the iron door into Hag Rock Redoubt Ruin. Inside, the Forsworn have erected sharpened wood spikes and attack viciously when you maneuver into their eating area. Clear this place of foes (or sneak by) before using the spiral stairs to reach an upper corridor and a circular storage room containing a Forsworn Briarheart. Then head southwest, around the corridor to the ruin's exit.

You arrive on the roof of the interior ruin. This stone plateau is dominated by steps to ascend and a small Forsworn camp to raze or ignore. Climb the steps until you reach the exterior of Dead Crone Rock, a granite fortification toward the slope's top. Head up the stairs to the first level, which consists of a corridor, more Forsworn, and spiral stairs up to the main floor. A circular chamber atop the spiral stairs has its main exit (to the southwest) blocked by a portcullis. Raise it by fighting through a chamber with a long, bloody sacrificial table and into a connecting room with a lever. Pull the lever to raise the portcullis before leaving by the now-open exit that ends in a wooden door.

You appear at the base of more steps. These lead to the top of Dead Crone Rock, where the Hagraven Drascua resides. Attack with your preferred weapons until she yields. Search her corpse for the pommel and the Dead Crone Rock Key, which opens the locked gate in the previous interior fortification you climbed through. Also, absorb another Word of Power from the nearby Word Wall.

CAUTION Beware of magic traps in this general area; fire shoots from Soul Gems on pedestals; rush and grab the gem to stop the fire or flee past.

➤ **Pommel stone of Mehrunes' Razor** ➤ **Dead Crone Rock Key**
➤ **Word of Power:** Dismaying Shout

◊ **OBJECTIVE:** Bring the pommel stone to Silus
♦ **TARGET:** Silus Vesuius's House, in Dawnstar

Part 2: Ghunzul's Blade Shards

Journey into Falkreath Hold and approach Cracked Tusk Keep. There are usually two Orcs standing guard on the watchtowers. Pick them off with arrows or spells from a distance to soften up the Keep's defenses. Then climb over the dilapidated fortifications, or use the front gate for a less-subtle entry if you aren't concerned about stealth. Expect a trio of Orc hunters and bandits on guard here. These shouldn't prove too difficult to overcome. Your main access point into the Keep is the door to the southwest, in the middle of the main inner Keep wall. An alternate entrance to the right (west) is locked (Adept) and allows you to avoid the confrontation with Ghunzul.

Once inside, prepare to attack more Orc enemies in the two-floor storage and dining area, with a door in the southeastern wall. This leads to a fireplace and bedroom, Ghunzul's usual location (although he may be wandering the Keep's interior). He's brandishing a particularly impressive two-handed weapon, so prepare for intense combat in a confined space. Continue fighting until you beat Ghunzul to death. Alternatively, you can try pickpocketing the Orc if your Sneak skills are truly impressive. Either way, Ghunzul is carrying an important key on him.

➤ **Cracked Tusk Vault Key**

TIP If you just want the Shards and can unlock the Expert-locked cage on your own, you can avoid Ghunzul completely. Or, defeat Ghunzul to make the unlocking a lot easier!

Return to the raised dining room. This time take the door on the lower level to the northwest, which leads down into a small barrel-storing cellar and passage. Ignore the door leading back outside (this is the western entrance from the exterior), and inspect the cage, which is blocking your path to the southwest. Use the Vault Key (or an exceptional Lockpick [Expert]) to unlock the cage, releasing the vertical spike bars. When the spikes recede, descend to and open the door to Cracked Tusk Vaults.

Head down the stairs and into the slightly soggy underground vault. The way ahead is blocked by several spear bars. Pull the two levers to either side of the passage to release both sets of spears. Then carefully walk forward, cutting instead of triggering the two trip wires that release darts up and into you. Or, run through and step to the side. Now approach the pedestal with the blade shards on it, and grab them before moving backward quickly, thus avoiding a flurry of additional darts. Now retrace your steps back out into Skyrim.

TIP If you stop after breaking each trip wire, the darts fire harmlessly in front of you. Avoid the dart traps entirely by sidestepping left just inside the door, but watch for a trip wire to the side that triggers a wall trap.

➤ **Shards of Mehrunes' Razor**

◊ **OBJECTIVE:** Bring the blade shards to Silus
♦ **TARGET:** Silus Vesuius's House, in Dawnstar

◊ **OBJECTIVE:** Kill Orchendor
♦ **TARGET:** Orchendor, in the Bthardamz Arcanex

Assault on the Afflicted

Bthardamz Exterior: Before you begin the trek to Bthardamz, optionally speak with Kesh the Clean again. He provides further information on Orchendor and the Dwarven ruins of a vast underground city, which you can actually see from this vantage point if you look due west. Then head down the mountain and climb the stone entrance steps to the pavilion domes that ushered in the Afflicted. Some still guard the area and will attack on sight. They are powerful warriors but have a weak constitution thanks to the pox Peryite infected them with. Work your way through the pavilion, and into the main entrance, complete with buttress domes on each side (you'll use one to exit from this place).

For the moment, head down the steps with the blade trap slit down the middle. The first golden lever you see activates these blades. The second lever to the right of the doorway blocked by spears removes this obstacle, allowing you through into the Bthardamz Upper District.

Bthardamz Upper District: Head down the ramped passage and around the corner to the right (north). Either open the gate (Novice) or navigate around two sleeping areas with Afflicted to pulverize. Continue along the corridors past an open storage room and down another slope to a large piston chamber where the Afflicted have gathered to breathe in the vapors of a bubbling ichor. Defeat or sneak around them, and head west into the main Upper District courtyard.

Amid the pipes and stonework is a central platform with green ooze bubbling. Take out the enemies, head north, climb the stairs to the balcony, and activate the lever. Spear bars retract from the balcony opposite, allowing you to leave via a stone path. Open the gold door and enter a passage heading west that ends in a pipe room. Dwarven Spheres are activated here if you enter. Take the sloping corridor on your right (south) with the whirring blade trap. Journey down a cobblestone street to a carved stone arch opening. Slay the Afflicted guarding this door to Bthardamz Workshop.

Bthardamz Workshop and Upper District (2): Move around the pipes, checking the gate on your right and left (north and south) to reach sleeping quarters. The second bedroom has a note revealing the exact location of Orchendor; he is inside the Bthardamz Arcanex. Continue along the green-tinged corridors to a stairwell where you fight your first Dwarven Spiders. The staircase allows you to enter the Upper District; gaze across the small maze of stonework and open a small chest. You can drop down from here (to the southeast, or you'll have to retrace your steps), or you can to return to the Workshop and head south into a steam pipe room with Afflicted and a second entrance back into the Upper District. Back in the Upper District, head southeast toward a series of stone steps. Climb them to the top. Along the way, there's a balcony you can check, as well as a separate Bthardamz Dwelling to scavenge. The stairs continue around to the southwest. Go up stone ramps offering a spectacular view back down and a corridor ending at a door to Bthardamz Lower District.

➤ **Afflicted's Note**

Bthardamz Lower District: Now in the Lower District, tread through the echoing gloom, past a gate (with a chest behind it), and through a gold door and Dwarven Spider attack. In a large, ruined coliseum is a central plinth on which rests a chest. The lever on the balcony activates a blade trap on the plinth. Battle the Afflicted here. The exit to the east leads to the main Lower District. Cross the curved courtyard, go through the open gate, and cross the two stone platforms that span a winding subterranean stream. Afflicted are active here.

Head through another open gate. Battle two Dwarven Spheres and a mass of Afflicted just after the arch with the lever on it. The lever drops a nasty spike just behind you; use it to skewer foes or stop them from following you. But it is better to sneak past or kill everyone. There are two sets of steps here. The ones to your left (north) lead to a circular platform; water pours from (currently inaccessible) upper walkways. The other staircase at the District's east end leads past Dwarven Spiders and into the Bthardamz Study.

Bthardamz Study: Through the gate to the east is a small study area. To your south is a golden door. Head through and go up the stairs (without setting off the pressure plate and activating the blade trap). Enter through a gate and into the Lower District once again.

Bthardamz Lower District (2): You're now on the upper walkways you could only see earlier. Head down the rooftop stone ramp. To your right (east) is a gate and a chest. To your left (west) is a large covered L-shaped walkway with a turret balcony in the middle. Expect combat with at least six Afflicted here, and watch your step; don't head off the platforms to a crushing fall below! Move through the second walkway heading south, and exit into the Bthardamz Arcanex.

> **NOTE** Don't worry; the fumes you're inhaling aren't at dangerous levels. You may also spot some ballistas. These can be fired but not aimed (so you can't use them on Dwarven Centurions unless they step right in front of the bolt's trajectory, and you only have one firing opportunity).

Bthardamz Arcanex: This is essentially a large watery grotto with Dwarven towers and platforms built inside it. Head along the platforms, preparing for combat with Dwarven Spheres. Climb the spiraling stone path to the upper corridor, at the end of which a Dwarven Centurion roars into life. You can try sprinting around him or backing up and tackling him from range. If you flee forward, you also meet Dwarven Spiders that can overwhelm you. Fight carefully, retreating if the Centurion becomes too much of a threat.

Once you flee from the mechanical foes or defeat them, climb the stairs beyond the Centurion and reach the upper balcony area. There are six more Dwarven Spiders to defeat before you sprint past a clanking pipe corridor that opens into a pipe-laden Arcanex chamber with two Dwarven Spheres. Defeat them before heading through the gap in the north wall to the rear of the Arcanex chamber, where you have a final confrontation with Orchendor.

Orchendor is in no mood to talk and attacks immediately. Use the scenery to your advantage. Use the gap in the wall or the stairs behind him to hide or fire from if necessary. Watch for his teleportation and for any Dwarven foes you haven't killed, as they tend to follow you into this combat. After you dispatch Orchendor, search him. Among his trinkets is a key allowing you to exit this place without having to retrace your steps.

➤ **Key to Bthardamz Elevator**

◊ **OBJECTIVE:** Report Orchendor's death to Peryite
♦ **TARGET:** Aspect of Peryite, Shrine to Peryite

Quest Conclusion

Head up the stairs at the Arcanex chamber's north end, using the key to reach the Bthardamz Elevator and activating the lever. Ride the elevator up to the exterior entrance. Run along the stone walkways and down to the pavilion to escape this Dwarven maze for good. Fast-Travel at any point or trek east, back to the shrine. Commune with Peryite by inhaling at the cauldron again. Peryite congratulates you, as your actions have sent Orchendor to roam the Pits; his betrayal will be punished and your obedience rewarded.

➤ **Spellbreaker**

Postquest Activities

Spellbreaker is as impressive as it is unique. It generates a Ward when you're blocking, making it very useful when you're fighting against magical enemies. Also beware of (random) retribution: There's a chance World Encounter: The Afflicted versus You* will occur, and you'll face Afflicted wishing you harm after your massacre here.

A NIGHT TO REMEMBER

PREREQUISITES: You must be Level 14 or higher

MINOR SPOILERS

INTERSECTING QUESTS: None

LOCATIONS: Markarth, Temple of Dibella, Morvunskar, Misty Grove, Rorikstead, Whiterun, Witchmist Grove

CHARACTERS: Ennis, Gleda the Goat, Sam Guevenne , Sanguine, Senna, Ysolda

ENEMIES: Conjurer, Fire Mage, Ice Mage, Moira, Necromancer, Pyromancer, Storm Mage, Giant

◊ **OBJECTIVES:** Participate in a drinking contest with Sam Guevenne, Find Sam Guevenne, Find the staff, Help clean up the Temple of Dibella, Apologize to the priestesses of Dibella, Ask about Sam and the staff in Rorikstead, Find Gleda the Goat, Bring Gleda the Goat back to Ennis in Rorikstead, Talk to Ysolda in Whiterun about the staff, Find the wedding ring in Witchmist Grove, Take the wedding ring, Return the wedding ring to Ysolda in Whiterun, Head to Morvunskar, Search Morvunskar for Sam and the staff

Drinking to Forget

Enter one of the many taverns in Skyrim. This could be the Bannered Mare in Whiterun or any of the other inns in any of the Hold Cities. Sometimes you're approached by a man wearing black robes named Sam Guevenne, who wonders if you'd like to play a drinking game in order to win a staff. If Sam isn't in the tavern, visit another watering hole; be patient until he appears. Sam produces some "special brew" and gets started immediately.

◊ **OBJECTIVE:** Participate in a drinking contest with Sam Guevenne

Sam downs a flagon and offers one to you. Swig it down. Sam brings out his flagon again and impressively downs another. Agree to the second drink. Sam tells you he's hit his limit and says that with one more drink, you'll win both the contest and the staff. You reply that you'll take that challenge. Down a third flagon. Sam tells you you're a fun person to drink with. He reckons you should join him at another place where the wine flows like water. You're about to respond when you black out.

The Day After: Recovery and Recollections

Part 1: Incoherently Blathering Drunken Blasphemer!

Your next memory is waking up to a tongue-lashing from a furious priestess. Unless you've remarkable knowledge of temple gods, you don't immediately realize where you are. Priestess Senna wonders why you don't remember blathering incoherently about marriage or a goat. Or indeed, losing your temper and throwing refuse across this sacred temple of Dibella. You can:

Ask about the man named Sam. This gets you nowhere until you've tidied up your mess.

(Persuade) You can apologize and tell her you don't remember how you got here.

(Bribe) You can ask how you got here and pay for any damages.

◊ **OBJECTIVE:** Find Sam Guevenne
◊ **OBJECTIVE:** Find the staff
◊ **OBJECTIVE:** Help clean up the Temple of Dibella

Begin tidying up the temple, collecting the rubbish listed below. Among the wine bottles is a note. Read it, and a list of three items are mentioned that can "repair the broken staff." The note is signed "Sam." You're fortunate that two of the three items on the list are among the trash you're clearing up! Now there's just the small matter of searching Skyrim for Sam. And the goat.

- ➤ **Alto Wine**
- ➤ **Repair Supplies Note**
- ➤ **Giant's Toe**
- ➤ **Holy Water**

◊ **OBJECTIVE:** Apologize to the priestesses of Dibella

If you didn't bribe or persuade Senna, return to her after the tidy-up and apologize. As Dibella preaches forgiveness, she grudgingly lets you leave and tells you that through your slurred ranting, you mentioned the town of Rorikstead.

◊ **OBJECTIVE:** Ask about Sam and the staff in Rorikstead

Part 2: Fermented Feed–Smelling Goat Rustler!

Exit the temple. You're in Markarth, in the Reach. Your next place to investigate is Rorikstead, to the east, on the edge of the Tundra plains. Wander into town and seek Ennis, who's tending to his vegetable patch or is locked behind closed doors (which you can pick, but it's better not to show clandestine behavior under these current conditions). Ennis angrily states you have a lot of nerve showing up here again. He proceeds to admonish you for stealing Gleda—his prized goat—and selling it to a giant. At this point, you can:

(Intimidate) Threaten Ennis to tell you everything so he doesn't end up like Gleda.

(Bribe) Ask him to help retrace your steps in return for some serious coin.

(Persuade) Tell him you need Sam and the staff to return Gleda.

Or ask what needs to be done. Ennis wants his prized goat back. Unharmed.

◊ **OBJECTIVE:** Find Gleda the Goat
◊ **OBJECTIVE:** Bring Gleda the Goat back to Ennis in Rorikstead

THE GREYBEARDS QUESTS

The following activities occur after you complete certain parts of the Main Quest. From this point on, High Hrothgar in Whiterun Hold is the main base of operations for the Greybeards. Providing you partner with Master Arngeir and Paarthurnax and do not complete Main Quest: Paarthurnax, you can help the Greybeards preserve the Way of the Voice. There are now two Radiant Quests you can attempt.

OVERVIEW

Sanctuary: High Hrothgar, in Whiterun Hold

High Hrothgar, on approach from the 7,000 steps.

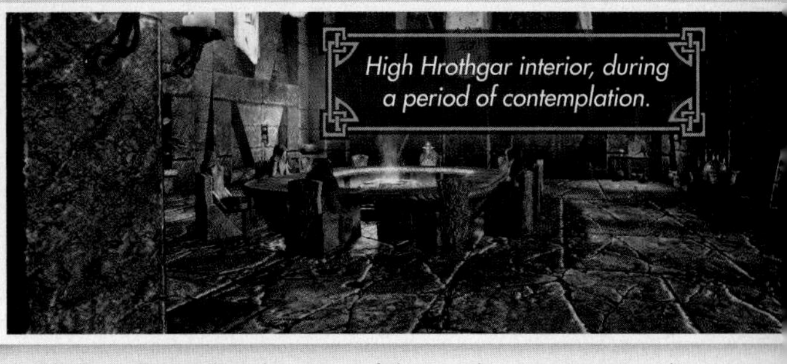
High Hrothgar interior, during a period of contemplation.

An ancient monastery high up on the slope of the Throat of the World, High Hrothgar is home to the Greybeards, masters of Thu'um—the voice powers made famous by Tiber Septim.

Important Characters

Leader: Paarthurnax

Paarthurnax lives above High Hrothgar, at the summit of the Throat of the World, and serves as the supreme master of the Greybeards. He remembers back to the days of the ancient Dragon War when Alduin was defeated and imprisoned. He views events from a distance and from a uniquely detached point of view.

Elder: Master Arngeir

Arngeir is the most powerful of the Greybeards, although this isn't immediately obvious to the rare visitors he receives. His initial reaction to you is cautious; he wants to believe that a Dragonborn has returned but hardly dares to hope it is true.

NOTE The other Greybeards—Masters Wulfgar, Einarth, and Borri—do not speak; their voices are too powerful. Only Master Arngeir is skilled enough to master his voice to the point of conversation. However, they have been known to attempt conversations with those powerful enough to withstand their voices. They excel in the training of Shouts by gestures and demonstration.

WORD WALL REVELATIONS*

NOTE * Quest names marked with this symbol do not appear in your Quest Menu list, although objectives may.

This Radiant Quest becomes available as soon as you complete Main Quest: The Horn of Jurgen Windcaller. You can complete it multiple times. It is always given to you by Master Arngeir.

Speak to Master Arngeir about the Greybeards, and he mentions that there are Words of Power scattered across Skyrim. Most are lost to the world, found only by those stumbling into underground passageways or snowy mountains not used for centuries. If you want, Master Arngeir can place a marker on your world map, randomly showing you a Word Wall you haven't yet discovered.

◊ **OBJECTIVE:** Find the Word of Power in [random location]

Quest Conclusion

Journey to a location that Arngeir marked, and absorb the Word of Power. This may involve battling any number of guardians, usually Draugr or a dragon. The Word Walls Arngeir reveals may be ones perched atop mountain peaks or hidden in deep dungeons. He usually won't reveal locations you've already been to, unless you've forgotten or missed the Word Wall at that location.

➤ **Word of Power**

Postquest Activities

You can return to Master Arngeir and begin this quest repeatedly. A section in the Training Chapter on page 47 lists the locations of all the Word Walls and their associated Shouts.

NOTE Sometimes this quest won't be available; this means that Arngeir hasn't discovered a location for you at the moment. It is wise to return later (try around three days) to see if his scrying has revealed any more locations.

MEDITATIONS ON WORDS OF POWER*

> **NOTE** This Radiant Quest becomes available as soon as you complete Main Quest: The Throat of the World. You can complete this multiple times. It is always given to you by Paarthurnax.

Trek to the summit of the Throat of the World and speak with Paarthurnax. He has much to tell you about the Words of Power and can even teach basic meditations to your Words of Power. Ask Paarthurnax if he trains people, and after the response, ask about the meditations. Paarthurnax grants you a single meditation. The exact one is up to you:

- **Perk:** Force Without Effort (Fus)
- **Perk:** Eternal Spirit (Feim)
- **Perk:** The Fire Within (Yol)

Quest Conclusion

Fus grants you 25 percent defense against stagger, and you stagger opponents 25 percent more often. Feim grants you 25 percent more health regeneration while you're ethereal. Yol grants you 25 percent bonus damage when you use the Fire Breath Shout.

Postquest Activities

You can return to Paarthurnax at any time and change the Meditation to another of the three perks. You can have only one Meditation at a time.

THE BLADES QUESTS

The following activities occur only after you complete Main Quest: Alduin's Wall. From this moment on, the Sky Haven Temple in the Reach is the main base of operations for the Blades. Providing you partner with Delphine and Esbern and complete Main Quest: Paarthurnax, you can help the Blades to gain a foothold in Skyrim once more. There are now four Radiant Quests you can attempt.

OVERVIEW

Sanctuary: Sky Haven Temple, in the Reach

Sky Haven Temple, entrance to the sacred interior.

Sky Haven interior, dominated by Alduin's Wall.

An ancient Akaviri sanctuary, Sky Haven Temple was built as a hidden outpost. The secret interior chambers are dominated by Alduin's Wall, the ancient mural that shows the history and future of Alduin—how he was defeated in ancient times and the prophecy of his return.

Important Characters

Blade Leader: Delphine

The last Blade left in Tamriel (as far as she knows), Delphine is hard-bitten and a survivor. Any idealism has been largely driven out of her during her years on the run. Competent, she tends toward paranoia. She hates the Thalmor above all and will stop at nothing to see them destroyed. Full of darkness and despair, she may yet be turned back toward idealism and the rebirth of the Blades.

Blade Archivist: Esbern

After the Blades' destruction, Esbern went underground, ignoring any messages for help from other Blades (having seen that this was often a Thalmor trap), which allowed him to survive. Esbern has been obsessed with the end of the world for decades. Now that Alduin has returned, he immediately recognizes this as the beginning of the end—without a Dragonborn, there is no hope to stop him.

REBUILDING THE BLADES*

NOTE * Quest names marked with this symbol do not appear in your Quest Menu list, although objectives may.

This Radiant Quest becomes available as soon as you complete Main Quest: Alduin's Wall. You can complete it multiple times. It is always given to you by Delphine.

Speak to Delphine about the Blades, and she mentions how few of them are left; in fact, there are only two in existence! To bolster the numbers, and because it is the Blades' sacred duty to protect the Dragonborn (you), Delphine asks if you know of any like-minded individuals who can give their hearts and minds to this course.

◊ **OBJECTIVE:** Bring a Follower to Delphine

Journey to a location where you left a Follower or where you can obtain one. Then return and speak to Delphine with the Follower accompanying you.

Quest Conclusion

Delphine welcomes your Follower into the fold. As time passes and you return to see your Follower, they are able to wear Blades armor and carry weapons used by the Blades, and they live in the Sky Haven Temple. They can accompany you on travels just as before. You can repeat this quest, turn in two additional Followers, and pick one to travel with you, just as before.

Postquest Activities

This is a good way to amass a small "pool" of Followers to take with you on journeys in the future.

DRAGONSLAYER'S BLESSING*

NOTE This Radiant Quest becomes available as soon as you complete Main Quest: Alduin's Wall. You can complete it multiple times. It is always given to you by Esbern.

Speak to Esbern and ask if the sage has any advice for you. Providing you're in good standing with the Blades, he mentions a blessing he can perform. Request this blessing, and he duly obliges.

Quest Conclusion

You are imbued with Esbern's Dragonslayer's Blessing, which gives you a +10 percent Critical Hit versus dragons for five days.

➤ **Dragonslayer's Blessing**

Postquest Activities

Once this wears off, ask Esbern to renew it if you wish.

DRAGON RESEARCH*

NOTE This Radiant Quest becomes available as soon as you complete the Blades Quest: Dragon Hunting.* You can complete it only once. It is always given to you by Esbern.

Once you've completed your first Dragon Hunting Quest for Esbern, report back to him. He's interested in you locating any Dragon Scales or Dragon Bones you may have pried off the corpses of the dragons you've slain previously.

◊ **OBJECTIVE:** Bring a Dragon Scale and a Dragon Bone to Esbern

Quest Conclusion

When you return with a Dragon Scale and a Dragon Bone to Esbern (which you may already have gathered, in which case, speak to him again), he concocts a strange potion and hands it to you. This potion imbues you with a 10 percent damage reduction from dragon attacks.

➤ **Esbern's Potion** ➤ **Perk: Dragon Infusion**

DRAGON HUNTING*

NOTE This Radiant Quest becomes available as soon as you complete The Blades Quest: Rebuilding the Blades.* You can complete it multiple times. It is always given to you by Esbern.

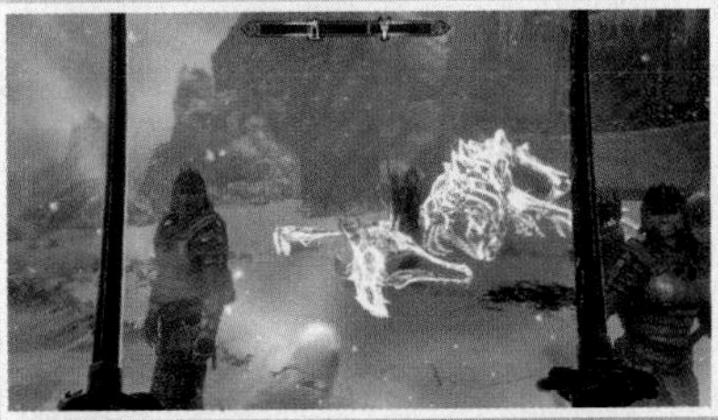

Once you've turned in three of your Followers to Delphine, and she's welcomed them into the fold, speak to Esbern, steering the conversation toward dragon lairs. When you ask Esbern if he has knowledge of any lairs, he informs you that he does and points out a [random] lair on your world map. If Esbern hasn't found a dragon lair, he'll mention the realm is quiet at the moment.

◊ **OBJECTIVE:** Kill the dragon in the [random] dragon lair

Quest Conclusion

Set off on your journey to slay the dragon, which is, after all, the raison d'être of the Blades. Begin combat with this hated beast. The Followers you have accrued will also stand and fight with you, making for an epic assault. Bring down the dragon and then report back to Esbern.

➤ **Dragon Bone** ➤ **Dragon Soul**
➤ **Dragon Scales**

Postquest Activities

Protect any Blades you wish to see live to fight another day; once Blades (your old Followers) die during battle, they cannot be replaced.

THE BARDS COLLEGE QUESTS

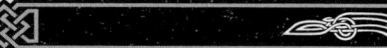

THE BARDS COLLEGE

Sanctuary: Bards College, in Solitude

This College has attracted the young, gifted, or rich and ungifted from across the realm of Skyrim. It is where Nords send the few sons and daughters without an aptitude for farmwork or battle.

Important Characters

Headmaster: Viarmo

Viarmo is totally apolitical when it comes to the Civil War. His only concern is the welfare of the Bards College. He is politically shrewd but has masterfully steered clear of taking sides or taking stands on any of the issues of the day. The Bards' role is to entertain and record the events of history, not to make them.

Dean of History: Giraud Gemane

Giraud also carries out many of the bureaucratic duties at the College. He is a mousy, quiet man, and not at all what one would expect from a bardic performer. In truth, he has a certain degree of stage fright. However, his mathematical precision and perfectionism have made him one of the best performers of the drums, piano, and several other "lesser" instruments.

Dean of Lutes: Inge Six-Fingers

Inge doesn't really have six fingers, but anyone who watches her play the lute believes she does. She is an old, crotchety woman who would rather burn her own lute than become headmaster because it would remove her from teaching. However, she will reluctantly put the needs of the College ahead of her own feelings if necessary.

Master Vocalist: Pantea Ateia

Pantea is one of the youngest masters of Voice that the Bards College in Solitude has ever had. Her performances are highly sought after, and she frequently plays at the palace for Elisif. Unlike Headmaster Viarmo, she is a supporter of the Imperial cause in Skyrim. In deference to the headmaster, she keeps her opinions largely to herself.

There are also students inside the College. These include the following:

Jorn: The most advanced student in the school. He is particularly enamored with the battle drum.

Aia Arria: The best singer. She is keenly aware of how she can enchant people with her voice, especially men.

At-Af-Alan: He has just started his lessons and spends more time with Giraud learning rhythm and beat.

Illdi: A recent enrollment and enthusiastic about memorizing the tales of old, her performances are timid and underwhelming.

PREREQUISITES: None
INTERSECTING QUESTS: None
LOCATIONS: Dead Men's Respite, Solitude, Bards College, Blue Palace
CHARACTERS: General Tullius, Giraud Gemane, Jarl Elisif the Fair, Jorn, Svaknir, Viarmo
ENEMIES: Draugr, Frostbite Spider, King Olaf One-Eye, Skeever
◊ **OBJECTIVES:** Find King Olaf's Verse, Return to the Bards College, Help Viarmo reconstruct Olaf's Verse, Meet Viarmo at the Blue Palace, Watch Viarmo perform Olaf's Verse, Speak to Viarmo, Speak to Jorn, Attend the Burning of King Olaf

Unearthing Arcane Edda

If you speak with any of the Bards who sing and play (usually in the main inn or tavern in any of Skyrim's main cities), they mention that you might be interested in becoming a member of the Bards College. These hints are optional to find but point you in the direction of the College.

When you're ready to become a Bard, visit the Avenues District. One of the fancier buildings houses the Bards College, as indicated by the door icon on your local map. The College Headmaster Viarmo is in the lobby of this building.

He warns you that the College accepts few applicants, but for your interview, he has a task that might be appropriate. He tells you that the Burning of King Olaf Festival, held by the College each year, has been forbidden by Solitude's Jarl Elisif. He believes he can change the Jarl's mind if he can perform a reading of King Olaf's Verse, a part of the living history of Skyrim called the Poetic Edda that the Bards College keeps.

The College historian, Giraud Gemane, believes that the only surviving copy of King Olaf's Verse was buried in the old king's tomb. Giraud's research leads him to believe that Dead Men's Respite is the location where the king still lies. Look here.

◊ **OBJECTIVE:** Find King Olaf's Verse
♦ **TARGET:** King Olaf's Verse, in Dead Men's Respite

A Ghost of a Chance

From Dragon Bridge, you can head south along the road to Robbers' Gorge, then follow the river east to the tomb, or take the longer (but safer) road past Fort Snowhawk before heading through the mountains. Enter the ancient barrow and head into the entry chamber, where you encounter the ghost of a bard. It turns and walks through the portcullis, fading out before you can interact with it. Return to the table and remove the Ruby Dragon Claw from the pressure plate, which raises the portcullis. You'll need the Claw later, but first, defend yourself from the restless Draugr. Your claw removal startled them out of slumber.

➤ **Ruby Dragon Claw**

With the Draugr temporarily thwarted, head through the doorway that opened and around to another sighting of the ghostly form; it bears the name Svaknir. Don't focus on it as you walk down the corridor; there's a floor pressure plate that triggers a spear trap for the unwary! Follow the narrow crypt corridor around and down, to a seemingly dead end. Look to the right for a chain that rotates the stone wall in front of you, opening up a way into the main crypt.

Svaknir walks out of sight, leaving you to fend off some Frostbite Spiders. Carefully pick your way past more cobwebs to another chain (in a crypt with fallen masonry) and pull it. The walls rotate once more, opening a new path through the tombs and unlocking several more chambers with Draugr. Fight or sneak through to the stairs heading down, avoiding the flame trap at the bottom.

You come out into a cobwebbed chamber with a floor grate, where more Frostbite Spiders descend to fight you. After looting the room, open the grate via the chain on the east wall, and drop into the water below. Wade into a damp burial chamber with spiral wooden steps that Svaknir wanders up while you deal with more Draugr and Skeever. Expect attacks from Draugr bowmen on the upper platform. Head up the steps, into the caged platform, and take stock of the path ahead of you.

On the floor to the door's right is a hinge trigger wire. Disarm it (Lockpicking: Adept) and you can open the door and safely cross the bridge.

Otherwise, open the door and carefully time your movements past the deadly swinging blades, stopping at the safe spots indicated by the candles (and lack of blood). Hurry! The longer you wait, the less synchronized the blades will be, making your run that much harder. You can also try a direct sprint (augmented with spells or a Shout if necessary), or leap to a side alcove and back onto the bridge, avoiding some of the blades. Activate the chain at the bridge's opposite end to stop the blades (allowing your followers to pass), and exit via an upper door.

Svaknir appears again near a sealed door in the next corridor. You cannot open the door for now, so continue deeper into the crypt. Deal with more Draugr along the way and a nasty magic caster trap as you move into a connecting chamber with a floor grate. Look down, and you see Svaknir descending the steps. Then look back up to see the Draugr rushing you from all sides.

After dealing with the ambush, activate the chain between the two carved dragon heads on the south wall to open the grate. Descend the spiral steps below, use the handle, and you come upon the final resting place of Svaknir, the bard who wrote King Olaf's Verse and who first began the festival so long ago. The specter sits next to his corpse, waiting for you to bear his masterwork out into the world. Pry it from his bony fingers.

➤ **King Olaf's Verse**

◊ **OBJECTIVE:** Return to the Bards College

Ascend the spiral stairs and retrace your steps, fighting off any surviving Draugr along the way. When you return to the sealed door, Svaknir is waiting for you. He beckons you to follow and casts a spell at the door, removing the barrier. He then draws his sword and races down the hall. Follow him.

At the hall's end is a Nordic Puzzle Door.

Puzzle Solution: Bring out the Ruby Dragon Claw you took in the entrance embalming room, and inspect the palm. The forms of a Wolf, a Hawk, and another Wolf are etched into the surface. Make sure the door's outer, middle, and inner rings have those carvings shown before you insert the Claw to unlock the door.

Head up the stairs beyond the door, where Svaknir waits with ghostly sword drawn as you enter the ceremonial burial chamber of King Olaf. Svaknir challenges the dead king, and the Draugr who protected him in life rise from their thrones to defend him once more. Join the bard in battle and cut down your foes as quickly as they rise.

Svaknir shouts a second challenge, and the Draugr on the middle level stand up one by one. These foes are tougher, but with the help of your spectral ally, you can beat them.

Finally, follow Svaknir up to the upper level, where the dead king's sarcophagus lies. The bard yells out his final challenge, and King Olaf One-Eye cracks open his sarcophagus and attempts to stop you. Fight the King, as he is carrying the key that allows you to exit this chamber—unless you wish to creep around and unlock the door (Master).

TIP **Defeating Old King Olaf:** It is important to note that Svaknir is invulnerable and cannot be hit by magic or weaponry. This makes him an excellent barraging machine to wade into the fray. If your own defenses are lacking, you can even stand behind him and cast your spells through him. Go ahead; he won't mind.

You don't have to fight the Draugr in the order shown previously. If Svaknir (or your Followers or summoned creatures) can handle the initial wave of Draugr, you can race to the Draugr that are still seated and slay them—ideally before they even finish standing up!

Before you leave, learn the new Word of Power from the Word Wall behind King Olaf's resting place. Then exit via the Iron Door, where Svaknir—his vengeance finally completed—vanishes in a bright light. Use the lever to remove the blocking stone, and exit Dead Men's Respite for good.

➤ **King Olaf's Treasury Key** ➤ **Word of Power:** Whirlwind Sprint

Return of the King

Present King Olaf's Verse to Viarmo. His jubilation quickly subsides as he reads the verse and finds some of it missing,and much of it less "poetic" than modern-day Edda. Offer to make up the missing parts of the verses. Viarmo is convinced.

◊ **OBJECTIVE:** Help Viarmo reconstruct Olaf's Verse
◊ **OBJECTIVE:** Meet Viarmo at the Blue Palace
◊ **OBJECTIVE:** Watch Viarmo perform Olaf's verse
◊ **OBJECTIVE:** Speak to Viarmo

Viarmo needs some story hooks and ideas that give the poem a more thrilling and weaving narrative than before. You are free to choose what happens in portions of the verses.

(Persuade) You can even choose a more fanciful and outlandish story for the poem. Complete the first Persuade, and a second Persuade option opens up. Choosing both of these increases the patronage paid by the court, and therefore your ultimate reward.

With the poem creatively polished, Viarmo sets off to see the Jarl of Solitude inside the Blue Palace. Follow him when the objective updates. Once inside the palace, ask Viarmo if he's ready. The objective updates again, and he climbs the stairs to gain an audience with Jarl Elisif the Fair.

After a thrilling (and some might say, unbelievable) recount of King Olaf's fable in verse form, Jarl Elisif the Fair recognizes that Solitude would be remiss if they forgo this traditional burning festival. She agrees to speak to General Tullius about the matter, and ensures that the College is well rewarded for such a stirring piece of poetry.

As soon as Viarmo leaves the Jarl's chamber, speak with him. Although you aren't a bard yet, you are set to be inducted during the festival. For now, you are to locate Jorn, who was preparing the effigy of King Olaf, and tell him to finish the preparations: The festival is back on!

◊ **OBJECTIVE:** Speak to Jorn
♦ **TARGET:** Jorn, in the Bards College

Jorn is usually in the Bards College and is an adept given responsibility for the effigy. Speak with Jorn now, and he asks you to return at 10:00 p.m. or later.

◊ **OBJECTIVE:** Attend the Burning of King Olaf

Quest Conclusion

Return to Jorn at the allotted time, and watch the festival. You can get some free food and hear some music here. Viarmo lights the effigy of King Olaf, which burns merrily. Then, in front of a crowd of Solitude citizens, Viarmo turns to you and welcomes you into the Bards College with the following rewards:

➤ **Leveled gold pieces** ➤ **Perk:** Gift of the Gab

Postquest Activities

You may now speak to any of the bards, who are now "friendly" to your cause. You can and should begin the instrument-collecting quests, detailed next.

She is angry about your unannounced visit, and especially annoyed if you're male, as this is a breach of Temple rules. Stay pleasant with your responses, and ask what the penalty is. You are tasked with locating Dibella's Sybil, a Reachwoman selected as a child to spend her whole life in devotion and communion with the goddess. Your transgression will be forgiven if you can find the next Sybil. Hamal tells you her location was foreseen in a vision. As an added incentive, you will receive the Blessing of Dibella if you're successful.

NOTE You can sneak through this Temple, secure the Statue of Dibella, and then speak to Hamal if you haven't been spotted yet.

CAUTION This quest and Degaine's Miscellaneous Objective are mutually exclusive—you can't do both. If you accept this quest, the priestesses take the statue back. If you reject it, or take the statue later, they become hostile and you fail the quest. This quest requires a little more work, but offers a far better reward.

◊ **OBJECTIVE:** Find the future Sybil of Dibella
♦ **TARGET:** Enmon in Karthwasten

A Father, Inferior

The settlement hewn into the rock that Mother Hamal saw in her vision is the mountain hamlet of Karthwasten. Journey there and wait until daylight hours to pester the townsfolk (as they don't appreciate you lockpicking and sneaking into their homes). Speak to either Mena, who is withdrawn and refers you to her husband, or Enmon. His daughter was taken by the Forsworn, and after you inform him that his daughter is the Sybil of Dibella, Enmon tells you where he thinks Fjotra is and offers to accompany you. Bring Enmon along or tell him to stay in Karthwasten.

➤ **Follower:** Enmon

◊ **OBJECTIVE:** Rescue Fjotra from the Forsworn
♦ **TARGET:** Fjotra in Broken Tower Redoubt

NOTE Enmon can come with you but is pretty pathetic when fighting against the Forsworn. He can die without this quest failing. Perhaps it is better for him to stay home...

Forsaking the Forsworn

Trek to the Broken Tower Redoubt and prepare for battle! Enter the stone structure, and fight through the Forsworn milling about inside. Open the wooden doors and avoid a swinging gate trap as you proceed deeper into the dwelling and up the two floors of spiral stairs inside the main tower. Beware of a boulder trap and more enemies as you ascend, and exit onto the upper battlements.

Enter the second tower atop the battlements, and engage the Forsworn Briarheart in the sacrificial chamber. Then inspect the prison door by the goat's head and candles. You can:

Search the gray corpse for the Prison Key, and use it to unlock the door.

Or pick the lock (Lockpick [Expert]).

Once you free Fjotra, explain that she has been chosen as the Sybil, and she agrees to accompany you back to Markarth.

➤ **Broken Tower Prison Key**

◊ **OBJECTIVE:** Bring Fjotra to the Temple
♦ **TARGET:** Inner Sanctum, Temple of Dibella, in Markarth

The Sybil Entranced

TIP Utilize Fast-Travel to minimize any problems getting Fjotra from the Broken Tower Redoubt to Markarth.

Return to Markarth with young Fjotra. Head up to the Temple of Dibella, enter the inner sanctum, and speak with Mother Hamal, who has made all the arrangements for Fjotra to begin her life of communing with the goddess. As a gesture of thanks, she requests you pray at Dibella's Altar, back in the entrance chamber where you met Senna.

◊ **OBJECTIVE:** Pray at Dibella's Altar
♦ **TARGET:** Temple of Dibella, in Markarth

Quest Conclusion

Once Fjotra is delivered to Mother Hamal, and you pray at the altar, you receive the following:

➤ **Perk:** Agent of Dibella

PREREQUISITES: None

INTERSECTING QUESTS: Thieves Guild Quest: Hard Answers

LOCATIONS: Gjukar's Monument, Greenspring Hollow, Ivarstead, Markarth, Understone Keep, Riften, Temple of Mara

CHARACTERS: Bassianus Axius, Boti, Calcelmo, Dinya Balu, Faleen, Fastred, Fenrig, Jofthor, Klimmek, Maramal, Ruki, Yngvar the Singer

ENEMIES: None

◊ **OBJECTIVES:** Talk to Fastred, Talk to Fastred's parents, Talk to Bassianus or Klimmek, Return to Dinya Balu, Talk to Calcelmo, Get advice from Yngvar, Deliver Poem, Deliver Faleen's letter, Return to Dinya Balu, Put on the Amulet of Mara, Talk to the long-dead lover, Find Fenrig, Bring Fenrig to Ruki, Return to Dinya Balu

Young Love

Enter the town of Riften. Sitting back from the main thoroughfare is the Temple of Mara. Head inside and speak to either Maramal (who may also be in the Bee and Barb); his priestess wife, Dinya Balu; or Briehl an acolyte. Any of them explain they are devoted to the goddess Mara, who gave mortals the gift of love. But to receive her blessing, you must first act as her hand in this world. Ask what you must do, and the priest explains the predicament of a young woman named Fastred. Her prayers were heard by her goddess and relayed to her servant; you must help her choose her suitor.

◊ **OBJECTIVE:** Talk to Fastred
♦ **TARGET:** Fastred, in Ivarstead

Travel to the fishing village of Ivarstead, which has seen better days. Locate the young lady named Fastred, who is usually chopping wood or working in her parents' allotment. She asks if you've been sent from Mara, then explains that her parents are being impossible: Fastred has two suitors, but her favorite—Bassianus—wants to marry and relocate to Riften, which her father has forbidden. She also has a soft spot for another man—Klimmek—who is less adventurous and wants to stay in Ivarstead.

◊ **OBJECTIVE:** Talk to Fastred's parents
♦ **TARGET:** Boti and Jofthor, in Ivarstead

Both Boti (Mother) and Jofthor (Father) should be close by or near their dwelling. Speak to both parents in either order. Boti tells you that she actually likes Bassianus and can perhaps persuade her husband to change his mind over her child's plans to leave for Riften. Talk with Jofthor, and he tells you that it isn't Fastred's plans to move that is upsetting him; she was supposedly "in love" with Klimmek until a few months ago, but he's a little spineless and needs a good shove to win Fastred over: That way the younger generation can help save the town. With these differing opinions, you have a choice to make.

◊ **OBJECTIVE:** Talk to Bassianus or Klimmek
♦ **TARGET:** Bassianus and Klimmek, in Ivarstead

You now have a choice to make and neither is "wrong"; you can speak to either Bassianus Axius or Klimmek: Both are likely to be near the river. Decide on Bassianus and suggest that he elopes. Decide on Klimmek and tell him Fastred probably appreciates a more assertive man and tell him to be bold. You can become more negative in your conversation with either suitor if you change your mind. Once you push either man into the arms of Fastred (who agrees to either suitor), your work here is done.

◊ **OBJECTIVE:** Return to Dinya Balu
♦ **TARGET:** Temple of Mara, in Riften

Unrequited Love

Back in Riften, enter the Temple and inform Dinya Balu that you've helped the young lovers in Ivarstead. Mara has another task for you to perform: An older man named Calcelmo must open up about his romantic troubles. Seek and help him on his path.

◊ **OBJECTIVE:** Talk to Calcelmo
♦ **TARGET:** Calcelmo, inside Understone Keep, in Markarth

Journey to Markarth, and venture into the Understone Keep. In the cathedral-sized interior chamber to the west, you're likely to find Calcelmo. Brush off his initial impoliteness, and inform him Mara sent you. He tells you he's been thinking about Faleen, Igmund's Housecarl (bodyguard). He longs for her but becomes tongue-tied when he tries to speak. Finding the right thing to say is the key here, and Calcelmo recommends you seek out Yngvar, who is more popular with the ladies. He may be able to help.

◊ **OBJECTIVE:** Get advice from Yngvar
♦ **TARGET:** Yngvar, in Markarth

Find Yngvar, who is usually leaning near a bridge in Markarth's main thoroughfare. Engage him in conversation, bringing the chatter around to Faleen. You'll find out that she secretly enjoys poetry, and Yngvar has just the verse, if you're ready to receive his golden words—which are going to cost you 200 gold pieces. You must pay the man to receive the poem.

➤ **200 gold pieces** ➤ **Love Poem**

◊ **OBJECTIVE:** Deliver Poem
♦ **TARGET:** Faleen, inside Understone Keep, in Markarth

Locate Faleen next to her master, in the throne chamber inside Understone Keep. You may reveal as much or little as you like about Calcelmo, but you must hand over the poem, which both surprises and impresses her greatly. In return, she gives you a letter to give back to him; it isn't as eloquent but is certain to please him.

➤ **Faleen's Letter to Calcelmo**

◊ **OBJECTIVE:** Deliver Faleen's letter
♦ **TARGET:** Calcelmo, inside Understone Keep, in Markarth

Hand Calcelmo the letter, and he leaves to join with Faleen and their love blossoms.

◊ **OBJECTIVE:** Return to Dinya Balu
♦ **TARGET:** Temple of Mara, in Riften

Deep Love

Dinya Balu has one last task to test you with in the final aspect of love, a strong love that can survive storms and even death. You must take the symbol of Mara and rejoin to wandering souls, binding them to this world.

➤ **Amulet of Mara**

◊ **OBJECTIVE:** Put on the Amulet of Mara
♦ **TARGET:** Yourself
◊ **OBJECTIVE:** Talk to the long-dead lover
♦ **TARGET:** Ruki, Gjukar's Monument

TIP Reach Gjukar's Monument by nightfall to ensure your ghosts are easy to spot.

Head to Gjukar's Monument and seek the ghost of Ruki. She has turned over every body in this long-forgotten battlefield but cannot find her soul mate. Mention the last battle was hundreds of years ago, but Ruki still believes she's witnessing the battle afresh. Begin the search anew.

◊ **OBJECTIVE:** Find Fenrig
♦ **TARGET:** Fenrig, south of Greenspring Hollow

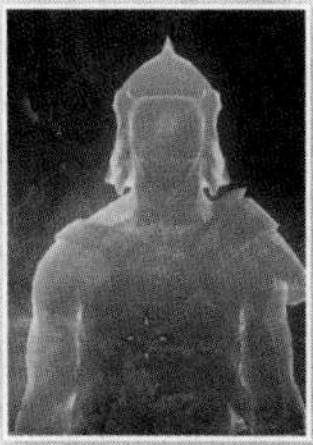

Ruki was searching in the wrong place; her lover's spirit resides on the heath to the south of Greenspring Hollow. Tell Fenrig that his wife is looking for him in the plains to the west. He agrees but must report back to camp by sunrise: Again, this is another spirit living in the past.

◊ **OBJECTIVE:** Bring Fenrig to Ruki
♦ **TARGET:** Ruki, Gjukar's Monument

Either Fast-Travel or trek back to Gjukar's Monument, where the couple embrace, then slowly rise into the air. Their spirits grow brighter as they ascend, until they become two bright points in the night sky, forever circling each other.

◊ **OBJECTIVE:** Return to Dinya Balu
♦ **TARGET:** Temple of Mara, in Riften

Quest Conclusion

Return one last time to Dinya Balu and explain that you helped the long-dead lovers find each other. She congratulates you on achieving the higher comprehension of love and says the Blessings of Mara will shine with you. You receive the following (which is different from the temporary Blessing of Mara if you pray at any of her shrines):

➤ **Perk:** Agent of Mara

THE BLESSINGS OF NATURE

PREREQUISITES: None
INTERSECTING QUESTS: None
MISCELLANEOUS QUEST: Barkeep Rumors
LOCATIONS: Eldergleam Sanctuary, Orphan Rock, Whiterun, The Bannered Mare, Gildergreen, Temple of Kynareth
CHARACTERS: Asta, Danica Pure-Spring, Hulda, Maurice Jondrelle, Enemies, Hagraven, Spriggan, Witch
◊ **OBJECTIVES:** Talk to Danica about the Goldergreen being destroyed, Retrieve Nettlebane, Bring Nettlebane to Danica, Retrieve Eldergleam sap, Return to Danica

The Slumbering Temple

Journey to the city of Whiterun, through the gates into the bailey, and visit the Bannered Mare. Engage the barkeep, Hulda, in some idle chatter, picking up on several rumors. Keep asking until she tells you about a withered tree by the Temple of Kynareth.

◊ **OBJECTIVE:** Talk to Danica about the Goldergreen being destroyed
♦ **TARGET:** Danica Pure-Spring, near the Gildergreen tree, in Whiterun

TIP You can start this quest by speaking to Danica Pure-Spring up at the Temple of Kynareth.

Search out Danica Pure-Spring, and ask her about the tree. It is an offshoot of the Eldergleam, a massive tree and the oldest living thing in Skyrim. Ask about reviving the tree, and she tells you that even if you reach the Eldergleam deep in its sanctuary, you couldn't tap its sap, as it cannot be cut by normal metal. Only one weapon is known to cut the tree's bark—Nettlebane—and it is carried by the Hagraven that prowls on Orphan Rock. Agree to retrieve this weapon hewn of dark magic from beyond the time of man.

◊ **OBJECTIVE:** Retrieve Nettlebane
♦ **TARGET:** Hagraven, Orphan Rock

Dark Arts on Orphan Rock

Brave traps, inclement weather, and a coven of witches that attack you on sight as you ascend and head across the tree branch to the top of Orphan Rock. Face the Hagraven in combat and slay her. Inspect the corpse, and secure the Nettlebane blade from it.

(Sneak) You may also try pickpocketing the blade from the Hagraven.

➤ **Nettlebane**

◊ **OBJECTIVE:** Bring Nettlebane to Danica
♦ **TARGET:** Danica Pure-Spring, the Temple of Kynareth, in Whiterun

Danica is probably inside the Temple of Kynareth. She isn't keen on touching the Nettlebane and asks if you're able to complete the next part of the task: to journey east to the Eldergleam Sanctuary grove and retrieve the sap from the ancient tree. Once the quest updates, you're stopped by Maurice Jondrelle, a pilgrim wishing to accompany you to the Sanctuary to witness the Eldergleam. You may agree to journey with him or ignore his request.

◊ **OBJECTIVE:** Retrieve Eldergleam sap
♦ **TARGET:** Eldergleam, in Eldergleam Sanctuary

NOTE Maurice may be holding you up, and you can ignore him or leave him to die whenever you tire of his company.

The Sting of Nettlebane

Hike the volcanic tundra until you find the rather unassuming cave entrance to Eldergleam Sanctuary. Enter it, and the cave opens into a gigantic grotto, where waterfalls tumble from the sky-high roof and hot springs belch from the ground. This interior wonder has pilgrims resting and watching in awe. Optionally speak to Asta for more information on the place and a warning not to harm the tree.

There are two ways to harvest the sap you need:

1. Some quick swipes to the tree's gigantic root structure, which is blocking the path to the tree trunk, shouldn't hurt the ancient entity. Despite Maurice's protests, produce Nettlebane and swipe once. The tree's roots creak and retract from the soil. Continue with this swiping until you reach the trunk, and pierce it with Nettlebane to siphon off some sap.

   ➤ **Eldergleam Sap**

2. Or, if Maurice is with you, agree to let him pray in front of the tree. A sapling grows from his devotion. You can return this to Danica instead.

   ➤ **Eldergleam Sapling**

◊ **OBJECTIVE:** Return to Danica
♦ **TARGET:** Danica Pure-Spring, the Temple of Kynareth, in Whiterun

Both Maurice Jondrelle and the Spriggans who guard the tree don't take kindly to sap stealing if you chose that option. They mount an offensive strike against you. Fight or flee from this place, and return swiftly to Danica Pure-Spring, presenting her with the sap. She is most grateful.

Quest Conclusion

Danica takes the sap (or sapling) from you. You are now on friendly terms with her, and she is available as a Trainer (a Master in Restoration).

Postquest Activities

After time passes and you return to the Temple of Kynareth, you witness the tree blooming again (if you returned with sap) or being replaced by the sapling (if Maurice prayed for you).

THE BONDS OF MATRIMONY

PREREQUISITES: None
◊ **OBJECTIVES:** Speak to Maramal about arranging your wedding, Attend your wedding ceremony, Visit your or your spouse's house

A Life Lived Alone Is No Life at All

Sometimes it is lonely on the mist-filled pathways of Skyrim. You may yearn for companionship. Or something more? If you feel your life is incomplete and must be shared with someone, make your way to Riften and check the Bee and Barb tavern or the Temple of Mara for a talk with Maramal the priest. He detests the drinking of mead and hopes the drunkards of Riften will eventually accept the teachings of the handmaiden of Kyne. Ask for more information about the Temple of Mara, and he tells you she is the goddess of love, tending to the sick, poor, and lost. The priests of Mara also perform wedding ceremonies for all the loving couples in Skyrim. Now ask how marriage works:

Life is hard and short, so there is little time for courtship. A person interested in looking for a spouse simply wears an Amulet of Mara around their neck, indicating their availability. After another shows interest and they agree to be together, they come to the temple and marry. You can purchase one of these Amulets for the low price of 200 gold pieces.

➤ **Amulet of Mara**

After you purchase an Amulet of Mara, check your Items > Apparel menu, and wear the necklace, or you'll never entice a spouse! At this point, you must find someone who wishes to marry you. To do this, you must strike up a friendship with any one of the following potential suitors. "Striking a friendship" means completing a favor for them, or otherwise getting into their good graces.

TIP Your gender, age, and race matters not: If you're attracted to someone, go out and catch their hearts!

☑	POTENTIAL SPOUSE	GENDER	RACE	OCCUPATION	HOLD	LOCATION	CONDITIONS FOR MARRIAGE
☐	Aela the Huntress	Female	Nord	Companion	Whiterun	Whiterun (Jorrvaskr)	Complete the Companions Quests
☐	Aeri	Female	Nord	Lumberjack	The Pale	Anga's Mill	Work for her by chopping firewood
☐	Ainethach	Male	Breton	Mine Owner	The Reach	Karthwasten	Complete their favor
☐	Angrenor Once-Honored	Male	Nord	Beggar	Eastmarch	Windhelm (Candlehearth Hall)	Take pity and give the beggar a gold piece
☐	Anwen	Female	Redguard	Priestess	The Reach	Markarth (Temple of Dibella)	Complete Temple Quest: The Heart of Dibella
☐	Argis the Bulwark	Male	Nord	Housecarl	The Reach	Markarth (Vlindrel Hall)	Become Thane of the Reach
☐	Athis	Male	Dark Elf	Companion	Whiterun	Whiterun (Jorrvaskr)	Complete the Companions Quests
☐	Avrusa Sarethi	Female	Dark Elf	Farmer	The Rift	Sarethi Farm	Complete their favor
☐	Balimund	Male	Nord	Blacksmith	The Rift	Riften	Complete their favor
☐	Belrand	Male	Nord	Hireling	Haafingar	Solitude (Winking Skeever)	Hire them at least once
☐	Benor	Male	Nord	Warrior	Hjaalmarch	Morthal	Challenge him to a brawl and win
☐	Borghak the Steel Heart	Female	Orc	Warrior	The Reach	Mor Khazgur	Convince her to become a Follower
☐	Brelyna Maryon	Female	Dark Elf	Student	Winterhold	Winterhold (College of Winterhold)	Complete both her favors
☐	Calder	Male	Nord	Housecarl	Eastmarch	Windhelm (Hjerim)	Become Thane of Eastmarch

✓	POTENTIAL SPOUSE	GENDER	RACE	OCCUPATION	HOLD	LOCATION	CONDITIONS FOR MARRIAGE
☐	Camilla Valerius	Female	Imperial	Merchant	Whiterun	Riverwood (Riverwood Trader)	Complete Side Quest: The Golden Claw
☐	Cosnach	Male	Breton	Drunk/Porter	The Reach	Markarth (Silver-Blood Inn)	Challenge him to a brawl and win
☐	Derkeethus	Male	Argonian	Fisherman	Eastmarch	Darkwater Crossing	Find and rescue him
☐	Dravynea the Stoneweaver	Female	Dark Elf	Mage	Eastmarch	Kynesgrove	Complete their favor
☐	Erik the Slayer	Male	Nord	Hireling	The Reach	Rorikstead	Complete his favor to make him a hireling
☐	Farkas	Male	Nord	Companion	Whiterun	Whiterun (Jorrvaskr)	Complete the Companions Quests
☐	Filnjar	Male	Nord	Blacksmith	The Rift	Shor's Stone	Complete Miscellaeous Objective: Mine or Yours
☐	Gat gro-Shargakh	Male	Orc	Miner	The Reach	Left Hand Mine /Kolskeggr Mine	Complete Pavo Attius's favor to liberate Kolskeggr Mine
☐	Ghorbash the Iron Hand	Male	Orc	Warrior	The Reach	Dushnikh Yal	Convince her to become a Follower
☐	Ghorza gra-Bagol	Female	Orc	Blacksmith	The Reach	Markarth (Blacksmith Shed)	Complete their favor
☐	Gilfre	Female	Imperial	Miller	Eastmarch	Mixwater Mill	Work for her by chopping firewood
☐	Gregor	Male	Nord	Housecarl	The Pale	White Hall (Dawnstar)	Complete Thane's Tasks: Thane of The Pale*
☐	Grelka	Female	Nord	Merchant	The Rift	Riften (Open Market)	Complete their favor
☐	Halbarn Iron-Fur	Male	Nord	Blacksmith	Solstheim	Thirsk Mead Hall	Complete Solstheim Regional Activity: Ore Inspired*
☐	Hilund	Female	Nord	Warrior	Solstheim	Thirsk Mead Hall	Complete Solstheim Regional Activity: Primitive Pointy Sticks*
☐	Iona	Female	Nord	Housecarl	The Rift	Riften (Honeyside)	Become Thane of the Rift
☐	Jenassa	Female	Dark Elf	Hireling	Whiterun	Whiterun (Drunken Huntsman)	Hire them at least once
☐	Jordis the Sword-Maiden	Female	Nord	Housecarl	Haafingar	Solitude (Proudspire Manor)	Become Thane of Haafingar
☐	Lydia	Female	Nord	Housecarl	Whiterun	Whiterun (Dragonsreach or Breezehome)	Become Thane of Whiterun
☐	Marcurio	Male	Imperial	Hireling	The Rift	Riften (Bee and Barb)	Hire them at least once
☐	Mjoll the Lioness	Female	Nord	Adventurer	The Rift	Riften	Complete their favor
☐	Morwen	Female	Nord	Blacksmith	Solstheim	Skaal Village	Complete Solstheim Regional Activity: Return to Falkreath*
☐	Moth gro-Bagol	Male	Orc	Blacksmith	The Reach	Markarth (Understone Keep)	Complete their favor
☐	Muiri	Female	Breton	Alchemist	The Reach	Markarth (Hag's Cure)	Complete Dark Brotherhood Quest: Mourning Never Comes
☐	Njada Stonearm	Female	Nord	Companion	Whiterun	Whiterun (Jorrvaskr)	Complete the Companions Quests
☐	Octieve San	Male	Breton	Citizen	Haafingar	Solitude	Complete their favor
☐	Omluag	Male	Breton	Miner	The Reach	Markarth (Markarth Smelter)	Complete their favor
☐	Onmund	Male	Nord	Student	Winterhold	Winterhold (College of Winterhold)	Complete their favor
☐	Orla	Female	Nord	Priestess	The Reach	Markarth (Temple of Dibella)	Complete Temple Quest: The Heart of Dibella
☐	Pavo Attius	Male	Imperial	Miner	The Reach	Left Hand Mine/Kolskeggr Mine	Complete his favor to liberate Kolskeggr Mine
☐	Perth	Male	Breton	Miner	The Reach	Soljund's Sinkhole	Complete their favor
☐	Quintus Navale	Male	Imperial	Alchemist	Eastmarch	Windhelm (The White Phial)	Complete Side Quest: Repairing the Phial
☐	Rayya	Female	Nord	Housecarl	Hjaalmarch	Highmoon Hall (Morthal)	Complete Thane's Tasks: Thane of Falkreath*
☐	Revyn Sadri	Male	Dark Elf	Merchant	Eastmarch	Windhelm (Sadri's Used Wares)	Complete their favor
☐	Ria	Female	Imperial	Companion	Whiterun	Whiterun (Jorrvaskr)	Complete the Companions Quests
☐	Roggi Knot-Beard	Male	Nord	Miner	Eastmarch	Kynesgrove	Complete their favor
☐	Romlyn Dreth	Male	Dark Elf	Meadery Worker	The Rift	Riften (Black-Briar Meadery)	Complete their favor
☐	Scouts-Many-Marshes	Male	Argonian	Dockworker	Eastmarch	Windhelm (Argonian Assemblage)	Complete their favor
☐	Senna	Female	Imperial	Priestess	The Reach	Markarth (Temple of Dibella)	Complete Temple Quest: The Heart of Dibella
☐	Shahvee	Female	Argonian	Dockworker	Eastmarch	Windhelm (Argonian Assemblage)	Complete their favor
☐	Sondas Drenim	Male	Dark Elf	Miner	Eastmarch	Darkwater Crossing	Complete their favor
☐	Sorex Vinius	Male	Imperial	Assistant Innkeeper	Haafingar	Solitude (Winking Skeever)	Complete their favor
☐	Stenvar	Male	Nord	Hireling	Eastmarch	Windhelm (Candlehearth Hall)	Hire them at least once
☐	Sylgja	Female	Nord	Miner	The Rift	Shor's Stone	Complete their favor
☐	Taarie	Female	High Elf	Tailor	Haafingar	Solitude (Radiant Raiments)	Complete their favor
☐	Temba Wide-Arm	Female	Nord	Miller	The Rift	Ivarstead	Complete their favor
☐	Torvar	Male	Nord	Companion	Whiterun	Whiterun (Jorrvaskr)	Complete the Companions Quests
☐	Uthgerd	Female	Nord	Warrior	Whiterun	Whiterun (Bannered Mare)	Challenge her to a brawl and win
☐	Valdimar	Male	Nord	Housecarl	Hjaalmarch	Highmoon Hall (Morthal)	Complete Thane's Tasks: Thane of Hjaalmarch*
☐	Vilkas	Male	Nord	Companion	Whiterun	Whiterun (Jorrvaskr)	Complete the Companions Quests
☐	Viola Giordano	Female	Imperial	Busybody	Eastmarch	Windhelm (Candlehearth Hall)	Start Revyn Sadri's favor, but then rat him out to Viola
☐	Vorstag	Male	Nord	Hireling	The Reach	Markarth (Silver-Blood Inn)	Hire them at least once
☐	Wilhelm	Male	Nord	Innkeeper	The Rift	Ivarstead (Vilemyr Inn)	Complete Dungeon Quest: Wilhelm's Specter
☐	Ysolda	Female	Nord	Citizen	Whiterun	Whiterun (Open Market)	Complete their favor

> **TIP** Opting for a quick marriage? Then approach Camilla Valerius over at the Riverwood Trader once Side Quest: The Golden Claw ends. She takes a shine to you after the quest is over.

When you're on friendly terms with your potential partner, they will notice—and mention—your Amulet of Mara and will usually express surprise that you're not spoken for. You can choose to ignore this advance or ask if they're interested in you. They answer that they are. But are you interested in them? Answer yes if you wish to continue down this road of happiness, or no to remain alone. You're tasked with arranging the marriage straight away...in case one of you dies.

◊ OBJECTIVE: Speak to Maramal about arranging your wedding

Return to Riften and find Maramel, either in the Temple of Mara or in the Bee and Barb. Tell him you'd like to have a wedding at the temple. He agrees, and sets the date for the next day, between dawn (5:00 a.m.) and dusk (7:00 p.m.).

◊ OBJECTIVE: Attend your wedding ceremony

> **NOTE** Whoops! Did a combination of adventuring and cold feet cause you to miss your wedding day? Then this previous objective fails. After a few hours, your jilted lover can be convinced to attempt the ceremony again. Speak to Maramal and arrange this; then wait another day and try getting to the temple on time!

Prosperity and Poverty, Joy, and Hardship

Oh, happy day! Tomorrow dawns, and you can head to the Temple of Mara at any time before dusk. Your spouse-to-be is already there and doesn't need to be told to turn up. As you enter, the ceremony begins. Maramal conducts the ceremony and eventually asks if you agree to be bound together in love, now and forever. You can:

Agree, for now and forever.

Or freak out slightly, halt the wedding, and tell Maramal you can't go through with it.

Or freak out completely and attack everyone. Doing this or leaving the temple during the ceremony fails this quest, and usually ups your Crime in the Rift considerably.

Assuming you didn't ruin your betrothed's day, he declares you to be wed.

➤ **The Bond of Matrimony**

◊ OBJECTIVE: Visit your or your spouse's house

At this point, your spouse asks where you both should live, now that you're married. They offer their own home to you. You can:

Agree, and visit the house (which should appear on your world map). Depending on who you've married, this could be anything from a sturdy-built stone dwelling to a small tent in the tundra.

Or, if you've already purchased a dwelling as part of the Thane Tasks (page 502), you can choose your spouse to live with you.

➤ **Spouse**

Quest Conclusion

The "happily ever after" part is next. Your spouse grants you the following benefits:

You can ask them to serve up a home-cooked meal for you once every 24 hours.

They set up a shop in the house you're living in. If your spouse was a merchant, they sell what they did before. If they weren't, they sell miscellaneous objects.

You may sleep close to your spouse and receive a bonus, feeling your Lover's Comfort when you awaken.

If your spouse is also a Follower, they can accompany you on adventures.

If your spouse is also a Trainer, you can train with them at your marital home.

If your spouse is a Follower and a Trainer, you can train with them anywhere you like!

If you've chosen to marry your Housecarl, you move into the abode that your spouse is already in charge of (one of the ones you've owned or built yourself before hiring them).

If you have an adopted child, your spouse also becomes their mother or father, and your betrothed may speak with you about your child.

➤ **Lover's Comfort**

SIDE QUESTS

OVERVIEW

Optimal Quest Start

Most Side Quests are available from the moment you begin your adventure, although it is wise to learn if there are prerequisites to complete first. As Side Quests aren't usually linked to one another (with a couple of exceptions), you can start them at your leisure.

> **NOTE** **Cross-Referencing:** Do you want to see maps and learn more about the traps, non-quest-related items, collectibles, crafting areas, and other important rooms of note in every location during these quests? Then cross-reference the location you travel to with the information on that location contained in this guide's Atlas.

Available Quests

There are a total of 25 different Side Quests available. Aside from the exceptions detailed below, most of these quests are independent of one another and can be completed whenever you encounter them.

✓	QUEST NAME	RELATED SETTLEMENT OR HOLD	PREREQUISITES
☐	Side Quest: Blood on the Ice	Windhelm	Enter and exit Windhelm four times
☐	Side Quest: The Ebony Warrior	None	You must be Level 80 or higher.
☐	Side Quest: Forbidden Legend	None	None
☐	Side Quest: The Forsworn Conspiracy	Markarth	None
☐	Side Quest: No One Escapes Cidhna Mine	Markarth	Complete Side Quest: The Forsworn Conspiracy
☐	Side Quest: The Golden Claw	Riverwood	None
☐	Side Quest: In My Time of Need	Whiterun	Complete Main Quest: Dragon Rising
☐	Side Quest: Kyne's Sacred Trials	None	None
☐	Side Quest: Laid to Rest	Morthal	None
☐	Side Quest: Lights Out!	Solitude	None
☐	Side Quest: Lost to the Ages	None	None
☐	Side Quest: The Man Who Cried Wolf	Solitude	None
☐	Side Quest: The Wolf Queen Awakened	Solitude	Complete Side Quest: The Man Who Cried Wolf
☐	Side Quest: Missing in Action	Whiterun	Enter and exit any of the buildings near the market in Whiterun
☐	Side Quest: Promises to Keep	Riften	None

✓	QUEST NAME	RELATED SETTLEMENT OR HOLD	PREREQUISITES
☐	Side Quest: A Return to Your Roots	Blackreach	Begin Daedric Quest: Discerning the Transmundane
☐	Side Quest: Rise in the East	Windhelm	None
☐	Side Quest: Rising at Dawn	Morthal	Contract Vampirism
☐	Side Quest: Unfathomable Depths	Riften	None
☐	Side Quest: The White Phial	Windhelm	None
☐	Side Quest: Repairing the Phial	Windhelm	Three days after completing both Main Quest: The Throat of the World and Side Quest: The White Phial
☐	Side Quest: Captured Critters*	None	None
☐	Side Quest: The Forgemaster's Fingers	Orc Strongholds	Non-Orc Race
☐	Side Quest: The Great Skyrim Treasure Hunt*	None	None
☐	Side Quest: Masks of the Dragon Priests*	None	Numerous (see quest)

> **NOTE** * Quest names marked with this symbol do not appear in your Quest Menu list, although objectives may.
>
> Note that not all of these quests will count towards the Sideways Achievement. Consult the Achievements Appendix on page 1079 for a list of relevant quests.

PREREQUISITES: Enter and exit Windhelm a total of four times

MINOR SPOILERS

INTERSECTING QUESTS: None

LOCATIONS: Windhelm, Calixto's House of Curiosities, Candlehearth Hall, Hall of the Dead, Hjerim, House of the Clan Shatter-Shield, Palace of the Kings, Bloodworks, Palace of the Kings Upstairs

CHARACTERS: Calixto Corrium, Friga Shatter-Shield, Helgird, Jorleif, Sidla the Unseen, Susanna the Wicked, Viola Giordano, Windhelm Guard, Wuunferth the Unliving

ENEMIES: None

◊ **OBJECTIVES:** Question the witnesses, Report to the guard, Talk to Jorleif, Get assistance from Jorleif, Examine the crime scene, Talk to Helgird, Get access to Hjerim, Investigate Hjerim for clues, Follow up on the clues from Hjerim, Meet Viola outside of Hjerim, Investigate Hjerium with Viola, Talk to Jorleif, Patrol the streets of the Stone Quarter at night, Speak to Wuunferth, Catch the murderer, Speak to Jorleif for reward

Murder Most Foul

NOTE This quest is available only after you enter Windhelm, leave this Hold City, head to a different location, return again, and complete this four times. Now enter at night, and look for a small group of townsfolk and a guard gathering in the graveyard.

When walking the Stone Quarter of Windhelm (west of the entrance gate), you stumble across a shocking scene. In the graveyard near the Hall of the Dead, the freshly slaughtered corpse of a woman lies draped over a grave. As the stunned onlookers assemble, go speak with the Windhelm Guard. He tells you another girl has been killed; this one is Susanna from Candlehearth Hall. When you ask, he admits she's the third young girl to be killed here, at night, and with her body cut and torn. Without time to investigate these heinous crimes, ask if he requires any help. He points you to the onlookers who might have some information to share.

◊ **OBJECTIVE:** Question the witnesses

There are three witnesses to speak to:

Calixto Corrium: The owner of the House of Curiosities in town. He thought he saw someone running away but didn't get a good look at him.

Sidla the Unseen: A beggar living in the Stone Quarter marketplace. She heard a scream and came running, but Susanna was already dead.

Helgird: The Priestess of Arkay from the Hall of the Dead. She noticed the woman's coinpurse was still on the body, so this wasn't a robbery.

Head back outside, and follow the trail of blood. This leads up the stone steps, around the corner to the north into the Valunstrad District, up more steps, and ends at a firmly locked (Master) front door to a building named Hjerim.

◊ **OBJECTIVE:** Get access to Hjerim
♦ **TARGET:** Hjerim front door, Valunstrad District, Windhelm

Accessing Hjerim can be tricky, as it can require a little asking around among the inhabitants of Windhelm. You can:

(Lockpick) Unlock the door (Master) using your considerable lockpicking prowess.

Ask around town. Speak to a guard or a local, and ask how you can enter Hjerim. You're told this used to belong to Friga Shatter-Shield and has been abandoned ever since she was killed. Apparently, her mother, Tova, has the key.

NOTE This horror house named Hjerim is actually for sale, but only after you've witnessed the murder scene. Consult the Thane Tasks on page 502 for further information.

◊ **OBJECTIVE:** Report to the guard

With nobody knowing (or saying anything), when you report back to the guard, he's suitably frustrated. Offer to investigate, and he points you in the direction of the Palace of the Kings, so you can talk to Jorleif. The steward of Windhelm will officially deputize you to conduct the investigation.

◊ **OBJECTIVE:** Talk to Jorleif
◊ **OBJECTIVE:** Get assistance from Jorleif
♦ **TARGET:** Jorleif, inside the Palace of the Kings, in Windhelm

Visit the Palace of the Kings, and contact Jorleif. Tell him you've heard about the murders. He gladly accepts your aid and tells the guards to assist you as necessary.

◊ **OBJECTIVE:** Examine the crime scene
◊ **OBJECTIVE:** Talk to Helgird
♦ **TARGET:** Victim's location, graveyard close to Hall of the Dead

TIP This objective is more easily completed during daylight hours. Note that you can follow the trail of blood and break into Hjerim and avoid a lot of investigative chatting to the locals, if you wish.

Return to the coffin where the body of Susanna was dumped. You notice there's blood pooling on the coffin lid and stains that match a dragging. The guard mentions the blood if you speak to him, too. Look west, and you'll see a trail of it. The guard also mentions that Helgird has taken the body into the Hall of the Dead to prepare it for burial. She might know something. The entrance to the Hall of the Dead is on your right (northwest) as you face the trail of blood. Head into the gloomy crypt, and after quizzing Helgird again, she reveals the cuts on the corpse were made with some kind of curved blade the Nords used to embalm their dead.

Tova Shatter-Shield is usually at the market in the southwest Stone Quarter or walking nearby. At night, she heads to the House of Clan Shatter-Shield. You can pick the lock (Master) to enter, or wait until morning until she unlocks the house; speak to her then or when she leaves. Tell her you have some questions about her daughter. Choose any conversation response regarding the finding of her daughter's killer, and let her know you need a key to investigate her house. She hands the key over. Take it, head back to Hjerim, and open the front door.

➤ **Key to Hjerim**

◊ **OBJECTIVE:** Investigate Hjerim for clues

A Butcher's Handiwork

Inside, the place has been cleared out, and cobwebs blanket the corners. The place is seemingly deserted, but a thorough inspection reveals the following:

Front room (north): The pots and pans here haven't been used for ages, judging by the skeever droppings and cobwebs inside.

Front room (entrance): The chest has splatters of blood and was recently pushed against the wall. Search it after inspecting it to reveal almost a dozen leaflets warning of a "butcher." The name "Viola Giordano" is mentioned on the leaflet. There is a journal to view, too. It makes grisly reading and seems to indicate necromantic activity.

Front room (entrance): The scattered mead bottles are from the previous occupants.

Front room (west wall): The low shelf by one of the wardrobes is filled with more leaflets warning about the Butcher. Remove the leaflets, as one of the piles is misshapen. Underneath, you find a strange (and exceptionally valuable) amulet! Inspect it in your Items > Apparel menu.

Front room (back wardrobe): One of the wardrobes at the back of the room has been nailed to the wall. Open it and slide the false panel back. You find a disgusting sight: a small makeshift altar and antechamber strewn with body parts. Check the altar, and you confirm it is being used for some unknown magic. A second Butcher Journal can be taken from here. It seems to contain ingredients, both body parts and an incantation.

Upstairs: Only the bed and chairs, which have been weirdly positioned, can be inspected.

➤ **Beware the Butcher! (19)** ➤ **Butcher Journal #2**
➤ **Butcher Journal #1** ➤ **Strange Amulet**

◊ **OBJECTIVE:** Follow up on the clues from Hjerim
♦ **TARGET:** Any Windhelm Guard, in Windhelm

TIP Only the first Butcher Journal and leaflets are needed to continue progress, although it is beneficial if you find everything listed here.

Leave the house and consult with any guard in Windhelm. Two new topics of conversation are available (assuming you found at least one leaflet and the Strange Amulet):

Ask about the "Butcher": Viola Giordano posts these all over the city, and someone keeps removing them.

Ask about the amulet. The guard hasn't seen anything like it, but Calixto at the House of Curiosities has a good eye for such trinkets.

Viola Giordano: Here Her Hearsay

Search for Viola wandering the streets of Windhelm. Ask her about the Butcher; she's been searching for him for months and then mentions the poster leaflet you found in Hjerim. She echoes the guard's information, that someone has been taking them down as quickly as she posts them around the city. She recommends you meet her at Hjerim for another inspection. You can follow her if you haven't uncovered the amulet. Otherwise, you are free to visit Calixto, too.

◊ **OBJECTIVE:** Meet Viola outside of Hjerim

Calixto Corrium: Curiouser and Curiouser

Head to the southeast part of the Stone Quarter and enter Calixto Corrium's House of Curiosities. Aside from taking a tour, you can ask him about the amulet you found. He cheerfully inspects the amulet, telling you it's a Wheelstone, an heirloom symbol of the power of Windhelm and traditionally carried by the court mage. He's interested in the piece and offers you 500 gold. You can:

Agree, and sell the piece.

Ask whether the court mage should have it instead, and keep it.

Or hold on to it.

➤ **500 gold pieces (if sold)**

Whatever your choice, the next place to head is Hjerim, where you should have agreed to meet Viola.

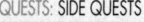

Puzzle Solution: There are two levers, one by each throne. Both of them rotate walls that block the nearby doors, allowing you to enter the chambers beyond. The right one currently allows you to access a semicircular chamber adjacent to the throne and lever. Battle the Draugr before inspecting the three large stone heads, each with an animal petroglyph in their maws. Working counterclockwise from the first petroglyph you see, the order is Snake, Whale, and Hawk. Return to the grating chamber, and pull the lever by the left throne until the rock wall shifts to open into a second, almost identical chamber. The difference is that there are three pillars. Rotate them so that the Snake faces out from the first pillar (facing the doorway), the Whale faces out from the second, and the Hawk faces from the third, mimicking the petroglyphs in the mirrored room you just came from. Now when you pull the chain, the grate opens.

Wind your way down the long spiral steps to a waterlogged tunnel with Frostbite Spiders to tackle. The open doors at the far end lead to a long hall, flanked with coffins. As you enter the hall, the doors slam shut behind you and the lights go out. Crypts to either side of the room open, and Draugr begin to emerge in the darkness. Quickly use a Nighteye spell or power if you can, then battle the guardians. When the foes are vanquished, the lights come back on. Step up to another Nordic Puzzle Door.

Puzzle Solution: Move the rings so the Hawk, Hawk, and Dragon appear on the outer, middle, and inner rings, respectively. Then insert the Ivory Dragon Claw into the keyhole. Venture forward, and open the doors leading into Folgunthur Crypt.

Brother Battle: Mikrul Gauldurson

The crypt is a massive chamber, flanked with coffins and a main tomb at the far (southeast) end. When you're about halfway across the crypt, the sarcophagus bursts open, and out clambers the fearsome Mikrul Gauldurson, now a Draugr of considerable power! Aside from his inherent toughness, he also wields the Gauldur Blackblade, a powerful sword with an Absorb Health enchantment. He is accompanied by Draugr Thralls: weak, unarmed Draugr that do little damage but crowd the space, making it hard for you to flee from Mikrul's reach.

Especially at low levels, you may find it harrowing to fight Mikrul in melee combat, as every blow he delivers rapidly refills his health. Followers and summoned creatures are best left behind, since Mikrul can drain their health just as easily. The safest bet is to refrain from being hit at all. Back away as best you can, dodge his blows, and use a bow or spells to whittle down his health. If desperate measures are called for, you can jump across the sarcophagi along the sides of the room to flee and regroup.

Once Mikrul falls, any surviving thralls also die. Be sure you pry Mikrul's bony fingers off his vampiric blade, which is an exceptional one-handed weapon. There are two other items of interest, too:

- **Gauldur Blackblade**
- **Writ of Sealing**
- **Gauldur Amulet Fragment**

Don't be fooled by the "fragment" part: Mikrul's amulet fragment is a full amulet in its own right and has a solid Fortify Health enchantment. The Writ has a curse against the Gauldurson brother written upon it. To exit the chamber, move to the far (southeast) end and insert the Ivory Dragon Claw into the right-side keyhole (the left leads to a rockfall). This removes the spear bars and allows access to the treasure chamber, which also contains a Word Wall. Now leave Folgunthur out of the southeast Iron Door, push out a sarcophagus lid for a shortcut into the banquet hall crypt, and retrace your steps back out. On your way, use the Ivory Claw in the first puzzle room to open a secret door with a chest.

- **Word of Power:** Frost Breath

Be Bound Here, Sigdis: Murderer, Betrayer

Travel to Geirmund's Hall, east of Ivarstead in the hilly forest close to Lake Geir. Enter the cave and crush the two Skeever; then peer down the massive sinkhole in the center of the room. Drop into the water below. Aside from the submerged crypt passage leading to a chest and a dead end, there are steps up to an Iron Door. Slash your way through Frostbite Spiders, watch for a trigger plate that launches darts, and head down into a waterlogged crypt. Aside from Draugr, there are Nordic puzzle pillars to inspect.

Puzzle Solution: Stand atop the steps and face down into the waterlogged crypt. On the left (south) wall are two small petroglyph plaques showing a Hawk and a Whale. On the right (north) wall, there are plaques showing a Whale and a Snake. Continue along the crypt's left side, and spin the two pillars to show the Hawk and the Whale. Backtrack, and continue along the crypt's right side, and spin the two pillars to show the Whale and the Snake (the first of these already shows the Whale and so doesn't need to be moved). Then pull the lever to open the portcullis doorway.

Head into the ruined hub chamber with a fallen bridge and steps up to an altar. You'll return here later, so simply check the corpse on the altar for a key and epitaph, where Lord Geirmund keeps his eternal vigil. To open the Iron Door behind the altar (Adept), use the key or pick it. Pass the Arcane Enchanter and turn left (west), as the direct route to Sigdis Gauldurson's sarcophagus is blocked. Climb the steps, kill the Draugr on the balcony overlooking the hub room, and ignore the easily spotted lever (unless you want spears in your sides). Instead, pull the hidden one just behind you to the right (southwest). This lowers the bridge.

Fight the Draugr as you cross (you can jump to the right and open a locked door [Expert] to reach a small treasure room, then retrace your steps). Use another lever on the middle "island" to lower the second bridge, and fight through into a small passage. Watch the floor trigger, or face swinging axes around the corner. Quickly step to the wall lanterns between the blades to avoid them.

- **Lord Geirmund's Key**
- **Geirmund's Epitaph**

Brother Battle: Sigdis Gauldurson

Follow the passage around and into the tomb of Sigdis Gauldurson. The moment he steps from his sarcophagus, he teleports away, and you suddenly have more than one Sigdis to deal with! His Illusory Duplicates spell means that two of these entities are magical doppelgangers. During the frenzy of combat, it may be difficult to tell, but Sigdis's duplicates have a few subtle differences:

The Gauldur Blackbow Signis uses dishes out significantly more damage and drains your Magicka.

The dopplegangers are wreathed in a slight blue glow.

The doppelgangers' helmets don't have horns, while Sigdis's helmet does.

The three foes fire from their platforms, forcing you to strike them using your favored weaponry. Sigdis teleports around and summons duplicates again periodically, speeding up if you destroy both duplicates or as his health falls.

Focus your attention on Sigdis, as he's the only one taking damage. After you kill him, any illusions are dispersed, and an exit doorway behind his coffin slides open once. Be sure you pry Sigdis's twitching fingers off his bow, which drains Magicka from targets. There are two other items of interest, too.

- **Gauldur Blackbow**
- **Writ of Sealing**
- **Gauldur Amulet Fragment**

Once again, Sigdis's amulet fragment is a real amulet, this time with a Fortify Stamina enchantment. The Writ has a curse against the Gauldurson brother written upon it. Exit via the newly opened corridor, leading to a large chest and a lever that opens a section of wall, leading you back into the initial chamber with the pit.

Be Bound Here, Jyrik: Murderer, Betrayer

At this point, or whenever you wish to explore Saarthal and face Jyrik Gauldurson, you must visit the College of Winterhold and begin the College of Winterhold questline. Consult the College of Winterhold Quests for all pertinent information. Here's what you need to do:

Complete College of Winterhold Quest: First Lessons, proving your magical aptitude and gaining admittance to the College, where you'll train with Tolfdir.

Begin College of Winterhold Quest: Under Saarthal, and explore the excavation. The route to take, and the Nordic Puzzle solutions, are detailed in that quest. This culminates in the discovery of a giant glowing orb that floats in a bubble of writhing magic, at the opposite end of the room. It is pulsing and made of some strange, unknown material. Tolfdir is transfixed by this but averts his gaze when a ferocious-looking Draugr rises from his eternal throne chair. You're about to face the third brother, Jyrik Gauldurson!

Brother Battle: Jyrik Gauldurson

Jyrik Gauldurson is coursing with evil magic, and for the first ten seconds of the battle, he is utterly impervious to any attacks. Use this time to step behind cover or let any summoned creatures you may have conjured or Followers bear the brunt of his attacks. Eventually, Tolfdir realizes that all your combined offensive capabilities aren't having an effect, so he turns to the Eye and focuses his attacks on the crackling globe. A few seconds later, he yells that Jyrik is vulnerable. Attack!

To further complicate matters, Jyrik is bathed in an elemental shield that cycles through the different elements and is impervious to attacks from the same element. So, if he's bathed in fire, then any Flame-based spells have no effect on him. Use attacks from any other element instead. If you have only one type of elemental magic (i.e., only Fire), wait a few seconds until Jyric's shielding changes elements, and then strike!

TIP Jyrik is extremely vulnerable to frost damage when he's on fire, and when encased in a frost shield, he's very vulnerable to fire. Use this to your advantage!

With Jyrik Gauldurson gurgling his last curse, turn your attention to his unique weapon, although not one he wields in the battle with you: the Staff of Jyrik Gauldurson, which lies on the altar in front of his throne. Grab it, and the other items of interest on his corpse:

- **Gauldur Amulet Fragment**
- **Writ of Sealing**
- **Staff of Jyrik Gauldurson**

As you might expect, his amulet fragment has a Fortify Magicka enchantment, while the Writ has a curse against him written upon it. Now use the Iron Door behind the orb to exit the chamber, which leads to a fern-filled grotto and an ancient Word Wall. Absorb the power before you exit back into the excavation site, releasing the portcullis with a wall handle and exiting Saarthal.

- **Word of Power:** Ice Form

Be Defeated Here, Gauldurson Brothers!

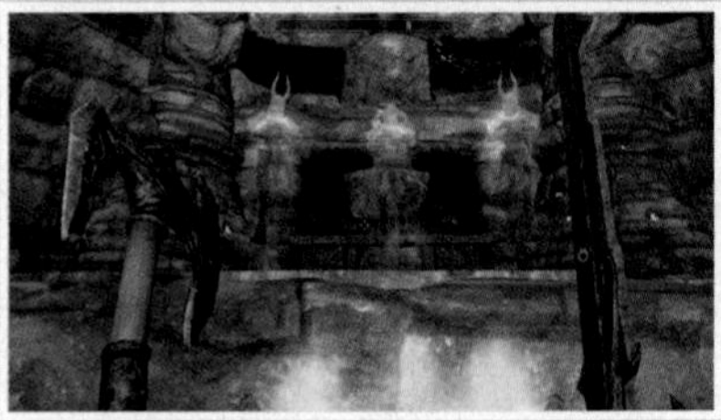

With the three Amulet Fragments in your possession, all that remains is to return to Reachwater Rock and enter the long hall that was sealed when you first visited this tomb. (If this is your first visit, see above for directions to the cave.)

Puzzle Solution: Move the rings so the Hawk, Hawk, and Dragon appear on the outer, middle, and inner rings, respectively. Then take the Ivory Dragon Claw you found on Daynas Valen's corpse in Folgunthur, and insert it into the keyhole. Continue down the steps beyond and enter the Arch-Mage Gauldur's tomb. Approach the altar at the far (northwest) end of the elaborately constructed room. Here you'll find three Amulet Pedestals.

As you set the final Amulet Fragment down on the pedestal, three spectral forms congeal from the ether on an inaccessible balcony above you. The power of the Gauldurson Brothers is strong enough to defy death—twice! Now you must face Mikrul, Sigdis, and Jyrik again, only this time they attack one after the other!

Mikrul is the first to step forward, teleporting to the room's far end as sarcophagi burst open around him. His thralls are back, stronger than before and now fully armed. This time, your best bet is to avoid Mikrul and go after the thralls first; you don't want to be surrounded by weapon-swinging Draugr. Once you slay them, Mikrul should be easier to defeat. Again, you may be better off attacking him from range: That strategy is even more effective here, since you can leap across the gaps in the platforms, but he must walk around them. When Mikrul falls, he returns to the upper platform and drops to a knee.

Sigdis steps forward next, this time joined by three ghostly duplicates. Again, their helmets are a telltale clue: The real Sigdis has curled horns on his helmet, while the duplicates have vertical horns. Ignore the duplicates and crush Sigdis as quickly as you can.

Finally, Jyrik steps forward. He is not invincible here, but he's still a powerful sorcerer. At several points in the battle, he teleports away to regain a little composure before attacking again. Use the same strategies as before to target his elemental weaknesses and bring him down.

After you deliver the final blow to Jyrik, the three brothers regroup at the altar. Suddenly, the sarcophagus behind them opens. The brothers turn, Sigdis lets out a shout, and a brilliant blast of light wipes them from existence. When the dust settles, a spectral figure (could this be Gauldur?) appears and grants you what you seek: In a flash of light, the Amulet Fragments combine!

◊ **OBJECTIVE:** Take the Gauldur Amulet

Quest Conclusion

Claim the reforged amulet and wear it proudly—you've earned it. While you may never wield its unique abilities as the brothers once did, the amulet is still immensely powerful, fortifying your Health, Magicka, and Stamina all in one.

- **Gauldur Amulet**

Postquest Activities

After claiming the amulet, jump up to the high platform and inspect the newly opened sarcophagus. Search Gauldur's skeleton, and you can find a sizable gold reward as well.

THE FORSWORN CONSPIRACY

PREREQUISITES: None

MINOR SPOILERS

INTERSECTING QUESTS: Side Quest: No One Escapes Cidhna Mine

LOCATIONS: Markarth, Nepos's House, Shrine of Talos, Silver-Blood Inn, Margret's Room, The Treasury House, The Warrens, Weylin's Room

CHARACTERS: Betrid Silver-Blood, Eltrys, Garvey, Kleppr, Margret, Markarth City Guard, Mulush gro-Shugurz, Rhiada, Thonar Silver-Blood

ENEMIES: Donnel, Dryston, Nana Ildene, Nepos the Nose, Uaile, Weylin

◊ **OBJECTIVES:** Read Eltrys' Note, Go to the Shrine of Talos, Find evidence about Margret, Find evidence about Weylin, (Optional) Obtain the key to Margret's room, Read Margret's Journal, Find evidence about Thonar, (Optional) Obtain the key to Weylin's room, Read Weylin's Note, Find out who "N" is, Find evidence about Nepos, Return to Eltrys

Murder in the Marketplace

On your first visit to Markarth, just after you enter the entrance gate, you immediately hear a man shouting, "The Reach belongs to the Forsworn!" before he murders a market patron in cold blood. The Markarth City Guard quickly overpower and slay the maniac (watch your own sword swings if the lunatic turns on you, as you don't want to accidentally strike a Markarth inhabitant). You can quickly speak to the other traders, before a man named Eltrys approaches you. He surreptitiously hands you a note. Read it; he is requesting a meeting in the Shrine of Talos.

➤ **Eltrys' Note**

◊ **OBJECTIVE:** Read Eltrys' Note
◊ **OBJECTIVE:** Go to the Shrine of Talos
♦ **TARGET:** Shrine of Talos, in Markarth

Before the body of Margret—the woman who was cut down—is carried away for rites and burial, quickly check her corpse; you'll find a key that can come in handy.

➤ **Key to Margret's Room**

Enter the shrine and locate Eltrys, who is attempting a clandestine investigation of a conspiracy within the city. This isn't the first brazen killing by the Forsworn; indeed, the City Guard seem to be actively covering up this slaughter. Eltrys tasks you with finding out more information about the folks involved: the attacker, Weylin, and the victim, Margret. For further hints, ask Eltrys exhaustive questions about the Forsworn and those involved. For more motivation, Eltrys says he'll pay you handsomely for what you uncover.

◊ **OBJECTIVE:** Find evidence about Margret
♦ **TARGET:** Silver-Blood Inn, in Markarth
◊ **OBJECTIVE:** Find evidence about Weylin
♦ **TARGET:** The Warrens, in Markarth

TIP You can undertake the following investigation in any order, and you can break off from one line of questioning to complete another. Each time your Quest Objective updates significantly, return to Eltrys (in the shrine) to inform him and receive a sizable reward (200 gold pieces each time).

TIP **No Murder in the Marketplace:** If you're quick, you can actually step in and kill Weylin before he has time to murder Margret. Should this occur, she offers the necklace she purchased just prior to being set upon as a way of thanking you. The quest continues with Eltrys handing you a note. Once you speak to him inside the Shrine of Talos, you can find Margret again (around the market or in the Silver-Blood Inn) and obtain more information about the attack, and why she is there.

Margret: Shadows Around Every Corner

Head into the Silver-Blood Inn, where Margret was staying, and have a quiet word with Kleppr the barkeep. Steer the conversation toward Margret, who Kleppr says prepaid an entire month's rent for the nicest room at the inn.

◊ **OBJECTIVE:** (Optional) Obtain the key to Margret's Room
♦ **TARGET:** Kleppr, in the Silver-Blood Inn, in Markarth

You obviously need to search Margret's Room, and for that you require a key or a Lockpick skill. There are various ways of entering Margret's Room:

Unlock the room using the key you uncovered from Margret's corpse, if you were quick-thinking at the start of this quest.

(Lockpick [Apprentice]) You can ignore Kleppr completely and—once the coast is clear—use Lockpicks to open the door.

(Persuade) You can sweet-talk Kleppr into giving you the key.

(Gold) Simple bribery does the trick, too.

(Intimidate) As does a not-so-veiled threat directed at the barkeep.

(Pickpocket) With an appropriate Pickpocket, you can ease the key into your possession.

➤ Key to Margret's Room

Inside Margret's Room, there's several trinkets to steal, but the real find is located inside the end table. Open it, and secure Margret's Journal.

➤ Margret's Journal

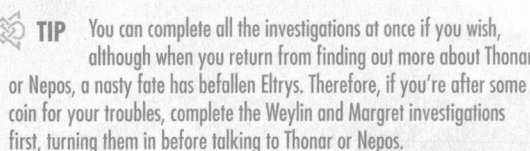

◊ **OBJECTIVE:** Read Margret's Journal
♦ **TARGET:** Margret's Room, Silver-Blood Inn, in Markarth

Open the journal: It seems Margret was an agent employed by General Tullius and was tasked to investigate the powerful Silver-Blood family, specifically Thonar Silver-Blood, the owner of Cidhna Mine. You have the information you seek; leave the inn. You're met outside by a city guard, who gives you what appears to be a threat if you continue poking your nose into the affairs of the Silver-Bloods.

◊ **OBJECTIVE:** Find evidence about Thonar
♦ **TARGET:** The Treasury House, in Markarth

TIP You can complete all the investigations at once if you wish, although when you return from finding out more about Thonar or Nepos, a nasty fate has befallen Eltrys. Therefore, if you're after some coin for your troubles, complete the Weylin and Margret investigations first, turning them in before talking to Thonar or Nepos.

Margret: The Spilling of Silver-Blood

Climb the hewn steps to the elaborate Treasury House, and enter. You're usually greeted by Rhiada, the Silver-Blood's maid, who challenges you on your antics after you ask to see Thonar. You can:

(Persuade) Pretend Thonar is expecting you.

(Bribe) Use some coin to win her over.

(Intimidate) Or attempt a fear-inducing utterance.

This allows you access into the dining room, where Thonar is usually eating. No matter your line of questioning, Thonar is the leader of this city, and he isn't happy at you butting into business that doesn't concern you. You're told to leave, just as you hear a commotion in an adjoining room. Thonar's servants, Donnel and Nana Ildene, reveal themselves to be Forsworn and have already killed Thonar's wife, Betrid, in cold blood! They now turn on you; defeat them both.

Thonar is shaken but ready to talk. He reveals he'd made a deal with the Forsworn. When the Nords conquered Markarth, Thonar spared King Madanach's life and locked him up in the Cidhna Mine. In exchange, the ousted king agreed to use his Forsworn to kill Thonar's enemies. But Thonar's grip on power is obviously slipping.

Weylin: A Subsistence Existence

◊ **OBJECTIVE:** (Optional) Obtain the key to Weylin's room
◊ **OBJECTIVE:** Read Weylin's Note
♦ **TARGET:** (Optional) Garvey, and Weylin's Room, the Warrens, in Markarth

Weylin the murderer worked as a miner and lived in the grim underbelly of Markarth, in a place known as the Warrens. Journey here, and gain some further insight into Weylin's grim life. Start with the bullying foreman of the smelter, Mulush gro-Shugurz. He won't tell you what he knows; he doesn't care enough to be involved in Weylin's antics. React by leaving or by:

(Persuade) Saying he must know something.

(Bribe) Bribing him to reveal some information.

(Intimidate) Telling him he'd better start caring.

If you're successful, Mulush reveals Weylin was slipped a piece of paper the last time he was paid. Now move into the Warrens.

The second person to interview is Garvey, who runs the Warrens where the poor make their pitiful existence. He isn't keen on just handing over Weylin's key to you. You have the following options:

(Persuade) Tell him it is important.

(Bribe) Press some gold into his filthy hands.

(Intimidate) Inform him this wasn't a request; it was an order.

(Pickpocket) Display your impressive Pickpocket skills and take the key by stealthy means.

When you reach Weylin's room inside the Warrens, you'll notice it is locked (Very Easy). However, picking the lock simply raises the alarm and isn't recommended if anyone is watching. Neither is striking Garvey, who holds the key.

➤ Key to Weylin's Room

Once inside Weylin's room, steal from his chest. There isn't much to line your pockets with, but the chest does contain an important clue: Weylin's Note.

➤ Weylin's Note

Open the note, which contains the order for the assassination in the market. It is simply signed "-N."

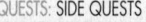

◊ **OBJECTIVE:** Find out who "N" is
♦ **TARGET:** Dryston, in Markarth

Weylin: On the Nose

The moment you step outside from the Warrens, an armored man by the name of Dryston strides up to you and threatens to teach you a lesson. There's no way out of this brawl; expect a pummeling if you don't retaliate. After you punch him down, he squeals the name of his employer: the city's old administrator, Nepos the Nose.

CAUTION

Retaliate with your fists and beat Dryston to his knees. Do not use weapons or kill him; this causes mass hostility across Markarth!

◊ **OBJECTIVE:** Find evidence about Nepos
♦ **TARGET:** Nepos's House, in Markarth

TIP You should definitely catch up with Eltrys and secure some gold pieces before uncovering more of this conspiracy!

With Nepos's thug beaten into submission, ascend the steps to reach the administrator's house, and step inside. You're stalled by Uaile, Nepos's protective housekeeper. She refuses to let you speak with Nepos but relents when the old man beckons you to his hearth. Nepos is wizened, and he confesses to directing Weylin in the murder, under orders from Madanach, who he describes as the "King in Rags." Madanach used to rule Markarth before the Nords drove out the Forsworn. Somehow, he still commands the Forsworn. Nepos's servants think you've heard enough and attack you. Stay and fight, or flee the dwelling.

◊ **OBJECTIVE:** Return to Eltrys
♦ **TARGET:** Shrine of Talos, in Markarth

Eltrys must be informed immediately! Unfortunately, as you enter the shrine and venture to his location, you see that Eltrys has been killed—almost certainly by the city guards milling about. Guards immediately accuse you of snooping and frame you for the recent murders, including that of Eltrys! You are to be banished to the Cidhna Mine. A place where *no one* escapes.

Quest Conclusion

Prior to Eltrys's demise, he rewards you with gold for your investigations of Weylin and Margret. Be sure to see him before your other investigations, or don't expect any coin!

➤ **Gold pieces [Leveled]**

Postquest Activities

Side Quest: No One Escapes Cidhna Mine begins immediately.

NO ONE ESCAPES CIDHNA MINE

MINOR SPOILERS

PREREQUISITES: Complete Side Quest: The Forsworn Conspiracy

INTERSECTING QUESTS: Side Quest: The Forsworn Conspiracy, Grisvar's Shiv*

LOCATIONS: Markarth, Cidhna Mine, Markarth Ruins

CHARACTERS: Borkul the Beast, Braig, Duach, Grisvar the Unlucky, Madanach, Markarth Guard, Odvan, Thonar Silver-Blood, Uraccen, Urzoga gra-Shugurz

ENEMIES: Dwarven Centurion, Frostbite Spider

◊ **OBJECTIVES:** Ask a prisoner about Madanach, Get past Borkul the Beast, Talk to Grisvar about getting a Shiv, Bring Grisvar the Skooma, Talk to Madanach, Hear Braig's story, Return to Madanach, Kill Grisvar the Unlucky, Return to Madanach, Follow Madanach, Kill Madanach, Search Madanach's body, Escape Cidhna Mine

NOTE * Indicates the secondary quest also available here has a name that does not appear in your Quest menu; the objectives are in the Miscellaneous section of your menu.

Imprisoned in a Forsaken Place

CAUTION

This quest does not commence if you're thrown into this mine due to your Crime level in the Reach!

◊ **OBJECTIVE:** Ask a prisoner about Madanach
♦ **TARGET:** Uraccen, in Cidhna Mine

You wake up to Urzoga gra-Shugurz shouting at you. He is the guard captain in charge of the prisoners in this mine, which is carved into the mountains of Markarth. Unlike prisons in other Hold Cities, you're expected to work, mining silver ore until you drop. You can reply with subservient or sarcastic remarks to Urzoga, before she opens up the cell door and you're allowed into the mine.

The quickest way to finding out more information about Madanach, who appears to run the prisoners on this side of the mine, is to speak with Uraccen. He's usually sitting by the campfire in the prison's middle chamber. You can make up whatever story you like about why you're here, and ask him about the prison's illicit Skooma trade, but be sure to ask him two important questions:

1. The location of Madanach. Unfortunately, nobody gets to speak with him without getting past Borkul the Beast. You may ask for more information about this Orc bodyguard, or step over to see him yourself.
2. Information on obtaining a Shiv a more subtle and cruel method of protecting yourself. A man named Grisvar has a spare one, if you're interested. This begins Side Quest: Grisvar's Shiv.

◊ **OBJECTIVE:** Get past Borkul the Beast

Borkul the Beast is standing guard by a locked gate close to the campfire. You can get on his good side by revealing your bloodlust, or offer a more measured response. When you ask to see Madanach, Borkul refuses until you pay the toll—a Shiv. You can:

Tell Borkul you don't have a Shiv. He suggests you get one. Complete Side Quest: Grisvar's Shiv from this point.

(Pickpocket) Use your impressive Pickpocket skill to pry Borkul's Key from his pocket without him knowing.

(Persuade) Tell Borkul that Madanach is expecting you.

(Brawl) Or offer to fight Borkul for access into Madanach's chamber. Fight the Orc, here by the campfire, and batter him with punches until he falls to his knees and tastes his own blood.

Once you succeed at any of these plans, Borkul hands over the key to Madanach's room, and you may progress.

➤ **Borkul's Key**

SIDE QUEST: GRISVAR'S SHIV*

◊ **OBJECTIVE:** Talk to Grisvar about getting a Shiv.

If you require a Shiv while in prison, head into the mine's southern part and hunt down Grisvar the Unlucky. He's here by the Jarl's request, due to his "problems." Ask for a Shiv, and he agrees—if you bring him back a bottle of Skooma from Duach.

Now head into the mine's north section and ask Duach about the Skooma. He isn't about to hand this over to just anyone, and your looks are beginning to annoy him. In that case, you should try:

(Persuade) Telling him you need the Skooma badly.

(Brawl) Demanding he hand the Skooma over and then fistfighting him for it. Remember, don't kill him!

When either of these plans is successful, you receive the Skooma from Duach.

➤ **Skooma**

CAUTION Did you drink the Skooma before realizing you need to hand it to Grisvar? Then this quest fails!

◊ **OBJECTIVE:** Bring Grisvar the Skooma

All that remains now is to return to Grisvar, hand him the Skooma, and accept a Shiv in return. You can use the Shiv to attack the prisoners (which is unwise, as they usually overwhelm you), or give it to Borkul the Beast if no other method of getting past him is working.

➤ **Shiv**

Mining the Mind of Madanach

◊ **OBJECTIVE:** Talk to Madanach

NOTE **Forsworn or Nord Alliance:** At this point, you can choose to side with Madanach, the leader of the Forsworn, against the Nords who have usurped his kingdom. Follow the quest sections marked with the alliance you wish to be associated with.

Forsworn Alliance: Madanach's Tasks

Forsworn Alliance: Open the barred door that Borkul was guarding, pass by a latrine and closed cell, and meet Madanach at his writing desk. He asks what it is that you want. You may answer in any way you wish, but Madanach points out that you are now a slave. The boot of the Nord steps on your throat. He mentions a man named Braig, who has been imprisoned almost as long as Madanach. You are to meet with him and ask why he's here. Madanach wants to know how widespread the injustice of Markarth really is. You can ask about the Forsworn and Thonar (the mine owner) before you leave.

◊ **OBJECTIVE:** Hear Braig's story

Search the mine's southern end for Braig, who greets you with a warning not to shiv him. Tell him Madanach has asked you to listen to his story, and he asks when you last had chains around your wrists. Answer him as you wish and again when he asks about your family. Then Braig tells of his daughter Aethra, an innocent caught up in recent entanglements when the Nords picked Braig up for being involved in the Forsworn uprising. Braig had only spoken to Madanach once, but that was enough for the Nords to execute her in front of him and throw him in this mine. You can ask Braig further questions, but this has satisfied Madanach's curiosity.

◊ **OBJECTIVE:** Return to Madanach

Journey back to Madanach, who seems to have used Braig's story to drill into you the injustices of the Nords. Your responses can be sympathetic or accusatory, but if you are to escape, Madanach needs a show of loyalty from you. He certainly doesn't want a Shiv in the back during any planned breakout. He tells you to visit Grisvar the Unlucky—a thief and a snitch—and dispatch him so only prisoners loyal to Madanach remain.

◊ **OBJECTIVE:** Kill Grisvar the Unlucky

You must kill Grisvar with your bare hands or with a Shiv if you previously received one from him. As he's the only prisoner not loyal to the Forsworn, he has to go. You can attack without even speaking to him, or tell him that Madanach says hello, which causes him to stand and fight for a bit, then flee. Hunt him down and kill him, again with a Shiv or your bare hands. Equip yourself with a Shiv from his corpse if you wish.

➤ **Shiv**

◊ **OBJECTIVE:** Return to Madanach
◊ **OBJECTIVE:** Follow Madanach

Your actions have proved to Madanach that you are one of them. He wishes you to accompany him so he can announce his plans to all his brothers. Follow Madanach into the main mine chamber with the campfire, where he informs his brethren that it is time to leave Cidhna Mine. There is a gate beside his quarters, and behind it is a tunnel. This leads right through the old Dwarven Ruins of Markarth and into the city. Duach, Odvan (the only prisoners you may not have met yet), and the others raucously approve.

Nord Alliance: Madanach's Death

◊ **OBJECTIVE:** Kill Madanach
◊ **OBJECTIVE:** Search Madanach's body

Nord Alliance: If you wish to side with the Nords and can't abide this Forsworn claptrap, you can ignore Madanach and instead begin to fight or pickpocket him. Killing him is obviously easier if you're carrying a Shiv rather than relying on your fists. Madanach is an accomplished mage, so this fight may be difficult to conclude in your favor. But if you do kill Madanach, you can skip any remaining conversations and search his body for the following important items:

➤ **Madanach's Note** ➤ **Madanach's Key**

The key unlocks the gate adjacent to Madanach's quarters, while the note informs you there's old Dwarven Ruins connecting this mine to Markarth, which is the only escape route. Time to earn an early pardon!

◊ **OBJECTIVE:** Escape Cidhna Mine
♦ **TARGET:** Markarth city exterior

An Early Pardon

Whether you're fleeing with your Forsworn brothers or you've killed Madanach, stolen his key, and used it to open the gate beside Madanach's quarters, the time has come to leave. Maneuver down the tunnel to a gold door that opens into Markarth Ruins. Dash in a northeastern direction along the remains of stone steps and metallic walkways, and into a Frostbite Spider–infested stone corridor. Stand and fight, or run past these large arachnids. If the Forsworn are with you, attack the spiders as a team.

Continue into a tight connecting tunnel that opens into a large two-level corridor with winding pipes and more dwarven automatons at the far end of it. Venture forward, and they grind into life (depending on your level, these enemies could be spheres or a dreaded Centurion!). When the dwarven mechanical beasts finally topple, continue heading northeast, scrambling up the earthen tunnel toward a golden door.

Forsworn Alliance: The Forsworn stop at the base of the steps, where a woman named Kaie calls for Madanach, bringing him all the equipment you were stripped of when you entered Cidhna Mine. In addition, you are granted an ancient outfit of the Forsworn that is blessed with the old magicks. Then the Forsworn pour out of the ruins and into Markarth.

➤ **Inventory Equipment**
➤ **Gauntlet of the Old Gods**
➤ **Armor of the Old Gods**
➤ **Helmet of the Old Gods**
➤ **Boots of the Old Gods**

Nord Alliance: Head up the steps to the gold doors. Madanach's Key opens them and you stumble out of the ruins and into Markarth.

Quest Conclusion

Forsworn Alliance: Thonar Silver-Blood is waiting to greet Madanach as he exits the ruins. He isn't about to let the Forsworn escape from his prison, especially after what they did to his family. The quest ends with the Forsworn swarming Thonar and killing him.

Nord Alliance: Thonar Silver-Blood is waiting to greet you as you exit the ruins. He isn't about to let the person responsible for killing Madanach out of his jurisdiction without giving him some kind of reward, especially after the peace you brought to his family. The quest ends with Thonar handing you all your equipment back, as well as a special ring—one that a smith would cut off seven fingers for! Remain calm during this time too; if you side with the Nords but kill Thonar, you don't receive his ring.

➤ **Inventory Equipment** ➤ **Silver-Blood Family Ring**

Postquest Activities

If you sided with the Forsworn, they begin a bloody rampage through the city, eventually reaching the gates and fleeing to Druadach Redoubt deep in the Reach. If you helped them, the Forsworn in Druadach (and only at this location) will be friendly.

PREREQUISITES: None

MINOR SPOILERS

INTERSECTING QUESTS: Main Quest: Bleak Falls Barrow

LOCATIONS: Bleak Falls Barrow, Riverwood

CHARACTERS: Camilla Valerius, Lucan Valerius

ENEMIES: Arvel the Swift, Bandits, Draugr, Frost Troll, Giant Frostbite Spider, Skeevers

◊ **OBJECTIVES:** Retrieve the Golden Claw, Cut Arvel down, Find the secret of Bleak Falls Barrow, Bring the claw to Lucan

Beneath the Barrow

Travel to Riverwood. You can overhear rumors about a recently robbed store; locate the Riverwood Trader. Inside, the proprietors Lucan and his sister, Camilla Valerius, are engaged in a heated discussion. It seems bandits have recently broken into their dried goods store and stolen a solid gold ornament in the shape of a dragon's claw. Offer your help to Lucan; the sibling bickering doesn't stop, but Camilla seems appeased and takes you out to the bridge on the edge of Riverwood.

◊ **OBJECTIVE:** Retrieve the Golden Claw
♦ **TARGET:** Golden Claw

TIP You can start this quest by simply adventuring into the Bleak Falls Barrow, without speaking to either Valerius sibling. You may also wish to cross-reference this quest with the Main Quest: Bleak Falls Barrow. Be on the lookout for a Dragonstone as you search.

Find your way up the mountain path north of Riverwood, passing the Riverwood Folly (where bandits roam), and to the summit, where the Nord tomb appears through the blizzard. Expect more bandit activity in this area. Locate the arched carved door leading into Bleak Falls Temple. Inside the first chamber, you hear two bandits around a campfire talking about a Dark Elf heading farther into the Barrow. End their conversation swiftly before venturing down the stairs.

Pass through the spiderwebs, the burial urns, and the dead Skeever, and engage another bandit on your way to a ceremonial entrance room. A portcullis blocks your path, and the lever nearby is currently inactive. In the alcoves to the left are a trio of three-sided pillars. Approach the first, and you'll notice they can be activated. Each side has a different animal carving: the Hawk, Whale, and Snake.

Puzzle Solution: Rotate the pillars so a Snake, Snake, and Whale face out. The carved Nord heads above the portcullis (and the fallen middle one) hold the answer in their maws.

Descend the spiral steps beyond, battling a few Skeevers on your way. As the thick spider silk begins to cover the walls, you hear a voice up ahead and to your left. Cut through the doorway covered in webbing, and enter the lair of a Giant Frostbite Spider. Attack the arachnid before venturing toward the trussed-up Dark Elf: one of the bandits from the raiding party you slaughtered previously. This is Arvel the Swift, who is carrying the Golden Claw. He quickly tells you he knows how it works, how it fits into the door in the Hall of Stories. The bandit is babbling. But he needs cutting down first. Oblige him.

◊ **OBJECTIVE:** Cut Arvel down
♦ **TARGET:** Arvel the Swift

TIP Having trouble dispatching such a large arachnid? Then search for a Potion of Paralysis on a shelf in the hallway before the puzzle chamber and a Fireball Scroll on the table in the room just after you descend the spiral steps. Use these if you need to.

After a couple of weapon swipes (or magical blasts), Arvel's sticky prison gives way. He immediately flees, laughing that he won't be sharing his treasure with the likes of you. This is correct, but that's because you'll be taking him out—use a quick arrow or two in the back or other ranged attack—or letting the denizens who lurk deeper into this crypt deal with him.

CAUTION It isn't wise to rush after Arvel; you'll soon catch up with him, and it is better to be prepared rather than rush headlong into an unknown chamber.

Follow Arvel's trail, passing through the crypt entrance and down into the catacombs. The swift soon meets the dead as Arvel falls under a flurry of Draugr attacks. The Nord undead now turn their attention to you. Battle them back using your combat mettle or run north toward the open spiked gate and pressure plate. Keep to the extreme left, and you can activate the swinging gate trap without being hit. Instead, use it as a skewering device against the Draugr. Then search Arvel. Among his belongings is the Golden Claw and the Dark Elf's journal. Read it for more clues on this Barrow's secret.

➤ **Golden Claw** ➤ **Arvel's Journal**

◊ **OBJECTIVE:** Find the secret of Bleak Falls Barrow
♦ **TARGET:** Hall of Stories

You have Lucan's trinket, but don't return it until you completely reconnoiter this Barrow. Continue down, battling Draugr and searching corpses, both resting and animated, as you go. At the swinging blades, sprint forward the moment the closest blade swings past you. Brandish your weaponry, but don't be overzealous with fire in the passageway with puddles; this is actually oil leaking from a hanging lamp, and the corridor erupts if flames touch the ground; use this as a trap against your bony foes.

Eventually, you climb steps into a tall chamber with a waterfall and another Draugr. Although a treasure chest can be ransacked, the Barrow's secret lies past a portcullis above the rushing stream. Locate the chain next to the portcullis and activate it, before splashing down the stream and into a larger, curved cavern with an opening at the far end. Ready any ranged attacks you can muster; a Draugr (or if you're at higher levels, a Frost Troll) is pacing the snow bridge directly below the waterfall opening. Strike it with as many projectiles as you can to weaken it, then engage it in a fierce battle throughout this upper cavern and lower bridge. Flee to regain Stamina or Magick if necessary. Another option is to simply flee entirely, although you'll miss the scavenging on the curved path below the bridge. Here you'll find the body of Thomas. Follow the path around and into the illuminated entrance to Bleak Falls Sanctum.

Open the Sanctum doors, and weave your way to another bladed corridor. Coax the Draugr beyond into this trap, before dashing through it, into the Great Chamber. Expect attacks from Draugr bowmen on the bridge above, as well as melee strikes from the ground. You can drop oil lamps and burn the decaying flesh of these foes as you head up and over the bridge, to the Iron Door leading into the Hall of Stories. The Hall is a long corridor with intricately carved Nord stonework on either side and an ornate door at the far end.

Puzzle Solution: The door consists of three "rings" that rotate when you activate them. Each has three animals plated into the structure, while the central keyhole is unlocked using the Golden Claw. This puzzle is inaccessible without it, as the solution is on the palm of the Golden Claw. Rotate it in your inventory to see the three circular petroglyph carvings on the Claw's palm. Move the rings so the Bear, Moth, and Owl appear on the outer, middle, and inner rings, respectively. Then insert the Golden Claw into the keyhole.

◊ **OBJECTIVE:** Bring the claw to Lucan
♦ **TARGET:** Lucan Valerius

This reveals the Barrow's secret at last: a ceremonial burial grotto with waterfalls surrounding the long-forgotten chamber. Move to the carved stone center and check the chest. Scavenge what you need; then inspect the Word Wall, where you're granted a Word of Power! However, this stirs a high-level Draugr Lord from his rest, and you must defend yourself from this final Barrow guardian.

After the fight, inspect the Draugr's corpse; he is carrying a Dragonstone! Now take the staircase on the chamber's left side, activating the handle to raise a secret stone slab door out into an upper Barrow alcove, a ceremonial alcove, and an exit out into Skyrim.

Now it is a simple matter of returning the Golden Claw heirloom to Lucan to complete this quest.

Quest Conclusion

➤ **Word of Power:** Unrelenting Force
➤ **Dragonstone**
➤ **Gold pieces (Leveled; if you return the Golden Claw to Lucan)**

Postquest Activities

The Dragonstone is a valuable item sought by the Wizard of Whiterun, Farengar Secret-Fire, as part of Main Quest: Bleak Falls Barrow.

PREREQUISITES: Complete Main Quest: Dragon Rising

MINOR SPOILERS

INTERSECTING QUESTS: None

LOCATIONS: Swindler's Den, Whiterun, The Bannered Mare, Dragonsreach Dungeon, Whiterun Stables

CHARACTERS: Alik'r Prisoner, Alik'r Warrior, Kematu, Saadia, Whiterun City Guard

ENEMIES: Alik'r Warrior, Bandit

◊ **OBJECTIVES:** Find the Redguard woman, Speak with Saadia or Inform the Alik'r of Saadia's location, Talk to the Alik'r Prisoner, Kill Kematu or Inform the Alik'r of Saadia's location, Kill Kematu or talk to him, Lead Saadia to the Whiterun Stables

A Wanted Woman

Once you've finished Main Quest: Dragon Rising and you enter the great city of Whiterun via the main gate, expect a commotion there. Cloaked Redguard warriors (who you find out are of the Alik'r Coterie) are in a heated discussion with the city guard. The Alik'r have already been banned from most of the city after an incident and jailing, but the men are determined to try and find a Redguard woman somewhere inside the walls. Speak to one of the Alik'r if you wish, or they stop and talk to you.

◊ **OBJECTIVE:** Find the Redguard woman

The woman in question is Saadia, who is a barmaid in the Bannered Mare. Enter this drinking establishment and let her know about the Alik'r warriors looking for Redguard women. Saadia appears agitated at this news and asks to speak to you privately.

◊ **OBJECTIVE:** Speak with Saadia
♦ **TARGET:** The Bannered Mare, in Whiterun
OR
◊ **OBJECTIVE:** Inform the Alik'r of Saadia's location
♦ **TARGET:** Redguard, on the road to or in Rorikstead

Siding with Saadia: Further Information

Whether you intend to side with Saadia or not, it is worth finding out more about this woman's predicament. Away from the main hearth of the place, Saadia pulls a knife and demands answers, but this is more in an act of desperation than violence. After answering her, she pleads with you to help her. Agree, or request a reward, and Saadia reveals she is a noble from Hammerfell who fled to Skyrim and has been forced into hiding after an attempt on her life. She says that her attackers are hired by a rival house to turn her blood into gold and drag her back to be executed.

Saadia wishes to hire you to drive the assassins out. Most of the Alik'r forces are mercenaries led by a man named Kematu. Remove him and the remaining forces are likely to scatter. You need to find the Alik'r hideout.

◊ **OBJECTIVE:** Talk to the Alik'r Prisoner
♦ **TARGET:** Dragonsreach Dungeon, in Whiterun

Siding with Saadia or the Alik'r: Base Location

If you spoke to Saadia, she will tell you the location of the Alik'r Prisoner: Speak to her to continue this quest. Then journey to Dragonsreach Dungeon, enter the cells, and speak to the Alik'r Prisoner through the bars. Ask about Kematu (which is possible only if you were told the leader's name in an earlier conversation). The prisoner will give up Kematu's whereabouts if you pay the fine for his release.

(100 Gold) Pay one of the guards the fine, and return to the cell to let the prisoner know. He then gives you instructions on the location of Kematu's base of operations. The guards intend to let the prisoner out "eventually."

TIP The other, less ingenious method of finding out where Kematu is located is to simply stumble across the Swindler's Den on your adventurers, once this quest is active.

◊ **OBJECTIVE:** Kill Kematu
OR
◊ **OBJECTIVE:** Inform the Alik'r of Saadia's location
♦ **TARGET:** Swindler's Den

Not Just a Pretty Face

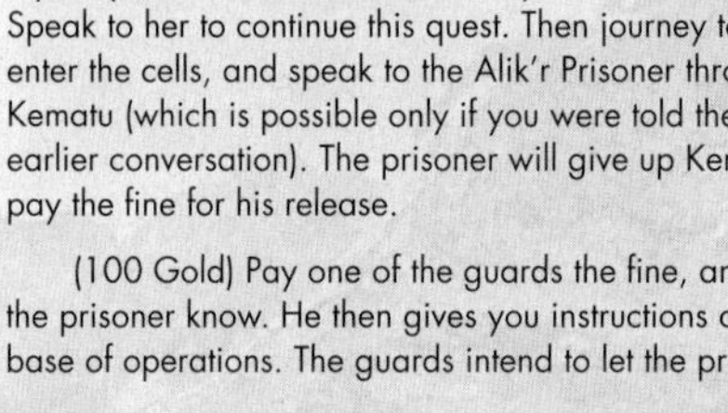

Due west of Whiterun, among the great granite protrusions, is a den hewn into the dense rocky Tundra. Enter the Swindler's Den and bring your offensive combat to bear on the bandits lurking within. You must defeat (or sneak past) these thugs whether you intend to side with the assassins or not. Pass through the rocky crags into a waterlogged corridor, deep into the tunnel system. Kematu and his troops are waiting above you.

No matter who you've sided with previously, Kematu allows you to speak and question him. You can find out why Saadia is being hunted. According to Kematu, she betrayed her people and a Redguard city fell during the war, and the Redguard houses wish to bring her back alive to face justice. At this point, you have a pivotal choice to make: Kill Kematu or talk to him.

◊ **OBJECTIVE:** Kill Kematu or talk to him
♦ **TARGET:** Swindler's Den

NOTE The more investigative of adventurers may wonder who is telling the truth: Kematu or Saadia. Alas, it is simply the word of one against another, and no firm evidence is ever found!

Siding with Saadia: Assassination!

If you are determined to save Saadia from the clutches of the Alik'r, you may attack them as soon as you can, or after another rather fruitless conversation with Kematu. Bring your best offensive weaponry to this slaughter! Gather any valuables you wish from the corpses, and then return to the Bannered Mare in Whiterun and inform Saadia of your success.

Siding with the Alik'r: A Wanted Woman

Speak again to Kematu, who informs you that his troops aren't assassins, but agents acting on behalf of Redguard Houses and ready to bring back a fugitive. Ask what they want you to do, and Kematu asks you to return to Saadia and convince her to meet you at the stables, where she'll be caught and brought to justice.

◊ **OBJECTIVE:** Lead Saadia to the Whiterun Stables
♦ **TARGET:** Saadia, the Bannered Mare, in Whiterun

Head back to the Bannered Mare and quickly speak with Saadia.

(Lie) Tell her you weren't able to defeat all the Alik'r forces, they are coming for her, and you have a horse ready for her.

Now exit Whiterun with Saadia following you. Move along the main cobbled road to Whiterun Stables and around to the side of the stable house, where Kematu is waiting for you both. He expertly immobilizes Saadia, and you may speak with him one final time to collect your reward.

Alternate Plans

At any point after speaking to Saadia, you can speak to the original Alik'r warriors you met at Whiterun's gate. They have moved to Rorikstead. Informing them that you've found Saadia completes the quest to the point where you're instructed to escort Saadia to the Whiterun Stables.

If you want to help Saadia but don't want to battle all of the Alik'r in Swindler's Den, there's always a cunning double cross you can pull (although the timing is difficult): Agree to help Kematu, and he'll appear in the stables alone, only after you've lied to Saadia and told her it is time to go. If you can kill Kematu before he paralyzes Saadia, she chastises you for using her as bait, but you can still claim the reward from her!

Quest Conclusion

If you slaughtered Kematu and saved Saadia, you receive the following:

- **500 gold pieces**

If you sided with Kematu of the Alik'r, you receive the following:

- **500 gold pieces**

Postquest Activities

If you helped Kematu capture Saadia, they are both gone the next time you return to Whiterun, and there is no further Alik'r presence in Skyrim. If you helped Saadia, she returns to her duties in the Bannered Mare, and no one is the wiser.

KYNE'S SACRED TRIALS

PREREQUISITES: None

MINOR SPOILERS

LOCATIONS: Bleakcoast Cave, Froki's Shack, Gjukar's Monument, Graywinter Watch, Loreius Farm, Mammoth Graveyard, Pinewatch, Twilight Sepulcher, Windward Ruins

CHARACTERS: Froki Whetted-Blade, Haming

ENEMIES: Guardian Troll Spirit, Mammoth Guardian Spirit, Mudcrab, Mudcrab Guardian Spirit, Sabre Cat Guardian Spirit, Skeever, Skeever Guardian Spirit, Troll, Ursine Guardian Spirit, Wolf, Wolf Guardian Spirit

◊ **OBJECTIVES:** Defeat the Guardian Mudcrab, Defeat the Guardian Skeever, Defeat the Guardian Wolf, Return to Froki, Defeat the Guardian Bear, Defeat the Guardian Mammoth, Defeat the Sabre Cat, Return to Froki, Defeat the Guardian Troll, Return to Froki

Honoring the Old Ways

Nestled just below the snow line, high in the Jerall Mountains, Froki's Shack overlooks the southwestern rim of the Rift. Froki Whetted-Blade himself is usually inside his modest dwelling, with his grandson Haming. Judging by the animal heads festooned about the shack walls, Froki is something of a hunter. He is also somewhat mocking of the city dwellers and their new beliefs in the Divines. Not Froki; he believes in the Nordic gods of yore, especially Kyne the Blessed Warrior-Wife and widow of Shor, the mother of men and beasts. The Sacred Trials are named for her. Ask about the trials, and Froki explains this is an old Nord tradition: a test to prove your worth in the eyes of Kyne. Agree to begin the trials, and you are told to defeat the guardian beasts blessed by Kyne. Froki anoints you with the symbol of the Wolf, the Crab, and the Skeever. You can ask Froki for further information on the trials, his child, and the worship of Kyne, before the great hunt begins.

◊ **OBJECTIVE:** Defeat the Guardian Mudcrab
♦ **TARGET:** Mudcrab Guardian Spirit, near Gjukar's Monument
◊ **OBJECTIVE:** Defeat the Guardian Skeever
♦ **TARGET:** Skeever Guardian Spirit, near Windward Ruins
◊ **OBJECTIVE:** Defeat the Guardian Wolf
♦ **TARGET:** Wolf Guardian Spirit, near Pinewatch

Defeat the following three Guardian animals in any order you wish.

Sacred Trial: Parts I, II, III

Mudcrab Guardian Spirit: Find this spirit in the marshy ground between Gjukar's Monument and Broken Fang Cave. Expect Mudcrabs to scuttle in and attack as you deal with the Spirit.

Skeever Guardian Spirit: Locate this spirit in the snowy cairn marking the entrance to Windward Ruins, just southwest of Dawnstar. Prepare for Skeever to nip at you as you defeat the spirit.

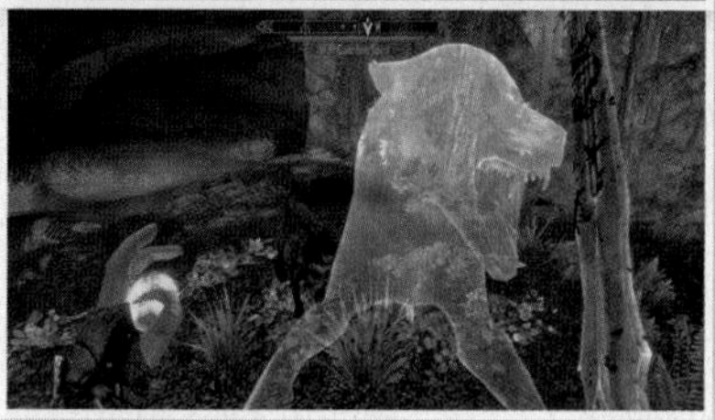

Wolf Guardian Spirit: Search for this spirit close to Lake Ilinalta, just northwest of Pinewatch. Combat is likely to include dispatching wolves, and sometimes cave bears as you finish the spirit.

◊ **OBJECTIVE:** Return to Froki

After you dispatch all three animal Guardian Spirits, return to Froki's Shack and speak to him. He softens his attitude to you slightly, realizing you're probably ready for a real challenge. He anoints you with the symbol of the Bear, Sabre Cat, and Mammoth. He warns you to tread carefully, as these are mighty beasts.

◊ **OBJECTIVE:** Defeat the Guardian Bear
♦ **TARGET:** Ursine Guardian Spirit, near the Twilight Sepulcher
◊ **OBJECTIVE:** Defeat the Guardian Mammoth
♦ **TARGET:** Mammoth Guardian Spirit, Mammoth Graveyard, near Loreius Farm
◊ **OBJECTIVE:** Defeat the Sabre Cat
♦ **TARGET:** Sabre Cat Guardian Spirit, near Bleakcoast Cave

Defeat the following three Guardian animals in any order you wish.

Sacred Trial: Parts IV, V, VI

Ursine Guardian Spirit: Find this spirit in the copse of trees above the rocky terrain northeast of Twilight Sepulcher. Unlike the previous Guardian Spirits, the bear is usually encountered alone.

Mammoth Guardian Spirit: Locate this spirit due west of Loreius Farm, north of Whiterun. Venture to the Mammoth's Graveyard (a Secondary Location), and slay this solitary spirit.

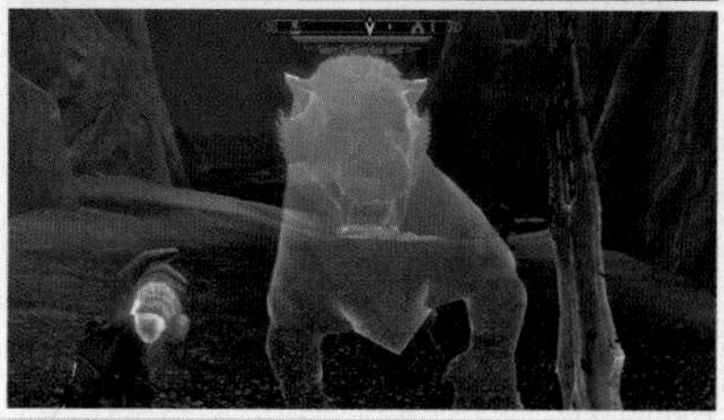

Sabre Cat Guardian Spirit: Search for this spirit at the base of the glaciers along the icy shores of the Sea of Ghosts, just southwest of Bleakcoast Cave. Other wild animals are close, but not with this spirit.

◊ **OBJECTIVE:** Return to Froki

Visit Froki's Shack once more, and inform the old man of your continued successes. You do Kyne proud, and only one challenge remains: to defeat the troll champion!

◊ **OBJECTIVE:** Defeat the Guardian Troll
♦ **TARGET:** Guardian Troll Spirit, in Graywinter Watch

Sacred Trial: Part VII

Guardian Troll Spirit: Prepare for a battle with three trolls, taking all necessary equipment, provisions, and precautions before you travel to Graywinter Watch in the foothills east of Whiterun. Try attracting the trolls one at a time once you're inside the cave, backing out of the entrance if combat becomes too dangerous. Do not rest until the Guardian Troll Spirit falls back into the ether. Then search the location for an impressive bow:

➤ **Froki's Bow**

NOTE This bow can be taken whether this quest is active or not. Should you speak to Froki after obtaining this weapon, he permits you to keep it.

◊ **OBJECTIVE:** Return to Froki

Quest Conclusion

Back at the shack for one final visit, inform Froki of your final triumph. He is pleased to call you a friend and that you finally know what it means to be a true hunter, in the Nordic tradition. For this, you earn an amulet imbued with the Blessing of Kyne.

➤ **Kyne's Blessing (-10% damage taken from wild animals)**

PREREQUISITES: None

MINOR SPOILERS

INTERSECTING QUESTS: None

LOCATIONS: Morthal, Alva's House, Highmoon Hall, Moorside Inn, Movarth's Lair, Hroggar's House, Morthal Cemetery

CHARACTERS: Alva, Helgi's Ghost, Hroggar, Jarl Idgrod Ravencrone or Sorli the Builder, Jonna, Thonnir

ENEMIES: Frostbite Spider, Laelette the Vampire, Movarth Piquine, Vampire, Vampire's Thrall, Alva

◊ **OBJECTIVES:** Talk to the Jarl, Investigate the burned house, Find Helgi after dark, Ask Thonnir about Laelette, Investigate Alva's house, (Optional) Tell the Jarl about Helgi, Show Alva's Journal to the Jarl, Kill the master vampire, Return to Morthal's Jarl

CAUTION

This quest involves you finding clues to convict Hroggar or prove his innocence. Although the townsfolk aren't fond of the man for his wanton ways so soon after a tragedy, they are even less happy with you murdering him and his new lover. So don't, unless you want this quest to be much shorter, and failed.

Answers in the Ash

The Hold City of Morthal has more than swamp critter encroachment to worry about; there's rumor around these parts about one of the homes in the city burning to the ground. Suspicions are rife. Nobody is trustworthy, and two villagers are arguing with the city steward Aslfur as you arrive. You can converse with the townsfolk, but a more elaborate version of the rumor can be gained when you visit the Moorside Inn and speak to the barkeep Jonna. Ask her about the story behind the burned down house. She refers to it as Hroggar's house. It burned recently; the dying screams of his wife and child woke half the town. Now people fear the place, thinking it is cursed. Hroggar claims it started as a hearth fire. Some folks started a rumor that Hroggar was to blame, especially since he took up with a new woman named Alva the day after the fire. Jonna thinks the Jarl might even pay someone to get to the bottom of this.

◊ **OBJECTIVE:** Talk to the Jarl
♦ **TARGET:** Jarl Idgrod Ravencrone, inside Highmoon Hall, in Morthal

It's only a few steps across to Highmoon Hall, and a few more to reach Jarl Idgrod Ravencrone (or Jarl Sorli if the Civil War has forced her from power), who is usually seated on her throne next to Aslfur, her husband and steward. Address the Jarl regarding the ruined house. She knows that Hroggar blames his wife for spilling bear fat in the fire, but most believe his lust for Alva resulted in the arson. Now with the rumors of the cursed dwelling, no one will touch the ashes. Except for you.

◊ **OBJECTIVE:** Investigate the burned house

The burned house is adjacent to the Moorside Inn. Head up the wooden steps and investigate the odd little glow in the corner. It turns out to be the spirit of the child who died in the fire, a girl named Helgi. The little mite is frightened and confused, but continue to ask her your preferred questions and she recalls the fire. She wants to know if you'll play with her. Agree, and she wants to play a game of hide-and-seek, but not until after dark. That's the time "the other one" comes out. She disappears before telling you anything else, although she seems afraid of this other entity.

◊ **OBJECTIVE:** Find Helgi after dark
♦ **TARGET:** Helgi's Ghost, graveyard in Morthal

Once darkness falls, after 8:00 p.m., journey to the western side of Morthal, to the small grave among the rocks with the coffin poking out. You won't have a quest target to it, but if you mention your conversation with Helgi to the Jarl, she can tell you where to look, which activates a quest target. Standing nearby is a woman. Laelette the Vampire comes at you with a vicious draining attack. Defeat her at once. Before she attacks you, she screams that Helgi is some kind of "reward." Slay her, and then inspect the child's coffin. Helgi's tiny voice tells you that Laelette was also playing this game, but she's glad you found her first. Helgi goes back to sleep in her ghostly world, leaving you to find Laelette's husband, Thonnir.

◊ **OBJECTIVE:** Ask Thonnir about Laelette
◊ **OBJECTIVE:** (Optional) Tell the Jarl about Helgi
♦ **TARGET:** Thonnir, in Morthal

A Morthal Enemy

Thonnir is an anxious-looking man who usually comes running to grieve over the dead body of his wife, Laelette, who vanished months ago. He had assumed his wife had joined the war effort. If you question Thonnir about his involvement in all of this, he tells you that Laelette and Alva (Hroggar's new lady) were good friends. Perhaps Alva is part of the arson?

◊ **OBJECTIVE:** Investigate Alva's house
♦ **TARGET:** Alva's House, in Morthal

Alva's house is one of the sturdy buildings of Nordic construction in Morthal. During the day, you may see Hroggar exiting the structure. You can tell him about Helgi's ghost or that Alva was the last person to see Laelette alive. Hroggar shows an amazing lack of compassion for his dead daughter and isn't too concerned about Laelette's fate, either. It seems the only way to gain more information is to search the dwelling. You can:

(Lockpick) Try the lock on the door to Alva's House (Adept) and pick it.

(Pickpocket) Or remove the key to Alva's House from Hroggar, ideally without being seen and fined by the Morthal Guards.

Once inside the residence, head down the stairs. During the day, you usually see Alva sleeping in the coffin. At night Hroggar might be sleeping in the bed upstairs. If she's awake, she viciously attacks you, revealing her vampiric nature to you. Bring her down if necessary, but don't leave the house without checking out her coffin. Alva's Journal is here and proves that Morthal is under attack from vampires under the command of a Vampire Lord named Movarth. But this isn't an assault using steel or spells; this is a subtle infiltration of the guards and residents, and Alva is one of the key succubi in this!

➤ **Alva's House Key** ➤ **Alva's Journal**

NOTE If you find Alva's Journal without killing her and show it to the Jarl, Alva flees town. She heads to a place of evil known as Movarth's Lair.

◊ **OBJECTIVE:** Show Alva's Journal to the Jarl
♦ **TARGET:** Highmoon Hall, in Morthal

Return to Highmoon Hall and approach the Jarl. Inform her that Alva is the murderer who set the fire. When you tell her Alva is a vampire, the Jarl understandably wants proof. After showing her Alva's Journal, the Jarl is both perturbed and in your debt, rewarding you with gold. Not wishing Morthal to become Movarth's feeding grounds once again after a hundred years of peace and quiet, Jarl asks whether you can clear out Movarth's lair and remove his presence for good this time. The townsfolk are assembling outside to help with this threat. This mob (which includes Thonnir) is yelling to slay the vampire and all his ilk. As soon as you move away from them, they head for Movarth's Lair.

➤ **Leveled gold pieces**

◊ **OBJECTIVE:** Kill the master vampire
♦ **TARGET:** Movarth, in Movarth's Lair

Massacring Movarth's Minions

Head north over the bridge and out of Morthal, with your weapon-wielding townsfolk following you. As you approach the lair, the residents' bravado begins to wane, and they falter, leaving only you and Thonnir to deal with the vampires. No matter; a more subtle approach (or coming in with a Follower or Thonnir, whom you can stop at the entrance if you wish to explore alone) is preferable anyway. Enter the cave and descend the curved earthen pathway down to an initial confrontation with Frostbite Spiders. Head through the small tunnel to the south, working your way into a long cavern with a Vampire's Thrall guarding a side tunnel. Slay the thrall before he assaults you. Then enter the side tunnel to the left (north), which leads to a foul-smelling chamber of corpses. A thrall is busily going over a dead villager's pockets. Dispatch this foe close to the mass grave. Take whatever stolen possessions you need, then exit to the north.

This passage leads around to either a ground tunnel or a wooden platform useful for long-range arrow or magical attacks or a place to retreat to. The main chamber is ahead of you, where two vampires, thralls, and Movarth Piquine reside. To stay alive, attack one at a time, coaxing foes into narrower tunnels instead of becoming surrounded. The vampires and Movarth are formidable opponents, so use your judgment and favored fighting implements to get the job done.

◊ **OBJECTIVE:** Return to Morthal's Jarl
♦ **TARGET:** Jarl Idgrod Ravencrone or Sorli the Builder, in Highmoon Hall, in Morthal

Quest Conclusion

With the vampiric threat over, feel free to explore the north chamber to grab Movarth's Boots (which add to your Sneak), and search the storage room with the Alchemy Lab and the connecting cavern. There's another thrall to optionally take down before the lair's chambers join, allowing you to head back up through the earthen entrance chamber, where a small ghostly figure thanks you for making her mother feel better. Back in Morthal, convene with the Jarl one final time, and tell her that the Master Vampire is dead. You are paid handsomely for your troubles and are congratulated by the Jarl and the townsfolk...who also take a rather large amount of credit for themselves.

➤ **Movarth's Boots** ➤ **Leveled gold pieces**

Postquest Activities

Veteran explorers may be interested to know that Movarth Piquine was previously seen as a character from the book *Immortal Blood* that appeared during adventures in Oblivion. In this book, he is a man betrayed by a vampire.

LIGHTS OUT!

MINOR SPOILERS

PREREQUISITES: None

INTERSECTING QUESTS: None

LOCATIONS: Broken Oar Grotto, East Empire Company Warehouse, Solitude, Solitude Lighthouse, Wreck of the Icerunner

CHARACTERS: Deeja, Jaree-Ra, Ma'zaka

ENEMIES: Bandit, Blackblood Marauder

◊ **OBJECTIVES:** Put out the fire in Solitude Lighthouse, Return to Jaree-Ra, Find Deeja at the Wreck of the Icerunner, Defeat Deeja, Find out where Jaree-Ra's bandits took the loot, Travel to Broken Oar Grotto, Defeat Jaree-Ra

Snuffing the Lights of Solitude

When you visit Solitude, be on the lookout for a shady Argonian character who usually lurks outside of Angeline's Aromatics, close to one of the city gates. He sometimes beckons you over. Step up to him and ask what he wants. He explains that he and his sister Deeja are treasure hunters. With the advent of the war, and as Solitude is one of the Empire's major ports, the Solitude Lighthouse serves a vital purpose keeping ships safe in the treacherous waters of the Northern Coast. Now, if the lighthouse went dark, one of the cargo ships that Jaree-Ra has had his eye on—the Icerunner—could run aground and yield some sizable plunder. Are you in?

If you are, agree to put out the lighthouse fire. You can also ask about the ship's crew or turn him over to the guards, but neither helps your success with this quest.

◊ **OBJECTIVE:** Put out the fire in Solitude Lighthouse
♦ **TARGET:** The top of Solitude Lighthouse

Beyond the giant arch of Solitude on the cusp of the Northern Coast is the Solitude Lighthouse. Climb the stairs in the exterior, being careful not to alert the lighthouse keeper, Ma'zaka. Although he sometimes confines himself inside his quarters within the Lighthouse, he may be wandering the building. Simply avoid him, or if you encounter Ma'zaka, kill him or sneak up the tower so you're not spotted. Ma'zaka won't spot that the Lighthouse fire is out until it is too late and the ship Jaree-Ra was eyeing runs aground. Once atop the Lighthouse tower, snuff the flames (there isn't any special equipment needed for this).

◊ **OBJECTIVE:** Return to Jaree-Ra
♦ **TARGET:** Jaree-Ra, near the East Empire Company Warehouse

Scuttled and Plundered!

Find Jaree-Ra on the docks outside the East Empire Company Warehouse. Speak to him: Your actions have already caused the Icerunner to run aground on the shoals across the bay. Jaree-Ra has already dispatched his sister and his gang, the Blackblood Marauders, to strip the ship of valuables. You are to join them.

◊ **OBJECTIVE:** Find Deeja at the Wreck of the Icerunner
♦ **TARGET:** Deeja, inside the Wreck of the Icerunner

TIP The Icerunner runs aground only during this quest; you cannot stumble upon it until you have extinguished the beacon for Jaree-Ra.

You can wade, swim, or Fast-Travel to a nearby location and clamber across the rugged terrain to the ship that has scraped the jagged rocks along the coast. As you draw near, you can see Blackblood Marauders are already stripping the cargo from the vessel. The corpses suggest that the ship's former crew have already been dealt with.

You can talk to one of the Marauders, who tells you Deeja is expecting you down in the hold of the ship. Enter the ship, and head south along the main corridor, opening the second door on your left. Wind your way down the steps to the waterlogged hold. Now head north to a storage alcove where Deeja is checking the contents of a large treasure chest.

Deeja says she's supposed to give you a cut of the loot. But as most of the loot has already been moved, she has another offering: a quick death!

◊ **OBJECTIVE:** Defeat Deeja
◊ **OBJECTIVE:** Find out where Jaree-Ra's bandits took the loot

The Argonian shouldn't be too terrifying an opponent for you; quickly cut her down and then search her still-twitching corpse. The note from Jaree-Ra refers to both the "fool who did our work at the lighthouse" and the location of the plundered loot: Broken Oar Grotto. Battle the remaining Blackblood Marauders who attempt to halt your progress from the Icerunner, and fight your way onto the exterior deck; expect to dispatch about five before the ship is empty of double-crossing cutthroats!

◊ **OBJECTIVE:** Travel to Broken Oar Grotto
◊ **OBJECTIVE:** Defeat Jaree-Ra
♦ **TARGET:** Broken Oar Grotto

When you get back outside, you'll notice that the rowboats loaded up with loot are already gone, as are most of the Marauders. Only one remains on the shore, with the boat that would have carried the last few stragglers away. Deal with him.

TIP **An Alternate Path—Violence Is Golden:** Did you suspect something was amiss when you arrived on the Icerunner's deck? Couldn't keep your hands off the rowboats loaded with treasure, could you? Or did you "accidentally" impale one of the Marauders on your blade? Then there's an alternate method of continuing: If you attack any Marauders or steal any of their loot, all the folks on the Icerunner turn hostile. You'll have to fight your way down to Deeja to claim the note from her corpse to continue this quest! The best part of this plan is that although you have a harder fight on your hands, your reward is greater, as the Marauders never leave with the loot, so you can claim it for yourself, either now or once the quest concludes!

Seeing the Light

Optimally Fast-Travel to Solitude Lighthouse and walk west along the Northern Coast, as the Broken Oar Grotto is nearby. There's a scuttled boat and two recently moored rowboats at the entrance. Enter the smuggler's hideout, fashioned from wood and cavern pathways, and maneuver through this large and looming place. Prepare for protracted combat at long and short ranges with Blackblood Marauders.

TIP Remember to locate the levers to lower the bridge sections to make your traversing a little easier. There are occasional oil lamps to strike and cause a ground fire, too. Better yet, simply submerge yourself and swim along the inlet (ideally while shrouding yourself using magic) to reach the rickety unloading building at the grotto's far end.

Farther into the grotto, Marauders guard a rickety building used for unloading ill-gotten gains. The end of the grotto, where a sunken ship decomposes in the turquoise water, is where Jaree-Ra is counting his loot. Battle up the wooden ramps to the top of the dock structure, and slay the dishonorable lizard with whatever death-dealing implements you consider most suitable. Then scour the Broken Oar Grotto for any remaining foes and any valuables you can scavenge.

TIP Fallen into the water? Then use the half-submerged jetty steps throughout this grotto to reach dry land. Fighting foes? Then utilize the jagged rock walls and passageways to hide in, if you're becoming overwhelmed.

Quest Conclusion

Consult the Atlas chapter for any valuables you can scavenge from the Wreck of the Icerunner or Broken Oar Grotto. Expect no other rewards.

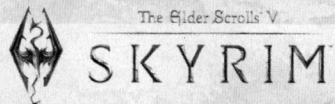

MINOR SPOILERS

PREREQUISITES: None

INTERSECTING QUESTS: Dark Brotherhood Quest: Mourning Never Comes, The College of Winterhold Quest: Revealing the Unseen

LOCATIONS: Arkngthamz, Deep Folk Crossing, Mzulft, Raldbthar, Ruins of Bthalft

CHARACTERS: Katria, Taron Dreth

ENEMIES: Chaurus, Dwarven Centurion, Dwarven Sphere, Dwarven Spider, Falmer, Forgemaster

◊ **OBJECTIVES:** (Miscellaneous): Identify the Crystal Shard, (Miscellaneous): Investigate the ruins of Arkngthamz, Reach the summit of Arkngthamz, (Optional) Retrieve Katria's Journal, Solve the Tonal Lock, Claim the treasure of Arkngthamz, Speak with Katria, Search for the Aetherium Shards (4), Locate the Aetherium Forge, Speak with Katria, Place the Aetherium Shards, Retrieve the Aetherium Crest, Stand Clear, Find the Aetherium Forge, Shut off the Steam, Defeat the Guardians of the Forge, Speak with Katria, (Optional) Search for Crafting Materials, Use the Aetherium Forge

In Preparation

You can start this quest in several different ways. There's no "optimal" way to begin, and you're most likely to simply stumble across it somewhere as part of your adventure. Here are the methods of learning about this quest:

1. Read a copy of a book called *The Aetherium Wars*, which starts the Miscellaneous Objective: Investigate the ruins of Arkngthamz.
2. Visit one of three Dwarven Ruins (Deep Folk Crossing, Raldbthar, or Mzulft), and find an Aetherium Shard without the knowledge gleaned from the book. The shard is initially known as a Glowing Crystal Shard, and once it is in your possession, you're prompted to locate a copy of *The Aetherium Wars*, which appears on your compass.

◊ **OBJECTIVE (MISCELLANEOUS):** Identify the Crystal Shard
♦ **TARGET:** The Aetherium Wars, located nearby

Find the book (usually on the corpse of an adventurer), and the objective updates.

◊ **OBJECTIVE (MISCELLANEOUS):** Investigate the ruins of Arkngthamz
♦ **TARGET:** Arkngthamz, the Reach

3. Or, visit the Dwarven Ruin Arkngthamz, gain entry, and speak to Katria directly. Optionally, you can secure (and read) a copy of the book from her corpse, as detailed later to this quest.

THE AETHERIUM WARS: BOOK NOW TO AVOID DISAPPOINTMENT

The book you're interested in looks like this. You can find 24 copies in fixed locations across Skyrim, although the book may also appear at random on bookshelves or in containers. The three easiest locations to try are:

Volkihar Keep (Haafingar Hold): On a small table, on the library balcony overlooking the main banquet chamber.

Dragonsreach (Whiterun Hold): On the bookshelf, inside Farengar's small antechamber study.

Fort Dawnguard (the Rift): On a corner bookshelf in the barracks room.

➤ The Aetherium Wars

NOTE Below is one of the paths you might take through this quest. There is no "correct" order for the places you visit (aside from the last one), but this route allows you to see all the locations in a logical progression, with minimal back-and-forth traveling.

Adventuring to Arkngthamz

Arkngthamz is a previously hidden Dwarven ruin located in the Reach. It is just southeast of the Orc Stronghold Dushnikh Yal, and also a short romp south from Reachwind Eyrie. As you approach its ancient exterior steps, you feel a slight vibration, an earthquake from down below. Push the imposing Dwarven doors open, and enter this ancient city.

A massive earthquake has recently decimated the ancient caverns and reinforcing structures. As you press forward, you must cross a fallen pillar over a fast-flowing stream. Continue down the hall, and listen carefully as a ghostly voice urges you to flee from this dangerous place. Moments later, as you emerge into the gigantic entry chamber, a pillar topples into the great watery chasm below. Stop for a moment, as a spectral entity named Katria approaches you.

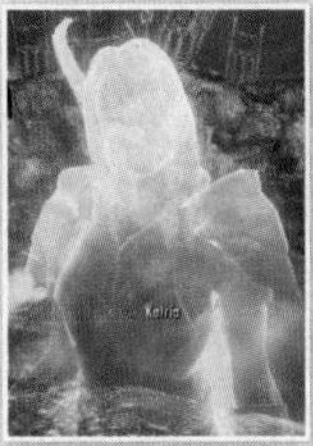

Listen to Katria as she asks why you're here—though she can already tell: You're after the treasure, just like all the others. If you've read *The Aetherium Wars*, you may recognize her name from the book's dedication. Ask her about it to learn a bit more of her history with the book's author. You can also ask about the treasure itself, which prompts her to explain her search for the Aetherium Forge and how she ended up here. She again asks you to turn back. You can:

(Persuade) Tell her you can handle yourself

Answer in any other way you wish

Ignore Katia completely.

When you make it clear that you intend to press on, she offers to accompany you. You can accept or decline this offer.

◊ **OBJECTIVE:** Reach the summit of Arkngthamz
♦ **TARGET:** Tonal Lock Chamber, Arkngthamz Summit

TIP Take her up on it! Katria is an accomplished archer and close-quarters specialist, and she's lost none of her prowess, despite her ethereal state. She also has a wide range of helpful commentary as you make your way through the ruins, from warning you of danger to pointing out hard-to-find treasure. Better yet, she won't replace your current follower (if any), so you have nothing to lose.

Shard 1: Arkngthamz Ascent

Approach the chasm, which has telltale signs of Falmer camps on the opposite side. For the moment, however, peer down over the precipice, to a fallen pillar that leads to a small island attached to a series of steaming pipes jutting out of the cliff wall opposite. Carefully climb down the pillar to the island and inspect the body you find there. This turns out to be Katria's corpse. Look up and you'll see she had quite the fall. She recommends you search her body for the journal she was keeping; she knows you're going to need it. Grab any other items she was carrying if you need them.

◊ **OBJECTIVE:** [Optional] Retrieve Katria's Journal
♦ **TARGET:** Katria's corpse

➤ Katria's Journal

Cross into the pipe vent tunnel, and make your way along as the entire structure continues to vibrate. Bring down a couple of Dwarven Spiders, then use the snaking golden pipe to navigate above the water-logged chamber and down past the metal fence. At the far end of the sagging corridor is a strange spinning device, which periodically rotates up and down, triggering the gate in front of you to open and close. Enter the cog room where Katria explains that these are Kinetic Resonators. When they're working properly, they trigger a mechanism nearby. To proceed, strike the second resonator (either with a bash or an arrow) and the nearby gate swings open. Onward!

Head southeast up the steps and around the corner to your first combat with the Falmer. There are two atop the steps and another lurking on this side of the pillared chasm. Cross the ground heading southeast, as another pillar crumbles under a fierce tremor. The pathway narrows to a snaking route across each side of the narrowing chasm. There is a Falmer to thwart on a high ridge opposite and two to tackle as they drop from their nests.

TIP Check the pathways all around and above you; occasionally there are Falmer you can strike from a long distance.

After the Falmer nests embedded in the chasm wall, there's a fallen pillar bridge to head over. However, if you inspect the sealed door to your left (south), Katria remarks that it's sealed tight. She's correct, although to open the chest behind the door, you can utilize the instability of this environment to your advantage. Head west to the cliff edge, looking down at the pile of pipes and giant carved dwarven head. Drop down to the riverbank, turn south, and trek up an inlet stream tunnel. This leads to the half-fallen rear of the chamber behind the door. Expect Dwarven Sphere combat before working your way around and to the east, to the chest. Use the lever to open the door from the chamber, and step back out onto the fallen pillar bridge.

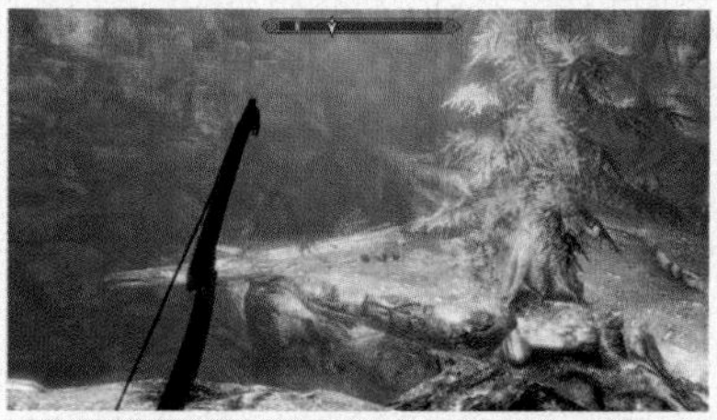

Cross the fallen pillar, then turn left (west) and head farther along the ledge as more of the rock wall detaches and plummets into the river below. Continue up the chasm ledges to a large grotto with several cascading waterfalls and a natural bridge spanning the chasm. Engage a couple of Falmer and a Chaurus, then head across the bridge, along a small winding tunnel to a Falmer hut and two more enemies. When they're both nullified, you have a choice of paths. The main route continues behind the hut, to your right (north).

However, there's a side tunnel to the southwest. Head up the narrow tunnel, face some more Chaurus in combat, and climb up the ledges leading to a tunnel stream. This brings you out among the grotto waterfalls. Watch your step! Tackle the Falmer that drops down on the narrow ledge with the chest to your left (north), loot the chest, then take the plunge: dive into the water here and look for an underwater tunnel that leads to a cavern with a chest. Then retrace your steps back to the hut room.

From the room with the hut, continue up the path on the right (north) to emerge into a large cavern dotted with pine trees. The sky of the Reach is visible above, while a gaping hole in the floor overlooks the chasm you crossed earlier. As the ground shakes, Katria remarks that her trusty bow, Zephyr, is lying on the log protruding halfway out above the increasingly deep chasm. She suggests you retrieve it. Carefully inch out onto the log, optionally crouching so you don't make any fast movements and fall, and grab the bow. Return to the relative safety of the ledge. Katria hopes you'll take good care of her beloved weapon.

➤ Zephyr

Look for the tunnel to the east. Follow it around to the north, and it opens out at the spectacular summit and the Tonal Lock Chamber. Descend under the dwarven arches, to a relatively flat lower area with a variety of crumbling masonry and scattered skeletal remains. Katria informs you that she mentioned "one more danger," and this is it: the Tonal Lock wall in front of you. She motions to the five resonators and tells you that hitting them (with an arrow) in the right order allows the doors to open. Get the order wrong, and you'll need to prepare for an earthquake...or worse.

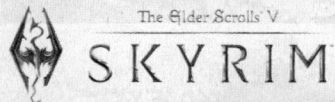

NOTE If you haven't met Katria yet, or refused her help earlier, she appears at this point and explains her current predicament. Which is also now yours.

◊ **OBJECTIVE:** Solve the Tonal Lock

Puzzle Solution: There are five resonators that make up the Tonal Lock. Bring out your favored bow (or Zephyr), utilize the scattered arrows on the ground if you run out of ammunition, and figure out the correct order to hit each resonator. There are two clues to help you:

The first clue is the correct listing of the first two resonators to hit. This is the sketch on the last page of Katria's Journal, which you found on her corpse earlier in the dungeon.

The second clue is on the corpse of the only non-skeletal Adventurer lying on the ground near your feet. Search him for a Scrap of Paper, which correctly lists the second and third resonator. Now take careful aim...

The correct order to strike the resonators is as follows: Lower row, left (directly above the left door). Then lower row, right (directly above the right door). Then upper row, left (of the dwarven head). Then upper row, right (of the dwarven head). Then finally, lower row, middle (below the dwarven head).

CAUTION It's a great idea to save your game before hitting any resonators. If you strike them in the wrong order, the dwarven head above the lock glows red, and something untoward occurs: The first failure causes Dwarven Spiders to emerge; fend them off before trying again. The second failure results in the appearance of Dwarven Spheres, while the third failure fires the ballistae, and the fourth causes the Dwarven Centurion behind the middle door to clank into life! Keep failing, and the ballistae keep firing. If you're still having problems, listen for Katria's hints.

◊ **OBJECTIVE:** Claim the treasure of Arkngthamz

Step through either the left or right open door, and around to the treasure room beyond. In front of the embedded dwarven chest is an Aetherium Shard. Pick it up, along with any other dwarven valuables you wish to gather.

➤ **Aetherium Shard (1 of 4)**

◊ **OBJECTIVE:** Speak with Katria

Katria is surprised that the Aetherium Shard is indeed real. She remarks that another piece, around the same size, would snap into place next to this one. So it seems there is more than one shard to find. In fact, she surmises there are three more, one for each of the cities that worked on the fabled Aetherium Forge. Together, they form the key needed to unlock the Forge. As your quest updates, she tells you to check her journal, which has more information on the places to look and reveals the location of the Forge. At this point, Katria disappears.

TIP Before you leave, pick up and read Katria's Journal, if you haven't already. Otherwise, the quest targets won't even appear on your compass.

◊ **OBJECTIVE:** Search for the Aetherium Shards (4)

♦ **TARGET:** Deep Folk Crossing (the Reach), Raldbthar (Winterhold Hold), and Mzulft (Eastmarch)

Exit the ruins of Arkngthamz by either retracing your steps or, better yet, by looking for the waterlogged tunnel in the western wall of the Tonal Lock chamber. Follow the tunnel to a frighteningly high drop down to the initial waterlogged chamber, and then dive off into the water below. Make sure you hit the river and not something solid, or this turns into a death plummet! Clamber back onto the small island where Katria's corpse is, then leave the same way you came in.

NOTE So where are the other shards? Depending on how thorough you've been in your exploration, you may have quest targets to none, one, two, or all three of them. You receive a quest target only after you've read Katria's journal and visited the location described by the journal. So you may well have quest targets to the shard in Raldbthar (the dungeon for Dark Brotherhood Quest: Mourning Never Comes) or Mzulft (for The College of Winterhold Quest: Revealing the Unseen), but you'll likely need to find at least Deep Folk Crossing by following the journal's map and clues.

Shard 2: Deep Folk Crossing

According to Katria's Journal, the second city is mentioned as "Bthar-zel" (which is Dwarven for "allied city"). It isn't Bthardamz but a smaller site north or northwest of there, on the river. The location is known colloquially as Deep Folk Crossing in the Reach and is a previously discoverable location. Head north from Bthardamz and locate the rushing river. Use the crossing bridge, heading north up the embankment on the other side, and pry the Aetherium Shard from its encasing. Katria appears to congratulate you before disappearing again. That was curiously straightforward....

➤ **Aetherium Shard (2 of 4)**

Shard 3: Raldbthar

Katria has listed the third shard as being hidden at the primary source of Aetherium and "extracted from some deeper mine." As this material has long since vanished from Tamriel, all you have to go on is Katria's scrawled map. Look carefully, as the number 3 is written just south of Lake Yorgrim. There are two previously discoverable Dwarven cities in these parts: Irkngthand and Raldbthar. Choose the latter, entering the ruins via one of three possible locations:

Enter from the Raldbthar elevator, if you've explored Raldbthar already.

Enter from Blackreach, if you've explored it already.

Or, you can clamber up the steep steps to quickly remove the local bandit population. Then enter the ruins via the main doors.

If this is your first time adventuring in Raldbthar, head down the slope to the fire trap, and dodge around the side corridor to the left (southeast), killing bandits as you go. At the end of the southwest corridor, you can unlock a gate [Master], allowing you to sneak around and strike three bandits from above with arrows or the dwarven ballista. Or you can head right and tackle three bandits around the campfire from the ground. Open the gate that's in the left (south) corner near the roasting fire, take down another bandit, and open the dwarven doors to the southwest.

Expect Dwarven Spiders and Spheres as you continue through another door, heading southwest to a left turn and a spinning blade trap. Navigate these rooms, watching for spilled oil as you head up through a pipe room with more automatons to dismantle. Locate the elevator and pull the switch, descending into a Falmer hive.

Dodge the spinning blade on the next slope, and the air fills with a strange mist. Bring down Falmer in or near their huts before rushing the steps to the northwest. Head up to the second floor, delivering death to more Falmer. Cross a small bridge to the northeast, en route to finding a button on a curved stone table in one corner of this upper level. This lowers a bridge to the southwest, allowing you to head across the rooftops above the first Falmer chamber, around a golden fence, through a door, and down into a pipe-filled steam room.

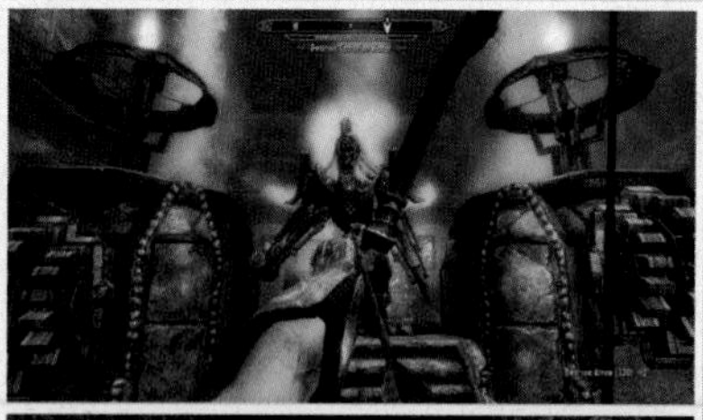

Watch for two pressure plates that set off crushing traps. Work through the automatons, heading north and then west, through a door and up a ramp to a corridor with four buttons to try. Ignore the other buttons and simply press the third one from the left; this one doesn't launch a trap. Pass the lowered bars, through the gate, and into another Falmer camp. After defeating all of the undesirables, inspect the grinding cogs close to the raised bridge. Four cogs have been jammed with bones or other implements, and they need to be released so both lamps to either side of the bridge button are lit. Find the following cogs:

Cog #1: Bone leg jammed into it. In front of the bridge, to the right (north) side, on a small lamp pillar.

Cog #2: Skull jammed into it. On the left (south) side of the water pool, attached to the perimeter wall.

Cog #3: Human spine jammed into it. On the right (north) side of the water pool, attached to the perimeter wall.

Cog #4: Dwarven Scrap jammed into it. In the pool underwater, below the button and section of bridge.

Return to the bridge and hit the button, but be prepared for combat with a Dwarven Centurion as the bridge connects and the door in the far wall opens. Head through, using the wall lever to drop the bars, and enter the inner chamber. As you enter, Katria appears to assist you in fighting off a swarm of automatons. Dispatch them, then claim the shard at the end of the nearby hall.

➤ **Aetherium Shard (3 of 4)**

TIP When leaving Raldbthar, exit via the lift in case you wish to quickly return here in the future. If you have the Attunement Sphere (from Daedric Quest: Discerning the Transmundane), you may wish to use it to activate the mechanism in this room so you can descend into Blackreach from here as well.

Shard 4: Mzulft

Katria's Journal mentions the final location as a storage site for raw Aetherium, just outside a Dwarven city. The city in question is Mzulft, on the far eastern edge of Eastmarch Hold. Mzulft is a previously discoverable location, but unlike the trek through Raldbthar, you don't need to enter the city itself. Instead, follow the journal's lead to search "just outside" the city, and enter the Dwarven Storeroom structure nearby.

Katria is already inside, wondering how best to break through the locked door. You have two choices:

Approach the gate [Expert], and pick the lock.

Locate the metal door to the right of it [Apprentice], open that, and then the second door [Apprentice] in the storage area beyond. Both allow you access into the shard storage area, where the final piece of this puzzle is found. Katria is elated and vanishes once again, heading for the Forge.

➤ **Aetherium Shard (4 of 4)**

◊ **OBJECTIVE:** Locate the Aetherium Forge
◊ **OBJECTIVE:** Speak with Katria
♦ **TARGET:** Ruins of Bthalft, the Rift

Forging Ahead: Ruins of Bthalft

Of course, you must utilize your cartographical skills and figure out from the Journal that the Forge seems to be below the Ruins of Bthalft, south of Lake Geir, just off the main east–west road from Ivarstead to Riften. When you reach the ruins, Katria is likely to be fending off bandits or other unfortunate fodder for your weapons. She urges you to inspect the strange device on the circle of flagstones. The gear in the middle of the device seems to fit the shards. Why not try it out?

◊ **OBJECTIVE:** Place the Aetherium Shards
◊ **OBJECTIVE:** Retrieve the Aetherium Crest
◊ **OBJECTIVE:** Stand Clear

After slotting in all four shards (which you can do one at a time, if you're not attempting this quest in any kind of succinct order)...nothing happens. Katria reckons you should retrieve the shards, which appear to have fused into some kind of crest. Yep! That seems to do the trick!

➤ **Aetherium Crest**

The ground beneath you rumbles violently as the device and the flagstones shift and ascend into the sky, forming the roof of a giant, circular tower and elevator entrance! This must be the entrance to the Forge. Head inside and pull the lever when you're ready.

> **TIP** **Preparation for Battle:** Come prepared! Health, Magicka, and Stamina Potions are vital when you face the final entity deep within the bowels of the Rift. You should also bring Fire Resistance potions; they are especially useful here.

◊ **OBJECTIVE:** Find the Aetherium Forge

Footfalls after Four Thousand Years

When you reach the bottom, Katria mentions that the ride down took longer than normal. Just how deep are you? Follow the pathway, and continue into a gigantic subterranean chamber, even after the lanterns flicker on automatically. Head across the connecting bridges and up the stone steps to the top of this massive forge entrance. Beyond the tree are two resonators. Aim and hit both of them (the order doesn't matter) to open the door. Then head down the slope, as the air becomes more acrid. Open the door to the south, and enter the Aetherium Forge.

◊ **OBJECTIVE:** Shut off the steam

With its ornate forge powered by the lava fires of Tamriel, this marvel of ancient technology is currently choked with harmful steam. Using the two steam valves on both of the raised platforms disperses the steam, allowing you to investigate the forge. But your investigation is interrupted by a familiar clanking. The guardians of the forge have appeared!

◊ **OBJECTIVE:** Defeat the Guardians of the Forge
♦ **TARGET:** Dwarven Spiders, Spheres, and the Forgemaster

Facing the Forgemaster

You're now locked in battle with the Guardians of the Forge. Below is advice on defeating them.

Initially, you're swarmed by a wave of Dwarven Spiders from the hatches on the lower grating level. These are followed by a wave of Dwarven Spheres from the upper hallways, along with additional Spiders. Prepare yourself for these waves with the weapons you choose, the incantations you prep, and the direction you're facing. Expect between four and six foes in each wave.

Be fleet of foot! Staying mobile, leaping from the upper platform near the valves, and sprinting across the lower grating allows you to outpace your enemies and swing around and prepare combat, potions, or ranged attacks more easily.

Don't get surrounded! Move to the opposite side of the chamber, leaving your foes trailing behind, and deal with them one at a time.

Beware of dead ends! Stay on either of the valve platforms, or the grating, and don't head up the passages where the foes appear, the alcoves to the sides of the grating, or down toward the lava; these are dead ends. If you make this mistake, expect to be overwhelmed easily.

It is worth turning the steam off when prompted, as it allows you to move around the chamber more freely. Do this as soon as you have an opportunity. Unlike you, the automatons aren't hurt or hindered by the steam.

In either the initial waves or the final battle, if you're close to death or having extreme difficulty in combat, step back and let Katria take most of the damage. Even if her ghost is snuffed out, she reforms moments later, none the worse for wear.

If you survive the initial waves, the Forgemaster clambers up out of the lava pool to one side of the forge. Check the compass so you know which side he's coming from.

As the Forgemaster emerges, you may wish to bombard him with long-range attacks, especially if you're hidden and can claim sneak bonuses.

Just before combat begins, it is most wise to consume your very best Fire Resistance potions. The steam also blasts forth again, so be sure to turn it off just like before, if you're set on rushing out to combat him, as you'll be damaged by the steam as well.

The Forgemaster is a unique Dwemer Automaton and glows red with heat. It is immune to fire but weak against frost. Frost spells and frost-enchanted weapons deal significant damage against him.

After emerging, the Forgemaster spends the first part of the battle close to the center of the chamber, alternating his Fire Breath and Fireball bellowing. Keep your distance, using ranged attacks or spells, and utilize the room's pillars for cover.

Once damaged below 50 percent, the Forgemaster tends to battle more aggressively, and actively searches for and attacks you. Also expect to feel the beast's two hammer arms if you try to engage in close combat. Once again, ranged attacks are safer.

If you're sure you want to face the Forgemaster in melee combat, be aware that he is constantly bathed in a Flame Cloak, so simply standing close to him is damaging to you!

> **CAUTION** Beware! That lava is as deadly as it looks!

Quest Conclusion

◊ **OBJECTIVE:** Speak with Katria
◊ **OBJECTIVE:** [Optional] Search for crafting materials
◊ **OBJECTIVE:** Use the Aetherium Forge

Once the Forgemaster finally topples, speak to Katria once more. She wants to confirm this is the real Aetherium Forge, and you're the smith to test it out! After optionally opening a dwarven chest in a nearby alcove, which contains the other necessary materials you need to craft a particularly impressive item from the Aetherium Crest you're carrying, approach the forge. You have a choice of three items and can craft only one.

Once the item has been forged, Katria seems satisfied that the quest she undertook in both life and death has been completed. She leaves you, and the quest completes.

Postquest Activities

Aside from utilizing your newly crafted item, the Wilderness Encounter: Taron Dreth (see page 682) may randomly occur. Here you meet Katria's treacherous former apprentice!

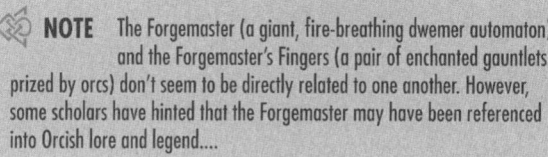

NOTE The Forgemaster (a giant, fire-breathing dwemer automaton) and the Forgemaster's Fingers (a pair of enchanted gauntlets prized by orcs) don't seem to be directly related to one another. However, some scholars have hinted that the Forgemaster may have been referenced into Orcish lore and legend....

AETHERIUM FORGE: CRAFTING TIPS

There are three items you can craft at the Aetherium Forge but only enough Aetherium to make one of them. It is therefore wise to figure out which item you value the most. Also, remember that you keep anything you don't forge: If none of them are of interest, you might think to craft the crown (as it has the highest value), but that's a mistake, as it requires two Flawless Sapphires (worth 1,000 gold) to make. Instead, pocket the Sapphires and craft one of the other items.

Katria's suspicions are also correct: There isn't any more Aetherium in Skyrim.

Aetherial Crown

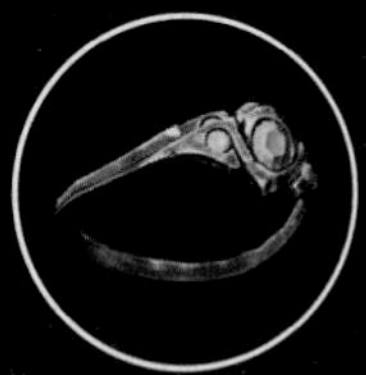

Retains the last Standing Stone ability you held, granting you its effects in addition to those of your current Stone.

The Aetherial Crown is the most versatile of the three items, and potentially the most powerful, but it also requires an investment on your part—it doesn't do anything by itself; you must track down the standing stones you want to empower it with.

The Crown also occupies your head armor slot, preventing you from wearing another helmet or a complete set of either light or heavy armor.

The skill improvement stones (Warrior, Mage, Thief, and Lover) are compatible with one another, and their abilities stack. So if you take both the Warrior Stone and the Lover Stone, your combat skills will increase 35 percent faster, and your magic and stealth skills increase 15 percent faster.

The Lord and Lady Stones make a good defensive combination, giving you 50 Armor, 25 percent Magic Resistance, and 25 percent faster Health and Stamina regen. If you use Heavy Armor, take the Steed Stone in place of one of these for its carry weight and movement benefits.

The Apprentice and Atronach stones work well for mages, giving you +50 Magicka, +100 percent Magicka Regen, and 50 percent Magicka Absorption, at a cost of being weak to magic in turn. Note that the Atronach's Magicka Regen penalty is *completely negated* when you have both Stones; you receive all of its benefits without the drawbacks!

If you prefer more active abilities, you can pick two of the Ritual, Serpent, Shadow, and Tower stones, and use each power once a day.

Aetherial Shield

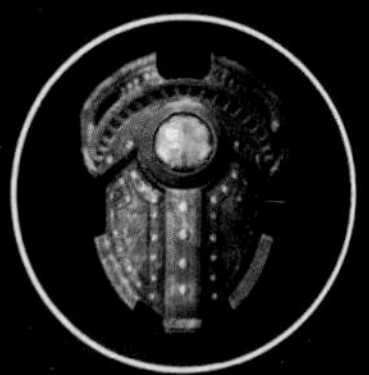

Enemies struck by this shield become ethereal for 15 seconds, making them unable to attack or be attacked.

The Aetherial Shield is a fast, effective way to take an enemy out of combat for a few seconds, at the cost of a little stamina (for the bash). It's easy to underestimate this ability, as it's actually surprisingly powerful.

Once made ethereal, most enemies will also flee from you, effectively extending the amount of time they remain out of combat. Only Daedra, Atronachs, and Dwarven Automatons will stand their ground.

Unlike most Illusion or undead-repelling spells, this effect works on all enemies regardless of level. Only dragons and a select few opponents (such as Lord Harkon) are immune to its effects. A few enemies (such as vampires) can break this spell by using their own magical abilities.

The Aetherial Shield is great for dealing with a crowd of foes, allowing you to take one or more enemies out of the fight for a few seconds so you can focus on other adversaries without distraction. The only limit to the number of enemies you can affect is your stamina.

The shield also works well against powerful single foes, such as Dragon Priests or Draugr Deathlords. If you find yourself on the verge of death, bash them, then take some time to heal up while they flee in terror.

Aetherial Staff

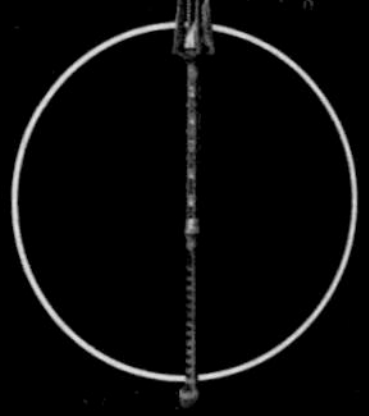

Summon a Dwarven Spider or Sphere for 60 seconds wherever the caster is pointing.

The Aetherial Staff allows you to conjure some interesting allies you can't otherwise obtain. Dwarven Automatons tend to have more health and better resistances than a comparably leveled Atronach. This is more beneficial still for adventurers who aren't focused on magic and want a tough ally for a fight. However, what you actually conjure from the staff is random and depends on your level.

Additionally, there is always a 15 percent chance of a "mishap." If your level is less than 15, this chance doubles to 30 percent. Mishaps include summoning a spider or sphere that dies immediately, or summoning in only scrap metal. Ack!

If your level is less than 15, you usually summon the basic Dwarven Spider Worker, although you have a small chance of a Dwarven Sphere appearing.

At Levels 15 to 29, you receive either the Dwarven Spider Worker or a Dwarven Sphere.

At Levels 30 to 44, you receive either the Dwarven Spider or Dwarven Sphere.

At Levels 45 and higher, you receive either the Dwarven Spider or Dwarven Sphere Guardian.

If you haven't put much effort into Conjuration magic or just want to have a cool Dwarven Sphere rolling around after you, the Aetherial Staff can be an entertaining choice. Experienced conjurers or those focused purely on making their adventurer as powerful as possible may want to choose another item.

THE MAN WHO CRIED WOLF

PREREQUISITES: None

MINOR SPOILERS

INTERSECTING QUESTS:
Side Quest: The Wolf Queen Awakened, Daedric Quest: The Mind of Madness

LOCATIONS: Solitude, Blue Palace, Wolfskull Cave, Wolfskull Ruins

CHARACTERS: Falk Firebeard, Jarl Elisif the Fair, Sybille Stentor, Varnius Junius

ENEMIES: Draugr, Necromancer, Necromancer Leader, Potema the Wolf Queen, Skeleton

◊ **OBJECTIVES:** Clear out Wolfskull Cave, Speak to Falk Firebeard

Malevolence Stirring

While you're in the spectacular city of Solitude, visit the Blue Palace, where Jarl Elisif the Fair is holding court. While listening to those seeking an audience with the Jarl, you may wish to strike up a conversation with Falk Firebeard, the Jarl's steward and manager of the housecarls. You can chat about General Tullius and Elisif's decisions regarding the war. Now wait for a man named Varnius Junius—a representative of the serfs of Haafingar Hold—to speak before the Jarl. He seems frightened and speaks of "unnatural magic," strange noises, and lights emanating from a place known as Wolfskull Cave. The Jarl promises to keep her population safe, but Court Wizard Sybille Stentor thinks this is just superstitious hokum. Falk agrees that a show of strength isn't necessary, but someone should investigate the cave system just to be safe.

Now speak with Falk Firebeard, asking him if he needs help with Wolfskull Cave. Falk was initially going to dismiss this as fanciful talk from an overly imaginative populous, but he agrees to pay you if you'll clear out the cave. You can also ask him about the cave's sordid past, when it was used for necromantic rituals. Nowadays, Falk reckons the place has a few brigands lurking inside.

◊ **OBJECTIVE:** Clear out Wolfskull Cave
♦ **TARGET:** Wolfskull Cave

Few Wolves but Plenty of Warlocks

Travel to the mountains north of Dragon Bridge and west of Solitude. As you reach the vertical fissure in the mountainside, you're attacked by a bony fiend. Defeat the skeletons guarding the cave entrance before disappearing inside. The initial cavern tunnels are suspiciously quiet, with a skeleton and Draugr likely to be roaming the otherwise-empty tunnels.

As you reach the first large chamber, tackle a couple of necromancers before passing through the wooden door. Undead Draugr and skeletons attack as you reach the top of a snowy fissure. Fight or flee from them, and enter Wolfskull Ruins.

As you reach the subterranean fortress, across the canyon-sized hole in the center of this vast natural cavern, something is frighteningly wrong. A gathering maelstrom of energy is congealing atop the central tower of the ruins. But there is no time for sightseeing; attack another incoming necromancer as you work through some craggy tunnels and oil lamp traps. As you reach the edge of the fortress ruins, you hear a chant. A group of necromancers are attempting to summon the spirit of Potema the Wolf Queen, an insane necromancer who challenged Uriel III for the throne of the Empire 500 years ago!

In the face of this evil, act swiftly: Head down the exterior steps and through the first tower archway, dispatching enemies as you go. Climb the tower and go out the eastern exit archway. Climb more steps as the Wolf Queen begins to stir and speak. Continue around the battlements, finishing more necromancers and Draugr. Potema warns her followers of an intruder. Enter the main tower as the maelstrom increases, and prepare for a fraught battle against more powerful necromancers and any undead they may conjure. With the leader dispatched and all enemies defeated, Potema becomes unbound, and the maelstrom dissipates.

TIP You can use the stairwell as cover during this fight, and coax the necromancers down to fight you one at a time.

◊ **OBJECTIVE:** Speak to Falk Firebeard

Quest Conclusion

Using the lever atop the tower, lower the drawbridge. This allows for a swift escape back into Wolfskull Cave and back outside, collecting any treasure as you go. Back inside the Blue Palace, inform Falk Firebeard that a group of necromancers were attempting to summon and bind Potema and that the ritual was interrupted. He is thankful this was stopped and rewards you almost appropriately for your troubles.

➤ **Leveled gold pieces**

Postquest Activities

Side Quest: The Wolf Queen Awakened begins shortly. This quest has the benefit of beginning a firm and friendly relationship with the Jarl of Solitude. If you speak to her after this quest, you can complete her Favor (see the Favors section starting on page 497 for more information) and place Torygg's Warhorn at a Shrine to Talos. This also aids in your relationship with Falk, allowing you to obtain a key from him that opens a wing of the Palace that is normally sealed, allowing you, in turn, to begin. Daedric Quest: The Mind of Madness.

PREREQUISITES: Complete Side Quest: The Man Who Cried Wolf, You must be Level 10 or higher.

MINOR SPOILERS

INTERSECTING QUESTS: Side Quest: The Man Who Cried Wolf

LOCATIONS: Solitude, Hall of the Dead, Potema's Catacombs, Potema's Refuge, Potema's Sanctum, Temple of the Divines

CHARACTERS: Falk Firebeard, Styrr

ENEMIES: Draugr, Vampire

◊ **OBJECTIVES:** Speak to Styrr, Defeat Potema, Retrieve Potema's remains, Give Potema's remains to Styrr, Return to Falk Firebeard

Malevolence Rising

Once you complete Side Quest: The Man Who Cried Wolf and continue your adventuring, the next time you enter a Hold City (such as Dawnstar or Whiterun), a courier runs up and hands you a message. It is an urgent communication from Falk requesting that you return to Solitude, as Potema's spirit is now free and a dangerous threat to Skyrim. There is one man who may be able to help you: Solitude's cemetery keeper, a wizard and Priest of Arkay named Styrr.

◊ **OBJECTIVE:** Speak to Styrr

♦ **TARGET:** Styrr, in the Hall of the Dead, in Solitude

Locate the Hall of the Dead in Solitude, and enter this eerie place. It is made even more strange by the slightly befuddled nature of the man you're meeting. Styrr beckons you over, and you may ask several questions about Potema, which he is happy to answer. Potema has been summoned in spirit form but fortunately was not raised from the dead; she will require help before she returns to the land of the living. For now, she lurks in a place where the dead eagerly serve her—the old catacombs. You are to find Potema's physical bones and bring them back to Styrr for sanctification. He hands you a key to enter the Catacombs.

➤ **Potema's Catacombs Key**

◊ **OBJECTIVE:** Defeat Potema

♦ **TARGET:** Potema, in Potema's Catacombs, within the Temple of the Divines, in Solitude

Wrecking a Resurrection

Brave the wintry weather and scale the battlements in the northern part of Solitude. Open the door to the Temple of the Divines, passing Freir at the shrine. Work your way past the temple nave and chancel, down some side steps, and through the barred door. Then open the door leading into Potema's Catacombs.

Venture down the corridor to the barred archway. Potema's spirit surrounds you, mocking you and promising to raise your corpse to serve her once she slays you. The bars recede, allowing you farther into the stone corridors, down more steps, and to your first encounters with a group of Draugr.

Descend the steps in the chamber with the hanging corpse cages, and slay your first vampire. Beware of more attacks from dark alcoves before activating the wall lever to open the portcullis in the archway to the northeast wall. Enter the sunken corridors, and head southeast, up into a large, natural cavern. Expect more Draugr and vampire incursions as you reach the flooded pillar chamber. Seek the exit to the south, which leads into a wider natural cavern and a large stone entrance flanked by Draugr.

The lever atop the circular plinth activates a rotating stone and iron grating; step through when there's a gap as the grating rises. A cauldron in the next room indicates the resurrection may be under way. Burst through the wooden doors and into Potema's Refuge.

Strike down more Draugr as you twist and turn around the stone tunnels. Locate the trio of levers on the plinth, and expect a vampire attack from the barred door to your right (north).

Puzzle Solution: The levers have three positions: The center one freezes the corresponding rotating stone disk, and left or right rotates the disk in either direction. The optimal plan is to set all of them to the center and then manually rotate and freeze each one in the open position, one by one, beginning with the nearest rotating stone.

Pass the rock column room and up steps into a throne room with a floor grating and a powerful Draugr and vampire to either battle or stealthily avoid. The double wooden doors (Master) can be easily opened if you take Potema's Sanctum Key, which rests on the right throne arm. This allows access down into the Sanctum.

➤ **Potema's Sanctum Key**

The frequency of foes (both vampiric and undead) increases now as you pass through an embalming room and past the slumped remains of a Draugr on a throne. He soon stirs. Dispatch any foes troubling you as you open more iron doors. Pass under the grating in the throne room, stepping over corpses as you go. Wait for Potema to mock you before raising the final portcullis that leads to her summoning chamber.

Potema is not yet fully formed but has a shock beam that emanates from her essence. Avoid this at all costs, as it is hazardous and inflicts shock damage upon you. The Wolf Queen has also summoned her inner council to stop you dead in your tracks. Summon your own power and remove any and all Draugr that advance out of their coffins or ceremonial alcoves. Expect to attack at least eight Draugr, with more appearing at once after you dispatch the first five or six. Once the Draugr are down, you can pass the deep purple glow and access the metal door at the far end of Potema's chamber. The skeletal spirit of Potema begins to congeal! Take her down immediately, before she can begin to resurrect more of her fallen lackeys. Then gather the bones from the throne beyond.

➤ **Potema's Skull**

Material 2: Among the Giants

Now travel to the mountains south and slightly west of Dawnstar, and climb to the large giants' camp of Stonehill Bluff. The place is surrounded by rocks on three sides, so the entrance and exit are the same. Head into the bluff, and check one of the grinding receptacles near a campfire; the Mammoth Tusk Powder is in there. You may take it without being attacked by the giants roaming this area, but you've got to be quick!

➤ **Mammoth Tusk Powder**

Material 3: Slaughter at Red Eagle Redoubt

The final ingredient is the magically enhanced heart of a Forsworn Briarheart. Any Briarheart will do; if you don't already have one, find one lurking atop the mountains on the Reach's eastern edge. You're heading to Red Eagle Redoubt, accessible via a lengthy ascent from the Karth River near Sky Haven Temple. Approach the entrance, and remove all Forsworn threats from the exterior before entering the interior, known as Red Eagle Ascent.

Pass the wooden stakes and skewered animals, and bring your weapons to bear on a couple of Forsworn in a gloomy grotto you can ignite if you blast the oily floor with fire. Climb up the sloping path and steps to an upper grotto, which features a flat stone plateau with an altar on it and four or five additional foes. Climb the wooden steps, then disappear up the exit corridor that leads back out to an iron door and the Reach.

Turn right (north) and begin a battling ascent up a large set of stone steps. Make sure the Forsworn are tumbling off here in a spectacular death plummet, and not you! Head under the three stone arches as you reach a sizable Forsworn camp and further enemies, clearing the area methodically so you aren't attacked from behind. Don't rush this assault. Continue around in a clockwise circle, and trot south up the steps to the south, leading into the Sundered Towers. The Briarheart is up here. Clear the area of other foes first, before killing the Briarheart and searching the corpse. Pluck the Briar Heart from it. Then search the area for any treasure you wish to scavenge.

➤ **Briar Heart**

◊ **OBJECTIVE:** Return to Quintus Navale
♦ **TARGET:** Quintus, in the White Phial, in Windhelm

Quest Conclusion

Return to the White Phial and tell Quintus of your success. He grabs the materials from you quickly concocts a gelling agent to seal the White Phial as he heads upstairs to Nurelion's bedchamber. As he demonstrates the solidity of the White Phial, the old elf smiles, uttering the word "marvelous" before lying still on the bed.

➤ **The White Phial**

Postquest Activities

Alas, Nurelion dies in his bed. Quintus gives the repaired Phial back to you, for your help. To use it, pick the type of potion you want it to contain, and thereafter when you drink that potion, the empty White Phial remains in your inventory, refilling every 24 hours. Quintus is now on friendly terms with you.

CAPTURED CRITTERS*

PREREQUISITES: None
INTERSECTING QUESTS: Thieves Guild Quest: Loud and Clear, Dungeon Quest: What Lies Beneath
LOCATIONS: Alchemist's Shack, Dushnikh Yal, Burguk's Longhouse, Duskglow Crevice, Frostflow Lighthouse, Goldenglow Estate
CHARACTERS: Aringoth, Burguk
ENEMIES: Chaurus, Falmer, Mercenary
◊ **OBJECTIVES:** None

◉ MINOR SPOILERS

NOTE * Quest names marked with this symbol do not appear in your Quest Menu list, although objectives may.

Bug Hunt

This is more of a curiosity than a real quest. Five of the insect species that inhabit Skyrim have been captured and placed into jars. A single example of each can be found hidden across this realm, in the following locations:

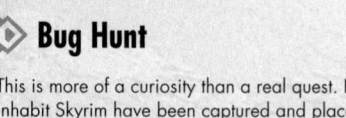

Moth in a Jar: Trek through the Pale until you reach and explore the Falmer Hive known as Duskglow Crevice. Battle through the connecting tunnels and crypts until you reach the raised stone chambers and portcullises. A room of refuse close to the final battle houses the jar.

➤ **Moth in a Jar**

Torchbug in a Jar: Locate Frostflow Lighthouse in Winterhold Hold, head inside (starting Dungeon Quest: What Lies Beneath), and move to the fireplace among the signs of the struggle. The fireplace mantel houses the glowing bug in the jar.

➤ **Torchbug in a Jar**

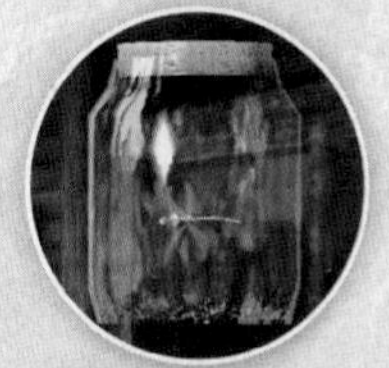

Dragonfly in a Jar: Journey to the Reach, and locate the Dushnikh Yal Orc stronghold (perhaps completing Side Quest: The Forgemaster's Fingers to win their approval). Enter Burguk's Longhouse, open the trapdoor to the cellar, and look for the jar on a cupboard under the platform.

➤ **Dragonfly in a Jar**

Butterfly in a Jar: While exploring the Rift, head along the edge of the forest on the southern foothills of the Throat of the World, and you'll stumble upon the Alchemist's Shack. There's a jar with a butterfly in it sitting on one of the shelves..

➤ **Butterfly in a Jar**

Bee in a Jar: During or after Thieves Guild Quest: Loud and Clear, enter the main building of Goldenglow Estate, head to the upper floor, and enter Aringoth's bedroom. Locate the jar on a dresser here.

➤ **Bee in a Jar**

Quest Conclusion

Once your critter collection reaches five, you have found them all.

Postquest Activities

Inspect the insects in your inventory, or put them on a shelf or table in a house you own. Aren't they pretty?

THE FORGEMASTER'S FINGERS

PREREQUISITES: Non-Orc Character

INTERSECTING QUESTS: None

◉ MINOR SPOILERS

LOCATIONS: Dushnikh Yal, Mor Khazgur, Narzulbur

CHARACTERS: Chief Burguk, Chief Larak, Chief Mauhulakh

ENEMIES: [Random]

◊ **OBJECTIVES:** Find the Forgemaster's Fingers, Bring the Forgemaster's Fingers to [Orc Chief]

Blood-Kin, or Bloodbath

NOTE To commence this quest, you must be a non-Orc; any other race is fine. Then visit any of the Orc strongholds listed in the table below and attempt to speak to one of the inhabitants. If you are an Orc, you can take advantage of the trading and training available in these strongholds without having to complete this trial.

✓	ORC STRONGHOLD LOCATION	HOLD	CHIEFTAIN NAME
☐	Mor Khazgur	The Reach	Chief Larak
☐	Dushnikh Yal	The Reach	Chief Burguk
☐	Narzulbur	Eastmarch	Chief Mauhulakh
☐	Largashbur	The Rift	Not applicable‡

NOTE ‡ If you approach Largashbur, you have to begin Daedric Quest: The Cursed Tribe to enter this stronghold. Completing that quest also makes you Blood-Kin to the Orcs, so you won't have to complete this quest.

During your travels, you may chance upon an Orc stronghold. If the location is listed above, you should be able to enter the place without being attacked (unless you strike first). However, when you approach one of the Orcs, he isn't welcome to your kind. He lives by the Code of Malacath, and outsiders have no place here. Answer that you're a traveler (you must keep your answers as pleasant as possible), and he tells you to stay out; you're not Blood-Kin. Politely ask how you can convince him to let you in, and he mentions whispers that he's heard regarding a pair of enchanted gauntlets, hidden away in a deep, dark dungeon. They are called the Forgemaster's Fingers. Return these to the Chief, and he'll decide whether you're worthy to be Blood-Kin to the Orcs.

◊ **OBJECTIVE:** Find the Forgemaster's Fingers

♦ **TARGET:** Forgemaster's Fingers, in [a random location]

Set off to the random location where the Forgemaster's Fingers are said to be kept, and battle through (or sneak past) the enemies guarding the Fingers, which are usually kept in a large treasure chest.

➤ **Forgemaster's Fingers**

◊ **OBJECTIVE:** Bring the Forgemaster's Fingers to [Orc Chief]

♦ **TARGET:** [Orc Chief], inside [an Orc stronghold]

Quest Conclusion

Return to the same Orc stronghold that you visited previously and locate the Chief, who may or may not have given you this quest to begin with. However, be sure the stronghold is the one from which you received the quest. Approach the Chief, and he's amazed that you managed to acquire this item. He welcomes you as a Blood-Kin, and the Orcs in the other strongholds know of your friendship with the Orcs, too.

Postquest Activities

From this point on, as long as you remain civil, you can trade and train with any of the Orcs in the strongholds throughout Skyrim.

NOTE * Quest names marked with this symbol do not appear in your Quest menu list, although objectives may.

Cartographical Evidence

During your adventuring, you may find a piece of parchment with a sketch on it. This is a treasure map, and there are 11 to find. Each leads to a particular location where a (usually well-hidden) small treasure chest can be opened and several valuable items pocketed.

CAUTION: You can't simply ignore the maps and trot off to find the treasure chests; they appear only once the map is in your possession.

➤ Treasure Map

Fort Neugrad Treasure Map

Falkreath Hold—Fort Neugrad: In the half-buried chest, on the main building rooftop (accessed via climbing up through the interior).

Fort Neugrad Treasure Map: Showing the rocky crevasse dead-end path east of the fort.

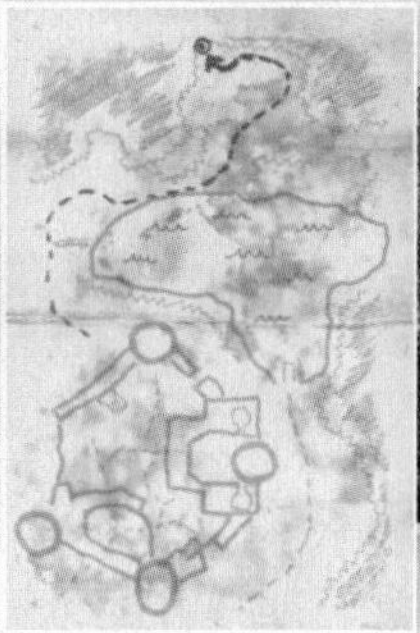

Falkreath Hold—Fort Neugrad: When you look at this map, the top of the page is east, not north. Situate yourself with this in mind, following the path around the lake and up into the crevasse.

Treasure Map I

Falkreath Hold—Bandit Camp: Ilinalta Foothills: On one of the bandits, just south of the guardian stones.

Treasure Map: Showing the settlement of Riverwood and the fallen tree.

Whiterun Hold: Inside the fallen tree, on the north bank of the river, west of Riverwood.

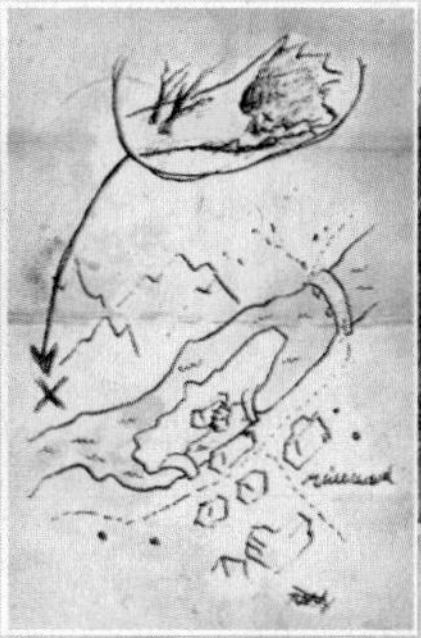

Treasure Map II

Winterhold Hold—Journeyman's Nook: Inside the knapsack, close to the fire and round table.

Treasure Map II: Showing Valtheim Towers and the river underneath.

Whiterun: Valtheim Towers, by the riverbank close to the waterfall, partly hidden by rocks on the south bank.

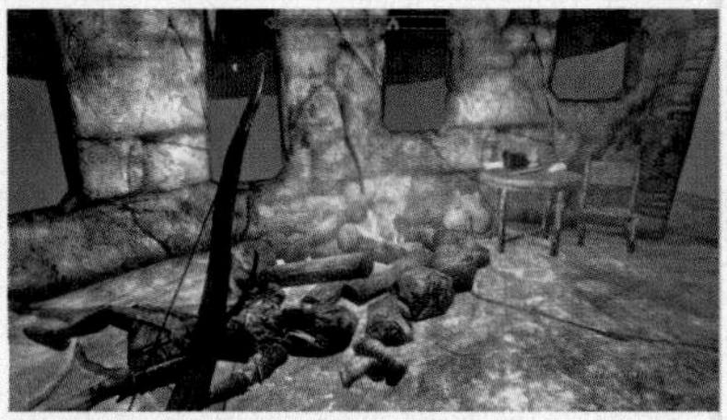
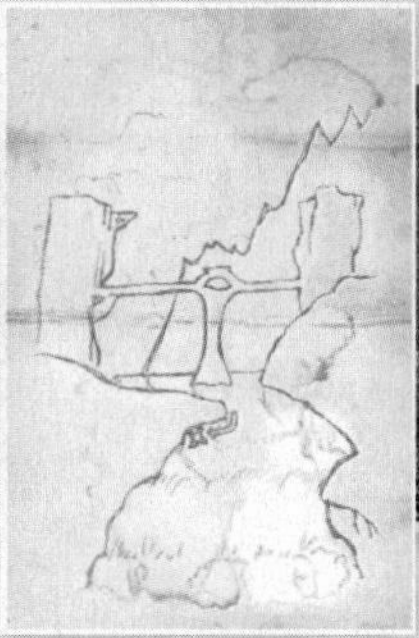
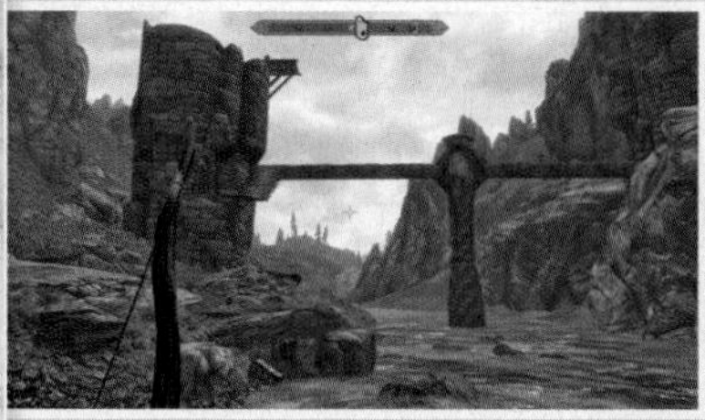

Treasure Map III

Eastmarch—Riverside Shack: In the chest, inside the shack.

Treasure Map III: Showing Solitude Lighthouse and the surrounding rocks.

Haafingar —Solitude Lighthouse: Below the northeast corner of the lighthouse and rocks, by the shore of the Sea of Ghosts.

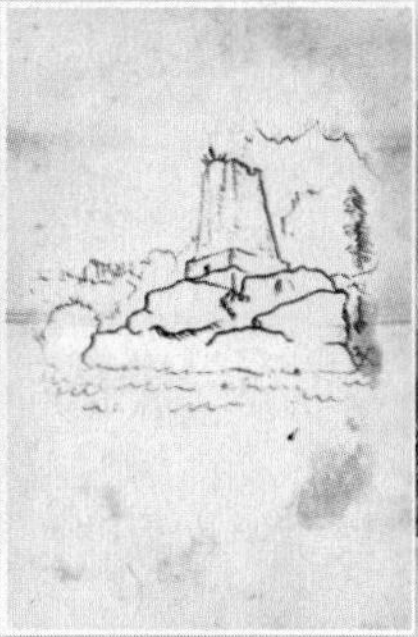
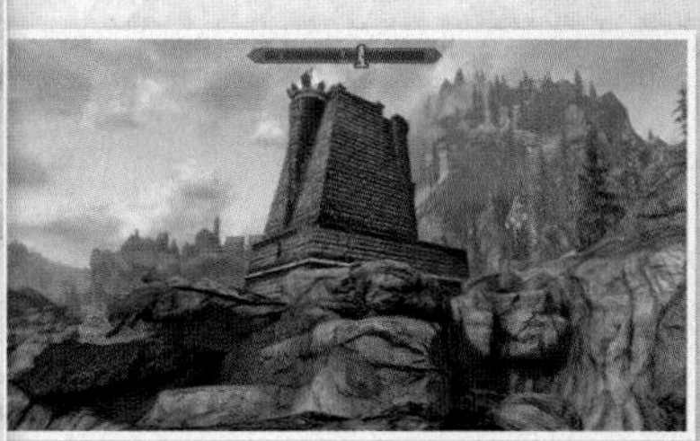

Treasure Map IV

Whiterun—Redoran's Retreat: Inside the large treasure chest close to the Bandit Chief, inside the mine.

Treasure Map IV: Showing Whiterun and the path up to the chest above the windmill.

Whiterun: The cliffs above Pelagia Farm. Follow the track around and up to the chest, half hidden by saplings.

Treasure Map V

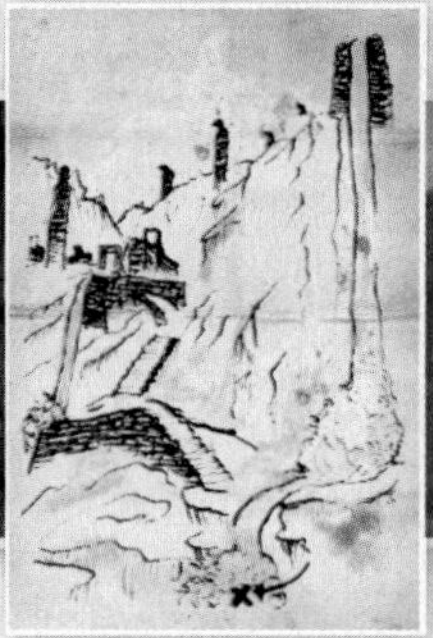

Falkreath Hold—Angi's Cabin: Inside the cabin, on the end table by the bed.

Treasure Map V: Showing the waterfalls of Lost Valley Redoubt.

The Reach: Just east of Gloomreach, at the very bottom of Lost Valley Redoubt, on the riverbank at the base of the waterfall. If you've already discovered Lost Valley Redoubt, Fast-Travel there and you're almost at the chest.

Treasure Map VI

The Pale – Secondary Location: A Bloody Trail. On the corpse of the female elf, among the rocky summit northwest of Volunruud. You can find a male Wood Elf close by and follow the trail of blood to her.

Treasure Map VI: Showing Korvanjund.

The Pale—Korvanjund. The exterior entrance, atop the barrow arch next to the gnarled tree.

Treasure Map VII

Eastmarch—Traitor's Post: In the chest, inside the bandit hideout.

Treasure Map VII: Showing Gallows Rock, within the outer walls.

Eastmarch—Gallows Rock: Within the outer wall ruins, near the main ground-level door, under the rock with the noose.

Treasure Map VIII

Winterhold—Secondary Location: Haul of the Horkers: On the corpse of a dead hunter.

Treasure Map VIII: Showing the town of Dragon Bridge.

Haafingar Hold—Dragon Bridge: In a satchel, next to the tree across from the bridge. This satchel holds the key to the chest, if you can't open it.

Haafingar Hold—Dragon Bridge: In a chest, in the river northeast of the bridge, underwater (Master).

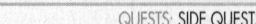

ANGI'S CAMP: COMPOSURE, SPEED, AND PRECISION*

TIP Before trekking to this remote locale, bring a few different bows with you to test which you prefer (although all bows work in the same way). It is beneficial to take the Eagle Eye or Steady Hand Archery perks in case the following training proves trickier than anticipated.

In the mountainous southwest corner of Falkreath Hold is a lone cabin. This is home to Angi. Listen to her story about her murdered family. Talk to her and request training, if you wish to improve your Archery skill.

Equip your favored bow, follow Angi down to the practice range, and listen to her instructions. Take the Practice Arrows tied to the front-right boundary post. If you require more during the course of this practice, request them from Angi. Now look ahead and spot all four of the practice targets (including the one in the distance, behind the three nearer ones). When you're completing a challenge, remain within the boundary or you'll fail.

➤ **Practice Arrow (10)**

First Challenge:

Hit the middle target (of the three closer targets in front of you)

Reward: Archery increased by 1

Hit the left target (of the three closer targets in front of you)

Reward: Archery increased by 1

Hit the right target (of the three closer targets in front of you)

Reward: Archery increased by 1

Second Challenge:

Hit the three closest targets within eight seconds (in any order), after Angi counts to three.

Reward: Archery Increased by 1

Third Challenge:

Hit the target far in the back, behind the front cluster of targets.

Reward: Archery increased by 1

Fourth Challenge:

Hit all four of the targets within ten seconds (in any order), after Angi counts to three.

Reward: Archery increased by 1

If you're having trouble with any of these challenges, try the following:

Zoom in to aim your shots to begin with, to gain a larger surface area. But don't do this during the two timed challenges, as this slows you down.

Crouch down so your bow is horizontal for increased accuracy.

You want to hit the tiny hole in the very center of each target. But you'll need to aim a little higher than the target so the arrow arcs through the air and strikes it accurately.

Move over the boundary, and inspect the targets at closer range if you wish, prior to an attempt.

During the fourth challenge, it is better to aim at the far target first, as this is most difficult to hit.

Aside from the increases to your Archery skill, once the fourth challenge is over, speak to Angi (using pleasant responses). She thanks you for keeping her company and not attempting to murder her. She then hands you a gift. After that, you can leave this windswept place (after checking her bedside table for the Treasure Map V).

➤ **Angi's Bow**

BARD'S LEAP SUMMIT: LEAP BEFORE YOU LOOK*

Fight the Forsworn to reach the top of Lost Valley Redoubt. The "Bard's Leap" itself is the precarious and breathtaking outlook over the waterfall. Here is the best way to survive the drop to the water below: use Whirlwind Sprint to make sure you get enough distance to clear the rocks, or use Ethereal Form before jumping off. The spectral shape of Azzadal, a Bardic Ghost, appears near the pool at the base of the Falls if you survive, and congratulates you for surviving the fall that he could not. He rewards you with an increase to your Speech skill.

➤ **Speech Skill increase**

BLIND CLIFF CAVE: MELKA AND PETRA*

Blind Cliff Bastion

Approach Blind Cliff Cave from the main road running north to south along the river. Clamber up through the giant cavern of collapsed follies, and exit to Blind Cliff Towers. Clamber up the exterior towers until you reach the ominous iron door leading to Blind Cliff Bastion. A caged Hagraven named Melka greets you. She is angry that another witch named Petra has caged her up. You can speak to her about being released and about her adversary. There is a "pretty staff" in it for you.

◊ **MISCELLANEOUS OBJECTIVE:** Kill the Hagraven Petra

To continue this quest, release Melka or explore on your own. Follow Melka to the rudimentary puzzle, which she tells you how to solve to avoid the dart traps (pull the middle handle). After passing through and up into another chamber (where Melka slays any Forsworn that you don't), she opens a stone wall panel leading to a lever. Pull the lever to stop the swinging blades in the corridor linking to Melka's parlor.

She waits for you to open the iron door connected to Petra's tower. Storm the chamber and defeat Petra here, along with her Forsworn bodyguards. Then return to Melka, demand a reward, and you're given the Hagraven's staff.

➤ **Eye of Melka**

DARKLIGHT TOWER: REPENTANCE

Darklight Tower (Interior)

Enter the initial chamber and you find the aftermath of a murder. A woman named Illia stands over the recently slain body and doesn't want you to jump to conclusions. Listen to her story, and she explains it was self-defense. Illia was attempting to flee the place, and the dead woman tried to stop her. She wants to leave, but suspects her own mother is set to become a Hagraven.

◊ **OBJECTIVE:** Help Illia reach the top of Darklight Tower

Ascend the tower, dealing with Frostbite Spiders and witches as you go. At the spear-barred door, pull the lever when you're ready to tackle a Hagraven.

Darklight Chambers

Kill more witches. At the lock (Master), Illia waits. Locate the corridor in the east wall, and face a Frostbite Spider and a second Hagraven in a fight for the key that unlocks the door.

➤ **Darklight Tower Key**

After a final ascent up spiral stairs to the tower's top, open a firmly locked door with the key Illia carries on her (if you kill her before reaching the top). The door leads back outside (Master). Wait for Illia, as she has a plan: to present you as a sacrifice to her mother and then kill her; the old crone is too far gone to be saved.

◊ **OBJECTIVE:** Defeat Illia's mother at the top of Darklight Tower

Darklight Tower (Exterior)

Step out into a small bailey on the upper crags. Illia's mother, Silvia, tells you to sit on the chair so your bloodletting can begin. Oblige Illia's mother as she is attacked by her daughter. You can stand and watch; intervene only if Illia is in danger of being killed. The quest concludes once Silvia falls. Afterward, approach Illia and invite her to join you as a Follower. She gladly accepts and mainly uses Frost magic on enemies.

➤ **Staff of Hag's Wrath** ➤ **Follower: Illia**

FORELHOST: SIEGE ON THE DRAGON CULT

Forelhost (Exterior)

Ascend the remains of the entrance tower until you spot a High Elf named Captain Valmir, who is wearing the officer's garb of the faction to which you are allied. He requires your assistance; he is on a mission to obtain a mask that a Dragon Priest named Rahgot used to own.

◊ **OBJECTIVE:** Obtain Rahgot's mask
◊ **OBJECTIVE:** (Optional) Find Skorm Snow-Strider's journal

Forelhost Stronghold (Interior)

Repel ghostly foes as the spirits of the dragon cultists appear to guard their old lair! Beware of floor triggers and traps. Pass the wall blades, entering the room to the northwest. Check the stone table, where Snow-Strider's journal is located. Now read this; it informs you why this location has so many blocked-off corridors.

➤ **Skorm Snow-Strider's Journal**

Work your way across the stronghold, down past the forge and kitchen. Locate the pair of wooden doors that lead to Forelhost Crypt. Before entering, watch for the fire-breathing dragon trap close to the barred doorway, and use the nearby lever to raise the portcullis blocking the doorway; this gives you quicker access to the entrance.

Forelhost Crypt

There is a cage surrounding the well (Master) close to the first main corridor. Come back here later if you can't open the cage door now.

Beware of runic floor traps as you travel farther underground and the light dwindles. Also expect a gate and dart traps prior to reaching a raised crypt. This is a dangerous location; expect a swarm of undead foes here!

Work your way to the platforms above, which lead to the other side of the barred wooden door (which you can now open if you wish). Pilfer the chest on the same raised tomb as the hardiest Draugr. This contains the Forelhost Well Key. Return to the well, unlock it, and drop into the icy water. Follow the waterlogged tunnels into a chamber where the remains of a poisoned warrior (mentioned in the journal) still lie among scattered poison bottles. In the adjacent room, beware the rising floor trap.

➤ **Forelhost Well Key**

Forelhost Refectory

The Refectory still bears the scars (and the dead) of the battle Snow-Strider wrote about. Open the iron door and enter the great hall, then open the double doors in the south wall. Traverse the oil-splattered stone corridor (burn it to defeat the Draugr if you wish), before entering the remains of a children's burial plot. There are Orders that confirm the mass burial, surrounded by flowers you can harvest.

➤ **Orders**

Above the burial garden is an alchemy chamber with more steps and Draugr; you can pull a lever to raise the portcullis leading back to the great hall, or press onward and upward, past the ruins of a throne and snow blown down from above. Beware the magic trap in the winding corridor beyond, which leads straight into Forelhost's library. But the prize to find isn't a book; it is a Glass Claw.

➤ **Glass Claw**

Take it, and the spear bars recede from the doorway farther into the library. Head through, past an embalming room, fire trap, and more Draugr, and head up to a hall and Nordic Puzzle Door.

Puzzle Solution: Open your inventory and look at the Glass Claw you just found. The palm bears the sign of the Wolf, Owl, and Snake. Working from the outer ring in, choose the same iconography on the door, and insert the Claw.

It takes only a few steps to reach the grand burial chamber of the Dragon Priest Rahgot. He is joined by a group of Draugr bodyguards, meaning this fight is both difficult and lengthy. But once over, the rewards are worth your anguish:

- **Rahgot**
- **Leveled Items and Weapons**
- **Staff of Wall of Flames**
- **Forelhost Balcony Key**
- **250 gold pieces**

TIP If you're gifted in One-Handed or Two-Handed skills, it is worth sprinting to Rahgot's tomb and hacking at the fearsome lich before he rises completely from his slumber; the more strikes you can inflict without retaliation, the better!

◊ **OBJECTIVE:** Return to Valmir

Forelhost (Exterior)

Use the Balcony Key to unlock the door in the southeast wall of the burial chamber. This leads back outside, to the balcony you couldn't reach when you first met Valmir. A Word Wall is just a few feet away! Once you learn the new phrase, drop down to Valmir's camp. It appears Valmir is an imposter (as he is clad in the attire of your enemy, unlike the first time you encountered him) and is now giving the same speech to convince an enemy soldier!

◊ **OBJECTIVE:** Kill the imposter Valmir

- **Word of Power:** Storm Call

NOTE You now have one of the eight Masks of the Dragon Priests. Consult the Side Quest of the same name for further information.

FROSTFLOW LIGHTHOUSE: WHAT LIES BENEATH*

Frostflow Lighthouse (Interior)

Inspect the corpse of Ramati, which has been savagely torn by claws. Near the fire is the body of a Chaurus. Ramati's corpse contains her husband's journal, which describes how the family came to own the lighthouse and the strange noises coming from the cellar. It also reveals a final, horrifying discovery.

In the northeast bedroom is Ramati's Journal, which details her rambunctious children Sudi and Mani and noises in the basement. It also tells how Ramati's husband made her promise to cremate him in the lighthouse torch when he died (this is important later).

In the north bedroom on a table is Sudi's Journal, which mentions the scratchings in the cellar, and a copy of the key Sudi hid in Mother's favorite keepsake.

Locate the Cellar Key in the burial urn above the fireplace, next to the collectible Torchbug in a Jar. (The Torchbug in a Jar is a unique item that can only be found here. It serves no purpose but makes for great house décor.)

- **Habd's Journal**
- **Ramati's Journal**
- **Sudi's Journal**
- **Mani's Cellar Key**
- **Torchbug in a Jar**

◊ **MISCELLANEOUS OBJECTIVE:** Find the source of the murders in Frostflow Lighthouse

Unlock the cellar door (Expert) using a lockpick or Mani's Cellar Key.

Frostflow Abyss

Open the gate to discover the corpse of Sudi. There are two notes nearby, and the insight into Sudi's last few days make grim reading.

- **Bloodstained Note**
- **Scrawled Page**
- **Habd's Lighthouse Key**

At the end of this waterlogged ice passage is a giant Chaurus Reaper; this is the source of the Frostflow Lighthouse murders.

After defeating it, you can use the Key to access the roof of the lighthouse. If you take Habd's remains from the belly of the giant Chaurus and burn them in the lighthouse torch, you receive a special blessing.

- **Perk:** Sailor's Repose (+10% to Health restored from Restoration magic)

Frostmere Crypt (Exterior)

As you approach the entrance to this ruin, a well-armored warrior races down the stairs before wheeling to face the bandits that pursue her. Help her (or not), then speak with the agitated Eisa Blackthorn. You can:

Speak to her and try to calm her down. She explains that she used to be a member of the gang here but was run out over a misunderstanding. As she storms off, the quest begins.

Provoke, ignore, or attack her, and she fights back—hard. She's every bit as tough as her attitude. Cut her down and take her journal from her body, hinting at the strange occurrences inside the crypt. This also starts the quest.

➤ **Eisa's Journal**

◊ **OBJECTIVE:** (Optional) Learn more about the theft in Frostmere Crypt
◊ **OBJECTIVE:** Find the stolen sword

NOTE Does Eisa's name sound familiar? If you've been to Cidhna Mine in Markarth, you might have heard her name mentioned. Eisa also figures in Hajvarr's journal in White River Watch. Skyrim's bandits really get around.

CAUTION If you kill Eisa and enter the crypt without reading her journal, the quest will never show up in your quest list. While everything still plays out as described below, because you didn't get the quest, completing it won't count toward the Sideways Achievement/Trophy.

WHISPERS IN THE RUINS

If you're sneaking (or just proceeding carefully), there's a good chance you'll hear some chatter from the bandits prior to engaging or avoiding them:

- Just inside the crypt entrance, two bandits question why Eisa and Ra'jiir would have stolen the sword.
- As you enter the central chamber, two bandits discuss Kyr's orders to seal up the mine until he gets back.
- In the dining hall, two bandits mention that Kyr has gone down to the tunnels, and something there has been "eerie" lately.
- When you activate the lever and return to the dining hall, bandits (having run up from the tunnels) are shocked at the carnage.
- As you enter the mine tunnels, two bandits discuss their concerns. Kyr has been gone for too long....

Frostmere Crypt (Interior)

After cutting down the bandits in the first room, take the scrap of paper (it appears a couple of times), confirming that the hunt for Ra'jiir and Eisa is on. As you step out onto the upper walkway in the main chamber, you can hear some bandits talking down below, and the quest updates.

◊ **OBJECTIVE:** Follow Kyr and Ra'jiir into the tunnels
♦ **TARGET:** Ra'jiir, in the Frostmere Depths

Follow the path around, but before descending into the dining hall, check the two bedrooms on the upper level. Kyr's Log is on a side table in his bedroom. If you allowed Eisa to leave quietly before, you find her journal in the other bedroom. Once you've read both, the optional objective is complete.

Continue deeper into the ruin and down through the tunnels to reach Frostmere Depths.

➤ **Kyr's Bounty (2)** ➤ **Kyr's Log**

Frostmere Depths

You emerge in a mist-shrouded subterranean forest, not far from the crumpled form of the bandit leader, Kyr. Hear his final words. When he dies, a strange glowing light manifests near his body and silently drifts down the path ahead of you.

Follow the light deeper into the woods, and watch as a lone figure—Ra'jiir—emerges from the fog and races for the altar in the center of the grove. Just before he reaches it, a fearsome ethereal form erupts in front of him and cuts him down. The Pale Lady then turns to thwart another tomb defiler: You!

◊ **OBJECTIVE:** Banish the Pale Lady

The Pale Lady is a powerful Wispmother, but if you have the strength, you can defeat her. Take out her wisps to reduce the bonuses they give her, then move in for the kill. The wide expanse around the tomb allows you to attack from a distance and hide between bouts of combat should you need to. If you're extremely quick, you can kill Ra'jiir, too.

Or, you can pick up the Pale Blade (the sword Ra'jiir carries and drops when he dies), approach the altar, and set the blade into the sword stand. This restores the seal on the Pale Lady's tomb, banishing her and her wisps in a blast of energy.

If you banish the Pale Lady by placing her blade atop the altar, you can take it again, breaking the seal and causing her to attack once more. You can repeat this until you decide to kill the Pale Lady, to flee, or to make the Pale Lady disappear again.

After dealing with the Pale Lady, approach the ruins to the north, where a Word Wall waits. Absorb the Word of Power, then take the exit here back to the crypts above.

➤ **The Pale Blade**

➤ **Word of Power:** Ice Form

NOTE The Pale Blade is a good weapon to use, with leveled Frost and Fear enchantments. If you're curious about the Pale Lady's nature, find the book called *Lost Legends*, which tells her story in passing, both as a children's fable and as the truth (which Ra'jiir finally realized too late during this exploration).

HIGH GATE RUINS: A SCROLL FOR ANSKA

High Gate Ruins (Interior)

Enter these old Draugr catacombs and meet up with a wizard named Anska. Speak with her, and she's quick to ask for help. This plucky adventurer and powerful fire mage has already begun advancing toward Vokun's Throne Room, where she believes she will find a scroll tying her family's history to that of the hero of yore, Ysgramor. Your reward for helping her? Any loot you wish, aside from the scroll. Agree, and the quest begins. Battle through more powerful Draugr, past a gate trap, and to a Nordic puzzle chamber.

◊ **OBJECTIVE:** Help Anska Retrieve Her Scroll

Puzzle Solution: Look up and to the south. Note the sequence of Hawk, Whale, Fox, Snake. The northern ceiling has the same sequence, but the third carving has fallen to the ground. Now match up the pedestals (which also contain a specific animal carving), and activate the lever of the Hawk, Whale, Fox, and Snake pedestals to match the ceiling order. There are two Hawk pedestals; it doesn't matter which one you activate first. If you're successful, the grating swings open. Descend the spiral stairs, and enter door to High Gate Ruins Catacombs.

High Gate Ruins Catacombs

There are more traps (and Draugr) as you progress, so beware of floor triggers. Head through the altar room, down the long hall to a second altar room, where three levers must be activated:

Puzzle Solution: Pull the lever in the center of the room. The next is in the right alcove, fight the Draugr guarding it, activate the lever, and face a second foe in the left alcove before activating the alcove lever behind it. This opens the portcullis allowing you into Vokun's Throne Room.

Step into the Throne Room, which seems to be honoring an ancient serpent god, and wait for the lich to appear. Be sure Anska survives this confrontation, and use the chamber's columns to hide from the fiend's more deadly attacks. Defeat Vokun, and then enter the chamber behind the throne room; this is a ceremonial altar chamber where the chanting reaches a crescendo, and you receive a Word of Power! Be sure you learn that and take the Sealed Scroll.

- **Vokun**
- **Word of Power:** Storm Call
- **Sealed Scroll**

◊ **OBJECTIVE:** Return the Scroll to Anska

TIP Removing Vokun's mask is imperative if you're also trying to finish Side Quest: Masks of the Dragon Priests*.

High Gate Ruins (Interior)

Exit the chamber via the north door at the end of the narrow corridor. Locate Anska, handing over the Scroll (which is otherwise useless to you and can't be sold). Anska is most grateful and gives you a gift.

- **Spell Tome:** Flaming Familiar

HILLGRUND'S TOMB: ANCESTRAL WORSHIP

Hillgrund's Tomb (Exterior)

Strike up a conversation at the entrance, and Golldir explains that he is worried for his aunt, who ventured into their family crypt to stop a necromancer. Agree to help Golldir rid the crypt of Vals Veran.

◊ **OBJECTIVE:** Defeat Vals Veran
◊ **OBJECTIVE:** (Optional) Protect Golldir

Hillgrund's Tomb (Interior)

Dispatch Draugr while keeping an eye on Golldir and stepping in if the undead are threatening to him. Descend to a connecting hallway, where Golldir's worst fears are confirmed; his aunt Agna lies in a pool of fresh blood. The nearby door is barred from the other side, so continue west, to a cave-in and through a Draugr-infested tomb corridor. The tomb opens into a deeper and much larger mausoleum where the dead rise again.

Puzzle Solution: When the coast is clear, pull the chain next to the bear carving, and an exit door opens. The double iron doors lead to the main crypt and an audience with the warlock Vals Veran.

Your tasks are twofold: killing Vals Veran and keeping Golldir alive (although this isn't necessary for quest completion). Strike at Vals Veran as often as you can, before backing off and dealing with the Draugr that have been summoned. The Draugr that close in on Golldir, or if Vals Veran focuses his attacks on the Nord, are your primary concerns. Continue the combat until both Draugr and Veran crumple to the ground.

Search Veran's corpse for a Crypt Key. A Chest Key is on Golldir, along with two missives; read them to gain a better understanding of the threats Vals Veran was imposing. The quest concludes after the battle.

Use the Crypt Key to open the iron door (Hard) atop the ceremonial stairs; this offers a quick exit. Golldir's chest in the antechamber beyond can be unlocked using the Chest Key. Assuming Golldir is alive, and you didn't start ransacking his family tomb, he is happy to become a Follower.

- **Hillgrund's Tomb Crypt Key**
- **Note from Agna**
- **Hillgrund's Tomb Chest Key**
- **Leveled gold reward**
- **Letter to Golldir**
- **Follower:** Golldir

NOTE Golldir is annoyed if you start stealing loot and opening chests, but not to the extent that this quest fails.

MISTWATCH: FORGETTING ABOUT FJOLA*

Mistwatch North Tower

Before the first wooden door, Christer calls to you, explaining that he believes his wife, Fjola, is being held in the tower somewhere. He gives you the key to Mistwatch and hopes you'll rescue her. Or, you can kill him and take the key, which opens the (otherwise sealed) wooden door.

➤ **Mistwatch Key**

◊ **MISCELLANEOUS OBJECTIVE:** Search Mistwatch for Fjola

Mistwatch East Tower

After battling bandits to the exterior lower balcony, up through the West Tower, out to the higher balcony, and finally to the top of the East Tower, you encounter the bandit leader herself. If you don't automatically attack her, you mention Fjola's name, and she reveals she's Fjola, leaving her husband and the boring life back at the farm for a career in banditry. She wants him to leave and pretend that she's dead; she hands you her wedding band to try and convince him to leave.

➤ **Fjola's Wedding Band**

◊ **MISCELLANEOUS OBJECTIVE:** Return to Christer

Mistwatch North Tower (Return)

Head back down to Christer and show him the wedding band. He now believes she's alive but not here, and leaves after giving you a small reward.

➤ **Leveled gold reward**

◊ **MISCELLANEOUS OBJECTIVE:** Report back to Fjola

Mistwatch East Tower (Return)

Back at the top of Mistwatch, tell Fjola that Christer won't bother her again, and she tells you she's in your debt and will repay it someday. For the moment, though, this quest is over.

MOSS MOTHER CAVERN: HUNTER AND HUNTED*

NOTE In order to receive rumors regarding the disappearance of Valdr's hunting party, you must be Level 16. If you aren't, you won't receive any information in Falkreath and must stumble upon the entrance to Moss Mother Cavern to begin this quest. Beware: The beasts may be too tough for you to overcome at lower levels!

Dead Man's Drink (Falkreath)

Stop by Dead Man's Drink and strike up a conversation inside. Among the other scuttlebutt, the innkeeper (Valga Vincia, or Narri) mentions that a hunting party has recently gone missing. It was led by a man named Valdr.

◊ **OBJECTIVE:** Locate Valdr's Hunting Party

Moss Mother Cavern (Exterior)

You hear several increasingly feeble shouts as you trudge down the path toward Moss Mother Cavern. Valdr waits on a log, bleeding heavily. You can:

- Hand him one or more healing potions; any standard healing potion will do.
- Cast a healing spell on him.
- Cast a healing spell with an area of effect, and catch Valdr in the area.
- Or leave him to his fate. If you enter the cavern without healing him, Valdr dies, and you miss this quest entirely.

◊ **OBJECTIVE:** Heal Valdr's Injuries

After you treat his injuries, Valdr explains his dilemma: The bodies of his friends are still inside the cave, being torn apart by beasts. You can offer to help him clear out the cavern, or tell him to stay outside while you head in alone. Valdr is a capable archer (especially if fully healed), but he can be killed, which causes you to fail the quest. The choice is yours. If you find the enemies inside too difficult, you can always leave and come back later. Valdr will remain at the entrance and wait for you indefinitely.

◊ **OBJECTIVE:** Return to Valdr

Moss Mother Cavern (Interior)

Enter this sun-dappled grotto, and you'll spot a fresh kill. Ari lies in a splatter of blood. There's little time to search her; expect a bear attack followed by a Spriggan. Try to edge into the cavern slowly so you aren't swarmed by too many enemies. Farther inside, you find the corpse of Niels, along with two additional Spriggans who emerge from the trees around you.

With all the enemies dispatched, speak with Valdr or return to him outside. He hands over a dagger Ari gave him when he first joined their hunting party.

➤ **Valdr's Lucky Dagger**

If you come back later, two small cairns have been set close to the cavern entrance: the graves of Ari and Niels. Valdr returns to the Dead Man's Drink in Falkreath, where he's always happy to see you again.

Understone Keep

Meet Calcelmo at the entrance to the excavation site, and tell him you wish to see Nchuand-Zel. In order to proceed, he asks you to defeat Nimhe, the "poisoned one," a giant Frostbite Spider. You receive the key to the dig site. Or, you can simply ignore Calcelmo and his spider problem (which isn't part of this quest), and unlock the giant bronze door to the Nchuand-Zel Excavation Site (Adept).

➤ Key to Nchuand-Zel

◊ **MISCELLANEOUS OBJECTIVE:** Kill Nimhe inside Nchuand-Zel

Nchuand-Zel Excavation Site

Head through the connecting chambers, down the pit chamber, through the cobwebbed spider chambers, to an excavation entrance room where Nimhe attacks. Fight her or flee. Defeating her completes the Miscellaneous Objective.

◊ **MISCELLANEOUS OBJECTIVE:** Tell Calcelmo that Nimhe is dead

On the platform slightly above Nimhe's intrusion point is a dead Imperial named Alethius. Check his corpse for some notes, which officially starts this quest. Read the note: It mentions chaperoning some researchers into these vast dwarven catacombs. Cut through the cobwebs, heading south into Nchuand-Zel.

➤ Alethius's Notes

◊ **OBJECTIVE:** Recover Stromm's journal

Nchuand-Zel

This is a giant open cavern with numerous towers and sloping paths linking them. Fight through the Falmer and down to the door leading to Nchuand-Zel Quarters.

Nchuand-Zel Quarters

Stromm's body is located near a small tree and fire runes on the floor. Avoid them, but inspect the corpse, and read the journal as the objectives update. There is more research to find.

➤ Stromm's Diary

◊ **OBJECTIVE:** Recover Erj's journal
◊ **OBJECTIVE:** Recover Krag's journal
◊ **OBJECTIVE:** Recover Staubs's journal

Nchuand-Zel Armory

Return to the main cavern, and descend to the bottom of the chamber. Wade over to the door and enter Nchuand-Zel Armory. Battle Falmer to the chamber with the two guardian Dwarven Spheres. Erj's corpse lies between them. Retrieve his journal.

➤ Erj's Notes

Nchuand-Zel

The other exit in the Armory leads you back into the main cavern, onto a previously inaccessible platform, where a Dwarven Centurion waits motionless, close to the body of Krag. Take his journal. Head up the slope into Nchuand-Zel Control.

➤ Krag's Journal

Nchuand-Zel Control

Staubin lies dead in a connecting corridor inside the Control district. Take his book; your search for the Lost Expedition is almost over.

➤ Staubin's Diary

◊ **OBJECTIVE:** Reactivate Nchuand-Zel's automated defenses

To switch the defenses on (which activates all the Dwarven Spiders, Spheres, and Centurions, who then clear the districts of Falmer), head into the control room with the grinding cogs and pistons, and pull the lever.

◊ **OBJECTIVE:** Find someone who knows about the expedition

Understone Keep

Exit the Nchuaud-Zel Control area and move back into the main cavern and up the earthen ledge, dropping down to the upper walkway. Flee north back into the excavation site, passing Nimhe and winding your way to Understone Keep. Speak to Calcelmo. Tell him you killed Nimhe (if this occurred), and then ask if he's researching the Dwemer. Calcelmo pays a good amount of coin for each research book you return. Don't forget to keep on asking him about researching the Dwemer to off-load all the books.

➤ Dwemer Museum Key ➤ 300 gold pieces (x4)

NILHEIM: THE NILHEIM SCAM*

Nilheim Exterior

Meet a wounded hunter named Telrav on the path just east of the bridge spanning the waterfall. He wants you to guide him safely to his camp in the nearby ruins of Nilheim, and you'll be rewarded.

◊ **MISCELLANEOUS OBJECTIVE:** Escort Telrav to his camp

Cross the bridge, following Telrav up and into the camp, where he tells you to wait, draws his bow, and assaults you along with four of his bandit mates. It's a trap!

◊ **MISCELLANEOUS OBJECTIVE:** Kill Telrav

Quickly quell this ambush, and slay Telrav and the other riffraff. Optionally, you can sneak into Nilheim and defeat all the bandits first, or slay Telrav when you meet him.

RAGNVALD: OTAR'S MAD GUARDIANS*

Ragnvald Temple

Battle Draugr and inspect a strange sarcophagus, which has two round divots into which to insert some kind of ceremonial key. Atop the stairs are spears barring your way.

◊ **MISCELLANEOUS OBJECTIVE:** Unlock the Sarcophagus in Ragnvald

Ragnvald Crypts

Fight more Draugr to reach a ceremonial crypt. Take Saerek's Skull Key from its pedestal to continue. Guardian Saerek is roused from slumber when you do; defeat him before returning to the Temple area.

➤ **Saerek's Skull Key**

Ragnvald Canal

Defeat more Draugr to reach a second ceremonial crypt. Remove Torsten's Skull Key from its pedestal to continue. Guardian Torsten is wakened from his rest and attacks you; defeat him before heading back to the Temple.

➤ **Torsten's Skull Key**

Ragnvald Temple (Return)

Once you are back at the sarcophagus, place each skull into the divot slot and prepare for battle. You've just released Otar the Mad, the dreaded Dragon Priest the Guardians laid to rest long ago. This is part of the Side Quest: Masks of the Dragon Priests*. Once you are able, run up through the retracting spears atop the steps and into the ceremonial chamber with a Word Wall at the far end. Learn this Word of Power before you leave.

➤ **Otar** ➤ **Word of Power:** Kyne's Peace

REBEL'S CAIRN: THE LEGEND OF RED EAGLE*

Rebel's Cairn (Interior)

Pedestal Cavern: Just inside the main cavern, locate the dead adventurer and pry the book from his hand. It tells the tale of Faolan Red Eagle, an ancient hero of the Reach. Read it to begin the following objective. The weapon slot in the pedestal will not accept any of your blades (unless you have Red Eagle's Fury already).

➤ **The Legend of Red Eagle**

◊ **MISCELLANEOUS OBJECTIVE:** Find Red Eagle's sword

TIP This quest can also be started by finding a copy of *The Legend of Red Eagle* elsewhere in Skyrim. This book appears in any number of locations, such as Farengar's study in Dragonsreach. Or, you can start the quest by clearing Red Eagle Redoubt first, claiming Red Eagle's Fury from the high-level enemy and reading the book (*Red Eagle's Rite*) on the altar nearby.

Red Eagle Redoubt (Exterior)

Follow the riverside trail up into the hills to reach your first objective, a cave entrance leading into Red Eagle Ascent. Head through the cave and back out into the exterior, then climb the stairs heading north, slaying Forsworn as you go. Continue up into the cliffside Forsworn Camp, looking for a Forsworn Briarheart on the stone altar plateau at the top, close to the entrance to the Sundered Towers. The Briarheart carries a key to the tower nearby and the sword you seek, Red Eagle's Fury.

➤ **Red Eagle's Fury** ➤ **Red Eagle Tower Key**

◊ **MISCELLANEOUS OBJECTIVE:** Unlock the secret of Red Eagle's Tomb

After defeating the boss, you can explore the Sundered Towers, scavenging for items and taking in the awesome view from atop the towers.

Rebel's Cairn

Pedestal Cavern: Return to Rebel's Cairn and insert Red Eagle's Fury into the weapon slot on the pedestal. A wall section slides away in front (east) of you.

Red Eagle's Tomb: Continue down the passage and enter the Red Eagle's secret crypt. As Red Eagle emerges from his sarcophagus, several skeletons rise around him. Cut them down and ransack the tomb for its treasures.

Pedestal Cavern: As you leave, you'll notice that the sword you placed in the weapon slot now glows with a brilliant light. Draw it forth, and claim the more powerful Red Eagle's Bane!

➤ **Red Eagle's Bane**

SHROUD HEARTH BARROW: WILHELM'S SPECTER*

Ivarstead (Vilemyr Inn)

Visit the Vilemyr Inn and speak to Wilhelm, who believes a ghost haunts Shroud Hearth Barrow, the ruin atop the hill. Offer to look into it for him.

◊ **MISCELLANEOUS OBJECTIVE:** Investigate Shroud Hearth Barrow

Shroud Hearth Barrow (Interior)

Head down the spiral steps to find a closed portcullis, where a specter urges you to leave. After he delivers his ghostly warning, move into the next room, which has four levers.

Puzzle Solution: Three of the four levers move one or more of the portcullises (there are three ahead of you in the junction). The fourth, on the far right, launches darts at you, so always ignore it. To open the two portcullises ahead (southwest) of you, make sure levers 1 and 3 are up and 2 and 4 are down.

As you head deeper into the ruins, the ghost you saw earlier attacks! Kill him...and notice that his body suddenly looks a lot more substantial. The "ghost" of the barrows turns out to be treasure hunter Wyndelius Gatharian, who Wilhelm may have mentioned. The journal on the table explains everything: Wyndelius has been using a unique potion, the Philter of the Phantom, to impersonate a ghost and keep the townsfolk at bay while he searched for a way into the ruins, but the potion seems to have driven him a bit mad. Take the journal, then return to Wilhelm at the Vilemyr Inn.

➤ **Wyndelius's Journal** ➤ **Philter of the Phantom (2)**

◊ **MISCELLANEOUS OBJECTIVE:** Bring Wyndelius's Journal to Wilhelm

NOTE The Philter of the Phantom is a unique item that briefly makes you look like a ghost! While fun, it doesn't have any functional effects.

Puzzle Solution: At the four levers, you'll notice the portcullis back to the surface is stopping your progress. Place all four levers in the down position to raise the portcullis, allowing you to exit.

Ivarstead (Vilemyr Inn)

Show Wyndelius's Journal to Wilhelm at the Vilemyr Inn to receive the Sapphire Dragon Claw you need to explore the interior of the barrows.

➤ **Sapphire Dragon Claw**

Shroud Hearth Barrow (Interior)

Retrace your steps, opening the portcullises as before, then head southwest to a Nordic Puzzle Door.

Puzzle Solution: The door consists of three large, rotating rings. Each ring has three animals symbols plated into it. The puzzle solution is actually on the palm of the Sapphire Dragon Claw; rotate it in your inventory to see the three circular petroglyph carvings on the Claw's palm. Move the rings so the Moth, Owl, and Wolf appear on the outer, middle, and inner rings, respectively. Then insert the Sapphire Dragon Claw into the keyhole.

In the next chamber, the portcullises slam shut on you as the Draugr begin climbing out of their sarcophagi. Fight them if you wish, but use the lever in the northeast alcove to open the portcullises, allowing you to continue.

After defeating the skeletons in the pool of oil and the trap-filled crypt, you'll enter another crypt where the doors shut and lock on you. Slay the last Draugr in front of the locked iron door to claim the key to the door, or just unlock it yourself (Expert). Then head into a canal area, with another puzzle to solve.

➤ **Shroud Hearth Barrow Key**

Puzzle Solution: To lower the bridge over the canal, open the double wooden doors. Step into the inner chamber and stand on the pressure plate. Four stone walls begin to turn, eventually revealing a carving in each alcove. Note the carvings, and turn the pillars outside to match that sequence. Or simply ignore this and twist the pillars so that the following are shown from left to right: Whale, Hawk, Snake, Whale.

Shroud Hearth Depths (Interior)

Inside the stepped tomb chamber, skeletons and Draugr emerge from their coffins to face you. As you cut them down, more emerge, until the final high-level Draugr clambers out of the tomb at the top of the structure.

Kill him, lowering the bridge and a stone door on the other side. Beyond is a large treasure chest and a Word Wall. Then exit via the iron door to the northwest.

➤ **Word of Power:** Kyne's Peace

SLEEPING TREE CAMP: THE SECRET AT THE SLEEPING TREE*

Begin this quest in two different ways:

- By listening to a rumor from any of the barkeeps dotted around Skyrim.
- Or by stumbling upon Sleeping Tree Camp, located west of Whiterun, in the Tundra plains.

Beware of lumbering mammoths and their giant shepherds. Give them a wide berth and they won't attack, or slay them if you wish. Your main concern here is the strange tree growing in a pond of eerie purple water. If you approach it and activate the spigot, you can drain a single potion of Sleeping Tree Sap. You aren't able to siphon off another bottle for another few days. A bottle isn't needed to accomplish this.

The small cave below the mammoth skull adjacent to the pond is another place to investigate, but watch for an irate giant inside. Locate the body of a dead Orc named Ulag. Among his possessions is another bottle of Sap and a note; take both and read Ysolda's Message. The message instructs the now-deceased Ulag to bring any Sleeping Tree Sap to a woman named Ysolda, at her stall in Whiterun. Before you leave, quickly open the treasure chest in the cave; there's usually some gold and a couple of bottles of Sleeping Tree Sap to gather. Don't leave camp without them!

➤ **Sleeping Tree Sap** ➤ **Ysolda's Message**

◊ **OBJECTIVE:** Speak to Ysolda about Sleeping Tree Sap

Ysolda is usually inside or near her house in the southern part of Whiterun's walled city or is walking to a stall. Speak with her, tell her you've some Sap to sell, and trade as many bottles as you wish. You can return to Sleeping Tree Camp and siphon off another batch of Sap, but don't expect the tree to regenerate sap immediately: This can take anywhere from three days to a month.

➤ **150 gold pieces (per Sap bottle)**

NOTE Sleeping Tree Sap is a powerful narcotic that fortifies a user's health by 100 for 45 seconds. However, it also blurs vision and slows down the recipient by 25 percent, so use it with caution! Such Sap is also available to purchase from certain Khajiit caravaneers on the roads of Skyrim. If you need another Sap fix, return to Sleeping Tree Camp in a month or so.

SOUTHFRINGE SANCTUM: THE SAVIOR OF SELVENI NETHRI*

Southfringe Sanctum

Entrance Cavern: Defeat the Spellsword at the entrance, and kill any other foes (except for Pumpkin the fox, in the small cage) as you head up the interior cavern slope.

Spider Cave: Continue through interlocking tunnels, and defeat all Frostbite Spiders when they swarm you.

Spider Warren: Selveni Nethri is tied up in spiderwebs in the center of the Sanctum. Hack or burn the web away. She explains that Bashnag's coven chased her out and left her for dead down here. Tell her to wait while you clear out the rest of the cave.

◊ **MISCELLANEOUS OBJECTIVE:** Help Selveni Nethri escape the cave

Bashnag's Coven: Kill anything you meet between Nethri and a confrontation with the Warlock Bashnag. Then explore the rest of the Sanctum and leave no enemy alive. Feel free to loot the place.

Spider Warren: Return to Selveni Nethri, tell her it is safe to exit, and follow her to the entrance cavern and out into Skyrim.

TREVA'S WATCH: INFILTRATION

Treva's Watch Exterior

Exterior Road: Meet Stalleo and his bodyguards camped out to the east of the fortification, close to the bridge. He has been forced out of his home by men loyal to Brurid, one of his rivals. Agree to help him, and begin this quest.

◊ **OBJECTIVE:** Use the back door to gain access to Treva's Watch

Treva's Watch

Entrance: You meet bandits on this sloped tunnel. Burn them all by firing an arrow at the oil lamp above them, or attack normally. Now work your way through this structure, slaying bandits along the way. A pile of corpses in the barrel room indicates where forces loyal to Stalleo have been slaughtered. There is a bandit chief to slay, but killing and exploring are optional.

Exterior Courtyard: Move to the ground-level exit to the east, open it, and pull the lever in the small wooden lean-to just outside the door. This opens the previously impenetrable main gates, retracting the spears blocking Stalleo and his men.

◊ **OBJECTIVE:** Meet up with Stalleo in the courtyard

Continue the fight in the courtyard (pulling the lever before or after you defeat the remaining bandits) and meet up with Stalleo when the coast is clear. He asks if you've seen his family (you haven't) and rewards you for your help.

➤ **Spell Tome:** Detect Life

Valthume Vestibule (Interior)

When you first enter this evil-stained place, a ghost named Valdar approaches. It explains that you stand in the tomb of Hevnoraak, and he may have returned. Valdar has been barely containing his power and hopes you'll explore the tomb and find three vessels that hold the power to vanquish Hevnoraak. Agree to this mission as Valdar sits back down on the throne where he died.

◊ **OBJECTIVE:** Collect the Vessels (3)

Expect numerous traps and attacks by Draugr and Frostbite Spiders as you search the interlocking chambers of this crypt. The specter of Hevnoraak intermittently appears and drifts off; you cannot affect this ethereal being, but its significance means you're making progress.

Valthume

The first Vessel is inside the coffin of a high-level Draugr, in a dead-end chamber to the east, with open (but inaccessible) wind tunnels up to the surface.

➤ **Opaque Vessel**

Valthume Catacombs

The second Vessel is through the portcullis (check the wall alcove to the right for the pull chain) in the northwest corner of the vertical Draugr crypt, toward the center of this section of Valthume.

➤ **Opaque Vessel**

Valthume Vestibule

Continue to fight your way through more Draugr and Frostbite Spiders. Your way is temporarily blocked by a Nordic Puzzle Door.

➤ **Iron Claw**

Puzzle Solution: The door consists of three rings that rotate when you activate them. Each of the them have three animals plated into the structure. The central keyhole is unlocked using the Iron Claw; this puzzle is inaccessible without it, as the puzzle solution is on the palm of the Iron Claw. Rotate it in your inventory to see the three circular petroglyph carvings on the Claw's palm. Move the rings so the Dragon, Hawk, and Wolf appear on the outer, middle, and inner rings, respectively. Then insert the Iron Claw into the keyhole.

Just beyond the door is a battle with Draugr guarding a pedestal with the last Vessel on it. Don't forget to approach the Word Wall to the west, and absorb a Word of Power.

➤ **Opaque Vessel** ➤ **Word of Power:** Aura Whisper

◊ **OBJECTIVE:** Perform the ritual with Valdar

Valthume

Back in the throne room close to the entrance, Valdar informs you that the vessels contain the Dragon Priest's blood. Emptying them into the nearby sconce is likely to remove any chance Havnoraak has of regaining his former powers. Oblige Valdar by pouring out the three vessels and then sit on the throne.

◊ **OBJECTIVE:** Defeat Hevnoraak

Slay this Dragon Priest, concentrating on cutting him down, rather than the Storm Thralls he summons. The quest concludes once this battle ends and Valdar has spoken to you, urging you to take the iron mask. This is part of Side Quest: Masks of the Dragon Priests*.

➤ **Hevnoraak**

VOLUNRUUD: SILENCED TONGUES

Volunruud (Interior)

◊ **OBJECTIVE:** Locate the Ceremonial Weapons

Enter the barrow. Beware of skeletons. Choose either path at the junction and search the entire area for a crypt containing an Archaic Nord Helmet sitting in a skull. The adjacent chamber has a Ceremonial Sword to take from the coffin. Watch for a Draugr ambush afterward.

➤ **Ceremonial Sword**

The path to the northwest leads to a tomb and a path leading down into a lower throne room with multiple floor traps and a Ceremonial Axe above the throne. Remove that from its wall coupling.

➤ **Ceremonial Axe**

◊ **OBJECTIVE:** Open the Elder's Cairn

Backtrack to the hub chamber and head north, to the Elder's Cairn door. Place both ceremonial weapons into their slots, and the door grinds open.

◊ **OBJECTIVE:** Defeat Kvenel

Head to the Elder's Cairn of Kvenel the Tongue, where the powerful Nord warrior's spirit still haunts. The ghost brandishes two very real versions of the ceremonial weapons you found earlier. Defeat the foe, watching out for his Shouts and Frost Thralls. Then search the corpse for the weapons themselves. Before leaving, check the upper steps that lead to a Word Wall.

➤ **Eduj** ➤ **Okin** ➤ **Word of Power:** Aura Whisper

NOTE One of Kvenel the Tongue's weapons may be lost to the ether when he dies, so don't expect to obtain both of them. The type of weapon is also randomly determined.

YNGOL BARROW: ASHORE IN A SEA OF GHOSTS*

Winterhold

Quest Start 1: Visit Birna's House in the Hold City of Winterhold first, and speak to her. She's done a bad deal on a trinket she wants rid of. Pay her 50 gold pieces. She tells you to come back if you find anything of interest inside Yngol Barrow, where this is supposed to be placed.

➤ Coral Dragon Claw

Quest Start 2: Or simply enter Yngol Barrow and locate the Coral Dragon Claw during your exploration. You never need speak to Birna (she won't have knowledge of the Claw if you find it this way).

Yngol Barrow (Exterior)

To further your knowledge of the tale of Yngol, read the book on the small shrine in front of the Barrow entrance.

➤ Yngol and the Sea-Ghosts

Yngol Barrow (Interior)

This tomb is suspiciously quiet. You are joined by an ever-increasing number of strange little spirit balls that bounce and seem to act with an otherworldly intelligence. Continue until you reach the portcullis chamber with the lever in front of it. Don't trigger the dart trap by moving the lever yet! Instead, search the dead scholar, removing his book and reading it.

➤ Notes on Yngol Barrow

Puzzle Solution: The book is the key here, as it refers to transcription of carvings in this room:

"Man in his throne, so should he be": This refers to the throne and skeleton to your right.

"Whale in the sea, so should he be": This refers to the pillar to the right of the throne, which is being splashed by water. Change it so the Whale is shown.

"Eagle in Sun's Sky, so should he be": This refers to the pillar bathed in light, left of you. Change it so the Hawk is shown.

"Snake in the weed, so should he be": This refers to the grass-covered pillar. Change that so the Snake is shown.

Now pull the lever. Enter the next chamber, where you'll find the Coral Dragon's Claw on a dais if you haven't received it at the start of this quest.

➤ Coral Dragon Claw

Continue deeper into the barrow until you reach a Nordic Puzzle Door.

Puzzle Solution: The door consists of three rings that rotate. Each of the them has three animals plated into the structure. The puzzle solution is on the palm of the Coral Dragon Claw; rotate it in your inventory to see the three circular petroglyph carvings on the Claw's palm. Move the rings so the Snake, Wolf, and Moth appear on the outer, middle, and inner rings, respectively. Then insert the Coral Dragon Claw into the keyhole.

Head into the resting place of Yngol. The spirit balls of energy congeal and form into Yngol's Shade, which must be fought. Then take Yngol's Helm from the skeletal remains of the warrior, and any other treasure you wish to ransack. Exit via the spiral steps to the southeast.

➤ Yngol's Helm

DUNGEON ACTIVITIES

Are you embarking on an exploration of a particularly strange or frightening cairn, barrow, fortification, or hole in the ground? Then consult the following chart, which lists every notable occurrence within a dungeon of Skyrim!

✓	LOCATION	HOLD	ASSOCIATED QUEST (AND POSSIBLE PREREQUISITE)	DESCRIPTION	REWARD
☐	Alftand	Winterhold	None (Daedric Quest: Discerning the Transmundane leads here but doesn't have to be active.)	You are sent here on your way to obtain an Elder Scroll. This is one connection to Blackreach. At the end of the exploration, you can obtain a Targe (shield) from Umana, a bandit explorer, in Alftand Cathedral.	Targe of the Blooded
☐	Anise's Cabin	Falkreath	None	A kindly old woman lives at this cabin in the woods, close to Riverwood. But enter her cellar, and you learn she's actually a witch. She attacks when you emerge.	Scavenged items
☐	Bard's Leap Summit	The Reach	None	Jumping off the overlook into the water below awakens a ghost named Azzadal. Beware of Forsworn and Hagravens, and converse with the spirit.	+2 Speech
☐	Blackreach	Blackreach (Other Realms)	Main Quest: Elder Knowledge or Daedric Quest: Discerning the Transmundane must be active to enter Blackreach	Launch any Dragon Shout at the central hanging "Sun" above the Debate Hall in the center of Blackreach, to summon a Dragon to fight.	Dragon Soul
☐	Bloated Man's Grotto	Falkreath	Before Daedric Quest: Ill Met by Moonlight	The Shrine to Talos at the back of the grotto was once an old Blades hideout. Find the note from a fallen Blade and the sword he left behind.	Bolar's Writ, Bolar's Oathblade
☐	Brinewater Grotto	Haafingar	None (Thieves Guild Quest: Scoundrel's Folly occurs here but doesn't have to be active)	This hidden bandit camp and Horker grotto can be reached through the Solitude East Empire Warehouse. Only the grotto section is available if you enter from the unmarked cave near Solitude Lighthouse.	Scavenged items
☐	Bronze Water Cave	The Pale	Thieves Guild Quest: Blindsighted is active	Normally, this strange cave with dwarven pipe-work is a dead end. However, it is a secret exit from Irkngthand at the zenith of this quest.	None
☐	Chillwind Depths	Hjaalmarch	None	Nearby Secondary Locations paint a grim picture. To the northeast is an attacked Caravan cart. At the base of the path leading to the cave lies an abandoned camp, once used by some adventurers who came to investigate. The adventurers themselves are found dead inside. Near the end of this Falmer and Frostbite Spider maze, a note on one of the prisoners tells what happened to those who were captured.	Merchant's Journal, Adventurer's Journal, Torn Note
☐	Clearpine Pond	Haafingar	None	Tread lightly: If you disturb the island (attacking the animals, harvesting the plants, or examining the dead alchemist), Spriggans emerge to attack.	Scavenged items

✓	LOCATION	HOLD	ASSOCIATED QUEST (AND POSSIBLE PREREQUISITE)	DESCRIPTION	REWARD
☐	Cronvangr Hall	Eastmarch	None	Before a fearful journey down into a chasm, fighting Frostbite Spiders, check the north wall of the entrance cavern to press a wall button, open a secret door, and venture into a vampire abode, the "Hall" itself, where few dare enter!	Scavenged items
☐	Crystaldrift Cave	The Rift	None	You can obtain Gadnor's Staff of Charming (which actually casts Fury) from his corpse, inside this animal den.	Gadnor's Staff of Charming
☐	Dead Men's Respite	Hjaalmarch	None (Bard's Quest: Tending the Flames occurs here but doesn't have to be active)	This is the tomb of King Olaf One-Eye. The bard Yrsarald was also entombed here; his ghost leads you through the dungeon and takes vengeance on Olaf during the final battle.	King Olaf's Verse (see quest for details)
☐	Druadach Redoubt	The Reach	None	You can find a map here that reveals the locations of all Forsworn camps. Madanach heads here if he survives the prison break, during Side Quest: No One Escapes Cidhna Mine.	Scavenged items
☐	Duskglow Crevice	The Pale	None	The Falmer that live here like to collect trinkets from the world of men. A group of bandits are down here to reclaim their stolen property; be quiet, and you can listen to their plotting.	Scavenged items
☐	Dwemer Museum (Understone Keep, in Markarth)	The Reach	None (Thieves Guild Quest: Hard Answers occurs here but doesn't have to be active)	See the quest for notes on how to gain legitimate access to the Museum, or for tips on sneaking through this space to the laboratory beyond.	See Quest
☐	Fallowstone Cave	The Rift	Daedric Quest: The Cursed Tribe is active	When the quest is active, another exit is available in this cave that connects to the otherwise-inaccessible Giant's Grove. You accompany Chief Yamarz here to kill an orc-eating giant and to retrieve Volendrung.	Volendrung (see quest for details)
☐	Fellglow Keep	Whiterun	College of Winterhold Quest: Hitting the Books is active	There are a number of interactions if this quest is active, compared to normal adventuring: You can release prisoners, try out the firing range, and battle a teleporting foe known as The Caller.	A number of important books (see quest for details)
☐	Folgunthur	Hjaalmarch	None (Side Quest: Forbidden Legend occurs here but doesn't have to be active)	Daynas Valen, a wizard investigating the Gauldur Legend (Side Quest: The Forbidden Legend) perished here along with his adventuring party. His journal and notes explain the truth behind this ancient mystery.	Gauldur Amulet Fragment, Gauldur Blackblade, Writ of Sealing (see quest for details)
☐	Forelhost	The Rift	Dungeon Quest: Siege on the Dragon Cult	One of eight lairs where a named Dragon Priest lies. You can obtain Rahgot's Mask here. The quest is automatically active.	Rahgot's Mask
☐	Geirmund's Hall	The Rift	Side Quest: Forbidden Legend is active	Named for Arch-Mage Geirmund, from the Gauldur Legend (Side Quest: The Forbidden Legend), who is entombed here along with one of the three brothers. Puzzle Solution (Pillars): Clockwise from the base of the steps: Hawk, Whale, Snake, Whale. Sigdis Gauldurson creates illusionary duplicates.	Gauldur Amulet Fragment, Gauldur Blackbow, Writ of Sealing (see quest for details)
☐	Gloombound Mine	Eastmarch	None	The Ebony mine is adjacent and connected to the Orc stronghold of Narzulbur.	Ebony Ore
☐	Hag's End	The Reach	Dark Brotherhood Quest: The Feeble Fortune*	The Hagraven here teleports after taking damage, until you eventually defeat her at the top of the ruins.	Scavenged items (see Dark Brotherhood Quest for most powerful items)
☐	Hall of the Vigilant	The Pale	None	The base of operations for the Vigil of Stendarr. The Vigilants attack if you are in werewolf form or if they sense you are a vampire. Otherwise, the Vigilants will gladly heal you of any nonpermanent diseases upon request.	Healing
☐	Halldir's Cairn	Falkreath	None	Halldir lures adventurers in here and compels them to sacrifice themselves on his cairn (Vidgrod, Raen, and Agrius have succumbed to him). Agrius's Journal (on the entrance room pedestal) tells the story. Puzzle Solution: Match the symbols on the stone heads in each room. Clockwise from the lever: Hawk, Snake, Whale. Halldir splits into three elemental forms in midbattle.	Halldir's Staff
☐	Halted Stream Camp	Whiterun	None	An old iron mine, now overrun by poachers. Beware the large pit located slightly to the east, and a trap filled interior where bandits are carving up a dead mammoth.	Poacher's Axe (with bandit at grindstone)
☐	Harmugstahl	The Reach	None	You encounter an adventurer fighting an enchanted Frostbite Spider at the entrance. Puzzle Solution (Levers): The four levers (A, B, C, D from left to right) trigger four bars (1, 2, 3, 4). Pulling a switch toggles its associated bar and the ones immediately next to them (pulling A toggles 1, 2. Pulling B toggles 2, 1, 3. Pulling C toggles 3, 2, 4. Pulling D toggles 4, 3). Simply pull levers A and D. Kornalus Frey is experimenting with these spiders. Find his key on his corpse that unlocks his bedroom (and Shrine of Julianos) and the door to the exit.	Scavenged items
☐	Irkngthand	The Pale	Thieves Guild Quest: Blindsighted is active	You accompany Karliah and Brynjolf through this expansive dwarven structure.	Eyes of the Falmer
☐	Kagrenzel	Eastmarch	None	If you find yourself falling, stay in the middle of the chasm you're falling through; you're more likely to survive. This connects to Stony Creek Cave (but only from this location).	None
☐	Katariah	Haafingar	Dark Brotherhood Quest: Hail Sithis! is active	The Emperor's ship only appears when the quest begins. Listen to conversations among the crew if you're sneaking. If you wish to avoid the top deck, pick the middeck door or take the key from the captain.	See Quest
☐	Knifepoint Ridge Interior	Falkreath	Daedric Quest: Boethiah's Calling is active	When this quest is active, you can enter a previously inaccessible inner chamber of the mine, where you can face and defeat the previous Champion of Boethiah.	Ebony Mail and Ebony Equipment
☐	Liar's Retreat	The Reach	None	This bandit hall and hideout has been recently attacked by Falmer, and both are waging a violent battle. There are dwarven ruin elements farther into this dungeon.	Rahd's Longhammer (next to Rahd's body on the altar.)

✓	LOCATION	HOLD	ASSOCIATED QUEST (AND POSSIBLE PREREQUISITE)	DESCRIPTION	REWARD
☐	Logrolf's House (Markarth)	The Reach	Daedric Quest: The House of Horrors is active	A strange house within the walls of Markarth, where odd occurrences are being investigated.	Mace of Molag Bal
☐	Lost Prospect Mine	The Rift	None	This mine was abandoned when one of the partners went missing. A Miner's Journal explains the story. The miner is, in fact, still here; his skeleton is in a secret chamber behind the waterfall, next to several gold veins. Use Whirlwind Sprint (or a lucky jump) to climb to this otherwise hard-to-reach ledge.	Gold Ore
☐	Lost Valley Redoubt	The Reach	None	This is a Forsworn encampment surrounding (both above and below) Bard's Leap Summit. If you're quiet, you can see Hagravens completing a ritual and creating a Briarheart. There is a Word Wall here, too.	Word of Power: Become Ethereal
☐	Mara's Eye Pond	Eastmarch	None	A trapdoor on the island leads to a smugglers' den claimed by a couple of vampires.	Scavenged items
☐	Meeko's Shack	Hjaalmarch	None	You find a dog, Meeko, by the side of the road, south of the shack. He leads you to the shack where his dead master lies. There is a Journal expressing the master's wishes.	Follower: Meeko
☐	Mzinchaleft	Hjaalmarch	None (Dark Brotherhood Side Contract: Maluril occurs here but doesn't have to be active)	An enterprising Dark Elf, Maluril, has hired a group of mercenary bandits to help excavate the ruins for valuable artifacts. Mzinchaleft Depths has an entrance into Blackreach (provided you have the Attunement Sphere from Daedric Quest: Discerning the Transmundane).	Scavenged Items
☐	Nightcaller Temple	The Pale	Daedric Quest: Waking Nightmare is active	This ruin is actually a former temple of Vaermina (only accessible during the quest). Together with Erandur, you fight your way through here to find the Skull of Corruption. Follower: Erandur, or Skull of Corruption	See Quest
☐	Orotheim	Hjaalmarch	None	If you kill the bandits here, they stop their raids on the giants of Talking Stone Camp to the south.	Scavenged items
☐	Orphan Rock	Falkreath	Temple Quest: The Blessings of Nature is active	You are sent here to retrieve Nettlebane from a Hagraven.	Nettlebane
☐	Pinewatch	Falkreath	None (Thieves Guild City Influence Quest: Silver Lining occurs here, but doesn't have to be active)	Press a button on the wall next to the table in the cellar, and access a hidden passage behind the bookshelf to find a bandit hideout. The bandits here have stolen Endon's Silver Mold, the quest item.	Endon's Silver Mold (and Scavenged items)
☐	Raldbthar	The Pale	None (Dark Brotherhood Quest: Mourning Never Comes occurs here but doesn't have to be active)	You are sent here to murder Alain Dufont. You can also obtain Aegisbane from him. This is one of the connections to Blackreach (provided you have the Attunement Sphere from Daedric Quest: Discerning the Transmundane).	Aegisbane, scavenged items
☐	Reachwater Rock	The Reach	Side Quest: Forbidden Legend is active	Puzzle Solution (Nordic Doors): If you have the necessary claws (one is found in Folgunthur), the first Puzzle Door's unlocking symbols are Bear, Whale, Snake. The second is Hawk, Hawk, Dragon. You fight Jyrik (Saarthal), Sigdis (Geirmund), and Mikrul (Folgunthur) again in sequence.	Gauldur Amulet
☐	Riften Jail (Mistveil Keep)	The Rift	None	Secret Exit: Note the Thieves Guild Shadowmark on the wall. Once only you can pull the broken shackle in your cell to open a secret door into the sewers and out into Lake Honrich.	None (you must retrieve your equipment, too!)
☐	Robbers' Gorge	Hjaalmarch	None	The bandits here demand a 100 gold toll each time you want to pass. If you refuse, they use their rockfall traps and attack from the high cliffs.	Scavenged items
☐	Serpent's Bluff Redoubt	Whiterun	None	This is a Forsworn hideout. Puzzle Solution: Put an item on the pressure plate on the altar to open the exit portcullis.	Scavenged items
☐	Shroud Hearth Barrow	The Rift	None (Miscellaneous Objective: Wilhelm's Specter occurs here but doesn't have to be active)	The "ghost" of the barrows turns out to be a treasure hunter named Wyndelius Gatharian, who is using a Philter of the Phantom. Show Wyndelius's Journal to Wilhelm at the Vilemyr Inn to receive the Sapphire Dragon Claw you need. Puzzle Solution (Nordic Door): Moth, Owl, Wolf. In the locked catacombs, the last Draugr has the Shroud Hearth Barrows Key. Puzzle Solution (Pillars): From left to right: Whale, Hawk, Snake, Whale. There is a Word Wall here, too.	Wyndelius's Journal, Sapphire Dragon Claw. Word of Power: Kyne's Peace
☐	Solitude Jail (Castle Dour)	Haafingar	None	Secret Exit: Break through the crumbling mortar in the back of your cell and exit behind Angeline's Aromatics.	None (you must retrieve your equipment, too!)
☐	Talking Stone Camp	Hjaalmarch	None	Bandits from Orotheim raid the camp periodically. Once you've cleared out that dungeon, the raids stop, and the giants lead their mammoths to a nearby stream, which gives you an opportunity to loot the camp more easily.	Scavenged items
☐	Tolvald's Cave	The Rift	Thieves Guild Side Quest: No Stone Unturned is active	A refuse pile just after the waterfall in Tolvald's Crossing is the final resting place of the Crown of Barenziah, a quest item for the Thieves Guild. You can only enter this cavern when the quest is active.	Crown of Barenziah (and scavenged items)
☐	Volskygge	Haafingar	Side Quest: Masks of the Dragon Priests*	Puzzle Solution: Activate Snake, Bear, Fox, Wolf in that order to raise the portcullis. One of eight lairs where a named Dragon Priest lies. You can obtain Volsung's Mask here. The quest is automatically active.	Volsung's Mask
☐	White River Watch	Whiterun	None	This bandit hideout has several notes to collect. You can talk your way past Ulfr the Blind instead of killing him. You can listen to the bandits' mutiny plans, and free a wolf to fight the bandits for you (pull the chain on the right wall before you reach the cage). Hajvarr Iron-Hand is on the exterior overlook.	Note to Rodulf, Ulif's Book, Hajvarr's Journal, Ironhand Gauntlets
☐	Whitewatch Tower	Whiterun	None	Some bandits attack this tower when you first approach. Help the guards fight them off, if you like.	Scavenged items

MISCELLANEOUS OBJECTIVES

This section of the guide deals with the dozens of Miscellaneous Objectives that appear in your Quest menu throughout your adventures. Like Favors, these are straightforward tasks with modest rewards, but some have unique elements, such as unlocking a dungeon or giving you access to a previously restricted area.

These are separated into Innkeeper Objectives (scuttlebutt and rumor you might hear at your favorite tavern) and Miscellaneous Objectives in each major settlement of Skyrim, separated by Hold. Note that each of these increases your relationship with the citizen you're doing the Favor for, which is important for your standing within a particular city (if you wish to complete any Thane Tasks).

Some Miscellaneous Objectives were important enough for us to flag with a quest name and the "*" symbol. The quest name won't appear in your Quest menu, but the Miscellaneous Objectives will be listed.

MISCELLANEOUS OBJECTIVES: INNKEEPERS

The following innkeepers are a good source for scuttlebutt across Skyrim. There is a (random) chance that they point you toward the start of a Side Quest or Daedric Quest, or contact with the Thieves Guild or Dark Brotherhood. They can also (randomly) provide you with Bounty Quests. Here are the innkeepers of Skyrim to check and the four types of Bounty Quests, which can be repeated:

INNKEEPERS OF SKYRIM

✓	HOLD LOCATION	SETTLEMENT	INN OR TAVERN	INNKEEPER
☐	Haafingar	Solitude	The Winking Skeever	Corpulus Vinius
☐	Haafingar	Dragon Bridge	Four Shields Tavern	Faida
☐	Hjaalmarch	Morthal	Moorside Inn	Jonna
☐	The Pale	Dawnstar	Windpeak Inn	Thoring
☐	The Pale	Nightgate Inn	Nightgate Inn (Interior)	Hadring
☐	Winterhold	Winterhold	The Frozen Hearth	Dagur
☐	The Reach	Markarth	Silver-Blood Inn	Kleppr
☐	The Reach	Old Hroldan Old Hroldan Inn	Eydis	Hulda
☐	Whiterun	Whiterun	The Bannered Mare	Hulda
☐	Whiterun	Rorikstead	Frostfruit Inn	Mralki
☐	Whiterun	Riverwood	Sleeping Giant Inn	Orgnar
☐	Eastmarch	Windhelm	Candlehearth Hall	Elda Early-Dawn
☐	Eastmarch	Windhelm	New Gnisis Cornerclub	Ambarys Rendar
☐	Eastmarch	Kynesgrove	The Braidwood Inn	Iddra
☐	Falkreath	Falkreath	Dead Man's Drink	Valga Vinicia
☐	The Rift	Riften	The Bee and Barb	Keerava
☐	The Rift	Ivarstead	Vilemyr Inn	Wilhem
☐	Solstheim	Raven Rock	The Retching Netch	Geldis Sadri

BOUNTY QUESTS

✓	QUEST NAME	PREREQUISITES	QUEST DESCRIPTION	TARGET OR LOCATION	REWARD*
☐	Bounty: Bandits*	None	Slay the leader of a bandit camp	Bandit leader, [a random bandit camp]	Leveled Gold
☐	Bounty: Forsworn*	None	Slay the leader of a Forsworn camp	Forsworn Briarheart, [a random Forsworn camp]	Leveled Gold
☐	Bounty: Giant*	Level 20	Slay a giant	[A random giant]	Leveled Gold
☐	Bounty: Dragon*	Level 10, Main Quest: Dragon Rising completed	Slay a dragon	[A random dragon]	Leveled Gold

NOTE * Rewards are given by the Hold's Jarl or Steward.

Four Shield Tavern, in Dragon Bridge.

Candlehearth Hall, in Windhelm.

Dead Man's Drink, in Falkreath.

MISCELLANEOUS OBJECTIVES: HAAFINGAR HOLD

Objectives: Dragon Bridge

✓	QUEST NAME	PREREQUISITES	QUEST GIVER	LOCATION	QUEST DESCRIPTION	TARGET OR LOCATION	REWARD
☐	Dragon's Breath Mead*	None	Olda	Horgeir's House	Retrieve the Dragon's Breath Mead from her drunk husband's stash	Dragon's Breath Mead, small cave overhang west of Dragon Bridge	Leveled Gold

Objectives: Solitude

✓	QUEST NAME	PREREQUISITES	QUEST GIVER	LOCATION	QUEST DESCRIPTION	TARGET OR LOCATION	REWARD
☐	No News is Good News *	None	Angeline Morrard	Angeline's Aromatics	Angeline hopes to know whether her daughter is safe. Ask, persuade, or intimidate Captain Aldis to learn that she died during an attack.	Captain Aldis, in or around Castle Dour courtyard.	None
☐	Fit for a Jarl *	None	Taarie	Radiant Raiment (or streets of Solitude)	Speak to Taarie and agree to wear an outfit while speaking to Jarl Elisif. Put on the Radiant Raiment Fine Clothes, and ask the Jarl what she thinks of your outfit. She agrees to purchase some dresses. Return to Taarie for your reward.	Radiant Raiment	Fine Clothes, Leveled Gold
☐	Return to Grace*	None	Svari	Streets of Solitude	Svari wants to convince her mother Greta to return to the Temple of the Divines. After speaking to Greta retrieve an amulet of Talos from the body of her brother Roggvir. Return to Greta with the Amulet for your reward.	Roggvir's Body (Executioner's Platform or Hall of the Dead)	Leveled Gold
☐	Delivery*	None	Sorex	Winking Skeever (or Streets of Solitude)	Sorex asks you to deliver Stros M'Kai Rum to Falk Firebeard. Deliver the rum directly to Falk in the Blue Palace and get your reward.	Leveled Gold	
☐	Spiced Wine Shipment*	None	Evette San	Market stalls	Evette is hoping that Vittoria Vici will release her Spiced Wine shipment. Persuade or bribe Vittoria Vici at the East Empire Company Warehouse to release the shipment, then return to Evette for the reward.	Vittoria Vici	2 Spiced Wine
☐	Elisif's Tribute*	Side Quest: The Man Who Cried Wolf	Elisif	Blue Palace	Elisif wants you to place Torygg's War Horn on a shrine of Talos as a tribute to her late husband. Take the War Horn to the specifed Shrine and place it at the foot of the statue of Talos, then return to Elisif for your reward.	Shrine of Talos: White River Valley [6.T]	Ability to Purchase Proudspire Manor

MISCELLANEOUS OBJECTIVES: HJAALMARCH HOLD

Objectives: Morthal

✓	QUEST NAME	PREREQUISITES	QUEST GIVER	LOCATION	QUEST DESCRIPTION	TARGET OR LOCATION	REWARD
☐	Falion's Nocturnal Habits*	None	Falion	Summoning Plinth, in the Marshes	Follow Falion northwest out of town during the night. He walks to a summoning circle to practice magic.	Falion; blackmail him, keep his secret, tell the Jarl, or blackmail and then tell the Jarl. You can uncover his activity, which he wants to keep quiet.	200 gold pieces (for blackmail only)
☐	Gorm's Letter*	Visit Moorside Inn in the evening	Gorm	Moorside Inn	Deliver his letter to Captain Aldis, as Gorm is concerned about Idgrod's ability to perform her duties as Jarl.	Captain Aldis, in Solitude (Castle Dour courtyard). Hand the message to the Captain	20 gold pieces

Objectives: Stonehills

✓	QUEST NAME	PREREQUISITES	QUEST GIVER	LOCATION	QUEST DESCRIPTION	TARGET OR LOCATION	REWARD
☐	Slow Shipments to Bryling*	None	Pactur	Rockwallow Mine	Bryling grows impatient regarding shipments from the mine. Speak to her on behalf of Pactur	Thane Bryling, near or in the Blue Palace of Solitude. Tell her the shipment is coming; there is no need to return to Pactur	Leveled Gold

MISCELLANEOUS OBJECTIVES: THE PALE

Objectives: Dawnstar

✓	QUEST NAME	PREREQUISITES	QUEST GIVER	LOCATION	QUEST DESCRIPTION	TARGET OR LOCATION	REWARD
☐	Salt of the Seas*	None	Captain Leif Wayfinder	Dawnstar (docked ship)	Wayfinder will pay gold for some special (and essential) Fine-Cut Void Salts.	Fine-Cut Void Salts, in a [random dungeon]	Leveled Gold

MISCELLANEOUS OBJECTIVES: WINTERHOLD

Objectives: Ahkari's Caravan

✓	QUEST NAME	PREREQUISITES	QUEST GIVER	LOCATION	QUEST DESCRIPTION	TARGET OR LOCATION	REWARD
☐	New Moon*	None	Kharjo	Ahkari's Caravan (see [10.00] Caravans, in the Atlas for the route, on page 980)	Kharjo hopes you'll retrieve the Amulet of the Moon for him	Find and give the Amulet of the Moon, from [a random dungeon]	Leveled Gold

Objectives: College of Winterhold

✓	QUEST NAME	PREREQUISITES	QUEST GIVER	LOCATION	QUEST DESCRIPTION	TARGET OR LOCATION	REWARD
☐	Lost Apprentices: Borvir*	Listen to Phinis' Lecture	Phinis Gestor	College of Winterhold	A number of apprentices have gone missing. Phinis is worried; find information on them.	Journeyman's Nook [4.26]	Leveled gold (for all four)
☐	Lost Apprentices: Ilas-tei*	Listen to Phinis' Lecture	Phinis Gestor	College of Winterhold	A number of apprentices have gone missing. Phinis is worried; find information on them.	Shrine of Talos: Ilas-tei's Last Stand [4.J]	Leveled gold (for all four)
☐	Lost Apprentices: Rundi*	Listen to Phinis' Lecture	Phinis Gestor	College of Winterhold	A number of apprentices have gone missing. Phinis is worried; find information on them.	Rundi's Mistake [4.N]	Leveled gold (for all four)
☐	Lost Apprentices: Yisra*	Listen to Phinis' Lecture	Phinis Gestor	College of Winterhold	A number of apprentices have gone missing. Phinis is worried; find information on them.	Yisra's Beachside Combustion [4.D]	Leveled gold (for all four)

Objectives: Winterhold

✓	QUEST NAME	PREREQUISITES	QUEST GIVER	LOCATION	QUEST DESCRIPTION	TARGET OR LOCATION	REWARD
☐	Finding Isabelle	Favor: A Good Talking To (Winterhold)	Dagur, Ranmir, then Haran	The Frozen Hearth	Complete Haran's Favor, then speak with Dagur, and then Haran. You learn why Ranmir is a drunk; he believes the love of his life ran off with some man named "Vex" from Riften. Visit the Ragged Flagon in Riften to find out Vex isn't male, and Isabelle wasn't unfaithful. Vex directs you to Hob's Fall Cave. Head there, find Isabelle's body, with a note for Ranmir. Return the note to him.	Isabelle Rolaine, Hob's Fall Cave	None

MISCELLANEOUS OBJECTIVES: THE REACH

Objectives: Dushnikh Yal

✓	QUEST NAME	PREREQUISITES	QUEST GIVER	LOCATION	QUEST DESCRIPTION	TARGET OR LOCATION	REWARD
☐	The Sword of Gharol	Orc or Complete Side Quest: The Forgemaster's Fingers	Gharol	Dushnikh Yal	Deliver Gharol's sword to her daughter Lash gra-Dushnikh	Deliver the Iron Sword to Lash, in Karthwasten	Leveled Gold

Objectives: Karthwasten

✓	QUEST NAME	PREREQUISITES	QUEST GIVER	LOCATION	QUEST DESCRIPTION	TARGET OR LOCATION	REWARD
☐	Sauranach's Mine!: Helping Atar*	None	Atar or Ainethach	Sauranach Mine/ Blacksmith's near Karthwasten Hall	Speak to Atar, who is being paid by Silver-Bloods to plunder this mine and tie up who owns it	Ainethach; persuade, bribe, or intimidate him into handing the deeds over, then report back to Atar	Leveled Gold
☐	Sauranach's Mine!: Helping Ainethach*	None	Atar or Ainethach	Blacksmith's near Karthwasten Hall/ Sauranach Mine	Speak to Ainethach, whose mine is being plundered by Silver-Bloods, and agree to force out the mercenaries and Atar	Atar; persuade, bribe, or attack them until they leave, then report back to Ainethach	Leveled Gold

Objectives: Kolskeggr Mine

✓	QUEST NAME	PREREQUISITES	QUEST GIVER	LOCATION	QUEST DESCRIPTION	TARGET OR LOCATION	REWARD
☐	Kolskeggr Clear Out*	None	Pavo	Left Hand Mine (Primary Location near Markarth)	Speak to Pavo at Left Hand Mine, where he fled. Forsworn have taken over his mine, Kolskeggr. Remove them.	Clear around five Forsworn from inside the mine (before or after speaking to Pavo)	Leveled Gold (and any scavenged gold from the mine)

Objectives: Markarth

✓	QUEST NAME	PREREQUISITES	QUEST GIVER	LOCATION	QUEST DESCRIPTION	TARGET OR LOCATION	REWARD
☐	Calcelmo's Ring*	None	Kerah	Market stall (close to Silver-Blood Inn)	Calcelmo requires a ring, and Kerah doesn't have time to deliver it. Will you?	Take Calcelmo's Ring into Understone Keep; Calcelmo rewards you	Leveled Gold
☐	Dibella's Shine*	None	Lisbet	Arnleif and Sons Trading Company	You're asked to retrieve a statue of Dibella taken by the Forsworn, to keep the store in business	Lisbet's Dibella Statue [a random Forsworn camp]	Leveled Gold
☐	The Steward's Potion*	None	Bothela	The Hag's Cure	Speak to Bothela about the name of her shop. She asks you to deliver a potion to the Steward Raerek, for his "stamina."	Give Stallion's Potion to Raerek	Leveled Gold
☐	The Last Scabbard*	None	Ghorza gra-Bagol	Markarth Blacksmiths Forge	Ghorza is looking for a long-forgotten Smithing book. Find one for her.	The Last Scabbard of Akrash, in the Fort Sungard Muster (though any copy will do)	+1 Smithing (from reading the book), +1 Smithing (from Ghorza after handing her the book)
☐	Triumph Over Talos*	None	Ondolemar	Understone Keep	The Thalmor advisor believes one of the population is secretly (and illegally) worshipping Talos. You're to find proof.	Ogmund's House (Novice), steal the Amulet of Talos inside, and bring it to Ondolemar	Leveled Gold
☐	The Heart of the Matter*	None	Moth gro-Bagol	Understone Keep Forge	Ask Moth about his armor, and he requests you find him a Daedra Heart. Return with one to receive one of his best pieces of armor	Daedra Heart	Leveled Armor Piece
☐	Neutralizing Nimhe*	Speak to Calcelmo about the excavation	Calcelmo	Understone Keep	A giant Frostbite Spider named Nimhe is troubling the excavation workers. Calcelmo agrees to let you into his museum if you kill the beast.	Use the Key to Nchuand-Zel, enter the excavation site, find and kill Nimhe, and report back.	Dwemer Museum Key

Objectives: Old Hroldan

✓	QUEST NAME	PREREQUISITES	QUEST GIVER	LOCATION	QUEST DESCRIPTION	TARGET OR LOCATION	REWARD
☐	The Ghost of Old Hroldan*	None	Eydis/Ghost of Old Hrolden	Old Hroldan	Head into Old Hroldan Inn, speak to Eydis the barkeep, and pay to sleep in Tiber Septim's room. You wake to screaming. Eydis mentions a Ghost of Old Hroldan that has appeared. Talk to him, and he mentions his old friend Hjalti, and his sword. Agree to bring him the sword. Speak to Eydis again for the location. Visit it, retrieve the sword, and return it; the ghost vanishes.	Hjalti's Sword, in [a random dungeon]	+1 One-Handed and +1 Block Skill

Objectives: Salvius Farm

✓	QUEST NAME	PREREQUISITES	QUEST GIVER	LOCATION	QUEST DESCRIPTION	TARGET OR LOCATION	REWARD
☐	Letter to Leonitus*	None	Rogatus Salvius	Salvius Farm	Rogatus has a letter he wants delivered to his son	Bring it to Leonitus Salvius at Old Hroldan	Leveled Gold

Objectives: Soljund's Sinkhole

✓	QUEST NAME	PREREQUISITES	QUEST GIVER	LOCATION	QUEST DESCRIPTION	TARGET OR LOCATION	REWARD
☐	Making It Hole Again*	None	Perth	Entrance to Sinkhole Mine	Perth tunneled into a Nordic crypt, and the mine is overrun by Draugr. Clear them out.	Defeat 10 Draugr and a high-level leader in the mine and crypt, then report back to Perth.	Leveled gold

MISCELLANEOUS OBJECTIVES: WHITERUN HOLD

Objectives: Rorikstead

✓	QUEST NAME	PREREQUISITES	QUEST GIVER	LOCATION	QUEST DESCRIPTION	TARGET OR LOCATION	REWARD
☐	Erik the Slayer	None	Erik	In the fields around town	Erik wants to live a life of an adventurer, but his father will not allow it. Speak to Mralki at the Frostfruit Inn; use Persuasion, Bribery, or Intimidation to approve of his son's new career.	Rorikstead	Leave town, then return. Erik the Slayer will be available as a hireling in the Frostfruit Inn.

Objectives: Riverwood

✓	QUEST NAME	PREREQUISITES	QUEST GIVER	LOCATION	QUEST DESCRIPTION AND TARGET/LOCATION	REWARD
☐	The Love Triangle: Helping Sven*	None	Sven	Riverwood	Talk to Sven. Ask him about Faendal. Take the fake letter from Faendal to Camilla and say it's from Faendal. Return to Sven.	25 gold pieces, Sven: Follower
☐	The Love Triangle: Betraying Sven*	None	Sven	Riverwood	Talk to Sven. Ask him about Faendal. Take the fake letter from Sven to Faendal. Tell him about Sven, and he hands you his own fake letter. Take the second letter to Camilla. Say it's from Sven. Return to Sven	25 gold pieces, Faendal: Follower
☐	The Love Triangle: Helping Faendal*	None	Faendal	Riverwood	Talk to Faendal. Ask him about Sven. Take the fake letter from Sven to Camilla and say it's from Sven. Return to Faendal.	25 gold pieces, Faendal: Follower
☐	The Love Triangle: Betraying Faendal*	None	Faendal	Riverwood	Talk to Faendal. Ask him about Sven. Take the fake letter from Faendal to Sven. Tell him about Faendal, and he hands you his own fake letter. Take the letter to Camilla. Say it's from Faendal. Return to Sven	25 gold pieces, Sven: Follower

NOTE During any of these plans, you can tell Camilla the truth or lie to her, depending on who you wish to side with.

Objectives: Whiterun

✓	QUEST NAME	PREREQUISITES	QUEST GIVER	LOCATION	QUEST DESCRIPTION	TARGET AND/OR LOCATION	REWARD
☐	Bullying Braith*	Between 8 a.m. and 8 p.m.	Lars Battle-Born	On the streets of Whiterun	Lars is fed up being bullied by Braith. Stop her bullying him	Braith; any threat succeeds	2 gold pieces (from Lars, even if you don't complete the Quest)
☐	Argonian Ale Extraction*	None	Brenuin	On the streets of Whiterun	Brenuin the beggar longs for the taste of Argonian Ale. Can you steal some for him?	The Bannered Mare	Potion of Vigorous Healing
☐	Greatsword for a Great Man*	None	Adrianne Avenicci	Warmaiden's Blacksmiths	Adrianne is busy, but has finished a sword for the Jarl. Can you take it to her father?	Proventus Avenicci, in Dragonsreach. Hand over Balgruuf's Greatsword to him for the reward	20 gold pieces
☐	Andurs' Arkay Amulet*	None	Anders, Priest of Arkay	Hall of the Dead	Anders has mislaid his Amulet, and hopes you can retrieve it from the crypt.	Hall of the Dead. Kill three Skeletons. Return with Amulet of Arkay	15 gold pieces
☐	Salt for Arcadia*	None	Farengar	Dragonsreach	Farengar asks you to deliver some Frost Salts to Arcadia, in Arcadia's Cauldron.	Arcadia, in Arcadia's Cauldron. See Ingredients locations, on page 147	Potion of Brief Invisibility, Potion of Enhanced Stamina, Potion of Illusion

MISCELLANEOUS OBJECTIVES: EASTMARCH HOLD

Objectives: Snapleg Cave/Darkwater Pass

✓	QUEST NAME	PREREQUISITES	QUEST GIVER	LOCATION	QUEST DESCRIPTION	TARGET OR LOCATION	REWARD
☐	Extracting an Argonian	None	Derkeethus	Darkwater Pass (Interior)	An Argonian named Derkeethus is trapped inside a Falmer Hive and needs rescuing.	Snapleg Cave/Darkwater Pass; open the wall section in the northeast corner in the grating room with Derkeethus below you. Open his gate (Expert) using the Darkwater Pit Key found in a jar, then escort Derkeethus to safety.	Follower: Derkeethus (and his friendship)

Objectives: Kynesgrove

✓	QUEST NAME	PREREQUISITES	QUEST GIVER	LOCATION	QUEST DESCRIPTION	TARGET OR LOCATION	REWARD
☐	Salt for the Stoneweaver*	None	Dravynea the Stoneweaver	Kynesgrove (around town)	Dravynea requires you to bring her some Frost Salts	See Ingredients Locations, on page 147	+1 Alteration skill

Objectives: Windhelm

✓	QUEST NAME	PREREQUISITES	QUEST GIVER	LOCATION	QUEST DESCRIPTION	TARGET OR LOCATION	REWARD
	Crew Cut*	None	Kjar	Windhelm docks (large docked ship)	Captain Kjar will pay handsomely if you slay an ex-crew mate who has been troubling him.	Bandit leader and bandits, in [a random bandit camp]	Leveled Gold
	Nightshade for the Unliving*	None	Hillevi Cruel-Sea	Stone Quarter Market Place	Hillevi hopes you'll have time to deliver Nightshade Extract to Wuunferth	Wuunferth the Unliving, in the Palace of the Kings (Upstairs)	100 gold pieces
	Malborn's Long Shadow*	Complete Main Quest: Diplomatic Immunity (Malborn survives)	Malborn	Gnisis Corner Club	Malborn (and Brelas, if she survived) heads here but is worried that a Khajiit Thalmor assassin is stalking him. Help him escape Windhelm.	Speak to the caravaneers who visit Windhelm until they tell you the name of the assassin: J'Datharr. You must kill J'Datharr. Then report back to Malborn	Leveled Gold

MISCELLANEOUS OBJECTIVES: FALKREATH HOLD

Objectives: Falkreath

✓	QUEST NAME	PREREQUISITES	QUEST GIVER	LOCATION	QUEST DESCRIPTION	TARGET OR LOCATION	REWARD
	Once a Thalmor...*	None	Runil	Falkreath graveyard (or around town)	Speak to Runil, then retrieve his journal and return it to him for your reward.	A [random dungeon]	Leveled gold reward
	Vighar the Vampire*	Complete: Favor: A Little Light Thievery*	Dengeir of Stuhn	Falkreath (Dengeir's Hall)	Kill Vighar's ancestor, a powerful vampire.	[A random vampire lair]	Medium amount of gold

MISCELLANEOUS OBJECTIVES: THE RIFT

Objectives: Heartwood Mill

✓	QUEST NAME	PREREQUISITES	QUEST GIVER	LOCATION	QUEST DESCRIPTION	TARGET OR LOCATION	REWARD
	Fight or Flight*	None	Grosta	Heartwood Mill	Grosta's good-for-nothing husband has gone missing. Find that layabout.	Nord corpse, inside Broken Helm Hollow	Leveled enchanted weapon

Objectives: Ivarstead

✓	QUEST NAME	PREREQUISITES	QUEST GIVER	LOCATION	QUEST DESCRIPTION	TARGET OR LOCATION	REWARD
	The Straw That Broke*	None	Narfi	Abandoned building (west of river), Vilemyr Inn	Speak to Narfi about his vanished sister, then ask Wilhelm about Narfi. Begin the search for her.	Reyda's satchel, in the river just southeast of town, then bring Reyda's Necklace to Narfi	Three [random] rare ingredients
	Grin and Bear It*	None	Temba Wide-Arm	Lumber Mill	Temba is constantly fending off bear attacks. Perhaps you can thin the herd out?	Hunt 10 bears and skin them for pelts or buy the pelts (anywhere in Skyrim, of any bear type: Snow, Cave, or normal), and return them to her	Leveled Enchanted War Axe
	Climb the Steps*	None	Kimmek	Kimmek's House or around town	Kimmek delivers supplies to the Greybeards, but his knees can't take the climb.	Drop (via inventory) Kimmek's supplies into the offering chest at High Hrothgar	Leveled Gold

Objectives: Merryfair Farm

✓	QUEST NAME	PREREQUISITES	QUEST GIVER	LOCATION	QUEST DESCRIPTION	TARGET OR LOCATION	REWARD
	Bow to the Master*	None	Dravin Llanith	Merryfair Farm	Dravin's Bow has been stolen, and he wishes it returned.	Dravin's Bow, in a locked treasure chest in the Ratway Warrens, under Riften. Return the bow to him.	Leveled Gems (5)

Objectives: Riften

✓	QUEST NAME	PREREQUISITES	QUEST GIVER	LOCATION	QUEST DESCRIPTION	TARGET OR LOCATION	REWARD
	The Lover's Requital*	None	Sibbi Black-Briar	Mistveil Keep (Riften Jail)	Discover Svidi's whereabouts	Lynly Star-Sung (pseudonym of Svidi; bard in Vilemyr Inn, in Ivarstead) Speak to her, return to Sibbi, and lie or tell her the truth regarding where she is (the reward is the same)	Sibbi's Chest Key (opens the chest in the Black-Briar Meadery)
	Under the Table*	None	Romlyn Dreth	Black-Briar Meadery	Deliver smuggled Black-Briar Keg, or turn Romlyn in	Wilhelm; innkeeper in Vilemyr Inn in Ivarstead, or Overseer Indaryn, at the Meadery	Gem or jewelry reward. Not repeatable.

✓	QUEST NAME	PREREQUISITES	QUEST GIVER	LOCATION	QUEST DESCRIPTION	TARGET OR LOCATION	REWARD
☐	Few and Far Between*	None	Ingun Black-Briar	Elgrim's Elixirs (wait for her to appear)	Collect 20 Deathbell, 20 Nightshade, and 20 Nirnroot for her experiments, then return to her	See Ingredients Locations, on page 146	Access to Ingun's Alchemy chest inside Elgrim's Elixirs
☐	Spread the Love*	Complete Temple Quest: The Book of Love	Dinya Balu	Temple of Mara	Deliver the "Warmth of Mara"; pamphlets praising the teachings of Mara	At least 20 citizens of Riften	Leveled Health Restore potion (5)
☐	Sealing the Deal*	None	Talen-Jei	The Bee and Barb	Talen-Jei wishes to show his love for Keerava by having a ring made with stones used in traditional Argonian wedding rings.	Three Flawless Amethysts	Leveled [Random] Potion
☐	Ice Cold*	None	Marise Aravel	Marketplace (cart next to the Bee and Barb)	Marise uses ground Ice Wraith Teeth to keep her foods fresh. She needs more.	Five Ice Wraith Teeth	Leveled Spell Tome and (delicious) Raw Pheasant
☐	Distant Memories*	None	Brand-Shei	Marketplace (Brand-Shei's stall)	Brand-Shei is hoping to recover memories of his past.	Lymdrenn Telvanni's Journal, in a waterlogged chest, in the Wreck of the Pride of Tel Vos	Brand-Shei's Strongbox Key (unlocks the strongbox inside his stall)
☐	Grimsever's Return*	None	Mjoll the Lioness	Marketplace, or around Riften	Mjoll laments the loss of her weapon, a fine longsword named "Grimsever"	Grimsever, in Mzinchaleft	Keep the weapon, or return it and have Mjoll as a Follower
☐	Stoking the Flames*	None	Balimund Iron-Boar	Scorched Hammer Blacksmiths	Balimund keeps his forge red-hot thanks to Fire Salts, but he's running low.	10 Fire Salts; see Ingredients Locations, on page 147	Leveled Gold
☐	Caught Red-Handed*	None	Svana Far-Shield	Haelga's Bunkhouse	Svana is angry at Haelga's promiscuous ways and wants you to retrieve three Marks of Dibella from her conquests	Bolli; at the Fishery. Hofgrir Horse-Crusher; at the stables. Overseer Indaryn; at Black-Briar Meadery, but all like to drink at the Bee and Barb. Use Persuasion, Intimidation, or Pickpocketing	Leveled Enchanted Heavy Armor (piece)
☐	Pilgrimage*	None	Alessandra	Hall of the Dead	Riften's Priest of Arkay has never made peace with her dead father. You are to make a pilgrimage for her	Hand Alessandra's Dagger to Andurs, inside Whiterun's Hall of the Dead, then return to her	Leveled Restoration Spell Tome
☐	Hunt and Gather*	None	Wylandriah	Mistveil Keep	Riften's Court Wizard, an eccentric crackpot, has mislaid some of her experimental gear. Collect them all.	Wylandriah's Spoon: Fellstar Farm in Ivarstead. Wylandriah's Ingot: The Frozen Hearth in Winterhold. Wylandriah's Soul Gem: The White Phial in Windhelm	Leveled [Random] Scroll
☐	Special Delivery*	None	Bolli	Riften Fishery	Bolli wishes to make a deal on behalf of the Fishery to sell fish to Kleppr in Markarth	Hand the Purchase Agreement from Bolli to Kleppr at Silver-Blood Inn	Leveled Ingot (4)
☐	Bring It!*	None	Harrald	Mistveil Keep	The spoiled son of the Jarl is too lazy to retrieve his own sword. You're told to bring it back to him	Steel Sword, from Balimund at the Scorched Hammer	Leveled Gem (2)
☐	Truth Ore Consequences*	None	Hafjorg	Elgrim's Elixirs	Hafjorg asks you to pick up an ore sample from Filnjar in Shor's Stone so it can be examined	Quicksilver Ore, from Filnjar	Leveled Skill Potions (a few; random)
☐	Ringmaker*	None	Madesi	Marketplace	Riften's jeweler has a short list of items needed to continue creating his exquisite Argonian-made jewelry	Gold Ore (1), Mammoth Tusk (1), Flawless Sapphire (2)	Leveled Jewelry
☐	Bloody Nose*	100 gold pieces	Hofgrir Horse-Crusher	Riften Stables	Hofgrir challenges you to a fistfight to test your mettle	Beat Hofgrir in a brawl (only use fists!)	200 gold pieces (100 of which was yours when betting)
☐	Toying with the Dead*	None	Vekel the Man	Ragged Flagon (Riften)	Vekel has found a buyer for a peculiar set of journals written by a long-dead necromancer. But he needs you to find them.	Arondil's Journals, Inside Yngvild (page 780)	Leveled Enchanted One-Handed Weapon
☐	Shardr and Sapphire*	None	Shadr	Around Riften	Sapphire (from the Thieves Guild) has bilked Shadr by lending him money to buy a shipment of goods that she also robbed, and she still wants the money!	(1) Pay off the debt in Shadr's stead, using Persuade or Intimidate against Sapphire. (2) Cut yourself into the deal with Sapphire if you're a member of the Thieves Guild, before returning to tell Shadr there's nothing you can do. (3) Threaten Sapphire to tell Brynjolf and she drops the debt. (4) If you're a Thieves Guild leader, choose plan 1 without any Persuasion or Intimidation, or plan 2.	Helping Shardr: Leveled Invisibility Potion. Helping Sapphire: Leveled Gold

✓	QUEST NAME	PREREQUISITES	QUEST GIVER	LOCATION	QUEST DESCRIPTION	TARGET OR LOCATION	REWARD
	Jarl's Quest Part 1: Helping Hand*	Potion of Minor Healing	Wujeeta	Riften Fishery	The Argonian is sick from a Skooma overdose, and pleads for a Healing potion to cleanse her system	Hand her a Healing potion (minor or otherwise)	Silver Amethyst Ring
	Jarl's Quest Part 2: The Raid*	Complete Jarl's Quest Part 1	Wujeeta, Jarl Laila	Riften Fishery/ Mistveil Keep	Speak to Wujeeta, and use Persuasion, Bribery, or Intimidation to find out about the Skooma dealer. Then speak to Jarl Laila Law-Giver in Mistveil Keep.	Riften Warehouse: Head to the Warehouse and slay Orini Dral and Sarthis Idren. Search Sarthis for his key to open the cellar door. Steal the Shipment's Ready note from his satchel.	None
	Jarl's Quest Part 3: Supply and Demand*	Complete Jarl's Quest Part 2	Jarl Laila	Mistveil Keep	Report the Skooma manufacturing operation to the Jarl, who sends you to kill the Dark Elves at Cragslane Cavern.	Wipe out everyone there (wolf kills are optional), then return to the Jarl.	Leveled Enchanted Weapon
	Erasing Vald's Debt*	Thieves Guild Quest: The Pursuit is active (and hasn't been completed)	Maven Black-Briar	The Bee and Barb/Black-Briar Manor	Speak to Maven once you wish to remove Vald's debt.	She needs you to locate the Quill of Germination Vald failed to retrieve. The Quill is in a strongbox beneath a small island, in Lake Honrich	Document absolving Vald of his debt (see quest for details)
	Gissur's Revenge*	Main Quest: A Cornered Rat is active	No one	The Ratway/ Ragged Flagon	If Gissur is alive at the end of Main Quest: Diplomatic Immunity, he may be spotted in the Ragged Flagon. Slay him or leave him alone. He eavesdrops if you speak to Dirge or Vekel. You can (sneak and) follow him into the Ratway, listening to Gissur telling Thalmor troops where you are. Attack or hide.	Gissur, the Ratway/Ragged Flagon	None
	Shavari the Assassin*	Main Quest: A Cornered Rat is active	No one	The Ratway/ Ratway Warrens	A Khajiit named Shavari is dispatched by Elenwen at the Thalmor Embassy to assassinate you. Kill her if you encounter her, or be killed.	Shavari, the Ratway	Note, signed by "E"

Objectives: Sarethi Farm

✓	QUEST NAME	PREREQUISITES	QUEST GIVER	LOCATION	QUEST DESCRIPTION	TARGET OR LOCATION	REWARD
	Smooth Jazbay*	None	Avrusa Sarethi	Sarethi Farm	Avrusa is a keen cultivator of Nirnroot but requires some ingredients for her farm.	Find 20 Jazbay Grapes; see Ingredients Locations, on page 148	Leveled Potions (a few, random)

Objectives: Shor's Stone

✓	QUEST NAME	PREREQUISITES	QUEST GIVER	LOCATION	QUEST DESCRIPTION	TARGET OR LOCATION	REWARD
	Mine or Yours*	None	Filnjar	Blacksmith's Forge	The Redbelly Mine is no longer in operation due to a Frostbite Spider infestation. Kill them for Filnjar	Redbelly Mine; kill six Frostbite Spiders, then return to Filnjar	Leveled Gold
	Letters for Mr. Rock-Chucker*	None	Sylgja	Sylgja's House	Sylgja asks if you'll mind delivering a satchel of letters to her parents	Take Sylgja's Satchel to Verner Rock-Chucker in Darkwater Crossing; bring Verner's Satchel back to her afterward	Leveled jewelry

FAVORS

Favors are miscellaneous objectives or small activities that you can find throughout Skyrim. Favors are controlled by the game's Radiant Story system, which uses a variety of factors to determine when to start a given quest. This means that not all Favors will be available at all times; in particular, you can only be on one Favor of each type at a time. For example, if you start one Rare Item Hunt, you must finish it before beginning another.

This section details all of the available Favors you can attempt during your exploration of Skyrim. Note that each of these increases your Relationship with the citizen you're doing the Favor for, which is important for your standing within a particular city. If the citizen isn't a resident of the city, then you perform the Favor simply to accrue a reward, to pass the time, or to be a pleasant person. This chapter is segmented into three parts:

Part 1—Activity Favors: Deals with manual labor you can do to earn an honest pay. Which you can then share with beggars if you wish.

Part 2—Favors for Citizens: Lists every resident in Skyrim who has a job for you to do if you speak to them.

Part 3—Thane Tasks: Reveals how to become a Thane (or a land-owning, respected resident) of each particular Hold, and the house you can purchase.

PART 1: ACTIVITY FAVORS

Favor (Activity): Chopping Wood*

NOTE * Quest names marked with this symbol do not appear in your Quest Menu list, although objectives may.

Visit one of the following locations and speak to the person specified (usually a lumbermill owner) in the table below. They will gladly pay for any firewood you chop. Find a Woodcutter's Axe (there should be one near the woodpile at this location), find a pile of wood, and continue to chop, before heading to the person for a reward.

- **Woodcutter's Axe**
- **Five gold pieces per piece of firewood chopped**

✓	HOLD	LOCATION	FIREWOOD PURCHASER
☐	Haafingar	Dragon Bridge	Horgeir
☐	Haafingar	Solitude Sawmill	Hjorunn
☐	Hjaalmarch	Morthal	Hroggar
☐	Hjaalmarch	Morthal	Jorgen
☐	The Pale	Anga's Mill	Aeri
☐	Eastmarch	Mixwater Mill	Gilfre
☐	Eastmarch	Kynesgrove	Ganna Uriel
☐	Whiterun	Riverwood	Hod
☐	Whiterun	Whiterun (The Bannered Mare)	Hulda
☐	Falkreath	Half-Moon Mill	Hert
☐	The Rift	Heartwood Mill	Grosta
☐	The Rift	Ivarstead	Temba Wide-Arm

Favor (Activity): Mining Ore*

Head to one of the following locations, and converse with the character specified (usually a mine owner) in the table below. They are happy to pay for any ore you mine. Find a Pickaxe (there should be a few inside any of the mines you visit) and locate a vein within the mine. Strike it, gather the ore, and head to the person for a reward.

- **Pickaxe**
- **25 gold pieces per Silver ore**
- **25 gold pieces per Quicksilver ore**
- **20 gold pieces per Orichalcum ore**
- **30 gold pieces per Moonstone ore**
- **30 gold pieces per Malachite ore**
- **7 gold pieces per Iron ore**
- **50 gold pieces per Gold ore**
- **60 gold pieces per Ebony ore**
- **20 gold pieces per Corundum ore**

✓	HOLD	LOCATION	ORE PURCHASER	ORE TYPE
☐	Hjaalmarch	Stonehills	Gestur Rockbreaker	Iron
☐	The Pale	Dawnstar	Beitild	Iron
☐	The Pale	Dawnstar	Leigelf	Quicksilver
☐	Winterhold	Whistling Mine	Thorgar	Iron
☐	The Reach	Dushnikh Yal	Gharol	Orichalcum
☐	The Reach	Left Hand Mine	Skaggi Scar-Face	Iron
☐	The Reach	Mor Khazgur	Shuftharz	Orichalcum
☐	Eastmarch	Darkwater Crossing	Verner Rock-Chucker	Corundum
☐	Eastmarch	Kynesgrove	Kjeld	Malachite
☐	Eastmarch	Narzulbur	Dushnamub	Ebony
☐	The Rift	Shor's Stone	Grogmar gro-Burzag	Iron

Favor (Activity): Harvesting Crops*

Trek over to any of the following farms and strike up a conversation with the character mentioned in the table below. They are grateful and pay for any crops you wish to harvest (from their property or anywhere else). Note the exact crops the character wishes to purchase; only pick those if you want to be paid for your labor, as there are usually more than these crop types in the locations.

- Five gold pieces per Wheat
- One gold piece per Potato
- One gold piece per Leek
- Two gold pieces per Cabbage
- One gold pieces per Gourd
- Ten gold pieces per Nirnroot

✓	HOLD	LOCATION	CROP PURCHASER	CROP TYPE
☐	Haafingar	Katla's Farm	Katla	Wheat, Potato, Leek
☐	The Reach	Salvius Farm	Vigdis Salvius	Potato
☐	Falkreath	Falkreath	Mathies	Cabbage, Gourd, Potato
☐	Whiterun	Rorikstead	Reldith	Wheat, Cabbage, Potato
☐	Whiterun	Rorikstead	Lemkil	Cabbage, Potato, Wheat
☐	The Rift	Ivarstead	Boti	Cabbage, Potato, Wheat
☐	Whiterun	Battle-Born Farm	Alfhild Battle-Born	Wheat, Leek, Gourds
☐	Eastmarch	Brandy-Mug Farm	Bolfrida Brandy-Mug	Wheat
☐	Eastmarch	Hlaalu Farm	Adisla , Belyn Hlaalu	Wheat
☐	Eastmarch	Hollyfrost Farm	Tulvur	Wheat
☐	Haafingar	Dragon Bridge	Azzada Lylvieve	Wheat, Cabbage, Potato
☐	The Rift	Sarethi Farm	Avrusa Sarethi	Potato, Nirnroot, Gourds
☐	The Rift	Snow-Shod Farm	Addvild	Wheat, Leek, Potato
☐	Whiterun	Pelagia Farm	Severio Pelagia	Cabbage, Potato
☐	The Rift	Merryfair Farm	Synda Llanith	Wheat, Cabbage, Gourd

Favor (Activity): A Drunk's Drink*

Mosey on over to your favorite inn or tavern, or the streets surrounding an inn, and you're likely to be accosted by a reasonably friendly drunk. If you purchase a drink for them, expect the rudiments of a dance (although it's more of a stagger) as your reward. The following drunks are particularly parched:

✓	HOLD	LOCATION	DRUNK
☐	Haafingar	Thalmor Embassy	Razelan‡
☐	The Pale	Dawnstar (Windpeak Inn)	Karl
☐	Winterhold	Winterhold (The Frozen Hearth)	Ranmir
☐	The Reach	Markarth (Silver-Blood Inn)	Cosnach
☐	The Reach	Markarth (Silver-Blood Inn)	Degaine
☐	Whiterun	Riverwood (Sleeping Giant Inn)	Embry
☐	Eastmarch	Windhelm	Torbjorn Shatter-Shield

NOTE ‡During Main Quest: Diplomatic Immunity only

Favor (Activity): The Gift of Charity*

Walk the streets of any Hold City, and you may be approached by a tattered or downtrodden beggar. You can ignore them or give them a gold piece as charity. The beggars you can give to are listed below, and your thoughtfulness is duly rewarded.

- **The Gift of Charity:** +10 to Speech for one hour

✓	HOLD	LOCATION	BEGGAR
☐	The Ragged Flagon	Riften	Gissur‡
☐	The Rift	Riften	Snilf
☐	Eastmarch	Windhelm	Angrenor Once-Honored
☐	Eastmarch	Windhelm	Silda the Unseen
☐	Whiterun	Whiterun	Brenuin
☐	The Rift	Ivarstead	Narfi
☐	The Reach	Markarth	Degaine
☐	The Rift	Riften	Edda
☐	Haafingar	Solitude	Svari
☐	Haafingar	Solitude	Noster Eagle-Eye
☐	Haafingar	Solitude	Dervenin

NOTE ‡ After Main Quest: Diplomatic Immunity, assuming Gissur is still alive.

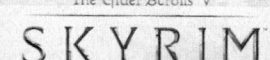

Favor: Special Delivery*

Visit the location specified, and converse with the Favor giver. They have an important item that needs to be delivered to someone in Skyrim. The recipient rewards you with a small amount of gold pieces. The following citizens of Skyrim have Delivery Favors for you:

➤ **Gold pieces (leveled, per delivery)**

✓	FAVOR GIVER	LOCATION FAVOR RECEIVED (HOLD/LOCATION NAME)	ITEM TO DELIVER	RECIPIENT	RECIPIENT LOCATION (HOLD/LOCATION NAME)
☐	Adonato Leotelli	Eastmarch/Windhelm (Candlehearth Hall)	Adonato's Book	Giraud Gemane	Haafingar/Solitude (Bard's College)
☐	Aeri	The Pale/Anga's Mill	Aeri's Note	Jarl Skald the Elder	The Pale/Dawnstar (The White Hall)
☐	Banning	The Reach/Markarth Stables	Spiced Beef	Voada	The Reach/Markarth (Understone Keep)
☐	Idgrod the Younger	Hjaalmarch/Morthal	Idgrod's Note	Danica Pure-Spring	Whiterun/Whiterun (Temple of Kynareth)
☐	Sondas Drenim	Eastmarch/Darkwater Crossing	Sondas's Note	Quintus Navale	Eastmarch/Windhelm (The White Phial)
☐	Thadgeir	Falkreath/Falkreath	Berit's Ashes	Runil	Falkreath/Falkreath (graveyard)

Favor: Sparring Partners*

If you think of yourself as an adventurer with lighting fists and a granite chin, you may wish to earn a swift 100 gold pieces by listening to the challenges of the following folk. They each have a reason for fighting you, and the combat is brawling only (just use fists, or risk enraging the entire settlement). Knock your opponent to their knees and win 100 gold pieces. Lose, and your adversary gains the gold.

➤ **100 gold pieces**

✓	PUGILIST	REASON FOR BRAWL	LOCATION (HOLD/LOCATION NAME)
☐	Benor	He's the strongest warrior and wants to prove it	Hjaalmarch/Morthal
☐	Burguk	A sparring partner is needed	The Reach/Dushnikh Yal
☐	Cosnach	To add excitement to his drunken day	The Reach/Markarth
☐	Larak	A sparring partner is needed	The Reach/Mor Khazgur
☐	Mauhulakh	A sparring partner is needed	Eastmarch/Narzulbur
☐	Rolff	You're an elf lover	Eastmarch/Windhelm
☐	Uthgerd	She's the strongest warrior and wants to prove it	Whiterun/Whiterun

Favor: A Good Talking To*

Locate the Favor giver and speak with them. It appears that they're having problems with a particular individual pestering, intimidating, or otherwise hassling them. Visit the instigator of this verbal assault, and attempt to sway them to the Favor giver's side. This is always achieved with a Persuasion, Bribe, Intimidation, or Brawl (fists only). After success with any of these, return to the Favor giver to receive a specific reward:

✓	FAVOR GIVER	LOCATION (HOLD/LOCATION NAME)	PROBLEM	INSTIGATOR	REWARD
☐	Carlotta Valentia	Whiterun/Whiterun (Bannered Mare)	Unwanted advances from a bard	Mikael	Small amount of gold
☐	Haran	Winterhold/Winterhold (The Frozen Hearth)	A significant tavern tab	Ranmir	Leveled weapon and armor
☐	Iddra	Eastmarch/Kynesgrove	Worrying about debts	Roggi Knot-Beard	Leveled weapon and armor
☐	Octieve San	Haafingar/Solitude	Gambling debts	Irnskar	+1 Two-Handed skill
☐	Omluag	The Reach/Markarth	A bullying smelter overseer	Mulush	Small amount of gold
☐	Scouts-Many-Marshes	Eastmarch/Windhelm Docks	A fare wage from a racist overseer	Torbjorn Shatter-Shield	Leveled potion

Favor: A Little Light Thievery*

Visit the person listed, who is in the same general vicinity as the location mentioned, and speak to them. They want you to visit a location and steal an important item. The item in question isn't on a person; it is in the location itself, allowing you to utilize Sneak or Magic to augment your stealth. Violence is inadvisable. Once you steal the item, you are to return and claim a specific reward.

✓	FAVOR GIVER	ITEM TO STEAL	LOCATION OF THEFT (HOLD/LOCATION NAME)	REWARD GIVEN
☐	Dengeir of Stuhn	Suspicious Letter	Falkreath/Falkreath (Lod's House)	Small amount of gold
☐	Malur Seloth	Nelacar's Staff	Winterhold/Winterhold (The Frozen Hearth)	+1 Speech skill
☐	Stands-in-Shallows	Double-Distilled Skooma	Eastmarch/Windhelm (Gnisis Cornerclub)	+1 Sneak Skill

Favor: A Little Light Burglary*

Locate Revyn Sadri (the only fellow who wants this Favor completed) in the Gray Quarter of Windhelm. He's usually in Sadri's Used Wares. Sadri has found out that a ring he purchased was stolen from Imperial Noblewoman Viola Giordano, who lives in her house in the swanky Valunstrad District. Break into her house, place the ring into her dresser, and return to Revyn.

➤ **Medium gold reward**

Favor: The Bandit Slayer*

Visit the Favor giver, who requires you to slay a troublesome bandit leader, located in a random bandit camp somewhere in Skyrim. Journey there, ignoring or slaying any other enemies that guard the place. Locate the bandit specified and kill him. Then return to the Favor giver for a reward.

✓	FAVOR GIVER	FAVOR GIVER LOCATION (HOLD/LOCATION NAME)	REASON FOR KILLING	REWARD GIVEN
☐	Ahtar	Haafingar/Solitude (Castle Dour Jail)	He let the bandit leader escape from jail.	Large amount of gold. Follower: Ahtar.
☐	Annekke	Eastmarch/Darkwater Crossing	She spotted them on her adventures.	+1 Light Armor skill
☐	Brunwulf Free-Winter	Eastmarch/Windhelm	Help against bandit marauders	Small amount of gold, and +1 Heavy Armor skill

Favor: The Vampire Slayer*

NOTE You must be Level 10 or higher to start this Favor.

Visit Sybille Stentor, the Court Wizard of Solitude, who stands with the Jarl in the Blue Palace. Unpleasant though she is, she offers you work to clear out a nearby vampire's lair (which is randomly determined). Journey there, ignoring or slaying any other enemies that guard the place. Locate the vampire specified and kill him or her. Then return to Sybille for the reward.

- **Leveled Jewelry Reward**
- **+1 Illusion skill**

Favor: Rare Item Hunt*

Journey to the Favor giver's location, and speak to them. They require you to find a specific and rare item located somewhere in Skyrim (the place is randomly determined but appears on your world map). Should you find this coveted item and return it to them, you receive a reward appropriate for the time spent looking.

✓	FAVOR GIVER	FAVOR GIVER LOCATION (HOLD/ LOCATION NAME)	RARE ITEM	REASON FOR ITEM RETRIEVAL	REWARD GIVEN
☐	Captain Aldis	Haafingar/Solitude	*The Mirror* (Book)	To help him train his men in blocking	Medium amount of gold
☐	Torbjorn Shatter-Shield	Eastmarch/Windhelm	Amulet of Arkay	To help his wife mourn the loss of their child	Medium amount of gold
☐	Ysolda	Whiterun/Whiteun (Ysolda's House)	Mammoth Tusk	To impress some Khajiit caravaneers	+1 Speech skill
☐	Jarl Siddgeir	Falkreath/Falkreath	Black-Briar Mead	As a tribute	Leveled Potion
☐	Rustleif	The Pale/Dawnstar	*Night Falls on Sentinel* (Book)	To read to his soon-to-be-born half-Redguard child	+1 Smithing skill
☐	Lami	Hjaalmarch/Morthal	*Song of the Alchemists* (Book)	The book she read as a girl, when studying alchemy	+1 Alchemy skill

Favor: Item Retrieval (Bandit Camp)*

Journey to where the Favor giver is and speak to them. They need you to journey to a [random] bandit camp, find a specific item stolen from them, and return it safely. When this occurs, you receive a reward appropriate for the time spent looking.

✓	FAVOR GIVER	FAVOR GIVER LOCATION (HOLD/LOCATION NAME)	STOLEN ITEM	REWARD GIVEN
☐	Amren	Whiterun/Whiterun	Amren's Father's Sword	+1 Block skill, +1 One-Handed skill
☐	Shahvee	Eastmarch/Windhelm Docks	Amulet to Zenithar (the Divine of Fortune)	+1 Light Armor skill, +1 Lockpicking skill

Favor: Item Retrieval (Cave)*

Head over to where the Favor giver is and chat with them. They require you to trek to a [random] cave, find a specific item they have mislaid or are looking for, and return it safely. When this occurs, you receive a reward appropriate for the time spent looking.

✓	FAVOR GIVER	FAVOR GIVER LOCATION (HOLD/LOCATION NAME)	REQUIRED ITEM	REWARD GIVEN
☐	Oengul War-Anvil‡	Eastmarch/Windhelm (Palace of the Kings)	High Queen Freydis's Sword	+1 Smithing skill
☐	Roggi	Eastmarch/Kynesgrove	Lenne's Ancestral Shield	+1 Block skill
☐	Runil	Falkreath/Falkreath (House of Arkay)	Runil's Journal	Large amount of gold
☐	Frida	The Pale/Dawnstar (The Mortar and Pestle)	Ring of Pure Mixtures	+1 Alchemy skill
☐	Noster Eagle-Eye	Haafingar/Solitude	Legion Helmet	+1 Sneak skill

Favor: Jobs for the Jarls*

The Jarl of a particular Hold has a task for you to complete. This usually involves killing some troublesome foes who are annoying or terrifying the Hold's population or retrieving a lost item of great importance. The enemy or item is located in a random place, usually within the Jarl's Hold. Complete the task, return to the Jarl, and expect an impressive payment for your time.

✓	FAVOR GIVER	PREREQUISITES	FAVOR GIVER LOCATION (HOLD/ LOCATION NAME)	TASK	TARGET LOCATION	REWARD GIVEN
	Jarl Igmund	None	The Reach/Markarth (Understone Keep)	Kill [a Forsworn leader] to prove yourself	A Forsworn camp	Large amount of gold
	Jarl Skald the Elder	Level 22	The Pale/Dawnstar (The White Hall)	Deal with [a giant] in the Pale	A giant camp	Large amount of gold
	Jarl Siddgeir	None	Falkreath/Falkreath (Jarl's Longhouse)	Kill [a bandit leader] he's had dealings with	A bandit camp	Large amount of gold
	Jarl Igmund	Level 20	The Reach/Markarth (Understone Keep)	Kill [a Hagraven] and bring back his father's shield	A Hagraven nest	Leveled armor, available house to purchase in Markarth
	Jarl Korir	None	Winterhold/Winterhold (Jarl's Longhouse)	Return with the Helm of Winterhold	A cave	Large amount of gold

CRAFTING TUTORIALS

Crafting Tutorial: Blacksmithing*

A Blacksmith of great prowess walks you through the smithing process. You must make a dagger and sharpen it. Then tan some leather, make a helm, and temper it.

✓	TUTORIAL GIVER	HOLD	TUTORIAL LOCATION	TASK
	Alvor	Whiterun	Riverwood Blacksmiths (Alvor and Sigrid's House)	Complete the smithing process
	Adrianne Avenicci	Whiterun	Whiterun Blacksmiths (Warmaiden's)	Complete the smithing process

Crafting Tutorial: Alchemy*

An Alchemist (er, bartender) of exceptional ability instructs you on how to make a potion.

✓	TUTORIAL GIVER	HOLD	TUTORIAL LOCATION	TASK
	Orgnar	Whiterun	Riverwood (Sleeping Giant Inn)	Make a potion
	Arcadia	Whiterun	Whiterun (Arcadia's Cauldron)	Make a potion
	Zaria	Falkreath	Falkreath (Grave Concoctions)	Make a potion

Crafting Tutorial: Enchanting*

A wizard of some considerable talent explains how to use the Arcane Enchanter.

✓	TUTORIAL GIVER	HOLD	TUTORIAL LOCATION	TASK
	Farengar Secret-Fire	Whiterun	Dragonsreach, inside Whiterun	Use the Arcane Enchanter

NOTE For more information on crafting, consult the Training Chapter, on page 70. Remember, there are far more Blacksmiths, Alchemists, and Enchanters in Skyrim, but only the ones in the preceding tables go through the crafting process with you.

Becoming a powerful and impressive member of Skyrim society culminates in the title "Thane." Follow our advice, and your good deeds pay off in the form of a piece of property you can purchase (and decorate) in eight of the nine Holds. In most Holds, you also get the services of your own Housecarl, a follower who waits for you in the same building as the Jarl or at your house (after purchase). You can be a Thane of multiple Holds, but there is no bonus if you're a Thane of Skyrim (that is, of all nine Holds).

NOTE "Good deeds" means helping the citizens of the Hold or Capital you're in, including the Jarl. Helping members of the Thieves Guild, Dark Brotherhood, or other guild does not count.

Thane of Haafingar*

Part 1—Friend of the Jarl: Jarl Elisif the Fair is the leader of Solitude. You must have finished Side Quest: The Wolf Queen Awakened, which is related to her Hold. You must also have completed the task she set for you. See Miscellaneous Objectives: Elisif's Tribute for more information.

Proudspire Manor: A fine example of Nord architecture, and a worthy prize for helping the population of Solitude.

Part 2—Friend of the City: You must now win the respect of the inhabitants of Solitude. Speak to Jarl Elisif, who asks you to assist the people of this Hold. Return to her once you've finished five (or more) Favors, tasks, or objectives that benefit the people. Consult the Miscellaneous Objectives and Favors sections of this guide, looking for "Solitude" as the location for tasks, Favors, and objectives.

Part 3—House in the City: Finally, you must purchase a piece of property in the city. Speak to the Jarl, and you're informed that a house is for sale. You're referred to Steward Falk Firebeard. The following residence is available:

House Name: Proudspire Manor
Cost: 25,000 gold pieces

- **Key to Proudspire Manor**

Visit the house and meet your Housecarl, Jordis the Sword-Maiden there. Return to the Jarl, who grants you the title of Thane and a reward. Guards in Haafingar now ignore one crime as long as your Bounty is less than 2,000.

- **Thane Title**
- **Blade of Haafingar (leveled enchanted sword)**
- **House:** Proudspire Manor
- **Follower:** Jordis the Sword-Maiden

Thane of Hjaalmarch*

Part 1—Friend of the Jarl: You must first befriend the Jarl of Morthal, achieved by completing either of the following:

Windstad Manor Grounds: A rather pleasing view across the salt marshes toward Solitude. Expect amazing sunsets.

Jarl Igrod Ravencrone is the leader of Morthal. In order to befriend her, you must finish Side Quest: Laid to Rest, which takes place in her Hold.

Jarl Sorli the Builder is the leader of Morthal once it has fallen into Stormcloak hands. To start this task with Sorli, you must have captured Hjaalmarch Hold, as part of the Civil War Quests.

Part 2—Friend of the City: You must now win the respect of the inhabitants of Morthal. Speak to the Jarl, who asks you to assist the people of this Hold. Return to the Jarl once you've finished three (or more) Favors, tasks, or objectives that benefit the people. Consult the Miscellaneous Objectives and Favors sections of this guide, looking for "Morthal" as the location for tasks, Favors, and objectives.

Return to the Jarl, who grants you the title of Thane and a reward. Guards in Hjaalmarch now ignore one crime as long as your Bounty is less than 2,000.

- **Thane Title**
- **Blade of Hjaalmarch (Leveled Enchanted Sword)**
- **Follower:** Valdimar

Part 3—Land in the Country: Although there is no house to purchase in this Hold, visit any settlement and look for a Courier to deliver a message stating that a plot of land has become available. Simply return to the Jarl's steward, and tell them "I'd like to purchase a house." There isn't one available, but there is a plot of land. Agree to pay the 5,000 gold for it, and you receive a charter for the land in question. Your world map updates to show the location of your plot.

- **Windstad Manor Charter (Hjaalmarch Hold)**

Thane of The Pale*

Part 1—Friend of the Jarl: You must first befriend the Jarl of Dawnstar, achieved by completing either of the following:

Heljarchen Hall Grounds: A swath of tundra with exceptional views of the Loreius Farm, Dragonsreach, and the Throat of the World in the distance.

Jarl Skald the Elder is the leader of Dawnstar. You must have finished Daedric Quest: Waking Nightmare, which is related to his Hold. You must also have completed the task he set for you. See the "Favor: Jobs for the Jarls" section of this guide for more information.

Jarl Brina Merilis is the leader of Dawnstar once it has fallen into Imperial hands. To start this task with Brina, you must have captured the Pale Hold, as part of the Civil War Quests.

Part 2—Friend of the City: You must now win the respect of the inhabitants of Dawnstar. Speak to the Jarl, who asks you to assist the people of this Hold. Return to the Jarl once you've finished three (or more) Favors, tasks, or objectives that benefit the people. Consult the Miscellaneous Objectives and Favors sections of this guide, looking for "Dawnstar" as the location for tasks, Favors, and objectives.

Return to the Jarl, who grants you the title of Thane and a reward. Guards in the Pale now ignore one crime as long as your Bounty is less than 2,000.

- **Thane Title**
- **Blade of the Pale (Leveled Enchanted Sword)**
- **Follower:** Gregor

Part 3—Land in the Country: Although there is no house to purchase in this Hold, visit any settlement and look for a Courier to deliver a message stating that a plot of land has become available. Simply return to the Jarl, and tell them "I'd like to purchase a house." There isn't one available, but there is a plot of land. Agree to pay the 5,000 gold for it, and you receive a charter for the land in question. Your world map updates to show the location of your plot.

➤ **Heljarchen Hall Charter (The Pale)**

Thane of Winterhold*

Only Jarl Korir of Winterhold lacks a house or a plot of land to grant you; he's still recovering from the decimation of his capital.

Part 1—Friend of the Jarl: You must first befriend the Jarl of Winterhold, achieved by completing either of the following:

Jarl Korir is the leader of Winterhold. You must have completed the task he set for you. See the "Favor: Jobs for the Jarls" section of this guide for more information.

Jarl Kraldar is the leader of Winterhold once it has fallen into Imperial hands. To start this task with Kraldar, you must have captured Winterhold Hold, as part of the Civil War Quests.

Part 2—Friend of the City: You must now win the respect of the inhabitants of Winterhold. Speak to the Jarl, who asks you to assist the people of this Hold. Return to the Jarl once you've finished three (or more) Favors, tasks, or objectives that benefit the people. Consult the Miscellaneous Objectives and Favors sections of this guide, looking for "Winterhold" as the location for tasks, Favors, and objectives.

Return to the Jarl, who grants you the title of Thane and a reward. Guards in Winterhold now ignore one crime as long as your Bounty is less than 2,000.

➤ **Thane Title**

➤ **Blade of Winterhold (Leveled Enchanted Sword)**

NOTE There is no Housecarl or house to purchase in this Hold.

Thane of the Reach*

The Vlindrels were a Colovian merchant family, driven from this home during the Reachmen Rebellion: Their former mansion has stood empty ever since.

Part 1—Friend of the Jarl: You must first befriend the Jarl of Markarth, achieved by completing either of the following:

Jarl Igmund is the leader of Markarth. You must have finished both the tasks he set for you. See the "Favor: Jobs for the Jarls" section of this guide for more information.

Jarl Thongvor Silver-Fish is the leader of Markarth once it has fallen into Stormcloak hands. To start this task with Thongvor, you must have captured the Reach Hold as part of the Civil War Quests.

Part 2—Friend of the City: You must now earn the respect of the inhabitants of Markarth. Speak to the Jarl, who asks you to assist the people of this Hold. Return to the Jarl once you've finished five (or more) Favors, tasks, or objectives that benefit the people. Consult the Miscellaneous Objectives and Favors of this guide, looking for "Markarth" as the location for tasks, Favors, and objectives.

Part 3—House in the City: Finally, you must purchase a piece of property in the city. Speak to the Jarl, and you're informed that a house is for sale. You're referred to the Steward: Raerek (Jarl Igmund) or Reburrus Quintilius (Jarl Thongvor). The following residence is available:

House Name: Vlindrel Hall
Cost: 8,000 gold pieces

➤ **Key to Vlindrel Hall**

Visit the house and meet your Housecarl, Argis the Bulwark. Return to the Jarl, who grants you the title of Thane and a reward. Guards in the Reach now ignore one crime as long as your Bounty is less than 2,000.

➤ **Thane Title**

➤ **Blade of the Reach (Leveled Enchanted Axe)**

➤ **House:** Vlindrel Hall

➤ **Follower:** Argis the Bulwark

Thane of Whiterun*

This compact but hardy dwelling is the least ostentatious of the Skyrim homes you can own, but it has undeniable charm.

Part 1—Dragon Rising: Jarl Balgruuf the Greater is the leader of Whiterun. When you aid his soldiers in fending off the dragon attack in Main Quest: Dragon Rising, he proclaims you Thane as a reward for your heroism. Your new Housecarl, Lydia, will wait for you in Dragonsreach until you find a home in the city. Guards in Whiterun will now ignore one crime as long as your Bounty is less than 2,000.

➤ **Thane Title**

➤ **Blade of Whiterun (Leveled Enchanted Axe)**

➤ **Follower:** Lydia

Part 2—House in the City: Although not required to become Thane of Whiterun, you can still purchase a house in the city. Speak to the Jarl, and you're informed that a house is for sale. You're referred to the Steward, Proventus Avenicci (Jarl Balgruuf) or Brill (Jarl Vignar). The following residence is available:

House Name: Breezehome
Cost: 5,000 gold pieces

➤ **Key to Breezehome**

Visit the house, where Lydia can now be found when not fighting at your side.

➤ **House:** Breezehome

House Name: Breezehome
Cost: 5,000 gold pieces

Thane of Eastmarch*

The blood of "the butcher of Windhelm" may have been wiped away, but have the spirits of the dead departed too? Yes, Hjerim isn't cursed, and is an exceptional residence.

Part 1—Friend of the Jarl: You must first befriend the Jarl of Windhelm, achieved by completing either of the following:

Jarl Ulfric Stormcloak is the leader of Windhelm. You must have conquered both Whiterun and Falkreath Holds for the Stormcloaks in order to become firm friends with him.

Jarl Brunwulf Free-Winter is the leader of Windhelm once it has fallen into Imperial hands. To start this task with Brunwulf, you must have captured Windhelm in the culmination of the Civil War Quests.

Part 2—Friend of the City: You must now win the respect of the inhabitants of Windhelm. Speak to the Jarl, who asks you to assist the people of this Hold. Return to the Jarl once you've finished five (or more) Favors, tasks, or objectives that benefit the people. Consult the Miscellaneous Objectives and Favors sections of this guide, looking for "Windhelm" as the location for tasks, Favors, and objectives.

Part 3—House in the City: Finally, you must purchase a piece of property in the city. Once Side Quest: Blood on the Ice sends you to Hjerim, speak to the Jarl, and you're informed that the house is for sale. You're referred to the Steward, Jorleif (Jarl Ulfric), or Captain Lonely-Gale (Jarl Brunwulf). The following residence is available:

House Name: Hjerim
Cost: 12,000 gold pieces

➤ **Key to Hjerim**

Visit the house and meet your Housecarl, Calder. Return to the Jarl, who grants you the title of Thane and a reward. Guards in Eastmarch now ignore one crime as long as your Bounty is less than 2,000.

➤ **Thane Title**

➤ **Blade of Eastmarch (Leveled Enchanted Axe)**

➤ **House:** Hjerim

➤ **Follower:** Calder

Thane of Falkreath*

Part 1—Friend of the Jarl: You must first befriend the Jarl of Falkreath, achieved by completing either of the following:

Lakeview Manor Grounds: The body of water is Lake Ilinalta. The view is fabulous, perched between the Shriekwind Hills.

Jarl Siddgeir is the leader of Falkreath. You must have completed the two tasks he set for you. See the "Favor: Jobs for the Jarls" and "Favor: Rare Item Hunt" sections for details.

Jarl Dengeir of Stuhn is the leader of Falkreath once it has fallen into Stormcloak hands. To start this task with Dengeir, you must have captured Falkreath as part of the Civil War Quests.

Part 2—Friend of the City: You must now win the respect of the inhabitants of Falkreath. Speak to the Jarl, who asks you to assist the people of this Hold. Return to the Jarl once you've finished three (or more) Favors, tasks, or objectives that benefit the people. Consult the Miscellaneous Objectives and Favors of this guide looking for "Falkreath" as the location for tasks, Favors, and objectives:

Return to the Jarl, who grants you the title of Thane and a reward. Guards in Falkreath now ignore one crime as long as your Bounty is less than 2,000.

➤ **Thane Title**

➤ **Blade of Falkreath (Leveled Enchanted Sword)**

➤ **Follower:** Valdimar

Part 3—Land in the Country: Although there is no house to purchase in this Hold, visit any settlement and look for a Courier to deliver a message stating that a plot of land has become available. This usually happens when you reach Level 9, whether you've completed any Thane Tasks or not. Once you've completed the previous parts, return to the Jarl's steward, and tell them "I'd like to purchase a house." There isn't one available, but there is a plot of land. Agree to pay the 5,000 gold for it, and you receive a charter for the land in question. Your world map updates to show the location of your plot.

➤ **Lakeview Manor Charter (Hjaalmarch Hold)**

Thane of the Rift*

Part 1—Friend of the Jarl: You must first befriend the Jarl of Riften, achieved by completing either of the following:

The only house to offer lake views and access to and from a Hold Capital, as well as a front garden and a copious cellar. Honeyside has it all!

Jarl Laila Law-Giver is the leader of Riften. You befriend her as part of the 'Deal with the Skooma Trade' objectives (Part 3).

Jarl Maven Black-Briar is the leader of Riften once it has fallen into Imperial hands. To start this task with Maven, you must have captured Riften as part of the Civil War Quests.

Part 2—Friend of the City: You must now win the respect of the inhabitants of Riften. Speak to the Jarl, who asks you to assist the people of this Hold. Return to the Jarl once you've finished five (or more) Favors, tasks, or objectives that benefit the people. Consult the Miscellaneous Objectives and Favors sections of this guide, looking for "Riften" as the location for tasks, Favors, and objectives.

Part 3—Deal with the Skooma Trade: Three of the Miscellaneous Objectives in Riften form a mini-questline in which you uncover the skooma trade in the city and deal with it. You must complete the objectives:

1. "Helping Hand"
2. "The Raid"
3. "Supply and Demand"

Note that the first two objectives do contribute toward the "Part 2—Friend of the City" portion of the Thane Quest (in case you haven't done enough yet).

Part 4—House in the City: Finally, you must purchase a piece of property in the city. Speak to the Jarl, and you're informed that a House is for sale. You're referred to the Steward, Anuriel (Jarl Laila) or Hemming Black-Briar (Jarl Maven). The following residence is available:

House Name: Honeyside
Cost: 8,000 gold pieces

➤ **Key to Honeyside**

Visit the house and meet your Housecarl, Iona. Return to the Jarl, who grants you the title of Thane and a reward. Guards in the Rift now ignore one crime as long as your Bounty is less than 2,000.

➤ **Thane Title**

➤ **Blade of the Rift (Leveled Enchanted Sword)**

➤ **House:** Honeyside

➤ **Follower:** Iona

For further details on improving the plots of land in Hjaalmarch, The Pale, and Falkreath Holds, consult the Hearthfire Chapter starting on page 112.

DAWNGUARD QUESTS

GENERAL OVERVIEW

Skyrim is under threat. The Vigilants of Stendarr are reeling after the massacre of their leaders and the burning of the sacred Hall of the Vigilant. Those who know tell of a force to the northwest, a brood of powerful night stalkers, and whisper of a prophecy called the *Tyranny of the Sun* that would bring perpetual darkness to the lands. Many ignore this peril out of fear or ignorance. But there is a small shaft of light in this eternal, damnable night: There is talk of the reformation of an ancient clan of vampire hunters—the Dawnguard—who will not cease until every one of the hated undead are driven from this land. Your adventuring takes you to the heart of both warring factions. But which one will you put a stake through?

This section reveals the sanctuaries and important characters from both the vampire and Dawnguard factions. After that, you will read up on the benefits of choosing to side with one over the other (which you must do during the course of the Dawnguard Main Quest), and we'll cover all of the associated quests you can attempt. Who will you side with? Is it time to draw your crossbow or sharpen your fangs?

NOTE **Cross-referencing:** Do you want to see maps and learn more about the traps, non-quest-related items, collectibles, crafting areas, and other important rooms of note in every location during these quests? Then cross-reference the location you travel to with the information on that location contained in the Atlas.

TIP **Whose side are you on?** The following information details the fortifications that the Dawnguard and the vampires use, as well as all characters who inhabit (or move to) the area. Next, we discuss the advantages of each faction (once you join one of them). Finally, we show characters who aren't strictly allied to either side. You actually don't choose a side until the end of Dawnguard Main Quest: Bloodline, but after that choice is made, there's no switching sides!

THE DAWNGUARD

The Dawnguard Sanctuary: Fort Dawnguard

Fort Dawnguard, from Dayspring Canyon.

Fort Dawnguard's crenellations.

The Circular Hall entrance.

The banquet hall, where mead freely flows.

Tucked away in the southeastern mountains of the Rift, in the hidden valley called Dayspring Canyon, towers the old fortification of Fort Dawnguard. Long fallen to disrepair, this massive fortress will become home to a new faction of vampire hunters born from the ashes of the Vigilants of Stendarr. It is here where the agents of the Dawnguard (led by Isran) have begun to gather, where new recruits dedicate themselves to the eradication of vampires, and where a solution to the growing menace must be found. But where is the line between pragmatism and fanaticism?

The grounds of the fort change slightly over the course of the Dawnguard quests (as detailed below), but the main fortification consists of two giant buttress towers connected to the main structure via an open walkway. The fort's main entrance is at the end of a curved path past an outside training area, which is used as a refugee camp as the vampires decimate the Vigilants of Stendarr and begin to attack the peaceful citizens of Skyrim.

Inside Fort Dawnguard, past the unfurled banners and large arched doorway, is an impressive circular hall with an upper balcony level. To the right (east) are two spiral staircases; one leads to the outside buttress tower walkway, and the other leads to the curved upstairs balcony. The northeast part of the fort has a third spiral staircase leading out to the second buttress tower walkway, and there's a natural cave where crossbow firing is practiced, and the Dawnguard's special breed of husky war dogs are raised. There is also an entrance to Dead Drop Falls (a small dungeon accessible only from the fort).

Back in the circular entrance hall, head north to reach the temporary barracks (around a large fireplace) and to access both "wings" of the castle. To the left (west) of the circular entrance hall are some storage and waiting rooms between the giant stone columns, and a spiral staircase leads up to the top of the fort—the upper crenellations. Staying on the ground floor, head northwest to the banquet hall where a considerable feast (and several mead barrels) keeps the Dawnguard in fighting shape. At the castle's west end is Gunmar's Forge, and a pen where his Armored Trolls are trained. Sorine Jurard and Florentius Baenius also perfect their talents in this area, close to a small target range.

Above the circular entrance hall is the balcony, which you access via spiral steps. Off the balcony are two corridors. One leads to a trophy and torture room and Isran's sleeping quarters. The other is a more lavish bedroom, saved for an adventurer who can truly lead the Dawnguard to victory.

NOTE Some of these Fort Dawnguard chambers become accessible only during or after the Dawnguard Main Questline has been completed.

The Dawnguard: Important Characters

Dawnguard Leader: Isran

Formerly a member of the Vigilants of Stendarr, Isran struck out on his own when he realized the Order was too soft and didn't really have what it took to defend against the evil in the world. He knew they'd be overrun one day, and he wasn't going to wait around for it to happen. He's very driven. While he won't discuss it with anyone, he lost his family to vampires years ago, and it's warped him. He now hates vampires far more than he cares about saving people and would willingly sacrifice just about anyone if it gave him a clear shot. In his mind, the ends justify the means every time.

➤ Trainer

Dawnguard Blacksmith: Gunmar

Gunmar lost most of his clan to vampires as a young man. While it was a similar experience to what Isran went through, his reaction was very different. He turned inward, speaking very little and acting only when necessary—but those actions were always clear, the goal being to spare others the same fate he suffered. His goal is the same as Isran's, and he will sign on to help the hunters, but he doesn't agree with the methods. Currently, he has little contact with Isran, preferring his own company and saving locals from troublesome encroaching animals.

➤ Trainer ➤ Vendor

Dawnguard Tinker: Sorine Jurard

A genius with gadgets, Sorine has been working on some new weaponry to defend herself. While she doesn't have the perspective deduction and knack for seeing the big picture that Isran does, she can relate to him. She has a peculiar quirk for assuming the worst-case scenario is bound to happen and so prepares for anything and everything. While never a member of the Vigilants, she's crossed paths with Isran in the past and appreciated his tenacity and survival instincts. She would have gladly worked with him again if necessary had they not parted on such unpleasant terms.

➤ Trainer ➤ Vendor

Dawnguard Mage: Florentius Baenius

Florentius used to be a priest of Arkay, the god of life and death, and seeing the repeated effects of vampire attacks (and fending off those he thought were dead friends) has driven him a little bit mad. He claims to speak directly to Arkay and says Arkay speaks back. He's made it a goal to destroy the vampire menace in Tamriel and believes that, with Arkay helping him, he's destined to succeed. Some think he's just playing at being mad so he can keep others at a distance, but if so, he's very good at maintaining the illusion.

➤ Trainer ➤ Vendor

Dawnguard Hunter: Durak

➤ Follower

Dawnguard Warrior: Celann

➤ Follower

Dawnguard Warrior: Ingjard

➤ Follower

Dawnguard Recruit: Agmaer

Agmaer has no personal stake in this conflict but wants to do the right thing. He's heard of vampires terrorizing Skyrim and wants to help. That means leaving his family farm and enlisting with the folks serving Isran, who Agmaer initially looks up to. As time goes on, though, his eagerness, honesty, and loyalty wobble, and he starts to question Isran's methods and whether the right thing is really being done.

➤ Follower

Dawnguard Recruit: Beleval

➤ Follower

Other Dawnguard Personnel

Dawnguard Warrior: Mogrul
Dawnguard Warrior: Ollrod
Dawnguard Warrior: Tilde
Dawnguard Warrior: Vori
Dawnguard Armored
Huskies: Bran and Sceolang

Dawnguard Advantages

Those choosing to side with the Dawnguard throughout the Dawnguard Main Quests can look forward to some changes in the construction of the fort and other benefits.

Fort Dawnguard Upgrades

Initially, the fort is filled with cobwebs and clutter, but it does have a few amenities, including a smelter and workbench.

After Dawnguard Main Quest: A New Order, Gunmar and Sorine settle in and set up full smithing and enchanting stations. You can now accept their Faction Quests, purchase items from them, and acquire the Armored Troll and Dawnguard Husky animal companions. The barracks area fills out to house the Dawnguard's new recruits.

During Dawnguard Main Quest: Prophet, a number of Dawnguard Agents return to the fort. You can now ask the members of the Dawnguard to join you on your missions.

Once you complete Dawnguard Faction Quest: Bolstering the Ranks, Florentius moves in, adding an Alchemy station.

During Dawnguard Main Quest: Beyond Death, a refugee camp is set up outside the fort.

After Dawnguard Main Quest: Kindred Judgment, you receive a private room on the fort's upper level.

Dawnguard-Only Benefits

If you side with the Dawnguard, you gain access to the following:

Dawnguard Weapons

Crossbows: The Dawnguard specialize in crossbows (such as the Steel Crossbow, as shown), which fire quickly and hit hard but take longer to reload than bows. While you can obtain basic crossbows by killing members of the Dawnguard (or requesting one from Durak the first time you visit the fort), you can only get enhanced versions of these weapons by siding with them and completing Dawnguard Faction Quest: Ancient Technology.

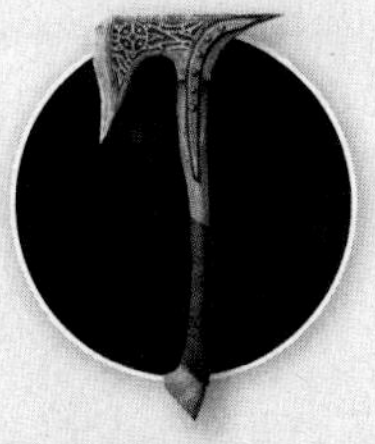

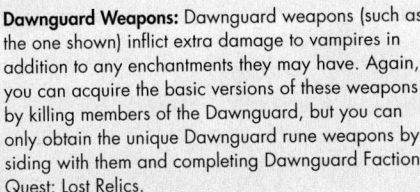

Dawnguard Weapons: Dawnguard weapons (such as the one shown) inflict extra damage to vampires in addition to any enchantments they may have. Again, you can acquire the basic versions of these weapons by killing members of the Dawnguard, but you can only obtain the unique Dawnguard rune weapons by siding with them and completing Dawnguard Faction Quest: Lost Relics.

Dawnguard Armor

Dawnguard Light and Heavy Armor: The Dawnguard have complete sets of both light and heavy armor (Heavy Armor shown here). Wearing a full set of Dawnguard armor provides additional protection from vampire melee attacks and Drain Life spells.

Dawnguard Spells

The Dawnguard's magic harnesses the power of the sun to damage the undead. These spells can be purchased from Florentius and Sorine once they have been recruited to your cause:

Sunfire: A ball of sunlight that inflicts 25 damage to undead.

Stendarr's Aura: For 60 seconds, nearby undead take 10 points of sun damage per second.

Vampire's Bane: A sunlight explosion that does 40 damage to undead in a 15-foot radius.

Dawnguard Animal Companions

Dawnguard Huskies: These are trained war dogs. With almost twice the health, stamina, and attack power of regular dogs, they are dependable companions.

Armored Trolls: These can be purchased from Gunmar for 500 gold each. While expensive, they make powerful allies, capable of causing and enduring enormous amounts of damage.

Dawnguard Followers

After completing Dawnguard Main Quest: Prophet, you can ask many of the Dawnguard recruits to join you on your missions. Equipped with full suits of Dawnguard armor, they are effective vampire hunters.

Dawnguard Followers

Those true to the cause of vanquishing vampires also heed your call to action and can be asked to follow you.

✓	NAME	PREREQUISITE	CLASS	SKILLS
☐	Agmaer	Dawnguard Main Quest: Prophet	Dawnguard Recruit	One-Handed, Two-Handed, Block, Light Armor, Heavy Armor
☐	Beleval	Dawnguard Main Quest: Prophet	Dawnguard Recruit	One-Handed, Two-Handed, Block, Light Armor, Heavy Armor
☐	Celann	Dawnguard Main Quest: Prophet	Dawnguard Warrior	One-Handed, Heavy Armor, Archery, Block
☐	Durak	Dawnguard Main Quest: Prophet	Dawnguard Hunter	Archery, One-Handed, Light Armor, Block
☐	Ingjard	Dawnguard Main Quest: Prophet	Dawnguard Warrior	Two-Handed, Heavy Armor, Archery, Block

Dawnguard Animal Companions

Fiercely loyal to their masters, you can bring along one of the two Fort Dawnguard Huskies or hire a troll for 500 gold from Gunmar.

✓	NAME	PREREQUISITE	TYPE
☐	Armored Frost Troll	Dawnguard Main Quest: A New Order	Armored Frost Troll
☐	Armored Troll	Dawnguard Main Quest: A New Order	Armored Troll
☐	Bran	Dawnguard Main Quest: A New Order	Dawnguard Husky
☐	Sceolang	Dawnguard Main Quest: A New Order	Dawnguard Husky

Dawnguard Trainers

Isran and some of his brethren are highly skilled. You could learn a thing or two from them!

✓	NAME	SKILL	LEVEL
☐	Florentius	Restoration	Master
☐	Gunmar	Smithing	Master
☐	Isran	Heavy Armor	Master
☐	Sorine	Archery	Master

Dawnguard Vendors

Your vampire-fighting friends also trade with you, offering reasonable prices and a few items you cannot purchase elsewhere.

✓	NAME	SERVICE	NOTES
☐	Florentius	Apothecary	Sells the unique spells Stendarr's Aura and Vampire's Bane.
☐	Gunmar	Blacksmith	Sells Dawnguard Armor.
☐	Sorine	General goods	Sells the unique spell Sunfire, as well as crossbows and bolts. Her inventory improves as you complete Dawnguard Faction Quest: Ancient Technology multiple times for her.

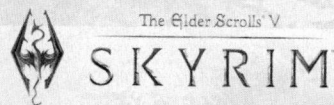

The Vampire Sanctuary: Castle Volkihar

Castle Volkihar, from a buzzard's-eye view.

The inner cathedral.

Castle Volkihar's main entrance.

The banquet hall, where blood flows freely.

Long thought lost to the eternal mists of the Sea of Ghosts, a sprawling castle on the rocky islands north of Icewater Jetty, on the northwest coast of Skyrim, has reportedly been spotted by fishermen. Little is known about the previous owners of the place, as it has changed hands countless times in history, but it has been home to the vampires and their leader, Lord Harkon, for centuries. Only practically reachable by boat, the castle is a formidable place, but once you manage to pass the vampire watchman, all the horror and decadence of the pure-blooded vampire is on display. This is a visit only for those brave or foolish enough to enter this lair of undeath, but there's a way of life that could spread all across this land....

Castle Volkihar's approach from Icewater Jetty is dominated by the castle, but there is a single watchtower by the boat mooring. Venture up the cobblestone bridge, passing the gargoyle statues, and you come to the watchman who guards the entrance, refusing to let anyone in he doesn't recognize. This is the only entrance to the keep proper, although those wishing to brave the rugged rocks to the left (north) side of the monumental castle walls will find an abandoned pier and a side entrance to the castle's undercroft.

Inside Castle Volkihar (in the area known as Volkihar Keep), the main hive of activity centers around a banqueting room, where "feasting" is part of the court's tradition (as is backstabbing, underhanded antics, and other unsavory practices designed to curry favor with Lord Harkon). To the left (west) is a laboratory and research room where Garan Marethi sometimes resides. The western corridor winds around to an armory and coffin chamber where the vampires can sleep like the dead. Both rooms connect up steps to a balcony and to the upper hall where Lord Harkon favors giving his proclamations, overlooking the banquet hall below.

To the right (east) of the banquet hall are three archways. The northernmost leads down to the kitchens and gaol, where Rargal Thrallmaster prepares his Vampire Cattle for feasting. The middle arch leads to an alcove where the fabled Bloodstone Chalice rests; once filled, it bestows great power on the vampire who drinks from it. The last arch leads down a short corridor to a combat training area where Fura Bloodmouth works and sleeps.

The more elegant chambers are on the elevated northern side of the keep. Up the steps and past the portcullis to the northwest is Volkihar Cathedral, where the vampire shrine and Harkon's inner sanctum is. North is a two-tiered bedroom (with torture chamber) where Harkon ponders his strategies. Behind the northern balcony are long-ruined steps that once led down into the castle's central courtyard, although you must clear these to reach this initially inaccessible place. The stairs to the northeast lead to a bedroom that used to belong to Serana.

NOTE Some of these Castle Volkihar chambers become accessible only during or after the Dawnguard Main Quest has been completed. Note that Volkihar undercroft, courtyard, ruins, and balcony are also part of this castle but aren't lived in by the vampires who frequent this place.

King of the Vampires: Lord Harkon

Lord Harkon

Long ago, Harkon ruled over a large part of Skyrim. He was a cruel tyrant who oppressed his people ruthlessly in his quest for wealth and power. Eventually, the realities of his mortal life began to sink in. So great was his appetite for power, he could not bear the thought of losing everything in death.

Despite the protests of his wife, Valerica, and his daughter Serana, Harkon began to explore the dark arts. When he learned of vampirism, he knew he had found a way to cheat death. But the immortal king quickly grew frustrated with the limitations of his newfound powers. He longed to walk the world in daylight with no fear of the sun's enfeebling effects. Harkon spent decades searching through ancient lore to find a solution to this problem, and so it was that he stumbled across an old prophecy that foretold of a day in which the vampires would gain power over the sun.

As he delved deeper into the prophecy, his wife became increasingly estranged. When she learned of his mad plan to fulfill the prophecy and darken the sun, she feared that he would kill every living thing in Nirn. He already acquired two of the Elder Scrolls that he needed, so she knew that Harkon was dangerously close to achieving his goal.

Valerica decided to take action. She arranged for Serana to be hidden away with one of the Elder Scrolls that Harkon had acquired. She took the other scroll and fled into the Oblivion plane known as the Soul Cairn. Since that time, Harkon has searched tirelessly for his wife and daughter and the lost Elder Scrolls.

Castigated Wife: Valerica

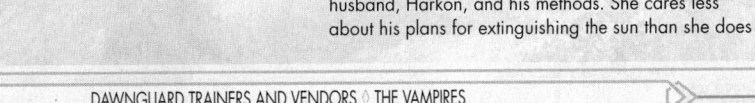

Valerica is one of the Daughters of Coldharbor, women who ritually sacrifice themselves to the Daedric Prince Molag Bal and receive the power of vampirism in exchange. She has always been at odds with her husband, Harkon, and his methods. She cares less about his plans for extinguishing the sun than she does about seeing him humiliated. When she learned that Harkon intended to use her daughter Serana's blood as part of a ritual to darken the sun, she enacted a desperate plan that involved hiding Serana away with one of the Elder Scrolls and then exiling herself to the Soul Cairn with another scroll (thus removing all of the elements Harkon needed to fulfill the prophecy).

Valerica fancies herself a necromancer, having dedicated her life to the study of the forbidden arts. She maintained a hidden laboratory in the ruined portion of the castle from which she would perform her summonings and experiments. In her studies, she unlocked the secrets of the Soul Cairn, the plane of Oblivion to which souls that are trapped within black Soul Gems are sent once their energy is expended. Over the course of several decades, Valerica was able to construct a portal to the Soul Cairn with which she intended to continue her studies. This portal became her escape from Harkon's grasp when she enacted her plan to foil the Tyranny of the Sun.

Valerica is a stern woman who places her hatred of Harkon above all other priorities. She cares for Serana, but not in an especially motherly way. This comes to the forefront when Serana confronts Valerica in the Soul Cairn and makes her mother realize that she's been used as a pawn in her parents' game.

Advisor: Garan Marethi

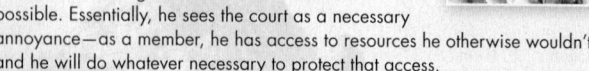

Garan is one of the older vampires in the court—he claims to have links to the Aundae clan from Morrowind, though no one has ever confirmed them. He's overly proud of his history and will name-drop famous associations whenever he can. He considers himself above the squabbles of the court, believing he is better than all of them, and so he keeps to himself, associating with the others as little as possible. Essentially, he sees the court as a necessary annoyance—as a member, he has access to resources he otherwise wouldn't, and he will do whatever necessary to protect that access.

Advisor: Feran Sadri

Feran was a powerful conjurer who was frustrated with the limitations of a normal life span. He saw vampirism as a way to escape the confines of that and allowed himself to be turned. He uses his immortality to learn as much as he can. As such, he's not terribly interested in the politics of the court; he provides services so he's seen as useful and can retain access to all of the resources at Harkon's disposal, but he keeps himself removed from the group at large. He's taken on Ronthil as an apprentice of sorts, largely because he knows that no one can stand Ronthil, thus deflecting attention away from himself.

Advisor: Orthjolf

Orthjolf was once a wealthy merchant in Riften and enjoyed his life. Turned by a member of Harkon's court, he's taken to life as a vampire and put his skills to use—now instead of buying and selling trinkets, he barters deals for Lord Harkon and keeps peace in the court. He loves having control over others and the ability to freely interpret his master's orders in a way that returns the most profit (and inflicts the most pain on others).

Advisor: Vingalmo

Once a member of the Thalmor, Vingalmo was turned by Harkon some hundred years ago and has found vampirism quite enjoyable. Already an accomplished diplomat, he has used his skills to work his way up in Harkon's court and made himself useful. Ultimately his goal is to be the man in charge, but he's in no hurry and is biding his time, attempting to move things into place to make it an easy transition.

Vampire Warrior: Fura Bloodmouth

Well known throughout the court for being vicious and brutal, Fura has gained quite a reputation. She has no capacity for leadership and knows it—she's more than willing to follow whoever is in charge, as long as it means she gets to maim and kill. She is devoted to her master but could be swayed to rebel if it would work out in her favor.

Feeder: Rargal Thrallmaster

Rargal's main role in the court is to make sure Lord Harkon and his underlings are constantly well fed, pulling from the stock of thralls (known as Vampire Cattle) kept in the castle to meet their needs. He prides himself on picking the right thrall for Harkon's mood and keeping the thrall pens well stocked at all times. His cruelty is matched only by his impulsiveness.

Vampire Smith: Hestla

Hestla spent her childhood dreaming of being one of the Companions. When she turned 20, her wish came true and she was invited to join. Unfortunately, her first assignment went badly, and she found herself left for dead in the woods. Even more unfortunate, she was preyed upon by a passing vampire and found herself turned into one. She's been accepted into the court and is glad to have the powers of a vampire, but she is concerned that she's out of her league. She's eager to please, with a slight undertone of concern for her well-being.

Vampire Adept: Ronthil

Once a wizard, Ronthil never really took to the idea of being a vampire. He was useful enough to weasel his way into the court and will now do whatever he must to stay there. He's a total sycophant and will gladly grovel at the feet of whatever master is in front of him so long as his needs are met. He annoys the majority of the other vampires, who have little or no respect for him, but he's good enough at what he does that they tolerate him.

Vampire Adept: Salonia Viria

Salonia won't talk about her past—her life before becoming a vampire. There are rumors that maybe she was part of the Penitus Oculatus, maybe an assassin.... Whatever it was, it wasn't pretty. No one in the court trusts her, especially due to her allegiance to Vingalmo. It's suspected that her presence is a response to Stalf, Vingalmo's answer to Orthjolf's apparent attempt to gain support by stacking the court.

Vampire Adept: Stalf

Stalf was a mountain of a man—all brawn and no brains. Orthjolf claims Stalf is from the same clan, though Stalf doesn't seem to remember that...or much of anything else for that matter. It's suspected that Orthjolf turned Stalf into a vampire to have a bit more muscle backing him up, should he ever attempt a coup against Lord Harkon. So far, neither of them have had the bravery or the opportunity to test this plan.

Other Vampire Adepts

Modhna

Namasur

Death Hounds

CuSith

Garmr

Vampire Advantages

Those choosing to side with the vampires and accept Harkon's "gift" throughout the Dawnguard Main Quest can look forward to some enhancements to their castle and other benefits.

Castle Volkihar Upgrades

Initially, the castle is entirely sealed off. When you bring Serana home during Dawnguard Main Quest: Bloodline, you gain access to the main hall, but the rest of the keep remains sealed until you decide whether to accept or reject Harkon's offer.

After Dawnguard Main Quest: Power of the Blood, you are free to explore the keep; use the smithing, enchanting, and alchemy stations; and feed on the castle's thralls. You can also trade and seek training from the other members of the court.

After Dawnguard Main Quest: The Bloodstone Chalice, Serana's room is refurnished. You can now accept Faction Quests from the members of the court and recruit Death Hounds. You can also drink from the Bloodstone Chalice to enhance your Drain Life abilities.

After Dawnguard Main Quest: Kindred Judgment, you take possession of Lord Harkon's quarters. Optionally, you can improve the castle further, if you wish:

- If you speak to Garan, you can order him to begin repairing the castle, which clears the rubble from a passage connecting the main banquet hall to the central courtyard.
- If you speak to Valerica (in the Soul Cairn), you can convince her to return to the castle. She takes up residence in her laboratory (the Volkihar Ruins area) and takes charge of both the laboratory and the courtyard garden, which are stocked with potions and alchemy ingredients, respectively.

Vampire-Specific Benefits

If you choose to side with the vampires, you gain access to the following:

Vampire Lord Form

Only those of Harkon's bloodline can call upon the power of the Vampire Lord. While it is possible to side with the Dawnguard and still receive this power from Serana, the Dawnguard will shun you if you do. Side with the vampires if you want to use this power to its fullest.

Blood of the Ancients

By completing Dawnguard Main Quest: The Bloodstone Chalice, you gain access to the Blood of the Ancients. This temporary ability enhances the power of your Drain Life spell in both your human and Vampire Lord forms.

Vampire Armor

Vampire Armor: Vampires have a stylish set of light armor that provides bonuses to magic skills and Magicka regeneration equivalent to the bonuses found on robes. Wearing this armor allows you to take advantage of Light Armor perks without sacrificing your casting prowess.

Vampire Lord Items: A number of Vampire Faction Quests will send you in search of enchanted items—such as fabled rings and amulets (Amulet of Bats, pictured)—that enhance your abilities as a Vampire Lord.

Vampire Spells

Vampire mages can use the dark arts of necromancy to strengthen their undead minions.

Necromantic Healing: Restores 10 Health and Stamina to the undead per second.

Heal Undead: Restores 75 Health and Stamina to the undead.

Vampire Animal Companions

Death Hounds are fearsome undead dogs with a powerful bite attack and a persistent Frost Cloak. While they do good damage, they have less health than common dogs at higher levels, so be ready to step in and heal them if necessary.

VAMPIRE TRAINERS AND VENDORS

Vampire Animal Companions

Castle Volkihar Death Hounds are fiercely loyal to their masters. You can bring along one of the two.

✓	NAME	PREREQUISITE	TYPE
☐	CuSith	Dawnguard Main Quest: The Bloodstone Chalice	Death Hound
☐	Garmr	Dawnguard Main Quest: The Bloodstone Chalice	Death Hound

Vampire Trainers

Some of Harkon's brethren are highly skilled. Seek their help before you take on the world of the living!

✓	NAME	SKILL	LEVEL
☐	Fura Bloodmouth	Two-Handed	Master
☐	Garan Marethi	Destruction	Expert
☐	Ronthil	Speech	Expert

Vampire Vendors

Your Dawnguard-dispatching friends also trade with you, offering reasonable prices and a few items you cannot purchase elsewhere:

✓	NAME	SERVICE	NOTES
☐	Feran Sadri	Apothecary	–
☐	Hestla	Blacksmith	Sells Vampire Armor.
☐	Ronthil	General Goods	Sells the unique spells Heal Undead and Necromantic Healing.

There are two additional characters who play a key role in the Dawnguard Quests, but they have a more pragmatic approach to the war between the living and undead or have learned to distrust both sides in this struggle.

Dexion Evicus

Dexion is a Moth Priest. A gentle man by nature, he is content to lose himself in books and readings of the Elder Scrolls. Scholarly pursuits are his passions, and he quails at the thought of danger. After all, he is quite old and sometimes forgetful, especially when preparing for the reading of Elder Scrolls are concerned. If he were to be captured, he would capitulate after being tortured briefly. He is not a strong man, though he is very dedicated to his craft.

Serana (Follower)

Serana is the daughter of Harkon and Valerica. Her mother sealed her away in Dimhollow Crypt to thwart her father's schemes. She grew up very close to her mother and distant from (but not opposed to) her father. Her relationship with her mother was as loving and nurturing as it could be, considering that they were both creatures of the dark. She learned necromancy and other sorts of magic at her mother's side, and she is a powerful mage in her own right.

Even as a child, hers was a fairly lonely life. She's naturally somewhat defensive, though not cold. She can deftly avoid difficult topics and turn the conversation back around into something you thought you wanted to talk about. She's built up these defenses because she has a quick temper and strong passion, so she doesn't let people get too close lest they fall victim to them. She's been taught to genuinely care about those who befriend her, but only so much as they prove worthwhile. She also has a touch of self-deprecating humor and awareness. She's smart, but a bit naive. After being sealed in Dimhollow Crypt for over a thousand years, she is curious about what the world has become. She remembers snow elves and dwarves and is somewhat sad to hear about their passing.

Serana's Powers

✓	NAME	PREREQUISITE	CLASS	SKILLS
☐	Serana	Dawnguard Main Quest: Awakening	Vampire Mage	Sneak, One-Handed, Light Armor, Conjuration, Destruction, Alteration

Like her parents, Serana is a vampire. This gives her the following abilities:

- Immunity to Disease
- Immunity to Poison
- Frost Resistance 50%
- Weakness to Fire 50%
- No Health, Magicka, or Stamina regeneration in sunlight.

Over time, her spells also improve based on your level:

✓	YOUR LEVEL	DRAIN LIFE	OTHER SPELLS
☐	Level 20 or Lower	Absorbs 8 Health per second from her target.	Raise Zombie, Ice Spike
☐	Level 20–27	Absorbs 10 Health and Stamina per second from her target.	Reanimate Corpse, Ice Spike
☐	Level 28–37	Absorbs 12 Health and Stamina per second from her target.	Reanimate Corpse, Ice Spike, Lightning Bolt
☐	Level 38–47	Absorbs 15 Health, Magicka, and Stamina per second from her target.	Revenant, Ice Spike, Lightning Bolt
☐	Level 48 or Higher	Absorbs 20 Health, Magicka, and Stamina per second from her target.	Revenant, Ice Storm, Chain Lightning

NOTE If you ally with the Dawnguard, you can convince Serana to cure herself of her vampirism after completing Dawnguard Main Quest: Kindred Judgment. This permanently removes her Drain Life ability and vampiric strengths and weaknesses, although she remains a formidable magic user.

PREREQUISITES: Complete Dawnguard Main Quest: Bloodline

MINOR SPOILERS

INTERSECTING QUESTS: Dawnguard Main Quest: Bloodline, Dawnguard Main Quest: Prophet

LOCATIONS: Castle Volkihar, Dayspring Canyon, Dwarven Rubble: Druadach, Fort Dawnguard, Random Animal Den

CHARACTERS: Gunmar, Isran, Sorine Jurard, Tilde, Vori

ENEMIES: Animals, Bear

◊ **OBJECTIVES:** Speak with Isran, Recruit Gunmar, Recruit Sorine Jurard, Help Gunmar defeat the bear, Return to Isran

Brazen Incursions at Fort Dawnguard

◊ **OBJECTIVE:** Speak with Isran
♦ **TARGET:** Isran, Fort Dawnguard, the Rift

NOTE This quest is available only to those who have sided with the Dawnguard against the vampire menace.

Once you've been dismissed from Lord Harkon's court and you're back at the castle's jetty, return to Fort Dawnguard via an extensive trek, or Fast-Travel there. As you near the castle, you may run into Vori (another of Isran's trusted forces, and a woman of few words). However, keep your wits about you as you reach the castle's entrance; a vampire menace has infiltrated Dayspring Canyon. Expect combat, with Isran showing his prowess with a mighty Dawnguard hammer against three vampire interlopers. Join the battle, then speak to Isran. He isn't confident you're bringing him good news.

You tell him about Serana, trapped in Dimhollow Crypt, and her bloodline. Isran's demeanor is even less jovial once you mention Serana's Elder Scroll—and your failure to obtain it. He curtly explains that the vampires "have everything they wanted, and we're left with nothing." But all is not lost: Isran knows people who he's met, worked with, and, astoundingly, hasn't alienated. He wants you to find a woman named Sorine Jurand, who is "whip-smart and good with tinkering." You're also tasked with locating Gunmar, a "big brute of a Nord" who is an accomplished blacksmith and animal trainer. Finish your conversation with Isran, and the quest updates.

◊ **OBJECTIVE:** Recruit Gunmar
♦ **TARGET:** Gunmar, [random Animal Den]
◊ **OBJECTIVE:** Recruit Sorine Jurard
♦ **TARGET:** Sorine Jurard, Dwarven Rubble: Druadach, the Reach

NOTE The following two objectives can be completed in either order.

Gunmar: Inducting the Trainer of Trolls

Look to your map to pinpoint the position of Gunmar, who can be found outside an Animal Den. When you approach, Gunmar immediately cautions you to hold fast, telling you he's been tracking a murderous bear for two weeks. When you mention Isran, Gunmar seems nonplussed; he's moved on with his life. Change his mind by mentioning the vampires and their Elder Scroll, and Gunmar realizes the predicament that could befall the realm. He agrees to help, but only after you both defeat the bear lurking within.

◊ **OBJECTIVE:** Help Gunmar defeat the bear

At this point, you can:

Enter the den, fend off any wild animals you encounter, hunt down the bear, and slay it in whatever method you deem appropriate.

Enter the den, wait for Gunmar, and follow him into combat, lending him support while he "bears" the brunt of the attacks.

Inform Gunmar that you've already killed the bear yourself (if you went in without speaking to him). He's suitably impressed.

Once the bear is dead, speak to Gunmar, and he agrees to meet you back at Fort Dawnguard. He will be there the next time you visit; there's no need to follow him.

Sorine Jurard: Drafting the Dwemer Tinkerer

Look to your map to pinpoint Sorine's location. She can be found in the Reach, in a remote location south of the Orc stronghold of Mor Khazgur and north of Druadach Redoubt, at Secondary Location: Dwarven Rubble: Druadach. As you begin talking with her, she seems a little preoccupied with a sack of Dwarven Gyros she has misplaced. After you inform her of Isran's request, she tells you Isran's hurtful comments at the end of their last meeting have dampened her enthusiasm for him, to say the least. But explain the dire situation regarding the vampires, and Sorine is a little more receptive. But she still requires at least one Dwarven Gyro for her research. At this point, you can:

(Persuade) Tell her there's little time to waste. Don't be surprised if Sorine doesn't share your urgency.

Hand over a Dwarven Gyro you may be carrying already.

Startle the Mudcrabs and beat back the odd Forsworn incursion as you search for her lost "sack" along the riverbed. The bag is actually a satchel, lying close to a tree on the riverbank (see picture). There are seven Dwarven Gyros inside Sorine's satchel, but you need give her only one.

Or go in search of a Dwarven Gyro on your own. You can visit any dwarven city in Skyrim (these locations are flagged throughout the Atlas) and manually search chests, tables, and shelves for a Dwarven Gyro. You can also pilfer them from Markarth's Understone Keep, including one right next to Calcelmo, the court wizard. Calcelmo also has several in his museum and quarters in the keep's upper levels. You need acquire only one, then return it to Sorine.

➤ **Dwarven Gyro**

With the Dwarven Gyro secured, return to Sorine Jurard and hand it over to her. She agrees to meet you back at Fort Dawnguard and will be there the next time you visit. There's no need to shadow her progress by following her.

Once both parties have been recruited, your quest updates:

◊ **OBJECTIVE:** Return to Isran
♦ **TARGET:** Fort Dawnguard, the Rift

An Unwelcome Guest

Upon your return to Fort Dawnguard, you'll see Isran and his cohorts have been busy setting up barricades and perimeter defenses. A Dawnguard agent named Tilde usually mans the gate. Speak to her and to Vori (who is patrolling nearby) if you wish. Enter the fort, and both Gunmar and Sorine are waiting in the circular entrance hall. Isran is on an upper balcony and bathes the ground in a strange writhing light. He is testing to see whether the three of you are tainted with vampirism:

If you haven't contracted vampirism, the quest continues.

If you have contracted vampirism, Isran refuses to let you into the fort, and the gates to the rest of the structure remain sealed. At this point, the only way to proceed is to cure yourself by completing Side Quest: Rising at Dawn (consult page 463) or being turned into a werewolf (see the Companions Quest: The Silver Hand on page 242).

When Isran has three healthy helpers, he instructs Gunmar to pen up some armored trolls to use as shock troops, while Sorine is to continue her research on improving the crossbow design. Meanwhile, you have more immediate concerns: A vampire has shown up at the fort, looking for you!

Postquest Activities

As soon as Isran mentions that a vampire is looking for you, Dawnguard Main Quest: Prophet begins.

TIP At this point, you can begin any of the Dawnguard's Faction Quests: In fact, it's recommended you help Sorine with her crossbow research as early as possible (improvements to this weapon make subsequent battles easier if you're employing this weapon), as well as any other ancillary quest Sorine, Gunmar, or Isran may have for you. Consult page 553 for further information.

PREREQUISITES: Complete Dawnguard Main Quest: The Bloodstone Chalice OR Complete Dawnguard Main Quest: A New Order

INTERSECTING QUESTS: Dawnguard Main Quest: The Bloodstone Chalice, Dawnguard Main Quest: A New Order, Dawnguard Main Quest: Seeking Disclosure, Dawnguard Main Quest: Scroll Scouting, Dawnguard Main Quest: Chasing Echoes

MINOR SPOILERS

LOCATIONS: Ambushed Caravan, Castle Volkihar, Dragon Bridge, Forebears' Holdout

LOCATIONS: Ambushed Caravan, Dragon Bridge, Forebears' Holdout, Fort Dawnguard

CHARACTERS: Dexion Evicus, Garan Marethi, Lord Harkon, Serana, (Optional) Urag gro-Shub, (Optional) Carriage drivers throughout Skyrim, (Optional) Innkeepers throughout Skyrim

CHARACTERS: Dexion Evicus, Isran, Serana, (Optional) Urag gro-Shub, (Optional) Carriage drivers throughout Skyrim, (Optional) Innkeepers throughout Skyrim

ENEMIES: Armored Husky, Armored Troll, Dawnguard, Death Hound, Malkus, Vanik

ENEMIES: Vampire, Vampire's Thrall

◊ **OBJECTIVES:** Speak to Harkon, Listen to Harkon's speech, (Optional) Ask carriage drivers about the Moth Priest, (Optional) Ask innkeepers in cities, bout the Moth Priest, Locate a Moth Priest, (Optional) Visit the College of Winterhold to ask about the Moth Priest, Ask people in Dragon Bridge if they saw the Moth Priest, Search along the road south of Dragon Bridge, Investigate the scene of the attack, Read the Vampire's Note, Rescue the Moth Priest, Deactivate the magic barrier, Defeat the enthralled Moth Priest, Use your Vampire's Seduction power on the Moth Priest, Feed on the Moth Priest to make him your thrall, Command the Moth Priest to go to Volkihar Castle, Report your success to Harkon, Command the Moth Priest to read the Elder Scroll, Speak to Harkon, Speak to Serana

◊ **OBJECTIVES:** Follow Isran, Speak to Serana, Speak to Isran, (Optional) Ask carriage drivers about the Moth Priest, (Optional) Ask innkeepers in cities about the Moth Priest, (Optional) Visit the College of Winterhold to ask about the Moth Priest, Locate a Moth Priest, Ask people in Dragon Bridge if they saw the Moth Priest, Search along the road south of Dragon Bridge, Investigate the scene of the attack, Read the Vampire's Note, Rescue the Moth Priest, Deactivate the magic barrier, Defeat the enthralled Moth Priest, Speak to the Moth Priest, Report your success to Isran, Speak to the Moth Priest, Speak to Serana

NOTE Although the objectives for this quest are largely the same for both factions, some events differ depending on which side you have chosen. Dawnguard- and Vampire-specific events are flagged as such throughout the quest.

Vampires: A Prequel to Prophecy

◊ **OBJECTIVE:** Speak to Harkon
♦ **TARGET:** Harkon's chamber, Castle Volkihar

Once you've spoken to Garan Marethi and explained your successes during Dawnguard Main Quest: The Bloodstone Chalice, the Dark Elf tells you to locate Lord Harkon, who wishes to speak with you. You'll find Harkon in one of his private chambers. Harkon reveals his true ambitions, stating that the vampire's greatest weakness is the sun, an enemy they've had no way to fight—that is, until he found an old prophecy written by a Moth Priest, the scholars who read the Elder Scrolls.

Harkon has been obsessed with the prophecy ever since, as it tells of a time when the vampires gain power over the sun itself. He believes Serana's Elder Scroll is the key to unraveling that prophecy. He has ordered his court to assemble and has a new task for all of them to carry out, including you.

◊ **OBJECTIVE:** Listen to Harkon's speech

Follow Lord Harkon to his balcony overlooking the banquet hall. He hails his scions of the night, proclaiming that the prophesied time is upon them. Now that the Elder Scroll is in their possession, Harkon requires a Moth Priest to read it. To this end, he has spread false rumors about the discovery of an Elder Scroll in Skyrim to lure a Moth Priest to these parts, and now his minions must search the land to see if one can be found. He wants his brood to look to the cities, speaking to innkeepers, carriage drivers, anyone who would meet a traveler. That is his command.

After the proclamation, Serana approaches you. Ask for her opinion, and she recommends asking a mage at the College of Winterhold. The quest updates with the following objectives, after which you can quiz Serana on her knowledge of the Elder Scrolls and on her life as a vampire.

◊ **(OPTIONAL) OBJECTIVE:** Ask carriage drivers about the Moth Priest
♦ **TARGET:** Any carriage driver, outside a Hold Capital or your house
◊ **(OPTIONAL) OBJECTIVE:** Ask innkeepers in cities about the Moth Priest
♦ **TARGET:** Any innkeeper in a Hold Capital
◊ **(OPTIONAL) OBJECTIVE:** Visit the College of Winterhold to ask about the Moth Priest
♦ **TARGET:** Urag gro-Shub, the College of Winterhold
◊ **OBJECTIVE:** Locate a Moth Priest
♦ **TARGET:** None

Dawnguard: An Uneasy Alliance

◊ **OBJECTIVE:** Follow Isran
♦ **TARGET:** Upper chambers, Fort Dawnguard

Once Isran has verified that none of his new brethren are night stalkers, he beckons you upstairs to a chamber with a rack and a collection of severed heads. Here you must deal with a vampire that actually had the gall to enter the fort looking for you. Lady Serana is waiting here, much to Isran's chagrin. Apparently, Serana has something really important to say to you.

◊ **OBJECTIVE:** Speak to Serana

Serana begs you to listen, before Isran loses his patience: She has important information regarding the Elder Scroll she was buried with. She explains that her father, an unpleasant character even by vampiric standards, has stumbled onto an obscure prophecy and lost himself in it. She doesn't know the details, except that Lord Harkon has become obsessed with part of the prophecy, stating that vampires would no longer need to fear the sun. He wishes to control the sun and wreck havoc across the world. Serana's mother wasn't happy with the prospect of a war with all of Tamriel, so she tried to stop him, which is why Serana was sealed away in the first place. Serana wants to finish what her mother started. But for that to happen, the Dawnguard need to embrace her. In a nonvampiric way, naturally.

◊ **OBJECTIVE:** Speak to Isran

Your conversation with Isran begins with him violently opposed to Serana. Respond as you wish, and Isran gives in just a little. Instead of out-and-out hostility, he figures Serana must have a death wish or is insane. Neither matters to him. But he'll tolerate her until the moment she lays a finger on anyone here.

After some barbed comments with Isran, Serana turns and explains that the Elder Scroll she carries cannot be read by either of you. Only the Moth Priests have this ability, but she has no idea where to find one. Isran interjects at this point, mentioning an Imperial scholar he saw in Skyrim a few days ago. But he isn't about to waste men trying to find him. However, he suggests you ask innkeepers, carriage drivers, and the like for clues as to the scholar's whereabouts. Ask Serana for her opinion, and she recommends asking a mage over at the College of Winterhold. The quest updates with the following objectives, after which you can quiz Serana on her knowledge of the Elder Scrolls and on her life as a vampire.

◊ **(OPTIONAL) OBJECTIVE:** Ask carriage drivers about the Moth Priest
♦ **TARGET:** Any carriage driver, outside a Hold Capital or your house
◊ **(OPTIONAL) OBJECTIVE:** Ask innkeepers in cities about the Moth Priest
♦ **TARGET:** Any innkeeper in a Hold Capital
◊ **(OPTIONAL) OBJECTIVE:** Visit the College of Winterhold to ask about the Moth Priest
♦ **TARGET:** Urag gro-Shub, The College of Winterhold
◊ **OBJECTIVE:** Locate a Moth Priest
♦ **TARGET:** None

To Catch a Moth Priest

NOTE The parallel faction paths now merge. Continue from this point no matter which faction you've sided with.

Optional Plan 1

Carriage drivers: One plan is to see whether a carriage driver has seen a Moth Priest on their travels. Simply approach one of them (say, Thaer outside of Solitude) and ask. He describes the scholar with impressive precision but then conveniently "forgets" any specific details. You can:

(Persuade) Try pleading, telling him it's vital you find him.

(Bribe) Offer a considerable sum of septims to reveal his knowledge.

Ignore him and try one of the other plans.

If either option is successful, you need not complete the other optional plans. Head to Dragon Bridge, where the driver mentions the Moth Priest was last seen.

Optional Plan 2

Innkeepers: Another option is to press the innkeepers in any of the cities for scuttlebutt about new Imperial arrivals. You can easily travel to any of them and ask about a Moth Priest passing through. Most haven't seen one, but Corpulus Vinius, owner of the Winking Skeever in Solitude, is more circumspect. You can:

(Persuade) Tell him it's important you find him straightaway.

(Bribe) Offer some coinage for his troubles.

Try your luck elsewhere with one of the other plans.

If one of the options is successful, you do not need to finish either of the other optional plans and can visit Dragon Bridge now.

Optional Plan 3

The College of Winterhold: This option is much easier if you've already completed College of Winterhold Quest: First Lessons (page 255) or Main Quest: Elder Knowledge (page 223) and you've already gained entrance to the College. If you haven't, read over the College Quest and prepare the spell for Faralda, who guards the bridge to the College. Once inside the College, head to the Arcanaeum and locate the Lorekeeper, Urag gro-Shub. Inform him you're trying to find a Moth Priest.

Urag gro-Shub tells you that the Priest stopped to research some texts in his library before setting out for Dragon Bridge. Head there now, as you don't need to complete the other two optional plans.

After you complete Optional Plans 1, 2, or 3 (you need finish only one or simply skip them and head straight to Dragon Bridge), the following objective becomes available:

◊ **OBJECTIVE:** Ask people in Dragon Bridge if they saw the Moth Priest
♦ **TARGET:** Citizens in Dragon Bridge, Haafingar Hold

Divulging at Dragon Bridge: Whether you've completed the optional objectives or not, set out for Dragon Bridge and ask around town about a Moth Priest visiting the place. The best bet is to stop and speak to an Imperial Soldier stationed here. He tells you the priest rode through town with an escort of soldiers not long ago. They were headed south.

◊ **OBJECTIVE:** Search along the road south of Dragon Bridge
◊ **OBJECTIVE:** Investigate the scene of the attack
◊ **OBJECTIVE:** Read the Vampire's Note

Move south across the Dragon Bridge and into Hjaalmarch Hold, following the cobblestone road. Your heart sinks as you spot an overturned carriage and bodies strewn near the next bridge. Your quest updates. Among the dead and a scattered copy of Effects of the Elder Scrolls is a vampire's corpse. Search it and read the Vampire's Note; it is from a man named Malkus giving orders for the ambush. The Moth Priest has been taken to the nearby Forebears' Holdout, a new location close by.

NOTE This ambushed caravan is just north of Secondary Location [2.D]: Ambushed Caravan, a location that has now disappeared.

◊ **OBJECTIVE:** Rescue the Moth Priest
♦ **TARGET:** Moth Priest, Forebear's Holdout

Over the bridge and in the low foothills is a collection of standing stones marking the entrance to Forebears' Holdout. The narrow rocky tunnel opens up to a much larger subterranean fortification (second picture), with a strange stone plateau upon which a shimmering barrier has been conjured. Take care, as the place is populated by enemies.

NOTE The parallel paths now split slightly, depending on the faction you sided with: Vampires or Dawnguard.

Vanquishing Vanik's Dawnguard

You may attack from range, at the initial balcony. Turn left (south), and walk through the giant stalagmites to the stone bridge, bringing down Armored Huskies as you go. Continue along the opposite riverbank, sneaking or battling your way into a large and roughly circular bailey, with a giant bonfire in the middle of it. Engage the Dawnguard and their Armored Troll as you fight up onto the crenellations, toward a strange and shimmering magical barrier. A vampire named Malkus has been slain by the Dawnguard's leader, a foe named Vanik; you must vanquish him at this upper stone summoning plateau. Then search Malkus's corpse for a Weystone Focus.

➤ **Weystone Focus**

◊ **OBJECTIVE:** Deactivate the magic barrier
♦ **TARGET:** Weystone Focus and Weystone Source, close by

Climb the stone steps to the balcony overlooking the magical barrier surrounded by open coffins, and press the Weystone Focus into the Source. The Weystones imprisoning the figure inside the vortex recede, releasing a man named Dexion Evicus, the fabled Moth Priest you've been searching for. He is quite hostile toward you and must be faced in combat. Fight him until he falls to his knees.

◊ **OBJECTIVE:** Defeat the enthralled Moth Priest
◊ **OBJECTIVE:** Use your Vampire's Seduction power on the Moth Priest
◊ **OBJECTIVE:** Feed on the Moth Priest to make him your thrall
◊ **OBJECTIVE:** Command the Moth Priest to go to Volkihar Castle

Dexion's Enthralled Ruminations

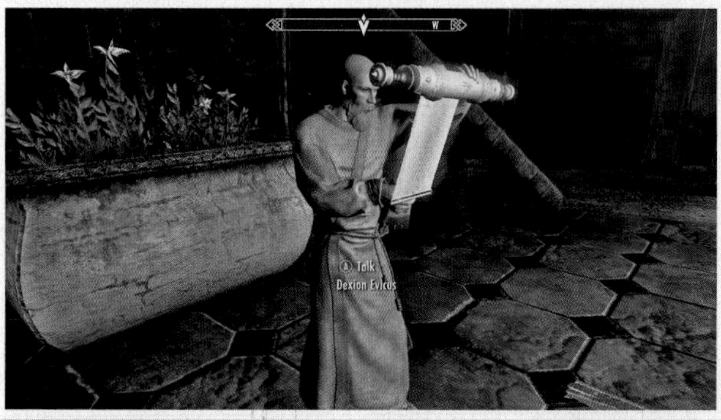

Once the Moth Priest yields but is still hostile to your actions, you are prompted to employ your Vampire's Seduction (Magic > Powers) on him. Once he's bathed in green light, talk to Dexion Evicus and feed on him. Once you've sunk your teeth into his neck and fed, speak to him again. He has been blinded by your majesty and must obey you! Command him to travel to Castle Volkihar. He agrees and sets off shortly. You may also wish to ask him about what exactly it is he does and about the Elder Scrolls. You need not chaperone him; he will be at the castle the next time you're there.

TIP Only Stage 2 (or higher) vampires have the Vampire's Seduction power. If you fed recently, you may need to wait a day to acquire this power and continue the quest.

◊ **OBJECTIVE:** Report your success to Harkon
◊ **OBJECTIVE:** Command the Moth Priest to read the Elder Scroll
♦ **TARGET:** Lord Harkon, Castle Volkihar, Haafingar Hold

Back inside Volkihar Castle's keep, stride toward Lord Harkon, who is already congratulating you and Serana on locating the Moth Priest. Tell Harkon you've made the Moth Priest your thrall, mentioning the Dawnguard you fought to reach him (any answer is fine). Harkon then wishes you would command your puppet to read the words of the prophecy.

Head over to the Moth Priest and request he read Serana's Elder Scroll. He unfurls the scroll parchment and begins his vision. He sees a great weapon called Auriel's Bow. He reads the scroll aloud, foretelling "darkness mingling with light and the night and day will be as one." The secret to the bow's power is written elsewhere, recorded in other scrolls. One contains the ancient secrets of the dragons, while the other speaks of the potency of ancient blood. Dexion's vision fades, and he tells you that to complete the prophecy, the other two scrolls must be obtained.

◊ **OBJECTIVE:** Speak to Harkon

Quest Conclusion: Three Scrolls to Find

Lord Harkon could best be described as "nonplussed" when you return to him, as the reading gave far less information than he was expecting. Ask him where these other scrolls are, and he admits his "traitor wife" stole one of them before disappearing. As for the other? He believes it was lost in the bowels of a Dwemer ruin. This quest now concludes.

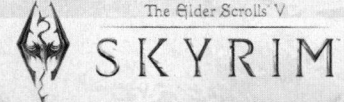

Vanquishing Malkus's Vampires

You can try ranged attacks from the initial balcony. Turn left (south), and walk down through the giant stalagmites to the stone bridge, bringing down Death Hounds as you go. Continue along the opposite riverbank, sneaking or battling into a large and roughly circular bailey, with a giant bonfire in the middle of it. Engage vampires and Vampire Thralls as you fight up onto the crenellations, toward a strange and shimmering magical barrier. An unclean vampire named Malkus is waiting to thwart you at this upper stone summoning plateau. Defeat him, then search his corpse for a Weystone Focus.

➤ Weystone Focus

◊ **OBJECTIVE:** Deactivate the magic barrier
♦ **TARGET:** Weystone Focus and Weystone Source, close by

Climb the stone steps to the balcony overlooking the magical barrier surrounded by open coffins, and press the Weystone Focus into the Source. The Weystones imprisoning the figure inside the vortex recede, freeing a man named Dexion Evicus, the fabled Moth Priest you've been searching for. Unfortunately, he is still under the power of the vampire and must be thwarted in combat. Fight him until he crumples to his knees.

◊ **OBJECTIVE:** Defeat the enthralled Moth Priest
◊ **OBJECTIVE:** Speak to the Moth Priest

Dexion's Imprecise Ponderings

Once the Moth Priest yields, he begs you to forgive him, saying that wasn't him you were fighting—he was being controlled by others. But now that you've broken the foul vampire's hold over him, Dexion Evicus is most grateful.

Ask him if he's all right, and inform him that you're after him for the same purpose. Answer how you wish, encouraging Dexion to visit Fort Dawnguard. He agrees and sets off shortly. You may also ask him about what it is he does exactly and about the Elder Scrolls. You need not chaperone him; he will be at the castle the next time you're there.

◊ **OBJECTIVE:** Report your success to Isran
◊ **OBJECTIVE:** Speak to the Moth Priest
♦ **TARGET:** Isran, Fort Dawnguard, the Rift

Back inside Fort Dawnguard's keep, walk toward Isran, who is already congratulating you and Serana on locating the Moth Priest. Ask Isran if he has the Scroll and if everything is ready, and Isran answers in the affirmative, telling you to speak to the Moth Priest when you're ready to listen to his ruminations.

Approach the Moth Priest and ask if he's ready to read the Elder Scroll. He appears to be, asking everyone to quiet down so he can concentrate. He unfurls the scroll parchment and begins his vision. He sees a great weapon called Auriel's Bow. He reads the scroll aloud, foretelling "darkness mingling with light and the night and day will be as one." The secret to the bow's power is written elsewhere, recorded in other scrolls. One contains the ancient secrets of the dragons, while the other speaks of the potency of ancient blood. Dexion's vision fades, and he tells you that to complete the prophecy, the other two scrolls must be obtained.

Quest Conclusion: A Trio of Scrolls to Source

The Moth Priest heads off to rest, and Isran leaves to attend to other matters, leaving you and Serana to ponder the location of the other scrolls. Serana admits her mother stole one of them before disappearing. As for the other? She believes it to be lost in the catacombs of an ancient Dwemer ruin. This quest now concludes.

Postquest Activities

◊ **OBJECTIVE:** Speak to Serana

As soon as you finish speaking with either Lord Harkon (Vampires) or Isran (Dawnguard), this quest concludes, and at least three new Dawnguard Main Quests may commence: Seeking Disclosure (which tracks when both remaining Elder Scrolls are found), Chasing Echoes (the quest to find the Elder Scroll [Blood]), and Scroll Scouting (the quest to find the Elder Scroll [Dragons], if you don't already have it). The latter two quests can be attempted in either order.

SEEKING DISCLOSURE

PREREQUISITES: Complete Dawnguard Main Quest: Prophet

MINOR SPOILERS

INTERSECTING QUESTS: Dawnguard Main Quest: Prophet, Dawnguard Main Quest: Scroll Scouting, Dawnguard Main Quest: Chasing Echoes, Dawnguard Main Quest: Beyond Death

◊ **OBJECTIVES:** Find the Elder Scroll (Blood), Find the Elder Scroll (Dragon), Bring both Elder Scrolls to Dexion

Unraveling the Elder Scrolls

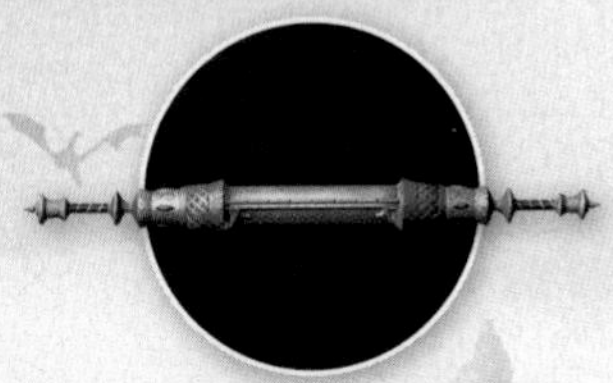

The Elder Scroll (Blood): Found with Serana's mother, deep within the otherworldly Soul Cairn, at the zenith of Dawnguard Main Quest: Beyond Death.

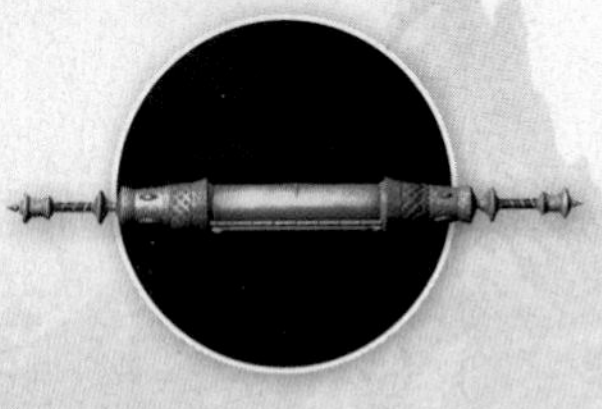

The Elder Scroll (Dragon): Found within the Dwemer Ruin known as the Tower of Mzark.

This is an "overview" quest, designed to help you keep track of your overall objectives from this point forward: To locate both remaining Elder Scrolls and bring them to Dexion Evicus. This runs concurrently with the specific quests related to each Elder Scroll in question. This quest concludes once both Elder Scrolls are in your possession and you've visited the Moth Priest. The specific quests to obtain both Scrolls can be completed in either order. Refer to the following quests to find each Scroll and conclude this quest:

✓	TYPE	QUEST NAME	RELEVANT ELDER SCROLL
☐	Dawnguard Main Quest	Scroll Scouting*	Dragon
☐	Main Quest	Elder Knowledge*	Dragon
☐	Daedric Quest	Discerning the Transmundane*	Dragon
☐	Dawnguard Main Quest	Chasing Echoes**	Blood
☐	Dawnguard Main Quest	Beyond Death**	Blood

NOTE * All three of these quests require you to access Blackreach (usually through Alftand or any other Dwarven ruin) and the Tower of Mzark to retrieve the Elder Scroll (Dragon). These are discussed in greater detail during Dawnguard Main Quest: Scroll Scouting.

** You must complete both of these quests in order to obtain Elder Scroll (Blood).

The section of this quest detailing what happens when you bring both Elder Scrolls to Dexion Evicus is detailed at the end of Dawnguard Main Quest: Beyond Death, later in this guide. Consult page 538 for all the information.

SCROLL SCOUTING

PREREQUISITES: Complete Dawnguard Main Quest: Prophet

MINOR SPOILERS

INTERSECTING QUESTS: Dawnguard Main Quest: Prophet, Dawnguard Main Quest: Scroll Scouting, Dawnguard Main Quest: Chasing Echoes, Dawnguard Main Quest: Beyond Death, Dawnguard Main Quest: Unseen Visions

LOCATIONS: Alftand, Alftand Animonculory, Alftand Cathedral, Alftand Glacial Ruins, Alftand Ruined Tower , Blackreach, College of Winterhold, The Arcanaeum, Hall of the Elements, Septimus Signus's Outpost, Tower of Mzark, Oculory

CHARACTERS: Septimus Signus, Serana, Urag gro-Shub

ENEMIES: Dwarven Centurion, Dwarven Sphere, Dwarven Spider, Falmer, Frostbite Spider , Horker, Ice Wolf, J'darr, Skeever, Sulla, Umana, Wolf

◊ **OBJECTIVES:** Ask Urag about the insane book, Daedric Quest Objective: Find Septimus Signus, Daedric Quest Objective: Transcribe the Lexicon, Recover the Elder Scroll, Buy back the Elder Scroll (Dragon) from Urag gro-Shub

Prelude: No Need to Repeat Yourself

NOTE This quest and Seeking Disclosure (which updates when you've secured each Elder Scroll) and Chasing Echoes (which begins the search for the Elder Scroll [Blood]) all begin concurrently. This quest and Chasing Echoes can be attempted in either order. This quest mirrors your search for the Scroll in Main Quest: Elder Knowledge (page 223) and Daedric Quest: Discerning the Transmundane (page 384).

In order to begin this quest, you must answer this all-important question: Have you already secured the Elder Scroll (Dragon)? There are three possible answers:

"No, I've never had it." This activates the following quest, and you must complete Plan 1 of it.

"Yes, I am carrying it." This quest does not activate; you skip it entirely. Begin Chasing Echoes instead.

"Yes, but I sold it." This quest activates, but you can skip to Plan 2 and buy back the Scroll from Urag gro-Shub.

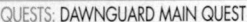

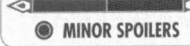

Plan 1: Hunting the Scroll—Scouting for Septimus Signus

After you talk with Serana, your map marker has flagged the College of Winterhold, where Serana believes you should begin your search. Journey to the College. At the bridge's near end, Faralda, a High Elf wizard, guards the entrance. She stops you, warning that it's not safe to cross the bridge and that you will be denied entrance to the College. Although she has some complaints about the College, which you can ask her about, you really just want to gain entry. Ask if this is possible, and she asks why. Choose the answer that best suits your demeanor. She requires that you take a test to show you're at least competent in the use of magic. You can:

Walk right in without dealing with Faralda, if you're already a member of the College of Winterhold.

(Persuade) Tell her that you both know you'll be successful.

Agree to take the test. When the test begins, Faralda requests you aim a spell at the seal on the ground near her.

Ask if she would grant entry to the Dragonborn. Faralda asks if you really have the Voice. If you have completed Main Quest: Dragon Rising (see page 205), simply demonstrate any Shout you have.

Spell Casting: Bring up your Magic inventory and choose the spell Faralda has requested. She can choose Firebolt, Magelight, Fury, Conjure Flame Atronach, or Healing Hands, depending on your available spells and knowledge of particular magic styles. Aim at the seal and cast the spell. After a successful casting, Faralda tells you to find Mirabelle Ervine inside the College. If you don't have the spell Faralda requests, simply purchase it from her.

Dragon Shouting: Bring up your Shout inventory, choose any Shout (a good choice is Fire Breath), aim it at the seal, and bellow. After you strike the seal, Faralda tells you there is much you both can learn from each other and that you'd be a superb addition to the College.

You can now ask Faralda more questions about Mirabelle and the College, or even receive training in the arts of Destruction Magic. The College of Winterhold Quest: First Lessons is now active, and you are told to report to Mirabelle Ervine. However, this is not required or even part of the Scroll Scouting Quest. Cross the bridge, enter the College's exterior courtyard, open the grand doors, and enter the Hall of the Elements. Immediately make a right (east) turn and enter the Arcanaeum.

CAUTION

Be extremely careful where you wave your fingers! Don't aim (accidentally or otherwise) at Faralda or choose a spell (or Shout) that has a large area of effect. If you cast a wider flame-based attack, you risk setting Faralda on fire, effectively ending your tryout as an apprentice mage!

TIP Do you want to mingle with other mages? Then consult the College of Winterhold Quests for further information on the denizens of this epicenter of magic in Skyrim.

Look for the Orc Mage named Urag gro-Shub, who runs the Arcanaeum; you may have already run into him during Dawnguard Main Quest: Prophet. Although you can ask to assist him in College business, you're really here to ask him about the Elder Scroll. Urag isn't too happy with you offhandedly inquiring about such a powerful artifact. You may listen to an overview of the Scrolls before asking if there's an Elder Scroll you could use. Urag laughs at this question; he wouldn't show the likes of you, even if he obtained one. Ask if he at least has any information on them. He agrees to locate a couple of arcane tomes that may have some clues. But mostly they contain lies leavened with rumors.

Urag gro-Shub locates and places two tomes on the nearby desk: *Effects of the Elder Scrolls* and *Ruminations on the Elder Scrolls.* After reading both books (which you may keep or leave on the desk), you find that the Ruminations tome is the work of a madman. Daedric Quest: Discerning the Transmundane is now active, providing its prerequisites have been met.

- *Effects of the Elder Scrolls*
- *Ruminations on the Elder Scrolls*

◊ **OBJECTIVE:** Ask Urag about the insane book

Speak with Urag again and let him know that the *Ruminations* book is incomprehensible. He doesn't seem surprised. After all, this book was the work of Septimus Signus. Although Signus is the world's leading scholar on the nature of the Elder Scrolls, Urag tells you he's "been gone for a long while." You suspect he means both mentally and physically. He currently resides north of the College in the treacherous Ice Fields. This quest now concludes, and Daedric Quest: Discerning the Transmundane starts. For your convenience, the rest of that quest is now detailed:

◊ **DAEDRIC QUEST OBJECTIVE:** Find Septimus Signus
♦ **TARGET:** Septimus Signus's Outpost

The Hermit of Hermaeus Mora

The giant chunks of ice floating off the Northern Coast are your next destination. Exit the College and run down to the frigid coastal waters. Hop across any floating ice that you can, navigating your way north. Expect to slice into a few Horkers along the way, and you may encounter wolves and Ice Wolves.

Septimus Signus's Outpost is cut into one of the hill-sized icebergs, close to a moored rowboat. Climb down the ladder and the slope to reach a lone mage in a chamber of ice. He appears to be guarding some kind of Dwemer box about the size of a house.

Asking Septimus about the Elder Scrolls results in a torrent of knowledge. Ask where the Scroll is, and after receiving moderately useless information, ask once more (either pleasantly or with a more threatening tone). Septimus agrees to tell you, but in return, you must venture into Blackreach, a strange underground Dwemer city that lies below Alftand.

Ask about getting into Blackreach. Septimus keeps up his riddle-based prattling and hands you two items: The first is an odd-edged lexicon, used by the Dwemer for inscribing. The second is an Attunement Sphere, which apparently "sings" when you near an important Dwemer door. Once these are in your grasp, your Main Quest updates. Stay and speak further with Septimus if your sanity can stand it.

➤ **Attunement Sphere** ➤ **Blank Lexicon**

◊ **DAEDRIC QUEST OBJECTIVE:** Transcribe the Lexicon
♦ **TARGET:** Daedric Quest, in Blackreach
◊ **OBJECTIVE:** Recover the Elder Scroll
♦ **TARGET:** Tower of Mzark

Trek to the Tower

TIP You must have the Attunement Sphere on your person in order to continue; otherwise, you cannot access the route necessary to reach the Elder Scroll. The following location is one of a few entrances to a giant underground city called Blackreach. This is the optimal path, but there are others. Consult the Atlas to see all the ways to enter this subterranean citadel and the Tower of Mzark.

Alftand is located on the glacial mountains southwest of Winterhold. Your trek there is usually interrupted by wild animal attacks. The exterior of Alftand is a series of dotted structures, both Dwarven and Nordic in nature. Below the glaciers is the Alftand Ruined Tower, which offers a dangerous route to the glacier's top. A much better way is to stay outside to reach the two windswept huts, an inaccessible Dwarven tower, and a precarious platform on the side of the glacier that winds down and around the rooftops. Head down the planked bridges near the shack on the glacier's edge until you reach the entrance to the Alftand Glacial Ruins. This is the way to go.

Wind through the glacial tunnels that have been mined out and left in a real mess, with debris and cooking equipment strewn about and the signs of fighting everywhere you look. Follow the tunnel down until you reach the beginnings of the Dwarven architecture, a stone tunnel that ends in a connecting room with a stone table and a large barred doorway to the north. This can only be unlocked from the other side. On the nearby table you'll find Research Notes. Whoever wrote it thought he saw a strange human figure on the other side of the barred doorway.

➤ **Research Notes**

At this point, the passage west heads up a ramp and down the other side, into another glacial intrusion. Watch for attacks from a Dwarven Spider as you go. A Skooma-addled Khajiit is shouting about being trapped here and attacks if he sees you. Drop him, and continue down into the start of the main Dwarven ruins. The ceilings tower above you as you reach a cog and piston room with a raised center and two Dwarven Spheres appearing from their wall holes to attack.

Continue north to a vent chamber with a locked gate (Novice) leading to a few scraps of treasure. Head through the gold door and up to a Dwarven Spider–infested passage stretching south. This leads to a locked (Apprentice) gold door with items to steal behind it and a main path around to the east, which brings you back into the cog and piston room. This time, you're above the raised center. Navigate the pistons (jump over them, or you risk being pushed off by them) in a counterclockwise route to the short corridor and door to the Alftand Animonculory.

TIP There are many trinkets of Dwemer origin to pick up (and sell once you leave). Among the vendors across Skyrim, a wizard named Calcelmo in Markarth's Understone Keep is most interested in these items and gives a good price, although you can sell them to any merchant or vendor who wants them.

Move through the green-tinged corridor to an opening on your left (east). This leads to a large pipeworks corridor. Avoid two Dwarven Spheres by staying on the low ground, and head through the gap in the gold fencing to the left of the stone steps. Otherwise, head up the steps, over the pipes, and up the ramp with the central slit. Walk on the slit so you don't trigger a blade trap by stepping on the pressure plates. At the barred doorway, use the lever on your right to lower the bars. The lever behind the bars raises them, which isn't necessary unless you're being pursued and want to halt your attackers. Step out into the grand Animonculory shaft—a long vertical drop you must descend without falling. Remove any Dwarven Spider threats, and head down the sloping stone walkway to an arched entrance platform. The gold door here (Apprentice) just leads to a dead end and more treasure.

Peer over the edge of the stone platform facing into the shaft. The walkway below has crumbled, forcing you to drop onto the jutting gold pipe and then the rubble platform. There is a walkway to the west that leads to a precarious ledge, a Dwarven Spider battle, and a piston that can push you over the edge. The way forward and down is to the northeast. Look for the lantern and falling water, as the sloping walkway is hidden.

As you descend, something horrific shuffles out of the shadows: an eyeless figure, thought to be myth. These are Falmer, the degenerate remnants of the original Elven inhabitants of Skyrim! Dispatch four of them as you follow the winding platform down. Take care not to lose your footing and fall to your death. Next, face the jet of fire blasting the entrance to a gold door. Dart through or around, and enter a Falmer nest.

Falmer appear from their huts, forcing you to fight or sneak by. Follow the passage down to a second set of Falmer in a boiler chamber. Watch for those rattling, hanging bones if you're sneaking, as these startle the Falmer into finding you. Head down the steps, watching for Skeever attacks, and look for a gold door on the southeast wall. This is the way onward, but you may wish to turn to the northwest, open a gate, and enter an ancient Dwarven Elevator. Pull the lever and you ascend to the Alftand Glacial Ruins.

Step around the rubble and to the barred doorway where you found the Research Notes. Pull a wall lever here so the bars retract. This allows you to easily navigate up and down the Animonculory if you explore here in the future. For now, use the elevator to head back down, and open the gold door in the southeast wall. This leads down to the shaft's bottom, where you encounter another Falmer attack and face a Frostbite Spider. From here, you have only one set of corridor steps and a claw trap (move around the trip wire) before you enter the Alftand Cathedral.

Battle a Falmer and navigate some floor trigger plates to reach a gold door that leads out into the main cathedral chamber—a massive echoing cavern with a central structure and a doorway barred with spears. Check the area for Falmer and the steps to your left (south) before heading to a gold lever above the entrance from which you came.

This raises the spears, enabling you to enter the cathedral platform, where a giant steam-powered mechanical monster roars to life. This Dwarven Centurion is a frightening form, but you should defeat it, as it carries a handy key.

➤ **Key to Alftand Lift**

Climb to the gate (southwest) at the platform's top, open it, and listen to the arguments of two thieves, Sulla and Umana. You must slay them, as there's no reasoning with them. Now open the gate beyond the strange Dwarven Mechanism. This leads to the top of the Alftand glacier, a tower you couldn't access when you first reached here.

Open the gate from the inside using the wall lever (so you can access the cathedral directly from the surface during future adventures); then travel back down to the cathedral. Approach the Dwarven Mechanism now, and insert the Attunement Sphere Septimus gave you. The floor parts, revealing stairs down to a hidden gold door and an entrance into the mysterious undercity of Blackreach.

NOTE Take a moment to adjust to the vastness of this cavern. Aside from firing a Dwarven ballista using an adjacent lever and investigating the small stone building to the southwest (Sinderion's Field Laboratory, where you can start collecting Crimson Nirnroot and begin Side Quest: A Return to Your Roots), there is a sprawling area to adventure through. Consult the Atlas for information on the entire area; this walkthrough points you directly to the exit necessary to reach the Elder Scroll.

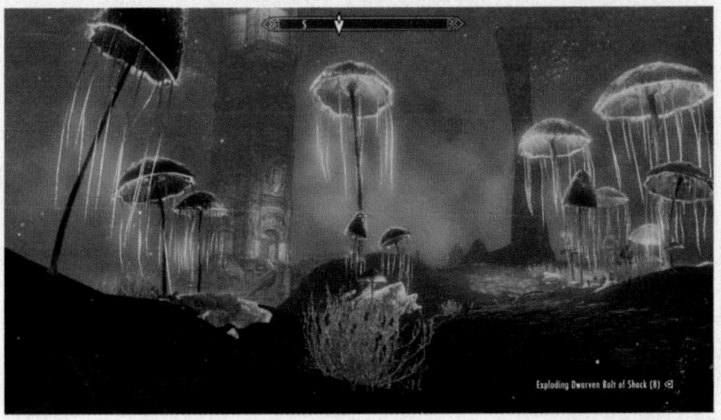

Head west to exit Blackreach using the appropriate Dwarven Elevator. First, though, you may wish to head southeast, to a golden button encased on a Dwarven head pedestal. Press it, and the elevator behind lights up, allowing you to ascend back to the exterior. Open the gate, allowing you to enter from the Great Lift at Alftand (a tower entrance northeast of Nightgate Inn). Return to Blackreach and find the cobblestone path heading roughly west. Follow it past ancient structures and towering luminescent fungi. Continue with a giant lake and cascading waterfalls to your left (south), heading over a stone bridge. Go west and turn left (south) to reach a colossal elevator that allows you to ascend into the Tower of Mzark, your destination.

Oculory Operation

Venture along a corridor with a burst steam pipe and small camping area, and go through gold doors into a gigantic, circular Aedrome chamber, which is dominated by a huge sphere. This appears to be some kind of massive Oculory, with a variety of focusing lenses and other golden machinery attached.

Head to the cluster of controls on the platform above the Oculory. The controls are comprised of five cylindrical devices: a lexicon receptacle and four positioning buttons embedded in pedestals. There is a certain way to use these devices to produce something hidden in one of the lenses.

Puzzle solution: Activate the lexicon receptacle, so the blank lexicon rests on top of it. The two pedestals to the receptacle's right—the only ones currently active—open and close the Oculory lenses. Press the taller of the two pedestals (right of the middle one with the lens chart on it) three or four times, until the pedestal with the blue button to the left of the middle one starts to glow. Move to this new pedestal (at this point, the blank lexicon may be glowing blue). The two pedestals to the receptacle's left—the taller of which is now active—control the ceiling lens array. Press the button of the taller, left pedestal twice, until the button on the far left, smaller pedestal begins to glow. Now press that button, and a large set of lens crystals descends from the ceiling and stops. The main crystal rotates and splits apart to reveal the Elder Scroll in a jeweled scroll holder.

Quest Conclusion

Drop from the balcony controls and approach the open lens crystal. Take the Elder Scroll from its elaborate compartment. Then exit using the door under the lexicon receptacle. This leads to one final Dwarven Elevator, which allows you to open the gate from the Tower of Mzark, step out into the exterior, and add another possible entrance to Blackreach, if you decide to return.

➤ **The Elder Scroll (Dragon)**

Plan 2: Buying the Scroll—Urag Drives a Hard Bargain

If you previously completed Main Quest: Elder Knowledge, used the Scroll during Main Quest: Alduin's Bane, and you've sold the Scroll to Urag gro-Shub, a new objective appears:

◊ **OBJECTIVE:** Buy back the Elder Scroll (Dragon) from Urag gro-Shub
♦ **TARGET:** Urag gro-Shub, College of Winterhold Arcanaeum

Visit the Lorekeeper, and explain your predicament to him. Somewhat understandably, he isn't happy to hand over such a precious piece of parchment. You'll need to pay for your mistake. You can:

Pay the 4,000 gold Urag gro-Shub is asking for the Elder Scroll.

(Persuade) Sweet-talk the Orc into lowering his asking price to 3,000 gold.

Or, if you've completed all the College of Winterhold Quests, and you've been granted the title of Arch-Mage, you can insist that Urag sell it back to you for its original purchase price of 2,000 gold.

➤ **The Elder Scroll (Dragon)**

Postquest Activities

Once you acquire the Elder Scroll, you are free to return to the giant underground city of Blackreach or continue Daedric Quest: Discerning the Transmundane. Consult that quest for further information. For now, though, you should rendezvous with Serana to begin Dawnguard Main Quest: Chasing Echoes (if the other Elder Scroll is yet to be found) or Dawnguard Main Quest: Unseen Visions (if you now have all three Elder Scrolls in your possession).

CHASING ECHOES

PREREQUISITES: Complete Dawnguard Main Quest: Prophet

MINOR SPOILERS

INTERSECTING QUESTS: Dawnguard Main Quest: Prophet, Dawnguard Main Quest: Scroll Scouting, Dawnguard Main Quest: Chasing Echoes, Dawnguard Main Quest: Beyond Death, Dawnguard Main Quest: Unseen Visions

LOCATIONS: Castle Volkihar, Volkihar Courtyard, Volkihar Ruins, Volkihar Undercroft, Soul Cairn

CHARACTERS: Serana, Valerica

ENEMIES: Death Hound, Feral Vampire, Gargoyle, Giant Frostbite Spider, Skeever, Skeleton

◊ **OBJECTIVES:** Speak to Serana, Explore Castle Volkihar's Courtyard, Locate Valerica's Journal, Investigate the moondial, Explore Castle Volkihar's Ruined Tower, Speak to Serana, Gather Soul Gem Shards, Gather Finely Ground Bone Meal, Gather Purified Void Salts, Place the ingredients in the vessel, Speak to Serana, Enter the Soul Cairn

A Rummage Through Valerica's Undercroft

NOTE This quest and Seeking Disclosure (which updates only as you secure each Elder Scroll) and Scroll Scouting (which begins the search for the Elder Scroll [Dragon]) all begin concurrently. You can attempt this quest and Scroll Scouting in either order. The Scroll Scouting Quest may not run if you already have the Elder Scroll (Dragon) in your inventory.

◊ **OBJECTIVE:** Speak to Serana

At the culmination of Dawnguard Main Quest: Prophet, when prying ears are away from the pair of you, Serana asks, "Do you have a moment to talk?" Indulge her. When you ask about the Elder Scroll, she says she firmly believes her mother, Valerica, holds the key to its whereabouts, but unfortunately, she only knows that Valerica left to go "somewhere safe." Prompt her to think of Castle Volkihar, and she excitedly tells you of a courtyard in the castle where she used to tend a garden. She also knows of a back way you can reach the courtyard without arousing suspicion.

◊ **OBJECTIVE:** Explore Castle Volkihar's Courtyard

♦ **TARGET:** Volkihar Courtyard, Castle Volkihar, Haafingar Hold

Return to the exterior of Castle Volkihar, then head to the left (northern) side of the bridge from the jetty watchtower, toward an unused inlet on the northern side of the island once used to bring supplies into the castle. It seems the previous owners left a skeleton crew—literally, as you're attacked by three or four bony fiends as you clamber onto the U-shaped jetty. Use the stone balconies to gain height and cover, before climbing the steps to enter Volkihar Undercroft.

An air of dank fetidness greets you as you head down a set of narrow steps and balconies, pausing to rid the ground of Skeever vermin. A look across the balcony (or via the door you open) reveals a gloomy interior dock filled with supporting buttresses and the soft, padded footsteps of Death Hounds. Bring your finest fiend-culling equipment to bear and begin defeating the hounds and their mistress, a Feral Vampire cast down from Harkon's court (you can read her scribblings on a Journal Fragment contained on her corpse). Pass by her shelves and small Alchemy Lab, up the steps to the west. Here you'll find an upper platform of mead barrels, a small table with a copy of the Aetherium Wars on it, and a nearby lever that opens a portcullis below and to your right (west). You can now progress deeper into the Undercroft.

➤ **Journal Fragment**

Serana warns you to take a left at the bridge, with exits left and right; her father has built a security measure to negotiate. Heading to the right (north) takes you through a tunnel of bear traps, down to the spiked watery lower level with no exit, and sometimes a lone Skeever to fight. Instead, head down the left (south) tunnel, avoiding the dangling spike traps, to engage a trio of Death Hounds sniffing around several bone piles in this waterlogged catacomb. Then step out into the bone pile room, sloshing about in the water and noting the open grating above from which prisoners were once dropped.

Not Your Mother's Keeper

Serana is ecstatic to finally see her mother. Valerica instantly thinks something is wrong, that Harkon has found a way to decipher the prophecy, but Serana assures her you're both here to stop him, to make everything right. The thought of strangers darkens Valerica's mood, and she orders you to speak with her.

◊ **OBJECTIVE:** Speak to Valerica

Valerica is suspicious you're here to kill her. You may answer her in any way you wish. Eventually, she reveals that the real key to the Prophecy of the Tyranny of the Sun is Serana herself. The second Elder Scroll that Valerica fled Castle Volkihar with declared that "the Blood of Coldharbour's Daughter will blind the eye of the Dragon." Both Serana and Valerica are "Daughters of Coldharbour" women who offer themselves to the Daedric Prince Molag Bal.

Other revelations abound: Serana's blood is integral to fulfilling the prophecy that Harkon seeks to complete, which is why both mother and daughter fled from Harkon in the first place. But now Harkon grows stronger. The conversation ends with you mentioning you're here for the Elder Scroll and Valerica telling Serana you're here for your own ends.

This talk infuriates Serana, who reveals how dedicated you've been to her in the short time you've known her, especially compared to being placed alive in a sarcophagus by her own mother! After more heated discussions, Valerica comes to an uneasy understanding with her daughter but agrees to assist you both. She has the Elder Scroll safely locked away in her prison, and you're fortunately in a position to breach the barrier that surrounds her.

You must locate the tallest of the rocky spires that surround these prison ruins. Each spire is tended by a Keeper, and destroying all three will release the barrier. Valerica also has one more word of warning: There is a dragon called Durnehviir roaming the Soul Cairn. You are to watch for him; the Ideal Masters have charged him with overseeing the Keepers, and he will intervene if he perceives you as a threat. Your quest updates, and you can ask Valerica for much more information (about her imprisonment, the Soul Cairn, and who the Ideal Masters are).

NOTE The plane of Coldharbour is Molag Bal's dominion within Oblivion. Great slave pens are said to lie in the oozing mud of this domain, while the skies burn in a continuous belch of fire, and a persistent chill envelops the air: This place is arguably more unpleasant than the Soul Cairn you're standing in!

TIP You can complete the following objective prior to finding Valerica, although there are no map markers showing their location if you find the Keepers first. We provide the optimal path to each of them.

◊ **OBJECTIVE:** Kill the Boneyard Keepers (3)

NOTE The Ideal Masters are mystic entities that lord over the Soul Cairn, controlling every aspect from its fabric to its appearance. Necromancers believe they are the crystalline structures dotting the Soul Cairn, but Valerica believes they've transcended their physical forms. Seek out Valerica for more information.

Freeing a Kept Woman

You may speak to Serana at length about her mother, then check your compass and notice three new markers: These are the locations of the three Keepers. If you're attempting to find the Keepers without the markers, look to the horizon for the tallest rocky spires in the Soul Cairn, with the disintegrating brickwork swirling into the sky.

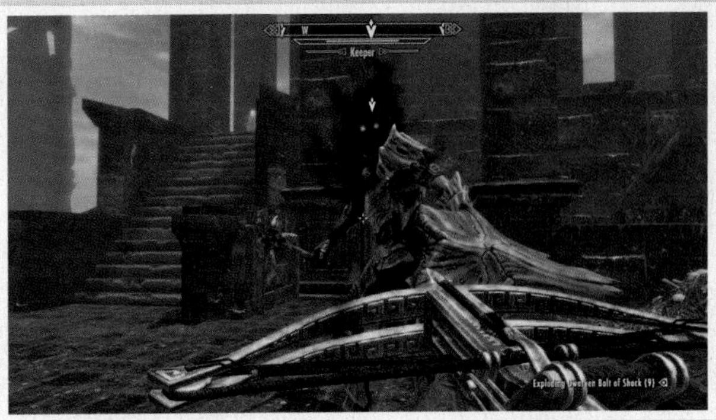

Keeper 1: The spire is located west of Valerica's location. The Keeper here sits on a massive throne in a large courtyard, surrounded by pillars and other structures. These obstacles provide plenty of hiding opportunities and allow you to duck behind cover to avoid his incredibly damaging weapon swings. Defeat the Keeper, claiming a Black Soul Gem (Grand) and potentially a Dragonbone weapon (at higher levels) from the dust he leaves behind.

Keeper 2: Take the path heading east from the first Keeper. Fight through the low hills of scrub and Bonemen to the next crumbling spire to the southeast. Before you reach the Keeper, deal with any Wrathmen appearing along the path prior to the spire. There are fewer structures to hide behind here, but the Keeper is visible at a greater distance, making ranged attacks much easier.

Keeper 3: Head northeast from the second Keeper. Among the twisted and gnarled trees, as well as the Bonemen and Wrathmen attacks, you may stumble across a soul named Jiub (Side Quest: Impatience of a Saint). Farther northeast is a small tower with an altar inside. Guarded by Mistmen (floating apparitions of skeletal blackness), and attracting lightning as you get close, this altar has Arvak's Skull atop it. Pick it up to complete Regional Activity: Arvak the Spectral Steed.

Continue on a rough path to the northeast, through more Bonemen and Wrathmen combat, toward a circular Teleporter guarded by foes. As the third Keeper's spire has already detached itself from the earth, you must step into the purple Teleporter to reach the spire. Do not fall at this point; instead, head counterclockwise around the edge of the spire and up the steps until you face down the third Keeper, who carries a bow that can drop you with a single arrow. Time ranged attacks to strike before the Keeper can fire his bow, or use the environment for cover. When the third Keeper bursts out of existence, return to Valerica.

Battle for the Boneyard

◊ **OBJECTIVE:** Speak to Valerica
◊ **OBJECTIVE:** Follow Valerica

Return to Valerica, who is impressed at your mettle. With the prison barrier down, Valerica warns you to keep an eye out for Durnehviir. You're then instructed to follow her. Pause at the Alchemy Lab or at Valerica's small collection of books before watching her open the giant doors that lead into her prison. This area, known as the Boneyard, is a massive graveyard sealed by a huge perimeter wall of black stone and spires. Suddenly, Serana spots movement. A giant, tattered dragon lands on an arch across the stone yard, enslaved by the Ideal Masters so it can challenge you to combat!

◊ **OBJECTIVE:** Slay Durnehviir

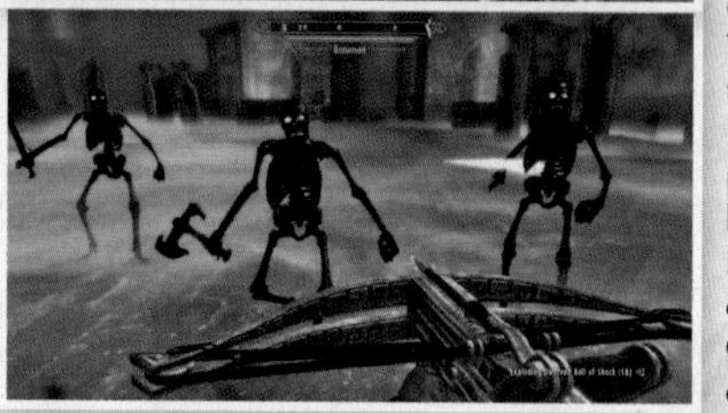

Durnehviir (picture 1) has attack patterns much like the other dragons you may have fought (and if you haven't, consult the tactics on page 205). His breath is more of a bolt of soul energy, which is just as damaging as fire or frost. The biggest problem are the Bonemen he conjures (shown in the second picture). Deal with them before they swarm you, ideally as Durnehviir circles overhead. Concentrate on the dragon when he lands or hovers close to your location. You may also wish to stay close to Serana and Valerica, letting them deal with the Bonemen or dragon while you provide supporting strikes at the other foe. Once Durnehviir is slain, his body collapses in on itself, but this is only one aspect of the beast, and you aren't rewarded with Durnehviir's soul.

◊ **OBJECTIVE:** Speak to Valerica
◊ **OBJECTIVE:** Follow Valerica
◊ **OBJECTIVE:** Retrieve the Elder Scroll

Valerica walks to an alcove on the lower wall on the Boneyard's eastern side. Speak with her, and she admits astonishment that Durnehviir was slain... unless the dragon's soul was more resilient than its host body. In fact, the beast may be reconstituting itself. Valerica suggests you take the Elder Scroll and be on your way. Oblige her, and walk to the alcove she's leading you to. Wait for her to unlock a long, ornate chest. Gather the Elder Scroll and any nearby potion concoctions you wish.

➤ **Elder Scroll (Blood)**

◊ **OBJECTIVE:** Speak to Valerica
◊ **SEEKING DISCLOSURE QUEST OBJECTIVE:** Bring both Elder Scrolls to Dexion
◊ **OBJECTIVE:** Return to Tamriel

At this point, if you had Serana trap part of your soul to allow you to enter the Soul Cairn, you can ask Valerica for help in retrieving it (Regional Activity: The Whole Soul*). Simply follow the marker on your compass to the soul fragment's location and reclaim it, restoring you to full health again.

Quest Conclusion

As a Daughter of Coldharbour, Valerica feels she must remain here, as returning to Tamriel increases Harkon's chances of bringing the Tyranny of the Sun to fruition. Say your good-byes, then begin to retrace your steps back to Tamriel. Head southwest out of the Boneyard and toward the devastated plains of the Soul Cairn. As you're about to leave, a large dragon startles you. Durnehviir has returned, only on this occasion, he wishes you to stay your weapons and listen awhile.

Durnehviir reveals he isn't dead but is trapped between "laas and dinok" (life and death). If you're willing to hear him out, Durnehviir honors you with the name "Qahnaarin" or "Vanquisher." At this point, Side Quest: Durnehviir begins, as the dragon asks a favor of you: to call him while you're in Tamriel, freeing him from this place. To this end, he gives you the three words of a Shout that will summon him.

➤ **Word of Power:** Curse, Summon Durnehviir

➤ **Word of Power:** Never, Summon Durnehviir

➤ **Word of Power:** Dying, Summon Durnehviir

Once you've finished speaking with Durnehviir, travel in a vaguely southwest direction through the Soul Cairn, retracing your steps back up into Volkihar Ruins to complete this quest.

> **NOTE** Once you've bade Valerica farewell, you can always speak to her again, learning more information through conversation, including information on how to retrieve the missing part of your soul, if Serana took it from you in order to enter the Soul Cairn. Consult Regional Activity: The Whole Soul* (page 578) for more information.

Postquest Activities: Seeking Disclosure

Dawnguard Quest: Seeking Disclosure is still active (as is Scroll Scouting if you haven't found the Elder Scroll [Dragon] yet). Exit the ruins via the door in the southwest corner of Valerica's laboratory and out onto the Castle Volkihar Balcony. From here, Fast-Travel to your next destination: to start the search for the Elder Scroll (Dragon) or, if you have both Elder Scrolls, to the fortress where Dexion Evicus awaits you.

◊ Return to your thrall in Castle Volkihar
◊ Dexion awaits you in Fort Dawnguard

When you meet with Dexion, his eyes are bandaged. This isn't a good sign, and the news gets worse: In his haste to read the first Elder Scroll (Sun), the Moth Priest neglected proper preparation. But you're not finished; it all depends on how much you're willing to risk to find Auriel's Bow. Dawnguard Main Quest: Unseen Visions now begins.

PREREQUISITES: Complete Dawnguard Main Quest: Seeking Disclosure

MINOR SPOILERS

INTERSECTING QUESTS: Dawnguard Main Quest: Seeking Disclosure, Dawnguard Main Quest: Scroll Scouting, Dawnguard Main Quest: Beyond Death, Dawnguard Main Quest: Touching the Sky

LOCATIONS: Ancestor Glade, Castle Volkihar, Fort Dawnguard

CHARACTERS: Dexion Evicus, Serana

ENEMIES: Dawnguard, Armored Troll, Master Vampire, Vampire's Thrall

◊ **OBJECTIVES:** Find a Moth Priest's knife, Gather bark from a Canticle Tree, Attract Ancestor Moth Swarms (7), Enter the column of light and read the Elder Scroll (Blood), Speak to Serana

Setting New Sights

NOTE This quest begins at the culmination of the previous three intertwined quests: Seeking Disclosure (which updates after you secure each Elder Scroll) Beyond Death (which has you retrieve the Elder Scroll [Blood] from the Soul Cairn), and Scroll Scouting (which begins the search for the Elder Scroll [Dragon]). Seeking Disclosure updates you to meet the Moth Priest Dexion Evicus, who has been stricken by blindness.

Back at the fortress, once you realize Dexion Evicus cannot read the Elder Scrolls you've assembled, ask him what you need to do to unlock the knowledge contained in the Scrolls. He tells you that Tamriel has a scattering of secluded locations known as Ancestor Glades. The one in Skyrim is located in the Pine Forest. Performing the "Ritual of the Ancestor Moth" within the glade should provide the answers you seek. The ritual involves carefully removing bark from a Canticle Tree, which then attracts Ancestor Moths to you. When seven swarms of moths are following, they provide you with second sight, which you need to decipher the Scrolls. You're welcome to ask Dexion additional questions about his blindness, but for now you have the location of the Ancestor Glade.

➤ **Elder Scroll (Blood)**

➤ **Elder Scroll (Dragon)**

➤ **Elder Scroll (Sun)**

◊ **OBJECTIVE:** Find a Moth Priest's knife

♦ **TARGET:** Draw Knife, in the Ancestor's Glade, Falkreath Hold

With all three Elder Scrolls on your person, set out from your fortress, heading toward Falkreath Hold and the Ancestor's Glade. It is located high in the southern mountains close to Pale Pass, near the Bloodlet Throne, and is easily accessible from Angi's Camp (but not from the woodland below Peak's Shade Tower). A small copse of trees and a stone route marker are the only clues to this hidden grove.

Enter the crack in the mountain and into a small cavern; step across the fallen log and through the small winding tunnel, and the glade's majesty soon becomes apparent. Although you're free to fully explore the turquoise mineral pools and splash about in the water, simply follow the ancient stone steps down and around to the glade itself. No one has been here for centuries. Duck under the three ancient henges to reach a carved pedestal shaped like the insignia of the Moth Priests. Floating in the middle of it is the Draw Knife. Take it.

➤ **Draw Knife**

◊ **OBJECTIVE:** Gather bark from a Canticle Tree

♦ **TARGET:** Any Canticle Tree in the Ancestor Glade

Locate one of the Canticle Trees (there's one just to the right of the pedestal, although any of the pink-blossoming trees within the Ancestor Glade will do), and begin to carefully scrape away, harvesting the Canticle Bark until you have enough and your quest updates.

➤ **Canticle Bark**

◊ **OBJECTIVE:** Attract Ancestor Moth Swarms (7)

♦ **TARGET:** Any Ancestor Moth Swarms in the Ancestor Glade

Elder Apparitions

Dotted about the glade are several Ancestor Moth swarms. They are friendly (very friendly, once you walk into their cloud of fluttering wings), and there are more than the seven swarms you need to attract.

Simply walk the rest of the path as it winds through the glade's rocky outcrops, looking for swarms as you go. You can retrace your steps back up to the glade entrance if you wish. But don't lose your footing on the slightly treacherous terrain if you decide to explore off the beaten track. Once the seventh swarm has found you, a beam of bright light emanates from the pedestal altar where you found the Draw Knife.

◊ **OBJECTIVE:** Enter the column of light and read the Elder Scroll (Blood)

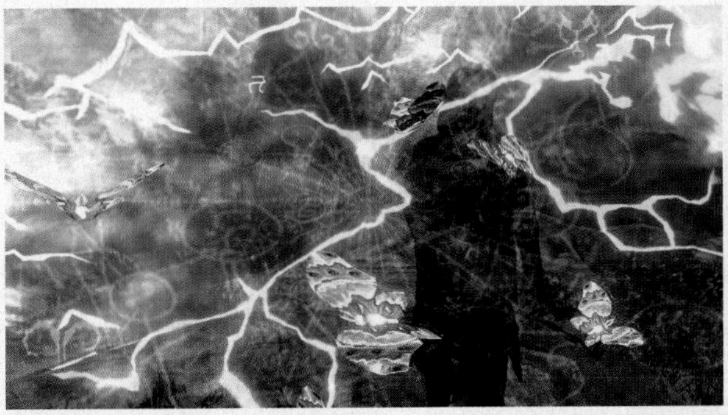

Stand in the middle of the light (you may wish to speak to Serana about the wondrous tranquility you're experiencing), and then access your Items > Books Menu and read the Elder Scroll (Blood). Your vision swims with light and ancient knowledge. You automatically bring out the other Scrolls and your vision changes. It is as if you're gazing down from the heavens, looking at the Reach and Haafingar Holds. The runes of Markarth (to the southwest) and Solitude (to the northeast) are visible, glowing red. Between the two, in the Druadach Mountains close to a Karth River tributary, is a third rune. The rune marks the place to uncover and the entrance to the location of Auriel's Bow!

◊ **OBJECTIVE:** Speak to Serana

Quest Conclusion

Serana was worried—you were as white as a Snow Elf—but after conversing with her, you are imbued with the knowledge of a place called Darkfall Cave. Serana reckons you both should set off immediately, before the forces against you are able to track you down. The quest now concludes.

Postquest Activities

Dawnguard Main Quest: Touching the Sky begins immediately. You can ask Serana about her knowledge of Auriel's Bow before leaving this place. On your way out, prepare for an ambush!

A complement of Dawnguard soldiers, including an Armored Troll, descend from the entrance, determined to thwart your deviant progress. Cull them or flee if their might becomes too much for you.

A half-dozen Vampire Thralls, controlled by a Master Vampire, head down from the entrance, with only one purpose in mind: to crush your hopes of progress. Defeat these night stalkers or flee before them.

TOUCHING THE SKY

PREREQUISITES: Complete Dawnguard Main Quest: Unseen Visions

◉ MAJOR SPOILERS

INTERSECTING QUESTS: Dawnguard Main Quest: Unseen Visions, Dawnguard Main Quest: Kindred Judgment

LOCATIONS: Ancestor's Glade, Darkfall Cave, Auriel's Chapel, Darkfall Grotto, Darkfall Passage, Forgotten Vale, Glacial Crevice, Inner Sanctum, Sharpslope Cave, Temple Balcony, Wayshrine of Illumination, Wayshrine of Learning, Wayshrine of Radiance, Wayshrine of Resolution, Wayshrine of Sight

CHARACTERS: Knight-Paladin Gelebor, Prelate Athring, Prelate Celegriath, Prelate Edhelbor, Prelate Sidanyis, Serana, Prelate Nirilor

ENEMIES: Ancient Frost Atronach, Arch-Curate Vyrthur, Chaurus, Chaurus Hunter, Chaurus Hunter Fledgling, Falmer, Falmer Shaman, Frostbite Spider, Frost Giant, Frost Troll, Frozen Chaurus, Frozen Falmer, Frozen Shaman, Giant Frostbite Spider, Naaslaarum, Troll, Vale Deer, Vale Sabre Cat, Voslaarum

◊ **OBJECTIVES:** Locate Auriel's Bow, Speak to Gelebor , Survive Darkfall Passage, Fill the Initiate's Ewer (5), Gain entry to the Inner Sanctum, Locate Arch-Curate Vyrthur, Confront Arch-Curate Vyrthur, Slay Arch-Curate Vyrthur, Speak to Gelebor, Retrieve Auriel's Bow

Auriel's Odyssey

◊ **OBJECTIVE:** Locate Auriel's Bow

♦ **TARGET:** Auriel's Bow, Temple Balcony, Forgotten Vale

TIP This quest is an epic expedition across a vast and previously unexplored wilderness. Therefore, it is worth preparing by gathering potions, lightening your inventory, and stocking up for the trek to come. You should also carry at least 40 Elven Arrows, but wait to use them until you reach the end of this quest.

After defeating (or fleeing from) the "unwelcoming committee" that confronts you as you leave Ancestor's Glade, head outside, then look to your world map. Your next destination, Darkfall Cave, is located south of Mor Khazgur and north of Druadach Redoubt, in the northern part of the Reach. The cave entrance protrudes from the snow level, above some sloping and uneven ground dotted with trees.

Once inside the cave, follow the narrow tunnel around the waterfall, past a Frostbite Spider and web-spun alcove, before heading west across a rickety wooden bridge. The trail goes cold here, until you look down. The way forward lies in the fast-flowing water below.

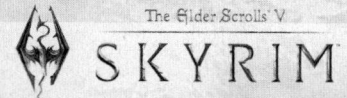

Face south and drop into the underground torrent, riding it into a plunge pool and over a waterfall to a pair of rushing streams. A few Frostbite Spiders follow you into this dark and dank environment. Deal with them now, as there's a Giant Frostbite Spider in an alcove to the east (it guards a skeleton draped over a chest), a little farther along the cavern. Continue north, following the tunnel as it narrows. Follow the trail of torches up to a campfire. A dead Breton lies here next to a chest. He carries a note detailing his inability to deal peaceably with trolls.

➤ Darkfall Cave Note

There's a tunnel that slopes up to the west (which returns you to Skyrim's surface), but you should head down, to the east. Avoid the trip wire (unless you enjoy being bruised by falling rocks), and follow the tunnel as it bends around to the north and opens into a larger, waterlogged cavern. Amid the gloom, stare north to some bloody remains, a torch, and a chest guarded by two trolls. Ignore or defeat them (a little too late for the Breton whose corpse you just rifled through), and splash through the rest of the cavern heading west. It is here you spot a very pale elf, standing in worship to an effigy of the sun. Gelebor beckons you forward; you have nothing to fear here.

> ◊ **OBJECTIVE:** Speak to Gelebor

Knight-Paladin Gelebor welcomes you to the Great Chantry of Auri-El, otherwise known as Alkosh, Akatosh, or Auriel; there are many names for the foremost of the gods. Gelebor is among the last of his race, a Snow Elf not "turned" or betrayed like the rest of the Falmer you have faced. Gelebor knows why you're here, but before he grants you clues to the Bow's location, he requires your assistance: You must kill Arch-Curate Vyrthur, his brother.

Gelebor believes the Betrayed (Falmer) have done something to Vyrthur, and previous Falmer incursions have resulted in much loss of life: The Falmer stormed the Inner Sanctum of the Chantry and (Gelebor believes) corrupted his brother. Gelebor cannot go to his brother's aid, as he has vowed never to leave the Wayshrines unguarded. With that, Gelebor conjures a ball of light and casts it at the carved sun in the center of the pool. A large, elven-made shrine rumbles out of the ground. Impressive. Gelebor explains that this Wayshrine was used for meditation and transport long ago, when the Chantry was a place of enlightenment.

Serana asks about the basin, which was used by initiates once their mantras were spoken. They dipped a ceremonial ewer into the basin at each Wayshrine before proceeding to the next. Upon reaching the sanctum, the initiates could present their ewer, filled with the water of all the Wayshrines, allowing them to enter the temple and gain an audience with the Arch-Curate himself. Serana isn't too interested in this symbolism. However, you'll have to be, as this is the only method of accessing the Sanctum to reach Vyrthur! There are five Wayshrines to find, and each requires you to use the ewer to retrieve and mix the sacred waters. You're handed the ewer, and Gelebor wishes you well.

➤ Initiate's Ewer

> ◊ **OBJECTIVE:** Survive Darkfall Passage
> ♦ **TARGET:** Western edge of Darkfall Grotto (Wayshrine)

Before you depart, you can speak to Gelebor at length about the spectral Prelates who guard each Wayshrine, find out more about the Chantry, and learn more about the Snow Elves. Then step into the first Wayshrine (which you don't need to extract water from) and into the Portal to Darkfall Passage.

Seeking Passage and Light

Stepping into Darkfall Passage, head down the narrow tunnel. The odd, luminous fungus plants recede as you approach, plunging you into gloom. These plants retract when you approach or strike them, reducing the light level in their immediate vicinity. Depending on your combat style, you may wish to keep your Vampire's Sight or a light spell active to improve visibility, or take advantage of the darkness by sneaking past the enemies that lie ahead. The Falmer, being blind, are unaffected by the light, but you may find it slightly easier to sneak by the Chaurus in darkness.

Keep your wits about you as a Chaurus Hunter bursts from its ground cocoon. Strike down two Falmer as you reach a small grotto where you must defeat another of the Betrayed, along with a couple of their Chaurus pets. Head down the tunnel to the west, turning north and avoiding the trip wire or you'll receive a Falmer claw trap to the face.

The tunnel turns to the southwest, opening up to a Falmer camp. Make short work of the four or five Falmer foes here, along with another Hunter as you close in on a subterranean waterfall. Then maneuver around to the waterfall's opposite side, edging along the ledge and heading north to a second Falmer camp. After you clear this immediate area of another couple of foes, inspect the chest below the Falmer bridge. Harvest the Gleamblossom if you wish, but remove the chest's trap trigger [Apprentice] or face a skewering from a trap.

Cross the bridge to the makeshift altar of skeletal remains, repelling four more Falmer foes as you head west, avoiding the bones that alert foes ahead. Pass the large glowing crystals, moving south and then east up a tunnel to another Falmer camp. This area has a Chaurus pen (attack the two beasts from range for easy takedowns) and a toughened Falmer to face. Then drop two more Falmer who enter via both of the two waterfall bridges behind the hut. With the coast clear, head through the water (or drop to a lower ledge, which is flagged in the Atlas on page 841). To the southeast is a dead-end chamber with a trip wire and claw trap and Chaurus Hunters to fight. You don't have to go this way; continue past the skeletal remains and down the windy tunnel.

Finally, you reach two rope releases, and some traps set into the ceiling. Serana comments that whatever is on the other side of this, the Falmer wanted to keep it there. Activate the left rope release, and a rock wall to the right (north) rumbles open. Ahead is a strange, catlike predator.

Either react and kill it immediately, or pull the other rope release and hope to skewer it with the multitude of traps (a claw, spears, and darts) it lets loose. You've brought down a Vale Sabre Cat. Now to find out what it was guarding....

Wayshrine of Illumination: Into the Gloomy Grotto

Step through into the giant Darkfall Grotto. Serana is suitably impressed. Stop at the initial vista point and look to the west. On the grotto's other side is a Wayshrine! To reach it, you can dive off into the water below, risking a death plummet, and then scramble onto dry land. Or, you can take a more sedate (and safer) route to the right (northeast), heading down the sloping path, past some glowing plants and crystals, and startling some Vale Deer (which are skittish but not hostile). Follow the narrow path across the grotto water and up to a shallow cave bathed in purple light, where you must face another Vale Sabre Cat. Wind your way north, to the grotto's opposite side, where your quest finally updates:

◊ **OBJECTIVE:** Fill the Initiate's Ewer (0/5)
♦ **TARGET:** Water Basin, at each of the five Wayshrines

You are greeted at the Wayshrine by spectral Prelate Sidanyis. He welcomes you to the Wayshrine of Illumination. Answer that yes, you are prepared to honor the mantras of Auri-El and fill your vessel with his enlightenment. He raises the Wayshrine. Step inside and draw water at the basin (this is very important!). Then step through the Portal to Forgotten Vale.

◊ **OBJECTIVE COMPLETE:** Fill the Initiate's Ewer (1/5)

Wayshrine of Sight: A Whole Other World

NOTE As you explore the Forgotten Vale, there are two Regional Activities that you can undertake and a multitude of side areas to explore. It is well worth reading up on what needs to be done so you don't miss anything. You should also check the Forgotten Vale map and Atlas information on page 996 to familiarize yourself with the topography of this incredible new land.

Regional Activity: Ancient Falmer Tomes* (page 579)
Regional Activity: Paragon of the Frost Giants* (page 580)

NOTE * Quest names marked with this symbol do not appear in your Quest Menu list, although objectives may.

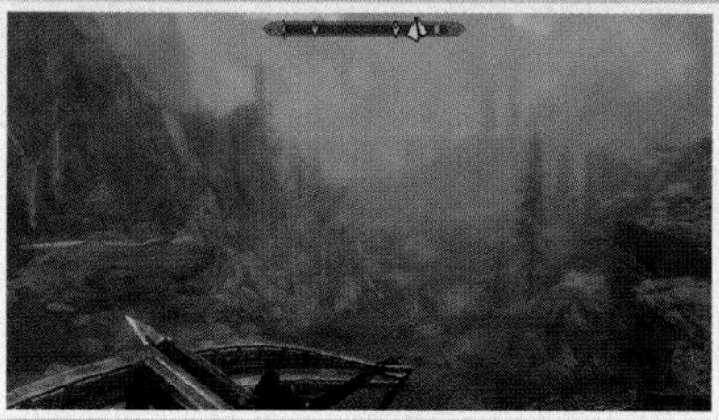

You're now in completely unfamiliar territory, somewhere beyond Skyrim's western borders and seemingly in the middle of a giant, rocky pit. Pass the luminous rocks and plants as you wind through the tunnel. You end up at the top of the pit and out into Forgotten Vale itself. The initial valley is usually shrouded in faint mist, with Vale Deer (and the odd Vale Sabre Cat) to do with as you wish. If you want to explore a bit, a Frost Troll lives in a small den up the snowy foothill to your left (southwest). But mainly stay on the valley floor, heading northwest through the old archway ruin and up the rough steps before turning right (northeast). Serana spots a second Wayshrine.

You are greeted by Prelate Athring, who welcomes you to the Wayshrine of Sight. Answer that you are ready to fill your vessel and the prelate opens the Wayshrine. Dip your ewer into the water basin before heading back down the hill. Don't return to Darkfall Cave; instead, press on, exploring farther into the Forgotten Vale.

◊ **OBJECTIVE COMPLETE:** Fill the Initiate's Ewer (2/5)

TIP As you progress, the Wayshrines you open provide portals to the previous Wayshrines, enabling a rudimentary "Fast-Travel" system between different areas. This is useful when exploring the Forgotten Vale after completing this quest.

Wayshrine of Learning: A Vale Revealed

Head down the hill to the southwest, through another archway and up a hill encased in snow. A group of Frostbite Spiders (and a bigger one behind them) stand between you and the opening to the rest of Forgotten Vale—a massive and sprawling ice-encrusted land dotted with the remains of Snow Elf architecture. It is easy to get lost in this huge valley, with a massive frozen lake to the southwest and many more surprises to come.

TIP With such a large area to explore, you are free to search everywhere and anywhere you wish. However, the following walkthrough shows you the optimal path, taking in all of the sights and combat opportunities. It is, however, but one of the many routes you may wish to take. Remember there are numerous Secondary Locations to discover. Find out more in the Atlas, on page 996.

DAWNGUARD FACTION QUESTS

The following nine Faction Quests become available after you complete Dawnguard Main Quest: A New Order. They can be completed during (or after) the Dawnguard Main Quest and typically offer you a task that results in strengthening the Dawnguard. Simply approach any resident of Fort Dawnguard and ask, "What can I do to help?"

NOTE Most of these quests are given out at random.

CAUTION These quests are available only to adventurers who have sided with the Dawnguard against the vampires. If you've thrown your lot in with Lord Harkon, expect open hostility and a sealed Fort Dawnguard!

TIP Remember you can utilize the talents of Serana (or any other Follower) and the Dawnguard's Armored Trolls to help you with these tasks. For more information on Armored Trolls, consult page 193.

ANCIENT TECHNOLOGY

Quest Giver: Sorine Jurard

Sorine is making good on her offer to improve Isran's crossbows, but she requires further inspiration and knowledge for this to happen—knowledge she believes the long-dead dwarves may have possessed. She wants you to find a particular Dwemer Schematic hidden somewhere in Skyrim.

◊ **OBJECTIVE:** Retrieve the Dwemer Schematic from [Dwarven Dungeon or Bandit Lair]
♦ **TARGET:** Dwemer Schematic, in a [random Dwarven Dungeon or Bandit Lair]

Journey to the location Sorine has indicated, and battle through the Dwarven automatons, bandits, or other foes blocking your path. The schematic in question is always located inside a large treasure chest. Some are hidden deep inside a lengthy dungeon, while others are closer to the surface; it all depends on the topography of the dungeon you're sent to.

◊ **OBJECTIVE:** Return to Sorine
◊ **TARGET:** Sorine Jurard, Fort Dawnguard, the Rift

Quest Conclusion

With the schematic in hand, return to Sorine, and she eagerly examines your find. Aside from a random weapon or item reward, Sorine also teaches you how to make the item described in the schematic at Gunmar's Forge. Once the quest concludes, you're also able to purchase it from Sorine.

NOTE Crafting Crossbows and Bolts: It is important to remember that if you want to craft your own crossbows and bolts, you'll need to learn the Steel Smithing and (eventually) Dwarven Smithing perks. For a complete list of raw Smithing materials needed to craft each item, consult page 81. If you're interested in fully enhancing a crossbow, aim to purchase (or craft) an Enhanced Dwarven Crossbow (which should be further tempered to Legendary quality) with a variety of Dwarven Bolts, depending on the enemies you're facing. Finally, remember that most crossbows and bolts can be made only at Gunmar's Forge inside the fort itself.

➤ **[Crossbow Improvement]**

Postquest Activities

You may now speak with another resident of Fort Dawnguard and take on a new Faction Quest. This quest can be completed a total of six times. Each time you accept it from Sorine, she will send you in search of a new schematic that unlocks a new crossbow or crossbow bolt technology, in the order listed below.

✓	SCHEMATIC	ITEM CREATED*	COMBAT ENHANCEMENT
☐	#1 Enhanced Crossbow Schematic	Enhanced Crossbow	Attacks with this crossbow ignore 50% of armor.
☐	#2 Exploding Fire Bolt Schematic	Exploding Steel Bolt of Fire	Explodes for 10 points of fire damage.
☐	#3 Exploding Ice Bolt Schematic	Exploding Steel Bolt of Ice	Explodes for 10 points of frost damage to Health and Stamina.
☐	#4 Exploding Shock Bolt Schematic	Exploding Steel Bolt of Shock	Explodes for 10 points of shock damage to Health and half that to Magicka.
☐	#5 Dwarven Crossbow Schematic	Dwarven Crossbow	Does more damage (and weighs slightly more) than a standard crossbow. Dwarven Bolts of Fire, Ice, and Shock can now be bought, crafted, and used (which cause 15 points of damage instead of 10).
☐	#6 Enhanced Dwarven Crossbow Schematic	Enhanced Dwarven Crossbow	Attacks with this crossbow ignore 50% of armor.

NOTE * These items can now be purchased from Sorine or crafted at Gunmar's Forge.

Quest Giver: Sorine Jurard. This quest occurs only once.

Finding Arkay's Voice

Once you learn that the Moth Priest was abducted by vampires during Dawnguard Main Quest: Prophet, Sorine Jurard may, during the course of your regular conversations, ask if you have a moment. She's been talking with Gunmar and is concerned about the severity of the vampire threat. She believes the Dawnguard will need Florentius, a Priest of Arkay, to help. Sorine thinks Isran may not want his help but wants you to find out anyway.

◊ **OBJECTIVE:** Speak with Isran

Find Isran and inform him that you "need to find someone named Florentius." Isran, as expected, is deeply concerned about the man and certainly doesn't trust him. Mention that Sorine thought he'd be able to help, and Isran swallows his feelings and gives you approval to find Florentius, who was last seen aiding the Vigilants of Stendarr at Ruunvald.

◊ **OBJECTIVE:** Find Florentius
♦ **TARGET:** Ruunvald Excavation, the Rift

Travel to Ruunvald Excavation in the snowy foothills of the Velothi Mountains, east of Shor's Watchtower and south of Tolvald's Cave. You need to trek south from the map marker to reach a gap in the mountainside that allows access up, then go north past the snow line to the excavation entrance. Close by is a tent with an interesting journal to read. It recounts the actions of Volk, a Vigilant guard who mentions that the excavation team was taking longer and longer to return to the surface, then disappeared entirely. Curious...

➤ **Volk's Journal**

A Charmed Life

Enter the Ruunvald Excavation and peer into the maw below. You should spot a Vigilant with a strange red haze about his head. This Vigilant, and all others in this part of Ruunvald, have been charmed and should be seen as hostile enemies. There's nothing you can do to save them, except to send them to Stendarr, courtesy of a quick death. Battle your way down the mine shaft and into a second mine cavern, engaging more Charmed Vigilants and their Husky hounds. Eventually, you reach a chamber with a rickety bridge. Here you'll find further adversaries, including Volk (pictured), who is possessed like the rest of them. Deal with all who oppose you before searching for a tunnel on the lowest level leading south to Runnvald Temple.

After a short passage, you enter the main temple room. This is where your primary adversaries, including a warlock named Minorne and the ill-fated expedition leader Moric Sidrey, have imprisoned Florentius close to the raised altar. Dispatch everyone who isn't called Florentius. Search the corpse of Minorne to discover the Ruunvald Key, which is handy to open the otherwise-inaccessible gate to the cage where Florentius is located.

➤ **Ruunvald Key**

Quest Conclusion

Once freed, Florentius Baenius asks what he (and Arkay, as he professes to have direct communication with the god of the cycle of birth and death) can do to help you. Once you mention Isran, Florentius thinks you're a joke, but once "Arkay" has instructed him that it's a good idea, he begrudgingly agrees to head off to Fort Dawnguard. You don't need to accompany him; he appears the next time you arrive at that destination. The quest now concludes.

Postquest Activities

Now head south, using the key to open the iron door. Enter a room with a treasure chest and an alcove lever in the southeast area near the bed; the lever raises a stone staircase leading to an exit into Skyrim.

When Florentius moves in to Fort Dawnguard, a new alchemy lab appears in the forge area. Florentius sells a variety of items (mainly potions) to help you and sometimes has a Faction Quest of his own: Lost Relic. You may now speak with another resident of Fort Dawnguard and take on a new Faction Quest.

➤ **Vendor (Apothecary):** Florentius Baenius

CLEANSING LIGHT

Quest Giver: Gunmar. This quest can occur more than once.

Gunmar has discovered the whereabouts of a vampire lair. He wants you to take out the head vampire inside the lair, which is usually sufficient to scatter its minions, although he'd prefer it if you destroy all of them. However, you aren't penalized if you fail to completely remove the vampiric presence.

◊ **OBJECTIVE:** Kill the Master Vampire at [a Vampire Lair]
♦ **TARGET:** Master Vampire, [random Vampire Lair]

Journey to the Vampire Lair and begin to systematically cull all of its inhabitants. The tactics you use are completely up to you. Find and face down the Master Vampire, slaughtering all those with fangs before this quest is complete.

◊ **OBJECTIVE:** Return to Gunmar

Quest Conclusion

With the hissing blood of the vanquished vampires still staining your weapon, return to Fort Dawnguard and seek out Gunmar. He has a small reward for your courage.

➤ **Leveled Weapon or Item**

Postquest Activities

You may now speak with another resident of Fort Dawnguard and take on a new Faction Quest.

HIDE AND SEEK

Quest Giver: Gunmar. This quest can occur more than once.

Gunmar has located the whereabouts of a vampire masquerading as a common citizen. This "citizen" is nothing but a parasite, ready to clamp down on the necks of any nearby innocent. Stop this deviancy right away! Gunmar requests a discreet kill; you can ask him further questions if you wish.

◊ **OBJECTIVE:** Discreetly kill [vampire masquerading as a traveling bard, pilgrim, or merchant]
♦ **TARGET:** The vampire, in [a settlement]

When you reach the settlement, seek out the vampire in citizen's clothing. You're able to ask him or her a few questions, which confirms your suspicions (as do those bloodred eyes). However, killing the beast in cold blood won't complete the quest and is seen as a crime. Instead, a spot of stealth is in order.

Sometimes, you can speak with your target and persuade or intimidate them into following you. Lead them somewhere out of the way, make sure you're alone, and then quickly take them out in a single strike.

Alternately, you can leave whatever establishment (usually a tavern) you may have found the vampire in and wait for your quarry to wander the settlement's streets. Survey the area to make sure you're alone, or cast magic so you're not seen. Then defeat the vampire without being seen (achieve this easily by crouching so you're hidden and striking the vampire with a ranged shot).

◊ **OBJECTIVE:** Return to Gunmar

Quest Conclusion

Once the pretend citizen is a very real corpse, journey back to Fort Dawnguard and meet up with Gunmar. He's happy there's one less monster to worry about, and you're rewarded forthwith.

➤ **Leveled Weapon or Item**

Postquest Activities

You may now speak with another resident of Fort Dawnguard and take on a new Faction Quest.

HUNTING THE MONSTER

Quest Giver: Gunmar. This quest can occur more than once.

Gunmar has learned of a possible vampire, and while he doesn't know its exact whereabouts, he has information on someone who does. You're to pay a visit to the beast's last known contact and "urge" them to reveal the vampire's location.

◊ **OBJECTIVE:** Find evidence of the vampire's whereabouts
♦ **TARGET:** [Vampire's friend], at a [random settlement]

Visit the person indicated in your quest log (or the place where they usually reside), and attempt one of the following:

Get straight to the point; tell them you're looking for a vampire. The friend doesn't know what you're talking about. Now you can:

- ◊ (Persuade) Ask them to tell you what you need to know.
- ◊ (Bribe) Offer some coin to jog their memory.
- ◊ (Intimidate) Threaten to get rough.
- ◊ (Brawl) Or bring out your fists and actually get rough.

One of these options is likely to work. Otherwise, you can:

- ◊ Pickpocket the friend for the information you need, or
- ◊ Search their residence for proof, which is sometimes found in one of their chests.

➤ **Letter from the Vampire**

◊ **OBJECTIVE:** Kill the Master Vampire at [a random bandit or warlock lair]

Locate the lair mentioned in the vampire's letter, and journey there ready to defeat this foul presence, along with any bandits or warlocks aligned with the monster. Once you kill the Master Vampire, your quest updates.

◊ **OBJECTIVE:** Return to Gunmar

Quest Conclusion

After the bloody battle, head back to Fort Dawnguard for a meeting with Gunmar. For those who cherish memories of loved ones, their compassion often conceals the beast. But your compassion compels you to destroy it. Good work!

➤ **Leveled Weapon or Item**

Postquest Activities

You may now speak with another resident of Fort Dawnguard and take on a new Faction Quest.

A JARL'S JUSTICE

Quest Giver: Isran. This quest can occur more than once.

Isran is concerned about a visiting "advisor" in the Jarl's court. He orders you to destroy this creature before it can infiltrate the Jarl's inner circle and complete whatever foul business it was contemplating. However, Isran warns you that the Jarl's guards are unaware of the threat and will treat violence against the advisor as a crime. You need to convince the Jarl that the threat is real. Or you can simply try not to get caught!

◊ **OBJECTIVE:** Warn [a Jarl] about the vampire threat
♦ **TARGET:** [a random Jarl], in [one of the Hold Capitals]

Visit the Jarl in question, and inform him that a vampire has infiltrated his court. The Jarl believes this to be a somewhat bold claim and requires some proof before he can possibly believe it. The only proof available is contained on the Advisor himself. Seek out this suspicious character and pickpocket him. On his person are Orders from his vampire masters.

➤ **Orders**

◊ **OBJECTIVE:** Bring evidence to [the Jarl]

At this point, continue not to attract attention, return to the Jarl, and present the evidence via a new conversation topic. The Jarl now entrusts you to take care of this unwanted visitor (as shown in the picture). The Jarl's guards won't interfere with you now that you're carrying out the Jarl's justice.

◊ **OBJECTIVE:** Destroy the vampire masquerading as a visiting advisor

Now simply return to the visiting advisor and kill him.

CAUTION

This quest can also be completed by finding the visiting advisor and slaying him without proof. However, this murder, if detected, is considered a major crime, and you'll suffer the consequences for your actions. However, this quest still completes.

◊ **OBJECTIVE:** Return to Isran

Quest Conclusion

With the Jarl's court back in order, return to Fort Dawnguard and locate Isran. He has a small reward for your dedication.

➤ **Leveled Weapon or Item**

Postquest Activities

You may now speak with another resident of Fort Dawnguard and take on a new Faction Quest.

LOST RELIC

Quest Giver: Florentius Baenius. This quest can occur up to three times.

Once you've freed Florentius during Dawnguard Faction Quest: Bolstering the Ranks, he requests that you help him (and Arkay) secure a fabled relic from the Dawnguard's past. Arkay has told Florentius where the relic is, but he requires you to retrieve it.

◊ **OBJECTIVE:** Retrieve the [Dawnguard Relic] from [a bandit, Falmer, Forsworn, vampire, or warlock dungeon]
♦ **TARGET:** [Dawnguard Relic], in [a random dungeon]

Enter the dungeon you're prompted to trek to, and battle or sneak your way to a large treasure chest somewhere within. Inside is the relic you seek. Take it!

➤ **[Dawnguard Relic]**

◊ **OBJECTIVE:** Return to Florentius Baenius

Quest Conclusion

Dawnguard Rune Axe

Dawnguard Rune Hammer

Dawnguard Rune Shield

Head back to Fort Dawnguard, and present the relic to Florentius. He (and Arkay) thank you for your service, and in addition to a small item reward, Florentius gifts you the relic itself. Use it wisely!

➤ **Leveled Weapon or Item** ➤ **Dawnguard Relic**

The following three relics are (randomly) available during this quest. For further information, consult pages 139 and 144.

✓	RELIC NAME	PROPERTIES
☐	Dawnguard Rune Axe	For every 10 undead you kill with this axe, the axe will do +10 Sun Damage to undead (up to +100).
☐	Dawnguard Rune Hammer	Bashing places a rune on a nearby surface; the rune explodes for 50 points of fire damage when enemies come near.
☐	Dawnguard Rune Shield	+10 Bash damage against vampires and sustained blocking creates a minor Sun Shield that does 10 points of damage while draining the wielder's Stamina.

Postquest Activities

You may now speak with another resident of Fort Dawnguard and take on a new Faction Quest.

PREEMPTIVE STRIKE

Quest Giver: Gunmar. This quest can occur more than once.

Gunmar has found another hated beast hiding from the light of day. It seems a vampire has infiltrated a group of bandits (or warlocks) and may be about to turn all the inhabitants into bloodsucking fiends. You are to dispatch the vampire and any other hostiles you see fit.

◊ **OBJECTIVE:** Kill the Master Vampire at [a bandit or warlock lair]
♦ **TARGET:** Master Vampire, [random bandit or warlock lair]

Commence your task by heading to the lair in question, and slay anyone who stands in your way. You need not defeat any of the usual inhabitants (although you can—they're always hostile toward you). However, you must find and defeat the Master Vampire, snuffing him from this realm, before this quest can conclude.

◊ **OBJECTIVE:** Return to Gunmar

Quest Conclusion

Once the Master Vampire has tasted your vengeance, trek back to Fort Dawnguard and find Gunmar. He offers a trinket or weapon for your services.

➤ **Leveled Weapon or Item**

Postquest Activities

You may now speak with another resident of Fort Dawnguard and take on a new Faction Quest.

RESCUE

Quest Giver: Florentius Baenius. This quest can occur more than once.

Florentius has some grave news. While you were adventuring, a group of bloodsuckers made off with your associate! This vicious night stalker seeks to gain leverage over the righteous, but there is hope: Your brethren is still alive. A rescue attempt must be undertaken at your earliest convenience.

◊ **OBJECTIVE:** Rescue [your spouse or friend] from [a bandit or warlock lair]

◊ **OBJECTIVE:** Kill the Master Vampire

♦ **TARGET:** [Random bandit or warlock lair]

NOTE The kidnapping is based on your previous friendship with certain denizens of Skyrim. The following citizens may be kidnapped:

Any nonessential person (so, not a Jarl) you've completed a task, quest, or favor for (in this case, Faendal of Riverwood).

Anyone who has previously been a Follower of yours.

Anyone you are currently married to.

You have a twofold task to accomplish: locate the loathsome lair, search out the Master Vampire within, and vanquish the beast. Once done, locate the victim and talk to them. This releases their bonds, and they are happy to return to their previous location without any further chaperoning.

◊ **OBJECTIVE:** Return to Florentius Baenius

Quest Conclusion

Florentius is awaiting your safe return. Naturally, Arkay has already told him of your triumph, and he offers you the following as a reward for ridding the lands of another vampire:

➤ **Leveled Weapon or Item**

Postquest Activities

You may now speak with another resident of Fort Dawnguard and take on a new Faction Quest.

VAMPIRE FACTION QUESTS

The following ten Faction Quests become available after you complete Dawnguard Main Quest: The Bloodstone Chalice. These can be completed during (or after) the Dawnguard Main Quest and typically offer you a task that results in strengthening the vampires of Castle Volkihar. You can have only one of these quests active at a time. Simply approach any resident of the castle and ask, "What can I do to help?"

NOTE Most of these quests are given out at random. The one exception is Vampire Faction Quest: Destroying the Dawnguard, which becomes randomly available only after you complete Dawnguard Main Quest: Kindred Judgment. Note the additional stipulations for Amulets of Night Power and The Gift (detailed below).

CAUTION These quests are available only to adventurers who have sided with the vampires against the Dawnguard. If you've joined Isran and fight against the Dawnguard, expect open hostility and a sealed Castle Volkihar.

TIP Remember you can utilize the talents of Serana (or any other Follower) and bring a Death Hound to help you in these tasks. For more information on Death Hounds, consult page 176. Finally, there's a small chance you may receive a Blood Potion as a reward at the end of any of these quests.

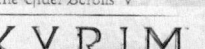

AMULETS OF NIGHT POWER

Quest Giver: Feran Sadri. This quest occurs only once. You must have the Vampire Lord perk "Summon Gargoyle" to receive this quest.

Once you've chosen the Vampire Lord perk "Summon Gargoyle" from the Perk constellation, visit Feran Sadri, who has located the last known resting place of a set of ancient Amulets of Night Power. He thinks they should be among vampires, not lying about unguarded for mortals to find. You can ask Feran what the amulets do, where they came from, and if you can keep them once you find them. The amulets are yours...if you can acquire them!

Amulet of the Gargoyle

Amulet of Bats

> ◊ **OBJECTIVE:** Retrieve the Amulet of the Gargoyle from [a random dungeon].
> ◊ **OBJECTIVE:** Retrieve the Amulet of Bats from [a random dungeon].
> ♦ **TARGET:** Amulet of the Gargoyle, in a [random dungeon]
> ♦ **TARGET:** Amulet of Bats, in a [random dungeon]

✓	AMULET NAME	PROPERTIES
☐	Amulet of the Gargoyle	While wearing this amulet, your Summon Gargoyle spell summons an additional gargoyle for 30 seconds. Vampire Lord form only.
☐	Amulet of Bats	While wearing this amulet, Bats will drain life from any nearby enemies. Vampire Lord form only.

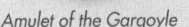

Journey to the location Feran Sadri has indicated, and battle through the foes blocking your path. The amulet you're searching for is sometimes located inside a treasure chest or is being carried by a particularly strong enemy (like a giant) or on the body of a slain corpse. Sometimes an amulet is hidden deep inside a lengthy dungeon, and sometimes it is closer to the surface. Be sure to visit both dungeons (in either order), and claim both amulets.

> ◊ **OBJECTIVE:** Return to Feran Sadri

Quest Conclusion

With both amulets stored in your inventory, head back to Castle Volkihar, and speak with Feran Sadri. He trusts you'll put those amulets to good use. He also rewards you.

- ➤ **Leveled Item**
- ➤ **Blood Potion (small chance)**

Postquest Activities

You may now speak with another resident of Castle Volkihar and take on a new Faction Quest.

ANCIENT POWER

Quest Giver: Feran Sadri. This quest can occur more than once.

Feran Sadri has been performing a little research on the Bloodstone Chalice you filled during Dawnguard Main Quest: The Bloodstone Chalice. He believes its salutary effects can be prolonged if it is infused with potent vampiric power. To this end, he's located the petrified remains of an elder vampire. You are to bring these remains to him.

> ◊ **OBJECTIVE:** Retrieve the Ancient Vampire [body part] from [a random dungeon].
> ♦ **TARGET:** Ancient Vampire [body part], in a [random dungeon]

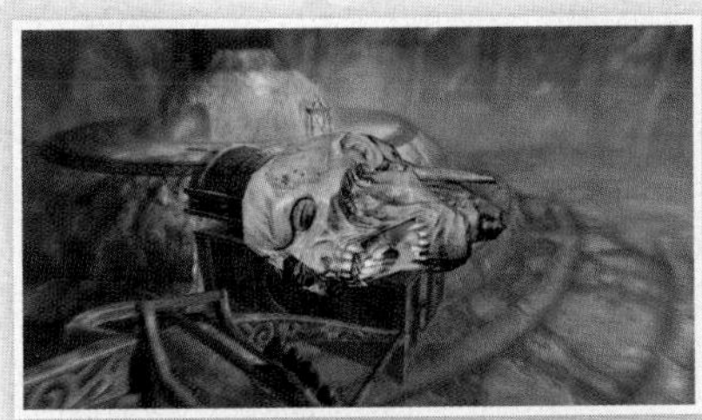

Locate the place Feran Sadri has mentioned, and explore it thoroughly until you reach the body part you're searching for. It is usually inside a treasure chest, deep in the dungeon. Claim these gruesome (and desiccated) remains.

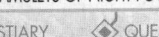

- ➤ **Ancient Vampire [body part]**

> ◊ **OBJECTIVE:** Return to Feran Sadri

Quest Conclusion

When you return to Castle Volkihar, Feran Sadri tells you he'll make the necessary preparations for the infusion into the Chalice. You're then rewarded.

- ➤ **Leveled Weapon or Item**
- ➤ **Blood Potion (small chance)**

Postquest Activities

You may now speak with another resident of Castle Volkihar and take on a new Faction Quest. In addition, you can return to the Bloodstone Chalice and drink from it. When you complete this Faction Quest, you receive the Blood of the Ancients ability (which causes your Vampiric Drain to absorb Magicka and Stamina), and the duration of this ability grows each time you complete this quest. So try to find as many body parts as Feran Sadri allows you to!

CULLING THE BEAST

Quest Giver: Fura Bloodmouth or Garan Marethi. This quest can occur more than once.

Fura (or Garan) has discovered a cluster of feral vampires running wild and upsetting the mortals. You are to cull these brutish beasts before the problem gets out of hand. You must take out the head vampire inside the lair, but any other vampires lurking there are also optional kills. However, you aren't penalized if you fail to completely remove the vampiric presence.

◊ **OBJECTIVE:** Kill the Master Vampire at [a Vampire Lair]
♦ **TARGET:** Master Vampire, [random Vampire Lair]

Journey to the vampire lair and begin systematically culling all of its inhabitants. The combat style you use is completely up to you. Find and face down the Master Vampire, slaughtering all that are feral and fanged of tooth, before this quest is complete.

◊ **OBJECTIVE:** Return to Fura Bloodmouth (or Garan Marethi)

Quest Conclusion

Stride back to Castle Volkihar and regale your task master with tales of your victory. You may have pitied those thin-bloods, but after disposing of a few, you realize they aren't worth the worry. Have a present:

- **Leveled Weapon or Item**
- **Blood Potion (small chance)**

Postquest Activities

You may now speak with another resident of Castle Volkihar and take on a new Faction Quest.

DECEIVING THE HERD

Quest Giver: Feran Sadri. This quest can occur more than once.

Feran Sadri has learned that the Dawnguard have increased their operations and have been aggressively recruiting. You are to put a damper on their efforts and give these troublemakers something to worry about. You are to murder someone and make a public display of it. The execution must happen in the streets, for all to see. The higher the profile of the victim, the better. To further change the public's opinion of the Dawnguard, you can optionally don their garb before committing the murder to make it seem as if you're a member of their sect, sowing confusion among the herd. Feran hands over Dawnguard armor and an Incriminating Note to plant on the victim you choose. You may ask Feran what he means by a "high-profile" target. Try the following:

A member of the Hold's ruling or exiled government, such as the Housecarl or Court Wizard
A priest, bard, or innkeeper
Any merchant (blacksmith, etc.)

- **Dawnguard Heavy Armor**
- **Dawnguard Boots**
- **Dawnguard Gauntlet**
- **Dawnguard Full Helmet**
- **Incriminating Letter**

◊ **OBJECTIVE:** Kill someone out in the streets of [a city]
◊ **[OPTIONAL] OBJECTIVE:** Make it a public kill while wearing Dawnguard armor
◊ **[OPTIONAL] OBJECTIVE:** Choose a high-profile victim
◊ **OBJECTIVE:** Plant letter on [victim]
♦ **TARGET:** Any citizen [a high-profile citizen is recommended], in [a city]

Don your Dawnguard Armor, Boots, Gauntlet, and Helmet. Then journey to the city and walk up to a high-profile target. If in doubt, choose the blacksmith or an innkeeper or merchant you don't normally patronize or receive training from. Then slaughter them. This instantly increases your crime, so attempt to plant the Incriminating Letter as soon after the murder as possible (before the objective updates, even). Then flee, fight, or pay your fine.

CAUTION
It is wise to leave Serana behind when completing this task, as she has the annoying knack of resurrecting the person you killed, making it difficult to immediately plant the evidence and retreat.

◊ **OBJECTIVE:** Return to Feran Sadri

Quest Conclusion

Once you've slain the high-profile citizen and placed a letter professing to be from the Dawnguard on the corpse, return to Castle Volkihar and tell Feran Sadri of your triumph. This should direct the people's anger toward the Dawnguard for a time. Now receive your reward.

- **Leveled Weapon or Item**
- **Blood Potion (small chance)**

Postquest Activities

You may now speak with another resident of Castle Volkihar and take on a new Faction Quest.

Durnehviir reveals he isn't dead but is trapped between "laas and dinok" (life and death). If you're willing to hear him out, Durnehviir honors you with the name "Qahnaarin" or "Vanquisher." At this point, Side Quest: Durnehviir begins, as the dragon asks a favor of you—to call him while you're in Tamriel and free him from this place. To this end, he gives you the three words of a Shout that will summon him.

- **Word of Power:** Curse, Summon Durnehviir
- **Word of Power:** Never, Summon Durnehviir
- **Word of Power:** Dying, Summon Durnehviir

◊ **OBJECTIVE:** Summon Durnehviir in Tamriel
◊ **OBJECTIVE:** Learn the first word of Durnehviir's Shout

TIP The location of your meeting with Durnehviir is shown in the Atlas for the Soul Cairn (see page 986).

Now conclude your adventures in the Soul Cairn, return to Skyrim, and begin this quest in earnest.

Torn from the Soul Cairn

You will need to spend three Dragon Souls to unlock all three words of Durnehviir's name. Then select this Shout and summon him back into the world of the living (Magic > Shouts > Summon Durnehviir).

Simply locate an area of land that is flat and wide enough to accommodate a dragon, such as the tundra plains west of Whiterun (as shown in the previous picture). You can call Durnehviir in any exterior location but not inside dungeons or spaces with high cliff walls (such as Eldergleam Sanctuary or the Ancestor's Glade).

TIP The crosshairs glow red if Durnehviir can't be summoned at a particular location. Move to a more suitable area and try again.

The tattered dragon breathes the free air of Vus once more and offers more than simple gratitude. He teaches you the first word of the Soul Tear Shout.

- **Word of Power:** Essence, Soul Tear

◊ **OBJECTIVE:** Learn the second word of Durnehviir's Shout

Now wait until you recover, and summon Durnehviir for a second time. He awards you the second word of the Soul Tear Thu'um.

- **Word of Power:** Tear, Soul Tear

◊ **OBJECTIVE:** Learn the third word of Durnehviir's Shout

Finally, summon the dragon one last time, after which he gathers enough strength to break free of the psychic control of the Ideal Masters. He also teaches you the final word:

- **Word of Power:** Zombie, Soul Tear

Your Thu'um cuts through flesh and shatters souls, commanding the will of the fallen.

Postquest Activities

Try out the Soul Tear Shout: Expend up to three Dragon Souls to gain the most potent form of this Thu'um, which damages foes, sucks their souls from their forms (and transfers them into any Soul Gems you may be carrying), and—at its most devastating—raises the foe you just slew to act as a zombified thrall!

FACE TO FACE*

PREREQUISITES: None
INTERSECTING QUESTS: None
LOCATIONS: Riften, The Ragged Flagon
CHARACTERS: Galathil
◊ **OBJECTIVES:** Locate the face sculptor in Riften

MINOR SPOILERS

NOTE * Quest names marked with this symbol do not appear in your Quest Menu list, although objectives may.

Under the Knife

On your journeys through Skyrim, you can speak to many a barkeep (such as Hulda in Whiterun) and learn much from their gossiping (Miscellaneous Objective: Innkeepers). Visit any innkeeper outside of Riften, and they may mention a rumor that someone living in Riften has the amazing ability to "change your face."

Or, if you're wandering through Riften, you may chance upon a city guard who mentions knowledge of the "face sculptor" visiting the Ragged Flagon. You receive a Miscellaneous Objective:

◊ **OBJECTIVE:** Locate the face sculptor in Riften
♦ **TARGET:** Galathil, the Ragged Flagon

Enter the Ratway, and make your way to the Thieves' Guild hideout and infamous tavern, the Ragged Flagon. The cowled Dark Elf sitting on the water deck is the infamous face sculptor Galathil, who utilizes a mixture of magic and deft cutting to rearrange your features for a (potentially) reasonable fee of 1,000 gold. Pay her the septims, and the following occurs:

- You can completely change your facial appearance, just like you did prior to your escape from Helgen at the very start of your adventure.
- You cannot change your race or sex. If you're a female Khajiit, you stay one.
- If you've contracted vampirism, Galathil notices this straightaway. Her techniques work only on the living, so you'll have to seek a cure before she agrees to work on you. Consult Side Quest: Rising at Dawn (page 463) if you wish to be cured.

Postquest Activities

You can change your face as often as you wish, as long as you have the funds to pay Galathil.

IMPATIENCE OF A SAINT

PREREQUISITES: Complete Dawnguard Main Quest: Chasing Echoes

MINOR SPOILERS

INTERSECTING QUESTS: Dawnguard Main Quest: Chasing Echoes, Dawnguard Main Quest: Beyond Death

LOCATIONS: Soul Cairn: Barrier Wall, Black Chapel, Black Church, Black Folly, Black Minster, Boneyard Citadel, Foundation Altar, Ideal Masters Crystal Folly, Morven Stroud: Soul Husk Merchant, Soul Pool Foundation

CHARACTERS: Jiub

ENEMIES: Boneman, Mistman, Wrathman

◊ **OBJECTIVES:** Find pages from Saint Jiub's Opus (10), Return to Jiub

NOTE This quest is open to both factions. It becomes available only after you enter the Soul Cairn as part of Dawnguard Main Quest: Beyond Death. Although every effort has been made to accurately pinpoint each location, it is well worth consulting the Soul Cairn Atlas and the Soul Cairn map (page 986), which has cartographical locations shown as well.

Important Character

Jiub (the Eradicator)

If you've ever adventured in Morrowind and woken up on a ship near a fellow prisoner, you'll already have met Jiub. After your initial introduction to the Dark Elf, you never see him again. However, during the time of Oblivion, he is referred to as Saint Jiub, a mysterious hero who tells you he somehow drove all the Cliff Racers from Vvardenfell. Jiub ended up in the Soul Cairn when his soul became trapped inside a Black Soul Gem.

Spending hundreds of years as a soul in the Soul Cairn has taken its toll on poor Jiub. He's now completely obsessed with authoring his books. Due to his current state (dead), he can never leave the Soul Cairn, nor can he be "slain." Once you make him aware of his predicament, Jiub hopes you'll spread the word of his face when you return to Tamriel.

The Rise and Fall of Saint Jiub

In order to find Jiub, see the walkthrough for Dawnguard Main Quest: Beyond Death, as Jiub is located on a main thoroughfare between the towers guarded by Keepers 2 and 3. Find the Location: Gnarled Glade where a lone ghost is waiting by a burned-out campfire. As you approach, the ghost is babbling about publishing books and becoming rich. Talk to him, and he speaks of his "opus." After further questioning, he informs you he's in quite the predicament, having lost all of the pages of his life's work. Carry on the chat, as he reveals more of his background, and you reveal that he's actually dead.

Crestfallen, Jiub realizes his writings can no longer be seen, until you both agree that you could carry his work out of the Soul Cairn for him. However, in order to write the second volume of his opus, he requires notes from his first volume. Those are the pages you are to gather for him.

◊ **OBJECTIVE:** Find pages from Saint Jiub's Opus (10)

♦ **TARGET:** Single pages, across the Soul Cairn

TIP You can gather pages before or after meeting Jiub; it is entirely up to you.

Page Gathering: The Patience of an Adventurer

What follows is a description of where each of the pages are located. They are listed from 1 to 10, although you won't find them in that order without significant backtracking across the Soul Cairn. In each case, three pictures are shown: They reveal the location from a distance, as you close in on the location, and finally at the location itself. Each location is also named: The names are references to the Atlas only (they don't appear on your local map). Check the compass direction on each picture so you know from which direction to approach. For precise map locations of each page and its number, check the map on page 986.

Jiub's Opus: Page 1

Steps of the Barrier Wall: These are located on the southern (initial side) of the barrier wall, just southeast of the stepped gap in the wall where the main path leads you from the start of the Soul Cairn. The page is next to the window atop the steps, to the right of a Soul. On the window's right side is *The Book of Life and Service* and a Soul Gem.

➤ **Jiub's Opus (Page 1)**

Jiub's Opus: Page 2

The Black Folly, Fallen Word Wall: The Black Folly, on the western side of the Boneyard wall, is just left (west) of where Valerica is imprisoned. Head through the entrance with the purple soul pools glowing on either side, and inspect the fallen Word Wall once you're inside. The page is next to a treasure chest, with a ruby and coin purse, half hidden in the low mist.

➤ **Jiub's Opus (Page 2)**

Jiub's Opus: Page 3

Ideal Masters Crystal Folly: Find this small Folly on the barrier wall's far left (northeast). This is accessed via an entrance just off the main path, on the wall's south side. Brave the Bonemen and climb to the chest with the Crystal above it. The page is located at the foot of the chest, next to a circlet.

➤ **Jiub's Opus (Page 3)**

Jiub's Opus: Page 4

Boneyard Citadel: Travel to the Boneyard entrance where Valerica is imprisoned. Head right (east), around the exterior Boneyard wall, to the fortification attached to the wall. Climb the steep steps, and locate the page beside a chest inside the highest of the small spires. It is guarded by a Mistman.

➤ **Jiub's Opus (Page 4)**

Jiub's Opus: Page 5

Soul Pool Foundation: This is on the route between Keepers 2 and 3, just south of where Jiub is located. The area consists of relatively flat scrubland, with low steps up to a stone foundation and circular soul pool. The page is on the ground, near an Elven Shield, a skull and some Soul Gems on the outside of the circular soul pool.

➤ **Jiub's Opus (Page 5)**

Jiub's Opus: Page 7

Foundation Altar: Southeast of the Boneyard Citadel and northeast of Arvak's Skull is a stepped area leading to an open altar, close to the perimeter barrier (to the east) and just east of the teleport to Keeper 3. Beware of Bonemen guarding this altar, which has Spell Tome: Conjure Mistman on it. Below it is the page, next to a coin purse and Soul Gem.

➤ **Jiub's Opus (Page 7)**

Jiub's Opus: Page 6

The Black Church: While on the main path from the Soul Cairn entrance, en route to the barrier wall, close to where the soul that lost Arvak is located, look to your right (east). Just north of the Black Chapel is the Black Church, an obsidian stone structure with four entrances into a small inner room. The the page lies here, next to a chest, coin purse, and Soul Gem.

➤ **Jiub's Opus (Page 6)**

Jiub's Opus: Page 8

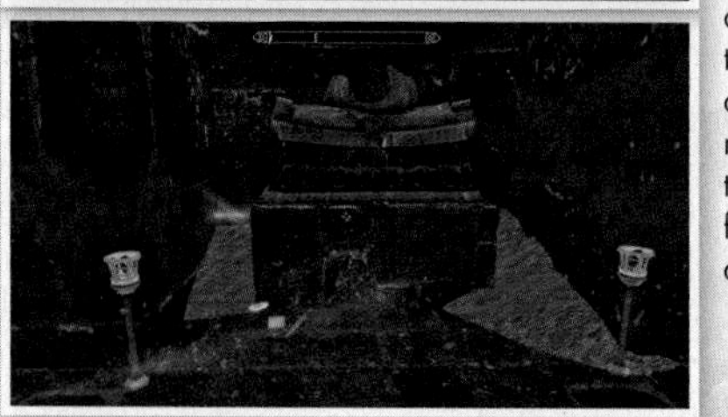

The Black Chapel: After climbing down the entrance steps from Volkihar Ruins, facing northeast and walking down the main path, the first building you see on your right (east) is the Black Chapel. Shoot an arrow into each turquoise orb so the bars at the chapel entrance recede. Then climb to the page inside, at the foot of a chest, next to a dagger and coin purse.

➤ **Jiub's Opus (Page 8)**

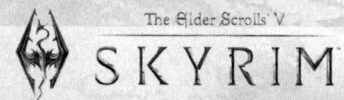

Jiub's Opus: Page 9

The Black Minster: After stepping across the barrier wall, locate the ruined foundations with four pathways off it. Face northwest and follow the path as it winds around to the north. Pass two black structures with Master Crystals atop them. Ignore those, and instead head for the largest structure on the northern edge of the Soul Cairn. It has a stepped entrance and a barred opening to the right of that. Enter the Minster, wandering the maze of corridors until you reach a teleport to the roof. The page is by a chest below the Crystal, near a Soul Gem.

➤ **Jiub's Opus (Page 9)**

Jiub's Opus: Page 10

Morven Stroud: Soul Husk Merchant: After you cross the barrier wall, turn right (east) and wander to the remains of a cart where a ghostly trader named Morven Stroud resides. The page is on one of the barrels close to his cart.

➤ **Jiub's Opus (Page 10)**

◊ **OBJECTIVE:** Return to Jiub

Quest Conclusion

After you gather all of Jiub's pages, revisit the poor fellow and offer the parchments to him. He is most excited and rewards you with a pristine copy of his first volume. Now his words can be read back in Tamriel! As an added bonus, Jiub also gives you his Locket.

➤ **Saint Jiub's Opus**

➤ **Locket of Saint Jiub**

Postquest Activities

You can read Saint Jiub's Opus or sell it for a tidy profit.

NOTE * Quest names marked with this symbol do not appear in your Quest Menu list, although objectives may.

A Lack of Cartographical Evidence

There are a huge number of Wilderness Encounters that can occur during your adventures in Skyrim (a complete list can be found on page 682). However, three of them (Dawnguard Novice, Dawnguard Outrider, and Dawnguard Remains) lead to this unmarked quest.

Like all Wilderness Encounters, these three are also random, so patience is necessary (and the encounters may take a while to occur). These particular encounters will occur only after you've completed Dawnguard Main Quest: The Bloodstone Chalice (Vampires) or Dawnguard Main Quest: A New Order (Dawnguard).

In each case, you find a member of the Dawnguard (or what's left of them) and a note, detailing the locations of three Wilderness Caches—dead drops set up by the Dawnguard to resupply their agents in the field. After reading the note, you can now find these hidden chests and claim the items they contain.

CAUTION You can't simply ignore the Wilderness Encounters or notes and wander off to find these Wilderness Caches; they appear only after you have experienced the Wilderness Encounter and read the corresponding note.

Caches 1–3: Dawnguard Novice

This Wilderness Encounter occurs only late at night (try between 11:00 p.m. and 1:00 a.m.) and only in Whiterun Hold. Dawnguard Novice Hakar is running from two vampires. Save him, and he abruptly resigns from the order, drops his items (which includes his Dawnguard Armor, orders, and a Cache Key), and flees for Rorikstead. Reading his note reveals the location of the Dawnguard Caches in Whiterun Hold (see below). You can also claim the orders and Cache Key from his corpse if he dies. You can now find Wilderness Caches 1, 2, and 3. If you don't take the Cache Key, the strongboxes are all locked [Expert]. The last of the three Caches you find contains a Scroll.

- **Dawnguard Orders:** Hakar
- **Dawnguard Cache Key**

Cache 1: "In Rorikstead, in the pasture behind Frostfruit Inn." Simple and direct. This cache is hidden between a fallen log and some large rocks in the pasture.

Cache 2: "Near Stendarr's Shrine in the center of the tundra." The shrine in question is Secondary Location [6.I]: Shrine of Stendarr: The Two Pillars. The cache is up against the rocks just behind the shrine.

Cache 3: "South of Whiterun's Western Watchtower." This cache is located on a small island in a stream south of the watchtower.

Caches 4–6: Dawnguard Outrider

This Wilderness Encounter occurs only in Hjaalmarch, the Pale, or Winterhold Holds. Dawnguard Saliah rides by you on horseback. If you try to talk to her, she quickly brushes you off—she has no time for conversation. Kill or pickpocket her for her orders (which reveal the Caches in Hjaalmarch, the Pale, and Winterhold) and a Cache Key. You can now search for Wilderness Caches 4, 5, and 6. If you don't take the Cache Key, the strongboxes are all locked [Expert]. The last of the three Caches you find contains a Scroll.

- **Dawnguard Orders:** Saliah
- **Dawnguard Cache Key**

Cache 4: "In Morthal, on the islet due east of the mill." It's easy to get lost in the marsh, but these directions are clear: carefully walk due east from the mill to find this cache up against a tree.

Cache 5: "Outside Nightgate Inn, at the foot of the pier." The cache is nestled among the rocks on the south side of the pier.

Cache 6: "Near Winterhold, under the great arch." The arch itself is not a marked location, but it's easy to spot from the road as you make your way south from Winterhold. The cache is buried in the snow at the foot of the arch.

Caches 7–9: Dawnguard Remains

This Wilderness Encounter occurs only in Haafingar or the Reach. Dawnguard Lynoit lies dead on the ground, surrounded by three smoldering vampire ash piles. Loot his body for his orders, which reveal the Caches in Haafingar and the Reach. You can now locate Wilderness Caches 7, 8, and 9. If you don't take the Cache Key, the strongboxes are all locked [Expert]. The last of the three Caches you find contains a Scroll.

➤ **Dawnguard Orders:** Lynoit ➤ **Dawnguard Cache Key**

Cache 7: "On the small island south of Solitude Sawmill." This is the island out in the middle of the Karth River. It requires a short swim, but it's not hard to find.

Cache 8: "Due east of the entrance to the ruin Volskygge." The cache is up against a fallen log east of Volskygge.

Cache 9: "On the east side of Karthwasten Bridge." After crossing the bridge, search the rocks around the dead tree to find this cache.

Quest Conclusion

Continue your adventuring until you've pried open all nine caches and recovered their treasure!

DAWNGUARD REGIONAL ACTIVITIES

OVERVIEW

Optimal Activity Start

The following activities are available during your time exploring two large areas: the Soul Cairn and the Forgotten Vale. Think of them as a subsection of Side Quests specific to these geographical areas. For quests that span more than these locations, consult the Side Quest chapter (page 564).

NOTE **Cross-Referencing:** Do you want to see maps and learn more about the traps, non-quest-related items, collectibles, crafting areas, and other important rooms of note in every location during these quests? Then cross-reference the location you travel to with the information on that location contained in this guide's Atlas.

Dawnguard: All of these activities are marked with the Dawnguard sign and are accessible only when Dawnguard is available.

Available Activities

There are a total of eight Regional Activities: seven in the Soul Cairn and two in Forgotten Vale. Aside from a few exceptions, most of these tasks are independent of one another and can be completed whenever you encounter them or if you return to either location.

✓	QUEST NAME	RELATED LOCATION	PREREQUISITES
☐	Regional Activity: Arvak the Spectral Steed*	Soul Cairn	Complete Dawnguard Main Quest: Chasing Echoes
☐	Regional Activity: Dark Conjurations*	Soul Cairn	Complete Dawnguard Main Quest: Chasing Echoes
☐	Regional Activity: (Don't Fear) The Reaper*	Soul Cairn	Complete Dawnguard Main Quest: Chasing Echoes
☐	Regional Activity: The Soul Husk Merchant*	Soul Cairn	Complete Dawnguard Main Quest: Chasing Echoes
☐	Regional Activity: Valerica's Concoction*	Soul Cairn	Complete Dawnguard Main Quest: Chasing Echoes
☐	Regional Activity: The Whole Soul*	Soul Cairn	Complete Dawnguard Main Quest: Beyond Death
☐	Regional Activity: Ancient Falmer Tomes*	Forgotten Vale	Complete Dawnguard Main Quest: Unseen Visions
☐	Regional Activity: Paragons of the Frost Giants*	Forgotten Vale	Complete Dawnguard Main Quest: Unseen Visions

NOTE * Quest names marked with this symbol do not appear in your Quest Menu list, although objectives may.

ARVAK THE SPECTRAL STEED*

PREREQUISITES: Complete Dawnguard Main Quest: Chasing Echoes

MINOR SPOILERS

INTERSECTING QUESTS: Dawnguard Main Quest: Chasing Echoes, Dawnguard Main Quest: Beyond Death

LOCATIONS: Soul Cairn

CHARACTERS: Arvak, Soul

◊ **OBJECTIVES:** Find Arvak's skull in the Soul Cairn, Return Arvak's Skull, *Quest names marked with this symbol do not appear in your Quest Menu list, although objectives may.

NOTE This unmarked quest is open to both factions. It becomes accessible only after you enter the Soul Cairn as part of Dawnguard Main Quest: Beyond Death.

A Good Deed for a Noble Steed

TIP The exact locations of the soul who once rode Arvak and Arvak's Skull are shown in the Atlas on page 986. Don't forget to check the map of the Soul Cairn, too.

Among the various oddities and general chaos that pervades the Soul Cairn, there are a couple of strange occurrences tied to a spectral steed named Arvak. You can:

Witness the spectral horse galloping across the Soul Cairn (as shown). You're unable to stop or interact with him. This is a Wilderness Special Encounter: Arvak (see page 682).

You can encounter a soul trapped in the Soul Cairn, just northeast along the path from the first Boneman encounter and black chapel, close to the entry portal. The soul pleads with you to "find my Arvak." The steed accompanied this soul into the Cairn but fled after they were attacked by monsters. The soul loves his horse dearly and wants his suffering to end. Your quest updates.

◊ **OBJECTIVE:** Find Arvak's skull in the Soul Cairn

The horse's skull is located on the direct route between the location of Keepers 2 and 3. Northeast of the second Keeper's location, look for a small tower with an altar inside. This altar has Arvak's Skull on it and is guarded by Mistmen (floating apparitions of skeletal blackness) and lightning.

➤ **Arvak's Skull**

◊ **OBJECTIVE:** Return Arvak's Skull

After you retrieve the skull, the soul you met earlier appears in a small graveyard just northeast of the altar (look for the compass waypoint with the Miscellaneous Objective active). The soul is ecstatic, as he can sense that Arvak's soul has been freed! In gratitude, the soul teaches you a spell that causes Arvak to appear before you.

➤ **Summon Arvak**

Postquest Activities

All that remains now is to summon Arvak to aid you on your travels. Select Magic > Conjuration > Summon Arvak, and with enough Magicka, you are able to conjure the spectral horse in the following locations:

Skyrim Exterior	Blackreach	Forgotten Vale Exterior
Soul Cairn	Dayspring Canyon	Solstheim

TIP The crosshairs glow red if Arvak can't be summoned in a particular area; move to a more suitable locale and try again. Arvak is useful to have if you prefer horses for travel and combat, want to conjure a loyal beast just before a battle, or want to travel on horseback through areas that other horses aren't able to reach. Arvak is especially well suited for mounted combat (see page 106), since, unlike other horses, he can't be permanently killed. Simply cast the spell to summon him once again.

PREREQUISITES: Complete Dawnguard Main Quest: Chasing Echoes

MINOR SPOILERS

INTERSECTING QUESTS: Dawnguard Main Quest: Chasing Echoes, Dawnguard Main Quest: Beyond Death

LOCATIONS: Soul Cairn, Foundation Altar, Keeper's Altar, Soul Graveyard

CHARACTERS: None

ENEMIES: Boneman, Mistman, Wrathman

◊ **OBJECTIVES:** None

NOTE This unmarked quest is open to both factions. It becomes accessible only after you enter the Soul Cairn as part of Dawnguard Main Quest: Beyond Death.

Summoning Men of Bone, Mist, and Wrath

Within the Soul Cairn, three special Spell Tomes have been left by unknown hands. They provide conjuration practitioners with everything they need to summon their own Bonemen, Mistmen, and Wrathmen to aid them in battle. These spell books can be found at the following locations:

Spell Tome: Conjure Boneman

Soul Graveyard: Once you've moved across the barrier wall, head northwest toward the cluster of larger and imposing buildings in the northeast corner of the Soul Cairn. Look for the Black Minster (the long building on the north horizon with a floating crystal above it). To the left (west) of that, close to where Keeper 1 rests, is a Soul Graveyard. In the middle is an altar. The Spell Tome rests on the obsidian plinth below it. Prepare for a Boneman ambush after you grab the book.

➤ **Spell Tome:** Conjure Boneman

Spell Tome: Conjure Wrathman

Keeper's Altar: This is located in the southeast corner of the Soul Cairn, along the eastern path just past the tower where the second Keeper resides, between the Keeper's tower and the Reaper's Lair. Enter this small, arched structure, and claim the Spell Tome from atop the altar. Beware of a Wrathman ambush once you take the tome.

➤ **Spell Tome:** Conjure Wrathman

Spell Tome: Conjure Mistman

Foundation Altar: Southeast of the Boneyard Citadel and northeast of Arvak's Skull is a stepped area leading to an open altar, close to the perimeter barrier (to the east) and just east of the teleport to Keeper 3. Beware of Bonemen guarding this altar, which has the Spell Tome: Conjure Mistman on it. Below it is Jiub's Opus (page 7), next to a coin purse and Soul Gem. Watch for a Mistman ambush after the book has been swiped.

➤ **Spell Tome:** Conjure Mistman

Postquest Activities

You can read all three books regardless of your Conjuration Skill level. If you have enough skill or Magicka to cast these spells, you can summon the denizens of the Soul Cairn to fight for you as your adventure continues.

PREREQUISITES: Complete Dawnguard Main Quest: Chasing Echoes

MINOR SPOILERS

INTERSECTING QUESTS: Dawnguard Main Quest: Chasing Echoes, Dawnguard Main Quest: Beyond Death

LOCATIONS: Soul Cairn, Black Temple, Keeper's Castle, Obsidian Hall, Reaper's Lair

CHARACTERS: None

ENEMIES: Boneman, Mistman, Reaper, Wrathman

◊ **OBJECTIVES:** None

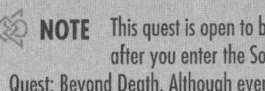

NOTE This quest is open to both factions. It becomes accessible only after you enter the Soul Cairn as part of Dawnguard Main Quest: Beyond Death. Although every effort has been made to accurately pinpoint each Reaper Gem Fragment, it is well worth consulting the Soul Cairn Atlas chapter and the Soul Cairn map (page 986), which has cartographical locations shown as well.

Initial Preparations

During your exploration of the Soul Cairn, you may chance upon a Reaper Gem Fragment. This is the only clue you have to the existence of something strangely terrifying that you can conjure to face in this realm (aside from the other oddities and foes to encounter).

Reaper Gem Gathering: Three Fragments of Power

What follows is a description of where each of the three Reaper Gem Fragments are located. They are listed from one to three, although you don't need to find them in that order. In each case, three pictures are shown: They reveal the location from a distance, as you close in on the location, and finally at the location itself. Each location is also named. The names are references to the Atlas section only (they don't appear on your local map). Check the compass direction on each picture so you know from which direction to approach.

Reaper Fragments: First Location

The Keeper's Castle: If you're completing Dawnguard Main Quest: Beyond Death, cross the barrier wall and turn left (northwest). Cross the undulating ground until you reach the fortification where the first Keeper resides. Or, if you've met Valerica and are starting your search for Keepers to fight, simply trek from the Boneyard to the first Keeper (as detailed in the quest). After fighting the Keeper in the courtyard, turn left (southwest). Fire an arrow or bolt through each of the turquoise orbs to release the gate ahead of you. This leads to an outer courtyard of standing stones, an Ideal Master Crystal that burns away at you, and a chest. Retrieve the Fragment from the chest.

➤ **Reaper Gem Fragment (1/3)**

Reaper Fragments: Second Location

The Obsidian Hall: South of the Boneyard is a very large ruin, with huge walled sides. It is directly north of the second Keeper location. Head around to the large opening and face north, wander inside (defeating any foes that appear), and locate the small, circular teleport in the smaller courtyard. You're transported to the upper roof (rather than the roof section you can reach via the nearby steps), where an Ideal Master Crystal hovers over a chest to the south. Grab the Fragments from the chest. Then carefully drop to the lower rooftop and escape.

➤ **Reaper Gem Fragment (2/3)**

Reaper Fragments: Third Location

The Black Temple: North of Arvak's Skull and just west of the floating citadel where the third Keeper is stationed is a medium-sized blocklike temple structure with an Ideal Master Crystal hovering above the roof. The structure is at the base of the hill on which the Boneyard is located. Enter the building, look for the open doorway to the right (north), and climb the steps to the roof. An Ideal Master Crystal hovers over a chest to the south. Take the Fragments from the chest and retrace your steps.

➤ **Reaper Gem Fragment (3/3)**

Quest Conclusion

Reaper's Lair: Journey to the Soul Cairn's southeast corner, east of the second Keeper's residence, and inspect the black structure. Look south for the imposing doors and enter the building. Step forward to the Reaper Shard Receptacle; insert the Soul Fragments you've collected into this altar. With all of the Fragments placed, a Reaper Gem is fused together. Moments later, the Reaper is summoned!

This ghostly stuff of nightmares is a hooded shadow armed with a massive axe. His glowing red eyes stare through you, and he's immediately hostile, as are the Bonemen minions that also appear. The first part of combat must include dodging the disgusting vomit he sprays across the chamber. Failure to step out of the flying acid results in some nasty damage.

Hopefully the Reaper will become preoccupied with slaying Serana, allowing you to attack from a different direction. Dodge or block those heavy axe swipes, and whittle down the Reaper's health until he falters and finally falls. Search his Ghastly Remains for your reward.

➤ **Black Soul Gem (3)**

Postquest Activities

Don't let the Reaper haunt your nightmares.

THE SOUL HUSK MERCHANT*

PREREQUISITES: Complete Dawnguard Main Quest: Chasing Echoes

MINOR SPOILERS

INTERSECTING QUESTS: Dawnguard Main Quest: Chasing Echoes, Dawnguard Main Quest: Beyond Death

LOCATIONS: Husk Pasture, Morven Stroud: Soul Husk Merchant, Soul Cairn

CHARACTERS: Morven Stroud

ENEMIES: None

◊ **OBJECTIVES:** None

NOTE This quest is open to both factions. It becomes accessible only after you enter the Soul Cairn as part of Dawnguard Main Quest: Beyond Death.

Husk Hunting for Morven

Located to the east of the main path through the Soul Cairn, just after you've stepped across the barrier wall, is the soul of a merchant named Morven Stroud. He's one of the few souls who can hold a conversation with you. Begin to talk, and you'll discover Morven wound up here after he sold an item with suspect ingredients to a necromancer coven. Morven was once a highly respected trader in High Rock (at least, according to Morven, he was), but now he waits here. Eternally. Offer to pass the time by collecting the only item he wants: Soul Husks. Return with 25 of them, and you can rummage through what he has left on his cart.

You may now begin collecting Soul Husks throughout the Soul Cairn (as this is the only place where they grow). You can find them in chests or growing in clusters. The largest concentration of them is in the Husk Pasture (shown).

When you have 25, return to Morven, and you're able to "purchase" one of the following (which is a random leveled item of the type you select):

- A sword (25 Husks)
- A battleaxe (25 Husks)
- Light armor (25 Husks)
- Heavy armor (25 Husks)
- A Spell Tome (25 Husks)

Or you can keep your Soul Husks, as Valerica also makes use of them (see Regional Activity: Valerica's Concoction).

TIP Soul Husks are actually edible and are found in your Food menu. For ten seconds, you gain 10 percent Magic Resistance and are protected from Soul Drain effects in the Soul Cairn.

Postquest Activities

You can continue to collect Soul Husks and exchange them for goods.

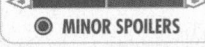

VALERICA'S CONCOCTION*

PREREQUISITES: Complete Dawnguard Main Quest: Beyond Death

MINOR SPOILERS

INTERSECTING QUESTS: Dawnguard Main Quest: Beyond Death

LOCATIONS: Soul Cairn, The Boneyard

CHARACTERS: Valerica

ENEMIES: Ideal Master Crystal

◊ **OBJECTIVES:** None

NOTE This quest is open to both factions. It becomes accessible only after you complete Dawnguard Main Quest: Beyond Death.

Hunting Husks for Valerica

Once you've helped Valerica, claimed the Elder Scroll, and have no further critical objectives to accomplish, you can speak to her again. Among the topics of conversation, you can request her help in dealing with the crystals around these parts. The crystals in question greatly drain you and can make life difficult when you're exploring. Valerica has spent decades perfecting an extract that increases the potency of Soul Husks. If you bring five of these Husks to her, she'd be happy to provide you with some.

You may now begin collecting Soul Husks throughout the Soul Cairn (as this is the only place where they grow). You can find them in chests or growing in clusters (shown). The largest concentration of them is in the Husk Pasture. When you have five, return to Valerica, who prepares and hands you the concoction.

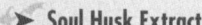

➤ **Soul Husk Extract**

Postquest Activities

Valerica continues to make Soul Husk Extract for as long as you return with Soul Husks. Once she leaves the Soul Cairn (as part of Postquest Activity: Valerica's Return*; see page 552), this option is no longer available.

THE WHOLE SOUL*

PREREQUISITES: Complete Dawnguard Main Quest: Chasing Echoes

MINOR SPOILERS

INTERSECTING QUESTS: Dawnguard Main Quest: Chasing Echoes, Dawnguard Main Quest: Beyond Death

LOCATIONS: Soul Cairn

CHARACTERS: Valerica

ENEMIES: None

◊ **OBJECTIVES:** Retrieve the Soul Essence Gem

NOTE This activity is available (and relevant) only if you allied yourself with the Dawnguard, then let Serana partially soul-trap you at the end of Dawnguard Main Quest: Chasing Echoes in order to enter the Soul Cairn. It becomes accessible only after you enter the Soul Cairn as part of Dawnguard Main Quest: Beyond Death.

Souled Out

Once you've met (and freed) Valerica, you can speak with her about your current condition. Valerica informs you that part of your soul is trapped here, and she's already found out where it is. She points this out to you, and your (Miscellaneous) quest updates:

◊ **OBJECTIVE:** Retrieve the Soul Essence Gem

♦ **TARGET:** Soul Essence Gem, inside a [random] chest

Flag the Miscellaneous Objective so that the location of the Soul Essence Gem appears on your compass, then follow it to the location shown. This is likely to be a chest under one of the Ideal Master Crystals, but the exact location varies. Open the chest in question, and quickly remove the Soul Essence Gem (Full). Your statistics now recover to their pre-soul-trapped levels.

➤ **Soul Essence Gem (Full)**

ANCIENT FALMER TOMES*

PREREQUISITES: Complete Dawnguard Main Quest: Unseen Visions

MINOR SPOILERS

INTERSECTING QUESTS: Dawnguard Main Quest: Unseen Visions, Dawnguard Main Quest: Touching the Sky

LOCATIONS: Forgotten Vale, Dead-End Ledge, Falmer Fissure, Snow Lake Entrance, Upper Falls Overlook

CHARACTERS: Urag gro-Shub

ENEMIES: Falmer, Frost Giant

◊ **OBJECTIVES:** Bring Ancient Falmer Tomes to Urag gro-Shub

NOTE * Quest names marked with this symbol do not appear in your Quest Menu list, although objectives may.

This quest is open to both factions. It becomes accessible only after you enter Forgotten Vale as part of Dawnguard Main Quest: Touching the Sky. Although every effort has been made to accurately pinpoint each location, it is well worth consulting the Forgotten Vale Atlas chapter and the Forgotten Vale map (page 996), which has cartographical locations shown.

Initial Preparations

To activate this unmarked quest (which is just a Miscellaneous Objective once you find the first book), simply find one of the four Ancient Falmer Tomes (as shown, also known as "Unknown Books") in the Forgotten Vale. These can be found in any order, and not all of them need to be found. However, you receive 1,000 gold for each book you find, so this is well worth your time.

◊ **OBJECTIVE:** Bring Ancient Falmer Tomes to Urag gro-Shub

♦ **TARGET:** Unknown Books I, II, III, and IV, Forgotten Vale

♦ **TARGET:** Urag gro-Shub, Arcanaeum, College of Winterhold

Tome Gathering: Four Books Forgotten

In this section, we tell you where each of the books are located. They are listed in numerical order, although you won't find them in that order without some backtracking through the Forgotten Vale. In each case, a picture of each location is shown, and each location is also named: The names are references to the Atlas section only (they don't appear on your local map). Check the compass on each picture so you know from which direction to approach.

Unknown Book, Vol. I

Snow Lake Entrance: The Sprawled Skeleton: When you reach the snowy hill and the Forgotten Vale lake, head south down the slope toward the water's edge. Along the way, you'll spot a skeletal corpse sprawled over a chest. Close to the chest is the book and a coin purse. This is usually the first book you'll find.

➤ **Unknown Book, Vol. I**

Unknown Book, Vol. II

Upper Falls Overlook: This is the most difficult book to find. First you must trek to the location of the third Frost Giant, which is in the northern Falmer cliffs area that you traverse before reaching the Glacial Crevice. The Frost Giant lives by a shallow cave high above the main river fissure, off a circular Falmer path (see page 1001). Slay this foe and claim the Emerald Paragon from its corpse. Then (usually after completing the Dawnguard Main Quest) journey to the Paragon Portal Platform (see page 1000), close to the second Frost Giant's location, and insert the Emerald Paragon. You emerge at Upper Falls Overlook, high above the Frozen Lake and close to the Temple Balcony. Head to the waterfall's edge and look right (east). The book is by some arrows, a bow, a chest, and a skeleton. This is usually the last book you'll find.

NOTE Consult Regional Activity: Paragons of the Frost Giants* for more information on the Emerald Paragon.

➤ **Unknown Book, Vol. II**

Unknown Book, Vol. III

Falmer Hut, Dead-End Ledge: Journey across the northern Falmer cliffs, the area you must traverse before reaching the Glacial Crevice. On your descent, with the river below you and the Glacial Crevice to the south, head across a couple of bridges (one Falmer-made and the other natural). There's a Falmer Hut with a mammoth skull adorning it. The book is on a table inside the hut, near some potions and other trinkets. This is usually the second book you'll find.

➤ **Unknown Book, Vol. III**

Unknown Book, Vol. IV

Falmer Hut, the Falmer Fissure: After emerging from the Glacial Crevice, enter the Falmer Fissure, and fight your way to the second part of this location, with four huts to ransack and a group of Chaurus Hunter Fledglings to remove from their nests below. Be sure to check the hut on the upper walkway at this area's far eastern end; the Unknown Book is here on a table near potions and a Falmer chest, just before you drop down and enter the sloping tunnel to the south. This is usually the third book you'll find.

➤ **Unknown Book, Vol. IV**

Quest Conclusion

When you have one or more of these tomes, visit the College of Winterhold and seek out Urag gro-Shub in the Arcanaeum. Ask him if he has any interest in ancient Falmer tomes, and he agrees to purchase them from you for 1,000 gold, plus a translated version of the book. Collect all four for the following rewards:

➤ **1,000 gold (per book)**

➤ **The Betrayed (translated version of Vol. I)**

➤ **Journal of Mirtil Angoth (translated version of Vol. II)**

➤ **Diary of Faire Agarwen (translated version of Vol. III)**

➤ **Touching the Sky (translated version of Vol. IV)**

Postquest Activities

Return to Urag gro-Shub if you missed any books, until you've found and sold all four and pocketed the translated copy and your "finder's fee."

PARAGONS OF THE FROST GIANTS*

PREREQUISITES: Complete Dawnguard Main Quest: Unseen Visions

MINOR SPOILERS

INTERSECTING QUESTS: Dawnguard Main Quest: Unseen Visions, Dawnguard Main Quest: Touching the Sky

LOCATIONS: Forgotten Vale Darkfall Grotto (Paragon Portal), Forgotten Vale Forest (Paragon Portal), Forgotten Vale Overlook (Paragon Portal), Frost Giant Lair, Falmer Cliffs: Circular Falmer Path, Inner Sanctum, Lower Lake, North Falmer Fissure, Paragon Portal Platform, Glacial Crevice (Paragon Portal), Inner Sanctum (Paragon Portal)

CHARACTERS: None

ENEMIES: Falmer, Frost Giant, Frost Troll

◊ **OBJECTIVES:** None

NOTE * Quest names marked with this symbol do not appear in your Quest Menu list, although objectives may.

This quest is open to both factions. It becomes accessible only after you enter Forgotten Vale as part of Dawnguard Main Quest: Touching the Sky. Although every effort has been made to accurately pinpoint each Frost Giant location, it is well worth consulting the Forgotten Vale Atlas chapter and the Forgotten Vale map (page 996), which shows cartographical locations and the hidden areas you can reach with each of the Paragons.

Initial Preparations

Hidden throughout the Forgotten Vale are shallow caves where Frost Giants dwell. These huge and sinewy beasts each carry a unique Paragon Stone. The first part of this task is to gather all of the Paragons. The second part of this task is to utilize the Paragons at a special Portal, which can transport you to otherwise-inaccessible parts of the Vale. Collect as many (or as few) Paragons as you wish.

This task requires little preparation; in fact, it is recommended that you undertake it during Dawnguard Main Quest: Touching the Sky, as all of the Frost Giant locations are close to the route you take through Forgotten Vale. This is an unmarked quest, so there are no objectives to watch for.

In the following section, we describe where each of the Frost Giants are located. They are listed one to five, although you can face them in any order you choose. In each case, a picture of the location is shown, along with its name: The names are references to the Atlas section only (they don't appear on your local map). Check the compass on each picture so you know from which direction to approach.

When facing a Frost Giant in combat, utilize the techniques you previously employed when fighting Giants. Beware of the Frost Giants' club smash, which is devastating, and don't get caught in the rocky terrain! It is wise to fire on these foes from a distance or let Serana (or any Armored Trolls, Huskies, or Death Hounds you've coaxed along with you) take the brunt of the hurting.

Part 1: Giant Killer—A Frosty Reception

Frost Giant 1

Frost Giant Lair (Lower Lake): From the entrance to the lower lake (where the first Unknown Book is located, just after the battle with the Frostbite Spiders), turn right (northwest) and work your way to the lake's northwest end. The Frost Giant is close to a waterfall, in a shallow cave. There's a snowy path northwest of here. Claim the Amethyst Paragon from its corpse.

➤ **Amethyst Paragon**

Frost Giant 2

Frost Giant Lair (Paragon Portal Platform): After traversing the Frozen Lake and activating the Wayshrine of Resolution, head north toward a natural bridge. At the bridge's other side, turn right (southeast), head along a previously unexplored path, and turn left (east) to an unexplored ridge. Move through rocky outcrops to a rushing river above the Lower Lake where you slew your first Frost Giant. This is where the snowy path (mentioned above) links to, and that's another route here. Slay the Frost Giant at the shallow cave, and remove the Sapphire Paragon from the body.

➤ **Sapphire Paragon**

> **TIP** This location has a Snow Elf Paragon Portal on the river's northwestern side. You insert each of the Paragons here. This can be done no matter how many you have.

Frost Giant 3

Frost Giant Lair (Falmer Cliffs—Circular Falmer Path): At the flapping banner marking the upper entrance to Sharpslope Cave, head southeast, down to a rickety bridge with a hut at the far end. Then climb the steep rocky path to the northeast. At the top is a circular path to the right (south) leading counterclockwise past the shallow cave with the third Frost Giant to face. Watch your step, as this path is precarious! Loot the Emerald Paragon from the dead giant.

➤ **Emerald Paragon**

Frost Giant 4

Frost Giant Lair (North Falmer Fissure): Having just navigated through the Glacial Crevice, enter the Falmer Fissure (a set of narrow crags where the Falmer have constructed numerous bridge pathways). Inspect the path leading north, past a bone rope and up through a gate to a steep ravine with a Frost Giant tending to his bone collection at the top. Slay him, and claim his Diamond Paragon.

➤ **Diamond Paragon**

Frost Giant 5

Frost Giant Lair (Inner Sanctum): Having entered the Inner Sanctum, in the initial chamber with the frozen Falmer, inspect an altar along the western wall of this temple entrance. Activate the altar and place your Ewer on it. This opens a secret door directly ahead of you. Step through, then turn around and grab the Ewer. Step back before the door closes.

Now investigate the secret passage you've found; it leads to an ice cave where you face the fifth and final Frost Giant. Claim the Ruby Paragon from its corpse before activating a second altar in the northern wall. Place the Ewer on the altar to access a second, smaller hidden chamber with a chest and a variety of potions and Elven Arrows. Check the entire area for skeletal remains and other items; then return to the first secret door, placing the Ewer on the side altar (grab it again afterward!) and stepping back through into the main temple entrance.

➤ **Ruby Paragon**

Part 2: The Really Forgotten Vale

With one or more Paragons in your possession, return to the site where you defeated the second Frost Giant and claimed the Sapphire Paragon (by the rushing river and two waterfalls). Look for this partially ruined Paragon Portal Platform (pictured). Activate the Paragon Socket, and insert the Paragon of your choice. The structure glows, and an archway to an otherwise-inaccessible part of the Forgotten Vale becomes accessible. Step on through to the following areas:

Amethyst Paragon

Darkfall Grotto (Paragon Portal): You're teleported to a high rock ledge overlooking the waterfall that leads (after some enforced swimming) into Darkfall Grotto. Search the area for a chest and potion. You can dive into the water below or use the paragon arch to safely teleport back.

➤ Chest and Potion

Sapphire Paragon

Inner Sanctum (Paragon Portal): You appear in a ruined section of the Inner Sanctum. On the other side of the room of arched windows are three chests, some well-made armor, and a scattering of valuable gems (including a diamond, amethysts, and various garnets). Now return to the Paragon Platform.

➤ Chest (3), and Gems

Emerald Paragon

Forgotten Vale Overlook (Paragon Portal): You emerge at the highest point in the Forgotten Vale—a rushing river tumbling from a waterfall. Follow the river downstream, to the edge of a second waterfall. Don't fall to your death here; instead, gaze out across the Frozen Lake (weather permitting) and check out Auriel's Chapel Balcony (which can't be reached either). Look east toward a small pillar ruin, a skeleton, a chest, arrows, a bow, and an Unknown Book (part of Regional Activity: Forgotten Vale: Ancient Falmer Tomes).*

➤ Chest, Arrows, and Bow ➤ Unknown Book, Vol. II

Diamond Paragon

Glacial Crevice (Paragon Portal): You're transported to a small, high ledge near the ceiling of the Glacial Crevice. Aside from a dangerous jump-off, there's a single chest to ransack before you return.

➤ Chest

Ruby Paragon

Forgotten Vale Forest (Paragon Portal): This location is the largest and consists of a sealed glade of thick woodland with sloping ground to the northwest that leads to a Frost Troll den. To the southwest, a powerful Falmer clad in fancy armor is finishing off the Frost Troll threat before turning his attention to you. Face the Falmer Warmonger in battle, and once you best him, peel off his armor and claim the legendary artifact he was carrying: Auriel's Shield. This is a fine prize!

➤ Falmer Hardened Armor ➤ Auriel's Shield
➤ Falmer Hardened Helm

Quest Conclusion

Slay any Frost Giants you may have missed, and fully investigate all five hidden areas to complete this quest.

Postquest Activities

The Ruby Paragon leads you to a location where you have the most to gain, as Auriel's Shield is an exceptional item. Remember you can sell the Paragons you don't want or need anymore, or you can display them in your home as a memento of this task.

DRAGONBORN QUESTS

GENERAL OVERVIEW

A new power – an ancient, creeping terror – is gradually enveloping the island of Solstheim off the coast of Morrowind. For it seems the long-forgotten tombs and sacred stones are resonating; grasped firmly by the machinations of the first Dragonborn: Scholars tell of a priest named Miraak, who served the dragons with a group of powerful acolytes, before finally turning against his dragon masters, and finding new strength and knowledge under the yoke of the Daedric Prince Hermaeus Mora. Miraak is demonstrating his fortitude by siphoning the island's All-Maker Stones, and enslaving its inhabitants. As his power grows, he has even sent his followers into the provinces of Skyrim in search of the 'false' Dragonborn, the only one who may be capable of stopping his return.

NOTE Cross-referencing: Would you like to see maps and learn more about the traps, non-quest-related items, collectibles, crafting areas, and other important rooms of note in every location during these quests? Then cross-reference the location you're in with the information on that location contained in this guide's Solstheim Atlas.

IMPORTANT LOCATIONS

Raven Rock

Raven Rock is a settlement located in the remains of the Hirstaang Forest. It's situated strategically in a small cove on the southern end of Solstheim. In Raven Rock's glory days, a pair of large docks jutted out into the cove, which provided access to the cargo ships the East Empire Company needed to send ebony out of and bring supplies into the colony. Now, only a single rickety dock remains. The eastern end of the city is dominated by the Bulwark, a massive stone fortification used to defend the town. A long, tall cliff protects the town's northern side, sheltering it from Solstheim's harsh conditions. Ever since Red Mountain's eruption, the once-lush pine forest has been transformed into ash waste. The Bulwark now serves as a different kind of barrier—protecting Raven Rock's inhabitants from ash storms.

Tel Mithryn

Dominated by the Telvanni tower along the island's southern coast, this Dunmeri settlement sits a little east of the ruins of Fort Frostmoth. It has a classic mushroom shape, with a fungal growth hollowed out into a top floor and a stalk holding it up off the ground. Currently, one section of it appears to be withered and dying. At the base of the stalk are bulbous growths that form secondary buildings. Tel Mithryn is home to Neloth, a Telvanni wizard who survived the Red Year of Vvardenfell. Neloth has been experimenting with the ash and other debris, such as heart stones, from the eruption of Red Mountain. He has multiple goals, but all of them involve returning to Vvardenfell and becoming Arch-Mage, although sometimes it just looks like accumulating power for power's sake.

Skaal Village

Skaal Village is located along the Felsaad Coast. The terrain is flat but rocky and dotted with pine trees and low scrub. There is no real economy here, as money has little value to the self-sufficient Skaal. Hunting is the main source of sustenance, as the Horkers on the northern coast and nearby Lake Fjalding are relative easy and lucrative prey. More adventurous Skaal seek the elusive Snow Wolf or Snow Bear, whose pelts are highly valued among their people.

The All-Maker Stones

The animistic Skaal hold these ancient carved stones to be evidence of their deity, part of a simple cosmology in which the All-Maker created all matter and the world. While these notions may seem primitive to Nords of Skyrim, the magic that courses through these stones is very real—so much so that Miraak seeks to siphon it and has tainted them with evil, compelling the weaker-willed people of Solstheim into constructing strange arched shrines for this purpose.

Temple of Miraak

In the distant past, one of the great temples of the Dragon Cult stood atop Solstheim's central mountains. It was destroyed by the dragons long ago, in the war fought over Miraak's betrayal, and forgotten. Now it is the site of the Tree Stone, one of the five All-Maker Stones sacred to the Skaal people. But a new temple is rising, with strange arches and an ornate. Its architects are the ordinary people of Solstheim, who have unknowingly fallen under the control of Miraak.

Nchardak

The dwarven city of Nchardak was built on a series of platforms extending out into the Sea of Ghosts. Thousands of years of disuse, and the cataclysmic Red Year, have decimated the ruin, causing most of it to sink into the sea. Only the tops of a few towers and the walkways connecting them still rise above the waterline. Many are tilted at precarious angles or have been ruined entirely, but a few, such as the domed Reading Room, remain intact.

Apocrypha

Amid a black ocean filled with writhing tentacles lies the endless library of forbidden knowledge. This realm of Oblivion is the domain of Hermaeus Mora. Black-covered books adorn every edifice. Pages flitter as if pulled by invisible string. And grotesque creatures malformed by Mora stalk the constantly elongating and retracting halls, feeding off the ghosts of those seeking knowledge. The laws of the mortal world hold no power here.

IMPORTANT CHARACTERS

Frea Crag-Strider

Frea is the daughter of Storn Crag-Strider. When Miraak began to seize control of Solstheim, she was with her father and was protected from Miraak's mind control. Her friends were not so fortunate and haven't been seen in quite some time. While her father focused on protecting the village, she devised a way to make that protection portable so that she could attempt to find out what has happened. With a special talisman to keep her safe, she's made it to the top of the strange temple in the center of Solstheim, looking for answers.

Storn Crag-Strider

Storn is the Skaal shaman, the spiritual advisor to the tribe. Stoic and patient, the Skaal look to him in times of difficulty for guidance and comfort. He communes with the land and calls upon the power of the All-Maker, the creator and sustainer, to protect them. Times have grown harder of late, and now his people have been shattered by the loss of most of the tribe to some unknown dark magic. At the last moment, Storn was able to shield the remaining few of his people from this spell, but it is taking all of his concentration to maintain the barrier, and he can't keep it up forever.

Neloth

Master Neloth is the Telvanni wizard who dwells in Tel Mithryn. Neloth seems to have difficultly with the concept that other people matter. He judges their health and well-being solely based on his personal comfort and needs. That said, he is no fool. He recognizes power and that power in others must be respected. At this point in his life, he has given up kidnapping women. He claims that it no longer interests him. Once you've kidnapped someone, you have to put up with their whining and complaining. It just isn't worth it.

Miraak

Miraak was the first Dragonborn. His destiny may have been to defeat Alduin back in the Mythic Era, but he chose a different path: to use his Dragonborn abilities to gain power for himself. Originally a dragon priest, he was seduced by Hermaeus Mora and secretly became his disciple. He gathered a cult to Hermaeus Mora at his temple on Solstheim.

Eventually, the other dragon priests discovered Miraak's heresy and led a crusade against him. He was defeated, his followers killed or scattered, and his temple razed. But Miraak was able to escape into Hermaeus Mora's realm of Apocrypha, where he has been growing in knowledge and power over the centuries while he waited for a chance to return.

Hermaeus Mora

Hermaeus Mora is the Daedric Prince of Knowledge, he who scryes the tides of Fate, weaving his way through the past and future. Always lurking, he is the void and the ever-seeing eyes. He resides everywhere and nowhere but takes glee in tormenting mortals from his realm in Oblivion, the plane called Apocrypha, where the infinite pages of countless books containing all forbidden knowledge are found.

AVAILABLE QUESTS

There are a total of seven Dragonborn Main Quests. Aside from Cleansing the Stones, which must be completed after The Fate of the Skaal but before the conclusion of The Gardener of Men, each quest leads directly into the next, as shown in the following table:

✓	QUEST NAME	PREREQUISITES
☐	Dragonborn Main Quest: Dragonborn	Complete Main Quest: The Way of the Voice
☐	Dragonborn Main Quest: The Temple of Miraak	Complete Dragonborn Main Quest: Dragonborn
☐	Dragonborn Main Quest: The Fate of the Skaal	Complete Dragonborn Main Quest: The Temple of Miraak
☐	Dragonborn Main Quest: Cleansing the Stones	Complete Dragonborn Main Quest: The Fate of the Skaal
☐	Dragonborn Main Quest: The Path of Knowledge	Complete Dragonborn Main Quest: The Fate of the Skaal
☐	Dragonborn Main Quest: The Gardener of Men	Complete Dragonborn Main Quest: The Path of Knowledge. You must also complete Dragonborn Main Quest: Cleansing the Stones to finish it.
☐	Dragonborn Main Quest: At the Summit of Apocrypha	Complete Dragonborn Main Quest: The Gardener of Men

DRAGONBORN MAIN QUEST

DRAGONBORN

PREREQUISITES: Complete Main Quest: The Way of the Voice

INTERSECTING QUESTS: Main Quest: The Way of the Voice, Main Quest: The Horn of Jurgen Windcaller, Dragonborn Main Quest: The Temple of Miraak

LOCATIONS: Earth Stone, High Hrothgar, Raven Rock, Temple of Miraak, Windhelm, Northern Maiden, Windhelm Docks

CHARACTERS: Adril Arano, Frea, Gjalund Salt-Sage, Neloth

ENEMIES: Cultist

◊ **OBJECTIVES:** Find out who sent the Cultists, Read Cultists' Orders, Travel to Solstheim, Search for information about Miraak, Investigate the shrine, Reach the Temple of Miraak

Called to Solstheim

NOTE The island of Solstheim is treacherous and unforgiving, and its more ferocious inhabitants are tough to slay without proper killing equipment. Once you begin this quest, gather enough provisions so you don't waste time traveling back and forth from Skyrim.

After your initial meeting with the Greybeards of High Hrothgar, unseen forces begin to conspire against you. To catch your first glimpse of your new and threatening foes, head to any town or city once Main Quest: The Horn of Jurgen Windcaller begins. In this example, your stroll through Riverwood was disrupted.

Enter any settlement and the regular jocularity with the town guards is silenced by the arrival of two strange figures wearing distinctively odd masks and clothing. One of the Cultists challenges you (head to another settlement if no challengers present themselves), mocking your supposed status as the true Dragonborn! Apparently, Lord Miraak is soon to appear, and you are but his shadow! The two Cultists then attack. Slay both of them, with or without the help of the townsfolk.

◊ **OBJECTIVE:** Find out who sent the Cultists

TIP Consider visiting a smaller settlement such as Dragon Bridge or Riverwood, as the Cultists are easier to spot, but the guard still offers effective backup to your own combat prowess.

CAUTION Such fighting inside a settlement can lead to the slaying of unimportant residents; this won't impact any major quests but may diminish the Favors you can attempt, so you may wish to draw the Cultists away from the villagers.

Once the fracas ends, inspect the corpses of the Cultists. Pick up the piece of paper marked "Cultists' Orders," which seems to be a missive from a Lord Miraak to his two minions, urging them to find and kill you. There's also a clue to their method of travel. You must retrace their steps by seeking out the ship the *Northern Maiden*, docked at Windhelm.

➤ Cultists' Orders

◊ **OBJECTIVE:** Read Cultists' Orders

◊ **OBJECTIVE:** Travel to Solstheim

♦ **TARGET:** Gjalund Salt-Sage, *Northern Maiden*, Windhelm Docks

Aboard the *Northern Maiden*

Head to Windhelm and descend to the dockside area near the East Empire warehouse. Locate the *Northern Maiden* and its forlorn-looking captain. Speak to Gjalund Salt-Sage, choosing your words how you like. It transpires that Gjalund was befuddled for most of the trip, losing whole days of his memory after agreeing to bring the Cultists aboard. He has little desire to return to Solstheim, though. Unless you:

(500 gold) Agree to pay him double his usual rate, or

(Persuade) Tell him he owes you for bringing those killers to your doorstep, or

(Intimidate) Let him know you're not taking no for an answer.

When you're successful, Gjalund agrees to set sail. Ready yourself for the voyage to Solstheim. As you arrive at the port of Raven Rock, Gjalund hopes you'll find out what's been going on around these parts.

TIP Plan your excursion to Solstheim wisely:

◊ If you lack proper attire, weapons, or supplies for such a lengthy trip, you might wish to make proper preparations before you speak with Gjalund.

◊ Consider traveling light; although there is a house you can acquire (see page 99), there's nowhere you can initially store your excess items.

◊ Solstheim (and in particular, the town of Raven Rock) has all of the usual merchants and services, so you need not return to Skyrim between every adventure. However, after you first arrive in Raven Rock, you can Fast-Travel back to the mainland (and vice versa) at any time or pay Gjalund to take you back.

◊ **OBJECTIVE:** Search for information about Miraak

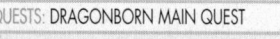

♦ **TARGET:** Adril Arano, Raven Rock docks

Rumors at Raven Rock

As you disembark, you're stopped by a Dunmer named Adril Arano. Ignore him if you want, but it's better to listen to what he has to say. He wants to know your intentions. You can:

Be as secretive as you like and investigate by speaking to other townsfolk.

Better yet, you can eke out some information from him; tell him you're looking for Miraak. Initially, he shrugs off your question and makes sure you know that House Redoran of Morrowind runs this sovereign territory. Ask him about Miraak again, and he stops to think. He's sure he doesn't know the name but reckons it may have something to do with the Earth Stone nestled on the high ground just outside of town. After he imparts this bit of information, you can quiz him about his suspicions regarding visitors and learn more about the town of Raven Rock.

◊ **OBJECTIVE:** Investigate the shrine
♦ **TARGET:** Neloth, at the Earth Shrine

Exit the docks and turn left, heading along the main thoroughfare. There are numerous merchants and other buildings of interest to check out (the Atlas on page 1037 has all this information), but aside from extra activities, you have a few options. You can:

Talk to the townspeople of Raven Rock. There are many to choose from, and they offer you variations on one of three pieces of information:

That Miraak sounds familiar, but the person can't remember why.

That the name has some connection to the shrine at the Earth Stone.

That this entity conjures up images of a temple near the middle of this island.

Ignore the townspeople and head directly to the Temple of Miraak if you're feeling antisocial or haven't the time for pleasantries.

TIP Ask about Miraak when speaking to Glover Mallory the blacksmith; then talk to Dreyla Alor, a merchant of general goods. You'll receive enough information to bypass the visit to the Earth Shrine and head straight to a strange temple. You don't have to pick those two; anyone with a full name is likely to give you some help.

If you head west and southwest along the main thoroughfare and around to a promontory overlooking the town, you can see some villagers hard at work erecting a strange monument around an odd glowing sacred stone the size of a frost giant. The majority of the workers seem transfixed and speak in short bursts as if possessed. Seek out a dark elf named Neloth, who ponders awhile on why you aren't in the same state as these drones. You can:

Ask him what these people are doing: He doesn't know but wants to leave them like this to find out.

Inquire about Morrowind, and he tells you a little more about the place.

If someone in Raven Rock hasn't mentioned the temple to you yet, Neloth will, and the quest updates.

NOTE This Earth Stone is one of six Sacred Stones to be found on Solstheim. Much like the Standing Stones of Skyrim, they grant great power to those who seek it. However, at the moment, the stones are consumed by a strange green energy. Try to activate any Stone and you will awake to find yourself helping in the construction. You will free the thralls forced to build these shrines for Miraak later in this quest.

◊ **OBJECTIVE:** Reach the Temple of Miraak

Enthralled at the Temple

Feel free to explore the large island of Solstheim, as there are multiple ways to reach the Temple of Miraak. You can choose to do that now or after partaking in a few side quests. The optimal path to the Temple—which is reasonably direct and takes in some of the scenery so you get your bearings—involves backtracking across Raven Rock along the main thoroughfare heading east, through the gatehouse.

After passing through the bulwark, follow the gray beach with the strange pentagonal rock column formations. In the far distance is Red Mountain (in Vvardenfell, the main island of Morrowind), spewing great plumes of volcanic ash, which explains much of Solstheim's ground coloration. Just up ahead is Old Attius Farm, where Captain Veleth is taking a hammering from a group of Ash Spawn. Help or avoid this fracas; find out more by starting Side Quest: March of the Dead (page 632).

Take a long left turn up the beach to the ashen, decimated forest, watching for intermittent savaging by Ash Hoppers. Weave around the gnarled stumps, rocky outcrops, and blighted trees in a roughly northern direction. Along the way, expect to run into a few nasty surprises, such as a Burnt Spriggan and a hunting party of Reavers.

Continue north up the rocky escarpment, until the gray ash gives way to tundra. Climb northeast, through the gaps in the crags; the skeletons of slain dragons appear, half buried in the snow. Locate the steep steps and archways, continuing your ascent up and into the Temple of Miraak. There's a splendid view from the wooden scaffolding at the top.

Quest Conclusion

Ignore the Reaver thralls chiseling new construction for their master, who have nothing to say but a monotonous chant about "his" return. As you descend into the central cloister, you should seek out Frea, a woman desperately attempting to free her friend Ysra from her mental bonds. Approach her to end this quest.

THE TEMPLE OF MIRAAK

PREREQUISITES: Complete Dragonborn Main Quest: Dragonborn

MINOR SPOILERS

INTERSECTING QUESTS: Dragonborn Main Quest: Dragonslayer, Dragonborn Main Quest: Dragonborn, Dragonborn Main Quest: Cleansing the Stones, Dragonborn Main Quest: The Fate of the Skaal

LOCATIONS: Temple of Miraak

CHARACTERS: Frea

ENEMIES: Cultists, Draugr, Gatekeeper, Miraak, Sahrotaar, Seeker

◊ **OBJECTIVES:** Talk to Frea, Find the source of Miraak's power, Read the Black Book, Talk to Frea

Down Among the Dead

NOTE This quest normally begins when you speak to Frea at the end of Dragonborn Main Quest: Dragonborn. However, there is another, very remote, possibility. If you never encountered the Cultists who begin that quest and instead traveled to Solstheim, visited the remote ruin of Saering's Watch, learned and unlocked the first word of the Bend Will Shout, and tried it out on the Wind Stone near Skaal village—all of this entirely on your own—you can free the Skaal "early." In that case, Storn will send you to find Frea at the temple, which begins this quest and skips over Dragonborn Main Quest: Dragonborn.

CAUTION From this point on, Miraak becomes an incredibly disruptive force on the isle of Solstheim (and throughout Skyrim). In particular, he may appear after you have killed a dragon and steal its soul away from you, making it significantly harder to unlock further Shouts. For more information, see World Interaction: Soul Stealing (page 683).

◊ **OBJECTIVE:** Talk to Frea
♦ **TARGET:** Frea, Temple of Miraak (exterior)

As the snow flurries dance around this circular arena, ignore Frea's mind-addled friend and talk to her yourself. She sternly explains she is one of the Skaal, the native people of this region, and that something has taken control of the minds of her tribe. Many work on great stone shrouds that corrupt the island's venerated and ancient standing stones. Her father is a shaman, who believes that Miraak has returned. You respond that you've already had a run-in with his cultists. You can ask Frea for:

More information about Miraak. This updates your objective.
Further knowledge of her people, the Skaal.
Why she's out here on her own.
And what exactly the Tree Stone is.

◊ **OBJECTIVE:** Find the source of Miraak's power
♦ **TARGET:** Black Book, the Temple of Miraak Sanctum

It doesn't take Miraak's cultists long to show themselves. Face them down with Frea's fearsome axe-work, and descend the curved ramp they came from. Open the door and enter the temple, working your way down the stone corridor and checking the antechambers on each side for supplies, as Frea advises. Aside from the burned and caged corpses, expect potions and poisons before you descend farther. Watch for the dart trap just before the narrow stairs where two more Cultists appear. Defeat them, and any Draugr you disturb if you stumble to the sides of this room.

TIP Frea is a tough Skaal warrior, and you can certainly let her lead the way into combat if you wish to conserve your potions, magic, or stamina.

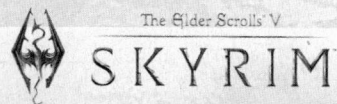

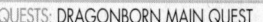

Pass through the small burial chamber where Frea warns of the many traps Miraak's minions may have prepared for you. Sure enough, there are floor plates to avoid in the subsequent connecting chamber (unless you're ready to receive a battering ram to the stomach), steps down to a portcullis that opens via the adjacent chain, and a vast pit chamber where Frea notices more poor souls trapped in hanging cages. She also spots a stone viewing abutment overlooking the vast steps in the chamber's center of.

Head clockwise around the chamber's edge, repelling Draugr threats that burst from their vertical coffins. After two or three Draugr, face three or four Cultists ascending from the pit steps. Once you and Frea cut down all foes, thoroughly inspect the chamber: As Frea predicted, there is a way to the stone abutment; maneuver up the rubble and coffins under the pillar and then clamber atop the pillar, where you find a large treasure chest. Return the way you came, and descend the pit steps into a Draugr crypt.

Activate the handle next to the small portcullis door and step through into a small tomb where the walled coffins contain a variety of long-dead Nords to cut down (you may wish to move around the pillars and rubble so Frea attacks from a different direction than you, splitting your enemies' focus). After you defeat the Draugr, clamber through to a long passageway heading north. Watch for the seated Draugr behind you.

Avoid the swinging blade trap's floor plates as the passage splits into two narrower corridors. Both meet up farther along the crypt, both have Draugr infesting them, and both have a floor plate and a battering ram to avoid as you enter. The lower chamber offers higher ground, making it slightly easier to navigate. The corridors merge at the entrance to a long hall. Beware the floor plate and fire trap as you reach the double doors.

Enter this long hall of swinging blade traps and make short, quick bursts of speed between the swings to avoid any nasty contusions. A Whirlwind Sprint Shout can see you to the hall's end, but don't dash too early and stop at a blade's arcing cut. Pull the lever to remove the spear bars, step over the remains of the inactive Nordic Puzzle Door, and descend to the wooden double doors.

Bars block the way to the west, so head down the narrow passage, ignoring the dead Draugr that collapses out of its tomb. Pull the handle to remove the barrier. As the wooden bridge falls into place, step down into the three-ramped chamber, where a Cultist and two Draugr minions are waiting to repel you. Watch the floor plate and dart trap as you descend to meet them. Tackle any ranged foes, then the Cultist, and split or combine your attacks with Frea if you wish. After the battle, locate the double doors leading to the Temple of Miraak Sanctum.

Keeper of the Dragon Cult

Proceed along a suspended cage bridge. Step across the scattered bones, into the connecting tunnel, and wind around, slaying four to six skeletons and a couple of Draugr who step out of their coffins and onto a floor plate that activates battering rams; attack these foes from above. Step into the cavern of the guardians, watching for active Draugr and bursting coffins as you go.

Head down the steps across the stone crypt, keeping to the cavern's right (northeast) side so you don't end up in a small dead-end pit. Watch for a floor plate and battering ram, and work your way around the stone ledge to face down further Cultist threats. A fiery cauldron has been lit at the top of the narrow steps down into an ancient burial site for members of a dragon cult. Frea is shocked that Miraak would display the skeletal remains of a dragon in such a disrespectful manner.

Animosity between Miraak and his dragon cult brethren is the least of your worries. Step up to the Word Wall on your left (south) and learn a word of the Dragon Aspect Shout. The transference of power from the wall triggers a Draugr ambush; expect two or three annoyances from the row of coffins and a particularly nasty foe known as the Gatekeeper to burst from the tomb below the dragon skeleton. Defeat everything that moves, and inspect the Gatekeeper's corpse to claim the key to go farther into the temple. The door to which the key belongs is behind the Gatekeeper's sarcophagus.

- **Word of Power:** Dragon Aspect
- **Temple of Miraak Key**

NOTE The Dragon Aspect Shout is powerful, giving you improved armor and a range of other benefits, but it isn't something you have to use as a part of this quest.

TIP The Gatekeeper has his own Shouts, and these may stall or disarm you. Circle him or head up the steps to more easily avoid these attacks.

Waking Dreams of a Starless Sky

Pass the banquet table and its long-dead feasters, opening a second iron door with the key. After a connecting corridor with a window, move into another feasting hall, devoid of foes but featuring strange carved totems you haven't seen before. Pass by these weird fishlike heads into the kitchens, which hold a few ingredients and a narrow windowed passage with a handle to pull. This opens a secret door between two sets of shelves in the feasting hall. Gather your resolve and head south, through the winding tunnel to a ruined reading nook.

This circular chamber has a large spiral staircase below, but it is currently barred. Frea points out there is nothing here but ruined books. But there's also a secondary chamber with a square-shaped trapdoor and menacing statuary. Activate the handle in front of the fish faces to open the trapdoor. Descend the spiral steps, which connect to the ones you could see if you looked down from the reading nook.

Descend to the connected circular corridors with the fiery maws lighting your path. At the end is a stone wall with a handle to pull, lowering a staircase. Go even lower, opening a wooden door. This leads to a massive and lengthy stepped chamber, adorned with dragon bones and falling boulders. Prepare to be embroiled in a fast-paced battle with some skeletons, three falling boulder traps (stay mobile and leap to the side if you trigger any), and a nasty veteran Draugr with a sharp blade. Once you bring this foe to his knees, climb the final steps to a large treasure chest near the odd, lumpy carving of the Keeper of Forbidden Knowledge, inspect it, then activate the chain in the alcove behind the chest.

◊ **OBJECTIVE:** Read the Black Book

Scramble down a winding tunnel to reach a particularly ominous final chamber. This circular area is dominated by a thick stone altar, upon which rests the weighty Black Book. Frea warns you there are dark magics at work here. When you are ready, pick up the book and read it.

➤ **Black Book:** Waking Dreams

Unlike other books you may have read, this one strangles you with a dark tentacle and transports you to a strange plane of existence. This is Apocrypha, the realm of Hermaeus Mora, where the crackling towers of learning mingle with archways of despair and confusion. Forced to kneel and unable to move, your appearance interrupts Miraak. Flanked by Seekers (and his own gigantic serpent dragon, Sahrotaar), he speaks to you as a pretender to his throne as the true Dragonborn. If you've completed Main Quest: Dragonslayer, he comes close to commending you on your prowess but insists you have no idea of the power a true Dragonborn can wield.

Yelling the Dragon Aspect Shout, his form is imbued with power—a power that you cannot hope to achieve. After further hubris, he commands two of his Seekers to return you to the mortal plane and sets off on his dragon mount.

TIP You can immediately reread Waking Dreams and explore the realm of Apocrypha within. The guidance through these strange and frightening otherworldly islands is contained in Dragonborn Main Quest: At the Summit of Apocrypha, which is the optimal time to attempt this.

Remember that whenever you pick up a Black Book, you can read it at any time by opening it in your inventory. Black Books work only on Solstheim, not in mainland Skyrim.

◊ **OBJECTIVE:** Talk to Frea

Quest Conclusion

You regain consciousness at the Black Book altar. Speak with Frea and answer her questions. Miraak has proven himself to be extremely dangerous, and the book you retrieved must be shown to her father. He might be able to further your knowledge.

NOTE This Black Book is one of six that link Tamriel to the plane of Apocrypha. If you wish to travel deeper into Hermaeus Mora's realm, consult the "Black Book" quests in the Solstheim Side Quests section. These begin on page 608.

PREREQUISITES: Complete Dragonborn Main Quest: The Temple of Miraak

MINOR SPOILERS

INTERSECTING QUESTS: Dragonborn Main Quest: The Temple of Miraak, Dragonborn Main Quest: Cleansing the Stones, Dragonborn Main Quest: The Path of Knowledge

LOCATIONS: Saering's Watch, Skaal Village, Shaman's Hut, Temple of Miraak, Wind Stone

CHARACTERS: Frea, Storn Crag-Strider

ENEMIES: Dragon, Draugr, Frost Troll, Lurker

◊ **OBJECTIVES:** Accompany Frea to Skaal Village, Talk to Storn Crag-Strider, Learn the Word of Power, Use the "Bend Will" Shout on the Wind Stone, Defeat the Lurker, Talk to Storn

Storn of the Skaal

◊ **OBJECTIVE:** Accompany Frea to Skaal Village
♦ **TARGET:** Storn Crag-Strider, Skaal Village

Follow Frea out of the exit tunnel, and back into the Solstheim wilderness. A few dozen footfalls farther down the snowy mountainside, Frea pauses and asks if you can see a green light down the valley. This is the Wind Stone, where her people work against their will. She beckons you on, away from that possessed place, to the village and her father, Storn.

Follow her across the wooden bridge heading east. Frea stops again with her village in the middle-distance. She explains Storn used magic to raise a barrier around the settlement, protecting the few remaining Skaal from Miraak's control. Continue to follow her into Skaal Village, where a group of elders are kneeling in prayer. She approaches them and tells them her news. It seems Storn has more stories to share.

◊ **OBJECTIVE:** Talk to Storn Crag-Strider

Approach Storn Crag-Strider and he asks that you speak quickly, as his powers of protection are dwindling. You mention Miraak, and Storn recalls reading about terrible battles fought at the temple. He asks if you are Dragonborn. Answer however you wish. Storn then tells you to journey to Saering's Watch. There is a Word of Power there that Miraak has already mastered. Knowing this Thu'um may help to break the spell Miraak has over the Skaal people. Before you go, you can:

- Ask for further information about Miraak.
- Ask what he means about freeing his people from control.
- Ask why you need to learn this Word of Power.

When Storn's answers have concluded, prepare to journey west, into the craggy, snowbound mountains of northern Solstheim.

◊ **OBJECTIVE:** Learn the Word of Power
◊ **TARGET:** Word Wall, Saering's Watch

Free Will

The trek to Saering's Watch is dangerous and difficult to traverse. The optimal path is to set out in a northwest direction, crossing back over the wooden bridge and skirting the edge of the Headwaters of Harstrad. Next, maneuver north, then northwest up the steep snowy slopes to pass by the entrance to Benkongerike. Turn right (north), heading under the stone henges as you reach the outskirts of Saering's Watch.

Pass under the henges (don't head farther up the mountain, as this places you away from the Word Wall) and head to the more open snowy cliffs where a great dragon is swooping down to attack a group of Draugr, recently resurrected from their tombs inside this ancient site. Other creatures may be prowling this area too (they are usually waiting among the rocky crags on the mountaintop, near the edge overlooking the ruins). Although not imperative, it is worth engaging in the battle here. You can:

Slay anything that moves, in no particular order. Wading in is fine. Firing down from a vantage point above these Draugr ruins is better.

Remember that you can also watch the dragon and Draugr battle it out, and then mop up any survivors if you aren't confident you can take them all on at the same time.

When you've thwarted the enemies in this vicinity, enter the ruins, looking for the three-headed stone serpent torch attached to the wall to the south. There is a set of stone steps to the left and right (heading southwest and northeast). Climb to the left to reach a secondary promontory with more steps up to the exterior Word Wall. Close by is a large treasure chest and the remains of a ritual involving candles and a long-dead skeleton. Approach the Word Wall, and learn your new Shout.

➤ **Word of Power:** Bend Will

NOTE If you have already learned this word before speaking with Storn, he sends you to the Wind Stone directly.

◊ **OBJECTIVE:** Use the "Bend Will" Shout on the Wind Stone
♦ **TARGET:** Wind Stone, in Solstheim

The Lurker at the Threshold

Before continuing, spend a Dragon Soul to unlock the Bend Will Shout (the dragon you just slew at the base of Saering's Watch will do nicely). Equip and Favorite the Shout before descending back the way you came, down the mountainside heading roughly southeast. Before you step onto the wooden bridge, go down the hillside, heading north toward the All-Maker's Wind Stone. The Skaal you speak to are beyond your ability to help and mumble praises to Miraak. Clear your throat and bellow the Bend Will Shout directly at the stone. The rock arches glow red and then explode, snapping the Skaal villagers from their malaise. As the pieces of masonry fall away, something is summoned from Hermaeus Mora's realm!

◊ **OBJECTIVE:** Defeat the Lurker

NOTE Did Miraak appear and steal the soul of the dragon you just slew? There's little you can do about this annoyance. If you're out of Dragon Souls to expend on Bend Will, travel back to Skyrim, locate a dragon lair, and slay another.

If you activate the Wind Stone before cleansing it, you'll join Miraak's other thralls in constructing the arches around this site. Fortunately, you have the willpower to snap out of this trance.

After cleansing the Wind Stone, you can commune with it. It grants you the power of the North Wind for a single day. Find out more information about the All-Maker Stones of Solstheim on page 94.

➤ **All-Maker Power:** North Wind (target takes 20 points of Frost damage for 10 seconds, plus Stamina damage)

The grim fish-headed statuary at Miraak's temple bears a resemblance to the unspeakable atrocity that appears to thwart you and the regrouping Skaal. Step forward and engage the Lurker, watching for its dark tendrils, ranged attack of black spittle, and foot-stomping splashes. This tough fellow is more easily contained if you utilize the Wind Stone to hide behind as you dodge its attacks. When the slimy beast is slain, your quest updates:

◊ **OBJECTIVE:** Talk to Storn
♦ **TARGET:** Storn Crag-Strider, Skaal Village

Quest Conclusion

Climb the hill with the freed Skaal tribe members, and head back to Skaal Village. Enter the shaman's hut if Storn isn't in the village exterior, and speak with him. He already knows you've prevailed. You can speak to him about the following matters:

Let him know his people are free. He mentions that you are now a friend of the Skaal. Ask him what to do next, and he asks if you might perform the same cleansing Shout on the rest of the stones of Solstheim.

Ask him for further information about Miraak.

Ask him what the All-Maker is.

Ask him what his role is among the Skaal.

Postquest Activities

Continue your conversation with Storn, and he asks you to remove Miraak's presence from the remaining All-Maker Stones. This starts Dragonborn Main Quest: Cleansing the Stones.

Tell Storn that isn't enough and that Miraak needs to be stopped now. He tells you this is beyond his power and understanding. You must learn more about the Black Book you're carrying. Storn won't read such unnatural tomes, but he recommends the Dark Elf Wizard Neloth to aid you in these matters. At this point, Dragonborn Main Quest: The Path of Knowledge begins. After this, you can quiz Storn about:

More information on the Black Books.

Neloth and his role in finding more Black Books.

After completing this quest, you can persuade Frea to join you as a Follower.

NOTE At this point, there are a few Regional Activities you can attempt at Skaal Village. These can be done at any time from this point on. Check page 671 for more information.

PREREQUISITES: Complete Dragonborn Main Quest: The Fate of the Skaal

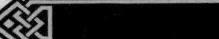

◉ MINOR SPOILERS

INTERSECTING QUESTS: Dragonborn Main Quest: The Fate of the Skaal, Dragonborn Main Quest: The Path of Knowledge

LOCATIONS: Beast Stone, Earth Stone, Sun Stone, Water Stone

CHARACTERS: Benkum, Bralsa Drel, Cindiri Arano, Dreyla Alor, Fethis Alor, Glover Mallory, Hjalfar, Liesl, Milore Ienth, Palevius Lex, Redoran Guard, Rirns Llervu, Ulves Romoran

ENEMIES: Cultist, Dragon, Lurker, Reaver, Riekling

◊ **OBJECTIVES:** Cleanse the Sun Stone, Cleanse the Beast Stone, Cleanse the Earth Stone, Cleanse the Water Stone

Before the Cleansing

NOTE This quest begins after you complete Dragonborn Main Quest: The Fate of the Skaal. With the Wind Stone already freed, there are four All-Maker Stones (other than the Tree Stone at Miraak's Temple) that you must remove from Miraak's influence. You may complete this quest at any time, but you must conclude it before you can finish Dragonborn Main Quest: The Gardener of Men.

◊ **OBJECTIVE:** Cleanse the Sun Stone
◊ **OBJECTIVE:** Cleanse the Beast Stone
◊ **OBJECTIVE:** Cleanse the Earth Stone
◊ **OBJECTIVE:** Cleanse the Water Stone

The following information may prove pertinent as you reach each of the All-Maker Stones:

- The encounters at each of the Stones can be attempted in any order.
- Once you utter the Bend Will Shout, the construction around the Stone glows brightly and explodes.
- Immediately afterward, a Lurker is summoned. Slay it to complete the objective.
- Some battles may involve additional Lurkers or other foes. However, you need slay only the Lurker indicated by the objective arrow for the objective to complete.
- These can be difficult fights, so bring a Follower or summoned creature to assist you. You can also take advantage of the landscape around the Stone (and even the Stone itself) for cover opportunities.
- The enthralled workers at each site sometimes help you by engaging the Lurkers. But do your best to protect them, as they can die and may cause you to miss out on some minor Favors.
- Once the Stones are freed of Miraak's disruptions, you can gain power from each of them. For complete details, consult page 52.

Sun Stone: Purging the Ashen and the Elvish

The Sun Stone is just north of Tel Mithryn. Bellow the Bend Will Shout, and prepare for combat with one (or more) Lurkers. The following information may prove helpful:

The Dark Elf Ulves Romoran, who works in the kitchens of Tel Mithryn, is currently enslaved here. Keep him alive if you wish to speak with him afterward.

The other stone workers are Reavers and are expendable.

Beware of Ash Spawn and Ash Hoppers in the vicinity: remove these threats first or your chances of victory are further hindered.

Watch your wild attacks when engaging Lurkers; accidentally slaying the Dark Elves helping your battle can increase your bounty on Solstheim.

➤ **All-Maker Power:** Sun Flare.

Beast Stone: Freeing the Weakling Rieklings

The Beast Stone is west of the Thirsk Mead Hall and southeast of the Temple of Miraak. Yell the Bend Will Shout, and ready your weapons for a Lurker incursion. Remember the following as you approach:

There are a small number of Rieklings working at the building site. They are expendable.

Beware of a Cultist or two in this area. They join in the battle against you, so try and place the Lurker between you and them. If you get lucky, their attacks may strike the beast, causing them to turn on each other.

➤ **All-Maker Power:** Conjure Werebear.

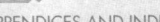

Earth Stone: Horror Near Raven Rock

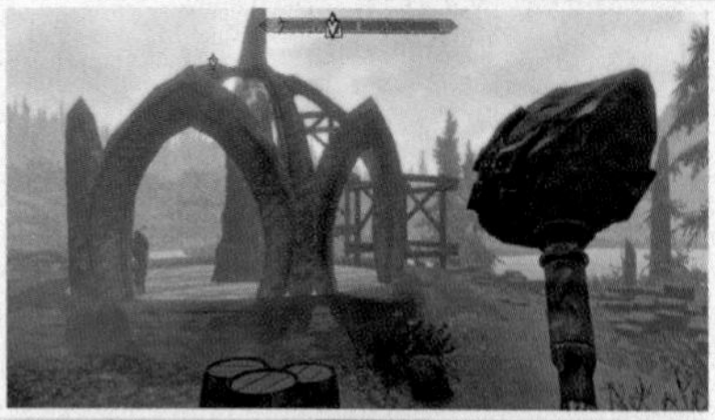

The Earth Stone is southwest of Raven Rock, on the overlook where you may have met Neloth during Dragonborn Main Quest: Dragonborn. Call upon the Bend Will Shout, then face the Lurker that emerges. Heed the following at this juncture:

Citizens of Raven Rock are working at this Stone. During daytime hours, expect Bralsa Drel and Rirns Llervu (both incidental during Solstheim Side Quest: The Final Descent) here.

During nighttime hours, expect to find Cindiri Arano (Raven Rock Favor), Dreyla Alor (incidental), Fethis Alor (merchant and Solstheim Side Quest: The Great Solstheim Strongbox Hunt*), Glover Mallory (merchant and Raven Rock Favors), and Milore Ienth (merchant and Raven Rock Favors). Since there is a high risk that some (or most) of these civilians will die, it's safer to cleanse this stone during the day.

There are two or three Redoran Guards working here during the day. They are expendable.

Although there are many Raven Rock citizens within fleeing distance, beware of who is attacking (and being slain by) the Lurkers.

➤ **All-Maker Power:** Bones of the Earth.

Water Stone: Untangling the Final Bonds

The Water Stone is north of Raven Rock and due west of Fahlbtharz, on a steep cliff path. Demolish the masonry with your Bend Will Shout, but watch for the following difficulties:

There are four sailors—Benkum, Hjalfar, Liesl, and Palevius Lex—enslaved at this Stone. Once freed, they may help in a fight but are expendable. Should any survive, they wander to the shore to wait for a ship and their freedom. They aren't involved in any other quests.

Expect a Cultist or two, and a dragon will fly in from a nearby island to the west. This can hamper your progress or help out considerably (if the Lurker and dragon end up fighting each other). But beware of lengthening odds if you're facing all three foes.

➤ **All-Maker Power:** Waters of Life.

Quest Conclusion

When all but the Tree Stone has been cleansed of Miraak's influence, this quest concludes. You should now continue with your Dragonborn Main Quest tasks (as completing this allows you to finish that quest line).

THE PATH OF KNOWLEDGE

PREREQUISITES: Complete Dragonborn Main Quest: The Fate of the Skaal

MINOR SPOILERS

INTERSECTING QUESTS: Dragonborn Main Quest: Cleansing the Stones, Dragonborn Main Quest: The Gardener of Men

LOCATIONS: Nchardak, Nchardak Aqueduct, Nchardak Great Chamber, Nchardak Reading Room, Nchardak Workshop, Tel Mithryn

CHARACTERS: Neloth

ENEMIES: Dwarven Ballista, Dwarven Centurion, Dwarven Sphere, Dwarven Spider, Reaver

◊ **OBJECTIVES:** Objective: Talk to Neloth, Travel to Nchardak with Neloth, Restore the steam supply to the Dwemer reading room, Release the book from the Dwemer contraption

An Insufferable Ally

This quest begins once you finish Dragonborn Main Quest: The Fate of the Skaal. You can complete it before, during, or after Dragonborn Main Quest: Cleansing the Stones.

◊ **OBJECTIVE:** Talk to Neloth

♦ **TARGET:** Neloth, in Tel Mithryn

You may have already met Neloth as part of Dragonborn Main Quest: Dragonborn or by visiting his tower at Tel Mithryn on your own. He has since returned to Tel Mithryn, in the southeast of the island. Beware of ash creatures as you approach.

Look for the lantern-lit root pathway that leads up to a circular door into the main structure of Tel Mithryn. Enter the tower, and then float up the magical lift to the upper floor where Neloth is practicing his magic. He doesn't recall inviting you here. Speak to him of the Black Book, after which you can converse on the following topics:

Your exploration to find more of these Black Books. Continue this line of questioning, mentioning you need to know what Miraak knows if you wish to stop him. Keep talking as Neloth reveals he knows the whereabouts of a Black Book connected to Miraak.

Questions regarding the Daedric Lord Hermaeus Mora.

The Black Book Neloth has learned the location of is sealed within a "reading room" in the dwarven ruin of Nchardak. He agrees to accompany you to see the tome, which is visible but firmly locked away.

◊ **OBJECTIVE:** Travel to Nchardak with Neloth

♦ **TARGET:** Nchardak Reading Room, Nchardak

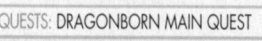

MINOR SPOILERS

PREREQUISITES: None

RELATED QUESTS: Solstheim Side Quest: Lost Knowledge, Solstheim Side Quest: Masks of the Acolyte Priests*, Solstheim Side Quest: Spider Crafting*

LOCATIONS: Apocrypha, White Ridge Barrow

ENEMIES: Albino Spider, Bandit, Draugr, Dukaan, Flame Spider, Lurker, Merilar Rendas, Seeker

◊ **OBJECTIVES:** Learn the Black Book's hidden knowledge

Dukaan's Dark Secret

In the five Black Book quests, you must check out one of five ancient books that teleport you to Hermaeus Mora's realm of Apocrypha. This specific book is hidden deep within White Ridge Barrow.

Reach the Black Book chamber by navigating through White Ridge Barrow. If you require a walkthrough, consult Solstheim Side Quest: Spider Crafting*. You do not need to finish that quest, but you must complete the following tasks:

Enter the spider-filled entrance passage, and descend the spiral steps. Move through the grand hall and defeat more spiders and parasitical arachnids with their Bandit victims.

Head roughly south, maneuvering toward the White Ridge Sanctum entrance. Activate the door bar, enter another huge hall, and engage (or avoid) Merilar Rendas and his spider friends.

Continue south to an iron door, which leads to a grand crypt with a Word Wall and a Dragon Acolyte Priest named Dukaan. Defeat or avoid this foe, then claim the Word of Power for the Cyclone Shout.

The Black Book is on a pedestal on the chamber's opposite side (below where you entered).

Reach the pedestal containing the Black Book, and read it. You are transported to Apocrypha.

➤ **Word of Power:** Cyclone ➤ **Black Book:** The Sallow Regent

NOTE This is an area of Apocrypha that does not overlap with the part of the realm you visit during the Dragonborn Main Quests.

TIP Neloth, a powerful Dunmeri mage in the settlement of Tel Mithryn, may request you locate and return this book so he can make a copy. This is Solstheim Side Quest: Lost Knowledge. Although you miss out on a monetary reward, you can obtain this book without seeking Neloth out first.

Seeker of Knowledge

◊ **OBJECTIVE:** Learn the Black Book's hidden knowledge

You are transported into the partial void, where strange hovering lanterns flit across a long and dark corridor. They are important, as they provide light in this forsaken place, and the darkness harms you. Watch out for the tentacles in the small pond near the pod, then set off down the dark and blackened path heading roughly south.

TIP You can also use a torch, or the Candlelight spell, to negate the effects of the darkness!

Continue south to a second tentacle pond, and a pod, then turn west and walk up the sloping tunnel to a larger, partially lit chamber with stacks of books and a possible Spell Tome. There are also a few gems and scrolls to search for. A Seeker appears to block your path, after which you must move to a second tunnel (south) and ascend it.

This seems to lead to a dead end, but continue south and a platform uncurls, linking to a well-lit area with a black table and a possible Spell Tome. When the lights go out, head up the steps to the south, attacking (or running past) a Lurker and winding your way up to the highest platform.

Quest Conclusion

This splits into two platforms before merging again. These narrow bridges have Lurkers to attack or avoid (there are a total of three), before you head south and up to the final platform. Here you find a vessel and two black tables with assorted items (including another possible Spell Tome). But you're here for this Black Book: open it, and you can select from among the following powers:

➤ **Seeker of Might (Combat skills are all 10% more effective)**

➤ **Seeker of Sorcery (All spells cost 10% less Magicka)**

➤ **Seeker of Shadows (Stealth skills are all 10% more effective)**

Postquest Activities

Choose your power, then open the book to return to Solstheim.

BLACK BOOK: THE WINDS OF CHANGE

PREREQUISITES: None

RELATED QUESTS: Solstheim Side Quest: Lost Knowledge, Solstheim Side Quest: Masks of the Acolyte Priests*, Solstheim Side Quest: The Great Solstheim Strongbox Hunt*

LOCATIONS: Apocrypha, Bloodskal Barrow, Raven Rock Mine

ENEMIES: Draugr, Lurker, Seeker, Zahkriisos

◊ **OBJECTIVES:** Learn the Black Book's hidden knowledge

MINOR SPOILERS

Buried Beneath Bloodskal Barrow

In the five Black Book quests, you must find and leaf through one of five archaic tomes that transport you to Hermaeus Mora's realm of Apocrypha. This particular book is nestled deep within Bloodskal Barrow, which you access from Raven Rock Mine.

Reach the Black Book chamber by completing Solstheim Side Quest: The Final Descent (see page 622 for the walkthrough for this quest). You need to finish some of this quest by completing the following tasks:

- Locate Raven Rock Mine and agree to help Crescius search for the secrets of his ancestors.
- Descend to the bottom of the mine, and make your way through the long Draugr crypt.
- This is Bloodskal Barrow; the Draugr-killing continues until you reach a grand basalt chasm.
- Approach the sealed door, and use the power attacks of the Bloodskal Blade to open it.
- Avoid the blade traps, then face off against and defeat the Dragon Acolyte Priest Zahkriisos.
- Learn the Word of Power from the Dragon Aspect Shout at the Word Wall before leaving.
- The chamber you must reach is a circular spiral stepped area with a small waterfall.
- Reach the pedestal containing the Black Book and read it. You are transported to Apocrypha.

➤ **Word of Power:** Dragon Aspect

➤ **Black Book:** The Winds of Change

NOTE This is an area of Apocrypha that does not overlap with the part of the realm you visit during the Dragonborn Main Quests.

TIP Neloth, a powerful Dunmeri mage in the settlement of Tel Mithryn, may request you locate and return this book so he can make a copy. This is Solstheim Side Quest: Lost Knowledge. Although you miss out on a monetary reward, you can obtain this book without seeking Neloth out first.

Adventurer's Insight

◊ **OBJECTIVE:** Learn the Black Book's hidden knowledge

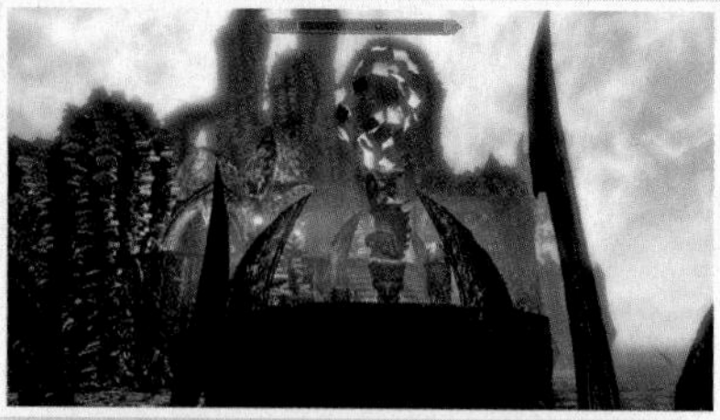

The great fetid seas of Apocrypha greet you. Focus on the path and head southeast, climbing the stepped platforms to your left as you turn east. Fight two or three Seekers as you go. Avoid the tentacle from the black pond as you reach a Scrye that opens a gate ahead (northeast) of you.

Head past a black table and a Magicka font, moving to a Stamina font, a black table, and a Scrye crammed together. The Scrye opens a second gate. Head southwest, engaging two more Seekers in the corridor beyond. Gather Magicka from a font as you continue south to a Scrye.

This opens a gate to the south, leading to a larger, open chamber with a ramp and a forming Lurker. Slay this atrocity, before or after you activate the Scrye to the west. There are two Magicka fonts to siphon here too. The Scrye on the ground elongates the steps. The Scrye atop the ramp opens the gate atop these steps.

Quest Conclusion

The gate allows access to the pedestal containing the tome and an adjacent vessel to ransack. Open the book and you can select from among the following powers:

➤ **Scholar's Insight (Reading Skill Books gives you an extra Skill Point)**

➤ **Companion's Insight (Your attacks, Shouts, and destruction spells do no damage to your Followers)**

➤ **Lover's Insight (Do 10% more damage and get 10% better prices from people of the opposite sex)**

Postquest Activities

Choose your power, then access the book to transport back to Solstheim.

PREREQUISITES: None

RELATED QUESTS: Solstheim Side Quest: Lost Knowledge, Solstheim Side Quest: The Great Solstheim Strongbox Hunt*

LOCATIONS: Apocrypha, Benkongerike

ENEMIES: Lurker, Mounted Riekling, Riekling, Seeker

◊ **OBJECTIVES:** Learn the Black Book's hidden knowledge

◉ MINOR SPOILERS

NOTE This is an area of Apocrypha that does not overlap with the part of the realm you visit during the Dragonborn Main Quests.

TIP Neloth, a powerful Dunmeri mage in the settlement of Tel Mithryn, may request you locate and return this book so he can make a copy. This is Solstheim Side Quest: Lost Knowledge. Although you miss out on a monetary reward, you can obtain this book without seeking Neloth out first.

Buried in Benkongerike

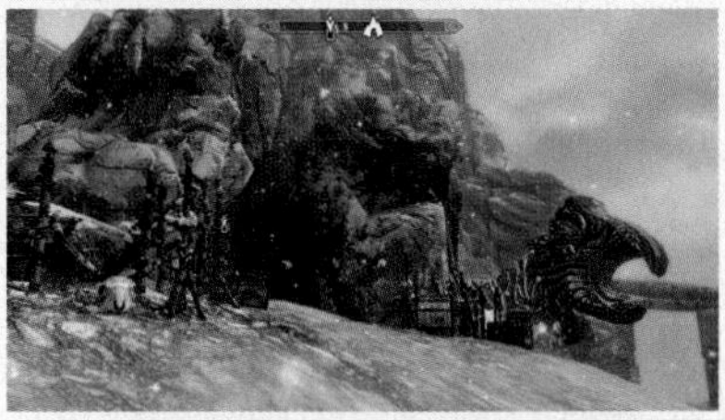

In the five Black Book quests, you must locate and pore over one of the strange books that whisk you into Hermaeus Mora's realm of Apocrypha. This specific book is hidden deep within Benkongerike.

Reach the Black Book chamber by weaving your way through Benkongerike. If you require a walkthrough, consult the Atlas entry for this cave complex and Draugr dungeon on page 1021. Here is a brief summary:

> Enter the large snowbound cave chamber and slay Rieklings that await you. Then head west and north through the icy passages, avoiding Riekling traps and foes leaping out from their strewn items.
>
> Maneuver east into the large cavern of rickety bridges, tearing through more Rieklings and leaving by the exit to the east. Watch for a final Riekling ambush before heading into Benkongerike Great Hall.

Move through the connecting passages and into the great hall, where a Bristleback-mounted Riekling Charger and a half-dozen infantry foes present a temporary problem. After you slay anything blue-skinned, head south to inspect the Nordic Puzzle.

Puzzle Solution: Ignore the pedestal with the handle (as you don't want to be struck by darts), and instead search the walls for petroglyphs corresponding to the pedestals below. The correct order, from left to right, is Hawk, Whale, Whale, and Serpent. The second petroglyph clue is missing; find it in a tent on the eastern upper ledge of this chamber.

Check the chest by the Word Wall, absorb the Cyclone Word of Power, then head east down a narrow tunnel and into a circular chamber where the Black Book awaits.

Reach the pedestal containing the Black Book, and read it. You are transported to Apocrypha.

➤ **Word of Power:** Cyclone

➤ **Black Book:** Untold Legends

Chapter and Perverse

◊ **OBJECTIVE:** Learn the Black Book's hidden knowledge

Pass the two Magicka fonts, heading north to a Stamina font, east to another Magicka font and black table, and north to Chapter II. You appear facing a stepped platform. Head onto it, turn left (west), cross the bridge, and face off against a Lurker just beyond two more Magicka fonts, on the far part of the bridge.

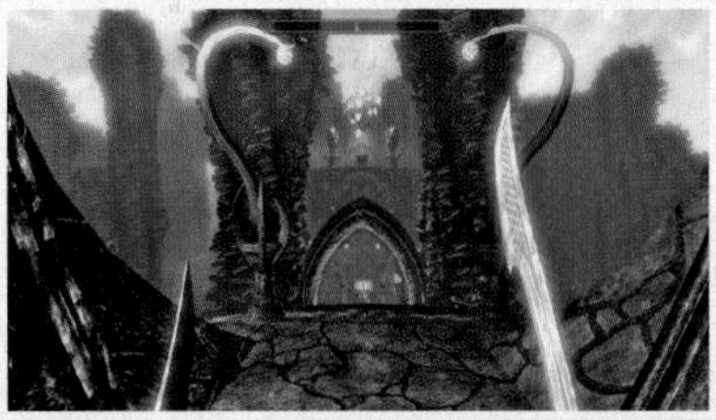

Continue west to the double exit; there is a ramp on either side. Head north, passing two Magicka fonts, and open Chapter III first. You appear in a cagelike chamber. Slay the Seeker, inspect the pod on the black table and a possible Spell Tome before opening Chapter II again. Head south, to the Magicka font and Chapter IV.

Head north, through a stepped tunnel with a Magicka font, and pass two Stamina fonts as the tunnel opens to a stepped cathedral chamber without a roof. Beware of two Seekers as you solve the way to open the exit.

Puzzle Solution:
In the center is a locked area with a Scrye. Surrounding this are six raised antechambers and the exit:

> **Antechamber 1 (northeast):** Stamina font and a Skill Book, Beggar (Pickpocket Skill Book).
>
> **Antechamber 2 (east):** Locked gate and Scrye, accessed from Antechamber 5.

Antechamber 3 (southeast): Stamina font.

Antechamber 4 (southwest): Magicka font.

Antechamber 5 (west): Scrye outside, which opens the gate leading to a Magicka font and Scrye inside, which opens the gate to Antechamber 2.

Antechamber 6 (northwest): Magicka font.

Simply head to Antechamber 5, activate the outside Scrye to open the adjacent door, and go inside this antechamber to a second Scrye; this opens Antechamber 2. Head there to the next Scrye and activate that. The north gate of the central locked area opens. Enter here, with its four Magicka fonts, and activate the final Scrye. The steps to the south extend, allowing access past two more Magicka fonts to a vessel and Chapter V.

Enter Chapter V, and head down the main corridor, peering ahead at what seems to be the Black Book at the end of this long tunnel. However, when you reach the middle, near the two Stamina fonts, the tunnel ahead grinds to the left, forcing you east to a black pond and a Lurker fight!

After the battle, follow the exit corridor north and west, activating a Scrye and opening a gate that leads back into the main tunnel. Dash south again, and the same trick is performed; the tunnel grinds right this time, forcing you west to a chamber with a Stamina font and a second Lurker to battle.

Quest Conclusion

Follow the exit corridor north (passing a Stamina font) and east, back once more into the main tunnel. Trek south one last time, and the corridor allows you access to two Stamina fonts and the Black Book. Open the book, and you can select from among the following powers:

- **Black Market (Summons a Dremora merchant to trade with you)**
- **Secret Servant (Summons a Dremora butler to carry your excess items)**
- **Bardic Knowledge (Summons a spectral drum that plays for you, increasing Stamina Regeneration for you and nearby allies)**

Postquest Activities

Choose your power, then open the book to return to Solstheim.

BRIARHEART NECROPSY

MINOR SPOILERS

PREREQUISITES: None

RELATED QUESTS: Solstheim Side Quests: Neloth's Quests (page 606).

LOCATIONS: Forsworn Redoubt (any), Tel Mithryn

CHARACTERS: Neloth

ENEMIES: Briarheart

◊ **OBJECTIVES:** Examine a Briarheart warrior, Talk to Neloth

A Briarheart out of Reach

NOTE This is one of many quests you complete by visiting and speaking to Neloth in his Tel Mithryn tower. For a complete list, consult page 606. Although randomly occurring, this quest usually becomes available once you complete Solstheim Side Quest: Heart Stones a couple of times.

That Dunmeri wizard all the folks in Raven Rock think of as an uptight loony has a problem. You'll know this if you visit him once you finish Dragonborn Main Quest: The Path of Knowledge. Return to his tower in Tel Mithryn, and he exclaims, "Curse these heart stones!" Ask if there's a problem, and he asks if you're familiar with the Briarhearts. Neloth seems keen on furthering his knowledge regarding the briar seeds they use in place of their hearts. You're to examine one of these fierce warriors of the Forsworn. Neloth casts a memory trace spell on you so he doesn't have to rely on your puny descriptive verbiage; therefore, there's no need to take notes. You can:

Set off immediately.

Or ask where Briarhearts can be found. His description points you in the direction of the Reach.

Or ask what Briarhearts have to do with Heart Stones. His explanations don't help this quest.

◊ **OBJECTIVE:** Examine a Briarheart warrior

♦ **TARGET:** Briarheart, [any Forsworn redoubt], the Reach

> **TIP** No Ancient Nordic Pickaxe? Then temporarily halt this quest and obtain one. There are several to choose from:
>
> Complete Solstheim Side Quest: A New Source of Stalhrim (see page 633), and free Baldor Iron-Shaper of the Skaal Village. He occasionally has one for sale.
>
> Complete Solstheim Side Quest: Unearthed (see page 645), and take the unique Ancient Nordic Pickaxe called "Hoarfrost" from Ralis Sedarys.
>
> Complete Solstheim Regional Activity: Favor for Glover Mallory (see page 669), and retrieve his Ancient Nordic Pickaxe from Crescius at the entrance to Raven Rock Mine.

Did you feel a stale breeze wafting? Head southeast toward the door, and open the double doors, entering the barrow treasure room. What a haul! Aside from armor, two chests, potions, precious stones, and weapons, there are numerous piles of Septims that total approximately 10,000 gold!

But be warned: the moment you touch the treasure, the portcullis behind you slams shut. It appears that Haknir's curse was no mere legend...

Open the second pair of iron doors and continue down a damp tunnel. What awaits you in the depths of this barrow?

➤ **Gold (approx. 10,000)**

Haknir Death-Brand: Leaving a Mark

The tunnel ends in a grand and eerie tomb chamber. As you edge toward the steps, and the ceremonial bier with the skeleton lying on it, a sword should catch your eye. Steel yourself, then take Bloodscythe from the altar. The moment you do, the doors to the chamber slam shut, and Haknir Death-Brand's ghost appears, urging you to join the dead!

◊ **OBJECTIVE:** Defeat Haknir Death-Brand

➤ **Bloodscythe**

As the Battle Begins

Haknir Death-Brand is a considerable force of fury and anger. You must meet his prowess with cunning and weather this storm. His attacks come in five waves:

Wave 1: Haknir Attacks! First, you confront Haknir. He is tough, fast, well armed, and well armored. He wears the complete set of Deathbrand Armor and wields both Bloodscythe (which saps your health and armor) and Soulrender (which siphons your Magicka and destroys magical defenses). You do have one advantage, though—Haknir is at the opposite end of the room. Use the time it takes for him to reach you to hit with your most powerful attacks, and try to cut him down as quickly as possible.

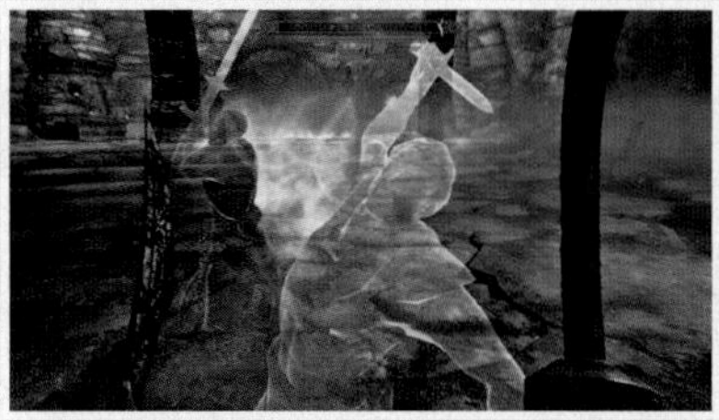

Wave 2: A Ghostly Crew. When Haknir's health falls below 70%, he disappears, and you face a swarm of weaker ghosts. Individually, the members of Haknir's crew are not difficult, but their sheer number can be a little overwhelming—two are generally in combat with you at all times, with a new one arising each time you cut down one of their companions.

Wave 3: Lieutenants Unleashed. After you fend off his crew, Haknir reappears by the altar, accompanied by his two lieutenants, Garuk Windrime and Thalin Ebonhand. Focus your attacks on Haknir, as he warps out as soon as his health falls below 40%. Eliminate one of the lieutenants, then stop to heal and recover if you need to—this is your best opportunity to do so during the battle. Then finish off the other to continue.

Wave 4: A Motley Crew. You then face a second wave of Haknir's crew. They're no more difficult than before, but you now fight three at a time instead of two. Followers or summoned allies are especially useful here to keep yourself from becoming surrounded and overwhelmed.

Wave 5: Haknir's Last Stand. Finally, you face Haknir again in a fight to the death. Finish him off and claim both Soulrender and his immense hoard of treasure.

Quest Conclusion

When Haknir Death-Brand finally vanishes, be sure to claim the blade he was wielding, as it amplifies the qualities of Bloodscythe. You are now free to loot from this barrow and return to the surface the way you came.

➤ **Soulrender**

Postquest Activities: The Deathbrand Treasure

The legendary treasure of the pirate despoiler Haknir Death-Brand is a worthy prize. In addition to a vast sum of gold and valuable gems, it includes some of the best gear available, especially for a Light Armor/Dual-Wielding specialist.

☑	NAME	TYPE	DESCRIPTION	FOUND
☐	Bloodscythe	One-Handed Sword	When dual-wielded with Soulrender, Absorb Health 15, Damage Armor (25% chance, 100/15s)	Gyldenhul Barrow
☐	Soulrender	One-Handed Sword	When dual-wielded with Bloodscythe, Absorb Magicka 15, Dispel Magic (25% chance)	Gyldenhul Barrow
☐	Deathbrand Gauntlets	Heavy Armor	Increases your dual-wielding damage by 10% for each Deathbrand item you wear.	[S.ND] Mudcrab Tidal Pools
☐	Deathbrand Boots	Heavy Armor	Increases your carry weight by 10% for each Deathbrand item you wear.	[SS.W] Basalt Causeway
☐	Deathbrand Helm	Heavy Armor	Waterbreathing. While wearing the full set of Deathbrand Armor, increases your Armor by 100.	[S.N28] Haknir's Shoal
☐	Deathbrand Armor	Heavy Armor	Increases your Stamina by 15 for each Deathbrand item you wear.	[SS.D] Bloodskal Copse

Postquest Activities

That treasure map, now used, would make a great conversation piece when displayed in your house. And if all that gold is burning a hole in your pocket, seek out Ralis Sedarys (in Solstheim Side Quest: Unearthed), who needs an investor with deep pockets in order to complete his work.

EXPERIMENTAL SUBJECT

PREREQUISITES: None

RELATED QUESTS: Solstheim Side Quests: Neloth's Quests (page 606).

LOCATIONS: Tel Mithryn

CHARACTERS: Neloth

◊ **OBJECTIVES:** Watch for side effects, Talk to Neloth

◉ MINOR SPOILERS

Water on the Brain

NOTE This is one of many quests you complete by visiting and speaking to Neloth in his Tel Mithryn tower. For a complete list, consult page 606.

The opinionated Dark Elf conjurer you took with you during Dragonborn Main Quest: The Path of Knowledge has a new task for you, one that is randomly assigned. Float up to his Tel Mithryn tower and ask, "Do you need help with your research?" Neloth asks if you're willing to be an experimental subject for him. Of course you are! Answer positively after requesting more information, and Neloth casts the spell on you. That's strange; you don't *feel* any stronger or more vigorous.

◊ **OBJECTIVE:** Watch for side effects
♦ **TARGET:** A rain or snowstorm or a body of water

Leave Tel Mithryn and go about your business. To prevent the side effects from this spell temporarily harming you when you're engaged in difficult combat, it's usually worth finding out what the problem is as soon as possible. It seems the spell weakens you when you're exposed to water. You can:

Go swimming in any body of water.

Or wait for it to rain.

At this point you should immediately notice the failings of this particular spell, as your health falls by around 25 points. You can continue your adventuring with this malaise affecting your water-based maneuvering, or seek out Neloth and allow him to remove this underdeveloped magical "gift."

◊ **OBJECTIVE:** Talk to Neloth
♦ **TARGET:** Neloth, Tel Mithryn

Quest Conclusion

Return to Neloth's quarters atop the floating lift inside the great trunk tower, and inform the spellcaster that his spell made you weaker once you got wet. Although Neloth mentions you could simply avoid water, that would lead to a lack of bathing. So he removes his spell and grants you a bit of coin to help mitigate your inconvenience.

➤ **Gold (250)**

Postquest Activities

Neloth has a second spell that he requires a willing target for. This is listed in the Solstheim Regional Activity: Tel Mithryn, on page 672.

PREREQUISITES: Complete Dragonborn Main Quest: The Fate of the Skaal

MINOR SPOILERS

LOCATIONS: Skaal Village

CHARACTERS: Torkild Wild-Blood, Wulf Wild-Blood

◊ **OBJECTIVES:** Look for Wulf's brother Torkild, Examine Torkild, Return to Wulf

Blood Brother

After cleansing the Wind Stone during Dragonborn Main Quest: The Fate of the Skaal, return to the Skaal Village and locate Wulf Wild-Blood. He's usually stirring a cooking pot as the Horker meat dries on hooks around his stall, near the central well in the settlement. Oh, and he has only one eye. Wulf is First Hunter of the Skaal. You can:

Ask if he's able to train you to better use two-handed weapons, as he's an impressive Trainer.

Ask what else a First Hunter does or how long he's been First Hunter.

Inquire about any wisdom he can share about hunting or the type of game he hunts.

The conversation meanders to the topic of his brother Torkild, with whom Wulf used to share the hunt. But long ago, Torkild was lost, and Wulf fears he fell in among the werebears. But he doesn't know where his brother is. If you happen to cross his path, you must be wary: He was a fierce warrior as a man; as a beast, he could be deadly! Your quest begins now.

◊ **OBJECTIVE:** Look for Wulf's brother Torkild

♦ **TARGET:** Torkild Wild-Blood, somewhere in Solstheim

Bear Brother

There are no compass directions to hint of Torkild's location. The werewolves of Frostmoon Crag do not know who this fellow is. So it falls to you to scour Solstheim and seek him out. Begin by trekking down to the coast, stopping at the eastern shores and turning north. Work your way along the shoreline, facing down possible Raider and Horker threats as you go. Torkild is often found somewhere along this stretch of rugged shore. However, he could be along the north or western shores and is occasionally found dead!

TIP To find Torkild, you must inspect the Solstheim World Map (pages 1008 and 1036) and find the markers that look like this: ●. These are Random Encounter locations, and Torkild can appear in any of them, except for the four most southerly markers. Essentially, make a counterclockwise tour of the coast until you find him.

When you eventually find Torkild, he's usually shirtless and ranting something about the All-Maker craving the night of the sun. You can:

Attempt to start a conversation. You don't get far, as Torkild turns large and hairy.

Or simply start to attack Torkild the moment you spot him. It allows you to land some strikes before he can retaliate.

Either way, you're in for a fight with a werebear. Batter the beast until it lies sprawling at your feet.

➤ **Letter to Wulf**

◊ **OBJECTIVE:** Examine Torkild

◊ **OBJECTIVE:** Return to Wulf

Quest Conclusion

On the corpse, you'll find a folded letter. Take it, and then examine it in the Item > Books menu. It is a sorrowful farewell to his brother, while Torkild was still mentally competent enough to write. Your objective updates, and you should return to Skaal Village and speak with Wulf again. Give him the letter from his brother, and Wulf recognizes the handwriting. He asks how Torkild died. Answer how you wish. Finally, Wulf imparts some of the wisdom of the Skaal (some skill increases), as you've done him a service, and the quest concludes.

➤ **Skill:** Archery +1

➤ **Skill:** Block +1

➤ **Skill:** One-Handed +1

➤ **Skill:** Heavy Armor +1

Postquest Activities

After this, providing your standing with the Skaal is favorable (it changes as you progress through the Dragonborn Main Quest), there are more Regional Activities (page 671) to complete here.

PREREQUISITES: None

RELATED QUESTS: Solstheim Side Quest: Masks of the Acolyte Priests*, Solstheim Side Quest: The Great Solstheim Strongbox Hunt*

LOCATIONS: Raven Rock, Bloodskal Barrow, Caerellius House, Raven Rock Mine

CHARACTERS: Aphia Velothi, Crescius Caerellius

ENEMIES: Draugr, Frostbite Spider, Skeever, Zahkriisos

◊ **OBJECTIVES:** Speak to Crescius Caerellius, Retrieve Gratian Caerellius's Journal, Escape Bloodskal Barrow, (Optional) Read Gratian Caerellius's Journal, Return to Crescius Caerellius

MINOR SPOILERS

The Caerellius Conspiracy

NOTE This is one of a few quests you can complete in Raven Rock. For a complete list, consult pages 606 and 668.

To the northwest of town, at the foot of the giant rock column formations, is the old Raven Rock Mine. Visit at any time, and once you pass the East Empire crates and boxes, there's a makeshift balcony under which Crescius Caerellius, an elderly Imperial, is arguing with his seemingly younger wife, Aphia Velothi. After their outbursts, you can speak to Crescius and he tells you he's busy. Inquire why, and after some suspicious verbal sparring, he tells you the mines below hold a secret that could put Raven Rock back on the map. The quest begins!

◊ **OBJECTIVE:** Speak to Crescius Caerellius
♦ **TARGET:** Crescius Caerellius, Raven Rock Mine

Continue your questioning: It seems that his great-grandfather, Gratian Caerellius, spent his entire life exploring ruins across Tamriel and met his end here almost 200 years ago. The East Empire Company explained it away as a rockfall, but Crescius reckons there was more to it. After a tidying up in their home, an unsent letter of Gratian's was discovered, as well as a key. Apparently, there was a great discovery—great enough for the East Empire to seal up the entrance. Unfortunately, Crescius hasn't been able to find it.

Answer how you wish; the old coot continues, adamant that there's something big down there that the East Empire Company doesn't want anyone to know about. He's telling you this because Aphia thinks him too old for such a dangerous exploration. He wants someone to find out what happened to Gratian and learn the East Empire Company's big secret. He hands over everything he has and asks you to emerge triumphantly so he can regain the respect he's lost.

➤ **Gratian's Letter** ➤ **Raven Rock Mine Key**

◊ **OBJECTIVE:** Retrieve Gratian Caerellius's Journal
♦ **TARGET:** Bloodskal chasm chamber, Raven Rock Mine

NOTE This is about the point you can request Glover's Ancient Nordic Pickaxe back, if the smith has sent you to reclaim it. Find out more about this task in the Solstheim Regional Activities, on page 669.

You can further delve into Crescius's world of conspiracy by asking about Gratian's death. You can also hear Aphia's side of the argument, how she met Crescius, and her opinion of her husband's story. Then, when you're ready for a (possibly terrifying) descent, step onto the wooden floor and peer down the steps. They are hooked by chains to a gigantic mine shaft with an almost bottomless drop. Nimbly descend onto the wooden platform to the west.

The Search for Gratian Caerellius

Follow the precarious floating balconies down to the opening in the south wall of this epic hole, watching for Skeever here. Continue past a Frostbite Spider and another alcove to the east, with a spider and some rickety platforms. Back in the central pit, continue north to a third alcove leading down a stepped tunnel to the west, then the south and east, with more spiders and planks and a web to cut through as you burst into a locked gate next to an East Empire strongbox. Open the gate using the key you received from Crescius.

Cross into a roughly mined area, which breaks through into a Draugr tomb that is ankle-deep in water. There's movement here. Draugr rise from their walled resting places to delay you. Fight four or five as you head through the crypt. Check the left area for a chest, then go east; avoid the floor plate and swinging gate trap. Head up the steps and around to the west.

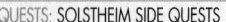

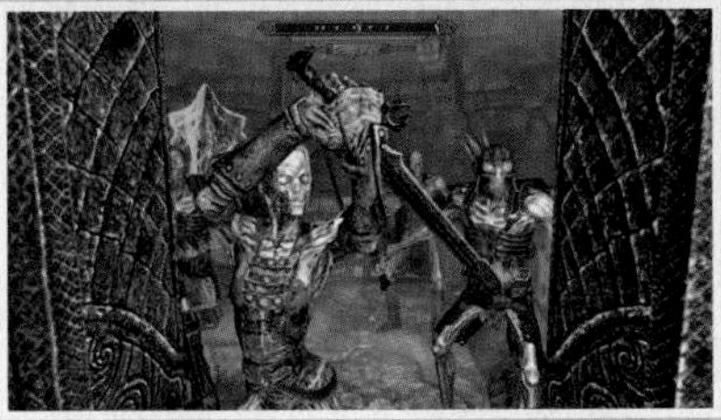

Here, four thrones are occupied by two slumbering dead (one on each side), who awaken to attack, along with a third foe farther along the hall and a locked chest [Master]. Defeat these enemies, as the circular chamber ahead features at least six Draugr of varying degrees of toughness. When the brutality is over, open the door to the west, wind your way through a narrow crypt corridor, and pass a tomb with a Stalhrim deposit embedded into it (which can only be mined if you have the Ancient Nordic Pickaxe).

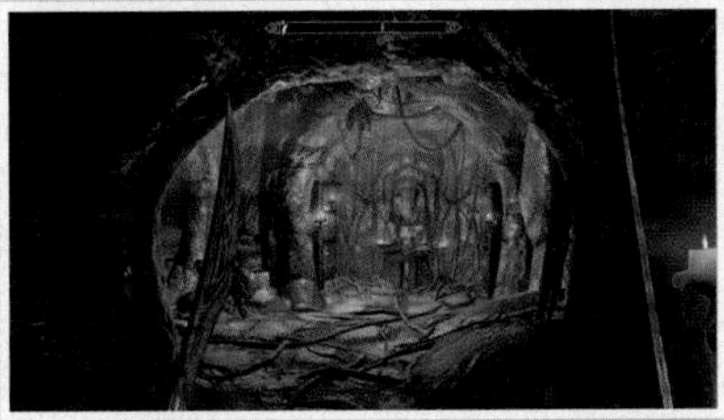

Pass the Alchemy Lab and shelves of ingredients (snag the Netch Jelly here if you're completing the Solstheim Regional Activity for Milore Ienth; see page 668), then move north along a stepped passage, watching for lightning traps in the shallow alcoves (race through or pry the Soul Gems off their pedestals). Back in the water, open the iron doors and ready yourself for combat with some particularly hardy Draugr.

➤ **Netch Jelly (2)**

Battle the Draugr around this interior canal and on the precarious wooden bridge. Behind the waterfall is a door that leads to a small alcove with a few scattered items and another Stalhrim deposit. Return and climb up to the alcoves and cross the wooden bridge to a high alcove with a chest [Expert] and an Arcane Enchanter. Yank the handle on the nearby pedestal, which opens a door on the chamber's eastern upper side. Move back across the bridge to reach it. Head south to a corridor junction. Left (east) is a pedestal surrounded by candles, where you find a Spell Tome for Ice Spike.

➤ **Spell Tome:** Ice Spike

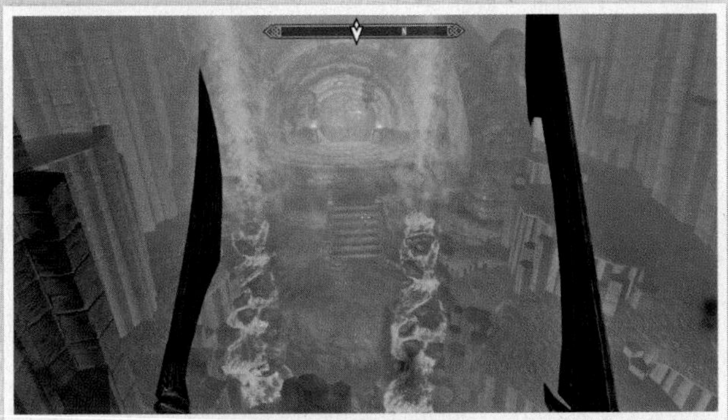

Head right (west), up the spiral steps to the balconies overlooking the Spell Tome pedestal. Dodge or remove the Soul Gem from the lightning trap, and work your way around to an open wooden door and a narrow cage bridge to the north. Carefully tread on the ground near the torch and steps, as a dart trap is easily activated. Rush through or avoid it before opening the wooden door, securing goods from a locked chest [Adept], heading back down the steps, and checking the low tunnel to the west. This brings you out onto a high chasm.

Breaking the Seal of the Bloodskal Clan

Two cave streams and numerous interlocking basalt columns offer a tremendous view of a strange and dimly lit wall of odd carvings. Could these be what Crescius was warbling about? Carefully descend to the ground and inspect the old bones of Gratian Caerellius, near the runic door. Aha! Gratian's Journal is on the corpse, along with a strange and wondrous blade. Grab both!

➤ **Gratian's Journal**

➤ **Bloodskal Blade**

◊ **OBJECTIVE:** Escape Bloodskal Barrow
◊ **OBJECTIVE:** (Optional) Read Gratian Caerellius's Journal
♦ **TARGET:** Bloodskal Barrow (exterior)

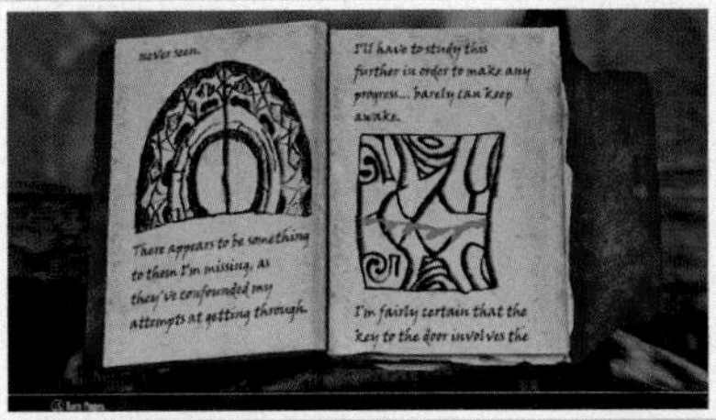

It is well worth your time to read Gratian's Journal. It mentions that miners broke through into a barrow belonging to the "Bloodskal Clan," the discovery of the sword, and their battles against Draugr where Gratian and his friend Millius were wounded terribly. The only survivor, Gratian became trapped and reached a strange door. In his malaise, he sketched the door and postulated that the use of the Bloodskal Blade (which emits a ribbon of mystical energy) may solve the puzzle.

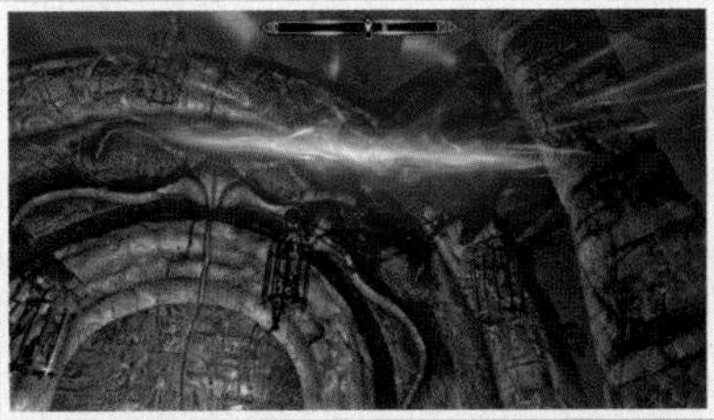

Puzzle Solution: Gratian was correct that the Bloodskal Blade is the key. Equip this two-handed weapon, stand so you're targeting the red slit in the outer arch, and make either a horizontal power attack with the blade (sidestep, hold down your Attack button, release), or a power attack while moving backward (which makes it easier to aim, as you aren't strafing). If you're successful, part of the arch will move up to connect with other moving sections, and a vertical glow appears.

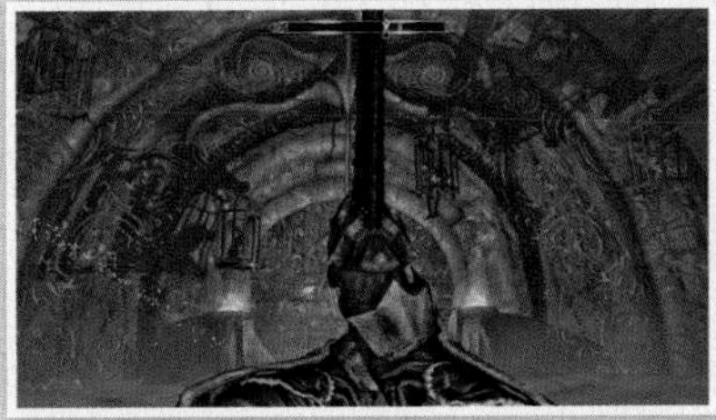

Puzzle Solution (continued): Make a vertical power attack (while holding still, hold down your Attack button, release), and be sure the ribbon of red hits close to the glow in the arch. A section indents, clicks, and the outer piece slides farther toward the apex of the arch. This time a horizontal glowing slit forms. Execute a horizontal power attack, and the entire left side of the outer arch slots into place!

Now move to view the right side of the outer arch. Perform exactly the same power attacks, and watch the sections of archway maneuver into new and unlocked positions. If you've correctly slashed, the entire arch glows red, and a massive vertical slit appears through the circular door. Launch a final, vertical power attack from your Bloodskal Blade, and the door opens!

Zahkriisos Rising

Head through the long Nord hall with the swinging blade traps and activate the lever at the far end to open the heavy gate. This grants you access into the lair of Zahkriisos, one of Miraak's Acolyte Priests. Check the large chest for him to appear. This fiend is able to summon Seekers and damage you with a powerful blast of lightning. Swap to your preferred weapons and engage this troublesome foe. If you're currently completing Solstheim Side Quest: Masks of the Acolyte Priests* (see page 662), he holds one of the masks you're looking for. Grab it from the ash pile you've reduced Zahkriisos to, and learn a Word of the powerful Dragon Aspect Shout.

TIP Is this battle becoming too difficult? Then feel free to pull the lever next to the portcullis on the way to the chamber's exit, allowing you to leave early and return to fight this foe at your convenience.

➤ **Zahkriisos**

➤ **Word of Power:** Dragon Aspect

Move west, through the arch you didn't come in from, and you'll notice a pedestal at the bottom of some spiral steps and small waterfall. Check the alcoves for a chest and Arcane Enchanter. On this plinth is a legendary Black Book! Pick this up, and you're transported into Apocrypha. You can:

Reread the book in your inventory to return to Tamriel.

Or complete your trek into this part of Apocrypha. This means finishing Solstheim Side Quest: Black Book: The Winds of Change (page 612). Consult that quest for the walkthrough of this realm.

➤ **Black Book:** The Winds of Change

Vindication and Celebration

Back in Raven Rock Mine, ascend the spiral steps to the door and enter Bloodskal Barrow. Move along the rough tunnel to the handle that reveals a secret rock door. Enter the subsequent Draugr tomb and engage a motley collection of Reavers. Slay them and pass an Alchemy Lab as you ascend past more plunderers and a couple of Altmer corpses. Exit through the door back into Solstheim, and the Bloodskal Barrow exterior.

◊ **OBJECTIVE:** Return to Crescius Caerellius

♦ **TARGET:** Caerellius House, Raven Rock

Quest Conclusion

Descend the two towers of Bloodskal, facing off against Reaver foes as you go and rummaging around for a chest [Adept] atop the second tower you reach. Once at the base of the towers, make a quick trip back to Raven Rock and search for the Caerellius House, close to the docks. Find Crescius and hand over the journal, vindicating his stories. He offers you a small gold reward for your troubles and can speak about the few Imperials in this town and his family.

➤ **[Leveled] Gold**

Postquest Activities

If you leave Raven Rock for a few days and then return to Crescius and Raven Rock Mine, the old man has convinced other miners that the area is safe to return, and the mine reopens. You can gather ebony ore from up to nine veins that are newly excavated.

➤ **Ebony Ore Vein (9)**

FROM THE ASHES

PREREQUISITES: None
LOCATIONS: Tel Mithryn
CHARACTERS: Neloth, Talvas Fathryon
ENEMIES: Ash Guardian
◊ **OBJECTIVES:** Destroy the Ash Guardian, Talk to Talvas

MINOR SPOILERS

A Pain in the Ash

NOTE This is one of many quests you can complete by visiting Tel Mithryn. For a complete list, consult pages 606 and 672.

Usually on your third or fourth trip into Tel Mithryn, you may see Neloth's apprentice, Talvas Fathryon, approach you. He's more than a little flustered, telling you that he conjured an Ash Guardian, and now it's running amok. You can:

Ignore him, which doesn't go down well.

Offer to destroy it for him.

Ask how this occurred.

Or tell him this is his mess to clean up.

Any of those responses is fine, as you're able to complete this quest with or without Talvas's approval. You can also report the matter to Neloth. He isn't happy about his foolish pupil's lack of conjuring skill but leaves the combat options up to you.

◊ **OBJECTIVE:** Destroy the Ash Guardian
♦ **TARGET:** Ash Guardian, Tel Mithryn

Search the settlement outside for signs of a ruckus, and then approach and defeat the whirling dust storm of rock and magic. The Ash Guardian fights with melee strikes, blasts of choking dust, and (more rarely) a powerful but short-range Fire Storm. Slay the boulder-beast while avoiding its more potent strikes.

◊ **OBJECTIVE:** Talk to Talvas

Quest Conclusion

Return to Talvas, who is usually in Neloth's tower, worrying about his master's wrath. Tell him of your success, and he rewards you with the Ash Guardian spell, if you have the skill to cast it, or a staff if you don't. He also realizes his summoning spell went awry because he cast it without a heart stone; to conjure an Ash Guardian and bind it to fight for you, a heart stone must be present or the creature runs amok.

➤ **Staff of Conjure Ash Guardian**

OR

➤ **Tome of Conjure Ash Guardian**

Postquest Activities

Talvas Fathryon will now join you as a Follower. His strengths are outlined on page 104. Talvas will also sell you a Tome of Conjure Ash Guardian, if he has one in stock.

➤ **Follower:** Talvas Fathryon

HEALING A HOUSE

PREREQUISITES: None
LOCATIONS: Headwaters of Harstrad, Tel Mithryn, Tel Mithryn Apothecary
CHARACTERS: Elynea Mothren, Neloth
ENEMIES: Spriggan
◊ **OBJECTIVES:** Get three taproots (3), Soak the taproots, Talk to Elynea, Plant the taproot, Talk to Elynea

MINOR SPOILERS

Getting to the Root of the Trouble

NOTE This is one of many quests you complete by visiting Tel Mithryn. For a complete list, consult pages 606 and 672

While you're visiting the Telvanni settlement of Tel Mithryn, you might wish to investigate the outbuildings in addition to Neloth's tower. Head up to the Tel Mithryn Apothecary, and you'll meet Elynea Mothren, the caretaker of the tower; she is also an apothecary and a mycologist. She isn't happy with her master Neloth. Inquire as to her perturbed nature. Neloth's tower is in need of repair, and Elynea needs three taproots soaked in the Headwaters of the Harstrad River to fix it. Perhaps you might be of service?

◊ **OBJECTIVE:** Get three taproots (3)
♦ **TARGET:** Taproots, from fallen Spriggan

You can complete this objective in several ways:

Locate any apothecary merchant and hope they have taproot to sell.

Scavenge in town or in a dungeon on the off-chance you find some. For example, your home in Riften, Honeyside, contains two specimens.

But by far the best plan is to hunt down Spriggan, slay them, and then search them for taproot. You'll usually find one on each corpse. That means facing three of them. In this example, we journeyed back to Skyrim, trekked to Haafingar Hold, and entered Shadowgreen Cavern, where a trio of Spriggan are known to reside. After slaying them, we Fast-Traveled back to Solstheim.

Or, if you wish to stay in Solstheim, you can wander the northern parts of the area, searching for Spriggan on a small island (Secondary Location: [S.NO] Giant Nirnroot Island) to the north and slightly northwest of Frossel. There are Spriggans there as well.

CAUTION Burnt Spriggans only offer Burnt Spriggan Wood on their charred corpses, so battling them isn't productive.

➤ **Taproot (3)**

Once you've secured three taproot, your objective updates:

◊ **OBJECTIVE:** Soak the taproots
♦ **TARGET:** Harstrad Cave, at the Headwaters of Harstrad

> **TIP** You need only two taproot before heading to the Headwaters of Harstrad, as there's a third Spriggan at the source where you soak your taproots.

The Headwaters of Harstrad is in the northern climbs of Solstheim, north of the Temple of Miraak and west of the Wind Stone. Locate this body of water and head west toward the waterfall and into Harstrad Cave through the cascading ice water. Once inside this grotto, prepare for another Spriggan attack. Slay it, optionally checking the crumpled skeleton and large chest it was guarding; then stand in the middle of the water and activate the headwaters. The taproots should now be soaked to Elynea's satisfaction.

◊ **OBJECTIVE:** Talk to Elynea
♦ **TARGET:** Elynea, Tel Mithryn Apothecary

Quest Conclusion

Back in Tel Mithryn, visit Elynea's Apothecary once more, and inform her of your soggy taproot status. She'll take two, but you must take the third taproot and plant it into the wall of the withered house.

◊ **OBJECTIVE:** Plant the taproot
♦ **TARGET:** Withered wall, Tel Mithryn tower

Traipse over to the Tel Mithryn tower, float up to Neloth's quarters, and survey the chamber. A bulbous and shiny protuberance on a wall to the northwest requires your taproot-planting skills. Once the taproot is inserted, your objective updates.

◊ **OBJECTIVE:** Talk to Elynea
♦ **TARGET:** Elynea, Tel Mithryn Apothecary

Back at the apothecary, tell Elynea her soaked taproot is planted, and you receive a curt thanks and a couple of potions for your troubles. The quest concludes.

➤ **[Leveled] Potion of Well-Being (2)**

Postquest Activities

If you return after a few days, Elynea is happy to sell you more potions of Well-Being, in addition to the usual alchemy supplies. If you look closely, you will see that the exterior of Neloth's home is looking better. Inside, Neloth has a new chamber and a few new test subjects.

HEART STONES

PREREQUISITES: This quest is repeatable.

MINOR SPOILERS

RELATED QUESTS: Solstheim Side Quests: Neloth's Quests (page 606).
LOCATIONS: Tel Mithryn
CHARACTERS: Neloth
◊ **OBJECTIVES:** Get a Heart Stone, Talk to Neloth

Rocks from Red Mountain

> **NOTE** This is one of many quests you complete by visiting and speaking to Neloth in his Tel Mithryn tower. For a complete list, consult page 606.

The aloof Dunmeri mage has another task for you to complete. Float up to his tower lair in Tel Mithryn and ask him, "Can I help with your research?" One (random) request Neloth has for you involves heart stones. He is running low on this precious resource and tells you:

If you have one on your person, he'll purchase it from you.

Otherwise, he can tell you where you might find one. Ask where, and he explains that every time Red Mountain belches, more land in the vicinity of Tel Mithryn. You should look for impact craters or exposed rock.

◊ **OBJECTIVE:** Get a Heart Stone
♦ **TARGET:** Heart Stone [a random location]

To the Heart of the Matter

Leave Neloth's tower and trudge through the silt and blowing ash heading left (south and west) out of town. Among the blasted tree stumps close to the beach are a few craters, as Neloth predicted. Or you can search for deposits around the upper edge of the town's exterior.

There are a few other places on the surface of Solstheim to find these deposits, but mainly look within the fallen ash of Red Mountain, in the southeastern part of the island. When you find a deposit, use a pickaxe to mine it until the vein is depleted.

➤ **Heart Stone**

◊ **OBJECTIVE:** Talk to Neloth
♦ **TARGET:** Neloth, Tel Mithryn

CAUTION Expect Burnt Spriggans, Flame Cloaked Spiders, and Ash Hoppers to temporarily prevent your mining activities during your search in these parts.

Quest Conclusion

Head back to Neloth, and the mage is relatively impressed by your locating and chipping skills, rewarding you with some septims for your troubles.

➤ **Gold (250)**

Postquest Activities

This quest is repeatable, although it occurs randomly. The Heart Stone is an expensive gemlike substance. It is useful to mine and is used when conjuring Ash Guardians (see page 172) or enchanting a staff (page 75)

LOST KNOWLEDGE

MINOR SPOILERS

PREREQUISITES: Complete Dragonborn Main Quest: The Gardener of Men, This quest is repeatable.

RELATED QUESTS: Solstheim Side Quest: Black Book: The Sallow Regent, Solstheim Side Quest: Black Book: The Winds of Change, Solstheim Side Quest: Black Book: Untold Legends, Solstheim Side Quest: The Great Solstheim Strongbox Hunt*, Solstheim Side Quest: Lost Legacy, Solstheim Side Quest: masks of the Acolyte Priests*, Solstheim Side Quest: Spider Crafting*, Solstheim Side Quest: The Final Descent, Solstheim Side Quests: Neloth's Quests (page 606)

LOCATIONS: Benkongerike, Bloodskal Barrow, Tel Mithryn, White Ridge Barrow

CHARACTERS: Neloth

◊ **OBJECTIVES:** Retrieve the Black Book, Talk to Neloth

Unspeakable Tomes

NOTE This is one of many quests you complete by visiting and speaking to Neloth in his Tel Mithryn tower. For a complete list, consult page 606.

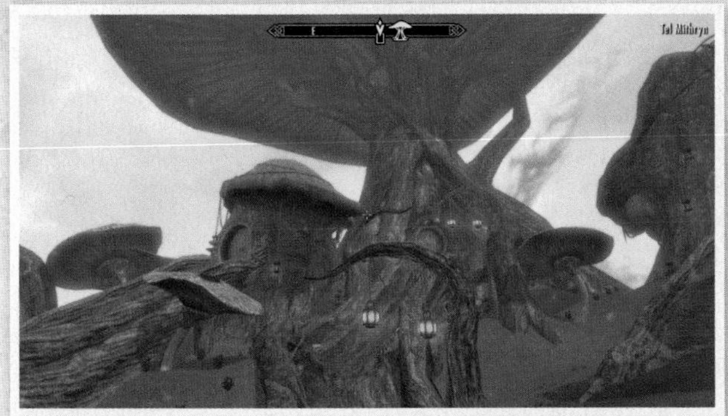

The haughty Dark Elf wizard you befriended during Dragonborn Main Quest: The Path of Knowledge is waiting to use you in his fungal tower—the largest structure in Tel Mithryn.

Float up to his quarters, and after some chatting about your heroics, Neloth brings up the Black Books. It seems Neloth has located another of them. He points out the location on your map and requests you obtain it for further study.

◊ **OBJECTIVE:** Retrieve the Black Book
♦ **TARGET:** [Random] Black Book, in [a random dungeon]

Forbidden Knowledge

The plan now is to head to the dungeon Neloth has indicated, battle your way through the many denizens in there, snag the tome, and then locate the dungeon's exit. However, there's just one issue, aside from the dangerous guardian each Black Book usually has protecting it: When you take the book, you automatically read it and you're transported to Apocrypha to begin one of the Black Book Side Quests. So prepare yourself for the journey (or open the book in your inventory and reread it to return to Tamriel). When you take the Black Book, this Side Quest objective updates too.

◊ **OBJECTIVE:** Talk to Neloth
♦ **TARGET:** Neloth, Tel Mithryn

There are seven Black Books. Four of these are not related to this quest:

- Two you retrieve during the Dragonborn Main Quest.
- One is already in Neloth's possession—it's in Tel Mithryn's Staff Enchanter room, which is locked until you complete Solstheim Side Quest: The Reluctant Steward.
- One is buried in the depths of Kolbjorn Barrow, so deep that even Neloth cannot locate it. To retrieve it, you must complete Solstheim Side Quest: Unearthed.

Neloth will send you to find the other three Black Books if you have not already found them.

➤ **Black Book:** The Hidden Twilight

Location: [S.N16] White Ridge Barrow

Black Book: The Sallow Regent

Solstheim Side Quest: Page 611

Related Solstheim Side Quest: Spider Crafting, page 665

Winding Draugr catacombs, with dangerous (and sometimes explosive and poisonous) Albino and Flame Cloaked Spiders await you. The bandits here have succumbed to the spiders' bites and are little more than puppets. The mage Merilar Rendas has been conducting experiments in White Ridge Sanctum. In its innermost chamber, you can also find the legendary Acolyte Priest Dukaan, who guards a Word Wall and the pedestal the Black Book rests on.

➤ **Black Book:** The Sallow Regent

Location: Raven Rock Mine (exit out to [S.S02] Bloodskal Barrow)

Black Book: The Winds of Change

Solstheim Side Quest: Page 612

Related Solstheim Side Quest: The Final Descent, page 622

You must be on Solstheim Side Quest: The Final Descent to explore most of this area. A long descent down a treacherous mine shaft leads to spiders, Draugr, and a conspiracy to solve. You must then wade through a waterlogged crypt, enter a grand basalt chasm, use the Bloodskal Blade to open a sealed door, slay the terrifying Acolyte Priest Zahkriisos, and finally enter a small chamber with a tumbling waterfall and spiral staircase, where the book is located.

➤ **Black Book:** The Winds of Change

Location: [S.N15] Benkongerike

Black Book: Untold Legends

Solstheim Side Quest: Page 613

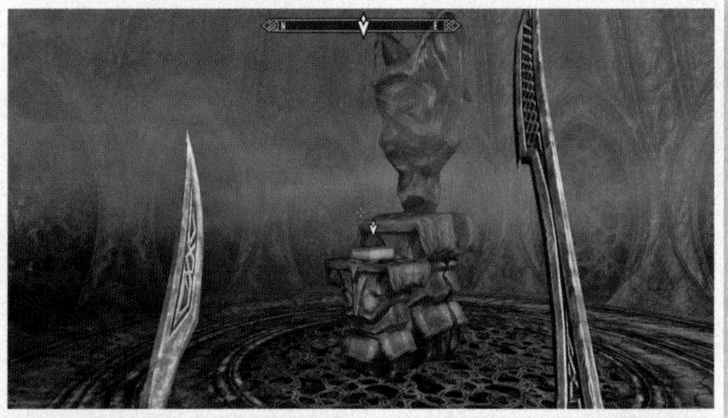

Benkongerike begins as a glacial cave system filled with multiple Riekling camps and traps and intermittent Riekling ambushes from their clusters of collected detritus. This changes to a Draugr dungeon as you reach the Great Hall. The place is teeming with Rieklings. Solve the Nordic puzzle, claim a Word of Power, and then read the Black Book in an adjacent chamber.

➤ **Black Book:** Untold Legends

Quest Conclusion

Trek back to Neloth, who is usually shouting at his apprentice Talvas or tinkering with his latest spells and other conjurings. Float up and mention that you have a Black Book in your possession. He eagerly takes it to make a copy before returning it. He also has a sizable gift for your efforts.

➤ **Gold (1,000)**

Postquest Activities

You can repeat this quest until you've found and showed Neloth all three Black Books. Simply look for "Can I help with your research?" in the conversation choices and this Side Quest may occur again.

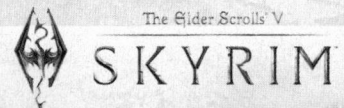

PREREQUISITES: Complete Solstheim Side Quest: A New Source of Stalhrim

MINOR SPOILERS

LOCATIONS: Skaal Village, Vahlok's Tomb

CHARACTERS: Tharstan

ENEMIES: Corrupted Shade, Draugr, Vahlok

◊ **OBJECTIVES:** Travel to Vahlok's Tomb, Talk to Tharstan, Explore Vahlok's Tomb, Find the main burial chamber, Talk to Tharstan

A Sacrifice Will Bring You Closer to That Which You Seek

> **NOTE** This is one of a few quests that begin when you discover and befriend the Skaal people of northeast Solstheim. This particular quest can start only after Solstheim Side Quest: A New Source of Stalhrim is over and Baldor is back at his anvil and forge.

A historian named Tharstan stops to speak with you, noting your bravery when you looked for Baldor. It is this very courage he seeks in a partner to aid his forays into the many ancient ruins that cover the island. Tharstan has recently discovered a new passage, opened by an earthquake after one of Red Mountain's eruptions. But the place may be dangerous, so he'll pay you to watch his back down there. The quest starts and continues when you decide to meet Tharstan at the ruins. Before then, you can question him about his background and his studies.

◊ **OBJECTIVE:** Travel to Vahlok's Tomb
♦ **TARGET:** Tharstan, Vahlok's Tomb (exterior)

> **NOTE** A wily adventurer such as yourself may recognize the name "Vahlok." Could this be one of Miraak's Acolytes, a Dragon Priest with a mask of power to pry from its ashes? No, Vahlok was vehemently opposed to Miraak and challenged him in ancient battle. But he's no friend of yours, either!

Vahlok's Tomb is southeast of Thirsk Mead Hall and is reasonably difficult to spot; it's a crack in the earth that's wide enough to slip into and reach a previously hidden door to Vahlok's Tomb. Open it, and head down the initial (south) tunnel to reach your new historian friend.

◊ **OBJECTIVE:** Talk to Tharstan
◊ **OBJECTIVE:** Explore Vahlok's Tomb
♦ **TARGET:** Amethyst Claw, Vahlok's Tomb

Tharstan is positively giddy about this newly uncovered crypt, and he's already had a look around. Up until your arrival, the only area of interest is an inscription and a switch in the grand main chamber. Move to the pedestal (pictured), where Tharstan reads off a cryptic riddle written in the dragon language. It translates as, "A sacrifice will bring you closer to that which you seek." Curious.

Tharstan descends to a glowing grate on the lower stone plateau, telling you to watch your step, as there are corpses strewn about the floor here. Tharstan wonders whether the fire beneath the grating has something to do with the inscription. Indeed it does:

Puzzle Solution: Locate one of the dead Draugr and pick it up (press and hold down the appropriate button or key), and drag it onto the glowing grating. Then move to the pedestal with the inscription and pull the switch. The grating opens, and the corpse tumbles into the fire below. Well done! Ceremonial torches flicker into life on either side of the stone plateau, and portcullises to the left (south) and right (north) open. You're able to head in either direction. Which way you go is up to you. Head left or right; you must solve puzzles on either side eventually.

All Men Must Die, Often by Their Own Means

Head up the steps, passing the torches and under the open portcullis into a tunnel heading south. Turn left (east), opening the iron door and moving down into a Draugr crypt. As expected, you have company. Tharstan is a historian, not a fighter, so tackle the four or five Draugr by yourself; then climb the steps to the east, encountering one or two more Draugr before reaching a pull chain and barred archway. Pull the chain and enter a rather puzzling chamber.

The exit arch opposite is currently sealed with a portcullis. Inside the chamber are three pillars around a central cylinder with odd, colored runes that glow with unnatural light. Tharstan inspects the pedestal plaque: "All men must die, often by their own means." Sounds rather grim to him.

Puzzle Solution: The central pillar has three sides, all differently colored and each with a different weapon resting on or nearby their own pedestal:

There is a green side with an Ancient Nord Bow.

There is a blue side with a Staff of Flames.

There is a red side with an Ancient Nord Sword.

The three smaller pillars have "impact stones" encased into them. These activate (glowing and changing color to match the part of the central pillar opposite) when a particular weapon is used to strike any part of the smaller pillar. However, the type of weapon is important:

Use the Ancient Nord Bow (or any other bow) and fire an arrow at the small pillar opposite the green side, so it lights up green.

Use the Staff of Flames (or any other staff) and unleash it at the small pillar opposite the blue side, so it lights up blue.

Use the Ancient Nord Sword (or any other blade) and slash at the small pillar opposite the red side, so it lights up red.

The portcullis rises, and Tharstan is ecstatic. What lies beyond in the next chamber?

A particularly nasty Draugr rises from his central coffin, flanked by two lesser Draugr who break free of their nearer tombs. After a protracted fight (on your own, as Tharstan isn't getting involved in this battle), inspect the Draugr corpses, the most troublesome of which is carrying the left half of an Amethyst Claw. Pry open two chests and gain a Word of Power. Meanwhile, Tharstan translates the runes on the wall, which describe a guardian who defeated someone named Miraak. Apparently this "Miraak" was a traitor. When you're ready to go, leave through the gap in one of the western sarcophagi. Pull the chain at the tunnel's end and step back into the initial grand chamber.

➤ **Amethyst Claw (left half)** ➤ **Word of Power:** Battle Fury

Continue Along the Path, Don't Tread Where You've Been

Head up the steps, passing the torches and through the open portcullis into a short tunnel heading north. Turn left (west) as the tunnel winds down, past a chest and into a rather puzzling chamber. Ahead are three archways, each with spears preventing your progress. Tharstan inspects the description on the raised pedestal near a group of nine pressure plates: "Continue along the path, don't tread where you've been." Interesting.

Puzzle Solution: Simply step onto the first plate in the near-right corner and sidestep left, zigzagging so you tread on each of the nine pressure plates only once. This is deceptively simple; as long as you don't step on any plate more than once, and you don't miss any plates, once you step on the ninth and last plate, the spears retract and progress is possible. Tharstan is excited. What lies beyond in the next chamber?

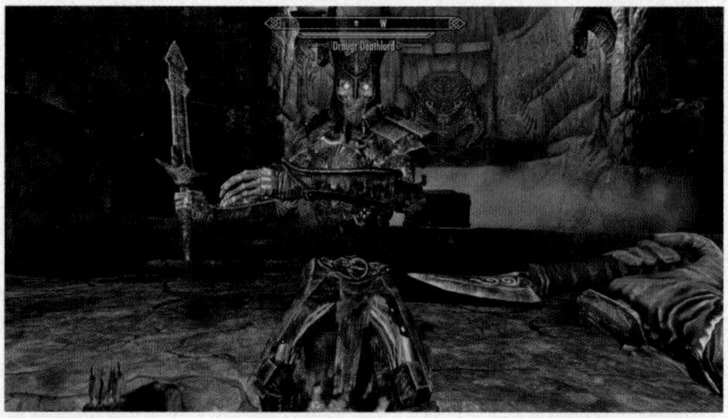

A powerful and troublesome Draugr clambers from his central coffin, and two lesser Draugr smash out of their nearer tombs. After a lengthy battle (by yourself, as Tharstan is paying you to remove all threats on his behalf), inspect the Draugr corpses, the most dangerous of which is holding the right half of an Amethyst Claw. Wrench open the chest and obtain a Word of Power. In the meantime, Tharstan ruminates on the wall runes, which refer to a guardian who inspired both men and dragons. He wonders if the guardian was himself a man or a dragon? When you're ready to proceed, leave through the gap in one of the southern sarcophagi. Pull the chain at the tunnel's end and step back into the initial grand chamber.

➤ **Amethyst Claw (right half)** ➤ **Word of Power:** Battle Fury

◊ **OBJECTIVE:** Find the main burial chamber
♦ **TARGET:** Vahlok's Tomb

Ethereal Above, Corruption Below

Move to the cage on the western side of the fiery stone plateau and inspect the indentations. These circular keyholes require you to place each of the Amethyst Claws into them, unlocking the cage in front of you. Pull the handle on the cage's pedestal, and a series of ethereal blue platforms appears, linking a path to the ledge and door on the opposite wall. Tharstan is suitably impressed.

> **TIP** These ethereal platforms of magic appear for a few seconds and then vanish, so you need to step on each of them quickly, moving to the next as it appears and stepping off before the platform disappears. If you fall, simply wade back and try again.

You may wish to trigger the platforms and watch how they appear (and disappear), and then activate the pedestal handle again. Follow the snaking path to the far ledge, drop down onto the dungeon passage heading west, and pass a barred door.

> **NOTE**
>
> 
>
> These barred doors are simply the exits from stairs you climb up if you fall during any of the subsequent platform-walking.
> If you fall into the water below, you face combat with Corrupted Shades; expect at least a dozen of these foes to cause you minimal threats. Then search any ground-level entrances for minor items, climb the steps and unlock the bar on the door, and return to the upper ledges to try again.

At the far end of the short tunnel is another pedestal and a handle. As expected, this releases another set of platforms, so quickly stand and follow each of them across the large waterlogged chamber to the upper tunnel across from you. This leads to another set of platforms, each time moving a little faster than before. Next comes a final set, moving so quickly you really need to run most of the time to reach the final ledge and double wooden doors.

> **TIP** Once you successfully navigate an ethereal bridge, it remains in place.

Through the doors is a Hall of Stories and a Nordic Puzzle Door at the far end.

Puzzle Solution: Those adventurers familiar with such a puzzle will know that the rings on this door correspond to a key on the palm of the claw the door opens. Not so this time! The palm of the Amethyst Claw is blank! While you're scratching your head, Tharstan arrives and studies the door, then heads to the wall carvings to ascertain a combination. Among the etchings are the following clues:

"A breeze, or maybe it's wind." This refers to the hawk, to be moved on the outer ring.

"The night sky, and the moon." This refers to the wolf, to be moved on the middle ring.

"Something to do with fire, and scales." This refers to the dragon, to be moved on the inner ring.

Vahlok Awakens

The door rumbles open. Pull the chain at the top of the steps to open a portcullis; this leads you out and into a high-status ceremonial tomb. As you edge forward, the stone sarcophagus ahead of you, near a large chest and Word Wall, cracks open as the Dragon Priest Vahlok the Jailer frees himself to face you!

The battle is frantic, and all the more tricky if you don't combat Vahlok's mainly fire-based attacks. Expect him to use Firebolt, Flame Cloak, Flames, and Incinerate, and he summons a Flame Atronach. Also watch for fire damage from the pressure plates dotted around the tomb; stay on the edges of the walkways or in the water, moving to the Word Wall to keep them from triggering.

> ◊ **OBJECTIVE:** Talk to Tharstan

Quest Conclusion

Tharstan is incredulous at seeing an actual Dragon Priest and believes there are numerous volumes to write based on this discovery alone! You're paid for your help and can additionally learn the final Word of the Battle Fury Shout before leaving the way you came.

➤ **Gold (1,000)** ➤ **Word of Power:** Battle Fury

Postquest Activities

Vahlok was a Dragon Priest but did not wear a mask. You can revisit Tharstan and ask him more about the details of Vahlok's life and his relationship with Miraak.

MARCH OF THE DEAD

PREREQUISITES: None

LOCATIONS: Fort Frostmoth, Old Attius Farm, Raven Rock

CHARACTERS: Captain Modyn Veleth

ENEMIES: Ash Spawn, General Falx Carius

◊ **OBJECTIVES:** Kill the ash spawn attacking Captain Veleth, Speak to Captain Veleth, Search the Attius Farm for clues, Kill General Falx Carius, Return to Captain Veleth

MINOR SPOILERS

Spawn on the Farm

The first time you leave Raven Rock through the southeastern gate under the Bulwark, be on the lookout for a group of lumpy, grotesque, human-sized monsters attacking a Dark Elf soldier outside of an abandoned farmhouse (Old Attius Farm). As you close, you'll discover Captain Veleth is valiantly defending himself against a trio of these misshapen Ash Spawn. The quest automatically starts now.

◊ **OBJECTIVE:** Kill the Ash Spawn attacking Captain Veleth

◊ **OBJECTIVE:** Speak to Captain Veleth

♦ **TARGET:** Ash Spawn outside Old Attius Farm

Charge in or attack from range, keep your strikes focused on the Ash Spawn, and try to avoid hitting Captain Veleth. Once all the foes lie in piles at your feet, head on over for a chat with the veteran guard. He laments his dead colleague and knows these Ash Spawn need to be stopped. You can:

Tell him you'd be glad to lend him a hand.

Tell him you'd be glad to accept payment for lending him a hand.

Or ignore him and the quest stalls. Either of the previous conversations allows you to progress.

Veleth tells you to look around and see if you can spot anything useful in the vicinity of the farm. The objective updates, and you can quiz Veleth further regarding these foul creatures.

◊ **OBJECTIVE:** Search the Attius Farm for clues

♦ **TARGET:** Old Attius Farm

One of the Ash Spawn that you or Veleth reduced to a pile of sand-colored ash is carrying something of interest: a Declaration of War! This couldn't have been written by these golems. Read the letter, which demands the unconditional surrender of Raven Rock! The writer is General Falx Carius, an Imperial who may have lost his mind. Veleth only confuses matters when you show him the letter; Carius was the garrison commander at Fort Frostmoth, but he died over 200 years ago during the eruption of Red Mountain.

➤ Declaration of War

Ask Veleth for further instructions, and he recommends you visit the fortress to see if Falx Carius is really dead, while Veleth returns to Raven Rock to prepare his men for more assaults.

◊ **OBJECTIVE:** Kill General Falx Carius

♦ **TARGET:** General Falx Carius, Fort Frostmoth interior

Fortress of the Mad General

Climb up the sandy promontory heading roughly east. You soon reach the perimeter of the fortress, now in a terrible state of disrepair. However, this hasn't fazed the current occupant, as you can hear General Falx Carius yell that an intruder has entered the fort, alerting the Ash Spawn guarding the battlements. Your fight into the fortress begins now!

Scrambling over the broken corner section in the fort's northwestern part is a good way to enter the area, as you have a height advantage and an easy way to escape. Use this route if you're focusing on long-range magic or arrow attacks.

Heading up the hill from the south isn't wise, as there are Ash Spawn with swords and ranged fireballs across the crenellations forcing you to hide or battle and shrug off numerous attacks.

Sneaking around to the lone southeast tower and slaying the Ash Spawn there is a possible plan. Then maneuver up onto the southern battlements or into the main ash-filled central area.

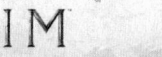

Deal with the Ash Spawn outside so they don't

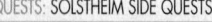

rush in behind you as you enter the fortress. There is a single access point—the door near the tattered banner along the western wall. Expect to fight around five or six Ash Spawn before you reach it.

The initial passageway heads north-south with three Ash Spawn to battle as you head east to join the passage. Remove all the threats, optionally checking the side chamber and ladder up to an exterior tower before turning and moving down the steps along the north tunnel.

Another two tough Ash Spawn appear in this lower training area. To the east is a sealed wooden door requiring a key, so locate the opening in the north wall and head down into the main crypt area. Expect another two Ash Spawn to waylay you before your exploration takes you west to a central tomb surrounded by coffin ledges. Atop and at the foot of the coffin are two items of great interest: Ildari's Journal (which details a sorcerer's ill-fated attempts to resurrect and control Falx) and a knapsack containing the Fort Frostmoth Key.

➤ **Ildari's Journal** ➤ **Fort Frostmoth Key**

> **TIP** Does that name sound familiar? You can learn more about Ildari in Solstheim Side Quest: Old Friends.
>
> While you're in Fort Frostmoth, it is worth exploring these catacombs a little more closely for some high-value items, especially in a spider-filled quarry area and the mead cellar (check page 1054 for the details).

Reduced to Ash

This key allows you to open the wooden door upstairs that you couldn't breach a moment ago. Ascend the steps heading east into an ash-filled hall where the resurrected but uncontrollable remains of General Falx Carius are waiting for you. Armed with a crushing Champion's Cudgel, Carius attacks immediately, prompting you into a fight with him and the four or five Ash Spawn that soon arrive to hamper your progress.

➤ **Fort Frostmoth Key**

➤ **Champion's Cudgel**

> ◊ **OBJECTIVE:** Return to Captain Veleth
> ♦ **TARGET:** Captain Veleth, Raven Rock

Quest Conclusion

With Carius dead (again), search his remains, loot the large treasure chest, and grab any other items you wish before leaving via the door in the south wall (unlocked using either of the Fort Frostmoth keys) and returning to Raven Rock. Captain Veleth is usually patrolling the battlements or central market area. Let him know you've dispatched General Carius, and he expresses regret, as the general helped found Raven Rock...before he was raised from the dead and went mad, obviously. Veleth mentions Councilor Morvayn has offered a gold reward for your help, and the quest concludes.

➤ **Gold [leveled]**

Postquest Activities

Captain Veleth has a Favor to offer now that you've finished this quest, as do many of Raven Rock's inhabitants. Find out about these tasks on page 668.

A NEW SOURCE OF STALHRIM

MINOR SPOILERS

PREREQUISITES: Complete Dragonborn Main Quest: The Fate of the Skaal

LOCATIONS: Abandoned Lodge, Northshore Landing, Skaal Village, Stalhrim Source

CHARACTERS: Ancarion, Baldor Iron-Shaper, Deor Woodcutter, Fanari Strong-Voice

ENEMIES: Mudcrab, Thalmor

◊ **OBJECTIVES:** Ask Deor about Baldor's disappearance, Search for Baldor Iron-Shaper, Retrieve the Stalhrim Source Map, Talk to Baldor Iron-Shaper

Hard as Iron and Cold as Death

This quest is accessible only after you complete Dragonborn Main Quest: The Fate of the Skaal and you've visited the Skaal Village. When you're there (or you leave and return one or two times), you'll overhear the village chief Fanari Strong-Voice discussing the disappearance of the village's blacksmith, Baldor Iron-Shaper. Deor is certain he saw two elves maneuvering something suspicious in the nearby woods. The following Miscellaneous Objective is now active:

> ◊ **OBJECTIVE:** Ask Deor about Baldor's disappearance
> ♦ **TARGET:** Deor Woodcutter, Skaal Village

You can now stop and speak with the gruff and curt Deor Woodcutter. He tells you Baldor forges Stalhrim, an art sacred to the Skaal. To make such weapons, others would need to learn that knowledge from Baldor. He reiterates the story of the two elves dragging something behind them in the forest. They were headed south and west. You're to search for any sign of Baldor; the Skaal would be grateful.

◊ **OBJECTIVE:** Search for Baldor Iron-Shaper
♦ **TARGET:** Baldor Iron-Shaper, Abandoned Lodge

Baldor's last known whereabouts were centered around an abandoned lodge to the southwest, close to Frostmoon Crag. When you finally reach this lodge, a group of four Thalmor impolitely dissuade you from any further progress. Engage them in combat, and loot each corpse after you defeat them. One of them is carrying the key to the lodge and a handwritten note. Curious...

➤ **Key to Abandoned Lodge** ➤ **Handwritten Note**

The note is a stern message from "A," regarding a severe displeasure at the lack of successful interrogation. The key opens up the lodge, which is otherwise sealed. Head inside, surveying an untidy huntsman's refuge, but don't forget to head down into the cellar; the missing smithy is trussed up in a corner yelling for help! Baldor remembers you and your help to the Skaal. Now these elves have taken him from his home and are interrogating him. Their leader Ancarion has a map, supposedly showing a hidden source of Stalhrim. The map belongs to the Skaal; Ancarion's fate is in your hands!

◊ **OBJECTIVE:** Retrieve the Stalhrim Source Map
♦ **TARGET:** Ancarion, Northshore Landing

Ancarion's Actions—Threatening the Thalmor

Along the rugged northwestern coast near the glacial caves and snowy mountains is a little-known windswept pier. Head to Northshore Landing, sheathing your weapons as you close in on an Altmer boat with three Thalmor soldiers guarding it. You're told to move along, as you're apparently trespassing. You can:

Tell the upstart that you have business to discuss with his leader. This affords you a conversation with Ancarion.

Tell the soon-dead High Elf to taste your blades and begin combat. End it after all three soldiers and Ancarion are bleeding into the water.

Assuming you didn't wade in thirsting for blood, board the vessel and speak with Ancarion. As expected, he is a haughty and objectionable High Elf. He doesn't seem interested in your request for the map and asks why he shouldn't kill you where you stand. You can:

Tell him the blacksmith won't talk. If successful, the Thalmor depart after handing you the map.

(Intimidate) Tell him his life is forfeit and to leave the island. If you're successful, the Thalmor give you the map and make preparations to flee.

(Persuade) Tell him that he wants Stalhrim weapons, and you can help him obtain some. You let him know Baldor told you he'd help teach you to make the weapons, which you can sell on to Ancarion. (Persuade) However, he'll need the map; otherwise Baldor won't divulge anything.

Or you can pickpocket the map if you're suitably and sneakily inclined.

Or you can stop this conversation and lay waste to these High Elves, positioning yourself a little better to land the first blow into Ancarion before combat becomes too messy.

There are three possible outcomes to this confrontation:

- ◊ Ancarion and his men give the map over to you and flee.
- ◊ Ancarion believes you'll sell him Stalhrim equipment, starting the Miscellaneous Objective: Sell Stalhrim Armor and Weapons to Ancarion. He buys only Stalhrim-based items, paying you for them (whether you've made them or not).
- ◊ You slay Ancarion and his men and take the map. He has it on his person.

◊ **OBJECTIVE:** Talk to Baldor Iron-Shaper
♦ **TARGET:** Baldor Iron-Shaper, Skaal Village

Quest Conclusion

Return to Skaal Village and locate the forge, which is working again now that Baldor is back in the village. Hand him the map (making sure you look at it first to see the location of the deposit). He's extremely grateful and tells you that if you bring Stalhrim to this forge (and only this forge), you can use his tools to craft any armor or weapons you wish—that is, providing you have the Ebony Smithing perk. For a list of items to craft, consult page 82.

Postquest Activities

➤ Stalhrim Source Map

As you can see from the map, the source isn't that far away from Northshore Landing, and once you read it, the marker for the Stalhrim Source appears on your world map. Visit this Draugr barrow entrance (before or after finishing the quest), which is filled with deposits to chip away at, provided you have the Ancient Nordic Pickaxe. There is a considerable haul here, as well as smaller deposits all over Solstheim (including Secondary Location: Horker Iceberg, northeast of Northshore Landing).

➤ Stalhrim Ore (30)

OLD FRIENDS

◉ MINOR SPOILERS

PREREQUISITES: Complete Solstheim Side Quest: Briarheart Necropsy, Complete Solstheim Side Quest: Healing a House

RELATED QUESTS: Solstheim Side Quests: Neloth's Quests (page 606).

LOCATIONS: Highpoint Tower, Tel Mithryn

CHARACTERS: Neloth

ENEMIES: Ash Guardian, Ash Spawn, Ildari Sarothril

◊ **OBJECTIVES:** Find the source of the attacks, Talk to Neloth, Kill Ildari, Talk to Neloth

Enemy Revealed

NOTE This is one of many quests you complete by visiting and speaking to Neloth in his Tel Mithryn tower. For a complete list, consult page 606. Although randomly occurring, this quest usually becomes available once you complete Solstheim Side Quests: Briarheart Necropsy and Healing a House.

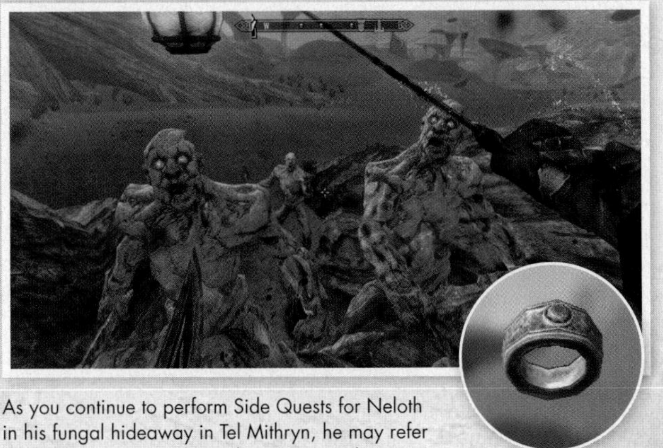

As you continue to perform Side Quests for Neloth in his fungal hideaway in Tel Mithryn, he may refer to attackers trying to thwart him. You may have disregarded this as paranoia, and he mentions it only infrequently as he orders you to finish different tasks. However, when you return to Tel Mithryn, you find a group of three or four Ash Spawn waiting to defeat you. Slay them and head in to speak with Neloth. Something more troubling is afoot!

Not surprisingly, Neloth says that he has legions of enemies back in Morrowind, but in this case, somebody in Solstheim is to blame. You can ask what needs doing (or if there's a bounty reward), and Neloth hands you a special ring. Wear it, walk around Tel Mithryn, and follow any strange clues it may impart. You may wish to ask Neloth about how the ring works (it follows a link back to the summoner of the Ash Spawn and provides a visual clue of their location). You can also ask about the threats he's received.

➤ Neloth's Ring of Tracking

◊ **OBJECTIVE:** Find the source of the attacks

♦ **TARGET:** Ildari's Sarcophagus, Tel Mithryn graveyard

Place Neloth's Ring of Tracking on your finger, step outside, head down to the ash grounds at the foot of the fungal root structures, and then look to your right (northeast). Head through the gaps in the rocky outcrops, and peer down toward the coast, with Nchardak in the distance. Something odd catches your eye in the small walled graveyard with the single pine tree. A strange purple glow emanates from one of the grave sites. Head closer and activate Ildari's Sarcophagus. After heaving back the lid, you'll find a staff and (more importantly) a Heart Stone inside. But no skeleton!

➤ Heart Stone

◊ **OBJECTIVE:** Talk to Neloth

♦ **TARGET:** Neloth, Tel Mithryn

Low-Life at Highpoint

Back at Neloth's tower, explain that the Heart Stone is the source of the attacks. You explain where you found it, and Neloth blames himself. The grave belongs to Ildari, his apprentice before Talvas. He found it annoying when she died. Reply regarding the lack of body in the grave. This continues the conversation.

Or ask more about the experiments he inflicted on her. He lets you know how he tried to emulate the Briarheart and implant a Heart Stone into Ildari's chest. It didn't take.

It seems Ildari may still live! He casts a divination, takes both the Heart Stone and his ring, and commands Ildari to reveal herself. A few moments later, he has her location. You'll find her in Highpoint Tower. The time for friendship seems to have passed; Neloth wants that thrice-cursed Heart Stone ripped from her chest.

◊ OBJECTIVE: Kill Ildari

♦ TARGET: Ildari Sarothril, Highpoint Tower

Head northwest from Tel Mithryn, until you find the cascading stream that used to be the Harstrad River before the choking ash falls from Red Mountain blocked much of the drainage. Move up the stream in the direction of Highpoint Tower, but don't continue to clamber up to the remains of the tower; the entrance is partially hidden. Instead, stay below the rocky area around the tower, and move clockwise around until you're slightly north of the location, facing south. A group of Ash Spawn are lurking near the dying pine trees and trama roots. Defeat the foes, locate the roughly hewn steps in the rocks that wind up to the southeast, and the stone tunnel entrance to the tower.

NOTE Highpoint Tower is half buried in ash and inaccessible until this quest is activated, so you can't explore it before this point.

Head down three levels of spiral steps (pausing at the table two floors down to secure the first of Ildari's Journals) to a curved stone tunnel that leads into a rocky cave attached to the base of the tower structure with numerous revolting egg sacs to your left (southwest). These burst as you head toward them, so slay any Flame Cloaked or Albino Spiders you find here or in the small cavern with the ruby geode deposits and the low caverns with sapphire and amethyst geodes and scattered bones.

➤ **Ildari's Journal, vol. I**

Back at the tower tunnel, move north into the next section of tunnel, plucking the Soul Gem from the magic caster trap so it doesn't spit shock bolts at you. Head past the Ash Spawn waiting to repel you, checking a circular side chamber for more foes. Back in the curved tunnel, rush the next caster trap and halt the electrical damage before continuing east to the tunnel exit.

A Sorcerer Scorned

Watch the explosive rune on the ground in the roughly circular chamber with the Arcane Enchanter. Head east down the large dungeon passage, watching for a wall rune at the far end. To the right (south) is a small dead-end passage with cells. One still has a prisoner inside—Niyya. If you unlock her door [Adept], she tells you Ildari sealed her and other miners into these cells and used them in her experiments. Ildari seems quite deranged. Just how deranged is detailed in the second of her journals, found on the table in the jail area.

➤ **Ildari's Journal, vol. II**

Backtrack to the wall rune and head north toward the bowl torch. Turn right (east) and follow the passage into a mine area. Drop down into the mine where veins of gold and sapphire ore can be depleted. Then head northwest, under the three hanging lanterns, and prepare for fraught combat as you reach a small fortification built within a large cave. Ildari Sarothril appears atop the battlements, telling you Neloth was a fool to send someone like you to finish her off. She's not the friendly sort, as indicated by the minions she summons before fleeing.

With a crackle from the gems surrounding her summoning plateau, she conjures an Ash Guardian, and three or four Ash Spawn also join in the throng. Back into the mine so you aren't swamped, and set about removing these initial threats. Then head toward the fortification, move up and around to the left onto the earthen walkways, and face four more Ash Spawn. There's a dead-end mine shaft nearby. Check it before climbing the wooden scaffold steps surrounding the old fort, passing the summoning circle and heading across to the interior of a partially ruined tower where Ildari yelled at you from.

Drop down and inspect the shelves and room, grabbing any items you wish. There are potions and ingredients, a book called Deathbrand (which launches the Solstheim Side Quest of the same name), Ildari's third journal, and a strongbox (not made by the East Empire Company).

➤ **Deathbrand**

➤ **Ildari's Journal, vol. III**

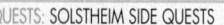

Exit the room via a southwest tunnel that winds up and turns into a fissure with Ash Spawn appearing as you progress. Deal with four or five of them before venturing down the fissure or climbing up the natural rock bridges if you wish to sneak past your foes. This leads to a castle corridor. The only way is to the right (southwest), over a bridge (which is actually above the initial chamber with the floor rune and Arcane Enchanter). This ends in a grand, two-story hall at the western end, where Ildari resides.

The Dunmeri apprentice has grown in competence (and insanity) since her time with Neloth. Face her ice storms and thunderbolts in an epic battle, disrupting her fast healing and other attempts to protect herself if you can. Long-range attacks may be more effective, as fighting on the narrow bridge to her balcony bedroom is tricky. When she finally drops to her knees, race in and rip her heart out, finally ending her malicious ways for good. Search her corpse for robes and a staff.

➤ **Heart Stone** ➤ **Telvanni Robes**

◊ **OBJECTIVE:** Talk to Neloth
♦ **TARGET:** Neloth, Tel Mithryn

Quest Conclusion

Activate the lever near the small bridge to her balcony, and a barred archway opens, allowing you to exit via a long path that ends at a pull chain that opens a section of wall leading back to the initial tower chamber. Exit, and return to Tel Mithryn. Tell Neloth of your victory, and he seems actually impressed by your prowess. He gives you a staff and makes you a member of House Telvanni.

➤ **[Random] Staff** ➤ **Bed and Chest**

Postquest Activities

Additional quests are available from Neloth. Ask what it means to be a member of his house, and Neloth mentions that when he returns to Vvardenfell in a few decades, you would be seen as nobility. In the meantime, you have your own bed and chest here to use as you please.

NOTE Ildari Sarothril was also involved in the experiments to resurrect General Falx Carius, the undead resident of Fort Frostmoth, who you must engage in Solstheim Side Quest: The March of the Dead. There's a separate journal in that location with more of her notes.

RELUCTANT STEWARD

PREREQUISITES: Second visit to Tel Mithryn (see below).

◉ **MINOR SPOILERS**

RELATED QUESTS: Solstheim Side Quest: A New Debt, Solstheim Side Quests: Neloth's Quests (page 606)

LOCATIONS: Raven Rock, The Retching Netch, Tel Mithryn

CHARACTERS: Dreyla Alor, Drovas Relvi, Elynea Mothren, Geldis Sadri, Grover Mallory, Neloth, Ulves Romoran, Varona

ENEMIES: Ash Spawn

◊ **OBJECTIVES:** Find Varona, Tell Neloth that Varona is dead, Find a new steward, Report back to Neloth

Haughty, Sardonic, and in Need of Sustenance

NOTE This is one of many quests you can complete by visiting and speaking to Neloth in his tower at Tel Mithryn. For a complete list, consult page 606. However, this particular Side Quest begins after you meet certain criteria:

Visit Tel Mithryn and speak to Varona Nelas. This isn't hard—she usually greets you when you first arrive, and you may have already forgotten about this meeting.

Then you must visit Raven Rock and return to Tel Mithryn.

While speaking with Neloth—sometimes after completing three or four previous Side Quests or minor tasks for the haughty Dunmer—he suddenly demands to know if you've seen Varona, as he's feeling peckish. Answer that you haven't seen his steward, and he demands you find her. You can answer Neloth regarding his attitude and receive put-downs in varying degrees of savage sarcasm, but the fact still remains: Varona is missing.

◊ **OBJECTIVE:** Find Varona
♦ **TARGET:** Rocky foothills of southern Solstheim

Exit Neloth's tower and make a few inquires among the other servants. The best places to engage in scuttlebutt are the two side structures.

Enter either Tel Mithryn Kitchen or Tel Mithryn Apothecary, and speak to Ulves Romoran or Elynea Mothren. Both mention that Varona went to Raven Rock to arrange for more supplies. This brings up a compass point to the northwest of your current location.

> **NOTE** Or, you can simply wander blindly until you uncover Varona's location.

Brilliant, Robust, and Blindingly Obedient

Varona's trip to Raven Rock was waylaid rather badly. She unfortunately didn't make it; she was attacked by the hated Ash Spawn who roam the southern foothills. Trek northwest from Tel Mithryn, passing the giant fungal growths until you find Varona's corpse and three or four Ash Spawn gathered around it, in the wilderness just east of the Harstrad River.

Deal out revenge to these Ash Spawn and then examine the still-fresh corpse of Varona Nelas. When you do, your quest updates. This might be a good opportunity to take the key she was carrying, too. It opens the modest dwelling in Tel Mithryn, which you can inspect at your leisure.

> ◊ **OBJECTIVE:** Tell Neloth that Varona is dead
> ♦ **TARGET:** Neloth, Tel Mithryn

As expected, when you return to Neloth in his high tower, he expresses breathtaking insensitivity toward the death of his steward. You also inform him that Ash Spawn were responsible. But there are more pressing matters, such as the brewing of tea—Neloth requires a new steward immediately, if not sooner! He believes that Raven Rock would be a great place to find a new servant, as "they are in awe" of him there. His requirements for a steward? Someone with a brilliant mind, robust physique, and blinding obedience. He seems to be describing a thrall, rather than a servant.

> ◊ **OBJECTIVE:** Find a new steward
> ♦ **TARGET:** Citizens of Raven Rock

Weak-Willed, Emaciated, and Exceptionally Insolent

Head over to Raven Rock and stroll the main thoroughfare, searching for a suitable replacement steward. Amazingly, Neloth's opinion of himself isn't shared by the citizens of this town. A few examples are listed:

Dreyla Alor isn't interested, as Neloth is as loony as a Skooma addict. He once wanted her father to import a live white mammoth. She may point you toward a fellow named Drovas.

Grover Mallory collapses in a fit of hysterics at the mention of such an idea. If you're a member of the Thieves Guild back in Skyrim, and you've completed Thieves Guild Quest: Taking Care of Business (see page 284), he points you toward a fellow named Drovas.

Geldis Sadri, the innkeeper in The Retching Netch believes Neloth to be soft in the head; apparently the lunatic wizard talks to Mudcrabs! However, Geldis has an apprentice who's hard up for coin: Try Drovas.

Desperate times call for desperate measures; locate Drovas Relvi, a shifty-looking character located in The Retching Netch, and ask him if he's interested in the job. After pondering employment with a crazed Telvanni wizard, he's happy to leave Raven Rock. Perhaps a little too happy? He'll gather his belongings and head there immediately. You don't need to chaperone him.

> ◊ **OBJECTIVE:** Report back to Neloth
> ♦ **TARGET:** Neloth, Tel Mithryn

Quest Conclusion

Back at Neloth's tower, inform Neloth you've found a new steward. Neloth is rarely impressed, and this isn't one of those occasions; Drovas makes dreadful canis root tea, but he'll do for now. As a reward, Neloth offers you the use of his staff enchanter, located in this chamber. You receive a reward of coin, too.

- **Staff Enchanter Key**
- **[Leveled] Gold**

Postquest Activities

Neloth is particularly taken with staffs, and has constructed a Staff Enchanter to allow him to create them without the usual hassle. For information on creating your own staffs, refer to page 75.

The Staff Enchanter room also contains an Arcane Enchanter, useful for enchanting your own items in between quests at Tel Mithryn. On top of it, you may find the Black Book known as "The Hidden Twilight." Reading it will transport you to Hermaeus Mora's realm of Apocrypha, beginning Solstheim Side Quest: Black Book: The Hidden Twilight.

You may also wish to inquire how Drovas is working out; it seems the new steward brought more than a few belongings with him from Raven Rock...Consult Solstheim Side Quest: A New Debt for further information.

MINOR SPOILERS

PREREQUISITES: 11,000 gold

RELATED QUESTS: Solstheim Side Quest: Black Book: Filament and Filigree, Solstheim Side Quest: Masks of the Acolyte Priests*

LOCATIONS: Kolbjorn Barrow

CHARACTERS: Miner , Ralis Sedarys

ENEMIES: Ahzidal, Draugr

◊ **OBJECTIVES:** Investigate Kolbjorn Barrow, Fund the excavation of Kolbjorn Barrow (1,000 gold), Wait for a message from Ralis, Visit the Kolbjorn Barrow Excavation, Clear the Draugr from Kolbjorn Barrow, Find a way deeper into the Barrow, Speak to Ralis, Fund the next phase of the excavation (2,000 gold), Wait for a message from Ralis, Return to Kolbjorn Barrow, Clear the Draugr from Kolbjorn Barrow, Search for the missing miners, Speak to Ralis, Fund the next phase of the excavation (3,000 gold), Wait for a message from Ralis, Return to Kolbjorn Barrow, Clear the Draugr from Kolbjorn Barrow, Speak to Ralis, Fund the next phase of the excavation (5,000 gold), Wait for a message from Ralis, Return to Kolbjorn Barrow, Locate Ralis, Defeat Ahzidal, Confront Ralis

Uncovering Kolbjorn Barrow

During your travels through Solstheim, you can learn about Kolbjorn Barrow from a variety of sources. There are several ways to begin this quest:

Read the book Ahzidal's Descent. There are a number of copies scattered around Solstheim. For example, in Tel Mithryn, on a table close to the floating lift in Neloth's chamber, or in Raven Rock, on Glover Mallory's bedroom shelf, on the second floor of his house.

Visit The Retching Netch in Raven Rock and speak to Geldis the innkeeper about rumors. He mentions a Dunmer named Ralis is up at the Barrow.

Or, you can simply stumble upon the Barrow, just southeast of Raven Rock, on the upper plateau overlooking the sea.

➤ **Book:** Ahzidal's Descent

◊ **OBJECTIVE:** Investigate Kolbjorn Barrow

Digging with a Dark Elf

As you approach Kolbjorn Barrow, buried by the ash from Red Mountain, you'll spot a Dunmer named Ralis Sedarys (and his nearby journal on a bed of hay). Ralis is an explorer from Mournhold who came to Solstheim in search of the Relics of Ahzidal, a set of powerful enchanted items said to have been entombed below.

As you progress with the conversation, asking why he toils with a pickaxe instead of hiring miners, he mentions his lack of funds to secure such workers. This is where a wealthy financier might come in handy. After asking more about the treasure, the quest starts and the objective updates:

➤ **The Journal of Ralis Sedarys, vol. 19**

◊ **OBJECTIVE:** Fund the excavation of Kolbjorn Barrow (1,000 gold)
♦ **TARGET:** Ralis Sedarys, Kolbjorn Barrow

Once you have the money, return to Ralis, and ask if he's looking for a partner. He's agreeable, as long as you manage the coin and he manages the dig. Offer him the 1,000 gold, giving him enough to hire a few lackeys and dig down deeper. But that will take time, so he'll send word when the tomb entrance is found.

◊ **OBJECTIVE:** Wait for a message from Ralis
♦ **TARGET:** Courier, any settlement

TIP Don't worry, Ralis may be a Dunmer, but he's an elf of his word: you aren't throwing your coin away. You will see dividends as the excavation continues...providing your septims keep coming!

If you return to Kolbjorn Barrow after paying Ralis but before he sends for you, you can watch the miners at work. However, you can't assist them; just stay out of their way and let them get back to their digging.

Journey away from the Barrow, to any main settlement on the island (such as Tel Mithryn or Raven Rock), and wait three days. Occupy yourself with other quests or simply sleep until the time has passed. Then Fast-Travel to a different settlement. A courier approaches with a parchment for your eyes only. Ralis seemed excited when he handed the message to the courier.

➤ **Letter from Ralis Sedarys 1**

◊ **OBJECTIVE:** Visit the Kolbjorn Barrow Excavation
♦ **TARGET:** Ralis Sedarys, Kolbjorn Barrow

Phase 1: Disturbing the Draugr Dead

Upon your return, it appears your money has been spent; there are miner tents and Ralis is on-site, moaning that something managed to wake the Draugr within the crypt. All the miners are dead, and only Ralis escaped. Unless you're prepared to deal with the draugr, the whole venture is over.

◊ **OBJECTIVE:** Clear the Draugr from Kolbjorn Barrow
◊ **OBJECTIVE:** Find a way deeper into the Barrow
♦ **TARGET:** Kolbjorn Barrow

The miners dug out the entrance, allowing you access down past their bloodied corpses and into an initial burial chamber, where they apparently hit a dead end. Expect at least six Draugr to contend with, both in the main path and from the four raised crypt corners. Once you've embedded your preferred weapons into their rotted hides, one of your objectives completes. But you still need to find a way onward.

Locate the main altar in the center of the burial chamber, and study the strange red skull. Lift it from its pressure plate, and a rotating wall arch ahead of you grinds open. Your objective updates, but don't leave just yet. Head into the newly opened chamber, and you'll see that a lot more digging is in your future. But Ralis's information appears to have been correct—a unique pair of boots sits on the pedestal directly ahead of you.

➤ **Skull**

➤ **Ahzidal's Boots of Waterwalking (Waterwalking ability, +10 Enchanting if four Relics of Ahzidal are worn)**

TIP Other than Vampire Lord form and the (exceedingly rare) Potions of Waterwalking, Ahzidal's Boots of Waterwalking are one of the only ways to acquire the Waterwalking ability. Being able to walk, sprint, Whirlwind Sprint, and even jump across the water can make exploring some waterlogged caves and crypts significantly easier. Remember that you can always take the boots off if you need to swim through a submerged passage.

◊ **OBJECTIVE:** Speak to Ralis
◊ **OBJECTIVE:** Fund the next phase of the excavation (2,000 gold)
♦ **TARGET:** Ralis Sedarys, Kolbjorn Barrow

Head back to the surface, and inform Ralis that his barrow is Draugr-free. He's moderately happy but needs to recruit more miners. This won't be an easy sell, as their friends recently perished here. When you're prepared (or able) to part with 2,000 gold, hand it to Ralis, who tells you it will take a few days to dig up more laborers. Why not swing back when you get a chance?

◊ **OBJECTIVE:** Wait for a message from Ralis
♦ **TARGET:** Courier, any settlement

Just as you did before, you must head away from the barrow and drum your fingers for three days. After 72 hours of occupying yourself with other tasks, head to a settlement and locate a courier, who has another message from Ralis.

➤ **Letter from Ralis Sedarys 2**

◊ **OBJECTIVE:** Return to Kolbjorn Barrow
♦ **TARGET:** Ralis Sedarys, Kolbjorn Barrow

Phase 2: Deeper with the Dead

As you arrive, it seems your cash injection has been spent; there's a cooking pot and two more tents, and the place is starting to look like an excavation site rather than a hunter's camp. Ralis isn't happy, though; more Draugr have emerged. At least six miners are dead, and the rest have fled. Perhaps a few are hiding or trapped down there?

◊ **OBJECTIVE:** Clear the Draugr from Kolbjorn Barrow
◊ **OBJECTIVE:** Search for the missing miners
♦ **TARGET:** Kolbjorn Barrow

Concern yourself first with eradicating the rotting Nords; head into the initial crypt area and lay waste to the foes appearing from the crypt walls and in the main corridor. Then head deeper (northwest) into the barrow. A toughened Draugr attacks from a circular platform; slay the fiend with ranged weapons or spells.

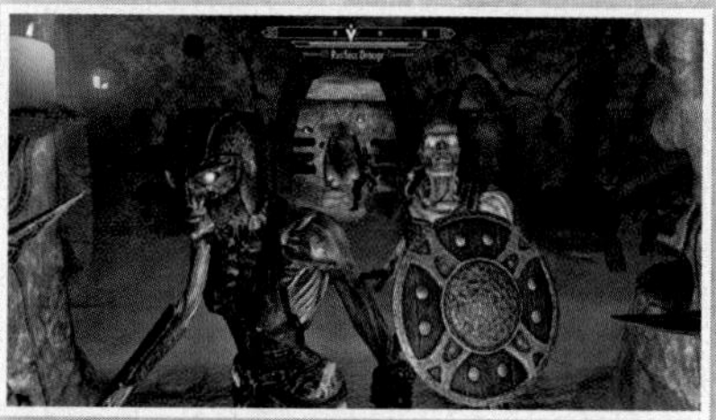

With the Draugr defeated, head under the narrow bridge to locate the two compass targets (the miners) in the crypt ahead. Bradyn is on the lower floor to your left (west). He's quite dead. However, prepare for more Draugr combat as you reach his corpse; kill three more foes and then venture farther (northwest) into the crypt, yanking the pull chain on the candlelit alcove ahead of you.

This opens a rotating door to your right (east), exposing a tough Draugr to tackle. Once he's down, pull a second chain in this new chamber's alcove, which opens a rotating door to the southwest, behind you. This leads to the upper crypt and another Draugr. Slay it, step around the pressure plate so the magic caster trap isn't triggered, then move to the portcullis puzzle with four handles to the right of it.

Puzzle Solution: The top handle releases the first portcullis. The second releases darts, so ignore it. The third and fourth handles together release the remaining portcullises, so pull them and continue up.

In the upper crypt area are the splattered remains of Mireli. Take the letter on her body if you wish, then inspect the blocked passageways up here. It isn't long before four additional Draugr show themselves. Wipe them out to complete the remaining objective. Before you leave, you might as well pocket another fabled item. Locate the seeming dead end to the northeast, hunting for a low handle on the protruding wall to your right, which slides open a secret alcove allowing you to pick up Ahzidal's Ring!

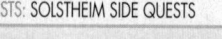

➤ **Mireli's Letter to Mother**

➤ **Ahzidal's Ring of Necromancy (whenever a creature you have reanimated takes damage, they explode for 50 points of Frost Damage and die)**

> **TIP** Is this ring worth it? It depends. Causing a weak creature to explode for 50 points of Frost Damage in a large radius may improve their damage output, but stronger creatures might have done more damage on their own. Also, wearing this ring prevents reanimated (but not summoned) creatures from taking damage on your behalf, since the first hit will kill them instantly.

◊ **OBJECTIVE:** Speak to Ralis
◊ **OBJECTIVE:** Fund the next phase of the excavation (3,000 gold)
♦ **TARGET:** Ralis Sedarys, Kolbjorn Barrow

> **NOTE** Can you hear the faint chant of a Word Wall? It is in the second chamber, buried under ash and rubble. You can't reach it yet.

Return to the surface and locate the dour Dunmer, informing him of the death down below. This hazard pay keeps piling up, and he now needs additional (some might say ludicrous) funds to continue this expedition. When your coffers can handle this outlay, hand it over and wait for Ralis to hire some brawny types to keep the new miners safe. Naturally, this will take a few days.

◊ **OBJECTIVE:** Wait for a message from Ralis
♦ **TARGET:** Courier, any settlement

You know the plan by now; move away from the barrow and attempt other tasks or wait for three days. After 72 hours, saunter into a settlement and locate a courier, who has another message from Ralis. Apparently Ralis is starting to scare the letter carriers.

➤ **Letter from Ralis Sedarys 3**

◊ **OBJECTIVE:** Return to Kolbjorn Barrow
♦ **TARGET:** Ralis Sedarys, Kolbjorn Barrow

Phase 3: Disturbing More Draugr

Upon your return, the barrow is almost bustling, with more tents and at least one living miner. So that's encouraging! However, Ralis is less than thrilled as he tells you of yet another disaster: More Draugr have been uncovered! Your objective is as clear as the sunken eyes on Ralis's face.

◊ **OBJECTIVE:** Clear the Draugr from Kolbjorn Barrow
♦ **TARGET:** Kolbjorn Barrow

Expect two foes in the initial chamber, another in the main chamber by the pedestal, and the excavation to have cleared out much of the room. Cross the bridge and head into the two-story crypt you explored last time and bring death to the Draugr inside. Continue down the stairs to the lower level where a sarcophagus has been uncovered (a Draugr bashes its way out to meet your blades), and a locked iron door blocks your progress [Expert]. Pick this lock to reach a hidden antechamber with spiders to crush and a chest to inspect. Head down the stairs and deal with another foe, and you can see back out to the central chamber.

Press on to explore more of the catacombs. In the newly opened room, locate a wall chain and pull it, which opens a hidden room to the northeast, where you find Ahzidal's Gauntlets.

➤ **Ahzidal's Gauntlets of Warding (your Wards are 25% less effective but absorb 50% of the Magicka from incoming spells)**

> **TIP** Although the gauntlets cause your Wards to block less damage, the increased Magicka absorption allows you to keep them up for longer. In a protracted battle with sorcerous foes, this may give you an edge.

Backtrack to the room with the wall chain and open the iron door. This leads to a wide tunnel with a rockfall trap that can remove Draugr threats ahead of you. Head down the stairs, turn southeast, then go up the steps and into a large sacrificial chamber. Expect to fight two or three Draugr at first, and then another three before you clear the barrow of foes. Before you leave, check the room for dead miners and guards, then look to the left (northeast), into a small antechamber with a pedestal, upon which rests a ring. You can open the portcullis by quickly sprinting across all of the pressure plates so they activate (light up), or simply snatch the ring through the closed grate using the Telekinesis spell.

➤ **Ahzidal's Ring of Arcana (allows you to cast the spells Freeze and Ignite)**

TIP Don't recognize those spells? Freeze and Ignite are unique to this ring and can't be acquired in any other way. Both have low casting costs and long-duration versions of their element's secondary effect, slowing or setting foes on fire for quite some time. Use Freeze on melee foes (especially bosses) to slow their movement and attack speed. Use Ignite to inflict heavy fire damage. Multiple castings of Ignite are cumulative, and each does the same damage as the powerful Incinerate spell, just over a longer duration.

NOTE Has your objective not updated? You may have missed a Draugr at the entrance or in an earlier chamber. Keep searching until you slay them all.

◊ **OBJECTIVE:** Speak to Ralis
◊ **OBJECTIVE:** Fund the next phase of the excavation (5,000 gold)
♦ **TARGET:** Ralis Sedarys, Kolbjorn Barrow

Head up the side steps in the sacrificial room and yank a chain to open the portcullis, watching for a subsequent blade trap and another chain that opens a quicker way back to the second chamber. Climb the wooden walkways and exit the barrow. Ralis is pleased at your Draugr dispatching but fears it's going to be everything he can do to find more miners. Got any spare change? Dig into your breeches and come up with an amazing amount of gold so he can hire some experienced muscle. Stop back in a few days to see what's been uncovered.

◊ **OBJECTIVE:** Wait for a message from Ralis
♦ **TARGET:** Courier, any settlement

Execute the "wait around for Ralis" plan once more. After three more days, a courier appears, telling you this is the last time he's visiting that place.

➤ **Letter from Ralis Sedarys 4**

◊ **OBJECTIVE:** Return to Kolbjorn Barrow
♦ **TARGET:** Ralis Sedarys, Kolbjorn Barrow

Phase 4: Curse of the Dragon Acolyte

The camp is more like a small settlement now, with numerous tents but few miners. Optionally, you may want to enter Ralis's tent and read some of his journals. Volume 23 is most illuminating, as the Dunmer appears to have been in league with (or driven mad by) Lord Ahzidal! No wonder there were so many deaths!

➤ **The Journal of Ralis Sedarys, vol. 23**

◊ **OBJECTIVE:** Locate Ralis
♦ **TARGET:** Ralis Sedarys, Kolbjorn Barrow

Descend into this barrow once more. This time, it isn't necessary to remove all Draugr you encounter, but your rage at paying for Ralis's sacrificial victims may have sent you into a fury. Gain some reward by descending the second chamber and approaching the Word Wall, learning the Word of Power before continuing and optionally taking the short route back to the sacrificial chamber. Yank the overhead pull chain to reactivate the blade traps and let them deal with some of the Draugr. Then press on and deal with the ones that await you in the sacrificial chamber.

Continue down the newly opened tunnel to a throne chamber with three Draugr to slay as they rise from their seats. After that, ponder a small puzzle:

Puzzle Solution I: There's a relic sealed in a small alcove here. Face north and south and pull each chain to rotate the wall so a whale petroglyph is exposed in opposite alcoves. Behind the two thrones are rotating pedestals. Shift both of them to the whale and pull the lever between them. The bars retract, allowing you to grab Ahzidal's Armor.

➤ **Ahzidal's Armor of Retribution (enemies who strike you with a melee attack have a small chance of being paralyzed)**

TIP The chance of actually paralyzing a foe in this way is small, but when it occurs, the unlucky enemy will be at your mercy.

Puzzle Solution II: Further progress is stalled. To continue you must open the central trapdoor. Opposite the pedestals are carvings of two hawk petroglyphs. Turn the pedestals so they are both hawks, pull the lever, and the trapdoor opens.

Descend the spiral steps, passing the scattered potions on the ceremonial table, then move into the lower crypts. Remove a Draugr to the right of the entrance before setting the floor ahead ablaze (via magic or a falling oil lamp shot by your bow). This helps remove the four Draugr in the main corridor and stops the forthcoming puzzle from burning you, if you're incorrect in your choices. Turn right (northeast).

Puzzle Solution: Ahead is a portcullis with a chain and two petroglyph pedestals. If you pull the chain, a fire trap engulfs you. Instead, turn the pedestals so the serpent petroglyph points at the ground marking on each pedestal. This is the third of the puzzles, and two serpents is the only remaining pair that hasn't been chosen. Pull the chain and claim Ahzidal's Helm. Watch for another fire trap as you take it!

➤ **Ahzidal's Helm of Vision (your Conjuration and Rune spells cost 25% more but can be cast at greater range)**

TIP The helm increases the range at which you can cast these spells by one range increment—about 30 feet. This is less than the increase offered by some Conjuration perks, but every bit helps. Note that you may want to unequip the helm if you regularly use other Conjuration spells (like bound weapons), as it increases their costs without giving you any corresponding benefit.

East Empire Pendant #27

Primary Location: [S.S07] Brodir Grove

Advance into this Reaver camp, and defeat the three foes around the campfire and hanging bones. After the fracas, move into the camp and locate the central fire. Turn north and walk to the stone column, and hanging hare and garlic, and find the half-buried East Empire crate with the strongbox atop it.

➤ **East Empire Pendant**

East Empire Pendant #28

Primary Location: [S.S09] Ramshackle Trading Post

Clamber up the scree and ashy foothills to this dilapidated structure. The East Empire Strongbox holding the pendant is on a crate, nestled in front of a smaller crate, just outside the entrance on the west side of the building.

➤ **East Empire Pendant**

East Empire Pendant #29

Primary Location: [S.S11] Fort Frostmoth (Interior)

Enter the fort's ash-filled courtyard and locate the entrance door along the western wall. Enter, head south, but turn left (east) before you reach the wooden ramp and the ladder. There is a side alcove chamber with a number of leaning cases. One of them has the strongbox. Beware of Ash Spawn!

➤ **East Empire Pendant**

East Empire Pendant #30

Primary Location: [S.S12] Ashfallow Citadel (Interior)

Head north up the steps, enter the main entrance, and look around the initial chamber. To your left (west) is a half-buried bookshelf with the East Empire Strongbox on it, to the left of the bloodstained stone pile and broken chair. Beware the Morag Tong who lurk at this location.

➤ **East Empire Pendant**

East Empire Pendant #31

Secondary Location: [SS.L] Gold Miners' Floodgate

Close to Ashfallow Citadel is a fast-moving stream. Follow it north to a closed gate, then clamber up the rocks and around, dropping down behind the gate to a makeshift platform where the corpse and note of an Argonian named Usha is lying. The strongbox is on the platform, to the right of the table.

➤ **East Empire Pendant**

East Empire Pendant #32

Secondary Location: [SS.M] Dunmeri Camp

Start at Vahlok's Tomb, climbing atop the mossy fissure and looking east. Head slightly southeast to this Dunmeri camp where the two slain Dark Elves lie. Watch for a Riekling ambush as you inspect the tent, which has a sleeping mat and the strongbox you seek.

➤ **East Empire Pendant**

East Empire Pendant #33

Secondary Location: [SS.O] Ashfallow Reaver Camp

From the exterior entrance to the Ashfallow Citadel, look directly west and move slightly southwest across the rocks above the river to this small camp. The East Empire Strongbox is close to the bed, under the lean-to, to the left of the chest. Beware the Reavers that are patrolling this location.

➤ **East Empire Pendant**

Quest Conclusion

Fethis Alor purchases each pendant for 500 gold. With 33 pendants to collect, that means up to 16,500 gold is available if you can find them all. Return to him with as many pendants as you wish to sell, as many times as you like.

➤ **Gold (500 x up to 33)**

KARSTAAG'S RESURRECTION*

PREREQUISITES: Level 50 (Recommended)

MINOR SPOILERS

LOCATIONS: Castle Karstaag Caverns, Castle Karstaag Ruins, Glacial Cave

CHARACTERS: None

ENEMIES: Horker, Karstaag, Mounted Riekling, Riekling

◊ **OBJECTIVES:** None

NOTE * Quest names marked with this symbol do not appear in your Quest menu list, although objectives may.

Headless and Furious

Solstheim's ancient tales speak of a frost giant lord both frightening and furious. This brute is said to have died more than 200 years ago, during the time of the Bloodmoon. Perhaps it is time for this gargantuan terror to stalk the northern lands once more? If you're keen on this idea, you should first visit the Glacial Cave, north of Saering's Watch below the glaciers along the northern shores of Solstheim. Expect lounging Horkers on the ice floes as you near.

Inside, an ice tunnel winds south, flanked by the trinkets of a Riekling clan. The cave is home to three easily defeated Rieklings. Search their belongings, but the real prize is at the eastern end of the cave. Embedded in the wall, as part of what looks like a very basic shrine, is a horned skull of a frost giant. Remove it from the ice.

➤ **Karstaag's Skull**

An Audience with Karstaag

Emerge from Glacial Cave and make your way up the steep snowy slopes toward Castle Karstaag Caverns and Castle Karstaag Ruins. These are massive mounds of ice and rock, rather than crenellations of stone, and look just like a mountain. You can enter Castle Karstaag Courtyard, where Karstaag's remaining bones can be found, in one of two ways:

The Short Way: Master of Unlocking

Travel to the south side of Castle Karstaag Ruins and face north. The entrance is an ice door to the north, with an infernal lock to pick [Master]. If you're able to open this door, you need not fight through the caverns.

The Long Way: Castle Cavern Slogging

Otherwise, you're in for a slog through the Castle Karstaag Caverns. Find the raging mountain stream and look to the west to find the cave entrance. Clamber to the top of the passage, look left (south), and venture into a massive ice cavern with at least five Rieklings. Head along the broken ice, passing the corpse of Esmond Tyne (who has an excellent formula for Bonemold Armor, part of

Raven Rock Regional Activity: Thievery and the Karstaag Connection). Now climb the icy banks, fighting Rieklings before crossing a bridge heading west into a narrow vertical fissure passage.

> **Bonemold Formula**

Navigate the ice chamber with the campfire and several more Rieklings. Open the ice door to the west, and unlock any of the other doors [Apprentice, Novice, and Novice] to reach small alcoves with minor items. Head east, through another ice door, up the passage to the top of the camp room, and head left (southeast) through the exit, back out onto an upper walkway of the massive ice cavern. Deal with three or four more Rieklings before crossing the long wooden bridge heading east.

Slay two more Rieklings on the far side of the bridge, then head up the ice tunnel, peering down to a Bristleback pen with four animals and a Riekling; ignore or slay it. Check the chest under the outcropping [Novice], then move back up the path to an ice door. This leads out to the highest part of the initial ice cavern. Dispatch two foes, cross the bridges heading southwest toward a couple more foes, and claim one more chest (plus two more nearby, if you can reach them; consult the Atlas for details). Head out the open ice door to a tunnel that brings you into Castle Karstaag Courtyard.

Summoning a Mighty Terror

NOTE This courtyard is the entirety of the interior of Castle Karstaag Ruins. You access this chamber via the short or long routes described above.

You emerge into the ruined shell of the once-great Castle Karstaag. A group of Rieklings immediately sets upon you; engage the Mounted Riekling first, then slay his two infantry lackeys. It is important to search the Mounted Riekling, as he is carrying the key allowing a swift exit through the ice door in the south wall [Master] (unless you picked that lock on your way in). Then approach the icy throne of Karstaag, where a scattering of giant bones rests between two ice torches. Are you ready to meet Karstaag? Then activate the Throne, place Karstaag's Skull, and prepare yourself!

> **Castle Karstaag Key**

CAUTION The following battle is fraught with difficulty! Remember that you can flee through the south ice door at any time if the fight isn't going your way.

Karstaag: The Glacial Guardian

Know Your Enemy

Before facing Karstaag, it's important to know what dangers you're up against and to have a plan for dealing with the threats this behemoth poses:

Almost Omnipotent: Karstaag is a high-level opponent, with massive reserves of health and devastating attacks. Although there's no "hard" level requirement, you should plan to be Level 50 or higher before you take him on.

Fire and Ice: Karstaag has high health (4,000) and rapidly regenerates his health—fast enough that some weapons and spells may not do any meaningful damage to him at all. However, he does have one weakness—fire damage will stop his regeneration for as long as it lasts. Most flame spells inflict Burning for a few seconds, but by far the most effective at this is Ignite (available only through Ahzidal's Ring of Arcana, found in Solstheim Side Quest: Unearthed), which deals its damage over 15 seconds. Use it, or your highest-damage fire weapons or flame spells, to wear him down. The Marked for Death Shout is also effective at weakening his defenses.

A Frosty Reception: Most of Karstaag's attacks and abilities inflict Frost damage—he has Frost Cloak, casts Blizzard, summons Ice Wraiths, and his club has a Frost enchantment. Armor and/or potions that increase your Frost and Magic resistance are critical.

Stay Away: Karstaag's attacks cause obscene damage—enough to slay a Dragon Priest in a few hits! Warriors with well-tempered Daedric Armor and high health may be able to stand up to him. Every other adventurer should plan to stay well out of his way—Karstaag is slow enough that if you keep moving and avoid backing yourself into a corner, you can generally avoid getting hit.

No Mean Feet: When Karstaag first appears, and each time he performs a stomp attack, a powerful blizzard is triggered at his location. If you are standing nearby, you will be flung backward—leaving you defenseless for several seconds. If you decide to fight Karstaag in melee, make sure to block when he prepares to stomp; this will negate the Blizzard's knockback, though not its damage.

The Cold Shoulder: Karstaag is constantly surrounded by a Frost Cloak that makes melee combat even more difficult. While it is possible to dispel his cloak for a time (using Soulrender, found in Solstheim Side Quest: Deathbrand), it will be renewed when Karstaag next performs his ground stomp.

Karstaag's Minions: When Karstaag's health falls below certain thresholds (80%, 40%, 15%), he will summon Ice Wraiths to harass you. Melee fighters may want to ignore them entirely—compared to Karstaag, they don't inflict much damage. Mages and ranged combatants should take them out quickly, as their speed and harassing attacks make it significantly harder to keep away from Karstaag.

Knocking Your Block Off: All of Karstaag's club attacks are power attacks and will break your block. While you can block his Stomp and Grab attacks effectively, dodge his club strikes.

Strengths and Weaknesses: Karstaag is immune to Frost and Resistant to Shock (75%). He's weak to Fire (25%). Karstaag is also immune to Poison, Disease, Paralysis, the Wabbajack, the Aetherial Shield, and Mora's Grasp.

Know Yourself

When fighting Karstaag, your tactics will depend largely on your play style:

Close Combat Savagery: Melee fighters should come heavily armed and armored. Make sure you have the best (preferably Daedric) weapons and armor you can get, temper them well, and imbue them with enchantments to resist frost, resist magic, and increase your one- or two-handed damage. Fire damage enchantments on your weapons are a must. Bring as many health potions as you can afford, focus your attacks on Karstaag, and try to cut him down as quickly as possible.

Stealth and Sprinting: Archers should come prepared to dodge and run. Equip armor that increases your Archery and Stamina—Frost resistance and Health are still useful but somewhat secondary, as you may not survive even a single hit. Stay mobile and try to remain as far away from Karstaag as possible, taking shots (preferably sneak attacks) whenever you can. If Karstaag's health regeneration is swamping the damage you do, consider casting Ignite on him (from Ahzidal's Ring of Arcana), which will allow you to shut down his regeneration for a time.

Incantations and Conjurations: Mages should bring their best Destruction spells and abilities to enhance them. While the other schools of magic are still useful, conjured allies won't distract Karstaag for long, and no amount of wards or armor spells will protect you from his attacks. Try to do as much damage to Karstaag as possible, as quickly as possible. One good combination is to wear the Zahkriisos Mask (increasing the potency of your Shock spells), use the Slow Time Shout, use either the Secret of Arcana Black Book Power or Root of Power Tree Stone ability, and then cast Lightning Storm for as long as you can. Despite Karstaag's shock resistance, the sheer damage of the spell will burn through most of his health. Then quickly switch over to the Ahzidal Mask, cast Ignite (from Ahzidal's Ring of Arcana) on Karstaag to stop his health regeneration, and finish him off with Incinerates.

Plan Ahead

As noted above, two Solstheim Side Quests have rewards that are especially useful when challenging Karstaag.

Deathbrand: Solstheim Side Quest: Deathbrand (page 617) is a treasure hunt that begins with the search for a suit of Stalhrim Armor (good, but not ideal for this battle). However, by the end of the quest, you will have earned about 10,000 gold and found two unique swords—Bloodscythe and Soulrender. These are effective at weakening Karstaag if you plan to fight him in melee. Once Bloodscythe has reduced his armor and Soulrender has dispelled his Frost Cloak, switch over to weapons with Flame enchantments for maximum damage.

Unearthed: In Solstheim Side Quest: Unearthed (page 645), you can use the gold from Deathbrand to cover the 11,000 gold cost of excavating Kolbjorn Barrow. The barrow contains a number of unique items, including Ahzidal's Ring of Arcana (which allows you to cast the Ignite spell, disabling Karstaag's health regeneration for the duration) and the Ahzidal Mask (which increases the damage done by your fire spells).

Quest Conclusion

When Karstaag is finally dispatched, you receive a mighty power: the ability to summon this ghostly (and ghastly) Frost Giant.

- **Summon Karstaag (Summons Karstaag to fight for you for 120 seconds. You may use this ability only three times, and only while outdoors.)**

Postquest Activities

Don't waste these opportunities; save Karstaag's next outing for when you're facing a particularly powerful foe, such as the Ebony Warrior (see page 430)!

MASKS OF THE ACOLYTE PRIESTS*

PREREQUISITES: None

MINOR SPOILERS

INTERSECTING QUESTS: Side Quest: Masks of the Dragon Priests*, Dragonborn Main Quest: At the Summit of Apocrypha, Solstheim Side Quest: Unearthed, Solstheim Side Quest: Spider Crafting*, Solstheim Side Quest: The Final Descent

LOCATIONS: Apocrypha, Bloodskal Barrow, Kolbjorn Barrow, White Ridge Barrow

ENEMIES: Ahzidal, Dukaan, Miraak, Zahkriisos

◊ **OBJECTIVES:** None

NOTE * Quest names marked with this symbol do not appear in your Quest menu list, although objectives may.

Awakening an Ancient Evil

Miraak and his Dragon Priest Acolytes have the same furious disposition as the Dragon Priests of Skyrim, who you may have encountered in Side Quest: Masks of the Dragon Priests* (see page 471).

NOTE Occasionally, the remnants of a powerful Nordic priest survive even death. Just like the Dragon Priests of Skyrim, Miraak was once a powerful ruler at the time of dragons, with three equally dangerous acolytes who guard his secrets from deep within sprawling barrows. Now that Miraak has returned to Solstheim, something is summoned within these silent crypts....

There is a fourth Dragon Priest on Solstheim: Vahlok the Jailor, who resides in Vahlok's Tomb. He has no mask, is not an acolyte, and has no affiliation with Miraak. Indeed, he fought against the Dragonborn Miraak, after learning of Miraak's traitorous behavior. Solstheim Side Quest: Lost Legacy (page 629) has more information on facing him.

Death to the Dragon Acolytes!

Acolyte Priest: Ahzidal (Bitter Destroyer)

Ahzidal

Location: [S.S04] Kolbjorn Barrow
Solstheim Side Quest: Unearthed (page 645)

This acolyte is powerful enough to control the actions of Ralis Sedarys, feeding off the miners the Dumner send to die at the hands of his Draugr brethren. Complete the quest to face Ahzidal (finding his relics along the way), and watch for his mainly fire-based attacks.

➤ **Ahzidal**

Acolyte Priest: Dukaan (Dishonored)

Dukaan

Location: [S.N17] White Ridge Barrow
Solstheim Side Quest: Spider Crafting* (page 665)

Dukaan is guarding a special tome—Black Book: The Sallow Regent. Reach his chamber by navigating your way through White Ridge Barrow. If you require a walkthrough, consult Solstheim Side Quest: Spider Crafting*. Beware his mainly frost-based attacks.

➤ **Dukaan**

Acolyte Priest: Zahkriisos (Blood Sword)

Zahkriisos

Location: [S.S02] Bloodskal Barrow
Solstheim Side Quest: The Final Descent (page 622)

This fiend, with his ability to summon Seekers and his predilection for shock-based attacks, is holed up deep in a section of Bloodskal Barrow, which is accessible only from Raven Rock Mine. Complete the quest to face Zahkriisos before rummaging through his ash pile to secure his mask for your collection.

➤ **Zahkriisos**

Dragonborn Priest: Miraak (Alliance Guide)

Miraak

Location: [S.A07] Apocrypha: Waking Dreams of a Starless Sky
Dragonborn Main Quest: At the Summit of Apocrypha (page 601)

The leader of these acolytes resides deep within Hermaeus Mora's realm of Apocrypha, leaving only briefly to steal souls from your battles with the dragons. His formidable powers, and how to defeat them, are discussed in Dragonborn Main Quest: At the Summit of Apocrypha. His mask, once you obtain it, may be either light or heavy armor (the mask will be whichever skill is a higher rank). It increases your Magicka by a leveled amount.

➤ **Miraak**

Quest Conclusion

Wear the mask of your preferred priest when the situation calls for it.

✓	HOLD	DUNGEON NAME	ACOLYTE PRIEST AND MASK NAME	MASK ABILITY	ASSOCIATED QUEST
☐	Solstheim	Kolbjorn Barrow	Ahzidal	Increases Fire Resistance by 50% and Fire spell damage by 25%	Solstheim Side Quest: Unearthed
☐	Solstheim	White Ridge Barrow	Dukaan	Increases Frost Resistance by 50% and Frost spell damage by 25%	Solstheim Side Quest: Spider Crafting*
☐	Solstheim	Bloodskal Barrow	Zahkriisos	Increases Shock Resistance by 50% and Shock spell damage by 25%	Solstheim Side Quest: The Final Descent
☐	Apocrypha	Summit of Apocrypha	Miraak	Increases your Magicka by 40–70 points, depending on your level	Dragonborn Main Quest: At the Summit of Apocrypha

Postquest Activities

You can also display these masks proudly in your abode. They are not part of Side Quest: Masks of the Dragon Priests* and have no power in Bromjunaar Sanctuary.

RINGS OF THE WEREWOLVES*

PREREQUISITES: None
INTERSECTING QUESTS: The Companions Quest: The Silver Hand
LOCATIONS: Frostmoon Crag
CHARACTERS: Akar, Hjordis, Majni, Rakel
◊ **OBJECTIVES:** Visit the [hunters or werewolves] of Frostmoon Crag

MINOR SPOILERS

NOTE * Quest names marked with this symbol do not appear in your Quest menu list, although objectives may.

Howling at the Frostmoon

During your travels through Solstheim, you may be told about the inhabitants of an icy overhang called Frostmoon Crag. You can:

Simply visit the place, which is southwest of the Altar of Thrond, north of Brodir Grove, and northeast of the Abandoned Lodge.

Or, visit Geldis the innkeeper in The Retching Netch in Raven Rock and ask for some rumors. One of these mentions the strange folk that make camp here. Time to pay them a visit?

Or, if you're a werewolf (after completing The Companions Quest: The Silver Hand, see page 242), you may encounter an explorer in Solstheim Wilderness Encounter: Hairy Hunter. He recognizes you as a fellow werewolf and tells you of Majni's pack.

◊ **OBJECTIVE:** Visit the [hunters or werewolves] of Frostmoon Crag

Rings and Things

The camp is a large underhang at the edge of the snowline, with views of Highpoint Tower to the southeast. Depending on your actions and attributes, the pack at this camp reacts in several different ways:

Rakel stops you as you approach the camp and speaks to you:

- If you are not a werewolf, she tells you to leave.
- If you are a werewolf but not in Beast Form, she recognizes it after a moment, and allows you to pass.
- If you are a werewolf in Beast Form, she welcomes you immediately.

At this point, if you're not a werewolf, you can:

- Leave forthwith to avoid any unpleasantness.
- Speak to Majni, Akar, Hjordis, or Rakel. They all tell you to go away.
- If you wait around the camp long enough, steal anything, or attack anyone, the pack turns hostile.

At this point, if you are a werewolf, you can:

- Speak to Majni to be formally welcomed. After speaking to Majni, you become friends with the pack, and you're free to sleep in the camp and take low-value items without it being considered a crime.
- Trade with Majni. In addition to some standard hunter's food and items, he also sells a unique set of werewolf rings (listed below).
- Speak to Majni, Akar, Hjordis, and Rakel to learn more about them and their pack.

If you commit a crime or otherwise cause the camp to become hostile:

- Majni and Akar turn to their Beast Forms immediately.
- Hjordis and Rakel remain in human form but will change if you kill the others.

Once all four are dead, you can take whatever you want from the camp, including a chest [Adept]. However, you can't get the rings this way. The only way to obtain them is to buy them from Majni.

NOTE If you cause the camp to become hostile, they always remain hostile (even if you later become a werewolf). If Rakel allows you to pass, the camp will no longer attack you just for being there (even if you later cease to be a werewolf). If Majni welcomes you, you will remain friends with the camp (even if you later cease to be a werewolf).

Quest Conclusion

Werewolf adventurers may purchase the following rings from Majni:

☑	RING	VALUE	POWER
☐	Ring of Bloodlust	1500	While in Beast Form, your attacks do 50% more damage, but you also take 50% more damage
☐	Ring of Instinct	3000	When you enter Beast Form, the world around you seems to slow for 20 seconds
☐	Ring of the Hunt	3500	While in Beast Form, your health regenerates
☐	Ring of the Moon	2250	Increases the duration of your Howls by 25%

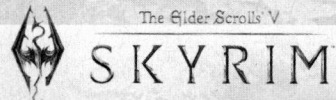

PREREQUISITES: None

INTERSECTING QUESTS: Solstheim Side Quest: Black Book: The Sallow Regent, Solstheim Side Quest: Lost Knowledge, Solstheim Side Quest: Masks of the Acolyte Priests*

LOCATIONS: White Ridge Barrow

ENEMIES: Albino Spider, Bandit, Draugr, Dukaan, Flame Spider, Merilar Rendas

◊ **OBJECTIVES:** None

MINOR SPOILERS

NOTE * Quest names marked with this symbol do not appear in your Quest menu list, although objectives may.

The Webs of White Ridge

While exploring Solstheim, you may have noticed the variety of spiders that inhabit the isle. The following activity has no objectives, but your exploration may give you some answers about these strange arachnids...and some interesting opportunities to control them.

Atop the snowy mountains of Solstheim, you may stumble across White Ridge Barrow, just west of Hrothmund's Barrow. Enter it, passing signs of violence at the entrance, where two dead Reavers have barred the wooden door shut. Remove the bar and open the door, passing two dead Albino Spiders and three dead Reavers before encountering live arachnids. Circle around the outside of spiral steps leading deeper into the tomb.

Head east down the tomb tunnel and engage more spiders (including Flame Cloaked Spiders) as the passage separates into two parallel corridors. Beware of exploding egg sacs, and mine any geodes you see; there are two Ruby Geodes to the north. Continue east down the corridors, past more egg sacs to a chain on one of the two end pillars, which releases a bridge platform ahead (east). If you have Whirlwind Sprint, use it to jump across the gap to the platform on the far side of the room, circle behind the wooden barriers, and search the area for items. Then drop down to the lower level and head toward the exit, fending off a bandit with a parasitical spider controlling it from its shoulders.

There are exits to the north and west. Head up the steps to the north first, cutting through thick cobwebs to open an iron door and a burial chamber with a nasty Draugr at the far end. There are two chests to pilfer from. Head to the sloping southeast of the room, working your way around to the west. Hack through more spiders, watching for egg sacs and possessed bandits. Continue down the corridor south, then east into a natural cavern with heart stone and ruby deposits and a door to White Ridge Sanctum.

Spider Scrolls

Move east and south, removing a bar from the door leading to a grand cavern where you're set upon by bandits, Flame Spiders, and a sorcerer named Merilar Rendas, who actually throws spiders at you! Remove the key and journal (revealing a difference of opinion with another mage) from her corpse before you move on. Slay her fast enough, and you can recover her supply of Flame Cloaked Spiders and Jumping Flame Spiders, then lob them back at your foes! Continue south to a Word Wall and a crypt with a frightening Acolyte Priest named Dukaan, who guards the Black Book: The Sallow Regent. Consult the Solstheim Side Quests for more information on them.

- **Merilar's Cage Door Key**
- **Merilar's Journal**
- **Dukaan**
- **Word of Power:** Cyclone
- **Black Book:** The Sallow Regent

To the west is a narrow winding crypt passage leading down and eventually out to a waterlogged well directly below the graven cavern with a chest. There's a fissure and stream running through it with more geodes to mine too. Of more interest is a wooden ramp to the northeast. Ascend it to the remains of a disused mining chamber, with further geodes, spiders, and possessed bandits to cull. In the north wall is a cell door [Adept], which Merilar's key opens. This leads you through some webs to a dead-end corridor with a chest at the end and a barred door into a circular chamber filled with possessed bandits and spiders.

Return to the mining chamber and climb the wooden ramps, which leads to a cage [Expert] that Merilar's key also opens. This is the place you need to reach to begin Spider Crafting. Once you have finished, you can head north to the ladder (the rest of the tunnel has some geodes to mine) and use Merilar's Key to open it. This leads to Secondary Location: White Ridge Barrow Hut, a small hut with spiders and a sapphire geode. This is a great alternate entrance to the Imbuing device on subsequent visits.

Quest Conclusion

The cage holds the remains of Servos Rendas, a Dunmeri mage with a journal explaining how badly wrong his friendship with Merilar went. Of greater importance is the odd metal device and Spider Experiment Notes near it. This is the Imbuing Chamber, where the Dark Elves' research can be put into practice!

- ➤ **Servos' Journal**
- ➤ **Spider Experiment Notes**

> **NOTE** The notes contain some recipes that explain how to create your own spiders! Activate the machine after you place the ingredients into it. Spiders show up as scrolls in your inventory. You throw them from your hands and create them in batches of three (for normal gems) or six (for flawless gems).

As you can see from the following recipe chart, the type of gem influences the elemental damage of the spider. Amethyst is Shock, Emerald is Poison, Ruby is Flame, and Sapphire is Frost.

Spider Crafting Recipes

Here is a complete list of spiders you can create and the ingredients you need to make them.

✓	INGREDIENTS	PRODUCES
☐	Damaged Albino Spider Pod, Ruby	Exploding Flame Spider
☐	Damaged Albino Spider Pod, Flawless Ruby	Exploding Flame Spider (2)
☐	Albino Spider Pod, Ruby, Salt Pile	Flame Cloaked Spider
☐	Albino Spider Pod, Flawless Ruby, Salt Pile	Flame Cloaked Spider (2)
☐	Albino Spider Pod, Ruby	Jumping Flame Spider
☐	Albino Spider Pod, Flawless Ruby	Jumping Flame Spider (2)
☐	Damaged Albino Spider Pod, Sapphire	Exploding Frost Spider
☐	Damaged Albino Spider Pod, Flawless Sapphire	Exploding Frost Spider (2)
☐	Albino Spider Pod, Sapphire, Salt Pile	Frost Cloaked Spider
☐	Albino Spider Pod, Flawless Sapphire, Salt Pile	Frost Cloaked Spider (2)
☐	Albino Spider Pod, Sapphire	Jumping Frost Spider
☐	Albino Spider Pod, Flawless Sapphire	Jumping Frost Spider (2)
☐	Damaged Albino Spider Pod, Emerald	Exploding Poison Spider
☐	Damaged Albino Spider Pod, Flawless Emerald	Exploding Poison Spider (2)
☐	Albino Spider Pod, Emerald, Salt Pile	Poison Cloaked Spider
☐	Albino Spider Pod, Flawless Emerald, Salt Pile	Poison Cloaked Spider (2)
☐	Albino Spider Pod, Emerald	Jumping Poison Spider
☐	Albino Spider Pod, Flawless Emerald	Jumping Poison Spider (2)
☐	Damaged Albino Spider Pod, Amethyst	Exploding Shock Spider
☐	Damaged Albino Spider Pod, Flawless Amethyst	Exploding Shock Spider (2)
☐	Albino Spider Pod, Amethyst, Salt Pile	Shock Cloaked Spider
☐	Albino Spider Pod, Flawless Amethyst, Salt Pile	Shock Cloaked Spider (2)
☐	Albino Spider Pod, Amethyst	Jumping Shock Spider
☐	Albino Spider Pod, Flawless Amethyst	Jumping Shock Spider (2)
☐	Albino Spider Pod, Dwarven Oil	Oil Spider
☐	Albino Spider Pod, Soul Gem	Mind Control Spider

Exploding Flame Spider

Exploding Frost Spider

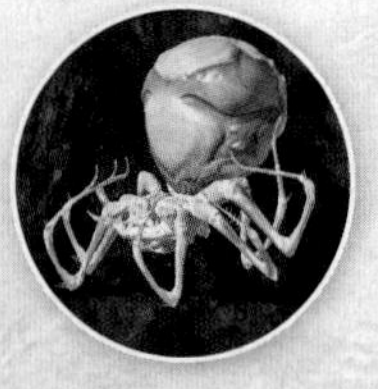
Exploding Poison Spider

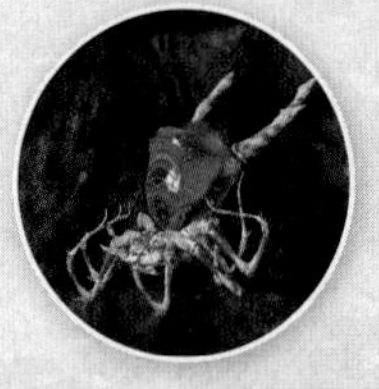
Exploding Shock Spider

Flame Cloaked Spider

Frost Cloaked Spider

Poison Cloaked Spider

Shock Cloaked Spider

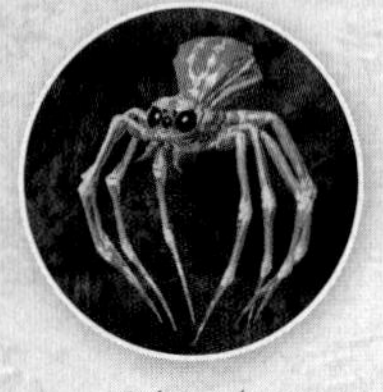
Oil Spider

Jumping Flame Spider

Jumping Frost Spider

Jumping Poison Spider

Jumping Shock Spider

Mind Control Spider

SOLSTHEIM REGIONAL ACTIVITIES

OVERVIEW

Optimal Activity Start

The following activities are available during your time exploring Solstheim. Think of them as a subsection of Side Quests specific to these settlements.

> **NOTE** **Cross-Referencing:** Do you want to see maps and learn more about the traps, non-quest-related items, collectibles, crafting areas, and other important rooms of note in every location during these quests? Then cross-reference the location you travel to with the information on that location contained in this guide's Atlas.

Available Activities

There are 16 Regional Activities: 8 in Raven Rock, 2 in Skaal Village, 2 in Tel Mithryn, and 4 at Thirsk Mead Hall. Aside from a few exceptions, most of these tasks are independent of one another and can be completed whenever you encounter them or if you return to either location.

RAVEN ROCK REGIONAL ACTIVITIES

☑	QUEST NAME	RELATED LOCATION	PREREQUISITES
☐	Solstheim Regional Activity: All Are Welcome*	Raven Rock (Bralsa Drel)	Complete Dragonborn Main Quest: Cleansing the Stones
☐	Solstheim Regional Activity: Emberbrand Embargo*	Raven Rock (Captain Veleth)	Complete Solstheim Side Quest: March of the Dead
☐	Solstheim Regional Activity: Jelly from Netch to Fetch*	Raven Rock (Milore Ienth)	None
☐	Solstheim Regional Activity: Sadri's Sujamma*	Raven Rock (Geldis Sadri)	None
☐	Solstheim Regional Activity: Take Your Pick*	Raven Rock (Glover Mallory)	None
☐	Solstheim Regional Activity: Thievery and the Karstaag Connection*	Raven Rock (Glover Mallory)	Complete Thieves Guild Quest: Taking Care of Business, and Meet the Family*
☐	Solstheim Regional Activity: Tomb Eradicator*	Raven Rock (Elder Othreloth)	None
☐	Solstheim Regional Activity: Tome Raider*	Raven Rock (Cindiri Arano)	None

SKAAL VILLAGE REGIONAL ACTIVITIES

☑	QUEST NAME	RELATED LOCATION	PREREQUISITES
☐	Solstheim Regional Activity: A Mother's Lament*	Skaal Village (Edla)	Complete Dragonborn Main Quest: Fate of the Skaal
☐	Solstheim Regional Activity: Return to Falkreath*	Skaal Village (Morwen)	Complete Dragonborn Main Quest: Fate of the Skaal

TEL MITHRYN REGIONAL ACTIVITIES

☑	QUEST NAME	RELATED LOCATION	PREREQUISITES
☐	Solstheim Regional Activity: Elynea's Ingredients*	Tel Mithryn (Elynea)	Complete Solstheim Side Quest: Healing a House
☐	Solstheim Regional Activity: Eyes and Ears*	Tel Mithryn (Neloth)	Randomly given

THIRSK MEAD HALL REGIONAL ACTIVITIES

☑	QUEST NAME	RELATED LOCATION	PREREQUISITES
☐	Solstheim Regional Activity: A Thirst in Thirsk*	Bujold's Retreat (Elmus)	Neither Solstheim Side Quest: The Chief of Thirsk Hall nor Retaking Thirsk have been completed.
☐	Solstheim Regional Activity: Berries out of Reach*	Thirsk Mead Hall (Elmus)	Complete Solstheim Side Quest: Retaking Thirsk
☐	Solstheim Regional Activity: Ore Inspired*	Thirsk Mead Hall (Halban)	Complete Solstheim Side Quest: Retaking Thirsk
☐	Solstheim Regional Activity: Primitive Pointy Sticks*	Thirsk Mead Hall (Hilund)	Complete Solstheim Side Quest: Retaking Thirsk

> **NOTE** * Quest names marked with this symbol do not appear in your Quest Menu list, although objectives may.

All Are Welcome*

NOTE This occurs once Dragonborn Main Quest: Cleansing the Stones has begun and the Earth Stone has been cleansed.

Bralsa Drel is a forlorn Dunmer who is enslaved at the Earth Stone just outside Raven Rock. She mumbles nonsense if you haven't cleansed this stone and carries rocks around. But after she's freed (and provided she survives the ensuing Lurker attack), she takes up residence inside the abandoned house in Raven Rock. Visit her and talk to her about her piteous existence. She tells you she's bad for business after her drinking at The Retching Netch got out of hand. Tell her you'll talk to Geldis Sadri for her.

◊ **MISCELLANEOUS OBJECTIVE:** Convince Geldis Sadri to admit Bralsa Drel to the inn

Head to the inn and ask why Bralsa Drel was banned. Sadri tells you he can't bring himself to watch her drown herself in drink anymore. Reply with one of the following:

(Persuade) That she has the right to do what she pleases.

(Intimidate) That she will be let in, or Sadri will answer to you!

(Gold) Or pay him gold to let her in.

When one of the three plans works, Sadri agrees.

◊ **MISCELLANEOUS OBJECTIVE:** Tell Bralsa Drel she's welcome at The Retching Netch

Quest Conclusion

Move back to Bralsa's location and inform her of the news. She seems a little happier and grants you the following:

➤ **Leveled item**

Emberbrand Embargo*

NOTE This occurs once Solstheim Side Quest: March of the Dead has concluded.

Locate Captain Veleth, who usually patrols the main thoroughfare of Raven Rock. Talk to him about the difficulties he has commanding the Redoran Guard, and he speaks of a particularly potent wine and a hidden stash his men have placed somewhere in town. Agree to find it for him.

◊ **MISCELLANEOUS OBJECTIVE:** Locate the hidden stash of Emberbrand Wine in Raven Rock

Captain Veleth recommends searching one of the abandoned houses on the outskirts of town. However, the structure with that name is empty of such contraband. Instead, continue southwest, to the gap between the two ruined structures with the trama root and a barrel, overlooking the docks. Search the barrel for the alcohol.

➤ **Emberbrand Wine (8)**

◊ **MISCELLANEOUS OBJECTIVE:** Report the stash of Emberbrand Wine to Captain Veleth

Quest Conclusion

Return to Captain Veleth with the wine, and he offers you a small reward for your troubles.

➤ **Gold (250)**

Jelly from Netch to Fetch*

Find Milore Ienth at her alchemy store in the main square of Raven Rock, and speak to her about the exotic ingredients she sells. She tells you she's trying to find a better source for netch jelly. Agree to locate some for her.

◊ **MISCELLANEOUS OBJECTIVE:** Retrieve netch jelly for Milore Ienth (5)

Netch jelly is particularly difficult to come by, so try one of the following plans:

Scour the coast of western Solstheim, where several small "pods" of Netch are located. Kill them and harvest the jelly from their remains.

Or, you can sneak into the dwellings in the main settlements (Raven Rock, Tel Mithryn, Skaal Village) and locate more jars of the stuff. Be careful with your stealing, though!

Or, during Solstheim Side Quest: The Final Descent, you can acquire two samples at an Alchemy Lab within the Raven Rock Mine exploration.

➤ **Netch Jelly (5)**

◊ **MISCELLANEOUS OBJECTIVE:** Bring the netch jelly to Milore Ienth

Quest Conclusion

Head back to Milore Ienth with the five jelly examples, and you're given some potent potions.

➤ **Potion of Ultimate Well-Being (2)**

Sadri's Sujamma*

Geldis Sadri, the proprietor of The Retching Netch, has a specialty of the house. Asking about it prompts him to mention a special sujamma. It's a taste sensation! Offer to spread the word of it, and you'll receive recompense. You're handed some samples to get rid of.

➤ **Sadri's Sujamma (10)**

◊ **MISCELLANEOUS OBJECTIVE:** Distribute Sadri's Sujamma (10)

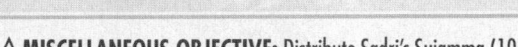

It falls to you to find interest among the townsfolk of Raven Rock for this elixir. Simply mosey up to any of the people of Raven Rock and ask if they wish to try. If they're interested, that's one fewer bottle you need to rid yourself of! Here are some plans to help you:

The following inhabitants are interested (although you may need to speak to them about their own woes first): Dreyla Alor, Fethis Alor, Cindiri Arano, Crescius Caerellius, Garyn Ienth, Milore Ienth, Glover Mallory, Gjalund Salt-Sage, Mirri Severin, Tilisu Severin, and Aphia Velothi.

Time your chats to after 8:00 p.m., inside The Retching Netch, as a large number of these folks head in here anyway, and you can rid yourself of at least five bottles without traipsing everywhere.

Time is also a factor, as waiting for 24 hours and then returning to someone you previously gave a bottle of sujamma to will cause them to take one again. This easily helps get rid of your stash!

◊ **MISCELLANEOUS OBJECTIVE:** Tell Geldis Sadri you've distributed his liquor samples

Quest Conclusion

Return to The Retching Netch, tell Geldis you've off-loaded the samples, and take his coin.

➤ **Gold (250)**

Take Your Pick*

Glover Mallory is the smith of Raven Rock, and he's an amenable fellow—that is, until you bring up the touchy subject of his lost pickaxe. He tells you that Crescius Caerellius, a crotchety (and possibly mad) old miner has this prized possession. He'd be happy if you retrieved it for him.

◊ **MISCELLANEOUS OBJECTIVE:** Retrieve the Ancient Nordic Pickaxe

Crescius is nearby, usually in the entrance chamber inside Raven Rock Mine, which is a short stroll to the northwest. When the subject comes up, demand the pickaxe back. He begrudgingly hands it over.

◊ **MISCELLANEOUS OBJECTIVE:** Return Ancient Nordic Pickaxe to Glover Mallory

Quest Conclusion

There is no modicum of coin for this task; Glover insists you use this special pickaxe yourself! Take it, as it's a rare item to find and the only type of pickaxe you can use to mine Stalhrim ore deposits.

➤ **Ancient Nordic Pickaxe**

Thievery and the Karstaag Connection*

NOTE This occurs once Solstheim Regional Activity: Take Your Pick* has concluded and you're a member of Skyrim's Thieves Guild, having completed Thieves Guild Quests: Taking Care of Business and Meet the Family*. Be sure to speak with Delvin Mallory (Glover's brother) and Vex regarding other jobs, and receive your Thieves Guild Armor from Tonilia.

Being a member of the Thieves Guild has its privileges. In this case, provided you've chatted at length with Delvin Mallory over in The Ragged Flagon under Riften and completed the prerequisites listed above, you can seek out Glover for a special additional job: to secure a special formula for constructing improved armor. A fellow named Esmond Tyne was carrying it.

TIP The note with the formula on it can be snagged before this activity becomes available.

◊ MISCELLANEOUS OBJECTIVE: Recover the Bonemold Formula for Glover Mallory

The formula is a note found on the corpse of Esmond Tyne. His bloodied body can be found on an ice floe at the water's edge, as soon as you enter the giant initial chamber in Castle Karstaag Caverns. If you read this note, you can create Improved Bonemold Armor at any forge, so check the note out before returning to Glover.

➤ **Bonemold Formula**

◊ MISCELLANEOUS OBJECTIVE: Bring the Bonemold Formula to Glover Mallory

Quest Conclusion

Back at the forge in Raven Rock, hand over the formula. For a fellow thief, Glover gladly provides you with additional compensation far beyond the usual handful of coins—a key to a secret cellar inside Mallory's home!

➤ **Key to Glover Mallory's House**

Postquest Activities

Enter Glover's house, head downstairs, and unlock the door. Inside is a thieves' treasure trove, which includes a weapon and shield on a rack [leveled]; poisons and potions; sweetrolls (all stolen, no doubt); a Thief Cache barrel with a shadowmark on it; a strongbox (not of the East Empire variety); a set of Blackguard's Armor; and Glover's Letter, which reveals his past and his daughter, the thief Sapphire. If you meet up with Sapphire in Riften's Ragged Flagon and talk to her about this note, she offers you an exquisite gem bearing her name.

➤ **Blackguard's Armor**

➤ **Blackguard's Boots**

➤ **Blackguard's Gloves**

➤ **Blackguard's Hood**

➤ **Sword and Shield [leveled]**

➤ **Thief Cache**

➤ **Glover's Letter**

➤ **Exquisite Sapphire**

Tomb Eradicator*

Elder Othreloth is located in or around the temple on the raised courtyard near the bulwark. Enter this sacred place, and ask more about the Ancestral Tombs. He's having troubles with abominations known as Ash Spawn that have risen from the remains of his own ancestors! Can you cleanse the tomb of this filth for him? Agree to receive a key that opens the otherwise-sealed crypts.

➤ **Raven Rock Tomb Key**

◊ MISCELLANEOUS OBJECTIVE: Clear the Temple's tomb of Ash Spawn

Head down the steps and north to the Temple Ancestral Tomb door, which only opens with the key. Then expect three waves of around four Ash Spawn, with more powerful variants appearing in the last wave, to attack you. They form from the cremated remains in the circular pyres throughout the tomb. Stay in one tomb or move between the different parts of the crypt; it doesn't matter. Keep the slaying going until the objective updates.

◊ MISCELLANEOUS OBJECTIVE: Tell Elder Othreloth that the Tomb has been cleansed

Quest Conclusion

Elder Otherloth is most pleased, as you honor the Reclamations with your actions. Have some coin!

➤ **Gold (250)**

Tome Raider*

The wife of Second Councilor Adril Arano is the well-to-do Cindiri Arano. Meet up with her in town, and she believes you can handle the recovery of a lost item. She never received an important folio she sent to the Imperial City. It was being returned aboard a ship called the *Strident Squall*, or something like that. Can you find it for her?

◊ MISCELLANEOUS OBJECTIVE: Locate Cindiri's Folio from the wreck of the *Strident Squall*

The *Strident Squall* has run aground, and the wreckage is now the base camp for an unruly gang of Reavers, in the southeastern coast of Solstheim. Travel there, slay the foes stopping you boarding the vessel, and work your way down into the hold and around to the large chest under the stairs. Take the saucy tome. Dare you read its shocking contents?

➤ **Lusty Argonian Maid Folio**

◊ MISCELLANEOUS OBJECTIVE: Return the Folio to Cindiri Arano in Raven Rock

Quest Conclusion

Cindiri Arano is most pleased with the return of her manuscript and offers you the following:

➤ **Ring [Leveled]**

A Mother's Lament*

NOTE This occurs once Dragonborn Main Quest: The Fate of the Skaal has concluded.

Speak to Edla, a trader who is usually wandering the village during the day, and she talks about her son. He's a good lad, but she's saddened at the prospect of him leaving the village. Tell her you'll talk to him for her, and she mentions she'd be most grateful.

◊ **MISCELLANEOUS OBJECTIVE:** Convince Nikulas to stay in Skaal Village

Nikulas is usually nearby, and he's full of vigor at the idea of adventuring. He's weary of village life and considers this a meager existence. You have a few options to convince him to stay. You can:

(Bribe) Tell him you're willing to help him get started, and hand over some gold. In return, he needs to give his mother some more time.

(Intimidate) Tell him the world is dangerous, and he isn't ready for it.

(Persuade) Ask him why he's abandoning his mother when she needs him the most.

When one of these options works, Nikulas agrees to stall his exploration.

◊ **MISCELLANEOUS OBJECTIVE:** Speak to Edla

Quest Conclusion

Edla is overjoyed at the news and offers some rare herbs as payment for your help.

- ➤ **Emperor Parasol Moss (5)**
- ➤ **Scathecraw (5)**
- ➤ **Ashen Grass Pod (5)**

Return to Falkreath*

NOTE This occurs once Dragonborn Main Quest: The Fate of the Skaal has concluded.

Find Morwen, who is usually clanging metal at the forge, or nearby. Strike up a conversation, and she mentions her mother once left the village. Morwen was born in Falkreath, where her mother's remains are still interred. She found a necklace belonging to her mother and wants it buried with her mother's bones.

- ➤ **Bera's Necklace**

◊ **MISCELLANEOUS OBJECTIVE:** Take Bera's Necklace to Runil in Falkreath

Travel back to Skyrim, and all the way to Falkreath, finding Runil the priest. He tends the graveyard and should be in that area. Speak to him of Morwen's favor, and he remembers her mother and father, Bera and Ulfarr. Present the necklace—a wedding gift—and Runil agrees to grant the request; it should bring joy to both parents as they walk in Aetherius.

◊ **MISCELLANEOUS OBJECTIVE:** Return to Morwen in Skaal Village

Quest Conclusion

Morwen is most pleased. Once again you are a true ally to the Skaal. A fine reward is then offered.

- ➤ **Nordic Carved Helmet**

Elynea's Ingredients*

NOTE This occurs once Solstheim Side Quest: Healing a House has concluded.

Head into Tel Mithryn Apothecary, and locate the owner Elynea Mothren. When she's not attempting to heal the fungal housing stock of this settlement, she's in need of particular ingredients for her alchemy. Can you bring back a [random] item for her?

◊ **MISCELLANEOUS OBJECTIVE:** Locate the [random ingredient] for Elynea Mothren

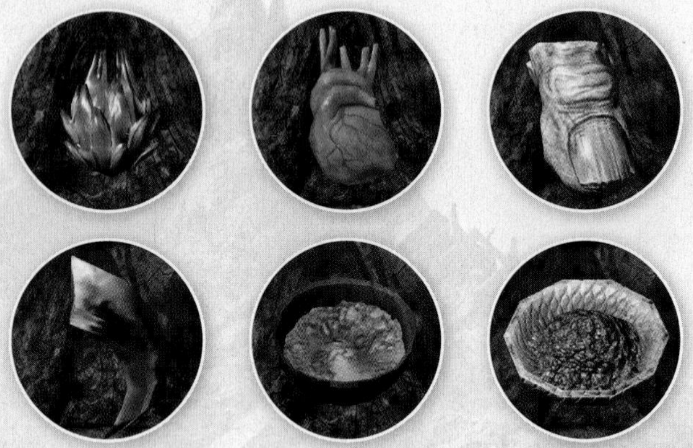

TIP The ingredient in question is chosen from the following list: Briarheart, Daedra Heart, Giant's Toe, Hagraven Claw, Vampire Dust, and Void Salts.

Obviously, the location of the ingredient depends on what it is. However, here is a sample location for each of them:

Briarheart: Found at Bard's Leap Summit, plucked from the foe of the same name.

Daedra Heart: Purchase from Enthir at the College of Winterhold.

Giant's Toe: Locate any Primary Location with Giants.

Hagraven Claw: Slay either Melka or Petra in Blind Cliff Cave.

Vampire Dust: Movarth's Lair has the undead foes you require.

Void Salts: Purchase from Sadri's Used Wares in Windhelm.

◊ **MISCELLANEOUS OBJECTIVE:** Return to Elynea

Quest Conclusion

Take the ingredient back to Elynea. This quest is repeatable, and you received gold for each item you hand over.

➤ **Gold [leveled]**

Eyes and Ears*

NOTE This occurs randomly, along with Neloth's many other Side Quests.

The infamous Neloth is always on the lookout for a test subject for spells he's working on. If you allow him to proceed through conversation, his incantation bathes you in light...before submerging you in darkness. You can hear him well enough, but this probably isn't helping your current mental state either, as he and his apprentice Talvas are shocked by the varied and unpleasant results. Tentacles coming out of your eyes? Unspeakable!

Quest Conclusion

Eventually, he returns you to normal, and you both vow never to speak of this again.

➤ **250 Gold**

THIRSK MEAD HALL REGIONAL ACTIVITIES

NOTE All four of these activities occur only if you side with Bujold the Unworthy and her motley band of incompetents, and not the Riekling Chief.

A Thirst in Thirsk*

NOTE This occurs prior to the completion of either Solstheim Side Quest: The Chief of Thirsk Hall, or Retaking Thirsk.

Visit the embarrassing ragtag collection of tents and Nords at Bujold's Retreat, and locate Elmus the mead maker. He's less concerned about the plight of his brethren and more interested in tasting some of that Ashfire Mead that they make at Thirsk. Of course, the place is overrun now, but if you could grab a bottle...

◊ **MISCELLANEOUS OBJECTIVE:** Bring Elmus some Ashfire Mead from Thirsk Mead Hall

Climb the hill and enter Thirsk Mead Hall, which, if neither related quest has begun, does not mean fighting the Rieklings (although you can certainly have a go at them). There are five bottles of Ashfire Mead scattered on the stone floor near the central fire pit. You only need one of them.

Quest Conclusion

Return to Elmus and hand over the mead. He considers you a true friend to Thirsk and pays for your troubles.

- **Gold [leveled]**

Berries out of Reach*

> **NOTE** This occurs once Solstheim Side Quest: Retaking Thirsk has been completed.

Once the Thirsk Mead Hall is back in the hands of Bujold's Nord crew and you haven't made them hostile or unfriendly by your actions at the end of that quest, search out the mead-master Elmus. He's keen to begin brewing again but requires juniper berries for the concoction. Do you have any?

> ◊ **MISCELLANEOUS OBJECTIVE:** Bring Elmus some Juniper Berries

If you don't, you can visit many of the apothecary merchants here or in Skyrim. But it is preferable to head to the Reach and locate the juniper trees that grow in abundance there. Gather some berries and return to Solstheim.

Quest Conclusion

Return to Elmus and give him the berries you've collected. He pays you for your troubles.

- **Gold [leveled]**

Ore Inspired*

> **NOTE** This occurs once Solstheim Side Quest: Retaking Thirsk has been completed.

Once Bujold's Nord crew has taken back Thirsk Mead Hall and you haven't made them hostile or unfriendly by your actions at the end of that quest, locate Halbarn Iron-Fur and speak about his work. As there's limited metal on Solstheim, and the Rieklings stole most of his ore, he asks if you'd mind finding him some more.

> ◊ **MISCELLANEOUS OBJECTIVE:** Bring 10 Stalhrim Ore and 15 Ebony Ingots to Halbarn

Be aware that Stalhrim is required in its ore form and ebony must be in ingots. Here are a few locations where you can find such deposits (and use any smelter to turn ebony ore into ingots).

Ebony Ingots: Head back to Skyrim and start mining in Gloombound Mine (Eastmarch) or Redbelly Mine (in Shor's Stone, in the Rift). Then smelt the ore into ingots.

Stalhrim Ore: The Stalhrim Source location has triple what is needed. Consult Solstheim Side Quest: A New Source of Stalhrim for details.

Quest Conclusion

Stagger back to Halbarn with your materials. He is impressed by your haul. He starts his blacksmith business, and you can purchase from him. In addition, you receive gold, and the prospect of his hand in marriage.

- **Gold [leveled]**
- **Marriage Prospect:** Halbarn Iron-Fur

Primitive Pointy Sticks*

> **NOTE** This occurs once Solstheim Side Quest: Retaking Thirsk has been completed.

Once Bujold's Nord crew has retaken Thirsk Mead Hall and you haven't made them hostile or unfriendly by your actions at the end of that quest, find Hilund, and she tells you she wants you to find a number of Riekling Spears for her.

> ◊ **MISCELLANEOUS OBJECTIVE:** Bring 50 Riekling Spears to Hilund

Such spears are commonly thrown by Rieklings. Consult this guide's Atlas for the many locations where Rieklings dwell (almost always in the snowy climbs of Solstheim). Search any you kill, and their camps, for the spears.

- **Riekling Spear**

Quest Conclusion

Return to Hilund and drop off the collected spears, which are subsequently displayed in the Mead Hall after three days. You receive gold as a reward.

- **Gold [leveled]**

WORLD INTERACTIONS AND ENCOUNTERS

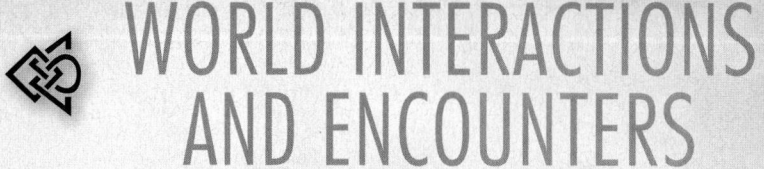

Unlike quests, Favors, and objectives, which typically involve a specific person or location, World Interactions and Encounters occur randomly and not all the time. And they almost never occur in the same place. Look for these small occurrences during your adventure.

World Interactions are random and usually very small-scale events that occur in populated areas, such as settlements, towns, or cities. They require you to perform an action, and the consequences are then detailed. Remember that you may perform the action, and it's possible that no one will notice or be interested in your antics. This is the random nature of World Interactions.

World Encounters are random events that may occur as you explore the roads and wilds of Skyrim. These events take a variety of forms, from simple combats to unique scenes that reflect the quests you've completed.

TIP You have very little control over when World Interactions and Encounters appear; just investigate or interact with the ones that interest you once you see them. The following tables show all the World Interactions and Encounters available across Skyrim.

WORLD INTERACTIONS

These are split up based on the actions you perform to get a reaction. These are listed in the following tables, along with a description of the interaction and any prerequisites (such as completing quests) you need to have accomplished.

Part 1: Items of Interest

These Interactions may commence any time you add an item to your inventory.

✓	WORLD INTERACTION	DESCRIPTION	PREREQUISITES
	1. An Interested Party	You pick something up. A nearby resident runs up and asks, "Did you find anything good?"	Inside a city, settlement, or town, but not inside a building.
	2. Watching the Rummager	You take something from a barrel, sack, crate, or container where "refuse" is usually placed. A nearby resident asks, "What's he/she doing rummaging around in there?" A second resident (if there is one nearby) replies, "Perhaps he/she is looking for food?"	You are not inside a building.
	3. Tailing the Thief	You steal an item. After a day or two, three thugs track you when you're in the wilderness, tell you they're here to punish you for stealing, and attack you. Search them for a note from the owner of the property you stole.	You must steal an item and not get caught.
	4. Calcelmo's Courier	After buying a dwarven item, you may receive a letter via courier (when you next visit a town or city) asking if you'll bring the item to Calcelmo; he will pay dearly for it.	You must buy [any dwarven item] from a merchant.

Part 2: Assaults with Consequences

These Interactions begin when you assault someone. This means striking them and then stopping before killing them (brawls don't count).

✓	WORLD INTERACTION	DESCRIPTION	PREREQUISITES
	1. It's All Relative	After you assault someone within view of others, the crime may be reported. Sometime in the future, you're stopped by a resident, a relative of the person you attacked. You can apologize (and the relative walks away) or remain unapologetic, resulting in an attack.	Attacking a resident of a town or city.
	2. An Impressive Assault	After you assault someone within view of others, inside a settlement, town, or city, you receive a letter from a courier. A [randomly determined resident] with an enemy has seen your assault and wants you to rough someone up for them. Meet the impressed party, agree, and then find the [randomly determined foe], roughing them up (but not killing them).	Attacking a resident of a town or city.
	3. A Memorable Assault	After you assault someone inside a settlement, town, or city, the next time you meet them, the victim remembers your assault and mentions this.	Attacking a resident of a town or city.

Part 3: Wizardry

These Interactions may begin once someone near to you witnesses you casting a magic spell.

✓	WORLD INTERACTION	DESCRIPTION	PREREQUISITES
☐	1. The Invisible Boy	Once you've cast a spell, a young boy runs up and asks you to cast invisibility on him. You can agree or refuse, but you can't really do this. If you agree, the boy, thinking he's invisible, heads off, sneaking up on people and trying to scare them	Casting magic within the vicinity of the witness.
☐	2. Lollygagging Looky-Loos	If you're inside a settlement, town, or city with a spell effect that creates a dangerous "sheen" or effect around your person, such as Flame Cloak, bystanders will murmur in alarm, and a crowd may start to form around you until you've dispelled the effect or it wears off.	Casting magic with a "dangerous" effect around you.
☐	3. Quiet, Please	Employ a Shout in a populated settlement, town, or city, and a nearby guard may run up and sternly warn you to stop, as it's making the locals nervous.	Utilizing a Shout.
☐	4. Quest, Please	Employ a Shout in a populated settlement, town, or city, and you may receive a Courier's letter soon afterwards, from a mysterious "friend" who gives directions to a nearby [random dungeon] that contains a Word Wall inside.	Utilizing a Shout.

Part 4: About Town

These Interactions may begin when you enter a settlement, town, or city.

✓	WORLD INTERACTION	DESCRIPTION	PREREQUISITES
☐	1. Courier Catch-Up	As you enter, you may be greeted by a courier with a letter or multiple letters. These may invite you to begin quests, locate areas of interest, or follow up on rumors you've heard, or they simply update your objectives. Consult the individual prerequisites of quests you may be interested in to find out more.	Entering a location.
☐	2. No Nudity	Enter a location without wearing any clothes, and the locals may comment on your appearance and ask you to put on some more appropriate attire.	Entering a location without clothing equipped.
☐	3. Careful, Now	Enter a location brandishing a weapon, and you may find locals asking you about it. Innkeepers and merchants may tell you to be careful brandishing such an implement. Sheath your weapon to stop this talk.	Entering a location with weapons unsheathed.
☐	4. The Enraged Mage	Enter a location, and [a random wizard] steps forward to challenge you to a duel. Kill the wizard (without accruing any Bounty, as you were challenged). You don't have to use magic, although the wizard may protest at this. Not after you kill him, though!	Entering a location.
☐	5. The Engaged Mage	Enter a location, and [a random student of magic] steps forward to ask you about learning ward spells. Oblige the student if you wish.	Entering a location.
☐	6. Gift Giving	Enter a location, and a person you've befriended (e.g., by completing a Favor) hands you a gift. This won't be the Jarl, though.	Entering a settlement, town, or city after befriending one or more of the population there.
☐	7. Games Without Frontiers	As you enter, you may see a group of children playing a game. Talk to them, and they may ask you to join them. The game will be either hide-and-seek or tag. Agree or decline. Play the game if you wish.	Entering a location, speaking to a child.
☐	8. Dragon Attack!	Enter a different location once the dragons return to Skyrim, and the guards yell out a warning as the residents scatter. A dragon swoops down into the settlement and attacks! Flee or fight.	Entering a location after Main Quest: Dragon Rising is complete.
☐	9. Other Talk	Merchants call out a greeting to you, as do friends welcoming you to your home if you own one. Those you haven't befriended may speak to you with suspicion.	Entering a location.

Part 5: Your Demeanor

These Interactions may begin once you visit a different settlement, town, or city in a particular visual state. These can occur as overheard murmuring, or as part of conversations you may have.

✓	WORLD INTERACTION	DESCRIPTION	PREREQUISITES
☐	1. The Spellcaster	Residents comment on your flowing robes, sometimes with suspicion.	Wear College of Winterhold robes.
☐	2. The Unclean One	Residents comment with disgust and sometimes sadness on your pox.	You have a disease.
☐	3. Pretty Colors	Residents are dazzled by the colorful aura you have surrounding your person.	Have a "colorful" magical effect.
☐	4. Pretty Dangerous	Residents are somewhat alarmed by the dangerous aura you have around you.	Have a "dangerous" magical effect, such as fire.
☐	5. Hands of Fire	Residents are a little taken aback by your flaming hands.	Have a Flame spell equipped and "unsheathed."
☐	6. The Immodest Adventurer	Residents are quick to comment on your lack of proper modesty.	Have no clothing on.
☐	7. On the Prowl	Residents aren't impressed by your strange crouching stance.	You're sneaking while spotted.

Part 6: Crafting

These Interactions may begin when you attempt to create an item at a crafting location.

✓	WORLD INTERACTION	DESCRIPTION	PREREQUISITES
	1. Friend of the Forge	A blacksmith comments on the item you're making (how rare it is, the type, or your competence).	You use a blacksmith's workbench to make or improve an item.
	2. Excellent Enchanting	A nearby Court Wizard comments on the item you're enchanting, or on your competence as an enchanter.	You use an Arcane Enchanter to enchant an item.
	3. Adept Alchemist	An apothecary merchant comments on the item you're making (if it's a poison or potion) or on your competence.	You use an Alchemy Lab to make an item.

Part 7: Dealing with the Dead

These Interactions may begin when you or a nearby person sees or interacts with a corpse.

✓	WORLD INTERACTION	DESCRIPTION	PREREQUISITES
	1. Suspicious Behavior	Residents step up to the corpse and look at it. A soldier usually tells folks to disperse and begins to interrogate you. Residents begin to wonder out loud if you're the murderer. You can protest your innocence (the guard leaves you alone) or offer an unpleasant response (which gets you arrested).	You're near a dead body (optionally with weapons unsheathed), but no one saw you kill this person.
	2. Dead Dragon	Residents step up to the remains of a dragon, remarking as you absorb the Dragon Soul.	You kill a dragon close to residents.

Part 8: Killing

These Interactions may begin when a nearby person is killed.

✓	WORLD INTERACTION	DESCRIPTION	PREREQUISITES
	1. A Friend's Inheritance	When you return to a settlement where a friend of yours was slain, a courier greets you and says your friend left you an inheritance. Collect the gold from the Jarl's Steward.	A friend of yours is killed (by you, without being caught, or by others).
	2. A Friend of Your Enemy	When you return to a settlement after you slay someone with a known enemy, a courier greets you to say the enemy of the deceased has a gift for you. Visit them to receive the reward (usually gold).	You kill a resident who has a known enemy.
	3. Not Going Out	A bereaved friend of a slain resident runs to their home or dwelling and locks themselves inside, refusing to come out.	The bereaved's friend was killed with them watching (by you or others).
	4. Hired Muscle	A relative of the deceased hires thugs to attack you.	A resident is killed by you, you're seen, and the deceased has a relative.
	5. Grave Digging	Residents of city's bodies may be disposed of, and any worldly goods you didn't loot from their corpse show up in their coffin in the hall of the dead.	Leave a civilian's corpse lying around a city and come back later.

Part 9: Items of Disinterest

These Interactions may begin if you discard an item (by dropping it, selling it, or giving it away).

✓	WORLD INTERACTION	DESCRIPTION	PREREQUISITES
	1. Dropping a Weapon	A guard stops you and reprimands you for leaving dangerous weapons lying around. Walk away or apologize and the guard leaves you alone. Converse and the guard asks for a fine (or bribe). If you refuse to pay, you're attacked or arrested.	Drop a weapon near a guard.
	2. I Think You Dropped This (I)	A resident stops you after picking up the discarded item, and hands it back to you (it now appears in your inventory)	Drop an item near a resident.
	3. Mine! Mine! Mine!	Two residents move to the item and begin to fight over whose it is. An audience may gather, commenting on the spectacle. The argument may escalate to a brawl (which you aren't involved in).	Dropping an item near two or more residents.
	4. No Littering, Please	A resident remarks with annoyance about your littering habits.	Dropping an item near a resident.
	5. I Think You Dropped This (II)	A resident stops you after picking up the discarded armor and asks if you meant to discard the piece.	Drop a piece of armor near a resident.

Part 10: Taverns

These Interactions may begin if you enter a tavern or inn in a Skyrim settlement.

✓	WORLD INTERACTION	DESCRIPTION	PREREQUISITES
	1. A Man Walks Into a Bar... (I)	The innkeeper welcomes you to the place.	You enter a tavern or inn.
	2. A Man Walks Into a Bar... (II)	The innkeeper yells for one of the waitstaff to serve you a drink.	You enter a tavern or inn and sit down.

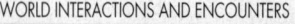

Part 11: Thievery

These interactions may begin if you enter a settlement and spot a thief.

✓	WORLD INTERACTION	DESCRIPTION	PREREQUISITES
	1. Caught Red-Handed	A Thieves Guild member attempts to flee if you (or another resident) approach them while they try to pick a door lock.	You see a thief try to pick a lock.

WORLD ENCOUNTERS

NOTE The following information notes whether the encounter takes place in one general location ("Scene") or if it continues along a path or into the wilderness ("Moving").

✓	WORLD ENCOUNTER	DESCRIPTION	MOVING ENCOUNTER OR A SCENE?	PREREQUISITES
	1. Bandit Battle	Two bandits and a bandit leader are about to kill another bandit.	Scene	None
	2. Elk Hunters	Two hunters chase after an elk. Once the elk has been slain, they patrol the area.	Moving	None
	3. Dragon versus Giant	A giant and a dragon engage in an epic fight.	Moving	Main Quest: Dragon Rising must be completed. Occurs only in the Pale or Whiterun Holds.
	4. Dragon Attack!	A dragon attacks you.	Moving	Main Quest: Dragon Rising must be completed.
	5. Orcs versus Forsworn	Five Forsworn are battling against three Orcs.	Moving	Occurs only in the Reach.
	6. Animals versus Bandit	A bandit is battling against a wild animal.	Scene	None
	7. Giant versus Bandits	Four bandits are battling against two giants and a mammoth.	Moving	Occurs only in the Pale and Whiterun Holds.
	8. Dragon Flight	A dragon flies past you without attacking, unless you provoke it.	Moving	Main Quest: Dragon Rising must be completed.
	9. Imperials and Captured Stormcloak	Three Imperial Soldiers lead a Stormcloak prisoner along the road.	Moving	Roads only
	10. Alduin's Emissary	A dragon flies to the nearest dragon lair and surveys the landscape.	Moving	Main Quest: Dragon Rising must be completed.
	11. Sabre Cats Hunting Mammoths	Two Sabre Cats prowl and attack a single mammoth	Moving	Occurs only in the Pale or Whiterun Holds.
	12. Wolves Hunting Elk	Two wolves prowl and attack two elk	Moving	None
	13. Spriggans versus Trolls	Two Spriggans are battling against one troll.	Moving	You must be Level 12 or higher. Occurs only in the Pale, Winterhold, or Eastmarch Holds.
	14. Skeevers versus Dogs	Four Skeever and three dogs fight each other.	Moving	None
	15. Atronach Mis-summoned	A [random] Atronach is seen wandering the landscape.	Moving	None
	16. Orcs Elk Hunters	Two Orc Hunters chase after an elk. Once the elk has been slain, they patrol the area.	Moving	None
	17. Imperial Impersonators	Three bandits are wearing the armor of three dead soldiers close by.	Scene	None
	18. Witch versus Atronach	One [random] Atronach is battling against a Witch	Moving.	You must be Level 5 or higher.
	19. Warlock versus Bandits	A conjurer is battling against three bandits.	Moving	You must be Level 5 or higher.
	20. Imperials versus Stormcloaks	Three Imperial Soldiers are battling against three Stormcloak Soldiers	Moving	None
	21. The Scavenger	A scavenger loots from the corpses of dead soldiers in a battlefield	Scene	None
	22. A Good Death	An old Orc is looking for an honorable death, to be slain by you.	Scene	None
	23. Hey You There! Take This!	A fugitive approaches you, shoves an item at you, and runs. Moments later a hunter approaches and asks about the fugitive. You can lie, tell the truth, keep the item, or return it to the hunter.	Moving	None

✓	WORLD ENCOUNTER	DESCRIPTION	MOVING ENCOUNTER OR A SCENE?	PREREQUISITES
	24. Imperial Scout Patrol	Imperial Soldiers are marching to an Imperial camp.	Moving	None
	25. Stormcloak Scout Patrol	Stormcloak Soldiers are marching to a Stormcloak camp.	Moving	None
	26. Courier on the Run	A courier is spotted dashing between settlements.	Moving	Roads only
	27. College Application Denied	A despondent young mage gives you his Staff of Resurrection and Black Soul Gem after speaking to you, dejected that he couldn't join the College of Winterhold.	Scene	You must be Level 15 or higher.
	28. Thalmor and Captured Prisoner	Three Thalmor lead a prisoner along the road.	Moving	Roads only
	29. Thalmor versus Stormcloaks	Three Thalmor are battling against three Stormcloak Soldiers	Moving	None
	30. Thalmor versus You	Three Thalmor attack you. Search the corpses for a note giving an order to look for you.	Moving	None
	31. M'aiq the Liar	You encounter a Khajiit named M'aiq the Liar and converse with him. You may have spoken with him elsewhere in Tamriel (see conversations in the separate section of this guide, on page 684). He'll say a few different things each time you find him.	Moving	None
	32. Bounty Hunters versus You	Three bounty hunters attack you. Search the corpses for a note giving an order to look for you.	Moving	None
	33. Hidden Treasure Hunt	You find the corpse of a dead treasure hunter with a letter leading you to a nearby [random] dungeon, and a valuable item inside a large treasure chest to find.	Scene	Side Quest: Treasure Maps is unrelated to this.
	34. Bard at Rest	Talsgar the Wanderer has stopped for a rest somewhere in the wilderness. You can request a song from him.	Scene	None
	35. Bard Attacked by Bandits	Talsgar the Wanderer is being attacked by bandits somewhere in the wilderness. Help if you wish.	Scene	None
	36. Bard Traveling	Talsgar the wanderer is walking along the road to the nearest settlement. If Talsgar dies, none of his specific encounters occur again.	Moving	Roads only
	37. On the Way to a Wedding	A pair of guests are traveling with a bodyguard to Vittoria Vici's wedding in Solitude.	Moving	Dark Brotherhood Quest: Bound Until Death not completed yet. Roads only.
	38. Lost After the Wedding	A pair of guests have become lost while returning home from the wedding in Solitude.	Moving	Dark Brotherhood Quest: Bound Until Death completed. Roads only.
	39. The Revenge of Louis Letrush	A thug sent by Louis Letrush attacks you.	Moving	Side Quest: Promises to Keep completed, and you decided to steal Frost the horse for yourself.
	40. The End of Louis Letrush	A thug and Louis Letrush are fighting in the wilderness.	Moving	Side Quest: Promises to Keep completed, and you decided to deliver Frost the horse but tell Maven about it.
	41. Ramblings of a Mad Woman	A madwoman approaches you, mumbling nonsense. She mentions the Blue Palace. If you've completed the quest indicated, she also talks about something called a "Wabbajack."	Scene	Daedric Quest: The Mind of Madness complete (for different conversation topic)
	42. The Drunken Dare	Somebody from your drunken night with Sanguine approaches and asks you for money you owe them. Pay, flee, or fight.	Scene	Daedric Quest: A Night to Remember completed
	43. Spriggans versus Lumberjacks	Two Spriggan are battling against two hunters in the wilderness.	Moving	You must be Level 8 or higher.
	44. Pain in the Neck	A hunter has been bitten by a vampire and asks for help. You can cure this disease, or ask where the [nearest] vampire den is.	Moving	None
	45. Looking to Join the Imperials	A farmer is on his way to sign up with the Imperials in Solitude.	Moving	None
	46. Looking to Join the Stormcloaks	A farmer is on his way to sign up with the Stormcloaks in Windhelm.	Moving	None
	47. Vigilants versus Atronach	Three Vigilants of Stendarr are battling against an Atronach.	Scene	None
	48. Vigilants versus Vampire	Two Vigilants of Stendarr are battling against a vampire.	Scene	Only occurs between 10:00 p.m. and 5:00 a.m.
	49. Vigilant versus Skeletons	A Vigilant of Stendarr is battling against three skeletons.	Scene	None
	50. Vigilants on Patrol	Two Vigilants of Stendarr are en route to the Hall of the Vigilant.	Moving	None
	51. Dead Woman's Pendant	A woman's corpse on the ground has a note mentioning a stolen pendant. The item in question can be found on one of the two nearby bandits.	Scene	None
	52. Finding the Gourmet	A traveler named Balbus is seeking the most famous chef in all of Skyrim. If you've completed the associated quest, you can pose as the Gourmet (with the correct identification papers taken from the quest) and receive a reward: a Daedra Heart, Troll Fat, a Spider Egg, and Balbus's prized fork!	Scene	Dark Brotherhood Quest: Recipe for Disaster completed (for reward only)
	53. Forsworn versus Merchant	Three Forsworn are battling against a merchant and a horse. If you defeat the Forsworn and the peddler survives, you can barter goods with him.	Moving	Occurs only in the Reach

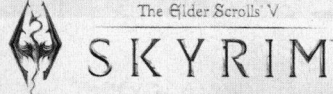

✓	WORLD ENCOUNTER	DESCRIPTION	MOVING ENCOUNTER OR A SCENE?	PREREQUISITES
☐	54. Forsworn versus Soldiers	Three Forsworn are battling against two Imperial Soldiers.	Moving.	Occurs only in The Reach.
☐	55. Bandits versus Traveling Merchant	Two bandits are battling against a merchant and a horse. If you defeat the bandits and the merchant survives, you can barter goods with him.	Moving	None
☐	56. Faldrus the Pilgrim	A Dark Elf named Faldrus is encountered on a pilgrimage to Azura's Shrine. Speak to Faldrus, and you receive an objective to travel to the shrine, as an introduction to Daedric Quest: The Black Star.	Moving	None
☐	57. Sharing a Bite to Eat	A beggar is close to a corpse. If you've completed Daedric Quest: The Taste of Death, you recognize the beggar as a Namira cultist, who offers you a bite on this found feast.	Scene	Share the meal only after Daedric Quest: The Taste of Death is complete.
☐	58. Necromancers versus You	Two necromancers attack and attempt to kill you. If you've completed Daedric Quest: The Black Star, one of them has a note ordering them to avenge the death of Malyn Varen.	Scene	Note found only after Daedric Quest: The Black Star is complete.
☐	59. Kynareth's Pilgrim	Once the Gildergreen has been restored, pilgrims begin to travel to Whiterun to see it. You pass one on your travels.	Moving	Complete Temple Quest: The Blessings of Nature.
☐	60. Peryite's Pilgrim	Before you start Daedric Quest: The Only Cure, you may encounter an Afflicted, a refugee with a pox fleeing from Bthardamz. You receive an objective to travel to Peryite's Shrine.	Scene	You must be Level 10 or higher. This does not happen once Daedric Quest: The Only Cure has started.
☐	61. The Afflicted versus You	Afflicted refugees spot and attack you for what you did.	Scene	You must be Level 10 or higher. Daedric Quest: The Only Cure must be completed.
☐	62. A Disturbed Spriggan	The corpse of a hunter is close to a live Spriggan, who attacks you.	Scene	You must be Level 8 or higher.
☐	63. Dragon Attack Aftermath	You stumble upon a cart and three charred corpses after a dragon attack.	Scene	Main Quest: Dragon Rising must be completed.
☐	64. Roaming Ice Wraiths	Ice Wraiths are winding through the air, back and forth. They attack as you near them.	Scene	You must be Level 10 or higher. Occurs only in Haafingar, the Pale, and Winterhold Holds.
☐	65. Spriggan versus Hagraven	A Spriggan is battling against a Hagraven in the wilderness.	Scene	You must be Level 20 or higher.
☐	66. A Hunter's Best Friend	You meet a Hunter and his dog wandering in the wilderness.	Scene	None
☐	67. Ice Wraiths verses Bandits	Ice Wraiths are battling against bandits in the snow.	Moving	You must be Level 10 or higher. Occurs only in Haafingar, the Pale, and Winterhold Holds.
☐	68. Dog versus Wolves	A dog is battling against two wolves. If you kill the wolves and the dog survives, it can become a Follower.	Moving	None
☐	69. Dead Bandit. Live Horse	A bandit corpse is lying on the ground, and a horse is wandering nearby. You can utilize this horse as a steed if you wish.	Scene	None
☐	70. Dueling Wizards	A Frost Mage and a Fire Mage are battling in the wilderness.	Scene	None
☐	71. Mistwatch Escapee	A prisoner has escaped from Mistwatch; he informs you where this fortification is.	Scene	Mistwatch must not already have been discovered.
☐	72. Thieves Guild Holdup	A member of the Thieves Guild holds you up for some gold. You can avoid this if you're already a member of this Guild.	Scene	Thieves Guild Quest: Taking Care of Business complete to avoid the holdup.
☐	73. Alik'r Accusation	Two Alik'r Warriors are accosting a woman.	Scene	This can occur before or during Side Quest: In My Time of Need, but not after it is completed.
☐	74. Dwemer Junk Peddlers	Two children offer to sell you some Dwemer artifacts. They also point you to a Dwemer Point of Interest (Secondary Location).	Scene	Occurs only in the Reach
☐	75. Blood Horkers' Revenge	The Blood Horkers from Side Quest: Rise in the East attack you in revenge.	Scene	Side Quest: Rise in the East completed
☐	76. Drinking Companions	Three drunks are reveling in the wilderness and offer you a drink. Offer them a bottle of Honningbrew mead; you receive a Gold Necklace.	Scene	None
☐	77. Vampire's Trick	You see a vampire attacking an innocent. Approach, and the "victim" is actually the vampire's thrall; both attack.	Scene	Only occurs between 10:00 p.m. and 4:00 a.m. Occurs anytime prior to Side Quest: Laid to Rest. Afterward, occurs anywhere except Hjaalmarch Hold.
☐	78. Vampires versus You	Two vampires attack you.	Scene	Only occurs between 10:00 p.m. and 4:00 a.m. Occurs anywhere prior to Side Quest: Laid to Rest. Afterward, occurs anywhere except Hjaalmarch Hold.
☐	79. The Companions Hunt (I)	Vilkas and Ria (members of the Companions) are out hunting Sabre Cats.	Moving	Occurs only prior to beginning or after completing all of the Companion Quests. Does not occur in Whiterun Hold.
☐	80. The Companions Hunt (II)	Skjor, Aela, and Njada (members of the Companions) are out hunting a mammoth.	Moving	Occurs only prior to beginning or after completing all of the Companion Quests. Does not occur in Whiterun Hold.
☐	81. The Companions Hunt (III)	Falkas, Athis, and Torvar (members of the Companions) are out hunting bears.	Moving	Occurs only prior to beginning or after completing all of the Companion Quests. Does not occur in Whiterun Hold.

✓	WORLD ENCOUNTER	DESCRIPTION	MOVING ENCOUNTER OR A SCENE?	PREREQUISITES
☐	82. Wolf Hunt	A fellow from Cragslane Cavern in Eastmarch was attempting to retrieve pit wolves that have bolted from their pens. He is found dead, with the pit wolves nearby. The note reveals the location of Cragslane Cavern.	Scene	Cragslane Cavern can already have been discovered.
☐	83. Bounty Killer	A Bounty Collector approaches you in the wilderness and offers you a chance to pay off your Bounty for a raised price "(the actual price depends on your bounty). Choose to pay, flee, or kill.	Scene	You must have a Bounty of 1,000+ in any Hold.
☐	84. Burned Crops	You meet two farmers displaced after a recent dragon attack. You can give them gold if you wish.	Moving	You must be at least Level 4. Roads only.
☐	85. The Nobles	Two noblemen are walking along the road escorted by two soldiers.	Moving	Roads only
☐	86. The Thalmor	Three Thalmor are walking along the road, eventually reaching the Thalmor Embassy.	Moving	Roads only
☐	87. The Stormcloaks	Three Stormcloaks are walking along the road, eventually reaching the nearest city.	Moving	Roads only. The Hold you see them in must be in Stormcloaks' control.
☐	88. The Imperials	Three Imperials are walking along the road, eventually reaching the nearest city.	Moving	Roads only. The Hold you see them in must be in Imperial control.
☐	89. The Adventurer	A mercenary adventurer is walking toward a nearby dungeon. You can speak to the adventurer and get them to reveal the location of the dungeon, which appears on your world map.	Moving	You must be at least Level 5. Roads only.
☐	90. The Taunting Adventurer	An adventurer taunts you on the road, spoiling for a fight. You can oblige, or talk your way out of it.	Moving	Roads only
☐	91. Not Your Courier	A courier is on the road, traveling to a nearby inn to deliver a message. You can steal the note (or kill the courier), which hints at [random] treasure inside a [random] nearby dungeon.	Moving	Roads only
☐	92. Skooma Dealer	A Skooma dealer offers you some of his stock. You can purchase or use intimidation to get your fix.	Moving	Roads only
☐	93. A Giant's Painted Cow	A giant is walking along the road with a painted cow close by. He heads to the nearest [random] giant's camp.	Moving	Roads only
☐	94. A Farmer's Painted Cow	A farmer is leading a painted cow along the road to a [random] giant's camp. This is part of a ritual so the giants and farmers live harmoniously together.	Moving	Roads only
☐	95. The Headless Horseman	Did you see a headless ghost riding a horse to Hamvir's Rest? You cannot stop or interact with this specter, as it appears to be on a different plane of existence than you. Perhaps the head of the horseman lies (attached to his helmet) within this graveyard?	Moving	Only occurs between 10:00 p.m. and 5:00 a.m.

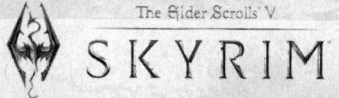

DAWNGUARD
WORLD INTERACTIONS AND ENCOUNTERS

One of the many strange, unique, or amazing encounters you may come across.

Just like World Interactions and Encounters in your original adventure, there are a whole host of randomly occurring small encounters to watch for during your new explorations.

TIP You have very little control over when World Interactions and Encounters appear; just investigate or interact with the ones that interest you, once you see them. The following tables show all the Dawnguard-related World Interactions and Encounters available across Skyrim.

DAWNGUARD WORLD INTERACTIONS

These are split up based on the actions you perform to get a reaction. We list them in table form, along with a description of the interaction and any prerequisites (such as quests) you need to have accomplished.

Part 1: Eclipse Attacks

The six events listed in the table can occur under two distinct sets of conditions:

Night Attacks: If your character is Level 8 or greater and you have not completed Dawnguard Main Quest: Kindred Judgment, these encounters can occur at night (21:00–05:00) when you enter any settlement with guards (such as a Hold Capital or village).

Eclipse Attacks: Once you've shot a Bloodcursed Arrow into the sun with Auriel's Bow after completing Dawnguard Main Quest: Touching the Sky, these encounters can occur when you enter any settlement with guards during the resulting eclipse.

✓	WORLD INTERACTION	DESCRIPTION	PREREQUISITES
☐	1. Gargoyle Attack	When you enter a city or town, a gargoyle is attacking.	Night or Eclipse Attack conditions.
☐	2. Vampire and Thralls	When you enter a city or town, a vampire and two Vampire Thralls are attacking.	Night or Eclipse Attack conditions.
☐	3. Vampires and Gargoyles	When you enter a city or town, a vampire and a gargoyle are attacking.	Night or Eclipse Attack conditions.
☐	4. Death Hounds	When you enter a city or town, three Death Hounds are attacking.	Night or Eclipse Attack conditions.
☐	5. Vampires and Death Hounds	When you enter a city or town, a vampire and two Death Hounds are attacking.	Night or Eclipse Attack conditions.
☐	6. Vampires, Gargoyles, and Death Hounds	When you enter a city or town, a vampire, gargoyle, and Death Hound are attacking.	Night or Eclipse Attack conditions.

Part 2: Other Attacks

The following three events occur only if you have completed Dawnguard Main Quest: Bloodline but *not* completed Dawnguard Main Quest: Kindred Judgment.

✓	WORLD INTERACTION	DESCRIPTION	PREREQUISITES?
☐	7. Vampire Summoner	When you enter a city or town, a vampire is skulking about. If it spots you, it approaches, summons a gargoyle, and attacks!	See above.
☐	8. Dawnguard Scouts	Outside Castle Volkihar, you encounter a couple of Dawnguard Scouts, who attack.	See above. You must also be allied to the vampires.
☐	9. Vampire Scouts	Outside Fort Dawnguard, you encounter a couple of Vampire Scouts, who attack.	See above. You must also be allied to the Dawnguard.

DAWNGUARD WORLD ENCOUNTERS

The following events occur throughout the Skyrim wilderness, either on roads or off the beaten track. The table also notes whether the encounter has any special conditions. Please be aware that as you progress through the Dawnguard Main Quest, the frequency of two Wilderness Encounters (Vampire Attack and Dawnguard Attack) increases.

☑	WILDERNESS ENCOUNTER	DESCRIPTION	SPECIAL NOTES
☐	1. Vigilants in Pursuit	1 to 3 Vigilants chase a fleeing vampire. Once the vampire is killed, they mention whether you helped in the fight.	Night only (22:00–5:00). Prior to starting Dawnguard Main Quest: Dawnguard.
☐	2. Vampire Masquerade	Two vampires (or three if you're above Level 15) have killed a group of Vigilants and stolen their robes. They call out to you, beckoning you over. They attack when you approach.	Once the vampires attack, this will not recur. Night only (22:00–5:00).
☐	3. Bats!	A large swarm of bats flies past you.	Wilderness only. Night only (22:00–5:00)
☐	4. Vampire Assassin	Two skeletons lie on the ground. When you approach, a Vampire Assassin teleports in and attacks. A note on her body names a nearby vampire lair that sent her to kill you; reading it adds that location to your map.	Dawnguard Main Quest: A New Order must be complete. There must be a (non-cleared) vampire lair in the Hold. Night only (22:00–5:00).
☐	5. Dawnguard Vampire Hunters	A Dawnguard Vampire Hunter patrols a section of road, possibly joined by one (if you're Level 10 or greater) or two (if you're Level 20 or greater) additional Dawnguard agents. They attack on sight. The Vampire Hunter has a writ authorizing your death for vampirism.	Dawnguard Main Quest: The Bloodstone Chalice must be complete. You must be a vampire.
☐	6. Dawnguard Novice	Dawnguard Novice Hakar is running from two vampires. Save him, and he resigns from the order, drops his items (Armor, Orders, Cache Key), and flees for Rorikstead. Reading the note reveals the caches in Whiterun Hold (see Side Quest: The Great Skyrim Cache Grab on page 570). You can also claim the Orders and Cache Key from his corpse if he dies.	This only takes place in Whiterun Hold, if Hakar has not previously been killed. Dawnguard Main Quest: The Bloodstone Chalice or A New Order must be complete. Night only (00:00–8:00).
☐	7. Dawnguard Outrider	Dawnguard Saliah rides by on horseback. Kill or pickpocket her for her Orders, which reveal the Caches in Hjaalmarch, the Pale, and Winterhold (see Side Quest: The Great Skyrim Cache Grab on page 570) and a Cache Key.	This only takes place in Hjaalmarch, the Pale, or Winterhold Hold, if Saliah has not previously been killed. Dawnguard Main Quest: The Bloodstone Chalice or A New Order must be complete.
☐	8. Dawnguard Remains	Dawnguard Lynoit lies dead on the ground, surrounded by smoldering vampire ash piles. Loot his body for his orders, which reveal the Caches in Haafingar and the Reach (see Side Quest: The Great Skyrim Cache Grab on page 570).	This only takes place in Haafingar or the Reach, if you haven't previously investigated Lynoit's corpse. Dawnguard Main Quest: The Bloodstone Chalice or A New Order must be complete.
☐	9. Taron Dreth	After completing Side Quest: Lost to the Ages, you may run across Taron Dreth (Katria's former apprentice) traveling to Markarth accompanied by his guards. If you speak to him (he'll stop to talk if you have one of the Aetherium items), you can confront him about his betrayal. He and his guards attack and must be killed.	Side Quest: Lost to the Ages completed; you have not previously spoken to or attacked Taron. Only occurs on a road.
☐	10. Werewolves versus Vampires	Three vampires and a werewolf appear at opposite sides of a clearing, wilderness area, or road, and charge at each other.	The Companions Quest: Proving Honor must be completed. Night only (22:00–5:00). Wilderness only.
☐	11. Werewolf Kills Loved One	A "naked" farmer stands nearby the corpse of a loved one (his wife). If you get close, he'll yell, "What have I done?" He'll then transform into a werewolf and attack. He also transforms if he's threatened.	The Companions Quest: Proving Honor must be completed. Night only (22:00–5:00). Wilderness only.
☐	12. Dawnguard Vampire Hunting	Three Dawnguard members are patrolling the area because of reports of vampires nearby. They'll greet you if you're close enough and ask if you've seen any. You can answer no, or, if you're a vampire, you can provoke them through conversation to attack.	Dawnguard Main Quest: The Bloodstone Chalice or A New Order must be complete. Late night only (00:00-5:00). Wilderness only.
☐	13. Vampire Feeding on a Vigilant	Two vampires are standing near the corpse of a Vigilant. They will attack on sight.	Dawnguard Main Quest: The Bloodstone Chalice or A New Order must be complete. Late night only (00:00–5:00). Wilderness only.
☐	14. Desperate Vampire Seeking Shelter from the Sun	A vampire out during the day is seeking shelter from the sun. The vampire is running to a cave and isn't hostile unless attacked first.	Daytime only (05:00–22:00). Wilderness only.
☐	15. Babette on the Road Near a Body	Babette from the Dark Brotherhood is standing near a fresh kill. You can inquire about it, and when you finish, she heads back to the Dawnstar Sanctuary (in the Pale).	Dark Brotherhood Quest: Hail Sithis! must be completed. Late night only (00:00–5:00). Road only.
☐	16. Giant Spider!	You encounter a Giant Frostbite Spider in the wild. The spider may be white or red depending on whether the environment is snowy or not.	You must be at least Level 14. Wilderness only.
☐	17. Dueling Giant Spiders!	You encounter two Giant Frostbite Spiders fighting over territory in the wild. The spiders may be white or red depending on whether the environment is snowy or not.	You must be at least Level 18. Wilderness only.
☐	18. Werewolves	Two werewolves run across the wilderness. They attack you if you're spotted.	The Companions Quest: Proving Honor must be completed. Night only (22:00–05:00). Wilderness only.
☐	19. Human Changes into Werewolf	A hunter transforms into a werewolf and attacks if you approach him.	The Companions Quest: Proving Honor must be completed. Night (22:00–05:00). Wilderness only.
☐	20. Gargoyles	Two gargoyles are on the prowl.	You must be Level 10 or higher. Night (22:00–05:00) or Eclipse (via Bloodcursed Arrows and Auriel's Bow fired at the sun) ongoing. Wilderness only.
☐	21. Death Hounds	A pack of three Death Hounds are out hunting.	Night (22:00–05:00) or Eclipse (via Bloodcursed Arrows and Auriel's Bow fired at the sun) ongoing. Wilderness only.
☐	22. Vampire and Death Hound	A vampire is traveling with his Death Hound.	Night (22:00–05:00) or Eclipse (via Bloodcursed Arrows and Auriel's Bow fired at the sun) ongoing. Wilderness only.
☐	23. Vampires versus Bandits	A gang of bandits are fending off an attack by some vampires.	Night (22:00–05:00) or Eclipse (via Bloodcursed Arrows and Auriel's Bow fired at the sun) ongoing. Wilderness only.
☐	24. Special Attack: Vampire Attack	You are attacked by a group of three vampires.	Dawnguard Main Quest: A New Order completed, but Dawnguard Main Quest: Kindred Judgment is not completed. Wilderness only. These attacks increase in frequency as you progress through the Dawnguard Main Quests. You must be allied with the Dawnguard.
☐	25. Special Attack: Dawnguard Attack	You are attacked by a group of three Dawnguard.	Dawnguard Quest: The Bloodstone Chalice completed, but Vampire Faction Quest: Destroying the Dawnguard is not completed. Wilderness only. These attacks increase in frequency as you progress through the Dawnguard Main Quests. You must be allied with the vampires.
☐	26. Special Encounter: Arvak	While wandering the Soul Cairn, you may see Arvak (a spectral horse) race by. If you chase him, he disappears.	Regional Activity: Soul Cairn: Arvak the Spectral Steed not completed. Soul Cairn only.

DRAGONBORN
WORLD INTERACTIONS AND ENCOUNTERS

One of the ferocious, surprising, or frightening encounters you may find yourself in.

Dragonborn introduces a number of new World Encounters and Interactions. Most of these will occur only on the isle of Solstheim, although many encounters from the mainland can be found there as well.

> **TIP** You have very little control over when World Interactions and Encounters will occur; just investigate or interact with the ones that interest you. The following tables list all of the new Dragonborn-related World Interactions and Encounters.

DRAGONBORN WORLD INTERACTIONS

Two new World Interactions can occur based on your actions in Dragonborn.

✓	WORLD INTERACTIONS	DESCRIPTION	PREREQUISITES
☐	1. Soul Stealing	When you kill a dragon, Miraak may appear and steal its soul. When you eventually kill him, you will recover all of the souls he stole from you in this way.	Dragonborn Main Quest: The Temple of Miraak completed; Dragonborn Main Quest: At the Summit of Apocrypha not completed. You must have just killed a dragon.
☐	2. Riekling Rescue	When fighting outdoors on Solstheim, several Rieklings may appear to aid you.	Solstheim Side Quest: The Chief of Thirsk Hall completed. Solstheim exterior only.

DRAGONBORN WORLD ENCOUNTERS

The following World Encounters may occur as you explore the isle of Solstheim whether on roads or off the beaten track. In addition to these encounters, many of the World Encounters from mainland Skyrim may (randomly) occur on Solstheim.

✓	WILDERNESS ENCOUNTER	DESCRIPTION	PREREQUISITES
☐	1. Hunters versus Elk	Two hunters pursue a fleeing elk.	Solstheim only.
☐	2. Animals versus Reaver	Two animals are attacking a lone Reaver.	Solstheim only.
☐	3. One Man and His Dog	A hunter and his dog are traveling through the wilderness.	Solstheim only.
☐	4. Reavers versus Ice Wraiths	Three Reavers are attacking a pair of Ice Wraiths.	Solstheim only. Level 10+
☐	5. Icarian Flight of Fancy	A wizard experimenting with a "Flight" spell has an unfortunate accident.	Solstheim only. Only occurs once.
☐	6. Unspeakable Madness	A madman is raving about the "secrets" a Black Book has shown him. He tells you its location, if you ask. He attacks when you try to leave.	Solstheim only.
☐	7. Lycanthrope Attack	Three men transform into werebears and attack.	Solstheim only.
☐	8. Assassin's Need	A band of Morag Tong assassins attack you for being a member of the Dark Brotherhood.	Solstheim only. Solstheim Side Quest: Served Cold completed; Dark Brotherhood Quest: Sanctuary completed.
☐	9. Death From Above	A Dragon or Serpentine Dragon attacks.	Solstheim only.
☐	10. Payment Is Due	Morgrul's thugs ambush you in the wilderness.	Solstheim only. Solstheim Side Quest: A New Debt has started but not concluded.
☐	11. The Rabbitting Reaver	A Reaver tells you that the gang at Frossel stole his treasure...then thinks better of it and attacks.	Solstheim only. Occurs only once. Frossel not discovered.
☐	12. Mutiny on the Mainland	A pirate orders a deserter to return to Haknir's Shoal with her. When he refuses, she attacks him (and you).	Solstheim only. Only occurs once. Level 36+. Solstheim Side Quest: Deathbrand not started.
☐	13. Hairy Hunter	A hunter recognizes you as a fellow werewolf and tells you about Majni's pack at Frostmoon Crag.	Solstheim only. You are a werewolf; Frostmoon Crag is not discovered.
☐	14. Hunters versus Netch	A band of hunters are preparing to try their luck against the fearsome Netch of Solstheim.	Solstheim only.
☐	15. Beast of the Wild	Wulf Wild-Blood's brother Torkild, now a werebear, attacks you.	Northern Solstheim only. Occurs during Solstheim Side Quest: Filial Bonds.

TALL TALES: THE UTTERANCES OF M'AIQ THE LIAR

Meet M'aiq the Liar. He's quite the talker:

"M'aiq's father was also called M'aiq. As was M'aiq's father's father. At least, that's what his father said."

"M'aiq wishes you well."

"M'aiq knows much, and tells some. M'aiq knows many things others do not."

"M'aiq carries two weapons, to be safe. What if one breaks? That would be most unlucky."

"M'aiq is always in search of calipers, yet finds none. Where could they have gone?"

"M'aiq hears many stories of war...yet few of them are true."

"How does anyone know there was a city of Winterhold? M'aiq did not see it with his eyes. Did you?"

"Too much magic can be dangerous. M'aiq once had two spells and burned his sweetroll."

"What does this mean, to combine magic? Magic plus magic is still magic."

"It does not matter to M'aiq how strong or smart one is. It only matters what one can do."

"Dragons were never gone. They were just invisible and very, very quiet."

"Werebears? Where? Bears? Men that are bears?"

"Much snow in Skyrim. Enough snow. M'aiq does not want any more."

"Snow falls. Why worry where it goes? M'aiq thinks the snowflakes are pretty."

"Skyrim was once the land of many butterflies. Now, not so much."

"M'aiq once walked to High Hrothgar. So many steps, he lost count."

"Once M'aiq got in trouble in Riften, and fled to Windhelm. It is good that nobody there cared."

"M'aiq can travel fast across the land. Some lazy types take carriages. It is all the same to M'aiq."

"M'aiq does not understand what is so impressive about shouting. M'aiq can shout whenever he wants."

"M'aiq saw a mudcrab the other day. Horrible creatures."

"M'aiq loves the people of Skyrim. Many interesting things they say to each other."

"Nords are so serious about beards. So many beards. M'aiq thinks they wish they had glorious manes like Khajiit."

"M'aiq does not remember his childhood. Perhaps he never had one."

"M'aiq is very practical. He has no need for mysticism."

"Nords' armor has lots of fur. This sometimes makes M'aiq nervous."

"M'aiq was soul trapped once. Not very pleasant. You should think about that once in a while."

"Some say Alduin is Akatosh. Some say M'aiq is a Liar. Don't you believe either of those things."

"Something strange happens to Khajiit when they arrive in Skyrim."

"M'aiq has heard the people of Skyrim are better-looking than the ones in Cyrodiil. He has no opinion on the matter. All people are beautiful to him."

"Why do soldiers bother with target practice? One learns best by hitting real people."

"M'aiq knows why Falmer are blind. It has nothing to do with the Dwemer disappearing. Really."

"M'aiq has heard it is dangerous to be your friend."

"The people of Skyrim are more open-minded about certain things than people in other places."

"Some like taking friends on adventures. M'aiq thinks being alone is better. Less arguing about splitting treasure."

"Don't try blocking if you have two weapons. You will only get confused. Much better to hit twice anyway."

"M'aiq knows many things, no?"

"M'aiq is tired now. Go bother somebody else."

"M'aiq is done talking."

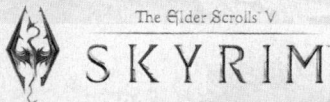

PRIMARY LOCATIONS

Total—30: Hold Capital, Blue Palace, and 28 Hold Locations

[1.00] Hold Capital City: Solitude
[1.00] Blue Palace
Jarl: Elisif the Fair
[1.01] Northwatch Keep
[1.02] Rimerock Burrow
[1.03] Pinefrost Tower
[1.04] Volskygge
[1.05] Steepfall Burrow and Lower Steepfall Burrow
[1.06] Lost Echo Cave
[1.07] Orphan's Tear
[1.08] Fort Hraggstad
[1.09] Widow's Watch Ruins
[1.10] Pinemoon Cave
[1.11] Clearpine Pond
[1.12] Ravenscar Hollow
[1.13] The Steed Stone
[1.14] Ironback Hideout
[1.15] Wolfskull Cave
[1.16] Statue to Meridia and Kilkreath Ruins
[1.17] Dragon Bridge
[1.18] Haafingar Stormcloak Camp
[1.19] Broken Oar Grotto
[1.20] Shadowgreen Cavern
[1.21] Thalmor Embassy
[1.22] Solitude Sawmill
[1.23] Katla's Farm
[1.24] East Empire Company Warehouse
[1.25] Brinewater Grotto
[1.26] Solitude Lighthouse
[1.27] Dainty Sload
[1.28] The Katariah

NOTE **Additional Locations:** These locations were added or modified by the Dawnguard, Hearthfire, or Dragonborn add-ons. New locations appear at the end of each Hold chapter.

SECONDARY LOCATIONS

Total—8 Points of Interest

[1.A] Clam Digger's Camp
[1.B] Forsworn Ambush Camp
[1.C] Howling Wolf's Folly
[1.D] Pinemoon Bear Lair
[1.E] Haafingar Sabre Cat's Lair
[1.F] Pincushion Peter
[1.G] Haafingar Nordic Burial Ruins
[1.H] Solitude Attack Camp

ADDITIONAL LOCATIONS

[DG.08] Icewater Jetty (see page 715)
[DG.09] Castle Volkihar (see page 715)
[HF.01] Proudspire Manor (Updated) (see page 695)

HOLD CAPITAL: SOLITUDE

Related Quests

Main Quest: Diplomatic Immunity
Main Quest: Season Unending
Civil War Quest: Joining the Legion
Civil War Quest: The Jagged Crown
Civil War Quest: Message to Whiterun
Civil War Quest: Reunification of Skyrim
Civil War Quest: A False Front
Civil War Quest: Rescue from Fort Kastav
Civil War Quest: The Battle for Fort Dunstad
Civil War Quest: The Battle for Fort Greenwall
Civil War Quest: Liberation of Skyrim
Civil War Quest: Battle for Solitude
Daedric Quest: The Mind of Madness
Side Quest: The Man Who Cried Wolf
Side Quest: The Wolf Queen Awakened
Side Quest: Lights Out!
Other Factions: Bards College Quest: Tending the Flames
Other Factions: Bards College Quest: Finn's Lute
Other Factions: Bards College Quest: Pantea's Flute
Other Factions: Bards College Quest: Rjorn's Drum
Dark Brotherhood Quest: Bound Until Death
Dark Brotherhood Quest: Breaching Security
Dark Brotherhood Quest: To Kill an Empire
Thieves Guild Quest: Scoundrel's Folly
Thieves Guild Radiant Quest: No Stone Unturned (x2)
Thieves Guild City Influence Quest: The Dainty Sload
Dungeon Activity (Solitude Jail)
Miscellaneous Objective: Innkeeper Rumors (the Winking Skeever)
Miscellaneous Objective: Angeline and Aldis* (Angeline Morrard)
Miscellaneous Objective: Looking Radiant* (Taarie)
Miscellaneous Objective: Spiced Wine Shipment* (Evette San)
Favor (Activity): The Gift of Charity* (Svari)
Favor (Activity): The Gift of Charity* (Noster One-Eye)
Favor (Activity): The Gift of Charity* (Dervenin)
Favor: A Good Talking To* (Octieve San)
Favor: The Bandit Slayer* (Ahtar)
Favor: The Vampire Slayer* (Sybille Stentor)
Favor: Rare Item Hunt* (Captain Aldis)
Favor: Item Retrieval (Cave)* (Noster One-Eye)
Thane Quest: Thane of Haafingar*

NOTE * Quest names marked with this symbol do not appear in your Quest Menu list, although objectives may.

Habitation: Hold Capital (Major)

Crafting

Alchemy Lab
Arcane Enchanters (2)
Blacksmith Forge
Grindstones (3)
Workbench

Services

Follower: Belrand [1/47]
Follower: Ahtar the Jailor [2/47]
Follower: Jordis the Sword-Maiden [3/47]
House for Sale: Proudspire Manor [1/5]
Marriage Prospect: Belrand [1/62]
Marriage Prospect: Sorex Vinius [2/62]
Marriage Prospect: Taarie [3/62]
Marriage Prospect: Jordis the Sword-Maiden [4/62]
Marriage Prospect: Octieve San [5/62]
Trader (Apothecary): Angeline Morrard [1/12]
Trader (Apothecary): Vivienne Onis [2/12]
Trader (Blacksmith): Beirand [1/33]
Trader (Carriage): Thaer [1/5]
Trader (Fence): Gulum-Ei [1/11] (after Thieves Guild Quest completion)
Trader (Fetcher): Fihada [1/3]
Trader (Food Vendor): Addvar [1/9]
Trader (Food Vendor): Jala [2/9]
Trader (Food Vendor): Evette San [3/9]
Trader (General Store Vendor): Endarie [1/19]
Trader (General Store Vendor): Sayma [3/19]
Trader (Innkeeper): Corpulus Vinius [1/15]
Trainer (Alteration: Journeyman): Melaran [1/3]
Trainer (Speech: Master): Giraud Gemane [1/4]
Trainer (Spell Vendor): Sybille Stentor [1/12]

Collectibles

Skill Book [Alchemy]: Song of the Alchemists [E1/10]
Skill Book [Archery]: The Gold Ribbon of Merit [C1/10]
Skill Book [Light Armor]: The Rear Guard [D1/10]
Skill Book [Light Armor]: The Refugees [E1/10]
Skill Book [Speech]: Biography of the Wolf Queen [D1/10]
Skill Book [Speech]: The Buying Game [E1/10]
Skill Book [Two-Handed]: Song of Hrormir [C1/10]
Unique Item: Asgeir's Wedding Band [1/112]
Unique Item: Vittoria's Wedding Band [2/112]
Unique Item: Shield of Solitude [3/112]
Unique Weapon: Headsman's Axe [1/80]
Unique Weapon: Firiniel's End [2/80]
Unusual Gem: [1/24]
Unusual Gem: [2/24]

Special Objects

Shrine of Akatosh [1/6]
Shrines of Arkay (2) [1/12; 2/12]
Shrine of Dibella [1/8]
Shrine of Julianos [1/5]
Shrine of Kynareth [1/6]
Shrine of Mara [1/5]
Shrine of Stendarr [1/5]
Shrine of Talos [1/17]
Shrine of Zenithar [1/5]
Business Ledgers
Civil War: Map of Skyrim
Chest(s)
Potions aplenty
Loose gear

Lore: City Overview

Solitude is the jewel of Imperial Skyrim. Ruled by Jarl Elisif the Fair, widow of the late High King, it is home to the headquarters of both the Legion and the Thalmor. Part of the reason for this is the eminently defensible nature of Solitude itself. Set upon a great stone arch that towers above the mouth of the Karth River, and surrounded by the soaring peaks of the Haafingar Mountains, Solitude is both a reinforced and breathtaking stronghold. Given the city's name, it may be ironic that over 80 percent of the Hold's population lives within Solitude's walls, but this is testament to the city's political importance, formidable defenses, and diverse population. The Bard's College is located here, as well as the sumptuous Blue Palace. Both are constructed atop the huge, natural arch that the city rests on, affording spectacular views over the Sea of Ghosts and Hjaalmarch to the east. Solitude's accessible docks and wharfs are in relatively calm waters, making trade one of the many reasons why the wealthiest Nords hail from this capital city. Solitude is the one, true cosmopolitan city of Skyrim.

Important Areas of Interest

① Lower Watchtower

Close to Katla's Farm and the Solitude Stables is a single watchtower at the base of the western (and main) entrance to Solitude. Thaer's carriage waits here for customers; you can take it to any other Hold City.

- Trader (Carriage): Thaer [1/5]

② Ma'dran's Caravan

When they aren't traveling, Ma'dran and his Khajiit brethren set up camp here. You can purchase a variety of wares from them. They also become Fences for you during the Thieves Guild Quests.

- Trader (Caravan Vendor): Ma'dran [19/19]
  - Weapons, Apparel, Potions, Food, Ingredients, Misc

③ Outer Gate

④ Main Gate

Market District

A variety of traders ply their wares in this southwestern district of the city. Aside from the traders, the marketplace is dominated by executioner's platform and the market stalls, which features a well said to be one of the oldest structures in Solitude.

A Main Gate: Exit to Skyrim

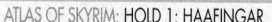

2 Swinging Wall Passage

Avoid the pressure plate on the ground in the center of this hall—take a side passage to avoid being impaled by a swinging wall of spikes. Slay a few more bandits and raid a chest at the hall's far end.

- ◊ Danger! Swinging Wall (pressure plate)
- ◊ Chest (Locked: Apprentice)

3 Lever Nook

Dispatch a couple of bandits at this dead end, then swipe a Skill Book off a shelf and unlock an Adept-level gate to access a lever that opens a secret passage in the nearby wall. Go through to discover some potions and a chest.

- ◊ Skill Book [Lockpicking]: Surfeit of Thieves
- ◊ Chest
- ◊ Potions

4 Dining Hall

A grotesque scene of a bloody Draugr splayed across an elegant dining table greets you here. Swipe a few potions from the shelves before entering the northern caverns to slay more bandits, score a few more potions, and loot some urns.

- ◊ Potions

5 Nordic Pillars Chamber

Gates slam shut as you enter the passage's end, trapping you near a sort of glyph puzzle and forcing you to solve it. The book on the pedestal provides clues as to the puzzle's solution. Activate the glyphs in the following order: Snake, Bear, Fox, Wolf. Don't miss the chest in the stairwell chamber beyond, and pull a lever before heading downstairs to open a secret passage. Explore the passage to reach a trapped room that features an urn and a few valuable potions.

- ◊ Danger! Battering Ram Trap (pressure plate)
- ◊ Chest
- ◊ Potions

B Door to Volskygge Passages

C Door to Volskygge

6 Lever Chamber

Pulling a lever in this quiet chamber opens a nearby holding cell, but there's no need to do so. Press onward and wipe out a Draugr so you may safely raid a chest in the next room. The chest is rigged with a trap hinge connected to the chest's left side. Unlock the hinge trap before opening the chest to avoid a dart trap.

- ◊ Chest

7 Trap Door Chambers

Avoid the pressure plate in the center of this odd chamber and avoid falling into the next room's central pit, or you'll have to take a dangerous Draugr-filled passage to the next chamber. Assuming you avoid the pitfall, look for the dead bandit next to a lever. This leads to a secret chamber with a chest and a health potion on a pedestal. Careful when grabbing the potion: it triggers a spear trap from the grate below.

- ◊ Danger! Swinging Blade Trap (pressure switch)
- ◊ Chest

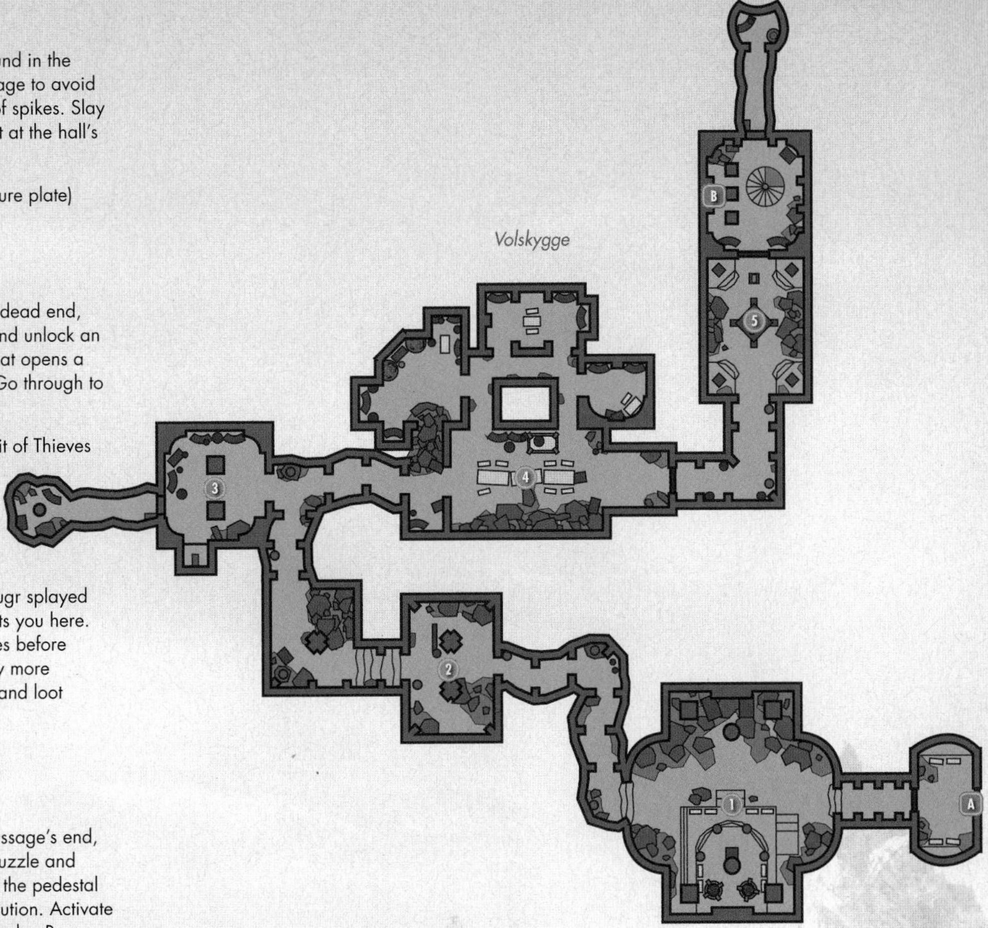

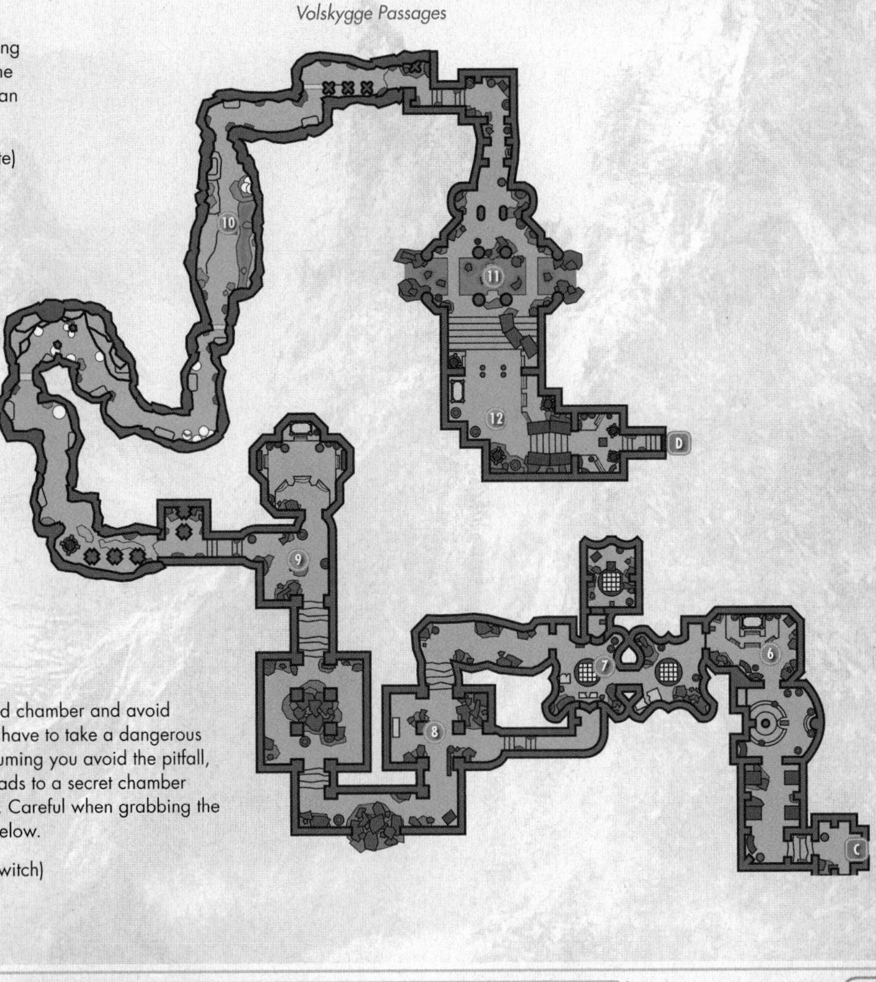

8 Burial Chamber

Loot the many urns and resting Draugr in this chamber, but beware the trap that's triggered by a central pressure plate. Don't miss the chest in the passage that follows, and beware a host of Dragur that ambush you on the way to [9].

- ◊ Danger! Swinging Wall (pressure plate)
- ◊ Chest (Locked: Apprentice)

9 Altar Chamber

A lone Draugr guards a quiet altar chamber here. Loot the many urns, then beware a battering ram trap as you scale the stairs that lead toward [10].

- ◊ Battering Ram Trap (pressure plate)
- ◊ Potion

10 Spider Passage

Slay a host of Frostbite Spiders and rip through thick webs on your way through this long, winding passage, harvesting ingredients from egg sacs as you go. Don't miss looting the chest or urns just before you arrive at [11].

- ◊ Chest

11 Brook Chamber

A gentle stream flows through this Draugr-filled chamber. Find a chest at one end of the brook along with an Orichalcum ore vein. Loot a few urns after laying the undead to rest here.

- ◊ Chest

12 Exit Chamber

Slay one final Draugr and loot several more urns and a large chest on your way out to the ruins' exterior peaks.

- ◊ Potions
- ◊ Loose gear

D Door to Volskygge Peak

Volskygge Peak

A mighty wizard named Volsung awaits you on the ruins' exterior peaks. Slay this powerful adversary to acquire the valuable gear that he owns, including a precious mask. Scale the nearby steps afterward to locate a Word Wall that bestows the Word of Power: Whirlwind.

- ◊ Dragon Priest Mask: Volsung [1/10]
- ◊ Word Wall: Whirlwind Sprint [1/2]
- ◊ Chest

[1.05] Steepfall Burrow and Lower Steepfall Burrow

Dungeon: Animal Den

Frost Troll
Ice Wolf

Collectibles

Skill Book [Destruction]: Mystery of Talara, v3 [C1/10]
Chest(s)

High in the northern peaks of Haafingar's central mountains lies the yawning mouth of a frozen cave. Steepfall Burrow also features a lower exit, which registers as a separate location on the world map. This connection can be exploited by travelers to facilitate their trek through Haafingar's treacherous mountains.

Upper Troll Cave

Beware when crossing the cavern's natural footbridge—it's a long way down. Attack the dangerous Frost Troll from range and see if you can knock the beast into the abyss for an easier kill (trolls carry little of value). Slay another troll in the far cave, then loot the chest in the nearby fissure for valuables. Don't miss the Skill Book by the skeleton.

- ◊ Skill Book [Destruction]: Mystery of Talara, v3 [C1/10]
- ◊ Chest

Lower Wolves' Lair

If you're feeling daring, drop from the natural footbridge and plummet into the icy water far below. The fall won't harm you, and you can potentially unlock a sunken chest down below for even more loot. To escape the watery cavern, search for an underwater passage to the west, which lies just below the waterline—this will lead you to an Ice Wolf lair, where another chest is located. Loot the wolves' lair and then step outside via the burrow's lower exit.

- ◊ Chest
- ◊ Chest (Locked: Apprentice)

[1.06] Lost Echo Cave

Recommended Level: 8

Dungeon: Falmer Hive

Animal
Falmer

Collectibles

Skill Book [One-Handed]: 2920, Morning Star, v1 [A2/10]
Chest(s)
Potions
Loose gear

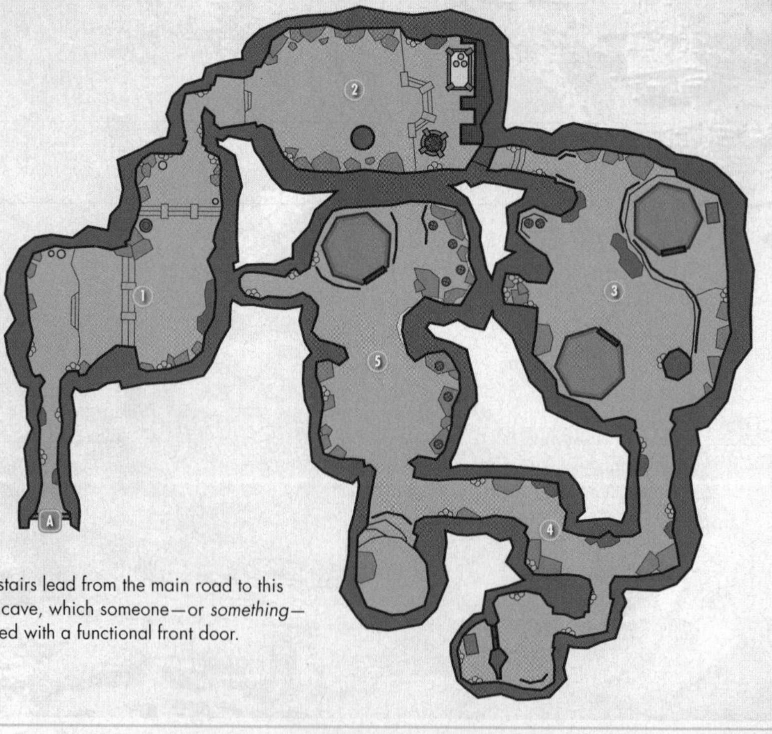

Wooden stairs lead from the main road to this mountain cave, which someone—or *something*—has outfitted with a functional front door.

Hold 3: The Pale

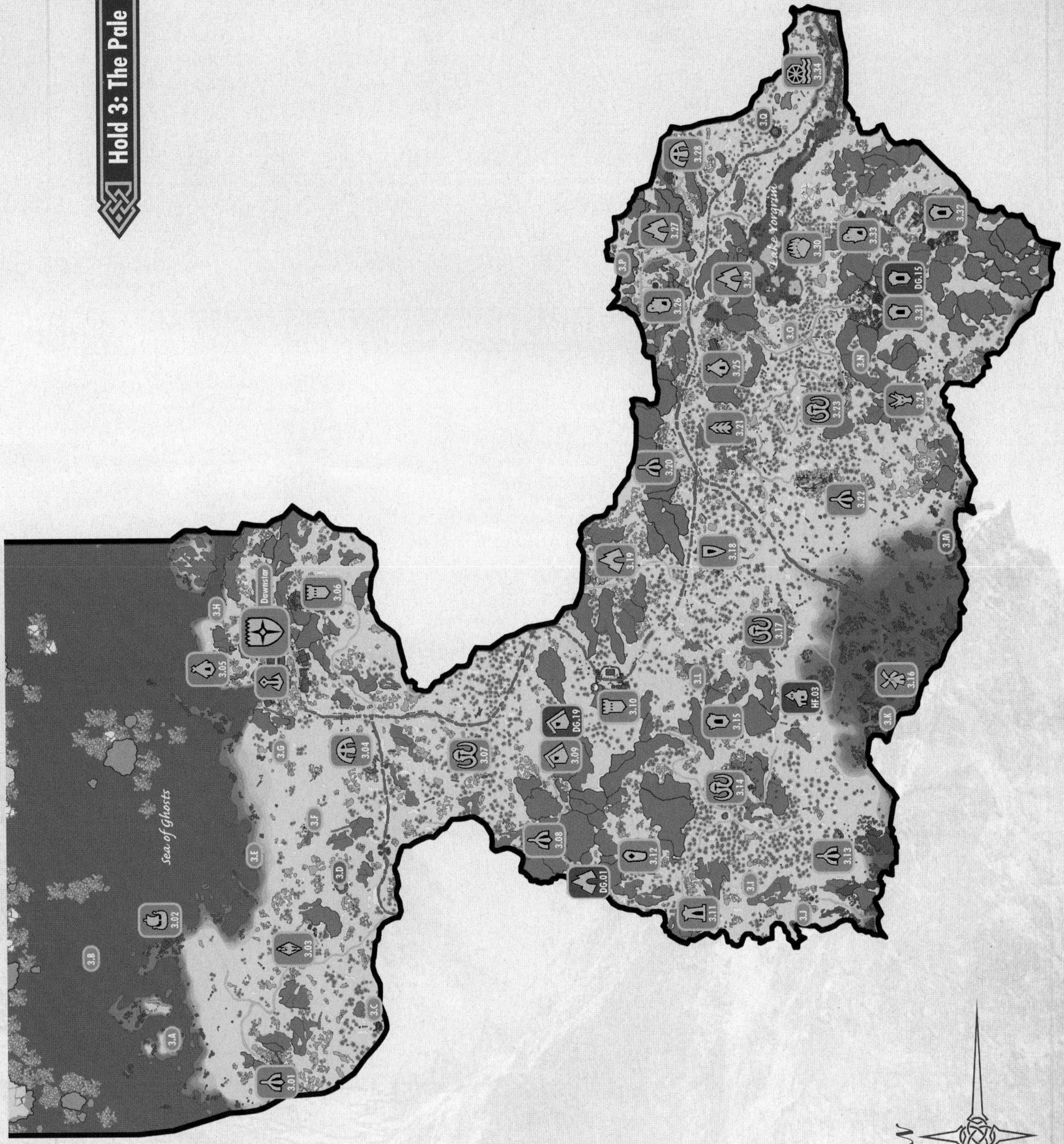

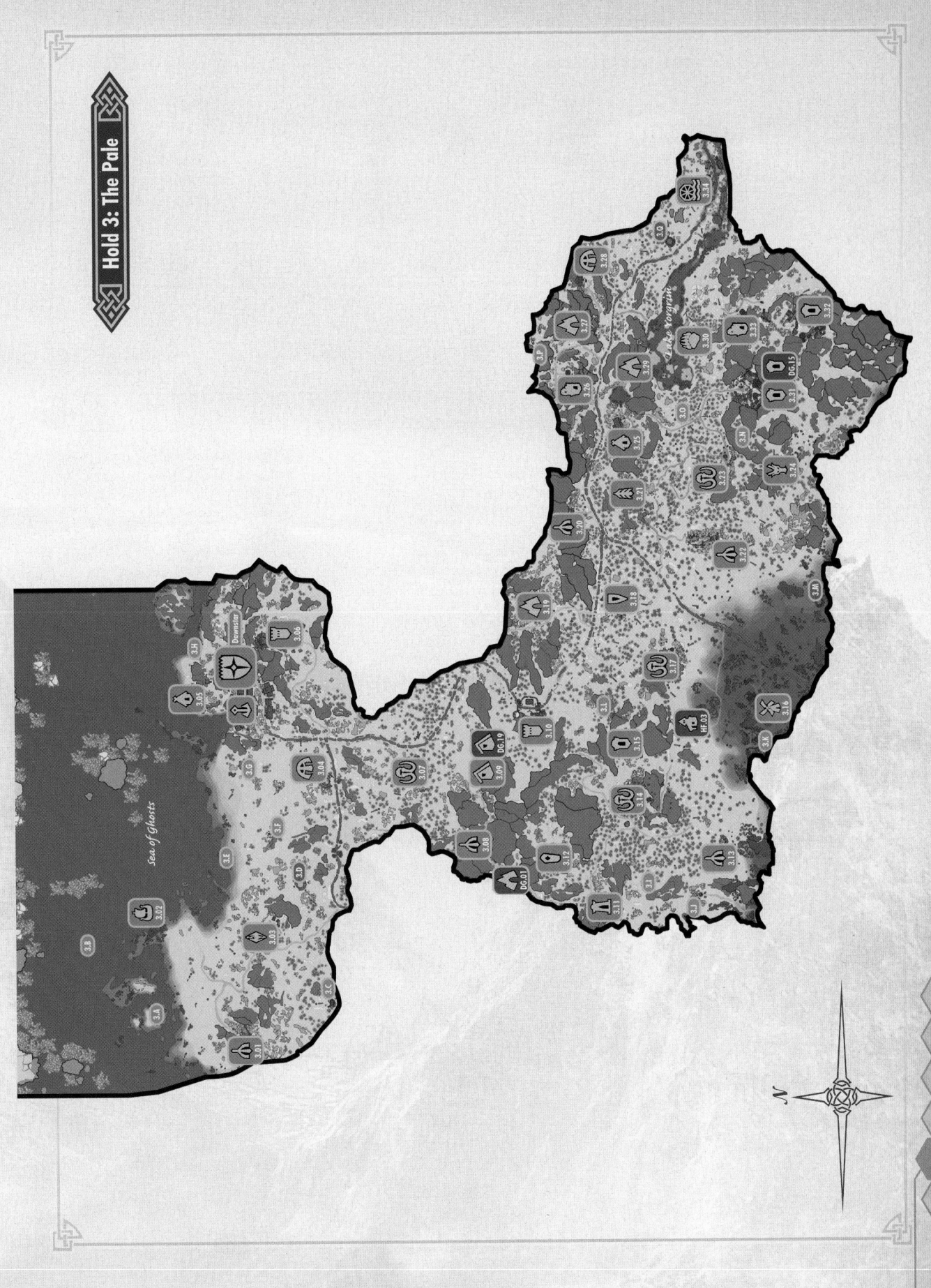

PRIMARY LOCATIONS

Total—35: Hold Capital and 34 Hold Locations

- [3.00] Hold Capital City: Dawnstar
  Jarl: Skald the Elder
- [3.01] High Gate Ruins
- [3.02] Wreck of the Brinehammer
- [3.03] Pale Imperial Camp
- [3.04] Windward Ruins
- [3.05] Dawnstar Sanctuary
- [3.06] Nightcaller Temple
- [3.07] Red Road Pass
- [3.08] Frostmere Crypt
- [3.09] Hall of the Vigilant
- [3.10] Fort Dunstad
- [3.11] Shrine of Mehrunes Dagon
- [3.12] The Lord Stone
- [3.13] Volunruud
- [3.14] Stonehill Bluff
- [3.15] Tower of Mzark
- [3.16] Loreius Farm
- [3.17] Blizzard Rest
- [3.18] Weynon Stones
- [3.19] Duskglow Crevice
- [3.20] Silverdrift Lair
- [3.21] Shrouded Grove
- [3.22] Korvanjund
- [3.23] Tumble Arch Pass
- [3.24] Shearpoint
- [3.25] Nightgate Inn
- [3.26] Blackreach Elevator (Alftand)
- [3.27] Forsaken Cave
- [3.28] Yorgrim Overlook
- [3.29] Bronze Water Cave
- [3.30] Pale Stormcloak Camp
- [3.31] Irkngthand
- [3.32] Raldbthar
- [3.33] Blackreach Elevator (Raldbthar)
- [3.34] Anga's Mill

SECONDARY LOCATIONS

Total—17 Points of Interest

- [3.A] Horker Standing Stones
- [3.B] Sunken Treasures
- [3.C] Bandit's Hovel
- [3.D] Dragon Mound: Sea Shore Foothills
- [3.E] Barnacle Boat
- [3.F] Shoreline Bandit Camp
- [3.G] Dawnstar Frost Troll Den
- [3.H] Shoreline Lovers' Tent
- [3.I] A Bloody Trail
- [3.J] Border Corner: Roadside Shrine of Mara
- [3.K] Mammoth Graveyard
- [3.L] Ice Shard Wild Animal Den
- [3.M] Dragon Mound: Shimmermist Hills
- [3.N] Julianos's Fallen
- [3.O] Yorgrim Forest Spider Trap
- [3.P] Wayward Peak Summit
- [3.Q] Dragon Mound: Yorgrim Resurrection

ADDITIONAL LOCATIONS

[DG.01] Dimhollow Crypt (see page 770)
[DG.15] Raldbthar (Updated) (see page 766)
[DG.19] Hall of the Vigilant (Updated) (see page 755)
[HF.03] Heljarchen Hall (see page 772)

HOLD CAPITAL: DAWNSTAR

Related Quests

Civil War Quest: Reunification of Skyrim
Civil War Quest: A False Front
Daedric Quest: Pieces of the Past
Daedric Quest: Waking Nightmare
Side Quest: Rise in the East
Dark Brotherhood Quest: Side Contract: Beitild
Miscellaneous Objective: Innkeeper Rumors (Windpeak Inn)
Miscellaneous Objective: Salt of the Seas* (Captain Leif Wayfinder)
Favor (Activity): Mining Ore* (Beitild)
Favor (Activity): Mining Ore* (Leigelf)
Favor (Activity): A Drunk's Drink* (Karl)
Favor: Rare Item Hunt* (Rustleif)
Favor: Item Retrieval (Cave)* (Frida)
Favor: Jobs for the Jarls* (Jarl Skald the Elder)
Thane Quest: Thane of The Pale*

Habitation: Hold Capital (Minor)

Crafting

Alchemy Lab
Arcane Enchanter
Blacksmith Forge
Grindstone
Smelters (2)
Tanning Rack

Services

Trader (Apothecary): Frida [4/14]
Trader (Blacksmith): Rustleif [5/33]
Trader (Blacksmith): Seren [6/33]
Trader (Innkeeper): Thoring [4/18]
Trader (Spells Vendor): Madena [3/12]

Special Objects

Civil War: Map of Skyrim

Collectibles

Skill Book [Conjuration]: 2920, Hearth Fire, v9 [B2/10]
Skill Book [Destruction]: Response to Bero's Speech [D1/10]
Skill Book [Destruction]: The Art of War Magic [E2/10]
Skill Book [Enchanting]: Catalogue of Weapon Enchantments [C1/10]
Skill Book [Lockpicking]: The Wolf Queen, v1 [E1/10]
Skill Book [Smithing]: Cherim's Heart [A1/10]
Chest(s)
Potions aplenty
Loose gear
Mineable ore (Iron, Quicksilver)

Lore: City Overview

Dawnstar, capital of the Pale Hold, sits on Skyrim's northern coastline, halfway between Winterhold and Solitude. Because of the glacial icefields just to the east, it is the last port before Windhelm that is not icebound. Dawnstar's economy is driven by its two mines, and the people of Dawnstar often find meaning in the stones. Like their leader, Jarl Skald the Elder, they stand unbreakable and firm despite all their troubles. Residents of the city fight the weather, the beasts, and raiders every day in order to keep goods and ore flowing into and out of their port and market.

Important Areas of Interest

1 Main Thoroughfare

The main road (packed with snow and dirt) is in two tiers, with the structures built around the inlet to the Sea of Ghosts. The upper track houses the main structures, while the lower road connects all the buildings owned by individuals. East and west of the roadways are the two mines that help bolster Dawnstar's economy. To the north, farther along the shoreline, is the entrance to an old, abandoned sanctuary. Dominating the town is the Nightcaller Temple, perched and ever watching over the rugged rocks.

2 Northstar Port (and the Sea Squall)

Captain Lief Wayfinder

Located at the base of the cliffs under the Nightcaller Temple, these docks host incoming trade ships. The vessel currently docked in these frigid waters is the Sea Squall.

Harlaug (Ferryman) [2/3]

3 The White Hall

The following leaders of Dawnstar are loyal to the Stormcloaks at the start of the Civil War.

Jarl Skald the Elder

Skald has ruled Dawnstar since his father's death on the battlefield 35 years ago. He came into his rule in his teenage years and has never really lost the arrogance and sense of invincibility that comes with that age. He is quick to judge and doesn't change his mind once he has decided something.

Jod (Housecarl)

Jod is Captain of the Dawnstar's Guard. He takes his duty and his loyalty to the town seriously. He served on a ship in the Great War, and because of his experiences, he is not anxious to fight the Empire. Skald's fervent animosity toward the Empire has made Jod doubt him.

Bulfrek

Bulfrek's family has served the Jarls of Dawnstar for generations. He is not pleased with being born into a life that he considers to be without honor. Although he would never speak it out loud, he would do almost anything to be free of his duty.

Madena (Court Wizard)

Madena is far from home. She is a Breton who served as a battle-mage in the Imperial Legion during the Great War. After seeing the horrors of a large war firsthand, she moved to Dawnstar, hoping that being a court mage in a small hold would be free of complication. She refuses to take sides, insisting that her job is to help the people of Dawnstar. She will support whoever is in power.

Frorkmar Banner-Torn

The following residents of Dawnstar arrive to take control of the capital, once this Hold has fallen during the Civil War.

Jarl Brina Merilis

Brina was once renowned throughout the Legion for her leadership and her tactical ability. She is a stern woman who tolerates no foolishness from those under her command. She does have a warm side that sometimes shows through, although it is rarely seen since the start of the war.

Horik Halfhand (Housecarl)

Horik has served with Brina nearly his whole life. With no command ambitions of his own, he is content to serve as her bodyguard. Horik has nothing but respect and admiration for his commander, and there are few things that would shake his loyalty to her.

The White Hall keep serves as both the Jarl's residence and the place where he holds court. The keep's main feature is the large combined throne room, mead hall, and council chamber that dominates the largest portion of the main floor. To the right are the Jarl's Bedchambers, while Madena, the Jarl's advisor (and excellent spell vendor), resides on the upper floor, along with his manservant Bulfrek. Madena's spell shop has been partly turned over to the Stormcloaks as a war room, with the blessing of Jarl Skald. Find a Skill Book on a small table upstairs and another tucked between a barrel and pony keg in the room with the training dummy.

- Crafting: Arcane Enchanter
- Trader (Spells Vendor): Madena [3/12]
  - Scrolls, Books, Misc
- Skill Book [Destruction]: The Art of War Magic [E2/10]
- Skill Book [Enchanting]: Catalogue of Weapon Enchantments [C1/10]
- Civil War: Map of Skyrim
- Chest
- Potions aplenty

4 Dawnstar Barracks

Jarl Skald's guards rest here after their patrols, murmuring about the nightmares all the inhabitants are suffering from. The Barracks has a main floor (where most of the drinking occurs) and an upper sleeping quarters leading to a balcony overlooking the shoreline. Down the stairs is the Dawnstar Jail. Remarkably, a Skill Book is tucked away in one corner of the jail.

- Skill Book [Lockpicking]: The Wolf Queen, v1 [E1/10]
- Evidence Chest
- Prisoner Belongings Chest
- Chest (3)
- Potions aplenty
- Loose gear

5 Windpeak Inn

Alesan
Thoring
Karita
Stig Salt-Plank
Erandur

Windpeak Inn is Dawnstar's only tavern and is run by Thoring and his young daughter Karita, who both live in the building. Karita serves as a bard, and their servant Abelone handles most of the menial chores, chopping wood or using the grindstone in the pen outside. Currently, the place is a meeting spot where anxious townsfolk (such as Fruki and Irgnir the miners) gather to gossip and worry about the strange nightmares that have been keeping them from their beds.

- Crafting: Grindstone
- Trader (Innkeeper): Thoring [4/15]
  - Room for the Night, Food, Innkeeper Rumors
- Chest (2)

6 Rustleif's House

Rustleif
Seren

Located overlooking the shoreline of Dawnstar, Rustleif has his smithy and home set up facing the main road. Rustleif is a renowned weaponsmith, and he is often called upon to arm and outfit the Jarl's men. His Redguard wife, Seren, assists him and is currently with child. Inside, their home is comfortable but a little spartan.

- Crafting: Blacksmith Forge, Tanning Rack
- Trader (Blacksmith): Rustleif [5/33]
  - Weapons, Apparel, and Misc
- Trader (Blacksmith): Seren [6/33]
  - Weapons, Apparel, and Misc.
- Chest

⑦ Leigelf's House

Leigelf Quicksilver

Because Leigelf manages Quicksilver Mine and spends most of his time obsessing about his work and his wife, his living arrangements are somewhat sparse.

- Chest

⑧ Brina's House

Brina (a respected Legion commander) retired to Dawnstar and has been living here for several years. She shares her dwelling with her bodyguard and friend Horik. Recently, when the Jarl of Dawnstar seceded from the Empire, she attempted to talk sense into him, but to no avail. Inside, their dwelling is where they sleep (in separate beds) and collect (rather than consume) a large amount of wine. Search the basket near the chest to discover a hidden Skill Book.

- Skill Book [One-Handed]: The Importance of Where
- Chest (2)

⑨ The Mortar and Pestle

Frida

The old widow Frida runs her modest alchemy shop from this building on the main road. A Skill Book is kept behind the counter.

- Crafting: Alchemy Lab
- Trader (Apothecary): Frida [3/12]
  - Potions, Food, Ingredients
- Skill Book [Conjuration]: 2920, Hearth Fire, v9 [B2/10]
- Unique Item: Ring of Pure Mixtures
- Chest (2)
- Potions aplenty

⑩ Beitild's House

Beitild Iron-Breaker

Beitild Iron-Breaker manages Iron-Breaker Mine. She's in constant competition with Leigelf Quicksilver, the owner of Quicksilver Mine and her former husband. Beitild lives in the house she used to share with her husband. She refuses to do much else but tend to her mine, eat, and sleep.

- Chest

⑪ Silus Vesuius's House (Locked: Requires Key)

Silus Vesuius

Also known as the Museum of the Mythic Dawn, the building is dedicated to the cult in Dawnstar. This is Silus's vain attempt to capture some attention and infamy for his family's past deeds. The pride of the collection is his impressive assortment of Mythic Dawn memorabilia, as well as a piece of Mehrunes' Razor that is kept in a secured display case. This building is only accessible once Daedric Quest: Pieces of the Past begins.

- Mehrunes' Razor Scabbard
- Mythic Dawn Commentaries 1, 2, 3, 4
- Mysterium Xarxes (Fragment; cannot be taken)
- Mythic Dawn Boots, Gloves, and Robes
- The Keepers of the Razor

⑫ Irgnir's House

Irgnir

Karl

Karl and Irgnir, the workers of Iron-Breaker Mine, live here in this modest dwelling. They have finally saved up enough gold to purchase from Beitild. They sometimes board with Gjak and Bodil, who take the other shifts to keep the mine constantly productive.

- Chest

⑬ Iron-Breaker Mine

This mine is located on the outskirts of town to the east. Karl, Irgnir, Gjak, and Bodil work here. This mine produces iron and has a smelter for extracting steel from the iron. Under the watchful (some might say, stern and overbearing) gaze of Beitild, the mine is producing a large amount of ore and is a boon to the local economy. Find a Skill Book resting atop a barrel near the firepit.

- Crafting: Smelter
- Skill Book [Destruction]: Response to Bero's Speech [D1/10]
- Mineable ore (Iron)

⑭ Fruki's House

Fruki

Lond Northstrider

Fruki and Lond, the miners working the Quicksilver veins, live here in this small structure in which Fruki was raised. They occasionally speak with Borgny and Edith, who take the other shifts to keep the mine productive—when Leigelf isn't running the operation into the ground.

- Chest

⑮ Quicksilver Mine

This mine is located on the outskirts of town to the west. Fruki, Lond, Borgny, and Edith work here. This is the only Quicksilver mine inside Skyrim's borders, but despite this, the mine is suffering—from marauders and falling production. In fact, it is practically shut down as Leigelf spends his time obsessing over his wife and the competing mine. More proud than sensible, Leigelf's negligence is causing all of his workers to consider quitting in frustration or fear of attack. The mine holds a Skill Book. Find it inside the small crate on the ground floor of the farthest cavern.

- Crafting: Smelter
- Skill Book [Smithing]: Cherim's Heart [A1/10]
- Mineable ore (Quicksilver)

[3.01] High Gate Ruins

Related Quests
- Side Quest: Masks of the Dragon Priests*
- Dungeon Quest: A Scroll for Anska

Recommended Level: 24

Dungeon: Dragon Priest Lair
- Anska
- Draugr
- Vokun

Dangers
- Dart Trap (pressure plates)
- Spear Trap (pressure plate)
- Swinging Spikes (pressure plates)

Quest Items
- Sealed Scroll

Collectibles
- Dragon Priest Mask: Vokun [5/10]
- Skill Book [Destruction]: A Hypothetical Treachery [A1/10]

Special Objects
- Word Wall: Storm Call [1/3]
- Chest(s)
- Potions aplenty
- Loose gear

High Gate Ruins

High Gate ruins is an old Draugr ruin inhabited by the Dragon Priest Vokun, wearer of the Iron Mask. The plucky adventurer and powerful Fire Mage Anska has already begun making her way toward Vokun's treasure, where she believes she will find a scroll tying her family's history to Ysgramor's.

A Exit to Skyrim

E Door to Vokun's Throne Room

1 Anska Encounter

Loot a few Draugr corpses on your way into this small chamber, where you encounter a woman named Anska. Speak with her to begin a new Side Quest that takes place in these ruins. Anska then assists you in clearing this dreary place.

2 Sacrificial Chamber

Slay a few Draugr in this large chamber, then raid the far chest and surrounding urns. Head upstairs and claim a number of potions from the balcony, along with a Skill Book that lies next to a skeleton in a dark corner. Don't miss looting another chest at the balcony's far end.

- ◊ Skill Book [Destruction]: A Hypothetical Treachery [A1/10]
- ◊ Chest (2)
- ◊ Potions aplentyv

3 Potion Room

Slay a group of Draugr on the way to this next chamber, which holds several more potions.

- ◊ Potions aplenty
- ◊ Loose gear

4 Stairwell Chamber

Sidestep a pressure plate trap in the passage that leads to this chamber. Look at the ceiling to find the pattern in which you must pull this chamber's four levers to open the central stairwell and descend to the catacombs below.

- ◊ Danger! Swinging Spikes (pressure plate)
- ◊ Potions

B Door to High Gate Ruins Catacombs

High Gate Ruins Catacombs

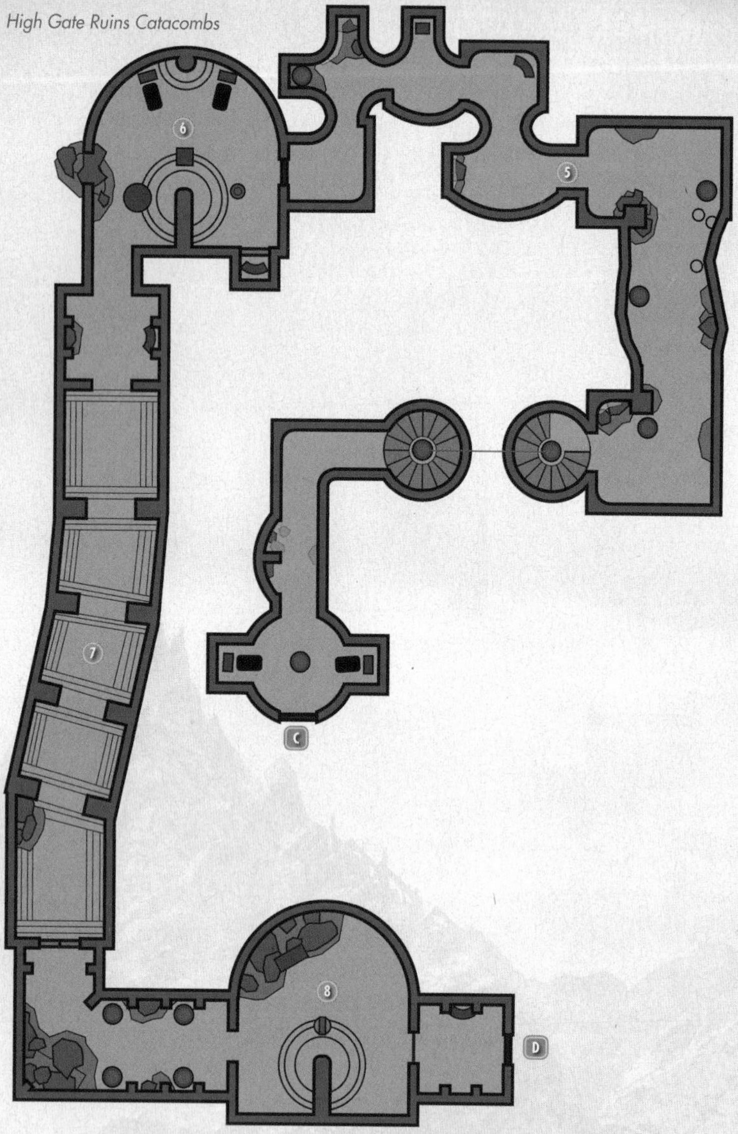

C Door to High Gate Ruins

5 Draugr Tunnels

Leap over a pressure plate that lies directly in a doorway in these passages—you'll be punctured by arrows if you touch it. Open the chest along the northernmost stretch without getting too close; you'll be impaled by spears if you touch the pressure plate on the ground near the chest.

- Danger! Dart Trap (pressure plate), Spear Trap (pressure plate)
- Chest
- Potions
- Loose gear

6 Treasure Room

After slaying this cavern's resident undead, open an Adept-level door to access a tiny closet with a chest. Removing the Soul Gem from the central pedestal causes two additional Draugr to emerge from the coffins behind you.

- Chest
- Loose gear

7 Trapped Passage

Avoid a myriad of pressure plates in this wide corridor—each one triggers a lethal trap.

- Danger! Dart Trap (pressure plates), Spear Trap (pressure plates)
- Potions

8 Lever Chamber

Slay a lone Draugr here, then pull the lever in the nearby alcove to open aonther small nook, freeing a powerful Draugr that quickly attacks. Pull the lever in the other nook to open the way to the throne room. The central lever can be ignored.

- Potions aplenty
- Loose gear

D Door to Vokun's Throne Room

Vokun's Throne Room

The doors swing open as you enter this wide chamber, and a demonic apparition rises from the central sarcophagus. It's Vokun. Slay the deadly Dragon Priest and collect his powerful mask, then head to the back room to locate a Word Wall. Open two chests along the upstairs balcony and loot a number of urns before claiming the scroll that Anska seeks from the central table. Take the upstairs passage back to the ruin's entrance and return the scroll to Anska, who now awaits you just outside.

- Dragon Priest Mask: Vokun [5/10]
- Word Wall: Storm Call [1/3]
- Sealed Scroll
- Chests (2)

[3.02] The Wreck of the *Brinehammer*

Recommended Level: 6

Dungeon: Shipwreck

Mudcrab

Collectibles

Skill Book [Archery]: Father of the Niben [A1/10]

Special Objects

Shrine of Kynareth [3/6]

Chest(s)

A merchant vessel called the *Brinehammer* has crashed along the Pale's brutal northern shoreline. Before heading below deck, enter the captain's quarters, where a chest and the remains of the captain await plundering.

- Captain Slaughterfish's Key (Captain Slaughterfish)
- Chest

Below Deck

Slay the odd Mudcrab as you scour the *Brinehammer*'s belly—the only items of interest are a chest near the vessel's center and the shrine that's nearby. There's no need to unlock the Novice-level door; you can simply circumvent it. Head down to the cargo hold after looting the chest. The north door to the cargo hold is unlocked as well.

- Shrine of Kynareth [3/6]
- Chest

Cargo Hold

Open the hold's locked chest and collect the nearby Skill Book, then dive underwater and find another locked chest that's sunken beneath the ship.

- Skill Book [Archery]: Father of the Niben [A1/10]
- Chests (Locked: Adept) (2)

[3.03] Pale Imperial Camp

Related Quests

Civil War Quest: Reunification of Skyrim
Civil War Quest: A False Front
Civil War Quest: The Battle for Fort Dunstad
Dungeon Activity

Habitation: Military: Imperial Camp

Imperial Quartermaster (Blacksmith)
Imperial Soldier
Legate Constantius Tituleius

Services

Trader (Blacksmith): Imperial Quartermaster [7/33]
Weapons, Apparel, Misc

Crafting

Anvil
Grindstone
Workbench

Special Objects

Civil War: Map of Skyrim
Chest(s)
Loose gear

This small military camp stands against the harshness of the Pale's frozen northern wastelands. Trade with the quartermaster, or use his many crafting workstations. Examine the map in the largest tent to potentially gain new map data. Loot a few chests within the smaller tents if you like before setting off.

[3.04] Windward Ruins

Related Quests

Side Quest: Kyne's Sacred Trials
College of Winterhold Radiant Quest: Destruction Ritual Spell

Recommended Level: 5

Dungeon: Animal Den

Animal
Chest (Locked: Adept)

A pair of lowly Skeevers guard this small collection of ruins. Head inside the small domed structure and utilize the pedestal in the back to advance the Destruction Ritual Spell Quest. Plunder the chest that's tucked away among rocks in the ruins' outer ring.

[3.05] Dawnstar Sanctuary

Related Quests

Dark Brotherhood Quest: The Cure for Madness
Dark Brotherhood Quest: Where You Hang Your Enemy's Head...
Dark Brotherhood Quest: Welcome to the Brotherhood
Dark Brotherhood Quest: Cicero's Return*
Dark Brotherhood Quest: The Dark Brotherhood Forever!
Dark Brotherhood Quest: The Torturer's Treasure: Parts I, II, III, IV*

Recommended Level: 8

Dungeon: Special/Habitation: Special

Cicero
Sanctuary Guardian
Udefrykte (Troll)

Services

Follower: Cicero [6/47]
Follower: Dark Brotherhood Initiate [7/47]

Dangers

Bear Traps
Oil Pool Trap
Spear Trap (proximity)

Collectibles

Skill Book [Alteration]: Sithis
Skill Book [Archery]: The Marksmanship Lesson [D1/10]
Skill Book [One Handed]: Fire and Darkness
Skill Book [Sneak]: Sacred Witness
Unique Item:Jester's Boots [10/112]
Unique Item:Jester's Clothes [11/112]
Unique Item:Jester's Gloves [12/112]
Unique Item:Jester's Hat [13/112]
Unique Item:Cicero'sBoots [14/112]
Unique Item:Cicero'sClothes [15/112]
Unique Item:Cicero'sGloves [16/112]
Unique Item:Cicero'sHat [17/112]
Unique Item:Worn Shrouded Armor [18/112]
Unique Item:Worn Shrouded Boots[19/112]
Unique Item:Worn Shrouded Cowl [20/112]
Unique Item:Worn Shrouded Gloves [21/112]
Unique Item:Tumblerbane Gloves[22/112]
Area Is Locked (quest required)
Chest(s)
Potions
Loose gear

Explore the coastline north of Dawnstar to discover an ominous door built into the rock face. This is the entrance to Dawnstar Sanctuary, which you cannot enter until you've advanced to Dark Brotherhood Quest: The Cure for Madness, during which you must chase a wounded person through this trap-filled place. The Dark Brotherhood eventually moves their hideout here after you complete their quest line.

A Exit to Skyrim

1 Training Chamber

Swipe a Sneak Skill Book off a small table on your way to this tall, circular chamber. Before maneuvering past the stabbing spears (Whirlwind Sprint may help), knock down two hanging lamps to ignite the oily floor below and singe a pair of Sanctuary Guardians. Get past the spears and then go downstairs to find a pair of Skill Books. Another book on a nearby shelf can potentially grant you a new quest.

- ◊ Danger! Oil Pool Traps, Spear Trap (proximity)
- ◊ Skill Book [Archery]: The Marksmanship Lesson [D1/10]
- ◊ Skill Book [One Handed]: Fire and Darkness
- ◊ Skill Book [Sneak]: Sacred Witness
- ◊ Potions
- ◊ Loose gear

2 No Access

These rooms are blocked by rubble until the Dark Brotherhood takes over the Dawnstar Sanctuary and removes the debris.

3 North Entry Hall

Moving through the training chamber lets you explore the north half of the sanctuary's entry hall. This section of the sanctuary has given way to the ravages of time. Collect a Skill Book from a shelf near the circular stained-glass window before proceeding into the snowy tunnel on your way to [4].

- ◊ Skill Book [Alteration]: Sithis
- ◊ Loose gear

4 Udefrykte's Lair

Dodge bear traps as you navigate the frigid tunnel, which leads to the den of an ill-tempered troll named Udefrykte. Raid a chest on a high ledge here as you continue to the trail of blood toward your quarry.

- ◊ Chest

5 Coffin Corridors

Slay a number of Sanctuary Guardians as you navigate this long passage. If you're skilled enough, loot the large locked chest in the southern nook as you go.

- ◊ Chest (Locked: Master)

6 Torture Chamber

Don't worry if you couldn't open that last chest—this gruesome chamber contains another. Unbar the nearby door to find yourself back at [3], your exploration of the Sanctuary complete. During Dark Brotherhood Quest: The Cure for Madness, you face Cicero here.

- ◊ Chest

Post–Dark Brotherhood Occupation

The Dark Brotherhood repurposes Dawnstar Sanctuary for their own base of operations after you complete the entire Dark Brotherhood quest line. Naturally, the place is much different after the Brotherhood moves in:

During Dark Brotherhood: Where You Hang Your Enemy's Head..., you can purchase New Banners (1,000 gold), a Poisoner's Nook (5,000 gold), a Torture Chamber (5,000), a Secret Entrance (5,000) that can be accessed from the hills above the Sanctuary, and a Master Bedroom (3,000 gold). All are bought from Delvin Mallory of the Thieves Guild, inside the Ragged Flagon in Riften.

During Dark Brotherhood: Welcome to the Brotherhood, Nazir has an initiate recruited for you.

- ◊ Follower: Dark Brotherhood Initiate [7/47]

During Dark Brotherhood: Cicero's Return,* you can elect to keep Cicero as a companion.

- ◊ Follower: Cicero [6/47]

During Dark Brotherhood: The Dark Brotherhood Forever!, you receive assassination orders from the Night Mother, who is also ensconced in these new surroundings.

During Dark Brotherhood: The Torturer's Treasure: Parts I, II, III, IV,* providing you've had the Torture Chamber installed, you can torture victims until they reveal the location of their treasure.

[3.06] Nightcaller Temple

Related Quests

Daedric Quest: Waking Nightmare
Dungeon Activity

Recommended Level: 18

Dungeon: Falmer Hive

Animal
Orcish Invader
Thorek
Vaermina Devotee
Veren Duleri

Services

Follower: Erandur [8/47]

Crafting

Alchemy Labs (3)
Arcane Enchanter

Quest Items

The Dreamscape
Skull of Corruption
Vaermina's Torpor

Collectibles

Skill Book [Alchemy]: Mannimaro, King of Worms [D1/10]
Unique Weapon: Skull of Corruption [12/80]

Special Objects

Shrine of Mara [2/5]
Area Is Locked (quest required)
Chest(s)
Potions aplenty
Loose gear

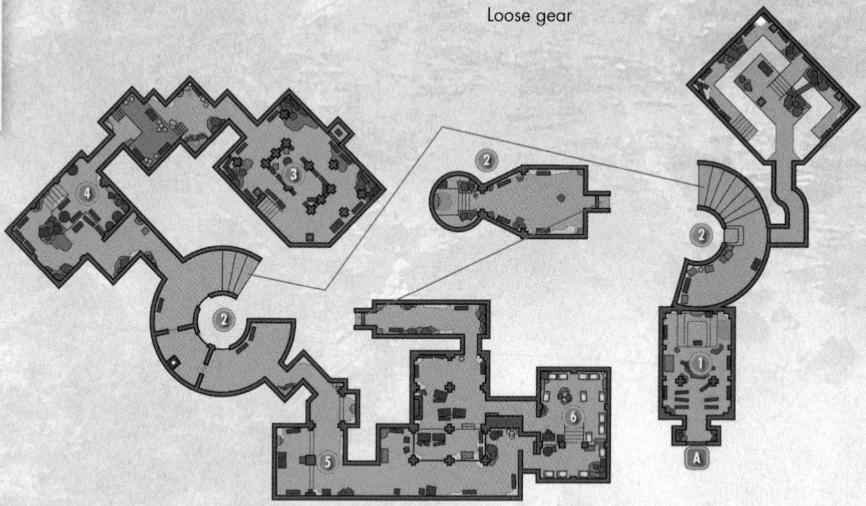

Just southeast of the Pale's capital city of Dawnstar, the single tower of an ancient temple rises up from the frozen rock. You visit this temple with Erandur as part of Daedric Quest: Waking Nightmare, hoping to solve the mystery of why Dawnstar's townsfolk have been suffering nightmares. Slay the beasts that guard the temple's entrance, then head inside.

A Exit to Skyrim

1 Shrine Chamber

The temple's entry chamber features a small shrine that instantly cures you of all diseases when touched. When you visit the temple as part of the "Waking Nightmare" quest, Erandur will open the way forward, allowing you to explore beyond this first room.

- Shrine of Mara [2/5]
- Chest (Locked: Novice)

2 Inner Sanctum

The Skull of Corruption is located here, which Erandur insists you must destroy to end the townsfolk's nightmares. Follow Erandur downstairs and slay the Orcish Invaders that awaken and attack. A barrier halts your progress; follow Erandur back upstairs and into the library.

- Skull of Corruption

3 Library

The library is in a terrible state. Cross a fallen pillar to locate a unique tome entitled *The Dreamstride*, which Erandur seeks.

- The Dreamstride

4 Laboratory

Secure the lab, then find a Skill Book near one of its three Alchemy Lab stations. Find the potion you seek downstairs, then speak to Erandur to advance the quest. Drink the potion to be whisked away to a vision of the past.

- Crafting: Alchemy Labs (3)
- Skill Book [Alchemy]: Mannimarco, King of Worms [D1/10]
- Vaermina's Torpor
- Apothecary's Satchels (2)
- Potions

Torpor Tantrum

After drinking Vaermina's Torpor, you must race through these rooms and passages to locate your objective: the Miasma release controls. At the end of the passage, pull the chain to release the Miasma and awaken from the dream.

- Potions aplenty
- Loose gear

2 Inner Sanctum Revisited

You emerge from the Torpor's effects back at the inner sanctum. Somehow you've gotten past the barriers. Take the Soul Gem that feeds them to deactivate the obstacles so that Erandur may join you. Follow Erandur to [5].

5 Passage to Sleeping Quarters

Use an Arcane Encanter and loot a chest as you navigate this passage.

- Crafting: Arcane Enchanter
- Chest
- Potions

6 Sleeping Quarters

Loot a chest on the balcony as you enter this room, and find another down below, near the stairs. Grab potions off a table and find more in the dining room that follows.

- Chest
- Chest (Locked: Adept)
- Potions
- Loose gear

2 Inner Sanctum, Third Visit

At last, you've reached the Skull of Corruption. Slay the final pair of priests after their brief chat with Erandur, then loot a large chest that's tucked away near the Skull's platform as your partner begins his ritual. A voice urges you to slay Erandur before the ritual is complete. If you do, the Skull of Corruption, an incredibly powerful and valuable staff, will be yours. Allowing Erandur to complete his ritual destroys the Skull and earns you Erandur's services as a follower.

- Unique Weapon: Skull of Corruption [12/80]
- Chest

[3.07] Red Road Pass

Dungeon: Giant Camp

Giant
Mammoth

In the northern section of the Pale, along the main road that runs between the east and west mountains, a giant has made camp. Bandits may attack this giant camp as you draw near. If this occurs, allow the conflict to play out, then slay the weakened victor (usually the giant) to claim some worthy plunder from the giant and the surrounding corpses.

[3.08] Frostmere Crypt

Related Quests

Dungeon Quest: The Pale Lady

Recommended Level: 6

Dungeon: Bandit Camp

Bandit
Eisa Blackthorn
Kyr
Ra'jirr
The Pale Lady

Crafting

Grindstone

Quest Items

Eisa's Log
Kyr's Log
Ra'jirr's Note

Collectibles

Skill Book [Sneak]: The Red Kitchen Reader [D1/10]
Unique Weapon: The Pale Blade [13/80]

Special Objects

Word Wall: Ice Form [1/3]
Chest(s)
Potions
Loose gear
Mineable ore: Iron

When you approach these mountain ruins, a warrior named Eisa flees down the steps, pursued by several bandits. Help her fight off the ruffians, then speak with her to begin a new quest that takes place within the nearby ruins.

A Exit to Skyrim

1 Guard Room

Slay a couple of bandits in this entry hall and loot a locked chest in the western nook. Pull the wall chain near the portcullis to open the way forward.

- Chest (Locked: Apprentice)
- Potions
- Loose gear

2 Connecting Tunnels

Claim a few valuables on your way through these short passages.

- Potion
- Loose gear

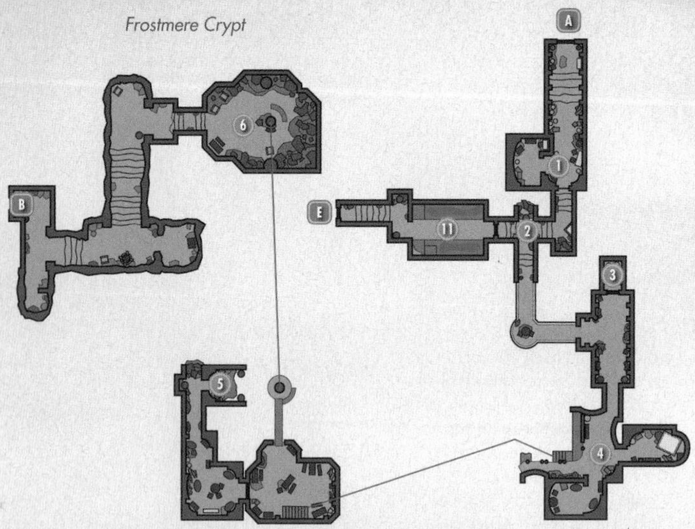

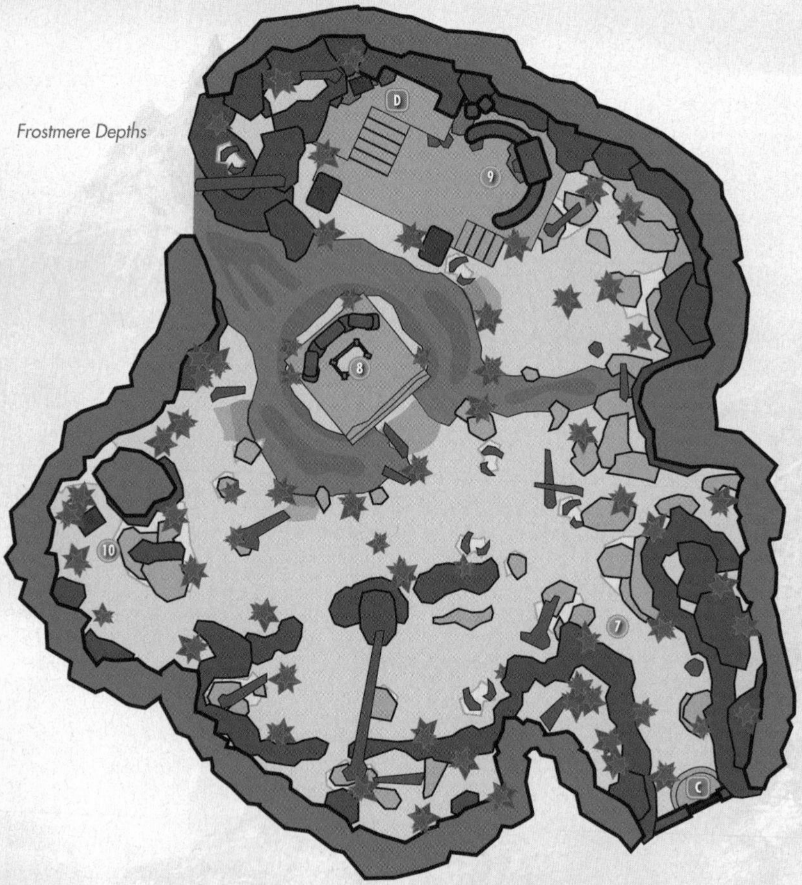

3 Grindstone Alcove

Grab a Skill Book from a shelf before picking a locked door to enter this small nook, where a crafting station and some valuable gear is found.

- ◊ Area Is Locked (Adept)
- ◊ Skill Book [Sneak]: The Red Kitchen Reader [D1/10]
- ◊ Crafting: Grindstone
- ◊ Loose gear

4 Upper Quarters

Search these small bedchambers to loot a chest and collect important quest-related documents.

- ◊ Eisa's Journal (if you didn't take it from outside)
- ◊ Kyr's Log
- ◊ Ra'jirr's Note
- ◊ Chest
- ◊ Potion
- ◊ Loose gear

5 Lever Overlook

Silence more bandits, then swipe a potion and loot an urn on your way to this overlook, where a Bandit Archer awaits. Pull the nearby lever to cause a drawbridge to fall, then head to [6] and head north across this new bridge.

- ◊ Potion

6 Drawbridge and Stairwell

Cross the drawbridge to enter this chamber from the south, then descend some stairs and slay a Bandit Mage in the lower chamber. Press onward through a winding mining tunnel, looting a chest and optionally mining some Iron Ore on your way to the crypt's lower depths.

- ◊ Chest
- ◊ Mineable ore: Iron
- ◊ Loose gear

B Door to Frostmere Depths

C Door to Frostmere Crypt

7 Shrouded Grove

A massive, overgrown cavern lies beneath the Frostmere Crypt. You find Kyr just inside—he's near death and gasps out a few final words before expiring. Continue deeper into the grove, and you'll spot Ra'jirr racing to the altar. The wraithlike form of the Pale Lady emerges and strikes him down before turning her wrath on you.

8 The Pale Blade

Claim the Pale Blade from Ra'jirr's corpse, then deal with the Pale Lady. Slay her or return the sword to the stand on the central altar to seal her away. Either choice completes this quest.

- ◊ Unique Weapon: The Pale Blade [13/80]

9 Word Wall

After defeating the Pale Lady, go upstairs and follow the sound of chanting to this location, where a Word Wall bestows you with an new Word of Power. Scale more steps and open a large chest near the exit door to the crypts. Don't leave just yet!

- ◊ Word Wall: Ice Form [1/3]
- ◊ Chest

10 Chest Nook

Raid a large locked chest that rests on a rise in this corner of the cavern. There's also some gear on a nearby skeleton that's just to the left as you step out into the grove proper.

- ◊ Chest (Locked: Master)
- ◊ Loose gear

D Door to Frostmere Crypt

E Door to Frostmere Depths

11 Watery Chamber

Take a quick dive underwater and try to open a chest for some loot before scaling this watery chamber's ramp. Unbar the far door and go through to return to the crypt's entrance.

- ◊ Chest (Locked: Adept)
- ◊ Loose gear

[3.09] and [DG.19] Hall of the Vigilant

Related Quests

Dungeon Activity

Recommended Level: 5

Dungeon: Special

Keeper Carcette (Restoration Trainer)
Vigilant of Stendarr

Services

Trainer (Restoration): Keeper Carcette [1/3]

Crafting

Alchemy Labs (2)
Tanning Rack

Collectibles

Skill Book [Heavy Armor]: The Knights of the Nine [E1/10]

Special Objects

Book: The Aetherium Wars
Chest(s)
Loose gear
Potions
Shrine of Stendarr [2/5]

Follow the main road south from Dawnstar, and you may notice this small meeting hall, located to the right of the road (first picture). This lodge is owned by the Vigilants of Stendarr—a group of monster hunters that specializes in fighting Daedra. Speak to any of the Vigilants here to have them cure you of any diseases or maladies you might be suffering, free of charge. Keeper Carcette runs the Hall and offers training in the Restoration skill.

As soon as the Dawnguard Main Quest begins, visit this location for a completely different experience: A recent and vicious battle between the Vigilants and a band of vampires has left the Hall in burning ruins, almost beyond repair. Bodies are strewn everywhere, and none of the Vigilants can be found. For this reason, avail yourself of Keeper Carcette's training for as long as you need to before the quest begins, or she (and the Skill Book) are likely to perish. However, there's a new book among the debris: The Aetherium Wars. When read, this begins Side Quest: Lost to the Ages.

[3.10] Fort Dunstad

Related Quests

Civil War Quest: Reunification of Skyrim
Civil War Quest: The Battle for Fort Dunstad

Recommended Level: 6

Habitation: Military Fort

Bandit or Civil War Soldiers

Crafting

Alchemy Labs (2)
Blacksmith Forge
Grindstone
Workbench

Dangers

Bear Traps
Oil Pool Traps
Wall Trap (lever)

Collectibles

Skill Book [Heavy Armor]: 2920, MidYear, V6 [A2/10]
Chest(s)
Potions aplenty
Loose gear

This Imperial fort was constructed around the Pale's main road as a highly effective checkpoint station and served as a prison for some of the worst criminals in Skyrim. Unfortunately, it's been overrun by vicious bandits! However, during the Civil War quest line, the bandits are banished from Fort Dunstad, and the place becomes a point of contention between the Stormcloaks and Imperials.

Exterior

Secure the exterior compound and tavern before breaching the keep, and snag a potion hidden inside a bucket atop the southern exterior watchtower.

- Crafting: Blacksmith Forge, Workbench
- Potion
- Loose gear

Stumbling Sabrecat (Tavern)

A pair of bandits lurk in this small tavern's basement. Clear out the place, then raid the basement chest.

- Chest (Locked: Apprentice)

Fort Dunstad (Interior)

Breach the stronghold's interior using either the main door or the second-story trapdoor. Inside, wipe out a host of bandits on the first floor, and optionally pull a lever to release a caged Skeever. Three more caged Skeevers are found upstairs, but beware of bear traps on the floor.

- Danger! Bear Traps
- Chest (Locked: Novice)
- Potion
- Loose gear

Commander's Quarters

This small barracks is loaded with potions of every sort, but a dangerous mage defends the place.

- Crafting: Alchemy Lab
- Potions aplenty

Prison

Enter the prison from the ground floor, and spy a potion that's mixed in with the booze on the wall. A large oil spill in the following hall gives you an opportunity to set the corridor ablaze with a fire-based attack. Loot a chest and free some caged Skeevers in the next room. If you wish, you can use the Wall Trap there by pulling a nearby lever. The chief of these villainous outlaws lurks upstairs, as does a ladder that leads up to a large chest.

- Danger! Oil Pool Trap, Wall Trap (lever)
- Crafting: Alchemy Lab, Grindstone
- Skill Book [Heavy Armor]: 2920, MidYear, V6 [A2/10]
- Chest (Locked: Apprentice)
- Potions
- Loose gear

[3.11] Shrine of Mehrunes Dagon

Related Quests

Daedric Quest: Pieces of the Past

Dungeon: Special

Dremora

Collectibles

Skill Book [Enchanting]: Catalogue of Armor Enchantments
Unique Weapon: Mehrunes' Razor [14/18]
Area Is Locked (quest required)
Chests (3)
Potion
Loose gear

High atop the frigid peaks of the Pale's western mountains, narrow stone stairs carved into the rock lead up to an ancient shrine. You visit this site during Daedric Quest: Pieces of the Past. Decide whether you wish to slay Silus and wield Mehrunes' Razor, a unique and powerful weapon, or allow Silus to keep the blade and be paid a large sum of coin in the process. Fight Dremora both inside and in this shrine, providing the Quest has reached its zenith.

[3.12] The Lord Stone

Recommended Level: 6

Dungeon: Special
Bandit

Special Objects
Standing Stone: The Lord Stone [3/13]

High atop the snowy mountains on the Pale's western edge, a small crew of bandits guards a tranquil shrine. Lay waste to the ruffians, then inspect the nearby stone to activate it and gain a new sign blessing. Those under the sign of the Lord are more resistant to both physical and magical damage. Note that you may have only one sign blessing at a time, so activating this Standing Stone will override any previous Stones you may have discovered.

[3.13] Volunruud

Related Quests

Dark Brotherhood Quest: The Silence Has Been Broken
Dark Brotherhood Quest: Hail Sithis!
Dungeon Quest: Silenced Tongues

Recommended Level: 14

Dungeon: Draugr Crypt

Dragon Priest
Draugr
Kvenel the Tongue
Skeleton

Dangers

Spear Trap (pressure plates)

Collectibles

Skill Book [One-Handed]: Mace Etiquette
Unique Item: Jeweled Amulet [23/112]
Unique Weapon: Ceremonial Sword [15/80]
Unique Weapon: Ceremonial Axe [16/80]
Unique Weapon: Eduj [17/80]
Unique Weapon: Okin [18/80]

Special Objects

Word Wall: Aura Whisper [1/3]
Chest(s)
Potions
Loose gear

Standing stones mark these sunken ruins, which lie at the far southwest reaches of the Pale. This small Draugr crypt is the personal mausoleum of a legendary Nord named Kvenel the Tongue and houses a pair of legendary weapons that he possessed in life. During Dark Brotherhood Quest: The Silence Has Been Broken, Amaund Motierre will give you a unique amulet here as well.

Exterior

Loot a chest and burial urn outside the ruins, then drop into the recessed area to raid another chest and urn before heading inside.

◊ Chests (2)

A Exit to Skyrim

1 Junction Chamber

Slay an unsuspecting skeleton as you descend into the central cavern, optionally stopping to read the book near the foot of its throne. Three side passage stretch off from this central hub. Scale the north steps to visit an altar room, and inspect the Elder's Cairn Door, which you cannot open until completing the Side Quest that plays out in these ruins.

2 Sleeping Nook

Visit this southwest nook first to loot a chest and urn.

◊ Chest

3 Weapon Chamber A

Slay a host of vile Draugr on your way to this far chamber, and head upward to where you find one of the two ceremonial weapons you seek in an open tomb. Claim a Skill Book that rests on a throne here as well. As you exit, beware the two mighty Draugr that guard the weapon.

◊ Skill Book [One-Handed]: Mace Etiquette
◊ Unique Weapon: Ceremonial Sword [15/80]

4 Weapon Chamber B

Dispatch many more undead and avoid dangerous traps as you head to this far room, where the second ceremonial weapon you're after is kept. Bring both weapons back to [2] and scale the north steps once more to at last open the Elder's Cairn Door.

◊ Danger! Spear Trap (pressure plate)
◊ Unique Weapon: Ceremonial Axe [16/80]

B Door to Volunruud Elder's Cairn

Knevel's Chamber

Battle some Draugr and a powerful undead chieftan called Knevel the Tongue in this cavernous lair. After the melee, search Knevel's remains to obtain two unique weapons, and follow the sound of chanting to locate an ancient Word Wall. Go north and cross a small footbridge to reach a treasure-filled alcove, then drop down to retrace your steps to the entrance.

◊ Unique Weapon: Eduj [17/80]
◊ Unique Weapon: Okin [18/80]
◊ Word Wall: Aura Whisper [1/3]
◊ Chests (4)
◊ Potions
◊ Loose gear

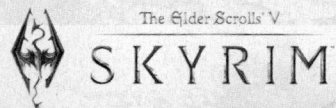

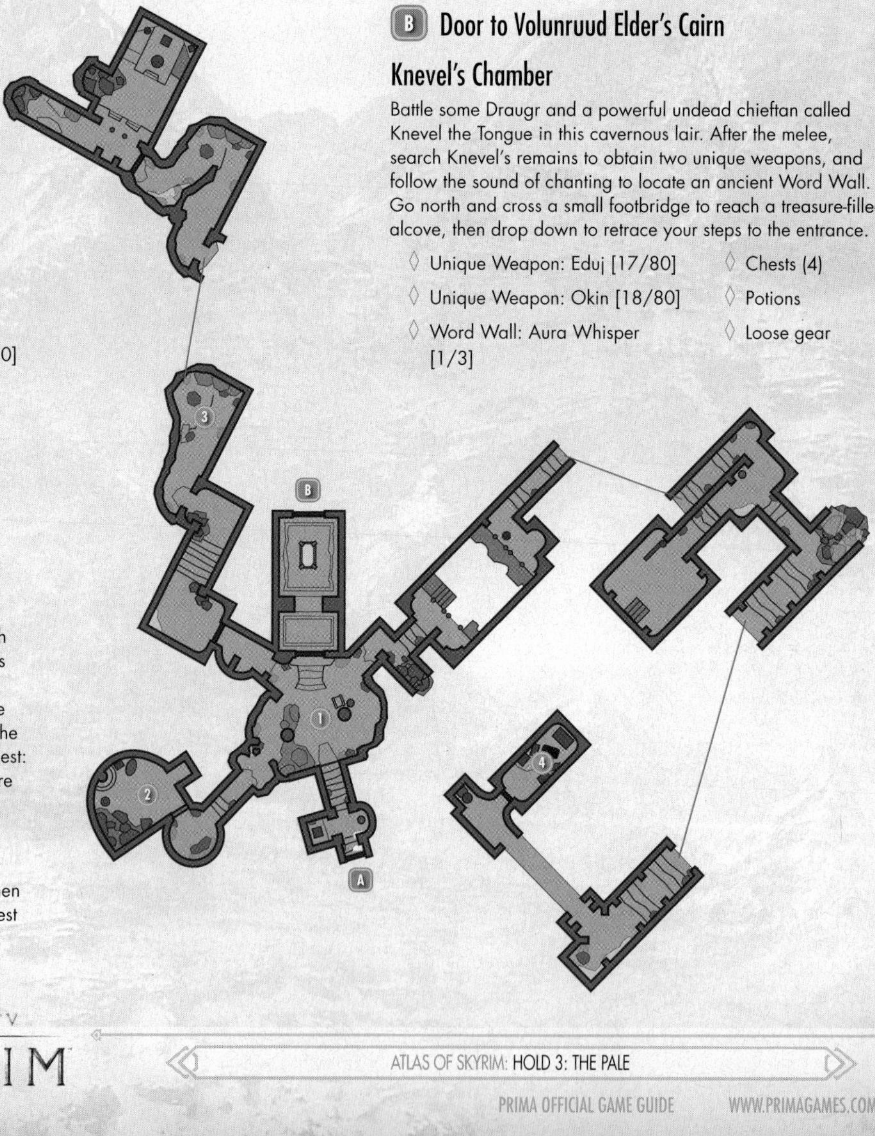

[3.14] Stonehill Bluff

Related Quests
Side Quest: Repairing the Phial

Dungeon: Giant Camp
Giant

Quest Items
Mammoth Tusk Powder
Chest(s)

The massive bones of slain mammoths decorate this giant's campsite, which is nestled amongst the Pale's southwest mountains. Slay the mighty giant if you dare, then raid his chest and corpse for plenty of treasure. During Side Quest: The White Phial, you'll find some needed Mammoth Tusk Powder here.

[3.15] Tower of Mzark

Related Quests
Main Quest: Elder Knowledge
Main Quest: Alduin's Bane
Daedric Quest: Discerning the Transmundane

Recommended Level: 18

Special Objects

Underground Connection: Blackreach [10.02]

Collectibles
Area Is Locked
Chest
Loose gear

This small tower, located just east of Stonehill Bluff [3.14], doesn't appear as a Primary Location on the in-game map, but it's important enough to consider it one. Beyond the tower's locked gate lies an elevator that ferries you down to the mythical Dwarven city of Blackreach [10.02], but you must pull the lever inside the tower to open its gate, making this a one-way ride until after you've used this elevator to exit Blackreach—then the gate remains unlocked.

[3.16] Loreius Farm

Related Quests
Side Quest: Kyne's Sacred Trials
Dark Brotherhood Quest: Delayed Burial

Habitation: Farm
Curwe
Vantus Loreius

Collectibles
Unique Item: Cicero's Boots [14/112]
Unique Item: Cicero's Clothes [15/112]
Unique Item: Cicero's Gloves [16/112]
Unique Item: Cicero's Hat [17/112]
Chest
Potion
Loose gear

Speak to the owner of this quaint farm to obtain Dark Brotherhood Quest: Delayed Burial, which plays out here. However, you can only obtain this quest prior to joining the Dark Brotherhood. You'll be rewarded no matter how you choose to resolve this quest, but note that if you choose to turn Cicero over to the guards, or if you're unable to convince Loreius to fix his cart's broken wheel, you will find Loreius and his wife murdered when you return here later. Pick a Novice-level lock to break into the farmhouse if you like. You can steal from a chest and swipe a potion from the floor within.

[3.17] Blizzard Rest

Dungeon: Giant Camp
Giant
Mammoth
Chest (Locked: Expert)

Beware when exploring the Pale's southern scrubland—an ill-tempered giant has made camp here. Exploit the difficult terrain to outmaneuver the lumbering brute when battling him, but beware his roaming mammoths. If you're able, unlock the campsite's chest afterward to obtain valuable plunder.

[3.18] Weynon Stones

Recommended Level: 18

Dungeon: Special
Ice Wraith

Special Objects
Shrine of Talos [2/17]
Chest (Locked: Novice)
Loose gear

Near the heart of the Pale, just south of the main road, a small collection of stones stands in the scrubland. The broken gear found here is largely worthless; loot a locked chest that's tucked away amongst the surrounding stones instead. You may also pray at the shrine at the base of the statue to receive Talos's blessing.

[3.19] Duskglow Crevice

This small cave is home to several vicious entities, but valuable treasure awaits the bold.

Related Quests

Side Quest: Captured Critters*

Dungeon Activity

Recommended Level: 18

Dungeon: Falmer Hive

Animal

Bandit

Falmer

Collectibles

Captured Critter: Moth in a Jar [1/5]

Skill Book [Lockpicking]: The Wolf Queen, v1

Skill Book [Pickpocket]: Purloined Shadows [C1/10]

Chest(s)

Potions

Loose gear

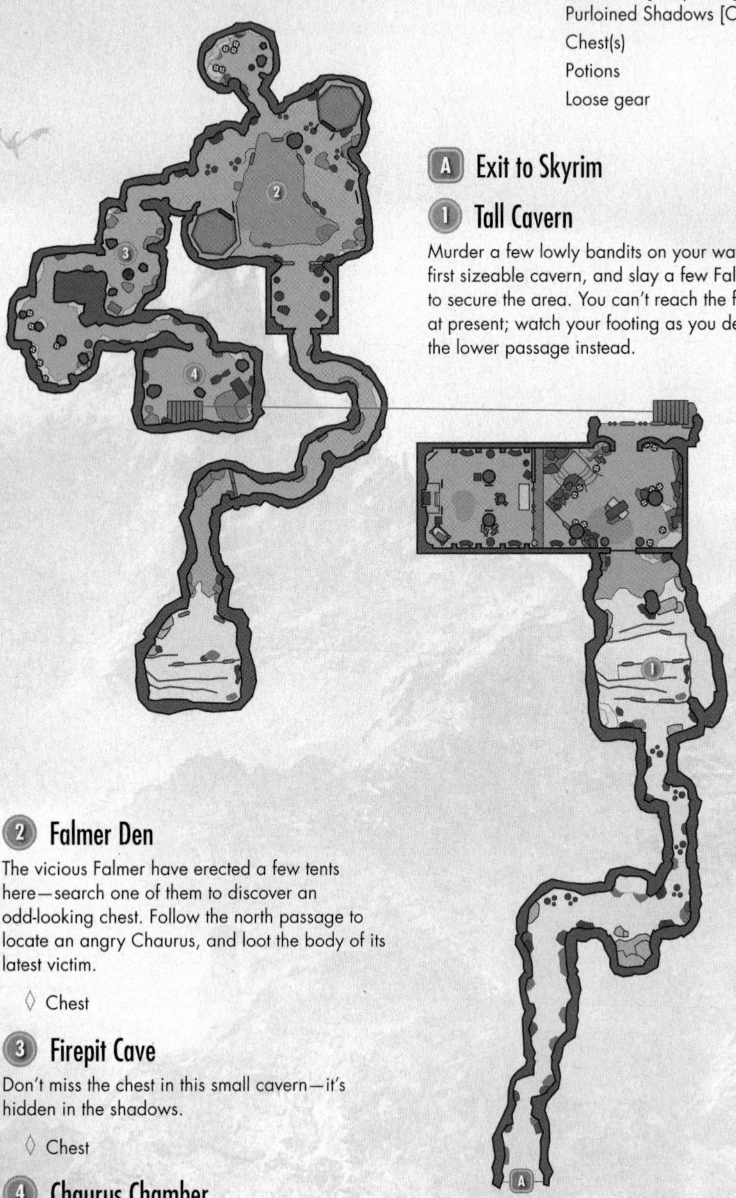

A Exit to Skyrim

1 Tall Cavern

Murder a few lowly bandits on your way into this first sizeable cavern, and slay a few Falmer here to secure the area. You can't reach the far ledge at present; watch your footing as you descend to the lower passage instead.

2 Falmer Den

The vicious Falmer have erected a few tents here—search one of them to discover an odd-looking chest. Follow the north passage to locate an angry Chaurus, and loot the body of its latest victim.

◊ Chest

3 Firepit Cave

Don't miss the chest in this small cavern—it's hidden in the shadows.

◊ Chest

4 Chaurus Chamber

Butcher another Chaurus on your way to this large chamber, then scale some stairs and squash yet another of the giant bugs. Proceed westward to locate a large chest and several valuable potions, along with a pair of Skill Books and a special Moth in a Jar that pertains to Side Quest: Captured Critters. Pull the chain on the wall in the corner near the potion shelf to open the downstairs portcullis, granting passage back to the cave's entrance.

◊ Captured Critter: Moth in a Jar [1/5]

◊ Skill Book [Lockpicking]: The Wolf Queen, v1

◊ Skill Book [Pickpocket]: Purloined Shadows [C1/10]

◊ Chest

◊ Potions

◊ Loose gear

[3.20] Silverdrift Lair

Recommended Level: 6

Dungeon: Draugr Crypt

Bandit

Draugr

Dangers

Battering Ram Trap (wall chain)

Oil Lamp Trap

Oil Pool Trap

Swinging Spikes (pressure plates)

Spear Trap (pedestal pressure plate)

Collectibles

Skill Book [Pickpocket]: Thief

Skill Book [Two-Handed]: Words and Philosophy

Special Objects

Word Wall: Disarm [2/3]

Chest(s)

Potions aplenty

Loose gear

These Nordic ruins, which lie along the southwest base of the Pale's eastern mountains, have become home to ruthless bandits. Dispatch a few exterior guards before investigating the ruins' interior.

A Exit to Skyrim

1 Entry Chamber

Loot an urn and the corpses of a few bandits in this first chamber before delving down into the Draugr-filled passages ahead. Don't miss the coin purse and piece of gear that's tucked away behind some rubble in the passage as you make your way to [2].

2 Central Chamber

Collect a number of potions from a table and a shelf as you enter this large, central chamber. Find a Skill Book on a stone table at the room's east end before heading downstairs to loot a couple of chests and turn a pair of handles in the oily western nook to open a passage leading toward [3].

◊ Danger! Oil Lamp Trap, Oil Pool Trap, Swinging Spikes (pressure plate)

◊ Skill Book [Two-Handed]: Words and Philosophy

◊ Chest

◊ Chest (Locked: Apprentice)

◊ Potions aplenty

2 Trapped Passage

Loot even more urns and skirt a pressure plate in this hall to avoid being perforated by arrows. Open a chest and beware the host of Draugr that lurk just ahead.

- Danger! Dart Trap (pressure plate)
- Chest

3 Burial Halls

Loot a number of burial urns in these passages, which are lined with the resting dead. Spy a Skill Book lying on a stone table, and unlock an Adept-level door to access a small room with a chest.

- Skill Book [Block]: The Mirror
- Chest
- Loose gear

4 Collapsing Chamber

Slay more Draugr in this chamber, and don't miss the chest that's hidden in the shadows among the southeast rubble. Jump a pressure plate in the passage that follows to avoid a trap, and proceed into the crypts.

- Danger! Battering Ram Trap (pressure plate)
- Chest
- Potions
- Loose gear

B Door to Forsaken Crypt

C Door to Forsaken Cave

5 Junction Chamber

Loot a few urns on your way into this tall, multitiered chamber. Slaughter all Draugr and navigate the east passages to reach this chamber's second level. Open a chest up here and then proceed north to [6].

- Chest
- Potions
- Loose gear

6 Trapped Floor Room

Beware the center of the floor in this small chamber—stepping on it causes it to rise, slamming you into lethal ceiling spikes. Unlock the Expert-level west door to access a treasure nook, then proceed through the other door to cut back through [5] and eventually arrive at [7].

- Danger! Rising Floor
- Chest

7 Curalmil's Chamber

Cut down more undead and loot more urns on your way to this chamber, where a mighty Draugr warrior awaits. Sprint past the swinging blades and slay Curalmil, then scale the nearby steps to reach a large chest and Word Wall.

- Word Wall: Marked for Death [1/3]
- Chest

8 Phial Chamber

Make your way to this quiet chamber, which opens after you use Nurelion's Mixture. Collect the Cracked White Phial from the pedestal, along with a Skill Book. Return to [7] and take the exit passage back to the cave's entrance.

- Crafting: Alchemy Lab
- Cracked White Phial
- Skill Book [Alchemy]: A Game at Dinner
- Apothecary's Satchel
- Potions

D Door to Forsaken Cave

E Door to Forsaken Crypt

[3.28] Yorgrim Overlook

Recommended Level: 5

Dungeon: Special

Skeleton

Collectibles

Chest(s)

At the Pale's southeast end, a shallow cave has been carved into the mountains that form the border to Winterhold. Slay a few skeletons up here, then see if you can unlock an Expert-level gate and claim the contents of a large chest.

[3.29] Bronze Water Cave

Related Quests

Thieves Guild Quest: Blindsighted
Dungeon Activity

Dungeon: Animal Den

Animal

Underground Connection: Irkngthand [3.31]

Collectibles

Unique Weapon: Nightingale Bow [19/80]

Along the Pale's southeast border, several thick metal pipes protrude from the ground near a widemouthed cave. Enter the cave with caution—a pair of ferocious beasts lurk within. You also visit this cave during a frantic escape from Irkngthand [3.31] at the climax of Thieves Guild Quest: Blindsighted. When you make good your escape, Karliah rewards your success with a unique bow.

[3.30] Pale Stormcloak Camp

Related Quests

Civil War Quest (when active, depending on who you side with)

Habitation: Military: Stormcloak Camp

Stormcloak Quartermaster (Blacksmith)
Stormcloak Soldier

Services

Trader (Blacksmith): Stormcloak Quartermaster [8/33]
Weapons, Apparel, Misc

Crafting

Anvil
Grindstone
Workbench

Special Objects

Civil War: Map of Skyrim
Chests (2)
Loose gear

The Stormcloaks have set up a samll encampment here, but this site may appear only during the Civil War quest line. Feel free to trade with the quartermaster or improve your weapons at his crafting workstations. Examine the map in the largest tent to potentially update your own.

[3.31] Irkngthand

Recommended Level: 12

Related Quests

- Thieves Guild Quest: Blindsighted
- Thieves Guild Additional Quest: Larceny Targets*
- Dungeon Activity

Dungeon: Dwarven City

- Animal
- Bandit
- Dwarven Sphere
- Dwarven Spider
- Dwarven Centurion
- Falmer
- Mercer Frey

Crafting

- Alchemy Lab
- Tanning Rack

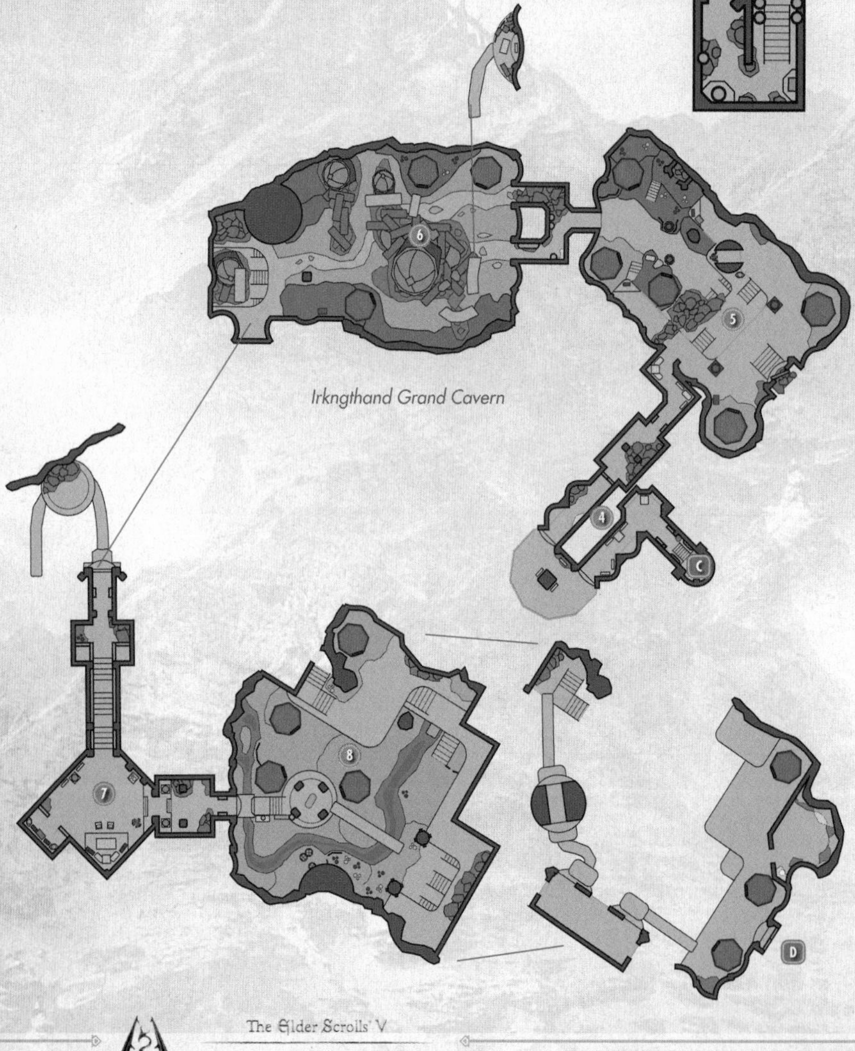

Dangers

- Bear Traps
- Bone Alarm Trap
- Dwarven Fire Pillar Trap (proximity)
- Dwarven Thresher (proximity)
- Dwarven Thresher (lever)
- Flail Trap (door)
- Flamethrower Trap (proximity)
- Flamethrower Trap (pressure plates)
- Spear Trap (pressure plate)

Underground Connection: Bronze Water Cave [3.29]

Quest Items

- Skeleton Key
- Right Eye of the Falmer

Collectibles

- Larceny Target: Left Eye of the Falmer [2/7]
- Unique Item: Skeleton Key [25/112]
- Area Is Locked (quest required)
- Chest(s)
- Potions aplenty
- Loose gear

This massive dwarven city remains largely sealed off until you venture here as part of Thieves Guild Quest: Blindsighted. Only the exterior ruins can be explored until then. Use stealth whenever possible here.

Exterior

Bandits have established a campsite at Irkngthand's exterior ruins. The front gate is sealed, so go west, pillaging a chest and swiping some potions from a wooden table. Go left and scale the stone steps, skirting bear traps and swiping some potions from a lean-to found at the top. Find a chest tucked away beneath another wooden table near some bedrolls, then avoid a pressure plate trap in the tunnel-like passage that follows. Pull the lever beyond the tunnel to open Irkngthand's front gate. Scale a series of narrow wooden stairs afterward to locate the bandits' leader. Loot two more chests that the chief guards. Scale the following ramps to reach the high door that leads to the Irkngthand Arcanex—these last few ramps appear only when the "Blindsighted" quest is active.

- Danger! Bear Traps, Spear Trap (pressure plate)
- Chests (2)
- Chest (Locked: Apprentice)
- Chest (Locked: Adept)
- Potions
- Loose gear

A Exit to Skyrim

1 Entry Chamber

Bandits lay slain near a firepit in this first chamber—likely the work of your quarry, Mercer Frey. Loot the large nearby chest if you're able to pick its tricky lock—an even more challenging dwarven chest sits nearby, tucked away near the middle of the west wall. Beware of a patrolling Dwarven Sphere as you make your way to [2].

- Chest (Locked: Expert)
- Chest (Locked: Master)

2 Pipeworks Passage

Sneak through this passage to reduce the odds of alerting reinforcement sentries. Find two small dwarven chests at the far south end of the passage—one on the lip of the outside wall, the other near the foot of the nearby stairs.

- Chest

3 Gate Chamber

Keep as close to the outside wall as possible to avoid this wide chamber's spinning Flame Pillars. Sneak or you'll alert Dwarven Spiders, which stand too short to be harmed by the traps. You can just barely circle past the final spout without being seared. Open the gate beyond and navigate a passage that leads up to a high east balcony, raiding a couple of chests as you go. Use the Alchemy Lab if you wish before taking the elevator down to the Grand Cavern.

- Danger! Dwarven Fire Pillar Trap (proximity)
- Crafting: Alchemy Lab
- Chests (Locked: Apprentice) (2)
- Potions

B Elevator to Irkngthand Grand Cavern

C Elevator to Irkngthand Arcanex

4 Entry Passage

After meeting up with Karliah and Brynjolf, stand back after opening the door here—Mercer has left it trapped, and a mace will come swinging your way. (Alternately, you can try and disable the trap's hinge.) Unlock an Expert-level gate a few paces farther to claim a chest and some potions. Continue out onto a balcony overlooking a huge cavern and you can spot Mercer offing a pair of Falmer. You cannot get to him yet, so continue down a sloping passage.

- Danger! Flail Trap (door)
- Chest
- Potion

5 Cavern A

Turn left as you enter this first massive cavern and creep across a pile of debris to locate a lever. Pull the lever, then creep back the way you came and loot a grotesque chest that sits near a Falmer tent with several potions. Continue sneaking around the balcony and, if possible, unlock an Expert-level gate so you may fire a ballista down at the dangerous Falmer below. Raid a chest at the balcony's other end and find the second lever there. You must pull one of the levers, then race to the other side to pull the other lever to open the gate below or the levers will reset. You can tell that the gate is open when the dwarven lamps on either side are both lit. Make your way downstairs, looting the chest that's tucked away near the steps. Avoid the road that follows—it's trapped with lethal spinning blades. Hop up and navigate the earthen ledges instead, finding a chest stashed near the north wall. Use stealth or you will alert the Sphere Centurions here.

- Danger! Dwarven Thresher (proximity)
- Crafting: Tanning Rack
- Chests (2)
- Chest (Locked: Novice)
- Chest (Locked: Adept)
- Potions

6 Cavern B

This second cavern is as big as the first. Sneak through here to avoid alerting the roaming Falmer. Scale a ramp as you enter to visit a small balcony with a few ingredients, as well as a good sniping position. Search the ledge to the left of the central road to discover a Falmer chest. A dwarven chest lies in the rubble at the trail's end. Follow a looping walkway around to reach the hallway that leads to the third cavern.

- Chest
- Chest (Locked: Apprentice)

7 Connecting Hallway

Mercer Frey has been here, looted the place, and scribbled a taunting message on the wall. Three scrolls of Detect Life can be found here, which can make the fight with Mercer much easier, so be sure to grab them.

- Danger! Bear Traps
- Loose gear

8 Cavern C

The third cavern is the largest of all, and it's teeming with powerful Falmer and a Dwarven Centurion. Do your best to avoid detection, and optionally jump off the bridge's right side, which you start on when entering the area. Press the button at the base of the entry stairs to unleash the Dwarven Centurion on the unsuspecting Falmer. Scale the east steps and cross a long walkway to advance toward the cavern's south end, where more Falmer and a nest of Frostbite Spiders threaten you. Watch out for Bear Traps left by Mercer along the way. Loot the two chests near the Falmer tents before proceeding through the door to the Slave Pens.

- Danger! Bear Traps
- Chest

D Door to Irkngthand Slave Pens

E Door to Irkngthand Grand Cavern

9 Entry and Torture Room

Ignore this area's locked gate—there's little of interest behind it. Check the south rubble to discover a chest, then sneak down and pull the lever on the east balcony to slice up the unsuspecting Falmer below. Go downstairs and collect an array of potions from a table. Search an unfortunate thief to discover his last words, which hint at riches ahead. Beware of the pressure plates in the passage that leads to [10].

- Danger! Bone Alarm Trap, Dwarven Thresher (lever), Flamethrower (pressure plates)
- Chest
- Potions aplenty
- Loose gear

10 Falmer Camp

Several powerful Falmer are camped here, making this a dangerous area. Sneak through by keeping close to the west wall. Two of their tents contain chests.

- Chests (2)

11 Chaurus Den

Stick close to the west wall to slip past the Falmer in this area, raiding a chest as you go. Beware of two hulking Chaurus that lurk to the south. A chest with a difficult lock sits in one of the southern tents, and a potion lies on the ground where the passage bends southeast. Pipes span the ceiling above the area with the Chaurus. Sneaking along here should allow you to bypass the enemies below or give you a great vantage to snipe them. A health potion can also be found at the opposite end of this cave.

- Chest (Locked: Apprentice)
- Chest (Locked: Expert)

12 Sanctuary Access

Loot one last chest—an ornate dwarven chest with an intricate lock—as you make your way through the Slave Pens' final stretch. Proceed through the nearby gate to reach the door to the Irkngthand Sanctuary.

- Chest (Locked: Master)

F Door to Irkngthand Sanctuary

Irkngthand Sanctuary

You finally catch up with your quarry in the sanctuary. Slay Mercer Frey in an epic battle (see Thieves Guild Quest: Blindsighted for complete strategies), then loot his body to obtain vast wealth, including the priceless Right Eye of the Falmer and the quest-related Skeleton Key. The cavern soon begins to collapse and fill with water. Exploit the rising tide to make your escape, but the way will open to you only if you possess the Skeleton Key. You will eventually emerge in Bronze Water Cave [3.29].

- ◊ Right Eye of the Falmer
- ◊ Larceny Target: Left Eye of the Falmer [2/7]
- ◊ Unique Item: Skeleton Key [25/112]

[3.32] and [DG.15] Raldbthar

Related Quests

Dark Brotherhood Quest: Mourning Never Comes
Side Quest: Lost to the Ages
A Dungeon Activity Is Available

Hold: The Pale

Recommended Level: 12

Dungeon: Dwarven City

Alain Dufont
Animal
Bandit
Dwarven Centurion
Dwarven Sphere
Dwarven Spider
Falmer
Katria

Crafting

Workbench (3)

Dangers

Dwarven Ballista Trap (pressure plate)
Dwarven Piston
Dwarven Thresher (proximity)
Dwarven Thresher (pressure plate)
Flamethrower
Flamethrower (buttons)
Oil Pool Traps

Underground Connection: Blackreach [10.02]

Collectibles

Chest(s)
Loose gear
Potions
Skill Book [Sneak]: 2920, Lost Seed, v8 [A1/10]
Unique Weapon: Aegisbane [20/81]

These ancient dwarven ruins, which run through the mountains at the Pale's southeast tip, have been overrun by treasure-seeking bandits.

A Exit to Skyrim

1 Bandit Den

Ignore the passage that's blocked by active fire spouts, and take a side passage to reach this chamber, which the bandits have secured as a base of operations. Dispatch the villains and loot an odd-looking dwarven chest that's tucked to one side of the room's entry doorway.

- ◊ Chest
- ◊ Crafting: Workbench
- ◊ Loose gear

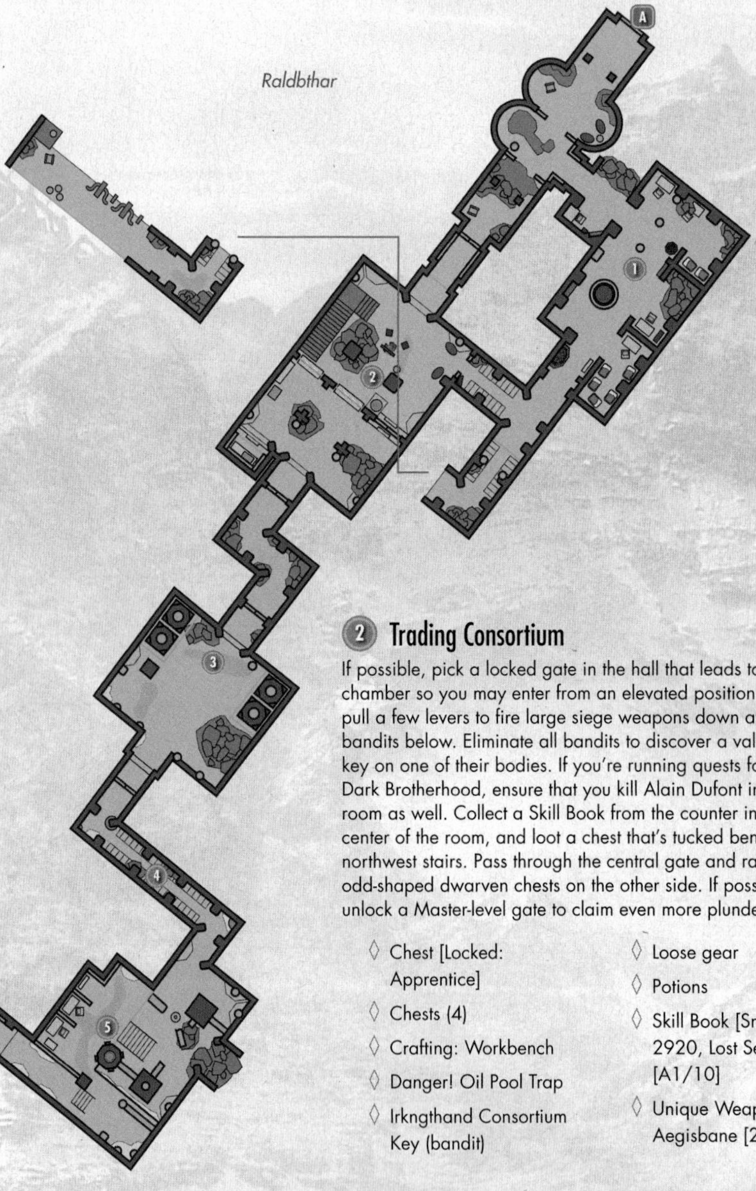

2 Trading Consortium

If possible, pick a locked gate in the hall that leads to this chamber so you may enter from an elevated position; then pull a few levers to fire large siege weapons down at the bandits below. Eliminate all bandits to discover a valuable key on one of their bodies. If you're running quests for the Dark Brotherhood, ensure that you kill Alain Dufont in this room as well. Collect a Skill Book from the counter in the center of the room, and loot a chest that's tucked beneath the northwest stairs. Pass through the central gate and raid the odd-shaped dwarven chests on the other side. If possible, unlock a Master-level gate to claim even more plunder.

- ◊ Chest [Locked: Apprentice]
- ◊ Chests (4)
- ◊ Crafting: Workbench
- ◊ Danger! Oil Pool Trap
- ◊ Irkngthand Consortium Key (bandit)
- ◊ Loose gear
- ◊ Potions
- ◊ Skill Book [Sneak]: 2920, Lost Seed, v8 [A1/10]
- ◊ Unique Weapon: Aegisbane [20/81]

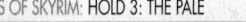

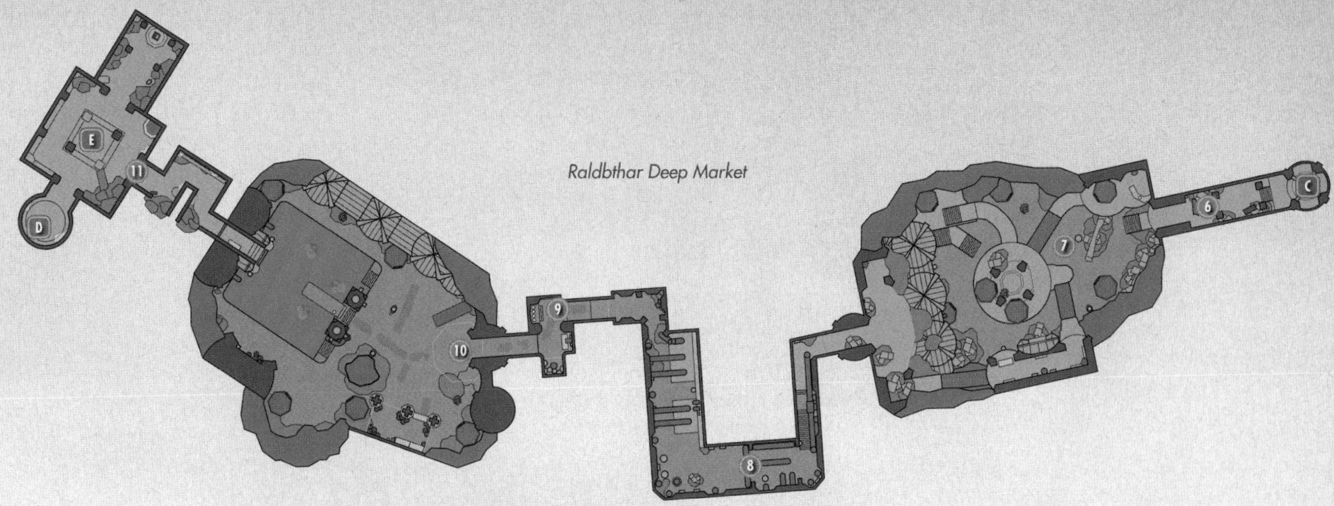

3 Oily Floor Chamber

Formidable Dwarven Spheres emerge from small holes in this second chamber's walls. Look to ignite the room's oil slicks to help defeat these foes. Secure the chamber and pillage the chest near the northwest wall. Find a coin purse tucked away near the southeast wall as well.

- Chest [Locked: Apprentice]
- Danger! Oil Pool Traps

4 Thresher Hallway

Carefully time the movement of the spinning blades as you scale this sloping passage, and keep close to the walls to avoid being sliced to ribbons.

- Danger! Dwarven Thresher (proximity)

5 Pipeworks

Search the wall near the stairs here to find a well-hidden dwarven chest. Find two more chests upstairs in the cubicles—one is long and rectangular and features a difficult lock. Beware of Dwarven Spiders that emerge from holes in the walls as you head for the far lift that ferries you to Raldbthar's Deep Market.

- Chest [Locked: Master]
- Chests [Locked: Novice] (2)
- Crafting: Workbench
- Danger! Dwarven Piston
- Danger! Flamethrower
- Danger! Oil Pool Trap
- Loose gear

B Door to Deep Market

C Door to Raldbthar

6 Deep Market Entry

Carefully move past the spinning blade that emerges from the ground as you descend this first sloping passage. Raid a chest that's tucked away in a corner at the bottom.

- Chest [Locked: Novice]
- Danger! Dwarven Thresher (proximity)

7 Fountain Square

Beware: vicious Falmer lurk in this massive cavern. Free a couple of Skeevers from a holding pen as you enter, then flee—they may attack their captors for you. Loot an odd-looking Falmer chest in the west tent, then scale the north steps and raid a locked dwarven chest. Slay a powerful Falmer on the high central balcony—believe it or not, you can circle around the Falmer tents up here to locate a chest that's cleverly hidden behind them. Cross a ramp afterward to locate another Falmer chest and a button. Press the button to lower a drawbridge that grants you access to the room's southern and western ledges. Loop around and take the west passage to [8].

- Chests (2)
- Chest [Locked: Apprentice]
- Loose gear
- Potion

8 Trapped Passage

Dodge pressure plate traps as you navigate this passage, slaying the odd Dwarven Automaton as you go. Loot a dwarven chest that's curiously affixed to the east wall. If you have Whirlwind Sprint, you can walk up the diagonal pipes in this room, then sprint across to the caged area you just walked under to find another hidden chest.

- Chest (2)
- Danger! Dwarven Ballista Trap (pressure plate)
- Danger! Swinging Blade Trap (pressure plate)

9 Button Puzzle Passage

Four buttons are lined up in a row in this passage. Simply press the third button from the left to open the way forward. Pressing any other button causes lethal flamethrowers to jet out from the surrounding walls.

- Danger! Flamethrower (buttons)

10 Jammed Gear Chamber

Battle several fierce Falmer in this sizeable chamber. If you are feeling tough, unlock the small trading post to battle the Chaurus and obtain the treasure lock in the cage. Find a chest at the chamber's west end and another within a Falmer tent that features an Expert-level locked gate. A third chest sits near another tent to the north. Remove obstructions from four gears around the room to restore power to the central button—search underwater to find one of the blocked gears. Press the button to lower the far drawbridge and unleash a fearsome Dwarven Centurion! Loot the rectangular chest across the drawbridge after defeating the Centurion.

- Chests (4)
- Potion

11 Mechanism Chamber

If you are on Side Quest: Lost to the Ages, Katria appears as you enter this chamber and helps you fend off a swarm of dwarven automatons. Raid the chest that lies among this final room's north rubble, along with the locked chest that's affixed to the west wall; then grab the Glowing Crystal Shard in the northern part of this chamber. If you've previously been to Blackreach [10.02], you can use the central mechanism here to return to the dwarves' subterranean city. Otherwise, the nearby lift will take you back out to Skyrim. Loot one last dwarven chest as you descend the outdoor steps that lead back to Raldbthar's main entrance.

- Aetherium Shard [3/4]
- Chest
- Chest (outdoors)
- Chest [Locked: Adept]
- Loose gear
- Potion

D Exit to Skyrim

E Elevator to Blackreach

[3.33] Blackreach Elevator (Raldbthar)

Underground Connection: Blackreach [10.02]

Collectibles

Area Is Locked

This small tower, located near the base of the mountain ruins of Raldbthar [3.32], doesn't appear as a Primary Location on the in-game map, but it's important enough to be considered one. Beyond the tower's locked gate lies an elevator that zips you down to the rumored dwarven city of Blackreach [10.02], but you must pull the lever inside the tower to open its gate. This makes it a one-way transport until after you've used this elevator to exit Blackreach. (The gate remains unlocked afterward.)

[3.34] Anga's Mill

Related Quests

Dark Brotherhood Quest: Side Contract: Ennodius Papius
Favor (Activity): Chopping Wood* (Aeri)
Favor: Special Delivery* (Aeri)

Habitation: Lumber Mill

Aeri (Marriage Prospect)
Kodrir
Leifur

Crafting

Grindstone

Services

Marriage Prospect: Aeri [7/62]

Collectibles

Skill Book [Speech]: Biography of the Wolf Queen
Chest(s)
Potions
Loose gear

At the Pale's southern end, a quiet lumber mill sits along the River Yorgrim, erected along the main road and near a bridge.

Exterior

Take advantage of the crafting stations located around the mill.

- Crafting: Grindstone

Aeri's House

Break into this small cabin to loot a chest and swipe a few potions, among other items of interest.

- Area Is Locked (Novice)
- Chest
- Potions
- Loose gear

Common House

Pick the lock of the common house's door to break in and plunder a few chests. A Skill Book rests on the end table by the bed.

- Area Is Locked (Novice)
- Skill Book [Speech]: Biography of the Wolf Queen
- Chests (2)
- Potion
- Loose gear

SECONDARY LOCATIONS

[3.A] Horker Standing Stones

On one of the tidal islands just north of High Gate Ruins is a cluster of dilapidated Nordic standing stones. Thieves have long since departed with anything of value (aside from a chiming Nirnroot at the water's edge). The place is now home to Horkers.

[3.B] Sunken Treasures

In the frigid waters of the Sea of Ghosts, north and a little west of the Wreck of the *Brinehammer*, are two tiny flat islands. Face due north on the smaller (western) one, and swim until you reach a sunken chest (Expert). Beware of Slaughterfish!

- Chest (Expert)

[3.C] Bandit's Hovel

A recently destroyed hunter's lodge is now home to a roaming bandit. The fire is still hot in the hearth, but the building itself is ruined and the contents picked clean aside from a chest with a dusting of snow on it.

- Chest

[3.D] Dragon Mound: Sea Shore Foothills

Related Quest: Main Quest: Elder Knowledge

This Dragon Mound is initially sealed. It opens during Main Quest: Elder Knowledge, and if you visit during or after this point in the Main Quest, the resurrected dragon will likely still be in the area. Engage!

[3.E] Barnacle Boat

Southwest from the Wreck of the *Brinehammer*, along the shore of the Sea of Ghosts, is a small upturned fishing boat. Now home to Mudcrabs, clear them out, and take the Fine Boots and Nordic Barnacle Clusters if you wish. But the real prize is the book.

- Skill Book [Alteration]: Daughter of the Niben
- Scimitar

[3.F] Shoreline Bandit Camp

On the northern shoreline side of a low rocky buttress north of the east-west path and northwest of Windward Ruins is a small fish-drying camp where three bandits are resting. Beware of bowmen here, and find a Skill Book resting atop a barrel.

- Skill Book [Destruction]: A Hypothetical Treachery
- Chest

[3.G] Dawnstar Frost Troll Den

If you're following the shoreline or taking the main road north to Dawnstar, then head along the rough snow path northwest and around to a shoreline overhang. Face down (or sneak behind) a Frost Troll for a chest with a Skill Book on it.

- Enemy: Frost Troll
- Skill Book [Block]: Death Blow of Abernanit
- Chest

[3.H] Shoreline Lovers' Tent

Follow the shoreline from Dawnstar Sanctuary to the east, passing Horkers, and step into an animal-skin tent with two bedrolls, some empty wine bottles, an Amulet of Mara, and a scattering of Red Mountain Flowers. The lovers who erected this tent are nowhere to be seen.

[3.I] A Bloody Trail

Side Quest: The Great Skyrim Treasure Hunt*

Approach this upper peak northward from Volunruud. Search the forested slopes for a bloodied male Wood Elf corpse. Follow the trail of blood upward, passing a long bow, into an area of rugged rocks, where another Wood Elf corpse lies.

- Treasure Map VI [1/11]
- Loose gear

[3.J] Border Corner: Roadside Shrine of Mara

Decorated with a sprig of Snowberry, this Shrine to Mara marks the general location of the borders between Hjaalmarch, the Pale, and Whiterun. Visit it easily if you head northeast from the path that takes you up and into Labyrinthian.

- Shrine of Mara [3/5]

[3.K] Mammoth Graveyard

Related Quests

Side Quest: Kyne's Sacred Trials

West of Loreius Farm, on the fringe of Whiterun Hold, lies a Mammoth Graveyard, where generations of these creatures have come to die. Giant stones and bone ornaments flank the entrance to this sacred site. A more recent corpse is being picked over by poachers when you arrive. If you are sent here for Kyne's Sacred Trials, you will face the Mammoth Guardian Spirit in this desolate place.

[3.L] Ice Shard Wild Animal Den

Off the beaten track and south of Fort Dunstad is a wooded area with deep snow and a wild animal den, usually populated with wolves. Shelter from the perpetual cold here, as the prey the wolves have dragged back have little worth looting.

[3.M] Dragon Mound: Shimmermist Hills

Related Quest: Main Quest: Elder Knowledge

This Dragon Mound is initially sealed. It opens during Main Quest: Elder Knowledge, and if you visit during or after this point in the Main Quest, the resurrected dragon will likely be circling this location. To battle!

[3.N] Julianos's Fallen

A half-buried skeleton is easy to miss, lying on a precarious abutment north of Shearpoint, overlooking the Lake Yorgrim basin below. This follower of Julianos was carrying a small shrine, which is also embedded in the ground.

- Shrine of Julianos [2/5]

[3.O] Yorgrim Forest Spider Trap

Among the trees just off the path that winds just northeast of Tumble Arch Pass are the remains of a section of dwarven masonry. Embedded into this stone is a chest. Approach, and around six Frostbite Spiders ambush you from the trees above!

- Chest

[3.P] Wayward Peak Summit

Above the tower to Blackreach and Forsaken Cave, you may be able to make out a tattered flag. If you manage to clamber up to the top, there's some equipment and an excellent view across the Yorgrim basin.

- Satchel
- Loose gear

[3.Q] Dragon Mound: Yorgrim Resurrection

Related Quest: Main Quest: Elder Knowledge

Related Quest: Main Quest: Alduin's Bane

This Dragon Mound is initially sealed. It opens during Main Quest: Elder Knowledge, once you learn that you need an Elder Scroll. After this point, but before you learn the Dragonrend Shout, Alduin will appear here and resurrect the dragon Viinturuth. Alduin cannot be harmed; he resurrects his brethren and flies off. But slay Viinturuth and claim his power for your own.

ADDITIONAL LOCATIONS

[DG.01] Dimhollow Crypt

Related Quests

Dawnguard Main Quest: Awakening

Dawnguard Main Quest: Bloodline

Recommended Level: 10

Faction: Vampire Lair

Death Hound
Draugr
Frostbite Spider
Lokil
Skeleton
Vampire
Vampire's Thrall

Special Area

Word Wall

Crafting

Arcane Enchanter

Puzzle

Ceremonial Crypt

Miscellaneous

Area is locked
Chest
Loose Gear
Potions

Exterior

The entrance to Dimhollow Crypt lies on a lonely, snowbound path that winds west and south up the mountain from the Hall of the Vigilant, in the Pale. You can also get there by trekking down from the Lord Stone.

Dimhollow Crypt

A Exit to Skyrim

1 Entrance Grotto

A short tunnel opens up into this grotto with a stream at its base. If Dawnguard Main Quest: Awakening is active, a group of vampires are speaking about the death of Vigilant Tolan. Expect combat with vampires, a thrall, and Death Hound. Then head south to the small stone tower and activate the chain inside to open the main entrance gate to the northeast.

If Dawnguard Main Quest: Awakening hasn't been started, only wolves are here, and a rockfall prevents you from progressing farther.

- Vigilant Tolan (Deceased)
- Chest
- Potions
- Loose Gear

2 Waterlogged Burial Chamber

After winding down a connecting stone corridor, expect four skeletons and a vampire to attack you here. To exit, pull the lever next to the gate in the western wall. Note the chest in the southeast corner.

- Chest

3 Draugr Catacombs

Expect combat between Draugr and a vampire, plus a Death Hound. The chamber has four portcullis gates leading to corridors. Three of the gates lead to a narrow dead end and a Draugr fight, a chest [Master], and a potion pedestal. The final, northwest gate has a passage leading deeper into the crypt.

- Arcane Enchanter
- Chest [Master]
- Potions

4 Waterlogged Cavern

Among the water and Namira's Rot mushrooms are a vampire and around four skeletons. To the south is Location #6 at the top of the waterfall.

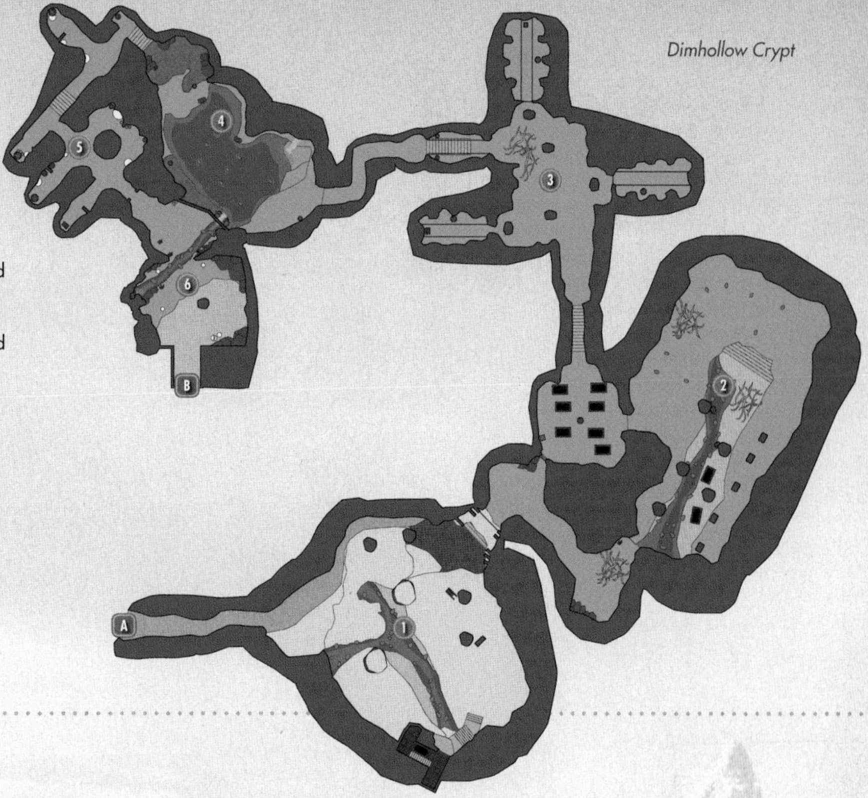

Dimhollow Crypt

5 Upper Draugr Catacombs

There are two vampire incursions here; the second vampire is accompanied by two Death Hounds. There are numerous dead Frostbite Spiders, urns to check, and a chest in one of the small dead-end corridors to the southwest.

◊ Chest

6 Cavern Gate

A strong vampire is usually finishing off a Giant Frostbite Spider in this chamber. Use the lever to open the gate, and rush the door to Dimhollow Cavern if the fight is unappealing.

B Door to Dimhollow Cavern

Dimhollow Cavern

B Door to Dimhollow Crypt

7 Lokil's Balcony

Although you may expect something to happen if you take the scroll from the pedestal, nothing does. Open the gate with the lever on the left. Gaze across the gloom at the central stone island, then descend and fight a vampire named Lokil and his brethren near a rock platform. The corpse they were talking about is that of a Vigilant of Stendarr named Adalvald. Claim his book, and check the chest tucked away in a corner behind the steps.

◊ Chest

◊ Adalvald's Journal

8 Ceremonial Crypt

This circular stone island is actually an elaborate sarcophagus. To open, solve the following puzzle:

Puzzle Solution: Follow the single line of flames back from the circle, and find the brazier it passes through. Push the brazier to the outer base it slides onto, channeling the fire around. This leads to another brazier to shift; continue to follow the fire around, channeling it onward using the braziers (there are five in total to push or pull; the fire won't move if you shove the brazier the wrong way). After the final brazier slots into place, a monolith is revealed. A Mysterious Woman, who was sealed in this crypt, falls out of it.

◊ Follower: Serana [DG1/13]

9 Gargoyle Ambush

This bridge and earthen slope allow exit from the circular crypt but is guarded by two ferocious gargoyles. Under the slope is a conjurer with a coin purse to check. On the upper balcony behind the gargoyles, above the graves, is a chest.

◊ Chest

10 Stepped Crypt Chamber

Head along the tunnel and up the steps to pull a lever, stirring a couple of Draugr and some skeletons; then raise the exit gate to the north. Check the table on the lower floor to the south for the following:

◊ Chest

◊ Spell Tome: Necromantic Healing

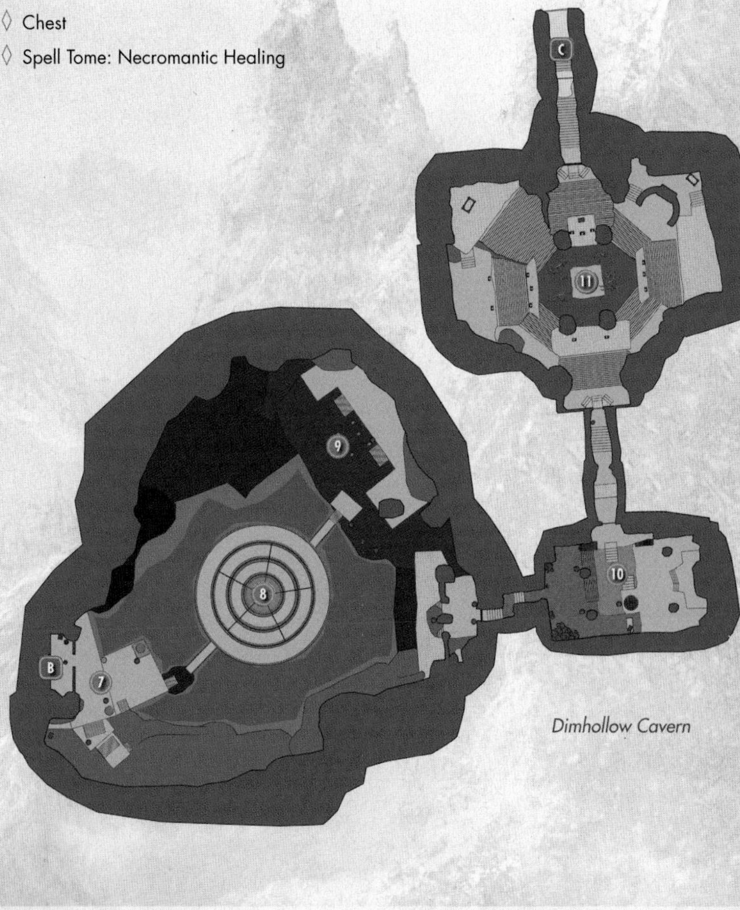

Dimhollow Cavern

Sacrificial Pit and Word Wall

The Nordic royals of yore sacrificed those who displeased them in this large pit. Expect combat with around four dangerous Draugr and skeletons here. Then check the entire stepped area for Deathbell flowers and Malachite Ore. Peek behind the Word Wall for coins and two leveled weapons, and loot the large chest. Or simply flee to the northern exit if combat becomes tricky.

- Malachite Ore Vein
- Chest
- Word of Power: Drain Vitality

Exit to Skyrim

Pull the chain on the right to exit into Skyrim. Now that the portcullis is up, you can enter Dimhollow Cavern from this entrance as well.

[HF.03] Heljarchen Hall

Related Quests

Hearthfire Task: Adoption
Hearthfire Task: Build Your Own House
Thane Task: Thane of Hjaalmarch

Services

Carriage Driver

Special Area

Shrine of Akatosh [HF2/3]
Shrine of Arkay [HF2/3]
Shrine of Dibella [HF2/3]
Shrine of Julianos [HF2/3]
Shrine of Kynareth [HF2/3]
Shrine of Mara [HF2/3]
Shrine of Stendarr [HF2/3]
Shrine of Talos [HF2/3]
Shrine of Zenithar [HF2/3]

Crafting

Alchemy Lab
Anvil or Blacksmith Forge
Arcane Enchanter
Carpenter's Workbench
Cooking Pot or Spit
Drafting Table
Grindstone
Oven
Smelter
Tanning Rack
Wood Chopping Block
Workbench

Miscellaneous

Area is locked
Chest
Loose gear
Potions Aplenty

A superb slice of land on the edge of the Pale, away from the most blistering of blizzards, this sits on firm tundra and offers exceptional views of Loreius Farm, Dragonsreach, and the Throat of the World in the far distance. Although there's a giant camp nearby, they've been quiet recently. The structure shown in the picture is simply one example of the property you could construct here, after finishing your Thane Task. This is the only buildable dwelling with a mill, which allows you to grind the flour required for most baking recipes.

- Follower: Gregor (Housecarl) [DG2/3]
- Land for Sale [2/3]
- Marriage Prospect: Gregor [DG2/3]

HOLD 4: WINTERHOLD HOLD

TOPOGRAPHICAL OVERVIEW

The northeastern coast of the Sea of Ghosts around the city of Winterhold is by far the least populated area of Skyrim, and the same can be said for the entire Hold. It has no towns or villages other than the capital, and many adventurers perish in the glacial fields that surround the city. Winterhold boasts a vast stretch of sharp and rugged coastline, and even the mouth of the White River, but it is otherwise devoid of flowing water. Instead, the vast majority of the Hold is either encased in snow or ice or part of the vast and treacherous Mount Anthor range, interspersed with strange or ancient burial sites, including the ominous Saarthal.

Routes and Pathways

There is but a single main road from Winterhold and its college of mages, which connects to the Pale. With no rivers, the only other pathways are the minor goat and hunting trails that weave through the mountains. These are recommended routes when first exploring such a vast and foreboding wilderness. The entire north and western part of the Hold is rugged coastline; don't forget your explorations can take you well into the Sea of Ghosts. To the west is Fort Fellhammer, a good marker since it is close to the border of the Pale. Should you refrain from using the main road, the Wayward Pass is another option, as the path it connects to weaves through the Mount Anthor range and takes in many locations. Otherwise, the edges of this Hold are less rocky and more glacial and feature a variety of lonely and lost barrows, including one said to be the tomb of the legendary warrior and founder of the Companions, Ysgramor.

AVAILABLE SERVICES, CRAFTING, AND COLLECTIBLES

Services
Followers: [4/47]
Houses for Sale: [0/5]
Marriage Prospects: [2/62]
Skill Trainers: [6/50]
- Alchemy: [0/3]
- Alteration: [1/3]
- Archery: [0/3]
- Block: [0/2]
- Conjuration: [1/3]
- Destruction: [1/3]
- Enchanting: [1/2]
- Heavy Armor: [0/3]
- Illusion: [1/2]
- Light Armor: [0/3]
- Lockpicking: [0/2]
- One-Handed: [0/3]
- Pickpocket: [0/3]
- Restoration: [1/3]
- Smithing: [0/3]
- Sneak: [0/3]
- Speech: [0/4]
- Two-Handed: [0/2]

Traders [13/133]:
- Apothecary [0/12]
- Bartender [0/5]
- Blacksmith [2/33]
- Carriage Driver [0/5]
- Fence [1/10]
- Ferryman [0/3]
- Fletcher [0/3]
- Food Vendor [0/9]
- General Goods [2/19]
- Innkeeper [0/15]
- Jeweler [0/2]
- Special [2/3]
- Spell Vendor [5/12]
- Stablemaster [0/5]

Collectibles
Captured Critters: [1/5]
Dragon Claws: [1/10]
Dragon Priest Masks: [0/10]
Larceny Targets: [1/7]
Skill Books: [12/180]
- Alchemy: [1/10]
- Alteration: [2/10]
- Archery: [0/10]
- Block: [2/10]
- Conjuration: [0/10]
- Destruction: [1/10]
- Enchanting: [1/10]
- Heavy Armor: [0/10]
- Illusion: [0/10]
- Light Armor: [0/10]
- Lockpicking: [2/10]
- One-Handed: [0/10]
- Pickpocket: [0/10]
- Restoration: [2/10]
- Smithing: [0/10]
- Sneak: [1/10]
- Speech: [0/10]
- Two-Handed: [0/10]

Treasure Maps: [2/11]
Unique Items: [15/112]
Unique Weapons: [6/80]
Unusual Gems: [3/24]

Special Objects
Shrines: [6/69]
- Akatosh: [0/6]
- Arkay: [2/12]
- Dibella: [1/8]
- Julianos: [0/5]
- Kynareth: [0/6]
- Mara: [0/5]
- Stendarr: [0/5]
- Talos: [3/17]
- Zenithar: [0/5]

Standing Stones: [2/13]
- The Serpent Stone
- The Tower Stone

Word Walls: [5/42]
- Animal Allegiance: [1/3]
- Aura Whisper: [0/3]
- Become Ethereal: [1/3]
- Disarm: [1/3]
- Dismaying Shout: [0/3]
- Elemental Fury: [0/3]
- Fire Breath: [0/2]
- Frost Breath: [0/3]
- Ice Form: [2/3]
- Kyne's Peace: [0/3]
- Marked for Death: [0/3]
- Slow Time: [0/3]
- Storm Call: [0/3]
- Throw Voice: [0/1]
- Unrelenting Force: [0/1]
- Whirlwind Sprint: [0/2]

CRAFTING STATIONS: WINTERHOLD

✓	TYPE	LOCATION A	LOCATION B
☐	Alchemy Lab	College of Winterhold (Hall of Countenance) [4.00]	College of Winterhold (Arch-Mage's Quarters) [4.00]
☐	Arcane Enchanter	College of Winterhold (Hall of Countenance) [4.00]	College of Winterhold (Arch-Mage's Quarters) [4.00]
☐	Anvil or Blacksmith forge	—	—
☐	Cooking Pot and Spit	Winterhold (Birna's Oddments) [4.00]	Winterhold (Kraldar's House) [4.00]
☐	Grindstone	Fort Kastav (Exterior) [4.19]	—
☐	Smelter	Fort Fellhammer [4.08]	—
☐	Tanning Rack	Wreck of the Pride of Tel Vos [4.22]	—
☐	Wood Chopping Block	—	—
☐	Workbench	—	—

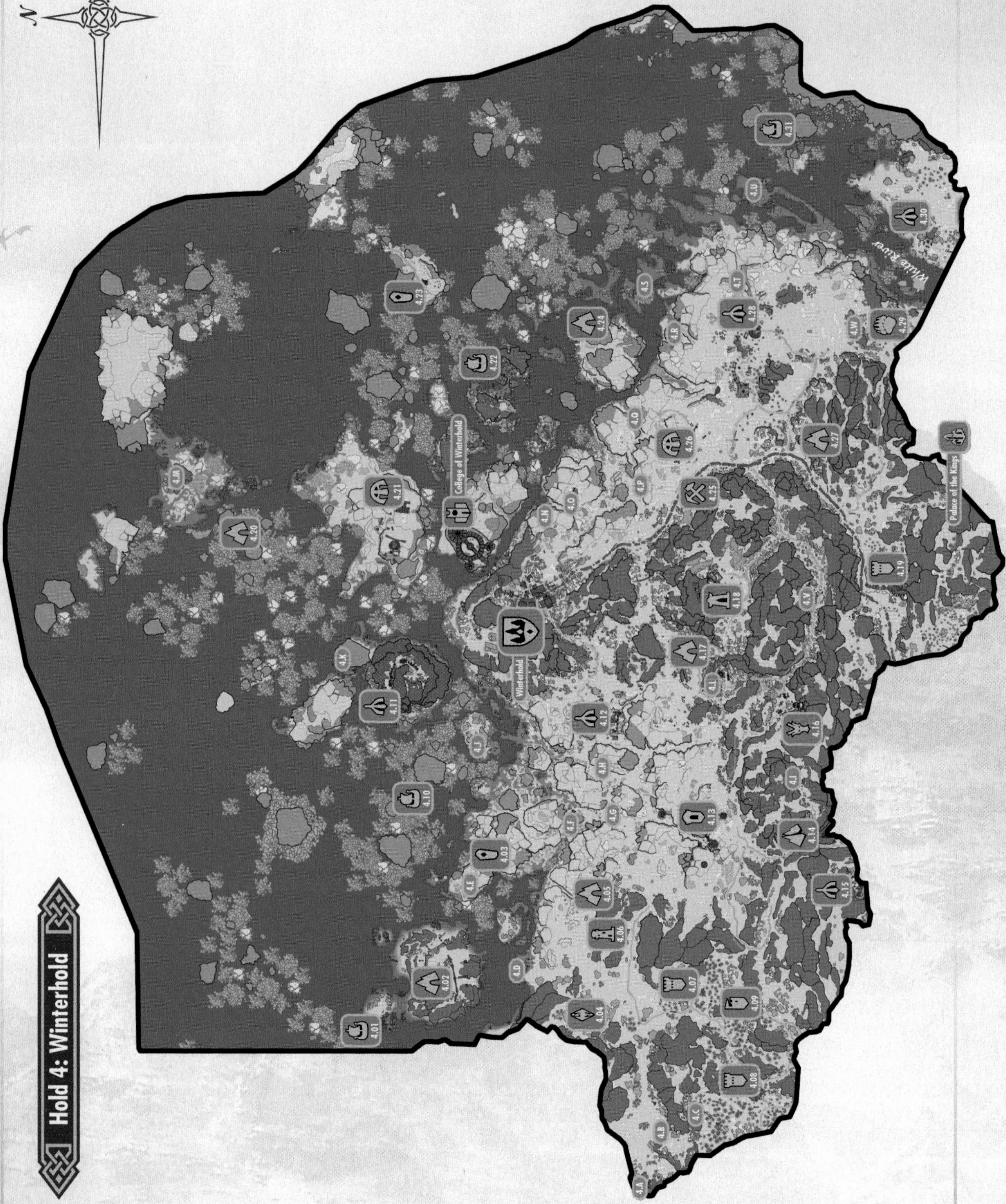

Hold 4: Winterhold

PRIMARY LOCATIONS

Total—33: Hold Capital, College of Winterhold, and 31 Hold Locations

- [4.00] Hold Capital City: Winterhold
- [4.00] College of Winterhold
  - Jarl: Korir
- [4.01] Hela's Folly
- [4.02] Yngvild
- [4.03] The Tower Stone
- [4.04] Winterhold Imperial Camp
- [4.05] Hob's Fall Cave
- [4.06] Frostflow Lighthouse
- [4.07] Driftshade Refuge
- [4.08] Fort Fellhammer
- [4.09] Snowpoint Beacon
- [4.10] Pilgrim's Trench
- [4.11] Ysgramor's Tomb
- [4.12] Saarthal
- [4.13] Alftand
- [4.14] Wayward Pass
- [4.15] Ironbind Barrow
- [4.16] Mount Anthor
- [4.17] Sightless Pit
- [4.18] Shrine of Azura
- [4.19] Fort Kastav
- [4.20] Septimus Signus's Outpost
- [4.21] Skytemple Ruins
- [4.22] Wreck of the Pride of Tel Vos
- [4.23] The Serpent Stone
- [4.24] Bleakcoast Cave
- [4.25] Whistling Mine
- [4.26] Journeyman's Nook
- [4.27] Stillborn Cave
- [4.28] Snow Veil Sanctum
- [4.29] Winterhold Stormcloaks Camp
- [4.30] Yngol Barrow
- [4.31] Wreck of the Winter War

SECONDARY LOCATIONS

Total—23 Points of Interest

- [4.A] Shrine of Dibella: Watching Dawnstar
- [4.B] Hunter's Overlook: Fellhammer Wastes
- [4.C] Wolf Den: Fellhammer Wastes
- [4.D] Yisra's Beachside Combustion
- [4.E] The Iceberg Explorer
- [4.F] Shrine of Talos: Winterhold Glaciers
- [4.G] Frozen Mammoth
- [4.H] Wet Bones
- [4.I] Dwarven Monument: Mount Anthor Summit
- [4.J] Shrine of Talos: Sea of Ghosts
- [4.K] Shrine of Talos: Ilas-Tei's Last Stand
- [4.L] Altar of Xrib
- [4.M] The Chill
- [4.N] Trapped for Eternity
- [4.O] Rundi's Mistake
- [4.P] Hunter's Camp: Glacier's Edge
- [4.Q] Haul of the Horkers
- [4.R] Hunters' Camp: Sea Shore of Ghosts
- [4.S] Hunter's Last Stand: Sea Shore of Ghosts
- [4.T] Ill-Gotten Gains: Sea Shore of Ghosts
- [4.U] Fisherman's Camp: Slaughterfish Bay
- [4.V] Avalanche Pass
- [4.W] Shrine of Arkay: Windhelm Hills

HOLD CAPITAL: WINTERHOLD

Related Quests

- Daedric Quest: The Black Star
- College of Winterhold Quest: First Lessons
- Thieves Guild Quest: Hard Answers
- Miscellaneous Objective: Innkeeper Rumors (The Frozen Hearth)
- Miscellaneous Objective: Finding Isabelle* (Dagur)
- Favor (Activity): A Drunk's Drink* (Ranmir)
- Favor: A Good Talking To* (Haran)
- Favor: A Little Light Thievery* (Malur Seloth)
- Favor: Jobs for the Jarls* (Jarl Korir)
- Thane Quest: Thane of Winterhold Hold*

Habitation: Hold Capital (Minor)

Services

- Trader (General Store Vendor): Birna [3/19]

Special Objects

- Civil War: Map of Skyrim

Collectibles

- Dragon Claw: Coral Dragon Claw [4/10]
- Skill Book [Alteration]: Breathing Water [A1/10]
- Skill Book [Destruction]: Mystery of Talara, v3 [C2/10]
- Skill Book [Restoration]: The Exodus [D1/10]
- Unique Item: The Black Star [26/112]
- Unique Weapon: Nightingale Blade [21/80]
- Unique Weapon: Staff of Arcane Authority [22/80]
- Chest
- Potions aplenty
- Loose gear

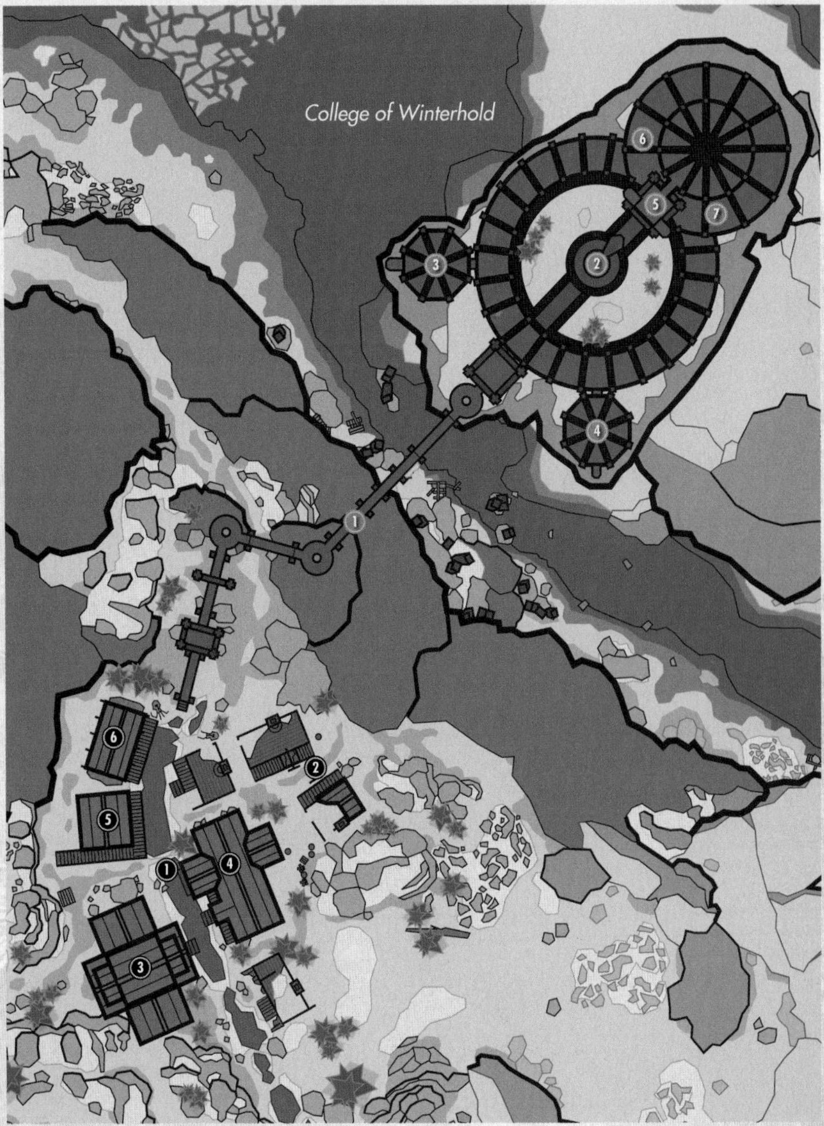

Hold Capital: Winterhold

Lore: City Overview

Once a great capital rivaling Solitude in power and importance, Winterhold is now little more than a shell of its former self. Eighty years ago, a seemingly never-ending series of storms lashed out at the northern coast of Skyrim, eventually causing most of the city to plummet into the Sea of Ghosts, an event now known as the Great Collapse. Strangely, the College of Winterhold was unaffected, remaining firm on a now freestanding spire of rock. Many inhabitants of Winterhold, both mages and magic-fearing Nords, were forced to abandon the city, and those who remained still eye the College with suspicion.

Since that time, the population of Winterhold has continued to dwindle. Other than the College, only a handful of buildings still stand. What remains of the town's economy is based around serving the needs of the College. As such, Winterhold has become something of a haven for mages in Skyrim, a safe refuge from distrustful Nords.

Important Areas of Interest

1 Main Thoroughfare

A single, snow-covered road winds past the dilapidated and collapsed structures of Winterhold, leading to the Winterhold Bridge and the domain of mages.

2 Ruins of the Cataclysm

Four of the town's main structures lie abandoned and rotting into the snowy ground. There are no items to snag of any worth.

3 Jarl's Longhouse

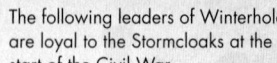

The following leaders of Winterhold are loyal to the Stormcloaks at the start of the Civil War.

Jarl Korir

Whatever optimism might have lived in Korir's heart was beaten down by decades of hearing how much better things used to be before the Great Collapse. Knowing nothing else, he carries on the grudges of his ancestors while refusing to abandon his home, so he's done everything he can to persevere. He'll maintain the traditions of his forefathers if it kills him, and he fails to realize the impact it's having on his son.

Thaena

Thaena's life isn't what it was supposed to be. The beautiful city she should've grown up in doesn't exist, her husband has turned into a bitter, cynical man, and the future for her son looks bleak. While Korir may stop short of assigning blame, Thaena has no problem pointing a finger at those responsible for her family's plight: the mages of Winterhold. Refusing to accept any responsibility for her situation, she's placed all the blame squarely on the shoulders of the College and spends every day cursing its existence.

Assur

Assur is confused by the reaction he gets when he repeats what his parents have always told him: mages can't be trusted, and anyone who uses magic is dangerous. He's been taught that warlocks and witches are even worse than elves, and no one but a Nord is a friend to Winterhold.

Malur Seloth

A slouch with few marketable skills, Melur has landed himself in what he perceives as a wonderful position. Korir is convinced that he's in cahoots with the mages of the College of Winterhold and therefore expects little of Malur in the way of servant's duties. Malur has done nothing to dissuade this misunderstanding; in fact, he's cultivating it to get away with as little work as possible. Naturally, he survives if the balance of power shifts to the Imperials.

Kai Wet-Pommel

The following residents arrive to take control of Winterhold, should this Hold fall during the Civil War.

Jarl Kraldar

Kraldar is, by all accounts, what may well be the last in a long line of nobility in Winterhold, due to the cataclysm. He understands that while the College may seem a bit of an eyesore to the rest of the province, being on good terms with the Arch-Mage is in Winterhold's best interest. Ever the optimist, he firmly believes that Winterhold will be restored to greatness someday, and often regales his Housecarl with his dreams for the future. He's less chatty with Malur Seloth.

Thonjolf (Housecarl)

Thonjolf's family has served the Kraldars for generations. It's all he knows. It doesn't matter that there's little for him to actually do or that the Great City of Winterhold doesn't exist anymore; he has a duty and he will perform it to the best of his ability. He's aware of Malur's abuse of his position and has repeatedly attempted to speak to Kraldar about it. Kraldar refuses to listen, so Thonjolf grows more frustrated with every passing day.

One of the buildings of old Winterhold has been repurposed as the Jarl's Longhouse, since the original home of the Jarl was lost in the Great Collapse. Korir rules from this new location, though currently there's very little "ruling" that actually takes place; the College remains separated from the mainland (both physically and socially), and the handful of residents left need little governing on a daily basis. Korir is convinced that without the Imperials or the College, Winterhold will someday regain its former glory. Jarl Korir is grateful for any protection and actively encourages the Stormcloaks to plan their attacks from his war room. In the downstairs bedroom, a Skill Book has been stashed in a woven basket that sits atop a barrel.

- Skill Book [Enchanting]: Twin Secrets
- Civil War: Map of Skyrim
- Chest
- Potions aplenty
- Loose gear

NOTE There is no jail in Winterhold, but that doesn't mean you can hack, steal, or annoy anyone you please. If you're caught committing a crime in Winterhold, you're taken to serve out your sentence on a remote glacial cave north of here in the Sea of Ghosts, aptly named the Chill. See the Secondary Location for the details.

4 The Frozen Hearth

Dagur	Nelacar
Haran	Angwe
Eirid	

The only profitable business left in Winterhold, the Inn serves as the sole place petitioners to the College may stay. As such, Dagur has put aside any personal feelings he may have toward wizards and does his best to look on the bright side. Nelacar is paying Dagur good money to maintain a small room in the Inn, where he can do some research on his own, away from the College. He also takes a cut of Enthir's questionable sales downstairs in the cellar. Enthir (a member of the College) stays here during the Thieves Guild Quests and becomes a Fence for you. Down in the cellar, a Skill Book is hidden among a collection of crates and sacks.

- Skill Book [Restoration]: The Exodus [D1/10]
- Unique Item: The Black Star [26/112]
- Unique Weapon: Nightingale Blade [21/80]
- Unique Weapon: Staff of Arcane Authority [22/80]
- Chest (3)

5 Birna's Oddments

Ranmir	Birna

Birna's family has lived there for generations beyond count, and no amount of natural disaster or weird magic is going to drive her out now.

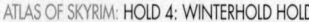

Her family's house is also a small shop selling a variety of items. She'll even part with a strange claw if the price is right.

- Trader (General Store Vendor): Birna [3/19]
  - Potions, Food, Misc
- Dragon Claw: Coral Dragon Claw [4/10]
- Skill Book [Destruction]: Mystery of Talara, v3 [C3/10]
- Potions aplenty
- Loose gear

6 Kraldar's House

One of the last few holdouts, Kraldar refuses to give up and move away from Winterhold.

Everything he has been through has instilled a great distrust for the mages of the College that borders on hatred. Kraldar is a pleasant sort, convinced that Winterhold will someday again be the shining jewel of Skyrim that it once was. Check inside the woven basket on the shelf to discover a hidden Skill Book.

- Skill Book [Alteration]: Breathing Water [A1/10]
- Chest

COLLEGE OF WINTERHOLD

Related Quests

Main Quest: Elder Knowledge
Daedric Quest: The Black Star
Daedric Quest: Discerning the Transmundane
Side Quest: Forbidden Legend
College of Winterhold Quest: First Lessons
College of Winterhold Quest: Under Saarthal
College of Winterhold Quest: Hitting the Books
College of Winterhold Quest: Good Intentions
College of Winterhold Quest: Revealing the Unseen
College of Winterhold Quest: Containment
College of Winterhold Quest: The Staff of Magnus
College of Winterhold Quest: The Eye of Magnus
College of Winterhold Radiant Quest: Rejoining the College
College of Winterhold Radiant Quest: Tolfdir's Alembic*
College of Winterhold Radiant Quest: Out of Balance*
College of Winterhold Radiant Quest: An Enchanted Journey*
College of Winterhold Radiant Quest: Restocking Soul Gems*
College of Winterhold Radiant Quest: Valuable Book Procurement*
College of Winterhold Radiant Quest: Shalidor's Insights
College of Winterhold Radiant Quest: The Atronach Forge*
College of Winterhold Radiant Quest: Tolfdir's Alembic*
College of Winterhold Radiant Quest: Forgotten Names*
College of Winterhold Radiant Quest: Aftershock*
College of Winterhold Radiant Quest: Rogue Wizard
College of Winterhold Radiant Quest: Arniel's Endeavor
College of Winterhold Radiant Quest: Apprentice: Brelyna's Practice
College of Winterhold Radiant Quest: Apprentice: J'Zargo's Experiment
College of Winterhold Radiant Quest: Apprentice: Onmund's Request
College of Winterhold Radiant Quest: Destruction Ritual Spell
College of Winterhold Radiant Quest: Illusion Ritual Spell
College of Winterhold Radiant Quest: Conjuration Ritual Spell
College of Winterhold Radiant Quest: Restoration Ritual Spell
College of Winterhold Radiant Quest: Alteration Ritual Spell
Thieves Guild Radiant Quest: No Stone Unturned
Miscellaneous Objective: Lost Apprentices: Borvir* (Phinis Gestor)
Miscellaneous Objective: Lost Apprentices: Ilas-tei* (Phinis Gestor)
Miscellaneous Objective: Lost Apprentices: Rundi* (Phinis Gestor)
Miscellaneous Objective: Lost Apprentices: Yisra* (Phinis Gestor)

Habitation: Special

Crafting

Alchemy Labs (3)
Arcane Enchanters (2)

Services

Follower: Brelyna Maryon [9/47]
Follower: J'Zargo [10/47]
Follower: Onmund [11/47]
Marriage Prospect: Brelyna Maryon [8/62]
Marriage Prospect: Onmund [9/62]
Trader (Fence): Enthir [2/11]
Trader (General Store Vendor): Enthir [4/19]
Trader (Special): Enthir [1/3]
Trader (Spell Vendor): Tolfdir [4/12]
Trader (Spell Vendor): Phinis Gestor [5/12]
Trader (Spell Vendor): Faralda [6/12]
Trader (Spell Vendor): Drevis Neloren [7/12]
Trader (Spell Vendor): Colette Marence [8/12]
Trainer (Tolfdir: Master): Alteration [2/3]
Trainer (Phinis Gestor: Expert): Conjuration [2/3]
Trainer (Faralda: Expert): Destruction [2/3]
Trainer (Sergius Turrianus: Expert): Enchanting [1/2]
Trainer (Drevis Neloren: Master): Illusion [1/2]
Trainer (Colette Marence: Expert): Restoration [2/3]

Collectibles

Skill Book [Alchemy]: De Rerum Dirennis [B2/10]
Unique Item: Arch-Mage's Robes [27/112]
Unique Item: Mage's Circlet [28/112]
Unique Item: Savos Aren's Amulet [29/112]
Unique Item: Mystic Tuning Gloves [30/112]
Unusual Gem: [5/24]
Chest
Potions aplenty

NOTE For more information on the College and biographies of the mages who live, teach, or learn there, please consult the College of Winterhold Quests, beginning on page 252.

Notable College Inhabitants

Savos Aren (Arch-Mage)

Unique Item: Arch-Mage's Robes [27/112]
Unique Item: Mage's Circlet [28/112]

Ancano (Thalmor Advisor)

Mirabelle Ervine (Master-Wizard)

Unique Item: Savos Aren's Amulet [29/112]

Enthir (Scholar)

Trader: Fence [2/11] (during Thieves Guild Quests only)
Trader: General Store Vendor [4/19]
Trader: Special [1/3]

Tolfdir (Wizard)

Trader: Spell Vendor [4/13]
Weapons, Scrolls, Books, Misc
Trainer: Alteration: Master [2/3]

Phinis Gestor (Wizard)

Trader: Spell Vendor [5/13]
Scrolls, Books, Misc
Trainer: Conjuration: Expert [2/3]

Faralda (Wizard)

Trader: Spell Vendor [6/13]
Weapons, Scrolls, Books, Misc
Trainer: Destruction: Expert [2/3]

Sergius Turrianus (Wizard)

Trainer: Enchanting: Expert [1/2]

Drevis Neloren (Wizard)

Trader: Spell Vendor [8/13]
Weapons, Scrolls, Books, Misc
Trainer: Illusion: Master [1/2]
Unique Item: Mystic Tuning Gloves [30/112]

Colette Marence (Scholar)

Trader: Spell Vendor [9/13]
Scrolls, Books, Misc
Trainer: Restoration: Expert [2/3]

Arniel Gane (Scholar)

Nirya (Scholar)

Urag gro-Shub (Lorekeeper)

Trader: Special [2/3]

Brelyna Maryon (Student)

Follower [9/47]
Marriage Prospect [8/62]

J'Zargo (Student)

Follower [10/47]

Onmund (Student)

Follower [11/47]
Marriage Prospect [9/62]

Augur of Dunlain

1 Winterhold Bridge

Many of the townsfolk in Winterhold think this bridge is being held up by magic alone, and they are correct. Faralda waits to greet (or halt) anyone thinking of entering the College, forcing them to prove they have an aptitude for magic. Ignore her, and the gates into the College remain closed to you. Fall from the bridge, and expect a long death plummet. Walk on the shores of the Sea of Ghosts below, and you'll find the remains of fallen masonry and stones, but only Clams, Nordic Barnacles, and Slaughterfish Eggs to collect.

2 Main Courtyard

Dominated by a statue of the first Arch-Mage of the College, this is the hub of the facility, offering access back out to the bridge and into the three Halls and one of the trapdoors into the murky depths of the Midden. The exterior windows offer exceptional views of the coastline.

> **NOTE** If you're looking for a specific member of the College, most move constantly throughout the Halls of Attainment, Countenance, and Elements. Any mages who are usually in a single location are mentioned below.

3 Hall of Attainment

This is to the west of the Courtyard and is where the students and some of the teachers rest. If you join the College, the first room on your right is where you can sleep. There are two floors and a door up onto the roof where you can access the other main parts of the College, which can be accessed from ground level as well.

◊ Chest (2)

4 Hall of Countenance

The senior members of the College have a home here, which is a tower laid out in the same fashion as the Hall of Attainment. Check the upper floor and the roof access. There are many staffs here, but stealing them isn't wise. The ingredients (and Soul Gems) on display near the Alchemy Lab (and Arcane Enchanter) can be used without penalty, so seek them out if you're looking for a particularly rare item (or gem) to craft. Also note the trapdoor entrance to the Midden at the base of the spiral steps.

Crafting: Alchemy Lab, Arcane Enchanter
◊ Tolfdir's Alembic
◊ Chest
◊ Potions aplenty
◊ Loose gear

5 Hall of the Elements

The College's grand central chamber is where students practice their magic and senior members discuss important matters. You attend your first lesson in magic here. Ancano usually mooches around these parts. This is a major location during the College of Winterhold Quests. The entrance is flanked by two doors, each leading to a higher level of the main tower.

6 Arch-Mage's Quarters

You can reach the Arch-Mage's Quarters from the Hall of the Elements or the Arcanaeum. These are the chambers of Savos Aren, where he spends some of his time. The circular chamber is lined with ingredients for mixing and features a fungal garden lit by magical floating lights. These aren't yours to take, unless you wish to incur the wrath of the College elders (or can manage it without being seen!) or you're patient enough to complete the College quest line, at which point the chamber becomes yours.

◊ Crafting: Alchemy Lab, Arcane Enchanter
◊ Unusual Gem: [5/24]

7 The Arcanaeum

You can reach the Arcanaeum from the Hall of the Elements or the roof parapets. This is the home to Urag gro-Shub the Lorekeeper and his extensive collection of tomes (although he's always on the lookout for more research materials). The Ysmir Collective, a selection of rare books, is on display, and many books are scattered about. If you want to read, you've come to the right place. The Investigator's Chest has rings to be used in the Midden, as part of College of Winterhold Radiant Quest: Forgotten Names.

◊ Investigator's Chest

The Midden

The Midden, a hidden underbelly where ancient and unspeakable magic has been practiced (and mostly forgotten about) isn't a place where College members usually go.

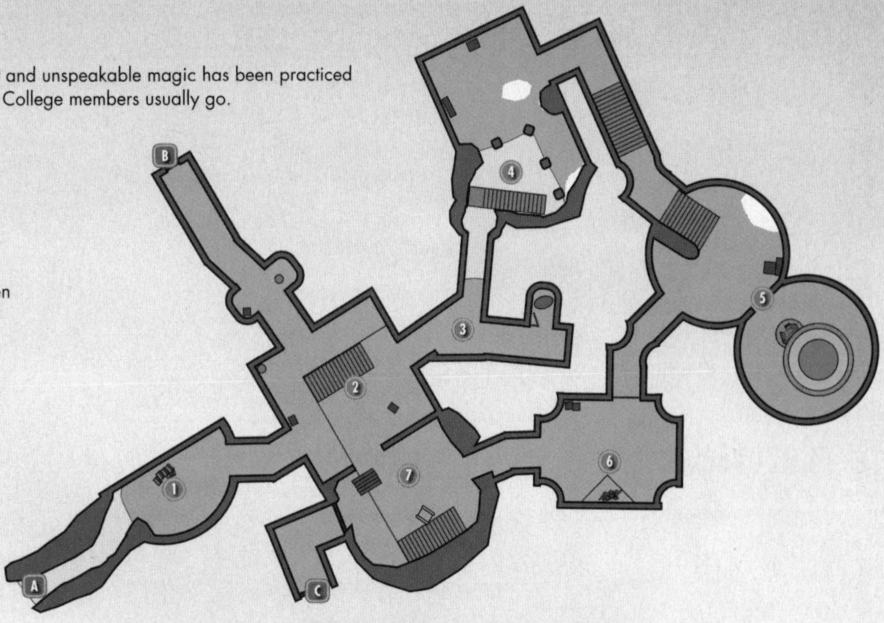

A Ladder to Main Courtyard

1 Semicircular Chamber

2 Torture Chamber Tower

Some rotting rugs lie at the bottom of the wooden steps, overlooked by two clamped skeletons. There are four exits to choose from here.

B Hagraven's Corridor

Pass the deer skull altar to reach this exit door.

3 Wet Bones and Blood

An unpleasant sacrifice was made here.

4 Snow Catacombs

5 Summoning Chamber

A large summoning circle is lit with an offering box to fill. This is the Atronach forge and used in the quest of that name.

6 Ancient Altar

7 Torture Chamber Tower (Waterfall)

This provides access to the Midden Dark.

C Door to Midden Dark

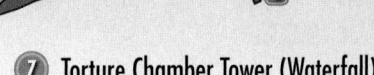

The Midden Dark

D Door to Midden

8 Chasm Bridge

Pass the skeletal design on the wall and watch your footing. Drop down if you wish.

◊ Chest

9 Catacombs Junction

10 Chamber of Augur of Dunlain (Locked: Requires Key)

The entity that lives in the depths of the Midden is holed up here. Speak to him only during specific quests.

11 Alchemy Offerings and Bone Pile

A small lab and an interesting book are available, prior to a skeleton skirmish.

◊ Crafting: Alchemy Lab

◊ Skill Book [Alchemy]: De Rerum Dirennis [B2/10]

12 Daedric Gauntlet

This bears the Sigil of Oblivion. It is the focus of Radiant Quest: Forgotten Names.

13 The Unlucky Goat

Slain in this snow cave, this is evidence of necromancy!

14 Spider Catacombs

E Exit to Skyrim

This exit is one-way and brings you out onto a rocky outcrop. From here you have a view of the Sea of Ghosts and the Skytemple Ruins.

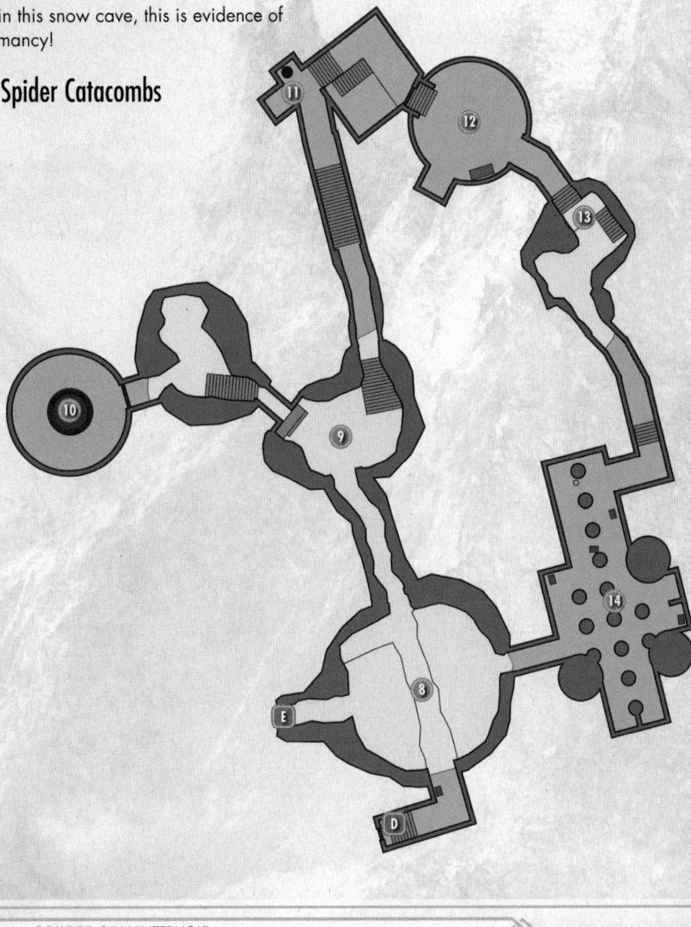

[4.01] Hela's Folly

Related Quests

Dark Brotherhood Quest: Side Contract: Deekus

Recommended Level: 6

Dungeon: Shipwreck

Deekus

Chest (Locked: Novice)

Chest (Locked: Apprentice)

A treasure-seeker named Deekus has made camp near a shipwreck along Winterhold's treacherous northern coastline. One of the Dark Brotherhood's side contracts marks this Argonian as a target. Deekus has amassed a hoard of precious gemstones and baubles. Steal these valuables to gain a small fortune, if you dare. Hop aboard the remnants of the nearby ship and dive underwater to discover a locked chest and additional gemstones aboard the ship's sunken half.

[4.02] Yngvild

Related Quests

Side Quest: No Stone Unturned

Miscellaneous Objective: Toying with the Dead*

Recommended Level: 8

Dungeon: Warlock Lair

Aroundil

Draugr

Yngvild Ghost

Collectibles

Skill Book [Alteration]: Reality & Other Falsehoods [C1/10]

Unusual Gem: [6/24]

Chest(s)

Potions

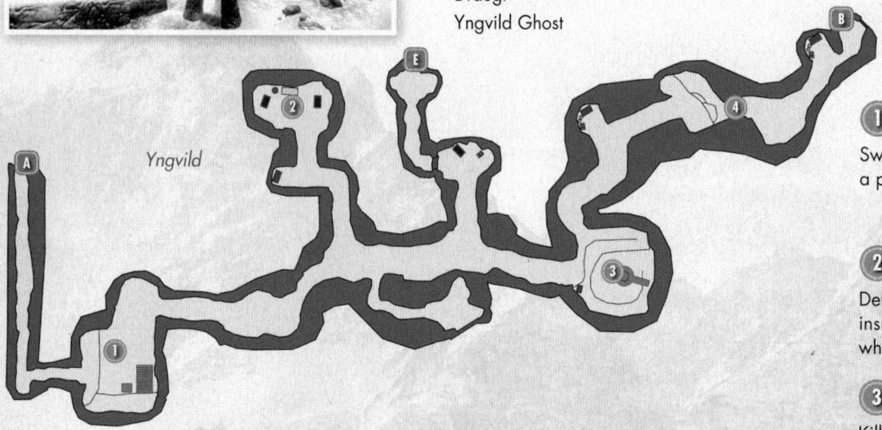

These ancient burial grounds lie on a frozen island in northeast Winterhold and are home to powerful undead. Arondil has been thrown out of Dawnstar and has unearthed and resurrected undead here. They are only female, however. His journals hint as his vile intentions.

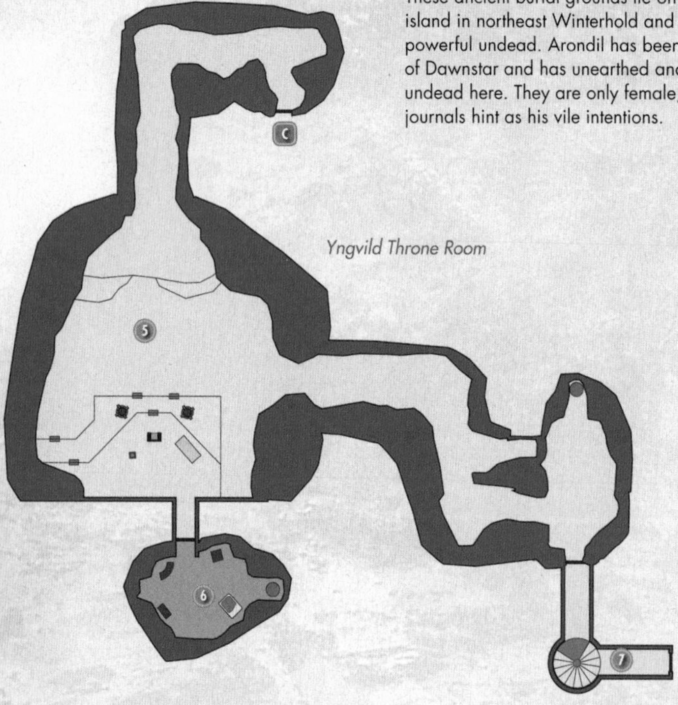

A Exit to Skyrim

1 Entry Cavern

Swipe a few potions in this first cavern, then battle a powerful Draugr on your way to [2].

◊ Potions

2 Urn Cavern

Defeat a deadly Yngvild Ghost and read an insightful journal on your way to this small cavern, where several urns beg looting.

3 Tall Cavern

Kill more ghosts and more mighty Draugr on your way to this tall cavern, then descend to the bottom, where a chest awaits.

◊ Chest

4 Passage to Throne Room

Slay another ghost and scan another two journals on your way to the Yngvild Throne Room.

◊ Potions

B Door to Yngvild Throne Room

C Door to Yngvild

5 Throne Room

A powerful mage named Arondil sits on a throne in this wide cavern. Slay him and collect a key from his corpse. Snatch the Skill Book that rests on a nearby table as well.

◊ Skill Book [Alteration]: Reality & Other Falsehoods [C1/10]

◊ Arondil's Key (Arondil)

6 Arondil's Quarters

Raid the giant chest in Arondil's private chamber, and collect the Unusual Gem from the table to gain a new Miscellaneous Objective.

- Unusual Gem: [6/24]
- Chest
- Potions

7 Exit Passage

Throw a lever in this final stretch to raise a portcullis, then use the key you found on Arondil to unlock the iron door and make your way back to Yngvild's entrance. Loot a locked chest on your way out.

- Chest (Locked: Apprentice)

D Door to Yngvild

E Door to Yngvild Throne Room

[4.03] The Tower Stone

Recommended Level: 6

Special Objects:

Standing Stone: The Tower Stone [4/13]

Ancient stones stand atop this glacial spire on Winterhold's frozen northwest coastline. Inspect the central Standing Stone to accept a new sign blessing. Those under the sign of the Tower can automatically open one Expert-level or lower lock once per day. Note that you can have only one sign blessing at a time, so activating this Standing Stone will override your current sign blessing (if any).

[4.04] Winterhold Imperial Camp

Related Quests

Civil War Quest: Reunification of Skyrim

Civil War Quest: Rescue from Fort Kastav

Habitation: Military: Imperial Camp

Imperial Quartermaster (Blacksmith)

Legate Sevan Telendas

Services

Trader (Blacksmith): Imperial Quartermaster [9/33]

Weapons, Apparel, Misc

Crafting

Alchemy Lab

Anvil

Grindstone

Workbench

Special Objects

Civil War: Map of Skyrim

Chests (2)

Potions

Loose gear

The Imperials have made camp in the frigid northwest mountains of Winterhold. Note that this Imperial campsite may only exist when you're playing through the Civil War quest line. Trade with the quartermaster if you like, or use his bevy of crafting stations. Inspect the tabletop map in the largest tent to potentially gain new map data. Loot a few chests before moving on.

[4.05] Hob's Fall Cave

Related Quests

Other Factions: Bards College Quest: Pantea's Flute

Side Quest: No Stone Unturned

Recommended Level: 8

Dungeon: Warlock Lair

Mage

Skeleton

Crafting

Alchemy Lab

Arcane Enchanter

Collectibles

Skill Book [Enchanting]: Enchanter's Primer [D1/10]

Skill Book [Restoration]: The Exodus

Unusual Gem: [7/24]

Chest(s)

Potions

Loose gear

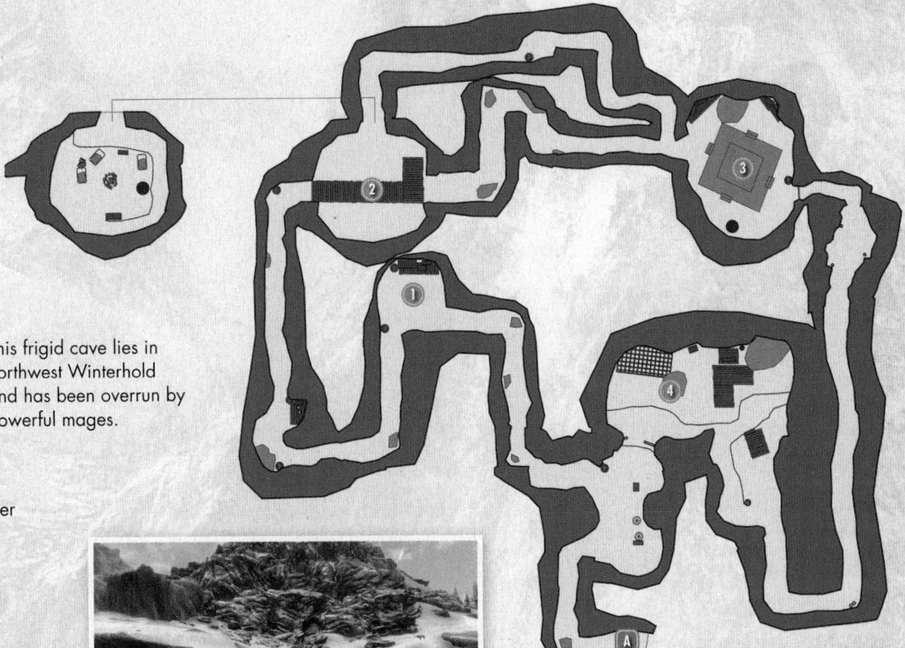

This frigid cave lies in northwest Winterhold and has been overrun by powerful mages.

Ⓐ Exit to Skyrim

① Mage's Cavern

Slay a skeleton on your way to this small cavern, where a mage defends several potions and a chest.

- ◊ Chest
- ◊ Potions

② Bridge Chamber

Avoid falling from this chamber's wooden rope bridge—it's a long way down. Instead, visit the bottom of this chamber by venturing down the north passage just before you reach [3]. Collect the Skill Book from the table here, along with the Unusual Gem that sits on the nearby cupboard—the latter begins a Side Quest.

- ◊ Crafting: Alchemy Lab
- ◊ Skill Book [Restoration]: The Exodus
- ◊ Unusual Gem: [7/24]
- ◊ Potions

③ Head Mage's Lair

A powerful spellcaster lurks in this wide chamber. Raid the place after slaying the mage, collecting a Skill Book from atop an Arcane Enchanter before pulling a wall chain to open the way forward. Steal Soul Gems from the pedestals in the passage that follows to deactivate the dangerous frost spout.

- ◊ Crafting: Arcane Enchanter
- ◊ Skill Book [Enchanting]: Enchanter's Primer [D1/10]
- ◊ Chest (Locked: Apprentice)
- ◊ Apothecary's Satchel
- ◊ Potions

④ Mage's Study

Several learned spellweavers guard this final cavern—slay them all to secure a large chest, then drop off the west cliff to return to the cave's first chamber.

- ◊ Chest ◊ Potion ◊ Loose gear

[4.06] Frostflow Lighthouse

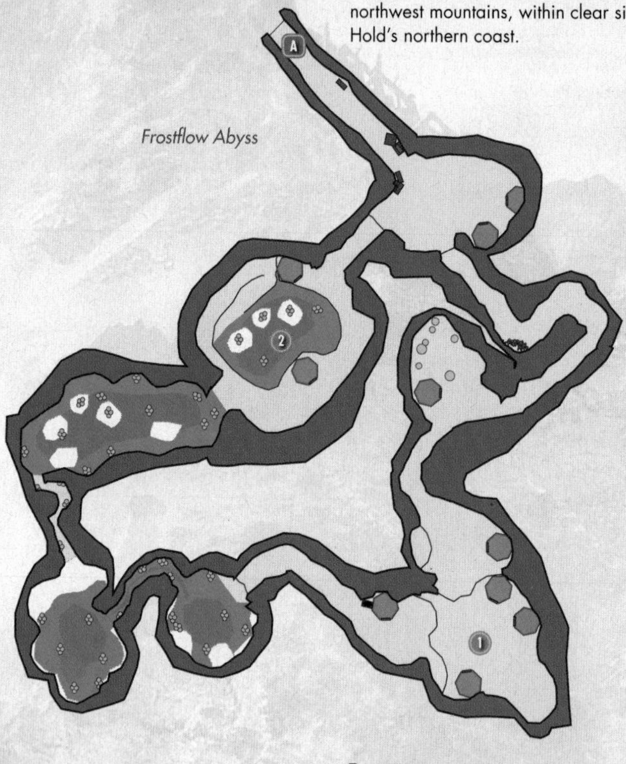

Dangers

Falmer Claw Trap (trip wire)

Collectibles

Captured Critter: Torchbug in a Jar [2/5]
Skill Book [Restoration]: Mystery of Talara, v2 [B2/10]
Chest(s)
Potions
Loose gear

This tall watchtower stands atop Winterhold's northwest mountains, within clear sight of the Hold's northern coast.

Related Quests

Side Quest: Captured Critters*
Dungeon Quest: What Lies Beneath*

Recommended Level: 18

Dungeon: Falmer Hive

Animal
Falmer

Exterior

Pick the Novice door lock to open the small storage shed that's attached to the lighthouse. A few potions are found within.

- ◊ Potions
- ◊ Loose gear

Frostflow Lighthouse (Interior)

Enter the tower to discover a butchered person. Search the corpse to gain a new Dungeon Quest and obtain an informative journal. A Torchbug in a Jar rests atop the mantel—this pertains to Side Quest: Captured Critters. In the northern room, you find Sudi's Journal on the desk, Mani's Letter in the knapsack under the bed, and a Skill Book. In the room adjacent, you find the journal of Ramati, the dead woman you just found. Piecing together the story from these journals will lead you to find Mani's Cellar Key, hidden in an urn on the mantel above the fireplace. Ramati's Journal also mentions a promise to cremate her husband in the lighthouse fire in the event of his death (this is important later).

Take the key and use it to reach the cellar where you can clear out a cluster of Chaurus and loot a locked chest. Venture through the large hole in the basement's southeast wall to proceed to the Frostflow Abyss.

- ◊ Captured Critter: Torchbug in a Jar [2/5]
- ◊ Skill Book [Restoration]: Mystery of Talara, v2 [B2/10]
- ◊ Chest (Locked: Adept)
- ◊ Mani's Cellar Key
- ◊ Mani's Letter
- ◊ Ramati's Journal
- ◊ Sudi's Journal
- ◊ Potions
- ◊ Loose gear

Ⓐ Path to Frostflow Lighthouse

① Falmer Den

Exterminate a Chaurus, Falmer, and Frostbite Spiders as you head to this chamber. Carefully trigger a trip wire from a safe distance to disable the Falmer Claw Trap as well. Dispatch all Falmer here, then search the tents to find two chests. Locate a third chest along the passage to [2].

- ◊ Danger! Falmer Claw Trap (trip wire)
- ◊ Chest (Locked: Novice)
- ◊ Chest (Locked: Apprentice)

② Chaurus Nest

Slay countless Chaurus on your way to this final cavern, where a monstrous Chaurus lurks—the source of the murders back in the lighthouse. Defeat the fiend to purify this place and complete the Miscellaneous Objective you acquired when you first entered the lighthouse. Collect the key you find within the giant Chaurus's remains, along with Habd's Remains (trust us); then take the exterior path to reach a chest with valuable loot.

- Habd's Lighthouse Key (Chaurus)
- Habd's Remains (Chaurus)
- Chest

Rooftop Loot

Now that you've solved the lighthouse's mystery, backtrack to the main level and use your newfound key to open the door that leads to the roof. Open the giant chest you find on the roof to obtain a nice haul of plunder. If you like, you may also throw Habd's Remains into the signal fire to receive a special blessing called Sailor's Repose, which permanently increases how much you heal with spells by 10 percent.

[4.07] Driftshade Refuge

Related Quests

The Companions Quest: Purity of Revenge

Recommended Level: 6

Dungeons: Vampire Lair

Silver Hand

Crafting

Anvil
Grindstone
Workbench

Dangers

Swinging Wall Trap (pressure plate)

Collectibles

Skill Book [Block]: Warrior [E1/10]
Skill Book [Light Armor]: The Rear Guard
Skill Book [One-Handed]: 2920, Morning Star, v1
Chest(s)
Potions
Loose gear

Though it appears to be a small barracks, the Driftshade Refuge features a sizeable tunnel network that's filled with ruthless ruffians known as the Silver Hand—hated enemies of the Companions. You must fight your way through this area during Companions Quest: Purity of Revenge.

Ⓐ Door to Skyrim

① Great Hall

Eliminate severeal Silver Hand and swipe a few minor valuables on your way to this chamber, where a chest awaits pillaging in a nook downstairs.

- Chest (Locked: Adept)
- Potions
- Loose gear

② Sleeping Quarters

Pick a locked door to enter this small sleeping area, then slay the groggy guard and plunder the place.

- Area Is Locked (Adept)
- Chest
- Potions

③ Cellar Access

Dispatch more Silver Hand in this far chamber and pillage a chest before pulling the wall lever to open a passage that leads to the cellar.

- Chest
- Potions

Ⓑ Door to Driftshade Cellar

Ⓒ Door to Driftshade Refuge

④ Barrel-Lined Passage

As you enter the cellar, search for a chest that's tucked away in a dark corner among barrels. Jump a pressure plate trap in this area, and don't bother picking the locked holding cell—the slain werewolf within has nothing of value.

- Danger! Swinging Wall Trap (pressure plate)
- Chest
- Potions
- Loose gear

⑤ Distillery

Dispatch several Silver Hand ruffians here, then collect the Skill Book on the far shelf.

- Skill Book [Light Armor]: The Rear Guard
- Potions

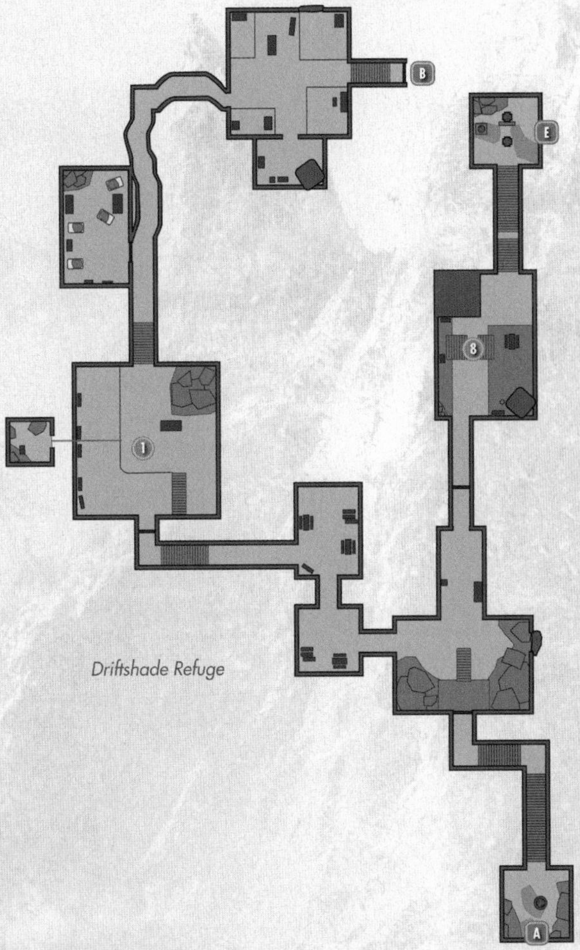

Driftshade Cellar

6 Holding Cells

Enter this snowy cavern, which features two giant holding cells, one of which contains a live werewolf. Free the creature if you dare, but be ready for a challenging battle.

7 Cellar Hearth

Check behind the large fireplace here to find some potions and a coin purse. Then head through the nearby door to return to the Refuge.

- ◊ Potions

D Door to Driftshade Refuge

E Door to Driftshade Cellar

8 Crafting Station

Lay waste to the final crew of Silver Hand bandits here, then locate two Skill Books and loot a large chest before unbarring the far door and making your way back outside.

- ◊ Crafting: Anvil, Grindstone, Workbench
- ◊ Skill Book [Block]: Warrior [E1/10]
- ◊ Skill Book [One-Handed]: 2920, Morning Star, v1
- ◊ Chest

[4.08] Fort Fellhammer

Recommended Level: 6

Dungeons: Bandit Camp
Bandit

Crafting
Smelter

Collectibles
Skill Book [Heavy Armor]: Orsinium and the Orcs
Chest(s)
Potions
Loose gear
Mineable ore (Iron)

This bandit-ridden keep stands at the west base of Winterhold's western mountains.

Garrison

Slay the bandit chief inside the small garrison and loot the large chest for valuables.

- ◊ Chest
- ◊ Potions
- ◊ Loose gear

Mines

A skilled hand is required to pick the lock to this fort's interior mines, where more bandits lurk and iron can be harvested in abundance. More importantly, a Skill Book rests on the far table.

- ◊ Area Is Locked (Expert)
- ◊ Skill Book [Heavy Armor]: Orsinium and the Orcs
- ◊ Mineable ore (Iron)

[4.09] Snowpoint Beacon

Recommended Level: 5

Dungeon: Bandit Camp
Bandit

Collectible
Chest (Locked: Novice)

Bandits have overrun this small tower, which stands atop Winterhold's west mountains. The chief awaits up top. Loot his body after the slaughter for plenty of plunder.

[4.10] Pilgrim's Trench

Recommended Level: 6

Dungeon: Shipwreck

Special Objects

Chests (2)

This small campsite is located along Winterhold's northern coastline. An interesting note rests atop a nearby barrel. Take a dip into the frigid ocean and swim out to a rowboat to the north. From here, dive straight underwater to discover a graveyard of ships that have wrecked against the ice and sunk. The largest ship, which features a topside cabin, still carries two chests within her hull.

[4.11] Ysgramor's Tomb

Related Quests

The Companions Quest: Glory of the Dead

Recommended Level: 6

Dungeon: Draugr Crypt

Animal

Companion Ghost

Kodlak Whitemane

Kodlak's Wolf Spirit

Collectibles

Skill Book [Two-Handed]: The Legendary City of Sancre Tor

Unique Item: Shield of Ysgramor [31/112]

Special Objects

Word Wall: Animal Allegiance [1/3]

Area Is Locked (quest required)

Chest(s)

Potions

Loose gear

This remote burial ground holds special significance to the Companions; you visit here during their "Glory of the Dead" quest. The area remains largely sealed off until you acquire that quest.

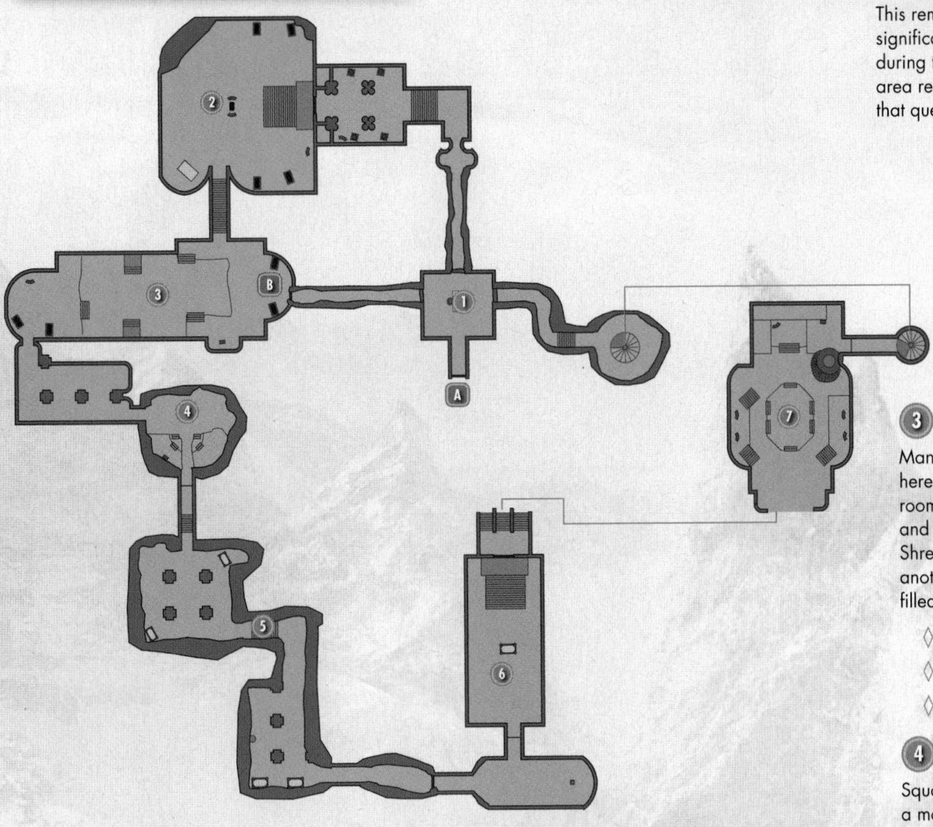

(A) Exit to Skyrim

(1) Entry Chamber

A statue to Ysgramor dominates the tomb's quiet entry chamber. If you're running Companions Quest: Glory of the Dead, place the axe Wuuthrad onto the statue at Vilkas's instruction to open the north passage and advance to [2]. If you haven't yet obtained that quest, then you cannot explore any farther.

- Potion
- Loose gear

(2) Sarcophagi Chamber A

Prove your valor to the Companions' ancestors by slaying the Companion Ghosts that emerge from sarcophagi in this sizable chamber.

- Potion
- Loose gear

(3) Sarcophagi Chamber B

Many more Companion Ghosts ambush you here—expect a challenging battle. Raid the room's southeast chest after things settle down, and find a potion in a nearby sarcophagus. Shred through thick cobwebs and snatch another potion on your way into a small room filled with ravenous Frostbite Spiders.

- Chest
- Potions
- Loose gear

(4) Giant Spider Den

Squash more spiders in this room, including a monstrous Giant Frostbite Spider that drops from the ceiling in ambush. Loot a locked chest and pull a wall chain to open the way forward.

- Chest (Locked: Adept)

(5) Burial Passages

Pocket a bit of plunder as you navigate these quiet halls. More Companion Ghosts attack as you near [6].

- Apothecary's Satchel
- Potions
- Loose gear

6 Shrine Chamber

Pull a handle to open the passage that leads into this chamber, where another host of Companion Ghosts descend upon you. Claim a Skill Book and potion from the central table before scaling the north stairs to [7].

- Skill Book [Two-Handed]: The Legendary City of Sancre Tor
- Potion

7 Burial Chamber

Speak with Kodlak's spirit in this large room, then examine the nearby Flame of the Harbinger to toss in one of the Glenmoril Witch Heads you obtained earlier in the Companions quest line. Slay Kodlak's Wolf Spirit when it emerges, then speak with Kodlak again to complete your quest. Raid the chamber's large northeast chest on your way upstairs, claiming a unique shield from within. You'll soon find your way back to the tomb's entry chamber.

- Unique Item: Shield of Ysgramor [31/112]
- Chest
- Loose gear

B Exit to Skyrim

Exterior World Wall

Upon returning to [1], take the west passage and exit out to Skyrim via the west door. Marvel at the view for a moment before sprinting up the snowy steps to discover a Word Wall.

- Word Wall: Animal Allegiance [1/3]

[4.12] Saarthal

Related Quests

College of Winterhold Quest: Under Saarthal
Side Quest: Forbidden Legend

Recommended Level: 6

Dungeon: Draugr Crypt

Arniel Gane
Draugr
Jyrik Gauldurson
Nerien

Crafting

Alchemy Lab

Dangers

Dart Trap (pressure plates)
Rune Traps (floor)

Puzzles

Nordic Pillars I
Nordic Pillars II

Quest Items

Enchanted Rings (3)
Saarthal Amulet

Collectibles

Skill Book [Two-Handed]: The Legendary Sancre Tor
Unique Item: Enchanted Ring [32/112]
Unique Item: Gauldur Amulet Fragment (Saarthal) [33/112]
Unique Item: Saarthal Amulet [34/112]
Unique Weapon: Staff of Jyrik Gauldurson [23/80]

Special Objects

Word Wall: Ice Form [2/3]
Area Is Locked (quest required)
Chest(s)
Potions
Loose gear

This snowy excavation site lies just southwest of Winterhold's capital and serves as the setting for the College of Winterhold's second quest.

Exterior

Loot a chest and several urns before speaking with Tolfdir at the excavation site as part of College of Winterhold Quest: Under Saarthal. Tolfdir unlocks the nearby door and urges you keep pace as he heads inside.

- Chest

A Exit to Skyrim

1 Chest Ledge

Chat up your colleagues as you follow Tolfdir deep into the excavation site. While navigating the high, narrow walkways here, boldly leap over to this north ledge and loot a chest.

- Chest
- Loose gear

PRIMARY LOCATIONS

Total—49: Hold Capital, Understone Keep, and 47 Hold Locations

- [5.00] Hold Capital City: Markarth
- [5.00] Understone Keep
  - Jarl: Igmund
- [5.01] Mor Khazgur
- [5.02] Deepwood Redoubt
- [5.03] Hag's End
- [5.04] Deep Folk Crossing
- [5.05] Bruca's Leap Redoubt
- [5.06] Bthardamz
- [5.07] Druadach Redoubt
- [5.08] Dragontooth Crater
- [5.09] Harmugstahl
- [5.10] Reach Stormcloak Camp
- [5.11] Liar's Retreat
- [5.12] Cliffside Retreat
- [5.13] Dragon Bridge Overlook
- [5.14] Ragnvald
- [5.15] Reach Imperial Camp
- [5.16] Shrine of Peryite
- [5.17] Karthwasten
- [5.18] Broken Tower Redoubt
- [5.19] Markarth Stables
- [5.20] Salvius Farm
- [5.21] Left Hand Mine
- [5.22] Kolskeggr Mine
- [5.23] The Lover Stone
- [5.24] Blind Cliff Cave
- [5.25] Four Skull Lookout
- [5.26] Red Eagle Redoubt
- [5.27] Sundered Towers
- [5.28] Rebel's Cairn
- [5.29] Karthspire Camp
- [5.30] Karthspire
- [5.31] Sky Haven Temple
- [5.32] Soljund's Sinkhole
- [5.33] Bleakwind Bluff
- [5.34] Old Hroldan
- [5.35] Hag Rock Redoubt
- [5.36] Dead Crone Rock
- [5.37] Purewater Run
- [5.38] Dushnikh Yal
- [5.39] Reachwater Rock
- [5.40] Reachwind Eyrie
- [5.41] Reachcliff Cave
- [5.42] Valthume
- [5.43] Gloomreach
- [5.44] Lost Valley Redoubt
- [5.45] Bard's Leap Summit
- [5.46] Cradle Stone Tower
- [5.47] Fort Sungard

SECONDARY LOCATIONS

Total—28 Points of Interest

- [5.A] Dwarven Rubble: Druadach
- [5.B] Dragon Mound: Reachward Pass
- [5.C] Dwarven Arch: Harmugstahl Falls
- [5.D] The Incautious Bather
- [5.E] A Bandit's Book
- [5.F] Dwarven Rubble: Karth River Confluence
- [5.G] Forsworn Camp: Bthardamz Outskirts
- [5.H] The Bloodied Bandit
- [5.I] Dragon Mound: Ragnvald Vale
- [5.J] Dwarven Ruins: Lair of the Wispmother
- [5.K] Sabre Cat Ravine
- [5.L] Totem to the Dragon
- [5.M] The Exposed Miner
- [5.N] Hagraven Camp: Ragnvald Scree
- [5.O] Dwarven Rubble: Salvius Farm Trail
- [5.P] Shrine of Zenithar: Four Skull Lookout
- [5.Q] Brush Strongbox: Riverside
- [5.R] Lost Treasure: Purewater Run
- [5.S] Forsworn Camp: Reachwater River
- [5.T] Dragon Mound: Karthspire Bluffs
- [5.U] Reachman's Altar: Red Eagle Redoubt
- [5.V] Lovers' Camp
- [5.W] River Rapids Treasure Chest
- [5.X] Reachwind Burial Mound
- [5.Y] Forsworn Camp: Gloomreach Pathway
- [5.Z] Shrine of Dibella: Bridge at Old Hroldan
- [5.AA] Juniper Tree Ruins
- [5.AB] Cradle Stong Crag

ADDITIONAL LOCATIONS

- [DG.11] Darkfall Cave (see page 839)
- [DG.13] Arkngthamz (see page 842)
- [HF.04] Vlindrel Hall (Updated) (see page 805)
- [DG.14] Deep Folk Crossing (see page 817)

HOLD CAPITAL: MARKARTH

Related Quests

- Civil War Quest: Liberation of Skyrim
- Civil War Quest: Compelling Tribute
- Daedric Quest: The House of Horrors
- Daedric Quest: Prelude: Hunger in the Hall*
- Daedric Quest: The Taste of Death
- Daedric Quest: A Night to Remember
- Side Quest: The Forsworn Conspiracy
- Side Quest: No One Escapes Cidhna Mine
- Temple Quest: The Heart of Dibella
- Temple Quest: The Book of Love
- Dark Brotherhood Quest: Mourning Never Comes
- Dark Brotherhood Quest: Breaching Security
- Dark Brotherhood Quest: Recipe for Disaster
- Thieves Guild Quest: Hard Answers
- Thieves Guild Radiant Quest: No Stone Unturned (x2)
- Thieves Guild Radiant Quest: Larceny Targets*
- Thieves Guild City Influence Quest: Silver Lining
- Dungeon Quest: The Lost Expedition
- Dungeon Activity (Understone Keep)
- Dungeon Activity (Abandoned House)
- Miscellaneous Objective: Innkeeper Rumors (Silver-Blood Inn)
- Miscellaneous Objective: Calcelmo's Ring* (Kerah)
- Miscellaneous Objective: Dibella's Shrine* (Lisbet)
- Miscellaneous Objective: The Steward's Potion* (Bothela)
- Miscellaneous Objective: The Last Scabbard* (Ghorza gra-Bagol)
- Miscellaneous Objective: Triumph Over Talos* (Ondolemar)
- Miscellaneous Objective: The Heart of the Matter* (Moth gro-Bagol)
- Miscellaneous Objective: Neutralizing Nimhe* (Calcelmo)
- Favor (Activity): A Drunk's Drink* (Cosnach)
- Favor (Activity): A Drunk's Drink* (Degaine)
- Favor (Activity): The Gift of Charity* (Degaine)
- Favor: A Good Talking To* (Omluag)
- Favor: Sparring Partners* (Cosnach)
- Favor: Jobs for the Jarls* (Jarl Igmund: 1)
- Favor: Jobs for the Jarls* (Jarl Igmund: 2)
- Thane Quest: Thane of The Reach*

Habitation: Hold Capital (Major)

Crafting

- Alchemy Labs (3)
- Anvils (2)
- Arcane Enchanters (3)
- Blacksmith Forges (2)
- Grindstones (2)
- Smelter
- Tanning Racks (2)
- Workbenches (4)

Services

- Follower: Cosnach [13/47]
- Follower: Vorstag [14/47]
- Follower: Argis the Bulwark [15/47]
- House for Sale: Vlindrel Hall [2/5]
- Marriage Prospect: Cosnach [10/62]
- Marriage Prospect: Vorstag [11/62]
- Marriage Prospect: Argis the Bulwark [12/62]
- Marriage Prospect: Anwen [13/62]
- Marriage Prospect: Orla [14/62]
- Marriage Prospect: Senna [15/62]
- Marriage Prospect: Omluag [16/62]
- Marriage Prospect: Muiri [17/62]
- Marriage Prospect: Ghorza gra-Bagol [18/62]
- Marriage Prospect: Moth gro-Bagol [19/62]
- Trader (Apothecary): Bothela [4/12]
- Trader (Blacksmith): Ghorza [11/33]
- Trader (Blacksmith): Mot gro-Bagol [12/33]
- Trader (Fence): Endon [3/10]
- Trader (Food Vendor): Hogni Red-Arm [4/9]
- Trader (General Store Vendor): Lisbet [5/19]
- Trader (Innkeeper): Kleppr [6/15]
- Trader (Jeweler): Kerah [1/2]
- Trader (Spell Vendor): Calcelmo [9/12]
- Trainer (Enchanting: Master): Hamal [2/2]
- Trainer (Smithing: Journeyman): Ghorza [1/3]
- Trainer (Sneak: Expert): Garvey [1/3]
- Trainer (Speech: Expert): Ogmund the Skald [2/4]
- Trader (Alchemy Vendor): Bothela [5/14]
- Trader (Alchemy Vendor): Muiri [6/14]
- Trader (Fence): Endon [3/4]
- Trader (General Store Vendor): Kerah [5/25]
- Trader (General Store Vendor): Hogni Red-Arm [6/25]
- Trader (General Store Vendor): Lisbet [7/25]
- Trader (Innkeeper): Kleppr [6/18]
- Trader (Innkeeper): Keerava [7/18]
- Trader (Weapons/Armor Vendor): Moth gro-Bagol [13/35]
- Trainer (Enchanting: Master): Hamal [2/2]
- Trainer (Smithing: Journeyman): Ghorza [1/3]
- Trainer (Sneak: Expert): Garvey [1/3]
- Trainer (Speech: Expert): Ogmund the Skald [2/4]

Special Objects

- Business Ledgers
- Civil War: Map of Skyrim
- Shrine of Arkay [5/12]
- Shrine of Dibella [3/8]
- Shrine of Talos [6/17]

Collectibles

- Larceny Target: Dwemer Puzzle Cube [4/7]
- Skill Book [Alchemy]: Herbalist's Guide to Skyrim [C1/10]
- Skill Book [Alteration]: Daughter of the Niben [B1/10]
- Skill Book [Alteration]: Sithis [D1/10]
- Skill Book [Conjuration]: The Warrior's Charge [E1/10]
- Skill Book [Heavy Armor]: Chimarvamidium [B1/10]
- Skill Book [Illusion]: 2920, Sun's Dawn, v2 [A1/10]
- Skill Book [Illusion]: Mystery of Talara, Part 4 [D1/10]
- Skill Book [Light Armor]: Ice and Chitin [A1/10]
- Skill Book [Lockpicking]: Proper Lock Design [B1/10]
- Skill Book [One-Handed]: The Importance of Where [E1/10]
- Skill Book [Restoration]: 2920, Rain's Hand, v4 [A2/10]
- Skill Book [Speech]: A Dance in Fire, v7 [C1/10]
- Unique Item: Calcelmo's Ring [41/112]
- Unique Item: Armor of the Old Gods [42/112]
- Unique Item: Boots of the Old Gods [43/112]
- Unique Item: Gauntlets of the Old Gods[44/112]
- Unique Item: Helmet of the Old Gods [45/112]
- Unique Item: Silver-Blood Family Ring [46/112]
- Unique Item: Muiri's Ring [47/112]
- Unique Item: Ogmund's Amulet of Talos [48/112]
- Unique Item: Raerek's Inscribed Amulet of Talos [49/112]
- Unique Weapon: Rusty Mace [50/80]
- Unique Weapon: Mace of Molag Bal [28/80]
- Unique Weapon: Shiv [29/80]
- Unique Weapon: Spider Control Rod [30/80]
- Unusual Gem: [8/24]
- Unusual Gem: [9/24]
- Chest(s)
- Potions aplenty
- Loose gear

Lore: City Overview

Markarth is an epic canyon city built eons ago by dwarven stonewrights in the Druadach Mountains. It is a defensive fortification constructed around the underground city of Nchuand-Zel. Primitive Reachmen were the first to repopulate the sprawling city after the dwarves' disappearance. Hundreds of years later, Markarth is in a state of turmoil stemming from what some historians (and Nord nationalists) call "the Markarth Incident."

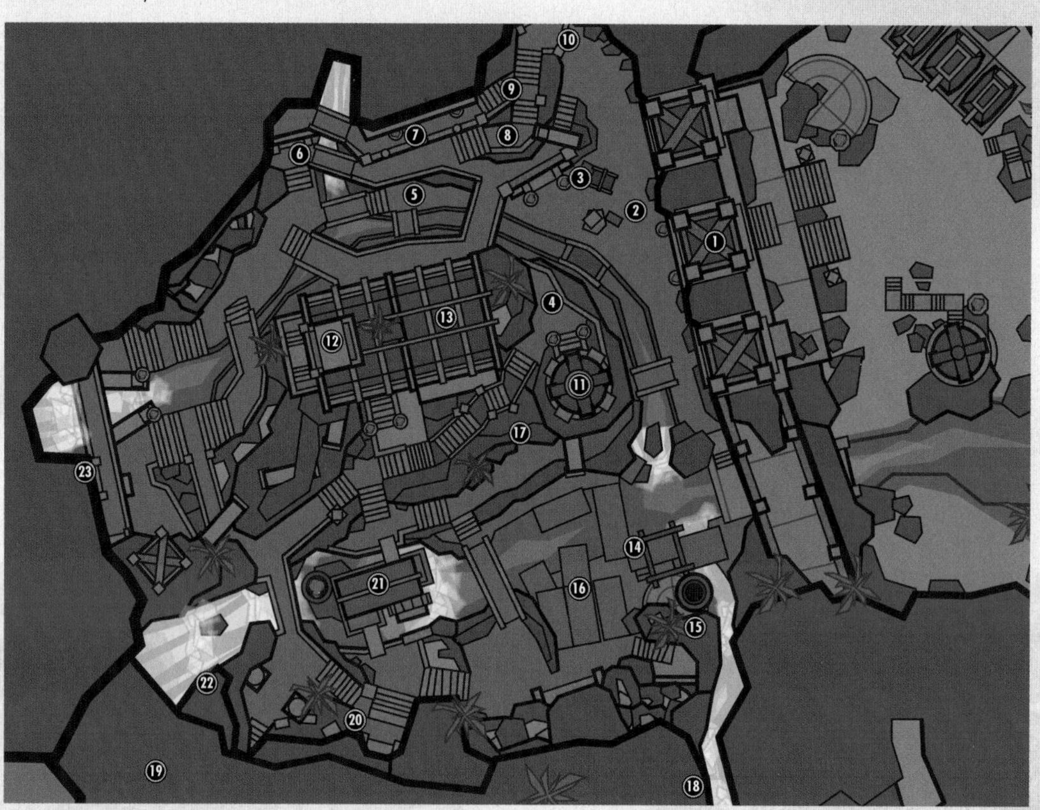

In 4E 174, at the height of the Great War, a tribe of native Reachmen called the Forsworn took advantage of the Empire's desperate straits by launching an open rebellion, wresting control of Markarth and declaring their independence from Skyrim. This was seen as a stab in the back by both the Empire and more radical Nord elements, but the Forsworn were left unchallenged for a time.

Two years later, in a short but very bloody war, Nord irregulars invaded the Reach and drove the Forsworn from Markarth. The Nords were led by the most vociferous adherents to Talos (whose worship had been outlawed by the terms of the White-Gold Concordat that ended the Great War), who claimed that they had been promised freedom of worship within the Reach in return for their help in retaking the Hold. While true, this secret agreement violated the terms of the treaty. Shortly thereafter, the Thalmor ambassador arrived in the Imperial City to confront the Emperor. Faced with the threat of a second war, the Emperor was forced to send the Imperial Legion to back the Thalmor Justiciars. The Nords refused to back down, and many were arrested or imprisoned. The Markarth Incident was a large step toward the eventual Civil War.

Aside from conflict and power struggles, Markarth is the center of silver mining in Skyrim. The city is a contrast between the beauty of its architecture, based on its dwarven heritage and the wealth of its silver mines, and the squalor and grime of the mining operation. Markarth simmers with tension between the ruling Nords and the native Reachmen who work the mines. Meanwhile, the surviving Forsworn hide in the hills, terrorizing the Reach and waiting for an opportunity to strike.

Important Areas of Interest

1 City Gates

The only way to enter Markarth (until you've visited Understone Keep and can Fast-Travel there) is to step through the giant dwarven doors. However, you can use the rocks to the north or the river to the south, and sneak into the guardhouse from either of these side entrances. There are some covered battlements from which the guards look out across the Reach and two watchtowers, one of which forms the side of the stables.

- Crafting: Workbench
- Loose gear

Highside

Located on the spur's north side, behind and above the market, Highside is where the most prominent members of the city (besides the Jarl and his advisors) live and work, mingling with the lower classes who stagger around the canal streets during let-out time at the Silver-Blood Inn.

2 Marketplace

Endon	Adara
Kerah	Hogni Red-Arm

An open-air market near the city gate, the Marketplace is where you'll watch a brazen Forsworn named Weylin attack one of the street traders (Margaret), meet Eltrys, and begin Side Quest: The Forsworn Conspiracy. One of the stalls has several necklaces to steal. Search Margaret's corpse for the key to her room inside the Silver-Blood Inn.

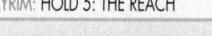

- Trader (Jeweler): Kerah [1/2]
- Trader (Food Vendor): Hogni Red-Arm [4/9]
- Unique Item: Calcelmo's Ring [41/112]
- Key to Margaret's Room
- Loose gear

③ Arnleif and Sons Trading Company

Lisbet   Imedhnain   Cosnach

Another of the ancient Markarth trading houses, this dwelling adjacent to the market functions as the general store for Markarth. Currently run by the widow Lisbet, the trading company has fallen on hard times due to the Forsworn situation.

- Follower: Cosnach [13/47]
- Marriage Prospect: Cosnach [10/62]
- Trader (General Store Vendor): Lisbet [5/19]
- Skill Book [Speech]: A Dance in Fire, v7 [C1/10]
- Business Ledger
- Strongbox [Adept]
- Chest

④ Silver-Blood Inn

Kleppr   Hroki and Hreinn
Frabbi   Ogmund

The Silver-Blood Inn is a relatively successful establishment considering the problems Markarth is facing and is perhaps the most welcoming of Markarth's social dwellings. It is comprised of a central bar and roaring fire, with rentable rooms on either side. Hire Vorstag to aid you in your adventures here, learn eloquence from Ogmund, and beckon Kleppr to ask him for the latest rumor around town and beyond. His wife, Frabbi, is a little more crabby. Search the rooms for loose gear, a few coins, and books. Continue Side Quest: The Forsworn Conspiracy by searching the only rented room that is locked (Adept), which belonged to the deceased Margaret. There's a journal in the end table that helps your progress.

- Follower: Vorstag [14/47]
- Marriage Prospect: Vorstag [11/62]
- Trader (Innkeeper): Kleppr [5/15]
  - Room for the night, food
- Trainer (Speech: Expert): Ogmund the Skald [2/4]
- Margaret's Journal
- Business Ledger
- Strongbox (Apprentice)
- Loose gear

⑤ Abandoned House (Locked: Requires Key)

Vigilant Tyranus

This dwelling is currently empty. It was the scene of a gruesome murder, and there's rumors of it being haunted. In order to explore this location and the passageways that run deep into the long-forgotten and unspeakable chambers, Daedric Quest: House of Horrors must be active.

- Unique Weapon: Rusty Mace [27/80]
- Unique Weapon: Mace of Molag Bal [28/80]
- Chest (2)
- Potions
- Loose gear

⑥ The Treasury House

Thonar Silver-Blood
Betrid
Rhiada
Ildene and Donnel

This is an impressive building befitting one of Markarth's most important families, who take charge of the Reach should it fall into Stormcloaks hands (Thongvor will move to Understone Keep with Reburrus and Yngvar, while Thonar, Betrid, Kolgrim, and the servants will remain in Treasury House). This family mansion of the Silver-Blood clan is the most elaborate dwelling in Markarth and also functions as a bank. It is where a frightening Forsworn insurrection is mounted during Side Quest: The Forsworn Conspiracy. Inside, a Skill Book rests on a stone shelf at the foot of the stairs. Behind the counter is a locked gate (Expert), behind which are some ingots and a safe. The rooms to the southeast are where the servants sleep. The locked door (Apprentice) to the northwest leads to Thonar's private chambers.

- Shadowmark: "Loot"
- Skill Book [Archery]: Vernaccus and Bourlor
- Unusual Gem: [8/24]
- Safe (Expert)
- Loose gear

⑦ Endon's House

This is a small but well-appointed house where Endon and Kerah work as silversmiths, along with their daughter Adara. One of them sells their wares in the market during the day. The shop contains a number of fine necklaces to steal.

- Crafting: Anvil, Workbench, Cooking Pot
- Display Cases (Adept) (2)
- Chest

⑧ Ogmund's House

A smaller but comfortable house where Ogmund lives. He follows the ancient teachings of a Nord skald; he plays in the Silver-Blood Inn and announces the news of the day in the market.

- Chest
- Loose gear

⑨ Nepos's House

Nepos the Nose
Uaile and Morven
Tynan

Nepos administers Cidhna Mine and the smelter. He's rather wealthy, for a native, and is collaborating with both the Silver-Bloods and Madanach in Side Quest: The Forsworn Conspiracy. His home consists of a large fireplace and a large feasting room with two tables. To the rear of the property are the bedrooms.

- Skill Book [Illusion]: Mystery of Talara, Part 4 [D1/10]
- Display Case (Apprentice)
- Chest
- Potions
- Loose gear

⑩ [HF.04] Vlindrel Hall (Markarth)

Related Quests

Hearthfire Task: Adoption
Thane Task: Thane of The Reach

Crafting	Miscellaneous
Alchemy Lab	Area is locked
Arcane Enchanter	Chest
Cooking Pot	Loose gear
	Potions aplenty

Should you become the Thane of the Reach (by completing Favors for the citizens and Jarl), you can purchase this abode from Jarl Thongvor's Steward, Reburrus Quintilius. Consult the Thane Quests for more information. This is a cliff house in the upper part of the city. The Vlindrels were a Colovian merchant family. During the Reachmen Rebellion, the Markarth Vlindrels were driven out, and their former mansion has stood empty ever since. Should you wish to purchase the children's bedroom, it replaces the Alchemy Laboratory.

- Follower: Argis the Bulwark (Housecarl) [15/47]
- House for Sale [2/5]
- Markarth Thief Caches [1/3]
- Marriage Prospect: Argis the Bulwark [12/62]
- Marriage Prospect: Argis the Bulwark [12/62]
- Follower: Lydia (Housecarl) [22/47]
- Marriage Prospect: Lydia [29/62]

Purchase Price: 8,000 gold

Jarl: Jarl Igmund or Jarl Thongvar Silverfish

Steward: Raerek or Reburrus Quintillius

Available Decorations

- Alchemy Laboratory (1,000 gold)
- Bedroom (800 gold)
- Children's Bedroom (700 gold)
- Enchanting Laboratory (1,000 gold)
- Entrance Hall (500 gold)
- Living room (900 gold)

Total cost: 12,900 gold

The Crag

This is the central spur of rock that splits the city into north (Highside) and south (Riverside) sections.

11 Guard Tower

This dwarven tower atop the central rock spur is now used as a barracks and lookout tower for the soldiers who patrol the city. Head down the spiral steps to the training room and sleeping quarters.

- ◊ Skill Book [Light Armor]: Ice and Chitin [A1/10]
- ◊ Skill Book [One-Handed]: The Importance of Where [E1/10]
- ◊ Loose gear

12 Temple of Dibella

Hamal   Orla and Anwen   Senna

The other main structure atop the Crag is the ancient Temple of Dibella. There is a Shrine of Dibella where you can get a Blessing Sybil's Antechamber: where the High Priestess sleeps. An Inner Sanctum (Locked: Expert) is where only women are allowed to go. A small number of priestesses wander the temple grounds. Inside the Sanctum, more priestesses pray and seek sensual contemplation, including Hamal, who is an exceptional enchantress. Aside from books (including a Skill Book on a shelf), ingredients, and a variety of trinkets, the following offerings are to be found. The door at the far end of the Inner Sanctum leads to an altar, where Dibella's fetish is prayed to and offerings are made.

- ◊ Marriage Prospect: Anwen [13/62]
- ◊ Marriage Prospect: Orla [14/62]
- ◊ Marriage Prospect: Senna [15/62]
- ◊ Trainer (Enchanting: Master): Hamal [2/2]
- ◊ Skill Book [Illusion]: 2920, Sun's Dawn, v2 [A1/10]
- ◊ Shrine of Dibella [3/8]
- ◊ Chest
- ◊ Potions
- ◊ Loose gear

13 Shrine of Talos

This is a relatively grand chapel. During Imperial control, it will be deserted and "closed," but even the Thalmor know not to desecrate this place for fear of fueling the rebellion. The shrine functions again if the Stormcloaks seize control. Eltrys usually hides out here.

- ◊ Shrine of Talos [6/17]

Riverside

This section of Markarth encompasses the area along the river, near the smelter, on the south side of the central spur. Reachmen laborers of Markarth live here; mainly they work in the smelter but are also maids and servants in other parts of the city. There's a slight feeling of despair cloaking the already-dirty air.

14 15 Smelter and Smelter Overseer's House

Mulush gro-Shugurz

The smelter is by the river, for all your ingot-creation needs. Above the smelter, by some half-hidden steps at the waterfall, is the locked entrance to Mulush's dwelling.

- ◊ Crafting: Anvil, Smelter
- ◊ Chest
- ◊ Knapsack
- ◊ Loose gear

16 The Stocks and Ducking Cage

For those who are unwilling or unable to work in Cidhna Mine to pay for their crimes, Markarth has another solution. The Stocks and Ducking Cage stands right outside the entrance to the mine, a reminder of the fate of any criminals who don't work or who talk back to their overseers. This can result in humiliation or death. Fortunately, you don't suffer either; you're put to work in the mines if you commit a crime in the Reach!

17 The Warrens

Degaine	Eltrys	Weylin
Hathrasil	Garvey	Dryston
Omluag	Cairine	

Most of the poor in Markarth live in the Warrens, an old crypt with run-down chambers for the poorest of the city's residents. Aside from the chambers that have suffered a cave-in, all six rooms are locked (Novice), and good practice for your Lockpicking skill. Only Weylin's room has anything more than a few pieces of food in it; there is a chest inside with a Note important for Side Quest: The Forsworn Conspiracy.

- ◊ Marriage Prospect: Omluag [16/62]
- ◊ Trainer (Sneak: Expert): Garvey [1/3]
- ◊ Weylin's Note
- ◊ Chest

18 Cidhna Mine

Urzoga gra-Shugurz	Odvan
Madanach	Uraccen
Braig	Borkul
Duach	Grisvar the Unlucky

This silver mine (*Cidhna* means "silver" in the Reach dialect) is the primary source of Markarth's wealth. It is also a prison where criminals work off their sentences. Many of the prisoners here are Forsworn, imprisoned for life after the Nords recaptured the city. The mine is owned and operated by the powerful Silver-Blood clan.

A Door to Markarth

1 Entrance Shaft

Urzoga gra-Shugurz and her Silver-Blood Guards patrol this area, which is usually off-limits to visitors. The main mine to the south has already been excavated and is sealed off.

2 Holding Cell (Locked: Adept)

This is where you collect your belongings and evidence should you try to escape.

- ◊ Skill Book [Lockpick]: Proper Lock Design [B1/10]
- ◊ Evidence Chest
- ◊ Unique Weapon: Shiv [29/80]
- ◊ Prisoner Belongings Chest
- ◊ Apothecary's Satchel
- ◊ Potions aplenty
- ◊ Loose gear

3 Early Excavations and Barracks

Urzoga's guards sleep here and use a couple of pull chains to open and close the mine entrance.

4 Mine Entrance (Locked: Requires Key)

Two connecting gates are opened by Urzoga when she ferries prisoners to and fro. You normally appear inside the prison only after committing crime or concluding Side Quest: The Forsworn Conspiracy.

5 Campfire

The large hub room has exits out of the mine, to the two tunnel areas. The entrance to Madanach's Quarters are guarded by Borkul the Beast and a moping man named Uraccen who usually sits by the fire.

6 South Tunnel

Mining occurs in these parts.

- ◊ Silver Ore Vein (2)

7 North Tunnel

Mining is coming to an end, and this area is home to more addicts than miners.

8 Madanach's Quarters (Locked: Requires Key)

The leader of the Forsworn Resistance is holed up in impressive surroundings given his imprisonment. He is the key to the Forsworn cause, during Side Quest: No One Escapes Cidhna Mine.

B Door to Markarth Ruins

This is only accessible during Side Quest: No One Escapes Cidhna Mine.

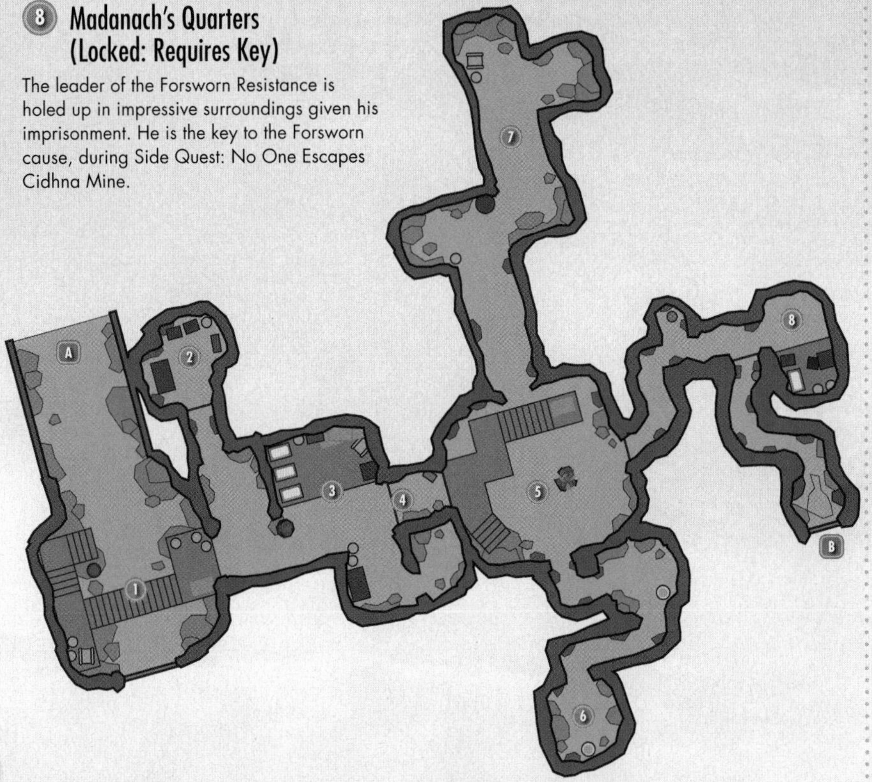

19 Markarth Ruins (Locked: Requires Key)

Part of an ancient dwarven city, these ruins have been slowly collapsing during earthquakes. No one ventures into these parts, due to the instability of the area and reports of mechanical monstrosities guarding the place. The only place with any items of worth is a ruined two-floor chamber with pipes and a dwaven automaton or two guarding. This area is used during Side Quest: No One Escapes Cidhna Mine. It connects Cidhna Mine to Markarth (Riverside).

- Unique Item: Armor of the Old Gods [42/112]
- Unique Item: Boots of the Old Gods [43/112]
- Unique Item: Gauntlets of the Old Gods[44/112]
- Unique Item: Helmet of the Old Gods [45/112]
- Unique Item: Silver-Blood Family Ring [46/112]
- Potions

20 The Hag's Cure

Bothela Muiri

Bothela is an old Reach woman who dispenses potions, poisons, and ingredients; tells your fortune; and runs the creepiest shop in Riverside. Aside from the ingredients to steal, you can always purchase a good amount of items. A Skill Book is kept behind the counter.

- Crafting: Alchemy Lab
- Marriage Prospect: Muiri [17/62]
- Trader (Apothecary): Bothela [5/14]
  - Potions, Food, Ingredients
- Skill Book [Alchemy]: Herbalist's Guide to Skyrim [C1/10]
- Unique Item: Muiri's Ring [47/112]
- Business Ledger
- Strongbox (Apprentice)
- Chest
- Potions aplenty

21 Lumber Mill and Forge

Ghorza gra-Bagol
Tacitus Sallustius

This overlooks Riverside, but the Blacksmith and her apprentice are well-respected members of the Understone Keep's staff and provide the Jarl with the best steel in the Reach.

- Crafting: Blacksmith Forge, Grindstone, Tanning Rack, Workbench
- Trader (Blacksmith): Ghorza [11/33]

22 Hall of the Dead [Locked: Adept]

Brother Verulus

The Hall of the Dead is in a side cavern accessed via Darkside or Understone Keep (both doors are locked), where the dead are buried in crypts and mausoleums are carved into the cave walls. Brother Verulus is the priest of Arkay who oversees the Hall of the Dead.

- Skill Book [Restoration]: 2920, Rain's Hand, v4 [A2/10]
- Shrine of Arkay [5/12]

23 Understone Keep

Jarl Igmund
Raerek (Steward)
Faleen (Housecarl)
Legate Emmanuel Admand
Thongvor Silver-Blood
Reburrus Quintilius (Steward)
Yngvar (Housecarl)
Calcelmo (Court wizard)
Aicantar
Anton Virane
Rondach and Voada
Blacksmith: Moth gro-Bagol
Ondolemar

The following leaders of Markarth are loyal to the Imperials at the start of the Civil War.

Jarl Igmund

Jarl Igmund, son of Hrolfdir and nephew of Raerek, recently took the throne when Hrolfdir was killed in battle with the Forsworn. Igmund is an Imperial supporter (some might say a puppet) and holds court all day and eats and sleeps in the Keep.

He sits upon the Mournful Throne, a relic and seat of power famous for centuries across the Reach.

Raerek (Steward)

Igmund's Steward and successor manages the household, serves as the treasurer, and commands the palace guard.

◊ Unique Item: Raerek's Inscribed Amulet of Talos [48/112]

Faleen (Housecarl)

She is completely loyal and very competent. She was Igmund's father's Housecarl and managed to escape from the ambush with the gravely wounded Igmund, although she blames herself for not being able to do more. As a result, she is almost paranoid about Igmund's security and will rarely allow him out of her sight.

Legate Emmanuel Admand

The following residents of Markarth arrive to take control once this Hold has fallen during the Civil War.

Thongvor Silver-Blood

Thongvor is the head of the Silver-Blood family, who controls the majority of Markarth's wealth. More involved in politics and Ulfric's rebellion, Thongvor leaves the business operations of the family to his brother Thonar.

Reburrus Quintilius (Steward)

Reburrus Quintilius is the steward to Thongvor. His family has served as the chief financial and political advisors to the Silver-Blood family for generations, and Reburrus has distilled the wisdom of the generations to a fine art.

Yngvar (Housecarl)

The huge housecarl to the Silver-Blood family, Yngvar has a reputation for cheerful brutality. He is completely loyal to the Silver-Blood clan and loves his job. He particularly loves it when he can beat someone to a pulp. But he is also surprisingly cultured; he attended the Bard's College as a youth, until he found better employment using his other talents.

The following citizens are staff of Understone Keep:

Calcelmo (Court wizard)

Calcelmo is here in order to study the Dwemer ruins in and around the city. He views his duties as the castle mage as a distraction from his main scholarly interest. He is completely uninterested (and mainly unaware) of politics. He has been quite put out by the Forsworn situation, which has prevented him from doing his usual wide-ranging travels. He is secretly in love with Faleen, although he has never told anyone else or done anything about it.

◊ Trader (Spell Vendor): Calcelmo [9/12]

Aicantar

Aicantar is Calcelmo's assistant and nephew. He is less than enthused by his uncle's plans to study more dangerous Dwemer Ruins and prefers they spend time studying spells and enchanting. Aicantar is aware of Calcelmo's secret love for Faleen but is unlikely to do anything about it directly. Faleen scares Aicantar, and the thought of her being around the laboratory more makes him nervous.

Anton Virane

Anton is a genuine Breton from High Rock in a city of Reachmen, a fact that constantly annoys him (because everyone assumes he's a Reachman). He is particularly bigoted toward Reachmen. He is an excellent cook, though, which is why the Jarl continues to tolerate him.

Rondach and Voada

Moth gro-Bagol

◊ Trader (Blacksmith): Moth gro-Bagol [12/33]

Ondolemar

Ondolemar is the head of the Thalmor Justiciars in Markarth, and a prime example of why most folk hate the Thalmor. Ondolemar is completely confident in the Dominion's ultimate victory over the Empire. He's a Thalmor true believer, and is not here if the Stormcloaks take this city during the Civil War.

Understone Keep (Interior)

Understone Keep is a gigantic dwarven structure, now used as the city's castle. Built by the Dwemer into the western wall of the canyon, the Castle Wizard, Calcelmo, has recently uncovered additional chambers (and worrying underground monstrosities) and a wealth of artifacts that he keeps in his museum. The sheer size of this place and ability to be well guarded negates some of the instability the location has recently suffered from.

A Door to Markarth

1 Entrance to the Mournful Throne

The first time you enter via the main doors, Thongvor Silver-Blood is having a heated discussion with Brother Verulus about the worship of the outlawed deity, Talos. At this huge intersection of stone and fire, head right to the Dwemer Museum, or move up to meet the Jarl, who is guarded by both Markarth Guards and Thalmor Soldiers. Jarl Igmund sits on the Mournful Throne, usually with his Steward and Housecarl by him. Outside, on the upper top of the stairs where Ondolemar and his guards like to stride about, are two stone tables. The one to the right (northwest) houses a Skill Book.

◊ Skill Book [Alteration]: Daughter of the Niben [B1/10]

2 Corridor to Nchuand-Zel

Head left to Nchuand-Zel's entrance.

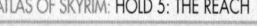

③ Nchuand-Zel Entrance

The epic cavern is usually where Calcelmo and Aicantar can be found, dedicating their lives to researching this mighty dwarven stronghold of historic significance. When you emerge from the entrance cavern close to the throne room, you are greeted by a rushing river, various curved passageways, and circular towers (one with seats to sit on and gaze down at the rushing water), as well as an entrance to the Hall of the Dead. Of more significance is the entrance to Nchuand-Zel itself. Enter here, either before speaking to Calcelmo (Locked: Adept) or after acquiring the key and agreeing to slay a large spider for him (Miscellaneous Objective: Neutralizing Nimhe*).

- ◊ Crafting: Alchemy Lab, Arcane Enchanter

Ⓑ Door to Nchuand-Zel Excavation Site

Ⓒ Door to Hall of the Dead

Ⓓ Door to Dwemer Museum [Adept]

④ Kitchens

To the left (south) of the throne room are the kitchens. The two hounds around here are large but friendly. Inside, you usually find Voada and Rondach and the short-tempered Anton Virane. As expected, there's a massive amount of food in here.

⑤ Jarl's Chamber (Locked: Adept)

Igmund rests here, behind the large golden door to the left (southeast) of the throne room. If you're going to sift through his personal belongings, remember to try the ones on the stone shelf facing the subterranean river that dominates the rear of the chamber.

- ◊ Skill Book [Conjuration]: The Warrior's Charge [E1/10]
- ◊ Loose gear

⑥ Understone Forge

This is located to the right (north) of the throne room. Moth gro-Bagol works here, while his sister Ghorza tends to the Blacksmith Forge outside.

- ◊ Crafting: Blacksmith Forge, Grindstone, Tanning Rack, Workbench
- ◊ Marriage Prospect: Ghorza gra-Bagol [18/62]
- ◊ Marriage Prospect: Moth gro-Bagol [19/62]
- ◊ Trader (Blacksmith): Moth gro-Bagol [12/34]
  - ○ Weapons, Apparel, Misc.
- ◊ Trainer (Smithing: Journeyman): Ghorza [1/3]
- ◊ Loose gear

⑦ Faleen's Room

To the right (northwest) are bedrooms for the more important members of the Jarl's council. Faleen's room (sometimes locked: Adept) is to the right, with the large dinner table, a Key to Markarth Keep that opens the two other nearby doors, and the Jarl's Quarters.

⑧ Raerek's Room

This room (sometimes locked: Adept) houses the steward, a Key, and his secret Talos-loving reading materials.

⑨ Imperial War Room

Up the stairs is a third room (sometimes locked: Apprentice) leading to the Imperial War Room, where Legate Emmanuel Admand is overseeing the Civil War in this territory.

- ◊ Civil War: Map of Skyrim
- ◊ Key to Markarth Keep (3)
- ◊ Display case (Novice)
- ◊ Loose gear

Understone Keep: Dwemer Museum

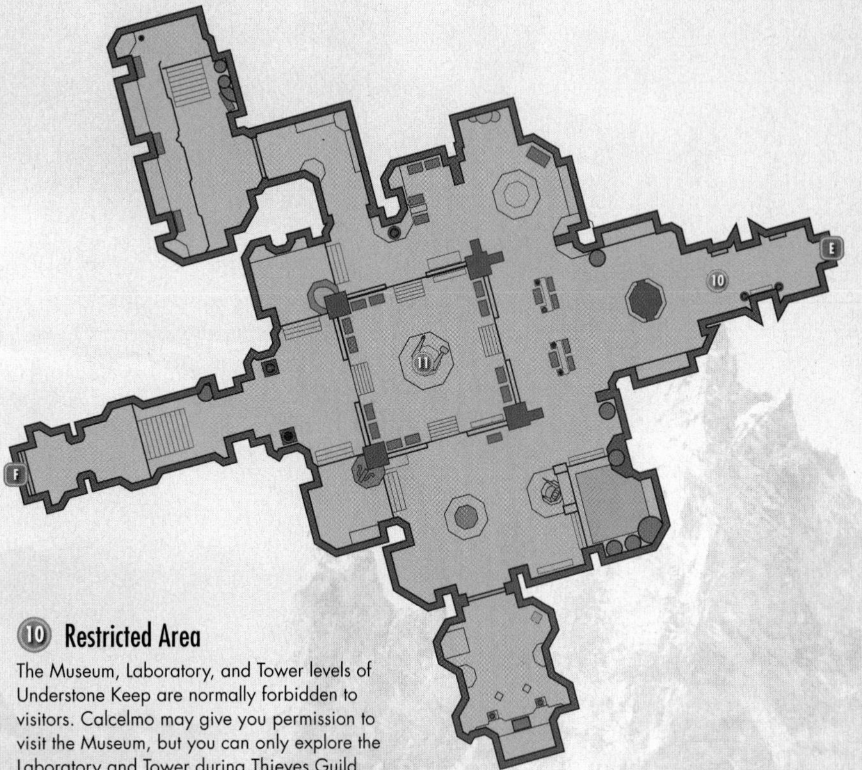

⑩ Restricted Area

The Museum, Laboratory, and Tower levels of Understone Keep are normally forbidden to visitors. Calcelmo may give you permission to visit the Museum, but you can only explore the Laboratory and Tower during Thieves Guild Quest: Hard Answers.

⑪ Dwemer Museum (Locked: Adept)

The Dwemer Museum showcases Calcelmo's collection of artifacts recovered from ruins across Skyrim. Only three guards patrol this area, keeping watch for intruders. This space is normally off-limits—the guards will aggressively arrest you if you trespass here—but you can get Calcelmo's permission to visit the museum in any number of ways; see Thieves Guild Quest: Hard Answers for details.

The Museum has the finest collection of Dwarven artifacts (weapons, armor, items, and books) in the entirety of Skyrim and the highest concentration of locked containers in any area of the game. There's even a small selection of Falmer items. To the south is a gate (Apprentice) leading to a small workshop with an Unusual Gem and locked chest (Expert). To the northwest is a locked gate (Adept) to a two-level storage room. Up the steps to the west is the laboratory door.

- ◊ Unusual Gem: [9/24]
- ◊ Display Case (3)
- ◊ Display Case (Novice) (5)
- ◊ Display Case (Apprentice) (2)
- ◊ Display Case (Adept) (7)
- ◊ Display Case (Expert) (14)
- ◊ Chest (Adept)
- ◊ Chest (Expert)
- ◊ Loose gear

Ⓔ Door to Understone Keep

Ⓕ Door to Calcelmo's Laboratory

Understone Keep: Calcelmo's Laboratory

This area is the main living and research quarters for Calcelmo and Aicantar, although they typically spend most of their time in the Keep, closer to the Nchuand-Zel Entrance. Most of this area is locked unless you're on Thieves Guild Quest: Hard Answers; see that quest for an exhaustive walkthrough of quest events in this space. The laboratory is divided into a number of chambers.

G Door to Dwemer Museum

12 Entry Room

The Entry Room has oil on the floor, a dart trap, and a gate you can't normally open to the southeast.

- Danger! Dart Trap, Oil Pool Trap
- Unique Weapon: Spider Control Rod [30/80] (quest only)

13 Throne Chamber

The Throne Chamber consists of a main room with a raised throne and guard. Dwarven junk (or is it research?) is scattered around, along with several traps you can activate. You cannot progress beyond the Throne door without a key, which you can only find during Thieves Guild Quest: Hard Answers.

14 Calcemo's Bedroom

To the northwest is Calcelmo's bedroom, which has some display cases (Apprentice) and scrolls to steal.

15 Aicantar's Bedroom

To the south is Aicantar's bedroom and food preparation area.

- Danger! Dwarven Ballista Trap, Dwarven Thresher Trap, Swinging Wall Trap
- Display Case (Apprentice)
- Loose gear

16 Steam Hall

Beyond the Throne Room is the Steam Hall. There's little to search for, except a few corpses of fallen foes. The valve at the far end activates the thresher traps in the floor, ideally against enemies following you.

- Danger! Dwarven Thresher Trap, Poison Gas Trap

17 Statue Room

Next is the Statue Room, whose exit is flanked by two Dwarven Spheres. There are two side chambers here; take advantage of the guard's patrol to slip through the door when he steps away from it.

18 Work Room

And finally, you emerge into a large work room. The valve in the control booth sets off a frightening number of traps in the room that will send even the most stout-hearted guard running for cover. This area has the following items and two exits.

- Danger! Dwarven Ballista Trap, Dwarven Thresher Trap, Flamethrower Trap
- Crafting: Arcane Enchanter
- Larceny Target: Dwemer Puzzle Cube [4/7]
- Skill Book [Enchanting]: Twin Secrets
- Chest
- Loose gear

H Barred Door

I Door to Markarth Wizards' Balcony

Markarth Wizards' Balcony (Exterior)

The great balcony atop the keep connects Calcelmo's laboratory to his tower, a separate structure off the main body of the Keep. There's a great view of the city from here. One section of the balcony wall has broken away, exposing a path around the cliffside that ends in a waterfall. If you were in a hurry, you might just be able to jump from here.

Understone Keep: Calcelmo's Tower

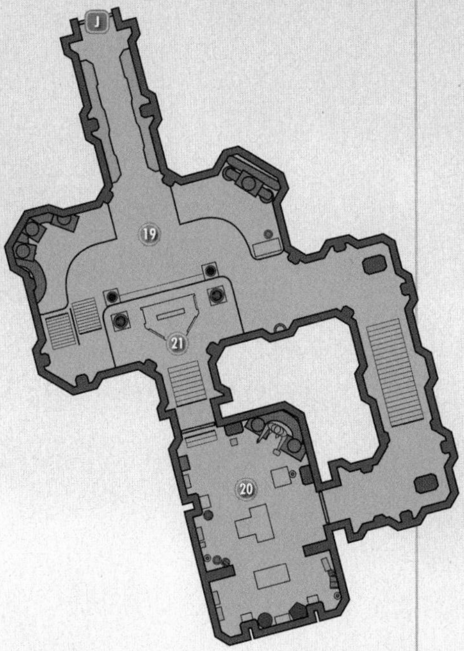

The tower (accessible only during Thieves Guild Quest: Hard Answers) has a lower-level entry hall, an upper-level office, and a massive stone relic containing a text in Dwemer and Falmer on the same granite slab!

J Door to Markarth Wizards' Balcony (Locked: Requires Key)

19 Entry Hall

20 Office

- Crafting: Alchemy Lab, Arcane Enchanter
- Skill Book [Heavy Armor]: Chimarvamidium [B1/10]
- Potions

21 Stone Relic

This stone is the key to Calcelmo's current research, a secret he jealously protects.

- Calcelmo's Stone

Nchuand-Zel Excavation Site

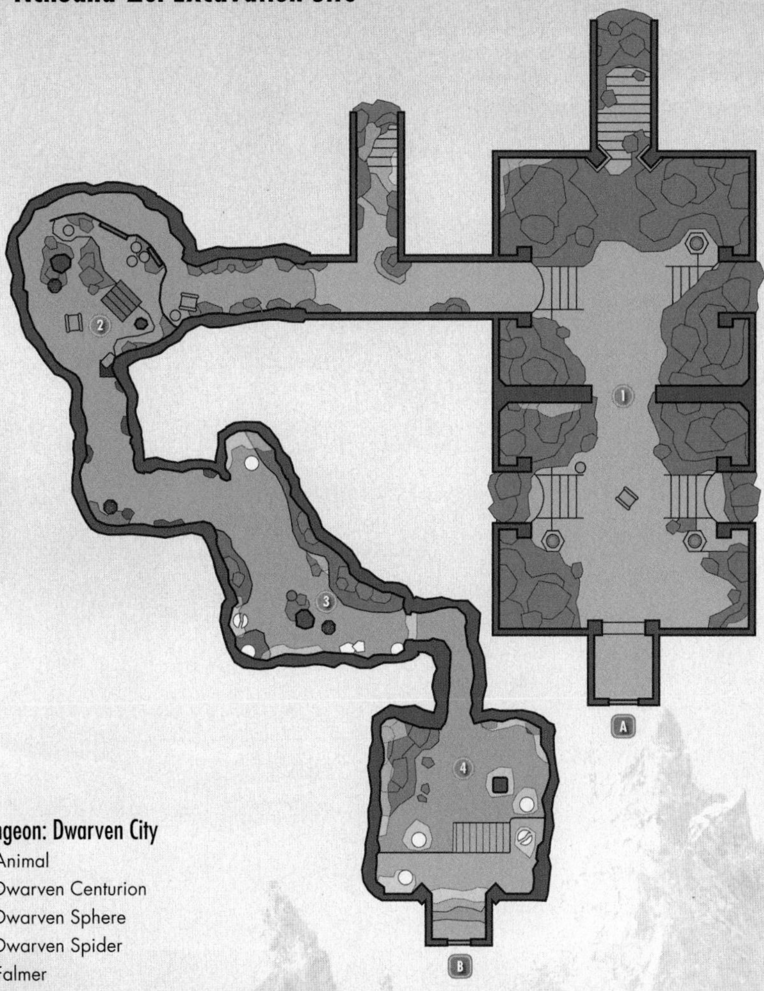

Dungeon: Dwarven City

- Animal
- Dwarven Centurion
- Dwarven Sphere
- Dwarven Spider
- Falmer
- Nimhe

Dangers

- Flamethrower Traps
- Rune Traps
- Spear Trap

Quest Items

- Alethius's Notes
- Krag's Journal
- Stromm's Diary
- Erj's Notes
- Staubin's Diary

Collectibles

- Skill Book [Alteration]: Sithis [D1/10]
- Area Is Locked (Adept)
- Chest(s)
- Potions
- Loose gear
- Mineable ore (Corundum, Iron, Moonstone)

A Door to Understone Keep

1 Entrance Corridor

Throughout this entire area, there's Dwemer artifacts to gather and sell later. Turn left (west) to break through the already-collapsed wall to where the excavation site was first discovered.

2 Excavation Drop

In this steam-filled drop, follow the mine working's ledges. Take that Potion of Plentiful Healing by the wagon before you descend. You'll need it! Try dropping onto the nearer stalagmite for a quicker drop down.

- Potion
- Loose gear

3 Mine Workings

These have been completely taken over by Frostbite Spiders. Slay them all here before continuing past the skeletons of the long-dead miners and cut through the webs.

- Mineable ore (Corundum, Iron)

4 Nimhe's Lair

A gigantic Frostbite Spider drops in to slay you as you reach the edge of the mining area. Face her or flee! Then inspect the dead Imperial named Alethius and read his Note. This begins Dungeon Quest: The Lost Expedition. Consult that quest for precise knowledge on completing this exploration.

- Alethius's Notes

B Door to Nchuand-Zel

Nchuand-Zel

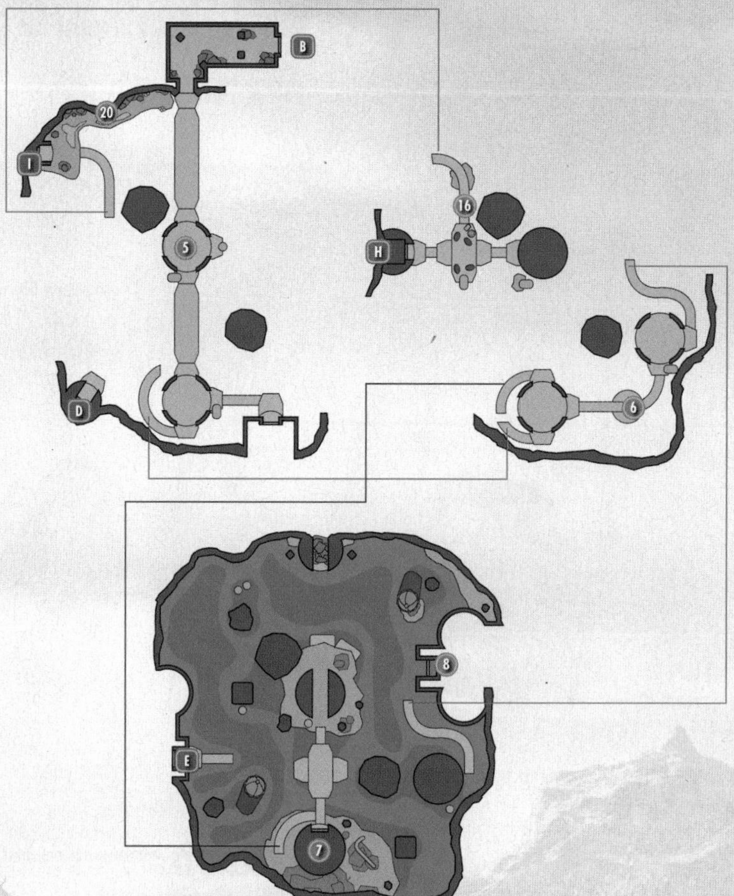

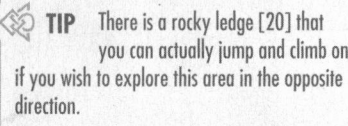

B Door to Nchuand-Zel Excavation Site

5 Upper Walkway (Upper Level)

After a short corridor ramp down, this opens up into a single, dramatic and gigantic chamber. This Upper Walkway has a couple of Falmer to face, and the southern tower has ramps down and a walkway across to the Nchuand-Zel Quarters. Find a Skill Book resting on an ornate bench as you go.

- Skill Book [Alteration]: Sithis [D1/10]

> **TIP** There is a rocky ledge [20] that you can actually jump and climb on if you wish to explore this area in the opposite direction.

C Door to Nchuand-Zel Quarters (Upper Level)

6 Lower Walkways (Lower Level)

Below the upper walkway are stone ramps down to a middle section, and down again to the base of the structure, which is waterlogged.

7 South Gate (Waterlogged Ground Area; Locked: Adept)

- Chest

8 Piston Building Door (Waterlogged Ground Area)

- Potions (underwater)

D Door from Nchuand-Zel Quarters (Lower Level)

This leads from the Quarters to an otherwise-inaccessible ledge.

- Chest

E Door to Nchuand-Zel Armory (Waterlogged Ground Area)

H Door from Nchaund-Zel Armory (Lower Level)

16 Krag's Walkway

The researcher Krag lies near blood splatters along this walkway and camping spot. The Dwarven Centurion roars into life only after you pull the switch inside the Control.

- Krag's Journal

I Door to Nchuand-Zel Control (Upper Level)

This is only accessed from this location, but only after you emerge from the Armory.

20 Escape Ledge (Upper Level)

The Dwarven mechanical entities may be moving (and attacking any Falmer you've left alive) if you fiddled with the Control. Use this ledge running around the northwest corner of this gigantic chamber to reach the exit and escape to the Excavation Site.

- Mineable ore (Moonstone)

Nchuand-Zel Quarters

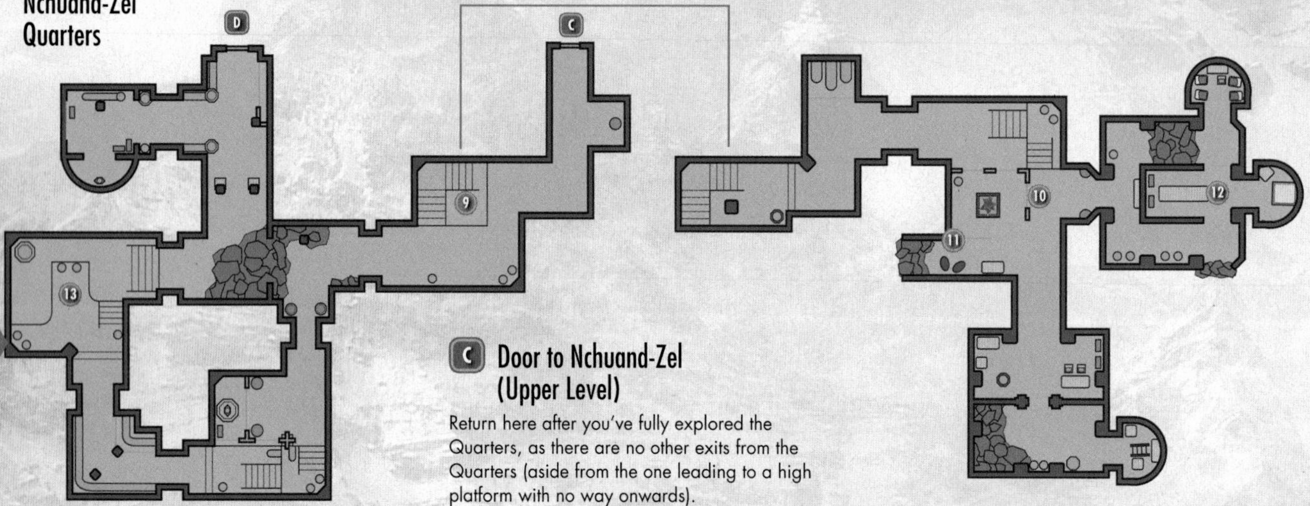

C Door to Nchuand-Zel (Upper Level)

Return here after you've fully explored the Quarters, as there are no other exits from the Quarters (aside from the one leading to a high platform with no way onwards).

9 Central Quarters Stairwell

This descends to corridors that run under the upper corridors above and the exit door [C], to another set of steps.

10 Eastern Quarters

Access this series of upper chambers from the Central Quarters Stairwell. When you reach the second ascending set of steps, watch for Fire Rune Traps at the top. Continue south down the corridor, passing Stromm's corpse, and check the dead bodies of the expedition's Imperial Guards and a torture chamber at the far end.

- ◊ Danger! Rune Traps
- ◊ Loose gear

11 Stromm

Search the corpse, and check the nearby stone table for his diary.

- ◊ Stromm's Diary

12 Far Eastern Living Areas

This collection of small rooms and a corridor are accessed after turning east at the steps with the Fire Rune Traps. Pass the pistons to reach a variety of dining, sleeping, and storage rooms.

- ◊ Loose gear

13 Western Chambers

These lower chambers are filled with Falmer foes. They lead you to the Door to Nchuand-Zel and a dead-end area with dwarven barrels and a chest.

- ◊ Chest

D Door to Nchuand-Zel (Upper Level)

Nchuand-Zel Armory

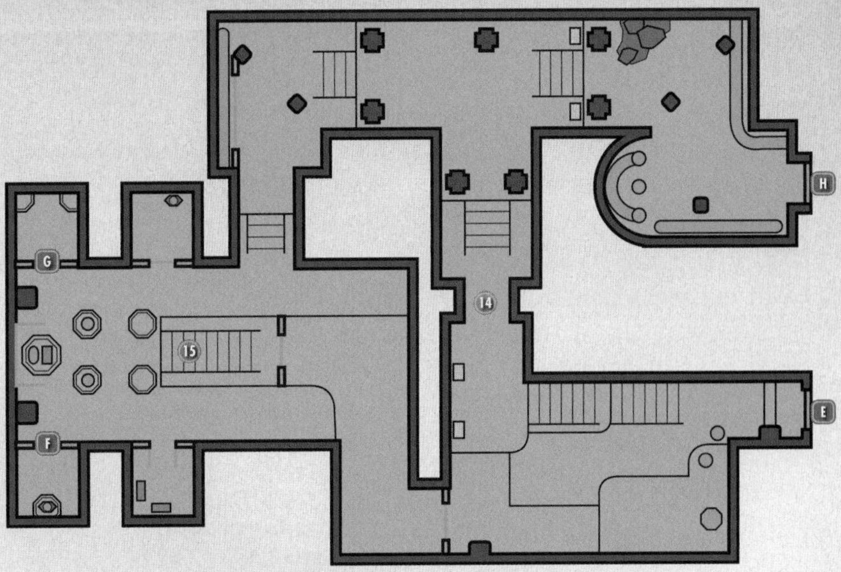

E Door to Nchuand-Zel (Waterlogged Ground Level)

14 Stone Corridors (Upper and Lower)

These wind through to the center of the Armory. Take the upper ramped corridors to the right turn (east) and to an exit door leading back into Nchuand-Zel [H]. Take the upper path and turn right (west), heading down past a Wall Fire and Wall Spear Trap (check the floor for a trigger and don't step on them!) to the Armory Hall. Take the lower path directly to the Armory Hall. There's a gate at the base of the steps to unlock (Adept).

- ◊ Danger! Flamethrower Trap, Spear Trap

15 Armory Hall and Erj

Statues of dwarven mechanical monsters stand frozen in time at the top of these steps. A dead Falmer and the remains of Erj the adventurer are also here. Close by are three gates, one of which is unlocked; behind it is a chest surrounded by Dwemer pots.

- ◊ Erj's Notes
- ◊ Chest

F Gate (Locked: Expert)

G Gate (Locked: Expert)

- ◊ Chest

H Door to Nchuand-Zel (Lower Level)

Nchuand-Zel Control

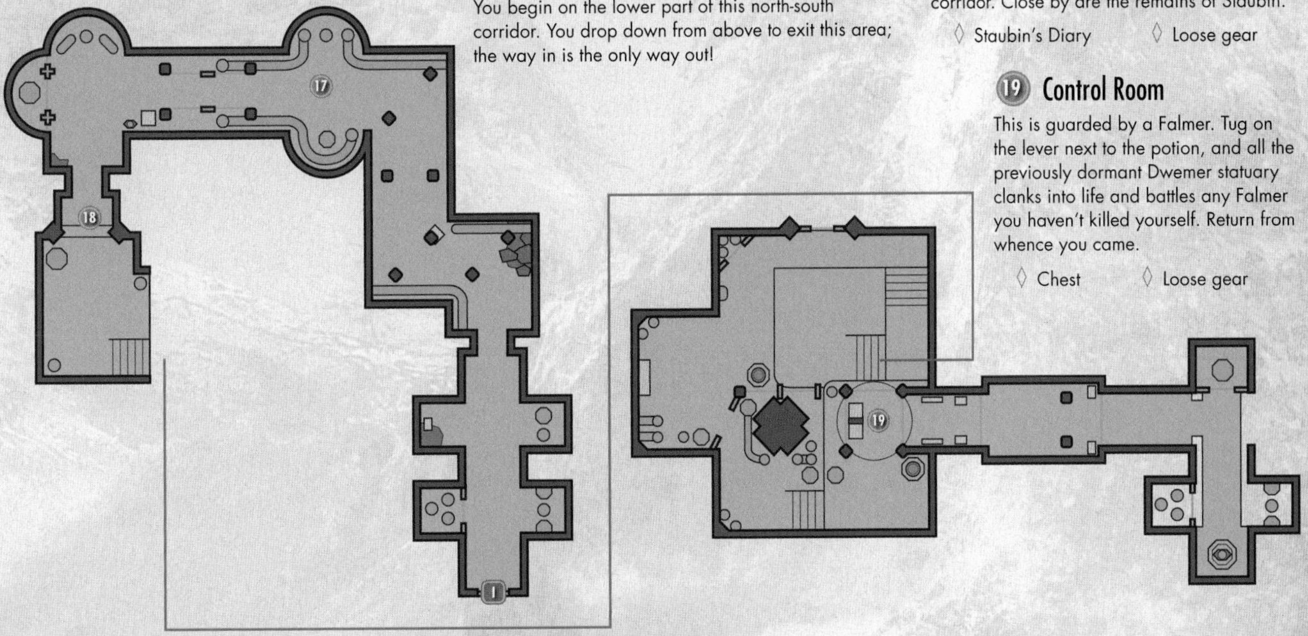

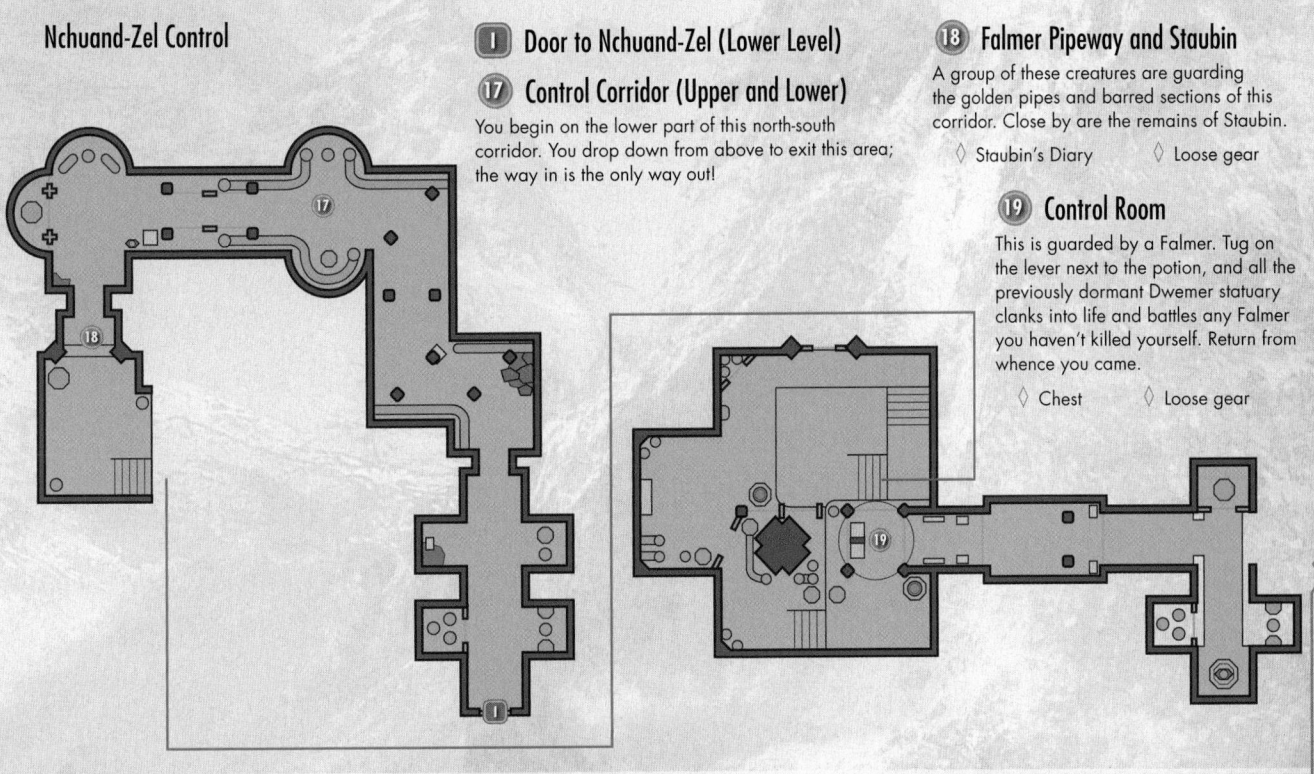

I Door to Nchuand-Zel (Lower Level)

17 Control Corridor (Upper and Lower)

You begin on the lower part of this north-south corridor. You drop down from above to exit this area; the way in is the only way out!

18 Falmer Pipeway and Staubin

A group of these creatures are guarding the golden pipes and barred sections of this corridor. Close by are the remains of Staubin.

- ◊ Staubin's Diary
- ◊ Loose gear

19 Control Room

This is guarded by a Falmer. Tug on the lever next to the potion, and all the previously dormant Dwemer statuary clanks into life and battles any Falmer you haven't killed yourself. Return from whence you came.

- ◊ Chest
- ◊ Loose gear

[5.01] Mor Khazgur

Related Quests

Side Quest: The Forgemaster's Fingers
Favor (Activity): Mining Ore* (Shuftharz)
Favor: Sparring Partners* (Larak)

Recommended Level: 6

Habitation: Orc Stronghold

Bagrak
Borgakh the Steel Heart (Follower, Marriage Prospect)
Chief Larak (Trainer: Block)
Ghamorz
Gul
Olur
Sharamph (Apothecary Vendor)
Shuftharz

Services

Follower: Borgakh the Steel Heart [16/47]
Marriage Prospect: Borgakh the Steel Heart [20/62]
Trader (Apothecary Vendor): Sharamph [7/14]
Potions, Food, Ingredients
Trainer (Block: Master): Chief Larak [1/2]

Crafting

Alchemy Lab
Blacksmith Forge
Grindstone
Smelter

Collectibles

Skill Book [Smithing]: The Armorer's Challenge [E1/10]
Chest(s)
Potions
Loose gear

This Orc stronghold stands at the Reach's far northwest tip, on the edge of Skyrim. The Orcs here are mistrustful, but the first guard that spots you will call out and offer you a Side Quest, which can help you curry favor with the Orcs. If you like, test your fistfighting aptitude in a friendly wager against the chief.

Exterior

Even if the Orcs are giving you the cold shoulder, you can still explore their stronghold and make use of several crafting stations. Grab a Skill Book off a shelf near the Blacksmith forge.

- Crafting: Alchemy Lab, Blacksmith Forge, Grindstone, Smelter
- Skill Book [Smithing]: The Armorer's Challenge [E1/10]
- Chest
- Apothecary's Satchel
- Potions

Larak's Longhouse

The Orc chief's longhouse holds some worthy loot, but you risk angering the Orcs if you break inside.

- Area Is Locked (Novice)
- Chests (2)
- Potions
- Loose gear

Mor Khazgur Cellar

Unlock the trapdoor near Larak's Longhouse to access a small cellar with a handful of valuables.

- Area Is Locked (Novice)
- Chest
- Potions

Mor Khazgur Mine

This small mine is worked by the Orcs and features thick veins of Orichalcum Ore.

- Chest
- Loose gear
- Mineable ore (Orichalcum)

[5.02] Deepwood Redoubt

Related Quests

Dark Brotherhood Quest: The Feeble Fortune*

Recommended Level: 14

Dungeon: Forsworn Redoubt

Forsworn

Crafting

Alchemy Lab
Arcane Enchanter
Anvil
Blacksmith Forge
Grindstone
Workbench

Dangers

Bone Alarm Trap
Dart Trap (pressure plate)
Rune Traps (floor)
Swinging Blade Trap (lever)
Swinging Wall Trap (pressure plate)

Collectibles

Skill Book [Sneak]: Sacred Witness [C1/10]
Trapped Chest
Chest(s)
Potions
Loose gear

Exterior

A band of Forsworn have taken over this ancient ruin, located atop a rocky rise at the northern tip of the Reach. Deepwood Redoubt leads to a larger Nordic ruin on the far side of a secret vale—Hag's End [5.03].

Fight your way up the outer stone steps to locate the entrance to the ruins. Swipe some potions from the nearby altar and lean-to before heading inside.

- Potions
- Loose gear

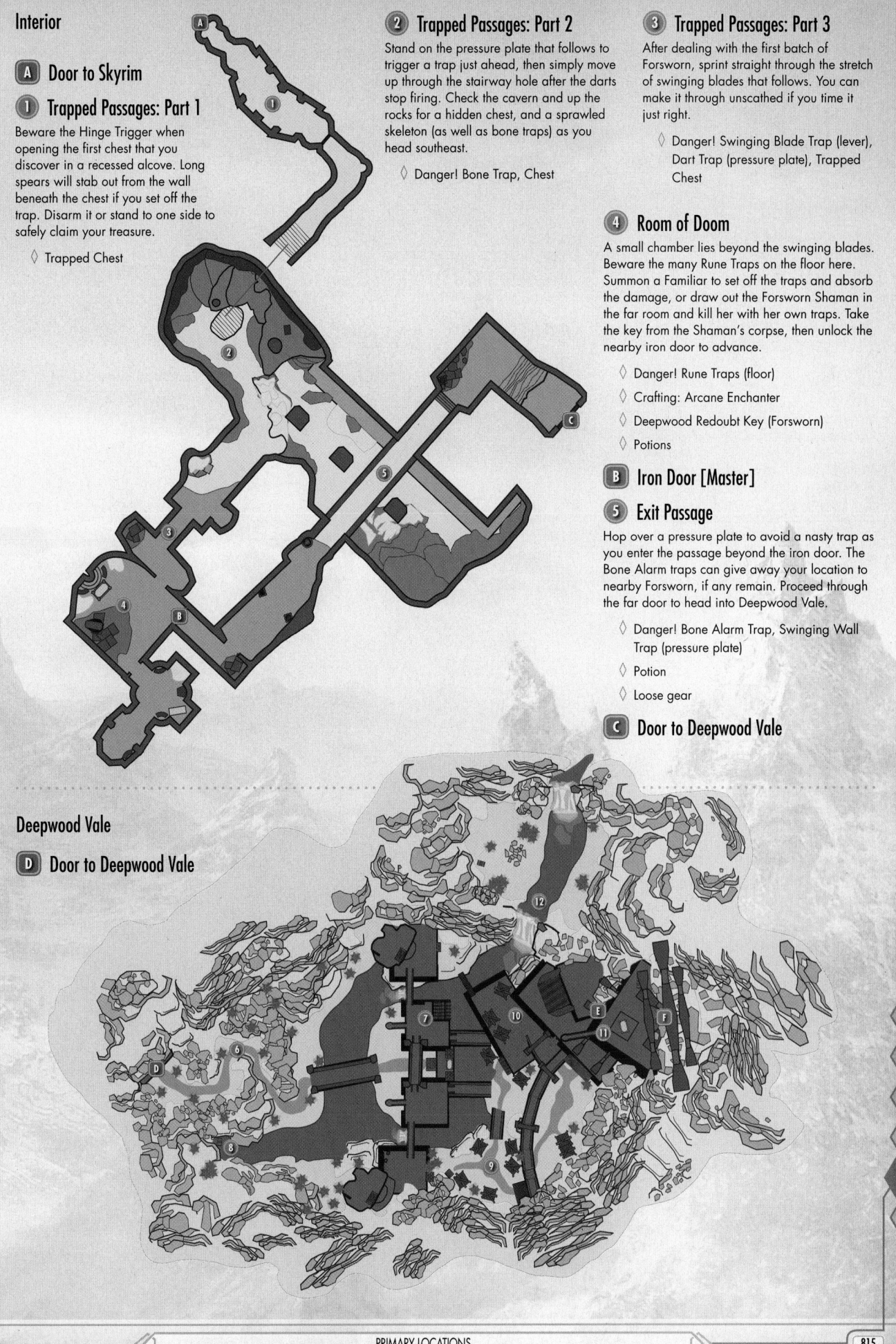

Interior

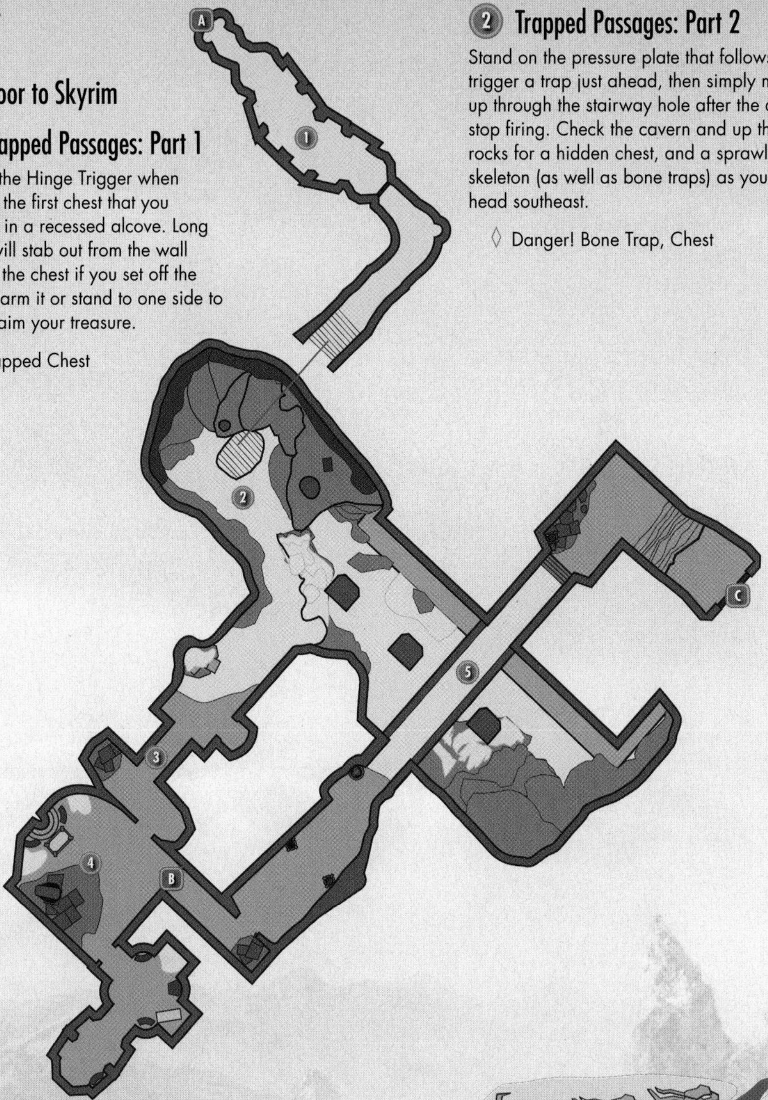

A Door to Skyrim

1 Trapped Passages: Part 1

Beware the Hinge Trigger when opening the first chest that you discover in a recessed alcove. Long spears will stab out from the wall beneath the chest if you set off the trap. Disarm it or stand to one side to safely claim your treasure.

◊ Trapped Chest

2 Trapped Passages: Part 2

Stand on the pressure plate that follows to trigger a trap just ahead, then simply move up through the stairway hole after the darts stop firing. Check the cavern and up the rocks for a hidden chest, and a sprawled skeleton (as well as bone traps) as you head southeast.

◊ Danger! Bone Trap, Chest

3 Trapped Passages: Part 3

After dealing with the first batch of Forsworn, sprint straight through the stretch of swinging blades that follows. You can make it through unscathed if you time it just right.

◊ Danger! Swinging Blade Trap (lever), Dart Trap (pressure plate), Trapped Chest

4 Room of Doom

A small chamber lies beyond the swinging blades. Beware the many Rune Traps on the floor here. Summon a Familiar to set off the traps and absorb the damage, or draw out the Forsworn Shaman in the far room and kill her with her own traps. Take the key from the Shaman's corpse, then unlock the nearby iron door to advance.

◊ Danger! Rune Traps (floor)

◊ Crafting: Arcane Enchanter

◊ Deepwood Redoubt Key (Forsworn)

◊ Potions

B Iron Door [Master]

5 Exit Passage

Hop over a pressure plate to avoid a nasty trap as you enter the passage beyond the iron door. The Bone Alarm traps can give away your location to nearby Forsworn, if any remain. Proceed through the far door to head into Deepwood Vale.

◊ Danger! Bone Alarm Trap, Swinging Wall Trap (pressure plate)

◊ Potion

◊ Loose gear

C Door to Deepwood Vale

Deepwood Vale

D Door to Deepwood Vale

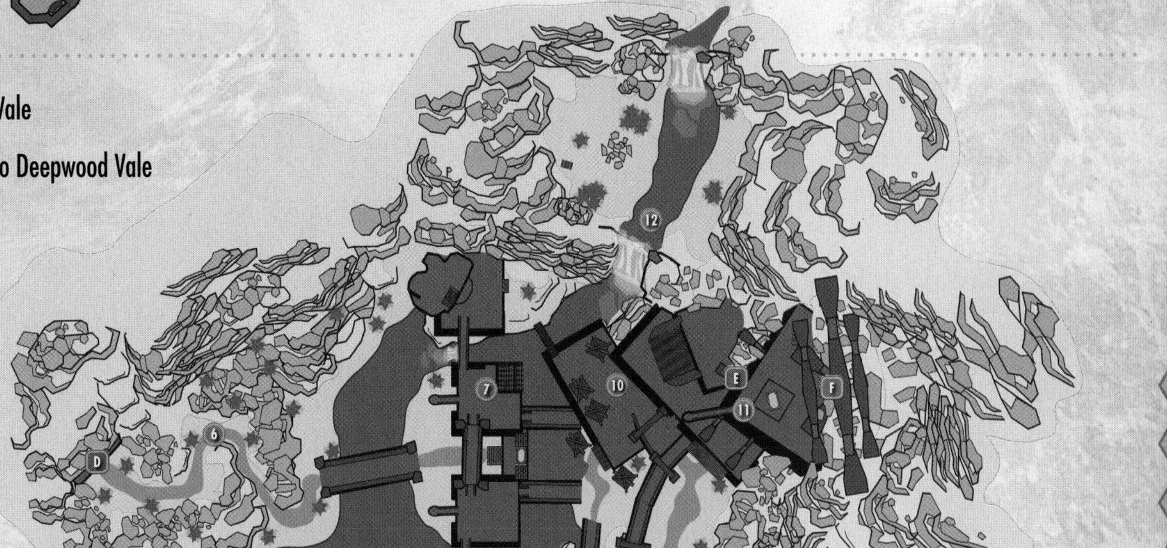

6 Deepwood Vale Entrance

Deepwood Redoubt leads out into a secret vale nestled in the mountains, where a much larger ruin awaits.

7 Vale Ramparts

Forsworn archers patrol the ramparts. The ramparts lead to Hag's End ([5.03]), the towering structure on the vale's east side.

8 Waterfall

River Channel – Look for a chest amid the rapids here.

9 Tent

There's also a Skill Book in the tent with the Alchemy Lab; one of many in this makeshift Forsworn camp.

10 The Towering Edifice: Hag's End

Make your way east toward Hag's End (see the next location in this Atlas for the interior information), slaying the Forsworn and claiming the treasure they guard. See Dark Brotherhood Radiant Quest: The Feeble Fortune for some strategies on assaulting this formidable fortress.

- ◊ Crafting: Alchemy Lab, Anvil, Blacksmith Forge, Grindstone, Workbench
- ◊ Skill Book [Sneak]: Sacred Witness [C1/10]
- ◊ Chests (2)
- ◊ Chest (Locked: Apprentice)
- ◊ Potions
- ◊ Loose gear

E Door to Hag's End

F Door to Hag's End

11 Deepwood Vale Summit

You exit out onto the upper level of Hag's End after navigating the interior of it, and overlook Deepwood Vale below. Face the Hagraven and her summoned minions for a final time and cut them down. Then claim the unique dagger from the corpse on the altar and the large chest nearby.

- ◊ Unique Weapon: Bloodthorn [31/80]
- ◊ Chest

12 Hidden Chest Atop Waterfall

If you have the Whirlwind Sprint Shout (or are good at rock climbing), head to the upper level of the Vale from which the waterfall descends. There, you can find one more chest and a unique pair of boots.

- ◊ Unique Item: Predator's Grace [54/112]
- ◊ Chest (Locked: Expert)

[5.03] Hag's End

Related Quests

Dark Brotherhood Quest: The Feeble Fortune*
Dungeon Activity

Recommended Level: 14

Dungeon: Hagraven Nest

Animal
Hagraven
Witch

Crafting

Alchemy Lab
Arcane Enchanter

Dangers

Battering Ram Trap (pressure plate)
Dart Trap
Flamethrower Trap
Rune Trap
Oil Lamp Trap
Oil Pool Trap

Collectibles

Skill Book [Illusion]: Mystery of Talara, Part 4
Unique Item: Ancient Shrouded Armor [50/112]
Unique Item: Ancient Shrouded Boots [51/112]
Unique Item: Ancient Shrouded Cowl [52/112]
Unique Item: Ancient Shrouded Gloves [52/112]
Unique Item: Predator's Grace [53/112]
Unique Weapon: Bloodthorn [31/80]

Special Objects

Word Wall: Slow Time [3/3]
Chest(s)
Potions
Loose gear

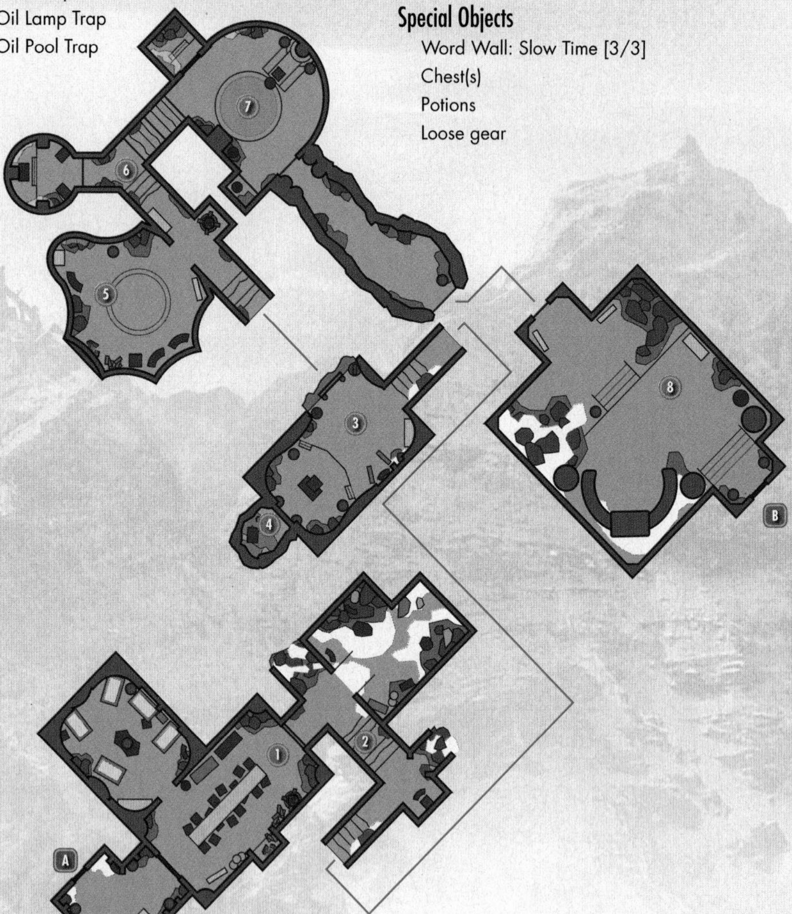

The ruins of Deepwood Redoubt [5.02] protect the tower of Hag's End, home to the formidable Hagraven that's revered by this band of Forsworn. You must brave Deepwood Redoubt in order to reach Deepwood Vale and challenge the Hagraven of Hag's End.

A Door to Deepwood Vale

1 Dining Room and Side Chambers

Slay vicious witches and battle the Hagraven in the first few chambers.

- ◊ Crafting: Alchemy Lab
- ◊ Potions
- ◊ Loose gear

[5.09] Harmugstahl

Related Quests
Dungeon Activity

Recommended Level: 8

Dungeon: Warlock Lair
Adventurer
Animal
Kornalus

Crafting
Alchemy Lab
Arcane Enchanter

Puzzles
Lever Puzzle

Collectibles
Skill Book [Alchemy]: A Game at Dinner

Special Objects
Shrine of Julianos [3/5]
Chest(s)
Potions aplenty
Loose gear

Exterior

This unassuming stronghold is built into the north side of the Reach's central mountains.

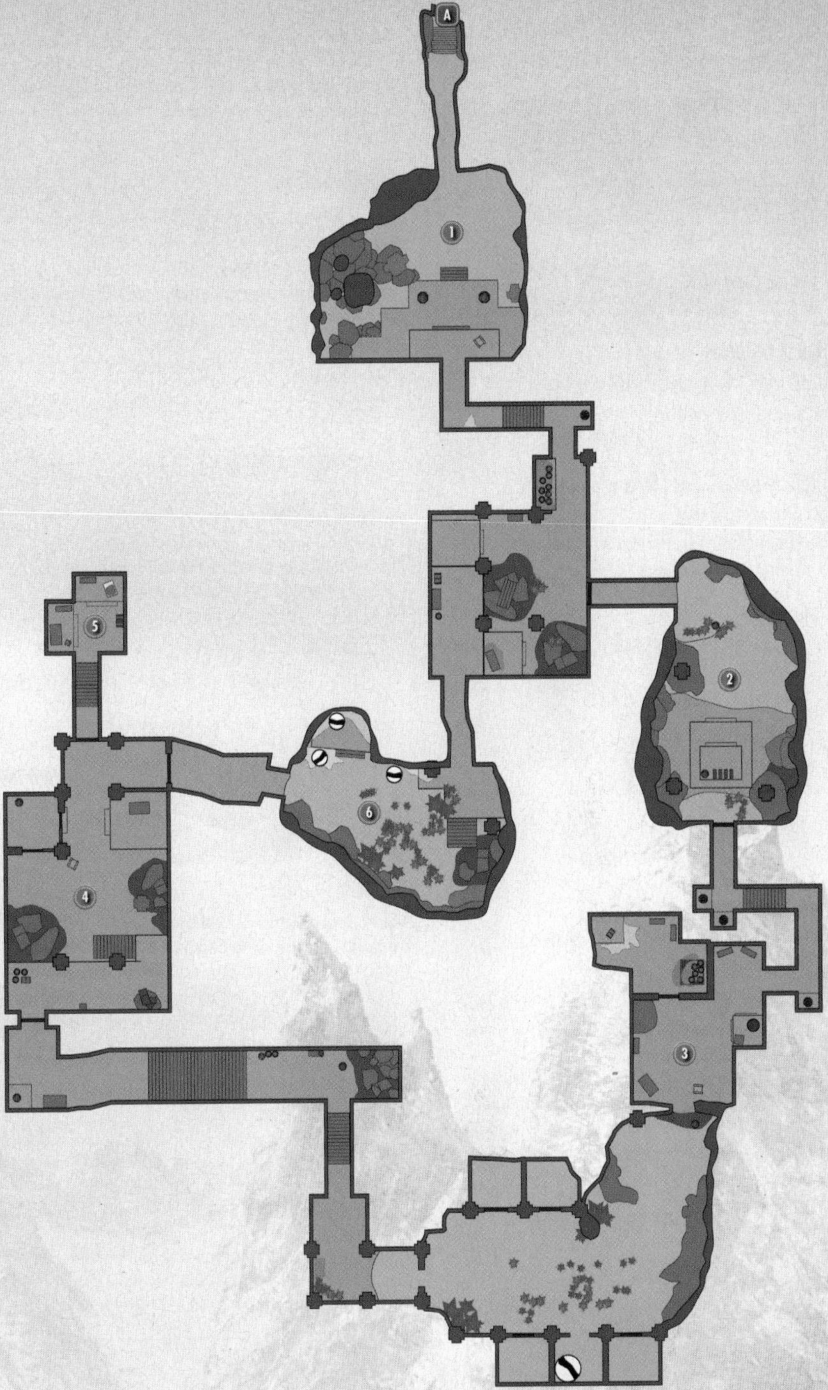

Interior

A Door to Skyrim

1 Entry Cavern

Witness an adventurer dispatch an overgrown spider in the first cavern, then speak to the man to learn that this place is supposedly overrun with the pests. You can loot a chest atop this room's balcony when you eventually make your way back around.

- Chest
- Satchel

2 Lever Cavern

Progress until you encounter a room with four levers. Pull only the far left and far right levers to open the way forward.

3 Alchemy Room

If you can, unlock this chamber's Expert-level door to access a small storage room filled with potions and a Skill Book.

- Crafting: Alchemy Lab
- Skill Book [Alchemy]: A Game at Dinner
- Chest
- Potions aplenty

4 Kornalus's Lab

Slay a dangerous mage named Kornalus in the next chamber, who's conducting some sort of nefarious study on the spiders. Claim a key from Kornalus's corpse and use it to open the nearby north door [Master].

- Crafting: Arcane Enchanter
- Kornalus Frey's Key (Kornalus)
- Potions

5 Kornalus's Quarters

Loot the giant chest in the small room beyond to claim valuable treasure. Touch the pyramid-shaped shrine to instantly cure any diseases you may have.

- Shrine of Julianos [3/5]
- Potions
- Chest

6 Giant Spider Cavern

This cavern's two Giant Frostbite Spiders are not only massive, but they've also been enchanted by Kornalus to make them even more formidable.

- Loose gear

[5.10] Reach Stormcloak Camp

Related Quests

- Civil War Quest: Liberation of Skyrim
- Civil War Quest: Compelling Tribute
- Civil War Quest: The Battle for Fort Sungard

Habitation: Military: Stormcloak Camp

- Kottir Red-Shoal
- Stormcloak Quartermaster (Blacksmith)
- Stormcloak Soldier

Services

- Trader (Blacksmith): Stormcloak Quartermaster [13/33]
  - Weapons, Apparel, Misc

Crafting

- Alchemy Lab
- Anvil
- Grindstone
- Workbench

Special Objects

- Civil War: Map of Skyrim Chests (2)
- Potions
- Loose gear

The Sons of Skyrim have erected a camp in the Reach's eastern mountains. Use the array of crafting stations here, and inspect the tabletop map in the largest tent to potentially gain new map data. If your stealth skills are sharp, loot a few chests before moving on.

[5.11] Liar's Retreat

Related Quests

- Dungeon Activity

Recommended Level: 18

Dungeon: Falmer Hive

- Animal
- Bandit
- Falmer

Collectibles

- Skill Book [Speech]: Biography of the Wolf Queen
- Unique Weapon: The Longhammer [32/80]
- Chest(s)
- Potions
- Loose gear

This medium-sized cave, which is situated within the Reach's eastern mountains, is being used as a bar and gambling hall by bandits. However, the bandits have recently found themselves faced with an overwhelming adversary—Falmer have invaded the cave!

Dining Hall

Sneak into the cave's first chamber to watch a few bandits battle against several Falmer. Slay the victors afterward, and beware of many more Falmer that emerge from the room's northern entrances. Claim a few potions from behind the bar.

- Potions
- Loose gear

Sleeping Quarters

Find a few potions and some loose gear in the various rooms that connect off the dining hall. Find a locked chest in the northwest room and pick the Novice-level southwest door to free a powerful bandit and obtain even more wealth. A Skill Book sits atop a high stone shelf near the locked chest.

- Skill Book [Speech]: Biography of the Wolf Queen
- Chest
- Chest (Locked: Adept)
- Potions
- Loose gear

Spider Tunnels

Slay a ravenous Frostbite Spider in the webbed passages that follow, and find a locked chest in a Falmer tent. Beware of additional spiders that may descend from the ceiling, as well as the Falmer archer who stands in an elevated position as you exit the tunnel. Loot the chest on the Falmer's perch.

- Chest
- Chest (Locked: Apprentice)
- Potions

Chaurus Den

Slay some poorly equipped bandit prisoners on your way to the cave's large, final chamber, where a massive Chaurus lurks. Loot a chest here, collect the Longhammer from near the bar owner's splayed body, then backtrack outside. Beware: a handful of powerful bandits will ambush you back in the dining hall, thinking that you're to blame for their hideout's destruction!

- Unique Weapon: The Longhammer [32/80]
- Chest
- Loose gear

[5.12] Cliffside Retreat

Recommended Level: 8

Habitation: Hunter Camp

- Hunter

Crafting

- Tanning Rack

Collectibles

- Skill Book [Archery]: The Marksmanship Lesson

A lone hunter makes his home at this humble shack, which stands on the Reach's eastern cliffs. A Skill Book is the main attraction here.

[5.13] Dragon Bridge Overlook

Recommended Level: 8

Dungeon: Forsworn Redoubt

- Forsworn
- Chest (Locked: Novice)
- Potion
- Loose gear

This Forsworn campsite overlooks Haafingar's infamous Dragon Bridge [1.17]. Slay the dangerous ruffians and then plunder their valuables.

[5.14] Ragnvald

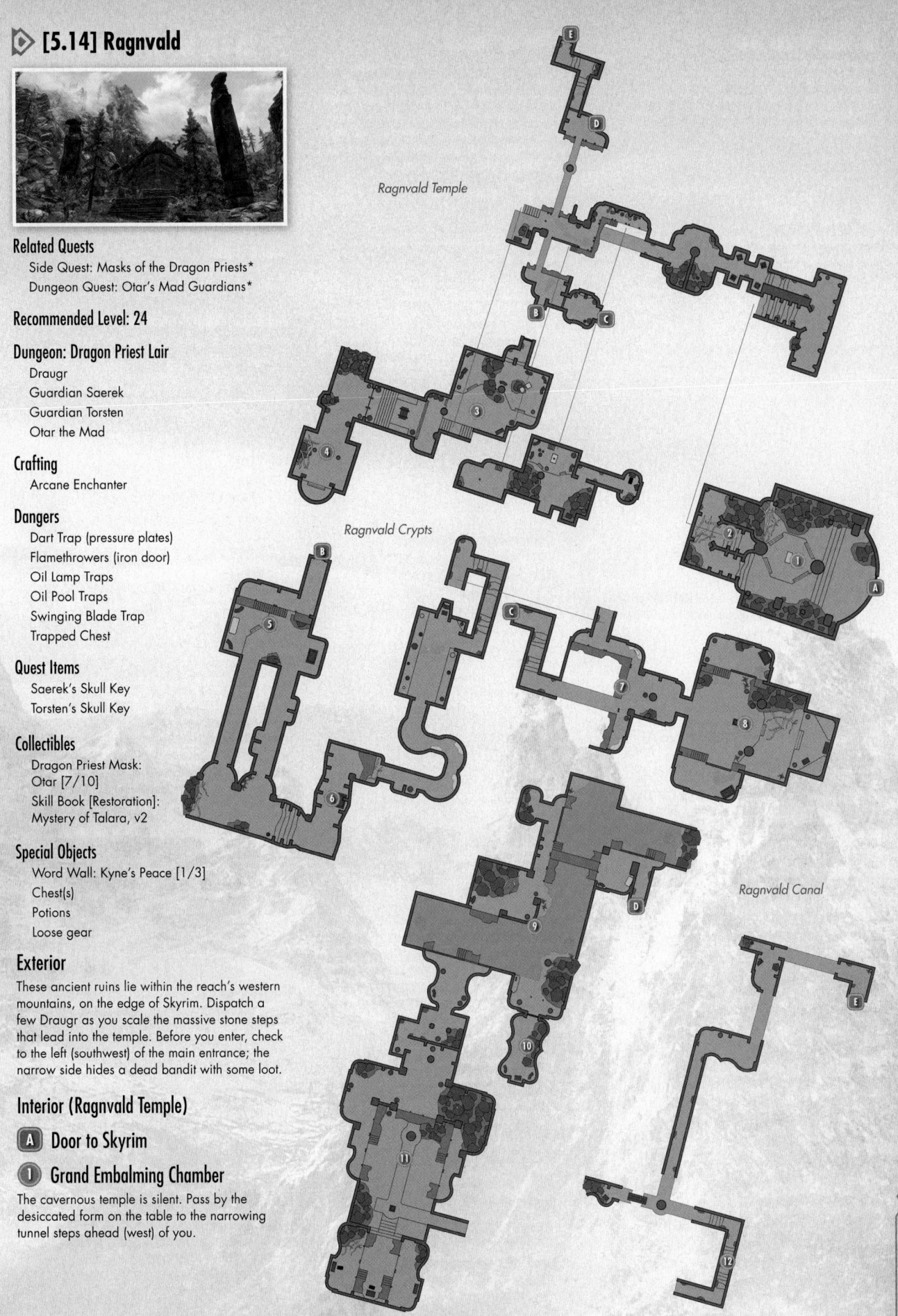

Related Quests

Side Quest: Masks of the Dragon Priests*
Dungeon Quest: Otar's Mad Guardians*

Recommended Level: 24

Dungeon: Dragon Priest Lair

Draugr
Guardian Saerek
Guardian Torsten
Otar the Mad

Crafting

Arcane Enchanter

Dangers

Dart Trap (pressure plates)
Flamethrowers (iron door)
Oil Lamp Traps
Oil Pool Traps
Swinging Blade Trap
Trapped Chest

Quest Items

Saerek's Skull Key
Torsten's Skull Key

Collectibles

Dragon Priest Mask: Otar [7/10]
Skill Book [Restoration]: Mystery of Talara, v2

Special Objects

Word Wall: Kyne's Peace [1/3]
Chest(s)
Potions
Loose gear

Exterior

These ancient ruins lie within the reach's western mountains, on the edge of Skyrim. Dispatch a few Draugr as you scale the massive stone steps that lead into the temple. Before you enter, check to the left (southwest) of the main entrance; the narrow side hides a dead bandit with some loot.

Interior (Ragnvald Temple)

A Door to Skyrim

1 Grand Embalming Chamber

The cavernous temple is silent. Pass by the desiccated form on the table to the narrowing tunnel steps ahead (west) of you.

2 Dead Draugr Steps

The tunnel steps lead to a small landing with a dead Draugr. The next landing (with the two ceremonial stone torch burners, and chest) has a further tunnel that's narrower still. This winds along to the large hub chamber of Otar.

- Potion
- Chest

3 Tomb of Otar

This sprawling chamber has exits to both side catacombs (the Crypts and Canal), and Draugr both on the walkways and the stone ground below (some are standing below Oil Lamps you can smash). Check this area for some scattered potions and two chests. Continue west to a strange and ornate sarcophagus with two odd slots in them. Return with two Skulls (one from each catacomb), insert them into the slots, and open the sarcophagus, summoning the mighty Dragon Priest Otar!

- Danger! Oil Lamp Traps, Oil Pool Traps
- Chest (2)
- Loose gear
- Potions
- Otar Mask

4 Word Wall of Kyne

Once Otar is defeated, the spears preventing you from accessing this chamber retract. Aside from the Word Wall, there are two chests (a locked one is found in a northern nook).

- Word Wall: Kyne's Peace [1/3]
- Chest
- Chest [Apprentice]

B Door to Ragnvald Crypts (upper)

C Door from Ragnvald Crypts (upper)

This has a door bar behind it, meaning you can only access it from the Crypts area, the first time you exit.

D Door to Ragnvald Canal (lower)

E Door from Ragnvald Canal (upper)

This has a door bar behind it, meaning you can only access it from the Canal area, the first time you exit.

Interior (Ragnvald Crypts)

B Door to Ragnvald Temple

5 Draugr Guard Chamber

Awaken the Draugr as you descend into this first chamber, then take the right (west) passage to avoid the left passage's traps.

Danger! Dart Trap (Pressure Plates)

6 Burial Passages

Slay a host of powerful Draugr as you progress.

7 Offering Chamber

Kill any foes, then watch out of the trapped chest that tempts you; open it from as far away as possible to avoid being impaled by spears. Then head to the walkways above this room to reach the final chamber, temporarily ignoring the upper tunnel and steps to the west, which lead you back into the Temple, after you face Saerek.

- Danger! Trapped chest
- Chest
- Skill Book (Restoration): Mystery of Talara, v2

8 Guardian Saerek's Tomb

This two-storey chamber has Draugr to slay first, before you inspect and take the strange skull on the pedestal in front of you. Then take it, and face the fearsome Guardian Saerek in combat!

- Danger! Oil Lamp Trap, Oil Pool Trap
- Saerek's Skull Key
- Chest

C Door to Ragnvald Temple

Interior (Ragnvald Canal)

D Door to Ragnvald Temple

9 North Canal Chamber

Search northwest to discover a chest. Then pull a southeast lever to lower a drawbridge ahead, but before you cross, open the nearby iron door from as far away as possible (or unlock the Trap Trigger [Expert]): a fire trap activates when the door opens.

- Chest
- Potions

10 Nook

Gather the items you need from the chest in here.

- Chest

11 Guardian Torsten's Tomb

12 Escape Route

Advance through the small maze of corridors and into this two-storey tomb. Swipe another skull from the central pedestal here to battle Guardian Torsten, who emerges from the far sarcophagus. Slay his brethren first, if you want fewer enemies to face at a time. Go upstairs to loot a locked chest, take the upper north corridor back to the previous cavern, jumping the pressure plate at the corridor's start to avoid activating a nasty trap. open one last chest near the arcane Enchanter before following the walkways back to the temple.

Danger! Flamethrowners (Iron Door), Swinging Blade Trap (Pressure Plate)

- Arcane Enchanter
- Chest
- Chest [Novice]
- Torsten's Skull Key

E Door to Ragnvald Temple

[5.15] Reach Imperial Camp

Related Quests

Civil War Quest (when active, depending on who you side with)

Habitation: Military: Imperial Camp

Imperial Quartermaster (Blacksmith)
Imperial Soldier

Services

Trader (Blacksmith): Imperial Quartermaster [14/33]
Weapons, Apparel, Misc

Crafting

Alchemy Lab
Anvil
Grindstone
Workbench

Special Objects

Civil War: Map of Skyrim Chests (2)
Potions
Loose gear

Imperial forces have erected a small camp in the Reach's eastern mountains, though this site may not exist, depending on the status of the Civil War quest line. Use the array of crafting stations here, and inspect the tabletop map in the largest tent to potentially gain new map data. If you like, loot a few chests before moving on.

[5.16] Shrine to Peryite

Related Quests

Daedric Quest: The Only Cure

Recommended Level: 12

Dungeon: Special

Kesh the Clean

Crafting

Alchemy Lab

Collectibles

Skill Book [Speech]: The Buying Game [E2/10]

This quaint shrine is perched high atop the Reach's northern mountains. Speak with the lone individual here, an alchemist named Kesh, to begin a Daedric Quest if you are Level 10 or higher. A Skill Book sits on the table near the Alchemy Lab.

[5.17] Karthwasten

Related Quests

Temple Quest: The Heart of Dibella

Miscellaneous Objective: Sauranach's Mine!: Helping Atar* (Atar or Ainethach)

Miscellaneous Objective: Sauranach's Mine!: Helping Ainethach* (Atar or Ainethach)

Habitation: Town

Ainethach (Marriage Prospect)

Atar

Belchimac

Enmon

Lash gra-Dushnikh

Mena

Ragnar

Crafting

Grindstone

Smelters (2)

Services

Marriage Prospect: Ainethach [21/62]

Collectibles

Chest(s)

Potions

Loose gear

Mineable ore (Silver)

This bustling mining community lies in the Reach's north-central region. You visit this village during "The Heart of Dibella" in search of an important child.

Exterior

When you first arrive at Karthwasten, you witness a verbal dispute between some Silver-Blood soldiers and a man named Ainethach, who owns the nearby Sanuarach mine. Speak to either person afterward to gain a Side Quest that involves the settling of their dispute.

- Crafting: Grindstone, Smelter (2)

1 Karthwasten Hall

This small area sports a chest and some loose coin, making it worth breaking into.

- Area Is Locked (Novice)
- Chest

2 Enmon's House

Pillage this humble abode for several potions and a chest.

- Area Is Locked (Novice)
- Chest
- Potions
- Loose gear

3 Miner's Barracks

Break into the barracks to raid a few chests.

- Area Is Locked (Novice)
- Chests (2)
- Loose gear

4 Fenn's Gulch Mine

This small silver mine has been largely mined out, but there's a bit of ore to be found in the northern nook.

- Loose gear
- Mineable ore (silver)

5 Sanuarach Mine

Silver-Blood soldiers guard this newer mine, and they won't let anyone harvest its precious silver until the situation between Atar and Ainethach here at Karthwasten has been resolved.

- Loose gear
- Mineable ore (Silver)

[5.18] Broken Tower Redoubt

Related Quests

Temple Quest: The Heart of Dibella

Recommended Level: 14

Dungeon: Forsworn Redoubt

Forsworn

Crafting

Grindstone

Dangers

Rockfall Trap (tripwire)
Rune Trap (floor)
Swinging Wall Trap (pressure plate)

Collectibles

Skill Book [Block]: The Mirror [D1/10]
Skill Book [Conjuration]: Liminal Bridges

Special Objects

Shrine of Dibella [4/8]
Chest(s)
Potions aplenty
Loose gear

This battered fortress stands in a valley between the Reach's rocky eastern hills. While Temple Quest: The Heart of Dibella is active, a band of Forsworn will be guarding an important child here, whom you must free.

Great Hall

Unlock the first chamber's Adept-level northwest door to access a stockroom with a chest. Proceed through the upstairs door and sidestep a pressure plate trap in the corridor on your way to the next room.

- Danger! Swinging Wall Trap (pressure plate)
- Chest
- Potions

Tower A

Unlock the chest within this circular chamber and swipe several potions off shelves. Claim a Skill Book from a table in the sleeping area before opening the east door and navigating a long passage to another tower.

- Skill Book [Block]: The Mirror [D1/10]
- Chest (Locked: Novice)
- Potions

Tower B

Slay more Forsworn in the second tower, and beware of a tripwire that's stretched across the stairs as you make your ascent. Loot a chest on the second level and then continue upstairs. Exit through the door at the top to access the fort's upper ramparts.

- Chest
- Potions

Exterior Ramparts

Exit the keep via any of its northern doors to visit the exterior ramparts, where more Forsworn await. Access the highest ramparts by exiting through the upstairs door in Tower B, then cut across and enter the top of Tower A.

- Crafting: Grindstone
- Potion
- Loose gear

Tower A (Top Level)

Beware: a powerful Forsworn mage lurks at the top of this tower, and the center of the room features a dangerous rune trap. Keep away from the room's center as you battle the mage. The key you find on his corpse opens the nearby holding cell, where the child you seek as part of "The Heart of Dibella" quest is imprisoned. Claim the Skill Book on the nearby table and touch the shrine near the altar to banish any diseases you might have.

- Danger! Rune Trap (floor)
- Skill Book [Conjuration]: Liminal Bridges
- Shrine of Dibella [4/8]
- Broken Tower Prison Key (Forsworn mage)
- Chest
- Potions aplenty

[5.19] Markarth Stables

Related Quests

Favor: Special Delivery* (Banning)

Habitation: Farm

Banning (Special)
Cedran (Stables)
Kibell (Carriage)

Services

Follower: Vigilance [17/47]
Trader (Carriage): Kibell [2/5]
Trader (Stables): Cedran [2/5]
Trader (Stablemasters): Cedran [2/5]

Stop by these fine stables to buy a steed or purchase a carriage ride to any Hold's capital. For 500 gold, you may also buy a trusty war dog named Vigilance to serve as your Follower – speak with Banning for assistance.

[5.20] Salvius Farm

Related Quests

Miscellaneous Objective: Letter to Leonitus* (Rogatus Salvius)
Favor (Activity): Harvesting Crops* (Vigdis Salvius)

Habitation: Farm

Rogatus Salvius
Vigdis Salvius

Collectibles

Area Is Locked [Novice]
Chest

This small farm stands just outside of Markarth's front gate. Speak with the farm's owner, Rogatus Salvius, to gain a new Side Quest. Break into the farmhouse and raid it for valuables if you dare.

[5.21] Left Hand Mine

Related Quests

Favor (Activity): Mining Ore* (Skaggi Scar-Face)

Habitation: Mine

Adeber
Daighre
Erith
Gat gro-Shargakh (Marriage Prospect)
Pavo Attius (Marriage Prospect)
Skaggi Scar-Face
Sosia Tremellia
Torom (dog)
Willem

Crafting

Smelter

Services

Marriage Prospect: Gat gro-Shargakh [22/62]
Marriage Prospect: Pavo Attius [23/62]

Collectibles

Chest(s)
Loose gear
Mineable ore (Iron)

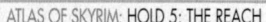

This bustling mining community is located just outside of Markarth's gates. It's busier than normal due to an influx of miners who have fled from the nearby Kolskeggr Mine [5.22], which has been overrun by Forsworn raiders.

Exterior

Chat with the villagers outside, including the mine's owner, Skaggi Scar-Face, to acquire a Side Quest involving another mine to the north. Skaggi will also purchase Iron Ore for a fair price.

- Crafting: Smelter

Miner's Barracks

If you like, raid a chest in the miner's barracks to claim some ill-gotten loot.

- Chest

Daighre's House

These humble miners don't have much, but you can steal what little they've got.

- Chest

Skaggi's House

The mine's owner isn't a rich woman, but you can break into her house and steal her life savings if you like.

- Area Is Locked (Novice)
- Chest

Left Hand Mine

There's plenty of iron to be claimed from this mine's thick ore veins.

- Loose gear
- Mineable ore (iron)

[5.22] Kolskeggr Mine

Related Quests

Miscellaneous Objective: Kolskeggr Clear Out* (Pavo)

Dungeon: Forsworn Redoubt

Forsworn

Crafting

Smelter	Loose gear
Potions	Mineable ore (Gold)

This valuable mining site has been overrun by Forsworn—its former workers have fled to the nearby Left Hand Mine [5.21]. Pick the easy front door lock to break into the cabin if you wish—you'll find pickaxes within. Go up the hill and enter the mine, slaying the remaining Forsworn there to secure it and its rich supply of valuable Gold Ore. Once the Forsworn are no more, the miners who fled to Left Hand Mine will return here to work.

[5.23] The Lover Stone

Recommended Level: 6

Dungeon: Special

Special Objects

Standing Stone: The Lover [6/13]

A small collection of ancient stones stands atop the mountains northeast of Markarth. Inspect the central Standing Stone to receive a new sign blessing. Those under the sign of the Lover can master all skills 15 percent faster. Note that you may only have one sign blessing at a time, so activating this Standing Stone will override your current sign blessing (if any).

[5.24] Blind Cliff Cave

Related Quests

Dungeon Quest: Melka and Petra*

Recommended Level: 14

Dungeon: Hagraven Nest

Forsworn
Melka

Crafting

Alchemy Lab

Dangers

Oil Lamp Traps
Oil Pool Traps

Puzzles

Handle Puzzle

Collectibles

Skill Book [Illusion]: Mystery of Talara, Part 4
Skill Book [Light Armor]: The Refugees [E2/10]
Unique Weapon: Eye of Melka [33/80]
Chest(s)
Potions
Loose gear

This small cave is located in the heart of the Reach, not far from the main road, and passing through it allows you to reach a pair of secluded, crumbling towers. The twisted Forsworn are using this area as a hideout.

Blind Cliff Cave (Interior)

Bring down a hanging lamp to ignite the oil in the cave's first passage and sear a lone Forsworn guard. Slay more Forsworn in the wide cavern that follows as you work your way up to a collapsed tower. Smiths should be on the lookout for ore veins throughout. Before entering the tower, check around behind it to locate a hidden chest, along with a Skill Book. Exit the cave via the tower's top door to return outside, near a pair of twin exterior towers.

- Skill Book [Light Armor]: The Refugees [E2/10]
- Danger! Oil Lamp Traps, Oil Pool Trap
- Chest

Blind Cliff Towers

Head to the top of the first exterior tower, slaying a few more Forsworn and looting a chest along the way. Cross the elevated walkway to reach the neighboring tower, looting a chest as you enter. Proceed into the bastion.

- Chests (2)
- Potion

Blind Cliff Bastion

You encounter a caged Hagraven named Melka in the bastion's entry passage. Speak to Melka to gain a new Side Quest, then pull the nearby chain to free Melka, who will guide you from this point forward. Melka can hold her own in most fights, but she is not invincible. Just ahead, turn the middle of three handles to safely raise a portcullis. Just beyond, allow Melka to expose a hidden lever, then pull it to deactivate the swinging blades in the next corridor. Just before Melka's alchemy parlor, you may spy a handle on the wall beyond the swinging blades and turn it to reveal a secret passage that leads to several urns and a chest. Backtrack out and proceed to the final cavern, where two Forsworn and a Hagraven named Petra await. Slay Petra to complete Melka's quest, and search Petra's remains to discover a Skill Book. Be sure to talk to Melka (or scavenge her corpse!) to claim your reward—a unique staff, the Eye of Melka.

- Crafting: Alchemy Lab
- Skill Book [Illusion]: Mystery of Talara, Part 4
- Unique Weapon: Eye of Melka [33/80]
- Chests (2)
- Potions
- Loose gear

[5.25] Four Skull Lookout

Related Quests

College of Winterhold Radiant Quest: Destruction Ritual Spell

Recommended Level: 8

Dungeon: Bandit Camp

Bandit

Collectibles

Chest(s)

Loose gear

Bandits have taken over this small stone ruin, located in the heart of the Reach. Clear out the villains, then loot the chest they're guarding. The special pedestal here is used during a College of Winterhold Quest.

[5.26] Red Eagle Redoubt

Related Quests

Side Quest: Repairing the Phial

Dungeon Quest: The Legend of Red Eagle

Recommended Level: 14

Dungeon: Forsworn Redoubt

Forsworn

Crafting

Alchemy Lab

Blacksmith Forge

Tanning Rack

Workbench

Dangers

Dart Trap

Oil Lamp Trap

Oil Pool Trap

Rockfall Trap

Quest Items

Red Eagle's Fury

Collectibles

Skill Book [Alteration]: Reality & Other Falsehoods

Unique Weapon: Red Eagle's Fury [34/80]

Chest(s)

Potions

Loose gear

Red Eagle Redoubt is perched on the precipice of the Tundra Plateau, just as the land plummets into the depths of the Reach. Millennia of erosion have all but destroyed the immense Nordic temple that once stood here, but a few remnants of its stairs and foundations remain. The Forsworn have built an impressive camp here, taking advantage of the area's natural defenses and commanding view of the Reach. The leader of this clan wields Red Eagle's Fury, an ancient blade that seals the tomb of Rebel's Cairn [5.28].

Exterior (Lower Area)

Slay the guards near the entrance and claim a few potions and a coin purse before continuing into the nearby cave.

- Potions

Red Eagle Ascent

This winding cave leads up to Red Eagle Redoubt's upper half. Avoid the oil pool (or shoot down the oil lamp above to ignite it), then look for a few potions next to a large brazier and a locked chest hidden behind some vines nearby. As you climb the first set of stairs, watch out for the rockfall and dart traps. A second chest can be found beneath the wooden stairs that lead up to the exit.

- Danger! Dart Trap, Oil Pool Trap, Oil Lamp Trap, Rockfall Trap
- Chest
- Chest (Locked: Adept)
- Potions

Exterior (Ascent Area)

As you emerge from the Red Eagle Ascent cave, travel south to find a lone chest sitting near a small yet unique statue that catches the eye [5.U]. Return to the cave exit entrance and scale a long flight of stone steps to reach a sizable Forsworn camp on the hill above. Find a Skill Book in a tent up here, along with a few crafting stations. Slay the mighty Forsworn leader to find a special key on his corpse, along with Red Eagle's Fury, a unique sword. When you have finished in the camp, use the key to open the nearby iron door and enter the Sundered Towers [5.27]. Pull a wall chain to lower the drawbridge and pillage the neighboring tower as well.

- Crafting: Alchemy Lab, Blacksmith Forge, Tanning Rack, Workbench
- Skill Book [Alteration]: Reality & Other Falsehoods
- Unique Weapon: Red Eagle's Fury [34/80] (Forsworn leader)
- Red Eagle Tower Key (Forsworn leader)
- Chests (2)
- Chest (Locked: Novice)
- Chest (Locked: Adept)
- Potions
- Loose gear

[5.27] Sundered Towers

Related Quests

Side Quest: Repairing the Phial

Dungeon: Forsworn Redoubt

Collectibles

Area Is Locked (Barred)

Chest (Locked: Novice)

Potions

Loose gear

These two towers are a major landmark, visible from much of the Reach and the western Tundra. The eastern tower is initially barred and all but inaccessible because of the surrounding cliffs. To explore them, claim the key from the boss in Red Eagle Redoubt [5.26], then enter the western tower from the entrance near the boss. Loot a few urns on your way up, then pull a wall chain to lower a drawbridge to the eastern tower. Raid a locked chest here, take in the spectacular view from atop both towers, and then unbar the eastern door as you leave.

[5.28] Rebel's Cairn

Related Quests

Dungeon Quest: The Legend of Red Eagle

Recommended Level: 14

Dungeon: Draugr Crypt

Red Eagle

Skeleton

Collectibles

Unique Weapon: Red Eagle's Bane [35/80]

Area Is Locked (Red Eagle's Fury required)

Chest

Potion

Loose gear

A common sword imbedded in a stone cairn marks the entrance to this secluded cave. Find the legendary blade called Red Eagle's Fury by slaughtering the Forsworn leader in nearby Red Eagle Redoubt [5.26], then place the sword into the pedestal in the main chamber to open a secret passage. Enter the tomb of Red Eagle, a powerful Draugr Warrior who raises skeletons to aid him. Lay Red Eagle to rest and loot his remains—along with a giant chest—to complete your quest and amass plenty of plunder. On your way out, reclaim Red Eagle's sword, which has been transfigured into an even more powerful blade—Red Eagle's Bane.

[5.29] Karthspire Camp

Related Quests

Main Quest: Alduin's Wall

Main Quest: The Throat of the World

Recommended Level: 14

Dungeon: Forsworn Redoubt

Dragon
Forsworn

Collectibles

Skill Book [Block]: A Dance in Fire, v2
Chest
Apothecary's Satchels (2)
Potion
Loose gear

Crafting

Blacksmith Forge
Grindstone
Tanning Rack
Workbench

This sprawling Forsworn encampment lies just outside of Karthspire [5.30]. This dangerous camp must be braved in order to reach Karthspire and explore Sky Haven Temple [5.31] as part of the Main Quest. Search the lower walkways and tents thoroughly to discover a Skill Book. Make your way up to a high platform, where a chest and a number of crafting stations are found. You also obtain a Dragon's Soul here during the Main Quest. Scale the west rocks afterward to locate a large cave entrance that leads into Karthspire.

[5.30] Karthspire

Related Quests

Main Quest: Alduin's Wall

Recommended Level: 14

Dungeon: Forsworn Redoubt

Forsworn

Dangers

Flamethrower (pressure plates)

Puzzles

Spinning Pillars Puzzle
Pressure Plates Puzzle
Underground Connection: Sky Haven Temple [5.31]
Chests (2)
Potions
Loose gear

Located due east of Markarth, Karthspire is a cave that you must navigate to reach Sky Haven Temple [5.31] during the Main Quest. Battle more Forsworn to secure the interior, finding a chest and several potions in the entry encampment. During the Main Quest, Esbern helps you solve a simple puzzle in the cavern that follows: spin the three pillars so that they each show the symbol of the Dragonborn, which resembles a circle. Cross the drawbridge that lowers and proceed to a room filled with pressure plates—step only on the path of Dragonborn tiles to safely reach a far wall chain that deactivates the trap. Proceed to the final chamber afterward to raid a large chest and locate the entrance to the Sky Temple, which Esbern helps you open.

[5.31] Sky Haven Temple

Related Quests

Main Quest: Alduin's Wall
Main Quest: The Throat of the World
Main Quest: Paarthurnax
Main Quest: Epilogue
Main Quest: Elder Knowledge
Other Factions: The Blades Quest: Rebuilding the Blades*
Other Factions: The Blades Quest: Dragon Hunting*
Other Factions: The Blades Quest: Dragonslayer's Blessing*
Other Factions: The Blades Quest: Dragon Research*

Habitation: Special

Delphine (the Blades)
Esbern (the Blades)

Underground Connection: Karthspire [5.30]

Collectibles

Skill Book [One-Handed]: Mace Etiquette
Unique Weapon: Dragonbane [36/80]

Special Objects

Alduin's Wall
Area Is Locked (quest required)
Chests (10)
Loose gear
Lots o'Gold!

This sacred sanctum lies east of Markarth and cannot be entered until you progress to Main Quest: Alduin's Wall. Inspect the central mural with Esbern to complete that quest and begin a new one. Search the west alcove to find a chest and Skill Book, then head upstairs and search the northwest sleeping area to discover a whopping seven more chests. Explore the armory to find a unique weapon lyinh on the table. Exit through any of the northeast doors to reach an exterior courtyard that offers breathtaking views, along with quick access to the world map's Fast-Travel option. Far below the upper exterior courtyard is the Karth River, and an abandoned rowboat containing scattered gems, an underwater chest, and a strongbox.

Blades Occupation

The Blades repurpose the Sky Haven Temple as their base of operations during the Main Quest. After finishing Main Quest: Alduin's Wall (and once you've sided with the Blades and completed Main Quest: Paarthurnax, meaning you're in good standing with them), you're able to return to Delphine and Esbern and commence the following:

During Other Factions Quest: Rebuilding the Blades,* you can bring up to three of your Followers (or Hirelings) and have Delphine train them to be Blades, after which they remain here.

During Other Factions Quest: Dragon Hunting, once you've brought three Followers to be trained, you can speak to Esbern and hunt a dragon with the newly trained Blades.

During Other Factions Quest: Dragonslayer's Blessing, you can receive a blessing from Esbern if you're in good standing with the Blades, which grants you +10 percent Critical Hit versus dragons for five days.

During Other Factions Quest: Dragon Research, bring back any Dragon Scales or Dragon Bones to Esbern and he concocts Esbern's Potion, imbuing you with a 10 percent damage reduction from dragon attacks.

[5.32] Soljund's Sinkhole

Related Quests

Miscellaneous Objective: Making It Hole Again* (Perth)

Recommended Level: 6

Dungeon: Draugr Crypt

Draugr
Perth (Marriage Prospect)

Crafting

Smelter

Services

Marriage Prospect: Perth [24/62]

Dangers

Dart Trap (lever)
Spear Trap (pressure plates)

Collectibles

Skill Book [Light Armor]: Jornibret's Last Dance
Chest(s)
Potions
Loose gear

Located in the heart of the Reach, this old mine has recently been invaded by Draugr and has since stopped working.

Exterior

Outside the mine, a man named Perth explains that the miners dug too deeply and accidently unearthed a Draugr-filled tomb. This gains you a Side Quest that you can satisfy by clearing out the undead within the mine.

◊ Crafting: Smelter

Miner's House

Breaking into the miner's house puts you within easy reach of two chests and a few potions.

◊ Area Is Locked (Novice)
◊ Chests (2)
◊ Potions

Soljund's Sinkhole (Interior)

These sizeable mines have been filled with undead ever since the miners accidentally tunneled into a forgotten crypt. Turn left at the first junction and slay the Draugr at the dead end, where a Skill Book sits atop a table on the overlook. Then backtrack and go right, dropping down a giant hole and slaughtering a host of powerful Draugr in the chamber below.

- Skill Book [Light Armor]: Jornibret's Last Dance
- Potion
- Loose gear

Draugr Tunnels

Wipe out undead on your way through the tunnels that follow, but don't touch the lever you soon locate—you'll only spring a nasty trap. Instead, pull two hidden levers that are affixed to the nearby walls to open the way forward. Scale some winding steps afterward and sidestep a couple of pressure plates upstairs. After passing the second pressure plate, climb more steps and search the dark west nook to discover an ornate chest. Slay a mighty Draugr in the large chamber that follows, then raid a large chest before following an elevated passage back to the mine's entrance.

- Danger! Spear Trap (pressure plates), Dart Trap (lever)
- Chests (2)
- Potions
- Loose gear

[5.33] Bleakwind Bluff

Dungeon: Hagraven Nest

Forsworn
Hagraven

Collectibles

Skill Book [Two-Handed]: King [B2/10]
Chest

Scale the crumbling stone steps that encircle this fallen tower, which protrudes from the Reach's eastern hills. Slay powerful Forsworn and Hagraven as you make your way up to the tower, where a large chest and Skill Book are found.

[5.34] Old Hroldan

Related Quests

Miscellaneous Objective: The Ghost of Old Hroldan* (Eydis/Ghost of Old Hrolden)

Habitation: Inn

Eydis (Innkeeper)
Leonitus Salvius
Skuli

Services

Trader (Innkeeper): Eydis [7/15]

Collectibles

Skill Book [Two-Handed]: Battle of Sancre Tor [A1/10]
Chest
Chests (Locked: Novice) (2)

Nestled along the west bank of the Reach's eastern hills, this small inn offers room and board to weary travelers. Speak to the innkeeper to buy a meal or rent a room, and search the place to loot a number of chests and discover a Skill Book on a nightstand.

[5.35] Hag Rock Redoubt

Related Quests

Daedric Quest: Pieces of the Past

Recommended Level: 14

Dungeon: Forsworn Redoubt

Forsworn

Crafting

Alchemy Lab
Anvil
Tanning Rack
Workbench

Collectibles

Skill Book [Sneak]: 2920, Last Seed, v8
Chest(s)
Potions aplenty
Loose gear

Dangers

Rockfall Trap (tripwire)

Located along the Reach's southwest edge, this large collection of mountainous ruins has been exploited by the Forsworn and fortified into a military encampment. You must pass through Hag Rock Redoubt in order to reach Dead Crone Rock [5.36] as part of Daedric Quest: Pieces of the Past.

Exterior

Scale the exterior tower, looting a chest and slaying a Forsworn on your way to the top. Cross the narrow aqueduct and dispatch more Forsworn, raiding a dome-shaped outdoor shack to obtain several potions and sack another chest. Beware the tripwire that's stretched across the steps of the east ruins, and keep going up to eventually reach Dead Crone Rock [5.36].

- Danger! Rockfall Trap (tripwire)
- Crafting: Alchemy Lab, Anvil, Tanning Rack, Workbench
- Chests (2)
- Chest (Locked: Adept)
- Apothecary's Satchels (2)
- Potions aplenty

Hag Rock Redoubt Ruin

Enter the west structure via any of its three entrances to explore a small network of interior ruins. Lay waste to more Forsworn here as you plunder even more loot. Search the shelves of the cupboard near the holding cells to find the key that unlocks them. Downstairs, find a Skill Book on a table that's covered with potions, along with a chest that's tucked away in a dark southeast nook.

- Skill Book [Sneak]: 2920, Last Seed, v8
- Hag Rock Ruin Jail Key
- Chest
- Chest (Locked: Adept)
- Potions
- Loose gear

[5.36] Dead Crone Rock

Related Quests

Daedric Quest: Pieces of the Past
Thieves Guild Radiant Quest: No Stone Unturned

Recommended Level: 14

Dungeon: Hagraven Nest

Drascua
Forsworn

Crafting

Arcane Enchanter

Dangers

Flamethrowers (floor)

Quest Items

Pommel Stone of Mehrunes' Razor

Collectibles

Skill Book [Alchemy]: A Game at Dinner
Unusual Gem: [10/24]

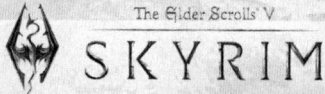

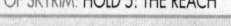

Special Objects

Word Wall: Dismaying Shout [2/3]
Chest(s)
Potions
Loose gear

To reach this remote Forsworn outpost, which lies at the southwest corner of the Reach, one must first deal with leagues of bloodthirsty Forsworn in the surrounding Hag Rock Redoubt [5.35].

Dead Crone Rock (Interior)

Loot a chest in the first passage, then slay Forsworn and snatch up potions on your way into a large cavern, where a large spiral staircase leads upstairs. Visit the west dining room to find another chest, more potions, and an Arcane Enchanter. Sprint down the following passage to avoid being burned by flamethrowers on the floor. Find a Skill Book in the next room and pull the nearby lever to raise a portcullis back in a previous chamber. Backtrack and take the southern stairs up to a door that leads outside.

- Danger! Flamethrowers (floor)
- Crafting: Arcane Enchanter
- Skill Book [Alchemy]: A Game at Dinner
- Chests (2)
- Potions

Exterior

Climb the exterior steps to find another chest, then keep going up to face a powerful Hagraven named Drascua on the hill. Slay the fiend and obtain a key from its corpse, along with a quest-related item. Then loot a giant chest before approaching the nearby Word Wall to gain a new Word of Power. Collect the Unusual Gem from the table to potentially gain a new Side Quest as well. Go back inside afterward and return to the spiral stairwell chamber. Unlock the southeast door with Drascua's key and head back outside to locate a third exterior chest.

- Pommel Stone of Mehrunes' Razor (Drascua)
- Unusual Gem: Stone of Barenziah [10/24]
- Word Wall: Dismaying Shout [2/3]
- Dead Crane Rock Key (Drascua)
- Chests (2)
- Potions

[5.37] Purewater Run

Dungeon: Animal Den

Animal

Collectibles

Chests (2)

Follow a stream into this watery cave, and swim quickly to the bottom of the deep water to loot a pair of dwarven chests before you're chewed up by aggressive Slaughterfish.

[5.38] Dushnikh Yal

Related Quests

Side Quest: The Forgemaster's Fingers
Side Quest: Captured Critters*
Miscellaneous Objective: The Sword of Gharol* (Gharol)
Favor (Activity): Mining Ore* (Gharol)
Favor: Sparring Partners* (Burguk)

Recommended Level: 6

Habitation: Orc Stronghold

Arob
Chief Burguk
Dulug
Ghak
Gharol (Blacksmith)
Ghorbash the Iron Hand (Follower, Marriage Prospect)
Mahk
Murbul (Apothecary)
Nagrub
Oglub
Umurn

Services

Follower: Ghorbash the Iron Hand [18/47]
Marriage Prospect: Ghorbash the Iron Hand [25/62]
Trader (Apothecary): Murbul [8/14]
  Potions, Food, Ingredients
Trader (Blacksmith): Gharol [15/33]
  Weapons, Apparel, Misc
Trainer (Heavy Armor: Expert): Gharol [1/3]
Trainer (One-Handed: Master): Burguk [1/3]

Crafting

Alchemy Labs (2)
Blacksmith Forge
Grindstone
Smelter
Tanning Racks (2)
Workbench

Collectibles

Captured Critter: Dragonfly in a Jar [3/5]
Skill Book [Heavy Armor]: Orsinium and the Orcs [D2/10]
Chest(s)
Potions
Loose gear
Mineable ore (Orichalcum)

The Reach boasts two Orc strongholds—this one lies far to the south, on the high cliffs of the southern Reach. As always, the Orcs will loathe your presence if you're an outsider, but you can gain their acceptance by completing a Side Quest that just about any of the local Orcs will bestow during conversation.

Exterior

Use any of the crafting stations outside. Check behind the chief's Longhouse to find a chest under some stairs. The blacksmith, Gharol, will buy any ore you collect from the nearby mine at a fair price. Test your fistfighting prowess in a friendly wager against the chief if you like.

- Crafting: Alchemy Lab, Blacksmith Forge, Grindstone, Smelter, Tanning Racks (2), Workbench
- Chest (Locked: Apprentice)
- Potions
- Loose gear

Burguk's Longhouse

If you dare, enter the Orc chief's Longhouse and plunder the place. Unlock the Novice-level trapdoor to enter the cellar and claim a Skill Book, along with a Dragonfly in a Jar that pertains to Side Quest: Captured Critters. Loop around the cellar's circuitlike tunnel to locate an Alchemy Lab and a locked chest that's hidden beneath the stairs.

- Area Is Locked (Novice)
- Crafting: Alchemy Lab
- Captured Critter: Dragonfly in a Jar [3/5]
- Skill Book [Heavy Armor]: Orsinium and the Orcs [D2/10]
- Chests (2)
- Chest (Locked: Apprentice)
- Apothecary's Satchel
- Potions
- Loose gear

Dushnikh Mine

Grab a pickaxe and collect Orichalcum Ore from the mine. There's a chest and a couple of potions here as well.

- Chest
- Potions
- Loose gear
- Mineable ore (Orichalcum)

[5.39] Reachwater Rock

Related Quests

Side Quest: Forbidden Legend
Dungeon Activity

Recommended Level: 15

Dungeon: Draugr Crypt

Gauldur
Jyrik Gauldurson
Mikrul Gauldurson
Sigdis Gauldurson

Puzzles

Nordic Puzzle Door (Emerald)
Nordic Puzzle Door (Ivory)

Collectibles

Dragon Claw: Emerald Dragon Claw [5/8]
Unique Item: Gauldur Amulet [56/112]
Chest(s)
Potion
Loose gear

Follow the main road east out of Markarth and you'll eventually reach a bridge. Look up to spy this waterfall cave, which is perched on a high cliff, hidden beneath a spray of water. Reachwater Rock is the long-forgotten tomb of the Arch-Mage Gauldur, a powerful First Era wizard. Visit this site after you've obtained all three Gauldur Amulet Fragments to reforge the Gauldur Amulet.

Reachwater Cavern

First, dive underwater to locate worthy gear and a locked chest. A second chest is perched on a high ledge on the room's east side; to reach it, stand by the Puzzle Door and use the Whirlwind Sprint Shout. Then climb the central spire and collect the Emerald Dragon Claw from the cavern's pedestal. Inspect the claw closely to notice three markings on it. Approach the nearby puzzle door and rotate its three rings to match the symbols on the claw: Bear, Whale, Snake. Examine the door's central keyhole to insert the claw and open the way forward.

- ◊ Dragon Claw: Emerald Dragon Claw [5/10]
- ◊ Chest
- ◊ Chest (Locked: Adept)
- ◊ Loose gear

Sealed Passage

Continue down the sealed passage as the doors open ahead of you until you reach another Puzzle Door. This one requires the Ivory Claw from Folgunthur [2.08] to solve. If you have the claw, inspect it to find the symbol sequence as you did before, then mimic the same pattern on the door: Hawk, Hawk, Dragon. Insert the Ivory Claw to open the way forward. Loot a few urns and grab a potion on your way to the final cavern.

- ◊ Potion

Amulet Chamber

Approach the altar and place the three Gauldur Amulet Fragments onto the pedestals to battle the three Gauldurson Brothers once more and receive the reforged Gauldur Amulet as a reward (see Side Quest: Forbidden Legend for tips). You'll find a secret nook has opened as you backtrack out of the chamber. Raid the large chest within.

- ◊ Unique Armor: Gauldur Amulet [55/112]
- ◊ Chest
- ◊ Loose gear

[5.40] Reachwind Eyrie

Recommended Level: 8

Dungeon: Special

Collectibles

Skill Book [Heavy Armor]: Chimarvamidium
Chest (Locked: Apprentice)
Chest (Locked: Expert)
Loose gear

This striking dwarven tower is visible for miles, standing tall among the Reach's rocky south-central hills. The tower is free of danger and contains a number of valuables. Stop by and have a look. The view from the balcony is spectacular.

[5.41] Reachcliff Cave

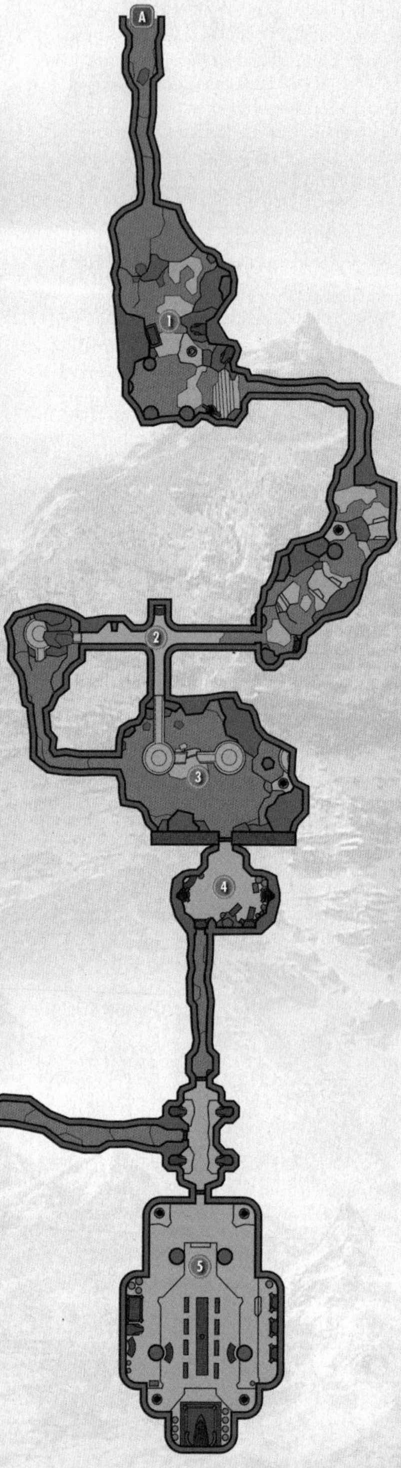

Related Quests

Daedric Quest: The Taste of Death

Recommended Level: 6

Dungeon: Draugr Crypt

Draugr

Services

Follower: Eola [19/47]

Dangers

Trapped Chest

Collectibles

Skill Book [Conjuration]: The Doors of Oblivion [D1/10]
Unique Item: Ring of Namira [57/112]
Area Is Locked
Chest(s)
Potions
Loose gear

Stone ruins line the path that leads to this sizable cave, where restless undead dwell. You cannot fully explore this site until you visit it as part of Daedric Quest: The Taste of Death, during which you can obtain a unique ring. Complete the quest, and Eola will offer to join you as a Follower.

A Exit to Skyrim

1 Entry Passages

Slay a handful of mighty Draugr as you navigate these winding passages.

2 Junction

Loot an urn and grab a potion and some gear in these burial passages. Beware of waking the resting dead.

◊ Potion ◊ Loose gear

8 9 Chasm Ledge and Falmer Nest

Take care as you progress up the chasm, as the rumbling continues. Before you cross the first bridge, edge to a small ledge and chest. Then cross the bridge. Expect three Falmer in this area. Remember to double back across the fallen pillar bridge to a ledge on the opposite side of the chasm with some Falmer fencing.

◊ Chest

10 Barred Chamber and Inlet Stream Tunnel

Inspect the sealed door to your left (south) and observe that there is a chest behind it. To reach it, head west to the cliff edge and drop down to the riverbank; then turn south and trek up an inlet stream tunnel. This leads to the half-fallen rear of the chamber behind the door and a fallen Dwarven Centurion at the foot of the waterfall. Expect Dwarven Sphere combat before the chest. Use the ground lever to open the door from the chamber.

◊ Chest

11 Waterfall Grotto

Pockmarked with Falmer nest holes, attack the foes (Falmer and a Chaurus) here. There are two secret areas (Locations 14 and 15) on the opposite side of the waterfall.

12 Falmer Camp

Slay the Falmer in this small camp, and journey southwest to reach the next location, or head north to continue toward your goal.

◊ Chest

13 Chaurus Tunnel

In this tight tunnel, expect Chaurus attacks as you ascend.

14 15 Waterfall Grotto (High Ledge and Secret Tunnel)

At the top of the Chaurus Tunnel is a stream leading to the top of the Waterfall Grotto. Watch for a Falmer dropping onto this precarious perch. Check the tiny ledge to the left (north) for a chest. Then (carefully) turn right (south), drop down the grotto wall to a lower ledge and to a second, lower stream. Inspect this secret tunnel for a chest. Then drop into the grotto water in search of one more secret, an underwater passage to the west. Dive into the pool at the base of the falls and search for this tunnel leading into a thin, secret cavern with another chest, close to the skeletal remains of a warrior.

◊ Chest (3) ◊ Loose gear ◊ Lots o' Gold

16 Zephyr's Glade

Sitting on the edge of a log over a nasty drop (where Katria fell from) is the ghost's trusty bow. Carefully reach for it before making your way up the cliffs here.

◊ Unique Weapon: Zephyr [DG6/7]

17 Tonal Lock Chamber

A spectacular summit with dwarven arches to descend through, and a flat lower area littered with dwarven arrows and skeletal remains (at least eight corpses are here, some of whom have gear to grab).

Puzzle Solution: There are five resonators that make up the Tonal Lock. Bring out your favored bow (or Zephyr), and utilize the scattered arrows on the ground if you run out of ammunition. Figure out the correct order to hit each resonator. There are two clues to help you:

The first clue provides the correct listing of the first two resonators to hit. This is the sketch on the last page of Katria's Journal.

The second clue is on the corpse of the only non-skeletal adventurer lying on the ground near your feet. Search him for a scrap of paper, which correctly lists the second and the third resonator. Now take careful aim...

The correct order to strike the resonators is as follows: lower row, left (directly above the left door). Then lower row, right (directly above the right door). Then upper row, left (of the dwarven head). Then upper row, right (of the dwarven head). Then, finally, lower row, middle (below the dwarven head).

CAUTION

If you strike the resonators in the wrong order, the dwarven head above the lock glows red, and Dwarven Spiders and Spheres are released. Three mistakes, and the Dwarven Centurion behind the middle door clanks into life!

Beyond the puzzle is the treasure room with an Aetherium Shard (called Glowing Crystal Shard if you haven't received this quest yet) and a chest and other items. Don't forget to find the chest on the ledge above the exit tunnel to Location 19 too!

◊ Aetherium Shard [1/4] ◊ Loose Gear
◊ Chest (2) ◊ Scrap of Paper

18 Waterlogged Tunnel

This is the preferred (and rather terrifying) exit back to the Grand Cavern. The long drop into the water is safe. Well, so long as you hit the water...

HOLD 6: WHITERUN HOLD

TOPOGRAPHICAL OVERVIEW

Whiterun Hold, named for the fortress city in the eastern part of its vast Tundra plain, is the most centrally located of the nine Holds. Roads are numerous and well maintained, and visibility across the plains is excellent. This Hold is relatively flat, surrounded by the mountains of the Reach to the west, Hjaalmarch and the Pale to the north, and Falkreath to the south. However, Whiterun's southeastern corner is dominated by the gigantic and soaring Throat of the World—the highest mountain in all of Tamriel. It is here that many climb the 7,000 steps to High Hrothgar, home to the mysterious and reclusive Greybeards.

Routes and Pathways

Whiterun is certainly one of the most well-tracked Holds, with main roads and excellent access west to the Reach, with a border road north through the town of Rorikstead and up toward Dragon Bridge. The Tundra plains have a number of odd barrows and giant camps to investigate, and the center is dominated by Fort Greymoor. The road here allows you to travel north, up through the mountains to reach the dreaded Labyrinthian in Hjaalmarch. Farther east is Whiterun and the roaring White River and town of Riverwood on the southern border with Falkreath. Another road stretches north from here, into the wilds of the Pale. There's yet another road that skirts the northern foothills of the Throat of the World, following White River valley into Eastmarch. And although the first of the 7,000 steps that pilgrims take to reach the summit of the Throat of the World begins in Ivarstead (in the Rift), the actual mountain lies within Whiterun's domain. However, only those possessing a Thu'um (Shout) powerful enough to impress the Greybeards of High Hrothgar will be allowed to finish the journey to the summit.

AVAILABLE SERVICES, CRAFTING, AND COLLECTIBLES

Services

- Followers: [14/47]
- Houses for Sale: [1/5]
- Marriage Prospects: [13/62]
- Skill Trainers: [8/50]
  - Alchemy: [1/3]
  - Alteration: [0/3]
  - Archery: [2/3]
  - Block: [1/2]
  - Conjuration: [0/3]
  - Destruction: [0/3]
  - Enchanting: [0/2]
  - Heavy Armor: [1/3]
  - Illusion: [0/2]
  - Light Armor: [0/3]
  - Lockpicking: [0/2]
  - One-Handed: [2/3]
  - Pickpocket: [0/3]
  - Restoration: [1/3]
  - Smithing: [1/3]
  - Sneak: [0/3]
  - Speech: [0/4]
  - Two-Handed: [1/2]
- Traders [22/133]:
  - Apothecary [1/12]
  - Bartender [1/5]
  - Blacksmith [6/33]
  - Carriage Driver [1/5]
  - Fence [1/10]
  - Ferryman [0/3]
  - Fletcher [1/3]
  - Food Vendor [3/9]
  - General Goods [3/19]
  - Innkeeper [3/15]
  - Jeweler [0/2]
  - Special [0/3]
  - Spell Vendor [1/12]
  - Stablemaster [1/5]

Collectibles

- Captured Critters: [0/5]
- Dragon Claws: [0/10]
- Dragon Priest Masks: [0/10]
- Larceny Targets: [1/7]
- Skill Books: [22/180]
  - Alchemy: [2/10]
  - Alteration: [0/10]
  - Archery: [2/10]
  - Block: [1/10]
  - Conjuration: [1/10]
  - Destruction: [1/10]
  - Enchanting: [2/10]
  - Heavy Armor: [1/10]
  - Illusion: [2/10]
  - Light Armor: [1/10]
  - Lockpicking: [0/10]
  - One-Handed: [2/10]
  - Pickpocket: [0/10]
  - Restoration: [1/10]
  - Smithing: [1/10]
  - Sneak: [2/10]
  - Speech: [1/10]
  - Two-Handed: [2/10]
- Treasure Maps: [1/11]
- Unique Items: [2/112]
- Unique Weapons: [12/80]
- Unusual Gems: [5/24]

Special Objects

- Shrines: [10/69]
  - Akatosh: [1/6]
  - Arkay: [1/12]
  - Dibella: [0/8]
  - Julianos: [1/5]
  - Kynareth: [1/6]
  - Mara: [0/5]
  - Stendarr: [1/5]
  - Talos: [3/17]
  - Zenithar: [2/5]
- Standing Stones: [1/13]
  - The Ritual Stone
- Word Walls: [2/42]
  - Animal Allegiance: [0/3]
  - Aura Whisper: [0/3]
  - Become Ethereal: [0/3]
  - Disarm: [0/3]
  - Dismaying Shout: [0/3]
  - Elemental Fury: [0/3]
  - Fire Breath: [1/2]
  - Frost Breath: [0/3]
  - Ice Form: [0/3]
  - Kyne's Peace: [1/3]
  - Marked for Death: [0/3]
  - Slow Time: [0/3]
  - Storm Call: [0/3]
  - Throw Voice: [0/1]
  - Unrelenting Force: [0/1]
  - Whirlwind Sprint: [0/2]

CRAFTING STATIONS: WHITERUN

✓	TYPE	LOCATION A	LOCATION B
☐	Alchemy Lab	Whiterun (Dragonsreach) [6.00]	Riverwood (Sleeping Giant Inn) [6.27]
☐	Arcane Enchanter	Whiterun (Dragonsreach) [6.00]	Riverwood (Sleeping Giant Inn) [6.27] (after Main Quest: The Horn of Jurgen Windcaller)
☐	Anvil or Blacksmith Forge	Whiterun (Warmaiden's) [6.00]	Riverwood (Exterior) [6.27]
☐	Cooking Pot and Spit	Whiterun (Warmaiden's) [6.00]	Riverwood (Exterior) [6.27] (after Main Quest: Before the Storm)
☐	Grindstone	Whiterun (Warmaiden's) [6.00]	Riverwood (Exterior) [6.27]
☐	Smelter	Whiterun (Warmaiden's) [6.00]	—
☐	Tanning Rack	Whiterun (Warmaiden's) [6.00]	Riverwood (Exterior) [6.27]
☐	Wood Chopping Block	Whiterun (Belethor's General Goods) [6.00]	Riverwood (Exterior) [6.27]
☐	Workbench	Whiterun (Warmaiden's) [6.00]	Riverwood (Exterior) [6.27]

Hold 6: Whiterun

PRIMARY LOCATIONS

Total—40: Hold Capital, Dragonsreach, and 38 Hold Locations

[6.00] Hold Capital City: Whiterun
[6.00] Dragonsreach
Jarl: Balgruuf the Greater
[6.01] Lund's Hut
[6.02] Rorikstead
[6.03] Serpent's Bluff Redoubt
[6.04] Whiterun Imperial Camp
[6.05] Swindler's Den
[6.06] Gjukar's Monument
[6.07] Broken Fang Cave
[6.08] Sleeping Tree Camp
[6.09] Rannveig's Fast
[6.10] Drelas' Cottage
[6.11] Greenspring Hollow
[6.12] Dustman's Cairn
[6.13] Hamvir's Rest
[6.14] Redoran's Retreat
[6.15] Fort Greymoor
[6.16] Silent Moons Camp
[6.17] Halted Stream Camp
[6.18] Bleakwind Basin
[6.19] Western Watchtower
[6.20] Whiterun Stables
[6.21] Pelagia Farm
[6.22] Honningbrew Meadery
[6.23] Chillfurrow Farm
[6.24] Battle-Born Farm
[6.25] Whitewatch Tower
[6.26] White River Watch
[6.27] Riverwood
[6.28] Shimmermist Cave
[6.29] Fellglow Keep
[6.30] Graywinter Watch
[6.31] The Ritual Stone
[6.32] Whiterun Stormcloak Camp
[6.33] Valtheim Towers
[6.34] Darkshade
[6.35] Guldun Rock
[6.36] Hillgrund's Tomb
[6.37] High Hrothgar
[6.38] Throat of the World

SECONDARY LOCATIONS

Total—24 Points of Interest

[6.A] Shrine of Akatosh: Rorikstead
[6.B] Dragon Mound: Rorikstead Resurrection
[6.C] The Expired Alchemist
[6.D] Hunter and Hunted
[6.E] Shrine of Zenithar: Ring of Boulders
[6.F] Fetid Pond
[6.G] Shrine of Zenithar: Crumbling Bastion
[6.H] King of the Mudcrabs
[6.I] Shrine of Stendarr: The Two Pillars
[6.J] Swallowed Skeleton: Greymoor Foothills
[6.K] Dragon Mound: Great Henge Resurrection
[6.L] Puzzling Pillar Ruins
[6.M] Necromancer's Bluff
[6.N] Bloodied Box: Sleeping Tree Camp
[6.O] Dragon Mound: Lone Mountain
[6.P] The Skeleton's Strong Box: Greymoor
[6.Q] The Lad of the Lake: Bleakwind Basin
[6.R] Smuggler's Den: Whiterun
[6.S] Whiterun Attack Camp
[6.T] Shrine of Talos: White River Valley
[6.U] Hunters' Camp: White River Hills
[6.V] Big Log Bridge
[6.W] Ruined Toll and Wispmother's Well
[6.X] The Seven Thousand Steps

ADDITIONAL LOCATIONS

[DG.18] Moldering Ruins (see page 869)

[HF.05] Breezehome (Updated) (see page 848)

HOLD CAPITAL: WHITERUN

Related Quests

Main Quest: Before the Storm
Main Quest: Bleak Falls Barrow
Main Quest: Dragon Rising
Main Quest: The Way of the Voice
Main Quest: The Fallen
Main Quest: Season Unending
Main Quest: The World-Eater's Eyrie
Civil War Quest: Message to Whiterun
Civil War Quest: Battle for Whiterun
Civil War Quest: Defense of Whiterun
The Companions Quest: Take Up Arms
The Companions Quest: Proving Honor
The Companions Quest: The Silver Hand
The Companions Quest: Blood's Honor
The Companions Quest: Purity of Revenge
The Companions Quest: Glory of the Dead
The Companions Radiant Quest: Animal Extermination (I)
The Companions Radiant Quest: Animal Extermination (II)
The Companions Radiant Quest: Hired Muscle
The Companions Radiant Quest: Trouble in Skyrim
The Companions Radiant Quest: Family Heirloom
The Companions Radiant Quest: Escaped Criminal
The Companions Radiant Quest: Rescue Mission
The Companions Radiant Quest: Striking the Heart
The Companions Radiant Quest: Stealing Plans
The Companions Radiant Quest: Retrieval
The Companions Radiant Quest: Totems of Hircine
The Companions Radiant Quest: Purity
The Companions Radiant Quest: Dragon Seekers
Daedric Quest: The Whispering Door
Daedric Quest: A Night to Remember
Side Quest: In My Time of Need
Side Quest: Missing in Action
Temple Quest: The Blessings of Nature
Dark Brotherhood Quest: Breaching Security
Dark Brotherhood Quest: Hail Sithis!
Dark Brotherhood Quest: The Feeble Fortune*
Dark Brotherhood Quest: Side Contract: Anoriath
Thieves Guild Quest: Dampened Spirits
Thieves Guild Radiant Quest: No Stone Unturned (x3)
Thieves Guild City Influence Quest: Imitation Amnesty
Miscellaneous Objective: Innkeeper Rumors (the Bannered Mare)
Miscellaneous Objective: Bullying Braith* (Lars Battle-Born)
Miscellaneous Objective: Argonian Ale Extraction* (Breniun)
Miscellaneous Objective: Greatsword for a Great Man* (Adrianne Avenicci)
Miscellaneous Objective: Andurs' Arkay Amulet* (Anders)
Miscellaneous Objective: Salt for Arcadia* (Arcadia)
Favor (Activity): Chopping Wood* (Hulda)
Favor (Activity): The Gift of Charity* (Brenuin)
Favor: A Good Talking To* (Carlotta Valentia)
Favor: Sparring Partners* (Uthgerd)
Favor: Rare Item Hunt* (Ysolda)
Favor: Item Retrieval (Bandit Camp)* (Amren)
Crafting Tutorial: Blacksmithing* (Adrianne Avenicci)
Crafting Tutorial: Alchemy* (Arcadia)
Crafting Tutorial: Enchanting* (Farengar Secret-Fire)
Thane Quest: Thane of Whiterun Hold*

Habitation: Hold Capital (Major)

Crafting

Alchemy Labs (2)
Arcane Enchanter
Blacksmith Forge
Grindstones (2)
Skyforge
Smelter
Tanning Rack
Workbench

Collectibles

Skill Book [Alchemy]: Herbalist's Guide to Skyrim [C2/10]
Skill Book [Archery]: The Black Arrow, v2 [B1/10]
Skill Book [Block]: Death Blow of Abernanit [C1/10]
Skill Book [Enchanting]: Enchanter's Primer [D2/10]
Skill Book [Heavy Armor]: Hallgerd's Tale [C1/10]
Skill Book [Illusion]: Before the Ages of Man [B1/10]
Skill Book [Restoration]: Withershins [E1/10]
Skill Book [Speech]: Biography of the Wolf Queen [D2/10]
Skill Book [Two-Handed]: Song of Hrormir [C2/10]
Unique Item: Andurs' Amulet of Arkay [58/112]
Unique Weapon: Balgruuf's Greatsword [39/80]
Unique Weapon: Wuuthrad [40/80]
Unique Weapon: Ebony Blade [41/80]
Unusual Gem: [11/24]
Unusual Gem: [12/24]
Unusual Gem: [13/24]
Chest
Potions aplenty
Loose Gear

Services

Follower: Jenassa [20/47]
Follower: Uthgerd the Unbroken [21/47]
Follower: Lydia [22/47]
Follower: Aela the Huntress [23/47]
Follower: Athis [24/47]
Follower: Farkas [25/47]
Follower: Njada Stonearm [26/47]
Follower: Ria [27/47]
Follower: Torvar [28/47]
Follower: Vilkas [29/47]
House for Sale: Breezehome [3/5]
Marriage Prospect: Jenassa [26/62]
Marriage Prospect: Uthgerd the Unbroken [27/62]
Marriage Prospect: Ysolda [28/62]
Marriage Prospect: Lydia [29/62]
Marriage Prospect: Aela the Huntress [30/62]
Marriage Prospect: Athis [31/62]
Marriage Prospect: Farkas [32/62]
Marriage Prospect: Njada Stonearm [33/62]
Marriage Prospect: Ria [34/62]
Marriage Prospect: Torvar [35/62]
Marriage Prospect: Vilkas [36/62]
Trader (Apothecary): Arcadia [7/12]
Trader (Blacksmith): Adrianne Avenicci [16/33]
Trader (Blacksmith): Ulfberth War-Bear [17/33]
Trader (Blacksmith): Eorlund Gray-Mane [18/33]
Trader (Fletcher): Elrindir [2/3]
Trader (Food Vendor): Carlotta Valentia [5/9]
Trader (Food Vendor): Anoriath [6/9]
Trader (General Store Vendor): Fralia Gray-Mane [9/25]
Trader (General Store Vendor): Belethor [6/19]
Trader (Innkeeper): Hulda [8/15]
Trader (Spell Vendor): Farengar Secret-Fire [10/12]
Trainer (Alchemy: Expert): Arcadia [2/3]
Trainer (Archery: Expert): Aela the Huntress [1/3]
Trainer (Block: Expert): Njade Stonearm [2/2]
Trainer (Heavy Armor: Master): Farkas [2/3]
Trainer (One-Handed: Journeyman): Amren [2/3]
Trainer (One-Handed: Expert): Athis [3/3]
Trainer (Restoration: Master): Danica Pure-Spring [3/3]
Trainer (Smithing: Master): Eorlund Gray-Mane [2/3]
Trainer (Two-Handed: Master): Vilkas [1/2]

Special Objects

Shrine of Arkay [7/12]
Shrine of Kynareth [5/6]
Shrine of Talos [8/17]
Business Ledger
Civil War: Map of Skyrim

Lore: City Overview

Whiterun is seen as the most "pure" Nordic city in Skyrim. In Whiterun, Nords live as they have for centuries: their lives are simple, harsh, and rooted in ancient traditions. Even the city's fortifications—wooden and stone palisade walls and the sheer defensive advantage offered by its position on a large bluff that raises the city above the surrounding Tundra—are archaic by contemporary standards. So while Windhelm may serve as the Stormcloaks' center of operations in the Civil War, it is the culture of Whiterun that best exemplifies what it means to be a "True Nord."

Whiterun is located on the eastern end of its Hold, a cold and windy Tundra that fills the center of Skyrim. It was constructed around the Companions' hall of Jorrvaskr, which, centuries ago, was the sole structure on the mountain. Now, Whiterun is a large city, albeit one that retains the feel of a smaller Nord village.

When approaching Whiterun, the towering fortress of Dragonsreach dominates the view. Its history can be traced back to the First Era, when King Olaf One-Eye subdued the great dragon Numinex in a legendary duel of Thu'ums atop Mount Anthor, and brought him back to the fledgling town as a captive. It was then that the magnificent keep was rebuilt and renamed to serve as a cage for Numinex, whose head still adorns the Great Hall.

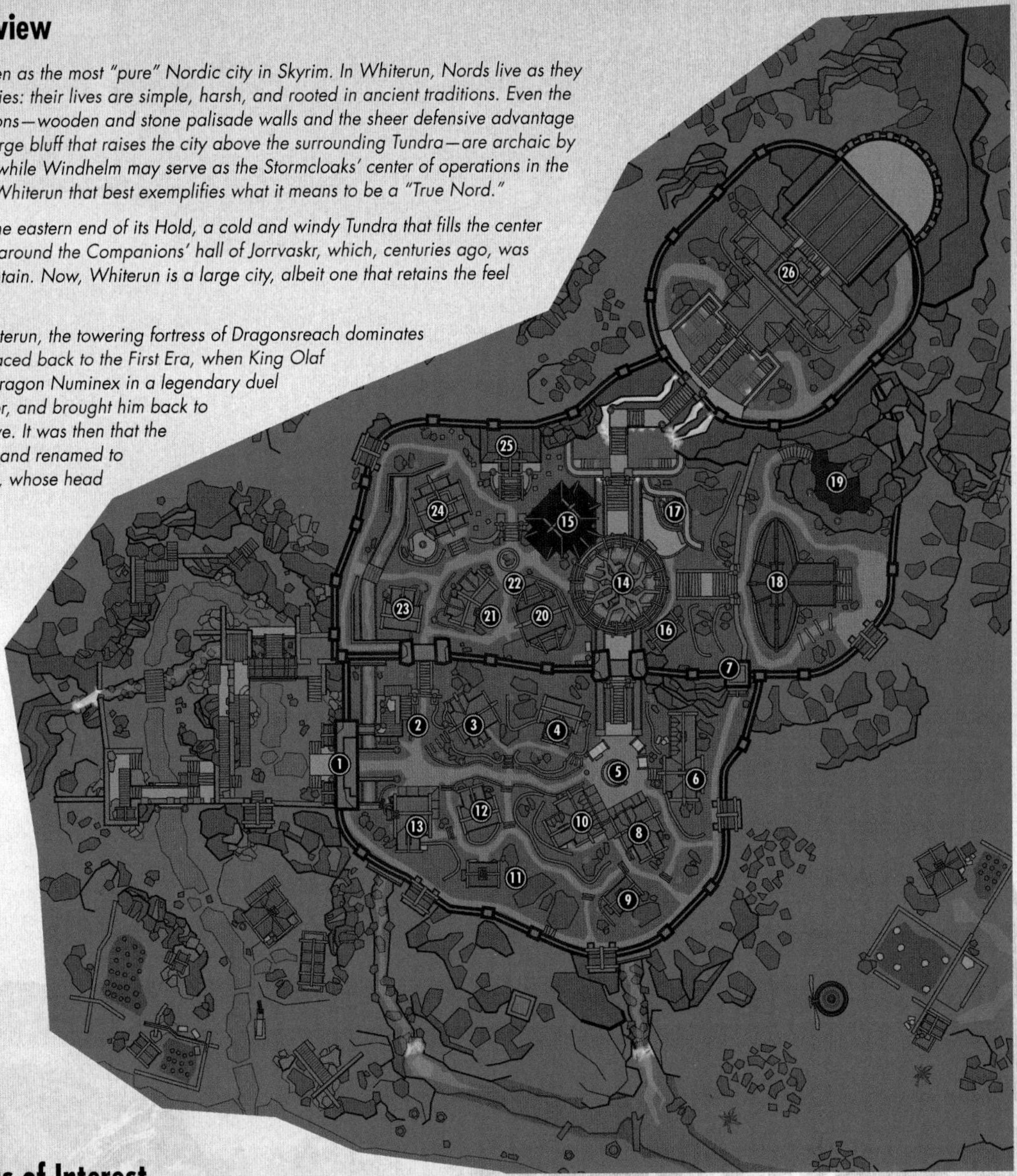

Important Areas of Interest

❶ City Gates and Drawbridge

The winding stone path that leads from the outer gate to the drawbridge and to the entrance to the Main Gate is designed to keep marauders at bay. The drawbridge is open and utilized in the Civil War Quests.

Plains District

This is the first district any visitor to Whiterun enters, so named because it is the lowest of the three and therefore closest to the plains outside the city. It contains all the major merchants and the marketplace.

❷ Main Gate and Guard Barracks (West)

Persuade, bribe, or otherwise insist that the guard lets you into Whiterun the first time you reach these gates. There is a small guard barracks just over the bridge and a couple of Alik'r Warriors (Side Quest: In My Time of Need) you can speak to. Explore the rushing canal water under the bridge or the platform on top of the guard barracks roof if you wish. Inside, there's little but food and Nordic pottery to steal.

◊ Chest

❸ The Drunken Huntsman

Anoriath Elrindir Nazeem Ahlam

The Drunken Huntsman is a unique shop specializing is the needs of hunters. It sells bows, arrows, clothing, suits of armor, and anything else that may be useful to those who stalk Skyrim's game. But the establishment is also set up as a small bar, and customers can buy a small selection of alcoholic drinks, including a specially made Wood Elven wine. The shop is run by the Wood Elf brothers Anoriath and Elrindir. Jenassa the Hireling is to be found here, too. There's also a Skill Book behind the counter. Check the back bedroom on the ground floor near the central cooking spit for a chest and strongbox. Upstairs is a single bedroom with an empty chest.

- ◊ Follower: Jenassa [20/47]
- ◊ Marriage Prospect: Jenassa [26/62]
- ◊ Trader (Fletcher): Elrindir [2/3]
  - ○ Weapons, Apparel, Food
- ◊ Skill Book [Archery]: The Black Arrow, v2 [B1/10]
- ◊ Business Ledger
- ◊ Strongbox (Apprentice)
- ◊ Chest

4 Severio Pelagia's House

Severio Pelagia

Nestled above the market is the residence of Severio Pelagia, who owns the Pelagia Farm just outside Whiterun's walls. Aside from a cooking pot and some delicious long taffy treat, there's very little worth stealing in this single-floor dwelling, which has a small bedroom and office on either side of the main dining area and fire pit.

- Shadowmark: "Loot"

5 Marketplace

Carlotta Valentia
Fralia Gray-Mane
Brenuin

The Whiterun Marketplace rivals the Bannered Mare as the most popular congregation spot in Whiterun. It is open during the day and closed at night. When the marketplace is open, stalls sells various items, including fresh fruits and vegetables. The stalls are run by Carlotta Valentia (fruits and vegetables), Fralia Gray-Mane (trinkets and jewelry), and Anoriah (fresh meat).

- Trader (Food Vendor): Carlotta Valentia [5/9]
  - Food
- Trader (Food Vendor): Anoriath [6/9]
  - Food
- Trader (General Store Vendor): Fralia Gray-Mane [6/19]
  - Apparel, Misc.

6 The Bannered Mare

Hulda
Uthgerd the Unbroken
Saadia
Sinmir
Mikael

The Bannered Mare is Whiterun's most popular gathering place, a tavern and inn that offers cold mead, fresh food, and a warm and welcoming fire. Its sign is that of a majestic horse carrying a banner. Hulda, the publican, is fond of telling the story of the horse, which belonged to a Nord king who died in battle; the king may have died, but his favorite filly carried his banner still, inspiring the leader's warriors to victory. The building has a central tavern area and a side kitchen with a business ledger and strongbox near the roasting spit. To the rear of the main bar area is a small bedroom and office where shady deals may be done. There are two sets of steps to separate bedroom areas.

- Shadowmark: "Loot"
- Follower: Uthgerd the Unbroken [21/47]
- Marriage Prospect: Uthgerd the Unbroken [27/62]
- Trader (Innkeeper): Hulda [8/15]
  - Room for the Night, Food
  - Innkeeper Rumors
- Skill Book [Heavy Armor]: Hallgerd's Tale [C1/10]
- Business Ledger
- Strongbox (Apprentice)
- Chest (2)

7 Guard Barracks (East)

This set of barracks bridges the gap between the Plains District and Dragonsreach. It is also where you exit after being jailed (or escaping from jail). The trapdoor in the side alcove leads to Dragonsreach Dungeon.

- Display case (Novice)
- Chest
- Loose gear

8 Arcadia's Cauldron

Arcadia

Arcadia's Cauldron is Whiterun's apothecary. It sells potions and potion ingredients of all kinds and is probably the most respected of the city's non-Nord-owned businesses. Aside from the goods she sells, she is an excellent trainer. Check the office at the back of the store for a Skill Book and the locked door (Adept) next to the lab; this leads to the area under the stairs and a chest. Upstairs is a landing balcony overlooking the shop and a cooking pot.

- Shadowmark: "Loot"
- Crafting: Alchemy Lab
- Trader (Apothecary): Arcadia [7/12]
  - Potions, Food, Ingredients, Books
- Trainer (Arcadia: Expert): Alchemy [2/3]
- Skill Book [Alchemy]: Herbalist's Guide to Skyrim [C2/10]
- Chest
- Potions aplenty

9 Ysolda's House

Ysolda

The young maid Ysolda lives in this house, making handcrafted goods that she hopes to sell. She is currently selling her goods to the Khajiit caravans, raising money to buy a shop of her own. Her dwelling is modest, locked, and has no loot to speak of, although there's a bowl of impressive potatoes.

- Shadowmark: "Empty"
- Marriage Prospect: Ysolda [28/62]

10 Belethor's General Goods

Belethor

The Wood Elf owner Belethor will buy and sell just about anything, and he's got a fair collection of items that could best be categorized as junk. From tomatoes to troll skulls, there's something here to steal, and a Skill Book on one of the shelves. In the back is a kitchen, and upstairs is a balcony, bed, and ledger with a strongbox.

- Shadowmark: "Loot"
- Trader (General Store Vendor): Belethor [7/19]
  - Apparel, Potions, Food, Books, Misc.
- Skill Book [Speech]: Biography of the Wolf Queen [D2/10]
- Business Ledger
- Strongbox (Apprentice)

11 Olava the Feeble's House

Olava the Feeble

Besides being a seer, Olava is also something of a hermit. She rarely leaves her house, and her residence is usually locked. Inside, there's a small table with a Petty Soul Gem and a setup for a reading, but otherwise the place is devoid of valuables.

- Chest

12 [HF.05] Breezehome

Related Quests

Hearthfire Task: Adoption
Thane Task: Thane of Whiterun

Crafting

Alchemy Lab
Arcane Enchanter
Cooking Pot

Miscellaneous

Area is locked
Chest
Loose gear
Potions aplenty

This dwelling is currently empty. Should you become the Thane of Whiterun (by completing Main Quest: Dragon Rising), you can purchase this abode from Jarl Balgruuf the Greater's Steward, Proventus Avenicci. Consult the Thane Quests for more information. Should you wish to purchase the children's bedroom, it replaces the Alchemy Laboratory.

- ◊ Follower: Lydia (Housecarl) [22/47]
- ◊ House for Sale [3/5]
- ◊ Marriage Prospect: Lydia [29/62]

Purchase Price: 5,000 gold

Jarl: Jarl Balgruuf the Greater or Jarl Vignar the Revered

Steward: Proventus Avenicci or Brill

Available Decorations

Alchemy Laboratory (500 gold)
Bedroom (300 gold)
Children's Bedroom (250 gold)
Dining room (250 gold)
Loft (200 gold)

Total cost: 6,500 gold

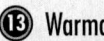

13 Warmaiden's

Adrianne Avenicci
Ulfberth War-Bear

This is the house and shop of Adrianne Avenicci and features a number of smithing locations, which is handy to use if you've purchased the adjacent Breezehome or you've entered the city. Inside, speak to Ulfberth War-Bear (or Adrianne, who also sells items) if you're interested in buying anything. Behind the counter is a door to a small kitchen and side exit. Upstairs is a landing overlooking the shop.

- ◊ Crafting: Blacksmith Forge, Grindstone, Smelter, Tanning Rack, Workbench
- ◊ Trader (Blacksmith): Adrianne Avenicci [16/33]
  - Weapons, Apparel, Misc
- ◊ Trader (Blacksmith): Ulfberth War-Bear [17/33]
  - Weapons, Apparel, Misc
- ◊ Unique Weapon: Balgruuf's Greatsword [39/80]
- ◊ Loose gear

Wind District

The Wind District is where most of Whiterun's residential buildings (including the mead hall Jorrvaskr) are located and was named because of the strong mountain winds that gust through the area.

14 15 Gildergreen Tree and Temple of Kynareth

Danica Pure-Spring — Maurice Jondrelle
Acolyte Jenssen — Lucia

The Temple of Kynareth is a tall wooden building with a central praying chamber. The sick and weary gather here, and Acolyte Jenssen and Danica Pure-Spring cast their healing spells. To the sides are an office stocked with books (one of them being a Skill Book found on a shelf) and a chest and a waiting area with an empty strongbox. The temple is receiving a steady flow of pilgrims, but these have started to wane as the ancient Gildergreen Tree in the main exterior gathering place and thoroughfare has begun to die.

- ◊ Trainer (Danica Pure-Spring: Master): Restoration [3/3]
- ◊ Skill Book [Restoration]: Withershins [E1/10]
- ◊ Shrine of Kynareth [5/6]
- ◊ Strongbox (empty)
- ◊ Chest
- ◊ Potions

16 17 Heimskr's House and Shrine of Talos

Heimskr

Heimskr's home is devoid of important or valuable possessions; it has been turned into a gathering place for illegal worship.

- ◊ Shrine of Talos [8/17]

18 Jorrvaskr

Harbinger: Kodlak Whitemane

The Circle: Aela the Huntress; Farkas, brother of Vilkas; Vilkas, brother of Farkas; Skjor, the scarred

Member: Athis, Njada Stonearm, Ria, Torvar, Vignar the Revered

Housekeeper: Tilma the Haggard

Blacksmith: Eorlund Gray-Mane

Jorrvaskr is the ancient and honored mead hall that has served as headquarters of the mercenary company the Companions for untold generations. According to local legend, Jorrvaskr is actually the oldest building in all of Whiterun and once existed by itself on the mountain, with the other buildings the town being built up around it over the centuries. Jorrvaskr is a place of honor and courage, and to walk into the hall is to proclaim, "I am a warrior and will die as I lived—in glorious battle!" The mead hall is also the place where you may join the Companions as a Shield-Brother or Sister. The exterior of the building features two front doors and a rear outside dining and training area.

Inside, the main floor is dominated by the mead hall and fire pit. A Skill Book rests on a low shelf here. At one end of the hall is a sparring area, and around the sides are various shelves stocked with books and food. The door at the north end leads to a bedroom with another chest. The stairs at the sound end lead down to the living quarters. Displayed on the wall here are the pieces of Wuuthrad, a powerful weapon wielded by their founder, Ysgramor. Check Kodlak Whitemane's bedroom chambers to find an Unusual Gem that pertains to Side Quest: No Stone Unturned.

- ◊ Follower: Aela the Huntress [23/47]
- ◊ Follower: Athis [24/47]
- ◊ Follower: Farkas [25/47]
- ◊ Follower: Njada Stonearm [26/47]
- ◊ Follower: Ria [27/47]
- ◊ Follower: Torvar [28/47]
- ◊ Follower: Vilkas [29/47]
- ◊ Marriage Prospect: Aela the Huntress [30/62]
- ◊ Marriage Prospect: Athis [31/62]
- ◊ Marriage Prospect: Farkas [32/62]
- ◊ Marriage Prospect: Njada Stonearm [33/62]
- ◊ Marriage Prospect: Ria [34/62]
- ◊ Marriage Prospect: Torvar [35/62]
- ◊ Marriage Prospect: Vilkas [36/62]
- ◊ Trainer (Archery: Expert): Aela the Huntress [1/3]
- ◊ Trainer (Block: Expert): Njade Stonearm [2/2]
- ◊ Trainer (Heavy Armor: Master): Farkas [2/3]
- ◊ Trainer (One-Handed: Expert): Athis [3/3]
- ◊ Trainer (Two-Handed: Master): Vilkas [1/2]
- ◊ Skill Book [Heavy Armor]: Hallgerd's Tale [C1/10]
- ◊ Unusual Gem: [11/24]
- ◊ Chest (2)
- ◊ Potions
- ◊ Loose gear

Living Quarters

The main corridor leading north begins with a dormitory where the new recruits sleep. At the far end are four bedrooms of the Circle members. Check for the Skill Book inside the display case. There's also a small bar in one of the bedrooms! At the far end of the corridor is Kodlak's private chambers, which has some rare items to steal:

- ◊ Skill Book [Archery]: The Marksmanship Lesson
- ◊ Skill Book [Two-Handed]: Song Of Hrormir [C2/10]
- ◊ Unusual Gem: [11/24]
- ◊ Chest (3)

19 Skyforge and the Underforge

The Skyforge is the great forge used by Eorlund Gray-Mane to craft his masterful weapons, shields, and armor. It got its name due to the fact that it's a large, ancient forge, located outside on a mountain, close to the sky. The forge is large, and unlike most forges is rather ornate. It is in the shape on an eagle, with wings spreading out from each side. Eorlund is happy to trade his wares with you, but will only train you after you join the Companions.

- Crafting: Skyforge, Grindstone
- Trader (Blacksmith): Eorlund Gray-Mane [18/33]
    - Weapons, Apparel, and Misc
- Trainer (Smithing: Master): Eorlund Gray-Mane [2/3]
- Skill Book [Smithing]: The Armorer's Challenge
- Unique Weapon: Wuuthrad [40/80]

Underneath the Skyforge is a hidden area known as the Underforge, where those welcomed into the Circle of the Companions observe a special blood ritual. This is only accessible during the Companions quest line. You can return here to deliver or utilize Totems; consult the quests starting on page 250 for more details.

20 House Gray-Mane

Olfina the Golden — Avulstein Gray-Mane

House Gray-Mane is the residence of Eorlund Gray-Mane and his children. It is a large, solid house, built by Eorlund over 35 years earlier. Recently, due to their differing stances on the Civil War, Clan Gray-Mane has bad relations with Clan Battle-Born, with whom they had always been friendly before the conflict started. Jon Battle-Born and Olfina the Golden are said to be in love, but the families certainly do not approve of such activities. Outside the house is a small paddock with a cow. Inside the house is a central fire pit and dining area, with a small entrance alcove and Avulstein's bedroom. Upstairs is a landing and two bedrooms with some books and valuables (usually necklaces) lying around.

- Shadowmark: "Loot"
- Chest (4)

21 Uthgerd's House

This is the house belonging to the violent Nord warmaiden that challenges you to fisticuffs in the Bannered Mare. Her home is locked, but once inside, is full of Nord pottery, a chest, and a small book collection in a nook under the stairs. Upstairs is an empty chest and a full display case.

- Chest
- Loose gear

22 Amren's House

Amren — Braith

Amren's House is attached to Uthgerd's. Amren is usually walking around the Wind District. His wife, Saffir, and daughter Braith may be inside the dwelling. There's very little worth stealing here.

- Shadowmark: "Danger"
- Trainer (One-Handed: Journeyman): Amren [2/3]

23 Carlotta Valentia's House

Mila Valentia

Carlotta Valentia lives in this house with her young daughter Mila. Find a couple of potions in one of the upstairs bedrooms, along with a Skill Book that's tucked between the bed and end table.

- Shadowmark: "Loot"
- Skill Book [Enchanting]: Enchanter's Primer [D2/10]

24 House of Clan Battle-Born

Olfrid Battle-Born — Jon Battle-Born
Bergritte Battle-Born — Alfhild Battle-Born
Idolaf Battle-Born — Lars Battle-Born

This large house holds three generations of the equally large Clan Battle-Born. This warrior family—owners of the Battle-Born Farm outside Whiterun—has lived in the city for centuries; their ties to Skyrim and the ancient Nord ways cannot be disputed. The Clan has come out vocally in support of the pro-Imperial forces in the ongoing Civil War. Recently, due to their differing stances on the Civil War, Clan Battle-Born has bad relations with Clan Gray-Mane, with whom they had always been friendly before the conflict started.

The rear door is usually unlocked, while the front door isn't (Novice). Inside, the ground floor is one large chamber with a cooking spit and dining table dominating the area. To the northwest is Olfrid's bedroom, which has some valuables on display (including a Skill Book) and a locked door (Adept) leading to a small office with books and an Imperial Missive, useful during Side Quest: Missing in Action. On the opposite side is a small bedroom with books to check, stairs up to the balcony, and two more bedrooms.

- Shadowmark: "Protected"
- Imperial Missive
- Skill Book [Two-Handed]: Battle of Sancre Tor
- Potions

25 Hall of the Dead

Andurs

The Whiterun Hall of the Dead is a single-story, high-ceilinged wooden structure and serves as Whiterun's mausoleum. The main floor has the sleeping quarters for Andurs (with a large collection of books and small collection of skulls) and a shrine to Arkay where the people of Whiterun can come and worship. Check one of the wall crypts to find an Unusual Gem lying near the foot of a skeleton—this pertains to Side Quest: No Stone Unturned.

- Unique Item: Andurs' Amulet of Arkay [58/112]
- Unusual Gem: [12/24]
- Shrine of Arkay [7/12]
- Chest

Whiterun Catacombs

These catacombs contain generations of Whiterun's dead, including the bodies of some of Skyrim's most honored departed—and not quite departed. There is also graveyard outside.

- Skill Book [Block]: Death Blow of Abernanit [C1/10]

Cloud District

The Cloud District is the smallest of Whiterun's three districts. It was so named because it is located atop the mountain Whiterun was built on and is therefore closer to the clouds than any other. It is dominated by the imposing form of Dragonsreach.

26 Dragonsreach

The following leaders of Whiterun are loyal to the Imperials at the start of the Civil War.

Jarl Balgruuf the Greater

Balgruuf believes that Skyrim should remain a part of the Empire. This has become something of a confusing situation for the people of Skyrim, many of whom are decidedly anti-Empire. Balgruuf embodies the very best of what it is to be a Nord, but at the same time he supports the Empire's presence. This has actually caused some of these same anti-Empire residents of Whiterun to at least reconsider their thinking. After all, if Balgruuf the Greater supports the Empire, then maybe they are the key to Skyrim's future. Balgruuf is very close to his younger brother Hrongar.

Hrongar

Hrongar is Balgruuf's younger brother and is something of a warmonger. He believes his brother should organize Imperial forces and wipe out any Stormcloaks presence in Whiterun Hold. Hrongar divides his time among a few activities, most notably advising (and sometimes arguing with) his brother Balgruuf and practicing with his sword and axe against the town guard.

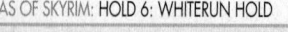

Frothar

Dagny

Nelkir

Farengar Secret-Fire (Court Wizard)

Farengar serves the Jarl because of duty, but Farengar has no interest in the Civil War and certainly has no love for the Empire. He is dedicated to the College of Winterhold and furthering the cause of magical research. So as long as he is able to maintain his laboratory and keep up his research, he really doesn't care what the Jarl believes.

Proventus Avenicci (Steward)

Proventus essentially tells Balgruuf whatever he wants to hear and is a politician through and through. In other words, Proventus is completely inept as a Steward. The only reason he's been able to achieve any manner of success and keep his position is because his daughter Adrianne is tactically brilliant and has been telling her father what to tell the Jarl.

Irileth (Housecarl)

Irileth is unusual for a Housecarl: She's female, a Dark Elf, and doesn't fit the role of muscle-bound protector. But that doesn't make her any less effective. Irileth is actually a skilled assassin, trained in Morrowind by the Morag Tong. She met Balgruuf several years prior and the two became fast friends and adventuring companions.

Commander Caius

The following residents arrive to take control of Whiterun, should this Hold fall during the Civil War.

Jarl Vignar Gray-Mane

Vignar was once a general and commander in the Legion during the Great War. He came to Whiterun to retire and be near his brother, the renowned smith Eorlund Gray-Mane. Because of his long experience as a soldier, Vignar holds a place of honor among the Companions, and the group welcomes his council. In the course of the Civil War, Vignar shifted loyalties to his home. He is angry at the Empire for surrendering to the Dominion and feels that Skyrim would be better off on its own, as in the ancient times. When the Stormcloaks control Whiterun, they call on Vignar's experience and wisdom to lead the city as its Jarl.

Brill (Steward)

Brill was once an adventurer who was injured by a Draugr axe a number of years ago. This brush with death left him shaken and broken. He took to drinking, spending much time and coin in the Bannered Mare. It was there he met Vignar, who he befriended. Vignar took Brill into his home, and he's never left.

Olfina Gray-Mane (Housecarl)

When Vignar is called upon to serve as Whiterun's Jarl, he names his niece Olfina as his Housecarl. Willful and determined, Olfina accepts the honorable duty and swears to defend her uncle's life with her own.

Sinmir

Dragonsreach is Whiterun's majestic keep. It was constructed in the ornate wooden style of the great Nord longhouses of old. Visually and politically, it is very much the focal point of the city. As is true of the keeps in other cities, Dragonsreach serves many important functions. There is an ornate bridge leading to the main double doors. Around to the side is an entrance to Dragonsreach Dungeon.

Dragonsreach (Interior)

A Door to Whiterun

1 Great Hall

The great hall is the main chamber of the keep and is where the Jarl holds court on his throne beyond the long tables and central fire pit. Check the shelves to the sides for all manner of books. There are balconies on the upper floor, accessed via the War Room, from which you can peer down.

2 Kitchens

Two large tables and an even bigger fireplace are where the Jarl's servants prepare the feasts of the long table.

3 Servant's Bedroom and Storage (Lower)

A rough-hewed, rock-walled chamber where the servant sleeps. There is a storage room behind the door.

B Door to Jarl's Quarters

C Old Wooden Door (Requires Key)

This odd door seems sealed from the other side. Consult Side Quest: The Whispering Door for more information.

5 War Room

This is where the Jarl and his advisors discuss matters of state, pouring over the Civil War map near the book-lined shelves. When needed, an Imperial Legate also plans from this location.

- Civil War: Map of Skyrim
- Display Case (Apprentice)
- Loose gear

D Door to Jarl's Quarters

E Door to Dragonsreach, Great Porch

Enter the Great Porch if you want an impressive view to the east. Legend has it that a dragon was trapped here, on this porch. Perhaps history might repeat itself? Consult the Main Quest for further information.

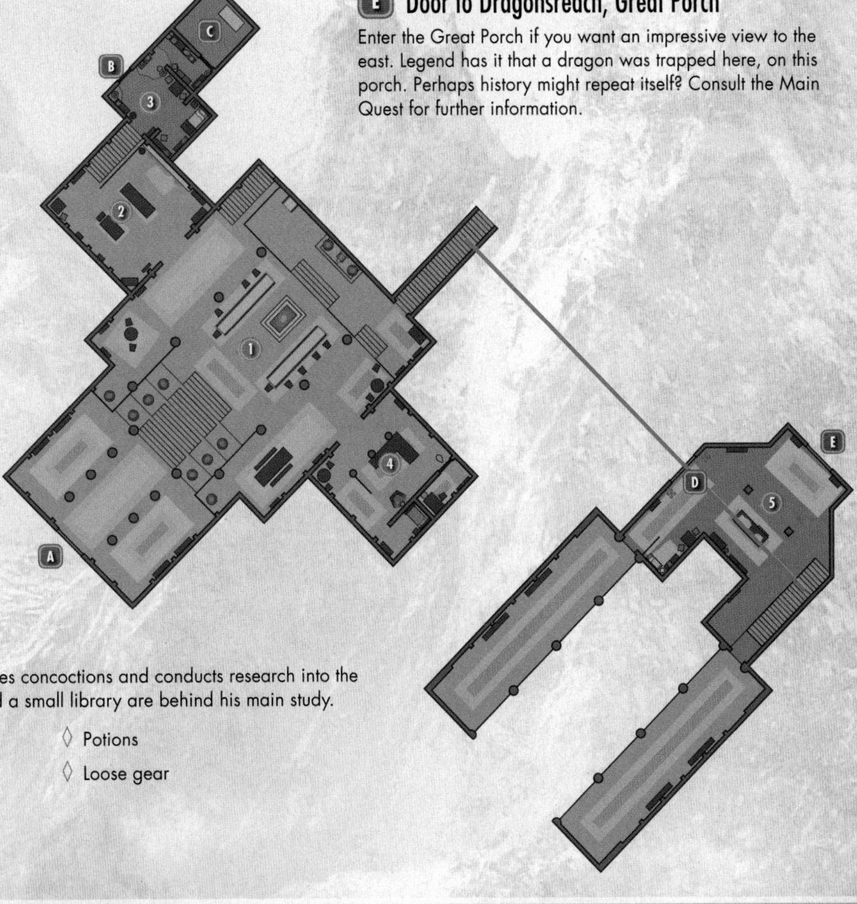

4 Farengar's Quarters

In this laboratory, the Court Wizard Farengar mixes concoctions and conducts research into the mysteries of the dragons' return. His bedroom and a small library are behind his main study.

- Crafting: Alchemy Lab, Arcane Enchanter
- Trader (Spell Vendor): Farengar Secret-Fire [10/12]
  - Apparel, Scrolls, Books, Misc
- Potions
- Loose gear

Dragonsreach Jarl's Quarters

This is the private quarters of the Jarl, and entering here without invitation results in you being removed, facing a fine, or worse. However, a special gem can be found here that pertains to Side Quest: No Stone Unturned.

- Unique Weapon: Ebony Blade [41/80]
- Unusual Gem: [13/24]

D Door to Dragonsreach

6 Inner Hall and Staircase

- Display Cases (Apprentice) (3)
- Display Case (Master)
- Loose gear

7 Proventus Avenicci's Chamber

Note the display case; it usually has something valuable inside.

- Display Case (Adept)
- Chest

8 Servant's Quarters

Fianna and Gerda usually rest here, in the tiny alcove bedrooms off the main food storage and wine vat area.

- Chest

B Door to Dragonsreach

9 Childrens' Bedroom

The Jarl's three children, Nelkir, Dagny, and Frothar, sleep here.

- Chest (3)

10 Hrongar's Bedroom

The Jarl's brother sleeps here. The study desk has shelves with books on them.

11 Jarl's Bedchamber

There are three connected chambers here: a dining area, bedroom, and book-filled study.

- Skill Book [Illusion]: Before the Ages of Man [B1/10]
- Loose gear

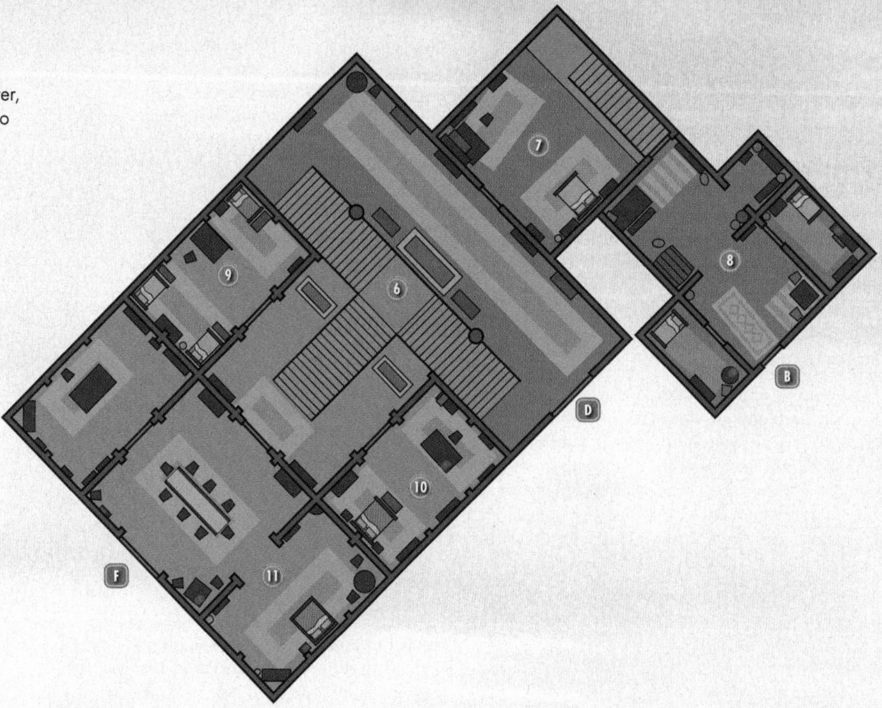

F Door to Whiterun

Exit onto a narrow parapet balcony and overlook the entirety of Whiterun.

Dragonsreach Dungeon

Cell Block

Arn

Home to a proportion of the city's guard and the jail. The entrance area has the chests you need to retrieve your items, either after you serve your time or if you reach in from the sewer grate behind the chests. The main cell block has cells on either side (Adept, unless a quest-related cell) and a door at the opposite end leading to Dragonsreach. The cell to the west is of particular interest, as it comes decked out with food and a variety of luxuries not normally associated with jails. This is where the more prominent miscreants are kept, usually after a drunken binge.

A man named Arn is imprisoned in this location, but only after you undertake Thieves Guild City Influence Quest; Imitation Amnesty.

- Evidence Chest
- Prisoner Belongings Chest

Dungeon Catacombs

Below the cells are the Catacombs, ideally explored only after you escape from your cell, and wish to weave your way to the small hub chamber, where you can climb a ladder and stand on some barrels to reach the chests which contain your belongings. Then open the barred door [Expert] or drop down the hole to reach a ladder leading up and into [7] Guard Barracks (East), down in the Plains District.

[6.01] Lund's Hut

Recommended Level: 12

Dungeon: Animal Den

Animal

Ravenous animals have swarmed this small cabin. Search poor Lund's remains, along with his chest, to relieve him of his final possessions.

Collectibles

- Chest(s)
- Potions

[6.02] Rorikstead

Related Quests

- Civil War Quest: Liberation of Skyrim
- Civil War Quest: A False Front
- Daedric Quest: A Night to Remember
- Side Quest: In My Time of Need
- Miscellaneous Objective: Innkeeper Rumors (Frostfruit Inn)
- Miscellaneous Objective: Erik the Slayer* (Erik)
- Favor (Activity): Harvesting Crops* (Reldith)
- Favor (Activity): Harvesting Crops* (Lemkil)

Habitation: Town

- Britte
- Ennis
- Erik the Slayer (Follower; Marriage Prospect)
- Jouane Manette
- Lemkil
- Mralki (Innkeeper)
- Reldith
- Rorik
- Sissel

Services

- Follower: Erik the Slayer [30/47]
- Marriage Prospect: Erik the Slayer [37/62]
- Trader (Innkeeper): Mralki [9/15]
- Food, Room and Board
- Quest Rumors

Crafting

- Tanning Rack
- Chest(s)
- Potions
- Loose gear

This small farming community lies at the west edge of Whiterun, near the Reach's border. A cozy inn offers food and comfort to weary travelers.

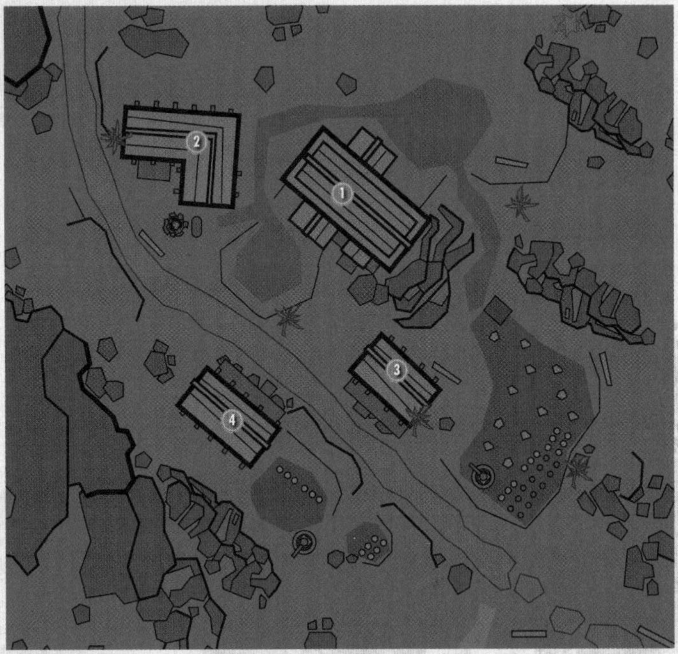

Exterior

There are plenty of crops to pluck up around the village, but little else of interest. Speak to Erik out in the fields to gain a Side Quest that you can fulfill right here.

Crafting: Tanning Rack

1 Frostfruit Inn

This small inn offers a warm bed and hot meal at a fair price.

- ◊ Chest

2 Rorik's Manor

Rorikstead's founder lives quite modestly. Still, his abode is worth looting.

- ◊ Chests (2)
- ◊ Potion
- ◊ Loose gear

3 Cowflop Farmhouse

Break into this farmhouse when no one's looking and steal from two chests.

- ◊ Area Is Locked (Novice)
- ◊ Chests (2)
- ◊ Potions

4 Lemkil's Farmhouse

This humble home has just one chest, but it's worth a peek if you can break in unseen.

- ◊ Area Is Locked (Novice)
- ◊ Chest

[6.03] Serpent's Bluff Redoubt

Related Quests

Dungeon Activity

Recommended Level: 14

Dungeon: Forsworn Redoubt

Forsworn
Hagraven

Crafting

Arcane Enchanter
Forge
Tanning Rack
Workbench

Dangers

Battering Ram Trap (pressure plate)
Dart Trap (pressure plate)
Spear Trap (tripwire)
Swinging Wall Trap (pressure plate)

Collectibles

Skill Book [Enchanting]: Twin Secrets [E1/10]
Chest(s)
Potions
Loose gear

Sharing a border with the Reach has its drawbacks—the Forsworn have established a formidable encampment in Whiterun's western flatlands.

Exterior

Slay a host of Forsworn as they pour forth to defend their camp, then begin looting their tents for valuables.

- Crafting: Forge, Tanning Rack, Workbench
- Chest
- Chest (Locked: Apprentice)
- Knapsack
- Potions
- Loose gear

Serpent's Bluff Redoubt (Interior)

The interior ruins begins with a trio of lethal traps: Sidestep a pressure plate at the foot of the stairs (which triggers a dart trap), jump the trip wire that lies just beyond (spear trap), and avoid the pressure plate beyond the wire (a swinging wall trap). Slay the Forsworn archer, then descend the stairs and avoid yet another pressure plate at the bottom (battering ram). Assail more Forsworn and a dangerous Hagraven in the main chamber, then unlock the Adept-level door under the platform to access a small room with a chest. Place any object (book, etc.) onto the pressure plate that sits atop the altar to open the passage on the upper level. Go through to discover a Skill Book sitting atop an Arcane Enchanter in the next area, along with a giant chest. Press a wall button to open the exit gate.

- Danger! Battering Ram Trap (pressure plate), Spear Trap (trip wire), Swinging Wall Trap (pressure plate), Dart Trap (pressure plate)
- Crafting: Arcane Enchanter
- Skill Book [Enchanting]: Twin Secrets [E1/10]
- Chest
- Chest (Locked: Apprentice)
- Potions
- Loose gear

[6.04] Whiterun Imperial Camp

Related Quests

Civil War Quest (when active, depending on who you side with)

Habitation: Military: Imperial Camp

Imperial Quartermaster (Blacksmith)
Imperial Soldier

Services

Trader (Blacksmith): Imperial Quartermaster [19/33]
Weapons, Apparel, Misc

Crafting

Alchemy Lab
Anvil
Grindstone
Workbench

Special Objects

Civil War: Map of Skyrim
Chest
Potions
Loose gear

Hardened Imperial soldiers have made camp at this site; however, the camp may or may not exist, depending on the state of the Civil War quest line. Trade with the quartermaster and feel free to utilize his numerous crafting stations. Inspect the tabletop map in the largest tent to potentially gain new map data as well.

[6.05] Swindler's Den

Related Quests

Side Quest: In My Time of Need

Recommended Level: 6

Dungeon: Bandit Camp

Bandit
Kematu
Alik'r

Dangers

Bear Traps

Collectibles

Skill Book [One-Handed]: Night Falls on Sentinel [D1/10]
Skill Book [Pickpocket]: Thief
Chest(s)
Potions
Loose gear

Tall rocks east of Rorikstead mark the entrance to a sizable underground cave. During Side Quest: In My Time of Need, this cave is used by the Alik'r Coterie as a base of operations. Bandits occupy the cave otherwise. Test your mettle against the drunken exterior guard before venturing inside.

Sunlit Cavern

Dispatch a bandit in the first cavern, then leap up to discover a chest on a sunlit ledge.

- Chest
- Loose gear

Firepit Cavern

Silence a few more bandits in the next cavern, then collect potions and loot a satchel that sits on a crate in the corner.

- Satchel
- Potions
- Loose gear

Mess

Fight hard to secure this cavern—more bandits are likely to emerge from the north passage. When you return to this cavern, navigating the high overlook on your way from the Sleeping Area to the Waterfall Cavern, you can claim a Skill Book that rests on a crate.

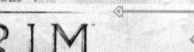

- Skill Book [One-Handed]: Night Falls on Sentinel [D2/10]
- Potion

Sleeping Area

Loot a chest on your way into this dimly lit cavern, where a Skill Book rests on a bedroll.

- Skill Book [Pickpocket]: Thief
- Chest

Waterfall Cavern

Avoid a pair of bear traps as you journey to this watery cavern, where the bandits' formidable leader lurks. Loot the cavern's giant chest after the battle, then simply continue along to come full circle and return to the first cavern.

- Danger! Bear Traps
- Chest
- Potion

[6.06] Gjukar's Monument

Related Quests

Side Quest: Kyne's Sacred Trials
Temple Quest: The Book of Love

Recommended Level: 12

Dungeon: Special

Ruki

Collectible

Loose gear

A small circle of rocks stands out among Whiterun's western flatlands, with one central pillar that's tall enough to catch one's eye from afar. Stop by this quiet shrine to collect some valuable gear. During Temple Quest: The Book of Love, you'll help reunite a pair of wayward souls here.

[6.07] Broken Fang Cave

Recommended Level: 6

Dungeon: Vampire Lair

Skeleton
Vampire

Crafting

Alchemy Lab
Arcane Enchanter

Collectibles

Skill Book [Illusion]: Mystery of Talara, v4 [D2/10]
Skill Book [Lockpicking]: The Wolf Queen, v1
Chest
Chest (Locked: Adept)
Potions
Loose gear

This shallow, rocky cave stands out among Whiterun's western flats. Inside lurks a powerful vampire and several lowly skeletons. Search the entry cavern's southeast corner to discover a locked chest, then take the west passage to a sleeping area, where another mighty vampire lurks, along with a large chest and a few crafting stations. Find a Skill Book on the metal shelf near the Arcane Enchanter, and another resting beside the Alchemy Lab.

[6.08] Sleeping Tree Camp

Related Quests

Dungeon Quest: The Secret at the Sleeping Tree*

Dungeon: Giant Camp

Giant
Mammoth
Ulag

Quest Items

Sleeping Tree Sap
Chest

A group of giants have made camp at this remote site, perhaps drawn by the mystifying glow of an unusual tree that grows from a steamy glowing pond. The tree has a sap spigot that you can turn to acquire some Sleeping Tree Sap, an unusual substance that greatly increases your health... with certain side effects. Returning here after a few days will allow another batch of Sap to be harvested. Enter the nearby cave afterward to face another formidable giant and a dead orc named Ulag. Read the note that Ulag carries to gain a new Side Quest to sell the Sleeping Tree Sap to Ysolda in Whiterun.

[6.09] Rannveig's Fast

Related Quests

Side Quest: No Stone Unturned

Recommended Level: 8

Dungeon: Warlock Lair

Sild the Warlock
Subjugated Ghost

Crafting

Alchemy Lab

Collectibles

Skill Book [Destruction]: Horrors of Castle Xyr [B1/10]
Unusual Gem: [14/24]

Special Objects

Word Wall: Kyne's Peace [2/3]
Chest(s)
Potions aplenty
Loose gear

A nefarious warlock named Sild is forcing a host of ghosts to defend these ancient ruins. Send the exterior ghosts to their eternal rest, or have pity and simply sprint past them, entering the large door that leads to an ancient crypt. Scaling the ruins' exterior steps leads to Cold Rock Pass [2.12] in Hjaalmarch.

Rannveig's Fast (Interior)

All is silent in the crypts' massive entry cavern. Proceed through the north passage, dispatching a ghost and swiping some potions on your way to the next chamber, where a giant chest tempts you from afar. Avoid the large, discolored trapdoor on the ground before the chest—the chest turns out to be empty, but you obtain a new Word of Power from the nearby Word Wall in the process. Take the north passage and scale a long staircase to reach the chamber's upper walkways; pull a lever to open the portcullis on the lower level that will lead you behind Sild as he still waits for you, or some other unlucky adventurer, to fall into the pit. Before you move on, cross the walkways to reach a high nook with a locked chest.

- Word Wall: Kyne's Peace [2/3]
- Chest
- Chest (Locked: Apprentice)
- Chest (Locked: Expert)
- Potions

Sild's Pit

If you've fallen through the trapdoor near the Word Wall, you will find yourself in a locked cage, with a madman named Sild the Warlock taunting you from just beyond the bars. Exploit Sild's hubris by crouching and pickpocketing a key off of him (you can also pick the lock, or loot another key out of Sild's Assistants Satchel that sits beside the cage), then escape the cage and slay the nefarious mage. Claim a number of potions from this frightening area, along with a Skill Book and an Unusual Gem that pertains to a Thieves Guild Radiant Quest. Then open the south door and scale some stairs that lead up to a chest and an exit door.

- Crafting: Alchemy Lab
- Skill Book [Destruction]: Horrors of Castle Xyr [B1/10]
- Unusual Gem: [14/24]
- Rannveigs Fast Key (Sild the Warlock)
- Chest
- Potions aplenty

[6.10] Drelas's Cottage

Recommended Level: 12

Dungeon: Warlock Lair

Drelas

Crafting

Alchemy Lab
Arcane Enchanter
Chest(s)
Potions aplenty

This quaint cottage is home to a seclusive mage named Drelas, who'll attack you on sight if you dare enter. Slaying Drelas is worthwhile, for the mage has amassed a wealth of valuable potions and ingredients.

[6.11] Greenspring Hollow

Related Quests

Temple Quest: The Book of Love

Dungeon: Animal Den

Animal

Crafting

Tanning Rack
Chest (Locked: Adept)
Loose gear

A hunter has become the hunted in Whiterun's western wilds, where a ferocious animal has slaughtered an unwary woodsman at his own camp. Avenge the poor hunter by dispatching the beast, then relieve the man of his final possessions.

[6.12] Dustman's Cairn

Scale the hill that lies northwest of Whiterun's capital to discover ancient ruins dug directly into the hilltop. You visit this site with your Shield-Sibling during Companion Quest: Proving Honor, in search of a fragment of Wuuthrad, the Blade of Ysgramor. Only a small portion of Dustman's Cairn can be explored until you visit the site as part of that quest.

Related Quests

The Companions Quest: Proving Honor
Dungeon Activity

Recommended Level: 6

Dungeon: Draugr Crypt

Animal
Draugr
Silver Hand

Crafting

Alchemy Lab

Dangers

Dart Trap (pressure plate)

Quest Items

Fragment of Wuuthrad

Collectibles

Skill Book [Two-Handed]: The Battle of Sancre Tor [A2/10]

Special Objects

Word Wall: Fire Breath [1/2]
Chest(s)
Potions
Loose gear

A Exit to Skyrim

1 Entry Chamber

Inspect the Skill Book on the entry chamber's central table, then loot the nearby chest before advancing.

◊ Skill Book [Two-Handed]: The Battle of Sancre Tor [A2/10]

◊ Chest (Locked: Novice)

2 Cavernous Chamber

Snag potions from a north nook in this quiet chamber, then pull a lever to open the south portcullis and advance the plot.

◊ Crafting: Arcane Enchanter

◊ Potions

3 Burial Hall

Dispatch several Silver Hand mercenaries on your way to this chamber, then raid the chest beneath the stairs. Find a larger chest hidden among the upstairs rubble, and open a secret nook in the upstairs north wall by pulling the nearby wall chain so you may access a third chest. Descend the south stairs and claim a bit of loot from a table on your way to [4].

◊ Chest

◊ Chest (Locked: Novice)

◊ Chest (Locked: Master)

◊ Potions

◊ Loose gear

4 Overgrown Passages

Slay a powerful Silver Hand mercenary and several Draugr in these passages. Loot the locked chest as you near [5].

◊ Chest (Locked: Adept)

5 Crumbling Hall

Dispatch worthy Silver Hand mercenaries in this wide, debris-filled chamber. You can just reach the coin purse on the south ledge by standing on the nearby stone.

6 Crypt Access

Avoid a pressure plate as you descend this

◊ Danger! Dart Trap (pressure plate)

◊ Chest

B Door to Dustman's Crypt

C Door to Dustman's Cairn

7 Walkway Chamber

You arrive just in time to witness a fierce battle between the Silver Hand and Draugr. Wait for the battle to play out, then slaughter the victors and cut across to [8].

8 Looping Passage

Loot a lone chest as you loop around this passage, heading back toward [7].

◊ Chest

9 Burial Preparation Area

Raid a chest that lies beneath this chamber's wooden stairs, then open the nearby door to find several potions.

◊ Chest (Locked: Adept)

◊ Potions

7 Walkway Chamber Revisited

Raid a chest on this chamber's ground floor, then search the nearby chest to discover a key that unlocks the north door.

◊ Dustman's Cairn Key (chest)

◊ Chest

10 Lab

Mix up a few potions at the Alchemy Lab here, and unlock the Novice-level door to access a closet with a potion.

◊ Crafting: Alchemy Lab

◊ Potion

11 Spider Den and Waterfall

Combat a Giant Frostbite Spider here, along with her young, then slaughter the Draugr that lie in the watery passage beyond.

12 Word Wall Chamber

Obtain a new Word of Power from this chamber's far Word Wall, then raid the nearby large chest and collect the Fragment of Wuuthrad from the nearby table to advance your quest. Beware: a host of powerful Draugr emerge from the surrounding sarcophagi after you claim the Fragment, and you've no choice but to slay them all. They will come at you in waves, so take your time and jump off the raised area and over the altar to give you space between you and your opponent if you need it. After the final Draugr emerges, a passage that leads back to the Dustman's Cairn is revealed.

◊ Fragment of Wuuthrad

◊ Word Wall: Fire Breath [1/2]

◊ Chest

◊ Potions

D Path to Dustman's Cairn

E Path to Dustman's Crypt

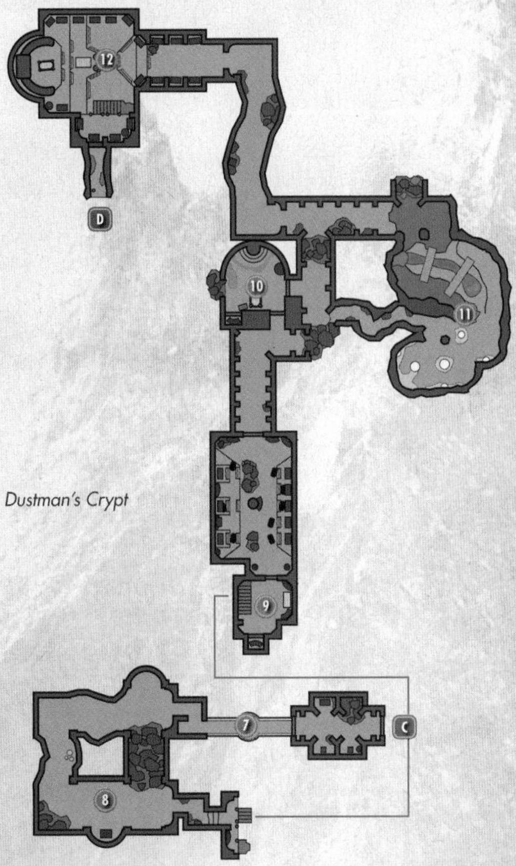

[6.13] Hamvir's Rest

Recommended Level: 6

Dungeon: Draugr Crypt

Draugr
Skeleton

Collectible

Chest (Locked: Master

Follow Whiterun's central road to its north end, and you'll find yourself standing before this plagued graveyard. Slay the undead here to cleanse the site and safely loot its giant—albeit locked—chest.

[6.14] Redoran's Retreat

Related Quests

Side Quest: The Great Skyrim Treasure Hunt*

Recommended Level: 6

Dungeon: Bandit Camp

Bandit
Dog

Dangers

Bear Trap
Bone Alarm Trap

Collectibles

Skill Book [Sneak]: 2920, Last Seed, v8 [A2/10]
Treasure Map IV [4/11]
Chest
Chest (Locked: Novice)
Potions
Loose gear

This shallow cave, which lies near Whiterun's central main road, has been occupied by ruthless bandits. Open a locked chest in the first cavern if you're able, then make your way into the rear cavern, where the bandit's chief lurks. Beware the bear trap that lies in front of the large chest. Open it from the side to claim a rare Treasure Map, among other spoils.

[6.15] Fort Greymoor

Related Quests

Dark Brotherhood Quest: Side Contract: Agnis

Recommended Level: 6

Habitation: Military Fort

Agnis
Bandit
Soldier (Stormcloak/Imperial, depending on your allegiance during the Civil War)

Crafting

Blacksmith Forge
Tanning Rack
Workbench

Dangers

Bear Traps
Flail Trap (trip wire)
Oil Pool Trap

Collectibles

Skill Book [Light Armor]: Rislav The Righteous [C1/10]
Chest(s)
Potions
Loose gear

Near the heart of Whiterun stands an imposing fortress that's been overrun by lawless bandits. Fort Greymoor also serves as a point of contention between the Stormcloaks and Imperials during the Civil War quest line, and therefore may be found populated by soldiers instead of bandits. A friendly old maid named Agnis also resides here—she's a person of interest to the Dark Brotherhood.

Exterior

Fight hard to secure the fort's exterior, then search the grounds thoroughly to find a chest tucked away near some hay to the east, along with a potion and coin purse near the west wooden lookout. A locked grate can be used to enter covertly from outside the walls. Enter the north tower to find another chest.

- Crafting: Blacksmith Forge, Tanning Rack, Workbench
- Chest
- Potion

Fort Greymoor (Interior)

The fort's interior consists of three multifloor towers. Find a chest in the middle tower's main floor, and avoid a trip wire and several bear traps as you head downstairs to explore its lower level. Take the passage to the north tower next, slaying bandits as you head upstairs to chat with a friendly maid named Agnis. Cut across to the south tower afterward and go upstairs to discover a large chest and a Skill Book.

- Danger! Bear Traps, Oil Pool Trap, Flail Trap (trip wire)
- Skill Book [Light Armor]: Rislav The Righteous [C1/10]
- Chest
- Chest (Locked: Novice)
- Potions
- Loose gear

Fort Greymoor Prison

Dispatch rugged bandits as you fight your way toward a chest that lies at the bottom of the prison. None of the cells are worth opening, unless you're simply after some lockpicking practice.

- Chest
- Loose gear

[6.16] Silent Moons Camp

Recommended Level: 6

Dungeon: Bandit Camp

Bandit

Crafting

Blacksmith Forge
Grindstone
Workbench

Collectibles

Skill Book [Smithing]: Heavy Armor Forging [B1/10]
Skill Book [Smithing]: Light Armor Forging
Unique Weapon: Lunar Iron Mace [42/80]
Unique Weapon: Lunar Iron Sword [43/80]
Unique Weapon: Lunar Iron War Axe [44/80]
Unique Weapon: Lunar Steel Mace [45/80]
Unique Weapon: Lunar Steel Sword [46/80]
Unique Weapon: Lunar Steel War Axe [47/80]
Chest(s)
Potions aplenty
Loose gear

These ancient ruins, located along Whiterun's northern border, have become home to ruthless bandits. Beware: these scoundrels' unique weapons deal additional fire damage, but only at night. This Silent Moons enchant can be disenchanted and put on other weapons!

Exterior

Slay some tough outer guards, then scale the ruins' exterior steps to reach a small enclosure at the top, where more bandits lurk. Loot a giant chest if you can manage to pick its tricky lock, then claim a pair of Skill Books and make use of some crafting stations before heading back downstairs and entering the door to the Silent Moons Camp.

- Crafting: Blacksmith Forge, Grindstone, Workbench
- Skill Book [Smithing]: Heavy Armor Forging [B1/10]
- Skill Book [Smithing]: Light Armor Forging
- Chest
- Chest (Locked: Master)
- Loose gear

Silent Moons Camp (Interior)

Slay bandits and loot a chest in the ruins' small interior. If you're able, pick an Adept-level door to access a storage room filled with potions and another chest. Climb the central ladder to return outside, then loot an exterior chest that you couldn't have reached before.

- Chests (2)
- Potions aplenty

[6.17] Halted Stream Camp

Related Quests

Dungeon Activity

Recommended Level: 6

Dungeon: Bandit Camp

Bandit

Crafting

Blacksmith Forge
Grindstone (2)
Tanning Rack (2)

Dangers

Bear Trap
Bone Alarm Trap
Oil Lamp Traps
Oil Pool Trap
Rockfall (pressure plate)
Trapped Chest

Collectibles

Unique Weapon: Poacher's Axe [49/80]
Chest(s)
Potions
Loose gear
Mineable ore (Iron)

Bandits have raised an impressive campsite just north of Whiterun. This is good place to acquire Iron Ore early in the game if you're into smithing.

Exterior

Avoid falling into the pit that lies just east of the camp; sharpened stakes will spell your end. Search beneath the wooden stairs to find two chests, but beware the trapped chest near the potions. Stand back and to the right when you open it to avoid being struck by a swinging flail, or lockpick the trigger attached to the chest to disarm it.

- Danger! Trapped Chest
- Crafting: Grindstone, Tanning Rack
- Chest (Locked: Apprentice)
- Potions
- Loose gear

Halted Stream Camp (Interior)

Beware a pressure plate trap as you enter the mine around which the bandits have built their camp. Slay a bandit within the mine and search his body to find a key that opens the following gate. Face the bandit chief in the large cavern beyond—sneak in and knock down the overhead lamps to start things off with a bang. Search the room afterward to secure multiple potions and pillage a pair of chests. Avoid the bear trap and hanging lamp in the exit passage as you make your way back outside. A bandit may be present sharpening a unique axe called the Poacher's Axe, which gives bonus damage against animals.

- Danger! Bear Trap, Oil Lamp Traps, Bone Alarm Trap, Oil Pool Trap, Rockfall (pressure plate)
- Crafting: Blacksmith Forge, Grindstone, Tanning Rack
- Unique Weapon: Poacher's Axe [48/80]
- Key to Halted Steam Mine (Bandit)
- Chest
- Chest (Locked: Novice)
- Potions aplenty
- Loose gear
- Mineable ore (Iron)

[6.18] Bleakwind Basin

Recommended Level: 2

Dungeon: Giant Camp

Giant
Mammoth

Collectible

Chest (Locked: Expert)

Two towering giants have made camp in the heart of Whiterun, tending to a herd of aggressive mammoths. Slay the brutes and their hulking livestock to secure the campsite. If you're able, unlock the giants' Expert-level chest to claim even more plunder from this site.

[6.19] Western Watchtower

Related Quests

Main Quest: Dragon Rising

Dungeon: Dragon Lair

Dragon (only during Main Quest visit)
Whiterun Guard

This tall tower lies west of Whiterun's capital and is patrolled by Whiterun Guards. Early in the Main Quest, a dragon attacks you here. This is your first battle against a dragon. Exploit the defensive nature of the tower to help you bring down the mighty beast.

[6.20] Whiterun Stables

Related Quests

Side Quest: In My Time of Need

Habitation: Farm

Bjorlam (Carriage Driver)
Skulvar Sable-Hilt (Stablemaster)

Services

Trader (Carriage Driver): Bjorlam [3/5]
Trader (Stablemaster): Skulvar Sable-Hilt [3/5]

Special Objects

Business Ledger
Chest
Strongbox (Locked: Expert)
Potions
Loose gear

Stop by the stables south of Whiterun's capital during daylight hours to buy a horse or buy a carriage ride to any other capital in Skyrim. If you're hard up for loot, pick the stable house's Novice-level lock to break in and raid the place.

[6.21] Pelagia Farm

Related Quests

The Companions Quest: Take Up Arms
Favor (Activity): Harvesting Crops* (Severio Pelagia)

Habitation: Farm

Nimriel
Severio Pelagia
Potion

A windmill draws the eye to this quaint farm, which lies just south of Whiterun's capital. There's little worth stealing from these humble folk—better to leave them be.

[6.22] Honningbrew Meadery

Related Quests

Thieves Guild Quest: Dampened Spirits
Thieves Guild Radiant Quest: Larceny Targets*

Recommended Level: 8

Habitation: Special

Animal
Hamelyn
Mallus Maccius
Sabjorn (Food Vendor)
Venomfang Skeever

Services

Trader (Fence): Mallus Maccius [5/10]
Trader (Food Vendor): Sabjorn [6/12]
Food

Crafting

Alchemy Lab

Dangers

Bear Traps
Flail Trap (trip wire)

Quest Items

Honningbrew Meadery Key (Sabjorn)
Pet Poison (Sabjor)
Promissory Note

Collectibles

Larceny Target: Honningbrew Decanter [5/7]
Skill Book [Alchemy]: A Game at Dinner [A1/10]
Skill Book [Sneak]: Three Thieves [E2/10]
Chests
Potions
Loose gear

Whiterun's renowned meadery lies just southeast of her capital. There's little of interest outside but quite a bit of drama and intrigue brewing within.

Honningbrew Meadery (Interior)

Speak with Sabjorn inside the meadery to purchase a variety of foodstuffs. You need special keys to enter the meadery's basement and upstairs office; these are obtained during Thieves Guild Quest: Dampened Spirits. The office holds most objects of value, including an informative note and Skill Book found on tables, as well as a locked chest that's further secured behind an Expert-level locked door (no key for this one). The office also contains one of seven Larceny Targets that pertain to a Thieves Guild Radiant Quest.

- Larceny Target: Honningbrew Decanter [5/7]
- Skill Book [Alchemy]: A Game at Dinner [A1/10]
- Honningbrew Meadery Key (Sabjorn)
- Pet Poison (Sabjor)
- Promissory Note
- Chest (Locked: Master)
- Loose gear

Honningbrew Basement

Beware of bear traps as you purge the brewery's basement of Skeevers during the "Dampened Spirits" quest. Beware: the Venomfang Skeevers can poison you. Stay sharp and safely trigger a trip wire from as far away as possible to disable a swinging flail. Surprisingly, a dangerous mage named Hamelyn lurks in the cavern that follows. Slay him and poison the nearby Skeever nest, then read the journal you find on Hamelyn's corpse to learn of his questionable motives. Loot a chest here as well before proceeding into the boilery.

- Danger! Bear Traps, Flail Trap (trip wire)
- Crafting: Alchemy Lab
- Skill Book [Sneak]: Three Thieves [E2/10]
- Chest (Locked: Novice)
- Potions

Honningbrew Boilery

You can only enter the boilery via the meadery's basement passage—the front door remains locked at all times. Head upstairs and optionally steal from a locked chest before nefariously poisoning the giant vat. Exit the boilery afterward with the key that hangs on the wall near the door.

- Chest (Locked: Apprentice)
- Honningbrew Brewhouse Key

[6.23] Chillfurrow Farm

Habitation: Farm

Wilmuth

Collectibles

Skill Book [One-Handed]: The Importance of Where [E2/10]
Chest
Loose gear

This small farm consists of a farmhouse, a windmill, and a small plot of wheat. Pick the Novice-level door to enter the farmhouse and steal from a chest if you like. A Skill Book rests on the nearby dresser as well.

[6.24] Battle-Born Farm

Related Quests

Favor (Activity): Harvesting Crops* (Alfhild Battle-Born)

Habitation: Farm

Alfhild Battle-Born
Gwendolyn

Collectible

Loose gear

Harvest Alfhild Battle-Born's crops and sell them back to her—she'll pay a fair wage for your work in her fields. If you don't feel like toiling out in the Skyrim sun, pick the farmhouse's Novice-level door and pilfer a couple of coin purses from within.

[6.25] Whitewatch Tower

Related Quests

Dungeon Activity

Recommended Level: 6

Dungeons: Special

Whiterun Guard

Collectibles

Chest

Chest (Locked: Novice)

Whiterun guards patrol this small tower, which lies on the road just north of the city. A small group of bandits are attacking the tower when you first approach; rush in, and you may be able to lend the guards a hand. Strip the bandits of their valuables, then scale the ruined western tower to claim a chest. If you're willing to take the risk, you can also loot the locked chest and weapon racks on the ground level, though the guards consider it theft if they catch you. Make sure to listen to the latest local gossip before moving on.

[6.26] White River Watch

Related Quests

Dungeon Activity

Recommended Level: 6

Dungeon: Bandit Camp

Bandit

Hajvarr Iron-Hand

Ulfr the Blind

Crafting

Alchemy Lab

Collectibles

Unique Item: Ironhand Gauntlets [59/112]

Chest(s)

Potions

Loose gear

This small bandit hideout lies east of Whiterun's capital, just across the White River. Pass through the small cave to face the bandits' leader, who prefers the cold embrace of the outdoor mountain air.

Exterior

Dispatch the exterior guards to secure a chest, then head inside.

- Chest (Locked: Novice)

White River Watch (Interior)

A blind guard sits just inside the cave—he'll call for reinforcements if you threaten him. Lie your way past the blind sentry and proceed upstairs. Dispatch or avoid the bandits in the sleeping area that follows. Loot the chest near the cupboard before heading upstairs to discover an Alchemy Lab. Bandits have been mistreating a wolf in the cavern that follows. Free the animal to have it attack its captors, then attack while they're distracted. Scale the winding ramp to reach a high passage that leads out to the White River Overlook.

- Crafting: Alchemy Lab
- Chest
- Potions
- Loose gear

Overlook

You emerge onto this rocky overlook, where the bandits' leader, Hajvarr Iron-Hand, awaits. Slay this worthy adversary to obtain valuable plunder from his corpse and from the nearby chest. Take in the view before Fast-Traveling away.

- Chest
- Potions
- Loose gear
- Unique Item: Ironhand Gauntlets [59/112]

[6.27] Riverwood

Related Quests

Main Quest: Before the Storm

Main Quest: The Horn of Jurgen Windcaller

Main Quest: A Blade in the Dark

Main Quest: Diplomatic Immunity

Main Quest: A Cornered Rat

Main Quest: Alduin's Wall

Main Quest: Paarthurnax

Side Quest: The Golden Claw

Miscellaneous Objective: Innkeeper Rumors (Sleeping Giant Inn)

Miscellaneous Objective: The Love Triangle: Helping Sven* (Sven)

Miscellaneous Objective: The Love Triangle: Betraying Sven* (Sven)

Miscellaneous Objective: The Love Triangle: Helping Faendal* (Faendal)

Miscellaneous Objective: The Love Triangle: Betraying Faendal* (Faendal)

Favor (Activity): Chopping Wood* (Hod)

Favor (Activity): A Drunk's Drink* (Embry)

Crafting Tutorial: Blacksmithing* (Alvor)

Crafting Tutorial: Alchemy* (Orgnar)

Habitation: Settlement

Alvor (Blacksmith)

Camilla Valerius (Marriage Prospect)

Delphine (Innkeeper)

Dorthe

Embry

Faendal (Follower; Trainer: Archery)

Frodnar

Gerdur

Hilde

Lucan Valerius (General Store Vendor)

Orgnar (Bartender)

Stump (dog)

Sigrid

Sven (Follower)

Services

Follower: Faendal [31/47]
Follower: Sven [32/47]
Marriage Prospect: Camilla Valerius [38/62]
Trader (Bartender): Orgnar [1/5]
Food, Ingredients
Trader (Blacksmith): Alvor [20/33]
Weapons, Apparel, Misc
Trader (General Store Vendor): Lucan Valerius [8/19]
Weapons, Apparel, Potions, Scrolls, Food, Books, Misc
Trader (Innkeeper): Delphine [10/15]
Room and Board
Innkeeper Rumors
Trainer (Archery: Journeyman): Faendal [2/3]

Crafting

Alchemy Lab
Blacksmith Forge
Grindstone (2)
Tanning Rack (2)
Workbench

Collectible

Chest(s)
Potions
Loose gear

Located in Whiterun's eastern valley, this small logging community is the first village that you're urged to visit following your escape from Helgen [8.32]. The friendly villagers here assist you and give advice during the early stages of your adventure.

Exterior

Speak with villagers to learn a little about Riverwood. Alvor will sell you fine weapons and armor and can also give you a Side Quest involving the use of his forge.

- Crafting: Blacksmith Forge, Grindstone (2), Tanning Rack (2), Workbench
- Loose gear

1 Sleeping Giant Inn

Rent a room for the night by talking to Delphine, or purchase food and drink from Orgnar. Gain a Miscellaneous Objective by asking Orgnar if you can use the inn's Alchemy Lab, and speak with Sven, the bard, to gain another Miscellaneous Objective involving the Bard's College. Delphine has a secret room beneath the inn with two chests, an Alchemy Lab, an Arcane Enchanter, and a lot of loose items. Once you befriend her in Main Quest: The Horn of Jurgen Windcaller, you have access to all of it.

- Crafting: Alchemy Lab
- Chest (3)
- Loose gear

2 Riverwood Trader

Speak with this humble shop's proprietor, Lucan Valerius, to gain a Side Quest involving the retrieval of a Golden Claw that's recently been stolen from his store. Then browse Lucan's impressive array of goods.

- Chest
- Chest (Locked: Novice) (2)
- Potions
- Loose gear

3 Alvor and Sigrid's House

If you followed Hadvar out of Helgen, you'll be welcomed into Alvor and Sigrid's home. The town blacksmith's house has a few items worth swiping, if you're that kind of adventurer.

- Area Is Locked (Novice)
- Chests (2)
- Potions
- Loose gear

4 Faendal's House

This wily elf has amassed several valuables that are well worth stealing if you think you can get away with it.

- Area Is Locked (Novice)
- Chests (2)
- Potions
- Loose gear

5 Hod and Gerdur's House

If you followed Ralof out of Helgen, after you speak with Gerdur, you'll be welcome to sleep at her humble home whenever you like.

- Area Is Locked (Novice)
- Chests (2)
- Potion

6 Sven and Hilde's House

Sven and Hilde have very little worth stealing, but you may rob them if you like.

- Area Is Locked (Novice)
- Chest
- Loose gear

[6.28] Shimmermist Cave

Recommended Level: 18

Dungeon: Falmer Hive

Animal
Dwarven Centurion
Falmer

Dangers

Swinging Wall Trap (trip wire)

Quest Items

Ebony Blade
Chest(s)
Loose gear

This sizeable cave is found at the foot of mountains that lie northeast of Whiterun's capital.

Shimmermist Cave (Interior)

Slay an overgrown Frostbite Spider in the first watery cavern, and beware the trip wire that's stretched across the end of the following passage. Slay a lone Falmer Archer in the next cavern with the Falmer tent, then proceed along the upper passage, dispatching another Falmer and looting an unusual chest on your way to the cave's inner grotto.

- Swinging Wall Trap (trip wire)
- Chest
- Loose gear

Shimmermist Grotto

Pick off more Falmer in the grotto's first tall cavern, and raid a tent to loot a chest before descending to the cavern's bottom. Dispatch an overgrown Chaurus in the passage that leads to the second chamber, where yet more Chaurus lurk. Loot a chest that rests near the mouth of the following passage, which leads to some long-forgotten dwarven ruins. Defeat a powerful Falmer here, along with a lumbering Dwarven Centurion, then loot one last chest before taking the east passage back to the cave's entrance.

- Chests (3)

[6.29] Fellglow Keep

Related Quests

College of Winterhold Quest: Hitting the Books
Side Quest: No Stone Unturned
Dungeon Activity

Recommended Level: 8

Dungeon: Warlock Lair

Animal
Mages
Atronachs
Orthorn

Crafting

Alchemy Lab
Anvil
Arcane Enchanter
Workbench

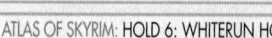

[7.01] Uttering Hills Cave

Related Quests

Thieves Guild City Influence Quest: Summerset Shadows

Recommended Level: 6

Dungeon: Bandit Camp

Bandit (prequest only)
Summerset Shadows (only during quest)

Collectibles

Skill Book [One-Handed]: Mace Etiquette
Unique Item: Fjotli's Silver Locket [63/112]
Chests
Potions
Loose gear

This small bandit cave is found within Eastmarch's northwest mountains. Slay a couple of exterior guards before venturing inside.

A Exit to Skyrim

1 Entry Tunnel

Grab a few items of value from a table as you descend the cave's snowy entry tunnel.

- Potions
- Loose gear

2 Campfire Cavern

Slay bandits as you make your way to this far cavern, where several bandits guard a chest near a campfire.

- Chest

3 Hideout Entry and Holding Cells

Loot the hideout's entry chamber, and discover a chest that's tucked away in a nook near the following corridor.

- Chest (Locked: Adept)
- Potions

4 Bandit Hideout

A powerful bandit lurks at the cave's end. Raid the place after securing the area, and burn the banner here as part of your quest. Find a Skill Book on a shelf in the bedroom with the chest, then make your way back outside.

- Skill Book [One-Handed]: Mace Etiquette
- Chest
- Knapsack
- Potion

[7.02] Gallows Rock

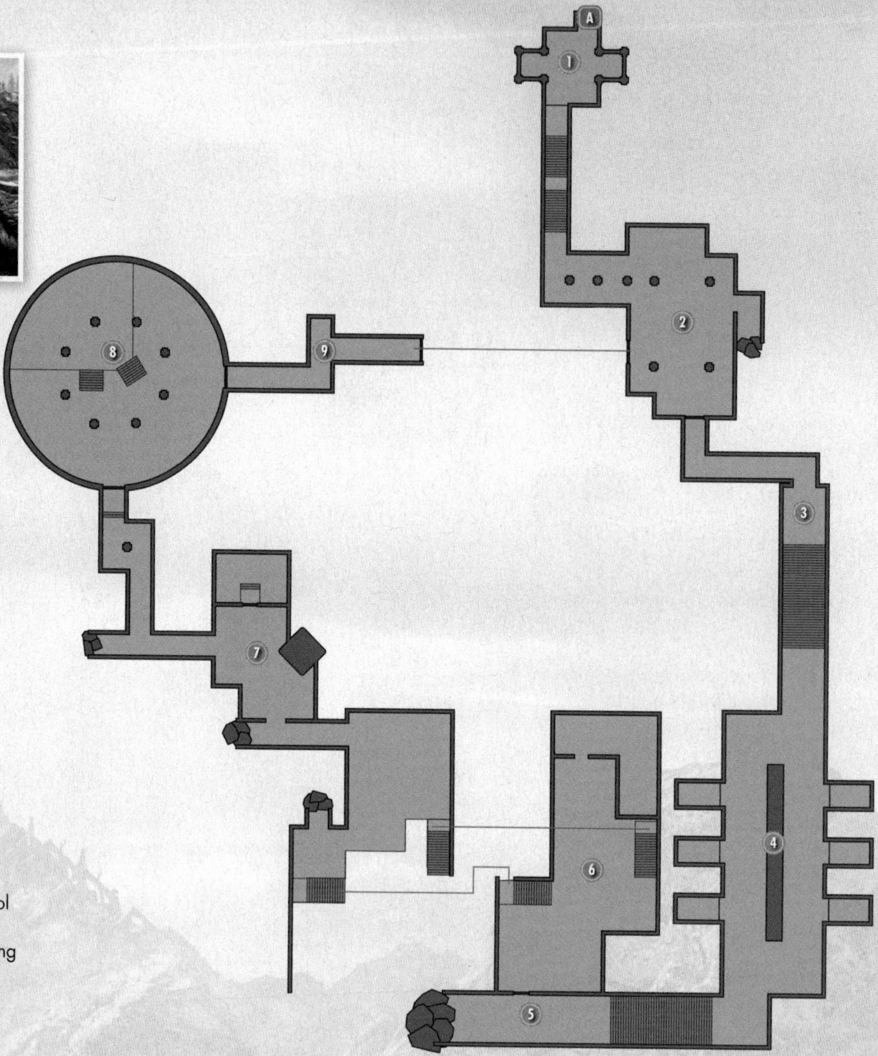

Related Quests

The Companions Quest: The Silver Hand

Recommended Level: 6

Dungeon: Bandit Camp

Animal
Silver Hand
Werewolf

Crafting

Tanning Racks (2)
Skill Book [One-Handed]: The Importance of Where
Skill Book [Smithing]: Last Scabbard of Akrash [C2/10]

Dangers

Swinging Wall Trap (pressure plate)
Chests
Potions
Loose gear

A group of bandits called the Silver Hand control a small fortress along Eastmarch's northwest border. You fight your way through this fort during Companions Quest: Silver Moon.

Exterior

Slay the outdoor guards, then search the top of the fort to discover a chest inside a small tower.

- Chest

A Exit to Skyrim

1 Entry Chamber

Pull a chain in the entry chamber to open the way forward.

- Loose gear

2 Mess

Slay a few more Silver Hand in this room, which contains a chest. The west door is barred, so go south instead.

- Chest
- Potions
- Loose gear

3 Corridor and Stairs

Slay a Skeever on your way upstairs, and avoid the pressure plate at the top of the steps—it triggers a nasty trap.

- Danger! Swinging Wall Trap (pressure plate)

4 Prison Cells

Defeat the Silver Hand bandits that guard a number of werewolves in this area. If you dare, pick the Adept-level locks on the cell doors to free and battle with the beasts.

- Potions
- Loose gear

5 South Stairs and Corridor

The primary item of interest here is a knapsack that contains valuable loot.

- Knapsack
- Loose gear

6 Great Hall

Kill more Silver Hand to secure the Great Hall, then explore the downstairs area thoroughly to discover a large chest with a tricky lock. A Skill Book rests on a table at the hall's north end.

- Crafting: Tanning Racks (2)
- Skill Book [One-Handed]: The Importance of Where
- Chest (Locked: Master)
- Potions
- Loose gear

7 Hearth and Sleeping Quarters

A roaring fireplace dominates the first chamber of this area. Find a Skill Book on a table near the hearth. Unlock the Adept-level north door to access a sleeping quarters filled with valuables.

- Skill Book [Smithing]: Last Scabbard of Akrash [C2/10]
- Chest
- Potions

8 Circular Chamber

Slay the final batch of Silver Hand here before looting the room and making your way back outside.

- Crafting: Tanning Racks (3)
- Chest
- Potions
- Loose gear

9 Barred Door Corridor

Claim an array of worthy gear from this corridor, then unbar the far door and take your leave of this place.

- Knapsack
- Loose gear

[7.03] Mara's Eye Pond

Related Quests

Dungeon Activity

Recommended Level: 6

Dungeon: Vampire Lair

Animal

Vampire

Collectibles

Skill Book [Pickpocket]: Wulfmare's Guide to Better Thieving [E2/10]

Chest(s)

Loose gear

This small, eerie pond lies on the west side of Eastmarch, just north of the Hold's larger and more prominent western hot springs. The pond derives its name from the tiny isle found in its center—when viewed from above, it resembles an eye.

Exterior

Exterminate the small cluster of Mudcrab near the pond's central "eye," then search for a trapdoor on the central isle, which leads into Mara's Eye Den. There's little else of interest around the pond.

Mara's Eye Den (Interior)

This small underground cavern was once a smugglers den but has since been taken over by a more blood chilling foe—vampires. Slay the cursed beings, then loot the place for loads of valuables, including a Skill Book that's mixed in with other books in a small crate. There's no need to pick the locked cage here—nothing of interest is found within.

- Skill Book [Pickpocket]: Wulfmare's Guide to Better Thieving [E2/10]
- Chest
- Chest (Locked: Apprentice)
- Loose gear

[7.04] Morvunskar

Related Quests

Daedric Quest: A Night to Remember

Recommended Level: 8

Dungeon: Warlock Lair

Mage

Naris the Wicked

Crafting

Blacksmith Forge

Tanning Rack

Workbench

Dangers

Swinging Wall Trap (pressure plate)

Collectibles

Skill Book [Destruction]: Mystery of Talara, v3

Skill Book [Smithing]: Cherim's Heart [A2/10]

Unique Weapon: Sanguine Rose [51/80]

Special Objects

Shrine of Dibella [6/8]

Chest(s)

Potions aplenty

Loose gear

A host of hostile mages practice their nefarious arts at this frigid fortress, which you visit during Daedric Quest: A Night to Remember. Slay the mob of mages that guard the grounds before heading inside. There's little of interest out in the cold.

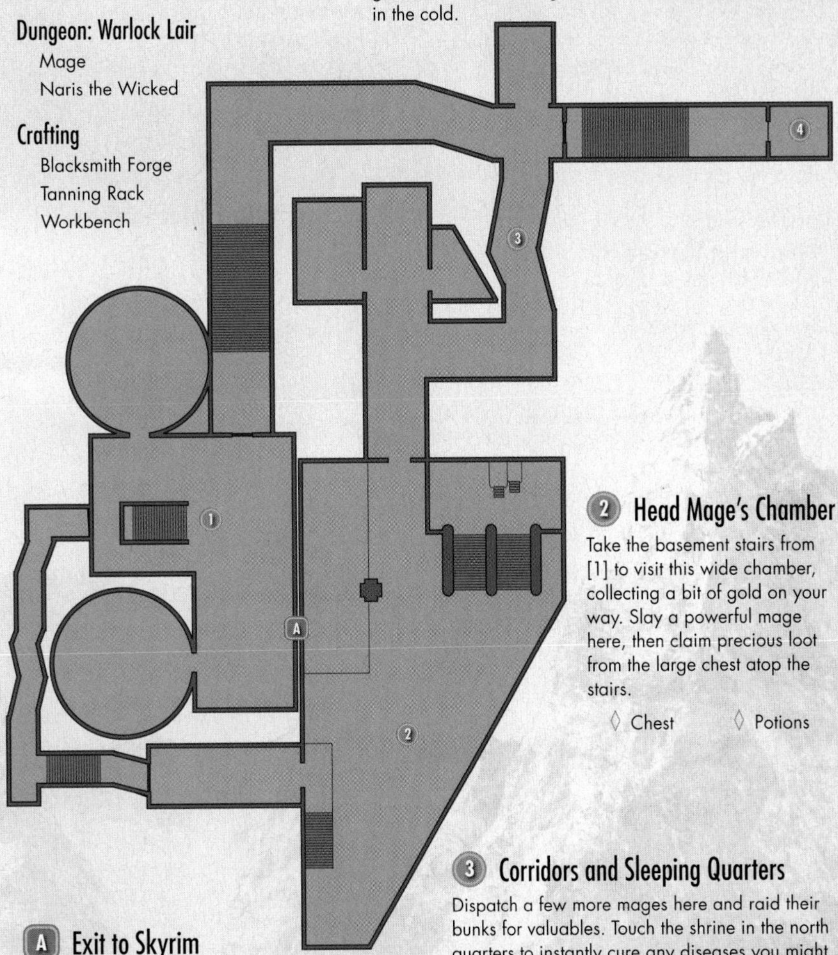

(A) Exit to Skyrim

(1) Crafthouse

Crafting opportunities abound in this first area of Morvunskar. Beware when engaging mages here—the sound of battle may bring reinforcements. Find a Skill Book resting on a table.

- Crafting: Blacksmith Forge, Tanning Rack, Workbench
- Skill Book [Smithing]: Cherim's Heart [A2/10]
- Potion
- Loose gear

(2) Head Mage's Chamber

Take the basement stairs from [1] to visit this wide chamber, collecting a bit of gold on your way. Slay a powerful mage here, then claim precious loot from the large chest atop the stairs.

- Chest
- Potions

(3) Corridors and Sleeping Quarters

Dispatch a few more mages here and raid their bunks for valuables. Touch the shrine in the north quarters to instantly cure any diseases you might be suffering.

- Danger! Swinging Wall Trap (pressure plate)
- Shrine of Dibella [6/8]
- Potions aplenty
- Loose gear

(4) Torture Chamber

Unlock Morunskar's northwest door and slay the twisted mage in the chamber beyond. A Skill Book sits on a shelf here. Pull a lever to access and loot the burnt corpses in the holding cell.

- Area Is Locked (Novice)
- Skill Book [Destruction]: Mystery of Talara, v3
- Chest
- Potions

[7.05] Kynesgrove

Related Quests

Main Quest: A Blade in the Dark
Miscellaneous Objective: Innkeeper Rumors (the Braidwood Inn)
Miscellaneous Objective: Salt for the Stoneweaver* (Dravynea the Stoneweaver)
Favor (Activity): Chopping Wood* (Ganna Uriel)
Favor (Activity): Mining Ore* (Kjeld)
Favor: A Good Talking To* (Iddra)
Favor: Item Retrieval (Cave)* (Roggi)

Habitation: Town

Dravynea the Stoneweaver (Marriage Prospect; Trainer: Alteration)
Ganna Uriel
Gemma Uriel
Iddra (Innkeeper)
Kjeld the Younger
Roggi Knot-Beard (Follower; Marriage Prospect)
Stormcloak Soldier

Services

Follower: Roggi Knot-Beard [37/47]
Marriage Prospect: Dravynea the Stoneweaver [47/62]
Marriage Prospect: Roggi Knot-Beard [48/62]
Trader (Innkeeper): Iddra [12/15]
- Food, Room and Board
- Innkeeper Rumors

Trainer (Alteration: Expert): Dravynea [3/3]

Crafting

Smelter

Collectibles

Skill Book [Enchanting]: Catalogue of Armor Enchantments [B2/10]
Chest(s)
Potion
Loose gear
Mineable ore (Malachite)

A short jaunt south of Windhelm lies a small mining community consisting of an inn that's been erected next to a working mine. You visit Kynesgrove during the Main Quest in search of Dragons.

Exterior

Chop wood outside the inn, or smelt ore by the mine.

- Crafting: Smelter
- Loose gear

Braidwood Inn

Chat up the locals in the inn to hear an array of gossip that leads to several Side Quests. Trade with Iddra if you like, or purchase a room if you're weary.

- Chests (2)

Steamscorch Mine

Kynesgrove's mine lies just up the hill from the Braidwood Inn. Inside, a woman named Ganna Uriel will purchase any firewood that you cut outside. If you like, use a pickaxe to mine some Malachite from the ore veins that run along the walls and floors. A Skill Book rests on the table at the tunnel junction.

- Skill Book [Enchanting]: Catalogue of Armor Enchantments [B2/10]
- Potion
- Loose gear
- Mineable ore (Malachite)

[7.06] Windhelm Stables

Habitation: Farm

Alfarinn (Carriage Driver)
Arivanya
Ulundil (Stablemaster)

Services

Trader (Carriage Draiver): Alfarinn [4/5]
Trader (Stablemaster): Ulundil [4/5]

Special Objects

Business Ledger
Strongbox (Expert)
Potion

The Windhelm Stables lie directly south of Eastmarch's capital city. The lone building here remains shut tight with a Novice-level locked door, but worthy services are available just outside. Break into the building and see if you can open the strongbox within.

[7.07] Brandy-Mug Farm

Related Quests

Favor (Activity): Harvesting Crops* (Bolfrida Brandy-Mug)

Habitation: Farm

Bolfrida Brandy-Mug
Faryl Atheron

Collectibles

Skill Book [Alteration]: Daughter of the Niben [B2/10]
Chest
Potion

This quaint farm lies just south of Windhelm. Harvest wheat and other ingredients from outside, then enter the farm and sell Bolfrida's wheat back to her for 5 gold a bundle.

[7.08] Hlaalu Farm

Related Quests

Favor (Activity): Harvesting Crops* (Belyn Hlaalu)

Habitation: Farm

Adisla
Belyn Hlaalu

Collectibles

Chest
Potions
Loose gear

This small farm lies southeast of Windhelm and is owned by a Dark Elf named Belyn Hlaalu. Harvest some wheat from outside, but you'll need to pick the door's Novice-level lock to enter and raid the farmhouse.

[7.09] Hollyfrost Farm

Related Quests

Favor (Activity): Harvesting Crops* (Tulvur)

Habitation: Farm

Tulvur
Tiber (dog)

Collectibles

Chest
Potion

This humble farm stands to the southeast of Eastmarch's capital. A feisty guard dog named Tiber guards the locked farmhouse.

[7.10] Traitor's Post

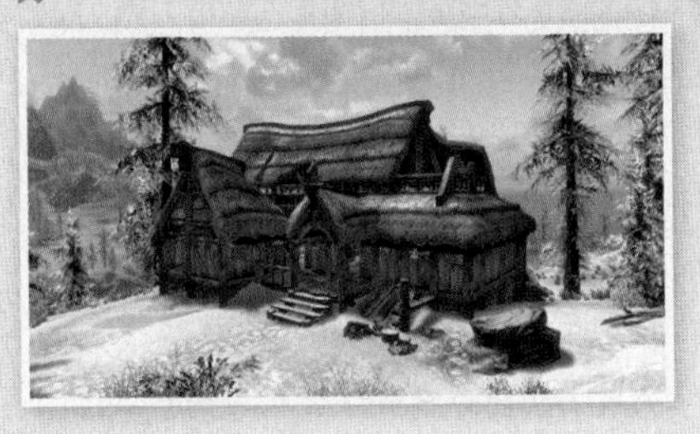

Related Quests
Side Quest: The Great Skyrim Treasure Hunt*

Recommended Level: 5

Dungeon: Bandit Camp
Bandit

Crafting
Tanning Rack

Collectibles
Skill Book [Block]: A Dance in Fire, v2 [A2/10]
Treasure Map VII [5/11]
Chest (Locked: Novice)
Chest (Locked: Master)
Loose gear

A small gang of bandits has taken refuge within a derelict inn located at Eastmarch's northeast corner. Find a Treasure Map inside the chest on the main floor, along with a Skill Book that's on a cupboard shelf. Then scale the rocks on the west side of the building, edge your way around the roof, and climb into the otherwise-inaccessible second floor to reach another, larger chest.

[7.11] Refugees' Rest

Dungeon: Animal Den
Animal

Collectible
Chest (Locked: Adept)

This remote station, which lies at Eastmarch's northeast tip along the northern road to Morrowind, consists of a ruined tower and unceremonious graveyard. A book found at the base of the nearby road sign reveals a little of this location's history.

[7.12] Sacellum of Boethiah

Related Quests
Daedric Quest: Boethiah's Calling

Recommended Level: 30

Habitation: Special
Boethiah Cultist
Priestess of Boethiah

Crafting
Alchemy Lab
Arcane Enchanter

Collectibles
Unique Weapon: Blade of Sacrifice [52/80]
Potions

You obtain the "Boethiah's Calling" quest upon discovering this unusual cult hideout, which lies at Eastmarch's northeast corner. Speak to the Priestess of Boethiah to learn of her cult and advance your quest. Watch the zealots practice their swordplay in the training area, and notice the pillar of sacrifice atop the snowy stairs—this comes into play later in the quest, after you lure an unfortunate soul here to their demise.

[7.13] Cradlecrush Rock

Dungeon: Giant Camp
Giant

Collectibles
Chest
Knapsack
Potions
Loose gear

A monstrous giant makes its home near these large, ominous rocks. One rock has apparently crushed some poor, unfortunate soul—loot the fool's surviving knapsack, which lies near a skeletal foot, for additional valuables.

[7.14] Abandoned Prison

This derelict prison's entrance can be seen from the road along Eastmarch's western boarder—cross a rushing river to get there.

A Exit to Skyrim

1 Leaky Chamber
Collect a host of hanging moss in this otherwise empty chamber, then take the lower passage to [2].

Recommended Level: 6

Dungeon: Special
Ghost

Collectibles
Skill Book [Two-Handed]: Song of Hrormir
Chest(s)
Loose gear

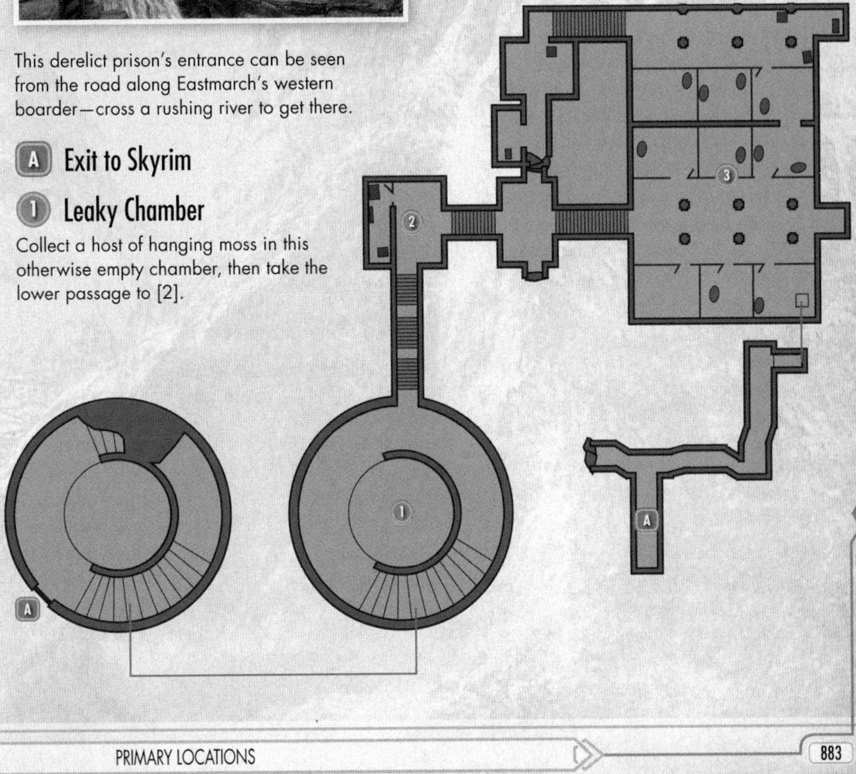

2 Guards' Office

A handful of valuables lie in the guards' small office, including a note that sheds some light on what may have happened here.

- Loose gear

3 Holding Cells

Search the skeletons here to find a handful of valuables. Take the Abandoned Prison Key from the far table and use it to open the cells. Find a chest to the north and claim the Skill Book that lies against it. Drop through the southeast cell's trapdoor to locate a sewer tunnel that leads back out to Skyrim.

- Skill Book [Two-Handed]: Song of Hrormir
- Abandoned Prison Key
- Chest (Locked: Master)
- Loose gear

[7.15] Mixwater Mill

Related Quests

Favor (Activity): Chopping Wood* (Gilfre)

Habitation: Lumber Mill

Gilfre (Marriage Prospect)

Services

Marriage Prospect: Gilfre [49/62]

Collectibles

Skill Book [Archery]: The Marksmanship Lesson [D2/10]
Chest(s)
Potions
Loose gear

Life moves at a slower pace here at this quaint lumber mill, which is located along the White River on the west side of Eastmarch, just north of where the Darkwater River branches off.

Exterior

If you like, enter the mill and slice up logs for Gilfre. Or grab a Woodcutter's Axe and chop wood to sell back to Gilfre for a bit of honest coin.

- Loose gear

Gilfre's House

Breaking into Gilfre's humble abode is worthwhile. Your unscrupulous actions can net you some decent coin, a few potions, and a Skill Book that rests on a small table.

- Area Is Locked (Novice)
- Skill Book [Archery]: The Marksmanship Lesson [D2/10]
- Chest
- Potions

Worker's House

No need to break into the Worker's House—the door is unlocked. Pop in, loot the place, and then head back out.

- Chests (3)
- Potions

[7.16] Broken Limb Camp

Dungeon: Giant Camp

Giant

Collectible

Chest

Two fearsome giants have made camp along Eastmarch's southwestern hills. While fighting giants is never wise, you can gain some decent loot and experience by clearing this campsite—if you're up to the task. If the brutes are too tough, try raiding their chest and then quickly fleeing before they realize they've been robbed.

[7.17] Cronvangr Cave

Related Quests

Dungeon Activity

Recommended Level: 6

Dungeon: Vampire Lair

Animal
Vampire

Collectibles

Chests
Potions
Loose gear

Near the heart of Eastmarch, massive egg sacks covered in thick webbing line the mouth of a forboding vampire cave.

Cronvangr Cave (Interior)

The cave's first cavern is overrun by Frostbite Spiders. Look for a button along the wall and press it to open a secret door. Go through to battle a small brood of vampires in a secret chamber, then raid the chest they guard. Exit the secret lair and continue to squash spiders as you proceed deeper into the cave, looting an underwater chest when you reach the bottom before advancing into the Broodlair.

- Chests (2)
- Apothecary's Satchel
- Potions
- Loose gear

Convangr Broodlair

Exterminate more spiders as you navigate the Broodlair's narrow passages. You soon reach a wide cavern, where a monstrous spider drops from the ceiling. Slay the brute and loot the nearby chest, then advance to loop around and find your way back outside.

- Chest

[7.18] Riverside Shack

Related Quests

Side Quest: The Great Skyrim Treasure Hunt*

Recommended Level: 6

Dungeon: Animal Den

Animal

Crafting

Tanning Rack

Collectibles

Skill Book [Light Armor]: Rislav the Righteous
Treasure Map III [6/11]
Chest (Locked: Apprentice)
Loose gear

As its name implies, this is a small, abandoned shack poised on the bank of the White River, somewhat near the middle of Eastmarch. If you can slay the vicious animal that lives inside the shack, you'll be free to loot the chest that's found here—and claim the Treasure Map within! A Skill Book is also found here, mixed in with a stack of other tomes.

[7.19] Witchmist Grove

Related Quests

Daedric Quest: A Night to Remember

Recommended Level: 14

Dungeon: Hagraven Nest

Witch

Quest Items

Wedding Ring

Collectibles

Skill Book [Destruction]: Response to Bero's Speech
Chest (Locked: Expert)

The woods in the center of Eastmarch are home to a vicious witch who lives in a small shack. If you manage to slay the spellcaster, see if you can also open the locked chest that she guards. You visit this site in search of a lost ring during Daedric Quest: A Night to Remember. Find a Skill Book stashed under the bed.

[7.20] Bonestrewn Crest

Dungeon: Dragon Lair

Dragon (after Main Quest: Dragon Rising)
Skeleton

Special Objects

Word Wall: Frost Breath [3/3]
Chest (Locked: Expert)

At the very center of Eastmarch, a handful of lowly skeletons guards a dismal hilltop, where the bones of great beasts lie strewn about. Defeat a monstrous dragon here if you've advanced past the "Dragon Rising" quest; then follow the sound of chanting to locate a Word Wall that bestows you with a new Word of Power. If possible, open the nearby locked chest to obtain valuable plunder.

[7.21] Steamcrag Camp

Dungeon: Giant Camp

Animal
Giant
Mammoth

Collectibles

Chest
Chest (Locked: Adept)
Knapsack
Potion

A towering giant has set up a campsite near the heart of Eastmarch. Attack the giant from the north ridge to gain a tactical advantage. Loot a chest here, then find another chest and a knapsack on a nearby smashed Khajiit wagon. Beware the wild animals that are nuzzling through the Khajiit's remains!

[7.22] Narzulbur

Related Quests

Side Quest: The Forgemaster's Fingers
Favor (Activity): Mining Ore* (Dushnamub)
Favor: Sparring Partners* (Mauhulakh)

Recommended Level: 6

Habitation: Orc Stronghold

Bolar
Chief Mauhulakh
Urog
Yatul

Crafting

Alchemy Lab
Tanning Rack

Collectibles

Skill Book [Heavy Armor]: The Knights of the Nine
Skill Book [Two-Handed]: Song of Hrormir
Chests
Potions aplenty
Loose gear

Nestled among the mountains that form Eastmarch's eastern border, this small Orcish mining community struggles to prosper by gathering ebony ore from the nearby Gloombound Mine.

Exterior

The Orcs are cold to outsiders, but they won't attack or force you away. Speak to the villagers to potentially gain a new quest that can help you earn their acceptance.

- Crafting: Alchemy Lab, Tanning Rack
- Potions
- Loose gear

Alchemy Workshop

Expert-level Lockpicking skill is required to enter the Narzulbur's alchemy workshop, where a vast array of potions and ingredients are kept.

- Area Is Locked (Expert)
- Crafting: Alchemy Lab
- Potions aplenty

Mauhulakh's Longhouse

The Longhouse features a roaring hearth, numerous food items, and sleeping quarters. A Skill Book sits on a table here, partially covered by other tomes.

- Skill Book [Heavy Armor]: The Knights of the Nine
- Chest (Locked: Adept)
- Chest (Locked: Master)
- Loose gear

Mauhulakh's Cellar

The cellar holds a few items of interest, particularly a chest with an Adept-level lock. A Skill Book is found on the shelf above.

- Skill Book [Two-Handed]: Song of Hrormir
- Chest (Locked: Adept)

[7.23] Gloombound Mine

Related Quests

Dungeon Activity

Recommended Level: 8

Services

Trader (Blacksmith): Dushamub [23/33]
Weapons, Apparel, Misc

Habitation: Mine

Bor
Dushamub (Blacksmith)
Gadba gro-Largash
Mogdurz
Mul gro-Largash

Crafting

Blacksmith Forge
Grindstone
Smelter
Workbench

Dangers

Oil Pool Trap

Collectibles

Skill Book [Smithing]: Heavy Armor Forging [B2/10]
Loose gear
Mineable ore (Ebony)

This small mine is located in Eastmarch's eastern mountains, just south of the Orcish stronghold of Narzulbur. A gifted blacksmith works nearby, and a variety of useful ore can be freely harvested within the mine. This is the only true ebony mine in Skyrim.

Exterior

Speak with an Orc blacksmith who works just outside the mine to purchase an array of superior weapons and arms. The blacksmith also has raw materials for sale and will pay top coin for any materials mined from the nearby site. Also feel free to use the blacksmith's crafting stations as you please. The Smelter requires a shovel to operate, which you can find in the mine. Discover a Skill Book in the open-air hut near the mine's entrance.

- Crafting: Blacksmith Forge, Grindstone, Smelter, Workbench
- Skill Book [Smithing]: Heavy Armor Forging [B2/10]

Gloombound Mine (Interior)

Many useful tools can be found within the Orcs' mine, such as Woodcutter Axes, Pickaxes, and Shovels. Scan the walls and floors of the mine to find Ebony Ore veins. Mine these for valuable ore that you can either sell or use to fashion weapons and armor.

- Danger! Oil Pool Trap
- Loose gear
- Mineable ore (Ebony)

[7.24] Cragwallow Slope

Dangerous mages reside in this small cave, which lies at the foot of Eastmarch's eastern mountain range. Nab a Soul Gem from the exterior ritual site on your way in.

Recommended Level: 6

Dungeon: Warlock Lair

Atronarch
Mage

Crafting

Alchemy Lab
Arcane Enchanter

Collectibles

Skill Book [Alteration]: The Lunar Lorkhan [E2/10]
Chest(s)
Potions aplenty
Loose gear

A Exit to Skyrim

1 Alchemy Station

Slay a lone mage in the cave's first small chamber, then collect some useful items from atop the nearby Alchemy Lab. Beware the Atronarchs and mages that lurk in the following tunnel.

◊ Crafting: Alchemy Lab
◊ Apothecary's Satchel
◊ Potion

2 Ruined Book Chamber

A long tunnel leads to this open chamber, where mining tools and a few Soul Gems are found among a host of worthless ruined books. Duck into the south sleeping quarters to snag a potion and loot a chest on your way to the next area.

◊ Chest
◊ Potion

3 Central Chamber

Slay more mages and Atronachs in the heart of this giant cavern before exploring the upper ledges to the north and south, which contain potions and other valuables. A Skill Book sits on a table here.

◊ Crafting: Alchemy Lab, Arcane Enchanter
◊ Skill Book [Alteration]: The Lunar Lorkhan [E2/10]
◊ Chest
◊ Potions aplenty

4 Exit Passage

One final mage lurks in the final passage, which deposits you back near the cave's entrance.

◊ Chest (Locked: Adept)
◊ Potions
◊ Loose gear

[7.25] Mzulft

Related Quests

College of Winterhold Quest: Revealing the Unseen

Recommended Level: 16

Dungeon: Dwarven City

Chaurus
Dwarven Sphere
Dwarven Spider
Falmer
Paratus Decimius

Crafting

Alchemy Lab

Dangers

Dwarven Piston Traps (pressure plate)
Rockfall Trap (trip wire)
Spear Trap (pressure plate)

Collectibles

Skill Book [Alteration]: The Lunar Lorkhan

Special Objects

Dwarven Armillary
Mineable ore (Moonstone) Ore
Area Is Locked (quest required)
Chests
Potions aplenty
Loose gear

This massive network of dwarven engineering has been carved into Eastmarch's eastern mountains. Its door remains securely locked until you acquire College of Winterhold Quest: Revealing the Unseen.

A Exit to Skyrim

1 Entry Corridor

There's little of note in this corridor, but beware of a dangerous trap that's triggered by a pressure plate. Dwarven Spiders lurk farther down the passage.

◊ Danger! Spear Trap (pressure plate)
◊ Potions

2 Treasure Room 1

Defeat more Dwarven Spiders, then pick an Adept-level door lock to access a northern treasure room that's guarded by a Dwarven Sphere.

◊ Chest
◊ Potion

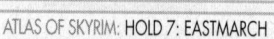

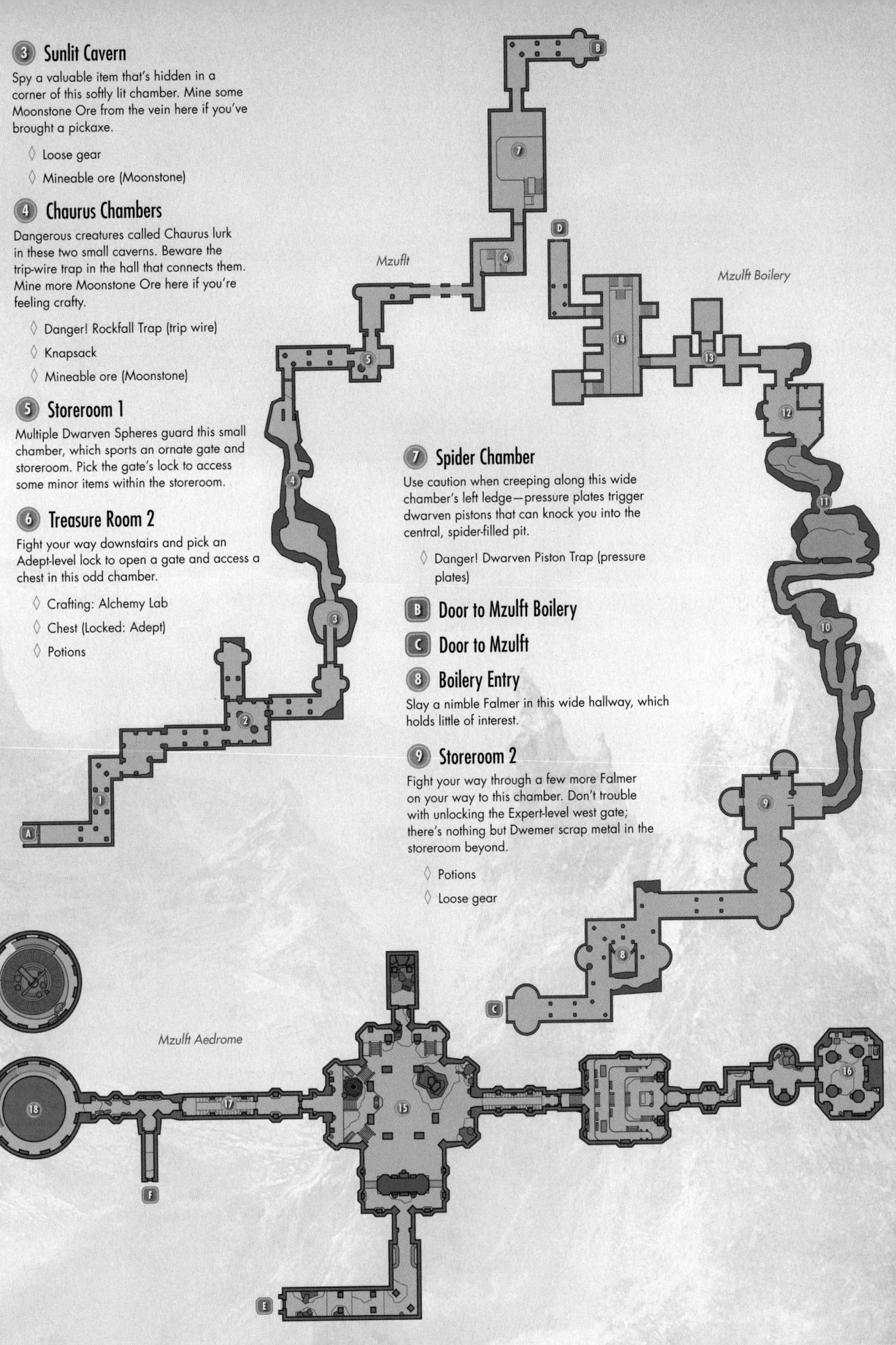

3 Sunlit Cavern

Spy a valuable item that's hidden in a corner of this softly lit chamber. Mine some Moonstone Ore from the vein here if you've brought a pickaxe.

- ◊ Loose gear
- ◊ Mineable ore (Moonstone)

4 Chaurus Chambers

Dangerous creatures called Chaurus lurk in these two small caverns. Beware the trip-wire trap in the hall that connects them. Mine more Moonstone Ore here if you're feeling crafty.

- ◊ Danger! Rockfall Trap (trip wire)
- ◊ Knapsack
- ◊ Mineable ore (Moonstone)

5 Storeroom 1

Multiple Dwarven Spheres guard this small chamber, which sports an ornate gate and storeroom. Pick the gate's lock to access some minor items within the storeroom.

6 Treasure Room 2

Fight your way downstairs and pick an Adept-level lock to open a gate and access a chest in this odd chamber.

- ◊ Crafting: Alchemy Lab
- ◊ Chest (Locked: Adept)
- ◊ Potions

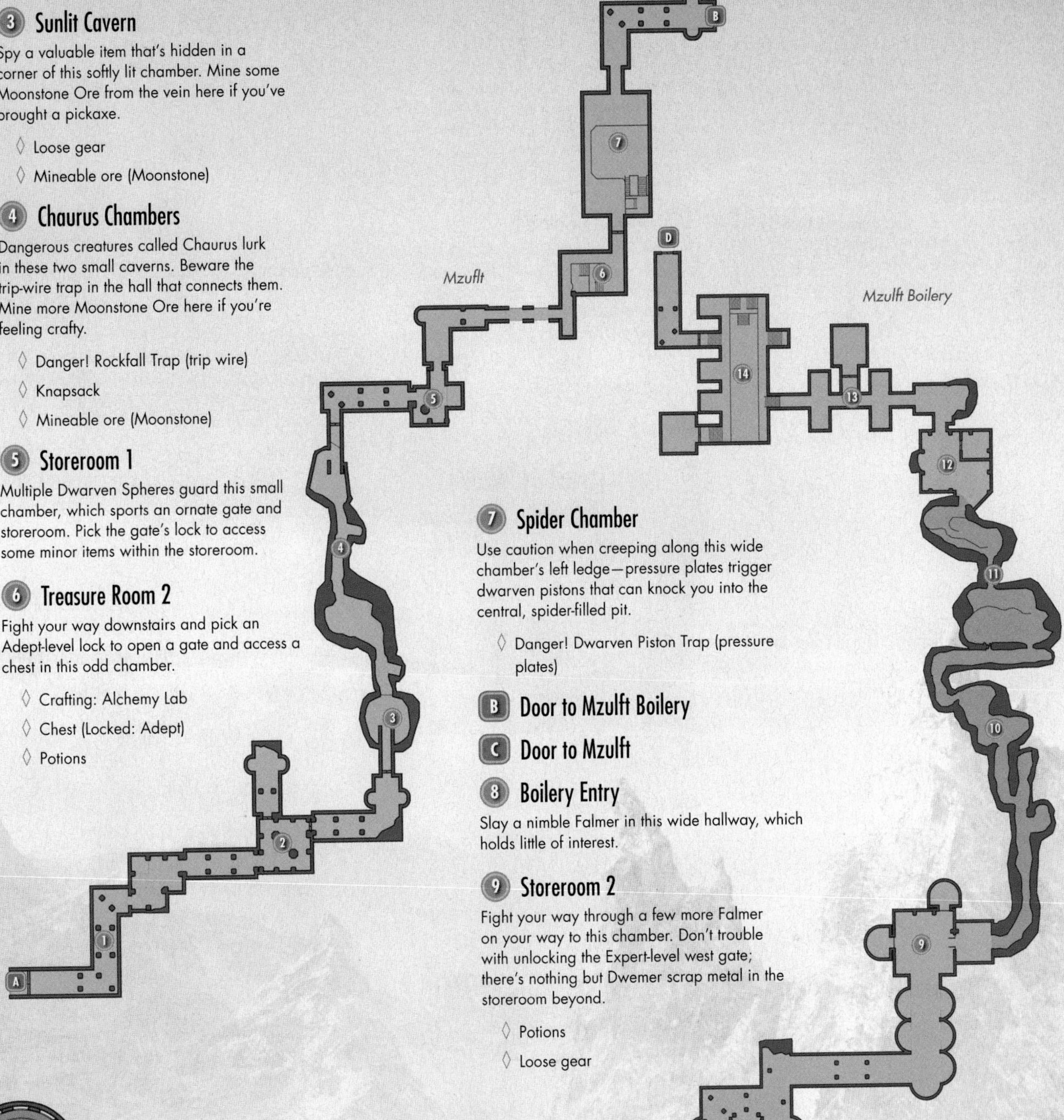

7 Spider Chamber

Use caution when creeping along this wide chamber's left ledge—pressure plates trigger dwarven pistons that can knock you into the central, spider-filled pit.

- ◊ Danger! Dwarven Piston Trap (pressure plates)

B Door to Mzulft Boilery

C Door to Mzulft

8 Boilery Entry

Slay a nimble Falmer in this wide hallway, which holds little of interest.

9 Storeroom 2

Fight your way through a few more Falmer on your way to this chamber. Don't trouble with unlocking the Expert-level west gate; there's nothing but Dwemer scrap metal in the storeroom beyond.

- ◊ Potions
- ◊ Loose gear

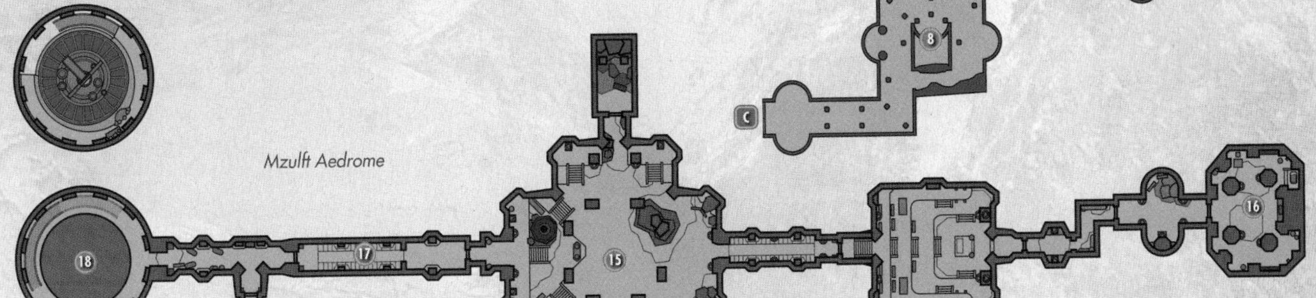

10 Earthen Passage

Don't overlook the odd-looking chests as you navigate this cavernous passage.

- Chests (2)
- Potion
- Loose gear

11 Iridescent Cavern

Harvest the many glowing mushrooms that lend an eerie light to these two caverns. Chaurus Eggs can be obtained by inspecting the various egg sacs as well.

- Chest
- Loose gear

12 Treasure Room 3

Pick the Expert-level door lock in this area to obtain an important key, along with treasure from a chest and a Skill Book.

- Skill Book [Alteration]: The Lunar Lorkhan
- Mzulft Room Key
- Chest

13 Treasure Room 4

Pick the Adept-level lock on the ornate door here to access a treasure room that's guarded by a Chaurus.

- Chest (Locked: Apprentice)
- Loose gear

14 Treasure Room 5

Beware: this large chamber's worthy treasures are guarded by multiple Falmer. Pick the Expert-level door in the southwest corner to access a small treasure room.

- Chest
- Chest (Locked: Novice)
- Potions aplenty

D Door to Mzulft Aedrome

E Door to Mzulft Boilery

15 Great Hall

This massive foyer is crawling with Falmer. Fight hard to secure the area, then pick the north door's Expert-level lock to access a treasure niche. The west door cannot be opened without the key you find inside a chest located in the eastern Cog Chamber. A Falmer Gloomlurker is carrying a Focusing Crystal, which is needed for location [18].

- Focusing Crystal
- Chests (3)

16 Cog Chamber

A lone Dwarven Sphere guards this far chamber. Open the chest and retrieve the Mzulft Observatory Key.

- Mzulft Observatory Key
- Chest
- Potions
- Loose gear

17 Locked Hall

You cannot access this hall without the Mzulft Observatory Key. The far door to [18] is locked as well—Paratus Deimius opens it when you retrieve the Focusing Crystal for him. The ruins' exit door is found here, accessed only after you complete the puzzle inside location [18]..

- Knapsack

18 Armillary Chamber

This large chamber houses a giant and mysterious dwarven mechanism. Paratus Decimius, and your knowledge of flame and frost spells, are the keys to solving this puzzle. Consult College of Winterhold Quest: Revealing the Unseen for the answers.

- Dwarven Armillary

F Exit to Skyrim

[DG.16] Mzulft: Dwarven Storeroom

Hold: Eastmarch

Related Quests

Side Quest: Lost to the Ages

Recommended Level: 16

Faction: Dwarven City
Katria

Miscellaneous
Loose gear

Search the nearby grounds for the Dwarven Storeroom and open the door. If you are on Side Quest: Lost to the Ages, Katria is waiting for you inside, wondering how best to break through the locked door. Otherwise, this is simply a small storage area.

You can unlock the gate [Expert] or locate the metal door to the right of it [Apprentice]. Open that and the second door [Apprentice] in the storage area beyond. Both allow you to reach the inner storeroom, which has a Glowing Crystal Shard (which you identify as an Aetherium Shard if you're on the quest). You can also claim a variety of dwarven items and scrap from this location, as well as several Dwarven Metal Ingots.

- Aetherium Shard [4/4]
- Loose gear

[7.26] Lost Knife Hideout

Recommended Level: 6

Dungeon: Bandit Camp
Animal
Bandit

Crafting
Grindstone
Cookpot

Dangers
Bone Alarm Trap
Rockfall Trap (trip wire)

Collectibles
Skill Book [Heavy Armor]: Orsinium and the Orcs
Skill Book [Two-Handed]: Words and Philosophy [E1/10]
Chest(s)
Potions
Loose gear

Bandits have set up a formidable hideout in this watery cavern. Make your way through Lost Knife Cave to reach the inner Lost Knife Hideout.

A Exit to Skyrim

1 Entry Tunnel

Kill the bandits at the end of the entry tunnel to obtain a key from one of their corpses.

- Lost Knife Cage Key (Bandit)
- Potions
- Loose gear

2 Watery Cavern

The cave's center is patrolled by more bandits, including archers that fire down from elevated walkways. A Skill Book sits on a table on the central wooden lookout.

- Danger! Bone Alarm Trap
- Skill Book [Two-Handed]: Words and Philosophy [E1/10]
- Loose gear

3 Waterfall Tunnel

Take a secret underwater passage, behind a waterfall, from [2] to reach a small tunnel with a treasure chest.

- Chest
- Loose gear

4 West Tunnel

This tunnel leads to the Lost Knife Hideout and features more bandits and a dangerous trip-wire trap. Scour the upstairs storeroom to find a chest.

- Danger! Rockfall Trap (trip wire)
- Chest
- Loose gear

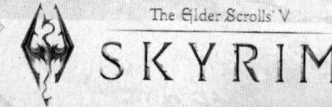

B Path to Lost Knife Hideout

C Path to Lost Knife Cave

5 Hideout Entry

Sneak your way past the talking bandits, then slip behind the far scaffolding to discover a hidden chest.

- Chest
- Potion

6 West Barracks

Beware: numerous bandits lurk in stone barracks to the west.

- Loose gear

7 West Corridors

Wipe out more bandits and claim more loot in these halls. Another Skill Book sits on a table atop the stairs here.

- Skill Book [Heavy Armor]: Orsinium and the Orcs
- Chest
- Potions
- Loose gear

8 Cage Chamber

Drop into the waterfall hole as you enter this area to discover a secret tunnel with a large, locked chest. The tunnel leads to several cages and a host of bandits. Open the cages with the key you found on the very first bandit—the same key can be found on another bandit here. Loot another large chest here as well.

- Danger! Bone Alarm Trap
- Crafting: Grindstone
- Lost Knife Cage Key (Bandit)
- Chests (2)
- Chest (Locked: Master)
- Potions
- Loose gear

D Path to Lost Knife Cave

E Path to Lost Knife Hideout

9 East Overlook

Dispatch a few more bandits and loot a chest on your way back through the cave after exiting the Lost Knife Hideout.

- Chest
- Potions
- Loose gear

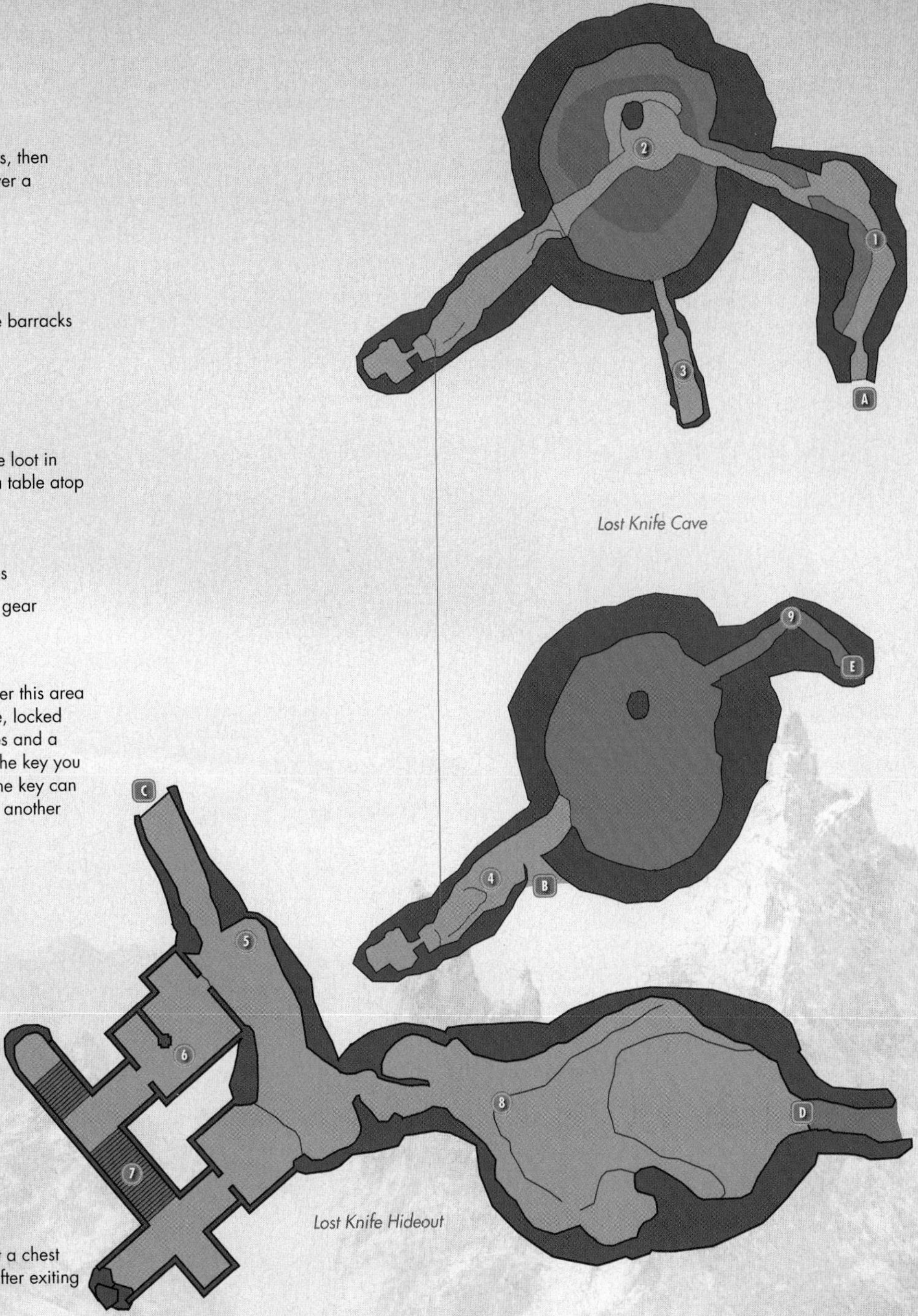

[7.27] Fort Amol

Related Quests

Civil War Quest: Reunification of Skyrim

Civil War Quest: The Battle for Fort Amol

Recommended Level: 6

Habitation: Military Fort

Mage (pre-Civil War)

Soldier (Imperial/Stormcloak, depending on the state of the Civil War)

Crafting

Alchemy Lab

Arcane Enchanter

Blacksmith Forge

Collectibles

Skill Book [Enchanting]: Catalogue of Armor Enchantments

Special Objects

Shrine of Julianos [5/5]

Chest(s)

Potions aplenty

Loose gear

This medium-sized fortress has been overrun by a group of hostile mages. Once the Civil War begins in earnest, the mages are driven out, and Fort Amol becomes a point of contention for Imperial and Stormcloak forces. A collapsed outer wall lets you infiltrate the fortress from the east.

Exterior

Secure the fort's exterior before exploring its small inner areas. A Shrine of Julianos rests on the Blacksmith Forge.

- Crafting: Alchemy Lab, Blacksmith Forge
- Shrine of Julianos [5/5]
- Chests (2)

Fort Amol (Interior)

Slay more mages and search every nook and cranny to find much more loot within Fort Amol's small interior. Don't miss the Skill Book on the shelf near the Arcane Enchanter.

- Crafting: Arcane Enchanter
- Skill Book [Enchanting]: Catalogue of Armor Enchantments
- Chest
- Chest (Locked: Adept)
- Potions aplenty
- Loose gear

Prison

Dispatch the mages in the prison's entry chamber, then loot the place.

- Potion

[7.28] Darkwater Pass

Related Quests

Miscellaneous Objective: Extracting an Argonian* (Derkeethus)

Recommended Level: 18

Dungeon: Falmer Hive

Animal
Derkeethus (Follower)
Falmer

Services

Follower: Derkeethus [38/47]

Dangers

Swinging Wall Trap (lever/trip wire)

Collectibles

Skill Book [Enchanting]: Catalogue of Weapon Enchantments
Chests
Potions

This watery pass runs through the Rift's northern mountains. An unfortunate Argonian named Derkeethus has become stuck in a sticky situation within...

> **NOTE** This walkthrough covers the pass as if you're heading from the bottom of the mountains and working your way up. However, it's also possible to enter from the top and work your way down.

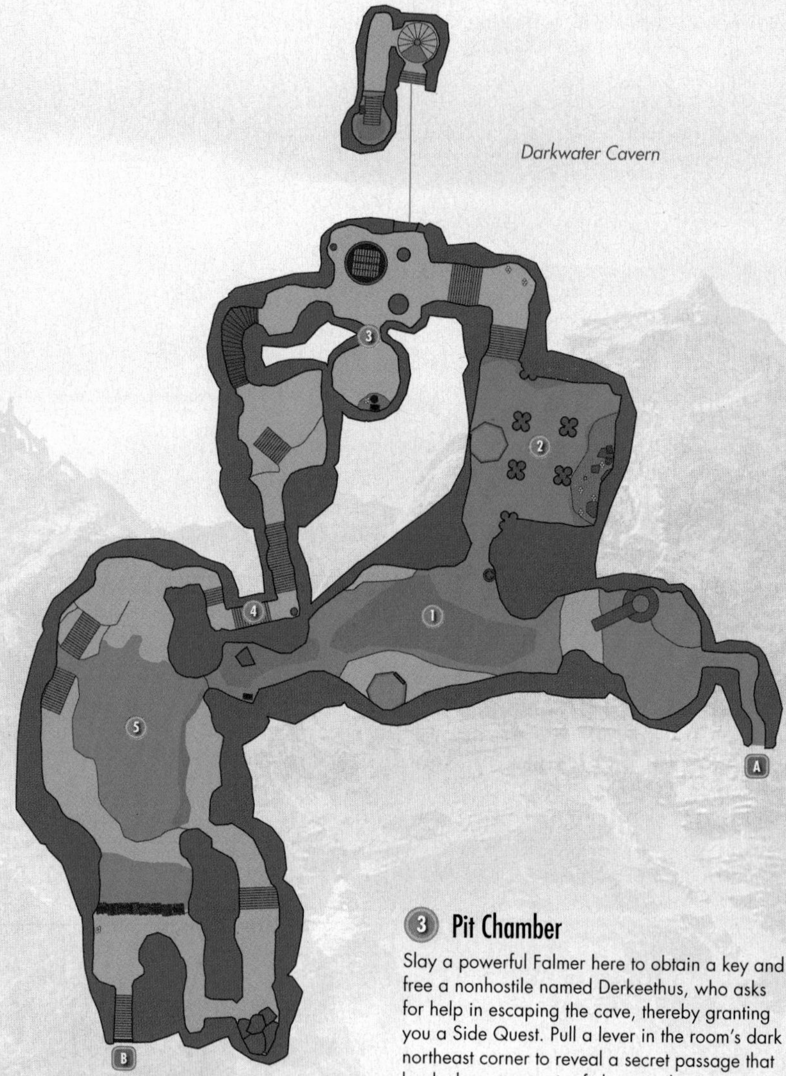

A Exit to Skyrim

1 Waterfall Cavern

Loot a chest and slay a few Falmer on your way to this first wide, watery cavern. Raid the Falmer chest by the far waterfall before proceeding into the north passage.

- Chests (2)

2 Chaurus Nest

Slay a number of Chaurus here, then search the east rubble to find more urns and another chest.

- Chest (Locked: Apprentice)

3 Pit Chamber

Slay a powerful Falmer here to obtain a key and free a nonhostile named Derkeethus, who asks for help in escaping the cave, thereby granting you a Side Quest. Pull a lever in the room's dark northeast corner to reveal a secret passage that leads down to a pair of chests in the watery pit below.

- Crafting: Arcane Enchanter
- Follower: Derkeethus [38/47]
- Skill Book [Enchanting]: Catalogue of Weapon Enchantments
- Darkwater Pit Key (Burial Urn)
- Shaman's Key (Falmer)
- Chests (3)
- Potion

④ Trapped Passage

Pull a lever to slay an unwary Falmer with a trap in this passage. Carefully deactivate the trip wire that also triggers the trap as you proceed to [5].

- Danger! Swinging Wall Trap (lever/trip wire)
- Potions

⑤ Rushing Rapids Cavern

Cut down multiple Falmer as you navigate this wide chamber. Scale the west ledges to locate a dark passage above the south waterfall, where you discover a chest. Climb the east ledges to reach a passage that leads back outside, but beware the trip wire that's stretched across the passage's entrance.

- Danger! Swinging Wall Trap (trip wire)
- Chest

Ⓑ Exit to Skyrim

[7.29] Snapleg Cave

Recommended Level: 14

Dungeon: Hagraven Lair

Animal
Hag
Witch

Crafting

Alchemy Lab
Arcane Enchanter

Dangers

Magic Caster Trap

Collectibles

Skill Book [Alteration]: Breathing Water
Chests
Potions
Loose gear

This medium-sized cave lies at the north base of the Rift's northern mountains and is home to vicious beasts and witches.

Ⓐ Exit to Skyrim

① Troll Cavern

Slay a few Skeevers in the cave's first tall chamber, then make your way to this wide cavern, where a few spell-slinging witches and a vicious predators lurk. Raid a chest inside a tent and find valuable loot in a box atop a rock; then take the south passage to [2], battling another troll along the way and snagging a Soul Gem from atop a pedestal to stop it from casting Ice Spikes at you.

- Danger! Magic Caster Trap
- Chest
- Potions
- Loose gear

② Giant Spider Lair

Dispatch a few Frostbite Spiders on your way to this web-covered cavern, where a Giant Frostbite Spider descends from the ceiling to feast.

- Chest

③ Hag's Cavern

Cut down a few more spiders on your way to this cavern, where a Hag lurks. Claim the Skill Book that rests on a barrel inside the tent here.

- Skill Book [Alteration]: Breathing Water
- Potions

④ Canal Cavern

Slay a vicious Hag and Hagraven in this cavern, which features a watery canal. If you release a Spriggan from its Apprentice-level holding cell here, it will battle these enemies for you. There's nothing of value underwater.

- Crafting: Arcane Enchanter

⑤ Loot Stash

Raid a giant chest as you navigate the cave's exit passage, making your way back to the first tall chamber.

- Crafting: Alchemy Lab
- Chest

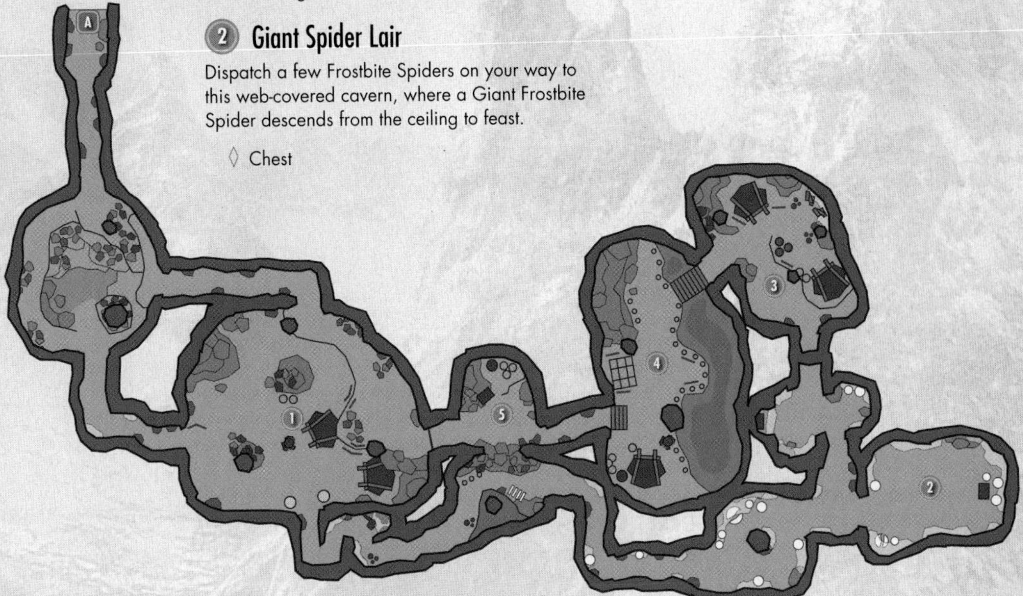

[7.30] Eldergleam Sanctuary

Related Quests

Temple Quest: The Blessings of Nature

Recommended Level: 8

Dungeon: Spriggan Grove

Asta
Sond
Spriggan

Collectible

Skill Book [Restoration]: Mystery of Talara, v2

This widemouthed cave is located within Eastmarch's southern territory. The interior of the cave consists primarily of one huge, sunlit cavern. Find a Skill Book leaning against a small pile of rocks near the path by the waterfall. A woman named Asta hints at a fearsome weapon being able to have some sort of effect on the roots of the cavern's great tree, the Eldergleam, which block the uphill path leading to the wondrous tree. You will return here with the necessary item during Temple Quest: Blessings of Nature.

[7.31] Darkwater Crossing

Related Quests

Favor (Activity): Mining Ore* (Verner Rock-Chucker)
Favor: Special Delivery* (Sonda Drenim)
Favor: The Bandit Slayer* (Annekke)

Habitation: Town

Annekke Crag-Jumper (Follower)
Derkeethus (Marriage Prospect)
Hrefna
Sondras Drenim (Marriage Prospect)
Stormcloak Soldier
Tormir
Verner Crag-Jumper

Crafting

Smelter

Services

Follower: Annekke Crag-Jumper [39/47]
Marriage Prospect: Derkeethus [50/62]
Marriage Prospect: Sondas Drenim [51/62]

Collectibles

Skill Book [Heavy Armor]: Chimarvamidium [B2/10]
Chest(s)
Loose gear
Minable ore (Corundum)

This picturesque town sits on either side of the wide, short waterfalls of the Darkwater River, at the southern border of Eastmarch. An ancient stone bridge spans the river—a remnant of an earlier age.

Exterior

Speak with an old miner named Sondas Drenim to gain a new Side Quest. If he isn't outside, then you'll find him in the nearby mine.

- Crafting: Smelter

Verner and Annekke's House

You must pick the lock of the farmhouse's door in order to gain entry, yet the place holds little worth stealing.

- Area Is Locked (Adept)
- Chest

Goldenrock Mine

The mine near Darkwater Passing is small, having been worked for only a few years by the locals. Grab a pickaxe and mine Corundum Ore from the veins that run along the mine's walls; then sell it to Verner Crag-Jumper, who gladly pays you for your efforts. A Skill Book rests atop a barrel at the end of the tunnel.

- Skill Book [Heavy Armor]: Chimarvamidium [B2/10]
- Loose gear
- Minable ore (Corundum)

[7.32] The Atronach Stone

Recommended Level: 6

Special Objects

Standing Stone: The Atronach Stone [8/13]

An ancient stone with peculiar markings stands on a small rise along the southern edge of Eastmarch. Touch the stone to gain the sign blessing of the Atronach. Those under the sign of the Atronach absorb Magicka from incoming spells and have a larger pool of Magicka, but they recover Magicka more slowly.

[7.33] Mistwatch

Related Quests

Dungeon Quest: Forgetting About Fjola*

Recommended Level: 6

Dungeon: Bandit Camp

Christer
Mistwatch Bandit
Bandit Leader (Fjola)

Quest Items

Fjola's Wedding Band

Crafting

Alchemy Lab

Collectibles

Skill Book [Heavy Armor]: Hallgerd's Tale
Unique Item: Fjola's Wedding Band [64/112]
Chests
Potions
Loose gear

This imposing stone fortress stands at the southern edge of Eastmarch, not far from the mountains along the Reach's north edge. A group of bandits have taken control of the fort and must be dealt with.

Exterior

Dispatch the handful of bandits who defend the fort's exterior, then pull a lever to lower the drawbridge and advance into the first of three interior towers.

North Tower

Speak with a man named Christer inside the tower to gain a new Side Quest and an important key that unlocks the nearby door. Make your way upstairs, then climb a ladder and use the key again to go outside. (Don't bother opening the upstairs holding cell—there's nothing of interest in the small room.)

- Mistwatch Key (Christer)
- Crafting: Alchemy Lab
- Chest
- Chest (Locked: Apprentice)
- Apothecary's Satchel
- Potions
- Loose gear

West Tower

Open a locked chest before entering the fort's second tower. More bandits await you inside, including one that's quite powerful. Fight your way upstairs and proceed through the high door.

- Chest
- Chest (Locked: Adept)
- Loose gear

[8.33] South Skybound Watch

Recommended Level: 6

Underground Connection: North Skybound Watch [8.34]

Chest (Locked: Novice)

This abandoned tower marks the southern entrance to Skybound Watch Pass, which runs through Falkreath's frosty eastern mountains. Navigate the pass to emerge at North Skybound Watch [8.34]. See that location's section for complete details on what awaits you within the pass.

Climb the tower to claim a chest and take in the amazing view of Falkreath to the west. When leaving, beware the Wispmother that haunts the woods just outside—you may find it easier to Fast-Travel away or return through the pass than to venture out along the cliffside.

[8.34] North Skybound Watch

Related Quests

College of Winterhold Radiant Quest: Destruction Ritual Spell

Dungeon: Bandit Camp

Animal

Bandit

Dangers

Battering Ram Trap (pressure plate)

Dart Trap (hinge trigger)

Underground Connection: South Skybound Watch [8.33]

Collectibles

Skill Book [Block]: Battle of Red Mountain [B1/10]

Chest(s)

Potions

Loose gear

An underground passage runs through Falkreath's frigid eastern mountains. This site, located north of Orphan Rock [8.35], marks the passage's north entrance, which is surrounded by ruins.

Exterior

Dispatch the bandits within the ruins, then open the wooden door behind them to exit onto the northern balcony. Take a moment to admire the view; if the weather is just right, you can even see the ocean in the distance. The pedestal here is the second of three you need for the College of Winterhold Radiant Quest: Destruction Ritual Spell.

Loot a chest to the left and swipe a Skill Book off the nearby shelf before descending some steps to locate the door that serves as the pass's northern entrance.

◊ Chest (Locked: Novice)

Skybound Watch Pass (Interior)

No matter which way you enter the pass, it's a straight sprint to the other end. Slaughter several bandits and a Giant Frostbite Spider as you navigate this relatively short passage, and beware the trapped chest at the tunnel's south end; disarm it or open it carefully to avoid the dart trap. Find another chest near the north campfire, along with a potion and Skill Book.

◊ Danger! Battering Ram Trap (pressure plate)

◊ Danger! Dart Trap (hinge trigger)

◊ Skill Book [Block]: Battle of Red Mountain [B1/10]

◊ Chest

◊ Potion

◊ Loose gear

[8.35] Orphan Rock

Related Quests

Temple Quest: The Blessings of Nature

Dungeon Activity

Dungeon: Hagraven Nest

Hag

Hagraven

Crafting

Arcane Enchanter

Dangers

Rune Trap (ground)

Spikes (ground)

Quest Items

Nettlebane (Hagraven)

Collectibles

Unique Weapon: Nettlebane [59/80]

Chest

Chest (Locked: Adept)

Loose gear

At the east edge of Falkreath, near the Throat of the World's [6.38] western base, a massive boulder towers over a mossy fallen log. Unless you're playing Temple Quest: Blessings of Nature, there's little to do here aside from looting a skeleton that lies inside the log. During the "Blessings of Nature" quest, beware of rune traps and sharp spikes placed around the boulder as you slay a few hags and a dangerous Hagraven to obtain a quest-related item—a fallen log now lets you reach the top of the boulder, where a chest and Arcane Enchanter are found. Loot a locked chest in one of the hags' surrounding tents as well.

[8.36] Falkreath Stormcloak Camp

Related Quests

Civil War Quest: Liberation of Skyrim

Civil War Quest: Rescue from Fort Neugrad

Habitation: Military: Stormcloak Camp

Stormcloak Quartermaster (Blacksmith)

Stormcloak Soldier

Services

Trader (Blacksmith): Stormcloak Quartermaster [27/33]

Weapons, Apparel, Misc

Crafting

Alchemy Lab

Anvil

Grindstone

Workbench

Special Objects

Civil War: Map of Skyrim

Chests (2)

Potions

Loose gear

The Sons of Skyrim have set up camp in the freezing eastern mountains of Falkreath, though this site may not exist, depending on your progress through the Civil War quest line. Trade with the quartermaster here if you like, or use his array of crafting stations. Inspect the tabletop map in the largest tent to potentially gain new map data. Steal goods from around the camp if your thieving skills are up to the task.

[8.37] Haemar's Shame

Related Quests

Daedric Quest: A Daedra's Best Friend

Recommended Level: 6

Dungeon: Vampire Lair

Animal

Vampire

Crafting

Alchemy Lab

Arcane Enchanter

Collectibles

Skill Book [Destruction]: Response to Bero's Speech [D2/10]

Unique Item: Masque of Clavicus Vile [79/112]

Chest(s)

Loose gear

This frozen cave lies at the eastern reaches of Falkreath. Traveling through it leads to Haemar's Shame—but you must contend with a number of vicious vampires in this forboding place. You visit this site during Daederic Quest: A Daedra's Best Friend.

Haemar's Cavern

Wipe out a vampire's thrall in the first cavern, then scale a ramp to discover a chest atop the wooden lookout. Avoid a lethal trap by sidestepping a pressure plate in the passage that follows, then slay a vampire and descend some wooden stairs. Battle several vampires in the following area, where you find another chest and an Alchemy Lab. Take a narrow passage to reach a wide cavern, where more vampires prowl. Find a Skill Book on a table in a nook surrounded by shelves, then descend more wooden stairs and proceed to Haemar's Shame.

- Crafting: Alchemy Lab
- Skill Book [Destruction]: Response to Bero's Speech [D2/10]
- Chests (2)
- Loose gear

Haemar's Shame

Squash a grotesque Frostbite Spider in the Shame's entry passage, then advance to a blood-soaked room with a chest and Arcane Enchanter. Navigate the winding passage that follows to reach a wide chamber with several lively vampires, including their powerful master. Clear the room, then check behind the large statue to find a giant chest. Pull a nearby wall chain to open an exit passage that leads outside.

- Crafting: Arcane Enchanter
- Chests (2)
- Loose gear

[8.38] Bonechill Passage

Dungeon: Animal Den

Animal

Underground Connection: Ancient's Ascent [8.39]

Collectibles:

Skill Book [Heavy Armor]: 2920, MidYear, v6

Knapsack

Potions

Loose gear

At the northern base of Falkreath's southern mountains, wide stone steps lead up to the mouth of a frozen cave. Enter to explore a short, icy passage that leads deeper into the mountains. This passage is the only means of reaching Ancient's Ascent [8.39]. Slay a few dangerous Ice Wraiths within Bonechill Passage, and collect the Skill Book that lies near a fallen bandit.

[8.39] Ancient's Ascent

Dungeon: Dragon Lair

Ice Wraith

Dragon (after Main Quest: Dragon Rising)

Special Objects

Word Wall: Animal Allegiance [2/3]

Chest

One must navigate through Bonechill Passage [8.38] to reach this remote site, which lies high among Falkreath's southern peaks. Dispatch gossamer Ice Wraiths as you ascend the snow-covered steps here, which lead up to an ancient Word Wall. After you complete the "Dragon Rising" quest, a great dragon will make its home here. Slay the beast and obtain your new Word of Power.

[8.40] Bloodlet Throne

Recommended Level: 6

Dungeon: Vampire Lair

Animal

Vampire

Crafting

Alchemy Lab

Arcane Enchanter

Dangers

Flamethrower Traps (pressure plate)

Oil Lamp Traps

Oil Pool Traps

Collectibles

Skill Book [Illusion]: Incident at Necrom [C2/10]

Chests

Potions aplenty

Loose gear

This ominous fortress stands at the edge of Skyrim, deep within Falkreath's southern mountains.

Exterior

Before heading inside, circle around the structure and explore the broken tower on its roof to discover a chest.

- Chest
- Loose gear

Entry Chambers

Avoid a pressure plate in the small entry chamber and progress until you reach a large chamber with a vampire and thrall. Knock down the hanging lamps here to ignite the oil on the floor and sear these foes. Go downstairs afterward and slay another vampire in the following chamber, which features several potions and an Arcane Enchanter.

- Danger! Flamethrower Traps (pressure plate), Oil Lamp Traps, Oil Pool Traps
- Apothecary's Satchel
- Potions

Rope Bridge Cavern

Proceed through a snowy passage to reach a sizable snowy cavern with a rope bridge. Dispatch the vampires and thralls here, then scale the north stairs and take a passage to reach the vampires' sleeping quarters.

- Crafting: Arcane Enchanter

Sleeping Area

A large pack of vampires and thralls reside in their sleeping quarters, which are located north of the rope bridge cavern. Slaughter them all to secure a chest, several potions, and an Alchemy

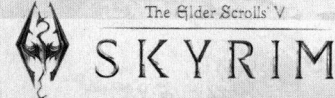

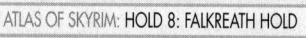

Lab. For a bit more sport, release a wolf from its cage here by picking the cage's Adept-level lock. Open another Adept-level gate in this area to access a storage room with several potions and a Skill Book. When you've finished looting the area, proceed across the rope bridge and pull a wall chain to open the gate you encounter.

- Crafting: Alchemy Lab
- Skill Book [Illusion]: Incident at Necrom [C2/10]
- Chests (2)
- Potions aplenty

Wolf Pit

Cross the Rope Bridge Cavern's hanging bridge and open a gate to enter a wide cavern filled with corpses. A nefarious Master Vampire sits on high and taunts you before releasing a few wolves. Slay the beasts and then pull the chain on the west wall to escape your predicament. Defeat the Master Vampire and then loot a large chest as you make your way south, unbarring a door and heading through to return to find yourself back at the entry chambers.

[8.41] Greywater Grotto

Dungeon: Animal Den

Animal

Collectibles

Chest

Loose gear

Bones and bloodstains litter the ground at the mouth of this frozen cave, which lies just south of Helgen [8.32]. Beware the dangerous Snowy Saber Cat that prowls outside—you'll face another inside the cave, along with several wolves and Ice Wolves. Loot the corpses of slain bandits and raid the chest at the cave's far end.

[8.42] Fort Neugrad

Related Quests

Civil War Quest: Liberation of Skyrim

Civil War Quest: Rescue from Fort Neugrad

Side Quest: The Great Skyrim Treasure Hunt*

Recommended Level: 6

Habitation: Military Fort

Bandit (pre-Civil War)

Soldier (Imperial/Stormcloak, depending on the state of the Civil War)

Crafting

Anvil

Forge

Workbench

Dangers

Bear Traps

Collectibles

Skill Book [Light Armor]: Jornibret's Last Dance [B1/10]

Treasure Map (Fort Neugrad Treasure Map): [10/11]

Chest(s)

Potions

Loose gear

This sizable stronghold stands among Falkreath's frigid southern mountains, close to the main road. This fort is a point of contention for the Imperials and Stormcloaks during the Civil War and is filled with ruthless bandits when the Civil War is not active. Attack the fort from the front like a warrior, or sneak around to discover a small gap in the north stockade wall to slip inside. You may also want to take a dip in the southeast lake, where you can find an underwater cave that leads into the prison.

Exterior

Loot the locked chest near the north wooden wall and use some crafting stations before entering the keep's interior or the prison. There's also a treasure chest on the roof of the main tower, though you must pass through the keep to reach it. This chest contains a Treasure Map.

- Crafting: Anvil, Forge, Workbench
- Treasure Map (Fort Neugrad Treasure Map): [10/11]
- Chest (Locked: Novice)
- Chest (Locked: Apprentice)
- Loose gear

Fort Neugrad Keep

There's only one way inside the Keep, and that's through the main door. Cut down the guards in the entry chamber, then enter either the east or west door and make your way upstairs. Secure the entry chamber's balcony, then go through the southeast door to face the bandits' leader, who carries a useful key and informative journal. Loot the giant chest in the chief's room and claim the nearby Skill Book, then return to the entry chamber and use his key to unlock the door to the library. Downstairs, deal with a powerful Bandit Mage, then claim a second giant chest. Finish exploring the fort to claim more loot, then take the ladder in the second-floor armory to reach a locked chest on the roof.

- Skill Book [Light Armor]: Jornibret's Last Dance [B1/10]
- Fort Neugrad Library Key (Bandit Chief)
- Chests (2)
- Potions
- Loose gear

Fort Neugrad Prison

If you're sneaking in through the prison, beware the bear trap at the end of the entry tunnel. More bandits lurk in the prison—loot a chest in an upstairs side room, along with a locked chest in the basement that's tucked behind a shelf with potions and a satchel.

- Danger! Bear Traps
- Chest
- Chest (Locked: Apprentice)
- Satchel
- Potions
- Loose gear

[8.43] Southfringe Sanctum

Related Quests

Dungeon Quest: The Savior of Selveni Nethri*

Recommended Level: 6

Dungeon: Special

Animal

Bashnag

Pumpkin

Selveni Nethri

Spellsword

Crafting

Alchemy Lab

Arcane Enchanter

Dangers

Rune Trap (gate)

Collectibles

Chests

Potions

Loose gear

This aptly named cave lies deep in Falkreath's southern mountains, on the fringe of Skyrim. A poor soul named Selveni Nethri has gotten herself into quite a sticky situation here...

Exterior

Slay a Spellsword to secure the cave's entrance. If you like, use the nearby Alchemy Lab to mix up some potions before entering the cave.

- Crafting: Alchemy Lab
- Apothecary's Satchel

Southfringe Sanctum (Interior)

Loot a chest that's hidden among growth as you navigate the cave's first passage. Beware the rune trap on the wooden gate that leads to the main, sunlit cavern. You now have a choice: either head uphill and slay more Spellswords or take a low, web-filled passage that's teeming with Frostbite Spiders (see the sections that follow). Both options lead toward the same destination: the cave's far end, where a nefarious mage named Bashnag awaits.

- Danger! Rune Trap (gate)
- Chest

Uphill Ascent

Dispatch several additional Spellswords as you scale the entry chamber's snowy slopes. If you like, release the caged fox named Pumpkin that you encounter after a short distance. Continue uphill, unlocking a wooden gate on your way to the cave's far end, where Bashnag awaits.

◊ Crafting: Arcane Enchanter

Spider Tunnel

As you might expect, the web-filled passage that stems from the sunlit entry cavern is filled with Frostbite Spiders. Loot a chest that's nestled near the wall as you go. After slaying a Giant Frostbite Spider, search the nearby nook to locate a poor soul named Selveni Nethri, who's stuck in a web. Carefully attack the web to free Selveni without harming him, then speak with Selveni to gain a new Objective that involves clearing the cave so that he can safely escape on his own. Tell Selveni to wait for now, and continue along to battle Bashnag.

◊ Chest

Bashnag's Chamber

Slay a cruel mage named Bashnag at the cave's far end, then raid the nearby chest and ensure that the entire cave is clear of hostiles before returning to Selveni and telling him that it's safe to leave. Follow Selveni out of the cave to ensure her survival and complete the quest.

◊ Chest

SECONDARY LOCATIONS

[8.A] Dragon Mound: Bilegulch Ridge

Related Quest: Main Quest: Alduin's Wall

This Dragon Mound is initially sealed. It opens during Main Quest: Alduin's Wall. If you visit during or after this point in the Main Quest, the mound will be open and empty.

[8.B] Toadstool Ring: Bilegulch Ridge

Whether you're collecting Bleeding Crown, Namira's Rot, or White Cap, there's an abundance of fungi in a strange ring—a perfect place to gather toadstool ingredients for your alchemy.

[8.C] Hunter's Camp: Sunderstone Gorge

A lone hunter with a slain elk is usually sitting by the fire or hunting the general location of the pathway close to Sunderstone Gorge. The hunter has a chest to steal from, but little else.

◊ Chest

[8.D] A Peddler's Misfortune

A peddler lies dead next to the remains of his overturned cart; his horse is just down the road. It looks like some bandits set an ambush here; the cart is stripped clean, though some bear traps still lie in the road.

◊ Danger! Bear Traps

[8.E] Toppled Tower: Knifepoint Woods

In the shallow grass valley to the north of Knifepoint Ridge are the remains of a small tower, tumbled to the ground years ago. It is now the den for some wild animals. Defeat them before they maul you.

[8.F] Burning Caravan: Evergreen Grove

Due west of Evergreen Grove, the aftermath of a dragon attack reveals two dead horses, burned corpses, and a smoldering caravan. Check the wagon to pry open a chest.

◊ Chest

[8.G] Shrine of Akatosh: Twilight Valley

On the rocky promontory above the entrance to the Twilight Sepulcher is a ceremonial ledge jutting out to a precarious edge, where the Shrine to Akatosh, a Skill Book, and some offerings can be found. Take what you need, receiving blessings if you wish.

◊ Skill Book [Enchanting]: A Tragedy in Black

◊ Shrine of Akatosh [6/6]

[8.H] Fisherman's Camp: Lake Ilinalta

A Fisherman is sitting on some stones close to his tent and boat, surveying the northwestern corner of Lake Ilinalta. Steal from his knapsack if you wish, and find a Skill Book lying on the ground inside the tent. Watch for Slaughterfish in the water.

◊ Skill Book [One-Handed]: Fire and Darkness

◊ Knapsack

[8.I] Sunken Fishing Boat: Lake Ilinalta

Swim southeast from the Fisherman's Camp, peering underwater at the first clump of rocks on the lake bed that you see. Hidden among the weeds is a sunken fishing boat with a locked chest inside.

- Chest (Locked: Adept)

[8.J] Dark Elf's Grave

A pauper's Nordic burial ground—a set of rocks and stones with a fluttering flag in the glade northwest of Half-Moon Mill—has the slumped corpse of a Dark Elf at its base. Steal the nearby purse and dagger if you wish.

[8.K] Alchemist's Camp: Evergreen Woods

On the higher ground above Evergreen Grove near a small waterfall is a deserted Alchemist's Camp. Check the Skill Book and read the journal; it gives clues to the whereabouts of the Alchemist: Follow the stream down to a pool where you'll find his corpse, a second Skill Book, and two Spriggans.

- Skill Book [Alchemy]: De Rerum Dirennis
- Skill Book [Alchemy]: Mannimarco, King of Worms
- Alchemist's Journal
- Apothecary's Satchel

[8.L] Dragon Mound: Evergreen Woods

Related Quest: Main Quest: Alduin's Wall

This Dragon Mound is initially sealed. It opens during Main Quest: Alduin's Wall. If you visit during or after this point in the Main Quest, the dragon will still be circling the area. Kill! Rend! Destroy!

[8.M] Sacrificial Altar: Evergreen Woods

Necromantic activity is to be expected as you close in on this altar surrounded by standing stones, south of Evergreen Grove. Kill any animated corpses if you must, but their controllers are your primary targets. Don't forget to read the Skill Book on the altar.

- Skill Book [Conjuration]: 2920, Frostfall, v10
- Apothecary's Satchel
- Potions

[8.N] Bear Cave: Halldir's Cairn

On the rocky slopes northwest of Halldir's Cairn is an alcove where two bears are on the prowl. Defeat them and inspect the dead hunter they've brought back to feast on.

[8.O] The Silvermoon: Lake Ilinalta

A sunken trading vessel named *Silvermoon* has been resting at the bottom of Lake Ilinalta for as long as the inhabitants of Riverwood can remember. Dive down where the mast is jutting out of the water. Among the clams and Nordic barnacle clusters is a chest that's still intact.

- Chest
- Loose gear

[8.P] Nordic Burial Grove

At the fork in the main road, close to the shore of Lake Ilinalta, is a pauper's burial stone with six graves surrounded by Nightshade plants. Two skeletons are guarding these unknown graves.

[8.Q] Fisherman's Island: Lake Ilinalta

Directly south of South Brittleshin Pass on the opposite (south) side of the lake is a small island with a fisherman's camp. Expect a boat, a tent, and some drying fish, as well as the fisherman, usually resting near the indigenous flowers.

- Knapsack

[8.R] Sunken Barrow: Lake Ilinalta

Southeast of South Brittleshin Pass on the lake's northern shore are three moss-covered standing stones that just break the lake's surface. Dive down, and you'll discover that they surround a submerged barrow with a chest at the bottom.

- Chest
- Loose gear

[8.S] The Indigestible Emerald

Southeast of Anise's Cabin, on a narrow grassy alcove among the rocky banks of White River, close to a single pine tree, lie the skeletal remains of an elk. It died with an extremely valuable Emerald, which can be picked from behind its rib cage.

[8.T] Riverwood Folly

Perched on the snowy rocks below and east of Bleak Falls Barrow is a dark stone folly, home to a small group of bandits. Access the area via the path from Riverwood or the steps from the north bank of the river. Head to the top for an amazing view and a chest.

- Chest
- Mineable ore (Iron)

[8.U] Wild Animal Den: Pinewatch Outcropping

Below a rocky outcrop facing the main road and lake, northwest of Pinewatch, is a wild animal den. Defeat the creatures and then inspect the den itself. Among the skeletal remains is a disintegrated old cart with a locked chest.

- Chest (Locked: Novice)

[8.V] The Conjurer's Altar: Lake Ilinalta

A strange mist shrouds this small cluster of standing stones and an altar within. Face down a mage and his familial forces before inspecting the Skill Book on the altar. Travel a handful of paces to the southwest to discover a woodsman who met his end felling trees. His trusty axe is the only of its kind.

- Skill Book [Conjuration]: 2920, Hearth Fire, v9
- Unique Weapon: The Woodsman's Friend [60/80]

[8.W] Hunter's Camp: The Guardian Stones

Follow the short path to the river's edge from the Guardian Stones, and you'll spot a hunter near a boat, tent, and campfire who's been hunting and fishing these parts for years. You may elect to steal from the locked chest.

- Chest (Locked: Novice)
- Mineable ore (Iron)

[8.X] Bandit Camp: Ilinalta Foothills

Side Quest: The Great Skyrim Treasure Hunt*

Along the winding road southwest of the Helgen Cave, due south of the Guardian Stones, a short trail leads up the hill to a small bandit camp. Expect attacks from three of these foes, a group of tents with some scattered food, and the following crafting locations and items:

- Crafting: Tanning Rack
- Skill Book [One-Handed]: Night Falls on Sentinel [D2/10]
- Treasure Map I [11/11]
- Satchel

[8.Y] Shrine of Talos: Ilinalta Foothills

Up a short path off the main road that winds down to the lake is a rocky promontory, upon which stands a statue of Talos. Three worshippers have been recently murdered by a Thalmor agent, who also lies dead here, with orders signed by Elenwen.

- Shrine of Talos [15/17]
- Note: Thalmor Orders
- Loose gear

[8.Z] Bandit Camp: Skybound Underhang

Follow the rough path across the snowy foothills toward Riverwood, and take the small switchback to reach a wooden platform with a bandit camp. Face down two foes, and rummage around for a few coins and the following:

- Skill Book [Block]: Warrior
- Chest

[8.AA] Bandit Bridge: Pinewatch

A little farther southwest along the main road from Pinewatch, two bandits stand atop a rickety wooden bridge, attacking you as you approach. Try to pass under the bridge, and they both release falling rocks; it is better to sneak from the east side along the second bridge, or drop them from range with spells or arrows.

- Danger! Rockfall Trap
- Loose gear

[8.AB] Bandit Camp: Pinewatch Heights

A group of bandits has killed a Dark Elf and taken over his camp. Now they come for you! Retaliate, and then search the small tent for a Skill Book.

- Crafting: Tanning Rack
- Skill Book [Alteration]: The Lunar Lorkhan

[8.AC] Hunter's Camp: Upper Pinewatch Ridge

Farther along the winding path, up into the snow, lies a windswept promontory with a hunter you can barter with. He has a few items that he's caught or skinned for sale.

- Trader (Food Vendor): Hunter [9/13]
  - Food, Misc
- Chest

[8.AD] Prospector's Shack: Bonechill Ridge

What appears to be a small prospector's shack is in fact the scene of gruesome carnage; two burned corpses bear witness to a recent dragon attack. Check inside the shack for a necklace and a note, which reveals the location of Ancient's Ascent.

- Note: Letter to Authorities
- Chest

[8.AE] Bandit Camp: Helgen Cliffs

On the main road west of Helgen is an overhang protecting what appears to be an empty campsite. Among the dead animals, there are a few loose items to steal, a Skill Book, and a locked chest. But be warned: touch the chest, and the bandits who dwell here will ambush you from behind! Watch for a few bear traps in the surrounding foliage.

- Danger! Bear Trap
- Skill Book [Light Armor]: The Refugees
- Chest (Novice)

[8.AF] The Mauled Refugees

Related Quest: Main Quest: Dragon Rising

Once you complete Main Quest: Dragon Rising, this rocky promontory just below and northwest of Helgen becomes a small camp with two dead refugees, a wolf to defeat, and a whole lot of spilled blood.

[8.AG] Khajiit Caravan Massacre

Five Khajiit caravaneers have been murdered on the steep snowy road just south of Orphan Rock. As you approach the fallen tree blocking the path, three or four bandits attack; beware of the bowmen! Massacre them, then gather any loose gear you wish (check the lead wagon). Note that if the Falkreath Stormcloak Camp [8.36] is present, the Stormcloaks have cleared the bandits from the road.

- Skill Book [Speech]: The Buying Game
- Chest
- Loose gear

[8.AH] Wild Animal Den: Orphan's Tear

Not far from the site of the Falkreath Stormcloak Camp [8.36] is an overhang where two snarling woodland predators (usually wolves) make their den. Their meals include a Nord corpse to loot for items. If the camp is present, the soldiers have driven the animals away, though you can still loot the den for any other loose items.

[6.AI] Dragon Mound: Bloodlet Peaks

Related Quest: Main Quest: Alduin's Wall

This Dragon Mound is initially sealed. It opens during Main Quest: Alduin's Wall. If you visit during or after this point in the Main Quest, the mound will be open and empty.

[8.AJ] The Headless Skeleton

North of the Southfringe Sanctum on the freezing rocky slopes is a pine tree overlooking Fort Neugrad. Someone has executed a long-dead Nord with an axe. The headless skeleton is slumped near a chest and Skill Book.

- Skill Book [Conjuration]: The Warrior's Charge
- Chest
- Loose gear

ADDITIONAL LOCATIONS

[DG.03] Ancestors Glade

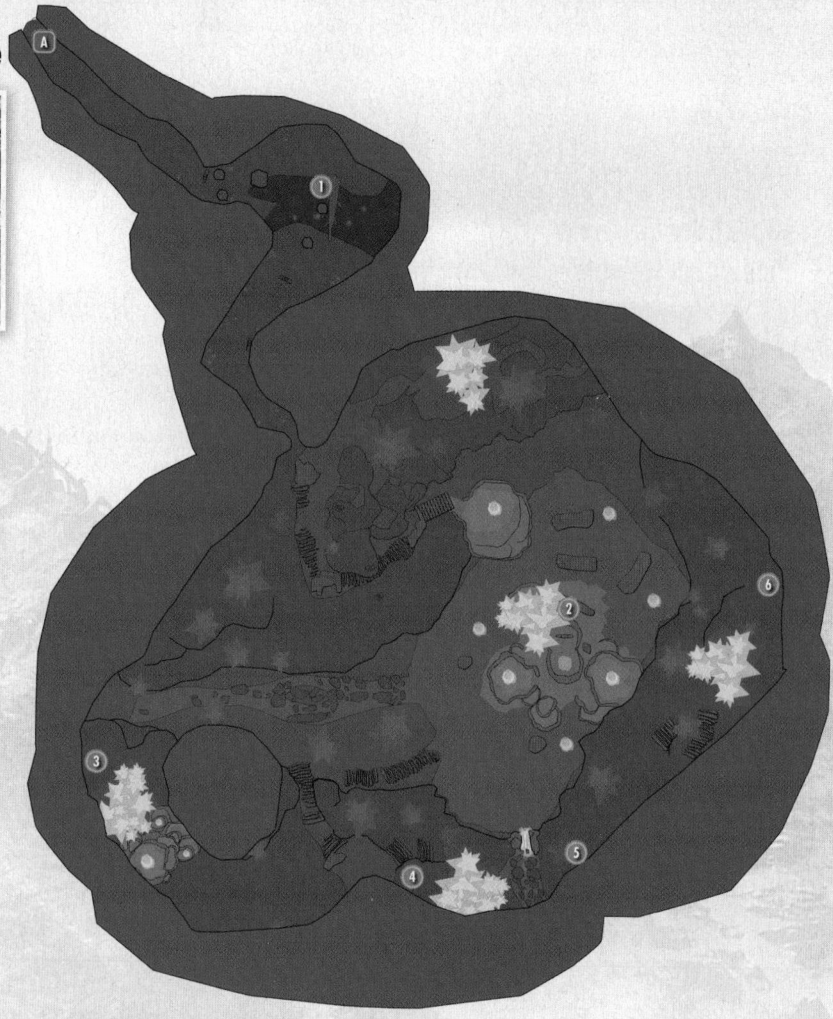

Related Quests

Dawnguard Main Quest: Unseen Visions

Recommended Level: 8

Faction: Spriggan Grove

Spriggan

Armored Troll
Dawnguard Agent

Vampire
Vampire Thrall

Miscellaneous

Area is Locked
Loose Gear

Exterior

Near a slit in the mountainside and a stone route marker, close to the windswept promontory of the Hunter's Camp, is the entrance to the Ancestor Glade. It is open regardless of whether the Dawnguard Main Quest is active.

Interior

A Exit to Skyrim

This is the entrance and exit to this area.

1 Spriggan Rockery

A narrow and plant-filled entrance greets you. If the quest for this area, Unseen Visions, isn't active, expect some sizable Spriggans to attempt to halt your progress. Cross the fallen tree trunk to head deeper toward the glade.

2 Glade Henge and Moth Priest Pedestal

There is a winding pathway throughout this glade to follow. Fluttering throughout are Ancestor Moths (which are harmless and not attracted to you unless the quest is active). Dotted about are Canticle Trees (with pink blossom) and special bark to remove if you have the Draw Knife (available from the pedestal only during the quest). The henges and pedestal serve an important role in the quest, as you read the Elder Scrolls here. Beware of your rivals; on your way out (during the quest only), there's a contingent of foes to face.

- Canticle Bark (quest only)
- Draw Knife (quest only)

3 Ancestral Offering

A leveled weapon is perched on the rocks here.

◊ Loose gear

4 Ancestral Offering

A leveled item and a gem are left on a carefully placed pile of rocks on the perimeter wall.

◊ Loose gear

5 Ancestral Offering

A few coins, an amulet, and a gem are left below a Soul Gem, against a carefully placed pile of rocks on the perimeter rock wall.

6 Ancestral Offering

A leveled weapon is perched on the rocks here.

◊ Loose gear

[HF.07] Lakeview Manor

Related Quests

Thane Task: Thane of Falkreath
Hearthfire Task: Adoption
Hearthfire Task: Build Your Own House

Services

Carriage Driver

Special Area

Shrine of Akatosh [HF3/3]
Shrine of Arkay [HF3/3]
Shrine of Dibella [HF3/3]
Shrine of Julianos [HF3/3]
Shrine of Kynareth [HF3/3]
Shrine of Mara [HF3/3]
Shrine of Stendarr [HF3/3]
Shrine of Talos [HF3/3]
Shrine of Zenithar [HF3/3]

Crafting

Alchemy Lab
Anvil or Blacksmith Forge
Arcane Enchanter
Carpenter's Workbench
Cooking Pot or Spit
Drafting Table
Grindstone
Oven
Smelter
Tanning Rack
Wood Chopping Block
Workbench

Miscellaneous

Area is locked
Chest
Potions aplenty
Loose gear

Perched between the Shriekwind Hills is this bright and sunny woodland glade. With ample clay and stone deposits, a good amount of iron ore to mine, and a bounty of woodland animals to kill and skin, this place is a huntsman's paradise! Overlooking Lake Ilinalta, and only a short romp from both Falkreath and Riverwood, this is a prime spot to make yourself at home. Note this picture is but an example of the type of property you could build here. This is the only buildable dwelling with an apiary.

◊ Follower: Rayya (Housecarl) [DG3/3]

◊ Land for Sale [3/3]

◊ Marriage Prospect: Rayya [DG3/3]

HOLD 9: THE RIFT

TOPOGRAPHICAL OVERVIEW

Nestled in the Autumnal Forest, high above the volcanic Tundra known as Eastmarch and bordering Cyrodill to the south and Morrowind to the east, is the prosperous and magical Hold known as the Rift. This is one of the four "old Holds" mentioned in history, and the majority of the Rift's population live and work around the lake port of Riften. The large forest of deciduous birch trees, interspersed with pine and smoother rocks (the result of a gigantic prehistoric glacial movement northward) makes the Rift habitable year-round; indeed, many Nords make their living on and around Lake Honrich. Two small towns lie within the Hold's borders: Shor's Stone, which is a small mining village north of Riften, and Ivarstead, which lies to the west, at the base of the towering Throat of the World.

Routes and Pathways

The Great Riften Road descends from the rugged mountain border with Falkreath to the west and winds east along the southern banks of the Treva River and Lake Honrich to Riften itself. Spurs from this road stretch north, connecting Riften to Ivarstead and Shor's Stone and beyond, descending the nearly sheer cliffs that form the border between the Rift and Eastmarch. To the east are the gates to Cyrodiil, which are currently sealed. Along the eastern edge of the Hold lie the Velothi Mountains, with a number of caves and secret retreats. The peak towering above Riften to the southeast is home to Forelhost, an ancient and vast Nordic temple. To the west are the steep and treacherous mountains that connect the Rift to Falkreath, and the town of Ivarstead where pilgrims begin their journey up the 7,000 steps that lead to High Hrothgar, high on the steep slopes of the gigantic Throat of the World. Delve into the Autumnal Forest of the Rift, and you'll find water mills, farms, and other more unspeakable places.

AVAILABLE SERVICES, CRAFTING, AND COLLECTIBLES

Services

- Followers: [7/47]
- Houses for Sale: [1/5]
- Marriage Prospects: [11/62]
- Skill Trainers: [6/50]
  - Alchemy: [0/3]
  - Alteration: [0/3]
  - Archery: [1/3]
  - Block: [0/2]
  - Conjuration: [0/3]
  - Destruction: [0/3]
  - Enchanting: [0/2]
  - Heavy Armor: [0/3]
  - Illusion: [1/2]
  - Light Armor: [0/3]
  - Lockpicking: [1/2]
  - One-Handed: [0/3]
  - Pickpocket: [1/3]
  - Restoration: [0/3]
  - Smithing: [1/3]
  - Sneak: [1/3]
  - Speech: [0/4]
  - Two-Handed: [0/2]
- Traders [24/133]:
  - Apothecary [2/12]
  - Bartender [3/5]
  - Blacksmith [6/33]
  - Carriage Driver [1/5]
  - Fence [1/10]
  - Fletcher [1/3]
  - Food Vendor [1/9]
  - General Goods [4/19]
  - Innkeeper [2/15]
  - Jeweler [1/2]
  - Special [0/3]
  - Spell Vendor [1/12]
  - Stablemaster [1/5]

Collectibles

- Captured Critters: [2/5]
- Dragon Claws: [2/10]
- Dragon Priest Masks: [1/10]
- Larceny Targets: [2/7]
- Skill Books: [23/180]
  - Alchemy: [0/10]
  - Alteration: [1/10]
  - Archery: [1/10]
  - Block: [1/10]
  - Conjuration: [0/10]
  - Destruction: [0/10]
  - Enchanting: [1/10]
  - Heavy Armor: [1/10]
  - Illusion: [2/10]
  - Light Armor: [1/10]
  - Lockpicking: [4/10]
  - One-Handed: [2/10]
  - Pickpocket: [3/10]
  - Restoration: [2/10]
  - Smithing: [1/10]
  - Sneak: [1/10]
  - Speech: [1/10]
  - Two-Handed: [1/10]
- Treasure Maps: [0/11]
- Unique Items: [24/112]
- Unique Weapons: [1/11]
- Unusual Gems: [2/24]

Special Objects

- Shrines: [9/69]
  - Akatosh: [0/6]
  - Arkay: [1/12]
  - Dibella: [1/8]
  - Julianos: [0/5]
  - Kynareth: [1/6]
  - Mara: [1/5]
  - Stendarr: [2/5]
  - Talos: [2/17]
  - Zenithar: [1/5]
- Standing Stones: [1/13]
  - The Shadow Stone
- Word Walls: [6/42]
  - Animal Allegiance: [1/3]
  - Aura Whisper: [1/3]
  - Become Ethereal: [0/3]
  - Disarm: [0/3]
  - Dismaying Shout: [1/3]
  - Elemental Fury: [0/3]
  - Fire Breath: [0/2]
  - Frost Breath: [0/3]
  - Ice Form: [0/3]
  - Kyne's Peace: [1/3]
  - Marked for Death: [1/3]
  - Slow Time: [0/3]
  - Storm Call: [1/3]
  - Throw Voice: [0/1]
  - Unrelenting Force: [0/1]
  - Whirlwind Sprint: [0/2]

CRAFTING STATIONS: THE RIFT

✓	TYPE	LOCATION A	LOCATION B
☐	Alchemy Lab	Riften (Mistveil Keep: Wylandriah's Room) [9.00]	Alchemist's Shack [9.09]
☐	Arcane Enchanter	Riften (Mistveil Keep: Wylandriah's Room) [9.00]	Riften (Honeyside) [9.00] (after Alchemy Lab Upgrade)
☐	Anvil or Blacksmith Forge	Riften (the Scorched Hammer) [9.00]	Shor's Stone [9.25]
☐	Cooking Pot and Spit	Riften (the Scorched Hammer) [9.00]	Riften (Temple of Mara) [9.00]
☐	Grindstone	Riften (the Scorched Hammer) [9.00]	Shor's Stone [9.25]
☐	Smelter	Shor's Stone [9.25]	—
☐	Tanning Rack	Riften (the Scorched Hammer) [9.00]	Shor's Stone [9.25]
☐	Wood Chopping Block	Riften (Mistveil Keep: Barracks) [9.00]	Ivarstead (9.01]
☐	Workbench	Riften (the Scorched Hammer) [9.00]	Shor's Stone [9.25]

Hold 9: The Rift

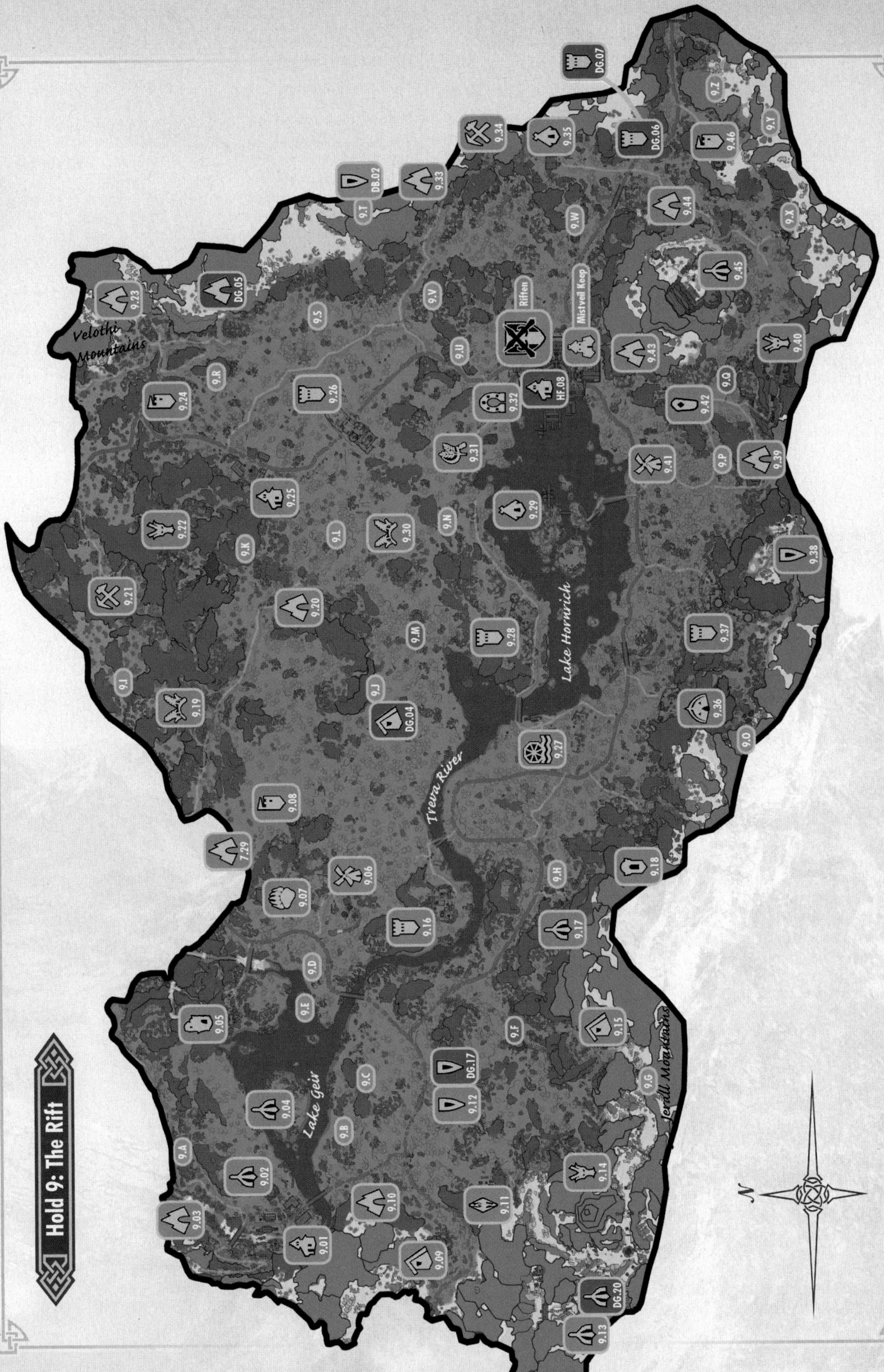

PRIMARY LOCATIONS

Total—48: Hold Capital, Mistveil Keep, and 46 Hold Locations

[9.00] Hold Capital City: Riften
[9.00] Mistveil Keep
Jarl: Laila Law-Giver
[9.01] Ivarstead
[9.02] Shroud Hearth Barrow
[9.03] Pinepeak Cavern
[9.04] Geirmund's Hall
[9.05] Nilheim
[9.06] Sarethi Farm
[9.07] Rift Stormcloak Camp
[9.08] Rift Watchtower
[9.09] Alchemist's Shack
[9.10] Honeystrand Cave
[9.11] Rift Imperial Camp
[9.12] Ruins of Bthalft
[9.13] Arcwind Point
[9.14] Autumnwatch Tower
[9.15] Froki's Shack
[9.16] Treva's Watch
[9.17] Angarvunde
[9.18] Avanchnzel
[9.19] Clearspring Tarn
[9.20] Boulderfall Cave
[9.21] Northwind Mine
[9.22] Northwind Summit
[9.23] Tolvald's Cave
[9.24] Shor's Watchtower
[9.25] Shor's Stone
[9.26] Fort Greenwall
[9.27] Heartwood Mill
[9.28] Faldar's Tooth
[9.29] Goldenglow Estate
[9.30] Autumnshade Clearing
[9.31] Merryfair Farm
[9.32] Riften Stables
[9.33] Fallowstone Cave and Giant's Grove
[9.34] Lost Prospect Mine
[9.35] Black-Briar Lodge
[9.36] Largashbur
[9.37] Darklight Tower
[9.38] Ruins of Rkund
[9.39] Crystaldrift Cave
[9.40] Lost Tongue Overlook
[9.41] Snow-Shod Farm
[9.42] The Shadow Stone
[9.43] Nightingale Hall
[9.44] Broken Helm Hollow
[9.45] Forelhost
[9.46] Stendarr's Beacon

SECONDARY LOCATIONS

Total—26 Points of Interest

[9.A] Darkwater Overhang
[9.B] Wood Cutter's Camp: Lake Geir
[9.C] The Poultry Reanimator: Lake Geir
[9.D] Treasure Hunter's Camp: Lake Geir
[9.E] Treasure Island: Lake Geir
[9.F] Dragon Mound: Autumnwatch Woods
[9.G] Shrine of Talos: Froki's Peak
[9.H] Medresi's Camp: Angarvunde
[9.I] Wild Animal Den: Mistwatch
[9.J] Bandit's Shack: Autumnshade
[9.K] Northwind Chest
[9.L] Altar in the Woods: Autumnshade
[9.M] Dragon Mound: Autumnshade Woods
[9.N] Hunters' Camp: Autumnshade Hills
[9.O] Troll Den: Rkund
[9.P] Wild Animal Den: Crystaldrift Cave
[9.Q] Dragon Mound: Lost Tongue Pass
[9.R] Wild Animal Den: Shor's Stone
[9.S] Trappers' Dilemma
[9.T] Miner's Camp: Velothi Mountains
[9.U] The Three Sentinels
[9.V] Shrine of Zenithar: Fallowstone
[9.W] Tumbledown Tower: Riften Outskirts
[9.X] Burning Farmhouse
[9.Y] Frost Troll Den: Jerall Mountain Ridge
[9.Z] Two Pine Ridge

ADDITIONAL LOCATIONS

[DG.04] Redwater Den (Updated) (see page 971)
[DG.05] Ruunvald Excavation (see page 973)
[DG.06] Dayspring Canyon (see page 974)
[DG.07] Fort Dawnguard (see page 974)
[DG.17] Ruins of Bthalft: The Aetherium Forge (Updated) (see page 947)
[DG.20] Arcwind Point (Updated) (see page 948)
[HF.08] Honeyside (Updated) (see page 937)
[DB.02] Last Vigil (see page 978)

HOLD CAPITAL: RIFTEN

Related Quests

Main Quest: A Cornered Rat
Main Quest: Alduin's Wall
Civil War Quest: Reunification of Skyrim
Civil War Quest: Compelling Tribute
Side Quest: Promises to Keep
Side Quest: Unfathomable Depths
Temple Quest: The Bonds of Matrimony
Temple Quest: The Book of Love
Dark Brotherhood Quest: Innocence Lost
Dark Brotherhood Quest: The Silence Has Been Broken
Dark Brotherhood Quest: Breaching Security
Dark Brotherhood Quest: Where You Hang Your Enemy's Head...
Thieves Guild Quest: A Chance Arrangement
Thieves Guild Quest: Taking Care of Business
Thieves Guild Quest: Loud and Clear
Thieves Guild Quest: Dampened Spirits
Thieves Guild Quest: Scoundrel's Folly
Thieves Guild Quest: Speaking With Silence
Thieves Guild Quest: The Pursuit
Thieves Guild Quest: Trinity Restored
Thieves Guild Radiant Quest: No Stone Unturned (Vex)
Thieves Guild Radiant Quest: No Stone Unturned (x2)
Thieves Guild Radiant Quest: Reparations
Thieves Guild Radiant Quest: Shadowmarks*
Thieves Guild Radiant Quest: Moon Sugar Rush*
Thieves Guild Radiant Quest: Armor Exchange*
Thieves Guild Radiant Quest: Larceny Targets (the Ragged Flagon)*
Thieves Guild Radiant Quest: Larceny Targets (Mercer's House)*
Thieves Guild Additional Jobs: The Numbers Job
Thieves Guild Additional Jobs: The Fishing Job
Thieves Guild Additional Jobs: The Bedlam Job
Thieves Guild Additional Jobs: The Burglary Job
Thieves Guild Additional Jobs: The Shill Job
Thieves Guild Additional Jobs: The Sweep Job
Thieves Guild Additional Jobs: The Heist Job
Thieves Guild City Influence Quest: Silver Lining
Thieves Guild City Influence Quest: The Dainty Sload
Thieves Guild City Influence Quest: Imitation Amnesty
Thieves Guild City Influence Quest: Summerset Shadows
Thieves Guild City Leadership Quest: Under New Management
Dungeon Activity (Riften Jail)
Miscellaneous Objective: Innkeeper Rumors (the Bee and Barb)
Miscellaneous Objective: Innkeeper Rumors (the Ragged Flagon)
Miscellaneous Objective: The Lover's Requital* (Sibbi Black-Briar)
Miscellaneous Objective: Under the Table* (Romlyn Dreth)
Miscellaneous Objective: Few and Far Between* (Ingun Black-Briar)
Miscellaneous Objective: Spread the Love* (Dinya Balu)
Miscellaneous Objective: Sealing the Deal* (Talen-Jei)
Miscellaneous Objective: Ice Cold* (Marise Aravel)
Miscellaneous Objective: Distant Memories* (Brand-Shei)
Miscellaneous Objective: Grimsever's Return* (Mjoll the Lioness)
Miscellaneous Objective: Stoking the Flames* (Balimund Iron-Boar)
Miscellaneous Objective: Caught Red-Handed* (Svana Far-Shield)
Miscellaneous Objective: Pilgrimage* (Alessandra)
Miscellaneous Objective: Hunt and Gather* (Wylandriah)
Miscellaneous Objective: Special Delivery* (Bolli)
Miscellaneous Objective: Bring It!* (Harrald)
Miscellaneous Objective: Truth Ore Consequences* (Hafjorg)
Miscellaneous Objective: Ringmaker* (Madesi)
Miscellaneous Objective: Bloody Nose* (Hofgrir Horse-Crusher)
Miscellaneous Objective: Toying with the Dead* (Vekel the Man)
Miscellaneous Objective: Shardr and Sapphire* (Shadr)
Miscellaneous Objective: Jarl's Quest Part 1: Helping Hand* (Wujeeta)
Miscellaneous Objective: Jarl's Quest Part 2: The Raid* (Wujeeta, Jarl Laila)
Miscellaneous Objective: Jarl's Quest Part 3: Supply and Demand* (Jarl Laila)
Miscellaneous Objective: Erasing Vald's Debt* (Maven Black-Briar)
Miscellaneous Objective: Gissur's Revenge* (Gissur)
Miscellaneous Objective: Shavari the Assassin* (Shavari)
Favor (Activity): The Gift of Charity* (Gissur)‡
Favor (Activity): The Gift of Charity* (Snilf)
Favor (Activity): The Gift of Charity* (Edda)
Thane Quest: Thane of The Rift*

Habitation Type: Hold Capital (Major)

Crafting

Alchemy Labs (5)
Arcane Enchanter
Forge
Grindstones (4)
Tanning Racks (3)
Workbenches (2)

Services

Follower: Mjoll the Lioness [40/47]
Follower: Marcurio [41/47]
Follower: Iona [42/47]
House for Sale: Honeyside [5/5]
Marriage Prospect: Mjoll the Lioness [52/62]
Marriage Prospect: Balimund [53/62]
Marriage Prospect: Gelka [54/62]
Marriage Prospect: Marcurio [55/62]
Marriage Prospect: Romlyn Dreth [56/62]
Marriage Prospect: Iona [57/62]
Trader (Apothecary): Elgrim [11/12]
Trader (Apothecary): Herluin Lothaire [12/12]
Trader (Bartender): Talen-Jei [3/5]
Trader (Bartender): Vekel the Man [4/5]
Trader (Blacksmith): Balimund [28/33]
Trader (Blacksmith): Arnskar Ember-Master [29/33]
Trader (Blacksmith): Vanryth Gatharian [30/33]
Trader (Fence): Tonilia [6/10]
Trader (Fletcher): Syndus [3/3]
Trader (Food Vendor): Ungrien [9/9]
Trader (General Store Vendor): Marise Aravel [13/19]
Trader (General Store Vendor): Brand-Shei [14/19]
Trader (General Store Vendor): Grelka [15/19]
Trader (General Store Vendor): Bersi Honey-Hand [16/19]
Trader (Innkeeper): Keerava [14/15]
Trader (Jeweler): Madesi [2/2]
Trader (Spell Vendor): Wylandriah [12/12]
Trainer (Archery: Master): Niruin [3/3]
Trainer (Light Armor: Expert): Grelka [3/3]
Trainer (Lockpicking: Master): Vex [1/2]
Trainer (Pickpocket: Master): Vipir [2/3]
Trainer (Smithing: Expert): Balimund [3/3]
Trainer (Sneak: Master): Delvin Mallory [2/3]

Collectibles

- Larceny Target: Bust of the Grey Fox [6/7]
- Skill Book [Lockpicking]: Advances in Lockpicking [A1/10]
- Skill Book [Lockpicking]: Advances in Lockpicking [A2/10]
- Skill Book [Lockpicking]: Surfeit of Thieves [C2/10]
- Skill Book [One-Handed]: Fire and Darkness [B2/10]
- Skill Book [Pickpocket]: Beggar [B1/10]
- Skill Book [Pickpocket]: Beggar [B2/10]
- Skill Book [Pickpocket]: Purloined Shadows [C2/10]
- Skill Book [Smithing]: The Armorer's Challenge [E2/10]
- Skill Book [Speech]: A Dance in Fire, v7 [C2/10]
- Skill Book [Two-Handed]: Words and Philosophy [E2/10]
- Unique Item: The Bond of Matrimony [80/112]
- Unique Item: Madesi's Silver Ring [81/112]
- Unique Item: Gloves of the Pugilist [82/112]
- Unique Item: Thieves Guild Armor [83/112]
- Unique Item: Thieves Guild Boots [84/112]
- Unique Item: Thieves Guild Gloves [85/112]
- Unique Item: Thieves Guild Hood [86/112]
- Unique Item: Amulet of Articulation [87/112]
- Unique Item: Guild Master's Armor [88/112]
- Unique Item: Guild Master's Boots [89/112]
- Unique Item: Guild Master's Gloves [90/112]
- Unique Item: Guild Master's Hood [91/112]
- Unique Item: Thieves Guild Armor (Improved) [92/112]
- Unique Item: Thieves Guild Boots (Improved) [93/112]
- Unique Item: Thieves Guild Gloves (Improved) [94/112]
- Unique Item: Thieves Guild Hood (Improved) [95/112]
- Unique Weapon: Chillrend [61/80]
- Unique Weapon: Alessandra's Dagger [62/80]
- Unique Weapon: Steel Sword [63/80]
- Unique Weapon: Dravin's Bow [64/80]
- Unusual Gem: [23/24]

Special Objects

- Business Ledger
- Civil War: Map of Skyrim
- Shrine of Arkay [12/12]
- Shrine of Dibella [8/8]
- Shrine of Mara [5/5]
- Shrine of Talos [16/17]
- Chest
- Potions aplenty
- Loose gear

Lore: City Overview

Riften is situated in the southeastern corner of the Rift, at the eastern end of Lake Honrich, with a good portion of the city actually spilling over the water atop large wooden piers. The entire city is bisected by a large canal that used to serve as access for small cargo boats but has lately fallen into disrepair and decay thanks to the lack of trade during the Civil War. But don't think that Riften isn't a bustling center of commerce; the Black-Briar Meadery has almost a monopoly on the sale and distribution of a Nord's favorite pastime: drinking.

However, the city of Riften is a paradox. The city is located in the beautiful Autumnal Forest region of Skyrim, and that beauty has encroached upon the city, in the form of wondrous foliage and generally pleasant weather. But most of the structures in Riften are wooden, and the city has a sort of old, run-down feel, which often takes visitors by surprise. Not that this bothers the people who live there, who see Riften for what it truly is—a bustling, energetic city with a strong economy fueled by hard-working fishermen and mead makers. The residents also understand that the city is, for all intents and purposes, owned and operated by the Maven Black-Briar, and in order to survive and thrive, everyone needs to adhere to her rules.

Important Areas of Interest

Dryside

The eastern edge of the city (which isn't built over the waters of Lake Honrich) is called Dryside. The bulk of the town is located on Dryside and is split by Riften's canal. Most of the more affluent homes are located on the eastern side of the canal, while most of Riften's shops and the marketplace are located on the western side. The southern portion of the city is dominated by Mistveil Keep and the jail.

A North Gate

The main gate of Riften, located along the northern wall, sees the most traffic of the city's three entrances. Foil the Riften guard's feeble attempts at shaking you down for money. Then speak with Maul, a gruff man waiting just inside the gates.

> **TIP** Talk to Maul. Afterward, the gates in this area are unlocked, once you enter an interior and return outside.

1 Bolli's House

Bolli Trout-Purse Nivenor

This three-floor structure is one of the more impressive houses in Riften, which speaks to Bolli's station. The Note you'll find on the bedside cabinet reveals Bolli's marriage isn't as successful.

- Shadowmark: "Loot"
- Chest
- Note: Requested Report

2 Aerin's House

Mjoll the Lioness Aerin

Aerin's home is small but tall, featuring three floors.

- Follower: Mjoll the Lioness [40/47]
- Marriage Prospect: Mjoll the Lioness [52/62]
- Loose Gear

3 Snow-Shod Manor

Vulwulf Snow-Shod
Nura Snow-Shod
Asgeir Snow-Shod

This three-floor wooden structure is the house of Clan Snow-Shod, a wealthy and influential family of Nord that owns the Snow-Shod Farm outside Riften. But even though the Clan has direct ties to the city's economy, it's their interest and involvement in the Civil War that really has people talking....

- Shadowmark: "Loot"
- Loose gear

4 Riftweald Manor (Locked: Special)

This property is owned by the current Guild Master of the Thieves Guild and is a fine structure. Mercer has cleverly integrated an isolated section of the Ratway into the sublevels of his home, which contains his private valued possessions. This hideaway includes a minivault, a study, and escape routes. Mercer Frey has paid several bandits to act as guards here and has given them the order to kill intruders.

Outside, the front and back doors are barred from the inside, and the back grounds are locked by three gates, two requiring a key and the other locked (Expert). You usually enter here during Thieves Guild Quest: The Pursuit and must shoot a mechanism to release a wooden ramp leading to an upper entrance (Expert). This cannot be done at any other time; exploration inside occurs only during or after this quest.

Riftweald Manor (Interior)

Upper Floor: A storage room leads to a landing, a smaller storage closet, and Mercer's bedroom. The door's bar in the landing can't be budged.

Ground Floor: A large living and dining room dominates this area, along with an adjacent foyer. The doors' bars here can't be removed either. The foyer table has a note mentioning the mechanism construction that has recently taken place outside. It is next to the front door (barred and sealed) that you find a suspicious cabinet leading to Mercer Frey's secret chambers.

Cellar: The cellar, accessed from the dining room, is a small area filled with foodstuffs.

- Note: To the Owner
- Potions
- Chest

Secret Cellar: Accessed via the false back panel of the suspicious cabinet on the ground floor (which can be closed using the pull bar on the other side). Watch for numerous traps as you navigate the sewer passages; there's a spear trap in front of you, triggered by a pressure plate. The next room has fire traps blasting up from the floor.

Puzzle Solution: Look at the floor and the nozzle holes where the fire blasts up from. These are divided into tiles. Each tile has a diamond shape; the fire traps that are activated are darker than those that are empty; simply step on the lighter-colored diamonds to avoid all fire damage.

There's a dart trap in the water-logged corridor (pressure plate) leading to a chest. At the corridor with the swinging blade and battering ram traps, dash between the blades and step left into the alcove. Wait for the battering ram to swing, then sprint to the left of the low chandelier, dodging the remaining blades. At the door, look down and unlock the trap trigger (Expert) or face darts when you open the door.

- Danger! Battering Ram Trap, Dart Trap, Fire Trap, Spear Trap, Swinging Blade Trap
- Chest

Mercer's Secret Study: There is a wealth of loot here, including an excellent weapon in a display case (Expert). The note from "R" is likely to be from Legate Rikke in Solitude. The exit tunnel leads to the Ratway Vaults, which connects back to the Warrens and the Ragged Flagon. Note the Shadowmark before you drop down into the Vaults.

- Shadowmark: "Danger"
- Mercer's Plans
- Skill Book [Sneak]: The Red Kitchen Reader
- Unique Weapon: Chillrend [61/80]
- Note: Many thanks
- Chest
- Larceny Target: Bust of the Gray Fox [6/7]

5 Temple of Mara

Maramal Dinya Balu

The Temple of Mara offers services to the people of Riften and is devoted to the worship of Mara, one of the Nine Divines and the recognized goddess of love. It is here that weddings are held (Side Quest: The Bonds of Matrimony). You can get a Blessing at the altar or at two smaller shrines on either side of the main chamber. The first Note is from Anuriel warning of disturbances in the Hall of the Dead. The second Note is from Talen-Jei, regarding his forthcoming wedding. The cellar has some food and drink, and an entrance to the Hall of the Dead.

- Unique Item: The Bond of Matrimony [80/112]
- Shrine of Mara [5/5]
- Note: Reports of a Disturbance
- Note: Argonian Ceremony
- Potions

6 Hall of the Dead

Alessandra

The Riften Hall of the Dead has two levels, underneath the Temple of Mara. The ground floor serves as a Shrine of Arkay; the bottom, underground level is actually a series of catacombs that contain some of Riften's most important dead. Connected to the mausoleum is a graveyard, containing even more of the city's departed. There are two entrances: from the outside under the Temple of Mara balcony and via the cellar inside the Temple. Inside, there are numerous skeletons from which you can remove a few coins, bone meal, and skulls.

- Unique Weapon: Alessandra's Dagger [62/80]
- Shrine of Arkay [12/12]

B The Ragged Flagon: Cistern Entrance

The secret entrance to the Ragged Flagon, Cistern, becomes available during the Thieves Guild Quest: Loud and Clear and becomes a world map marker (making it simple to return to the Guild). It can't be opened until then but provides a quicker return route to Brynjolf and Mercer Frey, instead of navigating the Ratway. Note the Shadowmark on the coffin (which you press to open) and on the surrounding Hall of the Dead entrance walls. If you're exiting from the Cistern, use the pull chain to open the coffin.

- Shadowmark: "The Guild"

7 Black-Briar Manor

Maven Black-Briar (Imperial Jarl)
Hemming Black-Briar (Imperial Steward)
Sibbi Black-Briar
Ingun Black-Briar

Black-Briar Manor is the home of the Black-Briar family, the wealthiest, most powerful family in all of Riften. The Black-Briar family are the owners of the Black-Briar Meadery, and as such control much of Riften's economy. It is accessed via the front door (note the Shadowmark), a leap over the garden fence, and through the back gate (Expert). Inside, the foyer end table has a Note regarding the loss of a mead shipment, and the rest of the ground floor has a dining table full of food and other stored items.

- Shadowmark: "Protected"
- Note: Regarding your Loss
- Potions

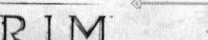

Cellar: There are three doors, two of which are unlocked. One leads to a small bedroom. One leads to a larger bedroom with an Alchemy Lab and a number of ingredients to steal. The third door (Expert) leads to a tiny chamber where the Black Sacrament has been performed. There is a letter from Maven here; she is unhappy with Astrid (from the Dark Brotherhood) about the lack of action regarding an assassination Maven requested!

◊ Crafting: Alchemy Lab ◊ Potions

◊ Note: To the Brotherhood

Upper Floor: Check the shelves in the hallway for a book on the Gaulder legends. On the bedside table are two letters, each containing a different tone from two business acquaintances. There is an exit onto an upper exterior balcony (a quick escape if need be!).

◊ Business Letters (2) ◊ Chest

8 Shrine of Talos

Nura Snow-Shod

Talos is worshipped openly when the Stormcloaks are in control of the city. When they are not, the shrine has less of a presence. Nura Snow-Shod is usually found here during the day, tending the Shrine.

◊ Shrine of Talos [16/17]

9 Dead Gate

The Dead Gate is so named for the number of people who died there thanks to repeated bandit raids of the city. The gate is now completely boarded up and no longer in use.

10 Mistveil Keep

The following leaders of Riften are loyal to the Stormcloaks at the start of the Civil War.

Jarl Laila Law-Giver

Laila is a fervent supporter of the Stormcloaks, strongly believing that the Empire can do nothing but steal the heritage of their city away if they come to power. She firmly believes in the old ways of Skyrim and is steeped in its traditions and mannerisms. Even though she rules quite a corrupt city, she is blissfully unaware of the more nefarious goings-on in town thanks to her Steward, Anuriel, who has been known to accept bribes and payoffs from the seedier inhabitants of Riften.

Harrald

Harrald is the youngest son of Laila Law-Giver. He is largely indifferent to the events of the Civil War but sides with the Stormcloaks because his mother does. This situation has driven a wedge between Saerlund and Harrald, who constantly chide each other for their stances on the situation.

Saerlund

Saerlund is the oldest son of Laila Law-Giver. When he publicly spoke in favor of the Imperial forces in the Civil War, Laila refused to recognize him as heir. There is a great deal of hostility between the two now, although Saerlund still lives in the Keep. Should Laila ever become exiled due to the Empire gaining control of Riften, Saerlund will remain behind and live in the Keep in defiance of his mother's beliefs.

Anuriel (Steward)

Anuriel's devotion to her Jarl is a guise for her true nature as a corrupt and greedy individual. She readily accepts bribes from influential people in the city and is extremely clever at covering her tracks (even if it means making loose ends disappear). She has no desire to actually become the Jarl, seeing her position as a stronger link to her corrupt ties. She has gained some reputation as someone not to be trifled with.

Unmid Snow-Shod (Housecarl)

Unmid is the second to youngest child of Vulwulf Snow-Shod. He has dedicated his life to the art of combat, becoming highly adept at all sorts of martial weaponry. Due to this incredible talent, he was hired as the Housecarl. On more than one occasion, Unmid has proved he cannot be bested in combat and has even put down several attempts on the Jarl's life. Unmid's single weakness is his infatuation for Anuriel, the Jarl's Steward.

Wylandriah (Court Wizard)

She spends most of her day in her laboratory performing experiments and only makes herself available to the Jarl when specifically summoned. She seems always scatterbrained, but this is an act, as Wylandriah would prefer to be doing her experimentation rather than matters of court. By acting this way, she believes people leave her to herself most of the time (which is true).

Gonnar Oath-Giver

The following residents of Riften arrive to take control of this city, once this Hold has fallen during the Civil War.

Maven Black-Briar, Imperial Jarl

As matron of the Black-Briar family and a powerful businesswoman, Maven is virtually unapproachable and elitist. She's cold, ruthless and calculating—and also well connected within the Empire and Skyrim alike. If the Empire takes control of Riften in the Civil War, Maven (thanks to powerful friends in Cyrodiil) is installed as the Imperial Jarl. She will also fill her court with family and allies.

Hemming Black-Briar, Imperial Steward

Hemming Black-Briar is the only son of Maven Black-Briar, and heir to family fortune. He is being groomed by Maven as a sort of protégé... someone to eventually take her place not only running the Meadery, but to also dabble in the same corrupt activities. Hemming is often an errand-boy, and has come to admire his mother's ways and fervently defends her whenever a family squabble should arise.

Maul (Housecarl)

Maul is a close friend of Hemming Black-Briar; when he was ambushed by bandits, Maul dove into the fray to save him. Ever since then, they have been partners in crime, with Maul assisting Hemming in his more nefarious activities assigned by Maven Black-Briar. He does not live within Riften, as he wants his identity to remain anonymous. Maul's brother is Dirge, part of the security at the Ragged Flagon.

Mistveil Keep (Exterior)

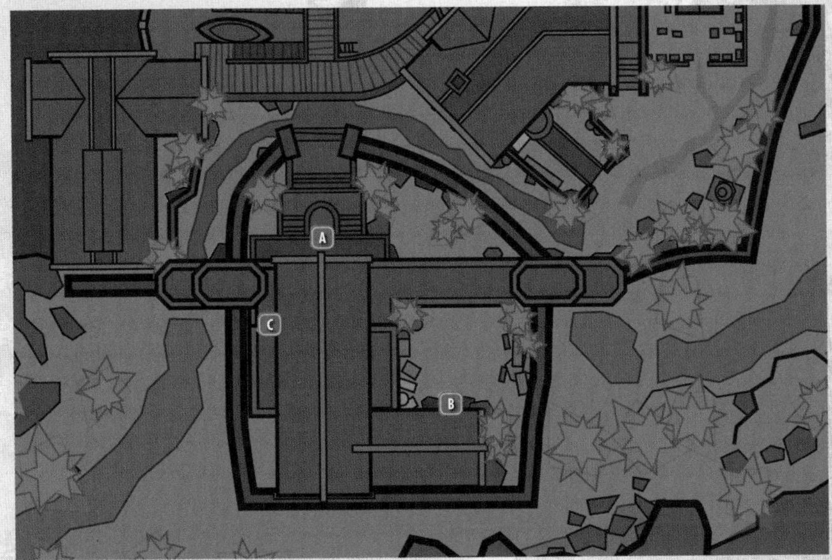

A Door to Mistveil Keep

B Door to Mistveil Keep Barracks

C Door to Riften Jail

This ominous stone keep is where Jarl Laila Law-Giver lives and rules, but this important building also contains the city's jail and barracks. The barracks are to your left (southeast) and the jail to the right (southwest) of the main door into the Keep, with the banners on each side. This is where the majority of the city's guards reside.

Mistveil Keep (Interior)

D Door to Riften

1 Banquest Hall and Throne Room

Guards, the Jarl, and her entourage are seated here. There's enough food here to feed a small army.

- Chest (2)

2 Wylandriah's Enchantments

The Court Wizard can usually be found here, in this two-room chamber off the Banquet Hall, which houses her shop and bed.

- Crafting: Alchemy Lab, Arcane Enchanter
- Trader (Spell Vendor): Wylandriah [12/12]
  - Weapons, Apparel, Scrolls, Books, Misc
- Chest
- Potions aplenty
- Loose gear

3 War Room and Armory

Gonnar Oath-Giver is plotting from this location (which was once a pantry) at the start of the Civil War. Open one door to head into the Barracks, and open the other into a bedroom armory filled with weapons.

- Civil War: Map of Skyrim
- Chest
- Loose gear

E Door to Mistveil Keep Barracks

4 Anuriel's Room

Located at the far end of the ground-floor corridor, this room has a number of precious gems and necklaces and a letter regarding the imprisonment of Sibbi Black-Briar. Head to this location during the Civil War Quest: Compelling Tribute (Imperials).

- Note: Sibbi Black-Briar
- Chest

F Door to Mistveil Keep Jarl's Quarters

Mistveil Keep Jarl's Quarters

G Door to Mistveil Keep

5 Upstairs Bedrooms

There are three doors at the top of the stairs, each leading to a bedroom. Check for the following, and a door from the Jarl's bedroom to a covered balcony offering views of Riften:

- Skill Book [Lockpicking]: Surfeit of Thieves [C2/10]
- Unusual Gem: [23/24]
- Display Cases [Adept] (3)
- Chests (3)
- Potions
- Loose gear

H Door to Riften

Mistveil Keep Barracks (Exterior)

A large yard where guards (and sometimes Harrald) come to practice.

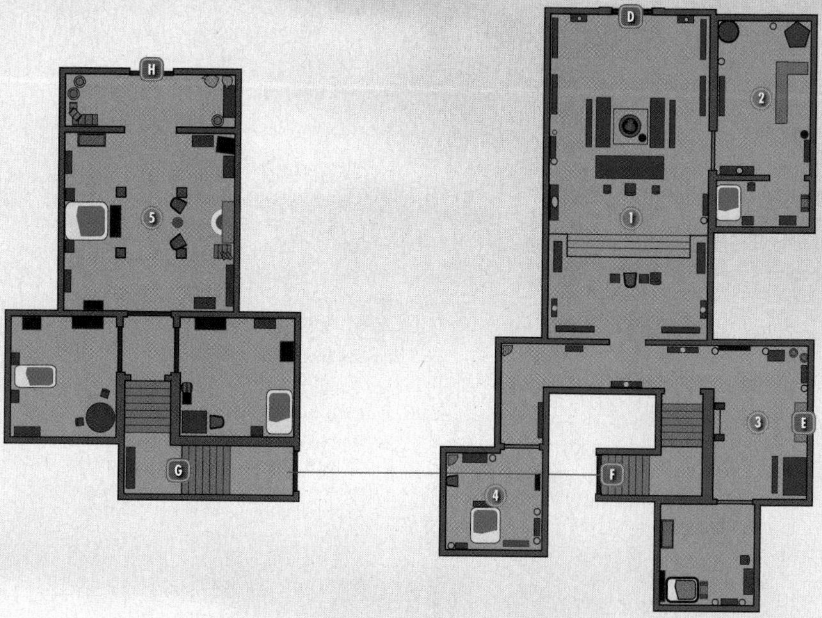

Mistveil Keep Barracks (Interior)

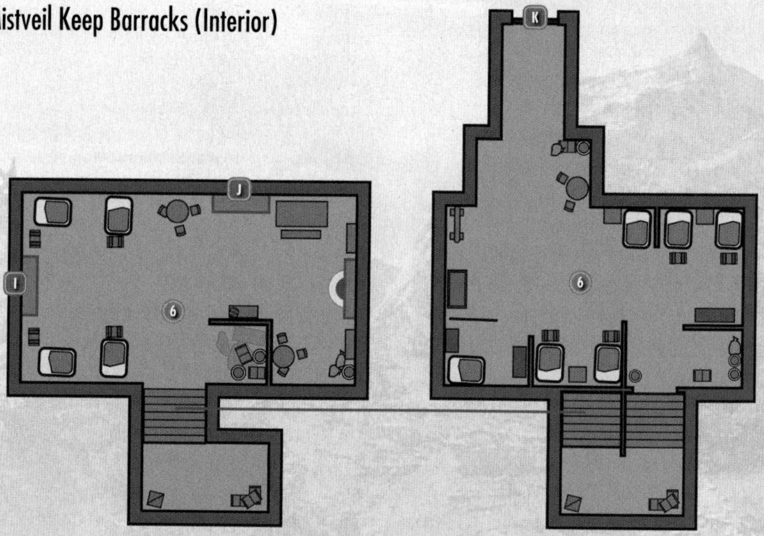

I Door to Mistveil Keep

6 Barracks Interior (Upper and Lower)

A large number of guards (and mead bottles) are inside this two-floor structure. The Riften Guards are well equipped and numerous. The lower exits lead out to the training yard and into Mistveil Keep. The upper exit leads out onto crenellations above the yard.

- Skill Book [Two-Handed]: Words and Philosophy [E2/10]
- Chests (8)
- Loose gear

J Door to Riften

K Door to Riften

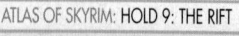

17 [HF.08] Honeyside

Related Quests
Thane Task: Thane of the Rift
Hearthfire Task: Adoption

Crafting
Alchemy Lab
Arcane Enchanter
Cooking Pot

Collectibles
Skill Book [Enchanting]

Miscellaneous
Area is locked
Chest
Loose gear
Potions aplenty

This dwelling is currently empty, save for a Skill Book that sits at the bottom of a leaning shelf in the basement. It features entrances from both Plankside and Dryside, enabling you to head to and from Riften without using the gates. Should you become the Thane of the Rift (by completing Favors for the Jarl), you can purchase this abode from Jarl Laila Law-Giver's Steward, Anuriel. Consult the Thane Quests for more information. Should you wish to purchase the children's bedroom, it replaces the Enchanting Laboratory.

- Follower: Iona (Housecarl) [42/47]
- House for Sale [5/5]
- Marriage Prospect: Iona [57/62]
- Skill Book [Enchanting]: Enchanter's Primer

Purchase Price: 8,000 gold

Jarl: Jarl Laila Lawgiver or Jarl Maven Black-Briar

Steward: Anuriel or Hemming Black-Briar

Available Decorations
Alchemy Laboratory (1,000 gold)
Bedroom (600 gold)
Children's Bedroom (550 gold)
Enchanting Laboratory (1,000 gold)
Garden (800 gold)
Kitchen (500 gold)
Porch (400 gold)

Total cost: 12,750 gold

18 Haelga's Bunkhouse

Haelga	**Fastred**
Svana Far-Shield	**Bassianus Axius**

Haelga's Bunkhouse provides long-term lodging for anyone who can keep up the rent and mostly caters to the fishermen and mead makers of Riften. There's something of a theme with many of the people who reside at the Bunkhouse: they do brutal, backbreaking work, and they're prone to abusing either alcohol or Skooma. It is a large building and has private rooms as well as a larger barracks-like common area with food on the tables. During Thieves Guild Quest: Taking Care of Business, a Statue of Dibella is on display on the bookcase in the main room. On the counter is a Note regarding an "experience" an anonymous patron had with Haelga. Behind the counter is Haelga's room, where she takes "clients" and writes in her ledger. Upstairs is a Skill Book, near the dormitory-style bedrooms, smaller bedroom, and storage room. More importantly is a Shrine of Dibella in Haelga's bedroom.

- Skill Book [Pickpocket]: Beggar [B1/10]
- Business Ledger
- Shrine of Dibella [8/8]
- Note: Until Next Time

Dryside: Canal Level

Aside from an old Alchemist's shop tucked away under the main thoroughfare, this less-desirable and impoverished part of town is damp, dark, and the entrance to the Ratway. It isn't plagued by violence, just those down on their luck.

19 Beggar's Row
When the beggars of Riften aren't hanging around the marketplace, they rest here. There's little to entice you, unless you like collecting cabbage.

- Shadowmark: "Empty"
- Skill Book [Speech]: A Dance in Fire, v7 [C2/10]

20 Elgrim's Elixirs

Elgrim	**Hafjorg**

Elgrim's Elixirs is Riften's lone apothecary. As it is located in the cramped and dangerous confines of the Canal Level, Elgrim's Elixirs usually caters to the members of the Thieves Guild and other unsavory types and specializes in poisons. The shop is filled with potions and ingredients. Find a Skill Book hidden inside a woven basket that sits atop the tall shelf near the fireplace. Behind the store is a bedroom, along with an alchemy chest belonging to Ingun Black-Briar, a strongbox, and a ledger. Favor Quest: Few and Far Between (given by Ingun) must be completed in order to open the Alchemy Chest here.

- Shadowmark: "Loot"
- Crafting: Alchemy Lab
- Trader (Apothecary): Elgrim [12/12]
  - Potions, Food, Ingredients, Books
- Skill Book [Alteration]: Reality & Other Falsehoods
- Business Ledger
- Ingun's Alchemy Chest (Requires Key)
- Strongbox (Adept)
- Potions aplenty

21 Marise Aravel's House
A homely hovel, with a good amount of food, this is where Marise the marketplace trader makes do.

- Shadowmark: "Loot"

22 Valindor's House
This is the dwelling of Valindor, who works part-time at the Meadery. This modest two-room chamber has little but food and a couple of books to steal.

- Shadowmark: "Loot"

23 Romlyn Dreth's House
The home of another Meadery worker, Romlyn's residence remains drab, even with a roaring fire.

- Potions

E Ratway (Entrance)
This is the initial entrance to the large underground sewer system where the Thieves Guild's tentacles have contracted to.

Plankside

The western edge of the city, known as Plankside, is actually built on the waters of Lake Honrich and serves as the city's center of mead production and distribution (which is, in fact, integral to Riften's economy) and its fishing industry (Riften's secondary economy). The buildings here have been built on wooden docks, and the district is very old and ramshackle. There are three main docks projecting from Plankside, one owned completely by Black-Briar Meadery and the other two used for general commerce and fishing boats.

F Honeyside (East Entrance)

This is the entrance to the House for Sale. Once you purchase Honeyside, you can enter and exit from this location instead of using any of the Dryside gates.

24 Riften Fishery

Tythis Ulen

Wujeeta

From-Deepest-Fathoms

Exterior: The structure has two entrances, locked during the night (Adept). There are fishing boats moored at the adjacent docks too; one has a tanning rack, and there are a number of fish barrels you can steal from.

- Crafting: Tanning Rack

Interior: The Riften Fishery is owned by Bolli Trout-Purse and is the center of all fishing in and around Riften. Inside, sections of the floor have been removed, allowing direct access to a salmon hatchery where the cellar used to be. But the fishery also serves as a general cleaning, storing, and processing area for all the fish that are caught on Lake Honrich. Most of the people who work in the Fishery reside at Haelga's Bunkhouse. There's an office off the balcony surrounding the hatchery with the following items:

- Business Ledger
- Note: Things to Do
- Strongbox (Apprentice)

G Black-Briar Meadery (East Entrance)

This entrance is used by the Dryside Meadery for loading and off-loading. It is an alternate entrance into the establishment.

D Dock Gate (East Entrance)

This allows quick and easy access to and from the blacksmith's and the marketplace; it is an often-overlooked gate.

25 Riften Warehouse (Locked: Requires Key)

Sarthis Idren

Orini

The large wooden building served as a warehouse and general storage facility for the Fishery but hasn't been used in years. It is firmly sealed. Instead, the main floor is musty, with old furniture scattered about. Another locked door (requires Key) down in the cellar leads to a Skooma and Moon Sugar den. To enter the Warehouse, consult the Jarl of Riften and begin her Favor: The Raid. Sarthis Idren and his accomplice Orini guard their makeshift Skooma lab. It can only be accessed by key during this quest (obtained from the Jarl)

- Sarthis's Satchel

H Sewer

This is where you arrive if you decide to escape from Riften Jail using the sewer escape route detailed at that location.

Ratway

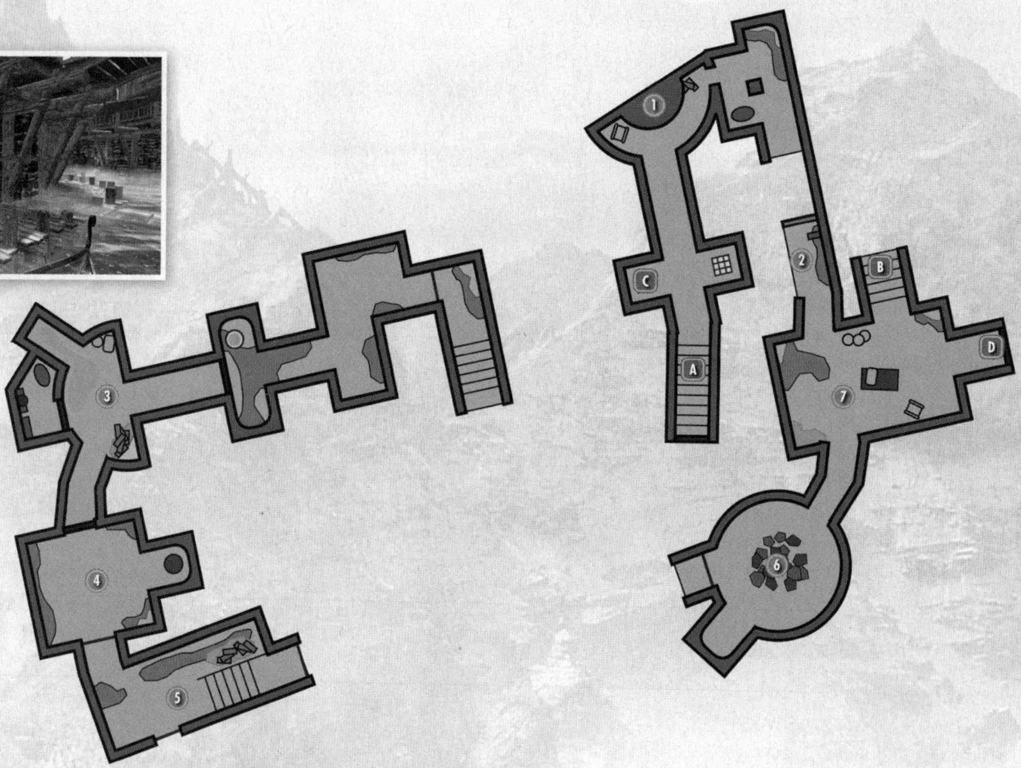

The Ratway is the area that runs beneath all of Riften. Comprised of interconnected basements and half-flooded sewer tunnels and dominated by a huge cistern in the center, the Ratway is a small city within a city. It is here that Riften's Thieves Guild plies its trade and the riffraff make their home.

The Ratway

A Door to Riften

1 Muggers' Tunnel

A pair of thugs prowl this initial tunnel (which has two side grates so you can peer down to Location [2]). Dodge or slay Hewnon Black-Skeever and Drahff.

2 The Bridge

The lever to lower this bridge is on the opposite (south) side, on the upper balcony. Approach it once you've finished initial explorations. Look up in the tunnel to the west, and you can see the tunnel grates from Location [1].

B Locked Gate (Expert)

Unlock this for a shortcut to the Ragged Flagon entrance (Location [7]), and the bridge balcony.

C Trapped Door (Apprentice)

The door at the end of the tunnel to the west is trapped. Unlock the trap trigger or face two spears in your chest from the left. Back up to avoid them just after opening the door, if you didn't disarm the trap.

- Danger! Spear Trap

3 Gian's Oily Ooze

This junction room has a Skeever and a madman named Gian the Fist to contend with. Use an arrow to drop the oil lamp and start a fire, or find other ways to defeat anyone attacking you.

- Danger! Oil Lamp Trap, Oil Pool Trap
- Unique Item: Gloves of the Pugilist [82/112]

4 Bear Trap Chamber

A low ceiling and bear traps on this paved floor await you. Gian's Alchemy Lab is in one alcove.

- Danger! Bear Trap (4)
- Crafting: Alchemy Lab

5 The Drunkard's Steps

Pass the mead barrel and watch for a pressure plate on the left side of the steps, as this triggers a battering ram in your back. Stay right instead.

- Danger! Battering Ram Trap!

6 Battleaxe Glade

A shaft of light allows plants to grow in this circular chamber.

- Loose gear

7 Ragged Flagon Entrance

Beware of lowlife attacks here. Lower the bridge from the balcony if you haven't done it already, enabling a quick exit back to Riften, when necessary. Check the table for a Skill Book. Skill Book [Pickpocket]: Beggar [B2/10]

D Door to the Ragged Flagon

The Ragged Flagon (Map Not Shown)

The following notable inhabitants of the Ragged Flagon and Cistern arrive during the Thieves Guild Quests:

Guild Master: Mercer Frey

Guild Second: Brynjolf

Guild Third: Delvin Mallory, Vex

Guild Member: Dirge, Vipir the Fleet, Niruin, Sapphire, Cynric Endell, Thrynn, Rune, Garthar, Ravyn Imyan

Guild Vendor: Vekel the Man, Syndus, Herluin Lothaire, Arnskar Ember-Master, Vanryth Gatharian

Guild Fence (Riften): Tonilia

The Ragged Flagon is the seediest, most dangerous tavern in all of Skyrim. It is located beneath the Riften city streets and serves as a meeting place for the province's criminal element. Strangers are not usually welcome, fights and even deaths are not uncommon, and most people in the place on any given night are involved in criminal activity in some capacity. It would be wise to enter here once you've befriended a thief named Brynjolf. One of the tables also contains a couple of notes, and there are two exits—one into the Vaults and a secret storage cabinet with a false back that opens up into the entrance to the Cistern. There's limited loot. The storage cabinet (requires Key) is opened by Brynjolf when he walks you into the Cistern.

- Trader (Apothecary): Herluin Lothaire [12/12]
  - Apparel, Potions, Misc
- Trader (Bartender): Vekel the Man [4/5]
- Trader (Fence): Tonilia [6/10]
  - Weapons, Apparel, Potions, Misc
- Trader (Fletcher): Syndus [3/3]
  - Weapons, Apparel, Misc
- Trader (Blacksmith): Arnskar Ember-Master [29/33]
  - Weapons, Apparel, Misc
- Trader (Blacksmith): Vanryth Gatharian [30/33]
  - Weapons, Apparel, Misc (Armor mending)
- Trainer (Archery: Master): Niruin [3/3]
- Trainer (Lockpicking: Master): Vex [1/2]
- Trainer (Pickpocket: Master): Vipir [2/3]
- Trainer (Sneak: Master): Delvin Mallory [2/3]
- Unique Item: Thieves Guild Armor [83/112]
- Unique Item: Thieves Guild Boots [84/112]
- Unique Item: Thieves Guild Gloves [85/112]
- Unique Item: Thieves Guild Hood [86/112]
- Unique Item: Amulet of Articulation [87/112]
- Unique Item: Guild Master's Armor [88/112]
- Unique Item: Guild Master's Boots [89/112]
- Unique Item: Guild Master's Gloves [90/112]
- Unique Item: Guild Master's Hood [91/112]
- Unique Item: Thieves Guild Armor (Improved) [92/112]
- Unique Item: Thieves Guild Boots (Improved) [93/112]
- Unique Item: Thieves Guild Gloves (Improved) [94/112]
- Unique Item: Thieves Guild Hood (Improved) [95/112]
- Note: A Warning
- Note: Timely Offer
- Chest

NOTE The quality of furnishings and frequency of items, banners, Guild members, and traders appearing in the empty alcoves opposite the Ragged Flagon bar area actually increases as you restore the Guild to its former glory by completing the City Influence Quests (see Thieves Guild Quests for more information). Aside from additional traders, this also occurs in the Cistern too.

The Ragged Flagon: Cistern

This more secretive and expansive main sewage hub is the stronghold for the Thieves Guild. It is only accessible once Brynjolf leads you here during Thieves Guild Quest: Loud and Clear.

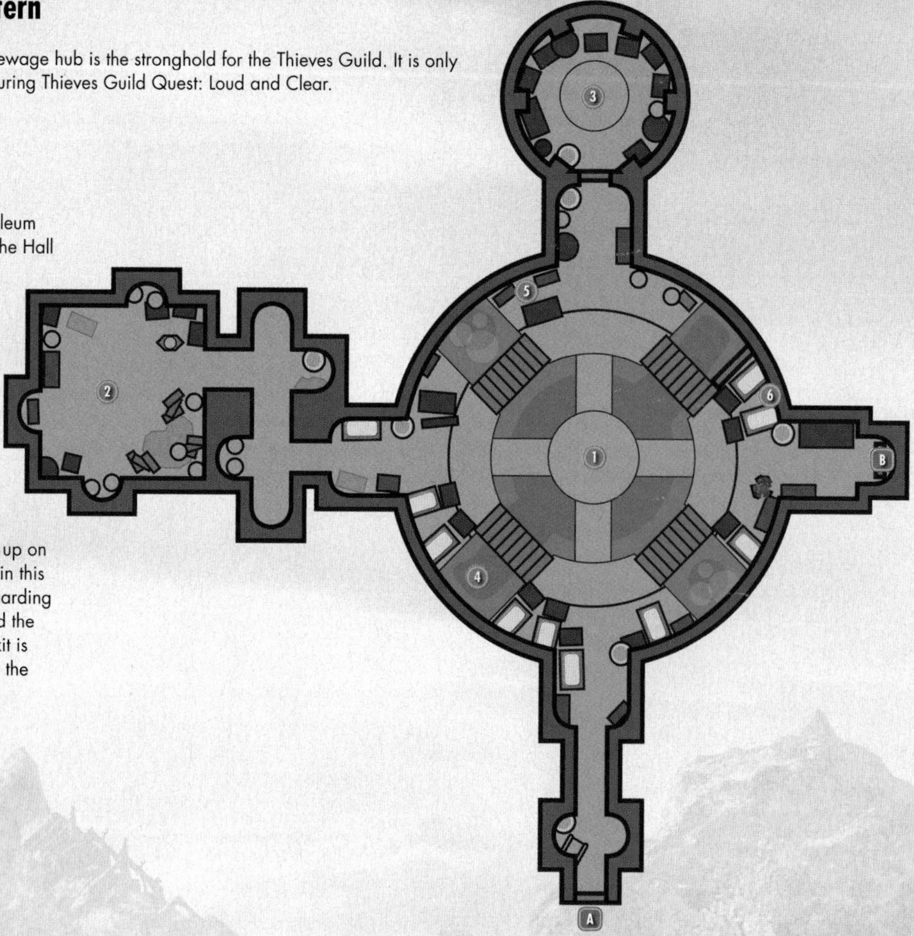

A Door to Ragged Flagon

B Ladder to Riften

This brings you up and through the mausoleum and into the small graveyard attached to the Hall of the Dead. When you first access this location, it is added to your world map, allowing quicker Fast-Travel back here between Thieves Guild Quests.

1 Main Cistern Chamber

Once you're a member, Guild chests are free for the opening. Otherwise they are inaccessible. These containers are also safe to store items in; deposit inventory items you wish to keep and return for them later. You should also read up on Shadowmarks by taking one of the books in this area. On Mercer Frey's table is a note regarding a tense relationship between the Guild and the East Empire Company. Near the ladder exit is a cupboard with another note, concerning the search for Rune's parents.

- Crafting: Grindstone
- Business Ledger
- Note: East Empire Connection
- Note: No Word Yet
- Guild Chests (7)
- Loose gear

2 Training Chamber

Pass the Alchemy Lab to reach this location. Niruin the master archer is usually practicing here. There are a variety of training chests to unlock, too, if you want to practice (and increase your Lockpicking skill). A Skill Book that rests on a barrel can help you quickly achieve the same.

- Crafting: Alchemy Lab
- Skill Book [Lockpicking]: Advances in Lockpicking [A2/10]
- Note: Training Chests
- Guild Chest
- Chest (Locked: Novice)
- Chest (Locked: Apprentice)
- Chest (Locked: Adept)
- Chest (Locked: Expert)
- Chest (Locked: Master)
- Loose gear

3 The Guild Vault

The entire wealth of the Thieves Guild is located in this chamber, which is firmly sealed and only unlocked during the Thieves Guild Quests.

- Loose gear

4 Shrine of Nocturnal

This shrine appears after you complete Thieves Guild Quest: Darkness Returns. The shrine provides the Blessing of Nocturnal, which adds +10 to your Sneak skill.

- Ability: Blessing of Nocturnal

5 Guild Leader's Office

This area of the Cistern contains two trophy shelves that help you track how many Radiant Quests you've completed. They also display all of the Larceny Targets you've found (see the Thieves Guild chapter for the details). The Crown of Queen Barenziah also appears here once all of the gems have been found and the crown located (Thieves Guild Side Quest: No Stone Unturned). Once you become Guild Leader (by completing the Thieves Guild quest line and all of the City Influence Quests), the Tribute Chest will appear at the base of the desk.

6 Your Bed

There is a bed here that is available for you to use whenever you wish.

The Ratway Vaults

A Door to the Ragged Flagon

◊ Shadowmark: "The Guild"

1 Hub Level and Balconies

You can drop down here, or follow the tunnels that weave through this central location.

B Door to Riftweald Manor

You can only drop down from here, which leads to an alcove close to the Hub Level.

◊ Shadowmark: "Danger"

2 Dead Nord's Campfire

The trip wire on the trapped doorway releases swinging flails. This has a campfire, a dead Nord, and Skeevers.

◊ Danger! Flail Traps

3 Spiral Steps

◊ Loose gear

4 Hub Level Gratings Tunnel

One of the side alcoves has an oil lamp you can drop on enemies below.

◊ Danger! Oil Lamp Trap

5 The Old Forge

◊ Crafting: Workbench ◊ Loose gear

◊ Chest

6 Vagrant's Hideout

Beyond this table and collection of loot is a corridor leading to the bottom of the Hub Level.

◊ Shadowmark: "Loot" ◊ Chest (Apprentice) (2)

◊ Chest ◊ Loose gear

C Door to the Ratway Warrens

There's oil on the floor and a potion to grab on your way here.

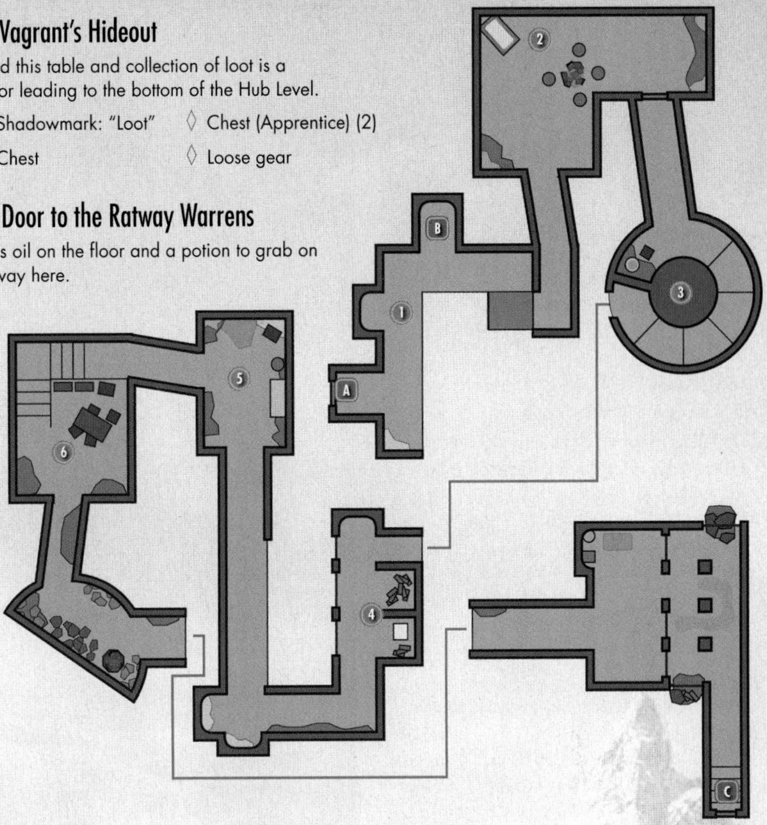

The Ratway Warrens

C Door to the Ratway Vaults

D Door to Warrens Hub Chamber (Apprentice)

7 Hub Chamber

All of the tunnels and cells in this location lead to and from this central location.

◊ Unique Weapon: Dravin's Bow [64/80]

8 Hefid's Cell (Locked: Apprentice)

This leads to a tiny dark cell where a maniac named Hefid the Deaf is babbling incoherently. She may have valuables on her corpse.

9 Salvianus's Cell

A man named Salvianus regales you with past talks. He may be an Imperial officer driven mad by war. He's no pushover if you decide to attack.

◊ Chest ◊ Loose gear

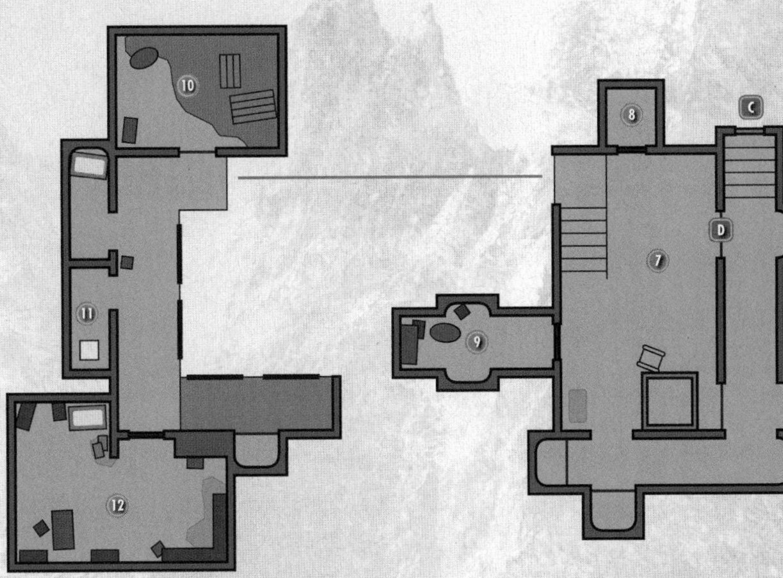

10 Knjakr's Cell

A mad chef is holed up in this cell.

◊ Crafting: Grindstone

11 Murder Hole

You can strike Salvianus from up above if you wish from here.

12 Esbern's Hideout

This secure underground chamber is the hiding place of Esbern, the Blades chronicler. You can only open the reinforced door during Main Quest: The Cornered Rat. Once inside, check through the multitude of books and a chest.

◊ Skill Book [One-Handed]: Fire and Darkness [B2/10]

◊ Chest

[9.01] Ivarstead

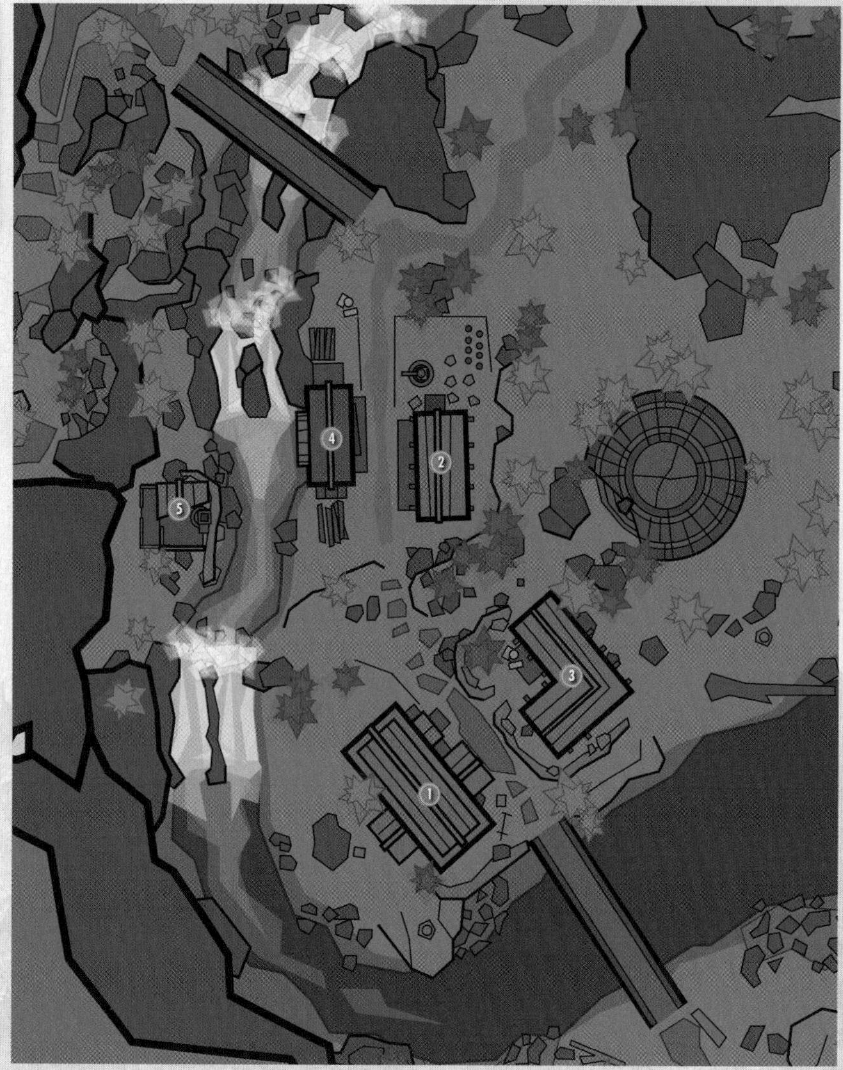

Related Quests

- Main Quest: The Way of the Voice
- Temple Quest: The Book of Love
- Dark Brotherhood Quest: Side Contract: Narfi
- Dungeon Quest: Wilhelm's Specter*
- Miscellaneous Objective: Innkeeper Rumors (Vilemyr Inn)
- Miscellaneous Objective: Lifting the Shroud* (Wilhelm)
- Miscellaneous Objective: The Straw That Broke* (Narfi)
- Miscellaneous Objective: Grin and Bear It* (Temba Wide-Arms)
- Miscellaneous Objective: Climb the Steps* (Kimmek)
- Favor (Activity): Harvesting Crops* (Boti)
- Favor (Activity): The Gift of Charity* (Narfi)

Habitation: Town

- Bassianus Axius
- Boti
- Fastred
- Gwilin
- Ivarstead Guard
- Jofthor
- Klimmek
- Lynly Star-Sung (Bartender)
- Narfi
- Temba Wide-Arm (Marriage Prospect)
- Wilhelm (Innkeeper; Marriage Prospect)

Crafting

- Tanning Rack

Services

- Marriage Prospect: Temba Wide-Arm [58/62]
- Marriage Prospect: Wilhelm [59/62]
- Trader (Bartender): Lynly Star-Sung [5/5]
  - Food
- Trader (Innkeeper): Wilhelm [15/15]
  - Food, Room and Board
  - Innkeeper Rumors

Quest Items

- Sapphire Dragon Claw
- Wylandriah's Spoon (Wylandria's Satchel)

Collectibles

- Dragon Claw: Sapphire Dragon Claw [8/10]
- Unique Item: Reyda's Necklace [96/112]
- Chest(s)
- Potions
- Loose Gear

This idyllic logging and fishing village sits along the west bank of Lake Geir, right near the foot of Skyrim's towering mountain, the Throat of the World [6.38]. Interesting things are occurring at Ivarstead, not the least of which being the supposedly haunted barrow that's just outside of town.

Exterior

Speak with Klimmek, Narfi, and Temba Wide-Arm to obtain a set of Miscellaneous Objectives. Temba will also pay you for any firewood you happen to chop outside, and you can gain the Gift of Charity by giving poor Narfi a gold piece.

◊ Crafting: Tanning Rack

1 Vilemyr Inn

The local innkeeper, Wilhelm, has plenty of information to impart. Chat him up to gain a new Side Quest involving the nearby haunted barrow, along with new map data and other random rumors. Bring the informative journal you discover within Shroud Hearth Barrow [9.02] to Wilhelm, and he'll hand you a special Sapphire Claw that lets you explore more of the place.

Lynly Star-Sung is also here. You can ask her to play an instrumental song for 5 septims (unless you can persuade her to play for free). Lynly is the woman who Sibbi Black-Briar is searching for in the quest "The Lover's Requital." Temba Wide-Arm and Gwilin both reside at the inn as well.

◊ Dragon Claw: Sapphire Dragon Claw [8/10]

◊ Chests (2)

◊ Loose Gear

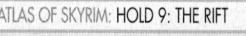

2 Fellstar Farm

The farmhouse is commonly locked, and a woman named Boti is usually found inside, keeping the place neat and orderly. Her husband, Jofthor, can usually be found outside working the grain mill or feeding the livestock. Her daughter, Fastred, can be found helping her mother in the fields or complaining about being stuck in this backwater village.

- Area Is Locked (Apprentice)
- Wylandriah's Satchel
- Wylandriah's Spoon (Wylandriah's Satchel)
- Chest

3 Klimmek's House

Bassianus Axius and Klimmek share this place. Klimmek allowed Bassianus to move in a long time ago, and their personalities have been clashing ever since.

- Area Is Locked (Apprentice)
- Chest
- Potion
- Loose Gear

4 Temba Wide-Arm's Mill

This is where Temba and Gwilin can be found during the day, chopping wood and working the mill.

5 Narfi's Ruined House

Narfi resides here, in the ruins of his family home. He can be found wandering around aimlessly calling for his sister or skulking about annoying the locals.

[9.02] Shroud Hearth Barrow

Related Quests

Dungeon Quest: Wilhelm's Specter*

Recommended Level: 6

Dungeon: Draugr Crypt

Draugr
Skeleton
Wyndelius Gatharian

Crafting

Alchemy Lab

Dangers

Battering Ram Trap (pressure plate)
Dart Trap (lever, pressure plate)
Flamethrower Trap (trapped door)
Oil Lamp Trap
Oil Pool Trap
Rockfall Trap (trip wire)
Swinging Blade Trap (trip wire, wall chain)
Spear Trap (pressure plate)
Swinging Wall Trap (pressure plates)

Puzzles

Claw Door (Sapphire Claw)
Nordic Pillars

Quest Items

Wyndelius' Journal

Collectibles

Skill Book [Illusion]: Before the Ages of Man [B2/10]

Special Objects

Word Wall: Kyne's Peace [3/3]
Chests
Potions
Loose gear

This barrow lies on the hill overlooking the village of Ivarstead. Speaking with Wilhelm, the town's innkeeper, provides you with a Dungeon Quest that entices you to investigate this haunted place in search of treasure.

A Exit to Skyrim

1 Lever Puzzle Passage

Obtain a bit of loot from a shelf on your way into this passage, where the ghost of Wyndelius Gatharian urges you to leave, then vanishes. Enter the nearby alcove, grab a Skill Book off the stone table, then face west, toward the far portcullis, so that two pairs of wall levers are visible. Looking at the portcullis, pull the leftmost lever, followed by the "inside" right lever, to manipulate the gates so that you may progress. Don't touch the far-right lever—it triggers a trap. Pull the wall chain that follows to raise the next few portcullises, and optionally unlock an Adept-level iron door to access a dangerous nook with a trapped chest and a pressure plate trap.

- Danger! Dart Trap (lever, trigger hinge), Spear Trap (pressure plate, wall chain)
- Skill Book [Illusion]: Before the Ages of Man [B2/10]
- Potion

2 Wyndelius's Study

Visit this room to catch up with the specter that warned you before. The ghost of Wyndelius Gatharian now lashes out at you. Lay it to rest to discover that it was never a ghost at all—just a man who'd been drinking a special potion to disguise himself as a specter. Collect the nearby journal and a few samples of the potion to gain new insight and advance the plot.

- Crafting: Alchemy Lab
- Wyndelius's Journal
- Philter of the Phantom
- Satchel
- Potions
- Loose gear

3 Hall of Stories

Bring the journal that you find at [2] back to Ivarstead's innkeeper, Wilhelm. In thanks, he'll give you the Sapphire Claw, which you need to open the Nordic Puzzle Door here. Beware of gouts of flame as you open the door and enter the passage (or look to the floor and disarm that particular trap), then inspect the Sapphire Claw and notice three symbols etched on its palm (Moth, Owl, Wolf). Rotate the door's three concentric rings to form the same pattern of symbols, then inspect the central keyhole to insert the claw and open the way forward.

- Danger! Flamethrower Traps (trapped door)

4 Draugr Ambush

A number of Draugr burst out of sarcophagi as you move through this chamber, and portcullises fall to trap you inside. Deal with the undead, then pull the lever in the east alcove to open the portcullises and continue on.

- Loose gear

5 Spiral Stairwell

A trapdoor plunges you into shallow water at the foot of this winding stairwell. Nab some gear from the bottom of the pool, then swim up and climb out (or pull the lever to lift yourself out). Go all the way upstairs to locate a Master-level locked door. If you can pick this tricky lock, you should have no trouble opening the large chest in the nook beyond.

- Chest (Locked: Expert)
- Loose gear

6 Oil Pit Chamber

Leap two pressure plates and slay a skeleton as you descend into this chamber, where a mob of skeletons are gathered in the center of the room below. Quickly knock down one of the central hanging lamps to ignite the oily floor beneath them and decimate all of the skeletons at once. Before going downstairs, spy a handle near a sarcophagus and pull it to allow you to enter the treasure room. More Draugr awaken when you reach the room's far side. Deal with them, then proceed through the northeast door. Beware of the trip wire stretched across the passage beyond.

- Danger! Battering Ram Trap (pressure plate), Dart Trap (pressure plate), Oil Lamp Trap, Oil Pool Trap
- Chest
- Potions
- Loose gear

7 Trapped Passage

Avoid triggering a trip wire and pressure plate as you battle a bow-wielding Draugr here. Jump the trip wire and sneak around the plate to avoid stirring more undead. Once again, you find yourself locked in the room. Pick the lock on the far door, or take it from the corpse of the Draugr near the door once you kill it—again.

- Danger! Swinging Blade Trap (trip wire/ wall chain), Swinging Wall Trap (pressure plate)

8 Drawbridge Chamber

A waterfall pushes a gentle stream through this long, enemy-free chamber. Pull a nearby wall chain to open the portcullis at the end of the stream, then claim a coin purse from the bottom of the small pool beyond. Find some gear behind the waterfall as well, then go upstairs and open the large southwest door to enter a chamber with a lone Draugr guard. Step on the pressure plate here to rotate the walls and catch glimpses of four glyphs. Spin the four glyph pillars outside the room to mimic the same pattern (Whale, Hawk, Snake, Whale), then step on the central pressure plate to lower a drawbridge.

- Potion
- Loose gear

9 Path to the Depths

Avoid the pressure plate just inside the door, then deliberately hit the trip wire to trigger a rockfall trap that smashes the Draugr in this passage.

See if you can open the Apprentice-level locked door to access a small nook with a gold bar, but beware the flamethrower trap that fires when you remove it.

- Danger! Flamethrower Trap (pressure pedestal), Rockfall Trap (trip wire), Swinging Wall Trap (pressure plate)
- Potion
- Loose gear

B Door to Shroud Hearth Depths

Your trip through the barrow has brought you to a cavernous underground temple. Slaughter all skeletons and Draugr that rise from their sarcophagi here—the last few are quite powerful. Proceed to the back room when the northwest passage opens, and disarm the trap on the large chest (or carefully stand to the side) to avoid being shot by darts. Gain a new Word of Power from the far Word Wall before taking your leave of this haunted barrow.

- Danger! Dart Trap
- Word Wall: Kyne's Peace [3/3]
- Potion
- Loose gear

C Door to Shroud Hearth Barrow

[9.03] Pinepeak Cavern

Dungeon: Animal Den

Animal

Collectibles

Skill Book [Smithing]: Heavy Armor Forging
Chest
Potion
Loose gear
Mineable ore (Corundum)

This small cave lies at the eastern base of Whiterun's towering mountain, the Throat of the World [6.38], landing it within the Rift's bounds. Slay the exterior Bear, then enter the cave and put down a second Bear to secure a Skill Book and a chest.

[9.04] Geirmund's Hall

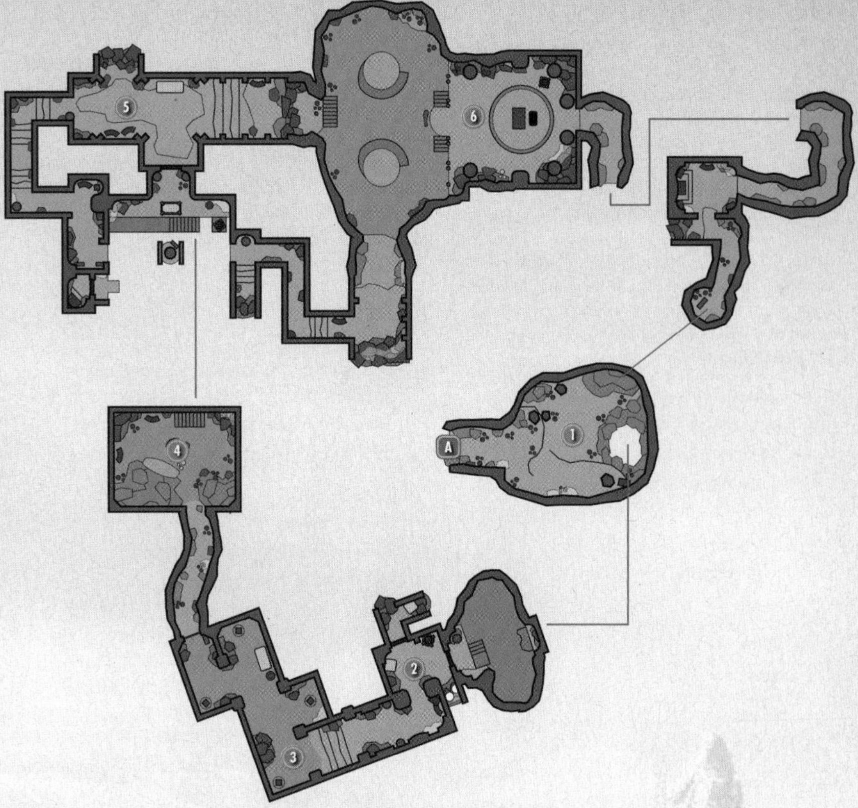

Related Quests

Side Quest: Forbidden Legend
Dungeon Activity

Recommended Level: 6

Dungeon: Draugr Crypt

Animal
Draugr
Sigdis Gauldurson

Crafting

Arcane Enchanter

Dangers

Dart Trap (pressure plate)
Flamethrower Trap (hinge trigger)
Magic Caster Trap
Mammoth Skull Trap (tabletop pressure plate)
Spear Trap (lever)
Swinging Blade Trap (pressure plate)

Puzzles

Nordic Puzzle Pillars

Collectibles

Skill Book [Two-Handed]: Words and Philosophy
Unique Item: Gauldur Amulet Fragment (Geirmund's Hall) [97/112] (Sigdis Gauldurson)
Unique Weapon: Gauldur Blackbow [65/80] (Sigdis Gauldurson)
Chests
Potions
Loose Gear

Explore the isle in the center of Lake Geir to discover this foreboding crypt. Geirmund's Hall is home to Sigdis Gauldurson, one of the three brothers sealed away in ancient times.

A Exit to Skyrim

1 Entry Cavern

Eliminate a few pesky Skeevers in the first small cavern, then search the body of a fallen adventurer to discover a book that hints at the history behind this tomb. Steel yourself, then leap into the nearby pit, landing in a watery chamber below. Search a short underwater passage to locate a sunken chest before climbing onto dry land and proceeding through and iron door.

◊ Chest

2 Spiderweb Hall

Slay a couple of Frostbite Spiders in this webbed corridor, and unlock an Adept-level iron door to access a small nook with some potions and gear. Disarm the trapped chest on the shelf, or stand off to one side as you open it to dodge the flamethrower trap. Then skirt a nearby pressure plate as you head toward [3].

◊ Danger! Dart Trap (pressure plate), Flamethrower Trap (hinge trigger)
◊ Chest
◊ Potions
◊ Gear

3 Flooded Catacombs

Cut down the Draugr that arise from these waterlogged burial passages, note the four glyphs on the walls near the stairs as you enter, two on each wall. Spin the four pillars in the passage ahead so that their glyphs match the ones near the stairs (Hawk, Whale, Snake, Whale). With the pillars properly rotated, pull the lever near the far portcullis to open the way forward. Beware of taking the Soul Gem from the table here—removing it causes the giant mammoth skull to swing at you like a battering ram!

◊ Danger! Mammoth Skull Trap (pressure pedestal)
◊ Potion

4 Lord Geirmund's Tomb

This tall chamber features plenty of Draugr and multiple tiers of walkways. Fight your way up some wooden stairs and collect an important key from the withered hand of Lord Geirmund on the altar. Inspect the nearby epitaph before using the key to open the nearby door and advance.

◊ Lord Geirmund's Key
◊ Potion
◊ Loose Gear

5 Crafty Passages

Slay a powerful Draugr and his animal companion here, then search around to find a couple of potions. Take the west passage and go upstairs to battle another mighty Draugr. Don't pull the lever by the bridge—it triggers a trap. Instead, turn around and pull a different lever that's mounted on the wall to lower to lower the bridge.

Back out on the upper level of Lord Geirmund's Tomb [4], look to your right to see a small ledge. Jump down and disarm the trap on the door, then enter the small alcove to find a locked chest.

Cross the bridge (pulling another lever on the far side of the central platform), then carefully avoid the pressure plate as you move on to the next chamber. It activates a nasty set of swinging blades that are difficult to dodge once triggered.

◊ Danger! Magic Caster Trap, Spear Trap (lever), Swinging Blade Trap (pressure plate)
◊ Crafting: Arcane Enchanter
◊ Chest (Locked: Expert)
◊ Potions
◊ Loose gear

6 Sigdis Gauldurson's Tomb

An incredibly powerful undead archer rises to combat you in this flooded chamber. Throughout the battle, Sigdis Gauldurson summons two illusory duplicates of himself to confuse you. The "real" enemy is the one that wears a horned helmet. Attack this version of the Sigdis to inflict damage, eventually slaying the fiend to attain two powerful items from its remains. When Sigdis falls, a secret door opens, allowing you to take the east passage to locate a giant chest and other valuables, including a Skill Book found on the top of the nearby bookshelf. Follow the passage to its end and pull a lever to open a secret door that connects back to [1].

- ◊ Unique Item: Gauldur Amulet Fragment (Geirmund's Hall) [97/112] (Sigdis Gauldurson)
- ◊ Unique Weapon: Gauldur Blackbow [65/80] (Sigdis Gauldurson)
- ◊ Skill Book [Two-Handed]: Words and Philosophy
- ◊ Chest
- ◊ Potions
- ◊ Loose Gear

[9.05] Nilheim

Related Quests

Dungeon Quest: The Nilheim Scam*

Recommended Level: 6

Dungeon: Bandit Camp

Guard

Telrav

Collectibles

Chests (2)

Apothecary's Satchel

Potion

Loose Gear

Little remains of this ruined fortress, which lies just east of Lake Geir, save some stone steps and a tower. An injured merchant named Telrav is found on the road outside of Nilheim. Agree to help Telrav, and he'll lead you to the camp—and then springs an ambush! Slay the villains and then raid their campsite in just retribution.

[9.06] Sarethi Farm

Related Quests

Side Quest: A Return to Your Roots

Miscellaneous Objective: Smooth Jazbay* (Avrusa Sarethi)

Favor (Activity): Harvesting Crops* (Avrusa Sarethi)

Habitation: Farm

Aduri Sarethi

Avrusa Sarethi (Marriage Prospect)

Rift Guard

Crafting

◊ Alchemy Lab

Tanning Rack

Services

Marriage Prospect: Avrusa Sarethi [60/62]

Collectibles

Potions

Loose Gear

This quaint farm stands in the Rift's central wilds, just north of the Treva River.

Exterior

Speak with the farm's owner, Avrusa Sarethi, to learn how she managed to grow so much rare Nirnroot in her garden and obtain a Side Quest. Avrusa is also your final destination in the "Return to Your Roots" quest (see quest for details), and the remains of Sinderion's living quarters can still be found in her basement.

- ◊ Crafting: Tanning Rack

Sarethi Farm (Interior)

Breaking into the farmhouse is profitable due to the many potions and additional Nirnroot found in the cellar.

- ◊ Area Is Locked (Novice)
- ◊ Crafting: Alchemy Lab
- ◊ Potions
- ◊ Loose Gear

[9.07] Rift Stormcloak Camp

Related Quests

Civil War Quest (when active, depending on who you side with)

Habitation: Military: Stormcloak Camp

Stormcloak Quartermaster (Blacksmith)

Stormcloak Soldier

Services

Trader (Blacksmith): Stormcloak Quartermaster [31/33]

Weapons, Apparel, Misc

Crafting

Alchemy Lab

Anvil

Grindstone

Workbench

Special Objects

Civil War: Map of Skyrim

Chests

Potions

Loose Gear

Depending on the status of the Civil War quest line, you may or may not be able to visit this small Stormcloak campsite. Here you may trade with the quartermaster or use his plethora of crafting stations. Examine the tabletop map in one of the tents to potentially gain new map data.

[9.08] Rift Watchtower

Related Quests

Side Quest: The Forgemaster's Fingers

Recommended Level: 6

Dungeon: Bandit Camp

Bandit

Orc

Crafting

Tanning Rack

Collectibles

Skill Book [Heavy Armor]: Hallgerd's Tale [C2/10]

Chest

Potions

Loose Gear

Orcish bandits occupy this tower, which stands in the Rift's northern mountains, east of Lake Geir. Slay the ruffians to steal their plunder.

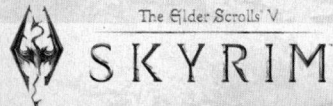

This large, forgotten temple runs deep into the Rift's southwest mountains, not far from the Dwarven ruins of Avanchnzel [9.18].

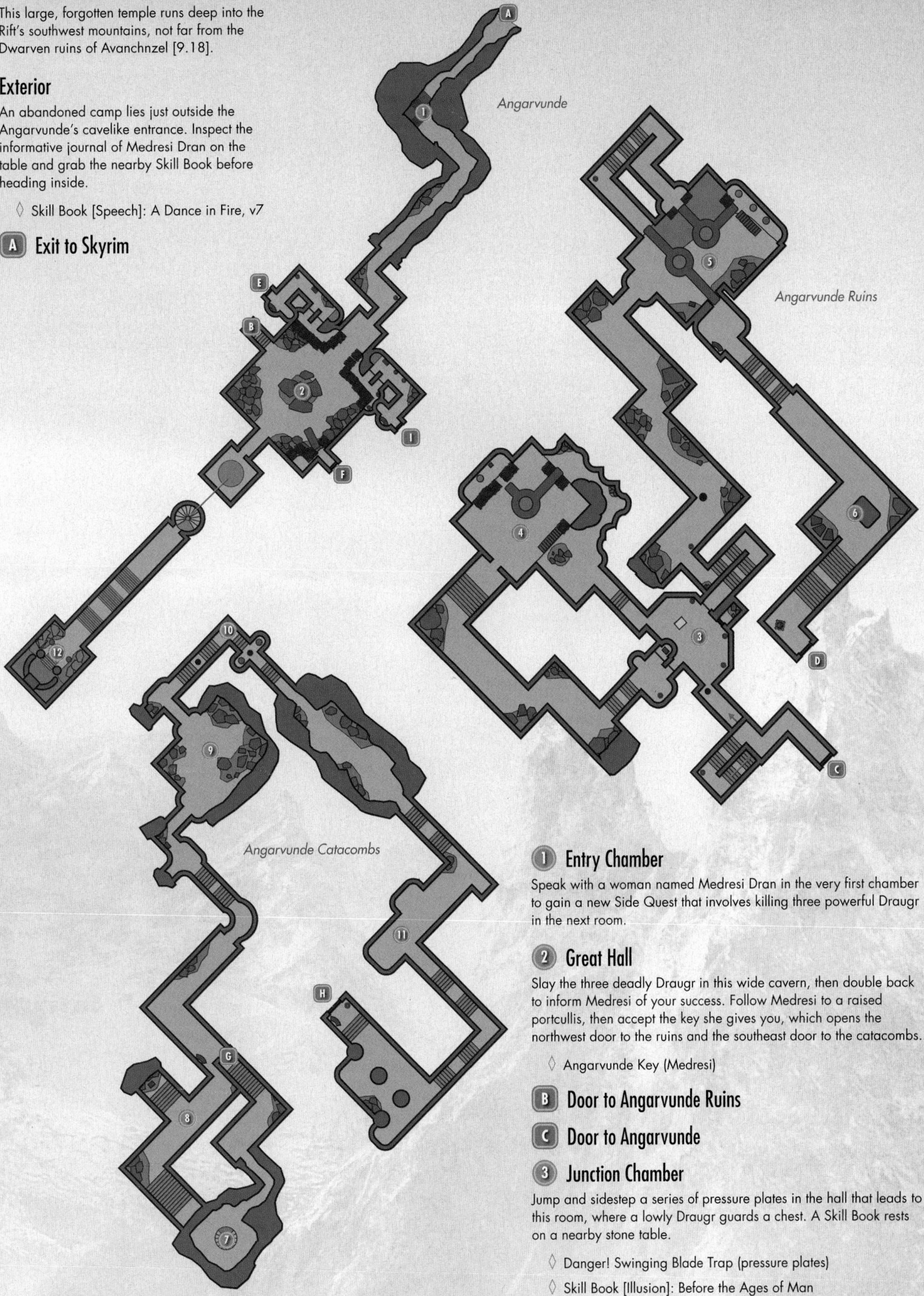

Exterior

An abandoned camp lies just outside the Angarvunde's cavelike entrance. Inspect the informative journal of Medresi Dran on the table and grab the nearby Skill Book before heading inside.

- ◊ Skill Book [Speech]: A Dance in Fire, v7

A Exit to Skyrim

1 Entry Chamber

Speak with a woman named Medresi Dran in the very first chamber to gain a new Side Quest that involves killing three powerful Draugr in the next room.

2 Great Hall

Slay the three deadly Draugr in this wide cavern, then double back to inform Medresi of your success. Follow Medresi to a raised portcullis, then accept the key she gives you, which opens the northwest door to the ruins and the southeast door to the catacombs.

- ◊ Angarvunde Key (Medresi)

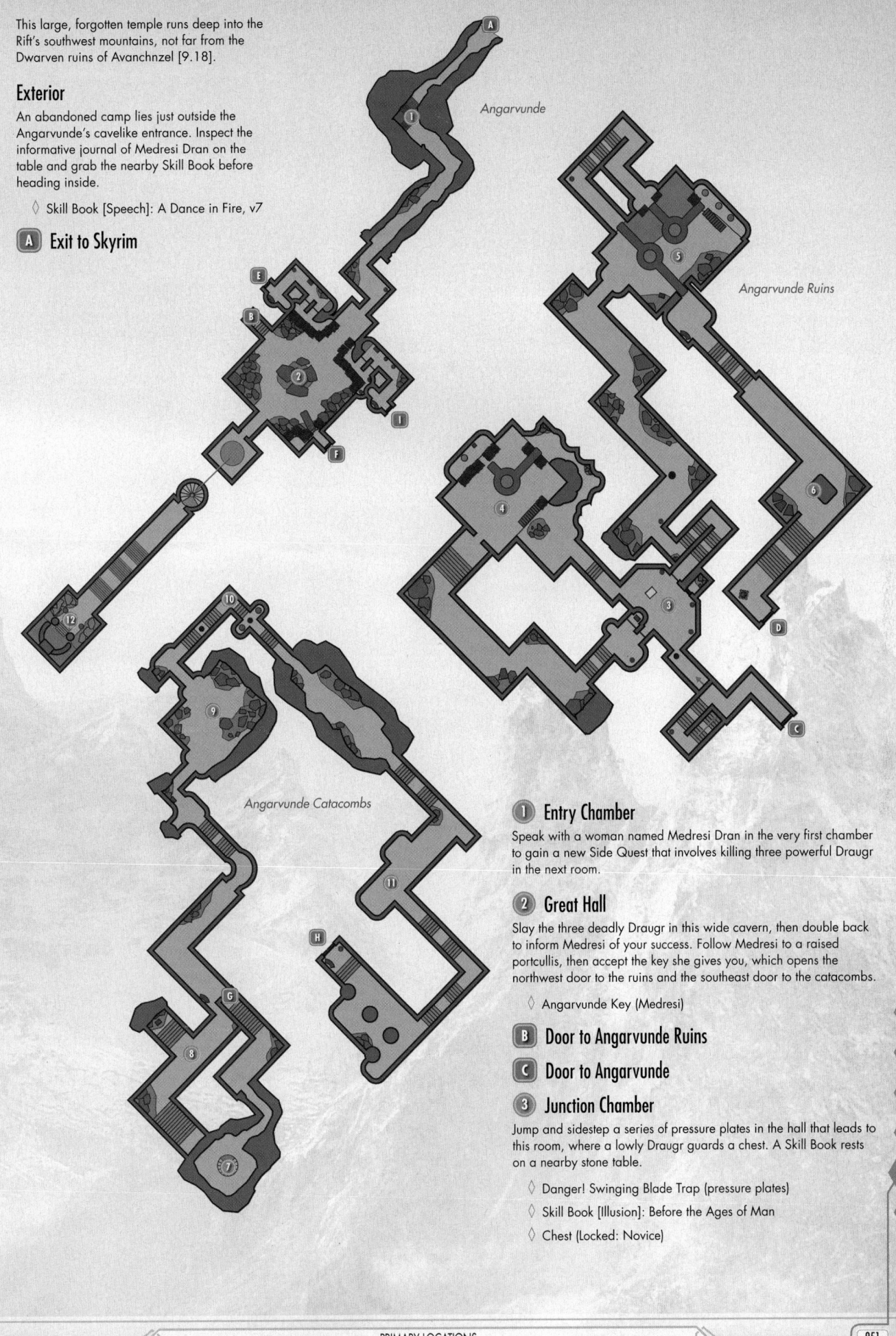

B Door to Angarvunde Ruins

C Door to Angarvunde

3 Junction Chamber

Jump and sidestep a series of pressure plates in the hall that leads to this room, where a lowly Draugr guards a chest. A Skill Book rests on a nearby stone table.

- ◊ Danger! Swinging Blade Trap (pressure plates)
- ◊ Skill Book [Illusion]: Before the Ages of Man
- ◊ Chest (Locked: Novice)

4 Broken Walkway Hall

Another group of powerful Draugr guards this chamber. Jump across the broken walkway to reach a valuable potion that sits atop a pedestal, but stand to one side of the pedestal when collecting the potion to avoid being impaled by spears. Take the lower passage to loop back around to [3].

- Danger! Spear Trap (pedestal pressure plate)
- Potion

3 Junction Chamber Revisited

Pull a lever to lower all of the portcullises in this chamber, then loot a locked chest you couldn't have reached before. Cut across the room and take the east passage to [5].

- Chest (Locked: Novice)

5 Sarcophagi Chamber

Avoid a pressure plate as you cut down powerful Draugr in the passages that lead to this large chamber, where another group of fearsome undead burst out from wall sarcophagi to attack. Loot a chest on the ground floor before heading upstairs and taking a winding passage to [6].

- Danger! Battering Ram Trap (pressure plate)
- Chest

6 Ruins Exit Passage

Collect a few valuables and slay one last formidable Draugr as you navigate this passage, which leads back to the Great Hall.

- Potions
- Loose Gear

E Door to Angarvunde

F Door to Angarvunde Ruins

2 Great Hall Revisited

Collect a bit of loot that you couldn't have reached before as you reenter the Great Hall, then scale the southeast fallen pillar to reach the door that leads into the catacombs.

- Chest
- Potions

G Door to Angarvunde Catacombs

H Door to Angarvunde

7 Broken Stairwell Chamber

Descend into this room, slaying a Draugr from an elevated vantage before dropping from the broken stairwell and proceeding to [8].

8 Burial Passages

Dispatch a few powerful Draugr in this passage, and stand to one side of the chest that lies atop the northwest stairs to avoid a nasty trap when opening it (or try disabling its trigger hinge).

- Danger! Trapped Chest

9 Canis Tree Chamber

Loot a chest on your way to this chamber, then raid another chest that lies near one of the gnarled Canis trees.

- Chest
- Chest (Locked: Novice)
- Potion

10 Arrow Trap Stairs

Beware of two pressure plates that trigger similar traps as you scale the stairs in this passage.

- Danger! Floor Arrows (pressure plates)

11 Catacombs Exit Passage

Cut through a host of Draugr as you navigate the catacombs' final passage, returning to the Great Hall.

- Potion
- Loose gear

H Door to Angarvunde

I Door to Angarvunde Catacombs

2 Great Hall (Third Visit)

Loot a chest and throw a lever to lower the portcullises as you did before. With all portcullises open, return to Medresi, who foolishly rushes off and is slain by a deadly trap. Enter the raised section of floor afterward, and you'll be lowered down to a secret passage.

- Chest

12 Word Wall Chamber

The temple's treasure is grand indeed, and there's nothing left to guard it. Obtain a new Word of Power from the ancient Word Wall here, and loot a large chest for vast wealth, completing your quest.

- Word Wall: Animal Allegiance [3/3]
- Chest

[9.18] Avanchnzel

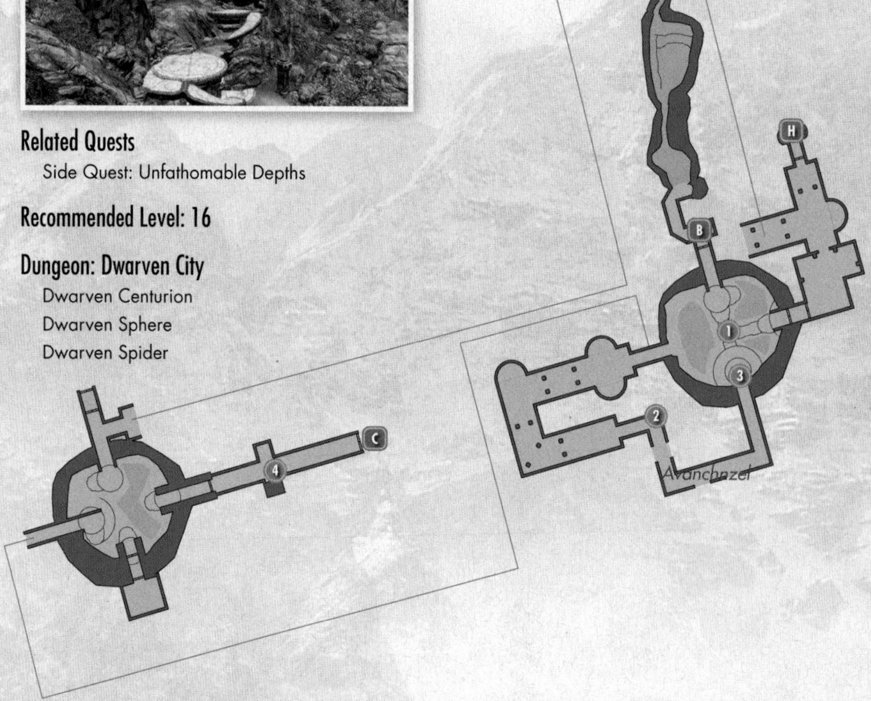

Related Quests

Side Quest: Unfathomable Depths

Recommended Level: 16

Dungeon: Dwarven City

Dwarven Centurion
Dwarven Sphere
Dwarven Spider

Crafting

Alchemy Lab

Dangers

Dwarven Thresher Trap (trapped door)
Dwarven Thresher Trap (pressure plate)
Spear Trap (trapped door)

Collectibles

Skill Book [Restoration]: Racial Phylogeny

Special Objects

Lexicon Receptacle
Chests
Potions
Loose Gear

This impressive collection of dwarven ruins stands among the Rift's southern mountains. This is a large area, for the ruins run deep into the rock. Scale a series of spiral pathways to locate Avanchnzel's cavelike entrance, and head inside.

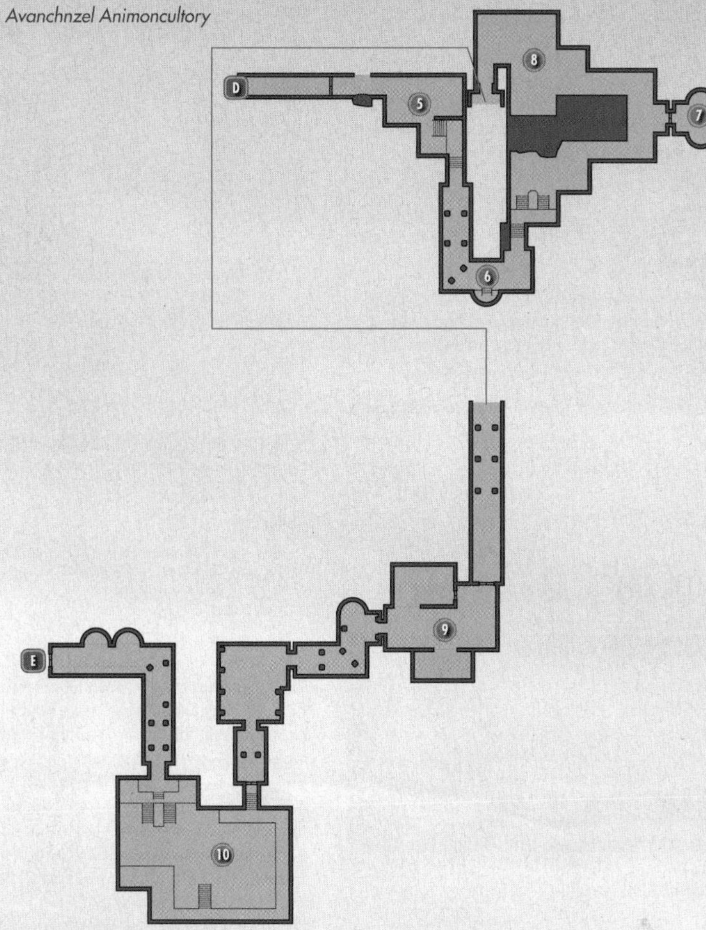

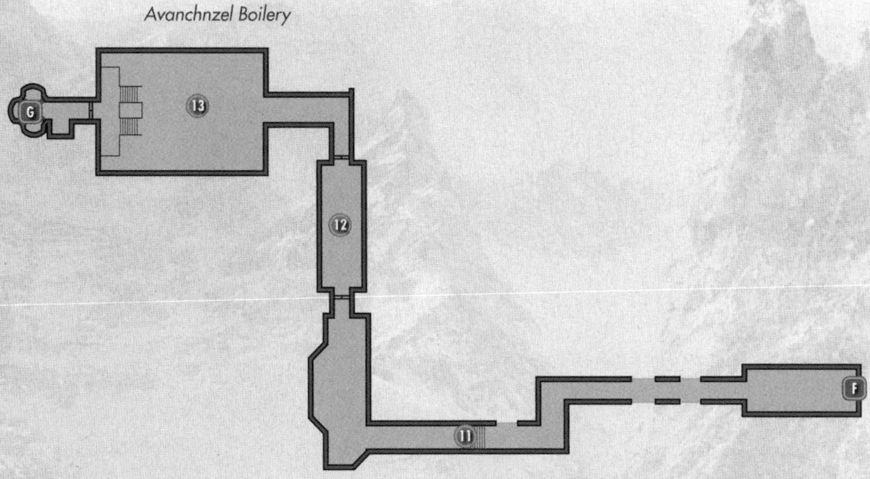

A Exit to Skyrim

1 Central Cavern

Destroy a couple of formidable Dwarven Spiders on your way to this massive, open-air cavern. Take the east passage and dismantle a Dwarven Sphere in the adjoining chamber, then scale a sloping passage and unbar a door so you may step out to the balcony and loot an outdoor chest. Head back inside and return to the large cavern. Loot another chest on a wall as you enter the south passage.

- Chest
- Chest (Locked: Apprentice)

B Door to Avanchnzel Balcony

2 South Passage

Dispatch more Dwarven Spheres and Spiders as you navigate the long passage that leads down to the main chamber's ground floor. Unlock an Apprentice-level gate along the way to access a nook with chest.

- Chest

3 Trapped Treasure Room

Annihilate a deadly group of Dwarven Spiders to secure the central chamber's ground floor, then approach the south door. Look up to notice several slots on the ceiling—spears will stab out from these when you open the door, so stand back and to one side to avoid this nasty surprise, or try to pick the door's trigger hinge. Loot two chests in the treasure room before backtracking out.

- Danger! Spear Trap (trapped door)
- Chests (2)
- Potion
- Loose Gear

4 Path to Animoncultory

From the base of the central chamber, take the east passage to locate the door that leads to the Avanchnzel Animoncultory. Raid a chest in the hall as you go.

- Chest

C Door to Avanchnzel Animoncultory

5 Treasure Room

Smash some Dwarven Sentries in this first chamber, then unlock the Adept-level gate to reach a chest.

- Chest

6 Connecting Corridor

Loot a locked chest as you navigate this winding hall.

- Chest (Locked: Adept)

7 Study

To safely enter this room, stand close to the door and run forward as you open it. You'll burst into the room before being hacked up by the blades that emerge from the ground when the door is opened.

- Danger! Dwarven Thresher Trap (trapped door)
- Skill Book [Restoration]: Racial Phylogeny
- Chest
- Loose Gear

8 Storage A

Make use of an Alchemy Lab here if you like.

- Crafting: Alchemy Lab
- Potion

9 Storage B

Bash through a few more dwarven automatons in this chamber, then unlock an Adept-level door and an Apprentice-level gate to access a pair of small treasure rooms.

- Chest
- Chest (Locked: Novice)
- Potions
- Loose Gear

10 Centurion Assembly

A large number of Dwarven Spiders guard this large chamber, where fearsome Dwarven Centurions were once built. Loot a chest that sits on a large shelf against the west wall on your way to the boilery.

- Chest

E Door to Avanchnzel Boilery

F Door to Avanchnzel Animoncultory

11 Access Corridor

Raid a pair of chests that sit on shelves as you move through this corridor, and grab a few potions from another shelf ahead.

- Chests (2)
- Potions

12 Spinning Blade Slope

Avoid the pressure plates that line this sloping hallway—stepping on one triggers a nasty spinning blade trap that must then be bypassed with care. Pull the lever at the bottom of the slope to deactivate the trap if need be.

- Danger! Dwarven Thresher Trap (pressure plates)

13 Centurion Chamber

A tower Dwarven Centurion guards this final chamber. Defeat the mechanical monster easily by simply backing away until the brute becomes stuck on thick pipes. You may then unleash ranged attacks to bring it down.

- Lexicon Receptacle

G Door to Avanchnzel

[9.19] Clearspring Tarn

Dungeon: Animal Den

Animal

Hunter (Food Vendor)

Services

Traders (Food Vendors): Hunters (2) [12/13; 13/13]

Food, Misc

Collectibles

Skill Book [Archery]: Vernaccus and Bourlor

Unique Weapon: Bow of the Hunt [66/80]

Chest(s)

Potions

This small, tranquil mountain lake is nestled among the Rift's northern mountains. Descend a dirt trail around the cliffside to reach a cave that lies just beneath the tarn.

Exterior

As you approach the pond, some hunters arrive and hunt the deer that gather here. If you like, trade with the hunters for food and pelts, then dive into the water to locate a sunken chest. Then follow the trail around the cliffside to enter a nearby cave.

- Chest (Locked: Apprentice)

Clearspring Cave

A lone predator guards this small cave. Kill the monster, then loot a chest here and claim a unique bow that inflicts bonus damage to animals. Check the Skill Book that also lies nearby.

- Skill Book [Archery]: Vernaccus and Bourlor
- Unique Weapon: Bow of the Hunt [66/80]
- Chest
- Potions

[9.20] Boulderfall Cave

Recommended Level: 6

Dungeon: Warlock Lair

Mage

Crafting

Alchemy Lab

Dangers

Bone Alarm Trap

Trapped Chest

Collectibles

Skill Book [Alchemy]: Herbalist's Guide to Skyrim

Potion

Loose Gear

This small, abandoned mine lies in the mountains to the west of Shor's Stone [9.25] and has become the home of a dangerous mage. Avoid the hanging rattles on your way in and, after slaying the mage, open the large chest from the side to dodge a dangerous flamethrower trap that fires from the wall above. Collect the Skill Book on the shelf before using the nearby Alchemy Lab.

[9.21] Northwind Mine

Recommended Level: 12

Dungeon: Special

Skeleton

Dangers

Rockfall (tripwire)

Underground Connection: Northwind Summit [9.22]

Collectibles

Skill Book [Block]: Death Blow of Abernanit

Chest

Knapsack

Loose Gear

This haunted mine has been tunneled into the Rift's northern mountains. Make your way to a tall chamber, then dispatch skeletons as you scale the wooden ramps that lead to the higher passages. Swipe the Skill Book on the ground-floor table, and find a chest and knapsack hidden beneath the scaffolding on the first ledge. Stand back and safely trigger the trip-wire trap in the upper passage to avoid a dangerous trap, then follow the passage to its end to exit the mine, arriving at Northwind Summit [9.22].

[9.22] Northwind Summit

Dungeon: Dragon Lair

Dragon (after Main Quest: Dragon Rising)

Skeleton

Crafting

Smelter

Underground Connection: Northwind Mine [9.21]

Special Objects

Word Wall: Aura Whisper [3/3]

Chest

Chest (Locked: Apprentice)

Loose Gear

This abandoned mining site sits high atop the Rift's northern mountains. You must navigate the Northwind Mine [9.21] to reach this summit, where plenty of treasure and an ancient Word Wall are found. And that's not all—after the "Dragon Rising" quest, an irritable dragon can be found and fought here as well!

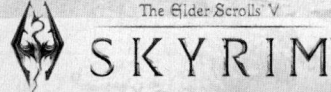

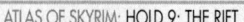

[9.23] Tolvald's Cave

Related Quests

Thieves Guild Radiant Quest: No Stone Unturned

Dungeon Activity

Recommended Level: 18

Dungeon: Falmer Hive

Animal

Falmer

Crafting

Alchemy Lab

Tanning Racks (3)

Dangers

Bear Traps

Bone Alarm Trap

Swinging Wall Trap (trip wire)

Trapped Chest

Quest Items

Crown of Barenziah

Collectibles

Skill Book [Block]: Battle of Red Mountain [B2/10]

Skill Book [Destruction]: Mystery of Talara, v3

Chest(s)

Potions

Loose Gear

This sizeable cave lies northeast of Shor's Stone [9.25] and runs deep into the Rift's eastern mountains, eventually giving way to ancient dwarven ruins. After collecting all of the Unusual Gems that are scattered throughout Skyrim, you're told to visit Tolvad's Cave in search of a special crown, to which the gems belong.

A Exit to Skyrim

1 Entry Cavern

Slaughter a few angry predators in the first cavern, then loot a locked chest near the central fire pit and flip through an informative journal that sits on a nearby stool. Beware of bear traps, hanging rattles, and many more predators as you make your way to the next room.

- Danger! Bear Traps, Bone Alarm Trap
- Chest (Locked: Apprentice)

2 Trapped Chest Chamber

An ornate metal door leads into this small, stone room. First, pull the chain on the west wall to open two side passages and slay a few Falmer. These villains would have ambushed you when you opened the room's tantalizing trapped chest. If you can't unlock the chest's trap hinge, stand atop the chest when opening it to avoid being shot by arrows. Then use the Falmer passages to visit a higher chamber, where you find an Alchemy Lab and several potions.

- Danger! Trapped Chest
- Crafting: Alchemy Lab
- Potions
- Loose Gear

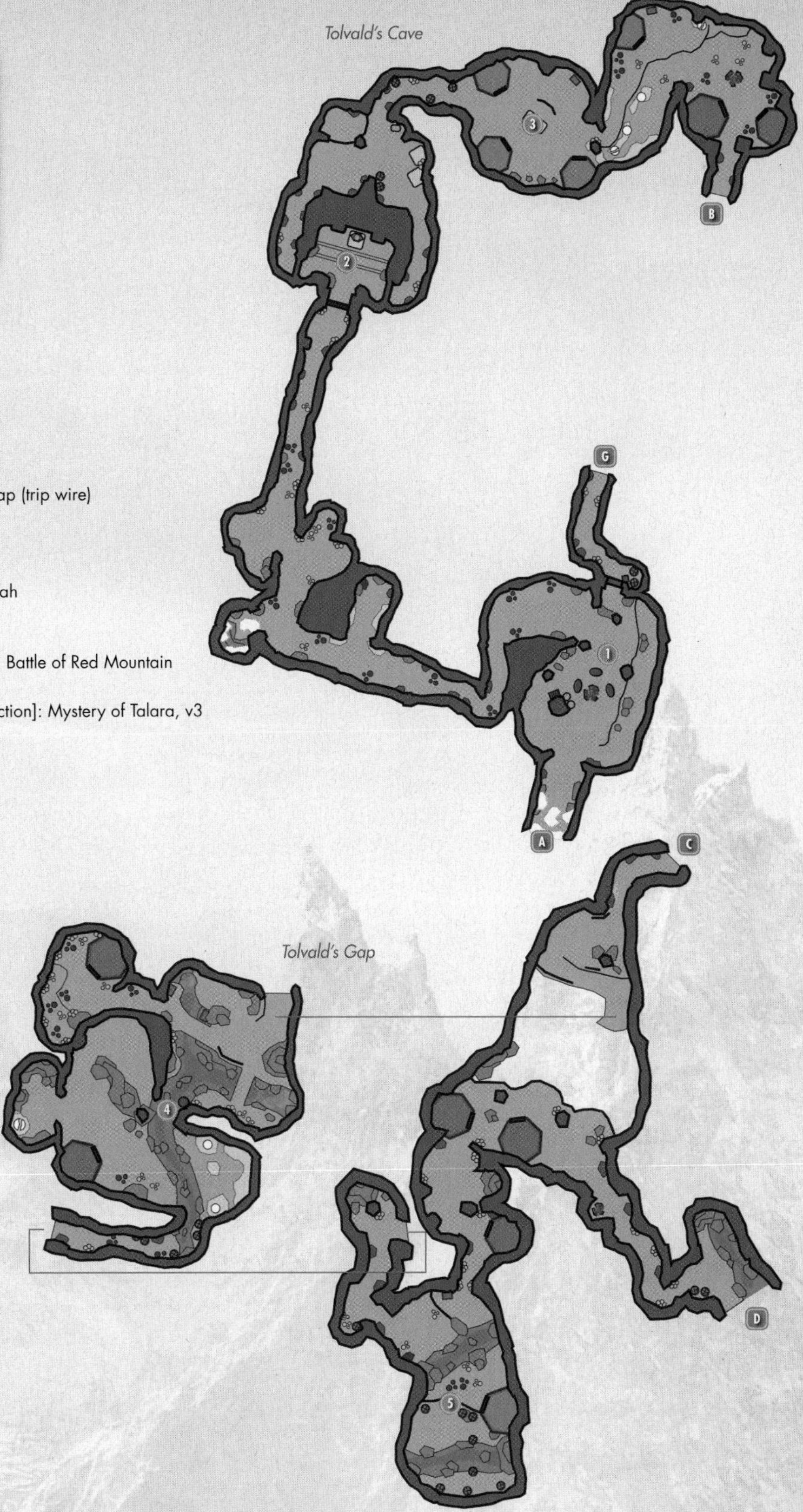

3 Falmer Lair

Kill the many Falmer in this cavern, then find a useful key on one of their bodies. Loot an odd-looking chest and then cut down an overgrown Frostbite Spider on your way to the back cavern, opening a locked chest along the way. Beware of additional Falmer emerging from small holes in the walls and find a third chest in a tent before taking the nearby passage to Tolvald's Gap.

- Crafting: Tanning Racks (2)
- Shaman's Key (Falmer)
- Chests (2)
- Chest (Locked: Adept)

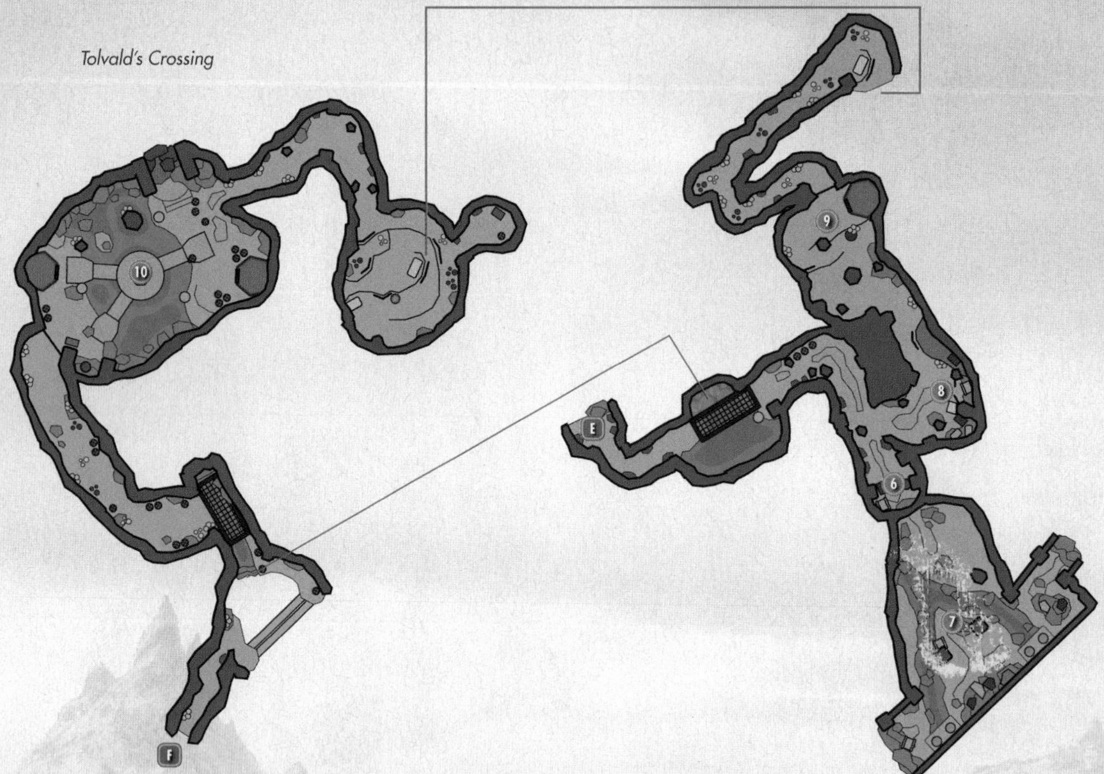

B Path to Tolvald's Gap

C Path to Tolvald's Cave

4 Divided Cavern

Dispatch several Falmer and a Skeever or two as you descend into the Gap's first cavern. Take a northwest passage to locate a small side cave with a chest in a Falmer tent and a large amount of mushrooms the Falmer have been cultivating. Backtrack out and locate another chest near a waterfall. Follow the stream to the cavern's southern half, where many more Falmer lurk. Follow the stream to its end, then take a side passage up to the next cavern.

- Chest
- Chest (Locked: Apprentice)
- Potions
- Loose Gear

5 Chaurus Den

Dangerous Chaurus lurk in this far chamber. Find a chest atop the waterfall here, then take the nearby passage to arrive at the previous chamber's high southern ledge, collecting a few potions from a nook along the way.

- Chest
- Potions

4 Divided Cavern Revisited

Loot another chest in a tent on this side of the cavern as you loop around to a passage that leads even deeper into the cave.

- Chest (Locked: Adept)

D Path to Tolvald's Crossing

E Path to Tolvald's Gap

6 Dead End

Beware of the powerful Falmer that lurks in the thick spray of the giant waterfall here, then head south when you reach a fork in the tunnel to reach this dead end, where a spirit materializes for a moment before vanishing. Inspect the interesting journal that lies near a skeleton here before looting the locked chest.

- Danger! Swinging Wall Trap (trip wire)
- Chest (Locked: Apprentice)

7 Old Road

If you've found all 24 Unusual Gems and are visiting this place as part of the "No Stone Unturned" quest, then the aforementioned dead-end passage will be opened, exposing a section of ancient underground dwarven road that's been caved in. Sift through the rubble here to locate the Crown of Barenziah.

- Crown of Barenziah

8 Caravan Junkyard

Stand as far back as possible before intentionally triggering the trip wire at the start of the junction's east passage, which leads to this treasure-filled passage. Treasured belongings pillaged from Dark Elf refugees lie heaped in a pile. You may not be able to open the giant locked chest here, but you can collect two valuable Skill Books, then explore an upper ramp to locate another locked chest before making your way to [8].

- Skill Book [Block]: Battle of Red Mountain [B2/10]
- Skill Book [Destruction]: Mystery of Talara, v3
- Chest (Locked: Expert)
- Chest (Locked: Master)
- Potion
- Loose Gear

9 Winding Ramp Cavern

Find a chest in a Falmer tent on your way to this tall cavern, where another mysterious Dark Elf spirit briefly appears to you once more. Inspect the nearby trailbook to uncover a bit more of the intrigue surrounding this place. Ascend the winding uphill path, being wary of the many overhead ledges from which Falmer archers can fire down at you. Find another chest in a tent before taking a high passage to [9].

- Crafting: Tanning Rack
- Chests (2)
- Loose Gear

10 Shallow Rapids Cavern

Several powerful Falmer and a hulking Chaurus lurk in this final cavern, which features a rushing stream. A large chest is attached to the wall near the makeshift throne the Falmer have erected here. Open the south gate and take a winding passage back to the Crossing's first cavern. Carefully navigate the ledges and steam pipes without falling to make your way to an exit path that leads back to the start of Tolvald's Cave.

F Path to Tolvald's Cave

G Path to Tolvald's Crossing

[9.24] Shor's Watchtower

Related Quests
- Civil War Quest: Reunification of Skyrim
- Civil War Quest: Compelling Tribute

Recommended Level: 6

Dungeon: Special

Collectible
- Chest (Locked: Novice)
- Potion
- Loose Gear

This wooden watchtower stands on the road north of Shor's Stone, on the precipice of the cliffs that descend from the Rift into Eastmarch. The guards here been slain, so feel free to loot the tower, including the chest on its highest tier. A note on the tower's ground floor hints at what befell the guards.

[9.25] Shor's Stone

This quiet mining community lies along the Rift's eastern road, making it a convenient stop for travelers heading between Eastmarch and the Rift. Unfortunately, the local mine has been overrun with giant spiders!

Related Quests
- Miscellaneous Objective: Mine or Yours* (Filnjar)
- Miscellaneous Objective: Letter for Mr. Rock-Chucker* (Sylgia)
- Favor (Activity): Mining Ore* (Grogmar gro-Burzag)

Habitation: Town
- Filnjar (Blacksmith; Marriage Prospect)
- Frostbite Spider
- Grogmar gro-Burzag
- Odfel
- Shor's Stone Guard
- Sylgja (Marriage Prospect)

Crafting
- Blacksmith Forge
- Grindstone
- Smelter
- Tanning Rack
- Workbench

Services
- Marriage Prospect: Filnjar [61/62]
- Marriage Prospect: Sylgja [62/62]
- Trader (Blacksmith): Filnjar [33/33]
  - Weapons, Apparel, Misc
- Chest(s)
- Potions
- Loose Gear
- Mineable ore (Ebony)

Exterior

Barter with Filnjar, the local blacksmith, or use his array of crafting stations. Speak with Filnjar to learn more about the trouble in the mine and gain a new Miscellaneous Objective.

- Crafting: Blacksmith Forge, Grindstone, Smelter, Tanning Rack, Workbench

1 Sylgja's House

Breaking into Sylgja's house is risky because she's usually home.

- Area Is Locked (Novice)
- Chests (2)

2 Filnjar's House

Filnjar has prospered over the years—raid his abode while he's busy working outdoors to claim valuable plunder.

- Area Is Locked (Novice)
- Chests (2)
- Potions
- Loose Gear

3 Odfel's House

With spiders overrunning the mine, Odfel just hangs at home. Clear out the mine so he can return to work—then plunder his vacant abode!

- Area Is Locked (Novice)
- Chest

4 Redbelly Mine

Slay a number of Frostbite Spiders as you descend this tall mine's winding ramps. Splatter every arachnid to clear out the infestation, then optionally mine some valuable Ebony Ore from the veins at the bottom before backtracking out to inform Filnjar of your success.

- Knapsack
- Loose Gear
- Mineable ore (Ebony)

[9.26] Fort Greenwall

Related Quests
- Civil War Quest: Reunification of Skyrim
- Civil War Quest: The Battle for Fort Greenwall

Recommended Level: 6

Habitation: Military Fort
- Animal
- Bandit (pre-Civil War)
- Soldier (Imperial/Stormcloak, depending on the state of the Civil War)

Crafting
- Blacksmith Forge
- Grindstone
- Workbench

Collectibles
- Skill Book [One-Handed]: Mace Etiquette [C2/10]

Special Objects
- Shrine of Stendarr [4/5]
- Chest(s)
- Potions
- Loose Gear

This imposing stronghold stands just south of the village of Shor's Stone [9.25]. The Rift's eastern road runs directly through the fort. You may therefore breach the fort quite easily, or opt to slip in through the cave. Fort Greenwall is a point of contention between the Stormcloaks and Imperials, so you may find soldiers occupying this space instead of bandits, depending on the status of the Civil War quest line.

Exterior
Dispatch a legion of bandits to secure the fort's outer grounds. Then begin raiding its various interior sections.

- ◊ Crafting: Blacksmith Forge, Workbench
- ◊ Loose Gear

Fort Greenwall (Interior)
Slay more bandits within Fort Greenwall's main interior. Find a grindstone in the basement and a knapsack near the tower's upper door.

- ◊ Crafting: Grindstone
- ◊ Loose Gear
- ◊ Knapsack

Prison
The prison connects to the Captain's Quarters, and its basement is infested with Frostbite Spiders. Cut through thick webs to make your way to the bottom, then unlock the Master-level door to access a chest.

- ◊ Chest
- ◊ Loose Gear

Captain's Quarters
The bandit's stalwart chief lies in the Captain's Quarters and won't go down without a fight. If you can't break into this area via its locked trapdoor entrance, enter through the fort's prison instead. Touch the small shrine you discover in here to instantly rid yourself of all diseases. A Skill Book sits on the shelf in the master bedroom.

- ◊ Area Is Locked (Master)
- ◊ Skill Book [One-Handed]: Mace Etiquette [C2/10]
- ◊ Shrine of Stendarr [4/5]
- ◊ Chest
- ◊ Potion
- ◊ Loose Gear

Cave
A small cave runs beneath Fort Greenwall. Enter via its northern mouth and pick an Expert-level gate to make your way through, emerging at a well within the fort. As you explore the cave, find a letter at the bottom of the southern pool that explains what fate befell the nearby floating corpse.

[9.27] Heartwood Mill

Related Quests
- Miscellaneous Objective: Fight or Flight* (Grosta)

Habitation: Lumber Mill
- Gralnach
- Grosta
- Rift Guard

Crafting
- Grindstone
- Tanning Rack

This small lumber mill, located at the west end of Lake Honrich, has fallen on hard times. Its owner has vanished, leaving his wife and child to run the place.

Exterior
Speak with Grosta to sell her any firewood you might be carrying and to gain a new Miscellaneous Objective.

- ◊ Crafting: Grindstone, Tanning Rack

Heartwood Mill (Interior)
The cabin sports a Novice-level lock, and there's little of value inside beyond foodstuffs, ingredients, and a coin purse.

- ◊ Area Is Locked (Novice)

[9.28] Faldar's Tooth

Recommended Level: 6

Dungeon: Bandit Camp
- Animal
- Bandit

Crafting
- Blacksmith Forge
- Grindstone
- Tanning Rack

Dangers
- Battering Ram Trap (trip wire)
- Bear Traps
- Bone Alarm Trap
- Oil Pool Trap
- Rockfall (trip wire)
- Spear Trap (pressure plates)
- Swinging Wall Trap (pressure plates/lever)
- Trapped Chest

Collectibles
- Skill Book [Alteration]: The Lunar Lorkhan
- Skill Book [Archery]: The Marksmanship Lesson
- Skill Book [Lockpicking]: Proper Lock Design [B2/10]
- Chests
- Potions aplenty
- Loose Gear

This mighty keep overlooks Lake Honrich from the north and has been overrun by lawless bandits who are running a wolf fighting ring.

Exterior
The bandits are quick to open the stronghold's front gate when they see you approach, but it isn't a warm welcome. They release vicious pit wolves to maul you! Slay the wicked beasts, then decide how you wish to enter the keep: either hurry inside the main gate and storm its interior, or remain outside the walls and circle around the fort's west side to unlock an Adept-level gate and bypass the keep's sizeable inner working altogether.

Later, after you've advanced to the fort's upper ramparts, fight your way up its wooden stairs and walkways until you reach a large tent with a chest and useful key. Go back downstairs a few levels and use the key to unlock the Expert-level door of the keep's eastern tower. Loot the chest within and proceed to the tower's top, then follow a rampart to reach the next tower. Go in and head up to battle the bandits' formidable leader, then loot the giant chest he was guarding and collect a couple of Skill Books.

- ◊ Skill Book [Alteration]: The Lunar Lorkhan
- ◊ Skill Book [Lockpicking]: Proper Lock Design [B2/10]
- ◊ Faldar's Tooth Key
- ◊ Chest (Locked: Novice)
- ◊ Chest (Locked: Apprentice)
- ◊ Loose Gear

A Exit to Skyrim (Lower Grounds)

1 Entry Tower

Avoid hanging rattles and pressure plates as you descend the keep's first stairwell. Don't free the caged pit wolf you encounter unless you wish to combat it. Simply go down to the lowest level and take the north passage to [2].

◊ Danger! Bone Alarm Trap, Spear Trap (pressure plates)

2 Cage Chamber

Ignite the oily floor here before you're detected by the patrolling bandits—one of them is a mage whose fireballs may set the room ablaze if you don't take advantage of the hazard first. Secure the room afterward, then optionally pick the Adept-level cages to free (and fight) a number of pit wolves. If you're swift, carefully step on the pressure plate to trigger a swinging wall trap, then deftly slip around the spiked gate to reach a locked chest in the small nook beyond. Pull the lever afterward to unhinge the spiked gate and escape the nook. Finally, unlock the Novice-level north door to access a small closet filled with potions.

◊ Danger! Oil Pool Trap, Swinging Wall Trap (pressure plate/lever)

◊ Crafting: Tanning Rack

◊ Chest (Locked: Adept)

◊ Potions aplenty

◊ Loose Gear

4 Waterlogged Chamber

A few feet of water cover the floor of this chamber. Search behind the stairs to discover a submerged chest, then scale the southern steps to find worthy loot and a satchel. Tug the pullbar on the southern balcony to open the far portcullis so you may proceed to [5].

◊ Chest

◊ Apothecary's Satchel

◊ Loose Gear

5 Kitchen and Quarters

Collect an interesting journal on your way to this area, where a slew of bandits await. Fight hard to slay this large group of scoundrels. Discover a Skill Book on a small table in the room with the firewood (west of the curved stairs).

◊ Skill Book [Archery]: The Marksmanship Lesson

◊ Potions

◊ Loose Gear

6 Exit Passage

Make a thorough search for loot as you navigate the keep's last few corridors, claiming plenty of potions. Beware of a trapped treasure chest, opening it from the side to avoid being shot by arrows or deactivating its trigger hinge. Dodge the pressure plate in the following passage on your way to the fort's final chamber.

◊ Danger! Bone Alarm Trap, Swinging Wall Trap (pressure plate), Trapped Chest

◊ Potions aplenty

◊ Loose Gear

7 Forge

Beware the trip wire that lies just underwater as you enter this final, waterlogged chamber. Numerous bear traps lie just beneath the water's surface as well, so keep an eye to the ground as you carefully creep through. Go upstairs and slay one final bandit to secure a crafting area. Carry on to find yourself back at [1], in an area you couldn't have reached before.

◊ Danger! Battering Ram Trap (trip wire), Bear Traps

◊ Crafting: Blacksmith Forge, Grindstone

◊ Chest (Locked: Novice)

◊ Loose Gear

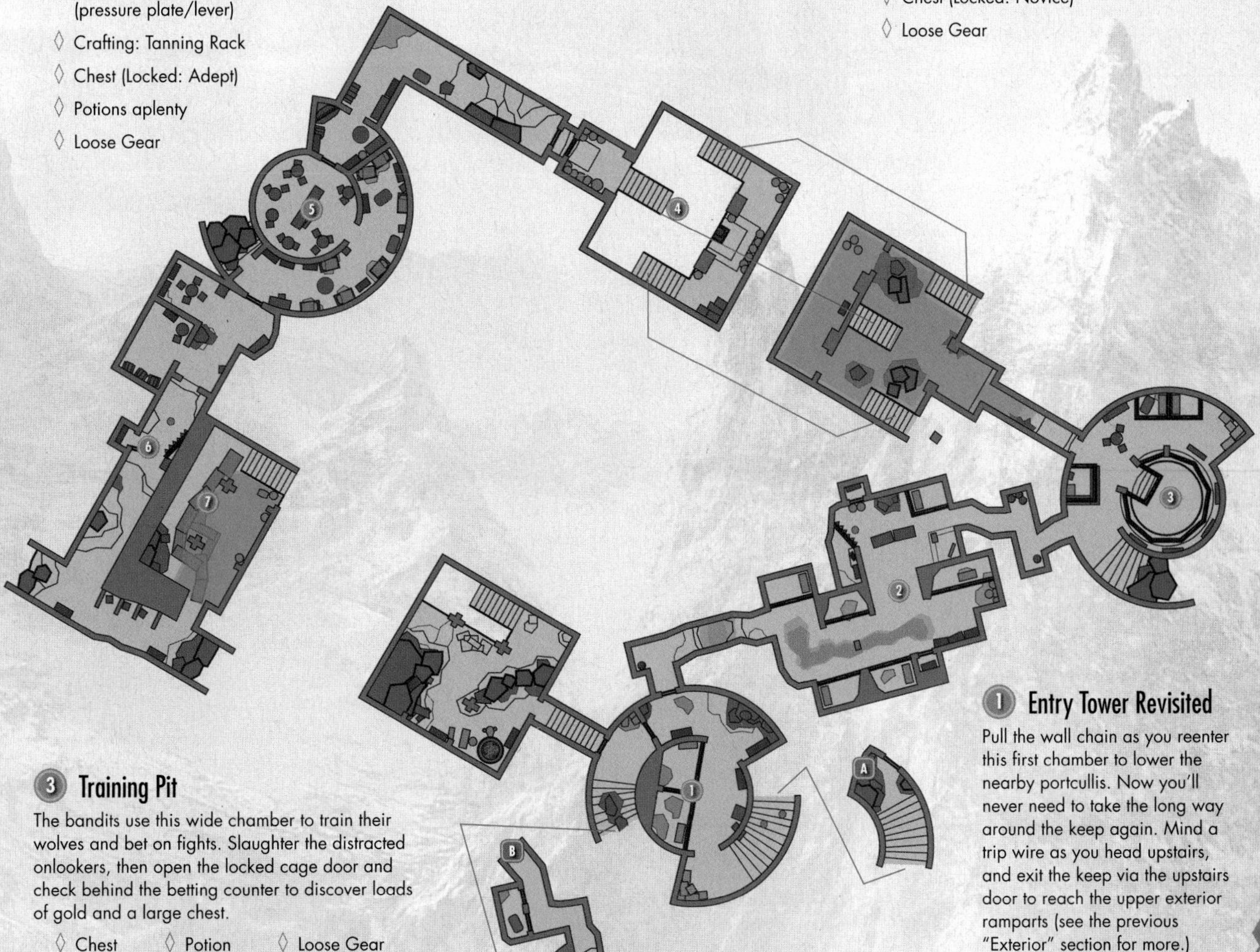

3 Training Pit

The bandits use this wide chamber to train their wolves and bet on fights. Slaughter the distracted onlookers, then open the locked cage door and check behind the betting counter to discover loads of gold and a large chest.

◊ Chest ◊ Potion ◊ Loose Gear

1 Entry Tower Revisited

Pull the wall chain as you reenter this first chamber to lower the nearby portcullis. Now you'll never need to take the long way around the keep again. Mind a trip wire as you head upstairs, and exit the keep via the upstairs door to reach the upper exterior ramparts (see the previous "Exterior" section for more.)

◊ Rockfall (trip wire)

B Exit to Skyrim (Upper Ramparts)

[9.29] Goldenglow Estate

Related Quests

- Side Quest: Captured Critters*
- Thieves Guild Quest: Loud and Clear
- Thieves Guild Radiant Quest: Larceny Targets*

Recommended Level: 6

Dungeon: Special	Dangers
Animal	Flail Trap (trip wire)
Aringoth	Oil Lamp Trap (trip wire)
Mercenary	Oil Pool Traps

Quest Items

- Goldenglow Bill of Sale

Collectibles

- Captured Critter: Bee in a Jar [5/5]
- Larceny Target: Queen Bee Statue [7/7]
- Skill Book [Pickpocket]: Guide to Better Thieving
- Area Is Locked (quest required)
- Chest(s)
- Potions
- Loose Gear

West of Riften, the sprawling Goldenglow Estate spans several islands across Lake Honrich. A small army of rugged Mercenaries guard the compound, and the south gate remains locked at all times; however, you discover means of slipping onto the premises during Thieves Guild Quest: Loud and Clear.

1 Main Gate

Goldenglow is a secure compound with only one entrance, and the guards aren't about to let anyone in.

2 Sewer Access

Approach Goldenglow Estate from the north to discover a low bank that you can climb onto, which is located here. This means of entry is only available during the "Loud and Clear" quest. Enter the nearby sewer to begin your infiltration.

3 Nirnroot Nook

Before entering the sewer, optionally swim over here to find a rare sprig of tingling Nirnroot growing down by the water.

Goldenglow Estate Sewer

Slay the Skeevers that scutter about the sewer, and safely trigger the trip wire near the oily floor with a ranged attack to ignite the oil and torch some more. If you can, unlock the Adept-level door that follows to claim a Skill Book and loot a chest. Beware of another trip-wire trap as you advance.

- Danger! Flail Trap (trip wire), Oil Lamp Trap (trip wire), Oil Pool Trap

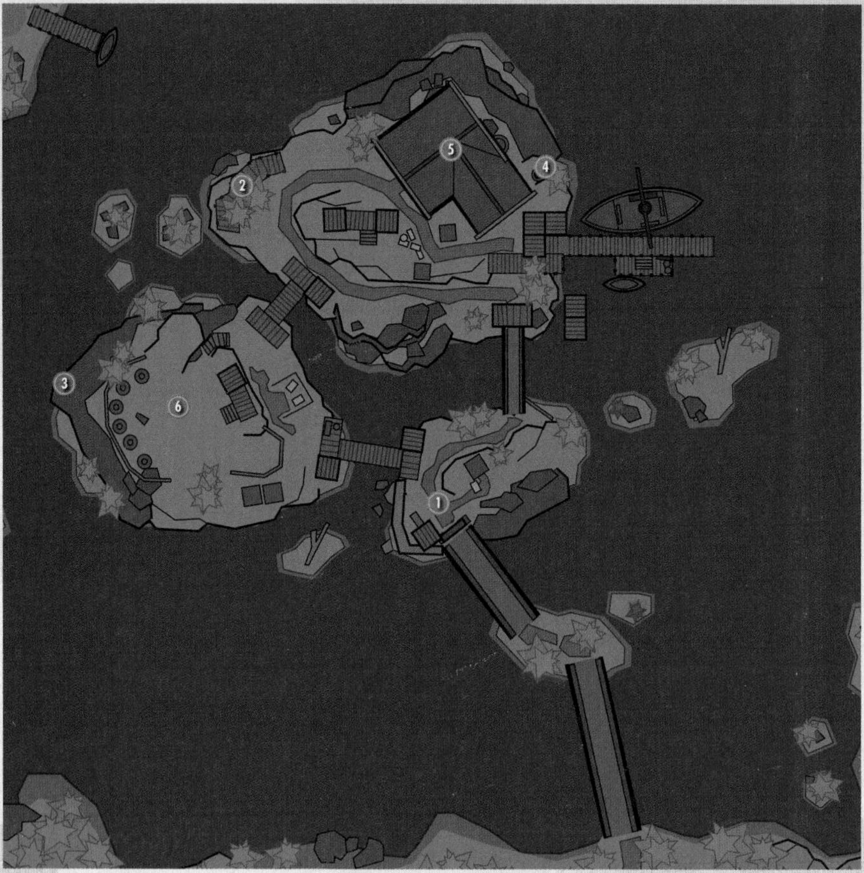

- Skill Book [Pickpocket]: Guide to Better Thieving
- Chest (Locked: Apprentice)
- Loose gear

4 Sewer Exit

The sewer spits you out behind the estate building, close to its rear door. Unfortunately, the door features an Expert-level lock—if you can't pick it, you'll need to risk sneaking around front and slipping in through the manor's unlocked front door.

5 Goldenglow Estate (Main Floor)

The estate's ground floor features two locked closets. Avoid the guards who patrol the halls and open both Adept-level doors to claim valuable loot from within. Cut through the central dining room to locate the stairs that lead up to the second floor, along with a Novice-level locked metal door that leads down to the basement.

- Strongbox (Adept)
- Chests (2)
- Knapsack
- Apothecary's Satchel
- Potions

5 Goldenglow Estate (Second Floor)

Visit the second floor in search of useful keys and loot. Sneak through the central bedroom to avoid detection and open an Adept-level door to raid a closet with an apothecary satchel hidden atop a shelf. Open the Novice-level door to Aringoth's bedchamber and quietly swipe a pair of keys from the wall hooks. Loot the chest by the bed as well, and take the unusual Bee in a Jar off the dresser. Lastly, nab the Queen Bee Statue from the nightstand—one of your fellow Thieves Guild comrades will be interested in this.

- Caged Critter: Bee in a Jar [5/5]
- Larceny Target: Queen Bee Statue [7/7]
- Goldenglow Cellar Key
- Goldenglow Safe Key
- Chest (Locked: Apprentice)
- Knapsack
- Apothecary's Satchel
- Loose gear

5 Goldenglow Estate (Basement)

Still more Mercenaries guard the basement. Continue to sneak through here, or slay the men so you may loot the chest they guard. Both men carry a Goldenglow Cellar Key, if you didn't obtain one from the second floor. Farther ahead, a seated guard can be barbecued by igniting a long patch of oil on the floor. Go downstairs to at last find the safe you seek, along with another chest.

- Danger! Oil Pool Trap
- Goldenglow Bill of Sale (Aringoth's Safe)
- Goldenglow Cellar Keys (Mercenaries)
- Aringoth's Safe (Locked: Expert)
- Chest (Locked: Novice)
- Chest (Locked: Apprentice)

6 Apiaries

Sneak over to this collection of beehives here—or simply sprint over at breakneck speed, hoping to outrun the guards—and use any fire-based attack to burn three of the apiaries. This completes a quest objective, but you'd better clear out of here fast!

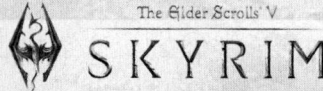

[9.30] Autumnshade Clearing

Recommended Level: 14

Dungeon: Spriggan Grove

Animal

Spriggan

Located north of Lake Honrich, this seemingly tranquil clearing is actually home to ferocious animals and reclusive forest spirits that may well attack trespassers. Loot the bodies of two slain hunters here, which lie in the brush near the west rock, to obtain some worthy gear.

[9.31] Merryfair Farm

Related Quests

Miscellaneous Objective: Bow to the Master* (Dravin Llanith)

Favor (Activity): Harvesting Crops* (Synda Llanith)

Habitation: Farm

Dravin Llanith

Rift Guard

Synda Llanith

This quiet farm lies just northwest of Riften. Speak with the farm's owner, Dravin Llanith, to gain a new Side Quest.

Merryfair Farm (Interior)

The farmhouse is locked, and there's little reason to break in. The only item of particular value is a coin purse tucked away near the basement bed.

◊ Area Is Locked (Novice)

[9.32] Riften Stables

Hofgrir Horse-Crusher (Stablemaster)

Sigaar (Carriage Driver)

Services

Trader (Carriage Driver): Sigaar [5/5]

Trader (Stablemaster): Hofgrir Horse-Crusher [5/5]

Potions

Swing by the stables that lie just outside Riften's main gate to purchase a horse or rent a carriage ride to another of Skyrim's bustling capitals. You can also speak with Hofgrir to participate in a challenging fistfight that can earn you 100 gold if you manage to KO the burly braggart.

Riften Stables (Interior)

Hofgrir's home is securely locked, but valuable treasure awaits those who manage to break in. Reading a certain book inside the cabin can potentially update your map with new locations.

◊ Area Is Locked (Adept)

◊ Strongbox (Apprentice)

[9.33] Fallowstone Cave
[9.33] Giant's Grove

Related Quests

Daedric Quest: The Cursed Tribe

Dungeon Activity

Dungeon: Animal Den/Giant Camp

Animal

Giant

Quest Items

Shagrol's Warhammer

Collectibles

Unique Weapon: Shagrol's Warhammer [67/80]

Unique Weapon: Volendrung [68/80]

Chest(s)

Potions

Loose Gear

This cavernous cave is located east of Riften, near the mountains that form Skyrim's border. Normally, Fallowstone Cave is filled with vicious predators, but during Daedric Quest: The Cursed Tribe, you'll find towering giants roaming the cave instead. You're also able to delve deeper into the cave during this quest, visiting a remote grove that's home to Giants.

Fallowstone Cave (Normal)

Beware of hungry predators as you follow the rushing stream. Stick to the south wall to discover a bandit's corpse inside a web-covered nook—collect the nearby potions after looting the body. Kill or avoid more predators as you follow the stream into an east passage. You can loot another slain bandit that lies in a southwest nook if you slay the nearby bear. Proceed up the path that follows, slaughtering more bears on your way up to a high, narrow trail that overlooks the main cavern. Unlock a large chest on this narrow ledge here as you proceed back to where you entered the cave.

◊ Chest (Locked: Apprentice)

◊ Potions

◊ Loose Gear

Fallowstone Cave (During "The Cursed Tribe")

All of the aforementioned goodies are still present within Fallowstone Cave when you visit the place with Chief Yamarz. Follow the Orc as he charges recklessly into the cave and battles a hulking giant. Help Yamarz bring down the brute, then loot the giant's remains, along with the chest near the firepit, which wasn't present in Fallowstone Cave before. Then simply continue following Yamarz as he battles another giant and a few Cave Bears. The Orc Chief leads you up a path to the Giant's Grove, which does not exist until you come here with Yamarz.

◊ Chest (Locked: Novice)

◊ Potions

Giant's Grove

The Giant's Grove is a large, outdoor area that can only be accessed by traveling through Fallowstone Cave; however, the trail that leads to the grove isn't present within Fallowstone until you come here with Chief Yamarz as part of "The Cursed Tribe" quest. Decide if you wish to slay the mighty giant here, or let Yamarz do it. The chief will die if you tell him to go, forcing you to finish his work, but he'll also attack you if you agree to slay the giant for him, hoping to keep your mouth shut about who really completed the task. If you choose to battle this mighty brute, exploit the rocks and trees here to keep distance from him. Relieve the Giant of Shagrol's Warhammer to advance the quest, then raid the large chest near the bloodstained altar before making your way back to Largashbur [9.36].

◊ Area Is Locked (quest required)

◊ Shagrol's Warhammer (Giant)

◊ Chest

◊ Potions

[9.34] Lost Prospect Mine

Related Quests

Dungeon Activity

Recommended Level: 6

Collectible

Potion
Loose Gear
Mineable ore (Gold)

This small mine, located in a valley on the Rift's far eastern edge, is believed to be depleted and has thus been abandoned. The intrepid explorer can still find value in this forgotten place, however.

Lost Prospect Mine (Interior)

Find an interesting journal on a table in the mine's central cavern, then locate some loose gear in the short side passages. Use the Whirlwind Sprint Shout (or make a very challenging jump) to reach the tunnel that stretches beyond the waterfall. Explore the tunnel's far end to discover a thick vein of precious Gold Ore, along with the skeletal remains of the missing miner.

[9.35] Black-Briar Lodge

Related Quests

Side Quest: Promises to Keep

Dungeon: Special

Black-Briar Mercenary
Frost (horse)

Quest Items

Frost's Identity Papers

Collectibles

Skill Book [Sneak]: Legend of the Krately House [B2/10]
Unusual Gem: [24/24]
Chest(s)
Potions

This sizable estate is nestled among the Rift's eastern mountains and is home to the Black-Briar family—a renowned lineage of proud brewers who have grown wealthy enough to hire formidable mercenaries to protect their interests. You must break into Black-Briar Lodge to steal a horse during Side Quest: Promises to Keep.

Exterior

Frost is kept in the southeast stables, but you first need to steal his Identity Papers. Wait for cover of night, then slip around and enter the lodge via the unlocked side door along its west wall—this leads into the manor's largely unguarded basement. Or take a more direct approach by slaying the exterior guards to obtain keys from their corpses, which unlock the lodge's Master-level front door. Once you've acquired Frost's Identity Papers, slip back out and sneak around behind the stables to approach Frost without being noticed.

- Black-Briar Lodge Key (Black-Briar Mercenaries)

Black-Briar Lodge (Basement)

A lone mercenary guards the basement. Wait a while and he'll go to sleep if it's late. Pick the nearby Adept-level wooden door, or pickpocket a key from the basement guard who opens it. Swipe Frost's Identity Papers from the end table in the small room beyond, which also features a chest.

- Black-Briar Lodge Key (Black-Briar Mercenary)
- Frost's Identity Papers
- Chest (Locked: Apprentice)
- Apothecary's Satchel
- Potions

Black-Briar Lodge (Upper Floors)

The lodge's main floor holds little of interest. Slay or slip past the guards in the dining hall, then go upstairs and visit the south bedroom to discover a Skill Book and an Unusual Gem that pertains to Thieves Guild Radiant Quest: No Stone Unturned. Lastly, backtrack out of the bedroom and search near the north upstairs door to spy a small chest that's tucked away on a shelf. The north door leads to a backyard area that's patrolled by more guards.

- Skill Book [Sneak]: Legend of the Krately House [B2/10]
- Unusual Gem: [24/24]
- Chest (Locked: Novice)

[9.36] Largashbur

Related Quests

Daedric Quest: The Cursed Tribe
Side Quest: The Forgemaster's Fingers

Recommended Level: 6

Habitation: Orc Stronghold

Atub (Trainer: Illusion)	Ogol
Garakh	Shagrol
Gularzob	Ugor
Lob	

Crafting

Alchemy Lab
Blacksmith Forge
Grindstone
Workbench

Services

Follower: Lob [43/47]
Follower: Ogol [44/47]
Follower: Ugor [45/47]
Trainer [Illusion: Expert]: Atub [2/2]

Collectibles

Skill Book [Block]: Battle of Red Mountain
Area Is Locked (quest required)
Chest(s)
Potions
Loose Gear

This Orc stronghold stands in the Rift's southern mountains, to the southwest of Lake Honrich. The Orcs here have fallen under a dreadful curse and will reluctantly accept the aid of an outsider.

Exterior

The first time you visit Largashbur, you'll witness the Orcs defending their stronghold from an enraged giant. Speak with the Orcs after the battle to learn of their current plight with the giants and gain a new Side Quest. The Orcs won't allow you to enter Largashbur until you've gathered several items that Atub needs to cure his cursed chief, Yamarz. (See the quest walkthrough for "The Cursed Tribe" for help in tracking these down.) Once you're granted entry, you can utilize a number of crafting stations and locate a locked chest near the entrance to the Largashbur Cellar.

- Crafting: Alchemy Lab, Blacksmith Forge, Grindstone, Workbench
- Chest (Locked: Master)
- Loose Gear

Longhouse

If you dare to steal from the Orcs, you'll find the Longhouse packed with valuables.

- Chests (2)
- Chest (Locked: Master)
- Potions
- Loose Gear

Cellar

Enter the Longhouse's cellar via an exterior trapdoor and loot the place without being seen. The middle book on the shelf is a Skill Book.

- Skill Book [Block]: Battle of Red Mountain
- Chest (Locked: Novice)
- Potions

[9.37] Darklight Tower

Related Quests
- Dungeon Quest: Repentance

Recommended Level: 8

Dungeon: Hagraven Nest
- Animal
- Hag
- Hagraven
- Illia (Follower)
- Silvia

Crafting
- Alchemy Lab
- Arcane Enchanter

Services
- Follower: Illia [46/47]

Dangers
- Swinging Wall Trap (pressure plate)

Collectibles
- Skill Book [Destruction]: Horrors of Castle Xyr
- Skill Book [Destruction]: Mystery of Talara, v3
- Skill Book [Illusion]: 2920, Sun's Dawn, v2 [A2/10]
- Unique Weapon: Staff of Hag's Wrath [69/80]
- Chests
- Potions aplenty
- Loose Gear

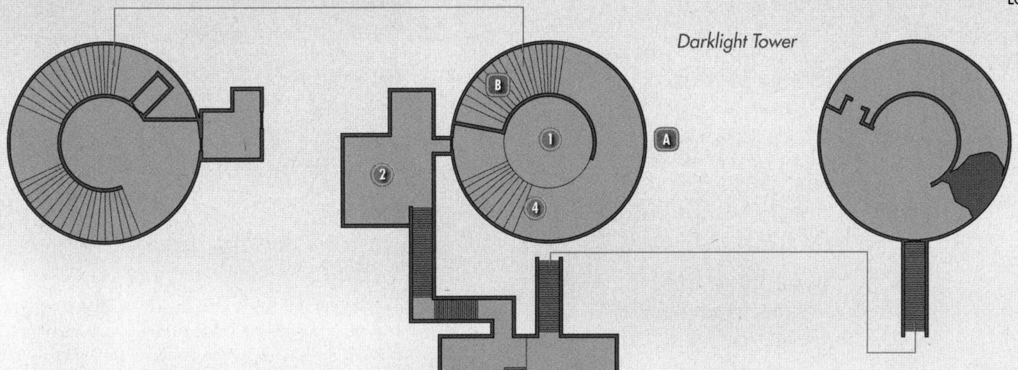

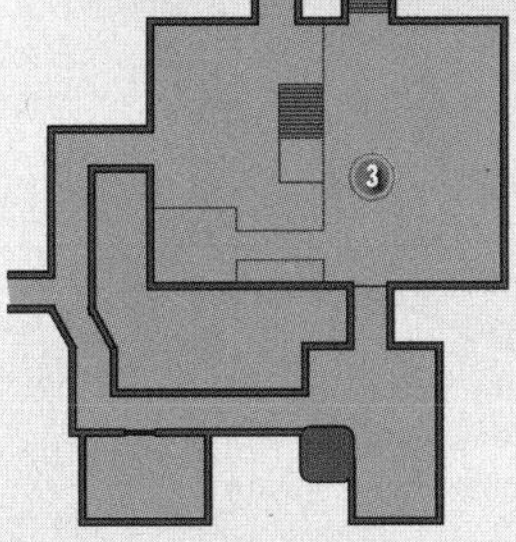

This stronghold, which stands nestled against the Rift's southern mountains to the southwest of Riften, derives its name from its tall central tower, which can be observed from a great distance. With the keep's outer wall in ruins, breaching the tower isn't nearly as challenging as it might have been in days of yore—simply scale the outer steps and head inside.

(A) Exit to Skyrim

(1) Entry Chamber

Speak with a woman named Illia in the tower's first cavern to learn that her mother is about to be made a part of some nefarious ritual. Agree to help Illia to gain a new Side Quest that involves rescuing her mother from the Darklight coven, then head upstairs to the room's balcony and slay a few Frostbite Spiders on your way to [2].

(2) Lab

Kill a skillful witch in this chamber, then loot the small chest that's tucked away in the northwest corner.

- ◊ Crafting: Alchemy Lab
- ◊ Chest
- ◊ Potions
- ◊ Loose Gear

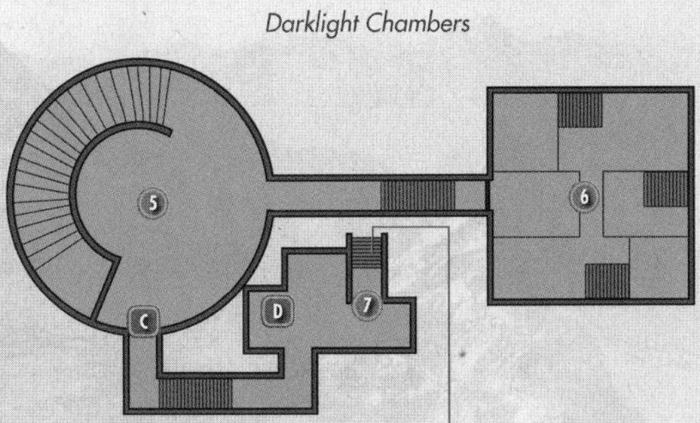

(3) Beast Chamber and West Passage

Another dangerous witch lurks in this large room, along with a fierce predator. Scale the steps and cross an arc to reach a platform with a few potions. Avoid the pressure plate here. Drop to the ground floor and follow Illia into the west passage. Destroy some thick webs as you go to expose a hidden chest. Open the locked south door that requires a special key by pickpocketing the needed key from Illia—you'll find valuable potions in the small closet beyond. Pull a lever to return to the main chamber, then cut straight across and head upstairs to find yourself in a high room that lies directly above [1].

- ◊ Danger! Swinging Wall Trap (pressure plate)
- ◊ Chest
- ◊ Potions aplenty

(4) Hagraven Chamber

Battle ferocious monsters and a Hagraven in this room, which lies directly above [1]. Raid the room after things settle down before proceeding through the door that leads to the Darklight Chambers.

- ◊ Skill Book [Illusion]: 2920, Sun's Dawn, v2 [A2/10]
- ◊ Chest

(B) Door to Darklight Chambers

(C) Door to Darklight Tower

(5) Locked Door Chamber

Cut down a pair of witches on your way up the initial staircase. The door that leads toward Illia's mother is locked. Take the east passage and enter the adjoining chamber instead. A Skill Book rests on a table that overlooks the central spike pit.

- ◊ Skill Book [Destruction]: Mystery of Talara, v3

6 Hagraven Lair

Defeat another dangerous Hagraven and a monster in this chamber to obtain a key, then raid a couple of chests and swipe several potions before returning to [5] to open the locked door.

- Darklight Tower Key (Hagraven)
- Chest
- Chest (Locked: Master)
- Potions

7 Study

Slay another witch in this crafting area, then loot a chest before proceeding upstairs. You soon emerge on high balcony back at [5]. Kill a Hag and two trolls up here, then proceed upstairs and head outside to face off against Illia's corrupted mother at the tower's apex.

- Crafting: Arcane Enchanter
- Chest
- Potions
- Loose Gear

D Exit to Skyrim

Tower Apex

Illia's mother, Silvia, awaits just outside the tower. Sit in the chair when instructed and wait for Illia to attack her mother by surprise, then join in and slay Silvia to complete Illia's quest. Invite Illia to continue adventuring with you if you like—she's a worthy companion. Raid a large chest in the nearby tent and claim the Skill Book on the table before setting off to new adventure.

- Skill Book [Destruction]: Horrors of Castle Xyr
- Unique Weapon: Staff of Hag's Wrath [69/80]
- Chest
- Potions

[9.38] Ruins of Rkund

Recommended Level: 6

Dungeon: Special

Wisp

Wispmother

Collectible

Chest

These remote Dwarven ruins lie within the Rift's southern mountains, on the edge of Skyrim. The best way to reach this site is by navigating Darklight Tower [9.37] and exiting in the mountains. The ruins here are guarded by several wisps and a formidable Wispmother. Slay these enemies so you may safely loot a dwarven chest that's tucked away in the far tower.

[9.39] Crystaldrift Cave

Related Quests

Dungeon Activity

Dungeon: Animal Den

Animal

Gadnor (deceased)

Collectibles

Unique Weapon: Gadnor's Staff of Charming [70/80]

Special Objects

Shrine of Kynareth [6/6]

Chest

Apothecary's Satchel

Potions

Loose Gear

This small animal cave lies in the mountains south of Riften. Slay the bear that lurks just outside, then go in to find several ravenous Sabre Cats and wolves. Kill the beasts and then inspect the body of Gadnor, who lies atop the central boulder, and collect the nearby staff to obtain a unique weapon. Raid a chest here as well, and touch the small Shrine of Kynareth to instantly cure any diseases you might have.

[9.40] Lost Tongue Overlook

Dungeon: Dragon Lair

Dragon (after Main Quest: Dragon Rising)

Master Necromancer (pre-Dragon Rising)

Skeleton

Dangers

Rune Traps

Special Objects

Word Wall: Dismaying Shout [3/3]

Chest

Potion

In the mountains south of Riften, on the very edge of Skyrim, long stone steps lead up to a breathtaking overlook. Use a ranged attack to detonate a rune trap from afar as you make your ascent. You may encounter a mage here unless you've advanced past the "Dragon Rising" quest—then you'll find a far more intimidating dragon on the premises! Cut down the beast so you may benefit from the nearby Word Wall, and loot the large chest that's also found here.

[9.41] Snow-Shod Farm

Related Quests

Favor (Activity): Harvesting Crops* (Addvild)

Habitation: Farm

Addvild

Leonara Arius

Riften Guard

Collectibles

Skill Book [Alteration]: Reality & Other Falsehoods [C2/10]

This small farm lies just southwest of Riften. Harvest the growing crops and then sell them back to the farm's owner, Addvild, for some honest coin.

Snow-Shod Farm (Interior)

The cabin's lock is easy enough to pick, and there's a Skill Book on the bottom of the shelf in the basement.

- Area Is Locked (Novice)
- Skill Book [Alteration]: Reality & Other Falsehoods [C2/10]

[9.42] The Shadow Stone

Recommended Level: 6

Dungeon: Special

Warlock

Special Objects

Standing Stone: The Shadow Stone [13/13]

South of Riften, these ancient stones stand atop a short hill. Defeat the guardian mage and inspect the central Standing Stone to accept a new sign blessing. Once a day, those under the sign of the Shadow can become invisible for 60 seconds. Note that you can have only one sign blessing at a time, so activating this Standing Stone will override your current sign blessing (if any).

[9.43] Nightingale Hall

Related Quests
Thieves Guild Quest: Trinity Restored

Recommended Level: 8

Dungeon: Special

Collectibles
Skill Book [Pickpocket]: Purloined Shadows
Skill Book [Sneak]: The Red Kitchen Reader
Unique Item: Nightingale Armor [100/112]
Unique Item: Nightingale Boots [101/112]
Unique Item: Nightingale Gloves [102/112]
Unique Item: Nightingale Hood [103/112]
Area Is Locked (quest required)
Chests (Locked: Novice) (2)

This derelict temple is the ancient home to the Nightingales—clandestine followers of the Daedric Prince Nocturnal. You can't enter this site until you gain Thieves Guild Quest: Trinity Restored. Follow Karliah through the area, claiming a Skill Book that lies near a bed in the waterfall cavern. Next, acquire and don the special armor of the Nightingales. After Karliah explains the terms involved in becoming a member of the Nightingales, search the east and west side rooms to locate a couple of chests and another Skill Book. Then follow Karliah to the far chamber and complete your initiation.

Once you complete the "Darkness Returns" quest (thus ending the Thieves Guild quest line), the living quarters overlooking the waterfall here is restored, and you may freely use this location as a place to rest and gather supplies. Karliah can also be found here postquest as well.

[9.44] Broken Helm Hollow

Recommended Level: 6

Dungeon: Bandit Camp
Bandit
Leifnarr (deceased)

Crafting
Tanning Rack

Dangers
Bone Alarm Trap
Trapped Chest

Collectibles
Skill Book [Two-Handed]: Battle of Sancre Tor
Potions
Loose Gear
Mineable ore (Corundum)

Bandits reside in this small cave, which lies in the Rift's southeast corner, on the east side of the tall peak that stands southeast of Riften. Dispatch the exterior guards, along with the bandits inside the cave, which include a formidable leader. Stand back before opening the giant chest on the ledge—it's trapped. Collect a nearby Skill Book from the nearby stand, then head back down the ramp and pull a chain on the south wall to open a secret passage that leads to the body of a slain Nord. This is Leifnarr's body, which you're sent to find by Grosta at Heartwood Mill [9.27].

[9.45] Forelhost

Related Quests
Side Quest: Masks of the Dragon Priests*
Dungeon Quest: Siege on the Dragon Cult
Dungeon Activity

Recommended Level: 24

Dungeon: Dragon Priest Lair
Animal
Captain Valmir
Dragon Cultist (ghost)
Draugr
Rahgot

Crafting
Alchemy Labs (2)
Arcane Enchanter

Dangers
Battering Ram Trap (pressure plate)
Dart Trap (pressure plates)
Flamethrower Traps (pressure plates)
Oil Lamp Traps
Oil Pool Traps
Rising Floor Trap
Rune Traps (wall/floor)
Spear Trap (pedestal pressure plates)
Swinging Blade Trap
Swinging Wall Trap (pressure plates)
Trapped Chests

Puzzles
Claw Door

Quest Items
Rahgot's Mask
Skorm Snow-Strider's Journal

Collectibles
Dragon Claw: Glass Claw [9/10]
Dragon Priest Mask: Rahgot [9/10]
Skill Book [Restoration]: The Exodus
Unique Weapon: Dragon Priest Staff [71/80]

Special Objects
Word Wall: Storm Call [2/3]
Chests
Potions aplenty
Loose Gear

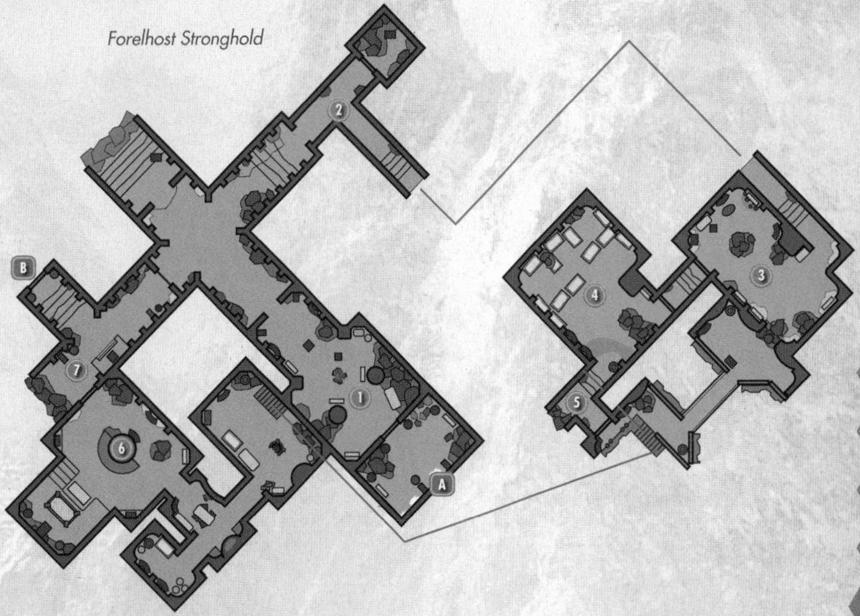

This massive stronghold stands in the snowy peaks of the mountains that lie southeast of Riften—a bit of climbing is required to get here. Forelhost is the tomb of one of eight fearsome Dragon Priests whose masks are part of a special quest.

Exterior

Speak with an soldier named Captain Valmir, who has made camp just outside the stronghold, to gain a new Side Quest that involves clearing the stronghold. (If you accidentally killed Captain Valmir before speaking with him, the key can be found on his body.) Don't let the captain catch you plundering his campsite before heading into the stronghold.

- Chest
- Potions

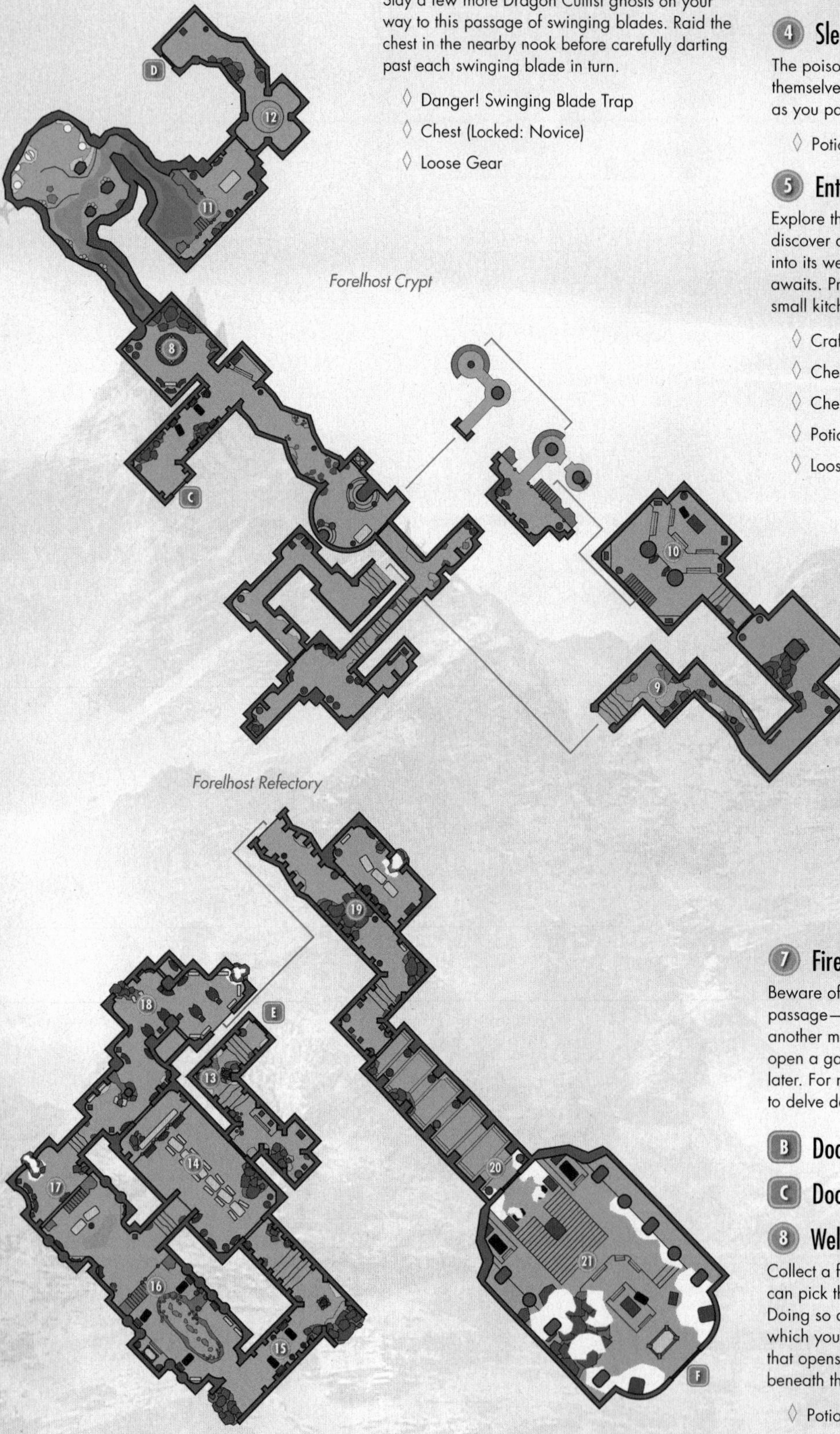

A Exit to Skyrim

1 Entry Hall

Dispatch the ghost of a Dragon Cultist in this first wide chamber. Carefully sidestep a pressure plate as you enter the north passage on your way to [2].

- Danger! Battering Ram Trap (pressure plate)

2 Swinging Blade Passage

Slay a few more Dragon Cultist ghosts on your way to this passage of swinging blades. Raid the chest in the nearby nook before carefully darting past each swinging blade in turn.

- Danger! Swinging Blade Trap
- Chest (Locked: Novice)
- Loose Gear

3 Journal Chamber

The informative journal that Captain Valmir hinted about is found in this quiet chamber. Collect it to complete an optional objective. If you return to Captain Valmir at this point, he'll give you a rundown of what he learns from the journal.

- Skorm Snow-Strider's Journal
- Chest (Locked: Apprentice)
- Potions aplenty

4 Sleeping Quarters

The poisons that the Dragon Cultists used to kill themselves long ago are still potent. Collect them as you pass through here.

- Potions

5 Entry Hall/Smithing Area: West Side

Explore the Entry Hall's upper walkways to discover a chest, then double back and descend into its western half, where a Dragon Cultist ghost awaits. Progress through the Smithing Area into a small kitchen.

- Crafting: Anvil, Grindstone, Workbench
- Chest
- Chest (Locked: Adept)
- Potions
- Loose gear

6 Worship Chamber

Swipe a few valuables from the kitchen on your way to this large chamber, which features a central stairwell. Slay a few powerful Draugr here, and skirt the pressure plate atop the central platform to avoid triggering a trap. Avoid standing directly in front of the room's chest when opening it—spikes will stab up from the floor below! Try disabling the chest's trigger hinge if you're skilled at lockpicking.

- Danger! Dart Trap (pressure plate), Trapped Chest
- Potions

7 Fire Trap Passage

Beware of a pair of pressure plates in this final passage—they trigger nasty fire traps. Slay another mighty Draugr here and throw a lever to open a gate so you may quickly exit this place later. For now, go downstairs and through a door to delve deeper into the keep.

B Door to Forelhost Crypt

C Door to Forelhost Stronghold

8 Well

Collect a few potions in this room, then see if you can pick the Master-level cage door in its center. Doing so allows you to skip areas [9] and [10], which you only need to visit to search for the key that opens the cage door. The watery passage beneath the trapdoor leads to [11].

- Potions

9 Burial Passages

Loot plenty of urns and slay a host of Draugr as you navigate this long, winding passage. Beware of removing items from pedestals, which triggers traps, and move with caution to avoid a variety of other traps along the way.

- Danger! Dart Trap (pressure plates), Rune Traps (wall/floor), Swinging Blade Trap, Spear Trap (pedestal pressure plates), Swinging Wall Trap (pressure plates)
- Chest (Locked: Master)
- Potions

10 Overlord's Tomb

A vastly powerful Draugr warrior rises from a central sarcophagus as you enter this large cavern. Slay it, along with its minions, to secure a needed key from a chest. Go upstairs and leap to a second chest afterward, then scale a winding ramp to reach a high door that leads back to the start of the burial passages, but watch out for the magic casting trap at the top! Dodge when it fires, then run across to loot the Soul Gem, or knock it off the pedestal with an arrow.

- Forelhost Well Key (chest)
- Danger Magic Trap
- Chests (2)
- Potions
- Loose Gear

11 Poison Chamber

Kill a few Skeevers on your way to this cavern, where the cultists who once lived here poisoned their water supply—don't worry, it's had several hundred years to dissipate. Collect a selection of leftover poisons and swipe a Skill Book off a shelf.

- Danger! Oil Pool Trap
- Skill Book [Restoration]: The Exodus
- Potions aplenty

12 Rising Floor Passage

The bend in this passage features a nasty trap—stepping in the middle causes a large section of floor to rise, slamming you into long spikes on the ceiling. Avoid the center of the passage while rounding the corner.

- Danger! Rising Floor Trap

D Door to Forelhost Refectory

E Door to Forelhost Crypt

13 Entry Passage

Dispatch powerful Draugr in the very first passage, and find a chest tucked away in the corner. Stand to one side of the pedestal near the chest when removing the item from it to avoid being shot by arrows.

- Danger! Dart Trap (pedestal pressure plate)
- Chest

14 Dining Area

This dining hall turned makeshift embalming area was used by the Cultists to hastily embalm their members after they destroyed the hallway during the siege. Loot a host of urns to pad your coin purse before taking the south passage to [15].

15 Oily Tunnel

Ignite the oil on the ground in this passage to help you kill the powerful Draugr that lurks here.

- Danger! Oil Lamp Traps, Oil Pool Trap

16 Open-Air Chamber

Dispatch more Draugr in this wide room, and loot the chest that lies beneath the wooden stairs. A large amount of deadly flowers can be harvested here, and the half-buried bodies of several Draugr can be looted as well. Go upstairs afterward and throw a lever in the east passage to open a portcullis, allowing for faster navigation of the floor. Backtrack out afterward and head north to [17].

- Chest (Locked: Adept)
- Potions

17 Lab

Lure a mighty Draugr toward the oil slick on the ground in this chamber, then knock down the overhead lamp to set the undead warrior ablaze. Read the informative note on the table near the Alchemy Labs and collect a host of potions before proceeding upstairs.

- Danger! Oil Lamp Trap, Oil Pool Trap
- Crafting: Alchemy Labs (2)
- Potions aplenty

18 Library

As you move into the Library, watch out for the magic casting trap that sits across the room. Either snipe the gem with a bow or time your movement and run from cover to cover to cross the room. Swipe a special Glass Claw off a pedestal as you move through this cluttered area. Stand back and to one side of other pedestals before removing their contents to avoid traps. Unlock Master and Expert-level doors here to access a small, potion-filled closet and a little alcove with a Soul Gem. Loot a locked chest on your way to [19].

- Danger! Spear Trap (pedestal pressure plate)
- Dragon Claw: Glass Claw [9/10]
- Chest (Locked: Apprentice)
- Potions aplenty
- Loose Gear

19 Arcane Workroom

Slay a deadly Draugr in this small chamber, then stand back and to one side when opening the far chest to avoid being stabbed by spears (or simply disable its trigger wire). Dodge a pressure plate in the south passage that follows, collecting a few potions on your way to [20].

- Danger! Flamethrower Trap (pressure plate), Trapped Chest
- Crafting: Arcane Enchanter
- Potions

20 Claw Door Passage

Inspect the Glass Claw you found back at [18] and notice three symbols on its palm. Rotate the three concentric rings of this passage's far door to imitate the same sequence of symbols, then inspect the central keyhole to insert the Glass Claw and gain access to the tomb's final chamber.

21 Rahgot's Tomb

An immensely powerful Dragon Priest named Rahgot rises from this chamber's central sarcophagus when you enter. Fight hard to slay the deadly villain, then obtain a valuable staff, key, and Dragon Priest Mask by sifting through Rahgot's remains. Use Rahgot's key to open the large door and head outside.

- Dragon Priest Mask: Rahgot [9/10] (Rahgot)
- Unique Weapon: Dragon Priest Staff [71/80]
- Forelhost Balcony Key (Rahgot)
- Chest

F Exit to Skyrim

Exterior (Balcony)

Back outside, cross a few snowy ramparts to locate an ancient Word Wall. Learn your new word of power, then descend to the fort's main courtyard to find Captain Valmir speaking with an enemy soldier. It turns out that Valmir is an imposter. Kill him to complete your quest, then inspect his corpse to discover an informative letter. Your work here is complete.

- Word Wall: Storm Call [2/3]

[9.46] Stendarr's Beacon

Recommended Level: 6

Habitation: Special

Vigilant of Stendarr (Blessing)

Collectibles

Skill Book [Restoration]: The Exodus [D2/10]

Special Objects

Shrine of Stendarr [5/5]
Chest
Knapsack
Satchel
Loose Gear

This sizeable tower, located in the far southeastern corner of Skyrim, has been occupied by the Vigil of Stendarr—zealous followers of the Divines who seek to eradicate the vile Daedra. Speak to any of the Vigilants here, or touch the small shrine on the interior altar, to instantly rid yourself of all diseases. Collect the Skill Book that lies on a bedroll here, and carefully loot the chest found atop the vigil without being caught. Find a valuable piece of gear near a skeleton that lies in the snow north of the tower as well.

[9.A] Darkwater Overhang

At the base of the steep waterfall and path to Ivarstead is an overhang with a troll inside. Amid the bones in the back of the overhang is a Stormcloak Soldier with a note detailing attacks in the area. The troll is possibly the culprit.

- Note

[9.B] Wood Cutter's Camp: Lake Geir

A murdered woodcutter lies slumped over his logs at this one-tent camp on the upper copse close to the road to Ivarstead. There's some food and a little coin to scrabble for.

[9.C] The Poultry Reanimator: Lake Geir

On top of the taller rocks, with the main road to the south, is a strange robed fellow attempting to resurrect a dead chicken. He succeeds in his creation and attacks as you close. Expect ingredients after you slaughter him.

[9.D] Treasure Hunter's Camp: Lake Geir

A small tent and a smoking fire off the main road indicates a small hunter's camp overlooking Lake Geir. Aside from some food, there's little to steal or scavenge, but a note on one of the barrels indicates there's treasure to be found on the island to the northwest.

- Note

[9.E] Treasure Island: Lake Geir

Just northwest of the Treasure Hunter's Camp by the stump of the ancient tree, two treasure hunters have dug up a chest. They don't take kindly to your presence, so face them in combat before removing any treasure you find.

- Chest

[9.F] Dragon Mound: Autumnwatch Woods

Related Quest: Main Quest: Diplomatic Immunity

This Dragon Mound is initially sealed. It opens during Main Quest: Diplomatic Immunity, and if you visit during or after this point in the Main Quest, the mound will be open and empty. Perhaps this dragon is the one that takes possession of nearby Autumnwatch Tower [9.14].

[9.G] Shrine of Talos: Froki's Peak

Above Froki's Shack is a steep pathway up to a mountaintop, where a stone Talos gazes across the Arcwind gorge. Receive a blessing, and search the offerings for the following:

- Skill Book [Two-Handed]: King
- Shrine to Talos [17/17]
- Satchel
- Loose gear

[9.H] Medresi's Camp: Angarvunde

Related Quest: Dungeon Quest: Medresi Dran and the Wandering Dead*

Adjacent to the entrance to Angarvunde is a small camp. This was the base of operations for Medresi Dran and her cowardly mercenaries. Search the place for her notes and a Skill Book. Visit Angarvunde to find her yourself.

- Skill Book [Speech]: A Dance in Fire, v7
- Medresi's Notes

[9.I] Wild Animal Den: Mistwatch

A trio of hungry wolves, or other wild animals, have made this rocky alcove home, dragging rabbits and other meat to feast on later. Aside from Nightshade, there's little here except the prospect of a savaging.

[9.J] Bandit's Shack: Autumnshade

This location has been modified or updated, and is also known as Redwater Den. See page 971.

A ruined shack is home to a couple of bandits and their dog. Don't try a frontal assault, as the door is boarded; attack from the holes in the side walls. They all come out fighting if you're spotted. Explore the building to find the following.

- Skill Book [Block]: Battle of Red Mountain
- Chest
- Loose gear

[9.K] Northwind Chest

At the base of the Northwind peak, just northeast of Boulderfall Cave, is a chest guarded by two skeletons of the nonanimated variety. Pry open the locked chest; there's usually gems and other baubles to stuff into your pockets.

- Chest (Locked: Novice)

[9.L] Altar in the Woods: Autumnshade

Deep in the Autumnshade forest, a Fire Mage is experimenting at an altar, surrounded by old and forgotten ceremonial stones. Slay the magician, picking up any of the Dwemer artifacts you wish, as well as a Skill Book.

- Skill Book [Restoration]: Racial Phylogeny

[9.M] Dragon Mound: Autumnshade Woods

Related Quest: Main Quest: Bleak Falls Barrow

This Dragon Mound is initially sealed. It opens during Main Quest: Bleak Falls Barrow, and if you visit during or after this point in the Main Quest, the mound will be open and empty.

[9.N] Hunters' Camp: Autumnshade Hills

On the higher and rockier terrain southeast of Autumnshade Clearing is a small hunters' camp tucked away in the hills. There are two hunters here, and a Skill Book rests inside one of their tents.

- Skill Book [Archery]: The Gold Ribbon of Merit
- Knapsack

[9.O] Troll Den: Rkund

Due west of the Ruins of Rkund is an old Nordic barrow entrance built into the side of the Jerall Mountains. However, this location hasn't been excavated and is home to a ferocious troll.

- Chest

[9.P] Wild Animal Den: Crystaldrift Cave

A little farther east from the Crystaldrift Cave entrance is another indent in the Jerall Mountains—an animal den with few items of note. You may be attacked by a Skeever during your brief exploration.

[9.Q] Dragon Mound: Lost Tongue Pass

Related Quest: Main Quest: Diplomatic Immunity

This Dragon Mound is initially sealed. It opens during Main Quest: Diplomatic Immunity. If you visit during or after this point in the Main Quest, the mound will be open and empty. Perhaps this is the dragon that now rules the ruin of Lost Tongue Overlook on the hill above?

[9.R] Wild Animal Den: Shor's Stone

Southeast of Shor's Watchtower, along the path that runs north-south along the base of the Velothi Mountains, is a rocky hillock with a wolf den. Expect some items to find on the corpse of a bandit in the back of the den.

[9.S] Trappers' Dilemma

In the woods to the east of Fort Greenwall is a rusting cage with a wolf in it. If you open the cage, the trappers return and attack! Fend them off with the wolf's help. If the wolf survives, it flees to the nearby wolf den [9.R].

[9.T] Miner's Camp: Velothi Mountains

> This location has been modified or updated, and is also known as Last Vigil. See page 978.

The vicious blizzards that race across the snow-swept peaks above the Rift have killed and half buried a lone miner. Nearby are two veins to attack with your pickaxe (or use the one nearby). Go west from the miner to find a Skill Book lying near the skeletal remains of another unfortunate soul.

- Skill Book [Destruction]: The Art of War Magic
- Mineable ore (Moonstone, Quicksilver)

[9.U] The Three Sentinels

The road leading north from Riften's North Gate and the Riften Stables is flanked by these three wooden watchtowers, where a small contingent of city guards keep watch for any sign of a bandit raid. At the top of each tower is a chest of items the guards have confiscated from brigands. Pick the lock, and you can help yourself.

- Chests (Locked: Adept) (3)

[9.V] Shrine of Zenithar: Fallowstone

Along the road north of Riften, just beyond the Three Sentinels [9.U], the road forks. Instead of taking either fork, look up the hill to the east, where you can find a small ruin. Defeat the wild animal that guards it, and you can pray at this makeshift Shrine to Zenithar. Take any offerings you wish.

- Shrine of Zenithar [5/5]
- Satchel

[9.W] Tumbledown Tower: Riften Outskirts

There's a reason one of Riften's gates has been sealed; farther along the old road east of town are the remains of a fallen tower, where you can find a couple of bandits picking through the rubble.

- Chest (Apprentice)

[9.X] Burning Farmhouse

Along the southern border, at the foot of the Jerall Mountains, is a small farmhouse burning merrily. Though you may think it the work of a dragon, inspect the summoning circle and the charred remains of a farmer clutching a Scroll of Conjure Flame Atronach to reveal how a familiar set fire to this abode. A Skill Book is hidden inside the hollow fallen log near the cabin.

- Skill Book [Destruction]: Horrors of Castle Xyr
- Chest

[9.Y] Frost Troll Den: Jerall Mountain Ridge

Look up at the precarious path, and you may see a flag up on a high ridge. Follow the bloodstained snow switchback around to an exposed Frost Troll's den. Slay the beast; the blood comes from the corpse of a miner. A Skill Book is hidden beneath an animal carcass. Skill Book [Block]: A Dance in Fire, v2

- Strongbox (Apprentice)
- Loose gear

[9.Z] Two Pine Ridge

Clamber the steep slopes from Stendarr's Beacon to find a pair of pine trees on a rocky ridge. Below one is a miner's bedroll. Look closely for a Skill Book.

- Skill Book [Sneak]: 2920, Last Seed, v8
- Mineable ore (Iron)

[DG.04] Redwater Den

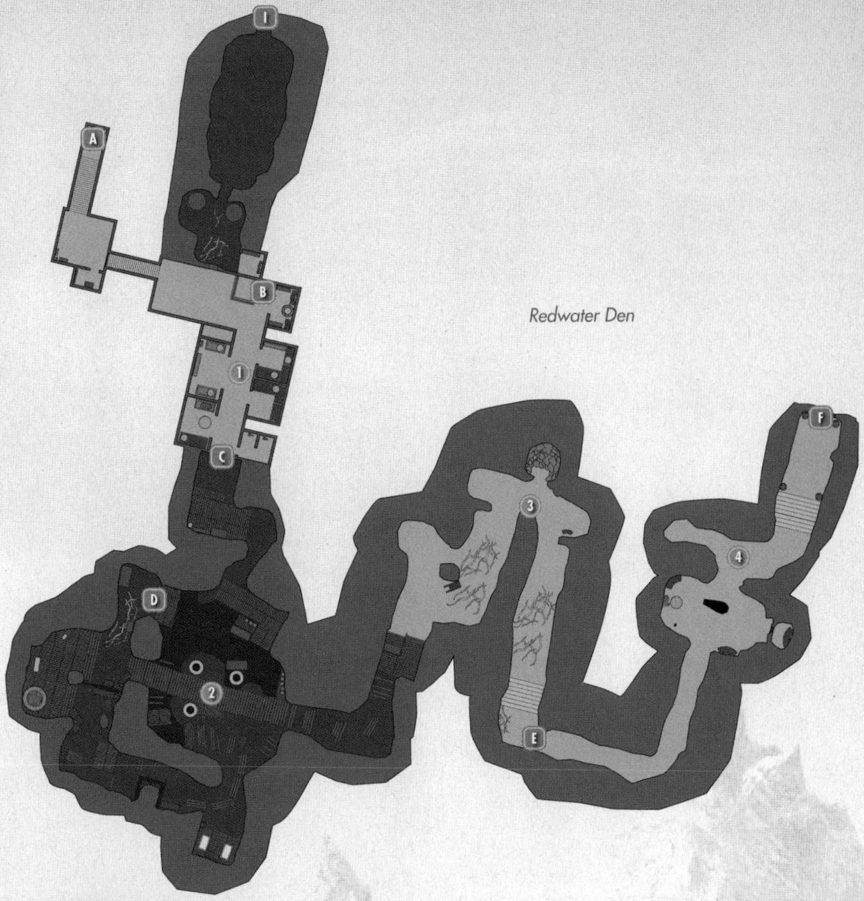

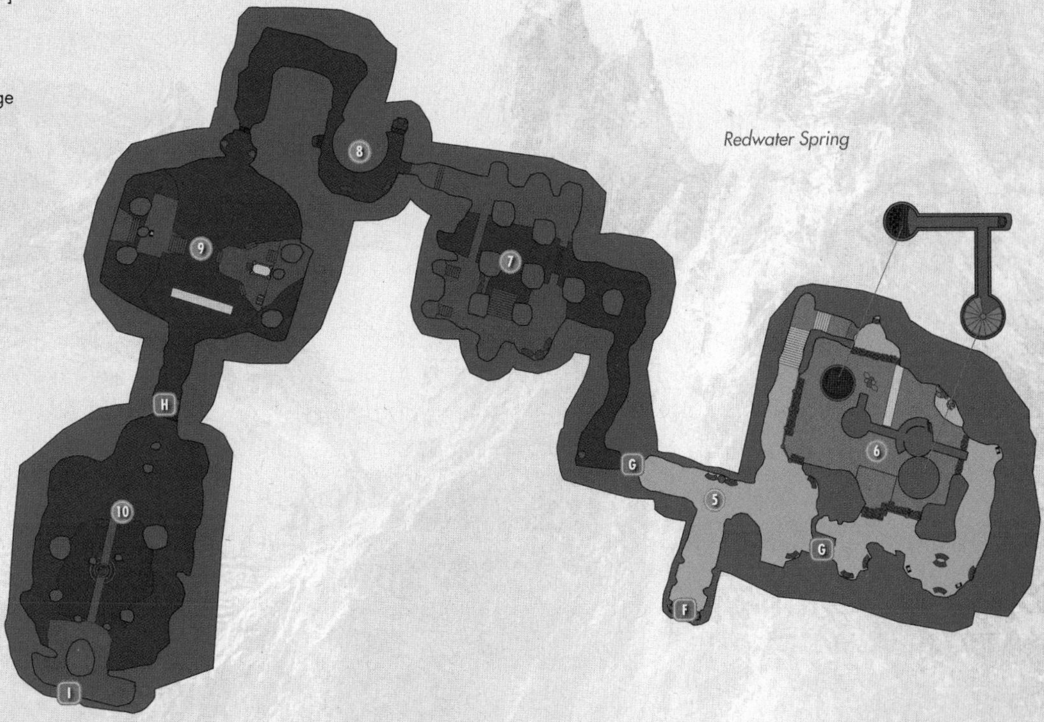

Related Quests

Dawnguard Main Quest: The Bloodstone Chalice

Recommended Level: 10

Faction: Vampire Lair

- Attendant
- Dealer
- Death Hound
- Doorman
- Master Vampire
- Skeleton
- Vampire
- Vampire's Thrall
- Venarus Vulpin

- Salonia Caelia
- Stalf

Services

Bartender: Dealer [DG1/1] [DG&HF 1/23]

Crafting

- Alchemy Lab
- Anvil or Blacksmith Forge
- Arcane Enchanter
- Cooking Pot
- Grindstone
- Workbench

Dangers

- Flamethrower Trap
- Oil Lamp Trap
- Oil Pool Trap
- Swinging Blade Trap
- Swinging Wall Trap

Miscellaneous

- Chest
- Loose Gear
- Potions

Exterior

> **NOTE** This location replaces Secondary Location [9.J] Bandit's Shack: Autumnshade.

A ruined shack is home to a couple of Redwater Lookouts and their dog. Don't try a frontal assault, as the lookouts are usually friendly and ask whether you're interested in "a fix." The front door is boarded; enter from the holes in the side walls. Explore the building to find a few items, then locate the trapdoor to descend into Redwater Den proper.

- Chest
- Loose gear
- Skill Book [Block]: Battle of Red Mountain

Redwater Den

A Trapdoor to Skyrim

A doorman requests you sheathe any weapons before he opens the door down to the Den. Check the alcove for the following:

- Chest
- Loose gear

1 Redwater Skooma Den

This murky bar is where deserters and bandits lie in small alcove rooms, feeling the aftereffects of Skooma consumption. The dealer can be persuaded to give you some Redwater Skooma, or you can pay to try some. If you'd prefer to fight, she is hostile, as is an attendant. The dealer, attendant, and vampires in the distillery all carry a Redwater Den Backrooms Key, which unlocks the hidden storeroom behind the bar, and the locked doors throughout this immediate area. The hidden storeroom to the north is the exit from this dungeon.

- Bartender: Dealer [DG1/1] [DG&HF 1/23]
- Loose Gear
- Redwater Den Backrooms Key
- Redwater Skooma
- Skooma

B Locked Door [Expert]

Or, unlock using the Redwater Den Backrooms Key.

C Locked Door [Adept]

You can pick this lock, or unlock it using the Redwater Den Backrooms Key. Either way, opening the door will cause the dealer and attendant to become hostile (if you haven't dealt with them already).

Behind the door, a passage leads past a bookcase with potions and a chest, to a balcony overlooking the distillery.

- Chest
- Potions

2 Skooma Distillery

This is where Redwater Skooma is fermented and distilled. The place is run by vampires, who use the potent magic of Redwater Spring to taint their Skooma. This is the first sign of their presence. If you consume Redwater Skooma in the den, you wake up in the cell in this chamber. The raised center of the ground floor has some Moon Sugar, other ingredients, and an Alchemy Lab. To the southwest is a tunnel up to a bridge that must be lowered via the nearby lever in order to continue forward. Watch for vampires and their thralls throughout.

- Alchemy Lab
- Book: The Aetherium Wars
- Cooking Pot
- Forge
- Grindstone
- Moon Sugar (5)
- Potions
- Skooma (12)
- Workbench

D Locked Cell Door [Adept]

If you drink Redwater Skooma while in the den, you black out and wake up behind this cell door. The body of a Novice Conjurer lies here, next to his Telekinesis Spell Tome (which you can read and use to fetch the key from the table just outside your cell).

- Spell Tome: Telekinesis

3 Mine and Draugr Tomb Entrance

Follow the path down to a mine and into a Draugr tomb as it turns back on itself to the south. Watch for the floor trigger in the small chamber with the fallen walls and half-buried urns. Drop the skeleton and thrall (using weapons or the flaming pots hanging above), then activate the chain to raise a section of wall.

- Chest
- Danger! Dart Trap
- Danger! Oil Lamp Trap
- Potions

E Chain and Secret Passage

4 Vampire's Coffin

A secret tunnel leads to a vampire's coffin. Slay the nightstalker and two Death Hounds in this area. Check the east wall for a chain to raise a section of wall, then head to a secret alcove with a leveled weapon and potions. Take the steps up to the large double doors leading to Redwater Spring.

- Arcane Enchanter
- Loose Gear
- Potions

F Door to Redwater Spring

I Door to Redwater Spring (Requires Key)

This door is accessible only after you visit Redwater Spring. It provides access back out of the spring, into the den to exit the dungeon.

Redwater Spring

F Door to Redwater Den

5 Venarus Vulpin's Altar to Arkay

An altar with Venarus Vulpin's Journal (charting his descent into Vampirism courtesy of the Redwater Spring) is here, between two gates, both of which open when you pull the chain in Location 6.

- Danger! Oil Pool Trap
- Venarus Vulpin's Journal

G Portcullis Gates

Unlock both via the chain to the southeast, in Location 6.

6 Draugr Crypt and Death Hound Pen

Defeat the two thralls in here, but watch your step—the entrance has a trapdoor down to a spiked pit. The pit has a lower corridor with swinging blade traps to a chest and steps up and out to the main floor, which houses two Death Hounds in a cage. Climb the spiral step column to an inaccessible chest alcove in the northwest corner (you can reach this only after using your Bats or Whirlwind Sprint abilities). Head around the upper edge of the room, past bookcases, benches, and another chest, to a chain that releases both portcullis gates.

- Chest (3)
- Cooking Pot
- Danger! Oil Lamp Trap
- Danger! Swinging Blade Trap
- Potions

7 Draugr Crypt (Vampire's Rest)

This large Draugr crypt has been recently reappropriated by vampires. Coffins line the alcoves of this tomb, and a Master Vampire, Death Hounds, and other nightstalkers await to attack. Exit in the northwest corner. Pull the chain to raise the gate.

- Alchemy Lab
- Danger! Oil Lamp Trap
- Danger! Oil Pool Trap
- Danger! Spike Trap

8 Embalming Antechamber

The door on the altar's right side simply flays spears in your face. The wooden door opens a small cupboard. The left side door opens to a passage with three nasty wall traps and a flamethrower trap to avoid (don't step on the floor plates).

- Chest
- Danger! Flamethrower Trap
- Danger! Spear Trap
- Danger! Swinging Wall Trap (3)

9 Grand Altar Chamber

It is here where you'll discover around three vampires and Venarus Vulpin's fate; he drank from the Bloodspring and is now a feral vampire! Pry the Redwater Wellspring Key from his corpse. It opens the door to the north [Master].

- Arcane Enchanter
- Loose Gear
- Redwater Wellspring Key
- Redwater Skooma (2)
- Venarus Vulpin's Research

F Door to Redwater Spring [Master]

⑩ Bloodspring

This is where you must dip the Bloodstone Chalice during the vampire-only Dawnguard Main Quest. Salonia Caelia and Stalf then set upon you.

> **NOTE** If you haven't activated this quest, or you're following the Dawnguard alliance, there is only the pool to inspect.

After drinking from the Bloodspring directly:

If you are a vampire, you receive the Tainted Blood of the Ancients ability. For one day, your Vampiric Drain will absorb Magicka and Stamina, but your maximum health will be reduced by 30.

If you are not a vampire, you have a chance of contracting *Sanguinare Vampiris* or another disease. Keep drinking from the spring, and you can contract any number of unpleasant poxes: This isn't exactly sanitary!

- ◊ Tainted Blood of the Ancients (vampire only)

Ⓘ Door to Redwater Spring (Requires Key)

This is accessible only after you visit Redwater Spring. It provides access back out of the spring, into the den to exit the dungeon.

[DG.05] Ruunvald Excavation

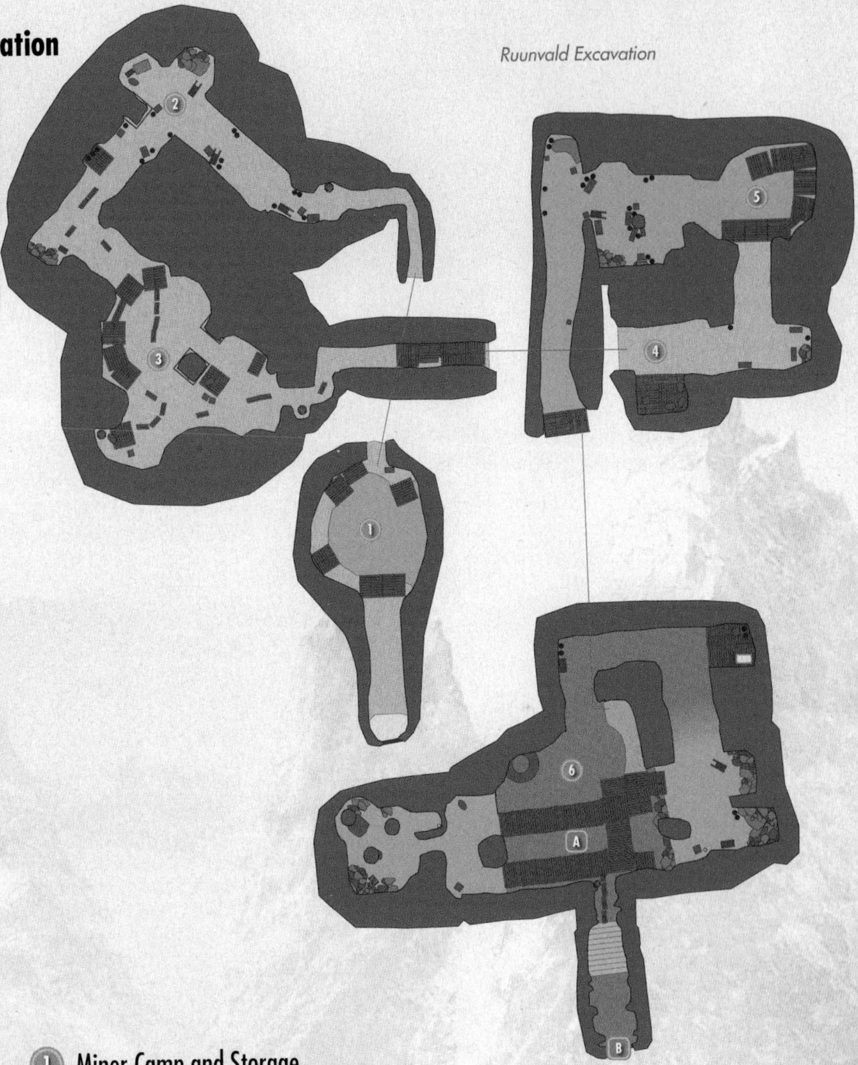

Related Quests
Dawnguard Faction Quest: Bolstering the Ranks

Recommended Level: 10

Faction: Vigilants of Stendarr

Dangers
- Crossbow Trap
- Oil Lamp Trap
- Oil Pool Trap

Collectibles
- Unique Weapon: Staff of Ruunvald [1/7]

Miscellaneous
- Area is locked
- Chest
- Loose gear

Exterior

> **NOTE** This location is completely sealed and does not appear until the quest is active.

Close by the mine door to this site is a large tent with an interesting journal to read. It charts the last known movements of Volk, a Vigilant guard who watched as the excavation team took longer to return to the surface, then disappeared entirely.

- ◊ Chest
- ◊ Volk's Journal

Ruunvald Excavation

Ⓐ Exit to Skyrim

① Miner Camp and Storage

Strange magic is at work. Vigilants of Stendarr patrol this pit but aren't in full control of their faculties. Charmed Vigilants are hostile throughout this dungeon. Enter the circular hole where miners (and the excavators) stored some of their equipment. Check the crate near the tunnel to the north for the first of explorer Moric Sidrey's books in this area: Discovering Ruunvald, vol. I.

- ◊ Book: Discovering Ruunvald, vol. I
- ◊ Chest [Apprentice]
- ◊ Malachite Ore Vein

② Mine Tunnel

There are a few Charmed Vigilants patrolling this old shaft. Check the table in the corner near the chest for some valuables, and you find a coin purse plus a Scroll after the Oil Lamp Trap.

- ◊ Chest (2)
- ◊ Danger! Oil Lamp Trap
- ◊ Danger! Oil Pool Trap
- ◊ Lots o' Gold
- ◊ Malachite Ore (2)
- ◊ Malachite Ore Vein
- ◊ Scroll

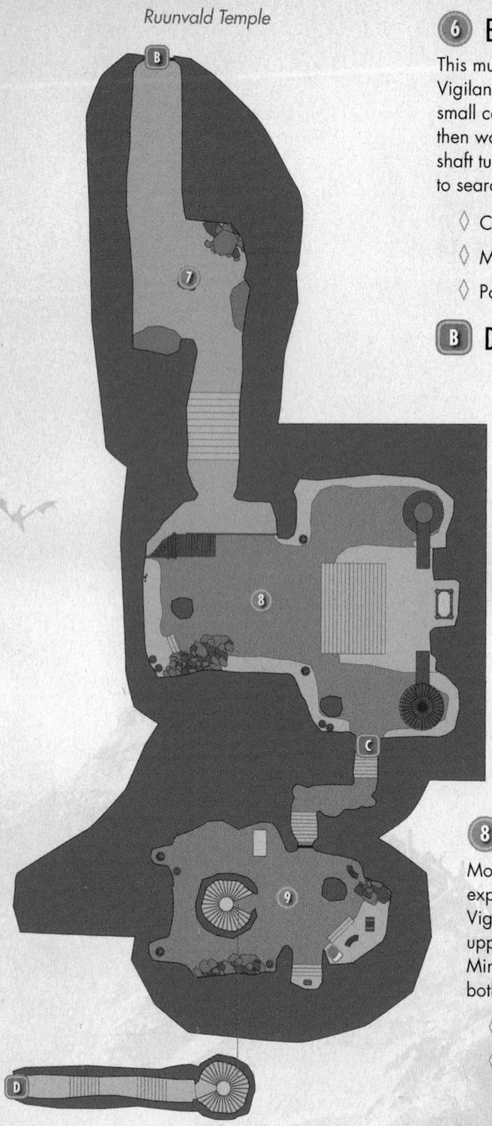

3 Mine Camp

A Husky and Charmed Vigilant guard this large cavern. Locate the second of Moric Sidrey's books on a crate near the tunnel exit.

- Book: Discovering Ruunvald, vol. II
- Loose Gear
- Malachite Ore Vein

4 Lower Mine Tunnel

Aside from watching for dogs and Charmed Vigilants, check the gap in the wooden decking for a chest [Adept].

- Chest [Adept]

5 Lower Mine Storage

The table and bookcase are of particular interest, as you'll find another of Moric Sidrey's writings and some other tomes. To the west is a storage tunnel; watch for pressure plates, as they activate crossbow traps.

- Book: Discovering Ruunvald, vol. III
- Danger: Crossbow Trap (2)

6 Excavation Entrance

This multilevel Nordic tomb entrance has several Vigilants to deal with, including Volk. Check the small cave across the first bridge for a chest, then work your way down. Check the lower mine shaft tunnel for some ore and a bed with a chest to search.

- Chest (2)
- Malachite Ore
- Potions

B Door to Ruunvald Temple

Ruunvald Temple

B Door to Ruunvald Excavation

7 Nordic Shrine Passage

Two ancient offering heads are present in this connecting passage. One has a journal on it, with a script (possibly) written by Volk, declaring his devotion to Minorne.

- Book: Minorne

8 Ruunvald Crypt

Moric Sidrey and Minorne are lurking in this expansive crypt room, along with a Charmed Vigilant,and Florentius, who is locked in the upper cage near the sarcophagus. Search Minorne for her staff and a key that opens both the cage and the iron door.

- Ruunvald Key
- Unique Weapon: Staff of Ruunvald [1/7]

C Iron Door (Requires Key)

Use the Ruunvald Key to open it.

9 Minorne's Study

To open the exit steps (which appear up through the floor), use the lever in the alcove. Note the book that begins Side Quest: Lost to the Ages on the table with the Alchemy Lab.

- Alchemy Lab
- Book: The Aetherium Wars
- Chest
- Potions

D Exit to Skyrim

Once you unlock the exit, you can return to this location from Skyrim.

[DG.06] Dayspring Canyon

[DG.07] Fort Dawnguard

Related Quests

Dawnguard Main Quest: Dawnguard
Dawnguard Main Quest: Awakening
Dawnguard Main Quest: Bloodline
Dawnguard Main Quest: A New Order
Dawnguard Main Quest: Prophet
Dawnguard Main Quest: Seeking Disclosure
Dawnguard Main Quest: Scroll Scouting
Dawnguard Main Quest: Chasing Echoes
Dawnguard Main Quest: Unseen Visions
Dawnguard Main Quest: Kindred Judgment
Dawnguard Faction Quest: Ancient Technology
Dawnguard Faction Quest: Bolstering the Ranks
Dawnguard Faction Quest: Cleansing Light
Dawnguard Faction Quest: Hide and Seek
Dawnguard Faction Quest: Hunting the Monster
Dawnguard Faction Quest: A Jarl's Justice
Dawnguard Faction Quest: Lost Relic
Dawnguard Faction Quest: Preemptive Strike
Dawnguard Faction Quest: Rescue

Recommended Level: 10

Faction: Dawnguard

Bear
Mudcrab
Vampire

Services

Apothecary
Blacksmith
General Goods Vendor

Crafting

Alchemy Lab
Anvil or Blacksmith Forge
Arcane Enchanter
Cooking Spit
Grindstone
Smelter
Tanning Rack
Wood Chopping Block
Workbench

Miscellaneous

Chest
Loose Gear
Potions Aplenty

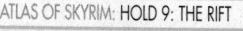

Entrance to Dayspring Canyon

A cave entrance northeast of Stendarr's Beacon in the southeast corner of the Rift is the only method of entering Dayspring Canyon and thus reaching Fort Dawnguard.

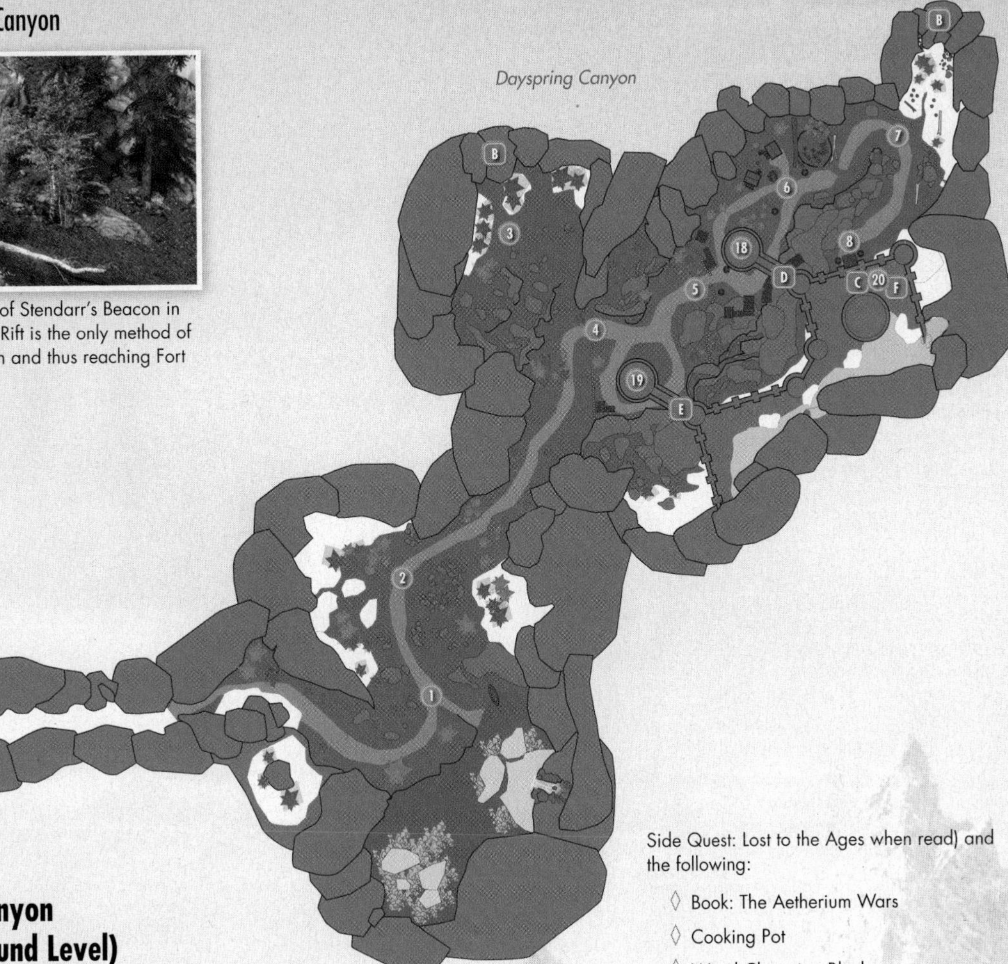

Dayspring Canyon (Exterior Ground Level)

A Exit to Skyrim

This leads back to the entrance to Dayspring Canyon.

1 Dayspring Falls

The snowmelt from the Velothi Mountains cascades into a peaceful and picturesque lake. On your first visit here, you'll meet Agmaer, who is also planning to join the Dawnguard. Although there are flowers to pick, a small fishing boat to inspect, salmon to grab in the lake, and a couple of Mudcrabs, there's little else to gather here.

- Loose gear

2 Dawnguard Gorge

Vampires sometimes attack from this point, later into the Dawnguard Main Quests. Otherwise, expect wildlife such as rabbits, deer, and butterflies in this small gorge where you can see the first of the buttress towers of Fort Dawnguard.

3 Mossy Glen

This area offers a good view of the exterior of Fort Dawnguard, if you look back as you climb this embankment. The overlook has one of the entrances to Mossy Glen Cave.

B Cave Entrance to Mossy Glen Cave

The interior of Mossy Glen Cave is detailed below. This is one of two entrances/exits to this cave.

4 Outer Wall Barricade

This location, around the base of the first Dawnguard tower buttress, is erected around the time of Dawnguard Main Quest: Bloodline, as the vampire attacks increase, before you return from meeting Harkon. It isn't here when you first discover the area. A watcher named Ollrod guards these defenses from his platform behind and above the thick wooden wall.

5 Inner Wall Barricade

This defensive point, around the base of the second Dawnguard tower buttress, is completed around the time of Dawnguard Main Quest: Prophet, after vampire attacks occur close to the main fort entrance, while you're out finding the Moth Priest. Only a simple wall is here when you first discover the area. Guards named Tilde, Mogrul, and Vori all patrol this area. Note the upper wooden platform just below the stone arch of the second tower buttress; this is another lookout spot.

6 Refugee Camp

Prior to Dawnguard Main Quest: Beyond Death, this is the small clearing where Durak practices with his crossbow (he gives a spare to you if you ask him). After the quest, a refugee camp is set up here, along with two tents. Alvide, Barknar, Jayri, and Sern all have their reasons for being here. Check the area for a book (which begins Side Quest: Lost to the Ages when read) and the following:

- Book: The Aetherium Wars
- Cooking Pot
- Wood Chopping Block

7 Dayspring Path

Vampires have been known to attack in this area, especially later in the Dawnguard Main Quest. The gap in the wooden wall leads to the second entrance (B) into Mossy Glen Cave.

8 Fort Dawnguard: Main Entrance

Expect to see Celann guarding this entrance on occasion, or another member of the Dawnguard. The imposing entrance is the only way into Fort Dawnguard.

C Doors to Fort Dawnguard

Mossy Glen Cave

Mossy Glen Cave is a small location with three chests to uncover. Both entrances lead to a large cave with four bears and a small side tunnel. Watch for the odd lurking Skeever too.

- Chest (3)

Fort Dawnguard (Interior)

Lore: Fort Dawnguard Overview

Tucked away in the southeastern Velothi Mountains of the Rift, in the hidden mountain valley called Dayspring Canyon, towers the old fortification of Fort Dawnguard. Long fallen to disrepair, this massive fortress will become home to a new faction of vampire hunters born from the ashes of the Vigilants of Stendarr. It is here where the agents of the Dawnguard, led by Isran, have begun to gather, where new recruits dedicate themselves to the eradication of vampires, and where a solution to the growing menace must be found.

Fort Dawnguard's interior is upgraded in stages throughout the Dawnguard Main Quest:

- Initially, the fort is filled with cobwebs and clutter, but it does have a few amenities, including a smelter and a workbench.
- After Dawnguard Main Quest: A New Order, Gunmar and Sorine settle in and set up full smithing and enchanting stations. You can now accept their Radiant Quests, purchase items from them, and acquire the Armored Troll and Dawnguard Husky animal companions. The barracks area fills out to house the Dawnguard's new recruits.
- During Dawnguard Main Quest: Prophet, several Dawnguard Agents return to the fort. You can now ask the members of the Dawnguard to join you on your missions.
- Once you complete Dawnguard Faction Quest: Bolstering the Ranks, Florentius moves in, adding an Alchemy Station.
- During Dawnguard Main Quest: Beyond Death, a refugee camp is set up outside the fort.
- After Dawnguard Main Quest: Kindred Judgment, you receive a private room on the fort's upper level.

Notable Inhabitants

- Dawnguard Leader: Isran
- Dawnguard Blacksmith: Gunmar
- Dawnguard Tinkerer: Sorine Jurard
- Dawnguard Priest: Florentius Baenius
- Dawnguard Hunter: Durak
- Dawnguard Warrior: Celann
- Dawnguard Warrior: Ingjard
- Dawnguard Warrior: Mogrul
- Dawnguard Warrior: Ollrod
- Dawnguard Warrior: Tilde
- Dawnguard Warrior: Vori
- Dawnguard Recruit: Agmaer
- Dawnguard Recruit: Beleval
- Vigilant of Stendarr: Vigilant Tolan
- Dawnguard Armored Huskies: Bran and Sceolang
- Dawnguard Refugee: Alvide
- Dawnguard Refugee: Barknar
- Dawnguard Refugee: Jayri
- Dawnguard Refugee: Sern

The following Dawnguard personnel (who may not arrive until later into the Dawnguard Main Quest) offer the following services to you:

Animal Companion

- Armored Frost Troll
- Armored Troll
- Bran [DG2/13]
- Sceolang [DG3/13]

Follower

- Agmaer [DG4/13]
- Beleval [DG5/13]
- Celann [DG6/13]
- Durak [DG7/13]
- Ingjard [DG8/13]

Trader

- Florentius Baenius (Apothecary) [DG1/2] [DG&HF 2/23]
- Gunmar (Blacksmith) [DG1/2] [DG&HF 3/23]
- Sorine Jurard (General goods) [DG1/1] [DG&HF 4/23]

Trainer

- Florentius Baenius (Restoration: Master) [DG1/1]
- Gunmar (Smithing: Master) [DG1/1]
- Isran (Heavy Armor: Master) [DG1/1]
- Sorine Jurard (Archery: Master) [DG1/1]

NOTE Traders here sell some unique items you cannot find anywhere else:

- Florentius sells the unique spells Stendarr's Aura and Vampire's Bane
- Gunmar sells Dawnguard Armor
- Sorine sells the unique spell Sunfire, Crossbows, Bolts, and Crossbow enhancements.

C Doors to Dayspring Canyon

These lead back out to the Dayspring Canyon exterior, by the main Dawnguard Fort entrance.

9 Circular Hall and Upper Balcony

This is where Isran first greets you and has an impassioned discussion with Vigilant Tolan. This room is the fort's main hub, with access in all directions. Head to the right (east) if you want to take the stairs to the upper balcony, which curves around the perimeter of this circular chamber.

◊ Loose gear

10 Eastern Corridor and Spiral Stairs

Linked to the Circular Hall, this north–south corridor allows access to the cave and the stairs (east) leading to the Upper Balcony. The other stairs (south, Location D) lead out to the exterior battlements.

D Doors to Dayspring Canyon

The doors atop the spiral steps lead to the exterior North Tower and Crenellations.

11 Training Cave and Husky Pen

A set of targets and some arrows and bolts are located in this large natural cave. In the kennel to the northeast, the Huskies are trained to hunt vampires. Take one of them with you (at no charge) if you wish. The entrance to Dead Drop Falls is to the north; this dungeon is accessible only from here.

- Chest
- Husky: Bran
- Husky: Sceolang
- Loose Gear

E Doors to Dayspring Canyon

The doors atop the spiral steps lead to the exterior South Tower and Crenellations.

12 Dawnguard Barracks

Isran has opened his hearth to his recruits, who have set up makeshift bunks in this room, once used as a reception and strategic planning area. During the night, many of the Dawnguard sleep here. As expected, there's a lot of Dawnguard equipment to make use of here, as well as a copy of the Aetherium Wars, a book that starts Side Quest: Lost to the Ages.

- Book: The Aetherium Wars
- Loose gear

13 Mead Storage and Waiting Area

Some members of the Dawnguard wait around in this area, which is dominated by the giant pillars and mead casks. There are a few books to read and a map of Skyrim, and the spiral steps to the south lead to the very top of the fort.

F Doors to Dayspring Canyon

The doors atop the spiral steps lead to the exterior upper battlements.

14 Banquet Hall

The mead tends to flow freely here, and you'll almost always encounter a Dawnguard agent in this chamber with the long table and roaring fire. If you're ever low on goblets, this is the place to look.

- Cooking Spit

15 Workshop and Troll Pens

Gunmar, Sorine Jurard, and Florentius Baenius all use this area to further the Dawnguard's chances at victory. There are several crafting stations here, as well as a Troll Pen (once Gunmar is brought into the Dawnguard fold) where you can hire an Armored Troll companion for 500 gold and practice your archery at a small range.

- Alchemy Lab
- Arcane Enchanter
- Book: The Aetherium Wars
- Forge
- Grindstone
- Iron Ingot (12)
- Loose gear
- Potions aplenty
- Smelter
- Tanning Rack
- Workbench

16 Isran's Room and Torture Chamber

Isran sleeps here, which may be one of the reasons why his personality is so...strained. The torture room is next to his bedroom.

- Chest
- Iron Ingot (3)

17 Lavish Bedroom

This bedroom can be yours if you side with the Dawnguard and put an end to Lord Harkon's schemes. There are weapon racks, a dummy, and a comfy bed here.

- Loose gear
- Steel Ingot (5)

G Cave to Drop Dead Falls

Dayspring Canyon (Fort Dawnguard Towers)

The upper crenellations overlooking Dayspring Canyon are all accessible from the spiral staircases inside the fort.

D Doors to Fort Dawnguard (Interior)

18 North Tower and Crenellations

This exterior battlement has a couple of books, Dawnguard equipment and weapons, a coin purse, and an empty chest.

- Loose Gear

E Doors to Fort Dawnguard (Interior)

19 South Tower and Crenellations

This exterior battlement has some storage areas where Dawnguard equipment, a scroll, potions, and a book or two can be found.

- Loose Gear
- Potions

F Doors to Fort Dawnguard (Interior)

20 Upper Battlements

The highest exterior location in Dayspring Canyon is atop the fort. Roam the battlements to find several fine pieces of Dawnguard equipment and weapons, two chests (one is empty), and the following:

- Chest
- Grindstone
- Loose gear
- Tanning Rack

Dead Drop Falls

Related Quests
None

Recommended Level: 8

Faction: Dawnguard

Dangers
- Bear Trap
- Dart Trap
- Spear Trap

Puzzle
Pressure Plates

Miscellaneous
- Chest
- Corundum Ore Vein
- Loose Gear
- Potions

Dead Drop Falls

This series of increasingly impressive natural caverns starts with a plunge down a waterfall hole. There are numerous ways to test your Crossbow-aiming throughout this location, which is one of the ways the Dawnguard utilize this cave complex.

A Exit to Fort Dawnguard

This leads back into the natural cavern and the Armored Troll pens area of Fort Dawnguard.

1 Drop Dead Falls Cavern and Grotto (Upper and Lower)

Upper: Water from the Velothi Mountains tumbles down a subterranean waterfall that dominates this cavern. The only way forward, is down, into the hole the cascading water has formed. Note the chest on the raised bank to the west, close to the exit door (D); scramble up or grab the chest on your way out.

- Chest

Lower: The lower grotto area is a large pool of water with natural pillars supporting the cavern above. There are two exits (to the north and west), but to fully explore this cave system, head north (as you'll find your way blocked at the top of Location 8 if you go west).

2 Isran's Cathedral: Eastern Walkway

Known colloquially as Isran's Cathedral (after the leader of the Dawnguard who discovered this cavernous chamber), the ground level is comprised of a winding natural path of bridges up from a ruined jetty. Note the chest behind the massive columns at the water's level, over on the western perimeter of this chamber. Watch for a bear trap (a Skeever didn't)—the pressure plate and dart trap on the top of the first bridge as you head northeast. Turn right (south), watching for a trip wire near the table with the empty chest on it (which launches spears at you). There's a second trip wire to the left (north) that triggers more darts.

- Chest
- Danger! Bear Trap
- Danger! Dart Trap (2)
- Danger! Spear Trap

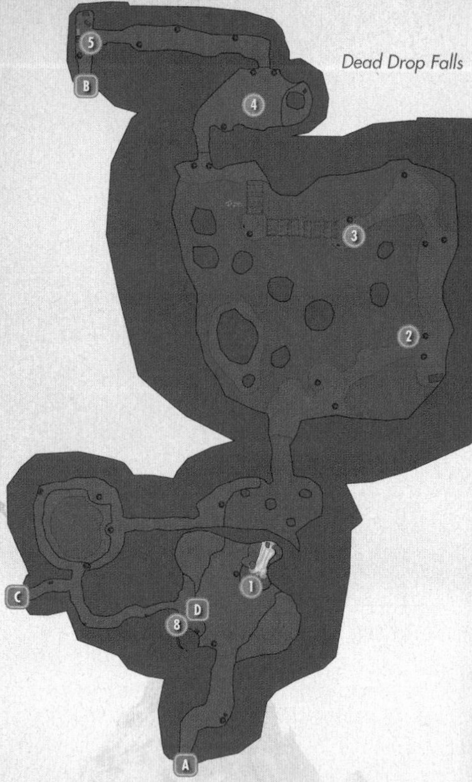

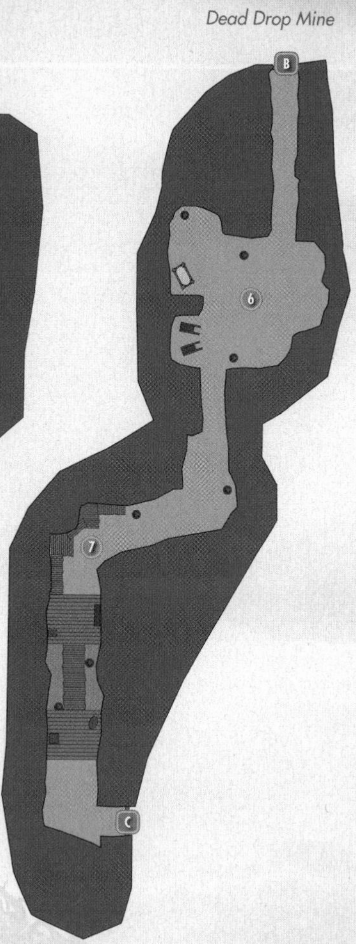

③ Isran's Cathedral: Northern Bridge

Farther along the ascending natural bridges is a group of wooden bridges that test your elementary puzzle-solving skills. There's a lever on the left that raises one of the bridges but not the other; either way you're left with a gap you can't cross.

Puzzle solution: Take the steel bolts (or use your own arrows), and fire at the target hanging from the huge stalagmite to the south. This raises (or lowers, depending on where the lever is positioned) both bridges. If both bridges are raised, use the lever to lower them before crossing.

Puzzle solution: At the second, ramped bridge, pull the lever to lower it, which also lowers the exit portcullis to Location 4. Move to the portcullis, turn around to face south, and fire an arrow or bolt at the second target to the south, raising both bridge and portcullis so you can escape. But wait! Step under the first open portcullis to a second one. Turn around and fire at the target again, raising the second portcullis and lowering the first. Then step into Location 4.

◊ Loose gear

④ Portcullis Puzzle Cave

Ahead (north) of you is a closed portcullis, three pressure plates on the floor (one with the book Uncommon Taste on it), and one above the portcullis. There's steel bolts on the barrel if you're running low on crossbow ammunition.

Puzzle solution: All four pressure plates need to be pressed in. For this to happen, simply place any object (such as the food from the barrel or large sack in the room) on each of the two pressure plates you can't stand on. Then fire an arrow at the fourth plate above the portcullis (while standing on the third, or positioning another item on it) to open it.

◊ Loose gear

⑤ Miners' Supply Cave

Head up the corridor from Location 4, pausing to fire at the target above the wooden support ceiling to raise the portcullis, and step into a supply cave with a chest, satchels, Ebony Ore, and various bolts on the table. Be sure to check out Confessions of a Khajiit Fur Trader.

◊ Chest (3) ◊ Ebony Ore (2) ◊ Loose gear

Ⓑ Door to Dead Drop Mine

Dead Drop Mine

Ⓑ Door to Dead Drop Falls

⑥ Mine Face

Check the table and straw for Corundum Ore and Ingots. Mine the veins here if you wish.

◊ Corundum Ore Vein (3)

⑦ Southern Passage

There's some Iron Ingots, loose gear, two crossbows, and a copy of a saucy read—The Sultry Argonian Bard, v1—on the upper platform where miners used to sleep. Below is a storage shelving area with many ingredients and a copy of The Aetherium Wars (which starts Side Quest: Lost to the Ages).

◊ Book: The Aetherium Wars

◊ Loose gear ◊ Potions

Ⓒ Door to Dead Drop Falls

(Return to) Dead Drop Falls

Ⓒ Door to Dead Drop Mine

⑧ The Dead Drop Sinkhole

This massive, ancient sinkhole is accessible from Location 1, but access to the mine is only available from the mine itself, as you need to activate a lever to open the portcullis in the upper tunnel. There's a second lever leading to a secret wall section that opens, allowing access back to Location 1, above the waterfall drop, so you can leave. There's nothing but a dangerous drop (and a ledge running around the perimeter) here.

Ⓓ Secret Door to Dead Drop Waterfall and Grotto

[DB.02] Last Vigil

Related Quests
Side Quest:
The Ebony Warrior

Recommended Level: 80+

Habitation:
Miner's Camp
The Ebony Warrior

Miscellaneous
Area is locked

> **NOTE** This location replaces Secondary Location [9.T] Miner's Camp: Velothi Mountains.

The Ebony Warrior

The vicious blizzards that race across the snow-swept peaks above the Rift have killed and half buried a lone miner. Nearby are two veins to attack with your pickaxe (or use the one nearby). Go west from the miner to find a Skill Book lying near the skeletal remains of another unfortunate soul. This windswept place of contemplation is the last vigil of an epic and powerful adventurer known as the Ebony Warrior. It is here that—assuming the Side Quest in question is active—you face him in ferocious mortal combat. Although his attire isn't unique, it is of the highest quality.

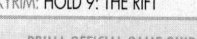

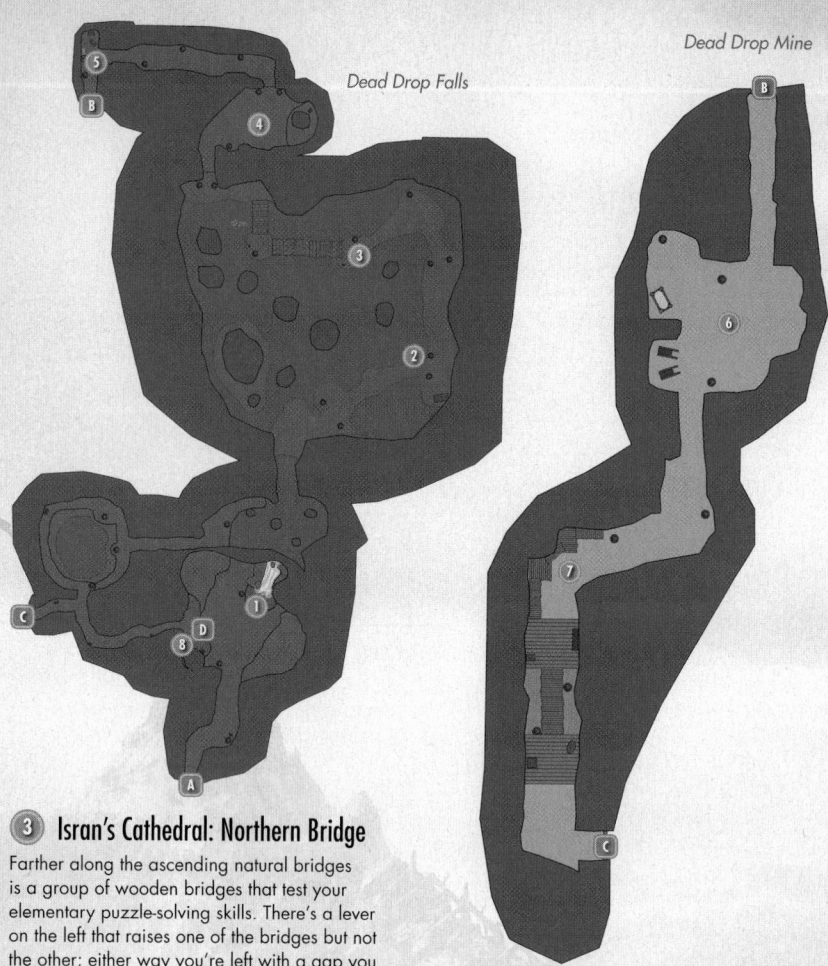

◊ Ebony Armor of Regeneration
◊ Ebony Boots of Frost Suppression
◊ Ebony Bow of Winter
◊ Ebony Gauntlets of Extreme Wielding
◊ Ebony Helmet of Waterbreathing
◊ Ebony Shield of Fire Suppression
◊ Ebony Sword of the Vampire
◊ Necklace of Shock Suppression
◊ Potion of Vigorous Healing (5)
◊ Ring of Peerless Wielding
◊ Skill Book [Destruction]: The Art of War Magic
◊ Moonstone Ore Vein
◊ Quicksilver Ore Vein

BLACKREACH AND OTHER REALMS

OVERVIEW

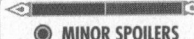

MINOR SPOILERS

The land of Skyrim brims with wondrous locales, yet some areas cannot easily be linked to any one Hold. In fact, certain areas can't even be said to exist within the confines of reality! From traveling caravans to the mind of a demented Emperor, all unusual and otherworldly locations are covered here, in "Other Realms."

AVAILABLE SERVICES, CRAFTING, AND COLLECTIBLES

Services

- Followers/Hirelings: [1/47]
- Houses for Sale: [0/5]
- Marriage Prospects: [0/62]
- Skill Trainers: [4/50]
  - Alchemy: [0/3]
  - Alteration: [0/3]
  - Archery: [0/3]
  - Block: [0/2]
  - Conjuration: [0/3]
  - Destruction: [0/3]
  - Enchanting: [0/2]
  - Heavy Armor: [0/3]
  - Illusion: [0/2]
  - Light Armor: [0/3]
  - Lockpicking: [1/2]
  - One-Handed: [0/3]
  - Pickpocket: [1/3]
  - Restoration: [0/3]
  - Smithing: [0/3]
  - Sneak: [1/3]
  - Speech: [1/4]
  - Two-Handed: [0/2]
- Traders [7/133]:
  - Apothecary: [0/12]
  - Bartender: [0/5]
  - Blacksmith: [0/33]
  - Carriage Driver: [0/5]
  - Fence: [4/10]
  - Fletcher: [0/3]
  - Food Vendor: [0/9]
  - General Goods: [3/19]
  - Innkeeper: [0/15]
  - Jeweler: [0/2]
  - Special: [0/3]
  - Spell Vendor: [0/12]
  - Stablemaster: [0/5]

Collectibles

- Captured Critters: [0/5]
- Dragon Claws: [1/10]
- Dragon Priest Masks: [1/10]
- Larceny Targets: [0/7]
- Skill Books: [6/180]
  - Alchemy: [1/10]
  - Alteration: [0/10]
  - Archery: [0/10]
  - Block: [1/10]
  - Conjuration: [0/10]
  - Destruction: [0/10]
  - Enchanting: [0/10]
  - Heavy Armor: [1/10]
  - Illusion: [0/10]
  - Light Armor: [0/10]
  - Lockpicking: [1/10]
  - One-Handed: [0/10]
  - Pickpocket: [0/10]
  - Restoration: [0/10]
  - Smithing: [1/10]
  - Sneak: [0/10]
  - Speech: [1/10]
  - Two-Handed: [0/10]
- Treasure Maps: [0/11]
- Unique Weapons: [2/80]
- Unique Items: [0/112]
- Unusual Gems: [0/24]

Special Objects

- Shrines: [0/69]
  - Akatosh: [0/6]
  - Arkay: [0/12]
  - Dibella: [0/8]
  - Julianos: [0/5]
  - Kynareth: [0/6]
  - Mara: [0/5]
  - Stendarr: [0/5]
  - Talos: [0/17]
  - Zenithar: [0/5]
  - Standing Stones: [0/13]
- Word Walls: [1/42]
  - Animal Allegiance: [0/3]
  - Aura Whisper: [0/3]
  - Become Ethereal: [0/3]
  - Disarm: [0/3]
  - Dismaying Shout: [0/3]
  - Elemental Fury: [0/3]
  - Fire Breath: [0/2]
  - Frost Breath: [0/3]
  - Ice Form: [0/3]
  - Kyne's Peace: [0/3]
  - Marked for Death: [0/3]
  - Slow Time: [0/3]
  - Storm Call: [1/3]
  - Throw Voice: [0/1]
  - Unrelenting Force: [0/1]
  - Whirlwind Sprint: [0/2]

ADDITIONAL LOCATIONS

[DG.10] Soul Cairn [DG.12] Forgotton Vale

Total—6

- [10.00] Khajiit Caravans (3)
- [10.01] Azura's Star
- [10.02] Blackreach
- [10.03] Blue Palace Pelagius Wing
- [10.04] Japhet's Folly
- [10.05] Skuldafn
- [10.06] Sovngarde

[10.00] Khajiit Caravans

Related Quests

Dark Brotherhood Quest: Side Contract: Ma'randru-jo

Thieves Guild Radiant Quest: Moon Sugar Rush* (Ri'saad)

Miscellaneous Objective: New Moon* (Kharjo)

Habitation: Special

Ahkari (General Store Vendor; Trainer: Journeyman)

Atahbah (Fence)

Dro'marash (Trainer: Speech)

Kharjo (Follower)

Khayla (Trainer: Sneak)

Ma'dran (Fence; General Store Vendor)

Ma'jhad (Fence; Trainer: Lockpicking)

Ma'randru-jo

Ra'zhinda

Ri'saad (Fence; General Store Vendor)

Zaynabi (Fence)

Services

Follower: Kharjo [47/47]

Trader (Fence): Ri'saad [7/10]

Trader (Fence): Atahba [8/10]

Trader (Fence): Ma'jahad [9/10]

Trader (Fence): Zaynabi [10/10]

Trader (General Store Vendor): Ri'saad [17/19]

Weapons, Apparel, Potions, Food, Ingredients, Misc

Trader (General Store Vendor): Ahkari [18/19]

Weapons, Apparel, Potions, Food, Ingredients, Misc

Trader (General Store Vendor): Ma'dran [19/19]

Weapons, Apparel, Potions, Food, Ingredients, Misc

Trainer (Lockpicking: Expert): Ma'jhad [2/2]

Trainer (Pickpocket: Journeyman): Ahkari [3/3]

Trainer (Sneak: Journeyman): Khayla [3/3]

Trainer (Speech: Journeyman 1): Dro'marash [4/4]

Crafting

Tanning Rack

Collectibles

Chest(s)

Potions

Loose gear

Three Khajiit caravans wander Skyrim, traveling from town to town and offering various goods and services. Each caravan is made up of an owner and his entourage, and each caravan travels its own route between two major cities.

Caravans will pause to do business with you while on the move but are more commonly found outside of Skyrim's larger capital cities, where they make camp for brief periods. Befriending each of the three savvy caravan owners can lead to special benefits!

Ri'saad's Caravan

Ri'saad is the patriarch of the Khajiit caravan merchants. He's the richest of the three and enjoys the best trade route, with exclusive contracts among Skyrim's wealthiest cities. Ri'saad's route takes him from Markarth [5.00] to Whiterun [6.00] and back again. Ri'saad offers a fine selection of wares, and Khayla can train you to be more stealthy.

◊ Crafting: Tanning Rack

Ahkari's Caravan

Ahkari has the monopoly on the north-south Dawnstar [3.00] to Riften [9.00] run—a very profitable passage. Speak with Ahkari to buy and sell a variety of goods or to receive training lessons in Pickpocket. Dro'marash can help you hone your Speech skill, while Kharjo will offer to serve as a Follower after you do him a special favor..

Ma'dran's Caravan

Ma'dran used to be the poorest of the three Khajiit merchants. Now, with the advent of the Civil War, his business is booming. Ma'dran's primary goods are weapons and armor, which are in high demand. Speak with Ma'dran to purchase some fresh gear, or pay Ma'jhad to help you improve your Lockpicking skill.

◊ Ma'dran's route is unique in that he shares a common stop with Ri'saad's caravan: Windhelm [7.00]. However, Ma'dran's route runs from Windhelm [7.00] to Solitude [1.00] instead of to Markarth [5.00].

[10.01] Azura's Star

Related Quests

Daedric Quest: The Black Star

Recommended Level: 6

Dungeon: Special

Dremora Churl

Malyn Varen

Collectibles

Unique Item: Azura's Star [36/112]

Unique Item: Black Star [26/112]

Area Is Locked (quest required)

Azura's Star is a unique location that's visited only during Daedric Quest: The Black Star. It is, in fact, the interior of the Star of Azura, the Daedric artifact you seek to recover during the quest. The person you seek out to assist you in repairing the Broken Star of Azura determines the reward you'll receive at the quest's end: You get Azura's Star (an infinite Grand Soul Gem) if you turn to Aranea Ienith, and you get the Black Star (an infinite Black Soul Gem) if you seek out Nelacar. Regardless of which person you turn to, you'll end up entering the star and chasing the nefarious Mayln Varen down a winding, crystalline pathway. Dremora will attempt to intercept you along the way. Defeat Varen when you reach the bottom to purify the star and claim a very valuable keepsake.

[10.02] Blackreach

Related Quests

Main Quest: Elder Knowledge

Daedric Quest: Discerning the Transmundane

Side Quest: A Return to Your Roots

Dungeon Activity

Recommended Level: 18

Dungeon: Dwarven City

Chaurus

Dwarven Sphere

Dwarven Spider

Giant

Falmer

Falmer Servant

Frost Troll

Frostbite Spider

Wisp

Wispmother

Crafting

Alchemy Lab

Arcane Enchanter

Workbench

Dangers

Dwarven Ballista Trap (lever)

Dwarven Thresher Trap (pressure plate)

Dwarven Thresher Trap (lever)

Swinging Blade Trap (pressure plates/lever)

Puzzles

Button Puzzle

NOTE Find additional Crimson Nirnroot plants inside of several of Blackreach's interior locations, such as Sinderion's Field Laboratory, the Silent Ruin, and the Derelict Pumphouse (among others).

The dwarves' capital city of Blackreach has been abandoned for ages and now serves as home to vicious Falmer. This great subterranean metropolis houses many secrets for those brave enough to probe its depths. Blackreach features multiple access elevators, but your first visit occurs during Daedric Quest: Discerning the Transmundane, in which you will likely travel through Alftand [4.13]. Therefore, the first time you enter Blackreach, you'll find yourself at [B], unless you chose one of the alternate routes.

Once you've accessed Blackreach, you may use any of the city's elevators to return to the surface. Some elevators connect to major dwarven ruins across Skyrim, such as Raldbthar [3.32] in the Pale. Others simply lead to lone elevator towers that stand in the wilderness. Ride each of Blackreach's elevators to open more and more surface connections to Blackreach—this makes moving to and from the great hidden city much easier.

Underground Connections

- Alftand [4.13]
- Blackreach Elevator (Alftand) [3.26]
- Blackreach Elevator (Raldbthar) [3.33]
- Mzinchaleft [2.18]
- Mzinchaleft Exterior [2.18]
- Raldbthar [3.32]
- Tower of Mzark [3.15]

Quest Items

- Crimson Nirnroot
- Elder Scroll
- Runed Lexicon

Collectibles

- Skill Book [Alchemy]: De Rerum Dirennis
- Skill Book [Block]: Warrior
- Skill Book [Heavy Armor]: 2920, MidYear, v6
- Skill Book [Smithing]: The Armorer's Challenge
- Skill Book [Speech]: A Dance in Fire, v6
- Area Is Locked (quest required)
- Chests
- Potions
- Loose gear
- Mineable ore (Corundum)

The terrain of Blackreach becomes tumultuous around the edges of the cavern but is otherwise quite level and easy. Expect to face a blend of dwarven security units, Falmer, and various cave dwellers like the Chaurus and Frostbite Spider. Encounters with other, more powerful creatures such as trolls and giants are rare.

Aside from exploring the Tower of Mzark [10] as part of the "Discerning the Transmundane" quest, you may also collect special Crimson Nirnroots as part of Side Quest: A Return to Your Roots. Around 50 of these special red plants grow throughout Blackreach. Many are labeled on the map provided here in this guide, while others are found inside of Blackreach's interior points of interest. Use this resource to track them down, then pinpoint their locations by the soft ringing sound each plant produces. Collect the requisite number of Crimson Nirnroot pants to advance the quest.

A Exit to Mzinchaleft Gatehouse [2.18]

B Elevator to Alftand Cathedral [4.13]

C Exit to Blackreach Elevator (Raldbthar) [3.33]

D Exit to Blackreach Elevator (Alftand) [3.26]

E Elevator to Raldbthar Deep Market [3.32]

F Exit to Great Lift AT Mzinchaleft [2.19]

1 Reeking Tower

Scale a rocky slope to reach this tall northern tower, then circle around to locate its door. Enter and slay a handful of overgrown Frostbite Spiders on your way to the far elevator, which takes you back out to Blackreach. You'll find yourself standing near a neighboring tower to the one you entered. Slay a few more spiders out here to cleanse this place.

2 Sinderion's Field Laboratory

This small lab is likely to be your first stop in Blackreach. Claim plenty of loot here and use the crafting stations to prepare yourself for the dangers that lurk in the dark. If you are planning on a long exploration of Blackreach, this is a great place to use as a base camp. Inspect the remains of Sinderion to acquire his informative journal and obtain a new quest that involves collecting Crimson Nirnroot from around Blackreach.

- Crafting: Alchemy Lab, Arcane Enchanter, Workbench
- Crimson Nirnroot
- Skill Book [Alchemy]: De Rerum Dirennis
- Chests (2)
- Knapsack
- Apothecary's Satchel
- Potions

3 Silent Ruin

Enter this small chamber to obtain a Skill Book and some Crimson Nirnroot, but avoid the pressure plate near the throne.

- Danger! Dwarven Thresher Trap (pressure plate)
- Crimson Nirnroot
- Skill Book [Block]: Warrior
- Chest

4 Hall of Rumination

The Hall of Rumination is one of three structures located at Blackreach's city center. Several lowly Falmer and Falmer Servants mill about the main chamber. Slay them and then notice a gate that you can't seem to open. Pull a lever on the balcony to the east of the gate to open it, but head through the nearby east doors first to secure a sleeping area and a room with a chest. Now go through the west gate and head upstairs to discover another chest. Take the nearby elevator up to a high exterior balcony, looping around to discover some Crimson Nirnroot outside.

- Crimson Nirnroot
- Chests (2)

5 Pumping Station

Exit the Debate Hall [6] via its northeast door and cross a walkway to enter this small workshop. The Pumping Station connects to the Silent City Catacombs [7] and houses a handful of poorly armed Falmer Servants. Exit through the northeast door so you may reenter via the northwest door and access a chest on the west balcony.

- Chest

6 Debate Hall

Plenty of Falmer and Falmer Servants lurk within the Debate Hall. The main attraction here is the Skill Book that lies on a small table near a skeleton in the east alcove.

- Skill Book [Speech]: A Dance in Fire, v6

7 Silent City Catacombs

Nab some Crimson Nirnroot on your way into this sewer network, which lies just east of Blackreach's city center. Slay a Falmer and loot a chest in the first hall, then jump the pairs of pressure plates in the hall that follow, or use the lever in the nook beyond the gate to trigger the blades and slice up any patrolling enemies. Proceed until you reach a watery chamber, then dive underwater to locate three submerged chests. Proceed through the next passage and slay another Falmer to obtain a useful key. Make your way through the south door to reach the final room, where you find more Falmer and a door that connects to Blackreach's Pumping Station [5].

- Danger! Swinging Blade Trap (pressure plates/lever)
- Crimson Nirnroot
- Shaman's Key (Falmer)
- Chests (4)

8 War Quarters

This small area sports plenty of beds to rest upon. Complete your circuit through the War Quarters to locate a pair of chests on the entry room's balcony.

- Chests (2)

9 Farm Overseer's House

This small abode offers you a place to rest and plenty of worthy plunder.

- Chest (Locked: Novice)
- Chest (Locked: Adept)
- Potions
- Loose gear

10 Tower of Mzark

This giant tower stands south of Blackreach's city center and houses an item of tremendous power. Ride up the elevator, then raid a couple of locked chests and inspect a Skill Book in the room at which you arrive. Scale a winding ramp to locate the remains of Drokt—read the nearby journal for some insight. Scale the remainder of the ramp to reach a control panel. Insert the Blank Lexicon into the Lexicon Receptacle, then press the third button from the left until the second button from the left becomes active. Now press the second button from the left until the first button on the left becomes active. Press this button until all of the buttons deactivate. Collect the Transcribed Lexicon from the Lexicon Receptacle and approach the central mechanism to obtain the mysterious Elder Scroll. Proceed through the nearby door and use the elevator beyond to quickly return to the surface of Skyrim.

- Elder Scroll
- Runed Lexicon
- Skill Book [Smithing]: The Armorer's Challenge
- Chests (Locked: Novice) (2)
- Potions
- Loose gear

11 Derelict Pumphouse

Destroy a dangerous Dwarven Spider here, then loot a chest that's affixed to the wall. Another chest lies underwater; jump the pipes and turn a submerged valve to access the chest, then surface for a moment to snag some Crimson Nirnroot before turning another valve to escape the water.

- Crimson Nirnroot
- Chest
- Chest (Locked: Adept)

Other Blackreach Locations

The following sites don't have quite as much going on as the aforementioned locations but are still worth exploring:

i Overpass

This overpass was presumably used to monitor the travel of workers to and from the city.

ii Wispmother Encounter

Beware of this clearing, where wisps flutter about. A dangerous Wispmother will attack if you draw near. Crimson Nirnroot grows by the planks that span the nearby stream to the east.

◊ Crimson Nirnroot

iii Guard Towers

Dwarven soldiers likely watched from these towers as workers traveled to and from the city.

iv Fungus Field

Blackreach's giant glowing mushrooms are growing strong here. Find some Crimson Nirnroot growing near the pipes to the north.

◊ Crimson Nirnroot

v Sleeping Chaurus

Get the drop on a pair of giant, snoozing Chaurus by sneaking up to this site.

vi Blackreach City: Main Gate

The gate to the dwarves' capital city lies here, allowing entry from the south.

vii Blackreach Arena

It is assumed that Falmer would have been made to fight at the small arena located here. Pulling the nearby lever causes a lethal spinning blade to stick up from the arena's floor. Collect the Skill Book that rests on the nearby stone table.

◊ Danger! Dwarven Thresher Trap (lever)

◊ Skill Book [Heavy Armor]: 2920, MidYear, v6

viii Troll Den

A pair of vicious Frost Trolls guard a sprig of Crimson Nirnroot on a high ledge here.

◊ Crimson Nirnroot

ix Shrine

Find a bit of loot at the small shrine near the water down here, but beware of a Dwarven Sphere that emerges from the wall.

◊ Crimson Nirnroot

◊ Potions

x Falmer Mining Camp

Dispatch a handful of dangerous Falmer here so you may raid the chests that they guard. If you like, mine some Corundum Ore from the vein near the leader's tent. Crimson Nirnroot grows by the water.

◊ Crimson Nirnroot

◊ Chests (2)

◊ Mineable ore (Corundum)

xi Vulthuryol's Gong

Notice the huge glowing orb floating above the Silent City at the center of Blackreach? Hit this distant target with your Unrelenting Force Shout and you'll summon the dragon Vulthuryol, who will soar out of his hidden lair to rain fire upon the city before setting down on the southern road.

[10.03] Blue Palace Pelagius Wing

Related Quests

Daedric Quest: The Mind of Madness

Recommended Level: 8

Dungeon: Special

Sheogorath

Pelagius the Mad

Collectibles

Skill Book [Lockpicking]: Surfeit of Thieves [C2/10]

Unique Weapon: Wabbajack [72/80]

Area Is Locked (quest required)

This special section of the Blue Palace in Solitude [1.00] remains locked at all times and is accessible only during Daedric Quest: The Mind of Madness. After a brief exploration of the long-unused wing, you're soon whisked away to unfamiliar surroundings—the deceptively verdant mind of Emperor Pelagius III! Speak with Sheogorath to advance the quest and receive a unique weapon called the Wabbajack—this is the only thing you can take with you when you leave this unusual place.

Travel down each of the three paths to encounter three very unusual situations, each a reflection of Pelagius's warped psyche. Use the Wabbajack to solve each of the situations as follows:

Arena: Shoot the spectating soldiers on the arena's far side, not the combatants.

Pelagius the Tormented: Shoot the sleeping Emperor to spawn a series of progressively more dangerous foes. Defeat them all.

Pelagius vs. Pelagius: Shoot the smaller version of Pelagius (named "Confidence") to make it grow. Shoot the Imperial Soldier named "Anger" to shrink it. Ensure that Pelagius's Confidence is as large as can be, then shoot the two specters of Self-Doubt that eventually appear to vanquish them.

Once you've returned from Pelagius's frightening mind, continue your search of the Pelagius Wing to discover a Skill Book on some crates downstairs.

[10.04] Japhet's Folly

Related Quests

Side Quest: Rise in the East

Dungeon: Bandit Camp

Blood Horker

Haldyn

Mudcrab

Crafting

Arcane Enchanter

Dangers

Swinging Spears (pressure plate)

Area Is Locked (quest required)

Chests

Potions

Loose gear

Japhet's Folly is a special island that only be reached only by ship. You visit Japhet's Folly during Side Quest: Rise in the East, with the goal of slaying a dangerous mage named Haldyn, who's raised an impressive pirate base here.

Once you arrive at Japhet's Folly, leap from your ship and cross the broken ice, heading for the tower that stands atop the nearby glacier. You can't actually reach the tower—follow your objective marker to locate the entrance to a small cave instead.

Sea Cave

Kill a few Mudcrab in the watery cave, and open a chest in the first cavern. Slay a lone Blood Horker bandit in the stone room you soon reach. Loot a second chest here, then grab the potions on the shelves before heading upstairs to the Japhet's Folly Towers.

◊ Chests (2) ◊ Potions

Japhet's Folly Towers

Avoid a pressure plate on the first landing as you go upstairs. Eliminate a couple of Blood Horker guards, then raid a chest as you cross a long hall to reach a neighboring tower. If you like, go downstairs to face a few more guards and discover more loot, including a locked chest. Unlock the Expert-level door down here to discover the final resting place of Japhet, whose remains lie next to an informative journal and a large chest. Go upstairs to slay Haldyn, raid his chest, and collect the key he carries. Then backtrack downstairs and use the Japhet's Folly Key to open the door in the connecting corridor, which leads outside.

◊ Danger! Swinging Spears (pressure plate)

◊ Crafting: Arcane Enchanter

◊ Japhet's Folly Key (Haldyn)

◊ Chests (2)

◊ Chest (Locked: Apprentice)

◊ Chest (Locked: Expert)

◊ Potions

◊ Loose gear

Japhet's Folly (Exterior)

Step outside to find the island being bombarded by cannon fire—your associates are doing their part! Slay the odd guard and loot a lone chest as you navigate the embattled encampment, but don't stray too far from the main path or you may be struck by friendly fire. Dispatch the final group of pirates down by the docks, then speak with Adelasia Vendicci to complete your quest and shove off.

◊ Chest

[10.05] Skuldafn

Related Quests

Main Quest: The World-Eater's Eyrie
Side Quest: Masks of the Dragon Priests*

Recommended Level: 24

Dungeon: Dragon Priest Lair

Dragon
Draugr
Frostbite Spider
Nahkriin

Dangers

Dart Trap (pressure plates)
Oil Lamp Trap (pressure plate)
Oil Pool Trap

Puzzles

Nordic Puzzle Door (Diamond Claw)
Nordic Pillars I
Nordic Pillars II

Collectibles

Dragon Claw: Diamond Claw [10/10]
Dragon Priest Mask: Nahkriin [10/10]

Special Objects

Word Wall: Storm Call [3/3]
Area Is Locked (quest required)
Chest(s)
Potions
Loose gear

Skuldafn is a special location that lies just outside the bounds of Skyrim's ninth Hold, the Rift. Once you've advanced to Main Quest: The World-Eater's Eyrie, you're able to visit Skuldafn by flying on the back of a dragon. Your goal is to access Skuldafn's portal to Sovngarde [10.06], the legendary underworld of the Nords.

Skuldafn (Exterior)

A Odahviing (to Skyrim)

1 Bridge Entrance

Slay a dragon that ambushes you in Skuldafn's large exterior ruins, while simultaneously battling multiple Draugr.

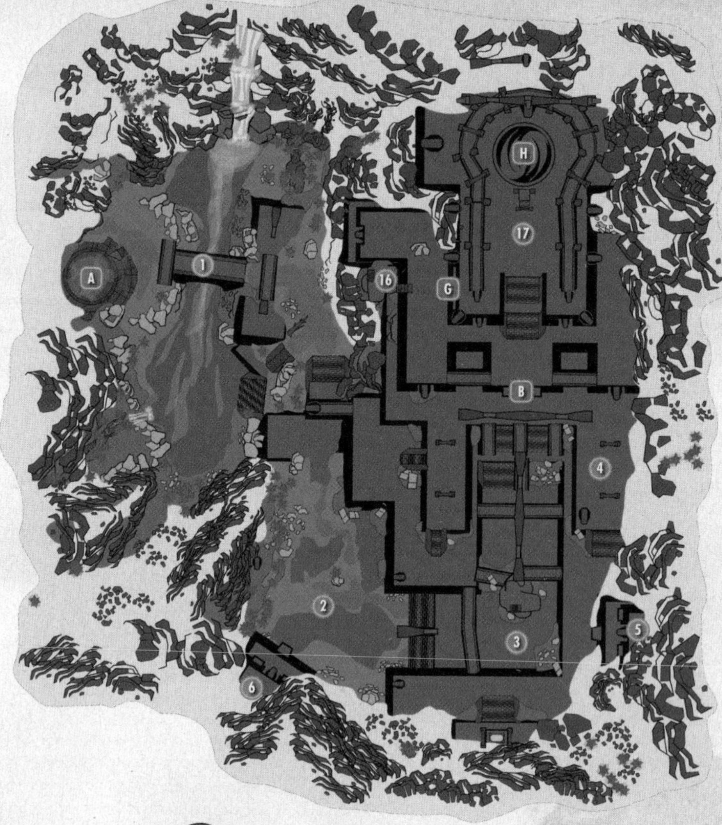

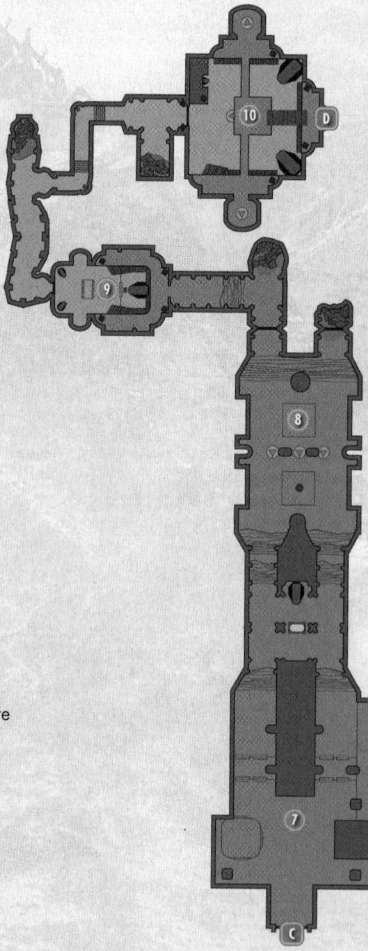

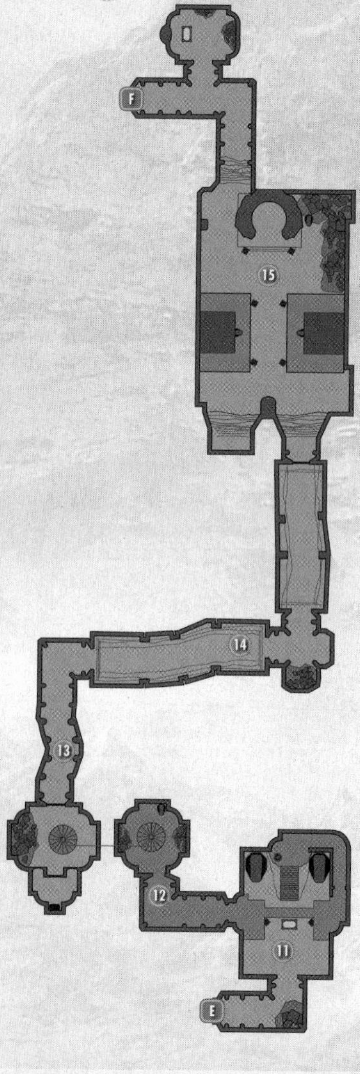

2 Lower Grounds

A second dragon strikes as you near the South Tower, and more Draugr are poised on the walkway beyond the east stairs.

3 Ruined Tower

Climb an open-air tower to locate a chest beyond the east stairs, then slay more Draugr as you scale the north stairs that follow.

4 Temple Walkways

If you like, loop around to visit the North Tower, and raid the exterior chest on the table atop the south steps, before entering Skuldafn Temple.

- Chests (2)

5 Skuldafn South Tower

This simple tower teems with Draugr, but there's a chest upstairs.

- Chest

6 Skuldafn North Tower

The North Tower's similar to its twin—full of undead and housing a chest on its upper level. Head outside through the upstairs door and reenter the tower via the other balcony door to discover a second chest in a small alcove.

- Chests (2)

B Door to Skuldafn Temple

Skuldafn Temple (Interior: Section I)

C Door to Skuldafn

7 Entry Hall

The legendary portal to Sovngarde is housed within this temple. Beware of pressure plate traps and Draugr as you explore the cavernous entry hall, looting a chest on the right.

8 Puzzle Chamber I

Spin the three Nordic pillars so that the two on the outside are mirroring the glyphs on the opposing walls (Snake, Whale). Then spin the central pillar so that its Hawk glyph faces toward the far porcullises. Pull the central lever to raise the Hawk portcullis, then raid the chest beyond. Change the central pillar again so that its Snake glyph is facing the portcullises; then pull the lever a second time to open the Snake portcullis and advance.

9 Draugr Crypt

Loot another chest at the bottom of the following chamber, then cut through Frostbite Spiders on your way to another room with a second Nordic Pillars Puzzle. Find a fourth chest here.

10 Puzzle Chamber II

Solve the simple puzzle by spinning the three pillars so that the bottom one shows a Snake, while the upper two show a Whale and a Hawk, matching the glyphs on the walls about the room. Pull the lever to lower the drawbridge that leads deeper into the temple.

- Danger! Dart Trap (pressure plates)
- Chests (4)

D Door to Skuldafn Temple

Skuldafn Temple (Interior: Section II)

E Door to Skuldafn Temple

11 Grand Stairs

Loop around the entry room, slaying Draugr on your way to a stairwell.

12 Spiral Steps

Beware the pressure plate near the stairwell—stepping on it causes a hanging lamp to fall and ignite the oily floor, while also causing arrows to fly out from the far wall! Go upstairs and raid a chest near more oil and another hanging lamp.

13 Oily Hall

Pull the nearby lever to open the north portcullis and sack another chest on your way down an oily hall, but beware another dangerous pressure plate.

14 Nordic Puzzle Door

Kill a powerful Draugr in the passage the follows to obtain the Diamond Claw, then use the claw to open the nearby puzzle door (Fox, Moth, Dragon).

15 Word Wall Chamber

Approach the Word Wall that follows to gain new power, then proceed toward the door that leads back outside to Skuldafn's exterior, swiping a few potions from a small embalming chamber along the way.

- Danger! Dart Trap (pressure plate), Oil Lamp Trap, Oil Lamp Traps (pressure plates), Oil Pool Trap
- Dragon Claw: Diamond Claw [10/10]
- Word Wall: Storm Call [3/3]
- Chests (2)
- Potions
- Loose gear

F Door to Skuldafn

Skuldafn (Exterior: Temple Apex)

G Door to Skuldafn Temple

16 West Tower

Cut down the Draugr outside the temple, then descend the wooden stairs of the west tower to plunder a large chest at the bottom.

17 Portal Threshold

Go back up and circle around the temple so you may scale its exterior stairs, at last arriving at the portal to Sovngarde. Slay the mighty Dragon Priest that guards this wondrous site so you may claim its valuable mask and staff. Inspect the Dragon Seal to replace the staff and open the portal once more. Gather your courage and jump into the beam to journey to Sovngarde [10.06]!

- Dragon Priest Mask: Nahkriin [10/10]
- Unique Weapon: Dragon Priest Staff [73/80]
- Chest
- Potion

H Portal to Sovngarde

[10.06] Sovngarde

Related Quests

Main Quest: Sovngarde
Main Quest: Dragonslayer
Main Quest: Epilogue

Recommended Level: 24

Dungeon: Dragon Lair

Alduin
Erlendr
Felldir the Old
Gormlaith Golden-Hilt
Hakon One-Eye
Hero of Sovngarde
Hunroor
Imperial Soldier
Jurgen Windcaller
Nikulas
Stormcloak Soldier
Tsun
Ulfgar the Unyielding
Ysgramor
Area Is Locked (quest required)

Sovngarde is the storied underworld of the Nords—the place where the greatest Nord heroes go when they die to enjoy an eternity of feasting and merriment. The only way a living mortal can visit this surreal realm is via the portal at Skuldafn [10.05], another special location that can only be visited during Main Quest: The World-Eater's Eyrie.

Sovngarde (Exterior)

Use the Clear Skies Shout to clear a path through Sovngarde's misty exterior. You can use Clear Skies to prevent Alduin from devouring the souls lost in the mist (they will aid you in the final battle against Alduin), but don't bother trying to attack Alduin—he's protected by his mist. You can turn right or left at the first junction; the steps straight ahead merely lead to an overlook. Wind around the central hill and approach Tsun, the guardian of this place. Defeat him to prove your worth, then cross the Whalebone Bridge and enter the towering Hall of Valor.

Hall of Valor

Skyrim's greatest heroes stroll the Hall of Valor. Ysgramor himself greets you when you first enter. Enjoy your peek at a true Nord's idea of paradise, then approach the three heroes of old to learn what you must do to defeat Alduin.

[DG.10] Soul Cairn

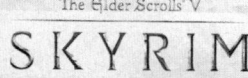

Related Quests

Dawnguard Main Quest: Chasing Echoes
Dawnguard Main Quest: Beyond Death
Side Quest: Impatience of a Saint
Side Quest: Durnehviir
Regional Activity: Arvak the Spectral Steed*
Regional Activity: Dark Conjurations*
Regional Activity: (Don't Fear) the Reaper*
Regional Activity: The Soul Husk Merchant*
Regional Activity: Valerica's Concoction*
Regional Activity: The Whole Soul*

Recommended Level: 13

Faction: Ideal Masters

Arvak	Mistman
Boneman	Morven Stroud
Durnehviir	Soul
Jiub	Valerica
Keeper	Wrathman

Services

Special: Morven Stroud (Special Vendor) [DG1/1] [DG&HF 8/23]

Crafting

Alchemy Lab

Dangers

Ideal Masters Crystal

Collectibles

Unique Item: Locket of Saint Jiub [DG12/17]

Miscellaneous

Area is locked
Chest
Loose gear
Lots o' Gold
Potions aplenty

Topographical Overview

Among the countless planes of Oblivion, the Soul Cairn has a particularly grim reputation. The plane of undeath is filled with lost, trapped, or accursed souls, bound to wander this place of despair and anguish for all eternity. The plane is ruled by mysterious beings known only as the Ideal Masters and is protected by their endless legions of undead Soul Guards. It is here that a powerful vampire named Valerica—Serana's mother and the wife of Lord Harkon—has dwelt for centuries in the colossal coliseum-like structure known as the Boneyard.

For the purposes of this guide, we have divided the Soul Cairn into three Parishes. The boundary lines are invisible and don't show up during your adventure; they have been created to aid you in locating the many small points of interest and secrets that the Soul Cairn holds. Here's what to look for:

3.2 **Major Location:** This is an area of the Soul Cairn that is critically important to Dawnguard Main Quest: Beyond Death. These are larger-scale locations and usually house a particularly hardy foe or impressive revelation.

3.A **Minor Location:** A section of the Soul Cairn that is optional to investigate. These may be as simple as waypoints to use as landmarks or buildings containing one or more of the many secrets that the Soul Cairn holds.

In addition to flagged locations, the following areas and items are shown on the map and are listed here (along with the number available):

Arvak's Skull (1): The skull of a spectral horse you can save as part of Regional Activity: Arvak the Spectral Steed.

Ideal Master Crystal (8): A strange, floating crystal that saps your energy as you enter its sphere of influence. These crystals are unbreakable and dangerous. Combat them with potions made by Valerica (Regional Activity: Valerica's Concoction) or by consuming Soul Husks (see below), and look for a chest under each one.

Jiub's Opus (10): The scattered pages of a renowned hero known as Saint Jiub. Gather them all as part of Side Quest: Impatience of a Saint.

Lightning Attractor (4): Place a Grand or Greater Soul Gem into the receptacle at this point, and a lightning strike transforms it into a Black Soul Gem.

Reaper Gem Fragments (3): Three locations where you may find fragments of the Eldritch Reaper Gem.

Reaper's Lair (1): The summoning place where you can call and fight the Reaper, as part of Regional Activity: (Don't Fear) the Reaper.

Spell Tome (3): The Spell Tomes needed to conjure Bonemen, Mistmen, and Wrathmen are scattered throughout the Cairn. Their locations are shown here.

Teleporter (9): A small circle of twisting purple light transports you to a nearby location (usually a rooftop).

In addition to the enemies you encounter and collectibles to find, there are three other items of interest:

Arvak: From time to time, you may see a skeletal horse with a spectral mane galloping in terror across this realm. This is Arvak, the lost but loyal steed. Find and ride him as part of Regional Activity: Arvak the Spectral Steed.*

Soul Husks: Dotted throughout the Soul Cairn (and also found in some chests) are Soul Husks. These desiccated growths are edible and are found in your Food menu. For ten seconds, you gain 10 percent Magic Resistance and are protected from Soul Drain effects (such as those of the Ideal Masters). Check the Regional Activities for more uses.

Soul Fissures: Throughout the Soul Cairn, you can also find several gaping cracks in the earth with a strange energy seeping from them. If you have an empty Soul Gem in your inventory, interact with these fissures to instantly fill the gem. Each fissure can be used only once.

Parish 1: The Threshold

This pathway leads from the portal to a large barrier wall that separates the inner and outer parts of the Cairn. This area has fewer foes and less danger, so explore it first, then search for the gap in the Barrier Wall to proceed. For quicker, less terrifying results, stay on the path!

Major Locations

[SC1.1] Portal to Volkihar Ruins

Related Quest: Dawnguard Main Quest: Beyond Death

This set of floating stone steps leads to a pulsating portal that leads back to Valerica's Laboratory, back in the Volkihar Ruins section of Castle Volkihar. This is the only entrance and exit to the Soul Cairn, and you can return here at any point once Dawnguard Main Quest: Beyond Death begins. Once opened, it will not close, so you can return to complete optional quests at your discretion.

Minor Locations

[SC1.A] Path of Souls

This winding pathway stretches out in a northeasterly direction, all the way to the Boneyard in Parish 2. The start of it has a baleful, ghostly figure standing on either side, among the dirt and stones. Speak to them and listen to their confused cries if you wish.

[SC1.B] The Black Chapel

Related Quest: Side Quest: Impatience of a Saint

The first charcoal structure you'll come across is this chapel, with tattered banners flapping and a mournful soul standing at the bottom of the steps. Shoot an arrow into each turquoise orb so the bars at the chapel entrance recede. Then head inside, looking for one of Jiub's pages, as well as the following:

- Chest
- Loose gear
- Jiub's Opus (Page 8) [1/10]

[SC1.C] Mournful Soul

Farther along the Path of Souls, you'll periodically encounter more trapped souls that are expressing sorrow, anger, and bewilderment. There are many scattered throughout the Cairn; speak to any you wish, but from this point on, the important ones are flagged. The two sitting on the side of the road are of no help to your cause.

[SC1.D] The Black Church

Related Quest: Side Quest: Impatience of a Saint

This ornate structure houses a Boneman on the ground, guarding a chest with another of Jiub's pages. Outside is a small, circular pool of light. Step into it, and you're whisked to the rooftop. Step around the grating (so you don't fall through) and claim a book and items from a second chest.

- Chest (2)
- Jiub's Opus (Page 6) [2/10]
- Teleporter [1/9]

> **NOTE** This is the first teleporter you may find in the Soul Cairn. All are flagged on the main map and are listed throughout.

[SC1.E] Arvak's Rider

Related Regional Activity: Arvak the Spectral Steed

The soul standing ankle-deep in the mist along this part of the pathway pleads with you to find his horse, Arvak. This steed is frightened, loyal, and must be rescued. Agree to help to begin the quest.

[SC1.F] The Barrier Wall

Bisecting the Parishes of the Soul Cairn is a giant black wall constructed by unknown hands. The steps and gap here is the only way through to the larger expanse of land beyond.

[SC1.G] The Black Gatehouse

This structure protrudes from an area of the Barrier Wall and provides an entrance to the small, self-contained area where the Crystal Folly stands. Pry open the chest along the way.

- Chest

[SC1.H] The Crystal Folly

Related Quest: Side Quest: Impatience of a Saint

Guarded by Bonemen, this small hillock has a folly to the Ideal Masters built on it. Deal with the bony foes before you close in, as the giant crystal floating above the chest atop the structure severely damages your energy. One of Jiub's pages is up here too.

- Chest
- Ideal Master Crystal [1/8]
- Jiub's Opus (Page 3) [3/10]

[SC1.I] Steps of the Barrier Wall (South)

Related Quest: Side Quest: Impatience of a Saint

Farther along the Barrier Wall to the east is a set of steps to a lost soul waiting near a book, a potion, and another of Jiub's pages. Through the window, you'll see a chest, on the north side. You can reach it only by trekking around to the wall's other side.

- Jiub's Opus (Page 1) [4/10]

[SC1.J] Totem to the Ideal Masters

A pile of bones arranged to form a strange totem is found among the gnarled trees here. Take the Black Soul Gem if you wish (there are three Bonemen to face if you do).

◊ Black Soul Gem

[SC1.K] Heaven's Arc Point

This stone pavement holds a strange altarlike collection of stones in its middle. Nearby is a Greater Soul Gem. Pick it up and place it in the receptacle of the Lightning Attractor. A crackle of lightning and a clap of thunder echo through the Cairn, transforming the gem into a Black Soul Gem. You'll find a Soul Husk here too (these aren't listed but can be collected for the quests listed previously).

◊ Greater Soul Gem

◊ Lightning Attractor [1/4]

◊ Soul Husk

[SC1.L] The Black Sanctuary

A set of half-buried stairs leads up to a teleporter. Check the ground level of the sanctuary structure first (there are Soul Gems among the skeletal rubble). You may wish to attack the Boneman patrolling the roof with a long-range attack, as the teleporter transports you there, to a chest and combat with a Wrathman.

◊ Chest

◊ Teleporter [2/9]

[SC1.M] The Black Monastery

This sizable structure dominates the southern part of the Cairn. Below the imposing tower is an interior courtyard with a wretched soul and steps to the roof area. Work your way around, past another prone soul, then head down the steps to the southwest and go to the tower. Fight fatigue from an Ideal Master Crystal, above a third soul and a chest.

◊ Chest ◊ Ideal Master Crystal [2/8]

TIP You can try using Whirlwind Sprint (Shout) or your Bats (Vampire Lord) powers to dash through the gap to the tower from the upper promontory.

Parish 2: The Cemetery

A large part of the Soul Cairn is given over to the countless piles of bones that have accumulated here throughout the centuries. These piles are everywhere, as are the wandering souls of the banished. This area is dominated by a cluster of large buildings to the northwest, where a Keeper lurks. However, to the north is the largest structure of all: the Boneyard where Valerica is imprisoned.

Major Locations

[SC2.1] The Boneyard (Entrance)

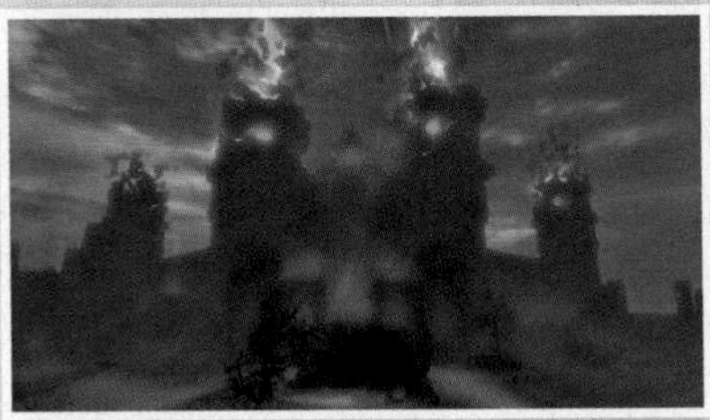

Related Quest: Dawnguard Main Quest: Beyond Death

Related Regional Activities

Dark Conjurations*
Valerica's Concoction*
The Whole Soul*

Trapped behind a barrier of energy, Valerica spends her time perfecting her alchemy and staving off the madness of loneliness. She is a font of knowledge about this place; speak to her if you want to learn more about her life, the Ideal Masters, and the origins of the Soul Cairn.

◊ Alchemy Lab

Boneyard (Interior)

The interior of the Boneyard is accessible only after all the Keepers have released their grip on Valerica, as part of the quest. Once inside, you face a troublesome dragon named Durnehviir, along with several Bonemen called upon by the Ideal Masters.

A Exit to Soul Cairn

1 Boneyard Arena

The battle begins here. Note the five clusters of standing stones around the arena, where four Bonemen (or other foes) are summoned during combat. Deal with them and the dragon.

2 Dragon Perch

Durnehviir begins his attack from this launching point. You can use the steps on either side to reach cover (away from the Bonemen) if combat isn't going your way.

3 Outer Battlements

Surrounding the boneyard (on all five sides) are steps to the upper battlements, where you are afforded some cover. Move up here if the battle in the arena is too hectic.

4 Valerica's Alcove

Between the steps to the arena's east is an alcove where Valerica stores her most precious items. Aside from the books and potions, there is a case containing the most valuable item of all: an Elder Scroll!

◊ Alchemy Lab

◊ Elder Scroll (Blood)

◊ Potions aplenty

[SC2.2] Keeper 1: Tabernacle of the Ideal Masters

Related Quest: Dawnguard Main Quest: Beyond Death

This sprawling structure is perhaps the largest outside of the Boneyard. Flanked by two adjoining wings, you can approach from the southeast (heading northwest) after navigating the cemetery, or move through the many gaps around the sides and rear of the structure. This is important, as a Keeper resides here, so cautious maneuvering is advisable.

To the northeast is a sunken courtyard with a teleporter that transports you to the roof. Here you find a Lightning Attractor (and a three-strong Boneman ambush) and a chest. To the southwest is a barred gate (to open it, fire at the two turquoise orbs above and to the right of the gate from the interior courtyard near the Keeper) leading to an exterior foundation area, where two Bonemen guard a chest and an Ideal Master Crystal. Finally, don't forget the teleporter to the northwest among the standing stones: It transports you to a section of roof you can't otherwise reach. Here, you'll find the skeletal remains of an adventurer, along with his gear and potions (and a Boneman to surprise you).

The Keeper sits on a massive throne in a large courtyard in the middle of this place. However, there are plenty of hiding places among the various pillars and structures surrounding him. Or you can attack and use the space provided by the courtyard to avoid his incredibly damaging weapon swings. Defeat the Keeper, claiming a Black Soul Gem (Grand) from the dust he leaves behind.

- Chest (3)
- Enemy: The Keeper
- Ideal Master Crystal [3/8]
- Lightning Attractor [2/4]
- Loose gear
- Potions
- Reaper Gem Fragment [2/3]
- Teleporter [3/9]
- Teleporter [4/9]

Minor Locations

[SC2.A] Black Gatehouse 1

Located on the Soul Path, with a damned spirit waiting at one of the entrances, this provides a landmark and cover as you explore.

[SC2.B] Black Gatehouse 2

This empty gatehouse has a pointed roof. Pass through it on the Soul Path, using it as a visual marker.

[SC2.C] Lost Structure

The unofficial "center" of the Soul Cairn, souls were placed here, at these crossroads, so they couldn't return to seek revenge on their captors. Now only the foundations and a few bone piles remain. Use this to situate yourself, as all the major roads lead from here.

[SC2.D] Black Gatehouse 3

Located at the foot of the hill on which the Boneyard is situated, you begin your climb up the hill from here. Watch for a few Bonemen to rise up and attack from the bones scattered near the structure to the south.

[SC2.E] Durnehviir's Rooftop Perch

Related Side Quest: Durnehviir

An enslaved dragon named Durnehviir stops you as you exit the Boneyard. Listen to what he says, and agree to his requests.

- Word of Power: Curse, Summon Durnehviir
- Word of Power: Dying, Summon Durnehviir
- Word of Power: Never, Summon Durnehviir

[SC2.F] The Black Folly

Related Quest: Side Quest: Impatience of a Saint

The occasional home of the enslaved dragon Durnehviir, this area has several crenellations and stairs to explore, but none lead to anything valuable. In fact, the only area of note is a partially destroyed Word Wall (that grants no Words of Power) that Durnehviir sometimes sits on. Below it, you'll find the following in the ankle-deep mist:

- Chest
- Jiub's Opus (Page 2) [5/10]
- Lots o' Gold

[SC2.G] Black Gatehouse 4

Don't confuse this with Location SC2.D, as the pathway this gatehouse marks takes you toward the second Keeper and into the main cemetery area.

[SC2.H] The Black Bethel

The reward for exploring this dangerous location is a chest guarded by the only Ideal Master Crystal hidden inside a structure. Heading north, approach from the south, past the two columns, and use the subterranean stairs and short tunnel for a fight with two Bonemen; then head inside. Or, clamber in from ground level, ignoring the tunnel. Alternatively, approach from the north (heading south), using your Bats (Vampire Lord) or Whirlwind Sprint (Shout) power to dash across the gap between the stone step slabs and the windowed interior.

- Chest
- Ideal Master Crystal [3/8]

[SC2.I] The Dark Battlements (Main)

If you're using the rudimentary pathway in your exploration, the entrance to the cemetery is via this ruined entrance, now merely half-sunk battlements silent in the stale air. Enter from either the north or south, moving quickly to step out of the Ideal Master Crystal's range. Engage the Boneman and Wrathmen that rise on the main platform. Remove the bars in the small spire that holds a soul and a chest by firing an arrow or bolt at both of the turquoise orbs (one above the bars, the other half hidden in an inaccessible alcove in the south corner of the platform).

- Chest
- Ideal Master Crystal [4/8]

[SC2.J] The Dark Battlements (Skeleton and Soul)

The edge of the battlements holds a soul watching over sprawled skeletal remains and a coin purse.

[SC2.K] The Dark Battlements (Wandering Soul)

If you speak to it, a soul babbles incoherently. It lives out eternity by wandering close to the battlements.

[SC2.L] The Black Mausoleum

A larger, tall structure close to the cemetery, this place coaxes you in with a barred entrance at the top of some steps, which can be removed by firing at the two turquoise orbs within the structure (or you can leap onto the soul pool and circumvent it entirely). The interior has nothing of value, except for a Boneman battle. But unlike the restless souls, only a moment of your time has been wasted.

[SC2.M] The Cemetery Gatehouse 1

One of five gatehouses that surround the cemetery. This is close to the rocky perimeter of the Soul Cairn, to the southwest.

[SC2.N] The Cemetery Gatehouse 2

The second gatehouse offers a path toward the domain of the second Keeper.

[SC2.O] The Cemetery Altar

Related Regional Activity: Dark Conjurations*

The eerie graveyard of lost souls dominates this Parish. In the middle is a black altar, upon which rests a Spell Tome you haven't read before. Take it before the five summoned Bonemen and Wrathman pick you apart.

- Spell Tome: Conjure Boneman [1/3]

[SC2.P] The Cemetery Gatehouse 3

This gatehouse is on the lower ground and offers a side path toward the large structure known as the Black Minster.

[SC2.Q] The Cemetery Gatehouse 4

Low down with the graves and ceremonial stones on either side, follow the path through this gatehouse.

[SC2.R] The Cemetery Gatehouse 5

The last gatehouse is on the outskirts of the second Keeper's territory, on the slightly higher ground on the edge of the cemetery.

[SC2.S] The Black Minster

Related Quest: Side Quest: Impatience of a Saint

Along the northern edge of this Parish is an ominous maze with an Ideal Master Crystal visible from the perimeter. A quick walk around this place reveals only one entrance, close to a barred section. Keep your wits about you as you work your way through the short maze, pausing to slay any Wrathmen that clamber out of bony piles. There's a chest in the southwest corner and a foe to face in the dead-end passage to the west.

Pass the Daedra Heart and Soul Husks to reach the middle thoroughfare, then head south and east into the second part of the maze. Follow the corridor until you notice a sack to the east. Then check that corridor for a chest to the south, along with a foe guarding a chest and a book. Find the next enemy near a teleporter. This transports you directly up onto the battlements. From here, sprint to the chest guarded by the Crystal and take another of Jiub's pages lying by the foot of the chest.

- ◊ Chest (2)
- ◊ Ideal Master Crystal [5/8]
- ◊ Jiub's Opus (Page 9) [6/10]
- ◊ Teleporter [5/9]

Parish 3: The Blasted Heath

A mist-filled twisting path cuts more scars through this parched and rancid land, where the remnants of forgotten buildings and the spirits of malevolent foes still linger. A shriveled forest dominated by a Keeper's spire gives way to more rocky ground and a collection of imposing structures to the northeast, dominated by a floating spire where the third Keeper watches over this realm.

Major Locations

[SC3.1] Keeper 2: The Shriveled Forest

Related Quest: Dawnguard Main Quest: Beyond Death

Fight through the low hills of scrub and deal with any Wrathmen that appear along the path leading to this location, an imposing spire slowly sinking into the shriveled forest. There are a few structures to hide behind, and the Keeper is visible at a good distance; this is helpful for ranged attacks.

- ◊ Enemy: Keeper

[SC3.2] Keeper 3: The Floating Citadel

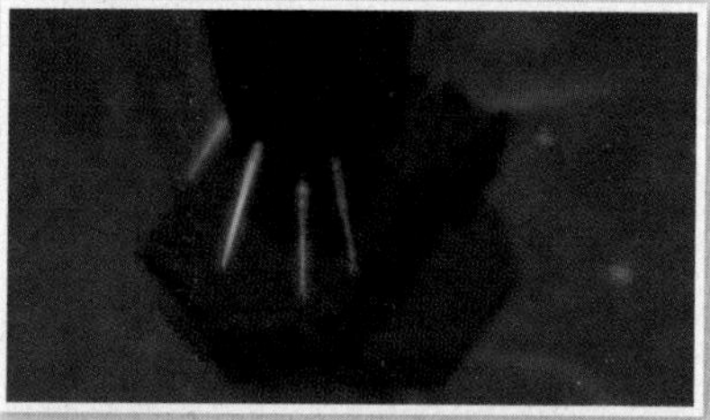

Related Quest: Dawnguard Main Quest: Beyond Death

The final Keeper resides in an ominous floating citadel offering the most impressive views and deadly plummets available in the Soul Cairn. Expect Boneman and Wrathman combat as you reach a teleporter under the hovering rock; this is the only way up to it. Climb the spire counterclockwise, and face down the third Keeper, who carries a bow that can drop you with a single arrow. Time ranged attacks to strike before the Keeper can fire his bow, or use the scenery as protection. The teleporter to return to the ground is on the uppermost ledge.

- ◊ Enemy: Keeper
- ◊ Teleporter [6/9]

Minor Locations

[SC3.A] Steps of the Barrier Wall (North)

Farther along the Barrier Wall to the east is a set of steps leading up to a chest. Through the window, you'll see a lost soul waiting near a book, a potion, and another of Jiub's pages, on the south side. You can reach it only by trekking around to the other side of the wall.

[SC3.B] Morven Stroud, the Soul Husk Merchant

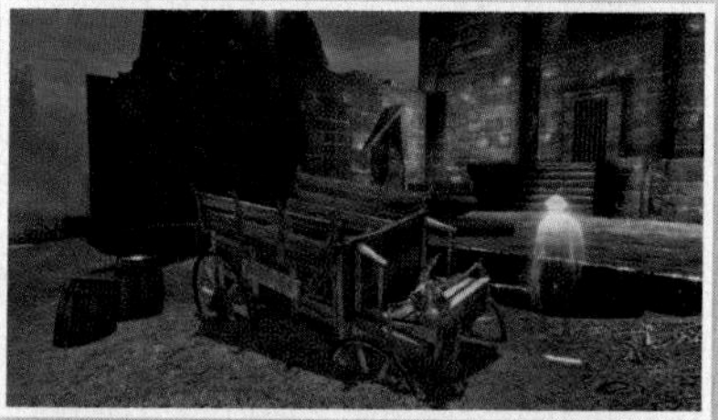

Related Quest: Side Quest: Impatience of a Saint

Related Regional Activity: The Soul Husk Merchant*

With his remains parked outside the Black Rectory, Morven Stroud is one of the few souls you can converse with. He ended up here after selling an item with suspect ingredients to a necromancer coven. No longer plying his wares in High Rock, he wants only Soul Husks. Return with 25 and you can claim a random leveled item from his collection. A nearby barrel has another one of Jiub's pages to take.

- ◊ Jiub's Opus (Page 10) [7/10]
- ◊ Vendor (Morven Stroud): Special Goods [DG1/1] [DG&HF 8/23]

[SC3.C] The Black Rectory

This is a smaller but imposing structure close to the two gatehouses in Parish 2. Access the barred entrance to an interior with a chest by firing an arrow or bolt at the turquoise orbs set into the building on either side. Next, climb the exterior steps to the south, leading to a teleporter up onto the roof. It is empty, but you can drop to the lower roof on the northern side and claim items from a second chest.

◊ Chest (2) ◊ Teleporter [7/9]

[SC3.D] Heaven's Wand Point

These foundations are slowly sinking into the heath, but the structure provides some aid; there is a Lightning Attractor to turn your Greater or Grand Soul Gems into Black ones. Note that a Boneman ambush (usually three strong) appear as you do this.

◊ Lightning Attractor [3/4]

[SC3.E] The Keeper's Chapel

East along the path, past a giant unnatural pillar, is a cluster of three buildings near location [SC3.1], the Shriveled Forest. Dominated by the second Keeper's domain, this side building holds little value, except as a place to hide or snipe from when fighting the Keeper.

[SC3.F] The Keeper's Altar

Related Regional Activity: Dark Conjurations*

The other building adjacent to the Keeper's throne is a sagged structure with pointed roof and crumbling foundations. Inside is a small altar with a book. Grab it, and prepare for two or three Wrathmen to rise and try to stop you.

◊ Spell Tome: Conjure Wrathman [2/3]

[SC3.G] Reaper's Lair

Related Regional Activity: (Don't Fear) the Reaper*

With scattered foundation stones and a raised foundation forecourt, this structure is short in stature but long on foreboding. You can enter this lair via the double arched doors. Inside is a strange altar crackling with arc lightning. If you have collected all the necessary Reaper Gem Fragments, you can fuse them at this Shard Receptacle and summon the fearsome Reaper himself! He attacks, along with a few Bonemen. Search his ghastly remains for the following:

◊ Black Soul Gem (3)

◊ Daedra Heart

[SC3.H] The Unwary Adventurer

A helmeted Nord skeleton lies slumped against a rock outcrop. His note tells of his hapless adventuring.

◊ Loose gear

[SC3.I] The Black Cloister

Featuring a Lightning Attractor (to turn Greater or Grand Soul Gems to Black) in its center and a five-strong Boneman ambush if you use the attractor, this three-tower ruin is otherwise dormant.

◊ Lightning Attractor [4/4]

[SC3.J] Soul Pool Foundation

Related Quest: Side Quest: Impatience of a Saint

Easy to find if you follow the paths of the Soul Cairn, this area of flat scrubland has a stone foundation and a circular soul pool. Take Jiub's page near some loose gear, watching for Wrathmen.

◊ Jiub's Opus (Page 5) [8/10]

◊ Loose gear

[SC3.K] Saint Jiub the Eradicator

Related Quest: Side Quest: Impatience of a Saint

Previously seen in Morrowind, this Dark Elf now resides here, seemingly oblivious to his fate. Speak to him to begin his Side Quest, and bring all ten of the found pages to him at this location, a small campfire on the path through the heath.

◊ Saint Jiub's Opus

◊ Unique Item: Locket of Saint Jiub [DG12/17]

[SC3.L] The Obsidian Hall

Related Regional Activity:
(Don't Fear) the Reaper*

This large ruin with huge walled sides is located south of the Boneyard but north of the second Keeper's location. Beware of foes as you investigate inside, finding a small, circular teleporter that allows you to move to the upper roof (rather than the roof section you can reach via the nearby stairs). Beware of an Ideal Master Crystal hovering above a chest to the south. Among other items, a Reaper Gem Fragment is found here.

- Ideal Master Crystal [7/8]
- Reaper Gem Fragment [2/3]
- Teleporter [8/9]

[SC3.M] Husk Pasture

A doleful farmer and the souls of his two cattle slowly move about this cluster of Soul Husks, lamenting their lot. This is the largest concentration of Soul Husks in the Cairn.

[SC3.N] Arvak's Altar

Related Regional Activity:
Arvak the Spectral Steed

The skeletal horse whose ghost you may see galloping across the Cairn from time to time is bound to this spot. The skull of Arvak rests atop the small altar, surrounded by Mistmen. Sometimes, four souls stop and pray from each opening of the stone structure covering the altar. Tackle the foes and claim the skull.

- Arvak's Skull

[SC3.O] Soul Pool Camp

Is there no end to this nightmare? Not for the three hapless souls seeking warmth from a soul pool among the thickets. Speak to them for a one-sided conversation.

[SC3.P] The Black Tower

The tallest structure that you can climb—at least, one that is attached to the ground—this tower is guarded by Wrathmen and Bonemen and has a teleporter at its base, transporting you to the top vantage point. Or, you can traipse up the stairs to the top instead. Aside from the views, there are no items to gather here.

- Teleporter [9/9]

[SC3.Q] Foundation Altar

Related Quest: Side Quest:
Impatience of a Saint
Related Regional Activity: Dark Conjurations*

East and a little north of Arvak's Skull is a stepped area leading to an open altar just east of the teleporter to Keeper 3. Beware of Bonemen guarding this altar, which has the Spell Tome: Conjure Mistman on it. Below it is Jiub's Opus (page 7), next to a coin purse and Soul Gem. Watch for a Mistman ambush after you swipe the book.

- Jiub's Opus (Page 7) [9/10]
- Spell Tome: Conjure Mistman [3/3]

[SC3.R] Boneyard Citadel

Related Quest: Side Quest:
Impatience of a Saint

On the opposite side of the Boneyard exterior wall from where Valerica is imprisoned is a fortification attached to the wall. Clamber up the steep steps, passing the three lost souls to find one of Jiub's pages beside a chest in the highest of the small spires. Watch for the Mistman guarding it and other foes close by.

- Chest
- Jiub's Opus (Page 4) [10/10]

[SC3.S] The Black Temple

Related Regional Activity:
(Don't Fear) the Reaper*

Just west of the floating citadel where the third Keeper lurks is a blocklike temple with an Ideal Master Crystal above the roof. Look for the open doorway on the ground, and climb the steps to reach it. The chest the Crystal guards contains the following:

- Reaper Gem Fragment [3/3]
- Ideal Master Crystal [8/8]

[FV2.F] Snowbound Skeletons

Two skeletons are half-buried in the snow, close to the arch. The potions are usually helpful if the lake dragons are readying their attacks.

- Loose gear
- Potions

[FV2.G] Emerald Paragon Portal

Related Regional Activity:
Paragons of the Frost Giants*

If you use the Emerald Paragon at the portal, you emerge at the highest point in Forgotten Vale—a rushing river tumbling from a waterfall.

[FV2.H] Forgotten Vale Overlook: Vista

Related Regional Activity:
Paragons of the Frost Giants*

Follow the river downstream from the portal to the edge of a second waterfall that plunges into the Frozen Lake. From the vista, you can check out the temple balcony of Auriel's Chapel. Look east to a small pillar ruin with a skeleton and the following:

- Chest
- Loose Gear
- Unknown Book, Vol. II [2/4]

[FV2.I] Waterfall Chest

At the base of the second waterfall from the Overlook is a hole in the ice. Plunge into the icy lake and search for a submerged chest.

- Chest

[FV2.J] Frozen Lakeshore

Far below the temple balcony, and periodically dotted around the edge of the lake, are a number of ore veins to mine.

- Malachite Ore Vein

[FV2.K] Lake Bed: The Heavy Chest

A swim along the base of the lake reveals that this area may have been dry land at one point; numerous Snow Elf ruins from the old pilgrim path are dotted throughout. Check this area in particular for a skeleton, crushed beneath a chest.

- Chest

[FV2.L] The Frozen Lake

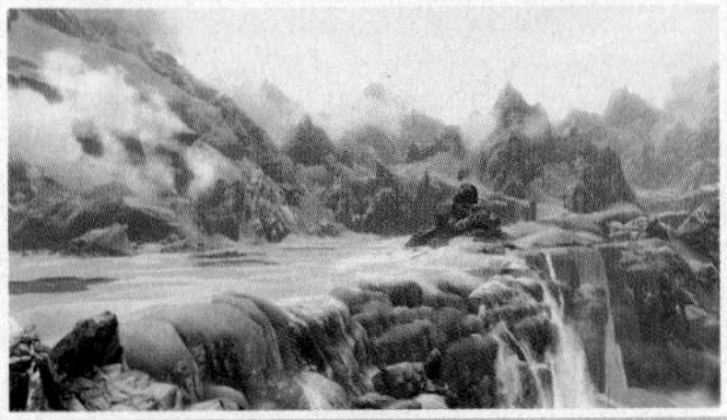

Related Main Quest: Dragon Rising

The Frozen Lake is sometimes quiet and serene. However, if you've completed Main Quest: Dragon Rising, two dragons—Naaslaarum and Voslaarum—burst up through the lake and begin their attack, dive-bombing the ice only to emerge from it a moment later! This combat is tricky, as you have two dragons to face, but it is otherwise the same as your previous experience defeating them (aside from the limited locations you can hide in).

- Dragon Soul (2)

NOTE These two dragons appear only if you've defeated your first dragon during Main Quest: Dragon Rising.

TIP Having problems avoiding these two monstrous flying fiends? You can always avoid their attacks by diving into the lake water and hiding while your Stamina, Health, or Magicka replenish.

[FV2.M] Word Wall: Frozen Lake

Perched on the edge of a lake is a carved rock with a single Word of Power set into it. Learn the Word, then search the skeletal remains for the following:

- Chest
- Potions
- Word of Power: Drain Vitality [DG1/3]

[FV2.N] Pilgrim's Path: Frozen Lake

At the north end of the Frozen Lake, the pilgrim's path begins again. Follow the rudimentary path under the arch, toward Area 3. At the start is a skeleton under the arch.

- Potions

> **TIP** Stop! There is a significant shortcut that circumvents almost all of Area 3, if you don't wish to traverse Forgotten Vale Fissure. Simply climb the hill, following the guide map over a ridge to Location [3.O]: Frozen Lake Ridge (Shortcut), and then down to the Glacial Crevice entrance! However, you'll miss out on the cave that has the Shellbug in it!

[FV2.O] Frost Giant Lair (Lower Lake)

Related Regional Activity:
Paragons of the Frost Giants*

The lake's northwest end has a waterfall with a Frost Giant close to it, in a shallow cave. There's a snowy path northwest of here. Defeat the giant, then claim the following from its corpse.

◊ Unique Item: Amethyst Paragon [1/5]

[FV2.P] Frost Giant Lair (Paragon Portal Platform)

Related Regional Activity:
Paragons of the Frost Giants*

Located at a shallow cave close to the rushing river above the Snow Lake waterfall. Take the Paragon from its body.

◊ Unique Item: Sapphire Paragon [2/5]

[FV2.Q] Paragon Portal Platform

Related Regional Activity:
Paragons of the Frost Giants*

This arch connects you to five other locations within the Forgotten Vale, allowing you to visit otherwise-inaccessible areas. Provided you have a Paragon (taken from each of the five Frost Giants), you can insert one into the socket, activate the Paragon Portal, and step through to the following locations:

✓	PARAGON	LOCATION
	Amethyst	[DG.11] Darkfall Grotto (Paragon Portal)
	Sapphire	[FV5.1] Inner Sanctum (Paragon Portal)
	Emerald	[FV2.G] Forgotten Vale Overlook (Paragon Portal)
	Diamond	[FV3.1] Glacial Crevice (Paragon Portal)
	Ruby	[FV6.A] Forgotten Vale Forest (Paragon Portal)

[FV2.R] Natural Bridge to Forgotten Vale Fissure

Enter Area 3 by crossing this natural rock bridge, then begin your trek through a large and twisting series of ledges and bridges all the way to the Glacial Crevice.

Area 3: Forgotten Vale Fissure and Glacial Crevice

Once you've explored the lake, you can make your way toward the lengthy and dangerous fissure, carved by the fast-flowing river. Here, you'll encounter numerous Falmer, cross bridges, and follow narrow ledges until you reach the Glacial Crevice (the Major Location, listed after the Minor ones in this case). You will traverse even more ledges until you reach the other side of the Forgotten Vale.

> **NOTE** The Glacial Crevice is Area 3's only major location. You enter this location after traversing through all of the minor locations. Look for the Glacial Crevice Interior map after the minor locations of Area 3.

Minor Locations

[FV3.A] Fissure Ledges

Cross from Area 2 and head down the ledge, the first of many you'll navigate on your journey to the Glacial Crevice.

[FV3.B] Falmer Camp (River)

Down at the river is a small Falmer camp with two huts. From here you can head along the river, or travel up through the gate, toward the next natural bridge.

◊ Potions

[FV3.C] Falmer Camp and Graveyard

Atop the short, steep path is another hut, with a chest in it. Above that is a small Falmer graveyard with a few weapons to scavenge.

◊ Chest ◊ Loose gear

[FV3.D] Natural Fissure Bridge (North)

The real expedition into the fissure begins now, as Falmer on the upper rock islands can see and fire down at you. Cross this bridge to begin your journey.

◊ Loose gear

[FV3.E] Path Ascent and Mining Remains

Continue up the natural ledges and bridges toward the entrance to Sharpslope Cave. Below it are skeletal remains, some Rock Warbler Eggs in a basket, and gold to grab.

- Gold Ore Vein and Gold Ore (2)
- Loose gear
- Lots o' Gold!

[FV3.F] Sharpslope Cave Entrance (Upper)

This connects to Location [3.G] via the Sharpslope Cave. This area is optional and leads to a large hole with a Falmer tower in the middle of it and a curved path that leads to a small cave camp with a hut and Falmer and Chaurus to face before exiting at Location [3.G]. However, halfway down the curved tower path is an easily missed opening in the perimeter wall. Step through into a side chamber with a Shellbug to mine.

- Chest
- Shellbug Chitin

[FV3.G] Sharpslope Cave Entrance (River)

This entrance to the cave is located close to the river rapids, where a number of Chaurus Hunters may hatch. You can also force your way up the river (south) and ignore the upper fissure area entirely.

- Orichalcum Ore Vein (3)

[FV3.H] Steep Slope

After crossing the Falmer bridge, check the hut (with potions inside) before ascending the steep rock path, past a chest.

- Chest
- Potions

[FV3.I] Frost Giant Lair: Falmer Cliffs

Related Regional Activity:
Paragon of the Frost Giants*

At the top of the steep rocky path is a circular path to the right (south) that leads counterclockwise past the shallow cave with the third Frost Giant to tackle. Watch your step, as this path is precarious! If you wish, you can climb atop the mountain the curved platform is fixed to and attack from range.

- Chest
- Unique Item: Emerald Paragon [3/5]

[FV3.J] Falmer Village: Rock Island (North)

A lone hut (usually with a shaman) is at the end of the natural bridge. Nearby is a Falmer bridge to the south.

- Chest
- Loose gear

[FV3.K] Falmer Village: Rock Island (South)

The collection of huts continues at the south end of the Falmer bridge. There are two huts (and a troll skull with gems above it on a high rock). After navigating the next Falmer bridge, there is a third hut and pen directly underneath. As always, Falmer are here to be thwarted.

- Loose gear
- Lots o' Gold

[FV3.L] Natural Bridges

The last part of the fissure consists of natural stone bridges down to the river level. Expect more Falmer trouble as you descend.

[FV3.M] Falmer Hut, Dead-End Ledge

Related Regional Activity:
Ancient Falmer Tomes*

Head across the two bridges (one natural, one made by the Falmer) to a hut with a mammoth skull on it. There's an Unknown Book to collect on the table, near some potions.

- Unique Item: Unknown Book, Vol. III [3/4]

[FV3.N] Fledgling Nest and River Rapids (River)

Below the final part of the pathway throughout the fissure is an optional area to investigate or to reach if you've slogged along the riverbed instead. Expect Chaurus Hunters to hatch and attack close to the rapids.

[FV3.O] Frozen Lake Ridge (Shortcut)

To circumvent almost this entire area, use this snowy slope to a ridge overlooking the Frozen Lake, if approached from the lake. Along the way, you can mine some Moonstone Ore.

- Moonstone Ore Vein (3)

[FV3.P] Entrance to Glacial Crevice

At the end of this exterior fissure, step into the river and fight two Falmer before heading through the open gate and into Area 4: Falmer Fissure (which is inside the mountain you're entering). The Forgotten Vale exterior continues on the other side of the Crevice.

[3.1] Glacial Crevice (Interior)

Related Quests

Dawnguard Main Quest: Touching the Sky

Regional Activity: Paragons of the Frost Giants

Recommended Level: 18

Faction: Falmer	Dangers	Miscellaneous
Chaurus	Claw Trap	Chest
Falmer		Loose gear
Frost Troll		

A glacial crevice formed during tens of thousands of years of water flow from the high peaks of the Haafingar Mountains, this area is now populated by Falmer and provides a critical path between two of the areas of Forgotten Vale.

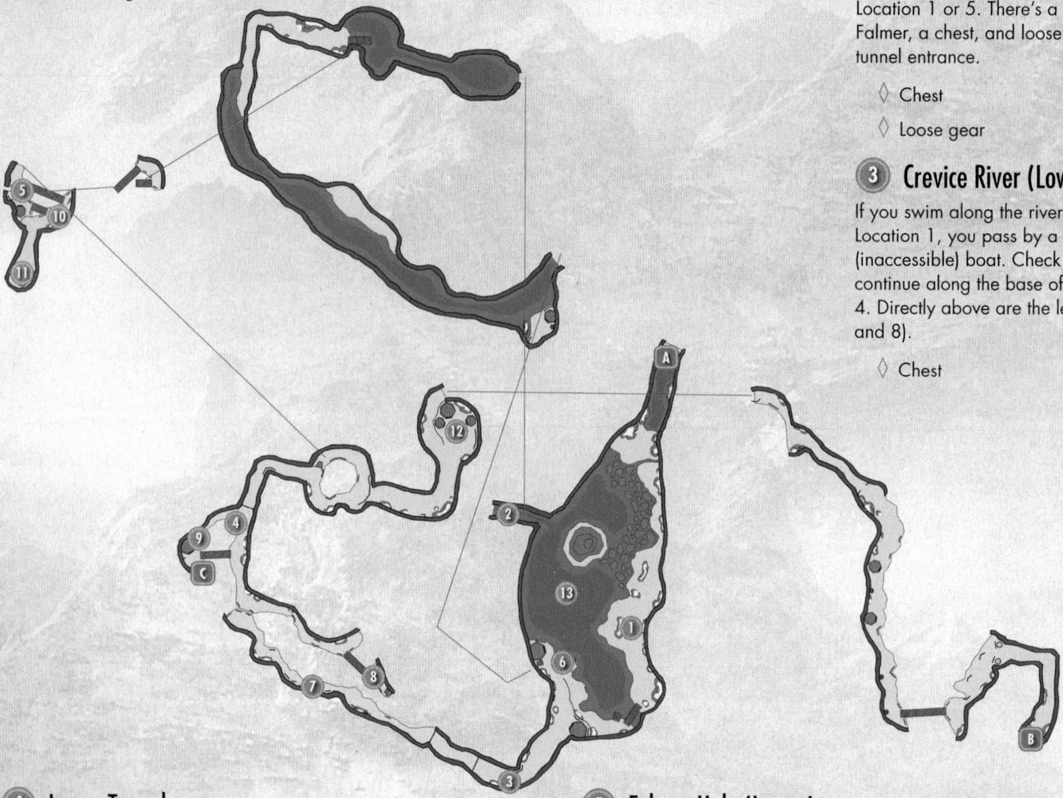

Interior

A Exit to Forgotten Vale

1 Iceberg Cavern (Lower)

This expansive cavern has a Frost Troll and a couple of Falmer to tackle along the icy ledges to the south (Location 6). This is the optimal path through the Crevice, although there's a lower river tunnel (Locations 3, 4, and 5) and a smaller, underwater tunnel to the west, which leads to Location 5.

2 Water Tunnel (Lower)

Swim through this narrow tunnel from either Location 1 or 5. There's a small cave with a dead Falmer, a chest, and loose gear to the west of the tunnel entrance.

- Chest
- Loose gear

3 Crevice River (Lower)

If you swim along the river's surface from Location 1, you pass by a Falmer tent and a small (inaccessible) boat. Check the hut, then optionally continue along the base of the crevice to Location 4. Directly above are the ledges (Locations 7 and 8).

- Chest

4 Lower Tunnel

Almost directly under the main exit tunnel from the first crevice is a tunnel leading up from the water's edge. It leads directly to Location 5.

5 Falmer Hole (Lower)

This large ice hole with Falmer bridges across it is accessible from the lower or middle levels. The middle level is Location 10. From here you can head farther east, up and into the deeper crevice areas.

6 Iceberg Cavern Promontory (Middle)

Check the tents before exiting along to the ledges above the river (Location 7).

- Chest
- Loose gear

7 Crevice Ledge (Middle)

Enter the narrow crevice ledges above Location 3, and watch for a trip wire as you enter. Continue along the ledge, fighting a Chaurus and Falmer as you go.

- Danger! Claw Trap

8 Crevice Outlook (Middle)

Halfway along the ledge, the fissure ledges connect. Investigate the ledge to the east on the opposite side to engage another Falmer.

- Chest

9 Crevice Falmer Hut (Middle)

The far end of the crevice holds a connecting tunnel to Location 10, a short bridge to a hut, a Falmer, and a chest. Enter the tunnel, watching for a trip wire as you step around the corner.

- Chest
- Danger! Claw Trap

10 Falmer Hole (Middle)

This large ice hole with Falmer bridges across it is accessible from the lower or middle levels. The lower level is Location 5. From here you can head farther east, up and into the deeper crevice areas. You can also access a small tunnel below you (Location 11). As you climb the ledge, enter a tunnel.

11 Falmer Tunnel (Middle)

A small tunnel with a hut and a Falmer at the end.

- Chest (2)

12 Falmer Lair (Middle and Upper)

Watch for foes, and climb the ledge up and around. Enter the narrow tunnel to the east, leading out to Location 13.

- Chest

13 Iceberg Cavern Ledge (Upper)

This ledge is actually above the first chamber you entered. Navigate a long ledge with four Falmers (and nests). Check one of the tents for a chest.

- Chest

14 Ruined Snow Elf Arch (Upper)

The remains of a stone arch marks the exit back to the next part of Forgotten Vale.

B Exit to Forgotten Vale

C Diamond Paragon Portal (Upper)

Enter the Paragon Portal (see Regional Activity: Paragons of the Frost Giants), and you're transported to a small, high ledge near the ceiling of the Glacial Crevice. Aside from a dangerous jump down, there's a single chest to ransack before you return.

- Chest

Area 4: Falmer Fissure

This is a tight and narrow fissure where the Falmer have made their home. Expect combat all along the maze of snaking bridgework, a long subterranean cave leading up to the final Wayshrine, and a final crossing above the fissure to the Snow Elf Inner Sanctum, where only those pilgrims who have attained enlightenment can enter.

Major Locations

[FV4.1] Wayshrine of Radiance

Related Quest: Dawnguard Main Quest: Touching the Sky

Prelate Edhelbor

Prelate Edhelbor allows you to commune with this Wayshrine (the fifth and final one to find), where your ewer is filled to brimming. Eventually, five locations can be accessed from here, depending on the other Wayshrines you have opened. Here's where you can be:

- Darkfall Passage
- Shrine of Learning
- Shrine of Resolution
- Shrine of Sight
- Temple Balcony
- Wayshrine [5/5]

[FV4.2] Entrance to the Inner Sanctum

Related Quest: Dawnguard Main Quest: Touching the Sky

The imposing Snow Elf Inner Sanctum, accessed at the end of this area, is a marvel of Snow Elf construction. Stride through the grand arch, and you're greeted by a towering statue of the great Auriel. To enter the Sanctum, ascend the steps, pour the water you've collected from the five Wayshrines into the receptacle, and the door will open. There are no other ways to pry open this door.

Minor Locations

[FV4.A] Glacial Crevice Exit

The main fissure route between here and Location [4.E] (along the ground) has you checking two raised Falmer Huts (one with a chest) and navigating a couple of trip wires along the ground as you pass under a third hut. The path splits here and has two stone ramps on either side at Location [4.E].

- Chest
- Danger! Claw Trap (2)

[FV4.B] Frost Giant Lair (North Falmer Fissure)

Related Regional Activity: Paragon of the Frost Giants*

After navigating the bone trap strung across the path, head through the gate and engage the Falmer, or wait for them to perish as they battle a Frost Giant. Defeat anything left alive, as the giant carries the Diamond Paragon you're after.

- Danger! Bone Trap
- Unique Item: Diamond Paragon [4/5]

[FV4.C] Upper Fissure Walls

If you continue to climb from the Frost Giant's location, past the mammoth skull to the remains of a Snow Elf arch, you reach the upper fissure. The going here is treacherous, but you can edge along above the Falmer huts, all the way to Location [4.D].

- Quicksilver Ore Vein (2)

[FV4.D] The Overexuberant Ore Extractor

With some careful maneuvering from Location [4.C], you can slowly step along the fissure walls, using Bats (Vampire Lord) or Whirlwind Sprint (Shout) to dash across to the opposite side if you're in the habit of gathering Bird Nests (there are 13 to find all along here). The real prize is under the Sanctum Bridge: a nook with a Gold Ore Vein and the skeletal remains of a miner who came a cropper here. Gather two Flawless Diamonds too!

- Bird's Nest (13)
- Diamond
- Flawless Diamond (2)
- Gold Ore (2)
- Gold Ore Vein
- Loose Gear
- Lots o' Gold!

[FV4.E] Falmer Fissure Village (Part 1)

[FV4.F] Falmer Fissure Village (Part 2)

Expect Falmer battles throughout. Two stone ramps appear along the bottom of the fissure; check each one. The left (north) ramp leads to a hut. The right (south) one enables you to reach the bridges crossing the huts, and the path on the ground leads to a Quicksilver Ore Vein. Check each hut (one has an Emerald, for example). Then the path narrows through to the second village area.

- Alchemy Lab
- Danger! Bone Trap
- Lots o' Gold!
- Potions
- Quicksilver Ore (2)
- Quicksilver Ore Vein

[FV4.G] Falmer Fissure Village (Part 3)

Related Regional Activity:
Ancient Falmer Tomes*

Expect Falmer battles throughout. This narrower fissure leads to a subterranean tunnel at Location [4.H], with huts to search along the ramped area and a Chaurus Hunter or three to fight on the ground below. Once you've secured the last Unknown Book from the farthest hut, drop down and enter the tunnel.

- Chest
- Potions
- Unique Item: Unknown Book Vol. IV [4/4]

[FV4.H] Fissure Tunnel (Part 1)

[FV4.I] Fissure Tunnel (Part 2)

This lengthy, uphill tunnel has Falmer burrows throughout and a trip wire to avoid (unless you wish to be buffeted by rocks). The tunnel's exit is close to the final Wayshrine [4.1].

- Danger! Falling Rocks
- Quicksilver Ore Vein (4)

[FV4.J] Wayshrine Falmer Camp

Above the last Wayshrine are a few bridges and Falmer huts to search through. Try the top one for the following:

- Potions aplenty

[FV4.K] Bridge to the Inner Sanctum

One of the few pieces of Snow Elf architecture that remain intact, this bridge spans the fissure you've just crossed. Optionally, you can take your life into your hands and try Whirlwind Sprinting to the bird nest on the broken column nearby. Or try some mining.

- Bird Nest
- Quicksilver Ore Vein

[FV4.L] Auriel's Lookout

A rocky promontory with a Snow Elf arch leads to a half-buried skeleton of a person who was once of some stature, as evidenced by the remains of a crown with three valuable gems. Keep the gems from rolling into the fissure! Then continue to Location [4.2].

- Flawless Ruby (2)
- Flawless Sapphire
- Loose Gear
- Lots o' Gold!

Area 5: Falmer Temple: Inner Sanctum and Chapel

These two interior areas (with their own maps) are the culmination of your expedition.

Major Locations

[5.1] Falmer Temple

Related Quests

Dawnguard Main Quest: Touching the Sky
Regional Activity: Paragons of the Frost Giants

Recommended Level: 20

Faction: Falmer Hive

Ancient Frost Atronach
Arch-Curate Vyrthur
Frozen Chaurus
Frozen Falmer
Frozen Shaman

Special Area

Shrine of Auriel [2/2]

Dangers

Falling Ceiling

Collectibles

Unique Item: Ancient Falmer Boots [DG5/17]
Unique Item: Ancient Falmer Cuirass [DG6/17]
Unique Item: Ancient Falmer Gauntlets [DG7/17]
Unique Weapon: Auriel's Bow [DG5/7]
Unique Item: Ruby Paragon

Miscellaneous

Area is locked
Chest
Loose gear
Lots o' Gold
Potions aplenty

Inner Sanctum

The most sacred temple of the Snow Elves, the Inner Sanctum is now reduced to a ruin and the lair of Arch-Curate Vyrthur. This is the culmination of your lengthy expedition across the Forgotten Vale and Dawnguard Main Quest: Touching the Sky.

A Exit to Forgotten Vale

1 Sanctum of the Betrayed

A host of frozen Falmer are gathered around a Shrine of Auriel. Seek the blessing of the shrine if you wish, and gather the numerous items still held by frozen foes and those you find around the room. But be warned: Taking these items may cause them to awaken. The doors to the north are your way forward, but there is a hidden chamber to the left (west). Place the ewer on the pedestal to reach it.

- Loose gear
- Potions
- Shrine of Auriel [2/2]

2 Frost Giant Lair

After a short corridor, the temple gives way to a cave where a Frost Giant lurks. It carries the last of the Paragons. Be sure to pick it up before inspecting the chests by the four skeletons.

- Chest
- Unique Item: Ruby Paragon

3 Hidden Antechamber

A pedestal in the northern wall (accessed with the ewer; return to claim it if you don't have it) unlocks a hidden chamber with the following items:

- Chest
- Loose gear
- Potions

4 Connecting Corridor

A corridor connecting the north and south sections of the Sanctum contains several frozen Falmer and skeletons. Collect the following along the way:

- Loose gear
- Potions

5 Northern Corridor

Visit the southeast corner of this area, which has an antechamber with a chest and potions. Then head north, passing a table and more frozen Falmer as the Sanctum gives way to an ice cave. Take the tunnel to the northwest.

- Chest
- Loose gear
- Potions

6 Ice Tunnel

On your way out of the Sanctum, take the side tunnel to the left (south) to reach a hidden area with a chest to open.

- Chest
- Potions

B Exit to Auriel's Chapel

C Sapphire Paragon Portal

7 Hidden Passage

The only way to reach this side chamber is to enter via the portal, having opened it using the Sapphire Paragon. Inside is a ruined passage with the following:

- Chest (3)
- Loose gear
- Lots o' Gold

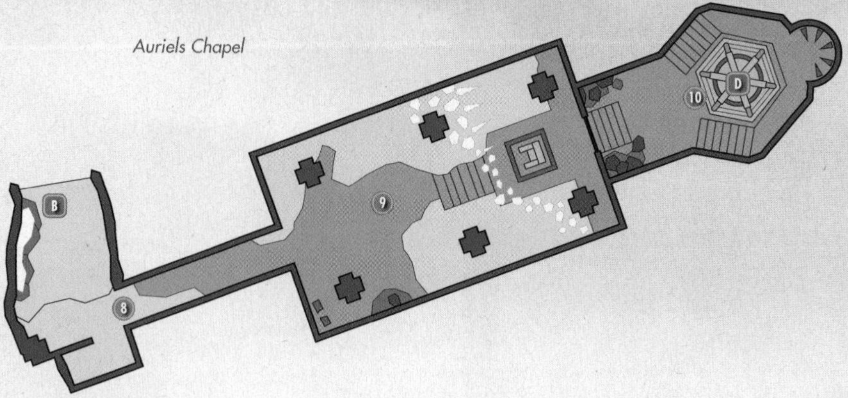

[5.2] Auriel's Chapel and Temple Balcony

B Exit to Inner Sanctum

8 Chapel Passage

A narrow passage leading into the chapel. You can also use this as a place to hide during the next battle.

9 Great Chapel

The battle within the chapel (which soon goes from indoors to outdoors) begins here. Expect heavy concentrations of foes, including Frozen Falmer and an Ancient Storm Atronach.

10 Temple Balcony

This is where you face Vyrthur in a battle to the death. Once the fight is over, the final Wayshrine opens, and you can claim Auriel's Bow from within. If you have Elven Arrows, you can ask Gelebor for a blessing (creating Sunhallowed Arrows) or ask Serana for her blood (creating Bloodcursed Arrows). Then spend a moment looking over the frozen lake from the vista balcony.

- Unique Item: Ancient Falmer Boots [DG5/17]
- Unique Item: Ancient Falmer Cuirass [DG6/17]
- Unique Item: Ancient Falmer Gauntlets [DG7/17]
- Unique Weapon: Auriel's Bow [DG5/7]

D Wayshrine Portal to Forgotten Vale

Area 6: Forgotten Vale Forest

Related Regional Activity: Paragons of the Frost Giants*

This sacred glade is unknown to all but the most meticulous of adventurers; it is accessible only after inserting the Ruby Paragon into the Paragon Platform socket. There are no critical Major Locations to find here.

Minor Locations

[FV6.A] Ruby Paragon Portal

This Snow Elf arch provides instant transportation between the Paragon Portal Platform and here, provided you have the Ruby Paragon.

[FV6.B] Frost Troll Den

If Frost Trolls haven't lumbered out of the thick woodland to intercept you, they can be found here, in a shallow cave with little debris but well hidden in this glade.

[FV6.C] Falmer Warmonger

To the southwest, a powerful Falmer clad in fancy armor is finishing off the Frost Troll threat. Face the Falmer Warmonger in battle. After you best him, peel off his armor and take the powerful artifact he was carrying. Auriel's Shield stores the energy of blocked attacks. Performing a power bash will release the stored energy.

- Chest
- Unique Item: Auriel's Shield [DG8/17]

TOPOGRAPHICAL OVERVIEW

In some ways, the northern climbs of Solstheim are slightly more hospitable than the southern wastes, since the ash storms do not reach them. Instead, adventurers are left to traverse rocky and snow-swept landscapes, with more scree and dirt along the coastline. Farther inland, there are soaring peaks and a grand temple to the new usurper of this realm, and farther north still is a large glacier field, within which an ancient castle to a long-dead frost giant still stands. Rieklings dominate many of the locations up here, but the Skaal people also call this home; their village is set amid the frozen peaks to the northeast. Finally, a number of islands, unmarked to the regular traveler, offer danger and treasure to those wishing to swim through the Sea of Ghosts to reach them.

Routes and Pathways

With no roads to find, you must rely on goat trails and the gaps between rocky ridges when maneuvering around the northern parts of Solstheim. It's helpful to work your way around the coast, perhaps starting at Bujold's Retreat and moving counterclockwise from there. Split the area into more manageable chunks: The far north offers treacherous movement over glaciers and a rugged coast with iceberg and rock islands. Farther inland are the high peaks and familiar barrow arches of Nordic crypts. Then there's the massive circular Temple of Miraak, where the bones of dragons rest and your main quest begins.

AVAILABLE SERVICES, CRAFTING, AND COLLECTIBLES

Services

- Followers: [DB2/7]
- Houses for Sale: [DB0/1]
- Marriage Prospects: [DB3/3]
- Skill Trainers: [DB2/5]
  - Alchemy: [0/0]
  - Alteration: [0/0]
  - Archery: [0/0]
  - Block: [0/0]
  - Conjuration: [DB0/1]
  - Destruction: [0/0]
  - Enchanting: [DB0/1]
  - Heavy Armor: [DB1/1]
  - Illusion: [0/0]
  - Light Armor: [0/0]
  - Lockpicking: [0/0]
  - One-Handed: [0/0]
  - Pickpocket: [0/0]
  - Restoration: [DB0/1]
  - Smithing: [0/0]
  - Sneak: [0/0]
  - Speech: [0/0]
  - Two-Handed: [DB1/1]
- Traders: [DB4/16]
  - Apothecary: [DB1/3]
  - Bartender: [0/0]
  - Blacksmith: [DB2/3]
  - Carriage Driver: [0/0]
  - Fence: [0/0]
  - Ferryman: [DB0/1]
  - Fletcher: [0/0]
  - Food Vendor: [DB0/1]
  - General Goods: [DB0/4]
  - Innkeeper: [DB0/1]
  - Jeweler: [0/0]
  - Special: [DB1/1]
  - Spell Vendor: [DB0/2]
  - Stablemaster: [0/0]

Collectibles

- Dragon Claws: [DB0/2]
- Acolyte Priest Masks: [DB1/4]
- East Empire Strongboxes: [DB14/33]
- Treasure Maps: [DB1/1]
- Unique Items: [DB9/31]
- Unique Weapons: [DB3/11]

Special Objects

- Shrines: [DB1/5]
  - Kynareth: [DB0/1]
  - Zenithar: [DB1/1]
  - Azura: [DB0/1]
  - Boethiah: [DB0/1]
  - Mephala: [DB0/1]
- Sacred Stones: [4/6]
  - Water Stone
  - Temple of Miraak (Tree Stone)
  - Beast Stone
  - Wind Stone
- Word Walls: [DB4/10]
  - Battle Fury: [DB0/3]
  - Bend Will: [DB1/1]
  - Cyclone: [DB2/3]
  - Dragon Aspect: [DB1/3]

SOLSTHEIM CRAFTING STATIONS: NORTHERN MOUNTAINS

✓	TYPE	LOCATION A	LOCATION B
☐	Alchemy Lab	Skaal Village (Shaman's Hut)	Skaal Village (Edla's House)
☐	Arcane Enchanter	Skaal Village (Shaman's Hut)	Altar of Thrond
☐	Anvil or Blacksmith Forge	Skaal Village (Baldor Iron-Shaper's House)	Thirsk Mead Hall
☐	Cooking Pot and Spit	Skaal Village (Greathall)	Skaal Village (Baldor Iron-Shaper's House)
☐	Grindstone	Skaal Village (Baldor Iron-Shaper's House)	None
☐	Smelter	Skaal Village (Baldor Iron-Shaper's House)	Damphall Mine
☐	Staff Enchanter	None	None
☐	Tanning Rack	Skaal Village (Barrier Focusing Stones and Well)	Skaal Village (Baldor Iron-Shaper's House)
☐	Wood Chopping Block	Skaal Village (Deor Woodcutter's House)	Damphall Mine
☐	Workbench	Skaal Village (Baldor Iron-Shaper's House)	None

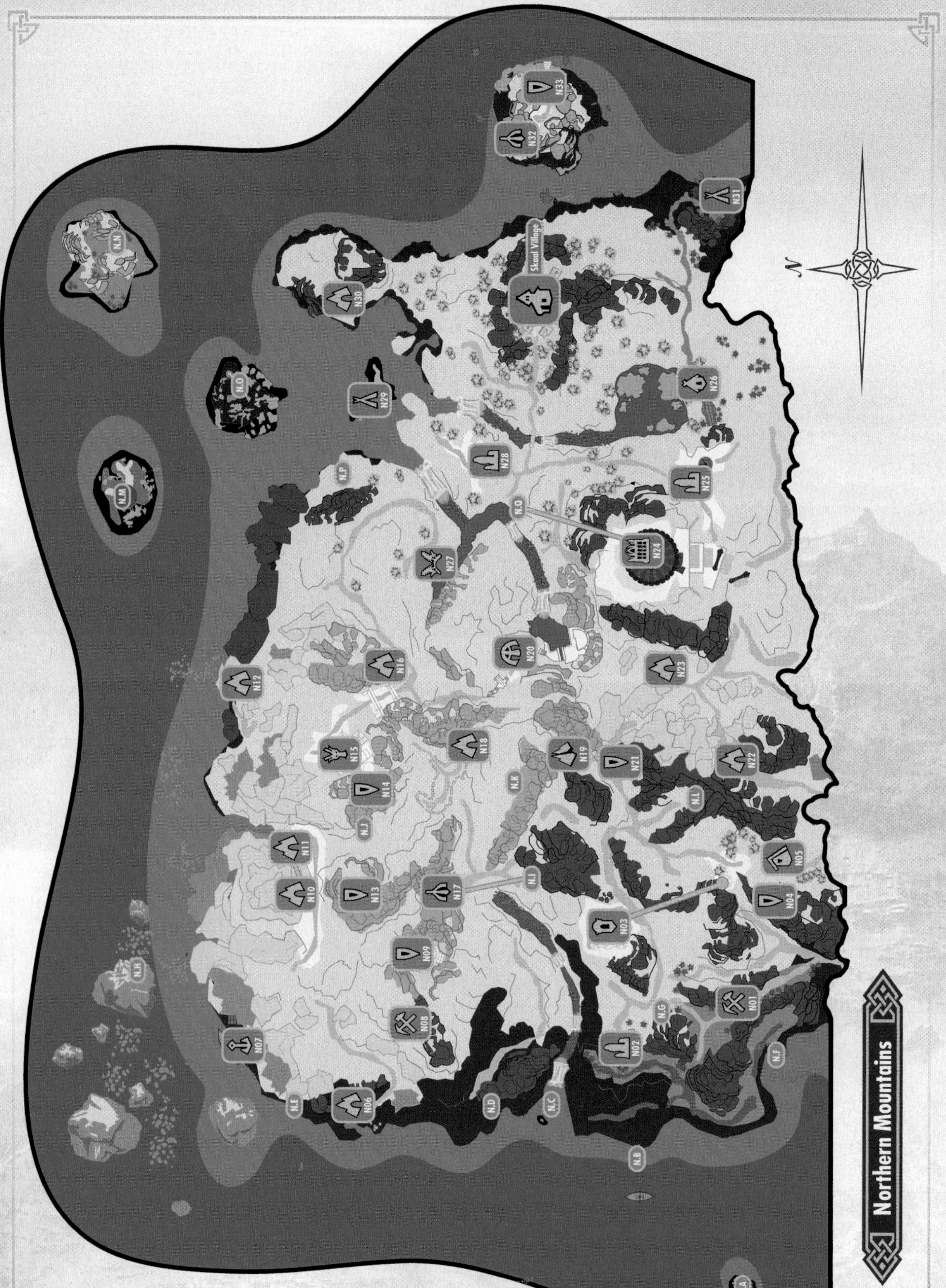
Northern Mountains
Skaal Village
N01
N02
N03
N04
N05
N06
N07
N08
N09
N10
N11
N12
N13
N14
N15
N16
N17
N18
N19
N20
N21
N22
N23
N24
N25
N26
N27
N28
N29
N30
N31
N32
N33
N.A
N.B
N.C
N.D
N.E
N.F
N.G
N.H
N.I
N.J
N.K
N.L
N.M
N.N
N.O
N.P

PRIMARY LOCATIONS

Total 34–Skaal Village and 33 locations

- [S.N00] Skaal Village
  - Chieftain: Fanari Strong-Voice
- [S.N01] Damphall Mine
- [S.N02] Water Stone
- [S.N03] Fahlbtharz
- [S.N04] Hvitkald Peak
- [S.N05] Abandoned Lodge
- [S.N06] Bristleback Cave
- [S.N07] Northshore Landing
- [S.N08] Broken Tusk Mine
- [S.N09] Stalhrim Source
- [S.N10] Castle Karstaag Ruins
- [S.N11] Castle Karstaag Caverns
- [S.N12] Glacial Cave
- [S.N13] Mortrag Peak
- [S.N14] Frykte Peak
- [S.N15] Saering's Watch
- [S.N16] Benkongerike
- [S.N17] White Ridge Barrow
- [S.N18] Hrothmund's Barrow
- [S.N19] Moesring Pass
- [S.N20] Snowclad Ruins
- [S.N21] Mount Moesring
- [S.N22] Frostmoon Crag
- [S.N23] Altar of Thrond
- [S.N24] Temple of Miraak (Tree Stone)
- [S.N25] Beast Stone
- [S.N26] Thirsk Mead Hall
- [S.N27] Headwaters of Harstrad
- [S.N28] Wind Stone
- [S.N29] Haknir's Shoal
- [S.N30] Frossel
- [S.N31] Bujold's Retreat
- [S.N32] Gyldenhul Barrow
- [S.N33] Horker Island

SECONDARY LOCATIONS

Total: 17 Points of Interest

- [S.NA] Spiky Grass Island
- [S.NB] The Ever-Abandoned Ship
- [S.NC] Waterfall and Grazing Netch
- [S.ND] Mudcrab Tidal Pools
- [S.NE] Riekling Chest
- [S.NF] The Fisherman's Haul
- [S.NG] Riekling Barrel Hoard
- [S.NH] Horker Iceberg
- [S.NI] White Ridge Barrow Hut
- [S.NJ] Forgotten Spoils
- [S.NK] Desolate Hunter's Camp
- [S.NL] Shrine of Zenithar
- [S.NM] Dragon Mound: Frozen Shoals
- [S.NN] Giant Nirnroot Island
- [S.NO] Riekling Outpost Island
- [S.NP] Lurker Ambush (Tidal Pool)
- [S.NQ] Temple of Miraak: Secret Exit

SKAAL VILLAGE

Related Quests

- Dragonborn Main Quest: The Fate of the Skaal
- Dragonborn Main Quest: Cleansing the Stones
- Dragonborn Main Quest: The Gardener of Men
- Dragonborn Main Quest: At the Summit of Apocrypha
- Solstheim Side Quest: Filial Bonds
- Solstheim Side Quest: A New Source of Stalhrim
- Solstheim Side Quest: Lost Legacy
- Solstheim Regional Activity (Skaal Village): A Mother's Lament*
- Solstheim Regional Activity (Skaal Village): Return to Falkreath*

Habitation: Skaal Village

Services

- Follower: Frea [DB1/7]
- Marriage Prospect: Morwen [DB3/3]
- Trader (Apothecary): Edla [DB1/16]
- Trader (Blacksmith): Baldor Iron-Shaper [DB4/16]
- Trainer (Master: Two-Handed): Wulf Wild-Blood [DB1/1]

Crafting

- Blacksmith Forge
- Cooking Pot
- Grindstone
- Smelter
- Tanning Rack
- Wood Chopping Block
- Workbench

Collectibles

- Unique Item: Bera's Necklace [DB6/31]

Miscellaneous

- Area is locked
- Chest
- Potions
- Loose gear

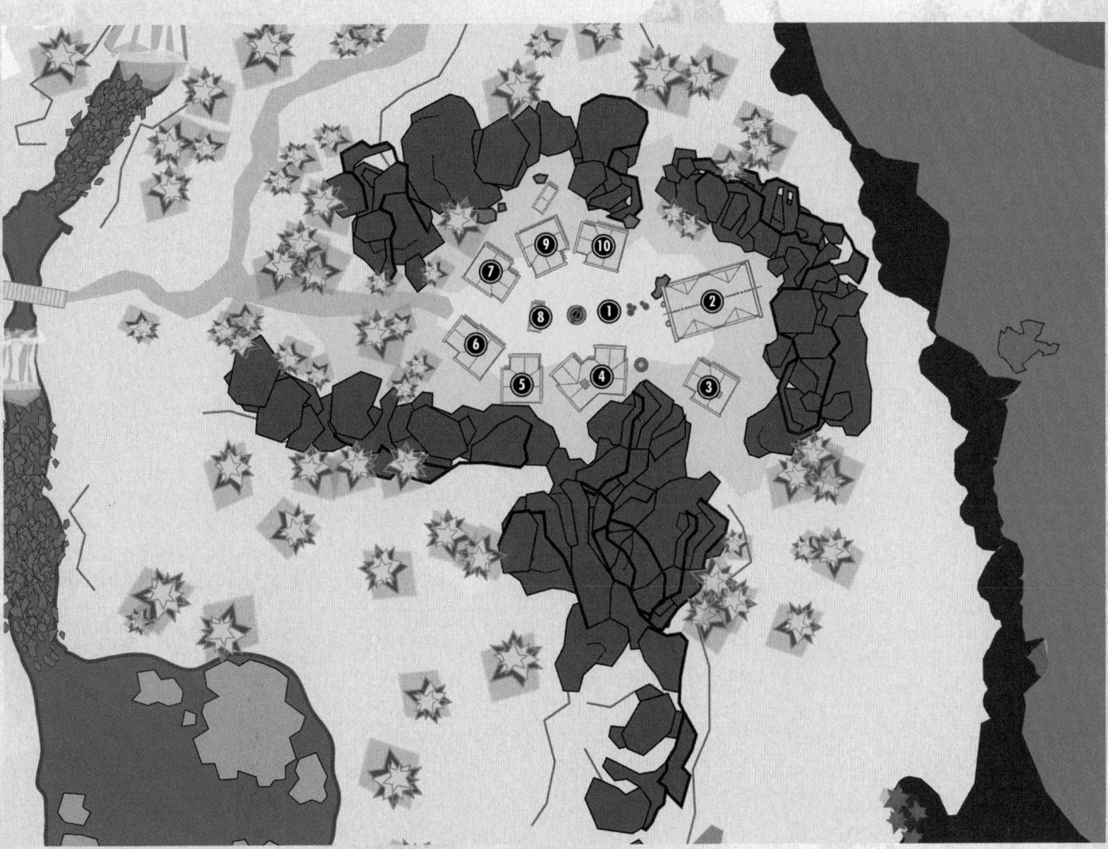

Lore: Settlement Overview

Skaal village is located in the Felsaad Coast region of Solstheim, north of Thirsk Mead Hall. The origin of the Skaal has been lost to the passage of time. Who founded this village, and why? What clues exist that might shed light on their history? And can this lost legacy provide insight into the events that are currently troubling Solstheim? These questions have been weighing heavily on the mind of Tharstan, a visiting scholar. He's always had a great passion for history, and the mystery of the village's origins is one he would very much like to solve.

There is no real economy in Skaal Village, as money is of little value to the self-sufficient Skaal. Hunting is the main source of sustenance for most; the Horkers on the northern coast and nearby Lake Fjalding are relatively easy and lucrative prey. More adventurous Skaal hunters go after the elusive Snow Wolf or Snow Bear, whose pelts are valued highly among them. The Skaal are skilled foresters as well, which makes sense since their village is surrounded by firs. A steady supply of firewood can mean the difference between life and death for these determined villagers.

Years of relative peace and prosperity for the Skaal have been shattered by the loss of most of the tribe to some unknown dark magic. At the last moment, the village shaman, Storn Crag-Strider, was able to shield the remaining few of his people from this spell, but it is taking all of his concentration and he can't keep it up forever.

Most of the town's population has been enslaved, and many are helping to build a strange arched shrine around the Wind Stone to the northwest of town. Free these villagers and they head back to the locations listed below. Consult the Dragonborn Main Quest: The Fate of the Skaal for further information. You cannot fully interact with the Skaal until you've befriended them.

Important Areas of Interest

1 Barrier Focusing Stones and Well

This is where Storn, Finna, and Nikulas remain on their knees, attempting to hold back Miraak's foul magic and keeping the minion of Hermaeus Mora from completing his subjugation of Solstheim.

◊ Crafting: Tanning Rack

2 Greathall

Fanari Strong-Voice

Ever since she was a child, Fanari has possessed a singular focus, always knowing what she wanted and doing whatever it took to get it. Seeing Fanari's determination to be the best hunter in the village, Wulf Wild-Blood was touched. He decided to take the young Nord woman under his wing, and with Wulf's guidance, Fanari eventually became a superb hunter. As she grew older, Fanari decided that she needed a new goal and she set her sights on becoming the village elder. She achieved this while still in her thirties, a remarkable feat for any of the Skaal. Her loyalty to the villagers, her fearless and unflappable nature, and a good dose of just being tired of hearing her go on about how she was meant to be the elder caused the other Skaal to name her as chieftain.

Tharstan

Tharstan is a visiting historian who has come to live with the Skaal in order to write a book about their culture and heritage. He now resides in a guest room in the village Greathall. Tharstan spends most of his days reading and writing in the Greathall and will be happy to talk to you about his research into the history of the Skaal.

This large lodge-style building serves as a gathering place for the villagers. It has traditionally also been the dwelling place of the village elder and his or her family. The current village elder is Fanari Strong-Voice, who succeeded Skaf the Giant in that role less than three years ago following Skaf's passing. Outspoken and opinionated, Fanari lets everyone around her know what she's feeling. However, her devotion to the villagers and her keen mind have made her a fine elder. She is also an expert hunter who has spent several years training under the tutelage of Wulf Wild-Blood.

Also living in the Greathall as a guest of the village is the visiting historian Tharstan, an enthusiastic scholar who has a great love for history and lore. All his life, he has been intrigued by the mysteries of Solstheim, and he has already written one volume about the island. He is living in Skaal Village mainly to study its people and learn about their history and culture.

The interior of the Greathall features a warm hearth with a cooking pot, various books of Tharstan's, and two sets of steps to a balcony bedroom, where Fanari keeps a small collection of pearls in a display case [Apprentice].

◊ Crafting: Cooking Pot

◊ Book: Ahzidal's Descent

3 Shaman's Hut

Storn Crag-Strider

Storn is the Skaal Shaman, the spiritual advisor to the tribe. Stoic and patient, the Skaal look to him in times of difficulty for guidance and comfort. He communes with the land and calls upon the All-Maker, the creator and sustainer of all things, to protect his people. Storn's daughter Frea has been groomed since childhood to succeed him as Shaman. Now in her early twenties, she is quietly rebelling against the idea. Storn believes this will pass and tries to maintain the calm that has served him so well over many years to wait until Frea realizes what she's truly meant for.

Frea

Frea is the daughter of Storn Crag-Strider, and she is conflicted about her future. Her father expects that she'll someday take his place as the village Shaman, but she's an accomplished warrior and hunter and thinks she might be chief material instead. You first meet Frea at the Temple of Miraak.

Storn, the village Shaman, makes his home here along with his daughter, Frea. One of the persistent mysteries of Skaal village is the identity of Frea's mother. Twenty-five years ago, before becoming the village Shaman, Storn set out to learn the ways of the world. When he returned five years later, he brought with him a four-year-old girl whom he introduced as his daughter, Frea. Storn refuses to speak about Frea's mother to anyone, including Frea. This has caused a rift between the two that prevents them from ever being truly close, but Storn has been a dutiful and loving father otherwise, so Frea cannot stay angry with him for long.

The house is decorated with pelts, various plants, herbs, and other shamanistic totems, as well as an Arcane Enchanter and an alchemy table. Tinkering with the creation of potions is one of Storn's hobbies.

◊ Crafting: Arcane Enchanter, Alchemy Lab

◊ Follower: Frea [DB1/7]

4 Baldor Iron-Shaper's House

Baldor Iron-Shaper

Baldor works the forge in Skaal village. He's a tough, hard-nosed, no-nonsense man who values hard work, honesty, and the weight of solid iron. He takes pride in his craft and will be quick to say so to anyone who will listen. The one thing Baldor wants most in life is to reclaim the lost art of forging Stalhrim. He knows how to do so, but he lacks the material itself.

Baldor Iron-Shaper lives in a modest house near the village center. He lives alone, having never married. Outside is his fine forge, where he can craft Stalhrim weapons and armor and Ancient Nordic Pickaxes. Inside, his house is usually locked [Adept] and features some displayed weapons, ore, a chest, cooking pot, and some ingots and more weapons upstairs.

- Crafting: Blacksmith forge, cooking pot, grindstone, smelter, tanning rack (2), workbench (2)
- Chest
- Loose gear
- Trader (Blacksmith): Baldor Iron-Shaper [DB4/16]

NOTE After the Skaal become friendly, Baldor isn't at his forge, and it falls to you to find him. Consult Solstheim Side Quest: A New Source of Stalhrim (page 633) for more information.

5 Deor Woodcutter's House

Deor Woodcutter

Deor is an unremarkable man, simple-minded and direct. He is, in many ways, the prototypical Skaal villager: He gets early up in the morning, works hard all day, eats a spare meal, and then sleeps through the night. He expects to spend all the rest of his days doing just that until he returns to the All-maker.

Yrsa

Yrsa is one of the younger women in Skaal Village. She is friendly and polite and likes baking. She is married to Deor and hopes they will soon have children, if she can get Deor to agree to it.

Deor and Yrsa are the youngest couple living in Skaal village. They have been married for eight years. Both are typical Skaal villagers, hard-working and self-sufficient. Their home is meager but well constructed, given Deor's supreme skills in the crafting of wood. Inside their house are the rough essentials for life: food, a cooking pot, and a copy of The Woodcutter's Wife, as well as another tome of interest.

- Crafting: Cooking pot, wood chopping block
- Book: Deathbrand

6 Oslaf's House

Oslaf

One of the many hunters in Skaal village, Oslaf would be very content if the rest of the world would just leave his village and his people alone. He is deeply mistrustful of outsiders, owing to an incident in his childhood where some Nords from Skyrim came to hunt in the land near Skaal Village. The Nords got drunk and picked a fight with Oslaf's father, wounding him badly. Oslaf is a devoted, if stern, father and husband. He thinks young Nikulas is a fool for wanting to leave the village, and he reminds his young daughter Aeta on a daily basis that her place is with her people.

Finna

Finna is a kindhearted villager who is almost the complete opposite of her stern husband, Oslaf. Where he dislikes strangers, she is welcoming and generous. She is good friends with Yrsa, and the two like to share idle gossip about the other villagers. Finna tries hard to instill positive qualities in her daughter, to provide a balance to her husband's more strict approach to parenting.

Aeta

Children in the Skaal Village are raised to contribute from an early age. The self-reliant Skaal do not have the resources to get by without everyone pitching in, so Aeta, the village's lone child, helps out where she can. Aeta is unlike many Nord children in Skyrim, having little time for play and no friends her own age. She has had to grow up more quickly and is surprisingly mature and level-headed for a child.

This building is home to Oslaf, Finna, and Aeta. It is a modest home with a fenced-in backyard that houses a few goats and planted potatoes, cabbage, and leeks. Finna has taken it upon herself to try to grow a meager crop here, although the climate and soil are less than ideal for farming. She spends most of her day outside tending to the garden while her husband, Oslaf, hunts game in the lands near the village. Inside the home is a cooking pot, some food and clothing, and very little else, save for a sweetroll in Aeta's bedroom.

- Crafting: Cooking Pot

7 Wulf Wild-Blood's House

Wulf Wild-Blood

One of the best hunters that the Skaal have ever known, Wulf Wild-Blood seems almost supernaturally attuned to nature. In truth, this is just the result of a lifetime spent tirelessly perfecting his art. Hunting is Wulf's great passion, and he only feels truly alive while on the trail, tracking game. His enthusiasm has waned slightly, after the disappearance of his brother Torkild.

For most of his long life, Wulf Wild-Blood has been the most accomplished hunter and trapper in Skaal village. Now facing his twilight years, Wulf wants to pass along his wisdom and teach a new generation of hunters. He will eagerly offer advice and wisdom. He wants nothing in exchange, save to keep his people strong by passing on what he has learned. His home features a variety of pelts, skinned meats, and mounted animal trophies.

- Crafting: Cooking pot
- Loose gear
- Trainer (Master: Two-Handed): Wulf Wild-Blood [DB1/1]

8 Wulf Wild-Blood's Butcher's Hut

This is where Wulf Wild-Blood prepares the meats and skins of the animals he and the other hunters bring back, before they are divided or sold on to traders from Raven Rock and Skyrim.

- Crafting: Cooking pot

9 Edla's House

Edla

Edla lost her husband, Heifnir, a few years ago and has been raising their son Nikulas alone ever since. The event made her reexamine her life and she decided that she wanted more for herself than the simple life of a villager. However, she could not deny that she was a Skaal, born and raised, and she had no desire to leave. Her compromise was to begin a new occupation as the village trader. In this new (and entirely self-appointed) role, she makes trades with travelers, selling off material the Skaal can spare, crafting her potions in exchange for septims, and using those to purchase supplies.

Nikulas

Nikulas might have the life of a typical Skaal villager were it not for the recent death of his father and the arrival of Tharstan in the village.

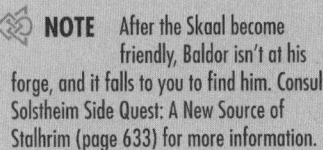

The loss of his father shook the young man greatly and made him question whether he really wanted to spend his entire life within the boundaries of the Skaal lands. Pouring fuel on the fire were Tharstan's exciting tales of his grand excursions exploring lost ruins across Skyrim and beyond.

This dwelling is home to Edla and Nikulas. Edla has tried hard to keep herself occupied since the tragic death of her husband, a hunter named Heifnir who was mauled by a bear three years ago. An unusually enterprising Skaal, she has taken to trading with travelers who pass through the village, taking gold in exchange for meat, furs, and other items that the villagers have in excess. She then uses that gold to buy whatever she thinks is useful or desirable. Inside her home are some simple foodstuffs and a few trinkets and potions.

- Crafting: Alchemy Lab, cooking pot
- Loose gear
- Potions
- Strong Box
- Trader (Apothecary): Edla [DB1/16]

⑩ Morwen's House

Morwen

Morwen's mother, Bera, was one of those rare Skaal who left the village to seek her fortunes elsewhere. She traveled to Skyrim with Ulfarr, a Nord sailor whose ship had wrecked near Skaal Village. Bera raised Morwen with tales of the Skaal Village, for in her heart she missed her home. Currently, Morwen works the smithy with Baldor.

After years as a mercenary, Morwen has chosen to put away her sword and live out her remaining years in peace. Morwen's mother was born in Skaal Village but left when she married a sailor from Skyrim and returned home with him. Morwen has had her fill of battle and now spends her days fishing and hunting to help provide food for the villagers. However, she will still pick up an axe should a threat to the village arise. Her house is a simple affair but cozy if you decide to marry and settle down with her (after completing Solstheim Regional Activity: Return to Falkreath*, page 671).

- Display case [Adept]
- Loose gear
- Marriage Prospect: Morwen [DB3/3]
- Unique Item: Bera's Necklace [DB6/31]

[S.N01] Damphall Mine

Related Quests
None

Recommended Level: 10

Dungeon: Mine
Reaver

Crafting
Alchemy Lab
Anvil
Smelter
Tanning Rack
Wood Chopping Block

Dangers
Danger! Oil Lamp Trap (5)
Danger! Rockfall Trap

Miscellaneous
Chest
Potions
Loose gear
Lots o' gold

Exterior

An abandoned iron and silver mine has been repurposed by a band of Reavers. It is located on the lower rocky abutments overlooking the Sea of Ghosts, just below the snow line. The entrance is slightly precarious; bring your best Reaver-killing equipment and slay the single foe outside, near the half-buried cart.

- Reaver

Interior

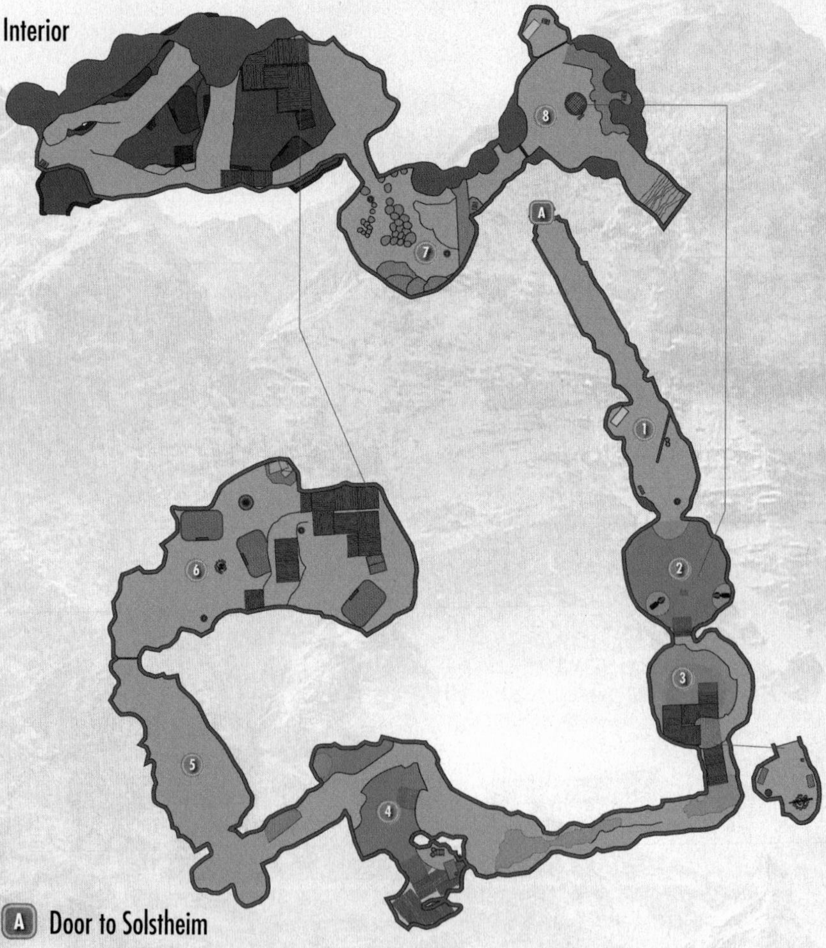

Ⓐ Door to Solstheim

① Grotto Entrance

Head down from the entrance, starting combat with two Reavers behind the fallen fencing. There's a single potion and purse to collect and some optional mining to attempt.

- Potions
- Pickaxe
- Iron Ore Vein

2 Grotto and Plunge Pool

This roughly circular and waterlogged mine shaft chamber is extremely steep. Look up at the square-shaped trapdoor two floors above you; this is your spectacular exit route! The pool is deep and has a chest, six skeletal remains, and two Reaver corpses to find.

- Chest

3 Lower Pool and Alchemist's Alcove

For a more stealthy and safer way to remove the Reaver threats in this area, use the ledge left of the waterfall and work your way around, passing a tunnel to your left; fight two foes here near an Alchemy Lab and shelf of potions. The rickety mine platforms lead down to a second tunnel directly under the first. The water below is devoid of items, save a Nordic Barnacle Cluster.

- Crafting: Alchemy Lab
- Pickaxe
- Potions
- Reaver

4 Bridge Cavern

Head through the lower tunnel, passing the spiky grass and an old campfire (watch for the tripwire trap!). Head into a cave with a low ceiling and a natural rock bridge ahead (west). Expect a silver ore vein and two Reavers on this bridge (shoot the oil lamp to splatter them with fire). Before continuing, take a dip in the water; there is a gap to swim through to the southeast leading to a cave alcove with the following:

- Danger! Oil Lamp Trap (2)
- Danger! Rockfall Trap
- Reaver
- Silver Ore Vein
- Book: Ahzidal's Descent
- Statue of Dibella
- Gold Ingot (3)
- Chest

5 Old Miners' Camp

Cross the bridge, climb over the skeletal feet of a crushed miner, and pass the wood chopping block and old Nordic carving to reach a cell door. Crafting: Wood Chopping Block

6 Reavers' Camp

Two pelt tents and at least five Reavers are waiting in this cavern, which grows vertically with two bridges ahead of you and ramps and ledges to ascend. The lower camp has a chest [Novice] and some potions in one tent and a smelter with iron ore behind it. Use the oil lamp traps if you wish. Climb the wooden ramps past a third and fourth tent to the ledge above and another ancient Nord carving. There's a narrow tunnel entrance ahead (southeast) and a moss-walled ledge to your right (west), leading to a natural arch where a skeletal victim paid the price for inaccurate Reaver archery! The ledges to the west lead to a bloody executioner's stump and another chest.

- Danger! Oil Lamp Trap (3)
- Reaver
- Crafting: Anvil, smelter, tanning rack
- Pickaxe
- Chest (2) [1 = Novice]
- Potions
- Loose Gear

7 Stalagmite Ascent

Climb the narrow, steep, and winding path with stalagmites around you, pausing to edge up the narrow path to your right (northeast) to a well-hidden chest. Slay the Reaver at the top. Then pull the chain to release the rock wall.

- Reaver
- Chest

8 Rock Waterfall and the Long Drop

The remaining Reavers (around three, including a leader carrying a Treasure Room Key) are in this final chamber, consisting of a rocky waterfall (which you can climb to reach a chest). The cell door [Master] is more easily opened with the key, leading to a chest and some excellent gear and valuables. When you're ready to leave, retrace your steps or fall down the trapdoor into the plunge pool (Location [2]), then head northwest.

- Reaver
- Loose gear
- Treasure Room Key
- Chest (2)
- Lots o' gold

[S.N02] Water Stone

Related Quests

Dragonborn Main Quest: Cleansing the Stones

Recommended Level: 25

Habitation: All-Maker Stone

Benkum
Hjalfar
Liesi
Palevius Lex

Special Area

Standing Stones

Miscellaneous

Area is locked

Once used in rituals during the time of the Bloodmoon, this is one of the All-Maker Stones sacred to the Skaal. Currently, its power is being siphoned by Miraak and stone arches constructed by four enthralled sailors who were only supposed to take a short shore leave on Solstheim. The Bend Will Shout is required to remove the trance the sailors are under and to cleanse the stone of Miraak's influence. After this, the sailors depart. Beware the dragon that is released out to the west, once the Lurker is summoned; both must be defeated or you must run from them.

- Power: Waters of Life

[S.N03] Fahlbtharz

Related Quests

Solstheim Side Quest:
The Challenges of Kagrumez*

Recommended Level: 25

Dungeon: Dwarven City

Albino Spider
Dwarven Ballista
Dwarven Centurion
Dwarven Sphere
Dwarven Spider
Oil Spider
Riekling

Dangers

Dwarven Fire Pillar Trap
Dwarven Swinging Trap

Puzzle

Dwarven Puzzle

Collectibles

Kagrumez Resonance Gem [DB2/5]
Unique Item: Visage of Mzund [DB20/31]

Miscellaneous

Chest
Loose gear
Lots o' gold

Fahlbtharz
Fahlbtharz Boilery
Fahlbtharz Grand Hall
Fahlbtharz Corridor
1
2
3
4
5
6
7
8
9
10
11
12
13
14
15
16
17
18
19
20
21
A
B
C
D
E
F
G
H
I
J
K
L

Exterior

This extensive Dwarven dungeon complex is guarded by new squatters, appropriated by Rieklings. Head through the high mountains to the northwest and approach the Rieklings heading north, or south from the sagging rooftops of the ruins. The nearby Fahlbtharz Elevator to the south is where you exit. Defeat the rider and three or four spear-throwing foes on the rickety battlements, check the area for a chest, then enter the door to the north.

- Chest
- Mounted Riekling
- Riekling

Interior

A Door to Solstheim

1 Riekling Camp

Enter the sloping stone corridor, fight through a Riekling camp with three or four foes, and descend south, passing the Riekling corpses and engaging Automatons farther down.

- Riekling
- Dwarven Sphere

2 Control Room

Besides a locked door [Novice] with some items behind it, this chamber features barred windows overlooking the gigantic cranking mechanisms of the waterlogged chamber, and also a shut gate. Activate the gate at the bank of buttons; look for the second button from the right side, along the bottom row, to open it (the rest launch traps or nothing at all).

- Danger: Dwarven fire pillar trap
- Loose gear

3 Connecting Passage

Check the dead end before you open the door for a chest.

- Chest [Adept]
- Dwarven Automatons

4 Kinetic Resonator

Hit the Kinetic Resonator with a weapon or arrow to unlock the gate around the corner. Then continue, looting a wall chest [Expert] as you wind around and down.

- Chest [Expert]

5 Leaking Oil Corridor

This is an oil-filled corridor with scuttling Oil Spiders to squash. Light the trail of oil first to avoid any potential dangers. Slash a second Kinetic Resonator encased in cobwebs to open a subsequent gate and access a lower set of chambers.

- Oil Spider

6 Fungal Chambers

These chambers contain glowing fungi and Dwarven Automatons. Deal with them, then head to the south, opening the door to reach the Water Chamber.

- Chest
- Dwarven Automaton

7 Water Chamber (First Visit: Entrance)

This area is initially bewildering, so stop and work out where you are in this chamber (check the adjacent map). Face south, and check your location; ahead is a pointed gatehouse with a gap you can't reach. So head right (west) and through a second (open) gatehouse to peer down to a set of giant cogs.

8 Water Chamber (First Visit: Lower Cogs)

Initially you can't access these from the water, so face south and drop down onto the cogs, heading southwest (ignoring or fighting the Automatons). Stay on the cogs until you reach the door to Fahlbtharz Corridor.

- Dwarven Automation

B Door to Fahlbtharz Corridor

Fahlbtharz Corridor

C Door to Fahlbtharz

9 Corridor Stairs and Storage

Ascend the steps, watching for the pressure plate that releases a swinging trap. Pass the gate [Adept] leading to an alcove chest, and ascend back to the door to Fahlbtharz.

- Danger! Dwarven swinging trap
- Chest
- Loose gear

D Door to Fahlbtharz

Fahlbtharz

E Door to Fahlbtharz Corridor

10 Water Chamber (Second Visit: Western Balcony)

Turn left (north), up the steps to a valve that lowers a ramp, allowing you quicker access back here if you fall. Pull the adjacent lever, opening up a bridge to the east.

11 Water Chamber (Second Visit: Connecting Bridges)

Head along the connecting bridges and gatehouses, then turn left (north) and engage a ballista. Now face east.

12 Water Chamber (Second Visit: Second Cogs)

Look down at the whirring cogs and drop to the bloody remains of a bandit adventurer named Eydis. Her journal reveals she was searching for an enchanted Dwarven Helm with her friend Ulyn. Head east along the cogs to the edge of the Water Chamber and up the steps to a door leading to Fahlbtharz Boilery.

- Dwarven Ballista
- Eydis's Journal

13 Water Chamber (Second Visit: Eastern Balcony)

Ignore the door for the moment, and head to the end of the balcony you're on to activate a valve that lowers two more ramps. This allows you to come back here if need be.

F Door to Fahlbtharz Boilery

Fahlbtharz Boilery

G Door to Fahlbtharz

14 Boilery Entrance Corridor

Enter the Boilery door, heading east, then north, and east again.

- Loose gear
- Dwarven Automaton

15 Boilery Piston Gate

Move around to the south through a strange chamber of pistons, pipes, and embedded machinery. Slay the ballista and climb the steps in the southeast corner. This leads to a balcony with a corpse clutching a bow; arrows are nearby. These are the remains of Ulyn, and his journal reveals clues to the secrets of the boilery puzzle you face.

Puzzle Solution: Face the circular piston lock to the west, and view the six kinetic resonators (the propeller devices glowing turquoise, three on either side of the main lock). To open the subsequent gate, you must pull all 20 fuel cylinders into place, activating the boiler. This is achieved by shooting an arrow at some of the resonators. Each resonator activates a specific number of cylinders. Shoot too few and nothing happens. Shoot too many and you release an increasingly dangerous number of Automatons and must defeat them. Each resonator has a set number of cylinders that it releases:

✓	RESONATOR	CYLINDERS RELEASED
☐	Far left	3
☐	Middle Left	4
☐	Near Left	6
☐	Near Right	9
☐	Middle Right	13
☐	Far Right	18

To reach 20 fuel cylinders, you need to shoot the far left (3), middle left (4), and middle right (13) tonal locks.

- Ulyn's Journal
- Dwarven Automation
- Loose gear

TIP You can also use ranged spells, or search the room for dwarven arrows if you run out of ammunition. Or, you can strike the pipes with a weapon..

16 Boilery Exit Corridor

Exit via the open gate to the southwest, climbing the stairs and swiping another resonator to open the adjacent gate (saving time if you have to retake this route), and move back into the Water Chamber of Fahlbtharz.

H Door to Fahlbtharz

Fahlbtharz

I Door to Fahlbtharz Boilery

17 Water Chamber (Third Visit: Upper Western Alcove)

Activate the lever and head across the bridge that grinds your way, moving west to the edge of the bridge, then turning right (north).

18 Water Chamber (Third Visit: Upper Cogs)

Jump onto the cogs, moving west.

19 Water Chamber (Third Visit: Second Bridge and Tonal Lock)

Leap to a second bridge and gatehouse section, heading west to a battle with a ballista near a chest and a resonator (in the gatehouse with a skeleton) to shoot (there's a bow by the skeleton in case you don't have ranged magic or weapons). This aligns the bridges you were on at the previous lever.

Wait! Make sure you're standing on the bridge section facing west, with the kinetic resonator diagonally left (southwest) of you! When you hit the resonator, ride the bridge. If you aren't standing correctly, you need to retrace your steps. Now turn and run south across the bridges to the Fahlbtharz Grand Hall.

- ◊ Dwarven Ballista
- ◊ Chest

J Door to Fahlbtharz Grand Hall

Fahlbtharz Grand Hall

K Door to Fahlbtharz

20 Grand Hall

Clear away the Albino and Oil Spiders, and battle two Dwarven Ballistas immediately. There are two Centurions in this chamber; it is wise to weed out your foes before you face them! Move to the walkway on the upper level and inspect three pedestals (known as Dynamo Actuators) that require a core to operate. If you already have two Dynamo Actuators, you can bypass the Dwarven Centurions; if not, you will need to wrench them from their corpses. Attack the nearby Centurions and scrounge a Centurion Dynamo Core from each, allowing you to raise the steps and remove two sets of bars to the treasure room.

- ◊ Albino Spider
- ◊ Oil Spider
- ◊ Dwarven Ballista
- ◊ Dwarven Centurion
- ◊ Centurion Dynamo Core (2)

21 Grand Hall Treasure Room

Inspect the treasure room thoroughly. Aside from piles of gold, chests, and the unique dwarven helm Visage of Mzund, a Kagrumez Resonance Gem is on a plate. Take what you wish, then leave via the dwarven elevator to the left (east), appearing outside at the Fahlbtharz Elevator.

- ◊ Unique Item: Visage of Mzund [DB20/31]
- ◊ Kagrumez Resonance Gem [DB2/5]
- ◊ Loose gear
- ◊ Lots o' gold

L Elevator to Solstheim

[S.N04] Hvitkald Peak

Dangers

Falling Adventurer!

Hvitkald Peak is one of four mountains on Solstheim you can climb. When you reach the summit, a landmark icon appears to reflect this (optional) accomplishment. Begin at the Abandoned Lodge and climb west, up behind the building to the sharp mountain ridge. Turn right (north) and maneuver up the ridgeline, then circle around to face south when you're almost at the top. Once at the summit, you have commanding views of the following locations:

North: Fahlbtharz elevator is very close, with the main entrance to Fahlbtharz a little farther away.

Northeast: Mount Moesring

East: The path up to Temple of Miraak. The circular indent is the entrance to Kagrumez.

Southeast: Abandoned Lodge, Brodir Grove, and Highpoint Tower.

South: Raven Rock

Southwest: Bloodskal Barrow

NOTE There are three other mountain peaks you can optionally climb: Frykte Peak, Mount Moesring, and Mortrag Peak.

CAUTION Beware! Heed the following before attempting this ascension:

It is exceptionally difficult to reach the top of this mountain without losing your footing and falling (which could kill you).

Save your progress before attempting the climb.

If you feel you are about to fall, use the Become Ethereal Shout to protect yourself from falling damage.

The Whirlwind Sprint Shout may assist you in your climb, although you're easily able to fly off the peak to a spectacular death if you overshoot your intended location!

Otherwise, head steadily forward while jumping continuously, strafing left and right when you reach an impasse; this is the easiest way to climb.

Mind the gap!

[SN.05] Abandoned Lodge

Related Quests

Solstheim Side Quest: A New Source of Stalhrim

Habitation: Thalmor

Baldor Iron-Shaper

Thalmor

Crafting

Grindstone

Miscellaneous

Chest

Exterior

A well-kept but sealed lodge with a grindstone, scattered barrels, and an impressive view of Red Mountain to the southeast. Normally, this place is silent. During the Side Quest, four Thalmor are guarding this location. Find a key on one of their corpses, allowing you to enter.

- ◊ Key to Abandoned Lodge

Interior

Inside are two beds, a few scattered coins, and steps down into a cellar bar area where Baldor Iron-Shaper is kept prisoner, near a chest [Novice].

- ◊ Baldor Iron-Shaper
- ◊ Chest [Novice]

[S.N06] Bristleback Cave

Related Quests

Solstheim Side Quest: The Great Skyrim Strongbox Hunt*

Recommended Level: 10

Dungeon: Riekling Camp

Bristleback

Mounted Riekling

Riekling

Collectibles

East Empire Strongbox [DB1/33]

Miscellaneous

Chest

Loose Gear

Exterior

Enter here to see how the Rieklings train their Bristlebacks and observe the Rieklings' hoarding tendencies. Your exploration begins at the rocky beach entrance, where the Rieklings have erected a rickety watchtower. Slay the three foes here before entering, and be on the lookout for an ambush if you approach the chest. It's empty.

- ◊ Riekling

Interior

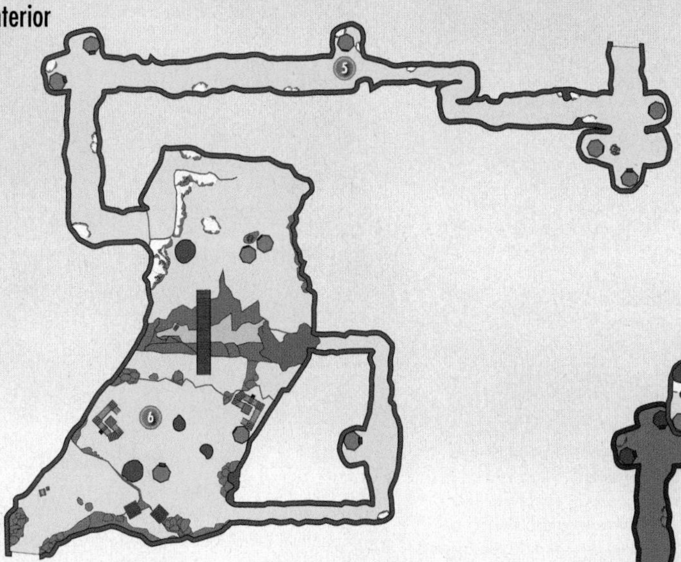

CAUTION

Beware of periodic Riekling ambushes from within barrels and other crates at the sides of the path throughout this location.

A Exit to Solstheim

1 Entrance Tunnel

Expect an ambush in the entrance tunnel, near the dead Reavers. Just after, the tunnel forks left (west) to the cave exit tunnel and drops north, farther into the icy cave system.

- ◊ Loose gear
- ◊ Riekling

2 Upper Camp

There are two ambushes and three or four foes here, along with a large number of low-value trinkets.

- ◊ Loose gear
- ◊ Riekling

3 Upper Village

Along with tents and huts, expect at least 12 Rieklings in this elongated ice cavern, which spreads out a little to the east. Search thoroughly for two chests and a Strongbox.

- ◊ Loose Gear
- ◊ Riekling
- ◊ Chest (2) [1 = Adept]
- ◊ Strongbox

4 East Tunnel Camps

Watch for two more ambushes in the tunnel and another one in the small camp. Don't overlook the tunnel continuing down and to the south; this leads to a lower camp where you'll find an East Empire Company Strongbox [Expert] on a barrel in the southeast item alcove.

- ◊ Loose gear
- ◊ Riekling
- ◊ East Empire Strongbox [Expert] [DB1/33]
- ◊ East Empire Pendant

5 Western Winding Tunnel

Beware of three ambushes as you make your way through the winding tunnels and occasional huts.

- ◊ Loose gear
- ◊ Riekling

6 Low Camp and Bristleback Pens

There is a sizable Riekling presence in this ice chamber, with at least four Bristlebacks, one Mounted Riekling, and five warriors ready to repel your advances. Navigate the fissure and the enemies to the exit tunnel in the southwest part of the chamber. If you fall down the fissure, there's a chest [Expert] and a narrow exit tunnel that leads back to the southeast part of this location, or you can venture down the tunnel into the fissure to avoid any falling damage.

- ◊ Loose gear
- ◊ Chest (2) [1 = Expert]
- ◊ Riekling
- ◊ Mounted Riekling
- ◊ Bristleback

7 Exit Tunnel

Climb this lengthy, winding tunnel with few enemies and a chest to open along the way, and you're able to drop down near the entrance and escape.

- ◊ Chest
- ◊ Loose Gear

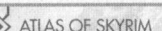

[S.N07] Northshore Landing

Related Quests

Solstheim Side Quest: A New Source of Stalhrim

Recommended Level: 25

Habitation: Dock

Ancarion
Mudcrab
Old Salty
Thalmor Soldier

Crafting

Tanning Rack

Collectibles

East Empire Strongbox [DB2/33]

Miscellaneous

Area is locked
Chest

Exterior

If Solstheim Side Quest: A New Source of Stalhrim isn't active, this small dock is deserted, save for a few Mudcrabs and a particularly huge specimen named Old Salty. Check the dock for a chest [Novice], and look under the dock in the water for a submerged boat with a chest [Apprentice] next to it. Inspect the small shack with the tanning rack outside; inside is a chest and an East Empire Strongbox [Expert], close to an ebony vein. There's an empty chest along the stream and another chest at the base of the rushing waterfall. If the quest is active, a Thalmor boat is moored here, along with three soldiers and a leader named Ancarion, all looking for Stalhrim on this blasted isle.

- Chest (5) [1 = Novice, 1 = Apprentice]
- East Empire Strongbox [Expert] [DB2/33]
- East Empire Pendant
- Ebony Ore
- Tanning Rack
- Ancarion
- Stalhrim Deposit (2)

[S.N08] Broken Tusk Mine

Recommended Level: 6

Dungeon: Mine

Riekling

Collectibles

East Empire Strongbox [DB3/33]

Miscellaneous

Chest   Lots o' gold

Exterior

A section of rickety ramparts guarded by five or six Rieklings (one mounted) await you on this snowy climb. Ascend from the entrance area below to the top watchtower, which has a chest and an East Empire Company Strongbox [Expert] to open.

- Chest
- East Empire Strongbox [Expert] [DB3/33]
- East Empire Pendant

Interior

The mine didn't yield much before it was abandoned by the Skaal. Now the single chamber is home to three Rieklings and their camp. However, they have collected some gold ingots, coin, silver, and gold rings and necklaces for your coffers. The back of the cave has the unpleasant remains of a Reaver.

- Chest (2)
- Ore: Heart Stone (2)

[S.N09] Stalhrim Source

Related Quests

Solstheim Side Quest: A New Source of Stalhrim

Recommended Level: 25

Habitation: Draugr Crypt

Hidden in a circular burial mound below (west of) White Ridge Barrow is a huge quantity of Stalhrim. If you wish to craft weapons and armor of immeasurable quantity, you may want to come here with an Ancient Nordic Pickaxe. Note that this area, when discovered as part of the Side Quest, will appear on your world map with a landmark icon.

- Stalhrim Deposit (10)

[S.N10] Castle Karstaag Ruins

[S.N11] Castle Karstaag Caverns

Related Quests

Solstheim Side Quest: Karstaag's Resurrection*
Solstheim Regional Activity: Thievery and the Karstaag Connection*

Recommended Level: 50

Dungeon: Riekling Camp

Karstaag
Mounted Riekling
Riekling

Miscellaneous

Area is locked
Chest
Loose gear

Exterior: Both Locations

Solstheim's ancient tales speak of a frost giant both frightening and furious. But this brute is said to have died more than 200 years ago, during the time of the Bloodmoon. Head up the steep snowy slopes toward Castle Karstaag Caverns and Castle Karstaag Ruins. The castle is a massive mound of sculpted ice and looks almost like a mountain.

Although the interior of Castle Karstaag has long since collapsed, its remains, worn down to glacial slabs, still form a near-impenetrable wall. Unless you can pick the lock on the massive front doors [Master], the only open path to the central courtyard (the Ruins) is through the icy, partially flooded tunnels under the castle (the Caverns), where a clan of Rieklings still defends its ancient home.

Interior: Castle Karstaag Caverns

A Exit to Solstheim

After following the raging mountain stream in the ravine to the castle's east, you enter the caverns here.

was able to use her healing arts to bring him back. Ever since that day, Aphia has remained by Crescius's side. Crescius was grateful for Aphia's support, and in time, they grew to care for each other quite deeply. Even though it broke Dunmer tradition, Lleril Morvayn allowed them to wed and they've been living together as man and wife ever since.

Aphia Velothi

Aphia Velothi was originally an acolyte at the Temple. Under the tutelage of Elder Othreloth, she studied the healing arts and was beginning to learn the traditions of the House of Reclamations. The idea that the Tribunal was gone was unbelievable to her; she firmly believed that the eruption of the Red Mountain wasn't a punishment from the Daedra but from the Tribunal. This view led to many arguments between Aphia and Elder Othreloth, which culminated in her being stripped of her duties and excommunicated from the temple. Elder Othreloth wished her exiled from Raven Rock altogether, but Lleril Morvayn refused his request, citing the fact that she had nowhere to go. She married Crescius after nursing him back to health.

This is the home of Crescius Caerellius, the sole remaining descendant of the Imperial settlers who once lived in the Raven Rock colony. His family has maintained this house since Raven Rock was founded in the Third Era. The house is strictly Imperial in design, bearing absolutely no Dunmer decoration or construction whatsoever. Crescius's wife, Aphia, is a Dunmer but has forsaken their ways and chosen to live a "purely Imperial lifestyle" in honor of her husband, whom she loves dearly. This has led to quite a bit of animosity with the rest of the town.

Inside the house there are various scattered books (read up on the history of Raven Rock here), along with a bounty of food, a cooking pot, and an East Empire Strongbox [Expert]. The stairwell has more food, while the small upstairs bedroom has coin purses, an owned bed, and a chest.

- Chest
- Cooking pot
- East Empire Strongbox [Expert] [DB16/33]
- East Empire Pendant
- Trainer (Restoration: Journeyman): Aphia Velothi [DB1/1]

3 Morvayn Manor

Lleril Morvayn

Lleril Morvayn is the son of Brara Morvayn, the House Redoran Councilor who settled in Raven Rock after the devastation of Vvardenfell. He took over as councilor from his mother when Brara died early in the Fourth Era. On more than one occasion, attempts on his life have been made by members of House Hlaalu, which has made Lleril quite paranoid. The dire economic and security situation has been weighing heavily on his shoulders.

Adril Arano

Adril Arano and Lleril Morvayn have been the best of friends ever since they rose through the ranks together in House Redoran. Whenever trouble threatened the warrior-house, the two of them could be found on the front lines, fighting back with everything they had. This bond persisted, and when the Red Year came, Adril was granted passage on Lleril's vessel that set out from Vvardenfell. Adril and Lleril remained close while living in Raven Rock, even helping out in the mines and patrolling the Bulwark when necessary. When Brara Morvayn finally passed away and Lleril was made councilor of Raven Rock, he immediately took Adril as his adviser. Even though Lleril is technically Adril's superior, he treats Adril as his equal, even allowing him to live in Morvayn Manor.

Cindiri Arano

Cindiri Arano is Adril Arano's wife. Cindiri arrived on one of the few refugee ships that escaped Vvardenfell and struck out for less "volcanic" pastures. Shortly after her arrival on Solstheim, she met Adril and they quickly fell in love. She's been quite supportive of her husband but takes exception to the danger he keeps placing himself in. She understands the close relationship between Lleril and Adril but fears that the violence targeting the councilor might bring harm to her husband as well. Cindiri can usually be found within Morvayn Manor or out on the streets when she needs some time to herself.

Once an opulent mansion, Morvayn Manor now serves as the government building for Raven Rock. In addition to Councilor Morvayn's hall, it also contains his living quarters and those of his advisor Adril. The banners of House Redoran are hung on the building's circular tower as a stark reminder of who's in charge.

Enter the manor to visit Lleril, sit on his throne, and check his local book collection. There's plenty of food, a Redoran Guard to ensure you don't eat any, an Arcane Enchanter, more food, and a cooking pot in the stairwell chamber. Upstairs are the Morvayn Manor Chambers [Adept]. Sneak in here to find a fair few bottles of wine and an East Empire Strongbox [Expert]. The private bed chambers include a display case [Expert] with Chitin Armor and a Helmet, a book called Deathbrand that begins a quest, gems, and Adril's Survey Results regarding the upkeep of the city, along with a reply from House Redoran.

- Arcane Enchanter
- Cooking pot
- East Empire Strongbox [Expert] [DB17/33]
- East Empire Pendant
- Book: Deathbrand

4 Temple

Elder Othreloth

Elder Othreloth has been the Elder (in actuality he's the only priest, but the title is honorary) at the Temple since he established it after arriving at the town at the beginning of the Fourth Era. The Temple honors "the House of Reclamations," the return to worship of the Daedra after the loss of the Tribunal. Elder Othreloth has been quite instrumental in stabilizing the beliefs of the residents in Raven Rock ever since the destruction of their homeland. He's convinced almost everyone that the eruption was punishment for forsaking the Daedra, making him quite feared and revered in town. This has kept the Temple completely free from the political mechanizations going on in Raven Rock, as neither House Redoran nor the remnants of House Hlaalu wish to anger him.

Galdrus Hlervu

Galdrus Hlervu is a relatively recent addition to the Temple. Hoping to pass along the "new old" ways of thinking to someone else, Elder Othreloth has taken Galdrus under his wing and has spent a good deal of his time prepping him for the inevitable. Unbeknownst to Elder Othreloth, Galdrus has been tampering with a bit of necromancy research on the side, using the ash pit in the lower level (where the Dunmer are interred) as his laboratory.

Raven Rock's temple is dedicated to the renewal of the ancient Dark Elven faith, with shrines to the three Daedra who traditionally aided the Dunmer: Azura, Mephala, and Boethiah. After the downfall of the Tribunal at the end of the Third Era, these temples have begun to replace the Tribunal temples as the Dark Elves return to the old ways. While these Daedric Princes were originally seen as the "Anticipations" to Almalexia, Vivec, and Sotha Sil, they have now been cast in a new light, as a part of the "House of Reclamations"...signifying the Dunmer's return to the old ways and an offset to the House of Troubles (the other Daedra). The city's Ancestral Tomb is located in the basement area (the lowest level) of the temple. This is where the Dunmer that have fallen are interred.

Enter the temple if you wish to speak to either Elder Othreloth or his equally haughty assistant. If you're collecting ash yams, there are over 60 between the urns outside and within these chambers. On the main floor are pyres and unique shrines to Azura, Boethiah, and Mephala. There are purses to steal here too. Downstairs in the tomb cellar are two chambers. To the left (west) is Otherloth's, with a number of bone meal servings, books, and a Strong Box [Expert], which you can open easily if you have the Raven Rock Temple Key (carried by both priests). To the right is Hlervu's room, with scattered books (including Deathbrand) and a chest. Ahead is a door to the Temple Ancestral Tomb (which is also accessible via the Morvayn Ancestral Tomb). You will visit the tomb during Solstheim Regional Activity: Tomb Eradicator*.

- Book: Deathbrand
- Chest
- Raven Rock Temple Key (2)
- Shrine of Azura [DB1/1]
- Shrine of Boethiah [DB1/1]
- Shrine of Mephala [DB1/1]
- Strong Box [Expert]

Interior: Temple Ancestral Tomb

These chambers are unlocked during Solstheim Regional Activity: Tomb Eradicator* (page 670), once you receive the Raven Rock Tomb Key from Otherloth. The pyres are laid out in a similar fashion to those in the upstairs temple area. The side exits to the Morvayn and Ulen ancestral tombs can be opened using the same key.

- ◊ Raven Rock Tomb Key
- ◊ Ash Spawn
- ◊ East Empire Strongbox [Expert] [DB18/33]

5 Morvayn Ancestral Tomb

You can enter this tomb by picking the lock [Expert] or using the Raven Rock Tomb Key. This is a smaller tomb with only a single door to the Temple Ancestral Tomb. Inspect the many urns for ash yams, and slay any Ash Spawn you see. Otherwise, this tomb is relatively empty.

- ◊ Ash Spawn

6 Ulen Ancestral Tomb

You can easily enter this crypt without a key, although you need the Raven Rock Tomb Key to unlock the door leading to the Temple Ancestral Tomb. Check the urns for ash yams, deal with any Ash Spawn, and wait for Tilisu Severin to arrive, as part of Solstheim Side Quest: Served Cold.

- ◊ Ash Spawn

7 The Bulwark

Captain Modyn Veleth

Modyn Veleth is the captain of the Redoran Guard, a job he takes extremely seriously. With the myriad of attempts on Lleril Morvayn's life, he's well aware that there are still forces out there aligning against the councilor. He's kept the Redoran Guard in good shape, teaching them how to maintain their weapons and armor and various battle techniques. Modyn previously served as a military officer in Vvardenfell and was sent here by the Redoran Council to protect Raven Rock (which it sees as one of its holdings). He wishes he was serving House Redoran back on the mainland but never complains about his current posting. When Modyn arrived at Raven Rock, the Bulwark was merely a shadow of how it appears today. Using his knowledge, he was able to enhance the wall's strength and suggest improvements, such as the massive protective gate.

The massive wall constructed after the eruptions on Vvardenfell serves multiple purposes. In addition to holding back the waves of ash and fell creatures that assault Raven Rock, the wall also houses the guard barracks, the captain of the guard's living quarters, and the city's jail. The wall also features a large set of steps that climbs the northern cliff face and ends in a watchtower with a large pyre. If the pyre is ever lit, this signals those on the wall below that a threat approaches from the north. The Bulwark has a large gate, one of the only defenses keeping the ash abominations from overrunning the small town.

The exterior of the Bulwark, accessed from the basalt cliffs above, the main gate below, or the balcony steps near the Temple, offers views of the Sea of Ghosts, Red Mountain, and the harbor.

The interior of the Bulwark, accessed from the main gate, has a guard presence. There are various (owned) cots and a bed, a fireplace with a cooking spit, an evidence chest should you need to retrieve belongings, and an East Empire Strongbox [Expert] sitting on the table at the end of the interior corridor.

- ◊ Cooking spit
- ◊ East Empire Strongbox [Expert] [DB19/33]
- ◊ East Empire Pendant
- ◊ Evidence Chest
- ◊ Redoran Guard

8A The Bulwark Jail

The Redoran Guard maintain the peace and see to the defense of Raven Rock. Crimes committed against the residents of Raven Rock are judged by Lleril, and prisoners are placed in the tiny prison in an antechamber of the massive Bulwark.

Aside from a couple of books, the jail cell features a solid door lock [Expert] and a guard who isn't the most perceptive of chaps. This allows you to sneak out if you wish, sleep in the cell's bed, or locate the hidden exit—the grate [Novice] in the fireplace. This leads to an ash and cobweb-lined passage to a second grate (under the belongings chest, allowing you to snag your stuff), which drops you down to a stone tunnel dug by Draugr. This ends at a door to Coldcinder Cave.

- ◊ Prisoner Belongings Chest
- ◊ Redoran Guard

8B Coldcinder Cave

This picture shows the exit trapdoor just outside Raven Rock. You can enter from here, but for a full exploration, begin inside Bulwark Jail.

A Door to the Bulwark Jail

1 Dry Bones

A set of ancient steps leads down, past the ruins of a nasty spike trap with scattered skeletons near it, and out into a narrow basalt corridor with a Skeever and a skeleton jammed up into the columns.

- ◊ Skeever

2 Netch Hatchery

A small group of Netch are floating about in the gloom of this basalt clearing.

- ◊ Betty Netch
- ◊ Netch Calf (2)

3 Draugr Causeway

B Trapdoor to Solstheim

Up a stone causeway is an exit ladder, bringing you out at location 8B on the Raven Rock map, a trapdoor just outside (and southeast) the main gates.

4 Coldcinder Barrow Ruins

Head through this easily overlooked narrow basalt passage to reach the tumbledown remains of a barrow. Approach and an Ash Spawn will appear, with two more foes emerging from alcoves as you approach the large chest. There's a second chest [Novice] on a circular platform to jump to and some Heart Stones to mine.

- ◊ Ash Spawn
- ◊ Chest [1, Novice]
- ◊ Heart Stone (3)

9 Main Thoroughfare

The main route from the bulwark gate to the east, around to the Earth Stone to the west, is where you'll find most of Raven Rock's inhabitants.

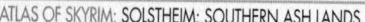

- ◊ Redoran Guard

Coldcinder Cave

⑩ Glover Mallory's House

Glover Mallory

Glover Mallory is one of the most prominent non-Dunmer citizens in Raven Rock. He arrived in town almost 20 years ago and constructed a full blacksmith's workshop with Lleril Morvayn's blessing. Glover quickly befriended many of the locals, who admired his earnestness in keeping Raven Rock alive and his prowess at the forge. Most of the residents treat Glover as a complete equal, including him in all of the town's decisions and even inviting him to some of their more personal ceremonies. He's integral to the Redoran Guard as well, providing equipment and repairs to the soldiers. Glover is very evasive about his past and has never publicly stated why he left the mainland and struck out for Solstheim. He's jovial and warm, and when he isn't at his anvil, he can be found hoisting a mug at The Retching Netch.

This is the home of the town's blacksmith, who works his smithy, known as the Ebony Anvil. Glover is a Breton, making him stand out a bit in this almost exclusively Dunmer town, but he has integrated quite well with everyone. He's proven to be quite adept at his trade and has even voluntarily contributed to the town's meager coffers. Outside, you can trade with Glover, ask about his Regional Activities, and use his crafting areas. Particularly observant members of the Thieves Guild might notice the Shadowmark displayed near the door to the interior of the home.

Inside his house is a variety of food, some books, a cooking pot, and an East Empire Strongbox [Expert]. Upstairs is a chest and a copy of Ahzidal's Descent, which begins Solstheim Side Quest: Unearthed.

After successfully completing Solstheim Regional Activity: Thievery and the Karstaag Connection* (see page 669), you're given the Key to Glover Mallory's House, which allows you to open the locked door downstairs. Inside is a thief's treasure trove, including a weapon and shield on a rack [leveled], poisons and potions, sweetrolls, a Thief Cache barrel with a Shadowmark on it, a generic strongbox, a set of Blackguard's Armor, and Glover's Letter, which reveals his past and his daughter, the thief Sapphire. If you meet up with Sapphire in Riften's Ragged Flagon and talk to her about this note, she offers you an exquisite gem bearing her name.

- ◊ Chest
- ◊ Crafting: Blacksmith's forge, cooking pot, grindstone, smelter, workbench
- ◊ Trader (Blacksmith): Glover Mallory [DB6/16]
- ◊ East Empire Strongbox [Expert] [DB20/33]
- ◊ East Empire Pendant
- ◊ Book: Ahzidal's Descent
- ◊ Key to Glover Mallory's House
- ◊ Unique Item: Blackguard's Armor [DB13/31]
- ◊ Unique Item: Blackguard's Boots [DB14/31]
- ◊ Unique Item: Blackguard's Gloves [DB15/31]
- ◊ Unique Item: Blackguard's Hood [DB16/31]
- ◊ Unique Item: Exquisite Sapphire (reward from Sapphire if Glover's letter is given to her) [DB17/31]
- ◊ Sword and Shield [leveled]
- ◊ Strong box
- ◊ Thief Cache
- ◊ Glover's Letter

⑪ Ienth Farm

Garyn Ienth **Milore Ienth**

Garyn and Milore Ienth are recent additions to Raven Rock. Seeking a home after theirs was lost, they wandered the mainland of Skyrim for a while until they settled in Windhelm. After staying there for a few years, they heard about the Dunmer settlement at Raven Rock and decided to take their chances. They packed up their things, boarded a boat, and never looked back. Garyn brought his knowledge of agriculture to Raven Rock and has become an integral part of the community. He provides quite a bit of grain and other dry goods to the town in exchange for other services, only keeping what he and Milore need to survive. Thanks in part to Milore's alchemical prowess, she's been able to accelerate the growth of some of the crops, producing higher yields.

Having descended from a long line of farmers, the Ieniths' struggle to raise their crops as they did when they lived in Morrowind. Fortunately, after years of trial and error, the farm is flourishing. This has provided quite the boon to the food supplies of the town, and Lleril Morvayn now considers the farm important enough to post a permanent guard there. Milore Ienth has taken on alchemy as a hobby and has recently converted the area in front of their home into a makeshift apothecary shop.

The grounds of the farm are filled with ash yam and scathecraw, and there are dozens more to steal at the stall in front of their home. There is also an Alchemy Lab where Milore trades (you can complete a Regional Activity for her). Inside the house are dozens more ash yams, a cooking pot, and a note to Milore from Nilara. Downstairs is where more ash yams are kept, along with an Alchemy Lab and various ingredients. Through the door is a bedroom with a few books and a chest.

- Crafting: Alchemy Lab (2), cooking pot
- Chest
- Note: To Milore from Nilara
- Trader (Apothecary): Milore Ienth [DB2/16]
- Trader (Food Vendor): Garyn Ienth [DB8/16]
- Trainer (Alchemy: Expert): Milore Ienth [DB1/1]

⑫ Alor House

Fethis Alor

Fethis owns this house and runs his general goods business from it. He's gained the reputation of being the town curmudgeon, but his presence is tolerated and his shop frequented due to the supply of decent goods he brings into Raven Rock through his old East Empire Company contacts. Fethis is quite proud of his connections within the company and constantly brings it up in conversation. He considers them an "ally" that would protect him if he ever needed it and uses this as leverage whenever a disagreement arises between himself and one of his customers.

Dreyla Alor

Dreyla is the daughter of Fethis and works at her father's shop doing mostly housekeeping and menial chores. Dreyla's mother recently died during an Ash Spawn attack on Raven Rock, so she's taken it upon herself to handle her mother's duties. She loves her father dearly but doesn't share his views of the East Empire Company.

This is a general goods shop that sells all sorts of supplies. It's seen its share of hard times, which is evidenced by the reduced inventory available. The owners do their best to maintain the shop, convinced that Raven Rock isn't finished yet. Outside the house is a tanning rack, a wood chopping block, and usually Fethis Alor, who offers an island-spanning Regional Activity: The Great Solstheim Strongbox Hunt*.

Enter the house to discover a cooking pot and a note: Dearest Dinya, as well as an assortment of books and a large number of barrels and crates. Downstairs is a second tanning rack, a grindstone, a workbench, and some iron ingots. The southwest bedroom has assorted apples and books and a chest. Remember to check the southeast bedroom of the cellar for a purse, chest, copy of Hallgerd's Tale (Heavy Armor Skill Book) on the bedside table, and an East Empire Strongbox [Expert] on the larger table.

- Chest (2)
- Crafting: Cooking pot, grindstone, tanning rack (2), wood chopping block, workbench
- Trader (General Goods): Fethis Alor [DB9/16]
- Skill Book: Hallgerd's Tale (Heavy Armor)
- East Empire Strongbox [Expert] [DB21/33]

⑬ The Retching Netch

Geldis Sadri

Geldis is one of the longest inhabitants of Raven Rock, arriving at the small town just after the mass exodus from Vvardenfell. Originally a miner in the ebony mines, Geldis earned a respectable amount of money and was able to amass a small fortune for himself. When the East Empire Company abandoned the town and as the population slowly changed from Imperial to Dunmer, he purchased the town's only inn. Lleril Morvayn provided some of his own funds to augment the inn to their liking.

Drovas Relvi

Drovas is friendly but a bit scatterbrained. He tends to be a bit naive and has made a couple of foolish decisions in his life. One of them was borrowing money from Mogrul. Drovas is apprenticing under Geldis Sadri, which basically means he's doing all of the jobs around the place that Geldis doesn't want to do. He does his job passably but has bigger aspirations. For the moment, he desperately wishes to flee Raven Rock before the orc that's after him demands pieces of flesh, rather than bags of coin.

Teldryn Sero

A Dunmeri Spellsword with a brash and boastful demeanor, Teldryn is resting up at The Retching Netch after his previous backer ordered an attack on a particularly large and well-defended lair of bandits. He is outfitted with light Chitin Armor, which he normally refuses to remove, and is skilled in both sword and magic. He spent his youth in Blacklight (in Morrowind) and professes to have met Saint Jiub (prior to the latter's disappearance) before plying his talents in Windhelm.

Mogrul

Slitter

Mogrul is a two-septim thug who usually runs a small-time gambling operation. But currently he's in Raven Rock with his murmuring associate Slitter to settle an outstanding debt. Mogrul is a heartless bastard. People who don't pay up tend to get hurt. If a debtor dies or flees the island, he has no compunctions about going after their relatives or friends to collect. He even has access to thugs and bandits to do some of the dirty work.

In recent years, The Retching Netch Cornerclub has served as Raven Rock's main watering hole. The meager common room can barely accommodate the small population of the town, but nevertheless, at night, the inn is filled with a good deal of the town's residents as they contemplate their bleak futures. A single room for rent is available here but hasn't been used in quite a long time. A Redoran Guard stands outside, in case of trouble.

Inside is a hearth (close to where Teldryn Sero usually sits) and cooking pot, and stairs lead down to the large cellar cornerclub itself, where Geldis is propped up behind the bar (guarding an East Empire Strongbox [Expert]). To the southwest and west are bedrooms, the larger of which has two chests and a large amount of cheese to steal. To the north is another bedroom (usually your room if you spend the night) with a chest and a copy of Deathbrand to read. The locked room [Apprentice] leads to another room with a chest.

- Book: Deathbrand
- Crafting: Cooking pot
- Chest (4)
- East Empire Strongbox [Expert] [DB22/33]
- East Empire Pendant
- Follower: Teldryn Sero [DB3/7]
- Trader (Innkeeper): Geldis Sadri [DB13/16]
- Food, room, and board
- Quest rumors

⑭ Abandoned Building

Bralsa Drel

Bralsa is a sujamma addict. She began drinking the potent beverage when she was in her teens and still imbibes the liquor today. She worked the mines for years before they were shut down, and then turned to the sujamma to drown her sorrows. Bralsa performs odd jobs around town occasionally (when she can remember), but instead of saving her coin or using it to clothe or feed herself, she plunks the money on the bar at the cornerclub and drinks it all away. Geldis Sadri usually cuts her off when he thinks she's had enough, and oftentimes she can be found sleeping on a bedroll in the back room of the tavern. On the rare occasions she is encountered sober, she's quite a bitter woman, lamenting about being stuck in Raven Rock and musing that she'd have been better off dying in the eruption like so many others.

Rirns Llervu

If every town has an odd man out, Rirns would be Raven Rock's. Arriving as a stowaway on the *Northern Maiden* a few decades ago, the Redoran Guard had to remove him from his hiding spot in a crate of supplies. He was shivering uncontrollably and talking in nonsensical whispers about "fish men" that walk the bottom of the sea. When pressed about this, he was unable to give a coherent answer. A few folks in Raven Rock have tried to give Rirns a chance at odd jobs, but he can barely form a sentence, let alone perform menial tasks.

You can find one run-down and two collapsed buildings on the outskirts of town. These are the remnants of homes and businesses that were left when the people and prosperity abandoned Raven Rock. The relatively intact home is occupied by some of the destitute members of the colony. One of them (Bralsa Drel) has a Regional Activity you can help her with (see page 668). A few tattered books and Nord mead bottles are the only items among the cobwebs in here.

15 Severin Manor (House to Own)

Vendil Severin **Tilisu Severin** **Mirri Severin**

The Severin family are an enigma to Raven Rock. Arriving in the small town only ten years ago, they brought large amounts of wealth with them and built their own manor house. No one in town is certain how the family attained their wealth, but since they've contributed so much of it to the town, most don't care. Lleril Morvayn has always been a bit wary of new faces in Raven Rock (because House Hlaalu has a price on his head), but after getting to know the family, his suspicions were averted. A few in town have noticed how oddly close in age Mirri Severin is to her father but haven't paid it much mind.

In actuality, all three Severin are not who they appear to be (his real name is Ulen, descendant of Vilur Ulen from House Hlaalu). They are aligned with House Hlaalu, specifically hired to kill Lleril Morvayn to avenge the death of Vilur Ulen. The Severin name had been created as a cover for the trio, whose sole purpose is to lay the groundwork for their plan. Knowing that the enterprise would be quite difficult, the trio has hired a small cadre of Morag Tong in a ruined fort not far from Raven Rock. When the time is right, they feel they'll be able to strike, taking out the Redoran Guard and Lleril at the same time.

This house becomes yours after the successful completion of Solstheim Side Quest: Served Cold. It cannot be furnished, but it does come with a full complement of helpful clutter to adorn your weapons, equipment, clothing, and other items. Enter the place to view the hearth, then head downstairs. To the southeast is a large bedroom with a chest and ash yam–growing area. To the northeast is a blacksmith's smelter, forge, and training area with a number of ingots and other crafting areas. To the east is an Alchemy Lab alcove and many ingredients. To the west is an Arcane Enchanter alcove and weapon drop plaques. To the west is the main bedroom with three chests, display cases, and a variety of pleasantly positioned skulls. Hidden near a bookcase is the Severin Family Safe [Expert], which you can unlock with a key Mirri carries. It contains an interesting note inside.

- ◊ Crafting: Cooking pot, Alchemy Lab, Arcane Enchanter, blacksmith forge, grindstone, smelter, tanning rack, workbench
- ◊ Chest (4)
- ◊ Potions
- ◊ Severin Safe Key
- ◊ Severin Family Safe
- ◊ The Ulen Matter

16 Raven Rock Mine

- ◊ Underground Connection

Gratian Caerellius (Deceased)

Millius (Deceased)

Evul Seloth*

Meden Maren*

Naris Mavani *

Tolenos Omoren *

> **NOTE** * These four miners return to Raven Rock Mine once you complete Solstheim Side Quest: The Final Descent.

Exterior

Raven Rock Mine, once one of the most abundant sources of ebony in Morrowind, was shut down in 4E 170. This led to a mass exodus from the town, cutting the population in half. Follow the path up behind Alor House, passing a wood chopping block, smelter, and various old East Empire crates. Then enter the mine.

- ◊ Crafting: Smelter, wood chopping block

Interior

A Door to Solstheim

1 Mine Entrance

In the gloom, you'll find Crescius Caerellius and his wife, Aphia Velothi, bickering about his precarious ventures deep in the mine. To progress farther into this mine, it's wise to speak to Crescius for his key and begin Solstheim Side Quest: The Final Descent. A quick check of the area finds a grindstone, pickaxes, and an East Empire Strongbox [Expert] under the balcony table upstairs. When you're ready for a descent, step onto the wooden floor and peer down the steps. They are hooked by chains to a gigantic mine shaft with an almost bottomless drop. Nimbly descend onto the wooden platform to the west.

- ◊ Crafting: Grindstone
- ◊ Pickaxe (3)
- ◊ East Empire Strongbox [Expert] [DB23/33]
- ◊ East Empire Pendant
- ◊ Raven Rock Mine Key
- ◊ Ebony Ore (9)

> **TIP** Once you complete the Solstheim Side Quest: The Final Descent, four miners (listed previously) return to the mine, and a total of nine Ebony Ore veins become accessible.

2 Floating Balconies and the Pit

B Planks

Follow the precarious floating balconies down to the opening in the south wall of this epic hole, watching for Skeever here before continuing past a Frostbite Spider and another alcove to the east, with a spider and some rickety platforms. Back in the central pit, continue north to a third alcove leading down a stepped tunnel to the west, then the south and east, with more spiders, escaping gas, planks, and a web to cut as you burst through into a locked gate next to an East Empire Strongbox. Open the gate using the key you received from Crescius.

- ◊ Danger! Explosive gas trap
- ◊ Pickaxe (3)
- ◊ Skeever
- ◊ Frostbite Spider
- ◊ East Empire Strongbox [Expert] [DB24/33]

> **TIP** You may wish to test your acrobatics and drop from ledge to ledge while descending.

3 Waterlogged Draugr Crypt

Cross into a roughly mined area, which breaks through into a Draugr tomb that is ankle-deep in water. There's movement here, as Draugr rise from their walled resting places to delay you. Fight four or five as you work your way through the crypt. Check the left area for a chest before heading east and avoiding the floor plate and swinging wall trap.

- ◊ Chest
- ◊ Draugr
- ◊ Danger! Swinging wall trap

④ The Dead Slumbering on Their Thrones

Head up the steps and around to the west. Here, four thrones are occupied by two slumbering dead (one on each side, with potions between them), who awaken to attack, along with a third foe farther along the hall and a locked chest [Master]. Be sure to defeat these enemies, as the circular chamber ahead features at least six Draugr of varying degrees of toughness.

- ◊ Chest [Master]
- ◊ Potions
- ◊ Draugr

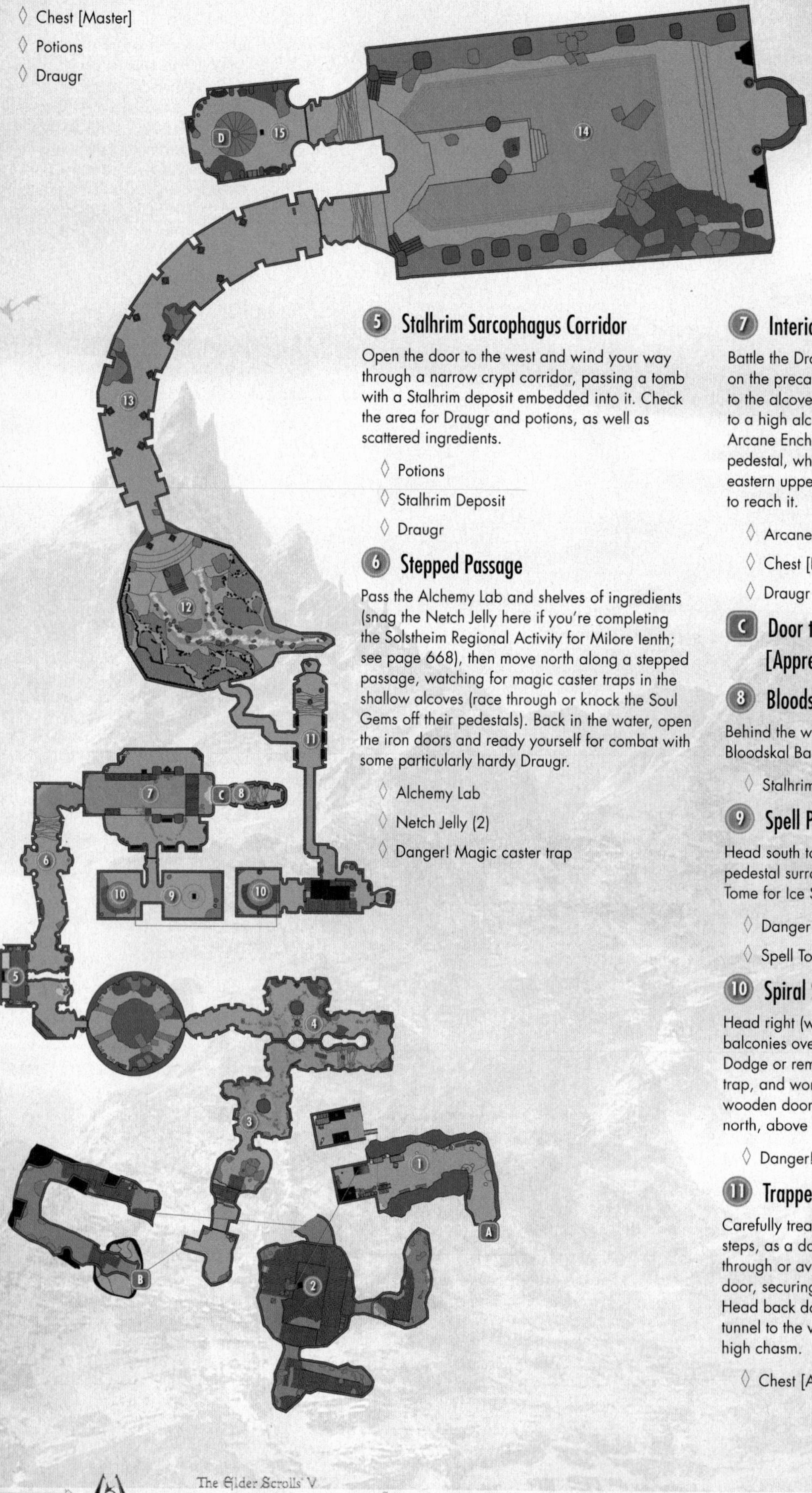

Raven Rock Mine and Bloodskal Barrow

⑤ Stalhrim Sarcophagus Corridor

Open the door to the west and wind your way through a narrow crypt corridor, passing a tomb with a Stalhrim deposit embedded into it. Check the area for Draugr and potions, as well as scattered ingredients.

- ◊ Potions
- ◊ Stalhrim Deposit
- ◊ Draugr

⑥ Stepped Passage

Pass the Alchemy Lab and shelves of ingredients (snag the Netch Jelly here if you're completing the Solstheim Regional Activity for Milore Ienth; see page 668), then move north along a stepped passage, watching for magic caster traps in the shallow alcoves (race through or knock the Soul Gems off their pedestals). Back in the water, open the iron doors and ready yourself for combat with some particularly hardy Draugr.

- ◊ Alchemy Lab
- ◊ Netch Jelly (2)
- ◊ Danger! Magic caster trap

⑦ Interior Canal

Battle the Draugr around this interior canal and on the precarious wooden bridge. Climb up to the alcoves and cross the wooden bridge to a high alcove with a chest [Expert] and an Arcane Enchanter. Yank the handle on the nearby pedestal, which opens a door on the chamber's eastern upper side. Move back across the bridge to reach it.

- ◊ Arcane Enchanter
- ◊ Chest [Expert]
- ◊ Draugr

Ⓒ Door to Bloodskal Barrow Alcove [Apprentice]

⑧ Bloodskal Barrow Alcove

Behind the waterfall is a door that leads to Bloodskal Barrow Alcove and the following:

- ◊ Stalhrim Deposit

⑨ Spell Pedestal

Head south to a corridor junction. Left (east) is a pedestal surrounded by candles, where a Spell Tome for Ice Spike is located.

- ◊ Danger! Magic caster trap
- ◊ Spell Tome: Ice Spike

⑩ Spiral Steps to Cage Bridge

Head right (west), up the spiral steps to the balconies overlooking the Spell Tome pedestal. Dodge or remove the Soul Gem from the lightning trap, and work your way around to an open wooden door and a narrow cage bridge to the north, above the interior canal.

- ◊ Danger! Magic caster trap

⑪ Trapped Alcove and Low Tunnel

Carefully tread on the ground near the torch and steps, as a dart trap is easily activated. Rush through or avoid it before opening the wooden door, securing goods from a locked chest [Adept]. Head back down the steps and check the low tunnel to the west. This brings you out onto a high chasm.

- ◊ Chest [Adept]

12 High Chasm and Runic Door of Bloodskal

Two cave streams and numerous interlocking basalt columns offer a tremendous view of a strange and dimly lit wall of odd carvings. Carefully descend to the ground and inspect the old bones of Gratian Caerellius, near the runic door. Gratian's Journal is on the corpse, along with a strange and wondrous blade. Grab both, check downstream for an alcove with a chest, then inspect the runic door.

- Gratian's Journal
- Unique Weapon: Bloodskal Blade [DB4/11]
- Chest

Puzzle Solution: The Bloodskal Blade is your key. Equip this two-handed weapon, stand so you're targeting the red slit in the outer arch, and make a horizontal power attack with the blade (sidestep, hold down your Attack button, release). If you're successful, you'll hear stone grinding and part of the arch will move up. A vertical glow appears.

Make a vertical power attack (hold down your Attack button, release), and be sure the ribbon of red hits close to the glow in the arch. A section indents, clicks, and the outer piece slides farther toward the apex of the arch. This time a horizontal glowing slit is formed. Execute a horizontal power attack, and the entire left side of the outer arch slots into place.

Now move to view the right side of the outer arch. Perform exactly the same power attacks, and watch the sections of archway maneuver into new and unlocked positions. Assuming you've correctly slashed, the entire arch glows red, and a massive vertical slit appears through the circular door. Launch a final, vertical power attack from the Bloodskal Blade and the door opens.

13 Nord Curved Hall of Traps

Head through the long Nord hall, deftly avoiding the swinging blade traps. Activate the lever at the far end to open the heavy gate, allowing access into the lair of Zahkriisos, one of Miraak's Acolyte Priests.

- Danger! Swinging blade trap

14 Lair of Zahkriisos

The powerful Acolyte Priest Zahkriisos confronts you in this chamber. This fiend can summon Seekers and strike you with a powerful blast of lightning. Swap to your preferred weapons and engage this troublesome foe. If you're currently completing Solstheim Side Quest: Masks of the Acolyte Priests* (see page 662), this is one of the masks you're looking for. Grab it from the ash pile you've reduced Zahkriisos to, and learn a Word of the Dragon Aspect Shout.

> **NOTE** Note that you are not locked into this room—if you find Zahkriisos too much of a challenge, you can flee and still claim the Black Book in the next room.

- Chest
- Seeker
- Zahkriisos
- Unique Item: Zahkriisos [DB19/31]
- Word Wall: Dragon Aspect [DB2/3]

15 Black Book: The Winds of Change

Move west, through the arch to a pedestal at the bottom of a spiral set of steps and small waterfall. Check the alcoves for a chest and Arcane Enchanter. On this plinth is a legendary Black Book.

- Arcane Enchanter
- Chest
- Black Book: The Winds of Change

D Door to Bloodskal Barrow

Ascend the spiral steps to the door and enter Bloodskal Barrow. Move along the rough tunnel to the handle, which reveals a secret rock door. Enter the subsequent Draugr tomb and engage a motley collection of Reavers, one singing a witty tune. This area is mapped and described in the Primary Location: Bloodskal Barrow (page 1047).

- Reaver

> **NOTE** Note that the tunnel from Raven Rock Mine into the Draugr tomb is accessible only from the mine. There is no pull chain on the Barrow side.

TEL MITHRYN

Related Quests

- Dragonborn Main Quest: The Path of Knowledge
- Solstheim Side Quest: Azra's Staffs
- Solstheim Side Quest: Black Book: The Hidden Twilight
- Solstheim Side Quest: Briarheart Necropsy
- Solstheim Side Quest: Experimental Subject
- Solstheim Side Quest: From the Ashes
- Solstheim Side Quest: Healing a House
- Solstheim Side Quest: Heart Stones
- Solstheim Side Quest: Lost Knowledge
- Solstheim Side Quest: Old Friends
- Solstheim Side Quest: Reluctant Steward
- Solstheim Side Quest: A New Debt
- Solstheim Side Quest: Telvanni Research
- Solstheim Side Quest: Wind and Sand
- Solstheim Regional Activity (Tel Mithryn): Eyes and Ears*
- Solstheim Regional Activity (Tel Mithryn): Elynea's Ingredients*

Habitation: Telvanni Tower

Services

- Follower: Talvas Fathryon [DB4/7]
- Trainer (Conjuration: Master): Talvas Fathryon [DB1/1]
- Trainer (Enchanting: Master): Neloth [DB1/1]
- Trader (Apothecary): Elynea Mothren [DB3/16]
- Trader (Spell Vendor): Neloth [DB15/16]
- Trader (Spell Vendor): Talvas Fathryon [DB16/16]

Special Area

- Black Book: The Hidden Twilight

Crafting

- Arcane Enchanter
- Cooking Pot
- Cooking Spit
- Staff Enchanter

Collectibles

- Unique Item: Neloth's Ring of Tracking [DB18/31]

Miscellaneous

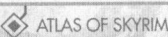

- Area is locked
- Chest
- Potions aplenty
- Loose gear
- Lots o' gold

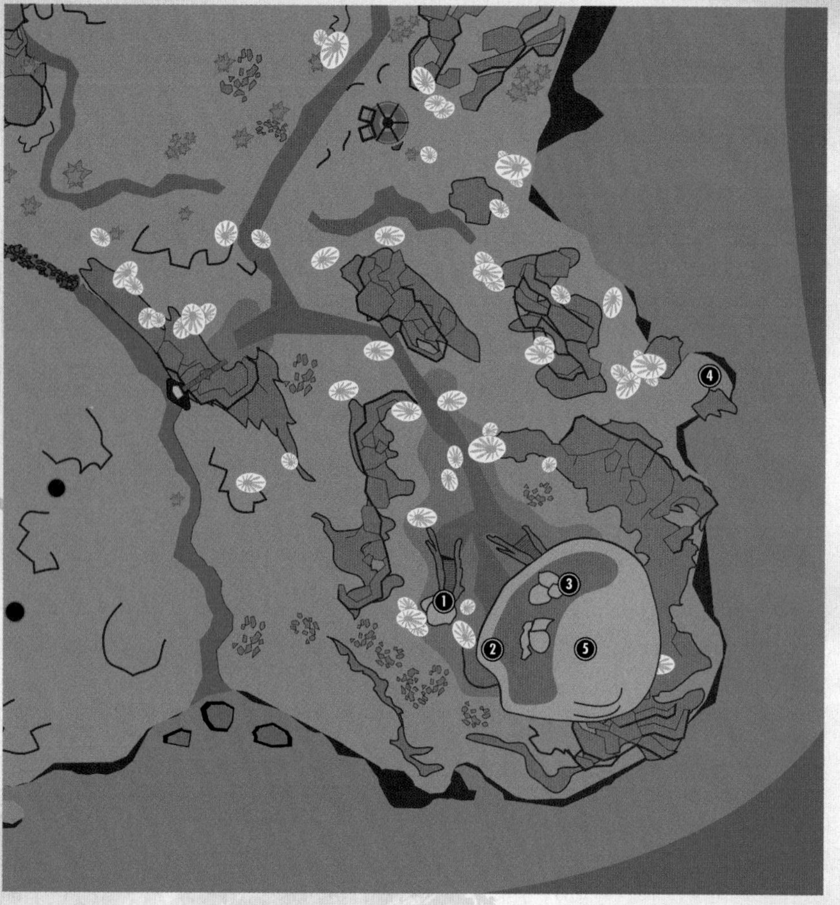

Lore: Settlement Overview

Tel Mithryn is a Telvanni Tower along the southern coast of the island, east of the ruined Fort Frostmoth. It has a classic mushroom shape, with a disk-shaped top floor and a stalk holding it up off the ground. Currently, a section of it appears to be withered and dying. At the base of the stalk are bulbous growths that form ground-floor dwellings. The master of Tel Mithryn is Neloth, a Telvanni wizard who survived the Red Year of Vvardenfell. Neloth has been experimenting with the ash and other debris from the eruption of Red Mountain, such as Heart Stones. He has multiple goals, but all of them involve returning to Vvardenfell and becoming Archmagister, although sometimes it just looks like accumulating power for power's sake.

> **NOTE** Some of Tel Mithryn's residents are currently enslaved and helping to build a strange arched shrine around the Sun Stone to the north of town. Free these folks and they head back to the locations listed below. Consult Dragonborn Main Quest: Cleansing the Stones for more information.

Important Areas of Interest

1 Tel Mithryn Kitchen

Ulves Romoran

Ulves Romoran is Tel Mithryn's cook and gardener. He is a surly, gruff man, who talks only a little and works very hard. It's not that he doesn't like you: he doesn't like anybody.

The preparation of Neloth's food is undertaken here. Most of the items here are owned and must be stolen if you want them.

- Crafting: Cooking pot, cooking spit
- Chest

2 Tel Mithryn Steward's House

Varona Nelas

Varona is the steward of Tel Mithryn. Haggard and giving the constant appearance of being overburdened, in truth there isn't much to be done as Neloth's steward, so most of it is an act to cover her inherent laziness. Elynea takes care of the tower and Uvyn prepares the meals, so Varona's biggest job is to procure supplies for the others. However, she makes this seem like a job that really requires ten people.

> **NOTE** You'll find the mildly incompetent Drovas Relvi here, once Solstheim Side Quest: Reluctant Steward is complete.

The Steward's House has several books and a chest to steal from. If Varona (or Drovas) isn't here, the place is locked [Novice].

- Book: Deathbrand
- Chest

3 Tel Mithryn Apothecary

Elynea Mothren

Elynea is the primary caretaker of the Tel Mithryn tower. She mostly ignores Neloth and Talvas. She would much rather just prune and water her fungi and concoct her potions and not have to deal with people. She has her own mushroom and toadstool patches and a potion-making table. A small bed sits off to one side.

- Crafting: Alchemy Lab
- Potions aplenty
- Trader (Apothecary): Elynea Mothren [DB3/16]

4 Tel Mithryn Graveyard

A small, informal cemetery overlooking the Sea of Ghosts. One of the graves is marked with the name "Ildari." Each sarcophagus can be robbed, for a few coins. Ildari's usually has a staff in it.

- Ash Spawn

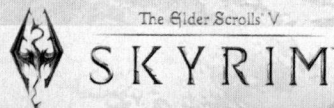

⑤ Tel Mithryn Tower

Neloth

Master Neloth is a Telvanni wizard and seems to have difficultly with the concept that other people matter. He judges their health and well-being solely based on his personal comfort and needs. That said, he is no fool. He recognizes power and that power in others must be respected. At this point in his life, he has given up kidnapping women. He claims it's because there are no suitable females in Solstheim, but the true reason is that it no longer interests him. Once you've kidnapped someone, you have to put up with their whining and complaining: it just isn't worth it.

Talvas Fathryon

Neloth's current apprentice, Talvas, is harried and somewhat put upon. At his core, he's really too pleasant a person to be in Tel Mithryn. When first encountered, he is attempting to summon an Ash Guardian, with what could only be described as "limited" success.

Neloth's home is the source of many quests. This towering mushroom structure, although partially withered, is still an impressive (and living) building. Ride up to the central chamber via a floating lift (use the lift, especially on the way down, to avoid an embarrassing death). Consult with Neloth (and Talvas, who moves in here after your initial outside encounter) whenever you want a new task.

Main Chamber: There's a large number of potions, scattered items (some dwarven in nature), maps of both Skyrim and Soltheim, and books to check. Stealing isn't encouraged, unless you wish to feel Neloth's wrath.

Talvas's Bedroom (north): A few cobwebs and little else.

Storage Room (east): Little more than crates and a few sacks.

Specimen Room (west): The blight that afflicts Tel Mithryn is most easily seen here; a diseased growth chokes off the western side of the main chamber. After completing Solstheim Side Quest: Healing a House, the blight is removed, and Neloth puts his new room to good use, capturing two Spriggans to assist him in his research.

Staff Enchanter Room (south): This chamber is firmly locked and can only be opened with the Staff Enchanter Key, your reward for completing Solstheim Side Quest: Reluctant Steward. Inside is an Arcane Enchanter, potions, a Black Book, and a method of easily crafting exceptionally potent staffs (see page 75).

- ◊ Crafting: Arcane Enchanter (3), Staff Enchanter
- ◊ Potions aplenty
- ◊ Chest (2)
- ◊ Black Book: The Hidden Twilight
- ◊ Book: Ahzidal's Descent
- ◊ Book: Deathbrand
- ◊ Staff Enchanter Key
- ◊ Follower: Talvas Fathryon [DB4/7]
- ◊ Trainer (Conjuration: Master): Talvas Fathryon [DB1/1]
- ◊ Trainer (Enchanting: Master): Neloth [DB1/1]
- ◊ Trader (Spell Vendor): Neloth [DB15/16]
- ◊ Trader (Spell Vendor): Talvas Fathryon [DB16/16]
- ◊ Unique Item: Neloth's Ring of Tracking [DB18/31]

TIP Talvas is a great asset to have as a Follower. Talvas also offers spells for sale that aren't available anywhere else. See page 131 for a complete list.

PRIMARY LOCATIONS

[S.S01] Earth Stone

Related Quests

Dragonborn Main Quest: Dragonborn
Dragonborn Main Quest: Cleansing the Stones

Recommended Level: 25

Habitation: All-Maker Stone

Bralsa Drel
Cindiri Arano
Dreyla Alor
Fethis Alor
Glover Mallory
Lurker
Milore Ienth
Redoran Guard
Rims Llervu

Special Area

Standing Stones

Miscellaneous

Area is Locked

This is one of the All-Maker Stones, nestled just outside and southwest of Raven Rock. You may meet the Dunmeri mage Neloth here in the initial stages of the Dragonborn Main Quest, before he moves to Tel Mithryn. Currently, the stone's power is being siphoned by Miraak, and stone arches are constructed by enthralled town citizens and Redoran Guards. At various times, Bralsa Drel, Cindiri Arano, Dreyla Alor, Fethis Alor, Glover Mallory, Milore Ienth, and Rims Llervu work here, and their quests aren't accessible until the stone is cleansed. The Bend Will Shout is required to remove the trance the population is under and to cleanse the stone of Miraak's influence. When this happens, expect a Lurker to appear, along with a second Lurker down by the water's edge.

- ◊ Pickaxe
- ◊ Power: Bones of the Earth

[S.S02] Bloodskal Barrow

Related Quests

Solstheim Side Quest: The Final Descent

Recommended Level: 10

Habitation: Reaver Camp

Reaver

Crafting

Alchemy Lab (2)
Cooking Pot (2)
Tanning Rack (3)
Wood Chopping Block

Miscellaneous

Area is locked
Chest
Potions
Loose gear

Underground Connection

Exterior

At the foot of the sharp, rocky slopes north of Raven Rock is the entrance to a Draugr tomb, now controlled by Reavers. There are two towers on the beach, one connected by an ancient stone bridge to the barrow interior.

Northern Tower

Expect around six Reavers as you investigate the ruins, heading for the lit torch at the base of the northern tower. This leads up to a second-floor stone bridge to the next tower and a wooden ramp up to sleeping quarters.

Southern Tower

Cross the stone bridge to reach a bed, chest, and steps up to a table with potions and an exit ramp that leads to the main stone bridge leading into Bloodskal Barrow. Or, continue into the tower, checking a living area with a cooking pot and a few bits of Chitin armor. Climb the stairs up to the roof. Here, you can find an Alchemy Lab, three tanning racks, and some books. Up more steps is a rickety wooden platform back to the otherwise inaccessible roof chamber of the Northern Tower.

- ◊ Crafting: Alchemy Lab, Cooking Pot, Tanning Rack (3)
- ◊ Chest
- ◊ Potions

Northern Tower (Return)

Drop down and check the bed, chest [Adept], and scrawled note on the table.

- Chest [Adept]
- Scrawled Note

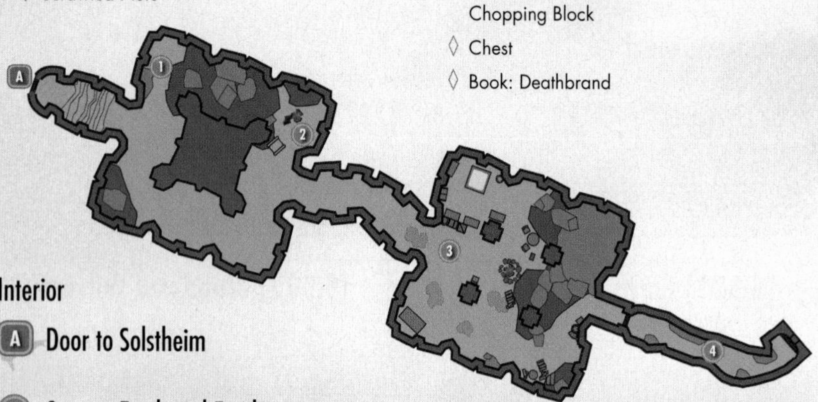

Interior

A Door to Solstheim

1 Corpses Fresh and Fetid

The initial part of this Draugr crypt, now overrun by three or four Reavers, has a couple of strewn corpses with common clothing on their backs.

- Reaver

2 Corpse Fire

The Reavers have been burning the dead.

3 Reaver Camp

Expect the majority of the combat to occur here. Check the area for a bed, assorted books and food, coin purses, and the following:

- Crafting: Alchemy Lab, Cooking Pot, Wood Chopping Block
- Chest
- Book: Deathbrand

4 Secret Tunnel (from Raven Rock Mine)

The barrow ends at a rock wall that looks like it may move. It is activated via a pull chain on the opposite side: This is actually the exit from Raven Rock Mine (see page 1043). You must complete Solstheim Side Quest: The Final Descent to fully explore this area

[S.S03] Old Attius Farm

Related Quests

Solstheim Side Quest: March of the Dead

Recommended Level: 20

Habitation: Farm

Ash Spawn
Captain Veleth

The first time you come across this decrepit structure by the Sea of Ghosts, Captain Veleth is valiantly fighting off three Ash Spawn, as Solstheim Side Quest: March of the Dead begins. Nearby is a slain Redoran Guard, who has some Bonemold Armor you can take if you wish.

- Bonemold Armor

[S.S04] Kolbjorn Barrow

Related Quests

Solstheim Side Quest: Black Book: Filament and Filigree
Solstheim Side Quest: Unearthed

Recommended Level: 50

Dungeon: Draugr Crypt

Ahzidal
Albino Spider
Draugr
Miner
Poison Spider
Ralis Sedarys

Special Area

Black Book: Filament and Filigree
Word Wall: Cyclone [DB3/3]

Crafting

Cooking Spit

Dangers

Battering Ram Trap
Magic Caster Trap
Rockfall Trap
Swinging Blade Trap

Puzzle

Nordic Puzzle Pillars
Rotating Walls

Services

Follower: Ralis Sedarys [DB5/7]

Collectibles

Unique Item: Ahzidal (Mask) [DB21/31]
Unique Item: Ahzidal's Armor of Retribution [DB22/31]
Unique Item: Ahzidal's Boots of Waterwalking [DB23/31]
Unique Item: Ahzidal's Gauntlets of Warding [DB24/31]
Unique Item: Ahzidal's Helm of Vision [DB25/31]
Unique Item: Ahzidal's Ring of Arcana [DB26/31]
Unique Item: Ahzidal's Ring of Necromancy [DB27/31]
Unique Item: Skull (Runic) [DB28/31]
Unique Weapon: Hoarfrost [DB5/11]

Miscellaneous

Area is locked
Chest
Potions
Loose gear

Exterior

> **NOTE** This location reveals its secrets over the course of several visits as you fund Ralis Sedarys's excavation. There are four phases, each allowing deeper progress into the barrow. The phase you must reach to access chambers is flagged below.

This location constantly changes throughout Solstheim Side Quest: Unearthed. The first time you arrive, a Dunmer named Ralis Sedarys is digging at a half-buried barrow entrance. The Journal of Ralis Sedarys, volume 19, is near a hay pile.

Phase 1: There are a few miner tents and Ralis is on-site, moaning about Draugr.

Phase 2: There is a cooking spit, two more tents, and Ralis lamenting the constant Draugr threat.

Phase 3: There are more tents, at least one living miner, and Ralis in one of his moods again.

Phase 4: The camp is more like a small settlement now, with numerous tents and several murdered miners. Optionally make a point to enter Ralis's tent, and read some of his journals. Volume 23 is most illuminating.

- Crafting: Cooking Spit
- Chest
- Kolbjorn Guard
- Miner
- Ralis Sedarys
- The Journal of Ralis Sedarys, volumes 19–23

Interior

Ⓐ Door to Solstheim

Accessible from Phase 1 onward.

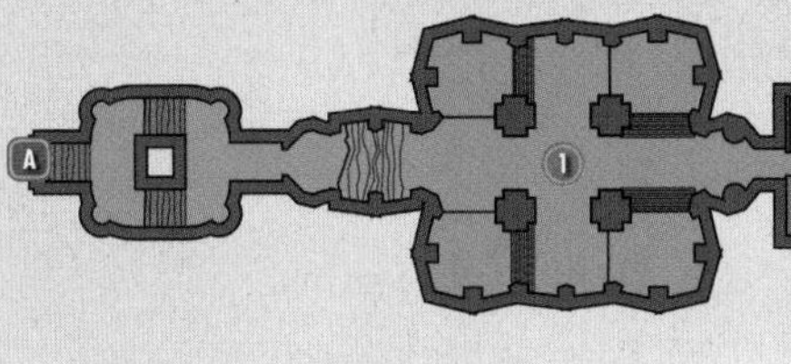

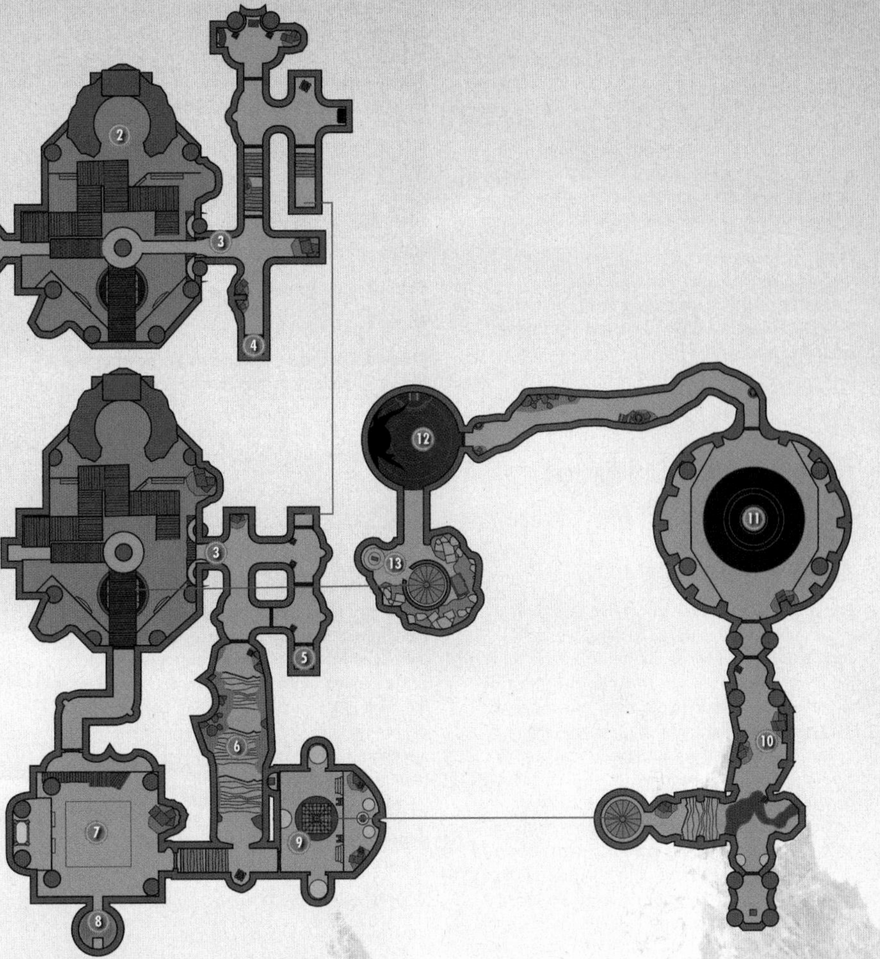

① Entryway and Initial Burial Chamber

Phase 1: Expect at least six Draugr to contend with, both in the entryway and from the four raised corners of the burial chamber. Locate the main altar in the center of the burial chamber, and study the red skull. Lift it from its pressure plate, and a rotating wall arch ahead of you grinds open.

Phase 2: In the entryway, take the first right to claim a chest at the dead end. Expect another Draugr ambush as you enter the burial chamber, including archers firing down at you from the four raised corners of the chamber.

Phase 3: Be prepared for two Draugr to rush you just inside the entrance. A third, more powerful foe awaits you in the chamber below.

Phase 4: Unchanged.

- Chest (3) [1 = Novice, 1 = Adept]
- Loose gear
- Draugr
- Unique Item: Skull (Runic) [DB28/31]

② Central Chamber

Phase 1: This chamber has almost completely collapsed and is filled with ash and rubble. However, a set of unique boots awaits you on the pedestal in the center of the room.

Phase 2: It looks like Ralis and the miners have made some progress here. A tough Draugr archer attacks from the circular platform in the center; strike with ranged spells or attacks to take him down quickly.

Phase 3: By now, most of the room has been excavated, although the Word Wall is still inaccessible (you can hear it but not reach it). Another Draugr awaits you on the central bridges.

Phase 4: Descend and approach the Word Wall, learning the Word of Power before continuing and optionally taking the short route back to the sacrificial chamber (Location [7]).

- Draugr
- Unique Item: Ahzidal's Boots of Waterwalking [DB23/31]
- Word Wall: Cyclone [DB3/3]

③, ④, and ⑤ Draugr Crypt

Phase 1: Inaccessible.

Phase 2: You must search these crypts for the corpses of two dead miners, Bradyn and Mireli. Bradyn is found on the lower floor to your left (west). He's quite dead. Kill three Draugr and then venture farther (northwest) into the crypt, yanking the pull chain on the candlelit alcove ahead of you. This opens a rotating door to your right (east), exposing a tough Draugr to tackle. Pull a second chain in this new chamber's alcove, which opens a rotating door to the southwest, behind you. This leads to the upper crypt and another Draugr to tackle. Optionally, step on the tripwire to trigger the battering ram trap (which often kills the Draugr), or slay it yourself. Avoid the pressure plate that sets off the magic caster trap, pluck the Soul Gem from the pedestal, then move to the portcullis puzzle with four handles to the right of it.

Puzzle Solution: The top handle releases only the first portcullis. The second releases darts, so ignore it. The third and fourth handles release the remaining portcullises, so pull them and continue up.

As you enter the upper crypt, the portcullis slam shut, trapping you in a small crypt with four Draugr. Deal with them, then examine the splattered remains of Mireli. Take the letter to her mother if you wish. Locate the seeming dead end to the northeast (Location [4]), hunting for a low handle to your right, which slides open a secret alcove allowing you to pick up Ahzidal's Ring of Necromancy!

Phase 3: Bring death to the Draugr inside this now fully excavated crypt. Head to the middle level where a sarcophagus has been uncovered (a Draugr bashes its way out to meet your blades), and an iron door [Expert] has been unsealed. Pick this lock to reach a hidden antechamber with spiders to crush and a chest to pilfer. Continue down the stairs (avoiding the traps if you didn't deal with them earlier), then continue back around to the chamber where you found Bradyn on your first visit. A new tunnel has been opened here, leading to a room with an iron door. Instead of continuing through it, kill the dormant Draugr in this room, then locate a wall chain in the alcove nearby. Yank it to expose a hidden room to the northeast (Location [5]) where Ahzidal's Gauntlets can be found. Taking them sets off a dart trap, so step back quickly to avoid being hit. Then head back and continue through the iron door.

Phase 4: Unchanged.

- Draugr
- Albino Spider
- Poison Spider
- Bradyn (Deceased)
- Mireli (Deceased)
- Mireli's Letter to Mother
- Potions
- Emerald Geode
- Chest (2)
- Loose Gear
- Danger! Battering Ram Trap
- Danger! Dart Trap
- Danger! Magic Caster Trap
- Unique Item: Ahzidal's Ring of Necromancy [DB27/31]
- Unique Item: Ahzidal's Gauntlets of Warding [DB24/31]

6 Grand Staircase and Corridor

Phase 1: Inaccessible.

Phase 2: Inaccessible.

Phase 3: Just inside the stairwell, hit the tripwire, then stop, allowing the rockfall trap to remove Draugr threats ahead of you. At the intersection, turn southeast, then continue up the steps and into a large sacrificial chamber.

Phase 4: After passing through the sacrificial chamber, descend the steps back to the intersection, where the other end of the corridor has been unblocked. Continue into the Throne Chamber (Location [9]).

- ◊ Draugr
- ◊ Danger! Rockfall Trap

7, 8 Sacrificial Chamber and Antechamber

Phase 1: Inaccessible.

Phase 2: Inaccessible.

Phase 3: Expect to face about five Draugr in this chamber, with several bursting out of the sarcophagi on the walls. Before you leave, check the room for dead miners and guards, then look to the left (northeast), into a small antechamber with a pedestal (Location [8]), upon which rests a ring. You can use the Telekinesis spell to pull the ring to you, or open the portcullis by running across the central pressure plates so they all activate. You have only a few seconds to do this before they reset, so aim carefully and make sure to sprint. Claim Ahzidal's Ring of Arcana from the pedestal, then optionally swim down into the water for some minor loot. To leave, head up the side steps in the sacrificial room and yank a chain to open the portcullis, watching for a subsequent blade trap and another chain that opens a quicker way back to the central chamber.

Phase 4: On your final visit to Kolbjorn Barrow, cross the Central Chamber's bridge and approach the hallway with the blade traps. A pair of Draugr will charge at you; pull the chain above the door to trigger the trap and cut them down. Then pull it again and proceed into the Sacrificial Chamber, where three more Draugr await you. Deal with them, then continue down the stairs into the corridor (Location [6]).

- ◊ Draugr
- ◊ Danger! Swinging Blade Trap
- ◊ Unique Item: Ahzidal's Ring of Arcana [DB26/31]

9 Throne Chamber

Phase 1: Inaccessible.

Phase 2: Inaccessible.

Phase 3: Inaccessible.

Phase 4: Head down to a throne chamber with three Draugr to slay as they rise from their seats. After that, ponder a small puzzle:

Puzzle Solution I: A suit of armor rests behind a barred arch. Face north and south and pull each chain to rotate the wall so a whale petroglyph is exposed in opposite alcoves. Behind the two thrones are rotating pedestals. Shift both of them to Whale and pull the lever between them. The bars retract, allowing you to grab Ahzidal's Armor.

Puzzle Solution II: Your progress is stalled. To continue, you must open the central trapdoor. In front of it is a carving with two Hawk petroglyphs. Turn the pedestals so they are both Hawks, pull the lever, and the trapdoor opens.

- ◊ Unique Item: Ahzidal's Armor of Retribution [DB22/31]

10 Lower Crypts

Phase 1: Inaccessible.

Phase 2: Inaccessible.

Phase 3: Inaccessible.

Phase 4: Descend the spiral steps, passing the scattered potions on the ceremonial table, then move into the lower crypts. Remove a Draugr to the right of the entrance before setting the floor ahead ablaze (via magic or a falling oil lamp shot by your bow). This helps remove the four Draugr in the main corridor and minimizes the damage from the forthcoming puzzle if you make a mistake. Turn right (north east).

Puzzle Solution: Ahead is a portcullis with a chain and two petroglyph pedestals. If you pull the chain, a fire trap engulfs you. Instead, turn the pedestals so the Serpent petroglyph points at the ground marking on each pedestal. This is the third of the puzzles, and two Serpents is the only remaining pair that hasn't been chosen. Pull the chain and claim Ahzidal's Helm. Watch for another fire trap as you take it!

Pass the sarcophagus with the Stalhrim deposit and move to the door opposite (southwest).

- ◊ Potions
- ◊ Loose gear
- ◊ Stalhrim deposit
- ◊ Unique Item: Ahzidal's Helm of Vision [DB25/31]

11 Ahzidal's Chamber

Phase 1: Inaccessible.

Phase 2: Inaccessible.

Phase 3: Inaccessible.

Phase 4: You enter the chamber just as Ralis finishes his dark ritual and the Dragon Acolyte Priest Ahzidal rises from the seal in the center of the room. Expect a constant stream of Draugr to pour from the wall crypts, with Ahzidal raising them to fight anew as combat progresses. Concentrate your attack on Ahzidal, countering his fire-based attacks and using the columns around the chamber as cover. When the fighting is over, check the ashes for his mask.

- ◊ Draugr
- ◊ Ahzidal
- ◊ Follower: Ralis Sedarys [DB5/7]
- ◊ Unique Item: Ahzidal (Mask) [DB21/31]
- ◊ Unique Weapon: Hoarfrost [DB5/11]

12 Hermaeus Mora's Chamber

Phase 1: Inaccessible.

Phase 2: Inaccessible.

Phase 3: Inaccessible.

Phase 4: Leave Kolbjorn Barrow via the gap in the sarcophagus to the southwest, passing a large chest in the tunnel before reaching a pull chain and allowing access into a strange and terrible chamber. Here you find an effigy of Hermaeus Mora, another huge chest and assorted items, and a fabled Black Book. This begins Solstheim Side Quest: Black Book: Filament and Filigree. Consult page 608 for more information.

- ◊ Chest (2)
- ◊ Loose gear
- ◊ Potions
- ◊ Black Book: Filament and Filigree

13 Rotating Staircase

Phase 1: Inaccessible.

Phase 2: Inaccessible.

Phase 3: Inaccessible.

Phase 4: Exit to the northeast, checking a Stalhrim deposit before activating a lever to summon a rotating staircase up to your level. Ascend, emerging in the central chamber.

- ◊ Stalhrim deposit

[S.S05] Wreck of the *Strident Squall*

Related Quests

Solstheim Regional Activity: Tome Raider*

Recommended Level: 10

Habitation: Reaver Camp

Reaver

Crafting

Cooking Pot

Collectibles

East Empire Strongbox [DB25/33]

Miscellaneous

Chest

Loose Gear

A band of five Reavers has succeeded in reinforcing the ruins of this merchant ship, constructing a walled encampment, with flayed and buried bodies of the previous crew on poles to put off potential invaders. On deck are battlements and the entrance to the wreck proper, with a chest [Adept] and sleeping rolls. Down into the hold, expect shelves with an East Empire Strongbox [Expert], a couple of skeletons, and steps leading underwater. Drowned in the bottom of the hold are an Alchemist, an Argonian, and in the otherwise-sealed area, a Redguard with a scimitar and knapsack. The hold also has a large chest that holds a special folio needed for a Regional Activity.

- ◊ Chest (2) [1 = Adept]
- ◊ Cooking Pot
- ◊ East Empire Strongbox [Expert] [DB25/33]
- ◊ East Empire Pendant
- ◊ Heart Stone
- ◊ The Lusty Argonian Maid Folio Edition

[S.S06] Hrodulf's House

Recommended Level: 20

Habitation: Hunter Camp

Ash Spawn
Reaver

Puzzle

Secret Bookcase Door

Collectibles

East Empire Strongbox [DB26/33]

Miscellaneous

Area is locked
Chest
Potions
Loose gear

Exterior

This hunter's hovel appears to have recently caught fire from the ashen rain that falls from Red Mountain's rumbling eruptions. As you explore this dwelling, expect two Ash Spawn to appear and attack. Find two Heart Stone deposits just east of the structure. By the missing wall where the Ash Spawn enter is an East Empire Strongbox [Expert], and opposite (south) is a chest and trapdoor into Hrodulf's House (cellar). The corpse of the resident, who appears to have been killed by Reavers, is on the shore directly south of here, at Secondary Location [S.SI] Hrodulf's Last Stand.

- Heart Stone (2)
- East Empire Strongbox [Expert] [DB26/33]
- East Empire Pendant

Interior

Two Reavers are chatting about their kills near a letter on the table, which was from Hrodulf's lover Bjornolfr. The cellar hold's Hrodulf's Journal, which hints at a hidden location off this chamber. There are scattered books and a bookshelf to activate, which opens a hidden tunnel to a Dwemer antechamber where Bjornolfr's corpse lies. Search the corpse for a bloodstained letter.

- Letter
- Hrodulf's Journal
- Potions aplenty
- Chest
- Dwarven Metal Ingot (3)
- Bloodstained Letter

[S.S07] Brodir Grove

Recommended Level: 10

Habitation: Bandit Camp (Reaver)

Reaver

Crafting

Cooking Pot
Grindstone

Dangers

Bear Trap

Collectibles

East Empire Strongbox [DB27/33]
Unique Weapon: Stormfang [DB6/11]

Miscellaneous

Chest

A circle of stones (without any magical abilities) stands near the edge of the woods northwest of Highpower Tower, within which is a Reaver camp. Expect three foes, the most troublesome of which is carrying a unique weapon: Stormfang. Watch for a bear trap in front of the large chest, look for various plant ingredients to pick, and claim the following:

- Chest (2)
- Cooking Pot
- East Empire Strongbox [Expert] [DB27/33]
- East Empire Pendant
- Grindstone
- Ore: Heart Stone (3)
- Unique Weapon: Stormfang [DB6/11]

[S.S08] Kagrumez

Related Quests

Solstheim Side Quest: The Challenges of Kagrumez*

Recommended Level: 25

Dungeon: Dwarven City

Dwarven Automaton
Reaver

Services

Follower: Steadfast Dwarven Sphere [DB6/7]
Follower: Steadfast Dwarven Spider [DB7/7]

Dangers

Trial Chamber

Puzzle

Dwarven Puzzle

Collectibles

Kagrumez Resonance Gem [DB4/5]
Kagrumez Resonance Gem [DB5/5]
Unique Weapon: Dwarven Black Bow of Fate [DB7/11]

Miscellaneous

Area is locked
Chest
Loose gear
Lots o' gold

Exterior

A dead Dunmeri mage is sprawled inside his tent, near a knapsack and a few dwarven parts. Otherwise, this area is desolate. The real entrance to Kagrumez is below. Excavation and rock slides have decimated one of the walls; there's a chest among the stonework. Activate the elevator to head inside.

- Chest
- Raleth Eldri (Deceased)

Interior

A Elevator to Solstheim

1 Corridor to the Golden Door

This is the entrance chamber, with dwarven metal and parts to take.

2 Trial Chamber

As you enter, a Reaver is talking about things coming out of the walls and suggests they return with more men. Another replies they have the mettle to slay a few spiders, before claiming the treasure of Kagrumez. Search the leader's corpse for two Kagrumez Resonance Gems; you need these to activate the strange pedestal receptacle in the middle of the chamber, which begins the forthcoming trials. There is a small journal to read, too, offering hints at what is to come.

- Kagrumez Resonance Gem [DB4/5]
- Kagrumez Resonance Gem [DB5/5]
- Raleth Eldri's Notes on Kagrumez

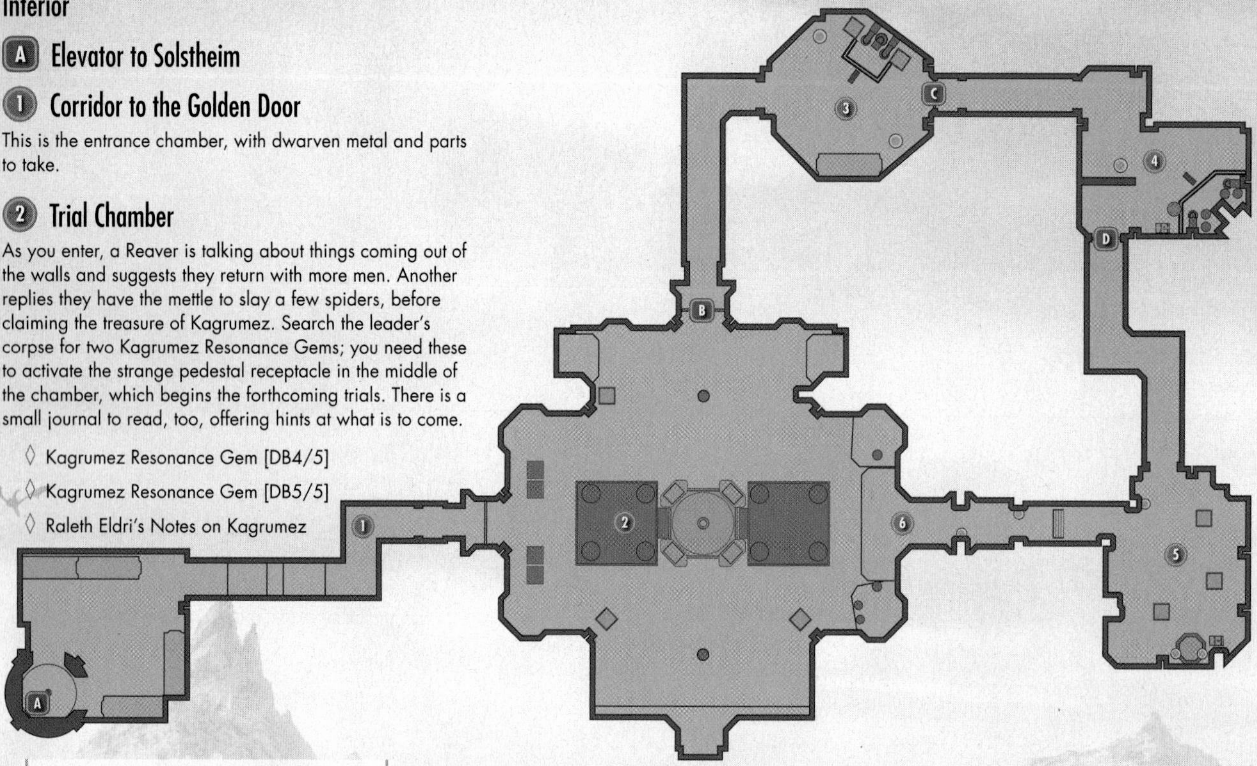

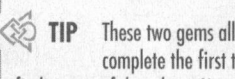

> **TIP** These two gems allow you to complete the first trial without finding any of the others. However, you must secure two more gems to access the remaining trials. Consult Solstheim Side Quest: The Challenges of Kagrumez* (page 650) for all Resonance Gem locations.

Trial 1: Automaton Attack

The resonance receptacle receives any Kagrumez Resonance Gems you wish to insert, and you can remove them without any problems. Look to the northern gate (Location B). Above it is a resonance marker, a golden plate with the fourth and ninth holes covered. Return to the receptacle and place the gems in that pattern to begin. You will face Dwarven Spiders (3) and Dwarven Ballistas (3).

Trial 2: Flame and Fireproof Spheres

In Location 3, locate the gate on the east wall (Location C). Above it is a resonance marker with the second, eighth, and ninth holes covered. Place the gems, and the trial begins. Two flame gouts shoot vertically, while steam blasts between the walls on the east and west sides. Toward the north and south edges of the arena are rotating fire pedestals that activate when you move near them; therefore, stay on the outer edges or the middle of the arena when fighting. You must defeat Dwarven Spiders (5) and Tempered Spheres (2), which are immune to fire damage.

Trial 3: A Short, Sharp Shock

In Location 4, locate the gate southwest of the room (Location D). Above it is a resonance marker with the first, fifth, seventh, and ninth holes covered. Place the gems to begin your final trial. The chamber fills ankle-deep in water, with islands in the center and around the edges. As you navigate the water, expect shock damage (which is extra-nasty if you're in the water) from Tempered Spheres (2), Dwarven Ballistas (2), and Dwarven Spiders (3).

B Northern Gate

3 Spider Storeroom

Head through the northern gate and up the passage. Among shelves of ingots is a lever that opens a strange cage. Inside is an automaton that acts in the same way as an Animal Companion. It can fight alongside you or "go home" (which is here). See page 104 for more information.

- Dwarven Metal Ingot (15)
- Follower: Steadfast Dwarven Spider [DB6/7]

C Eastern Gate

4 Sphere Storeroom

This is another storage chamber with a chest and a lever to pull. This reveals a new automaton to control, the Steadfast Dwarven Sphere! Choose this or the Spider to aid you, if you wish.

- Chest
- Follower: Steadfast Dwarven Sphere [DB7/7]

D Southwestern Gate

5 Upper Chamber

Head up to a long hall. Among the other treasures is the Dwarven Black Bow of Fate, an impressive haul for your final prize.

- Chest
- Flawless Diamond
- Diamond (2)
- Gold Ingot (7)
- Unique Weapon: Dwarven Black Bow of Fate [DB7/11]

6 Viewing Balcony

Although you can use Whirlwind Sprint to access balconies overlooking the trial chamber, they lead nowhere. This location has two stone seats but little else.

[S.S09] Ramshackle Trading Post

Recommended Level: 10

Habitation: Trading Post

Falas Selvayn

Services

Trader (General Goods): Falas Selvayn [DB10/16]

Collectibles

East Empire Strongbox [DB28/33]

Unique Weapon: Glass Bow of the Stag Prince [DB8/11]

What looks to be an abandoned (and certainly ruined) trading post is actually still used by Falas Selvayn. Enter the structure, looking for an arrow that pins a note to the northwest corner wall. It reads "Meet me here at midnight." Just outside is an East Empire Strongbox [Expert]. Falas turns up just after midnight (stay away from the location, then return to meet him). He remains here until around 4:00 a.m. Purchase (or pickpocket) a unique bow from him.

- East Empire Strongbox [Expert] [DB28/33]
- East Empire Pendant
- Trader (General Goods): Falas Selvayn [DB10/16]
- Unique Weapon: Glass Bow of the Stag Prince [DB8/11]

NOTE Highpoint Tower is half buried in ash and inaccessible until Solstheim Side Quest: Old Friends begins.

[S.S10] Highpoint Tower

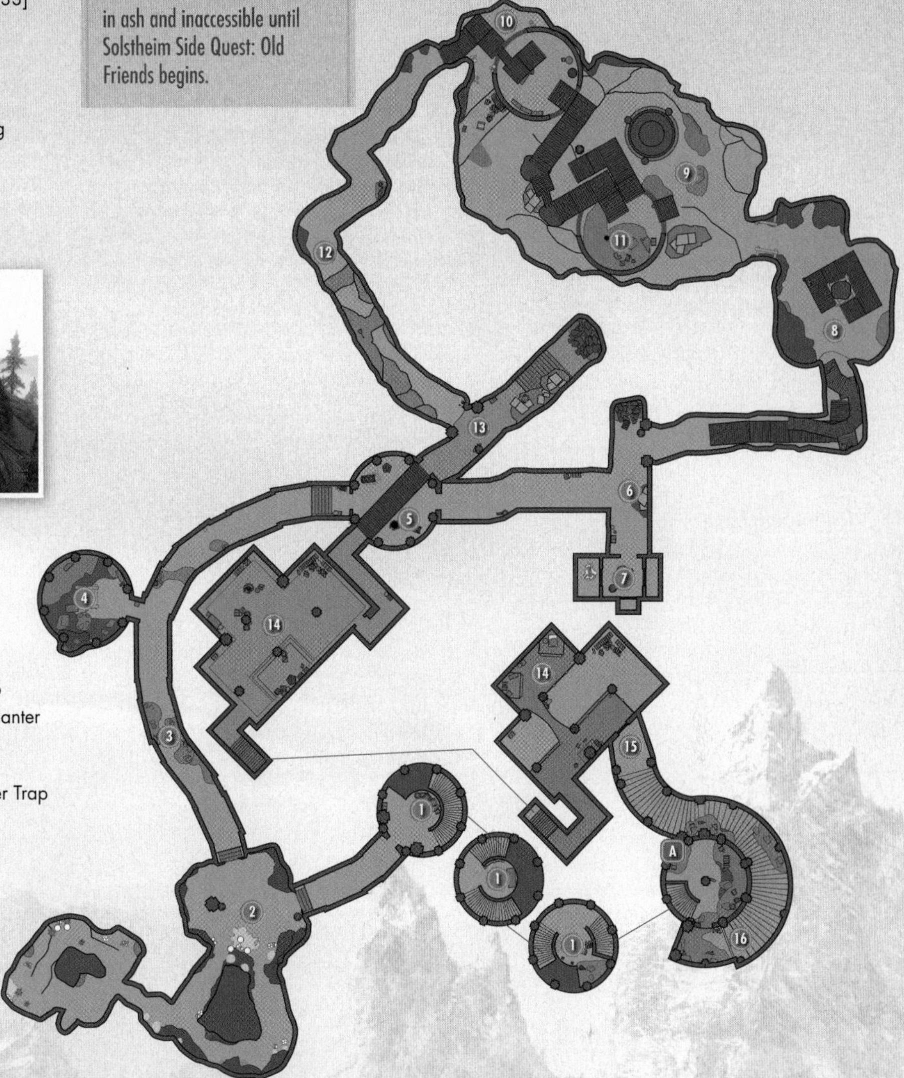

Related Quests

Solstheim Side Quest: Old Friends

Recommended Level: 20

Dungeon: Ash Spawn Lair

Ash Spawn
Flame Cloaked Spider
Albino Spider
Niyya
Ildari Sarothril

Crafting

Alchemy Lab
Arcane Enchanter

Dangers

Magic Caster Trap
Rune Trap

Collectibles

Unique Item: Telvanni Robes [DB29/31]

Miscellaneous

Area is locked
Chest
Potions
Loose gear
Lots o' gold

Exterior

Highpoint Tower is a lonely ruin with commanding views of the southern ashlands. The exterior is devoid of life, aside from the hated Ash Spawn. The tower turret has a chest you can scramble up to (use the lip edge to maneuver around) and a deposit of Heart Stone. But the entrance is under the tower, cunningly hidden and guarded by Ash Spawn. To find it, stay below the rocky area around the tower and move clockwise around until you're slightly north of the location, facing south. A group of Ash Spawn are lurking near the dying pine trees and trama roots. Defeat the foes, locate the roughly hewn steps in the rocks that wind up to the southeast, and approach the stone tunnel entrance to the tower.

- Chest
- Heart Stone Deposit

Interior

A Door to Solstheim

This is firmly sealed until the aforementioned Side Quest is active.

1 Tower Chamber

The entrance area is half filled with rubble and ash; there's little of worth here or in the caved-in entrance to the south. Head down three levels of spiral steps, pausing at the table two floors down to secure the first of Ildari's Journals.

- Ildari's Journal, vol. I

2 Rocky Cave and Low Caverns

A curved stone tunnel leads into a rocky cave attached to the base of the tower structure with numerous revolting egg sacs to your left (southwest). These burst as you head toward them, so slay any Flame Cloaked or Albino Spiders here or in the small cavern with the ruby geode deposits. The low caverns have more geodes and scattered bones.

- Amethyst Geode
- Emerald Geode
- Ruby Geode (2)
- Sapphire Geode
- Flame Cloaked Spider
- Albino Spider

3 Curved Stone Tunnel

Move north into the next section of tunnel, plucking the Soul Gem from its focusing cradle so it doesn't spit shock bolts at you. Head past the partial collapse and Ash Spawn waiting to repel you. Rush the next magic caster trap and halt the electrical damage before continuing east to the tunnel exit.

- Danger: Magic Caster Trap
- Ash Spawn

4 Circular Side Chamber

Check here for more foes, scattered iron ingots, and a bird's nest.

- Ash Spawn

5 Circular Torture Room and Bridge

Watch the fire rune on the ground in the roughly circular chamber with the Arcane Enchanter and woodcutter's axe. You return here when navigating the wooden bridge above.

- Crafting: Arcane Enchanter
- Danger: Rune Trap

6 Dungeon Passage

Head east down the large dungeon passage, watching for a wall rune at the far end. To the right (south) is a small dead-end passage with cells. To the left (north) is a blocked area and bowl torch. A gap to the right (east) allows access into a mine area. Grab the flawless diamond and coin purses protruding from a half-buried chest in the ceiling!

- ◊ Flawless Diamond
- ◊ Danger: Rune Trap

7 Cells

One still has a prisoner inside: Niyya. If you unlock her door [Adept], she tells you Ildari sealed her and other miners into these cells and used them in her experiments. Ildari seems quite deranged. Just how deranged is detailed in the second of her journals, found on the table in the jail area. The other two cells [Novice] have prisoners a little too bony to be of any use to you.

- ◊ Ildari's Journal, vol. II
- ◊ Niyya

8 Orichalcum Mine Workings

Drop down into the mine where veins of gold, Orichalcum, and sapphire ore are located. Then head northwest, under the three hanging lanterns, and prepare for fraught combat.

- ◊ Gold Vein
- ◊ Orichalcum Ore (3)
- ◊ Sapphire Geode (2)

9 Summoning Battlements (Lower)

A small fortification built within a large cave. Ildari Sarothril appears atop the battlements: She's not the friendly sort, as indicated by the minions she summons before fleeing. She conjures an Ash Guardian, and three or four Ash Spawn also join in the throng.

- ◊ Ash Guardian
- ◊ Ash Spawn

10 Dead-End Mine Shaft

If you collect toadstools and cheese, prepare to be pleased.

11 Summoning Battlements (Upper)

Climb the wooden scaffold steps surrounding the old fort, passing the summoning circle and an apothecary satchel. Cross to the interior of a partially ruined tower where Ildari yelled at you from. Drop down and inspect the shelves and room, grabbing any items you wish. The area has potions; ingredients; several books of interest, including Ahzidal's Descent, Deathbrand, and Ildari's third journal; and a strongbox (not made by the East Empire Company).

- ◊ Crafting: Alchemy Lab
- ◊ Book: Ahzidal's Descent
- ◊ Book: Deathbrand
- ◊ Ildari's Journal, vol. III
- ◊ Potions
- ◊ Strongbox

12 Mine Fissure

Cross to the exit and southwest tunnel that winds up and turns into a fissure with Ash Spawn appearing as you progress.

13 Castle Corridor

The only way is to the right (southwest), over a bridge (above Location [5]). There's a chest at the opposite end, in the rubble, already opened.

- ◊ Potions
- ◊ Loose gear

14 Ildari Sarothril's Chamber

This chamber is a grand, two-story hall where Ildari resides. Face her ice storms and thunderbolts in an epic battle, watching for her fast healing and other possible magical enhancements. Long-range attacks may be easier, as fighting on the narrow bridge to her balcony bedroom is tricky. When she finally drops to her knees, race in and rip her heart out, finally ending her malicious ways for good. Search her corpse for robes and a staff. The room also contains a variety of ingredients and loose gear.

- ◊ Crafting: Arcane Enchanter, Wood Chopping Block
- ◊ Chest
- ◊ Loose gear
- ◊ Potions
- ◊ Ildari Sarothril
- ◊ Heart Stone
- ◊ Unique Item: Telvanni Robes [DB29/31]

15 Barred Archway Exit

Activate the lever near the small bridge, and a barred archway opens, allowing you to exit via a long second tower staircase.

16 Secret Exit

A pull chain here opens a section of wall leading back to the initial tower chamber.

[S.S11] Fort Frostmoth

Related Quests

Solstheim Side Quest: March of the Dead

Solstheim Side Quest: The Great Solstheim Strongbox Hunt*

Recommended Level: 25

Dungeon: Military Fort

Ash Spawn

General Falx Carius

Collectibles

East Empire Strongbox [DB29/33]

Unique Weapon: Champion's Cudgel [DB9/11]

Miscellaneous

Area is locked

Potions

Chest

Loose gear

Exterior

This was once a sizable Imperial garrison, where unruly soldiers were sent as penance. Now it is a ghostly shell. Ash Spawn patrol the walls, and the booming voice of General Falx Carius instructs his minions to attack. Expect around six foes to contend with along the battlements and in the southeast tower (where you find skeletal remains and a knapsack). To the south is a sunken Nord merchant boat with a few mead barrels and a skeleton, and a three-tiered harbor wall with steps up to the main southern entrance.

The fort proper is half buried by the ash, and there are numerous gaps in the battlements that allow you into the central courtyard. The western tower is accessible, with a foe at the top and a good vantage point for long-range attacks. But the most intact sections of the fort lie along the north and west walls. The north wall door is accessible only from the inside, leaving you with one entrance—to the west. Heading inside is the only way to reach the western and northern rooftops, where you find a chest along the western side.

- ◊ Chest
- ◊ Ash Spawn

Interior

A Door to Solstheim

1 Western Entrance Corridor

The choking ash is everywhere, as are three or four Ash Spawn to contend with, throughout Locations 1, 2, and 3. Adjacent to the door is a small guard chamber with a couple of potions. Move to the main north-south corridor and check the nearby small armory to the southeast for Imperial equipment, some books, and an East Empire Strongbox [Expert]

- ◊ Ash Spawn
- ◊ Potions
- ◊ Book: The Legend of Red Eagle
- ◊ East Empire Strongbox [Expert] [DB29/33]
- ◊ East Empire Pendant
- ◊ Loose gear

2 Imperial Barracks

The ruined remains of beds and imperial equipment are located here. Watch out for the foe and the chest [Adept].

- ◊ Ash Spawn
- ◊ Chest [Adept]

3 Training Room

A ramp to a ladder and trapdoor allows access to the western roof, where you'll find a chest. The room has scattered items and a few potions.

- ◊ Ash Spawn
- ◊ Potions

B Trapdoor to Solstheim

4 Ruined Hallway

Including the steps down you've taken to reach here, there are five separate exits and one blocked-off alcove in this chamber, along with two Ash Spawn. There's scattered equipment and a cobwebbed entrance to the west. There's a locked cell door [Master] to the north (you can also unlock it with the Fort Frostmoth key, found in Location [6]). Inside is a chest, some hidden moon sugar, and a variety of drinks. The other exit north leads down to the crypt. To the east is a wooden door requiring the Fort Frostmoth Key to

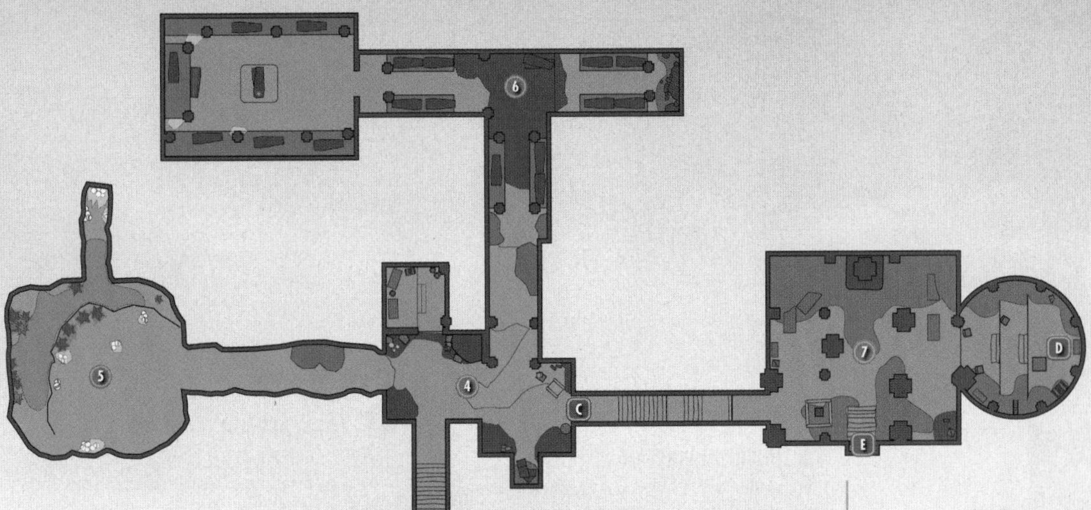

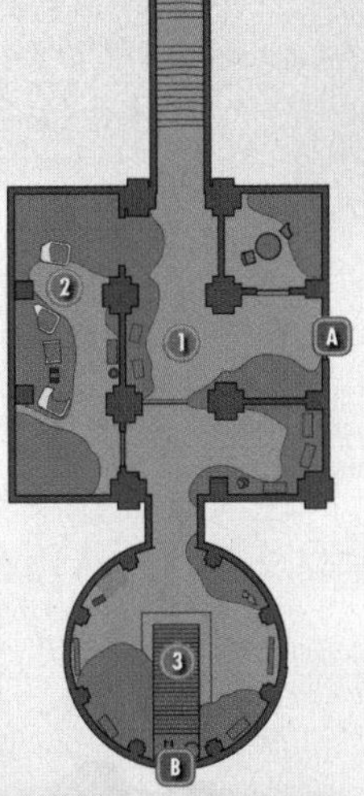

open (which is in the crypt). To the south, a wall has fallen on the skeletal remains of Maximian Axius, with a letter and knapsack nearby. Check the knapsack for three more letters.

- ◊ Ash Spawn
- ◊ Loose Gear
- ◊ Chest
- ◊ Maximian's Knapsack
- ◊ A Letter to Selina, I–IV

5 Geode Chamber

Five nasty little spiders guard seven egg clusters in this gloomy rock cave, with Heart Stone and ruby geodes to mine afterward.

- ◊ Albino Spider
- ◊ Flame Cloaked Spider
- ◊ Jumping Flame Spider
- ◊ Heart Stone Deposit (2)
- ◊ Ruby Geode (3)

6 Crypt

Face Ash Spawn in this narrow crypt lined with Imperial coffins, with two stacked atop each other at the chamber's west end. Aside from a chest and a few potions, there's a knapsack with a key inside that opens the wooden door to the east in Location [4]. Ildari's Journal is atop the coffins, detailing Neloth's old apprentice Ildari Sarothril and her attempts to raise the dead (for more about Ildari, see Solstheim Side Quest: Old Friends, on page 635).

- ◊ Ash Spawn
- ◊ Chest
- ◊ Potions
- ◊ Knapsack
- ◊ Fort Frostmoth Key
- ◊ Ildari's Journal
- ◊ Loose Gear

C Wooden Door [Requires Key]

Use the Fort Frostmoth Key to open this door.

7 General Falx Carius's Chamber

If you're here for Solstheim Side Quest: March of the Dead, the resurrected remains of the general fight you here, along with four Ash Spawn minions. There's a chest, some books, and potions to obtain.

- ◊ Ash Spawn
- ◊ Book: Ahzidal's Descent
- ◊ Book: Deathbrand
- ◊ Chest
- ◊ General Falx Carius
- ◊ Unique Weapon: Champion's Cudgel [DB9/11]

D Trapdoor to Solstheim

This leads up to the roof for a quick escape.

E Door to Solstheim [Requires Key]

Use the Fort Frostmoth Key to open this door.

[S.S12] Ashfallow Citadel

Related Quests

Solstheim Side Quest: Served Cold

Solstheim Side Quest: The Great Solstheim Strongbox Hunt*

Recommended Level: 25

Dungeon: Military Fort

Mirri Severin

Morag Tong

Tilisu Severin

Vendil Severin

Dangers

Bear Trap (5)

Swinging Wall Trap (3)

Spear Trap (2)

Crafting

Alchemy Lab

Arcane Enchanter

Collectibles

East Empire Strongbox [DB30/33]

Miscellaneous

Area is locked

Chest

Potions

Loose gear

Exterior

An old Imperial fort now controlled by the Morag Tong (an ancient assassins guild from Morrowind who pray to Mephala), Ashfallow Citadel is an unassuming ruin from the outside. The fort is half buried in ash, and enemies prowl only the stone battlements if Solstheim Side Quest: Served Cold is active. Stone piles stained with blood and bone dissuade you from exploration, but aside from the steep ground, there's little to threaten you here (until you enter).

- ◊ Morag Tong
- ◊ Heart Stone Deposit (2)

Interior

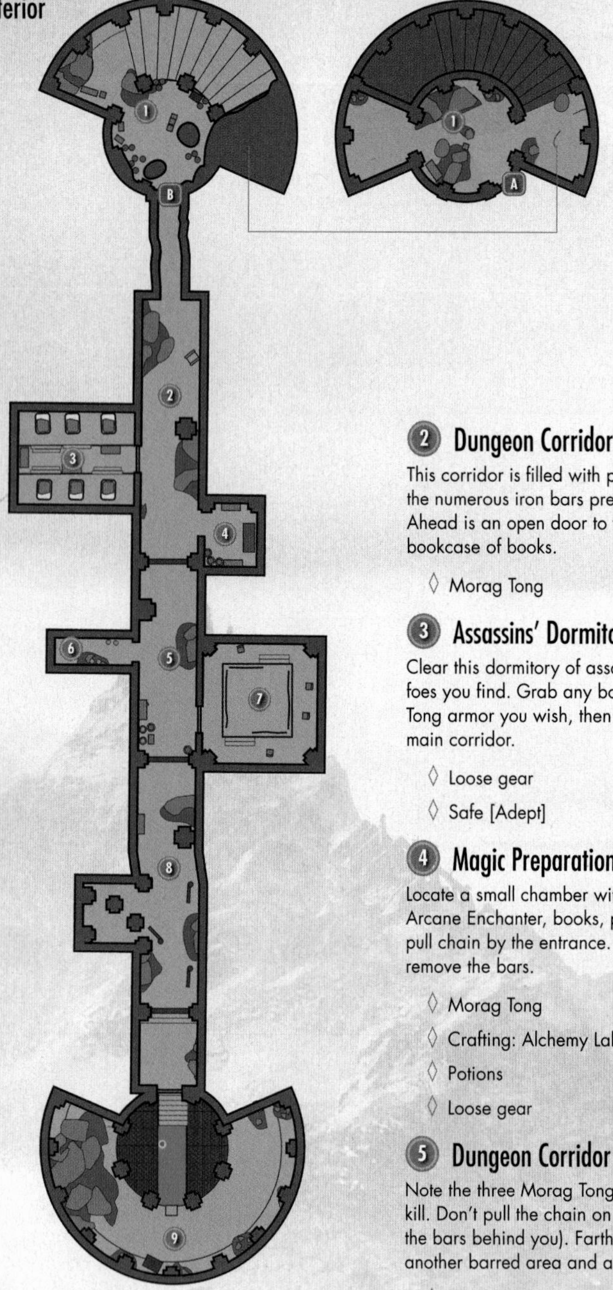

A Door to Solstheim

1 Tower Room

Check the bookshelf to your left (west), where an East Empire Strongbox [Expert] sits on the middle shelf. There's a skeleton to loot and steps down to the north. These lead to a storage room with a chest and a narrow tunnel, which is sealed unless Solstheim Side Quest: Served Cold is active. Morag Tong appears only during this quest.

- ◊ Morag Tong
- ◊ East Empire Strongbox [Expert] [DB30/33]
- ◊ East Empire Pendant
- ◊ Chest

B Rock Wall Entrance

There are no levers or chains to pull; this rock wall only recedes during Solstheim Side Quest: Served Cold.

2 Dungeon Corridor (Part 1)

This corridor is filled with pull chains to remove the numerous iron bars preventing your progress. Ahead is an open door to your right (west) and a bookcase of books.

- ◊ Morag Tong

3 Assassins' Dormitory

Clear this dormitory of assassins and any other foes you find. Grab any books, chitin, or Morag Tong armor you wish, then head back to the main corridor.

- ◊ Loose gear
- ◊ Safe [Adept]

4 Magic Preparation Nook

Locate a small chamber with an Alchemy Lab, Arcane Enchanter, books, potions, and a pull chain by the entrance. Yank the chain to remove the bars.

- ◊ Morag Tong
- ◊ Crafting: Alchemy Lab, Arcane Enchanter
- ◊ Potions
- ◊ Loose gear

5 Dungeon Corridor (Part 2)

Note the three Morag Tong assassins you must kill. Don't pull the chain on the left wall (it raises the bars behind you). Farther down the corridor is another barred area and a bookcase.

- ◊ Morag Tong
- ◊ Book: Ahzidal's Descent

6 Bear Trap Passage

Watch out for bear traps before you reach another chain. Pull that, which removes the first set of bars farther down the corridor.

- ◊ Danger! Bear Trap (5)

7 Training Room.

Outside this door is a third chain, which opens the next part of the corridor. Inside is a training ring and some loose gear. If you didn't kill Mirri Severin back in Raven Rock, she will confront you here.

- ◊ Mirri Severin
- ◊ Morag Tong
- ◊ Loose gear

8 Dungeon Corridor (Part 3)

In the next part of the corridor are eight pressure plates linked to three separate swinging wall traps and two wall spear traps, so take extreme care as you tread forward. The safest way to reach the two pull chains in the alcove to your right (west) is to look down and avoid all pressure plates; maneuver past the alcove, turn right, and edge between the left wall of the alcove and a swinging trap. Watch for more plates as you look for two pull chains, both on the pillars in this alcove. They open the two remaining bars.

- ◊ Danger! Swinging Wall Trap (3)
- ◊ Danger! Spear Trap (2)

9 Vendil Severin's Quarters

Ignore the pull chain to your right, just before the final arched entrance, as this simply raises the bars directly behind you, cutting off your only retreating route. You must slay Vendil Severin, along with his fellow assassins, including Tilisu, if she still lives. When Vendil finally yields, check his corpse for the key to his manor in Raven Rock.

- ◊ Tilisu Severin
- ◊ Vendil Severin
- ◊ Severin Manor Key
- ◊ Morag Tong
- ◊ Chest

[S.S13] Vahlok's Tomb

Related Quests

Solstheim Side Quest: Lost Legacy

Recommended Level: 30

Dungeon: Draugr Crypt

Corrupted Shade
Draugr
Thartan
Vahlok the Jailor

Special Area

Word Wall: Battle Fury [DB1/3]
Word Wall: Battle Fury [DB2/3]
Word Wall: Battle Fury [DB3/3]

Dangers

Flamethrower Trap

Puzzle

Nordic Puzzle Door
Nordic Puzzles

Miscellaneous

Area is locked
Chest
Loose gear
Lots o' gold

> **TIP** Remember, there are no doors here. Simply complete the exploration, read any Black Book you're carrying, or succumb to death and be transported back to Tamriel. You can return here at any time by rereading the Black Book in your inventory.

1 Chapter I: Fetid Pier and Lookout

The great fetid seas of Apocrypha greet you. Focus on the path and head southeast, climbing the stepped platforms to your left as you turn east. Fight two or three Seekers as you go. Avoid the tentacle from the black pond, as you reach a Scrye that opens a gate ahead (northeast) of you.

- Seeker

2 Chapter I: Side Passage

Move past a black table and a Magicka font. A Stamina font, a black table, and a Scrye are crammed together. The Scrye opens a second gate.

- Font of Magicka
- Font of Stamina

3 Chapter I: Corridor of Whirling Pages

Head southwest, engaging two more Seekers in the corridor beyond. Gather Magicka from a font as you continue south to a Scrye. This opens a gate to the south.

- Font of Magicka (2)
- Seeker

4 Chapter I: Lurker Pool

This leads to a larger, open chamber with a ramp and a forming Lurker. Slay this atrocity, before or after you activate the Scrye to the west. There are two Magicka fonts to siphon here too. The Scrye on the ground elongates the steps. The Scrye atop the ramp opens the gate atop these steps.

- Font of Magicka (2)
- Lurker

5 Chapter I: Black Book: The Winds of Change

The gate allows access to the pedestal containing the tome, and there is an adjacent vessel to ransack. Open the book to claim one of the following abilities:

- Scholar's Insight (reading Skill Books gives you an extra skill point)
- Companion's Insight (your attacks, shouts, and destruction spells do no damage to your followers)
- Lover's Insight (do 10% more damage and get 10% better prices from people of the opposite sex)
- Vessel

[S.A07] Apocrypha: Waking Dreams of a Starless Sky

Related Quests

Dragonborn Main Quest: The Temple of Miraak

Dragonborn Main Quest: At the Summit of Apocrypha

Recommended Level: 35

Dungeon: Apocrypha

Kruziikrel	Relonikiv
Lurker	Sahrotaar
Miraak	Seeker

Special Area

Black Book: Waking Dreams of a Starless Sky

Word of Power: Dragon Aspect [DB3/3]

Collectibles

Unique Weapon: Miraak's Staff [DB10/11]

Unique Weapon: Miraak's Sword [DB11/11]

Unique Item: Miraak's Boots [DB1/31]

Unique Item: Miraak's Gloves [DB2/31]

Unique Item: Miraak's Mask [DB3/31]

Unique Item: Miraak's Robes [DB4/31]

Miscellaneous

Area is locked

Chest

Black Book: Waking Dreams of a Starless Sky

This book rests on a pedestal deep within the Temple of Miraak [S.N24], which you will find during Dragonborn Main Quest: The Temple of Miraak. After slaying the Gatekeeper, traverse the large stepped chamber and pass a statue of Hermaeus Mora before scrambling down a winding tunnel to a circular chamber. Take the Black Book and read it. You are transported to Apocrypha. You read it again at the start of Dragonborn Main Quest: At the Summit of Apocrypha.

Interior: Apocrypha

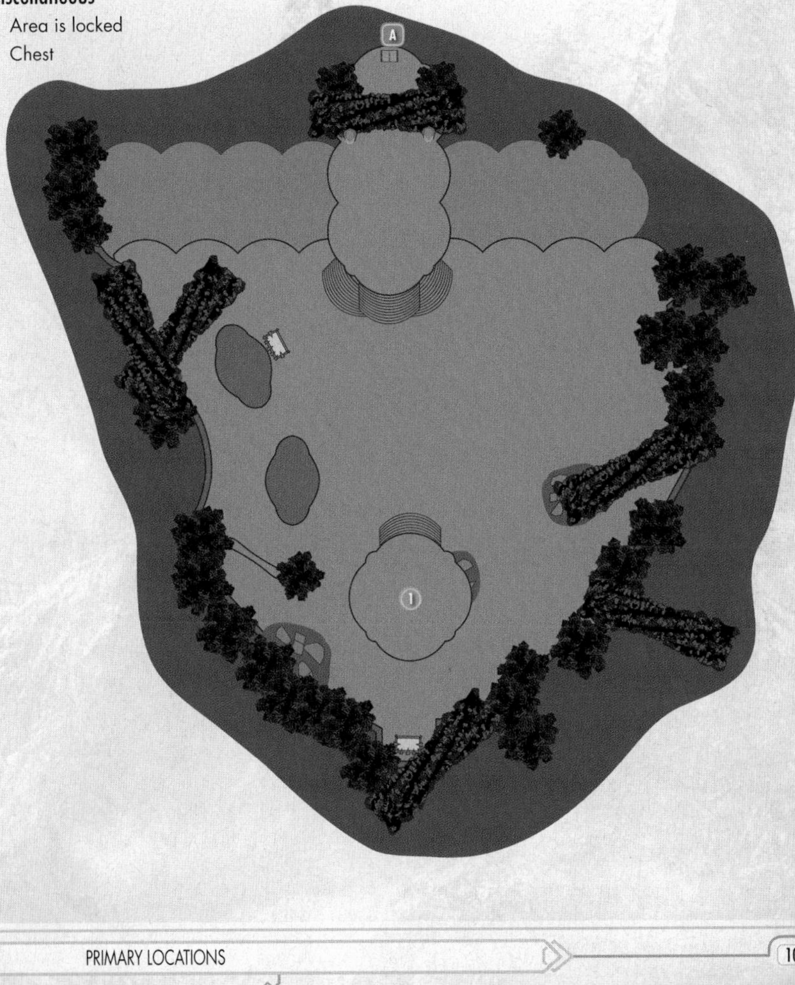

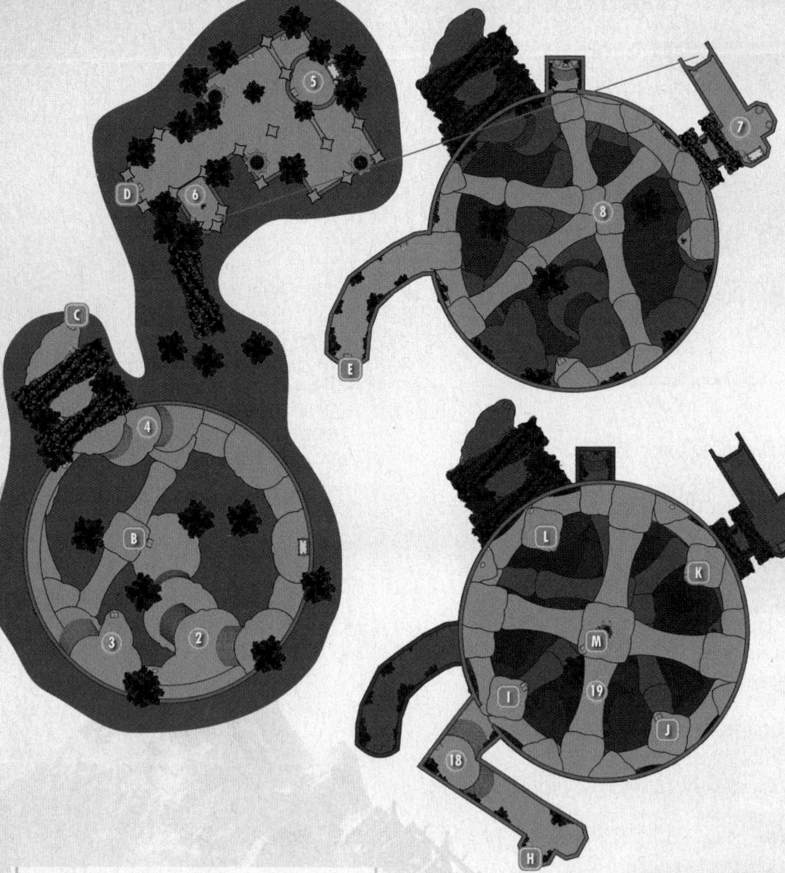

> **TIP** Remember, there are no doors here. Simply complete the exploration, read any Black Book you're carrying, or succumb to death and be transported back to Tamriel. You can return here at any time by rereading the Black Book in your inventory.

1 Chapter I: Plateau on the Stinking Sea

Check the table to the south for a trio of books. There is also a pod to open along the left and right (east and west) walls. Scan a second table for a Soul Gem, and then head north, passing two Magicka fonts and open Chapter II.

- ◊ Font of Magicka (2)
- ◊ Pod (2)

A Book to Chapter II

B Book to Chapter I

2 Chapter II: Miraak's Tower: Entrance Steps

Climb the first set of stone steps, watching Seekers. Check the nearby table for a book before ascending farther and heading left (north) around the edge of this large, cylindrical chamber: Miraak's Tower. Pass the table with Heavy Armor Forging (a Smithing Skill Book) and around to a small bridge to your left (south). There are some steps not yet elongated into a staircase position.

- ◊ Skill Book: Heavy Armor Forging (Smithing)

3 Chapter II: Miraak's Tower: Entrance Bridges

Cross the bridge, go up the steps, and head around to the plinth that holds a cracked and ancient book called Boneless Limbs.

- ◊ On Apocrypha: Boneless Limbs [1/4]

4 Chapter II: Miraak's Tower: Archway Doors

The gathering of this book elongates the steps at the initial side of the bridge, so cross over, head up the steps to the north, and go out of the open archway doors to view a vast ocean of filth. Turn right (northeast) and open Chapter III.

C Book to Chapter III

D Book to Chapter II

5 Chapter III: Corridors of Books

Enter the tunnel that leads roughly northeast, passing a door to your right that you can't open yet. The corridor splits to the left and right, with two or three Seekers and a couple of pools with whipping tentacles to dodge. There are two Magicka fonts if you need them. Both corridors merge at some steps up to a platform and a table with Song of the Alchemists (an Alchemy Skill Book). Turn around, and on a stone plinth lies another ancient book called Delving Pincers. Gather the book to open the door you passed earlier.

- ◊ Seeker
- ◊ Font of Magicka (2)
- ◊ Skill Book: Song of the Alchemists (Alchemy)
- ◊ On Apocrypha: Delving Pincers [2/4]

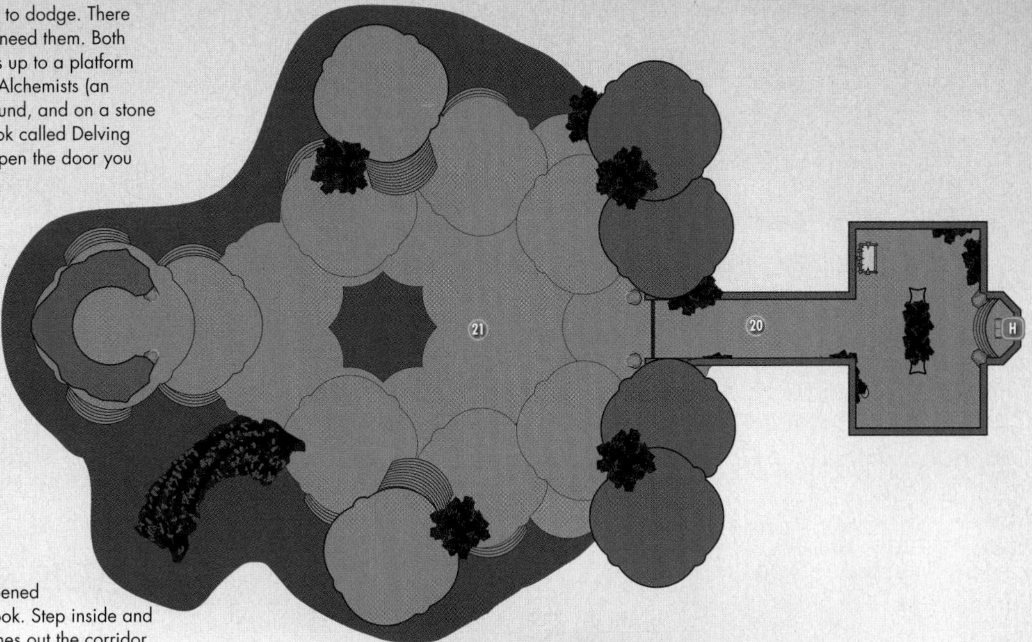

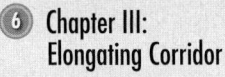

6 Chapter III: Elongating Corridor

Retrace your steps along the corridor (southwest), as the previously closed door opened when you took the ancient book. Step inside and activate the Scrye. This stretches out the corridor ahead of you.

7 Chapter III: Corridor Junction

Head past a Magicka font, then another, stopping at the junction to inspect a table with Catalogue of Weapon Enchantments (an Enchanting Skill Book) and other books on it. Pass a Stamina font and head right (southwest), back into Miraak's tower chamber.

- ◊ Font of Magicka
- ◊ Font of Stamina
- ◊ Skill Book: Catalogue of Weapon Enchantments (Enchanting)

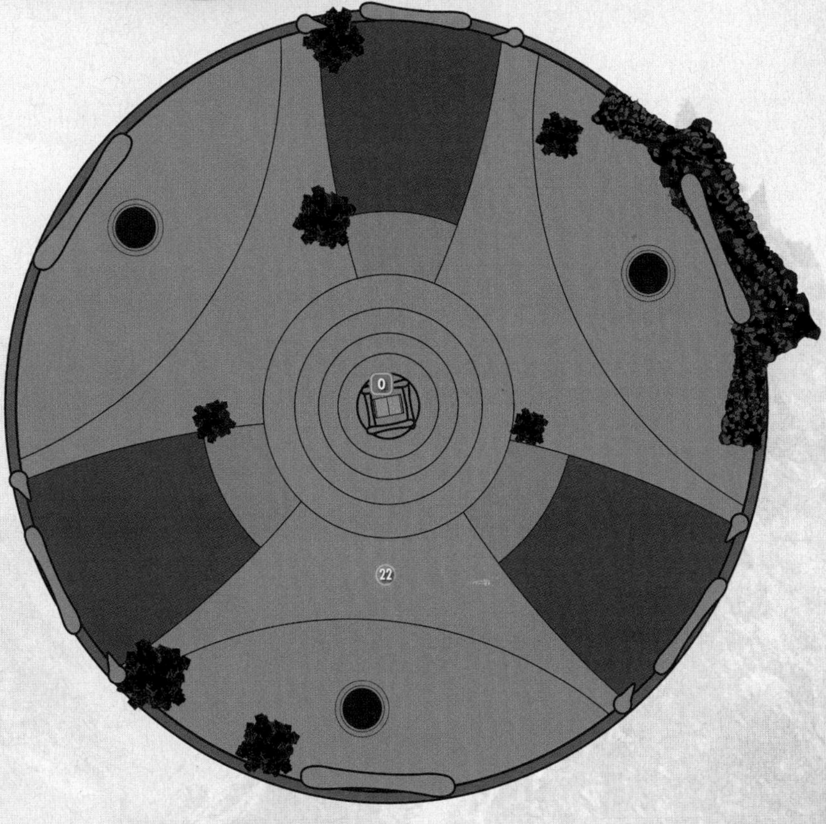

8 Chapter III: Miraak's Tower: Crisscrossing Platforms

Head left (south), opening a pod and activating a nearby Scrye, which opens a door to the northwest (leading to a small alcove with a vessel you can search for items). Now head south along the main bridge platform, then go right, passing a pod to a plinth with a Magicka font and another ancient tome, Prying Orbs. Taking the book opens a gate on the western part of the chamber, allowing further progress. After a Magicka and Stamina font, you reach Chapter IV.

- ◊ Font of Magicka (2)
- ◊ Font of Stamina
- ◊ Pod (2)
- ◊ Vessel
- ◊ On Apocrypha: Prying Orbs [3/4]
- ◊ Seeker

E Book to Chapter IV

F Book to Chapter III

9 Chapter IV: Stepped Courtyard

From your high position above a multitude of steps and shifting tunnel walls, turn right (west) and head down the steps, pausing to grab at the Stamina font above you. Directly ahead is a low balcony fence below which is a second Stamina font; access that from the top of the steps, then descend on either side, facing down two or three Seekers as you go. Don't forget a pod on a southwest platform.

- ◊ Font of Stamina (2)
- ◊ Pod
- ◊ Seeker

10 Chapter IV: Retracting Tunnels

Head past the black table and the selection of books, then down to the lower ground and a tattered banner. Enter the tunnel to the south, moving around the long left curve to a junction with a black table and two very long passages ahead (east) and right (south). The tunnel ahead with the Magicka and Stamina fonts retracts as you move down it, forcing you right, where a similar retraction occurs.

- ◊ Font of Magicka
- ◊ Font of Stamina
- ◊ Seeker

11 Chapter IV: Open and Stepped Area

Backtrack to the initial tunnel; it has turned to the opposite (south) direction, allowing you to move into an open area, where you face two more Seekers. There is a stepped area to the west.

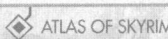

Climb the steps, passing two tables (one houses some scrolls) and a Magicka font near your fourth and final ancient book, Gnashing Blades. As you gather this tome, the books around you will shift and expose a new passage.

- Font of Magicka
- Seeker
- On Apocrypha: Gnashing Blades [4/4]

12 Chapter IV: Elongating Tunnel

Move down the steps and head right (southeast) into the newly opened tunnel. This ends in a junction with an alcove to your right (south) with two black tables and a corridor that expands when you enter it. Nearby are two additional tables with more books to leaf through.

13 Chapter IV: Long Corridor

Move ahead (east) down the long corridor to a pair of Stamina fonts and a pod, before continuing down the left turn and into another chamber with a Stamina font under a walkway.

- Font of Stamina
- Pod

14a Chapter IV: Frothing Pool

14b Chapter IV: Secret Vessels

Avoid the black tentacles as you head northwest across the ground bridge, and engage two or three Seekers on the initial stepped balcony. Pass a black table, working your way along an upper bridge heading south, and up more steps to a Scrye. This moves the tunnel you passed through to a new position.

Look closely at the map on page 1074, and you'll discover a small, narrow plinth with two strange vessels on it. This is normally inaccessible during your exploration. To reach it, "die" partway through (just after taking On Apocrypha: Gnashing Blades; by succumbing to an enemy or stepping into the fetid waters). Then re-read Black Book: Waking Dreams. This resets the moving hallways into a configuration allowing you to reach the plinth!

- Seeker
- Vessel (2)

15 Chapter IV: Eastern Tunnel

Descend and enter the tunnel now heading east, down the long left curve past a small tentacle pool.

16 Chapter IV: Lurker-Summoning Chamber

One of these beasts is summoned as you near the circular black ooze in the middle. There's a Scrye in the northwest corner of the chamber that opens an alcove with a vessel and black table in an adjacent corridor farther northwest (head around the corridor entrance to access it). Just before that alcove is a second Scrye. Activate that, and the chamber's main door to the north swings open. Slay the horror before proceeding.

- Font of Stamina (2)
- Lurker

17 Chapter IV: Stepped Exit

At the end of the corridor to the north is a Magicka font and access to Chapter V.

- Font of Magicka

G Book to Chapter V

H Book to Chapter IV

18 Chapter V: Book Tunnel

Siphon the Magicka font near the open book before following the corridor up the steps, past a Stamina font, and out into the upper walkways of the central tower chamber.

- Font of Magicka
- Font of Stamina

19 Chapter V: Miraak's Tower: Book Pedestals

Slay the Seekers first. The focus of the room is a plinth in the central spine of the chamber, which houses access to Chapter VI. Place each of the four Apocrypha Books on their correct pedestals. Simply read the clues from the books and the books' names and lay the tome on the image best associated with each book. Or, follow this plan:

I Gnashing Blades Pedestal

The pedestal with the fishlike maw is closest to you. Place "Gnashing Blades" here.

J Delving Pincers Pedestal

The pedestal with the two claws is nearby. Place "Delving Pincers" here. Expect Seekers to attack you at this point.

K Boneless Limbs Pedestal

The pedestal with the mass of writhing tentacles is opposite the entrance. Place "Boneless Limbs" here.

L Prying Orbs Pedestal

The pedestal with the strange evil fishlike eye is the last of the plinths. Place "Prying Orbs" here.

If you've placed the books on the correct pedestals, the opening to Chapter VI glows green. If not, remove the books and try again. When you're ready for the final chapter, head to Chapter VI and open it.

- Seeker
- Pod (3)

> **TIP** It is possible to have opened Black Book: Waking Dreams and completed all the chapters up to this point as soon as you receive the book, during Dragonborn Main Quest: The Temple of Miraak. If you did this, you begin your trek at Chapter VI, rather than earlier.

M Book to Chapter VI

N Book to Chapter V

20 Chapter VI: Double Corridor Entrance

Exit via a small double-corridor leading to a single tunnel. Grab the Art of War Magic (a Destruction Skill Book) from the black table as you go.

- Skill Book: The Art of War Magic (Destruction)

21 Chapter VI: Promontory Amid the Unspeakable Ocean

This is bereft of life until you pass the Stamina fonts and approach the curved stone edifice at the opposite end. This is a Word Wall! Approach the Word Wall and defeat the two Seekers that are summoned to prevent your progress. Learn the powerful new Thu'um, part of the Dragon Aspect Shout.

- Seeker
- Sahrotaar
- Word Wall: Dragon Aspect [DB3/3]

Final Chapter: Summit of Apocrypha

At this point, assuming you're completing the Dragonborn Main Quest, Sahrotaar appears. You must tame him so you can ride him to the final confrontation with Miraak atop Apocrypha. The confrontation occurs on a huge, circular plateau.

> **NOTE** Sahrohtaar only appears if you have reached here during the Dragonborn Main Quest. Otherwise, you must use (any) Black Book to return to the mortal world. This is also the case if you haven't completed prior quests in the Dragonborn Main Quest. When you do, then read the book and return, you appear by the Word Wall and Sahrohtaar soon appears.

23 Miraak's Tower: Summit

When Miraak finally yields, you can claim your just rewards from Hermaeus Mora:

- Dragon Souls
- Unique Weapon: Miraak's Staff [DB10/11]
- Unique Weapon: Miraak's Sword [DB11/11]
- Unique Item: Miraak's Boots [DB1/31]
- Unique Item: Miraak's Gloves [DB2/31]
- Unique Item: Miraak's Mask [DB3/31]
- Unique Item: Miraak's Robes [DB4/31]

After taking Miraak's equipment, approach the Black Book: Waking Dreams in the center of the summit. Read this tome, and green light envelops you. Look around, and you'll see shimmering images of the Skill Constellations arrayed around you. You can approach any of these mirages, activate them, and expend a Dragon Soul to clear all of the perks in a particular Skill Constellation. You can:

Recover all of the Perk Points you have spent in a single constellation, then spend them elsewhere.

Do this as many times as you wish, as long as you have enough Dragon Souls.

Read the Black Book a second time to return to Solstheim.

O Book to Solstheim

APPENDICES

Keeping track of your progress across the Province of Skyrim can be overwhelming at times. The following Appendices attempt to summarize the information you need to know and restore a feeling of calm, knowledgeable ease to your journey. Or, they reference other tables in this guide where information is readily available. At the end of these Appendices is a brief section with research and information on the language of the dragons, a glossary, and finally an index.

MINOR SPOILERS

CAUTION This chapter has highly secret information; read with care!

NOTE Aside from Appendix I, and unless otherwise specified, information contained within these Appendices is also listed within the Atlas.

Color-coding: The following tables feature elements present from Dawnguard, Hearthfire, and Dragonborn. Such elements are color-coded accordingly. Original elements are in white and gray.

☐ [DG1/1] Dawnguard/Hearthfire ☐ [DB1/1] Dragonborn

APPENDIX I: ACHIEVEMENTS AND TROPHIES

This table lists all the Achievements (PC or Xbox) or Trophies (PlayStation 4) that you can accrue during the game.

✓	ICON	INDEX	ACHIEVEMENT	POINTS	TROPHY	DESCRIPTION	NOTES
☐		1	Unbound	10	Bronze	Complete "Unbound"	Complete Main Quest: Unbound
☐		2	Bleak Falls Barrow	10	Bronze	Complete "Bleak Falls Barrow"	Complete Main Quest: Bleak Falls Barrow
☐		3	The Way of the Voice	20	Bronze	Complete "The Way of the Voice"	Complete Main Quest: The Way of the Voice
☐		4	Diplomatic Immunity	20	Bronze	Complete "Diplomatic Immunity"	Complete Main Quest: Diplomatic Immunity
☐		5	Alduin's Wall	20	Bronze	Complete "Alduin's Wall"	Complete Main Quest: Alduin's Wall
☐		6	Elder Knowledge	20	Bronze	Complete "Elder Knowledge"	Complete Main Quest: Elder Knowledge
☐		7	The Fallen	20	Bronze	Complete "The Fallen"	Complete Main Quest: The Fallen
☐		8	Dragonslayer	50	Gold	Complete "Dragonslayer"	Complete Main Quest: Dragonslayer
☐		9	Take Up Arms	10	Bronze	Join the Companions	Complete your first Companions Radiant Quest
☐		10	Blood Oath	10	Bronze	Become a member of the Circle	Become a Werewolf, at the start of The Companions Quest: The Silver Hand
☐		11	Glory of the Dead	30	Silver	Complete "Glory of the Dead"	Complete The Companions Quest: Glory of the Dead
☐		12	Gatekeeper	10	Bronze	Join the College of Winterhold	Complete College of Winterhold Quest: First Lessons
☐		13	Revealing the Unseen	10	Bronze	Complete "Revealing the Unseen"	Complete College of Winterhold Quest: Revealing the Unseen
☐		14	The Eye of Magnus	30	Silver	Complete "The Eye of Magnus"	Complete College of Winterhold Quest: The Eye of Magnus
☐		15	Taking Care of Business	10	Bronze	Join the Thieves Guild	Complete Thieves Guild Quest: A Chance Arrangement
☐		16	Darkness Returns	10	Bronze	Complete "Darkness Returns"	Complete Thieves Guild Quest: Darkness Returns
☐		17	One with the Shadows	30	Silver	Returned the Thieves Guild to its former glory	Complete Thieves Guild Quest: Darkness Returns and all four City Influence Quests
☐		18	With Friends Like These…	10	Bronze	Join the Dark Brotherhood	Complete Dark Brotherhood Quest: With Friends Like These…
☐		19	Bound Until Death	10	Bronze	Complete "Bound Until Death"	Complete Dark Brotherhood Quest: Bound Until Death
☐		20	Hail Sithis!	30	Silver	Complete "Hail Sithis!"	Complete Dark Brotherhood Quest: Hail Sithis!
☐		21	Taking Sides	10	Bronze	Join the Stormcloaks or the Imperial Army	Complete Civil War Quest: Joining the Legion OR Joining the Stormcloaks
☐		22	War Hero	10	Bronze	Capture Fort Sungard or Fort Greenwall	Complete Civil War Quest: The Battle for Fort Greenwall (Imperial) OR The Battle for Fort Sungard (Stormcloak)
☐		23	Hero of Skyrim	30	Silver	Capture Solitude or Windhelm	Complete Civil War Quest: Battle for Windhelm (Imperial) OR Battle for Solitude (Stormcloak)
☐		24	Sideways	20	Bronze	Complete 10 side quests	Complete 10 of the Side Quests listed below.
☐		25	Hero of the People	30	Bronze	Complete 50 Misc Objectives	These include Quests flagged with a "*" in this guide, Miscellaneous Objectives, or Favors.
☐		26	Hard Worker	10	Bronze	Chop wood, mine ore, and cook food	Complete these three activities using the approprate stations.
☐		27	Thief	30	Silver	Pick 50 locks and 50 pockets	There are no restrictions on this, aside from the Crimes you're committing.
☐		28	Snake Tongue	10	Bronze	Successfully persuade, bribe, and intimidate	Consult the Quests sections to find opportunities for this.
☐		29	Blessed	10	Bronze	Select a Standing Stone blessing	Activate any of the 13 Standing Stones
☐		30	Standing Stones	30	Silver	Find 13 Standing Stones	Activate all of the 13 Standing Stones
☐		31	Citizen	10	Bronze	Buy a house	Purchase any of the five houses listed in the Training section.
☐		32	Wanted	10	Bronze	Escape from jail	Pick the lock, or find a secret escape route. See Crime and Punishment in the Training section for options.
☐		33	Married	10	Bronze	Get married	Complete Temple Quest: The Bonds of Matrimony. Potential spouses are listed with that quest.
☐		34	Artificer	10	Bronze	Make a smithed item, an enchanted item, and a potion	Consult the Training section on Crafting (page 70) for more information.
☐		35	Master Criminal	20	Bronze	Bounty of 1000 gold in all nine holds	Consult Crime and Punishment in the Training section (page 64) for more information.

Achievements and Trophies Continued

✓	ICON	INDEX	ACHIEVEMENT	POINTS	TROPHY	DESCRIPTION	NOTES
		36	Golden Touch	30	Silver	Have 100,000 gold	Barter, trade, complete quests, and craft weapons, armor, and potions to sell.
		37	Delver	40	Silver	Clear 50 dungeons	Consult the Atlas for all appropriate locations flagged as "Dungeons".
		38	Skill Master	40	Silver	Get a skill to 100	Consult the Training section for more information on Skills and Perks (page 12).
		39	Explorer	40	Silver	Discover 100 Locations	Consult the Atlas for all 350+ Primary Locations.
		40	Reader	20	Bronze	Read 50 Skill Books	Consult page 1091 for sample Skill Book Locations.
		41	Daedric Influence	10	Bronze	Acquire a Daedric Artifact	See the Daedric Quests (page 378), and the notes below for more information.
		42	Oblivion Walker	30	Silver	Collect 15 Daedric Artifacts	See the Daedric Quests (page 378), and the notes below for more information.
		43	Dragon Soul	10	Bronze	Absorb a dragon soul	This will occur during Main Quest: Dragon Rising.

✓	ICON	INDEX	ACHIEVEMENT	POINTS	TROPHY	DESCRIPTION	NOTES
		44	Dragon Hunter	20	Bronze	Absorb 20 dragon souls	After completing Main Quest: Dragon Rising, begin fighting Dragons, searching for Dragon Mounds (page 92), and exploring Dragon Lairs (see Atlas).
		45	Words of Power	10	Bronze	Learn all three words of a shout	
		46	Thu'um Master	40	Silver	Learn 20 shouts	
		47	Apprentice	5	Bronze	Reach Level 5	Consult the Training section on page 44 for tips on leveling.
		48	Adept	10	Bronze	Reach Level 10	Consult the Training section on page 44 for tips on leveling.
		49	Expert	25	Bronze	Reach Level 25	Consult the Training section on page 44 for tips on leveling.
		50	Master	50	Silver	Reach Level 50	Consult the Training section on page 44 for tips on leveling. Patience is also key!
			TOTAL	1,000			

✓	ICON	INDEX	ACHIEVEMENT	POINTS	TROPHY	DESCRIPTION	NOTES
		51	Awakening	20	Bronze	Complete "Awakening"	Complete Dawnguard Main Quest: Awakening
		52	Beyond Death	20	Bronze	Complete "Beyond Death"	Complete Dawnguard Main Quest: Beyond Death
		53	Kindred Judgement	40	Silver	Complete "Kindred Judgment"	Complete Dawnguard Main Quest: Kindred Judgment
		54	Ancient Power	30	Silver	Gather five chalice ingredients, or find five ancient technologies	Complete Dawnguard Faction Quest: Ancient Technology five times, or complete Vampire Faction Quest: Ancient Power five times.
		55	Soul Tear	20	Bronze	Learn all three words of Soul Tear	Complete Side Quest: Durnehviir
		56	Auriel's Bow	20	Bronze	Use the special power of Auriel's Bow	Complete Dawnguard Main Quest: Touching the Sky, then use Auriel's Bow to shoot the sun with a Sunhallowed or Bloodcursed Arrow.
		57	Werewolf Mastered	20	Bronze	Acquire 11 werewolf perks	Complete the Werewolf Perk Tree.
		58	Vampire Mastered	20	Bronze	Acquire 11 vampire perks	Complete the Vampire Lord Perk Tree.
		59	A New You	20	Bronze	Change your face	Complete Misc Objective: Surgery
		60	Legend	40	Silver	Defeat a Legendary Dragon	Legendary Dragons will only appear after you reach Level 57.
			TOTAL	250			

✓	ICON	INDEX	ACHIEVEMENT	POINTS	TROPHY	DESCRIPTION	NOTES
		61	Proud Parent	10	Bronze	Adopt a child	Adopt any child.
		62	Landowner	10	Bronze	Buy a plot of land	Become a friend of the Jarl of Falkreath, Hjaalmarch, or the Pale, then purchase land from them.
		63	Architect	10	Bronze	Build three wings on a house	Build the main hall and all three wings of any house.
		64	Land Baron	10	Bronze	Buy three plots of land	As Landowner, but buy land from all three Jarls.
		65	Master Architect	10	Bronze	Build three houses	As Architect, but complete all three houses.
			TOTAL	50			

APPENDIX III: SHRINES

All of the shrines to each of the Nine Divines are listed below. The Training section (page 55) and Other Factions Quests (page 417) have more information on shrines and their Blessings.

✓	NUMBER	ZONE #	LOCATION	DESCRIPTION
			SHRINE OF AKATOSH	
☐	[1/6]	[1.00]	Solitude	Temple of the Divines, in the main chamber.
☐	[2/6]	[2.25]	Skyborn Altar	On the altar in front of the Word Wall (prior to Main Quest: Dragon Rising).
☐	[3/6]	[5.47]	Fort Sungard	Fort Sungard Shrine Interior, if the Imperials control the fort.
☐	[4/6]	[6.A]	Shrine of Akatosh: Rorikstead	Sitting next to the ruin stones.
☐	[5/6]	[7.R]	Shrine of Akatosh: Steamcrag Hillock	On the altar.
☐	[6/6]	[8.G]	Shrine of Akatosh: Twilight Valley	On the edge of the stone overlook.
			SHRINE OF ARKAY	
☐	[1/12]	[1.00]	Solitude	Temple of the Divines, in the main chamber.
☐	[2/12]	[1.00]	Solitude	In the Hall of the Dead, on a table in the side area beyond the metal door.
☐	[3/12]	[4.14]	Wayward Pass	On the narrow platform halfway through the pass.
☐	[4/12]	[4.W]	Shrine of Arkay: Windhelm Hills	On the altar in the circle of stones, if the Stormcloak Camp is not present.
☐	[5/12]	[5.00]	Markarth	In the Hall of the Dead, on the circular pedestal in the back room.
☐	[6/12]	[5.07]	Druadach Redoubt	Sitting on a rock ledge near the wall by the ramps at the back of the cave.
☐	[7/12]	[6.00]	Whiterun	In the Hall of the Dead, on an altar in the chapel area downstairs.
☐	[8/12]	[7.00]	Windhelm	In the catacombs, in the center of the main hall.
☐	[9/12]	[8.00]	Falkreath	On the porch outside the Hall of the Dead.
☐	[10/12]	[8.00]	Falkreath	On the porch outside the Hall of the Dead.
☐	[11/12]	[8.00]	Falkreath	In the Hall of the Dead, against the far wall.
☐	[12/12]	[9.00]	Riften	In the Mausoleum, sitting on a narrow wooden table.
			SHRINE OF DIBELLA	
☐	[1/8]	[1.00]	Solitude	Temple of the Divines, in the main chamber.
☐	[2/8]	[4.A]	Shrine of Dibella: Watching Dawnstar	Exterior; on the altar near the statue.
☐	[3/8]	[5.00]	Markarth	In the Temple of Dibella, on the altar near the wall.
☐	[4/8]	[5.18]	Broken Tower Redoubt	Inside the tower atop the keep, at the base of the statue.
☐	[5/8]	[5.Z]	Shrine of Dibella: Bridge at Old Hroldan	On the altar at the base of the stone pillar.
☐	[6/8]	[7.04]	Morvunskar	In the small sleeping area off of the long corridor.
☐	[7/8]	[7.A]	Lucky Lorenz's Shack	In one corner of the ruined shack.
☐	[8/8]	[9.00]	Riften	In Haelga's Bunkhouse, at the foot of the bed in Haelga's bedroom.
			SHRINE OF JULIANOS	
☐	[1/5]	[1.00]	Solitude	Temple of the Divines, in the main chamber.
☐	[2/5]	[3.N]	Julianos' Fallen	Sitting in the snow near a skeleton up in the mountains.
☐	[3/5]	[5.09]	Harmugstahl	On the dresser in Kornalus Frey's quarters.
☐	[4/5]	[6.29]	Fellglow Keep	During College of Winterhold Quest: Hitting the Books, behind the locked door at the foot of the stairs leading up to the Ritual Chamber.
☐	[5/5]	[7.27]	Fort Amol	Before the Civil War begins, on a stone block in the courtyard.
			SHRINE OF KYNARETH	
☐	[1/6]	[1.00]	Solitude	Temple of the Divines, in the main chamber.
☐	[2/6]	[2.M]	Shrine of Kynareth: Hjaalmarch Hills	On the ruined stone platform.
☐	[3/6]	[3.02]	Brinehammer	On the floor near the chest in the center of the ship.
☐	[4/6]	[5.47]	Fort Sungard	Fort Sungard Shrine Interior, before the Civil War begins.
☐	[5/6]	[6.00]	Whiterun	In the Temple of Kynareth, on the altar opposite the door.
☐	[6/6]	[9.39]	Crystaldrift Cave	On a rock along the wall inside the cave.
			SHRINE OF MARA	
☐	[1/5]	[1.00]	Solitude	Temple of the Divines, in the main chamber.
☐	[2/5]	[3.06]	Nightcaller Temple	On Erandur's altar, on one side of the entry chamber.
☐	[3/5]	[3.J]	Border Corner: Roadside Shrine of Mara	On the stone planter.
☐	[4/5]	[5.V]	Lovers' Camp	After killing the animal here, leave the area and then return. The shrine will appear on the rock, by the two stone cairns.
☐	[5/5]	[9.00]	Riften	In the Temple of Mara, on the central altar and several side altars.
			SHRINE OF NOCTURNAL	
☐	[1/1]	[9.00]	Riften: The Ragged Flagon Cistern	Appears once Thieves Guild Quest: Darkness Returns is complete
			SHRINE OF STENDARR	
☐	[1/5]	[1.00]	Solitude	Temple of the Divines, in the main chamber.
☐	[2/5]	[3.09]	Hall of the Vigilant	On the altar table inside the Hall.
☐	[3/5]	[6.I]	Shrine of Stendarr: The Two Pillars	On the small stone altar.
☐	[4/5]	[9.26]	Fort Greenwall	On a dresser between two shelves inside the Captain's Quarters.
☐	[5/5]	[9.46]	Stendarr's Beacon	On the small stone altar inside the tower.
			SHRINE OF TALOS	
☐	[1/17]	[1.00]	Solitude	Temple of the Divines, in the main chamber, if the Stormcloaks have won the Civil War.
☐	[2/17]	[3.18]	Weynon Stones	At the base of the statue.
☐	[3/17]	[4.F]	Shrine of Talos: Winterhold Glaciers	At the base of the statue.
☐	[4/17]	[4.J]	Shrine of Talos: Sea of Ghosts	On the ground behind the statue.
☐	[5/17]	[4.K]	Shrine of Talos: Ilas-Tei's Last Stand	At the base of the statue.
☐	[6/17]	[5.00]	Markarth	In the Shrine of Talos, at the base of the statue.
☐	[7/17]	[5.47]	Fort Sungard	Fort Sungard Shrine Interior, if the Stormcloaks control the fort.
☐	[8/17]	[6.00]	Whiterun	At the foot of the statue near the Gildergreen Tree.
☐	[9/17]	[6.29]	Fellglow Keep	On the ruined altar in the chapel area, half-buried amid the rubble.
☐	[10/17]	[6.T]	Shrine of Talos: White River Valley	On the altar near the statue.
☐	[11/17]	[7.00]	Windhelm	In the Temple of Talos, at the base of the statue.
☐	[12/17]	[7.B]	Shrine of Talos: Cradlecrush Pond	At the base of the statue.
☐	[13/17]	[7.E]	Shrine of Talos: Watcher of Windhelm	On the circular pedestal behind the statue.
☐	[14/17]	[8.12]	Bloated Man's Grotto	Prior to Daedric Quest: Ill Met by Moonlight, on the altar in the shrine area at the back of the grotto.
☐	[15/17]	[8.Y]	Shrine of Talos: Ilinalta Foothills	On the rocks near the statue.
☐	[16/17]	[9.00]	Riften	In the southeast corner of the city, near the graveyard.
☐	[17/17]	[9.G]	Shrine of Talos: Froki's Peak	On the ground near the statue.
			SHRINE OF ZENITHAR	
☐	[1/5]	[1.00]	Solitude	Temple of the Divines, in the main chamber.
☐	[2/5]	[5.P]	Shrine of Zenithar: Four Skull Lookout	At the edge of the stone lookout.
☐	[3/5]	[6.E]	Shrine of Zenithar: Ring of Boulders	On the stone platform at the base of the largest stone.
☐	[4/5]	[6.G]	Shrine of Zenithar: Crumbling Bastion	On the crude stone altar under the archway.
☐	[5/5]	[9.V]	Shrine of Zenithar: Fallowstone	On the altar in the remnants of the tower.

✓	NUMBER	ZONE#	LOCATION	DESCRIPTION
			SHRINE OF AURIEL	
	[DG1/2]	[DG.11]	Darkfall Cave	Near Knight-Paladin Gelebor's post.
	[DG2/2]	[DG.12]	Forgotten Vale: Falmer Temple – Inner Sanctum	In the center of the Inner Sanctum, surrounded by frozen Falmer.
			SHRINE OF AKATOSH	
	[HF1/3]	[HF.02]	Windstad Manor	Can be constructed in your home's cellar.
	[HF2/3]	[HF.03]	Heljarchen Hall	Can be constructed in your home's cellar.
	[HF3/3]	[HF.07]	Lakeview Manor	Can be constructed in your home's cellar.
			SHRINE OF ARKAY	
	[HF1/3]	[HF.02]	Windstad Manor	Can be constructed in your home's cellar.
	[HF2/3]	[HF.03]	Heljarchen Hall	Can be constructed in your home's cellar.
	[HF3/3]	[HF.07]	Lakeview Manor	Can be constructed in your home's cellar.
			SHRINE OF DIBELLA	
	[HF1/3]	[HF.02]	Windstad Manor	Can be constructed in your home's cellar.
	[HF2/3]	[HF.03]	Heljarchen Hall	Can be constructed in your home's cellar.
	[HF3/3]	[HF.07]	Lakeview Manor	Can be constructed in your home's cellar.
			SHRINE OF JULIANOS	
	[HF1/3]	[HF.02]	Windstad Manor	Can be constructed in your home's cellar.
	[HF2/3]	[HF.03]	Heljarchen Hall	Can be constructed in your home's cellar.
	[HF3/3]	[HF.07]	Lakeview Manor	Can be constructed in your home's cellar.

✓	NUMBER	ZONE#	LOCATION	DESCRIPTION
			SHRINE OF KYNARETH	
	[HF1/3]	[HF.02]	Windstad Manor	Can be constructed in your home's cellar.
	[HF2/3]	[HF.03]	Heljarchen Hall	Can be constructed in your home's cellar.
	[HF3/3]	[HF.07]	Lakeview Manor	Can be constructed in your home's cellar.
			SHRINE OF MARA	
	[HF1/3]	[HF.02]	Windstad Manor	Can be constructed in your home's cellar.
	[HF2/3]	[HF.03]	Heljarchen Hall	Can be constructed in your home's cellar.
	[HF3/3]	[HF.07]	Lakeview Manor	Can be constructed in your home's cellar.
			SHRINE OF STENDARR	
	[HF1/3]	[HF.02]	Windstad Manor	Can be constructed in your home's cellar.
	[HF2/3]	[HF.03]	Heljarchen Hall	Can be constructed in your home's cellar.
	[HF3/3]	[HF.07]	Lakeview Manor	Can be constructed in your home's cellar.
			SHRINE OF TALOS	
	[HF1/3]	[HF.02]	Windstad Manor	Can be constructed in your home's cellar.
	[HF2/3]	[HF.03]	Heljarchen Hall	Can be constructed in your home's cellar.
	[HF3/3]	[HF.07]	Lakeview Manor	Can be constructed in your home's cellar.
			SHRINE OF ZENITHAR	
	[HF1/3]	[HF.02]	Windstad Manor	Can be constructed in your home's cellar.
	[HF2/3]	[HF.03]	Heljarchen Hall	Can be constructed in your home's cellar.
	[HF3/3]	[HF.07]	Lakeview Manor	Can be constructed in your home's cellar.

✓	NUMBER	ZONE#	LOCATION	DESCRIPTION
			SHRINE OF KYNARETH	
	[DB1/1]	[S.SE]	Wilderness Shrine to Kynareth	Northwest of Raven Rock; follow the path up the steep slope to a tree and shrine.
			SHRINE OF ZENITHAR	
	[DB1/1]	[S.NL]	Shrine of Zenithar	On the rocky, snow-clad ground south of Moesring Pass, above Frostmoon Crag.
			SHRINE OF AZURA	
	[DB1/1]	[S.S00]	Raven Rock	Inside Raven Rock Temple.
			SHRINE OF BOETHIAH	
	[DB1/1]	[S.S00]	Raven Rock	Inside Raven Rock Temple.
			SHRINE OF MEPHALA	
	[DB1/1]	[S.S00]	Raven Rock	Inside Raven Rock Temple.

C

M

N

O

P

Q

R

S

T

U

V

W

Y

Z

QUESTS INDEX

NOTE * Quest names marked with an asterisk do not appear in your Quest Menu list, although objectives may.

The Elder Scrolls V

SKYRIM®

SPECIAL EDITION

PRIMA OFFICIAL GAME GUIDE

Written by

David S.J. Hodgson, Steve Stratton & Steve Cornett

Prima Games
6081 East 82nd Street, Suite #400
Indianapolis, IN 46250

www.primagames.com

Product Manager: Paul Giacomotto

Design & Layout: In Color Design

Maps: 99 Lives, Loren Gilliland

Copy Editor: Carrie Andrews

Tech Editor: Josef Frech, Dominic Ricci

BASED ON A GAME RATED BY THE ESRB MATURE 17+ M

ISBN:

Standard Edition: 9780744017847
Collector's Edition 9780744017830

Printing Code: The rightmost double-digit number is the year of the book's printing; the rightmost single-digit number is the number of the book's printing. For example, 16-1 shows that the first printing of the book occurred in 2016.

19 18 17 16 4 3 2 1

001-305278-Oct/2016

Printed in the USA.

ADDITIONAL WRITING

Alan Nanes
Andrew Langlois
Brian Chapin
Bruce Nesmith
Daryl Brigner
Emil Pagliarulo
Jeff Browne
Jeff Gardiner
Joel Burgess
Jon Paul Duvall
Justin Schram
Kurt Kuhlmann
Matt Daniels
Nate Ellis
Philip Nelson
Ryan Jenkins
Shane Liesegang
Steve Cornett
William Shen

SPECIAL THANKS

Todd Howard
Paul Graber
Liz Rapp
Clara Struthers
Robert Wisnewski
Ashley Cheng
Craig Lafferty
Matt Carofano
Natalia Smirnova
Nate McDyer
Paris Nourmohammadi
Erin Losi
Pete Hines
Chris Krietz
Andrew Scharf
Marcia Mitnick
Lisa Cole
Chandi Abey
Carlos Guice

EDITORS-IN-CHIEF

Steve Cornett
Jeff Gardiner
Craig Lafferty

THE ELDER SCROLLS V: SKYRIM GAME DIRECTOR

Todd Howard

THE ELDER SCROLLS V: SKYRIM CREATED BY:

Bethesda Game Studios

PRIMA GAMES STAFF

VP & PUBLISHER

Mike Degler

EDITORIAL MANAGER

Tim Fitzpatrick

DESIGN AND LAYOUT MANAGER

Tracy Wehmeyer

LICENSING

Christian Sumner
Paul Giacomotto

MARKETING

Katie Hemlock

DIGITAL PUBLISHING

Julie Asbury
Tim Cox
Shaida Boroumand

OPERATIONS MANAGER

Stacey Ginther

Acknowledgements – David S. J. Hodgson

To Bethesda: Firstly, this guide wouldn't have been anywhere nearly as thorough if it wasn't for the generosity of knowledge and help I received from all at Bethesda. Thanks to Jeff Gardiner, Bruce Nesmith, Jeff Browne, Pete Hines, Erin Losi, and all those that helped me. In particular, the fastidious and meticulous prowess of Steve Cornett in helping wrangle statistics, quests, and making mind-bogglingly comprehensive documentation deserves (and has) my eternal gratitude.

Special thanks to: My loving wife Melanie; Mum, Dad, and Ian; Loki; Steve "Authorkiin" Stratton, Sonja and all at 99 Lives, Mark and Targa of In Color Design, Pappa G, Shaida Boroumand; The Moon Wiring Club, Laibach, and Kraftwerk; Ron and Fez, Eastside Dave, Bill Tetley; and M for Miskatonic University. An Ivy League school over 200 years old, Housing the largest occult collection in the western world, And the most varied alumni, I'm told.

Acknowledgements – Steve Stratton

Steve Cornett and Jeff Gardiner at Bethesda for their outstanding help and support, without which this guide would not have been possible. Thanks to Paul G. at Prima, Carrie Andrews, and Mark and Targa of In Color Design for transforming our crazy manuscript into this breathtaking tome. Special thanks to David S.J. Hodgson, the Authorborn.

Acknowledgements – Steve Cornett

To the team: No book, not even the longest guide ever published, can do justice to the years of hard work, late nights, and long weekends you put into Skyrim. Thank you, and congratulations. Special thanks to Todd, Jeff, Craig, Bruce, Jeff, and Joel, for your advice and support; and to the design team for your help with a host of obscure questions and document reviews.

Thanks to everyone in the ZeniMax family who helped make Skyrim and this guide a success. Special thanks to Paris, Erin, and Pete; Harald and Ruth; and to our entire QA team, who deserve far more credit than they receive.

Thanks to Paul, Shaida, and everyone at Prima for coordinating this massive project.

To David and Steve, who in two years of searching, Unearthed every secret and left No Stone Unturned (pages 645 and 302, respectively).

And most importantly, to our players and fans: Thanks for making all of this possible.

Acknowledgements – Paul Giacomotto

To the Prima family: What started off as an egg is now a full grown 1,100 page fire breathing dragon! Special thanks to Debra, Andy, Mark, and Aaron for direction, encouragement, and support. Thanks to my fellow Product Managers and co-workers– Don, Jesse, JJ, Fernando, and Jim for picking up the slack while I tried to wrangle this beast. To Rick, Melissa, and Jamie for knocking out many design requests and your advice. To Jeff and Terry for selling it and Veronika for chasing me for info.

Special thanks to: David, Steve S., and Steve Cornett...I'm in awe. More than 785,000 words, thousands of hours, hundreds of sleepless nights, and a barrage of emails/phone calls...yet you still stand, more distinguished than ever with battle scars and dented armor- "Hun, Kaal, Zoor". In Color Design (Mark and Targa), 99 Lives, Loren 'Evil Drew', Carrie, and Shaida you are true champions surviving arrows to the knee and a 'legendary' amount of information. Robin, Brandon, and Gianna who make me smile. Pops, Mom, and Dre for my core values.

To Bethesda Game Studios: Paris, Erin, Steve, Craig, Marcia Mitnick, Lisa Cole, Chandi Abey, Carlos Guice and the rest of the committed team you've been tremendous partners and supportive to this project.

To the fans and players: We work tirelessly for you, thanks!